P9-BAV-325

Rating system

★★★★★ Excellent

★★★★ Very Good

★★★ Good

★★ Fair

★ Poor

🦃 Turkey

Also by Mick Martin & Marsha Porter
Published by Ballantine Books:

VIDEO MOVIE GUIDE FOR KIDS: A BOOK FOR PARENTS

VIDEO MOVIE GUIDE 1990

Mick Martin
& Marsha Porter

BALLANTINE BOOKS • NEW YORK

Copyright © 1989 by Mick Martin and Marsha Porter

All rights reserved under International and Pan-American Copyright Conventions. Published in the United States of America by Ballantine Books, a division of Random House, Inc., New York, and simultaneously in Canada by Random House of Canada Limited, Toronto.

Library of Congress Catalog Card Number: 89–91657

ISBN 0-345-36329-9

Manufactured in the United States of America

First Ballantine Books Edition: November 1989

CONTENTS

CHIEF CONTRIBUTORS

DERRICK BANG
HARVEY BURGESS
M. FAUST
JEAN FOURNIER
PAUL FREEMAN
JACK GARNER
RICH GARRISON
WILLIAM GLINES
RON GLUCKMAN
ROBERT HOLMAN
PHIL HOOVER
SCOTT HUNTER
JIM LANE
RICHARD LEATHERS
GREG LEIS
BILL MCLEOD
DON NORRIS
DENNIS ROOD
BOB SHAW
LISA SMITH-YOUNGS
TOM TOLLEY
ROBERT YOUNG JR.

FOREWORD

You hold in your hands the most comprehensive critical guide to movies on video available. Where other movie-review books contain films that may never be released to video stores, *Video Movie Guide* concentrates only on what you can rent at your local shop or purchase through the mail. Even so, that still puts this edition at over 9,000 titles.

It is also a book written *by* people who love movies *for* people who love movies. We treat this annual publication like a kind of holy quest, searching out obscure titles and oddball distributors in order to pack *VMG* with as many available titles as possible. This is why you'll find more B movies, foreign films, concert videos, cartoon collections, comedy performances, early sound-era westerns, TV movies, direct-to-video releases, and TV series covered here than in any other movie guide.

As with last year's Foreign Language Films chapter, we have continued to expand our coverage and categories. This year marks the debut of our Documentaries chapter. The Musicals chapter is now called Music & Musicals, and contains performance videos in all fields, including dance and opera.

Rock-concert videos are dealt with in depth. We don't see the difference between a theatrically released concert movie such as The Rolling Stones' *Let's Spend the Night Together* and a video original like the Police's *Synchronicity Concert*. Both are the same type of film, even though other movie-review books only cover concert movies that have played theatrically. We have expanded the chapter to include feature-length concert videos of all kinds.

In addition, there have been substantial increases in our Children's Viewing/Family Films and Westerns chapters. Numerous cartoon collections and animated adaptations of literary classics have been added to the former category, while B Westerns from the genre's heyday have been added to the latter.

As in previous years, we have covered all of the major movie releases available in stores as well as several months of upcoming titles, which we reviewed while they were in theatrical release. Also, we have gone backward as much as forward, catching up on whatever obscure or previously released titles we may have missed in earlier editions. We honestly believe that you cannot find a more complete critical review of movies on videocassette.

To help you find movies reviewed in this book, we have several features: a complete alphabetical listing of titles at the back of the book, a cast index, a director index, and a special list of movies for family viewing. In the complete title index, an asterisk has been placed next to all new additions. Alternate titles have also been listed so that a film like *The Asphyx*, for example, can be found under its video title, *Spirits of the Dead*, and so on.

A few readers have expressed dismay because we reevaluate films from edition to edition. We feel this is necessary. A good movie might catch us on a bad day, or vice versa, and lead to a less than objective analysis. Some of the better-known film critics balk at being considered consumer guides, but that is exactly what we strive to be. Not everyone is going to like everything. But if a film has merit, even if we don't particularly care for it, we have striven to call attention to its attributes. We want this book to be, given the capriciousness of opinion, the most accurate and useful critical guide to movies.

This is why we rate genre movie against genre movie. For example, dramas are rated against dramas, mysteries against mysteries, and so on. There is no way Buck Jones's *Gunman from Bodie* could be compared to *Citizen Kane*, for example, so we try to keep things in perspective.

Video Movie Guide is meant to function as a viewing guide to what is available in video stores for rent and a buyer's guide to titles available by mail order. As with books, some movies may go out of print and become unavailable for purchase. However, many films that can no longer be purchased can be found for rent in many stores.

A number of Disney titles—*Swiss Family Robinson*, for example—are placed on moratorium, which means you can find them for viewing purposes at a rental store but cannot currently buy them—although they will be rereleased eventually. More and more video companies are using this approach.

In addition, as we go to press, several Errol Flynn adventure films—*Captain Blood* and *Sea Hawk*, for example—exist in some kind of never-never land, as rights have been transferred from one company to another. This is why we do not list distributors in *Video Movie Guide*. Other titles, like *The Last Picture Show* and *The Private Life of Sherlock Holmes*, were pulled some time ago by their respective distributors and are not generally available. But they *have* been released on video, so we include them in our book.

We regret any inconvenience a reader might have in attempting to buy a particular title listed in this book, and we'd like to help. We have received letters asking us where to buy a given movie, even though we have listed numerous mail-order houses each year in the foreword. As much as we would like to assist, we do not have the time to find movies for readers who want to buy them.

TO ORDER VIDEOS

However, we have arranged with Mike Antonaros, at Mr. Dickens Books and Tapes, to offer *Video Movie Guide* readers mail-order services. To find a movie reviewed in this book, write to Mr. Dickens Books and Tapes, 5323-A Elkhorn Boulevard, Sacramento, CA 95842. They will do their best to locate a particular title for you.

Other sources for movies on video include—for classic and creaky oldies: Video Yesteryear (Box C, Sandy Hook, CT 06482), Blackhawk Films (1 Old Eagle Brewery, P.O. Box 3990, Davenport, IA 52808), and Shokus Video (P.O. Box 8434, Van Nuys, CA 91409). For foreign films, write to Facets Multimedia (1517 Fullerton Avenue, Chicago, IL 60614). Sinister Cinema (P.O. Box 777, Pacifica, CA 94044) specializes in horror flicks, while Discount Video (P.O. Box 7122, Burbank, CA 91510) and Budget Video (1534 N. Highland, Los Angeles, CA 90028) have inventories that go beyond what is generally available, including those hard-to-find B Westerns. Video West (1901 Paige Place, NE, Albuquerque, NM 87112) offers hundreds of Westerns for collectors.

We welcome comments from our readers but can only answer those that come with a self-addressed stamped envelope. Our mailing address is Video Movie Guide, P.O. Box 189674, Sacramento, CA 95818. Until next year, happy viewing!

INTRODUCTION

In creating the *Video Movie Guide* we have attempted to give you the most up-to-the-minute book, with a clear rating system and easy access to the titles covered. Only movies that had been scheduled for release as videos at the time of publication are included in this edition. You will find movies listed in alphabetical order at the end of the book and then discussed in depth in their respective genres:

- Action/Mystery/Adventure
- Children's Viewing/Family Films
- Comedy
- Drama
- Foreign Language
- Horror/Suspense
- Music/Musicals
- Science-Fiction/Fantasy
- Westerns
- Documentaries

In addition, you will find indexes on pages 1213–1583, organized by directors and performers, as well as a list of films recommended for family viewing.

The rating system runs from five stars to a turkey. We feel a five-star film is a must; a four-star rating means it's well worth watching. The desirability of a film with a lesser rating depends on your liking for a particular type of film or movie star. A turkey by any other name is still a bad movie. If a film is particularly offensive, even though it has a big-name star, we want you to know why. Likewise, if a little-known gem has special attributes, we've done our best to call your attention to it.

Certain kinds of movies have been purposely ignored. For example, we do not feel that hardcore sex films have a place in a book of this kind.

We've included kung fu movies featuring well-known stars such as Bruce Lee and Chuck Norris. However, the all-the-same Chinese imports with lots of bang-pow fist-and-foot action but no plot don't vary much above mediocre in quality. So we've left them out.

We have, however, been more lenient about the inclusion of horror films. Since there is a huge audience for them and they are readily available, we've attepted to include even the lowest of the low to help prevent you from getting stuck with a turkey.

When a film has been rated G, PG, PG-13, R, or X by the Motion Picture Association of America we have noted it. Only theatrically released films distributed after November 1967 were considered by the MPAA ratings board, so we have attempted to indicate the potentially objectionable content in films released before then, as well as in made-for-cable and video-only products. Even the MPAA ratings are confusing at times, so, wherever appropriate, we have explained these as well.

Overall, we feel this is the most practical guide to what's available on video. We hope you agree.

ACKNOWLEDGMENTS

The authors are grateful to a number of wonderful people without whose help *Video Movie Guide* would not be a reality. Cary Nosler, whose radio program on health and nutrition is heard nationwide, planted the seed. Our first editor, Marilyn Abraham, helped define the book's form and nurture its growth, and our current editor, Joe Blades, is a consistent source of support, sage advice, and inspiration.

Our chief contributors, a splendid crew of film critics, movie buffs, and historians, have also contributed greatly to this tome. Allow us to introduce them:

Derrick Bang, a founding contributor, is the film critic for the *Daily Democrat* and a columnist for *Tower Video Collector* magazine.

Jean Fournier is an independent filmmaker and the author of several short stories.

Paul Freeman's writings on movies and movie stars appear frequently in the *San Mateo Times*, *The San Francisco Chronicle*, and *S.F. Weekly* as well as in a number of other publications across the country.

Rich Garrison is a free-lance writer and movie buff whose Old J Cinema revived numerous classics in its time.

Ron Gluckman, now a staff member at the *Sacramento Union*, is a longtime rock-music reviewer and columnist whose work has appeared in a number of papers across the country.

Robert Holman is an actor and movie buff whose life has been devoted to the appreciation of movies.

Phil Hoover and Scott Hunter are horror-film buffs who are covering their field of expertise while keeping a critical eye on the contributions of others in that vein.

Richard Leathers is a free-lance writer from Seattle, one of the—if not *the*—biggest movie towns in the country.

Greg Leis is heard on KNCO radio in Grass Valley, California. In addition to reviewing movies, he has helped to keep the authors sane with his invaluable assistance and research.

Bill McLeod is a life-long movie buff whose work as a film publicist in San Francisco involves him with stars and filmmakers. He sneaks time to write reviews.

Don Norris, formerly of the *Sacramento Union*, is a key writer on the subject of family films.

Dennis Rood is one of the founding contributors to *Video Movie Guide*: a filmmaker, an expert reviewer of classic science-fiction and horror films, and someone who also keeps us up-to-date with research.

Bob Shaw is the film reviewer for KTVU Channel 2's *10 O'Clock News* in San Francisco and a funny guy.

Lisa Smith-Youngs is masterminding our deeper foray into children's programs.

Motion-picture historian and collector Tom Tolley is another founding contributor whose amazing knowledge of movies has been a key factor in shaping the book.

Another chief contributor since the beginning, Robert Young Jr., is currently working on a book about the career of silent comedy star Roscoe "Fatty" Arbuckle. His past work includes writing *Movie Memo*, a short history of the MGM studios, ghostwriting the autobiography of Sessue Hayakawa, and being contributing editor for *American Classic Screen* magazine.

Joining us this year are Harvey Burgess, film critic for the *Charlotte Leader*; Jack Garner, chief film critic for *Gannett News Service*; M. Faust, who has contributed to *Movies on TV* and *Video Digest* magazine; actor–film fan William Glines; and Jim Lane, film critic for *Sacramento News and Review* weekly.

In addition, Ethan Aronson, Tim Eldred, Roy Engoron, Jack Keaton, Nancy Klasky, Bill Smith, Bill Webb, Wendy Welker, and Gary Zilaff have made substantial contributions to *Video Movie Guide* over the years.

Also writing about movies in their fields of expertise: Mike Antonaros, Gayna Lamb-Bang, Dave Barkai, Matias Bombal, John Bridges, Mitchell Cohen, Steve Connell, Mike Fleiss, Del Forsythe, J. Douglas Halford, Scott Howe, Susanne Kocher, Sherry Kramer, John Lidicoat, Linda Logsden, Boyd Magers, Steve Martarano, Rick Meyers, Ed Morrisroe, Paul C. Plain, Don Radovich, Linda Rajotte, Fritz Rodrigues, Vicki and Marc Sazaki, Jack Schwab, Ed Slofkosky, Mark Steensland, Jimmy Summers, Joe Svogar, John Tibbetts, Gerry Watt, Sam Beau Webb, and Ross Woodbury.

Staff members of the *Sacramento Union* contributed capsule reviews to our first edition. Peter Anderson, Alison ApRoberts, Jim Carnes, Cathy Cassinos, Steve Connell, Mark Halverson, Tom Miner, Ana Sandoval, Richard Simon, Lou Thelen, Kevin Valine, and Twila J. Walker added to the foundation on which this book was originally built.

Thanks also to our families for their support and patience. Eileen and Chuck Porter, Hada Martin, Matt and Norma Condo, and Diane Martin have pitched in to help on numerous occasions. Even Francesca Martin has done her bit.

Jerry Cox, Jim Dixon, Jerry Sterchi, Pat Still, Walt von Hauffee, and Bob Wilkins gave us moral support during tough times, and Carol Johnson has been our guardian angel from the beginning. We are also grateful to Wade M. Kent, Gary R. Rose and Robert Schmidt for their voluntary research on our behalf.

Others who made this book possible include Dennis Ambrose, Bob Badgley, Don Besse, Elizabeth A. Bird, Mark Brown, Shannon Byrony, Catherine Coulter, George Davidson, Elise Donner, Phyllis Donovan, Steve Elias, Mike Farrace, Vicki Fischer, Stan Goman, Lisa Green, Hope Hilandera, Paul Hodgkins, Susan Hunt, Steve Johnson, Robert J. Kantor, Heidi

Keller, Jeff Kepley, Bob Kronenberg, Duncan Mandrill, Neil Matsuoka, David Miller, Dr. Patrick O'Donoghue, Amy Parmeter, Jan "Short" Patrick, Patricia Pausner, Virgil and Linda Phillips, Jerry Pompei, Marsha Raphael, Nora Reichard, Walter and Pat Rice, Les Rosen, Erik Sakach, Kris Sazaki, Charles A. Schrade, Mary Scott, Russ Solomon, Jon Souza, Lee Stacy, John Sudman, Cynthia Wright, Janet Wygal, and Lorie Young.

ACTION/MYSTERY/ ADVENTURE

ABDUCTION (1985) ★★½
DIR: Boon Collins. **CAST:** Roberta Weiss, Lawrence King Phillip, Dan Haggerty.
This action flick is not as sleazy as the video box art would have you believe. A backwoods jogger (Roberta Weiss) is abducted by a crazed mountainman and taken back to his cabin. Nothing new, but some good chase scenes. Not rated, but has violence, profanity, and adult subject matter. 1985; 87m.

ABOVE THE LAW ★★★½
DIR: Andrew Davis. **CAST:** Steve Seagal, Pam Grier, Sharon Stone, Daniel Faraldo, Henry Silva.
Director Andrew Davis, who gave credibility to Chuck Norris in *Code of Silence*, teams up with karate expert Steve Seagal (who cowrote the story and coproduced with Davis) for this tough, action-filled cop thriller. Seagal is a Chicago cop and Vietnam veteran who takes on the CIA when he stumbles across a smuggling operation. The result is a strong entry for action buffs. Rated R for lots of violence, profanity, and drug use. 1988; 97m.

ACCESS CODE ★
DIR: Mark Sobel. **CAST:** Martin Landau, Michael Ansara, Macdonald Carey.
Dreadful action film about an Orwellian Big Brother surveillance system that takes over the country's national security complex through the computer systems of the government. A compelling story completely botched by the acting and direction. Not rated, has profanity. 1984; 90m.

ACE DRUMMOND ★★½
DIR: Ford Beebe, Cliff Smith. **CAST:** John King, Jean Rogers, Noah Beery Jr., Lon Chaney Jr.
An archvillain known as The Dragon has thwarted every effort by an international group attempting to establish a round-the-world airline service. Aviation whiz Ace Drummond jumps from the Sunday funnies to the silver screen. Laughable in many respects, this is still a pretty good serial and the only filming of this character's adventures. 1936; B&W; 250m.

ACROSS 110TH STREET ★★★½
DIR: Barry Shear. **CAST:** Anthony Quinn, Yaphet Kotto, Anthony Franciosa, Richard Ward.

This one is a real sleeper! An action-packed, extremely violent film concerning gang warfare between the Mafia and its black counterparts. Entire cast is very good, as are the action scenes. Rated R for violence, language. 1972; 102m.

ACTION IN ARABIA ★★½
DIR: Leonide Moguy. **CAST:** George Sanders, Virginia Bruce, Gene Lockhart, Robert Armstrong, Michael Ansara.

George Sanders fights against time and Nazi agents as he attempts to inform the Allied authorities about German plans for a pact with the Arabs in this wartime romance-adventure. The love of a woman helps to turn the tide for the western powers in this sandy adventure. 1944; B&W; 75m.

ACTION JACKSON ★★
DIR: Craig R. Baxley. **CAST:** Carl Weathers, Craig T. Nelson, Vanity, Sharon Stone, Thomas F. Wilson, Bill Duke.

A maverick cop (Carl Weathers) is on the trail of a corrupt auto tycoon (Craig T. Nelson). Unfortunately, *Action Jackson* is a gabfest punctuated by not-so-hot sex scenes. Even with all the talk, screenwriter Robert Reneau has to introduce a character in the last 20 minutes to explain what is happening. There are a couple of good stunt scenes, though. Rated R for violence, drug use, simulated sex, nudity, and profanity. 1988; 95m.

ADVENTURES OF CAPTAIN FABIAN
DIR: William Marshall. **CAST:** Errol Flynn, Vincent Price, Agnes Moorehead.

The career of Errol Flynn was a roller-coaster ride to be sure, but seldom did it get as low as this turkey. Flynn doesn't have the heart needed to rise above this lackluster swashbuckler. A sad sight for fans of the genre and Errol Flynn alike. 1951; 100m.

ADVENTURES OF CAPTAIN MARVEL, THE ★★★★
DIR: William Witney, John English. **CAST:** Tom Tyler, Frank Coghlan Jr., William Benedict, Louise Currie.

Fawcett Comics' Captain Marvel is splendidly brought to life by Republic Studios in what is generally regarded as the best serial of all time, certainly the best superhero chapterplay ever produced. Sincerely acted by all involved, this serial set the standards for flying stunts for years to come. 1941; B&W; 12 chapters.

ADVENTURES OF DON JUAN, THE ★★★★
DIR: Vincent Sherman. **CAST:** Errol Flynn, Viveca Lindfors, Robert Douglas, Alan Hale, Romney Brent, Ann Rutherford, Robert Warwick, Jerry Austin, Douglas Kennedy, Una O'Connor.

Despite the obvious use of footage from *The Adventures of Robin Hood* and *The Private Lives of Elizabeth and Essex*, this is a solid swashbuckler. Errol Flynn plays the great lover and swordsman of the title with tongue planted firmly in cheek. The years of drinking were beginning to show on his once boyishly handsome face. Yet this is quite appropriate to his portrayal of the famous libertine, who comes to the aid of a queen (Viveca Lindfors) in his later years. 1949; 110m.

ADVENTURES OF ROBIN HOOD, THE ★★★★★
DIR: Michael Curtiz, William Keighley. **CAST:** Errol Flynn, Basil Rathbone, Ian Hunter, Olivia De Havilland, Claude Rains, Alan Hale, Eugene Pallette.

This classic presents Errol Flynn at his swashbuckling best. He is backed up in this color spectacular by a perfect cast of supporting actors. Olivia De Havilland is Maid Marian. Alan Hale and Eugene Pallette are Little John and Friar Tuck. The bad guys are also at their evil best, as played by Basil Rathbone and Claude Rains. Lavish sets and a stirring musical score help place *Robin Hood* among the very best adventure films. 1938; 106m.

ADVENTURES OF SHERLOCK HOLMES, THE ★★★★½
DIR: Alfred Werker. **CAST:** Basil Rathbone, Nigel Bruce, Ida Lupino, George Zucco.

The best of all the Basil Rathbone–Nigel Bruce Sherlock Holmes movies, this pits the great detective against his arch-nemesis, Dr. Moriarty (played by George Zucco). The period setting, atmospheric photography, and the spirited performances of the cast (which includes a young Ida Lupino as Holmes's client) make this a must-see for mystery fans. 1939; B&W; 85m.

ADVENTURES OF SHERLOCK HOLMES, THE (SERIES) ★★★★★
DIR: Paul Annett, John Bruce, David Carson, Ken Grieve, Alan Grint, Derek Marlowe. **CAST:** Jeremy Brett, David Burke.

Jeremy Brett portrays Holmes as twitchy, arrogant, wan, humorless, and often downright rude—in short, everything Conan Doyle's hero was described to be. David Burke's Dr. Watson brings youthful dash and intelligent charm to this most famous of detectives' sidekicks. Each episode in this baker's dozen of cases is impeccably scripted and superbly acted; high points include "The Red-Headed League," "The Speckled Band," "A Scandal in Bohemia" (wherein Holmes meets Irene Adler), and "The Final Problem." Unrated, but contains frank discussions of violence and drug abuse. 1984–1986; 52 minutes each.

ADVENTURES OF SHERLOCK HOLMES, THE (TELEVISION SERIES) ★★★
DIR: Steve Previn, Sheldon Reynolds. **CAST:** Ronald Howard, H. Marion Crawford, Archie Duncan.

Producer-director Sheldon Reynolds generated the world's first Sherlock Holmes television series for the European market, and the 36 episodes hold up reasonably well. Ronald Howard (son of Leslie) is a bit young and overly enthusiastic as Holmes, but H. Marion Crawford makes a solid Watson. The original scripts are much lighter than Conan Doyle's stories, resulting in a finished tone that suggests the cast had a good time. However trivial the mysteries, Howard and Crawford still bring honor to two of fiction's most enduring characters. Suitable for family viewing. 1955; B&W; 52m.

ADVENTURES OF TARTU ★★½
DIR: Harold S. Bucquet. **CAST:** Robert Donat, Valerie Hobson, Glynis Johns, Walter Rilla, Phyllis Morris.

Robert Donat steals the show as a British spy entrusted with the crippling of a poison gas factory behind enemy lines. He is joined in this blend of comedy and suspense by lovely Valerie Hobson and perky Glynis Johns. Nothing really special about this one, but it's fun. 1943; B&W; 103m.

ADVENTURES OF TARZAN, THE ★★½
DIR: Robert Hill. **CAST:** Elmo Lincoln, Louise Lorraine, Percy Pembroke.

Early action star Elmo Lincoln dons a wig for the third time to portray the Lord of the Jungle in this ambitious chapterplay. Lincoln finds himself fighting unscrupulous Bolsheviks, wild animals, a claimant to his family name, and the hordes of the lost city of Opar. Loosely adapted from two Tarzan novels. Silent. 1921; B&W; 15 chapters.

ADVENTURES OF THE FLYING CADETS ★★
DIR: Ray Taylor, Lewis D. Collins. **CAST:** Johnny Downs, Bobby Jordan, Ward Wood, Billy Benedict, Eduardo Ciannelli, Robert Armstrong.

A mysterious figure known as the Black Hangman has located a secret deposit of helium in Africa and plans to sell it to the Nazis. The young Flying Cadets have been falsely implicated in a series of murders and set out to clear their names and bring the traitorous agent to justice. Not a great serial, but even an excess of stock footage is offset by a good cast and some thrilling action sequences. 1943; B&W; 13 chapters.

AFRICA—TEXAS STYLE! ★★
DIR: Andrew Marton. **CAST:** Hugh O'Brian, John Mills, Tom Nardini.

The idea of a movie about cowboys rounding up animals in Africa must have sounded good in theory. But in practice, it's pretty dull going. Even the location photography doesn't help. Give us *Hatari!* any day. 1966; 106m.

AFRICAN RAGE ★★★½
DIR: Peter Collinson. **CAST:** Anthony Quinn, John Phillip Law, Marius Weyers, Sandra Prinsloo, Ken Gampu.

Anthony Quinn is a nurse in an African hospital where a tribal leader is admitted amid heavy security. Quinn's kidnapping of the leader, played with great dignity and warmth by Simon Sabela, takes some very unusual and interesting turns. A surprisingly moving film. Unrated. 1985; 105m.

AFTER THE THIN MAN ★★★★½
DIR: W. S. Van Dyke. **CAST:** William Powell, Myrna Loy, James Stewart, Elissa Landi, Joseph Calleia, Sam Levene.

Second of the six wonderful *Thin Man* films made with William Powell and Myrna Loy, following on the heels of 1934's *The Thin Man*. Powell, Loy, and Asta, the incorrigible terrier, trade quips and drinks in this decent murder mystery. Rising star James Stewart merely adds to the fun. The dialogue is fast-paced and quite droll, and Powell and Loy demonstrate a chemistry that explains the dozen hits they had together. Not to be missed. Followed, in 1939, by *Another Thin Man*. 1936; B&W; 113m.

AGAINST ALL FLAGS ★★★
DIR: George Sherman. **CAST:** Errol Flynn, Maureen O'Hara, Anthony Quinn, Mildred Natwick.

Though Errol Flynn's energy and attractiveness had seriously ebbed by this time, he still possessed the panache to make this simple swashbuckler fun to watch. He portrays a dashing British soldier who infiltrates a pirate stronghold, pausing only to romance the fiery Maureen O'Hara. 1952; 83m.

AGENT ON ICE ★★★½
DIR: Clark Worswick. **CAST:** Tom Ormeny, Clifford David, Louis Pastore, Matt Craven.

This exciting action film features Tom Ormeny as John Pope, a former CIA agent who has become a target for both the CIA and the Mafia. Clifford David plays the corrupt CIA official who has been laundering money for Mafia leader Frank Matera (Louis Pastore). Rated R for violence and obscenities. 1985; 96m.

AIR FORCE ★★★★
DIR: Howard Hawks. **CAST:** John Garfield, John Ridgely, Gig Young, Charles Drake, Harry Carey, Arthur Kennedy, George Tobias.

This is essentially wartime propaganda about a flying fortress and its crew taking on the enemy at Pearl Harbor, Manila, and the Coral Sea. However, the direction by Howard Hawks puts the film head and shoulders above similar motion pictures. 1943; B&W; 124m.

AL CAPONE ★★★½
DIR: Richard Wilson. **CAST:** Rod Steiger, Fay Spain, James Gregory, Martin Balsam, Nehemiah Persoff.

Rod Steiger is mesmerizing as Al Capone in this perceptive portrait of the legendary Chicago gangster. The film covers Capone's life from his first job for seventy-five dollars a week to his ultimate fate behind prison walls. Filmed in black and white with a documentary-style narrative, which heighten the quality of this film. The supporting cast—Fay Spain in particular—is just right. 1959; B&W; 104m.

ALFRED HITCHCOCK PRESENTS (TELEVISION SERIES) ★★★★
DIR: Alfred Hitchcock. **CAST:** Barbara Bel Geddes, Tom Ewell, John Williams.
This classic anthology series featured a broad range of mystery and suspense. First-rate casts added to the fun. During breaks, Alfred Hitchcock himself drolly commented on the action. One of the four episodes on the initial video release, "Lamb to the Slaughter," stars Barbara Bel Geddes in a deliciously ironic tale of murder. Black humor and surprise endings were trademarks of the show. 1955–1962; 120m.

ALICE TO NOWHERE ★★★★
DIR: John Power. **CAST:** John Waters, Steve Jacobs, Rosie Jones, Ruth Cracknell.
A bungled jewel heist sets in motion this fast-paced adventure. A nurse assigned to a job in central Australia is unknowingly carrying the stolen jewels. The action never lets up as she is pursued by the robbers to the outback. Made for Australian television and shown on independent stations in the United States. 1986; 210m.

ALIEN FROM L.A. ★★½
DIR: Albert Pyun. **CAST:** Kathy Ireland, Linda Kerridge, William R. Moses.
When a nerdy valley girl goes in search of her archaeologist father, she embarks on the adventure of her life. She follows her father's trail down a bottomless pit to the center of the Earth, where she finds the sunken city of Atlantis. A paranoid culture, the Atlanteans brand her an alien and send death squads to apprehend her. Although this is a low-budget film, it has enough action and humor to be appropriate for most family members. Rated PG for light violence. 1983; 88m.

ALL QUIET ON THE WESTERN FRONT ★★★★★
DIR: Lewis Milestone. **CAST:** Lew Ayres, Louis Wolheim.
Despite some dated moments and an "old movie" look, this film still stands as a powerful statement against war and man's inhumanity to man. Lew Ayres and Louis Wolheim star in this story, set during World War I, which follows several young men into battle, examining their disillusionment and eventual death. 1930; B&W; 130m.

ALLAN QUATERMAIN AND THE LOST CITY OF GOLD
DIR: Gary Nelson. **CAST:** Richard Chamberlain, Sharon Stone, James Earl Jones, Henry Silva, Robert Donner, Cassandra Peterson.
As if they weren't bad enough in the original, Richard Chamberlain and Sharon Stone reprise their roles from the tongue-in-beak turkey, *King Solomon's Mines*. This equally awful sequel also wastes the considerable talents of James Earl Jones. Rated PG. 1987; 95m.

ALOHA, BOBBY AND ROSE ★★
DIR: Floyd Mutrux. **CAST:** Paul LeMat, Dianne Hull, Tim McIntire.
B-movie treatment of two kids on the lam for a murder they didn't mean to commit. Paul LeMat's first starring role after *American Graffiti*. He is interesting, but the film is downbeat and uninspired. Rated R. 1975; 88m.

AMAZING SPIDERMAN, THE ★★
DIR: E. W. Swackhamer. **CAST:** Nicholas Hammond, David White, Michael Pataki, Hilly Hicks, Lisa Eilbacher.
Marvel Comics's popular character makes his live-action debut in this made-for-TV adaptation that involves Spidey's origin and a villain who uses mind control to force people to rob banks. Although fairly well-acted, it's missing many of the wisecracking elements that made the comic-book character popular. The production values and special effects are decent, though, especially the wall-crawling

scenes. Not rated, but appropriate for all ages. 1977; 93m.

AMAZONS
DIR: Alex Sessa. **CAST:** Windsor Taylor Randolph, Penelope Reed, Joseph Whipp, Danitza Kingsley, Willie Nelson.
The ridiculousness of the fight scenes in this film rivals that of the worst kung-fu flick. Two Amazon warriors (Windsor Taylor Randolph and Penelope Reed) must recover an ancient sword to defeat the evil Kalungo (Joseph Whipp), who is threatening their people. This silly film is rated R for nudity, violence, and sex. 1986; 76m.

AMBUSHERS, THE ★
DIR: Henry Levin. **CAST:** Dean Martin, Senta Berger, Janice Rule, James Gregory, Albert Salmi, Kurt Kasznar, Beverly Adams.
Only hardcore Dean Martin fans will want to bother with this one, the third movie in the Matt Helm secret-agent series. The weak story has America's first flying saucer in danger of being sabotaged by enemy agents. 1968; 102m.

AMERICAN JUSTICE ★★½
DIR: Gary Grillo. **CAST:** Gerald McRaney, Jameson Parker, Wilford Brimley.
Small-town cops near the Mexican border become involved in an illegal alien/slavery ring. It's brutal and violent and probably truer than you'd think. A fair attempt by TV's *Simon and Simon* to work together in different roles. Rated R for violence, sex, and language. 1986; 79m.

AMERICAN NINJA ★
DIR: Sam Firstenberg. **CAST:** Michael Dudikoff, Guich Koock, Judie Aronson, Steve James.
Dumb, dumb comic book–style adventure film about an American-soldier (Michael Dudikoff) who single-handedly takes on an army of martial arts mercenaries in the Philippines. Chuck Norris does it better. Rated R for profanity and violence. 1985; 95m.

AMERICAN NINJA II ★★
DIR: Sam Firstenberg. **CAST:** Michael Dudikoff, Steve James, Larry Poindexter, Gary Conway.
Michael Dudikoff continues to set new standards for nonacting in this mindless but enjoyable-for-fans martial arts movie. Dudikoff and Steve James, who is as watchable as ever, play army rangers who come to the aid of the marines and wipe out a passel of heroin dealers. Rated R. 1987; 96m.

AMERICAN NINJA III
DIR: Cedric Syndstrom. **CAST:** Steve James, David Bradley, Marjoe Gortner.
Martial-arts fans will be thoroughly disappointed with the latest entry in the *American Ninja* series. Michael Dudikoff is replaced by David Bradley, a real no-talent. Comic-book movie filled with cartoon characters. Rated R for violence and profanity. 1989; 89m.

AMERICAN ROULETTE ★★
DIR: Maurice Hatton. **CAST:** Andy Garcia, Kitty Aldridge, Robert Stephens.
Political thriller about a deposed president (Andy Garcia) of a South American nation, living in exile in London. The ex-president's life is constantly in jeopardy from Latin death squads—and the CIA and KGB play a tug of war with his loyalities. Robert Stephens gives a fine performance as a sleazy British agent. Light on action, long on talk, with a sappy ending. Rated R. 1988; 102m.

AMSTERDAM KILL, THE ★
DIR: Robert Clouse. **CAST:** Robert Mitchum, Bradford Dillman, Richard Egan, Leslie Nielsen, Keye Luke.
Fresh from his successes in *Farewell My Lovely* and *The Yakuza*, Robert Mitchum dived into this dud about an international drug conspiracy. He's a retired narcotics agent who comes to the aid of an old buddy accused of smuggling. It sounds exciting, but it's terribly dull. Rated R. 1977; 90m.

AND THEN YOU DIE ★★★★
DIR: Francis Mankiewicz. **CAST:** Kenneth Welsh, R. H. Thompson, Wayne Robson, Tom Harvey, George Bloomfield, Graeme Campbell.

Canadian version of *The Long Good Friday*. Kenneth Welsh is Eddie Griffin, drug czar for Canada's coke freaks. His kingdom starts unraveling around him after the Mafia don in his area is murdered. Eddie gets caught in a squeeze play between the don's successor, an up-and-coming coke dealer, and the police. The film grabs you right from the opening frame and keeps you guessing right up to the final scene. 1987; 115m.

ANDERSON TAPES, THE ★★★★
DIR: Sidney Lumet. **CAST:** Sean Connery, Dyan Cannon, Martin Balsam, Ralph Meeker, Margaret Hamilton.

Sean Connery is perfectly cast in this exciting film about an ex-con under surveillance who wants to pull off the Big Heist. Slickly done, with tight editing and direction to keep the viewer totally involved, it holds up extremely well on video. Rated PG. 1972; 98m.

ANGEL ★
DIR: Robert Vincent O'Neil. **CAST:** Cliff Gorman, Susan Tyrrell, Dick Shawn, Donna Wilkes.

Bad, low-budget flick about a 15-year-old who moonlights as a Hollywood Boulevard hooker and is menaced by a psychotic killer. Rated R for nudity, violence, suggested sex, and profanity. 1983; 94m.

ANGEL OF DEATH
DIR: A. Frank Drew White. **CAST:** Susan Andrews, Howard Vernon.

Even among the lowly subgenre of Nazi revival movies, this rates near the bottom of the list. (Okay, it's better than *They Saved Hitler's Brain*, though not by much). Dr. Josef Mengele is alive and well in South America, trying to revive the Third Reich through artificial insemination. Rated R for violence, profanity. 1986; 90m.

ANGEL OF H.E.A.T. ★
DIR: Myrl A. Schreibman. **CAST:** Marilyn Chambers, Dan Jesse, Mary Woronov, Stephen Johnson.

Marilyn Chambers appears as Angel Harmony, head of Harmony's Elite Attack Team...which should be renamed Hardly Ever Any Talent. Not enough sex and skin for the hardcore crowd, and not enough plot, good acting, or production values for the spy flick lovers. Rated R. 1982; 93m.

ANGELS DIE HARD ★★
DIR: Richard Compton. **CAST:** William Smith, Tom Baker, R. G. Armstrong, Dan Haggerty.

The bikers turn out to help a community during a mining disaster. Less ridiculous than most of its predecessors and contemporaries. Look for Dan Haggerty in an early role. Violence; adult situations. Rated R. 1970; 86m.

ANGELS WITH DIRTY FACES ★★★★½
DIR: Michael Curtiz. **CAST:** James Cagney, Pat O'Brien, Humphrey Bogart, Ann Sheridan, George Bancroft, Bobby Jordan.

This is thoroughly enjoyable entertainment. The plot is that old Hollywood standby about two childhood friends, the one who goes bad (James Cagney) and the other who follows the right path (Pat O'Brien, as the priest), and the conflict between them. Yet, as directed by Warner Bros.' stalwart Michael Curtiz, it often seems surprisingly fresh. 1938; B&W; 97m.

ANGKOR: CAMBODIA EXPRESS ★
DIR: Alex King. **CAST:** Robert Walker Jr., Christopher George, Woody Strode, Nancy Kwan.

In this subpar variation on *The Killing Fields*, Robert Walker Jr. plays an American journalist who left his girlfriend (Nancy Kwan) behind in Cambodia as its government fell to the Khmer Rouge and returns to Cambodia to bring her out. 1985; 86m.

ANNIHILATORS, THE ★
DIR: Charles E. Sellier Jr. **CAST:** Christopher Stone, Andy Wood, Lawrence Hilton-Jacobs, Jim Antonio, Gerrit Graham.
Another film in which Vietnam veterans reunite, organize a vigilante group, annihilate the sadistic gangs, and return to their normal lives. The only difference this time is that not all of the "heroes" survive. Christopher Stone stars in the Chuck Norris–style lead role. Rated R for grotesque violence and language. 1985; 87m.

ANOTHER THIN MAN ★★★★
DIR: W. S. Van Dyke. **CAST:** William Powell, Myrna Loy, Virginia Grey, Otto Kruger, C. Aubrey Smith, Ruth Hussey, Nat Pendleton, Tom Neal.
Nick and Nora Charles (William Powell and Myrna Loy) contend with a gentleman who dreams about catastrophes before they take place. As usual, the plot is secondary to the interaction between the two leads. Follows *After the Thin Man* (1936) and precedes *Shadow of the Thin Man* (1941). Suitable for family viewing. 1939; B&W; 105m.

ANZIO ★★
DIR: Edward Dmytryk. **CAST:** Robert Mitchum, Peter Falk, Robert Ryan, Earl Holliman, Arthur Kennedy, Patrick Magee, Mark Damon, Reni Santoni.
Would-be blockbuster about the Allied invasion of Italy during World War II doesn't make the grade as either history or spectacle and ultimately wastes the talents of a great cast and an often inspired director. This mediocre big-budget bust never pulls things together enough to rise above endless shots of troops, tanks, smoke, and amphibious landings. 1968; 117m.

APOCALYPSE NOW ★★★★
DIR: Francis Ford Coppola. **CAST:** Marlon Brando, Martin Sheen, Robert Duvall, Harrison Ford.
An exceptional war film in every sense, this work pulsates with artistic ambition. It reaches for truth, struggles for greatness—and almost succeeds. The central character, Captain Willard (Martin Sheen), tells the story of his danger-filled journey toward a fateful meeting with a man named Kurtz, a highly decorated officer who the army contends has gone mad. Rated R. 1979; 153m.

APPOINTMENT IN HONDURAS ★★½
DIR: Jacques Tourneur. **CAST:** Glenn Ford, Ann Sheridan, Zachary Scott, Jack Elam.
Good cast helps this far-fetched story of an idealistic American (Glenn Ford) helping local misfits free their country from political tyranny. The actors do their best, but rather silly material gets in their way. Plot and dialogue are somewhat laughable. Ann Sheridan is highly watchable, as usual. 1953; 79m.

APPOINTMENT WITH DEATH ★★
DIR: Michael Winner. **CAST:** Peter Ustinov, Lauren Bacall, Carrie Fisher, John Gielgud, Piper Laurie, Hayley Mills, Jenny Seagrove, David Soul, Amber Bezer.
Standard Agatha Christie mystery made boring by poor editing and pedestrian direction. Peter Ustinov is Hercule Poirot again (bringing competency if not vivaciousness to the part), trying to unravel a murder at an archaeological dig in the Holy Land. Rated PG for adult situations. 1988; 102m.

APPOINTMENT WITH FEAR
DIR: Alan Smithee. **CAST:** Michelle Little, Michael Wyle, Kerry Remsen, Douglas Rowe, Garrick Dowhen.
Cancel this appointment! All there is here is bad acting, gratuitous nudity, and a wigged-out Egyptian king driving around Los Angeles in a Ford van. Not rated, but contains sex, nudity, and profanity. 1987; 96m.

ARABESQUE ★★★
DIR: Stanley Donen. **CAST:** Gregory Peck, Sophia Loren, Kieron Moore,

Alan Badel, Carl Duering, George Coulouris.

Fast-paced espionage adventure about college professor Gregory Peck and his nightmarish involvement with death-dealing secret agents is an entertaining "chase" film and a conscious effort to capture the "now" look of the 1960s. Beautiful Sophia Loren keeps Peck company. 1966; 118m.

ARE YOU IN THE HOUSE ALONE? ★★½

DIR: Walter Grauman. **CAST:** Kathleen Beller, Blythe Danner, Tony Bill, Robin Mattson, Dennis Quaid, Ellen Travolta, Tricia O'Neil.

In this substandard made-for-television treatment of Richard Peck's Edgar Award–winning mystery novel, a beautiful high-school student becomes the target of a campaign of terror that eventually leads to a sexual attack and mental torture. It's been done better before, but Kathleen Beller is exceptional as the heroine. 1978; 96m.

ARIZONA HEAT ★

DIR: John G. Thomas. **CAST:** Michael Parks, Denise Crosby, Hugh Farrington.

Run-of-the-mill cop story about a tough but good policeman (Michael Parks) inheriting a female partner (Denise Crosby) and tracking down a crazed cop-killer. Rated R for language, violence, and sex. 1988; 91m.

ARK OF THE SUN GOD... TEMPLE OF HELL, THE

DIR: Anthony M. Dawson. **CAST:** David Warbeck, John Steiner, Susie Sudlow, Alan Collins.

A big-time thief is commissioned to steal an ancient artifact from an ark buried thousands of years ago. Not only are the title and story a ripoff of *Raiders of the Lost Ark*, we are also subjected to anti-Arabic sentiment and a hero who mutters pseudocool 007-style wisecracks. Not rated; violence. 1986; 92m.

ARMED RESPONSE ★½

DIR: Fred Olen Ray. **CAST:** David Carradine, Lee Van Cleef, Mako, Lois Hamilton, Ross Hagen, Brent Huff, Laurene Landon.

In Los Angeles's Chinatown, a Vietnam vet and his family fight a Japanese mob for possession of a jade statue. *Armed Response* starts out parodying the action-adventure genre, but loses its sense of humor in the middle and bogs down for too long, becoming boring and jingoistic. Rated R. 1986; 86m.

AROUND THE WORLD UNDER THE SEA ★★

DIR: Andrew Marton. **CAST:** Lloyd Bridges, Shirley Eaton, David McCallum, Brian Kelly, Keenan Wynn, Marshall Thompson.

Volcanoes, a giant eel, a submarine, scuba gear, and a quarrel over who's in charge make this lackluster, harmless viewing. Shirley Eaton was in *Goldfinger*, in case you're a James Bond fan. 1966; 117m.

ARREST BULLDOG DRUMMOND ★★½

DIR: James Hogan. **CAST:** John Howard, Heather Angel, George Zucco, H. B. Warner, E. E. Clive, Reginald Denny, John Sutton.

Bulldog Drummond and his cronies pursue a murderer to a tropical island where he has taken refuge along with a death ray he has stolen. Fifth in the popular series featuring John Howard. Available on a double-bill video with *Bulldog Drummond in Africa*. 1938; B&W; 57m.

ARSON INC. ★½

DIR: William Berke. **CAST:** Robert Lowery, Anne Gwynne.

Robert Lowery is an arson-squad investigator and Anne Gwynne is his romantic interest. They perform capably, but the script is at best predictable, and stock footage of fires is quite evident. Inferior. 1950; B&W; 64m.

ASHANTI ★★½
DIR: Richard Fleischer. **CAST:** Michael Caine, Peter Ustinov, Beverly Johnson, William Holden, Omar Sharif, Rex Harrison.

A shopping trip turns into a tale of horror when the black wife (Beverly Johnson) of a white doctor (Michael Caine) in Africa is kidnapped and turned over to a slave trader (Peter Ustinov). Thus begins a fairly exciting chase across various exotic locales. Rated R. 1979; 118m.

ASSASSINATION ★
DIR: Peter R. Hunt. **CAST:** Charles Bronson, Jill Ireland, Stephen Elliott, Jan Gan Boyd, Randy Brooks, Michael Ansara.

In this predictable, poorly written action flick, Charles Bronson plays a seasoned secret service agent who is called upon to guard the first lady (Jill Ireland) after several mysterious "accidents" have nearly taken her life. Because the president is impotent, the agent and the lady fall in love. Rated R for profanity and violence. 1987; 105m.

ASSAULT OF THE REBEL GIRLS (A.K.A. CUBAN REBEL GIRLS)
DIR: Barry Mahon. **CAST:** Errol Flynn, Beverly Aadland, John McKay.

When dealing with a cinema legend like Errol Flynn, there's a tendency to soft-pedal and glamorize his weaker vehicles. In truth, Flynn's last film is a cheaply made bargain-basement production. This sad exit for a great star got some low-octane mileage out of Flynn's visit to Cuba and the mild topicality of Castro's overthrow of the dictator Batista, but only Flynn completists will be able to finish this one. 1959; B&W; 68m.

ASSAULT ON AGATHON ★
DIR: Laslo Benedek. **CAST:** Nico Minardos, Nina Van Pallandt, John Woodvine, Marianne Faithfull.

While investigating a series of robberies of Greek banks, a British and an American Interpol agent uncover a plot by a World War II underground leader to start a new revolution. The writers and director tried to cram too much story into an hour and a half. Nice Greek scenery, though. 1976; 96m.

ASSAULT ON PRECINCT 13 ★★★★½
DIR: John Carpenter. **CAST:** Austin Stoker, Laurie Zimmer, Tony Burton, Nancy Loomis, Darwin Joston.

Here's director John Carpenter's riveting movie about a nearly deserted L.A. police station that finds itself under siege by a youth gang. It's a modern-day version of Howard Hawks's *Rio Bravo*, with exceptional performances by its entire cast. Rated R. 1976; 90m.

ASSISI UNDERGROUND, THE ★★
DIR: Alexander Ramati. **CAST:** Ben Cross, James Mason, Irene Papas, Maximilian Schell, Karl Heinz Hackl, Delia Boccardo, Edmund Purdom.

There is very little suspense in this melodrama tracing the activities of a Franciscan monastery as part of the Jewish liberation network in World War II Italy. Ben Cross struggles valiantly to bring some life to this dreary fact-based tale; hard work considering the poor dialogue and unrealistic behavior of the Jews he is trying to help escape from Europe. Rated PG. 1985; 115m.

AT BERTRAM'S HOTEL ★★★★½
DIR: Mary McMurray. **CAST:** Joan Hickson, Caroline Blakiston, Helena Michell, George Baker, James Cossins, Preston Lockwood, Joan Greenwood.

Miss Marple (Joan Hickson) takes a London vacation, courtesy of her nephew Raymond, in this superior installment of the Agatha Christie series. Miss Marple encounters some old friends during her stay at Bertram's Hotel, where she discovers that surface appearances are just a little too good to be true. Costumes and set design are luxurious. Unrated; suitable for family viewing. 1986; 102m.

AT SWORD'S POINT ★★★
DIR: Lewis Allen. **CAST:** Cornel Wilde, Maureen O'Hara, Alan Hale Jr., Dan O'Herlihy, Blanche Yurka, Robert Douglas.

Colorful story of the offspring of the Three Musketeers joining forces to rid the country of villainy is familiar but harmless. Cornel Wilde displays his Olympic-caliber skill with the sword and Maureen O'Hara is as beautiful and feisty as ever, but this time she backs it up with swordplay. 1952; 81m.

ATOM MAN VS. SUPERMAN ★★
DIR: Spencer Gordon Bennet. **CAST:** Kirk Alyn, Noel Neill, Lyle Talbot, Tommy Bond, Pierre Watkin, Jack Ingram, Don Harvey, Terry Frost.

The second and final serial based on the adventures of Superman reunites most of the principal cast from the first chapterplay and throws in the Man of Steel's nemesis, Lex Luthor, for good measure. Competently played by the talented and often-seen Lyle Talbot, Luthor is out to blackmail Metropolis by threatening the city with destruction from a variety of sources including the inevitable disintegrating machine. 1950; B&W; 15 chapters.

ATTACK FORCE Z ★★
DIR: Tim Burstall. **CAST:** John Phillip Law, Sam Neill, Mel Gibson, Chris Haywood, John Waters.

Okay Australian film concerning a group of commandos on a secret mission against the Japanese in World War II. Most notable is a young Mel Gibson as the leader of the commandos. Unrated. 1981; 84m.

AVALANCHE
DIR: Corey Allen. **CAST:** Rock Hudson, Mia Farrow, Robert Forster, Jeanette Nolan.

It's movies like this bomb that gave disaster pictures a bad name. Rock Hudson, Mia Farrow, Robert Forster, and Jeanette Nolan are among those fooling around and fighting before the catastrophe of the title. Rated PG. 1978; 91m.

AVENGERS, THE (TELEVISION SERIES) ★★★½
DIR: Don Leaver, Robert Day. **CAST:** Patrick Macnee, Diana Rigg, Linda Thorson.

Patrick Macnee stars in the finest British secret agent series ever as quintessential agent, John Steed. Diana Rigg as the rugged, leather-garbed Emma Peel was followed by Linda Thorson's Tara King for the program's final year. Charming, witty, and absolutely ageless, this program will remain loved for generations to come. Suitable for family viewing. 1965–1969; 52 minutes each.

AVENGING ANGEL
DIR: Robert Vincent O'Neil. **CAST:** Betsy Russell, Rory Calhoun, Susan Tyrrell, Ossie Davis.

Remember *Angel*, the high-school student who doubled as a Hollywood hooker? Well, she's back. Only this time our heroine is out to avenge the murder of the cop who acted as her mentor. Dumb. Rated R for nudity, profanity, and violence. 1985; 96m.

AVENGING FORCE ★★★
DIR: Sam Firstenberg. **CAST:** Michael Dudikoff, Steve James, James Booth, Bill Wallace, John P. Ryan, Marc Alaimo.

A better-than-average action-adventure flick about a former secret service agent forced out of retirement when his best friend, a black southern politician, is involved in an assassination attempt in which his son is killed. The acting is admittedly dry, but the action is top-notch, with plenty of opportunity to cheer for the hero. Rated R for violence and profanity. 1986; 104m.

AWAY ALL BOATS ★½
DIR: Joseph Pevney. **CAST:** Jeff Chandler, George Nader, Julie Adams, Lex Barker, Keith Andes, Richard Boone, Jock Mahoney, William Reynolds, Charles McGraw, John McIntire.

In this lackluster war film, Jeff Chandler plays Captain Hanks, commander of an attack transport unit in the South Pacific during World War II. We follow Chandler and his men as they train for heavy combat awaiting them. 1956; 114m.

BACK TO BATAAN ★★★
DIR: Edward Dmytryk. **CAST:** John Wayne, Anthony Quinn, Richard Loo, Beulah Bondi.
A fun World War II action film with John Wayne at his two-fisted best. Good script, photography, acting, and battle action make this film well worth your time. Video quality is quite good. 1945; B&W;.95m.

BACKLASH ★★★
DIR: Bill Bennett. **CAST:** David Argue, Gia Carides, Lydia Miller, Brian Syron.
Subtle story of two cops (David Argue, Lydia Miller) escorting an accused murderess (Gia Carides) across the Australian desert. Argue turns in a fine performance as an embittered, abrasive policeman. Rated R for language and nudity. 1988; 85m.

BAD GUYS ★★
DIR: Joel Silberg. **CAST:** Adam Baldwin, Mike Jolly, Michelle Nicastro, Ruth Buzzi, Sgt. Slaughter.
A somewhat contrived story about two police officers who are suspended indefinitely, without pay. After having no luck with interim jobs, they decide to become professional wrestlers. Rated PG. 1985; 87m.

BADGE 373 ★½
DIR: Howard W. Koch. **CAST:** Robert Duvall, Verna Bloom, Eddie Egan, Henry Darrow.
This very low-rent police drama casts Robert Duvall as a cop out to nab his partner's killer and break the mob in New York City. Pretty routine stuff is thrown together in an even more routine fashion. For hard-core fans of the genre only. Rated R. 1973; 116m.

BAND OF THE HAND ★★½
DIR: Paul Michael Glaser. **CAST:** Stephen Lang, Michael Carmine, Lauren Holly, John Cameron Mitchell, Daniele Quinn, Leon Robinson, James Remar.
A Vietnam vet (Stephen Lang) takes a group of incorrigible Florida teens and turns them into an anti-drug squad. That's right, it's *Mod Squad* for the 1980s and just as silly as it sounds. Rated R for profanity, brief nudity, cocaine use, and violence. 1986; 109m.

BARE KNUCKLES ★★★
DIR: Don Edmonds. **CAST:** Robert Viharo, Sherry Jackson, Michael Heit, Gloria Hendry, John Daniels.
A fun martial arts thriller about a modern-day bounty hunter on the trail of a vicious killer stalking women on the streets of the city. Rated R for brief nudity, violence, and adult language. 1984; 90m.

BAT 21 ★★★★
DIR: Peter Markle. **CAST:** Gene Hackman, Danny Glover, Jerry Reed, David Marshall Grant.
In a typically effective performance, Gene Hackman is a military mastermind who is shot down during a reconnaissance mission in Vietnam, where he is trapped behind enemy lines. It's up to pilot Danny Glover to keep Hackman safe and sane until he can be rescued. Fine telling of a heroic, true-life story guarantees to keep you on the edge of your seat. Rated R for violence and profanity. 1988; 105m.

BATAAN ★★★★½
DIR: Tay Garnett. **CAST:** Robert Taylor, George Murphy, Thomas Mitchell, Lloyd Nolan, Robert Walker, Desi Arnaz Sr., Barry Nelson.
One of the best films about World War II chronicles the exploits of an army patrol attempting to stall the Japanese onslaught in the Philippines. 1943; B&W; 114m.

BATMAN (1989) ★★★½
DIR: Tim Burton. **CAST:** Jack Nicholson, Michael Keaton, Kim Basinger, Pat Hingle, Billy Dee Williams, Jack

Palance, Robert Wuhl, Michael Gough.

So much of *Batman* is exciting, darkly funny and awe-inspiring that one cannot help being disappointed when this ambitious production all but collapses under its own weight in the last half hour. Still, there's much to enjoy in Jack Nicholson's bizarre, over-the-top performance as the villainous Joker, Michael Keaton's underplayed but effective dual role as millionaire-playboy Bruce Wayne and Batman, and the spectacular, *Blade Runner*-like sets. Director Tim Burton may not have known when to stop, but no one can say he didn't give it his all. Rated PG-13 for profanity and violence. 1989; 130m.

BATTLE BENEATH THE EARTH ★★½

DIR: Montgomery Tully. **CAST:** Kerwin Mathews, Robert Ayres, Martin Benson, Viviane Ventura, Bessie Love.

Stalwart Kerwin Mathews leads the fight against the Chinese hordes who intend to invade the United States via underground tunnels. Pretty good adventure fantasy in the comic book/pulp magazine tradition. 1967; 91m.

BATTLE CRY ★★★

DIR: Raoul Walsh. **CAST:** Van Heflin, Tab Hunter, Dorothy Malone, Anne Francis.

A platoon of marines is followed into battle during World War II. The conflicts they face on the islands of the Pacific are contrasted to the emotional conflicts faced by their girlfriends at home. All in all, it is a successful piece of wartime fluff. 1955; 149m.

BATTLE FORCE ★★

DIR: Humphrey Longon. **CAST:** Henry Fonda, John Huston, Stacy Keach, Helmut Berger, Samantha Eggar.

The effect of war on the lives and destinies of two families, one American, the other German, is chronicled in this passable World War II adventure. 1976; 92m.

BATTLE HELL ★★

DIR: Michael Anderson. **CAST:** Richard Todd, Akim Tamiroff, Keye Luke, William Hartnell, Donald Houston, Robert Urquhart, James Kenney.

More British stiff upper lip in this tale of the H.M.S. *Amethyst* battling the communist Chinese on the Yangtze River. Pretty standard war flick, overly long, but with some good battle footage. Not rated: some violence. 1956; 112m.

BATTLE OF AUSTERLITZ, THE ★

DIR: Abel Gance. **CAST:** Claudia Cardinale, Leslie Caron, Vittorio De Sica, Orson Welles.

This attempt to re-create the epic battle of the Napoleonic wars is slow, dull, abysmally dubbed, and generally uninspired. Too bad because writer-director Abel Gance, in 1927, created a masterpiece dealing with this same era, the superb silent *Napoleon*. 1960; 123m.

BATTLE OF BRITAIN ★★½

DIR: Guy Hamilton. **CAST:** Michael Caine, Ralph Richardson, Robert Shaw, Trevor Howard, Susannah York, Curt Jurgens, Edward Fox, Kenneth More, Christopher Plummer, Laurence Olivier, Harry Andrews, Nigel Patrick.

It's a shame that a film that has a $12 million budget, a cast of characters straight from the British Who's Who of film and stage, great aerial photography, and a subject matter that deals with a vital period of British history could not have been better than this semi-epic. We see only occasional glimpses of the great actors plus the aerial shots and that's it. 1969; 132m.

BATTLE OF EL ALAMEIN, THE ★★★

DIR: Calvin Jackson Padget. **CAST:** Michael Rennie, Robert Hossein, Frederick Stafford, Ettore Manni, George Hilton.

A re-creation of the famous twelve-day 1942 turning point clash between the artillery, tanks, and infantry of the British Eighth Army under General

Montgomery and the German army's fabled Afrika Korps commanded by Field Marshal Rommel in the windswept Libyan Desert southwest of Alexandria. We know the outcome, but getting there makes for exciting watching. Rated PG. 1968; 96m.

BATTLE OF THE BULGE ★★
DIR: Ken Annakin. **CAST:** Henry Fonda, Robert Shaw, Robert Ryan, Dana Andrews.
This is a fairly decent war film. It has solid acting and exciting battle sequences but suffers on video for two reasons: the small screen hurts the epic scale and 23 minutes are cut from the original print, with some important footage missing. 1965; 140m.

BATTLE OF THE COMMANDOS ★
DIR: Umberto Lenzi. **CAST:** Jack Palance, Curt Jurgens, Tomas Hunter, Diana Largo, Wolfgang Preiss.
Jack Palance stars in this boring World War II adventure of commandos attacking the Germans on the eve of D-Day. Lots of phony battle scenes, bad acting, and a poor script all add up to a big bomb. 1969; 94m.

BEAST, THE ★★
DIR: Kevin Reynolds. **CAST:** Steven Bauer, George Dzundza.
A clichéd war film, unique only for its adversaries: Soviet soldiers and Afghan rebels in the deserts of Afghanistan. Though the Afghans speak subtitled native language, the Soviets speak in slang-laced Americanized English. They sound more like California surfers than Russian soldiers. Rated R, with profanity and violence. 1988; 109m.

BEAU GESTE ★★★★½
DIR: William Wellman. **CAST:** Gary Cooper, Robert Preston, Ray Milland, Brian Donlevy, J. Carrol Naish, Susan Hayward, Broderick Crawford, Albert Dekker, Donald O'Connor, James Stephenson.
Gary Cooper fulfilled every idealistic boy's dream of honor, sacrifice, and brotherly love in this splendid adaptation of P. C. Wren's adventure classic. Director William Wellman took a handpicked cast to the desert wasteland near Yuma, Arizona, and painstakingly re-created the arid setting of the world's most famous Foreign Legion adventure using the silent-film version as his blueprint. The action is brisk, the characters are unforgettable. 1939; B&W; 114m.

BEDROOM EYES ★★★
DIR: William Fruet. **CAST:** Kenneth Gilman, Dayle Haddon, Barbara Law, Christine Cattel.
A young stockbroker peers into a window one evening and sees a woman so tantalizing he feels compelled to return every night. When the object of his voyeurism is murdered, the man must try to prove his innocence, with the help of a female psychologist. A silly but undeniably erotic mystery. 1986; 90m.

BEHIND THE RISING SUN ★★½
DIR: Edward Dmytryk. **CAST:** Margo, Tom Neal, J. Carrol Naish, Robert Ryan.
The versatile J. Carrol Naish plays a Japanese publisher whose political views bring him into conflict with his son, educated in the U.S. It all takes place when Japan was fighting China, not long before World War II. 1943; B&W; 89m.

BELARUS FILE, THE ★★½
DIR: Robert Markowitz. **CAST:** Telly Savalas, Suzanne Pleshette, Max von Sydow, Herbert Berghof, George Savalas.
Telly Savalas returns as the lollipop-sucking police detective Kojak in this made-for-television movie about a maniac murdering Russian survivors of a Nazi concentration camp. For fans of the series only. 1986; 95m.

BEN-HUR (1959) ★★★★★
DIR: William Wyler. **CAST:** Charlton Heston, Jack Hawkins, Sam Jaffe.
In this film, which won eleven Oscars, a wealthy Jewish nobleman during the time of Christ incurs the hostility of the Roman military governor,

who was his childhood friend. He is reduced to manning an oar on a slave galley, and his family is sent to prison. Years later he returns to seek vengeance upon his Roman tormentor. This culminates in a spectacular chariot race. Charlton Heston won an Oscar for his first-rate performance in the title role. 1959; 211m.

BENEATH THE 12-MILE REEF ★★★
DIR: Ted Post. **CAST:** Robert Wagner, Gilbert Roland, Terry Moore, Richard Boone.
Here is some good old-fashioned Hollywood entertainment. Film deals with sponge divers off the Florida coast. Light, enjoyable fluff. 1953; 102m.

BERLIN EXPRESS ★★★½
DIR: Jacques Tourneur. **CAST:** Merle Oberon, Robert Ryan, Charles Korvin, Paul Lukas, Robert Coote.
A taut, crisply edited espionage thriller from the director of the original *Cat People*. Filmed in semidocumentary style, *Berlin Express* takes full advantage of post–World War II Germany, incorporating actual footage of bombed-out Frankfurt and Berlin into the drama. Thrown together on a train to Berlin, Robert Ryan as an American nutrition expert, Paul Lukas as a marked German statesman trying to reunite his war-torn country, and Merle Oberon as Lukas's aide all give standout performances. 1948; B&W; 86m.

BERLIN TUNNEL 21 ★★
DIR: Richard Michaels. **CAST:** Richard Thomas, Horst Buchholz, José Ferrer, Jacques Breuer, Nicolas Farrell, Ute Christensen.
Richard Thomas stars as an American soldier in Berlin in 1961. His girlfriend cannot leave the eastern section of Berlin to join him. The solution: sneak her out of East Berlin with the help of Horst Buchholz, an engineer who also has loved ones trapped in the East. Predictable. 1981; 141m.

BEST KEPT SECRETS ★★★½
DIR: Jerrold Freedman. **CAST:** Patty Duke, Frederic Forrest, Peter Coyote, Meg Foster.
When a police officer is not promoted to the Special Information Unit, his wife (Patty Duke) decides to find out why. She discovers a secret file that the police department has been using for blacklisting purposes. This TV movie is guaranteed to keep your interest. 1989; 94m.

BEST REVENGE ★★½
DIR: John Trent. **CAST:** John Heard, Levon Helm, Alberta Watson, John Rhys-Davies.
Granger (John Heard) has come to Spain to team up with Bo (Levon Helm), who has promised him the contacts for a $4 million hashish deal. This fast-moving action adventure has some good acting, but fails to rise above its pedestrian plot. 1984; 92m.

BEVERLY HILLS COP ★★★★
DIR: Martin Brest. **CAST:** Eddie Murphy, Lisa Eilbacher, Judge Reinhold, John Ashton.
In this highly entertaining cops-and-comedy caper, Eddie Murphy plays a street-wise policeman from Detroit who takes a leave of absence to track down the men who killed his best friend. This quest takes him to the unfamiliar hills of ritzy Southern California, where he's greeted as anything but a hero. Rated R for violence and profanity. 1984; 105m.

BEVERLY HILLS COP II ★★½
DIR: Tony Scott. **CAST:** Eddie Murphy, Judge Reinhold, Jurgen Prochnow, Ronny Cox, John Ashton, Brigitte Nielsen, Allen Garfield, Dean Stockwell.
This sequel to *Beverly Hills Cop* lacks most of the charm and freshness of the first film, choosing instead to unwind as a thunderous, pounding assault on the senses. Eddie Murphy needs all his considerable talent to enliven this confusing mess, and he just manages to pull it off. Rated R for profanity and brief nudity. 1987; 102m.

BEYOND ATLANTIS ★★
DIR: Eddie Romero. **CAST:** Patrick Wayne, John Ashley, Leigh Christian, Sid Haig.
Unexciting movie about a motley bunch of adventurers looking for a fabulous treasure on an uncharted isle. Rated PG for mild violence. 1973; 89m.

BEYOND THE POSEIDON ADVENTURE ★
DIR: Irwin Allen. **CAST:** Michael Caine, Sally Field, Telly Savalas, Jack Warden, Peter Boyle.
Probably one of the weakest ideas yet for a sequel. Michael Caine heads one of two salvage crews (his being the good one, of course) that race each other and time to probe the upside-down wreck of the *Poseidon.* An incredible waste of a talented cast. Rated PG for mild violence and language. 1979; 114m.

BIG BAD MAMA ★★
DIR: Steve Carver. **CAST:** Angie Dickinson, Tom Skerritt, William Shatner, Joan Prather.
Here's an okay film concerning a mother (Angie Dickinson), sort of a second-rate Ma Barker, leading her daughters on a robbery spree during the Depression. It's not a classic by any means, but the action keeps things moving along. Rated R for violence, nudity, and sex. 1974; 83m.

BIG BAD MAMA II
DIR: Jim Wynorski. **CAST:** Angie Dickinson, Robert Culp, Danielle Brisebois, Julie McCullough, Bruce Glover.
A shabby sequel to a so-so movie. Angie Dickinson, leader of a family of female bank robbers, is still trying to avenge her husband's murder. But this time she and her daughters find love, and this film gets about as sappy as can be. Rated R for violence and nudity. 1987; 85m.

BIG BIRD CAGE, THE ★½
DIR: Jack Hill. **CAST:** Pam Grier, Anitra Ford, Sid Haig.
Some of the women-in-prison movies that producer Roger Corman cranked out in the Seventies were worth seeing because some talented filmmakers brought a high level of ability and excitement to them. This, however, is one of the boring ones. The prisoners work a sugar plantation in Manila, plotting to escape with the aid of a group of revolutionaries. Rated R for nudity and violence. 1972; 88m.

BIG BRAWL, THE ★★★
DIR: Robert Clouse. **CAST:** Jackie Chan, José Ferrer, Kristine DeBell, Mako.
Director Robert Clouse again fails to reach the heights attained with his *Enter the Dragon.* Nevertheless, this kung-fu comedy has its moments—most provided by its agile star, Jackie Chan. 1980; 95m.

BIG BUST OUT, THE
DIR: Richard Jackson. **CAST:** Vonetta McGee, Karen Carter, Linda Fox, Monica Taylor.
Four female convicts escape from a prison somewhere in the Middle East when they are sent to do janitorial work at a convent. Idiotic. 1973; 75m.

BIG CAT, THE ★★★
DIR: Phil Karlson. **CAST:** Lon McCallister, Preston Foster, Forrest Tucker.
A marauding mountain lion complicates feuding between high country ranchers in this enjoyable adventure film. 1949; 75m.

BIG COMBO, THE ★★★
DIR: Joseph H. Lewis. **CAST:** Cornel Wilde, Jean Wallace, Richard Conte.
A classic American gangster film done in the *film noir* style. Cornel Wilde has the starring role as a half-crazed policeman who is after gangsters and will do whatever is necessary to get them. Quite violent for its time and very well photographed, with an exciting climax. 1955; B&W; 89m.

BIG EASY, THE ★★★★
DIR: Jim McBride. **CAST:** Dennis Quaid, Ellen Barkin, Ned Beatty, John Goodman, Lisa Jane Persky, Ebbe Roe Smith, Tom O'Brien, Charles Ludlam.

Everything is easy in the Big Easy (a.k.a. New Orleans) for slick and only slightly sleazy police lieutenant Remy McSwain (Dennis Quaid). That is, until Anne Osbourne (Ellen Barkin), an upright and uptight assistant district attorney, comes along. *The Big Easy* is a wild, southern-style variation on the old-fashioned cop films of the Thirties and Forties. Rated PG-13 for profanity, nudity, simulated sex, and violence. 1987; 100m.

BIG FIX, THE ★★★½
DIR: Jeremy Paul Kagan. **CAST:** Richard Dreyfuss, Susan Anspach, Bonnie Bedelia.

Novelist Roger Simon's laid-back detective, Moses Wine, comes to the screen in this flawed thriller. The setting—which harkens back to the revolutionary Sixties—has become dated, but a murder mystery of any stripe is still suspenseful. Rated PG. 1978; 108m.

BIG HEAT, THE ★★★★
DIR: Fritz Lang. **CAST:** Glenn Ford, Gloria Grahame, Jocelyn Brando, Alexander Scourby, Lee Marvin, Jeanette Nolan, Carolyn Jones.

A crackerjack classic of crime *film noir*. Homicide detective Dave Bannion (Glenn Ford) is bent on solving the puzzle of an unexpected suicide of a fellow police officer, even though he is told by his superiors to leave bad enough alone. Exceptional acting, especially by Lee Marvin and Gloria Grahame. 1953; B&W; 90m.

BIG RED ONE, THE ★★★★½
DIR: Samuel Fuller. **CAST:** Lee Marvin, Mark Hamill, Robert Carradine, Bobby DiCicco.

This release gave Lee Marvin his best role in years. As a grizzled sergeant leading a platoon of "wetnoses" into the dangers of battle, he's excellent. Based on writer-director Sam Fuller's personal reminiscences of World War II. It's a terrific war movie. Rated PG. 1980; 113m.

BIG SCORE, THE ★★½
DIR: Fred Williamson. **CAST:** Fred Williamson, John Saxon, Richard Roundtree, Nancy Wilson, Ed Lauter, Joe Spinell, Michael Dante.

Fred Williamson breaks all the rules in going after drug king Joe Spinell. Williamson, the director, doesn't make the story move fast enough. Rated R for violence and profanity. 1983; 85m.

BIG SLEEP, THE (1946) ★★★★½
DIR: Howard Hawks. **CAST:** Humphrey Bogart, Lauren Bacall, Martha Vickers, Bob Steele, Elisha Cook Jr., Dorothy Malone.

Raymond Chandler's fans couldn't complain about this moody, atmospheric rendition of Philip Marlowe's most bizarre case. Bogart's gritty interpretation of the tough-talking P.I. is a high point in his glorious career, and sultry Lauren Bacall throws in enough spark to ignite several city blocks. Unrated; adult themes and violence. 1946; B&W; 114m.

BIG SLEEP, THE (1978)
DIR: Michael Winner. **CAST:** Robert Mitchum, James Stewart, Sarah Miles, Oliver Reed, Candy Clark, Edward Fox.

Director Michael Winner came up with a loser in this remake of the classic screen detective yarn. Rated R for violence, profanity, and nudity. 1978; 100m.

BIG STEAL, THE ★★★½
DIR: Don Siegel. **CAST:** Robert Mitchum, Jane Greer, William Bendix, Ramon Novarro, Patric Knowles.

Four sets of desperate and disparate characters chase each other over bumpy roads in the Southwest and Mexico following a robbery. An intriguing film, somewhat difficult to follow but great fun to watch. 1949; B&W; 71m.

BIG SWITCH, THE ★
DIR: Pete Walker. **CAST:** Sebastian Breaks, Virginia Wetherell.
When a stylish, jet-setting gambler gets caught up in a one-night stand with a mysterious and beautiful female, he unwittingly becomes the central figure in a story of intrigue. The protagonist slowly unravels the mystery surrounding an underworld kingpin. Rated R. 1969; 68m.

BIG TREES, THE ★★½
DIR: Felix Feist. **CAST:** Kirk Douglas, Eve Miller, Patrice Wymore, Edgar Buchanan, John Archer, Alan Hale.
Lumberman Kirk Douglas wants the redwoods on homesteaders' land in this colorful adventure set in northwest California in 1900. A remake of 1938's *Valley of the Giants*. 1952; 89m.

BIG TROUBLE IN LITTLE CHINA ★★★½
DIR: John Carpenter. **CAST:** Kurt Russell, Kim Cattrall, Dennis Dun, James Hong, Victor Wong, Kate Burton.
An adventure fantasy with Kurt Russell as a pig trucker unwittingly swept into a mystical world underneath San Francisco's Chinatown. It's an empire ruled by a sinister 2,000-year-old ghost who must marry a green-eyed woman to restore his youth. The movie is a lighthearted special-effects showcase designed to look a bit silly, in the style of old serials. Rated PG-13. 1986; 99m.

BILLY JACK ★★½
DIR: Tom Laughlin. **CAST:** Tom Laughlin, Delores Taylor, Clark Howat, Bert Freed, Julie Webb.
A film that seems to suggest that a good kick in the groin will bring "peace and love," *Billy Jack* was a box-office sensation. The star, Tom Laughlin, produced and directed. Rated PG. 1971; 114m.

BIRD OF PARADISE ★★½
DIR: King Vidor. **CAST:** Joel McCrea, Dolores Del Rio, John Halliday, Skeets Gallagher, Lon Chaney Jr.
Even the reliable Joel McCrea can't save this bit of South Sea island silliness. Amid sacrifices and angry volcano gods, the seafaring McCrea attempts to woo native princess Dolores Del Rio. This kind of thing was fairly typical (and popular) in the 1930s, but it looks awfully dumb today. 1932; B&W; 80m.

BIRDS OF PREY ★★★★
DIR: William A. Graham. **CAST:** David Janssen, Ralph Meeker, Elayne Heilvell.
Ex–World War II fighter pilot turned peacetime Salt Lake City traffic helicopter jockey (David Janssen) hears the siren song of war anew when he witnesses a bank heist in progress and chases the robbers, who make their getaway in their own 'copter. An aerial battle of wits follows. Terrific flying sequences. 1973; 81m.

BLACK ARROW, THE ★★★½
DIR: Gordon Douglas. **CAST:** Louis Hayward, George Macready, Janet Blair, Edgar Buchanan.
Hero Louis Hayward is in fine form as he fights the evil George Macready in this highly enjoyable entry into the swashbuckler genre. Some fine action scenes, with a slam-bang finale. 1948; B&W; 76m.

BLACK BELT JONES ★★★
DIR: Robert Clouse. **CAST:** Jim Kelly, Scatman Crothers, Gloria Hendry.
A likable kung-fu action film about a self-defense school in Watts combatting a "mafioso"-type group. Not a classic film, but an easy pace and good humor make this a fun action movie. Rated PG for violence. 1974; 87m.

BLACK CAESAR ★★
DIR: Larry Cohen. **CAST:** Fred Williamson, Art Lund, Val Avery, Julius W. Harris, William Wellman Jr., D'Urville Martin, Gloria Hendry.

In this passable gangster flick, Fred Williamson stars as Tommy Gibbs, bloodthirsty, gun-wielding Godfather of Harlem. Gibbs eliminates anyone who stands in his way on his rise to the top. The soundtrack by the Godfather of Soul, James Brown, doesn't hurt. Rated R. 1973; 92m.

BLACK EAGLE ★★½
DIR: Eric Carson. **CAST:** Sho Kosugi, Jean Claude Van Damme, Vladimir Skomarovsky, Doran Clark.

A decent martial-arts flick about a CIA agent (Sho Kosugi) sent to recover a top-secret laser-tracking device from a U.S. fighter downed in the Mediterranean. The KGB has also sent a man (Jean Claude Van Damme), and the two agents do the international tango. Rated R for violence. 1988; 93m.

BLACK GESTAPO, THE ★
DIR: Lee Frost. **CAST:** Rod Perry, Charles P. Robinson, Phil Hoover.

Violent blaxploitation movie set in the Watts section of L.A. during 1965, when it was the location of rioting. The gestapo of the title is an underground army formed to get rid of the drug dealers and slumlords in black neighborhooods. Sociological content is nil; this is just an excuse for a lot of cheap, mindless violence. Rated R. 1975; 88m.

BLACK JACK ★★★
DIR: Julien Duvivier. **CAST:** George Sanders, Herbert Marshall, Agnes Moorehead, Patricia Roc, Marcel Dalio.

George Sanders is soldier of fortune Michael Alexander who has a drug-smuggling scheme in Tangiers aboard his yacht, the *Black Jack*. Despite the initial feeling that this is a dated film, the twists in plot will hold viewers' attentions. 1949; B&W; 103m.

BLACK KLANSMAN, THE ★
DIR: Ted V. Mikels. **CAST:** Richard Gilden, Rima Kutner.

This exploitative but mild melodrama follows the efforts of a light-skinned black musician to avenge the death of his daughter, killed when the Ku Klux Klan bombed a church. He passes for white, joins the Klan, and seduces the leader's daughter. Unrated, but includes violence and sexual situations. 1966; B&W; 88m.

BLACK MOON RISING ★★
DIR: Harley Cokliss. **CAST:** Tommy Lee Jones, Linda Hamilton, Robert Vaughn, Richard Jaeckel, Lee Ving, Bubba Smith.

The only redeeming point of this little car theft number is its occasional accent on humor. The cast is top-notch, but the material is mostly pedestrian. Rated R for language, nudity, sex, and some rather gruesome violence. 1986; 93m.

BLACK PIRATE, THE ★★★½
DIR: Albert Parker. **CAST:** Douglas Fairbanks Sr., Donald Crisp, Billie Dove, Anders Randolph.

One of superstar Douglas Fairbanks's most popular films, this early color production packs enough thrills for a dozen pictures. Written by Fairbanks, *Pirate* contains a duel to the death with cutlasses on the beach, a daring underwater raid on a pirate ship, and one of the most famous of all movie stunts: Fairbanks's ride down the ship's sail on a knife, cleverly achieved with an apparatus hidden from the camera. Silent. 1926; B&W; 122m.

BLACK RAVEN, THE ★½
DIR: Sam Newfield. **CAST:** George Zucco, Wanda McKay, Glenn Strange, I. Stanford Jolley.

Poorly made suspense movie from PRC, the cheapest of Hollywood's Poverty Row studios of the Thirties and Forties. Set in a country inn, the Black Raven, the movie juggles subplots about embezzlement, elopement, murder, and revenge. Nostalgia fans with an hour to kill may enjoy it for the cast of familiar faces. 1943; B&W; 64m.

BLACK SUNDAY ★★★
DIR: John Frankenheimer. **CAST:** Robert Shaw, Bruce Dern, Marthe Keller, Fritz Weaver.

An Arab terrorist group attempts to blow up the president at a Superbowl in Miami's Orange Bowl. Tension is maintained throughout. Rated R. 1977; 143m.

BLACK WINDMILL, THE ★★★½
DIR: Don Siegel. **CAST:** Michael Caine, Joseph O'Conor, Donald Pleasence, John Vernon, Janet Suzman, Delphine Seyrig.

Straightforward story is enhanced by Don Siegel's razor-sharp direction and Michael Caine's engrossing performance as an intelligence agent whose son has been kidnapped. The suspense builds carefully to a satisfying climax. Rated R. 1974; 106m.

BLACKBEARD THE PIRATE ★★★
DIR: Raoul Walsh. **CAST:** Robert Newton, Linda Darnell, William Bendix, Keith Andes.

Entertaining pirate yarn with some good action and fine characterizations. Gorgeous Linda Darnell is the charming damsel in distress. In the title role, Robert Newton is a bit overzealous at times, but puts in a fine performance. Go for it. 1952; 99m.

BLACKOUT (1978) ★★★
DIR: Eddy Matalon. **CAST:** Jim Mitchum, Robert Carradine, Belinda Montgomery, June Allyson, Jean-Pierre Aumont, Ray Milland.

At times, this movie, about a New York City apartment building attacked by a gang of escaped criminals during a blackout, reeks of a disaster film. Still, there are good action scenes and enough drama to make you almost forget the shortcomings. Rated R for violence. 1978; 86m.

BLADE ★★★
DIR: Ernest Pintoff. **CAST:** John Marley, Jon Cypher, Kathryn Walker, William Prince, Michael McGuire, Joe Santos, John Schuck, Keene Curtis, Ted Lange, Marshall Efron, Steve Landesberg.

Middle-aged New York detective Blade (John Marley) stalks the psycho who murdered the daughter of a powerful right-wing congressman. Along the way he uncovers a lot of other goings-on in the naked city. The story's not much, but TV addicts can count the faces that later went on hit shows (*Barney Miller*'s Steve Landesberg, *The Love Boat*'s Ted Lange, *McMillan and Wife*'s John Schuck). Rated R for violence. 1973; 90m.

BLADE MASTER, THE ★
DIR: David Hills. **CAST:** Miles O'Keeffe, Lisa Foster.

This is one of those action-packed slice-and-dice adventures that may entertain if not taken seriously. Muscleman Miles O'Keeffe, along with his small band of followers, chops his way across the countryside battling nasty sorcerers and spirits in a quest to conquer evil. Rated PG. 1984; 92m.

BLAKE OF SCOTLAND YARD ★★½
DIR: Robert Hill. **CAST:** Ralph Byrd, Lloyd Hughes, Joan Barclay, Herbert Rawlinson, Dickie Jones, Bob Terry, Nick Stuart.

A power-mad count offers a king's ransom to the man who helps him to obtain a death-dealing device, and a mysterious cloaked character called The Scorpion begins a reign of terror in his campaign to secure the weapon. Made by Victory Pictures, a bargain-basement independent producer, this cliffhanger lacks the values that Universal or Republic put into their product, but it's still fun. 1937; B&W; 15 chapters.

BLASTFIGHTER
DIR: John Old Jr. **CAST:** Michael Sopkiw, Valerie Blake, George Eastman, Mike Miller.

Michael Sopkiw is Jake "Tiger" Sharp, a dull ex-convict who returns to his hometown in the Appalachians, where he becomes a Rambo trying to clean up an immoral populace. Not rated, but contains violence. 1984; 93m.

BLIND RAGE ★
DIR: Efren C. Pinion. **CAST:** D'Urville Martin, Leo Fong, Tony Ferrer, Dick Adair, Darnell Garcia, Charlie Davao, Leila Hermosa, Fred Williamson, Jessie Crowder.

If you really believe that four blind men could rob a bank during business hours, you deserve this film. Fred Williamson fans, beware; his appearance is very brief. Rated R for violence and profanity. 1978; 81m.

BLINDSIDE ★★
DIR: Paul Lynch. **CAST:** Harvey Keitel, Lori Hallier, Allen Fawcett.

Only the acting talent of Harvey Keitel distinguishes this would-be suspense film yawner. Keitel stars as a former surveillance expert who discovers a murder plot. Rated R for violence and profanity. 1988; 102m.

BLOOD AND GUNS ★
DIR: Giulio Petroni. **CAST:** Orson Welles, Tomas Milian, John Steiner.

Orson Welles's screen presence is at a loss in this dull action yarn about three men whose lives intertwine after the Mexican revolution. What could have been an interesting character study falls apart due to poor direction. Rated R for profanity and violence. 1968; 90m.

BLOOD IN THE STREETS ★★
DIR: Sergio Sollima. **CAST:** Oliver Reed, Fabio Testi, Agostina Belli.

In this French-Italian film, a prison warden (Oliver Reed) is forced to release a prisoner as ransom for his kidnapped wife. There are some exciting chase scenes in this overall so-so film. Rated R for sex, nudity, language, and violence. 1974; 111m.

BLOOD ON THE SUN ★★★½
DIR: Frank Lloyd. **CAST:** James Cagney, Robert Armstrong, Wallace Ford, Sylvia Sidney.

This hard-hitting action drama finds James Cagney fighting Japanese military and government men in Japan just before World War II. An unusual plot and good pace make this worth watching. 1945; B&W; 98m.

BLOOD SIMPLE ★★★★½
DIR: Joel Coen. **CAST:** John Getz, Frances McDormand, Dan Hedaya, M. Emmet Walsh.

A slyly suspenseful, exciting (and sometimes agonizing) edge-of-your-seat story of how a bar owner (Dan Hedaya) hires a private eye (M. Emmet Walsh) to follow his wife (Frances McDormand) to find out if she's cheating on him. *Blood Simple*, is defined as a "state of confusion that follows the commission of a murder, i.e., 'He's gone blood simple.' " Rated R for suggested sex, violence, and profanity. 1984; 96m.

BLOODSPORT ★★
DIR: Newt Arnold. **CAST:** Jean Claude Van Damme, Donald Gibb, Leah Ayres, Normann Burton, Forest Whitaker, Bolo Yeung.

Kung-fu expert Jean Claude Van Damme plays a martial arts master who arrives in Hong Kong to compete in the *kumite*, a violent championship contest. The fighting sequences are tremendous, and the action surrounding the contest is great, but the framing story offers only clichés. Rated R for violence and language. 1987; 100m.

BLOODSTONE ★★
DIR: Dwight H. Little. **CAST:** Brett Stimely.

An adventure film in the tradition of *Raiders of the Lost Ark*, this falls short of the mark. The story involves newlyweds who become involved in a jewel heist in the Middle East. Loaded with humor and lots of action, but marred by poor performances. Rated PG-13 for violence. 1988; 90m.

BLOODY MAMA ★★½
DIR: Roger Corman. **CAST:** Shelley Winters, Don Stroud, Pat Hingle, Robert Walden, Bruce Dern, Robert De Niro.

Shelley Winters plays Ma Barker in this gangster flick. Her four sons share her notoriety as Depression-era bandits. Rated R. 1970; 90m.

BLOWING WILD ★
DIR: Hugo Fregonese. **CAST:** Gary Cooper, Barbara Stanwyck, Anthony Quinn, Ruth Roman, Ward Bond.
Wildcat Barbara Stanwyck lusts almost in vain for Gary Cooper in this foul tale of bandits in the Mexican oilfields. An exceptionally poor script brings a good cast to its knees. 1953; 90m.

BLUE CITY
DIR: Michelle Manning. **CAST:** Judd Nelson, Ally Sheedy, David Caruso, Paul Winfield, Scott Wilson, Anita Morris.
Estranged son Judd Nelson returns to his hometown and learns that his father, previously the mayor, has been killed. Determined to avenge this murder, Nelson goes on a ludicrous destructive spree against the local crime lord. Rated R for language and violence. 1986; 83m.

BLUE LIGHTING, THE ★★
DIR: Lee Phillips. **CAST:** Sam Elliott, Robert Culp, Rebecca Gilling.
Lightweight action movie starring Sam Elliott as a hired gun sent to Australia to retrieve a precious gem from I.R.A. renegade Robert Culp. Culp knows Elliott's coming and sets a series of traps for him. A passable timewaster. Rated PG. 1986; 95m.

BLUE MAX, THE ★★★
DIR: John Guillermin. **CAST:** George Peppard, James Mason, Ursula Andress, Jeremy Kemp.
For those with a yen for excellent aerial-combat gymnastics, superb photography, and a fine Jerry Goldsmith music score, this is the film. The storyline is quite a different matter. Seen from the eyes of Kaiser Wilhelm II, air aces, and their superior officers, the plot is very standard material. The cast is fine but somewhat restrained. See it for the marvelous dogfights. You can tolerate the story. 1966; 156m.

BLUE SUNSHINE ★★½
DIR: Jeff Lieberman. **CAST:** Zalman King, Deborah Winters, Mark Goddard, Robert Walden, Charles Siebert.
Oddball mystery-thriller dealing with a series of random killings committed by former college students suffering the side effects of a drug taken ten years previously. Low-budget film is both ridiculous and terrifying at the same time. Rated PG for mild language and violence. 1976; 97m.

BLUE THUNDER ★★★★½
DIR: John Badham. **CAST:** Roy Scheider, Malcolm McDowell, Candy Clark, Warren Oates.
A state-of-the-art helicopter is the centerpiece of this action-paced police melodrama. Piloted by Roy Scheider, the craft—a.k.a. "Blue Thunder"—battles combat jets commanded by villain Malcolm McDowell high above the crowded streets of downtown Los Angeles. The result is a gripping and immensely entertaining—if somewhat implausible—adventure thriller. Rated R for violence, nudity, and profanity. 1983; 109m.

BOBBIE JO AND THE OUTLAW ★½
DIR: Mark L. Lester. **CAST:** Marjoe Gortner, Lynda Carter, Jesse Vint, Merrie Lynn Ross, Belinda Belaski, Gerrit Graham.
Lynda Carter, hungry for excitement, tags along with Marjoe Gortner and his gang. An orgy of murders and robberies ensues. Lots of violence, little credibility. Rated R for nudity, violence, and profanity. 1976; 89m.

BODY IN THE LIBRARY, THE ★★★½
DIR: Silvio Narizzano. **CAST:** Joan Hickson, Gwen Watford, Andrew Cruickshank, Moray Watson, Valentine Dyall.
Agatha Christie's Miss Marple (Joan Hickson) stays close to home in this mystery when she is summoned by a good friend with the misfortune to have found a body in her library at

Gossington Hall, St. Mary Mead. Careful armchair sleuths will find this one solvable, but red herrings abound. Unrated; suitable for family viewing. 1984; 153m.

BODY SLAM ★★
DIR: Hal Needham. **CAST:** Dirk Benedict, Tanya Roberts, Roddy Piper, Lou Albano, Barry Gordon.
A down-and-out rock 'n' roll promotional manager signs up a couple of renegade professional wrestlers to go on a barnstorming tour. The tour is so successful that they turn the wrestling world on its ear. Although this film is silly, it has a lot of heart. Rated PG for mild violence. 1987; 92m.

BOMBARDIER ★★★½
DIR: Richard Wallace. **CAST:** Pat O'Brien, Randolph Scott, Eddie Albert, Robert Ryan, Anne Shirley, Barton MacLane.
This is a solid action film dealing with the training of flyers during World War II. There is nothing new in the familiar formula of this film, but a good cast and fast pace make it enjoyable. 1943; B&W; 99m.

BONNIE AND CLYDE ★★★★★
DIR: Arthur Penn. **CAST:** Warren Beatty, Faye Dunaway, Gene Hackman, Estelle Parsons, Michael J. Pollard, Gene Wilder.
This still fresh and innovative gangster film was one of the first to depict graphic violence, turning the genre inside-out, combining comedy, bloodshed, pathos, and social commentary with fascinating results. 1967; 111m.

BONNIE'S KIDS ★★½
DIR: Arthur Marks. **CAST:** Tiffany Bolling, Steve Sandor, Robin Mattson, Scott Brady.
Two amoral girls molested by their stepfather kill him and move in with their criminal uncle. They plan to rob their uncle but are pursued by thugs. Lots of action, but all rather pointless. Rated R for simulated sex, nudity, adult themes, and violence. 1982; 105m.

BORDER, THE ★★★½
DIR: Tony Richardson. **CAST:** Jack Nicholson, Harvey Keitel, Valerie Perrine, Warren Oates, Elpidia Carrillo.
Jack Nicholson is first-rate in this often effective drama about a border patrol officer who rebels against the corruption in his department and the rampant greed of his wife, Valerie Perrine. Rated R. 1982; 107m.

BORDER HEAT ★
DIR: Tony Gaudioz. **CAST:** Darlanne Fluegel, John Vernon.
This action flick, set in Texas, has all the excitement of a siesta. Darlanne Fluegel gives an uninspired performance as a field worker who tries to make her life easier by becoming the boss's woman and then changes her mind. The extremely slow pace and uneventful script don't help. Rated R for violence. 1988; 93m.

BORDERLINE ★★★½
DIR: Jerrold Freedman. **CAST:** Charles Bronson, Bruno Kirby, Bert Remsen, Ed Harris, Wilford Brimley.
Charles Bronson gives one of his better portrayals in this release, which got the jump on the similar *The Border*, with Jack Nicholson, by nearly two years. As in the later film, the central character—a border guard—becomes involved with the problems of an illegal alien and her child. The result is a watchable action film. Rated R. 1980; 105m.

BORN AMERICAN ★
DIR: Renny Harlin. **CAST:** Mike Norris, Steve Durham, David Coburn, Albert Salmi, Thalmus Rasulala.
This low-budget film features a mostly ridiculous and sometimes morbid story in the tradition of *Red Dawn*. It involves three high-school buddies who cross the Russian border while on summer vacation in Lapland. Rated R for sex and violence. 1986; 103m.

BORN LOSERS ★★★
DIR: T. C. Frank. **CAST:** Tom Laughlin, Elizabeth James, Jeremy Slate, William Wellman Jr., Robert Tessier.

This biker exploitation movie is better than the celebrated *Billy Jack*, which also starred Tom Laughlin. Granted, we still have to sit through scenes with terrible amateur actors, but at least there is no girl singing off-key about her brother being dead. 1967; 112m.

BORN TO RACE ★
DIR: James Fargo. **CAST:** Joseph Bottoms, Robert F. Logan, Marc Singer, George Kennedy.

This clunker of a film couldn't get off the starting line. The plot, what little there is of it, concerns a top-notch racing-circuit driver getting ready for the big race. Along the way he gets involved with a female Italian engineer. Don't bother. Rated R for nudity, simulated sex, violence, and profanity. 1988; 95m.

BOTANY BAY ★★½
DIR: John Farrow. **CAST:** Alan Ladd, James Mason, Patricia Medina.

Alan Ladd stars as an unjustly accused criminal aboard a ship about to establish a penal colony in British-occupied Australia. He finds himself confronting a cruel captain (James Mason) and romancing a beautiful young actress (Patricia Medina). Atmospheric costume drama. 1953; 94m.

BOUNTY, THE ★★★★
DIR: Roger Donaldson. **CAST:** Mel Gibson, Anthony Hopkins, Laurence Olivier, Edward Fox.

Mel Gibson is Fletcher Christian, and Anthony Hopkins is Captain William Bligh in this, the fourth and most satisfying screen version of *The Mutiny on the Bounty*. This sweeping seafaring epic from the director of *Smash Palace* is the first movie to present the historic events accurately—and to do so fascinatingly. Rated PG for nudity and violence. 1984; 132m.

BOXCAR BERTHA ★★½
DIR: Martin Scorsese. **CAST:** David Carradine, Barbara Hershey, Barry Primus, Bernie Casey, John Carradine.

Small-town girl (Barbara Hershey) hooks up with a gang of train robbers (led by David Carradine) in this *Bonnie and Clyde* coattailer. Martin Scorsese buffs will be disappointed. Rated R. 1972; 97m.

BOYS IN COMPANY C, THE ★★★
DIR: Sidney J. Furie. **CAST:** Stan Shaw, Andrew Stevens, James Canning, James Whitmore Jr.

The film opens with the arrival of various draftees in the Marine Corps induction center and comes close, at times, to being the powerful film the subject of the Vietnam war suggests. The combat scenes are particularly effective, and the deaths of soldiers are gory without being overdone. Rated R for violence. 1978; 127m.

BOYS OF THE CITY ★★
DIR: Joseph H. Lewis. **CAST:** Bobby Jordan, Leo Gorcey, Dave O'Brien, Donald Haines.

Somewhere between their incarnations as the Dead End Kids and the Bowery Boys, the Forties version of the Brat Pack turned up as the East Side Kids in low-budget movies that were equal parts drama and comedy. In this one, the gang takes a trip to the mountains, where they solve the murder of a judge by gangsters. 1940; B&W; 68m.

BRADDOCK: MISSING IN ACTION III ★★
DIR: Aaron Norris. **CAST:** Chuck Norris, Aki Aleong.

After the war has ended, Colonel Braddock (Chuck Norris) returns to Vietnam to rescue a group of Amerasian children held captive in a POW camp. A dark, grainy, low-budget film cowritten by Norris. It's shallow and brainless with offensive racial stereotypes, but if you liked the first two films, you'll probably enjoy this one, too. Rated R for violence. 1987; 90m.

BRADY'S ESCAPE ★★★
DIR: Pal Gabor. **CAST:** John Savage, Kelly Reno.

A minor HBO-produced film concerning an American attempting to escape the Nazis in Europe during WWII. Nothing original is added to the familiar plot. 1984; 96m.

BRANNIGAN ★★★½
DIR: Douglas Hickox. **CAST:** John Wayne, Richard Attenborough, Judy Geeson, Mel Ferrer, Ralph Meeker, John Vernon.

John Wayne travels to London to bring back a fugitive in this enjoyable cops-and-robbers chase film. It's fun to see the Duke in jolly old England and the cast is outstanding. Rated PG. 1975; 111m.

BRASS MONKEY, THE ★★
DIR: Thornton Freeland. **CAST:** Carole Landis, Carroll Levis, Herbert Lom, Avril Angers, Ernest Thesiger.

In this British thriller we get a not-very-effective story based on a radio program. Carole Landis is a radio singer who prevents the theft of a Buddhist religious icon. The script is weak and Landis and the other players seem bored. 1948; B&W; 84m.

BRASS TARGET ★★
DIR: John Hough. **CAST:** Sophia Loren, George Kennedy, John Cassavetes, Robert Vaughn, Max von Sydow, Bruce Davison.

Pure Hollywood hokum at its most ridiculous would ask us to believe that Gen. George Patton (George Kennedy) was murdered after World War II because of a large gold robbery committed by his staff. Not much to recommend this boring film. Rated PG for moderate language and violence. 1978; 111m.

BREAKER! BREAKER! ★
DIR: Don Hulette. **CAST:** Chuck Norris, George Murdock, Terry O'Connor, Don Gentry.

A quickie thrown together to cash in on the CB craze, this Chuck Norris flick promises, but does not deliver, a slam-bang ending. Rated PG. 1977; 86m.

BREAKER MORANT ★★★★★
DIR: Bruce Beresford. **CAST:** Edward Woodward, Jack Thompson, John Waters, Bryan Brown.

This is one Australian import you won't want to miss. Imagine the high adventure of the original *Gunga Din*, the wisecracking humor of *To Have and Have Not*, and the character drama of *The Caine Mutiny* all rolled into one super movie. Rated PG. 1979; 107m.

BREAKOUT ★★★
DIR: Tom Gries. **CAST:** Charles Bronson, Robert Duvall, Jill Ireland, John Huston, Sheree North, Randy Quaid.

While not exactly Charles Bronson at his best, this action-adventure film does have its moments as the star, playing a devil-may-care helicopter pilot, rescues Robert Duvall, an American businessman framed for murder and held captive in a Mexican jail. Rated PG. 1975; 96m.

BREAKTHROUGH ★
DIR: Andrew V. McLaglen. **CAST:** Richard Burton, Robert Mitchum, Rod Steiger, Curt Jurgens.

This dull war film—a sequel to Sam Peckinpah's *Cross of Iron*—stars Richard Burton as Sergeant Steiner, a heroic German officer who saves the life of an American colonel (Robert Mitchum) after the Nazis thwart an attempt on Hitler's life. Rated PG. 1978; 115m.

BREED APART, A ★★★½
DIR: Philippe Mora. **CAST:** Rutger Hauer, Kathleen Turner, Powers Boothe, Donald Pleasence.

When a billionaire collector hires an adventurous mountain climber to steal the eggs of an endangered pair of nesting eagles, the result is a nicely paced film that manages to combine drama, suspense, romance, and even a touch of post-Vietnam commentary.

Rutger Hauer plays the strange recluse who lives in a tent-palace in the loneliest reaches of the Blue Ridge Mountains. Rated R for sex, nudity, and violence. 1984; 95m.

BRIDE AND THE BEAST, THE ★

DIR: Adrian Weiss. **CAST:** Charlotte Austin, Lance Fuller, Johnny Roth, Steve Calvert, William Justine.

Stock jungle footage is used to pad out this tale of the new bride of a big-game hunter who, under hypnosis, discovers that she lived a past life as a gorilla. This explains why she spends her wedding night making eyes at the gorilla that her new husband keeps caged in the basement. Third-rate monkeyshines with an anticlimactic ending. 1958; 78m.

BRIDGE ON THE RIVER KWAI, THE ★★★★★

DIR: David Lean. **CAST:** William Holden, Alec Guinness, Jack Hawkins, Sessue Hayakawa, James Donald.

Considered by many to be David Lean's greatest work, this war epic brought the British director his first Oscar. The powerful, dramatic story centers around the construction of a bridge by British and American prisoners of war under the command of Japanese colonel Sessue Hayakawa. Alec Guinness, a Lean semiregular since *Great Expectations*, is the stiff-upper-lipped British commander who uses the task as a way of proving British superiority. 1957; 161m.

BRIDGE TO HELL ★½

DIR: Umberto Lenzi. **CAST:** Andy J. Forest.

After a group of World War II POWs escape, they must fight their way home. A bridge is their last obstacle and they decide to take it out after crossing. (Sound familiar?) Lots of shooting and explosions. Unfortunately, not much of a plot. Not rated, but contains violence and profanity. 1989; 94m.

BRIDGE TOO FAR, A ★★★½

DIR: Richard Attenborough. **CAST:** Dirk Bogarde, James Caan, Michael Caine, Sean Connery, Laurence Olivier, Robert Redford.

Here's another story of a famous battle with the traditional all-star cast. In this case it's World War II's "Operation Market Garden," a disastrous Allied push to get troops behind German lines and capture an early bridgehead on the Rhine. Rated PG. 1977; 175m.

BRIDGES AT TOKO-RI, THE ★★★★½

DIR: Mark Robson. **CAST:** William Holden, Fredric March, Grace Kelly, Mickey Rooney, Earl Holliman, Charles McGraw, Robert Strauss, Willis Bouchey, Gene Reynolds.

With this picture, screenwriter Valentine Davies and director Mark Robson created one of the cinema's most authentic depictions of war. It is certainly the best motion picture about the Korean War. James Michener's novel, as adapted here, centers on a bomber pilot and his crew, part of an aircraft-carrier force assigned to destroy vital North Korean bridges. 1954; 103m.

BRING ME THE HEAD OF ALFREDO GARCIA ★★½

DIR: Sam Peckinpah. **CAST:** Warren Oates, Isela Vega, Gig Young, Robert Webber, Emilio Fernandez, Kris Kristofferson, Helmut Dantine.

Warren Oates gives an outstanding performance as a piano player in Mexico who becomes mixed up with vicious bounty hunters. Hard-core Sam Peckinpah fans will appreciate this one more than the casual viewer. Rated R. 1974; 112m.

BROTHERHOOD OF DEATH

DIR: Bill Berry. **CAST:** Roy Jefferson, Le Tari, Haskell V. Anderson.

Satanic Ku Klux Klansmen battle gun-toting black Vietnam veterans in the pre–civil-rights-movement South. This is a typical black exploitation film with low production values and below-average acting. Rated R for violence and language. 1976; 85m.

BUCCANEER, THE ★★

DIR: Anthony Quinn. **CAST:** Yul Brynner, Charlton Heston, Claire Bloom, Charles Boyer, Douglas Dumbrille, Lorne Greene, Ted de Corsia.

Studio-bound remake of C. B. De Mille's 1938 romance of pirate Jean Lafitte and his involvement in the War of 1812 boasts a cast capable of hamming *and* acting, but that's not enough to make this stiff color creaker come alive. 1958; 121m.

BUCKTOWN

DIR: Arthur Marks. **CAST:** Fred Williamson, Pam Grier, Thalmus Rasulala, Tony King, Bernie Hamilton, Art Lund.

This mindless blaxploitation flick finds Fred Williamson journeying to a southern town to bury his brother, who has been killed by corrupt cops. Fred calls in reinforcements from Philadelphia, a gang war ensues, and the corrupt cops are wiped out. Rated R. 1975; 95m.

BULLDOG DRUMMOND ★★★

DIR: F. Richard Jones. **CAST:** Ronald Colman, Joan Bennett, Lilyan Tashman.

Ronald Colman smoothly segued from silent to sound films playing the title's ex–British army officer adventurer in this exciting, witty, definitive first stanza of what became a popular series. 1929; B&W; 89m.

BULLDOG DRUMMOND COMES BACK ★★★

DIR: Louis King. **CAST:** John Howard, John Barrymore, Louis Campbell, E. E. Clive, Reginald Denny, J. Carrol Naish.

The first of seven films starring John Howard as the adventurer-sleuth is an atmospheric tale of revenge. The crazed widow of one of Bulldog Drummond's former enemies makes off with our hero's girl, Phyllis. A gem available on tape with *Bulldog Drummond Escapes*. 1937; B&W; 59m.

BULLDOG DRUMMOND ESCAPES ★★

DIR: James Hogan. **CAST:** Ray Milland, Guy Standing, Heather Angel, Porter Hall, Reginald Denny, E. E. Clive, Fay Holden.

Famed ex–British army officer Bulldog Drummond comes to the aid of his ladylove when she becomes embroiled in an international espionage ring. Young Ray Milland stars in his only outing as the World War I hero in this okay series entry. Paired on tape with *Bulldog Drummond Comes Back*. 1937; B&W; 65m.

BULLDOG DRUMMOND IN AFRICA ★★½

DIR: Louis King. **CAST:** John Howard, Heather Angel, J. Carrol Naish, H. B. Warner, Anthony Quinn.

An international spy ring has struck again. This time they've kidnapped Colonel Neilson and hidden him somewhere in North Africa, and Hugh "Bulldog" Drummond isn't going to stand for it. Good fun. Double-billed with *Arrest Bulldog Drummond* on tape. 1938; B&W; 58m.

BULLDOG DRUMMOND'S BRIDE ★★½

DIR: James Hogan. **CAST:** John Howard, Heather Angel, Reginald Denny, H. B. Warner, Eduardo Ciannelli.

The last of Paramount's Bulldog Drummond series finds John Howard combating evil close at hand when a crack bank robber uses Drummond's honeymoon flat as a hideout for himself and his explosives. Not the best of the series, but it's still a rousing adventure. On tape with *Bulldog Drummond's Secret Police*. 1939; B&W; 56m.

BULLDOG DRUMMOND'S PERIL ★★★

DIR: James Hogan. **CAST:** John Howard, John Barrymore, Louise Campbell, H. B. Warner, Reginald Denny.

Bulldog Drummond has a personal stake in a chase that takes him from London to Switzerland—the synthetic diamond that was stolen is a wedding gift intended for our hero and his patient fiancée, Phyllis. Full of close calls, witty dialogue, and an injection of controlled lunacy by the great John Barrymore. On tape with *Bulldog Drummond's Revenge*. 1938; B&W; 66m.

BULLDOG DRUMMOND'S REVENGE ★★★

DIR: Louis King. **CAST:** John Howard, John Barrymore, Louise Campbell, Reginald Denny, E. E. Clive.

The second film in Paramount's Drummond series featuring John Howard, this entry focuses on the hero's attempts to recover a powerful explosive and to bring to justice the people responsible for stealing it. Aided by the colorful Colonel Neilson (John Barrymore at his most enjoyable), Drummond fights evildoers at every turn. Released on a double bill with *Bulldog Drummond's Peril*. 1937; B&W; 55m.

BULLDOG DRUMMOND'S SECRET POLICE ★★½

DIR: James Hogan. **CAST:** John Howard, Heather Angel, Reginald Denny, Leo G. Carroll, H. B. Warner.

Stylish entry in the long-running series finds gentleman adventurer Bulldog Drummond searching a forbidding castle for hidden treasure while matching wits with a crazed murderer. Double billed with *Bulldog Drummond's Bride* on videotape. 1939; B&W; 54m.

BULLETPROOF ★★½

DIR: Steve Carver. **CAST:** Gary Busey, Darlanne Fluegel, Henry Silva, Thalmus Rasulala, L. Q. Jones, Rene Enriquez, R. G. Armstrong, Luke Askew.

Gary Busey plays a one-man army named Frank "Bulletproof" McBain, an ex-CIA agent who singlehandedly takes on a band of multinational terrorists. It's silly, but fun—thanks to Busey and a strong cast of character actors. Rated R for profanity, nudity, and violence. 1988; 95m.

BULLFIGHTER AND THE LADY, THE ★★★★

DIR: Budd Boetticher. **CAST:** Robert Stack, Joy Page, Gilbert Roland, Katy Jurado.

Many of the themes explored in the superb series of low-budget westerns director Budd Boetticher later made with Randolph Scott (*Decision at Sundown*; *The Tall T*) are evident in this first-rate drama. A skeet-shooting champ (Robert Stack) decides to become a bullfighter and enlists the aid of a top professional (Gilbert Roland). 1951; B&W; 87m.

BULLITT ★★★★

DIR: Peter Yates. **CAST:** Steve McQueen, Robert Vaughn, Jacqueline Bisset, Norman Fell, Don Gordon.

Although a bit dated now, this police drama directed by Peter Yates still features one of star Steve McQueen's best screen performances. The San Francisco car-chase sequence is still a corker. 1968; 113m.

BUNCO ★★½

DIR: Alexander Singer. **CAST:** Robert Urich, Tom Selleck, Donna Mills, Michael Sacks, Will Geer, Arte Johnson, James Hampton, Bobby Van.

Passable made-for-television crime thriller has Robert Urich and Tom Selleck as a pair of police detectives out to bust a confidence ring. Typical TV fare. 1976; 90m.

BUSHIDO BLADE

DIR: Tom Kotani. **CAST:** Richard Boone, Frank Converse, James Earl Jones, Toshiro Mifune, Mako.

Top-billed Richard Boone gives an outrageously hammy performance in this Japanese-made answer to *Shogun* as Commander Matthew Perry, whose mission is to find a valuable sword. Frank Converse (in the action-hero role), James Earl Jones, Toshiro Mifune, and Mako fare little better in this poorly directed adventure. Rated R for violence. 1979; 104m.

CABO BLANCO ★
DIR: J. Lee Thompson. **CAST:** Charles Bronson, Dominique Sanda, Jason Robards Jr.

A miserable suspense-thriller remake of *Casablanca.* As good as he can be when he wants to, Charles Bronson is no Humphrey Bogart. And we shouldn't expect him to be. So why is he playing a nightclub owner saving a damsel in distress (Dominique Sanda) from a modern-day Nazi (Jason Robards Jr.)? We don't know—and neither will you. Rated R. 1982; 87m.

CAGED WOMEN
DIR: Vincent Dawn. **CAST:** Laura Gemser, Gabrielle Tinti.

A typical sexploitation flick about a female journalist who poses as a prostitute to get thrown into jail and expose the corrupt prison system. Full of brutality and unnecessary violence, the movie meanders through gang rapes and group tortures. Only the sadistic will be entertained by this garbage. Not rated, but contains nudity, violence, and profanity. 1984; 97m.

CALL OF THE WILD ★★★½
DIR: Ken Annakin. **CAST:** Charlton Heston, Michele Mercier, Maria Rohm, Rik Battaglia.

Charlton Heston stars in this adaptation of Jack London's famous novel. A domesticated dog is stolen and forced to pull a snow sled in Alaska as John (Charlton Heston) searches for gold. Some profanity and violence. Rated PG. 1972; 100m.

CAME A HOT FRIDAY ★★
DIR: Ian Mune. **CAST:** Peter Bland, Philip Gordon, Billy T. James, Michael Lawrence.

Mildly amusing film set in 1949 New Zealand, where two con men make their fortune cheating bookmakers all across the country. Rated PG for language and adult situations. 1985; 101m.

CANNIBAL WOMEN IN THE AVOCADO JUNGLE OF DEATH ★★½
DIR: J. D. Athens. **CAST:** Shannon Tweed, Adrienne Barbeau, Bill Maher, Barry Primus.

Playboy playmate Shannon Tweed stars in this comedic adventure about a feminist anthropologist who takes her ditzy student and a bumbling guide in search of the infamous cannibal women, a group of ultraleft feminists who eat their mates. Some great sight gags, with most of the funny bits belonging to semimacho guide Bill Maher. Rated PG-13 for nudity. 1988; 90m.

CANNONBALL ★½
DIR: Paul Bartel. **CAST:** David Carradine, Veronica Hamel, Gerrit Graham, Sylvester Stallone, Robert Carradine, Carl Gottlieb, Belinda Balaski.

This plays like a poor man's *Cannonball Run* or *Gumball Rally*, executed by somebody having neither the skill nor the understanding of complex vehicular stunts. David Carradine plays an unpleasant antihero out to beat the rest of the cast in an exotic race. Rated R for violence. 1976; 93m.

CAPER OF THE GOLDEN BULLS, THE ★
DIR: Russell Rouse. **CAST:** Stephen Boyd, Yvette Mimieux, Giovanna Ralli, Vito Scotti, J. G. Devlin, Arnold Moss, Walter Slezak.

Stephen Boyd plays a wealthy American who is blackmailed by his old accomplice (Giovanna Ralli) into robbing the Royal Bank of Spain. The heist is okay and the plot is believable, but the comedic one-liners and the performances are below average. Not rated, has some violence. 1966; 106m.

CAPTAIN AMERICA (1944) ★★★
DIR: John English, Elmer Clifton. **CAST:** Dick Purcell, Lorna Gray, Lionel Atwill, Charles Trowbridge, Rus-

sell Hicks, John Davidson, Frank Reicher, Hugh Sothern.

Joe Simon and Jack Kirby's comic-book character is brought to movie life to tangle with the fiendishly refined Lionel Atwill, who has not only a destructive ray machine but a machine capable of bringing dead animals back to life! Two-fisted District Attorney Dick Purcell manfully pursues Atwill. 1944; B&W; 15 chapters.

CAPTAIN AMERICA (1979) ★★
DIR: Rod Holcomb. **CAST:** Reb Brown, Len Birman, Heather Menzies, Steve Forrest.

A criminal genius plots to extort millions from the government by threatening to blow up a major city with a stolen nuclear device. Of course the only man who can stop him is the star-spangled avenger. This is average TV fare with a disappointingly simple plot. Not rated, but suitable for all viewers. 1979; 90m.

CAPTAIN AMERICA II: DEATH TOO SOON ★½
DIR: Ivan Nagy. **CAST:** Reb Brown, Christopher Lee, Connie Selleca, Len Birman.

Ridiculous made-for-television adventure of the comic-book hero. Joe Simon and Jack Kirby's red, white, and blue avenger, Captain America (Reb Brown), is pitted against a supervillain (Christopher Lee) who has perfected a fast-aging process. Plodding. 1979; 100m.

CAPTAIN BLOOD ★★★★½
DIR: Michael Curtiz. **CAST:** Errol Flynn, Olivia De Havilland, Basil Rathbone, Lionel Atwill, Ross Alexander, Guy Kibbee, Henry Stephenson.

Errol Flynn's youthful enthusiasm, great character actors, realistic miniature work, and Erich Wolfgang Korngold's score all meld together under Michael Curtiz's direction and provide audiences with perhaps the best pirate film of all time. 1935; B&W; 95m.

CAPTAIN CAUTION ★★½
DIR: Richard Wallace. **CAST:** Victor Mature, Louise Platt, Bruce Cabot, Leo Carrillo, Vivienne Osborne, El Brendel, Robert Barrat, Miles Mander, Roscoe Ates.

In command of a ship during the War of 1812 with England, Victor Mature, in the title role, is taken for a coward when he urges prudence. Richard Wallace's fast-paced, cannon-bellowing direction quells all restlessness, however. 1940; B&W; 85m.

CAPTAIN GALLANT—FOREIGN LEGION ★★½
DIR: Sam Newfield. **CAST:** Buster Crabbe, Fuzzy Knight, Cullen "Cuffy" Crabbe.

Baby boomers should remember this Saturday-morning television series involving the adventures and escapades of Captain Gallant of the French Foreign Legion who, with his son "Cuffy" and comical sidekick Fuzzy Knight, rode the North African deserts outwitting black-turbaned villains. This video release is a compilation of two of the best episodes. Nostalgic fun. 1956; B&W; 60m.

CAPTAIN KIDD ★★
DIR: Rowland V. Lee. **CAST:** Charles Laughton, Randolph Scott, Reginald Owen, John Carradine, Sheldon Leonard, Barbara Britton, Gilbert Roland.

Not even Charles Laughton's mugging and posturing can redeem this swashbuckling yarn about the pirate whose treasure is still being sought. 1945; 89m.

CAPTAIN SCARLETT ★★½
DIR: Thomas Carr. **CAST:** Richard Greene, Leonora Amar, Nedrick Young.

A dashing hero thought to be dead returns to France after the Napoleonic Wars to discover his estate has been confiscated by a nasty nobleman. Saving ladies in distress and righting wrongs becomes his life. Simple, predictable, and good clean fun. 1953; 75m.

CAPTIVE RAGE

DIR: Cedric Sundstrom. **CAST:** Oliver Reed, Robert Vaughn.

A plane carrying American citizens is hijacked. This film revels in its degradation of women. Whenever things get dull, a female hostage is beaten and raped. Although Oliver Reed tries hard to give a good performance, even he can't elevate this movie from the sewer. Rated R for violence, profanity, and nudity. 1988; 99m.

CARAVAN TO VACCARES

DIR: Geoffrey Reeve. **CAST:** David Birney, Charlotte Rampling, Michel Lonsdale, Marcel Bozzuffi.

David Birney is an American drifter in southern France who is hired to bring a mysterious Hungarian to the United States. If this cliché-ridden film had followed the plot of Alistair MacLean's novel, it might have been exciting. Read the book instead. Rated PG. 1974; 98m.

CARDIAC ARREST ★½

DIR: Murphy Mintz. **CAST:** Garry Goodrow, Mike Chan, Max Gail.

Garry Goodrow, maverick detective, investigates a series of grisly murders that has the cops puzzled and the citizens of San Francisco living in fear. The killer's specialty is carving the hearts out of his victims. Low-budget thriller that starts out with a quick pace but ultimately fails. Rated R for violence and adult situations. 1980; 90m.

CARIBE ★★

DIR: Michael Kennedy. **CAST:** John Savage, Kara Glover, Stephen McHattie.

Two federal agents are out of their league in dealing with a sinister arms smuggler in this bland spy thriller. CIA agent Kara Glover and her partner arrange a weapons sale for their own personal gain. But the contact, Stephen McHattie, has no intention of fulfilling his part of the bargain. He kills Glover's partner and confiscates the weapons. Beautiful photography of the Belize jungles and mountains rescue this tired spy thriller. 1987; 90m.

CASINO ROYALE (1954) ★★★★

DIR: William H. Brown. **CAST:** Barry Nelson, Peter Lorre, Linda Christian.

007 fans who believe Sean Connery to have been the first screen incarnation of their favorite secret agent will be surprised and thrilled by this Bonded treasure, originally aired live on an American television anthology series. Barry Nelson stars as an Americanized "Jimmy" Bond who faces the menacing Le Chiffre (Peter Lorre, in a deliciously evil role) across a gambling table. Although greatly compressed from the Ian Fleming novel which had been published only the year before, this remains a surprisingly faithful adaptation of its source material. 1954; B&W; 55m.

CAST A GIANT SHADOW ★★

DIR: Melville Shavelson. **CAST:** Kirk Douglas, Senta Berger, Angie Dickinson.

The early history of Israel is told through the fictionalized biography of American Col. Mickie Marcus (Kirk Douglas). Marcus, an expatriate army officer, is cajoled into aiding Israel in its impending war to wrest independence from its hostile Arab neighbors. Highly romanticized piece of historical fluff. 1966; 142m.

CASTLE IN THE DESERT ★★★

DIR: Harry Lachman. **CAST:** Sidney Toler, Arleen Whelan, Richard Derr, Douglas Dumbrille, Henry Daniell.

Charlie Chan travels to the middle of the Mojave Desert as the guest of a millionaire whose wife is descended from the infamous Borgias. By some odd coincidence, people begin to die by poison, and Honolulu's answer to Sherlock Holmes must solve the mystery. Full of secret panels, mysterious shadows, and close-ups of gloved hands, this is one of the best remembered and most satisfying of the later Chans, the last in the series made by Twentieth Century Fox. 1942; B&W; 61m.

CAT AND THE CANARY, THE (1927) ★★★½
DIR: Paul Leni. **CAST:** Laura LaPlante, Tully Marshall, Flora Finch, Creighton Hale.
This is an exceptional silent version of a mystery that has been subsequently remade several times. The entire cast is wonderful as a spooky group that spends the night in a mysterious old house. Laura LaPlante is in top form. 1927; B&W; 75m.

CATCH ME A SPY ★★★
DIR: Dick Clement. **CAST:** Kirk Douglas, Marlene Jobert, Trevor Howard.
This is a good suspense thriller with, surprisingly, a few laughs. The story is built around an East-West espionage theme in which both sides trade for their captured spies. Rated PG. 1971; 93m.

CATCH THE HEAT ★★
DIR: Joel Silberg. **CAST:** David Dukes, Tiana Alexander, Rod Steiger, Brian Thompson, Jorge Martinez, John Hancock.
Tiana Alexander is a narcotics cop in San Francisco who is sent undercover to South America to bust up a drug empire headed by Rod Steiger. Even Alexander's kung-fu prowess is routine with these cardboard characters. Rated R. 1987; 88m.

C.C. & COMPANY ★★½
DIR: Seymour Robbie. **CAST:** Joe Namath, Ann-Margret, William Smith, Sid Haig, Jennifer Billingsley, Greg Mullavey.
Basically idiotic action film has Broadway Joe Namath (in his first feature) cast as C.C. Ryder, misfit member of a rowdy biker gang, attempting to "split" when he falls for top fashion photographer Ann-Margret. Rated R for mild language and nudity. 1970; 90m.

CERTAIN FURY
DIR: Stephen Gullenhaal. **CAST:** Tatum O'Neal, Irene Cara, Nicholas Campbell, George Murdock, Moses Gunn, Peter Fonda.
Somebody certainly should be furious about this tasteless, stupid movie. Tatum O'Neal is Scarlet ("Scar")—a dumb white street woman; Irene Cara is Tracy—a dumb pampered black woman. They're thrown together in an opening-scene bloodbath and through the rest of the movie run for their lives from police and drug dealers. Rated R for violence. 1985; 87m.

CHAIN REACTION ★★★
DIR: Ian Barry, George Miller. **CAST:** Steve Bisley, Anna-Maria Winchester.
Engrossing drama following a nuclear power plant employee (Ross Thompson) accidentally exposed to a lethal dose of radiation during a near meltdown. Rated R. Some explicit sex, nudity, and violence. 1980; 87m.

CHAINED HEAT ★
DIR: Paul Nicolas. **CAST:** Linda Blair, John Vernon, Nita Talbot, Stella Stevens, Sybil Danning, Tamara Dobson.
The story of women in prison, this cheapo offers few surprises. Only those who like cheap laughs, nudity, sex, violence, profanity, and bad acting will enjoy this exploitation flick. Rated R. 1983; 95m.

CHALLENGE, THE ★★★½
DIR: John Frankenheimer. **CAST:** Scott Glenn, Toshiro Mifune, Calvin Young.
An American (Scott Glenn) gets caught in the middle of a decades-old private war between two brothers in modern-day Japan. This movie has ample rewards for both samurai film aficionados and regular moviegoers. Rated R for profanity and violence. 1982; 112m.

CHANDU THE MAGICIAN ★★½
DIR: William Cameron Menzies, Marcel Varnel. **CAST:** Edmund Lowe, Bela Lugosi, Irene Ware, Henry B. Walthall.
Stylishly produced and full of exotic sets, sleight of hand, and special effects, this imaginative fantasy suffers from a stolid performance by Edmund

Lowe. Bela Lugosi, however, is in rare form as the gleefully maniacal Roxor, master of the black arts. An enjoyable curiosity. 1932; B&W; 70m.

CHARADE ★★★★½

DIR: Stanley Donen. **CAST:** Cary Grant, Audrey Hepburn, Walter Matthau, James Coburn, George Kennedy.

A comedy-mystery directed in the Alfred Hitchcock suspense style, this features the ever-suave Cary Grant helping widow Audrey Hepburn find the fortune stashed by her late husband. Walter Matthau, George Kennedy, and James Coburn are first-rate in support. 1963; 114m.

CHARGE OF THE LIGHT BRIGADE, THE ★★★★

DIR: Michael Curtiz. **CAST:** Errol Flynn, Olivia De Havilland, Patric Knowles, Donald Crisp, David Niven, Henry Stephenson.

October 25, 1854: Balaclava, the Crimea; military minds blunder, and six hundred gallant Britishers, sąbers flashing, ride to their deaths. The film, which climaxes with one of the most dramatic cavalry charges in history, is based on Tennyson's famous poem. 1936; B&W; 116m.

CHARLEY VARRICK ★★★★

DIR: Don Siegel. **CAST:** Walter Matthau, Joe Don Baker, Felicia Farr, Andy Robinson, John Vernon.

A bank robber (Walter Matthau) accidentally steals money from the mob (he hits a bank where its ill-gotten gains are laundered). Matthau is superb as Varrick, the "last of the independents," and Joe Don Baker sends chills up the spine as the hit man relentlessly pursuing him. Rated PG. 1973; 111m.

CHARLIE CHAN AT THE OPERA ★★★½

DIR: H. Bruce Humberstone. **CAST:** Warner Oland, Boris Karloff, Charlotte Henry, Keye Luke, Thomas Beck, William Demarest.

Charlie Chan is called in to help solve the mysterious disappearance of a mental patient who becomes the suspect in two murders during an opera. Crazed baritone Boris Karloff chews up the scenery magnificently as the odds-on killer, but sly Warner Oland as Chan and Keye Luke as his number-one son hold their own in this often confusing mystery. The thirteenth film in the Fox series, this is considered by many devotees to be one of the best. 1936; B&W; 68m.

CHARLIE CHAN AT THE WAX MUSEUM ★★★

DIR: Lynn Shores. **CAST:** Sidney Toler, C. Henry Gordon, Marc Lawrence, Marguerite Chapman.

A radio broadcast from a wax museum means murder—as Charlie Chan weaves his way through false clues, false faces, and poison darts to unravel the eerie goings-on. Spooky settings and top character actors like Marc Lawrence make this one of the best of the Sidney Toler Chans made for Twentieth Century Fox. This one is compact and tantalizing. 1949; B&W; 64m.

CHARLIE CHAN IN PARIS ★★½

DIR: Lewis Seiler. **CAST:** Warner Oland, Mary Brian, Erik Rhodes, John Miljan, Thomas Beck, Keye Luke.

Former Fu Manchu Warner Oland drew on almost twenty years of cinematic experience playing Oriental menaces to make the character of Charlie Chan uniquely his own. This seventh entry in the series shows why he succeeded so well. The Honolulu sleuth seeks the knife-wielding killer who murdered one of his agents. Chan's oldest son Lee (Keye Luke) makes his initial appearance and aids his father in an adventure that climaxes in a chase through the sewers of Paris. The Swedish-born Oland died in 1937 after making sixteen Chan films and will always be remembered as the definitive Charlie Chan. 1935; B&W; 72m.

CHARLIE CHAN IN RIO ★★½
DIR: Harry Lachman. **CAST:** Sidney Toler, Mary Beth Hughes, Cobina Wright Jr., Victor Jory, Harold Huber, Richard Derr.
The last of the better-budgeted Charlie Chans, this film was an improvement over the previous efforts. Chan (Sidney Toler) arrives in Rio de Janeiro to bring back a murderess, only to discover that she has been killed. After sorting through false leads and encountering bad-news characters like Victor Jory and Harold Huber, Chan brings the killer to bay with the aid of a psychic. 1941; B&W; 60m.

CHARLIE CHAN'S SECRET ★★½
DIR: Gordon Wiles. **CAST:** Warner Oland, Rosina Lawrence, Charles Quigley, Astrid Allwyn, Jonathon Hale.
Charlie Chan travels from Honolulu to San Francisco in search of a missing heir. When the heir is murdered and then mysteriously appears during a séance, Chan nabs the culprit. Sliding panels, supernatural overtones, and plenty of red herrings highlight this tenth entry in the long-running series. 1936; B&W; 72m.

CHESTY ANDERSON, U.S. NAVY (A.K.A. ANDERSON'S ANGELS)
DIR: Ed Forsyth. **CAST:** Shari Eubank, Scatman Crothers, Fred Willard, Frank Campanella.
This dated, low-budget, tasteless crime thriller features Shari Eubank as the title character. When her sister disappears, she (accompanied by her WAVE friends) becomes involved with a crooked senator and the Mafia. Rated R for nudity, obscenities, and violence. 1975; 83m.

CHINA GIRL ★
DIR: Abel Ferrara. **CAST:** James Russo, David Caruso, Richard Panebianco, Sari Chang, Russell Wong, Joey Chin, James Hong.
Romeo and Juliet on Friday the 13th. The story concerns the star-crossed love affair of an Italian boy (Richard Panebianco) and a China Girl (Sari Chang). As a result of their relationship, gang warfare breaks out and the innocent couple is caught in the middle. Rated R for violence and profanity. 1987; 90m.

CHINA SEAS ★★★½
DIR: Tay Garnett. **CAST:** Clark Gable, Jean Harlow, Wallace Beery, Lewis Stone.
Clark Gable is the captain of a Chinese river steamer in pirate-infested waters. Jean Harlow is once again the lady with a spotted past, who we all know is the perfect mate for Gable if he'd only realize it himself. An enjoyable screen romp. 1935; B&W; 90m.

CHINATOWN ★★★★½
DIR: Roman Polanski. **CAST:** Jack Nicholson, Faye Dunaway, John Huston, Perry Lopez, Diane Ladd.
One of the great detective films, this stars Jack Nicholson as a 1940s Los Angeles private eye who stumbles on to a crooked land deal as well as a murder. Rated R for language, violence, nudity. 1974; 131m.

CHINESE CONNECTION, THE ★★★
DIR: Lo Wei. **CAST:** Bruce Lee, Miao Ker Hsio.
This action-packed import, in which Bruce Lee plays a martial arts expert out to avenge the death of his mentor, is good, watchable fare. But be forewarned: It's dubbed, and not all that expertly. Rated R. 1979; 107m.

CHINESE WEB, THE ★
DIR: Don McDougall. **CAST:** Nicholas Hammond, Robert F. Simon, Benson Fong, John Milford, Ted Danson.
Typical TV-cartoon, only this time it's a live-action feature-length movie. When a Chinese official seeks protection from his publisher friend in New York, newspaper photographer Peter Parker (alias Spiderman) wards off the corrupt businessman who is after said official. No moral here, just superhero action. 1978; 95m.

CHOKE CANYON ★
DIR: Chuck Ball. **CAST:** Stephen Collins, Janet Julian, Lance Henriksen, Bo Svenson.
A two-fisted physicist (Stephen Collins) takes on an evil industrialist in this absurd action-adventure movie. Even the superb stunt work and spectacular scenery do not make up for the lack of a believable story. Rated PG. 1986; 96m.

CHRISTINA ★★
DIR: Paul Krasny. **CAST:** Barbara Parkins, Peter Haskell, James McEachin, Marlyn Mason.
Contrived mystery film about a wealthy foreigner (Barbara Parkins) who pays an unemployed aircraft engineer (Peter Haskell) twenty-five thousand dollars to marry her so she can acquire a U.S. passport...or so we think. 1974; 95m.

CINCINNATI KID, THE ★★★★
DIR: Norman Jewison. **CAST:** Steve McQueen, Ann-Margret, Edward G. Robinson, Karl Malden.
Steve McQueen had one of his earliest acting challenges in this study of a determined young poker player on his way to the big time. He lets nothing stand in his way, especially not the reigning king of the card tables, Edward G. Robinson. 1965; 113m.

CIRCLE OF IRON ★★★
DIR: Richard Moore. **CAST:** David Carradine, Jeff Cooper, Christopher Lee, Roddy McDowall, Eli Wallach, Erica Creer.
Bruce Lee was preparing the screenplay for this martial arts fantasy shortly before he died as the follow-up to his tremendously successful first American film *Enter the Dragon.* Ironically, the lead role fell to David Carradine, who had also been chosen over Lee for the lead in the television series *Kung Fu*. Fans of the genre will love it. Rated R for violence. 1979; 102m.

CITY OF SHADOWS ★★
DIR: David Mitchell. **CAST:** John P. Ryan, Paul Coufas, Tony Rosato.
It's the old story of Cain and Abel, set in the not-so-distant future. The first brother is a cop who lives by his own rules and deals out justice in like fashion, and the other is a maniac outlaw who kidnaps little boys and kills them. Some good action sequences along with satisfactory acting make this a passable film. 1986; 92m.

CLAY PIGEON, THE ★★★
DIR: Richard Fleischer. **CAST:** Bill Williams, Barbara Hale, Richard Quine, Richard Loo, Frank Fenton, Frank Wilcox, Martha Hyer.
It is just after World War II. Sailor Bill Williams comes out of a coma to find he is going to be court-martialed for treason. When he is also accused of murder, he gets on the trail of the real killer. Tight plot and taut direction make this a seat-edge thriller. 1949; B&W; 63m.

CLEOPATRA JONES
DIR: Jack Starrett. **CAST:** Tamara Dobson, Shelley Winters, Bernie Casey, Brenda Sykes.
Secret agent Cleopatra Jones returns from an overseas assignment to save her old neighborhood, including a halfway house run by her ex-boyfriend, from an evil drug queen gang leader (Shelley Winters) known as "Mommy." Rated PG for violence. 1973; 80m.

CLIMB, THE ★★★
DIR: Donald Shebib. **CAST:** Bruce Greenwood, James Hurdle, Kenneth Walsh, Ken Pogue, Thomas Hauff.
Straightforward account of the 1953 German assault on Nanga Parbat, the world's fifth highest peak. David Greenwood is Herman Buhl, the arrogant climber who reached the summit alone. Rated PG, but suitable for the whole family. 1988; 86m.

CLOAK AND DAGGER (1984) ★★★
DIR: Richard Franklin. **CAST:** Henry Thomas, Dabney Coleman, Michael Murphy, John McIntire, Shelby Leverington.

A highly imaginative boy (Henry Thomas, of *E.T.*) who often plays pretend games of espionage with his fantasy friend, Jack Flack (Dabney Coleman), finds himself involved in a real life-and-death situation when he stumbles on to the evil doings of a group of spies (led by Michael Murphy). It's suspenseful and fast-paced enough to keep adults interested and entertained, but not so scary and violent as to upset the kiddies. Rated PG. 1984; 101m.

CLOUD DANCER ★★★½
DIR: Barry Brown. **CAST:** David Carradine, Jennifer O'Neill, Joseph Bottoms, Colleen Camp.

A story about competing stunt flyers, this film features one of David Carradine's best performances. As the king of daredevil pilots, he struggles to keep ahead of his ambitious protégé (Joseph Bottoms) as well as fighting his love for Jennifer O'Neill. Rated PG. 1980; 108m.

CLUB LIFE ★½
DIR: Norman Thaddeus Vane. **CAST:** Tony Curtis, Dee Wallace, Michael Parks, Yana Nirvana.

Neon lovers! May we have your attention please. This is just the film for you. The neon used in the disco surpasses anything you've ever seen. Lovers of good filmmaking will find this picture dull and uninspired. Rated R. 1987; 93m.

CLUTCHING HAND, THE ★★½
DIR: Albert Herman. **CAST:** Jack Mulhall, Marion Shilling, Yakima Canutt, Reed Howes, Ruth Mix, William Farnum, Rex Lease, Mae Busch, Bryant Washburn, Robert Frazer, Franklyn Farnum, Snub Pollard.

This independent chapterplay pits Craig Kennedy, the Scientific Detective, against a shadowy figure known only as the Clutching Hand. This villain has kidnapped an eminent scientist who claims to have made synthetic gold. A veritable Who's Who of former silent-film heroes and heroines appears here. The plot is standard and the resolution not that earthshaking, but the stunts and circumstances make this a fun serial to watch. 1936; B&W; 15 chapters.

COBRA ★★
DIR: George Pan Cosmatos. **CAST:** Sylvester Stallone, Brigitte Nielsen, Reni Santoni, Andrew Robinson.

Sylvester Stallone comes back for more *Rambo*-like action as a tough city cop on the trail of a serial killer in this unrelentingly grim and gruesome thriller. It is packed with action and violence. Rated R for violence, gore, and profanity. 1986; 95m.

COCAINE COWBOYS
DIR: Ulli Lommel. **CAST:** Jack Palance, Tom Sullivan, Andy Warhol, Suzanna Love.

Abysmal attempt at cult filmmaking. This inept thriller concerns the exploits of a struggling rock band whose members resort to drug smuggling in order to finance their music career. They end up in deep trouble with mobsters and hired killers. This movie was shot at Andy Warhol's Montauk home, where it should have stayed. Rated R for nudity and graphic violence. 1979; 86m.

COCAINE WARS ★½
DIR: Hector Olivera. **CAST:** John Schneider, Kathryn Witt, Federico Luppi, Royal Dano.

This heavy-duty-violence action film contains predictably poor acting and dialogue. John Schneider plays an undercover agent in a South American country who takes on a drug lord's empire as well as the country's military establishment. Rated R for violence, profanity, sex, and nudity. 1986; 82m.

COCKFIGHTER ★★
DIR: Monte Hellman. **CAST:** Warren Oates, Harry Dean Stanton, Richard B. Shull, Troy Donahue, Millie Perkins.

Title says it all. Warren Oates and Harry Dean Stanton can't breathe life into this simplistic look at the illegal sport of cockfighting. For Oates fans only. Rated R. 1974; 83m.

CODE NAME: EMERALD ★★★½
DIR: Jonathan Sanger. **CAST:** Ed Harris, Max von Sydow, Horst Buchholz, Helmut Berger, Cyrielle Claire, Eric Stoltz.

Better-than-average World War II espionage film about a double agent (Ed Harris) who attempts to rescue a U.S. Army officer (Eric Stoltz) held for interrogation in a French prison. The plot moves along at a good clip despite the lack of action. Rated PG for violence and sex. 1985; 95m.

CODE NAME: WILD GEESE ★½
DIR: Anthony M. Dawson. **CAST:** Lewis Collins, Lee Van Cleef, Ernest Borgnine, Mimsy Farmer, Klaus Kinski.

Marginal action-adventure is set in the Golden Triangle of Asia. A group of mercenaries hire out as a task force to destroy the opium trade for the Drug Enforcement Administration. Rated R. 1984; 101m.

CODE OF SILENCE ★★★★
DIR: Andrew Davis. **CAST:** Chuck Norris, Henry Silva, Bert Remsen, Dennis Farina, Mike Genovese, Ralph Foody, Nathan Davis.

With this film, Chuck Norris proved himself the heir to Charles Bronson as the king of the no-nonsense action movie. In *Code of Silence*, the star gives a right-on-target performance as tough cop Sgt. Eddie Cusack, who takes on warring mob families and corrupt police officers. Rated R for violence and profanity. 1985; 102m.

COFFY ★½
DIR: Jack Hill. **CAST:** Pam Grier, Booker Bradshaw, Sid Haig, Allan Arbus, Robert DoQui.

Pam Grier is wasted in this feeble blaxploitation action flick. She plays a nurse posing as a junkie so that she can put the hurt on the drug dealers who hooked her sister. Rated R. 1973; 91m.

COLD STEEL ★
DIR: Dorothy Ann Puzo. **CAST:** Brad Davis, Adam Ant, Sharon Stone, Jonathan Banks.

Brainless rehash about a cop, Brad Davis, out for revenge for the murder of his father. Lots of technical mistakes: boom mikes appearing out of nowhere, skylines changing from night to day in one scene, blown dialogue. Rated R for violence, nudity, and profanity. 1988; 91m.

COLD SWEAT ★
DIR: Terence Young. **CAST:** Charles Bronson, Liv Ullmann, Jill Ireland, James Mason, Gabriele Ferzetti, Michel Constantin.

Some old Charles Bronson movies are more comic than action-packed. *Cold Sweat*, a dated, offensively sexist piece of machismo, has Charlie shooting his way through an irrelevant plot and yelling at his whining wife to do what he commands. Rated R. 1970; 94m.

COLUMBO: MURDER BY THE BOOK ★★★½
DIR: Steven Spielberg. **CAST:** Peter Falk, Jack Cassidy, Martin Milner, Rosemary Forsyth.

Steven Spielberg steers a winning cast through a provoking "perfect crime" script tailored by writer Steven Bochco (*Hill Street Blues*, *L.A. Law*, *Hooperman*). As homicide detective Columbo, Peter Falk is hard-pressed to trip up smug murderer Jack Cassidy. One of the best episodes of the long-running television series. 1971; 79m.

COMBAT KILLERS ★★
DIR: Ken Loring. **CAST:** Paul Edwards, Marlene Dauden.

The captain of an American platoon in the Philippines during the closing days of WWII is tormented by a desire for glory. He puts his men through unnecessary dangers in fighting Japanese forces. Straightforward adventure will please war fans, though others may find it routine. The movie is unrated and contains some violence and profanity. 1980; 96m.

COME AND GET IT ★★★½
DIR: Howard Hawks, William Wyler. **CAST:** Edward Arnold, Joel McCrea, Frances Farmer, Walter Brennan.
Based on Edna Ferber's novel, this involving film depicts life in Wisconsin's lumber country. It captures the robust, resilient nature of the denizens. Edward Arnold is perfectly cast as the grasping capitalist who needs to have his eyes opened. Walter Brennan's performance earned an Oscar for best supporting actor. 1936; B&W; 105m.

COMMANDO ★★★½
DIR: Mark L. Lester. **CAST:** Arnold Schwarzenegger, Rae Dawn Chong, Dan Hedaya, James Olson, Alyssa Milano.
"Commando" John Matrix makes Rambo look like a wimp. As played by big, beefy Arnold Schwarzenegger, he "eats Green Berets for breakfast." He soon goes on the warpath when his 11-year-old daughter is kidnapped by a South American dictator (Dan Hedaya) he once helped depose. Rated R for violence and profanity. 1986; 90m.

COMMANDO SQUAD ★★
DIR: Fred Olen Ray. **CAST:** Brian Thompson, Kathy Shower, William Smith, Sid Haig, Robert Quarry, Ross Hagen, Mel Welles.
Lots of action but no substance in this standard tale of American drug agents operating undercover in Mexico. Kathy Shower is a tough female agent who tries to rescue her lover/coagent (Brian Thompson) from the clutches of an evil drug king. Rated R for strong language and violence. 1987; 90m.

COMMANDOS ★½
DIR: Armando Crispino. **CAST:** Lee Van Cleef, Jack Kelly, Marino Masé.
Italian World War II film with dubbed English and not enough action to make it worth looking in on. Jack Kelly and Lee Van Cleef lead a small special force into North Africa to spy on the German army. Rated PG for violence and sex. 1968; 89m.

COMMANDOS STRIKE AT DAWN ★★½
DIR: John Farrow. **CAST:** Paul Muni, Lillian Gish, Cedric Hardwicke, Anna Lee, Alexander Knox, Ray Collins.
Okay WWII tale of underground fighter Paul Muni, who goes up against the Nazis after they invade his Norwegian homeland. The great cast deserved a better script than this, though it is nice to watch Muni and Lillian Gish practice their art. Some good action sequences keep things moving. 1942; B&W; 96m.

CONFIDENTIAL ★½
DIR: Bruce Pittman. **CAST:** August Schellenberg, Chapelle Jaffe, Neil Munro.
A film that starts off well but quickly strangles on its own *film noir* style. A newspaper reporter investigating an old murder in 1949 Los Angeles is slain, and a hard-bitten detective tries to find the reasons why. Visually promising but narratively dull. Rated R for nudity, language, and violence. 1988; 95m.

CONQUEROR, THE 🦃
DIR: Dick Powell. **CAST:** John Wayne, Susan Hayward, Pedro Armendariz, Agnes Moorehead.
John Wayne plays Genghis Khan, and the results are unintentionally hilarious as the Duke spouts stilted, clichéd barbarian dialogue in his familiar drawling fashion. 1956; 111m.

CONVOY ★★
DIR: Sam Peckinpah. **CAST:** Kris Kristofferson, Ali MacGraw, Ernest Borgnine, Madge Sinclair, Burt Young.
Truckers, led by Kris Kristofferson, go on a tri-state protest over police brutality, high gas prices, and other complaints. An uneven script and just fair acting mar this picture. Rated PG. 1978; 110m.

COOGAN'S BLUFF ★★★★
DIR: Don Siegel. **CAST:** Clint Eastwood, Lee J. Cobb, Susan Clark, Tisha Sterling, Don Stroud, Betty Field, Tom Tully.
Clint Eastwood and director Don Siegel in their first collaboration. The squinty-eyed star hunts down a murderous fugitive (Don Stroud) in the asphalt jungle. Rated PG. 1968; 100m.

COOL HAND LUKE ★★★★★
DIR: Stuart Rosenberg. **CAST:** Paul Newman, George Kennedy, J. D. Cannon, Lou Antonio, Robert Drivas, Strother Martin.
One of Paul Newman's greatest creations is the irrepressible Luke. Luke is a prisoner on a southern chain gang and not even the deprivations of these subhuman conditions will break his spirit. George Kennedy's performance is equally memorable and won him a supporting Oscar. 1967; 126m.

COP ★★
DIR: James B. Harris. **CAST:** James Woods, Lesley Ann Warren, Charles Durning, Charles Haid, Raymond J. Barry, Randi Brooks.
A supercharged performance by James Woods is not enough to make this crime thriller succeed. The film was based on the novel *Blood on the Moon* by James Ellroy and all too quickly goes from being a fascinating character study to just another sleazy and mindless slasher flick. Rated R for violence, gore, simulated sex, nudity, and profanity. 1988; 110m.

COP IN BLUE JEANS, THE ★
DIR: Bruno Corbucci. **CAST:** Tomas Milian, Jack Palance, Maria Rosaria Omaggio, Guido Mannari.
This film about an undercover cop (Thomas Milian) trying to take out an underworld boss (Jack Palance) has plenty of action scenes. But after enduring the shoddy voice dubbing and the poorly developed characters, the viewer is all too relieved to push the rewind button. Not rated; contains violence. 1978; 92m.

CORLEONE ★★
DIR: Pasquale Squiteri. **CAST:** Giuliano Gemma, Claudia Cardinale, Francisco Rabal.
Dull Italian drama about two childhood friends in Sicily who decide to fight the powerful landowners who control their homeland. One does so politically, the other by joining the Cosa Nostra. Aside from the title, which is the name of the Sicilian town where they live, this has no connection to the *Godfather* movies. Rated R for profanity, violence. 1985; 115m.

CORNERED ★★★
DIR: Edward Dmytryk. **CAST:** Dick Powell, Walter Slezak, Micheline Cheirel, Luther Adler, Morris Carnovsky.
Fresh from his success as hardboiled sleuth Philip Marlowe in *Murder, My Sweet*, former song-and-dance man Dick Powell continued to score as a dramatic actor in this thriller about a discharged Canadian airman on the trail of Nazi collaborators who murdered his French wife. The hunt takes him from France to Switzerland to Argentina and a rendezvous within a nest of corrupt Europeans. 1946; B&W; 102m.

CORRUPT ★½
DIR: Roberto Faenza. **CAST:** Harvey Keitel, John Lydon, Sylvia Sidney, Nicole Garcia.
Turtle-paced psychological thriller featuring Harvey Keitel as a corrupt narcotics officer. Suspicion and paranoia run rampant in his department because someone is killing undercover cops. Not rated, but equivalent to an R for violence and profanity. 1984; 99m.

CORRUPT ONES, THE ★★★
DIR: James Hill. **CAST:** Robert Stack, Nancy Kwan, Elke Sommer, Werner Peters.
Robert Stack plays a photographer who receives the key to a Chinese treasure. Not surprisingly, he soon finds that he's not alone in his search for the goodies. This is a good—but

not great—adventure film. 1966; 92m.

CORSICAN BROTHERS, THE (1941) ★★★½
DIR: Gregory Ratoff. **CAST:** Douglas Fairbanks Jr., Ruth Warrick, J. Carrol Naish, Akim Tamiroff, H. B. Warner, Henry Wilcoxon.

Alexandre Dumas's classic story of twins who remain spiritually tied, though separated, crackles in this lavish old Hollywood production. Intrigue and swordplay abound. Douglas Fairbanks Jr. is fine, backed by two of the best supporting players ever: J. Carrol Naish and Akim Tamiroff. 1941; B&W; 112m.

CORVETTE SUMMER ★
DIR: Matthew Roberts. **CAST:** Mark Hamill, Kim Melford, Annie Potts.

This mindless car-chase film finds Mark Hamill in Las Vegas hunting car thieves who have ripped off his Corvette. This film is not even up to par with *Cannonball Run.* Rated PG. 1978; 105m.

COTTON CLUB, THE ★★★★
DIR: Francis Ford Coppola. **CAST:** Richard Gere, Diane Lane, James Remar, Gregory Hines, Lonette McKee.

Despite all the scandal, an inflated budget of more than $50 million, and some ragged last-minute trimming, *The Cotton Club* is a winner. The story about two pairs of brothers, one black and one white, is set at Harlem's most famous nightclub. Cornet player Gere and moll Diane Lane make love while gangster James Remar (as Dutch Schultz) fumes, and Gregory Hines dances his way into the heart of songbird Lonette McKee in this flawed but brilliant film. Rated R for violence, nudity, profanity, and suggested sex. 1984; 128m.

COUNT OF MONTE CRISTO, THE (1934) ★★★★
DIR: Rowland V. Lee. **CAST:** Robert Donat, Elissa Landi, Irene Hervey, Louis Calhern, Sidney Blackmer, Raymond Walburn, O. P. Heggie.

In the title role, Robert Donat heads a superb, fine-tuned cast in this now classic film of Dumas's great story. Innocent sailor Edmond Dantes, falsely accused of aiding the exiled Napoleon and infamously imprisoned for fifteen years, escapes to levy revenge on those who framed him. A secret cache of treasure makes it all very sweet. 1934; B&W; 119m.

COUNT OF MONTE CRISTO, THE (1975) ★★★½
DIR: David Greene. **CAST:** Richard Chamberlain, Tony Curtis, Louis Jourdan, Donald Pleasence, Taryn Power.

Solid TV adaptation of the Alexandre Dumas classic. Richard Chamberlain cuts a dashing figure as the persecuted Edmond Dantes. The casting of Tony Curtis as the evil Mondego works surprisingly well. 1975; 100m.

CRASHOUT ★★½
DIR: Lewis R. Foster. **CAST:** William Bendix, Arthur Kennedy, Luther Adler, William Talman, Marshall Thompson.

Okay story about the odyssey of six convicts who crash out of prison. Unfortunately, the fine character development is hurt by a sometimes static plot and disappointing climax. William Bendix, however, is wonderfully unsympathetic as the self-serving ringleader. 1955; B&W; 82m.

CRAZY MAMA ★★★
DIR: Jonathan Demme. **CAST:** Stuart Whitman, Cloris Leachman, Ann Sothern, Jim Backus.

Vibrant film blends crime, comedy, and finely drawn characterizations in this story of three women on a crime spree from California to Arkansas and their experiences with the various men they pick up along the way. Successful mixture of music and atmosphere of the 1950s, coupled with a 1970s attitude, makes this an enjoyable film. Rated PG. 1975; 82m.

CRIME KILLER, THE ★
DIR: George Pan-Andreas. **CAST:** George Pan-Andreas, Leo Morrell, Athan Karras.

A confusing plot has a no-nonsense cop getting suspended, teaming up with two of his ex–Vietnam buddies, and smashing a guns-and-airplane deal with an Arab connection. Insipid. Unrated. 1985; 90m.

CRIME STORY ★★★½
DIR: Abel Ferrara. **CAST:** Dennis Farina, Anthony Denison, Stephen Lang, Darlanne Fluegel, Bill Smitrovich, John Santucci, Steve Ryan, Bill Campbell, Paul Butler.

Former Chicago cop Dennis Farina makes a believable and charismatic hero in this pilot for the Michael Mann–produced TV series. As Mike Torello, Farina attempts to stop the rise of ambitious hood Lucca (Anthony Denison) in the Mafia hierarchy. Strong character performances by an offbeat supporting cast make this an exceptional film of its kind. Made for TV. 1986; 96m.

CRIMSON GHOST, THE ★★½
DIR: William Witney, Fred Bannon. **CAST:** Charles Quigley, Linda Stirling, Clayton Moore, Kenne Duncan, I. Stanford Jolley, Tom Steele, Dale Van Sickel.

Yet another death-dealing device falls into the wrong hands when a physicist loses his counteratomic Cyclotrode to henchmen of the mysterious Crimson Ghost, a villain dressed in a black cape with skeletal hands and a death's-head face. Criminologist Duncan Richards (Charles Quigley) comes to the rescue. 1946; B&W; 12 chapters.

CRIMSON PIRATE, THE ★★★★½
DIR: Robert Siodmak. **CAST:** Burt Lancaster, Nick Cravat, Eva Bartok, Torin Thatcher, Christopher Lee.

One of the all-time great swashbucklers, this follow-up to *The Flame and the Arrow* features the incredibly agile Burt Lancaster besting villains and winning fair maids in high style. Lancaster's partner from his circus days, Nick Cravat, joins in for some rousing action scenes. It's part adventure story, part spoof, and always entertaining. 1952; 104m.

CROSS MISSION ★★
DIR: Al Bradley. **CAST:** Richard Randall.

There's lots of shooting, some martial arts, even a little voodoo in this predictable tale about a pretty photographer and a handsome soldier of fortune in a banana republic. They are taken prisoner by the rebels, then converted to the cause. Rated R. 1989; 90m.

CROSS OF IRON ★★★½
DIR: Sam Peckinpah. **CAST:** James Coburn, Maximilian Schell, James Mason, David Warner.

With this action-packed war film, director Sam Peckinpah proved that he hadn't lost the touch that made *Ride the High Country* and *The Wild Bunch* such memorable movies. Still, *Cross of Iron* did not receive much acclaim when released. Perhaps it was the theme: the heroics of weary German soldiers in World War II. A precursor of *Das Boot*, this film is an interesting work by one of Hollywood's more original directors. Rated R. 1977; 119m.

CRUSOE ★★½
DIR: Caleb Deschanel. **CAST:** Aidan Quinn, Ade Sapara.

This film by noted cinematographer-turned-director Caleb Deschanel is an attractive but incomplete examination of *Robinson Crusoe*, with a twist: the Defoe classic has been updated to the early nineteenth century, and Crusoe is now a young slave trader living and working in Virginia. Aidan Quinn makes an appealing title character. Rated PG-13. 1989; 97m.

CRY OF BATTLE ★½
DIR: Irving Lerner. **CAST:** James MacArthur, Van Heflin, Rita Moreno, Leopoldo Salcedo, Sidney Clute.

The son (James MacArthur) of a wealthy businessman gets caught in the Philippines during the Japanese occupation and has to resort to guerrilla warfare. Poorly directed, but does address the ethical questions of racism and the conduct of war. Not rated; with violence. 1957; B&W; 99m.

CRY OF THE INNOCENT ★★★½
DIR: Michael O'Herlihy. **CAST:** Rod Taylor, Joanna Pettet, Nigel Davenport, Cyril Cusack, Jim Norton, Alexander Knox.

This exciting made-for-TV suspense thriller has Rod Taylor playing the grieving husband and father who loses his wife and children when a plane crashes into their summer home in Ireland. When a Dublin detective tells Taylor the crash was no accident, Taylor is determined to find out who planted the bomb in the plane. 1980; 93m.

CUBA ★★★
DIR: Richard Lester. **CAST:** Sean Connery, Brooke Adams, Jack Weston, Hector Elizondo, Denholm Elliott, Chris Sarandon, Lonette McKee.

A thinly veiled remake of *Casablanca*, this Richard Lester film is nonetheless far superior to J. Lee Thompson's similar *Cabo Blanco* (which starred Charles Bronson). Sean Connery and Brooke Adams play one-time lovers renewing their passion amid the dangerous doings during the fall of Batista in 1959. As usual, Lester invests his tale with memorable bits. Rated R. 1979; 121m.

CYCLONE ★
DIR: Fred Olen Ray. **CAST:** Heather Thomas, Martin Landau, Jeffrey Combs, Troy Donahue, Martine Beswick, Robert Quarry, Huntz Hall.

Stupid action flick about a top-secret military experiment—a militarized motorcycle—that is leaked to a group of arms smugglers. When the head scientist of the project is killed, his girlfriend steps in to guard the two-wheeled tank from the bad guys. Rated R for violence and profanity. 1986; 89m.

DAIN CURSE, THE ★
DIR: E. W. Swackhamer. **CAST:** James Coburn, Hector Elizondo, Jason Miller, Jean Simmons.

A poor, two-hour version of a just passable TV miniseries based on the Dashiell Hammett mystery classic. James Coburn is fine as the dapper detective hero but is thwarted by a muddled screenplay. Unrated. 1978; 123m.

DAM BUSTERS, THE ★★★★½
DIR: Michael Anderson. **CAST:** Richard Todd, Michael Redgrave, Ursula Jeans, Basil Sydney.

Richard Todd and Michael Redgrave star in this British film about the development and use of a specially designed bomb to destroy a dam in Germany during World War II. An outstanding cast and great script. 1954; 102m.

DAMN THE DEFIANT! ★★★★
DIR: Lewis Gilbert. **CAST:** Alec Guinness, Dirk Bogarde, Maurice Denham, Anthony Quayle.

Authenticity is the hallmark of this sea saga of the Napoleonic period. This British production pits the commanding officer of a British warship against a hated second officer. The performances are superb. 1962; 101m.

DANCE OR DIE ★½
DIR: Richard W. Munchkin. **CAST:** Ray Kieffer, Rebecca Barrington.

Another listless made-for-video thriller, from the same folks who gave the world *L.A. Crackdown* (Parts 1 and 2), *The Killing Game*, and other forgettable programs. This one pits a drug-addicted Las Vegas choreographer against mob drug dealers and federal drug agents. 1988; 81m.

DANDY IN ASPIC, A ★★
DIR: Anthony Mann. **CAST:** Laurence Harvey, Tom Courtenay, Mia Farrow, Lionel Stander, Harry Andrews.

Who's on whose side? That's the question that pops up most often in this confusing, rather flat spy thriller. Laurence Harvey plays a double agent based in Berlin who is ordered to kill himself. This was director Anthony Mann's last film; he died during production and Harvey completed the direction. 1968; 107m.

DANGER ZONE, THE ★
DIR: Henry Vernon. **CAST:** Michael Wayne, Jason Williams, Suzanne Tara, Robert Canada, Juanita Ranney.

Contrived low-budget flick with not one, but three lurid stories. One concerns a drug ring, another deals with a female singing group, and the third is about a hell-raising motorcycle gang. There's also a psychopathic murderer on the loose. Rated R for language, nudity, and violence. 1986; 90m.

DANGEROUS CHARTER ★
DIR: Robert Gottschalk. **CAST:** Chris Warfield, Sally Fraser, Chick Chandler.

Three fishermen find an abandoned yacht with a corpse on board. They set out to find the murderers, and soon they're involved in heroin smuggling. Yawn. Further proof that anything that was ever put on film will sooner or later wind up on video. 1962; B&W; 74m.

DANGEROUS LOVE
DIR: Marty Ollstein. **CAST:** Elliott Gould, Lawrence Monoson, Anthony Geary.

A video dating service offers more than romance when a maniac killer with a camera begins murdering his dates and taping their deaths. When a yuppie computer whiz is framed for the murders, he hacks his way to the killer. There's hacking of every sort in this one, both in front of and behind the camera. Rated R for nudity, profanity, and violence. 1988; 96m.

DANGEROUS MISSION ★★
DIR: Louis King. **CAST:** Victor Mature, Piper Laurie, Vincent Price, William Bendix.

In this below-average movie, Piper Laurie witnesses a mob killing in New York City and has to flee the city because the killers are after her. The chase ends at Glacier National Park. A good cast but an overdone plot. 1954; 75m.

DAREDEVILS OF THE RED CIRCLE ★★★
DIR: William Witney, John English. **CAST:** Charles Quigley, Bruce Bennett, David Sharpe, Carole Landis.

One of the most action-packed serials of all time pits three college athletes (including former Tarzan Bruce Bennett and ace stunt man David Sharpe) against the evil #39013, a former convict who disguises himself in order to gain power and exact vengeance on the society that imprisoned him. Fast-paced and well-acted. 1939; B&W; 12 chapters.

DARING DOBERMANS, THE ★★½
DIR: Byron Chudnow. **CAST:** Charles Knox Robinson, Tim Considine, David Moses, Joan Caulfield.

Fun sequel to *The Doberman Gang* is a little more kiddy-oriented, but it's still okay, featuring another well-planned caper for the canine stars. Rated PG for very light violence and language. 1973; 90m.

DARING GAME ★★½
DIR: Laslo Benedek, Ricou Browning. **CAST:** Lloyd Bridges, Nico Minardos, Michael Ansara, Joan Blackman, Shepperd Strudwick.

Ivan Tors, producer of TV's *Sea Hunt* and *Flipper*, heads back into the water for this unsuccessful series pilot. It's about a team of commandos nicknamed The Flying Fish who are proficient on land, air, and sea. No better or worse than a lot of stuff that *did* make it to TV. 1968; 101m.

DARK AGE ★★½

DIR: Arch Nicholson. **CAST:** John Jarratt, Nikki Coghill, Max Phipps.

What begins as a blatant *Jaws* rip-off becomes an entertaining thriller about a giant killer crocodile that may also be the spirit of an Aboriginal tribe. A bit tough to follow due to Australian accents, but this flick offers a tolerable way to kill an hour and a half. Rated R for violence. 1987; 90m.

DARK PASSAGE ★★★

DIR: Delmer Daves. **CAST:** Humphrey Bogart, Lauren Bacall, Bruce Bennett, Agnes Moorehead.

This is an okay Humphrey Bogart vehicle in which the star plays an escaped convict who hides out at Lauren Bacall's apartment while undergoing a face change. The stars are watchable, but the uninspired direction (including some disconcerting subjective camera scenes) and the outlandish plot keep the movie from being a real winner. 1947; B&W; 106m.

DARKSIDE, THE ★★

DIR: Constantino Magnatta. **CAST:** Tony Galati, Cyndy Preston.

A rookie cab driver picks up a porn star who is being pursued by thugs. She has a reel of film that proves her producers are actually making snuff films. There's some good suspense here, but melodramatic acting holds it back. Rated R for nudity, violence, and profanity. 1987; 95m.

DAWN PATROL, THE ★★★★

DIR: Edmund Goulding. **CAST:** Errol Flynn, Basil Rathbone, David Niven, Melville Cooper, Barry Fitzgerald, Donald Crisp.

Basil Rathbone is excellent as a commanding officer of a frontline British squadron during World War I who has no choice but to order raw replacements into the air against veteran Germans. Errol Flynn and David Niven shine as gentlemen at war. A fine film. 1938; B&W; 103m.

DAWSON PATROL, THE ★

DIR: Peter Kelly. **CAST:** George R. Robertson, Tim Henry, Neil Dainaro, James B. Douglas.

A Royal Canadian Mounted Police dogsled expedition turns tragic in this feeble docudrama set at the turn of the century. A voice-over narration tries to cover the poor production values and makes the movie much worse. Not rated, but contains violence. 1985; 75m.

DAY OF THE ASSASSIN ★

DIR: Brian Trenchard Smith, Carlos Vasallo. **CAST:** Chuck Connors, Glenn Ford, Richard Roundtree, Jorge Rivero, Henry Silva, Andres Garcia.

Chuck Connors plays a James Bond–type hero in this dull action film. The shah of Iran's yacht blows up and sinks in a South American bay. In its hull is the exiled leader's treasure—thus sparking international interest in the booty. Not rated; contains violence and profanity. 1979; 94m.

DAY OF THE JACKAL, THE ★★★★

DIR: Fred Zinnemann. **CAST:** Edward Fox, Alan Badel, Tony Britton, Cyril Cusack.

Edward Fox is a cunning assassin roaming Europe in hopes of a crack at General Charles de Gaulle. High suspense and a marvelous performance by Fox underscore a strong storyline. Rated PG. 1973; 141m.

DAYS OF HELL

DIR: Anthony Richmond. **CAST:** Conrad Nichols, Kiwako Harada.

Good luck staying awake through this yawner about a group of mercenaries sent into Afghanistan to rescue a scientist, only to find that they're really pawns in another scheme to seize a nerve-gas formula. As one character puts it, "This whole business stinks like a flounder." Unrated. 1984; 88m.

DAYTON'S DEVILS ★½

DIR: Jack Shea. **CAST:** Leslie Nielsen, Rory Calhoun, Lainie Kazan, Barry Sadler, Georg Stanford Brown.

Leslie Nielsen leads a group of has-beens and ex-cons—or, as the video box says, "a melting pot of losers"—in a robbery of an Air Force base bank. 1968; 107m.

DEAD-BANG ★★★½
DIR: John Frankenheimer. **CAST:** Don Johnson, Penelope Ann Miller, William Forsythe, Bob Balaban, Tim Reid.

Don Johnson stars as real-life L.A. detective Jerry Buck, whose investigation into the murder of a police officer leads to the discovery of a chilling conspiracy. Johnson's strong performance is supported by an excellent cast. John Frankenheimer directs with authority and adds texture to the familiar plot. Rated R for violence, profanity, nudity, and simulated sex. 1988; 109m.

DEAD HEAT ON A MERRY-GO-ROUND ★★★½
DIR: Bernard Girard. **CAST:** James Coburn, Camilla Sparv, Aldo Ray, Ross Martin, Severn Darden, Robert Webber.

This thoroughly engrossing film depicts the heist of an airport bank. Not a breezy caper flick, it unfolds a complex plot in a darkly intelligent manner. The cast is impeccable. James Coburn delivers one of his most effective performances. 1966; 104m.

DEAD POOL, THE ★★★★
DIR: Buddy Van Horn. **CAST:** Clint Eastwood, Patricia Clarkson, Liam Neeson, Evan Kim.

Clint Eastwood's fifth Dirty Harry adventure is a surprisingly strong entry in the long-running series. Action and chuckles are in abundance as our hero tracks down a weirdo who is murdering celebrities on a list that also carries Harry's name. It's good fun for fans. Rated R for violence and profanity. 1988; 92m.

DEAD RECKONING ★★★
DIR: John Cromwell. **CAST:** Humphrey Bogart, Lizabeth Scott, Morris Carnovsky, Charles Cane, Marvin Miller, Wallace Ford, George Chandler.

World War II veteran Humphrey Bogart is caught in a web of circumstance when he seeks the solution to an old army buddy's disappearance. Lizabeth Scott and Morris Carnovsky tell too many lies trying to cover it all up. A brutal yet sensitive example of *film noir*. Bogart is excellent. 1947; B&W; 100m.

DEADLINE (1988) ★★★
DIR: Richard Stroud. **CAST:** John Hurt, Imogene Stubbs, Robert McBain, Greg Hicks.

John Hurt gives a moving performance as an alcoholic British journalist who becomes involved in a doomed love affair with a beautiful noblewoman (Imogene Stubbs). Together they weather a revolution on an island estate in the Persian Gulf. Rated R for nudity, profanity, and graphic violence. 1988; 110m.

DEADLINE AT DAWN ★★
DIR: Harold Clurman. **CAST:** Susan Hayward, Paul Lukas, Lola Lane, Bill Williams, Jerome Cowan.

Penned by Clifford Odets, this film is predictable and anticlimactic. While on liberty, sailor Bill Williams is slipped a mickey by Lola Lane and, upon awakening, he finds her dead. With the help of a dancer (Susan Hayward) and a cabbie (played flatly by Paul Lukas), he sets out to clear himself. 1946; B&W; 83m.

DEADLY EMBRACE ★
DIR: Ellen Cabot. **CAST:** Jan-Michael Vincent, Jack Carter, Ken Abraham.

Jan-Michael Vincent is a tycoon who wishes to divorce his wife for his new lover. That being too expensive, he looks for other means. Sexual decadence ends in murder. There's lots of nudity and simulated sex in this unrated, but definitely soft-core, porn dud. 1988; 82m.

DEADLY ENCOUNTER ★★★½
DIR: William A. Graham. **CAST:** Larry Hagman, Susan Anspach, James Gammon, Michael C. Gwynne.

Hounded by mobsters, Susan Anspach enlists the aid of her old lover Larry Hagman, an ex–combat helicopter pilot. Great aerial stunts are a treat and help keep the action moving right along. Pretty good for television. 1972; 100m.

DEADLY FORCE ★★★
DIR: Paul Aaron. **CAST:** Wings Hauser, Joyce Ingalls, Paul Shenar.

Wings Hauser (*Vice Squad*) plays "Stony" Jackson Cooper, an ex-cop who returns to his old Los Angeles stomping grounds to stomp people until he finds the maniac who stomped a buddy's daughter to death. Rated R for violence, nudity, and profanity. 1983; 95m.

DEADLY HERO ★★★½
DIR: Ivan Nagy. **CAST:** Don Murray, Diahn Williams, Lilia Skala, George S. Irving, Conchata Ferrell, Ron Weyand, James Earl Jones, Treat Williams.

Strange yet engaging bad-cop film with Don Murray as a New York police officer struggling to stay on the force after an incident's repercussions threaten his upcoming pension. The film is dated by the trendy mid-Seventies fashions and popular art, yet that is ironically one of its more interesting qualities. Rated PG for violence, profanity. 1975; 102m.

DEADLY ILLUSION ★
DIR: William Tannen, Larry Cohen. **CAST:** Billy Dee Williams, Vanity, Morgan Fairchild, John Beck, Joe Cortese.

An unbelievable plot and an idiotic script are saved from pure turkeydom by some good action. Billy Dee Williams plays an unlicensed private detective on the trail of a murderer. Avoid. Rated R for violence, nudity, and profanity. 1987; 90m.

DEADLY IMPACT ★★
DIR: Larry Ludman. **CAST:** Fred Williamson, Bo Svenson.

Fred Williamson and Bo Svenson work well together in this otherwise contrived, Italian-made action film about an attempt to rip off Las Vegas gambling houses. Rated R. 1985; 90m.

DEADLY INTENT ★★
DIR: Nigel Dick. **CAST:** Lisa Eilbacher, Steve Railsback, Maud Adams, Lance Henriksen, Fred Williamson.

A murderous archaeologist returns from an expedition with a priceless jewel and blood on his hands. He's soon murdered and everybody who knew him is after his widow in hopes of finding the jewel. Although the cast is talented, none of them can get this thriller off the ground. The film is flawed by poor pacing and bad logic. Rated R for violence and language. 1988; 83m.

DEADLY PREY
DIR: David A. Prior. **CAST:** Cameron Mitchell, Troy Donahue.

Absolutely wretched piece of celluloid about a secret mercenary boot camp (located conveniently in southeast Los Angeles) that abducts innocent citizens from the streets and uses them as prey for the secret soldiers' training. Yet another nail for Cameron Mitchell's film-career coffin. Rated R for violence and profanity. 1987; 87m.

DEADLY REVENGE ★
DIR: Juan Carlos Sesanzo. **CAST:** Rodolfo Ranni, Julio de Grazia.

Talky crime drama (dubbed in English) about a mild-mannered writer who agrees to take over a nightclub after its owner, a childhood friend, is killed. What he doesn't know is that his friend was killed because he was using the club for drug smuggling. Rated R for profanity, violence, nudity, and sexual situations. 1984; 90m.

DEADLY STRANGER ★½
DIR: Max Kleven. **CAST:** Darlanne Fluegel, Michael J. Moore, John Vernon.

A drifter (Michael J. Moore) takes a job as a farm laborer on a plantation where the owner and a local union leader are conspiring to exploit migrant workers. The owner's mistress (Darlanne Fluegel) tries to get Moore's help in reclaiming some of the union's dirty money. Clichéd movie wastes the talents of Fluegel and the time of the viewer. Unrated; nudity. 1988; 93m.

DEADLY TWINS
DIR: Joe Oaks. **CAST:** Judy Landers, Audrey Landers.

A typical revenge flick about twin sisters who are gang-raped. When the wheels of justice don't turn for them, they turn their own wheels and go after their attackers themselves. Extremely low production values make this one a chore to watch. Not rated, but contains adult themes. 1985; 87m.

DEADLY VENGEANCE
DIR: A. C. Qamar. **CAST:** Arthur Roberts, Alan Marlowe, Bob Holden.

The poor acting, editing, and lighting in this insipid film make one wonder if it was planned by a couple of beginning film students over a keg of beer. Contains obscenities, simulated sex scenes, and violence. 1985; 84m.

DEAR DETECTIVE ★★½
DIR: Dean Hargrove. **CAST:** Brenda Vaccaro, Arlen Dean Snyder, Ron Silver, Michael MacRae, Jack Ging, M. Emmet Walsh.

A lighthearted film with moments of quality about a female homicide detective involved in a series of murdered local government officials, counterpointed by an amusing love interest with a mild-mannered university professor. Unrated with mild violence. Made for TV. 1979; 92m.

DEATH BEFORE DISHONOR
DIR: Terry Leonard. **CAST:** Fred Dryer, Brian Keith, Joanna Pacula, Paul Winfield.

Grade Z war film has Fred Dryer as a Marine Corps sergeant in an unnamed Middle Eastern country. His commanding officer, Brian Keith, is kidnapped by Arab terrorists and most of his men are killed. Rated R for violence and profanity. 1986; 112m.

DEATH CHASE ★½
DIR: David A. Prior. **CAST:** William Zipp, Paul Smith, Jack Starrett, Bainbridge Scott.

An innocent jogger is caught up in a shoot-out, given a gun by a dying man, and suddenly finds himself in the midst of an elaborate chase game being controlled by a shadowy corporate head. The premise is intriguing, but the execution is uninspired in this shoddily made thriller. 1988; 88m.

DEATH HUNT ★★★½
DIR: Peter R. Hunt. **CAST:** Charles Bronson, Lee Marvin, Andrew Stevens, Angie Dickinson, Carl Weathers, Ed Lauter.

Based on the true story of a hazardous manhunt in the Canadian Rockies, *Death Hunt* pits trapper Charles Bronson against Mountie Lee Marvin. This gritty adventure film, directed by Peter Hunt, also features vicious dogfights and bloody shootouts set against the spectacular scenery of the Yukon Territory. Rated R. 1981; 97m.

DEATH KISS, THE ★★★
DIR: Edwin L. Marin. **CAST:** Bela Lugosi, David Manners, Adrienne Ames, John Wray, Vince Barnett, Edward Van Sloan.

Entertaining movie-within-a-movie whodunit is a treat for fans of early 1930s films and a pretty well-paced mystery to boot as Bela Lugosi (in fine, hammy form) is embroiled in the investigation of a murder that took place during filming. 1933; B&W; 75m.

DEATH ON THE NILE ★★★½
DIR: John Guillermin. **CAST:** Peter Ustinov, Bette Davis, David Niven, Mia Farrow, Angela Lansbury, George Kennedy, Jack Warden.

The second in the series of films based on the Hercule Poirot mysteries, written by Agatha Christie, is good, but nothing special. Peter Ustinov stars as the fussy Belgian detective adrift in Africa with a set of murder suspects. Despite a better-than-average Christie plot, this film, directed by John Guillermin tends to sag here and there. Rated PG. 1978; 140m.

DEATH SQUAD, THE ★★
DIR: Harry Falk. **CAST:** Robert Forster, Michelle Phillips, Claude Akins, Melvyn Douglas.

A self-appointed coterie of cops is rubbing out criminals beating the rap on legal technicalities. A former officer is given the job of finding out who's doing it and cleaning house. Clint Eastwood did it all infinitely better in *Magnum Force*. Made for television. 1974; 78m.

DEATH TARGET ★★
DIR: Peter Hyams. **CAST:** Jorge Montesi, Elaine Lakeman.

Three soldiers for hire reunite in one last bid for fortune. But when one of the guys falls for a drug-addict hooker, her loony pimp gets into the act, putting a wrench in the works for everyone. Macho. No rating. 1983; 72m.

DEATH WISH ★★★★
DIR: Michael Winner. **CAST:** Charles Bronson, Hope Lange, Vincent Gardenia, Jeff Goldblum.

Charles Bronson gives an excellent performance as Paul Kersey, a mild-mannered New Yorker moved to violence when his daughter is raped and his wife killed by sleazy muggers. It's a gripping story of one man's revenge. Rated R because of nudity and violence (includes a graphic rape scene). 1974; 93m.

DEATH WISH II ★
DIR: Michael Winner. **CAST:** Charles Bronson, Jill Ireland, Vincent Gardenia, J. D. Cannon, Anthony Franciosa.

This carbon-copy sequel to the successful *Death Wish* is a revolting, violent crime chiller. Picking up where the first left off, Paul Kersey (Charles Bronson) now lives in Los Angeles, where his daughter and his housekeeper are murdered. Rated R because of nudity and violence. 1982; 93m.

DEATH WISH III
DIR: Michael Winner. **CAST:** Charles Bronson, Deborah Raffin, Ed Lauter, Martin Balsam.

Paul Kersey (Charles Bronson), loses a loved one and then goes on another rampage. Someone should go on a rampage and destroy all the copies of this piece of trash. Rated R for violence, profanity, drug use, nudity, and sex. 1985; 99m.

DEATH WISH 4: THE CRACKDOWN ★
DIR: J. Lee Thompson. **CAST:** Charles Bronson, Kay Lenz, John P. Ryan, Perry Lopez, Soon-Teck Oh, George Dickerson, Dana Barron.

Emotional attachments and logical reasoning have been completely tossed out the window in the fourth *Death Wish* entry. Charles Bronson is back as the vigilante, but this time he's hired by a newspaper magnate to destroy two drug families operating in Los Angeles. Rated R for violence and language. 1987; 98m.

DEATHMASK ★★
DIR: Richard Friedman. **CAST:** Farley Granger, Lee Bryant, Arch Johnson.

This talky, confusing screenplay is interesting in concept but is never sure where it's going. The plot involves a medical investigator who, after his daughter drowns, pours all his obsessive energy into investigating the death of a young boy. Not rated. 1984; 103m.

DEATHSHOT
DIR: Mitch Brown. **CAST:** Richard C. Watt, Frank Himes.

Two Illinois detectives will stop at nothing to break up a drug ring, leaning on an assortment of pimps and junkies to get information. This depressing (doesn't the sun ever shine in Illinois?) tale with a cast of greasy-haired, pimply-faced actors could have been the basis for a *Saturday Night Live* skit, except it's played straight. 1973; 90m.

DECEIVERS, THE ★★½
DIR: Nicholas Meyer. **CAST:** Pierce Brosnan, Shashi Kapoor, Saeed Jaffrey.
Melodramatic yarn set in 1820s India and based on the true story of the murderous Thuggee cult. Pierce Brosnan stars as Lt. William Savage, a young British officer who goes undercover and joins the cult. This slow-going film has its moments. Rated PG-13. 1988; 103m.

DEEP, THE ★★
DIR: Peter Yates. **CAST:** Robert Shaw, Jacqueline Bisset, Nick Nolte, Louis Gossett Jr., Eli Wallach, Robert Tessier.
The success of *Jaws* prompted this screen adaptation of another Benchley novel, but the results weren't nearly as satisfying. A good cast founders in this waterlogged tale of treasure-hunting. Rated PG. 1977; 123m.

DEFENSE PLAY ★
DIR: Monte Markham. **CAST:** David Oliver, Monte Markham.
Substandard spy story about a group of newly graduated high-school geniuses taking on some nasty Russian spies. Too complicated for its own good. Not rated; contains profane language, violence, and nudity. 1988; 95m.

DEFIANCE ★★★
DIR: John Flynn. **CAST:** Jan-Michael Vincent, Art Carney, Theresa Saldana, Danny Aiello, Fernando Lopez.
Potent story depicts savage New York street gang terrorizing helpless neighborhood. Outsider Jan-Michael Vincent reluctantly gets involved. This well-directed film packs quite a wallop. Rated R for violence and profanity. 1980; 102m.

DELIVERANCE ★★★★★
DIR: John Boorman. **CAST:** Jon Voight, Burt Reynolds, Ned Beatty, Ronny Cox, James Dickey.
Jon Voight, Burt Reynolds, and Ned Beatty are superb in this first-rate film about a canoe trip down a dangerous river that begins as a holiday but soon turns into a weekend of sheer horror. Based on the novel by James Dickey. Rated R for profanity, sex, and violence. 1972; 109m.

DELOS ADVENTURE, THE
DIR: Joseph Purcell. **CAST:** Roger Kern, Jenny Neuman, Kurtwood Smith, Kevin Brophy.
Scientists stumble on a secret Soviet military operation on an island and are hunted down by snipers. Sounds interesting, huh? Unfortunately, the poor acting and script prevent it from being more than a time waster. Rated R for gratuitous nudity and excessive violence and gore. 1987; 98m.

DELTA FORCE, THE ★★
DIR: Menahem Golan. **CAST:** Chuck Norris, Lee Marvin, Martin Balsam, Joey Bishop, Robert Forster, Lainie Kazan, George Kennedy, Hanna Schygulla, Susan Strasberg, Bo Svenson, Robert Vaughn, Shelley Winters.
In this disappointing action film, which is perhaps best described as "The Dirty Dozen at the Airport," Chuck Norris and Lee Marvin are leaders of an anti-terrorist group charged with saving the passengers on a hijacked airliner. Rated R for profanity and violence. 1986; 126m.

DELTA FOX
DIR: Ferd Sebastian, Beverly Sebastian. **CAST:** Priscilla Barnes, Richard Lynch, Stuart Whitman, John Ireland, Richard Jaeckel.
A hired assassin finds that he himself has been set up to be killed while making a run from Florida to California. Another turkey from the husband and wife team who gave the world *Gator Bait* and other exploitation drivel, this one isn't as violent as their usual, which only makes it more boring. Rated R. 1977; 92m.

DESERT FOX, THE ★★★★
DIR: Henry Hathaway. **CAST:** James Mason, Jessica Tandy, Cedric Hardwicke, Luther Adler, Desmond Young.

A tour-de-force performance by James Mason marks this film biography of German Field Marshal Rommel. His military exploits are glossed over in favor of the human story of the disillusionment and eventual involvement in the plot to assassinate Hitler. 1951; B&W; 88m.

DETECTIVE, THE (1954) ★★★½
DIR: Robert Hamer. **CAST:** Alec Guinness, Joan Greenwood, Peter Finch, Bernard Lee, Sidney James.

The versatile Alec Guinness is sublime in this deft film presentation of G. K. Chesterton's priest-detective in action. Here Father Brown seeks out purloined art treasures and the culprits responsible. Joan Greenwood, of the ultrathroaty voice, and the rest of the cast fit like Savile Row tailoring. Intelligent, highly entertaining fare from Britain. 1954; B&W; 91m.

DEVASTATOR, THE ★½
DIR: Cirio H. Santiago. **CAST:** Richard Hill, Katt Shea, Crofton Hardester, Kaz Garas, Terence O'Hara, Bill McLaughlin.

Lousy acting and writing ravage this movie about a Vietnam vet (Richard Hill) who assembles a squad of buddies to battle an evil marijuana plantation owner. Rated R for violence and language. 1985; 89m.

DIAMONDS ★★★
DIR: Menahem Golan. **CAST:** Robert Shaw, Richard Roundtree, Barbara Hershey, Shelley Winters.

Well-planned plot and good chemistry between Robert Shaw and Richard Roundtree make this an enjoyable film of action and intrigue. When a British entrepreneur hires an ex-con and his girlfriend to assist him in a $100 million diamond heist the stage is set for an amazing number of plot twists, filmed in the blazing landscapes of Israel. 1975; 108m.

DIAMONDS ARE FOREVER ★★★★
DIR: Guy Hamilton. **CAST:** Sean Connery, Jill St. John, Charles Gray, Bruce Cabot.

This release was supposed to be Sean Connery's last appearance as James Bond before he decided to *Never Say Never Again*. It's good fun for 007 fans and far superior to most of the Roger Moore films that followed it. Rated PG. 1971; 119m.

DICK TRACY ★★★
DIR: Ray Taylor, Alan James. **CAST:** Ralph Byrd, Kay Hughes, Smiley Burnette, Lee Van Atta, Francis X. Bushman.

Chester Gould's comic-strip detective Dick Tracy (Ralph Byrd) chases a mysterious criminal known as *The Spider* who has kidnapped his brother and turned him into a slave. Great stunts and plenty of action in this one. 1937; B&W; 15 chapters.

DICK TRACY, DETECTIVE ★½
DIR: William Berke. **CAST:** Morgan Conway, Anne Jeffreys, Mike Mazurki, Jane Greer.

Standard second-feature fare with Morgan Conway as an unconvincing Dick Tracy tangling with the denizens of the underworld. 1945; B&W; 62m.

DICK TRACY MEETS GRUESOME ★★½
DIR: John Rawlins. **CAST:** Ralph Byrd, Boris Karloff, Anne Gwynne, Edward Ashley, June Clayworth.

Everybody's favorite Dick Tracy, Ralph Byrd, returns to the role he originated in serials for Republic Studios just in time to do battle with Gruesome, played with his usual style by the great Boris Karloff. 1947; B&W; 65m.

DICK TRACY RETURNS ★★★
DIR: William Witney, John English. **CAST:** Ralph Byrd, Lynne Roberts (Mary Hart), Charles Middleton, David Sharpe, Jerry Tucker, Ned Glass.

Ralph Byrd's second outing as comic-strip detective Dick Tracy finds the unbeatable G-man hot on the trail of the murderous Stark gang, an evil family that has killed one of Tracy's men. 1938; B&W; 15 chapters.

DICK TRACY VS. CRIME INC. ★★★

DIR: William Witney, John English. **CAST:** Ralph Byrd, Michael Owen, Jan Wiley, John Davidson, Ralph Morgan.

Dick Tracy is called in to help stop the mysterious "Ghost," a ruthless member of the Council of Eight, a group of influential citizens attempting to rid the city of crime. 1941; B&W; 15 chapters.

DICK TRACY VERSUS CUEBALL ★½

DIR: Gordon Douglas. **CAST:** Morgan Conway, Anne Jeffreys, Lyle Latell, Rita Corday, Dick Wessel.

Dick Tracy chases a bald strangler who made off with a fortune in jewelry in this low-budget feature film. Morgan Conway's anemic Dick Tracy holds this one back, but Dick Wessel as Cueball peps up this modest programmer. 1946; B&W; 62m.

DICK TRACY'S DILEMMA ★★½

DIR: John Rawlins. **CAST:** Ralph Byrd, Lyle Latell, Kay Christopher, Jack Lambert, Ian Keith.

Two-fisted detective Dick Tracy (Ralph Byrd) finds himself up against a maniacal killer with an iron hook. 1947; B&W; 60m.

DICK TRACY'S G-MEN ★★★

DIR: William Witney, John English. **CAST:** Ralph Byrd, Irving Pichel, Ted Pearson, Jennifer Jones, Walter Miller.

FBI agent Dick Tracy is forced to pursue the evil Zarnoff, the head of an international spy ring, after already capturing him and witnessing his execution. The ruthless spy lord is revived by drugs and redoubles his efforts at sabotage, putting Tracy and his men in one tight spot after another. 1939; B&W; 15 chapters.

DIE HARD ★★★★½

DIR: John McTiernan. **CAST:** Bruce Willis, Alan Rickman, Bonnie Bedelia, Alexander Godunov, Paul Gleason, William Atherton, Hart Bochner, James Shigeta.

If this rip-roaring action picture doesn't recharge your batteries, you're probably dead. Alan Rickman and Alexander Godunov play terrorists who invade an L.A. high-rise. The direction of John McTiernan packs a wallop. Bruce Willis is more human, not to mention chattier, than most action heroes. Also unusual is the strength and independence of the female lead, Bonnie Bedelia. This adventure lends itself to repeated viewing. Rated R for violence, nudity, profanity, and drug use. 1988; 131m.

DILLINGER (1945) ★★★

DIR: Max Nosseck. **CAST:** Edmund Lowe, Anne Jeffreys, Lawrence Tierney, Eduardo Ciannelli, Marc Lawrence, Elisha Cook Jr.

This look at the life and style of archetypal American gangster-antihero John Dillinger bids fair to be rated a *film noir*. Tough guy off-screen Lawrence Tierney is perfect in the title role. 1945; B&W; 89m.

DILLINGER (1973) ★★★★

DIR: John Milius. **CAST:** Warren Oates, Ben Johnson, Cloris Leachman, Michelle Phillips, Richard Dreyfuss, Harry Dean Stanton, Geoffrey Lewis, Steve Kanaly, Frank McRae.

John Milius made an explosive directorial debut with this rip-roaring gangster film featuring Warren Oates in his best starring role. As a jaunty John Dillinger, he has all the charisma of a Cagney or a Bogart. In many ways, this is a gangster version of Sam Peckinpah's *The Wild Bunch*, with a superb supporting cast energizing every scene. Rated R for profanity and violence. 1973; 96m.

DINNER AT THE RITZ ★★½

DIR: Harold Schuster. **CAST:** David Niven, Paul Lukas, Annabella, Romney Brent.

Good cast makes British whodunit about Annabella seeking her father's murderer an enjoyable diversion. Well-produced, with just a light enough touch to balance out all the familiar elements of crime melodrama. Early David Niven effort displays his unique qualities at comedy and light drama. 1937; B&W; 77m.

DIRTY DOZEN, THE ★★★★½
DIR: Robert Aldrich. **CAST:** Lee Marvin, Ernest Borgnine, Charles Bronson, Jim Brown, John Cassavetes, Donald Sutherland, Clint Walker.

Lee Marvin is assigned to take a group of military prisoners behind German lines and strike a blow for the Allies. It's a terrific entertainment—funny, star-studded, suspenseful, and even touching. 1967; 145m.

DIRTY HARRY ★★★★½
DIR: Don Siegel. **CAST:** Clint Eastwood, Harry Guardino, John Mitchum, Reni Santoni, Andy Robinson, John Vernon.

This is the original and still the best screen adventure of Clint Eastwood's maverick San Francisco detective. Outfoxed by a maniacal killer (Andy Robinson), "Dirty Harry" Callahan finally decides to deal out justice in his own inimitable and controversial fashion for an exciting, edge-of-your-seat climax. Rated R. 1971; 102m.

DIRTY MARY, CRAZY LARRY ★★★
DIR: John Hough. **CAST:** Peter Fonda, Susan George, Vic Morrow, Adam Roarke, Roddy McDowall.

Race-car driver Peter Fonda and his two accomplices lead Vic Morrow and a small army of law enforcement officers on a frantic, nonstop chase in this satisfying low-budget action film. Rated R for language, violence. 1974; 93m.

DISAPPEARANCE, THE ★★★★
DIR: Stuart Cooper. **CAST:** Donald Sutherland, Francine Racette, David Hemmings, John Hurt, Christopher Plummer.

This exciting film has Donald Sutherland portraying a professional hit man who can't do his job properly after his wife disappears. He pursues a top man in the organization (Christopher Plummer) because he believes that he is responsible for his wife's disappearance. Rated R for sex and violence. 1977; 80m.

DISHONORED LADY ★
DIR: Robert Stevenson. **CAST:** Hedy Lamarr, Dennis O'Keefe, John Loder, William Lundigan.

Beautiful and glamorous magazine executive Hedy Lamarr is accused of killing her former boyfriend and refuses to testify at her trial. Ponderous adaptation of a successful Broadway drama. 1947; B&W; 85m.

DISORGANIZED CRIME ★★
DIR: Jim Kouf. **CAST:** Hoyt Axton, Corbin Bernsen, Rubén Blades, Fred Gwynne, Ed O'Neil, Lou Diamond Phillips, Daniel Roebuck, William Russ.

Misadventures of five ex-cons trying to pull a bank heist in a small Montana town. When their leader is busted by a couple of New Jersey cops, the other four decide to rob the bank anyway. Some fine performances are wasted in this disorganized mess that can't decide whether it's a comedy or an action drama. Rated R for violence and profanity. 1989; 98m.

DISTANT DRUMS ★★
DIR: Raoul Walsh. **CAST:** Gary Cooper, Mari Aldon, Richard Webb, Ray Teal, Arthur Hunnicutt, Robert Barrat, Clancy Cooper.

Good old laconic Gary Cooper tracks down gun smugglers who are selling firesticks to renegade Seminole Indians in the Everglades. A tired story and screenplay manage to get by on Cooper, good photography, and music. 1951; 101m.

DIXIE DYNAMITE ★½
DIR: Lee Frost. **CAST:** Warren Oates, Christopher George, Jane Anne Johnstone, R. G. Armstrong.

Imagine one of those cheesy Burt Reynolds good-ol'-boys movies, where he and some buddies raise heck in revenge for mistreatment from the local deputy. Now imagine it without Burt Reynolds. The ever-watchable Warren Oates isn't enough to make this one worth wasting your time. Rated PG. 1976; 89m.

DOBERMAN GANG, THE ★★½
DIR: Byron Chudnow. **CAST:** Byron Mabe, Julie Parrish, Simmy Bow, Hal Reed.

A vicious pack of Doberman pinschers are trained as bank robbers in this implausible but well-made action tale. Rated PG for language, mild violence. 1972; 87m.

DR. KILDARE'S STRANGE CASE ★★★
DIR: Harold S. Bucquet. **CAST:** Lew Ayres, Lionel Barrymore, Laraine Day, Nat Pendleton, Samuel S. Hinds, Emma Dunn.

Friendly old Dr. Gillespie and his medical whiz junior, Dr. Kildare, are featured in this tale of the deranged. Lew Ayres deals with a cuckoo; nurse Laraine Day provides love interest; Lionel Barrymore is at the ready to counsel as Dr. Gillespie. This is one of the best of the Kildare series. 1940; B&W; 76m.

DR. NO ★★★★
DIR: Terence Young. **CAST:** Sean Connery, Ursula Andress, Jack Lord, Bernard Lee.

The first of the James Bond movie sensations, it was in this film that Sean Connery began his ascent to stardom as the indomitable British secret agent 007. Bond is sent to Jamaica to confront the evil Dr. No, a villain bent on world domination. Ursula Andress was the first of the (now traditional) sensual Bond heroines. As with most of the series' films, there is a blend of nonstop action and tongue-in-cheek humor. 1962; 111m.

DR. SYN ★★½
DIR: Roy William Neill. **CAST:** George Arliss, Margaret Lockwood, John Loder, Roy Emerton, Graham Moffatt.

Master character actor George Arliss's final film has him playing a traditional English vicar who blossoms into a pirate when the sun goes down. Nothing earthshaking here, but direction and rich atmosphere make it all palatable. 1937; B&W; 80m.

DOG DAY ★
DIR: Yves Boisset. **CAST:** Lee Marvin, Jean Carmet, Victor Lanoux, Miou-Miou, Tina Louise.

Lee Marvin is an American fugitive on the run with millions of dollars in this maudlin and often offensive tale of intrigue set in France. Hiding out in a farmhouse, he is exploited by the vulgar and mercenary family that lives there. Sex, profanity, and violence. 1985; 101m.

DOGS OF WAR, THE ★★
DIR: John Irvin. **CAST:** Christopher Walken, Tom Berenger, Colin Blakely, Hugh Millais.

A graphic account of the coup d'etat of a West African dictatorship (starring Christopher Walken as the leader of a band of mercenaries), this film depicts a senseless act of violence totally motivated by the lust for wealth and power. Unfortunately, this movie doesn't quite hold together. Rated R for violence. 1980; 102m.

$ (DOLLARS) ★★★★★
DIR: Richard Brooks. **CAST:** Warren Beatty, Goldie Hawn, Gert Fröbe, Robert Webber.

Simply one of the best heist capers ever filmed. Warren Beatty, bank employee, teams with Goldie Hawn, hooker, to duplicate critical safe deposit keys for a cool $1.5 million. Intriguing concept, deftly directed in a fashion that reveals continuous unexpected plot twists. Rated R for violence and sexual situations. 1972; 119m.

DON IS DEAD, THE ★★★½
DIR: Richard Fleischer. **CAST:** Anthony Quinn, Frederic Forrest, Robert Forster, Al Lettieri, Angel Tompkins, Charles Cioffi.

Director Richard Fleischer gives us yet another story of a Mafia family struggling for control of Las Vegas interests (à la *The Godfather*). Well-acted performances make for better-than-average viewing. Rated R for violence. 1973; 115m.

DON Q, SON OF ZORRO ★★★½

DIR: Donald Crisp. **CAST:** Douglas Fairbanks Sr., Mary Astor, Jack McDonald, Donald Crisp.

Derring-do in old California as the inimitable Douglas Fairbanks fights evildoers and greedy oppressors while saving ladylove Mary Astor from a fate worse than death. Well-mounted, inventive, and fast-paced. Silent. 1925; B&W; 111m.

DON WINSLOW OF THE COAST GUARD ★★

DIR: Ford Beebe, Ray Taylor. **CAST:** Don Terry, Elyse Knox.

Popular comic-strip hero Don Winslow returns to the screen to guard America's coastline from saboteurs and fifth columnists. Pretty standard serial stuff with a lot of stock footage and narrow escapes aplenty. 1943; B&W; 13 chapters.

DOOMED TO DIE ★★

DIR: William Nigh. **CAST:** Boris Karloff, Grant Withers, Marjorie Reynolds, Melvin Lang, Guy Usher.

Monogram's popular series about the aged Chinese detective, Mr. Wong, was running out of steam by the time this film, the fourth in the series, was released. Wong (Boris Karloff) is called in by hard-boiled homicide captain Grant Withers after a millionaire is murdered and his ship, which is carrying a fortune in negotiable bonds, is sunk. 1940; B&W; 68m.

DOUBLE DEAL ★½

DIR: Abby Berlin. **CAST:** Richard Denning, Marie Windsor, Carleton Young, Fay Baker, Taylor Holmes, Paul E. Burns, James Griffith.

Casual direction and a poor adaptation of a story that wasn't very good in the first place resulted in this dull programmer from RKO. A tough oil engineer accepts a rush job to bring in an oil well owned by driller Carleton Young. After the driller is killed, brave engineer Richard Denning stays on to help Marie Windsor, who has inherited the oil field. 1950; B&W; 83m.

DOWN TWISTED ★★

DIR: Albert Pyun. **CAST:** Carey Lowell, Charles Rocket, Thom Matthews, Linda Kerridge.

Stylish *Romancing the Stone*–type thriller about an innocent waitress who agrees to help her roommate out of a jam. Before she knows it, she's stuck in Central America with a disreputable soldier of fortune and a lot of people shooting at her. The convoluted plot is needlessly overcomplicated; it gets better as it goes along, though you may not find it worth the effort. Rated PG-13. 1987; 88m.

DOWN UNDER ★

DIR: Not Credited. **CAST:** Don Atkinson, Donn Dunlop, Patrick Macnee.

Patrick Macnee narrates this crudely shot tale of two Southern California surfers who catch gold fever in Australia. Stale and pointless. 1984; 90m.

DRAGNET (1954) ★★★★

DIR: Jack Webb. **CAST:** Jack Webb, Ben Alexander, Richard Boone, Ann Robinson, Dennis Weaver.

Dragnet is the feature-length (color!) version of the popular detective series with director-star Jack Webb as the no-nonsense Sgt. Joe Friday, and Ben Alexander as his original partner, Frank Smith. In the story, based as always on a true case, Friday and Smith are assigned to solve the murder of a mobster. All clues seem to lead to his former associates. 1954; 89m.

DRESSED TO KILL ★★★

DIR: Roy William Neill. **CAST:** Basil Rathbone, Nigel Bruce, Patricia Morison, Edmund Breon, Frederic Worlock, Harry Cording.

Final entry in Universal's popular Rathbone/Bruce Sherlock Holmes series. This one involves counterfeiting, specifically a Bank of England plate hidden in one of three music boxes. After filming was completed, Rathbone—fearing typecasting—had had enough; his concerns clearly were genuine, as he did not work again for nearly nine years. Unrated—suitable for family viewing. 1946; B&W; 72m.

DRIVER, THE ★★★★
DIR: Walter Hill. **CAST:** Ryan O'Neal, Bruce Dern, Isabelle Adjani, Ronee Blakley, Matt Clark.
High-energy crime drama focuses on a professional getaway driver (Ryan O'Neal) and his police pursuer (Bruce Dern). Walter Hill's breakneck pacing and spectacular chase scenes make up for the lack of plot or character development. It's an action movie pure and simple. Rated PG for violence and profanity. 1978; 90m.

DROWNING POOL, THE ★★½
DIR: Stuart Rosenberg. **CAST:** Paul Newman, Joanne Woodward, Anthony Franciosa, Richard Jaeckel, Murray Hamilton, Melanie Griffith, Gail Strickland, Linda Haynes.
Poor follow-up to *Harper*, with Paul Newman re-creating the title role. Director Stuart Rosenberg doesn't come up with anything fresh in this stale entry into the detective genre. Rated PG—violence. 1976; 108m.

DRUMS ★★★½
DIR: Zoltán Korda. **CAST:** Sabu, Raymond Massey, Valerie Hobson, Roger Livesey, David Tree.
Stiff-upper-lip British Empire epic starts slow but builds to an exciting climax as soldiers of the queen aid young Prince Sabu in his struggle against usurping uncle Raymond Massey. 1938; 99m.

DRUMS ALONG THE MOHAWK ★★★★
DIR: John Ford. **CAST:** Claudette Colbert, Henry Fonda, Edna May Oliver, John Carradine, Jessie Ralph, Robert Lowery, Ward Bond.
Claudette Colbert and Henry Fonda are among a group of sturdy settlers of upstate New York during the Revolutionary War. Despite the episodic nature of its story, *Drums Along the Mohawk* emerges as another richly detailed film from director John Ford. Beautifully photographed in color, this work benefits from vibrant supporting performances by Edna May Oliver, Jessie Ralph, John Carradine, and Ward Bond. 1939; 103m.

DRUMS OF FU MANCHU ★★★½
DIR: William Witney, John English. **CAST:** Henry Brandon, Robert Kellard, Gloria Franklin, Olaf Hytten, Tom Chatterton, Luana Walters, George Cleveland, Dwight Frye.
This exciting serial presents the definitive Fu Manchu interpretation with smooth, sinister Henry Brandon splendidly cast as the greatest of all Far Eastern menaces. Sir Dennis Nayland Smith and his associates tackle the deadly doctor and his fierce Dacoit slaves in an effort to keep him from finding the scepter of the great Genghis Khan. 1940; B&W; 15 chapters.

DUEL OF CHAMPIONS ★
DIR: Ferdinando Baldi. **CAST:** Alan Ladd, Robert Keith, Franco Fabrizi.
Alan Ladd is a weary centurion leader in ancient Rome fighting for the glory that once was. Forgettable. 1961; 105m.

DUELLISTS, THE ★★★★
DIR: Ridley Scott. **CAST:** Keith Carradine, Harvey Keitel, Albert Finney, Edward Fox, Cristina Raines, Robert Stephens, Tom Conti.
The Duellists traces a long and seemingly meaningless feud between two soldiers in the Napoleonic Wars. This fascinating study of honor among men is full of irony and heroism. Rated R. 1977; 101m.

DYNASTY OF FEAR ★★
DIR: Jimmy Sangster. **CAST:** Joan Collins, Peter Cushing, Judy Geeson, Ralph Bates.
A slow-paced British murder mystery. An emotionally disturbed young lady is set up with psychological traps to take the blame for murder by a devious and greedy pair of lovers.

Rated PG for relatively mild violence. 1985; 93m.

EACH DAWN I DIE ★★★★
DIR: William Keighley. **CAST:** James Cagney, George Raft, George Bancroft, Jane Bryan, Maxie Rosenbloom.

Energetic Warner Bros. film occasionally slips the bounds of believability but never fails to be entertaining. James Cagney is terrific as the youthful reporter who is framed for murder after exposing a crooked district attorney. 1939; B&W; 92m.

EAGLE HAS LANDED, THE ★★★
DIR: John Sturges. **CAST:** Michael Caine, Donald Sutherland, Robert Duvall.

Michael Caine is a Nazi agent who is given orders to plan and carry out the kidnapping or murder of Prime Minister Churchill. This movie gets started on a promising note, but it is sabotaged by a weak, contrived ending. Rated PG. 1977; 123m.

EARTHQUAKE ★
DIR: Mark Robson. **CAST:** Charlton Heston, Genevieve Bujold, Lorne Greene, Ava Gardner, Walter Matthau, George Kennedy.

Once you get past the special-effects mastery of seeing Los Angeles destroyed, you've got a pretty weak film on your hands. The old classic *San Francisco* did it better. Rated PG. 1974; 129m.

EAST OF BORNEO ★★★
DIR: George Melford. **CAST:** Rose Hobart, Charles Bickford, Georges Renavent, Noble Johnson.

Intrepid and tenacious Rose Hobart searches the teeming Borneo jungle for her supposedly lost doctor husband Charles Bickford, who isn't lost at all but living it up as personal physician to native prince Georges Renavent. Filled with wildlife, this jungle adventure is lots of fun and ends with a bang. 1931; B&W; 77m.

EAST OF KILIMANJARO ★★
DIR: Arnold Belgard. **CAST:** Marshall Thompson, Gaby André.

A deadly virus has affected the cattle of the area in Africa east of Kilimanjaro. A daring photographer throws his weight into the fight against the microbe. Routine adventure. 1957; 75m.

EAT MY DUST ★
DIR: Charles B. Griffith. **CAST:** Ron Howard, Christopher Norris, Dave Madden, Warren Kemmerling.

A low-budget 1976 race yarn notable only for the fact that it gave Ron Howard the power to direct his next starring vehicle, *Grand Theft Auto*, which, in turn, led to such treats as *Night Shift* and *Splash*. Rated PG. 1976; 90m.

EDDIE MACON'S RUN ★★½
DIR: Jeff Kanew. **CAST:** John Schneider, Kirk Douglas, Lee Purcell, Leah Ayres.

John Schneider is a prison escapee who manages to stay one step ahead of the law. Kirk Douglas co-stars as the hard-nosed policeman on his trail. It's a predictable, lightweight movie. Rated PG for vulgar language and violence. 1983; 95m.

EDGE OF DARKNESS ★★★★½
DIR: Martin Campbell. **CAST:** Bob Peck, Joe Don Baker, Jack Woodson, John Woodvine, Joanne Whalley.

A complex mystery produced as a miniseries for British television. The story revolves around a nuclear processing plant and its covert government relations. Bob Peck offers an intense portrayal of a British police detective who, step by step, uncovers the truth as he investigates the murder of his daughter. 1986; 307m.

EIGER SANCTION, THE ★★½
DIR: Clint Eastwood. **CAST:** Clint Eastwood, George Kennedy, Jack Cassidy, Thayer David, Vonetta McGee.

Laughable but entertaining adaptation of Trevanian's equally laughable but entertaining novel. Clint Eastwood is a college professor by day (named Hemlock, no less) and supersecret agent by night sent to expose a killer during a dangerous mountain climb. Outrageously overblown characters and plenty of opportunities for Eastwood to strut his macho stuff. Rated R for violence and sex. 1975; 128m.

8 MILLION WAYS TO DIE ★★
DIR: Hal Ashby. **CAST:** Jeff Bridges, Rosanna Arquette, Alexandra Paul, Andy Garcia.
An alcoholic ex-cop, Jeff Bridges, attempts to help a high-priced L.A. prostitute get away from her boss and crazed Colombian coke dealer boyfriend, Andy Garcia. Considering the talent involved, this one should have been a real killer, but there are too many holes in the script and several dead spots throughout. Rated R for violence, nudity, and language. 1986; 115m.

EL CID ★★★
DIR: Anthony Mann. **CAST:** Charlton Heston, Sophia Loren, Raf Vallone, Hurd Hatfield.
Some of the best battle action scenes ever filmed are included in this 1961 spectacle about the medieval Spanish hero El Cid. Unfortunately, on smaller home screens much of the splendor will be lost. You will be left with the wooden Charlton Heston and the beautiful Sophia Loren in a love story that was underdeveloped due to the movie's emphasis on spectacle. 1961; 184m.

ELECTRA GLIDE IN BLUE ★★★★
DIR: James William Guercio. **CAST:** Robert Blake, Billy Green Bush, Mitchell Ryan, Elisha Cook Jr., Jeannine Riley, Royal Dano.
Robert Blake plays an Arizona cop with aspirations of being a detective. This extremely violent melodrama features good performances by the entire cast with several twists and turns to keep the viewer guessing. Rated R. 1973; 106m.

ELEPHANT BOY ★★★
DIR: Robert Flaherty, Zoltán Korda. **CAST:** Sabu, W. E. Holloway, Walter Hudd, Bruce Gordon.
Sabu made his film debut and became a star in this drama about a boy who claims to know where elephants go to die. Robert Flaherty's co-direction gives the film a travelogue quality, but it interests and delights just the same. 1937; B&W; 80m.

11 HARROWHOUSE ★★½
DIR: Aram Avakian. **CAST:** Charles Grodin, Candice Bergen, James Mason, John Gielgud.
Confused heist caper which vacillates too wildly between straight drama and dark comedy. Diamond salesman Charles Grodin is talked into stealing valuable gems. Too farfetched to be taken seriously, yet that seems to be the intent. An excellent cast goes to waste. Rated PG—mild sexual overtones. 1974; 95m.

EMERALD FOREST, THE ★★★★
DIR: John Boorman. **CAST:** Powers Boothe, Meg Foster, Charley Boorman.
In this riveting adventure film based on a true story, Powers Boothe stars as Bill Markham, an American engineer who, with his family, goes to the Amazon jungle to build a dam. There, his 5-year-old son is stolen by a native tribe known as the Invisible People. Markham spends the next ten years trying to find his son. Rated R for nudity, suggested sex, profanity, and violence. 1985; 110m.

EMPIRE STATE ★½
DIR: Ron Peck. **CAST:** Martin Landau, Ray McAnally, Catherine Harrison.
Visually stunning film collapses under the weight of a leaden plot and shallow performances. Powerful real-estate magnate Martin Landau becomes involved with some shady dealings in London. Rated R for nudity, and violence. 1987; 104m.

ENCHANTED ISLAND ★
DIR: Allan Dwan. **CAST:** Dana Andrews, Jane Powell, Arthur Shields, Don Dubbins.

This dull adaptation of Herman Melville's *Typee* has Dana Andrews as a deserter from a whaling ship who lands on a beautiful island where he falls in love with the perfect native girl, Jane Powell. Sure! 1958; 95m.

ENDLESS NIGHT ★★
DIR: Sidney Gilliat. **CAST:** Hayley Mills, Hywel Bennett, Britt Ekland, George Sanders, Per Oscarsson, Lois Maxwell.

A film adaptation of one of Agatha Christie's stories packaged on video in the *Murderer's Row* collection, *Endless Night* is more soap opera than murder mystery. Hywel Bennett is unspectacular as a lower-class English chauffeur who marries rich heiress Hayley Mills. Too many flashbacks make the story choppy and unintelligible. Not rated; contains profane language, violence, and brief nudity. 1972; 95m.

ENDLESS SUMMER, THE ★★★★
DIR: Bruce Brown. **CAST:** Mike Hynson, Robert August.

The only surfing documentary ever to gain an audience outside the Beach Boy set, this is an imaginatively photographed travelogue that captures the joy, danger, and humor of two youths searching worldwide for the perfect wave. Much of the success is attributable to the whimsical narration. 1966; 95m.

ENEMY TERRITORY ★★
DIR: Peter Manoogian. **CAST:** Gary Frank, Ray Parker Jr., Jan-Michael Vincent, Frances Foster.

This film features a good premise but suffers from poor acting, writing, and production values. Gary Frank is an insurance salesman trapped inside a ghetto apartment building and battling a vicious gang. Ray Parker Jr. is his accidental partner. Although handled well in spots, the film has huge lapses of nonaction. Rated R for language, extreme violence, and brief nudity. 1987; 89m.

ENFORCER, THE (1951) ★★★½
DIR: Bretaigne Windust. **CAST:** Humphrey Bogart, Zero Mostel, Everett Sloane, Ted de Corsia, Roy Roberts.

A big-city district attorney, Humphrey Bogart, attempts to break up the mob in this effective crime drama. At under ninety minutes, it moves like lightning and is refreshingly devoid of most of the clichés of the genre. 1951; B&W; 87m.

ENFORCER, THE (1976) ★★★★
DIR: James Fargo. **CAST:** Clint Eastwood, Tyne Daly, Harry Guardino, Bradford Dillman, John Mitchum.

A step up from the muddled *Magnum Force* and a nice companion piece to *Dirty Harry*, this third entry in the popular series has detective Harry Callahan grudgingly team with a female cop (Tyne Daly) during his pursuit of a band of terrorists. John Mitchum gives a standout performance in his final series bow as tough cop Frank DiGeorgio. It'll make your day. Rated R. 1976; 96m.

ENIGMA ★★
DIR: Jeannot Szwarc. **CAST:** Martin Sheen, Brigitte Fossey, Sam Neill, Derek Jacobi, Michel Lonsdale, Frank Finlay.

Espionage yarn succumbs to lethargy. The KGB sics an elite group of assassins on five Soviet dissidents. A CIA agent (Martin Sheen) attempts to thwart the insidious scheme by entangling his former lover with the top Russian agent. Rated PG. 1982; 101m.

ENTER THE DRAGON ★★★★
DIR: Robert Clouse. **CAST:** Bruce Lee, John Saxon, Jim Kelly, Ahna Capri, Yang Tse, Angela Mao.

Bruce Lee soared to international superstardom with this fast-paced, tongue-in-cheek kung-fu film. A big-budget American version of the popular Chinese genre, it has a good plot and strong performances—from Lee,

John Saxon, and Jim Kelly. Rated R, due to violence. 1973; 97m.

ENTER THE NINJA ★★

DIR: Menahem Golan. **CAST:** Franco Nero, Susan George, Sho Kosugi, Alex Courtney.

A passable martial arts adventure about practitioners of an ancient Oriental art of killing. Rated R. 1981; 94m.

ESCAPE FROM ALCATRAZ ★★★★

DIR: Don Siegel. **CAST:** Clint Eastwood, Patrick McGoohan, Roberts Blossom, Jack Thibeau.

Any movie that combines the talents of star Clint Eastwood and director Don Siegel is more than watchable. This is a gripping and believable film about the 1962 breakout from the supposedly perfect prison. Patrick McGoohan is also excellent as the neurotic warden. Rated PG. 1979; 112m.

ESCAPE FROM NEW YORK ★★★½

DIR: John Carpenter. **CAST:** Kurt Russell, Lee Van Cleef, Ernest Borgnine, Donald Pleasence, Adrienne Barbeau.

The year is 1997. *Air Force One*—with the president (Donald Pleasence) onboard—is hijacked by a group of revolutionaries and sent crashing into the middle of Manhattan, which has been turned into a top-security prison. It's up to Snake Plissken (Kurt Russell), a former war hero gone renegade, to get him out in twenty-four hours. It's fun, surprise-filled entertainment Rated R. 1981; 99m.

ESCAPE FROM THE KGB

DIR: Harald Phillipe. **CAST:** Thomas Hunter, Marie Versini, Ivan Desny, Walter Barnes.

Badly duplicated to video, this tale of intrigue offers an excellent example of slipshod editing. A jet-setting CIA agent is sent to infiltrate a Siberian spaceport to find out what the Russkies are up to now. Insipid. Not rated. 1987; 99m.

ESCAPE TO ATHENA ★★★

DIR: George Pan Cosmatos. **CAST:** Roger Moore, Telly Savalas, David Niven, Claudia Cardinale, Stefanie Powers, Richard Roundtree, Elliott Gould, Sonny Bono.

Roger Moore as a Nazi officer? Sonny Bono as a member of the Italian Resistance? Elliott Gould as a hippie in a World War II concentration camp? Sound ridiculous? It is. It's a *Hogan's Heroes* for the big screen but, in a dumb sort of way, entertaining. Rated PG. 1979; 101m.

EVEL KNIEVEL ★★½

DIR: Marvin J. Chomsky. **CAST:** George Hamilton, Sue Lyon, Rod Cameron.

Autobiography of motorcycle stunt man Evel Knievel. George Hamilton is surprisingly good as Knievel. Some nice stunts. Rated PG. 1972; 90m.

EVIL THAT MEN DO, THE ★★½

DIR: J. Lee Thompson. **CAST:** Charles Bronson, Theresa Saldana, José Ferrer, Joseph Maher.

Believe it or not, Charles Bronson has made a watchable film for a change. He plays a professional killer who comes out of retirement to avenge the brutal murder of an old friend. Rated R for violence and profanity. 1984; 90m.

EVIL UNDER THE SUN ★★★★

DIR: Guy Hamilton. **CAST:** Peter Ustinov, Jane Birkin, Colin Blakely, James Mason, Roddy McDowall, Diana Rigg, Maggie Smith, Nicholas Clay.

This highly entertaining mystery, starring Peter Ustinov as Agatha Christie's Belgian detective Hercule Poirot, is set on a remote island in the Adriatic Sea where a privileged group gathers at a luxury hotel. Of course, someone is murdered and Poirot cracks the case. Rated PG because of a scene involving a dead rabbit. 1982; 102m.

EXECUTIONER, THE ★★

DIR: Sam Wanamaker. **CAST:** George Peppard, Joan Collins, Judy

Geeson, Oscar Homolka, Keith Michell, Nigel Patrick.

This British spy picture features George Peppard as an intelligence agent who believes he is being compromised by fellow spy Keith Michell. Joan Collins is the love interest. Average. Rated PG. 1970; 107m.

EXPRESS TO TERROR ★

DIR: Dan Curtis. **CAST:** George Hamilton, Steve Lawrence, Stella Stevens, Don Meredith, Fred Williamson, Don Stroud.

This mystery set on a supertrain will come in handy for those times when you're missing those old NBC *Wednesday Night at the Movies* flicks. In this case, a collection of superstars must solve a series of murders on an express from New York to Los Angeles. As blasé as *The Love Boat*, but entertainingly ridiculous. Stirring disco music soundtrack. 1979; 120m.

EXTERMINATOR, THE ★★

DIR: James Glickenhaus. **CAST:** Christopher George, Samantha Eggar, Robert Ginty, Steve James, Tony DiBenedetto.

The Exterminator is a low-budget, extraordinarily violent film. It's the story of a vigilante who takes the law into his own hands when the law refuses to punish the gang members who made a cripple of his best friend during a mugging. Rated R. 1980; 101m.

EXTERMINATOR 2, THE

DIR: Mark Buntzman. **CAST:** Robert Ginty, Deborah Gefner, Frankie Faison, Mario Van Peebles.

In this disgusting cheapo, Robert Ginty returns as the one-man vigilante force set on cleaning up New York City à la *Death Wish*. This time, though, our "hero" has graduated from using a gun to using a blowtorch. Rated R for violence, nudity, and profanity. 1984; 104m.

EXTREME PREJUDICE ★★★★

DIR: Walter Hill. **CAST:** Nick Nolte, Powers Boothe, Maria Conchita Alonso, Michael Ironside, Rip Torn, Clancy Brown, William Forsythe.

Nick Nolte is in peak form in this modern-day western as a two-fisted Texas Ranger whose boyhood friend, Powers Boothe, has become a drug kingpin across the border in Mexico. The federal government sends six high-tech agents to nail Boothe with "extreme prejudice." Rated R for profanity, drug use, nudity, and violence. 1987; 96m.

EYE FOR AN EYE ★★½

DIR: Steve Carver. **CAST:** Chuck Norris, Christopher Lee, Richard Roundtree, Matt Clark, Maggie Cooper.

This surprisingly entertaining kung-fu movie features Chuck Norris as a human weapon battling a variety of bullies. Shawn Kane (Norris) is an ex-cop trying to crack a narcotics-smuggling ring. With the help of a lovely news editor (Maggie Cooper) and a martial arts master (Matt Clark) who doubles as a walking fortune cookie, Kane confronts a sinister Christopher Lee and, finally, a human tank called The Professor. Rated R. 1981; 106m.

EYE OF THE EAGLE ★

DIR: Cirio H. Santiago. **CAST:** Brett Clark, Robert Patrick, Ed Crick, William Steis.

Purports to be Vietnam action flick in the mold of *Platoon* and *Rambo*, but this cheap shoot-'em-up focuses instead on three do-gooders who combat a renegade band of U.S. soldiers called the Lost Command. The good guys are led by Brett Clark, a mondo-muscular hunk who outshoots entire squadrons with only a pistol. Rated R for violence. 1987; 84m.

EYE OF THE NEEDLE ★★★½

DIR: Richard Marquand. **CAST:** Donald Sutherland, Ian Bannen, Kate Nelligan, Christopher Cazenove.

In this adaptation of Ken Follett's novel, Donald Sutherland stars as the deadly Nazi agent who discovers a ruse by the Allies during World War

II. Plenty of suspense and thrills for those new to the story. Rated R because of nudity, sex, and violence. 1981; 112m.

EYE OF THE TIGER ★★★
DIR: Richard C. Sarafian. **CAST:** Gary Busey, Yaphet Kotto, Seymour Cassel.

Buck Mathews (Gary Busey) stands up against a motorcycle gang and the corrupt law enforcement that have plagued a small town in Texas. When the motorcycle gang kills Mathews's wife, he takes revenge. Busey and Yaphet Kotto give quality performances that save this formula vengeance film. Rated R for violence and language. 1986; 90m.

FALCON IN MEXICO, THE ★★
DIR: William Berke. **CAST:** Tom Conway, Mona Maris, Nestor Paiva, Bryant Washburn.

The ninth film in the long-running series finds the suave sleuth south of the border as he tries to recover a woman's portrait. The owner of the gallery where the painting was displayed has been murdered and the artist responsible for the painting was reportedly killed fifteen years earlier, but Tom Conway as the smooth Falcon untangles the mystery. 1944; B&W; 70m.

FALCON TAKES OVER, THE ★★★
DIR: Irving Reis. **CAST:** George Sanders, James Gleason, Ward Bond, Hans Conried, Lynn Bari.

Early entry in the popular *Falcon* mystery film series sets star George Sanders in a search for a missing woman. During the course of this search he encounters a good many of Hollywood's favorite character actors and actresses as well as much of the plot from Raymond Chandler's *Farewell My Lovely*, of which this is the first filmed version. 1942; B&W; 63m.

FALCON'S BROTHER, THE ★★★
DIR: Stanley Logan. **CAST:** George Sanders, Tom Conway, Don Barclay, Jane Randolph, Amanda Varela.

The sophisticated Falcon (played by former Saint, George Sanders) has decoded a Nazi spy message and races against time to prevent the assassination of a South American diplomat. Aided by his brother (in fact Sanders's real-life brother, Tom Conway), the Falcon realizes his goal but pays with his life at the end. Brother Tom vows to bring the guilty to justice and to continue the work his martyred sibling has left undone. This well-made, nicely acted little detective film is a true oddity. 1942; B&W; 63m.

FAMILY, THE (1970) ★★★
DIR: Sergio Sollima. **CAST:** Charles Bronson, Jill Ireland, Telly Savalas, Michael Constantine, George Savalas.

Charles Bronson is mad. Some creep framed him and, what's worse, stole his girl! Bronson is out for revenge. This film has plenty of action, but nothing new to offer. Rated R. 1970; 100m.

FAREWELL MY LOVELY ★★★★½
DIR: Dick Richards. **CAST:** Robert Mitchum, Charlotte Rampling, John Ireland, Sylvia Miles, Harry Dean Stanton.

This superb film adaptation of Raymond Chandler's celebrated mystery novel stands as a tribute to the talents of actor Robert Mitchum. In director Dick Richards's brooding classic of *film noir*, Mitchum makes a perfect, world-weary Philip Marlowe, private eye. The detective's search for the long-lost love of gangster Moose Malloy takes us into the nether world of pre–World War II Los Angeles for a fast-paced, fascinating period piece. Rated R. 1975; 97m.

FAREWELL TO THE KING ★★★½
DIR: John Milius. **CAST:** Nick Nolte, Nigel Havers, Frank McRae, James Fox.

In this old-fashioned, boy's-eye-view adventure epic from writer-director John Milius, Nick Nolte plays a World War II soldier who deserts following Gen. Douglas MacArthur's retreat form Corregidor. Nolte ends up in the jungles of Borneo, where he becomes a king who unifies the island's various tribes of headhunters. Nigel Havers is excellent as the British officer who incites the natives to battle. *Farewell to the King* is in the style of Edgar Rice Burroughs's *Tarzan* stories, with a touch of *Gunga Din* thrown in. Rated R for violence and profanity. 1989; 114m.

FAST LANE FEVER ★★½

DIR: John Clark. **CAST:** Terry Serio, Deborah Conway, Max Cullen, Graham Bond.

A street gang with souped-up street cars bullies others into racing for money. An underdog good guy loses to the bad guys, then comes back against all odds. Interesting cars and a fascinating look at Australia through the camera lens. Rated R for profanity, sex, and violence. 1982; 94m.

FAST MONEY 🦃

DIR: Douglas Holloway. **CAST:** Sammy Allred, Sonny Carl Davis, Lou Perry, Marshall Ford, Doris Hargrave.

This low-quality bore introduces a group of young men who are getting high and smuggling drugs from Mexico—while being pursued by a sheriff and his undercover agents. Sadly, these miscreants are supposed to be the heroes. Rated R for obscenities, drug use, and lawlessness. 1985; 92m.

FASTER PUSSYCAT! KILL! KILL! ★★★½

DIR: Russ Meyer. **CAST:** Tura Satana, Haji, Jori Williams, Juan Bernard.

This movie has everything you could want from a Russ Meyer film. Beautiful girls, fast-paced action, and lots of wild and wacky humor. In its day it was considered fairly hard-core, yet today it could even be shown on late-night television. 1962; B&W; 83m.

FATAL BEAUTY 🦃

DIR: Tom Holland. **CAST:** Whoopi Goldberg, Sam Elliott, Rubén Blades, Harris Yulin, John P. Ryan, Jennifer Warren, Brad Dourif.

This excremental action flick panders to the basest human elements of senseless violence, relentlessly foul language, and ludicrously exaggerated drug use. Whoopi Goldberg stars as an improbably resourceful cop who takes repeated lickin's but keeps on tickin' while pursuing several smarmy drug pushers. The usually capable Sam Elliott is lost in a supporting performance. Rated R for language and excessive violence. 1987; 104m.

FATAL HOUR, THE ★★½

DIR: William Nigh. **CAST:** Boris Karloff, Grant Withers, Marjorie Reynolds, Charles Trowbridge.

Boris Karloff is cast as homicide detective Mr. Wong in this suspenseful thriller about murder and jewel smuggling. Grant Withers is solid as police Captain Street. 1940; B&W; 68m.

FEAR (1988) ★★★

DIR: A. Ferretti. **CAST:** Cliff De Young, Kay Lenz, Frank Stallone.

Vicious, brutal story of four escaped convicts who go on a rampage of murder and kidnapping. Cliff De Young and Kay Lenz star as a married couple whose vacation is terrifyingly interrupted when the cons take them hostage. A surprisingly fine performance by Frank Stallone highlights this impressive study in terror. Rated R for violence and profanity. 1988; 96m.

FEAR CITY ★★

DIR: Abel Ferrara. **CAST:** Tom Berenger, Billy Dee Williams, Rae Dawn Chong, Melanie Griffith, Rossano Brazzi, Jack Scalia.

After a promising directorial debut with *Ms. 45*, Abel Ferrara backslid with this all-too-familiar tale about a psychopath killing prostitutes in New York City. Some good performances and action sequences still can't save this one. Rated R for violence, nudity, and profanity. 1985; 93m.

FFOLKES ★★★
DIR: Andrew V. McLaglen. **CAST:** Roger Moore, James Mason, Anthony Perkins, Michael Parks, David Hedison.

Of course, no movie with Roger Moore is a classic, but this tongue-in-cheek spy thriller with the actor playing against his James Bond stereotype provides some good, campy entertainment. This film features Moore as a woman-hating, but cat-loving, gun for hire who takes on a band of terrorists. Rated PG. 1980; 99m.

FIELD OF HONOR (1986) ★★
DIR: Hans Scheepmaker. **CAST:** Everett McGill, Ron Brandsteder, Hey Young Lee.

Tale of a Dutch infantryman in the Korean War left for dead after a surprise attack by the Chinese. Everett McGill is the survivor who hides out with two shell-shocked kids until the Chinese forces are pushed back. Rated R for violence, profanity, and nudity. 1986; 93m.

FIFTH MUSKETEER, THE ★★
DIR: Ken Annakin. **CAST:** Beau Bridges, Sylvia Kristel, Ursula Andress, Cornel Wilde, Olivia De Havilland, José Ferrer, Rex Harrison, Lloyd Bridges, Alan Hale.

An uninspired retelling of *The Man in the Iron Mask*. Beau Bridges is watchable enough as King Louis XIV and his twin brother, Philipe, who was raised as a peasant by D'Artagnan (Cornel Wilde) and the three musketeers (Lloyd Bridges, José Ferrer, and Alan Hale). The film never springs to life. Rated PG. 1979; 103m.

FIGHTING BACK ★★★
DIR: Lewis Teague. **CAST:** Tom Skerritt, Patti LuPone, Michael Sarrazin, Yaphet Kotto, David Rashe, Ted Ross.

A deli owner decides to organize a neighborhood committee against crime after his wife and mother are victims of violence. Unfortunately, his emotionalism gets in the way of his professionalism, but he still makes his mark—and you can't help but cheer him on. A rapid succession of violent acts, lots of profanity, and occasional nudity make this R-rated film questionable for young audiences. 1982; 98m.

FIGHTING MARINES, THE ★★
DIR: Joseph Kane, B. Reeves "Breezy" Eason. **CAST:** Grant Withers, Adrian Morris, Ann Rutherford, Jason Robards Sr., Pat O'Malley.

A detachment of U.S. Marines runs up against the sabotage of a modern-day pirate when it tries to establish a landing field on Halfway Island in the Pacific. The plot's thin, the acting forced, but the special effects are remarkable. Pieced together from twelve serial chapters. 1936; B&W; 69m.

FIGHTING SEABEES, THE ★★★
DIR: Edward Ludwig. **CAST:** John Wayne, Dennis O'Keefe, Susan Hayward, William Frawley, Duncan Renaldo.

John Wayne and Dennis O'Keefe are construction workers fighting the Japanese in their own way while each attempts to woo Susan Hayward away from the other. This 1944 war film, which co-stars William Frawley, is actually better than it sounds. 1944; B&W; 100m.

FINAL CHAPTER—WALKING TALL ★
DIR: Jack Starrett. **CAST:** Bo Svenson, Margaret Blye, Forrest Tucker, Lurene Tuttle, Morgan Woodward, Libby Boone.

The original *Walking Tall* was a cheaply made, often amateurish film with only graphic violence, a basis in truth, and a powerful performance by Joe Don Baker. Apparently that was enough. The film spawned many imitators, some starring Baker, and two sequels that, oddly enough, did not. The last one is titled *Final Chapter*. While it is not as bad technically as the first, it is flawed just the same, because the script has nothing new to tell us about the life of the protagonist, Buford T. Pusser (Bo Svenson). Rated R for violence. 1977; 112m.

FINAL COMBAT, THE ★★★★
DIR: Luc Besson. **CAST:** Pierre Jolivet, Fritz Wepper, Jean Bouise, Jean Reno.

In a post-apocalypse world, a lonely man makes an attempt to break away and find a kind of happiness. He soon discovers that he must fight for what he desires rather than try to run away. This may sound like any one of the *Mad Max* films, but there are really very few similarities. This is a much more sensitive and cerebral story. The performances are good and the story is compelling, and all this is accentuated by the fact that there is no dialogue in the movie. Rated R for violence. 1984; B&W; 93m.

FINAL COMEDOWN, THE ★
DIR: Oscar Williams. **CAST:** Billy Dee Williams, D'Urville Martin, Celia Kaye, Raymond St. Jacques.

Dated, heavyhanded film about a disgruntled young black man who becomes involved with a group of militants. The group takes on the police, and after being shot, the young man reflects on his prejudice-ridden past. Rated R for violence, profanity, and nudity. 1972; 84m.

FINAL JUSTICE
DIR: Greydon Clark. **CAST:** Joe Don Baker, Venantino Venantini, Helena Abella, Bill McKinney.

In this incoherent ripoff of the Clint Eastwood cops-and-robbers film *Coogan's Bluff*, Joe Don Baker plays a rural sheriff who travels to Italy to take on the Mafia and halt criminal activities. Poor dubbing and mindless violence make this a repelling movie. Rated R for nudity, violence, and language. 1984; 90m.

FINAL MISSION
DIR: Cirio H. Santiago. **CAST:** Richard Young, John Dresden, Kaz Garas, Christine Tudor.

In this stupid *First Blood* ripoff, a Vietnam veteran comes back to the States to become a cop and fight the American traitor he had to deal with back in Southeast Asia. The final scene is a blatant copy of the Sly Stallone film. Not rated, but with profanity, violence, and nudity. 1984; 101m.

FINAL OPTION, THE ★★★★
DIR: Ian Sharp. **CAST:** Judy Davis, Lewis Collins, Richard Widmark, Robert Webber, Edward Woodward.

Judy Davis stars in this first-rate British-made suspense thriller as the leader of a fanatical anti-nuclear group that takes a group of U.S. and British officials hostage and demands that a nuclear missile be launched at a U.S. base in Scotland. If not, the hostages will die. And it's up to Special Air Services undercover agent Peter Skellen (Lewis Collins) to save their lives. Rated R for violence and profanity. 1982; 125m.

FIRE AND ICE (1987) ★
DIR: Willy Bogner. **CAST:** John Eaves, Suzy Chaffee.

When the musical theme of a film offers only the words of the title sung over and over again, you know you're in for an ordeal. Such is the case with *Fire and Ice*, a silly cross-country chase flick in which boy falls for girl and girl doesn't know boy exists! Only the superb ski sequences, set in some of the world's finest ski resorts, make this watchable. No rating. 1987; 80m.

FIRE OVER ENGLAND ★★★
DIR: Alexander Korda. **CAST:** Laurence Olivier, Vivien Leigh, Flora Robson.

A swashbuckling adventure of Elizabethan England's outnumbered stand against the Spanish Armada. Made in the 1930s, it wasn't released in this country until 1941, in order to evoke American support and sympathy for Britain's plight against the Nazi juggernaut during its darkest days. This is only one of the three films that united husband and wife, Laurence

Olivier and Vivien Leigh. 1936; B&W; 92m.

FIREFOX ★★★½
DIR: Clint Eastwood. **CAST:** Clint Eastwood, Freddie Jones, David Huffman, Warren Clarke, Ronald Lacey, Stefan Schnabel.

Clint Eastwood doffs his contemporary cowboy garb to direct, produce, and star in this action-adventure film about an American fighter pilot assigned to steal a sophisticated Russian aircraft. The film takes a while to take off, but when it does, it's good, action-packed fun. Rated PG for violence. 1982; 124m.

FIREPOWER ★★
DIR: Michael Winner. **CAST:** Sophia Loren, James Coburn, O. J. Simpson, Eli Wallach, Vincent Gardenia, Anthony Franciosa.

Firepower is a muddled, mindless mess. A research chemist is blown up by a letter bomb while his wife, Adele Tasca (Sophia Loren), watches helplessly. The chemist was about to prove to the world that a company owned by the third-richest man in the world, Carl Stegner (George Touliatos), has been distributing contaminated drugs responsible for causing the cancerous deaths of a great many people. The widow joins Justice Department agent James Coburn in trying to bring Stegner out of seclusion. Rated R. 1979; 104m.

FIREWALKER ★
DIR: J. Lee Thompson. **CAST:** Chuck Norris, Louis Gossett Jr., Melody Anderson, John Rhys-Davies.

Two soldiers of fortune search for hidden treasure and end up in a Mayan temple of doom. Along the way, they murder Native Americans trying to protect sacred Indian burial grounds. Believe it or not, we're supposed to root for these pinheads. The only thing funny or scary about the movie is that they left room for a sequel. Rated PG. 1986; 96m.

FIRST BLOOD ★★★½
DIR: Ted Kotcheff. **CAST:** Sylvester Stallone, Richard Crenna, Brian Dennehy, David Caruso, Jack Starrett.

Sylvester Stallone is top-notch as a former Green Beret who is forced to defend himself from a redneck cop (Brian Dennehy) in the Oregon mountains. The action never lets up. A winner for fans. Rated R for violence and profanity. 1982; 97m.

FIRST DEADLY SIN, THE ★★
DIR: Brian G. Hutton. **CAST:** Frank Sinatra, Faye Dunaway, James Whitmore, David Dukes, Brenda Vaccaro, Martin Gabel, Anthony Zerbe.

Lawrence Sanders's excellent mystery is turned into a so-so cop flick with Frank Sinatra looking bored as aging Detective Edward X. Delaney, who is on the trail of a murdering maniac (David Dukes). He, however, fares much better than co-star Faye Dunaway, who spends the entire picture flat on her back in a hospital bed. Rated R. 1980; 112m.

FIRST YANK INTO TOKYO ★½
DIR: Gordon Douglas. **CAST:** Tom Neal, Barbara Hale, Richard Loo, Keye Luke, Benson Fong.

Tom Neal has plastic surgery so he can pose as a Japanese soldier and help an American POW escape. As usual, Hollywood casts some fine Asian actors as sinister types. This low-budget melodrama is not worth the time. 1945; B&W; 82m.

FISTS OF FURY ★★★
DIR: Lo Wei. **CAST:** Bruce Lee, Maria Yi, James Tien, Nora Miao.

Bruce Lee's first chop-socky movie (made in Hong Kong) is corny, action-filled, and violent. It's no *Enter the Dragon*, but his fans—who have so few films to choose from—undoubtedly will want to see it again. Rated R. 1972; 102m.

FIVE FOR HELL 🦃
DIR: Frank Kramer. **CAST:** Klaus Kinski, John Garko, Margaret Lee, Nick Jordan, Luciano Rosi, Sam Burke.

In this Italian-made World War II bomb, a special unit of American soldiers goes behind enemy lines to copy the plans of an all-out German offensive. The gimmick in this film is that every soldier has an expertise in one thing or another—none of them having anything to do with combat. Not rated; has sex and violence. 1985; 88m.

FIVE GOLDEN DRAGONS ★½
DIR: Jeremy Summers. **CAST:** Robert Cummings, Rupert Davies, Margaret Lee, Brian Donlevy, Christopher Lee, George Raft, Dan Duryea.

An innocent man runs into an international crime ring in Hong Kong. This British production was Bob Cummings's last feature film. It's a boring, poorly made adventure, featuring cameo appearances by fading stars who would do anything for a free trip. 1967; 93m.

FIVE WEEKS IN A BALLOON ★★★
DIR: Irwin Allen. **CAST:** Red Buttons, Barbara Eden, Fabian, Cedric Hardwicke, Peter Lorre, Herbert Marshall, Billy Gilbert, Reginald Owen, Henry Daniell, Barbara Luna, Richard Haydn.

Up, up, and away on a balloon expedition to Africa, or, Kenya here we come! Author Jules Verne wrote the story. Nothing heavy here, just good, clean fun and adventure in the mold of *Around the World in Eighty Days*. 1962; 101m.

FIX, THE 🦃
DIR: Will Zens. **CAST:** Vince Edwards, Tony Dale, Richard Jaeckel, Julie Hill, Byron Cherry, Charles Dierkop, Don Dubbins, Leslie Leah, Robert Tessier.

Tedious film about drug dealers and the country-and-western performers (Vince Edwards and Tony Dale) who get caught up in the smuggling. Cheaply made. Not rated, has violence. 1984; 95m.

FLAME AND THE ARROW, THE ★★★★
DIR: Jacques Tourneur. **CAST:** Burt Lancaster, Virginia Mayo, Nick Cravat.

Burt Lancaster is at his acrobatic, tongue-in-cheek best in this film as a Robin Hood–like hero in Italy leading his oppressed countrymen to victory. It's a rousing swashbuckler. 1950; 88m.

FLAME OF THE BARBARY COAST ★★½
DIR: Joseph Kane. **CAST:** John Wayne, Ann Dvorak, William Frawley, Joseph Schildkraut.

John Wayne plays a Montana rancher who fights with a saloon owner (Joseph Schildkraut) over the affections of a dance hall girl (Ann Dvorak). This romantic triangle takes place against the backdrop of the San Francisco earthquake. It's watchable, nothing more. 1945; B&W; 91m.

FLAME TO THE PHOENIX, A ★★
DIR: William Brayne. **CAST:** Frederick Treves, Ann Firbank.

On the eve of Hitler's invasion of Poland, British diplomats plan their strategy while the Polish underground prepares for a long, bloody struggle. This talky drama is hard to follow, with characters of various nationalities all speaking with British accents. Unrated, the movie contains brief nudity and sexual situations. 1983; 80m.

FLASH AND THE FIRECAT ★
DIR: Ferd Sebastian, Beverly Sebastian. **CAST:** Richard Kiel, Roger Davis, Tricia Sembera.

Flash (Roger Davis) and Firecat (Tricia Sembera) blaze across the California beaches, stealing cars and robbing banks and doing other dumb things. Nevertheless, surprisingly, they outwit the authorities and eventually get away with their crime spree, proving once again that crime pays—but only in trashy movies like this one. 1975; 94m.

FLASHPOINT ★★★½
DIR: William Tannen. **CAST:** Kris Kristofferson, Treat Williams, Rip Torn, Kevin Conway, Tess Harper.
Kris Kristofferson and Treat Williams star in this taut, suspenseful, and action-filled thriller as two Texas border officers who accidentally uncover an abandoned jeep containing a skeleton, a rifle, and $800,000 in cash—a discovery that puts their lives in danger. Rated PG-13 for profanity and violence. 1984; 95m.

FLAT TOP ★★
DIR: Lesley Selander. **CAST:** Richard Carlson, Sterling Hayden, Keith Larsen, Bill Phillips.
A mediocre World War II action film following the exploits of an aircraft carrier battling the Japanese forces in the Pacific. Most of the battle scenes are taken from actual combat footage. 1952; B&W; 83m.

FLATBED ANNIE AND SWEETIE PIE: LADY TRUCKERS ★★½
DIR: Robert Greenwald. **CAST:** Annie Potts, Kim Darby, Harry Dean Stanton, Arthur Godfrey, Rory Calhoun.
Annie Potts is Flatbed Annie, a veteran trucker who trains a novice named Sweetie Pie (Kim Darby). The two team up in an effort to support their costly rig. A mildly entertaining diversion with a few chuckles along the way. Made for TV. 1979; 104m.

FLESH AND BLOOD ★★★½
DIR: Paul Verhoeven. **CAST:** Rutger Hauer, Jennifer Jason Leigh, Tom Burlinson, Susan Tyrrell, Ronald Lacey, Jack Thompson.
Set in medieval Europe, *Flesh and Blood* follows the lives of two men—mercenary soldier Rutger Hauer and the son of a feudal lord (Tom Burlinson)—and their love for the same woman (Jennifer Jason Leigh). The cast is stellar, the sets are lavish, and the plot turns will keep the viewer guessing, but not in the dark. Rated R for violence, sex, nudity, profanity. 1985; 126m.

FLETCH ★★★★
DIR: Michael Ritchie. **CAST:** Chevy Chase, Joe Don Baker, Tim Matheson, Dana Wheeler-Nicholson, Richard Libertini, M. Emmet Walsh.
Chevy Chase is first-rate as Gregory Mcdonald's wisecracking reporter, I. M. "Fletch" Fletcher, who starts out doing what seems to be a fairly simple exposé of drug dealing in Los Angeles and ends up taking on a corrupt cop (Joe Don Baker), a tough managing editor (Richard Libertini), and a powerful millionaire (Tim Matheson) who wants Fletch to kill him. The laughs are plenty and the action almost nonstop. Rated PG for violence and profanity. 1985; 96m.

FLETCH LIVES ★★★½
DIR: Michael Ritchie. **CAST:** Chevy Chase, Cleavon Little, Hal Holbrook, Julianne Phillips, Richard Libertini, Randall "Tex" Cobb, George Wyner.
Chevy Chase returns to the role of I. M. Fletcher and scores another triumph. Chase was born to play the wisecracking reporter. In this one, Fletch finds himself heir to a southern plantation and quits his newspaper job—only to become both a murder suspect and a target for unscrupulous villains. If you enjoyed the original *Fletch*, this sequel is guaranteed to satisfy. 1989; 98m.

FLIGHT OF THE PHOENIX, THE ★★★★
DIR: Robert Aldrich. **CAST:** James Stewart, Richard Attenborough, Peter Finch, Ernest Borgnine, Hardy Krüger, Ronald Fraser, Christian Marquand, Ian Bannen, George Kennedy, Dan Duryea.
An all-star international cast shines in this gripping adventure about the desert crash of a small plane and the grueling efforts of the meager band of passengers to rebuild and repair it against impossible odds, not the least of which are starvation and/or heat prostration. 1966; 143m.

FLORIDA STRAITS ★★½
DIR: Mike Hodges. **CAST:** Raul Julia, Fred Ward, Daniel Jenkins, Jaime Sanchez, Victor Argo, Ilka Tanya Payan, Antonio Fargas.

Raul Julia is a Cuban refugee who enlists the aid of charter boaters Fred Ward and Daniel Jenkins to help him get back to Cuba and rescue the woman he loves. Although a bit contrived in spots, this is watchable. An unrated HBO production that contains some violence and rough language. 1986; 98m.

FLYING BLIND ★★★
DIR: Frank McDonald. **CAST:** Richard Arlen, Jean Parker.

This is the third release of upscale B pictures from the William H. Pine–William C. Thomas production unit that operated at Paramount Pictures from 1941 through 1945. The previous films were *Power Dive* and *Forced Landing*, and all three share the same topic: aviation. The script here is by Maxwell Shane and deals with heroes versus evil foreign agents in the United States. 1941; B&W; 70m.

FLYING LEATHERNECKS ★★★½
DIR: Nicholas Ray. **CAST:** John Wayne, Robert Ryan, Jay C. Flippen.

John Wayne is the apparently heartless commander of an airborne fighting squad, and Robert Ryan is the caring officer who questions his decisions in this well-acted war film. The stars play off each other surprisingly well, and it's a shame they didn't do more films together. 1951; 102m.

FLYING TIGERS, THE ★★½
DIR: David Miller. **CAST:** John Wayne, John Carroll, Mae Clarke, Gordon Jones.

Exciting dogfight action scenes make this low-budget John Wayne World War II vehicle watchable, but the story sags a bit. 1942; B&W; 102m.

FOLLOW THAT CAR ★
DIR: Daniel Haller. **CAST:** Dirk Benedict, Tanya Tucker, Teri Nunn.

Typical good-ol'-boy action-adventure with our three stars, Dirk Benedict, Tanya Tucker, and Teri Nunn, joining forces with Uncle Sam to get bad guys who are running booze and tobacco without paying any taxes. Lots of singing for Tucker fans and car chases and corny dialogue for the *Cannonball Run* crowd. Nothing new here. Rated PG for language and violence. 1980; 96m.

FOR YOUR EYES ONLY ★★★½
DIR: John Glen. **CAST:** Roger Moore, Carole Bouquet, Lynn-Holly Johnson, Topol.

For the first time since Roger Moore took over the role of 007 from Sean Connery, we have a film in the style that made the best Bond films—*From Russia with Love* and *Goldfinger*—so enjoyable. *For Your Eyes Only* is genuine spy adventure, closer in spirit to the novels by Ian Fleming. Rated PG. 1981; 127m.

FORCE FIVE ★★
DIR: Walter Grauman. **CAST:** Gerald Gordon, Nick Pryor, Bradford Dillman.

In this action-packed but predictable martial arts film, a soldier of fortune and his four buddies rescue a woman held against her will by an evil cult leader on a remote island. Rated R for violence, nudity, and profanity. 1975; 78m.

FORCE OF ONE ★★★
DIR: Paul Aaron. **CAST:** Chuck Norris, Jennifer O'Neill, James Whitmore, Pepe Serna.

This is the sequel to *Good Guys Wear Black*. In this karate film, Chuck Norris cleans up a California town that has drug problems. As always, it only takes one good guy (Norris) to kick and/or punch some sense into the bad guys. Rated PG. 1979; 90m.

FORCE TEN FROM NAVARONE ★
DIR: Guy Hamilton. **CAST:** Robert Shaw, Harrison Ford, Edward Fox, Franco Nero, Barbara Bach, Carl Weathers, Richard Kiel.

This is a poor sequel to the classic *Guns of Navarone*. Decent acting is the only good thing you can say about this World War II film about a commando group out to destroy a bridge. 1978; 118m.

FORCED VENGEANCE ★★½

DIR: James Fargo. **CAST:** Chuck Norris, Mary Louise Weller, Camilla Griggs, Michael Cavanaugh, David Opatoshu, Seiji Sakaguchi.

Even pacing and a somewhat suspenseful plot are not enough to make this film a must-see—unless you're a die-hard Chuck Norris fan, that is. This time, our martial arts master plays an ex–Vietnam vet turned casino security chief living in the Far East. Rated R for violence, nudity, and profanity. 1982; 90m.

FOUR DEUCES, THE ★★

DIR: William H. Bushnell Jr. **CAST:** Jack Palance, Carol Lynley, Warren Berlinger, Adam Roarke, Gianni Russo, H. B. Haggerty, John Haymer, Martin Kove, E. J. Peaker.

Jack Palance is a gang leader during Prohibition times in this high-camp action film about gangsters. The movie is poorly conceived, with an odd mixture of blood and spoof. Not a black comedy; not a serious drama, either. *The Four Deuces* does not have an MPAA rating, but it contains sex, nudity, violence, and profanity. 1975; 87m.

FOUR FEATHERS, THE (1939) ★★★★

DIR: Zoltán Korda. **CAST:** Ralph Richardson, John Clements, June Duprez, C. Aubrey Smith.

A young man (John Clements) from a military background is branded a coward when he forsakes military duty for a home and family during time of war. Rejected by his family, friends, and fiancée, he sets out to prove his manhood. This motion picture was one of the few English productions of its era to gain wide acceptance. It still holds up well today. 1939; 115m.

FOUR FEATHERS, THE (1978) ★★★

DIR: Don Sharp. **CAST:** Beau Bridges, Robert Powell, Simon Ward, Jane Seymour, Harry Andrews.

Solid television retelling of the A. E. W. Mason story, with plenty of action and derring-do. Beau Bridges portrays the Britisher who must prove his bravery to his friends by secretly fighting against Sudanese tribesmen in nineteenth-century Africa. Although the transition of the story from British to American ideals is shaky, the story itself is powerful. 1978; 110m.

FOUR HORSEMEN OF THE APOCALYPSE ★★

DIR: Vincente Minnelli. **CAST:** Glenn Ford, Ingrid Thulin, Charles Boyer, Lee J. Cobb, Paul Henreid, Paul Lukas.

The 1921 silent version of this complex anti-war tale of two brothers who fight on opposite sides during World War I is still the best. When Rudolph Valentino played Julio, you cared. This one, updated to World War II, falls flat, despite a fine cast. 1961; 153m.

FOUR MUSKETEERS, THE ★★★★★

DIR: Richard Lester. **CAST:** Oliver Reed, Raquel Welch, Richard Chamberlain, Frank Finlay, Michael York, Christopher Lee, Faye Dunaway, Charlton Heston.

In this superb sequel to Richard Lester's *The Three Musketeers*, the all-star cast is remarkably good, and the director is at the peak of his form. The final duel between Michael York and Christopher Lee is a stunner. Rated PG. 1975; 108m.

FOURTH PROTOCOL, THE ★★★

DIR: John Mackenzie. **CAST:** Michael Caine, Pierce Brosnan, Joanna Cassidy, Ned Beatty.

Michael Caine is the best component of this stiff screen version of Frederick Forsyth's thriller. Caine is a British agent who suspects "something big" is being smuggled into England; his guess is accurate, and he discovers an atomic-bomb delivery is being supervised by ultra-cool Russian agent Pierce Brosnan. Rated R for violence, nudity, and language. 1987; 119m.

FOXTRAP ★
DIR: Fred Williamson. **CAST:** Fred Williamson, Christopher Connelly, Arlene Golonka.
Another vanity project for ex-athlete Fred Williamson, who writes, produces, and directs these flabby action vehicles for himself. In this one, he plays a bodyguard sent to Europe to find a missing heiress. Rated R for violence, drug use, and sexual situations. 1986; 88m.

FRAMED ★
DIR: Phil Karlson. **CAST:** Joe Don Baker, Conny Van Dyke, Gabriel Dell, Brock Peters, John Marley.
Thoroughly nauseating and graphically violent story of a man (Joe Don Baker) framed for a crime he did not commit, and the outrageous lengths to which he resorts in order to clear his name. Rated R for gory violence and language. 1975; 106m.

FRANTIC ★★★½
DIR: Roman Polanski. **CAST:** Harrison Ford, Emmanuelle Seigner, Betty Buckley, John Mahoney, David Huddleston.
Director Roman Polanski bounces back with this clever and often darkly funny Hitchcockian thriller, which makes Harrison Ford a stranger in the very strange underbelly of Paris. He's a surgeon visiting the city to lecture at a medical conference; when his wife (Betty Buckley) vanishes from their hotel room, he confronts indifference through official channels before trying to puzzle things out on his own. Inexplicably rated R for minimal violence. 1988; 120m.

FREEWAY ★★★
DIR: Francis Della. **CAST:** Darlanne Fluegel, James Russo, Richard Belzer, Michael Callan.
A fad film mirroring the real-life series of freeway killings in the Los Angeles area. A nurse (Darlanne Fluegel), dissatisfied with the police investigation of the murder of her boyfriend by a freeway sniper, pursues the killer on her own. Good acting, exciting direction, and some great action sequences make up for the threadbare plot. Rated R for violence, profanity, and nudity. 1988; 95m.

FRENCH CONNECTION, THE ★★★★★
DIR: William Friedkin. **CAST:** Gene Hackman, Fernando Rey, Roy Scheider, Eddie Egan, Sonny Grosso.
Gene Hackman is an unorthodox New York narcotics cop in this Oscar-winning performance. He and his partner (Roy Scheider) are investigating the flow of heroin coming into the city from France. The climactic chase is the best in movie history. Rated R. 1971; 104m.

FRENCH CONNECTION II, THE ★★
DIR: John Frankenheimer. **CAST:** Gene Hackman, Fernando Rey, Bernard Fresson, Jean-Pierre Castaldi, Charles Millot.
Disappointing sequel to the 1971 winner for best picture has none of the thrills, chills, and action of the original. Instead, New York detective Popeye Doyle (Gene Hackman), who has journeyed to Paris to track the drug trafficker who eluded him in the States, finds himself addicted to heroin and suffering withdrawal. He isn't the only one who suffers. . . . There's the viewer, too. Rated R. 1975; 119m.

FRESH KILL
DIR: Joseph Merhi. **CAST:** Flint Keller, Tricia Parks.
A would-be actor becomes involved with a not-so-innocent woman and her ex-boyfriend, a vicious Mexican gangster who will stop at nothing to get her back. Made-for-video junk marked by some truly repulsive violence. 1987; 90m.

FRIDAY FOSTER ★★½
DIR: Arthur Marks. **CAST:** Pam Grier, Julius W. Harris, Thalmus Rasulala, Carl Weathers, Eartha Kitt, Godfrey Cambridge, Yaphet Kotto.
In this blaxploitation effort, based on a comic strip, Pam Grier plays the title character, a fashion photographer who doubles as a two-fisted avenger—this time taking on anti-black terrorists. A strong supporting cast helps. Rated R. 1975; 90m.

FROM HELL TO BORNEO ★★
DIR: George Montgomery. **CAST:** George Montgomery, Torin Thatcher, Julie Gregg, Lisa Moreno.
George Montgomery owns an island. Crooks and smugglers want in. He defends it. Sweat and jungle. 1964; 96m.

FROM HELL TO VICTORY ★½
DIR: Hank Milestone. **CAST:** George Peppard, George Hamilton, Capucine, Horst Buchholz, Sam Wanamaker.
This hokey story of a bunch of strangely allied friends during the early stages of World War II has next to nothing to offer. An exception must be made for the lovely Capucine, who is really quite good. Rated PG. 1979; 100m.

FROM RUSSIA WITH LOVE ★★★★½
DIR: Terence Young. **CAST:** Sean Connery, Lotte Lenya, Robert Shaw, Daniela Bianchi.
The definitive James Bond movie. Sean Connery's second portrayal of Agent 007 is right on target. Lots of action, beautiful women, and great villains. Connery's fight aboard a passenger train with baddy Robert Shaw is as good as they come. 1963; 118m.

FUGITIVE GIRLS
DIR: A. C. Stephen. **CAST:** Jabee Abercrombie, Rene Bond, Edward D. Wood Jr.
Here's a video treasure for camp buffs—a women's prison movie written by Ed *(Plan 9 from Outer Space)* Wood! Actually, these oh-so-tough gals bust out of the big house and set off in search of their hidden loot. It's terribly made, with many inept day-for-night shots in which you can barely see what's going on. But the hardboiled dialogue is pretty funny, and Wood even has a cameo role as a hillbilly gas-station attendant! Rated R for nudity and sexual situations. 1975; 90m.

FUGITIVE: THE LAST EPISODE, THE (TELEVISION SERIES) ★★★½
DIR: Don Medford. **CAST:** David Janssen, Barry Morse, Bill Raisch, Diane Brewster.
Based on circumstantial evidence, Dr. Richard Kimble (David Janssen) is sentenced to death for the murder of his wife. He escapes from the grasp of Indiana police lieutenant Philip Gerard (Barry Morse) and goes in search of the one-armed man he believes was the real culprit. After four outstanding seasons of adventures on the run, the series ends in run-of-the-mill fashion. Kimble, still pursued by the obsessive Gerard, finally encounters the one-armed man. Though somewhat disappointing as the climax to a classic series, this two-part episode is a must for fans. 1967; 120m.

FUNERAL IN BERLIN ★★★½
DIR: Guy Hamilton. **CAST:** Michael Caine, Oscar Homolka, Eva Renzi, Paul Hubschmid, Guy Doleman.
Second in Michael Caine's series of three "Harry Palmer" films, following *The Ipcress File* and preceding *The Billion-Dollar Brain.* This time, working-class spy Palmer assists in the possible defection of a top Russian security chief (Oscar Homolka). As usual, Caine can do no wrong; his brittle performance and the authentic footage of the Berlin Wall add considerably to the film's bleak tone. Unrated; suitable for family viewing. 1967; 102m.

FURTHER ADVENTURES OF TENNESSEE BUCK, THE ★½
DIR: David Keith. **CAST:** David Keith, Kathy Shower, Sidney Lassick.

Yet another cheap imitation of Indiana Jones, with David Keith playing an incorrigible jungle adventurer hired as a guide by a young couple. Kathy Shower, a 1987 *Playboy* playmate, is the female side of the couple; she can't act worth a lick. Rated R for violence, language, nudity, and simulated sex. 1988; 90m.

F/X ★★★½
DIR: Robert Mandel. **CAST:** Bryan Brown, Brian Dennehy, Diane Venora, Cliff De Young, Mason Adams, Jerry Orbach.

In this fast-paced, well-acted suspense thriller, Bryan Brown plays special effects wizard Rollie Tyler, who accepts thirty thousand dollars from the Justice Department's Witness Relocation Program to stage the fake assassination of a mob figure who has agreed to name names. After he successfully fulfills his assignment, Tyler is double-crossed and must use his wits and movie magic to survive. Rated R for profanity, suggested sex, and violence. 1986; 110m.

GALLAGHER'S TRAVELS ★½
DIR: Michael Caulfield. **CAST:** Ivar Kants, Joanne Samuel, Stuart Campbell, Jennifer Hagan.

This comedy-adventure concerns an English reporter who teams up with an Australian photographer to track down an animal-smuggling ring. There's not much adventure, and Joanne Samuel as the photographer is the most obnoxious sidekick in recent cinema history. 1987; 94m.

GAME FOR VULTURES ★★
DIR: James Fargo. **CAST:** Joan Collins, Richard Harris, Richard Roundtree, Ray Milland.

A long, dusty, and violent trek through the agonies of South Africa's ongoing black and white conflict. Strong cast, strong theme, weak movie. Rated R for lots of machine-gun violence. 1986; 113m.

GAME OF DEATH
DIR: Robert Clouse. **CAST:** Bruce Lee, Kareem Abdul-Jabbar, Danny Inosanto, Gig Young, Hugh O'Brian, Colleen Camp, Dean Jagger, Chuck Norris.

The climactic twenty minutes of Bruce Lee in action fighting Kareem Abdul-Jabbar and Danny Inosanto are thrilling. The rest of the film is not. Though top-billed, Lee only appears in those few scenes. He died shortly after their completion. It was left to film producer Raymond Chow and his associates to build a film around them to capitalize on Lee's popularity. Rated R. 1979; 102m.

GANG BUSTERS ★½
DIR: Bill Karan. **CAST:** Myron Healey, Sam Edwards, Don Harvey, Frank Gerstle.

As a film about prison life and various attempts at breakout, this picture simply doesn't measure up. 1955; B&W; 78m.

GANGS, INC. ★★
DIR: Phil Rosen. **CAST:** Joan Woodbury, Jack LaRue, Alan Ladd, John Archer, Vince Barnett.

Low-budget crime drama about an anguished woman with an unhappy past who seeks justification in a life of crime. Also titled *Paper Bullets*. 1941; B&W; 72m.

GANGSTER WARS ★★½
DIR: Richard C. Sarafian. **CAST:** Michael Nouri, Brian Benben, Joe Penny.

This movie traces the lives of mobsters "Lucky" Luciano, "Bugsy" Siegel, and Meyer Lansky from their childhood friendship to becoming the most powerful leaders in organized crime during the 1920s. This is an action-packed gangster movie, which at times is difficult to follow and tends to lead the viewer down some dead ends. Rated PG for violence. 1981; 121m.

GATOR ★★
DIR: Burt Reynolds. **CAST:** Burt Reynolds, Jack Weston, Lauren Hutton, Jerry Reed, Alice Ghostley, Mike Douglas, Dub Taylor.

Burt Reynolds directed this mildly entertaining sequel to *White Lightning*. In it, Burt plays an ex-con out to get revenge—with the help of undercover agent Jack Weston—on some nasty southern politicians. Rated PG. 1976; 116m.

GATOR BAIT ★
DIR: Ferd Sebastian, Beverly Sebastian. **CAST:** Claudia Jennings, Sam Gilman, Clyde Ventura.

Claudia Jennings plays a Cajun alligator poacher in the Louisiana bayou who is wrongfully blamed for a murder. She is pursued by the authorities and the slain man's surviving family. A lot of action here, but the direction and performances are poor. Rated R for violence, profanity, and nudity. 1973; 91m.

GATOR BAIT II—CAJUN JUSTICE ★★
DIR: Ferd Sebastian, Beverly Sebastian. **CAST:** Jan MacKenzie.

A revenge flick with a twist: a happy ending. Cajun newlyweds are ravaged by a group of bayou inbreds. The low-budget look and poor acting rate only two stars, but this is a decent entry in the revenge category. Rated R for violence. 1988; 95m.

GAUNTLET, THE ★½
DIR: Clint Eastwood. **CAST:** Clint Eastwood, Sondra Locke, Pat Hingle, William Prince.

One of actor-director Clint Eastwood's few failures, this release features the squinty-eyed star as an alcoholic, barely capable cop assigned to bring a prostitute (Sondra Locke) to trial. Corrupt officials do everything they can to stop him, which leads to a completely preposterous and violent showdown. Rated R. 1977; 109m.

GENERAL DIED AT DAWN, THE ★★★
DIR: Lewis Milestone. **CAST:** Gary Cooper, Akim Tamiroff, Madeleine Carroll, Porter Hall, Dudley Digges.

Nicely turned story of adventurer Gary Cooper battling Chinese warlord Akim Tamiroff. Film is a bit short on action but draws some fine character studies. Madeleine Carroll is good as Cooper's love interest, but it is Tamiroff who steals the show. 1936; B&W; 97m.

GETAWAY, THE ★★★★
DIR: Sam Peckinpah. **CAST:** Steve McQueen, Ali MacGraw, Ben Johnson, Sally Struthers.

Top-notch adventure and excitement occur when convict Steve McQueen has his wife seduce the Texas Parole Board chairman (Ben Johnson) in exchange for his early freedom. McQueen becomes jealous and resentful after the deal is consummated and kills the chairman, setting off a shotgun-charged chase. Rated PG. 1972; 122m.

GETTING EVEN ★½
DIR: Dwight H. Little. **CAST:** Edward Albert, Audrey Landers, Joe Don Baker.

This is a fast-paced but unspectacular action-adventure film. The hero is a wealthy industrialist with a passion for danger. Fighting terrorism for the U.S. government, he attempts to stop a rival from killing the people of Texas with nerve gas. Rated R for violence and nudity. 1986; 89m.

GHOST PATROL ★★
DIR: Sam Newfield. **CAST:** Tim McCoy, Claudia Dell, Walter Miller, Wheeler Oakman, Slim Whitaker.

Colonel Tim McCoy takes a commanding lead in this low-budget film about a government agent investigating the strange crashes of airplanes carrying top-secret information. This pseudoscience-fiction story appears to have been an effort to cash in on the unexpected success of Gene Autry's

Phantom Empire and Tom Mix's *Miracle Rider*. 1936; B&W; 57m.

GHOST WARRIOR ★★½
DIR: Larry Carbol. **CAST:** Hiroshi Fujioka, John Calvin, Janet Julian, Andy Wood.

In Japan, two skiers exploring a cave find a four-hundred-year-old samurai warrior entombed in ice. He is taken to the United States in a hush-hush operation and revived. Although slow at times and obviously derivative of the film *Iceman*, *Ghost Warrior* is an entertaining, though violent, diversion. Rated R for violence. 1984; 86m.

GLADIATOR, THE ★★
DIR: Abel Ferrara. **CAST:** Ken Wahl, Nancy Allen, Robert Culp, Stan Shaw, Rosemary Forsyth, Bart Braverman.

Competent but attenuated TV film about a mechanic (Ken Wahl) who goes on the vengeance trail against drunk drivers in Los Angeles after his younger brother is killed by a deranged DUI. Some of the drama works, but often the narrative becomes repetitious. 1986; 94m.

GLASS KEY, THE ★★★★
DIR: Stuart Heisler. **CAST:** Brian Donlevy, Alan Ladd, Veronica Lake, William Bendix.

Solid version of Dashiell Hammett's excellent novel has Alan Ladd as the bodyguard to politician Brian Donlevy, who is accused of murder. It's up to Ladd to get him off, and he has to take on vicious gangsters to get the job done. Fine work by everyone involved makes this a cinematic gem. 1942; B&W; 85m.

GLEAMING THE CUBE ★★★
DIR: Graeme Clifford. **CAST:** Christian Slater, Steven Bauer, Richard Herd, Ed Lauter.

Better-than-average murder-mystery aimed at the teenage crowd. Christian Slater stars as a skateboard ace who kick-starts a murder investigation when his adopted Vietnamese brother is found hanged in a motel. His investigation reveals that his brother's employer is involved with a weapons-smuggling ring. Spectacular, exciting skateboard stunts and an appealing performance by Slater help glide over the holes in the plot. Rated PG. 1989; 104m.

GLITTER DOME, THE ★★½
DIR: Stuart Margolin. **CAST:** James Garner, Margot Kidder, John Lithgow, Colleen Dewhurst, John Marley.

Made-for-HBO cable version of Joseph Wambaugh's depressingly downbeat story concerning two police detectives in Los Angeles, James Garner and John Lithgow, out to solve a murder. Both cops appear on the edge of losing control. 1985; 90m.

GLORIA ★★★½
DIR: John Cassavetes. **CAST:** Gena Rowlands, Buck Henry, John Adames, Julie Carmen, Lupe Guarnica.

After his family is executed by the Mafia, a little boy hides out with a female neighbor. Together they must flee or be killed. Gena Rowlands is very good in the title role as the streetwise Gloria, whose savvy and brains keep the two alive. Rated R—language, violence. 1980; 121m.

GLORY BOYS, THE ★★½
DIR: Michael Ferguson. **CAST:** Rod Steiger, Anthony Perkins, Alfred Burke, Joanna Lumley.

A many-sided Middle Eastern, terrorist/counterterrorist plot and counterplot. Solid production values, but the overfamiliar scenario is a waste. No rating but contains violence and profanity. 1984; 130m.

GO TELL THE SPARTANS ★★★★
DIR: Ted Post. **CAST:** Burt Lancaster, Craig Wasson, Marc Singer.

In one of the best Vietnam war films, Burt Lancaster is a commander who begins to wonder "what we're doing over there." It's a very honest portrayal of America's early days in Vietnam, with Lancaster giving an excellent performance. Rated R. 1978; 114m.

GOLDEN CHILD, THE ★★
DIR: Michael Ritchie. **CAST:** Eddie Murphy, Charlotte Lewis, Charles Dance, Randall "Tex" Cobb, Victor Wong, James Hong.

Eddie Murphy stars as a Los Angeles social worker who is stunned when members of a religious sect call him "The Chosen One" and expect him to save a magical child from the forces of evil. You'll be even more stunned when you watch this cheesy comedy-adventure and realize it was one of the biggest hits of its year. Rated PG-13 for violence and profanity. 1986; 96m.

GOLDFINGER ★★★★
DIR: Guy Hamilton. **CAST:** Sean Connery, Gert Fröbe, Honor Blackman, Harold Sakata.

Goldfinger is so enjoyable to watch that it's easy to forget the influence of the film on the spy-adventure genre. From the precredits sequence (cut out of most TV versions) to the final spectacular fight with Goldfinger's superhuman henchman, Oddjob (Harold Sakata), the film firmly establishes characters and situations that measured not only future Bond films but all spy films to follow. Sean Connery is the ultimate 007, John Barry's music is unforgettable, and Oddjob made bowler hats fashionable for heavies. 1964; 108m.

GOLIATH AND THE BARBARIANS ★★
DIR: Carlo Campogalliani. **CAST:** Steve Reeves, Bruce Cabot, Giulia Rubini, Chelo Alonso.

Steve Reeves plays Goliath in this so-so Italian action film. In this episode, he saves Italy from invading barbaric tribes. As in many of Reeves's films, the only object of interest is the flexing of his muscles. 1960; 86m.

GONE IN 60 SECONDS ★
DIR: H. B. Halicki. **CAST:** H. B. Halicki, Marion Busia, George Cole, James McIntyre, Jerry Daugirda.

Stuntman-turned-film-auteur H. B. Halicki can wreck a bunch of cars faster than you can say Hal Needham, but when it comes to making a watchable action film, George Miller he ain't. This movie, about a ring of car thieves working under the front of an insurance adjustment firm, is bone dull except for the forty-minute car chase finale, which is twenty minutes too long. Rated PG for violence. 1974; 97m.

GOOD GUYS WEAR BLACK ★★
DIR: Ted Post. **CAST:** Chuck Norris, Anne Archer, James Franciscus, Lloyd Haynes, Jim Backus, Dana Andrews.

This Chuck Norris action film starts out well but quickly dissolves into a routine political action-thriller that really goes nowhere. Lightweight entertainment. Rated PG. 1979; 96m.

GOONIES, THE ★★★
DIR: Richard Donner. **CAST:** Sean Astin, Josh Brolin, Jeff Cohen, Corey Feldman, Kerri Green, Martha Plimpton, Ke Huy-Quan.

This "Steven Spielberg production" is a mess. But it's sometimes an entertaining mess. The screenplay, taken from a story by Spielberg, concerns a feisty group of underprivileged kids—whose housing project is about to be destroyed—spending one last adventure-filled Saturday afternoon together. This happens after they find a treasure map, which could be the solution to all their problems. Rated PG for profanity. 1985; 111m.

GORDON'S WAR ★★½
DIR: Ossie Davis. **CAST:** Paul Winfield, Carl Lee, David Downing, Tony King, Gilbert Lewis.

Competent but uninspiring variation on *Death Wish* with an all-black cast. Paul Winfield is a Vietnam vet who avenges his wife's drug death, teaming up with three other vigilantes along the way to rid Harlem of drugs. Rated R for violence, language, graphic drug use, and nudity. 1978; 90m.

GORKY PARK ★★½
DIR: Michael Apted. **CAST:** William Hurt, Lee Marvin, Joanna Pacula, Brian Dennehy, Ian Bannen, Alexander Knox.
In this maddeningly uninvolving screen version of Martin Cruz Smith's best-selling mystery novel, three mutilated bodies are found in the Moscow park, and it's up to Russian policeman Arkady Renko (a miscast William Hurt) to find the maniacal killer. Lee Marvin is quite good as a suave bad guy, as are Joanna Pacula and Brian Dennehy. Rated R for nudity, sex, violence, and profanity. 1983; 128m.

GOTCHA! ★★★★
DIR: Jeff Kanew. **CAST:** Anthony Edwards, Linda Fiorentino, Alex Rocco, Nick Corri, Marla Adams, Klaus Lowitsch.
In this entertaining mixture of coming-of-age comedy and suspense thriller, a college boy (Anthony Edwards) goes to Paris in search of romance and adventure. He gets both when he meets a beautiful, mysterious woman (Linda Fiorentino) who puts both of their lives in danger. Rated PG-13 for slight nudity, suggested sex, profanity, and violence. 1985; 97m.

GRAND THEFT AUTO ★★½
DIR: Ron Howard. **CAST:** Ron Howard, Nancy Morgan.
The basic plot of *It's a Mad Mad Mad Mad World* is given a retread by first-time director—and star—Ron Howard in this frantic 1977 car-chase comedy. Sadly, little of the style that made *Night Shift* and *Splash* such treats is evident here. Rated PG. 1977; 89m.

GRAY LADY DOWN ★★★½
DIR: David Greene. **CAST:** Charlton Heston, David Carradine, Stacy Keach, Ned Beatty, Ronny Cox, Rosemary Forsyth.
This adventure film starring Charlton Heston is action-packed and well-acted. The story concerns a two-man rescue operation of a sunken nuclear sub that has accidentally collided with a freighter. Beautiful photography and special effects highlight the drama pitting man and machine against time and underwater dangers. 1977; 111m.

GREASED LIGHTNING ★★★
DIR: Michael Schultz. **CAST:** Richard Pryor, Pam Grier, Beau Bridges, Cleavon Little, Richie Havens.
Greased Lightning is a funny and exciting film. Richard Pryor is a knockout in the lead role, and the film is a real audience pleaser. Because the story is true, it carries a punch even *Rocky* couldn't match. While Rocky Balboa remains a stirring character of fiction, Wendell Scott's story is the more dramatic of the two. Scott was the first black man to win a NASCAR Grand National stock car race. Rated PG. 1977; 96m.

GREAT CHASE, THE ★★★★
DIR: Frank Gallop. **CAST:** Buster Keaton, Douglas Fairbanks Sr., Lillian Gish, Pearl White.
Silent film chases from several classics comprise the bulk of this compilation, including the running acrobatics of Douglas Fairbanks in *The Mark of Zorro*, the escape of Lillian Gish over the ice floes in *Way Down East*, and car chases and stunts of all descriptions from silent comedies. A large part of the film is devoted to Buster Keaton's locomotive chase from *The General*. 1963; B&W; 79m.

GREAT ESCAPE, THE ★★★★★
DIR: John Sturges. **CAST:** Steve McQueen, James Garner, Charles Bronson, Richard Attenborough, James Coburn.
If ever there was a movie that could be called pure cheer-the-heroes entertainment, it's *The Great Escape*. The plot centers around a German prison camp in World War II. The commandant has received the assignment of housing all the escape-minded Allied prisoners, or, as he puts it, "putting all the rotten eggs in one basket." The

Germans are obviously playing with fire with this all-star group, and, sure enough, all hell breaks loose with excitement galore. 1963; 168m.

GREAT RIVIERA BANK ROBBERY, THE ★★★½

DIR: Francis Megahy. **CAST:** Ian McShane, Warren Clarke, Stephen Greif, Christopher Malcolm.

In 1976, a group of French right-wing terrorists called "The Chain," with the assistance of a gang of thieves, pulled off one of the largest heists in history. The step-by-step illustration of this bold operation proves to be interesting, and the fact that this incident really happened makes this film all the more enjoyable. 1979; 98m.

GREAT SMOKEY ROADBLOCK, THE ★★½

DIR: John Leone. **CAST:** Henry Fonda, Eileen Brennan, John Byner, Dub Taylor, Susan Sarandon, Austin Pendleton.

Entertaining if somewhat hokey comedy-drama casts Henry Fonda as a trucker on the verge of losing his rig, when along comes a homeless entourage of prostitutes (led by Eileen Brennan), who persuade Henry to take them for a ride. Rated PG for language. 1976; 84m.

GREAT TEXAS DYNAMITE CHASE, THE ★½

DIR: Michael Pressman. **CAST:** Claudia Jennings, Jocelyn Jones, Johnny Crawford, Chris Pennock.

Bullets and bodies fly in this low-budget cult film about two female bank robbers who blast their way across the countryside. Former Playmate Claudia Jennings adds the extra zest to this otherwise routine drive-in feature. Look for Johnny Crawford, of *The Rifleman* fame, in a featured role. Violence, some nudity, suggestive scenes. Rated R. 1977; 90m.

GREAT TRAIN ROBBERY, THE ★★★★

DIR: Michael Crichton. **CAST:** Sean Connery, Lesley-Anne Down, Donald Sutherland, Alan Webb.

Based on a true incident, this suspense-filled caper has plenty of hooks to keep you interested. Sean Connery is dashing and convincing as mastermind Edward Pierce. Lesley-Anne Down is stunning as his mistress, accomplice, and disguise expert. Add a pinch of Donald Sutherland as a boastful pickpocket and cracksman and you have a trio of crooks that can steal your heart. Rated PG. 1979; 111m.

GREAT WALDO PEPPER, THE ★★★

DIR: George Roy Hill. **CAST:** Robert Redford, Bo Svenson, Susan Sarandon, Bo Boundin.

The daredevil barnstorming pilots of the era between the world wars are sent a pleasant valentine by director George Roy Hill in this flying film. Robert Redford, in a satisfying low-key performance, is Waldo Pepper, a barnstormer who yearns for the action of the World War I dogfights. Rated PG. 1975; 108m.

GREEN ARCHER ★★

DIR: James W. Horne. **CAST:** Victor Jory, Iris Meredith, James Craven, Robert Fiske.

Detective Spike Holland tries to unravel the mystery of Garr Castle after he is called in to investigate the disappearance of Valerie Howett's sister, Elaine. A jealous claimant to the castle as well as a gang of jewel thieves thicken the plot in this venerable old Edgar Wallace story. Lots of sliding panels and silhouettes of the phantom bowman in this slow-moving chapterplay. 1940; B&W; 15 chapters.

GREEN BERETS, THE ★★★

DIR: John Wayne, Ray Kellogg. **CAST:** John Wayne, David Janssen, Jim Hutton, Aldo Ray, Raymond St. Jacques, Bruce Cabot, Jack Soo, George Takei, Patrick Wayne.

John Wayne's Vietnam war movie is better than its reputation would suggest. We were fully prepared to hate the film after having avoided it when originally released. However, it turned out to be an exciting and enjoyable (albeit typical) Wayne vehicle. Rated G. 1968; 141m.

GREEN ICE ★½

DIR: Ernest Day. **CAST:** Ryan O'Neal, Anne Archer, Omar Sharif.

Unconvincing tale of an emerald theft in Colombia. Ryan O'Neal engineers the robbery. Rated PG. 1981; 115m.

GREYSTOKE: THE LEGEND OF TARZAN, LORD OF THE APES ★★★½

DIR: Hugh Hudson. **CAST:** Christopher Lambert, Andie MacDowell, Ian Holm, Ralph Richardson, James Fox, Cheryl Campbell.

Director Hugh Hudson made one of the few Tarzan movies to remain faithful to the books and original character created by Edgar Rice Burroughs. Tarzan in one dramatic leap, goes from the dank, dangerous rain forests of West Africa to claim his rightful heritage—a baronial mansion in Scotland and a title as the seventh Earl of Greystoke. Rated PG for nudity and violence. 1984; 129m.

GUMBALL RALLY, THE ★★½

DIR: Chuck Bail. **CAST:** Michael Sarrazin, Gary Busey, Tim McIntire, Raul Julia, Normann Burton.

First film based on an anything-goes cross-country road race. Featuring some excellent stunt driving, with occasional laughs, it's much better than *Cannonball Run.* Rated PG for language. 1976; 107m.

GUNG HO! ★★½

DIR: Ray Enright. **CAST:** Randolph Scott, Grace McDonald, Alan Curtis, Noah Beery Jr., J. Carrol Naish, David Bruce, Robert Mitchum, Sam Levene.

Although not meant to be funny, this ultrapatriotic war film has its truly outrageous moments. It must have been a real booster for wartime filmgoers in America. Today it's almost embarrassing—particularly during the scene in which a recruit is accepted into a special team of commandos simply because he "hates Japs." 1943; B&W; 88m.

GUNGA DIN ★★★★★

DIR: George Stevens. **CAST:** Cary Grant, Victor McLaglen, Douglas Fairbanks Jr., Joan Fontaine, Sam Jaffe, Eduardo Ciannelli.

An acknowledged classic, this release has it all: laughs, thrills, and chills. Howard Hawks was originally set to direct it and played a large part in its creation. Plot: Three soldiers in nineteenth-century India put down a native uprising with the help of an Indian water carrier. 1939; B&W; 117m.

GUNS OF NAVARONE, THE ★★★★

DIR: J. Lee Thompson. **CAST:** Gregory Peck, David Niven, Anthony Quinn, Stanley Baker, Anthony Quayle, James Darren.

Along with *The Great Escape*, this film is one of the best World War II adventure yarns. Gregory Peck, David Niven, and Anthony Quinn are part of a multinational task force that is sent to Greece with a mission to destroy two huge German batteries that threaten a fleet of Allied troop transports. 1961; 145m.

GYMKATA ★

DIR: Robert Clouse. **CAST:** Kurt Thomas, Tetchie Agbayani, Richard Norton.

Gold medal–winning World Champion gymnast Kurt Thomas stars in this disappointing fist-and-foot actioner as a secret agent who must compete in a deadly athletics competition to retrieve U.S. secrets. Rated R for violence. 1985; 90m.

GYPSY WARRIORS, THE ★★

DIR: Lou Antonio. **CAST:** James Whitmore Jr., Tom Selleck, Joseph Ruskin, Lina Raymond, Michael Lane, Ted Gehring, Albert Paulsen, Kenneth Tiger.

James Whitmore Jr. and Tom Selleck are two American soldiers in World War II who go behind enemy lines to capture a formula for germ warfare.

The humor is bland and the action is déjà vu. Not rated. Has violence. 1978; 77m.

HAMMETT ★★
DIR: Wim Wenders. **CAST:** Frederic Forrest, Peter Boyle, Marilu Henner, Elisha Cook Jr., R. G. Armstrong.
A disappointing homage to mystery writer Dashiell Hammett, this Wim Wenders–directed and Francis Ford Coppola–meddled production was two years in the making and hardly seems worth it. The plot is nearly incomprehensible, something that could never be said of the real-life Hammett's works (*The Maltese Falcon*; *The Thin Man*; etc.). Rated PG. 1982; 97m.

HANGMEN ★★
DIR: J. Christian Ingvordsen. **CAST:** Rick Washburne, Jake La Motta, Doug Thomas.
Extremely violent, poorly acted, and poorly written time-killer. An ex-CIA operative (Rick Washburne) is hunted by another agency man (Jake La Motta) who has gone bad. Washburne's family is dragged into the mess. Rated R for violence and language. 1987; 88m.

HARD TICKET TO HAWAII 🦃
DIR: Andy Sidaris. **CAST:** Dona Speir, Hope Marie Carlton, Ronn Moss.
This adventure tries to be tongue-in-cheek, but it's more likely to make you gag. The plot has to do with two drug enforcement agents tracking down smugglers in Hawaii, and there's a subplot about a giant rabid snake, but that's all just filler between scenes in which the female cast members, most of them ex-*Playboy* models, display their charms. Rated R for plentiful nudity and sexual situations. 1987; 96m.

HARD TIMES ★★★★½
DIR: Walter Hill. **CAST:** Charles Bronson, James Coburn, Jill Ireland, Strother Martin.
This release is far and away one of Charles Bronson's best starring vehicles. In it he plays a bare-knuckles fighter who teams up with a couple of hustlers, James Coburn and Strother Martin, to "sting" some local hoods. Bronson's wife, Jill Ireland, is surprisingly good as the love interest. Rated PG. 1975; 97m.

HARD WAY, THE ★★
DIR: Michael Dryhurst. **CAST:** Patrick McGoohan, Lee Van Cleef, Donal McCann, Edna O'Brien.
Patrick McGoohan is an international terrorist who wants out of the business. His wife has taken the children, so he decides to quit before he loses his freedom or his life. Unfortunately for him, a former associate (Lee Van Cleef) wants him to do one more job and will have him killed if he doesn't. 1979; 88m.

HARPER ★★★★½
DIR: Jack Smight. **CAST:** Paul Newman, Lauren Bacall, Shelley Winters, Arthur Hill, Julie Harris, Janet Leigh, Robert Wagner.
Ross MacDonald's detective, Lew Archer, undergoes a name change but still survives as a memorable screen character in the capable hands of Paul Newman. This one ranks right up there with *The Maltese Falcon*, *The Big Sleep* (the Humphrey Bogart version), *Farewell My Lovely*, and *The Long Goodbye* as one of the best of its type. 1966; 121m.

HATARI! ★★★
DIR: Howard Hawks. **CAST:** John Wayne, Elsa Martinelli, Red Buttons, Hardy Krüger.
If only Howard Hawks had been able to do as he wanted and cast Clark Gable along with John Wayne in this story of zoo-supplying animal hunters in Africa, this could have been a great film. As it is, it's still enjoyable, with a fine blend of action, romance, and comedy. 1962; 159m.

HAWK THE SLAYER ★★
DIR: Terry Marcel. **CAST:** Jack Palance, John Terry.
In this sword-and-sorcery adventure, John Terry plays the good Hawk, who, with his band of warriors—a

dwarf and an elf among them—fights Jack Palance, his evil older brother. Palance's performance saves the film from mediocrity. Not rated; has violence. 1980; 90m.

H-BOMB
DIR: P. Chalong. **CAST:** Chris Mitchum, Olivia Hussey, Krung Srmlai.
Stupid martial arts film about two missing U.S. nuclear missiles and the attempts by various rogue bands to obtain them. Not rated, but there are scenes with violence, profanity, and nudity. 1971; 98m.

HEART LIKE A WHEEL ★★★★
DIR: Jonathan Kaplan. **CAST:** Bonnie Bedelia, Beau Bridges, Leo Rossi, Hoyt Axton, Bill McKinney, Dean Paul Martin, Dick Miller.
A first-rate film biography of racing champion Shirley Muldowney, this features a marvelous performance by Bonnie Bedelia as the first woman to crack the National Hot Rod Association's embargo against female competitors. Rated PG for language. 1983; 113m.

HEARTBREAK RIDGE ★★★
DIR: Clint Eastwood. **CAST:** Clint Eastwood, Marsha Mason, Everett McGill, Bo Svenson, Mario Van Peebles, Moses Gunn.
Whoever thought Grenada would be the subject of cinematic war heroics? Though the film could use some trimming, the story of a hard-nosed marine sergeant whipping a hopeless-looking unit into a crack fighting team is still compelling. Actually, the most intriguing element of the movie is the rocky romance between Clint Eastwood and Marsha Mason, who plays his skeptical ex-wife. Eastwood is both amusing and touching as a macho military dinosaur trying to be a sensitive, '80s kind of guy. Rated R. 1986; 126m.

HEARTS AND ARMOUR ★★½
DIR: Giacomo Battiato. **CAST:** Zenda Araya, Barbara de Rossi, Rick Edwards, Ronn Moss, Tanya Roberts.
Warrior Orlando (Rick Edwards) seeks victory over the Moors and the rescue of his love (Tanya Roberts), while his female comrade-in-arms, Bradamante (Barbara de Rossi), falls in love with Ruggero (Ron Moss), the Moor whom Orlando is fated to kill. This film is loosely based on the legend of Orlando Furioso. Unfortunately, the script is not strong enough to do justice to the complex plot. Not rated; has violence and nudity. 1983; 101m.

HEAT (1987) ★★½
DIR: Dick Richards. **CAST:** Burt Reynolds, Karen Young, Peter MacNicol, Howard Hesseman, Neill Barry, Diana Scarwid.
A good try at an action thriller that doesn't succeed because of awkward pacing, uneven direction, and a mood that swings wildly from raw violence to good-buddy playfulness. Burt Reynolds is a Las Vegas–based troubleshooter with two problems: an old girlfriend who craves revenge and a mousy young executive (Peter MacNicol, stealing every scene he shared with Reynolds) who craves the ability to protect himself. Rated R for language and violence. 1987; 101m.

HEATED VENGEANCE ★★
DIR: Edward Murphy. **CAST:** Richard Hatch, Michael J. Pollard, Dennis Patrick, Mills Watson, Cameron Dye, Robert Walker Jr.
A U.S. serviceman (Richard Hatch) returns to Southeast Asia years after the Vietnam War to bring back his old flame (Jolina Mitchell-Collins). Former enemies abduct him and bring him back to their camp, where he finds that they are dealing with drugs. Unrated, has violence, profanity, sex and nudity. 1987; 91m.

HELL ON FRISCO BAY ★★★
DIR: Frank Tuttle. **CAST:** Alan Ladd, Joanne Dru, Edward G. Robinson, William Demarest, Fay Wray.
A 1930s-type hardboiled crime story of a framed cop who does his time, is released from prison, and goes after

the bigwig gangster who set him up. Lots of action on San Francisco's streets and its famous bay. 1955; 98m.

HELL SQUAD

DIR: Kenneth Hartford. **CAST:** Bainbridge Scott, Glen Hartford, William Bryant, Marvin Miller.

Low-budget, poorly acted action film concerns a group of Las Vegas showgirls who are recruited by the CIA. Their mission: rescue an American kidnapped by Arab terrorists. Rated R for nudity and gore. 1985; 88m.

HELL UP IN HARLEM ★

DIR: Larry Cohen. **CAST:** Fred Williamson, Julius W. Harris, Gloria Hendry, Margaret Avery, D'Urville Martin.

This violent, cheaply made sequel to *Black Caesar* has Fred Williamson exacting revenge on his former girlfriend (Gloria Hendry), along with those who deposed him as mob kingpin in the first flick and seemingly everyone else in New York. Not for the weak of stomach. Rated R. 1973; 98m.

HELLCATS, THE

DIR: Robert F. Slatzer. **CAST:** Ross Hagen, Dee Duffy.

The brother of a slain police detective seeks revenge. He tracks down a gang of female drug-smuggling bikers that his brother was investigating. Even within the lowly subgenre of biker movies, this one is the pits. Unrated, it features violence. 1967; 90m.

HELLCATS OF THE NAVY ★★★

DIR: Nathan Juran. **CAST:** Ronald Reagan, Nancy Davis, Arthur Franz, Harry Lauter.

This none-too-exciting drama has one thing to attract viewers: President Ronald Reagan and First Lady Nancy co-star. 1957; B&W; 82m.

HELLDORADO (1934) ★½

DIR: James Cruze. **CAST:** Richard Arlen, Madge Evans, Henry B. Walthall, Ralph Bellamy, James Gleason, Helen Jerome Eddy.

A penniless hitchhiker discovers a ghost town with a gold mine. The picture boasts an acclaimed director and a highly professional cast, but it is feebly and unpersuasively produced. 1934; B&W; 75m.

HELLFIGHTERS ★★

DIR: Andrew V. McLaglen. **CAST:** John Wayne, Katharine Ross, Vera Miles, Jim Hutton, Bruce Cabot.

Once again the talents of John Wayne have been squandered. The Duke is cast as a high-priced fireman sent around the world to put out dangerous oil rig fires. Even hard-core Wayne fans may wince at this one. Rated PG. 1969; 121m.

HELL'S ANGELS '69 ★★

DIR: Lee Madden. **CAST:** Tom Stern, Jeremy Slate, Conny Van Dyke, Sonny Barger, Terry the Tramp.

Two rich kids devise a plan to rob a gambling casino by infiltrating the Hell's Angels and then using the gang to create a diversion. The plan works until the bikers retaliate and swap their choppers for dirt bikes to pursue the robbers across rugged terrain. Mediocre. 1969; 97m.

HELL'S ANGELS ON WHEELS ★★½

DIR: Richard Rush. **CAST:** Adam Roarke, Jack Nicholson, Sabrina Scharf, John Garwood, Jana Taylor.

This is one of the better 1960s biker films, most notably because Jack Nicholson has a big role in it. Not a great work by any means, but if you like biker movies... 1967; 95m.

HELL'S BRIGADE ★

DIR: Henry Mankiewirk. **CAST:** Jack Palance, John Douglas.

Fairly rotten film concerning a commando raid on Hitler's Germany during World War II. Low budget, poorly acted. 1980; 99m.

HELL'S HOUSE ★★

DIR: Howard Higgin. **CAST:** Junior Durkin, Bette Davis, Pat O'Brien, Frank Coghlan Jr., Charley Grapewin, Emma Dunn.

Gangster and prison films in the 1930s had their junior counterparts. In this barely so-so example, an innocent boy does time in a harsh reformatory because he won't rat on an adult crook friend. Junior Durkin is the poor kid, Pat O'Brien is the crook—a bootlegger—and Bette Davis is his girl. 1932; B&W; 72m.

HERO AND THE TERROR ★★½
DIR: William Tannen. **CAST:** Chuck Norris, Jack O'Halloran, Brynn Thayer, Jeffrey Kramer, Steve James.
Chuck Norris gives a good performance in this otherwise disappointing thriller. He's a police officer suffering from deep trauma after confronting a brutal, demented killer called the Terror (Jack O'Halloran). When the Terror escapes from a mental ward, our hero must battle the monster again. Rated R for violence and profanity. 1988; 90m.

HEROES IN HELL
DIR: Michael Wotruba. **CAST:** Klaus Kinski, Stan Simon, Lars Block, George Manes, Carlos Ewing, Luis Joyce, Rosemary Lindt.
Lame World War II battle picture has captured Allied prisoners of war escaping from a Nazi POW camp, joining a group of partisans, and taking on the Germans. Unrated, but PG for violence would be proper. 1974; 90m.

HIDING OUT ★★
DIR: Bob Giraldi. **CAST:** Jon Cryer, Keith Coogan, Annabeth Gish, Oliver Cotton, Claude Brooks, Ned Eisenberg.
Jon Cryer does some top-notch acting in this comedy-drama, but the film overall lets him down. Screenwriter Joe Menosky and Jeff Rothberg can be commended for avoiding the obvious clichés in their story of a Boston stockbroker (Cryer) hiding from the mob in a suburban Delaware high school. The result, however, is a collection of bits and pieces rather than a cohesive whole. Rated PG-13 for profanity and violence. 1987; 98m.

HIGH-BALLIN' ★★
DIR: Peter Carter. **CAST:** Peter Fonda, Jerry Reed, Helen Shaver, Chris Wiggins, David Ferry.
Peter Fonda and Jerry Reed are good old boys squaring off against the bad boss of a rival trucking company. The film has enough action and humor to make it a passable entertainment. Helen Shaver is its most provocative element. Rated PG. 1978; 100m.

HIGH COMMAND, THE ★★★
DIR: Thorold Dickinson. **CAST:** Lionel Atwill, Lucie Mannheim, James Mason.
Rebellion, a new murder, and a 16-year-old killing absorb the interest of officers and men at an isolated British outpost on an island off the coast of Africa. Honor, integrity, and the tradition of the Colonial Service are at stake in this adventure during the fading days of the British empire. 1937; B&W; 84m.

HIGH COUNTRY, THE ★★
DIR: Harvey Hart. **CAST:** Timothy Bottoms, Linda Purl, George Sims, Jim Lawrence, Bill Berry, Walter Mills.
So-so production values drag down this tale of a chance meeting between an escaping convict (Timothy Bottoms) and a wide-eyed girl (Linda Purl) in the Canadian Rockies. It's a clichéd story, although Bottoms turns in his usual accomplished performance. Not rated, but has violence and brief nudity. 1980; 99m.

HIGH CRIME ★★
DIR: Enzo G. Castellari. **CAST:** Franco Nero, James Whitmore, Fernando Rey.
Narcotics cop vs. Mafia kingpin in the picturesque Italian seaport of Genoa. Full of action, but no surprises. Rated PG. 1973; 100m.

HIGH RISK ★★½
DIR: Stewart Raffill. **CAST:** James Brolin, Cleavon Little, Bruce Davison, Chick Vennera, Anthony Quinn, James Coburn, Ernest Borgnine, Lindsay Wagner.

While snatching $5 million from a South American drug smuggler (James Coburn), four amateur conspirators (James Brolin, Cleavon Little, Bruce Davison, and Chick Vennera) blaze their way through numerous shootouts, crossing paths with a sleazy bandit leader (Anthony Quinn), hordes of Colombian soldiers, and plenty of riotous trouble. This preposterous comic-strip adventure offers diversion, but a lot of it is just plain awful. Rated R. 1981; 94m.

HIGH ROAD TO CHINA ★★★
DIR: Brian G. Hutton. **CAST:** Tom Selleck, Bess Armstrong, Jack Weston, Wilford Brimley, Robert Morley, Brian Blessed.

Tom Selleck stars as a World War I flying ace who, with the aid of his sidekick/mechanic, Jack Weston, helps a spoiled heiress (Bess Armstrong) track down her missing father (Wilford Brimley). It's just like the B movies of yesteryear: predictable, silly, and fun. Rated PG for violence. 1983; 120m.

HIGH ROLLING
DIR: Igor Auzins. **CAST:** Joseph Bottoms, Grigor Taylor, Sandy Hughs, Judy Davis, John Clayton.

Two out-of-work carnival workers hitchhike through Australia until they are picked up by a drug runner. They end up stealing the runner's dope, money, and his car—a hot Corvette. Rated PG for profanity and brief nudity, this feature is a big disappointment. 1977; 88m.

HIGH SCHOOL CAESAR ★½
DIR: O'Dale Ireland. **CAST:** John Ashley, Gary Vinson, Lowell Brown.

A rich high-school kid (John Ashley) is ignored by the father he idolizes, so he spends his time running a protection racket, selling exams, and rigging school elections. The video distributor is marketing this as one of a series of "campy" juvenile-delinquent features from the 1950s, but it's neither good nor bad enough to be memorable. 1960; B&W; 72m.

HIGH SIERRA ★★★★½
DIR: Raoul Walsh. **CAST:** Humphrey Bogart, Ida Lupino, Alan Curtis, Arthur Kennedy, Joan Leslie, Henry Hull.

Humphrey Bogart is at his best as a bad guy with a heart of gold in this 1941 gangster film. Bogart pays for the operation that corrects pretty Joan Leslie's crippled foot, but he finds his love is misplaced. One of the finest of the Warner Bros. genre entries. 1941; B&W; 100m.

HIGH VELOCITY ★½
DIR: Remi Kramer. **CAST:** Ben Gazzara, Britt Ekland, Paul Winfield, Keenan Wynn, Alejandro Rey, Victoria Racimo.

Run-of-the-mill feature made in Manila about two ex-Vietnam buddies hired to rescue the head of a big corporation from Asian terrorists. Everyone gets doublecrossed, including the viewer who rents this. It gets an extra half-star for the actors, though most of them are wasted. Rated PG. 1977; 106m.

HIGH VOLTAGE ★★½
DIR: Howard Higgin. **CAST:** William Boyd, Carole Lombard, Owen Moore, Diane Ellis, Billy Bevan.

Elements of *Stagecoach* are evident in this early Pathé sound film (made ten years before John Ford's classic) that teams a pre–Hopalong Cassidy William Boyd and a lovely, young Carole Lombard as a world-wise couple who fall for each other while snowbound during a bus trip in California's Sierra Nevada Mountains. Worth watching for Lombard's fine performance. 1929; B&W; 57m.

HIGHEST HONOR, THE ★★★★★
DIR: Peter Maxwell. **CAST:** John Howard, Atsuo Nakamura, Stuart Wilson.

A World War II story of a unique friendship between two enemies: Captain Robert Page, an Australian Army officer, and Winoyu Tamiya, a security officer in the Japanese army. This great war film, packed with high adventure and warm human drama, is also a true story. Rated R. 1984; 99m.

HIGHPOINT ★
DIR: Peter Carter. **CAST:** Richard Harris, Christopher Plummer, Beverly D'Angelo, Kate Reid, Peter Donat, Saul Rubinek.

Confusing comedy-thriller about an accountant (Richard Harris) who becomes mixed up in a CIA plot and international intrigue. This poorly produced caper fails to deliver any genuine thrills. Rated R; contains profanity and violence. 1980; 88m.

HIS KIND OF WOMAN ★★★½
DIR: John Farrow. **CAST:** Robert Mitchum, Jane Russell, Vincent Price, Tim Holt, Charles McGraw, Raymond Burr, Jim Backus, Marjorie Reynolds.

Entertaining chase film as two-fisted gambler Robert Mitchum breezes down to South America to pick up fifty thousand dollars only to find out he's being set up for the kill. Jane Russell is in fine shape as the worldly-looking gal with a good heart, and Vincent Price steals the show as a hammy Hollywood actor who is thrilled to be involved in *real* danger and intrigue. 1951; B&W; 120m.

HIT, THE ★★★★
DIR: Stephen Frears. **CAST:** John Hurt, Terence Stamp, Tim Roth, Fernando Rey, Laura Del Sol, Bill Hunter.

The British seem to have latched on to the gangster film with a vengeance. First, they made the superb film *The Long Good Friday*, and now they've scored again with this gripping character study. John Hurt gives an unusually restrained (and highly effective) performance as a hit man assigned to take care of a squealer (Terence Stamp) who has been hiding in Spain after testifying against the mob. Rated R for violence. 1984; 97m.

HIT AND RUN ★★½
DIR: Charles Braverman. **CAST:** Paul Perri, Claudia Cron, Bart Braverman.

A New York cab driver, obsessed with the death of his wife in a hit-and-run accident, becomes a pawn in a murder plot. Mystery fans will appreciate the nighttime atmosphere and carefully (if slowly) developed plot. Rated PG. 1982; 96m.

HIT LADY ★★½
DIR: Tracy Keenan Wynn. **CAST:** Yvette Mimieux, Dack Rambo, Clu Gulager, Joseph Campanella, Keenan Wynn.

Entertaining twist on an old story has Yvette Mimieux as a hit lady who tries to retire, only to be blackmailed into taking on just one more job. Televison movie; contains some cleaned-up-violence. 1974; 74m.

HITLER'S CHILDREN ★★★★
DIR: Edward Dmytryk, Irving Reis. **CAST:** Tim Holt, Bonita Granville, Kent Smith, Otto Kruger.

A great love story is created with the horror of Nazi Germany as a background. This film shows a young German boy who falls in love with an American girl. The boy gets caught up in Hitler's enticing web of propaganda, while his girlfriend resists all of Hitler's ideas. 1942; B&W; 83m.

HOLCROFT COVENANT, THE ★★
DIR: John Frankenheimer. **CAST:** Michael Caine, Anthony Andrews, Victoria Tennant, Mario Adorf, Lilli Palmer.

In the closing days of World War II, three infamous Nazi officers deposit a large sum of money into a Swiss bank account to be withdrawn years later by their children. This slow but intriguing film, based on the novel by Robert Ludlum, will undoubtedly please spy film enthusiasts, although others may find it tedious and contrived. Rated R for adult situations. 1985; 105m.

HOLLYWOOD COP ★
DIR: Amir Shervan. **CAST:** David Goss, Jim Mitchum, Cameron Mitchell, Troy Donahue, Aldo Ray, Lincoln Kilpatrick.

Undercover cop David Goss battles the mob when they kidnap a young boy. Though the movie is set in Los Angeles, the locations look more like Oklahoma. The presence of such B movie regulars as Cameron Mitchell, Aldo Ray, and Troy Donahue might lead you to expect something entertainingly bad, but it's just a bore. Rated R for nudity and violence. 1987; B&W; 100m.

HOLLYWOOD VICE SQUAD ★
DIR: Penelope Spheeris. **CAST:** Ronny Cox, Frank Gorshin, Leon Isaac Kennedy, Trish Van Devere, Carrie Fisher.

A tepid affair about a woman (Trish Van Devere) who goes searching for her runaway daughter in the sleazoid areas of Hollywood. Rated R for nudity, profanity, and violence. 1986; 93m.

HOLT OF THE SECRET SERVICE ★★
DIR: James W. Horne. **CAST:** Jack Holt, Evelyn Brent, C. Montague Shaw, Tristram Coffin, John Ward, Ted Adams, Joe McGuinn, Ray Parsons.

Iron-jawed Jack Holt had become such an institution after almost thirty years as a matinee and action star that Columbia decided to bill him as a secret service agent under his own name. The result is a middling serial with a formula plot. There aren't any mysterious masked menaces or hooded phantoms in this cliff-hanger, just agent Holt and his pretty partner Evelyn Brent against a gang of counterfeiters. 1941; B&W; 15 chapters.

HONOR AMONG THIEVES ★★½
DIR: Jean Herman. **CAST:** Charles Bronson, Alain Delon, Brigitte Fossey.

Charles Bronson plays a mercenary who is locked in a French bank over the weekend with Alain Delon, a doctor. Bronson is there to rob the bank of its 200 million francs, while Delon is there to replace some misappropriated securities. This is a little different type of picture for Bronson—a bit more subtle, a little slower-paced, and with more dialogue than action. Rated R. 1983; 93m.

HOPSCOTCH ★★★★
DIR: Ronald Neame. **CAST:** Walter Matthau, Ned Beatty, Glenda Jackson.

Walter Matthau is wonderful in this fast-paced and funny film as a spy who decides to extract a little revenge on the pompous supervisor (Ned Beatty) who demoted him. Glenda Jackson has a nice bit as Matthau's romantic interest. Rated R. 1980; 104m.

HORSEMEN, THE ★
DIR: John Frankenheimer. **CAST:** Omar Sharif, Jack Palance, Leigh Taylor-Young, Peter Jeffrey, Eric Pohlmann.

In this dull action film, Omar Sharif, as an Afghan tribesman, attempts to outride his father, who is an expert horseman. Though there is action aplenty, you never get a sense of who the characters are and why they are so crude and frankly dumb. It's a second-rate *Taras Bulba.* Rated PG. 1970; 109m.

HOSTAGE ★
DIR: Hanro Möhr. **CAST:** Wings Hauser, Karen Black, Kevin McCarthy, Nancy Locke.

Idiotic story of a simple South African farmer (Wings Hauser) who must rescue his wife and child from evil Arabs who hijack the wife's plane. But wait—Hauser was a member of a secret American military squad, which comes to his rescue (sort of). A lesson on how not to make a movie. Rated R for language and violence. 1987; 94m.

HOSTAGE TOWER, THE ★★½
DIR: Claudio Guzman. **CAST:** Peter Fonda, Maud Adams, Billy Dee Williams, Rachel Roberts, Douglas Fairbanks Jr.

A successful international criminal sought by major police organizations puts together a special team of experts for his next spectacular crime, broadly hinted at in the title. Intrigue and private purposes abound in this action film, wherein the cast successfully outweighs the movie. Rated PG for violence. 1980; 97m.

HOT BOX, THE ★½
DIR: Joe Viola. **CAST:** Margaret Markov, Andrea Cagen, Charles Dierkop.
Low-budget Filipino-shot women's-prison film was cowritten and produced by Jonathan Demme. It features the standard plot of brutalized female inmates who break out and start a local revolution. Rated R; contains nudity, profanity, and violence. 1972; 85m.

HOT CHILD IN THE CITY ★½
DIR: John Florea. **CAST:** Leah Ayres Hendrix, Shari Shattuck, Antony Alda, Ronn Moss.
This small-cast whodunit about the murder of a record-company owner has some suspense, but an insufficient number of suspects. A hot soundtrack by Billy Idol and Lou Reed isn't enough. Not rated, has violence, profanity, sex, and nudity. 1987; 85m.

HOT ROCK, THE ★★★★
DIR: Peter Yates. **CAST:** Robert Redford, George Segal, Ron Leibman, Paul Sand, Zero Mostel, Moses Gunn, William Redfield, Charlotte Rae.
A neatly planned jewelry heist goes awry and the fun begins. Peter Yates's direction is razor sharp. The cast is absolutely perfect. This movie is a crowd-pleasing blend of action, humor, and suspense. Rated PG. 1972; 105m.

HOT TARGET ★
DIR: Denis Lewiston. **CAST:** Simone Griffeth, Bryan Marshall, Steve Marachuk.
The bored wife of a British business tycoon finds herself being extorted after having a one-night stand with a stranger she meets in the park. Though her husband becomes suspicious—and this leads to a fairly intriguing plot development—an unimaginative directorial style turns this film into a sleepwalk-through-suspense drama. Explicit nudity. Rated R. 1984; 93m.

HOTEL COLONIAL ★
DIR: Cinzia Torrini. **CAST:** John Savage, Robert Duvall, Rachel Ward, Massimo Troisi.
In this uncredited adaptation of Joseph Conrad's "Heart of Darkness," John Savage searches the jungles of Colombia for his brother (Robert Duvall), a terrorist who has faked his own death. The two are supposed to be Italian, though Savage looks about as Italian as a mayonnaise sandwich. Rated R for nudity and violence. 1987; 107m.

HOUND OF THE BASKERVILLES, THE (1939) ★★★★
DIR: Sidney Lanfield. **CAST:** Basil Rathbone, Nigel Bruce, John Carradine, Lionel Atwill, Mary Gordon, E. E. Clive, Richard Greene.
The second best of the Basil Rathbone–Nigel Bruce Sherlock Holmes movies, this 1939 release marked the stars' debut in the roles for which they would forever be known. While *The Adventures of Sherlock Holmes*, which was made the same year, featured the on-screen detective team at its peak, this 20th Century Fox–produced adaptation of Sir Arthur Conan Doyle's most famous mystery novel still can be called a classic. For those unfamiliar with the story, Holmes and Watson are called upon by Henry Baskerville (Richard Greene) to save him from a curse—in the form of a hound from hell—that has plagued his family for centuries. 1939; B&W; 84m.

HOUND OF THE BASKERVILLES, THE (1959) ★★★★
DIR: Terence Fisher. **CAST:** Peter Cushing, Christopher Lee, Andre Morell, Maria Landi, Miles Malleson.
One of the better adaptations of A. Conan Doyle's moody novel, and particularly enjoyable for its presentation of Peter Cushing (as Sherlock Holmes) and Christopher Lee to-

gether in non-horror roles. This British entry (from the Hammer House of Horror) caught more of the murky atmosphere than any other version of any other Holmes tale. Intelligent scripting, compelling acting, and spooky cinematography. 1959; 84m.

HOUR OF THE ASSASSIN ★½
DIR: Luis Llosa. **CAST:** Erik Estrada, Robert Vaughn.

Action thriller set in the fictional South American country of San Pedro where Erik Estrada has been hired by the military forces to kill the president. Robert Vaughn plays the CIA agent who has to stop him. Although this film has its share of car crashes, gunfire, and explosions, it lacks any real suspense. Rated R. 1986; 96m.

HOUSE OF FEAR ★★★★
DIR: Roy William Neill. **CAST:** Basil Rathbone, Nigel Bruce, Aubrey Mather, Dennis Hoey.

The last of the high-quality entries in the Universal Sherlock Holmes series has Holmes (Basil Rathbone) and Watson (Nigel Bruce) attempting to solve a series of murders among the guests at a Scottish mansion. It was based on Conan Doyle's "The Adventure of the Five Orange Pips" and combines atmosphere, pacing, fine acting, and sure direction. 1945; B&W; 69m.

HOUSE OF THE RISING SUN ★★
DIR: Greg Gold. **CAST:** Frank Annese, Jamie Barrett, Tawny Moyer, Deborah Wakeham, James Daughton, John J. York.

Technically sound but artistically soulless film that attempts to give an Eighties look to a Thirties murder mystery. Jamie Barrett is an aspiring reporter, willing to do anything to get the lowdown on pimp Frank Annese, even posing as one of his girls to expose his murdering ways. Not rated, but contains adult situations. 1987; 86m.

HUNTER ★★½
DIR: Leonard Horn. **CAST:** John Vernon, Steve Ihnat, Fritz Weaver, Edward Binns.

A brainwashed agent is programmed to release a deadly virus. The scheme is discovered, and a good guy takes his place to catch the bad guys. Made for television. 1971; 73m.

HUNTER, THE ★★
DIR: Buzz Kulik. **CAST:** Steve McQueen, Eli Wallach, LeVar Burton, Ben Johnson, Kathryn Harrold.

The Hunter, an uneven action film, focuses on a modern-day bounty hunter. Steve McQueen plays real-life troubleshooter Ralph "Papa" Thorson. Though old and a bit awkward, Thorson leads—at least on screen—a dangerous, action-filled life. Traveling from one state to another in pursuit of fugitives, he is constantly putting his life on the line. Rated PG. 1980; 97m.

HURRICANE (1979)
DIR: Jan Troell. **CAST:** Jason Robards Jr., Mia Farrow, Dayton Ka'ne, Max von Sydow, Trevor Howard.

Another Dino de Laurentiis misfire, this awful remake of the John Ford classic details a love affair between Charlotte Bruckner (Mia Farrow), daughter of the governor (Jason Robards) of Pago Pago, and the young native chief, Matangi (Dayton Ka'ne). Rated PG. 1979; 119m.

HURRICANE EXPRESS ★★
DIR: Armand Schaefer, J. P. McGowan. **CAST:** John Wayne, Tully Marshall, Conway Tearle, Shirley Grey.

Big John Wayne stars in his second serial for Mascot Pictures and plays an aviator on the trail of the mysterious "Wrecker," who has been wreaking havoc with the local trains and is responsible for the death of his father. This feature, edited down from a twelve-chapter serial, displays a high level of energy and excitement, a great deal of it as a direct result of young Wayne's whole-hearted involvement in this basically simple chase film. 1932; B&W; 80m.

HUSTLE ★★½

DIR: Robert Aldrich. **CAST:** Burt Reynolds, Catherine Deneuve, Eddie Albert, Ernest Borgnine, Jack Carter, Ben Johnson.

Hustle reteams director Robert Aldrich and actor Burt Reynolds after their box-office success with *The Longest Yard.* Fine character performances from Eddie Albert, Ernest Borgnine, and Jack Carter help to elevate the macho/action yarn, but it is Academy Award–winner Ben Johnson who provides the real show. Rated R. 1975; 120m.

I COVER THE WATERFRONT ★★★

DIR: James Cruze. **CAST:** Claudette Colbert, Ernest Torrence, Ben Lyon, Wilfred Lucas, George Humbert.

One, and one of the better, of a spate of newspaper stories that vied with gangster films on 1930s screens. In this one, a ruthless fisherman who smuggles Chinese into the United States doesn't think twice about pushing them overboard when approached by the Coast Guard. Claudette Colbert is his innocent daughter. Ace reporter Ben Lyon courts her in an effort to get at the truth. 1933; B&W; 70m.

I SEE A DARK STRANGER ★★★½

DIR: Frank Launder. **CAST:** Deborah Kerr, Trevor Howard, Raymond Huntley, Liam Redmond.

Known in Great Britain as *The Adventuress,* this delightful picture tells of a high-strung yet charming Irish girl who, hating the British, helps a Nazi spy during World War II. Wry humor serves as counterpoint to the suspense. A class act. 1947; B&W; 98m.

I SPY (TELEVISION SERIES) ★★★★

DIR: Richard C. Sarafian, Paul Wendkos. **CAST:** Robert Culp, Bill Cosby.

Remember Bill Cosby before terminal cuteness and a bank account the size of Guam overwhelmed him? This classic TV series will remind you of his charm and dramatic ability. It also focuses much-deserved attention on the colossally cool and clever Robert Culp. There's plenty of fun and suspense as spies Kelly Robinson and Alexander Scott, under the guise of tennis pro and trainer, do battle against the international forces of evil. 1965–1968; Each episode runs 60 minutes.

I, THE JURY ★

DIR: Richard T. Heffron. **CAST:** Armand Assante, Barbara Carrera, Alan King.

In the mid-1940s, Mickey Spillane wrote *I, the Jury,* introducing Mike Hammer, his no-nonsense private eye. For this updated version, Spillane's basic plot—Hammer out to find the killer of his old army buddy—has been kept intact. However, the film is a disappointing and sleazy hybrid of James Bond and *Death Wish II*. Rated R. 1982; 111m.

ICE STATION ZEBRA ★★★

DIR: John Sturges. **CAST:** Rock Hudson, Ernest Borgnine, Patrick McGoohan, Jim Brown, Tony Bill, Lloyd Nolan.

This long cold war cliff-hanger about a submarine skipper awaiting orders while cruising to the North Pole under the ice was eccentric billionaire Howard Hughes's favorite film. The suspense comes with a British agent's hunt for the usual Russian spy. Rated G. 1968; 148m.

IF LOOKS COULD KILL ★★

DIR: Chuck Vincent. **CAST:** Kim Lambert, Tim Gail.

A photographer is hired to videotape a woman's apartment to gather evidence against her on an embezzlement charge. Suspense and duplicity follow. But the dialogue is poor and the direction is mediocre. Rated R for violence, profanity, nudity, and sex. 1986; 90m.

IMPOSSIBLE SPY, THE ★★★★
DIR: Jim Goddard. **CAST:** John Shea, Eli Wallach, Sasson Gabay.

This video is based on the true exploits of Elie Cohen, a spy for Israel's Mossad. Cohen, played by John Shea, is recruited by the Mossad in 1959 and sent to Argentina, where he works his way into the good graces of a group that is plotting to overthrow the Syrian government. He participates while sending information to Israel. The results of his work affect not only his family but the future of Israel. Made for British television, this is unrated. 1987; 96m.

IN HARM'S WAY ★★
DIR: Otto Preminger. **CAST:** John Wayne, Kirk Douglas, Patricia Neal, Tom Tryon, Paula Prentiss, Brandon de Wilde, Stanley Holloway, Jill Haworth, Burgess Meredith, Henry Fonda, Dana Andrews, Franchot Tone, Patrick O'Neal.

With its incredibly talented cast, you would think this war film couldn't miss. Miss it does. John Wayne leads the United States Navy into a monumental struggle against the Japanese. Kirk Douglas is the antihero who stirs up a fuss. The ships are models and the battles are conducted in a bathtub. It's too big and too long. 1965; B&W; 167m.

INSIDE MAN, THE ★★★½
DIR: Tom Clegg. **CAST:** Dennis Hopper, Hardy Krüger, Gosta Ekman, Cella Gregory.

Inspired by a 1981 incident in which a Soviet submarine ran aground in Sweden, this exciting adventure film really moves. A CIA agent (Dennis Hopper) sets up a young ex-marine (Gosta Ekman) as the inside man who must investigate the theft of a laser-submarine search device. Check this one out. It's unrated, but contains some strong language. 1984; 90m.

INSIDE OUT ★★★
DIR: Peter Duffell. **CAST:** Telly Savalas, Robert Culp, James Mason, Aldo Ray.

An unlikely trio (Telly Savalas, Robert Culp, and James Mason) band together to recover $6 million in gold that Hitler had hidden. Only one man knows where the gold is, so the trio must get this ex-Nazi out of a maximum-security prison so that he can lead them to it. The action and suspense in this film should hold most viewers' attention. Rated PG. 1975; 98m.

INSTANT JUSTICE 🦃
DIR: Craig T. Rumar. **CAST:** Michael Paré, Tawny Kitaen, Charles Napier.

Instant Justice is the worst of the one-man-army movies. Michael Pare plays marine Sergeant Youngblood, an overblown Stallone/Eastwood/Bronson amalgam who has a penchant for head-butting. When on leave in Madrid to visit his sister, he finds she's been murdered by drug dealers. He then goes on a vengeful rampage. Rated R. 1986; 101m.

INTO THE FIRE ★
DIR: Graeme Campbell. **CAST:** Art Hindle, Olivia D'Abo, Lee Montgomery, Susan Anspach.

A young drifter (Lee Montgomery) finds himself in the middle of deceit and treachery when he stops at a roadside diner. He becomes a patsy in an insurance scam that leads to murder. Take a hint from the title and dispose of this one properly. Rated R for nudity and violence. 1988; 88m.

INTO THE HOMELAND ★★★
DIR: Lesli Linka Glatter. **CAST:** Powers Boothe, C. Thomas Howell, Paul LeMat, Cindy Pickett.

This HBO release is a topical but predictable story starring Powers Boothe as an ex-cop who endeavors to rescue his kidnapped daughter from a white supremacist organization headed by Paul LeMat. The shockingly real portrayal of the supremacists' ethics and the conflict between Boothe and C. Thomas Howell (as LeMat's son and would-be successor) make this movie worth viewing. Unrated, but contains violence and strong language. 1987; 120m.

INVASION U.S.A. ★★★

DIR: Joseph Zito. **CAST:** Chuck Norris, Richard Lynch, Melissa Prophet.

Chuck Norris plays a one-man army (as always) who comes to the rescue of the good ol' U. S. A. and pummels the minions of psychotic spy Richard Lynch. Rated R for violence, gore, and profanity. 1985; 107m.

INVINCIBLE SWORD, THE

DIR: Hsu Tseng Hung. **CAST:** Wang Yu.

A band of traveling acrobats takes on an evil tyrant in order to save a captured general. Bad dubbing—and the stunts are either too stupid or too incredible. Not rated but contains violence and profanity. 1978; 93m.

IPCRESS FILE, THE ★★★★

DIR: Sidney J. Furie. **CAST:** Michael Caine, Nigel Green, Guy Doleman, Gordon Jackson, Sue Lloyd.

First and by far the best of Michael Caine's three Harry Palmer films, this one introduces Len Deighton's reluctant thief-turned-secret agent. Caine, relentlessly serious behind owllike spectacles, investigates the mystery of specialists kidnapped behind the iron curtain. John Barry's moody jazz score superbly counterpoints the action, and Sidney J. Furie's direction is taut and suspenseful. Unrated, suitable for family viewing. 1965; 108m.

IRON EAGLE ★★

DIR: Sidney J. Furie. **CAST:** Louis Gossett Jr., Jason Gedrick, Tim Thomerson, David Suchet.

A better name for this modern war movie might have been *Ramboy*, so shamelessly does it attempt to be a *Rambo* for the teen-age set. Jason Gedrick stars as an 18-year-old would-be pilot who steals an F-16 fighter plane to rescue his father (Tim Thomerson), a prisoner of war in the Middle East. A terminally dull fantasy of bloodlust. Rated PG-13 for violence and profanity. 1986; 115m.

IRON EAGLE II ★

DIR: Sidney J. Furie. **CAST:** Louis Gossett Jr., Mark Humphrey, Stuart Margolin, Alan Scarfe.

In this ridiculous sequel to the preposterous original, Louis Gossett Jr. returns as Charles "Chappy" Sinclair. Chappy's new assignment is to lead a combined unit of American and Soviet pilots in a raid on a nuclear missile base in a hostile Middle Eastern country. You'll be hostile, too, if you make the mistake of renting this moronic mess. Rated PG for violence and profanity. 1988; 105m.

IRON MASK, THE ★★★½

DIR: Allan Dwan. **CAST:** Douglas Fairbanks Sr., Nigel de Brulier, Marguerite de la Motte.

The last of Douglas Fairbanks's truly memorable series of historical adventures is a rousing version of the Dumas story of the later adventures of D'Artagnan and his efforts to restore the rightful king to the throne of France. One by one the famous Three Musketeers fail in their valiant quest, leaving only the ever-agile Fairbanks to uncover the secret of the iron mask. Well-budgeted and full of good stunts and deadly encounters, this film was released with sound effects and a synchronized score. 1929; B&W; 87m.

ISLAND TRADER ★★

DIR: Howard Ruble. **CAST:** John Ewart, Ruth Cracknell, Eric Oldfield.

A young boy on an island finds a wrecked airplane laden with gold bullion. He is then pursued by a dangerous criminal and a tugboat skipper, both of whom want the treasure. This potentially exciting adventure film is marred by amateurish direction, a low budget, and uninspired acting. 1970; 95m.

IVANHOE ★★★★

DIR: Richard Thorpe. **CAST:** Robert Taylor, Elizabeth Taylor, Joan Fontaine, George Sanders, Sebastian Cabot.

Robert Taylor stars as Sir Walter Scott's dashing knight Ivanhoe. His mission is to secure the ransom for King Richard the Lionhearted, who has been captured while returning from the Crusades. Action and swordplay abound as Ivanhoe strives for Richard's release and protects two very fair maidens (Elizabeth Taylor and Joan Fontaine) from the lecherous grasp of archvillain George Sanders. 1952; 106m.

JACKSON COUNTY JAIL ★★★½

DIR: Michael Miller. **CAST:** Yvette Mimieux, Tommy Lee Jones, Robert Carradine.

This chase film is pretty good. Yvette Mimieux escapes from jail with fellow inmate Tommy Lee Jones. Audiences can't help but sympathize with Mimieux, because she was unfairly arrested and then raped by her jailer. Rated R. 1976; 89m.

JAIL BAIT

DIR: Edward D. Wood Jr. **CAST:** Timothy Farrell, Dolores Fuller, Lyle Talbot, Herbert Rawlinson, Steve Reeves.

Delightfully awful crime melodrama from everyone's favorite bad auteur, Ed *(Plan 9 From Outer Space)* Wood. Hardboiled punk Tim Farrell, whose face must hurt from sneering so much, involves the son of a famous plastic surgeon in a robbery, then forces the doctor to help him escape from the police. There's lots of ridiculous dialogue, cheap sets, and a final plot twist you'll spot a mile away. Also includes one of the most godawful droning musical scores you'll ever hear. A must-see for camp aficionados. 1954; B&W; 70m.

JAKE SPEED ★★★½

DIR: Andrew Lane. **CAST:** Wayne Crawford, Dennis Christopher, Karen Kopins, John Hurt, Leon Ames, Donna Pescow, Barry Primus, Monte Markham.

This quirky little adventure thriller, from the folks involved with the equally deft *Night of the Comet*, postulates that the book adventures of a pulp hero named Jake Speed actually are biographical chapters in the life of a real person. When Karen Kopins's younger sister is kidnapped and threatened with white slavery by John Hurt's delightfully oily villain, Speed (Wayne Crawford) and his associate Remo (Dennis Christopher) materialize and offer to help. Rated PG for mild violence. 1986; 100m.

JEWEL OF THE NILE, THE ★★★½

DIR: Lewis Teague. **CAST:** Michael Douglas, Kathleen Turner, Danny DeVito, Avner Eisenberg.

This generally enjoyable sequel to *Romancing the Stone* details the further adventures of novelist Joan Wilder (Kathleen Turner) and soldier of fortune Jack Colton (Michael Douglas) in the deserts of North Africa. Danny DeVito supplies the laughs. Rated PG. 1985; 106m.

JOHNNY ANGEL ★★★

DIR: Edwin L. Marin. **CAST:** George Raft, Claire Trevor, Signe Hasso, Hoagy Carmichael.

Above-average gangster film provides some nice moments. George Raft seeks the killer of his father while busting up the mob. Nothing special, but fun to watch. 1945; B&W; 79m.

JUGGERNAUT (1974) ★★★★½

DIR: Richard Lester. **CAST:** Richard Harris, Omar Sharif, David Hemmings, Anthony Hopkins, Shirley Knight, Ian Holm, Roy Kinnear.

Here's a first-rate, suspenseful thriller about demolitions expert Richard Harris attempting to deactivate a bomb aboard a luxury liner. Richard Lester elevates the familiar plot line with inspired direction, and Lester regular Roy Kinnear is on hand to add some deft bits of comedy. Rated PG. 1974; 109m.

JUNGLE HEAT ★½

DIR: Gus Trikonis. **CAST:** Peter Fonda, Deborah Raffin, John Amos.

Although this film is considered to be an adventure tale, it tries to please everyone with a little horror and romance thrown in. Unfortunately, it fails to use any of these elements effectively. Dr. Evelyn Howard (Deborah Raffin), an anthropologist from L.A., hires an alcoholic ex–Vietnam vet (Peter Fonda) to fly her into the jungles of South America. There she looks for an ancient tribe of pygmies but finds instead monsters that greatly resemble the Creature from the Black Lagoon. Rated PG for language and gore. 1984; 93m.

JUNGLE MASTER, THE 🦃
DIR: Miles Deem. **CAST:** Johnny Kissmuller, Simone Blondell, Edward Mann.

An expedition journeys to Africa in search of the legendary ape-man, Karzan, no, not Tarzan—Karzan. Somebody must have been sued for this movie, if not for copyright infringement, then bad film-making. This movie is not a total loss, though; there is quite a bit of unintentional humor. A gem for bad film buffs. 1985; 90m.

JUNGLE PATROL ★★
DIR: Joseph M. Newman. **CAST:** Kristine Miller, Arthur Franz, Ross Ford, Tommy Noonan, Gene Reynolds, Richard Jaeckel, Harry Lauter.

This is a routine World War II story about a squadron of fliers commanded by a young officer who has been ordered to hold an airfield against the Japanese. The subplot is a silly romance between the officer and a USO performer. Best ingredient: the music score by Emil Newman and Arthur Lange. 1948; B&W; 72m.

JUNGLE RAIDERS ★★
DIR: Anthony M. Dawson. **CAST:** Christopher Connelly, Marina Costa, Lee Van Cleef.

Christopher Connelly plays an adventurer–con man hired to find the Ruby of Gloom in Malaysia. This *Raiders of the Lost Ark* ripoff is too plodding for most viewers. It includes a few fun, action-filled moments but stick to the Lucas-Spielberg classic. Rated PG for violence and profanity. 1985; 102m.

JUNGLE WARRIORS ★★½
DIR: Ernst R. von Theumer. **CAST:** Sybil Danning, Marjoe Gortner, Nina Van Pallandt, Paul Smith, John Vernon, Alex Cord, Woody Strode, Kai Wulfe, Dana Elcar.

The idea of a group of female models in Peru for a shoot in the jungle is quite absurd. If you can overlook the premise, though, this action film about a cocaine producer and his perverted sister is modestly satisfying. It's rather like an episode of *Miami Vice* but with scantily dressed women packing machine guns. Rated R for violence, profanity, and nudity. 1983; 96m.

JUNIOR G-MEN ★★
DIR: Ford Beebe, John Rawlins. **CAST:** Billy Halop, Huntz Hall, Gabriel Dell, Bernard Punsley, Phillip Terry, Russell Hicks, Cy Kendall, Kenneth Howell.

Politely dropped from the Warner Brothers stable after a few years of service, the Dead End Kids split forces and inflicted their obnoxious personae on a wider audience than ever. Do-gooder G-man Jim Bradford and his insufferable Junior G-Man companion Harry Trent do their best to reform the hard-boiled gang and involve them in the search for leader Bill Barton's father, a famous inventor who has been kidnapped by greedy traitors. 1940; B&W; 12 chapters.

JUNKMAN, THE ★
DIR: H. B. Halecki. **CAST:** Christopher Stone, Susan Shaw, Lang Jeffries, Lynda Day George.

From the makers of *Gone in 60 Seconds*, this sequel is tagged as the "chase film for the '80s." What this story lacks in plot and acting, it makes up for in action. There are so many crash scenes that it actually becomes boring. Rated PG. 1982; 99m.

KANSAS CITY MASSACRE, THE ★★★
DIR: Dan Curtis. **CAST:** Dale Robertson, Bo Hopkins, Robert Walden, Mills Watson, Scott Brady, Harris Yulin.
Dale Robertson reprises his role of the outlandish Melvin Purvis that he originated in 1974's *Melvin Purvis, G-Man.* Practically every notorious gangster who ever lived meets the unstoppable G-man in this made-for-TV film. Watch for the acting debut of the notorious ex-governor of Georgia, Lester Maddox. Here he's governor of Oklahoma. 1975; 120m.

KASHMIRI RUN, THE
DIR: John Peyser. **CAST:** Pernell Roberts, Alexandra Gasteda, Julian Mateos, Gloria Camara.
Pernell Roberts is an American adventurer in the Far East who is commissioned to take two scientists to India and bring back a load of yak skins. On the way he faces communist Chinese soldiers, bandits, and wild animals. If you can watch further than this, you have the world's strongest stomach. 1969; 93m.

KEEPING TRACK ★★★½
DIR: Robin Spry. **CAST:** Michael Sarrazin, Margot Kidder, Alan Scarfe, Ken Pogue.
Superior action thriller follows Michael Sarrazin and Margot Kidder as two innocent bystanders who witness a murder and a robbery. Once they find the five million dollars, they must learn to trust one another because everyone is after them, including the CIA and Russian spies. This one will keep you guessing. Rated R. 1985; 102m.

KELLY'S HEROES ★★★
DIR: Brian G. Hutton. **CAST:** Clint Eastwood, Telly Savalas, Donald Sutherland, Don Rickles, Gavin MacLeod, Carroll O'Connor.
An amiable ripoff of *The Dirty Dozen*, this 1970 war comedy was funnier at the time of its original release. Stoic Clint Eastwood is stuck with a bunch of goof-offs (Telly Savalas, Donald Sutherland, Don Rickles, and Gavin McLeod) as he searches for Nazi treasure. Sutherland's World War II hippie ("Give me those positive waves, man") is a little tough to take these days, but this caper picture still has its moments. Rated PG. 1970; 145m.

KENNEL MURDER CASE, THE ★★★★
DIR: Michael Curtiz. **CAST:** William Powell, Mary Astor, Eugene Pallette, Ralph Morgan, Jack LaRue.
A classic detective thriller, this features William Powell as the dapper Philo Vance solving a locked-door murder. The supporting players complement his suave characterization perfectly. Dated, but good. 1933; B&W; 73m.

KEY LARGO ★★★★
DIR: John Huston. **CAST:** Humphrey Bogart, Lauren Bacall, Edward G. Robinson, Claire Trevor, Lionel Barrymore.
Humphrey Bogart is one of a group of dissimilar individuals held in a rundown Florida Keys hotel by a band of hoodlums on the lam. Lauren Bacall looks to him as her white knight, but as a disillusioned war vet he has had enough violence. That is, until a crime kingpin (Edward G. Robinson) pushes things a little too far. 1948; B&W; 101m.

KIDNAPPED ★
DIR: Howard Avedis. **CAST:** David Naughton, Barbara Crampton, Kim Evenson, Lance LeGault, Chick Vennera, Charles Napier, Kin Shriner, Jimmie Walker.
Hokey melodrama that casts Barbara Crampton as a woman who goes after the kidnappers of her 16-year-old sister. David Naughton is a sympthetic cop. A.J. the Chimp, who appears as Naughton's pet, no doubt wrote the screenplay and composed the music. Rated R for language, nudity, and violence. 1988; 90m.

KILL, THE ★★
DIR: Rolf Bamer. **CAST:** Richard Jaeckel.
Richard Jaeckel plays a world-weary, womanizing private eye in this overly familiar story of a hunt for stolen money in the byways of the Orient. The locale is Macao, famed gambling haven across the bay from Hong Kong. No rating, but contains violence and nudity. 1973; 81m.

KILL AND KILL AGAIN ★★
DIR: Ivan Hall. **CAST:** James Ryan, Anneline Kriel.
Kung-fu champ James Ryan repeats his starring role from *Kill or Be Killed* in this sequel to that box-office winner. This time, martial arts master Steve Chase (Ryan) has been hired to rescue a Nobel Prize–winning chemist from the clutches of a demented billionaire who wants his victim's formula for synthetic fuel. Rated R. 1981; 100m.

KILL CASTRO 🦃
DIR: Peter Barton. **CAST:** Stuart Whitman, Caren Kaye, Robert Vaughn, Woody Strode, Albert Salmi, Michael Gazzo, Sybil Danning, Raymond St. Jacques.
Espionage and murder are the formulas for this implausible adventure yarn. Captain Tony (Stuart Whitman) is a Key West boat skipper who is "blackmailed" into helping a CIA agent named Hud (Robert Vaughn) carry out an assassination plot against Fidel Castro. Rated R. 1978; 90m.

KILL OR BE KILLED ★★
DIR: Ivan Hall. **CAST:** James Ryan, Norman Combes, Charlotte Michelle.
A former Nazi pits himself against the Japanese master who defeated him in an important tournament during World War II. Run-of-the-mill martial arts nonsense. James Ryan shows a glimmer of personality to go with his physical prowess. Rated PG. 1980; 90m.

KILL POINT ★
DIR: Frank Harris. **CAST:** Leo Fong, Richard Roundtree, Cameron Mitchell, Stack Pierce, Hope Holliday.
Incredibly bloody tale of gang warfare, revenge, and justice in L.A. Leo Fong plays a police detective whose brother is murdered by a gang of hoods. Fong is out to get the killers. Weak performances and gratuitous violence mar this low-budget thriller. Rated R for violence and language. 1984; 89m.

KILLER ELITE, THE ★★½
DIR: Sam Peckinpah. **CAST:** James Caan, Robert Duvall, Arthur Hill, Bo Hopkins, Mako, Burt Young, Gig Young.
Secret service agent James Caan is double-crossed by his partner (Robert Duvall) while guarding a witness. Disabled by a bullet wound, he has to begin a long process of recovery. He wants revenge. The story seems to have a lot of promise, but this is never realized. There are some good action scenes. However, considering all the top-flight talent involved, it is a major disappointment. Rated PG. 1975; 120m.

KILLER FISH 🦃
DIR: Anthony M. Dawson. **CAST:** Lee Majors, Karen Black, Margaux Hemingway, Marisa Berenson, James Franciscus.
Thieves steal jewels from a Latin American dictatorship and bury them at the bottom of a lake to be picked up at a later date. To prevent his hirelings from pulling a fast one with the gems, the mastermind behind the theft floods the lake with a variety of flesh-eating fish. You can guess the rest of the story. Bad acting and lousy Spanish accents help to make this a total bust. Rated PG, but contains violence and some nudity. 1978; 101m.

KILLERS, THE ★★★
DIR: Don Siegel. **CAST:** Lee Marvin, John Cassavetes, Angie Dickinson, Ronald Reagan.

Two hitmen piece together a story on the man they've just killed. A tense thriller loosely based on a short story by Ernest Hemingway. This remake of the 1946 classic emphasizes violence rather than storytelling. Ronald Reagan is excellent as an unscrupulous business tycoon. Rated PG; contains graphic violence. 1964; 95m.

KILLING AT HELL'S GATE ★★★
DIR: Jerry Jameson. **CAST:** Robert Urich, Deborah Raffin, Lee Purcell, Joel Higgins, George DiCenzo, Paul Burke, Brion James, John Randolph.
Made-for-TV action film about a group of people, including a controversial U.S. senator, who take a raft trip only to find that the bullets are harder to dodge than the jagged rocks. This ain't no *Deliverance*, but it's watchable. 1981; 96m.

KILLING GAME, THE ★
DIR: Joseph Merhi. **CAST:** Chad Hayward, Cynthia Killion.
A free-lance Las Vegas hitman (Chad Hayward) is blackmailed by a mobster who wants him to extend his services into dealing drugs. Made-for-video movie tries to evoke a cynical, hardboiled style but lacks the talent behind (and in front of) the camera. Unrated, but featuring nudity and substantial violence. 1988; 83m.

KILLING TIME, THE ★★★★
DIR: Rick King. **CAST:** Beau Bridges, Kiefer Sutherland, Wayne Rogers, Joe Don Baker.
Kiefer Sutherland is a killer posing as a new deputy sheriff in a small resort town. Beau Bridges is to be the new sheriff upon the retirement of Joe Don Baker. But there is much more to be discovered in this tense drama of murder, deception, and suspicion. Rated R for violence and profanity. 1987; 94m.

KIM ★★★½
DIR: Victor Saville. **CAST:** Errol Flynn, Dean Stockwell, Paul Lukas, Thomas Gomez, Cecil Kellaway.
Rudyard Kipling's India comes to life in this colorful story of the young son of a soldier and his adventures with a dashing secret operative in defense of queen and country. Dean Stockwell is one of the finest and most believable of child stars, and the great Errol Flynn is still capable of personifying the spirit of adventure and romance in this one-dimensional but entertaining story. 1951; 113m.

KING ARTHUR, THE YOUNG WARLORD ★½
DIR: Sidney Hayers, Pat Jackson, Peter Sasdy. **CAST:** Oliver Tobias, Michael Gothard, Jack Watson, Brian Blessed, Peter Firth.
King Arthur, the Young Warlord follows the English legend in his early years through subplots that lead nowhere. The acting is second-rate, and while some of the action scenes are good, it must be noted that the violence displayed may not be some people's idea of good ol' G-rated fun despite the MPAA approval. 1975; 96m.

KING OF THE KONGO ★★
DIR: Richard Thorpe. **CAST:** Walter Miller, Jacqueline Logan, Richard Tucker, Boris Karloff.
Historically important as the first serial released in both silent and sound versions, this early Mascot serial features veteran chapterplay hero Walter Miller as a secret service agent searching both for his brother and for the secret of a temple's treasure. Boris Karloff is a standout as the heavy. 1929; B&W; 10 chapters.

KING OF THE ROCKETMEN ★★★
DIR: Fred Bannon. **CAST:** Tristram Coffin, Mae Clarke, Dale Van Sickel, Tom Steele.
This chapterplay precursor to the *Commando Cody* television series has longtime baddie Tristram Coffin joining the good guys for a change. Strapping on his flying suit, he does battle with evil conspirators. Good fun for serial fans, with highly implausible last-minute escapes. 1949; B&W; 12 chapters.

KING SOLOMON'S MINES (1937) ★★★½

DIR: Robert Stevenson. **CAST:** Cedric Hardwicke, Paul Robeson, Roland Young, John Loder, Anna Lee.

H. Rider Haggard's splendid adventure story received its first sound-film treatment here. Cedric Hardwicke lacks the flair of a matinee-idol lead but makes a very realistic Allan Quatermain, while Paul Robeson gives perhaps the best performance of his screen career as King Umbopa. 1937; B&W; 79m.

KING SOLOMON'S MINES (1950) ★★★★★

DIRS: Compton Bennett, Andrew Morton. **CAST:** Stewart Granger, Deborah Kerr, Hugu Haas.

The "great white hunter" genre of adventure films has been a movie staple for ages, yet only this one rates as a cinema classic. Stewart Granger guides a party through darkest Africa in search of a lady's husband. On the way, the hunter and the lady (Deborah Kerr) become fast friends. 1950; 102m.

KING SOLOMON'S MINES (1985)

DIR: J. Lee Thompson. **CAST:** Richard Chamberlain, Sharon Stone, John Rhys-Davies, Herbert Lom, Ken Gampu.

A crime against H. Rider Haggard's classic adventure novel. Starring Richard Chamberlain as Allan Quatermain, the film is an embarrassment—a compendium of cornball clichés and stupid slapstick. Rated PG for violence. 1985; 100m.

KING SOLOMON'S TREASURE ★

DIR: Alvin Rakoff. **CAST:** David McCallum, Britt Ekland, Patrick Macnee, John Colicos.

This mindless adventure features John Colicos, Patrick Macnee, and a stuttering David McCallum pursuing treasure in Africa's Forbidden City. Britt Ekland makes a silly Phoenician queen. No need to rent this one, folks! 1976; 90m.

KINGS AND DESPERATE MEN: A HOSTAGE INCIDENT ★★★

DIR: Alexis Kanner. **CAST:** Patrick McGoohan, Alexis Kanner, Andrea Marcovicci, Margaret Trudeau.

Improbable but engrossing account of terrorists taking over a radio talk show to present their case to the public. Patrick McGoohan lends his commanding presence as the abrasive, cynical talk-show host. A strange, almost cinema vérité portrayal. Rated PG-13 for language and violence. 1989; 117m.

KINJITE (FORBIDDEN SUBJECTS) ★

DIR: J. Lee Thompson. **CAST:** Charles Bronson, Perry Lopez, Peggy Lipton.

Again Charles Bronson plays a vigilante who deals out his own brand of justice. This film is a disgustingly ugly comment on contemporary law-and-order issues–and it's extremely racist as well. Rated R for nudity, profanity, and violence. 1989; 96m.

KIROSHI ★★½

DIR: Michael Truman, Peter Yates. **CAST:** Patrick McGoohan, Kenneth Griffith, Amanda Barrie, Ronald Howard.

Patrick McGoohan's popular *Secret Agent* television series is poorly represented by this attempt to string two episodes into a full-length feature. The color photography—the series was B&W—is the only legitimate appeal; the episodes themselves are rather weak. The linking element is an Oriental death cult, which agent John Drake battles with his usual intelligence and quick wit. Unrated; suitable for family viewing. 1966; 100m.

KISS ME DEADLY ★★★½

DIR: Robert Aldrich. **CAST:** Ralph Meeker, Albert Dekker, Cloris Leachman, Paul Stewart.

Robert Aldrich's adaptation of Mickey Spillane's Mike Hammer novel. Brutal and surrealistic, it has Hammer attempting to protect a woman (Cloris Leachman) from the men who want to kill her. 1955; B&W; 105m.

KISS TOMORROW GOODBYE ★½

DIR: Gordon Douglas. **CAST:** James Cagney, Barbara Payton, Ward Bond, Barton MacLane, Luther Adler, John Litel.

This loser brought the popularity of gangster pictures to a screeching halt. A grapefruit in Barbara Payton's face would not have helped this story of crooked cops and hoodlums. James Cagney tries hard but the Warner Bros. gangster fire is almost out. 1950; B&W; 102m.

KNIGHTRIDERS ★★★

DIR: George A. Romero. **CAST:** Ed Harris, Tom Savini, Amy Ingersoll.

What was supposed to be a modern-day look at the lost Code of Honor comes across on screen as a bunch of weirdos dressed in armor riding motorcycles in a traveling circus. At a length of almost two-and-a-half hours, there isn't enough to hold the viewer's interest. Rated PG. 1981; 145m.

KNIGHTS OF THE ROUND TABLE ★★½

DIR: Richard Thorpe. **CAST:** Robert Taylor, Ava Gardner, Mel Ferrer, Stanley Baker, Felix Aylmer, Robert Urquhart.

Colorful wide-screen epic of King Arthur's court is long on pageantry but lacks the spirit required to make this type of film work well. 1953; 115m.

KUNG FU ★★★

DIR: Jerry Thorpe. **CAST:** David Carradine, Keye Luke, Philip Ahn, Keith Carradine, Barry Sullivan.

The pilot of the 1970s television series starring David Carradine has its moments for those who fondly remember the show. Carradine plays a Buddhist monk roaming the Old West. When his wisdom fails to mollify the bad guys, he is forced to use martial arts to see justice done. 1971; 75m.

L.A. CRACKDOWN ★★

DIR: Joseph Merhi. **CAST:** Pamela Dixon, Tricia Parks.

An undercover cop (Pamela Dixon) battles crack dealers and blows away bad guys by the dozen, but she has a soft spot in her heart for women who have been forced into prostitution and crime. Made-for-video cheapie that is more concerned with showing sexy women than exploring their problems (no surprise there), but it's pretty much what you'd expect from this kind of unapologetic programmer. The sequel followed so fast, it was probably made at the same time. Unrated; nudity, violence. 1988; 84m.

L.A. CRACKDOWN II ★½

DIR: Joseph Merhi. **CAST:** Pamela Dixon, Anthony Gates.

More of the same, with Pamela Dixon and her new partner stalking a serial killer with a penchant for bar girls (which provides the excuse for otherwise gratuitous nudity). Starts out okay, but the middle is obviously just padding. Unrated; nudity, strong violence. 1988; 87m.

LADIES CLUB ★★

DIR: A. K. Allen. **CAST:** Karen Austin, Diana Scarwid, Christine Belford, Beverly Todd.

A policewoman and a female doctor organize a support group to help rape victims deal with their feelings of rage and disgust. The club of the title soon turns into a vigilante group with the women punishing repeat offenders who commit rape and are freed on a technicality or by a lenient court. Rated R for violence and gore. 1987; 86m.

LADY FROM SHANGHAI ★★★½

DIR: Orson Welles. **CAST:** Rita Hayworth, Orson Welles, Everett Sloane, Glenn Anders, Erskine Sanford, Ted de Corsia.

Orson Welles and Rita Hayworth were husband and wife when they made this taut, surprising thriller about a beautiful, amoral woman, her crippled, repulsive lawyer husband, his partner, and a somewhat naive Irish sailor made cat's-paw in a murder scheme. Under Welles's inventive direction, Everett Sloane and the camera steal the show with a climactic scene in the hall of mirrors at San Francisco's old oceanfront Playland. 1948; B&W; 87m.

LADY IN RED ★★★½
DIR: Lewis Teague. **CAST:** Pamela Sue Martin, Robert Conrad, Robert Forster, Louise Fletcher, Robert Hogan.

A splendid screenplay by John Sayles energizes this telling of the Dillinger story from the distaff side, with Pamela Sue Martin as the gangster's moll enduring the results of a life of crime. Director Lewis Teague keeps things moving right along. Rated R for profanity, nudity, and violence. 1979; 93m.

LADY IN THE LAKE ★★★
DIR: Robert Montgomery. **CAST:** Robert Montgomery, Audrey Totter, Lloyd Nolan, Jayne Meadows, Tom Tully, Leon Ames.

Director-star Robert Montgomery's adaptation of Raymond Chandler's mystery is a failed attempt at screen innovation. Montgomery uses a subjective camera to substitute for detective Philip Marlowe's first-person narrative of his efforts to find a missing wife. A clever but ineffectual whodunit. 1946; B&W; 103m.

LADY OF BURLESQUE ★★★
DIR: William Wellman. **CAST:** Barbara Stanwyck, Michael O'Shea, J. Edward Bromberg, Iris Adrian, Pinky Lee.

Slick and amusing adaptation of Gypsy Rose Lee's clever mystery novel of top bananas, blackouts, and strippers, *The G-String Murder*. Interesting look into an aspect of show business that now exists only in fading memories. 1943; B&W; 91m.

LADY SCARFACE ★★½
DIR: Frank Woodruff. **CAST:** Judith Anderson, Dennis O'Keefe, Frances Neal, Eric Blore, Marc Lawrence.

Role reversal is the order of the day for this story of a hardened dame who spits lead and asks questions later, ruling her gang with a velvet glove and leading the police and authorities on a grim chase. Atmospheric but pretentious, this offbeat attempt to inject new life into a basic crime story isn't as good as it could have been despite the presence of classy Judith Anderson. 1941; B&W; 66m.

LADYHAWKE ★★★½
DIR: Richard Donner. **CAST:** Matthew Broderick, Rutger Hauer, Michelle Pfeiffer, Leo McKern, John Wood.

In this seven-hundred-year-old legend of love and honor, Rutger Hauer and Michelle Pfeiffer are lovers separated by an evil curse. Hauer, a valiant knight, is aided by a wisecracking thief, Matthew Broderick, in his quest to break the spell by destroying its creator. This is a lush and lavish fantasy that will please the young and the young at heart. Rated PG-13 for violence. 1985; 124m.

LAGUNA HEAT ★★★½
DIR: Simon Langton. **CAST:** Harry Hamlin, Jason Robards Jr., Rip Torn, Catharine Hicks, Anne Francis, James Gammon.

This well-written script was made for HBO cable. Harry Hamlin is an ex–L.A. cop who lives with his father in Laguna Beach. He soon gets involved in a murder investigation. Director Simon Langton keeps the action moving and the plot twisting. 1987; 110m.

LAS VEGAS LADY ½
DIR: Noel Nosseck. **CAST:** Stella Stevens, Stuart Whitman, George DiCenzo, Lynne Moody, Linda Scruggs.

Made-for-TV fodder, but racier and with less substance than *Magnum, P.I.* reruns. Characters who are bored with their jobs at a big casino must find a way to salvage a lame plot about a big money heist. 1976; 87m.

LASSITER ★★★
DIR: Roger Young. **CAST:** Tom Selleck, Jane Seymour, Lauren Hutton, Bob Hoskins.

Tom Selleck stars in yet another period adventure film as a jewel thief in the 1930s who attempts to steal a cache of uncut diamonds from the Nazis. This could be called good-but-not-great entertainment. Rated R for nudity, suggested sex, violence, and profanity. 1984; 100m.

LAST AMERICAN HERO, THE ★★★★
DIR: Lamont Johnson. **CAST:** Jeff Bridges, Valerie Perrine, Geraldine Fitzgerald, Ned Beatty, Gary Busey, Art Lund, Ed Lauter, William Smith.

An entertaining action film about the famous whiskey runner from North Carolina who becomes a legend when he proves himself a great stock-car driver. Jeff Bridges's portrait of the rebel Johnson is engaging, but Art Lund steals the show as Johnson's bootlegger father. Rated PG for profanity and sex. 1973; 95m.

LAST CONTRACT, THE ★★
DIR: Allan A. Buckhantz. **CAST:** Jack Palance, Rod Steiger, Bo Svenson, Richard Roundtree, Ann Turkel.

In this violent film, Jack Palance stars as an artist and a hit man who is hired to kill his best friend. Unable to do it, he is ordered to assassinate a rival crime lord. When he kills the wrong man, the deadly game of hit and counterhit gets out of hand. Rated R. 1986; 85m.

LAST DAYS OF POMPEII ★★
DIR: Mario Bonnard. **CAST:** Steve Reeves, Fernando Rey, Christine Kaufmann, Barbara Carroll, Angel Aranda.

A different scenario than the 1935 original. Steve Reeves plays a hero in the Roman army stationed in Greece who tries to save a group of Christians that has been jailed and condemned to death. The story is interesting, but the action scenes are rather dumb. 1960; 93m.

LAST DRAGON, THE ★★★½
DIR: Michael Schultz. **CAST:** Taimak, Vanity, Christopher Murney.

Produced by Motown Records man Berry Gordy, this is lively, unpretentious nonsense about a shy karate champ (Taimak) fending off villains threatening a disc jockey (Vanity). A combined music video and comic strip, it's good, silly fun. Rated PG-13 for violence. 1985; 109m.

LAST EMBRACE, THE ★★★½
DIR: Jonathan Demme. **CAST:** Roy Scheider, Janet Margolin, Sam Levene, Marcia Rodd, Christopher Walken, John Glover, Charles Napier.

A CIA agent must track down an obsessed, methodical killer. A complex, intelligent thriller in the Hitchcock style with skilled performances, a lush music score, and a cliff-hanging climax at Niagara Falls. Rated R for nudity and violence. 1979; 102m.

LAST OF SHEILA, THE ★★★★
DIR: Herbert Ross. **CAST:** James Coburn, Dyan Cannon, James Mason, Raquel Welch, Richard Benjamin.

A cleverly planned, very watchable whodunit. Because of some unusual camera angles and subtle dialogue, the audience is drawn into active participation in the mystery. A sundry collection of Hollywood types are invited on a yachting cruise by James Coburn. It seems one of them has been involved in the murder of Coburn's wife. Rated PG. 1973; 120m.

LAST PLANE OUT
DIR: David Nelson. **CAST:** Jan-Michael Vincent, Lloyd Batista, Julie Carmen.

Poor ripoff of *Under Fire*, with Jan-Michael Vincent playing a news reporter in Nicaragua during the final days of the Somoza regime in 1979. 1983; 98m.

LAST RITES ★★

DIR: Donald P. Bellisario. **CAST:** Tom Berenger, Daphne Zuniga, Paul Dooley.

A young Italian priest (Tom Berenger) runs afoul of the Mafia when he grants sanctuary to a woman (Daphne Zuniga) who has witnessed a gangland murder. It's an interesting premise, but the story turns silly when priest and witness begin to fall in love. Rated R for violence, nudity, and profanity. 1988; 103m.

LAST SEASON, THE

DIR: Raja Zahr. **CAST:** Christopher Gosch, Louise Dorsey, David Cox.

A gosh-awful film shot on video to really hammer home the overall poverty. A bunch of redneck hunters invades a peaceful forest and shoots up everything in sight, prompting young Christopher Gosch to fight back. Not rated: contains offensive language, nudity, and violence. 1987; 90m.

LAST VALLEY, THE ★★★

DIR: James Clavell. **CAST:** Michael Caine, Omar Sharif.

Impressive and thought-provoking adventure epic about a warrior (Michael Caine) who brings his soldiers to a peaceful valley that, in the seventeenth century, has remained untouched by the Thirty Years War. Rated R. 1971; 128m.

LATE SHOW, THE ★★★★½

DIR: Robert Benton. **CAST:** Art Carney, Howard Duff, Lily Tomlin, Bill Macy, John Considine.

Just prior to directing *Kramer vs. Kramer*, Robert Benton created this little gem. It stars Art Carney as an aging private eye out to avenge the death of his partner (Howard Duff) with the unwanted help of wacky Lily Tomlin. Loosely lifted from Sam Peckinpah's *Ride the High Country* and John Huston's *The Maltese Falcon*, this detective story is a bittersweet, sometimes tragic, takeoff on the genre. That it works so well is a credit to all involved. Rated PG. 1977; 94m.

LAUGHING POLICEMAN, THE ★★★½

DIR: Stuart Rosenberg. **CAST:** Walter Matthau, Bruce Dern, Louis Gossett Jr., Albert Paulsen, Cathy Lee Crosby, Anthony Zerbe.

Little-known police thriller that deserved far better than it got at the box office. Walter Matthau and Bruce Dern are a pair of cops seeking a mass murderer who preys on bus passengers. Taut drama, taken from the superb thriller by Maj Sjowall and Per Wahloo...although characterization suffers a bit in the transition from book to screen. Rated R for violence. 1974; 111m.

LAURA ★★★★★

DIR: Otto Preminger. **CAST:** Gene Tierney, Dana Andrews, Vincent Price, Judith Anderson, Clifton Webb.

A lovely socialite (Gene Tierney) is apparently murdered, and the police detective (Dana Andrews) assigned to the case is up to his neck in likely suspects. To compound matters, he has developed a strange attraction for the deceased woman through her portrait. So starts one of the most original mysteries ever to come from Hollywood. 1944; B&W; 88m.

LAWRENCE OF ARABIA ★★★★★

DIR: David Lean. **CAST:** Peter O'Toole, Alec Guinness, Anthony Quinn, Arthur Kennedy, Omar Sharif.

Director David Lean brings us an expansive screen biography of T. E. Lawrence, the complex English leader of the Arab revolt against Turkey in World War I. This is a tremendous accomplishment in every respect. Peter O'Toole is stunning in his first major file role as Lawrence. A definite thinking person's spectacle. 1962; 222m.

LEFT HAND OF GOD, THE ★★★½

DIR: Edward Dmytryk. **CAST:** Humphrey Bogart, Lee J. Cobb, Gene Tierney, Agnes Moorehead.

Humphrey Bogart is an American forced to pose as a priest while on the run from a renegade Chinese warlord (Lee J. Cobb). It's not the fastest-moving adventure story, but Bogart and Cobb are quite good, and Gene Tierney is an effective heroine. The result is worthy entertainment. 1955; 87m.

LEGAL EAGLES ★★★½
DIR: Ivan Reitman. **CAST:** Robert Redford, Debra Winger, Daryl Hannah, Brian Dennehy, Terence Stamp, Steven Hill, Jennie Dundas, Roscoe Lee Browne.
This droll comedy-mystery succeeds due to the engaging presence of Robert Redford as an assistant district attorney and Debra Winger as a defense attorney. The two become uneasy partners in a complex case involving art theft and a loopy performance artist, played by Daryl Hannah. The story doesn't bear close examination, but Redford and Winger keep things moving with energy and charisma. Rated PG for mild adult situations. 1986; 114m.

LEGEND OF BILLIE JEAN, THE ★
DIR: Matthew Robbins. **CAST:** Helen Slater, Keith Gordon, Christian Slater, Peter Coyote.
Another one of those teen rebel flicks. This one is about a girl from Texas (Helen Slater) who becomes an outlaw and ends up with all the youths in Corpus Christi backing her up. There are few subtleties here and the obvious is exploited for the dim of wit. Rated PG-13 for language and (only a little) violence. 1985; 92m.

LEPKE ★★★
DIR: Menahem Golan. **CAST:** Tony Curtis, Anjanette Comer, Michael Callan, Warren Berlinger, Milton Berle, Vic Tayback.
Tony Curtis gives an effective performance in the lead role of this gangster drama. He's the head of Murder Inc. The story sticks close to the facts. It's no classic, but watchable. Rated R. 1975; 110m.

LETHAL OBESSION ★
DIR: Peter Patzack. **CAST:** Tahnee Welch, Elliott Gould, Michael York, Peter Maffay.
Contrived suspense yarn about a group of professional criminals who deal in drugs and murder while having to control the streets of New York City. Rock star Peter Maffay plays an undercover cop confined to a wheelchair. In brief cameo appearances, Elliott Gould and Michael York couldn't have turned in more wooden performances. Rated R; contains nudity, profanity, and violence. 1987; 100m.

LETHAL WEAPON ★★★★
DIR: Richard Donner. **CAST:** Mel Gibson, Danny Glover, Gary Busey, Mitchell Ryan, Tom Atkins, Darlene Love.
This fast, frantic, and wholly improbable police thriller owes its success to the chemistry between the two leads. Mel Gibson is fine as the cop on the edge (the weapon of the title), Danny Glover is equally good as his laid-back, methodical partner. Richard Donner directs with a lot of zip, and the result is a lot of fun. Rated R for violence. 1987; 105m.

LETHAL WEAPON 2 ★★★
DIR: Richard Donner. **CAST:** Mel Gibson, Danny Glover.
Mel Gibson and Danny Glover return as odd-couple police officers Riggs and Murtaugh in this enjoyable action sequel, which is packed with laughs and suspense. This time, our mismatched heroes are up against some bad guys from South Africa. Predictable but fun. Rated PG. 1989; 110m.

LICENCE TO KILL ★★★★
DIR: John Glen. **CAST:** Timothy Dalton, Robert Davi, Carey Lowell.
Timothy Dalton, in his second outing as James Bond, seeks revenge when his pal, former CIA-agent-turned-DEA-man Felix Leiter, is maimed and Leiter's bride is murdered. Uncommonly serious tone is a boost to the once-formulaic series, and Dalton

comes into his own as the modern 007. Rated PG-13. 1989; 120m.

LIFETAKER, THE
DIR: Michael Papas. **CAST:** Terence Morgan.
A boring sex thriller about a lonely housewife who entices a young man into her home and seduces him. When her jealous husband finds out, they all play a deadly game of cat and mouse to eliminate one another. Not rated, but contains violence and sexual scenes. 1989; 97m.

LIGHT AT THE END OF THE WORLD, THE ★
DIR: Kevin Billington. **CAST:** Kirk Douglas, Yul Brynner, Samantha Eggar, Jean-Claude Druout, Fernando Rey.
Tedious adaptation of the Jules Verne story. Kirk Douglas is a lighthouse keeper whose isolated island is invaded by ruthless pirates led by Yul Brynner. Douglas doesn't even fight the pirates until the very end of the film, and by then the audience has fallen asleep. Not rated, contains violence and sexual suggestions. 1971; 126m.

LIGHTHORSEMEN, THE ★★★½
DIR: Simon Wincer. **CAST:** Jon Blake, Peter Phelps, Tony Bonner, Bill Kerr, John Walton, Sigrid Thornton.
Vivid dramatization of the encounter between the Australian and Turkish forces at the city of Beersheba in the North African desert during World War I. Film's main focus is on a young recruit who cannot bring himself to kill another man in battle. Beautiful cinematography and fine performances by the entire cast make this one a winner. Rated PG. 1988; 110m.

LION AND THE HAWK, THE ★★★
DIR: Peter Ustinov. **CAST:** Peter Ustinov, Herbert Lom, Simon Dutton, Leonie Mellinger, Denis Quilley, Michael Elphick.
Turkey in 1923, with its social, religious, and economic revolution picking up steam, is the backdrop for this film about a young rebel (Simon Dutton) who defies cultural tradition and runs off with a woman betrothed to a powerful regional governor's nephew. Not rated; has sex, nudity, and violence. 1983; 105m.

LION OF AFRICA, THE ★★
DIR: Kevin Connor. **CAST:** Brian Dennehy, Brooke Adams, Don Warrington, Carl Andrews, Katharine Schofield.
This HBO action film is long-winded and anticlimactic, as well as being a tad too derivative of *Romancing the Stone*. Odd couple Brian Dennehy and Brooke Adams race across Africa with a hot rock that attracts a host of bad guys. Not rated, has violence and profanity. 1987; 110m.

LION OF THE DESERT ★★★½
DIR: Moustapha Akkad. **CAST:** Anthony Quinn, Oliver Reed, Rod Steiger.
This epic motion picture gives an absorbing portrait of the 1929–31 war in the North African deserts of Libya when Bedouin troops on horseback faced the tanks and mechanized armies of Mussolini. Anthony Quinn is Omar Mukhtar, the desert lion who became a nationalist and a warrior at the age of 52 and fought the Italians until they captured and hanged him twenty years later. Rated PG. 1981; 162m.

LISBON ★★
DIR: Ray Milland. **CAST:** Ray Milland, Claude Rains, Maureen O'Hara, Francis Lederer, Percy Marmont.
Maureen O'Hara's husband is in a communist prison. International gentleman thief Claude Rains hires Ray Milland to rescue him. Not James Bond caliber. Not *To Catch a Thief* classy. Not really worth much. 1956; 90m.

LIST OF ADRIAN MESSENGER, THE ★★★★½
DIR: John Huston. **CAST:** George C. Scott, Dana Wynter, Clive Brook, Herbert Marshall.

Excellent suspenser has a mysterious stranger visiting an English estate and the puzzling series of murders that coincide with his arrival. Crisp acting, coupled with John Huston's taut direction, makes this crackerjack entertainment. With cameo appearances by Kirk Douglas, Tony Curtis, Burt Lancaster, Robert Mitchum, Frank Sinatra. 1963; B&W; 98m.

LITTLE CAESAR ★★★
DIR: Mervyn LeRoy. **CAST:** Edward G. Robinson, Douglas Fairbanks Jr.

Historically, this is an important film. Made in 1930, it started the whole genre of gangster films. As entertainment, this veiled biography of Al Capone is terribly dated. Edward G. Robinson's performance is like a Warner Bros. cartoon in places, but one has to remember this is the original; the rest are imitators. 1930; B&W; 80m.

LITTLE DRUMMER GIRL, THE ★★½
DIR: George Roy Hill. **CAST:** Diane Keaton, Yorgo Voyagis, Klaus Kinski.

Director George Roy Hill did everything he could to make this adaptation of John Le Carré's bestseller a fast-paced, involving political thriller. However, his work is thwarted by an unconvincing lead performance by Diane Keaton, who plays an actress recruited by an Israeli general (Klaus Kinski) to help trap a Palestinian terrorist. Rated R for violence, profanity, suggested sex, and nudity. 1984; 130m.

LITTLE LAURA AND BIG JOHN ♥
DIR: Luke Moberly, Bob Woodburn. **CAST:** Karen Black, Fabian, Ivy Thayer, Ken Miller.

A very cheap response to the popular outlaw films of the late 1960s (*Bonnie and Clyde*; *Butch Cassidy and the Sundance Kid*; etc.). *Little Laura and Big John* is about the Ashley Gang, a bunch of losers who can put you to sleep by just saying "Stick 'em up." Rated R for violence, nudity, and profanity. 1972; 82m.

LITTLE NIKITA ★★★½
DIR: Richard Benjamin. **CAST:** Sidney Poitier, River Phoenix, Richard Jenkins, Caroline Kava, Richard Bradford, Richard Lynch, Loretta Devine, Lucy Deakins.

Well-crafted, old-fashioned espionage story about the awakening of "sleeper" agents (planted by the Soviets twenty years earlier in San Diego). Sidney Poitier is the FBI agent tracking the situation, and River Phoenix plays a teenager caught in the middle. Richard Bradford is great as a manipulative but likable KGB agent. Rated PG for language and violence. 1988; 98m.

LITTLE TREASURE ★★★
DIR: Alan Sharp. **CAST:** Margot Kidder, Ted Danson, Burt Lancaster.

While the synopsis on the back of the box may give one the impression this release is a ripoff of *Romancing the Stone*, only the rough outline of the story is lifted from the 1984 hit. The Margot Kidder/Ted Danson team is not a copy of the Kathleen Turner/Michael Douglas couple; these characters are more down-home. And the concentration on domestic drama almost fills the gap left by the absence of action. R for nudity and language. 1985; 95m.

LIVE AND LET DIE ★★
DIR: Guy Hamilton. **CAST:** Roger Moore, Jane Seymour, Yaphet Kotto, Geoffrey Holder.

The first Roger Moore (as James Bond) adventure is a hodgepodge of the surrealistic and the slick that doesn't quite live up to its Sean Connery–powered predecessors. The chase-and-suspense formula wears thin in this series entry. Rated PG. 1973; 121m.

LIVES OF A BENGAL LANCER, THE ★★★★½
DIR: Henry Hathaway. **CAST:** Gary Cooper, Franchot Tone, Richard Cromwell, Guy Standing, C. Aubrey Smith, Monte Blue, Kathleen Burke.

One of the great adventure films, this action-packed epic stars Gary Cooper and Franchot Tone as fearless friends in the famed British regiment. Their lives become complicated when they take the commander's son (Richard Cromwell) under their wings and he turns out to be less than a model soldier. 1935; B&W; 109m.

LIVING DAYLIGHTS, THE ★★★½
DIR: John Glen. **CAST:** Timothy Dalton, Maryam D'Abo, Jeroen Krabbé, Joe Don Baker, John Rhys-Davies, Art Malik, Desmond Llewellyn.

Timothy Dalton adds a dimension of humanity to Ian Fleming's famous creation in his screen bow as the ultimate spy hero. The silly set pieces and gimmicks that marred even the best Roger Moore entries in the series are gone. Instead, the filmmakers have opted for a strong plot about a phony KGB defector (Jeroen Krabbé) and a renegade arms dealer (Joe Don Baker) who wreak all sorts of havoc until 007 steps in. Rated PG. 1987; 130m.

LOADED GUNS
DIR: Fernando Di Leo. **CAST:** Ursula Andress, Woody Strode, Isabella Biagin.

Thoroughly stupid espionage flick from Italy that tries to be comical when it's not and is a laugh riot when it's supposed to be serious. Ursula Andress is a spy who tries to bust up a cocaine-smuggling ring. Not rated, but would be an R by MPAA standards due to sex, nudity, violence, and profanity. 1975; 90m.

LONE RUNNER ★
DIR: Roger Deodato. **CAST:** Miles O'Keeffe, Savina Gersak, Donal Hodson, Ronald Lacey.

Ho-hum, another Miles O'Keeffe dud. In this one our hero runs around a desert with a Rambo crossbow (complete with exploding arrows) and saves a damsel in distress (Savina Gersak). Rated PG for violence and profanity. 1986; 84m.

LONE WOLF MCQUADE ★★★½
DIR: Steve Carver. **CAST:** Chuck Norris, L. Q. Jones, R. G. Armstrong, David Carradine, Barbara Carrera.

Chuck Norris plays a maverick Texas ranger who forgets the rules in his zeal to punish the bad guys. Norris meets his match in David Carradine, the ruthless leader of a gun-smuggling ring. The worth-waiting-for climax is a martial arts battle between the two. Rated PG for violence and profanity. 1983; 107m.

LONG GOOD FRIDAY, THE ★★★★★
DIR: John MacKenzie. **CAST:** Bob Hoskins, Helen Mirren, Pierce Brosnan.

This superb British film depicts the struggle of an underworld boss (Bob Hoskins, in a brilliant performance) to hold on to his territory. It's a classic in the genre on a par with *The Godfather*, *The Public Enemy*, and *High Sierra*. Rated R for nudity, profanity, and violence. 1980; 114m.

LONG JOHN SILVER ★★★
DIR: Byron Haskin. **CAST:** Robert Newton, Connie Gilchrist, Kit Taylor, Grant Taylor.

Avast me hearties, Robert Newton is at his scene-chewing best in this otherwise unexceptional (and unofficial) sequel to Disney's *Treasure Island*. 1954; 109m.

LONGEST DAY, THE ★★★★★
DIR: Ken Annakin, Andrew Marton, Bernhard Wicki. **CAST:** John Wayne, Robert Mitchum, Henry Fonda, Richard Burton, Rod Steiger, Sean Connery, Robert Wagner.

A magnificent re-creation of the Allied invasion of Normandy in June of 1944 with an all-star cast, this epic war film succeeds where others may fail—*Midway* and *Tora! Tora! Tora!*, for example. A big-budget film that shows you where the money was spent, it's first-rate in all respects. 1963; B&W; 180m.

LONGEST YARD, THE ★★★★
DIR: Robert Aldrich. **CAST:** Burt Reynolds, Eddie Albert, Michael Conrad, Bernadette Peters, Ed Lauter.

An ex-professional football quarterback (Burt Reynolds) is sent to a Florida prison for stealing his girlfriend's car. The warden (Eddie Albert) forces Reynolds to put together a prisoner team to play his semipro team made up of guards. Great audience participation film with the last third dedicated to the game. Rated R for language and violence. 1974; 123m.

LOOPHOLE ★★½
DIR: John Quested. **CAST:** Albert Finney, Martin Sheen, Susannah York, Colin Blakely.

In yet another heist film, unemployed architect Albert Finney concocts an ambitious plan to break into a highly guarded and impenetrable London bank. There is a bit of snap in the scenario and dialogue, but ultimately *Loophole* loses its freshness. Susannah York gives a fine performance. Not rated. 1980; 105m.

LORD JIM ★★★★
DIR: Richard Brooks. **CAST:** Peter O'Toole, James Mason, Eli Wallach.

Joseph Conrad's complex novel of human weakness has been simplified for easier appreciation and brought to the screen in a lavish visual style. Peter O'Toole is Jim, a sailor in Southeast Asia who is adopted by a suppressed village as its leader in spite of a past clouded by allegations of cowardice. The belief shown in him by the native villagers is put to the test by a group of European thugs. 1965; 154m.

LOSERS, THE ★
DIR: Jack Starrett. **CAST:** William Smith, Bernie Hamilton, Adam Roarke.

Imagine *Rambo* made as a biker film and you'll have *The Losers*. You'll also be a loser if you rent it. The CIA sends a motorcycle gang riding armored bikes into Cambodia on a rescue mission. A sense of humor would have helped. Rated R for violence and nudity. 1970; 95m.

LOST CITY OF THE JUNGLE ★½
DIR: Ray Taylor, Lewis D. Collins. **CAST:** Russell Hayden, Lionel Atwill, Jane Adams, Keye Luke, Helen Bennett, Ted Hecht, John Eldredge, John Miljan, Ralph Lewis.

Sir Eric Hazarias (Lionel Atwill) wants to rule the world and he thinks he's discovered the way with Meteorium 245, the only defense against the atomic bomb. Phony temples, stock footage, familiar car chases, and cheating chapter endings are common to this minor chapterplay—the only outstanding thing about it is the presence of Atwill in his last screen role. 1946; B&W; 13 chapters.

LOST COMMAND ★★★
DIR: Mark Robson. **CAST:** Anthony Quinn, Alain Delon, George Segal, Michele Morgan, Claudia Cardinale.

A good international cast and fine direction bring to vivid life this story of French-Algerian guerrilla warfare in North Africa following World War II. Anthony Quinn is especially effective as a peasant who has earned a position of command. Great action scenes. 1966; 130m.

LOST EMPIRE, THE ★½
DIR: Jim Wynorski. **CAST:** Melanie Vincz, Raven De La Croix, Angela Aames, Paul Coufos, Robert Tessler.

Inept, hokey film about busty gals who infiltrate the island stronghold of a mysterious and powerful ruler is just one excuse for the female leads to model skimpy outfits. Rated R for some nudity, violence. 1983; 86m.

LOST JUNGLE, THE ★★
DIR: Armand Schaefer, David Howard. **CAST:** Clyde Beatty, Cecilia Parker, Syd Saylor, Warner Richmond, Wheeler Oakman, Mickey Rooney.

Clyde Beatty's first serial for Mascot Studios. Our hero's girlfriend and her father are lost on an uncharted jungle island during an expedition and

Beatty joins the rescue team. This would be pretty standard fare except for some spectacular animal stunts peformed by the inimitable Beatty, one of the finest daredevil peformers of all time. 1934; B&W; 12 chapters.

LOST PATROL, THE ★★★★
DIR: John Ford. **CAST:** Victor McLaglen, Boris Karloff, Wallace Ford, Reginald Denny, Alan Hale, J. M. Kerrigan, Billy Bevan.

An intrepid band of British cavalrymen lost in the Mesopotamian desert are picked off by the Arabs, one by one. Brisk direction and top-notch characterizations make this a winner—though it is grim. 1934; B&W; 65m.

LOST SQUADRON ★★★
DIR: George Archainbaud. **CAST:** Richard Dix, Mary Astor, Erich Von Stroheim, Joel McCrea, Dorothy Jordan, Robert Armstrong.

Mystery-adventure about the "accidental" deaths of former World War I pilots engaged as stunt fliers for the movies. Full of industry "in-jokes," breezy dialogue, and good stunts, this is a fun film—especially for anyone with an interest in stunt flying or aviation in general. 1932; B&W; 79m.

LOVE AND BULLETS ★½
DIR: Stuart Rosenberg. **CAST:** Charles Bronson, Rod Steiger, Strother Martin, Bradford Dillman, Henry Silva, Jill Ireland.

Incredibly dull Charles Bronson thriller. Bronson is hired to snatch Ireland from crime lord Rod Steiger. An absolute waste of a good cast. Rated PG for violence. 1979; 103m.

LOVE SPELL ★
DIR: Tom Donavan. **CAST:** Richard Burton, Kate Mulgrew, Nicholas Clay, Cyril Cusack.

In this film based on the legend of Tristan and Isolde and their doomed love, Richard Burton portrays Mark, king of Cornwall, who sends his nephew, Tristan, to fetch Mark's intended bride. Unfortunately, the two fall in love, creating the most difficult of triangles. The chase and battle scenes are unimaginatively filmed, and most of the acting mediocre. 1979; 90m.

LOW BLOW
DIR: Frank Harris. **CAST:** Leo Fong, Cameron Mitchell, Troy Donahue, Akosua Busia, Stack Pierce.

Wooden acting, sloppy editing, and poor direction earn this one a place in turkeydom. Leo Fong plays a private investigator who tries to rescue a millionaire's daughter from a religious cult. Rated R for violence and profanity. 1986; 85m.

LUCKY LUCIANO ★★
DIR: Francesco Rosi. **CAST:** Gian Maria Volonté, Rod Steiger, Edmond O'Brien, Vincent Gardenia, Charles Cioffi.

This U.S.-Franco-Italian production deals with the last years of one of crimeland's most "influential" bosses. The film started out to be an important one for Francesco Rosi, but the distributors of the English edition went in for the sensationalism with too graphic subtitles and/or dubbing, depending on the version. Not a bad film if you know Italian. If you don't, stick with *The Godfather*. Rated R for profanity and violence. 1974; 110m.

MACAO ★★
DIR: Josef von Sternberg. **CAST:** Jane Russell, Robert Mitchum, William Bendix, Gloria Grahame, Thomas Gomez.

Jane Russell is a singer in the fabled Oriental port and gambling heaven of Macao, across the bay from Hong Kong. She's in love with Robert Mitchum, a good guy caught in a web of circumstance. Russell is the only thing about this film that isn't flat. 1952; B&W; 80m.

MACKINTOSH MAN, THE ★★★
DIR: John Huston. **CAST:** Paul Newman, James Mason, Dominique Sanda, Ian Bannen, Nigel Patrick.

A cold war spy thriller with all the edge-of-seat trimmings: car chases, beatings, escapes, and captures. Trouble is, it has been done before, before, and before. Paul Newman is the agent; wily and wonderful James Mason is the communist spy he must catch. Rated PG. 1973; 98m.

MACON COUNTY LINE ★★★

DIR: Richard Compton. **CAST:** Alan Vint, Max Baer Jr., Geoffrey Lewis.

A very effective little thriller based on a true incident. Set in Georgia in the 1950s, the story concerns three youths hunted by the law for a murder they did not commit. Producer Max Baer Jr. has a good eye for detail and the flavor of the times. Rated R. 1974; 89m.

MAD DOG MORGAN ★★½

DIR: Philippe Mora. **CAST:** Dennis Hopper, Jack Thompson, David Gulpilil, Michael Pate.

Dennis Hopper plays an Australian bush ranger in this familiar tale of a man forced into a life of crime. Good support from aborigine David Gulpilil and Australian actor Jack Thompson help this visually stimulating film, but Hopper's excesses and a muddled ending weigh against it. Early prison sequences and scattered scenes are brutal. Rated R. 1976; 102m.

MADAME SIN ★★★

DIR: David Green. **CAST:** Robert Wagner, Bette Davis, Roy Kinnear, Paul Maxwell, Denholm Elliott, Gordon Jackson.

Undistinguished film in which Bette Davis plays a female Fu Manchu opposite Robert Wagner's sophisticated hero. Written expressly for the actress, it was the most expensive made-for-TV movie of its time and won high ratings. 1971; 73m.

MADIGAN ★★★½

DIR: Don Siegel. **CAST:** Richard Widmark, Henry Fonda, Harry Guardino, James Whitmore, Inger Stevens, Michael Dunn, Steve Ihnat, Sheree North.

Well-acted, atmospheric police adventure-drama pits tough Brooklyn cop Richard Widmark and New York's finest against a crazed escaped murderer. Realistic and exciting, this is still one of the best of the "behind-the-scenes" police films. 1968; 101m.

MAGNUM FORCE ★★★

DIR: Ted Post. **CAST:** Clint Eastwood, Hal Holbrook, David Soul, Tim Matheson, Robert Urich.

This is the second and least enjoyable of the five Dirty Harry films. Harry (Clint Eastwood) must deal with vigilante cops as well as the usual big-city scum. Body count is way up there, Clint is iron-jawed and athletic, but the film still lacks something. Rated R for language, violence, nudity, and gore. 1973; 124m.

MALONE ★★★½

DIR: Harley Cokliss. **CAST:** Burt Reynolds, Cliff Robertson, Kenneth McMillan, Scott Wilson, Lauren Hutton, Cynthia Gibb.

In this modern-day western, Burt Reynolds is in top form as Malone, an ex-CIA hit man on the run. Underneath all the car chases, big-bang explosions, and the blitz fire of automatic weapons is the simplest of all B-western plots—in which a former gunfighter is forced out of retirement by the plight of settlers forced off their land by black-hatted villains. Rated R for profanity, violence, and suggested sex. 1987; 92m.

MALTESE FALCON, THE ★★★★★

DIR: John Huston. **CAST:** Humphrey Bogart, Mary Astor, Sydney Greenstreet, Peter Lorre, Elisha Cook Jr., Ward Bond.

One of the all-time great movies, John Huston's first effort as a director is the definitive screen version of Dashiell Hammett's crime story. In a maze of double-crosses and back-stabbing, Humphrey Bogart, as Sam Spade, fights to get hold of a black bird, "the stuff that dreams are made of." 1941; B&W; 100m.

MANIAC COP ★

DIR: William Lustig. **CAST:** Tom Atkins, Bruce Campbell, Richard Roundtree, William Smith, Sheree North.

A deranged killer cop is stalking the streets of New York, murdering innocent people. Hysteria sweeps the city as the public begins to fear the police. The film starts strong but disintegrates into just another bad slasher flick. Rated R for violence, nudity, and adult situations. 1988; 92m.

MAN, A WOMAN AND A BANK, A ★★

DIR: Noel Black. **CAST:** Donald Sutherland, Brooke Adams, Paul Mazursky.

An odd little caper flick which never quite gets off the ground. A couple of guys decide to rob a bank via computer, and—of course—things don't work out as planned. Rated PG. 1979; 100m.

MAN IN THE EIFFEL TOWER, THE ★★★★

DIR: Burgess Meredith. **CAST:** Charles Laughton, Franchot Tone, Burgess Meredith, Robert Hutton, Jean Wallace.

A rarely seen little gem of suspense: an intriguing plot, a crafty police inspector (Charles Laughton), an equally crafty murderer (Franchot Tone), and an exciting conclusion played out against the backdrop of Paris's most famous landmark. Uniformly well-acted, this intelligent mystery is worth tracking down in video stores with a more extensive library of older, lesser-known titles. 1949; 97m.

MAN IN THE IRON MASK, THE (1939) ★★★

DIR: James Whale. **CAST:** Louis Hayward, Joan Bennett, Warren William, Alan Hale, Joseph Schildkraut.

Louis Hayward plays twin brothers—a fop and a swashbuckler—in this first sound version of Dumas's classic novel of malice, mayhem, intrigue, and ironic revenge in eighteenth-century France. Separated at birth, one brother becomes the king of France, the other a sword-wielding cohort of the Three Musketeers. Their clash makes for great romantic adventure. 1939; B&W; 110m.

MAN IN THE IRON MASK, THE (1977) ★★★

DIR: Mike Newell. **CAST:** Richard Chamberlain, Patrick McGoohan, Louis Jourdan, Jenny Agutter, Ralph Richardson.

This is the Alexandre Dumas tale of twin brothers, separated at birth. One becomes the wicked king of France, the other, a heroic peasant. The story receives a top-drawer treatment in this classy TV movie. Richard Chamberlain proves he's the most appealing swashbuckler since Errol Flynn retired his sword. 1977; 100m.

MAN INSIDE, THE ★★½

DIR: Gerald Mayer. **CAST:** James Franciscus, Stefanie Powers, Jacques Godin, Len Birman, Donald Davis, Allan Royale.

In this so-so film, James Franciscus is a Canadian vice squad agent who works his way into the organization of a major heroin dealer. In the course of his assignment he has the opportunity to split with $2 million, and is tempted to do so. This Canadian film is unrated. 1984; 96m.

MAN ON FIRE ★

DIR: Elie Chouraqui. **CAST:** Scott Glenn, Brooke Adams, Danny Aiello, Joe Pesci, Jonathan Pryce.

Scott Glenn plays an ex-CIA agent hired to protect the daughter of a wealthy American couple. Trouble is, the story is so confusingly presented that you're not sure why the daughter needs protecting or why she is ultimately kidnapped, and the relationship between Glenn and the little girl is made so solid so fast that it is totally unbelievable. Glenn is the film's only redemption. Rated R for language and graphic violence. 1987; 92m.

MAN WHO WOULD BE KING, THE ★★★★½

DIR: John Huston. **CAST:** Sean Connery, Michael Caine, Christopher Plummer.

A superb screen adventure, this is loosely based on Rudyard Kipling's story and was made at the same time Sean Connery and John Huston starred in the other sand-and-camel flick, the excellent *The Wind and the Lion*. Both are classics in the adventure genre. Rated PG. 1975; 129m.

MAN WITH BOGART'S FACE, THE ★★½

DIR: Robert Day. **CAST:** Robert Sacchi, Michelle Phillips, Olivia Hussey, Franco Nero, Misty Rowe, Victor Buono, Herbert Lom, Sybil Danning, George Raft, Mike Mazurki.

A modern-day Humphrey Bogart–type mystery. Film has fun with the genre while avoiding outright parody. A warm-hearted homage. Enjoyable, but of no great importance. Rated PG. 1980; 106m.

MAN WITH THE GOLDEN GUN, THE ★½

DIR: Guy Hamilton. **CAST:** Roger Moore, Christopher Lee, Britt Ekland, Maud Adams, Herve Villechaize, Bernard Lee, Lois Maxwell.

In spite of the potentially sinister presence of Christopher Lee as the head baddie, this is the most poorly constructed of all the Bond films. Roger Moore sleepwalks through the entire picture, and the plot tosses in every cliché, including the (then) obligatory nod to kung fu. Rated PG—some violence. 1974; 125m.

MANHUNT ★★

DIR: Fernando Di Leo. **CAST:** Mario Adorf, Henry Silva, Woody Strode, Adolfo Celi, Luciana Paluzzi, Sylva Koscina, Cyril Cusack.

Unbeknownst to him, a small-time Milano crook is framed as a big-time drug dealer, which results in the murder of his wife. He sets out in search of an explanation and revenge. Mediocre action picture was retitled *The Italian Connection* to cash in on the success of *The French Connection*. Dubbed in English. Rated R. 1973; 93m.

MANHUNT IN THE AFRICAN JUNGLE (SECRET SERVICE IN DARKEST AFRICA) ★★

DIR: Spencer Gordon Bennet. **CAST:** Rod Cameron, Joan Marsh, Duncan Renaldo, Lionel Royce.

American undercover agent Rod Cameron, posing as a Nazi, joins forces with United Nations agent Joan Marsh, posing as a journalist, to defeat the Axis in North Africa. Not the most thrill-laden of serials. 1943; B&W; 15 chapters.

MANHUNTER ★★★★½

DIR: Michael Mann. **CAST:** William L. Petersen, Kim Greist, Brian Cox, Dennis Farina, Joan Allen.

Thoroughly engrossing tale of an FBI man (William Petersen) following a trail of blood through the Southeast left by a ruthless, calculating psychopath known only as "The Tooth Fairy," for reasons made shockingly clear. Rated R for violence and various adult contents. 1986; 118m.

MARATHON MAN ★★★★

DIR: John Schlesinger. **CAST:** Dustin Hoffman, Laurence Olivier, Roy Scheider, William Devane, Marthe Keller.

A young student (Dustin Hoffman) unwittingly becomes involved in the pursuit of an ex–Nazi war criminal (Laurence Olivier) in this chase-thriller. The action holds your interest throughout. Rated R. 1976; 125m.

MARCH OR DIE ★★½

DIR: Dick Richards. **CAST:** Gene Hackman, Terence Hill, Max von Sydow, Catherine Deneuve.

Old-fashioned epic adventure that reminds us of *Beau Geste* and *The Charge of the Light Brigade*, but it lacks the credibility and style of these classics. Gene Hackman stars as an iron-willed major in the French Foreign Legion, who defends a desert outpost in Africa from marauding Arabs. Catherine Deneuve provides the romance for an obsessive Hackman. Not rated, but equivalent to an R for violence and mature situations. 1977; 104m.

MARK OF ZORRO, THE ★★★½
DIR: Fred Niblo. **CAST:** Douglas Fairbanks Sr., Marguerite de la Motte, Noah Beery Sr., Robert McKim.

Douglas Fairbanks took a chance in 1920 and jumped from comedy-adventures to *costumed* comedy-adventures; with this classic film, he never turned back. Fairbanks made the character of Zorro his own and quickly established himself as an American legend. Silent. 1920; B&W; 90m.

MARKED WOMAN ★★★
DIR: Lloyd Bacon. **CAST:** Bette Davis, Humphrey Bogart, Eduardo Ciannelli, Lola Lane, Isabel Jewell, Allen Jenkins.

Iron-hided district attorney Humphrey Bogart, in one of his early good-guy roles, convinces Bette Davis and a coterie of other ladies of the evening to squeal on their boss, crime kingpin Eduardo Ciannelli. The film is based on the downfall of New York racketeer Lucky Luciano. 1937; B&W; 99m.

MASCARA ★
DIR: Patrick Conrad. **CAST:** Charlotte Rampling, Michael Sarrazin, Derek de Lint.

Luridly exploitative film starring Charlotte Rampling and Michael Sarrazin as a sister and brother with a very kinky relationship. A costume designer falls for Rampling and finds himself in a secret underworld of private passions and insane obsessions. Someone is murdering transvestites, and the designer soon becomes a prime suspect. Rated R for nudity, profanity, and violence. 1987; 99m.

MASKED MARVEL, THE ★★½
DIR: Spencer Gordon Bennet. **CAST:** William Forrest, Louise Currie, Johnny Arthur.

The mysterious Masked Marvel comes to the aid of the World-Wide Insurance Company to battle the evil Sakima, a former Japanese envoy, and his gang of saboteurs, who are threatening the security of America. Practically nonstop action and top stunt work highlight this wartime Republic serial, which is about as patriotic as a serial can be. 1943; B&W; 12 chapters.

MASKS OF DEATH ★★★
DIR: Roy Ward Baker. **CAST:** Peter Cushing, John Mills, Anne Baxter, Ray Milland.

Twenty-seven years after playing Sherlock Holmes in the Hammer Films version of *The Hound of the Baskervilles,* Peter Cushing returned to the role for this enjoyable thriller. This time, the Great Detective and Dr. Watson (John Mills) investigate a series of bizarre murders, which leave their victims' faces frozen in expressions of terror. 1986; 80m.

MASSIVE RETALIATION ★
DIR: Thomas Cohen. **CAST:** Tom Boyer, Karlene Crockett, Peter Donat, Marilyn Hassett, Jason Gedrick.

A group of friends gathers at their own civil-defense fort during a national emergency. This action film takes itself so seriously, it comes off like a cold-war State Department instructional film. Not rated; has profanity and violence. 1984; 90m.

MASTER BLASTER ★
DIR: Glenn Wilder. **CAST:** Jeff Moldovan, Donna Rosae, Joe Hess, Peter Lunblad.

A survival-game competition gets out of hand when someone substitutes various devices of death for a supposedly harmless paintball gun. The acting is totally without conviction, especially the dispirited veteran who looks too young to have had a driver's permit when he was "doin' his hitch in Nam," and the stereotypical stupid redneck southerners. Rated R for violence, profanity, and nudity. 1985; 94m.

MATA HARI ★★
DIR: Curtis Harrington. **CAST:** Sylvia Kristel, Christopher Cazenove, Oliver Tobias.

Liberally sprinkled with action, erotica, and existentialism, *Mata Hari* is one of Sylvia (*Emmanuelle*) Kristel's better works. A departure from the more familiar tales of Mata Hari, this story traces the erotic dancer from Indonesia as she unwittingly becomes the tool of the German government during World War II. Rated R for sex and nudity. 1985; 103m.

MCQ ★★★½

DIR: John Sturges. **CAST:** John Wayne, Al Lettieri, Eddie Albert, Diana Muldaur, Clu Gulager, Colleen Dewhurst.

The success of *Dirty Harry* and the slow death of the western prompted John Wayne to shed his Stetson and six guns for cop clothes. While this John Sturges film doesn't quite match the Clint Eastwood–Don Siegel production that inspired it, there are some good scenes and suspense. Rated PG. 1974; 116m.

MEAN JOHNNY BARROWS

DIR: Fred Williamson. **CAST:** Fred Williamson, Roddy McDowall, Stuart Whitman, Elliott Gould.

Fred Williamson plays Johnny Barrows, a Vietnam war hero, dishonorably discharged for striking an officer. Trying to make it as a civilian, he becomes involved in a gang war. Bad acting and horrible music. Rated R. 1976; 80m.

MEAN SEASON, THE ★★★½

DIR: Phillip Borsos. **CAST:** Kurt Russell, Richard Jordan, Mariel Hemingway, Richard Masur.

Miami crime reporter Kurt Russell finds himself the unwilling confidant of a maniacal killer in this exciting thriller. The film occasionally relies on stock shocks. Still, it is fast-paced and inventive enough to overcome the clichés. Rated R for violence. 1985; 109m.

MECHANIC, THE ★★½

DIR: Michael Winner. **CAST:** Charles Bronson, Jan-Michael Vincent, Jill Ireland, Keenan Wynn.

A professional hit man (Charles Bronson) teaches his craft to a young student (Jan-Michael Vincent). Slow-moving for the most part, with a few good action scenes. The ending has a nice twist to it, but the film is generally much ado about nothing. Rated R for violence and language. 1972; 100m.

MELVIN PURVIS: G-MAN ★★★

DIR: Dan Curtis. **CAST:** Dale Robertson, Harris Yulin, Margaret Blye, Dick Sargent.

In the tradition of the Warner Bros. gangster films of the Thirties, Melvin Purvis (Dale Robertson) holds nothing back in this fictionalized account of the all-consuming search for Machine Gun Kelly. Wild and fast-paced, this made-for-TV film is exciting and entertaining. 1974; 78m.

MEMORIES OF MANON (THE EQUALIZER) ★★★

DIR: Tony Wharmby. **CAST:** Edward Woodward, Melissa Sue Anderson, Anthony Zerbe, Robert Lansing, Jon Polito, Keith Szarabajka.

Edward Woodward's commanding performance as *The Equalizer* gives weight to this made-for-TV release about a New York avenger and his discovery of danger stalking the daughter (Melissa Sue Anderson) he didn't know he had. Fans of Woodward and his series will enjoy a second look. 1988; 96m.

MEN IN WAR ★★★★

DIR: Anthony Mann. **CAST:** Robert Ryan, Aldo Ray, Vic Morrow.

This outstanding Korean War action film with Robert Ryan and Aldo Ray fighting the Chinese and each other is one of the very best "war is hell" films. 1957; B&W; 104m.

MERCENARY FIGHTERS ★★

DIR: Riki Shelach. **CAST:** Peter Fonda, Reb Brown, Ron O'Neal, Jim Mitchum, Robert DoQui.

U.S. mercenaries (Peter Fonda and company) are hired by the ruler of an African nation to get rid of the tribesmen who are blocking the building of a new dam. When they discover that the dam would force the tribe off its ancestral homeland, the mercenaries begin to fight among themselves as to whether or not they're doing the right thing. The actors took some heat for participating in this film, which was made in South Africa and the results are certainly nothing you'd want to put your career on the line for. 1986; 91m.

MESSENGER OF DEATH ★★½
DIR: J. Lee Thompson. **CAST:** Charles Bronson, Trish Van Devere, John Ireland, Jeff Corey, Laurence Luckinbill, Marilyn Hassett.

Middling Charles Bronson vehicle features the star in a convincing portrayal of a newspaper reporter investigating the bizarre murder of a Mormon family. A strong, suspenseful opening degenerates into a routine thriller. However, one must credit screenwriter Paul Jarrico with keeping the viewer guessing, and director J. Lee Thompson does elicit believable performances from the cast. Rated R for violence and profanity. 1988; 98m.

MIAMI VICE ★★★★
DIR: Thomas Carter. **CAST:** Don Johnson, Philip Michael Thomas, Saundra Santiago, Michael Talbott, John Diehl, Gregory Sierra, Bill Smitrovich, Belinda Montgomery, Martin Ferrero, Mykel T. Williamson, Olivia Brown, Miguel Pinero.

This pilot for the popular NBC series is slam-bang entertainment. A New York City cop (Philip Michael Thomas) on the trail of the powerful drug kingpin who killed his brother traces him to Miami, running into a vice cop (Don Johnson) who's after the same guy. All the trademarks of the series are here: great music, rapid-fire editing, gritty low-key performances, and bursts of sporadic violence. The only real flaw in this tape is the sound quality, which, even in hi-fi stereo, is muffled. 1984; 97m.

MIAMI VICE: "THE PRODIGAL SON" ★★★
DIR: Paul Michael Glaser. **CAST:** Don Johnson, Philip Michael Thomas, Edward James Olmos, Olivia Brown, Penn Jilette, Pam Grier.

The pastel duo, Crockett (Don Johnson) and Tubbs (Philip Michael Thomas), trek up to New York in search of the bad guys in this watchable second-season opener. 1985; 99m.

MIDNIGHT CROSSING ★
DIR: Roger Holzberg. **CAST:** Faye Dunaway, Daniel J. Travanti, Kim Cattrall, John Laughlin, Ned Beatty.

Poorly written and realized film about four people on a treasure hunt into Cuba to retrieve $1 million in cash hidden when Castro took over. The plot twists can be seen a mile away, and the actors' accents fade in and out. Rated R for language, violence, and nudity. 1988; 104m.

MIDNIGHT LACE ★★★
DIR: David Miller. **CAST:** Doris Day, Rex Harrison, John Gavin, Myrna Loy, Roddy McDowall, Herbert Marshall, Natasha Perry.

A fine mystery with a cast that makes the most of it. Doris Day is an American living in London and married to successful businessman Rex Harrison. She soon finds her life in danger. Some viewers may find it less sophisticated than present-day thrillers, but there's plenty of suspense and plot twists to recommend it. 1960; 100m.

MIDNIGHT RUN ★★★★
DIR: Martin Brest. **CAST:** Robert De Niro, Charles Grodin, Yaphet Kotto, John Ashton, Dennis Farina.

Robert De Niro is wonderfully funny as a bounty hunter charged with bringing in fugitive Charles Grodin. The latter is hiding out after stealing $15 million from a crime boss and giving it to charity. Mixing laughs, surprises, and oodles of action, Martin Brest has come up with the perfect follow-up to his megahit, *Beverly*

Hills Cop. Rated R for profanity and violence. 1988; 125m.

MIDWAY ★★★
DIR: Jack Smight. **CAST:** Henry Fonda, Charlton Heston, Robert Mitchum, Hal Holbrook, Edward Albert, Cliff Robertson.
An all-star cast was assembled to bring to the screen this famous sea battle of World War II. Midway became famous as the site of the overwhelming victory of American carrier forces, which shifted the balance of power in the Pacific. As a historical drama, this film is accurate and maintains interest. However, a romance subplot is totally out of place. Rated PG. 1976; 132m.

MIGHTY QUINN, THE ★★★★
DIR: Carl Schenkel. **CAST:** Denzel Washington, Robert Townsend, James Fox, Sheryl Lee Ralph, Mimi Rogers.
A quirky, entertaining mystery story, set in the reggae world of a Caribbean island (presumably Jamaica). Denzel Washington plays the local police chief—"The Mighty Quinn"—who is on the trail of a murderer. Director Carl Schenkel contributes an inventive visual style and makes ample use of a wonderful reggae score by Rita Marley, Sister Carol, the Neville Brothers, Yellowman, and others. Rated R, with profanity, violence, and mild sexual situations. 1989; 95m.

MINES OF KILIMANJARO ★½
DIR: Mino Guerrini. **CAST:** Tobias Hoesl, Elena Pompei, Christopher Connelly.
Raiders of the Lost Ark imitation with an American college student in Africa searching for the lost diamond mines of Kilimanjaro. Trying to stop him are the Nazis, Chinese gangsters, and native tribesmen. The action footage is badly choreographed, the music is strident, and the historical accuracy is a laugh. Not rated, but contains violence. 1987; 88m.

MIRROR CRACK'D, THE ★½
DIR: Guy Hamilton. **CAST:** Elizabeth Taylor, Kim Novak, Tony Curtis, Angela Lansbury, Edward Fox, Rock Hudson.
Elizabeth Taylor, Kim Novak, and Tony Curtis seem to be vying to see who can turn in the worst performance in this tepid adaptation of the Agatha Christie murder mystery. Angela Lansbury makes an excellent Miss Marple, and Edward Fox is topnotch as her Scotland Yard inspector nephew. Rated PG. 1980; 105m.

MISFIT BRIGADE, THE ★★★
DIR: Gordon Hessler. **CAST:** Bruce Davison, David Patrick Kelly, D. W. Moffett, Oliver Reed, David Carradine, Jay O. Sanders.
Oliver Reed and David Carradine have cameo roles in this takeoff on *The Dirty Dozen*. Bruce Davison, David Patrick Kelly, and their buddies are assorted criminals from a Nazi penal brigade. They are offered their freedom if they go on a dangerous mission and survive. The cast has a lot of fun with the tongue-in-cheek action. Rated R. 1987; 99m.

MISSING IN ACTION ★★★½
DIR: Joseph Zito. **CAST:** Chuck Norris, M. Emmet Walsh, Lenore Kasdorf, James Hong.
Chuck Norris is a one-man army in this Vietnam-based action film. Anyone else might be laughable in such a role. But the former karate star makes it work. The story focuses on an attempt by Col. James Braddock (Norris), a former Vietnam prisoner of war, to free the other Americans he believes are still there. Rated R for profanity, violence, and brief nudity. 1984; 101m.

MISSING IN ACTION 2: THE BEGINNING ★★½
DIR: Lance Hool. **CAST:** Chuck Norris, Cosie Costa, Soon-Teck Oh, Steven Williams.
Following on the heels of the previous year's surprise hit, this "prequel" is really the same movie, only it tells the

story of how Colonel Braddock (Chuck Norris) and his men escaped their Vietnam prison camp after ten years of torture. The acting is nonexistent, the action predictable and violent. Rated R for violence. 1985; 95m.

MR. ACE ★½
DIR: Edwin L. Marin. **CAST:** George Raft, Sylvia Sidney, Stanley Ridges, Sara Haden, Jerome Cowan.

Potboiler about spoiled society woman (Sylvia Sidney) who uses gangster (George Raft) to win congressional election goes through the motions but very little else. The acting is okay, but the story is too familiar and the ending too trite to be taken seriously. 1946; B&W; 84m.

MR. BILLION ★★½
DIR: Jonathan Kaplan. **CAST:** Terence Hill, Valerie Perrine, Jackie Gleason, Slim Pickens, William Redfield, Chill Wills, Dick Miller.

Sappy but seductive story about a humble Italian mechanic (Terence Hill) who will inherit a financial empire if he can get to the signing over of his uncle's will before a gang of kidnappers or the corporation's chairman (Jackie Gleason) gets to him first. Rated PG for violence and sex. 1977; 89m.

MR. INSIDE/MR. OUTSIDE ★★
DIR: William A. Graham. **CAST:** Hal Linden, Tony LoBianco, Phil Bruns, Paul Benjamin, Stefan Schnabel.

Hal Linden and Tony LoBianco are fine in this made-for-television cop thriller as two New York City detectives attempting to foil a smuggling ring. Director William Graham's pacing makes you forget how much this movie is like so many other works created for TV. 1973; 74m.

MR. LUCKY ★★★
DIR: H. C. Potter. **CAST:** Cary Grant, Laraine Day.

Cary Grant is a gambler attempting to bilk money from a charity relief program. He changes his tune when he falls for a wealthy society girl, Laraine Day. This is a slick piece of wartime fluff. The plot has nothing you haven't seen before, but the charm of Grant makes it watchable. 1943; B&W; 100m.

MR. MAJESTYK ★★★½
DIR: Richard Fleischer. **CAST:** Charles Bronson, Al Lettieri, Linda Cristal, Lee Purcell, Paul Koslo.

In this better-than-average Charles Bronson vehicle, he's a watermelon grower (!) coming up against gangster Al Lettieri (in a first-rate performance). Rated R. 1974; 103m.

MR. MOTO'S LAST WARNING ★★★
DIR: Norman Foster. **CAST:** Peter Lorre, Ricardo Cortez, Virginia Field, John Carradine, George Sanders.

One of the last in the low-budget series that produced eight films in less than three years. This time out, the detective gets involved with terrorist spies intent on blowing up the French fleet in the Suez Canal. Enjoyable, quaint entertainment with a good supporting cast. 1939; B&W; 71m.

MR. ROBINSON CRUSOE ★★★
DIR: A. Edward Sutherland. **CAST:** Douglas Fairbanks Sr., William Farnum, Maria Alba.

Dashing Douglas Fairbanks Sr. bets he can survive like Crusoe on a South Sea island. Just how he does it makes for great fun. Fairbanks was just short of 50 when he made this film, but he was still the agile, athletic swashbuckler whose wholesome charm made him the idol of millions. 1932; B&W; 76m.

MR. WONG, DETECTIVE ★★★
DIR: William Nigh. **CAST:** Boris Karloff, Grant Withers, Evelyn Brent, Maxine Jennings, Lucien Prival.

First of five Mr. Wong films starring Boris Karloff as Hugh Wiley's black-suited sleuth is a notch above most of Mascot Pictures programmers. Mr. Wong attempts to solve the deaths of three industrialists, which have baffled the authorities and have the government and media in an uproar. Fun for mystery and detective fans. 1938; B&W; 69m.

MIXED BLOOD ★★½

DIR: Paul Morrissey. **CAST:** Marilia Pera, Richard Ulacia, Linda Kerridge, Geraldine Smith, Angel David, Rodney Harvey.

Paul Morrissey, the same man who brought you Andy Warhol's versions of *Frankenstein* and *Dracula*, has made a serious film about the Alphabet City drug subculture and its inherent violent nature. The lack of emotion in the characters shifts the focus from the actor to the landscape to which he or she is reacting. Here the surroundings are brutal and unforgiving, and the cheap film stock gives the movie a newsreel feeling. Not rated, but contains violence and profanity. 1985; 98m.

MOBY DICK ★★★★½

DIR: John Huston. **CAST:** Gregory Peck, Richard Basehart, Leo Genn, Orson Welles.

Director John Huston's brilliant adaptation of Herman Melville's classic novel features Gregory Peck in one of his best performances as the driven Captain Ahab. 1956; 116m.

MOGAMBO ★★★

DIR: John Ford. **CAST:** Clark Gable, Grace Kelly, Ava Gardner.

This remake of the film classic *Red Dust* stars Clark Gable as the great white hunter who dallies with a sophisticated married woman (Grace Kelly), only to return to the arms of a jaded lady (Ava Gardner, who is quite good in the role of the woman with a past). It's not great John Ford, but it'll do. 1953; 115m.

MOONLIGHTING (1985) ★★★★

DIR: Robert Butler. **CAST:** Cybill Shepherd, Bruce Willis, Allyce Beasley.

This is the pilot film for the delightfully offbeat ABC series. Maddie, a supersuccessful model, suddenly finds herself facing poverty, thanks to an embezzler. She decides to sell off all her assets, including a money-losing detective agency. David, a fast-talking, irresistible eccentric, tries to talk her into making a career of sleuthing instead. Bruce Willis is dazzling as David. And the chemistry beween Willis and Cybill Shepherd heats up to just the right temperature. 1985; 97m.

MOONRAKER ★

DIR: Lewis Gilbert. **CAST:** Roger Moore, Lois Chiles, Michel Lonsdale.

The James Bond series hit absolute rock bottom in 1979 with this outer-space adventure featuring Roger Moore as the famed secret agent. It's a groaner for 007 fans and nonfans alike. Rated PG. 1979; 126m.

MOONSHINE COUNTY EXPRESS ★★

DIR: Gus Trikonis. **CAST:** John Saxon, Susan Howard, William Conrad, Dub Taylor.

In this bogus action flick, William Conrad has his hands full with the three vengeful daughters of a man he just murdered. Rated PG for mild language and violence. 1977; 95m.

MORGAN THE PIRATE ★★★

DIR: André de Toth, Primo Zeglio. **CAST:** Steve Reeves, Valerie Lagrange, Ivo Garbani.

This fictionalized account of the adventures of the historical Henry Morgan (with muscleman Steve Reeves in the title role) is perhaps the most entertaining of that actor's many Italian-made features. Even by current standards, there is plenty of action and romance. 1961; 93m.

MORITURI ★★½

DIR: Bernhard Wicki. **CAST:** Marlon Brando, Yul Brynner, Janet Margolin, Trevor Howard, Wally Cox, William Redfield.

Marlon Brando portrays a spy working for the British who, through a series of moral equations involving anti-Nazism versus Nazism, convinces the captain of a German freighter on a voyage from Japan to Germany to side with the Allies. The concept is good, but the script gets weaker and weaker as the film progresses. 1965; B&W; 128m.

MOTHER LODE ★★
DIR: Charlton Heston. **CAST:** Charlton Heston, John Marley, Nick Mancuso, Kim Basinger.

Although this modern-day adventure yarn about a search for gold boasts a feasible plot and fine acting by Charlton Heston (who also directed) and John Marley, its liabilities far outweigh its assets. Rated PG, the film contains occasional obscenities and violence. 1982; 101m.

MOTOR PSYCHO ★★
DIR: Russ Meyer. **CAST:** Haji, Alex Rocco, Steven Oliver.

A woman and a man whose spouses were attacked by a vicious gang of desert bikers team up for revenge. Russ Meyer made this as a second feature for his cult classic *Faster, Pussycat! Kill! Kill!* Meyer aficionados will find it pretty tame. Unrated, the movie contains comparatively mild violence. 1965; B&W; 73m.

MOVING FINGER, THE ★★★½
DIR: Roy Boulting. **CAST:** Joan Hickson, Michael Culver, Sandra Payne, Richard Pearson, Andrew Bicknell.

The sleepy village of Lymston loses its serenity when residents begin receiving nasty anonymous letters; the situation so upsets the vicar's wife that she summons her good friend Miss Marple (Joan Hickson). This tale is highlighted by its engaging characters. Unrated; suitable for family viewing. 1984; 102m.

MOVING VIOLATION ★★½
DIR: Charles S. Dubin. **CAST:** Stephen McHattie, Kay Lenz, Eddie Albert, Lonny Chapman, Will Geer, Dick Miller.

Another southern car-chase movie from the Roger Corman factory, this one features some pretty good high-speed pyrotechnics. (Those scenes were done by second-unit director Barbara Peeters.) The plot, which is merely an excuse for the chases, has an innocent couple being pursued by a corrupt sheriff. Rated PG. 1976; 91m.

MS. .45 ★★★★
DIR: Abel Ferrara. **CAST:** Zoe Tamerlis.

An attractive mute woman is raped and beaten twice in the same evening. She slips into madness and seeks revenge with a .45 pistol. A female version of *Death Wish* with an ending at a Halloween costume party that will knock your socks off. Not for all tastes. Rated R for violence, nudity, rape, language, and gore. 1981; 90m.

MURDER AHOY ★★½
DIR: George Pollock. **CAST:** Margaret Rutherford, Lionel Jeffries, Stringer Davis, Charles Tingwell.

Threadbare mystery has Miss Marple (Margaret Rutherford) investigating murder aboard ship. This was the last film in the British series, although it was released in America before the superior *Murder Most Foul*. Despite her considerable talents, Rutherford could not raise this sinking ship above the level of mediocrity. 1964; B&W; 74m.

MURDER AT THE GALLOP ★★★★
DIR: George Pollock. **CAST:** Margaret Rutherford, Robert Morley, Flora Robson, Stringer Davis.

Margaret Rutherford has her best Miss Marple outing in this adaptation of Agatha Christie's Hercule Poirot mystery, *After the Funeral*. She and Robert Morley play off each other beautifully in this comedy-laced tale, which has Marple insinuating herself into a murder investigation. Her assistant, Mr. Stringer, is played by Rutherford's real-life husband, Stringer Davis. 1963; B&W; 81m.

MURDER BY DECREE ★★★½
DIR: Bob Clark. **CAST:** Christopher Plummer, James Mason, Donald Sutherland, Genevieve Bujold, Susan Clark, David Hemmings, John Gielgud, Anthony Quayle.

Excellent cast stylishly serves up this Sherlock Holmes mystery. Christopher Plummer and James Mason are well suited to the roles of Holmes and Dr. Watson. The murky story deals with Jack the Ripper. Rated R for violence and gore. 1979; 121m.

MURDER IS ANNOUNCED, A ★★★½

DIR: David Giles. **CAST:** Joan Hickson, Ursula Howells, Renée Asherson, John Castle, Sylvia Syms, Joan Sims.

The sedate Personals column of Chipping Cleghorn's *North Benham Gazette*, usually filled with pleas regarding lost dogs and bicycles for sale, is enlivened by a classified announcing a murder, which then takes place, as scheduled. Miss Marple (Joan Hickson) is summoned by the village constabulary. This is one of Agatha Christie's more convoluted stories. Unrated; suitable for family viewing. 1984; 153m.

MURDER MOST FOUL ★★★½

DIR: George Pollock. **CAST:** Margaret Rutherford, Ron Moody, Charles Tingwell, Stringer Davis, Francesca Annis, Dennis Price.

Like *Murder at the Gallop*, this is another Miss Marple adventure fashioned out of a Hercule Poirot mystery (*Mrs. McGinty's Dead*). The plot is only a framework for Margaret Rutherford's delightful antics. This time, she is the only dissenting member of a jury in a murder case. 1964; B&W; 91m.

MURDER MY SWEET ★★★★

DIR: Edward Dmytryk. **CAST:** Dick Powell, Claire Trevor, Anne Shirley.

In the mid-1940s, Dick Powell decided to change his clean-cut crooner image by playing Raymond Chandler's hard-boiled detective, Philip Marlowe. It worked marvelously, with Powell making a fine white knight in tarnished armor on the trail of killers and blackmailers. 1944; B&W; 95m.

MURDER ON FLIGHT 502 ★★

DIR: George McCowan. **CAST:** Ralph Bellamy, Polly Bergen, Robert Stack, Theodore Bikel, Sonny Bono, Dane Clark, Laraine Day, Fernando Lamas, George Maharis, Farrah Fawcett, Hugh O'Brian, Brooke Adams, Walter Pidgeon, Molly Picon.

A mad bomber threatens to blow an international airliner into pieces. He is thwarted by Robert Stack and other reluctant heroes. Reminiscent of *Airport* and a half-dozen sequels. The cast alone keeps this made-for-TV potboiler from falling flat on its baggage carousel. 1975; 120m.

MURDER ON THE ORIENT EXPRESS ★★★★½

DIR: Sidney Lumet. **CAST:** Albert Finney, Ingrid Bergman, Lauren Bacall, Sean Connery, Vanessa Redgrave, Michael York, Jacqueline Bisset.

Belgian detective Hercule Poirot solves a murder on a train in this stylish prestige picture based on the Agatha Christie mystery. Albert Finney is terrific as the detective and is supported by an all-star cast. Rated PG. 1974; 127m.

MURDER ONE ★

DIR: Graeme Campbell. **CAST:** Henry Thomas, James Wilder, Stephen Shellen.

The year is 1973. Two brothers and a friend bust out of jail. The brothers and friend head for home, only to find the police waiting for them and a younger brother eager to join them. Looking for kicks and thrills, the four of them set out on an odyssey of madness, mayhem, and murder. A morose, soulless film that says very little about the characters' motivation and goes nowhere with its conclusions. Based on a true story. Rated R for nudity, profanity, and violence. 1988; 82m.

MURDER OVER NEW YORK ★★

DIR: Harry Lachman. **CAST:** Sidney Toler, Marjorie Weaver, Robert Lowery, Ricardo Cortez, Donald MacBride, Melville Cooper, Kane Richmond, Clarence Muse, John Sutton.

The world's most famous Oriental detective, Charlie Chan (Sidney Toler), goes after a gang of saboteurs plaguing the airways after a Scotland Yard Inspector is felled by poisonous gas. Although cast with plenty of top-flight character actors, this one falls a little flat. The formula was wearing pretty thin after twenty-four films. 1940; B&W; 64m.

MURDER SHE SAID ★★★★

DIR: George Pollock. **CAST:** Margaret Rutherford, Arthur Kennedy, Charles Tingwell, Muriel Pavlow, James Robertson Justice, Thorley Walters.

Now that Joan Hickson has brought Agatha Christie's Miss Marple to life in the superb BBC series, it has become common for mystery buffs to denigrate the four films starring Margaret Rutherford as Marple. We beg to differ. While they may not be faithful to the original novels, Rutherford makes a delightful screen sleuth, and this adaptation of *4:50 to Paddington* is quite enjoyable. The first entry in the series, it has Marple witnessing a murder on a train. 1961; B&W; 87m.

MURDERERS' ROW ★★½

DIR: Henry Levin. **CAST:** Dean Martin, Ann-Margret, Karl Malden, James Gregory.

This entry into the Matt Helm secret-agent series is pretty dismal. Dean Martin has been much better in other films. The Matt Helm series was an attempt to grab the Bond and Flint audience, but Martin just couldn't cut it as a superspy. 1966; 108m.

MURPH THE SURF ★★½

DIR: Marvin J. Chomsky. **CAST:** Robert Conrad, Don Stroud, Donna Mills, Luther Adler.

In this based-on-real-life thriller, two Florida beachniks connive to do the impossible: steal the fabled 564-carat Star of India sapphire out of New York's American Museum of Natural History. Re-creation of the 1964 crime induces sweat, along with a good speedboat chase, but the picture never really catches a wave. 1975; 101m.

MURPHY'S LAW ★

DIR: J. Lee Thompson. **CAST:** Charles Bronson, Carrie Snodgress, Kathleen Wilhoite.

Charles Bronson is a cop framed for the murder of his ex-wife, who escapes from jail handcuffed to the teenage girl who stole his car. It's a plot line used before in *The Defiant Ones*, *The Gauntlet*, and *48 Hrs*. all of which are better films. The only thing *Murphy's Law* does well is prove Murphy's Law. Rated R. 1986; 101m.

MURPHY'S WAR ★★★

DIR: Peter Yates. **CAST:** Peter O'Toole, Sian Phillips, Horst Janson, Philippe Noiret, John Hallam.

World War II sea drama follows a British seaman, sole survivor of a brutal massacre of his ship's crew by a German U-boat, as he seeks revenge. Peter O'Toole gives a hard-hitting, no-holds-barred performance as the outraged, bloodthirsty Murphy. Rated PG. 1971; 108m.

MUTINY ON THE BOUNTY (1935) ★★★★

DIR: Frank Lloyd. **CAST:** Charles Laughton, Clark Gable, Franchot Tone, Dudley Digges, Eddie Quillan, Donald Crisp, Henry Stephenson.

The first and best known of three versions of the now classic account of mutiny against the tyranny of Captain William Bligh during a worldwide British naval expedition in 1789. Charles Laughton is superb as the merciless Bligh, Clark Gable unquestionably fine as the leader of the mutiny, Fletcher Christian. The film won an Oscar for best picture and still entertains today. 1935; B&W; 132m.

MUTINY ON THE BOUNTY (1962) ★★

DIR: Lewis Milestone. **CAST:** Marlon Brando, Trevor Howard, Richard Harris, Hugh Griffith, Richard Haydn, Gordon Jackson.

This years-later remake hits the South Seas with a gigantic belly flop. The color is beautiful, Trevor Howard is commanding as the tyrannical Captain Bligh, but Marlon Brando as mutiny leader Fletcher Christian? Yucko! 1962; 179m.

MYSTERIOUS DR. SATAN ★★★
DIR: William Witney, John English. **CAST:** Eduardo Ciannelli, Robert Wilcox, William Newell, C. Montague Shaw, Dorothy Herbert, Ella Neal, Jack Mulhall, Edwin Stanley.

Eduardo Cianelli unleashes his death-dealing robot upon a helpless public. Chockful of great stunts, last-minute escapes, and logic that defies description, this prime chapterplay from Republic's thrill factory had just about everything a juvenile audience could ask for and then some. Put your mind on hold and lose yourself in this fifty-year-old fun. 1940; B&W; 15 chapters.

MYSTERIOUS MR. WONG, THE ★★
DIR: William Nigh. **CAST:** Belá Lugosi, Wallace Ford, Arline Judge.

Not to be confused with the Mr. Wong detective series that starred Boris Karloff, this low-budget mystery has Bela Lugosi in the title role, portraying a fiendish criminal bent on possessing twelve coins connected with Confucius. 1935; B&W; 68m.

MYSTERY SQUADRON ★★½
DIR: Colbert Clark, David Howard. **CAST:** Bob Steele, Guinn Williams, Lucille Brown, Jack Mulhall, Purnell Pratt.

Mascot Studios continued its effort to be the best producer of serials with this fast-moving story of the sinister Mystery Squadron and its fanatical leader, the Black Ace. Flying daredevils Bob Steele and "Big Boy" Williams trade in their chaps and horses for parachutes and planes as they do their utmost to apprehend the Black Ace, a deadly saboteur. 1933; B&W; 12 chapters.

NAKED AND THE DEAD, THE ★★★
DIR: Raoul Walsh. **CAST:** Aldo Ray, Joey Bishop, Cliff Robertson, Raymond Massey.

This action-packed World War II film is based on Norman Mailer's famous book. Not nearly as good as the book, nevertheless the film is still quite powerful and exciting. Worth a watch. 1958; 131m.

NAKED CAGE, THE ★½
DIR: Paul Nicholas. **CAST:** Shari Shattuck, Angel Tompkins, Lucinda Crosby.

An innocent young girl finds herself mistakenly arrested for bank robbery. The first half of this film borders on soft-core pornography. The plot is the same as any other women-in-prison movie, but the truly hideous villains make this movie worth seeing. Rated R for violence, harsh language, and loads of nudity. 1982; 97m.

NAKED JUNGLE, THE ★★
DIR: Byron Haskin. **CAST:** Charlton Heston, Eleanor Parker, Abraham Sofaer, William Conrad, Romo Vincent, Douglas Fowley.

In this studio soap opera made from the short story *Leninnen Versus the Ants*, Charlton Heston is slightly out of place but still powerful as the South American plantation owner who stands up to a horde of voracious soldiers ants. Eleanor Parker is ridiculous as his new wife, and a young, thin William Conrad is along for the ride. Not rated, contains slight violence. 1953; 95m.

NAKED PREY, THE ★★★★
DIR: Cornel Wilde. **CAST:** Cornel Wilde, Gert Van Den Bergh, Ken Gampu.

An African safari takes a disastrous turn and Cornel Wilde winds up running naked and unarmed through the searing jungle as a large band of native warriors keeps on his heels, determined to finish him off. This is an amazingly intense adventure of man versus man and man versus nature.

Wilde does a remarkable job, both as star and director. 1966; 94m.

NAKED VENGEANCE ★

DIR: Cirio H. Santiago. **CAST:** Deborah Tranelli, Kaz Garas, Bill McLaughlin, Nick Nicholson.

Unpleasant exploitation flick about a woman who seeks vengeance after she is raped and her parents murdered. This is extremely violent, both in showing the woman being gang-raped and her revenge. It's a case of two wrongs most definitely not making a right. Available in both R and unrated versions; we'd suggest that you avoid both. 1986; 97m.

NAKED YOUTH ★★

DIR: John Schreyer. **CAST:** Robert Hutton, John Goddard, Carol Ohmart.

A good kid gets involved with a bad apple and together they wind up in prison—and then break out. Filmed mostly in the desert of New Mexico, this movie has its share of cheap thrills, but it's hardly the camp classic the distributors would have you believe. 1961; B&W; 80m.

NAME OF THE ROSE, THE ★★★

DIR: Jean-Jacques Annaud. **CAST:** Sean Connery, F. Murray Abraham, Christian Slater, Elya Baskin, Feodor Chaliapin, William Hickey, Michel Lonsdale, Ron Perlman.

In this passable screen adaptation of Umberto Eco's bestseller, Sean Connery stars as a monkish Sherlock Holmes trying to solve a series of murders in a fourteenth-century monastery. Connery is fun to watch, but the plot is rather feeble. Rated R for nudity, simulated sex, and violence. 1986; 118m.

NATE AND HAYES ★★★

DIR: Ferdinand Fairfax. **CAST:** Tommy Lee Jones, Michael O'Keefe, Max Phipps.

Tommy Lee Jones as a good pirate, Michael O'Keefe as his missionary accomplice, and Max Phipps as their cutthroat nemesis make this a jolly movie. Set in the South Seas of the late nineteenth century, it's unpretentious, old-fashioned movie fun. Rated PG for violence. 1983; 100m.

NEMESIS ★★★½

DIR: David Tucker. **CAST:** Joan Hickson, Margaret Tyzack, Anna Cropper, Valerie Lush, Peter Tilbury, Bruce Payne, Helen Cherry.

Joan Hickson's Miss Marple beomes the "unbeatable rival no man may escape" in this adaptation of Agatha Christie's last novel. The attractive English countyside forms the backdrop for this clever story. Unrated; suitable for family viewing. 1986; 102m.

NEVER CRY WOLF ★★★★★

DIR: Carroll Ballard. **CAST:** Charles Martin Smith, Brian Dennehy.

Carroll Ballard made this breathtakingly beautiful, richly rewarding Disney feature about a lone biologist (Charles Martin Smith) learning firsthand about the white wolves of the Yukon by living with them. It's an extraordinary motion picture in every sense of the word. Rated PG for brief nudity. 1983; 105m.

NEVER SAY NEVER AGAIN ★★★★½

DIR: Irvin Kershner. **CAST:** Sean Connery, Klaus Maria Brandauer, Max von Sydow, Barbara Carrera, Kim Basinger, Edward Fox, Bernie Casey, Alec McCowen.

Sean Connery makes a triumphant return to the role of James Bond in this high-style, tongue-in-cheek remake of *Thunderball*. Once again, agent 007 goes up against the evil Largo (exquisitely played by Klaus Maria Brandauer), the sexy and deadly Fatima (Barbara Carrera), and the ever-present head of SPECTRE, Blofeld (Max von Sydow). Action-packed and peppered with laughs, *Never Say Never Again* falters a bit during the climax, but nevertheless emerges as a solid entry in the Bond film canon. Rated PG for violence and nudity. 1983; 137m.

NEVER SO FEW ★★★
DIR: John Sturges. **CAST:** Frank Sinatra, Gina Lollobrigida, Peter Lawford, Steve McQueen, Paul Henreid, Charles Bronson, Richard Johnson, Brian Donlevy, Dean Jones.

Adroitly led by a group of American officers, a band of Burmese guerrillas fight a series of vicious battles against invading Japanese troops in this World War II action picture. The battle scenes are quite good, but the film is marred at times by the philosophizing of U.S. Army officer Frank Sinatra. It's good, but talky. 1959; 124m.

NEVER TOO YOUNG TO DIE ★
DIR: Gil Bettman. **CAST:** John Stamos, Vanity, Gene Simmons, George Lazenby.

A really rotten film that steals everything it can from the James Bond and *Road Warrior* series. John Stamos plays the son of George Lazenby, an American secret agent who is murdered by a gang of crazies, led by Gene Simmons. Unbelievably bad dialogue, and boring action scenes make this a real bomb. Rated R for language, sex, and violence. 1986; 90m.

NEW ADVENTURES OF CHARLIE CHAN, THE (TELEVISION SERIES) ★★★
DIR: Charles Haas. **CAST:** J. Carrol Naish, James Hong.

What do you get when you have an Irish actor (J. Carrol Naish) playing a retired Chinese detective? Unintentional but nonetheless delightful camp. Each of the three volumes released thus far contains three episodes of this British TV mystery series. In each adventure, Chan spouts old Chinese proverbs while unraveling convoluted murder or espionage cases. 1957; B&W; 90m.

NEW ADVENTURES OF TARZAN ★★½
DIR: Edward Kull, W. F. McGaugh. **CAST:** Bruce Bennett, Ula Holt, Frank Baker, Dale Walsh, Harry Ernest.

For the first time on film, Edgar Rice Burroughs's immortal jungle lord spoke and behaved the way he had been created. This sometimes slow, but basically enjoyable twelve-episode chapterplay wove a complex story about a search for Tarzan's missing friend and a treacherous agent intent on stealing an ancient Mayan stone. 1935; B&W; 12 chapters.

NEWMAN'S LAW ★
DIR: Richard T. Heffron. **CAST:** George Peppard, Roger Robinson, Abe Vigoda, Eugene Roche.

George Peppard plays a good cop accused of corruption and suspended from the force, who privately pursues the case he is on. Sound familiar? It is, with all the clichés intact. Rated PG for violence. 1974; 98m.

NIGHT CROSSING ★★★½
DIR: Delbert Mann. **CAST:** John Hurt, Jane Alexander, Beau Bridges, Ian Bannen.

This Disney film is about a real-life escape from East Germany by two families in a gas-filled balloon. Unfortunately, minor flaws, such as mismatched accents and Americanized situations, prevent it from being a total success. Rated PG for violence. 1981; 106m.

NIGHT FLIGHT FROM MOSCOW ★★★
DIR: Henri Verneuil. **CAST:** Henry Fonda, Yul Brynner, Farley Granger, Dirk Bogarde, Virna Lisi, Philippe Noiret.

A decent, if overly talky, espionage film with a strong cast. Yul Brynner is a Russian diplomat who engages in a complicated plan to defect to the West. Rated PG. 1973; 113m.

NIGHT FRIEND
DIR: Peter Gerretsen. **CAST:** Art Carney, Chuck Shamata.

A crusading priest becomes involved in organized crime. This is a preachy and boring film that masquerades as an action-oriented drama. Rated R for profanity, nudity, and violence. 1987; 94m.

NIGHT MOVES ★★★★
DIR: Arthur Penn. **CAST:** Gene Hackman, Susan Clark, Melanie Griffith.

A dark and disturbing detective study with Gene Hackman superb as the private eye trying to solve a baffling mystery. This release was unfairly overlooked when in theaters—but you don't have to miss it now. Rated R. 1975; 95m.

NIGHT OF THE GENERALS ★
DIR: Anatole Litvak. **CAST:** Peter O'Toole, Omar Sharif, Tom Courtenay, Donald Pleasence, Joanna Pettet, Christopher Plummer.

This lurid WWII murder mystery, revolving around a group of Nazi generals, has very little to offer. It will leave you bored, confused, and slightly repulsed. 1967; 148m.

NIGHT OF THE JUGGLER ★★
DIR: Robert Butler. **CAST:** James Brolin, Cliff Gorman, Richard Castellano, Abby Bluestone, Linda G. Miller, Mandy Patinkin.

Psychopath kidnaps little girl for ransom. It's the wrong little girl. Her daddy's an ex-cop with no money and lots of rage. The movie, buoyed by James Brolin's potent performance, initially grabs viewers' attention. Eventually, a cruel streak undermines the drama as it wheezes to a predictable conclusion. Rated R. 1980; 101m.

NIGHT TRAIN TO MUNICH ★★★★½
DIR: Carol Reed. **CAST:** Rex Harrison, Margaret Lockwood, Paul Henreid, Basil Radford, Naunton Wayne.

Based on Gordon Wellesley's novel *Report on a Fugitive*, this taut thriller concerns a British agent (Rex Harrison) trying to rescue a Czech scientist who has escaped from the Gestapo. Along with a fine cast and superb script and direction, this film is blessed with the moody and wonderful photography of Otto Kanturek. Also known under the title *Night Train*. 1940; B&W; 93m.

NIGHTHAWKS ★★★★½
DIR: Bruce Malmuth. **CAST:** Sylvester Stallone, Billy Dee Williams, Rutger Hauer, Lindsay Wagner.

From its explosive first scene to the breathtakingly suspenseful denouement, *Nighthawks*, about a police detective hunting a wily terrorist, is a thoroughly enjoyable, supercharged action film. Rated R for violence, nudity, and profanity. 1981; 99m.

NIGHTKILL ★★★
DIR: Ted Post. **CAST:** Jaclyn Smith, Robert Mitchum, James Franciscus.

Largely unreleased in theaters, this is a tidy little cat-and-mouse thriller with former Charlie's Angel Jaclyn Smith as a conniving widow and Robert Mitchum as the world-weary investigator who gets caught up in her scheme. Despite some inept direction, the last half-hour is a nail-biter, particularly scenes in a bathroom shower. Rated R for violence, nudity, and profanity. 1983; 97m.

NIGHTSTICK ★★★
DIR: Joseph L. Scanlan. **CAST:** Bruce Fairbairn, Robert Vaughn, Kerrie Keane, John Vernon, Leslie Nielsen.

A fast-paced thriller with Bruce Fairbairn as an unorthodox cop who is hunting down two ex-convict brothers. The deadly duo are placing bombs in banks and threatening to blow them up unless a ransom is met. A good cast and above-average script make this one worth renting. Equivalent to an R, violent! 1987; 94m.

NINE DEATHS OF THE NINJA
DIR: Emmet Alston. **CAST:** Sho Kosugi, Brent Huff, Emilia Lesniak, Blackie Dammett.

Sho Kosugi (*Enter the Ninja*) stars in yet another grunt-and-groan, low-budget martial arts mess. This time, he attempts to rescue a congressman who has been kidnapped by terrorists. Rated R. 1985; 94m.

99 AND 44/100 PERCENT DEAD ★

DIR: John Frankenheimer. **CAST:** Richard Harris, Chuck Connors, Edmond O'Brien, Bradford Dillman, Ann Turkel.

A hit man is hired to rub out a gangland boss. The first five minutes are stylish, and Bradford Dillman's impersonation of Elmer Fudd is sort of fun, but the rest of the film is a bore. Rated PG for violence. 1974; 98m.

99 WOMEN ★

DIR: Jess (Jesus) Franco. **CAST:** Maria Schell, Mercedes McCambridge, Herbert Lom, Luciana Paluzzi.

Eurojunk set in a women's prison with all the usual stereotypes. Differs only slightly from others of this genre by concentrating more on the wardens who run the prison than on the actual prisoners, but it's still a poor excuse to exhibit floggings of underdressed women and soft-core lesbian trysts. Rated R. 1969; 90m.

NINJA III: THE DOMINATION

DIR: Sam Firstenberg. **CAST:** Lucinda Dickey, Sho Kosugi.

Best described as *The Exorcist* meets *Enter the Dragon*, this turkey stars Lucinda Dickey as a young woman possessed by the spirit of an evil revenge-seeking Ninja. And only Sho Kosugi can bring her bloody rampage to an end. Rated R for violence and profanity. 1984; 95m.

NO DEAD HEROES

DIR: J. C. Miller. **CAST:** John Dresden, Max Thayer, Dave Anderson, Nick Nicholson, Mike Monte, Toni Nero.

Another post–Vietnam War film where our heroes go in and kick some commie tail. A lot of fire and explosions, but so what? Hilarious comic book dialogue. Not rated, has violence and profanity. 1986; 86m.

NO MAN'S LAND ★★½

DIR: Peter Werner. **CAST:** Charlie Sheen, D. B. Sweeney, Randy Quaid, Lara Harris, Bill Duke, Arlen Dean Snyder.

Predictable police melodrama, with D. B. Sweeney as a young undercover cop tracking a Porsche theft ring in Los Angeles, headed by smoothie Charlie Sheen. Randy Quaid is Sweeney's boss, a lieutenant with a vendetta against Sheen. The dialogue is sometimes childish, but the film has pace and economy. Rated R for language and violence. 1987; 107m.

NO MERCY ★½

DIR: Richard Pearce. **CAST:** Richard Gere, Kim Basinger, Jeroen Krabbé, George Dzundza, William Atherton, Terry Kinney, Bruce McGill, Ray Sharkey, Gary Basaraba.

No Mercy is a predictable, rapid-paced thriller about a Chicago cop (Richard Gere) who travels to New Orleans to avenge the murder of his partner. Kim Basinger is the Cajun woman who is Gere's link to the villain. Rated R for violence, language, and sexual situations. 1986; 107m.

NO RETREAT, NO SURRENDER

DIR: Corey Yuen. **CAST:** Kurt McKinney, J. W. Fails, Ron Pohnel, Jean Claude Van Damme.

An uninspired cross between *The Karate Kid* and *Rocky IV* about a teenager who keeps getting beaten up by kung-fu students. Tired of bloody noses, this living punching bag finds an instructor, but instead of being taught by a karate expert from Okinawa, his teacher is the ghost of Bruce Lee. Dumb. 1985; 85m.

NORSEMAN, THE

DIR: Charles B. Pierce. **CAST:** Lee Majors, Charles B. Pierce Jr., Cornel Wilde, Mel Ferrer.

This low-budget story of the Vikings landing in America in A.D. 1022 is so full of stupid historical errors and unbelievable elements that it should never have been released. Rated PG. 1978; 90m.

NORTH STAR, THE ★★★★
DIR: Lewis Milestone. **CAST:** Ruth Gordon, Walter Huston, Anne Baxter, Dana Andrews.

This is a well-done World War II film about Russian peasants battling Nazi invaders during the early days of the German invasion of Russia in 1941. It's a bit corny and sentimental in places, but the battle scenes have the usual Milestone high-quality excitement. 1943; B&W; 105m.

NORTHEAST OF SEOUL ★½
DIR: David Lowell Rich. **CAST:** Anita Ekberg, John Ireland, Victor Buono.

Three unlikely down-and-outers join forces and end up double-crossing each other in their pursuit of an ancient mystical sword that promises wealth and power to the owner. This poorly dubbed movie is very routine. Rated PG for violence. 1972; 84m.

NORTHERN PURSUIT ★★★
DIR: Raoul Walsh. **CAST:** Errol Flynn, Julie Bishop, Tom Tully.

Despite Raoul Walsh's capable direction, this film, about a German heritage Canadian Mountie (Errol Flynn) who feigns defection and guides a party of Nazi saboteurs to their secret base, is pure claptrap. It marked the beginning of Flynn's slow descent into obscurity and, eventually, illness. 1943; B&W; 94m.

NORTHVILLE CEMETERY MASSACRE, THE ★
DIR: William Dear. **CAST:** David Hyry, Carson Jackson.

Although director William Dear later went on to make *Harry and the Hendersons*, this cheaply made biker movie is about as far from a family film as you can get. A motorcycle gang—falsely accused of rape—clashes with the residents of a small town. Violent and unpleasant. Rated R. 1976; 81m.

NOWHERE TO HIDE ★★★★
DIR: Mario Azzopardi. **CAST:** Amy Madigan, Michael Ironside, John Colicos, Daniel Hugh Kelly.

Amy Madigan stars in this exciting adventure of relentless pursuit. Her husband, a marine officer, has uncovered a defective part that is causing accidents in his helicopter squadron. Before he can go public, he is killed. The assassins believe Madigan has the damaging evidence, and the chase is on. An exhilarating climax. Not rated. 1987; 100m.

NUMBER ONE WITH A BULLET ★½
DIR: Jack Smight. **CAST:** Robert Carradine, Billy Dee Williams, Valerie Bertinelli, Peter Graves, Doris Roberts.

Uninspired police thriller–buddy movie suffers from a total lack of chemistry between the two stars, Billy Dee Williams and Robert Carradine, and a contrived script. There is no logic or credibility to any of the events as Carradine and Williams pursue a drug kingpin in between cutesy set pieces. Rated R for violence, profanity, and nudity. 1987; 103m.

NYOKA AND THE TIGER MEN (PERILS OF NYOKA) ★★½
DIR: William Witney. **CAST:** Kay Aldrige, Clayton Moore, William Benedict, Lorna Gray.

Nyoka, the Jungle Girl, aids archeologist Clayton Moore in saving and deciphering the long-lost Tablets of Hippocrates, which contain the medical knowledge of the ancient Greeks. The evil Vultura does everything possible to obtain them and do away with her competitors. Plenty of stunts make this an enjoyable afternoon diversion. 1942; B&W; 15 chapters.

OBSESSION: A TASTE FOR FEAR
DIR: Piccio Raffanini. **CAST:** Virginia Hey, Gerard Darmon.

Tacky, tasteless, disgusting Italian film about an investigation into the brutal murders of women starring in bondage-type porno films. Contains nudity, violence, and sexual deviance. Has absolutely no redeeming social value. 1989; 90m.

OCEAN'S ELEVEN ★★★
DIR: Lewis Milestone. **CAST:** Frank Sinatra, Dean Martin, Sammy Davis Jr., Peter Lawford, Angie Dickinson, Cesar Romero.

A twist ending, several stars, and good production values save this tale of an attempted robbery in Las Vegas. Frank Sinatra is the leader of the gang, and his now-famous "rat pack" are the gang members. Lightweight but pleasant. 1960; 127m.

OCEANS OF FIRE ★★
DIR: Steve Carver. **CAST:** Gregory Harrison, Billy Dee Williams, Lyle Alzado, Tony Burton, Ray "Boom Boom" Mancini, Ken Norton, Lee Ving, Cynthia Sikes, David Carradine.

Predictable formula adventure-saga about five ex-cons and head honcho, Gregory Harrison, putting up an oil rig off the South American coast. Everyone gets a chance to do his stuff as the men overcome mother nature, corporate greed, and personal vendettas to accomplish their dangerous mission. Only a star-studded cast saves this one from the depths of mediocrity. Rated PG. 1987; 93m.

OCTAGON, THE ★★
DIR: Eric Karson. **CAST:** Chuck Norris, Karen Carlson, Lee Van Cleef, Jack Carter.

This "kung-fu" flick stars Chuck Norris as a bodyguard for Karen Carlson. Norris naturally takes on multiple opponents and beats them easily. Rated R. 1980; 103m.

OCTOPUSSY ★★★½
DIR: John Glen. **CAST:** Roger Moore, Maud Adams, Louis Jourdan.

Roger Moore returns as James Bond in the thirteenth screen adventure of Ian Fleming's superspy. It's like an adult-oriented *Raiders of the Lost Ark*: light, fast-paced, funny, and almost over before you know it—almost, because the film tends to overstay its welcome just a bit. Rated PG for violence and suggested sex. 1983; 130m.

ODESSA FILE, THE ★½
DIR: Ronald Neame. **CAST:** Jon Voight, Maximilian Schell, Derek Jacobi, Maria Schell.

Frederick Forsyth wrote the bestselling novel, but little of the zip remains in this weary film adaptation. German journalist Jon Voight learns of a secret file that may expose some former Nazis. That's about all there is to tell. Rated PG for violence. 1974; 128m.

OFF LIMITS ★★★
DIR: Christopher Crowe. **CAST:** Willem Dafoe, Gregory Hines, Fred Ward, Amanda Pays, Scott Glenn.

Saigon, 1968, makes a noisy and violent background for this murder mystery. Willem Dafoe and Gregory Hines are a pair of military investigators assigned to find the high-ranking killer of local prostitutes. The two leads have good chemistry, Amanda Pays is credible as a sympathetic nun, and Scott Glenn is superb as a warped, messianic infantry colonel. Don't expect the plot to make much sense. Rated R for extreme language, violence, and brief nudity. 1988; 102m.

OKEFENOKEE ★½
DIR: Roul Haig. **CAST:** Peter Coe, Henry Brandon.

The Florida swamplands are the setting for this forgettable story about smugglers who use the Seminole Indians to help bring drugs into the country. When the Indians are pushed too far, they strike back. What swamp did they dig this one out of? 1960; 78m.

OLD IRONSIDES ★
DIR: James Cruze. **CAST:** Charles Farrell, Esther Ralston, Wallace Beery, George Bancroft, Fred Kohler Sr., Boris Karloff.

This big-budget, action-packed yarn of wooden ships and iron men besting pirates in the Mediterranean has a big director, big stars, big scenes, and was ballyhooed at its premiere, but it was scuttled by a lackluster script. Far from a golden silent, it bombed at the box office. Silent. 1926; B&W; 88m.

OMEGA SYNDROME ★★
DIR: Joseph Manduke. **CAST:** Ken Wahl, George DiCenzo, Doug McClure, Ron Kuhlman, Patti Tippo.

Ken Wahl is a single parent who teams up with his old Vietnam war buddy to track down his daughter's abductors. They find that a white supremist group is behind the kidnapping. A very manipulative screenplay makes the film hard to take seriously. Rated R for violence and profanity. 1986; 90m.

ON HER MAJESTY'S SECRET SERVICE ★★★★
DIR: Peter R. Hunt. **CAST:** George Lazenby, Diana Rigg, Telly Savalas.

With Sean Connery temporarily out of the James Bond series, Australian actor George Lazenby stepped into the 007 part for this entry—and did remarkably well. Director Peter Hunt keeps this moving at an incredibly fast pace, and this story about everyone's favorite superspy falling in love with an heiress (Diana Rigg) is one of author Ian Fleming's best. Rated PG. 1969; 140m.

ON THE LINE ★★½
DIR: José Luis Borau. **CAST:** David Carradine, Scott Wilson, Victoria Abril, Jeff Delger, Paul Richardson, Jesse Vint, Sam Jaffe.

David Carradine smuggles aliens across the Mexican border. Scott Wilson pledges to nail Carradine and his operation. This mediocre adventure is not rated. 1987; 103m.

ON THE YARD ★★
DIR: Raphael D. Silver. **CAST:** John Heard, Mike Kellin, Richard Bright, Thomas D. Waites, Joe Grifasi.

Subpar prison melodrama pits John Heard against a prison-yard boss. Some good peformances by Mike Kellin and Richard Bright help, but this addition to the prison-film genre never gets going, nor does it ring true. Rated R. 1979; 102m.

ONCE A HERO ★★
DIR: Claudia Weill. **CAST:** Jeff Lester, Robert Forster, Milo O'Shea.

Yesteryear's comic-book superhero, Captain Justice, is slowly fading away. His fans are deserting him for Rambo-style heroes, and his creator is running on empty. So he decides to cross the forbidden zone from his world of fantasy to our world of today with predictable but occasionally amusing results. Not rated. 1988; 74m.

ONCE UPON A TIME IN AMERICA (LONG VERSION) ★★★★
DIR: Sergio Leone. **CAST:** Robert De Niro, James Woods, Elizabeth McGovern, Tuesday Weld, Treat Williams, Burt Young.

Italian director Sergio Leone's richly rewarding gangster epic; a $30 million production starring Robert De Niro in a forty-five-year saga of Jewish gangsters in New York City. Leone is best known for his spaghetti westerns *A Fistful of Dollars*, *The Good, the Bad and the Ugly*, and *Once Upon a Time in the West*. This release culminates ten years of planning and false starts by the filmmaker. It was well worth the wait. Rated R for profanity, nudity, suggested sex, and violence. 1984; 225m.

ONE BODY TOO MANY ★★½
DIR: Frank McDonald. **CAST:** Bela Lugosi, Jack Haley, Jean Parker, Blanche Yurka, Lyle Talbot, Douglas Fowley.

Snappy dialogue and a memorable cast of good performers make this fast-paced whodunit worth a watch. Wise-cracking Jack Haley is mistaken for a private investigator and finds himself in the thick of murder and intrigue. Bela Lugosi is again typecast as a menace, but this caricature role isn't nearly as offensive as many he was forced into in the 1940s. Nothing special, but not too bad for a low-budget programmer. 1944; B&W; 75m.

ONE DOWN, TWO TO GO ★★
DIR: Fred Williamson. **CAST:** Fred Williamson, Jim Brown, Jim Kelly, Richard Roundtree.
Kung-fu fighter (Jim Kelly) suspects a tournament is fixed and calls on his buddies (Jim Brown and director Fred Williamson) for help in this low-budget, theatrically unreleased sequel to *Three the Hard Way*. Some actors are hopelessly amateurish, and the story is a mere sketch. Unrated, the film has violence. 1983; 84m.

ONE MINUTE TO ZERO ★★
DIR: Tay Garnett. **CAST:** Robert Mitchum, Ann Blyth, William Talman, Charles McGraw, Richard Egan.
Sluggish film about the Korean War benefits from some good acting by the male leads. The romantic subplot doesn't help much, but then not much could help this barely serviceable story about servicemen. 1952; B&W; 105m.

ONE OF OUR AIRCRAFT IS MISSING ★★★★
DIR: Michael Powell, Emeric Pressburger. **CAST:** Godfrey Tearle, Eric Portman, Pamela Brown, Hugh Williams, Googie Withers, Peter Ustinov.
This British production is similar to *Desperate Journey* (1942) with Errol Flynn and Ronald Reagan. The story concerns an RAF crew who are shot down over Holland during World War II and who try to escape to England. High-caliber suspense. 1941; B&W; 106m.

ONE SHOE MAKES IT MURDER ★★½
DIR: William Hale. **CAST:** Robert Mitchum, Angie Dickinson, Mel Ferrer, Jose Perez, John Harkins, Howard Hesseman.
In this made-for-television movie, reminiscent in plot of *Out of the Past*, Robert Mitchum plays a world-weary detective who is hired by a crime boss (Mel Ferrer) to find his wayward wife (Angie Dickinson). Mitchum is watchable in a variation on his Philip Marlowe characterization from *Farewell My Lovely*, but the story and direction never achieve a level of intensity. 1982; 97m.

ONE STEP TO HELL ★★
DIR: Sandy Howard. **CAST:** Ty Hardin, Pier Angeli, Rossano Brazzi, George Sanders.
On their way to a South African jail, a trio of killers escape and head for the jungle in search of a hidden gold mine, with police officer Ty Hardin hot on their trail. Not bad, but you wouldn't want to expend a lot of effort looking for it. 1968; 94m.

ONE THAT GOT AWAY, THE ★★★★
DIR: Roy Baker. **CAST:** Hardy Krüger, Colin Gordon, Michael Goodliffe.
Excellent adaptation of the book by Kendal Burt and James Leasor about a captured German aviator who keeps escaping from a multitude of British prisoner-of-war camps. Based on a true story and especially well directed and performed, this adventure is highly recommended. 1958; B&W; 106m.

OPERATION AMSTERDAM ★★★
DIR: Michael McCarthy. **CAST:** Peter Finch, Eva Bartok, Tony Britton, Alexander Knox.
It's 1940 and Allied spies penetrate Holland to prevent the invading Nazis from getting their hands on Amsterdam's rich cache of diamonds. Filmed in a semidocumentary style, this movie is standard but well acted and produced. 1960; B&W; 105m.

OPERATION C.I.A. ★★½
DIR: Christian Nyby. **CAST:** Burt Reynolds, Kieu Chinh, Danielle Aubry, John Hoyt.
Political intrigue in Vietnam before the United States' full involvement finds a youthful Burt Reynolds at his physical peak as an agent assigned to derail an assassination attempt. Good location photography and Reynolds's enthusiasm and believability mark this film as one of the best chase films of the mid-1960s. 1965; B&W; 90m.

OPERATION 'NAM ★★
DIR: Larry Ludman. **CAST:** Oliver Tobias, Christopher Connelly, Manfred Lehman, John Steiner, Ethan Wayne, Donald Pleasence.
Run-of-the-mill tale about a group of bored Vietnam vets going back to Vietnam to rescue their leader, still held in a POW camp. Notable only for the appearance of Ethan Wayne, one of John's sons. Not rated, but contains violence, language, and nudity. 1985; 85m.

OPERATION THUNDERBOLT ★½
DIR: Menahem Golan. **CAST:** Yehoram Gaon, Klaus Kinski, Assaf Dayan.
Another film, like *The Raid on Entebbe*, dealing with the Israeli commando raid in Uganda in 1976 to free 104 hijacked airline passengers. Overly sentimental, with poor performances and rather routine action sequences. No MPAA rating. 1977; 125m.

OPPOSING FORCE ★★½
DIR: Eric Carson. **CAST:** Tom Skerritt, Lisa Eichhorn, Anthony Zerbe, Richard Roundtree, John Considine.
In this average action-adventure movie, a group of soldiers undergo simulated prisoner-of-war training. When the commanding officer (Anthony Zerbe) goes insane, he rapes the sole female soldier (Lisa Eichhorn) and sets into motion a chain of violent events. Rated R for profanity and violence. 1986; 97m.

ORDEAL BY INNOCENCE ★★
DIR: Desmond Davis. **CAST:** Donald Sutherland, Sarah Miles, Christopher Plummer, Ian McShane, Diana Quick, Faye Dunaway.
In this production of yet another Agatha Christie novel, the cast may be stellar, but the performances are almost all phoned in. Donald Sutherland plays a man who is certain that justice has been ill served in a small British community. Rated PG-13 for language and nudity. 1984; 91m.

ORDER OF THE BLACK EAGLE ★½
DIR: Worth Keeter. **CAST:** Ian Hunter, Charles K. Bibby, William T. Hicks, Jill Donnellan, Anna Rappagna, Flo Hyman.
Ian Hunter is the James Bond-ish main character, Duncan Jax, abetted in destroying a neo-Nazi group by his sidekick, a baboon, and a band of misfits who look suspiciously like Rambo, Indiana Jones, and a few other stars of the adventure genre. Decent action sequences, though. Rated R for violence and language. 1987; 93m.

ORGANIZATION, THE ★★★
DIR: Don Medford. **CAST:** Sidney Poitier, Barbara McNair, Raul Julia, Sheree North.
This is the third and last installment of the Virgil Tibbs series based on the character Sidney Poitier originated in *In the Heat of the Night*. Tibbs is out to break up a ring of dope smugglers. A pretty good cop film, with some exciting action scenes. Rated PG; some strong stuff for the kids. 1971; 107m.

OSTERMAN WEEKEND, THE ★★
DIR: Sam Peckinpah. **CAST:** Rutger Hauer, John Hurt, Burt Lancaster, Dennis Hopper, Chris Sarandon, Meg Foster.
Sam Peckinpah's last is a confusing action movie with scarce viewing rewards for the filmmaker's fans. Based on Robert Ludlum's novel, it tells a complicated and convoluted story of espionage, revenge, and duplicity. Rated R for profanity, nudity, sex, and violence. 1983; 102m.

OUT ★½
DIR: Eli Hollander. **CAST:** Peter Coyote, Danny Glover, O-Lan Shephard, Gail Dartez, Jim Hoynie, Scott Beach.
You may want out before the final countdown of this offbeat, surrealistic action film. Peter Coyote is an urban guerrilla who starts out in Greenwich Village and goes cross-country on as-

signments from a mysterious commander. This comedy-action pastiche tries very hard to be artsy. Rated PG. 1983; 88m.

OUT OF BOUNDS ★½
DIR: Richard Tuggle. **CAST:** Anthony Michael Hall, Jenny Wright, Jeff Kober, Glynn Turman, Raymond J. Barry.
In this incomprehensible thriller, Anthony Michael Hall plays a naïve Iowa boy who journeys to Los Angeles and accidentally switches luggage with a nasty heroin smuggler. Tony Kayden's script assumes lunatic proportions: the story progresses only because every character behaves like a total idiot at all times. Rated R for extreme violence. 1986; 93m.

OUT OF THE PAST ★★★★½
DIR: Jacques Tourneur. **CAST:** Robert Mitchum, Jane Greer, Kirk Douglas, Richard Webb, Rhonda Fleming, Dickie Moore, Steve Brodie.
This film, which stars Robert Mitchum, is perhaps the quintessential example of *film noir*. A private eye (Mitchum, in a role intended for Bogart) allows himself to be duped by the beautiful but two-faced mistress (Jane Greer) of a big-time gangster (Kirk Douglas). It's a forgotten masterwork. 1947; B&W; 97m.

OUTLAW FORCE ★★
DIR: David Heavener. **CAST:** David Heavener, Paul Smith, Frank Stallone, Warren Berlinger.
It had to happen. Somebody crossed *Rambo* with *Urban Cowboy*. A gang of punks run out of town by a handsome country singer (David Heavener) gets revenge when they rape and kill his wife, then kidnap his young daughter and return home to (where else?) Hollywood. Heavener, a Vietnam vet, takes justice into his hands. Rated R for violence. 1987; 95m.

OUTPOST IN MOROCCO ★★
DIR: Robert Florey. **CAST:** George Raft, Marie Windsor, Akim Tamiroff.
George Raft is out of his element as a French legionnaire assigned to stop the activities of desert rebels only to find himself falling in love with the daughter (Marie Windsor) of their leader (Akim Tamiroff). Pure hokum and slow moving, too. 1949; B&W; 92m.

OVERKILL ★
DIR: Ulli Lommel. **CAST:** Steve Rally, John Nishio, Laura Burkett, Allen Wisch, Roy Summersett, Antonio Caprio.
Racist, violent *Miami Vice*–type of crime story: all flash and no substance. Steve Rally plays a shirtless stud cop who, along with a Tokyo policeman, tries to break up the *yakuza* (Japanese Mafia) operating in Los Angeles' Little Tokyo. Rated R for extreme violence, extreme language, sex, and nudity. 1986; 81m.

PACIFIC INFERNO ★★½
DIR: Rolf Bayer. **CAST:** Jim Brown, Richard Jaeckel, Tim Brown, Tad Horino, Wilma Redding, Vic Diaz.
This war adventure film is set in the Philippines during the final fall and capture of U.S. and Filipino soldiers. General MacArthur ordered the dumping of $16 million in silver in Manila Bay to avoid seizure by the enemy. Jim Brown and Richard Jaeckel are American navy prisoners who are forced to dive for its recovery. Good, steady action follows. Unrated. 1985; 90m.

PALAIS ROYALE ★★
DIR: Martin Lavut. **CAST:** Dean Stockwell, Kim Cattrall, Matt Craven.
The Hollywood gangster is viewed through a peculiarly Canadian prism in this Toronto-made *film noir*. Matt Craven plays an ambitious advertising executive, circa 1959, who stumbles into a world of gangsters and goons. Slovenly. 1988; 100m.

PAPER TIGER ★★
DIR: Ken Annakin. **CAST:** David Niven, Toshiro Mifune, Ando, Hardy Krüger.
Stiffly British David Niven is tutor to the son (Ando) of a Japanese ambas-

sador (Toshiro Mifune). He and his young charge are kidnapped by terrorists for political reasons. Derring-do follows, but it's all lukewarm and paplike. Rated PG. 1976; 99m.

PAPILLON ★★★★½
DIR: Franklin J. Schaffner. **CAST:** Steve McQueen, Dustin Hoffman, Victor Jory, Don Gordon.

Unfairly criticized, this is a truly exceptional film biography of the man who escaped from Devil's Island. Steve McQueen gives an excellent performance, and Dustin Hoffman is once again a chameleon. Director Frank Schaffner invests the same gusto here that he did in *Patton*. Rated PG. 1973; 150m.

PARADISE ★½
DIR: Stuart Gillard. **CAST:** Willie Aames, Phoebe Cates, Tuvia Tavi.

Willie Aames and Phoebe Cates star as two teenagers who, as members of a caravan traveling from Bagdad to Damascus in the nineteenth century, escape a surprise attack by a sheik intent on adding Cates to his harem. While fleeing the villain and looking for help, they have time to diddle à la Brooke Shields and Christopher Atkins in *Blue Lagoon*. Rated R for frontal male and female nudity. 1982; 100m.

PARIS EXPRESS, THE ★★½
DIR: Harold French. **CAST:** Claude Rains, Marta Toren, Anouk Aimée, Marius Goring, Herbert Lom.

Based on acclaimed mystery writer Georges Simenon's novel, this film details the exploits of a finance clerk (Claude Rains) who turns embezzler. Hoping to travel the world with his ill-gotten gains, he runs into more trouble and adventure than he can handle. 1953; 80m.

PARTNERS IN CRIME: THE AFFAIR OF THE PINK PEARL ★★★½
DIR: Tony Wharmby. **CAST:** Francesca Annis, James Warwick, Reece Dinsdale.

Six years have passed since the events of *The Secret Adversary*, during which Tommy and Tuppence (James Warwick and Francesca Annis) have become husband and wife. A Scotland Yard friend suggests they buy the defunct Blunt Detective Agency to utilize their skills as amateur sleuths; their cinema-struck young butler, Albert (Reece Dinsdale), becomes the office boy. The "guaranteed 24-hour service" is tested by their first client, who wants them to locate a missing person. 1982; 51m.

PARTNERS IN CRIME: THE AMBASSADOR'S BOOTS ★★★½
DIR: Paul Annett. **CAST:** Francesca Annis, James Warwick, Reece Dinsdale.

Tommy and Tuppence adopt the alter egos of Mr. Blunt and Miss Robinson when hired by the American ambassador to England. What begins as a mundane investigation leads to death and intrigue in this fast-paced and engaging episode. 1982; 51m.

PARTNERS IN CRIME: THE CASE OF THE MISSING LADY ★★★½
DIR: Paul Annett. **CAST:** Francesca Annis, James Warwick, Reece Dinsdale.

Tommy and Tuppence (James Warwick and Francesca Annis) are hired by a famous explorer to find his fiancée. The trail leads to The Grange, a hospital employing very unusual treatments for "nerve cases," where Tuppence's attempts to work undercover become particularly amusing. 1982; 51m.

PARTNERS IN CRIME: THE CLERGYMAN'S DAUGHTER ★★★½
DIR: Paul Annett. **CAST:** Francesca Annis, James Warwick, Reece Dinsdale.

Tommy and Tuppence find their Christmas reminiscences interrupted by a clergyman's daughter with a vexing problem: Her recent inheritance, a mansion dubbed Red House, appears to be haunted. The young woman has been approached by a mysterious stranger who wishes to buy the place. Another superb entry. 1982; 51m.

PARTNERS IN CRIME: THE CRACKLER ★★★½
DIR: Christopher Hodson. **CAST:** Francesca Annis, James Warwick, Reece Dinsdale, Shane Rimmer.

Tommy and Tuppence go undercover while investigating a case involving forged bank notes. Agatha Christie borrowed the flavor of Edgar Wallace's 1920s mystery novels, with their emphasis on multiple secret identities, for this final case in the series. 1982; 51m.

PARTNERS IN CRIME: FINESSING THE KING ★★★½
DIR: Christopher Hodson. **CAST:** Francesca Annis, James Warwick, Reece Dinsdale.

Tuppence is intrigued by an unusual message in a newspaper personals column, so she and Tommy follow the trail to a charity costume ball (which they attend dressed as Holmes and Watson). Sharp-eyed viewers will find all the clues necessary to match wits with our amateur sleuths as they discover a much bigger mystery than expected. Pay particular attention to the period cars and elaborate costumes. 1982; 51m.

PARTNERS IN CRIME: THE HOUSE OF LURKING DEATH ★★★
DIR: Christopher Hodson. **CAST:** Francesca Annis, James Warwick, Reece Dinsdale.

This atypically somber entry finds Tommy and Tuppence investigating a poisoning case, only to find their client dead within the first twenty-four hours. The mansion standing in for the story's Thurnly Grange makes an appropriately spooky setting for this eerie and atmospheric tale. 1982; 51m.

PARTNERS IN CRIME: THE MAN IN THE MIST ★★★½
DIR: Christopher Hodson. **CAST:** Francesca Annis, James Warwick, Reece Dinsdale.

Tommy (disguised as a priest) and Tuppence are on their way home after having failed to solve a case, when a suggested shortcut to the railway station proves providential; a scream from a nearby house launches them into their next mystery. As usual, Agatha Christie's lighthearted sleuths are up to the challenge. 1982; 51m.

PARTNERS IN CRIME: THE SECRET ADVERSARY ★★★★
DIR: Tony Wharmby. **CAST:** Francesca Annis, James Warwick, George Baker, Honor Blackman, Reece Dinsdale.

This feature-length World War I–era tale, based on Agatha Christie's second novel, introduces the characters of Tommy and Tuppence (James Warwick and Francesca Annis). Lacking personal finances or steady jobs after having left war service, they band together and advertise their services as amateur sleuths; their first case involves a missing treaty between world powers. This excellent story makes a heartwarming introduction to the *Partners in Crime* series. 1983; 100m.

PARTNERS IN CRIME: THE SUNNINGDALE MYSTERY ★★★½
DIR: Tony Wharmby. **CAST:** Francesca Annis, James Warwick, Reece Dinsdale.

Business is quiet at the Blunt Detective Agency, so Tommy and Tuppence travel to Sunningdale to investigate an unsolicited case: the fatal stabbing, with a woman's hatpin, of a man on a golf course. The sleuths apply their unique talents to the solution of the murder. 1982; 51m.

PARTNERS IN CRIME: THE UNBREAKABLE ALIBI ★★★½

DIR: Christopher Hodson. **CAST:** Francesca Annis, James Warwick, Reece Dinsdale.

A woman seeming to have been in two places at the same time forms the crux of this extremely witty entry in Agatha Christie's lighthearted detective series. Tommy and Tuppence are hired by a man who has been challenged by the woman he loves; unless her apparently solid alibi can be broken, he cannot marry her. 1982; 51m.

PARTY LINE ★

DIR: William Webb. **CAST:** Richard Hatch, Leif Garrett, Richard Roundtree.

Disconnected nonsense about telephone party–line callers who turn up dead with their throats cut. Leif Garrett is the mama's boy killer, at the beck and call of his sadistic sister. Hang up on this wrong number. Rated R for violence, profanity, and nudity. 1988; 91m.

PASSAGE TO MARSEILLES ★★★

DIR: Michael Curtiz. **CAST:** Humphrey Bogart, Claude Rains, Sydney Greenstreet, Peter Lorre.

The performances of Humphrey Bogart, Claude Rains, Sydney Greenstreet, and Peter Lorre are all that's good about this muddled film about an escape from Devil's Island during World War II. Directed by Michael Curtiz, its flashback-within-flashback scenes all but totally confuse the viewer. 1944; B&W; 110m.

PASSION ★★

DIR: Allan Dwan. **CAST:** Cornel Wilde, Yvonne De Carlo, Raymond Burr, Lon Chaney Jr., John Qualen.

Colorful hokum about a hot-blooded adventurer (Cornel Wilde) and his quest for vengeance in old California. Directed by veteran filmmaker Allan Dwan, this okay adventure boasts a nice cast of character actors. 1954; 84m.

PATRIOT

DIR: Frank Harris. **CAST:** Gregg Henry, Simone Griffeth, Michael J. Pollard, Jeff Conaway, Stack Pierce, Leslie Nielsen.

Underwater commandos fighting terrorists over nuclear weapons sounds like a good idea for an action-adventure film, but you wouldn't know it from watching this one. Rated R for nudity and violence. 1986; 90m.

PEARL OF DEATH, THE ★★★★

DIR: Roy William Neill. **CAST:** Basil Rathbone, Nigel Bruce, Evelyn Ankers, Miles Mander, Dennis Hoey, Mary Gordon, Ian Wolfe, Rondo Hatton.

Director Roy William Neill fashions Arthur Conan Doyle's "The Six Napoleons" into a rip-snorting screen adventure for Holmes (Basil Rathbone) and Watson (Nigel Bruce). They're tracking a trio of criminals: Giles Conover (Miles Mander), Naomi (Evelyn Ankers), and the Creeper (Rondo Hatton). Good stuff. 1944; B&W; 69m.

PENDULUM ★★

DIR: George Schaefer. **CAST:** George Peppard, Richard Kiley, Jean Seberg, Charles McGraw.

In this rather confusing mystery, police captain George Peppard must acquit himself of a murder charge and catch the real culprit. A good cast perks things up some, but the story is too full of holes to be taken seriously. Some violence, adult situations. Rated PG. 1969; 106m.

PENITENTIARY ★★

DIR: Jamaa Franaka. **CAST:** Leon Isaac Kennedy, Thommy Pollard.

Leon Isaac Kennedy dons boxing gloves as the black Rocky to triumph over pure evil in this lurid, but entertaining, movie. Rated R for violence and profanity. 1979; 94m.

PENITENTIARY II ★

DIR: Jamaa Fanaka. **CAST:** Leon Isaac Kennedy, Glynn Turman, Ernie Hudson, Mr. T.

Basically a retread of the first film, but the action scenes inside and outside of the ring can't hold up the limp plot. Rated R for violence and profanity. 1982; 108m.

PENITENTIARY III
DIR: Jamaa Fanaka. **CAST:** Leon Isaac Kennedy, Anthony Geary, Steve Antin, Ric Mancini, Jim Bailey.
This is a wimp of a movie: listless acting, unmotivated direction, silly dialogue, and worse—terrible, phony fight scenes. Lock this one up in solitary confinement. 1987; 91m.

PERILS OF GWENDOLINE, THE ★
DIR: Just Jaeckin. **CAST:** Tawny Kitaen, Brent Huff.
Adapting this film from the 1940s comic strip "The Adventures of Sweet Gwendoline," Just Jaeckin, who is also responsible for *Emmanuelle* and *The Story of O*, claims to have made a sexy comedy adventure. What he's made instead is a poorly acted escapade that tries to titillate through glorification of sadomasochistic forays into sex. Rated R for violence, profanity, and sexual content. 1985; 96m.

PERILS OF PAULINE, THE (1933) ★½
DIR: Ray Taylor. **CAST:** Evalyn Knapp, Robert Allen, James Durkin, John Davidson, Sonny Ray.
Sound serial version of the famous Pearl White cliffhanger retains only the original title. The daughter of a prominent scientist and her companion struggle to keep the formula for a deadly gas out of the hands of evil Dr. Bashan and his slimy assistant Fang. This so-so serial lacks the charisma of later efforts from Universal Studios. 1933; B&W; 12 chapters.

PERMISSION TO KILL ★★
DIR: Cyril Frankel. **CAST:** Dirk Bogarde, Ava Gardner, Bekim Fehmiu, Timothy Dalton, Nicole Calfan, Frederic Forrest.
An exiled politician (Bekim Fehmiu) from an Eastern bloc nation living in Austria decides to return to his native country. A Western intelligence agent (Dirk Bogarde) must stop him. Rated PG for violence, profanity, and nudity. 1975; 96m.

PERSUADERS, THE (TELEVISION SERIES) ★★★
DIR: Basil Dearden, Val Guest. **CAST:** Roger Moore, Tony Curtis, Laurence Naismith.
This tongue-in-cheek adventure series lasted just one season on ABC, but it offers a fair bit of action, humor, and style. Set in the glamor spots of Europe, the show follows two dashing playboys: Brett Sinclair (Roger Moore), a British lord, and Daniel Wilde (Tony Curis), a self-made millionaire from the Bronx. A retired judge has tricked them into joining forces and fighting for justice. Moore and Curtis are fun to watch in these tailor-made roles, smoothly handling the roughhousing, rivalry, and romance. The first two episodes to be released on tape are "Overture," guest starring Imogen Hassal, and "Five Miles to Midnight," with Joan Collins. 1972; 60m.

PHANTOM EMPIRE ★★★
DIR: Otto Brewer, B. Reeves "Breezy" Eason. **CAST:** Gene Autry, Frankie Darro, Betsy King Ross, Smiley Burnette.
Gene Autry, with the aid of Frankie Darro, champion rider Betsy King Ross, and the Junior Thunder Riders, overcomes threats from above ground (greedy crooks who want his radium-riddled Radio Ranch and do their best to interrupt his frequent radio broadcasts) and the deadly threat of Murania, the futuristic city twenty thousand feet beneath the ground. Plenty of action, the wonders of the "city of the future," and good special effects (including a death ray) make this one of Mascot Films's best serials. 1935; B&W; 12 chapters.

PHANTOM EXPRESS ★★
DIR: Emory Johnson. **CAST:** J. Farrell MacDonald, Sally Blane, William Collier Jr., Hobart Bosworth.

J. Farrell MacDonald loses his job and his pension with the railroad after his own engine is ruined in a wreck with a mysterious train. Shunned by his friends and co-workers, the salty old engineer decides to bring the villains to justice himself and does so with the help of young Sally Blane. Nothing new here, but the vintage trains are a treat to look at. 1932; B&W; 65m.

PHILIP MARLOWE, PRIVATE EYE: FINGER MAN ★★★★
DIR: Sidney Hayers. **CAST:** Powers Boothe, William Kearns, Gayle Hunnicutt, Ed Bishop, William Hootkins.

Another installment in the HBO series featuring Powers Boothe's delicious interpretation of Raymond Chandler's square-jawed detective. This time out, Philip Marlowe has his own life to worry about, as the sole witness to the killing of a government investigator who was poking into mob activities. Chandler would have been pleased. Unrated; brief violence. 1983; 55m.

PHILIP MARLOWE, PRIVATE EYE: THE PENCIL ★★★★
DIR: Peter R. Hunt. **CAST:** Powers Boothe, William Kearns, Kathryn Leigh Scott, David Healy, Stephen Davies.

First in the series of absolutely gorgeous made-for-cable adaptations of Raymond Chandler's famed detective. Production values are superb, from the meticulous attention paid to period authenticity, to the mournful wail of John Cameron's music. Powers Boothe is perfect as the cynical, world-weary, hard-boiled dick. In this episode, Marlowe is hired to protect a stoolie who's been sent a pencil by the mob (signaling their intention to kill him). 1983; 55m.

PHYSICAL EVIDENCE ★★½
DIR: Michael Crichton. **CAST:** Burt Reynolds, Theresa Russell, Ned Beatty, Kay Lenz.

Polished performances by Theresa Russell and Burt Reynolds are wasted in this convoluted police thriller. Russell is a public defender assigned to defend Reynolds, a cop accused of murder. A threadbare, erratic plot and haphazard direction by Michael Crichton ruin what could have been a first-rate film. Rated R for adult situations, violence, and profanity. 1989; 100m.

PIMPERNEL SMITH ★★★
DIR: Leslie Howard. **CAST:** Leslie Howard, David Tomlinson, Philip Friend, Hugh McDermott, Mary Morris.

Star Leslie Howard, who also produced, brought his 1934 role in *The Scarlet Pimpernel* up to modern times in this anti-Nazi thriller involving a daring rescue of important scientists from prison. 1942; B&W; 122m.

PINK CADILLAC ★★
DIR: Buddy Van Horn. **CAST:** Clint Eastwood, Bernadette Peters, John Dennis Johnston, William Hickey, Geoffrey Lewis, Bill McKinney.

Clint Eastwood returns to the *Every Which Way But Loose*–style action comedy with this mediocre effort, in which he plays a skip tracer out to nab the bail-jumping Bernadette Peters. She's on the run from some speed-freak white supremacists, so of course Clint decides to help her out. There are some good lines in this formula film, but it is predictable, overdone, and ultimately boring. Rated PG-13 for violence, profanity, and suggested sex. 1989; 122m.

PLATOON LEADER ★
DIR: Aaron Norris. **CAST:** Michael Dudikoff, Robert F. Lyons, Rick Fitts, William Smith.

Recipe for a bad movie: take all the best scenes from recent Vietnam war films, mash them together, add nonactor Michael Dudikoff as a fearless *Platoon Leader*, and you have this leaden bore. Rated R for violence. 1988; 93m.

PLUNDER ROAD ★★
DIR: Hubert Cornfield. **CAST:** Gene Raymond, Wayne Morris, Jeanne Cooper.
This ingenious update to *The Great Train Robbery* leaves five men on the run with ten million dollars in gold. The crime-does-not-pay theme prevails. The acting is not the greatest. 1957; B&W; 76m.

POCKETFUL OF RYE, A ★★½
DIR: Guy Slater. **CAST:** Joan Hickson, Peter Davison, Fabia Drake, Timothy West, Tom Wilkinson, Clive Merrison.
Agatha Christie's Miss Marple (Joan Hickson) arrives late in this mystery, which concerns a murder that is somehow connected with a nursery rhyme. The bulk of the story centers around one of Miss Marple's former protégées, now working as a parlormaid. Unrated; suitable for family viewing. 1984; 102m.

POPPY IS ALSO A FLOWER, THE ★½
DIR: Terence Young. **CAST:** E. G. Marshall, Trevor Howard, Gilbert Roland, Rita Hayworth, Anthony Quayle, Angie Dickinson, Yul Brynner, Eli Wallach, Marcello Mastroianni, Omar Sharif, Grace Kelly.
James Bond creator Ian Fleming wrote the original story for this movie about efforts to put an end to an international drug ring. Many in the huge cast worked for scale as a protest against drug abuse, but it backfired. There are so many stars popping up in small roles that they overwhelm the plot. Originally made for television, later released theatrically with added footage. Unrated, the film contains violence. 1966; 105m.

POSEIDON ADVENTURE, THE ★★★
DIR: Ronald Neame. **CAST:** Gene Hackman, Ernest Borgnine, Shelley Winters, Roddy McDowall, Red Buttons, Stella Stevens.
It's New Year's Eve on the passenger liner *Poseidon*. A tidal wave overturns the ship, and from here on out the all-star cast, special effects, and imaginative sets take over. It's a fairly watchable disaster flick, nothing more. Rated PG. 1972; 117m.

P.O.W.: THE ESCAPE ★★½
DIR: Gideon Amir. **CAST:** David Carradine, Mako, Charles R. Floyd, Steve James.
David Carradine's considerable acting talents are wasted once again in this *Rambo* ripoff that is missing everything but action. Carradine plays battle-hardened vet Col. Jim Cooper, who leads a group of POWs through enemy lines to freedom during the closing days of the Vietnam war. Rated R for profanity and violence. 1986; 90m.

PRAY FOR THE WILDCATS ★½
DIR: Robert Michael Lewis. **CAST:** Andy Griffith, William Shatner, Angie Dickinson, Janet Margolin, Robert Reed, Marjoe Gortner, Lorraine Gary.
An evil Andy Griffith is the only thing that stands out in this terrible movie. Three businessmen try to land a big account from their deranged client (Griffith) while on a macho motorcycle trip in the desert. Made for TV. 1974; 100m.

PRESIDIO, THE ★★★
DIR: Peter Hyams. **CAST:** Sean Connery, Mark Harmon, Meg Ryan, Jack Warden, Dana Gladstone, Mark Blum.
An old-fashioned star vehicle, this murder mystery features Sean Connery as a military provost marshal at San Francisco's Presidio. Police detective Mark Harmon, who once served under Connery and still bears a grudge, is assigned to work with his former commanding officer. Forget the plot and enjoy seeing Connery excel in a tailor-made role. Rated R for violence and profanity. 1988; 97m.

PRIME CUT ★★
DIR: Michael Ritchie. **CAST:** Lee Marvin, Gene Hackman, Angel Tompkins, Gregory Walcott, Sissy Spacek.

Sissy Spacek made her film debut in this sleazy but energetic crime thriller about big-time gangsters and the slaughterhouse they use to convert their enemies into sausage. The talents of Lee Marvin and Gene Hackman elevate this essentially tasteless offering. Rated R for nudity, gore, and violence. 1972; 86m.

PRIME RISK ★★★½
DIR: Michael Frakas. **CAST:** Lee Montgomery, Sam Bottoms, Toni Hudson, Keenan Wynn, Clu Gulager.

Two frustrated young people (Lee Montgomery and Samuel Bottoms) devise a scheme to rip off automatic-teller machines. Trouble arises when they stumble on to a greater conspiracy involving foreign agents planning to sabotage the Federal Reserve System. There is nonstop action in this entertaining thriller, with Keenan Wynn as a suitable villain. Rated PG-13 for mature situations and language. 1984; 98m.

PRISONER OF ZENDA, THE ★★★
DIR: Richard Thorpe. **CAST:** Stewart Granger, Deborah Kerr, Jane Greer, Louis Calhern, James Mason, Lewis Stone.

An innocent traveler in a small European country is the exact double of its king and gets involved in a murder plot. This is a flashy Technicolor remake of the famous 1937 Ronald Colman version. 1952; 101m.

PRIVATE FILES OF J. EDGAR HOOVER, THE ★★½
DIR: Larry Cohen. **CAST:** Broderick Crawford, Michael Parks, José Ferrer, Celeste Holm, Rip Torn, Ronee Blakley, James Wainwright, Dan Dailey, Lloyd Nolan.

A soap-opera style account of the life and times of J. Edgar Hoover, concentrating on the seamier side of the FBI man's investigations. James Wainwright plays the young protagonist with low-key (some would say boring) intensity, while Broderick Crawford growls his way through Hoover's elder years. Rated PG for language and gangster violence. 1977; 111m.

PRIVATE INVESTIGATIONS 🦃
DIR: Nigel Dick. **CAST:** Clayton Rohner, Ray Sharkey, Paul LeMat, Talia Balsam, Anthony Zerbe.

One more time with an overworked plot: young Los Angeles architect is chased around town by bad guys who think he knows something that could expose their schemes. The details rely on foolish coincidences. A pointless use of film stock. It's rated R for language and violence. 1987; 91m.

PRIVATE LIFE OF SHERLOCK HOLMES, THE ★★★★½
DIR: Billy Wilder. **CAST:** Robert Stephens, Colin Blakely, Genevieve Page, Christopher Lee, Irene Handl, Clive Revill, Stanley Holloway.

Director Billy Wilder's affectionately satirical pastiche of the Conan Doyle stories reveals the "secrets" allegedly shared by Sherlock Holmes (Robert Stephens) and Dr. John H. Watson (Colin Blakely). It does so with wit, humor, taste, and even suspense. Rated PG. 1970; 125m.

PROFESSIONALS, THE ★★★★½
DIR: Richard Brooks. **CAST:** Lee Marvin, Burt Lancaster, Robert Ryan, Woody Strode, Claudia Cardinale, Ralph Bellamy.

A rip-snorting adventure film with Lee Marvin, Burt Lancaster, Robert Ryan, and Woody Strode as the title characters out to rescue the wife (Claudia Cardinale) of a wealthy industrialist (Ralph Bellamy) from the clutches of a Mexican bandit (Jack Palance) who allegedly kidnapped her. Directed with a fine eye for character and action by Richard Brooks. 1966; 117m.

PROTECTOR, THE ★★½
DIR: James Glickenhaus. **CAST:** Jackie Chan, Danny Aiello, Roy Chiao.

Standard kung-fu film distinguished by nicely photographed action sequences and a sense of humor. Story has Jackie Chan as an undercover

New York cop traveling to Hong Kong to break up a big heroin ring that is shipping its goods to New York City. Rated R for violence, nudity, and language. 1985; 94m.

PUBLIC ENEMY ★★★★½
DIR: William Wellman. **CAST:** James Cagney, Jean Harlow, Mae Clarke, Eddie Woods, Beryl Mercer.

Public Enemy, with a snarling, unredeemable James Cagney in the title role, is still a highly watchable gangster film. William A. Wellman expertly directed this fast-paced and unpretentious portrait of the rise and fall of a vicious hoodlum. 1931; B&W; 84m.

PURSUIT OF THE GRAF SPEE ★★★½
DIR: Michael Powell, Emeric Pressburger. **CAST:** John Gregson, Anthony Quayle, Peter Finch, Bernard Lee, Ian Hunter, Patrick Macnee, Christopher Lee.

Highly enjoyable account of the World War II sea chase and eventual battle involving British naval forces and the German's super warship, the *Graf Spee*. Featuring a solid cast, the film benefits from attention to detail and a realistic building of tension. 1957; 106m.

PURSUIT TO ALGIERS ★★★
DIR: Roy William Neill. **CAST:** Basil Rathbone, Nigel Bruce, John Abbott, Marjorie Riordan, Martin Kosleck, Rosalind Ivan.

Basil Rathbone's Holmes and Nigel Bruce's Watson become bodyguards accompanying the young heir to a royal throne on a hazardous sea voyage. Their client disguises himself as Watson's nephew, which makes for some droll dialogue. One of the few Rathbone/Bruce films that borrows nothing from the canon. Unrated—suitable for family viewing. 1945; B&W; 65m.

PYX, THE
DIR: Harvey Hart. **CAST:** Karen Black, Christopher Plummer, Donald Pilon.

A nearly incomprehensible murder mystery about a dead prostitute and the police investigation mounted to uncover her killer. It's told mostly in flashbacks. The soundtrack, most of which is sung by star Karen Black, is out-and-out annoying. Rated R for violence. 1973; 111m.

QUIET COOL ★
DIR: Clay Borris. **CAST:** James Remar, Adam Coleman Howard, Daphne Ashbrook, Jared Martin, Nick Cassavettes.

This amateurishly directed action-adventure film casts veteran heavy James Remar as a New York cop who journeys to the Pacific Northwest to take on the maniacal marijuana growers who have killed the parents of sweet-natured Joshua (Adam Coleman Howard). The setting is beautiful; the story, ludicrous. Rated R. 1986; 80m.

QUIET THUNDER ★
DIR: David Rice. **CAST:** Wayne Crawford, June Chadwick.

Inane cross between *Raiders of the Lost Ark* and *Crocodile Dundee*, with Wayne Crawford playing a lunkheaded African adventurer who is forced to flee across the desert after witnessing the secret assassination of an African president. The budget is so low that the "African" desert has cactus, rattlesnakes, and burros. No rating, but contains offensive language, violence, and brief nudity. 1988; 94m.

QUILLER MEMORANDUM, THE ★★★½
DIR: Michael Anderson. **CAST:** George Segal, Alec Guinness, Max von Sydow, George Sanders, Senta Berger, Robert Helpmann.

First-rate espionage film abandons the gadgets and gimmickry that marked most of the spy movies of the 1960s and concentrates on Harold Pinter's intelligent script. An American secret agent (George Segal) goes undercover to shatter a neo-Nazi hate organization that is gaining strength in Berlin. 1966; 105m.

RACKETEER ★★½
DIR: Howard Higgin. **CAST:** Robert Armstrong, Carole Lombard, John Loder, Paul Hurst, Hedda Hopper.
This early sound gangster film finds gang leader Robert Armstrong involved in the familiar eternal triangle as he falls for Carole Lombard. She, in turn, pines for ailing concert violinist Roland Drew. Though the story has been done with some variations dozens of times, this primitive talkie has some snappy dialogue and features lively performances. 1930; B&W; 68m.

RAD ★★½
DIR: Hal Needham. **CAST:** Bill Allen, Lori Laughlin, Talia Shire, Ray Walston, Jack Weston.
Staunch character players Talia Shire, Ray Walston, and Jack Weston support a cast of youthful actors in this film about a daredevil bicyclist (Bill Allen) who competes to win a thousand dollars at Hell Track, "the most dangerous bicycle race in the world." *Rad* turns out to be fairly entertaining, thanks to the exciting race sequences. Rated PG. 1986; 95m.

RADAR MEN FROM THE MOON ★★
DIR: Fred Brannon. **CAST:** George Wallace, Aline Towne, Roy Barcroft.
Commando Cody, Sky Marshal of the Universe and inventor of a flying suit and a rocket ship, uses all the means at his disposal to aid America in combating Retik, the ruler of the moon, who is bent on (what else?) invading the Earth. The bullet-headed hero chases villains on land, in the air, and all the way to the moon and back and gets his fair share of abuse along the way. Lots of fisticuffs and stock footage. 1952; B&W; 12 chapters.

RADIO PATROL ★½
DIR: Ford Beebe, Cliff Smith. **CAST:** Grant Withers, Catherine Hughes, Mickey Rentschler, Adrian Morris, Monte Montague, Silver Wolf.
This testimonial to the police radio cop is okay for the kids who are bound to fall in love with young Pinky Adams and his canine helper Irish (played by Mickey Rentschler and Silver Wolf, respectively), but adults will be bored. There's not much here plot-wise: international crooks kill an inventor to gain his formula for flexible bulletproof steel and then try to pry the secret out of his young son. 1937; B&W; 12 chapters.

RAGE OF HONOR
DIR: Gordon Hessler. **CAST:** Sho Kosugi, Robin Evans.
Sho Kosugi is an able martial artist, but his fight choreography is dull to watch. Even worse, he speaks English with such a thick accent that he's completely incomprehensible; he'd be better off dubbed! The movie's highlight is a pair of ninja midgets, if that's your idea of an evening's entertainment. Rated R for strong violence. 1987; 91m.

RAID ON ROMMEL ★
DIR: Henry Hathaway. **CAST:** Richard Burton, John Colicos, Clinton Greyn, Wolfgang Preiss.
Veteran director Henry Hathaway must have had his mind somewhere else when he was making this substandard war film. Richard Burton plays a British Intelligence officer who leads a small group of Allied POWs behind enemy lines in North Africa. His mission: destroy the big guns at Tobruk before the British invasion fleet lands. Rated PG for violence. 1971; 98m.

RAISE THE TITANIC ★
DIR: Jerry Jameson. **CAST:** Jason Robards Jr., David Selby, Richard Jordan, Anne Archer, Alec Guinness, J. D. Cannon.
In this disastrously dull disaster flick, a marine research foundation headed by Jason Robards Jr. has developed a laser protective screen that could be installed around the perimeter of the United States to make it impregnable to missile attack. But to power the screen, the government needs byzanium, a precious radioactive metal

whose only known world supply reportedly went down as contraband aboard the *Titanic*. Rated PG. 1980; 112m.

RAMBO: FIRST BLOOD II ★★★
DIR: George Pan Cosmatos. **CAST:** Sylvester Stallone, Richard Crenna, Charles Napier, Steven Berkoff, Julia Nickson, Martin Kove.

This sequel to *First Blood* is an old-fashioned war movie. Its hero is larger than life, and the villains are pure mule-mean. In other words, it's an action fan's delight. Sylvester Stallone returns as Johnny Rambo, who goes back to Vietnam to rescue American prisoners of war. Rated R. 1985; 94m.

RAMBO III ★★
DIR: Peter MacDonald. **CAST:** Sylvester Stallone, Richard Crenna, Marc de Jonge, Kurtwood Smith.

Sylvester Stallone's hammer-handed tendencies operate at overdrive in this second sequel to *First Blood*. As co-writer, Stallone is responsible for the jingoistic story that makes child-killing sadists of the Russians (led by Marc de Jonge's near-hysterical Soviet colonel) who control a particular sector of Afghanistan. This is button-pushing, lowest-common-denominator filmmaking all the way. Rated R for extreme violence. 1988; 101m.

RANSOM ★★½
DIR: Richard Compton. **CAST:** Oliver Reed, Stuart Whitman, Deborah Raffin, John Ireland, Jim Mitchum, Paul Koslo.

When a psycho begins killing people in a small town and refuses to stop until he receives a $4 million ransom, Stuart Whitman (the richest man in town) hires a mercenary (Oliver Reed) to kill the extortionist. There are some slow moments, but worse than these are the unanswered questions about why the murderer dresses like an American Indian and what his motive really is. Rated PG for violence. 1977; 90m.

RAPE OF THE SABINES
DIR: Richard Pottier. **CAST:** Mylene Demongeot, Roger Moore.

Roger Moore plays Romulus, founder of Rome, in this cheesy epic whose budget wouldn't have paid the catering bill on one of Moore's James Bond movies. Rome lacks women, the neighboring Sabines have lots of 'em, and therein hangs what passes for a tale. This Italian-French coproduction is dubbed (poorly) in English. 1961; 100m.

RAW COURAGE ★★★★
DIR: Robert L. Rosen. **CAST:** Ronny Cox, Tim Maier, Art Hindle, M. Emmet Walsh, William Russ, Lisa Sutton, Lois Chiles.

Three cross-country runners must fend for themselves when they run into a group of weekend warriors in the Colorado desert lands. Ronny Cox is excellent as one of the runners. However, Cox, who wrote the screenplay, has taken a few too many pages from James Dickey's *Deliverance*. Still, *Raw Courage* has enough white-knuckle moments to make you forget about the lack of originality. Rated R for violence and profanity. 1983; 90m.

RAW DEAL ★★★½
DIR: John Irvin. **CAST:** Arnold Schwarzenegger, Kathryn Harrold, Darren McGavin, Sam Wanamaker, Paul Shenar, Steven Hill, Joe Regalbuto, Ed Lauter, Robert Davi.

Big Arnold Schwarzenegger stars in this fast-paced action film as a former FBI agent who is recruited by his former boss (Darren McGavin) to infiltrate the Chicago mob as an act of revenge. It's predictable, even formula. But the formula works. Rated R for profanity and violence. 1986; 107m.

REAP THE WILD WIND ★★★½
DIR: Cecil B. DeMille. **CAST:** John Wayne, Ray Milland, Raymond Massey, Paulette Goddard, Robert Preston, Charles Bickford, Susan Hayward.

Bawdy tale of the shipping and salvage business off the coast of Georgia during the early nineteenth century. John Wayne is a robust sea captain and Ray Milland is a well-to-do owner of a shipping company. Plenty of old-fashioned action and humor with the typical Cecil B. De Mille touches. Entire cast is first-rate, especially the villainous Raymond Massey. The final underwater action scenes are classics. 1942; 124m.

REBEL (1973) ★★

DIR: Robert Schnitzer. **CAST:** Sylvester Stallone, Anthony Page, Henry G. Sanders.

This early Sylvester Stallone movie casts him as a student radical who begins to ponder his future. This low-budget production only proves that Stallone started out mumbling. It is unrated. 1973; 80m.

REBEL ROUSERS ★★

DIR: Martin B. Cohen. **CAST:** Cameron Mitchell, Jack Nicholson, Bruce Dern, Diane Ladd, Harry Dean Stanton.

This drive-in biker film from the late 1960s would barely rate a second look if it weren't for a crop of future big-name stars and character performers who inhabit it. The ill-mannered-youth-on-motorcycles versus uptight-establishment-straights story takes a backseat to flamboyant characterizations in this one. 1967; 78m.

RED ALERT ★★★½

DIR: William Hale. **CAST:** William Devane, Michael Brandon, Ralph Waite, Adrienne Barbeau, David Hayward, M. Emmet Walsh, Don Wiseman.

This 1977 made-for-TV film about a nuclear power plant is just as timely today as when it first aired. An incident at the plant has killed fourteen workers. Was it an accident, sabotage, or computer fault? A fine cast lends an air of reality and immediacy to this gripping mystery. 1977; 95m.

RED DAWN ★★★½

DIR: John Milius. **CAST:** Patrick Swayze, C. Thomas Howell, Ron O'Neal, Lea Thompson, Ben Johnson, Harry Dean Stanton, William Smith, Powers Boothe.

Some viewers undoubtedly will feel that right-wing writer-director John Milius (*The Wind and the Lion* and *Conan the Barbarian*) has gone too far with this tale of the Russians invading a small American town. But we took this film as a simple "what if?" entertainment and, really enjoyed it. Rated PG-13 for violence and profanity. 1984; 114m.

RED FLAG: THE ULTIMATE GAME ★★½

DIR: Don Taylor. **CAST:** Barry Bostwick, Joan Van Ark, Fred McCarren, George Coe.

The air force has a jet-fighter combat course located near Las Vegas that over the years has fine-tuned thousands of the best pilots in the air force. The combat game is called Red Flag. It's an older and weaker version of *Top Gun* and suffers by comparison. 1981; 90m.

RED HEAT (1988) ★★★★

DIR: Walter Hill. **CAST:** Arnold Schwarzenegger, James Belushi, Peter Boyle, Ed O'Ross, Larry Fishburne, Gina Gershon, Richard Bright.

Director Walter Hill has taken his biggest hit, *48 Hrs.*, and reworked it as a vehicle for Arnold Schwarzenegger and James Belushi. Big Arnold plays a Soviet police officer forced to team up with a wisecracking Chicago cop (Belushi) to track down a Russian drug dealer (Ed O'Ross). It's fast and exciting; a best bet for action buffs. Rated R for violence, profanity, and nudity. 1988; 107m.

RED SONJA

DIR: Richard Fleischer. **CAST:** Arnold Schwarzenegger, Brigitte Nielsen, Sandahl Bergman, Paul Smith, Ernie Reyes Jr.

Agony, agoneee...this dreadful sword-and-sorcery film introduces us to Red Sonja (Brigitte Nielsen), pulp author Robert E. Howard's female counterpart to Conan. With the help of superswordsman Kalifor (Arnold Schwarzenegger), our heroine takes on the evil minions of cruel Queen Gedren (Sandahl Bergman). It's all to save the world from a powerful green light bulb. Rated PG-13 for violence. 1985; 89m.

REDNECK ♥

DIR: Silvio Narizzano. **CAST:** Telly Savalas, Franco Nero, Mark Lester.

Vile crime story about two criminals who take a young boy hostage. Not only is the film particularly nasty with gratuitous violence, it's poorly written as well. Hard to believe that this was directed by the same man who did *Georgy Girl*! Unrated. 1972; 89m.

REFLECTION OF FEAR ★★½

DIR: William Fraker. **CAST:** Robert Shaw, Mary Ure, Sally Kellerman, Signe Hasso, Sondra Locke.

Confusing, uninspired story of a beautiful young girl who becomes the central figure in a cobweb of crime and murder. Should have been better, considering the cast. Rated R. 1973; 102m.

REFORM SCHOOL GIRLS ★★

DIR: Tom DeSimone. **CAST:** Wendy O. Williams, Sybil Danning, Pat Ast, Linda Carol.

"So young. So bad. So what?" That was the promo line for this spoof of the women-in-prison genre. Writer-director Tom DeSimone manages to get in the usual exploitative ingredients—women taking showers, etc.—while simultaneously making fun of them. Rated R for violence, profanity, nudity, and simulated sex. 1986; 94m.

REHEARSAL FOR MURDER ★★★½

DIR: David Greene. **CAST:** Robert Preston, Lynn Redgrave, Jeff Goldblum, Patrick Macnee, William Daniels, Lawrence Pressman.

Richard Levinson and William Link, those clever fellows behind the creation of *Columbo*, occasionally stray into the realm of made-for-television movies; this is one of the best. Robert Preston leads his stage friends through the reading of a play designed to ferret out the killer of star Lynn Redgrave. The excellent cast does a fine job with the witty material, and Levinson and Link deliver another of their surprise conclusions. 1982; 100m.

REMO WILLIAMS: THE ADVENTURE BEGINS ★★★

DIR: Guy Hamilton. **CAST:** Fred Ward, Joel Grey, Wilford Brimley, J. A. Preston, George Coe, Charles Cioffi, Kate Mulgrew.

This adaptation of the *Destroyer* novels is like a second-rate James Bond adventure. It offers pleasant diversion and nothing more. Fred Ward is fine as the hero of the title and Joel Grey is a kick as his Asian martial arts mentor, but the film takes too much time establishing the characters and too little giving us the adventure promised in the title. Rated PG-13 for violence and profanity. 1985; 121m.

RENEGADES ★

DIR: Jack Sholder. **CAST:** Kiefer Sutherland, Lou Diamond Phillips, Jami Gertz.

Kiefer Sutherland is a Philadelphia cop. Lou Diamond Phillips is a Lakota Indian. When an undercover operation goes sour, they join forces to track down a vicious band of thieves. Disappointing, lackluster thriller from the director of *The Hidden*. Rated R for profanity and violence. 1989; 110m.

RENT-A-COP ★

DIR: Jerry London. **CAST:** Burt Reynolds, Liza Minnelli, James Remar, Richard Masur, Bernie Casey, Robby Benson, John P. Ryan.

When a drug bust goes awry and both cops and crooks are killed by a masked thief (James Remar), a police detective (Burt Reynolds) is accused of masterminding the hit by his nasty boss (John P. Ryan). The only witness to the crime is a kooky prostitute (Liza Minnelli), so she and the cop set off to find the killer. Minnelli is absolutely grating as a supposedly sexy working girl, Reynolds looks bored and tired. Rated R for violence and profanity. 1988; 95m.

RESCUE, THE ★★
DIR: Ferdinand Fairfax. **CAST:** Kevin Dillon, Kristina Harnos, Marc Price, Charles Haid, Edward Albert.

As if *Iron Eagle* wasn't bad enough, here's another dopey movie about a group of teens who set out to rescue their dads from a prisoner-of-war camp. To his credit, Ferdinand Fairfax achieves some genuine excitement and suspense along the way, but the basic premise is preposterous. Rated PG for profanity and violence. 1988; 99m.

RETURN OF CHANDU (THE MAGICIAN) ★★½
DIR: Ray Taylor. **CAST:** Bela Lugosi, Maria Alba, Clara Kimball Young, Lucien Prival, Bryant Washburn.

Crackerjack fantasy-adventure serial has enough action, trickery, and plot twists for two chapterplays as Bela Lugosi plays Chandu, Master of White Magic, hot on the trail of evil Lemurians who have stolen his beloved Princess Nadji. Hokey but fun family fare. 1934; B&W; 12 chapters.

RETURN OF FRANK CANNON, THE ★★½
DIR: Corey Allen. **CAST:** William Conrad, Arthur Hill, Diana Muldaur, Ed Nelson.

When an ex-CIA agent is murdered, portly detective Frank Cannon (William Conrad) comes out of retirement. The sappy story has Cannon agreeing to leave his life of pleasure as a restaurateur-fisherman to tackle the case because the victim's wife is an old flame. Made for television. 1980; 96m.

RETURN OF THE DRAGON ★★★½
DIR: Bruce Lee. **CAST:** Bruce Lee, Chuck Norris, Nora Miao.

After seeing *Return of the Dragon*, we have no doubt that Bruce Lee, not Robert Clouse, directed *Enter the Dragon*. Lee was credited with staging the fight scenes, but our guess is that he was well aware of the latter film's possible impact and exercised control over the creative nonacting facets of the film whenever he could. *Return of the Dragon* was made before *Enter*, and it shows Lee's considerable directorial talent. A delightful film, brim-full of comedy, action, and acrobatics. Rated R. 1973; 91m.

RETURN OF THE MAN FROM U.N.C.L.E., THE ★★★
DIR: Ray Austin. **CAST:** Robert Vaughn, David McCallum, Patrick Macnee, Tom Mason, Gayle Hunnicutt, Geoffrey Lewis, Anthony Zerbe, Keenan Wynn, George Lazenby.

Secret agents Napoleon Solo (Robert Vaughn) and Illya Kuryakin (David McCallum) are called out of a fifteen-year retirement by U.N.C.L.E. to battle their nemesis Justin Sepheran (Anthony Zerbe) and the evil organization T.H.R.U.S.H. Fans of the original series will find this light-hearted spy adventure especially entertaining. 1983; 109m.

RETURN TO MACON COUNTY ★
DIR: Richard Compton. **CAST:** Don Johnson, Nick Nolte, Robin Mattson.

Two fun-loving boneheads run afoul of the law in the rural south. No style or substance. A lame sequel to the surprisingly good thriller *Macon County Line*. Interesting only to see Nick Nolte in his first film and Don Johnson before *A Boy and His Dog* and *Miami Vice*. Rated PG. 1975; 104m.

REVENGE OF THE NINJA
DIR: Sam Firstenberg. **CAST:** Sho Kosugi, Keith Vitali, Arthur Roberts, Mario Gallo.

Japanese karate experts take on the mob in this kung-fu flick, which is a cut or so above most of the Hong Kong–made martial arts junk. Rated R for violence and nudity. 1983; 88m.

RIDDLE OF THE SANDS ★★★★
DIR: Tony Maylam. **CAST:** Michael York, Jenny Agutter, Simon MacCorkindale.

Based on the spy novel by Erskine Childers, this is the story of two young Englishmen (Michael York, Simon MacCorkindale) who set sail on a holiday just prior to World War I and stumble upon political intrigue and adventure in the North Sea. The result is an absorbing adventure film. Rated PG for slight violence and profanity. 1984; 102m.

RIDER ON THE RAIN ★★★★
DIR: René Clement. **CAST:** Charles Bronson, Marlene Jobert, Jill Ireland.

Charles Bronson gives one of his finest screen performances in this gripping, Hitchcock-style thriller made in France. The story deals with the plight of a woman (Marlene Jobert) who kills an unhinged rapist and dumps his body into the sea. She is soon pursued by a mysterious American (Bronson). Thus begins a fascinating game of cat and mouse. Rated R for violence. 1970; 115m.

RIFIFI ★★★★
DIR: Jules Dassin. **CAST:** Jean Servais, Carl Mohner, Perlo Vita, Robert Manuel, Magali Noel.

A milestone that begat a continuing breed of films hinging on the big, carefully planned robbery that falls apart—usually just as the criminals and the audience are convinced of success. This one is sure to have you pumping adrenaline from start to finish, especially during the brilliant twenty-minute silent robbery sequence that is its selling point, and the falling out of thieves which follows. 1955; B&W; 115m.

RIOT IN CELL BLOCK ELEVEN ★★★½
DIR: Don Siegel. **CAST:** Neville Brand, Leo Gordon, Emile Meyer, Frank Faylen.

This taut prison drama with a message depicts an aborted prison escape that ends with the convicts barricaded and demanding to be heard. Made at the height of the "exposé" and true-crime wave in the mid-fifties, this film avoids the sensational and documentary style of its contemporaries and focuses on the action and the characterizations of the convicts, the prison staff, and the media. 1954; B&W; 80m.

ROAD HOUSE ★★
DIR: Rowdy Herrington. **CAST:** Patrick Swayze, Ben Gazzara, Sam Elliott.

Hot on the heels of *Dirty Dancing*, Patrick Swayze turns to a rowdy, rough-house movie about a bar bouncer who cleans out a Missouri saloon. A male action film with lots of fistfights, a high body count, and a disappointing level of sexist humor. Rated R. 1989; 108m.

ROADHOUSE 66 ★★★½
DIR: John Mark Robinson. **CAST:** Willem Dafoe, Judge Reinhold, Kaaren Lee, Kate Vernon, Stephen Elliott, Alan Autry.

As teen exploitation films go, this one is pretty good. Judge Reinhold plays a yuppie stuck in a small New Mexico town with car trouble. Willem Dafoe is an ex-rock-and-roller and all-around tough guy who helps the young executive in dealing with his existential crisis. The film drags a bit and Dafoe overplays his role, but there are some good moments to be had. Rated R for sex, nudity, violence, and profanity. 1984; 94m.

ROARING TWENTIES, THE ★★★★½
DIR: Raoul Walsh. **CAST:** James Cagney, Humphrey Bogart, Priscilla Lane, Gladys George, Jeffrey Lynn, Frank McHugh, Joe Sawyer.

James Cagney and Humphrey Bogart star in this superb Warner Bros. gangster entry. Produced by Mark Hellinger and directed by Raoul Walsh (*White Heat*), it's one of the best of its kind, with Cagney featured as a World War I veteran who comes back to no job and no future after fighting for his country. Embittered by all this, he turns to crime. 1939; B&W; 104m.

ROBBERS OF THE SACRED MOUNTAIN ★★

DIR: Bob Schulz. **CAST:** John Marley, Simon MacCorkindale, Louise Vallance, George Touliatos.

This action-adventure film could have been another *Raiders of the Lost Ark*. Unfortunately, poor acting and choppy editing leave it in the mediocre range. Simon MacCorkindale does, however, stand out as a determined British reporter who wants to interview a famous anthropologist (John Marley). Rated R for sex, nudity, and violence. 1982; 90m.

ROBBERY ★★★½

DIR: Peter Yates. **CAST:** Stanley Baker, Joanna Pettet, James Booth.

Suspenseful crime drama about the complex heist of the British Royal Mail. Solid direction and excellent performances surpass the predictable script. 1967; 114m.

ROBIN AND MARIAN ★★★★½

DIR: Richard Lester. **CAST:** Sean Connery, Audrey Hepburn, Richard Harris, Ian Holm, Robert Shaw, Nicol Williamson, Denholm Elliott, Kenneth Haigh.

Take the best director of swashbucklers, Richard Lester; add the foremost adventure film actor, Sean Connery; mix well with a fine actress with haunting presence, Audrey Hepburn; and finish off with some of the choicest character actors. You get *Robin and Marian*, a triumph for everyone involved. Rated PG. 1976; 112m.

ROBIN HOOD AND THE SORCERER ★★★★

DIR: Ian Sharp. **CAST:** Michael Praed, Anthony Valentine, Nickolas Grace, Clive Mantle, Peter Williams.

While the telling of the Robin Hood legend in this film may be less straightforward than most, the added element of the mysticism enhances the all-too-familiar story and gives the dusty old characters new life. Michael Praed plays the legendary English outlaw with conviction. 1983; 115m.

ROLLING THUNDER ★★★★

DIR: John Flynn. **CAST:** William Devane, Tommy Lee Jones, Linda Haynes, James Best, Dabney Coleman, Lisa Richards, Luke Askew.

William Devane delivers a fine performance as a Vietnam POW returned home to a small town in Texas. For his courage and endurance under torture, he is honored with two thousand silver dollars by the local merchants. (A dollar for every day served as a POW.) A gang of vicious killers attempts to rob him, but his conditioning to pain under the Vietnamese will not let him tell them where the silver is, even when they begin to torture him. After some hospitalization, Devane recruits his Vietnam buddy (played superbly by Tommy Lee Jones) and the hunt is violently and realistically played out. Rated R. 1977; 99m.

ROLLING VENGEANCE ★★½

DIR: Steven H. Stern. **CAST:** Don Michael Paul, Lawrence Dane, Ned Beatty, Lisa Howard.

A young trucker avenges the murder of his family and the rape of his girlfriend. A cross between a trucker movie and *Rambo*. Rated R for violence and language. 1987; 92m.

ROMANCING THE STONE ★★★★½

DIR: Robert Zemeckis. **CAST:** Kathleen Turner, Michael Douglas, Danny DeVito, Alfonso Arau, Zack Norman.

A rip-snorting adventure film that combines action, a love story, suspense, and plenty of laughs, this movie stars Kathleen Turner as a timid romance novelist who becomes involved in a situation more dangerous, exciting, and romantic than anything she could ever dream up. Michael Douglas plays the shotgun-wielding soldier of fortune who comes to her aid while Danny DeVito, Alfonso Arau, and Zack Norman add delightful bits of comedy. Rated PG for violence, nudity, and profanity. 1984; 105m.

ROSARY MURDERS, THE ★★★
DIR: Fred Walton. **CAST:** Donald Sutherland, Charles Durning, Belinda Bauer, Josef Sommer, James Murtaugh.

Donald Sutherland is a priest who hears the confession of a killer who is murdering nuns and priests. An interesting film, thanks to strong performances by Sutherland and Charles Durning as the bishop. Slow pacing by director Fred Walton and a needlessly murky denouement keep this murder mystery from being top-rank. Rated R for violence and nudity. 1987; 107m.

ROUGH CUT ★★★
DIR: Don Siegel. **CAST:** Burt Reynolds, Lesley-Anne Down, David Niven, Patrick Magee.

The screenplay, by Francis Burns, is a welcome return to the stylish romantic comedies of the 1930s and 1940s with the accent on witty dialogue, action, and suspense. Burt Reynolds and Lesley-Anne Down are a perfect screen combination. As two sophisticated jewel thieves who plot to steal $30 million in uncut diamonds, they exchange quips, become romantically entwined, and are delightful. Rated R. 1980; 112m.

RUCKUS ★★★½
DIR: Max Kleven. **CAST:** Dirk Benedict, Linda Blair, Ben Johnson, Richard Farnsworth, Matt Clark.

This lighthearted adventure film is like *Rambo* without the killing. That's one of the appealing things about this tale of a Vietnam soldier, Dirk Benedict, who escapes from an army psycho ward in Mobile and ends up in a little southern town where he is harassed by the locals—but not for long. PG for violence and language. 1984; 91m.

RUMOR OF WAR, A ★★★
DIR: Richard T. Heffron. **CAST:** Brad Davis, Keith Carradine, Stacy Keach, Michael O'Keefe.

A well-made television movie about a marine combat unit in Vietnam. Brad Davis plays a young officer who bravely leads his men into combat. He eventually gets charged with murder. The video version is about an hour and a half shorter than the original television print. Too bad. 1980; 105m.

RUN SILENT, RUN DEEP ★★★★
DIR: Robert Wise. **CAST:** Clark Gable, Burt Lancaster, Jack Warden, Don Rickles.

Clark Gable becomes the captain of a submarine that Burt Lancaster was to command. Although he resents his new boss, Lancaster stays on. Tensions rise among Lancaster, Gable, and the crew as they set out from Pearl Harbor to destroy a Japanese cruiser. This film is noted as one of the finest World War II submarine movies. 1958; B&W; 93m.

RUNAWAY NIGHTMARE
DIR: Michael Cartel. **CAST:** Michael Cartel, Al Valletta.

The best that can be said about this movie is that the camera remains in focus, a mixed blessing at best. Two Nevada worm ranchers are kidnapped by a gang of beautiful women, who torture them, initiate them into their gang, and tell them about their plot to rip off the mob. A hideous talkfest. 1984; 104m.

RUNAWAY TRAIN ★★★★
DIR: Andrei Konchalovsky. **CAST:** Jon Voight, Eric Roberts, Rebecca DeMornay, John P. Ryan, Kenneth McMillan, Kyle T. Heffner, T. K. Carter.

In this riveting, pulse-pounding adventure movie, two convicts escape from prison and, accompanied by a hostage (Rebecca DeMornay), make the mistake of hopping a train speeding straight for disaster. While the story gets a bit too allegorical and philosophical for its own good on occasion, the film's unrelenting intensity more than makes up for it. Rated R for violence, gore, and profanity. 1986; 112m.

RUNNING SCARED (1980) ★★★
DIR: Paul Glicker. **CAST:** Ken Wahl, Judge Reinhold, Bradford Dillman, Pat Hingle, Lonny Chapman, John Saxon.

Ken Wahl and Judge Reinhold are servicemen returning home after two years in the Panama Canal Zone. Reinhold has appropriated some military property, including cameras and guns. He takes an aerial photo to check out the camera. Unknowingly, he has filmed a secret base that is to be used in the Bay of Pigs operation. When their plane lands, authorities find negatives and the chase is on. Unrated. 1980; 82m.

RUNNING SCARED (1986) ★★★★
DIR: Peter Hyams. **CAST:** Gregory Hines, Billy Crystal, Steven Bauer, Darlanne Fluegel, Joe Pantoliano, Dan Hedaya, Jimmy Smits, Jonathan Gries, Tracy Reed.

Fast, funny, and exciting, this *Beverly Hills Cop*–style comedy–cop thriller features inspired on-screen teamwork from Gregory Hines and Billy Crystal as a pair of wisecracking detectives on the trail of a devious drug dealer. Rated R for violence, nudity, and profanity. 1986; 107m.

RUSSIAN ROULETTE ★★
DIR: Lou Lombardo. **CAST:** George Segal, Cristina Raines, Bo Brudin, Denholm Elliott, Richard Romanus, Gordon Jackson, Peter Donat, Nigel Stock, Louise Fletcher.

George Segal plays a Royal Canadian Mountie sucked into a secret service plot to kidnap a Russian dissident prior to a visit from the Soviet premier. The KGB, however, has its own plans to use the dissident to assassinate the premier and blame everything on the CIA. Good premise, but no action or thrills. Rated PG. 1975; 100m.

RUTHERFORD COUNTY LINE ★
DIR: Thom McIntyre. **CAST:** Earl Owensby, Terry Loughlin.

Wooden acting dampens an otherwise decent script about real-life Rutherford County, North Carolina, Sheriff Damon Husky (Earl Owensby) and his efforts to police the rural Blue Ridge community. The actors appear to read their lines from cue cards. Not rated; the film contains episodes of profanity and graphic violence. 1985; 98m.

SAHARA (1943) ★★★½
DIR: Zoltán Korda. **CAST:** Humphrey Bogart, Bruce Bennett, Lloyd Bridges, Dan Duryea, J. Carrol Naish.

One of the better war films, this production contains plenty of action, suspense, and characterization. Humphrey Bogart plays the head of a British-American unit stranded in the desert. The soldiers must keep the ever-present Nazi forces at bay while searching for the precious water they need to stay alive. It's a down-to-the-bone, exciting World War II drama. 1943; B&W; 97m.

SAHARA (1984)
DIR: Andrew V. McLaglen. **CAST:** Brooke Shields, Lambert Wilson, Horst Buchholz, John Rhys-Davies, John Mills.

Brooke Shields stars in this turkey of an adventure picture as a young heiress who, in order to fulfill a promise to her dying father, enters "the world's most treacherous auto race" (across the Sahara Desert), gets kidnapped by an Arab sheik (Lambert Wilson), and eventually falls in love with him. Sound awful? It is! Rated PG for violence and profanity. 1984; 104m.

SAIGON COMMANDOS ★★½
DIR: Clark Henderson. **CAST:** Richard Young, P. J. Soles, John Allen Nelson.

In Vietnam, U.S. military cop Richard Young investigates the murders of local drug dealers. Okay action drama, with more than a passing resemblance to *Off Limits* (though this was made earlier). Rated R for strong violence, profanity. 1987; 91m.

SAINT, THE (TV SERIES) ★★
DIR: Roy Baker, Leslie Norman. **CAST:** Roger Moore, Winsley Pithey, Norman Pitt, Ivor Dean, Percy Herbert, Ronald Radd, Lois Maxwell.

Before essaying the role of James Bond, Roger Moore honed his suavity in the series *The Saint*. He sparkled as international adventurer Simon Templar, a connoisseur of fine wine and women. The devilishly daring troubleshooter continually aided the police, who considered him a foe. Made in England, the production could usually be relied on to provide intriguing mysteries, witty dialogue, and solid action. Two episodes per tape. 1963–1969; 100 minutes each.

SAINT IN LONDON, THE ★★★
DIR: John Paddy Carstairs. **CAST:** George Sanders, Sally Gray, David Burns, Ralph Truman.

George Sanders as the Saint is up to his halo in spies, murder, and intrigue in this entertaining series entry, the second to star Sanders as Simon Templar. Entrusted to protect a foreign ambassador from hired killers, the Saint fails and feels honor-bound to track down the culprits. Based on a short story by Leslie Charteris, this handsome programmer is fun to watch and features a charming and witty lead in Sanders. 1939; B&W; 72m.

SAINT IN NEW YORK, THE ★★★
DIR: Ben Holmes. **CAST:** Louis Hayward, Kay Sutton, Jonathan Hale, Jack Carson, Sig Ruman.

The first of Leslie Charteris's popular crime novels to hit the screen, this smooth adventure features Louis Hayward as the Saint, gentleman crimefighter, and his efforts to clean up the city. Simon Templar has been called in by concerned citizens who want him to put an end to six gangsters who have been plaguing their metropolis. Hayward is fine in the title role of the continental adventurer. 1938; B&W; 71m.

ST. IVES ★★★½
DIR: J. Lee Thompson. **CAST:** Charles Bronson, Jacqueline Bisset, John Houseman, Maximillian Schell, Harry Guardino, Dana Elcar, Dick O'Neill, Elisha Cook Jr.

This is a good Charles Bronson film about a former police reporter who becomes involved in a murder. Director J. Lee Thompson pulls an understated and believable performance out of the star. Rated PG. 1976; 93m.

SAINT STRIKES BACK, THE ★★★
DIR: John Farrow. **CAST:** George Sanders, Wendy Barrie, Jonathan Hale, Jerome Cowan, Neil Hamilton, Barry Fitzgerald.

A good cast, a good story, and a charming performance by George Sanders as Simon Templar, debonair crimefighter, make this one of the best of a very pleasant series. Sanders, in his first appearance as the suave adventurer, pulls out all the stops in his efforts to clear the name of a dead policeman and straighten out his wayward daughter. 1939; B&W; 67m.

ST. VALENTINE'S DAY MASSACRE, THE ★★
DIR: Roger Corman. **CAST:** Jason Robards Jr., George Segal, Ralph Meeker, Jean Hale, Frank Silvera, Joseph Campanella, Bruce Dern.

Watching the leads ham it up provides sporadic fun, but this gaudy gangster picture is long on violence and short on dramatic impact. The massacre itself has been depicted in more exciting style in other films. Where's Eliot Ness when you need him? 1967; 100m.

SAINT'S VACATION, THE ★★
DIR: Leslie Fenton. **CAST:** Hugh Sinclair, Sally Gray, Arthur Macrae, Cecil Parker, Gordon McLeod.

Simon Templar finds mystery and adventure instead of peace and quiet when he encounters spies and intrigue on his vacation attempt. Hugh Sinclair plays the sophisticated Saint for the first time in this programmer filmed in England with a British cast. Passable, but not up to the earlier entries in the series. 1941; B&W; 60m.

SALAMANDER, THE ★
DIR: Peter Zinner. **CAST:** Franco Nero, Anthony Quinn, Martin Balsam, Sybil Danning, Christopher Lee, Cleavon Little, Paul Smith, Claudia Cardinale, Eli Wallach.
Abysmal political action-thriller about a colonel who attempts to prevent a fascist coup d'état in Italy. Great veteran cast cannot rise above the idiotic script. Rated R; contains violence and profanity. 1981; 101m.

SALZBURG CONNECTION, THE ★
DIR: Lee H. Katzin. **CAST:** Barry Newman, Anna Karina, Joe Maross, Wolfgang Preiss, Helmut Schmid, Udo Kier, Klaus Maria Brandauer.
This incredibly bad spy film set in Europe has Barry Newman playing an American lawyer on vacation who gets mixed up with Nazi spies, double agents, and a pretty girl (Anna Karina). The story is almost incoherent, with acting to match. Rated PG for violence and language. 1972; 93m.

SAND PEBBLES, THE ★★★½
DIR: Robert Wise. **CAST:** Steve McQueen, Richard Crenna, Richard Attenborough, Candice Bergen, Mako, Simon Oakland, Gavin MacLeod.
Steve McQueen gives his most compelling performance as Hollman, an ordinary seaman on an American warship stationed off China in 1925. He prefers to remain below deck with his only love, the ship's engines. That way he avoids involvement or decisions, and as long as he obeys orders his life will flow smoothly, yet uneventfully, along. Hollman is forced by changes in China to become involved with the world outside his engine room. The result is an enjoyable, sweeping epic with unforgettable characters. 1966; 179m.

SANDERS OF THE RIVER ★★½
DIR: Zoltán Korda. **CAST:** Paul Robeson, Leslie Banks, Nina Mae McKinney, Robert Cochran.
"Sandy the lawgiver" is the heavy right hand of the British Empire in this action drama of colonialism in darkest Africa. Paul Robeson rises above demeaning circumstances and fills the screen with his commanding presence. Great footage of the people and terrain of Africa adds to the mood of this adventure and gives it an aura lacking in many jungle films. 1935; B&W; 98m.

SANDS OF IWO JIMA ★★★★½
DIR: Allan Dwan. **CAST:** John Wayne, John Agar, Forrest Tucker, Richard Jaeckel, Arthur Franz.
Superb war film. The Duke was never better than as the haunted Sergeant Stryker, a man hated by his men (with a few exceptions) for his unyielding toughness, but it is by that attitude that he hopes to keep them alive in combat. Watch it and see how good the Duke really was. 1949; B&W; 110m.

SAPPHIRE ★★★
DIR: Basil Dearden. **CAST:** Nigel Patrick, Yvonne Mitchell, Michael Craig, Paul Massie, Bernard Miles.
This mystery about Scotland Yard detectives searching for the murderer of a young black woman was judged a failure at the time because of the reticent way it addressed then current racial tensions. Now it can be enjoyed as a solid police procedural. 1959; 92m.

SATAN'S SATELLITES ★½
DIR: Fred Brannon. **CAST:** Judd Holdren, Aline Towne, Wilson Wood, Lane Bradford, John Crawford, Leonard Nimoy.
Heroic Judd Holdren of the Inter-Planetary Patrol, aided by his two assistants and his flying suit, battles otherworldly villains Lane Bradford and Leonard Nimoy, who want to blow the Earth out of its orbit. Originally released by Republic Studios as a

twelve-episode serial entitled *Zombies of the Stratosphere*, this sequel to *Radar Men from the Moon* is a cheaply done paste-up job. 1958; B&W; 70m.

SAVAGE DAWN ★

DIR: Simon Nuchtern. **CAST:** George Kennedy, Richard Lynch, Lance Hendriksen, Karen Black, William Forsythe.

A motorcycle gang takes over a small town in the desert. Retired weapons expert George Kennedy and former CIA agent Lance Hendriksen come to the town's rescue. Tired retread. Rated R for violence, nudity, and profanity. 1984; 102m.

SAVAGE JUSTICE

DIR: Joey Romero. **CAST:** Julie Montgomery, Steve Memel.

The daughter of an American ambassador is caught up in a revolution in a foreign country. Her parents are killed, and she is taken hostage by the rebels. Ludicrous revenge melodrama. Unrated, the film has nudity and violence. 1988; 90m.

SAVAGE STREETS

DIR: Danny Steinmann. **CAST:** Linda Blair, Robert Dryer, Sal Landi, John Vernon.

That *Exorcist* kid, Linda Blair, is at it again. This time, she's the tough leader of a street gang that stops terrorizing tourists and senior citizens when her sister is raped by a rival gang. Poor sis is a deaf-mute, which makes it all the more disgusting a scene, and Blair decides "this means war." But it really means bore. Rated R for everything imaginable. 1985; 90m.

SCANDALOUS (1988)

DIR: Robert W. Young. **CAST:** Lauren Hutton, Albert Fortell, Capucine.

Scandalously incomprehensible suspense film. A penniless playboy is hired to find a secretary who has witnessed the murder of a renowned author. Not rated, but equivalent to PG-13 for mature audiences. 1988; 90m.

SCARAMOUCHE ★★★★

DIR: George Sidney. **CAST:** Stewart Granger, Eleanor Parker, Mel Ferrer, Janet Leigh.

This big-screen adaptation of the Rafael Sabatini story is first-class entertainment for the whole family. Stewart Granger is perfectly cast as the swashbuckling Scaramouche, who sets out to avenge his brother's murder by a villainous master swordsman (Mel Ferrer). A wonderfully witty script, splendid cinematography, fine performances, and outstanding action scenes. 1952; 118m.

SCARFACE (1932) ★★★★½

DIR: Howard Hawks. **CAST:** Paul Muni, Ann Dvorak, George Raft, Boris Karloff, Osgood Perkins.

Subtitled "Shame of the Nation" when released in the 1930s, this thinly veiled account of the rise and fall (the latter being fictional) of Al Capone easily ranks as one of the very best films in the gangster genre—right up there with *The Public Enemy*, *The Roaring Twenties*, *High Sierra*, and *White Heat*. Paul Muni is first-rate as the Chicago gangster and receives excellent support from Ann Dvorak, George Raft, and, outstanding as a rival gangster, Boris Karloff. See it. 1932; B&W; 93m.

SCARFACE (1983) ★★★★½

DIR: Brian De Palma. **CAST:** Al Pacino, Steven Bauer, Robert Loggia, Paul Shenar.

One-time "Godfather" Al Pacino returns to his screen beginnings with a bravura performance in the title role of this updating of Howard Hawks's 1932 gangster classic. Rather than bootleg gin as Paul Muni did in the original, Pacino imports and sells cocaine. Directed by Brian De Palma, it's the most violent, thrilling, revolting, surprising, and gruesome gangster movie ever made. Rated R for nudity, violence, sex, and profanity. 1983; 170m.

SCARLET AND THE BLACK, THE ★★½

DIR: Jerry London. **CAST:** Gregory Peck, Christopher Plummer, John Gielgud.

The action in this film is centered around the Vatican during the time of the German occupation of Rome in 1943. Based on a story entitled "The Scarlet Pimpernel of the Vatican," it chronicles the adventures of an Irish priest who manages to elude the German captors in true Pimpernel fashion. Moderately entertaining. 1983; 143m.

SCARLET CLAW, THE ★★★★

DIR: Roy William Neill. **CAST:** Basil Rathbone, Nigel Bruce, Gerald Hamer, Paul Cavanaugh, Arthur Hohl, Miles Mander, Ian Wolfe.

Stunningly atmospheric entry in the Universal series of Sherlock Holmes mysteries has the detective journeying to Canada to find the culprit in a bizarre series of murders. This is a true whodunit, which keeps you guessing right to the end. 1944; B&W; 74m.

SCARLET PIMPERNEL, THE (1934) ★★★

DIR: Harold Young. **CAST:** Leslie Howard, Raymond Massey, Merle Oberon, Nigel Bruce.

Leslie Howard plays Sir Percy, an English aristocrat engaged in the underground effort to snatch out from under the blade of the guillotine Frenchmen caught in the Reign of Terror. In the tradition of many swashbucklers, he hides his activities under the guise of a fop. His ruse may throw off the French authorities, as ably represented by a sinister Raymond Massey, but he is also turning off his beautiful wife, Merle Oberon. 1934; B&W; 95m.

SCARLET PIMPERNEL, THE (1982) ★★★½

DIR: Clive Donner. **CAST:** Anthony Andrews, Jane Seymour, Ian McKellen, James Villiers, Eleanor David.

This is the made-for-TV version of the much-filmed (seven times) adventure classic. Anthony Andrews makes a dashing hero leading a double life aiding French revolutionaries while posing as a foppish member of British society. Jane Seymour is breathtakingly beautiful as his ladylove. This lavish production proves that remakes, even for television, can be worthwhile. 1982; 150m.

SCARLET SPEAR, THE ★

DIR: George Breakston, Ray Stahl. **CAST:** Ray Bentley, Martha Hyer.

The son of an African chief undertakes a series of ritual tasks to prove his manhood. He is watched by a British official who fears that one of the tasks may provoke a tribal war. The story is merely an excuse to present Technicolor scenes of the African terrain, which you can see better elsewhere. 1954; 78m.

SCENE OF THE CRIME (1985) ★½

DIR: Walter Grauman, Harry Falk. **CAST:** Orson Welles, Markie Post, Alan Thicke, Ben Piazza.

A cross between a game show and a murder mystery, this film is cut into three episodes, narrated by Orson Welles, that ask the viewers to try to solve the murder at the end of each. Welles is there to reveal the necessary clues, in case you miss them. Originally made for network TV. 1985; 74m.

SCENES FROM A MURDER ★

DIR: Alberto De Martino. **CAST:** Telly Savalas, Anne Heywood.

Inept thriller stars Telly Savalas as a killer who stalks an actress (Anne Heywood). Murder and mayhem in the theater world couldn't be duller. Filmed in Italy. 1972; 90m.

SCORCHY ★

DIR: Hinkel Avedis. **CAST:** Connie Stevens, Cesare Danova, William Smith, Marlene Schmidt, Normann Burton, Joyce Jameson.

Connie Stevens is an undercover cop trying to bust a major drug ring. You won't check this out for its acting ability, so you won't be surprised. However, you will get some action and lots of gratuitous gore. Rated R. 1976; 99m.

SCORPION
DIR: William Riead. **CAST:** Tonny Tulleners, Don Murray.
Dimwitted martial arts film stars nonactor Tonny Tulleners, who takes on a band of terrorists. But his dreadful performance is only one of the dismal ingredients in this grade-Z gobbler. Rated R. 1987; 98m.

SEA DEVILS ★★
DIR: Ben Stoloff. **CAST:** Victor McLaglen, Preston Foster, Ida Lupino, Donald Woods.
Victor McLaglen and Ida Lupino play father and daughter in this soggy tale of Coast Guard trial and tribulation. McLaglen and Preston Foster are service rivals given to settling problems with their fists. Unfortunately, the audience can't fight back. 1937; B&W; 88m.

SEA HAWK, THE ★★★★
DIR: Michael Curtiz. **CAST:** Errol Flynn, Flora Robson, Claude Rains, Donald Crisp, Alan Hale, Henry Daniell, Gilbert Roland.
Errol Flynn was the best of the screen's costumed adventurers. *The Sea Hawk* shows him at his swashbuckling peak. He plays a buccaneer sea captain who is given tacit approval by Queen Elizabeth I (Flora Robson) to wreak havoc on the Spanish fleet and their cities in the New World. 1940; B&W; 109m.

SEA SHALL NOT HAVE THEM, THE ★★★
DIR: Lewis Gilbert. **CAST:** Michael Redgrave, Dirk Bogarde, John Mitchell.
Nicely done World War II film about British air rescue operations. Main story follows an RAF bomber crew shot down over the North Sea and their rescue from the ocean. 1955; B&W; 92m.

SEA WOLVES, THE ★★★
DIR: Andrew V. McLaglen. **CAST:** Gregory Peck, Roger Moore, David Niven, Trevor Howard, Barbara Kellerman, Patrick Macnee.
A World War II version of *The Over the Hill Gang*. Gregory Peck and Roger Moore play two British officers who recruit a bunch of Boer War veterans now in their autumn years to do some espionage against the Germans along the coast of India. While the film relies too heavily on comedy that doesn't work, the last twenty minutes has enough spirit to redeem it. The film is based on a true story. Rated PG for violence and sex. 1980; 120m.

SEARCH AND DESTROY ★½
DIR: William Fruet. **CAST:** Perry King, Don Stroud, Tisa Farrow, George Kennedy, Park Jong Soo.
Search and Destroy is a pain to watch—the continuity problems are so serious that the viewer may get a headache by watching the camera's subject jump from one side of the screen to the other. Perry King is an American Vietnam veteran who is being chased by a Vietnamese villain seeking revenge. Not rated, the film has violence and profanity. 1981; 93m.

SECOND CHANCE ★★½
DIR: Rudolph Maté. **CAST:** Robert Mitchum, Linda Darnell, Jack Palance, Reginald Sheffield, Roy Roberts.
Robert Mitchum plays protector to a former gangster's girlfriend (Linda Darnell) as they are pursued through South America by hit man Jack Palance. This passable chase melodrama was Howard Hughes's first excursion into wide screen, and the often-imitated climax aboard the gondola cars suspended above a deep chasm is the centerpiece of the film. 1953; 82m.

SECRET AGENT, THE ★★★
DIR: Alfred Hitchcock. **CAST:** John Gielgud, Madeleine Carroll, Robert Young, Peter Lorre, Percy Marmont, Lilli Palmer.

Off-beat espionage film by the master of suspense contains many typical Alfred Hitchcock touches, but lacks the pacing and characterizations that set his best efforts apart from those of his contemporaries. Alternately grim and humorous, this uneven film (based on a novel by Somerset Maugham) is still watchable and comparable with many of the best films in the genre. 1936; B&W; 93m.

SECRET AGENT (TELEVISION SERIES) ★★★½

DIR: Don Chaffey, Peter Maxwell, Michael Truman. **CAST:** Patrick McGoohan, Peter Madden.

The suave, debonair, and resourceful John Drake (Patrick McGoohan) turned out to have more than one life; after the limited success of his 1961 series, *Danger Man*, he returned in 1965 with the far more flamboyant—and popular—*Secret Agent*. In spite of a faithful following, the new show disappeared after forty-five episodes had been aired. (But Drake would appear again—in a sense—as *The Prisoner*.) Creator and executive producer Ralph Smart, who wore the same hats during *Danger Man*, changed the format a bit for this second outing; now Drake worked for the specifically British agency known as M.I.9 and took orders from an "M"-like figure named Hobbs (Peter Madden). The hour-length dramas, many written by Smart, were far grittier and more realistic than their American counterparts. 1965–1966; B&W; 53 minutes each.

SECRET WEAPONS ★

DIR: Don Taylor. **CAST:** James Franciscus, Sally Kellerman, Linda Hamilton, Geena Davis.

Sleazy made-for-TV potboiler about a Russian espionage training camp. At the school, beautiful young girls are taught to pass as Americans and to use their sexual charms to obtain secret information. Substandard. 1985; 96m.

SELL-OUT, THE ★★½

DIR: Peter Collinson. **CAST:** Richard Widmark, Oliver Reed, Gayle Hunnicutt, Sam Wanamaker.

Double agent Oliver Reed screws up and finds that both the Soviets and the Americans have put out contracts on him. He seeks helps from his former mentor, retired CIA agent Richard Widmark. Okay spy stuff, though a bit heavy on the shootouts and car chases toward the end. Filmed in Israel. Rated PG. 1976; 88m.

SERGEANT YORK ★★★

DIR: Howard Hawks. **CAST:** Gary Cooper, Walter Brennan, George Tobias, Ward Bond, Noah Beery Jr., June Lockhart.

A World War II morale booster that succeeded beyond mere propaganda and is still good entertainment today. Gary Cooper got an Academy Award as the deeply religious young farmer from backwoods Tennessee who tries to avoid service in World War I because of his religious convictions only to become the war's most decorated American hero! 1941; B&W; 134m.

SEVEN HOURS TO JUDGMENT ★★

DIR: Beau Bridges. **CAST:** Beau Bridges, Ron Leibman, Julianne Phillips, Reggie Johnson, Al Freeman Jr.

An action-thriller that loses much of its thrill due to its baby-faced star (and his jumpy direction). Bridges is a judge who, after letting a gang of thugs off on a technicality, must run a gauntlet through their territory. Ron Leibman steals the film as the distraught (and psychotic) husband of the gang's victim. Rated R for violence and profanity. 1988; 89m.

SEVEN MAGNIFICENT GLADIATORS, THE ★

DIR: Bruno Mattei. **CAST:** Lou Ferrigno, Sybil Danning, Brad Harris, Dan Vadis, Mandy Rice-Davies.

In this umpteenth resetting of *The Seven Samurai*, seven gladiators defend the people of a small village against barbarians. With a cast like this, you wouldn't exactly expect high drama, but you'll be disappointed if you're looking for campy fun or lots of action. Rated PG. 1983; 86m.

SEVEN SINNERS ★★★
DIR: Tay Garnett. **CAST:** John Wayne, Marlene Dietrich, Albert Dekker, Broderick Crawford, Mischa Auer, Anna Lee.

A brawling story of saloon life in the steamy tropics, as John Wayne and Albert Dekker vie for sultry Marlene Dietrich, who walks through this slight story with good humor as a heartbreaking "entertainer." A serviceable action tale. 1940; B&W; 87m.

SEVEN-PER-CENT SOLUTION, THE ★★★★
DIR: Herbert Ross. **CAST:** Nicol Williamson, Alan Arkin, Robert Duvall, Laurence Olivier, Vanessa Redgrave, Joel Grey.

Sherlock Holmes (Nicol Williamson) attempts to get rid of his cocaine addiction by getting treatment from Sigmund Freud (Alan Arkin). This is a fast-paced adventure with touches of humor. Robert Duvall's portrayal of Dr. Watson nearly steals the show. Great fun. Rated PG; okay for everyone. 1976; 113m.

SEVEN-UPS, THE ★★
DIR: Philip D'Antoni. **CAST:** Roy Scheider, Tony LoBianco, Richard Lynch.

Hoping to cash in on the popularity of *The French Connection*, the producer of that film directs this slam-bang action flick in an intellectual vacuum. All that's missing are William Friedkin, Gene Hackman, and an intelligent story…but what the hey, we've got a better car chase! Roy Scheider is, as always, quite appealing, but he can't make something out of this nothing. Rated PG for violence. 1973; 103m.

SHADOW OF THE EAGLE ★★½
DIR: Ford Beebe. **CAST:** John Wayne, Dorothy Gulliver, Walter Miller, Kenneth Harlan, Yakima Canutt.

John Wayne's second serial for Mascot Pictures is another one of those stolen inventions–kidnapped scientist affairs, this time masterminded by a mysterious criminal known as The Eagle, who likes to write his threats in the sky with an airplane. Although a bit creaky, this is fun to watch. 1932; B&W; 12 chapters.

SHADOW OF THE THIN MAN ★★★★
DIR: W. S. Van Dyke. **CAST:** William Powell, Myrna Loy, Sam Levene, Donna Reed, Barry Nelson.

Fourth in the series, with sleuths Nick and Nora Charles (William Powell and Myrna Loy) dividing their time between mysteries, Asta the wonder dog, and a stroller-bound Nick Jr. (who arrived in the previous film). Barry Nelson and Donna Reed are among the innocents this time around, and the story concerns dire deeds at the local race track. Another sumptuous serving of sophisticated fun. 1941; B&W; 97m.

SHADOW STRIKES, THE ★½
DIR: Lynn Shores. **CAST:** Rod La Rocque, Lynn Anders, Norman Ainsley.

Loosely based on *The Ghost of the Manor*, one of hundreds of stories featuring the mysterious Shadow, this lackluster effort finds Rod La Rocque on the trail of a gang of crooks who have murdered his father, a prominent attorney. 1937; B&W; 61m.

SHAFT ★★★
DIR: Gordon Parks Jr. **CAST:** Richard Roundtree, Charles Cioffi, Moses Gunn.

One of the best black films from the late 1960s and early 1970s. There is plenty of action and raw energy as private eye Shaft (Richard Roundtree) battles the bad guys in order to rescue a kidnapped woman. Great musical score by Isaac Hayes. Rated PG for violence. 1971; 100m.

SHAKEDOWN ★½
DIR: James Glickenhaus. **CAST:** Peter Weller, Sam Elliott, Patricia

Charbonneau, Antonio Fargas, Blanche Baker.

The talents of Peter Weller and Sam Elliott are all but wasted in this loud, sleazy action-thriller. Weller plays a public defender assigned to defend a crack dealer accused of killing an undercover cop. His investigation into the case leads him to suspect corruption in the New York Police Department. Elliott is the maverick cop who helps him prove it. Rated R for violence, nudity, and profanity. 1988; 112m.

SHAKER RUN ★½

DIR: Bruce Morrison. **CAST:** Cliff Robertson, Leif Garrett, Lisa Harrow, Shane Briant.

A New Zealand laboratory accidentally creates a deadly virus that the military wants as a weapon. But the culture is lifted by a conscientious doctor (Lisa Harrow) who commissions a daredevil driver and his mechanic (Cliff Robertson and Leif Garrett, respectively) to transport it across the country. Not rated, but the equivalent of a PG for violence and profanity. 1985; 91m.

SHALLOW GRAVE ★

DIR: Richard Styles. **CAST:** Tony March, Lisa Stahl, Tom Law.

A low-budget action film about four college girls who witness a killing and are locked up in the slammer by a corrupt sheriff. Derivative. Not rated, but contains violence and nudity. 1987; 90m.

SHAME ★★★★

DIR: Steve Jodrell. **CAST:** Deborra-Lee Furness, Tony Barry, Simone Buchanan.

While on a motorcycling vacation, a lawyer (Deborra-Lee Furness) ends up in an out-of-the-way Australian town where young women are terrorized and ritually raped by a gang of young toughs. So the two-fisted Furness decides to make them pay for their crimes. It sounds corny, but *Shame* is really quite effective. Rated R for violence and profanity. 1987; 90m.

SHAMUS ★★½

DIR: Buzz Kulik. **CAST:** Burt Reynolds, Dyan Cannon, John P. Ryan.

An okay detective thriller, with Burt playing Burt. Nothing new to add to the genre, but lots of action keeps things moving along in this story of a private eye investigating a weapons-smuggling ring. Rated PG. 1973; 106m.

SHARK! (A.K.A. MANEATERS!) ★

DIR: Samuel Fuller. **CAST:** Burt Reynolds, Barry Sullivan, Arthur Kennedy, Silvia Pinal, Enrique Lucero.

Waterlogged undersea adventure about Burt Reynolds and the boys braving man (and ham)-eating sharks to retrieve sunken loot is nothing new and loaded with scenic and stock footage to pad out the tired storyline. Director Samuel Fuller disavowed his association with this joint Mexico-U.S. production. Rated PG. 1969; 92m.

SHARK HUNTER, THE

DIR: Enzo G. Castellari. **CAST:** Franco Nero, Jorge Luke, Mike Forrest.

Franco Nero stars as a Caribbean island recluse who beats up sharks and searches for buried treasure. Good for a laugh, thanks to the lame voice dubbing. Otherwise, feed this one to the you-know-what. Not rated, but the equivalent of a PG for violence and brief nudity. 1984; 92m.

SHARK'S TREASURE

DIR: Cornel Wilde. **CAST:** Cornel Wilde, Yaphet Kotto, John Neilson, Cliff Osmond.

Good guys and bad guys search for sunken treasure while Cornel Wilde and tiger sharks mete out justice. This was the first film to cash in on the success of *Jaws*, though these sharks look downright anemic. Silly and pompous, with jarring homosexual overtones. A complete embarrassment. Rated PG for violence. 1975; 95m.

SHARKY'S MACHINE ★★★★½
DIR: Burt Reynolds. **CAST:** Burt Reynolds, Rachel Ward, Brian Keith, Bernie Casey, Vittorio Gassman, Charles Durning.
This is one of the best cop thrillers ever made. It's exciting, suspenseful, funny, and intelligent, so good it joins *48 Hrs.*, *Dirty Harry*, and *Tightrope* as the best of the genre. Burt Reynolds stars under his own direction as an undercover cop who has a compulsion to crack down on a new wave of crime in his city. Rated R because of violence and profanity. 1981; 119m.

S.H.E. ★★★
DIR: Robert Lewis. **CAST:** Omar Sharif, Cornelia Sharpe, Robert Lansing, Anita Ekberg.
This average made-for-TV spy/action thriller has one twist...a female James Bond. Beautiful Cornelia Sharpe is S.H.E. (Security Hazards Expert). She pursues Robert Lansing, the U.S. syndicate boss, throughout Europe. Omar Sharif makes an appearance as a wine baron. 1979; 105m.

SHEENA ★
DIR: John Guillermin. **CAST:** Tanya Roberts, Ted Wass, Donovan Scott.
Tanya Roberts stars as the comic book heroine Sheena, Queen of the Jungle. In this dull adventure film, an evil African prince tries to take over his brother's kingdom while our heroine, with the help of reporters Ted Wass and Donovan Scott, attempts to stop him. Rated PG. 1984; 117m.

SHERLOCK HOLMES AND THE SECRET WEAPON ★★★
DIR: Roy William Neill. **CAST:** Basil Rathbone, Nigel Bruce, Lionel Atwill, Karen Verne, Dennis Hoey, Mary Gordon.
Although the contemporary (1940s) setting makes the Baker Street sleuth seem oddly out of place, Basil Rathbone remains one of the definitive Holmeses. In this case, he once again faces the ruthless Professor Moriarty (Lionel Atwill). A code that appears in this film is borrowed from *The Adventure of the Dancing Man*. This also is the first Rathbone Holmes to be rereleased in color, a dubious distinction that won't improve it a bit; these films were made for the shadowy world of black and white. 1942; 68m.

SHERLOCK HOLMES AND THE SPIDER WOMAN ★★★½
DIR: Roy William Neill. **CAST:** Basil Rathbone, Nigel Bruce, Gale Sondergaard, Dennis Hoey.
Originally released under the abridged title *Spider Woman*, this Sherlockian adventure is one of the better modernized versions of the Conan Doyle stories. In this one, the villain is the fiendishly evil Adrea Spedding (Gale Sondergaard), a woman who drives gambling men to suicide in order to increase her personal fortune. It's full of sexual attitudes that are now archaic, but it has tension and fine performances. 1944; B&W; 62m.

SHERLOCK HOLMES AND THE VOICE OF TERROR ★★★
DIR: John Rawlins. **CAST:** Basil Rathbone, Nigel Bruce, Evelyn Ankers, Henry Daniell, Montague Love, Thomas Gomez, Hillary Brooke, Mary Gordon.
After starring in the classics *The Hound of the Baskervilles* and *The Adventures of Sherlock Holmes* at Twentieth Century Fox, Basil Rathbone and Nigel Bruce moved to Universal to continue in the roles of Holmes and Watson. This first entry in the series is enjoyable. Set during World War II, it has our heroes going after spies who are using radio broadcasts to sabotage Allied efforts. A strong cast helps. 1942; B&W; 65m.

SHERLOCK HOLMES FACES DEATH ★★★
DIR: Roy William Neill. **CAST:** Basil Rathbone, Nigel Bruce, Dennis Hoey, Hillary Brooke.
Holmes (Basil Rathbone) and Watson (Nigel Bruce) find themselves back in the shadows and fog—albeit in modern times—as they attempt to solve a

murder. Based on Conan Doyle's "The Musgrave Ritual," this is a good entry in the series. 1943; B&W; 68m.

SHERLOCK HOLMES IN WASHINGTON ★★½
DIR: Roy William Neill. **CAST:** Basil Rathbone, Nigel Bruce, Marjorie Lord, Henry Daniell, George Zucco.
Cornball wartime propaganda has Sherlock Holmes (Basil Rathbone) and Dr. Watson (Nigel Bruce) chasing after spies in Washington, D.C. Strong villainy from George Zucco and Henry Daniell helps, and the stars are as watchable as ever. 1943; B&W; 71m.

SHOGUN (FULL-LENGTH VERSION) ★★★★
DIR: Jerry London. **CAST:** Richard Chamberlain, Toshiro Mifune, Yoko Shimada, Damien Thomas.
Forget about the shortened version that is also out on video; this ten-hour original is the only one that does justice to James Clavell's sweeping novel. Richard Chamberlain began his reign as king of the miniseries with his portrayal of Blackthorne, the English sailor shipwrecked among the feudal Japanese. Rarely has television been the original home for a program of this epic scope, and it all works, from the breathtaking cinematography to the superb acting. 1980; 600m.

SHOOT ★★★½
DIR: Harvey Hart. **CAST:** Cliff Robertson, Ernest Borgnine, Henry Silva.
A group of buddies spending a weekend hunting are attacked by another group of hunters who are after game more interesting than deer. When one of their party is wounded, the attacked hunters, led by Cliff Robertson and Ernest Borgnine, want revenge and mount a military-style campaign to get it. Rated R for violence and profanity. 1976; 98m.

SHOOT TO KILL ★★★½
DIR: Roger Spottiswoode. **CAST:** Sidney Poitier, Tom Berenger, Kirstie Alley, Clancy Brown, Richard Masur, Andrew Robinson.
Sidney Poitier returns to the screen after a ten-year absence to portray a streetwise FBI agent determined to track down a ruthless killer. The chase leads to the mountains of the Pacific Northwest, where Poitier teams with tracker Tom Berenger. A solid thriller. Rated R for language and violence. 1988; 110m.

SHOUT AT THE DEVIL ★★
DIR: Peter R. Hunt. **CAST:** Lee Marvin, Roger Moore, Barbara Parkins, Ian Holm.
Good action scenes elevate this otherwise distasteful and overly complicated film about a hard-drinking American adventurer (Lee Marvin) and an upper-crust Englishman (Roger Moore) who join forces to blow up a German battleship before the breakout of World War I. Rated PG. 1976; 119m.

SHRIEK IN THE NIGHT, A ★★★
DIR: Albert Ray. **CAST:** Ginger Rogers, Lyle Talbot, Arthur Hoyt, Purnell Pratt.
Ginger Rogers and Lyle Talbot play two fast-talking reporters competing for a juicy scoop on a murder case in this entertaining low-budget whodunit. Full of mysterious goings-on and creaking doors, this tidy thriller makes up for its lack of production quality by the spunky, enthusiastic performances by the two leads. 1933; B&W; 66m.

SICILIAN, THE ★
DIR: Michael Cimino. **CAST:** Christopher Lambert, Terence Stamp, Joss Ackland, John Turturro, Richard Bauer, Barbara Sukowa, Giula Boschi, Barry Miller, Andreas Katsulas, Ramon Bieri.
At first, *The Sicilian* appears to be a flamboyant gangster epic on a par with Francis Coppola's *The Godfather* and Sergio Leone's *Once Upon a Time in America*. But this adaptation of Mario Puzo's novel becomes a tedious bore thanks to heavy-handed and pretentious direction. Rated R for violence and profanity. 1987; 105m.

SIDEWINDER 1 ★★
DIR: Earl Bellamy. **CAST:** Marjoe Gortner, Michael Parks, Susan Howard, Alex Cord.
Michael Parks is a quiet, reclusive motocross racer who becomes a partner in developing a new dirt bike. *Sidewinder 1* has good racing scenes—motocross fans will love them—but the story is studded with sexist remarks and attitudes about women as sex objects and professional women as frigid and misguided. Rated PG. 1977; 97m.

SIEGE OF FIREBASE GLORIA, THE ★★★
DIR: Brian Trenchard-Smith. **CAST:** Wings Hauser, Lee Ermey.
Outnumbered five to one, our marines defended the hilltop outpost called Firebase Gloria during the Tet offensive in 1968. This is the dramatization of their seemingly hopeless struggle. Grisly scenes of death and destruction bring the Vietnam War close to home. Rated R. 1988; 95m.

SILENT ASSASSINS
DIR: Lee Doo Young, Scott Thomas. **CAST:** Sam Jones, Linda Blair, Jun Chong, Phillip Rhee, Bill Erwin, Mako.
Stupid action flick about a CIA biggie gone bad and a good cop (Sam Jones) assigned to prevent him from getting a germ-warfare formula. Linda Blair plays Jones's wife. Not rated, but has violence and profanity. 1987; 91m.

SILENT RAGE ★
DIR: Michael Miller. **CAST:** Chuck Norris, Ron Silver, Stephen Furst.
A Texas sheriff is pitted against a psychotic killer who has become virtually indestructible through genetic engineering in this karate-horror-thriller-western. Rated R for nudity, profanity, sex, and violence. 1982; 105m.

SILVER BLAZE ★★★
DIR: Thomas Bentley. **CAST:** Arthur Wontner, Ian Fleming, Lyn Harding, John Turnbull, Robert Horton, Arthur Goulet.
Beginning with *Sherlock Holmes' Fatal Hour*, in 1931, Arthur Wontner starred as Holmes in five handsome but low-budget films, of which *Silver Blaze* was the last. Ironically, this movie was not released in America until after the 1939 *Hound of the Baskervilles* introduced Basil Rathbone as the screen's most famous detective. So impressive was Rathbone's debut as Holmes, the American distributor retitled *Silver Blaze* as *Murder at the Baskervilles*. Indeed, Sir Henry Baskerville himself pops up in this loose adaptation of the original story about the disappearance of a prized racehorse. In a further variation, Professor Moriarty (Lyn Harding) and Colonel Moran (Arthur Goulet) are behind the nefarious goings-on. It may not be faithful, but *Silver Blaze* is fun for mystery fans. 1937; B&W; 60m.

SINBAD THE SAILOR ★★★
DIR: Richard Wallace. **CAST:** Douglas Fairbanks Jr., Walter Slezak, Maureen O'Hara, Jane Greer, Anthony Quinn, Sheldon Leonard.
Aping his father, Douglas Fairbanks Jr., as Sinbad, sails forth in search of Alexander the Great's fabled treasure and hits a variety of reefs. Unfortunately, the plot not only thickens but gets murky, to boot. Some say it's all tongue-in-cheek, but it's really more foot-in-mouth. Nonetheless, it is fun. 1947; 117m.

SINISTER URGE, THE
DIR: Edward D. Wood Jr. **CAST:** Kenne Duncan, James Moore, Jean Fontaine.
Ed *(Plan 9 From Outer Space)* Wood's last film as a writer-director is one his fans won't want to miss. The police battle a ring of pornographers and a killer who gets so worked up by looking at these "dirty pictures" that he then goes to the park to kill innocent young women. In the best early-Sixties fashion, Wood got away with flashes of nudity by claiming social significance. Look for him in a brief appearance as a participant in a fistfight outside the candy store where the evil pornographers sell their insidious wares! 1961; B&W; 75m.

SIROCCO ★★★
DIR: Curtis Bernhardt. **CAST:** Humphrey Bogart, Marta Toren, Lee J. Cobb, Everett Sloane, Zero Mostel.
Humphrey Bogart plays a successful crook operating in postwar Syria. He is forced to intercede in a terrorist-police situation and gets himself in trouble with both factions. One of Bogart's best later works and a representative sample of the darker side of romance and intrigue, poles apart from, but structurally related to films like *Casablanca* and *Beat the Devil.* Give it a try. 1951; B&W; 98m.

SKY BANDITS
DIR: Zoran Perisic. **CAST:** Scott McGinnis, Jeff Osterhage, Ronald Lacey.
An uninspired mixing of *Butch Cassidy and the Sundance Kid* and *The Blue Max*, this British production features Scott McGinnis and Jeff Osterhage as outlaws from the Old West who end up as flying aces in World War I. It isn't worth the price of an off-night video rental. Rated PG for violence. 1986; 95m.

SKY PIRATES
DIR: Colin Eggleston. **CAST:** John Hargreaves, Meredith Phillips, Max Phipps.
In 1945 a plane takes off from Australia heading to Bora Bora with a mystical stone on board. The stone, when combined with two other stones in a cave on Easter Island, will give a person unlimited power for either good or evil. Terrible acting, a stupid plot, and poorly executed stunts. Rated PG-13 for violence. 1988; 89m.

SLAM DANCE ★★½
DIR: Wayne Wang. **CAST:** Tom Hulce, Mary Elizabeth Mastrantonio, Virginia Madsen, Harry Dean Stanton, Adam Ant, Don Opper.
An L.A. artist (Tom Hulce) becomes embroiled in two murders of high-priced call girls in this Hitchcockian thriller. The standard situations involving an innocent man trying to clear himself are given some fresh approaches, but there are several holes in the plot, and some events make little sense. Rated R. 1987; 99m.

SLAUGHTER IN SAN FRANCISCO
DIR: William Lowe. **CAST:** Chuck Norris, Robert Jones, Daniel Ivan.
Another abysmal martial arts chop-socky fest. A police officer tries to uncover the killers of his fellow cop and finds a crime ring along the way. Top-billed Chuck Norris appears only briefly. Rated R for violence and profanity. 1974; 87m.

SLAVE OF THE CANNIBAL GOD
DIR: Sergio Martino. **CAST:** Stacy Keach, Ursula Andress.
A woman (Ursula Andress) encounters a cult of flesh-eaters while attempting to find her missing husband in New Guinea. Her resourceful guide (Stacy Keach) helps her through one close call after another. The low budget and inept production team—look for the occasional intrusion of a boom mike in the dialogue scenes—offer a few laughs, but the groans greatly outnumber them. Rated R for violence and nudity. 1979; 87m.

SLAVERS ★½
DIR: Jurgen Goslar. **CAST:** Trevor Howard, Ron Ely, Britt Ekland, Ray Milland, Cameron Mitchell.
This German production is a cut above the wretched *Mandingo*, though it's still an exploitative excuse for entertainment. Ray Milland plays an Arab slave trader in nineteenth-century Africa who treats his charges like cattle. Rated R for violence, nudity, and sexual situations. 1977; 102m.

SLEEPING DOGS ★★½
DIR: Roger Donaldson. **CAST:** Sam Neill, Warren Oates, Nevan Rowe, Ian Mune.
Here's a "what if?" film set in New Zealand during a time of economic crisis. Sam Neill plays a husband and father who discovers his wife is having an affair, so he goes off to live by

himself for a while. Meanwhile, a group of government agents manufacture a revolution by killing innocent bystanders during demonstrations and making it look like the work of the protesters. No MPAA rating. 1977; 107m.

SLEEPING MURDER ★★★★
DIR: John Davies. **CAST:** Joan Hickson, Geraldine Alexander, John Moulder-Brown, Frederick Treves, Jack Watson.

Two newlyweds fall in love with a strange old house in an English seaside town. Into this well-established mood of foreboding comes Miss Marple (Joan Hickson), who helps the young couple decipher the events behind an unsolved murder. Unrated, suitable for family viewing. 1986; 102m.

SLIPPING INTO DARKNESS ★½
DIR: Eleanor Gawer. **CAST:** Michelle Johnson, Neill Barry.

An ex–motorcycle gang member's brother is murdered. So the biker gets his former buddies together to find out whodunit. Give this one the slip. Rated R for violence, nudity, and profanity. 1988; 87m.

SLOANE
DIR: Dan Rosenthal. **CAST:** Robert Resnik, Debra Blee, Raul Aragon.

On the box of this video, the sales pitch begins: "In the action-packed tradition of *Rambo*..." But Stallone never looked as wimpy as Robert Resnik, who stars in this dreadful film about organized crime in Manila. Wholly unbelievable, even without the cannibalistic pygmies. Not rated, but has plenty of sex, violence, and profanity. 1984; 95m.

SMALL TOWN IN TEXAS, A ★★
DIR: Jack Starrett. **CAST:** Timothy Bottoms, Susan George, Bo Hopkins, Art Hindle, Morgan Woodward.

Fairly effective B picture pits a revenge-lusting Timothy Bottoms against the crooked sheriff (Bo Hopkins) who framed him in a drug bust and stole his wife (Susan George). Car crashes, fights, and even a little suspense. Rated R. 1976; 95m.

SNATCHED ★★½
DIR: Sutton Roley. **CAST:** Howard Duff, Leslie Nielsen, Sheree North, Barbara Parkins, Robert Reed, John Saxon, Tisha Sterling, Anthony Zerbe, Richard Davalos.

In this mediocre made-for-television film, the wives of three rich men are kidnapped and held for ransom. The crime is complicated when one of the husbands refuses to pay his share of the ransom. 1973; 73m.

SNO-LINE ★½
DIR: Douglas F. O'Neans. **CAST:** Vince Edwards, Paul Smith, June Wilkinson.

Everyone talks really tough in this film about a crooked DA (Vince Edwards) whose Texas cocaine operation is threatened by the mob. Tough talk doesn't mask the fact that the writing and acting are substandard, though. Rated R for violence and language. 1984; 89m.

SNOWS OF KILIMANJARO, THE ★★★★
DIR: Henry King. **CAST:** Gregory Peck, Susan Hayward, Ava Gardner, Leo G. Carroll, Hildegarde Neff, Torin Thatcher.

A broad and colorful canvas of foreign adventure with author-hero (Gregory Peck) lying injured on the slope of Africa's famous mountain reflecting on his life. From Africa to Spain to the Riviera and back again. One of the better renderings of a Hemingway novel. 1952; 117m.

SOLDIER, THE
DIR: James Glickenhaus. **CAST:** Ken Wahl, Klaus Kinski, William Prince.

In this boring, stupid, and disgusting "thriller" by writer-director James Glickenhaus, Russian agents pretending to be a terrorist group steal enough plutonium for a large nuclear explosion, and it is up to the soldier (Ken Wahl, of TV's *Wiseguy* to sabotage their plan without the official sanction or support of the United States government. Rated R for blood, gore, violence, and profanity. 1982; 96m.

SOLDIER'S STORY, A ★★★★★
DIR: Norman Jewison. **CAST:** Howard Rollins Jr., Adolph Caesar.

A murder mystery, a character study, and a deeply affecting drama rolled into one, *A Soldier's Story*, based on Charles Fuller's 1981 Pulitzer Prize–winning play, is an unforgettable viewing experience. This riveting movie examines man's inhumanity to man in one of its most venal forms: racial hatred. Rated PG for violence and profanity. 1984; 102m.

SOMETHING OF VALUE ★★★
DIR: Richard Brooks. **CAST:** Rock Hudson, Dana Wynter, Sidney Poitier, Wendy Hiller, Frederick O'Neal, Juano Hernandez, William Marshall, Michael Pate.

White settlers in Kenya are preyed upon by bloodthirsty Mau Mau tribesmen sick of oppression in this often too-graphic drama, which opens with a specially filmed foreword from Winston Churchill. 1957; B&W; 113m.

SON OF MONTE CRISTO, THE ★★★
DIR: Rowland V. Lee. **CAST:** Louis Hayward, Joan Bennett, George Sanders, Florence Bates, Montague Love, Ian Wolfe, Clayton Moore, Ralph Byrd.

True to established swashbuckler form, masked avenging hero Louis Hayward crosses wits, then swords, with would-be dictator George Sanders. Honoring tradition, he then frees imprisoned fair lady Joan Bennett from the villain's clutches. 1941; B&W; 102m.

SON OF THE SHEIK ★★½
DIR: George Fitzmaurice. **CAST:** Rudolph Valentino, Vilma Banky, Bull Montana, Montague Love, George Fawcett, Karl Dane.

This sequel to the 1921 adventure *The Sheik*, proved to be bedroom-eyed, ex-gardener Rudolph Valentino's final film. Made shortly before his death at age 31, it was released to coincide with his funeral and was an immediate hit. In the title role, the legendary Valentino acquitted himself with confidence and flair, foiling his enemies and winning the heart of nomadic dancer Vilma Banky. Silent. 1926; B&W; 62m.

SONG OF THE THIN MAN ★★★½
DIR: Edward Buzzell. **CAST:** William Powell, Myrna Loy, Keenan Wynn, Dean Stockwell, Gloria Grahame, Patricia Morison.

Sixth and final entry in the series, a cut above the previous one because of its involvement in jazz music circles. Nick and Nora Charles (William Powell and Myrna Loy) match wits with a murderer this time out, and the setting helps their dialogue regain its crisp sparkle. All in all, a worthy effort with which to conclude things. 1947; B&W; 86m.

SOUL HUSTLER
DIR: Burt Topper. **CAST:** Fabian, Nai Bonet, Tony Russell.

A drug-using wanderer swindles gullible hicks. Execrable. Rated PG for strong language. 1986; 81m.

SOUTH OF PAGO PAGO ★★
DIR: Alfred E. Green. **CAST:** Victor McLaglen, Jon Hall, Frances Farmer, Olympe Bradna, Gene Lockhart.

A good title is wasted on this so-so action tale of pirates heisting native-harvested pearls and being pursued and engaged by the locals. Typical South Sea fare. 1940; B&W; 98m.

SOUTHERN COMFORT ★★★★
DIR: Walter Hill. **CAST:** Keith Carradine, Powers Boothe, Fred Ward, Brion James.

Director Walter Hill's 1981 "war" film focuses on the plight of a National Guard unit lost in Cajun country while on routine training maneuvers. Armed only with M-16 rifles loaded with blanks, the soldiers (who include Keith Carradine and Powers Boothe) find themselves ill-equipped to deal with the hostile locals—and an edge-of-your-seat entertainment is the result. Rated R for violence. 1981; 106m.

SPARTACUS ★★★★½
DIR: Stanley Kubrick. **CAST:** Kirk Douglas, Jean Simmons, Laurence Olivier, Peter Ustinov, Charles Laughton, Tony Curtis.
One of the more rewarding big-budget epics that marked the late 1950s and 1960s. Even though this fictional story of an actual slave revolt against the Roman Empire is large-scale in every detail, it never lets the human drama get lost in favor of spectacle. 1960; 196m.

SPECKLED BAND, THE ★★★
DIR: Jack Raymond. **CAST:** Raymond Massey, Lyn Harding.
In his motion-picture debut, Raymond Massey makes a sturdy Sherlock Holmes, who must bring to justice the evil villain, Dr. Grimesby Roylott (Lyn Harding). Harding, who later played Professor Moriarty in the Arthur Wontner series of Holmes mysteries, is a superb villain, and the sets are decidedly gothic. Time has not been kind to the overall production, but *The Speckled Band* has much to offer fans of the canon. 1931; B&W; 48m.

SPEED ZONE ★
DIR: Jim Drake. **CAST:** John Candy, Donna Dixon, Joe Flaherty, Eugene Levy, Tom Smothers, Tim Matheson, Jamie Farr, Peter Boyle, Brooke Shields.
Another dismal yawner about the *Cannonball Run* cross-country road race. As in the previous two entries in the series, an assortment of fading stars act like morons as they attempt to beat each other in a supposedly funny and exciting coast-to-coast contest. A mindless bore. Rated PG for profanity. 1989; 87m.

SPY SMASHER ★★★
DIR: William Witney. **CAST:** Kane Richmond, Sam Flint, Marguerite Chapman, Hans Schumm, Tristram Coffin.
The costumed radio hero (Kane Richmond) takes on the Nazis in this fun-for-fans cliff-hanger serial. 1942; B&W; 12 chapters.

SPY WHO LOVED ME, THE ★★★★
DIR: Lewis Gilbert. **CAST:** Roger Moore, Barbara Bach, Curt Jurgens, Richard Kiel, Bernard Lee, Lois Maxwell, Desmond Llewellyn, Caroline Munro.
This, the tenth James Bond epic, is Roger Moore's third, and he finally hits his stride. Directed with a blend of excitement and tongue-in-cheek humor, the film teams Bond with Russian agent XXX (Barbara Bach) in an effort to stop an industrialist (Curt Jurgens) from destroying the surface world so he can rule an undersea kingdom. Rated PG for violence, sexual situations. 1977; 125m.

SQUIZZY TAYLOR ★★½
DIR: Kevin Dobson. **CAST:** David Atkins, Jacki Weaver, Alan Cassell, Michael Long.
Fairly interesting film about the notorious Australian gangster of the 1920s who rose to fame in Melbourne because of his keen wit and flamboyant style. David Atkins gives a convincing performance. But the story begins to lose its edge after a while. Not rated. Has sex, nudity, and violence. 1983; 103m.

STAKEOUT ★★★★½
DIR: John Badham. **CAST:** Richard Dreyfuss, Emilio Estevez, Madeleine Stowe, Aidan Quinn, Dan Lauria, Forest Whitaker.
The fastest and funniest cop thriller since the original *Beverly Hills Cop*. A pair of detectives (Richard Dreyfuss and Emilio Estevez) strive to apprehend psychotic killer Aidan Quinn, who has escaped from prison. Rated R for profanity, nudity, suggested sex, and violence. 1987; 116m.

STALAG 17 ★★★★★
DIR: Billy Wilder. **CAST:** William Holden, Robert Strauss, Peter Graves, Otto Preminger.

Many critics felt William Holden's Academy Award for *Stalag 17* was a gift for failing to give him proper recognition in *Sunset Boulevard*. Those critics should view this prison camp comedy-drama again. This film still holds up brilliantly today. Billy Wilder successfully alternated between suspense and comedy in this story of a World War II prison camp. Holden plays an opportunistic and cynical sergeant whose actions make him a natural suspect as the spy in the POWs' midst. 1953; B&W; 120m.

STAR OF MIDNIGHT ★★½

DIR: Stephen Roberts. **CAST:** William Powell, Ginger Rogers, Paul Kelly, Gene Lockhart, Ralph Morgan.

William Powell, in a role cloned from his *Thin Man* series, is a debonair, urbane lawyer accused of murder. Abetted by Ginger Rogers, he sallies forth, repartee in mouth, to catch the real culprit. The police and gangsters alike make it difficult. Not bad. 1935; B&W; 90m.

STEEL ★★★

DIR: Steve Carver. **CAST:** Lee Majors, Jennifer O'Neill, Art Carney, George Kennedy, Harris Yulin, Terry Kiser, Richard Lynch, Roger E. Mosley, Albert Salmi, R. G. Armstrong.

Plenty of action and stunts keep this minor film popping along surprisingly well. Lee Majors stars as the head of a construction crew struggling to complete a skyscraper on schedule. Majors is almost convincing, and a strong cast of character actors are great fun to watch. Rated R. 1980; 99m.

STEELE JUSTICE ★

DIR: Robert Boris. **CAST:** Martin Kove, Sela Ward, Ronny Cox, Bernie Casey, Joseph Campanella, Sarah Douglas, Soon-Teck Oh.

One-man-army Martin Kove is hired to wipe out the Vietnamese mafia in Los Angeles. He succeeds, of course. The film doesn't. Rated R for profanity and violence. 1987; 94m.

STICK ★★★

DIR: Burt Reynolds. **CAST:** Burt Reynolds, Charles Durning, George Segal, Candice Bergen.

Stick is an odd mixture of comedy and violence that more than once strains the viewer's suspension of disbelief. Fans of the original novel, by Elmore Leonard, will be shocked at how far Reynolds's film strays from its source. What should have been a tough, lean, and mean movie contains a surprising amount of clowning by its stars. Despite all this, it has enough action and genuine laughs to please Reynolds's fans. Rated R for profanity and violence. 1985; 109m.

STILETTO ★½

DIR: Bernard Kowalski. **CAST:** Alex Cord, Britt Ekland, Patrick O'Neal, Barbara McNair.

Alex Cord has the starring role in this weak picture about a rich jet-setter who also happens to be a professional killer who decides to quit his job. The Mafia doesn't like that idea, so they decide to kill him. Lots of violent action and sexy situations, but it all adds up to a disappointment. Harold Robbins wrote the story. Rated R. 1969; 98m.

STING, THE ★★★★½

DIR: George Roy Hill. **CAST:** Paul Newman, Robert Redford, Robert Shaw, Charles Durning, Ray Walston, Eileen Brennan, Harold Gould, Dana Elcar.

Those *Butch Cassidy and the Sundance Kid* stars, Paul Newman and Robert Redford, were reunited for this fast-paced entertainment as two con men who outcon a con. Winner of seven Academy Awards—including best picture—this film, directed by George Roy Hill (*A Little Romance* and *Butch Cassidy*) revived Scott Joplin's music. For that, and the more obvious reasons, it is not to be missed. Rated PG. 1973; 129m.

STING II, THE ★★

DIR: Jeremy Paul Kagan. **CAST:** Jackie Gleason, Mac Davis, Teri

Garr, Karl Malden, Oliver Reed, Bert Remsen.

You could hardly expect a sequel to such a joyously entertaining film as *The Sting* to measure up. True to those expectations, this film, starring Jackie Gleason, Mac Davis, Teri Garr, and Karl Malden, doesn't come close. Rated PG for violence. 1983; 102m.

STINGRAY ★

DIR: Richard Taylor. **CAST:** Chris Mitchum, Sherry Jackson, Bill Watson.

Highly uneven action yarn that mixes violence and comedy. Two young men buy a Stingray, unaware that it's filled with stolen cash and drugs. Filmed in and around St. Louis. Rated R for violence and profanity. 1978; 100m.

STONE COLD DEAD ★★

DIR: George Mendeluk. **CAST:** Richard Crenna, Belinda Montgomery, Paul Williams, Linda Sorenson.

This fair film, based on the novel *Sin Sniper* by Hugh Garner, centers on the investigation by Sergeant Boyd (Richard Crenna) into a bizarre series of prostitute killings. Rated R. 1980; 97m.

STONE KILLER, THE ★★★½

DIR: Michael Winner. **CAST:** Charles Bronson, Martin Balsam, David Sheiner, Norman Fell, Ralph Waite.

A *Dirty Harry*–style cop thriller, this casts Charles Bronson as a no-nonsense New York cop who gets transferred to Los Angeles because of his direct way of dealing with gun-toting criminals…he shoots them. It packs a wallop. Rated R. 1973; 95m.

STOPOVER TOKYO ★★

DIR: Richard L. Breen. **CAST:** Robert Wagner, Edmond O'Brien, Joan Collins, Ken Scott.

Based on a story by John P. Marquand, this ho-hum espionage tale has an American spy (Robert Wagner) chasing a communist undercover agent all over Tokyo, making this a combination spy/travelogue movie. Wagner is earnest, as usual, but even the cast's enthusiasm can't put life into this one. Joan Collins is worth watching, as always. 1957; 100m.

STORM ★

DIR: David Winning. **CAST:** David Palfy, Stan Kane.

Slow, predictable thriller about two college students who play assassination tag with paint guns at school. One is a reckless, careless hunk, the other, a likable nerd. Dreadful ripoff of *Gotcha*, a vastly superior film. No storm here, just a miserable little dribble. Rated PG-13 for violence and profanity. 1987; 100m.

STRANGE SHADOWS IN AN EMPTY ROOM

DIR: Martin Herbert. **CAST:** Stuart Whitman, John Saxon, Martin Landau, Tisa Farrow.

When a cop investigates his sister's mysterious death, he's drawn into a conspiracy involving college students and faculty. There is no real suspense. The actors seem to wish they were somewhere else, and who knows where the director was. Not rated but contains violence. 1976; 97m.

STRANGER ON THE THIRD FLOOR ★★★★

DIR: Boris Ingster. **CAST:** Peter Lorre, John McGuire, Elisha Cook Jr., Margaret Tallichet.

Peter Lorre gives yet another singular performance as a disinterested murderer, a character truly alien yet strangely sympathetic. A great hallucination sequence and good performances all the way around make this a compelling treat. 1940; B&W; 64m.

STREET PEOPLE ★½

DIR: Maurizio Lucidi. **CAST:** Roger Moore, Stacy Keach.

Whatever casting director decided to use Roger Moore in the part of a Sicilian hitman ought to seek a different line of work. Moore and sidekick Stacy Keach travel from Italy to San Francisco to rub out the rival mobster who has been cutting in on the heroin trade. Of course, the San Francisco scenes of this Italian movie include plenty of car chases over those hilly streets. Rated R for violence. 1976; 92m.

STREETHAWK ★
DIR: Virgil Vogel. **CAST:** Rex Smith, Jayne Modean, Christopher Lloyd, Joe Regalbuto, Lawrence Pressman, Robert Beltran.

Only kiddies—and fans of the short-lived television series, if there are any—will find much to enjoy in this story of a police officer (Rex Smith) left for dead by drug dealers. He is "resurrected" by the FBI to become a black-costumed, undercover crime fighter who rides a souped-up motorcycle. 1986; 60m.

STREETS OF FIRE ★★★
DIR: Walter Hill. **CAST:** Diane Lane, Michael Paré, Rick Moranis, Amy Madigan, Willem Dafoe.

Taken on its own terms, this comic book–style movie is a diverting compendium of nonstop action and stylized storytelling set to a rocking backbeat. In it a famous rock singer (Diane Lane) is captured by a motorcycle gang in Walter Hill's mythic world, which combines 1950s attitudes and styles with a futuristic feel. It's up to her two-fisted former boyfriend, Tom Cody (Michael Paré) to save her. Rated R for profanity and violence. 1984; 93m.

STRIKE FORCE ★★
DIR: Barry Shear. **CAST:** Richard Gere, Cliff Gorman, Donald Blakely, Edward Grover, Joe Spinell.

A *French Connection* rehash, this made-for-television movie stars Richard Gere as a cop out to make a big drug bust. Lots of action, not much story. 1975; 74m.

STRIKER'S MOUNTAIN ★★
DIR: Allen Simmonds. **CAST:** Leslie Nielsen, August Schellenberg, Mimi Kuzyk, Bruce Greenwood.

Predictable plot with suspenseless conflicts. A small-time resort owner alternately courts and repels the big corporate backing that Leslie Nielsen, as a ruthless millionaire, controls. The ski scenes are the best part of the film. Unrated. 1987; 99m.

STRIPPED TO KILL ★★★
DIR: Katt Shea Ruben. **CAST:** Kay Lenz, Greg Evigan, Norman Fell.

This generally impressive terror film has nearly an hour of tense excitement but wastes thirty minutes on strip tease acts. Two undercover cops (Kay Lenz and Greg Evigan) investigate the murder of a young stripper. Norman Fell plays the jaded strip joint owner. Rated R for excessive nudity, erotic dancing, and violence. 1987; 83m.

STUDY IN SCARLET, A ★
DIR: Edwin L. Marin. **CAST:** Reginald Owen, Anna May Wong, Alan Dinehart, June Clyde, Alan Mowbray.

Bearing absolutely no resemblance to the first of Arthur Conan Doyle's Sherlock Holmes stories, this low-budget entry is perhaps the most lackluster of all the sound Holmes films. Reginald Owen plays Holmes as a portly gadfly, drawing conclusions that can't possibly be explained through the action (or lack of it) in the film. Slow and creaky, this is of interest *only* as a seldom-seen title. 1933; B&W; 70m.

STUDY IN TERROR, A ★★★★
DIR: James Hill. **CAST:** John Neville, Donald Houston, Georgia Brown, John Fraser, Anthony Quayle, Barbara Windsor, Robert Morley, Cecil Parker.

This superior Sherlock Holmes adventure pits "the original caped crusader," as the ads called him, against Jack the Ripper. John Neville is an excellent Holmes. And Donald Houston is perhaps the screen's finest Dr. John Watson. 1965; 94m.

SUDDEN DEATH 🦃
DIR: Sig Shore. **CAST:** Denise Coward, Frank Runyeon, Jaime Tinelli.

While on her way to meet her fiancé, a woman is kidnapped by two men in a stolen cab, brutally beaten, raped, and left for dead. With the police unable to apprehend the criminals and with her fiancé shunning her, she buys a gun and begins to deal out her own justice. Cheaply made rehash of *Death Wish* and *Ms. .45*. Predictable, exploitative trash. Rated R. 1986; 93m.

SUDDEN IMPACT ★★★★
DIR: Clint Eastwood. **CAST:** Clint Eastwood, Sondra Locke, Pat Hingle, Bradford Dillman.

"Dirty Harry" Callahan (Clint Eastwood) is back, and he's meaner, nastier, and—surprise!—funnier than ever in this, his fourth screen adventure. In the story, a killer (Sondra Locke, in a rare, effective performance) is methodically extracting bloody revenge on the sickos who raped her and a younger sister. It becomes Harry's job to track her down, but not until he's done away with a half-dozen villains and delivered twice as many quips including, "Go ahead, make my day." Rated R for violence and profanity. 1983; 117m.

SUMMER CITY ★★
DIR: Christopher Fraser. **CAST:** Mel Gibson, Phil Avalon, Steve Bisley.

Mel Gibson stars in this Australian teen rebel flick that lacks a fresh approach to one of the oldest stories in film: four wild and crazy teens go on a surfing weekend at a sleepy little seaside community only to find trouble when one of the delinquents messes around with a local's daughter. A few intense moments, and the acting is not bad, but even some of the dialogue is indistinguishable in the muddy audio, and the Aussie dialect only aggravates the problem. Not rated, but the equivalent of PG for some sex, partial nudity, and violence. 1976; 83m.

SUMMERTIME KILLER, THE ★★½
DIR: Antonio Isasi. **CAST:** Chris Mitchum, Karl Malden, Olivia Hussey, Raf Vallone, Claudine Auger, Gerard Tichy.

A 6-year-old boy witnesses the beating and drowning of his father by a gang of hoods. Twenty years pass, and we follow the grown-up son (Christopher Mitchum) as he systematically pursues and kills these men in New York, Rome, and Portugal. While a police detective (Karl Malden) is investigating one of the murders, a Mafia boss hires him to privately track down the killer. There are some exciting motorcycle pursuits along the way before the ending takes a slight twist. Rated R for violence and language. 1972; 100m.

SUNBURN ★
DIR: Richard C. Sarafian. **CAST:** Farrah Fawcett, Charles Grodin, Art Carney, William Daniels, Joan Collins.

Farrah Fawcett-Majors's second feature film is worse than her first (*Somebody Killed Her Husband*). This time she pretends to be the wife of insurance investigator Charles Grodin to get the real scoop on a suicide case in Acapulco. Breathy acting and ham-handed scripting do not help the paper-thin plot. Rated PG. 1979; 94m.

SUNSET ★★★½
DIR: Blake Edwards. **CAST:** James Garner, Bruce Willis, Malcolm McDowell, Mariel Hemingway, Kathleen Quinlan, Jennifer Edwards, Patricia Hodge, M. Emmet Walsh, Joe Dallesandro.

Writer-director Blake Edwards begins this charming little *soufflé* with an intriguing notion: what if legendary lawman Wyatt Earp (James Garner) had met silent-screen cowboy Tom Mix (Bruce Willis) and the two had become fast friends? The boys get involved in a seamy murder case reminiscent of Hollywood's famed William Desmond Taylor scandal. Rated R for language and violence. 1988; 107m.

SUPERCARRIER ★★★
DIR: William A. Graham. **CAST:** Robert Hooks, Paul Gleason, Ken Olandt, Richard Jaeckel.

This is the TV-movie premiere of the short-lived series of the same name.

The action takes Top Gun graduates on a mission aboard a supercarrier. The Russians have a plane in U.S. air space and two pilots are assigned to escort it out. The flight and action scenes are engrossing, but on the ground *Supercarrier* is pretty routine. 1988; 90m.

SUPERFLY ★★★
DIR: Gordon Parks Jr. **CAST:** Ron O'Neal, Carl Lee, Sheila Frazier, Julius W. Harris.

This exciting film follows a Harlem drug dealer's last big sale before he attempts to leave the drug world for a normal life. Rated R. 1972; 96m.

SUPERVIXENS ★★½
DIR: Russ Meyer. **CAST:** Shari Eubank, Charles Napier.

If you've never seen a Russ Meyer movie, this isn't the one to start with. This frenzied, campy tale of sex and violence is meant to be taken in the spirit of a Road Runner cartoon, but the brutality is extremely strong. That aside, the movie features plenty of the usual Meyer Amazons and a suitably sneering performance by Charles Napier as an evil Southwestern sheriff. Unrated, but for adults *only!* 1975; 105m.

SURF NAZIS MUST DIE ★★½
DIR: Peter George. **CAST:** Barry Brenner, Gail Neely, Dawn Wildsmith.

The Surf Nazis are a gang of weirdos who rule the Los Angeles beaches. The action scenes are badly staged and the dialogue is inane. Vile, stupid, and pointless, but there's something about this film...Rated R for violence, language, sex, nudity. 1987; 83m.

SURFACING ★
DIR: Claude Jutra. **CAST:** Joseph Bottoms, Kathleen Beller, R. H. Thompson.

This adventure film is essentially *Deliverance* stirred with pyschological mumbo jumbo and kinky sex. The result is unsavory and illogical. Kathleen Beller and friends search for traces of her father and an ancient Indian civilization in a beautiful but brutal wilderness. You'll root for Mother Nature. Rated R. 1984; 90m.

SURVIVAL GAME ★
DIR: Herb Freed. **CAST:** Mike Norris, Deborah Goodrich, Seymour Cassel, Arlene Golonka.

Mike Norris, Chuck's son, fails to fill his father's boots either as an actor or a fighter in this action tale. He befriends a girl whose father, a famous Sixties drug guru, has just gotten out of prison. His old friends believe that he has hidden $2 million, and they want it. The R rating for mild profanity is not really warranted. 1987; 89m.

SUSPECT ★★★½
DIR: Peter Yates. **CAST:** Cher, Dennis Quaid, Joe Mantegna, Liam Neeson, Philip Bosco, John Mahoney, Fred Melamed.

Cher is just fine as a public defender assigned to prove a deaf and mute street bum (Liam Neeson) innocent of the murder of a Washington, D.C., secretary. One of the jurors, lobbyist Dennis Quaid, takes a liking to Cher and begins helping her with the seemingly impossible case, thus putting her career and their lives in danger. Rated R for violence and profanity. 1987; 128m.

SWASHBUCKLER, THE 🦃
DIR: Jean-Paul Rappeneau. **CAST:** Jean-Paul Belmondo, Marlene Jobert, Laura Antonelli, Michel Auclair, Julien Guiomar.

Stupid story about a naturalized American who gets caught up in the French Revolution while delivering grain and seeking a divorce from his wife. This is not the Robert Shaw movie of the same name, but a French export that has been dubbed in English. Beware! 1984; 100m.

SWEET REVENGE ★★
DIR: Mark Sobel. **CAST:** Nancy Allen, Ted Shackelford, Martin Landau.

Nancy Allen plays a Los Angeles newswoman investigating the disappearance of several young women. She gets her story the hard way when she is kidnapped and taken to a slave market in Southeast Asia. Average action tale is marred by a disappointing ending and the miscasting of Allen, who isn't believable when she switches into Rambo gear. Rated R for violence, nudity, and sexual situations. 1987; 99m.

SWEET SIXTEEN ★½

DIR: Jim Sotos. **CAST:** Aliesa Shirley, Bo Hopkins, Patrick Macnee, Susan Strasberg, Don Stroud.

In this static mystery, which is surprisingly "clean" by today's mad-slasher movie standards, a young woman (Aliesa Shirley) from the big city reluctantly spends her summer—and her sixteenth birthday—in a small Texas town and becomes the chief suspect in a series of murders. Rated R for profanity and partial nudity. 1984; 96m.

SWEET SWEETBACK'S BAADASSSSS SONG ★★★½

DIR: Melvin Van Peebles. **CAST:** Melvin Van Peebles, Rhetta Hughes, Simon Chuckster, John Amos.

Minor cult black film about a man running from racist white police forces. Melvin Van Peebles plays the title character, who will do anything to stay free. Very controversial when released in 1971. Lots of sex and violence gave this an X rating at the time. Probably the best of the black-produced and -directed films of the early 1970s. Rated R. 1971; 97m.

SWORD OF LANCELOT ★★★

DIR: Cornel Wilde. **CAST:** Cornel Wilde, Jean Wallace, Brian Aherne, George Baker.

Colorful production and location photography highlight this pre-*Camelot* version of life at the court of King Arthur and the forbidden love between Lancelot and Queen Guinevere (Mr. and Mrs. Cornel Wilde in real life). Long on pageantry, action, and chivalrous acts of derring-do, this is a "fun" film in the same vein as *Ivanhoe* and *The Vikings*. 1963; 116m.

TAI-PAN ★★

DIR: Daryl Duke. **CAST:** Bryan Brown, John Stanton, Joan Chen, Tim Guinee.

Pretentious, overblown adaptation of James Clavell's bestseller, this disjointed mess plays like a television miniseries chopped from eight hours to two. Bryan Brown is properly stoic as the "Tai-Pan," chief trader, who dreams of establishing a colony of commerce to be named Hong Kong. Joan Chen is ludicrous as his concubine, a woman given to superlatives such as "fantastical-good" and "terrifical-bad." Rated R for brief nudity and violence. 1986; 127m.

TAKING OF PELHAM ONE TWO THREE, THE ★★★★

DIR: Joseph Sargent. **CAST:** Walter Matthau, Robert Shaw, Martin Balsam, Tony Roberts.

Walter Matthau is at his growling, grumbling, gum-chewing best in this edge-of-your-seat movie. He plays the chief detective of security on the New York subway who must deal with the unthinkable: the hijacking of a commuter train by four men (with a fine Robert Shaw as their leader) and a demand by them for a $1 million ransom to prevent their killing the passengers one by one. Rated PG. 1974; 104m.

TAMARIND SEED, THE ★★★

DIR: Blake Edwards. **CAST:** Omar Sharif, Julie Andrews, Anthony Quayle.

A sudsy melodrama in the old tradition, but still a lot of fun. Julie Andrews falls in love with a foreign emissary played by Omar Sharif, only to be told (by her own State Department) to stay away from him. The cold war intrigue seems pretty absurd these days, but Andrews and Sharif generate a playful chemistry that overlooks many sins. Rated PG. 1974; 123m.

TANK ★★½

DIR: Marvin J. Chomsky. **CAST:** James Garner, Shirley Jones, C. Thomas Howell, G. D. Spradlin.

The always likeable James Garner plays Sgt. Maj. Zack Carey, an army career soldier who has to use his privately owned Sherman tank to rescue his family (Shirley Jones and C. Thomas Howell) from the clutches of a mean country sheriff (G. D. Spradlin). It's all a bunch of hokum, but a sure audience pleaser. Rated PG. 1984; 113m.

TARAS BULBA ★★★

DIR: J. Lee Thompson. **CAST:** Tony Curtis, Yul Brynner.

Tony Curtis and Yul Brynner give top-notch performances in this action-packed adventure centering on Cossack life during the sixteenth century in the Ukraine. Great location photography in Argentina by Joe MacDonald, and a fine musical score by Franz Waxman. Solid entertainment. 1962; 122m.

TARGET ★★★

DIR: Arthur Penn. **CAST:** Gene Hackman, Matt Dillon, Gayle Hunnicutt, Josef Sommer, Victoria Fyodora, Herbert Berghof.

In this fast-paced, entertaining suspense-thriller directed by Arthur Penn (*Bonnie and Clyde*), a father (Gene Hackman) and son (Matt Dillon) put aside their differences when they become the targets of an international spy ring. *Target* is a tad predictable, but it is the kind of predictability that adds to the viewer's enjoyment rather than detracting from it. Rated R for violence, profanity, and nudity. 1985; 117m.

TARGET EAGLE

DIR: J. Anthony Loma. **CAST:** Jorge Rivero, Maud Adams, George Peppard, Max von Sydow, Chuck Connors.

Dreadful action film. Jorge Rivero plays a mercenary who is hired by a Spanish police department to infiltrate a drug-smuggling ring. Max von Sydow and George Peppard are believable as the chief of police and drug-ring leader, respectively, but the rest of the performances are incredibly poor. Not rated, has violence. 1982; 101m.

TARZAN AND THE GREEN GODDESS ★★

DIR: Edward Kull. **CAST:** Bruce Bennett, Ula Holt, Frank Baker.

Olympic champion Herman Brix (a.k.a. Bruce Bennett) makes one of the best-looking of all movie Tarzans as he journeys to South America with an expedition to help secure a priceless stone image with destructive powers known as the "Green Goddess." Edited down from the serial *New Adventures of Tarzan* (released in 1935), this disjointed film and its companion, *Tarzan's New Adventures*, did all right at the box office despite competition from MGM's Johnny Weissmuller films. However, primitive filming conditions and a horrible soundtrack severely hinder the jungle nonsense. 1938; B&W; 72m.

TARZAN AND THE TRAPPERS ★½

DIR: H. Bruce Humberstone. **CAST:** Gordon Scott, Evelyn Brent, Rickie Sorenson, Maurice Marsac.

This oddity is actually three television pilots that producer Sol Lesser was unable to sell to networks back in 1958. The trappers of the title are poachers that Tarzan deals with during the first episode. This is pretty ordinary, uninspired stuff, but it's a one-of-a-kind Tarzan film, unavailable for years. 1958; B&W; 74m.

TARZAN OF THE APES ★★★½

DIR: Scott Sidney. **CAST:** Elmo Lincoln, Enid Markey, George French.

The first filmed version of Edgar Rice Burroughs's classic tells the story of Lord and Lady Greystoke, their shipwreck and abandonment on the African coast, and the fate of their boy child, John. Raised by Kala the she-ape, infant John becomes Tarzan of the Apes. Barrel-chested Elmo Lincoln portrayed Tarzan as an adult and actually killed the lion he fights in one of the film's more exciting moments. Enhanced with a synchronized musical score, this silent extravaganza is well worth the watch. Silent. 1918; B&W; 130m.

TARZAN THE APE MAN (1932) ★★★½

DIR: W. S. Van Dyke. **CAST:** Johnny Weissmuller, Maureen O'Sullivan, Neil Hamilton.

Tarzan the Ape Man is the film that made Johnny Weissmuller a star and Tarzan an idiot. That classic "Me Tarzan, you Jane" blasphemy is here in its original splendor. Maureen O'Sullivan seduces the dumb beast, and it's all great fun. Hollywood at its peak...but no relation to Edgar Rice Burroughs's hero. 1932; B&W; 99m.

TARZAN THE APE MAN (1981)

DIR: John Derek. **CAST:** Bo Derek, Richard Harris, Miles O'Keeffe, John Phillip Law.

One suggestion for anyone planning to watch this movie: grab a book. That way, you'll have something interesting to do while it's on the screen. Even counting the lowest of the low-budget Tarzan flicks, this one is the absolute worst. Rated R for profanity, sex, and nudity. 1981; 112m.

TARZAN THE FEARLESS ★

DIR: Robert Hill. **CAST:** Buster Crabbe, Jacqueline Wells, E. Alyn Warren, Edward Woods.

Buster Crabbe stars as the Lord of the Jungle in this low, low-budget feature. Johnny Weissmuller he ain't. Crabbe fared much better in the now campy "Flash Gordon" and "Buck Rogers" serials. Leave this one on the vine. 1933; B&W; 85m.

TARZAN THE MIGHTY ★★½

DIR: Jack Nelson. **CAST:** Frank Merrill, Natalie Kingston, Al Ferguson.

Tarzan number five Frank Merrill once earned the title of "World's Most Perfect Man" and his jungle heroics made this Universal serial the hit of 1928. It was expanded from twelve to fifteen episodes by astute executives who correctly gauged a receptive audience. Merrill was the most athletic of all previous screen Tarzans and pioneered many of the stunts associated with the series, especially the vine swinging and aerial acrobatics. Silent. 1928; B&W; 15 chapters.

TARZAN THE TIGER ★★

DIR: Henry McRae. **CAST:** Frank Merrill, Natalie Kingston, Lillian Worth, Al Ferguson.

Based loosely on Edgar Rice Burroughs's *Tarzan and the Jewels of Opar*, this serial was shot as a silent but released with sychronized musical score and sound effects. Frank Merrill as Tarzan inaugurated the popular vine-swing used by later ape-men and was the first to give his rendition of the famous cry of the bull ape—sans mixer and dubbers. This sequel to *Tarzan the Mighty* was long considered a lost film. 1929; B&W; 15 chapters.

TARZAN'S REVENGE ★

DIR: D. Ross Lederman. **CAST:** Glenn Morris, Eleanor Holm, George Barbier, C. Henry Gordon, Hedda Hopper, George Meeker.

Back-lot nonsense with Olympic champions Glenn Morris as the Lord of the Jungle and Eleanor Holm as his Jane gives the hammy supporting actors plenty of opportunity to chew on the scenery. The 1930s saw four screen Tarzans, but Sol Lesser's choice of Morris as the fourth was less than inspired. 1938; B&W; 70m.

TELEFON ★★★

DIR: Don Siegel. **CAST:** Charles Bronson, Lee Remick, Donald Pleasence, John Mitchum, Patrick Magee.

In this good suspense film, Charles Bronson is a KGB agent who, with the help of the CIA's Lee Remick, is out to stop some preprogrammed Soviet spies from blowing up the United States. Rated PG. 1977; 102m.

TEN LITTLE INDIANS

DIR: Peter Collinson. **CAST:** Oliver Reed, Richard Attenborough, Elke Sommer, Herbert Lom, Gert Fröbe.

Absolutely dismal third version of the Agatha Christie classic. This one completely mucks up the plot, switching from an isolated island mansion to a hotel deep in the Iranian desert(!). The entire cast overacts abysmally, and the script must have been written with a purple pen. The plot concerns an unseen killer who sequentially knocks off the visitors. Avoid at all costs and stick with the original, 1945's *And Then There Were None.* Rated PG—mild violence. 1975; 98m.

TEN TO MIDNIGHT ★

DIR: J. Lee Thompson. **CAST:** Charles Bronson, Andrew Stevens, Lisa Eilbacher, Cosie Costa.

They might as well have titled this one *Charles Bronson Meets the Slasher.* Old "Death Wish" himself goes up against a *Friday the 13th*–type killer in this disappointing action film. It's all rather disgusting, and Bronson looks bored. Rated R for sex, nudity, profanity, and violence. 1983; 101m.

10 VIOLENT WOMEN ★

DIR: Ted V. Mikels. **CAST:** Sherri Vernon, Dixie Lauren, Georgia Morgan.

There are fewer thrills than violent women in this low-budget action film; for that matter, there only seem to be seven or eight violent women. Female coal miners land in jail after a jewel robbery and a cocaine deal go bad. Director Ted Mikels has a juicy cameo as a fence who comes to a bad end: death by spiked heel! Rated R for violence and a little nudity. 1982; 95m.

TENNESSEE STALLION ★★★

DIR: Don Hulette. **CAST:** Audrey Landers, Judy Landers, James Van Patten.

Interesting background, beautiful photography, and more than competent acting save this otherwise ordinary action-adventure film set in the world of the Tennessee walking horse show circuit. Jimmy Van Patten is excellent as a man from the wrong circles of society who makes it to the big time with his outstanding horse and the help of the woman who loves him. 1978; 87m.

TEQUILA SUNRISE ★★★★½

DIR: Robert Towne. **CAST:** Mel Gibson, Kurt Russell, Michelle Pfeiffer, Raul Julia.

In his second film as a director, legendary screenwriter Robert Towne *(Chinatown, The Last Detail)* takes an oft-used plot and makes it new. Mel Gibson and Kurt Russell play two childhood friends who end up on opposite sides of the law. Michelle Pfeiffer is the beautiful object of their affections. Because Towne makes his characters seem real and the situations believably low-key, *Tequila Sunrise* emerges as a fascinating and often surprising movie. Rated R for profanity, violence, suggested sex, and drug use. 1988; 116m.

TERMINAL ISLAND

DIR: Stephanie Rothman. **CAST:** Phyllis Davis, Tom Selleck, Don Marshall, Marta Kristen.

Don't be fooled by the fact that Tom Selleck's name has been moved up in the credits. He has very little to do in this trite piece of exploitation, made very early in his career. No matter. It's an awful movie, anyway, one of those would-be titillating flicks about two groups of male prisoners fighting over the favors of the only females on an island penal colony. Rated R. 1977; 88m.

TERROR BY NIGHT ★★★

DIR: Roy William Neill. **CAST:** Basil Rathbone, Nigel Bruce, Alan Mowbray, Renee Godfrey, Billy Bevan, Dennis Hoey.

Penultimate entry in the Rathbone/Bruce Sherlock Holmes series, with the master sleuth and his loyal companion up against a series of murders on a train bound from London to Edinburgh. The culprit ultimately turns out to be Col. Sebastian Moran, but you'll have to watch the film to discover which of the passengers he impersonates! 1946; B&W; 69m.

TERROR SQUAD ★★★
DIR: Peter Maris. **CAST:** Chuck Connors, Kerry Brennan.

Better-than-average action movie about small-town Indiana police chief Chuck Connors battling Libyan terrorists who are after a nearby nuclear plant. This offers some thrills and style despite the obvious low budget. Unrated. 1987; 92m.

TERRORISTS, THE ★★★★
DIR: Caspar Wrede. **CAST:** Sean Connery, Ian McShane, James Maxwell, Isabel Dean, Jeffrey Wickham, John Quentin, Robert Harris.

Solid suspense thriller has Sean Connery as the bullheaded commander of Norway's national security force, which is galvanized into action when a group of English terrorists takes over the British embassy. Rated PG for violence. 1975; 100m.

THARUS, SON OF ATTILA
DIR: Roberto Montero. **CAST:** Jerome Courtland, Lisa Gastoni, Rik Von Nutter.

A tacky historical drama so disjointed and so badly produced that any semblance of a story is lost in poorly staged battles and stupid (and badly dubbed) dialogue. Not rated. 1987; 89m.

THEY CALL ME MISTER TIBBS ★★★
DIR: Gordon Douglas. **CAST:** Sidney Poitier, Barbara McNair, Martin Landau.

An inferior follow-up, this contains the further adventures of the character Sidney Poitier created for the film *In the Heat of the Night*. Detective Virgil Tibbs is again investigating a murder and trying to clear his friend, as well. Rated PG—contains strong language and some violence. 1970; 108m.

THEY DRIVE BY NIGHT ★★★★
DIR: Raoul Walsh. **CAST:** George Raft, Humphrey Bogart, Ann Sheridan, Ida Lupino.

Here's a Warner Bros. gem! George Raft and Humphrey Bogart star as truck-driving brothers who cope with crooked bosses while wooing Ann Sheridan and Ida Lupino. The dialogue is terrific, and the direction by Raoul Walsh is crisp. 1940; B&W; 93m.

THEY WERE EXPENDABLE ★★★★½
DIR: John Ford. **CAST:** John Wayne, Robert Montgomery, Donna Reed, Jack Holt, Ward Bond, Marshall Thompson, Louis Jean Heydt.

First-rate action drama about American PT boat crews fighting a losing battle against advancing Japanese forces in the Philippines. Director John Ford based this film, his most personal, on his war experiences and the people he knew in the conflict. No phony heroics or glory here, but a realistic, bleak, and ultimately inspiring picture of men in war. 1945; B&W; 136m.

THIEF ★★★★
DIR: Michael Mann. **CAST:** James Caan, Tuesday Weld, James Belushi, Willie Nelson.

James Caan stars in this superb study of a jewel thief. Caan's character tries desperately to create the life he visualized while in prison—one complete with a car, money, house, wife, and kids. But as soon as he manages to acquire these things, they start slipping away. It's an interesting plot, and Michael Mann's direction gives it a sense of realism. Visually stunning, with a great score by Tangerine Dream. Rated R for violence, language, and brief nudity. 1981; 122m.

THIN MAN, THE ★★★★½
DIR: W. S. Van Dyke. **CAST:** William Powell, Myrna Loy, Edward Brophy, Porter Hall, Maureen O'Sullivan.

Viewers and critics alike were captivated by William Powell and Myrna Loy in this first (and best) of a series based on Dashiell Hammett's mystery novel about his "other" detective and wife, Nick and Nora Charles. The thin man is a murder victim. But never mind. The delight of this fun film is the banter between its stars. You'll like their little dog, too. 1934; B&W; 89m.

THIN MAN GOES HOME, THE ★★½

DIR: Richard Thorpe. **CAST:** William Powell, Myrna Loy, Lucile Watson, Gloria De Haven, Anne Revere, Helen Vinson, Harry Davenport, Leon Ames, Donald Meek, Edward Brophy.

Fifth and weakest entry in the series. Nick Charles (William Powell) returns to his old hometown, accompanied by Nora (Myrna Loy) and young Nick Jr. The mystery this time around just doesn't have the same spark, and the witty dialogue sounds a bit wilted. Still entertaining, but a lesser effort. 1944; B&W; 101m.

13 RUE MADELEINE ★★★

DIR: Henry Hathaway. **CAST:** James Cagney, Annabella, Walter Abel, Frank Latimore, Melville Cooper, E. G. Marshall, Karl Malden, Sam Jaffe, Richard Conte.

Espionage thriller, inspired by *March of Time* series, shot in semidocumentary style. James Cagney is OSS chief who goes to France to complete a mission when one of his men is killed. 1946; B&W; 95m.

THIRTY-NINE STEPS, THE (1978) ★★★½

DIR: Don Sharp. **CAST:** Robert Powell, David Warner, Eric Porter, Karen Dotrice, John Mills.

An innocent man stumbles on to a spy plot in pre-WWI London. Hunted by enemy agents who think he has intercepted an important communiqué, and civil authorities who believe he is a murderer, the man has nowhere to turn. The best of several Hitchcock remakes in the 1970s. It can't compete with the original, of course, but the cast is good. The script is witty, and the climax atop Big Ben is exciting. Rated PG. 1978; 102m.

THIRTY SECONDS OVER TOKYO ★★★★

DIR: Mervyn LeRoy. **CAST:** Spencer Tracy, Van Johnson, Robert Walker, Phyllis Thaxter, Scott McKay, Robert Mitchum, Stephen McNally.

Spencer Tracy is in top form as General Doolittle, who led the first bombing attack on Tokyo during World War II. Robert Mitchum and Van Johnson give effective supporting performances as air crew chiefs. We follow Doolittle and his men as they train for the big mission, bomb Tokyo, and make their way home on foot through China. A true-life adventure that, despite its length, never bogs down. 1944; B&W; 138m.

THIS GUN FOR HIRE ★★★★

DIR: Frank Tuttle. **CAST:** Alan Ladd, Robert Preston, Veronica Lake.

Alan Ladd made his first big impression in this 1942 gangster film as a bad guy who turns good guy in the end. Robert Preston and Veronica Lake co-star in this still enjoyable revenge film. 1942; B&W; 80m.

THOMAS CROWN AFFAIR, THE ★★★★

DIR: Norman Jewison. **CAST:** Steve McQueen, Faye Dunaway, Paul Burke.

Combine an engrossing bank-heist caper with an offbeat romance and you have the ingredients for a fun-filled movie. Steve McQueen and Faye Dunaway are at their best as the sophisticated bank robber and unscrupulous insurance investigator who happens to be tracking him. The emotional tricks and verbal sparring between these two are a joy. This is one of the few films where the split-screen technique really moves the story along. 1968; 102m.

THRASHIN'

DIR: David Winters. **CAST:** Josh Brolin, Robert Rusler, Chuck McCann.

Hotshot skateboarder Josh Brolin comes to L.A. for a competition and gets on the bad side of a gang of street skaters. The usual teen fodder, not rendered any livelier by the nonstop skateboarding stunts. Rated PG-13 for sexual situations. 1986; 92m.

THREE DAYS OF THE CONDOR ★★★★

DIR: Sydney Pollack. **CAST:** Robert Redford, Cliff Robertson, Max von Sydow, Faye Dunaway, John Houseman.

Robert Redford is a CIA information researcher who is forced to flee for his life when his New York cover operation is blown and all of his co-workers brutally murdered. What seems at first to be a standard man-on-the-run drama gradually deepens into an engrossing mystery as to who is chasing him and why. Faye Dunaway expertly handles a vignette as the stranger Redford uses to avoid capture. Rated R. 1975; 117m.

THREE KINDS OF HEAT

DIR: Leslie Stevens. **CAST:** Robert Ginty, Victoria Barrett, Shakti, Sylvester McCoy, Barry Foster.

Low-budget spy adventure cheapie. Robert Ginty is the mush-mouthed, simpering Interpol agent who attempts to break up some sort of nefarious criminal organization. Rated R for language, but take out a few bad words and this movie could play on Saturday-morning TV. 1987; 87m.

THREE MUSKETEERS, THE (1933) ★★

DIR: Armand Schaefer, Colbert Clark. **CAST:** John Wayne, Ruth Hall, Jack Mulhall, Raymond Hatton, Francis X. Bushman Jr., Noah Beery Jr., Creighton Chaney (Lon Chaney Jr.).

The weakest and least-seen of John Wayne's three serials for Mascot Studios. This desert-bound story presents four friends who fight against a harsh environment and the evil Devil of the Desert. Standard Foreign Legion stuff. 1933; B&W; 12 chapters.

THREE MUSKETEERS, THE (1948) ★★

DIR: George Sidney. **CAST:** Gene Kelly, Lana Turner, June Allyson, Van Heflin, Vincent Price, Gig Young, Angela Lansbury, Keenan Wynn.

MGM's all-star version of the classic swashbuckler by Alexandre Dumas gets its swords crossed up. This is primarily due to some blatant miscasting. Gene Kelly as D'Artagnan and his co-star June Allyson playing the queen's seamstress are never convincing as French citizens during the reign of Louis XIII. Fans of Lana Turner may find the movie worthwhile, because hidden in this fluff is one of her finest performances as the villainous Lady DeWinter. 1948; B&W; 128m.

THREE MUSKETEERS, THE (1973) ★★★★★

DIR: Richard Lester. **CAST:** Michael York, Oliver Reed, Raquel Welch, Richard Chamberlain, Faye Dunaway, Charlton Heston.

Alexandre Dumas's oft-filmed swashbuckler classic—there may have been as many as ten previous versions—finally came to full life with this 1973 release. It is a superb adventure romp with scrumptious moments of comedy, character, and action. Throughout, director Richard Lester injects throwaway bits of slapstick and wordplay—you have to pay careful attention to catch them, and it's well worth it. Rated PG. 1973; 105m.

THREE THE HARD WAY ★★★

DIR: Gordon Parks Jr. **CAST:** Fred Williamson, Jim Brown, Jim Kelly, Sheila Frazier, Jay Robinson.

A white supremacist (Jay Robinson) attempts to wipe out the black race by putting a deadly serum in the country's water supply. Fred Williamson, Jim Brown and Jim Kelly team up to stop him in this action-packed movie. Rated PG for violence. 1974; 93m.

THROUGH NAKED EYES ★★★

DIR: John Llewellyn Moxey. **CAST:** David Soul, Pam Dawber, Rod McCary.

A pretty good made-for-TV mystery thriller with voyeurism in high-rise apartments as the pivotal plot line.

David Soul is watching Pam Dawber across the way, but she's also been watching him. When a series of murders occurs in their buildings, it appears some one else is watching, too. Unrated. 1983; 91m.

THUNDER AND LIGHTNING ★★
DIR: Corey Allen. **CAST:** David Carradine, Kate Jackson, Roger C. Carmel, Sterling Holloway.

Weak "action film" about moonshiners and their misadventures. Stars David Carradine and Kate Jackson are watchable enough, but a few touches of originality wouldn't have hurt. Rated PG for profanity and violence. 1977; 95m.

THUNDER BAY ★★★½
DIR: Anthony Mann. **CAST:** James Stewart, Dan Duryea, Joanne Dru, Jay C. Flippen, Gilbert Roland.

James Stewart plays an oil driller forced to take on a nasty group of Louisiana shrimp fishermen. The story is full of action and fine characterizations from a talented cast. 1953; 102m.

THUNDER ROAD ★★★★
DIR: Arthur Ripley. **CAST:** Robert Mitchum, Gene Barry, Keely Smith, Jim Mitchum.

Robert Mitchum wrote the original story and hit theme song for this fast-paced, colorful tale of a bootlegger (Mitchum) who attempts to outwit revenuer Gene Barry. It's one of Mitchum's few all-around, big-screen successes and a tribute to his talents in front of and behind the camera. The star's son, Jim Mitchum, made his film debut as Robert's younger brother. 1958; B&W; 92m.

THUNDER RUN
DIR: Gary Hudson. **CAST:** Forrest Tucker, John Ireland, John Shepherd, Jill Whitlow, Cheryl M. Lynn.

Forrest Tucker stars in this grade Z action flick as a truck driver who is persuaded by an old army pal (John Ireland) to act as bait in a scheme to catch terrorists. He is to haul plutonium so they can be caught trying to steal it. Therefore, this movie is a bomb in more ways than one. Rated R for nudity, profanity, suggested sex, and violence. 1986; 89m.

THUNDER WARRIOR
DIR: Larry Ludman. **CAST:** Mark Gregory, Bo Svenson.

In this shameless ripoff of the action scenes in *First Blood*, a tough Indian goes on a one-man rampage in protest against a treaty-breaking white man. Rated R for profanity, violence, and nudity. 1983; 84m.

THUNDER WARRIOR II
DIR: Larry Ludman. **CAST:** Mark Gregory, Bo Svenson.

Sleazy, Italian-made action flick that's a real yawner from beginning to end. A young Indian returns to his native reservation to find a constuction crew building on a sacred tribal burial ground. When he finds that all legal avenues are blocked, he goes on the warpath. Cheapo dubbing and mindless plot labels this as a real hatchet job. Rated R. 1985; 84m.

THUNDERBALL ★★★
DIR: Terence Young. **CAST:** Sean Connery, Claudine Auger, Adolfo Celi.

When originally released in 1965, this fourth entry in the James Bond series suffered from comparison to its two admittedly superior predecessors, *From Russia with Love* and *Goldfinger*. However, time has proved it to be one of the more watchable movies based on the books by Ian Fleming, with Sean Connery in top form as 007 and assured direction by Terence Young. 1965; 129m.

THUNDERBOLT AND LIGHTFOOT ★★★★
DIR: Michael Cimino. **CAST:** Clint Eastwood, Jeff Bridges, George Kennedy, Geoffrey Lewis, Gary Busey.

Clint Eastwood's right-on-target performance is equaled by those of co-stars Jeff Bridges, George Kennedy, and Geoffrey Lewis in this decidedly offbeat caper picture. The stoic top-lined actor plays an ex-con who hooks up with petty thief Bridges to hunt down the hidden spoils of a heist committed several years before. The only problem is that his ex-partners in the crime, Kennedy and Lewis, have the same idea, but no intention of sharing the loot. *Thunderbolt and Lightfoot* is a little-known action gem that proved a little too offbeat for Clint's fans when originally released in 1974. However, movie buffs have since proclaimed it a cinematic gem, a reputation it deserves. Rated R. 1974; 114m.

TIME TO DIE, A ★★

DIR: Matt Cimber. **CAST:** Rex Harrison, Rod Taylor, Edward Albert, Raf Vallone.

Despite the name actors and source material by Mario Puzo, this vengeance flick has a story as dog-eared as they come. An American spy returns to Europe after World War II to hunt the Nazis who killed his French wife and friends. He also plays cat and mouse with U.S. Intelligence. The twists unravel too easily to make for a thrilling affair. Rated R for nudity and violence. 1983; 89m.

TIMERIDER

DIR: William Dear. **CAST:** Fred Ward, Belinda Bauer, Peter Coyote, L. Q. Jones, Ed Lauter.

There are the films that just sort of sit there, never achieving anything. This is one of those films. A motorcycle rider and his motorcycle break the time barrier and end up being chased by cowboys in the Old West. It sounds far more interesting than it is. If you're having difficulty sleeping, this is the cure. Rated PG. 1983; 94m.

TNT JACKSON ★

DIR: Cirio H. Santiago. **CAST:** Jeanne Bell, Stan Shaw, Pat Anderson.

Jeanne Bell stars as a sexy kung-fu expert who comes to Hong Kong to exact revenge on her brother's killer. She gets involved with heroin dealers and must fight her way out of their clutches. This kung-fu/blaxploitation flick will appeal to only a few select viewers. Rated R for nudity, profanity, and violence. 1975; 73m.

TO HAVE AND HAVE NOT ★★★★½

DIR: Howard Hawks. **CAST:** Humphrey Bogart, Lauren Bacall, Walter Brennan.

Director Howard Hawks once bet Ernest Hemingway he could make a good film from one of the author's worst books. Needless to say, he won the bet with this exquisite entertainment, which teamed Humphrey Bogart and Lauren Bacall for the first time. The story takes place before the events of the book and concerns the decision of an apathetic soldier of fortune (Bogart) to fight the Nazis. 1944; B&W; 100m.

TO HELL AND BACK ★★½

DIR: Jesse Hibbs. **CAST:** Audie Murphy, Marshall Thompson, Charles Drake, Gregg Palmer, Jack Kelly, Paul Picerni, Susan Kohner, David Janssen.

Real-life war hero Audie Murphy plays himself in this sprawling World War II action film. We follow Audie Murphy and his buddies (Marshall Thompson, Jack Kelly, and David Janssen) from North Africa to Berlin. Murphy received twenty-four medals, including the Congressional Medal of Honor, which made him the most decorated soldier in World War II. Good performances and true-life drama make up for a static script and rather routine battle sequences. 1955; 106m.

TO LIVE AND DIE IN L.A.

DIR: William Friedkin. **CAST:** William L. Petersen, Willem Dafoe, John Pankow, Dean Stockwell, Debra Feuer, John Turturro, Darlanne Fluegel.

This vile and violent exercise in bloody self-indulgence is one of the bleakest cinema statements mankind ever produced. There is no way to distinguish bad from good; every character is equally insensitive, manipulative, and emotionally bankrupt in this overly violent account of lone wolf William L. Petersen's attempt to shut down counterfeiter Willem Dafoe. Rated R for sex, nudity, and excessive violence. 1985; 114m.

TOBRUK ★★★
DIR: Arthur Hiller. **CAST:** Rock Hudson, George Peppard, Guy Stockwell, Nigel Green.

Rock Hudson, Nigel Green, and George Peppard lead a ragtag group of British soldiers and homeless Jews against the Nazi and Italian armies in the North African desert during World War II. To do so, they must sneak through Axis lines disguised as German soldiers escorting Allied prisoners through the desert. An exciting climax, beautiful photography, and good performances help offset a farfetched script. 1966; 110m.

TOMBOY ★
DIR: Herb Freed. **CAST:** Betsy Russell, Kristi Somers, Jerry Dinome.

Mindless nonsense (with plenty of skin) about a female race car driver named Tommy (Betsy Russell) who takes on the man of her dreams (Jerry Dinome) on and off the track. Rated R. 1985; 91m.

TOO LATE THE HERO ★★★½
DIR: Robert Aldrich. **CAST:** Michael Caine, Cliff Robertson, Henry Fonda.

Great World War II action drama about two reluctant soldiers who are sent on a suicide mission to an island in the Pacific Ocean. Shown on network TV as *Suicide Run*. Rated PG. 1970; 133m.

TOP GUN ★★★½
DIR: Tony Scott. **CAST:** Tom Cruise, Kelly McGillis, Val Kilmer, Anthony Edwards, Tom Skerritt, Michael Ironside, John Stockwell, Rick Rossovich, Barry Tubb, Whip Hubley.

Tom Cruise stars as a student at the navy's Fighter Weapons School, where fliers are turned into crack fighter pilots. While competing for the title of Top Gun there, he falls in love with an instructor (Kelly McGillis of *Witness*). Rated PG for light profanity, suggested sex, and violence. 1986; 110m.

TOPKAPI ★★★★★
DIR: Jules Dassin. **CAST:** Peter Ustinov, Melina Mercouri, Maximilian Schell.

This is one of the finest and funniest of the "big heist" genre. Director Jules Dassin assembled a highly talented international cast. They are members of a charming group of jewel thieves whose target is a priceless jeweled dagger in a Turkish museum. The execution of their clever plan is both humorous and exciting. 1964; 120m.

TORA! TORA! TORA! ★★★★
DIR: Richard Fleischer, Toshio Masuda, Kinji Fakasaku. **CAST:** Jason Robards Jr., Martin Balsam, James Whitmore, Joseph Cotten.

An American-Japanese cooperative venture reenacts the events up to and including the December 7 attack on Pearl Harbor. Although many well-known actors contribute their skills, they are overshadowed by the technical brilliance of the realistic re-creation of the climactic attack. Rated G. 1970; 143m.

TOUGH ENOUGH ★★½
DIR: Richard Fleischer. **CAST:** Dennis Quaid, Warren Oates, Stan Shaw, Pam Grier, Wilford Brimley.

Dennis Quaid plays the "Country-and-Western Warrior," a singer-fighter who slugs his way through taxing "Toughman" contests from Fort Worth to Detroit in a quest for fame and fortune. It's *Rocky* meets *Honeysuckle Rose*, yet still mildly enjoyable. Rated PG for profanity and violence. 1983; 106m.

TOUGHER THAN LEATHER ★
DIR: Rick Rubin. **CAST:** Run DMC, The Beastie Boys.

Popular rap group Run-DMC stars in this below-par, low-budget quickie about murder and revenge in the music industry. Rated R for violence, profanity, and nudity. 1988; 92m.

TOUR OF DUTY ★★★
DIR: Bill L. Norton. **CAST:** Terence Knox, Stephen Caffrey, Joshua Maurer, Kevin Conroy.
Pilot for the TV series of the same name, *Tour of Duty* is like a 90-minute course in Vietnam War history with prime-time cleanliness. And while the cleanliness hinders the film's credibility, the action scenes make it worth watching. Not rated, has violence. 1987; 93m.

TOWERING INFERNO, THE ★★★★
DIR: John Guillermin, Irwin Allen. **CAST:** Steve McQueen, Paul Newman, William Holden, Faye Dunaway, Fred Astaire, Richard Chamberlain.
This is the undisputed king of the disaster movies of the 1970s. An all-star cast came together for this big-budget thriller about a newly constructed San Francisco high-rise hotel and office building that is set ablaze due to substandard materials. Rated PG. 1974; 165m.

TOWN CALLED HELL, A
DIR: Robert Parrish. **CAST:** Robert Shaw, Telly Savalas, Stella Stevens.
This confusing action yarn about a manhunt for a Mexican revolutionary features an impressive cast in a full-scale stinker. Short on thrills and long on snores. Rated R. 1971; 95m.

TOY SOLDIERS ★
DIR: David Fisher. **CAST:** Jason Miller, Cleavon Little, Rodolfo DeAnda.
This is an inept and poorly acted film about a group of vacationing college students in Latin America. As the unconvincing story unfolds, we find our young heroes attempting to rescue a captured friend. Rated R. 1983; 85m.

TRAIN, THE ★★★★
DIR: John Frankenheimer. **CAST:** Burt Lancaster, Paul Scofield, Michel Simon, Jeanne Moreau.
A suspenseful World War II adventure about the French Resistance's attempt to stop a train loaded with fine art, seized from French museums, from reaching its destination in Nazi Germany. Burt Lancaster is fine as the head of the French railway system, but he is far outclassed by the performance of Paul Scofield as the unrelenting German commander. 1965; B&W; 113m.

TRAXX ★★★
DIR: Jerome Gray. **CAST:** Shadoe Stevens, Priscilla Barnes, Robert Davi, John Hancock.
Wacky, often funny tale about a mercenary turned cookie maker who cleans the criminal element out of Hadleyville, Texas. Shadoe Stevens is Traxx, a man who derives simple pleasure from shooting people, causing mayhem—and baking the oddest-flavored cookies he can imagine. Rated R for cartoon violence and slight nudity. 1988; 85m.

TREASURE OF THE AMAZON ★
DIR: Rene Cardona Jr. **CAST:** Stuart Whitman, Bradford Dillman, Donald Pleasence, John Ireland.
Mexican-made action flick about a group of adventurers fighting the elements and each other as they sail the Amazon in search of a fortune in diamonds. Completely unmemorable. Unrated, the film contains some violence. 1983; 105m.

TREASURE OF THE FOUR CROWNS
DIR: Ferdinando Baldi. **CAST:** Tony Anthony, Ana Obregon, Gene Quintano.
In this ripoff of *Raiders of the Lost Ark* by the folks who created the dreadful *Comin' at Ya*, a group of adventurers attempt to steal invaluable Visigoth treasures from a crazed cult leader. The story is boring. The acting is pitiful. Rated PG for violence and gore. 1983; 97m.

TREASURE OF THE SIERRA MADRE, THE ★★★★★
DIR: John Huston. **CAST:** Humphrey Bogart, Tim Holt, Walter Huston, Bruce Bennett.
Humphrey Bogart gives a brilliant performance in this study of greed.

The setting is rugged mountains in Mexico where Bogart, with Tim Holt and a grizzled prospector, played marvelously by Walter Huston, set out to make a fortune in gold prospecting. They do, with their troubles getting worse. Seamless script and magnificent performances add up to a classic. 1948; B&W; 126m.

TREASURE OF THE YANKEE ZEPHYR ★★½

DIR: David Hemmings. **CAST:** Ken Wahl, Lesley Ann Warren, Donald Pleasence, George Peppard, Bruno Lawrence.

When an old animal trapper (Donald Pleasence) discovers a sunken treasure of military medals and liquor, he enlists the aid of his partner (Ken Wahl) and his daughter (Lesley Ann Warren) to bring in the haul. A ruthless claim jumper (George Peppard) and his henchmen follow in hopes of getting the shipment of gold that Pleasence is unaware of. Rated PG for violence. 1981; 97m.

TRIUMPH OF SHERLOCK HOLMES, THE ★★★½

DIR: Leslie S. Hiscott. **CAST:** Arthur Wontner, Ian Fleming, Lyn Harding, Leslie Perrins.

A candle is the clue that unlocks the secret of a murder in this superior Sherlock Holmes film featuring Arthur Wontner and Ian Fleming as the infallible consulting detective and his friend and assistant Dr. John Watson. Made by an independent production company on a limited budget, this rendering of Conan Doyle's "Valley of Fear" retains much of the story's original dialogue. 1935; B&W; 75m.

TROMA'S WAR ★★½

DIR: Michael Herz, Samuel Weil. **CAST:** Carolyn Beauchamp, Sean Bower.

A slam-bang shoot-em-up about a group of air-crash survivors stranded on a deserted island. This rag-tag bunch soon find themselves fighting terrorists bent on taking over the United States by infecting all levels of society with the AIDS virus. Made by the people responsible for *The Toxic Avenger*, this frequently tasteless flick combines violent action with totally deadpan comedy. Unrated. 1988; 105m.

TRUCKSTOP WOMEN ★

DIR: Mark L. Lester. **CAST:** Claudia Jennings, Lieux Dressler, John Martino.

No-good Claudia Jennings teams up with mafia hitman John Martino to take over a truck-stop prostitution racket run by her mother. Joyless drive-in fodder, with plot secondary to shootouts and undressed women. Rated R. 1974; 82m.

TRY AND GET ME ★★★½

DIR: Cy Endfield. **CAST:** Frank Lovejoy, Lloyd Bridges, Kathleen Ryan, Richard Carlson.

A desperate, unemployed husband and father (Frank Lovejoy) teams up with a ruthless thief and murderer (Lloyd Bridges) but can't live with his guilt after their crime spree. Interesting analysis of criminality, yellow journalism, and mob rule. Unrated, but contains violence. 1950; 91m.

TUXEDO WARRIOR ★★

DIR: Andrew Sinclair. **CAST:** John Wyman, Carol Royle, Holly Palance, James Coburn Jr.

Trite story about a bar owner/soldier of fortune (John Wyman) who becomes embroiled with diamond thieves in South Africa. Two stars for the British accents and some decent action. Not rated, but contains violence and profanity. 1982; 93m.

TWELVE O'CLOCK HIGH ★★★★

DIR: Henry King. **CAST:** Gregory Peck, Dean Jagger, Gary Merrill, Hugh Marlowe.

Gregory Peck is the flight commander who takes over an England-based bomber squadron during World War II. He begins to feel the strain of leadership and becomes too involved with the men in his command. This is a well-produced and well-acted film. Dean Jagger won an Oscar for supporting actor for his fine performance. 1950; B&W; 132m.

20,000 LEAGUES UNDER THE SEA ★★★★

DIR: Richard Fleischer. **CAST:** Kirk Douglas, James Mason, Paul Lukas, Peter Lorre.

In this Disney version of the famous Jules Verne adventure-fantasy, a sailor (Kirk Douglas) and a scientist (Paul Lukas) get thoroughly involved with Captain Nemo, played by James Mason, and his fascinating submarine of the future. The cast is great, the action sequences ditto. 1954; 127m.

TWILIGHT'S LAST GLEAMING ★★★

DIR: Robert Aldrich. **CAST:** Burt Lancaster, Paul Winfield, Burt Young, William Smith, Charles Durning, Richard Widmark, Melvyn Douglas, Joseph Cotten.

Although this is another maniac-at-the-button doomsday chronicle, it is so convincing that it makes the well-worn premise seem new. From the moment a group of ex-cons (Burt Lancaster, Paul Winfield, Burt Young, and William Smith) seize control of an air force pickup truck, it becomes obvious the audience is in the front seat of a nonstop roller coaster. Rated R for violence and profanity. 1977; 146m.

TWO LOST WORLDS ★

DIR: Norman Dawn. **CAST:** James Arness, Laura Elliot, Bill Kennedy, Gloria Petroff, Tom Hubbard, Pierre Watkin, James Guilfoyle.

Pointless story involving pirates and kidnapping, shipwreck and rescue. This is one of half a dozen or so films from the early 1950s that rented stock footage from Hal Roach's *One Million B.C.* and built a loose story around prehistoric lizards and erupting volcanoes. This one was a dud when it was released, and time hasn't done it any favors. 1950; B&W; 61m.

TWO TO TANGO ★★½

DIR: Hector Olivera. **CAST:** Don Stroud, Adrienne Sachs, Michael Cavanaugh, Dulio Marzio.

Satisfying little thriller starring Don Stroud as a burned-out hit-man for an ominous organization called the Company. He's terminated one too many targets and bargains with his superior to do one last hit in Buenos Aires, Argentina; then he'll retire to Nepal. Rated R for violence and nudity. 1988; 87m.

TYCOON ★

DIR: Richard Wallace. **CAST:** John Wayne, Laraine Day, Cedric Hardwicke, Judith Anderson, Anthony Quinn, James Gleason.

A would-be epic about the building of a railroad through the Andes. John Wayne stinks as the headstrong and reckless engineer who feuds with tycoon Cedric Hardwicke while listlessly romancing his daughter, Laraine Day. It's all overblown, ridiculous, and unconvincing. 1947; 128m.

ULYSSES ★★

DIR: Mario Camerini. **CAST:** Kirk Douglas, Silvana Mangano, Anthony Quinn, Rossana Podesta, Sylvie.

One of Kirk Douglas's least successful independent productions, this heavily dubbed Italian epic emphasizes dialogue over thrills. Kirk Douglas does his best, but he gets mired down in this slow retelling of Ulysses's long voyage home after the Trojan War. 1955; 104m.

UNCOMMON VALOR ★★★★

DIR: Ted Kotcheff. **CAST:** Gene Hackman, Fred Ward, Reb Brown, Randall "Tex" Cobb, Harold Sylvester, Robert Stack.

In this action-packed adventure film, retired marine Gene Hackman learns that his son may still be alive in a Vietnamese prison camp ten years after being listed as missing in action. He decides to go in after him. Rated

R for profanity and violence. 1983; 105m.

UNDER FIRE ★★½
DIR: Roger Spottiswoode. **CAST:** Nick Nolte, Gene Hackman, Joanna Cassidy, Ed Harris, Jean-Louis Trintignant.
Nick Nolte, Gene Hackman, and Joanna Cassidy are journalists covering political upheaval in Central America circa 1979. While *Under Fire* has its moments (found primarily in the superb supporting performances of Ed Harris and French actor Jean-Louis Trintignant), you have to wade through a bit of sludge to get to them. Rated R for profanity, violence, and gore. 1983; 128m.

UNDERCOVER ★
DIR: John Stockwell. **CAST:** David Neidorf, Jennifer Jason Leigh, Barry Corbin, David Harris, Kathleen Wilhoite.
Cliché-ridden cop story. David Neidorf is a policeman who goes undercover in a South Carolina high school to break up a drug ring. Neidorf looks at least 25, which is one of the many inconsistencies in this film. Rated R for language, nudity. 1987; 92m.

UNDERWATER! ★★
DIR: John Sturges. **CAST:** Jane Russell, Gilbert Roland, Richard Egan, Jayne Mansfield, Lori Nelson.
The best stories about this sopping-wet adventure center around the elaborate publicity launched by reclusive millionaire Howard Hughes to sell it to the public. Hughes's original idea of supplying the press with aqualungs and screening the film in an underwater theater didn't help the reviews and only made this costly, overblown story of sea scavengers more of a hoot than it already was. 1955; 99m.

UNTOUCHABLES, THE ★★★★½
DIR: Brian De Palma. **CAST:** Kevin Costner, Sean Connery, Robert De Niro, Charles Martin Smith, Andy Garcia, Billy Drago, Richard Bradford.
An absolutely superb retelling of the events made famous by the beloved television series, with director Brian De Palma working his stylish magic in tandem with a deft script from Pulitzer-winning playwright David Mamet. Prohibition-era Chicago has been beautifully re-created to emphasize big-city decadence. Al Capone (a grand seriocomic performance by Robert De Niro) was the populist hero for providing alcohol for the masses; Eliot Ness was the arrow-straight federal agent who rose to the challenge. Kevin Costner plays Ness as the ultimate *naif* who fails miserably until taken under the protective wing of an honest beat cop (Sean Connery, in the performance of his career). Rated R for language and extreme violence. 1987; 119m.

UNTOUCHABLES: SCARFACE MOB, THE ★★★
DIR: Phil Karlson. **CAST:** Robert Stack, Keenan Wynn, Barbara Nichols, Pat Crowley, Neville Brand, Bruce Gordon, Anthony George, Abel Fernandez, Nick Giorgiade.
This violence-ridden film was released theatrically in 1962 but was actually the original two-part pilot for this popular series, first telecast in 1959. Steely-eyed Robert Stack as Eliot Ness gets the government's go-ahead to form his own special team of uncorruptible agents and leads them in forays against the enemy: bootleggers, racketeers, and especially the minions of kingpin Al "Scarface" Capone and his enforcer, Frank Nitti. 1962; B&W; 90m.

URBAN WARRIORS
DIR: Joseph Warren. **CAST:** Karl Landgren.
A group of scientists survive a nuclear holocaust and find they must fight for their continued survival in a violent world. These so-called urban warriors seem to be fighting in a deserted warehouse in the middle of a desert and couldn't act even if it meant a drink of water. The overdubbed soundtrack never matches their lips,

anyway. Who funds these things? Rated R for violence. 1989; 90m.

UTU ★★★★★
DIR: Geoff Murphy. **CAST:** Anzac Wallace, Bruno Lawrence, Kelly Johnson, Tim Elliot.
This stunner from New Zealand contains all the action of the great American westerns, but with a moral message that leaves most of that genre's best in the dust. Anzac Wallace plays Te Wheke, a Maori corporal in the nineteenth-century British army who finds his family slaughtered by his own army. It is there at his burning village that he vows "utu" (Maori for revenge) and goes on a march with fellow Maori rebels to rid his land of white people. Rated R for violence. 1985; 100m.

VANISHING POINT ★★½
DIR: Richard C. Sarafian. **CAST:** Cleavon Little, Barry Newman, Dean Jagger.
Interesting story of a marathon car chase through Colorado and California. Cleavon Little gives a standout performance as the disc jockey who helps a driver (Barry Newman) elude the police. Richard Sarafian's direction is competent, but the story eventually runs out of gas before the film ends. Rated PG. 1971; 107m.

VEGA$ ★★½
DIR: Richard Lang. **CAST:** Robert Urich, Judy Landers, Tony Curtis, Will Sampson, Greg Morris.
A few days in the life of a high-flying, T-Bird-driving private eye whose beat is highways, byways, and gambling casinos of Las Vegas. Robert Urich, an ex-cop, is hired to find a runaway teen-age girl who's gotten in too deep with the sleazy side of Fortune Town. 1978; 104m.

VENDETTA [turkey]
DIR: Bruce Logan. **CAST:** Karen Chase, Sandy Martin, Roberta Collins, Kin Shriner.
This is a laughably bad women's prison flick. *Vendetta* is the story of a stuntwoman who purposely commits several crimes so that she'll be thrown in the slammer—the same one her younger sister was unjustly put in—where she can then avenge the death of that sister, who was murdered by a jail gang. Pure low-budget slime. Rated R. 1985; 89m.

VENGEANCE [turkey]
DIR: Antonio Isasi. **CAST:** Jason Miller, Lea Massari, Marisa Peredes.
What can you say about a film in which the most compelling actor is a German shepherd? That's the problem with this dull account of an escape from a Latin American prison camp. Unrated, the film has graphic violence and sex. 1987; 114m.

VENGEANCE IS MINE ★★
DIR: John Trent. **CAST:** Ernest Borgnine, Michael J. Pollard, Hollis McLaren.
A stark and brutal story of back-country justice. Some murderous bank robbers invade a farm and run into Ernest Borgnine, who matches brutality with brutality. A bleak and stilted movie. Not rated; contains violence and profanity. 1976; 90m.

VENUS IN FURS ★
DIR: Jess Franco. **CAST:** James Darren, Barbara McNair, Klaus Kinski, Dennis Price.
British, Italian, and German talents joined to make this pitifully poor mystery involving a musician and a mutilated woman who washes ashore. Almost, but not quite, a turkey. Rated R. 1970; 86m.

VERNE MILLER ★½
DIR: Rod Hewitt. **CAST:** Scott Glenn, Barbara Stock, Thomas G. Waites, Lucinda Jenney, Sonny Carl Davis, Andy Robinson.
Scott Glenn stars as the infamous gunman who masterminded and executed the violent Kansas City massacre at the insistence of crime czar Al Capone. This ridiculous gangster yarn features too many dull gunfights and too little storyline or character development. Rated R for nudity and violence. 1988; 95m.

VICE SQUAD ★★★½

DIR: Gary A. Sherman. **CAST:** Season Hubley, Wings Hauser, Gary Swanson, Beverly Todd.

Slick, fast-paced thriller set in the seamy world of pimps and prostitutes. Season Hubley is an adorable mom by day and a smart-mouthed hooker by night forced to help cop Gary Swanson capture a sicko killer, played with frightening intensity by Wings Hauser. A total fairy tale, but it moves quickly enough to mask improbabilities. Not for the squeamish. Rated R. 1982; 97m.

VICIOUS ★★

DIR: Paul Zwicky. **CAST:** Tamblyn Lord, Craig Pearce.

In this bland Australian film a young man is unwittingly the provocateur of a sadistic attack on his wealthy girlfriend and her parents by a trio of thugs. The ensuing revenge is predictable. Rated R for graphic violence. 1988; 90m.

VICTORY ★★★

DIR: John Huston. **CAST:** Sylvester Stallone, Michael Caine, Pelé, Max von Sydow.

Sylvester Stallone and Michael Caine star in this entertaining but predictable World War II drama about a soccer game between Allied prisoners of war and the Nazis. Germany intends to cheat. But our boys want to strike a blow for democracy. With a title like *Victory*, guess who wins. Rated PG. 1981; 110m.

VIEW TO A KILL, A ★★★

DIR: John Glen. **CAST:** Roger Moore, Tanya Roberts, Christopher Walken, Grace Jones.

Despite a spectacular opening sequence and some dandy little moments along the way, the James Bond series is starting to look a little old and tired—just like its star, Roger Moore. Christopher Walken co-stars as the maniacal villain who plans to corner the world's microchip market by flooding the San Andreas Fault. Good for fans only. Rated PG for violence and suggested sex. 1985; 131m.

VIKINGS, THE ★★★½

DIR: Richard Fleischer. **CAST:** Kirk Douglas, Tony Curtis, Ernest Borgnine, Janet Leigh.

Well-done action film following the exploits of a group of Vikings (led by Tony Curtis and Kirk Douglas). Many good battle scenes and beautiful photography and locations make the picture a standout. Ernest Borgnine gives a great performance. Don't miss it. 1958; 114m.

VILLAIN STILL PURSUED HER, THE ★

DIR: Eddie Cline. **CAST:** Anita Louise, Richard Cromwell, Hugh Herbert, Alan Mowbray, Buster Keaton, Billy Gilbert, Margaret Hamilton.

Dull, old-fashioned melodrama is pretty thick sledding even with a veteran crew of character actors and actresses to break the monotony. Buster Keaton adds a little pep to this otherwise tired production, but the overall tone of this movie is that of tedium. 1940; B&W; 66m.

VIOLATED

DIR: Richard Cannistraro. **CAST:** J. C. Quinn, John Heard.

Soap-opera starlets are invited to Mafia parties, where they are brutally raped. This violent and degrading film is full of lousy acting and even worse direction. Rated R for violence and nudity. 1984; 90m.

VIOLENT BREED, THE

DIR: Fernando Di Leo. **CAST:** Henry Silva, Harrison Muller, Woody Strode, Carole André.

The CIA goes into Vietnam to stop a guerrilla gang that is importing drugs to America. Impossible situations, terrible acting, rotten dubbing, gratuitous nudity, and violence galore. 1983; 91m.

VIOLENT YEARS, THE

DIR: Franz Eichorn. **CAST:** Jean Moorehead, Barbara Weeks, Glenn Corbett, I. Stanford Jolley.

The screenwriter of this camp classic was Edward D. Wood Jr., and it bears his unmistakable touch. A gang of rich girls, ignored by their parents, don men's clothing and rob gas stations. In their spare time, they pet heavily at a combination pajama-cocktail party, rape a lover's-lane Lothario, and even get involved in an international communist conspiracy! Their response to every query is a sneered "So What?" A must-see for buffs of bad movies! 1956; 65m.

VIPER ★
DIR: Peter Maris. **CAST:** Linda Purl, James Tolkan, Jeff Kober, Chris Robinson.

A CIA operation breaks into a university and kills the members of the administration, blaming it on Middle Eastern terrorists. The government is then justified in taking military action against an Arab nation. An operative threatens to expose the plan and is promptly terminated, leaving his wife to unravel the circumstances behind her husband's death. As a political statement, this falls flat on its face. Rated R for language and violence. 1988; 96m.

VIVA KNIEVEL ★
DIR: Gordon Douglas. **CAST:** Evel Knievel, Marjoe Gortner, Leslie Nielsen, Gene Kelly, Lauren Hutton.

Evel Knievel (playing himself) is duped by a former buddy, Jessie (Marjoe Gortner), into doing a stunt tour of Mexico. What Evel doesn't know is that Jessie's boss, Stanley Millard (Leslie Nielsen), plans to murder him during the climax of one of his feats of daring. Rated PG, the film has no profanity, sex, or nudity, and very little violence. 1977; 106m.

VON RYAN'S EXPRESS ★★★★
DIR: Mark Robson. **CAST:** Frank Sinatra, Trevor Howard, Edward Mulhare, James Brolin, Luther Adler.

This is a first-rate World War II tale of escape from a prisoner-of-war camp aboard a German train to neutral Switzerland. Trevor Howard is the officer in charge until a feisty Frank Sinatra takes over the escape plan. This is a great action story, with Sinatra playing the hero's role perfectly. 1965; 117m.

WAKE ISLAND ★★★★
DIR: John Farrow. **CAST:** Brian Donlevy, Macdonald Carey, Robert Preston, Albert Dekker, William Bendix, Walter Abel.

Hard-hitting tale of a small gallant detachment of U.S. marines holding out against attack after attack by the Japanese army, navy, and air force. A true story from the early dark days of World War II when there had been no American victories. Brian Donlevy commands the troops, and William Bendix and Robert Preston fight each other as much as they fight the Japanese. *Wake Island* received four Academy Award nominations and was the first realistic American film made about World War II. 1942; B&W; 88m.

WAKE OF THE RED WITCH ★★★★
DIR: Edward Ludwig. **CAST:** John Wayne, Gail Russell, Gig Young, Luther Adler.

Good, seafaring adventure tale with John Wayne outstanding as a wronged ship's captain seeking justice and battling an octopus for sunken treasure. 1948; B&W; 106m.

WALK IN THE SUN, A ★★★★½
DIR: Lewis Milestone. **CAST:** Dana Andrews, Richard Conte, Sterling Holloway, John Ireland.

Based on Harry Brown's novel, this picture really gets to the heart of the human reaction to war. The story of an American army unit's attack on a German stronghold in World War II Italy is a first-rate character study. 1945; B&W; 117m.

WALK INTO HELL ★★★
DIR: Les Robinson. **CAST:** Chips Rafferty, Françoise Christophe, Reg Lye.

Popular Australian star Chips Rafferty is something of a precursor to "Crocodile" Dundee in this Outback adventure. He plays a bush explorer who helps a businessman find oil in New Guinea. Of course, the aborigines aren't all too happy about this. Plenty of *National Geographic*–type footage pads out this okay adventure. 1957; 93m.

WALKING TALL ★★½
DIR: Phil Karlson. **CAST:** Joe Don Baker, Elizabeth Hartman, Noah Beery Jr., Rosemary Murphy.

Poor Joe Don Baker never outran his one-note performance as Buford Pusser, the baseball bat–toting southern sheriff who decided to take the law into his own hands in his fight against the cancerous scum of society. Unpleasantly brutal and difficult to enjoy for any reason; good guy Baker is almost worse than the outrageously stereotyped baddies he reduces to pulp. Talented Elizabeth Hartman is completely wasted. Not a family picture. Rated R. 1973; 125m.

WALKING TALL PART II ★½
DIR: Earl Bellamy. **CAST:** Bo Svenson, Luke Askew, Richard Jaeckel, Noah Beery Jr.

In this sequel, there is more baseball than justice from Sheriff Buford T. Pusser (Bo Svenson). This follow-up to the successful *Walking Tall* proves that sequels are better off not being made at all. This storyline gives Svenson a chance to flex his muscles and look mean, but that's about it. Rated R for violence and language. 1975; 109m.

WANDA NEVADA ★★½
DIR: Peter Fonda. **CAST:** Peter Fonda, Brooke Shields, Fiona Lewis.

Interesting little film with Peter Fonda as a shifty, amoral gambler who wins Brooke Shields in a poker game. They come into the possession of a map that marks a gold strike. If you watch carefully, you'll see Henry Fonda as a gold prospector. It's the only film that father and son ever did together. Rated PG for violence and mature situations. 1979; 105m.

WANTED: DEAD OR ALIVE ★★★
DIR: Gary A. Sherman. **CAST:** Rutger Hauer, Gene Simmons, Robert Guillaume, Mel Harris, William Russ.

In this lean and mean action thriller, Rutger Hauer stars as Nick Randall, the great-grandson of Old West bounty hunter Josh Randall (who was played by Steve McQueen in the *Wanted: Dead or Alive* television series). Nick is a former CIA agent who is brought out of retirement by the company when an international terrorist (Gene Simmons) begins leaving a bloody trail across Los Angeles. Rated R for profanity and violence. 1987; 104m.

WAR BOY, THE ★★★½
DIR: Allan Eastman. **CAST:** Helen Shaver, Kenneth Welsh, Jason Hopely.

A 12-year-old boy (Jason Hopely) living in World War II Germany suffers the experiences of growing up amid the brutalities of conflict. Hopely's performance is terrific. The story and production are nowhere near as ambitious as *Hope and Glory* or *Empire of the Sun*, but *The War Boy* is a good film in its own right. Rated PG for violence and some sex. 1985; 96m.

WAR PARTY ★★
DIR: Franc Roddam. **CAST:** Kevin Dillon, Billy Wirth, Tim Sampson, M. Emmet Walsh.

An interesting idea, but not suitably developed, this film details what happens when a group of disgruntled, modern-day native Americans go on the warpath. They disrupt a summer festival by taking the cowboy-and-Indian war games seriously—and use real ammunition. Rated R, with strong violence. 1988; 100m.

WARBIRDS 🦃
DIR: Ulli Lommel. **CAST:** Jim Eldbert.

Woefully inept action flick concerns American intervention in a Middle Eastern revolution. Pilots recruited by the CIA find themselves in deep trouble when their mission is jeopardized by a traitor. Rated R for violence and profanity. 1988; 88m.

WARBUS ★★
DIR: Ted Kaplan. **CAST:** Daniel Stephen, Rom Kristoff, Urs Althaus, Gwendoline Cook, Ernie Zarte, Don Gordon.

A Vietnam adventure about a motley crew fleeing a mission in a school bus, heading south during the closing days of the war. Hardly a realistic portrayal of the war, but the characters are likable and the action is tightly paced. Rated R for violence and profanity. 1985; 90m.

WARLORDS OF HELL
DIR: Clark Henderson. **CAST:** Brad Henson, Jeffrey D. Rice.

Somebody, somewhere, with money to waste came up with the idea of making this stupid excuse for a movie. The plot (what little there is of it) has two dirt bike–riding brothers who accidentaly wander into a marijuana plantation south of the border. This film should have been titled *Jerks on Mopeds*. Watching this garbage *is* pure hell. Rated R for nudity, violence, and profanity. 1987; 76m.

WARNING, THE
DIR: Damiano Damiani. **CAST:** Martin Balsam, Giuliano Gemma, Giancarlo Zanetti.

Convoluted dirty-cop flick from Italy. The folks who dubbed this thing must not have been up on the really emotionally loaded colloquialisms of modern English—to be really insulted in this flick is to be called a "turd." Martin Balsam's performance is pure paycheck and everyone else takes the whole affair far too seriously. Not rated, but probably equal to an R for violence, profanity, and nudity. 1985; 101m.

WARRIOR QUEEN
DIR: Chuck Vincent. **CAST:** Sybil Danning, Donald Pleasence, Richard Hill, Josephine Jacqueline Jones.

This celluloid stinker robs footage from an old Italian epic about the eruption of Mount Vesuvius and pads it out with a nonstory about Sybil Danning as an emissary from Rome inspecting the city of Pompeii. She speaks about fifteen words in the whole movie, and therefore embarrasses herself less than Donald Pleasence, who looks foolish as the drunken mayor Clodius. There are two different versions, an R-rated one with nudity and violence and an unrated one with more nudity and less of Pleasence. 1987; 69/79 minutes.

WARRIORS, THE (1955) ★★★
DIR: Henry Levin. **CAST:** Errol Flynn, Joanne Dru, Peter Finch, Yvonne Furneaux, Michael Hordern.

In this, his last swashbuckling role, Errol Flynn looks older than his 46 years. Cast as a British prince, he seems more qualified to battle the bulge and the bottle than the murderous hordes of nasty Peter Finch. Nevertheless, even in his decline, Flynn was more adept with a sword and a leer than anyone else in Hollywood. Though the movie is predictable, it's also quite entertaining. 1955; 85m.

WARRIORS, THE (1979) ★★★★
DIR: Walter Hill. **CAST:** Michael Beck, James Remar, Thomas Waites.

Comic book–style violence and sensibilities made this Walter Hill film an unworthy target for those worried about its prompting real-life gang wars. It's just meant for fun, and mostly it is, as a group of kids try to make their way home through the territories of other, less-understanding gangs in a surrealistic New York. Rated R. 1979; 94m.

WATCHED! ★
DIR: John Parsons. **CAST:** Stacy Keach, Harris Yulin, Brigid Polk, Tony Serra.

Stacy Keach stars as a former U.S. attorney who suffers a drug-related mental breakdown and kills a narcotics agent. Amateur direction by Parsons, who also wrote the tedious story. Unrated. 1973; 95m.

WE OF THE NEVER NEVER ★★★★½

DIR: Igor Auzins. **CAST:** Angela Punch McGregor, Arthur Dignam, Tony Barry.

The compelling story of a woman's year in the Australian Outback, where she learns about aborigines and they learn about her, is based on a true-life account written by Jeannie Gunn and published in 1908. Rated G. 1983; 132m.

WET GOLD ★

DIR: Dick Lowry. **CAST:** Brooke Shields, Burgess Meredith, Tom Byrd, Brian Kerwin.

Brooke Shields plays a waitress who follows an old alcoholic's (Burgess Meredith) lead to sunken gold. Along the way, she dumps her spoiled boyfriend for a handsome diver. A substandard made-for-TV film. 1984; 95m.

WHEELS OF FIRE

DIR: Cirio H. Santiago. **CAST:** Gary Watkins, Laura Banks, Lynda Wiesmeiser, Linda Grovenor.

Shameless ripoff of *The Road Warrior* lacks the taste of most of the films that have come in the wake of George Miller's action masterpiece. Nudity, violence, and rape dominate this story about a gang of nomadic bad guys with a leader named Scourge. Rated R for sex, nudity, violence, and profanity. 1984; 81m.

WHEN LIGHTNING STRIKES ★

DIR: Burton King. **CAST:** Francis X. Bushman Jr.

That's Lightning as in Lightning, the Wonder Dog, star of this ridiculous Rin Tin Tin ripoff that Video Yesteryear has revived for its Golden Turkey series. Lightning and his master battle bad guys in the Pacific Northwest who want to seize their land for its timber. 1934; B&W; 51m.

WHERE EAGLES DARE ★★★

DIR: Brian G. Hutton. **CAST:** Richard Burton, Clint Eastwood, Mary Ure, Michael Hordern, Patrick Wymark, Anton Diffring, Robert Beatty, Donald Houston, Ingrid Pitt.

Clint Eastwood and Richard Burton portray Allied commandos in this World War II adventure film which is short on realism. Instead we have far-fetched but exciting shootouts, explosions, and mass slaughter. Our heroes must break out an American general being held captive in a heavily fortified German castle before the Nazis can get highly secret information out of him. 1969; 158m.

WHILE THE CITY SLEEPS ★★½

DIR: Fritz Lang. **CAST:** Dana Andrews, Ida Lupino, Rhonda Fleming, George Sanders, Vincent Price, John Drew Barrymore, Thomas Mitchell, Howard Duff, Mae Marsh.

An impressive cast and the talents of director Fritz Lang can't transform this standard newspaper-crime story into a great film, although so many of the necessary elements seem to be present. Rival newspaper executives compete with each other and the police in an effort to come up with the identity of a mad killer who has been stalking the city, but this convoluted gabfest quickly bogs down and wastes the considerable acting talents involved. 1956; B&W; 100m.

WHISTLE STOP ★

DIR: Leonide Moguy. **CAST:** George Raft, Ava Gardner, Tom Conway, Victor McLaglen, Charles Drake, Jimmy Conlin.

Small-town girl Ava Gardner returns from the big city. She loves town drunk George Raft but opts for suave gambler Tom Conway, who gets murdered. Raft is implicated, but is cleared at the last minute. Tripe as false as cheap pearls from start to finish. 1946; B&W; 85m.

WHITE DAWN, THE ★★★★

DIR: Phil Kaufman. **CAST:** Warren Oates, Louis Gossett Jr., Timothy Bottoms.

This is a gripping and thought-provoking adventure film. Three whalers (Warren Oates, Louis Gossett Jr., and

Timothy Bottoms) get lost in the Arctic and are rescued by Eskimos, whom they end up exploiting. Rated PG. 1974; 109m.

WHITE GHOST
DIR: B. J. Davis. **CAST:** William Katt, Rosalind Chao, Martin Hewitt, Wayne Crawford, Reb Brown.
William Katt does an embarrassing Rambo imitation in this miserable ripoff. He plays an American soldier who stays behind after the withdrawal of troops from Vietnam, wreaking his own style of revenge on his enemies while searching for MIAs in the jungle. Rated R for violence and profanity. 1988; 93m.

WHITE HEAT ★★★★½
DIR: Raoul Walsh. **CAST:** James Cagney, Margaret Wycherly, Virginia Mayo, Edmond O'Brien, Steve Cochran.
James Cagney gives one of his greatest screen performances as a totally insane mama's boy and gangster, Cody Jarrett, in this film. Margaret Wycherly is chillingly effective as the evil mom, and Virginia Mayo is uncommonly outstanding as the badman's moll. But it is Cagney's picture pure and simple as he ironically makes it to "the top of the world, Ma!" 1949; B&W; 114m.

WHITE HOT ★★½
DIR: Robby Benson. **CAST:** Robby Benson, Tawny Kitaen, Danny Aiello.
A quick-paced drama about a yuppie couple's fall from grace through the trapdoor of drugs. Robby Benson (in his directorial debut) and Tawny Kitaen take over a drug lord's trade and become hopelessly immersed in the high life. Benson's clean-cut look is the only drawback to an otherwise entertaining, if lightweight, drug flick. Rated R for violence and drug use. 1989; 95m.

WHITE LIGHTNING ★★
DIR: Joseph Sargent. **CAST:** Burt Reynolds, Jennifer Billingsley, Ned Beatty, Bo Hopkins, Matt Clark, Louise Latham, Diane Ladd.
Good old boy Burt Reynolds as a speed-loving moonshiner fights the inevitable mean and inept cops and revenue agents in this comic-book chase and retribution film. A good cast of character actors makes this stock drive-in movie entertaining, although it is just like the majority of Burt Reynolds's car films—gimmicky and predictable. Rated PG. 1973; 101m.

WHITE LINE FEVER ★★★
DIR: Jonathan Kaplan. **CAST:** Jan-Michael Vincent, Kay Lenz, Slim Pickens, L. Q. Jones, Leigh French, Don Porter.
Jan-Michael Vincent plays an incorruptible young trucker in this film. He is angered when forced to smuggle goods in his truck. He fights back after he and his pregnant wife (Kay Lenz) are attacked. Rated PG. 1975; 92m.

WHITE WATER SUMMER ★★★
DIR: Jeff Bleekner. **CAST:** Kevin Bacon, Sean Astin, Jonathan Ward, Matt Adler.
Kevin Bacon plays a ruthless wilderness guide who intends to transform four boys into men. Sean Astin is the boy most abused by Bacon and he must decide what to do when Bacon is seriously injured. Interesting coming-of-age adventure. Rated PG for profanity. 1987; 87m.

WHO KILLED MARY WHAT'S 'ER NAME? ★★½
DIR: Ernest Pintoff. **CAST:** Red Buttons, Sylvia Miles, Conrad Bain, David Doyle, Ron Carey, Alice Playten, Sam Waterston.
Gritty detective melodrama about an ex-boxer who solves the murder of a prostitute when no one else seems to care. Above average low-budget thriller. Rated PG. 1971; 90m.

WHO'LL STOP THE RAIN ★★★★½
DIR: Karel Reisz. **CAST:** Nick Nolte, Michael Moriarty, Tuesday Weld, Anthony Zerbe, Richard Masur, Ray

Sharkey, David Opatoshu, Gail Strickland.

In this brilliant film, Nick Nolte gives one of his finest performances as a hardened vet who agrees to smuggle drugs for a buddy (the always effective Michael Moriarty). What neither of them knows is that it's a setup, so Nolte and Moriarty's neurotic wife, played to perfection by Tuesday Weld, have to hide out from the baddies (Anthony Zerbe, Richard Masur, and Ray Sharkey) who want to steal their stash and then kill them. Rated R. 1978; 126m.

WICKED LADY, THE (1983)

DIR: Michael Winner. **CAST:** Faye Dunaway, Alan Bates, John Gielgud, Denholm Elliott, Prunella Scales, Oliver Tobias, Glynis Barber.

An absolutely awful swashbuckler, this wastes the talents of stars Faye Dunaway and Alan Bates. Despite the presence of two such high-powered acting talents, this period adventure film about an aristocrat who gets her kicks robbing travelers is a real groaner, and it's easy to see why the production company (Cannon Films) decided not to release it to the theaters. Rated R. 1983; 98m.

WILD ANGELS, THE ★★

DIR: Roger Corman. **CAST:** Peter Fonda, Nancy Sinatra, Bruce Dern, Michael J. Pollard, Diane Ladd, Gayle Hunnicutt.

It's 1960s hip, low-budget Hollywood style. If they gave Oscars for cool, Peter Fonda—in shades, three-day growth of beard, and leather—would win for sure. This cool motorcycle gang leader needs a hot mama. Unfortunately, he has to make do with Nancy ("These Boots Are Made for Walkin") Sinatra. But the movie's greatest asset is "Blue's Theme," which revs up the proceedings with wonderfully tacky fuzz-tone guitar. 1966; 93m.

WILD GEESE, THE ★★★

DIR: Andrew V. McLaglen. **CAST:** Richard Burton, Roger Moore, Richard Harris, Stewart Granger, Hardy Krüger, Jack Watson, Frank Finlay.

The Wild Geese features the unlikely combination of Richard Burton, Roger Moore, and Richard Harris as three mercenaries hired by a rich British industrialist (Stewart Granger) to go into Rhodesia and free a captured humanist leader so the millionaire's company can again have the copper rights to the country. Better than you would expect. Rated R. 1978; 134m.

WILD GEESE II ★

DIR: Peter R. Hunt. **CAST:** Scott Glenn, Barbara Carrera, Edward Fox, Laurence Olivier, Stratford Johns.

In this contrived and vastly inferior sequel a new group of mercenaries attempts to break into a Berlin prison to free Nazi war criminal Rudolf Hess. Even more ludicrous, this operation is backed by an American television network. Gone from this film are the earlier film's believable situations and three-dimensional characters. Rated R for violence and language. 1985; 118m.

WILD MAN

DIR: F. J. Lincoln. **CAST:** Don Scribner.

In this low-rent production with lousy actors and a lame plot, Don Scribner plays ex-CIA agent Eric Wild who is pressured by his former boss to take on one more assignment. Yawn. Rated R for nudity, profanity, and violence. 1989; 105m.

WILD ONE, THE ★★★½

DIR: Laslo Benedek. **CAST:** Marlon Brando, Mary Murphy, Robert Keith, Lee Marvin, Jay C. Flippen, Jerry Paris, Alvy Moore.

This classic film (based loosely on a real event in Hollister, California) about rival motorcycle gangs taking over a small town is pretty tame stuff these days and provides more laughs than thrills. Marlon Brando and his brooding Johnny are at the heart of this film's popularity; that coupled with the theme of motorcycle nomads have assured the film a cult following. 1953; B&W; 79m.

WILD PAIR, THE ★★
DIR: Beau Bridges. **CAST:** Beau Bridges, Bubba Smith, Lloyd Bridges, Raymond St. Jacques, Gary Lockwood, Danny De La Paz.
Beau Bridges, a yuppie FBI agent, and Bubba Smith, a streetwise city cop, are assigned to investigate a drug-related murder. The two personalities clash as they find organized crime and other surprises around each corner. Bridges's acting, even as Smith's, is fine, but his directing is wanting. Rated R for profanity, violence, and nudity. 1987; 89m.

WIND AND THE LION, THE ★★★★
DIR: John Milius. **CAST:** Sean Connery, Brian Keith, Candice Bergen, John Huston, Geoffrey Lewis, Steve Kanaly, Vladek Sheybal.
In the 1970s, Sean Connery made a trio of memorable adventure movies, one being this release, impressively directed by John Milius. As in the other two films—*The Man Who Would Be King* and *Robin and Marian*—*The Wind and the Lion*, in which Connery plays a dashing Arab chieftain, is a thoroughly satisfying motion picture. Rated PG. 1975; 119m.

WINGS ★★★★
DIR: William Wellman. **CAST:** Clara Bow, Charles "Buddy" Rogers, Richard Arlen, Jobyna Ralston, Gary Cooper, Arlette Marchal, El Brendel.
The first recipient of the Academy Award for best picture, this is a silent film with organ music in the background. The story concerns two buddies who join the Air Corps in World War I and go to France to battle the Germans. War scenes are excellent, even by today's standards. Anti-war message is well done, although the love story tends to bog the film down a bit. Look for a young Gary Cooper. Much of the story rings true. 1927; B&W; 139m.

WINNERS TAKE ALL ★★½
DIR: Fritz Kiersch. **CAST:** Don Michael Paul, Kathleen York, Robert Krantz.
Spurred by jealousy at the success of an old friend, a California teen decides to compete in a Texas regional motocross competition. All of the usual sports-movie clichés are present and accounted for, though the final grudge race is full of high-spirited stunts that even nonracing fans should enjoy. Rated PG-13. 1986; 103m.

WINNING ★★★½
DIR: James Goldstone. **CAST:** Paul Newman, Joanne Woodward, Robert Wagner, Richard Thomas.
Paul Newman is very good as a race car driver who puts winning above all else, including his family. Some very good racing sequences and fine support from Joanne Woodward and Richard Thomas. Rated PG. 1969; 123m.

WISDOM ★
DIR: Emilio Estevez. **CAST:** Emilio Estevez, Demi Moore, Tom Skerritt, Veronica Cartwright, William Allen Young.
Writer-director Emilio Estevez plays a modern-day Robin Hood who comes to the aid of America's farmers in a bank-robbing spree with girlfriend Demi Moore. *Wisdom* is at its best when played as a light-hearted, tongue-in-cheek romp. Too bad Estevez, who wrote an outstanding screenplay for *That Was Then—This Is Now*, is unable to maintain this tone throughout. Instead, he assaults the viewer with violence, angst, and overlong mood shots of scenery and lovemaking. Rated R for violence, profanity, and sex. 1986; 109m.

WITNESS ★★★★½
DIR: Peter Weir. **CAST:** Harrison Ford, Kelly McGillis, Josef Sommer, Lukas Haas, Alexander Godunov, Danny Glover.
This is three terrific movies in one: an exciting cop thriller, a touching romance, and a fascinating screen study of a modern-day clash of cultures.

Harrison Ford is superb in the starring role as a police captain who must protect an 8-year-old Amish boy, the only witness to a drug-related murder. Rated R for violence, profanity, and nudity. 1985; 112m.

WOMAN HUNT, THE
DIR: Eddie Romero. **CAST:** John Ashley, Pat Woodell, Sid Haig.

Every couple of years, someone decides that the world needs a remake of *The Most Dangerous Game*, the classic about a madman who hunts human beings for sport. They're almost always lousy, and this one, made in the Philippines, is no exception. In fact, it's one of the lousiest. Rated R for nudity and violence. 1975; 80m.

WOMAN IN GREEN, THE ★★★
DIR: Roy William Neill. **CAST:** Basil Rathbone, Nigel Bruce, Hillary Brooke, Henry Daniell, Paul Cavanagh.

This is a grisly little entry in the Rathbone/Bruce Sherlock Holmes series, with the master sleuth investigating a series of severed fingers sent to Scotland Yard. The culprit is, once again, Professor Moriarty (Henry Daniell), this time masterminding a hypnosis-blackmail-murder scheme. Careful viewers will detect moments from *The Adventure of the Empty House*. 1945; B&W; 68m.

WORLD WAR III ★★★½
DIR: David Greene. **CAST:** Rock Hudson, David Soul, Brian Keith, Cathy Lee Crosby, Katherine Helmond, Jeroen Krabbé.

In this made-for-TV thriller, Rock Hudson, as a U.S. president, must send a crack military unit to Alaska to stop the Russians from capturing the Alaska pipeline. The battle scenes are tense and effective, and Brian Keith, as the Russian secretary-general, is terrific. It's long but certainly worth a view. 1982; 200m.

YAKUZA, THE ★★★★★
DIR: Sydney Pollack. **CAST:** Robert Mitchum, Brian Keith, Ken Takakura, Herb Edelman, Richard Jordan.

In this superb blending of the American gangster and Japanese samurai genres, Robert Mitchum plays Harry Kilmer, an ex-G.I. who returns to Japan to do a dangerous favor for a friend, George Tanner (Brian Keith). The latter's daughter has been kidnapped by a Japanese gangster—a Yakuza—who is holding her for ransom. This forces Kilmer to call on Tanaka (Ken Takakura), a one-time enemy who owes him a debt. Thus begins a clash of cultures and a web of intrigue that keep the viewers on the edge of their seats. Rated R. 1975; 112m.

YANKEE CLIPPER ★★½
DIR: Rupert Julian. **CAST:** William Boyd, Elinor Fair, Frank Coghlan Jr., John Miljan, Walter Long.

Future Hopalong Cassidy William Boyd plays a tough seadog determined to win a race against a British ship as they sail from China to Boston. Plenty of good sea footage is interspersed with a sticky love story between Boyd and an English girl, Elinor Fair, but a near mutiny and Walter Long as the villainous Iron-Head Joe help offset the mush. Silent, with soundtrack. 1927; B&W; 51m.

YEAR OF LIVING DANGEROUSLY, THE ★★★★½
DIR: Peter Weir. **CAST:** Mel Gibson, Sigourney Weaver, Linda Hunt, Michael Murphy, Bill Kerr, Noel Ferrier.

The Year of Living Dangerously is set in 1965 Indonesia when the Sukarno regime was toppling from pressures left and right. Mel Gibson and Sigourney Weaver star as an Australian journalist and a British diplomatic attaché, respectively. The film, however, belongs to Linda Hunt, in her Academy Award–winning role as free-lance photographer Billy Kwan. Rated R for profanity, nudity, and violence. 1983; 115m.

YEAR OF THE DRAGON ★
DIR: Michael Cimino. **CAST:** Mickey Rourke, John Lone, Ariane, Leonard Termo.

This film about the attempts of a New York police officer (Mickey Rourke) to stop the violence caused by youth gangs in Chinatown has some exciting and effectively dramatic moments. Overall, however, it's racist, sexist, foul-mouthed, overly violent, and just plain disgusting, another study in excess from director Michael Cimino. Rated R for violence, profanity, gore, simulated sex, and nudity. 1985; 136m.

YOU ONLY LIVE TWICE ★★★

DIR: Lewis Gilbert. **CAST:** Sean Connery, Akiko Wakabayashi, Tetsuro Tamba, Mie Hama, Karin Dor, Bernard Lee, Lois Maxwell, Desmond Llewellyn, Donald Pleasence.

Sean Connery as James Bond—who could expect more, especially in these days of cheap imitations? Well, a better plot and more believable cliffhanger situations come to mind. Still, this entry isn't a bad 007, and it does star the best Bond. 1967; 116m.

YOU TALKIN' TO ME ★★★

DIR: Charles Winkler. **CAST:** Jim Youngs, Faith Ford, Mykel T. Williamson, James Noble.

A struggling young New York actor whose idol is Robert De Niro (particularly De Niro's performance in *Taxi Driver*) moves to Los Angeles seeking his big break. He finds rejection and frustration instead. Finally he dyes his hair blond and adapts his personality to southern California taste and style. Quirky offbeat film that eventually succeeds despite weak direction and clumsy dialogue. Rated R for violence and profanity. 1987; 97m.

YOUNG AND INNOCENT ★★★

DIR: Alfred Hitchcock. **CAST:** Derrek de Marney, Nova Pilbeam, Percy Marmont, Edward Rigby, Mary Clare, Basil Radford.

Reputedly director Alfred Hitchcock's favorite of the films he made in Great Britain, this chase-within-a-chase film employs one of his favorite devices, that of an innocent man avoiding the police while attempting to catch the real criminal and prove his innocence. Not as well known as many of his other films, this seldom-seen movie is vintage Hitchcock and on a par with much of his best work. 1937; B&W; 80m.

YOUNG SHERLOCK HOLMES ★★½

DIR: Barry Levinson. **CAST:** Nicholas Rowe, Alan Cox, Sophie Ward, Anthony Higgins, Freddie Jones.

This disappointingly derivative Steven Spielberg production speculates on what might have happened if Sherlock Holmes (Nicholas Rowe) and Dr. John H. Watson (Alan Cox) had met during their student days in 1870 England. A better name for it might be *Sherlock Holmes and the Temple of Doom.* While youngsters are likely to enjoy it, most adults—especially frequent filmgoers or video viewers—are cautioned to avoid it. Rated PG-13 for violence and scary stuff. 1985; 115m.

YOUNG WARRIORS, THE ★½

DIR: Lawrence D. Foldes. **CAST:** Ernest Borgnine, Richard Roundtree, Lynda Day George, James Van Patten, Anne Lockhart, Mike Norris, Dick Shawn, Linnea Quigley.

Revenge exploitation with James Van Patten leading his college-frat brothers on a hunt for the psychos who raped and killed his sister. On the way, they practice vigilante justice on any other scumbags who cross their path. Competently produced, but it makes us uncomfortable that anyone out there might be taking this trashy genre seriously. Rated R for violence. 1983; 105m.

ZOMBIES OF THE STRATOSPHERE (SATAN'S SATELLITES) ★★

DIR: Fred Brannon. **CAST:** Judd Holdren, Aline Towne, Wilson Wood, Lane Bradford.

Judd Holdren, representing the Inter-Planetary Patrol, dons a flying suit and tracks down part-human zombies who have enlisted the aid of a renegade scientist to construct a hydrogen bomb that will blow Earth off its orbit and enable them to conquer what's left of the world. Balsa wood rocket ships and stock footage from the other "Rocket Man" serials make this one of the more ludicrous entries from Republic Studios in the last years of the movie serial. Enjoy the stunts in this one and skip the story. 1952; B&W; 12 chapters.

ZULU ★★★★½

DIR: Cy Endfield. **CAST:** Stanley Baker, Michael Caine, Jack Hawkins, Nigel Green.

Several films have been made about the British army and its exploits in Africa during the nineteenth century. *Zulu* ranks with the finest. A stellar cast headed by Stanley Baker and Michael Caine who charge through this story of an outmanned British garrison laid to siege by several thousand Zulu warriors. Based on fact, this one delivers the goods for action and tension. 1964; 138m.

ZULU DAWN ★★★

DIR: Douglas Hickox. **CAST:** Burt Lancaster, Peter O'Toole, Simon Ward, John Mills, Nigel Davenport.

This prequel to the film *Zulu*, which was made fifteen years earlier, seems quite pale when compared with the first. Based on the crushing defeat of the British army at the hands of the Zulu warriors, *Zulu Dawn* depicts the events leading up to the confrontation portrayed in *Zulu*. Considering all involved, this is a disappointment. Rated PG for violence. 1979; 121m.

CHILDREN'S VIEWING/ FAMILY FILMS

ABSENT-MINDED PROFESSOR, THE ★★★★
DIR: Robert Stevenson. **CAST:** Fred MacMurray, Nancy Olson, Tommy Kirk, Ed Wynn, Keenan Wynn.

One of Disney's best live-action comedies, this stars Fred MacMurray in the title role of a scientist who discovers "flubber" (flying rubber). Only trouble is, no one will believe him—except Keenan Wynn, who tries to steal his invention. 1961; B&W; 104m.

ACROSS THE GREAT DIVIDE ★★
DIR: Stewart Raffill. **CAST:** Robert Logan, George (Buck) Flower, Heather Rattray, Mark Edward Hall.

Across the Great Divide is family entertainment at its most unchallenging. Two kids (Heather Rattray and Mark Hall) meet up with a shifty gambler (Robert Logan), and the three eventually unite for safety on their monotonous trek through valleys, mountains, and rivers. Rated G. 1976; 89m.

ADVENTURES OF AN AMERICAN RABBIT, THE ★★★
DIR: Steward Moskowitz. **CAST:** Animated.

In this enjoyable-for-kids feature-length cartoon, mild-mannered and sweet-natured Rob Rabbit becomes the heir to the Legacy, which magically transforms him into the star-spangled protector of all animalkind, the American Rabbit. Rated G. 1986; 85m.

ADVENTURES OF BULLWHIP GRIFFIN, THE ★★
DIR: James Neilson. **CAST:** Roddy McDowall, Suzanne Pleshette, Karl Malden, Harry Guardino, Richard Haydn, Hermione Baddeley, Cecil Kellaway.

Typical, flyweight Disney comedy, this ripoff of *Ruggles of Red Gap* is textured with unique character performers, such as Richard Haydn and Karl Malden, but fails to offer anything original. Roddy McDowall plays a proper English butler who finds himself smack-dab in the wilds of California during the Gold Rush and helps save the day for his young "master," Brian Russell. Okay for the kids but not much to recommend for a discriminationg audience. 1966; 110m.

ADVENTURES OF DROOPY ★★★½

DIR: Tex Avery. **CAST:** Animated.

Next to Tom and Jerry, Tex Avery's Droopy was MGM's most famous cartoon character. The slow-talking, sad-eyed pooch is represented here in a half-dozen animated shorts, including "Dumb-Hounded," "Wags to Riches," "The Shooting of Dan McGoo," "Droopy's Good Deed," "Dragalong Droopy," and "Deputy Droopy." The stories and gags are sometimes repetitive, but a few bits are priceless. 1985; 53m.

ADVENTURES OF FELIX THE CAT, THE ★

DIR: Joseph Oriolo. **CAST:** Animated.

Made for television by Paramount Pictures, these cheesy and cheap works of unimagination can't hold a candle to Pat Sullivan's original cartoons from the Twenties. Felix manages to escape from every tough situation with his magic bag of tricks. In this collection, the feisty feline combats King Blob, Martin the Martian, dinosaurs, and a man-eating plant. Interesting to younger kids only. 1960; 54m.

ADVENTURES OF HUCKLEBERRY FINN, THE ★★

DIR: Jack B. Hively. **CAST:** Forrest Tucker, Larry Storch, Brock Peters.

This drawn-out version of Mark Twain's classic has its moments but lacks continuous action. In it, young Huck fakes his own drowning to avoid attendance at a proper eastern school for boys. When his friend, Slave Jim (Brock Peters), is accused of his murder, he must devise a plan to free him. Huck and Jim find themselves rafting down the Mississippi with two likable con artists (Larry Storch and Forrest Tucker). 1978; 97m.

ADVENTURES OF MARK TWAIN, THE ★★

DIR: Will Vinton. **CAST:** Animated.

Animated clay figures are used to illustrate this fairy tale, and a very interesting and different illustration it makes. Too much time is spent, however, on the framing story, which has Mark Twain flying in a dirigible into outer space. Huck Finn, Tom Sawyer, and Becky Thatcher stow away on the blimp and spend the time exploring Twain's magical balloon. Viewers not familiar with Mark Twain or his works will be lost. Rated G. 1985; 86m.

ADVENTURES OF MILO IN THE PHANTOM TOLLBOOTH, THE ★★★

DIR: Chuck Jones, Abe Levitow, Dave Monahan. **CAST:** Butch Patrick, Animated.

An assortment of cartoon talents, including director Chuck Jones and voice greats like Mel Blanc, Hans Conried, Daws Butler, and June Foray, make this unusual but entertaining film coalesce. Live-action footage combines with animation to tell the story of a young boy who enters a booth that takes him into the Land of Wisdom. Rated G. 1969; 89m.

ADVENTURES OF SINBAD, THE ★½

DIR: Richard Slapczynski. **CAST:** Animated.

Slow re-telling of a tale from *The Thousand and One Nights*. Sinbad the sailor sets out to retrieve the proverbial magic lamp when it is stolen by the Old Man of the Sea. Colorless. 1979; 48m.

ADVENTURES OF THE WILDERNESS FAMILY ★★★½

DIR: Stewart Raffill. **CAST:** Robert Logan, Susan D. Shaw, Ham Larsen, Heather Rattray, George (Buck) Flower, Hollye Holmes.

This is a variation on the Swiss Family Robinson story. A family (oddly enough named Robinson) moves to the Rocky Mountains to escape the frustrations and congestion of life in Los Angeles. They're sick of smog, hassles, and crime. And, more important, the daughter, Jenny (Heather

Rattray), has a serious respiratory problem that only fresh, clean air can rectify. They build a cabin and brave the dangers of the wild. Rated G. 1975; 100m.

ADVENTURES OF TOM SAWYER, THE ★★★★
DIR: Norman Taurog. **CAST:** Tommy Kelly, Jackie Moran, Victor Jory, May Robson, Walter Brennan, Ann Gillis.

One of the better screen adaptations of Mark Twain's works. Tommy Kelly is a perfect Tom Sawyer, but it's Victor Jory as the villainous Indian Joe who steals the show. Good sets and beautiful cinematography make this one work. Fine family entertainment for young and old. 1938; B&W; 93m.

ALADDIN ★★
DIR: Bruno Corbucci. **CAST:** Bud Spencer, Luca Venantini, Janet Agren.

Update of the Aladdin tale, with Bud Spencer as the genie from the lamp, discovered this time by a boy in a junk shop in a modern city. A little too cute at times, and the humor is forced. Not rated; contains some violence. 1987; 95m.

ALADDIN AND HIS MAGIC LAMP ★★★
DIR: Jean Image. **CAST:** Animated.

Artful animation helps to make this an engrossing version of the classic story. Young Aladdin finds the magic lamp and rescues the genie, but things go amiss when a black-hearted sorcerer puts the genie's power to evil use. 1985; 70m.

ALADDIN AND HIS WONDERFUL LAMP ★★★½
DIR: Tim Burton. **CAST:** Valerie Bertinelli, Robert Carradine, James Earl Jones, Leonard Nimoy.

This *Faerie Tale Theatre* interpretation of the classic Arabian Nights tale adds a few twists. One is the offer of the genie (James Earl Jones) to rearrange Aladdin's (Robert Carradine) face when Aladdin makes demands on him. The second surprise is the TV the genie produces to satisfy the sultan and win the princess (Valerie Bertinelli) for Aladdin. The whole family can enjoy this one. 1985; 60m.

ALAKAZAM THE GREAT ★★½
DIR: James H. Nicholson, Samuel Z. Arkoff. **CAST:** Animated.

Musical morality play for kids about the evils of pride and the abuse of power. When naïve little Alakazam the monkey is made king of the animals, he quickly develops an abusive personality that can only be set to rights through an arduous pilgrimage. Somewhat muddled, but watchable. 1961; 84m.

ALICE IN WONDERLAND ★★★½
DIR: Clyde Geronimi, Hamilton Luske, Wilfred Jackson. **CAST:** Animated.

The magic of the Walt Disney Studio animators is applied to Lewis Carroll's classic in this feature-length cartoon with mostly entertaining results. As with the book, the film is episodic and lacking the customary Disney warmth. But a few absolutely wonderful sequences—like the Mad Hatter's tea party and the appearances of the Cheshire cat—make it worth seeing. Rated G. 1951; 75m.

ALICE'S ADVENTURES IN WONDERLAND ★★
DIR: William Sterling. **CAST:** Fiona Fullerton, Dudley Moore, Peter Sellers, Ralph Richardson, Spike Milligan.

This British live-action version of Lewis Carroll's classic tale is too long and boring. It is a musical that employs an endless array of silly songs, dances, and riddles. Although it sticks closely to the book, it's not as entertaining as Disney's fast-paced animated version of 1951. Rated G. 1973; 97m.

ALL CREATURES GREAT AND SMALL ★★★½
DIR: Terence Dudley. **CAST:** Christopher Timothy, Robert Hardy, Peter Davison.

This feature-length film picks up where the popular British television series left off, with veterinarian James Herriot (Christopher Timothy) returning to his home and practice after having served in World War II. Although he has been away for years, things quickly settle into a comfortable routine. The animal stories are lifted from Dr. Herriot's poignant, bittersweet books, with a few moments likely to require a hanky or two. 1986; 94m.

ALMOST ANGELS ★★½
DIR: Steve Previn. **CAST:** Peter Weck, Hans Holt, Fritz Eckhardt, Bruni Lobel, Sean Scully.

Schmaltzy film focusing on the Vienna Boys' Choir and the problems one boy encounters when his voice cracks and he can no longer sing in the choir. Rated G. 1962; 93m.

AMAZING DOBERMANS ★★
DIR: David Chudnow, Byron Chudnow. **CAST:** James Franciscus, Barbara Eden, Fred Astaire, Jack Carter.

Third in a series of films about do-gooder dogs pits a treasury agent (James Franciscus) against inept crooks who can dodge the long arm of the law but can't compete with the dogged determination of the Dobermans. Harmless, but hardly inspired. Rated G. 1976; 94m.

AMAZING MR. BLUNDEN, THE ★★★
DIR: Lionel Jeffries. **CAST:** Laurence Naismith, Lynne Frederick, Garry Miller, Dorothy Alison, Diana Dors.

Neat little ghost story about children from the 20th century (Lynne Frederick, Garry Miller) helping right a wrong done 100 years previously. Laurence Naismith is the mysterious (and amazing) Mr. Blunden, a 19th-century lawyer who is at home in the 20th century. The children seem a little old to be involved in this type of adventure, but on the whole the story is delightful. Rated PG. 1972; 100m.

AMERICAN TAIL, AN ★★★
DIR: Don Bluth. **CAST:** Dom DeLuise, Phillip Glasser, Madeline Kahn, Nehemiah Persoff, Christopher Plummer (voices).

An immigrant mouse becomes separated from his family while voyaging to the United States. The execution and lavish animation make up for the trite and predictable story. Film picks up steam with the introduction of Dom DeLuise, as a vegetarian cat. Rated G. 1986; 82m.

AMY ★★★½
DIR: Vincent McEveety. **CAST:** Jenny Agutter, Barry Newman, Kathleen Nolan, Chris Robinson, Margaret O'Brien, Nanette Fabray.

Disney warmth runs though this sensitive story. Jenny Agutter is Amy, a young woman who leaves her domineering husband after the death of their deaf son. She decides to teach at a school for the deaf. Since the movie is set in the 1900s, there are many barriers and prejudices for her to overcome. A film for the whole family. Rated G. 1981; 100m.

ANIMALYMPICS ★★★
DIR: Steve Lysberger. **CAST:** Animated.

Featuring the voices of Billy Crystal, Gilda Radner, and Harry Shearer, this feature brings the Olympics to life with animals from around the world. Though the production seems somewhat overlong, there are bright spots: a news commentator called Ba Ba Wawa and a pole-vaulting hippo. 1980; 78m.

ANNIE OAKLEY ★★★
DIR: Michael Lindsay-Hogg. **CAST:** Jamie Lee Curtis, Brian Dennehy, Cliff De Young, Nick Ramus, Joyce Van Patten.

This first episode of Shelley Duvall's new series, *Tall Tales and Legends*, deals with true-life character Annie Oakley. Jamie Lee Curtis convincingly plays the sharp-shooting Annie with Brian Dennehy as her Wild West show boss, Buffalo Bill. 1985; 52m.

ANT AND THE AARDVARK, THE ★★★

DIR: Friz Freleng, George Gordon, Gerry Chiniqy. **CAST:** Animated.

Relying on dialogue and characterizations that are obviously aimed at adults, this laugh-filled cartoon series is strongly reminiscent of the Warner Bros. Road Runner cartoons. Here, a hungry aardvark is continually confounded by an inventive red ant. Five episodes are offered on this tape. 1969; 32m.

ANY FRIEND OF NICHOLAS NICKLEBY IS A FRIEND OF MINE ★★★½

DIR: Ralph Rosenblum. **CAST:** Fred Gwynne.

A charming period piece by author Ray Bradbury. Fred Gwynne shines as a mysterious stranger who comes to a small Illinois town where he takes an imaginative schoolboy under his wing. This is a poignant and humorous drama comparable to PBS's award-winning *Anne of Green Gables*. 1981; 55m.

APPLE DUMPLING GANG, THE ★★

DIR: Norman Tokar. **CAST:** Bill Bixby, Tim Conway, Don Knotts, Susan Clark, David Wayne, Slim Pickens, Harry Morgan.

A gambler (Bill Bixby) inherits three children who find a huge gold nugget in a supposedly played-out mine in 1870. Tim Conway and Don Knotts trip and foul up as left-footed bad guys. The best word for this is "innocuous." Good, clean, unoriginal, predictable fare from Disney. The kids will love it. Rated G. 1975; 100m.

APPLE DUMPLING GANG RIDES AGAIN, THE ★½

DIR: Vincent McEveety. **CAST:** Tim Conway, Don Knotts, Harry Morgan, Jack Elam, Kenneth Mars, Ruth Buzzi, Robert Pine.

A cast composed of comic actors, each of whom is top-notch in solo spots, is no guarantee of hilarious ensemble playing. In this sequel to the 1975 original, Tim Conway and Don Knotts again play bumbling, inept outlaws in the Old West. Not quite a turkey, but close! Even so, the kids will enjoy it—once. Rated G. 1979; 88m.

ARCHER'S ADVENTURE ★★★

DIR: Denny Lawrence. **CAST:** Brett Climo, Robert Coleby, Tony Barry.

The two-hour running time may be a bit long for young children, but otherwise this adventure makes for good family viewing. In nineteenth-century Australia, a young man crosses the country with an untried horse that he wants to enter in a race. Based on a true story (or, as a title notes, "It probably didn't happen this way, but it should have"), *Archer's Adventure* has plenty of engaging characters and incidents. Unrated. 1985; 120m.

AROUND THE WORLD IN 80 DAYS (1974) ★★★

DIR: Arthur Rankin Jr., Jules Bass. **CAST:** Animated.

A turn-of-the-century English gentleman, Phileas Fogg, undertakes a wager to go around the globe in eighty days despite endless obstacles. This is well paced for youngsters, but includes dialogue that even adults will find amusing. Made for television. 1974; 60m.

ASTERIX: THE GAUL (SERIES) ★★★

DIR: René Goscinny. **CAST:** Animated.

Walt Disney Productions picked up this series of history-spoofing cartoons from a talented French cartoon maker for release on videocassette. Asterix, a mysteriously powerful Gallic warrior, tromps through a variety of notable periods in history, telling the tales from a whimsical, action-filled perspective. 1967; 67m.

BABES IN TOYLAND ★★

DIR: Jack Donohue. **CAST:** Ray Bolger, Tommy Sands, Ed Wynn, Annette Funicello, Tommy Kirk.

A disappointing Disney version of the Victor Herbert operetta. In Mother

Goose Land, Barnaby (Ray Bolger) kidnaps Tom the Piper's Son (Tommy Sands) in order to marry Mary (Annette Funicello). The Toymaker (Ed Wynn) and his assistant (Tommy Kirk) eventually provide the means for Tom to save the day. Despite a good Disney cast, this film never jells. Rated G. 1961; 105m.

BABY TAKE A BOW ★★½
DIR: Harry Lachman. **CAST:** Shirley Temple, James Dunn, Claire Trevor.

In Shirley Temple's first starring vehicle, she helps her dad, who's accused of stealing a valuable necklace. Shirley must outthink the investigators in order to clear Dad's name. She pouts a lot but makes up for it with her charming rendition of "On Accounta' I Love You." 1934; B&W; 76m.

BACH AND BROCCOLI ★★
DIR: André Melançon. **CAST:** Andrée Pelletier.

Slow-moving family-fare film made in Quebec. A 12-year-old girl is forced to live with her bachelor uncle. The two establish an uneasy relationship. Not rated, but equivalent to G. 1986; 96m.

BAMBI ★★★★★
DIR: David Hand. **CAST:** Animated.

This lush adaptation of Felix Salten's beloved story represents the crowning achievement of Walt Disney's animation studio. Never again would backgrounds be delineated with such realistic detail, with animation so precise that it resembled live photography. The screenplay, too, has a bit more bite than the average Disney yarn, with equal helpings of comedy and tragedy fueling a confrontation between forest animals and that most horrific of two-legged interlopers: man. 1942; 69m.

BAREFOOT EXECUTIVE, THE ★★
DIR: Robert Butler. **CAST:** Kurt Russell, Joe Flynn, Harry Morgan, Wally Cox, Heather North, Alan Hewitt, John Ritter.

Mild Disney comedy about an individual (Kurt Russell) who finds a chimpanzee that can select top television shows. Rated G. 1971; 92m.

BARNEY BEAR CARTOON FESTIVAL ★★½
DIR: Rudolf Ising, Michael Lah, Preston Blair, Hugh Harman. **CAST:** Animated.

This collection of Barney Bear cartoons is interesting because the main character is different in three of the four features. Nevertheless, he never fails to come out a loser in each episode. These cartoons find him coping with everything from a leaky roof to insomnia to the pursuit of a wild Mexican jumping bean. 1939–1948; 32m.

BARON MUNCHAUSEN ★★★
DIR: Karel Zeman. **CAST:** Milos Kopecky, Jana Brejchova.

The adventures of the German folkhero, noted for the tallest tales ever told, are recounted here in a blend of live action and inventive animation. Unfortunataely, the story itself is rather boring, so while adults may enjoy the unique special effects, kids are likely to get antsy. Also known as *The Fabulous Baron Munchausen*. In German with English subtitles. 1961; 110m.

BATMAN (1966) ★★★
DIR: Leslie Martinson. **CAST:** Adam West, Burt Ward, Frank Gorshin, Burgess Meredith, Lee Meriwether, Cesar Romero.

Holy success story! The caped crusader and his youthful sidekick jump from their popular mid-1960s television series into a full-length feature film. Adam West and Burt Ward keep quip in cheek as they battle the Fearsome Foursome: the Riddler (Frank Gorshin), the Penguin (Burgess Meredith), the Catwoman (Lee Meriwether), and the Joker (Cesar Romero). Very silly material played with ludicrous seriousness, resulting in a lot of fun. 1966; 105m.

BATTERIES NOT INCLUDED ★★★
DIR: Matthew Robbins. **CAST:** Hume Cronyn, Jessica Tandy, Frank McRae, Elizabeth Peña.

Pleasant fantasy feature about tenement dwellers who are terrorized by thugs hired by a land developer. All seems lost until a group of tiny aliens comes to their aid. The screenplay by Mick Garris has its moments, but often the movie is simply too derivative and predictable. That said, the younger set will love it. Rated PG. 1987; 106m.

BE MY VALENTINE, CHARLIE BROWN ★★★
DIR: Phil Roman. **CAST:** Animated.
Writer Charles Schulz goes overboard with his cruelty toward Charlie Brown in this holiday saga, which finds our hero dragging a suitcase to school in anticipation of all the cards he'll receive during a classwide valentine exchange. Linus, meanwhile, empties his piggy bank to purchase an elaborate chocolate heart for his favorite teacher, Miss Othmar. 1975; 25m.

BEANY AND CECIL ★★★★
DIR: Bob Clampett. **CAST:** Animated.
Baby boomers will love the references to 1960s television shows and events in this classic series of cartoons on tape, though today's kids may find it somewhat confusing. Nevertheless, the adventures of Beany and Cecil offer enough fun-filled entertainment for viewers of all ages to enjoy. Each of the ten volumes in this series offers six pun-filled adventures. 1984; 60m.

BEAR WHO SLEPT THROUGH CHRISTMAS, THE ★★½
DIR: Hawley Pratt, Gerry Chiniqy. **CAST:** Animated.
Tommy Smothers is the voice of Ted E. Bear, who, defying the mandate of his employer at the honey factory, skips winter hibernation to find out what all the hubbub behind Christmas is. He's rewarded for his cheeky endeavors in the end. Other voices you'll recognize include those of Barbara Feldon and Arte Johnson. 1983; 60m.

BEAUTY AND THE BEAST (1983) ★★★★
DIR: Roger Vadim. **CAST:** Klaus Kinski, Susan Sarandon.
A merchant's daughter takes her father's place as the prisoner of a melancholy beast and finds that love can change all things. Klaus Kinski is marvelous as the Beast and Susan Sarandon a fine Beauty in this *Faerie Tale Theatre* production. 1983; 52m.

BEDKNOBS AND BROOMSTICKS ★★★½
DIR: Robert Stevenson. **CAST:** Angela Lansbury, David Tomlinson, Roddy McDowall.
Angela Lansbury is a witch who uses her powers to aid the Allies against the Nazis during World War II. She transports two children to faraway and strange locales during which they meet and play soccer with talking animals, among other things. This Disney film is an effective combination of special effects, animation, and live action. Rated G. 1971; 117m.

BELSTONE FOX, THE ★★
DIR: James Hill. **CAST:** Eric Porter, Jeremy Kemp, Bill Travers, Rachel Roberts.
An orphaned fox cub is raised in captivity and cleverly eludes both hounds and hunters. Although the plot and dialogue are somewhat lacking, the film is worth watching for the animal photography. Unrated, but contains some violence to animals. 1973; 103m.

BEN AND ME ★★★★
DIR: Hamilton Luske. **CAST:** Animated.
Walt Disney's entire animation team contributed to the luxurious look of this short, which follows the adventures of Amos the Mouse (voiced by Sterling Holloway), companion and unknown confidant to Benjamin Franklin. Apparently Amos helped ol' Ben come up with his most famous ideas! 1954; 25m.

BENIKER GANG, THE ★★½
DIR: Ken Kwapis. **CAST:** Andrew McCarthy, Jennie Dundas, Charles Fields, Jeff Alan-Lee, Danny Pintauro.

Pleasant family film has Andrew McCarthy as Arthur Beniker, 18-year-old orphanage inmate who leads an "orphanage break" of four other incorrigibles. Not too cutesy, and the story even makes some sense. Rated G; suitable for the entire family. 1985; 87m.

BENJI ★★★★
DIR: Joe Camp. **CAST:** Peter Breck, Deborah Walley, Edgar Buchanan, Frances Bavier, Patsy Garrett.

Benji parallels *Lassie* and *Rin Tin Tin* by intuitively doing the right thing at the right time. In this film, a dog saves two children who get kidnapped. Unlike Lassie or Rin Tin Tin, Benji is a small, unassuming mutt, which makes him all the more endearing. Rated G. 1974; 86m.

BENJI THE HUNTED ★★★
DIR: Joe Camp. **CAST:** Benji.

Most kids will love this adventure featuring everyone's favorite sweet-faced mutt slogging his poor little lost way through the wilderness of the Pacific Northwest to civilization. Rated G. 1987; 90m.

BEST OF BUGS BUNNY AND FRIENDS, THE ★★★★
DIR: Tex Avery, Bob Clampett, Arthur Davis, Friz Freleng, Chuck Jones. **CAST:** Animated.

Some of the best pre-1947 Warner Bros. cartoons have been collected for this long overdue package. Highlights include Bob Clampett's "What's Cookin' Doc?" (in which Bugs Bunny campaigns shamelessly for an Oscar) and Friz Freleng's Oscar-winning "Tweetie Pie," as well as Chuck Jones's touching and clever "Bedtime for Sniffles." A treasure for fans of classic cartoons. For all ages. 1986; 53m.

BEST OF LITTLE LULU ★★★
DIR: Seymour Kneitel, I. Sparber. **CAST:** Animated.

This is a fine collection of six of the original Famous Studios Lulu cartoons. Particularly delightful is "Lulu Gets the Birdie," in which our heroine drives a photographer nuts as she tries to get her picture taken. 1943; 55m.

BETTY BOOP—A SPECIAL COLLECTOR'S EDITION ★★★★
DIR: Dave Fleischer. **CAST:** Animated.

The zany, often bizarre Boop cartoons of the 1930s, with lecherous villains drooling over wide-eyed, luscious-legged, skimpily clad Betty, are best suited for older children or adults. The special collector's edition offers a winning array of the best adventures featuring the "oop poop a doop" girl, including "Betty Boop's Rise to Fame" with special live action provided by "Uncle" Max Fleischer. Other segments include the talents of Cab Calloway and Louis Armstrong. 1930; 90m.

BIG RED ★★★
DIR: Norman Tokar. **CAST:** Walter Pidgeon, Gilles Payant, Emile Genest, Janette Bertrand.

This pleasant family film drawn from the beloved children's book of the same title features Walter Pidgeon as the owner of a sleek Irish setter named Big Red, which spends its formative years in loving companionship with young Gilles Payant. When the dog grows older and is groomed for professional shows, it escapes and tries to find its youthful friend. 1962; 89m.

BILLION DOLLAR HOBO, THE ★★
DIR: Stuart E. McGowan. **CAST:** Tim Conway, Will Geer.

This film has Tim Conway playing a sympathetic hobo. Conway does his familiar down-and-out bumpkin role, but the rest of the cast is wasted. The slow pace is a further drawback. Rated G for family viewing. 1978; 96m.

BIRCH INTERVAL, THE ★★★
DIR: Delbert Mann. **CAST:** Eddie Albert, Rip Torn, Susan McClung, Ann Wedgeworth, Anne Revere.
Engaging, poignant 11-year-old Susan McClung learns lessons of life and love while living with relatives in Amish Pennsylvania. An excellent cast makes this sadly neglected film a memorable viewing experience. 1976; 104m.

BLACK ARROW ★★★½
DIR: John Hough. **CAST:** Oliver Reed, Georgia Slowe, Benedict Taylor, Fernando Rey, Donald Pleasence.
In this enjoyable Disney adventure film, Sir Daniel Brackley (Oliver Reed), a corrupt and wealthy landowner, is robbed by the Black Arrow, an outlaw. He then conceives of a plan to marry his ward, Joanna (Georgia Slowe), and send his nephew (Benedict Taylor) to his death. The tide turns when his nephew and the Black Arrow combine forces to rescue Joanna. 1984; 93m.

BLACK BEAUTY (1946) ★★★
DIR: Max Nosseck. **CAST:** Mona Freeman, Richard Denning, Evelyn Ankers, J. M. Kerrigan, Terry Kilburn.
Based on Anna Sewell's novel that is about a little girl's determined effort to find her missing black colt. Though pedestrian at times, the treatment is still effective enough to hold interest and bring a tear or two. 1946; B&W; 74m.

BLACK BEAUTY (1971) ★★
DIR: James Hill. **CAST:** Mark Lester, Walter Slezak, Patrick Mower.
One of the world's most-loved children's books, *Black Beauty* has never been translated adequately to the screen. This version is passable at best, an international coproduction. Kids who've read the book may want to see the movie, though this movie won't make anyone want to read the book. 1971; Great Britain/Germany/Spain; 106m.

BLACK PLANET, THE 🦃
DIR: Paul Williams. **CAST:** Animated.
Though promoted on its packaging as "delightful animation with a contemporary theme," this sophomorically animated feature is too cynical for some children. Two warring factions of the mythical planet Terra Verte consider destroying each other with doomsday weapons in order to gain control of dwindling resources. 1984; 78m.

BLACK STALLION, THE ★★★★★
DIR: Carroll Ballard. **CAST:** Kelly Reno, Mickey Rooney, Teri Garr, Hoyt Axton, Clarence Muse.
Before taking our breath away with the superb *Never Cry Wolf*, director Carroll Ballard made an impressive directorial debut with this gorgeous screen version of the well-known children's story. Kelly Reno plays the young boy stranded on a deserted island with "The Black," a wild, but very intelligent, horse who comes to be his best friend. It's a treat the whole family can enjoy. Rated G. 1979; 118m.

BLACK STALLION RETURNS, THE ★★★★
DIR: Robert Dalva. **CAST:** Kelly Reno, Vincent Spano, Teri Garr, Allen Garfield, Woody Strode.
A sequel to the 1979 film *The Black Stallion*, this is first-rate fare for the young and the young at heart. The story, based on the novel by Walter Farley, picks up where the first film left off. Alec Ramsey (Kelly Reno) is a little older and a little taller, but he still loves his horse, The Black. And this time, Alec must journey halfway around the world to find the stallion, which has been stolen by an Arab chieftain. Rated PG for slight violence. 1983; 93m.

BLACKBEARD'S GHOST ★★★
DIR: Robert Stevenson. **CAST:** Peter Ustinov, Dean Jones, Suzanne Pleshette, Elsa Lanchester.
This fun Disney comedy has Peter Ustinov playing a ghost who must prevent his ancestors' home from be-

coming a gambling casino. 1968; 107m.

BLUE BIRD, THE ★★½

DIR: Walter Lang. **CAST:** Shirley Temple, Spring Byington, Nigel Bruce.

Following on the success of *The Wizard of Oz*, this extravagant fantasy features Shirley Temple as a spoiled brat who seeks true happiness by leaving her loving parents' home. She meets some remarkable characters before realizing that there's no place like home. Film is remarkable for the star's characterization of a spiteful little crab, which contrasts markedly with her usual sunny roles. 1940; 88m.

BLUE FIN ★★

DIR: Carl Schultz. **CAST:** Hardy Krüger, Greg Rowe, Liddy Clark, Hugh Keays-Byrne.

The son of a commercial fisherman finds that growing up is hard to do, especially when he has to do so before he's ready. On a fishing trip with his father, the boy is caught in a storm. With the fishing boat nearly destroyed and his father seriously injured, the young hero must act responsibly for the first time in his life. 1977; 93m.

BLUE FIRE LADY ★★½

DIR: Ross Dimsey. **CAST:** Catherine Harrison, Mark Holden, Peter Cummins.

The story of racetracks and horse racing, the trust and love between an animal and a person are well handled in this family film. It chronicles the story of Jenny (Cathryn Harrison) and her love for horses, which endures despite her father's disapproval. 1983; 96m.

BLUE YONDER, THE ★★★½

DIR: Mark Rosman. **CAST:** Peter Coyote, Huckleberry Fox, Art Carney, Dennis Lipscomb, Joe Flood, Mittie Smith, Frank Simons.

Heartfelt tale of a boy (Huckleberry Fox) who goes back in time via a time machine to warn his late grandfather (Peter Coyote) of his unsuccessful attempt at a nonstop transatlantic flight. Good performances keep the creaky plot airborne. 1985; 89m.

BOATNIKS, THE ★★½

DIR: Norman Tokar. **CAST:** Robert Morse, Stefanie Powers, Phil Silvers, Norman Fell, Mickey Shaughnessy.

Disney comedy in which Robert Morse plays a heroic Coast Guard officer who manages a romantic relationship with Stefanie Powers while pursuing bumbling thieves (Phil Silvers, Norman Fell, and Mickey Shaughnessy). Rated G. 1970; 99m.

BOB THE QUAIL ★

DIR: Not Credited. **CAST:** Animated.

This collection of three episodes featuring Bob the Quail and his woodland friends offers viewers some lessons on the lives of wild creatures. Storytelling goes in-depth here to explain the way these birds mate, build nests, raise their young, and relate to other animals in the food chain. A subsequently produced video, *Chatterer the Squirrel*, provides essentially the same information from a squirrel's perspective. 1978; 60m.

BON VOYAGE ★½

DIR: James Neilson. **CAST:** Fred MacMurray, Jane Wyman, Michael Callan, Deborah Walley.

This Walt Disney production about an American family's misadventures on a European holiday is close to a dud. The cast is okay but the script is slow and far from intelligent. 1962; 130m.

BON VOYAGE, CHARLIE BROWN ★★★

DIR: Bill Melendez. **CAST:** Animated.

An animated film starring the "Peanuts" gang, this is well suited for viewing by the younger generation. It's basically a "Peanuts" guide to world travel. Rated G. 1980; 75m.

BONGO ★★

DIR: Jack Kinney, Bill Roberts, Hamilton Luske. **CAST:** Animated.

Originally part of a Disney feature-length blend of live action and animation called *Fun and Fancy Free*, this cartoon short follows the adventures of a little circus bear who flees the big top for the wonders of the open woods. The flimsy story is further marred by pathetic songs and endless countryside vistas, but historians will note an early appearance by the chipmunks who would shortly become Chip 'n' Dale. 1947; 36m.

BORN FREE ★★★★★

DIR: James Hill. **CAST:** Virginia McKenna, Bill Travers, Geoffrey Keen, Peter Lukoye.

An established family classic, this is the tale of Elsa the lioness and her relationship with an African game warden and his wife. 1966; 96m.

BOY GOD, THE ★

DIR: J. Erastheo Navda. **CAST:** Niño Muhlach.

Too childish for adults and too adult for children, *The Boy God* concerns Rocco, the boy god (good name for a god) and his fight against the forces of the netherworld. Rocco makes a very pudgy deity and spends more time in the film dealing with regular life than with fighting fantastical enemies. Poorly dubbed and not rated, but contains some violence. 1986; 100m.

BOY NAMED CHARLIE BROWN, A ★★★★

DIR: Bill Melendez. **CAST:** Animated.

Charles Schulz's "Peanuts" gang jumps to the big screen in this delightful, wistful tale of Charlie Brown's shot at fame in a national spelling bee. Rated G. 1969; 85m.

BOY TAKES GIRL ★★

DIR: Michal Bat-Adam. **CAST:** Gabi Eldor, Hillel Neeman, Dina Limon.

A young girl learns to adapt when her parents leave her at a farming cooperative one summer and fly away for a vacation. Some adult themes and more romance than may be acceptable for younger viewers, but this comedy-drama is passable for older kids. 1983; 93m.

BOY WHO LEFT HOME TO FIND OUT ABOUT THE SHIVERS, THE ★★★½

DIR: Graeme Clifford. **CAST:** Peter MacNicol, Dana Hill, Christopher Lee, David Warner, Frank Zappa, Jeff Corey.

In this *Faerie Tale Theatre* production narrated by Vincent Price, a boy (Peter MacNicol, of *Sophie's Choice*) goes off to a Transylvanian castle (operated by Christopher Lee, no less) to find out about fear. Good moments overcome a rather protracted mid-section. Not for young children. 1985; 54m.

BRAVE ONE, THE ★★★★

DIR: Irving Rapper. **CAST:** Michel Ray, Rodolfo Hoyos, Elsa Cardenas, Joi Lansing.

Above-average family film about a Mexican boy whose pet bull is sold. Knowing that its fate is to die in the bullfighting ring, the boy tracks his pet to Mexico City, where he does everything he can to save it. Winner of an Academy Award for best original story, which went unclaimed for almost twenty years because screenwriter, "Robert Rich" was really the blacklisted Dalton Trumbo. 1956; 102m.

BRIGHT EYES ★★★½

DIR: David Butler. **CAST:** Shirley Temple, James Dunn, Jane Withers, Judith Allen.

Delicious melodrama finds Shirley Temple living in a fine mansion as the maid's daughter. After her mom's untimely death, three people vie for her adoption rights. Curly Shirley is irresistible as the ever-cheerful little bright eyes. 1934; 83m.

BRIGHTY OF THE GRAND CANYON ★★

DIR: Norman Foster. **CAST:** Joseph Cotten, Dick Foran, Karl Swensen, Pat Conway.

Acceptable little film for the family. Brighty is a desert mule who teams up with Dick Foran, a prospector who has discovered a large vein of gold in the Grand Canyon. The photography is quite good. 1967; 89m.

BROTHERS LIONHEART, THE ★★½

DIR: Olle Hellbron. **CAST:** Staffan Gotestam, Lars Soderdahl, Allan Edwall.

This slow-moving children's fantasy filmed in Sweden, Denmark, and Finland features two brothers who are reunited after death in a medieval world where they fight dragons and villains in an attempt to free their war leader, Ulva, who will rid the country of tyrants. If you don't fall asleep within the first forty-five minutes, you will be rewarded with a fine fairy tale. Rated G. 1977; 108m.

BUGS AND DAFFY: THE WARTIME CARTOONS ★★★★★

DIR: Bob Clampett, Friz Freleng, Chuck Jones, Frank Tashlin. **CAST:** Animated.

This is a tape you'll want to own. Due to their war-theme content and blatant propaganda, most of these eleven cartoons haven't been seen in decades. The classic standouts include Chuck Jones's "Super Rabbit" and Bob Clampett's "Drafty Daffy" (with our daft hero attempting to escape the draft board) and "Falling Hare" (featuring Bugs's frantic battle with an airplane gremlin). Chaotic pacing and inspired animation make these must-see cartoons, no matter *what* their subject. And you truly haven't lived until you've seen how a certain Herr Hitler fares in these shorts.... 1943–1945; 120m.

BUGS AND DAFFY'S CARNIVAL OF THE ANIMALS ★★★

DIR: Chuck Jones. **CAST:** Animated.

The Saint-Saëns is given an animated twist by director Chuck Jones, who uses Bugs Bunny and Daffy Duck to introduce each of the individual themes. For once, the limited animation found in these late-entry made-for-television specials is appropriate; the simpler style blends nicely with the music and generates fond memories of Disney's *Fantasia*. 1976; 26m.

BUGS BUNNY AND ELMER FUDD CARTOON FESTIVAL FEATURING "WABBIT TWOUBLE" ★★★★

DIR: Tex Avery, Bob Clampett, Friz Freleng. **CAST:** Animated.

Another winning collection of vintage Warner Bros. cartoons, this tape features some real classics. For example, Bob Clampett's "The Big Snooze" has Elmer Fudd quitting the studio because of a contract dispute. It's a riot. So is Friz Freleng's "Slick Hare," in which tough-guy Humphrey Bogart demands a rabbit dinner from restauranteur Elmer. 1940–1946; 54m.

BUGS BUNNY CARTOON FESTIVAL FEATURING "HOLD THE LION PLEASE" ★★★

DIR: Bob Clampett, Friz Freleng, Chuck Jones. **CAST:** Animated.

Two of the cartoons in this collection—Friz Freleng's "Racketeer Rabbit" and Chuck Jones's "Super Rabbit"—are recognized classics in the wascally wabbit's career; the former, in particular, is a showcase for Bugs's impressive abilities at chaotic improvisation. (It also includes an early appearance by the Edward G. Robinson–type baddie who later evolved into the semiregular dubbed Rocky.) The others, Jones's "Hold the Lion Please" and Bob Clampett's "Buckaroo Bugs," are worth a chuckle or two. 1942–1946; 34m.

BUGS BUNNY CLASSICS ★★★★★

DIR: Tex Avery, Friz Freleng, Chuck Jones, Robert McKimson. **CAST:** Animated.

Absolutely the finest collection of Bugs Bunny cartoons currently available. Beginning with a fast-paced early entry—Tex Avery's "Heckling Hare"—this tape moves up to Marvin the Martian's first appearance, in Chuck Jones's "Haredevil Hare." Friz Freleng also contributes a related pair, with "Hare Trigger" (Yosemite Sam's debut) and "Bugs Bunny Rides Again" (Sam's third appearance). Throw in Robert McKimson's "Acrobatty Bunny" and one more each from Freleng and Jones, and you've got a great hour's entertainment. 1941–1948; 60m.

BUGS BUNNY IN KING ARTHUR'S COURT ★★★
DIR: Chuck Jones. **CAST:** Animated.
Improper travel advice ". . . from Ray Bradbury" sends Bugs Bunny on a decidedly wrong turn in this special, originally made for network television. Although King Arthur's territory has been mined by earlier and better Warner Bros. cartoons, writer-director Chuck Jones manages to produce a few genuine chuckles. 1977; 25m.

BUGS BUNNY/ROAD RUNNER MOVIE, THE ★★★★
DIR: Chuck Jones, Phil Monroe. **CAST:** Animated.
Classic cartoons made by Chuck Jones for Warner Bros. are interwoven into this laugh fest; the first and best of the 1970s and '80s feature-length compilations. Includes such winners as "Duck Amuck" and "What's Opera, Doc?" Rated G. 1979; 92m.

BUGS BUNNY, SUPERSTAR ★★★★
DIR: Larry Jackson. **CAST:** Animated.
A delightful collection of nine classic Warner Bros. cartoons from the Thirties and Forties. Produced mainly as a tribute to director Bob Clampett, this tape is a must-see if only for the hilarious *Fantasia* parody "Corny Concerto." Rated G. 1975; 90m.

BUGS BUNNY'S HARE-RAISING TALES ★★★
DIR: Friz Freleng, Chuck Jones, Abe Levitow, Robert McKimson. **CAST:** Animated.
Bugs Bunny tackles the classics in this amusing collection, from the three little pigs and the big, bad wolf (Robert McKimson's "The Wind-Blown Hare") to William Shakespeare (Abe Levitow's "A Witch's Tangled Hare"). The two standouts are Friz Freleng's "Rabbitson Crusoe," co-starring a shipwrecked Yosemite Sam, and Chuck Jones's "Rabbit Hood," which features a last-minute appearance by a most unexpected Robin Hood. 1948–1959; 45m.

BUGS BUNNY'S WACKY ADVENTURES ★★★★
DIR: Friz Freleng, Chuck Jones. **CAST:** Animated.
Warner Home Video pulled out all the stops on its Golden Jubilee 14-Karat Collection. Included are such Chuck Jones–directed classics as "Duck! Rabbit! Duck!," "Ali Baba Bunny," "Bunny Hugged," and "Long-Haired Hare." This is cartoon fun for all ages. 1985; 59m.

BUGSY MALONE ★★★½
DIR: Alan Parker. **CAST:** Scott Baio, Florrie Augger, Jodie Foster, John Cassisi, Martin Lev.
The 1920s gangsters weren't really as cute as these children, who run around shooting whipping cream out of their pistols. But if you can forget that, this British musical provides light diversion. Rated G. 1976; 93m.

CANDLESHOE ★★½
DIR: Norman Tokar. **CAST:** David Niven, Helen Hayes, Jodie Foster, Leo McKern, Vivian Pickles.
Confused Disney comedy about a street kid (Jodie Foster) duped by shady Leo McKern into posing as an heir to Helen Hayes. Marred by typically excessive Disney physical "humor" (read: slapstick). Rated G. 1977; 101m.

CANINE COMMANDO ★★★★½
DIR: Walt Disney. **CAST:** Animated.
Pluto goes to war in this impeccable trio of cartoons drawn from Disney's World War II years, serving hitches in the army ("The Army Mascot"), the navy ("Dog Watch"), and the coast guard ("Canine Patrol"). The first is the funniest, with Pluto's attempt to

chew tobacco; the last is the cutest, with an early appearance by the little turtle with the spring in its step. 1942–1945; 23m.

CANNON MOVIE TALES: THE EMPEROR'S NEW CLOTHES ★★★

DIR: David Irving. **CAST:** Sid Caesar, Robert Morse, Clive Revill.

Excellent big-budget version of Hans Christian Andersen's classic. Sid Caesar lends his broad comedic presence as the Emperor, and Robert Morse hams it up as the con man–tailor who designs the Emperor's new clothes. Not rated, but suitable for the family. 1989; 85m.

CANNON MOVIE TALES: RED RIDING HOOD ★★

DIR: Adam Brooks. **CAST:** Craig T. Nelson, Isabella Rossellini.

Ho-hum version of the fairy tale "Little Red Riding Hood" presents some major changes in the familiar story. Our heroine must deal with an absent father, a sleazy wolfman, and a grandmother who turns out to be a witch. Rated G. 1989; 84m.

CANNON MOVIE TALES: SLEEPING BEAUTY ★★★

DIR: David Irving. **CAST:** Morgan Fairchild, Tahnee Welch, Nicholas Clay, Sylvia Miles, Kenny Baker, David Holliday.

Impressive but overly long re-telling of the children's classic fairy tale. Morgan Fairchild is the queen; Tahnee Welch is her beautiful daughter who falls under the evil spell. Rated G. 1989; 90m.

CANNON MOVIE TALES: SNOW WHITE ★★★½

DIR: Michael Berz. **CAST:** Diana Rigg, Sarah Peterson, Billy Barty.

Diana Rigg is outstanding as the evil queen–wicked stepmother in this enjoyable live-action version of the Brothers Grimm fairy tale. Rigg plots to do away with Snow White so that she will remain "the fairest in the land," but a septet of dwarfs and a handsome prince thwart her plans. 1989; 85m.

CANTERVILLE GHOST, THE ★★★

DIR: Paul Bogart. **CAST:** John Gielgud, Ted Wass, Andrea Marcovicci, Alyssa Milano, Harold Innocent, Lila Kaye.

Modern retelling of the classic Oscar Wilde short story, with John Gielgud as the blowhard ghost who tries to terrorize a spunky American family. Gielgud is excellent as the ghost, but Ted Wass is highly unsatisfactory as the father, and the ghostly shenanigans have a dangerous quality about them that was not present in the original. Unrated; suitable for older children. 1986; 96m.

CAPTAIN JANUARY ★★★

DIR: David Butler. **CAST:** Shirley Temple, Guy Kibbee, Buddy Ebsen, Jane Darwell.

Swept overboard, orphan Shirley Temple is taken in by a lonely lighthouse keeper (Guy Kibbee). The incredible dance number featuring Shirley and a local fisherman (Buddy Ebsen) is worth the price of the rental. 1936; B&W; 75m.

CAPTAIN SCARLET VS. THE MYSTERONS ★★★½

DIR: David Lane, Alan Perry, Desmond Saunders, Ken Turner. **CAST:** Animated.

Captain Scarlet, along with the Spectrum organization, must fight back when Martian invaders, the Mysterons, attack the planet Earth. Instead of standard animation, the film uses sophisticated puppets and technique called Supermarionation, which should fascinate young viewers. Rated G. 1967; 90m.

CARE BEARS MOVIE, THE ★★★

DIR: Aran Selznick. **CAST:** Mickey Rooney, Georgia Engel (voices).

Poor animation mars this children's movie about bears who cheer up a pair of kids. Rated G, no objectionable material. 1985; 80m.

CARTOON MOVIESTARS: BUGS! ★★★½

DIR: Bob Clampett, Friz Freleng, Chuck Jones, Robert McKimson. **CAST:** Animated.

Bugs Bunny performs without his regular co-stars in this collection, which includes first appearances by lesser lights in the Warners animated rogues' gallery: the Three Bears (in Chuck Jones's wonderful "Bugs Bunny and the Three Bears") and Beaky Buzzard (in Bob Clampett's superb "Bugs Bunny Gets the Boid"). Of the others, Robert McKimson's "Gorilla My Dreams" has become a minor classic, with its use of hilarious gags. A good collection. 1942–1948; 60m.

CARTOON MOVIESTARS: DAFFY! ★★★★

DIR: Tex Avery, Bob Clampett, Arthur Davis, Friz Freleng, Robert McKimson. **CAST:** Animated.

Bob Clampett's classic "The Great Piggybank Robbery" is the showpiece in this octet of Daffy Duck cartoons, and it's a chaotic blend of *film noir* and Dali-esque art that could only have come from Clampett's fevered imagination. Other high points include Clampett's "Book Revue" and a rare World War II–era entry, Friz Freleng's "Yankee Doodle Daffy." Historians will also appreciate Tex Avery's "Daffy Duck and Egghead," featuring an early appearance of the character who would mature into Elmer Fudd. 1938–1948; 60m.

CARTOON MOVIESTARS: ELMER! ★★★★

DIR: Arthur Davis, Friz Freleng, Chuck Jones. **CAST:** Animated.

Historians eager to follow the progress of Elmer Fudd will be delighted by this collection. A high point is Friz Freleng's "The Hare-Brained Hypnotist," in which Elmer and Bugs Bunny swap minds and bodies, and Mr. Fudd gets to torment his old foe in a new form. Also included are two later entries with Daffy Duck: Arthur Davis's "What Makes Daffy Duck?" and Chuck Jones's "A Pest in the House." Both are hysterical. 1940–1948; 60m.

CARTOON MOVIESTARS: PORKY! ★★★½

DIR: Tex Avery, Bob Clampett, Friz Freleng, Chuck Jones, Robert McKimson, Frank Tashlin. **CAST:** Animated.

Travel with us all the way back to 1935 and the birth of the Warners animation studio's first "modern" star: Porky Pig, in Friz Freleng's "I Haven't Got a Hat." Most of the other cartoons in this collection showcase Porky's excellent ability as a supporting player, including three wonderful team-ups with Daffy Duck: Chuck Jones's "My Favorite Duck," Bob Clampett's "Baby Bottleneck," and Robert McKimson's "Daffy Doodles." The best, however, is Jones's "Little Orphan Airedale." 1935–1947; 60m.

CARTOON MOVIESTARS: STARRING BUGS BUNNY ★★★★

DIR: Friz Freleng, Chuck Jones, Robert McKimson. **CAST:** Animated.

Bugs Bunny's second team-up with Yosemite Sam—Friz Freleng's "Buccaneer Bunny"—is the high point of this seven-cartoon collection, which also features a rare World War II–era title: Freleng's "Hare Force" (co-starring an early rendition of Tweety Pie's owner, Granny). Of the three by Chuck Jones, "Hare Tonic" is easily the funniest, with Bugs making a sap (yet again) of Elmer Fudd. 1944–1948; 54m.

CASEY AT THE BAT ★★½

DIR: David Steinberg. **CAST:** Elliott Gould, Bill Macy, Hamilton Camp, Carol Kane, Howard Cosell.

One of Shelley Duvall's *Tall Tales and Legends*. Howard Cosell narrates this embellishment of the Casey legend, with Elliott Gould's Casey as the father of baseball and Hamilton Camp as Boss Undercrawl, the evil landowner out to destroy the national pastime. Fairly imaginative. 1986; 52m.

CASEY'S SHADOW ★★½
DIR: Martin Ritt. **CAST:** Walter Matthau, Alexis Smith, Robert Webber, Murray Hamilton.
Only the droll playing of star Walter Matthau makes this family film watchable. Matthau is a horse trainer deserted by his wife and left to raise three sons. It lopes along at a slow pace, and only the star's fans will want to ride it out. Rated PG. 1978; 116m.

CASPER'S FIRST CHRISTMAS
DIR: Carl Urbano. **CAST:** Animated.
Cheap production values, including a new (not to mention, irritating) voice for Casper, make this a chore to watch. The classic cartoon character is joined by Hanna-Barbera's cavalcade of animated stars to help an old ghost save his condemned home for the holidays. A laugh track is included in case children don't find this amusing. They won't. 1987; 28m.

CASTAWAY COWBOY, THE ★★★½
DIR: Vincent McEveety. **CAST:** James Garner, Vera Miles, Robert Culp, Eric Shea.
James Garner plays a Texas cowboy in Hawaii during the 1850s. There he helps a lovely widow (Vera Miles) start a cattle ranch despite problems created by a land-grabbing enemy (played by Robert Culp). Good family entertainment. Rated G. 1974; 91m.

CAT, THE ½
DIR: Ellis Kadison. **CAST:** Peggy Ann Garner, Barry Coe, Roger Perry, Dwayne Rekin.
Poor story of a lost boy who is rescued by a wildcat. This may hold marginal interest for very small children. Walt Disney it isn't. 1966; 87m.

CAT FROM OUTER SPACE, THE ★★½
DIR: Norman Tokar. **CAST:** Ken Berry, Sandy Duncan, Harry Morgan, Roddy McDowall.
Disney comedy/sci-fi about a cat from outer space with a magical collar. The cat needs the United States to help it return to its planet. Rated G. 1978; 103m.

CHALLENGE TO BE FREE ★★
DIR: Tay Garnett, Ford Beebe. **CAST:** Mike Mazurki, Vic Christy, Jimmy Kane.
This forgettable film features a fur trapper being chased across one thousand miles of frozen Arctic wasteland by twelve men and one hundred dogs. Rated G. 1974; 88m.

CHARLEY AND THE ANGEL ★★
DIR: Vincent McEveety. **CAST:** Fred MacMurray, Cloris Leachman, Harry Morgan, Kurt Russell, Vincent Van Patten.
Time-worn plot about a guardian angel who teaches an exacting man (Fred MacMurray) a few lessons in kindness and humility before his time on Earth is up is reminiscent of many better, more sincere films. The kids won't mind, but chances are you've seen a better version already. 1973; 93m.

CHARLIE BROWN AND SNOOPY SHOW, THE (VOLUME I) ★★★
DIR: Bill Melendez, Sam Jaimes. **CAST:** Animated.
These eight vignettes, all taken from the Saturday-morning series of the same name, are marred by some weak material. The better episodes include Snoopy's Foot, in which the wounded beagle is traded for Marcie in a baseball exchange; "Vulture," a quickie with Snoopy's imitation of that bird of prey; and "Peppermint Patty," during which she finally learns that Snoopy *isn't* the "funny-looking kid with the big nose." 1983–1985; 45m.

CHARLIE BROWN AND SNOOPY SHOW, THE (VOLUME II) ★★★★
DIR: Bill Melendez, Sam Jaimes. **CAST:** Animated.
This collection of seven vignettes features some of the funnier tales drawn from Charles Schulz's newspaper strip. Peppermint Patty goes undercover to find the "Gold Stars" mis-

placed by her teacher; Lucy throws Schroeder's piano into the dreaded kite-eating tree; and Charlie Brown's misthrown bowling ball proves a surprise to Linus and Sally while they await the "Great Pumpkin." 1983–1985; 45m.

CHARLIE BROWN CELEBRATION, A ★★★★½

DIR: Bill Melendez. **CAST:** Animated.

Charles Schulz introduces this potpourri of tales lifted directly from his newspaper strip (a format later used on Saturday morning's *The Charlie Brown and Snoopy Show*). Peppermint Patty enrolls in the Ace (Dog) Obedience School in the belief that a diploma there will eliminate her need for conventional education; Lucy throws Schroeder's piano down a sewer; and Charlie Brown checks himself into a hospital after "feeling woozy." 1981; 50m.

CHARLIE BROWN CHRISTMAS, A ★★★★★

DIR: Bill Melendez. **CAST:** Animated.

The Peanuts cast made its animated debut in this adorable seasonal special, which should be required viewing for anybody concerned about losing the Christmas spirit. Charlie Brown searches through aluminum monstrosities and finds a forlorn wooden tree that needs "a little love," and Snoopy jumps on the commercial bandwagon by entering an outdoor decoration contest. Vince Guaraldi's jazz themes, which immediately became a series trademark, are a highlight. 1965; 25m.

CHARLIE BROWN THANKSGIVING, A ★★★★

DIR: Bill Melendez, Phil Roman. **CAST:** Animated.

Marcie and Woodstock make their animated debuts in this holiday fable that allows Linus (ever the sage) to explain the true meaning of Thanksgiving. Peppermint Patty invites herself and several friends to Charlie Brown's house for what she imagines to be a feast, but chef Snoopy has other ideas: buttered toast, popcorn, pretzels, and jelly beans. Vince Guaraldi's jazz background is particularly splendid. 1973; 25m.

CHARLIE BROWN'S ALL-STARS ★★★★★

DIR: Bill Melendez. **CAST:** Animated.

After a previous season with 999 losses and an opening game with a score of 123–0, Charlie Brown's baseball team decides to quit, in this second animated Peanuts outing. Chuck wins them back by promising team uniforms but then learns the sponsor won't endorse a team with (shudder) several girls and a dog. What will poor Charlie Brown do? As always, Vince Guaraldi's music is dazzling. 1966; 26m.

CHARLIE, THE LONESOME COUGAR ★★★

DIR: Not Credited. **CAST:** Ron Brown, Brian Russell, Linda Wallace, Jim Wilson, Rex Allen (narrator).

A misunderstood cougar comes into a lumber camp in search of food and companionship. After adopting the animal, the men are not certain whether it will adapt back to its wild habitat, or even if they want it to. This entertaining Disney animal film is more believable than the storyline would suggest. Rated G. 1968; 75m.

CHARLOTTE'S WEB ★

DIR: Charles A. Nichols, Iwao Takamoto. **CAST:** Debbie Reynolds, Paul Lynde, Henry Gibson (voices).

Absolutely wretched adaptation of E. B. White's beloved children's book. Charlotte the spider, Wilbur the pig, and Templeton the rat lose all their charm and turn into simpering participants in a vacuous musical. Blocky animation, typical of Hanna-Barbera's Saturday-morning drivel, and insipid songs. Only for those under age four. Rated G. 1973; 85m.

CHILD OF GLASS ★★

DIR: John Erman. **CAST:** Steve Shaw, Katy Kurtzman, Barbara Barrie, Biff McGuire, Nina Foch, Anthony Zerbe, Olivia Barash.

When a boy's parents buy an old New Orleans mansion, he discovers that it is haunted by the ghost of a young girl. He sets about solving the mystery of her death so that her spirit can rest. Inoffensive Disney made-for-TV movie with a hammy performance by Olivia Barash as the ghost. 1978; 93m.

CHILD'S CHRISTMAS IN WALES, A ★★

DIR: Don McBrearty. **CAST:** Denholm Elliott, Mathonwy Reeves.

Dylan Thomas's holiday classic gets a tasteful but disappointingly clumsy treatment in this made-for-public-television special. Director Don McBrearty's images do not complement Thomas's brilliantly evocative words, and often actually contradict them. A plot of sorts is imposed on the story that makes the film seem more like Walton Mountain than Thomas's mythical Welsh town of Llareggub. Not rated. 1987; 55m.

CHIP 'N' DALE AND DONALD DUCK ★★★★

DIR: Walt Disney. **CAST:** Animated.

The scruffier, less refined chipmunks of "Chip 'n' Dale" (1947) are the high point of this collection. There's a freshness to the cartoon that is absent in the later, more formulaic clashes between Donald Duck and the chipmunks. Still, "Out of Scale" is quite clever, as Chip 'n' Dale invade Donald's backyard train layout; and the creative use of tar in "Out on a Limb" is quite funny. 1947–1955; 48m.

CHIPMUNK ADVENTURE, THE ★★

DIR: Janice Karman. **CAST:** Animated.

Alvin, Simon, and Theodore go on a round-the-world adventure in this uninspired feature-length cartoon. What made the original, scruffy chipmunks so appealing is missing here, replaced by a sort of ersatz Disney plot about jewel-smuggling villains. The kids may get a kick out of this, but anyone over the age of nine is advised to find something else to do. Rated G. 1987; 76m.

CHITTY CHITTY BANG BANG ★★½

DIR: Ken Hughes. **CAST:** Dick Van Dyke, Sally Ann Howes, Anna Quayle, Lionel Jeffries, Benny Hill.

This musical extravaganza, based on a book by Ian Fleming, is aimed at a children's audience. In it, a car flies, but the flat jokes and songs leave adult viewers a bit seasick as they hope for a quick finale. However, the kiddies will like it. Rated G. 1968; 142m.

C.H.O.M.P.S. ★★

DIR: Don Chaffey. **CAST:** Wesley Eure, Valerie Bertinelli, Conrad Bain, Chuck McCann, Red Buttons, Jim Backus.

A small-town enterprise is saved from bankruptcy when a young engineer (Wesley Eure) designs a computer-controlled watchdog. *C.H.O.M.P.S.*, has a lot of the absurdity of a cartoon (Joseph Barbera, of Hanna-Barbera fame, conceived and produced the film). Kids under twelve may enjoy it, but the profanity thrown in for the PG rating is purely gratuitous. 1979; 90m.

CHRISTIAN THE LION ★★½

DIR: Bill Travers, James Hill. **CAST:** Bill Travers, Virginia McKenna, George Adamson.

A lion born in a London zoo is returned to the wilds in Kenya. This pleasant film is also interesting for the real-life drama. Bill Travers portrayed George Adamson, the wildlife expert, in *Born Free*. Now, Adamson is seen helping Christian adapt to his natural habitat. Rated G for family viewing. 1976; 89m.

CHRISTMAS CAROL, A (1938) ★★★½

DIR: Edwin L. Marin. **CAST:** Reginald Owen, Gene Lockhart, Kathleen Lockhart, Leo G. Carroll, Terry Kilburn.

This film version of Charles Dickens's Christmas classic is a better-than-average retelling of Ebenezer Scrooge's transformation from a greedy malcontent to a generous, compassionate businessman. Reginald Owen is fine as Scrooge, and so is the rest of the cast. 1938; B&W; 69m.

CHRISTMAS CAROL, A (1951) ★★★★★

DIR: Brian Desmond Hurst. **CAST:** Alastair Sim, Kathleen Harrison, Jack Warner, Michael Hordern.

Starring Alastair Sim as Ebenezer Scrooge, the meanest miser in all of London, this is a wondrously uplifting story—as only Charles Dickens could craft one. Recommended for the whole family, *A Christmas Carol* is sure to bring a tear to your eye and joy to your heart. 1951; B&W; 86m.

CHRISTMAS COAL MINE MIRACLE, THE ★★★

DIR: Jud Taylor. **CAST:** Mitchell Ryan, Kurt Russell, Andrew Prine, John Carradine, Barbara Babcock, Melissa Gilbert, Don Porter, Shelby Leverington.

In this made-for-television film a crew of striking coal miners, threatened by their union-busting bosses, enter a mine and are trapped by an explosion. The action is good, but the tone is too sweet. Also known as *Christmas Miracle in Caulfield, U.S.A.* 1977; 100m.

CHRISTMAS LILIES OF THE FIELD ★★★

DIR: Ralph Nelson. **CAST:** Billy Dee Williams, Maria Schell, Fay Hauser.

A handyman (Billy Dee Williams) returns to help nuns and orphans once again, in this sequel to the award-winning 1963 film. A solid, well-intentioned movie with the original director, yet not quite achieving the charm of the original. Not rated, but suitable for all ages. 1984; 98m.

CHRISTMAS STORY, A ★★★★

DIR: Bob Clark. **CAST:** Peter Billingsley, Darren McGavin, Melinda Dillon, Ian Petrella.

Both heartwarming and hilarious, this is humorist Jean Shepherd's wacky recollections of being a kid in the 1940s and the monumental Christmas that brought the ultimate longing—for a regulation Red Ryder air rifle. Problem is, his parents don't think it's such a good idea. But our hero isn't about to give up. Peter Billingsley is marvelous as the kid. Melinda Dillon and Darren McGavin also shine as the put-upon parents. A delight for young and old. Rated PG. 1983; 98m.

CINDERELLA (1950) ★★★★

DIR: Wilfred Jackson, Hamilton Luske, Clyde Geronimi. **CAST:** Animated.

In this underappreciated Disney delight, a pretty youngster, who is continually berated and abused by her stepmother and stepsisters, is given one night to fulfill her dreams by a fairy godmother with the help of some animal friends. The mice characters are among the studio's best, and the story moves along at a good clip. Almost in the league of *Snow White and the Seven Dwarfs* and *Pinocchio*, this animated triumph is sure to please the young and the young-at-heart. Rated G. 1950; 75m.

CINDERELLA (1985) ★★★★

DIR: Mark Cullingham. **CAST:** Jennifer Beals, Matthew Broderick, Jean Stapleton, Eve Arden, Edie McClurg.

This is one of the most entertaining of producer Shelley Duvall's *Faerie Tale Theatre* entries. Jennifer Beals is a shy, considerate, and absolutely gorgeous Cinderella; Matthew Broderick does his aw-shucks best as the smitten Prince Henry. Sweetly romantic, a treat for all. Unrated—family fare. 1985; 60m.

COLD RIVER ★★★★

DIR: Fred G. Sullivan. **CAST:** Suzanna Weber, Pete Teterson, Richard Jaeckel.

In the autumn of 1932, an experienced guide takes his 14-year-old daughter and his 12-year-old stepson on an extended camping trip. Far out in the wilderness, the father dies of a heart attack, and the children must survive a blizzard, starvation, and an encounter with a wild mountain man. A fine family movie. Rated PG. 1981; 94m.

COLUMBIA PICTURES CARTOON CLASSICS ★★★★½

DIR: John Hubley, Robert Cannon, Pete Burness. **CAST:** Animated.

Superb collection of cartoons produced by the UPA Studios for Columbia Pictures is highlighted by a sensational version of Edgar Allan Poe's chilling "The Tell-Tale Heart," which is read by James Mason. Other classics include "Gerald McBoing-Boing" (from the story by Dr. Seuss), "Ragtime Bear" (the first Mr. Magoo cartoon), James Thurber's wryly funny "A Unicorn in the Garden," and "Robin Hoodlum," a selection from the seldom seen Fox and Crow series. For all ages. 1948–1956; 56m.

COMPUTER WORE TENNIS SHOES, THE ★★

DIR: Robert Butler. **CAST:** Kurt Russell, Cesar Romero, Joe Flynn, William Schallert.

A student accidentally becomes a genius after being short-circuited with a computer. The movie is weak, with the "excitement" provided by a group of mobsters and gamblers which attempts to use the student for its nefarious purposes. 1969; 87m.

CONDORMAN ★½

DIR: Charles Jarrott. **CAST:** Michael Crawford, Oliver Reed, James Hampton, Barbara Carrera.

This Disney film has everything you've ever seen in a spy film—but it was better the first time. A comic book writer (Michael Crawford) gets his chance to become a spy when he goes after a beautiful Russian defector (Barbara Carrera). The best thing that can be said is that it's a watchable film that you can show your kids. Rated PG. 1981; 90m.

CONNECTICUT YANKEE IN KING ARTHUR'S COURT, A (1970) ★

DIR: Zoran Janjic. **CAST:** Animated.

Bland re-telling of the Mark Twain time-travel yarn is further destroyed by even blander animation. No doubt children and adults alike would be more interested in the cinematic version starring Bing Crosby. The fact that the makers of this cartoon tried to update the character into our century doesn't help. 1970; 74m.

CONTINUING ADVENTURES OF CHIP 'N' DALE, THE ★★★½

DIR: Walt Disney. **CAST:** Animated.

Contrary to this collection's theme, its best cartoon doesn't feature the chipmunks at all, but is instead a solo performance by Donald Duck: "Modern Inventions," which lets Donald loose in a futuristic museum full of gorgeously rendered labor-saving devices. Chip 'n' Dale make their best appearance in a rare team-up with Pluto, "Food for Feudin'." 1937–1951; 50m.

CRICKET IN TIMES SQUARE, A ★★★½

DIR: Chuck Jones. **CAST:** Animated.

This Chuck Jones production is the delightful tale of a country cricket named Chester who finds himself in the relatively unfriendly city of New York. A Parent's Choice award winner, recommended for all ages. 1973; 30m.

CRYSTALSTONE ★★½

DIR: Antonio Pelaez. **CAST:** Frank Grimes, Kamlesh Gupta.

Although it has a magical undercurrent, *Crystalstone* is more about the very down-to-earth adventures of two children escaping from a wicked guardian than about the fantastical Crystalstone, the fabled stone of happiness, which the kids are seeking. A good film for older children, with just enough action and ghoulishness to amuse them. Rated PG. 1987; 103m.

DAFFY DUCK CARTOON FESTIVAL: AIN'T THAT DUCKY ★★★★

DIR: Bob Clampett, Friz Freleng, Chuck Jones, Robert McKimson. **CAST:** Animated.

Fans must not miss this collection's prize—Bob Clampett's "The Wise Quacking Duck"—because it represents one of the most hilarious teamups between Warners Studio's most frenetic talent (Daffy) and its most manic animator (Clampett). Robert McKimson's "Daffy Duck Slept Here" is another standout, as it signifies one of the first partnerships with the mature, post–World War II Porky Pig. 1942–1948; 35m.

DAFFY DUCK: THE NUTTINESS CONTINUES ★★★★½

DIR: Tex Avery, Bob Clampett, Chuck Jones. **CAST:** Animated.

Chuck Jones's superb "Duck Amuck," in which the vain and selfish Daffy Duck gets more than his just deserts from an animated witch with a rather wicked sense of humor, is but one of many treats in this absolutely first-rate cartoon collection. 1985; 59m.

DAFFY DUCK'S MADCAP MANIA ★★★

DIR: Friz Freleng, Chuck Jones, Robert McKimson. **CAST:** Animated.

These late-period entries in Daffy Duck's canon feature numerous supporting faces, but the cartoons themselves are only average. Friz Freleng's "A Star Is Bored" is the best, with Daffy taking a new job as Bugs Bunny's stand-in. Chuck Jones's "You Were Never Duckier" is intriguing, as it also features Henry Hawk, usually associated with Foghorn Leghorn. The only other noteworthy selection is Freleng's "Golden Yeggs," with guest appearances by gangsters Rocky and Mugsy. 1948–1956; 45m.

DAFFY DUCK'S MOVIE: FANTASTIC ISLAND ★★

DIR: Friz Freleng. **CAST:** Animated.

This pedestrian compilation is for Warner Bros. cartoon fanatics and toddlers only. Chunks of fairly funny shorts are strung together with a weak, dated parody of TV's *Fantasy Island.* Daffy deserved better. Rated G. 1983; 78m.

DAFFY DUCK'S QUACKBUSTERS ★★★★

DIR: Greg Ford, Terry Lennon. **CAST:** Animated.

The best feature-length-film compilation of Warner Bros. cartoons since Chuck Jones's *Bugs Bunny/Road Runner Movie,* this release from Greg Ford and Terry Lennon features two new cartoons—"Quackbusters" and "Night of the Living Duck"—as well as classics from Jones ("Claws for Alarm," "Transylvania 6-5000," and "The Abominable Snow Rabbit") and Friz Freleng ("Hyde and Go Tweet"). The wraparound story was animated with as much care as the original cartoons, and the result is a delight for young and old. Rated G. 1988; 80m.

DAISY (LIMITED GOLD EDITION 1) ★★★½

DIR: Walt Disney. **CAST:** Animated.

Daisy Duck, never one of Disney's better stars, plays only a marginal role in these seven cartoons, most of which are nearly solo vehicles for Donald Duck. The animation is superb in "Mr. Duck Steps Out," which follows Donald and his nephews as they get ready for a date with Daisy. Of the remaining entries—marred by the noticeably weaker post–World War II art—"Sleepytime Donald" and "Donald's Dilemma" are the funniest. 1940–1950; 48m.

DANCING PRINCESSES, THE ★★★★

DIR: Peter Medak. **CAST:** Lesley Ann Warren, Peter Weller, Roy Dotrice.

This enchanting *Faerie Tale Theatre* production features Roy Dotrice as an overprotective king who locks his daughters in their room each night. When the shoe cobbler insists the princesses are wearing out a pair of dancing slippers each day, the king offers one of his daughters to any man who can discover where the girls go each night. A charming tale which is suitable for the entire family. 1984; 50m.

DANNY ★★★
DIR: Gene Feldman. **CAST:** Rebecca Page, Janet Zarish.

A warm, touching, predictable story of an unhappy little girl who obtains a horse that has been injured and then sold off by the spoiled daughter of the wealthy stable owners. A fine family film. Rated G. 1977; 90m.

DARBY O'GILL AND THE LITTLE PEOPLE ★★★½
DIR: Robert Stevenson. **CAST:** Albert Sharpe, Janet Munro, Sean Connery, Jimmy O'Dea.

Darby O'Gill is an Irish storyteller who becomes involved with some of the very things he talks about, namely leprechauns, the banshee, and other Irish folk characters. Darby tricks the leprechaun king into granting him three wishes but soon regrets his trickery. This wonderful tale is one of Disney's best films and a delightful fantasy film in its own right. It features a young and relatively unknown Sean Connery as Darby's future son-in-law. 1959; 93m.

DAVY CROCKETT AND THE RIVER PIRATES ★★★
DIR: Norman Foster. **CAST:** Fess Parker, Buddy Ebsen, Kenneth Tobey, Jeff York.

Fess Parker, as idealized Davy Crockett, takes on Big Mike Fink (Jeff York) in a keelboat race and tangles with Indians in the second Walt Disney–produced Davy Crockett feature composed of two television episodes. Thoroughly enjoyable and full of the kind of boyhood images that Disney productions evoked so successfully in the late 1940s and '50s. Fun for the whole family. 1956; 81m.

DAVY CROCKETT (KING OF THE WILD FRONTIER) ★★★½
DIR: Norman Foster. **CAST:** Fess Parker, Buddy Ebsen, Hans Conried, Kenneth Tobey.

Finely played by all involved, this is actually a compilation of three episodes that appeared originally on television and were then released theatrically. 1955; 88m.

DAYDREAMER, THE ★★★
DIR: Jules Bass. **CAST:** Paul O'Keefe, Burl Ives, Tallulah Bankhead, Terry-Thomas, Victor Borge, Ed Wynn, Patty Duke, Boris Karloff, Ray Bolger, Hayley Mills, Jack Gilford, Margaret Hamilton.

This *Children's Treasures* presentation combines live action with puppetry to bring a young Hans Christian Andersen and his tales to life. 1966; 80m.

DIAMONDS ON WHEELS ★★
DIR: Jerome Courtland. **CAST:** Peter Firth, Patrick Allen.

Subpar Disney adventure pits a group of teenage auto-racing enthusiasts against a mob of jewel thieves. This being a Disney movie, the kids have no trouble bringing the bad guys to justice. Strictly formula; even toddlers will realize they've seen it before. Unrated. 1973; 87m.

DIRT BIKE KID, THE
DIR: Hoite C. Caston. **CAST:** Peter Billingsley, Stuart Pankin, Anne Bloom, Patrick Collins.

A ridiculous story about a boy who buys an old dirt bike that turns out to have a life of its own. Youngsters may like this film but almost everyone else will absolutely hate it. Rated PG for vulgarity. 1985; 91m.

DISNEY CHRISTMAS GIFT, A ★★★★
DIR: William Robert Yates. **CAST:** Animated.

A collection of memorable scenes from Disney's animated classics, including *Peter Pan*, *Cinderella*, and *Bambi*, in addition to a variety of yuletide short subjects. Made for cable TV. 1982; 47m.

DISNEY'S BEST: 1931–1948 ★★★★

DIR: Walt Disney. **CAST:** Animated.

Two of the finest cartoons Disney ever produced highlight this collection, but the other four entries fall far short of that mark. The standout is the Oscar-winning "Ugly Duckling" (1939), luxuriously rendered with Dick Lundy's animation of the central character; this one'll draw tears from granite. The other classic is "Truant Officer Donald," wherein the badge-toting duck attempts to drag his free-spirited nephews back to school. 1931–1948; 48m.

DISNEY'S DREAM FACTORY: 1933–1938 (LIMITED GOLD EDITION 2) ★★★

DIR: Walt Disney. **CAST:** Animated.

Although most of these song-laden fairy tales are aimed at the small fry, adults will be impressed by the sumptuous animation of "Wynken, Blynken, and Nod" (1938). The Disney studios never made a more luxurious short cartoon. Albert Hurter's design work on the Shakespeare-themed "Music Land" is also quite lush. 1933–1938; 50m.

DISNEY'S HALLOWEEN TREAT ★★★

DIR: William Robert Yates. **CAST:** Animated.

Little of this cable-TV production has to do with Halloween although it does have its moments. Highlights include the complete *Legend of Sleepy Hollow* and a portion of *Fantasia*. Enthusiasts of Disney animation will enjoy this regardless of its somewhat misleading title. 1982; 47m.

DISNEY'S TALL TALES ★★½

DIR: Walt Disney. **CAST:** Animated.

Lesser American folk legends take the spotlight in this weak collection of Disney cartoons, which is highlighted only by a spirited rendition of "Casey at the Bat" (extracted from the 1946 feature, *Make Mine Music*). King Midas and his "Golden Touch" provide a strong conclusive moral, but the rest of these tales are only average. 1934–1961; 50m.

DOCTOR DOLITTLE ★★½

DIR: Richard Fleischer. **CAST:** Rex Harrison, Samantha Eggar, Anthony Newley, Richard Attenborough.

Rex Harrison plays the title role in this children's tale, about a man who finds more satisfaction being around animals than people. Children may find this film amusing, but for the most part, the acting is weak, and any real script is nonexistent. 1967; 152m.

DR. SEUSS: HORTON HEARS A WHO/THE GRINCH WHO STOLE CHRISTMAS ★★★★

DIR: Chuck Jones. **CAST:** Animated.

Veteran cartoon director Chuck Jones brings his talent to the telling of these made-for-television Dr. Seuss tales. Children will be engrossed in the story of Horton the elephant who must save the tiny society living on a speck of dust, while all those around him balk at his absurd notions. *The Grinch Who Stole Christmas* follows with a warm tale made especially for holiday viewing. 1974; 51m.

DR. SEUSS: THE CAT IN THE HAT/DR. SEUSS ON THE LOOSE ★★★★

DIR: Hawley Pratt, Alan Zaslove. **CAST:** Animated.

Parents and children familiar with Dr. Seuss's *Cat in the Hat* book will notice some changes in this story, which still has two kids stuck in a house on a rainy day. The Cat in the Hat shows up and turns their home upside-down looking for his moss-covered, three-handled grendenza. Even better are the shorts in *Dr. Seuss on the Loose*, which include "The Sneetches," "The Zax," and the delightful "Green Eggs and Ham." 1974; 51m.

DR. SEUSS: THE GRINCH GRINCHES THE CAT IN THE HAT/PONTOFFEL POCK ★★★★

DIR: Joe Baldwin. **CAST:** Animated.

Two of Dr. Seuss's most famous characters go head-to-head in part one of this delightful children's tape, in which the Cat teaches the grouchy Grinch a few lessons in manners. *Pontoffel Pock* features a lonely boy who gets a magical piano. 1982; 49m.

DR. SEUSS: THE LORAX/THE HOOBER BLOOB HIGHWAY ★★★★

DIR: Hawley Pratt, Alan Zaslove. **CAST:** Animated.

The enticingly bizarre world of Dr. Seuss is colorfully brought to the screen in this collection of two made-for-TV specials. *The Lorax* relates the importance of our environment, while *The Hoober Bloob Highway* brims with sound principles about self-worth. This makes for good family-time viewing. 1974; 48m.

DR. SYN, ALIAS THE SCARECROW ★★½

DIR: James Neilson. **CAST:** Patrick McGoohan, George Cole, Tony Britton, Geoffrey Keen, Kay Walsh.

Showcased in America as a three-part television program in 1964, this colorful tale of a man who poses as a minister by day and a champion of the oppressed by night is a variation on Disney's popular *Zorro* show of the late 1950s. Patrick McGoohan brings style and substance to the legendary Dr. Syn. 1962; 129m.

DOG OF FLANDERS, A ★★★★

DIR: James B. Clark. **CAST:** David Ladd, Donald Crisp, Theodore Bikel.

Ouida's world-famous 1872 tear-jerking novel about a boy and his dog and their devotion to each other tastefully filmed in its European locale. Nello (David Ladd) delivers milk from a cart pulled by the dog Patrasche. Donald Crisp and Theodore Bikel shine in character roles, but the picture belongs to Ladd and the scene-stealing mutt fans will recall from *Old Yeller*. Have Kleenex handy. 1960; 96m.

DONALD (LIMITED GOLD EDITION 1) ★★★★

DIR: Walt Disney. **CAST:** Animated.

These early adventures of Donald Duck are noteworthy for the richer animation of Disney's World War II years, and all are solo vehicles for Disney's famous duck. "Autograph Hound" is the most ambitious, with Donald trying to crash a movie studio to collect signatures. Donald seeks gainful employment in "The Riveter" and then enjoys himself in an arcade in "Good Time for a Dime." Amid these gems, the poor quality of "The New Neighbor" makes its inclusion something of a mystery. 1939–1953; 51m.

DONALD DUCK IN MATHEMAGIC LAND ★★★★

DIR: Walt Disney. **CAST:** Animated.

This clever instructional feature marks one of Donald Duck's final appearances in a theatrical animated short. Donald serves as a guide through a mystical land filled with numbers and inventive explanations of simple mathematical principles. In pre–*Sesame Street* times, this was the closest children got to creative teaching, and the tape remains engaging to this day. 1959; 27m.

DONALD DUCK: THE FIRST 50 YEARS ★★★½

DIR: Walt Disney. **CAST:** Animated.

The need to feature highlights from Donald Duck's career makes this an uneven and disappointing collection. "The Wise Little Hen" is noteworthy only for Donald's debut, complete with trademark sailor suit. Daisy Duck is introduced in "Don Donald," and Huey, Dewie, and Louie in "Donald's Nephews," but both cartoons are shrill and obnoxious. The highlight is the Oscar-nominated "Rugged Bear" (1953), with Humphrey absolutely hilarious as a bear who masquerades as a rug to escape hunters. 1934–1953; 45m.

DONALD'S BEE PICTURES (LIMITED GOLD EDITION 2) ★★★½

DIR: Walt Disney. **CAST:** Animated.

This collection wears thin pretty quickly, since all seven cartoons feature Donald Duck's battles with a remarkably persistent honeybee. Most also employ the noticeably limited animation of Disney's later period; the one exception is the bee's debut in "Window Cleaners" (1940), which showcases stunning artwork to tell its story of Donald and Pluto as inept high-rise window cleaners. 1940–1952; 50m.

DOT AND THE BUNNY ★★★
DIR: Yoram Gross. **CAST:** Animated.

A little girl falls asleep, dreaming of her adventures with a lop-eared rabbit as they search for a missing baby kangaroo. Real-life backgrounds make this a unique production that involves animated characters parading about the Australian jungle. 1982; 79m.

DOUBLE MCGUFFIN, THE ★★★½
DIR: Joe Camp. **CAST:** Ernest Borgnine, George Kennedy, Elke Sommer, Rod Browning, Lisa Whelchel, Vincent Spano, Lyle Alzado.

Here's another family (as opposed to children's) movie. It's full of Hitchcock references in a story about some smart kids who uncover a plot to kill the leader of a Middle Eastern country. The three nominal stars only have supporting parts; they get top billing just for marquee value. From Joe Camp, the one-man movie factory who created the *Benji* films. Rated PG. 1979; 101m.

DREAM FOR CHRISTMAS, A ★★
DIR: Ralph Senensky. **CAST:** George Spell, Hari Rhodes, Beah Richards.

Overwhelmed by a soundtrack far too dramatic for its simple settings, this tale of a black pastor and his family who decide to move to California to start a congregation is full-fledged Americana. A very basic good-guy-beats-the-odds production that parallels the television hit, *The Waltons*. And it came from the very same creator: Earl Hamner. 1973; 100m.

DUMBO ★★★★
DIR: Ben Sharpstein. **CAST:** Animated.

Disney's cartoon favorite about the outcast circus elephant with the big ears is a family classic. It has everything: personable animals, a poignant story, and a happy ending. It is good fun and can still invoke a tear or two in the right places. 1941; 64m.

DUSTY ★★★
DIR: John Richardson. **CAST:** Bill Kerr, Noel Trevarthen, Carol Burns, Nicholas Holland, John Stanton.

An emotional story of a retired, lonely shepherd in Australia who is adopted by Dusty, a stray sheepdog. 1985; 89m.

EARTHLING, THE ★★★½
DIR: Peter Collinson. **CAST:** William Holden, Ricky Schroder, Jack Thompson, Olivia Hamnett, Alwyn Kurts.

A dying man (William Holden) and an orphaned boy (Ricky Schroder) meet in the Australian wilderness in this surprisingly absorbing family film. A warning to parents: There is a minor amount of profanity, and a scene in which the boy's mother and father are killed may be too shocking for small children. Rated PG. 1980; 102m.

ELMER FUDD CARTOON FESTIVAL: AN ITCH IN TIME ★★★½
DIR: Bob Clampett, Friz Freleng, Chuck Jones. **CAST:** Animated.

Elmer Fudd sheds his image as a hunter in this lively quartet of cartoons, which includes two recognized classics: Bob Clampett's "An Itch in Time," and Friz Freleng's "Back Alley Oproar." In both cases, poor Elmer is befuddled by obnoxious house pets. One of the other cartoons—Chuck Jones's "Elmer's Pet Rabbit"—is a golden oldie: the second team-up between Mr. Fudd and an early Bugs Bunny. 1940–1948; 33m.

ELMER FUDD'S COMEDY CAPERS ★★★★

DIR: Friz Freleng, Chuck Jones, Robert McKimson. **CAST:** Animated.

An outstanding collection of Warner Bros. cartoons, this set is highlighted by a quartet of Chuck Jones gems: "The Rabbit of Seville," "Bugs' Bonnets," "What's Opera, Doc?," and "Rabbit Seasoning." 1950–1957; 57m.

EMIL AND THE DETECTIVES ★★★½

DIR: Peter Tewksbury. **CAST:** Roger Moseby, Walter Slezak, Brian Russell, Heinz Schubert.

Another of the excellent live-action adventures made by the Disney Studios in the early 1960s, this grand little tale follows the escapades of a young boy who hires a gang of young, amateur sleuths after he's been robbed. Wholly improbable, but neatly constructed from the classic children's novel by Erich Kastner. 1964; 99m.

EMPEROR'S NEW CLOTHES, THE ★★

DIR: Peter Medak. **CAST:** Alan Arkin, Art Carney, Dick Shawn, Timothy Dalton (narrator).

Lavishly costumed (as one might expect from such a title), this *Faerie Tale Theatre* production presents a narcissistic king (Dick Shawn) whose vanity eventually makes him the laughingstock of his country. Alan Arkin and Art Carney have to deliver some painfully banal lines—in modern argot and out of sync with the story's time and setting. 1984; 54m.

ENCHANTED FOREST, THE ★★★

DIR: Lew Landers. **CAST:** Edmund Lowe, Harry Davenport, Brenda Joyce, Billy Severn, John Litel.

Pleasant fantasy about an old hermit who teaches a young boy to love the forest and its creatures lacks a big-studio budget but is fine family fare. 1945; 77m.

ERNEST SAVES CHRISTMAS ★★★

DIR: John R. Cherry III. **CAST:** Jim Varney, Douglas Seale, Oliver Clark, Billie Bird.

In this family movie, a vast improvement over *Ernest Goes to Camp*, TV pitchman Jim Varney returns as Ernest P. Worrell. This time the obnoxious but well-meaning Ernest attempts to help Santa Claus (Douglas Seale) find a successor. If they fail, there will be no Christmas! The script is funny without being moronic, and sentimental without being maudlin. Rated G. 1988; 95m.

ESCAPADE IN FLORENCE ★½

DIR: Steve Previn. **CAST:** Ivan Desny, Tommy Kirk, Annette Alliotto, Nino Castelnuovo.

Uninspired story about two young men and their misadventures in picturesque Italy contains the obligatory chases and seemingly perilous situations that seem to be a prerequisite for movies about art theft and forgery. 1962; 80m.

ESCAPADE IN JAPAN ★★★½

DIR: Arthur Lubin. **CAST:** Jon Provost, Roger Nakagawa, Cameron Mitchell, Teresa Wright.

Little Jon Provost, his friend Roger Nakagawa, and Japan itself are the stars of this charming film about a young boy who survives an airplane crash in Japan and is taken in by a family of isolated fishers. This is one of the all-time best kids-on-the-run films. 1957; 93m.

ESCAPE ARTIST, THE ★★

DIR: Caleb Deschanel. **CAST:** Griffin O'Neal, Raul Julia, Teri Garr, Joan Hackett, Desi Arnaz Sr.

Confusing, rambling account of a boy (Griffin O'Neal, who might be appealing with better material) who uses a love of magic and escape artistry to frame the city politicos responsible for killing his father. Rated PG—mild violence and profanity. 1982; 96m.

ESCAPE TO WITCH MOUNTAIN ★★★½

DIR: John Hough. **CAST:** Eddie Albert, Ray Milland, Kim Richards, Ike Eisenmann.

In this engaging Disney mystery-fantasy, two children with strange powers are pursued by men who want to use them for evil purposes. It's good! Rated G. 1975; 97m.

FABULOUS FIFTIES (LIMITED GOLD EDITION-1), THE ★★★★½

DIR: Walt Disney. **CAST:** Animated.

This eclectic quartet represents some of the finest experimental animation produced by the Disney studio, and every short included here captured at least an Oscar nomination. The stop-motion stick figures of "Noah's Ark" are a technical standout, but older viewers will no doubt prefer Ward Kimball's Oscar-winning history of music: "Toot, Whistle, Plunk, and Boom," Disney's first Cinemascope cartoon. Rounding out the package are the traditionally cute "Lambert, the Sheepish Lion" and the wacky "Pigs Is Pigs." 1951–1959; 49m.

FABULOUS FLEISCHER FOLIO, THE (VOLUME ONE) ★★★

DIR: Max Fleischer, Dave Fleischer. **CAST:** Animated.

Max and Dave Fleischer ran neck and neck with Disney in terms of animation quality in the 1930s. Some of their more adorable efforts are on view here. "Small Fry" is a bubbly cartoon about a young catfish playing hooky. In "Hunk and Spunky," our heroes are a pair of donkeys. Also included are "The Golden State," "Play Safe," "Ants in the Plants," and the lovely "Song of the Birds." 1930s; 50m.

FABULOUS FLEISCHER FOLIO, THE (VOLUME TWO) ★★★

DIR: Dave Fleischer. **CAST:** Animated.

This is a nicely balanced package that should please all ages. "Snubbed by a Snob" features Hunk and Spunky. There's an entertaining version of the children's rhyme in "Greedy Humpty Dumpty." Other enchanting features include "The Hawaiian Birds" and "Somewhere in Dreamland." 1930s; 50m.

FABULOUS FLEISCHER FOLIO, THE (VOLUME THREE) ★★★

DIR: Dave Fleischer. **CAST:** Animated.

There's everything from supercuteness to black comedy on this tape. "Cobweb Hotel" is the frighteningly funny tale of a cunning spider running a hotel for flies (yum-yum). "Fresh Vegetable Mystery" is a winner that features a cuddly cast of veggies. "The Stork Market" takes viewers to a baby factory and lets us sing along to "Pretty Baby." Also on this tape are "Farm Foolery," "The Little Stranger," and "A Kick in Time." 1930s; 50m.

FABULOUS FLEISCHER FOLIO, THE (VOLUME FOUR) ★★½

DIR: Dave Fleischer. **CAST:** Animated.

More cartoons crafted by Max and Dave Fleischer in the Thirties and Forties are featured in this edition. Among the highlights are "Toys Will Be Toys," an old-fashioned sing-along featuring "Oh! You Beautiful Doll," and a Mother Goose takeoff, "The Kids in the Shoe." Other titles include: "To Spring," "Funshine State," "Musical Memories," and "An Elephant Never Forgets." 1934–1949; 43m.

FABULOUS FLEISCHER FOLIO, THE (VOLUME FIVE) ★★

DIR: Dave Fleischer. **CAST:** Animated.

The Christmas cartoons of Max and Dave Fleischer are featured in this Disney video release, which is for animation buffs and youngsters only. Included are: "Rudolph the Red-Nosed Reindeer," "The Ski's the Limit," "Peeping Penguins," "Bunny Mooning," "Snow Fooling," and "Christmas Comes But Once a Year." 1937–1949; 43m.

FAMILY CIRCUS CHRISTMAS, A ★★½

DIR: Al Kouzel. **CAST:** Animated.

Lighthearted holiday fare involving the characters of the popular comic strip. One of the children wishes for Santa to bring their dead grandfather home for Christmas. Of course, Santa comes through. Made for television. 1986; 60m.

FAMOUS FIVE GET INTO TROUBLE, THE ★

DIR: Trine Hedman. **CAST:** Astrid Villaume, Ova Sprogoe, Lily Broberg.

Four kids go on an unchaperoned camping trip, where they meet a fifth boy on the run from crooks. This film suffers from terminal blandness. 1987; 90m.

FAST TALKING ★★

DIR: Ken Cameron. **CAST:** Rod Zuanic, Steve Bisley, Tracy Mann, Petter Hehir, Denis Moore, Toni Allaylis, Chris Truswell.

This Australian comedy stars Rod Zuanic as a little punk that you'd love to shake and put on the straight and narrow. The fact that he has a miserable home life, a brother who forces him to push drugs at school, a system that doesn't hold much of a future for him doesn't make this fast talker any more endearing. 1986; 93m.

FATTY FINN ★★★

DIR: Maurice Murphy. **CAST:** Ben Oxenbould, Bert Newton.

This film seems to borrow from the Little Rascals comedy series. In it, young Fatty Finn is desperately trying to earn money to buy a radio. But every time he tries, the neighborhood bully and his gang sabotage Fatty's efforts. The happy ending makes up for all the hardships 10-year-old Fatty has endured along the way. 1984; 91m.

FELIX'S MAGIC BAG OF TRICKS ★

DIR: Joseph Oriolo. **CAST:** Animated.

Though this little guy provided plenty of entertainment for his audience in the 1920s, he seems to have completely lost his charm in the transition to the modern age. Perhaps it might be blamed on an assembly-line production that repeats the same plot line over and over: the evil Professor's attempts to steal Felix's magic bag of tricks. 1960; 60m.

FIGHTING PRINCE OF DONEGAL, THE ★★½

DIR: Michael O'Herlihy. **CAST:** Peter McEnery, Susan Hampshire, Tom Adams, Gordon Jackson.

A rousing adventure-action film set in sixteenth-century Ireland. When Peter McEnery succeeds to the title of Prince of Donegal, the Irish clans are ready to fight English troops to make Ireland free. This is a Disney British endeavor that is often overlooked but definitely worth watching. 1966; 110m.

FLIGHT OF DRAGONS, THE ★★★★

DIR: Arthur Rankin Jr., Jules Bass. **CAST:** Animated.

Stop-motion animation and the voices of John Ritter, James Earl Jones, Harry Morgan, and James Gregory bring this fantasy to life. Good wizards select a man to stop the evil reign of the Red Wizards. Grade-schoolers will be fascinated by this tale. 1982; 98m.

FLIPPER'S ODYSSEY ★★½

DIR: Paul Landres. **CAST:** Flipper, Brian Kelly, Luke Halpin, Tommy Norden.

Rin Tin Tin with fins heroically saves a photographer, a lonely fisherman's dog, and his own young master. Flipper out-acts the rest of the cast. Underwater shots are the highlight. 1965; 77m.

FOGHORN LEGHORN'S FRACTURED FUNNIES ★★★½
DIR: Robert McKimson. **CAST:** Animated.
Robert McKimson made some hilarious Bugs Bunny, Daffy Duck, and Porky Pig cartoons, but his best work was to be found in this series about a cantankerous country rooster and a young chicken hawk with the mannerisms of a big-city kid. 1948–1955; 58m.

FOLLOW ME, BOYS! ★★★½
DIR: Norman Tokar. **CAST:** Vera Miles, Fred MacMurray, Lillian Gish, Kurt Russell.
Heartwarming Disney film in which Fred MacMurray plays the new Boy Scout leader in a small 1930s town. 1966; 131m.

FOR BETTER OR FOR WORSE: THE BESTEST PRESENT ★★★★
DIR: Lynn Johnston. **CAST:** Animated.
Lynn Johnston, winner of several awards for cartooning and comic strips, brings her comic-strip family to animated life in this Christmas tale. The family, which is modeled after Johnston's own, faces a crisis when little Elizabeth loses her beloved stuffed bunny. Surprisingly effective and affecting. 1985; 23m.

FOR THE LOVE OF BENJI ★★★½
DIR: Joe Camp. **CAST:** Benji, Patsy Garrett, Cynthia Smith, Allen Fulzat, Ed Nelson.
The adorable mutt cleverly saves the day again when he takes on a spy ring in Athens. The whole family can enjoy this one together. Rated G. 1977; 85m.

FRASIER THE LOVABLE LION (A.K.A. FRASIER THE SENSUOUS LION) ★★½
DIR: Pat Shields. **CAST:** Michael Callan, Katherine Justice.
Cute film about a zoology professor who discovers he can talk with Frasier, the oversexed lion at the Lion Country Safari Theme Park in Irvine, California. It is a children's film, even though the subject matter does border on being adult. 1973; 97m.

FREAKY FRIDAY ★★★½
DIR: Gary Nelson. **CAST:** Jodie Foster, Barbara Harris, John Astin, Ruth Buzzi, Kaye Ballard.
One of Disney's better comedies from the 1970s, this perceptive fantasy allows mom Barbara Harris and daughter Jodie Foster to share a role-reversing out-of-body experience. Adapted with wit by Mary Rodgers from her own book. Rated G. 1977; 95m.

FROM PLUTO WITH LOVE (LIMITED GOLD EDITION 2) ★★★★
DIR: Walt Disney. **CAST:** Animated.
Seen here without his regular co-stars, Pluto proves quite capable on his own. "T-Bone for Two," in which he tries to snatch a bone from a nasty bulldog, remains one of Disney's funniest cartoons. A frisky little seal turns up in "Pluto's Playmate" (with gorgeous animation by Grant Simmons), and a little turtle comes COD in "Pluto's Surprise Package." The collection is slightly marred by two late-period entries—"Cold Turkey" and "Plutopia"—but all the others are enchanting. 1941–1951; 50m.

FUN AND FANCY FREE ★★★½
DIR: Walt Disney. **CAST:** Edgar Bergen and Charlie McCarthy, Mortimer Snerd, Luana Patten, Dinah Shore.
The first segment of this Disney feature is the story of Bongo, a circus bear who runs off into the forest and falls for a female bear. It's a moderately entertaining tale. When Edgar Bergen narrates the clever version of "Jack and the Beanstalk," pitting Mickey, Donald, and Goofy against Willie the Giant, things pick up considerably. 1947; 96m.

GALAXY EXPRESS, THE
DIR: Taro Rin. **CAST:** Animated.
This Japanese production seems too chilling for youngsters. An actual locomotive moves through the solar system carrying its passengers in

search of their dreams. A young boy tracks the murderer of his mother; a mysterious lady seeks eternal life. Odd. Rated PG. 1980; 94m.

GARBAGE PAIL KIDS MOVIE, THE ★
DIR: Rod Amateau. **CAST:** Anthony Newley, Mackenzie Astin, Katie Barberi.

Disgusting would-be comedy featuring the Muppet-like Garbage Pail Kids. The scanty costumes, constant sexual overtones and violence are totally inappropriate for youngsters. Rated PG-13. 1987; 100m.

GENTLE GIANT ★★★
DIR: James Neilson. **CAST:** Dennis Weaver, Vera Miles, Gentle Ben, Clint Howard, Ralph Meeker.

A touching, Disneyesque story of a lonely boy and an orphaned black bear cub. The latter then grows to full half-ton size. Mildly awkward acting and editing, but the film's heart is pure and the animal scenes are very good. Unrated, with only minimal violence. 1967; 93m.

GEORGE AND THE CHRISTMAS STAR ★★½
DIR: Gerald Potterton. **CAST:** Animated.

George lives out in space on a desolate planetoid, but the Christmas spirit lives on in his heart. While decorating his Christmas tree, he dreams of capturing a real star to adorn the topmost branches. He sets off in a self-made spaceship to get the star. Songs written and performed by Paul Anka. 1985; 25m.

GERALD MCBOING-BOING (COLUMBIA PICTURES CARTOONS VOLUME THREE) ★★★
DIR: Robert Cannon. **CAST:** Animated.

This little guy helped to establish his studio of origin, UPA, as a predominant force in the cartoon business of the 1950s. Gerald, created by Dr. Seuss, is an unusual character who communicates only with a series of noises, which is acceptable, since he is only a toddler. First-time viewers will enjoy the opening episode but will notice, as audiences did at the time of his popularity, that his adventures become somewhat repetitive. 1950–1954; 30m.

G.I. JOE: THE MOVIE ★
DIR: Don Jurwich. **CAST:** Animated.

The famous action figure takes on his evil rival COBRA in this feature-length cartoon. The animation is as economical as in the Saturday-morning series and the violence might be objectionable to some parents. Not rated. 1987; 93m.

GIRL WHO SPELLED FREEDOM, THE ★★★★½
DIR: Simon Wincer. **CAST:** Wayne Rogers, Mary Kay Place, Jade Chinn, Kathleen Sisk.

Disney does an excellent job of adapting the Yann family's true story, dramatizing their flight from Cambodia to find refuge with a Tennessee family. Made for TV, this fine film is unrated. 1985; 90m.

GNOME-MOBILE, THE ★★½
DIR: Robert Stevenson. **CAST:** Walter Brennan, Ed Wynn, Mathew Garber, Karen Dotrice.

This one is kid city. From Disney, of course. Walter Brennan doubles as a wealthy businessman and a gnome who must find a wife for his grandson-gnome. The Gnome-Mobile is one fancy Rolls-Royce. 1967; 104m.

GOING BANANAS 🦃
DIR: Boaz Davidson. **CAST:** Dom DeLuise, Jimmie Walker, David Mendenhall, Herbert Lom.

Even Dom DeLuise can't soak a laugh out of this idiotic safari film. In it, he chaperones a spoiled brat (David Mendenhall) while a wacky guide (Jimmie Walker) shows them the sights in Africa. The plot (?!) thickens when a talking chimpanzee tags along. Rated PG. 1988; 95m.

GOLDEN SEAL, THE ★★★½
DIR: Frank Zuniga. **CAST:** Torquil Campbell, Steve Railsback, Penelope Milford.
A young boy (Torquil Campbell) living with his parents (Steve Railsback and Penelope Milford) on the Aleutian Islands makes friends with a rare golden seal and her pup, and tries to protect them from fur hunters. It's a good story, predictably told. Rated PG. 1983; 95m.

GOLDILOCKS AND THE THREE BEARS ★
DIR: Gilbert Cates. **CAST:** Tatum O'Neal, Hoyt Axton, Alex Karras, John Lithgow, Donovan Scott.
Although it features a well-known and talented cast, this *Faerie Tale Theatre* production is a lifeless adaptation of the story about a little girl who trespasses into the home of three bears and creates havoc. Its attempts at humor fall flat. 1982; 51m.

GOOD GRIEF, CHARLIE BROWN ★★★★
DIR: Bill Melendez, Sam Jaimes, Phil Roman. **CAST:** Animated.
Linus and his blanket are the subject of these five tales, all drawn from *The Charlie Brown and Snoopy Show*. Poor Linus can't get much respect; Lucy locks the blanket in a closet for two weeks, Sally ransoms it for a marriage proposal, and it winds up in the claws of the neighborhood cat. 1983–1985; 30m.

GREAT EXPECTATIONS (1983) ★★
DIR: Jean Tych. **CAST:** Animated.
Spotty though interesting-enough adaptation of Charles Dickens's classic tale about a young man's lessons in maturity. There's a lot of tragedy here (as expected), which may catch the attention of older children, but small youngsters will no doubt find this too low-key. 1983; 72m.

GREAT LAND OF SMALL, THE ★★
DIR: Vojta Jasny. **CAST:** Karen Elkin, Michael Blouin, Michael J. Anderson, Ken Roberts.
Beautifully photographed but slightly disjointed tale of a magical dwarf who can only be seen by those who believe in him, i.e., children. Rated G; should appeal to children, but nothing in it for adults. 1987; 94m.

GREAT LOCOMOTIVE CHASE, THE ★★★½
DIR: Francis D. Lyon. **CAST:** Fess Parker, Jeffrey Hunter, Jeff York, John Lupton.
Fess Parker and his band of spies infiltrate the South and abscond with a railroad train. Jeffrey Hunter is the conductor who chases them to regain possession of the train. This is a straightforward telling of the events, emphasizing action and suspense. 1956; 85m.

GREAT MUPPET CAPER, THE ★★★★
DIR: Jim Henson. **CAST:** Muppets, Diana Rigg, Charles Grodin, Peter Falk, Peter Ustinov, Jack Warden, Robert Morley.
Miss Piggy, Kermit the Frog, Fozzie Bear, and the Great Gonzo attempt to solve the mysterious theft of the fabulous Baseball Diamond in this, the second feature-length motion picture Muppet outing. Rated G. 1981; 95m.

GREAT SPACE CHASE ★★
DIR: Ralph Bakshi. **CAST:** Animated.
In this feature-length cartoon, Mighty Mouse must battle the evil Harry the Heartless when he tries to steal the Dreaded Doomsday Machine from a peace-loving Kingdom. Along for the ride are a number of other evildoers. So-so Terrytoons animation and feeble plotting. 1983; 88m.

GREENSTONE, THE ★★★
DIR: Kevin Irvine. **CAST:** Joseph Corey, John Riley, Kathleen Irvine, Jack Mauck.
A young boy and his family live on the edge of an enchanted forest. But

the forest and the Greenstone inside call to the young boy. Despite his family's warnings, he goes into the forest and finds the stone, which transports him to a magical fantasy world. A good family film for all ages. Rated G. 1985; 48m.

GREYFRIARS BOBBY ★★★
DIR: Don Chaffey. **CAST:** Donald Crisp, Laurence Naismith, Alex Mackenzie, Kay Walsh.
Somewhat lethargic tale of a dog that is befriended by an entire town after his owner dies. The plot drags, but the cast and the atmosphere of the settings make it worth watching. 1961; 91m.

GULLIVER'S TRAVELS (1939) ★★½
DIR: Dave Fleischer. **CAST:** Lanny Ross, Jessica Dragonette (voices).
Made and issued as an answer to Disney's *Snow White and the Seven Dwarfs*, this full-length cartoon of the famous Jonathan Swift satire about an English sailor who falls among tiny people in a land called Lilliput is just so-so. 1939; 74m.

GULLIVER'S TRAVELS (1977) ★★
DIR: Peter R. Hunt. **CAST:** Richard Harris, Catherine Schell.
Richard Harris seems lost in this meager re-telling of the Jonathan Swift satire about an English sailor whose bizarre adventures take him to a land of tiny people, Lilliput, and a country of giants. The combination of live action and animation further detracts from the story. Rated G. 1977; 80m.

GUMBY AND THE WILD WEST (VOLUME FOUR) ★★
DIR: Art Clokey. **CAST:** Animated.
While there are a few out West selections in this volume, the title is somewhat misleading because Gumby and Pokey find more to do here than spend time with cowboys and Indians. Shorts included: "The Glob," "The Kachinas," "School for Squares," and "The Golden Iguana." 1956; 60m.

GUMBY CELEBRATION, A (VOLUME TEN) ★½
DIR: Art Clokey. **CAST:** Animated.
Most certainly a collection of Gumby adventures that would have even our little clay hero crimson with embarrassment. Only for those with a masochistic admiration for the lesser adventures of Gumby. 1956; 60m.

GUMBY FOR PRESIDENT (VOLUME NINE) ★★
DIR: Art Clokey. **CAST:** Animated.
Long-term Gumby constituents will be disappointed in viewing this assortment, which includes: "Candidate for President," "Little Lost Pony," "Toy Joy," "Yard Work Made Easy," "Point of Honor," "Mysterious Fires," "Do-It-Yourself Gumby," "Siege of Boonesboro," "Gold Rush Gumby," and "Wishful Thinking." 1956; 60m.

GUMBY MAGIC (VOLUME TWO) ★★
DIR: Art Clokey. **CAST:** Animated.
A tape for true Gumby purists, including the first three (Gumby in his primitive period) Gumby adventures, which for some strange reason finds Old Pointy Head on a "Moon Trip," "Trapped on the Moon," and just plain old "Gumby on the Moon" (Is there something we don't know?) Six other adventures, including the somewhat unsettling "Robot Rumpus," round out the menu. 1956; 60m.

GUMBY RIDES AGAIN (VOLUME FIVE) ★★
DIR: Art Clokey. **CAST:** Animated.
Run-of-the-mill Gumby fare here in ten different features, including "How Not to Trap Lions," "Odd Ball," "Toy Capers," and "The Ferris Wheel Mystery." May be too tame for older youngsters, and most adults will tire of this one quickly. 1956; 60m.

GUMBY SUMMER, A (VOLUME EIGHT) ★★
DIR: Art Clokey. **CAST:** Animated.
Though hardier Gumby fans may be able to recall one or two offerings in this collection of adventures, most of this is bottom-of-the-clay barrel. This

volume includes "The Blue Goo," "Gumby League," "The Missile Bird" (mildly entertaining), "Shady Lemonade," "Motor Mania," "Making Squares," "Pokey Express," and three additional adventures. 1956; 60m.

GUMBY'S FUN FLING (VOLUME ELEVEN) ★½
DIR: Art Clokey. **CAST:** Animated.
More scrapings from the bottom of the Gumby archives. These were better left a little dusty. 1956; 30m.

GUMBY'S HOLIDAY SPECIAL (VOLUME SEVEN) ★★★
DIR: Art Clokey. **CAST:** Animated.
A collection of Gumby adventures with holiday themes, such as "Son of Liberty," "Santa Witch," "The Golden Gosling," "Gumby Crosses the Delaware," "Scrooge Loose," and "Pilgrims on the Rocks," in addition to two other featurettes. 1956; 60m.

GUMBY'S INCREDIBLE JOURNEY (VOLUME SIX) ★★
DIR: Art Clokey. **CAST:** Animated.
Here's an easy-to-pass-up collection of adventures with Old Pointy-head and his Day-Glo partner, Pokey. Titles include: "Fantastic Farmer," "Too Loo," "The Racing Game," "Treasure for Henry," "Who's What?," and by far the most interesting adventure, "The Small Planets," in which Gumby and his pal run away from home in a spaceship. 1956; 60m.

GUS ★★★½
DIR: Vincent McEveety. **CAST:** Edward Asner, Don Knotts, Gary Grimes, Dick Van Patten.
This Disney comedy has a mule named Gus delivering the winning kicks for a losing football team. Naturally, the rival team kidnaps the mule before the big game, and the search is on. Lots of slapstick comedy for the kids to enjoy in this one. Rated G. 1976; 96m.

HANS BRINKER ★★★
DIR: Robert Scheerer. **CAST:** Robin Askwith, Eleanor Parker, Richard Basehart, Roberta Torey, John Gregson, Cyril Ritchard.
This is the well-known tale of Hans Brinker and his silver skates. Made this time as a musical, it stars Robin Askwith as Hans with Eleanor Parker and Richard Basehart as his mother and invalid father. Cyril Ritchard has a cameo musical number, and there are some pleasant skating sequences. This film would make particularly good family viewing for the holidays. It is not rated, but would be considered a G. 1979; 103m.

HANSEL AND GRETEL ★★★
DIR: James Frawley. **CAST:** Joan Collins, Ricky Schroder, Paul Dooley, Bridgette Anderson.
Joan Collins is a perfectly wicked stepmother-cum-witch in this *Faerie Tale Theatre* production of the classic tale of two children (Ricky Schroder, and Bridgette Anderson) who learn a valuable lesson when they take candy from a stranger. 1982; 51m.

HAPPIEST MILLIONAIRE, THE ★★★
DIR: Norman Tokar. **CAST:** Fred MacMurray, Tommy Steele, Greer Garson, Geraldine Page, Gladys Cooper, John Davidson.
The Disney version of a factual memoir of life in the Philadelphia household of eccentric millionaire Anthony J. Drexel Biddle. Lively light entertainment that hops along between musical numbers. 1967; 118m.

HAPPY NEW YEAR, CHARLIE BROWN ★★★
DIR: Bill Melendez, Sam Jaimes. **CAST:** Animated.
Charlie Brown's hopes of a carefree Christmas vacation are dashed when he is assigned the task of turning *War and Peace* into a book report. His resolve weakens further when Peppermint Patty hosts a New Year's Eve party that includes Heather (the little red-haired girl) as a guest. Desiree Goyette and Ed Bogas bring events to a crashing halt with their banal music and lyrics. 1985; 25m.

HE-MAN AND THE MASTERS OF THE UNIVERSE (SERIES) ★
DIR: Hal Sutherland. **CAST:** Animated.

A very popular but poorly produced cartoon series about the heroic exploits of Prince Adam of the planet Eternia. Adam is transformed into super-hero He-Man whenever he raises his sword. His nemesis is the evil Skeletor, and in this tape (the first of a series, each around 45 minutes in length with several episodes) he sets a ferocious horde of dragons loose on Eternia in "The Dragon Invasion." Also included is "Curse of the Spellstone." 1983; 45m.

HEARTBEEPS ★★★
DIR: Allan Arkush. **CAST:** Andy Kaufman, Bernadette Peters, Dennis Quaid.

Andy Kaufman and Bernadette Peters play robots who fall in love, leave a factory, and decide to explore the world around them. It's a good family film by director Alan Arkush, and the kids will probably love it. Rated PG. 1981; 79m.

HEATHCLIFF—THE MOVIE ★
DIR: Bruno Bianchi. **CAST:** Animated.

An example of everything that is wrong with cartoons today, this release is sloppily drawn, poorly scripted, and generally pointless. Rated G. 1986; 89m.

HEIDI (1937) ★★★★
DIR: Allan Dwan. **CAST:** Shirley Temple, Jean Hersholt, Arthur Treacher.

This classic stars a spunky Shirley Temple as the girl who is taken away from her kind and loving grandfather's home in the Swiss Alps and forced to live with her cruel aunt. 1937; B&W; 88m.

HEIDI (1965) ★★★★
DIR: Werner Jacobs. **CAST:** Eva Maria Singhammer.

Shirley Temple fans will disagree, but we think that the beautiful location scenes filmed in the Swiss Alps and the generally high level of production and performances make this the best version on video of the classic children's tale. It's been updated to the present day, but otherwise it is faithful to Johanna Spyri's book. Dubbed in English. 1965; 95m.

HEIDI'S SONG ★½
DIR: Robert Taylor. **CAST:** Animated.

Only those 5 years old and younger will enjoy this feature-length cartoon adaptation of Johanna Spyri's classic children's tale. Rated G. 1982; 94m.

HERBIE GOES BANANAS ★★½
DIR: Vincent McEveety. **CAST:** Cloris Leachman, Charles Martin Smith, John Vernon, Stephan W. Burns, Harvey Korman.

This is the corniest and least funny of Disney's "Love Bug" series. This time Herbie is headed for Brazil to compete in the Grand Primio. Rated G. 1980; 93m.

HERBIE GOES TO MONTE CARLO ★★★½
DIR: Vincent McEveety. **CAST:** Dean Jones, Don Knotts, Julie Sommars, Eric Braeden, Roy Kinnear, Jacque Marin.

Herbie the VW falls in love with a sports car as they compete in a race from Paris to Monte Carlo. There are lots of laughs in this one. Rated G. 1977; 104m.

HERBIE RIDES AGAIN ★★★½
DIR: Robert Stevenson. **CAST:** Helen Hayes, Ken Berry, Stefanie Powers, Keenan Wynn.

This Disney comedy-adventure is a sequel to *The Love Bug*. This time, Helen Hayes, Ken Berry, and Stefanie Powers depend on Herbie, the magical Volkswagen, to save them from an evil Keenan Wynn. Rated G. 1974; 88m.

HERE COMES SANTA CLAUS
DIR: Christian Gion. **CAST:** Karen Cheryl, Armand Meffre.

This dud is not even adequate for small children. Two kids visit Santa at the North Pole to make a personal plea for the return of the boy's parents on Christmas. Santa looks all right, but doesn't say Santa-like things, and gets into some ridiculous situations with African rebels. 1984; 78m.

HERE'S DONALD ★★★★
DIR: Walt Disney. **CAST:** Animated.
The avian star of the luxuriously rendered "Donald's Ostrich" is clearly an ancestor of the stars used in the "Dance of the Hours" sequence in *Fantasia;* aside from that historical reference, the cartoon itself is marvelous, as poor Donald tries to prevent the waddling bird from swallowing everything that isn't nailed down. Donald and Goofy also go "Crazy With the Heat" during a desert trek for gasoline. 1937–1947; 22m.

HERE'S GOOFY ★★★½
DIR: Walt Disney. **CAST:** Animated.
The rubberized Goofy is best represented in this trio of cartoons by "Knight for a Day," which proves that underdogs can sometimes beat the best. "For Whom the Bull Toils" is the better of the remaining two entries, both of which employ the more limited post–World War II artwork. 1945–1953; 22m.

HERE'S MICKEY ★★★½
DIR: Walt Disney. **CAST:** Animated.
Donald Duck's frantic attempts to complete a nursery rhyme in "Orphan's Benefit" are the best part of the finest cartoon in this trio; Dick Lundy's rendering of the mumbling mallard is simply priceless. A surrealistic touch is employed for "Mickey's Garden," which finds the famous mouse battling house-size insects. By contrast, "Mickey's Birthday Party" is lethargic and boring. 1935–1941; 27m.

HERE'S PLUTO ★★★
DIR: Walt Disney. **CAST:** Animated.
The needlessly infantile "Springtime for Pluto," complete with mawkish songs, mars this trilogy; fortunately, the luxurious artwork of "Pantry Pirate" (as Pluto tries for a roast ham) is compensation of sorts. "Mail Dog," with supporting lunacy by a snowshoe hare, is moderately amusing. 1941–1947; 23m.

HE'S YOUR DOG, CHARLIE BROWN ★★★★½
DIR: Bill Melendez. **CAST:** Animated.
Snoopy misbehaves and is ordered back to the Daisy Hill Puppy Farm in this delightful entry, the last to employ the original character voices first heard in *A Charlie Brown Christmas*. Our hero postpones his fate by hiding out with Peppermint Patty, who still—at this point—thinks of him as the "funny-looking kid with the big nose." 1968; 25m.

HEY THERE, IT'S YOGI BEAR ★★★
DIR: William Hanna, Joseph Barbera. **CAST:** Mel Blanc, J. Pat O'Malley, Julie Bennett, Daws Butler, Don Messick (voices).
With this movie, Hanna-Barbera Studios made the jump from TV to feature-length cartoon. The result is consistently pleasant. Rated G. 1964; 89m.

HIDEAWAYS, THE ★★★
DIR: Fielder Cook. **CAST:** Ingrid Bergman, Sally Prager, Johnny Doran, George Rose, Richard Mulligan, Madeline Kahn.
Two bored suburban kids spend a week hiding out in the Metropolitan Museum of Art. Interested in one of the statues, the duo tracks down its donor, an eccentric rich woman (Ingrid Bergman) who lives in a mansion in New Jersey. Fanciful tale won't appeal to all children, but it has a legion of admirers. Originally titled *From the Mixed-Up Files of Mrs. Basil E. Frankweiler*. Rated G. 1973; 105m.

HOBBIT, THE ★★
DIR: Arthur Rankin Jr., Jules Bass. **CAST:** Animated.
Disappointing cartoon version of the classic J. R. R. Tolkien fantasy. Orson Bean provides the voice of the dwarf-like Hobbit, Bilbo Baggins, and John Huston, at his stentorian best, is the mighty wizard Gandalf. Unfortunately, all the strange creatures have a

cutesy look, which doesn't jell with the story. An unrated TV movie. 1978; 78m.

HOBSON'S CHOICE (1983) ★★★½

DIR: Gilbert Cates. **CAST:** Sharon Gless, Jack Warden, Richard Thomas, Bert Remsen, Robert Englund, Lillian Gish.

Sharon Gless is the main attraction in this quaint period drama, set in 1914 New Orleans. She's the spirited and capable eldest daughter of the irascible Henry Horatio Hobson (Jack Warden), seller of shoes and self-proclaimed "pillar of the community." Stung by her fathers's belief that she'll forever remain an old maid, Gless methodically arranges a marriage with his finest shoemaker (Richard Thomas). Unrated; suitable for family viewing. 1983; 100m.

HONEY, I SHRUNK THE KIDS ★★★½

DIR: Joe Johnston. **CAST:** Rick Moranis, Jared Rushton, Matt Frewer.

Old-fashioned Disney fun in the *Absent-Minded Professor* tradition gets contemporary special effects and solid bits of comedy. Rick Moranis is the scientist who invents a machine that, when accidentally triggered, shrinks his and the neighbors' kids to ant-size. Rated PG for slight profanity. 1989; 100m.

HOPPITY GOES TO TOWN ★★★

DIR: Dave Fleischer. **CAST:** Kenny Gardner, Gwen Williams, Jack Mercer, Ted Pierce (voices).

Max and Dave Fleisher, of Betty Boop and Popeye fame, brought their distinctive style of animation to this feature about the insect residents of Bugtown, faced with destruction from the encroachment of human civilization. The Fleischers were better at making short cartoons—there's not enough plot or characterization here to justify a feature—but their style is always delightful. Adults may enjoy it more than kids. 1941; 77m.

HORSE IN THE GRAY FLANNEL SUIT, THE ★★

DIR: Norman Tokar. **CAST:** Dean Jones, Diane Baker, Lloyd Bochner, Fred Clark, Kurt Russell.

This Disney film takes you back to America's early awareness of Madison Avenue and the many games and gimmicks it devises to get the almighty dollar. Dean Jones is an ad executive who develops an ad campaign around his daughter's devotion to horses. The gray flannel suit refers to the typical businessman's apparel of the period. 1968; 113m.

HORSE WITHOUT A HEAD, THE ★★★

DIR: Don Chaffey. **CAST:** Leo McKern, Jean-Pierre Aumont, Herbert Lom, Pamela Franklin, Vincent Winter.

Good old Disney fun as a group of boys give more trouble to a band of thieves than they can handle. An excellent cast headed by Leo McKern as a devious no-gooder. The whole family will enjoy this unrated film. 1963; 89m.

HORSEMASTERS ★★

DIR: Bill Fairchild. **CAST:** Annette Funicello, Janet Munro, Tommy Kirk, Donald Pleasence, Tony Britton.

Annette and Tommy team up once again in this average story about young Americans pursuing their careers in horse training among the great riding academies of Europe. 1961; 77m.

HOT LEAD AND COLD FEET ★★

DIR: Robert Butler. **CAST:** Jim Dale, Karen Valentine, Don Knotts, Jack Elam, Darren McGavin.

This predictable, occasionally funny western stars Jim Dale as twin brothers who are forced to race to determine which will receive their father's legacy of a town; one is a drunk who terrorizes the town and the other a missionary. Rated G. 1978; 89m.

HOW THE BEST WAS WON (LIMITED GOLD EDITION 2) ★★★

DIR: Walt Disney. **CAST:** Animated.

Look for Ward Kimball's caricatures of Disney-studio animators (as picadors) in the Oscar-winning "Ferdinand the Bull" (1938), but don't expect much from the four other cartoons. This collection will appeal mostly to the very young. "Three Orphan Kittens" and "Funny Little Bunnies" are overbearingly cute, and the one Mickey Mouse entry—"Building a Building"—is a routine black-and-white adventure. 1933–1960; 48m.

HUCKLEBERRY FINN ★★★★

DIR: Robert Totten. **CAST:** Ron Howard, Donny Most, Antonio Fargas, Merle Haggard, Jack Elam, Royal Dano, Sarah Selby.

Ron Howard does a fine job as Mark Twain's mischievous misfit. This made-for-TV film is well worth watching. The supporting actors are fun to watch too. 1975; 74m.

HURRAY FOR BETTY BOOP ★

DIR: Max Fleischer, Dave Fleischer. **CAST:** Animated.

This Warner Bros. tribute to the classic cartoon character is an insult to the Fleischers. Snippets of classic cartoons (in their artificially recolored state) are clumsily strung together with all new narration featuring the voices of a miscast Tommy Smothers as Pudgy and an annoying Victoria D'Orazi as Betty. 1980; 81m.

IN SEARCH OF THE CASTAWAYS ★★★★

DIR: Robert Stevenson. **CAST:** Hayley Mills, Maurice Chevalier, George Sanders, Wilfrid Hyde-White, Michael Anderson Jr.

A young Hayley Mills plays the kidnapped daughter of a sea captain (Maurice Chevalier). There are lots of great special effects depicting natural disasters for them to overcome. 1962; 100m.

IN SEARCH OF THE WOW WOW WIBBLE WOGGLE WAZZLE WOODLE WOO! ★★★★

DIR: Barry Callller. **CAST:** Tim Noah.

An infectiously scored, engagingly staged musical, featuring Tim Noah in what is virtually a one-man show. The talented Noah is assisted by a company of Muppet-like soft-sculpture creatures, such as Musty Moldy Melvin and Greasy Grimy Gerty. A celebration of the imagination, this film will appeal to the child in everyone. Rated G. 1985; 55m.

INCREDIBLE JOURNEY, THE ★★★★½

DIR: Fletcher Markle. **CAST:** Emile Genest, John Drainie.

This live-action Walt Disney film, is the story of two dogs and a cat that make a treacherous journey across Canada to find their home and family. It's impossible to dislike this heartwarming tale. 1963; 80m.

INSPECTOR GADGET (SERIES) ★★★

DIR: Jean Chalopin, Bruno Bianchi. **CAST:** Animated.

Don Adams supplies the voice for the title hero, whom adults will find strikingly reminiscent of Adams's Maxwell Smart character. Children seem to have a particular fondness for the inspector's "gadgets," which he always has on hand to get him out of a fix. Animated in Japan, tapes provide an hour and a half of entertainment (3–4 episodes) with a likable hero. 1983; 90m.

INTERNATIONAL VELVET ★★

DIR: Bryan Forbes. **CAST:** Tatum O'Neal, Christopher Plummer, Anthony Hopkins.

A disappointing sequel to *National Velvet* (1944), with Tatum O'Neal only passable as the young horsewoman who rides to victory. Rated PG. 1978; 127m.

IS THIS GOODBYE, CHARLIE BROWN? ★★★

DIR: Phil Roman. **CAST:** Animated.

Snoopy takes over the psychiatric booth and inherits the blanket when Linus and Lucy are forced to move, victims of a father with changing jobs. The kids' world is inappropriately invaded by adults (a rare miscalculation in this series). 1983; 25m.

IT CAME UPON A MIDNIGHT CLEAR ★★

DIR: Peter H. Hunt. **CAST:** Mickey Rooney, Scott Grimes, Barrie Youngfellow, George Gaynes, Hamilton Camp.

Cornball story about a New York cop (Mickey Rooney) who dies from a heart attack but arranges with heavenly higher-ups to spend one last Christmas with his grandson (Scott Grimes). *It's a Wonderful Life* this is not. Made for television. 1984; 99m.

IT WAS A SHORT SUMMER, CHARLIE BROWN ★★★★

DIR: Bill Melendez. **CAST:** Animated.

Lucy signs everybody up for summer camp, where the girls easily beat the boys at every sporting event—until a climactic wrist-wrestling challenge from the mysterious Masked Marvel. The flashback framing device (a school assignment) is quite clever. 1969; 26m.

IT'S A MYSTERY, CHARLIE BROWN ★★★½

DIR: Phil Roman. **CAST:** Animated.

When Woodstock's nest mysteriously disappears, Sherlock Snoopy—complete with dripping bubble-pipe—interrogates the Peanuts gang in an effort to uncover the culprit. To the amazement of everybody, it turns up at a school science exhibit. Vince Guaraldi contributes appropriately eerie music. 1974; 26m.

IT'S AN ADVENTURE, CHARLIE BROWN ★★★★

DIR: Bill Melendez. **CAST:** Animated.

Charlie Brown gets to shine in new surroundings in this compilation of tales lifted directly from Charles Schulz's newspaper strip. When the EPA threatens action after he bites the kite-eating tree, Charlie Brown flees to another neighborhood and becomes a hero to a gaggle of peewee baseball players. Schulz appears in a brief introduction. 1983; 50m.

IT'S ARBOR DAY, CHARLIE BROWN ★★★½

DIR: Phil Roman. **CAST:** Animated.

Charles Schulz turns conservationist in this timely tale, which also marks the animated debut of Re-run Van Pelt (Linus and Lucy's younger brother). Lucy plants a tree on the pitcher's mound of Charlie Brown's ballfield while the other kids fill the area with other assorted shrubs and vines; the chaotic greenery then gives them an edge when Peppermint Patty's team shows up for the first baseball game of the season. This was jazz composer Vince Guaraldi's final bow in the series. 1976; 25m.

IT'S FLASHBEAGLE, CHARLIE BROWN ★

DIR: Bill Melendez. **CAST:** Animated.

Blame *Flashdance* for this animated aberration that inappropriately crams the Peanuts gang into an exercise video (led by Lucy, no less). Blame Ed Bogas and Desiree Goyette for the abysmal music with inane lyrics. Mostly, though, blame Charles Schulz for approving this ill-advised travesty, definitely the series' lowest point. 1984; 25m.

IT'S MAGIC, CHARLIE BROWN ★★★★

DIR: Phil Roman. **CAST:** Animated.

The "Great Houndini" (a.k.a. Snoopy) performs a magic show with lamentable results; every trick misfires except one—which makes Charlie Brown invisible. While Snoopy cracks the books to solve this dilemma, Chuck recognizes his golden opportunity: Lucy won't know when to pull the football away if she *can't see him kick it!* 1981; 25m.

IT'S THE EASTER BEAGLE, CHARLIE BROWN ★★★★

DIR: Phil Roman. **CAST:** Animated.

A running gag involving Peppermint Patty's attempts to explain egg coloring to Marcie is merely one of this holiday tale's treats; others involve Snoopy's construction of a birdhouse for Woodstock and a wicked jab from writer Charles Schulz at the avarice of stores with pre-pre-pre-Christmas sales. 1974; 25m.

IT'S THE GREAT PUMPKIN, CHARLIE BROWN ★★★★★
DIR: Bill Melendez. **CAST:** Animated.

In this third animated Peanuts outing, Linus persuades Sally to forgo trick-or-treating by joining him in a "sincere" pumpkin patch wait for the Great Pumpkin. Great in all respects. 1966; 26m.

IT'S THREE STRIKES, CHARLIE BROWN ★★★★
DIR: Bill Melendez, Robert E. Balzer, Sam Nicholson, Phil Roman. **CAST:** Animated.

Eight vignettes lifted from Charles Schulz's newspaper strip—all with a baseball theme. By far the best story finds Re-Run joining Charlie Brown's team, which then wins a game...under clouded circumstances. Another tale finds Snoopy quitting his playing position in disgust and then returning as the team manager. 1983–1985; 41m.

IT'S YOUR FIRST KISS, CHARLIE BROWN ★★★
DIR: Phil Roman. **CAST:** Animated.

This weak entry will be remembered as the story that gave the little red-haired girl a name: Heather. After suffering through a football game, Charlie Brown is selected to escort the homecoming queen, a responsibility that culminates with a task he approaches with mixed feelings: a kiss on her cheek. 1977; 25m.

JACK AND THE BEANSTALK ★★★
DIR: Lamont Johnson. **CAST:** Dennis Christopher, Elliott Gould, Jean Stapleton, Mark Blankfield, Katherine Helmond.

This *Faerie Tale Theatre* production sticks more to the original story than most. Katherine Helmond plays Jack's complaining mom. Jean Stapleton plays a kind giantess, while Elliott Gould is a very dumb giant. Jack sells the family cow (named Spot) for five magic beans and manages to acquire great wealth while learning about his past. 1982; 60m.

JACOB TWO-TWO MEETS THE HOODED FANG ★★★½
DIR: Theodore J. Flicker. **CAST:** Stephen Rosenberg, Alex Karras.

Delightful tale of a boy nicknamed Jacob Two-Two because he has to say everything twice when talking to grownups. (They never listen to him the first time.) Fed up with adults, he dreams that he is sentenced to Slimer's Island, a children's prison where his guard is the Hooded Fang (a funny performance by Alex Karras). The low budget shows, but most of the humor of Mordecai Richler's book is retained. Rated G. 1979; 80m.

JETSONS MEET THE FLINTSTONES, THE ★★★
DIR: Ray Patterson. **CAST:** Animated.

There are a surprising number of laughs when the family from the future travels back to Bedrock in a time machine. Comic complications develop when the Flintstones and the Rubbles jet to the twenty-fifth century, leaving the Jetsons to cope with Stone Age situations. Predictable fare perhaps, but fun for the whole family nonetheless. Rated G. 1988; 100m.

JIMMY THE KID ★★
DIR: Gary Nelson. **CAST:** Paul LeMat, Gary Coleman, Cleavon Little, Fay Hauser, Dee Wallace.

Paul LeMat leads a band of bungling criminals in an attempt to kidnap the precocious son (Gary Coleman) of some extremely wealthy country-western singers (Cleavon Little and Fay Hauser). To everyone's surprise, Jimmy doesn't mind being kidnapped; in fact, he sort of likes it. Yawn. Rated PG. 1983; 85m.

JOHNNY APPLESEED/PAUL BUNYAN ★★
DIR: Arthur Rankin Jr., Jules Bass. **CAST:** Animated.
One in the series of the Rankin/Bass Festival of Family Classics—you may have seen the American Legend Series on television. If so, neither you nor older children will enjoy it again. With less than poor animation and plot development, only small children will find this duo entertaining. In "Johnny Appleseed" the hero proves that Doc Staywell's medicine isn't as good as an apple a day. "Paul Bunyan" provides an account of the giant's beginnings as an orphan (raised by two lumberjacks). Undated; 60m.

JOHNNY SHILOH ★★★½
DIR: James Neilson. **CAST:** Brian Keith, Kevin Corcoran, Darryl Hickman, Skip Homeier.
After his parents are killed during the Civil War, young Johnny Shiloh joins up with a group of soldiers led by the crusty Brian Keith. The performances are good and it's pure Walt Disney adventure. 1963; 90m.

JOHNNY TREMAIN ★★★½
DIR: Robert Stevenson. **CAST:** Hal Stalmaster, Luana Patten, Sebastian Cabot, Richard Beymer.
Colorful Walt Disney Revolutionary War entry is a perfect blend of schoolboy heroics and Hollywood history, with young Johnny Tremain an apprentice silversmith caught up in the brewing American Revolution. Heavy on the patriotism, with picture-book tableaus of the Boston Tea Party, Paul Revere's ride, and the battles at Concord. Infectious score throughout. 1957; 80m.

JOURNEY BACK TO OZ ★★½
DIR: Hal Sutherland. **CAST:** Animated; Liza Minnelli, Milton Berle, Paul Lynde, Ethel Merman, Mickey Rooney, Danny Thomas (voices).
This cartoon version sequel to *The Wizard of Oz* leaves the Wizard out. The voices of famous stars help maintain adult interest. Rated G. 1974; 90m.

JOURNEY OF NATTY GANN, THE ★★★★★
DIR: Jeremy Paul Kagan. **CAST:** Meredith Salenger, Ray Wise, John Cusack, Lainie Kazan, Scatman Crothers.
With this superb film, the Disney Studios returned triumphantly to the genre of family films. Meredith Salenger stars as Natty, a 14-year-old street urchin who must ride the rails from Chicago to Seattle during the Depression to find her father (Ray Wise). Rated PG for light violence. 1985; 101m.

JUNGLE BOOK ★★★★
DIR: Zoltán Korda. **CAST:** Sabu, Joseph Calleia, John Qualen.
This one's for fantasy fans of all ages. Sabu stars in Rudyard Kipling's tale of a boy raised by wolves in the jungle of India. Beautiful color presentation holds the viewer from start to finish. Rated G. 1942; 109m.

JUNGLE CAT ★★★★
DIR: James Algar.
This Disney True Life Adventure won the best feature documentary award at the Berlin International Film Festival in 1960. It follows the life of a spotted female jaguar in a South American jungle. Fascinating and educational. 1960; 69m.

JUST PLAIN DAFFY ★★★½
DIR: Bob Clampett, Friz Freleng, Robert McKimson, Frank Tashlin. **CAST:** Animated.
Most of the cartoons on this tape have been released in previous MGM/UA Daffy Duck and Porky Pig collections, so it doesn't win points for originality. The new material includes two World War II–era entries: Frank Tashlin's "Nasty Quacks" and Friz Freleng's "Duck Soup to Nuts," the latter once more teaming Daffy and Porky. 1943–1948; 60m.

JUST WILLIAM'S LUCK ★★
DIR: Val Guest. **CAST:** William Graham, Garry Marsh.

Based on a series of children's books that were popular in Great Britain, this isn't likely to do as well with American kids. William and his pals are mischief-makers who spend most of the film getting into various sorts of trouble. At the end, they make up for it by helping the police capture a gang of thieves. 1947; 87m.

JUSTIN MORGAN HAD A HORSE ★★★
DIR: Hollingsworth Morse. **CAST:** Don Murray, Lana Wood, Gary Crosby.

Agreeable Disney film focuses on the ingenuity and foresight of a poor Vermont schoolteacher following the Revolutionary War. He trained and bred the first Morgan horse, which was noted for its speed, strength, and stamina. 1972; 91m.

KAVIK THE WOLF DOG ★★★
DIR: Peter Carter. **CAST:** Ronny Cox, John Ireland, Linda Sorenson, Andrew Ian McMillan, Chris Wiggins.

This average made-for-TV movie is the story of Kavik, a brave sled dog who journeys back to the boy he loves when a ruthless, wealthy man transports him from Alaska to Seattle. 1980; 104m.

KID FROM LEFT FIELD, THE ★★★
DIR: Adell Aldrich. **CAST:** Gary Coleman, Tab Hunter, Gary Collins, Ed McMahon.

Gary Coleman plays a batboy who leads the San Diego Padres to victory through the advice of his father (a former baseball great). Ed McMahon co-stars in this remake of the 1953 Dan Dailey version. Made for TV. 1979; 100m.

KID WITH THE 200 I.Q., THE ★★
DIR: Leslie Martinson. **CAST:** Gary Coleman, Robert Guillaume, Dean Butler, Karl Michaelson, Harriet Nelson.

In this predictable TV movie, Gary Coleman plays a 13-year-old genius who enters college. Academics present no problem. Social life does. It's mildly amusing at best. 1983; 96m.

KIDNAPPED ★★★
DIR: Robert Stevenson. **CAST:** James MacArthur, Peter Finch.

Walt Disney takes a shot at filming this Robert Louis Stevenson eighteenth-century adventure. A young man (James MacArthur) is spirited away to sea just as he is about to inherit his family's estate. Plenty of swashbuckling swordplay for children of all ages. 1960; 94m.

KIDS IS KIDS ★★★½
DIR: Walt Disney. **CAST:** Animated.

The Oscar-nominated "Good Scouts," from 1938, with Donald Duck and his nephews battling a bear in Yellowstone Park, stands far above the other four cartoons in this collection. The rest pit Donald against the boys (who grow into spoiled teens with cars in "Lucky Number") in a variety of nasty revenge schemes that show all four ducks in a rather unflattering light. 1938–1953; 50m.

KING OF THE GRIZZLIES ★★½
DIR: Ron Kelly. **CAST:** Wahb, John Yesno, Chris Wiggins, Hugh Webster.

Wahb, a grizzly cub, loses his mother and sister to cattlemen protecting their herd. He quickly gets into trouble but is rescued by John Yesno, a Cree Indian. Average animal adventure film in the Disney mold. Rated G. 1969; 93m.

LADY AND THE TRAMP ★★★★
DIR: Hamilton Luske, Clyde Geronimi, Wilfred Jackson. **CAST:** Animated.

One of the sweetest animated tales from the Disney canon, this fantasy concerns a high-bred cocker spaniel (Lady) and the adventures she has with a raffish mongrel stray (The Tramp). Since Disney originally had the film released in CinemaScope, more attention has been given to the lush backgrounds. Unrated; suitable for family viewing. 1955; 75m.

LAND BEFORE TIME, THE ★★★★
DIR: Don Bluth. **CAST:** Animated.

This terrific animated film from director Don Bluth follows the journey of five young dinosaurs as they struggle to reach the Great Valley, the only place on Earth as yet untouched by a plague that has ravaged the world. On the way, they have several funny, suspenseful, and life-threatening adventures. The result is a wonderful film for the younger set. Rated G. 1988; 66m.

LAND OF FARAWAY, THE ★★
DIR: Vladimir Grammatikor. **CAST:** Timothy Bottoms, Susannah York, Christopher Lee.

A joint international effort—combining talents from the Soviet Union, Sweden, Norway, Great Britain, and the United States—doesn't infuse this fairy-tale film with anything special. An orphaned 11-year-old boy is rescued from his dreary, dismal existence and spirited away to *The Land of Faraway*. The boy's father turns out to be the king of Faraway, and he finds the joy in life that he's been missing. But there's a catch: He has to earn his new inheritance by seeking out and destroying the evil knight, Kato. Poor production values and sloppy direction spoil an otherwise good fairy tale. Rated PG. 1987; 95m.

LAST FLIGHT OF NOAH'S ARK ★★★
DIR: Charles Jarrott. **CAST:** Elliott Gould, Genevieve Bujold, Ricky Schroder, Vincent Gardenia.

This is the story of an unemployed pilot (Elliott Gould) who, against his better judgment, agrees to fly a plane full of farm animals to a Pacific island for a young missionary (Genevieve Bujold). This film, while not one of Disney's best, does offer clean, wholesome fun for the younger (and young-at-heart) audience. Rated G. 1980; 97m.

LAST UNICORN, THE ★★★½
DIR: Arthur Rankin Jr., Jules Bass. **CAST:** Animated.

Well-written and nicely animated feature about a magical unicorn who goes on a quest to find and rescue the rest of her kind. Strong characters and a sprightly pace make this a little gem, which features the voices of Alan Arkin, Jeff Bridges, Mia Farrow, Tammy Grimes, Robert Klein, Angela Lansbury, Christopher Lee, and Keenan Wynn. It's a class act. Rated G. 1982; 85m.

LEGEND OF HILLBILLY JOHN, THE ★★
DIR: John Newland. **CAST:** Hedge Capers, Severn Darden, Denver Pyle.

When a young man's grandfather challenges the devil and loses, he decides to take on the master of hell himself, armed with only his guitar. Flawed low-budget production with intermittent charms. 1973; 86m.

LEGEND OF SLEEPY HOLLOW, THE ★★★★
DIR: Jack Kinney, Clyde Geronimi, James Algar. **CAST:** Animated.

One of the finest of the Disney "novelette" cartoons, this adaptation of the spooky Washington Irving tale is given a properly sepulchral tone by narrator Bing Crosby. Reasonably scary, particularly for small fry, who might get pretty nervous during poor Ichabod Crane's final, fateful ride. 1949; 49m.

LT. ROBIN CRUSOE, U.S.N. ★
DIR: Byron Paul. **CAST:** Dick Van Dyke, Nancy Kwan, Akim Tamiroff.

Modern-day story of Robinson Crusoe, poorly done and with few laughs. Dick Van Dyke is stranded on a tropical island and gets involved with a female revolt against the island's male chauvinist ruler. Van Dyke's talents are totally wasted in a film that started with an idea by Walt Disney and ended without a decent script. Rated G. 1966; 113m.

LIFE AND TIMES OF GRIZZLY ADAMS, THE ★½

DIR: Dick Friedenberg. **CAST:** Dan Haggerty, Don Shanks, Lisa Jones, Marjory Harper, Bozo.

Fur trapper Dan Haggerty heads for the hills when he's unjustly accused of a crime. There he befriends an oversized bear and they live happily ever after. This sloppy, syrupy film inspired (?) the TV series. Rated G. 1976; 93m.

LIFE IS A CIRCUS, CHARLIE BROWN ★★½

DIR: Phil Roman. **CAST:** Animated.

Snoopy runs off and joins Miss Molly and her trained poodles in this lightweight entry, notable only for Charlie Brown's recollection of how he first met his faithful (?) beagle. Charles Schulz's script is unusually thin. 1980; 25m.

LIFE WITH MICKEY (LIMITED GOLD EDITION 2) ★★★★½

DIR: Walt Disney. **CAST:** Animated.

Three 1936 cartoons are the treasures of this collection. "Alpine Climbers" teams Mickey Mouse with Donald Duck and Pluto. Artist Art Babbitt contributes great caricatures of Hollywood luminaries in "Mickey's Polo Team," and Donald Duck has a great time with trained seals in "Mickey's Circus." The tape also includes "Shanghaied," an early black-and-white adventure with Minnie Mouse. 1934–1951; 51m.

LIGHT IN THE FOREST, THE ★★½

DIR: Herschel Daugherty. **CAST:** James MacArthur, Fess Parker, Wendell Corey, Joanne Dru, Carol Lynley.

James MacArthur stars as a young man who had been captured and raised by the Delaware Indians and is later returned to his white family. Generally a good story with adequate acting, the ending is much too contrived and trite. 1958; 92m.

LIGHTNING, THE WHITE STALLION ★

DIR: William A. Levey. **CAST:** Mickey Rooney, Susan George.

In this disappointing family film, Mickey Rooney plays a down-on-his-luck gambler who owns a champion jumper. The horse is stolen. With the aid of two young people, he recovers the horse for one last make-or-break race. Rated PG. 1986; 93m.

LION, THE WITCH AND THE WARDROBE, THE ★★★½

DIR: Bill Melendez. **CAST:** Animated.

Four children pass through a wardrobe into a wondrous land of mythical creatures where an evil Ice Queen has been terrorizing her subjects. This enjoyable made-for-television cartoon was based on C.S. Lewis's *Chronicles of Narnia*. 1979; 95m.

LITTLE HOUSE ON THE PRAIRIE (TELEVISION SERIES) ★★★

DIR: Michael Landon. **CAST:** Michael Landon, Karen Grassle, Melissa Gilbert, Melissa Sue Anderson, Lindsay and Sidney Greenbush, Victor French, Dean Butler, Matthew Laborteaux.

The long-running series was based on Laura Ingalls Wilder's novels about her family's adventures on the Kansas frontier. Michael Landon, who had creative control over the show, made people forget Little Joe Cartwright with his strong portrayal of Charles Ingalls, the idealistic, sensitive husband and father. Though you need a high tolerance for sentimentality to watch this moralistic series, episodes tended to be genuinely heartwarming, rather than sappy. 1974–1984; 60 minutes (special TV-movies are 100 minutes).

LITTLE LORD FAUNTLEROY (1980) ★★★★

DIR: Jack Gold. **CAST:** Ricky Schroder, Alec Guinness, Eric Porter, Colin Blakely, Connie Booth.

This is the made-for-television version of the heartwarming classic about a poor young boy (Ricky Schroder) whose life is dramatically changed when his wealthy grandfather (Alec Guinness) takes him in. Well done. 1980; 120m.

LITTLE MATCH GIRL, THE ★★
DIR: Mark Hoeger, Wally Broodbent. **CAST:** Monica McSwain, Nancy Duncan, Matt McKim, Dan Hays.

This *Children's Treasures* production was originally a stage play. Unfortunately, the pageantry and emotion of the live-action production are lost in the video translation. In it, a poor girl's grandmother, about to die, reveals a magic in the matches that they sell. After the grandmother's death, the girl (Monica McSwain) gets so caught up in the magic that she neglects to sell her wares. *Not* advised for children under 10. 1983; 54m.

LITTLE MERMAID, THE ★★★½
DIR: Robert Iscove. **CAST:** Pam Dawber, Karen Black, Treat Williams, Brian Dennehy, Helen Mirren.

In this segment of Shelley Duvall's *Faerie Tale Theatre*, Pam Dawber plays Pearl, a mermaid daughter of King Neptune. She falls hopelessly in love with a human and sacrifices all to win his love. Although this is a low-budget production, it still manages to keep its viewers entertained. 1984; 50m.

LITTLE MISS MARKER (1934) ★★★★
DIR: Alexander Hall. **CAST:** Adolphe Menjou, Shirley Temple, Dorothy Dell, Charles Bickford, Lynne Overman.

Delightful Shirley Temple vehicle has our little heroine left as an I.O.U. on a gambling debt and charming hard-hearted racetrack denizens into becoming better people. This is the best of the screen adaptations of Damon Runyon's story. 1934; B&W; 88m.

LITTLE MISS MARKER (1980) ★
DIR: Walter Bernstein. **CAST:** Walter Matthau, Julie Andrews, Tony Curtis, Bob Newhart, Sara Stimson, Lee Grant.

Even the star power of Walter Matthau, Julie Andrews, and Bob Newhart can't save this turgid remake. Rated PG. 1980; 103m.

LITTLE MISS TROUBLE AND FRIENDS ★★
DIR: Trevor Bond, Terry Ward. **CAST:** Animated.

With an animation style reminiscent of Terrytoon's "Tom Terrific," this collection of episodes offers youngsters an education in proper social behavior. However, tiny tykes may become confused since Little Miss Trouble and her friends, who are named after various aspects of their own personalities (Mr. Small, etc.), spend a lot of time displaying poor ethics before learning their lessons. Unimaginative, though based on bestselling children's fiction. 1983; 43m.

LITTLE ORPHAN ANNIE ★★½
DIR: John S. Robertson. **CAST:** Mitzi Green, Edgar Kennedy, Buster Phelps, May Robson.

The first sound version featuring the adventures of Harold Gray's pupilless, precocious adolescent. A good cast and engaging score by Max Steiner add to the charm of this undeservedly neglected comic strip adaptation. 1932; B&W; 60m.

LITTLE PRINCE, THE (SERIES) ★★½
DIR: Jameson Brewer. **CAST:** Animated.

Recommended by the National Educational Association, this takeoff of the Antoine de Saint-Exupéry story will bore older kids to tears. Little viewers may be fascinated by the adventures of the little humanoid hero who lives on the faraway planet of B-612 and travels through the galaxy on a variety of comets. Five volumes compose this series. 1986; 60m.

LITTLE PRINCESS, THE ★★★½
DIR: Walter Lang. **CAST:** Shirley Temple, Richard Greene, Anita Louise, Ian Hunter, Cesar Romero, Arthur Treacher.

The 1930s supertyke Shirley Temple had one of her very best vehicles in this Victorian era tearjerker. In it, she's a sweet-natured child who is mistreated at a strict boarding school when her father disappears during the Boer War. Get out your handkerchiefs. 1939; B&W; 93m.

LITTLE RED RIDING HOOD ★★★★

DIR: Graeme Clifford. **CAST:** Mary Steenburgen, Malcolm McDowell, Darrell Larson.

Malcolm McDowell plays a brazenly wicked wolf to a perky Red Riding Hood (Mary Steenburgen). Frances Bay makes for a rather zany grandmother. Although this production is highly entertaining, don't expect it to stick to the tale as most would remember it. 1983; 51m.

LITTLE TWEETY AND LITTLE INKI CARTOON FESTIVAL ★★★½

DIR: Bob Clampett, Friz Freleng, Chuck Jones. **CAST:** Animated.

Tweety Pie, that little yellow bird whose size belies impressive wit and agility, remains one of animator Bob Clampett's greatest creations. This collection begins with Tweety's second appearance (although the first in which he was so named): Clampett's "Birdy and the Beast." Fans will also appreciate Friz Freleng's "I Taw a Putty Tat." Animator Chuck Jones is barely remembered today, in light of his later achievements, for the creation of Inki, a youthful African warrior whose great courage comes packed in a small body. Inki's first appearance—in "Little Lion Hunter"—is one of three cartoons rounding out this package. 1939–1948; 50m.

LITTLE WOMEN (1981) ★★

DIR: John Matsuura, Kazuya Miyazaki. **CAST:** Animated.

Parents who wish to expose their children to a timeless classic may be fooled by the packaging of this video, which presents only a small portion of Louisa May Alcott's famous book. Run-of-the-mill Japanese animation belies the fact that this production was simplified for a young audience and further simplified for translation to a foreign culture. 1981; 23m.

LITTLEST ANGEL, THE ★

DIR: Joe Layton. **CAST:** Johnny Whitaker, Fred Gwynne, Connie Stevens, James Coco, E. G. Marshall, Tony Randall.

Though tolerably charming when it was broadcast, this made-for-TV musical fantasy loses something in its video translation. A young shepherd finds his transition into heaven difficult to accept after having fallen to his death from a cliff. 1969; 77m.

LITTLEST HORSE THIEVES, THE ★★★

DIR: Charles Jarrott. **CAST:** Alastair Sim, Peter Barkworth, Maurice Colbourne, Susan Tebbs, Andrew Harrison, Chloe Franks.

At the turn of the century, some children become alarmed when they learn that the pit ponies working in the coal mines are to be destroyed. To prevent the deaths, the children decide to steal the ponies. Rather predictable but with good characterizations and a solid period atmosphere. Rated G. 1976; 104m.

LITTLEST OUTLAW, THE ★★★

DIR: Roberto Gavaldon. **CAST:** Pedro Armendariz, Joseph Calleia, Rodolfo Acosta, Andres Velasquez.

This Walt Disney import from Mexico tells a familiar but pleasant story of a young boy who befriends a renegade horse and saves him from destruction. The kids should like it, and this one will appeal to the adults as well. 1954; 73m.

LIVING FREE ★★

DIR: Jack Couffer. **CAST:** Susan Hampshire, Nigel Davenport, Geoffrey Keen.

Disappointing sequel to *Born Free*, with Elsa the lioness now in the wilderness and raising three cubs. The chemistry just isn't here in this film. 1972; 91m.

LOONEY, LOONEY, LOONEY BUGS BUNNY MOVIE ★★★½
DIR: Friz Freleng. **CAST:** Animated.

This followup to the *Bugs Bunny/Road Runner Movie* lacks the earlier film's inventiveness, but then Chuck Jones was always the most cerebral of the Warner Bros. cartoon directors. Friz Freleng, on the other hand, only tried to make people laugh. This collection of his cartoons—which feature Daffy Duck, Porky Pig, Tweety Pie, and Yosemite Sam, among others, in addition to Bugs—does just that with general efficiency. Rated G. 1981; 79m.

LOONEY TUNES VIDEO SHOW, THE (VOLUME 1) ★★★½
DIR: Friz Freleng, Chuck Jones, Robert McKimson. **CAST:** Animated.

By far the best in this series, this collection is highlighted by Chuck Jones's "The Ducksters," a frenetic masterpiece that stands as one of the best Daffy Duck–Porky Pig teamings. Robert McKimson's "Devil May Hare" introduces Bugs Bunny to the Tasmanian Devil, and Friz Freleng's "Mexican Shmoes" (a Speedy Gonzales vehicle) is noteworthy, too. Finally, Jones's "Zipping Along" is one of his earlier Road Runner shorts. 1950–1961; 49m.

LOONEY TUNES VIDEO SHOW, THE (VOLUME 2) ★★
DIR: Friz Freleng, Chuck Jones, Robert McKimson. **CAST:** Animated.

It's filler time. Post-1960 entries mar this collection, which contains only one decent cartoon: Chuck Jones's Pepe Le Pew romp titled "Two Scents Worth." Although most of the regular stars are represented, the selections leave much to be desired. 1950–1965; 48m.

LOONEY TUNES VIDEO SHOW, THE (VOLUME 3) ★★★
DIR: Chuck Jones, Rudy Larriva, Robert McKimson. **CAST:** Animated.

A mixed bag of the reasonably good and the extremely bad. The former is represented by one of the better Foghorn Leghorn shorts, Robert McKimson's "Fractured Leghorn"; the latter is covered by Rudy Larriva's wretched "Quacker Tracker," one of Daffy Duck's post-1960 limited-animation duels with Speedy Gonzales. 1950–1967; 48m.

LOVE BUG, THE ★★★½
DIR: Robert Stevenson. **CAST:** Michele Lee, Dean Jones, Buddy Hackett, Joe Flynn.

This is a delightful Disney comedy. A family film about a Volkswagen with a mind of its own and some special talents as well, it was the first of the four "Herbie" films. Rated G. 1969; 107m.

LUCKY LUKE: THE BALLAD OF THE DALTONS ★★
DIR: René Goscinny. **CAST:** Animated.

Overlong yarn of the Old West starring an all-American cowboy (complete with immovable cigarette on the lower lip): Lucky Luke. This is part of a series of Lucky Luke adventures featuring the legendary (and here, bungling) Dalton gang. References to killing are taken in stride, but for the most part this is harmless cartoon fare. Not rated. 1978; 82m.

MAD MONSTER PARTY ★★½
DIR: Jules Bass. **CAST:** Boris Karloff, Phyllis Diller, Ethel Ennis, Gale Garnett (voices).

An amusing little puppet film; a lot more fun for genre buffs who will understand all the references made to classic horror films. Worth seeing once, as a novelty. 1967; 94m.

MAGIC CHRISTMAS TREE, THE
DIR: Richard C. Parish. **CAST:** Chris Kroegen, Valerie Hobbs, Robert Maffei, Dick Parish, Terry Bradshaw.

A laughable effort, with only the most tenuous connection to Christmas. Chris Kroegen is a boy who falls out of a witch's tree on Halloween afternoon (yes, most of the story takes place on Halloween) and has an eerie dream. Not rated. 1966; 70m.

MAGIC OF LASSIE, THE ★★½
DIR: Don Chaffey. **CAST:** James Stewart, Mickey Rooney, Pernell Roberts, Stephanie Zimbalist, Michael Sharrett, Alice Faye, Gene Evans, Lane Davies, Mike Mazurki, Lassie.

Like the Disney live-action films of yore, *The Magic of Lassie* tries to incorporate a little of everything: heartwarming drama, suspense, comedy and even music. But here the formula is bland. The story is okay, as far as cute kids pining for their dogs go, but it is all too long. Rated G. 1978; 100m.

MAGIC SWORD, THE ★★
DIR: Bert I. Gordon. **CAST:** Gary Lockwood, Anne Helm, Basil Rathbone, Estelle Winwood, Liam Sullivan.

Young Gary Lockwood is on a quest to free an imprisoned princess and fights his way through an ogre, dragon, and other uninspired monsters with the help of the witch in the family, Estelle Winwood. It's Basil Rathbone who makes the show work, and he makes a fine old evil sorcerer, relishing his foul deeds and eagerly planning new transgressions. The kids might like it, but it's laughable. 1962; 80m.

MAN CALLED FLINTSTONE, A ★★★½
DIR: William Hanna, Joseph Barbera. **CAST:** Animated.

The Ralph Kramden and Ed Norton of the kiddie-set, Fred Flintstone and Barney Rubble are featured in this full-length animated cartoon. Fred takes over for lookalike secret agent, Rack Slag, and goes after the "Green Goose" and his henchmen, SMIRK agents. The whole Bedrock gang goes along as Fred and company travel from Paris to Rome on their spy-chasing adventure. Great fun for the kids. 1966; 87m.

MAN IN THE SANTA CLAUS SUIT, THE ★★★
DIR: Corey Allen. **CAST:** Fred Astaire, John Byner, Nanette Fabray, Gary Burghoff, Bert Convy, Harold Gould.

In one of his last performances, Fred Astaire plays seven characters who enrich the lives of everybody in a small community. This made-for-TV production is a delightful Christmastime picture. 1978; 100m.

MANNY'S ORPHANS ★
DIR: Sean S. Cunningham. **CAST:** Richard Lincoln.

This is another *Bad News Bears* movie, but of course not within striking distance of the original. Why do they bother, and how do they get the money to do it? (Originally released as *Here Come the Tigers.*) 1978; 90m.

MAN'S BEST FRIEND ★★★½
DIR: Walter Lantz, Tex Avery. **CAST:** Animated.

The creations of Walter Lantz, including Woody Woodpecker, Andy Panda, and Chilly Willy, cavort with canines in this loose-knit collection. But the best "cartune" (as Lantz spelled it) in this group has nothing to do with his more famous characters. Instead Tex Avery's wild and crazy "Dig That Dog" takes the prize. It's an old bit where the man thinks he's a dog and vice versa, but watch what Avery does with it. 1985; 51m.

MARK TWAIN'S CONNECTICUT YANKEE IN KING ARTHUR'S COURT ★★
DIR: David Tapper. **CAST:** Richard Basehart, Roscoe Lee Brown, Paul Rudd.

A pedestrian adaptation of Mark Twain's story in which a Connecticut blacksmith dreams that he has been transported to the England of King Arthur. Made for television. 1978; 60m.

MARTIN'S DAY ★★½
DIR: Alan Gibson. **CAST:** Richard Harris, Lindsay Wagner, John Ireland, James Coburn, Justin Henry, Karen Black.

Richard Harris plays an escaped convict who kidnaps young Justin Henry but ends up being his friend in this Canadian production. A good idea with a pedestrian resolution. Rated PG. 1984; 98m.

MARVEL COMICS VIDEO LIBRARY ★★½

DIR: Various. **CAST:** Animated.

It's hard for us to say whether comic-book fans will enjoy these often slapdash and uninspired cartoons featuring the superheroes from the Marvel line of comics. The animation is generally poor, and all of the cartoons look insipid next to Max and Dave Fleischer's Superman cartoons of the 1940s. That said, some of Ralph Bakshi's Spiderman cartoons are okay, and the Captain America series gets around the problems of limited animation by using what look like comic-book panels combined with slight animation. 1985–1986; each tape 60m.

MARY POPPINS ★★★★★

DIR: Robert Stevenson. **CAST:** Julie Andrews, Dick Van Dyke, David Tomlinson, Glynis Johns, Karen Dotrice, Matthew Garber, Jane Darwell, Ed Wynn, Arthur Treacher, Hermione Baddeley.

Here's Julie Andrews in her screen debut. She plays a nanny who believes that "a spoonful of sugar makes the medicine go down." Andrews is great in the role and sings ever so sweetly. The song and dance numbers are attractively laid on, with Dick Van Dyke, as Mary's Cockney beau, giving an amusing performance. Rated G. 1964; 140m.

MASTERMIND (TELEVISION SERIES) ★★★½

DIR: Don Sharp. **CAST:** Sam Waterston, Julian Glover, Barrie Houghton.

This British TV adventure series features Sam Waterston as Professor Quentin E. Deverill, an American inventor and scientist in 1912, who leaves Harvard to pursue his studies in London. The "Target London" episode has Deverill solving a kidnapping case. In "The Great Motor Race" archvillain Kilkiss (Julian Glover) tries to create a global empire. "The Infernal Devise" episode is about a remote-control system Deverill has invented to better mankind. It's a little like Saturday-matinee material, but the acting, set decoration, costumes, and gadgetry make it a lot of fun. 1981–1982; 48–51 minutes.

MASTERS OF THE UNIVERSE ★★½

DIR: Gary Goddard. **CAST:** Dolph Lundgren, Frank Langella, Courteney Cox, James Tolkan, Meg Foster.

Those toy and cartoon characters come to life on the silver screen, and all things considered, the translation is fairly successful. He-Man and friends are exiled to Earth, where they befriend a teenage couple and battle Skeletor's evil minions. Kids should find all this entertaining, although a small amount of foul language and one scene of graphic violence may be deemed unsuitable for young children by some parents. Rated PG. 1987; 106m.

MEDICINE HAT STALLION, THE ★★

DIR: Michael O'Herlihy. **CAST:** Leif Garrett, Mitchell Ryan, Bibi Besch, John Anderson, Charles Tyner, John Quade, Milo O'Shea, Ned Romero.

Decent TV movie about a young lad (Leif Garrett) who, with the help of Indian Chief Red Cloud (Ned Romero) runs off to join the Pony Express. Well acted, but overlong, and the commercial breaks are jarring and obvious. 1977; 85m.

MELODY ★½

DIR: Waris Hussein. **CAST:** Jack Wild, Mark Lester, Tracy Hyde, Roy Kinnear, Kate Williams, Ken Jones.

A cute story, completely destroyed by montage after montage set to a musical score by the Bee Gees. Not enough dialogue here to carry this innocent tale about two 10-year-olds who fall in love and decide to get married. Slow. 1972; 130m.

MGM CARTOON MAGIC ★★★½

DIR: Tex Avery, George Gordon. **CAST:** Animated.

Droopy and Tom & Jerry weren't the only cartoon characters at MGM in the Forties and Fifties, as demonstrated by this enjoyable collection. Barney Bear is represented here by "Unwelcome Guest." The Captain and Kids put on "The Captain's Christmas," while "The Lonesome Stranger" fights for truth, justice, and his own survival in the Old West. Director Tex Avery brings this collection's greatest chuckles in "Screwball Squirrel," "Little Rural Riding Hood" (which is almost for adults only), and "King Size Canary." For all ages. 1983; 53m.

MICKEY (LIMITED GOLD EDITION 1) ★★★★½

DIR: Walt Disney. **CAST:** Animated.

Mickey Mouse's first appearance, in "Steamboat Willie" (1928), is reason enough to view this tape; the impressively inventive animation, entirely the work of Ub Iwerks, remains enchanting to this day. Of the remaining entries, most from Disney's classic period, "Symphony Hour" is the standout. 1928–1953; 51m.

MICKEY AND THE BEANSTALK ★★★★½

DIR: Walt Disney. **CAST:** Animated.

This gorgeous rendition of the classic fairy tale is a must-see for all Disney animation fans. It's the most ambitious adventure created for the Terrific Trio—Mickey Mouse, Donald Duck, and Goofy—as they struggle to free the Magic Harp from the shape-changing clutches of Willie the Giant. 1947; 29m.

MICKEY AND THE GANG ★★★★½

DIR: Walt Disney. **CAST:** Animated.

This trio of cartoons is highlighted by 1938's "Boat Builders," which teams Mickey Mouse, Donald Duck, and Goofy in an effort to assemble a full-sized boat from a rather complex kit. The threesome also gets together for "Moose Hunters," and Pluto battles a gopher while working as Mickey's "Canine Caddy." 1937–1941; 25m.

MICKEY KNOWS BEST ★★★★★

DIR: Walt Disney. **CAST:** Animated.

Fred Spencer's animation of Donald Duck, as he attempts to extricate himself from a plumber's helper, is just one of the high points in "Moving Day." Donald also generates plenty of laughs trying to recite "Twinkle, Twinkle, Little Star" in "Mickey's Amateurs," and Pluto takes an immediate dislike to a most endearing pachyderm in "Mickey's Elephant." 1936–1937; 26m.

MICKEY'S CHRISTMAS CAROL ★★★★

DIR: Burney Matinson. **CAST:** Animated.

Mickey Mouse plays Bob Cratchit in this pleasant adaptation of the Dickens classic. Rated G. 1984; 26m.

MICKEY'S CRAZY CAREERS ★★★★½

DIR: Walt Disney. **CAST:** Animated.

Forget this collection's one weak black-and-white entry ("The Mail Pilot") and concentrate on the other five cartoons, every one a classic. "The Band Concert," Disney's first Technicolor Mickey Mouse vehicle, is hilarious as a young Donald Duck ruins a performance of "The William Tell Overture." The famous trio—Mickey, Donald, and Goofy—are put to work in "Clock Cleaners," "Tugboat Mickey," "Magician Mickey," and "Mickey's Fire Brigade." 1933–1940; 48m.

MILLION DOLLAR DUCK, THE ★★

DIR: Vincent McEveety. **CAST:** Dean Jones, Sandy Duncan, Joe Flynn, Tony Roberts.

A duck is accidentally given a dose of radiation that makes it produce eggs with solid gold yolks. Dean Jones and Sandy Duncan, as the owners of the duck, use the yolks to pay off bills until the Treasury Department gets wise. Mildly entertaining comedy in the Disney tradition. Rated G. 1971; 92m.

MINNIE (LIMITED GOLD EDITION 1) ★★★½
DIR: Walt Disney. **CAST:** Animated.

The phenomenal perspective animation of Ub Iwerks in the black-and-white "Plane Crazy" makes it this collection's most visually impressive entry. "Mickey's Rival" features the only appearance of Mortimer Mouse, who also desires Minnie Mouse's love. Most of the others employ Minnie as a lesser supporting character for insipidly cute tales featuring Pluto, Figaro the cat, and Frankie the bird. 1928–1947; 52m.

MINOR MIRACLE, A ★★½
DIR: Raoul Lomas. **CAST:** John Huston, Pelé, Peter Fox.

A heartwarming story about a group of orphaned children and their devoted guardian (John Huston), who band together to save the St. Francis School for Boys. If you liked *Going My Way* and *Oh God!* you'll like this G-rated movie. 1983; 100m.

MIRACLE DOWN UNDER ★★★½
DIR: George Miller. **CAST:** Dee Wallace, John Waters, Charles Tingwell, Bill Kerr, Andrew Ferguson.

This moving drama is actually *A Christmas Carol* Australian style. Only a small boy's kindness can rekindle an evil miser's Christmas spirit. This fine family film contains no objectionable material. 1987; 106m.

MIRACLE OF THE WHITE STALLIONS ★★
DIR: Arthur Hiller. **CAST:** Robert Taylor, Lilli Palmer, Curt Jurgens, Eddie Albert, James Franciscus, John Larch.

True story of the evacuation of the famed Lipizzan stallions from war-torn Vienna doesn't pack much of a wallop, but the kids and horse fans should enjoy it. 1963; 92m.

MIRACLE ON 34TH STREET ★★★★★
DIR: George Seaton. **CAST:** Natalie Wood, Edmund Gwenn, Maureen O'Hara.

In this, one of Hollywood's most delightful fantasies, the spirit of Christmas is rekindled in a young girl (Natalie Wood) by a department store Santa. Edmund Gwenn is perfect as the endearing Macy's employee who causes a furor when he claims to be the real Kris Kringle. Is he or isn't he? That is for you to decide in this heartwarming family classic. 1947; B&W; 96m.

MISADVENTURES OF GUMBY, THE (VOLUME THREE) ★★★
DIR: Art Clokey. **CAST:** Animated.

Better-than-average Gumby tales highlight this package, which includes "Baker's Tour," "Gumby Concerto," "The Black Knight" (an example of the more unpleasant side of Gumby stories), and six other misadventures. 1956; 60m.

MISADVENTURES OF MERLIN JONES, THE ★★½
DIR: Robert Stevenson. **CAST:** Tommy Kirk, Annette Funicello, Leon Ames, Stu Erwin, Alan Hewitt.

Tommy Kirk stars in this Disney family programmer as a boy genius whose talents for mind reading and hypnotism land him in all sorts of trouble. Entertaining for the young or indiscriminate; pretty bland for everybody else. 1964; 88m.

MISS ANNIE ROONEY ★★
DIR: Edwin L. Marin. **CAST:** Shirley Temple, William Gargan, Guy Kibbee, Dickie Moore, Peggy Ryan, Gloria Holden.

The highlight of this film comes when Dickie Moore gives Shirley Temple her very first screen kiss. The rest of this average picture involves a poor girl who falls madly in love with a rich dandy. No sparks here. 1942; 84m.

MR. MAGOO IN SHERWOOD FOREST ★★★½
DIR: Abe Levitow. **CAST:** Animated.
Mr. Magoo, as the jolly Friar Tuck, joins Robin Hood and his merry men to thwart the evil designs of King John and the sheriff of Nottingham. Appealing entry in the Magoo series. 1964; 85m.

MR. MAGOO IN THE KING'S SERVICE ★★★
DIR: Abe Levitow. **CAST:** Animated.
A trio of tales featuring Mr. Magoo as D'Artagnan, Cyrano de Bergerac, and Merlin the magician. An average installment in the long-running series. 1964; 97m.

MR. MAGOO, MAN OF MYSTERY ★★★
DIR: Abe Levitow. **CAST:** Animated.
Mr. Magoo, as Dr. Watson, aids supersleuth Sherlock Holmes. As Dr. Frankenstein, he creates a man from the parts of dead bodies and must suffer the consequences. As the Count of Monte Cristo, Magoo exacts revenge against his enemies. And finally, as Dick Tracy, he fights a bevy of bizarre baddies. 1964; 96m.

MR. MAGOO'S CHRISTMAS CAROL ★★★★★
DIR: Abe Levitow. **CAST:** Animated.
Mr. Magoo is Ebenezer Scrooge in this first-rate animated musical of Charles Dickens's holiday classic, which remains the best animated adaptation to date. The songs by Jule Styne and Bob Merrill are magnificent. 1962; 53m.

MR. MAGOO'S STORYBOOK ★★★★
DIR: Abe Levitow. **CAST:** Animated.
Magoo is all seven dwarfs in "Snow White"; portrays the idealistic knight, Don Quixote of La Mancha; and plays Puck in William Shakespeare's *A Midsummer Night's Dream*. 1964; 117m.

MR. SUPERINVISIBLE ★★
DIR: Anthony M. Dawson. **CAST:** Dean Jones, Gastone Moschin, Ingeborg Schoener, Rafael Alonso, Peter Carsten.
Disney-like comedy with Dean Jones as the scientist who stumbles upon a virus that causes invisibility. Cute in spots; kids should like it. 1973; 90m.

MONKEYS GO HOME ★½
DIR: Andrew V. McLaglen. **CAST:** Maurice Chevalier, Dean Jones, Yvette Mimieux.
Stupid even for a Walt Disney film (and that covers a lot of territory), this is a low-water mark for action director Andrew McLaglen. Disney regular Dean Jones plays an American who inherits a French farm and is stymied in picking the delicate fruit until he hits on the idea of using "retired" air force test chimps! Rated G. 1966; 89m.

MONKEY'S UNCLE, THE ★★
DIR: Robert Stevenson. **CAST:** Tommy Kirk, Annette Funicello, Leon Ames, Arthur O'Connell, Frank Faylen.
This sequel to *The Misadventures of Merlin Jones* finds whiz kid Tommy Kirk up to no good with a flying machine and a sleep-learning technique employed on a monkey. More of the same from Disney, really: bumbling scientific high-jinks, mild slapstick, and G-rated romance with Annette Funicello. For young minds only. 1965; 87m.

MOON PILOT ★★★½
DIR: James Neilson. **CAST:** Tom Tryon, Brian Keith, Edmond O'Brien, Dany Saval.
Tom Tryon gets volunteered to become the first astronaut to circle the moon. Good script, with satire and laughs in ample quantities. Rated G. 1962; 98m.

MOONCUSSERS ★★½
DIR: James Neilson. **CAST:** Oscar Homolka, Kevin Corcoran, Robert Emhardt, Joan Freeman.
Kevin Corcoran stars as a boy who discovers the secrets of the Mooncussers—pirates who work on moonless nights to draw ships to their doom

by means of false signal lamps on shore. 1962; 85m.

MOONSPINNERS, THE ★★★
DIR: James Neilson. **CAST:** Hayley Mills, Eli Wallach, Pola Negri, Peter McEnery, Joan Greenwood.

A young girl (Hayley Mills) becomes involved in a jewel theft in Crete. A young man is accused of the theft and has to work with the girl to prove his innocence. The best features of this film are the appearance of a "grown-up" Hayley Mills and the return to the screen of Pola Negri. The film is essentially a lightweight melodrama in the Hitchcock mold. 1964; 118m.

MORE OF DISNEY'S BEST: 1932–1946 ★★★★★
DIR: Walt Disney. **CAST:** Animated.

This sextet, which is vastly superior to its companion collection, includes three "Silly Symphonies" and three cartoons with the better-known stars. "The Brave Little Tailor" is one of Mickey Mouse's best solo vehicles. The Oscar-winning "The Old Mill" (1937) draws considerable drama from the plight of forest creatures trying to ride out a fierce storm, and 1933's "Three Little Pigs" (also an Oscar winner) proves just who's "...afraid of the Big, Bad Wolf." 1932–1946; 50m.

MOUNTAIN FAMILY ROBINSON ★★½
DIR: John Cotter. **CAST:** Robert Logan, Susan D. Shaw, Heather Rattray, Ham Larsen.

Mountain Family Robinson delivers exactly what it sets out to achieve. It does not purport to have any other message than that of the value of familial love, understanding, and togetherness. Predictable and a bit corny. The cast displays an affability that should charm the children and make this film a relaxing, easy time-passer for parents as well. Rated G. 1979; 100m.

MOUSE AND HIS CHILD, THE ★★
DIR: Fred Wolf, Chuck Swenson. **CAST:** Animated.

Muddled cartoon feature about a pair of wind-up toys who attempt to escape from the tyranny of an evil rat after falling off a toy-store shelf and ending up in a dump. It's an uneasy combination of a simple children's story with a heavy-handed metaphor. The voices are provided by Peter Ustinov, Cloris Leachman, Andy Devine, and Sally Kellerman. Rated G. 1977; 82m.

MOWGLI'S BROTHERS ★★★★
DIR: Chuck Jones. **CAST:** Animated.

The classic tale by Rudyard Kipling is brought to life by animator Chuck Jones and the voices of Roddy McDowall and June Foray. Though the animation here is far simpler than Jones's earlier "Rikki Tikki Tavi," this story of a foundling who is raised by the law of the jungle and a pack of wolves will be a delight to viewers of all ages. 1977; 30m.

MUPPET MOVIE, THE ★★★½
DIR: James Frawley. **CAST:** Muppets, Edgar Bergen and Charlie McCarthy, Milton Berle, Mel Brooks, James Coburn, Dom DeLuise, Elliott Gould, Bob Hope, Madeline Kahn, Carol Kane, Cloris Leachman, Steve Martin, Richard Pryor, Telly Savalas, Orson Welles, Paul Williams.

Though there is a huge all-star guest cast, the Muppets are the real stars of this superior family film in which the characters trek to Hollywood in search of stardom. Rated G. 1979; 94m.

MUPPETS TAKE MANHATTAN, THE ★★★
DIR: Frank Oz. **CAST:** Muppets, Art Carney, Dabney Coleman, Joan Rivers, Elliott Gould, Liza Minnelli, Brooke Shields.

Jim Henson's popular puppets take a bite of the Big Apple in their third and least effective screen romp. The screenplay is of the old "let's put on a show" genre, with playwright Kermit and his pals trying to get their musical on the Broadway stage. Rated G. 1984; 94m.

MY FRIEND LIBERTY ★★★½
DIR: Jimmy Picker. **CAST:** Animated.
An entertaining and enlightening look at the history of America's most famous statue in a claymation perspective by Academy Award winner Jimmy Picker. Viewers of all ages will find this an enjoyable lesson about who we are and where we came from. 1986; 30m.

MY LITTLE PONY: THE MOVIE ★★★
DIR: Michael Joens. **CAST:** Danny DeVito, Madeline Kahn, Cloris Leachman, Rhea Perlman, Tony Randall (voices).
Darling ponies are threatened by the evil witch family (Cloris Leachman, Madeline Kahn, and Rhea Perlman). Children under 7 should enjoy this, but older children and adults may feel it's too long. Rated G. 1986; 85m.

MY SIDE OF THE MOUNTAIN ★★★★
DIR: James B. Clark. **CAST:** Teddy Eccles, Theodore Bikel.
File this in that all-too-small category of films that both you and your kids can enjoy. A 13-year-old Toronto boy decides to prove his self-worth by living in a Quebec forest for one year with no resources other than his own wits. Gus the Raccoon steals the show, but you'll be charmed and entertained by the rest of the movie as well. Rated G. 1969; 100m.

MYSTERY ISLAND ★★★
DIR: Gene Scott. **CAST:** Jayson Duncan, Niklas Juhlin.
When four children whose boat has run out of gas discover what appears to be a deserted island, they promptly name it Mystery Island. There is actually an old pirate who lives there. The children find a case of counterfeit money which belongs to villains, who later return to the island for it. The old pirate's timely intervention saves the kids. The best part about this children's film is the beautiful underwater photography. 1981; 75m.

MYSTERY MANSION ★
DIR: David F. Jackson. **CAST:** Dallas McKennon, Greg Wynne, Jane Ferguson.
An absolutely unremarkable film about a girl with strange but true dreams, two escaped convicts, a harried father in danger of losing his land to an evil tycoon, and hidden treasure—all involved with an old Victorian mystery house. It's all been done before, and better, in countless other films. Rated G. 1986; 95m.

NAPOLEON AND SAMANTHA ★★★½
DIR: Bernard McEveety. **CAST:** Johnny Whitaker, Jodie Foster, Michael Douglas, Will Geer, Arch Johnson, Henry Jones.
This Disney film features Johnny Whitaker as Napoleon, an orphan who decides to hide his grandpa's body when the old man dies and care for their pet lion, Major. When a college student/goat herder named Danny (Michael Douglas) helps bury Grandpa, Napoleon decides to follow him to his flock. Samantha (Jodie Foster) joins him and the lion as they cross mountains and streams and face the dangers of a fierce mountain lion and a bear. Rated G. 1972; 91m.

NATIONAL VELVET ★★★★
DIR: Clarence Brown. **CAST:** Mickey Rooney, Elizabeth Taylor, Donald Crisp, Anne Revere, Angela Lansbury, Reginald Owen.
This heartwarming tale of two youngsters determined to train a beloved horse to win the famed Grand National Race is good for the whole family, and especially good for little girls who love horses and sentimentalists who fondly recall Elizabeth Taylor when she was young, innocent, and adorable. Have Kleenex on hand. 1944; 125m.

NELVANAMATION (VOLUME ONE) ★★★
DIR: Clive Smith. **CAST:** Animated.

Four made-for-television cartoons. In "A Cosmic Christmas," a kindhearted boy attempts to explain the celebration to some friendly aliens. "The Devil and Daniel Mouse" is an outstanding short about a folk singing rodent (music by John Sebastian). A robotic version of the Shakespearean love story is brought to life in "Romie-0 and Julie-8." The last episode, "Please Don't Eat the Planet," is subtitled "An Intergalactic Thanksgiving." 1980; 100m.

NELVANAMATION (VOLUME TWO) ★★½
DIR: Ken Stephenson, Gian Celestri, Greg Duffell. **CAST:** Animated.

More enjoyable cartooning from Canada's Nelvana Studios. This well-written collection includes "Take Me Out to the Ball Game," a sci-fi baseball story with music by Rick Danko of The Band, and "The Jack Rabbit Story," with music by John Sebastian. 1980; 100m.

NEVER A DULL MOMENT ★
DIR: Jerry Paris. **CAST:** Dick Van Dyke, Edward G. Robinson, Dorothy Provine, Henry Silva.

Undoubtedly one of the weakest of all Disney feature films, this dismal effort has all the finesse one would expect from Dick Van Dyke doing his sophisticated version of Jerry Lewis at his worst. Rated G. 1968; 100m.

NEW ADVENTURES OF PIPPI LONGSTOCKING, THE ★
DIR: Ken Annakin. **CAST:** Tami Erin, Eileen Brennan, Dennis Dugan, Dianne Hull.

Something has been lost in the film adaptation of Astrid Lindgren's tale. This time spunky but lovable Pippi is an anarchistic brat who manages to give adult viewers a headache and children ideas about driving adults over the edge. A few catchy tunes remind one of *Annie*, but there is nothing else to recommend this. Rated G. 1988; 100m.

NIGHT THEY SAVED CHRISTMAS, THE ★★★★
DIR: Jackie Cooper. **CAST:** Jaclyn Smith, Art Carney, Paul LeMat, Mason Adams, June Lockhart, Paul Williams.

In this excellent made-for-television film, three kids strive to protect Santa's toy factory from being destroyed by an oil company. Art Carney is delightful as Saint Nick. 1984; 100m.

NIGHTINGALE, THE ★★★½
DIR: Ivan Passer. **CAST:** Mick Jagger, Bud Cort, Barbara Hershey, Edward James Olmos.

An emperor (Mick Jagger) survives court intrigue to discover true friendship from a lowly maid (Barbara Hershey) with the help of a nightingale in this enjoyable *Faerie Tale Theatre* production. 1983; 51m.

NIKKI, WILD DOG OF THE NORTH ★★★
DIR: Jack Couffer. **CAST:** Don Haldane, Jean Coutu, Emile Genest.

The rugged wilderness of northern Canada provides the backdrop to this story of a dog that is separated from his owner. 1961; 73m.

NO DEPOSIT, NO RETURN ★★
DIR: Norman Tokar. **CAST:** David Niven, Don Knotts, Darren McGavin, Herschel Bernardi, Barbara Feldon.

Two kids decide to escape from their multimillionaire grandfather (David Niven) and visit their mother in Hong Kong. On their way to the airport, they end up in a getaway car with two incompetent safecrackers with (surprise!) a soft spot in their hearts for kids. It is unrealistic and not very believable, with occasional bits of real entertainment. Rated G. 1976; 115m.

NORTH AVENUE IRREGULARS, THE ★★½
DIR: Bruce Bilson. **CAST:** Edward Herrmann, Barbara Harris, Cloris Leachman, Susan Clark, Karen Val-

entine, Michael Constantine, Patsy Kelly, Virginia Capers.

Average Disney film about a young priest (Edward Herrmann) who wants to do something about crime. He enlists a group of churchgoing, do-good women to work with him. Quality cast is wasted on marginal script. Rated G. 1979; 100m.

NOW YOU SEE HIM, NOW YOU DON'T ★★

DIR: Robert Butler. **CAST:** Kurt Russell, Joe Flynn, Jim Backus, Cesar Romero, William Windom.

Kurt Russell discovers a formula that will make a person or item invisible. Bad guy Cesar Romero attempts to hijack the discovery for nefarious purposes, which leads to disastrous results. Rated G. 1972; 85m.

NUTS ABOUT CHIP 'N' DALE ★★★

DIR: Walt Disney. **CAST:** Animated.

Pluto's attempts to bury a bone cause problems with the two chipmunks in "Food for Feudin'," easily the best cartoon of this collection. In "Two Chips and a Miss" both chipmunks fall in love with Clarice (in her only appearance). The noisy and somewhat cruel struggles with Donald Duck in "Trailer Horn" end things on an unfortunate note. 1950–1952; 22m.

OFF ON A COMET ★½

DIR: Richard Slapczynski. **CAST:** Animated.

A boring re-creation of the Jules Verne fantasy. A French captain must solve the riddle of what's happened to the world when it collides with a comet. The characters' accents are somewhat bothersome and may get in the way of understanding for younger viewers. 1979; 52m.

OFFICER AND A DUCK, AN (LIMITED GOLD EDITION 2) ★★★★½

DIR: Walt Disney. **CAST:** Animated.

Six exceptional animated treats. Donald Duck turns unwilling soldier in these rarely seen entries, from his first days of "Donald Gets Drafted" to his ambitious scheme to go AWOL in "The Old Army Game," a plan that backfires with hilarious results. 1942–1943; 50m.

OH, HEAVENLY DOG! ★

DIR: Joe Camp. **CAST:** Benji, Chevy Chase, Jane Seymour, Omar Sharif, Robert Morley.

Chevy Chase should have known better. This movie is an overly silly cutesy about a private eye (Chase) who is murdered and then comes back as a dog (Benji) to trap his killers. Kids, however, should enjoy it. Rated PG. 1980; 103m.

OLD YELLER ★★★★

DIR: Robert Stevenson. **CAST:** Dorothy McGuire, Fess Parker, Tommy Kirk, Chuck Connors.

Here's a live-action Walt Disney favorite. A big yellow mongrel is taken in by a Southwestern family. The warm attachment and numerous adventures of the dog and the two boys of the family are sure to endear this old mutt to your heart. A few tears are guaranteed to fall at the conclusion, so you'd best have a hankie. 1957; 83m.

ON THE RIGHT TRACK ★★

DIR: Lee Philips. **CAST:** Gary Coleman, Maureen Stapleton, Michael Lembeck, Norman Fell.

Gary Coleman (of television's "Diff'rent Strokes") plays a tyke who sets up residence in a railroad station to escape the hustle and bustle of the city. Once the word gets around that he has a talent for picking the winners in horse races, his life becomes complicated all over again. Without Coleman, this would be an awful movie. Even with him, it is nothing to shout about. Rated PG. 1981; 98m.

ONCE UPON A MIDNIGHT SCARY ★★½

DIR: Neil Cox. **CAST:** Vincent Price, René Auberjonois, Severn Darden.

Interesting television production of a trilogy of children's classic ghost stories, hosted by Vincent Price. *The Ghost Belongs to Me*, *The Legend of Sleepy Hollow*, and *The House with a*

Clock in its Walls are presented in that order, with the first two stories the standouts. All are given a preteen treatment, which means no gore and no bad language, just some old-fashioned scares. 1979; 50m.

ONE AND ONLY, GENUINE, ORIGINAL FAMILY BAND, THE ★★½

DIR: Michael O'Herlihy. **CAST:** Walter Brennan, Buddy Ebsen, Lesley Ann Warren, John Davidson, Goldie Hawn.

This period comedy, set in the Dakota territories, features Walter Brennan—who struggles to keep his family's band together in order to get invited to the Democratic convention in St. Louis. This is a lightweight movie made shortly after Walt Disney's death. It misses his touch but is, nonetheless, moderately enjoyable for the whole family. Rated G. 1967; 110m.

ONE OF OUR DINOSAURS IS MISSING ★★½

DIR: Robert Stevenson. **CAST:** Peter Ustinov, Helen Hayes, Derek Nimmo, Clive Revill.

In this moderately entertaining comedy spy film, Peter Ustinov plays a Chinese intelligence agent attempting to recover some stolen microfilm. Helen Hayes plays a nanny who becomes involved in trying to get the film to the British authorities. The film is in a dinosaur skeleton that Hayes and other nannies take to the streets of London. Rated G. 1975; 101m.

1001 RABBIT TALES ★★★★

DIR: Friz Freleng, Chuck Jones. **CAST:** Animated.

Fourteen classic cartoons are interwoven with new footage to make another feature-length film out of the well-known Warner Bros. characters. This time the theme is fairy tales. Bugs and the gang spoof "Goldilocks and the Three Bears," "Jack and the Bean Stalk," and "Little Red Riding Hood," among others. This one also contains Chuck Jones's "One Froggy Evening," one of the greatest cartoons ever! Rated G. 1982; 76m.

OUR LITTLE GIRL ★★★

DIR: John S. Robertson. **CAST:** Shirley Temple, Rosemary Ames, Joel McCrea, Lyle Talbot.

Curly-top Shirley's physician father (Joel McCrea) is away so much that his lovely wife (Rosemary Ames) seeks solace from neighbor Lyle Talbot. Shirley is so distressed by this turn of events that she runs away, forcing her parents to reunite in their search for her. Fine melodrama. 1935; B&W; 63m.

PACKIN' IT IN ★★★½

DIR: Jud Taylor. **CAST:** Richard Benjamin, Paula Prentiss, Molly Ringwald, Tony Roberts, Andrea Marcovicci.

When Gary and Dianna Webber (Richard Benjamin and Paula Prentiss) flee from the pollution and crime of Los Angeles, they find themselves living among survivalists in Woodcrest, Oregon. The laughs begin as these city folks, including their punked-out daughter (played by Molly Ringwald), try to adjust to life in the wilderness. 1982; 92m.

PADDINGTON BEAR (SERIES) ★★★

DIR: Michael Bond. **CAST:** Animated.

This British production successfully uses a charming stuffed bear and stop-action along with flat, cut-out human figures. Paddington is a darling bear who came to England from Peru. He manages to get into many scrapes (each volume in the series of tapes has eleven featurettes) and somehow comes out on top by virtue of his wit and imagination. Children under seven will find this entertaining. 1983; 50m.

PARENT TRAP, THE ★★★★

DIR: David Swift. **CAST:** Hayley Mills, Brian Keith, Maureen O'Hara, Joanna Barnes.

Walt Disney doubled the fun in this comedy when he had Hayley Mills play twins. Mills plays sisters who meet for the first time at summer camp and decide to reunite their divorced parents (Brian Keith and Maureen O'Hara). 1961; 124m.

PEANUT BUTTER SOLUTION, THE ★★½
DIR: Michael Rubbo. **CAST:** Mathew Mackay, Siluk Saysanasy, Helen Hughes.
Remember sitting around a campfire when you were a kid and creating a story that just went on and on? This is a campfire movie. Part of the *Tales for All* series, it combines old houses, ghosts, an evil madman, enforced child labor, and a main character with a real hairy problem, all mixed together in sort of a story. 1985; 96m.

PECK'S BAD BOY ★★★
DIR: Sam Wood. **CAST:** Jackie Coogan, Wheeler Oakman, Doris May, Raymond Hatton, Lillian Leighton.
Jackie Coogan shines as the mischievous scamp who commits all manner of mayhem upon anyone who happens to cross his path, yet miraculously escapes the lethal designs his victims must harbor. Silent. 1921; B&W; 54m.

PECK'S BAD BOY WITH THE CIRCUS ★★
DIR: Eddie Cline. **CAST:** Tommy Kelly, Ann Gillis, Edgar Kennedy, Billy Gilbert, Benita Hume, Spanky MacFarland, Grant Mitchell.
Tommy Kelly, the mischievous Peck's Bad Boy, and his ragamuffin gang of troublemakers (including an aging Spanky MacFarland) wreak havoc around the circus. Comedy greats Edgar Kennedy and Billy Gilbert are the best part of this kids' film. 1938; B&W; 78m.

PECOS BILL, KING OF THE COWBOYS ★★★½
DIR: Howard Storm. **CAST:** Steve Guttenberg, Martin Mull, Dick Schaal, Rebecca DeMornay, Claude Akins.
This episode from Shelley Duvall's *Tales and Legends* is fun for the whole family. Steve Guttenberg is irresistible as Bill, the wild man raised by coyotes. A truly entertaining hour! 1986; 60m.

PEPE LE PEW'S SKUNK TALES ★★★
DIR: Chuck Jones, Arthur Davis, Abe Levitow. **CAST:** Animated.
Once again, Warner Bros. director Chuck Jones takes top honors in a Warner Bros. cartoon release. His 1949 Oscar-winning "For Scent-imental Reasons" features the amorous skunk, Pepe Le Pew, at his cat-wooing best. 1948–1960; 56m.

PETE'S DRAGON ★★½
DIR: Don Chaffey. **CAST:** Mickey Rooney, Jim Dale, Helen Reddy, Red Buttons, Jim Backus, Sean Marshall.
Only the kiddies will get a kick out of this Disney feature, which combines live action with animation. The story takes place in Maine circa 1908 when a 9-year-old boy (Sean Marshall) escapes his overbearing foster parents with the aid of the pet dragon that only he can see. Sort of a children's version of *Harvey*, it's generally lackluster and uninspired. Rated G. 1977; 134m.

PETRONELLA ★★★★
DIR: Rick Locke. **CAST:** Sylvia, Mayf Nutter, James Arrington, Jerry Maren, David Jensen, David E. Morgan.
This live-action production of *Enchanted Musical Playhouse* stars the lovely country-pop singer Sylvia as a liberated princess who sets out to rescue an imprisoned prince. The whole family can enjoy this delightful tale with its cheerful songs and humorous moments. 1985; 30m.

PIED PIPER OF HAMELIN, THE ★★★★★
DIR: Nicholas Meyer. **CAST:** Eric Idle, Tony Van Bridge, Keram Malicki-Sanchez, Peter Blaise.
Nicholas Meyer, who also directed *The Day After* and *Star Trek III*, does a terrific job of adapting Robert

Browning's eerie poem for this *Faerie Tale Theatre* episode. 1985; 60m.

PINK AT FIRST SIGHT ★★★★
DIR: Friz Freleng, David H. DePatie. **CAST:** Animated.

This was a Valentine's Day TV special in which the Pink Panther, Blake Edwards's lovable and zany cartoon character, longs to have a lady panther and enough money to buy her a special present. To this end, he attempts to make some money as a singing messenger. Also included on this tape are four shorter features. 1964–1981; 49m.

PINK PANTHER CARTOON FESTIVAL: A FLY IN THE PINK, THE ★★★½
DIR: Friz Freleng, David H. DePatie. **CAST:** Animated.

The featured short on this nine-cartoon tape has the Pink Panther pursuing a fruit fly. Among the other installments: "Pink-a-Rella," in which our hero finds a magic wand, and "Pink Plasma," depicting a less than enjoyable stay in Transylvania. 1968–1975; 57m.

PINK PANTHER CARTOON FESTIVAL: PINK-A-BOO, THE ★★★
DIR: Friz Freleng, David H. DePatie. **CAST:** Animated.

The featured short on this tape has the Pink Panther desperately trying to rid his house of a pesky mouse that constantly outwits him. Also offered are "Slink Pink," "Pink Aye," "In the Pink of the Night," and four other titles. 1964–1979; 56m.

PINOCCHIO (1940) ★★★★★
DIR: Walt Disney. **CAST:** Animated.

In this timeless Walt Disney animated classic, a puppet made by a lonely old man gets the chance to become a real boy. *Pinocchio* is one of those rare motion pictures that can be enjoyed over and over again by adults as well as children. If you remember it as a "kid's show," watch it again. You'll be surprised at how wonderfully entertaining it is. Rated G. 1940; 87m.

PINOCCHIO (1983) ★★★★
DIR: Peter Medak. **CAST:** James Coburn, Carl Reiner, Pee-wee Herman, James Belushi, Lainie Kazan, Don Novello.

An excellent adaptation of the classic tale about the adventures of a wooden puppet who turns into a real boy. This *Faerie Tale Theatre* production, as with most of the others, will be best appreciated—and understood—by adults. It's blessed with just the right touch of humor, and Lainie Kazan is wonderful as the "Italian" fairy godmother. 1983; 51m.

PINOCCHIO AND THE EMPEROR OF THE NIGHT ★★
DIR: Hal Sutherland. **CAST:** Edward Asner, Tom Bosley, James Earl Jones, Don Knotts, William Windom (voices).

This scary continuation of the classic tale features an incorrigible Pinocchio who manages to lose his father's prized jewel box as well as his own right to be a real boy. Animation is okay, but somehow you feel as though you're watching an overlong Saturday-morning cartoon. Rated G. 1987; 91m.

PIPPI LONGSTOCKING, PIPPI IN THE SOUTH SEAS, PIPPI ON THE RUN, PIPPI GOES ON BOARD ★★
DIR: Olle Hellbron. **CAST:** Inger Nilsson.

These four movies about the little Swedish girl with the red pigtails and the magical powers were all made at the same time but released in this country over several years. Each has Pippi and her friends annoying grownups and having adventures, mostly dealing with her sea-captain father in faraway lands. Young kids seem to like the movies, even though adults will be appalled at how poorly made and atrociously dubbed they are. Be warned, though, that active children emulating the obnoxious antics of Pippi are even worse than kids shouting Pee-wee Herman's "secret word" all day. Rated G. 1969; 99/85/99/84 minutes.

PLUTO ★★★★
DIR: Walt Disney. **CAST:** Animated.
"The Pointer" is the treasure of this uneven collection. While both "Bone Trouble" and "Private Pluto" (featuring early appearances by the as-yet-unnamed Chip 'n' Dale) are the other highlights, the tape also includes the weaker storylines and limited animation of "Camp Dog" and "The Legend of Coyote Rock." 1939–1950; 52m.

PLUTO (LIMITED GOLD EDITION 1) ★★★★
DIR: Walt Disney. **CAST:** Animated.
Dinah the dachshund plays the romantic lead, with Butch the bulldog a constant threat, in many of these delightful Pluto cartoons. Still, his best adventures are a pair of richly animated World War II–era cartoons: "Pluto at the Zoo" and "Pluto Junior" (which proves the dangers of fathering a child who resembles the parent *too* much). All seven of these entries are quite enjoyable. 1942–1950; 47m.

POGO'S SPECIAL BIRTHDAY SPECIAL, THE ★★★
DIR: Chuck Jones. **CAST:** Animated.
Walt Kelly's beloved characters from the popular comic strip come to life here in the expected nonsensical fashion. Keep on your toes in order to catch the masterful Kelly adaptation of Cajun dialects, as director Chuck Jones takes a sideways look at American holidays and their origins. 1986; 26m.

POLLYANNA (1920) ★★★½
DIR: Paul Powell. **CAST:** Mary Pickford, Katharine Griffith, Howard Ralston.
Mary Pickford (at age 27 in 1920) portrays 12-year-old Pollyana, and she melts the hearts of everyone. If you admire silent films or Pickford, or both, you should see this one. 1920; B&W; 78m.

POLLYANNA (1960) ★★★½
DIR: David Swift. **CAST:** Hayley Mills, Jane Wyman, Agnes Moorehead, Adolphe Menjou, Karl Malden, Nancy Olson.
Walt Disney's version of this classic childhood book is good entertainment for the whole family. Hayley Mills is the energetic and optimistic young girl who improves the lives of everyone she meets. Jane Wyman, Agnes Moorehead, and Adolphe Menjou head an exceptional supporting cast for this film. 1960; 134m.

PONCE DE LEON AND THE FOUNTAIN OF YOUTH ★
DIR: Sheldon Larry. **CAST:** Michael York, Sally Kellerman, Paul Rodriguez, Dr. Ruth Westheimer.
This forgettable production of Shelley Duvall's *Tall Tales and Legends* wastes the talents of Michael York by reducing him to an unbelievably vain Ponce de Leon. This is too corny for children or adults. 1986; 50m.

POPEYE ★★★
DIR: Robert Altman. **CAST:** Robin Williams, Shelley Duvall, Ray Walston, Paul Smith, Paul Dooley, Richard Libertini, Wesley Ivan Hurt.
This adaptation of the famous comic strip by director Robert Altman is the cinematic equivalent of the old "good news, bad news" routine. The good news is that Robin Williams makes a terrific Popeye, and Shelley Duvall was born to play Olive Oyl. The bad news is that it's often boring. Still, it's hard to really dislike *Popeye*—it's so wonderfully weird to look at and so much fun at times. Rated PG. 1980; 114m.

POPEYE CARTOONS ★★★★
DIR: Dave Fleischer. **CAST:** Animated.
Popeye the Sailor Man gets his finest treatment in this trio of classic big-screen cartoons from Max and Dave Fleischer: "Popeye Meets Sinbad," "Aladdin and His Wonderful Lamp," and "Popeye Meets Ali Baba." 1930s–1940s; 56m.

PORKY PIG AND DAFFY DUCK CARTOON FESTIVAL FEATURING "TICK TOCK TUCKERED" ★★★★

DIR: Bob Clampett, Chuck Jones, Robert McKimson. **CAST:** Animated.

Bob Clampett takes the top prizes for the sheer hilarity of his contributions: "Baby Bottleneck," in which Porky and Daffy go boom in the baby boom; "Wagon Heels"; and "Tick Tock Tuckered," in which our guys play Beat the Clock. It's a cartoonaholic's dream come true. 1943–1947; 57m.

PORKY PIG CARTOON FESTIVAL FEATURING "NOTHING BUT THE TOOTH" ★★½

DIR: Bob Clampett, Arthur Davis, Chuck Jones, Frank Tashlin. **CAST:** Animated.

Porky Pig's star vehicle "The Swooner Crooner" is the only noteworthy entry in this otherwise unremarkable collection. "Crooner" is a World War II–era short, in which farmer Porky employs roosters resembling Bing Crosby and Frank Sinatra to move a group of hens to complete eggs-haustion. Bob Clampett's "Kitty Kornered" features a team-up with Sylvester the cat. 1944–1948; 36m.

PORKY PIG TALES ★★★★

DIR: Arthur Davis, Chuck Jones, Robert McKimson. **CAST:** Animated.

Animator Chuck Jones is well represented by this late-period sextet of Porky Pig cartoons, the best being "Jumpin' Jupiter," in which campers Porky and Sylvester the cat are "spacenapped" by a rather exotic alien. The collection concludes with one of Porky's last appearances: with Daffy Duck in Robert McKimson's "China Jones," originally released in 1959. 1948–1959; 44m.

PORKY PIG'S SCREWBALL COMEDIES ★★★

DIR: Friz Freleng, Chuck Jones, Robert McKimson. **CAST:** Animated.

A fun collection with two delightful Friz Freleng–directed cartoons the standouts: "You Ought to Be in Pictures," in which Porky lets Daffy Duck talk him into quitting cartoons for feature films; and the "Dough for Do-Do," in which Porky goes after the priceless dodo in Africa amidst surreal backgrounds. 1985; 59m.

PRINCE AND THE PAUPER, THE (1937) ★★★½

DIR: William Keighley. **CAST:** Errol Flynn, Claude Rains, Barton MacLane, Alan Hale, Billy Mauch, Bobby Mauch.

Enjoyable story of the young Prince of England trading places with his identical look-alike, a street beggar. One of Errol Flynn's lesser-known films. Erich Wolfgang Korngold wrote the music. 1937; B&W; 120m.

PRINCE AND THE PAUPER, THE (1978) ★★★½

DIR: Richard Fleischer. **CAST:** Charlton Heston, Oliver Reed, George C. Scott, Rex Harrison, Mark Lester.

An all-star cast brings Mark Twain's novel of mistaken identity in not-so-jolly old England to life. Edward, the only son of King Henry VIII (Charlton Heston), trades places with his double, a child from the London slums. The young prince has trouble reclaiming his crown even with the aid of a swashbuckling soldier-of-fortune (Oliver Reed). Nothing pretentious here, just a costumed adventure that should satisfy young and old. Rated PG. 1978; 113m.

PRINCE OF CENTRAL PARK, THE ★★

DIR: Harvey Hart. **CAST:** T. J. Hargrave, Lisa Richards, Ruth Gordon, Marc Vahanian.

Ruth Gordon is, as usual, a bright spot in this made-for-TV children's film about an orphaned brother and sister who flee their foster home for a tree house in Central Park. The script is a bit cynical for a story aimed at children, but Gordon's charm serves to turn that around to her benefit. 1976; 76m.

PRINCESS AND THE PEA, THE ★★★½

DIR: Tony Bill. **CAST:** Liza Minnelli, Tom Conti, Beatrice Straight, Tim Kazurinsky.

One of the most interesting *Faerie Tale Theatre* productions, this film features fine performances from Liza Minnelli and Tom Conti. In a way, it's sort of a takeoff on *Arthur*, in which Minnelli starred with Dudley Moore. The actress delivers some rather familiar lines of dialogue as she plays a princess tested for her royal qualities, which include a special kind of sensitivity. 1983; 53m.

PRINCESS WHO HAD NEVER LAUGHED, THE ★★★★

DIR: Mark Cullingham. **CAST:** Howie Mandel, Ellen Barkin, Howard Hesseman.

In this funny Grimm's fairy tale, laughter does prove to be the best medicine for the forlorn princess (Ellen Barkin). Growing up with her father (Howard Hesseman), who prefers to be called "Your Seriousness," she has never had a happy or amusing moment. When she locks herself in her room, her father decrees a Royal Laugh-off to make his daughter happy. At this point Howie Mandel appears as Weinerhead Waldo and the fun begins. 1984; 51m.

PRIZEFIGHTER, THE ★★½

DIR: Michael Preece. **CAST:** Tim Conway, Don Knotts, David Wayne.

In addition to starring in this goofy comedy, Tim Conway wrote the story. In it, we get a glimpse of 1930s boxing, with Conway playing a stupid boxer who has Don Knotts for his manager. Children may find the corny gags amusing, but most adults will be disappointed. Rated PG. 1979; 99m.

PURPLE PEOPLE EATER ★★½

DIR: Linda Shayne. **CAST:** Ned Beatty, Shelley Winters, Neil Patrick Harris, Peggy Lipton.

A sappy family flick about an alien (the title character) who comes to Earth to join a rock 'n' roll band. He is aided by an aspiring young musician, and in turn helps the local seniors hold on to their retirement complex. The fine cast, headed by Ned Beatty, is overshadowed by a sickeningly sweet alien puppet. Rated PG. 1988; 91m.

PUSS IN BOOTS ★★★★

DIR: Robert Iscove. **CAST:** Ben Vereen, Gregory Hines, George Kirby, Brock Peters, Alfre Woodard.

To ensure himself an easy life, a wily feline carries out a plan to turn his impoverished master into a rich marquis by winning him an ogre's castle and the hand of the king's daughter in marriage. Ben Vereen is purringly convincing as the cat and Brock Peters a standout as the ogre in this *Faerie Tale Theatre* production. 1984; 53m.

RACE FOR YOUR LIFE, CHARLIE BROWN ★★★

DIR: Bill Melendez. **CAST:** Animated.

Third entry in the "Peanuts" film series has moved further away from the poignant sophistication of *A Boy Named Charlie Brown* and closer to the mindless pap of Saturday-morning cartoon fare. Rated G. 1977; 75m.

RAFFI AND THE SUNSHINE BAND ★★★★½

DIR: David Devine. **CAST:** Raffi.

This delightfully tuneful follow-up to *A Young Children's Concert with Raffi* is guaranteed to keep the young ones happy. This time, the Canadian folk singer is accompanied by a four-piece band on old favorites and new songs, including "Day-O," "Time to Sing," "Rise and Shine," and "Five Little Ducks." 1988; 60m.

RAILWAY CHILDREN, THE ★★★★½

DIR: Lionel Jeffries. **CAST:** Dinah Sheridan, Bernard Cribbins, William Mervyn, Ian Cuthbertson, Jenny Agutter, Sally Thomsett, Gary Warren.

Wonderful family fare from Great Britain. Set in 1905, this tale focuses on a family whose idyllic life is shattered. Director Lionel Jeffries, a popular British comic actor, also wrote the screenplay based on the novel by E. Nesbit. Warmth, comedy, and adventure—must-see. 1972; 104m.

RAINBOW BRITE AND THE STAR STEALER ★★★
DIR: Bernard Deyries, Kimio Yabuki. **CAST:** Animated.

When the Dark Princess tries to steal Spectra (the world's light source), Rainbow Brite teams up with a chauvinistic, but admittedly brave, little boy named Krys to prevent the theft. This is Rainbow Brite's first feature-length film, and should continue to thrill the little girls who tend to be her most avid fans. 1985; 85m.

RAPUNZEL ★★★½
DIR: Gilbert Cates. **CAST:** Jeff Bridges, Shelley Duvall, Gena Rowlands.

A pregnant woman's desire for radishes results in her having to give her baby daughter to the witch who owns the radish garden. Shelley Duvall is amusing as both the mother and a grown Rapunzel. Jeff Bridges makes a fine, put-upon husband and a handsome prince who must rescue Rapunzel from the man-hating witch, delightfully played by Gena Rowlands. Another *Faerie Tale Theatre* production. 1982; 51m.

RARE BREED, A ★
DIR: David Nelson. **CAST:** George Kennedy, Forrest Tucker, Tracy Vaccaro, Don DeFore, Tom Hallick.

This film tries too hard to be cute and inspiring. It's the story of the abduction of an Italian racehorse. Try *National Velvet* instead. 1981; 94m.

RED BALLOON, THE ★★★★★
DIR: Albert Lamorisse. **CAST:** Pascal Lamorisse, Georges Sellier.

This fanciful, endearing tale of a giant balloon that befriends a small boy in Paris is a delight for children and adults alike. Outside of a catchable word or two here and there, the film is without dialogue. The story is crystal clear in the visual telling, punctuated by an engaging musical score. 1956; 34m.

RED PONY, THE ★★
DIR: Lewis Milestone. **CAST:** Myrna Loy, Robert Mitchum, Peter Miles, Louis Calhern, Shepperd Strudwick, Margaret Hamilton.

It is very hard to make a dull movie from a John Steinbeck novel. This rendition manages to accomplish that. Myrna Loy and Robert Mitchum are wasted in this story of a young Northern California boy who is given a colt, which runs away. 1948; 89m.

RELUCTANT DRAGON, THE ★★★★½
DIR: Charles A. Nichols. **CAST:** Animated.

This delightful, though somewhat unorthodox, medieval dragon tale is a must-see for anyone! Director Charles Nichols orchestrates a fast-paced, hilarious romp—a droll encounter between a bard and a dragon. This is truly a Disney gem. Not rated. Suitable for the entire family. 1957; 28m.

RETURN FROM WITCH MOUNTAIN ★★
DIR: John Hough. **CAST:** Bette Davis, Christopher Lee, Kim Richards, Ike Eisenmann.

Christopher Lee and Bette Davis capture Ike Eisenmann to use his supernatural powers to accomplish their own purposes. Sequel to *Escape to Witch Mountain,* in which Eisenmann and Kim Richards discover their powers and the effect they can have on humans. Lee wants to conquer the world, while Davis just wants to get rich. A good children's film, but weak Disney. Rated G. 1978; 93m.

RETURN OF GUMBY, THE (VOLUME ONE) ★★★½
DIR: Art Clokey. **CAST:** Animated.

Though Gumby will always in some respects represent a certain aspect of Americana, he seems to have lost some of his initial charm in the transfer to videocassette. This tape, however, offers the best collection of Gumby's through-the-storybook episodes, such as "King for a Day" and "Hot Rod Granny." 1956; 60m.

RETURN TO OZ ★★★★
DIR: Walter Murch. **CAST:** Fairuza Balk, Nicol Williamson, Jean Marsh, Piper Laurie, Matt Clark.
In this semi-sequel to *The Wizard of Oz*, viewers will hear no songs nor see any Munchkins. It is a very different, but equally enjoyable, trip down the Yellow Brick Road, with young star Fairuza Balk outstanding as Dorothy. It gets pretty scary at times and isn't all fluff and wonder like the Oz of yore. This is nevertheless a magical film for the child in everyone. Rated PG for scary stuff. 1985; 110m.

RETURN TO TREASURE ISLAND ★★★½
DIR: Piers Haggard. **CAST:** Brian Blessed, Christopher Guard, Kenneth Colley.
This five-tape series was produced for the Disney Channel. It is a sequel to Disney's 1950 film *Treasure Island*, based on Robert Louis Stevenson's classic novel. The action here takes place ten years later with young Jim Hawkins (Christopher Guard) now an educated young man being reunited with the scheming Long John (Brian Blessed). 1985; each tape 101m.

RIDE A WILD PONY ★★★
DIR: Don Chaffey. **CAST:** Michael Craig, John Meillon.
This entertaining Disney film is the tale of a horse and the two children who want to own him. One is a poor boy who needs him to ride to school and the other is a rich girl with polio who needs him to help regain her strength and independence. The setting is Australia. Rated G. 1976; 86m.

RIKKI-TIKKI-TAVI ★★★★
DIR: Chuck Jones. **CAST:** Animated.
An outstanding feature from landmark cartoonist Chuck Jones detailing the adventures of a brave mongoose. This is a first-rate adaptation of the story by Rudyard Kipling. 1975; 30m.

RIP VAN WINKLE ★★½
DIR: Francis Ford Coppola. **CAST:** Harry Dean Stanton, Talia Shire, Ed Begley Jr., Mark Blankfield, Tim Conway, Hunter Carson.
This episode of *Faerie Tale Theatre* will probably not grab most viewers. Francis Ford Coppola does not seem suited to directing fantasies. The story remains basically unchanged as Rip falls asleep for twenty years in the Catskill Mountains only to awaken as an old man. 1985; 60m.

ROAD RUNNER VS. WILE E. COYOTE: THE CLASSIC CHASE ★★★★
DIR: Chuck Jones. **CAST:** Animated.
Although Chuck Jones deserves credit for some of the funniest Bugs Bunny/Daffy Duck cartoons and for creating Pepe Le Pew, for many the cliff-hanging (and falling) attempts of Wile E. Coyote to catch the uncatchable Road Runner stand as his greatest achievements. This first-rate collection includes several of his best shorts. 1985; 54m.

ROB ROY, THE HIGHLAND ROGUE ★★
DIR: Harold French. **CAST:** Richard Todd, Glynis Johns, James Robertson Justice, Michael Gough, Finlay Currie.
Slow-moving historical saga is not up to the usual Walt Disney adventure film and is perhaps the weakest of the three films made in England with sturdy Richard Todd as the heroic lead. The few battle scenes are enjoyable enough and the scenery is lovely, but the pace is erratic and there is just too much dead time. 1954; 85m.

ROBIN HOOD ★★★
DIR: Wolfgang Reitherman. **CAST:** Animated.
A feature-length cartoon featuring the adventures of Robin Hood and his gang, this is one of the lesser animated works from the Walt Disney

Studios, but still good entertainment for the kiddies. Rated G. 1973; 83m.

RUDOLPH THE RED-NOSED REINDEER (AND OTHER WONDERFUL CHRISTMAS STORIES) ★★★
DIR: Max Fleischer, Rene Bras. **CAST:** Animated.

The title episode on this tape of four holiday featurettes will be a real treat for those who enjoy vintage animation. It's a 1944 effort by Max Fleischer. Two black-and-white live-action shorts accompany the cartoon portions of this offering, which also includes a story called "Madeline's Christmas," a French holiday classic that is marred by continual drop-outs in the picture. 1944; 30m.

RUMPELSTILTSKIN (1980) ★★★½
DIR: Emile Andolino. **CAST:** Herve Villechaize, Shelley Duvall, Ned Beatty, Jack Fletcher, Bud Cort.

In this *Faerie Tale Theatre* production, a poor miller's daughter (Shelley Duvall, the series' executive producer) becomes a queen by outwitting a dwarf (Herve Villechaize) and fulfilling her boastful father's promise that she can spin straw into gold. Villechaize is great as a rather unsavory Rumpelstiltskin, and Ned Beatty is convincing as the selfish king who learns to think about others as well as himself. The sets are especially beautiful. 1982; 53m.

RUMPELSTILTSKIN (1986) ★★½
DIR: Pino VanLamsweerde. **CAST:** Animated.

Run-of-the-mill cartoon adaptation of the classic fairy tale about a pesky little man who aids a lovely young maiden in her attempt to spin straw into gold in order to serve his own selfish ends. Animation style here is comparable to the taste of fast food. 1986; 30m.

RUMPELSTILTSKIN (1987) ★★★½
DIR: David Irving. **CAST:** Amy Irving, Billy Barty, Clive Revill, Priscilla Pointer, John Moulder-Brown.

This musical, based on the Brothers Grimm fairy tale, will delight most viewers under the age of 12. In it, Amy Irving plays a poor daydreamer who wishes she could marry a prince. When her father brags that everything she touches turns to gold, she is summoned by the greedy king (Clive Revill) to spin straw into gold. Rumpelstiltskin (Billy Barty) rescues her from this impossible task but expects her to repay him with her firstborn child. Rated G. 1987; 85m.

RUN FOR THE ROSES ★★½
DIR: Henry Levin. **CAST:** Vera Miles, Stuart Whitman, Sam Groom, Panchito Gomez.

Originally titled *Thoroughbred*, this is a *Rocky*-ish saga about a horse that eventually competes in the Kentucky Derby. A Puerto Rican boy, staying with his stepfather, devotes himself to making the nearly lame horse a winner. Rated PG. 1978; 93m.

RUN, REBECCA, RUN ★★★★
DIR: Peter Maxwell. **CAST:** Henri Szeps, Simone Buchanan, John Stanton.

This action-filled adventure finds a brave young girl captured by an illegal alien on an Australian island. Her fear of him soon dissolves as she helps him face the Australian authorities in order to be legally admitted to their country. 1983; 81m.

SALUTE TO CHUCK JONES, A ★★★★½
DIR: Chuck Jones. **CAST:** Animated.

This terrific package includes "One Froggy Evening" (perhaps the best cartoon of all time), along with "Duck Dodgers in the 25½ Century," "What's Opera, Doc?" (a superb Wagnerian takeoff) and the Oscar-winning "For Scent-imental Reasons," among others. 1985; 56m.

SALUTE TO FRIZ FRELENG, A ★★★½
DIR: Friz Freleng. **CAST:** Animated.

Three Academy Award–winning shorts—"Knighty Knight Bugs," "Speedy Gonzales," and "Birds

Anonymous" (with Sylvester and Tweety Pie)—highlight this tribute to Friz Freleng. 1985; 57m.

SALUTE TO MEL BLANC, A ★★★★

DIR: Friz Freleng, Chuck Jones, Robert McKimson. **CAST:** Animated.

The main voice behind the Warner Bros. cartoons gets a fitting tribute in this superb collection of animated shorts, particularly "The Rabbit of Seville." 1985; 58m.

SAMMY, THE WAY-OUT SEAL ★★½

DIR: Norman Tokar. **CAST:** Jack Carson, Robert Culp, Patricia Barry, Billy Mumy, Ann Jillian, Michael McGreevey, Elisabeth Fraser.

Better than the title would imply. This series of misadventures involves two young brothers and the seal they attempt to keep as a pet. The film moves along briskly and features larger-than-life comic Jack Carson in one of his last performances. 1962; 89m.

SANTA CLAUS—THE MOVIE ★★★★

DIR: Jeannot Szwarc. **CAST:** Dudley Moore, John Lithgow, David Huddleston, Burgess Meredith, Judy Cornwell.

In this enjoyable family film, one of Santa's helpers, an elf named Patch (Dudley Moore), visits Earth and innocently joins forces with an evil toy manufacturer (delightfully played by John Lithgow). It is up to Santa (David Huddleston) to save him—and the spirit of Christmas in children everywhere. Rated PG for light profanity and adult themes. 1985; 105m.

SAVAGE SAM ★★½

DIR: Norman Tokar. **CAST:** Brian Keith, Tommy Kirk, Kevin Corcoran, Dewey Martin, Jeff York, Marta Kristen.

Officially a sequel to *Old Yeller*, the film has little in common with its predecessor, except for some of the character names. Captured by Indians, the only hope of rescue for three children lies with Savage Sam, Old Yeller's son. This is an entertaining action film, albeit without the characterizations and depth of its predecessor. 1963; 103m.

SAVANNAH SMILES ★★★½

DIR: Pierre DeMoro. **CAST:** Bridgette Anderson, Mark Miller, Donovan Scott, Peter Graves, Chris Robinson, Michael Parks.

In this surprisingly good, independently made family film, a 6-year-old runaway named Savannah (Bridgette Anderson) accidentally hides in the backseat of a car operated by two small-time crooks, Alvie (Mark Miller) and Boots (Donovan Scott). It's love at first sight for the trio, who decide to try to be a real family. The authorities, however, have other ideas. Rated G. 1982; 107m.

SAVE THE LADY ★★★

DIR: Leon Thau. **CAST:** Matthew Excell, Robert Clarkson, Miranda Cartledge, Kim Clifford.

Four kids set out to fight City Hall after a bureaucrat orders the historic *Lady Hope* steam ferry to be destroyed. The kids rescue *Lady Hope*'s former skipper from a retirement home. Together with an expert engineer, the team valiantly repairs and repaints the boat. The action picks up when the ferry must elude a fleet of police boats. 1981; 76m.

SCANDALOUS JOHN ★★★

DIR: Robert Butler. **CAST:** Brian Keith, Alfonso Arau, Michele Carey, Rick Lenz, Harry Morgan, Simon Oakland.

Brian Keith stars as an eccentric ranch owner fighting to maintain his way of life. In his world, a cattle drive consists of one steer, and gunfights are practiced in the house with live ammunition. He must battle with the law, the world in general, and reality to keep his ranch and the life he loves. Laughs and poignancy are combined in this movie. Rated G. 1971; 113m.

SCARY TALES ★★★½

DIR: Walt Disney. **CAST:** Animated.

This collection contains two superb Donald Duck vehicles: "Donald's

Lucky Day" (with its affectionate black cat) and "Duck Pimples" (an unusually chaotic cartoon for Disney, quite reminiscent of a Bob Clampett Daffy Duck cartoon). The balance of the tape includes two early black-and-white shorts, both sadly dated: "Skeleton Dance" and "Haunted House." 1928–1945; 43m.

SEA GYPSIES, THE ★★★
DIR: Stewart Raffill. **CAST:** Robert Logan, Mikki Jamison-Olsen, Heather Rattray.

Director Stewart Raffill wrote this adventure movie which tells of five castaways in the Pacific who end up on a remote Aleutian island. This Disney-style tale takes the survivors through many difficulties and is climaxed by a race against the approaching Alaskan winter to build a makeshift escape craft. 1978; 102m.

SEABERT: THE ADVENTURE BEGINS ★★½
DIR: John Armstrong, Al Lowenheim. **CAST:** Animated.

This feature provides a mild ecological message when a baby seal is saved from destruction by a young Eskimo girl and her American companion. Seabert and his new pals set off on a series of adventures that lead them all over the Arctic. Youngsters will find this as entertaining as Saturday-morning television, but not much more. 1987; 90m.

SECRET GARDEN, THE ★★½
DIR: Katrina Murray. **CAST:** Sarah Hollis Andrews, David Patterson.

Slow BBC production about a little girl uprooted from India and placed in the care of her cold, stern uncle in his manor house in England. Of course the girl thaws her uncle because of her resemblance to his dear, late wife. Pretty standard stuff, although it's well acted at least. Not rated; suitable for all. 1984; 107m.

SECRET OF NIMH, THE ★★★★★
DIR: Don Bluth. **CAST:** Dom DeLuise, Peter Strauss, John Carradine (voices).

Lovers of classic screen animation, rejoice! Don Bluth's *The Secret of Nimh* is the best feature-length cartoon to be released since the golden age of Walt Disney. This movie, about the adventures of a widow mouse, is more than just a children's tale. Adults will enjoy it, too. Rated G. 1982; 82m.

SECRET OF THE SWORD, THE ★
DIR: Bill Reed, Gwen Wetzler, Ed Friedman, Lou Kachivas, Marsh Lamore. **CAST:** Animated.

Characters from the television series *He-Man and the Masters of the Universe* are featured in this poorly animated, ineptly written feature-length cartoon. Rated G. 1985; 90m.

SESAME STREET PRESENTS FOLLOW THAT BIRD ★★★★
DIR: Ken Kwapis. **CAST:** Sandra Bernhard, Chevy Chase, John Candy, Dave Thomas, Joe Flaherty, Waylon Jennings.

Although this kiddie film has an impressive "guest cast," the real stars are *Sesame Street* TV show regulars Big Bird, the Cookie Monster, Oscar the Grouch, Count von Count, the Telly Monster, etc. Children will love this story about Big Bird being evicted from Sesame Street. Rated G. 1985; 88m.

SHAGGY D.A., THE ★
DIR: Robert Stevenson. **CAST:** Dean Jones, Tim Conway, Suzanne Pleshette.

Feeble sequel to Disney's far superior *The Shaggy Dog*, this retread stars Dean Jones as the victim of an ancient curse that turns him into a canine at the worst of moments. Rated G. 1976; 91m.

SHAGGY DOG, THE ★★★½
DIR: Charles Barton. **CAST:** Fred MacMurray, Jean Hagen, Tommy Kirk, Annette Funicello.

An ancient spell turns a boy into a sheepdog, and the fur flies in this slapstick Disney fantasy. Many of the gags are good, but the film sometimes drags. 1959; 104m.

SHE LIKES YOU, CHARLIE BROWN ★★★½

DIR: Bill Melendez, Sam Jaimes, Sam Nicholson, Phil Roman. **CAST:** Animated.

Puppy love is the theme of these ten stories, all taken from *The Charlie Brown and Snoopy Show*. Many are brief blackout sketches; the longer pieces include a wry date involving Peppermint Patty and Snoopy. 1983–1985; 41m.

SHE-RA, PRINCESS OF POWER (VOLUME ONE) ★

DIR: Hal Sutherland. **CAST:** Animated.

It's obvious only a modicum of imagination went into this companion series to *He-Man*. Here, his twin sister, Adora, also has a magic sword that changes her into She-Ra, defender of the crystal castle. Aided by her horse, Spirit, She-Ra saves a kidnapped woodcutter in "The Missing Axe." In "The Crystal Castle," Castle Bright Moon is under attack by the evil Shadow Weaver. (Other volumes in this series of tapes provide similar plots at the same length.) 1985; 45m.

SHERLOCK HOLMES AND THE BASKERVILLE CURSE ★★

DIR: Eddy Graham. **CAST:** Animated.

We weren't very impressed by this feature-length cartoon version of Sir Arthur Conan Doyle's oft-filmed "The Hound of the Baskervilles." The animation is way below par, and the story trifled with a bit too much for our tastes. It may be an effective introduction for youngsters to the joys of the canon. Rated G. 1984; 60m.

SHE'S A GOOD SKATE, CHARLIE BROWN ★★★½

DIR: Phil Roman. **CAST:** Animated.

Snoopy trains Peppermint Patty for a skating competition, and Marcie gets in over her head while sewing a skating dress for her friend. Woodstock's involvement in the climactic sequence is particularly touching. Faithful fans will also object to adults who actually speak (rather than *blat* like a muted trumpet). 1980; 25m.

SIGN OF ZORRO, THE ★★½

DIR: Norman Foster, Lewis R. Foster. **CAST:** Guy Williams, Henry Calvin, Gene Sheldon, Britt Lomond, George J. Lewis, Lisa Gaye.

Baby boomers, beware. If you have fond memories of this swashbuckling Disney television series about the Z-slashing Robin Hood of Old Mexico, you might want to skip this uneven feature compilation of original episodes. It's still fine for the kiddies, however. 1960; B&W; 91m.

SILLY SYMPHONIES ★★★

DIR: Walt Disney. **CAST:** Animated.

Ward Kimball's animation for "Toby Tortoise Returns" makes this entry the high point of the trio; the tortoise and the hare get together for one more round—this time in a boxing ring. Animator Fred Moore brings some energy to another variation on an old theme with "Three Little Wolves." "Water Babies," by contrast, is an attractive, but pointless, piece of fluff. 1935–1936; 25m.

SILLY SYMPHONIES (LIMITED GOLD EDITION 1) ★★½

DIR: Walt Disney. **CAST:** Animated.

Only the very young will sit still for these syrupy and badly dated fairy tales, most of which hang the thinnest of stories on what was then an experimental art form. The one exception is "The Flying Mouse," with its emphasis on character and personality rather than stock gags and silliness. 1933–1938; 54m.

SILLY SYMPHONIES: ANIMAL TALES ★★½

DIR: Walt Disney. **CAST:** Animated.

Although this collection is highlighted by "Elmer Elephant," most of the other cartoons are lamentably uninvolving. Two are little more than early black-and-white animation exercises; "Cock o' the Walk" and "More Kittens" are the best of what remains. 1930–1936; 50m.

SILLY SYMPHONIES: ANIMALS TWO BY TWO ★★★½

DIR: Walt Disney. **CAST:** Animated.

"The Tortoise and the Hare," a 1935 Oscar winner, is the classic in this trio of early Disney cartoons; the luxurious animation is blended with a strong story that manages to be exciting in spite of its (by now) foregone conclusion. By comparison, "Father Noah's Ark" and "Peculiar Penguins" are pretty, but uninvolving. 1933–1935; 26m.

SILLY SYMPHONIES: FANCIFUL FABLES ★½

DIR: Walt Disney. **CAST:** Animated.

Only historians will find this tape appealing, since several of its six cartoons go all the way back to the primitive black-and-white days of the late 1920s. Even youngsters will yawn through most of the simplistic scripts. 1928–1937; 50m.

SLEEPING BEAUTY (1959) ★★★★½

DIR: Clyde Geronimi. **CAST:** Animated.

This Disney adaptation of Charles Perrault's seventeenth-century version of the famous fairy tale features storybook-style animation that may surprise those accustomed to the softer style of the studio's other feature-length cartoons. Nevertheless, it is the last genre classic to be supervised by Walt Disney himself and belongs in any list of the best children's films (while having the added asset of being enjoyable for adults, as well). Rated G. 1959; 75m.

SLEEPING BEAUTY (1983) ★★★★

DIR: Jeremy Paul Kagan. **CAST:** Beverly D'Angelo, Bernadette Peters, Christopher Reeve, Sally Kellerman.

This is one of the funniest *Faerie Tale Theatre* episodes. Christopher Reeve is excellent as the handsome prince, and Bernadette Peters makes a sweet and pretty princess. Sally Kellerman is wonderful as the queen. 1983; 60m.

SMURFS AND THE MAGIC FLUTE, THE ★

DIR: John Rust. **CAST:** Animated.

Those little blue people from the popular Saturday-morning television cartoon show are featured in their first movie. The kiddies will probably love it, but parents should read a book. Rated G. 1983; 80m.

SNIFFLES THE MOUSE CARTOON FESTIVAL FEATURING "SNIFFLES BELLS THE CAT" ★★★★

DIR: Chuck Jones. **CAST:** Animated.

The sweet-natured Sniffles the Mouse was created during Warner Bros. cartoon-director Chuck Jones's Disneyesque period. Three of the four cartoons in this package, "Sniffles Bells the Cat," "The Brave Little Mouse," and "Toy Trouble," feature exquisite animation and inventive stories that will particularly charm the younger set. 1940–1944; 36m.

SNOOPY, COME HOME ★★★½

DIR: Bill Melendez. **CAST:** Animated.

Charming second entry in the "Peanuts" film series doesn't contain the childhood *angst* of the first but maintains the irreverent view of life found in the best of Charles Schulz's comic strips. Snoopy decides life at home ain't all it's cracked up to be, so he and Woodstock set off to find America. Needless to say, there's no place like home. Rated G. 1972; 70m.

SNOOPY'S GETTING MARRIED, CHARLIE BROWN ★★★½

DIR: Bill Melendez. **CAST:** Animated.

While guarding Peppermint Patty's house one night, Snoopy meets Genevieve, the poodle of his dreams (both agree that *Citizen Kane* is the best movie ever made), and he decides to get hitched. Snoopy's brother, Spike (in his animated debut), turns up as best beagle, but things don't turn out the way our favorite dog expects. 1985; 25m.

SNOW QUEEN ★★

DIR: Peter Medak. **CAST:** Melissa Gilbert, Lance Kerwin, Lee Remick,

Lauren Hutton, Linda Manz, David Hemmings.

This film is an exceedingly dull *Faerie Tale Theatre* tale of the Snow Queen (played by Lee Remick), who teaches an unruly boy a valuable lesson. The sets and special effects are second only to the actors' lines for their banality. 1983; 48m.

SNOW WHITE AND THE SEVEN DWARFS ★★★★

DIR: Peter Medak. **CAST:** Elizabeth McGovern, Vanessa Redgrave, Vincent Price, Rex Smith.

Both Vincent Price and Vanessa Redgrave are wickedly wonderful in this splendid adaptation of the Grimm's tale. Price plays the evil queen's (Redgrave) advising mirror. Lovely Elizabeth McGovern plays a sweet Snow White. 1983; 51m.

SNOW WHITE AND THE THREE STOOGES

DIR: Walter Lang. **CAST:** The Three Stooges, Patricia Medina, Carol Heiss, Guy Rolfe, Buddy Baer, Edgar Barrier.

Just about as bad as a film can be, this sad entry from what was left of the Three Stooges just lumbers on like a bad grammar-school play done on movie sets. This one is for Three Stooges completists *only*—the kids will hold it against you if you rent them this one. 1961; 107m.

SNOWBALL EXPRESS ★★

DIR: Norman Tokar. **CAST:** Dean Jones, Nancy Olson, Harry Morgan, Keenan Wynn, Johnny Whitaker.

This formula comedy stars the Disney stable of players from the 1960s and 1970s. Dean Jones inherits a run-down hotel and attempts to turn it into a ski resort. This is standard family viewing with a ski chase to help the pace and provide some laughs. Rated G. 1972; 99m.

SO DEAR TO MY HEART ★★★★

DIR: Harold Schuster. **CAST:** Burl Ives, Beulah Bondi, Harry Carey, Luana Patten, Bobby Driscoll, Matt Willis.

One of the finest of all feature-length Walt Disney films, this loving re-creation of small-town life in the early years of this century is wonderful entertainment. Young Bobby Driscoll (one of the finest of all child actors) has taken a notion to enter his black lamb Danny in the county fair. A singing blacksmith (Burl Ives in his film debut) encourages him in his dreams. This gentle film presents a beautiful evocation of a time that has passed, and is loaded with love, goodwill, and sentiment. 1949; 84m.

SOMEDAY YOU'LL FIND HER, CHARLIE BROWN ★★½

DIR: Phil Roman. **CAST:** Animated.

Lamentable values pervade this tale, when Charlie Brown falls in love with a girl seen briefly during a "honey shot" of a televised ball game. (So much for the little red-haired girl.) 1981; 25m.

SOMEWHERE, TOMORROW ★★★

DIR: Robert Weimer. **CAST:** Sarah Jessica Parker, Nancy Addison, Tom Shea, Rick Weber.

The Ghost and Mrs. Muir for a teen audience, this film is about a girl, played by Sarah Jessica Parker, who learns how to deal with her father's death by falling in love with the ghost of a teenage boy. The result is good family entertainment. 1986; 91m.

SON OF FLUBBER ★★★½

DIR: Robert Stevenson. **CAST:** Fred MacMurray, Nancy Olson, Keenan Wynn, Tommy Kirk, William Demarest, Paul Lynde.

This Disney sequel to *The Absent-Minded Professor* once again stars Fred MacMurray as the inventor of Flubber. Two new discoveries are featured: "dry rain" and "flubbergas." While not as good as the original "Flubber" film, it does have some moments reminiscent of the original. 1963; B&W; 100m.

SORCERER'S APPRENTICE, THE ★★

DIR: Peter Sander. **CAST:** Animated.

The greatest merits of this re-telling of the renowned Brothers Grimm tale are its narration by Vincent Price and its brevity. Stilted, almost scary animation and backdrops make this an awfully dark version of the story about a youngster who becomes the hostage apprentice of a black-hearted sorcerer. 1985; 22m.

SPEEDY GONZALES' FAST FUNNIES ★★½
DIR: Friz Freleng, Robert McKimson. **CAST:** Animated.

Subtle racism always makes this character an uncomfortable experience under the best of conditions, and many of the entries in this collection are far from the best. Speedy's debut is included ("Cat-Tails for Two," an amusing reworking of Steinbeck's *Of Mice and Men*), although he looks nothing like his later dashing self. Also noteworthy are "Tabasco Road" and "Pied Piper of Guadalupe." 1953–1961; 54m.

SPORT GOOFY ★★★★
DIR: Walt Disney. **CAST:** Animated.

Do-it-yourselfers will love this tape, which employs Goofy as a foil to demonstrate everything you *never* wanted to know about various sporting events. "Olympic Champ" and "Hockey Homicide" are the acknowledged classics. The other entries feature lessons in golf, baseball, and tennis. 1942–1949; 43m.

SPORT GOOFY'S VACATION ★★★½
DIR: Walt Disney. **CAST:** Animated.

As usual, Goofy's World War II–era adventures are vastly superior to those that followed, and this collection includes only two of the classics: "How to Fish" and "Tiger Trouble." Later entries turn the Goof into a family man, complete with young son, and the results simply aren't as satisfying. 1942–1961; 43m.

STAND UP AND CHEER ★★★
DIR: Hamilton MacFadden. **CAST:** Warner Baxter, Shirley Temple, Madge Evans, James Dunn, Stepin Fetchit.

Depression-plagued Americans need something to bring them out of their slump. Is it jobs, money, a chicken in every pot? No! The president says it's the curly-headed little dynamo he appoints as the Secretary of Amusement. Little Shirley manages to buoy spirits through her songs, dances, and sage advice. 1934; B&W; 80m.

STAR FOR JEREMY, A ★★★½
DIR: Barry Mowat. **CAST:** Animated.

Thoughtful animation and a thought-provoking storyline make this a video parents will enjoy sharing with children. Young Jeremy wonders about the origins of the Christmas star and is treated to a wonderful adventure. 1985; 22m.

STARBIRDS ★½
DIR: Michael Part, Tadao Nagahama. **CAST:** Animated.

Refugees from a destroyed solar system plot to invade Earth in order to survive. The fact that these aliens look suspiciously like angels is somewhat disturbing. Mediocre. 1986; 75m.

STARRING CHIP 'N' DALE ★★★★½
DIR: Walt Disney. **CAST:** Animated.

The clever wordplay of Chip 'n' Dale's best cartoon, "Donald Applecore," makes this trio of cartoons the most satisfying of the chipmunk collections. "Working for Peanuts" pits the critters against a nut-loving elephant, and the chipmunks don protective armor to battle the tree-destroying earth-mover of "Dragon Around." 1951–1954; 22m.

STARRING DONALD AND DAISY ★★
DIR: Walt Disney. **CAST:** Animated.

This shrill and unpleasant trio of cartoons does little for Donald or Daisy (and two of these shorts can be found in other, better collections). Daisy makes her debut in "Don Donald" as Donald's look-alike and sound-alike in high heels; no feminine charm for *this* duck! 1936–1953; 23m.

STARRING MICKEY AND MINNIE ★★★★★
DIR: Walt Disney. **CAST:** Animated.
No doubt about it, Walt Disney used his best scripters and animators on the pre–World War II cartoons featuring his trademark star, Mickey Mouse. All three of these shorts are gems. The best is "Hawaiian Holiday," with its interludes between Pluto and a crab. Mickey also makes a stalwart "Brave Little Tailor" and encounters an unusual pest while trying to clean Minnie's yard in "The Little Whirlwind." 1937–1941; 25m.

STORY OF BABAR, THE ★★★★½
DIR: Bill Melendez, Ed Levitt. **CAST:** Animated.
This delightfully narrated (featuring the voice characterizations of Peter Ustinov) featurette does well by following closely to the form of the classic children's book by Jean de Brunhoff. Little Babar is left an orphan after a hunter kills his mother in the jungle. He flees to Paris, where he learns the ways of gentility and is made King of the Elephants upon his return to the wild. No rating. 1986; 30m.

STORY OF ROBIN HOOD, THE ★★★
DIR: Ken Annakin. **CAST:** Richard Todd, Joan Rice, Peter Finch, James Hayter, James Robertson Justice, Michael Hordern.
This is Disney's live-action version of the Robin Hood legend, and it holds to the well-known legend of the outlaw of Sherwood Forest but has elements that give the movie its own identity. One nice touch is the use of a wandering minstrel, who draws the story together. Richard Todd is a most appealing Robin Hood, while James Robertson Justice, as Little John, and Peter Finch, as the Sheriff of Nottingham, are first-rate. 1952; 83m.

STORYBOOK SERIES, THE (VOLUME ONE) ★★★
DIR: Sam Weiss. **CAST:** Animated.
Hayley Mills hosts this made-for-television program that features three moralistic stories for kiddies. Entertaining for adults, too! Other volumes are hosted by Michael York, Mickey Rooney, and John Carradine. 1986; 30m.

STRAWBERRY SHORTCAKE AND PETS ON PARADE (TELEVISION SERIES) ★★½
DIR: Fred Wolf. **CAST:** Animated.
To steal a pet-show prize, the conniving Purple Pieman frames Strawberry Shortcake on a bribery charge. Her fruity friends come to her rescue. A number of Strawberry Shortcake cartoons are available on video. They're wonderful...for the preschool crowd. Older kids might gag on the sweetness. CUTE! CUTE! CUTE! Making the shows more palatable for grownups who happen to walk by the set are songs by such Baby Boomer favorites as John Sebastian and Flo & Eddie. 1982; 60 minutes (including shorts at the show's conclusion).

SUMMER MAGIC ★★½
DIR: James Neilson. **CAST:** Hayley Mills, Burl Ives, Dorothy McGuire, Deborah Walley, Eddie Hodges, Peter Brown.
Dorothy McGuire is a recent widow who finds out she has no money available. She moves her family to Maine, where they live in a fixer-upper house but are charged no rent by Burl Ives. Deborah Walley, a snobbish cousin, comes to visit and causes trouble. Lightweight and enjoyable. Rated G. 1963; 100m.

SUPER POWERS COLLECTION ★
DIR: Various. **CAST:** Animated.
These made-for-television cartoons featuring DC Comic heroes Superman, Batman, Aquaman, and Superboy are just pitiful. The stories are dull and the animation is dreadful. 1985; 60 minutes each.

SUPERDAD ★★½
DIR: Vincent McEveety. **CAST:** Bob Crane, Barbara Rush, Kurt Russell, Joe Flynn.

Bob Crane doesn't approve of his daughter's boyfriend (Kurt Russell) or the crowd she runs with. She claims that he just doesn't understand them. He decides to find out about the kids first-hand and to prove to his daughter that he's not hopelessly behind the times. Rated G. 1973; 94m.

SUPERMAN CARTOONS ★★★★
DIR: Dave Fleischer, Seymour Kneitel, Isadore Sparber. **CAST:** Animated.

All other superhero cartoons pale in comparison to this collection of excellent "Man of Steel" shorts from the Max Fleischer Studios. Made between 1941 and 1943, these actually constitute the company's finest work, its Popeye cartoons notwithstanding. There are several tapes available with a selection of seven or eight shorts (approximately 75 minutes) made from 16mm prints of varying quality. One company (Video Rarities) offers a 150-minute tape with all seventeen Superman shorts taken from mint-condition 35mm Technicolor prints, and the difference is amazing. 1940s; 75–150 minutes.

SUSANNAH OF THE MOUNTIES ★★★
DIR: William A. Seiter. **CAST:** Shirley Temple, Randolph Scott, Margaret Lockwood.

After her parents are killed in an Indian attack, curly Shirley is raised by a kind Canadian Mountie (Randolph Scott). Not one to hold a grudge, Shirley decides to play peacemaker for the whites and Indians by befriending the chief's son. 1939; B&W; 78m.

SWISS FAMILY ROBINSON, THE ★★★½
DIR: Ken Annakin. **CAST:** John Mills, Dorothy McGuire, James MacArthur, Tommy Kirk, Sessue Hayakawa.

Walt Disney's comedy-adventure film, adapted from the classic children's story by Johann Wyss about a family shipwrecked on a desert island. 1960; 128m.

SWORD AND THE ROSE, THE ★★½
DIR: Ken Annakin. **CAST:** Richard Todd, Glynis Johns, James Robertson Justice, Michael Gough.

Romance, intrigue, and heroic acts of derring-do are the order of the day in this colorful Walt Disney adaptation of *When Knighthood Was in Flower*. Richard Todd is adept with both the lance and the ladies and makes an ideal lead and Michael Gough is a truly malevolent heavy. 1953; 93m.

SWORD IN THE STONE, THE ★★★½
DIR: Wolfgang Reitherman. **CAST:** Animated.

The legend of King Arthur provided the storyline for this animated feature film from the Walt Disney studios. Although not up to the film company's highest standards, it still provides fine entertainment for the young and the young at heart. Rated G. 1963; 80m.

SWORD OF THE VALIANT ★★★½
DIR: Stephen Weeks. **CAST:** Miles O'Keeffe, Sean Connery, Trevor Howard.

The Old English tale of Sir Gawain and the Green Knight is brought to the screen with an appealing blend of action-adventure and tongue-in-cheek humor. Miles O'Keeffe plays Sir Gawain, a rookie knight in the court of King Arthur sent out on a quest brought on by a challenge issued by the magical Green Knight (Sean Connery). Rated PG. 1984; 162m.

SYLVESTER AND TWEETY'S CRAZY CAPERS ★★★
DIR: Friz Freleng, Robert McKimson. **CAST:** Animated.

More Warner Bros. madness with that "bad old puddy tat" and the ready-for-anything little birdy. Sylvester goes solo in "Mouse-Taken Identity," but those cartoons pitting him against Tweety Pie are the best. For all ages. 1985; 54m.

TALE OF THE FROG PRINCE ★★★★

DIR: Eric Idle. **CAST:** Robin Williams, Teri Garr, René Auberjonois, Candy Clark.

Perhaps the best of the *Faerie Tale Theatre* presentations, this story about a slighted fairy godmother who exacts revenge by turning a prince (Robin Williams) into a frog was inventively written and directed by Eric Idle, of Monty Python fame. It's witty and well-acted. 1982; 51m.

TALE OF TWO CHIPMUNKS, A ★★

DIR: Walt Disney. **CAST:** Animated.

Chip 'n' Dale are badly served by this inferior trio of cartoons, which hits a low point with "The Lone Chipmunks," a rather clumsy attempt to imitate the Road Runner series. Donald Duck co-stars in the equally weak "Chips Ahoy," which leaves "Chicken in the Rough" (wherein Dale imagines hen's eggs to be larger, tastier acorns) as the only attraction. 1951–1956; 24m.

TALES OF BEATRIX POTTER ★★★

DIR: Brian MacNamara. **CAST:** Animated.

Produced in a quietly fascinating storybook fashion with little movement on the part of the characters, this production utilizes Potter's original illustrations to tell the stories. Each tale reinforces the folly that occurs when the central characters fail to stay on the straight and narrow. 1986; 43m.

TARO, THE DRAGON BOY ★★★★

DIR: K. Urayama. **CAST:** Animated.

Distinctive animation, reminiscent of Japanese silkscreens, provides an engaging forum for introducing young viewers to Japanese mythology and culture. Here, young Taro makes a pilgrimage to a faraway lake to rescue his mother, who has been turned into a dragon. 1985; 75m.

TEENAGE MUTANT NINJA TURTLES: THE EPIC BEGINS ★★★½

DIR: Yoshikasu Kasai. **CAST:** Animated.

Those bestselling comic-book heroes in a half shell make their entrance into the video world. The story tells of their origins and of their first battle with their archenemy, Shredder. There's lots of action and suspense and some fair animation. Its only drawback is having been edited down from five half-hour episodes into little over an hour. Still, it holds together pretty well. Not rated, but contains light violence. 1988; 72m.

TEN WHO DARED ★

DIR: William Beaudine. **CAST:** Brian Keith, John Beal, James Drury, David Stollery.

In 1869, Major John Wesley Powell and nine other explorers set out to explore the wild Colorado River. A poorly crafted script, one-dimensional characters, and obvious studio and matte shots make this a movie to be missed by the entire family. 1960; 92m.

TEX AVERY'S SCREWBALL CLASSICS ★★★★

DIR: Tex Avery. **CAST:** Animated.

Anybody wondering about the origins of the voluptuous Jessica in *Who Framed Roger Rabbit* need look no further than "Swing Shift Cinderella," a 1945 cartoon classic that perfectly captures Tex Avery's chaotic and frantic imagination. Seven entries of this collection are exceptional; the eighth, "A Symphony in Slang," is quite weak—so you're advised to limit viewing to small doses. 1943–1954; 59m.

THANKSGIVING STORY, THE ★★½

DIR: Philip Leacock. **CAST:** Richard Thomas, Ralph Waite, Michael Learned, Ellen Corby, Will Geer.

Originally a TV holiday special, this features the wholesome Walton family. John-boy (Richard Thomas) tries to impress the girl of his dreams while applying for a college scholarship. An accident causing brain damage threatens his future. Of course, the whole family joins together in the crisis. A bit slow-paced and overly sweet. 1973; 95m.

THAT DARN CAT ★★½
DIR: Robert Stevenson. **CAST:** Dean Jones, Hayley Mills, Dorothy Provine, Roddy McDowall, Elsa Lanchester, Neville Brand, William Demarest, Ed Wynn, Frank Gorshin.

Trust Disney to take a great book—*Undercover Cat*, by Gordon and Mildred Gordon—and turn it into a moronic slapstick farce. Hayley Mills and Dorothy Provine are owners of a fulsome feline christened "DC" (for Darn Cat). One evening DC returns from his nightly rounds with a watch belonging to a woman taken hostage in a recent bank robbery. Enter Dean Jones as an ailurophobic FBI agent who attempts to tail DC. 1965; 116m.

THEIR ONLY CHANCE ★★
DIR: David Siddon. **CAST:** Jock Mahoney, Steve Hoddy.

True-life adventure film about a young man (Steve Hoddy) who has a way with wild animals. Former Tarzan Jock Mahoney has a dual role as a rancher and a mountain man. A nice, quiet wildlife film suitable for the entire family. 1975; 84m.

THERE'S NO TIME FOR LOVE, CHARLIE BROWN ★★★½
DIR: Bill Melendez. **CAST:** Animated.

This misnamed adventure concerns Charlie Brown's efforts to earn a good grade on a classroom report written about a field trip to an art museum. Alas, he and Peppermint Patty get separated from the others and mistakenly wind up in a supermarket. 1973; 25m.

THEY WENT THAT-A-WAY AND THAT-A-WAY ★★
DIR: Edward Montagne, Stuart E. McGowan. **CAST:** Tim Conway, Chuck McCann, Reni Santoni, Richard Kiel, Dub Taylor.

Tim Conway wrote and stars in this prison-escape comedy. He plays a small-town deputy who follows the governor's orders by being secretly placed in a maximum-security prison as an undercover agent posing as a hardened criminal. Fellow deputy (Chuck McCann) is his partner on the mission. When the governor suddenly dies, the two must escape from the prison. There are some silly gags, but this film does provide fair entertainment if you are looking for a few laughs and no deep plots. Rated PG. 1978; 106m.

THIRD MAN ON THE MOUNTAIN ★★★
DIR: Ken Annakin. **CAST:** Michael Rennie, James MacArthur, Janet Munro, Herbert Lom.

James MacArthur stars as a young man whose father was killed in a climbing accident. The Citadel (actually the Matterhorn) has never been scaled, and the boy's father died in an attempt. Miraculously, he finds the secret passage his father had been seeking. Breathtaking scenery and an excellent script make this film an excellent adventure story for the family. Not rated. 1959; 106m.

THOSE CALLOWAYS ★★★★
DIR: Norman Tokar. **CAST:** Brian Keith, Vera Miles, Brandon de Wilde, Linda Evans.

Sensitive, sentimental film about a family in New England. Man battles townspeople and nature to preserve a safe haven for geese. Marvelous scenes of life in a small town and the love between individuals. Rated G. 1965; 131m.

THREE CABALLEROS, THE ★★★
DIR: Walt Disney. **CAST:** Animated.

In Walt Disney's first attempt at combining animation and live action, Donald Duck is joined by two Latin feathered friends for a trip down to Rio. Originally, this cartoon travelogue was designed as a World War II propaganda piece promoting inter-American unity. It still holds up well today and remains a timeless learning experience for the kids. 1942; 72m.

THREE LITTLE PIGS, THE ★★★★
DIR: Howard Storm. **CAST:** Billy Crystal, Jeff Goldblum, Valerie Perrine.
Billy Crystal plays the industrious little pig who proves that "haste makes waste" when he takes his time building a sturdy house to keep the big, bad wolf away. Jeff Goldblum makes a hilarious, cigar-chomping wolf. 1984; 51m.

THREE LIVES OF THOMASINA, THE ★★★★
DIR: Don Chaffey. **CAST:** Patrick McGoohan, Susan Hampshire, Karen Dotrice, Vincent Winter.
An excellent cast and innovative ways of telling the story highlight this tale of love and caring. A young girl's cat is brought back to life by a woman who also teaches the girl's father to let others into his life. The cat's trip to cat heaven is outstandingly executed. 1964; 97m.

THROUGH THE LOOKING GLASS ★★½
DIR: Andrea Bresciani, Richard Slapczynski. **CAST:** Animated.
A likable adaptation of the further adventures of Alice after her trip to Wonderland. This production loses some of its charm due to a more contemporary telling, but voice characterizations by Phyllis Diller, Mr. T, and Jonathan Winters help. No rating. 1987; 70m.

THUMBELINA ★★★★
DIR: Michael Lindsay-Hogg. **CAST:** Carrie Fisher, William Katt, Burgess Meredith, narration by David Hemmings.
This is an *Alice in Wonderland*–type tale of a thumb-size girl (Carrie Fisher) and her adventures as she tries to find her way home. The creatures she meets along the way are well characterized. This is one of the more rewarding *Faerie Tale Theatre* productions. 1983; 48m.

TIGER TOWN ★★½
DIR: Alan Shapiro. **CAST:** Roy Scheider, Justin Henry.
In this passable movie, made for the Disney Channel, Roy Scheider stars as a legendary baseball player whose final year with the Detroit Tigers looks dismal until a young boy (Justin Henry) "wishes" him to success. At least, that's what the boy believes. Both Scheider and Henry give good performances, but the overall effect is not as impressive as it could have been. Rated G. 1984; 76m.

TIGER WALKS, A ★★½
DIR: Norman Tokar. **CAST:** Brian Keith, Vera Miles, Pamela Franklin, Sabu, Kevin Corcoran, Peter Brown, Una Merkel, Frank McHugh.
This Disney drama about an escaped circus tiger and the impact his fate has on a small town boasts a good cast of veteran film personalities as well as a jaundiced view of politics and mass hysteria. In the best Walt Disney tradition, the cooler heads in the community fight an uphill battle to capture the runaway tiger, only to be thwarted at every turn by the fearful majority who want to shoot the animal on sight. 1964; 88m.

TOBY MCTEAGUE ★★★
DIR: Jean Claude Lord. **CAST:** Winston Rekert, Yannick Bisson, Timothy Webber.
Solid children's story about Canadian teenager Toby McTeague, who has to take over the reins of his father's dog-racing team for the big race. Some profane language, but otherwise suitable for almost everyone. 1987; 94m.

TOBY TYLER ★★★½
DIR: Charles Barton. **CAST:** Kevin Corcoran, Henry Calvin, Gene Sheldon, Bob Sweeney, Mr. Stubbs, James Drury.
Disney version of the popular juvenile book about a young runaway and his adventures with the circus is breezy entertainment and a showcase for young Kevin Corcoran (Moochie of

many Disney television shows and the *Mickey Mouse Club*). 1960; 96m.

TOM AND JERRY CARTOON FESTIVALS (VOLUME ONE) ★★★
DIR: William Hanna, Joseph Barbera. **CAST:** Animated.

The sometimes violent slapstick adventures of Tom the cat and Jerry the mouse won several Oscars for MGM. In this collection, titles include the Academy Award–winning "Cat Concerto," "The Flying Cat," "The Little Orphan," "Jerry's Cousin," "Dr. Jekyll and Mr. Mouse," "The Bodyguard," "Mouse Follies," and "The Cat and the Mermouse." For all ages. 1940–1960; 58m.

TOM AND JERRY CARTOON FESTIVALS (VOLUME TWO) ★★½
DIR: William Hanna, Joseph Barbera. **CAST:** Animated.

This okay collection has "Mouse in Manhattan," "Hic-Up Pup," "The Milky Waif," "Cat Napping," "Mouse Trouble," "Jerry and the Lion," "Saturday Evening Puss," and "Invisible Mouse." 1940–1960; 58m.

TOM AND JERRY CARTOON FESTIVALS (VOLUME THREE) ★★★
DIR: William Hanna, Joseph Barbera. **CAST:** Animated.

Featured in this collection are "Million Dollar Cat," "The Night Before Christmas," "Polka Dot Puss," "Two Little Indians," "Trap Happy," "Tom and Jerry at the Hollywood Bowl," "Cue Ball Cat," and "Little Runaway." 1940–1960; 59m.

TOM EDISON—THE BOY WHO LIT UP THE WORLD ★★★★
DIR: Henning Schellerup. **CAST:** David Huffman, Adam Arkin, Michael Callan, Rosemary DeCamp, James Griffith.

A fine cast makes this film enjoyable. Tom Edison (David Huffman) and Cole Bogardis (Adam Arkin) begin working for the telegraph company at the same time. In Tom's spare time, he works on an assortment of inventions, including a cockroach electrocutor and a direct telegraph machine. Mr. Craner (Michael Callan) is threatened by Edison's inventiveness and tries to sabotage his efforts. 1983; 49m.

TOM SAWYER ★★
DIR: James Nielson. **CAST:** Josh Albee, Jeff Tyler, Jane Wyatt, Buddy Ebsen, Vic Morrow, John McGiver.

Mark Twain's classic story loses its satirical edge in this homogenized made-for-television production about the adventures of Tom Sawyer (Josh Albee) and Huckleberry Finn (Jeff Tyler). The kids may enjoy it, but adults will want to reread the book. Better yet, read the book to your kids. Rated G. 1973; 78m.

TOM THUMB ★★★½
DIR: George Pal. **CAST:** Russ Tamblyn, June Thorburn, Peter Sellers, Terry-Thomas, Alan Young, Jessie Matthews, Bernard Miles.

This underrated George Pal fantasy is a treat for young and old viewers. Good effects, pleasant tunes, and a distinguished cast of veteran British performers combine with Russ Tamblyn's infectious lead to make this a surefire choice for the kids. 1958; 98m.

TONKA ★★★
DIR: Lewis R. Foster. **CAST:** Sal Mineo, Philip Carey, Jerome Courtland.

Sal Mineo is White Bull, a Sioux Indian who captures and tames a wild stallion and names it Tonka Wakan—The Great One. Tribal law requires him to give the horse to his older Indian cousin, a bully who would mistreat the animal. Rather than do so, Mineo frees the horse. The horse is captured again and sold to the U.S. cavalry. Mineo tracks down the horse. 1958; 97m.

TRANSFORMERS, THE MOVIE
DIR: Nelson Shin. **CAST:** Animated.

In this animated vehicle for violence and destruction, the "good" autobots (who convert or transform into cars) and the dinobots (who change into dinosaurs) must battle the evil forces of Unicrom (Orson Welles) and Megatron (who later becomes Galvatron). Rated PG for violence and occasional obscenities, and we do not recommend it for children under 12. 1986; 80m.

TREASURE ISLAND (1934) ★★★★

DIR: Victor Fleming. **CAST:** Wallace Beery, Lionel Barrymore, Jackie Cooper, Lewis Stone.

This is an MGM all-star presentation of Robert Louis Stevenson's children's classic of a young boy's adventure with pirates, buried treasure, and that delightful rogue of fiction Long John Silver. It seems all the great character actors of the 1930s put in an appearance, including Wallace Beery, as Silver, and Lionel Barrymore, as Billy Bones. 1934; B&W; 105m.

TREASURE ISLAND (1950) ★★★★

DIR: Byron Haskin. **CAST:** Robert Newton, Bobby Driscoll, Basil Sydney.

Disney remake of the Robert Louis Stevenson pirate adventure is powered by a memorable Robert Newton as Long John Silver. 1950; 87m.

TUCK EVERLASTING ★★★½

DIR: Frederick King Keller. **CAST:** Margaret Chamberlain, Fred A. Keller, James McGuire, Sonia Raimi.

Entertaining family film about a 12-year-old girl who discovers a family of immortals living in the woods on her father's property. She becomes involved in their lives and is eventually entrusted with their secret. Rated G. 1980; 100m.

TUKIKI AND HIS SEARCH FOR A MERRY CHRISTMAS ★★½

DIR: Vic Atkinson. **CAST:** Animated.

Featuring the voices of Sterling Holloway and Adam Rich, this richly animated tale follows the trek of an Eskimo boy in his search for a deeper meaning to Christmas. Along the way, viewers are treated to lessons about the traditions and cultures of many lands. 1979; 30m.

TWEETY AND SYLVESTER ★★★★½

DIR: Bob Clampett, Friz Freleng, Robert McKimson. **CAST:** Animated.

This tape is a joy, beginning with three of Tweety Bird's solo adventures: "A Tale of Two Kitties," "Birdie and the Beast," and "A Gruesome Twosome" (with a Jimmy Durante cat). Sylvester the cat solos in his debut, "Life with Feathers," along with two other cartoons; the two team up in "Tweety Pie," which won the Warners animation department its first Oscar. 1942–1948; 60m.

TWELVE MONTHS ★★½

DIR: Kimio Yabuki. **CAST:** Animated.

A good-hearted waif is rewarded for her kindness by the incarnations of each month of the year when she is sent on an impossible errand by her evil stepmother. What might have been an entertaining tale is marred by a dragging pace. 1985; 90m.

TWENTY THOUSAND LEAGUES UNDER THE SEA ★½

DIR: Arthur Rankin Jr., Jules Bass. **CAST:** Animated.

Less than thrilling adaptation of the Jules Verne classic. Here, Captain Nemo and his amazing submarine, the *Nautilus*, are the centerpiece of a number of deep-sea adventures. 1972; 60m.

UB IWERKS CARTOON FESTIVAL VOL. I–V ★★

DIR: Ub Iwerks. **CAST:** Animated.

Ub Iwerks was a Disney animator who left in 1930 to start his own studio. Ten years later, he returned as director of technical research for Disney, where he stayed for the rest of his career. In between, he made a series of so-so cartoons, generally derived from fairy tales. 1930s; 23–57 minutes each.

UGLY DACHSHUND, THE ★★
DIR: Norman Tokar. **CAST:** Dean Jones, Suzanne Pleshette, Charlie Ruggles, Parley Baer, Kelly Thordsen.
In this Disney movie, Dean Jones and Suzanne Pleshette are husband and wife; she loves dachshunds and owns a number of puppies. Charlie Ruggles convinces Jones to take a Great Dane puppy to raise. Since all of its peers are dachshunds, the Great Dane assumes it is one, too, and tries to act like them. Somewhat entertaining along the lines of a made-for-TV-movie. Not rated. 1966; 93m.

UNDERGRADS, THE ★★★½
DIR: Steven H. Stern. **CAST:** Art Carney, Chris Makepeace, Jackie Burroughs, Len Birman, Alfie Scopp.
Billed as a comedy, this made-for-cable Disney film has only sporadic funny moments. Art Carney plays a spunky senior citizen whose son would like to put him into a rest home. Chris Makepeace (Carney's movie grandson) refuses to allow this. Instead, he and his grandfather become college roommates. A good film with a message, this one has some heavy moments. 1984; 102m.

UNIDENTIFIED FLYING ODDBALL ★★½
DIR: Russ Mayberry. **CAST:** Dennis Dugan, Jim Dale, Ron Moody, Kenneth More.
Inept astronaut is transported to the court of King Arthur in his spacecraft. Once there, he discovers that Merlin and a knight are plotting against the king and sets out to expose them with his modern technology. Uneven script with situations not fully developed or explored hampers this Disney trifle. Rated G. 1979; 92m.

UNSINKABLE DONALD DUCK, THE ★★★½
DIR: Walt Disney. **CAST:** Animated.
Donald Duck meets Jaws the shark in the impeccably animated "Sea Scouts," one of the finest examples of Disney's pre–World War II cartoons. By comparison, "Lion Around" (1950) is woefully inadequate. The middle entry, "Donald's Off Day," is an average example of the trouble caused by Donald's temper. 1939–1950; 24m.

VERY FUNNY, CHARLIE BROWN ★★★½
DIR: Bill Melendez, Sam Nicholson, Phil Roman. **CAST:** Animated.
Snoopy is the star in this baker's dozen of short stories taken from Charles Schulz's newspaper strip. The famed beagle extorts endorsements from the Peanuts gang in his attempt to win the Daisy Hill Puppy Cup. 1983–1985; 39m.

VERY MERRY CRICKET, A ★★★
DIR: Chuck Jones. **CAST:** Animated.
The sequel to Jones's earlier production, *A Cricket in Times Square*. Here, the talented virtuoso bug is drawn back to the Big Apple by a cat-and-mouse team who serve as his best friends. Fast-paced and entertaining. 1973; 26m.

WALTZ KING, THE ★★½
DIR: Steve Previn. **CAST:** Kerwin Mathews, Brian Aherne, Senta Berger, Peter Kraus, Fritz Eckhardt.
The wonderful music of Johann Strauss Jr. is the real star of this Walt Disney biography filmed on location in Vienna. A treat to the eyes and ears, this is a good family film. 1963; 94m.

WATER BABIES, THE ★★★
DIR: Lionel Jeffries. **CAST:** James Mason, Billie Whitelaw, Bernard Cribbins, Joan Greenwood, David Tomlinson.
If your kids are big fans of *Mary Poppins*, they should enjoy this. In Victorian England a chimney sweep's apprentice has a series of adventures with animated characters who live underwater. Designed more for kids than for families, though adults can enjoy the cast of fine British character actors. Rated G. 1979; 93m.

WEE WILLIE WINKIE ★★★★

DIR: John Ford. **CAST:** Shirley Temple, Victor McLaglen, C. Aubrey Smith, Cesar Romero, Constance Collier.

The best of Shirley Temple's features from her star period is this adaptation of a Rudyard Kipling tale. Temple and her screen mother Constance Collier go to live with her disapproving grandfather C. Aubrey Smith in India. It's a real charmer and fine adventure film to boot. 1937; B&W; 100m.

WESTWARD HO THE WAGONS ★★½

DIR: William Beaudine. **CAST:** Fess Parker, Kathleen Crowley, Jeff York, David Stollery, Sebastian Cabot, George Reeves.

Episodic film about a wagon train traveling west. The basic appeal is seeing Fess Parker in another Davy Crockett–type role and four of the Mouseketeers as children in the train. Devoid of a real beginning or end, this movie just rambles along for its entire running time. Not rated. 1956; 90m.

WHAT A NIGHTMARE, CHARLIE BROWN ★★

DIR: Phil Roman, Bill Melendez. **CAST:** Animated.

Snoopy eats too much pizza and dreams of being an Alaskan sled dog, where his "civilized upbringing" makes him no match for the environment. Boring and repetitious saga. 1978; 25m.

WHAT HAVE WE LEARNED, CHARLIE BROWN? ★★★★

DIR: Bill Melendez. **CAST:** Animated.

This somber and moving tribute to fallen war heroes acts as a postscript to the Peanuts feature film, *Bon Voyage, Charlie Brown.* While in France, Linus explains the history of the World War II invasion at Omaha Beach and World War I's legend of the white-crossed red poppies. Judy Munsen's haunting background themes contribute greatly to this most unusual Peanuts offering. 1983; 24m.

WHAT NEXT, CHARLIE BROWN? ★★★

DIR: Bill Melendez, Sam Jaimes, Sam Nicholson, Phil Roman. **CAST:** Animated.

Poor Charlie Brown has a mighty tough time in these thirteen tales battling kite-eating trees and Lucy's big mouth. Several of the vignettes (all taken from *The Charlie Brown and Snoopy Show*) are rather cruel, and others are quickie blackouts united by common themes such as snow fights and Schroeder's piano. The resulting mix is somewhat uneven. 1983–1985; 47m.

WHERE THE RED FERN GROWS ★★★★

DIR: Norman Tokar. **CAST:** James Whitmore, Beverly Garland, Jack Ging, Lonny Chapman, Stewart Peterson.

Fine family fare about a boy's love for two hunting dogs and his coming of age in Oklahoma in the 1930s. Rated G. 1974; 90m.

WHISTLE DOWN THE WIND ★★★½

DIR: Bryan Forbes. **CAST:** Hayley Mills, Alan Bates, Bernard Lee, Norman Bird, Elsie Wagstaff.

Bryan Forbes's first film is a thoughtful, allegorical tale about three children who encounter an accused murderer hiding in a barn and take him to be a Christ figure fleeing from his persecutors. Based on Mary Hayley Bell's popular novel, this is one of the best films ever made dealing with the fragile nature of childhood trust and beliefs. 1961; B&W; 99m.

WHITE FANG AND THE HUNTER ★★

DIR: Alfonso Brescia. **CAST:** Robert Wood, Pedro Sanchez.

A dog, White Fang, and his master, Daniel (Robert Wood), are attacked by wolves, and only White Fang's protection saves Daniel. They are taken in by a young widow who is being forced to marry. So Daniel and the dog come to her aid. Poor acting and directing hamper this familiar story. Rated G. 1985; 87m.

WHITEWATER SAM ★★½
DIR: Keith Larsen. **CAST:** Keith Larsen.
Keith Larsen wrote, directed, co-produced, and stars in this family film of a wilderness adventure. He plays the legendary Whitewater Sam, the first white man to survive the harsh Rocky Mountain winters. The real star, however, seems to be his darling, intelligent dog, Sybar. The beautiful scenery makes this film more than watchable. Rated PG for violence. 1978; 85m.

WILBUR AND ORVILLE: THE FIRST TO FLY ★★★★
DIR: Henning Schellerup. **CAST:** James Carroll Jordon, Chris Beaumont, John Randolph, Louise Latham, Edward Andrews.
This entertaining biography of the Wright brothers shows their determination in the face of ridicule and harassment.The moral of this delightful film lies in sticking to something when you know you're right. 1973; 47m.

WILD AND WOODY ★★
DIR: Walter Lantz. **CAST:** Animated.
Woody Woodpecker wanders the West in search of feeble laughs in this collection of Walter Lantz "cartunes." Some of the gags work well, but this grouping suffers from repetition, especially due to the lack of any other Lantz characters (such as Andy Panda or Chilly Willy). 1951–1963; 51m.

WILD HORSE HANK ★★½
DIR: Eric Till. **CAST:** Linda Blair, Richard Crenna, Al Waxman, Michael Wincott.
Linda Blair is a horse lover pitted against a family that is stampeding wild horses. Richard Crenna plays her father. This Canadian feature is not rated. 1978; 94m.

WILDERNESS FAMILY, PART 2, THE ★★★
DIR: Frank Zuniga. **CAST:** Robert Logan, Susan D. Shaw, Heather Rattray, Ham Larsen, George (Buck) Flower, Brian Cutler.
Taken on its own terms, *The Wilderness Family, Part 2* isn't a bad motion picture. Film fans who want thrills and chills or something challenging to the mind should skip it. Rated G. 1978; 105m.

WILLY WONKA AND THE CHOCOLATE FACTORY ★★★
DIR: Mel Stuart. **CAST:** Gene Wilder, Jack Albertson, Peter Ostrum, Roy Kinnear.
Gene Wilder plays a candy company owner who allows some lucky kids to tour the facility. However, a few of his guests get sticky fingers (pun intended) and suffer the consequences. This essentially entertaining movie has its memorable moments—as well as bad. Rated G. 1971; 98m.

WIND IN THE WILLOWS, THE ★★★★★
DIR: Wolfgang Reitherman. **CAST:** Animated.
One of Disney's finest. This adaptation of Kenneth Grahame's classic deals with the adventures of J. Thaddeus Toad and his friends Cyril, Mole, Rat, and Mac Badger. Basil Rathbone narrates this classic short. 1949; 75m.

WOODY WOODPECKER AND HIS FRIENDS (VOLUME ONE) ★★★★
DIR: Walter Lantz. **CAST:** Animated.
The first in a series of classic cartoons. The eight in this collection include the first Woody Woodpecker cartoon, "Knock Knock," plus "Ski for Two" and "The Bandmaster." 80m.

WOODY WOODPECKER AND HIS FRIENDS (VOLUME TWO) ★★★
DIR: Walter Lantz. **CAST:** Animated.
This collection of eight cartoons features "The Poet and the Peasant," "Fish Fry," "The Screwdriver," "Wacky Bye Baby," "Woody Dines Out," "Loose Nut," "S-H-H-H," and "Convict Concerto." 59m.

WOODY WOODPECKER AND HIS FRIENDS (VOLUME THREE) ★★★★

DIR: Walter Lantz. **CAST:** Animated.

The excellent "The Barber of Seville" and "Dog Tax Collector" are among the cartoons in this collection, which features Woody Woodpecker, Andy Panda, Wally Walrus, and Chilly Willy. 55m.

WORLD ACCORDING TO GOOFY, THE (LIMITED GOLD EDITION 2) ★★★★

DIR: Walt Disney. **CAST:** Animated.

Two classics from the early 1940s highlight this collection. Goofy attempts to deal with a magician's trunk in "Baggage Buster"; "Goofy's Glider" finds the poor guy becoming airborne by every means except that suggested by the cartoon's title. "Home Made Home" can be viewed as the animated answer to "Mr. Blandings Builds His Dream House," and "They're Off" illustrates the folly of track betting. 1940–1953; 50m.

WORLD OF ANDY PANDA, THE ★★½

DIR: Walter Lantz. **CAST:** Animated.

The black-and-white Micky Mouse look-alike, Andy Panda, went through a number of changes in appearance, and these cartoons from 1941 to 1946 reflect this. Since Andy has always been rather light in the area of charisma, many of his animated adventures often feature other, less bland critters. That said, "Apple Andy" is a near classic, and the rest aren't bad. 62m.

WORLD'S GREATEST ATHLETE, THE ★★★

DIR: Robert Scheerer. **CAST:** Jan-Michael Vincent, John Amos, Tim Conway, Roscoe Lee Browne.

John Amos is the athletics instructor at Merrivale College. He and his assistant, Tim Conway, travel to Africa to get away from their toubles and come across Nanu (Jan-Michael Vincent), the greatest natural athlete in the world. One of the better Disney college films. Rated G. 1973; 89m.

YEARLING, THE ★★★★½

DIR: Clarence Brown. **CAST:** Gregory Peck, Jane Wyman, Claude Jarman Jr., Chill Wills.

A beautiful film version of Marjorie Kinnan Rawlings's sensitive story of a young boy's love for a pet fawn that his father must destroy. Simply told, this emotionally charged drama has been rated one of the finest films ever made. 1946; 134m.

YOU CAN'T WIN, CHARLIE BROWN ★★★½

DIR: Bill Melendez, Sam Jaimes, Phil Roman. **CAST:** Animated.

These ten stories, all taken from Charles Schulz's newspaper strip, find the Peanuts gang at school. Sally takes Snoopy to class as a show-and-tell exhibit (and the other kids jeer that he's a chicken or a small moose), and Charlie Brown and Peppermint Patty wind up in a shoving match when forced to share the same desk. 1983–1985; 36m.

YOUNG CHILDREN'S CONCERT WITH RAFFI, A ★★★★

DIR: David Devine. **CAST:** Raffi.

Put on this tape and watch the magic happen. Canadian folksinger Raffi has a way with children, and his delightful, lighthearted tunes are easy on adult ears as well. Not only do his songs—which include "Down by the Bay," "Baby Beluga," "Wheels on the Bus," "Bumping Up and Down," and "Shake My Sillies Out"—teach youngsters to rhyme and reason, they also give them things to do while watching. 1984; 50m.

YOUNG MAGICIAN, THE ★★

DIR: Waldemar Dziki. **CAST:** Rusty Jedwab.

Trite tale of a young man (Rusty Jedwab) who discovers he has magical powers and has a run-in with society. Special effects are good, but the dubbing in this Polish-Canadian production detracts a lot from the story.

Not rated; suitable for the entire family. 1986; 99m.

YOU'RE A GOOD MAN, CHARLIE BROWN ★★★
DIR: Sam Jaimes. CAST: Animated.

The famous Broadway musical is given the animated treatment, with mixed results. Several of Clark Gesner's witty songs are garbled and difficult to understand, and the notion of an animated Snoopy with a voice—after lacking one for twenty years—doesn't quite work. 1985; 60m.

YOU'RE A GOOD SPORT, CHARLIE BROWN ★★★½
DIR: Phil Roman. CAST: Animated.

Anybody tired of seeing poor Charlie Brown constantly winding up with the fuzzy end of the lollipop will *love* this story. Peppermint Patty challenges Chuck to a motocross race—his bike, naturally, is number 13—but both of them must work hard to keep up with the mystery contestant: the Masked Marvel. 1975; 26m.

YOU'RE IN LOVE, CHARLIE BROWN ★★★★★
DIR: Bill Melendez. CAST: Animated.

Charlie Brown first spots the little red-haired girl in this fourth animated Peanuts short, and he loses his already shaky abilities of coherent thought and rational behavior. Peppermint Patty (in her animated debut) mistakes his interest and sets him up for a late-night rendezvous with Lucy. 1967; 26m.

YOU'RE THE GREATEST, CHARLIE BROWN ★★★
DIR: Phil Roman. CAST: Animated.

Hoping to bring honor to his school, Charlie Brown trains hard and enters the Junior Olympics Decathlon; his opponents include Marcie, Freddy Fabulous (the previous year's all-city champ), and a mysterious entrant dubbed the Masked Marvel. The thin story doesn't allow much of the gang's personalities to emerge. 1979; 25m.

ZIGGY'S GIFT ★★★½
DIR: Richard Williams. CAST: Animated.

Tom Wilson's comic-strip character is brought to delightful life in this holiday special made for television. Ziggy naïvely goes to work as a street-corner Santa for a bogus charity. This has a certain contemporary charm that can be enjoyed by young and old alike. 1982; 30m.

COMEDY

ABBOTT AND COSTELLO IN HOLLYWOOD ★★
DIR: S. Sylvan Simon. **CAST:** Bud Abbott, Lou Costello, Frances Rafferty, Robert Stanton.
Lesser Abbott and Costello effort has Bud and Lou trying to make it big as movie stars. Best scenes occur early in the film, with Lou playing a barber. 1945; B&W; 83m.

ABBOTT AND COSTELLO MEET CAPTAIN KIDD ★½
DIR: Charles Lamont. **CAST:** Bud Abbott, Lou Costello, Charles Laughton, Hillary Brooke, Leif Erickson.
One of Abbott and Costello's few color films, this is strictly preschooler fare. As the title suggests, the boys play a pair of jerks who get chased around uncharted islands, pirate ships, etc., by the infamous Captain Kidd, as portrayed by Charles Laughton, who makes every effort to retain his dignity. 1952; 70m.

ABBOTT AND COSTELLO MEET DR. JEKYLL AND MR. HYDE ★★★½
DIR: Charles Lamont. **CAST:** Bud Abbott, Lou Costello, Boris Karloff.
Fun mixture of comedy and horror has the team up against the smooth Dr. Jekyll and the maniacal Mr. Hyde. The laughs come fast and furious in this, one of the boys' better films of the 1950s. Boris Karloff is in top form in the dual role, and don't miss the hilarious scene in which Lou is turned into a mouse! 1953; B&W; 77m.

ABBOTT AND COSTELLO MEET FRANKENSTEIN ★★★★
DIR: Charles Barton. **CAST:** Bud Abbott, Lou Costello, Lon Chaney Jr., Bela Lugosi.
Whenever someone writes about the Universal horror classics, they always cite this film as evidence of how the series fell into decline. Likewise, screen historians call it the beginning of the end for the comedy team. It deserves neither rap. For Bud Abbott and Lou Costello, it meant a resurgence of popularity after a slow fall from favor as the 1940s box-office champs. Yet it never compromises the characters of Dracula (Bela Lugosi), the Wolfman (Lon Chaney), or the Frankenstein monster (Glenn Strange). Director Charles Barton mixes fright and fun without sacrificing either. 1948; B&W; 83m.

ABBOTT AND COSTELLO MEET THE KILLER, BORIS KARLOFF ★★★

DIR: Charles Barton. **CAST:** Bud Abbott, Lou Costello, Boris Karloff, Lenore Aubert, Gar Moore, James Flavin.

Second in the duo's *Abbott and Costello Meet...* series, brought on by the tremendous popularity of their *Frankenstein* send-up the year before. In this enjoyable outing, Bud and Lou match wits with Boris Karloff, in classic form as a sinister swami doing away with his enemies at a posh hotel. 1949; B&W; 84m.

ABBOTT AND COSTELLO SHOW, THE (TELEVISION SERIES) ★★★

DIR: Various. **CAST:** Bud Abbott, Lou Costello, Sidney Fields, Hillary Brooke, Joe Besser.

Set in Hollywood, this comedy series depicts Bud Abbott's and Lou Costello's efforts to improve their financial situation. Inevitably, they get into hot water with their landlord, the local cop, and lady friends. Though the comics appear somewhat weary and the humor is often forced, enough of the gags work to make the episodes worth a glance. Many of Abbott and Costello's classic routines are incorporated into the shows, boosting the slim plots. 1952–1954; 53m.

ABDULLA THE GREAT ★

DIR: Gregory Ratoff. **CAST:** Gregory Ratoff, Kay Kendall, Sydney Chaplin.

An Egyptian nobleman sets out to win the affections of an English girl. Dull is the best word to describe this silly satire that attempts to lampoon King Farouk. A waste of talent. 1954; 103m.

ADAM'S RIB ★★★★½

DIR: George Cukor. **CAST:** Spencer Tracy, Katharine Hepburn, Judy Holliday, Tom Ewell, David Wayne.

The screen team of Spencer Tracy and Katharine Hepburn was always watchable, but never more so than in this comedy. As husband-and-wife lawyers on opposing sides of the same case, they remind us of what movie magic is really all about. The supporting performances by Judy Holliday, Tom Ewell, David Wayne, and Jean Hagen greatly add to the fun. 1949; B&W; 101m.

ADVENTURE OF SHERLOCK HOLMES' SMARTER BROTHER, THE ★★½

DIR: Gene Wilder. **CAST:** Gene Wilder, Madeline Kahn, Marty Feldman, Dom DeLuise.

Even discounting the effrontery of writer-director-star Gene Wilder's creating a smarter sibling, Sigerson Holmes (Gene Wilder), one is still left with a less-than-hilarious, highly uneven romp. Though the principals—who also include Marty Feldman and Dom DeLuise—try hard, the film's soggy structure (and Wilder's poor research into the canon) plunge the whole thing into mediocrity. Rated PG. 1975; 91m.

ADVENTURES BEYOND BELIEF

DIR: Marcus Tompson. **CAST:** Skyler Cole, Jill Whitlow, Elke Sommer, Stella Stevens, Edie Adams, John Astin, Larry Storch.

In this incoherent excuse for madcap comedy, Skyler Cole plays an Elvis Presley fan who helps a mobster's daughter (Jill Whitlow) escape from an all-girls' school run by the sadistic Elke Sommer. A cast of familiar faces can't save this hodgepodge. Unrated. 1987; 95m.

ADVENTURES IN BABYSITTING ★★★½

DIR: Chris Columbus. **CAST:** Elisabeth Shue, Keith Coogan, Anthony Rapp, Maia Brewton, Penelope Ann Miller, Vincent D'Onofrio.

A sort of *After Hours* for the teen crowd, this is a surprisingly entertaining film about what happens when 17-year-old Chris Parker (Elisabeth Shue) accepts a baby-sitting assignment. There are a number of hilarious moments—our favorite being a sequence in a blues club presided over by superguitarist Albert Collins. Rated PG-13 for profanity and violence. 1987; 100m.

ADVENTURES OF A PRIVATE EYE ★★

DIR: Stanley Long. **CAST:** Christopher Neil, Suzy Kendall, Harry Corbett, Diana Dors, Fred Emney, Liz Fraser, Irene Handl, Ian Lavender, Jon Pertwee, Adrienne Posta.

Boring British comedy about a detective's assistant who tries his hand at investigating a blackmail case while his boss is on vacation. The film has plenty of nudity and some scenes of rather explicit sex. Not rated. 1987; 96m.

ADVENTURES OF OZZIE AND HARRIET, THE (TELEVISION SERIES) ★★★★

DIR: Ozzie Nelson. **CAST:** Ozzie Nelson, Harriet Nelson, Ricky Nelson, David Nelson, Kris Nelson, June Nelson, Don DeFore, Lyle Talbot.

This is the prototypical family sitcom. Though it's primarily remembered for its all-American wholesomeness, the show was genuinely funny on a consistent basis for 14 years. That remarkable accomplishment must be primarily credited to Ozzie Nelson, who produced, directed, and cowrote, as well as starred as the earnest father who could create chaos out of the simplest situations. Real-life wife Harriet and sons Ricky and David added warmth and naturalness. 1952–1966; B&W; 60m.

ADVENTURES OF PICASSO, THE ★★★

DIR: Tage Danielsson. **CAST:** Gosta Eckman, Hans Alfredson, Margaretha Krook, Bernard Cribbins, Wilfred Brambell.

Witty, off-the-wall Swedish comedy about the life of Picasso. The rubber-faced Gosta Eckman looks like Buster Keaton playing Picasso, and Bernard Cribbins is a scream in drag as Gertrude Stein. Some truly funny moments make this semislapstick film shine. In overly simplistic Spanish, French, and English, so no subtitles are needed. Not rated; contains some ribald humor. 1988; 94m.

ADVENTURES OF TOPPER, THE ★★★

DIR: Phillip Rapp. **CAST:** Anne Jeffreys, Robert Sterling, Leo G. Carroll, Lee Patrick, Thurston Hall, Kathleen Freeman.

This television comedy consistently earned chuckles, if not an abundance of belly laughs as this video compilation attests. Leo G. Carroll is delightful as Cosmo Topper, the henpecked bank vice-president who is the only one who can see a trio of ghosts—Marion Kirby (Anne Jeffreys), her husband George (Robert Sterling), "that most sporting spirit," and their booze-swilling Saint Bernard, Neil. 1953–1956; 93m.

AFFAIRS OF ANNABEL, THE ★★★★

DIR: Ben Stoloff. **CAST:** Jack Oakie, Lucille Ball, Ruth Donnelly, Fritz Feld, Thurston Hall.

The pre–*I Love Lucy* Lucille Ball is very funny in this fast-paced comedy as a none-too-bright movie star whose manager (Jack Oakie) is continually dreaming up outrageous publicity stunts for her. The supporting cast of familiar Thirties faces also provides plenty of laughs, especially Fritz Feld as a supercilious foreign director. 1937; 73m.

AFRICA SCREAMS ★★

DIR: Charles Barton. **CAST:** Bud Abbott, Lou Costello, Hillary Brooke, Shemp Howard, Max Baer, Clyde Beatty, Frank Buck.

Bud and Lou are joined by circus great Clyde Beatty and Frank (*Bring 'Em Back Alive*) Buck in this thin but enjoyable comedy, one of their last feature films. Most of the jungle and safari clichés are evident in this fast-paced, oddball film but they work acceptably, especially with plenty of familiar and capable players in support.

Fun for the kids as well as the adults. 1949; B&W; 79m.

AFTER HOURS ★★★★
DIR: Martin Scorsese. **CAST:** Griffin Dunne, Rosanna Arquette, Teri Garr, John Heard, Linda Fiorentino, Richard "Cheech" Marin, Tommy Chong, Catherine O'Hara, Verna Bloom.
After Hours is the most brutal and bizarre black (as in dark) comedy we are ever likely to see—a mixture of guffaws and goose pimples. Griffin Dunne stars as a computer operator who unwillingly spends a night in the SoHo area of downtown Manhattan. A trio of strange women (played by Rosanna Arquette, Teri Garr, and Linda Fiorentino) mystify, seduce, and horrify our hapless hero, and his life soon becomes a total nightmare. Rated R for profanity, nudity, violence, and general weirdness. 1985; 94m.

AFTER THE FOX ★
DIR: Vittorio De Sica. **CAST:** Peter Sellers, Victor Mature, Britt Ekland, Martin Balsam.
Peter Sellers is at his worst, playing an Italian movie director in this flat farce. Victor Mature gives an amusing portrayal of a leading man whose ego remains mammoth, though his screen popularity is declining rapidly. The script for this fiasco was written by none other than Neil Simon. 1966; 103m.

AIRPLANE! ★★★★
DIR: Jim Abrahams, David Zucker, Jerry Zucker. **CAST:** Robert Hays, Julie Hagerty, Leslie Nielsen, Kareem Abdul-Jabbar, Lloyd Bridges, Peter Graves, Robert Stack.
This is a hilarious spoof of the *Airport* series—and movies in general. While the jokes don't always work, there are so many of them that this comedy ends up with enough laughs for three movies. Rated PG. 1980; 88m.

AIRPLANE II: THE SEQUEL ★★★½
DIR: Ken Finkleman. **CAST:** Robert Hays, Julie Hagerty, Peter Graves, William Shatner.
Viewers who laughed uncontrollably through *Airplane!* will find much to like about this sequel. The stars of the original are back, with silly jokes and sight gags galore. However, those who thought the original was more stupid than funny undoubtedly will mutter the same about the sequel. Rated PG for occasional adult content. 1982; 85m.

ALFIE ★★★★
DIR: Lewis Gilbert. **CAST:** Michael Caine, Shelley Winters, Millicent Martin, Julia Foster, Shirley Anne Field.
Wild and ribald comedy about a Cockney playboy (Michael Caine) who finds "birds" irresistible. Full of sex and delightful charm, this quick-moving film also tells the poignant tragedy of a man uncertain about his lifestyle. Nominated for five Oscars, including best picture and best actor. 1966; 113m.

ALL IN A NIGHT'S WORK ★★★
DIR: Joseph Anthony. **CAST:** Shirley MacLaine, Dean Martin, Charlie Ruggles, Cliff Robertson, Gale Gordon, Jack Weston.
The heir to a publishing empire falls in love with a girl he believes has, at one time, been the mistress of his own uncle. This comedy starts well but lags before the finale. Harmless fun. 1961; 94m.

ALL NIGHT LONG ★★★
DIR: Jean-Claude Tramont. **CAST:** Gene Hackman, Barbra Streisand.
Praised by some for its offbeat style and story, this comedy, starring the odd couple of Gene Hackman and Barbra Streisand, is only occasionally convincing. Hackman stars as an executive demoted to the position of managing a twenty-four-hour grocery store. There, he meets a daffy housewife (played by a miscast Streisand)

and love blooms. This picture has its partisans, but it is still unlikely to satisfy most viewers. 1981; 95m.

ALL OF ME ★★★★½
DIR: Carl Reiner. **CAST:** Steve Martin, Lily Tomlin, Victoria Tennant, Richard Libertini.
Steve Martin finds himself haunted from within by the soul of a recently deceased Lily Tomlin when an attempt to put her spirit in another woman's body backfires. This delightful comedy gives its two stars the best showcase for their talents to date. Rated PG for suggested sex, violence, and profanity. 1984; 93m.

ALL OVER TOWN ★★½
DIR: James W. Horne. **CAST:** Chic Johnson, Ole Olson, Franklin Pangborn, Mary Howard, James Finlayson.
Stage favorites of the 1920s and 1930s, Olson and Johnson display their zany patter and antics as they try to produce a show in a theater on which a hex has been put. Some funny moments, but most of this low-budget comedy is antiquated. 1937; B&W; 62m.

ALL-STAR TOAST TO THE IMPROV, AN ★★★½
DIR: Walter C. Miller. **CAST:** Robert Klein, Billy Crystal, Richard Lewis, Martin Mull, Paul Rodriguez, Robin Williams.
Robert Klein hosts this hour of outrageous comedy from the famous Improv club in Los Angeles. On view are some of the most gifted funny men to grace the stand-up spotlight. Originally produced for HBO cable television. Not rated. 1988; 60m.

ALL THE MARBLES
DIR: Robert Aldrich. **CAST:** Peter Falk, Vicki Frederick, Laurene Landon, Burt Young, Tracy Reed.
Peter Falk stars as the unscrupulous manager of two female wrestlers in this dreadful movie, directed by Robert Aldrich (*The Dirty Dozen*). Bad taste...total waste. Rated R because of nudity, violence, and profanity. 1981; 113m.

ALLNIGHTER, THE
DIR: Tamar Simon Hoffs. **CAST:** Susanne Hoffs, John Terlesky, Joan Cusack, Dedee Pfeiffer, James Anthony Shanta, Janelle Brady.
Rock star Susanna Hoffs (of the Bangles) stars in this terminally dumb 1980s beach movie as a college student who goes on one last fling before graduating. After about 10 minutes, you'll want to fling the tape out the window. This, by the way, was a family affair. Director Tamar Simon Hoffs is the star's mother. What some parents do to their kids! Rated PG. 1987; 90m.

ALMOST PERFECT AFFAIR, AN ★★★
DIR: Michael Ritchie. **CAST:** Keith Carradine, Monica Vitti, Raf Vallone.
A very human love triangle evolves amidst the frenzy of film politics that surrounds the Cannes Film Festival. This romantic comedy about a young American filmmaker and the worldly but lovable wife of a powerful Italian film mogul is slow to start, but leaves you with a warm feeling. Rated PG with suggested sex and partial nudity. 1979; 92m.

ALMOST YOU ★★★★
DIR: Adam Books. **CAST:** Brooke Adams, Griffin Dunne, Karen Young, Marty Watt.
Brooke Adams and Griffin Dunne give excellent performances in this film about a restless husband and his down-to-earth wife. Dunne perfectly emulates the frustrated over-30 businessman and husband with comic results. Adams plays his wife, who is recovering from a car accident that gives her a new perspective on life. Rated R for language, sex, and nudity. 1985; 91m.

ALWAYS ★★★
DIR: Henry Jaglom. **CAST:** Henry Jaglom, Patrice Townsend, Joanna Frank, Alan Rachins, Melissa Leo.

Largely autobiographical, *Always* follows Henry Jaglom and Patrice Townsend through their breakup and their reckoning of the relationship. This movie has a bittersweet feeling that is reminiscent of some of Woody Allen's films dealing with romance. Unfortunately, the movie doesn't have the laughs that Allen provides, so the melancholy moments seem a bit long. Rated R for profanity and nudity. 1984; 105m.

AMAZING ADVENTURE ★★★
DIR: Alfred Zeisler. **CAST:** Cary Grant, Mary Brian, Peter Gawthorne, Henry Kendall, Leon M. Lion.

Feeling guilty after inheriting a fortune, Cary Grant sets out to earn his living in this comedy of stout hearts among the poor-but-honest in England during the Depression. 1936; B&W; 70m.

AMAZON WOMEN ON THE MOON ★★★
DIR: John Landis, Joe Dante, Carl Gottlieb, Peter Horton, Robert K. Weiss. **CAST:** Rosanna Arquette, Ralph Bellamy, Carrie Fisher, Sybil Danning, Steve Allen, Griffin Dunne, Steve Guttenberg, Ed Begley Jr., Arsenio Hall, Howard Hesseman, Russ Meyer, B. B. King, Henny Youngman.

This silly scrapbook send-up of Saturday morning, sci-fi, and sitcom TV schlock stitches together star-strewn skits, but many of the plots are threadbare. When on the mark the chuckles come easily. More often, it's like the Not Ready for Prime Time Players on a not-so-prime night. Rated R for nudity. 1987; 85m.

AMBASSADOR'S DAUGHTER, THE ★★★
DIR: Norman Krasna. **CAST:** Olivia De Havilland, John Forsythe, Myrna Loy, Adolphe Menjou, Tommy Noonan, Edward Arnold.

A beautiful Olivia De Havilland and a handsome John Forsythe star in this sophisticated romantic comedy about a congressman (Edward Arnold) attempting to curtail the amorous adventures of G. I.s in Paris. Winningly performed by all. 1956; 102m.

AMERICA
DIR: Robert Downey. **CAST:** Zack Norman, Tammy Grimes, Michael J. Pollard, Richard Belzer, Laura Ashton, Liz Torres.

No, not the TV miniseries, and even more boring. This mess has a down-and-out cable station trying to get financial support from New York's latest $10 million lottery winner, who happens to be a janitor. Nothing funny here. Rated R. 1986; 90m.

AMERICAN DREAMER ★★★
DIR: Rick Rosenthal. **CAST:** JoBeth Williams, Tom Conti, Giancarlo Giannini.

JoBeth Williams plays Cathy Palmer, a would-be novelist who, in a short story contest, successfully captures the style of a series of adventure stories that feature a superspy named Rebecca Ryan and thereby wins a trip to Paris. But once there, Palmer is hit by a car and wakes up believing she is the fictional character. The picture is sort of a *Romancing the Stone II*, but never quite shines as brightly as one expects. Rated PG for violence. 1984; 105m.

AMERICAN GRAFFITI ★★★★½
DIR: George Lucas. **CAST:** Richard Dreyfuss, Ron Howard, Paul LeMat, Cindy Williams, Candy Clark, Mackenzie Phillips, Harrison Ford, Bo Hopkins, Charles Martin Smith.

Star Wars creator George Lucas discovered his talent for creating lighthearted, likable entertainment with this film about the coming of age of a group of high-school students in Northern California. Blessed with a superb rock 'n' roll score and fine performances it's the best of its kind and inspired the long-running television series *Happy Days*. Rated PG. 1973; 110m.

AMERICANIZATION OF EMILY, THE ★★★½

DIR: Arthur Hiller. **CAST:** James Garner, Julie Andrews, Melvyn Douglas, James Coburn, Joyce Grenfell, Keenan Wynn, Judy Carne.

Who would think of turning the Normandy invasion into a massive publicity event? According to screenwriter Paddy Chayefsky, the American military brass would drool over the possibilities. James Garner winningly plays the naval officer designated to be the first casualty on the beach. The script, intelligently handled by director Arthur Hiller, bristles with hard-edged humor. 1964; B&W; 117m.

AMERICATHON

DIR: Neal Israel. **CAST:** John Ritter, Harvey Korman, Nancy Morgan, Peter Riegert, Zane Buzby, Fred Willard, Chief Dan George.

Before managing to entertain audiences with such questionable movies as *Bachelor Party* and *Moving Violations*, director Neal Israel made this absolutely abysmal comedy about a bankrupt American government staging a telethon to save itself. Rated R for profanity and sleaze. 1979; 86m.

AMOS AND ANDY (TELEVISION SERIES) ★★★

DIR: Charles Barton. **CAST:** Tim Moore, Spencer Williams Jr., Alvin Childress, Ernestine Wade, Amanda Randolph.

Amos is the narrator. He runs a cab company. Andy is his amiable, slow-witted partner. Kingfish is an inept con man who tries to get Andy involved in an endless series of often hilarious get-rich-quick schemes. The first major television show with an all-black cast, *Amos and Andy* features sharp writing, energetic humor, and witty, memorable performances. CBS pulled the show in 1966 amid charges of racism, and rightfully so in that era. Now these surprisingly timeless comedies have been released on video, and they can be enjoyed if taken in the proper context. 1951–1953; B&W; 30m.

AND NOW FOR SOMETHING COMPLETELY DIFFERENT ★★★½

DIR: Ian McNaughton. **CAST:** John Cleese, Eric Idle, Terry Jones, Michael Palin, Graham Chapman, Terry Gilliam.

Fitfully funny but still a treat for their fans, this was the first screen outing of the Monty Python comedy troupe. It's a collection of the best bits from the team's television series. With delightful ditties, such as "The Lumberjack Song," how can you go wrong? Rated PG. 1972; 89m.

ANDROCLES AND THE LION ★★½

DIR: Chester Erskine. **CAST:** Alan Young, Jean Simmons, Victor Mature, Robert Newton, Maurice Evans, Elsa Lanchester, Reginald Gardiner, Gene Lockhart, Alan Mowbray, John Hoyt, Jim Backus.

An incredible cast still can't save this plodding story of a mild-mannered tailor (Alan Young) whose act of kindness toward a lion helps to save a group of Christians doomed to die in the Coliseum. George Bernard Shaw's pointed retelling of an old fable loses its bite in this rambling production, and Young is ineffectual in the leading role. Jean Simmons made her American debut in this movie, one of the least successful of all adaptations of Shaw's works. 1952; B&W; 105m.

ANDY GRIFFITH SHOW, THE (TELEVISION SERIES) ★★★★

DIR: Various. **CAST:** Andy Griffith, Don Knotts, Ron Howard, Jim Nabors, Frances Bavier, Howard McNear, George Lindsey, Hal Smith, Howard Morris.

As of this writing, six volumes have been released of one of television's most fondly remembered situation comedies. This series takes place in fictitious Mayberry, North Carolina, a sleepy little town looked after by laid-back sheriff Andy Taylor (Andy Griffith) and his manic deputy, Barney Fife (Don Knotts, winner of numerous Emmy Awards for his portrayal). The volumes now available are *The Best of Barney*, *The Best of Floyd*, *The Best of Otis*, *The Best of Gomer*, *The Best of Ernest T. Bass*, and *The Vintage Years*. Each volume contains four episodes spotlighting a particular character's most memorable moments. 1960–1965; B&W; 100m.

ANDY HARDY GETS SPRING FEVER ★★★
DIR: W. S. Van Dyke. **CAST:** Mickey Rooney, Lewis Stone, Fay Holden, Cecilia Parker, Ann Rutherford.

Another in the long-running series about all-American life in a small town. This installment finds Andy Hardy (Mickey Rooney) saddled with the trials and tribulations of producing his high-school play. 1939; B&W; 85m.

ANDY HARDY MEETS A DEBUTANTE ★★★
DIR: George B. Seitz. **CAST:** Mickey Rooney, Lewis Stone, Cecilia Parker, Fay Holden, Judy Garland.

Mickey Rooney again portrays the all-American teenager who dominated the long-running series. Good, wholesome family-film fare. 1940; B&W; 86m.

ANDY HARDY'S DOUBLE LIFE ★★★
DIR: George B. Seitz. **CAST:** Mickey Rooney, Lewis Stone, Cecilia Parker, Fay Holden, Ann Rutherford, Esther Williams, William Lundigan.

Fresh from championship swimming, Esther Williams got her studio start in this warm and sentimental addition to the hit series. 1942; B&W; 92m.

ANDY HARDY'S PRIVATE SECRETARY ★★★
DIR: George B. Seitz. **CAST:** Mickey Rooney, Lewis Stone, Fay Holden, Ian Hunter, Kathryn Grayson, Gene Reynolds, Ann Rutherford.

Kathryn Grayson is the focus in this slice of wholesome Americana from the innocent days just before World War II. Fun for the whole family. 1940; B&W; 101m.

ANIMAL CRACKERS ★★★★
DIR: Victor Heerman. **CAST:** The Marx Brothers, Margaret Dumont, Lillian Roth.

Animal Crackers is pure Marx Brothers, a total farce loosely based on a hit play by George S. Kaufman. Highlights include Groucho's African lecture—"One morning I shot an elephant in my pajamas. How he got into my pajamas, I'll never know"—and the uproariously funny card game with Harpo, Chico, and the ever-put-upon Margaret Dumont. 1930; B&W; 98m.

ANIMAL HOUSE ★★★★½
DIR: John Landis. **CAST:** John Belushi, Tim Matheson, Karen Allen, Peter Riegert, John Vernon, Tom Hulce.

Although it has spawned a seemingly relentless onslaught of inferior carbon copies, this comedy is still one of the funniest movies ever made. If you're into rock 'n' roll, partying, and general craziness, this picture is for you. We gave it a 95, because it has a good beat and you can dance to it. Rated R. 1978; 109m.

ANNIE HALL ★★★★★
DIR: Woody Allen. **CAST:** Woody Allen, Diane Keaton, Tony Roberts, Paul Simon, Shelley Duvall, Carol Kane.

Woody Allen's exquisite romantic comedy won the 1977 Academy Awards for best picture, actress (Diane Keaton), director (Allen), and screenplay (Allen and Marshall Brickman)—and deserved every one of them. This delightful semi-autobiographical romp features Allen as Alvy Singer, a more assured version of Alan Felix, from *Play It Again, Sam*, who falls in love (again) with Keaton (in the title role). Rated PG for profanity and bedroom scenes. 1977; 94m.

ANY WEDNESDAY ★★
DIR: Robert Ellis Miller. **CAST:** Jane Fonda, Jason Robards Jr., Dean

Jones, Rosemary Murphy, Ann Prentiss.

The spiciness of the original Broadway script gets lost in this film adaptation. Jason Robards plays the New York businessman who deducts his paramour's (Jane Fonda) apartment as a business expense. A poor man's *The Apartment*. 1966; 109m.

ANY WHICH WAY YOU CAN ★
DIR: Buddy Van Horn. **CAST:** Clint Eastwood, Sondra Locke, Geoffrey Lewis, William Smith, Ruth Gordon.

Another comedy clinker from Clint Eastwood and company, this features the same cast and story (about the adventures of a streetfighter and his pet orangutan) from *Every Which Way But Loose*, a movie that wasn't very good to begin with. Rated PG. 1980; 116m.

APARTMENT, THE ★★★★★
DIR: Billy Wilder. **CAST:** Jack Lemmon, Shirley MacLaine, Fred MacMurray, Ray Walston, Jack Kruschen, Edie Adams.

Rarely have comedy and drama been satisfyingly blended into a cohesive whole. Director Billy Wilder does it masterfully in this film. With career advancement in mind, Jack Lemmon permits his boss (Fred MacMurray) to use his apartment for illicit love affairs. Then he gets involved with the boss's emotionally distraught girlfriend (Shirley MacLaine). Lemmon sparkles. MacLaine is irresistible. And MacMurray, playing a heel, is a revelation. 1960; B&W; 125m.

APRIL FOOLS, THE ★
DIR: Stuart Rosenberg. **CAST:** Jack Lemmon, Catherine Deneuve, Peter Lawford, Sally Kellerman, Myrna Loy, Charles Boyer.

A failed attempt at a serious romantic comedy that veers too often into awkward slapstick. This is the sort of film best left to the French; director Stuart Rosenberg just doesn't know what to make of the genre. Jack Lemmon falls in love with his boss's wife...and that's it. An excellent—and completely wasted—supporting cast cannot disguise the thin script. Rated PG for adult situations. 1969; 95m.

ARMED AND DANGEROUS ★
DIR: Mark L. Lester. **CAST:** John Candy, Eugene Levy, Robert Loggia, Kenneth McMillan, Meg Ryan, Jonathan Banks, Brion James.

Comedy fizzle from two talented SCTV graduates whose theatrical films have consistently fallen short of their usually hilarious TV sketches and bits. The story concerns fired cop Frank Dooley (John Candy) and former lawyer Norman Kane (Eugene Levy), who meet and become partners at their new jobs as private security guards for a firm known as Guard Dog. Rated PG-13 for language. 1986; 89m.

ARMY BRATS
DIR: Ruud van Hemert. **CAST:** Frank Schaafsma, Geert DeJong, Akemay, Peter Faber.

This ridiculous comedy centers around the war taking place within the Gisbert family. Mr. Gisbert has been the paranoid commander at his home while his apathetic wife amused herself with her tennis coach. Meanwhile, their four children have armed themselves to overthrow their parents. Foreign, it is dubbed and unrated. The obscene language and nudity make it comparable to an R. 1984; 103m.

AROUND THE WORLD IN 80 DAYS (1956) ★★★
DIR: Michael Anderson. **CAST:** David Niven, Cantinflas, Shirley MacLaine, Marlene Dietrich, Robert Newton.

An all-star extravaganza with David Niven, Cantinflas, and Shirley MacLaine in the pivotal roles, this inflated travelogue was a spectacular success when originally released. However, it seems hopelessly dated today and loses all too much on the small screen. Even picking out the dozens of stars in cameo roles doesn't yield as much joy under the plodding direction of Michael Anderson as it could have. It's a curiosity at best. 1956; 167m.

AROUND THE WORLD IN 80 WAYS ★★
DIR: Stephen MacLean. **CAST:** Philip Quast.
Despite a wonderfully goofy premise, this comedy from Down Under is just not very funny. Philip Quast is a young tour guide who must take his decrepit father on a world tour, but lacks the money so he fakes it, never leaving his neighborhood. Rated R for language and crudity. 1988; 90m.

ARSENIC AND OLD LACE ★★★★½
DIR: Frank Capra. **CAST:** Cary Grant, Priscilla Lane, Jack Carson, James Gleason, Peter Lorre, Raymond Massey, Jean Adair, Josephine Hull.
Two sweet old ladies have found a solution for the loneliness of elderly men with no family or friends—they poison them! Then they give them a proper Christian burial in their basement. Their nephew, Mortimer (Cary Grant), an obvious party pooper, finds out and wants them to stop. This delightful comedy is crammed with sparkling performances. 1944; B&W; 118m.

ARTHUR ★★★★
DIR: Steve Gordon. **CAST:** Dudley Moore, Liza Minnelli, Stephen Elliott, John Gielgud.
Dudley Moore is Arthur, the world's richest (and obviously happiest) alcoholic. But all is not well in his pickled paradise. Arthur will lose access to the family's great wealth if he doesn't marry the uptight debutante picked out for him by his parents. He doesn't love her…in fact, he doesn't even like her. And what's worse, he's in love with a wacky shoplifter (Liza Minnelli). Most of the time, it's hilarious, with John Gielgud as a sharp-tongued butler providing the majority of the laughs. Rated PG because of profanity. 1981; 97m.

ARTHUR 2: ON THE ROCKS ★★
DIR: Bud Yorkin. **CAST:** Dudley Moore, Liza Minnelli, John Gielgud, Cynthia Sikes, Stephen Elliot, Paul Benedict, Geraldine Fitzgerald, Barney Martin.
Some sequels simply don't take characters in the directions imagined by those who loved the original film, and *Arthur 2* is a case in point. Although scripter Andy Breckman captures each performer's individual quirks, his overall story is morose, uncomfortable, and marred by its badly contrived conclusion. Call this one a good try. Rated PG for mild profanity. 1988; 99m.

AS YOU LIKE IT ★★★
DIR: Paul Czinner. **CAST:** Elisabeth Bergner, Laurence Olivier, Felix Aylmer, Leon Quartermaine.
Laurence Olivier is commanding as Orlando to beautiful Elisabeth Bergner's stylized Rosalind in this early filming of Shakespeare's delightful comedy. Lovers of the Bard will be pleased. 1936; B&W; 96m.

AT THE CIRCUS ★★★½
DIR: Edward Buzzell. **CAST:** The Marx Brothers, Margaret Dumont, Kenny Baker, Eve Arden.
The Marx Brothers were running out of steam as a comedy team by this time. Still, any film with Groucho, Harpo, and Chico is worth watching, although you'll probably feel like punching the comedy's "hero" (or is that a zero?), Kenny Baker, when he sings that highly forgettable ditty "Step Up, Take a Bow." 1939; B&W; 87m.

AT WAR WITH THE ARMY ★★★★
DIR: Hal Walker. **CAST:** Dean Martin, Jerry Lewis, Polly Bergen, Angela Greene, Mike Kellin.
Dean Martin and Jerry Lewis were still fresh and funny at the time of this comedy release, but a classic it isn't (though some scenes are gems). 1950; B&W; 93m.

ATOLL K (UTOPIA) 🦃
DIR: Léo Joannon. **CAST:** Stan Laurel, Oliver Hardy.
The final screen outing of the great comedy team of Stan Laurel and Oliver Hardy is a keen disappointment.

Laurel became ill during its making and looks just awful (making his crying scenes more sad than funny). It's a regrettable final bow for two of the screen's greatest clowns. 1950; B&W; 80m.

ATTACK OF THE KILLER TOMATOES
DIR: John DeBello. **CAST:** David Miller, Sharon Taylor, George Wilson, Jack Riley.

In this campy cult film, the tomatoes are funnier than the actors, most of whom are rank amateurs. The plot? Killer tomatoes begin terrorizing the western United States while the military plans inept strategies. Rated PG. 1980; 87m.

AUDIENCE WITH MEL BROOKS, AN ★★★½
DIR: Mel Brooks. **CAST:** Mel Brooks.

This is a reserved, delightfully anecdotal evening with the comic genius. Filmed in England, it features Brooks answering questions from the audience about his career, life, and famous collaborators. 1984; 55m.

AUNTIE MAME ★★★½
DIR: Morton Da Costa. **CAST:** Rosalind Russell, Forrest Tucker, Coral Browne, Fred Clark.

Rosalind Russell, in the title role, plays a free-thinking eccentric woman whose young nephew is placed in her care. Russell created the role on the stage; it was a once-in-a-lifetime showcase that she made uniquely her own. 1958; 143m.

AUTHOR! AUTHOR! ★★★
DIR: Arthur Hiller. **CAST:** Al Pacino, Dyan Cannon, Alan King, Tuesday Weld.

Al Pacino stars as a playwright whose wife (Tuesday Weld) leaves him with five kids (not all his) to raise in this nicely done bittersweet comedy. Dyan Cannon plays the actress with whom he falls in love. Rated PG for brief profanity. 1982; 110m.

AWFUL TRUTH, THE ★★★★
DIR: Leo McCarey. **CAST:** Irene Dunne, Cary Grant, Ralph Bellamy, Molly Lamont.

Irene Dunne and Cary Grant divorce so that they can marry others. Then they do their best to spoil one another's plans. Leo McCarey won an Oscar for directing this prime example of the screwball comedies that made viewing such a delight in the 1930s. Grant—a master of timing—is in top form, as is co-star Dunne. It's hilarious all the way. 1937; B&W; 92m.

BABY BOOM ★★★½
DIR: Charles Shyer. **CAST:** Diane Keaton, Harold Ramis, Sam Wanamaker, Pat Hingle, Sam Shepard.

Yuppie fairy tale about a career woman (Diane Keaton) who finds her eighty-hour-per-week corporate job interrupted by the untimely arrival of a babe-in-arms. It seems Keaton is the poor tot's only surviving relative, so she attempts to juggle job responsibility and parenting while boyfriend and boss recoil in disgust. The laughs are frequent, but the film doesn't find any warmth until Keaton flees to the country and meets local veterinarian Sam Shepard. Rated PG for language. 1987; 103m.

BABY LOVE
DIR: Dan Wolman. **CAST:** Yftach Katzur, Zachi Noy, Jonathan Segall.

This poorly dubbed Israeli-German teen sex comedy has no redeeming value. Strangely, the last fifteen minutes make a stab at drama as the only virgin around (Baby Love) tries to commit suicide. Unrated, this is equivalent to an R for nudity and sexual situations. 1983; 81m.

BACHELOR AND THE BOBBY-SOXER, THE ★★½
DIR: Irving Reis. **CAST:** Cary Grant, Myrna Loy, Shirley Temple, Rudy Vallee.

Lady judge Myrna Loy cleverly sentences playboy Cary Grant to baby-sit

Shirley Temple, her sister, a panting nubile teenager with a crush on him. There are some hilarious moments, but the comedy gets thin as Loy's lesson begins to cloy. Best bit is the play on words about the Man with the Power, Voodoo and Youdo. 1947; B&W; 95m.

BACHELOR MOTHER ★★★
DIR: Garson Kanin. **CAST:** Ginger Rogers, David Niven, Charles Coburn, Frank Albertson, Ernest Truex.
The old story about a single woman who finds a baby on a doorstep and is mistaken for its mother has never been funnier than in this witty film by writer-director Garson Kanin. Ginger Rogers as the shop girl who finds her job in jeopardy and her whole life upside-down as a result of the confusion shows her considerable skill for comedy. David Niven, in an early starring role, is just great as the store owner's son who attempts to "rehabilitate" the fallen Rogers. 1939; B&W; 82m.

BACHELOR PARTY ★★
DIR: Neal Israel. **CAST:** Tom Hanks, Tawny Kitaen, Adrian Zmed, George Grizzard, Robert Prescott.
Even Tom Hanks (of *Splash*) can't save this "wild" escapade into degradation when a carefree bus driver who has decided to get married is given an all-out bachelor party by his friends. Rated R for profanity and nudity. 1984; 106m.

BACK TO SCHOOL ★★★½
DIR: Alan Metter. **CAST:** Rodney Dangerfield, Sally Kellerman, Burt Young, Keith Gordon, Robert Downey Jr., Ned Beatty, M. Emmet Walsh, Adrienne Barbeau, William Zabka, Severn Darden.
A true surprise from the usually acerbic Rodney Dangerfield, who sheds his lewd-'n-crude image in favor of one more sympathetic and controlled. He stars as the self-made owner of a chain of "Tall and Fat" stores who decides to return to college for a never-achieved diploma. He selects the college attended by his son in order to spend more time with the boy (well played by Keith Gordon). Rated PG-13 for occasionally vulgar humor. 1986; 96m.

BAD MEDICINE ★★★½
DIR: Harvey Miller. **CAST:** Steve Guttenberg, Julie Hagerty, Alan Arkin, Bill Macy, Curtis Armstrong, Julie Kavner, Joe Grifasi, Robert Romanus, Taylor Negron.
Steve Guttenburg and Julie Hagerty play students attending a "Mickey Mouse" med school in Central America. When they find the health conditions in a nearby village unacceptable, they set up a medical clinic, stealing the needed drugs from the school's pharmacy. The all-star cast does not disappoint. Rated PG-13 for profanity, sex, and adult situations. 1985; 97m.

BAD NEWS BEARS, THE ★★★★★
DIR: Michael Ritchie. **CAST:** Walter Matthau, Tatum O'Neal, Vic Morrow, Alfred Lutter, Jackie Earle Haley.
An utterly hilarious comedy directed by Michael Ritchie, this film focuses on the antics of some foul-mouthed Little Leaguers, their beer-guzzling coach (Walter Matthau), and girl pitcher (Tatum O'Neal). But be forewarned, the sequels, *Breaking Training* and *The Bad News Bears Go to Japan*, are strictly no-hitters. Rated PG. 1976; 102m.

BAD NEWS BEARS GO TO JAPAN, THE ★
DIR: John Berry. **CAST:** Tony Curtis, Jackie Earle Haley, Tomisaburo Wakayama, George Wyner, Lonny Chapman.
Worst of the *Bad News Bears* trio of films, this features Tony Curtis as a small-time promoter with big ideas, which involve taking the unpredictable (but now sanitized) pint-size ball team to Japan. Unfunny and too

cutesy, it was their last screen romp. Rated PG. 1978; 91m.

BAD NEWS BEARS IN BREAKING TRAINING, THE ★★
DIR: Michael Pressman. **CAST:** William Devane, Jackie Earle Haley, Clifton James.
Without Walter Matthau, Tatum O'Neal, and director Michael Ritchie, this sequel to *The Bad News Bears* truly is bad news...and rather idiotic. How many kids do *you* know who'd be allowed to hop into a minibus and drive to Houston *sans* adult supervision? Jackie Earle Haley returns as the team star, and William Devane has a reasonable part as Haley's footloose father. Don't expect much. Rated PG for mild profanity. 1977; 100m.

BAGDAD CAFÉ ★★★★
DIR: Percy Adlon. **CAST:** Marianne Sägebrecht, H. C. Pounder, Jack Palance.
This delightfully offbeat comedy-drama concerns a German businesswoman who appears in the minuscule desert town in California called Bagdad. She and the highly-strung owner of the town's only diner-hotel have a major culture and personality clash. Jack Palance as a bandanna-wearing artist is so perfectly weird he practically walks off with the film. Rated PG. 1988; 91m.

BALL OF FIRE ★★★½
DIR: Howard Hawks. **CAST:** Gary Cooper, Barbara Stanwyck, Dana Andrews, Oscar Homolka, S. Z. Sakall, Richard Haydn, Henry Travers, Tully Marshall, Allen Jenkins.
Stuffy linguistics professor Gary Cooper meets hotch-cha dancer Barbara Stanwyck. He and seven lovable colleagues are putting together an encyclopedia. She's recruited to fill them in on slanguage. She does this, and more! Gangster Dana Andrews and motor-mouthed garbage man Allen Jenkins add to the madcap antics in what has been dubbed the last of the prewar screwball comedies. Good show! 1941; B&W; 111m.

BALLOONATIC, THE/ONE WEEK ★★★
DIR: Buster Keaton, Eddie Cline. **CAST:** Buster Keaton, Phyllis Haver, Sybil Seely.
The comedic invention and physical stamina of the Great Stone Face, as Buster Keaton was called, are shown to perfect advantage in these early 1920s silent shorts. In *The Balloonatic* Buster is "skyjacked" by a runaway balloon and dropped into the wilderness. In *One Week* he constructs a kit house from fouled-up assembly plans. An ample demonstration of why Keaton was one of the great silent comics. Silent. 1920–1923; B&W; 48m.

BALTIMORE BULLET, THE ★★½
DIR: Robert Ellis Miller. **CAST:** James Coburn, Bruce Boxleitner, Omar Sharif, Ronee Blakley.
In this tale of big-league pool hustling, clever cuesters James Coburn and Bruce Boxleitner carefully build up to scoring big in a nail-biting shootout with suave Omar Sharif. Rated PG. 1980; 103m.

BANANAS ★★★★
DIR: Woody Allen. **CAST:** Woody Allen, Louise Lasser, Carlos Montalban, Howard Cosell.
Before he started making classic comedies, such as *Annie Hall*, *Zelig*, and *Broadway Danny Rose*, writer-director-star Woody Allen made some pretty wild—though generally uneven—wacky movies. This 1971 comedy, with Woody's hapless hero becoming involved in a South American revolution, does have its share of hilarious moments. Rated PG. 1971; 82m.

BANANAS BOAT, THE
DIR: Sidney Hayers. **CAST:** Doug McClure, Hayley Mills, Lionel Jeffries, Warren Mitchell.
Often a film comes along that raises important questions, such as "Why was it made?" This purported comedy has no plot, no acting, and no laughs, unless old men getting beat up and

Doug McClure's bare rear end are considered funny. Rated PG for naughty language and nudity. 1974; 91m.

BANG BANG KID, THE ★★½
DIR: Stanley Prager. **CAST:** Guy Madison, Sandra Milo, Tom Bosley, Riccardo Garrone.

Goofy comedy-Western with Tom Bosley as Merriweather Newberry, the inventor of a robot gunfighter (dubbed The Bang Bang Kid). The residents of a mining community hope that they can use it to defeat Bear Bullock (Guy Madison), the town boss who treats the townies as his serfs. (He even lives in a castle he imported from Spain!) Good for kids; passable for grownups in a silly mood. 1968; 90m.

BANK DICK, THE ★★★★★
DIR: Eddie Cline. **CAST:** W. C. Fields, Cora Witherspoon, Una Merkel, Shemp Howard.

W. C. Fields is at his best in this laugh-filled comedy. In it, Fields plays a drunkard who becomes a hero. But the story is just an excuse for the moments of hilarity—of which there are many. 1940; B&W; 74m.

BAREFOOT IN THE PARK ★★★★½
DIR: Gene Saks. **CAST:** Robert Redford, Jane Fonda, Charles Boyer, Mildred Natwick, Herb Edelman.

A young Robert Redford and Jane Fonda team up as newlyweds in this adaptation of Neil Simon's Broadway play. The comedy focuses on the adjustments of married life. Ethel Banks and Mildred Natwick play the mothers-in-law, and Charles Boyer is a daffy, unconventional neighbor. 1967; 105m.

BASIC TRAINING ★½
DIR: Andrew Sugerman. **CAST:** Ann Dusenberry, Rhonda Shear, Angela Aames, Walter Gotell.

A small-town girl with the mission of cleaning up our government ends up at the Pentagon. Rooming with two other girls in Washington, D.C., she manages to become involved in endless hijinks. This movie is intermittently tasteless, and the attempts at comedy are old and tired. It ends up being mainly a vehicle for T&A. Rated R for sex and language. 1984; 86m.

BATTLE OF THE SEXES, THE ★★★½
DIR: Charles Crichton. **CAST:** Peter Sellers, Robert Morley, Constance Cummings, Jameson Clark.

Peter Sellers is wonderful as an elderly Scottish Highlander bent on murder. Robert Morley, always a favorite, is simply delightful and helps keep this British comedy on a fast and funny track. 1960; B&W; 88m.

BAWDY ADVENTURES OF TOM JONES, THE ★
DIR: Cliff Owen. **CAST:** Nicky Henson, Trevor Howard, Joan Collins, Arthur Lowe, Georgia Brown, Madeleine Smith, Jeremy Lloyd.

This ridiculous romp features Trevor Howard as the lecherous Squire Western. Young Tom Jones (played by an innocent-looking Nick Henson), an outcast due to his illegitimate birth, is in love with Western's daughter and spends the entire film hoping to win her hand. Along the way he is "forced" to cavort with an assortment of other ladies. Rated R for nudity and a multitude of sexual situations. 1976; 89m.

BEACH GIRLS, THE ★½
DIR: Pat Townsend. **CAST:** Debra Blee, Val Kline, Jeana Tomasina.

Dumb sex comedy about a couple of teen-age girls who throw a big party at their uncle's Malibu beach house while he's away. Typical unrealistic nonsense. Rated R for nudity. 1982; 91m.

BEACH HOUSE ★
DIR: John Gallagher. **CAST:** Ileana Seidel, John Cosola.

Mirthless comedy about a feud between Italian kids from Brooklyn and snobs from Philadelphia, all vacationing at the same beach house. This is a movie that would actually be *improved* by the presence of Frankie and Annette! Rated PG, which means that it's lacking anything that audiences for this kind of movie pay to see. 1982; 75m.

BEACHBALLS
DIR: Joe Ritter. **CAST:** Phillip Paley, Heidi Helmer.

Another sleazy teen tumble. Charlie Harrison's folks go out of town leaving their home in the hands of Charlie and his sister. Charlie pursues a "10," but has trouble getting her attention since he's only about a "2." This will appeal only to slow 15-year-olds. Rated R for nudity and profanity. 1988; 79m.

BEAT THE DEVIL ★★★★
DIR: John Huston. **CAST:** Humphrey Bogart, Robert Morley, Peter Lorre, Jennifer Jones, Gina Lollobrigida.

Because it's all played straight, critics and audiences alike didn't know what to make of this delightful though at times baffling satire of films in the vein of *The Maltese Falcon* and *Key Largo* when it first hit screens. Sadly, some still do not. Nonetheless, this droll comedy, cobbled on location in Italy by John Huston and Truman Capote, is a twenty-four-carat gem. 1954; B&W; 93m.

BEAUTIFUL BLONDE FROM BASHFUL BEND, THE ★★½
DIR: Preston Sturges. **CAST:** Betty Grable, Cesar Romero, Rudy Vallee, Olga San Juan, Sterling Holloway, Hugh Herbert, Porter Hall, Margaret Hamilton.

Sharpshooter-schoolmarm Betty Grable has boyfriend trouble and must deal with a kidnapping and a philandering Cesar Romero in this wacky Western farce. A select collection of comic character players helps her resolve it all. Tolerable family fun, but not a highlight in director Preston Sturges's career. 1949; 77m.

BEDAZZLED ★★★★
DIR: Stanley Donen. **CAST:** Peter Cook, Dudley Moore, Raquel Welch, Eleanor Bron.

A cult favorite, this British comedy stars Dudley Moore as a fry cook tempted by the devil (played by his one-time comedy partner, Peter Cook). Co-starring Raquel Welch, it's an often-hilarious updating of the Faust legend. 1967; 107m.

BEDTIME FOR BONZO ★★★
DIR: Frederick de Cordova. **CAST:** Ronald Reagan, Diana Lynn, Walter Slezak, Jesse White.

This sweet-natured film is worth watching. Ronald Reagan plays a young college professor who uses a chimpanzee to prove that environment, not heredity, determines a person's moral fiber. He hires a young woman (Diana Lynn) to pose as the chimp's mom while he plays father to it. Not surprisingly, Mom and Dad fall in love. 1951; B&W; 83m.

BEER ★★★★
DIR: Patrick Kelly. **CAST:** Loretta Swit, Rip Torn, Kenneth Mars, David Alan Grier, William Russ, Peter Michael Goetz, Dick Shawn.

Hilarious comedy that examines the seamy side of the advertising industry. Loretta Swit plays a cold-blooded advertising agent who tries to turn three ordinary guys (David Alan Grier, William Russ, and Saul Stein) into beer-drinking American heroes. The plan works, and soon they are the talk of the country. Dick Shawn's impression of Phil Donahue must be seen to be believed. Rated R for profanity, sex, and adult subject matter. 1985; 83m.

BEING THERE ★★★★½
DIR: Hal Ashby. **CAST:** Peter Sellers, Shirley MacLaine, Melvyn Douglas, Jack Warden.

This sublimely funny and bitingly satiric comedy features Peter Sellers's last great screen performance. His portrayal of a simple-minded gardener—who knows only what he sees on television yet rises to great political heights—is a classic. Shirley MacLaine and Melvyn Douglas are also excellent in this memorable film, directed by Hal Ashby. Rated PG. 1979; 130m.

BELL, BOOK AND CANDLE ★★★½

DIR: Richard Quine. **CAST:** James Stewart, Kim Novak, Jack Lemmon, Ernie Kovacs.

A modestly entertaining bit of whimsy about a beautiful witch (Kim Novak) who works her magic on an unsuspecting publisher (James Stewart). Although the performances (including those in support by Jack Lemmon, Ernie Kovacs, and Hermione Gingold) are fine, this comedy is only mildly diverting. 1958; 103m.

BELLBOY, THE ★★

DIR: Jerry Lewis. **CAST:** Jerry Lewis, Alex Gerry, Sonny Sands.

A typical hour-plus of Jerry Lewis mugging and antics so dear to those who find him funny. This time around, Jerry is a bellboy at a swank Miami Beach hotel. Years ago, "Fatty" Arbuckle made a film of the same name that was funny. This, unfortunately, is plotless drivel seasoned with guest appearances by Milton Berle and Walter Winchell. Rated G when rereleased in 1972. 1960; B&W; 72m.

BELLES OF ST. TRINIAN'S, THE ★★★½

DIR: Frank Launder. **CAST:** Alastair Sim, Joyce Grenfell, Hermione Baddeley, George Cole.

Alastair Sim doubles as the dotty headmistress of a bonkers school for girls and her crafty bookie brother, who wants to use the place as a cover for his nefarious operations. Joyce Grenfell adds to the hilarity in this British comedy based on English cartoonist Ronald Searle's schoolgirls with a genius for mischief. 1955; B&W; 90m.

BENEATH THE VALLEY OF THE ULTRA-VIXENS ★½

DIR: Russ Meyer. **CAST:** Francesca "Kitten" Natividad, Anne Marie, Ken Kerr, June Mack.

A chaotic sexual odyssey concerning neurotic behavior among the residents of a small Southern California community. A big disappointment, as the film suffers from incomprehensible editing, leaving the viewer confused. This film contains extremely explicit nudity and language and is recommended for adults only. 1979; 93m.

BERNICE BOBS HER HAIR ★★★★

DIR: Joan Micklin Silver. **CAST:** Shelley Duvall, Veronica Cartwright, Bud Cort, Dennis Christopher, Gary Springer, Lane Binkley, Polly Holliday.

The perceptions of self-worth and personal integrity form the core of this droll adaptation of F. Scott Fitzgerald's ode to a shy young girl. Bernice (Shelley Duvall) sacrifices her luxuriously long hair for a shot at the inner circle of popularity jealously guarded by her hedonistic Jazz Era friends. Veronica Cartwright is wonderfully malignant as the fickle society girl who plays *Pygmalion* with her shy, unassuming cousin. Introduced by Henry Fonda. 1976; 49m.

BEST DEFENSE ★★★

DIR: Willard Huyck. **CAST:** Dudley Moore, Eddie Murphy, Kate Capshaw, George Dzundza, Helen Shaver.

Any movie that features the talents of Dudley Moore and Eddie Murphy has to be funny. Sometimes, however, laughs aren't enough. It's very easy to get confused in this film, as the story jumps back and forth between the 1982 segment, featuring Moore as the inept inventor of a malfunctioning piece of defense equipment, and the 1984 footage, with Murphy as the hapless soldier forced to cope with it. The liberal use of profanity and several sex scenes make this R-rated romp unfit for youngsters. 1984; 94m.

BEST FRIENDS ★★
DIR: Norman Jewison. **CAST:** Burt Reynolds, Goldie Hawn, Ron Silver, Jessica Tandy.

Burt Reynolds and Goldie Hawn star in this disappointingly tepid romantic comedy as a pair of successful screenwriters who decide to marry—thus destroying their profitable working relationship. A mess. Rated PG for profanity and adult situations. 1982; 116m.

BEST LEGS IN THE 8TH GRADE, THE ★★★
DIR: Tom Patchett. **CAST:** Tim Matheson, Annette O'Toole, James Belushi, Kathryn Harrold.

Bittersweet made-for-TV comedy focusing on the complexities of modern romance. Tim Matheson is a yuppie lawyer who gets some much needed advice on the affairs of the heart. Annette O'Toole plays his girlfriend. 1984; 48m.

BEST OF CHEVY CHASE, THE ★★★½
DIR: Lorne Michaels. **CAST:** Chevy Chase, Dan Aykroyd, John Belushi, Jane Curtin, Garrett Morris, Bill Murray, Laraine Newman, Gilda Radner, Candice Bergen, Ron Nessen, Richard Pryor.

Though he only appeared on *Saturday Night Live* for one year, Chevy Chase was the series' first star and this compilation of skits shows why. Chase was the most self-conscious performer on the show. He never sank deep into character like Dan Aykroyd or John Belushi; rather, he basically played himself. This tape contains some of Chase's most memorable pieces of comedy: Gerald Ford in the Oval Office, the sneaky land-shark in a *Jaws* sequel.... The "Weekend Update" segments, though, are pulled from several different broadcasts, which throws off their pacing. 1987; 60m.

BEST OF COMIC RELIEF, THE ★★
DIR: Walter C. Miller. **CAST:** Robin Williams, Billy Crystal, Whoopi Goldberg, Martin Short, Harold Ramis, George Carlin, Sid Caesar, Carl Reiner, Steve Allen.

A very disappointing concert tape by some of the great names of stand-up comedy, past and present, who banded together on March 29, 1986, in a benefit concert for the homeless of Los Angeles. The original HBO show was three hours long, yet the tape is only two hours. The editor went after the older comedians with a chain saw, thereby desecrating some classic bits, and left some unfunny stuff by the new wave of comics. Unrated, but contains adult situations and profanity. 1986; 120m.

BEST OF DAN AYKROYD, THE ★★★★
DIR: Lorne Michaels. **CAST:** Dan Aykroyd, John Belushi, Chevy Chase, Jane Curtin, Garrett Morris, Bill Murray, Laraine Newman, Gilda Radner, Shelley Duvall, Madeline Kahn, Margot Kidder, Steve Martin.

The title notwithstanding, this is a collaborative effort; some of the best skits of *Saturday Night Live* from 1975 to 1979. As in *The Best of John Belushi*, the namesake is not always the center of attention. Also, some of these pieces ("The Two Wild and Crazy Guys: the Festrunk Brothers" and "The Final Days of the Nixon Presidency") haven't worn well over the last half-decade. Even so, the shortcomings really don't matter when you are rolling on the floor. 1986; 56m.

BEST OF GILDA RADNER, THE ★★★★
DIR: Dave Wilson. **CAST:** Gilda Radner, John Belushi, Chevy Chase, Dan Aykroyd, Jane Curtin, Bill Murray, Steve Martin, Candice Bergen, Madeline Kahn, Buck Henry.

Of all the *Saturday Night Live* stars, none shone brighter on the series than Gilda Radner. Her characterizations—of Baba Wawa, Emily Litella, Roseanne Rosannadanna, and Lisa Loopner—were classics, and these are all well represented in this package produced by the show's creator, Lorne Michaels. Also included is her brilliant bit with Steve Martin, "Dancing in the Dark," and an homage to *I Love Lucy*. Hilarious and poignant reminder of a great talent. 1989; 59m.

BEST OF JOHN BELUSHI, THE ★★★½

DIR: Lorne Michaels. **CAST:** John Belushi, Dan Aykroyd, Chevy Chase, Jane Curtin, Garrett Morris, Bill Murray, Laraine Newman, Gilda Radner, Elliott Gould, Buck Henry, Robert Klein, Rob Reiner.

A collection of skits from *Saturday Night Live* shows between 1975 and 1979. From "Samurai Delicatessen" to his hilarious Joe Cocker impression, this is John Belushi at his best. The tape ends with Tom Schiller's short subject "Don't Look Back in Anger," the now-ironic piece that is set in the future where Belushi visits the graves of his fellow Not Ready for Prime Time Players who he "outlived." 1985; 60m.

BEST OF NOT NECESSARILY THE NEWS, THE ★★★★

DIR: John Moffitt, Holte C. Caston. **CAST:** Anne Bloom, Danny Breen, Rich Hall, Mitchell Laurance, Stuart Pankin, Lucy Webb.

A first-rate collection of some of the wittiest and funniest moments from the HBO comedy series, which satirizes network news and its commercials. Bits range from cerebral to pure slapstick as the zany cast covers everything from Reagan to feminine hygiene products. Unrated. 1988; 57m.

BEST OF SPIKE JONES, VOLUMES 1 & 2, THE ★★★

DIR: Bud Yorkin. **CAST:** Spike Jones & His City Slickers, Earl Bennett, Billy Barty.

Compilations from Jones's 1954 TV show, these tapes are a nostalgic record of the star's manic comedy style. There are truly funny, if sporadic, moments. Jones's humor derived from comedically destroying a well-known piece of music with outrageous sight and sound gags. He and his band, the City Slickers, had a successful live show in the early 1940s, as well as a hit radio show, which produced two memorable songs: "Der Fuehrer's Face"(1942) and "Cocktails for Two" (1944). 1954; B&W; 51 and 53 minutes.

BEST OF THE BIG LAFF OFF, THE ★★★½

DIR: Various. **CAST:** Eddie Murphy, Sandra Bernhard, Ronn Lucas, Harry Anderson, Mike Davis, Steve Mittleman, Paul Rodriguez, David Steinberg.

Hundreds of hungry comics have competed in the annual Laff Off contests around the country. This collection features more losers than winners, although Paul Rodriguez, Harry Anderson, Sandra Bernhard, and an already shocking, green but confident 19-year-old Eddie Murphy appear. David Steinberg ties the performance clips together with a mixture of warmth and wit. Rated R for language. 1983; 60m.

BEST OF THE FESTIVAL OF CLAYMATION, THE ★★

DIR: Will Vinton. **CAST:** Animated.

A visually stunning but unfulfilling and overlong collection of Claymation shorts. Claymation is the word coined by Will Vinton to describe the cartoon animation of sculpted clay (the singing raisins from the TV ad are examples). The framing story is good, lampooning film critics Gene Siskel and Roger Ebert, and the "Dinosaur" short is entertaining. The film's limited scope, however, inhibits it from becoming more than a simple showcase of effects. Unrated. 1987; 53m.

BEST OF TIMES, THE ★★★

DIR: Roger Spottiswoode. **CAST:** Robin Williams, Kurt Russell, Pamela Reed, Holly Palance, Donald Moffat, Margaret Whitton, M. Emmet Walsh, R. G. Armstrong, Dub Taylor.

This comedy starts off well, then continues to lose momentum right up to the *Rocky*-style ending. That said, it is an amiable enough little movie which benefits from likable performances by its lead players. Robin Williams and Kurt Russell star as two former football players who dropped the ball when their moment for hometown glory came and went. But they get a second chance to win one for the folks in Taft (formerly Moron), California. Rated PG-13 for profanity and suggested sex. 1986; 100m.

BETTE MIDLER'S MONDO BEYONDO ★★★★
DIR: Thomas Schlamme. **CAST:** Bette Midler, Bill Irwin.

Bette Midler has created another outrageous and hilarious character: an Italian sexpot who is hostess to a cable variety show. The avant-garde performers who support her are a delight. Trivia note: Midler's husband is one of the Kipper Kids. 1988; 60m.

BETTER LATE THAN NEVER ★★½
DIR: Richard Crenna. **CAST:** Harold Gould, Larry Storch, Strother Martin, Tyne Daly, Harry Morgan, Victor Buono, George Gobel, Donald Pleasence, Lou Jacobi.

Your average made-for-television comedy about a motley mixture of nursing home inhabitants who revolt against house rules that limit their freedom. The premise is good, the execution so-so. Theft of a train is a nice touch. Rated PG. 1979; 100m.

BETTER OFF DEAD ★★
DIR: Savage Steve Holland. **CAST:** John Cusack, David Ogden Stiers, Diane Franklin, Kim Darby, Amanda Wyss.

A mixture of clever ideas and awfully silly ones, this comedy focuses on the plight of teenage Everyman, Lance Meyer (John Cusack), who finds his world shattered when the love of his life, Beth (Amanda Wyss), takes up with a conceited jock. Lance figures he is "Better Off Dead" than Bethless. The film is at its best when writer-director Savage Steve Holland throws in little sketches that stand out from the familiar plot. Little gems of hilarity scattered throughout. Rated PG for profanity. 1985; 97m.

BETWEEN THE LINES ★★★★
DIR: Joan Micklin Silver. **CAST:** John Heard, Jeff Goldblum, Lindsay Crouse, Stephen Collins, Jill Eikenberry, Bruno Kirby, Gwen Welles, Lewis J. Stadlen, Jon Korkes, Michael J. Pollard, Lane Smith, Joe Morton, Richard Cox, Marilu Henner.

Very good post-Sixties film in the tradition of *Return of the Secaucus 7* and *The Big Chill*. Staff of a once-underground newspaper has to come to terms with the paper's purchase by a large publisher. Superb ensemble acting. Rated R for profanity and nudity. 1977; 101m.

BEVERLY HILLBILLIES, THE (TELEVISION SERIES) ★★★
DIR: Ralph Levy. **CAST:** Buddy Ebsen, Irene Ryan, Donna Douglas, Max Baer, Raymond Bailey, Nancy Kulp.

Selected episodes from the long-running TV series. The gags, corny but effective, lampoon everything from banks to doctors to Hollywood studios to wealthy matrons. The immensely popular series was finally canceled not because of sagging ratings but because CBS decided to upgrade its network image. 1962–1971; three 30-minute episodes per cassette.

BEYOND THERAPY ★★
DIR: Robert Altman. **CAST:** Julie Hagerty, Jeff Goldblum, Glenda Jackson, Tom Conti, Christopher Guest, Cris Campion.

Robert Altman is a hit-and-miss director and his *Beyond Therapy* (adapted from Christopher Durang's play) qualifies as a miss. The movie, which pokes fun at psychiatrists and their patients, really is a mess filled with unconnected episodes. Most of the performances and much of the dialogue are salvageable and hilarious, however. Most notable are Tom Conti and, as a bizarre psychiatrist, Glenda

Jackson. Cris Campion as a brooding, ponytailed waiter is humorous in a sensually mysterious way. Rated R. 1987; 93m.

BIG ★★★★
DIR: Penny Marshall. **CAST:** Tom Hanks, Elizabeth Perkins, Robert Loggia, John Heard, Jared Rushton, David Moscow.

This endearing fantasy is enlivened by a deft performance from Tom Hanks and an unusually intelligent script from Gary Ross and Anne Spielberg (one of the few in this genre, in fact, which has the *chutzpah* to resolve itself properly). Hanks stars as the "big person" embodiment of young David Moscow, who wishes for a creaky amusement-park fortune-telling machine to make him "big." Hanks, as the result, performs brilliantly as the 13-year-old in a 35-year-old body; he's ably assisted by spunky Elizabeth Perkins as an associate at the children's toy company (what else?) where he's able to land a job. Forget all the other soul-transference films that sprouted in late 1987 and early 1988; this is the only one that matters. Rated PG-13 for mild sexual themes. 1988; 102m.

BIG BET, THE ★
DIR: Bert I. Gordon. **CAST:** Lance Sloane, Kimberley Evanson, Sylvia Kristel, Ron Thomas.

Lurid sex comedy that tries to cash in on the high-school-film craze. Lance Sloane portrays a sex-starved teenage stud who makes a bet that he can score with the new girl in a week. Unrated, this film contains nudity, sexual situations, and some strong language. 1985; 90m.

BIG BUS, THE ★★★
DIR: James Frawley. **CAST:** Joseph Bologna, Stockard Channing, John Beck, Lynn Redgrave, José Ferrer, Ruth Gordon, Richard B. Shull, Sally Kellerman, Ned Beatty, Richard Mulligan, Larry Hagman, Howard Hesseman, Harold Gould.

A super-luxurious nuclear-powered bus runs into trouble while carrying a group of misfits from New York to Denver. This spoof of disaster movies appeared four years before *Airplane!* It's not as funny or as tightly paced, but it does have a silly and sarcastic playfulness that grows on you. One of those few films that work better on the small screen. Rated PG. 1976; 88m.

BIG BUSINESS ★★★½
DIR: Jim Abrahams. **CAST:** Bette Midler, Lily Tomlin, Fred Ward, Edward Herrmann, Michele Placido, Daniel Gerroll, Barry Primus, Michael Gross, Deborah Rush, Nicolas Coster.

Bette Midler and Lily Tomlin play two sets of mismatched twins, one raised in a West Virginia country setting and another accustomed to wealth and power in New York City. Despite the unoriginal, one-joke plot, the stars manage some genuinely hysterical moments. Rated PG for light profanity. 1988; 95m.

BIG CITY COMEDY ★★
DIR: Mark Warren. **CAST:** John Candy, Billy Crystal, McLean Stevenson, Martin Mull, Tim Kazurinsky, Fred Willard.

This is a compilation of skits from a 1980 John Candy syndicated TV series. Even with funny guys Billy Crystal, Martin Mull, and Tim Kazurinsky on hand as guests, this is a disappointing tape. Candy can be very funny but, unfortunately, not here. He is quite a sight to behold as Queen Victoria, but you can see that on the cassette box. 1986; 56m.

BIG GAG, THE ★
DIR: Yuda Barkan, Igal Shilon. **CAST:** Danuta, Caroline Langford.

This adult version of *Candid Camera* is an exercise in boredom. Supposed comedy skits and practical jokes focus on flirting nuns, testing a new deodorant, a woman in a very short skirt soliciting help, a woman who pinches men in public. Humiliating people in public places and rude, obnoxious behavior is not our idea of humor. PG-13. 1988; 87m.

BIG MOUTH, THE ★★
DIR: Jerry Lewis. **CAST:** Jerry Lewis, Harold J. Stone.

The bloom was off the rose by this point in Jerry Lewis's solo career, and this standard gangster comedy is a profound disappointment. Title character Jerry (an apt description in a film where everybody shouts all the time) gets involved in a witless search for stolen diamonds. Lewis's character bits and attempts at disguise are pretty flimsy. For true fans only. 1967; 107m.

BIG SHOTS ★★★½
DIR: Robert Mandel. **CAST:** Ricky Busker, Darius McCrary, Robert Joy, Robert Prosky, Paul Winfield, Jerzy Skolimowski.

A funny and exciting film about kids, but not just for kids. After the death of his father, an 11-year-old boy from the suburbs strikes up a friendship with a young black boy who teaches him the ways of the street. Rated PG-13. 1988; 91m.

BIG STORE, THE ★★
DIR: Charles F. Riesner. **CAST:** The Marx Brothers, Tony Martin, Virginia Grey, Margaret Dumont, Douglass Dumbrille.

Singer (and nonactor) Tony Martin inherits a department store and calls on the Marx Brothers to save him from swindler Douglass Dumbrille. The last and weakest of the Marx Brothers' movies for MGM, this misfire is woefully understocked in laughs. Even so, Groucho manages some good bits, often in scenes with his classic foil, Margaret Dumont, and Chico and Harpo team for a delightful piano duet. 1941; 103m.

BIG TALK ★★
DIR: Amy Heckerling. **CAST:** John Travolta, Kirstie Alley, Olympia Dukakis.

Would someone please tell John Travolta to wipe that goofy look off his face? Perhaps that's why Kirstie Alley fights off his attentions for so long in this moderately funny tale of a single woman who decides to go it alone and raise a child in New York. Alley is impressive as the independent mother battling intrusive help from cab driver Travolta and her mother (Olympia Dukakis). Bruce Willis has the most demanding role of his career as the voice of spermatozoa. Not rated. 1989; 110m.

BIG TOP PEE-WEE ★★
DIR: Randal Kleiser. **CAST:** Pee-wee Herman, Kris Kristofferson, Susan Tyrrell, Valeria Golino.

Pee-wee Herman plays a simple country bumpkin whose greatest pleasure in life is his pet hog. The circus comes to town, and when local folks protest, Pee-wee invites them to pitch the Big Top on his land. Film contains the longest kiss in screen history. Rated PG for hog and human love rites. 1988; 86m.

BIG TROUBLE ★★
DIR: John Cassavetes. **CAST:** Peter Falk, Alan Arkin, Beverly D'Angelo, Charles Durning, Robert Stack, Paul Dooley, Valerie Curtin, Richard Libertini.

Big Trouble has its moments, but alas, they are few and far between. Alan Arkin is an honest insurance salesman trying to put his three talented sons through Yale. When he meets up with a rich married woman (Beverly D'Angelo), the two plot against her husband (Peter Falk). Crazy plot twists abound, but none of them are all that funny. Rated R for profanity and adult subject matter. 1985; 93m.

BILL COSBY: 49 ★★★½
DIR: David Lewis, Camille Cosby. **CAST:** Bill Cosby.

This recorded stage performance is a perfect follow-up to Bill Cosby's hugely entertaining *Bill Cosby—Himself*. It reflects the years that have passed since his earlier video, which dealt with childbirth and child rearing. Now we get Cosby's special insight into the everyday adventures of advancing into middle age. This master funnyman does not disappoint. 1987; 67m.

BILL COSBY—HIMSELF ★★★★
DIR: William H. Cosby Jr. **CAST:** Bill Cosby.

The wit and wisdom of Bill Cosby on the subjects of childbirth, raising a family (and being raised), going to the dentist, taking drugs and drinking, and life in general provide laughs and food for thought in this excellent comedy video. One can see how the hugely successful television series *The Cosby Show* evolved from his family and observations of their behavior. Rated G. 1985; 104m.

BILLY CRYSTAL: A COMIC'S LINE ★★★★
DIR: Bruce Gowers. **CAST:** Billy Crystal.

This HBO special released on tape features an innovative and very funny performance by Billy Crystal. Using the premise of a Broadway musical audition, he presents various characters trying out for the part. There is also an amusing yet wonderfully warm sequence with Crystal as a small boy being left at home for the first time. He shows much more than just a flair for comedy and timing. 1984; 59m.

BILLY CRYSTAL: DON'T GET ME STARTED ★★★
DIR: Paul Flaherty, Billy Crystal. **CAST:** Billy Crystal, Rob Reiner, Christopher Guest, Eugene Levy, Brother Theodore.

In the first part of this video, Rob Reiner takes the role of interviewer in a "yockumentary" on the making of a Billy Crystal special. Eugene Levy is manager and promoter, and Crystal shows up as Sammy Davis Jr., Whoopi Goldberg, and himself as they attempt to show us what happens behind the scenes prior to showtime. The second half is the actual live performance with Crystal inviting Fernando ("You look mahvelous!") to the stage. 1986; 60m.

BILOXI BLUES ★★★★
DIR: Mike Nichols. **CAST:** Matthew Broderick, Christopher Walken, Matt Mulhern, Casey Siemaszko.

As second in Neil Simon's loosely autobiographical trilogy (after *Brighton Beach Memoirs*), this witty glimpse of growing up in a Deep South World War II boot camp stars Matthew Broderick as Simon's observant alter ego. When not clashing with Christopher Walken's sly drill sergeant or learning about the birds and bees from an amused wartime prostitute, Broderick makes perceptive comments about life, the war, and his army buddies. Rated PG-13 for language and sexual themes. 1988; 106m.

BINGO LONG TRAVELING ALL-STARS AND MOTOR KINGS, THE ★★★
DIR: John Badham. **CAST:** Billy Dee Williams, James Earl Jones, Richard Pryor, Ted Ross.

This is a comedy-adventure of a barnstorming group of black baseball players as they tour rural America in the late 1930s. Billy Dee Williams, Richard Pryor, and James Earl Jones are three of the team's players and must resort to conniving, clowning, and conning to ensure their team's survival. Only the lack of a cohesive script keeps this from receiving more stars. Rated PG. 1976; 110m.

BIRDS AND THE BEES, THE ★★
DIR: Norman Taurog. **CAST:** George Gobel, Mitzi Gaynor, David Niven.

This poor remake of the 1941 Barbara Stanwyck–Henry Fonda comedy hit, *The Lady Eve*, has military cardsharp David Niven setting daughter Mitzi Gaynor on playboy millionaire George Gobel in hopes of getting rich from the marriage. "Lonesome George" wiggles free, but falls for her anyway. Don't settle for imitations. Insist on the original. 1956; 94m.

BIRTHDAY BOY, THE ★★
DIR: Claude Conrad. **CAST:** James Belushi, Michelle Riga, Dennis Fa-

rina, Ron Dean, Jim Johnson, Ed Blatchford, Fred Kaz.

A Cinemax Comedy Experiment that proves once again how difficult it is to produce an even moderately funny film. James Belushi (who also wrote the script) is a sporting-goods salesman who journeys cross-country on his birthday in an attempt to sell his old gym coach a load of basketballs. Unrated, but contains adult language. 1986; 30m.

BISHOP'S WIFE, THE ★★★

DIR: Henry Koster. **CAST:** Cary Grant, Loretta Young, David Niven, James Gleason.

Harmless story of debonair angel (Cary Grant) sent to Earth to aid a bishop (David Niven) in his quest for a new church. The kind of film they just don't make anymore. No rating, but okay for the whole family. 1947; B&W; 108m.

BLACK BIRD, THE ★★★

DIR: David Giler. **CAST:** George Segal, Stéphane Audran, Lionel Stander, Lee Patrick.

Surprisingly enjoyable comedy produced by and starring George Segal as Sam Spade Jr. The visual gags abound, and an air of authenticity is added by the performances of 1940s detective film regulars Lionel Stander, Elisha Cook, and Lee Patrick. The latter two co-starred with Humphrey Bogart in *The Maltese Falcon*, on which the film is based. It's funny, with a strong performance from Segal. Rated PG. 1975; 98m.

BLACKSMITH, THE/COPS ★★★½

DIR: Buster Keaton. **CAST:** Buster Keaton, Virginia Fox.

Two shining examples of deadpan silent comedian Buster Keaton at his best. What he does to a white luxury limo in *The Blacksmith* is a hilarious crime. His antics in *Cops* bid fair to prove him Chaplin's master. The chase scene is a classic of timing and invention. Silent. 1922; B&W; 38m.

BLAME IT ON RIO ★★½

DIR: Stanley Donen. **CAST:** Michael Caine, Joseph Bologna, Valerie Harper, Michelle Johnson.

A middle-aged male sex fantasy directed by Stanley Donen (*Lucky Lady*; *Charade*), this film—which equally combines both good and bad elements—features Michael Caine as a befuddled fellow who finds himself involved in an affair with the teenage daughter (Michelle Johnson) of his best friend (Joseph Bologna). Although essentially in bad taste, *Blame It on Rio* does have a number of very funny moments. Rated R for nudity, profanity, and suggested sex. 1984; 110m.

BLAZING SADDLES ★★★½

DIR: Mel Brooks. **CAST:** Cleavon Little, Gene Wilder, Harvey Korman, Madeline Kahn, Mel Brooks, Slim Pickens.

Mel Brooks directed this sometimes hilarious, mostly crude spoof of westerns. The jokes come with machine-gun rapidity, and the stars race around like maniacs. If it weren't in such bad taste, it would be perfect for the kiddies. Rated R. 1974; 93m.

BLIND DATE

DIR: Blake Edwards. **CAST:** Bruce Willis, Kim Basinger, John Larroquette, William Daniels, George Coe, Mark Blum, Phil Hartman.

A tasteless exercise in slapstick that sends Bruce Willis (in his film debut) on a last-minute blind date with Kim Basinger, an attractively gift-wrapped bundle that comes with one explicit instruction: do not let her drink. Naturally, Willis can't wait to pour champagne down her throat. By way of retribution, Willis loses his job, his car, and his self-esteem, and we lose our patience with the forced, mind-numbing attempts at physical humor. Rated PG-13 for adult situations. 1987; 93m.

BLISS ★★★★
DIR: Ray Lawrence. **CAST:** Barry Otto, Lynette Curran, Helen Jones, Jeff Truman.

In this biting black comedy from Australia, a business executive (Barry Otto) nearly dies from a heart attack. By managing to survive, he finds himself in a hellish version of the life he once had. Not everyone will appreciate this nightmarish vision of modern life, but it is one of the most original motion pictures of recent years. Rated R. 1986; 93m.

BLOCK-HEADS ★★★★
DIR: John G. Blystone. **CAST:** Stan Laurel, Oliver Hardy, Patricia Ellis, Minna Gombell, Billy Gilbert, James Finlayson.

Twenty years after the end of World War I, Stan Laurel is discovered still guarding a bunker. He returns to a veterans' home, where Oliver Hardy comes to visit and take him to dinner. A well-crafted script provides the perfect setting for the boys' escapades. Their characters have seldom been used as well in feature films. 1938; B&W; 55m.

BLOODBATH AT THE HOUSE OF DEATH ★★
DIR: Ray Cameron. **CAST:** Vincent Price, Kenny Everett, Pamela Stephenson, Gareth Hunt, Don Warrington, John Fortune, Sheila Steafel.

Although advertised as one, this British movie is not all that much of a spoof on horror films. There is realistic gore (especially in the opening scene, where the film lives up to its not-so-ironic title), and near the film's end the camp antics turn serious. In the story, a team of paranormal specialists investigates a house that was the scene of a mysterious massacre. Vincent Price plays a nutty devil worshiper who plots to get rid of the snoopy scientists who are inhabiting this house of Satan. Not rated, but equivalent to an R for violence, gore, sex, nudity, and profanity. 1985; 92m.

BLOOPERS FROM STAR TREK AND LAUGH-IN ★★½
DIR: Various. **CAST:** William Shatner, Leonard Nimoy, DeForest Kelley, Dan Rowan, Dick Martin, Martin Milner, Kent McCord, Sammy Davis Jr., Dean Martin.

Don't try to explain the melding of these two television shows. Just sit back and enjoy the *Star Trek* bloopers and ignore the *Laugh-In* gaffes. It's genuinely funny to see the unemotional Spock (Leonard Nimoy) dissolve into laughter when he walks into one of the sliding *Enterprise* doors that is supposed to open smoothly at his approach. *Rowan and Martin's Laugh-In* depended on its topicality for humor, and many of the bloopers will leave people of the Eighties wondering what was so funny about this Sixties telehit. 1966; 26m.

BLUE IGUANA ★★
DIR: John Lafia. **CAST:** Dylan McDermott, Jessica Harper, James Russo, Tovah Feldshuh, Dean Stockwell.

For his first film, writer-director John Lafia attempted a *Raising Arizona*–style spoof of the hard-boiled detective story—and failed. The story concerns a "recovery specialist" (Dylan McDermott) who is coerced by IRS agents Tovah Feldshuh and Dean Stockwell into going after $40 million in contraband money stored in a south-of-the-border bank. The supporting actors are allowed to overact to bizarre proportions. Rated R for violence. 1988; 90m.

BLUE MONEY ★★★
DIR: Colin Bucksey. **CAST:** Tim Curry, Debby Bishop, Billy Connolly, Frances Tomelty.

Larry Gormley (Tim Curry) discovers a suitcase with half a million dollars in his cab. The money turns out to belong to the mob, and they want it back. Not a very original idea, but well written, acted, and directed, this comedy provides plenty of fast-moving fun. Made for British television. 1984; 82m.

BLUE MOVIES ★★
DIR: Ed Fitzgerald. **CAST:** Steve Levitt, Larry Poindexter, Lucinda Crosby, Darian Mathias, Christopher Stone, Don Calfa, Larry Linville.
Poorly directed, cheaply made comedy about two young entrepreneurs and their quest to make a pornographic movie. It has some funny moments. Rated R for profanity and nudity. 1988; 92m.

BLUES BROTHERS, THE ★★★½
DIR: John Landis. **CAST:** John Belushi, Dan Aykroyd, John Candy, Carrie Fisher.
Director John Landis attempted to film an epic comedy and came pretty darn close. In it, the musicians of the title, John Belushi and Dan Aykroyd, attempt to save an orphanage. The movie's excesses—too many car crashes and chases—are offset by Belushi and Aykroyd as the Laurel and Hardy of backbeat; the musical turns of Aretha Franklin, James Brown, and Ray Charles; and Landis's flair for comic timing. Rated R. 1980; 132m.

BOARDING SCHOOL ★★★½
DIR: André Farwagi. **CAST:** Nastassja Kinski, Gerry Sundquist, Kurt Raab.
A European boarding school for girls, located next to an all-boys boarding school, creates the setting for sexual hijinks and young love in this sexy comedy. The 1956 theme is enhanced by some Bill Haley music. Rated R for nudity. 1978; 100m.

BOB & CAROL & TED & ALICE ★★★★½
DIR: Paul Mazursky. **CAST:** Natalie Wood, Robert Culp, Elliott Gould, Dyan Cannon.
In this comedy, Natalie Wood and Robert Culp (Carol and Bob) play a modern couple who believe in open marriage, pot-smoking, etc. Their friends, conservative Elliott Gould and Dyan Cannon (Ted and Alice), are shocked by Bob and Carol's behavior. Meanwhile, Bob and Carol try to liven up Ted and Alice's marriage by introducing them to their way of life. Lots of funny moments. Rated R. 1969; 104m.

BOB & RAY, JANE, LARAINE & GILDA ★★★
DIR: Dave Wilson. **CAST:** Bob Elliott, Ray Goulding, Jane Curtin, Laraine Newman, Gilda Radner, Willie Nelson.
The low-key humor of Bob & Ray takes center-stage in this summer replacement special from the *Saturday Night Live* folks. As far as these two fellows are concerned, you either love 'em or hate 'em. If routines like "House of Toast," in which Bob & Ray introduce a restaurant that specializes in you-know-what, or a deadpan reading of the lyrics of Rod Stewart's "If You Think I'm Sexy" by the middle-aged humorists sound like fun to you, this is the tape you've been waiting for. 1979; 75m.

BOBO, THE ★
DIR: Robert Parrish. **CAST:** Peter Sellers, Britt Ekland, Rossano Brazzi.
A bumbling matador (Peter Sellers) has to seduce a high-priced courtesan (Britt Ekland) in order to get employment as a singer. If this plot sounds stupid, then you have reached the core of this hopeless movie. 1967; 105m.

BOHEMIAN GIRL, THE ★★★
DIR: James W. Horne, Charles Rogers. **CAST:** Stan Laurel, Oliver Hardy, Thelma Todd, Antonio Moreno.
Laurel and Hardy portray gypsies in this typical tale of the gypsy band versus the country officials. A variety of misadventures occur, and the film is entertaining, especially with the hilarious scene of Stan attempting to fill wine bottles and becoming more and more inebriated. 1936; B&W; 70m.

BONNIE SCOTLAND ★★★
DIR: James W. Horne. **CAST:** Stan Laurel, Oliver Hardy, James Finlayson, June Vlasek (June Lang), William Janney.
Stan Laurel and Oliver Hardy venture to Scotland so that Stan can reap a "major" inheritance—which turns out

to be merely bagpipes and a snuffbox. By mistake, they join the army and are sent to India, where they help to quell a native uprising. The thin plot offers the boys an opportunity to play off each other's strengths: Ollie's reactions and Stan's fantasy world that keeps becoming reality. 1935; B&W; 80m.

BORN IN EAST L.A. ★★★½

DIR: Richard "Cheech" Marin. **CAST:** Richard "Cheech" Marin, Daniel Stern, Paul Rodriguez, Jan-Michael Vincent.

Cheech, minus Chong, had a surprise box-office hit with this comedy, which started off as a video takeoff of Bruce Springsteen's "Born in the U.S.A." While not a comedy classic, this low-budget film has a number of funny moments. Rated R for profanity. 1987; 85m.

BORN YESTERDAY ★★★★½

DIR: George Cukor. **CAST:** Judy Holliday, William Holden, Broderick Crawford, Howard St. John.

Judy Holliday is simply delightful as a dizzy dame who isn't as dizzy as everyone thinks she is, in this comedy directed by George Cukor. William Holden is the professor hired by a junk-dealer-made-good (Broderick Crawford) to give Holliday lessons in how to be "high-toned." The results are highly entertaining—and very funny. 1950; B&W; 103m.

BOSS' WIFE, THE ★★★½

DIR: Ziggy Steinberg. **CAST:** Daniel Stern, Christopher Plummer, Arielle Dombasle, Fisher Stevens, Melanie Mayron, Martin Mull.

After the first twenty minutes, this comedy starts rolling. Daniel Stern and Melanie Mayron play Joel and Janet, a two-career couple trying to make time for a baby. When Joel's boss (Christopher Plummer) finally notices him, he expects Joel to spend the weekend at the company resort where he will compete with slick, sleazy Tony (Martin Mull) for a coveted promotion. Laughs abound when Joel is pursued by the boss's nymphomaniac wife (beautiful Arielle Dombasle). Rated R for nudity, obscenities and sexual situations. 1986; 83m.

BOY, DID I GET A WRONG NUMBER!

DIR: George Marshall. **CAST:** Bob Hope, Elke Sommer, Phyllis Diller.

When you get a wrong number, hang up and dial again. Too bad the cast and director didn't. This one is a bomb! 1966; 99m.

BRAZIL ★★★★

DIR: Terry Gilliam. **CAST:** Jonathan Pryce, Robert De Niro, Katherine Helmond, Ian Holm, Bob Hoskins, Michael Palin, Ian Richardson.

A savage blend of *1984* and *The Time Bandits* from Monty Python director Terry Gilliam. Jonathan Pryce stars as a bemused paper shuffler in a red tape–choked future society at the brink of collapsing under its own bureaucracy. Definitely not for all tastes, but a treat for those with an appreciation for social satire. Were it not for a chaotic conclusion and slightly overlong running time, this would be a perfect picture. Rated R for language and adult situations. 1985; 131m.

BREAKFAST CLUB, THE ★★★★

DIR: John Hughes. **CAST:** Emilio Estevez, Molly Ringwald, Paul Gleason, Anthony Michael Hall, Ally Sheedy.

A group of assorted high-school misfits gets to be friends while serving weekend detention in this terrific comedy, directed by John Hughes, the king of watchable teen films. Rated R. 1985; 100m.

BREAKFAST IN HOLLYWOOD ★½

DIR: Harold Schuster. **CAST:** Bonita Granville, Beulah Bondi, Tom Breneman.

This is a romantic comedy based on the radio series of the same name. The plot is thin, but there are some nice musical moments from Nat King Cole and Spike Jones. On radio it's fine.

On film, the imagination is gone. 1946; B&W; 91m.

BREAKING ALL THE RULES ★
DIR: James Orr. **CAST:** Carl Marotte, Thor Bishorpric, Carolyn Dunn.

Typical teen sex comedy. This time four teenagers look for love (translation: lust) and adventure on the last day of summer vacation. They find both at an amusement park when they become involved with a gang of jewel thieves. Rated R for profanity and nudity. 1984; 91m.

BREAKING AWAY ★★★★★
DIR: Peter Yates. **CAST:** Dennis Christopher, Dennis Quaid, Daniel Stern, Jackie Earle Haley.

There comes a time in every young man's life when he must loose the ties of home, family, and friends and test his mettle. Dennis Christopher is the young man who retains an innocence we too often mistake for naïveté; Paul Dooley and Barbara Barrie are the often humorously confused parents who offer subtle, sure guidance. This is a warm portrayal of family life and love, of friendships, of growing up and growing away. Rated PG for brief profanity. 1979; 100m.

BREATH OF SCANDAL, A ★★
DIR: Michael Curtiz. **CAST:** Sophia Loren, John Gavin, Maurice Chevalier, Angela Lansbury.

This intended high-style romantic comedy set in Austria in the gossip-rife court of Franz Joseph has little going for it. Beautiful princess scorns mama's wish that she marry a prince. Instead, encouraged by papa, she conveniently opts for a visiting American mining engineer. The script, taken from the Molnar play that poor John Gilbert adapted for his disastrous first talkie, is uninspired. The casting is uninspired. The directing is uninspired. But the scenery and costumes are nice. 1960; 98m.

BREWSTER MCCLOUD ★★★
DIR: Robert Altman. **CAST:** Bud Cort, Sally Kellerman.

If you liked Robert Altman's *M*A*S*H* (the movie) and *Harold and Maude*, and your humor lies a few degrees off-center, you'll enjoy this "flight of fantasy" about a boy (Bud Cort) who wants to make like a bird. Rated R. 1970; 104m.

BREWSTER'S MILLIONS (1945) ★★½
DIR: Allan Dwan. **CAST:** Dennis O'Keefe, Helen Walker, June Havoc, Mischa Auer, Eddie "Rochester" Anderson, Gail Patrick.

This is the fifth of seven film versions of the 1902 novel and stage success about a young man who will inherit millions if he is able to spend $1 million quickly and quietly within a set period of time. Dennis O'Keefe and company perform this Tinsel Town stalwart in fine fashion, making for a bright, entertaining comic romp. 1945; B&W; 79m.

BREWSTER'S MILLIONS (1985) ★★★
DIR: Walter Hill. **CAST:** Richard Pryor, John Candy, Lonette McKee, Stephen Collins, Pat Hingle, Tovah Feldshuh, Hume Cronyn.

It took director Walter Hill to bring Richard Pryor out of his movie slump with this unspectacular, but still entertaining, comedy about a minor-league baseball player who stands to inherit $300 million if he can fulfill the provisions of a rather daffy will. It's no classic, but still much, much better than *The Toy* or *Superman III*. Rated PG for profanity. 1985; 97m.

BRIGHTON BEACH MEMOIRS ★★★½
DIR: Gene Saks. **CAST:** Jonathan Silverman, Blythe Danner, Bob Dishy, Brian Drillinger, Stacey Glick, Judith Ivey, Lisa Waltz.

Neil Simon's reminiscences of his adolescence make for genuinely enjoyable viewing. Refreshingly free of Simon's often too-clever dialogue, it aims for the heart and, more often than not, hits its mark. Rated PG-13 for sexual references. 1986; 110m.

BRINGING UP BABY ★★★★★
DIR: Howard Hawks. **CAST:** Cary Grant, Katharine Hepburn, Charlie Ruggles, May Robson.

A classic screwball comedy, this Howard Hawks picture has lost none of its punch even after fifty years. Katharine Hepburn plays a daffy rich girl who gets an absentminded professor (Cary Grant) into all sorts of trouble. *Bringing Up Baby* is guaranteed to have you falling out of your seat with helpless laughter. 1938; B&W; 102m.

BRINKS JOB, THE ★★★½
DIR: William Friedkin. **CAST:** Peter Falk, Peter Boyle, Allen Garfield, Warren Oates, Paul Sorvino, Gena Rowlands.

Peter Falk stars in this enjoyable release in which a gang of klutzy crooks pulls off "the crime of the century." It's a breezy caper film reminiscent of George Roy Hill's *Butch Cassidy and the Sundance Kid* and *The Sting*. Rated PG. 1978; 103m.

BRITANNIA HOSPITAL ★★★
DIR: Lindsay Anderson. **CAST:** Leonard Rossiter, Graham Crowden, Malcolm McDowell, Joan Plowright.

A wildly inadequate hospital serves as a metaphor for a sick society in this okay black comedy by British director Lindsay Anderson (*If; O Lucky Man*). Rated R. 1982; 115m.

BROADCAST NEWS ★★★★★
DIR: James L. Brooks. **CAST:** William Hurt, Albert Brooks, Holly Hunter, Jack Nicholson, Robert Prosky, Joan Cusack.

Writer-director-producer James L. Brooks tackles the flashy emptiness of contemporary television journalism and takes no hostages. William Hurt stars as the coming trend in news anchors—all enthusiasm and no education—who clashes amiably with Albert Brooks as the reporter's reporter: blessed with insight and a clever turn of phrase, but no camera presence. Both are attracted to dedicated superproducer Holly Hunter, an overachiever who schedules brief nervous breakdowns into her workday. Deft scripting and superb performances are just a few of the attractions in this great film. Not to be missed. Rated R for profanity. 1987; 131m.

BROADWAY DANNY ROSE ★★★★½
DIR: Woody Allen. **CAST:** Woody Allen, Mia Farrow, Milton Berle, Sandy Baron.

The legendary talent agent Broadway Danny Rose (Woody Allen) takes on an alcoholic crooner (Nick Apollo Forte) and carefully nurtures him to the brink of stardom in this hilarious comedy, also written and directed by Allen. Mia Farrow is delightful as a gangster's moll who inadvertently gets Rose in big trouble. Rated PG for brief violence. 1984; B&W; 86m.

BRONCO BILLY ★★★
DIR: Clint Eastwood. **CAST:** Clint Eastwood, Sondra Locke, Geoffrey Lewis, Scatman Crothers, Sam Bottoms, Bill McKinney, Dan Vadis.

This warm-hearted character study centers around Clint Eastwood as Bronco Billy, the owner of a rundown Wild West show. Sondra Locke is deserted on her honeymoon by her husband (Geoffrey Lewis). Desperate, she agrees to join the show as Eastwood's assistant and that's when the lightweight tale takes a romantic turn. Rated PG. 1980; 119m.

BUCK PRIVATES ★★★
DIR: Arthur Lubin. **CAST:** Bud Abbott, Lou Costello, Lee Bowman, Alan Curtis, Jane Frazee.

Abbott and Costello are at their best in their first starring film, but it's still no classic. On the lam, the two are forced to enlist during WWII. 1941; B&W; 82m.

BUDDY, BUDDY ★★
DIR: Billy Wilder. **CAST:** Jack Lemmon, Walter Matthau, Paula Prentiss, Klaus Kinski.

Jack Lemmon is a clumsy would-be suicide who decides to end it all in a hotel. Walter Matthau is a hit man who rents the room next door and finds the filling of his contract difficult. The results are less than hilarious but do provoke a few smiles. Rated R because of profanity and brief nudity. 1981; 96m.

BULL DURHAM ★★★★

DIR: Ron Shelton. **CAST:** Kevin Costner, Susan Sarandon, Tim Robbins, Trey Wilson, Robert Wuhl.

Tim Robbins plays a rookie pitcher for a minor-league baseball team. He has a lightning-fast throw, but he's apt to hit the team mascot as often as the strike zone. Kevin Costner is a dispirited catcher brought in to "mature" Robbins. A quirky, intelligent comedy with plenty of surprises, the film contains some of the sharpest jabs at sports since *Slap Shot*. Rated R for profanity and sexual content. 1988; 104m.

BULLFIGHTERS, THE ★★★

DIR: Malcolm St. Clair. **CAST:** Stan Laurel, Oliver Hardy, Margo Woode, Richard Lane, Carol Andrews.

While not a classic, this latter-day Laurel and Hardy film is surprisingly good—especially when you consider that the boys had lost all control over the making of their pictures by this time. The story has Laurel resembling a famous bullfighter, and, of course, this leads to chaos in the ring. 1945; B&W; 61m.

BULLSHOT ★★½

DIR: Dick Clement. **CAST:** Alan Shearman, Diz White, Ron House, Frances Tomelty, Michael Aldridge.

Sometimes a movie can be fun for a while, then overstay its welcome. Such is the case with this spoof of Herman Cyril "Scapper" McNiele's *Bulldog Drummond* mystery/spy adventures. Everything is played to the hilt, and the characters go beyond stereotypes to become caricatures. Although this is occasionally irritating, the star-screenwriters do create some funny moments. Rated PG for profanity, sex, and violence. 1985; 95m.

BUNDLE OF JOY ★★★

DIR: Norman Taurog. **CAST:** Debbie Reynolds, Eddie Fisher, Adolphe Menjou, Tommy Noonan.

In this breezy remake of Ginger Rogers's *Bachelor Mother*, Debbie Reynolds portrays a department-store salesgirl who takes custody of an infant. (Eddie Fisher is suspected of being the father.) A scandal ensues. 1956; 98m.

'BURBS, THE ★★

DIR: Joe Dante. **CAST:** Tom Hanks, Bruce Dern, Carrie Fisher, Rick Ducommun, Corey Feldman, Wendy Schaal, Henry Gibson.

In this weird and ultimately unsatisfying comedy, Tom Hanks plays a suburbanite who decides to hang around the house during his vacation. He becomes more and more concerned about the bizarre family who has moved in next door. Essentially it's *Neighbors* all over again, with Hanks, Carrie Fisher, Rick Ducommun, and Bruce Dern turning in strong performances. Despite some inspired touches from director Joe Dante, it falls flat in the final third. Rated R for violence and profanity. 1989; 102m.

BURGLAR ★★★

DIR: Hugh Wilson. **CAST:** Whoopi Goldberg, Bobcat Goldthwait, G. W. Bailey, Lesley Ann Warren.

Whoopi Goldberg stars in this amiable but unspectacular caper comedy as a retired cat burglar forced back into a life of crime by a crooked cop (G. W. Bailey) who is blackmailing her. In doing his bidding, she ends up the prime suspect in a rather messy murder case. Goldberg does well in a role originally written for Bruce Willis, but one wishes she would find a comedy script tailored specifically for her impressive talents. Rated R for profanity and violence. 1987; 91m.

BUS STOP ★★★★½

DIR: Joshua Logan. **CAST:** Marilyn Monroe, Don Murray, Arthur O'Connell, Betty Field, Casey Adams.

Marilyn Monroe plays a distraught showgirl who is endlessly pursued by an oaf of a cowboy named Bo (Don Murray). He even kidnaps her when she refuses to marry him. Lots of laughs as Bo mistreats his newly found "angel." Arthur O'Connell is excellent as Verg, Bo's older and wiser friend who advises Bo on the way to treat women. 1956; 96m.

BUSTER KEATON FESTIVAL: VOL. 1 ★★★
DIR: Buster Keaton, Eddie Cline, Malcolm St. Clair. **CAST:** Buster Keaton, Virginia Fox, Joe Roberts, Eddie Cline.
The legendary Buster Keaton shines in these three short slapstick comedies first released in the roaring 1920s: *Paleface*, *The Blacksmith*, and *Cops*. The last, in particular, is a gem of silent-film shenanigans contrived around Keaton's pursuit by an entire city police force. 1921–1922; B&W; 55m.

BUSTER KEATON FESTIVAL: VOL. 2 ★★★
DIR: Buster Keaton, Eddie Cline. **CAST:** Buster Keaton, Sybil Seely, Eddie Cline, Bonnie Hill, Freeman Wood, Joe Roberts, Virginia Fox, Joseph Keaton, Myra Keaton, Louise Keaton.
Conjuring warm silent-comedy memories, the unique Buster Keaton cavorts sublimely in this trio of short features: *The Boat*, *The Frozen North*, and *The Electric House*. The titles alone indicate the hilarious mayhem and madness that fill the screen. The premise of the third film is priceless, the technical execution pure genius. 1921–1922; B&W; 55m.

BUSTER KEATON FESTIVAL: VOL. 3 ★★★
DIR: Buster Keaton, Eddie Cline. **CAST:** Buster Keaton, Virginia Fox, Phyllis Haver, Renée Adorée, Joe Roberts.
Another hilarious collection of Keaton's slapstick comedies: *Daydreams*, *The Balloonatic*, and *The Garage*. Keaton at the mercy of a folding boat in a raging river in *The Balloonatic* is outstanding. Good, clean fun, all around. 1921–1922; B&W; 54m.

BUSTER KEATON SCRAPBOOK, VOL. I ★★★★
DIR: Buster Keaton. **CAST:** Buster Keaton, Eddie Cline.
The Paleface, *Daydreams*, *The Blacksmith*—three silent-comedy gems from the fertile mind of one of film's most inventive and innovative actor-directors. Standout scenes include the paddle-wheel sequence in *Daydreams*, and the magnet and Rolls-Royce destruction in *The Blacksmith*. 1921–1922; B&W; 58m.

BUSTER KEATON: THE GOLDEN YEARS ★★★
DIR: Buster Keaton, Eddie Cline. **CAST:** Buster Keaton, Joe Roberts, Renée Adorée, Virginia Fox.
The incomparable "Great Stone Face" Buster Keaton and his often imperious and domineering co-star Joe Roberts once more create good, clean laughter in three of Keaton's early silents: *The Paleface*, *Daydreams*, and *The Blacksmith*. The viewer is double-dared to keep a straight face. Great, timeless, nostalgic movie memories for everyone. Silent with musical score. 1921–1922; B&W; 60m.

BUSTER KEATON: THE GREAT STONE FACE ★★★½
DIR: Buster Keaton. **CAST:** Buster Keaton, Roscoe "Fatty" Arbuckle, Mabel Normand, Phyllis Haver, Marlon Mack, Joseph Keaton, Al St. John.
Narrated by comedian Henry Morgan, this roundup brings together these Keaton classics: *Daydreams*, *Cops*, *The Balloonatic*, *The General*, and *Fatty at Coney Island*. Gags in *Cops* and *The General* alone document the genius of the Great Stone Face. 1968; B&W; 60m.

BUSTIN' LOOSE ★★½
DIR: Oz Scott. **CAST:** Richard Pryor, Cicely Tyson, Robert Christian, Alphonso Alexander, Janet Wong.
You take super-bad ex-con Richard Pryor, stick him on a school bus with goody-two-shoes teacher Cicely Tyson and eight ornery schoolchildren, and what have you got? A cross-country, comic odyssey as long as the bus is rolling and Pryor is up to his madcap antics. But *Bustin' Loose* bogs down in its last half-hour. Rated R for profanity and violence. 1981; 94m.

BUY AND CELL ★
DIR: Robert Boris. **CAST:** Robert Carradine, Michael Winslow, Randall "Tex" Cobb, Fred Travalena, Ben Vereen, Malcolm McDowell.
Robert Carradine stars as a Wall Street broker who takes the rap for his boss's insider trading. While in the slammer, he enlists the help of a ragtag group of prisoners, and together they form a company and get rich. Some funny bits, but this is mostly an overblown screwball comedy. Rated R. 1989; 91m.

CACTUS FLOWER ★★★
DIR: Gene Saks. **CAST:** Walter Matthau, Ingrid Bergman, Goldie Hawn.
Watch this one for Goldie Hawn's performance that earned her an Academy Award as best supporting actress. She's the slightly wonky girlfriend of dentist Walter Matthau, who actually loves his nurse (Ingrid Bergman). Although adapted from a hit Broadway play by Abe Burrows, this film version is pretty short on laughs. Ingrid Bergman is far too serious in her role, and Matthau simply doesn't make a credible dentist. Rated PG for adult situations. 1969; 103m.

CADDY, THE ★★★
DIR: Norman Taurog. **CAST:** Dean Martin, Jerry Lewis, Donna Reed, Fred Clark.
In this lesser comedy from the Martin and Lewis team the fellas enter the world of golf. Jerry plays a would-be golf pro who can't stand the attention of all the inquisitive fans. Strictly formulaic, but highlighted by several entertaining clashes between the two stars. 1953; 95m.

CADDYSHACK ★★
DIR: Harold Ramis. **CAST:** Chevy Chase, Rodney Dangerfield, Ted Knight, Michael O'Keefe, Bill Murray.
Only Rodney Dangerfield, as an obnoxious refugee from a leisure-suit collectors' convention, offers anything of value in this rip-off of the *Animal House* formula. Chevy Chase and Bill Murray sleepwalk through their poorly written roles, and Ted Knight looks a little weary of imitating his Ted Baxter routine from *The Mary Tyler Moore Show*. Rated R for nudity and sex. 1980; 99m.

CADDYSHACK II ★
DIR: Allan Arkush. **CAST:** Jackie Mason, Chevy Chase, Dan Aykroyd, Robert Stack, Dyan Cannon, Randy Quaid, Jonathan Silverman.
Deciding to pass on this abysmal sequel may be the smartest career move Rodney Dangerfield ever made. Jackie Mason is wasted in the hopelessly contrived (and unfunny) lead role of a philanthropic construction magnate who takes on the cruelly snobbish members of an exclusive country club. Even worse, Chevy Chase and Dan Aykroyd completely embarrass themselves in the kind of sappy supporting roles they once viciously lampooned on *Saturday Night Live*. Only Randy Quaid, as Mason's maniacally aggressive lawyer, adds any sparkle. Rated PG for profanity. 1988; 103m.

CALIFORNIA SUITE ★★★½
DIR: Herbert Ross. **CAST:** Jane Fonda, Alan Alda, Maggie Smith, Richard Pryor, Bill Cosby.
This enjoyable adaptation of the Neil Simon play features multiple stars.The action revolves around the various inhabitants of a Beverly Hills hotel room. We are allowed to enter

and observe the private lives of the various guests in the room during the four watchable short stories within this film. Rated PG. 1978; 103m.

CALL OUT THE MARINES ★★½
DIR: Frank Ryan. **CAST:** Victor McLaglen, Edmund Lowe, Binnie Barnes, Paul Kelly, Robert Smith, Franklin Pangborn.

The prime attraction here is the team of Victor McLaglen and Edmund Lowe in their last comedy together. As always, they play a pair of battling marine buddies, this time engaged in a rivalry over saloon singer Binnie Barnes. Several songs (by Mort Greene and Harry Revel) are no great shakes. 1942; 66m.

CAMPUS MAN ★★
DIR: Ron Casden. **CAST:** John Dye, Kim Delaney, Kathleen Wilhoite, Steve Lyon, Morgan Fairchild, Miles O'Keeffe.

In this well-intended and generally watchable movie, a college student (John Dye) produces and markets an all-male, pinup calendar and strikes it rich. His roommate (Steve Lyon) agrees to be one of the hunks of the month and ends up becoming a celebrity. Rated PG. 1987; 95m.

CAN I DO IT 'TIL I NEED GLASSES?
DIR: I. Robert Levy. **CAST:** Robin Williams, Roger Behr, Debra Klose, Moose Carlson, Walter Olkewicz.

A follow-up to *If You Don't Stop, You'll Go Blind*. A trash-heap of prehistoric naughty jokes acted out by hopped-up extras in need of a buck. Robin Williams appears for all of a minute, enough for the filmmakers to cash in on his success. Rated R for nudity and profanity. 1980; 72m.

CAN SHE BAKE A CHERRY PIE? ★★★
DIR: Henry Jaglom. **CAST:** Karen Black, Michael Emil.

Karen Black plays a woman whose husband leaves her before she has fully awakened one morning. She meets Eli, played by Michael Emil, a balding character actor whose body is slowly sliding into his knees. They're both a little neurotic, and pretty dippy in the bargain. This is a small film, and its appeal is quiet. It also is an example of what can be right with American movie-making, even when the money isn't there. No rating, but considerable vulgar language, sexual situations. 1984; 90m.

CANNERY ROW ★★★
DIR: David S. Ward. **CAST:** Nick Nolte, Debra Winger, Audra Lindley, M. Emmet Walsh, Frank McRae.

It's hard to really dislike this film, starring Nick Nolte and Debra Winger, even though it has so many problems. Despite its artificiality, halting pace, and general unevenness, there are so many marvelous moments—most provided by character actor Frank McRae as the lovable simpleton Hazel—that you don't regret having seen it. Rated PG for slight nudity, profanity, and violence. 1982; 120m.

CANNONBALL RUN ★
DIR: Hal Needham. **CAST:** Burt Reynolds, Roger Moore, Farrah Fawcett, Dom DeLuise, Dean Martin, Sammy Davis Jr.

This star-studded bore is the story of an unsanctioned, totally illegal cross-country car race in which there are no rules and few survivors. Director Hal Needham and writer Brock Yates team up once again with Burt Reynolds to make another action-comedy, but laughs have never been so rare nor stunts so unspectacular. Rated PG for profanity. 1981; 95m.

CANNONBALL RUN II
DIR: Hal Needham. **CAST:** Burt Reynolds, Dom DeLuise, Shirley MacLaine, Marilu Henner, Telly Savalas, Dean Martin, Sammy Davis Jr., Frank Sinatra.

Take an Arab fortune, a pair of bogus nuns, inept underworld warfare, and a bunch of crazies willing to risk their necks in a mad cross-country race with no rules or regulations, and you have the starting line-up for this typically awful Hal Needham rehash of *Cannonball Run*. What a waste of talent. Rated PG for simulated violence and profanity. 1984; 108m.

CAN'T BUY ME LOVE ★★
DIR: Steve Rash. **CAST:** Amanda Peterson, Patrick Dempsey, Courtney Gains, Tina Caspary, Seth Green, Sharon Farrell, Dennis Dugan, Ami Dolenz, Steve Franken.
The title song is the Beatles' classic tune. Unfortunately, this film is all downhill from there. Patrick Dempsey plays a nerd who learns that popularity isn't all it's cracked up to be. The message is delivered in heavy-handed style and the laughs are few. Still, teens will love it. Rated PG-13 for profanity. 1987; 94m.

CAPTAIN'S PARADISE, THE ★★★★
DIR: Anthony Kimmins. **CAST:** Alec Guinness, Celia Johnson, Yvonne De Carlo, Bill Fraser.
From the opening shot, in which he is "shot," Alec Guinness displays the seemingly artless comedy form that marked him for stardom. He plays the bigamist skipper of a ferry, a wife in each port, flirting with delicious danger. Timing is all, and close shaves—including a chance meeting of the wives—yields edge of seat entertainment. Lotsa fun. 1953; B&W; 77m.

CAPTAIN'S TABLE ★★½
DIR: Jack Lee. **CAST:** John Gregson, Peggy Cummins, Donald Sinden, Nadia Gray.
This is a delightful comedy about a skipper of a cargo vessel who is given trial command of a luxury liner. He is met with chaos while trying to see his passengers and crew safely through the voyage. Has some wildly funny moments. Not rated. 1960; B&W; 90m.

CAR WASH ★★★½
DIR: Michael Schultz. **CAST:** Richard Pryor, Franklin Ajaye, Sully Boyar, Ivan Dixon.
This is an ensemble film that features memorable bits from Richard Pryor, George Carlin, Franklin Ajaye, Ivan Dixon, and the Pointer Sisters. There are plenty of laughs, music, and even a moral in this fine low-budget production. Rated PG. 1976; 97m.

CARBON COPY ★★★½
DIR: Michael Schultz. **CAST:** George Segal, Susan Saint James, Jack Warden, Dick Martin.
This amiable, lightweight comedy of racial manners stars George Segal as a white corporate executive who suddenly discovers he has a teenage black son just itching to be adopted in lily-white San Marino, California. Rated PG. 1981; 92m.

CARLIN AT CARNEGIE ★★★½
DIR: Steven Santos. **CAST:** George Carlin.
This Home Box Office–backed video may not be as consistently funny as other comedy videos, but it has that special quality of having come from the heart—as well as hard-earned experience and deep thought. It's funny and sad at the same time. Carlin has found that you can't always have a nice day and does a very funny, brilliant routine on how being told to have one can be irritating. And, as always, Carlin uses the English language—and our taboos on certain parts of it—against itself in several bits. 1983; 60m.

CARLIN ON CAMPUS ★★★½
DIR: Steve Santos. **CAST:** George Carlin.
An uproarious show by one of America's funniest men, George Carlin, recorded live for HBO. Carlin has some classic bits on this tape, including "A Place for My Stuff" and observations on driving. The only drawback is the infantile and ribald cartoons that are plugged in at odd moments. Unrated, but contains raw language. 1984; 59m.

CARLTON-BROWNE OF THE F.O. ★★½

DIR: Jeffrey Dell. **CAST:** Terry-Thomas, Peter Sellers, Luciana Paluzzi.

A British foreign-office secretary is assigned to a small island nation, formerly of the empire. A series of misunderstandings, conspiracies, and counterplots befuddle Terry-Thomas as Carlton-Browne. For serious buffs this is an interesting, but not classic, bit of movie history. Not rated and only mildly ribald. 1958; B&W; 88m.

CARRY ON AT YOUR CONVENIENCE ★½

DIR: Gerald Thomas. **CAST:** Sidney James, Kenneth Williams, Charles Hawtrey, Joan Sims.

The British *Carry On* comedy players were still carrying on in 1971, but they were starting to run out of breath. It's hard to imagine anything funny coming out of a story about a strike at a toilet factory, and precious little does here. Unrated, but full of innuendoes. 1971; 86m.

CARRY ON BEHIND ★

DIR: Gerald Thomas. **CAST:** Elke Sommer, Kenneth Williams, Sidney James, Joan Sims.

Archaeologists and holiday campers stumble over each other while trying to share the same location. By this point, the *Carry On* series had become merely smutty, as the title indicates; the level of humor makes *Three's Company* look like Molière by comparison. Unrated. 1975; 90m.

CARRY ON CLEO ★★★½

DIR: Gerald Thomas. **CAST:** Amanda Barrie, Sidney James, Kenneth Williams, Kenneth Connor, Joan Sims, Charles Hawtrey, Jim Dale, Jon Pertwee.

It's a matter of personal taste, but we find this to be the funniest of the *Carry On* series. (Of course, you might not find any of them funny.) It's designed as a spoof of the then-current Burton-Taylor *Cleopatra. Dr. Who* fans will spot Jon Pertwee in a small role. 1965; 92m.

CARRY ON COWBOY ★★½

DIR: Gerald Thomas. **CAST:** Sidney James, Kenneth Williams, Joan Sims, Angela Douglas, Jim Dale.

Another in a very long, and weakening, line of British farces—*Carry on Doctor, Carry On Nurse*—many of them spoofs of highly popular films. Replete with the usual double-entendre jokes and sight gags, this one sends up *High Noon.* 1966; 91m.

CARRY ON CRUISING ★★★

DIR: Gerald Thomas. **CAST:** Sidney James, Kenneth Williams, Kenneth Connor, Liz Fraser.

One of the earlier, and therefore better, entries in the long-lived British series. The jokes are more energetic, less forced. In this one, the players try desperately to fill in for the regular crew of a Mediterranean cruise ship. Unrated. 1962; B&W; 99m.

CARRY ON DOCTOR ★★★

DIR: Gerald Thomas. **CAST:** Frankie Howerd, Sidney James, Kenneth Williams, Charles Hawtrey, Jim Dale, Hattie Jacques, Joan Sims, Peter Butterworth.

Adding veteran British comic Frankie Howerd to the cast helped perk up this *Carry On* entry a bit. The usual gang play the bumbling staff of a hospital, caught up in a battle over a secret weight-loss formula. Unrated. 1968; 95m.

CARRY ON EMMANUELLE ★

DIR: Gerald Thomas. **CAST:** Suzanne Danielle, Kenneth Williams, Kenneth Connor, Joan Sims, Peter Butterworth, Beryl Reid.

The last of the *Carry On* series, and not a moment too soon. The cast could have been doing them in their sleep by this point, and at times it looks as if they were. Unrated, but an R equivalent for nudity and smirky sex jokes. 1978; 88m.

CARRY ON NURSE ★★★

DIR: Gerald Thomas. **CAST:** Kenneth Connor, Kenneth Williams, Charles Hawtrey, Terence Longden.

Daffy struggle between patients and hospital staff. It's one of the most consistently amusing entries in this distinctive British comedy series. 1960; 90m.

CARTIER AFFAIR, THE ★½
DIR: Rod Holcomb. **CAST:** Joan Collins, David Hasselhoff, Telly Savalas, Jay Gerber, Hilly Hicks.
Less than funny comic romance that involves a male secretary (David Hasselhoff) falling in love with his soap-opera-legend boss (Joan Collins). The twist is that he's actually an ex-con planted in her employ to set up a heist of her fabulous jewels. Basically boring, unbelievable story with uninspired acting. 1985; 96m.

CASANOVA'S BIG NIGHT ★★½
DIR: Norman Z. McLeod. **CAST:** Bob Hope, Joan Fontaine, Basil Rathbone, Audrey Dalton, Frieda Inescort, Hope Emerson, Hugh Marlowe, John Carradine, John Hoyt, Robert Hutton, Raymond Burr, Lon Chaney Jr.
The evergreen Bob Hope is a lowly tailor's assistant masquerading as the great lover Casanova in this costume comedy set in plot-and-intrigue-ridden Venice. Old Ski Nose is irrepressible, as always, sets are sumptuous, and costumes lavish, but the script and direction don't measure up. Funny, but not *that* funny. 1954; 86m.

CASINO ROYALE ★★
DIR: John Huston, Ken Hughes, Robert Parrish, Joe McGrath, Val Guest. **CAST:** Peter Sellers, Ursula Andress, David Niven, Orson Welles, Joanna Pettet, Woody Allen, Deborah Kerr, William Holden, Charles Boyer, John Huston, George Raft, Jean-Paul Belmondo.
What do you get when you combine the talents of this all-star ensemble? Not much. This is the black sheep of the James Bond family of films. The rights to *Casino Royale* weren't part of the Ian Fleming package. Not wanting to compete with the Sean Connery vehicles, this film was intended to be a stylish spoof. It's only sporadically amusing. For the most part, it's an overblown bore. 1967; 130m.

CASUAL SEX? ★★★
DIR: Genevieve Robert. **CAST:** Lea Thompson, Victoria Jackson, Stephen Shellen, Mary Gross.
Oddball, likable comedy about two single girls (Lea Thompson and Victoria Jackson) who go hunting for men at a health resort. Although not providing roll-in-the-aisles laughter, *Casual Sex?* is a real attempt at making some sense of the safe-sex question. Rated R for sexual frankness, language and nudity. 1988; 90m.

CATCH AS CATCH CAN ★★
DIR: Franco Indovina. **CAST:** Vittorio Gassman, Martha Hyer, Gila Golan, Claudio Gora, Massimo Serato.
Vittorio Gassman plays a television-commerical actor who finds the animal kingdom out to get him. From chickens to bulls to a pesky fly, they all contribute to the actor's downfall. If this all sounds too silly, it is. And the dubbed English makes it worse. Not rated, has sex and nudity. 1968; 92m.

CATCH-22 ★★★
DIR: Mike Nichols. **CAST:** Alan Arkin, Martin Balsam, Richard Benjamin, Anthony Perkins, Art Garfunkel.
This release stars Alan Arkin as a soldier in World War II most interested in avoiding the insanity of combat. Its sarcasm alone is enough to sustain interest. Rated R. 1970; 121m.

CAVEMAN ★
DIR: Carl Gottlieb. **CAST:** Ringo Starr, Barbara Bach, John Matuszak, Shelley Long, Dennis Quaid.
Ex-Beatle Ringo Starr plays the prehistoric hero in this silly, vulgar, and sometimes outright stupid spoof of *One Million Years B.C.* Because of the amount of sexual innuendo, it is definitely not recommended for kids, although they are perhaps the only people who would really think it was funny. Rated PG. 1981; 92m.

CHAMPAGNE FOR CAESAR ★★★★

DIR: Richard Whorf. **CAST:** Ronald Colman, Celeste Holm, Vincent Price, Barbara Britton, Art Linkletter.

Satire of early television and the concept of game shows is funnier now than when it was originally released. A treasure trove of trivia and great one-liners, this intelligent spoof features actor Ronald Colman as Beauregarde Bottomley, self-proclaimed genius and scholar who exacts his revenge on soap tycoon Vincent Price by appearing on his quiz show and attempting to bankrupt his company by winning all their assets. 1950; B&W; 99m.

CHANCES ARE ★★★½

DIR: Emile Ardolino. **CAST:** Cybill Shepherd, Robert Downey Jr., Ryan O'Neal, Mary Stuart Masterson, Christopher McDonald, Josef Sommer.

In this derivative but generally charming romantic comedy, a surprisingly effective Robert Downey Jr. plays the reincarnated soul of Cybill Shepherd's husband (Christopher McDonald). As the result of a mistake in the soul-recycling center in heaven, Downey has retained a dormant memory of his past life. It returns during a visit to Shepherd's home just as he is about to seduce "their" daughter (Mary Stuart Masterson). It's good silly fun from then on—even if you've seen *Here Comes Mr. Jordan* or *Heaven Can Wait*. Rated PG for mild profanity. 1989; 108m.

CHANGE OF SEASONS, A 🦃

DIR: Richard Lang. **CAST:** Shirley MacLaine, Anthony Hopkins, Bo Derek, Michael Brandon.

Poor Shirley MacLaine. She seems destined to make the same movie over and over again. The only difference between this film and *Loving Couples*, which closely followed it into release, is that Anthony Hopkins and Bo Derek co-star as the ultramodern mate-swappers who discover the real meaning of love just in the nick of time. Miss it. Rated R. 1980; 102m.

CHAPLIN REVUE, THE ★★★★

DIR: Charles Chaplin. **CAST:** Charlie Chaplin, Edna Purviance, Tom Wilson, Sydney Chaplin.

Assembled and scored by Charlie Chaplin for release in 1959, this revue is composed of three of his longer, more complex and polished films: *A Dog's Life*, which established Chaplin's reputation as a satirist; *Shoulder Arms*, a model for *The Great Dictator*; and *The Pilgrim*, in which escaped convict Chaplin assumes the garb of a minister. 1959; B&W; 121m.

CHARLIE CHAN AND THE CURSE OF THE DRAGON QUEEN ★★

DIR: Clive Donner. **CAST:** Peter Ustinov, Lee Grant, Angie Dickinson, Richard Hatch.

Although there are moments in this tongue-in-cheek send-up of the 1930s Charlie Chan mystery series that recapture the fun of yesteryear, overall it's just not a very good movie. The only thing that saves this film is that the stars seem to be having so much fun it's hard not to get caught up in it, even though afterward you may regret laughing. Rated PG. 1981; 97m.

CHARLIE CHAPLIN CARNIVAL ★★★

DIR: Charles Chaplin. **CAST:** Charlie Chaplin, Edna Purviance, Eric Campbell, Lloyd Bacon.

One of a number of anthologies made up of two-reel Chaplin films, this one is composed of *The Vagabond*, *The Count*, *Behind the Screen*, and *The Fireman*. Charlie Chaplin, Edna Purviance (his forever leading lady), and the giant Eric Campbell provide most of the hilarious, romantic, touching moments. Bedrock fans will find *The Vagabond* a study for the longer films that followed in the 1920s—*The Kid*, in particular. 1916; B&W; 80m.

CHARLIE CHAPLIN CAVALCADE ★★★

DIR: Charles Chaplin. **CAST:** Charlie Chaplin, Henry Bergman, Edna Purviance, John Rand, Wesley Ruggles, Frank J. Coleman, Albert Austin, Eric Campbell, Lloyd Bacon, Leo White.

Another in a series of anthologies spliced up out of two- and three-reel Chaplin comedies. This features four of his best: *One A. M., The Pawnshop, The Floorwalker, The Rink.* As in most of Chaplin's short comedies, the sidesplitting action results mainly from underdog Chaplin clashing with the short-fused giant Eric Campbell. 1916; B&W; 81m.

CHARLIE CHAPLIN FESTIVAL ★★★

DIR: Charles Chaplin. **CAST:** Charlie Chaplin, Eric Campbell, Edna Purviance, Albert Austin, Henry Bergman.

The third in a number of Chaplin film anthologies. Featuring *Easy Street*, one of his best-known hits, this group contains *The Cure, The Adventurer*, and *The Immigrant*, and gives viewers the full gamut of famous Chaplin emotional expressions. The coin sequence in the last is sight-gag ingenuity at its best. 1917; B&W; 80m.

CHARLIE CHAPLIN—THE EARLY YEARS, VOL. 1 ★★★★★

DIR: Charles Chaplin. **CAST:** Charlie Chaplin, Edna Purviance, Eric Campbell, Albert Austin.

In this collection of early Charlie Chaplin shorts, we get three outstanding stories. *The Immigrant* finds Charlie, who meets Edna Purviance on the boat to America, in love and broke. The story is how they survive in the land of dreams. *The Count* has Charlie trying to lead the high life with no money. *Easy Street* finds Charlie "saved" by missionary Purviance and out to save everyone else. All three episodes are quite funny and heartwarming. If you like old silent comedies, you'll love these. 1917; B&W; 62m.

CHARLIE CHAPLIN—THE EARLY YEARS, VOL. 2 ★★★★★

DIR: Charles Chaplin. **CAST:** Charlie Chaplin, Edna Purviance, Eric Campbell, Albert Austin.

Volume Two of the Charlie Chaplin series presents three more classic shorts. The first is *The Pawnbroker*, with Charlie running a pawnshop. As you might expect, nothing is quite normal in this pawnshop. The second feature is called *The Adventure*, as Charlie plays an escaped con who gets mistaken for a high-society man and finds himself in the middle of wealthy society. And *One A.M.* ends the collection as Charlie tries desperately to get some sleep after a long night of boozing it up. Everything in his room keeps moving. A must for Chaplin fans. 1916; B&W; 61m.

CHARLIE CHAPLIN, THE EARLY YEARS, VOL. 3 ★★★★★

DIR: Charles Chaplin. **CAST:** Charlie Chaplin, Edna Purviance, Eric Campbell, Henry Bergman.

In Volume Three of this great series, we get three more classic Chaplin shorts. First off is *The Cure*, where Charlie plays a drunk who goes to a health spa to dry out. He also happens to bring a trunkload of booze with him; the result is a spa full of smashed people. Next Charlie shows up as *The Floorwalker* in a large department store who catches his boss trying to make off with the store's money. Last Charlie is *The Vagabond*, a wandering violinist who saves a young girl's life and also falls in love with her. Unfortunately for Charlie, her mother takes her away from him. Don't miss these wonderful treasures from the past. 1917; B&W; 64m.

CHARLIE CHAPLIN—THE EARLY YEARS, VOL. 4 ★★★★★

DIR: Charles Chaplin. **CAST:** Charlie Chaplin, Edna Purviance, Eric Campbell, Albert Austin, Lloyd Bacon, Charlotte Mineau, James T. Kelly, Leo White.

In Volume Four of the Charlie Chaplin series, we start out with *Behind the*

Screen, as Charlie plays a movie studio stagehand who goes crazy from being overworked. The final pie-throwing clash is a classic. Next is *The Fireman*, with Charlie a brave firefighter who must rescue Edna Purviance, his girlfriend, from a fire. The final story is *The Ring*, with Charlie playing a bumbling waiter in a high-class restaurant. All three stories are in the great Chaplin tradition. 1916; B&W; 63m.

CHATTANOOGA CHOO CHOO ★★
DIR: Bruce Bilson. **CAST:** George Kennedy, Barbara Eden, Joe Namath, Melissa Sue Anderson.

A sillier and cornier movie you'll probably never see. The story deals with a bet to make a New York–to–Chattanooga train trip within a deadline. George Kennedy plays the comedy villain and owner of a football team on which Joe Namath is the coach. Barbara Eden starts out as Kennedy's girlfriend but soon falls in love with the "good guy"—Namath. Rated PG for mild profanity. 1984; 102m.

CHEAPER TO KEEP HER ★
DIR: Ken Annakin. **CAST:** Mac Davis, Tovah Feldshuh, Art Metrano, Ian McShane.

Mac Davis plays a sexist private detective whose investigations are confined to tracking down ex-husbands who haven't paid their alimony. Despite an advertising claim that it's about women's rights, this film cares as little about women as it does about good comedy. Rated R. 1980; 92m.

CHECK AND DOUBLE CHECK ★
DIR: Melville Brown. **CAST:** Freeman Gosden, Charles Correll, Sue Carol, Charles Norton.

This sad comedy starring radio's Amos 'n Andy in blackface was RKO's biggest hit for the 1930 season and made Freeman Gosden and Charles Correll the top stars for that year—but by that time they weren't even with the studio anymore and never made another film. Very popular in the Midwest and the South when it was first released, this clinker looks its age and then some. 1930; B&W; 80m.

CHECK IS IN THE MAIL, THE
DIR: Joan Darling. **CAST:** Brian Dennehy, Anne Archer, Hallie Todd, Chris Herbert, Michael Bowen, Dick Shawn, Beau Starr.

This unfunny comedy tells the lamentable story of a man (Brian Dennehy) who is tired of the capitalist system. A hard-luck case, he decides to rebel, all the while not realizing that he is part of the same system he so disdains. Rated R for profanity and adult situations. 1986; 83m.

CHEECH AND CHONG'S NEXT MOVIE ★★
DIR: Thomas Chong. **CAST:** Cheech and Chong, Evelyn Guerrero, Betty Kennedy.

This is Cheech and Chong's (Richard Marin and Thomas Chong) in-between movie—in between *Up in Smoke*, their first, and *Nice Dreams*, number three. If you liked either of the other two, you'll like *Next Movie*. But if you didn't care for the duo's brand of humor there, you won't in this one either. Rated R for nudity and profanity. 1980; 99m.

CHEERLEADERS
DIR: Paul Glicker. **CAST:** Stephanie Fondue, Denise Dillaway, Jovita Bush, Debbie Lowe.

Dated sex farce that was racy in the early Seventies, but now seems tired. The lame plot centers around the last virgin in California. Sound stupid? Well, it is. Rated X at one time; now equivalent to an R for nudity and profanity. 1972; 84m.

CHICKEN CHRONICLES, THE ★
DIR: Francis Simon. **CAST:** Steve Guttenberg, Ed Lauter, Lisa Reeves, Meredith Baer, Phil Silvers.

This witless comedy centers on the carnal pursuits of Steve (*Police Academy*) Guttenberg, a charmless high school senior. Even Phil Silvers can't scare up many laughs in this one. Rated PG. 1977; 95m.

CHRISTMAS IN CONNECTICUT ★★★½

DIR: Peter Godfrey. **CAST:** Barbara Stanwyck, Dennis Morgan, Sydney Greenstreet, S. Z. Sakall, Reginald Gardiner, Una O'Connor.

In this spirited comedy, a successful newspaper family-advice columnist (Barbara Stanwyck) arranges a phony family for herself—all for the sake of publicity. The acting is good and the pace is quick, but the script needs polishing. Nonetheless, it's a Christmas favorite. 1945; B&W; 101m.

CHRISTMAS IN JULY ★★★½

DIR: Preston Sturges. **CAST:** Dick Powell, Ellen Drew, Raymond Walburn, William Demarest, Ernest Truex, Franklin Pangborn.

Touching, insightful comedy-drama about a young couple's dreams and aspirations. Dick Powell is fine as the enthusiastic young man who mistakenly believes that he has won a contest and finds all doors opening to him—until the error is discovered. This one is a treat for all audiences. Once you've seen it, you'll want to see all of Preston Sturges's films. 1940; B&W; 67m.

CHU CHU AND THE PHILLY FLASH ★★

DIR: David Lowell Rich. **CAST:** Alan Arkin, Carol Burnett, Jack Warden, Ruth Buzzi.

This is another bittersweet comedy about a couple of losers. It's supposed to be funny. It isn't. The stars, Alan Arkin and Carol Burnett, do manage to invest it with a certain wacky charm, but that isn't enough to make up for its shortcomings. Rated PG. 1981; 100m.

CHUMP AT OXFORD, A ★★★

DIR: Alf Goulding. **CAST:** Stan Laurel, Oliver Hardy, Wilfred Lucas, Forrester Harvey, James Finlayson, Anita Garvin.

Stan Laurel receives a scholarship to Oxford, and Oliver Hardy accompanies him. Not accepted by the other students, they are the butt of pranks and jokes until Stan receives a blow on the head and becomes a reincarnation of a college hero. A fair script, but the Stan and Ollie characters never seem to fit well into it. 1940; B&W; 63m.

CIRCUS, THE/A DAY'S PLEASURE ★★★

DIR: Charles Chaplin. **CAST:** Charlie Chaplin, Allan Garcia, Merna Kennedy, Harry Crocker, Betty Morrisey, George Davis, Henry Bergman.

This double feature admirably showcases Charlie Chaplin's world-famous gifts for comedy and pathos. In the first, vagabond Charlie hooks up with a traveling circus and falls for the bareback rider, who loves a muscle-bound trapeze artist. The film earned Chaplin a special Oscar at the first Academy Awards ceremony for writing, acting, directing, and producing. In the second feature, Charlie and his family try in vain to have Sunday fun. Silent. 1928; B&W; 105m.

CITIZEN'S BAND ★★★★

DIR: Jonathan Demme. **CAST:** Paul LeMat, Candy Clark, Ann Wedgeworth, Marcia Rodd, Charles Napier, Alix Elias, Roberts Blossom, Bruce McGill, Ed Begley Jr.

Delightful character study centers around a group of people who use citizen's band radios. Screenwriter Paul Brickman and director Jonathan Demme turn this slight premise into a humorous and heartwarming collection of vignettes with Paul LeMat appealing as the central character and Charles Napier screamingly funny as a philandering truck driver. Rated PG. 1977; 98m.

CITY HEAT ★★★

DIR: Richard Benjamin. **CAST:** Clint Eastwood, Burt Reynolds, Jane Alexander, Madeline Kahn, Irene Cara, Richard Roundtree, Rip Torn, Tony LoBlanco.

Clint Eastwood and Burt Reynolds portray a cop and a private eye, respectively, in this enjoyable action comedy, directed by Richard Benjamin. Despite a few clashes while pursuing gangsters, the two have a grudging mutual respect. It's fun for fans of the stars. Rated PG for violence. 1984; 94m.

CITY LIGHTS ★★★★★
DIR: Charles Chaplin. **CAST:** Charlie Chaplin, Virginia Cherrill, Harry Myers, Hank Mann.

In his finest film, Charlie Chaplin's little tramp befriends a blind flower-seller, providing her with every kindness he can afford. Charlie develops a friendship with a drunken millionaire and takes advantage of it to help the girl even more. Taking money from the millionaire so the girl can have an eye operation, he is arrested and sent to jail. His release from jail and the subsequent reunion with the girl may well be the most poignant ending of all his films. 1931; B&W; 81m.

CLASS
DIR: Lewis John Carlino. **CAST:** Rob Lowe, Jacqueline Bisset, Andrew McCarthy, Stuart Margolin.

This is a generally unfunny and offensive comedy about two preppies, one of whom unwittingly falls in love with the other's alcoholic mother (Jacqueline Bisset). Rated R for nudity, profanity, sex, and violence. 1983; 98m.

CLASS REUNION
DIR: Michael Miller. **CAST:** Gerrit Graham, Stephen Furst, Zane Buzby, Michael Lerner.

The graduating class of 1972 returns to wreak havoc on its alma mater, Lizzie Borden High School, in this awful *Animal House*–style comedy. Rated R for nudity, leering sexual references, profanity, and drug-taking. 1982; 84m.

CLOCKWISE ★★★½
DIR: Christopher Morahan. **CAST:** John Cleese, Penelope Wilton, Alison Steadman, Stephen Moore, Sharon Maiden, Joan Hickson.

No one plays a pillar of pomposity better than John Cleese. In *Clockwise*, written expressly for Cleese, he gets a perfect role for his patented persona. Brian Stimpson, a headmaster, runs everything by the clock—in the extreme. However, his complete control is soon shattered by a misunderstanding—and hilarity is the result. Rated PG. 1987; 96m.

CLUB PARADISE
DIR: Harold Ramis. **CAST:** Robin Williams, Peter O'Toole, Jimmy Cliff, Twiggy, Rick Moranis, Adolph Caesar, Eugene Levy, Joanna Cassidy.

Lame, witless, boring, and offensive attempt to use adult stars in a concept overdone by moronic teen comedies. Robin Williams and Jimmy Cliff start their own little Club Med–style resort; other cast members play tourists who arrive for a vacation. This is filmmaking at the top of its lungs, everybody shouts and screams. PG-13 for language and drug humor. 1986; 104m.

CLUE ★★½
DIR: Jonathan Lynn. **CAST:** Eileen Brennan, Tim Curry, Madeline Kahn, Christopher Lloyd, Michael McKean, Martin Mull, Lesley Ann Warren.

Inspired by the popular board game, the movie is a pleasant spoof of whodunits. The delightful ensemble establishes a suitably breezy style. Silliness eventually overwhelms the proceedings. As a gimmick, the film was originally shown in theatres with three different endings. All versions are included on the videocassette. Rated PG-13. 1985; 100m.

COAST TO COAST ★★
DIR: Joseph Sargent. **CAST:** Dyan Cannon, Robert Blake, Quinn Redeker, Michael Lerner, Maxine Stuart, Bill Lucking.

Dyan Cannon stars as a wacko blonde who's been railroaded into a mental hospital by her husband. He has had her declared insane so he can avoid an expensive divorce. Cannon escapes by bopping her psychiatrist over the head with a bust of Freud, and the chase is on. A trucker (Robert Blake) gives Cannon a lift, and they romp from Pennsylvania to California. Rated PG for profanity. 1980; 95m.

COCA COLA KID, THE ★★★
DIR: Dusan Makavejev. **CAST:** Eric Roberts, Greta Scacchi, Bill Kerr.
A nude scene between Eric Roberts and Greta Scacchi in a bed covered with feathers is enough to make anyone's temperature rise, but as a whole this little film doesn't have enough bite to it. Roberts plays a gung-ho troubleshooter from the popular beverage company who comes to Australia to sell the drink to a hard-nosed businessman (Bill Kerr) who has a monopoly on a stretch of land with his own soft drink. Worth a look. Rated R for nudity. 1985; 90m.

COCOANUTS ★★★½
DIR: Joseph Santley, Robert Florey. **CAST:** The Marx Brothers, Kay Francis, Margaret Dumont.
The Marx Brothers' first movie was one of the earliest sound films and suffers as a result. Notice how all the maps and newspapers are sopping wet (so they wouldn't crackle into the supersensitive, primitive microphones). The romantic leads are laughably stiff, and even the songs by Irving Berlin are forgettable. However, the Marxes—all four of them, Groucho, Harpo, Chico, and Zeppo—supply some classic moments, making the picture well worth watching. 1929; B&W; 96m.

COLD FEET ★★★½
DIR: Bruce Van Dusen. **CAST:** Griffin Dunne, Marissa Chibas, Blanche Baker.
This enjoyable low-key romance features a film writer (Griffin Dunne) who has just left his complaining, childlike wife (Blanche Baker) and vowed to go it alone. Enter an attractive scientist (Marissa Chibas) who has just dumped her overbearing boyfriend. Rated PG for slight profanity. 1984; 91m.

COLLEGE ★★★½
DIR: James W. Horne. **CAST:** Buster Keaton, Anne Cornwall, Flora Bramley, Grant Winters.
An anti-athletics bookworm, Buster Keaton, goes to college on a scholarship. His girl falls for a jock, and Keaton decides to prove he can succeed in athletics to win her back. He fails hilariously in every attempt, but finally rescues her from the evil-intentioned jock by unwittingly using every athletic skill. 1927; B&W; 65m.

COLONEL EFFINGHAM'S RAID ★★½
DIR: Irving Pichel. **CAST:** Charles Coburn, Joan Bennett, William Eythe, Allyn Joslyn, Elizabeth Patterson, Donald Meek.
Slight small-town story about Charles Coburn's efforts to preserve a local monument and save the community's pride is pleasant enough and has marvelous characters populating it. Not a great film, but harmless fun and at times thought-provoking. 1945; B&W; 70m.

COMFORT AND JOY ★★★★½
DIR: Bill Forsyth. **CAST:** Bill Paterson, Eleanor David, C. P. Grogan, Alex Norton.
Scottish filmmaker Bill Forsyth scores again with this delightful tale of a disc jockey (Bill Paterson) whose life is falling apart. His girlfriend walks out on him, taking nearly everything he owns. Birds seem to like decorating his pride and joy: a red BMW. And what's worse, he gets involved in a gangland war over—are you ready for this?—the control of ice cream manufacturing and sales. It's one you'll want to see. Rated PG. 1984; 90m.

COMIC CABBY
DIR: Carl Lindahl. **CAST:** Bill McLaughlin, Al Lewis, Frank Guy.
This has to be one of the worst hours of video you could rent. Based on Jim Pietsch's book *The New York City Cab Driver's Joke Book*, it's an extended skit that dramatizes a day in

the life of a rookie cabby. The jokes are bad and the acting worse. You'll want to take the bus from now on. 1986; 60m.

COMING TO AMERICA ★★★½
DIR: John Landis. **CAST:** Eddie Murphy, Arsenio Hall, James Earl Jones, John Amos, Madge Sinclair.
Eddie Murphy deserves credit for trying to do something different in *Coming to America.* Instead of his usual wisecracking character, Murphy, who also wrote the story, stars as a pampered African prince who refuses to marry the pretty and pliable queen his father (James Earl Jones) has picked for him, opting instead to journey to New York City to find an intelligent, independent woman to be his lifelong mate. The film is a little slow at times, but the laughs are frequent enough to hold one's interest. Rated R for profanity, nudity and suggested sex. 1988; 116m.

COMMIES ARE COMING, THE COMMIES ARE COMING, THE ★★
DIR: George Waggner. **CAST:** Jack Kelly, Jean Cooper, Peter Brown, Patricia Woodell, Andrew Duggan, Robert Conrad.
Jack Webb narrates this 1950s anticommunist pseudodocumentary about what would happen if the Russians captured the United States. It's easy to laugh at this silly film. Unrated. 1984; B&W; 60m.

COMPLEAT "WEIRD AL" YANKOVIC, THE ★★½
DIR: Jay Levey, Robert K. Weiss. **CAST:** "Weird Al" Yankovic.
This is all that you ever wanted to know about "Weird Al" Yankovic. At 100 minutes, it's probably more than most people want to know. Filmed in documentary fashion, it traces Al's birth on October 23, 1959, through school, early jobs, and finally his entertainment career. In the process, eight of his videos are shown, including *Eat It*, *I Love Rocky Road*, *I Lost on Jeopardy*, and *Like a Surgeon*. The two best sequences show Al going to Michael Jackson for permission to do a parody of *Beat It* and a Devo send-up entitled *Dare to Be Stupid.* Weird Al—the man, the myth, the legend? You decide. 1985; 100m.

COMPROMISING POSITIONS ★★
DIR: Frank Perry. **CAST:** Susan Sarandon, Raul Julia, Edward Herrmann, Judith Ivey, Mary Beth Hurt, Anne DeSalvo, Josh Mostel.
In the first half-hour, this is a hilarious and innovative takeoff on murder mysteries and a devastatingly witty send-up of suburban life. However, it soon descends into the clichés of the mystery genre. That's too bad, because the plot, about an overly amorous dentist who is murdered, has great possibilities. But it eventually collapses into a not-very-suspenseful whodunit. Rated R for nudity, profanity, and violence. 1985; 98m.

CONNECTICUT YANKEE IN KING ARTHUR'S COURT, A (1948) ★★★
DIR: Tay Garnett. **CAST:** Bing Crosby, Rhonda Fleming, Cedric Hardwicke, William Bendix, Henry Wilcoxon, Murvyn Vye.
The third film version of Mark Twain's intriguing social satire, this costly but profitable production presents Bing Crosby as the blacksmith who dreams himself back to Camelot and is proclaimed a wizard because of his modern knowledge. It's good, clean, happy fun for all. 1948; 107m.

CONSUMING PASSIONS ★★
DIR: Giles Foster. **CAST:** Tyler Butterworth, Jonathan Pryce, Freddie Jones, Sammi Davis, Prunella Scales, Vanessa Redgrave, Thora Hird.
Morbid, gross, and sometimes amusing movie about a go-getting, nerdish junior executive who accidentally discovers a "secret ingredient"—human beings—that saves a sagging candy company. Adapted from a play written by Michael Palin and Terry Jones of *Monty Python's Flying Circus*

fame, the film suffers from the one-joke premise. Rated R for language, sexual situations, and overall grossness. 1988; 95m.

CONTINENTAL DIVIDE ★★★½
DIR: Michael Apted. **CAST:** John Belushi, Blair Brown, Allen Garfield, Carlin Glynn.
As light-hearted romantic comedies go, this one is tops. John Belushi stars as Ernie Souchak, a Chicago newspaper columnist unexpectedly sent into the Rockies to write a story about an ornithologist (Blair Brown). Just as unexpectedly, they fall in love. Rated PG because of slight amounts of nudity. 1981; 103m.

COPACABANA ★
DIR: Alfred E. Green. **CAST:** Groucho Marx, Carmen Miranda, Andy Russell, Steve Cochran, Abel Green.
Not even Groucho Marx can save this slight comedy about the problems caused by a woman applying for two jobs at the same nightclub. Carmen Miranda does her "banana hat bit" and the viewer eventually falls asleep. 1947; B&W; 92m.

CORSICAN BROTHERS, THE (1984)
DIR: Thomas Chong. **CAST:** Cheech and Chong, Roy Dotrice.
The comedy team of Cheech and Chong apparently enjoyed working on the Monty Python–powered period pirate comedy *Yellowbeard* so much they decided to do a silly swashbuckler of their own. Loosely based on the book by Alexandre Dumas, this forgettable film features Tommy Chong and Richard "Cheech" Marin as twins dueling to the death with dastardly villains. Rated R. 1984; 90m.

COUCH POTATO WORKOUT TAPE ★
DIR: Brian Cury. **CAST:** Larry "Bud" Melman.
Larry "Bud" Melman, of *Late Night with David Letterman* fame, is the ultimate couch potato, a tuber who treats inertia as exercise. Conceived as a parody of Jane Fonda–style workout tapes (with a Jane look-alike), this spoof never gets off the cutting-room floor. The gags fall flat and the best routine is the remote-control thumb press, which you can use to turn this novelty item off. Unrated. 1989; 35m.

COUCH TRIP, THE ★★½
DIR: Michael Ritchie. **CAST:** Dan Aykroyd, Walter Matthau, Charles Grodin, Donna Dixon, Richard Romanus, Mary Gross, David Clennon, Arye Gross.
Dan Aykroyd and Walter Matthau offer a few moments of mirth in this middling comedy about a computer hacker (Aykroyd) who escapes from a mental institution, impersonates the head of the facility, and becomes a hugely successful media shrink. Charles Grodin is exceptional as the neurotic radio doctor Aykroyd replaces, and Mary Gross has some terrific scenes as Grodin's wacky wife. Rated R for profanity and suggested sex. 1988; 95m.

COUNTRY GENTLEMEN ★★
DIR: Ralph Staub. **CAST:** Ole Olson, Chic Johnson, Joyce Compton, Lila Lee.
Fast-talking confidence men Ole Olson and Chic Johnson sell shares in a worthless oilfield to a group of World War I veterans, then learn thar's oil in them thar hills! Humorous, but what a weary plot! This flick did little for the comic duo, who always fared better on the stage. 1936; B&W; 54m.

COURT JESTER, THE ★★★
DIR: Norman Panama, Melvin Frank. **CAST:** Danny Kaye, Glynis Johns, Basil Rathbone, Angela Lansbury, Mildred Natwick, Robert Middleton.
Romance, court intrigue, a joust, and in the middle of it all the one and only Danny Kaye as a phony court jester full of double-takes and double-talk. This is one funny film of clever and complicated comic situations superbly brought off. 1956; 101m.

COUSINS ★★★★½

DIR: Joel Schumacher. **CAST:** Ted Danson, Isabella Rossellini, Sean Young, William L. Petersen, Lloyd Bridges, Norma Aleandro, Keith Coogan.

Cousins is an utter delight; a marvelously acted, written, and directed romance. Ted Danson, Isabella Rossellini, Sean Young, and William Petersen star as star-crossed spouses, cousins, and lovers in this Americanized takeoff on the 1975 French comedy hit, *Cousin, Cousine. Cousins* is about love rather than sex, making it a rare modern movie with heart. Rated PG-13 for profanity and suggested sex. 1989; 109m.

CRACKERS ★½

DIR: Louis Malle. **CAST:** Donald Sutherland, Jack Warden, Sean Penn, Wallace Shawn.

Crackers is a nearly unwatchable film directed by Louis Malle. It isn't often Malle comes up with a turkey, but when he does, it comes complete with all the trimmings. Even the high-powered talents of stars Donald Sutherland, Sean Penn, and Jack Warden can't lift this caper "comedy" above mediocrity. It's about a bunch of down-and-out San Franciscans who decide to turn to crime in order to survive. Rated PG. 1984; 92m.

CRACKING UP

DIR: Jerry Lewis. **CAST:** Jerry Lewis, Herb Edelman, Zane Buzby, Dick Butkus, Milton Berle.

A relatively new Jerry Lewis comedy. Translation: No laughs here. Lewis plays an accident waiting to happen with numerous other characters. Rated R. 1983; 83m.

CRIME & PASSION ★★

DIR: Ivan Passer. **CAST:** Omar Sharif, Karen Black, Joseph Bottoms, Bernhard Wicki.

A weak comedy of sex and money that gives us Omar Sharif as a rich businessman who becomes sexually aroused when bad things happen to him. Karen Black provides the zany aggressive sexuality that makes some moments zing with her particular brand of oddness. Her seduction of Joseph Bottoms is a classic. Weird and wild. Rated R. 1975; 92m.

CRIMES OF THE HEART ★★★★½

DIR: Bruce Beresford. **CAST:** Diane Keaton, Jessica Lange, Sissy Spacek, Sam Shepard, Tess Harper, David Carpenter, Hurd Hatfield.

In this superb screen adaptation of Beth Henley's Pulitzer Prize–winning play, Diane Keaton, Jessica Lange, and Sissy Spacek star as three eccentric sisters who stick together despite an onslaught of extraordinary problems. It is a film of many joys. Not the least of which are the performances of the stars, fine bits by Sam Shepard and Tess Harper in support, the biting humor, and the overall intelligence. Rated PG-13 for subject matter. 1986; 105m.

CRITICAL CONDITION ★★½

DIR: Michael Apted. **CAST:** Richard Pryor, Rachel Ticotin, Rubén Blades, Joe Mantegna, Bob Dishy, Joe Dallesandro, Garrett Morris, Randall "Tex" Cobb.

Mishmash of a comedy has some funny moments but ultimately tests the viewer's patience. Richard Pryor stars as a hustler who runs afoul of the law and the mob. He must feign insanity to stay out of prison. While under observation in a psychiatric ward of a big hospital, Pryor surprisingly finds himself in charge of the institution. Rated R for profanity, violence, and scatological humor. 1987; 105m.

"CROCODILE" DUNDEE ★★★★½

DIR: Peter Faiman. **CAST:** Paul Hogan, Linda Kozlowski, John Meillon, Mark Blum, David Gulpilil, Michael Lombard.

Those folks who moan that they don't make movies like they used to will be delighted by this hilarious Australian import. Paul Hogan plays the title character, a hunter who allegedly crawled several miles for help after a king-size crocodile gnawed off a leg. This slight exaggeration is enough to persuade an American newspaper reporter (Linda Kozlowski) to seek him out and persuade him to join her on a trip to New York, where the naïve outbacker faces a new set of perils (and deals with them in high comic style). Rated PG-13 for profanity and violence. 1986; 98m.

"CROCODILE" DUNDEE II ★★★½

DIR: John Cornell. **CAST:** Paul Hogan, Linda Kozlowski, John Meillon, Charles Dutton, Hector Ubarry, Juan Fernandez.

This follow-up to the wildly successful release from Down Under adds action to the winning formula of laughs, surprises, romance, and adventure. Mick Dundee (Paul Hogan) and Sue Charlton (Linda Kozlowski) are living a relatively quiet life in New York City until some Colombian drug dealers step in. The results should please fans of the first film. Rated PG for violence and light profanity. 1988; 110m.

CROOKS AND CORONETS (SOPHIE'S PLACE) ★★

DIR: Jim O'Connolly. **CAST:** Edith Evans, Telly Savalas, Cesar Romero, Warren Oates, Harry H. Corbett.

This picture had only a limited release in the United States and for good reason. It wasn't cunning and bold enough for a good crime picture, and certainly not funny enough for a quality comedy. Dame Edith Evans owns a large estate and the other characters are villains trying to steal the valuable property from her. The robbers fall under her magical spell and the crime goes out the window. Not rated. 1970; 102m.

CROSS MY HEART ★★

DIR: Armyan Bernstein. **CAST:** Martin Short, Annette O'Toole, Paul Reiser, Joanna Kerns.

Interminable comedy about the disastrous third date of two vulnerable people trying to keep silly secrets from each other. Martin Short and Annette O'Toole are unmemorable as the couple. Rated R for nudity and language. 1987; 88m.

CURSE OF THE PINK PANTHER, THE ★★★

DIR: Blake Edwards. **CAST:** Ted Wass, David Niven, Robert Wagner, Harvey Korman, Herbert Lom.

No, this isn't another trashy compilation of outtakes featuring the late Peter Sellers. Instead, series producer-writer-director Blake Edwards has hired Ted Wass (of TV's *Soap*) to play a bumbling American detective searching for the still-missing Jacques Clouseau, and he's a delight. When Wass is featured, *Curse* is fresh and diverting—and, on a couple of memorable occasions, it's hilarious. Rated PG for nudity, profanity, violence, and scatological humor. 1983; 109m.

DANCING MOTHERS ★★★

DIR: Herbert Brenon. **CAST:** Clara Bow, Alice Joyce, Dorothy Cumming, Norman Trevor.

Bee-sting-lipped Jazz Age flapper Clara Bow romps through this exuberant verge-of-sound silent about flaming youth. Enthusiastic performances work to offset the simple plot. 1926; B&W; 60m.

DANGEROUS CURVES ★★★½

DIR: David Lewis. **CAST:** Tate Donovan, Danielle von Zerneck, Robert Stack, Robert Klein, Robert Romanus.

A college senior gets a chance to earn a position with a corporation if he can deliver a birthday present to the boss's daughter. The present is a bright red Porsche. This zany comedy, aimed at the younger set, actually is above average for this genre and has a wider appeal. The young leads are appealing, and the support of Robert Klein and Robert Stack add to the enjoyment immensely. Rated PG. 1988; 93m.

DATE WITH AN ANGEL ★
DIR: Tom Loughlin. **CAST:** Michael E. Knight, Phoebe Cates, Emmanuelle Beart, David Dukes.

In this hopelessly inept comedy, a beautiful angel (Emmanuelle Beart) loses control of her wings and lands in the arms of a mortal (Michael E. Knight). The supposedly zany complications are, of course, that Knight and Beart fall in love. Knight's girlfriend, played by Phoebe Cates, becomes jealous and attempts to wreak revenge. You've seen it before and executed with more imagination and taste. Rated PG for profanity. 1987; 105m.

DAY AT THE RACES, A ★★★½
DIR: Sam Wood. **CAST:** The Marx Brothers, Allan Jones, Maureen O'Sullivan, Margaret Dumont.

The Marx Brothers—Groucho, Harpo, and Chico, that is—were still at the peak of their fame in this MGM musical-comedy. Though not as unrelentingly hilarious and outrageous as the films they made at Paramount with Zeppo, it is nonetheless an enjoyable film. The first to follow *A Night at the Opera*, their biggest hit, and use a variation on its formula, it works very well—which, sadly, did not prove to be the case with most of the Marx Brothers movies that followed. 1937; B&W; 111m.

DAY IN THE DEATH OF JOE EGG, A ★★★
DIR: Peter Medak. **CAST:** Alan Bates, Janet Suzman, Peter Bowles.

This competent British production features the wonderful Alan Bates and Janet Suzman as a married couple whose small son, physically and mentally disabled since birth, causes them to consider euthanasia. Doesn't sound too funny, but in a strange way it is. 1972; 106m.

DAYS OF THRILLS AND LAUGHTER ★★★½
DIR: Robert Youngson. **CAST:** Buster Keaton, Stan Laurel, Oliver Hardy, Charlie Chaplin, Harold Lloyd, Douglas Fairbanks Sr., The Keystone Kops.

A homage to classic silent-film comedians and daredevils, this collection of clips includes, among other winners, Charlie Chaplin's dinner-roll dance from *Gold Rush*. Stuntmen and daredevils are also saluted. A worthwhile nostalgia film. 1961; B&W; 93m.

D.C. CAB 🦃
DIR: Joel Schumacher. **CAST:** Gary Busey, Mr. T, Adam Baldwin, Max Gail.

A mindless "madcap" comedy with Gary Busey and Mr. T. Don't pay the fare. A down and out crew of cabdrivers is inspired by the new kid. Rated R. 1983; 99m.

DEAD MEN DON'T WEAR PLAID ★★★★
DIR: Carl Reiner. **CAST:** Steve Martin, Rachel Ward, Reni Santoni, Carl Reiner, George Gaynes.

In this often hilarious and always entertaining comedy, Steve Martin plays a private eye who confronts the suspicious likes of Humphrey Bogart, Burt Lancaster, Alan Ladd, Bette Davis, and other stars of Hollywood's Golden Age, with the help of tricky editing and writer-director Carl Reiner. Rachel Ward co-stars as Martin's sexy client. Rated PG for adult themes. 1982; B&W; 89m.

DEAL OF THE CENTURY ★★
DIR: William Friedkin. **CAST:** Chevy Chase, Sigourney Weaver, Gregory Hines, Vince Edwards.

A two-bit arms hustler (Chevy Chase) peddles an ultrasophisticated superweapon to a Central American dictator. This black comedy has its good moments. Unfortunately, it also has its bad moments and, as a result, ends up in that nether world of the near misses. Rated PG for violence and profanity. 1983; 99m.

DEAR BRIGITTE ★★½
DIR: Henry Koster. **CAST:** James Stewart, Fabian, Glynis Johns, Billy

Mumy, Cindy Carol, Jesse White, Ed Wynn, Brigitte Bardot.

A clever premise gone wrong. Ten-year-old boy genius who handicaps horses won't play unless he gets to go to France and meet Brigitte Bardot. What could have been charming comes across as contrived pap. 1965; 100m.

DEAR WIFE ★★½

DIR: Richard Haydn. **CAST:** Joan Caulfield, William Holden, Mona Freeman, Edward Arnold, Billy deWolfe.

The second of three amusing films involving the same cast of characters, and mostly the same players. This sequel to *Dear Ruth* has fresh-faced younger sister (to Joan Caulfield) Mona Freeman conniving to elect heartthrob William Holden to the state senate seat sought by her politician father Edward Arnold. Billy deWolfe fills it all out with his peculiar brand of haughty humor. 1949; B&W; 88m.

DEATHROW GAMESHOW

DIR: Mark Pirro. **CAST:** Robin Blythe, John McCafferty.

Incredibly dull comedy about a detestable gameshow host who's on the run from mobsters. He hosts *Live or Die*, a program that allows death-row cons to play for their lives. Rated R for nudity and overall crudeness. 1988; 78m.

DECAMERON NIGHTS ★★★

DIR: Hugo Fregonese. **CAST:** Joan Fontaine, Louis Jourdan, Joan Collins, Binnie Barnes, Marjorie Rhodes, Godfrey Tearle.

Louis Jourdan is Boccaccio, the poet, storyteller, and humanist best known for *The Decameron*. Three of his tales are told within the overall frame of his trying to win the love of a recent widow (Joan Fontaine). Each story features the cast members as various characters. The sets and costumes add greatly to this period comedy. 1953; 75m.

DELIVERY BOYS ★★½

DIR: Ken Handler. **CAST:** Jody Olivery, Joss Marcano, Mario Van Peebles.

This average teen comedy features pizza delivery boys who breakdance during their time off. They plan to compete in a breakdance contest that offers a $10,000 prize but encounter problems in getting there on time. Rated R. 1984; 94m.

DESPERATE LIVING

DIR: John Waters. **CAST:** Mink Stole, Edith Massey, Jean Hill, Liz Renay, Susan Lowe.

A "monstrous fairy tale," director John Waters calls it. And that may be an understatement. This story about a murderess (played by Mink Stole) and her escapades through a village of criminals who are ruled by a demented queen (Edith Massey) is a bit redundant. But various scenes provide enough humor and wit for anyone with a taste for the perverse and a yen for some good old-fashioned misanthropy. This is unrated, but it is the equivalent of an X, due to violence, nudity, and unbridled gore. 1977; 95m.

DESPERATE MOVES ★★★

DIR: Oliver Hellman. **CAST:** Steve Tracy, Eddie Deezen, Isabel Sanford, Paul Benedict, Christopher Lee.

Steve Tracy plays a young nerd from a small Oregon town traveling to California to pursue his dreams. How he copes with his naïveté and the culture shock of inner-city San Francisco is touching and amusing, if occasionally silly. Good effort by supporting cast. Not rated, but would probably fall near the PG-13 category. 1986; 106m.

DESPERATELY SEEKING SUSAN ★★★★½

DIR: Susan Siedelman. **CAST:** Rosanna Arquette, Madonna, Robert Joy, Mark Blum, Laurie Metcalf.

A delightfully daffy, smart, and intriguing comedy made from a feminine perspective. Rosanna Arquette stars as a bored housewife who adds spice to her life by following the personal column love adventures of the mysterious Susan (Madonna). One day, our heroine decides to catch a glimpse of her idol and, through a set of unlikely but easy-to-take plot convolutions, ends up switching places with her. Rated PG-13 for violence. 1985; 104m.

DETECTIVE SCHOOL DROPOUTS ★★★★

DIR: Filippo Ottoni. **CAST:** David Landsberg, Lorin Dreyfuss, Christian De Sica, Valeria Golino, George Eastman.

David Landsberg and Lorin Dreyfuss co-star in this hilarious comedy. (The two wrote the screenplay as well.) Landsberg plays Wilson, whose obsession with detective stories loses him a string of jobs. Finally, he goes to P.I. Miller (Dreyfuss) for lessons in investigation. The two accidentally become involved in an intrigue with star-crossed lovers. Rated PG for obscenities. 1985; 92m.

DEVIL AND MAX DEVLIN, THE ★★

DIR: Steven H. Stern. **CAST:** Elliott Gould, Bill Cosby, Susan Anspach, Adam Rich.

This is visible proof that it takes more than just a few talented people to create quality entertainment. Despite Elliott Gould, Bill Cosby, and Susan Anspach, this Disney production—another takeoff on the Faustian theme of a pact made with the devil—offers little more than mediocre fare. It's basically a waste of fine talent. Rated PG. 1981; 96m.

DEVIL AND MISS JONES, THE ★★★★

DIR: Sam Wood. **CAST:** Jean Arthur, Robert Cummings, Charles Coburn, Spring Byington, S. Z. Sakall, William Demarest.

One of those wonderful comedies Hollywood used to make. Witty, sophisticated, poignant, and breezy, this one has millionaire Charles Coburn going undercover as a clerk in his own department store in order to probe employee complaints and unrest. Delightful doings. 1941; B&W; 92m.

DIARY OF A YOUNG COMIC ★★½

DIR: Gary Weis. **CAST:** Richard Lewis, Stacy Keach, Dom DeLuise, Nina Van Pallandt, Bill Macy, George Jessel.

This watchable low-budget comedy follows the adventures of a young New York comic, Richard Lewis, who thinks that by moving to Hollywood he'll be an instant hit. Along the way we are given vignettes as he finds an apartment, encounters an agent, gets a booking, takes odd jobs, and finally performs at the Improvisation in Los Angeles. 1979; 67m.

DIE LAUGHING

DIR: Jeff Werner. **CAST:** Robby Benson, Linda Grovenor, Charles Durning, Bud Cort.

Robby Benson stars as Pinsky, a young cabbie with aspirations of becoming a rock recording star. He gets mixed up in a conspiracy that involves the changing of nuclear waste into weapons-grade plutonium. It's neither very funny nor exciting. Rated PG. 1980; 108m.

DINER ★★★★½

DIR: Barry Levinson. **CAST:** Steve Guttenberg, Daniel Stern, Mickey Rourke, Kevin Bacon, Ellen Barkin.

Writer-director Barry Levinson's much-acclaimed bittersweet tale of growing up in the late 1950s, unlike *American Graffiti*, is never cute or idealized. Instead, it combines insight, sensitive drama, and low-key humor. Rated R for profanity and adult themes. 1982; 110m.

DINNER AT EIGHT ★★★★★

DIR: George Cukor. **CAST:** John Barrymore, Jean Harlow, Marie Dressler, Billie Burke, Wallace Beery.

A sparkling, sophisticated, and witty comedy of character written by George S. Kaufman and Edna Ferber for the Broadway stage, this motion picture has a terrific all-star cast and lots of laughs. It's an all-time movie classic. 1933; B&W; 113m.

DIRTY LAUNDRY
DIR: William Webb. **CAST:** Leigh McCloskey, Jeanne O'Brien, Frankie Valli, Sonny Bono.
Stupid chase film involving a handsome young man (Leigh McCloskey) and his new girl (Jeanne O'Brien), and a group of drug-dealing thugs trying to recoup a million dollars. Rated PG-13 for profanity. 1987; 81m.

DIRTY ROTTEN SCOUNDRELS ★★★★½
DIR: Frank Oz. **CAST:** Steve Martin, Michael Caine, Glenne Headly, Barbara Harris.
Here's one of those rare instances where the remake is far better than the original. In retooling *Bedtime Story*, which starred Marlon Brando and David Niven, director Frank Oz came up with a genuine laugh riot. Michael Caine plays the Niven role of a sophisticated con man whose successful bilking of wealthy female tourists is endangered by upstart Steve Martin. Their battle of wits reaches true comic highs when they duel over the fortune and affections of American heiress Glenne Headly. Rated PG for profanity. 1988; 110m.

DIRTY TRICKS
DIR: Alvin Rakoff. **CAST:** Elliott Gould, Kate Jackson, Rich Little, Arthur Hill, Nicholas Campbell.
This Canadian-made movie brings the comedy-thriller genre to an all-time low. The story is ridiculous, the dialogue insipid, and the characters unappealing. Worse than that, this movie is incredibly dull. Rated PG. 1980; 91m.

DISORDERLY ORDERLY, THE ★★★
DIR: Frank Tashlin. **CAST:** Jerry Lewis, Glenda Farrell, Susan Oliver, Everett Sloane, Jack E. Leonard, Kathleen Freeman.
Jerry Lewis is out of control at a nursing home in a good solo effort directed by comedy veteran Frank Tashlin, who reached his peak here. Comic gems abound in this film, which isn't just for fans. In fact, if you've never been one of Jerry's faithful, give this one a try to see if you can't be swayed. You just might be surprised. 1964; 90m.

DIVORCE OF LADY X, THE ★★★★
DIR: Tim Whelan. **CAST:** Merle Oberon, Laurence Olivier, Binnie Barnes, Ralph Richardson.
In this British comedy, Laurence Olivier plays a lawyer who allows Merle Oberon to spend the night at his place. Although nothing actually happened that night, Olivier finds himself branded "the other man" in her divorce. A series of hilarious misunderstandings are the result. 1938; 90m.

DIXIE CHANGING HABITS ★★★½
DIR: George Englund. **CAST:** Suzanne Pleshette, Cloris Leachman, Kenneth McMillan, John Considine.
Suzanne Pleshette plays Dixie, who runs a highly successful prostitution ring. When she's busted, she must spend time in a convent directed by Cloris Leachman as the Mother Superior. The sisters learn about business and making a profit, and Dixie learns to respect herself. All in all, this made-for-TV comedy is highly entertaining. 1982; 96m.

DIXIE LANES ★
DIR: Don Cato. **CAST:** Hoyt Axton, Karen Black, Art Hindle, Tina Louise, Ruth Buzzi, Moses Gunn, John Vernon.
Chaotic comedy revolving around the bad luck of a family named Laid Law. Most of the film takes place in a bowling alley called Dixie Lanes. Save yourself the trouble of watching this mess, and if you need to kill some time, go bowling. Not rated, but equivalent to a PG-13. 1988; 90m.

DOCTOR AT LARGE ★★★
DIR: Ralph Thomas. **CAST:** Dirk Bogarde, James Robertson Justice, Shirley Eaton.

Young Dr. Simon Sparrow wants to join the hospital staff, but the grumpy superintendent isn't buying. Comic conniving ensues as Sparrow seeks a place. Third in a series of six films featuring Dr. Sparrow. 1957; 98m.

DOCTOR AT SEA ★★★
DIR: Ralph Thomas. **CAST:** Dirk Bogarde, Brigitte Bardot, Brenda de Banzie, James Robertson Justice.

Fed up with the myriad complications of London life and romance, young, handsome Dr. Simon Sparrow seeks a rugged man's world by signing up on a passenger-carrying freighter as ship's doctor. He goes from the frying pan into the fire when he meets Brigitte Bardot on the high seas! Second in the highly successful British comedy series. 1955; 92m.

DOCTOR DETROIT ★★½
DIR: Michael Pressman. **CAST:** Dan Aykroyd, Howard Hesseman, Nan Martin, T. K. Carter.

Dan Aykroyd (*Trading Places*; *The Blues Brothers*) stars in this comedy as a soft-spoken English professor who becomes a comic book–style pimp and takes on the local mob. Aykroyd has some genuinely funny moments, but the movie is uneven overall. Rated R for profanity, nudity, and violence. 1983; 89m.

DR. HECKYL AND MR. HYPE ★★★½
DIR: Charles B. Griffith. **CAST:** Oliver Reed, Sunny Johnson, Mel Welles, Jackie Coogan, Corinne Calvet, Dick Miller.

Oh, no, not another *Dr. Jekyll and Mr. Hyde* parody! But this is quite funny, right up there with Jerry Lewis's *The Nutty Professor*. Oliver Reed is hilarious as both an ugly podiatrist and his alter ego, a handsome stud. Writer-director Charles B. Griffith, who wrote the original *Little Shop of Horrors*, has a field day here. Rated R for nudity. 1980; 99m.

DOCTOR IN DISTRESS ★★★
DIR: Ralph Thomas. **CAST:** Dirk Bogarde, Samantha Eggar, James Robertson Justice.

In this high jinks–jammed British comedy of medical student and young physician trials and tribulations, head of hospital Sir Lancelot Spratt reveals he is human when he falls in love. Hero Dr. Simon Sparrow has trouble romancing a beautiful model. It's all fast-pace and very funny. Fourth in a series of six that began with *Doctor in the House*. 1963; B&W; 103m.

DOCTOR IN THE HOUSE ★★★½
DIR: Ralph Thomas. **CAST:** Dirk Bogarde, Muriel Pavlow, Kenneth More, Donald Sinden, Kay Kendall, James Robertson Justice, Donald Houston.

This well-paced farce features a superb British cast. It's about the exploits of a group of medical students intent on studying beautiful women and how to become wealthy physicians. This low-key comedy of manners inspired six other *Doctor* movies and eventually led to a TV series. Not rated. 1954; 92m.

DR. OTTO AND THE RIDDLE OF THE GLOOM BEAM ★★★
DIR: John R. Cherry III. **CAST:** Jim Varney.

A fun and wacky journey into the mind of Jim Varney. Dr. Otto has a deranged plan for taking over the world and Lance Sterling is the only person who can stop him. Varney plays both Otto and Sterling and most of the other leading roles in this refreshingly strange comedy. A must for Varney fans. Rated PG. 1986; 97m.

DR. STRANGELOVE OR HOW I LEARNED TO STOP WORRYING AND LOVE THE BOMB ★★★★★
DIR: Stanley Kubrick. **CAST:** Peter Sellers, Sterling Hayden, George C. Scott, Slim Pickens, Keenan Wynn.

Stanley Kubrick's black comedy masterpiece about the dropping of the "bomb." Great performances from an all-star cast, including Peter Sellers in three hilarious roles. Don't miss it. 1964; B&W; 93m.

DOCTOR TAKES A WIFE, THE ★★★½

DIR: Alexander Hall. **CAST:** Ray Milland, Loretta Young, Reginald Gardiner, Edmund Gwenn, Gail Patrick.

This delightful comedy employs an oft-used plot. Through a series of misadventures, Ray Milland is incorrectly identified as Loretta Young's handsome husband. So he takes advantage of the misunderstanding. All ends happily. 1940; B&W; 89m.

DOGPOUND SHUFFLE ★

DIR: Jeffrey Bloom. **CAST:** Ron Moody, David Soul, Raymond Sutton, Pamela McMyler, Ray Stricklyn.

Movies don't get much worse than this piece of sentimental slop. Story has Ron Moody and David Soul as two drifters who rescue a dog from the pound and spend the rest of the movie working up a song-and-dance team with their four-legged friend. Even kids will be bored with this mess. Rated PG for language. 1974; 98m.

DOIN' TIME ★

DIR: George Mendeluk. **CAST:** Jeff Altman, Dey Young, Richard Mulligan, John Vernon, Judy Landers, Colleen Camp, Melanie Chartoff, Graham Jarvis, Pat McCormick, Eddie Velez, Jimmie Walker.

Doin' Time is a bum rap: It resorts to the worst toilet humor and uses physical comedy that was rendered trite years ago. A pie fight within the first 15 minutes of this film should be an effective "we told you so" if you decide to ignore this review. We must admit, however, that there are some funny moments—like flotsam in a swamp of bad taste. Rated R for profanity and sex. 1984; 84m.

DOIN' TIME ON PLANET EARTH ★★½

DIR: Charles Matthau. **CAST:** Nicholas Strouse, Adam West, Candy Azzara, Martha Scott, Matt Alden, Andrea Thompson.

A teenage nerd living in Sunnydale, Arizona ("Prune Capital of the World"), feels so out of place that he wonders if he isn't really from another planet. His unique "adoption fantasy" is fed by the arrival of two weirdos (Adam West and Candace Azzara) who may or may not be from outer space themselves. First-time director Charles Matthau (son of Walter) shows knack for off-the-wall comedy and makes the most of a meager budget and an uneven cast. Rated PG. 1988; 83m.

DON RICKLES: BUY THIS TAPE YOU HOCKEY PUCK ★½

DIR: Barry Shear. **CAST:** Don Rickles, Jack Klugman, Don Adams, Michele Lee, James Caan, Michael Caine, José Ferrer, Arthur Godfrey, Elliott Gould.

With Don Rickles cracking the same tired jokes in a Las Vegas lounge setting, one may ask: Why has he put out this video of his 1975 television special? Besides the obvious monetary reason, there is another. When the camera is not on Rickles insulting his audience, it is used to showcase the comedian's talent as an actor. There are scenes of him impersonating Dustin Hoffman's Ratso from *Midnight Cowboy* and an excellent reenactment of a scene from the Lee–Lawrence play *Inherit the Wind*. But the segment with Michele Lee is a shameless Las Vegas commercial. 1975; 51m.

DONOVAN'S REEF ★★★

DIR: John Ford. **CAST:** John Wayne, Lee Marvin, Elizabeth Allen, Jack Warden, Dorothy Lamour.

Director John Ford's low, knockabout style of comedy prevails in this tale of two old drinking, seafaring buddies—John Wayne and Lee Marvin—forced to set aside their playful head-knocking to aid another pal, Jack Warden, in putting on an air of respectability to impress the latter's visiting daughter (Elizabeth Allen). 1963; 109m.

DON'S PARTY ★★★½

DIR: Bruce Beresford. **CAST:** John Hargreaves, Pat Bishop, Graham Kennedy.

Don's Party is a hilarious, and at times vulgar, adult comedy. Like the characters in *Who's Afraid of Virginia Woolf?*, the eleven revelers at Don's party lose all control, and the evening climaxes in bitter hostilities and humiliating confessions. With no MPAA rating, the film has nudity and profanity. 1976; 91m.

DON'T DRINK THE WATER ★★★★½

DIR: Howard Morris. **CAST:** Jackie Gleason, Estelle Parsons, Ted Bessell, Joan Delaney, Michael Constantine, Howard St. John, Danny Meehan, Richard Libertini.

Jackie Gleason plays a caterer on a vacation with his wife (Estelle Parsons) and daughter (Joan Delaney). When the plane taking them to Greece is hijacked behind the Iron Curtain, Gleason is accused of spying and finds asylum in the U.S. embassy. Gleason's cranky *Honeymooners* attitude is perfectly balanced by Parsons's bubbleheaded comments. Time hasn't worn the screenplay, based on Woody Allen's wacky play. Rated G. 1969; 100m.

DON'T RAISE THE BRIDGE, LOWER THE RIVER ★

DIR: Jerry Paris. **CAST:** Jerry Lewis, Terry-Thomas, Jacqueline Pearce, Bernard Cribbins.

Weak vehicle for Jerry Lewis concerns the once-outstanding comedian's efforts to keep his marriage alive, even as everything seems to be going against him. This just isn't funny. Rated G. 1968; 99m.

DORF AND THE FIRST GAMES OF MOUNT OLYMPUS ★★★

DIR: Lang Elliott. **CAST:** Tim Conway.

Tim Conway reprises his amusing character, Dorkus Dorf, in this followup to *Dorf on Golf*. This time, more variety is given as Dorf demonstrates some twelve events in the first Olympian meet. Some are quite innovative; some just silly. 1988; 35m.

DORF ON GOLF ★★½

DIR: Roger Beatty. **CAST:** Tim Conway.

Tim Conway has created a humorous character, measuring approximately three feet tall, called Dorkus Dorf. In this video he gives tips on playing and enjoying golf. As with most comedy skits, some of them work and some of them fall short. This spawned a sequel, *Dorf and the First Games of Mount Olympus*, which is more fun. 1987; 30m.

DOUBLE DYNAMITE ★★½

DIR: Irving Cummings. **CAST:** Frank Sinatra, Jane Russell, Groucho Marx.

Disappointing comedy about a bank teller (Frank Sinatra) who receives a generous reward for saving a gangster's life completely by accident. Sinatra and Groucho Marx can't rise above the weak script and direction. 1951; B&W; 80m.

DOUBLE EXPOSURE ★★★

DIR: Nico Mastorakis. **CAST:** Mark Hennessy, Scott King, John Vernon.

Two aspiring Venice Beach photographers divide their time between trying to impress the local bathing beauties and solving a murder that they accidentally photographed (shades of *Blow-up*!). Standard comedy thriller done with a little more panache than most of these low-budgeters. Director Nico Mastorakis manages to breathe some life into the clichés. Rated R for nudity. 1987; 100m.

DOUGH AND DYNAMITE/ THE KNOCKOUT ★★★

DIR: Mack Sennett, Charles Chaplin. **CAST:** Roscoe "Fatty" Arbuckle, Charlie Chaplin, Chester Conklin, Fritz Schade, Phyllis Allen, Charlie Chase, Slim Summerville, Edgar Kennedy, Minta Durfee, Hank Mann, Mack Swain, Al St. John, Mack

Sennett, Joe Bordeaux, Eddie Cline, The Keystone Kops.

Two of the best slapstick two-reelers Mack Sennett's famous Keystone Studios churned out during the heyday of fast-and-furious, rough-and-tumble comedies. *The Knockout*, actually a Fatty Arbuckle film, has Charlie Chaplin playing the referee, the third man in the ring, in a fight sequence between behemoths (to him) Edgar Kennedy and Arbuckle. *Dough and Dynamite* is set in a French restaurant. 1914; B&W; 54m.

DOWN AMONG THE "Z" MEN ★
DIR: Maclean Rogers. **CAST:** Peter Sellers, Harry Secombe, Michael Bentine, Spike Milligan, Carol Carr.

Before there was a Monty Python there were the Goons, a British comedy team that featured Peter Sellers, among others (see cast). This comedy troupe was not all that funny, as this film so vividly illustrates. An absent-minded professor misplaces his formula for a special combat gas. What follows is a madcap and tired race between the professor, the military, as well as a couple of crooks to find the secret formula. 1961; B&W; 82m.

DOWN AND OUT IN BEVERLY HILLS ★★★½
DIR: Paul Mazursky. **CAST:** Nick Nolte, Bette Midler, Richard Dreyfuss, Little Richard, Tracy Nelson, Elizabeth Peña, Evan Richards.

When a Los Angeles bum (Nick Nolte) loses his dog to a happy home, he decides to commit suicide in a Beverly Hills swimming pool. The pool's owner (Richard Dreyfuss) saves the seedy-looking character's life and thereby sets in motion a chain of events that threatens to destroy his family's rarefied existence. The result is an uneven but often funny and always outrageous adult sex comedy. Rated R for profanity, violence, nudity, and simulated sex. 1986; 102m.

DOWN BY LAW ★★★★½
DIR: Jim Jarmusch. **CAST:** John Lurie, Tom Waits, Roberto Benigni, Ellen Barkin.

Stranger Than Paradise director Jim Jarmusch improves on his static deadpan style by allowing his *Down by Law* characters a bit more life. In fact, he appears to be leaning more optimistically toward activity. He gives the film an energetic Italian comedian (Roberto Benigni), who looks like a dark-haired Kewpie doll. This lively imp inspires his lethargic companions (John Lurie, Tom Waits) to speak, sing, and generally loosen up a little. The three meet in the same jail cell and eventually end up escaping together. Rated R for nudity and profanity. 1986; 90m.

DRAGNET (1987) ★★½
DIR: Tom Mankiewicz. **CAST:** Dan Aykroyd, Tom Hanks, Alexandra Paul, Harry Morgan, Christopher Plummer, Dabney Coleman, Elizabeth Ashley, Jack O'Halloran, Kathleen Freeman.

Dan Aykroyd's deliriously funny impersonation of Jack Webb can only carry this comedy so far. While Tom Hanks adds some funny moments of his own, the contrived screenplay about political double-dealing in Los Angeles tends to bog down. Rated PG-13 for profanity and violence. 1987; 107m.

DREAM A LITTLE DREAM ★★
DIR: Marc Rocco. **CAST:** Jason Robards Jr., Corey Feldman, Meredith Salenger, Piper Laurie.

An obnoxious teen has the hots for Miss Unattainable (Meredith Salenger). When the two get caught up in Jason Robards's dream, he gets his chance to be with her. Problems arise when her crazy boyfriend reacts and Robards wants to end the dream. Mediocre. Rated PG-13 for language. 1989; 115m.

DREAM TEAM, THE ★★★★½
DIR: Howard Zieff. **CAST:** Michael Keaton, Christopher Lloyd, Peter

Boyle, Stephen Furst, Lorraine Bracco, Dennis Boutsikaris.

When a psychiatrist (Dennis Boutsikaris) takes four mental patients on a field trip to Yankee Stadium, he is unexpectedly waylaid and his quartet of lovable loonies is let loose in the Big Apple. This gem of a comedy features terrific ensemble performances. It'll steal your heart—guaranteed. Rated PG for profanity and violence. 1989; 113m.

DREAMING OUT LOUD ★★½

DIR: Harold Young. **CAST:** Chester Lauck, Norris Goff, Frances Langford, Robert Wilcox, Irving Bacon, Frank Craven, Phil Harris.

Chester Lauck and Norris Goff, better known as radio's Lum and Abner, fare well in this first of a film series based on their misadventures at the Jot-em Down Store in Pine Ridge, Arkansas. The crackerbarrel philosophers quietly, and with humor, exert a variety of influences on their fellow citizens. It's corn, but clean corn. 1940; B&W; 65m.

DRIVE-IN ★★★

DIR: Rod Amateau. **CAST:** Lisa Lemole, Glen Morshower, Gary Cavagnaro, Trey Wilson.

Enjoyable film about a day in the life of a small Texas town. At dusk all the citizens head off for the local drive-in theatre. With as many as three plots developing, *Drive-In* is like a Southern *American Graffiti.* Rated PG. 1976; 96m.

DUCK SOUP ★★★★★

DIR: Leo McCarey. **CAST:** The Marx Brothers, Margaret Dumont, Louis Calhern, Raquel Torres, Edgar Kennedy.

Groucho, Harpo, Chico, and Zeppo in their best film: an antiestablishment comedy that failed miserably at the box office at the time of its release. Today, this Leo McCarey–directed romp has achieved its proper reputation as the quintessential Marx Brothers classic. 1933; B&W; 70m.

EAGLE, THE ★★★

DIR: Clarence Brown. **CAST:** Rudolph Valentino, Vilma Banky, Louise Dresser, Clark Ward, Spottiswoode Aitken.

Produced to boost the legendary Rudolph Valentino's then-sagging popularity, this satirical romance of a Russian Cossack lieutenant who masquerades as a do-gooder bandit to avenge his father's death proved a box-office winner for the star. Valentino is at his romantic, swoon-inducing, self-mocking best in the title role. Silent. 1925; B&W; 72m.

EASY MONEY ★½

DIR: James Signorelli. **CAST:** Rodney Dangerfield, Joe Pesci, Geraldine Fitzgerald, Candy Azzara.

Nothing is worse than an unfunny comedy—except maybe an unfunny comedy with someone who is ordinarily hilarious. So it is with this film, starring Rodney Dangerfield as a high-living, good-time guy who has to give up all his vices or forfeit a $10 million inheritance. After seeing it, you understand how the comic put-upon stage character feels; in the case of *Easy Money*, it's viewers who get no respect. Rated R for profanity and suggested sex. 1983; 95m.

EAT OR BE EATEN ★★★

DIR: Phil Austin. **CAST:** Firesign Theatre Players.

This spoof centers around newscasters Haryll Hee and Sharyll Shee as they cover the crisis in Labyrinth County. There, the deadly Koodzoo threatens to cover the city with its vine if a virgin is not sacrificed to him. Between news coverage we see clever commercials that poke fun at those we normally see, as well as takeoffs on TV evangelists and sitcoms. This one has lots of laughs. Unrated, it deals with adult topics and is comparable to a PG. 1985; 30m.

EAT THE PEACH ★★

DIR: Peter Ormrod. **CAST:** Stephen Brennan, Eamon Morrissey, Catherine Byrne, Niall Toibin.

Eat the Peach takes place in an Irish village and tells the story of Vinnie and Arthur, two friends who see the Elvis Presley film *Roustabout* in which a cyclist rides the carnival Wall of Death, and decide to create their own. A slight and subtle movie. You want to like it, but it just never kicks in. Rated PG. 1987; 90m.

EAT THE RICH
DIR: Peter Richardson. **CAST:** Lanah Pellay, Ronald Allen, Sandra Dorne.
This ludicrous exercise in bad taste uses profanity, violence, and toilet jokes to elicit laughs. An asexual waiter gets fired, so he wreaks havoc on the British welfare office before starting a people's revolt. Everyone who appears to be rich—or even just employed—is shown as a subversive, perverted, or greedy pig. Nothing makes sense. Rated R for profanity and violence. 1987; 92m.

EATING RAOUL ★★★★
DIR: Paul Bartel. **CAST:** Paul Bartel, Mary Woronov, Robert Beltran, Susan Saiger.
A hilarious black comedy cowritten and directed by Paul Bartel, this low-budget film presents an inventive but rather bizarre solution to the recession. When Mary Bland (Mary Woronov) is saved by her frying-pan-wielding husband, Paul (Bartel), from a would-be rapist, the happily married couple happily discover that the now-deceased attacker was rolling in dough—so they roll him and hit on a way to end their economic woes. Rated R for nudity, profanity, sexual situations, and violence. 1982; 83m.

EDDIE MURPHY—DELIRIOUS ★★★
DIR: Bruce Gowers. **CAST:** Eddie Murphy, The Bus Boys.
Stand-up comedy performance by the superstar at Constitution Hall, Washington, D.C., runs more hot than cold, as Eddie hurls barbs at gays, Michael Jackson, Ralph Kramden and Ed Norton of *The Honeymooners*, his parents, Mr. T, etc. Most of the gags are obscene and often hilarious, but there are also occasional stretches of boredom as the show progresses. Be forewarned: contains strong language. 1983; 70m.

EDDIE MURPHY RAW ★★
DIR: Robert Townsend. **CAST:** Eddie Murphy.
Little of Eddie Murphy's talent comes across in this live-performance film. While there are some funny bits, the comedian too often relies on shock and plain bad taste. The show ends on a flat note with a silly routine about his family having to eat toys because they were poor. Rated R for profanity, scatological humor, and sexual descriptions. 1987; 91m.

EDUCATING RITA ★★★★½
DIR: Lewis Gilbert. **CAST:** Michael Caine, Julie Walters, Michael Williams.
A boozing, depressed English professor (Michael Caine) takes on a sharp-witted, eager-to-learn hairdresser (Julie Walters) for Open University tutorials and each educates the other, in this delightful romantic comedy based on a London hit play. Rated PG for profanity. 1983; 110m.

EGG AND I, THE ★★★
DIR: Chester Erskine. **CAST:** Claudette Colbert, Fred MacMurray, Louise Allbritton, Marjorie Main, Percy Kilbride, Donald MacBride, Samuel S. Hinds, Fuzzy Knight.
Hayseed Fred MacMurray spirits his finishing-school bride Claudette Colbert away from the snooty atmosphere of Boston to cope with chicken farming in the rural Pacific Northwest. Everything goes wrong. Marjorie Main and Percy Kilbride as Ma and Pa Kettle made comic marks bright enough to earn them their own film series. Not a laugh riot, but above-average funny. 1947; B&W; 108m.

18 AGAIN ★½
DIR: Paul Flaherty. **CAST:** George Burns, Charlie Schlatter, Tony Roberts, Anita Morris, Miriam Flynn, Jennifer Runyon, Red Buttons.

Yet another unsuccessful attempt to portray the older man magically switching into a young man's body. George Burns is the crusty grandfather who inhabits grandson Charlie Schlatter's body to fulfill a birthday wish. Schlatter does a terrible, drawn-out George Burns impersonation, and the film is clumsily written and cliché-filled. Even George Burns can't save this one. Rated PG for language and sexual suggestion. 1988; 100m.

ELECTRIC DREAMS ★★★
DIR: Steve Barron. **CAST:** Lenny Von Dohlen, Virginia Madsen, Bud Cort (voice).

An ingenious blending of the motion picture with the rock music video, this release deals with the complications that arise when an absentminded architect, Miles (Lenny Von Dohlen), buys his first home computer. It's a wonderful convenience—at least at first. But it isn't long before the computer (the voice for which is supplied by Bud Cort, of *Harold and Maude* fame) begins to develop a rather feisty personality and even starts wooing Miles's cellist girlfriend, Madeline (Virginia Madsen). Rated PG for profanity. 1984; 96m.

ELVIRA, MISTRESS OF THE DARK ★★★½
DIR: James Signorelli. **CAST:** Elvira, Morgan Shepherd, Daniel Greene, Jeff Conaway, Susan Kellerman.

The late-night TV scream queen of B-film horror makes her debut as a movie star. It was well worth the wait! Elvira descends upon a midwestern town to sell her late aunt's estate. The puritanical townsfolk have other plans once they see the scantily clad mistress of the dark. What ensues is a laugh riot, albeit with more breast jokes than you can count. You'll scream when you see Elvira as a baby. Rated PG for foul language. 1988; 90m.

EMANON ★
DIR: Stuart Paul. **CAST:** Stuart Paul, Cheryl M. Lynn, Jeremy Miller.

The Messiah comes to New York City. He wears rags and lives among the bums, and "respectable" people ignore him until a crippled boy (Jeremy Miller) discovers that Emanon (no name, spelled backwards), played by writer-director Stuart Paul, can perform miracles. So the boy asks Emanon to help his mother's foundering dress business. The poor script, unbelievable dialogue, and talentless actors transform a spiritual drama into a bad comedy. Rated PG-13 for minor obscenities. 1986; 98m.

EMO PHILIPS LIVE ★★★★
DIR: Cynthia L. Sears. **CAST:** Emo Philips.

A high-level comedy concert. Emo Philips has the delivery of a frightened three-year-old and the body movements of an android. He may act strange, but he possesses a unique, off-center perception that crashes through the boundaries of normal comedy into a netherworld of twisted humor. Not rated; free of profanity. 1987; 55m.

END, THE ★★★½
DIR: Burt Reynolds. **CAST:** Burt Reynolds, Sally Field, Dom DeLuise, Joanne Woodward, David Steinberg, Pat O'Brien, Myrna Loy, Kristy McNichol, Robby Benson.

The blackest of black comedies, this stars Burt Reynolds (who also directed) as an unfortunate fellow who is informed he's dying of a rare disease. Poor Burt can hardly believe it. What's worse, his friends and family don't seem to care. So he decides to end it all. In the process, he meets a maniac (Dom DeLuise) who is more than willing to lend a hand. It's surprisingly funny. Rated R. 1978; 100m.

ENSIGN PULVER ★★★
DIR: Joshua Logan. **CAST:** Robert Walker Jr., Burl Ives, Walter Matthau, Tommy Sands, Millie Perkins, Kay

Medford, Larry Hagman, Jack Nicholson.

This sequel to *Mr. Roberts* doesn't quite measure up. The comedy, which takes place aboard a World War II cargo ship, can't stay afloat despite the large and impressive cast. Robert Walker Jr. is no match for Jack Lemmon, who played the original Ensign Pulver in 1955. 1964; 104m.

ENTER LAUGHING ★★½

DIR: Carl Reiner. **CAST:** Reni Santoni, José Ferrer, Shelley Winters, Elaine May, Jack Gilford, Janet Margolin, Michael J. Pollard, Don Rickles, Rob Reiner, Nancy Kovack.

Carl Reiner's semiautobiographical comedy, about a young man who shucks his training and ambitions as a pharmacist to become a comedian, is studded with familiar faces and peopled by engaging personalities—but doesn't really leave a lasting memory. There are more than a few genuinely funny scenes, but overall the film is bland. 1967; 112m.

ENTERTAINING MR. SLOANE ★★

DIR: Douglas Hickox. **CAST:** Beryl Reid, Peter McEnery, Harry Andrews, Alan Webb.

Joe Orton, the young British playwright whose short life formed the basis of *Prick Up Your Ears,* wrote the play from which this film was made. Neither play nor film has aged well. An amoral young man is taken in at a house where both a grotesque middle-aged woman and her brother, a latent homosexual, have romantic designs on him. Well performed, but no longer shocking enough to be effective. Unrated. 1970; 94m.

ERIC BOGOSIAN–FUNHOUSE ★★★★

DIR: Lewis MacAdams. **CAST:** Eric Bogosian.

Eric Bogosian is one of the most imaginative and versatile performers currently working in theatre and motion pictures. His sensational one-man show taped in Los Angeles features the actor doing a cross-section of characters including derelicts, street hoods, evangelists, radio announcers, television newsmen, and prison inmates. This journey through the American psychological landscape is hilarious, poignant, terrifying, and thought-provoking. Rated R for strong language and subject matter. 1988; 80m.

ERNEST FILM FESTIVAL ★★

DIR: John R. Cherry III. **CAST:** Jim Varney.

This appears to be a promo tape used to secure future commercials for Jim Varney's character, Ernest. On it you will see, if you can stand it, 101 commercials and bloopers of the Ernest and Vern variety. He sells everything from cars to eggs using his country-hick lingo. 1986; 55m.

ERNEST GOES TO CAMP ★

DIR: John R. Cherry III. **CAST:** Jim Varney, Victoria Racimo, John Vernon, Iron Eyes Cody, Lyle Alzado.

Fans of the many commercials starring Ernest (Hey, Vern!) will enjoy some of Jim Varney's comedy antics, but the film could have been called *Meatballs XI* for all the originality it contains. The story revolves around a dim-witted groundskeeper (Varney) who becomes the counselor for a group of juvenile delinquents being given a second chance by attending a posh summer camp. Rated PG for profanity and scatological humor. 1987; 95m.

ERNIE KOVACS: TELEVISION'S ORIGINAL GENIUS ★★★★

DIR: Keith Burns. **CAST:** Ernie Kovacs, Edie Adams, Jack Lemmon, Steve Allen, Chevy Chase, John Barbour.

This tribute to the late Ernie Kovacs was produced for cable television. It is a series of clips from Kovacs's television career along with comments from friends (Jack Lemmon and Steve Allen) and family (wife Edie Adams and daughter). Narration is provided by John Barbour of *Real People.* Those familiar with Kovacs's work will fondly remember his innovative creations: Percy Dovetonsils, Eugene, and the Nairobi Trio. For others, this serves as an introduction to Kovacs's comic genius. 1982; 86m.

ERRAND BOY, THE ★★★
DIR: Jerry Lewis. **CAST:** Jerry Lewis, Brian Donlevy, Sig Ruman.
One of Jerry Lewis's better solo efforts, as he proceeds (in his own inimitable style) to make a shambles of the Hollywood movie studio where he is employed as the local gofer. Very funny. 1961; B&W; 92m.

EUROPEAN VACATION
DIR: Amy Heckerling. **CAST:** Chevy Chase, Beverly D'Angelo, Dana Hill, Jason Lively, Eric Idle, Victor Lanoux, John Astin.
The sappy sequel to *Vacation*, this moronic mess has three laughs. Two of them are provided by Eric Idle as a veddy, veddy polite British bicyclist mangled by the vacationing Griswalds (Chevy Chase, Beverly D'Angelo, Dana Hill, and Jason Lively). They win an all-expense (but decidedly low-budget) European vacation grand prize on the television game show *Pig in a Poke*. Rated PG-13 for nudity, violence, and profanity. 1985; 95m.

EVENING WITH BOB GOLDTHWAIT: SHARE THE WARMTH, AN ★★★★
DIR: Anthony Eaton. **CAST:** Bob Goldthwait.
Bob Goldthwait lashes out at Ronald and Nancy Reagan, Bruce Willis, Bob Hope, Lucille Ball, *Rolling Stone* magazine, and the world in general, with a delivery so maniacal, it's downright scary. This is caustic comedy at its funniest. See Goldthwait before someone sues him or locks him away. Not rated, but filled with profanity. 1987; 55m.

EVENING WITH ROBIN WILLIAMS, AN ★★★★
DIR: Don Mischer. **CAST:** Robin Williams.
Here's a remarkably good comedy video with Robin Williams going back to his stand-up comedy roots. He's totally unpredictable when improvising on stage, and this adds to his charm. Filmed at San Francisco's Great American Music Hall, it provides ample proof why Williams was considered one of the finest live comedians of his era before scoring on television (with *Mork and Mindy*) and in the movies. Unrated, it contains profanity. 1983; 60m.

EVERY GIRL SHOULD BE MARRIED ★★½
DIR: Don Hartman. **CAST:** Cary Grant, Betsy Drake, Franchot Tone, Diana Lynn, Alan Mowbray.
A bit of light comic froth balanced mostly on Cary Grant's charm and polish. He plays a baby doctor. Betsy Drake, who later got him off-screen, plays a salesgirl bent on leading him to the altar. The title is irksome, but the picture's diverting, innocent fun. 1948; B&W; 85m.

EVERY WHICH WAY BUT LOOSE ★★★
DIR: James Fargo. **CAST:** Clint Eastwood, Sondra Locke, Geoffrey Lewis, Clyde (the ape), Ruth Gordon.
After *Smokey and the Bandit* cleaned up at the box office, Clint Eastwood decided to make his own modern-day cowboy movie. This 1978 release proved to be one of the squinty-eyed star's biggest moneymakers. The film is far superior to its sequel, *Any Which Way You Can*. Rated R. 1978; 114m.

EVERYTHING YOU ALWAYS WANTED TO KNOW ABOUT SEX BUT WERE AFRAID TO ASK ★★★★
DIR: Woody Allen. **CAST:** John Carradine, Woody Allen, Lou Jacobi, Louise Lasser, Anthony Quayle, Lynn Redgrave, Tony Randall, Burt Reynolds, Gene Wilder.
Everything You Always Wanted to Know about Sex But Were Afraid to Ask gave Woody Allen, scriptwriter, star, and director, an opportunity to stretch out without having to supply

all the talent himself. Several sequences do not feature Woody at all. The film is broken up into vignettes supposedly relating to questions asked. Rated R. 1972; 87m.

EXPERIENCE PREFERRED...BUT NOT ESSENTIAL ★★★★★
DIR: Peter Duffell. **CAST:** Elizabeth Edmonds, Sue Wallace, Geraldine Griffith, Karen Meagher, Ron Bain, Alun Lewis, Robert Blythe.

This delightful British import, which is somewhat reminiscent of Scottish director Bill Forsyth's *Gregory's Girl* and *Local Hero*, follows the awkward and amusing adventures of a young woman during her first summer job at a Welsh coastal resort in 1962. She comes to town insecure and frumpy and leaves at the end of the summer pretty, sexy, and confident. Can you guess why? Right! Rated PG for language. 1983; 80m.

EXPERTS, THE ★
DIR: Dave Thomas. **CAST:** John Travolta, Arye Gross, Kelly Preston, Deborah Foreman, James Keach, Charles Martin Smith.

John Travolta and Arye Gross star as two hip nightclub entrepreneurs from New York City. Charles Martin Smith is a KGB agent who whisks the boys off to a secret American-like community in Russia. Top-notch cast is wasted in this implausible mess. Rated PG-13 for violence and profanity. 1988; 94m.

EXTRA GIRL, THE ★★★
DIR: Dick Jones. **CAST:** Mabel Normand, Ralph Graves.

Madcap silent comedienne Mabel Normand's last film—and a winner! Normand plays a naïve, starstruck Midwestern girl who fantasizes about fame in films. She wins a beauty contest, goes to Hollywood, and winds up a no-name extra. Silent with music score. 1923; B&W; 87m.

FALLING IN LOVE AGAIN ★★½
DIR: Steven Paul. **CAST:** Elliott Gould, Susannah York, Michelle Pfeiffer, Stuart Paul.

Elliott Gould stars as a middle-aged dreamer who is obsessed with his younger days in the Bronx. Gould and wife (Susannah York) are on vacation and headed east to recapture the past. The film suffers from countless long flashbacks of his youthful romance with WASP princess (Michelle Pfeiffer) and is a poor attempt at romantic comedy. Rated R. 1980; 103m.

FAMILY JEWELS, THE ★★½
DIR: Jerry Lewis. **CAST:** Jerry Lewis, Donna Butterworth, Sebastian Cabot.

Jerry Lewis tries to outperform Alec Guinness (from *Kind Hearts and Coronets*) in this syrupy tale of a wealthy young heiress (Donna Butterworth) forced to select a guardian from among six uncles. Lewis plays all six, but his seventh—the family chauffeur—is the only one with any credibility. It's a long stretch for thin material. 1965; 100m.

FANDANGO ★★
DIR: Kevin Reynolds. **CAST:** Kevin Costner, Judd Nelson, Sam Robards, Chuck Bush, Brian Cesak.

This is an unfunny comedy about a group of college chums (led by Kevin Costner and Judd Nelson) going on one last romp together before being inducted into the army—or running away from the draft—in 1971. Slow-going and a bit too angst-ridden, *Fandango* seems as if it's going to get better any minute, but it doesn't. Rated PG for profanity. 1984; 91m.

FAR NORTH ★★★
DIR: Sam Shepard. **CAST:** Jessica Lange, Charles Durning, Tess Harper, Donald Moffat, Ann Wedgeworth, Patricia Arquette.

Actor-playwright Sam Shepard's first film as a director is a surprisingly funny comedy-drama about three generations of a farming family. Yet underlying the humor is a typically Shepardian sense of tragedy as wayward daughter Jessica Lange comes home after her father is hurt in a farming accident. She wants desperately to make some sort of a connection with him before he dies. Rated PG-13 for profanity and sexy scenes. 1988; 87m.

FARMER'S DAUGHTER, THE ★★★

DIR: H. C. Potter. **CAST:** Loretta Young, Joseph Cotten, Ethel Barrymore, Charles Bickford, Lex Barker, Keith Andes, James Arness.

Loretta Young won the best actress Oscar for her delightful performance in this charming comedy about a Swedish woman who clashes with the man she loves over a congressional election. 1947; B&W; 97m.

FARMER'S OTHER DAUGHTER, THE 🦃

DIR: John Patrick Hayes. **CAST:** Judy Pennebaker, Bill Michael, Ernest Ashworth.

Incredibly lame film about a family trying to save their farm from the mean old banker who wants to foreclose on the place. Totally insufferable. 1965; 84m.

FAST BREAK ★★½

DIR: Jack Smight. **CAST:** Gabe Kaplan, Harold Sylvester, Mike Warren, Bernard King, Reb Brown.

As a basketball coach, Gabe Kaplan resurrects some of the laughs he got with his sweathogs on *Welcome Back, Kotter*. Kaplan plays a New York deli worker who quits to coach a college basketball team in Nevada. He brings four blacks from his New York ghetto to help the team, and one turns out to be a girl. Kaplan must beat a tough rival team in order to get a $30,000-a-year contract at the university, so he whips the unpromising team into shape. Rated PG. 1979; 107m.

FAST TIMES AT RIDGEMONT HIGH ★★½

DIR: Amy Heckerling. **CAST:** Sean Penn, Jennifer Jason Leigh, Judge Reinhold, Brian Backer, Phoebe Cates, Ray Walston.

In 1979, Cameron Crow went back to high school to discover what today's teens are up to and wrote about his experiences. From his excellent book, they've made a kind of *Animal House* of the teenage set. Youngsters will love it, but adults will probably want to skip the movie and read the book. Rated R for nudity, profanity, and simulated sex. 1982; 92m.

FATAL GLASS OF BEER, A/POOL SHARKS ★★★

DIR: Clyde Bruckman, Edwin Middleton. **CAST:** W. C. Fields, George Chandler, Rosemary Theby, Bud Ross.

This pairing brings together two distinct examples of the unique comedy of W. C. Fields. The first, produced by Mack Sennett, finds Fields practicing his peculiar art in the frozen North, complete with snow on cue and misplaced Indians. *Pool Sharks*, made 18 years earlier, is the comedian's first distributed film. In it, he is pitted against Bud Ross in the pool game of all pool games—played for the love of a mutually sought girl. Fields's bizarre brand of humor highlights both. 1915–1933; B&W; 60m.

FATHER GOOSE ★★★

DIR: Ralph Nelson. **CAST:** Cary Grant, Leslie Caron.

A bedraggled, unshaven, and unsophisticated Cary Grant is worth watching even in a mediocre comedy. Grant plays a hard-drinking Australian coast watcher during the height of World War II. His reclusive lifestyle on a remote Pacific island is interrupted when he is forced to play nursemaid to a group of adolescent schoolgirls and their prudish teacher (Leslie Caron). 1964; 115m.

FATHER GUIDO SARDUCCI GOES TO COLLEGE ★★

DIR: Steve Binder. **CAST:** Don Novello, Billy Vera and The Beaters.

Don Novello re-creates his *Saturday Night Live* character of Father Guido Sarducci during a live concert at U.C. Santa Barbara. He touches on birthdays, life insurance, his years at DooDa U., and President Reagan. His priestly character is sometimes lost in his more worldly comments. We guess you had to be there to really enjoy it. 1985; 59m.

FATHER OF THE BRIDE ★★★½
DIR: Vincente Minnelli. **CAST:** Spencer Tracy, Elizabeth Taylor, Joan Bennett, Leo G. Carroll, Don Taylor, Billie Burke.
Spencer Tracy's proud and frantic papa is the chief attraction in this droll examination of last-minute preparations prior to daughter Elizabeth Taylor's wedding. Writers Frances Goodrich and Albert Hackett include a few too many scenes of near-slapstick hysteria, but the quieter moments between father and daughter are wonderful (if a bit dated). 1950; 93m.

FATHER'S LITTLE DIVIDEND ★★★
DIR: Vincente Minnelli. **CAST:** Spencer Tracy, Elizabeth Taylor, Joan Bennett, Don Taylor, Billie Burke.
In *Father of the Bride*, the marriage of daughter Elizabeth Taylor to Don Taylor made a wreck out of Spencer Tracy. Now, in the sequel, she's expecting, and Tracy is not exactly overjoyed at the prospect of being a grandfather. This play off of a winner doesn't measure up to the original, but it's entertaining fare anyway. Spencer Tracy could bluster and be flustered with the best. 1951; 82m.

FATSO ★★½
DIR: Anne Bancroft. **CAST:** Dom DeLuise, Anne Bancroft, Candy Azzara, Ron Carey.
Too many juvenile toilet jokes mar what might have been a humorous study of a man's confrontation with his own obesity. Dom DeLuise stars as the chubby Italian-American who wrestles with a variety of diets. Messages get lost amid the shrill performances. Rated PG for language and questionable humor. 1980; 94m.

FATTY AND MABEL ADRIFT/MABEL, FATTY AND THE LAW ★★★
DIR: Roscoe Arbuckle. **CAST:** Roscoe "Fatty" Arbuckle, Mabel Normand, Frank Hayes, May Wells, Al St. John.
Solo and as a duet, Fatty Arbuckle and Mabel Normand were near peerless in the halcyon days of silent comedies. These two Mack Sennett features are outstanding examples of why the public held them both in admiration. The kiss-good-night sequence in *Fatty and Mabel Adrift* is reason enough to see the film. 1915–1916; B&W; 40m.

FATTY'S TIN-TYPE TANGLE/OUR CONGRESSMAN ★★★
DIR: Roscoe Arbuckle, Rob Wagner. **CAST:** Roscoe "Fatty" Arbuckle, Mabel Normand, Al St. John, Will Rogers, Mollie Thompson.
This is a curious pairing of a Mack Sennett Keystone comedy and a Hal Roach satire made a decade apart and totally unrelated in subject matter. In the first, Fatty gets Mabel's goat by making goo-goo eyes at the maid. In the second, newly elected congressman Will Rogers, straight from the sticks, bombs in Washington society. 1915–1924; B&W; 44m.

FAWLTY TOWERS ★★★★
DIR: John Cleese, Connie Booth. **CAST:** John Cleese, Prunella Scales, Connie Booth.
This British television series is a true comedy classic. Written by Monty Python's John Cleese and his ex-wife Connie Booth, the show is a situation comedy about the problems of running a small seaside inn. The characters are typical (harried husband, shrewish wife, incompetent help) and the storylines mundane (guest loses money; fire drill; restaurant critics arrive), but in the hands of Cleese and company, each episode is a near-perfect ballet of escalating frustration. For sheer, double-over belly laughs, this series has never been equalled. 1975; 75m.

FEDS ★★

DIR: Dan Goldberg. **CAST:** Mary Gross, Rebecca DeMornay, Ken Marshall.

A second-string comedy about two women (Mary Gross and Rebecca DeMornay) who work to beat the odds and graduate from the FBI's training academy. Some good laughs, but not enough. Rated PG-13 for mild language. 1988; 83m.

FEEL MY PULSE ★★½

DIR: Gregory La Cava. **CAST:** Bebe Daniels, Richard Arlen, William Powell.

Silent screwball comedy boasts a hypochondriac heiress who inherits a sanitarium that is used by bootleggers as a front and a hideout. Bebe Daniels, armed with a stethoscope to keep track of her heartbeat, does a fine job as the germ-wary, sheltered young girl who encounters a life she didn't dream existed. Silent. 1928; B&W; 86m.

FEMALE TROUBLE

DIR: John Waters. **CAST:** Divine, Edith Massey, Cookie Mueller, David Lochary, Mink Stole, Michael Potter.

The story of Dawn Davenport (Divine) from her days as a teenage belligerent through her rise to fame as a criminal and then to her death as a convicted murderer. As in other films by Waters, the theme here is the Jean Genet–like credo "crime equals beauty." Also, as in other films by the enfant terrible from Baltimore, *Female Trouble* will offend just about anyone. Though it is unrated, this film is the equivalent of an X, due to sex, nudity, and violence. 1973; 90m.

FERRIS BUELLER'S DAY OFF ★★★★

DIR: John Hughes. **CAST:** Matthew Broderick, Alan Ruck, Mia Sara, Jeffrey Jones, Jennifer Grey, Charlie Sheen, Cindy Pickett, Lyman Ward.

Writer-director John Hughes strikes again, this time with a charming tale of a high-school legend in his own time (Matthew Broderick, playing the title character) who pretends to be ill in order to have a day away from school. The expressive Broderick owns the film, although he receives heavy competition from Jeffrey Jones, whose broadly played dean of students has been trying to nail Ferris Bueller for months. Rated PG-13 for mild profanity. 1986; 104m.

FIENDISH PLOT OF DR. FU MANCHU, THE

DIR: Piers Haggard. **CAST:** Peter Sellers, Helen Mirren, Sid Caesar, David Tomlinson.

Peter Sellers plays a dual role of "insidious Oriental villain" Fu Manchu, who is out to rule the world, and his arch-enemy, the Holmes-like Nayland Smith of Scotland Yard. It's unfunny, racist, and just plain awful. Sellers's last movie. Rated PG. 1980; 108m.

FIFTH AVENUE GIRL ★★

DIR: Gregory La Cava. **CAST:** Ginger Rogers, Walter Connolly, Verree Teasdale, Tim Holt, James Ellison, Kathryn Adams.

Limp social comedy features Ginger Rogers as a homeless but levelheaded young lady who is taken in by Walter Connolly, one of those unhappy movieland millionaires who is just dying to find someone to lavish gifts on. 1939; B&W; 83m.

FIND THE LADY ★★★

DIR: John Trent. **CAST:** John Candy, Mickey Rooney, Peter Cook, Lawrence Dane, Alexandra Bastedo.

In this slapstick rendition of a cops-and-robbers spoof, John Candy, as the cop, and Mickey Rooney, as a kidnapper, create lots of laughs. The story is filled with car crashes, disasters on the pistol range, and every kind of general catastrophe on the way to a very funny finish. 1986; 90m.

FINDERS KEEPERS ★★½

DIR: Richard Lester. **CAST:** Louis Gossett Jr., Michael O'Keefe, Beverly D'Angelo.

Director Richard Lester went back to his comedy roots with this disappointingly uneven slapstick chase film, which stars Louis Gossett Jr., Michael O'Keefe, and Beverly D'Angelo as a trio of wacky characters. The story deals with a missing $5 million and a wild train ride at the end of which the winner takes all. Rated PG for profanity and violence. 1983; 96m.

FINE MADNESS, A ★★★
DIR: Irvin Kershner. **CAST:** Sean Connery, Joanne Woodward, Jean Seberg.
Whimsical story of a daffy, radical poet, well portrayed by Sean Connery (proving that, even in the 1960s, he could stretch further than James Bond). Many of the laughs come from his well-developed relationship with wife Joanne Woodward, although the film occasionally lapses into lurid slapstick. Unrated; adult themes. 1966; 104m.

FINE MESS, A ★
DIR: Blake Edwards. **CAST:** Ted Danson, Howie Mandel, Richard Mulligan, Stuart Margolin, Maria Conchita Alonso, Jennifer Edwards, Paul Sorvino.
Supposedly inspired by the Laurel and Hardy classic, *The Music Box*, this movie is totally lacking in originality. The illogical plot has Ted Danson and Howie Mandel winning a bundle on a fixed horse race and spending the rest of the picture running from gangster Paul Sorvino's henchmen. Gag after gag falls embarrassingly flat. Rated PG. 1986; 100m.

FINNEGAN BEGIN AGAIN ★★★★
DIR: Joan Micklin Silver. **CAST:** Mary Tyler Moore, Robert Preston, Sam Waterston, Sylvia Sidney.
In this endearing romance, Robert Preston plays Michael Finnegan, an eccentric retired advice columnist who befriends schoolteacher Elizabeth (Mary Tyler Moore) after learning of her secret affair with a married undertaker (Sam Waterston). Their eventual romance becomes a warm, funny, and tender portrayal of love blossoming in later life. Made for cable. 1985; 97m.

FIREHOUSE
DIR: J. Christian Ingvordsen. **CAST:** Barrett Hopkins, Shannon Murphy, Violet Brown, John Anderson, Peter Onorati.
Cheap sets, bad dialogue, and choppy editing offer little support to this *Charlie's Angels* clone set in a firehouse. Setting fire to the script would have been a better notion. Rated R. 1987; 91m.

FIRST FAMILY
DIR: Buck Henry. **CAST:** Bob Newhart, Gilda Radner, Madeline Kahn, Richard Benjamin, Harvey Korman, Bob Dishy, Rip Torn.
The superior comic talents of Bob Newhart, Madeline Kahn, Gilda Radner, Richard Benjamin, and Harvey Korman are totally wasted in this unfunny farce about an inept president, his family, and his aides, written and directed by Buck Henry. It's a mess. Rated R. 1980; 104m.

FIRST HOWIE MANDEL SPECIAL, THE ★★½
DIR: Maurice Abraham. **CAST:** Howie Mandel.
This Howie Mandel concert was filmed live in Toronto, Canada. Mandel is from Canada and his countrymen give him a surprisingly lukewarm reception. They seem to like his comedy, but they are reluctant to participate in the performance. This makes for strained viewing—something you don't need in comedy. If you like Mandel's screaming, his nervous off-the-wall delivery, and X-rated material meant to shock, you'll enjoy this one. 1983; 57m.

FIRST TIME, THE ★★½
DIR: Charlie Loventhal. **CAST:** Tim Choate, Krista Erickson, Wallace Shawn, Wendie Jo Sperber.
With parents pushing poor Charlie into a relationship with a girl—any girl!—he resists. But when he gets into filmmaking, the opposite sex goes mad for him. This campus com-

edy is rated PG-13 for mature situations and language. 1982; 96m.

FISH CALLED WANDA, A ★★★★½

DIR: Charles Crichton. **CAST:** John Cleese, Jamie Lee Curtis, Kevin Kline, Michael Palin, Tom Georgeson, Patricia Hayes.

Monty Python veteran John Cleese wrote and starred in this hilarious caper comedy. Jamie Lee Curtis and Kevin Kline are American crooks who plot to double-cross their British partners in crime (Michael Palin and Tom Georgeson) with the unwitting help of barrister Cleese. Be forewarned: *Wanda* has something in it to offend everyone. Rated R for profanity and violence. 1988; 108m.

FISH THAT SAVED PITTSBURGH, THE ★★½

DIR: Gilbert Moses. **CAST:** Stockard Channing, Flip Wilson, Jonathan Winters, Julius Irving.

Curious mixture of disco, astrology, and comedy. A failing basketball team turns to a rather eccentric medium for help, and the resulting confusion makes for a few amusing moments. Features a veritable smorgasbord of second-rate actors, from Jonathan Winters to basketball great Julius Irving (Dr. J.). Proceed at your own risk. Rated PG for profanity. 1979; 102m.

FLAMINGO KID, THE ★★★½

DIR: Garry Marshall. **CAST:** Matt Dillon, Richard Crenna, Jessica Walter, Janet Jones, Hector Elizondo.

A teen comedy-drama with more on its mind than stale sex jokes. Matt Dillon stars as Jeffrey Willis, a Brooklyn kid who discovers how the other half lives when he takes a summer job at a beach resort. A good story which explores the things (and people) that shape our values as we reach adulthood. A genuine pleasure, and you'll be glad you tried it. Rated PG-13 for frank sexual situations. 1984; 100m.

FLASK OF FIELDS, A ★★★★½

DIR: Monte Brice, Clyde Bruckman, Leslie Pearce. **CAST:** W. C. Fields, Rosemary Theby, George Chandler.

The Golf Specialist, A Fatal Glass of Beer, and *The Dentist*—three short comedy gems—amply display the matchless talents of W. C. Fields. This is an entertaining tribute. Don't be misled by the credits; Fields directed himself. Hilarious. Bawdy is the only word for the tooth-pulling sequence in *The Dentist*. 1930; B&W; 61m.

FLICKS ★½

DIR: Peter Winograd. **CAST:** Pamela Sue Martin, Joan Hackett, Martin Mull, Richard Belzer, Betty Kennedy.

Aside from "Cat and Mouse," a hilarious cartoon about a retirement home for elderly cartoon characters, *Flicks* is a structureless string of movie parodies that's long on mediocre satire and short on laughs. Rated R. 1985; 79m.

FLYING DEUCES ★★★

DIR: A. Edward Sutherland. **CAST:** Stan Laurel, Oliver Hardy, Jean Parker.

Stan Laurel and Oliver Hardy join the Foreign Legion to help Ollie forget his troubled romantic past. Their attempts at adjusting to Legion life provide many laugh-filled situations, although the script has weak areas and the movie occasionally drags. 1939; B&W; 65m.

FOLLOW THAT CAMEL ★★★½

DIR: Gerald Thomas. **CAST:** Phil Silvers, Jim Dale, Peter Butterworth, Charles Hawtrey, Anita Harris, Joan Sims, Kenneth Williams.

This British comedy, part of the *Carry On* series, features Phil Silvers as the conniving Sgt. Knockers. Lots of laughs, mostly derived from puns and sexist jokes. Some dialogue is a bit racy for young children. Unrated. 1967; 91m.

FOLLOW THAT DREAM ★★★½
DIR: Gordon Douglas. **CAST:** Elvis Presley, Arthur O'Connell, Joanne Moore, Anne Helm, Jack Kruschen.

Elvis is almost too sweet as the naïve hillbilly who, along with his family, moves to a Florida beach. Some laughs result from their inability to fit in and the reactions of the local folk to them. The story is based on Richard Powell's novel *Pioneer Go Home*. Unrated, but contains no objectionable material. 1962; 110m.

FOOLIN' AROUND ★★★
DIR: Richard T. Heffron. **CAST:** Gary Busey, Annette O'Toole, John Calvin, Eddie Albert, Cloris Leachman, Tony Randall.

Gary Busey went from his acclaimed title performance in *The Buddy Holly Story* to starring in this amiable ripoff of *The Graduate* and *The Heartbreak Kid*. Still, Busey, as a working-class boy who falls in love with rich girl Annette O'Toole, is always watchable. He and O'Toole make an appealing screen team, and this makes the movie's lack of originality easier to take. Rated PG. 1980; 111m.

FOR LOVE OF IVY ★★★★
DIR: Daniel Mann. **CAST:** Sidney Poitier, Abbey Lincoln, Beau Bridges, Nan Martin, Carroll O'Connor, Lauri Peters.

Sidney Poitier delivers a terrific performance as Jack Parks, trucking company owner by day and gambling operator by night. Ivy (Abbey Lincoln) is a maid for a wealthy family. When she decides to leave their employ, the family's children (Beau Bridges and Lauri Peters) connive to get Parks to take her out and make her happy. Carroll O'Connor and Nan Martin play Ivy's employers. This is a fine comedy-drama with a wonderful ending. 1968; 101m.

FOR PETE'S SAKE ★★★
DIR: Peter Yates. **CAST:** Barbra Streisand, Michael Sarrazin, Estelle Parsons, Molly Picon.

Lightweight comedy vehicle tailor-made to fit the talents of Barbra Streisand. In this one she plays the wife of cab driver Michael Sarrazin, trying to raise money for him while becoming involved with underworld thugs. Strictly for Streisand fans. Rated PG. 1974; 90m.

FOR THE LOVE OF IT ★★½
DIR: Hal Kanter. **CAST:** Don Rickles, Deborah Raffin, Jeff Conaway, Tom Bosley, Henry Gibson, Barbi Benton, Adam West, Norman Fell, Noriyuki "Pat" Morita.

This would-be wacky comedy is so confusing you'll find yourself absorbed in figuring out who's chasing who and why. Don Rickles wants the Russians' secret plans to take over the Middle East to create a new video game called "Doom's Day," but the CIA and FBI are also interested in them. Some of the chase scenes become so involved that the viewer forgets this is a comedy. Rated PG for violence and adult themes. 1980; 98m.

FOREVER LULU ★½
DIR: Amos Kollek. **CAST:** Hanna Schygulla, Deborah Harry, Alec Baldwin, Paul Gleason, Annie Golden, Dr. Ruth Westheimer, Charles Ludlam.

Ridiculous ripoff of *Desperately Seeking Susan* that's desperately in need of a cohesive plot and a leading lady who can act. Hanna Schygulla portrays a would-be writer at the end of her rope. She's so irritatingly naïve that the viewer never really cares what happens to her. By chance she stumbles on to a drug deal, and the rest is history. As usual, ripoffs like this never measure up. Don't settle for an imitation; get the original. Rated R for nudity, profanity, and violence. 1987; 86m.

FORTUNE COOKIE, THE ★★★★½
DIR: Billy Wilder. **CAST:** Jack Lemmon, Walter Matthau, Ron Rich, Cliff Osmond.

Jack Lemmon is accidently injured by a player while filming a football game from the sidelines. His brother-in-law, Walter Matthau, sees this as an ideal attempt to make some lawsuit money. So starts the first of the usually delightful Lemmon-Matthau comedies. Matthau is at his scene-stealing best in this Oscar-winning role. 1966; B&W; 125m.

FORTY CARATS ★★★½
DIR: Milton Katselas. **CAST:** Liv Ullmann, Edward Albert, Gene Kelly, Nancy Walker, Deborah Raffin.

This comedy has Liv Ullmann playing a 40-year-old divorcée being pursued by a rich 22-year-old, Edward Albert. Laughs abound as Ullmann's grown daughter (Deborah Raffin) and ex-husband (Gene Kelly) react to her latest suitor. Rated PG. 1973; 110m.

48 HRS. ★★★★½
DIR: Walter Hill. **CAST:** Eddie Murphy, Nick Nolte, Annette O'Toole, Frank McRae, James Remar, David Patrick Kelly.

Add *48 Hrs.* to the list of the best cops-and-robbers movies ever made. It's so action-packed, it'll keep you on the edge of your seat from beginning to end. There's more good news: It's funny too. In the story, a cop (Nick Nolte) goes looking for a psychotic prison escapee (James Remar) with the help of a fast-talking con man (Eddie Murphy). It's a dangerous mission, and there's never a dull moment. Rated R for violence, profanity, and nudity. 1982; 96m.

FOUL PLAY ★★★
DIR: Colin Higgins. **CAST:** Goldie Hawn, Chevy Chase, Dudley Moore, Burgess Meredith, Marilyn Sokol.

Gloria Mundy (Goldie Hawn) accidentally becomes involved in a plot to assassinate the Pope. Detective Tony Carlson (Chevy Chase) tries to protect and seduce her. Hawn is good as the damsel in distress, but Chase is hardly the Cary Grant type. Still it's fun. Rated PG. 1978; 116m.

FRANCIS IN THE NAVY ★★
DIR: Arthur Lubin. **CAST:** Donald O'Connor, Martha Hyer, Jim Backus, David Janssen, Clint Eastwood, Martin Milner, Paul Burke.

Sixth of the seven-picture series starring Francis, the talking mule. (Chill Wills provides his voice.) Silly, but the kids will enjoy it. 1955; B&W; 80m.

FRANCIS, THE TALKING MULE ★★★½
DIR: Arthur Lubin. **CAST:** Donald O'Connor, Patricia Medina, ZaSu Pitts, Tony Curtis, Ray Collins, Chill Wills (voice).

First in a series from Universal, this well-known comedy tells the story of how a dimwitted student at West Point (Donald O'Connor) first met up with the famous talking mule of the title. The gags really fly as Francis proceeds to get O'Connor in all sorts of outrageous predicaments, consistently pulling him out just in the nick of time. Some screamingly funny scenes. Followed by six sequels. 1950; B&W; 91m.

FRANKEN AND DAVIS AT STOCKTON STATE ★★★
DIR: Randy Cohen. **CAST:** Al Franken, Tom Davis.

The weird, cerebral humor of Al Franken and Tom Davis is undoubtedly an acquired taste. Those who enjoyed their occasional stints—with "The Franken and Davis Show"—on the original *Saturday Night Live* will find much to appreciate in this live comedy concert, taped at Stockon College in New Jersey. Others may be a little perplexed by what they see at first. But we suggest you stick it out; there are some gems here. 1984; 55m.

FRATERNITY VACATION
DIR: James Frawley. **CAST:** Stephen Geoffreys, Sheree Wilson, Cameron Dye, Leigh McCloskey.

A teen-lust comedy with no laughs, no imagination, and no point for existing, *Fraternity Vacation* stars Stephen Geoffreys as a world-class nerd who somehow scores during vacation time in Palm Springs. He scores while the viewer snores. Rated R for profanity and nudity. 1985; 95m.

FREE RIDE ★½
DIR: Tom Trbovich. **CAST:** Gary Herschberger, Reed Rudy, Dawn Schneider, Peter DeLuise, Warren Berlinger, Mamie Van Doren, Frank Campanella.

Disjointed, cheap rip-off of *Animal House*, with Gary Herschberger playing a supercool professional student, and Reed Rudy as his bunkie. Fitfully funny but not recommended. Rated R for language and nudity. 1986; 92m.

FREEBIE AND THE BEAN ★★★
DIR: Richard Rush. **CAST:** Alan Arkin, James Caan, Valerie Harper, Loretta Swit.

Before astounding filmgoers with the outrageous black comedy *The Stunt Man*, director Richard Rush twisted the cop genre around with this watchable (but not spectacular) release. James Caan and Alan Arkin play San Francisco detectives who wreak havoc while on the trail of gangster Jack Kruschen. Rated R. 1974; 113m.

FRENCH LESSONS ★★★½
DIR: Brian Gilbert. **CAST:** Jane Snowden, Diana Blackburn, Françoise Brion.

Romantic comedy about an English teenager who goes to Paris to study French for the summer. She is determined to fall in love and learns more out of the classroom than in. Rated PG. 1986; 90m.

FRENCH POSTCARDS ★★★½
DIR: Willard Huyck. **CAST:** David Marshall Grant, Blanche Baker, Miles Chapin, Debra Winger.

Written, produced, and directed by the couple who gave us *American Graffiti*, Gloria Katz and Willard Huyck, this film benefits greatly from the skillful supporting performances by two noted French film stars, Marie-France Pisier (*Love on the Run*) and Jean Rochefort (*Till Marriage Do Us Part*). The younger set of characters are well played by David Marshall Grant, Miles Chapin, Valerie Quennessen, and Blanche Baker. *French Postcards* is an enjoyable way to spend a couple of hours. Rated PG. 1979; 92m.

FRITZ THE CAT ★★★
DIR: Ralph Bakshi. **CAST:** Animated.

This is an X-rated rendition of Robert Crumb's revolutionary feline and it's the most outrageous cartoon ever produced. Fritz the Cat has appeared in Zap Comix and Head Comix, as well as in other underground mags. It's sometimes funny and sometimes gross, but mostly just so-so. 1972; 77m.

FROM THE HIP ★★★
DIR: Bob Clark. **CAST:** Judd Nelson, Elizabeth Perkins, John Hurt, Ray Walston, Darren McGavin.

Thoroughly unrealistic but nonetheless entertaining courtroom comedy that works in spite of director Bob Clark's tendency to forget that he's no longer making *Porky's*. Judd Nelson stars as a brash young attorney (Robin "Stormy" Weathers, no less) whose histrionic flair nets him the opportunity to defend John Hurt, a man accused of murder. Hurt delivers a particularly fine, high-powered performance as a ruthless egomaniac who considers himself better than the rest of humanity. Rated PG for language. 1987; 111m.

FRONT PAGE, THE ★★★★
DIR: Lewis Milestone. **CAST:** Pat O'Brien, Adolphe Menjou, Mary Brian, Edward Everett Horton.

A newspaper editor and his ace reporter do battle with civic corruption and each other in the first version of this oft-filmed hit comedy. The fast-paced, sparkling dialogue and the performances of the Warner Bros. stable of character actors have not aged after more than fifty years. This classic movie retains a great deal of charm. 1931; B&W; 99m.

FULL MOON IN BLUE WATER ★★
DIR: Peter Masterson. **CAST:** Gene Hackman, Teri Garr, Burgess Meredith, Elias Coteas, Kevin Cooney.
Gene Hackman and Teri Garr bring wonderful moments to this offbeat comedy-drama. Otherwise, the film is corny and uneven. The story is the basic B-Western plot about a poor fellow who is about to lose his property to evil land-grabbers. In this case, it's Hackman, as a bar owner whose place has gone downhill since the disappearance of his wife. Rated R for profanity and light violence. 1988; 94m.

FULLER BRUSH GIRL, THE ★★★
DIR: Lloyd Bacon. **CAST:** Lucille Ball, Eddie Albert, Jerome Cowan, Lee Patrick.
Lucy's in typical form as a dizzy cosmetics salesgirl up to her mascara in murder and hoodlums. Wisecracking dialogue and familiar character faces help this one out. Harmless fun. 1950; B&W; 85m.

FULLER BRUSH MAN, THE ★★★
DIR: S. Sylvan Simon. **CAST:** Red Skelton, Janet Blair, Don McGuire, Adele Jergens, Buster Keaton.
Red Skelton slapsticks along his route as a door-to-door salesman and gets involved with murder. Sadly unsung master gagster Buster Keaton deserves a lot of credit for the humor he adds to many other Skelton films. 1948; B&W; 93m.

FUN WITH DICK AND JANE ★★★★
DIR: Ted Kotcheff. **CAST:** Jane Fonda, George Segal, Ed McMahon.
How does one maintain one's lifestyle after a sacking from a highly paid aerospace position? George Segal and Jane Fonda have a unique solution. They steal. This comedy caper is well named, because once they begin their career in crime, some quality fun is in store for the audience. Rated PG. 1977; 95m.

FUNNY FARM ★★
DIR: George Roy Hill. **CAST:** Chevy Chase, Madolyn Smith, Joseph Maher, Brad Sullivan, MacIntyre Dixon.
Chevy Chase and Madolyn Smith star as Andy and Elizabeth Farmer, a sportswriter and schoolteacher, who give up the city life for greener pastures in Vermont. Andy plans to write a novel, but their idyllic country life goes awry with a series of predictable disasters, laboriously dramatized. Rated PG for adult language and situations. 1988; 101m.

FUNNY THING HAPPENED ON THE WAY TO THE FORUM, A ★★★★
DIR: Richard Lester. **CAST:** Zero Mostel, Phil Silvers, Jack Gilford, Michael Crawford, Buster Keaton.
Ancient Rome is the setting for this fast-paced musical comedy. Zero Mostel is a never-ending source of zany plots to gain his freedom and line his toga with loot as a cunning slave. He is ably assisted by Phil Silvers and Jack Gilford in this bawdy romp through classic times. Look for Buster Keaton in a nice cameo. 1966; 99m.

FUZZ ★★★
DIR: Richard A. Colla. **CAST:** Raquel Welch, Burt Reynolds, Yul Brynner, Tom Skerritt.
Raquel Welch and Burt Reynolds star as police in this comedy-drama. Yul Brynner plays a bomb-happy villain. It has a few good moments, but you'd have to be a member of the Burt Reynolds fan club to really love it. Rated PG. 1972; 92m.

GALACTIC GIGOLO ★★
DIR: Gorman Bechard. **CAST:** Carmine Capobianco, Debi Thibeault, Frank Stewart, Ruth Collins.
Brainless, relentlessly silly movie about an alien (Carmine Capobianco) who wins a trip to Prospect, Connecticut. Prospect has the reputation for being the horniest place in the galaxy.

Rated R for language and nudity. 1987; 80m.

GALLAGHER—MELON CRAZY ★★★★

DIR: Joe Hostettler. **CAST:** Gallagher, Bill Kirchenbauer.

Mr. Smash and Splash considers his favorite fruit in all its various incarnations. Things get as wild as three-piece melon suits, melon blimps, and giant, 30-foot melons. All this is climaxed by a Super-Sledge-o-Matic smashing spree. It's funny stuff. 1984; 58m.

GALLAGHER—OVER YOUR HEAD ★★★★

DIR: Joe Hostettler. **CAST:** Gallagher.

Gallagher performs in the Lone Star state. The Texas audience goes wild when he enters wearing a 20-gallon hat and carrying a pistol with a 10-foot barrel. It gets better from there. He takes sarcastic swipes at politicians, ancient history, and gun control. 1984; 58m.

GALLAGHER—STUCK IN THE 60S ★★★★

DIR: Wayne Orr. **CAST:** Gallagher.

If you're a product of the 1960s, and even if you're not, you'll love this hilarious comedy video. It's all playfully honest and enjoyably silly. 1983; 58m.

GALLAGHER—THE BOOKKEEPER ★★★★

DIR: Joe Hostettler. **CAST:** Gallagher.

Gallagher takes a potshot at what seems to matter most in our society: the almighty dollar. In this concert performance, he whimsically attacks the IRS, banking, and what we spend our money on. And, of course, be prepared for the Sledge-o-Matic! 1985; 58m.

GALLAGHER—THE MADDEST ★★★½

DIR: Wayne Orr. **CAST:** Gallagher.

Here's more inspired Gallagher-style madness for comedy fans. Bits include the introduction of a mutant sofa, a treatise on hats with and without handles, and, of course, everything ends with the gush of Gallagher's Sledge-o-Matic. Filmed live in concert. 1984; 59m.

GAMBIT ★★★½

DIR: Ronald Neame. **CAST:** Michael Caine, Shirley MacLaine, Herbert Lom.

An engaging caper comedy that teams Michael Caine's inventive but unlucky thief with Shirley MacLaine's mute and mysterious woman of the world...or *is* she? The target is a valuable art treasure, jealously guarded by ruthless owner Herbert Lom, and Caine's plan is—to say the least—unusual. Naturally, things don't work out as expected, and that's when the fun begins. Caine and MacLaine make a grand pair; it's a shame they didn't get together for another film of this sort. Unrated; suitable for family viewing. 1966; 108m.

GARBO TALKS ★★★★

DIR: Sidney Lumet. **CAST:** Anne Bancroft, Ron Silver, Carrie Fisher, Howard DaSilva, Dorothy Loudon, Hermione Gingold.

In this often funny and touching contemporary comedy, Anne Bancroft is delightful as an outspoken crusader against the small injustices in the world. But she has her fantasies, too, and enlists the aid of her son (Ron Silver) in finding Greta Garbo, who at age 79 can occasionally be spotted walking around New York. Rated PG for profanity. 1984; 103m.

GARRY SHANDLING: ALONE IN VEGAS ★★★★

DIR: William Dear. **CAST:** Garry Shandling.

Nothing seems especially funny about stand-up comic Garry Shandling—not his clothes, not his expression, not even his material. He's just an average guy, and that's his charm. In a world where every other comedian wants to be cooking like a gourmet chef, Shandling is like mama's recipes—warm and familiar. 1984; 60m.

GARRY SHANDLING SHOW, THE ★★★

DIR: Tom Trbovich. **CAST:** Garry Shandling, Paul Willson, Rose Marie, Doug McClure, Donny Osmond, Johnny Carson.

Garry Shandling spoofs late-night talk shows, specifically Johnny Carson's anniversary shows. He looks back over the last twenty-five years of this mock variety show, with clips featuring Mr. Ed, the world's fattest man, and some very funny bits about the Beatles. Zany comedy abounds with guest stars coming out of the walls. 1985; 60m.

GAS

DIR: Les Rose. **CAST:** Sterling Hayden, Peter Aykroyd, Susan Anspach, Donald Sutherland, Howie Mandel, Helen Shaver.

America's past petroleum shortages (whether real or conspiratorial) have not been laughing matters, and neither is this tasteless, tedious comedy about an artificial gas-crisis in a Midwest city. Rated R because of sex and rough language. 1981; 94m.

GAS PUMP GIRLS ★

DIR: Joel Bender. **CAST:** Kirsten Baker, Dennis Bowen, Huntz Hall, Rikki Marin, Bill Smith.

This teen comedy features four beautiful girls who take on the big oil company across the street in an all-out gas war. The little gas station picks up business when the sexy girls offer service with a smile. Rated PG for nudity. 1978; 102m.

GENERAL, THE ★★★★★

DIR: Buster Keaton. **CAST:** Buster Keaton, Marion Mack, Glen Cavender, Jim Farley, Joseph Keaton.

The General is a film based on an incident in the Civil War. Buster Keaton is an engineer determined to recapture his stolen locomotive. Magnificent battle scenes are mere backdrops for Keaton's inspired acrobatics and comedy. Solid scripting, meticulous attention to detail, and ingenious stunt work make this picture excellent. 1927; B&W; 74m.

GENERATION ★★★

DIR: George Schaefer. **CAST:** David Janssen, Kim Darby, Peter Duel, Carl Reiner, Andrew Prine, James Coco, Sam Waterston.

Remember the generation gap? If not, then you're not likely to enjoy this dated but modestly amusing comedy about a businessman (David Janssen) trying to cope with his pregnant daughter and hippie son-in-law, who want to have their upcoming baby at home. (Home in this case is an East Village loft.) Rated PG. 1969; 104m.

GENEVIEVE ★★★½

DIR: Henry Cornelius. **CAST:** Kenneth More, Kay Kendall, Dinah Sheridan, John Gregson, Arthur Wontner.

Captivating, low-key comedy about friendly rivals who engage in a race after finishing a sports car rally in England. No pretenses or false claims in this charming film, just great performances, beautiful countryside, and a spirit of fun and camaraderie. Originally shown as the second half of a double bill in America, this stylish feature gave Kenneth More one of his best roles and showcased the charm and comedy flair of Kay Kendall, one of Britain's top talents. 1954; 86m.

GENTLEMEN PREFER BLONDES ★★

DIR: Howard Hawks. **CAST:** Jane Russell, Marilyn Monroe, Charles Coburn, Tommy Noonan, Elliott Reid, George Winslow.

Howard Hawks gets surprisingly good performances from his stars, Jane Russell and Marilyn Monroe, in this 1953 musical comedy. As usual, Hawks does his best to make good scenes, but this time the silly plot—about two women searching for husbands—thwarts his esteemable talents. 1953; 91m.

GEORGE BURNS AND GRACIE ALLEN SHOW, THE (TELEVISION SERIES) ★★★½
DIR: Ralph Levy. **CAST:** George Burns, Gracie Allen, Harry Von Zell, Ronnie Burns, Bea Benaderet, Hal March, Bob Sweeney, Fred Clark, Larry Keating.

In this classic series, George Burns plays a nearly imperturbable entertainer, married to madcap Gracie Allen. Allen turns everyday life into a nonstop adventure by innocently causing a whirlwind of confusion. She's endlessly endearing. Burns is dryly delightful, puffing on his cigar and looking into the camera, commenting on the developing plot. 1950–1958; B&W; 120m.

GEORGE BURNS—HIS WIT AND WISDOM ★★★
DIR: Mort Fallick. **CAST:** George Burns.

A day in the life of George Burns. If you like Burns, there is a lot of pleasant diversion to be had in this short program. Burns's dry-witted charm is the main attraction; the "special appearances," which are trotted out like surprise celebrity guests on a talk show, range from delightful (Carol Channing) to pointless (Emma Samms). Not rated. 1989; 45m.

GEORGE BURNS IN CONCERT ★★★★
DIR: Jim Shaw. **CAST:** George Burns.

George Burns is at his funniest in this live, onstage performance produced for Home Box Office. It's all standup jokes and stories that Burns aims at himself. He spends a lot of time talking in a hilarious fashion about his part in the film *Oh, God* and of his extraordinary lifespan. Combined with a number of delightfully silly songs that sound suspiciously like vaudeville, *George Burns in Concert* makes for thoroughly enjoyable entertainment. 1982; 55m.

GEORGE CARLIN LIVE! WHAT AM I DOING IN NEW JERSEY? ★★★★
DIR: Bruce Gowers. **CAST:** George Carlin.

George Carlin is at his hilarious best in this HBO special taped before a live audience in New Jersey. Carlin blasts away at politics, stupid motorists, the FCC, and FM radio. Hysterical insights in this unpredictable hour of caustic, no-holds-barred humor. Not rated; contains some profanity. 1988; 60m.

GEORGE CARLIN—PLAYIN' WITH YOUR HEAD ★★
DIR: Rocco Urbishi. **CAST:** George Carlin, Vic Tayback.

There's little of the classic Carlin character to be seen in this comedy video. The one redeeming factor is a black-and-white short at the beginning—"The Envelope," in which Carlin plays a Sam Spade character named Mike Holder. Vic Tayback costars as the ringleader of a bunch of hooligans. No rating, but there's an ample helping of raw language. 1986; 58m.

GEORGY GIRL ★★★½
DIR: Silvio Narizzano. **CAST:** Lynn Redgrave, James Mason, Alan Bates, Charlotte Rampling.

Generations clash as suave, patient fairy-godfather James Mason works to make chubby London mod girl Lynn Redgrave his mistress in this totally engaging British comedy. Charlotte Rampling is a standout as the chubby's tough-bitch roommate. Mason, of course, gives another of his flawless characterizations. 1966; B&W; 100m.

GET CRAZY ★★★½
DIR: Allan Arkush. **CAST:** Malcolm McDowell, Allen Garfield, Daniel Stern, Ed Begley Jr., Miles Chapin, Lou Reed, Stacey Nelkin, Bill Henderson, Franklin Ajaye, Bobby Sherman, Fabian.

Here's the wildest, weirdest, and most outrageous rock 'n' roll comedy any of us is likely to see. It's a story about a rock concert on New Year's Eve, Malcolm McDowell plays a Mick Jagger–style rock singer, Allen Goorwitz is a Bill Graham–ish promoter, and Daniel Stern is his lovesick stage manager. Rated R for nudity, profanity, violence, and suggested sex. 1983; 92m.

GET OUT OF MY ROOM ★

DIR: Richard "Cheech" Marin. **CAST:** Cheech and Chong, John Paragon, Elvira, Jan-Michael Vincent.

The only good thing about this tape is Cheech's "Born in East L.A." musical video, featuring Elvira and Jan-Michael Vincent. Unfortunately, the rest of the tape is boring. Cheech and Chong talk about how to make videos and decide that the main thing to do is to hire lots of beautiful girls. Other songs include: "Get Out of My Room," "I'm Not Home Right Now," and "Love Is Strange." 1985; 53m.

GETTING IT RIGHT ★★★★½

DIR: Randal Kleiser. **CAST:** Jesse Birdsall, Helena Bonham Carter, Peter Cook, John Gielgud, Jane Horrocks, Lynn Redgrave.

Surrounded by a wonderful cast of endearing eccentrics, Jesse Birdsall sails through his role as a 31-year-old virgin who becomes a sensitive lover (to Lynn Redgrave's madcap neglected socialite). Something of an updated version of the British social comedies of the Sixties (*Georgy Girl, Alfie*). Highly recommended. Rated R for nudity and sexual situations. 1989; 102m.

GHOST FEVER

DIR: Alan Smithee. **CAST:** Sherman Hemsley, Luis Avalos.

Southern cops Hemsley and Avalos investigate strange happenings at Magnolia Mansion, where the two beautiful owners are being haunted by their great-great-grandfather. The only humor in this cheapster comes from watching the visible wires moving props around. Hemsley, who put up $3 million of the budget, also sings two songs on the soundtrack. Director Alan Smithee doesn't exist; it's a fake name applied when the real director (in this case, Lee Madden) doesn't want his name on the final product. Rated PG. 1985; 86m.

GHOST GOES WEST, THE ★★★★

DIR: René Clair. **CAST:** Robert Donat, Jean Parker.

A millionaire buys a Scottish castle and transports it stone by stone to America only to discover that it comes complete with a ghost. Robert Donat gives a memorable performance in this bit of whimsy. 1935; B&W; 100m.

GHOST IN THE NOONDAY SUN ★½

DIR: Peter Medak. **CAST:** Peter Sellers, Anthony Franciosa, Peter Boyle, Spike Milligan, Clive Revill.

Too silly pirate parody features a Peter Sellers so demented that his dialogue is almost indistinguishable. Sellers and his fellow pirates go searching for lost treasure and are haunted by a ghost. Not rated. Appropriate for children. 1974; 90m.

GHOSTBUSTERS ★★★★

DIR: Ivan Reitman. **CAST:** Bill Murray, Dan Aykroyd, Sigourney Weaver, Harold Ramis, Annie Potts, Ernie Hudson, William Atherton, Rick Moranis.

Bill Murray, Dan Aykroyd, Sigourney Weaver, and Harold Ramis are terrific in this very funny and often frightening comedy-horror film about a special organization that fights evil spirits. Is it *The Exorcist* meets *Saturday Night Live*? That's pretty close—but it's better. Rated PG for profanity and scary scenes. 1984; 107m.

GHOSTBUSTERS II ★★½

DIR: Ivan Reitman. **CAST:** Bill Murray, Dan Aykroyd, Sigourney Weaver, Harold Ramis, Rick Moranis, Ernie Hudson, Annie Potts.

In this watchable sequel to the 1984 box-office blockbuster, the original cast returns to take on an explosion of evil spirits on a fateful New Year's

Eve. The formula now seems fairly tired, despite some funny moments at the outset. Older kids are more likely to enjoy the shenanigans than adults. Rated PG. 1989; 110m.

GHOSTS OF BERKELEY SQUARE ★★½
DIR: Vernon Sewell. **CAST:** Robert Morley, Felix Aylmer, Ernest Thesiger, Wilfrid Hyde-White.

After accidentally killing themselves while plotting to murder a superior officer, two British officers are condemned to haunt an old mansion until it is visited by royalty. Routine ghost comedy made palatable by a good cast. 1947; B&W; 85m.

GHOSTS ON THE LOOSE ★½
DIR: William Beaudine. **CAST:** The East Side Kids, Bela Lugosi, Ava Gardner, Rick Vallin.

Silly movie pits Monogram's moronic East Side Kids against a bored Bela Lugosi and his German henchmen in this pallid variation on the "old haunted house" theme. No real thrills, no real laughs in this tired creaker. Even a youthful Ava Gardner can't perk this pooch up. 1943; B&W; 65m.

GIDGET ★★½
DIR: Paul Wendkos. **CAST:** Sandra Dee, James Darren, Arthur O'Connell, Cliff Robertson, Doug McClure.

The eternal beach bunny, Gidget (Sandra Dee), becomes involved with Cliff Robertson in order to make the man she's infatuated with (James Darren) notice her. This is the first and the best of a sub-par surfer series. 1959; 95m.

GIDGET GOES HAWAIIAN ★★
DIR: Paul Wendkos. **CAST:** Deborah Walley, James Darren, Michael Callan, Carl Reiner, Peggy Cass, Eddie Foy Jr.

Everyone's favorite "girl-midget" (played here by Deborah Walley, taking over from Sandra Dee) returns to the screen in this inoffensive, brainless sequel to the 1959 box-office hit. 1961; 102m.

GIDGET GOES TO ROME ★½
DIR: Paul Wendkos. **CAST:** Cindy Carol, James Darren, Jeff Donnell, Jessie Royce Landis.

Glendon Swarthout's irrepressible beach bunny presses onward, if not upward, in this below-average sequel to *Gidget*. Strictly a time-passer. 1963; 101m.

GIG, THE ★★★
DIR: Frank D. Gilroy. **CAST:** Wayne Rogers, Cleavon Little, Joe Silver, Andrew Duncan, Daniel Nalbach.

Very nicely done comedy-drama concerning a group of men who get together once a week to play Dixieland jazz and their reactions to being hired for a two-week stint at a resort in the Catskill Mountains of New York. Film admirably avoids the clichés associated with this type of buddy film. Nice ensemble acting, with Cleavon Little and Joe Silver leading the way. Give this one a try. 1985; 92m.

GILDA LIVE ★★
DIR: Mike Nichols. **CAST:** Gilda Radner, Don Novello, Paul Shaffer.

We've always loved Gilda Radner's characters from *Saturday Night Live*, and they're all represented in *Gilda Live*. But something is missing in her live show. The result is very few laughs. Rated R. 1980; 96m.

GIRL, A GUY AND A GOB, A ★★★
DIR: Richard Wallace. **CAST:** Lucille Ball, George Murphy, Edmond O'Brien, Henry Travers.

A silly, predictable comedy that tends to grow on you; it focuses on a working girl, her happy-go-lucky sailor boyfriend, and an upper-crust executive. Dated, of course, but cute and polished. Movie buffs will be interested to note the producer was legendary Harold Lloyd. Not rated, but contains nothing offensive. 1941; B&W; 90m.

GIRL CAN'T HELP IT, THE ★★★
DIR: Frank Tashlin. **CAST:** Tom Ewell, Jayne Mansfield, Edmond O'Brien, Julie London, Henry Jones, Fats

Domino, The Platters, The Trenlers, Little Richard, Gene Vincent and His Blue Caps, Eddie Cochran, Barry Gordon, Ray Anthony, Nino Tempo, The Chuckles.

Tom Ewell is given the task of turning squealing Jayne Mansfield into a singer on the clear understanding that he keep his hands to himself, a tough request when faced with the would-be singer's winning ways and obvious charms. Great rock 'n' roll by some of its premier interpreters is the real reason for watching this film. 1957; 99m.

GIRL IN EVERY PORT, A ★½

DIR: Chester Erskine. **CAST:** Groucho Marx, William Bendix, Marie Wilson, Don DeFore, Gene Lockhart.

Silly film about sailors involved in horse-racing scheme milks the old hide-the-horse-on-the-ship gag for all that it's worth (which isn't much) and then some. Only the presence of Groucho Marx makes this tired story worthy of note. 1952; B&W; 86m.

GIRL IN THE PICTURE, THE ★★★

DIR: Cary Parker. **CAST:** John Gordon-Sinclair, Irina Brook, David McKay, Gregor Fisher, Paul Young, Rikki Fulton.

The Girl in the Picture is a slight but very charming movie from Scotland. John Gordon-Sinclair plays a Glasgow photographer who's feeling stagnant in his relationship with his live-in design-student girlfriend. The film charts their breakup and what ensues because of it. The problems they face are never dealt with, but it doesn't seem to matter because the going is so enjoyable. The lovers are an amusing pair—Gordon-Sinclair, with his trademark understated manner and Irina Brook, with her intelligence and graceful strength. Rated PG. 1985; 90m.

GIRL RUSH ★★½

DIR: Gordon Douglas. **CAST:** Robert Mitchum, Frances Langford, Wally Brown.

Mildly amusing comedy about a group of vaudeville performers who attempt to stage a show called *The Frisco Follies* for a group of miners. Unfortunately, their efforts are met with resistance by a cool, menacing gambler played by Robert Mitchum. 1944; B&W; 65m.

GIRLS JUST WANT TO HAVE FUN

DIR: Alan Metter. **CAST:** Sarah Jessica Parker, Lee Montgomery, Morgan Woodward, Jonathan Silverman.

Sarah Jessica Parker stars as a young woman whose family moves to Chicago, where the popular television show *Dance TV* is filmed. She just lovvves to dance, and it just so happens the show is holding auditions for new dancers. She's going to give it a try, but will she be picked? This is a predictable, boring, and dumb movie. Rated PG for profanity. 1985; 90m.

GLORY YEARS ★½

DIR: Arthur Allan Seidelman. **CAST:** George Dzundza, Archie Hahn, Tim Thomerson, Tawny Kitaen, Michael Fairman, Sandy Simpson, Beau Starr, Donna Pescow.

Three old high-school buddies on their twenty-year reunion use their alumni fund to gamble in Las Vegas. They lose it all and then attempt to win it all back. The whole film reeks of a bad *Big Chill* rip-off. Originally an HBO miniseries. Not rated, has profanity, sex, and nudity. 1987; 150m.

GO WEST ★★★½

DIR: Edward Buzzell. **CAST:** The Marx Brothers, John Carroll, Diana Lewis, Walter Woolf King.

Far from prime-screen Marx Brothers, this is still one of their best MGM movies and a treat for their fans. Good comedy bits combine with a rip-roaring climax (stolen by screenwriter Buster Keaton from *The General*) for a highly watchable star comedy. 1940; B&W; 81m.

GODS MUST BE CRAZY, THE ★★★★★
DIR: Jamie Uys. **CAST:** Marius Meyers, Sandra Prinsloo.
This work, by South African filmmaker Jamie Uys, is a hilarious, poignant, exciting, thought-provoking, violent, and slapstick concoction that involves three separate stories. One is about a Bushman whose tribe selects him to get rid of an evil thing sent by the gods: a Coke bottle. The second features the awkward love affair of a teacher and a klutzy scientist. The last involves a band of terrorists fleeing for their lives. These all come together for a surprising and satisfying climax. Unrated, the film has violence. 1980; 109m.

GOING APE! ★
DIR: Jeremy Jue Kronsberg. **CAST:** Tony Danza, Jessica Walter, Stacey Nelkin, Danny DeVito, Art Metrano, Joseph Maher.
Tony Danza plays the heir to a million-dollar fortune-with-a-catch: In order to get the money, he has to care for three unpredictable simians. Because the film is padded with all-too-familiar material, very little fun shines through. Rated PG. 1981; 87m.

GOING BERSERK ★
DIR: David Steinberg. **CAST:** John Candy, Joe Flaherty, Eugene Levy, Alley Mills, Pat Hingle, Richard Libertini.
This is an unfunny comedy starring former *SCTV* regulars John Candy, Joe Flaherty, and Eugene Levy. Written and directed by David Steinberg (a former stand-up comedian who made his film-making debut with *Paternity*, starring Burt Reynolds), it never really goes anywhere, and its collection of supposedly "zany" bits just isn't funny. Rated R. 1983; 85m.

GOING IN STYLE ★★★★
DIR: Martin Brest. **CAST:** George Burns, Art Carney, Lee Strasberg, Charles Hallahan, Pamela Payton-Wright.
Three retirees who gather daily on a park bench need to add some spice to their empty existence. One of their sons needs help in paying his bills, so they decide to pitch in by robbing a bank. This crime caper has some unexpected plot twists mixed with a perfect sprinkling of humor. It is a delight throughout. Rated PG. 1979; 96m.

GOING UNDERCOVER ★
DIR: James Kenelm Clarke. **CAST:** Jean Simmons, Lea Thompson, Chris Lemmon.
Poor excuse for a sex comedy. There's nothing sexy or funny in this time-waster. Chris Lemmon plays an airhead gumshoe hired by Jean Simmons to protect her stepdaughter. Rated PG-13 for violence. 1988; 89m.

GOLD RUSH, THE ★★★★★
DIR: Charles Chaplin. **CAST:** Charlie Chaplin, Mack Swain, Georgia Hale.
Charlie Chaplin's classic comedy is immortal for the scrumptious supper of a boiled boot, the teetering Klondike cabin, and the dance of the dinner rolls. Some parts are very sentimental, but these give the viewer time to catch his or her breath after laughing so much. 1925; B&W; 100m.

GOLDEN AGE OF COMEDY, THE ★★★★
COMPILER: Robert Youngson. **CAST:** Stan Laurel, Oliver Hardy, Will Rogers, Harry Langdon, Ben Turpin, Carole Lombard, Snub Pollard.
First and most popular of Robert Youngson's tributes to silent film comedy, this compilation of highlights introduced new generations of moviegoers to the great years of silent comedy and continues to do so. Many of the shorts with Laurel and Hardy (including the classic "Two Tars") will be familiar to viewers due to their popularity and availability, but the segments with Will Rogers spoofing silent film greats Douglas Fairbanks and Tom Mix, and the footage with Harry Langdon (who was at one time

considered a comedic equal to Charlie Chaplin, Buster Keaton, and Harold Lloyd) are seldom seen and well worth the wait. 1957; B&W; 78m.

GONE ARE THE DAYS ★★★
DIR: Gabrielle Beaumont. **CAST:** Harvey Korman, Susan Anspach, Robert Hogan.

After witnessing a gangland-style shooting, the Daye family is assigned to a witness relocation agent (Harvey Korman), who is creatively unsuccessful in a long-distance game of hide-and-seek. This wacky comedy is pleasantly acted and well photographed. Some fairly clever situations arise from an otherwise predictable premise. A Disney made-for-cable production. Good fun for the family. 1984; 90m.

GOOD NEIGHBOR SAM ★★★
DIR: David Swift. **CAST:** Jack Lemmon, Romy Schneider, Dorothy Provine, Edward G. Robinson.

This comedy is similar to many of the lightweight potboilers given to Jack Lemmon in the 1960s. It is an overlong farce about a married advertising designer who pretends marriage to his foreign neighbor next door so she can secure an inheritance. He must continue the charade to avoid offending his firm's puritanical client who chanced to see them together. 1964; 130m.

GOOD SAM ★★
DIR: Leo McCarey. **CAST:** Gary Cooper, Ann Sheridan, Edmund Lowe.

Gary Cooper plays a guy who can't say no in this barely watchable "comedy." He's Mr. Nice-Guy to everyone but his own family. He feels he has to help everyone, so he lends all his money to "friends" and the "needy." Unfortunately, when it comes to buying things for his family (such as a house) he has no money left. 1948; B&W; 114m.

GOODBYE COLUMBUS ★★★★
DIR: Larry Peerce. **CAST:** Richard Benjamin, Ali MacGraw, Jack Klugman.

This film marked the start of Ali MacGraw's and Richard Benjamin's movie careers. Ali plays a rich, spoiled Jewish-American princess who meets a college dropout (Benjamin) at her country club. They have an affair, and we get to see her flaws through his "average guy" eyes. Rated R. 1969; 105m.

GOODBYE GIRL, THE ★★★★½
DIR: Herbert Ross. **CAST:** Richard Dreyfuss, Marsha Mason, Quinn Cummings.

Neil Simon's sparkling screenplay and the acting of Marsha Mason and Richard Dreyfuss combine to produce one of the best pure comedies since Hollywood's golden '30s. Mason and Dreyfuss are a mismatched pair of New Yorkers forced to become roommates. Rated PG. 1977; 110m.

GOODBYE NEW YORK ★★★
DIR: Amos Kollek. **CAST:** Julie Hagerty, Amos Kollek, David Topaz, Shmuel Shiloh.

In this amusing comedy, an insurance salesperson (Julie Hagerty) becomes fed up with her job and husband and leaves for Paris. After falling asleep on the plane, she wakes up in Israel with no money and no luggage. Rated R for language and very brief nudity. 1984; 90m.

GOOF BALLS ★½
DIR: Brad Turner. **CAST:** Ben Gordon.

This lame comedy opens with a bungled robbery performed by a bunch of inept losers. Some are caught and sent to prison. One guy gets away and ends up on a remote tropical island, where he opens a golf resort. Gangsters, oil sheiks, bikinied girls, and a number of other stupid characters abound. Unrated. 1987; 89m.

GORILLA, THE ★★
DIR: Allan Dwan. **CAST:** The Ritz Brothers, Bela Lugosi, Lionel Atwill.

This is another one of those horror comedies that takes place in an old mansion and again wastes poor Bela Lugosi's acting talents. The Ritz Brothers were an acquired taste, to be sure, and this is not their best vehicle by any stretch of the imagination. 1939; B&W; 66m.

GORP

DIR: Joseph Ruben. **CAST:** Michael Lembeck, Philip Casnoff, Dennis Quaid, David Huddleston, Rosanna Arquette.

Particularly unfunny summer-camp flick that relies on stupid sight gags and toilet jokes. (This time, it's Camp Oskemo for wealthy Jewish children.) Rated R for nudity and profanity. 1980; 91m.

GOSPEL ACCORDING TO VIC, THE ★★★½

DIR: Charles Gormley. **CAST:** Tom Conti, Helen Mirren, David Hayman, Brian Pettifer, Jennifer Black.

In this delightful comedy from Scotland, a teacher (Tom Conti) at a Glasgow parochial school finds that he can create miracles—even though he doesn't believe in them. Those who have reveled in the subtle, sly humor of *Gregory's Girl*, *Local Hero*, and other Scottish films will find similar joys in this. Rated PG-13 for adult content. 1986; 92m.

GRACE QUIGLEY ★★½

DIR: Anthony Harvey. **CAST:** Katharine Hepburn, Nick Nolte, Elizabeth Wilson, Chip Zien, Christopher Murney.

After witnessing the murder of her landlord, spinster Katharine Hepburn enlists the aid of freelance hit man Nick Nolte. Hepburn wants Nolte to end her life, but not before he puts to rest some of her elderly friends who feel it is time for them to die. Extremely black comedy doesn't have enough humor and warmth to rise above its gruesome subject matter. Rated R. 1985; 87m.

GRASS IS ALWAYS GREENER OVER THE SEPTIC TANK, THE ★★★½

DIR: Robert Day. **CAST:** Carol Burnett, Charles Grodin, Alex Rocco, Linda Gray.

Carol Burnett and Charles Grodin shine in this tale of the domestic horrors of suburban life taken from Erma Bombeck's bestseller. The comedy doesn't always work, but when it does it rivals Grodin's *The Heartbreak Kid* and some of the best moments of Burnett's TV show. No rating, but the equivalent of a PG for language. 1978; 98m.

GRASS IS GREENER, THE ★★★½

DIR: Stanley Donen. **CAST:** Cary Grant, Deborah Kerr, Jean Simmons, Robert Mitchum.

Cary Grant and Deborah Kerr star as a married couple experimenting with extramarital affairs in this comedy. Jean Simmons plays Grant's girlfriend, while Robert Mitchum courts Kerr. Some funny moments, but it's not hilarious. 1960; 105m.

GREAT BANK HOAX, THE ★★½

DIR: Joseph Jacoby. **CAST:** Richard Basehart, Burgess Meredith, Paul Sand, Ned Beatty, Michael Murphy, Arthur Godfrey.

It is doubtful that viewers today will think of Watergate when watching this comedy caper, but it was originally intended as a parable. When the pillars of the community find out that the bank has been embezzled they decide to rob it. Great characterizations by all-star cast. Rated PG. 1977; 89m.

GREAT DICTATOR, THE ★★★★★

DIR: Charles Chaplin. **CAST:** Charlie Chaplin, Jack Oakie, Paulette Goddard.

Charlie Chaplin stars in and directs this devastating lampoon of the Third Reich. The celebrated clown's first all-talking picture, it casts him in two roles—as his famous Little Tramp and as Adenoid Hynkel, the Hitler-like ruler of Tomania. As with the similarly themed *Duck Soup*, starring the Marx Brothers, the comedy was a little too whimsical for wartime audiences. But it has to be regarded as a classic. 1940; B&W; 128m.

GREAT GUNS ★★
DIR: Monty Banks. **CAST:** Stan Laurel, Oliver Hardy, Sheila Ryan.

Although it's a cut below their classics, Sons of the Desert will love it, and so will most—especially the young. Stan and Ollie have jobs guarding a rich man's playboy son, Dick Nelson. He gets drafted; the fellows join up to continue their work. The playboy gets along just fine in khaki. The boys get up to their ears in trouble with an archetypical sergeant. 1941; B&W; 74m.

GREAT LOVER, THE ★★★★
DIR: Alexander Hall. **CAST:** Bob Hope, Rhonda Fleming, Roland Young, Jim Backus, Roland Culver, George Reeves.

This is top-notch Bob Hope. The story, as usual, is simple. While on a transatlantic steamship, a timid Boy Scout leader romances lovely Rhonda Fleming and tracks down a strangler. Comedic suspense is well played. 1949; B&W; 80m.

GREAT MCGINTY, THE ★★★½
DIR: Preston Sturges. **CAST:** Brian Donlevy, Akim Tamiroff, Muriel Angelus, Louis Jean Heydt, Arthur Hoyt.

The ups and downs of hobo Brian Donlevy and his crooked cohort Akim Tamiroff make for very funny satire in this refreshing gem from the inventive Preston Sturges. The action is secondary to the great dialogue. The leads are fine and the rapport they share on screen is truly engaging. 1940; B&W; 83m.

GREAT OUTDOORS, THE ★★½
DIR: Howard Deutch. **CAST:** Dan Aykroyd, John Candy, Stephanie Faracy.

Another screwball comedy featuring former members of *Saturday Night Live* and *SCTV*, this stars Dan Aykroyd and John Candy as brothers-in-law battling to take charge of a family vacation in the country, where almost everything goes wrong. Screenwriter John Hughes and director Howard Deutch have scattered a few genuine guffaws among predictable gags about bears, bats, and boats. Aside from Aykroyd, spectacular as the jerky know-it-all, all the characters are shallow. Rated PG for profanity. 1988; 90m.

GREAT RACE, THE ★★★½
DIR: Blake Edwards. **CAST:** Tony Curtis, Natalie Wood, Jack Lemmon, Peter Falk, Keenan Wynn, Larry Storch, Arthur O'Connell, Vivian Vance.

Set in the early 1900s, this film comically traces the daily events of the first New York–to–Paris car race. Unfortunately, two-and-a-half hours of silly spoofs will have even the most avid film fan yawning. 1965; 147m.

GREAT ST. TRINIAN'S TRAIN ROBBERY, THE ★★★
DIR: Frank Launder, Sidney Gilliat. **CAST:** Frankie Howerd, Reg Varney, Dora Bryan.

The last in the series of British comedies based on Ronald Searle's cartoons depicting a girls' school populated by monstrously awful brats. In this one, the students prove more than a match for thieves who have hidden loot on the school premises. Not the best of the series, but fun nonetheless. 1966; 94m.

GREAT WALL, A ★★★½
DIR: Peter Wang. **CAST:** Peter Wang, Sharon Iwai, Kelvin Han Yee.

A Great Wall is not a documentary about the 1,500-mile structure that rolls wavelike through northern China. Instead, it is a warm comedy about the clash of cultures that results when a Chinese-American family returns to its homeland. It is also the first American movie to be made in the People's Republic of China. As such, it gives some fascinating insights into Chinese culture and often does so in a marvelously entertaining way. Rated PG. 1986; 100m.

GREATEST MAN IN THE WORLD, THE ★★★★
DIR: Ralph Rosenblum. **CAST:** Brad Davis, Reed Birney, John McMartin,

Howard DaSilva, Carol Kane, William Prince, Sudie Bond.

A droll adaptation of James Thurber's wry tale. Brad Davis is an uncouth amateur barnstormer who outperforms Charles Lindbergh by flying nonstop around the *world*...aided by a brilliant method of fuel conservation, and fortified—during the four-day trip—by a hunk of salami and a gallon of gin. Thurber understood the true purpose of journalism: to share the news that's fit *for* print. Introduced by Henry Fonda; suitable for family viewing. 1980; 51m.

GREGORY'S GIRL ★★★★½

DIR: Bill Forsyth. **CAST:** Gordon John Sinclair, Dee Hepburn, Chic Murray, Jake D'Arcy, Alex Norton, John Bett, Clare Grogan.

In this utterly delightful movie from Scotland, a gangly, good-natured kid named Gregory—who has just gone through a five-inch growth spurt that has left him with the physical grace of a drunken stilt walker and made him a problem player on the school's winless soccer team—falls in love with the team's newest and best player: a girl named Dorothy. Unrated, the film has no objectionable content. 1981; 91m.

GROOVE TUBE, THE ★★½

DIR: Ken Shapiro. **CAST:** Ken Shapiro, Lane Sarasohn, Chevy Chase, Richard Belzer.

A sometimes funny and most times just silly—or gross—1974 takeoff on television by writer-director Ken Shapiro. The V.D. commercial is a classic, however. Look for Chevy Chase in his first, brief screen appearance. Rated R. 1974; 75m.

GUIDE FOR THE MARRIED MAN, A ★★★½

DIR: Gene Kelly. **CAST:** Walter Matthau, Inger Stevens, Robert Morse, Sue Ane Langdon, Lucille Ball, Jack Benny, Joey Bishop, Art Carney, Jayne Mansfield, Carl Reiner, Sid Caesar, Phil Silvers, Jeffrey Hunter, Sam Jaffe.

Worldly Robert Morse tries to teach reluctant Walter Matthau the fundamentals of adultery. His lessons are acted out by a dazzling roster of top comedy stars. This episodic film provides a steady stream of laughs. The bit in which Joey Bishop is caught red-handed and practices the "deny, deny, deny" technique is a classic. 1967; 89m.

GUIDE FOR THE MARRIED WOMAN, A ★★½

DIR: Hy Averback. **CAST:** Cybill Shepherd, Charles Frank, John Hillerman, Elaine Joyce, Peter Marshall, Eve Arden.

In this made-for-television movie, Cybill Shepherd plays a frustrated housewife who decides that life must hold more excitement than her current predictable situation. Though the cast includes many big names, this film never really takes off and is no match for the earlier *Guide for the Married Man*. 1978; 100m.

GULLIVER IN LILLIPUT ★★

DIR: Barry Letts. **CAST:** Andrew Burt, Elizabeth Sladen.

This British TV movie stays fairly close to the Jonathan Swift classic satire of small-minded people. Probably too close because it's not long before these bickering people stop being funny and start getting on your nerves. Not rated, but contains no objectionable material. 1982; 107m.

GUMSHOE ★★★½

DIR: Stephen Frears. **CAST:** Albert Finney, Billie Whitelaw, Frank Finlay, Janice Rule, Caroline Seymour.

Every hard-bitten private-eye film and *film noir* is saluted in this crime-edged comedy. Liverpool bingo caller Albert Finney finds himself in deep, murky water when he tries to live his fantasy of being a Humphrey Bogart–type shamus. Raymond Chandler and Dashiell Hammett fans will love every frame. Rated PG. 1972; 88m.

GUNG HO ★★★★

DIR: Ron Howard. **CAST:** Michael Keaton, Gedde Watanabe,

George Wendt, Mimi Rogers, John Turturro, Clint Howard.

Another winner from director Ron Howard and writers Lowell Ganz and Babaloo Mandel, who previously teamed on *Night Shift* and *Splash.* This is a pointed and relevant study of the cultural chaos that occurs when small-town Hadleyville's automobile plant is rescued from closure by imported Japanese management. Michael Keaton holds things together as the fast-talking liaison between employees and management. Rated PG-13 for language. 1985; 111m.

HAIRSPRAY
DIR: John Waters. **CAST:** Sonny Bono, Divine, Colleen Fitzpatrick, Deborah Harry, Ricki Lake, Leslie Ann Powers, Clayton Prince, Jerry Stiller, Mink Stole, Shawn Thompson, Pia Zadora.

Writer-director John Waters's ode to the dance craze of the Sixties features some outrageously campy performances. The story revolves around the desire of a pudgy teen (Ricki Lake) to be one of the featured stars on a Baltimore TV show in 1963. Forget the story and enjoy the soundtrack, which features some great songs from the era. In fact, unless you're a Waters fan, the soundtrack is all you'll ever want to experience of this intentionally awful movie. Rated PG. 1988; 87m.

HALF-SHOT AT SUNRISE ★
DIR: Paul Sloane. **CAST:** Bert Wheeler, Robert Woolsey, Dorothy Lee, Edna May Oliver.

Straight man Bert Wheeler and his lecherous, wisecracking partner Robert Woolsey inflicted themselves on the public for most of the 1930s. This dated story of World War I doughboys trying to score with the gals was stale even when it was released. 1930; B&W; 78m.

HAMBURGER—THE MOTION PICTURE
DIR: Mike Marvin. **CAST:** Leigh McCloskey, Sandy Hackett, Randi Brooks, Charles Tyner, Chuck McCann, Dick Butkus.

A very funny comedy could be made about the fast-food industry, but this isn't it. The story involves a promiscuous fellow (Leigh McCloskey) who has to clean up his act or lose a $250,000 inheritance. We are supposed to care about this, but McCloskey's character is so one-dimensional we can hardly stand him. Rated R for profanity, nudity, suggested sex, and violence. 1986; 90m.

HAMMERED: THE BEST OF SLEDGE ★★
DIR: Jackie Cooper, Gary Walkow, Martha Coolidge. **CAST:** David Rasche, Anne-Marie Martin, Harrison Page, John Vernon.

Well-intentioned but flat takeoff of tough cop movies and TV shows, *Hammered* stars David Rasche as Detective Sledge Hammer of the SFPD, a man who talks to his gun and loves extreme and senseless violence. This is a compilation of four *Sledge Hammer* TV shows. The best segment is the last, the pilot for the series, in which Hammer searches for the mayor's kidnapped daughter. The funny moments are there, but poor writing and uninspired delivery by the actors makes the satire limp. 1986; 104m.

HAMMERSMITH IS OUT ★★★½
DIR: Peter Ustinov. **CAST:** Elizabeth Taylor, Richard Burton, Peter Ustinov, Beau Bridges, George Raft, John Schuck.

In this black comedy an insane criminal is sprung from an asylum by an ambitious attendant. Sinister purpose abounds, with farce and black humor mixed in freely. Gaining strength and polish as the plot unfolds, the film promises a bit more than it actually offers. Rated R for profanity, sexual situations, and mild violence. 1971; 108m.

HANKY PANKY ★
DIR: Sidney Poitier. **CAST:** Gene Wilder, Gilda Radner, Richard Widmark, Kathleen Quinlan, Robert Prosky.

In an obvious takeoff on the Hitchcock suspense formula, this seldom funny comedy features Gene Wilder as an innocent man caught up in international intrigue and murder. Gilda Radner is Wilder's confused helpmate, and Richard Widmark leads the baddies in this ultimately disappointing and, in the last half, boring film. Rated PG for violence and gore. 1982; 110m.

HANNAH AND HER SISTERS ★★★★★
DIR: Woody Allen. **CAST:** Woody Allen, Michael Caine, Mia Farrow, Carrie Fisher, Barbara Hershey, Maureen O'Sullivan, Dianne Wiest, Max von Sydow, Daniel Stern, Lloyd Nolan, Sam Waterston.

One of Woody Allen's very best, a two-year study of a family held together by house-mother Mia Farrow. Hannah is best friend, trusted confidante, and sympathetic peacemaker for sisters Barbara Hershey and Dianne Wiest, husband Michael Caine, and parents Maureen O'Sullivan and Lloyd Nolan. Woody's along for a glib part as a hypochondriac who may get his fondest wish: a fatal disease. Rated PG-13 for sexual situations. 1986; 106m.

HAPPY HOOKER, THE ★★★
DIR: Nicholas Sgarro. **CAST:** Lynn Redgrave, Jean-Pierre Aumont, Elizabeth Wilson, Tom Poston, Lovelady Powell, Nicholas Pryor.

After Xaviera Hollander's novel became a bestseller, Lynn Redgrave was cast as Hollander in this offbeat comedy. Redgrave adds a wry touch as she recounts Hollander's rise from free-lance prostitute to one of New York's most infamous madams. Additionally, viewers get a peek at the kinky scenes one gets into when they play the sex-for-hire game. Rated R for nudity and sex. 1975; 96m.

HAPPY HOOKER GOES TO WASHINGTON, THE
DIR: William A. Levey. **CAST:** Joey Heatherton, George Hamilton, Ray Walston, Jack Carter.

Xaviera Hollander (Joey Heatherton) is innocently pursuing her career as a madam when she is surprised by a process server and called to Washington. Once there, she is forced to give testimony to a Senate committee sworn to uphold the morals of America. Naturally, she finds that all the senators use call girls and are unfit to judge her. Rated R for profanity, nudity, and sex. 1977; 89m.

HAPPY HOUR ★★
DIR: John DeBello. **CAST:** Richard Gilliland, Jamie Farr, Tawny Kitaen, Rich Little.

Blah comedy about a chemist's discovery of a secret ingredient that makes beer irresistible. A lot of T&A, and a good peformance by Rich Little as a superspy, but the premise keeps the film's comedic stock low. Not rated, coarse language. 1986; 88m.

HAPPY NEW YEAR ★★★½
DIR: John G. Avildsen. **CAST:** Peter Falk, Charles Durning, Tom Courtenay, Wendy Hughes.

Another film that was the victim of the studio system; it received only a marginal theatrical release. Peter Falk deserves to be seen in his multirole performance. He and Charles Durning are a couple of con men planning a jewel heist in Florida. (Based on Claude Lelouch's 1973 French film of the same name.) Rated PG. 1987; 86m.

HARD COUNTRY ★★★½
DIR: David Greene. **CAST:** Jan-Michael Vincent, Michael Parks, Kim Basinger, Tanya Tucker, Ted Neeley.

Though it tries to make a statement about the contemporary cowboy lost in the modern world and feminism in the boondocks, this is really just lighthearted entertainment. A rockabilly love story of the macho man (Jan-Michael Vincent) versus the liberated woman (Kim Basinger). Rated PG. 1981; 104m.

HARDBODIES 🦃

DIR: Mark Griffiths. **CAST:** Grant Cramer, Teal Roberts, Gary Wood, Michael Rappaport, Roberta Collins.

In this disgusting, insulting, and degrading-to-women sexploitation flick, three middle-aged, successful, but far-from-sexy men rent a summer beach house in hopes of seducing teenage girls. They have no luck until Scotty Palmer (Grant Cramer), "the hottest guy on the beach," according to the press kit, decides to help them score. Rated R for nudity, simulated sex, and profanity. 1984; 90m.

HARDBODIES TWO 🦃

DIR: Mark Griffiths. **CAST:** Brad Zutaut, James Karen.

All about the sexual antics of a group of students on an academic cruise. This vulgar sequel is aimed at satisfying the curiosity of its target audience of teenage males. Rated R for nudity and profanity. 1986; 89m.

HARDLY WORKING ★★

DIR: Jerry Lewis. **CAST:** Jerry Lewis, Susan Oliver, Roger C. Carmel, Deanna Lund, Harold J. Stone, Steve Franken.

Jerry Lewis's 1980s screen comeback is passable family fare. As a middle-aged, out-of-work clown, he tries his hand at a number of jobs and flubs them all. His fans will love it; others need not apply. Rated PG. 1981; 91m.

HAROLD AND MAUDE ★★★★★

DIR: Hal Ashby. **CAST:** Bud Cort, Vivian Pickles, Ruth Gordon, Cyril Cusack, Charles Tyner, Ellen Geer.

Hal Ashby directed this delightful black comedy about an odd young man named Harold (Bud Cort) who devises some rather elaborate fake deaths to jar his snooty, manipulative mother (Vivian Pickles). Soon his attention turns to an octogenarian named Maude (Ruth Gordon), with whom he falls in love. Featuring a superb soundtrack of songs by Cat Stevens, this is one of the original cult classics—and deservedly so. Rated PG. 1972; 90m.

HAROLD LLOYD'S COMEDY CLASSICS ★★★

DIR: Harold Lloyd. **CAST:** Harold Lloyd, Bebe Daniels, Snub Pollard.

This nostalgic retrospective combines four of Harold Lloyd's prestardom shorts: *The Chef*, *The Cinema Director*, *Two Gun Gussie*, and *I'm On My Way*. Silent with musical score. Compiled after Lloyd's death. 1919; B&W; 47m.

HARPER VALLEY P.T.A. ★

DIR: Richard Bennett. **CAST:** Barbara Eden, Ronny Cox, Nanette Fabray, Susan Swift, Ron Masak.

Based on the popular country song, this silly piece of fluff features Barbara Eden as the sexy woman who gives her gossiping neighbors their proper comeuppance. Rated PG. 1978; 102m.

HARRY AND WALTER GO TO NEW YORK ★★½

DIR: Mark Rydell. **CAST:** James Caan, Elliott Gould, Michael Caine, Diane Keaton, Charles Durning.

James Caan and Elliott Gould appear to be having the time of their lives portraying two inept con men. Michael Caine and Diane Keaton are, as always, excellent. Mark Rydell directs this unusually light film with an invisible touch. *Harry and Walter* is sort of like Chinese food—an hour later, you feel as if you haven't had anything. Rated PG. 1976; 123m.

HARRY'S WAR ★½

DIR: Kieth Merrill. **CAST:** Edward Herrmann, Geraldine Page, Karen Grassle, David Ogden Stiers, Salome Jens, Elisha Cook Jr.

In this cornball comedy, Harry Johnson (Edward Herrmann) takes on the Internal Revenue Service, which made a mistake on his return. As a result, Harry is left homeless and broke. Unfortunately, the script is more dumb than funny. A few bright moments are provided by character actor Elisha Cook Jr. Rated PG. 1981; 98m.

HAUNTED HONEYMOON ★

DIR: Gene Wilder. **CAST:** Gene Wilder, Gilda Radner, Dom DeLuise, Jonathan Pryce, Paul Smith, Peter Vaughan.

Writer-director-star Gene Wilder fails to scare up a single solid laugh in this sadly limp chiller spoof. He even squanders the talents of his wife, Gilda Radner. They play 40s radio stars who plan to wed at an ominous family estate, which is populated by loonies, werewolves, and transvestites. Rated PG. 1986; 90m.

HAVING A WONDERFUL TIME

DIR: Alfred Santell. **CAST:** Ginger Rogers, Douglas Fairbanks Jr., Red Skelton, Lucille Ball, Eve Arden, Lee Bowman, Jack Carson.

Based on a Broadway stage hit, this was supposed to be romance and comedy at a famed Catskills resort hotel. It proved to be a big waste of a big cast that produced a big loss ($276,000) while misusing and abusing some great talent. Not the best way to remember Red Skelton's screen debut. 1938; B&W; 71m.

HAVING IT ALL ★★★

DIR: Edward Zwick. **CAST:** Dyan Cannon, Hart Bochner, Barry Newman, Sylvia Sidney, Melanie Chartoff.

Dyan Cannon makes up for any script deficiencies with sheer exuberance. In this remake of *The Captain's Paradise*, the roles are reversed, and it is Cannon who plays the bigamist. As a fashion designer, she is constantly traveling between New York and Los Angeles. She has a home and husband in each of the two cities and manages to juggle the two. Made for TV, this is unrated. 1982; 100m.

HAWMPS!

DIR: Joe Camp. **CAST:** James Hampton, Christopher Connelly, Slim Pickens, Denver Pyle, Jack Elam.

An extremely unfunny movie from the director of *Benji*, centering on an Old West cavalry unit that uses camels instead of horses. The cast is made up of familiar faces who appear uninspired. A very dumb film. Rated G. 1976; 120m.

HEAD OFFICE ★★

DIR: Ken Finkleman. **CAST:** Judge Reinhold, Lori-Nan Engler, Eddie Albert, Merritt Butrick, Ron Frazier, Richard Masur, Rick Moranis, Jane Seymour, Danny DeVito.

A sometimes funny comedy about the son of an influential politician who upon graduating from college gets a high-paying job with a major corporation. He then begins scaling the business ladder at an incredible rate, no matter how badly he fouls up. Rated PG-13. 1985; 90m.

HEARTBREAK HOUSE ★★★½

DIR: Anthony Page. **CAST:** Rex Harrison, Amy Irving, Rosemary Harris.

Rex Harrison is ideally cast as George Bernard Shaw's Captain Shotover. At Shotover's house the guests include his two daughters and a visiting young woman, each in the grip of some romantic trauma. As in many of Shaw's plays, what is presented is essentially an ongoing collision of philosophies, but the able cast keeps the debate lively. Unrated, but with no objectionable material. 1985; 122m.

HEARTBREAK KID, THE ★★★★

DIR: Elaine May. **CAST:** Charles Grodin, Cybill Shepherd, Jeannie Berlin, Eddie Albert, Audra Lindley.

The lack of care or commitment in the modern marriage is satirized in this comedy. Charles Grodin plays a young man who's grown tired of his wife while driving to their honeymoon in Florida. By the time he sees beautiful Cybill Shepherd on the beach, his marriage has totally disintegrated. Jeannie Berlin, director Elaine May's daughter, is the big scene stealer as Grodin's whining bride. Rated PG. 1972; 104m.

HEARTBURN ★★★½

DIR: Mike Nichols. **CAST:** Meryl Streep, Jack Nicholson, Jeff Daniels, Maureen Stapleton, Stockard

Channing, Richard Masur, Catherine O'Hara, Milos Forman.

Uneven adaptation of Nora Ephron's novel (she also wrote the screenplay) and a thinly disguised account of her own separation from Watergate journalist Carl Bernstein. Jack Nicholson and Meryl Streep fall in love, get married, and drift apart. Little explanation is given for this eventual drift, which is the film's weakness; its strength, comes from the superb performances by the stars and an incredible supporting cast. Needlessly rated R for language. 1986; 108m.

HEARTS OF THE WEST ★★★

DIR: Howard Zieff. **CAST:** Jeff Bridges, Alan Arkin, Blythe Danner, Andy Griffith.

Pleasant little comedy-drama about an aspiring writer from Iowa (Jeff Bridges) who, determined to pen masterful westerns, winds up in Hollywood as a most reluctant cowboy. The setting is the early 1920s, and the story playfuly explodes many of those classic western myths—such as the notion that a cowboy would leap from a second-story balcony onto his horse and then ride off into the sunset. Rated PG. 1975; 103m.

HEATHERS ★★★★

DIR: Michael Lehmann. **CAST:** Winona Ryder, Christian Slater, Kim Walker.

A *Dr. Strangelove* or *Blue Velvet* of the teen set, this brash black comedy tackles such typically adolescent issues as peer pressure, high school cliques, heterosexuality, and homosexuality—and even teen suicide—in ways that are inventive, irreverent, startling, and occasionally offensive. Rated R; with violence and profanity. 1989; 110m.

HEAVEN CAN WAIT ★★★★½

DIR: Warren Beatty, Buck Henry. **CAST:** Warren Beatty, Julie Christie, Jack Warden, Dyan Cannon, Charles Grodin, James Mason, Buck Henry, Vincent Gardenia.

In this charming, thoroughly entertaining remake of *Here Comes Mr. Jordan* (1941), Warren Beatty stars as quarterback Joe Pendleton, who meets a premature demise when an overzealous angel (Buck Henry) takes the athlete's spirit out of his body after an accident. As it turns out, it wasn't Joe's time to die. However, in the interim, his body is cremated. Thus begins a quest by Joe, the angel, and his superior (James Mason) to find a proper earthly replacement. Rated PG. 1978; 100m.

HEAVEN HELP US ★

DIR: Michael Dinner. **CAST:** Andrew McCarthy, Kevin Dillon, Malcolm Dunarie, Stephen Geoffreys, Donald Sutherland, John Heard, Wallace Shawn, Kate Reid.

Donald Sutherland, John Heard, Wallace Shawn, and Kate Reid support the youthful cast of this generally unfunny and often repulsive comedy about a group of schoolboys (played by Andrew McCarthy, Kevin Dillon, Malcolm Dunarie, and Stephen Geoffreys) discovering the opposite sex and other adolescent pursuits. Rated R. 1985; 90m.

HEAVENLY BODIES ★½

DIR: Lawrence Dane. **CAST:** Cynthia Dale, Richard Rebiere, Laura Henry.

More sweaty dancing bodies à la *Flashdance* are featured in this dull, low-budget release about a secretary who is tired of her nine-to-five existence and opens her own aerobics exercise club in a warehouse. Rated R for nudity, profanity, and sexual innuendo. 1985; 90m.

HEAVENLY KID, THE ★★

DIR: Cary Medoway. **CAST:** Lewis Smith, Jason Gedrick, Jane Kaczmarek, Richard Mulligan.

The Heavenly Kid is earthbound. Cocky Bobby Fontana (Lewis Smith) bit the big one in a chicken race seventeen years ago: which would make it 1968, but the soundtrack and the wardrobe are definitely 1955—a basic problem rendering this otherwise simply stupid film completely unintelligible. Rated PG-13 for language, situations, and bare body parts. 1985; 90m.

HEAVENS ABOVE ★★★½
DIR: John Boulting, Roy Boulting. **CAST:** Peter Sellers, Cecil Parker, Isabel Jeans, Eric Sykes.

Another low-key gem from the late Peter Sellers, this irreverent story of a clergyman with the common touch spoofs just about everything within reach, some of it brilliantly. Sellers shows his congregation the error of their selfish ways and engages them in some odd charities, often with hilarious results. 1963; B&W; 105m.

HELLO AGAIN ★★½
DIR: Frank Perry. **CAST:** Shelley Long, Judith Ivey, Gabriel Byrne, Corbin Bernsen, Sela Ward, Austin Pendleton.

Suburban housewife Shelley Long chokes to death on a Korean meatball only to find herself brought back to life via a magic spell cast by her wacky sister (Judith Ivey). Long then must cope with the changes that occurred during her absence. Screenplay by Susan Isaacs. Rated PG for profanity. 1987; 95m.

HER ALIBI ★★★
DIR: Bruce Beresford. **CAST:** Tom Selleck, Paulina Porizkova, William Daniels, Tess Harper, Patrick Wayne, Hurd Hatfield.

This clever comedy-mystery presents Tom Selleck as a suspense writer who provides an alibi for a beautiful murder suspect (Paulina Porizkova). He then finds himself the victim of a number of mysterious accidents. Is she trying to kill him? It's fun finding out. Fans of director Bruce Beresford may think this ditty is beneath him, but only a curmudgeon can resist its daffy charms. Rated PG for profanity and comic violence. 1989; 110m.

HERCULES GOES BANANAS ★
DIR: Arthur Allan Seidelman. **CAST:** Arnold Schwarzenegger, Arnold Stang.

Ridiculous piece of celluloid starring a very young Arnold Schwarzenegger as Hercules. (His voice is dubbed.) Hercules, it so happens, is being punished by Zeus: the mighty man's physical power is taken away from him and he's left on his own to survive in New York City. It's a sure bet that Schwarzenegger would love to forget this one. 1972; 73m.

HERE COMES MR. JORDAN ★★★★★
DIR: Alexander Hall. **CAST:** Robert Montgomery, Evelyn Keyes, Claude Rains, Rita Johnson, Edward Everett Horton, James Gleason.

We all know that bureaucracy can botch up almost anything. Well, the bureaucrats of heaven can really throw a lulu at boxer Joe Pendleton (Robert Montgomery). The heavenly administrators have called Joe up before his time, and they've got to set things straight. That's the basis for the delightful fantasy *Here Comes Mr. Jordan.* 1941; B&W; 93m.

HERE COMES TROUBLE ★★★
DIR: Lewis Seller. **CAST:** Paul Kelly, Arline Judge, Mona Barrie, Gregory Ratoff.

Jewel thief Mona Barrie mistakenly involves Paul Kelly in a crime when she gives him a cigarette case containing some loot. A mixture of comedy and crime—a perfect hourlong time-filler. 1936; B&W; 62m.

HERO AT LARGE ★★★½
DIR: Martin Davidson. **CAST:** John Ritter, Anne Archer, Bert Convy, Kevin McCarthy.

In this enjoyably lightweight film, John Ritter plays Steve Nichols, an out-of-work actor who takes a part-time job to promote a movie about a crusading superhero, *Captain Avenger*. Along with thirty or so other young men, he dresses up like the film's title character and signs autographs for youngsters who see the movie. Unlike the other impersonators, who grumble about how degrading the job is, Nichols finds pleasure in representing, if only in the minds of children, the powers of justice. Rated PG. 1980; 98m.

HE'S MY GIRL 🦃
DIR: Gabrielle Beaumont. **CAST:** T. K. Carter, David Hallyday.

Ridiculously awful trash about two musicians who win a trip to Los Angeles and a chance at a recording contract. There's just one catch: The trip calls for one male contestant and one female contestant. So T. K. Carter dons heels, wig, and dress. Rated PG-13 for profanity. 1987; 104m.

HEY ABBOTT! ★★★★
DIR: Jim Gates. **CAST:** Bud Abbott, Lou Costello, Joe Besser, Phil Silvers, Steve Allen.

This is a hilarious anthology of high points from Abbott and Costello television programs. Narrated by Milton Berle, the distillation includes the now-legendary duo's classic routines: "Who's on First?," "Oyster Stew," "Floogle Street," and "The Birthday Party." 1978; B&W; 76m.

HIGH ANXIETY ★★
DIR: Mel Brooks. **CAST:** Mel Brooks, Madeline Kahn, Cloris Leachman, Harvey Korman, Dick Van Patten, Ron Carey.

Mel Brooks successfully spoofed the horror film with *Young Frankenstein* and the western with *Blazing Saddles*. However, this takeoff of the Alfred Hitchcock suspense movies falls miserably flat. Rated PG. 1977; 94m.

HIGH HOPES ★★★★★
DIR: Mike Leigh. **CAST:** Ruth Sheen, Philip Davis.

A biting satire of Margaret Thatcher's England, as viewed by three distinct, combative couples in modern London. Ruth Sheen and Philip Davis are memorable as two latter-day hippie leftists who name their cactus Thatcher because it's a pain in the you-know-where. 1989; 100m.

HIGH SCHOOL, USA ★★
DIR: Rod Amateau. **CAST:** Michael J. Fox, Dwayne Hickman, Angela Cartwright.

The fact that the dancing robot is the best actor in this film should tell you something. This made-for-TV feature is your typical teen flick, which is exceptional only because it doesn't rely on nudity and foul language to hold its audience's attention. Michael J. Fox and his pals fight back against the rich preppies who run the school. 1983; 96m.

HIGH SEASON ★★★★
DIR: Clare Peploe. **CAST:** Jacqueline Bisset, Irene Papas, James Fox, Kenneth Branagh, Sebastian Shaw, Robert Stephens.

This delightfully pixilated comedy-mystery presents a group of people feuding, faking, laughing, and loving on a breathtaking Greek isle. Co-written and directed by Clare Peploe, the wife of Bernardo Bertolucci, *High Season* offers Jacqueline Bisset as a photographer and James Fox as her sculptor husband. Rated R for brief nudity and adult themes. 1988; 104m.

HIGH SPIRITS ★
DIR: Neil Jordan. **CAST:** Peter O'Toole, Steve Guttenberg, Daryl Hannah, Beverly D'Angelo, Jennifer Tilly, Liam Neeson.

Writer-director Neil Jordan, who succeeded so brilliantly with *Mona Lisa*, fails just as impressively with this misfired attempt to blend comedy with a gentle ghost story. Peter O'Toole, who spends most of the film either drunk or attempting suicide, tries to generate revenue for the ancient family castle by proclaiming it a haunted tourist trap. Naturally, his feeble attempts arouse some genuine spooks. Ill-defined and badly executed, but the castle is quite impressive. Rated PG-13 for language and mild sexual themes. 1988; 97m.

HIGH STAKES ★★
DIR: Larry Kent. **CAST:** David Foley, Roberta Weiss, Winston Rekert.

Hoping to become a star reporter, a young daydreamer gets his chance when he uncovers a criminal plot to unearth a hidden Nazi treasure. His Walter Mitty–ish fantasies are the least appealing part of the movie, but some funny supporting characters and one-liners compensate. Unrated. 1986; 82m.

HILLBILLYS IN A HAUNTED HOUSE ★
DIR: Jean Yarbrough. **CAST:** Ferlin Husky, Joi Lansing, Don Bowman, John Carradine, Lon Chaney Jr., Basil Rathbone, Molly Bee, Merle Haggard, Sonny James.
Unbelievably bad mishmash of country corn and horror humor is an insult to both genres and deserves its star only because of the appearance of great horror film veterans (including Basil Rathbone's last film role). 1967; 88m.

HIPS, HIPS, HOORAY ★★★
DIR: Mark Sandrich. **CAST:** Bert Wheeler, Robert Woolsey, Thelma Todd, Ruth Etting, George Meeker, Dorothy Lee.
Clowns Bert Wheeler and Robert Woolsey liven up this early, somewhat blue, comedy-musical. The pair play havoc as they invade Thelma Todd's ailing cosmetic business. 1934; B&W; 68m.

HIS DOUBLE LIFE ★★★
DIR: Arthur Hopkins, William C. de Mille. **CAST:** Lillian Gish, Roland Young.
Edwardian novelist Arnold Bennett's comedy about a wealthy recluse who finds a better life by becoming a valet when his valet dies and is buried under his name. Remade with Monty Woolley and Gracie Fields as *Holy Matrimony* in 1943. 1933; B&W; 67m.

HIS GIRL FRIDAY ★★★★★
DIR: Howard Hawks. **CAST:** Cary Grant, Rosalind Russell, Ralph Bellamy, Gene Lockhart, Helen Mack, Ernest Truex.
Based on Ben Hecht and Charles MacArthur's *The Front Page*, which was filmed on three other occasions, this is undoubtedly the best of Howard Hawks's comedies. Originally with two male leads, Hawks converted this gentle spoof of newspapers and reporters into a hilarious battle of the sexes. Rosalind Russell is the reporter bent on retirement, and Cary Grant is the editor bent on maneuvering her out of it—and winning her heart in the process. 1940; B&W; 92m.

HIS PICTURE IN THE PAPERS ★★★½
DIR: John Emerson. **CAST:** Douglas Fairbanks Sr.
This clever film has Douglas Fairbanks performing a variety of Herculean feats—all aimed at getting his picture on the front pages of the New York papers. This comedy helped to define Fairbanks's motion-picture persona as the boisterous, buoyant, devil-may-care, ultra-athletic young go-getter. Silent. 1916; B&W; 68m.

HIS ROYAL SLYNESS/HAUNTED SPOOKS ★★★½
DIR: Hal Roach, Alf Goulding. **CAST:** Harold Lloyd, Mildred Davis, Harry Pollard, Wallace Howe, Gaylord Lloyd.
Silent comedy star Harold Lloyd spreads his considerable talent in this pair of bellybusters from Hal Roach's fun factory. In the first, Lloyd impersonates the king of a small monarchy; in the second, he is maneuvered into living in a haunted mansion. Sight gags and double takes highlight both these shorts. Silent, with music. 1920; B&W; 52m.

HISTORY OF THE WORLD, PART ONE, THE
DIR: Mel Brooks. **CAST:** Mel Brooks, Dom DeLuise, Madeline Kahn, Harvey Korman, Gregory Hines, Cloris Leachman.
Without the thematic unity of *Blazing Saddles* or *Young Frankenstein*, Mel

Brooks is lost in this collection of bits that emerge like unused footage from *Monty Python's The Meaning of Life.* Brooks apparently feels that five-year-old "poo-poo jokes" are the height of humor, but their frequent overuse does not mask the complete absence of wit in this episodic glance at life in ancient Rome, during the French Revolution, and other note-worthy (?) stops along the way. Rated R for crude language. 1981; 86m.

HISTORY OF WHITE PEOPLE IN AMERICA, THE ★★★½
DIR: Harry Shearer. **CAST:** Martin Mull, Mary Kay Place, Fred Willard, Steve Martin.

Martin Mull narrates this hilarious spoof documentary on white heritage, current hobbies, and food preferences. He takes us to the Institute for White Studies and into the home of a very white family. We get to know the Harrison family (with Mary Kay Place and Fred Willard as Mom and Dad). Made for cable TV, this is unrated, but it contains obscenities and sexual topics. 1985; 48m.

HISTORY OF WHITE PEOPLE IN AMERICA, THE (VOLUME II) ★★★½
DIR: Harry Shearer. **CAST:** Fred Willard, Mary Kay Place, Martin Mull, Michael McKean, Amy Lynn, George Gobel, Christian Jacobs, Eileen Brennan, Stella Stevens.

Martin Mull returns in four hilarious new episodes with the very white Harrison family. In "White Religion," Mr. and Mrs. Harrison (Fred Willard and Mary Kay Place) must deal with their daughter's teen pregnancy. "White Stress" features Mr. Harrison coming unglued, seeing a psychiatrist, and trying to relax. In "White Politics," Mr. Harrison runs for water commissioner because their water is polluted. The last episode, "White Crime," finds Mr. Harrison, his son, and Martin Mull in court with Eileen Brennan as the judge. Unrated, this does contain obscenities. 1986; 100m.

HIT THE ICE ★★★
DIR: Charles Lamont. **CAST:** Bud Abbott, Lou Costello, Patric Knowles, Elyse Knox.

Abbott and Costello play a pair of photographers in this outing, eluding assorted crooks. Gags abound, but so do musical numbers, which always seem to grind these films to a halt. On a par with most of their other efforts, it guarantees a great time for A & C fans. 1943; B&W; 82m.

HOBSON'S CHOICE (1954) ★★★★★
DIR: David Lean. **CAST:** Charles Laughton, John Mills, Brenda de Banzie, Daphne Anderson.

Charles Laughton gives one of his most brilliant performances as a turn-of-the-century London shoemaker whose love for the status quo and his whiskey is shattered by the determination of his daughter to wed. This is the original 1954 movie version of the British comedy. Laughton is expertly supported by John Mills and Brenda de Banzie as the two who wish to marry. 1954; B&W; 107m.

HOLD THAT GHOST ★★★½
DIR: Arthur Lubin. **CAST:** Bud Abbott, Lou Costello, Richard Carlson, Joan Davis.

Abbott and Costello score in this super comedy about two goofs (guess who) inheriting a haunted house where all kinds of bizarre events occur. You may have to watch this one a few times to catch all the gags. 1941; B&W; 86m.

HOLE IN THE HEAD, A ★★★
DIR: Frank Capra. **CAST:** Frank Sinatra, Edward G. Robinson, Eleanor Parker, Eddie Hodges, Carolyn Jones, Thelma Ritter, Keenan Wynn, Joi Lansing.

Frank Sinatra plays a Florida motel owner who never quite manages to get his life together, torn between his adoring son (Eddie Hodges) and his nagging brother (Edward G. Robinson). Ironically, one indication of his impractical nature is (supposedly) his idea of building a Disneyland in the Florida Swamps! The veteran cast keeps this wispy comedy afloat, and its virtues include the Oscar-winning song "High Hopes." Not rated; suitable for the whole family. 1959; 120m.

HOLIDAY ★★★★½
DIR: George Cukor. **CAST:** Katharine Hepburn, Cary Grant, Doris Nolan, Lew Ayres, Edward Everett Horton, Binnie Barnes, Henry Daniell.

This delightful film was adapted from the Broadway play by Phillip Barry and features Cary Grant as a nonconformist, who, for love's sake, must confront New York City's upper-class society. Indeed, he must make the ultimate sacrifice to please his fiancée (Doris Nolan) and join her father's banking firm. Only her sister (Katharine Hepburn) seems to understand Grant's need to live a different kind of life. 1938; B&W; 93m.

HOLLYWOOD BOULEVARD ★★★
DIR: Joe Dante, Allan Arkush. **CAST:** Candice Rialson, Mary Woronov, Rita George, Jeffrey Kramer, Dick Miller, Paul Bartel.

A would-be actress goes to work for inept movie-makers in this comedy. This is the first film that Joe Dante (*Gremlins*) directed. Rated R. 1976; 83m.

HOLLYWOOD HARRY ★★★½
DIR: Robert Forster. **CAST:** Robert Forster, Joe Spinell, Shannon Wilcox, Kathrine Forster, Marji Martin, Mallie Jackson, Read Morgan.

Robert Forster stars in this comedy about a down-and-out detective who is forced to take his runaway niece on his investigations. Forster also directed this entertaining low-budget feature. Rated PG-13 for profanity. 1985; 99m.

HOLLYWOOD HIGH
DIR: Patrick Wright. **CAST:** Marcy Albrecht, Sherry Hardin.

Easily one of the century's ten worst films, this unfunny sex comedy follows four girls in their quest for a place to "get it on." The girls are airheads and their so-called sexy dialogue is enough to induce nausea. Avoid at all costs! Rated R for profanity and nudity. 1976; 81m.

HOLLYWOOD HIGH, PART II
DIR: Caruth C. Byrd, Lee Thomburg. **CAST:** April May, Donna Lynn, Camille Warner, Drew Davis, Bruce Dobos.

Teen sexploitation at its worst, this pornographic tape features nonactors with ridiculous dialogue, cruising, partying, skinny-dipping, and making out. Rated R for profanity and nudity. 1981; 86m.

HOLLYWOOD HOT TUBS
DIR: Chuck Vincent. **CAST:** Paul Gunning, Donna McDaniel.

In this ludicrous video a young man wangles a job at a local hot tub firm in L.A. Lots of imbecilic jokes, naked girls, and a frenetic climax all help *not* to distinguish this quickie from the rest of the crowd. Somebody pull the drain plug, please. Rated R for nudity. 1984; 103m.

HOLLYWOOD ON PARADE ★★
DIR: Louis Lewyn. **CAST:** Fredric March, Ginger Rogers, Jean Harlow, Jeanette MacDonald, Maurice Chevalier, Mary Pickford, Jackie Cooper.

The most interesting aspects of this collection of short films from Paramount are the brief glimpses of some of Hollywood's best-known stars of the period. The practically nonexistent plot is tepid. Watch for the stars and forget the rest. 1934; B&W; 59m.

HOLLYWOOD OR BUST ★★½
DIR: Frank Tashlin. **CAST:** Jerry Lewis, Dean Martin, Pat Crowley, Anita Ekberg.

One of Dean Martin and Jerry Lewis's lesser efforts concerns the boys' misadventures on a trip to Hollywood where movie nut Jerry hopes to meet his dream girl, Anita Ekberg (who plays herself). Starts off well, but stalls as soon as Dean meets Pat

Crowley and the musical interludes begin. The final teaming of Martin and Lewis. 1956; 95m.

HOLLYWOOD OUTTAKES ★★½
DIR: Bruce Goldstein. **CAST:** Humphrey Bogart, Bette Davis, Errol Flynn, George Raft, James Cagney, Judy Garland, Mickey Rooney.

This is a sometimes terrific, most times passable, collection of blooper and newsreel footage from the 1930s, 1940s, and 1950s. No MPAA rating. 1984; 90m.

HOLLYWOOD SHUFFLE ★★★½
DIR: Robert Townsend. **CAST:** Robert Townsend, Anne-Marie Johnson, Starletta Dupois.

In the style of *Kentucky Fried Movie*, writer-director-star Robert Townsend lampoons Hollywood's perception of blacks—and racial stereotypes in general. It's not always funny, but some scenes are hilarious. A private-eye spoof called "Death of a Break Dancer," a parody of television movie-review shows called "Sneakin' into the Movies," and something entitled "Black Acting School" are the standouts. Rated R for profanity and adult content. 1987; 82m.

HOLLYWOOD ZAP
DIR: David Cohen. **CAST:** Ivan E. Roth, Ben Frank.

If this so-called comedy doesn't offend you, you probably can't be offended. A country bumpkin goes off to Los Angeles to find his long-lost father and runs into characters and situations so tasteless that they're better left undescribed. Rated R. 1986; 85m.

HOME IS WHERE THE HART IS ★
DIR: Rex Bromfield. **CAST:** Valri Bromfield, Stephen E. Miller, Eric Christmas, Leslie Nielsen, Martin Mull.

Lethargic, unfunny attempt at a black comedy. A gold-digging crook-turned-nurse (Valri Bromfield) murders a bedridden old lady in order to get her husband, the rich and senile Slim Hart (hence the cute title). Leslie Nielsen co-stars as a bumbling sheriff. Rated PG-13. 1987; 85m.

HOME MOVIES ★★
DIR: Brian De Palma. **CAST:** Nancy Allen, Keith Gordon, Kirk Douglas, Gerrit Graham, Vincent Gardenia.

A little film produced with the help of Brian De Palma's film-making students at Sarah Lawrence College. A director, played by Kirk Douglas, gives "star therapy" to a young man who feels he is a mere extra in his own life. The film is quirky and fun at times, but more often it's simply pointless. Interesting as an experiment by an established talent, but as entertainment, it's quite tedious. Rated PG. 1980; 90m.

HONKY TONK FREEWAY ★★★
DIR: John Schlesinger. **CAST:** William Devane, Beverly D'Angelo, Beau Bridges, Geraldine Page, Teri Garr.

Director John Schlesinger captures the comedy of modern American life in a small Florida town. The stars keep you laughing. Rated R. 1981; 107m.

HOOPER ★★★★
DIR: Hal Needham. **CAST:** Burt Reynolds, Sally Field, Jan-Michael Vincent, Brian Keith.

Fresh from their success with *Smokey and the Bandit*, director Hal Needham and stars Burt Reynolds and Sally Field are reunited for this humorous, knockabout comedy about Hollywood stuntmen. Jan-Michael Vincent adds to the film's impact as an up-and-coming fall guy out to best top-of-the-heap Reynolds. Good fun. Rated PG. 1978; 99m.

HORSE FEATHERS ★★★★★
DIR: Norman Z. McLeod. **CAST:** The Marx Brothers, Thelma Todd, David Landau.

The funniest of the films starring the four Marx Brothers, this features Groucho as the president of Huxley College, which desperately needs a winning football team. So Groucho hires Chico and Harpo to help him fix the season. Meanwhile, Groucho is competing for the attentions of the sexy college widow, Thelma Todd. The team's most outrageous and hilarious gagfest. 1932; B&W; 69m.

HORSE'S MOUTH, THE ★★★½
DIR: Ronald Neame. **CAST:** Alec Guinness, Kay Walsh, Renee Houston, Michael Gough.
Star Alec Guinness, who also penned the script, romps in high comic style through this film version of Joyce Cary's mocking novel about an eccentric painter. 1958; 93m.

HOSPITAL, THE ★★★★½
DIR: Arthur Hiller. **CAST:** George C. Scott, Diana Rigg, Barnard Hughes.
You definitely don't want to check in. But if you like to laugh, you'll want to check it out. This 1971 black comedy did for the medical profession what...*And Justice for All* did for our court system and *Network* did for television. Paddy Chayefsky's Oscar-winning screenplay casts George C. Scott as an embittered doctor battling against the outrageous goings-on at the institution of the title. Rated PG. 1971; 103m.

HOT DOG...THE MOVIE ★★
DIR: Peter Markle. **CAST:** David Naughton, Patrick Houser, Shannon Tweed.
David Naughton co-stars with one-time Playboy Playmate of the Year Shannon Tweed in this comedy about high jinks on the ski slopes that will no doubt delight its youthful target audience. Rated R for nudity, profanity, and suggested sex. 1984; 96m.

HOT MOVES
DIR: Jim Sotos. **CAST:** Michael Zorek, Adam Blair, Jeff Fishman, Johnny Timko.
Here's another rip-off of *Animal House*; a teen lust comedy with little lust and less laughs. Rated R. 1985; 80m.

HOT PURSUIT ★
DIR: Steven Lisberger. **CAST:** John Cusack, Robert Loggia, Wendy Gazelle, Jerry Stiller, Monte Markham.
In this unfunny comedy, a college student (John Cusack) misses the plane on which he was to join his girlfriend (Wendy Gazelle) and her wealthy parents on a vacation cruise. He then finds himself embarking on a series of wildly improbable misadventures as he attempts to catch up with them. Rated PG-13 for profanity and violence. 1987; 90m.

HOT RESORT ★½
DIR: John Robins. **CAST:** Tom Parsekian, Michael Berz, Bronson Pinchot, Marcy Walker, Frank Gorshin.
Airplane style takeoff on the resort industry is a classic example of what happens when there's just not enough script to work with. Lots of improvising and empty plot holes overwhelm the attractive cast. Make no reservations. Rated R for nudity, profanity, and simulated sex. 1984; 92m.

HOT STUFF ★★★½
DIR: Dom DeLuise. **CAST:** Dom DeLuise, Jerry Reed, Suzanne Pleshette, Ossie Davis.
A entertaining, old-fashioned comedy that whips right along. Director-star Dom DeLuise makes the most of his dual role. His is a good-natured kind of comedy. The story concerns a government fencing operation for capturing crooks and the results are humorous. Rated PG. 1979; 87m.

HOT TO TROT ★★½
DIR: Michael Dinner. **CAST:** Bob Goldthwait, Dabney Coleman, Virginia Madsen, Cindy Pickett, Mary Gross.
Cute update on the Francis the Talking Mule comedies of the Fifties. This time we have a witty horse. What gets tiresome is the horse's dumb friend Fred (Bob Goldthwait). Fred tries to match wits with his evil stepfather (Dabney Coleman), but doesn't stand a chance until Don the horse steps in to help out. The best lines go to John Candy as the horse's voice. Rated PG for profanity. 1988; 83m.

HOUND OF THE BASKERVILLES, THE (1977)
DIR: Paul Morrissey. **CAST:** Dudley Moore, Peter Cook, Denholm Elliott, Joan Greenwood, Hugh Griffith, Terry-Thomas, Roy Kinnear.

Truly abysmal send-up of the novel by Conan Doyle has the British comedy team of Dudley Moore and Peter Cook embarrassing themselves as Watson and Holmes, respectively. Yet they have only themselves to blame, as the duo collaborated on the screenplay with director Paul Morrissey, who shows absolutely no flair for comedy. 1977; 84m.

HOUSE CALLS ★★★★½
DIR: Howard Zieff. **CAST:** Walter Matthau, Glenda Jackson, Richard Benjamin, Art Carney.

Here's a romantic comedy reminiscent of films Spencer Tracy and Katharine Hepburn made together mostly because of the teaming of Walter Matthau and Glenda Jackson. A recently widowed doctor (Matthau) finds his bachelor spree cut short by a romantic encounter with a nurse (Jackson) who refuses to be just another conquest. A delightful battle of the sexes with two equally matched opponents. Rated PG. 1978; 96m.

HOUSEBOAT ★★★
DIR: Melville Shavelson. **CAST:** Cary Grant, Sophia Loren, Martha Hyer, Harry Guardino.

A minor entry in Cary Grant's *oeuvre* of romantic fluff, largely unremarkable because of its ho-hum script. With this sort of insubstantial material coming his way, it's little wonder Grant chose to retire eight years later. He lives on a houseboat *sans* wife; Sophia Loren is the housekeeper-maid with whom he falls in love. Unrated; suitable for family viewing. 1958; 110m.

HOW I GOT INTO COLLEGE ★
DIR: Savage Steve Holland. **CAST:** Anthony Edwards, Corey Parker.

Uninspired and dull adolescent comedy that throws away a promising premise: the antics high schoolers use to get into good colleges, and the manipulations colleges use to get certain students. There are a few funny fantasy sequences, but the movie is generally unimaginative, superficial, and poorly paced. Rated PG-13. 1989; 98m.

HOW I WON THE WAR ★★★½
DIR: Richard Lester. **CAST:** Michael Crawford, John Lennon, Michael Hordern, Jack MacGowran.

John Lennon had his only solo screen turn (away from the Beatles) in this often hilarious war spoof. Directed by Richard Lester, it features Michael Crawford as a military man who has a wacky way of distorting the truth as he reminisces about his adventures in battle. 1967; 109m.

HOW TO BEAT THE HIGH CO$T OF LIVING ★★
DIR: Robert Scheerer. **CAST:** Jessica Lange, Susan Saint James, Jane Curtin, Richard Benjamin, Fred Willard, Dabney Coleman.

A great cast all dressed up with no place to go...except Jane Curtin, whose shopping-mall strip-tease is a marginal high point in a caper comedy not even up to the substandards of an average made-for-television movie. Curtin, Jessica Lange, and Susan Saint James are a trio of housewives who decide to heist a large display of cash in order to meet the grocery payments. Tiresome and taxing. Rated PG. 1980; 110m.

HOW TO BREAK UP A HAPPY DIVORCE ★★★
DIR: Jerry Paris. **CAST:** Hal Linden, Barbara Eden, Harold Gould.

Ex-wife Barbara Eden wants ex-husband Hal Linden back. To make him jealous, she dates a well-known playboy. Comic mayhem follows. Lots of sight gags. This is an unrated TV movie. 1976; 78m.

HOW TO MARRY A MILLIONAIRE ★★★
DIR: Jean Negulesco. **CAST:** Lauren Bacall, Marilyn Monroe, Betty

Grable, William Powell, Cameron Mitchell, David Wayne, Rory Calhoun.

The stars, Marilyn Monroe, Lauren Bacall, and Betty Grable, are fun to watch in this comedy. However, director Jean Negulesco doesn't do much to keep our interest. The story in this slight romp is all in the title—with William Powell giving the girls a run for his money. 1953; 96m.

HOWIE FROM MAUI 🦃

DIR: Walter C. Miller. **CAST:** Howie Mandel.

Howie Mandel can be a charming goofball, a laughable bumbler like Jerry Lewis. But as a solo act, Mandel's self-centered style of comedy is funny for a mere five minutes. He fills the other 55 minutes of this one-man show with vulgar, banal, and boring material. Rated R for profanity. 1987; 60m.

HOWIE MANDEL'S NORTH AMERICAN WATUSI TOUR ★★★½

DIR: Jerry Kramer. **CAST:** Howie Mandel.

This Howie Mandel concert was filmed in Chicago and shows how much he has improved in his timing and delivery since his first special in 1983. His screaming and sight-gag props are still here, but his improvisation and interplay with the audience are now the highlights of his act. This group of fans really gets into the performance and you will, too. 1986; 52m.

HUNK 🦃

DIR: Lawrence Bassoff. **CAST:** John Allen Nelson, Steve Levitt, Rebeccah Bush, Robert Morse, James Coco, Avery Schreiber, Deborah Shelton.

A social outcast (John Allen Nelson) makes a deal with the devil (James Coco) to get a sexy, muscular body and then has to suffer the consequences in this dull, unfunny comedy. Rated PG. 1987; 90m.

HURRY UP OR I'LL BE 30 ★★★

DIR: Joseph Jacoby. **CAST:** John Lefkowitz, Linda De Coff, Danny DeVito.

Somewhat aimless comedy-drama will appeal to those with a fondness for slice-of-life movies. Set in Brooklyn, the movie follows an almost-thirty single guy (John Lefkowitz) who is frustrated over the lack of love and business success in his life. Danny DeVito has a supporting part as a fellow Brooklynite. Rated R for sexual situations and profanity. 1973; 88m.

HYSTERICAL ★½

DIR: Chris Bearde. **CAST:** William Hudson, Mark Hudson, Brett Hudson, Cindy Pickett, Richard Kiel, Julie Newmar, Bud Cort, Robert Donner, Murray Hamilton, Clint Walker.

Zany horror spoof generates only a sprinkling of laughs as the bulk of its off-the-wall humor thuds embarrassingly. This movie was supposed to make the Hudson Brothers the Marx Brothers of the 1980s. The Hudsons have an undeniable charm, but their film debut is more like chicken poop than *Duck Soup*. Rated PG. 1983; 87m.

I LOVE LUCY (TELEVISION SERIES) ★★★★★

DIR: William Asher. **CAST:** Lucille Ball, Desi Arnaz Sr., Vivian Vance, William Frawley.

The archetypical TV sitcom. Domestic squabbles have never been more entertaining. Ricky's accent and temper, Lucy's schemes and ambitions, Ethel's submissiveness, Fred's parsimoniousness, all added up to surefire hilarity. The chemistry among the cast members was incredible. Episodes bear innumerable viewings. Classic moments include Lucy and Ethel toiling in a chocolate factory, Lucy stomping grapes, Lucy meeting William Holden, Ricky getting the news that he's a father, and Lucy selling a health tonic which happens to have a high alcohol content. 1951–1956; 48 minutes each tape.

I LOVE MY WIFE ★½
DIR: Mel Stuart. **CAST:** Elliott Gould, Brenda Vaccaro, Angel Tompkins, Dabney Coleman, Joan Tompkins.
Barely laughable sex comedy dealing with the problems of an upper-class couple (Elliott Gould, Brenda Vaccaro) and their ridiculous attempts to solve them. Rather daring for the time and far too tame for today's audiences, this film would have been silly no matter when it was released. Rated PG. 1970; 95m.

I LOVE YOU ALICE B. TOKLAS! ★★★
DIR: Hy Averback. **CAST:** Peter Sellers, Leigh Taylor-Young, Jo Van Fleet.
Peter Sellers plays a lawyer-cum-hippie in this far-out comedy about middle-age crisis. Rated PG. 1968; 93m.

I MARRIED A WOMAN ★½
DIR: Hal Kanter. **CAST:** George Gobel, Diana Dors, Adolphe Menjou, Jessie Royce Landis, Nita Talbot, William Redfield, John McGiver.
Is that the best title they could come up with? George Gobel plays an advertising man who is having difficulty holding on to both his biggest account and his wife, who feels he's not paying her enough attention. "Lonesome George" plays his standard character here, and it doesn't translate well into a full-length movie. Angie Dickinson and John Wayne have walk-on parts. 1958; B&W/color; 80m.

I OUGHT TO BE IN PICTURES ★★★★
DIR: Herbert Ross. **CAST:** Walter Matthau, Ann-Margret, Dinah Manoff.
Neil Simon's best work since *The Goodbye Girl*, this heartwarming story stars Walter Matthau as a father who deserts his Brooklyn family. Dinah Manoff is the daughter who wants to be a movie star, and Ann-Margret is the woman who brings the two together. Rated PG for mild profanity and brief nudity. 1982; 107m.

I WANNA HOLD YOUR HAND ★★★
DIR: Robert Zemeckis. **CAST:** Nancy Allen, Bobby DiCicco, Marc McClure, Theresa Saldana, Eddie Deezen, Will Jordan, Wendie Jo Sperber.
A group of New Jersey teens try to get tickets to the Beatles' first appearance on the *Ed Sullivan Show*. This was one of the biggest money losers of 1978, but it's not that bad. Fast-paced and energetic, with a nice sense of period and some fine performances. Rated PG. 1978; 104m.

I WAS A TEENAGE TV TERRORIST ★
DIR: Stanford Singer. **CAST:** Julie Hanlon, Adam Nathan.
A teenager and his girlfriend who work in the supply room of a cable television station decide to get even with their employers by pulling a series of pranks designed to look like the work of terrorists. A laughless comedy. Unrated, with profanity. 1985; 85m.

I WILL, I WILL...FOR NOW ★
DIR: Norman Panama. **CAST:** Elliott Gould, Diane Keaton, Paul Sorvino, Victoria Principal, Robert Alda, Warren Berlinger.
This is one of those mid-1970s trashers complete with mistaken-identity plot and a Santa Barbara sex clinic where "nothing is unnatural." Diane Keaton is the only one who comes out of this mess without looking ridiculous. A star for her ability to float above the wreckage. Rated R. 1976; 96m.

IF... ★★★★
DIR: Lindsay Anderson. **CAST:** Malcolm McDowell, David Wood, Richard Warwick.
This is British director Lindsay Anderson's black comedy about English private schools and the revolt against their strict code of behavior taken to the farthest limits of the imagination. Malcolm McDowell's movie debut. Rated R. 1969; 111m.

IF I WERE RICH ★★★
DIR: Zoltán Korda. **CAST:** Robert Donat, Wendy Hiller, Edmund Gwenn.
How to live and avoid paying bills while waiting for prosperity to return is the theme of this entertaining British comedy. Robert Donat falls for Wendy Hiller when he arrives to shut off her once-rich-but-now-bankrupt father Edmund Gwenn's electricity. The debonair Donat is a delight in this early pairing with Hiller. 1933; B&W; 63m.

I'M ALL RIGHT JACK ★★★½
DIR: John Boulting. **CAST:** Peter Sellers, Terry-Thomas, Ian Carmichael.
British comedies can be marvelously entertaining, especially when they star Peter Sellers, as in this witty spoof of the absurdities of the labor movement carried to its ultimate extreme. This is humor at its best. 1960; B&W; 101m.

I'M GONNA GIT YOU SUCKA! ★★★★
DIR: Keenen Ivory Wayans. **CAST:** Keenen Ivory Wayans, Bernie Casey, Jim Brown, Isaac Hayes, Antonio Fargas, Steve James, John Vernon, Clu Gulager.
Keenen Ivory Wayans wrote and directed this uproariously funny parody of the blaxploitation flicks of the early Seventies. Wayans culls his cast from the very films he so brilliantly satirizes. The gags run fast and loose, and the result is a satisfying laughfest. Rated R for language. 1989; 88m.

IMMORAL MR. TEAS, THE ★★★
DIR: Russ Meyer. **CAST:** W. Ellis Teas.
After receiving an anesthetic at the dentist's office, middle-aged Mr. Teas discovers that he has the ability to see through women's clothing. Surprisingly well made, this was a huge hit and ushered in a whole era of nudie cuties, most with variations on the same plot. The nudity is tame by modern standards, and anyone who remembers the Fifties and Sixties should enjoy this as a nostalgic curiosity. 1959; 63m.

IMPORTANCE OF BEING EARNEST, THE ★★★½
DIR: Anthony Asquith. **CAST:** Michael Redgrave, Edith Evans, Margaret Rutherford, Joan Greenwood, Michael Denison, Dorothy Tutin, Richard Wattis.
A peerless cast of stage professionals brings this version of Oscar Wilde's classic Victorian Era comedy of manners to vivid life in high style. Once again, the problem of Mr. Worthing's cloakroom origins delights with hilarious results. A very funny film. 1952; 95m.

IMPROPER CHANNELS ★
DIR: Eric Till. **CAST:** Alan Arkin, Mariette Hartley, Monica Parker.
Is this comedy...or bureaucratic nightmare? The two should mix, but unfortunately don't, in this story of an overeager social worker who accuses a father (Alan Arkin) of child abuse. Rated PG for language. 1981; 92m.

IMPURE THOUGHTS ★★½
DIR: Michael A. Simpson. **CAST:** Brad Dourif, Lane Davies, Terry Beaver, John Putch.
A group of friends who attended the same Catholic grammar school in the early Sixties meet after death and reminisce about their youths. This satire will work best for those who either attended such schools or who vividly remember the Kennedy era; others will find it puzzling. Rated PG. 1986; 87m.

IN PERSON ★★★
DIR: William A. Seiter. **CAST:** Ginger Rogers, George Brent, Alan Mowbray, Grant Mitchell, Samuel S. Hinds, Edgar Kennedy.
Vivacious, shrewish film star flees to a resort incognito and meets a handsome stranger who is totally unimpressed when he learns who she really is. Enjoyable. 1935; B&W; 85m.

IN THE MOOD ★★½
DIR: Phil Alden Robinson. **CAST:** Patrick Dempsey, Talia Balsam, Beverly D'Angelo, Michael Constantine, Kathleen Freeman.

Patrick Dempsey plays a conniving teenager who becomes a media star by repeatedly marrying older women. Although this period (1940's) comedy has some funny bits and lines, the story is slapdash. Talia Balsam and Beverly D'Angelo are fine as the "older" women (21 and 25), and Michael Constantine is funny as Dempsey's father. Rated PG-13. 1987; 100m.

INCREDIBLE ROCKY MOUNTAIN RACE, THE ★★★
DIR: James L. Conway. **CAST:** Christopher Connelly, Forrest Tucker, Larry Storch, Jack Kruschen, Mike Mazurki.

This western with a comic touch is about a race used by townspeople to get rid of two troublemakers. These troublemakers include Mark Twain (Christopher Connelly) and his arch enemy, Mike Fink (Forrest Tucker). They are to race to the West Coast and retrieve five rare relics. There is more comedy as the snags increase and the problems get out of hand. Rated G. 1985; 97m.

INCREDIBLE SHRINKING WOMAN, THE ★★
DIR: Joel Schumacher. **CAST:** Lily Tomlin, Ned Beatty, Henry Gibson, Elizabeth Wilson, Charles Grodin, Pamela Bellwood, Mike Douglas, Mark Blankfield.

This comedy, starring Lily Tomlin, falls prey to the law of diminishing returns. But to simply dismiss it as a failure would be inaccurate and unfair. This comic adaptation of Richard Matheson's classic science-fiction novel (*The Shrinking Man*) is not a bad movie. It's more like...well...the perfect old-fashioned Disney movie—a little corny and strained at times but not a total loss. Rated PG. 1981; 88m.

INDISCREET ★
DIR: Leo McCarey. **CAST:** Gloria Swanson, Ben Lyon, Arthur Lake.

Near-boring comedy-drama in which Gloria Swanson spends most of her time trying to conceal her questionable past from Ben Lyon. That she sings three songs does not help things a bit. Not to be confused with 1958's fine film of same title starring Ingrid Bergman and Cary Grant. 1931; B&W; 92m.

IN-LAWS, THE ★★★★
DIR: Arthur Hiller. **CAST:** Peter Falk, Alan Arkin, Penny Peyser, Michael Lembeck.

This delightful caper comedy mixes mystery and action with the fun. Vince Ricardo (Peter Falk) is the mastermind behind a bold theft of engravings of U.S. currency from a Treasury Department armored car. Sheldon Kornpett (Alan Arkin), is a slightly neurotic dentist. After just a few minutes with Vince, he is convinced the man is completely out of his mind, and soon they're off on a perilous mission. Falk and Arkin make a great team, playing off each other brilliantly. Rated PG. 1979; 103m.

INSPECTOR GENERAL, THE ★★★★
DIR: Henry Koster. **CAST:** Danny Kaye, Walter Slezak, Elsa Lanchester.

In this classic comedy set in Russia of the 1800s, Danny Kaye is the town fool who is mistaken for a confidant of Napoleon. The laughs come when Danny is caught up in court intrigue and really has no idea what is going on. Kaye's talents are showcased in this film. 1949; 102m.

INTERNATIONAL HOUSE ★★★½
DIR: A. Edward Sutherland. **CAST:** W. C. Fields, Peggy Hopkins Joyce, Baby Rose Marie, Cab Calloway, Stu Erwin, George Burns, Gracie Allen, Bela Lugosi, Franklin Pangborn, Sterling Holloway.

An offbeat, must-see film involving a melting pot of characters gathered at the luxurious International House

Hotel to bid on the rights to the radioscope, an early version of television. As usual, a Russian muddies the waters with cunning and craft, while an American bumbles to the rescue. W. C. Fields and Burns and Allen are in rare form throughout. 1933; B&W; 70m.

INVASION OF THE GIRL SNATCHERS

DIR: Lee Jones. **CAST:** Elizabeth Rush.

This apparently never released comedy has been resurrected on video as a so-bad-it's-good item. But really it's just bad. Somewhere in the Midwest an assistant detective, several greasy kids, and a cult leader in the service of aliens from outer space do battle. Unrated; the film contains nudity and sexual suggestiveness. 1973; 90m.

INVITATION TO THE WEDDING ★★

DIR: Joseph Brooks. **CAST:** John Gielgud, Ralph Richardson, Paul Nicholas, Elizabeth Shepherd.

A feeble little British tale about a young American college student who falls in love with his best friend's sister, who just so happens to be engaged to an English war hero. The student is invited to the wedding in England, and during the rehearsal he's accidentally married to the girl by her bungling uncle, the village vicar (played with great style by Ralph Richardson). John Gielgud offers the only comic relief as an Englishman-turned-Southern evangelist. 1973; 89m.

IRMA LA DOUCE ★★★

DIR: Billy Wilder. **CAST:** Shirley MacLaine, Jack Lemmon, Lou Jacobi, Herschel Bernardi.

Gendarme Jack Lemmon gets involved with prostitute Shirley MacLaine in what director Billy Wilder hoped would be another MacLaine/Lemmon hit like *The Apartment*. It isn't. It's raw humor in glorious color. Send the "Silver Spoons" set off to bed before you screen this one. 1963; 142m.

ISHTAR ★

DIR: Elaine May. **CAST:** Warren Beatty, Dustin Hoffman, Isabelle Adjani, Charles Grodin, Jack Weston, Tess Harper, Carol Kane.

A bloated, disjointed, and ponderous megabuck vanity production that might have been satisfying as a smaller film but sinks under its own weight. Warren Beatty and Dustin Hoffman star as a pair of inept, would-be singer-songwriters who travel all the way to north Africa to get a booking. Once there, this latter-day *Road* picture completely derails. Rated PG-13 for language and brief nudity. 1987; 107m.

IT ★★★

DIR: Clarence Badger. **CAST:** Clara Bow, Antonio Moreno, William Austin, Lloyd Corrigan, Jacqueline Gadsden, Gary Cooper.

Advance promotion about *It* (read: sex appeal) made this clever little comedy about shopgirl Clara Bow chasing and catching her boss Antonio Moreno a solid hit. It also boosted red-haired Brooklyn bombshell Clara to superstardom. Rising star Gary Cooper appears only briefly. Silent. 1927; B&W; 71m.

IT CAME FROM HOLLYWOOD ★★★

DIR: Malcolm Leo, Andrew Solt. **CAST:** Dan Aykroyd, John Candy, Cheech and Chong, Gilda Radner.

Dan Aykroyd, John Candy, Cheech and Chong, and Gilda Radner appear in comedy vignettes as the hosts of this watchable *That's Entertainment*–style compilation of the worst all-time (but hilarious) losers in *Plan 9 from Outer Space*, *Robot Monster*, *Batmen of Africa*, and *Untamed Women*. Rated PG for sexual references and scatological humor. 1982; 80m.

IT HAPPENED ONE NIGHT ★★★★★

DIR: Frank Capra. **CAST:** Clark Gable, Claudette Colbert, Ward Bond.

Prior to *One Flew over the Cuckoo's Nest*, this 1934 comedy was the only film to capture all the major Academy Awards. Clark Gable stars as a cynical reporter on the trail of a runaway heiress, Claudette Colbert. They fall in love, of course, and the result is vintage movie magic. 1934; B&W; 105m.

IT SHOULD HAPPEN TO YOU ★★★½

DIR: George Cukor. **CAST:** Judy Holliday, Peter Lawford, Jack Lemmon, Michael O'Shea, Vaughn Taylor.

Judy Holliday plays an actress who's desperate to garner publicity and hopes splashing her name across billboards all over New York City will ignite her career. The movie provides a steady stream of chuckles. Jack Lemmon makes an amusing screen debut. Holliday is hard to resist. 1954; B&W; 81m.

IT TAKES TWO ★★

DIR: David Beaird. **CAST:** George Newbern, Kimberly Foster.

This young boy's fantasy features George Newbern as a reluctant bridegroom who has an affair with a fast car and a hot blond car dealer. Then he must choose between the blonde and his childhood sweetheart, who just happens to be waiting (and waiting!) at the altar. Only teens may fully appreciate this trite sex comedy. Rated PG-13 for profanity and sexual situations. 1988; 79m.

IT'S A GIFT ★★★★★

DIR: Norman Z. McLeod. **CAST:** W. C. Fields, Kathleen Howard, Baby LeRoy.

In a class with the best of the comedies of the 1930s (including *Duck Soup*, *I'm No Angel*, *My Man Godfrey*), this classic was produced during the peak of Fields's association with Paramount and is his archetypal vehicle, peopled with characters whose sole purpose in life seems to be to annoy his long-suffering Harold Bissonette. A side-splitting series of visual delights. 1934; B&W; 73m.

IT'S A JOKE, SON! ★★

DIR: Ben Stoloff. **CAST:** Kenny Delmar, Una Merkel, June Lockhart, Kenneth Farrell, Douglass Dumbrille.

Radio's Senator Claghorn comes to life in the form of Kenny Delmar, whose bombastic talk and Old South attitude entertained millions on Fred Allen's popular network show. The blustering politician is hijacked by some underhanded rivals and only the strains of his beloved "Dixie" give him the strength to win the day. Cornball but fun. 1947; B&W; 63m.

IT'S A MAD MAD MAD MAD WORLD ★★★★

DIR: Stanley Kramer. **CAST:** Spencer Tracy, Milton Berle, Jonathan Winters, Buddy Hackett, Sid Caesar, Phil Silvers, Mickey Rooney, Peter Falk, Dick Shawn, Ethel Merman, Buster Keaton, Jimmy Durante, Edie Adams, Dorothy Provine, Terry-Thomas, William Demarest, Andy Devine.

Spencer Tracy and a cast made up of "Who's Who of American Comedy" are combined in this wacky chase movie to end all chase movies. Tracy is the crafty police captain who is following the progress of various money-mad citizens out to beat one another in discovering the buried hiding place of 350,000 stolen dollars. 1963; 154m.

IT'S IN THE BAG ★★★

DIR: Richard Wallace. **CAST:** Fred Allen, Jack Benny, Binnie Barnes, Robert Benchley, Victor Moore, Sidney Toler, Rudy Vallee, William Bendix, Don Ameche.

The plot (if there ever was one) derives from the Russian fable about an impoverished nobleman on a treasure hunt. Continuity soon goes out the window, however, when the cast starts winging it in one hilarious episode after another. This is Fred Allen, acerbic and nasal as always, in his best screen comedy. 1945; B&W; 87m.

I'VE HEARD THE MERMAIDS SINGING ★★★

DIR: Patricia Rozema. **CAST:** Sheila McCarthy, Paule Viallargeon, Anne-Marie Macdonald.

A slight but often engaging story about a naïve photographer (Sheila McCarthy) who longs to be a part of the elitist art world. She takes a job as a secretary in an art gallery and becomes hopelessly infatuated with its female curator. The cloyingly whimsical ending is the only thunk in this nifty debut from director Patricia Rozema. Rated PG. 1987; 83m.

IZZY & MOE ★★★½

DIR: Jackie Cooper. **CAST:** Jackie Gleason, Art Carney, Cynthia Harris, Zohra Lampert.

Together for the last time, Jackie Gleason and Art Carney are near perfect as ex-vaudevillians who become New York Prohibition agents in this made-for-TV movie based on actual characters. The two stars still work beautifully together after all these years. 1985; 100m.

JABBERWOCKY ★★½

DIR: Terry Gilliam. **CAST:** Michael Palin, Max Wall, Deborah Fallender.

Monty Python fans will be disappointed to see only one group member, Michael Palin, in this British film. Palin plays a dim-witted peasant during the Dark Ages. A monster called Jabberwocky is destroying villages all over the countryside, so Palin tries to destroy the monster. There are some funny moments but nothing in comparison with true Python films. No MPAA rating. 1977; 100m.

JACK BENNY PROGRAM, THE (TELEVISION SERIES) ★★★★

DIR: Frederick de Cordova. **CAST:** Jack Benny, Mary Livingstone, Eddie "Rochester" Anderson, Dennis Day, Don Wilson, Mel Blanc.

Following the formula that had made him a smash on radio, Jack Benny became a fixture on TV. Bolstered by the top-notch character actors who popped up on the show, Benny held the spotlight with a pregnant pause, a hand on the chin, or a shift of the eyes. Comic bits frequently revolved around Benny's stinginess and deadly violin playing. A host of stars visited the show over the years, appearing in songs and/or sketches. The roster on video includes Ernie Kovacs, Jayne Mansfield, Johnny Carson, Connie Francis, The Smothers Brothers, George Burns, Humphrey Bogart, Kirk Douglas, Fred Allen, Ann-Margret, and Bob Hope. 1950–1965; B&W; 30m.

JACKIE CHAN'S POLICE FORCE

DIR: Jackie Chan. **CAST:** Jackie Chan, Brigitte Lin.

A lame, comedic kung-fu mixture. Jackie Chan plays a bumbling policeman, assigned to protect the star witness in a drug case who is (surprise) a beautiful woman. Poorly dubbed, with ho-hum action footage. Rated PG-13 for violence. 1986; 101m.

JANE AND THE LOST CITY ★★★½

DIR: Terry Marcel. **CAST:** Kristen Hughes, Maud Adams, Sam Jones.

World War II British comic-strip heroine, Jane, comes to life in the form of lovely Kristen Hughes. She must help England's war effort by finding the diamonds of Africa's Lost City before the Nazis get them. Handsome Sam Jones plays Jungle Jack, an American guide for the British. A treasure trove of chuckles. Rated PG for profanity. 1987; 94m.

JANE AUSTEN IN MANHATTAN ★★

DIR: James Ivory. **CAST:** Anne Baxter, Robert Powell, Sean Young, Tim Choate.

The team responsible for *A Room with a View* and other literary adaptations comes up empty with this satire about two off-Broadway producers battling for the rights to a little-known play written by Jane Austen when she was 12 years old. The in-fighting among the theatrical community is amusing, but the movie is predominantly cold and unmoving. Unrated. 1980; 108m.

JAY LENO'S AMERICAN DREAM ★★★½

DIR: Ira Wohl. **CAST:** Jay Leno.

Talented comedian Jay Leno takes an irreverent look at all that is Americana as he saunters through much of this video in a glossy silver sports coat. His commentary is salty and enjoyable because it hits so close to home. 1986; 49m.

JEKYLL & HYDE—TOGETHER AGAIN ★★★

DIR: Jerry Belson. **CAST:** Mark Blankfield, Bess Armstrong, Krista Erickson.

If you like offbeat, crude, and timely humor, you'll enjoy this 1980s-style version of Robert Louis Stevenson's horror classic. Though the film needs some editing, Mark Blankfield is a riot as the mad scientist who can't snort enough of the powdery white stuff he's invented. Rated R for heavy doses of vulgarity and sexual innuendo. 1982; 87m.

JERK, THE ★★★★

DIR: Carl Reiner. **CAST:** Steve Martin, Bernadette Peters, Bill Macy, Jackie Mason.

Steve Martin made a very funny film debut in this wacky comedy. Nonfans probably won't like it, but then Martin has always had limited appeal. For those who think he's hilarious, the laughs just keep on coming. Rated R. 1979; 94m.

JERRY LEWIS LIVE

DIR: Arthur Forrest. **CAST:** Jerry Lewis.

One of the worst stand-up comedy tapes we've viewed so far. Jerry Lewis's comedy is dull and pointless. His pantomime is poor and his singing even worse. Lewis is straining to prove himself—as if we didn't know who he is. And when he caps almost every shtick with an obnoxious cackle and a comment on how dumb his jokes are, the viewer is only too aware of how miserable an unfunny comedy can be. 1984; 73m.

JINXED ★★½

DIR: Don Siegel. **CAST:** Bette Midler, Ken Wahl, Rip Torn, Benson Fong.

Bette Midler is in peak form as a would-be cabaret singer who enlists the aid of a blackjack dealer (Ken Wahl) in a plot to murder her gambler boyfriend (Rip Torn) in this often funny black comedy, directed by Don Siegel. If it weren't for Midler, you'd notice how silly and unbelievable it all is. However, she's so watchable you don't mind suspending your disbelief. Rated R for profanity and sexual situations. 1982; 103m.

J-MEN FOREVER ★★

DIR: Richard Patterson. **CAST:** Peter Bergman, Philip Proctor.

Firesign Theatre's Peter Bergman and Philip Proctor have taken footage from old films of the Thirties and Forties and dubbed in their own comic dialogue. It's funny at times but way too long for this type of treatment. Rated PG for profanity and violence. 1979; 75m.

JOCKS

DIR: Steve Carver. **CAST:** Scott Strader, Perry Lang, Mariska Hargitay, Richard Roundtree, Christopher Lee.

Discounting Christopher Lee's brief appearance in this stupid film, Richard Roundtree is the only one with true acting ability. Roundtree plays a tennis coach at L.A. College, who must make his goofy team champions in order to keep his job. Rated R for nudity and obscenities. 1986; 90m.

JOE PISCOPO LIVE! ★★★

DIR: David Grossman. **CAST:** Joe Piscopo, George Wallace.

This HBO concert was taped on the UCLA campus. Joe Piscopo showcases some of his characterizations as Robert De Niro (*Taxi Driver, Raging Bull*) and as Phil Donahue (to George Wallace's Oprah Winfrey). It's an uneven show and Piscopo sometimes appears to be entertaining himself more than the fans. 1987; 60m.

JOE PISCOPO VIDEO, THE ★★½

DIR: Jay Dubin. **CAST:** Joe Piscopo, Eddie Murphy, Joseph Bologna, Jan Hooks.

This HBO special has some funny moments, most deriving from Joe Piscopo's impressions. But aside from a Frank Sinatra look-alike singing in a heavy-metal rock band and a "Thriller" spinoff where the ghouls popping up out of the graveyard are Jerry Lewis clones *à la The Nutty Professor*, the moments are delivered in a quick montage and then disappear for good. 1984; 60m.

JOHNNY BE GOOD ★

DIR: Bud Smith. **CAST:** Anthony Michael Hall, Robert Downey Jr., Paul Gleason, Uma Thurman, Steve James, Seymour Cassel, Michael Greene, Robert Downey Sr.

Disjointed, repetitive stab at moralistic comedy. Anthony Michael Hall is Johnny Taylor, a tremendous high-school football player who is heavily (and illegally) recruited by every major college in the United States. Hall's innocent-boy persona fails in this role. Rated R for language, partial nudity, and sexual situations. 1988; 86m.

JOHNNY DANGEROUSLY ★½

DIR: Amy Heckerling. **CAST:** Michael Keaton, Joe Piscopo, Marilu Henner, Maureen Stapleton.

In this fitfully funny spoof of 1930s gangster movies, Michael Keaton and Joe Piscopo play rival crime lords. Directed by Amy Heckerling, it leaves the viewer with genuinely mixed feelings. That's because many of its gags rely on shock laughs and others never seem to make it to the punchline. Rated PG-13 for violence and profanity. 1984; 90m.

JOSEPH ANDREWS ★★

DIR: Tony Richardson. **CAST:** Ann-Margret, Peter Firth, Beryl Reid, Michael Hordern, Jim Dale, John Gielgud, Hugh Griffith, Wendy Craig, Peggy Ashcroft.

The adventures of Joseph Andrews (Peter Firth) as he rises from lowly servant to personal footman. This is director Tony Richardson's second attempt to transform a Henry Fielding novel to film. Unfortunately, the first-rate cast cannot save this ill-fated attempt to restage *Tom Jones*. Rated R for sex and profanity. 1977; 99m.

JOSHUA THEN AND NOW ★★★★½

DIR: Ted Kotcheff. **CAST:** James Woods, Alan Arkin, Gabrielle Lazure, Michael Sarrazin, Linda Sorenson.

Based by screenwriter Mordecai Richler (*The Apprenticeship of Duddy Kravitz*) on his autobiographical novel of the same name, this little-known gem is blessed with humor, poignancy, and insight. James Woods is wonderful as Jewish writer, Joshua Shapiro, whose life seems to be in shambles. He is a hard guy to keep down. Surviving an embarrassing upbringing by a gangster father (Alan Arkin in his funniest performance ever), Joshua nearly meets his match in the snobbish high society of his WASP wife (Gabrielle Lazure). Rated R for profanity, nudity, suggested sex. 1985; 118m.

JOY OF SEX, THE ★★

DIR: Martha Coolidge. **CAST:** Michelle Meyrink, Cameron Dye, Lisa Langlois.

This comedy, about the plight of two virgins, male and female, unhappy with their status in a sex-crazy age, has few offensive elements. But there is one problem: it isn't funny. Rated R for profanity, suggested sex, and scatological humor. 1984; 93m.

JOY STICKS

DIR: Greydon Clark. **CAST:** Joe Don Baker, Leif Green, Logan Ramsey.

The alleged story in *Joy Sticks* is that a wealthy businessman (Joe Don Baker) wants to shut down the local video gameroom frequented by his teenage daughter. Little of interest happens. Rated R. 1983; 88m.

JUMPIN' JACK FLASH ★★½
DIR: Penny Marshall. **CAST:** Whoopi Goldberg, Stephen Collins, John Wood, Carol Kane, James Belushi, Annie Potts, Peter Michael Goetz, Roscoe Lee Browne, Jeroen Krabbé, Jonathan Pryce.
Whoopi Goldberg's inspired clowning is the only worthwhile element in her first big-screen comedy. She plays a computer operator who breaks the monotony of her job by sending personal messages. Then she gets one from an endangered undercover agent and finds herself involved in international intrigue. Rated R for profanity and violence. 1986; 100m.

JUST ONE OF THE GUYS ★★★
DIR: Lisa Gottlieb. **CAST:** Joyce Hyser, Clayton Rohner, Billy Jacoby, Toni Hudson.
A sort of reverse *Tootsie*, this surprisingly restrained teen-lust comedy stars Joyce Hyser as an attractive young woman who switches high schools and sexes to overcome an imagined prejudice against her writing and win a journalism prize. The premise is flimsy and forced, but director Lisa Gottlieb and her cast keep the viewer entertained. Rated PG-13 for nudity, violence, and profanity. 1985; 88m.

JUST TELL ME WHAT YOU WANT ★½
DIR: Sidney Lumet. **CAST:** Alan King, Ali MacGraw, Peter Weller, Myrna Loy, Keenan Wynn, Tony Roberts, Dina Merrill.
Alan King gives a fine performance in this otherwise forgettable film as an executive who attempts to get his mistress (Ali MacGraw) back. She's in love with a younger man (Peter Weller), and King will do anything to get her back. Rated R. 1980; 112m.

JUST YOU AND ME, KID ★★
DIR: Leonard Stern. **CAST:** George Burns, Brooke Shields, Ray Bolger, Lorraine Gary, Burl Ives.
The delights of George Burns as an ex–vaudeville performer do not mask the worthless plot in this tale of Burns's attempt to hide a young runaway (Brooke Shields) fleeing a drug dealer. Shields's inability to move with Burns's rhythm rapidly becomes annoying. Rated PG for mild language and brief nudity. 1979; 93m.

K-9 ★★★
DIR: Rod Daniel. **CAST:** James Belushi, Mel Harris, Kevin Tighe.
James Belushi is terrific as a maverick cop whose singleminded pursuit of a drug dealer (Kevin Tighe) makes him a less-than-desirable partner for other officers. Enter Jerry Lee, a feisty police dog who proves to be more than a match for Belushi in the pursuit of criminals and females. Rated PG for profanity and violence. 1989; 95m.

KEATON RIDES AGAIN/RAILROADER ★★★★
DIR: John Spotton, Gerald Potterton. **CAST:** Buster Keaton.
Coupled delightfully in this Buster Keaton program are a biographical profile with interviews, and a solo opus of Buster in trouble on a handcar rolling along the seemingly endless tracks of the Canadian National Railway. Both were lovingly produced by the National Film Board of Canada less than a year before the great comic's life ended. 1965; B&W; 81m.

KENTUCKY FRIED MOVIE ★★★
DIR: John Landis. **CAST:** Evan Kim, Master Bong SooHan, Bill Bixby, Donald Sutherland.
The first film outing of the creators of *Airplane!* is an on-again, off-again collection of comedy skits. Directed by John Landis, the best bits involve a Bruce Lee takeoff and a surprise appearance by Wally and the Beaver. Rated R. 1977; 78m.

KEYSTONE COMEDIES, VOL. 1 ★★★
DIR: Roscoe Arbuckle. **CAST:** Roscoe "Fatty" Arbuckle, Minta Durfee, Al St. John, Louise Fazenda, Edgar Kennedy, Joe Bordeaux.

Fatty's Faithful Fido, Fatty's Tintype Tangle, and *Fatty's New Role*—three fast-moving bop-and-bash comedies in the celebrated Fatty series produced by Mack Sennett at Keystone Studios in 1915—compose this first of five volumes devoted to the famed silent comedian's artistry. *Fatty's Faithful Fido* is a comedy action gem. The dog comes close to stealing the show. Slapstick humor in the classic mold. 1915; B&W; 46m.

KEYSTONE COMEDIES, VOL. 2

★★★

DIR: Roscoe Arbuckle. **CAST:** Roscoe "Fatty" Arbuckle, Mabel Normand, Minta Durfee, Al St. John, Alice Davenport, Joe Bordeaux.

Mack Sennett hit real reel paydirt when he teamed rotund comic Roscoe Arbuckle and elfin comedienne Mabel Normand in a film series. These three examples—*Fatty and Mabel at the San Diego Exposition, Fatty and Mabel's Simple Life,* and *Mabel's Washday*—amply show why. 1915; B&W; 42m.

KEYSTONE COMEDIES, VOL. 3

★★★

DIR: Roscoe Arbuckle. **CAST:** Roscoe "Fatty" Arbuckle, Mabel Normand, Minta Durfee, Dora Rogers, Alice Davenport, Al St. John, Owen Moore.

Four more stanzas in the screen lives of two of silent film's great comedic performers: Roscoe Arbuckle and Mabel Normand. They're all "watch springs and elastic" as they create marvelous mayhem in *Mabel Lost and Won, Wished on Mabel, Mabel, Fatty and the Law* and *Fatty's Plucky Pup.* 1915; B&W; 58m.

KEYSTONE COMEDIES: VOL. 4

★★★

DIR: Roscoe Arbuckle. **CAST:** Roscoe "Fatty" Arbuckle, Mabel Normand, Edgar Kennedy, Glenn Cavender, Ford Sterling, Mae Busch, Al St. John, Alice Davenport.

Three stanzas in the sidesplitting Fatty-and-Mabel slapstick series Mack Sennett connived and contrived between 1912 and 1916: *Mabel's Willful Way, That Little Band of Gold,* and *Mabel and Fatty's Married Life.* Mayhem and mirth only past masters of the double take and pratfall can muster. 1915; B&W; 44m.

KEYSTONE COMEDIES: VOL. 5

★★★

DIR: Roscoe Arbuckle. **CAST:** Roscoe "Fatty" Arbuckle, Bill Bennett, Walter Reed, Edgar Kennedy, Harold Lloyd, Joe Bordeaux, Minta Durfee, Ford Sterling, Charles Arling, Joe Swickard, Dora Rogers, Nick Cogley, Charles Chase, W. C. Hauber.

Fabled Mack Sennett's madcap mob of laugh-catchers dish up three more hilarious happy helpings of classic silent comedy: *Miss Fatty's Seaside Lovers, Court House Crooks,* and *Love Loot and Crash.* Keystone Studio's pride, roly-poly Roscoe Arbuckle, is a tubby terror in drag. 1915; B&W; 45m.

KID, THE/THE IDLE CLASS

★★★★

DIR: Charles Chaplin. **CAST:** Charlie Chaplin, Edna Purviance, Jackie Coogan.

A skillful blend of comedy and pathos, *The Kid,* the first of Charles Chaplin's silent feature films, has his famous tramp alter ego adopting an abandoned baby boy whose mother, years later, suddenly appears to claim him. Chaplin is magnificent. Coogan's performance in the title role made him the first child superstar. Also on the bill: *The Idle Class,* a satire on the leisure of the rich involving mistaken identity. Silent. 1921; B&W; 86m.

KID FROM BROOKLYN, THE

★★★

DIR: Norman Z. McLeod. **CAST:** Danny Kaye, Virginia Mayo, Vera-Ellen, Steve Cochran, Eve Arden.

Danny Kaye is fine as the comedy lead in this remake of Harold Lloyd's *The Milky Way.* He plays the milkman who becomes a prizefighter. Good family entertainment. 1946; 104m.

KIND HEARTS AND CORONETS ★★★★

DIR: Robert Hamer. **CAST:** Dennis Price, Alec Guinness, Valerie Hobson.

A young man (Dennis Price) thinks up a novel way to speed up his inheritance—by killing off all the other heirs. This is the central premise of this arresting black comedy, which manages to poke fun at mass murder and get away with it. Alec Guinness plays all eight of his victims. 1949; 104m.

KING IN NEW YORK, A ★★½

DIR: Charles Chaplin. **CAST:** Charlie Chaplin, Dawn Addams, Michael Chaplin.

Supposedly anti-American, this 1957 film by Charles Chaplin, not seen in the United States until 1973, was a big let-down to his fans, who had built their worship on *Easy Street*, *City Lights*, *Modern Times*, and *The Great Dictator*. It pokes fun at the 1950s, with its witch hunts and burgeoning post-war technology. It is not the Chaplin of old, but just old Chaplin, and too much of him. 1957; B&W; 105m.

KISS ME GOODBYE ★★★

DIR: Robert Mulligan. **CAST:** Sally Field, James Caan, Jeff Bridges, Claire Trevor.

Sally Field plays a widow of three years who has just fallen in love again. Her first husband was an electrifying Broadway choreographer named Jolly (James Caan). Her husband-to-be is a slightly stuffy Egyptologist (Jeff Bridges). Before her wedding day she receives a visit from Jolly's ghost, who is apparently upset about the approaching wedding. Rated PG for profanity and sexual situations. 1982; 101m.

KNIGHTS AND EMERALDS ★★★½

DIR: Ian Emes. **CAST:** Christopher Wild, Beverly Hills, Warren Mitchell.

A young drummer in a marching band in working-class Birmingham defies the racism of his family and friends when he takes up with a competing band of black youths. This genial British comedy about integration among the young is original and endearing, sidestepping countless clichés into which it could easily have fallen. A good family item. Rated PG. 1986; 94m.

KNOWHUTIMEAN? ★★★

DIR: John R. Cherry III. **CAST:** Jim Varney.

A fun, if slightly repetitive, collection of Ernest commercials followed by a series of skits featuring Varney as a variety of Ernest's colorful ancestors. A must for Jim Varney fans. 1983; 57m.

KOTCH ★★★★

DIR: Jack Lemmon. **CAST:** Walter Matthau, Deborah Winters, Felicia Farr, Charles Aldman.

Walter Matthau is in top form as a feisty senior citizen who takes to the road when his family tries to put him in a retirement home. First-time director Jack Lemmon does himself proud with this alternately witty and warmly human comedy. Rated PG. 1971; 113m.

LADY EVE, THE ★★★★

DIR: Preston Sturges. **CAST:** Barbara Stanwyck, Henry Fonda, Charles Coburn, William Demarest.

Barbara Stanwyck, Henry Fonda, and Charles Coburn are first-rate in this romantic comedy, which was brilliantly written and directed by Preston Sturges. Fonda is a rather simple-minded millionaire, and Stanwyck is the conniving woman who seeks to snare him. The results are hilarious. 1941; B&W; 94m.

LADYKILLERS, THE ★★★★½

DIR: Alexander Mackendrick. **CAST:** Alec Guinness, Peter Sellers, Cecil Parker.

England had a golden decade of great comedies during the 1950s. *The Ladykillers* is one of the best. Alec

Guinness and Peter Sellers are teamed as a couple of small-time criminals who have devised what they believe to be the perfect crime. Unfortunately, their plans are thwarted by the sweetest, most innocent little old landlady you'd ever want to meet. Great fun! 1955; 87m.

LAS VEGAS HILLBILLYS ★
DIR: Arthur C. Pierce. **CAST:** Ferlin Husky, Jayne Mansfield, Mamie Van Doren, Sonny James, Richard Kiel.

Hillbilly Ferlin Husky inherits a failing Las Vegas bar and makes it a success by turning it into Vegas' only country and western nightclub. The story is a thin frame on which to hang a lot of country performers indifferently lip-synching their songs. The 1967 sequel *Hillbillys in a Haunted House*, is equally dismal. 1966; 90m.

LAST AMERICAN VIRGIN, THE ★
DIR: Boaz Davidson. **CAST:** Lawrence Monoson, Diane Franklin, Steve Antin, Joe Rubbo, Louisa Moritz.

Tawdry teen-sex flick with one of the worst morals ever captured on film: don't bother to help a friend, 'cause he (or she) will burn you every time. Writer-director Boaz Davidson must have led one miserable childhood. Rated R for sex. 1982; 92m.

LAST MARRIED COUPLE IN AMERICA, THE ★
DIR: Gilbert Cates. **CAST:** Natalie Wood, George Segal, Arlene Golonka, Bob Dishy, Priscilla Barnes, Dom DeLuise, Valerie Harper.

Lamebrained little sex farce about one perfect couple's struggle to hold their own marriage together amid the divorces and separations around them. Tries desperately to be hip but ends up as nothing more than a smutty little dirty joke with a lot of very annoying characters. Rated R for profanity and nudity. 1980; 103m.

LAST OF THE RED HOT LOVERS ★½
DIR: Gene Saks. **CAST:** Alan Arkin, Paula Prentiss, Sally Kellerman.

Alan Arkin plays a married man trying to sneak around in this 1972 comedy. He uses his mother's apartment for his rendezvous and cracks us up with his unsuave manner. Rated PG. 1972; 98m.

LAST POLKA, THE ★★★★
DIR: John Blanchard. **CAST:** John Candy, Eugene Levy, Catherine O'Hara, Rick Moranis.

This made-for-HBO special features the unique Second City comedy of Yosh (John Candy) and Stan (Eugene Levy) Schmenge, a delightful pair of polka bandleaders, as they reminisce about their checkered musical careers. Fellow *SCTV* troupe members Catherine O'Hara and Rick Moranis add to the hilarity in this adept send-up of *The Last Waltz*, Martin Scorsese's documentary chronicling the final concert of real-life rock legends The Band. 1984; 60m.

LAST REMAKE OF BEAU GESTE, THE ★
DIR: Marty Feldman. **CAST:** Marty Feldman, Michael York, Ann-Margret, Trevor Howard.

We have Marty Feldman's success in *Young Frankenstein* to thank for this vapid Foreign Legion comedy, Feldman's first (and last) attempt at the triple crown of writing, directing, and starring. If you try for the long haul, watch for Feldman's sequence with "co-star" Gary Cooper in footage intercut from the 1939 classic. Rated PG—sexual situations. 1977; 84m.

LAST RESORT ★★½
DIR: Zane Buzby. **CAST:** Charles Grodin, Jon Lovitz, Robin Pearson Rose, Megan Mullally, John Ashton.

Charles Grodin and family are off on vacation to Club Sand, which turns out to be Army cots, marauding armed guerrillas, and horny club counselors. Amid slapstick jokes and Grodin's exasperated yelling is an intermittently entertaining movie. Rated R for sex and language. 1985; 80m.

LAUREL AND HARDY CLASSICS, VOLUME 1 ★★★

DIR: James Parrott, Charles Rogers. **CAST:** Stan Laurel, Oliver Hardy, Billy Gilbert, Charlie Hall.

This collection contains *The Music Box*, *County Hospital*, *The Live Ghost*, and *Twice Two*. *The Music Box* won an Oscar as the Best Short of 1932. In it, Stan Laurel and Oliver Hardy attempt to deliver a piano up a long flight of stairs to the home of Theodore Swarzenhoffen (Billy Gilbert). Other than that outstanding offering, this is a mediocre collection of L&H comedy. 1930s; B&W; 90m.

LAUREL AND HARDY CLASSICS, VOLUME 2 ★★★★★

DIR: James Parrott, George Marshall. **CAST:** Stan Laurel, Oliver Hardy, Stanley Sanford, Charlie Hall.

Packed with laughs in every minute, this collection contains *Blotto*, *Towed in a Hole*, *Brats*, and *Hog Wild*, four of the best short comedies produced by this classic team. While some of the situations might seem dated (sneaking out to drink booze during Prohibition and putting up a radio antenna), the development of the plots is flawless and transcends time. This is the best of the short-subject collections. 1930s; B&W; 80m.

LAUREL AND HARDY CLASSICS, VOLUME 3 ★★½

DIR: Lloyd French, George Marshall. **CAST:** Stan Laurel, Oliver Hardy, Mae Busch, Charlie Hall.

Four more Laurel and Hardy short subjects: *Oliver the Eighth*, *Busy Bodies*, *Their First Mistake*, and *Dirty Work*. *Busy Bodies* is by far the best of the bunch, with a lumber-factory setting. 1930s; B&W; 80m.

LAUREL AND HARDY CLASSICS, VOLUME 4 ★★★

DIR: James W. Horne, James Parrott. **CAST:** Stan Laurel, Oliver Hardy, Charlie Hall, James Finlayson, Walter Long, Mae Busch.

In *Another Fine Mess*, Stan Laurel and Oliver Hardy are trapped in a house when escaping from the police. *Laughing Gray* has them attempting to hide a forbidden dog in their room. *Come Clean* starts with a simple trip for ice cream, but after saving Mae Busch's life, Stan and Ollie can't get rid of her. *Any Old Port* pits them against Walter Long twice; once as the manager of a hotel and again as a boxer. This collection contains a consistently entertaining group of short subjects. 1930s; B&W; 90m.

LAUREL AND HARDY CLASSICS, VOLUME 5 ★★★

DIR: James Parrott. **CAST:** Stan Laurel, Oliver Hardy, Edgar Kennedy, Anita Garvin.

Two good and two moderate comedies—*Perfect Day*, *Helpmates*, *Be Big*, and *Night Owls*, respectively—make up this tape. In *Helpmates*, the action develops from a simple idea: Ollie has to clean up the house so that his wife won't know he's hosted a party in her absence. From this simple beginning, laughs are many and well earned. 1930s; B&W; 80m.

LAUREL AND HARDY CLASSICS, VOLUME 6 ★★★★

DIR: James W. Horne, Charles Rogers. **CAST:** Stan Laurel, Oliver Hardy, Mae Busch, Charlie Hall.

A collection of top-notch comedies all: *Our Wife*, *The Fixer-Uppers*, *Them Thar Hills*, and *Tit for Tat*. *Them Thar Hills* is a marvelous blend of logic and silliness, with Stan and Ollie going to the mountains for Ollie's health and ending up in a tit-for-tat duel with Charlie Hall. The duel is resumed in *Tit for Tat*, the only sequel ever made by L&H. *Our Wife*, the weakest of the group, has a scene that forecasts the stateroom sequence in the Marx Brothers' *A Night at the Opera*. 1930s; B&W; 80m.

LAUREL AND HARDY CLASSICS, VOLUME 7 ★★½

DIR: James Parrott, James W. Horne, Lloyd French, Charles Rogers. **CAST:** Stan Laurel, Oliver Hardy, Charlie Hall, James Finlayson.

A collection of two moderately funny films, *Thicker Than Water* and *Midnight Patrol*, and two well-done films, *Below Zero* and *Me and My Pal*. *Patrol* places Stan and Ollie in the police force. It may bear the distinction of having the most gruesome ending of any of their films. 1930s; B&W; 80m.

LAUREL AND HARDY CLASSICS, VOLUME 8 ★★½

DIR: Lewis R. Foster, James W. Horne, James Parrott. **CAST:** Stan Laurel, Oliver Hardy, Stanley Sanford, Billy Gilbert.

Men o' War is the standout of this collection. As sailors on leave, Laurel and Hardy attempt to impress two young ladies in Los Angeles' MacArthur Park. *One Good Turn* has them attempting to help an older woman save her home. *The Laurel and Hardy Murder Case*, the weakest film here, is a parody of murder mysteries. 1930s; B&W; 70m.

LAUREL AND HARDY CLASSICS, VOLUME 9 ★★★½

DIR: James W. Horne, Charles Rogers, Lewis R. Foster. **CAST:** Stan Laurel, Oliver Hardy, Mae Busch, Charlie Hall, Jean Harlow, James Finlayson, Walter Long.

In *Beau Hunks*, Stan Laurel and Oliver Hardy join the Foreign Legion. *Going Bye Bye!* has Stan and Ollie attempting to leave town after offering testimony that convicts Walter Long; their escape includes the totally logical and classic line "Excuse me, please—my ear is full of milk." *Chickens Come Home* is an election-year saga. *Berth Marks* is the first Laurel and Hardy sound film. Despite its audio awkwardness, this video has some fine comedy pieces. 1930s; B&W; 108m.

LAVENDER HILL MOB, THE ★★★★★

DIR: Charles Crichton. **CAST:** Alec Guinness, Stanley Holloway, Sidney James, Alfie Bass.

Fun, fun, and more fun from this celebrated British comedy. Alec Guinness is a mousy bank clerk. He has a plan for intercepting the bank's armored-car shipment. With the aid of a few friends he forms an amateur robbery squad. Lo and behold, they escape with the loot. After all, the plan was foolproof. Or was it? 1951; B&W; 82m.

LEADER OF THE BAND ★★★

DIR: Nessa Hyams. **CAST:** Steve Landesberg, Gallard Sartain, Mercedes Ruehl.

In this charming comedy Steve Landesberg plays an unemployed musician who becomes the band instructor for a group of misfits. Gailard Sartain plays the school-board chairman whom Landesberg must woo in order to keep his job. Too much footage is devoted to marching-band performances, but all in all this film has general appeal. Rated PG for profanity. 1987; 90m.

LEAGUE OF GENTLEMEN, THE ★★★★

DIR: Basil Dearden. **CAST:** Jack Hawkins, Nigel Patrick, Roger Livesey, Richard Attenborough, Bryan Forbes, Kieron Moore.

A British army officer, dismayed at being forced into early retirement, assembles a group of other military retirees and plots a perfect robbery. One of those lighthearted thrillers where the joy comes from watching professionals pull off an incredibly detailed crime. 1961; B&W; 114m.

LEMON DROP KID, THE ★★★

DIR: Sidney Lanfield. **CAST:** Bob Hope, Marilyn Maxwell, Lloyd Nolan, Jane Darwell, Andrea King, Fred Clark, Jay C. Flippen, William Frawley.

Great group of character actors makes this Damon Runyon story of an incompetent bookie, who has to cough up some money quick or breathe his last, work like a charm. Fast-talking Bob Hope has the tailor-made leading role. Deadly Lloyd Nolan plays the guy putting the screws to Hope, and Marilyn Maxwell plays the girl caught in the middle. 1951; B&W; 91m.

LENNY BRUCE PERFORMANCE FILM, THE ★★★★
DIR: John Magnuson. **CAST:** Lenny Bruce.

This simple, straightforward solo showcases Lenny Bruce, the master of bitter satire in all his gritty brilliance. Bruce was an original, a pioneer who paved the way for George Carlin, Richard Pryor, and all the rest. Also included is Bruce's color-cartoon parody of the Lone Ranger, "Thank You Masked Man." Otherwise, black and white. Rated R for language. 1968; 70m.

LEONARD PART 6 ★
DIR: Paul Weiland. **CAST:** Bill Cosby, Tom Courtenay, Joe Don Baker, Moses Gunn.

Bill Cosby plays a retired secret agent. A supersecret device that controls and turns the most benign creatures into killing machines is in the hands of a heinous, evil person. Cosby, forced into saving the world, does so, but he can't save the picture. Rated PG. 1987; 83m.

LET'S DO IT AGAIN ★★★½
DIR: Sidney Poitier. **CAST:** Sidney Poitier, Bill Cosby, Jimmie Walker, Calvin Lockhart, John Amos.

After scoring with *Uptown Saturday Night*, Sidney Poitier and Bill Cosby decided to reteam for another enjoyable comedy in 1975. Jimmie Walker, Calvin Lockhart, and John Amos are also on hand to add to the fun in this tale of a couple of lodge brothers taking on the gangsters. Rated PG. 1975; 112m.

LETTER TO BREZHNEV ★★★½
DIR: Chris Bernard. **CAST:** Alexandra Pigg, Alfred Molina, Peter Firth, Margi Clarke.

This wistful, spunky little movie presents two young women of Liverpool who decide to forgo their usual night out at the local Kirby disco in favor of a night in town, where they befriend a couple of Russian sailors. Teresa (played by Liverpool's stand-up comedienne Margi Clarke) is just after some fun, but Elaine (Alexandra Pigg) falls in love with her sailor. Peter Firth plays Elaine's love and he's the quintessence of sweetness. Alexandra Pigg gives the film some street-talking sass and Firth imbues it with adorable innocence. 1985; 95m.

LIBELED LADY ★★★★★
DIR: Jack Conway. **CAST:** William Powell, Myrna Loy, Spencer Tracy, Jean Harlow.

Their fame as Nick and Nora Charles in the *Thin Man* series notwithstanding, this is the finest film to have paired William Powell and Myrna Loy. They take part in a deliciously funny tale of a newspaper that, when faced with a libel suit from an angered woman, attempts to turn the libel into irrefutable fact. Spencer Tracy and Jean Harlow lend their considerable support, and the result is a delight from start to finish. 1936; B&W; 98m.

LICENSE TO DRIVE ★★★
DIR: Greg Beeman. **CAST:** Corey Haim, Corey Feldman, Carol Kane, Richard Masur, Heather Graham.

Wildly improbable yet frenetically funny account of how young Les (Corey Haim) flunks his driver's license exam yet steals his grandfather's Cadillac for a hot date. A slickly made film which deals with every high school fantasy. Richard Masur is perfect as the quiet, sane father trying to deal with insanity. Rated PG for swearing and slight sexual suggestions. 1988; 88m.

LIFE BEGINS FOR ANDY HARDY ★★★
DIR: George B. Seitz. **CAST:** Mickey Rooney, Judy Garland, Lewis Stone, Fay Holden, Ann Rutherford, Sara Haden.

Andy Hardy, fresh out of high school, tries on New York City for size, comes to grips with a mature woman, and learns a few big-city lessons before deciding college near home and hearth is best. The eleventh and one of the best in the series. 1941; B&W; 100m.

LIFE OF BRIAN ★★★★
DIR: Terry Jones. **CAST:** Terry Jones, John Cleese, Eric Idle, Michael Palin, Terry Gilliam, Graham Chapman.

Religious fanaticism gets a real drubbing in this irreverent and often sidesplitting comedy, which features and was created by those Monty Python crazies. Graham Chapman plays the title role of a reluctant "savior" born in a manger just down the street from Jesus Christ's. Rated R for nudity and profanity. 1979; 93m.

LIFE WITH FATHER ★★★★
DIR: Michael Curtiz. **CAST:** William Powell, Irene Dunne, Edmund Gwenn, ZaSu Pitts, Jimmy Lydon, Elizabeth Taylor, Martin Milner.

A warm, witty, charming, nostalgic memoir of life and the coming of age of author Clarence Day in turn-of-the-century New York City. Centering on his staid, eccentric father (William Powell), the film is a 100 percent delight. Based on the long-running Broadway play. 1947; 118m.

LIKE FATHER, LIKE SON ★★
DIR: Rod Daniel. **CAST:** Dudley Moore, Kirk Cameron, Margaret Colin, Catharine Hicks, Sean Astin, Patrick O'Neal.

Father and son (Dudley Moore and Kirk Cameron) accidentally transfer brains. Take that premise and stretch it out and you've pegged this movie. The film too often sinks to tasteless and juvenile stunts to spice up the lone idea. Rated PG-13. 1987; 99m.

LI'L ABNER ★½
DIR: Albert S. Rogell. **CAST:** Granville Owen, Martha O'Driscoll, Buster Keaton, Kay Sutton, Edgar Kennedy, Chester Conklin, Billy Bevan, Al St. John.

The first of two filmed versions of Al Capp's popular comic strip boasts a great cast of silent film's best clowns but comes across with a thud—no timing, no suspense, no laughs. The bizarre make-up and outlandish costumes alone are almost enough to recommend this oddity, one of a handful of movies based on the Sunday pages and aimed at general audiences. 1940; B&W; 78m.

LILY IN LOVE ★★★★
DIR: Karoly Makk. **CAST:** Christopher Plummer, Maggie Smith, Elke Sommer, Adolph Green.

Christopher Plummer is superb as an aging, egocentric actor who disguises himself as a younger man in an attempt to snag a plum role in a film written by his wife (Maggie Smith), and succeeds all too well. *Lily in Love* is a marvelously warm and witty adult comedy. Unrated, the film has some profanity. 1985; 105m.

LIMELIGHT ★★★½
DIR: Charles Chaplin. **CAST:** Charlie Chaplin, Claire Bloom, Buster Keaton, Sydney Chaplin, Nigel Bruce.

Too long and too much Charlie Chaplin (who trimmed Buster Keaton's part when it became obvious he was stealing the film), this is nevertheless a poignant excursion. Chaplin is an aging music hall comic on the skids who saves a ballerina (Claire Bloom) from suicide and, while bolstering her hopes, regains his confidence. The score, by Chaplin, is haunting. 1952; B&W; 145m.

LISTEN TO YOUR HEART ★★★
DIR: Don Taylor. **CAST:** Kate Jackson, Tim Matheson, Cassie Yates, George Coe, Tony Plana.

This cute but predictable romantic comedy features a book editor (Tim Matheson) falling in love with his art director (Kate Jackson). Naturally, problems and embarrassing situations arise when coworkers realize that they're having an affair. Made for TV, this is unrated. 1983; 104m.

LITTLE DARLINGS ★★
DIR: Ronald F. Maxwell. **CAST:** Tatum O'Neal, Kristy McNichol, Matt Dillon.

A story of the trials and tribulations of teen-age virginity, this film too often lapses into chronic cuteness, with characters more darling than realistic. *Little Darlings* follows the antics of two 15-year-old outcasts—rich, sophisticated Ferris Whitney (Tatum O'Neal) and poor, belligerent Angel Bright (Kristy McNichol)—as they compete to "score" with a boy first. Rated R. 1980; 95m.

LITTLE MURDERS ★★★★
DIR: Alan Arkin. **CAST:** Elliott Gould, Marcia Rodd, Vincent Gardenia, Elizabeth Wilson, Donald Sutherland, Lou Jacobi, Alan Arkin.

Jules Feiffer's savagely black comedy details the nightmarish adventures of a mild-mannered New Yorker (Elliott Gould) who finds the world becoming increasingly insane and violent. What seemed like bizarre fantasy when *Little Murders* was originally released is today all too close to reality. Strangely, this makes the film easier to watch while taking away none of its bite. Terrific supporting performances by Vincent Gardenia, Elizabeth Wilson, and director Alan Arkin. Rated PG for violence and profanity. 1971; 107m.

LITTLE ROMANCE, A ★★★★½
DIR: George Roy Hill. **CAST:** Thelonious Bernard, Diane Lane, Laurence Olivier, Sally Kellerman, Broderick Crawford, David Dukes.

Everyone needs *A Little Romance* in their life. This absolutely enchanting film by director George Roy Hill has something for everyone. Its story of two appealing youngsters (Thelonious Bernard and Diane Lane) who fall in love in Paris is full of surprises, laughs, and uplifting moments. Rated PG. 1979; 108m.

LITTLE SEX, A ★½
DIR: Bruce Paltrow. **CAST:** Tim Matheson, Kate Capshaw, Edward Herrmann.

A New York director of television commercials can't keep his hands off his actresses, even though he's married to a beautiful, intelligent woman. This is a tepid romantic comedy. Rated R. 1982; 95m.

LITTLE TOUGH GUYS ★★
DIR: Harold Young. **CAST:** Billy Halop, Huntz Hall, Gabriel Dell, Bernard Punsley, David Gorcey, Helen Parrish, Robert Wilcox, Marjorie Main.

Offshoot of the popular Dead End Kids films for Warner Bros., this was the first in a series for Universal that would eventually redefine the gang's hard edges and turn them into the bumbling East Side Kids and finally the hopelessly inept Bowery Boys. Not as good as the earlier entries, this film is still far superior to the treatment the boys would receive from Monogram Pictures in the years ahead. 1938; B&W; 63m.

LIVE AT HARRAH'S ★★
DIR: Greg Stevens. **CAST:** Bill Cosby, Rip Taylor, Elaine Boozler, Dick Shawn, Sammy King.

Rip Taylor is the host for the on-and off-stage routines of Bill Cosby, Elaine Boozler, Dick Shawn and Sammy King. This is a curiously uneven selection of material. Boozler and Shawn deliver adult humor and then Cosby comes onstage with an overly long routine with kids from the audience. 1981; 60m.

LIVE FROM WASHINGTON—IT'S DENNIS MILLER ★★★½
DIR: Paul Miller. **CAST:** Dennis Miller.

This is the concert that Dennis Miller gave in Washington, D.C., during his U.S. tour in 1988. Miller, who is best known for Weekend Update on *Saturday Night Live*, is given no restrictions on language or subject matter and takes full advantage of it. His routine is well paced, and he makes some very funny observations. TV newscaster Edwin Newman has a cameo at the beginning, advising the comedian about going to D.C. and playing to a tough audience. 1988; 60m.

LOCAL HERO ★★★★½
DIR: Bill Forsyth. **CAST:** Burt Lancaster, Peter Riegert, Fulton MacKay.

A wonderfully offbeat comedy by Bill Forsyth. Burt Lancaster plays a Houston oil baron who sends Peter Riegert to the west coast of Scotland to negotiate with the natives for North Sea oil rights. As with *Gregory's Girl*, which was about a gangly, good-natured boy's first crush, this film is blessed with sparkling little moments of humor, unforgettable characters, and a warmly human story. Rated PG for language. 1983; 111m.

LONELY GUY, THE ★★★
DIR: Arthur Hiller. **CAST:** Steve Martin, Robyn Douglass, Charles Grodin, Merv Griffin, Dr. Joyce Brothers.

Steve Martin stars in this okay comedy as a struggling young writer who makes his living working for a greeting card company. One day he comes home to find his live-in mate (Robyn Douglass) in bed with another man and becomes the "Lonely Guy" of the title. Only recommended for Steve Martin fans. Rated R for brief nudity and profanity. 1984; 90m.

LONGSHOT, THE
DIR: Paul Bartel. **CAST:** Tim Conway, Harvey Korman, Jack Weston, Ted Wass, Anne Meara, Stella Stevens, Jonathan Winters.

An embarrassment from beginning to end, at every level of production, and upon every word uttered. A Tim Conway–Harvey Korman venture is always somewhat suspect, but this dreck about small-time horse players and big-time losers, and the smarmy types who are in the margins, is mind-numbing and depressing. Rated PG. 1985; 110m.

LOOKIN' TO GET OUT ★★★
DIR: Hal Ashby. **CAST:** Jon Voight, Burt Young, Ann-Margret, Bert Remsen.

This offbeat comedy stars Jon Voight and Burt Young as a couple of compulsive gamblers out to hit the fabled "big score" in Las Vegas. It'll keep you interested for most of its running time, although it does drag a bit in the middle. However, the first hour zips by before you know it, and the ending is a humdinger. Rated R for violence and profanity. 1982; 104m.

LOOSE CONNECTIONS ★★★½
DIR: Richard Eyre. **CAST:** Stephen Rea, Lindsay Duncan.

In this cult comedy, an Englishwoman (Lindsay Duncan) builds a car with two female friends so that they can attend a feminist convention in Germany. At the last minute, her friends back out, and she is forced to accept a goofy substitute (Stephen Rea) as her traveling companion. Offbeat entertainment. Rated PG for profanity. 1984; 90m.

LOOSE SHOES ★
DIR: Ira Miller. **CAST:** Buddy Hackett, Howard Hesseman, Bill Murray, Susan Tyrrell, Avery Schreiber.

Failed attempt to spoof B movies. The successful gags are very few and the whole outing reeks of a *Kentucky Fried Movie* ripoff. At least with that film the sex, nudity, and profanity were used to poke fun at sexploitation flicks. Here, these qualities are exposed simply for the drive-in audience's satisfaction. Rated R. 1977; 73m.

LOOT ★½
DIR: Silvio Narizzano. **CAST:** Lee Remick, Richard Attenborough, Milo O'Shea, Hywel Bennett.

A hearse driver and his friend rob a bank and store the loot inside a coffin, setting off a slapstick, cliché-ridden comedy complete with a runaway funeral procession racing through city streets—and every graveyard quip in the book. The humor is black and very British. Dated now, this was probably racy in its day. Not rated. 1972; 102m.

LOSIN' IT ★★★
DIR: Curtis Hanson. **CAST:** Tom Cruise, Shelley Long, Jackie Earle Haley, John Stockwell.

Better-than-average teen exploitation flick, this one has four boys off to Tijuana for a good time. Shelley Long ("Cheers") adds interest as a runaway wife who joins them on their journey. Rated R. 1982; 104m.

LOST AND FOUND ★
DIR: Melvin Frank. **CAST:** Glenda Jackson, George Segal, Maureen Stapleton.
After teaming up successfully for *A Touch of Class*, writer-director Melvin Frank and his stars, Glenda Jackson and George Segal, tried again. But the result was an unfunny comedy about two bickering, cardboard characters. Rated PG. 1979; 112m.

LOST IN AMERICA ★★★★½
DIR: Albert Brooks. **CAST:** Albert Brooks, Julie Hagerty, Garry Marshall.
Writer-director-star Albert Brooks is one of America's great natural comedic resources. *Lost in America* is his funniest film to date. Some viewers may be driven to distraction by Brooks's all-too-true study of what happens when a "successful" and "responsible" married couple chucks it all and goes out on an *Easy Rider*–style trip across the country. Brooks makes movies about the things most adults would consider their worst nightmare. He cuts close to the bone and makes us laugh at ourselves in a very original way. If you can stand the pain, the pleasure is well worth it. Rated R for profanity and adult situations. 1985; 92m.

LOTS OF LUCK ★★
DIR: Peter Baldwin. **CAST:** Martin Mull, Annette Funicello, Fred Willard, Polly Holliday, Mia Dillon, Tracey Gold.
Made for Disney's cable channel, this mildly funny family film exposes the darker side of striking it rich. A down-on-its-luck family (Martin Mull and Annette Funicello play dad and mom) suddenly wins the lottery as well as every other contest it enters. Unfortunately they lose their friends and privacy. 1985; 88m.

LOVE AND DEATH ★★★★
DIR: Woody Allen. **CAST:** Woody Allen, Diane Keaton, Harold Gould, Alfred Lutter, Zvee Scooler.
This comedy set in 1812 Russia is one of Woody Allen's funniest films. Diane Keaton is the high-minded Russian with assassination (of Napoleon) in mind. Allen is her cowardly accomplice with sex on the brain. The movie satirizes not only love and death, but politics, classic Russian literature (Tolstoy's *War and Peace*), and foreign films, as well. Use of Prokofiev music enhances the piece. Rated PG. 1975; 82m.

LOVE AT FIRST BITE ★★★★
DIR: Stan Dragoti. **CAST:** George Hamilton, Susan Saint James, Richard Benjamin, Dick Shawn, Arte Johnson.
The Dracula legend is given the comedy treatment in this amusing parody of horror films. George Hamilton plays the campy Count, who has an unorthodox way with the ladies. (In this case, it's Susan Saint James, much to the chagrin of her boyfriend, Richard Benjamin.) Even though the humor is heavy-handed in parts, you find yourself chuckling continually in spite of yourself. Rated PG. 1979; 96m.

LOVE AT FIRST SIGHT
DIR: Rex Bromfield. **CAST:** Mary Ann McDonald, Dan Aykroyd, Barry Morse.
On the original *Saturday Night Live*, Dan Aykroyd used his boyish charm to pull outrageous humor out of material that was in extremely poor taste. In this pre-*SNL* Canadian comedy, he tries for laughs as a blind man in love with a girl whose family won't have him for a son-in-law. The charm isn't there and all that's left is bad taste. Even Aykroyd's most rabid fans should avoid it. Rated PG. 1977; 85m.

LOVE AT STAKE ★
DIR: John Moffitt. **CAST:** Barbara Carrera, Bud Cort, Dave Thomas, Patrick Cassidy, Stuart Pankin.

Attempted spoof of witchcraft and black-magic films is a dismal failure. The mayor and the judge of Salem, Massachusetts devise a scheme to accuse innocent townspeople of being witches so that they can attach their property. Enter real witch Barbara Carrera, who adds little to this cauldron of mush. Rated R for nudity and profanity. 1988; 88m.

LOVE FINDS ANDY HARDY ★★★

DIR: George B. Seitz. **CAST:** Mickey Rooney, Lewis Stone, Fay Holden, Judy Garland, Cecilia Parker, Lana Turner, Ann Rutherford.

In this fourth film of the series, the love that finds Mickey Rooney as Andy Hardy is then-teenager Lana Turner. As usual, it's an all-innocent slice of small-town American family life. 1938; B&W; 90m.

LOVE HAPPY ★★

DIR: David Miller. **CAST:** The Marx Brothers, Marilyn Monroe, Raymond Burr.

The last Marx Brothers movie, this 1949 production was originally set to star only Harpo, but Chico and, later, Groucho were brought in to beef up its box-office potential. They should've known better. This "Let's put on a show" retread doesn't even come close to their lesser works at MGM. Only Groucho's ogling of then-screen-newcomer Marilyn Monroe makes it interesting for movie buffs. 1949; B&W; 91m.

LOVE IN THE AFTERNOON ★★★★

DIR: Billy Wilder. **CAST:** Gary Cooper, Audrey Hepburn, Maurice Chevalier, John McGiver.

Audrey Hepburn shares fantastic chemistry with both Maurice Chevalier and Gary Cooper in this film classic, which explores the love interests of an American entrepreneur and his lopsided involvement with a young French ingenue. When her doting father (a detective) is asked to investigate the American's love life, it makes for a touching, charming bit of entertainment that never loses its appeal. 1957; 130m.

LOVE LAUGHS AT ANDY HARDY ★★

DIR: Willis Goldbeck. **CAST:** Mickey Rooney, Lewis Stone, Fay Holden, Sara Haden, Bonita Granville.

America's all-American, lovable, irritating, well-meaning wimp comes home from World War II and plunges back into the same adolescent rut of agonizing young love. The change of times has made this cookie-cutter film very predictable, but it's fun anyway. 1946; B&W; 93m.

LOVELINES

DIR: Rod Amateau. **CAST:** Michael Winslow, Greg Bradford, Mary Beth Evans.

Michael Winslow, the sound-effects cop in *Police Academy*, is the only recognizable face in this dreadful teen comedy. The film is supposed to be about a teen telephone service and an all-girl rock band attempting to break into the big time. But there are so many plot digressions, it ends up being about how not to make a movie. Rated R for nudity, suggested sex, violence, and profanity. 1984; 93m.

LOVER COME BACK ★★★★

DIR: Delbert Mann. **CAST:** Rock Hudson, Doris Day, Tony Randall, Edie Adams, Jack Oakie, Jack Kruschen, Ann B. Davis, Joe Flynn, Jack Albertson.

Rock Hudson and Doris Day are rival advertising executives battling professionally, psychologically, and sexually. A bright comedy that builds nicely. One of their best. Silly, innocent fun with a great supporting cast. 1961; 107m.

LOVERBOY ★½

DIR: Joan Micklin Silver. **CAST:** Patrick Dempsey, Kate Jackson, Carrie Fisher, Barbara Carrera, Kirstie Alley, Robert Ginty.

If you can believe that a pizza delivery boy could use his job as a front for a stud service, you are on your way to swallowing this lame sex farce. The talented Joan Micklin Silver, whose previous films include *Hester Street* and *Crossing Delancey*, seems to have little flair for this kind of it's-all-a-silly-misunderstanding comedy. Or perhaps her heart just wasn't in the clumsy gags, unpleasant characters, and incredible situations. Rated PG-13 for profanity and sexual situations. 1989; 98m.

LOVERS AND LIARS ★★½
DIR: Mario Monicelli. **CAST:** Goldie Hawn, Giancarlo Giannini, Laura Betti.

The first thing that occurs to you while watching this film is a question: What's Goldie Hawn doing in a dubbed Italian sex comedy? Co-starring Giancarlo Giannini it is a modestly entertaining piece of fluff tailored primarily for European tastes and, therefore, will probably disappoint most of Hawn's fans. Rated R. 1979; 96m.

LOVERS AND OTHER STRANGERS ★★★½
DIR: Cy Howard. **CAST:** Gig Young, Diane Keaton, Bea Arthur, Bonnie Bedelia, Anne Jackson, Harry Guardino, Richard Castellano, Michael Brandon, Cloris Leachman, Anne Meara.

A funny film about young love, marriage, and their many side effects on others. Marks Diane Keaton's debut in pictures. The late Gig Young is a delight. 1970; 106m.

LOVES AND TIMES OF SCARAMOUCHE, THE ★
DIR: Enzo G. Castellari. **CAST:** Michael Sarrazin, Ursula Andress, Aldo Maccioni, Gian Carlo Prete.

Michael Sarrazin, as Scaramouche, stumbles through this ridiculous swashbuckler in the tradition of *The Three Musketeers*. Scaramouche is a young Lothario who unwittingly becomes a draftee in Napoleon's army while fleeing from the irate husband of one of his many loves. Of course, Napoleon's true love also has an eye on him, which only makes matters worse. 1976; 92m.

LOVESICK ★★★
DIR: Marshall Brickman. **CAST:** Dudley Moore, Elizabeth McGovern, Alec Guinness, John Huston.

This is a sweet romantic comedy that tugs at your heart as it tickles your funny bone. You won't fall out of your seat laughing or grab a tissue to dab away the tears. But this movie, about a psychiatrist's (Dudley Moore) obsession with his patient (Elizabeth McGovern), does have its moments. Rated PG. 1983; 95m.

LOVING COUPLES ★★
DIR: Jack Smight. **CAST:** Shirley MacLaine, James Coburn, Susan Sarandon, Stephen Collins.

The plot is that old and tired one, about two couples who swap partners for a temporary fling only to reunite by film's end happier and wiser for the experience. It's a premise that's been worn thin by filmmakers and especially television since the swinging 1960s and is badly in need of retirement. Rated PG. 1980; 97m.

LUCKY JIM ★★★
DIR: John Boulting. **CAST:** Ian Carmichael, Terry-Thomas, Hugh Griffith.

Hijinks and antics at a small British university as a young lecturer tries to improve his lot by sucking up to his superior, but continually goofs. Acceptable adaptation of the Kingsley Amis novel. 1957; 95m.

LUCKY PARTNERS ★★★
DIR: Lewis Milestone. **CAST:** Ginger Rogers, Ronald Colman, Spring Byington, Jack Carson, Harry Davenport.

Artist Ronald Colman wishes passing errand girl Ginger Rogers good luck, thereby touching off a chain of events ending in romance. Lightweight comedy with, for the time, raw touches. Ginger's naïve charm and Ronald's urbanity make for interesting interplay. 1940; B&W; 99m.

LUGGAGE OF THE GODS ★½
DIR: David Kendall. **CAST:** Mark Stolzenberg, Gabriel Barr, Gwen Ellison.
This obvious rip-off of *The God's Must Be Crazy* has every opportunity to be hilarious, but manages to blow most of the lines and sight gags. A primitive tribe, unaware of the advances of man, is both delighted and frightened by an airplane emptying its cargo pit over their territory. Rated G. 1983; 78m.

LUPO ★★★
DIR: Menahem Golan. **CAST:** Yuda Barkan, Gabi Amrani, Esther Greenberg.
In this warmhearted comedy from Israel, Yuda Barkan is charming as Lupo, a cart driver. Like a modern Fiddler on the Roof, he's caught in the currents of change. His horse is killed by a car, his daughter is wooed by a rich banker's son, and the city plans to demolish the old shack he calls home. Rated G. 1970; 100m.

LUST IN THE DUST ★★
DIR: Paul Bartel. **CAST:** Tab Hunter, Divine, Lainie Kazan, Geoffrey Lewis, Henry Silva, Cesar Romero.
Tab Hunter and female impersonator Divine (who's anything but), who first teamed in *Polyester*, star in this so-so spoof of spaghetti westerns, directed by Paul Bartel. The ad blurb tells all: "He rode the West. The girls rode the rest. Together they ravaged the land." Rated R for nudity, suggested sex, and violence. 1985; 86m.

LUV ★★
DIR: Clive Donner. **CAST:** Jack Lemmon, Elaine May, Peter Falk, Severn Darden.
When talent the caliber of Jack Lemmon, Peter Falk, and Elaine May cannot breathe life into a film, then nothing can. The plot concerns three New York intellectuals and their tribulations through life. Who cares? 1967; 95m.

MABEL AND FATTY ★★★
DIR: Roscoe Arbuckle, Mack Sennett. **CAST:** Roscoe "Fatty" Arbuckle, Mabel Normand.
"He Did and He Didn't," "Mabel and Fatty Viewing the World's Fair at San Francisco," and "Mabel's Blunder" comprise this boffo trio of silent comedies in the classic Mack Sennett tradition. The fabled "Fatty" and Mabel are perfectly paired in the first and second features; Mabel goes it alone in the third. Silent with music. 1914–1916; B&W; 61m.

MACARONI ★★★★½
DIR: Ettore Scola. **CAST:** Jack Lemmon, Marcello Mastrolanni, Daria Nicolodi.
Wonderful Italian comedy-drama from the director of *A Special Day* and *Le Bal*. This one concerns an American executive (Jack Lemmon) who returns to Naples for a business meeting forty years after his stay there with the army. He is visited by an old friend (Marcello Mastroianni). Both Lemmon and Mastroianni deliver brilliant performances. Rated PG for profanity. 1985; 104m.

MAD MISS MANTON, THE ★★★
DIR: Leigh Jason. **CAST:** Barbara Stanwyck, Henry Fonda, Sam Levene, Frances Mercer, Stanley Ridges.
A group of high-society ladies led by Miss Manton (Barbara Stanwyck) help solve a murder mystery with comic results—sometimes. The humor is pretty outdated, and the brand of romanticism, while being in step with the 1930s, comes off rather silly in the latter part of the twentieth century. Henry Fonda plays a newspaper editor who falls in love with the mad Miss Manton. 1938; B&W; 80m.

MAD WEDNESDAY ★★½
DIR: Preston Sturges. **CAST:** Harold Lloyd, Frances Ramsden, Jimmy Conlin, Raymond Walburn, Arline Judge, Lionel Stander, Rudy Vallee, Edgar Kennedy.

The great silent comedian Harold Lloyd stars in an update of his famous brash, go-getting 1920s straw-hatted, black-rimmed-glasses character. A good, but not well executed, idea. Originally issued in 1947 as *The Sin of Harold Diddlebock* in the director's version. This was producer Howard Hughes's "improved" version. 1950; B&W; 90m.

MADE FOR EACH OTHER ★★★★
DIR: John Cromwell. **CAST:** Carole Lombard, James Stewart, Charles Coburn, Lucile Watson, Harry Davenport.

This is a highly appealing comedy-drama centering on the rocky first years of a marriage. The young couple (Carole Lombard and James Stewart) must do battle with interfering in-laws, inept servants, and the consequences of childbirth. The real strength of this film lies in the screenplay, by Jo Swerling. It gives viewers a thoughtful and tasteful picture of events that we can all relate to. 1939; B&W; 100m.

MADE IN HEAVEN ★★
DIR: John Paddy Carstairs. **CAST:** David Tomlinson, Petula Clark, Sonja Ziemann, A. E. Matthews.

This silly English comedy stars a very young Petula Clark. Following a tradition started by Henry VI, a local village holds an annual contest to determine if a couple can survive one year of unmarried married bliss. The hiring of a flirtatious, Hungarian maid complicates the matter. 1948; 90m.

MADIGAN'S MILLIONS
DIR: Stanley Prager. **CAST:** Dustin Hoffman, Elsa Martinelli, Cesar Romero.

Only the most fanatical Dustin Hoffman fans need bother with this tedious spy farce. Hoffman plays a buffoonish treasury agent sent to recover some dirty money in Italy. This clumsy film offers neither laughs nor suspense. It was filmed before *The Graduate* but not released until well after Hoffman's success was established. You'll have to look hard to find any glimmer of star potential here. 1967; 86m.

MAGIC CHRISTIAN, THE ★★★
DIR: Joseph McGrath. **CAST:** Peter Sellers, Ringo Starr, Christopher Lee, Raquel Welch, Richard Attenborough, Yul Brynner.

A now-dated comedy about the world's wealthiest man (Peter Sellers) and his adopted son (Ringo Starr) testing the depths of degradation to which people will plunge themselves for money still has some funny scenes and outrageous cameos by Christopher Lee (as Dracula), Raquel Welch, and Richard Attenborough. Rated PG. 1970; 93m.

MAID TO ORDER ★★½
DIR: Amy Jones. **CAST:** Ally Sheedy, Beverly D'Angelo, Michael Ontkean, Valerie Perrine, Dick Shawn, Tom Skerritt.

This modern retelling of the Cinderella fable isn't much of a star vehicle for Ally Sheedy, who's constantly upstaged by the supporting players. She's a spoiled little rich girl whose hip fairy godmother (Beverly D'Angelo) turns her into a nonentity, forced to work for an honest dollar. Rated PG for language and brief nudity. 1987; 96m.

MAID'S NIGHT OUT, THE ★★
DIR: Ben Holmes. **CAST:** Joan Fontaine, Hedda Hopper, Allan "Rocky" Lane, Cecil Kellaway.

This energetic comedy tells of a millionaire's son (Allan Lane) who becomes a milkman for a month to win a bet with his self-made millionaire father (George Irving). Along the way, he meets Joan Fontaine. Lowbrow but fun. 1938; B&W; 64m.

MAIN EVENT, THE ★
DIR: Howard Zieff. **CAST:** Barbra Streisand, Ryan O'Neal, Paul Sand.

A limp boxing comedy that tried unsuccessfully to reunite the stars of *What's Up Doc?*, Barbra Streisand and Ryan O'Neal. This movie will put you to sleep the hard way. Rated PG. 1979; 112m.

MAIN STREET TO BROADWAY ★★
DIR: Tay Garnett. **CAST:** Tom Murton, Mary Murphy, Agnes Moorehead, Rosemary de Camp, Tallulah Bankhead.
The story of a young playwright's rise to success on Broadway is nothing you haven't seen before. The only attraction here is an endless array of cameo appearances by Ethel and Lionel Barrymore, Shirley Booth, Rex Harrison, Rodgers and Hammerstein, Mary Martin, Lilli Palmer, Cornel Wilde, and other notables of the theater world. 1953; B&W; 102m.

MAJOR BARBARA ★★★½
DIR: Gabriel Pascal. **CAST:** Wendy Hiller, Rex Harrison, Robert Morley, Robert Newton, Emlyn Williams, Sybil Thorndike, Deborah Kerr.
In the title role as a Salvation Army officer, Wendy Hiller heads a matchless cast in this thoughtful film of George Bernard Shaw's comedy about the power of money and the evils of poverty. Rex Harrison, as her fiancé, and Robert Newton, as a hardcase with doubts about the honesty and motives of do-gooders, are excellent. 1941; B&W; 136m.

MAJOR LEAGUE ★★★½
DIR: David S. Ward. **CAST:** Tom Berenger, Charlie Sheen, Corbin Bernsen, Margaret Whitton, James Gammon.
In this often funny but clichéd baseball comedy, the Cleveland Indians find themselves headed for oblivion when the new owner, former showgirl Margaret Whitton, decides to put together the worst possible team so as to break her lease with the league and move the team to Miami. Tom Berenger, Charlie Sheen, and Corbin Bernsen are fine as three inept players, and character actor James Gammon shines as their coach. Rated R for profanity and violence. 1989; 95m.

MAKE A MILLION ★★★
DIR: Lewis D. Collins. **CAST:** Charles Starrett, Pauline Brooks.
In this Depression comedy, college economics professor Charles Starrett's radical ideas for sharing the wealth get him fired. He develops a plan that soon has him rolling in money—and attracting a greedy banker and others bent on getting in on the gravy. The student whose lies got him fired, the daughter of the banker, switches sides to help him carry the day against the power of position and wealth. 1935; B&W; 66m.

MAKE MINE MINK ★★★★
DIR: Robert Asher. **CAST:** Terry-Thomas, Athene Seyler, Billie Whitelaw.
Bright dialogue and clever situations make this crazy comedy from Britain highly enjoyable. An ex-officer, a dowager, and a motley crew of fur thieves team to commit larceny for charity. Gap-toothed Terry-Thomas is in top form in this one. 1960; 100m.

MAKING MR. RIGHT ★★½
DIR: Susan Seidelman. **CAST:** John Malkovich, Ann Magnuson, Ben Masters, Glenne Headly, Laurie Metcalf, Polly Bergen, Hart Bochner.
This mild satire, about a female image consultant who falls for the android she's supposed to be promoting, doesn't come close to the energy level of director Susan Seidelman's *Desperately Seeking Susan.* John Malkovich shows impressive comedic dexterity in the dual role of the ingenuous android and the antisocial scientist who created him. Rated PG-13. 1987; 98m.

MAKING THE GRADE ★★½
DIR: Dorian Walker. **CAST:** Judd Nelson, Jonna Lee, Carey Scott.
A rich kid pays a surrogate to attend prep school for him. Typical teen-exploitation fare. Rated R. 1984; 105m.

MALCOLM ★★★★½
DIR: Nadia Tess. **CAST:** Colin Friels, John Hargreaves, Lindy Davies, Chris Haywood.

An absolutely charming Australian entry that swept that country's Oscars the year it was released. Colin Friels has the title role as an emotionally immature young man who, after he loses his job with a local rapid-transit company (for building his own tram with company parts), finds himself among thieves and loves it. 1986; 90m.

MALIBU BIKINI SHOP, THE
DIR: David Wechter. **CAST:** Michael David Wright, Bruce Greenwood, Barbara Horan, Debra Blee, Jay Robinson.

An exploitative romp about two brothers who inherit a bikini shop. Shades of *The Graduate* and *The Heartbreak Kid* but with none of the style of either. Rated R for nudity and profanity. 1985; 90m.

MALIBU EXPRESS
DIR: Andy Sidaris. **CAST:** Darby Hinton, Sybil Danning, Shelley Taylor Morgan, Brett Clark, Art Metrano.

Darby Hinton plays a millionaire turned private eye. He narrates the events *à la Magnum, P.I.*, but the similarities between this film and any decent movie or TV show end there. The amazing thing about this film is how it managed to get an R rating when it is clearly soft porn. Not recommended for anyone! 1984; 101m.

MAN IN THE WHITE SUIT, THE ★★★★★
DIR: Alexander Mackendrick. **CAST:** Alec Guinness, Joan Greenwood, Cecil Parker.

In *The Man in the White Suit*, Alec Guinness is the perfect choice to play an unassuming scientist who invents a fabric that can't be torn, frayed, or stained! Can you imagine the furor this causes in the textile industry? This uniquely original script pokes fun at big business and big labor as they try to suppress his discovery. Joan Greenwood is a treasure in a supporting role. 1952; B&W; 84m.

MAN OF FLOWERS ★★★★★
DIR: Paul Cox. **CAST:** Norman Kaye, Alyson Best, Chris Haywood, Werner Herzog.

Kinky, humorous, and touching, this winner from Australia affirms Paul Cox (of *Lonely Hearts* fame) as one of the wittiest and most sensitive directors from Down Under. Norman Kaye is terrific as an eccentric old man who collects art and flowers and watches pretty women undress. To him these are things of beauty that he can observe but can't touch. Rated R for nudity. 1984; 90m.

MAN THAT CORRUPTED HADLEYBURG, THE ★★★★★
DIR: Ralph Rosenblum. **CAST:** Robert Preston, Fred Gwynne, Frances Sternhagen, Tom Aldredge.

Robert Preston shows up in Hadleyburg with a sack of gold. Would-be saints and holier-than-thou guardians of public decency are exposed as ordinary people with quite human failings in this delightfully sly adaptation of Mark Twain's acerbic story. Henry Fonda's introduction includes rare film footage of Twain. Unrated and suitable for family viewing. 1980; 40m.

MAN WHO LOVED WOMEN, THE (1983) ★★★
DIR: Blake Edwards. **CAST:** Burt Reynolds, Julie Andrews, Marilu Henner, Kim Basinger, Barry Corbin.

The first collaboration of Burt Reynolds, Julie Andrews, and her director hubby, Blake Edwards, didn't sound like the kind of thing that would make screen history. And it isn't. But, surprise of surprises, it is a pleasantly entertaining—and sometimes uproariously funny—adult sex comedy. The always likable Reynolds plays a guy who just can't say no to the opposite sex. Rated R for nudity and profanity. 1983; 110m.

MAN WHO WASN'T THERE, THE

DIR: Bruce Malmuth. **CAST:** Steve Guttenberg, Jeffrey Tambor, Lisa Langlois, Art Hindle, Vincent Baggetta.

Clumsy comedy involves Steve Guttenberg in espionage and invisibility. This was originally released in 3-D, but the characters are barely one-dimensional. The film disappeared quickly from movie theaters, making it *The Movie That Wasn't There.* Rated R for nudity, language. 1983; 111m.

MAN WITH ONE RED SHOE, THE ★★★½

DIR: Stan Dragoti. **CAST:** Tom Hanks, Dabney Coleman, Charles Durning, Lori Singer, James Belushi, Carrie Fisher, Edward Herrmann.

An American remake of the French comedy *The Tall Blond Man with One Black Shoe*, this casts Tom Hanks as a concert violinist who is pursued by a group of spies led by Dabney Coleman. Hanks is nearly the whole show. However, Jim Belushi (as his practical-joke-loving buddy) and Carrie Fisher (as an overly amorous flute player) also provide some hearty laughs. Rated PG for profanity and violence. 1985; 96m.

MAN WITH TWO BRAINS, THE ★★★★

DIR: Carl Reiner. **CAST:** Steve Martin, Kathleen Turner, David Warner, Paul Benedict.

Steve Martin stars in this generally amusing takeoff of 1950s horror-sci-fi flicks as a scientist involved with two women: a nasty wife (Kathleen Turner, of *Body Heat*) and a sweet patient (the voice of Sissy Spacek). There's only one problem in his relationship with the latter: all that's left of her is her brain. Rated R for nudity, profanity, and violence. 1983; 93m.

MANHATTAN ★★★★★

DIR: Woody Allen. **CAST:** Diane Keaton, Woody Allen, Michael Murphy, Mariel Hemingway, Meryl Streep.

Reworking the same themes he explored in *Play It Again, Sam* and *Annie Hall*, Woody Allen again comes up with a masterpiece perhaps his greatest. Diane Keaton returns as the object of his awkward but well-meaning affections. It's heartwarming, insightful, screamingly funny, and a feast for the eyes. The black-and-white cinematography of long-time Allen collaborator Gordon Willis recalls the great visuals of *Citizen Kane* and *The Third Man.* Rated R. 1979; B&W; 96m.

MANIFESTO ★★★½

DIR: Dusan Makavejev. **CAST:** Camilla Soeberg, Alfred Molina, Eric Stoltz, Simon Callow, Lindsay Duncan.

A colorful, eccentric comedy from the director of *Montenegro* and *The Coca-Cola Kid.* It's a wacky tale of revolutionaries trying to alter the political system in a picturesque European country, circa 1920. Romance, misguided idealism, and ineptitude get in the way of all their efforts, but viewers have a lot of fun along the way. 1988; 96m.

MANNEQUIN

DIR: Michael Gottlieb. **CAST:** Andrew McCarthy, Kim Cattrall, Estelle Getty, G. W. Bailey.

A boy-meets-girl film with a twist: it's actually boy makes girl. Andrew McCarthy plays a sensitive window shop dresser who builds a mannequin that comes to life only around him. *Mannequin* is a very stupid, unfunny film that is a boring mixture of MTV glitz and worn-out comedy bits. Rated PG. 1987; 90m.

MAN'S FAVORITE SPORT? ★★★

DIR: Howard Hawks. **CAST:** Rock Hudson, Paula Prentiss, John McGiver, Roscoe Karns, Maria Perschy, Charlene Holt.

Comedy about a nonfishing outdoor-sports columnist who finds himself entered in an anglers' contest is fast and funny and provides Rock Hudson with one of his best roles. Screwball Paula Prentiss spends most of her time gumming up the works for poor Rock. The situations and dialogue are clever and breezy, employing director Howard Hawks's famous overlapping dialogue to maximum advantage. 1964; 120m.

MARATHON ★★½

DIR: Jackie Cooper. **CAST:** Bob Newhart, Herb Edelman, Dick Gautier, Anita Gillette, Leigh Taylor-Young, John Hillerman.

In this comic examination of midlife crisis, Bob Newhart becomes enamored with a woman he sees at a local running event. With his wife busy with her career, he eventually travels to the New York marathon, only to discover his true feelings. The uninspired direction and screenplay weaken the efforts of a veteran cast. Rated PG for mild language. 1985; 97m.

MARCH OF THE WOODEN SOLDIERS ★★★★

DIR: Gus Meins. **CAST:** Stan Laurel, Oliver Hardy, Charlotte Henry.

Originally titled *Babes in Toyland*, this film features Stan Laurel and Oliver Hardy as the toymaker's assistants in the land of Old King Cole. Utterly forgettable songs slow down an otherwise enjoyable fantasy film. Stan and Ollie are integrated well into the storyline, finally saving the town from the attack of the boogeymen. 1934; B&W; 73m.

MARRIED TO THE MOB ★★★★½

DIR: Jonathan Demme. **CAST:** Michelle Pfeiffer, Matthew Modine, Dean Stockwell, Mercedes Ruehl.

Imagine the amazing *Something Wild* with less menace, more humor, oddball set design to the nth degree, eccentric characters galore, and, as usual in a Jonathan Demme movie, music that sets the scene and the audience in motion. Michelle Pfeiffer plays a beautiful, innocent-yet-fatal femme, here doing her darnedest to extricate herself from the Long Island mob scene after her mobster husband is "iced"; Dean Stockwell is the threatening Don Juan don; Matthew Modine is the savior-nerd. Rated R for language and adult situations. 1988; 106m.

MARY HARTMAN, MARY HARTMAN (TELEVISION SERIES) ★★★★

DIR: Joan Darling, Jim Drake. **CAST:** Louise Lasser, Greg Mullavey, Mary Kay Place, Graham Jarvis, Victor Killan, Debralee Scott, Martin Mull.

This series was too off-the-wall for the networks, so producer Norman Lear sold it in syndication. Full of whimsy and satire, the show plunged into subjects considered taboo by normal sitcoms, such as impotence and marijuana, not to mention waxy yellow build-up. Louise Lasser, as Mary, fashioned a unique character with which a wide audience empathized. Volumes I and II deal with such provocative and hilarious storylines as the search for the Fernwood Flasher. This series is definitely worth another look. 1976; 70m.

M*A*S*H ★★★★½

DIR: Robert Altman. **CAST:** Elliott Gould, Donald Sutherland, Sally Kellerman, Tom Skerritt, Robert Duvall, JoAnn Pflug, Bud Cort, Gary Burghoff.

Fans of the television series of the same name and *Trapper John, M.D.* may have a bit of trouble recognizing their favorite characters, but this is the original. One of eccentric film director Robert Altman's few true artistic successes, this release is outrageous good fun. Rated PG. 1970; 116m.

M*A*S*H: GOODBYE, FAREWELL, AMEN ★★★★

DIR: Alan Alda. **CAST:** Alan Alda, Henry Morgan, Loretta Swit, Jamie Farr.

A beautiful send-off to one of the great television series. Alan Alda and company have finally seen the end of the Korean War and are headed home. This last episode is handled with the usual excellence that one has come to associate with the series. A must for "M*A*S*H" fans and those who think there is nothing worth watching on television. 1983; 120m.

MATILDA ★★★½
DIR: Daniel Mann. **CAST:** Elliott Gould, Robert Mitchum, Clive Revill, Harry Guardino, Roy Clark, Lionel Stander, Art Metrano.

A cute comedy about a boxing kangaroo who becomes a legend in the sport. Elliott Gould plays a small-time booking agent who becomes the manager of the heavyweight marsupial. Despite some problems in the directing, the film is watchable and humorous. Sentimental at times and a bit corny, too, but worth the time. Recommended for family viewing. Rated G. 1978; 105m.

MATING SEASON, THE ★★★
DIR: John Llewellyn Moxey. **CAST:** Lucie Arnaz, Laurence Luckinbill, Swoosie Kurtz, Diane Stilwell, Joel Brooks.

An enjoyable romantic comedy set among the flora and fauna commonly inhabited by bird-watchers. When an emotional lady attorney resorts to bird-watching for relaxation she meets a charming businessman. Affable little TV movie. 1986; 96m.

MATTER OF PRINCIPLE, A ★★★★
DIR: Gwen Arner. **CAST:** Alan Arkin, Barbara Dana, Tony Arkin.

Delightful tale about a selfish tyrant (Alan Arkin) who is suddenly overthrown by his much-put-upon wife (Barbara Dana, Arkin's real-life wife). She takes their eleven children after he destroys their first Christmas tree. Finally, he must wake up and think about someone besides himself. Unrated, but fine family entertainment. 1983; 60m.

MAXIE ★★
DIR: Paul Aaron. **CAST:** Glenn Close, Mandy Patinkin, Ruth Gordon, Barnard Hughes, Valerie Curtin.

Cute but not particularly impressive fantasy about a conservative secretary (Glenn Close) who becomes possessed by the spirit of a flamboyant flapper (Close, too). The star is wonderful, but the predictable plot and the uninspired direction let her—and the viewer—down. Few laughs and no surprises. Rated PG for suggested sex. 1985; 98m.

MEATBALLS ★★★½
DIR: Ivan Reitman. **CAST:** Bill Murray, Harvey Atkin, Kate Lynch, Chris Makepeace.

Somehow, this *Animal House*–style comedy's disjointedness is easier to swallow than it should be. Elmer Bernstein's music gets sentimental in the right places, and star Bill Murray is fun to watch. Rated PG. 1979; 92m.

MEATBALLS PART II
DIR: Ken Weiderhorn. **CAST:** Richard Mulligan, Kim Richards, John Mengatti, Misty Rowe.

This lame sequel to *Meatballs* should never have been made. Pitifully unfunny high jinks at summer camp, with an alien getting in on the action this time. In fact, he has all three of the good lines. Rated PG for sexual references. 1984; 87m.

MEATBALLS III ★
DIR: George Mendeluk. **CAST:** Sally Kellerman, Patrick Dempsey, Al Waxman, Shannon Tweed.

Poor Sally Kellerman. She deserves better than this lousy sex comedy. Bearing little relationship to the Bill Murray charmer and its dreadful follow-up, this yawner cast Kellerman as the ghost of a porno star who has to do a good deed in order to get into heaven. So she sets about trying to get the nerdy Patrick Dempsey laid. No more *Meatballs*, please. Rated R for nudity, profanity, and suggested sex. 1987; 94m.

MELVIN AND HOWARD ★★★★★
DIR: Jonathan Demme. **CAST:** Paul LeMat, Jason Robards Jr., Mary Steenburgen, Pamela Reed.
This brilliantly directed slice-of-life film works marvelously well on two levels. On the surface, it's the entertaining tale of how Melvin Dummar (Paul LeMat) met Howard Hughes (Jason Robards)—or did he? Underneath, it's a hilarious spoof of our society. Mary Steenburgen co-stars in this triumph of American filmmaking, a rare gem that deserves to be seen and talked about. Rated R. 1980; 95m.

MEMED MY HAWK ★★
DIR: Peter Ustinov. **CAST:** Peter Ustinov, Herbert Lom, Simon Dutton, Denis Quilley, Michael Gough, Michael Elphick, Siobhan McKenna.
Wonderful character actor Peter Ustinov wrote, directed, and starred in this comedy-drama set in 1923 Turkey. He plays the incompetent ruler of several small villages who is faced with a guerrilla rebellion and the indifference of the Turkish government, which correctly considers him a pompous buffoon. Ustinov and other excellent actors do what they can to prevent this from being as dry as the desert setting. PG-13 for some brief nudity. 1984; 105m.

MEMORIES OF ME ★
DIR: Henry Winkler. **CAST:** Billy Crystal, Alan King, JoBeth Williams.
A New York doctor (Billy Crystal) has a heart attack and decides to reevaluate his priorities as well as his stormy relationship with his father (Alan King). This Jewish male version of *Terms of Endearment* seems like one long inside joke. The script (co-written by Billy Crystal) wanders all over the place. Rated PG-13 for profanity and adult situations. 1988; 104m.

MEXICAN SPITFIRE ★★★½
DIR: Leslie Goodwins. **CAST:** Lupe Velez, Donald Woods, Leon Errol.
This is one of a series of second-feature comedies about a youngish businessman and his temperamental Mexican wife. Though the stars are Lupe Velez and Donald Woods, the simplistic plot shifts early on to the young man's accident-prone uncle Matt and his rich and proper boss Lord Epping, both of whom were played by the spaghetti-legged Ziegfeld comic Leon Errol. He's in top form here. 1939; B&W; 75m.

MICKI & MAUDE ★★★★½
DIR: Blake Edwards. **CAST:** Dudley Moore, Amy Irving, Ann Reinking, George Gaynes, Wallace Shawn.
In this hysterically funny comedy Dudley Moore stars as a television personality who tries to juggle marriages to two women, Amy Irving and Ann Reinking. Directed by Blake Edwards, it's a triumph for filmmaker and cast alike. Rated PG-13 for profanity and suggested sex. 1984; 96m.

MIDDLE-AGE CRAZY ★★★
DIR: John Trent. **CAST:** Bruce Dern, Ann-Margret, Graham Jarvis.
Bruce Dern lives the lyrics of this pop song–turned-film, playing a fellow who shorts out upon reaching the midlife crisis of his fortieth birthday. Wife Ann-Margret is abandoned for a football cheerleader, conservative clothes give way to snazzy threads, and the family car is pushed aside by a Porsche. Director John Trent resists the easy opportunity for cheap comedy, however, and treats the material with surprising compassion. Rated PG. 1980; 95m.

MIDNIGHT MADNESS
DIR: David Wechter, Michael Nankin. **CAST:** David Naughton, Debra Clinger, Eddie Deezen, Stephen Furst.
Absolutely awful post–*Animal House* Disney production about a bunch of teen-age idiots going on a midnight scavenger hunt. Rated PG. 1980; 110m.

MIDSUMMER NIGHT'S SEX COMEDY, A ★★½

DIR: Woody Allen. **CAST:** Woody Allen, Mia Farrow, José Ferrer, Julie Hagerty, Tony Roberts, Mary Steenburgen.

Woody Allen's sometimes dull cinematic treatise—albeit sweet-natured, and beautifully photographed by Gordon Willis—on the star-writer-director's favorite subjects: sex and death. That's not to say *A Midsummer Night's Sex Comedy* doesn't have its humorous moments. Allen's fans will undoubtedly enjoy it. Rated PG for adult themes. 1982; 88m.

MIKEY AND NICKY ★★★

DIR: Elaine May. **CAST:** Peter Falk, John Cassavetes, Ned Beatty, Joyce Van Patten.

The story of a fateful day and the relationship of two small-time crooks who have been best friends since childhood. This hauntingly funny film slowly builds to its climax in the Elaine May tradition. Great acting from Peter Falk and John Cassavetes. Rated R for profanity. 1976; 119m.

MILKY WAY, THE (1936) ★★★★

DIR: Leo McCarey. **CAST:** Harold Lloyd, Adolphe Menjou, Helen Mack.

In this superb compendium of gags flowing from his character of a milkman who innocently decks the champion during a brawl, the great Harold Lloyd amply proves why he was such a success. Lloyd was a master comic craftsman. This is the finest of his few talking films. 1936; B&W; 83m.

MILLION DOLLAR MYSTERY ★

DIR: Richard Fleischer. **CAST:** Jamie Alcroft, Royce D. Applegate, Tom Bosley, Eddie Deezen, Rich Hall, Mack Dryden.

A gimmick film that originally offered $1 million to the first audience member who could put the movie's clues together. Composed mostly of banal and immature dialogue and chase scenes. *Million Dollar Mystery* is greatly reminiscent of *Scavenger Hunt* and other mindless films of that ilk. Rated PG. 1987; 95m.

MIRACLE OF MORGAN'S CREEK, THE ★★★★½

DIR: Preston Sturges. **CAST:** Betty Hutton, Eddie Bracken, William Demarest, Diana Lynn, Brian Donlevy, Akim Tamiroff, Jimmy Conlin, Porter Hall.

All comic hell breaks loose when Betty Hutton finds herself pregnant following an all-night party, can't recall who the father is, and eventually gives birth to sextuplets. An audacious, daring Bronx cheer at American morals and ideals, this rollicking farce, cram-jammed with comic lines, is a real winner. 1944; B&W; 99m.

MIRACLES ★★½

DIR: Jim Kouf. **CAST:** Tom Conti, Teri Garr, Paul Rodriguez, Christopher Lloyd.

This film involves a sick little girl in a remote Mexican jungle, a doctor and his recently divorced wife in L.A., and a bungling burglar. The story revolves around the sometimes funny circumstances that bring all these characters together. Rated PG for language and mild violence. 1986; 90m.

MISCHIEF ★★★

DIR: Mel Damski. **CAST:** Doug McKeon, Catherine Mary Stewart, Chris Nash, Kelly Preston, D. W. Brown.

In this disarming coming-of-age comedy, Doug McKeon (*On Golden Pond*) plays Jonathan, whose hopes of romance are thwarted until Gene (Chris Nash, in an impressive debut), a kid from the big city, shows him how. Rated R for violence, profanity, nudity, and simulated sex. 1985; 93m.

MISS FIRECRACKER ★★★★

DIR: Thomas Schlamme. **CAST:** Holly Hunter, Mary Steenburgen, Tim Robbins, Alfre Woodard, Scott Glenn.

A wacky, colorful, feel-good movie about a young Mississippi woman whose hunger for self-respect takes her through the rigors of her hometown Yazoo City Miss Firecracker

Contest. Holly Hunter is marvelous as the misguided woman, while Mary Steenburgen shines as her cousin, a former beauty queen who returns for the contest. From the off-Broadway play by Beth (*Crimes of the Heart*) Henley. Rated PG. 1989; 102m.

MISS RIGHT ★½
DIR: Paul Williams. **CAST:** William Tepper, Karen Black, Margot Kidder, Virna Lisi, Marie-France Pisier, Clio Goldsmith.

This vignettish, uneven sex comedy strongly resembles TV's *Love American Style*. A UPI correspondent in Rome (William Tepper) becomes involved with several beautiful women but decides to break up with each of them in order to find—and be with—the perfect woman (Margot Kidder?). Rated R for profanity and nudity. 1988; 98m.

MISSIONARY, THE ★★★½
DIR: Richard Loncraine. **CAST:** Michael Palin, Maggie Smith, Denholm Elliott, Trevor Howard, Michael Hordern.

Monty Python's Michael Palin, who also wrote the script, plays a well-meaning American minister assigned the task of saving the souls of London's fallen women. Not a non-stop, gag-filled descent into absurdity like the Monty Python movies. It is, instead, a warmhearted spoof with the accent on character and very sparing but effective in its humor. Rated R. 1982; 90m.

MR. AND MRS. SMITH ★★★★
DIR: Alfred Hitchcock. **CAST:** Carole Lombard, Robert Montgomery, Gene Raymond, Jack Carson.

This film deals with the love-hate-love relationship of Carole Lombard and Robert Montgomery, who play a couple who discover their marriage isn't legal. The bouncy dialogue by Norman Krasna is justly famous and includes some of the most classic comedy scenes ever. Directing this enjoyable farce, in his only pure comedy, is Alfred Hitchcock. 1941; B&W; 95m.

MR. BILL LOOKS BACK ★★★
DIR: Walter Williams. **CAST:** Animated.

This is a collection of shorts taken from *Saturday Night Live* episodes. In each, Mr. Bill and his dog Spot are tormented by Mr. Hands and the evil Sluggo. Bill's adventures take him to Coney Island, Skid Row, a psychiatrist's office, the police station, and Sing Sing. There are some hilarious moments. 1980; 30m.

MR. BILL'S REAL LIFE ADVENTURES ★★½
DIR: Jim Drake. **CAST:** Peter Scolari, Valerie Mahaffey, Lenore Kasdorf, Michael McAnus.

The hilarity of the clay figure's misfortunes doesn't quite translate with real-life characters. Peter Scolari as Mr. Bill, however, is terrific. Mr. Bill, his sweet wife Sally (Valerie Mahaffey), their son Billy, and dog Spot are tiny people who must battle not only the huge world around them but also their neighbors. 1986; 43m.

MR. BLANDINGS BUILDS HIS DREAM HOUSE ★★★★
DIR: H. C. Potter. **CAST:** Cary Grant, Myrna Loy, Melvyn Douglas.

In this screwball comedy, Cary Grant plays a man tired of the hustle and bustle of city life. He decides to move to the country, construct his private Shangri-La, and settle back into what he feels will be a serene rural lifestyle. His fantasy and reality come into comic conflict. Myrna Loy is cast as his ever-patient wife in this very fine film. 1948; B&W; 94m.

MR. HOBBS TAKES A VACATION ★★★
DIR: Henry Koster. **CAST:** James Stewart, Maureen O'Hara, Marie Wilson, Fabian, John Saxon.

Somewhat against his better judgment, ever-patient James Stewart takes his wife Maureen O'Hara and their children and grandchildren on vacation. They wind up in a ramshackle old house on the Pacific Coast, and he winds up more hassled than when home or at work. Good acting and a clever script make this thin-plotted comedy amusing. 1962; 116m.

MR. MIKE'S MONDO VIDEO ★★★

DIR: Michael O'Donoghue. **CAST:** Michael O'Donoghue, Dan Aykroyd, Jane Curtin, Carrie Fisher, Teri Garr, Deborah Harry, Margot Kidder, Bill Murray, Laraine Newman, Gilda Radner, Julius LaRosa, Paul Schaffer, Sid Vicious.

This comedy special by former *Saturday Night Live* writer Michael O'Donoghue was originally slated to run on late-night network television, but NBC decided it was too outrageous—even offensive in some parts—to be broadcast. *Mr. Mike's Mondo Video* was then briefly released to theaters where it did little box-office and received negative reviews. In fact, it is kind of a time capsule of comedy and pop figures from the 1970s. It stands as a reminder of how far-out comedy got on television after years of safe, insipid sitcoms. 1979; 75m.

MR. MOM ★★★★

DIR: Stan Dragoti. **CAST:** Michael Keaton, Teri Garr, Ann Jillian, Martin Mull.

Michael Keaton is hilarious as an engineer who loses his job at an automobile manufacturing plant and, when wife Teri Garr gets a high-paying job at an advertising agency, becomes a hopelessly inept househusband. The story is familiar and the events somewhat predictable, but Keaton's off-the-wall antics and boyish charm make it all seem fresh and lively. Rated PG for light profanity. 1983; 91m.

MR. NORTH ★★★½

DIR: Danny Huston. **CAST:** Anthony Edwards, Robert Mitchum, Lauren Bacall, Harry Dean Stanton, Anjelica Huston.

In this fantasy a young Yale graduate arrives in elite Newport, Rhode Island as a tutor and ends up touching the citizens in seemingly magical ways. Based on Thornton Wilder's novel, *Theophilus North*, and directed by the late John Huston's son, Danny, this small-scale piece of whimsy is a winner. Rated PG. 1988; 92m.

MR. PEABODY AND THE MERMAID ★★

DIR: Irving Pichel. **CAST:** William Powell, Ann Blyth, Irene Hervey.

This is *Splash*, 1940s-style. A married New Englander (William Powell) snags an amorous mermaid while fishing and transfers her to his swimming pool, with the expected results. 1948; B&W; 89m.

MR. ROBERTS ★★★★½

DIR: John Ford, Mervyn LeRoy. **CAST:** Henry Fonda, James Cagney, Jack Lemmon, William Powell, Ward Bond.

A Navy cargo ship well outside the World War II battle zone is the setting for this hit comedy-drama. Henry Fonda is Lieutenant Roberts, the first officer who helps the crew battle their ceaseless boredom and tyrannical captain (James Cagney). Jack Lemmon began his road to stardom with his sparkling performance as the irrepressible con-man Ensign Pulver. 1955; 123m.

MR. SYCAMORE ★

DIR: Pancho Kohner. **CAST:** Jason Robards Jr., Sandy Dennis, Jean Simmons, Mark Miller.

We'd love to know how actors like Jason Robards, Sandy Dennis, and Jean Simmons were persuaded to appear in this completely inane comedy-drama about a mailman who, tired of his nagging wife, decides to turn into a tree. Robards spends much of the movie standing in a hole on his lawn, waiting for his leaves to sprout. Peculiar and pointless. Unrated. 1975; 87m.

MR. WINKLE GOES TO WAR ★★★
DIR: Alfred E. Green. **CAST:** Edward G. Robinson, Ruth Warrick, Richard Lane, Robert Armstrong.

Edward G. Robinson is a henpecked bookkeeper who gets drafted into the army during World War II. As the saying goes, the army makes a man out of him. Like so many films of its time, *Mr. Winkle Goes to War* was part of the war effort, and as such, hasn't worn very well; what was considered heartfelt or patriotic back in the 1940s is now rendered maudlin or just corny. Still, the acting is excellent. 1944; B&W; 80m.

MODERN GIRLS ★★★
DIR: Jerry Kramer. **CAST:** Cynthia Gibb, Virginia Madsen, Daphne Zuniga, Clayton Rohner, Stephen Shellen, Chris Nash.

Cynthia Gibb, Virginia Madsen, and Daphne Zuniga turn in fine individual performances as the *Modern Girls*, but this well-edited and visually striking film has some slow scenes among the funny. This teen comedy about a night in L.A.'s rock clubs begins better than it ends. However, younger viewers should find it enjoyable overall. Rated PG-13 for profanity and sexual situations. 1987; 82m.

MODERN PROBLEMS ★★
DIR: Ken Shapiro. **CAST:** Chevy Chase, Patti D'Arbanville, Mary Kay Place.

In this passable comedy, directed by Ken (*The Groove Tube*) Shapiro, Chevy Chase plays an air traffic controller who may be permanently out to lunch. His girlfriend has left him, and a freak nuclear accident has endowed him with telekinetic powers. Rated PG because of its brief nudity and sexual theme. 1981; 91m.

MODERN ROMANCE ★★★★
DIR: Albert Brooks. **CAST:** Albert Brooks, Kathryn Harrold, Bruno Kirby.

Love may be a many-splendored thing for some people, but it's sheer torture for Robert Cole (Albert Brooks) in this contemporary comedy. Brooks wrote, directed, and starred in this very entertaining, often hilarious story about a self-indulgent, narcissistic Hollywood film editor whose love life has the stability of Mount St. Helens. Rated R. 1981; 93m.

MODERN TIMES ★★★★
DIR: Charles Chaplin. **CAST:** Charlie Chaplin, Paulette Goddard.

Charlie Chaplin must have had a crystal ball when he created *Modern Times*. His satire of life in an industrial society has more relevance today than when it was made. Primarily it is still pure Chaplin, with his perfectly timed and edited sight gags. The story finds the Little Tramp confronting all the dehumanizing inventions of a futuristic manufacturing plant. 1936; B&W; 89m.

MODERNS, THE ★★
DIR: Alan Rudolph. **CAST:** Keith Carradine, Linda Fiorentino, John Lone, Wallace Shawn, Genevieve Bujold, Geraldine Chaplin, Kevin J. O'Connor.

This ironic look at the Paris art scene of the Twenties just isn't funny *enough*. Director Alan Rudolph is always poised at the crossroads of humorous seriousness, but in *The Moderns* he's got his vision in limbo too much of the time. You know it's intended to be for laughs, but it comes off too stilted. Keith Carradine is good as an expatriate painter, and Wallace Shawn has the best lines as a gossip columnist. Unrated. 1988; 126m.

MONDO TRASHO
DIR: John Waters. **CAST:** Divine, Mary Vivian Pearce, Mink Stole, David Lochary.

Director John Waters's longest film—and you can feel every minute of it. This is not a sync-sound movie, and the 1950s rock 'n' roll, along with the occasional wild dubbed-over dialogue, gets tiresome after twenty minutes. Waters put it best—this is a "gutter film." Unrated, but this is equivalent to an X for violence, gore, and sex. 1971; 130m.

MONEY PIT, THE ★★

DIR: Richard Benjamin. **CAST:** Tom Hanks, Shelley Long, Alexander Godunov, Maureen Stapleton, Joe Mantegna, Philip Bosco, Josh Mostel.

In this gimmicky, contrived Steven Spielberg production, Tom Hanks plays a rock 'n' roll lawyer who falls in love with musician Shelley Long. When these lovebirds buy a fixer-upper, they encounter all sorts of problems. Rated PG for profanity and suggested sex. 1986; 90m.

MONKEY BUSINESS (1931) ★★★★½

DIR: Norman Z. McLeod. **CAST:** The Marx Brothers, Thelma Todd, Ruth Hall.

The Marx Brothers are stowaways on a cruise ship, deflating pomposity and confusing authority. This movie dispenses with needless subplots and stagy musical numbers. It's undiluted Marx zaniness, and one of the team's best films. 1931; B&W; 77m.

MONKEY BUSINESS (1952) ★★★★

DIR: Howard Hawks. **CAST:** Cary Grant, Marilyn Monroe, Ginger Rogers, Charles Coburn, Hugh Marlowe, Larry Keating.

A romping screwball comedy about a genius chemist (Cary Grant) who invents a formula that delays the aging process. A chimpanzee in the lab pours the formula in the public water fountain, causing all concerned to revert to adolescence. A minor classic. 1952; B&W; 97m.

MONSIEUR VERDOUX ★★★★

DIR: Charles Chaplin. **CAST:** Charlie Chaplin, Martha Raye, Isobel Elsom, Marilyn Nash, William Frawley.

A trend-setting black comedy in which a dandified, Parisian Bluebeard murders wives for their money. Wry humor abounds. Charlie Chaplin is superb in the title role. But it's Martha Raye who steals the film—most decidedly in the rowboat scene. The genius that made Charles Spencer Chaplin famous the world over shows throughout. 1947; B&W; 123m.

MONSTER A GO-GO 🦃

DIR: Bill Rebane, Sheldon Seymour. **CAST:** Phil Morton, June Travis.

Herschell Gordon Lewis (of *Blood Feast* infamy) bought the rights to an unfinished movie about an astronaut who is turned into a giant by radiation. He quickly shot a few scenes and added some narration to give it the barest continuity and released it to drive-ins as camp. It's just boring garbage. 1965; B&W; 70m.

MONTY PYTHON AND THE HOLY GRAIL ★★★½

DIR: Terry Gilliam. **CAST:** Terry Jones, Graham Chapman, John Cleese, Terry Gilliam, Michael Palin.

The Monty Python gang assault the legend of King Arthur and his knights in this often uproariously funny, sometimes tedious, movie. Rated PG. 1974; 90m.

MONTY PYTHON LIVE AT THE HOLLYWOOD BOWL ★★★★

DIR: Terry Hughes. **CAST:** John Cleese, Eric Idle, Graham Chapman, Terry Jones, Michael Palin, Terry Gilliam.

Hold on to your sides! Those Monty Python crazies are back with more unbridled hilarity. Rated R for profanity, nudity, and the best in bad taste. 1982; 73m.

MONTY PYTHON'S FLYING CIRCUS (TELEVISION SERIES) ★★★★

DIR: Ian MacNaughton. **CAST:** Graham Chapman, John Cleese, Terry Gilliam, Eric Idle, Terry Jones, Michael Palin.

This is a series of videos featuring highlights from the popular English TV show of the early 1970s. All the madcap characters remain intact along with the innovative and trendsetting animation by Terry Gilliam. You don't have to be British to enjoy the various political asides and lampoons. You do have to like fast-paced, off-the-wall craziness. The talented cast also conceived and wrote all of the material. 1970–1972; 60 minutes each.

MONTY PYTHON'S THE MEANING OF LIFE ★★★★
DIR: Terry Jones. **CAST:** John Cleese, Eric Idle, Graham Chapman, Terry Jones, Terry Gilliam.

Those Monty Python goons perform a series of sketches on the important issues of life. According to Michael Palin, the film "ranges from philosophy to history to medicine to halibut—especially halibut." It's the English troupe's finest feature film to date—a heady mixture of satiric and surreal bits about the life cycle from birth to death. It may prove offensive to some and a sheer delight to others. Rated R for all manner of offensive goings-on. 1983; 103m.

MOON IS BLUE, THE ★★
DIR: Otto Preminger. **CAST:** William Holden, David Niven, Maggie McNamara, Tom Tully, Dawn Addams.

It's hard to believe this comedy, based on a stage hit, was once considered highly controversial. We doubt that even your grandmother would be offended by the sexual innuendos in this very moral film. The thin plot concerns a young woman who fends off two slightly aging playboys by repeatedly vowing to remain a virgin until married. 1953; B&W; 95m.

MOON OVER PARADOR ★★½
DIR: Paul Mazursky. **CAST:** Richard Dreyfuss, Raul Julia, Sonia Braga, Jonathan Winters, Fernando Rey, Polly Holliday.

This misfired comedy thrusts Richard Dreyfuss, who plays a modestly successful actor, into the role of his career: impersonating the recently deceased dictator of one of those anonymous Caribbean countries that crop up in stories like this. Political strongman Raul Julia wants the charade to continue until he can take over smoothly. Light comedy, alas, turns uncomfortably real when terrorist tactics begin, and everything rattles to a most unconvincing conclusion. Rated PG-13 for language and mild sexual themes. 1988; 105m.

MOONSTRUCK ★★★★½
DIR: Norman Jewison. **CAST:** Cher, Nicolas Cage, Vincent Gardenia, Olympia Dukakis, Danny Aiello, Julie Bovasso, John Mahoney, Feodor Chaliapin.

Cher, Nicolas Cage, and a superb supporting cast enliven this delightful comedy about a group of Italian-Americans who find amore when the moon shines bright. *Moonstruck*, with its quirky humor and ensemble playing, reminds one of a Woody Allen comedy. Director Norman Jewison and screenwriter John Patrick Shanley manage to make one hilarious complication follow another. Rated PG for profanity and suggested sex. 1987; 102m.

MORGAN ★★★★
DIR: Karel Reisz. **CAST:** Vanessa Redgrave, David Warner, Robert Stephens, Irene Handl.

In this cult favorite, Vanessa Redgrave decides to leave her wacky husband (David Warner). He's a wild man who has a thing for gorillas (this brings scenes from *King Kong*). Nevertheless, he tries to win her back in an increasingly unorthodox manner. Deeply imbedded in the 1960s, this film still brings quite a few laughs. 1966; B&W; 97m.

MORGAN STEWART'S COMING HOME ★
DIR: Alan Smithee. **CAST:** Jon Cryer, Lynn Redgrave, Viveka Davis, Paul Gleason, Nicholas Pryor.

Made before *Pretty in Pink* but released after it to take advantage of the impression Jon Cryer made in that John Hughes teen comedy. The young actor stars in this tepid comedy as a preppie who tries to reorder his family's priorities. Cryer has some good moments, and Lynn Redgrave is top-notch as his mom, but the laughs just aren't there. Rated PG-13. 1987; 92m.

MORONS FROM OUTER SPACE ★★½

DIR: Mike Hodges. **CAST:** Griff Rhys Jones, Mel Smith, James B. Sikking, Dindsdale Landen.

Four aliens from a distant planet crash-land on Earth, but unlike most of the recent films dealing with this idea, their arrival is not a secret and they soon become international celebrities. The comedy comes from the fact that they're idiots and act accordingly. Unfortunately, the morons are not as funny as the viewer would hope. Rated PG for language. 1985; 78m.

MOSCOW ON THE HUDSON ★★★★½

DIR: Paul Mazursky. **CAST:** Robin Williams, Maria Conchita Alonso, Cleavant Derricks.

Robin Williams stars in this sweet, funny, sad, and sexy comedy as a Russian circus performer who, while on tour in the United States, decides to defect after experiencing the wonders of Bloomingdale's department store in New York. Paul Mazursky cowrote and directed this touching character study. Rated R for profanity, nudity, suggested sex, and violence. 1984; 115m.

MOTHER, JUGS, AND SPEED ★★★

DIR: Peter Yates. **CAST:** Bill Cosby, Raquel Welch, Larry Hagman, Harvey Keitel.

Hang on tight! This is a fast and furious black comedy about a run-down ambulance service that puts body count ahead of patient welfare in the race to the hospital. Bill Cosby and Raquel Welch make an odd combination that clicks. There's also some scene-stealing hilarity from Larry Hagman as an oversexed driver. Rated R. 1976; 95m.

MOUSE THAT ROARED, THE ★★★★

DIR: Jack Arnold. **CAST:** Peter Sellers, Jean Seberg, Leo McKern.

Any film that features the comic talents of Peter Sellers at his peak can't help but be funny. In this British movie, a tiny European nation devises a foolproof method of filling its depleted treasury. It declares war on the United States, then loses and collects war reparations from the generous Americans. Even foolproof plans don't always go as expected...in this case with hilarious results. 1958; 83m.

MOVERS AND SHAKERS ★★

DIR: William Asher. **CAST:** Walter Matthau, Charles Grodin, Vincent Gardenia, Tyne Daly, Bill Macy, Gilda Radner, Steve Martin, Penny Marshall.

This star-studded film starts off well but quickly falls apart. Walter Matthau plays a Hollywood producer who, through loyalty to an old friend and business associate, begins work on a movie project with only the title, *Love in Sex*, to start with. Charles Grodin plays the screenwriter who is commissioned to write the script, which is intended as a tribute to love. But with serious marital problems, Grodin is hardly the proper candidate. Rated PG for profanity. 1985; 80m.

MOVIE MOVIE ★★★½

DIR: Stanley Donen. **CAST:** George C. Scott, Trish Van Devere, Eli Wallach, Red Buttons, Barry Bostwick, Harry Hamlin, Barbara Harris, Art Carney, Ann Reinking, Kathleen Beller.

Clever, affectionate spoof of 1930s pictures presents a double feature: *Dynamite Hands* is a black-and-white boxing story; *Baxter's Beauties of 1933* is a lavish, Busby Berkeley–type extravaganza. This nostalgic package even includes a preview of coming attractions. Rated PG. 1978; 107m.

MOVIE STRUCK (A.K.A. PICK A STAR) ★★
DIR: Edward Sedgwick. **CAST:** Stan Laurel, Oliver Hardy, Jack Haley, Patsy Kelly.

Typical story about a young girl trying to break into pictures is brightened by a brief appearance by Stan Laurel and Oliver Hardy, who demonstrate the effectiveness of breakaway glass during a barroom confrontation with a tough. Strange musical numbers and some witty dialogue buoy this thin story a little, but Stan and Ollie are still the main reasons to catch this one—and there just isn't that much of them. 1937; B&W; 70m.

MOVING ★
DIR: Alan Metter. **CAST:** Richard Pryor, Beverly Todd, Dave Thomas, Dana Carvey, Randy Quaid, Rodney Dangerfield.

Chalk this up as another disappointment from Richard Pryor. In a story about as funny as oral surgery, Pryor plays an out-of-work mass-transit engineer. After a near-hopeless search for employment, he finds a job in Idaho and must move his family from their home in New Jersey. Rated R for profanity and violence. 1988; 90m.

MOVING VIOLATIONS ★★
DIR: Neal Israel. **CAST:** John Murray, Jennifer Tilly, James Keach, Wendie Jo Sperber, Sally Kellerman, Fred Willard.

Neal Israel and Pat Proft, who brought us *Police Academy* and *Bachelor Party*, writhe again with another "subject" comedy—this time about traffic school. The team has come up with more laughs than usual, and star John Murray does a reasonable job of imitating his older brother, Bill. Rated PG-13 for profanity and suggested sex. 1985; 90m.

MUGSY'S GIRLS ★
DIR: Kevin Brodie. **CAST:** Ruth Gordon, Laura Branigan, Eddie Deezen.

A predictable bit of fluff about a sorority out to earn rent money through mud wrestling. A lame *Animal House* with little redeeming value. Rated R for nudity and profanity. 1985; 87m.

MUNSTERS' REVENGE, THE ★★★
DIR: Don Weiss. **CAST:** Fred Gwynne, Yvonne De Carlo, Al Lewis, Sid Caesar.

More schlock than shock and chock full of predictable puns, this munster mash is super Saturday-morning fun. Most of the original players from the TV series are back, with outstanding guests like Sid Caesar as the curator of a wax museum. 1981; 96m.

MURDER BY DEATH ★★★★
DIR: Robert Moore. **CAST:** Peter Sellers, Peter Falk, David Niven, Maggie Smith, James Coco, Alec Guinness.

Mystery buffs will get a big kick out of this spoof of the genre, penned by Neil Simon. Peter Sellers, Peter Falk, David Niven, Maggie Smith, and James Coco play thinly disguised send-ups of famed fictional detectives who are invited to the home of Truman Capote to solve a baffling murder. Rated PG. 1976; 94m.

MUSCLE BEACH PARTY ★★
DIR: William Asher. **CAST:** Frankie Avalon, Annette Funicello, Buddy Hackett, Luciana Paluzzi, Don Rickles, John Ashley, Jody McCrea, Morey Amsterdam.

Everyone's favorite surfing couple, Frankie and Annette, and their beach buddies return for more fluff in the sun. The gang's beach has been invaded by body-building hunks. This features the first screen appearance of Little Stevie Wonder. 1964; 94m.

MY AMERICAN COUSIN ★★★★
DIR: Sandy Wilson. **CAST:** Margaret Langrick, John Wildman, Richard Donat.

This delightful Canadian comedy-drama focuses on what happens when the dull life of 12-year-old Sandra (played by feisty newcomer Margaret Langrick) is invaded by her high-spirited 17-year-old relative, Butch (John Wildman), from California. A warm character study with a number of funny moments, this is a refreshing antidote to the mindless teen flicks so common today. Rated PG for mild sexuality. 1986; 110m.

MY BEST FRIEND IS A VAMPIRE ★★

DIR: Jimmy Huston. **CAST:** Robert Sean Leonard, Cheryl Pollak, René Auberjonois, Fannie Flagg.

Teen romance with a twist: Our hero has just become a vampire. Comic bits revolve around his unwelcome physiological changes. Abundant car-chase scenes should intrigue teen viewers. Rated PG for Jeremy's seduction by the sexy vampire. 1986; 90m.

MY BEST GIRL ★★½

DIR: Sam Taylor. **CAST:** Mary Pickford, Charles "Buddy" Rogers, Lucien Littlefield, Hobart Bosworth.

Typical sweet, sunshiny Mary Pickford fare, this is a small-town romantic comedy about a tried-and-true shop girl who falls in love with the new clerk. He's really the boss's son. Virtue is rewarded, of course. Silent. 1927; B&W; 60m.

MY BREAKFAST WITH BLASSIE ★½

DIR: Johnny Legend, Linda Lautrec. **CAST:** Andy Kaufman, Fred Blassie.

Former professional wrestling champion Fred Blassie and protegé Andy Kaufman discuss life, breakfast, and various ways of insulting people during a breakfast at a Southern California coffee shop. Spoof on *My Dinner with Andre* is mildly amusing at first and the concept is reasonably clever, but even fans of the two performers will find the film tedious. 1983; 60m.

MY CHAUFFEUR ★★½

DIR: David Beaird. **CAST:** Deborah Foreman, Sam Jones, Howard Hesseman, E. G. Marshall, Sean McClory.

In this better-than-average (for the genre) softcore sex comedy, an aggressive, slightly kooky young woman upsets things at an all-male limousine company. Rated R for oodles of nudity, leering dirty old men by the truckload, suggested sex, and profanity. Don't let the kids rent this while you're out playing poker. 1986; 97m.

MY DEAR SECRETARY ★★½

DIR: Charles Martin. **CAST:** Laraine Day, Kirk Douglas, Helen Walker, Keenan Wynn, Alan Mowbray.

A comedy battle of quips and wits between writer Kirk Douglas and bestselling author Laraine Day. Both lose the picture to Keenan Wynn, who is a droll delight. 1948; B&W; 94m.

MY DEMON LOVER ★★★½

DIR: Charlie Loventhal. **CAST:** Scott Valentine, Michelle Little, Robert Trebor, Gina Gallego, Alan Fudge.

Scott Valentine is delightful as a lovable bum who is possessed by the devil. His infatuation with a very gullible Denny (Michelle Little) becomes complicated when he is transformed into a demon every time he gets amorous. Rated PG for simulated sex and mild gore. 1987; 87m.

MY FAVORITE BRUNETTE ★★★★½

DIR: Elliott Nugent. **CAST:** Bob Hope, Dorothy Lamour, Peter Lorre, Lon Chaney Jr., John Hoyt.

Classic Bob Hope comedy with Bob as a photographer who, thanks to a case of mistaken identity, makes No. 1 on the death list of a gang of thugs, played beautifully by Peter Lorre, Lon Chaney Jr., John Hoyt, and Elisha Cook Jr. The gags fly one after another as Bob tries every trick in the book to save his neck, as well as Dorothy Lamour's. A scream! 1947; B&W; 87m.

MY FAVORITE WIFE ★★★★★

DIR: Garson Kanin. **CAST:** Cary Grant, Irene Dunne, Randolph Scott.

Cary Grant and Irene Dunne teamed up for many hilarious films, but the best is this often-copied comedy. Grant is a widower about to be remarried when his long-lost and presumed-dead wife (Dunne) is rescued after years on an island with a handsome young scientist (Randolph Scott). The delightful complications that result make this one of the 1940s' best comedies. 1940; B&W; 88m.

MY FAVORITE YEAR ★★★★½
DIR: Richard Benjamin. **CAST:** Peter O'Toole, Mark Linn-Baker, Joseph Bologna, Lainie Kazan, Bill Macy.
This warmhearted, hilarious comedy is an affectionate tribute to the frenzied Golden Age of television, that period when uninhibited comics like Sid Caesar faced the added pressure of performing live. With superb performances all around and on-the-money direction by Richard Benjamin, it's a real treasure. Rated PG for slight profanity and sexual situations. 1982; 92m.

MY LITTLE CHICKADEE ★★★★★
DIR: Eddie Cline. **CAST:** W. C. Fields, Mae West, Dick Foran, Joseph Calleia.
W. C. Fields and Mae West enter a marriage of convenience in the Old West. It seems the card sharp (Fields) and the tainted lady (West) need to create an aura of respectability before they descend upon an unsuspecting town. That indicates trouble ahead for the town, and lots of fun for viewers. 1940; B&W; 83m.

MY LOVE FOR YOURS ★★★
DIR: Edward H. Griffith. **CAST:** Madeleine Carroll, Fred MacMurray, Allan Jones, Helen Broderick, Akim Tamiroff, Osa Massen, John Qualen.
An eager cast and a witty script make a passable entertainment of this otherwise trite story of a cool, self-assured career girl thawed by love. It's also known as *Honeymoon in Bali*. 1939; B&W; 99m.

MY MAN GODFREY ★★★★★
DIR: Gregory La Cava. **CAST:** Carole Lombard, William Powell, Gail Patrick, Alice Brady, Eugene Pallette.
My Man Godfrey is one of the great screwball comedies of the 1930s. Carole Lombard plays the most eccentric member of an eccentric family. William Powell is the relatively sane portion of the formula. Carole finds him when she is sent to find a "lost man." Powell seems to fit the bill, since he's living a hobo's life on the wrong side of the tracks. 1936; B&W; 95m.

MY STEPMOTHER IS AN ALIEN ★★½
DIR: Richard Benjamin. **CAST:** Dan Aykroyd, Kim Basinger, Jon Lovitz, Alison Hannigan.
A beautiful alien (Kim Basinger) comes to Earth to reverse the effects of a ray that has changed the gravity of her planet. Unfortunately, the creator of the ray (Dan Aykroyd) doesn't know how to re-create it. Thinking he is lying, she marries him to get the secret. A so-so farce with a predictably sweet ending. Rated PG-13. 1988; 108m.

MY TUTOR ★
DIR: George Bowers. **CAST:** Matt Lattanzi, Caren Kaye, Kevin McCarthy.
It looks like a dumb exploitation movie. It sounds like a ripoff of *Private Lessons*. It's advertised like sleazoid trash. Put it all together and that's exactly what you get in this film—in which a young man gets an education in more than just reading, writing, and 'rithmetic. Rated R for nudity and implied sex. 1983; 97m.

NADINE ★★★
DIR: Robert Benton. **CAST:** Jeff Bridges, Kim Basinger, Rip Torn, Gwen Verdon, Glenne Headly, Jerry Stiller.
A cute caper comedy. Kim Basinger is a not-so-bright hairdresser who finds herself involved in murder and mayhem. She enlists the aid of her estranged husband (Jeff Bridges), a saloon owner with big ideas and few brains. Rip Torn gives a fine performance as the chief villain. Rated PG for light violence and profanity. 1987; 95m.

NAKED GUN, THE ★★★★
DIR: David Zucker. **CAST:** Leslie Nielsen, George Kennedy, Priscilla Presley, Ricardo Montalban, O. J. Simpson, Nancy Marchand.

Fans of the short-lived television series *Police Squad!* will love this full-length adventure featuring Leslie Nielsen's stiff-lipped Frank Drebin, the toughest—and clumsiest—cop in the universe. The writing and producing team of David Zucker, Jim Abrahams, and Jerry Zucker, also responsible for *Airplane,* have riddled this parody of 1960s television cop shows with countless sight gags, outrageous puns, and over-the-top characterizations. Rated PG-13 for language and mild sexual coarseness. 1988; 85m.

NAKED TRUTH ★★½

DIR: Mario Zampi. **CAST:** Terry-Thomas, Dennis Price, Peter Sellers, Shirley Eaton.

This oddball comedy involves a group of loonies who are brought together to get rid of the editor of a smutty magazine. Peter Sellers is good as a disgusting television celebrity and Terry-Thomas is very effective as a racketeer. This British picture was originally titled *Your Past Is Showing*. 1957; 92m.

NASTY HABITS ★★

DIR: Michael Lindsay-Hogg. **CAST:** Glenda Jackson, Sandy Dennis, Susan Penhaligon, Edith Evans, Melina Mercouri.

Nasty Habits promises much more than it delivers. As a satire of the Watergate conspiracy, placed in a convent, it relies too heavily on the true incident for its punch. Philadelphia is the setting for the confrontation between Alexandra (Glenda Jackson) and Felicity (Susan Penhaligon), who are vying for the position of abbess after the sudden death of the incumbent, Hildegarde (Edith Evans). Rated PG, with some profanity. 1977; 96m.

NEIGHBORS ★★★½

DIR: John G. Avildsen. **CAST:** John Belushi, Dan Aykroyd, Cathy Moriarty, Kathryn Walker, Tim Kazurinsky.

This is a strange movie. John Belushi plays a suburban homeowner whose peaceful existence is threatened when his new neighbors (played by Dan Aykroyd and Cathy Moriarty turn out to be complete wackos. It isn't a laugh-a-minute farce, but there are numerous chuckles and a few guffaws along the way. Rated R because of profanity and sexual content. 1981; 94m.

NEVER GIVE A SUCKER AN EVEN BREAK ★★★★

DIR: Eddie Cline. **CAST:** W. C. Fields, Gloria Jean, Leon Errol.

This is a wild and wooly pastiche of hilarious gags and bizarre comedy routines revolving around W. C. Fields's attempt to sell an outlandish script to a movie studio. Some of the jokes misfire, but the absurdity of the situations makes up for the weak spots. 1941; B&W; 71m.

NEW HOMEOWNER'S GUIDE TO HAPPINESS, THE ★★★

DIR: Jonathan Cutler. **CAST:** Judge Reinhold, Demi Moore.

In this black comedy, Judge Reinhold is a new resident of suburbia who finds various means to silence the endless yapping of the neighborhood dogs that disrupt his paradise. As his pregnant wife, Demi Moore also knows how to handle the neighbors. This is the last half of a one-hour tape coupled with *Ron Reagan Is the President's Son,* which you should fast-forward through. 1988; 60m.

NEW LEAF, A ★★★★

DIR: Elaine May. **CAST:** Walter Matthau, Elaine May, Jack Weston, James Coco, William Redfield.

A rare (and wonderful) triple play from an American female talent: writer-director-star Elaine May makes an impressive mark with this latter-day screwball comedy, about a bankrupt rogue (Walter Matthau) who must find a rich woman to marry—within six weeks. His target turns out to be a clumsy botanist (May) seeking immortality by finding a new specimen of plant life (hence one element of the title). Rated PG for adult situations. 1971; 102m.

NEW LIFE, A ★★★

DIR: Alan Alda. **CAST:** Alan Alda, Ann-Margret, Hal Linden, Veronica Hamel, John Shea, Mary Kay Place, Beatrice Alda.

This amusing examination of life after divorce will please writer-director Alan Alda's fans, but others may find the brew too reminiscent of Neil Simon and Woody Allen (both of whom have done better with similar material). After a fairly agreeable separation, Alda and Ann-Margret stumble into other relationships, he with Veronica Hamel's crisp and efficient doctor, she with John Shea's enthusiastic artist. Hal Linden gives a standout performance as Alda's happily promiscuous best friend. Rated PG-13 for language and sexual themes. 1988; 104m.

NEW WAVE COMEDY ★

DIR: Michael Kriegman. **CAST:** Mark Weiner, Eric Bogosian, Margaret Smith, John Kassir, Wayne Federman, Patty Rosborough, Jefferey Essman, Steve Sweeny.

A comical hodgepodge offering everything from breakdancing hand puppets to an overly worldly Barbie Doll impersonation. The only familiar faces in this eight-part comedy tape are those of Mark Weiner (*Saturday Night Live*), Margaret Smith, a deadpan stand-up comic who frequents the David Letterman set, and John Kassir, the 1985 comedy champ from *Star Search.* Strong language. 1986; 60m.

NEW YORK STORIES ★★★★½

DIR: Woody Allen, Francis Ford Coppola, Martin Scorsese. **CAST:** Woody Allen, Rosanna Arquette, Mia Farrow, Giancarlo Giannini, Julie Kavner, Heather McComb, Nick Nolte, Don Novello, Patrick O'Neal, Talia Shire.

Here's a wonderful creation that provides discriminating video viewers with three terrific movies for the price of one. Woody Allen's *Oedipus Wrecks* marks his long-awaited return to comedy. Starring Allen as a lawyer who cannot escape his mother's overbearing influence, it's a hilarious vignette. Francis Coppola's *Life Without Zoe* is a light but charming fantasy about a sophisticated youngster named Zoe (Heather McComb) and her adventures in New York City. The best of this splendid trio is Martin Scorsese's *Life Lessons*, about the obsessive love of a celebrated painter (Nick Nolte) for his protégée (Rosanna Arquette). Rated PG for profanity. 1989; 119m.

NICE DREAMS ★★★

DIR: Thomas Chong. **CAST:** Cheech and Chong, Evelyn Guerrero, Peewee Herman, Stacy Keach.

Cheech and Chong, the counterculture kings of drug-oriented comedy, haven't run out of steam yet. Their third feature film doesn't have quite as many classic comic gems as its predecessors, but it's more consistently entertaining. Rated R for nudity and profanity. 1981; 87m.

NICE GIRL LIKE ME, A ★

DIR: Desmond Davis. **CAST:** Barbara Ferris, Harry Andrews, Gladys Cooper.

A young woman (Barbara Ferris) straight out of boarding school decides to experience life firsthand. After the death of her diplomat father, she inherits an estate whose caretaker is a retired British seaman (Harry Andrews). Dated Sixties comedy that was considered risqué for its time, but now seems silly and contrived. Rated PG. 1969; 91m.

NICE GIRLS DON'T EXPLODE ★★

DIR: Chuck Martinez. **CAST:** Barbara Harris, Michelle Meyrink, William O'Leary, Wallace Shawn.

Droll, slow-moving comedy about a girl (Michelle Meyrink) who causes spontaneous combustion of objects around her when she's out on a date. William O'Leary as her current boyfriend is exceptional. Rated PG, the film contains some strong language and mild nudity. 1987; 92m.

NICK DANGER IN THE CASE OF THE MISSING YOLK

DIR: William Dear. **CAST:** Firesign Theatre Players, Wendy Cutler, Christy Kaatz.

The usually funny Firesign Theatre Players (Phil Austin, Peter Bergman, and Phil Proctor) don't quite make it with this one. A hillbilly family, the Yolks, are transported to a futuristic home. Private eye Nick Danger becomes involved with the family when their son runs away with a TV commercial star and both are kidnapped. 1983; 60m.

NIGHT AT THE OPERA, A ★★★★★

DIR: Sam Wood. **CAST:** The Marx Brothers, Margaret Dumont, Kitty Carlisle, Allan Jones, Sig Ruman.

Despite the songs and sappy love story, the Marx Brothers (minus Zeppo) are in peak form in this classic musical comedy, which co-stars the legendary Margaret Dumont. 1935; B&W; 92m.

NIGHT BEFORE, THE ★★★

DIR: Thom Eberhardt. **CAST:** Keanu Reeves, Lori Laughlin, Theresa Saldana, Trinidad Silva.

A senior prom date turns into a hilarious nightmare in this riveting, offbeat comedy. After waking up in an alley in East L.A., a young man (Keanu Reeves) finds his date and wallet missing along with his father's sports car. And then things get surreal—in the style of *After Hours*. Rated R for language and violence. 1988; 85m.

NIGHT IN CASABLANCA, A ★★★

DIR: Archie Mayo. **CAST:** The Marx Brothers, Charles Drake, Lisette Verea, Lois Collier.

Although the Marx Brothers' formula was wearing thin by 1946, Groucho's wisecracks and the incomparable antics of Chico and Harpo still carry the film. Joining forces to foil Nazi treasure thieves in post-WWII Casablanca, the brothers anarchize the staid Hotel Casablanca. 1946; B&W; 85m.

NIGHT IN THE LIFE OF JIMMY REARDON, A ★

DIR: William Richert. **CAST:** River Phoenix, Meredith Salenger, Ione Skye, Louanne, Ann Magnuson.

Jimmy Reardon is a teenage sex fiend in 1962 Evanston, Illinois. He sleeps with his best friend's girl; he sleeps with his mother's best friend; and he treats his own girl like dirt because she refuses to give in to his urges. Though promoted as a comedy, this flim is a stark view of American youth. Rated R for profanity and leering sexual content. 1988; 92m.

NIGHT OF THE LIVING BABES

DIR: Jon Valentine. **CAST:** Michelle McClellan, Connie Woods, Andrew Nichols.

Sexually saturated and totally idiotic film about two men who check out a new whorehouse only to be abducted by the prostitutes, tormented by strippers, and threatened by a transvestite. While this might be found on the comedy shelf in your local video store, it comes closer to soft-core porn. 1987; 60m.

NIGHT PATROL ★

DIR: Jackie Kong. **CAST:** Linda Blair, Pat Paulsen, Jaye P. Morgan, Jack Riley, Billy Barty, Murray Langston.

In this dumb variation on *Police Academy*, screenwriter Murray Langston plays a bumbling rookie policeman who doubles at night as "The Unknown Comic," cracking jokes in Los Angeles comedy clubs while wearing a paper bag over his head. The jokes often are offensive and the plot even worse. Rated R for the usual garbage. 1985; 84m.

NIGHT SHIFT ★★★★

DIR: Ron Howard. **CAST:** Henry Winkler, Shelley Long, Michael Keaton.

When a nerdish morgue attendant (Henry Winkler) gets talked into becoming a pimp by a sweet hooker (Shelley Long) and his crazed co-worker (Michael Keaton), the result is uproarious comedy. While the concept is a little weird, director Ron Howard packs it with so many laughs and such appealing characters that you can't help but like it. Rated R for nudity, profanity, sex, and violence. 1982; 105m.

NIGHT THEY RAIDED MINSKY'S, THE ★★★½

DIR: William Friedkin. **CAST:** Britt Ekland, Jason Robards Jr., Elliott Gould.

Director William Friedkin's tale of a religious girl's (Britt Ekland) involvement, much to her father's dismay, with a burlesque comic (Jason Robards). It's a nice look at what early burlesque was like, with good performances by all. Rated PG. 1968; 99m.

NIGHT TO REMEMBER, A (1943) ★★★★

DIR: Richard Wallace. **CAST:** Loretta Young, Brian Aherne, Jeff Donnell, William Wright, Sidney Toler, Gale Sondergaard.

This is a very interesting comedy-whodunit about a Greenwich Village mystery author and his wife who try to solve a real murder. Performances are wonderful and the direction is taut. 1943; B&W; 91m.

NINE LIVES OF FRITZ THE CAT ★★½

DIR: Robert Taylor. **CAST:** Animated.

A streetwise alley cat tries to escape his mundane existence in the sequel to the 1972 cult favorite, *Fritz the Cat.* Fritz is his usual witty, horny self. The animation is excellent and the film is written with a hip sense of humor. This is not Saturday-morning material, however, as there is a distinctly erotic tone to virtually every scene. Rated R for adult theme and language. 1974; 77m.

NINE TO FIVE ★★★★

DIR: Colin Higgins. **CAST:** Jane Fonda, Lily Tomlin, Dolly Parton, Dabney Coleman.

In this delightful comedy, Jane Fonda almost ends up playing third fiddle to two marvelous comediennes, Lily Tomlin and Dolly Parton. (That's right, Dolly Parton!) The gifted singer-songwriter makes one of the brightest acting debuts ever in this hilarious farce about three secretaries who decide to get revenge on their sexist, egomaniacal boss (Dabney Coleman). Rated PG. 1980; 110m.

1941

DIR: Steven Spielberg. **CAST:** John Belushi, Dan Aykroyd, Toshiro Mifune, Christopher Lee, Slim Pickens, Ned Beatty, John Candy, Nancy Allen, Tim Matheson, Murray Hamilton, Treat Williams.

Steven Spielberg laid his first and (so far) only multimillion-dollar egg with this unfunny what-if comedy about the Japanese attacking Los Angeles during World War II. An all-star cast is all but completely wasted in this—pardon the pun—bomb. Rated PG. 1979; 118m.

90 DAYS ★★★

DIR: Giles Walker. **CAST:** Stefas Wodoslavsky, Sam Grana.

A fine little comedy shot in documentary style. The narrator has sent for a Korean pen pal to come to be his wife in Canada. On the eve of her arrival, his best friend is thrown out by a live-in lover and lands on their doorstep. The resultant cultural differences are humorously explored. Not rated. 1986; 100m.

92 IN THE SHADE ★★★

DIR: Thomas McGuane. **CAST:** Peter Fonda, Warren Oates, Margot Kidder, Harry Dean Stanton, Burgess Meredith, Elizabeth Ashley, Sylvia Miles.

This wild and hilarious adaptation of first-time director Thomas McGuane's prize-winning novel concerns rival fishing-boat captains in

Florida. Entire cast is first-rate in this sleeper. Rated R. 1975; 93m.

NINOTCHKA ★★★★★
DIR: Ernst Lubitsch. **CAST:** Greta Garbo, Melvyn Douglas, Bela Lugosi.

"Garbo laughs," proclaimed the ads of its day; and so will you in this classic screen comedy. Greta Garbo is a soviet commissar sent to Paris to check on the lack of progress of three bumbling trade envoys who have been seduced by the decadent trappings of capitalism. Melvyn Douglas, as a Parisian playboy, meets Garbo at the Eiffel Tower and plans a seduction of his own, in this most joyous of Hollywood comedies. 1939; B&W; 110m.

NO MAN OF HER OWN ★★★★
DIR: Wesley Ruggles. **CAST:** Clark Gable, Carole Lombard.

A big-time gambler marries a local girl on a bet and tries to keep her innocent of his activities. This vintage film has everything the average film fan looks for—drama, romance, and comedy. 1932; B&W; 85m.

NO SMALL AFFAIR ★★½
DIR: Jerry Schatzberg. **CAST:** Jon Cryer, Demi Moore.

A 16-year-old amateur photographer named Charles Cummings (Jon Cryer) falls in love with an up-and-coming 23-year-old rock singer, Laura Victor (Demi Moore), and his passion for her eventually leads to the performer's big break. A mixture of delightfully clever and unabashedly stupid elements, *No Small Affair* ultimately fails. Rated R for nudity, violence, and profanity. 1984; 102m.

NO SURRENDER ★★
DIR: Peter Smith. **CAST:** Michael Angelis, Avis Bunnage, James Ellis, Tom Georgeson, Bernard Hill, Ray McAnally, Joanne Whalley, Elvis Costello.

Eccentric British film about a New Year's Eve party at a run-down nightclub in Liverpool. There is a moral subtext here, but little else that is engaging. Rated R. Contains violence and profanity. 1986; 100m.

NO TIME FOR SERGEANTS ★★★★
DIR: Mervyn LeRoy. **CAST:** Andy Griffith, Nick Adams, Myron McCormick, Murray Hamilton, Don Knotts.

In this hilarious film version of the Broadway play by Ira Levin, young Andy Griffith is superb as a country boy drafted into the service. You'll scream with laughter as good-natured Will Stockdale (as portrayed by Andy on stage as well as here) proceeds to make a complete shambles of the U.S. Air Force through nothing more than sheer ignorance. 1957; B&W; 119m.

NOBODY'S FOOL ★
DIR: Evelyn Purcell. **CAST:** Rosanna Arquette, Eric Roberts, Mare Winningham, Jim Youngs, Louise Fletcher.

Despite its pedigree—a screenplay by playwright Beth Henley *(Crimes of the Heart)*—this film is a real disappointment that wastes the talents of its stars, Rosanna Arquette and Eric Roberts. Arquette plays a small-town klutz who is fated to fall in love with the lighting director (Roberts) of a traveling theatrical company. Because both characters are such oddballs, we couldn't care less whether they get together or not. Rated PG-13 for mild violence. 1986; 107m.

NOBODY'S PERFEKT ★
DIR: Peter Bonerz. **CAST:** Gabe Kaplan, Alex Karras, Robert Klein, Susan Clark, Paul Stewart, Alex Rocco.

Three friends all undergoing psychoanalysis (Gabe Kaplan, Robert Klein, and Alex Karras) decide to extort $650.00 from the city of Miami to pay for their car, which was totaled because they ran into a large pothole. Along the way, they become heroes by capturing armored-car robbers. This unfunny comedy is one embarrassing flat joke after another. 1981; 96m.

NOCTURNA ★
DIR: Harry Tampa. **CAST:** Nai Bonet, John Carradine, Yvonne De Carlo, Sy Richardson.

This fourth-rate imitation of *Old Dracula* and *Love at First Bite* has Dracula's granddaughter tiring of Transylvania and moving to Manhattan, with her grandfather in pursuit. Bet you can't guess who John Carradine plays. (Oh, you did.) Pretty feeble, though *David Letterman* regular Brother Theodore provides a few laughs. Rated R for nudity. 1979; 85m.

NORMAN CONQUESTS, THE EPISODE 1: TABLE MANNERS ★★★½
DIR: Herbert Wise. **CAST:** Richard Briers, Penelope Keith, Tom Conti, David Troughton, Fiona Walker, Penelope Wilton.

Alan Ayckbourn's clever trilogy is set in a family home in a small English town. The three segments each take place in a different part of the house but encompass the same span of time. Furthermore, each part is complete in itself, but blends with the others for a delightful experience. In the dining room, Norman (Tom Conti) tries to seduce his two sisters-in-law and draws the rest of the family into the tangle with surprising results. Sara (Penelope Keith) is a treat as she tries to organize meals and control the others. 1980; 108m.

NORMAN CONQUESTS, THE EPISODE 2: LIVING TOGETHER ★★★½
DIR: Herbert Wise. **CAST:** Richard Briers, Penelope Keith, Tom Conti, David Troughton, Fiona Walker, Penelope Wilton.

The parlor is the setting as the family gathers for the weekend. Norman (Tom Conti) keeps everyone on the run as he drinks, manipulates, and seduces. 1980; 93m.

NORMAN CONQUESTS, THE EPISODE 3: ROUND AND ROUND THE GARDEN ★★★½
DIR: Herbert Wise. **CAST:** Richard Briers, Penelope Keith, Tom Conti, David Troughton, Fiona Walker, Penelope Wilton.

A garden setting rounds out a zany weekend at an English house. As Norman (Tom Conti) pursues his wife's sister, Tom (David Troughton), the visiting vet, misinterprets the goings-on and embarrasses himself in the bargain. 1980; 106m.

NORMAN LOVES ROSE ★★★½
DIR: Henri Safran. **CAST:** Carol Kane, Tony Owen, Warren Mitchell.

In this Australian-made comedy, Tony Owen plays a love-struck teenager who is enamored of his sister-in-law, Carol Kane. When she gets pregnant, the question of paternity arises. Lots of laughs in this one! Rated R. 1982; 98m.

NOT FOR PUBLICATION ★★½
DIR: Paul Bartel. **CAST:** Nancy Allen, David Naughton, Laurence Luckinbill.

A writer and a photographer attempt to break out of sleazy tabloid journalism by doing an investigative piece about high-level corruption. Amusing story starts off well but loses momentum. Playful, but not as distinctive as Paul Bartel's other works, such as *Eating Raoul* and *Lust in the Dust*. Rated PG for profanity. 1984; 87m.

NOTHING PERSONAL ★
DIR: George Bloomfield. **CAST:** Donald Sutherland, Suzanne Somers, Lawrence Dane, Roscoe Lee Browne, Dabney Coleman, Saul Rubinek, John Dehner.

A romantic comedy about the fight to stop the slaughter of baby seals? This is how Suzanne Somers decided to launch her motion picture career? Sure, Donald Sutherland is a dependable leading man, but even he looks silly in this mishmash of message and entertainment. It should have been called *Nothing Playing*. Rated PG. 1980; 97m.

NOTHING SACRED ★★★★
DIR: William Wellman. **CAST:** Carole Lombard, Fredric March, Walter Connolly, Charles Winninger.

Ace scriptwriter Ben Hecht's cynical mixture of slapstick and bitterness, perfectly performed by Fredric March and Carole Lombard, makes this satirical comedy a real winner. Vermont innocent, Lombard, is mistakenly thought to be dying of a rare disease. A crack New York reporter (March) pulls out all the stops in exploiting her to near national sainthood. The boy-bites-man scene is priceless. 1937; 75m.

NUMBER ONE OF THE SECRET SERVICE ★★★
DIR: Lindsay Shonteff. **CAST:** Nicky Henson, Richard Todd, Aimi MacDonald, Geoffrey Keen, Sue Lloyd, Dudley Sutton, Jon Pertwee.

In this enjoyable spoof of James Bond films, secret agent Charles Blind attempts to stop evil Arthur Loveday from killing prominent international financiers. Rated PG. 1970; 87m.

NUTCASE
DIR: Roger Donaldson. **CAST:** Nevan Rowe, Ian Watkin, Michael Wilson, Ian Mune.

The kids are the only ones who aren't complete idiots in this silly movie. The plot, which is extremely far-fetched, has a group of wacky villains threatening to blow up New Zealand's volcanoes if they don't receive $5 million. 1983; 49m.

NUTTY PROFESSOR, THE ★★★★
DIR: Jerry Lewis. **CAST:** Jerry Lewis, Stella Stevens, Kathleen Freeman.

Jerry Lewis's funniest self-directed comedy, this release—a takeoff on Robert Louis Stevenson's *Dr. Jekyll and Mr. Hyde*—is about a klutz who becomes a smoothie when he drinks a magic formula. Reportedly, this was Lewis's put-down of former partner Dean Martin. 1963; 107m.

O.C. & STIGGS ★★★
DIR: Robert Altman. **CAST:** Daniel H. Jenkins, Neill Barry, Paul Dooley, Jane Curtin, Martin Mull, Dennis Hopper, Ray Walston, Jon Cryer, Melvin Van Peebles.

Inspired by characters from *National Lampoon*, this offbeat film has two teenagers whose goal is to make life completely miserable for the local bigot (Paul Dooley), an obnoxious insurance magnate. Jane Curtin is the alcoholic wife with the running gag of finding unusual hiding places for her bottle. Another energetic iconoclastic comedy from Robert Altman. Not rated. 1987; 109m.

ODD COUPLE, THE ★★★★
DIR: Gene Saks. **CAST:** Walter Matthau, Jack Lemmon, John Fiedler, Herb Edelman.

Walter Matthau as Oscar Madison and Jack Lemmon as Felix Unger bring Neil Simon's delightful stage play to life in this comedy. They play two divorced men who try living together. The biggest laughs come from the fact that Felix is "Mr. Clean" and Oscar is a total slob—they're constantly getting on each other's nerves. Rated G. 1968; 105m.

ODD JOB, THE ★★½
DIR: Peter Medak. **CAST:** Graham Chapman, David Jason, Diana Quick, Bill Paterson, Simon Williams.

Monty Python's Graham Chapman wrote and starred in this comedy about a depressed businessman who hires a hitman to kill him. When he decides that life is worth living after all, he finds that he can't cancel his contract. Full of oddball characters and silly situations, but somehow it never builds up a full head of steam. Unrated. 1978; 86m.

ODDBALLS
DIR: Miklos Lente. **CAST:** Foster Brooks, Michael Macdonald.

Beefing up character actor Foster Brooks's role might have saved this confusing comedy, but we doubt it. Brooks plays the alcoholic owner of a boys' summer camp. Naturally, his camp is directly across from Camp Bountiful, which is a retreat for sexy young women. The plot (?!) thickens when Brooks agrees to sell his camp to a man who'd like to use it for a shopping mall. Rated PG for obscenities and sexual situations. 1984; 92m.

OFF BEAT ★★
DIR: Michael Dinner. **CAST:** Meg Tilly, Judge Reinhold, Cleavant Derricks, Harvey Keitel.

This attempt at an old-fashioned romantic comedy succeeds as a romance, but as a comedy, it elicits only an occasional chuckle. One gains instant sympathy for captivating Meg Tilly's vulnerable big-city police officer. She finds herself falling for her partner, Judge Reinhold, while trying out for a mixed precinct police dance program. Rated PG. 1986; 100m.

OFF LIMITS ★½
DIR: George Marshall. **CAST:** Bob Hope, Mickey Rooney, Marilyn Maxwell, Marvin Miller.

Marilyn Maxwell adds a little "oomph" to this otherwise silly story of two army buddies and their inane and seldom hilarious antics. Yet another of those limp comedies about an ineffectual loser who winds up a boxing contender. Only the presence of Bob Hope and Mickey Rooney makes this film worth watching, and both are represented on video in much better films. 1953; B&W; 89m.

OFF THE MARK ★★★
DIR: Bill Berry. **CAST:** Mark Neely, Terry Farrell, Virginia Capers, Jon Cypher, Barry Corbin.

This off-the-wall comedy centers around Mark Neely, who once hosted a Russian boy (Terry Farrell) in his home for a year. Now they're both grown up and competing in a triathlon. The two leads are a delight. 1986; 81m.

OFF THE WALL
DIR: Rick Friedberg. **CAST:** Paul Sorvino, Patrick Cassidy, Rosanna Arquette, Billy Hufsey, Mickey Gilley, Monte Markham.

A Tennessee speed demon (Rosanna Arquette) picks up two handsome hitchhikers (Billy Hufsey and Patrick Cassidy) and leaves them to take the rap for her joyriding. When they're sentenced to six months in Snake Canyon Prison, they must deal with Arquette's attempts to rescue them. This low-budget farce would be best forgotten. Rated R. 1982; 86m.

OH! CALCUTTA! ★★
DIR: Guillaume Martin Aucion. **CAST:** Raina Barrett, Mark Dempsey, Samantha Harper, Bill Macy.

Only historians of the 1960s will have any reason to watch this, a videotaped performance of the musical revue that became infamous because it dealt with sex and featured onstage nudity. The show was never erotic to begin with, and none of the sketches retain any humor or bite, a disappointment considering that the writers included Sam Shepard, John Lennon, Jules Feiffer, and Dan Greenberg. Unrated. 1972; 108m.

OH DAD, POOR DAD—MAMA'S HUNG YOU IN THE CLOSET AND I'M FEELING SO SAD ★★★½
DIR: Richard Quine. **CAST:** Rosalind Russell, Robert Morse, Barbara Harris, Jonathan Winters, Lionel Jeffries.

A cult favorite, and deservedly so. The plot has something to do with an odd young man (Robert Morse) whose mother (Rosalind Russell) drags him off on a vacation in the tropics with the boy's dead father. Morse excels in this unique, well-written, often hilarious film. 1967; 86m.

OH, GOD! ★★★★
DIR: Carl Reiner. **CAST:** George Burns, John Denver, Teri Garr, Ralph Bellamy.

God is made visible to a supermarket manager in this modern-day fantasy. The complications that result make for some predictable humor, but the story is kept flowing by some inspired casting. Ageless George Burns is a perfect vision of a God for Everyman in his tennis shoes and golf hat. John Denver exudes the right degree of naïveté as the put-upon grocer. Rated PG. 1977; 104m.

OH, GOD! BOOK II ★★
DIR: Gilbert Cates. **CAST:** George Burns, Suzanne Pleshette, David Birney, Louanne, Howard Duff.

George Burns, as God, returns in this fair sequel and enters a little girl's life, assigning her the task of coming up with a slogan that will revive interest in him. So she comes up with "Think God" and begins her campaign. It's passable family fare. Rated PG. 1980; 94m.

OH, GOD, YOU DEVIL! ★★★½
DIR: Paul Bogart. **CAST:** George Burns, Ted Wass, Roxanne Hart, Ron Silver, Eugene Roche.

George Burns is back as the wisecracking, cigar-smoking deity. Only this time he plays a dual role—appearing as the devil. Ted Wass is the songwriter who strikes a Faustian bargain with Burns's bad side. This delightful comedy-with-a-moral is guaranteed to lift your spirits. Rated PG for suggested sex and profanity. 1984; 96m.

OKLAHOMA ANNIE ★
DIR: R. G. Springsteen. **CAST:** Judy Canova, John Russell, Grant Withers, Allen Jenkins, Almira Sessions, Minerva Urecal.

This moronic movie is little more than an excuse for Judy Canova to ham it up and inflict a few tunes on the audience as she chases the varmints out of town and brings decency to her community. Mercifully, this was one of the last films Canova made America suffer through and is almost redeemed by a great cast of familiar character actors. 1952; 90m.

ON APPROVAL ★★★
DIR: Clive Brook. **CAST:** Beatrice Lillie, Clive Brook, Googie Withers, Roland Culver.

Former Sherlock Holmes Clive Brook displays a confident hand at directing in this enjoyable farce about women who exchange boyfriends. Fun and breezy with terrific performances by some of England's best talents, this film gave beloved Beatrice Lillie one of her best screen roles and proved popular on both sides of the Atlantic. 1943; B&W; 80m.

ONCE BITTEN ★★★
DIR: Howard Storm. **CAST:** Lauren Hutton, Jim Carrey, Karen Kopins, Cleavon Little.

Sly little vampire film about an ancient bloodsucker (Lauren Hutton) who can remain young and beautiful only by periodically supping on youthful male virgins. Likable Jim Carrey is her latest target, and their first few encounters (three's the magic number) leave him with an appetite for raw hamburgers and a tendency to sleep during the day so as to avoid sunlight. Rated PG-13 for sexual situations. 1985; 92m.

ONCE UPON A HONEYMOON ★★½
DIR: Leo McCarey. **CAST:** Ginger Rogers, Cary Grant, Walter Slezak, Albert Dekker, Albert Basserman, Harry Shannon, John Banner.

In this travesty, one Cary Grant preferred to forget, he plays a newspaperman trying to get innocent stripteaser Ginger Rogers out of Europe as the German army advances. Complicating matters is her marriage to Nazi officer Walter Slezak. This amusing adventure-comedy is a bit dated, but Grant fans won't mind. 1942; B&W; 117m.

ONE CRAZY SUMMER ★★½
DIR: Savage Steve Holland. **CAST:** John Cusack, Demi Moore, Curtis Armstrong, Bobcat Goldthwait, Joe Flaherty, Tom Villard.

Star John Cusack and writer-director Savage Steve Holland of *Better Off Dead* are reunited in this weird, slightly sick, and sometimes stupidly funny comedy about a college hopeful (Cusack) who must learn about love to gain entrance to an institute of higher learning. If you accept that silly premise, then you may get a few laughs out of *One Crazy Summer*. Rated PG. 1986; 94m.

ONE MORE SATURDAY NIGHT ★★★½
DIR: Dennis Klein. **CAST:** Al Franken, Tom Davis, Moira Harris.

Al Franken and Tom Davis, who were writers and semiregulars on the original *Saturday Night Live* TV show, star in this enjoyable comedy, which they also wrote, about the problems encountered by adults and teenagers when trying to get a date on the most important night of the week. In its humane and decidedly offbeat way, *One More Saturday Night* is about the human condition in all its funny/sad complexity. Rated R for profanity and simulated sex. 1986; 95m.

ONE RAINY AFTERNOON ★★
DIR: Rowland V. Lee. **CAST:** Francis Lederer, Ida Lupino, Roland Young, Hugh Herbert, Erik Rhodes, Mischa Auer.

Silly movie about a young man who causes a furor when he kisses the wrong girl during a performance in the theater. It's a pretty slight premise to build a film on, but under the skillful hands of director Rowland V. Lee (*The Count of Monte Cristo*, *Son of Frankenstein*), it becomes entertaining fare. A fine supporting cast helps flesh out the thin story, and a young Ida Lupino makes for a lovely leading lady. 1936; B&W; 79m.

ONE TOUCH OF VENUS ★★
DIR: William A. Seiter. **CAST:** Robert Walker, Ava Gardner.

The Pygmalion myth gets the Hollywood treatment, long before *My Fair Lady*, although this is a wee bit diluted. Robert Walker plays a department store window decorator who becomes smitten, predictably, when a display statue of Venus comes to life in the form of Ava Gardner. The potentially entertaining premise is left flat by a script that lacks originality and wit. 1948; B&W; 90m.

ONE, TWO, THREE ★★★½
DIR: Billy Wilder. **CAST:** James Cagney, Arlene Francis, Horst Buchholz, Pamela Tiffin, Lilo Pulver, Red Buttons.

James Cagney's "retirement" film (and his only movie with famed director Billy Wilder) is a nonstop, madcap assault on the audience. Wilder's questionable humor and odd plot about the clash between capitalism and communism and its effect on a young couple could have spelled catastrophe for any other leading man, but veteran Cagney pulls it off with style. 1961; B&W; 108m.

ONLY TWO CAN PLAY ★★★½
DIR: Sidney Gilliat. **CAST:** Peter Sellers, Mai Zetterling, Richard Attenborough, Virginia Maskell.

Peter Sellers is fabulous as a frustrated but determined Don Juan with aspirations of wooing society woman Mai Zetterling. As in so many of his roles, Sellers is funny and appealing in every move and mood. And Zetterling is the perfect choice for the haughty object of his attentions. 1962; 106m.

ONLY WITH MARRIED MEN ★★
DIR: Jerry Paris. **CAST:** David Birney, Michele Lee, Dom DeLuise, Judy Carne, Gavin MacLeod.

This TV movie is a pleasant yet thoroughly predictable light sex comedy about a woman (Michele Lee) who decides she will only date married men. After an initial mixup at an attorney's office she mistakes a bachelor (David Birney) for his married partner. 1974; 74m.

OPERATION PETTICOAT ★★★★
DIR: Blake Edwards. **CAST:** Cary Grant, Tony Curtis, Dina Merrill, Gene Evans, Arthur O'Connell, Dick Sargent.

The ageless Cary Grant stars with Tony Curtis in this wacky service comedy. They are captain and first officer of a submarine that undergoes a madcap series of misadventures during World War II. Their voyage across the Pacific is further complicated when a group of Navy women is forced to join the crew. 1959; 124m.

OUR MISS BROOKS (TELEVISION SERIES) ★★★
DIR: Al Lewis. **CAST:** Eve Arden, Gale Gordon, Robert Rockwell, Richard Crenna, Gloria McMillan, Jane Morgan.

Desilu, basking in the success of *I Love Lucy,* adapted this likable vehicle for comedienne Eve Arden. The show, previously a hit on radio, stars Arden as Connie Brooks, a well-meaning English teacher at Madison High. Miss Brooks goes to extremes to earn the affection—or even the attention—of biology instructor Philip Boynton (Robert Rockwell). She constantly clashes with the blustering principal, Osgood Conklin (Gale Gordon). Richard Crenna is endearingly goofy as problem student Walter Denton. 1952–1957; 30 minutes each episode.

OUR RELATIONS ★★★½
DIR: Harry Lachman. **CAST:** Stan Laurel, Oliver Hardy, James Finlayson, Alan Hale, Sidney Toler.

Stan Laurel and Oliver Hardy play two sets of twins. One set are sailors; the other are happily married civilians. When the boys' ship docks in the same city, a hilarious case of mistaken identity occurs. Highly enjoyable, the film doesn't lag at all. It features excellent performances by James Finlayson, Alan Hale, and Sidney Toler. 1936; B&W; 74m.

OUT OF CONTROL
DIR: Allan Holzman. **CAST:** Martin Hewitt, Betsy Russell, Jim Youngs.

Filmed in Yugoslavia and the USA, this movie seems unable to decide whether it should be a comedy, a romance, or a thriller. A group of teenagers take off for an exciting weekend on a private island. When their plane crashes, they must survive on a seemingly deserted island. Rated R for obscenities, nudity, and violence. 1984; 78m.

OUT OF THE BLUE ★★★
DIR: Leigh Jason. **CAST:** George Brent, Virginia Mayo, Ann Dvorak, Turhan Bey, Carole Landis.

A not-very-innocent young woman passes out in a naïve married man's apartment, making all sorts of trouble in this entertaining romantic comedy of errors and such. 1947; B&W; 84m.

OUT OF TOWNERS, THE ★★★
DIR: Arthur Hiller. **CAST:** Jack Lemmon, Sandy Dennis, Sandy Baron, Anne Meara, Billy Dee Williams.

Jack Lemmon and Sandy Dennis star in this Neil Simon comedy of a New York City vacation gone awry. It's a good idea that doesn't come off as well as one would have hoped. Rated PG for language. 1970; 97m.

OUTLAW BLUES ★★½
DIR: Richard Heffron. **CAST:** Peter Fonda, Susan Saint James, James Callahan, Michael Lerner.

Yet another of Peter Fonda's harmless but rather bland light comedies. He's an ex-con with a talent for song-writing but little in the way of industry smarts; he naïvely allows established country-western star James Callahan to make off with a few hits. Aided by backup singer Susan Saint James, in a charming little part, Fonda figures out how to outfox the Establishment and succeed on his own. Rated PG for light violence and brief nudity. 1977; 100m.

OUTRAGEOUS ★★★★
DIR: Richard Benner. **CAST:** Craig Russell, Hollis McLaren, Richert Easley.

A very offbeat and original comedy drama concerning a gay nightclub performer's relationship with a pregnant mental patient. A different kind of love story, told with taste and compassion. Female impersonator Craig Russell steals the show. Take a chance on this one. Rated R. 1977; 100m.

OUTRAGEOUS FORTUNE ★★★★
DIR: Arthur Hiller. **CAST:** Bette Midler, Shelley Long, Peter Coyote, Robert Prosky, John Schuck, George Carlin.

Yet another delightfully inventive adult comedy from Disney's Touchstone arm, highlighted by a show-stealing performance by the Mae West of the 1980s: Bette Midler. Her strutting, strident would-be actress is a scream, a word that also describes the level at which she delivers her rapid-fire dialogue. Rated R for profanity. 1987; 100m.

OUTTAKES ★
DIR: Jack M. Sell. **CAST:** Forrest Tucker, Bobbi Weyler, Joleen Lutz.

Forrest Tucker is the narrator of this collection of blackouts and vignettes, but he would have been better advised to just lend his name to the production and not appear at all. Stupid beyond belief. Not rated, but contains sex, nudity, ridiculous violence, language, and questionable taste. 1985; 75m.

OVER THE BROOKLYN BRIDGE ★★½
DIR: Menahem Golan. **CAST:** Elliott Gould, Shelley Winters, Sid Caesar, Carol Kane, Burt Young, Margaux Hemingway.

Elliott Gould stars in this occasionally interesting but mostly uneven slice-of-life story about a slovenly, diabetic Jewish luncheonette owner who dreams of getting out by buying a restaurant in downtown Manhattan. Standing in the way are his strict but loony relatives and his chic fashion-model girlfriend, who isn't Jewish. Rated R for nudity and profanity. 1983; 108m.

OVERBOARD ★
DIR: Garry Marshall. **CAST:** Goldie Hawn, Kurt Russell, Edward Herrmann, Katherine Helmond.

The irresistible Goldie Hawn can't even begin to save this wreck of a movie about a haughty heiress who falls off her yacht and loses her memory. Muscle-bound Kurt Russell plays the penniless carpenter who devises a scam to benefit from her amnesia. Sluggish. Rated PG. 1988; 106m.

OWL AND THE PUSSYCAT, THE ★★★★
DIR: Herbert Ross. **CAST:** Barbra Streisand, George Segal, Robert Klein.

Barbra Streisand plays a street-smart but under-educated prostitute who teams up with intellectual snob and bookstore clerk George Segal. The laughs abound as the two express themselves, through numerous debates. Rated R. 1970; 95m.

PACK UP YOUR TROUBLES ★★★
DIR: George Marshall. **CAST:** Stan Laurel, Oliver Hardy.

Stan Laurel and Oliver Hardy join the army in World War I, with the usual disastrous results. After being discharged, they assume responsibility for a fallen comrade's young daughter and search for her grandparents. The plot line and scripting aren't as solid as in other films, but the boys squeeze out every laugh possible. 1932; B&W; 68m.

PADDY ★★½
DIR: Daniel Haller. **CAST:** Des Cave, Milo O'Shea, Peggy Cass.

Excellent performances by all the actors, especially Des Cave in the title role, cannot save this rather confused coming-of-age comedy. Despite moments of true hilarity, the film remains at best mildly amusing. 1969; 97m.

PALEFACE, THE ★★★★
DIR: Norman Z. McLeod. **CAST:** Bob Hope, Jane Russell, Robert Armstrong.

Hope stars as a cowardly dentist who marries Calamity Jane (Jane Russell in rare form) and becomes, thanks to her quick draw, a celebrated gunslinger. It inspired a sequel, *Son of Paleface*, and a remake, *The Shakiest Gun in the West*, with Don Knotts, but the original is still tops. 1948; 91m.

PALM BEACH STORY, THE ★★★★

DIR: Preston Sturges. **CAST:** Claudette Colbert, Joel McCrea, Rudy Vallee, Mary Astor, Sig Arno, William Demarest, Franklin Pangborn, Jimmy Conlin.

Preston Sturges was perhaps the greatest of all American writer-directors. This light story of an engineer's wife (Claudette Colbert) who takes a vacation from marriage in sunny Florida and encounters one of the oddest groupings of talented characters ever assembled may well be his best film. 1942; B&W; 90m.

PANAMA LADY ★★

DIR: Jack B. Hively. **CAST:** Lucille Ball, Allan "Rocky" Lane, Donald Briggs, Evelyn Brent, Abner Biberman.

Lucille Ball does her best to liven up this tired story about a saloon dancer stuck in the tropics with her pick of the local sweat-soaked swains. Future Saturday-matinee cowboy favorite Allan "Rocky" Lane plays the two-fisted hombre who whisks everybody's favorite redhead off to the romantic oil fields in the jungle that he calls home. This is a remake of *Panama Flo* (1932). 1939; B&W; 65m.

PANDEMONIUM ★★★

DIR: Alfred Sole. **CAST:** Carol Kane, Tom Smothers, Debralee Scott, Candy Azzara, Miles Chapin, Tab Hunter.

After a mass murder of cheerleaders in 1962 and continued attacks on cheerleading camps across the nation, there is only one place left to learn—Bambi's Cheerleading School. In this parody of slasher movies, Carol Kane steals the show as Candy, a girl with supernatural powers who just wants to have fun and fit in. Tom Smothers is a displaced Canadian Mountie; Paul Reubens (currently Pee-Wee Herman) plays his assistant. Rated PG for obscenities. 1980; 82m.

PAPER MOON ★★★★★

DIR: Peter Bogdanovich. **CAST:** Ryan O'Neal, Tatum O'Neal, Madeline Kahn, John Hillerman.

Critic-turned-director Peter Bogdanovich ended his four-film winning streak—which included *Targets*, *The Last Picture Show*, and *What's Up Doc?*—with this comedy, starring Ryan O'Neal and Tatum O'Neal as a con man and a kid in the 1930s who get involved in some pretty wild predicaments and meet up with a variety of wacky characters. It's delightful entertainment from beginning to end. Rated PG. 1973; B&W; 102m.

PARADISE MOTEL ★★★

DIR: Cary Medoway. **CAST:** Gary Herschberger, Robert Krantz, Joanna Leigh Stack.

Another teen romp, but with a surprise: the appealing cast can act. Gary Hershberger is a student whose father keeps moving the family around in pursuit of his get-rich schemes. The latest venture is the Paradise Motel. To gain acceptance quickly at his new school, Hershberger loans out one of the rooms to the class stud. Rated R for language and nudity. 1985; 87m.

PARADISIO ★½

DIR: none credited. **CAST:** Arthur Howard, Eva Waegner.

One of dozens of early Sixties nudie movies that went to ridiculous lengths to show naked women. Like many others, this one revolves around a pair of magic glasses that enable its wearer to see through clothing. Unlike most of the genre, though, it has a ridiculously convoluted spy plot along with the nudity. Star Arthur Howard was Leslie's brother. 1961; B&W; 82m.

PARAMEDICS ★★½

DIR: Stuart Margolin. **CAST:** George Newbern, Christopher McDonald, Lawrence Hilton-Jacobs, John Pleshette, James Noble, John P. Ryan.

A good guys–bad guys flick disguised as a sex comedy. Two paramedics are transferred to a nasty part of the city where a vicious gang is killing people to sell their organs. The comedy comes in the form of a mysterious beauty with a rather fatal sex drive. Rated PG-13 for sexual references. 1987; 91m.

PARAMOUNT COMEDY THEATRE, VOL. 1: WELL DEVELOPED ★★★★

DIR: Joe Hostettler. **CAST:** Howie Mandel, Bob Saget, Judy Carter, Philip Wellford, Bruce Mahler.

Howie Mandel hosts this very funny comic review filmed live at the Magic Club in Hermosa Beach, California. A big plus is that the material is new, and in many cases it is quite hilarious. Bob Saget is very funny with a fast-paced off-the-wall delivery. Judy Carter combines magic and comedy. Bruce Mahler uses an accordion and piano effectively. Our favorite is Philip Wellford, whose juggling and unicycle skills are perfect complements for his witty delivery. There is some adult-oriented material. 1986; 65m.

PARAMOUNT COMEDY THEATRE, VOL. 2: DECENT EXPOSURES ★★★

DIR: Joe Hostettler. **CAST:** Howie Mandel, Marsha Warfield, Doug Ferrari, Paul Feig, Joe Alaskey.

Howie Mandel once again hosts live performances by four up-and-coming comedians. Marsha Warfield, from the *Night Court* cast, is a standout. Doug Ferrari makes a couple of good observations on modern hangups. Paul Feig comes off as a well-dressed Pee-wee Herman. The best performance is by Joe Alaskey. His impressions are outstanding. 1987; 67m.

PARDON US ★★★★

DIR: James Parrott. **CAST:** Stan Laurel, Oliver Hardy, Wilfred Lucas.

Stan Laurel and Oliver Hardy are sent to prison for selling home-brewed beer. They encounter all the usual prison stereotypical characters and play off them to delightful comedy effect. During an escape, they put on black faces and pick cotton along with blacks and Ollie sings "Lazy Moon." 1931; B&W; 55m.

PARENTHOOD ★★★★★

DIR: Ron Howard. **CAST:** Steve Martin, Mary Steenburgen, Tom Hulce, Jason Robards Jr., Dianne Wiest, Rick Moranis, Martha Plimpton, Keanu Reeves.

Director Ron Howard returns to the kind of movie he does best, with emphasis on character and comedy, and the result is a heartwarming and hilarious winner. Steve Martin and Mary Steenburgen are superb as model parents coping with career and kids. There's fine support from Rick Moranis as a yuppie who pushes his three-year-old daughter to learn Kafka and karate, Dianne Wiest as a Woodstock-goer coping with three troubled teens, and Jason Robards as the granddad who discovers that parenthood is a job for life. Rated PG. 1989; 110m.

PARENTS ★

DIR: Bob Balaban. **CAST:** Randy Quaid, Mary Beth Hurt, Sandy Dennis, Bryan Madorsky.

Actor-turned-director Bob Balaban has created a black comedy in search of laughs. It's a slick, gross-out movie about a cannibalistic couple and their relationship with their suspicious young son. The film aspires to the rarefied air of low-budget camp like *Eating Raoul*, but it falls far short. Rated R. 1989; 90m.

PARIS HOLIDAY ★★

DIR: Gerd Oswald. **CAST:** Bob Hope, Fernandel, Anita Ekberg, Martha Hyer, Preston Sturges.

Film-within-a-film show business story featuring Bob Hope and French comic Fernandel never gets off the ground. Statuesque Anita Ekberg succeeds in diverting attention from the two uncomfortable comedians and the hokey subplot involving a gang of counterfeiters. 1957; 101m.

PARIS WHEN IT SIZZLES ★★★
DIR: Richard Quine. **CAST:** William Holden, Audrey Hepburn, Noel Coward, Gregoire Aslan, Marlene Dietrich.
Uneven story-within-a-story about a screenwriter (William Holden) who "creates" a Parisian fantasyland for himself and the assistant (Audrey Hepburn) with whom he's fallen in love. As the story progresses, they—and the viewer—have an increasingly difficult time distinguishing fact from scripted fiction. 1954; 110m.

PARLOR, BEDROOM AND BATH ★★★
DIR: Edward Sedgwick. **CAST:** Buster Keaton, Charlotte Greenwood, Reginald Denny, Cliff Edwards, Dorothy Christy, Joan Peers, Sally Eilers, Natalie Moorhead, Edward Brophy.
Some genuine belly laughs buoy this slight comedy about a bewildered bumpkin (Buster Keaton) at the mercy of some society wackos. Charlotte Greenwood works well with the Great Stone Face. 1932; B&W; 75m.

PARTNERS ★★★
DIR: James Burrows. **CAST:** Ryan O'Neal, John Hurt.
Ryan O'Neal and John Hurt are two undercover detectives assigned to pose as lovers in order to track down the murderer of a gay man in this warm, funny, and suspenseful comedy-drama written by Francis Veber (*La Cage aux Folles*). Rated R for nudity, profanity, violence, and adult themes. 1982; 98m.

PARTY ANIMAL
DIR: Harvey Hart. **CAST:** Mathew Causey, Robin Harlan.
Not even a great rock soundtrack can save this despicable piece of sludge. Another one of those sex-crazed frat-boy films—a genre that could use a moratorium. Rated R for sex, nudity, and profanity. 1983; 78m.

PARTY CAMP ★★
DIR: Gary Graver. **CAST:** Andrew Ross, Kerry Brennan, Peter Jason.
Andrew Ross takes a job as a camp counselor with the object of turning the militarylike operation into party time for all. Just another teen romp with the usual caricatures, obligatory nudity, and titillation. Rated R. 1986; 96m.

PASS THE AMMO ★★★½
DIR: David Beaird. **CAST:** Tim Curry, Bill Paxton, Linda Kozlowski, Annie Potts, Glenn Withrow, Dennis Burkley.
Tim Curry's deliciously scheming evangelist is merely one of the delights in this inventive satire of television sermonizing. Bill Paxton and Linda Kozlowski play a couple of good ol' folks who plot to "steal back" some inheritance money the televangelist bilked from her family. Rated PG-13 for language and violence. 1987; 93m.

PASSPORT TO PIMLICO ★★★½
DIR: Henry Cornelius. **CAST:** Margaret Rutherford, Stanley Holloway, Hermione Baddeley, Basil Radford, Naunton Wayne.
One of a number of first-rate comedies turned out by Britain in the wake of World War II. A salty group of characters raise hell when they invoke an ancient treaty giving them the right to form their own self-governing enclave smack in the middle of London. Sly Margaret Rutherford and Stanley Holloway divide comedy chores with cricket-crazy Basil Radford and Naunton Wayne. 1948; B&W; 85m.

PAT AND MIKE ★★★
DIR: George Cukor. **CAST:** Spencer Tracy, Katharine Hepburn, Aldo Ray, William Ching.
Cameo appearances by a host of tennis and golf greats, including Babe Didrikson and Don Budge, stud this five-iron tale of athlete Katharine Hepburn and promoter-manager Spencer Tracy at odds with each other on a barnstorming golf and tennis tour. As always, the Tracy and Hepburn chemistry assures good comedy. 1952; B&W; 95m.

PATERNITY ★★½
DIR: David Steinberg. **CAST:** Burt Reynolds, Beverly D'Angelo, Norman Fell, Elizabeth Ashley, Lauren Hutton.

Buddy Evans (Burt Reynolds) decides to have a son—without the commitment of marriage—and recruits a music student working as a waitress (Beverly D'Angelo) to bear his child in this adult comedy. The first two-thirds provide belly laughs and chuckles. The problem comes with the unoriginal and predictable romantic ending. Rated PG because of dialogue involving sex and childbirth. 1981; 94m.

PATSY, THE ★★½
DIR: Jerry Lewis. **CAST:** Jerry Lewis, Everett Sloane, Ina Balin, Keenan Wynn, Peter Lorre, John Carradine.

A very minor Jerry Lewis comedy, though the stellar supporting cast is fun to watch. This one is for Lewis fans only; new viewers to Jerry's type of comedy should take in *The Errand Boy* or *The Nutty Professor* first. 1964; 101m.

PAUL REISER OUT ON A WHIM ★★★½
DIR: Carl Gottlieb. **CAST:** Paul Reiser, Belinda Bauer, Brooke Adams, Elliott Gould, Carol Kane, Carrie Fisher, Teri Garr, Michael J. Pollard, Desi Arnaz Jr.

Paul Reiser, the star of the TV series *My Two Dads*, combines his standup comedy routine with a minimovie. The movie is about a fantasy in which Reiser searches for a beautiful dreamlike lady who keeps reappearing and wanting to know the meaning of "the real thing." This featurette breaks the usual comedian-standup mold and makes *Out on a Whim* worth a viewing. 1988; 60m.

PEE-WEE HERMAN SHOW, THE ★★½
DIR: Marty Callner. **CAST:** Pee-wee Herman, Phil Hartman, Brian Seff.

Adult fans of Pee-wee Herman will fit right into his childish but risqué playhouse. Others will no doubt wonder what planet he's from. This live comedy-variety show has Pee-wee entertaining a host of friends: Mailman Mike, Hammie and Susan, Captain Carl, Hermit Annie, and a sexy singer. Unrated, but some of the humor is sexual in nature. 1981; 58m.

PEE-WEE'S BIG ADVENTURE ★★★½
DIR: Tim Burton. **CAST:** Pee-wee Herman, Elizabeth Daily, Mark Holton, Diane Salinger.

You want weird? Here it is. Pee-wee Herman makes the jump from television to feature films with this totally bizarre movie about a man-size, petulant, 12-year-old goofball (Herman) going on a big adventure after his most prized possession—a bicycle—is stolen by some nasties. Rated PG for a scary scene and some daffy violence. 1985; 90m.

PEGGY SUE GOT MARRIED ★★★★½
DIR: Francis Ford Coppola. **CAST:** Kathleen Turner, Nicolas Cage, Barry Miller, Catharine Hicks, Joan Allen, Kevin J. O'Connor, Lisa Jane Persky, Barbara Harris, Don Murray, Maureen O'Sullivan, Leon Ames, John Carradine.

Some have called this film a *Back to the Future* for adults. This description is fine as far as it goes, but there is much more to the film. Wistful, and often joyously funny, it features Kathleen Turner as Peggy, a 43-year-old mother of two who is facing divorce. When she attends her twenty-fifth annual high-school reunion, she is thrust back in time and gets a chance to change the course of her life. Rated PG-13 for profanity and suggested sex. 1986; 103m.

PEOPLE ARE FUNNY ★★½
DIR: Sam White. **CAST:** Jack Haley, Rudy Vallee, Ozzie Nelson, Art Linkletter, Helen Walker, Frances Langford.

From the Pine-Thomas B unit at Paramount comes this agreeable little comedy. Jack Haley is a small-town radio announcer who has aspirations to be a big-time radio personality. Inspired by the radio program that later became a successful television series with Art Linkletter as the host. 1946; B&W; 94m.

PERFECT FURLOUGH ★★
DIR: Blake Edwards. **CAST:** Tony Curtis, Janet Leigh, Keenan Wynn, Linda Cristal, Elaine Stritch, Troy Donahue.
Perfectly forgettable fluff about soldier Tony Curtis (who is taking the leave for his entire unit, which is stationed in the Arctic) and his "perfect" vacation in Paris. The usual setbacks and misunderstandings plague poor Tony's furlough, but at least he gets to meet and eventually win Janet Leigh (Mrs. Tony Curtis at that time). 1958; 93m.

PERFECT MATCH, THE ★★
DIR: Mark Deimel. **CAST:** Marc McClure, Jennifer Edwards, Diane Stilwell, Rob Paulsen, Karen Witter.
Although Marc McClure and Jennifer Edwards create some funny moments, the pacing and the dialogue are frequently iffy in this romantic hodgepodge. The couple meets through a misleading personal ad—with both parties claiming to be something they're not. Rated PG for no apparent reason. 1987; 93m.

PERILS OF PAULINE, THE (1947) ★★★
DIR: George Marshall. **CAST:** Betty Hutton, John Lund, Billy DeWolfe, William Demarest, Constance Collier, Frank Faylen.
Betty Hutton plays Pearl White, the queen of the silent serials, in this agreeable little movie. The old-style chase scenes and cliff-hanger situations make up for the overdose of sentimentality. 1947; 96m.

PERSONAL SERVICES ★★★
DIR: Terry Jones. **CAST:** Julie Walters, Alec McCowen, Shirley Stelfox.
The true-life story of Christine Painter, a British waitress who happened into a very successful career as a brothel madam, catering to gentlemen with kinky interests. Julie Walters gives an all-out performance that's fascinating, but the movie's overall bluntness about its subject matter may be offputting to most American viewers. It's rated R for language. 1987; 105m.

PERSONALS, THE ★★★½
DIR: Peter Markle. **CAST:** Bill Schoppert, Karen Landry, Paul Elding, Michael Laskin.
Entertaining light comedy about a recently divorced Minneapolis man (Bill Schoppert) trying to get back in the dating game. Schoppert has the characteristics of Woody Allen, showing both pathos and a knack for one-liners. Rated PG for profanity. 1983; 90m.

PHILADELPHIA STORY, THE ★★★★★
DIR: George Cukor. **CAST:** Katharine Hepburn, Cary Grant, James Stewart, Ruth Hussey, John Howard.
This is one of the best comedies to come out of Hollywood. From the first scene, where Tracy Lord (Katharine Hepburn) deposits her ex-husband's (Cary Grant) golf clubs in a heap at her front door and in return, Grant deposits Hepburn in a heap right next to the clubs, the 1940s version of *The Taming of the Shrew* proceeds at a blistering pace. Grand entertainment. 1940; B&W; 112m.

PICK-UP ARTIST, THE ★½
DIR: James Toback. **CAST:** Molly Ringwald, Robert Downey Jr., Dennis Hopper, Harvey Keitel.
Robert Downey Jr. is a young man with a line for every occasion, and Molly Ringwald the spirited young woman who turns him into a one-woman man. An absolute mess. Rated PG-13 for language and sexual content. 1987; 81m.

PICKWICK PAPERS, THE ★★★
DIR: Noel Langley. **CAST:** James Hayter, James Donald, Joyce Grenfell, Nigel Patrick, Hermione Baddeley.

Arguably the best cinema condensation of Charles Dickens. Here recorded are the clever antics of Samuel Pickwick, Alfred Jingle, and Sam Weller as they move through their corner of mid-ninteenth-century England. 1954; 109m.

PIECE OF THE ACTION, A ★★★
DIR: Sidney Poitier. **CAST:** Sidney Poitier, Bill Cosby, Denise Nicholas, James Earl Jones.

Third entry in the Bill Cosby–Sidney Poitier partnership (after *Uptown Saturday Night* and *Let's Do It Again*), this one showing Poitier's greater comfort on both sides of the camera. The story concerns a pair of rascals given one of Life's Awful Choices: prison, or a team-up with some social workers to help a group of ghetto kids. Rated PG. 1977; 135m.

PILLOW TALK ★★★★
DIR: Michael Gordon. **CAST:** Doris Day, Rock Hudson, Tony Randall, Thelma Ritter.

If you like the fluffy light comedy of Doris Day and Rock Hudson, this is their best effort. The ever-virginal Miss Day is keeping the wolves at bay. In the tradition of Ralph Bellamy and Gig Young, Tony Randall is excellent as the suitor who never wins the girl. 1959; 105m.

PINK CHIQUITAS, THE
DIR: Anthony Currie. **CAST:** Frank Stallone, Bruce Pirrie, Elizabeth Edwards, Eartha Kitt.

A truly infantile comedy that gives even infants a bad name. Frank Stallone (who also wrote the original music for the film) is a super private eye battling an army of women, turned sex-starved by a pink meteor that has crashed to earth. Rated PG-13 for language and sexual situations. 1987; 85m.

PINK FLAMINGOS
DIR: John Waters. **CAST:** Divine, Mink Stole, David Lochary, Mary Vivian Pearce, Edith Massey.

Pink Flamingos is the story of Babs Johnson (Divine), the "filthiest person alive," and Connie and Raymond Marble (Mink Stole and David Lochary), two challengers who are jealous of Babs's notoriety. As in all of Waters films, don't look for brilliant acting or sophisticated plot turns—the point here is to shock. If this doesn't, nothing will. Due to violence, nudity, and very poor taste, we'd rate this one an X. 1972; 95m.

PINK MOTEL
DIR: Mike MacFarland. **CAST:** Phyllis Diller, Slim Pickens, Terri Berland, Squire Fridell.

This crummy sex comedy features Phyllis Diller and Slim Pickens as owners of a less than prosperous motel. The entire film centers around the people who rent a cheap room there on a Friday night. Unrated, this contains nudity and sexual situations. 1982; 90m.

PINK NIGHTS ★½
DIR: Phillip Koch. **CAST:** Shaun Allen, Kevin Anderson.

Yet another teen sex comedy with a few yucks and nothing much else. The film follows the antics of a high-school boy who suddenly finds himself living with three teenage girls, and he doesn't know what to do about the situation. Rated PG for profanity. 1985; 87m.

PINK PANTHER, THE ★★★½
DIR: Blake Edwards. **CAST:** Peter Sellers, David Niven, Capucine, Claudia Cardinale, Robert Wagner.

Peter Sellers is featured in his first bow as Inspector Jacques Clouseau, the inept French detective, on the trail of a jewel thief known as the Phantom in this, the original *Pink Panther*. This release has some good—and even hilarious—moments. But the sequel, *A Shot in the Dark*, is better. 1964; 113m.

PINK PANTHER STRIKES AGAIN, THE ★★★½
DIR: Blake Edwards. **CAST:** Peter Sellers, Herbert Lom, Lesley-Anne Down, Burt Kwouk, Colin Blakely.

Peter Sellers's fourth time out as the clumsy Inspector Clouseau. Clouseau's former supervisor, Herbert Lom, cracks up and tries to destroy the world with a superlaser. Meanwhile, he's hired a team of international killers to do away with Clouseau. One turns out to be Lesley-Anne Down, who falls in love with the diminutive Frenchman. Rated PG. 1976; 103m.

PIRATES

DIR: Roman Polanski. **CAST:** Walter Matthau, Cris Campion, Charlotte Lewis, Roy Kinnear.

A turgid, overblown mess which doesn't even succeed as the pirate comedy it's intended to be. Walter Matthau is horribly miscast as Captain Red, a luckless scoundrel. He sets his eyes on a golden throne and spends most of this interminable picture trying to steal it. Director and coscripter Roman Polanski has no business even attempting this genre, and the performers should strike it from their résumés. Rated PG-13 for vulgarity. 1986; 117m.

PLAIN CLOTHES ★★★½

DIR: Martha Coolidge. **CAST:** Arliss Howard, Suzy Amis, George Wendt, Seymour Cassel, Abe Vigoda, Robert Stack, Harry Shearer.

A 24-year-old police detective (Arliss Howard) goes undercover as a high-school student to prove his younger brother innocent of the murder of a teacher. From this not-very-promising plot, director Martha Coolidge and screenwriter A. Scott Frank have fashioned a marvelously tongue-in-cheek hybrid of mystery, teen comedy, and suspense thriller. Rated PG for profanity and violence. 1988; 100m.

PLANES, TRAINS AND AUTOMOBILES ★★★★

DIR: John Hughes. **CAST:** Steve Martin, John Candy, Michael McKean, Laila Robins, Martin Ferrero, Charles Tyner.

Although it tends to lose momentum in the last half, this screamingly funny film features Steve Martin and John Candy at the peak of their comedic powers. Martin is an uptight marketing executive en route from New York to Chicago to celebrate Thanksgiving with his family, only to end up on a bizarre cross-country odyssey with an obnoxious bozo played by Candy. Rated R for profanity. 1987; 100m.

PLAY IT AGAIN, SAM ★★★★½

DIR: Herbert Ross. **CAST:** Woody Allen, Diane Keaton, Tony Roberts, Jerry Lacy, Susan Anspach.

Woody Allen plays a movie columnist and feature writer who lives his life watching movies. Humphrey Bogart is his idol, and the film commences with the final scenes from *Casablanca.* Allen's wife leaves him for a life of adventure, and the film revolves around some unsuccessful attempts by his friends (Diane Keaton and Tony Roberts) to set him up with a girl. In an age when funny movies may make you smile at best, this is an oasis of sidesplitting humor. Rated PG. 1972; 87m.

PLAYBOY OF THE WESTERN WORLD ★★★★

DIR: Brian Desmond Hurst. **CAST:** Siobhan McKenna, Gary Raymond, Michael O'Brian.

Everything about this story is fresh and inspiring, especially the dialogue and accents. A wonderful adaptation of the classic Irish play about a young woman and her fellow villagers falling in love with a handsome roguish stranger. 1962; 100m.

PLAYING FOR KEEPS

DIR: Bob Weinstein, Harvey Weinstein. **CAST:** Daniel Jordano, Matthew Penn, Leon W. Grant, Harold Gould, Jimmy Baio.

In this achingly familiar movie, a group of teenagers inherit a dilapidated hotel and attempt to turn it into a rock 'n' roll resort for kids. However, a chemical company wants the property for waste dumping and pulls every dirty trick possible to get it. Rated PG-13 for profanity, violence, nudity, and suggested sex. 1986; 103m.

PLAYMATES ★★★★

DIR: Theodore J. Flicker. **CAST:** Alan Alda, Connie Stevens, Barbara Feldon, Doug McClure, Severn Darden, Roger Bowen, Eileen Brennan.

This is a very good romantic comedy about two divorced men who become friends and then secretly begin to date each other's ex-wife, with crazy results. Good cast, fine direction, and an energized screenplay by Richard Baer make this TV movie sparkle. 1972; 73m.

PLAZA SUITE ★★★★½

DIR: Arthur Hiller. **CAST:** Walter Matthau, Maureen Stapleton, Barbara Harris, Lee Grant.

Walter Matthau is at his comic best as he re-creates three separate roles from Neil Simon's stage comedy. The movie is actually three tales of what goes on in a particular suite. Rated PG. 1971; 115m.

POCKETFUL OF MIRACLES ★★★

DIR: Frank Capra. **CAST:** Bette Davis, Glenn Ford, Hope Lange, Thomas Mitchell, Peter Falk, Edward Everett Horton, Jack Elam, Ann-Margret.

The term Capra-Corn could have been coined in response to this overly sentimental picture, basically a remake of the director's 1933 *Lady for a Day*. But Bette Davis is a delight as Apple Annie and Glenn Ford is winningly earnest as the producer who tries to turn her into a lady. Ann-Margret's film debut. 1961; 136m.

POISON IVY ★★

DIR: Larry Elikann. **CAST:** Michael J. Fox, Nancy McKeon, Robert Klein, Caren Kaye, Jason Bateman, Adam Baldwin.

Top talents save this banal TV movie about life at a summer camp. Michael J. Fox is the hip couselor; Nancy McKeon is Camp Pinewood's assistant nurse and Fox's love interest; and Robert Klein is the bombastic camp director. All right for star watching. 1985; 97m.

POLICE ACADEMY ★★

DIR: Hugh Wilson. **CAST:** Steve Guttenberg, George Gaynes, Kim Cattrall, Bubba Smith, Michael Winslow, Andrew Rubin.

Here's another *Animal House*–style comedy that tries very hard to be funny. Sometimes it is, and sometimes it isn't. But overall, it's highly forgettable. Rated R for nudity, violence, and profanity. 1984; 95m.

POLICE ACADEMY II: THEIR FIRST ASSIGNMENT ★★

DIR: Jerry Paris. **CAST:** Steve Guttenberg, Bubba Smith, David Graf, Michael Winslow, Bruce Mahler, Colleen Camp, Marion Ramsey, Howard Hesseman, George Gaynes.

Those inept would-be police officers from Hugh Wilson's *Police Academy* (which was written by Neal Israel and Pat Proft, of *Bachelor Party*) return in this less funny but still box office–potent production. Episodic and silly, it has no story to speak of, just more mindless high jinks with the boys in blue. Rated PG-13 for profanity. 1985; 90m.

POLICE ACADEMY III: BACK IN TRAINING

DIR: Jerry Paris. **CAST:** Steve Guttenberg, Bubba Smith, David Graf, Michael Winslow, Marion Ramsey, Leslie Easterbrook, Art Metrano, Tim Kazurinsky, Bobcat Goldthwait, George Gaynes.

The graduates from the original *Police Academy* return to their alma mater to aid their muddle-headed mentor (George Gaynes), who is engaged in a pitched battle with his rival (Art Metrano). One moronic joke follows another in this nearly plotless and poorly edited series of set pieces. Rated PG for silly violence and references to body parts. 1986; 90m.

POLICE ACADEMY 4: CITIZENS ON PATROL ★½

DIR: Jim Drake. **CAST:** Steve Guttenberg, Bubba Smith, Michael Winslow, David Graf, Tim Kazurinsky, Sharon Stone, G. W. Bailey, Bobcat Goldthwait.

It's like a curse. Each spring a new *Police Academy* movie is released. And each year, for several weeks, it becomes the number-one film in America. Let's just say that if you liked the first three, there's no reason you shouldn't like the fourth. Rated PG for mild profanity. 1987; 87m.

POLICE ACADEMY 5—ASSIGNMENT: MIAMI BEACH ★½

DIR: Alan Myerson. **CAST:** Bubba Smith, David Graf, Michael Winslow, Leslie Easterbrook, Marion Ramsey, Janet Jones, Matt McCoy, René Auberjonois.

Silly fifth entry in the *Police Academy* series, which sends the academy gang to the drug capital of the world to save the job and reputation of their beloved school commandant. Bubba Smith, now the leader of the pack, looks lost (but he always looks that way), and René Auberjonois wastes his talent as a bumbling mobster. Rated PG for language and ribald humor. 1988; 90m.

POLICE ACADEMY SIX: CITY UNDER SIEGE ★

DIR: Peter Bonerz. **CAST:** Bubba Smith, Kenneth Mars, George Gaynes, David Graf, Michael Winslow, G. W. Bailey.

Those bungling cops return in this, the sixth entry in what seems like a never-ending series. The city is reeling from the shock of a crime wave headed by a mastermind who somehow knows every move the cops make. Mr. Big and his outlaw band have the city in the palms of their hands until our addlebrained heroes come to the rescue. Rated PG for violence and profanity. 1989; 87m.

POLICE SQUAD! ★★★★

DIR: Jim Abrahams, David Zucker, Jerry Zucker, Joe Dante, Reza S. Badiyi. **CAST:** Leslie Nielsen, Alan North.

Originally a 1982 summer TV show, with only six episodes aired, this is now a minor cult classic. The folks who made *Airplane!* went all out on this. Each one of the episodes is hilarious, much funnier than the popular film *Police Academy*. 1982; 75m.

POLISH VAMPIRE IN BURBANK, A ★★½

DIR: Mark Pirro. **CAST:** Mark Pirro, Lori Sutton, Eddie Deezen.

Low-budget, sophomoric horror-comedy that, nonetheless, provides a few laughs. Mark Pirro plays a "virgin" vampire. His sultry sister, another vampire, takes him out one night for a bite. One of those films that you giggle at, then feel very sheepish. Not rated, but contains sexual suggestion and some ghoulish violence. 1985; 84m.

POLYESTER

DIR: John Waters. **CAST:** Divine, Tab Hunter, Edith Massey, Mary Garlington.

Anyone for bad taste? Female impersonator Divine and 1950s heartthrob Tab Hunter play lovers in this film by writer-producer-director John Waters (*Pink Flamingos*). A special gimmick called "Odorama" allowed viewers to experience the story's various smells via a scratch-and-sniff card. That's just one reason why *Polyester* really stinks, and it's all intentional. Rated R for bad taste. 1981; 86m.

POOR LITTLE RICH GIRL, THE ★★★

DIR: Maurice Tourneur. **CAST:** Mary Pickford.

Mary Pickford's main claim to fame was her uncanny ability to convincingly portray females many years her junior. She stunted her range by doing so again and again, but the public loved it and willingly paid for it. She earned high critical acclaim demonstrating her range in this sentimental comedy-drama. One critic said that she was 8 years old, then a haughty 16, with no warning or motivation for the mercurial change. Silent, with organ music. 1917; B&W; 64m.

PORKY'S ★½

DIR: Bob Clark. **CAST:** Dan Monahan, Mark Herrier, Wyatt Knight, Roger Wilson, Kim Cattrall, Scott Colomby.

The ads lied when they called this the "funniest movie about growing up ever made." (Dumbest is a better description.) Bob Clark wrote and directed this "comedy" about teenagers in the 1950s whose hormones and hot tempers lead them into all kinds of strange situations, including a fateful trip to a redneck dive called Porky's. Rated R for vulgarity, nudity, and adult themes. 1981; 94m.

PORKY'S II: THE NEXT DAY

DIR: Bob Clark. **CAST:** Dan Monahan, Wyatt Knight, Mark Herrier, Roger Wilson, Kaki Hunter, Scott Colomby, Nancy Parsons, Edward Winter.

Bob Clark wrote and directed this sequel to his hit comedy. This time, the lustful kids of Angel Beach High battle with the Ku Klux Klan, which is trying to prevent (of all things) a Shakespeare festival. Dumb. Rated R for the usual garbage. 1983; 95m.

PORKY'S REVENGE

DIR: James Komack. **CAST:** Dan Monahan, Wyatt Knight, Tony Ganios, Mark Herrier, Kaki Hunter, Scott Colomby.

It's just more of the same stupidity. This time, the owner of the redneck dive that gave the series its name attempts to get even with the goons from Angel Beach High. This turkey gives new meaning to the word *sleeper*. Rated R for profanity, suggested sex, and nudity. 1985; 90m.

PRAY TV (1980) ★★½

DIR: Rick Friedberg. **CAST:** Dabney Coleman, Archie Hahn, Joyce Jameson, Nancy Morgan, Roger E. Mosley, Marcia Wallace.

Dabney Coleman plays Marvin Fleece, penny-ante con man, who takes faltering TV station KRUD and turns it into K-GOD, with some novel ideas about religious programming. A really funny satire on religion and television, betrayed only by a weak ending. Rated PG for language and general tastelessness. 1980; 92m.

PREP SCHOOL ★★½

DIR: Paul Almond. **CAST:** Leslie Hope, Andrew Sabiston.

This comedy-drama about a coed prep school in New England has the usual cast of characters. There's the obnoxious rich girl, the misfit, the macho jock, and at least two pranksters. Familiar, but nicely performed. Rated PG-13 for profanity. 1981; 97m.

PREPPIES

DIR: Chuck Vincent. **CAST:** Nitchie Barrett, Dennis Drake, Steven Holt, Katt Shea.

Adult movie king Chuck Vincent, attempted to make the minor leap from porno to R-rated sexploitation flicks with this teen sex comedy. He didn't make it. The screenplay he coauthored with Rick Marx about three women of easy virtue is just as insipid as those normally found in the substandard explicit sex films with which Vincent made his reputation. Rated R for nudity, simulated sex, and profanity. 1984; 90m.

PRESIDENT'S ANALYST, THE ★★★★

DIR: Theodore J. Flicker. **CAST:** James Coburn, Godfrey Cambridge, Pat Harrington, Will Geer.

Vastly underappreciated satire from writer-director Theodore J. Flicker, who concocts a wild tale concerning a psychiatrist (James Coburn) selected to be our president's "secret shrink." Coburn walks away with the picture, his wicked smile and piercing eyes becoming more and more suspicious as he falls prey to the paranoia of his elite assignment. Unrated; adult themes. 1967; 104m.

PRETTY SMART
DIR: Dimitri Logothetis. **CAST:** Tricia Leigh Fisher, Lisa Lorient, Dennis Cole, Patricia Arquette.

Claptrap about a rebellious new student at an exclusive girls' school. She tries to organize everyone against the headmaster, who is using innocent girls to smuggle drugs—and making videotapes of them taking showers (which he sells to his drug connections). You'll want a shower, too, after watching this descent into sleaze. Rated R. 1986; 84m.

PRINCE AND THE SHOWGIRL, THE ★★½
DIR: Laurence Olivier. **CAST:** Laurence Olivier, Marilyn Monroe, Sybil Thorndike, Jeremy Spencer.

In a romantic comedy about the attraction of a nobleman for an American showgirl, you'd want to stress the attraction of opposites. Marilyn Monroe and Laurence Olivier's acting talents are in full flower, and they are fun to watch; however, they are so dissimilar that they never click. 1957; 117m.

PRINCE OF PENNSYLVANIA ★
DIR: Ron Nyswander. **CAST:** Fred Ward, Bonnie Bedelia, Keanu Reeves, Amy Madigan.

Keanu Reeves portrays a morbid, morose teenager in a small Pennsylvania mining town. He feels trapped by his surroundings and his family, so he stages a rebellion—involving the kidnapping of his father. Director Ron Nyswander's script strives for comedy at one moment, then veers toward drama the next, with aggravating results. Rated R for nudity, violence, and profanity. 1988; 93m.

PRINCESS AND THE PIRATE, THE ★★★
DIR: David Butler. **CAST:** Bob Hope, Virginia Mayo, Victor McLaglen, Walter Brennan, Walter Selzak.

A happy, hilarious Bob Hope howler. He and the beautiful Virginia Mayo are pursued by pirates and trapped by potentate Walter Slezak. Victor McLaglen is properly menacing as a buccaneer bent on their destruction. Walter Brennan is something else—a pirate? This one's lots of fun for all! 1944; 94m.

PRINCESS ACADEMY, THE
DIR: Bruce Block. **CAST:** Eva Gabor, Lar Park Lincoln.

Another girls' school movie, in which the entire point is to cram in as many extraneous shower and bedroom scenes as possible. Innocent young Cindy (Lar Park Lincoln) is sent to the exclusive Von Pupsin finishing school in Switzerland. There she gets a crash course in sex from her rich schoolmates. Eva Gabor has a few befuddled comic moments as the head of the school, but her appearances are brief and one can only hope that she didn't know what was going on in the rest of the script. Rated R. 1987; 90m.

PRISONER OF SECOND AVENUE, THE ★★★★
DIR: Melvin Frank. **CAST:** Jack Lemmon, Anne Bancroft, Gene Saks, Elizabeth Wilson, Florence Stanley.

Neil Simon blends laughter with tears in this film about an executive (Jack Lemmon) who loses his job and has a nervous breakdown. Anne Bancroft plays Lemmon's wife. Rated PG. 1975; 105m.

PRISONER OF ZENDA, THE ★★★½
DIR: Richard Quine. **CAST:** Peter Sellers, Lionel Jeffries, Elke Sommer, Lynne Frederick.

Zany rendition of the classic tale of a look-alike commoner who stands in for the endangered king of Ruritania. A warm and hilarious film despite the lack of critical acclaim. Rated PG for language. 1979; 108m.

PRIVATE BENJAMIN ★★★★
DIR: Howard Zieff. **CAST:** Goldie Hawn, Eileen Brennan, Armand Assante, Robert Webber, Sam Wanamaker.

This comedy is at its best in the first half, when Goldie Hawn, as a spoiled Jewish princess, joins the army. Thanks to the sales pitch of a double-crossing army recruiter, she expects her hitch to be like a vacation in the Bahamas. The last part of the movie gets a little heavy on the message end, but Hawn's buoyant personality makes it easy to take. Rated R for profanity, nudity, and implicit sex. 1980; 110m.

PRIVATE EYES, THE ★

DIR: Lang Elliott. **CAST:** Tim Conway, Don Knotts, Trisha Noble, Bernard Fox.

If Tim Conway and Don Knotts had depended on movies like this to make it in show business, they could easily have wound up on unemployment rather than television. This Holmes and Watson send-up is neither consistently funny nor engaging. In short, a waste of time. Rated PG. 1980; 91m.

PRIVATE FUNCTION, A ★★★★

DIR: Malcolm Mowbray. **CAST:** Michael Palin, Maggie Smith, Denholm Elliott, Richard Griffiths.

The Michael Palin/Maggie Smith team repeat the success of *The Missionary* with this hilarious film about a meek foot doctor and his socially aspiring wife who become involved with the black market during the food rationing days of post–World War II England when they acquire an unlicensed pig. The humor is open to those who like Monty Python, but is also accessible to audiences who do not find that brand of humor funny. Rated R. 1985; 96m.

PRIVATE LESSONS ★

DIR: Alan Myerson. **CAST:** Sylvia Kristel, Howard Hesseman, Eric Brown, Pamela Bryant.

This soft-porn comedy, about a wealthy, virginal teenage boy being seduced by his sexy, conniving 30-year-old housekeeper, is a seedy movie, run through with amateurish acting, cheap production values, and silly dialogue. Rated R because of nudity and sexual content. 1981; 87m.

PRIVATE POPSICLE ★

DIR: Boaz Davidson. **CAST:** Yftach Katzur, Zachi Noy, Jonathan Segall.

In this fourth film featuring the Lemon Popsicle gang, a popular comedy team in Europe, we find the trio joining the Israeli army. The attempts at comedy fall flat. The inept dubbing just makes it all the worse. The picture is unrated, but there is much nudity and sex in it. 1982; 100m.

PRIVATE RESORT ★★

DIR: George Bowers. **CAST:** Rob Morror, Johnny Depp, Tony Azito, Dody Goodman, Hector Elizondo.

This teen comedy features two young men (Rob Morror and Johnny Debb) seeking romance and excitement at a luxurious resort. The few funny moments come from slapstick chases and Three Stooges–type routines. Rated R for nudity, obscenities, and sexual situations. 1985; 82m.

PRIVATE SCHOOL

DIR: Noel Black. **CAST:** Phoebe Cates, Martin Mull, Sylvia Kristel, Ray Walston, Julie Payne, Michael Zorek.

If *Porky's*, *Porky's II*, *Bachelor Party*, *Class*, etc., haven't sated your appetite for slobbering sexploitation comedies geared to adolescents, this awful film offers more of the same: skin, stupidity, and more skin. Enroll at your own risk. Rated R for nudity and profanity. 1983; 97m.

PRIVATES ON PARADE ★★★½

DIR: Michael Blakemore. **CAST:** John Cleese, Denis Quilley, Michael Elphick, Simon Jones, Joe Melia, John Standing, Nicola Pagett.

While this story of a gay USO-type unit in the British army is a comedy, it has its serious moments. These come when the unit accidentally runs into a gang of gunrunners. John Cleese is hilarious as the pathetic army major who's ignorant of the foul play that goes on under his nose. Rated PG-13 for adult situations and profanity. 1983; 107m.

PRIZZI'S HONOR ★★★★★
DIR: John Huston. **CAST:** Jack Nicholson, Kathleen Turner, Robert Loggia, John Randolph, William Hickey, Anjelica Huston.

This totally bent comedy is perhaps best described as *The Godfather* gone stark, raving mad. Jack Nicholson plays a Mafia hit man who falls in love with a mystery woman (Kathleen Turner), who turns out to be full of surprises. Perhaps the blackest black comedy ever made. It's a real find for fans of the genre. Rated R for nudity, suggested sex, profanity, and violence. 1985; 130m.

PRODUCERS, THE ★★★★
DIR: Mel Brooks. **CAST:** Zero Mostel, Gene Wilder, Kenneth Mars, Dick Shawn, Lee Meredith, Christopher Hewett.

Mel Brooks's first film as a director remains a laugh-filled winner. Zero Mostel stars as a sleazy Broadway promoter who, with the help of a neurotic accountant (Gene Wilder), comes up with a scheme to produce an intentional flop titled *Springtime for Hitler* and bilk its backers. The plan backfires, and the disappointed duo ends up with a hit and more troubles than before. Rated PG. 1968; 88m.

PROJECTIONIST, THE ★★
DIR: Harry Hurwitz. **CAST:** Chuck McCann, Ina Balin, Rodney Dangerfield.

A projectionist in a New York movie palace escapes his drab life by creating fantasies, casting himself as the hero in various films. The movie intercuts new footage into old classics, a technique used later by Steve Martin in *Dead Men Don't Wear Plaid*. While interesting as a low-budget experiment, the film has surprisingly little entertainment value. Rated R for profanity and partial nudity. 1970; 85m.

PROMISES, PROMISES ★
DIR: King Donovan. **CAST:** Jayne Mansfield, Marie McDonald, Tommy Noonan, Mickey Hargitay, Fritz Feld.

The only thing going for this film is the scenes of a next-to-totally-naked Jayne Mansfield. About two women trying to find out who made them pregnant, the movie is silly and crude. A monumental waste of film and time. 1963; 75m.

PROMOTER, THE ★★★
DIR: Ronald Neame. **CAST:** Alec Guinness, Glynis Johns, Valerie Hobson, Petula Clark.

Alec Guinness is clever, conniving, and all innocence in this comedy centering on a penniless young man who exploits every opportunity to get ahead in the world. Glynis Johns is delightful as the girl who believes in him. 1952; B&W; 88m.

PROTOCOL ★★★½
DIR: Herbert Ross. **CAST:** Goldie Hawn, Chris Sarandon, Richard Romanus, Cliff De Young, Gail Strickland.

In this film, directed by Herbert Ross, Goldie Hawn is a lovable airhead who goes through a startling metamorphosis to become a true individual. Sound a little like *Private Benjamin*? You bet your blond movie actress. As unoriginal as it is, this comedy-with-a-message works surprisingly well. It's no classic. However, viewers could do a lot worse. Rated PG for violence, partial nudity, and adult situations. 1984; 96m.

PULP ★★½
DIR: Michael Hodges. **CAST:** Michael Caine, Mickey Rooney, Lionel Stander, Lizabeth Scott, Al Lettieri.

Sometimes funny, sometimes lame black comedy casts Michael Caine as a pulp mystery writer hired to pen the biography of retired film star and reputed mobster Mickey Rooney. Caine carries the film well enough, with his voice-over narration a nice Chandleresque touch, and Rooney is excellent in his few scenes, but the film never really catches fire. Rated PG for profanity and violence. 1972; 95m.

PURLIE VICTORIOUS ★★★½

DIR: Nicholas Webster. **CAST:** Ossie Davis, Ruby Dee, Sorrell Booke, Alan Alda, Godfrey Cambridge, Beah Richards.

Alan Alda made his film debut as a southern liberal in this good-humored comedy written by Ossie Davis. Davis and his wife, Ruby Dee, play an evangelist couple who try to convert an old barn into an integrated church. Their chief opposition comes from the bigot (Sorrel Booke) who owns the barn. Godfrey Cambridge is especially funny as a farm worker who feigns servitude to Booke. Also known as *Gone Are the Days*. 1963; B&W; 93m.

PURPLE ROSE OF CAIRO, THE ★★★★

DIR: Woody Allen. **CAST:** Mia Farrow, Jeff Daniels, Danny Aiello, Edward Herrmann, John Wood.

Woody Allen's clever screen creation recalls his story for *Play It Again, Sam*. The latter had Allen's character interacting with the specter of Humphrey Bogart, who sagely advised him on his love life. In *The Purple Rose of Cairo*, Mia Farrow is a Depression-era housewife who finds her dreary day-to-day existence enlivened when a dashing, romantic hero walks off the screen and sweeps her off her feet. Like Allen's *Zelig* and *Broadway Danny Rose*, it mixes humor with very human situations. The result, as in the two previous cases, is a very satisfying work of celluloid. Rated PG for violence. 1985; 85m.

PURSUIT OF D. B. COOPER ★★½

DIR: Roger Spottiswoode. **CAST:** Treat Williams, Robert Duvall, Kathryn Harrold, Ed Flanders, Paul Gleason, R. G. Armstrong.

The famous skyjacker is turned into a fun-loving good old boy in this hit-and-miss comedy starring Treat Williams, Robert Duvall, and Kathryn Harrold. If you liked *Smokey and the Bandit*, you'll probably enjoy this. Otherwise, avoid it. Rated PG because of minimal violence and sexuality. 1981; 100m.

PUTNEY SWOPE ★★★★

DIR: Robert Downey. **CAST:** Alan Abel, Mel Brooks, Allen Garfield, Pepi Hermine, Ruth Hermine, Antonio Fargas.

This wildly funny film concerns a black man who takes over a Madison Avenue advertising firm. Alan Abel, Mel Brooks, and Allen Garfield appear in this zany parody of American lifestyles. Rated R. 1969; 88m.

PYGMALION ★★★★½

DIR: Anthony Asquith, Leslie Howard. **CAST:** Leslie Howard, Wendy Hiller, Wilfrid Lawson, Marie Lohr, David Tree.

This is an impeccable adaptation of George Bernard Shaw's classic play. The comedy is deliciously sophisticated. The performances are exquisite, particularly that of Leslie Howard, who'll make you forget Rex Harrison's Henry Higgins in an instant. As the professor's feisty Cockney pupil, Wendy Hiller is a delight. 1938; B&W; 95m.

QUICK, LET'S GET MARRIED 🦃

DIR: William Dieterle. **CAST:** Ginger Rogers, Ray Milland, Barbara Eden, Walter Abel, Michael Ansara, Elliott Gould.

Made in 1964 but not released for seven years, this feeble farce has Ginger Rogers as the madam of a bordello conspiring with an adventurer, played laconically by Ray Milland, to pull off a hoax on a supposedly innocent prostitute (Barbara Eden). Good cast. Respected director. Very bad film. 1971; 96m.

QUIET MAN, THE ★★★★★

DIR: John Ford. **CAST:** John Wayne, Maureen O'Hara, Victor McLaglen, Barry Fitzgerald, Mildred Natwick, Arthur Shields, Ward Bond, Jack MacGowran.

John Ford's easygoing and marvelously entertaining tribute to the people and the land of Ireland. The story centers around an American ex-boxer

(John Wayne) who returns to his native land, his efforts to understand the culture and people of a rural village, and especially his interest in taming a spirited colleen (Maureen O'Hara) in spite of the disapproval of her brother (Victor McLaglen). 1952; 129m.

RABBIT TEST
DIR: Joan Rivers. **CAST:** Billy Crystal, Roddy McDowall, Joan Prather.
Horrible comedy about the world's first pregnant man. Joan Rivers borrows her leaden stage persona for her directing debut, and even the occasionally talented Billy Crystal can't do anything with this wretched material. Rated R—profanity. 1978; 84m.

RADIO DAYS ★★★
DIR: Woody Allen. **CAST:** Mia Farrow, Seth Green, Julie Kavner, Josh Mostel, Michael Tucker, Dianne Wiest.
One of writer-director Woody Allen's gentler fables, a pleasant little fantasy about people whose lives revolved around the radio during the days prior to World War II. This affectionate overview does for radio what *The Purple Rose of Cairo* did for the movies; unfortunately, Allen's intentions in *Radio Days* are a bit *too* ambitious. Many of the characters in his large ensemble cast get lost, and too much time is spent with others. Rated PG. 1987; 85m.

RAFFERTY AND THE GOLD DUST TWINS ★★½
DIR: Dick Richards. **CAST:** Sally Kellerman, Mackenzie Phillips, Alan Arkin, Alex Rocco, Charles Martin Smith, Harry Dean Stanton.
Amusing and entertaining little film with Sally Kellerman and Mackenzie Phillips kidnapping a hapless Alan Arkin and forcing him to drive them to New Orleans from California. Good cast and pacing make up for simple plot. Rated PG for profanity. 1975; 92m.

RAGE OF PARIS, THE ★★★
DIR: Henry Koster. **CAST:** Danielle Darrieux, Douglas Fairbanks Jr., Mischa Auer, Helen Broderick, Glenda Farrell, Louis Hayward, Harry Davenport, Samuel S. Hinds.
Famed French star Danielle Darrieux made her U.S. film debut in this airy romantic comedy about mistaken identity and artful conniving for the sake of love and money. Deft direction steered the excellent cast through an engaging script. Good, clean fun all around. 1938; B&W; 78m.

RAISING ARIZONA ★★★★
DIR: Joel Coen. **CAST:** Nicolas Cage, Holly Hunter, Randall "Tex" Cobb, Trey Wilson, John Goodman, William Forsythe.
An almost indescribable lunatic comedy from the makers of *Blood Simple*. Nicolas Cage plays an ex-convict married to policewoman Holly Hunter. Both want children but cannot have any. So they decide to help themselves to one. What follows is a delightful, offbeat comedy that is extremely fast-paced, with eye-popping cinematography and decidedly different characters. Rated PG-13. 1987; 94m.

RAP MASTER RONNIE—A REPORT CARD ★★★
DIR: Jay Dubin. **CAST:** Jim Morris, Jon Cryer, Carol Kane, Tom Smothers.
As indicated by the title, this is a look back at the Ronald Reagan presidency as seen through the eyes of writer Garry Trudeau. Jim Morris, who makes his living imitating Reagan, does a fine job here with the help of a supporting cast. This HBO special is unrated. 1988; 47m.

RAT PFINK A BOO BOO
DIR: Ray Dennis Steckler. **CAST:** Vin Saxon, Carolyn Brandt.
The title was supposed to be *Rat Pfink and Boo Boo*, but the titlemaker screwed it up and director Ray Dennis Steckler couldn't afford to have the credits redone, so he let the name stand. That'll clue you in as to what to expect in this lunatic movie that Steckler literally made up as he went along. A loose parody of *Batman*, it

has everything a bad-movie lover could ever want, and more: ridiculous superhero costumes, terrible acting (mostly improvised, and it shows), and atrocious rock 'n' roll songs. 1965; 72m.

RATINGS GAME, THE ★★★★
DIR: Danny DeVito. **CAST:** Danny DeVito, Rhea Perlman, Gerrit Graham, Louis Giambalvo, Ronny Graham, Huntz Hall, Kevin McCarthy, John Megna, Michael Richards, Mark L. Taylor.

Danny DeVito directs and leads an amiable cast in this comedy about a millionaire trying to break into the Hollywood scene with his rotten screenplays. When he falls in love with an employee from the Computron company (Rhea Perlman), they fix the TV ratings. Not rated, has profanity. 1984; 102m.

RAVISHING IDIOT, THE
DIR: Edouard Molinaro. **CAST:** Anthony Perkins, Brigitte Bardot.

A big bomb of a comedy that can be recommended only for insomniacs. Thin plot concerns a spy out to steal NATO plans of ship movements. Skip it. 1965; B&W; 110m.

REACHING FOR THE MOON ★★★
DIR: Edmund Goulding. **CAST:** Douglas Fairbanks Sr., Bebe Daniels, Edward Everett Horton.

Robust and energetic Douglas Fairbanks plays a financier on whom liquor has an interesting effect. Edward Everett Horton is his valet and Bebe Daniels is the girl. 1931; B&W; 62m.

REAL GENIUS ★★★
DIR: Martha Coolidge. **CAST:** Val Kilmer, Gabe Jarret, Michelle Meyrink, William Atherton, Ed Lauter.

This is a mildly amusing comedy about a group of science prodigies (led by Val Kilmer) who decide to thwart the plans of their egomaniacal mentor (William Atherton) who is secretly using their research to build a rather nasty little laser weapon for the CIA. Director Martha Coolidge does her best to keep things interesting, but she can't overcome the predictability of the climax. Rated PG for profanity. 1985; 105m.

REAL LIFE ★★★
DIR: Albert Brooks. **CAST:** Albert Brooks, Charles Grodin, Frances Lee McCain, J. A. Preston.

Albert Brooks's fans will eat up this tasty satire parodying an unrelenting PBS series that put the day-to-day life of an American family under the microscope. In Brooks's film the typical family comes hilariously unglued under the omnipresent eye of the camera. The script (written by Brooks) eventually falters, but not before a healthy number of intelligent laughs are produced. Rated PG. 1979; 99m.

REAL MEN ★★★
DIR: Dennis Feldman. **CAST:** James Belushi, John Ritter, Bill Morey, Gail Barl, Barbara Barrie.

This action-filled comedy features James Belushi as an infallible Bond-like CIA agent. His latest mission is to protect his wimpish new partner (John Ritter) and make contact with powerful aliens. Ritter's confidence soars as Belushi repeatedly convinces him that he's a hero. Rated PG-13 for profanity, violence, and brief nudity. 1987; 86m.

REALLY WEIRD TALES ★★★
DIR: Paul Lynch, Don McBreaty, John Blanchard. **CAST:** Joe Flaherty, John Candy, Catherine O'Hara, Martin Short, Dan Harron, Olivia D'Abo, Sheila McCarthy.

For cable fodder, these three odd short stories produced for HBO have their moments. Martin Short plays a hack lounge singer at a playboy's swank party in "All's Well That Ends Strange." "Cursed with Charisma" features John Candy as a hustler who takes the citizens of a small town for all they have. The last story, featuring Catherine O'Hara, is the best. "I'll Die Loving" is about a woman from a Catholic orphanage who is cursed with the odd power of loving people to death. Not rated, has profanity. 1986; 85m.

RECRUITS
DIR: Rafal Zielinski. **CAST:** Alan Deveau, Annie McAuley.

In this dismal, low-budget takeoff on the *Police Academy* movies, which were bad enough to begin with, a sheriff hires hookers, thieves, and bums as deputies. That's when the "fun" starts. Save us. Rated R. 1987; 90m.

REEFER MADNESS ★★½
DIR: Louis J. Gasnier. **CAST:** Dave O'Brien, Dorothy Short, Warren McCollum, Lillian Miles, Carleton Young.

This 1930s anti-marijuana film is very silly, and sometimes funny. It's a cult film that really isn't as good as its reputation suggests. 1936; B&W; 67m.

REIVERS, THE ★★★★
DIR: Mark Rydell. **CAST:** Steve McQueen, Rupert Crosse, Will Geer, Sharon Farrell, Mitch Vogel, Michael Constantine.

Grand adaptation of the William Faulkner tale concerning a young boy (Mitch Vogel) who, with the help of his mischievous older friends (Steve McQueen and Rupert Crosse), "borrows" an automobile and heads for fun and excitement in 1905 Mississippi. The charming vignettes include a stopover in a brothel and a climactic horse race that could spell doom for the adventurers. Rated PG. 1969; 107m.

RENTED LIPS
DIR: Robert Downey. **CAST:** Martin Mull, Dick Shawn, Jennifer Tilly, Robert Downey Jr., June Lockhart, Pat McCormick, Eileen Brennan.

A talented cast is wasted—make that embarrassed—in this pitiful excuse for a comedy. Martin Mull and Dick Shawn play inept documentary filmmakers (*Aluminum, Our Friend*, etc.) who agree to complete a porno film called *Halloween in the Bunker*. Not since Chuck Barris's self-promoting *Gong Show Movie* has a film been so monumentally bad. Robert Downey Jr. is directed by his father in a performance that is breathtakingly awful. Rated R for profanity, nudity, and violence. 1988; 85m.

REPO MAN ★★★★
DIR: Alex Cox. **CAST:** Emilio Estevez, Harry Dean Stanton, Vonetta McGee, Sy Richardson, Tracey Walter.

Wild, weird, and unpredictable, this film stars Emilio Estevez as a young man who gets into the repossession racket. Under the tutelage of Harry Dean Stanton (in a typically terrific performance), Estevez learns how to steal cars from people who haven't kept up their payments. Meanwhile, bizarre events lead them to an encounter with what may be beings from space. *Repo Man* is not for every taste. However, those who occasionally like to watch something different will enjoy it. Rated R. 1984; 92m.

RESTLESS NATIVES ★★★½
DIR: Michael Hoffman. **CAST:** Vincent Friell, Joe Mulloney, Teri Lolly, Ned Beatty.

Okay, so it's not perfect—the humor and the characterizations are broad and the thick, Scottish accents sometimes make the dialogue difficult to decipher. But that doesn't stop this film from being thoroughly entertaining. Two young Scots, disguised as a clown and a wolfman, rob tourist buses and become national heroes in the process. Rated PG. 1986; 90m.

RETURN OF CAPTAIN INVINCIBLE, THE ★★½
DIR: Phillippe Mora. **CAST:** Alan Arkin, Christopher Lee.

Camp send-up of old comic-book-hero serials of the Thirties and Forties. Arkin is Captain Invincible, fighting crime and Nazis and preserving the American way of life. During the communist witchhunt of the Fifties, though, the captain is accused of being a red and quickly becomes a national disgrace. Alan Arkin flies high as Captain Invincible, who must combat Christopher Lee and his evil minions. Songs, special effects, and corny melodrama all combine to get you through the occasional dull bits. Rated PG for profanity and violence. 1984; 101m.

RETURN OF THE KILLER TOMATOES ★★½
DIR: John DeBello. **CAST:** Anthony Starke, George Clooney, John Astin.
The mad scientist, whose experiments caused the first tomato war, perfects his process that creates intelligent vegetable life. He can now change tomatoes into human replicas. Although it lacks the spontaneous humor the original exhibited, this *Return* has its moments. Language may not be suitable for a younger audience. Rated PG. 1988; 99m.

RETURN OF THE PINK PANTHER, THE ★★★★
DIR: Blake Edwards. **CAST:** Peter Sellers, Christopher Plummer, Herbert Lom, Catherine Schell, Burt Kwouk, Peter Arne.
Writer-director Blake Edwards and star Peter Sellers revived their Inspector Clouseau character for a new series of comic adventures beginning with this slapstick classic. There are many funny scenes as Sellers attempts to track down the Phantom (Christopher Plummer) while making life intolerable for the chief inspector (Herbert Lom). Rated PG. 1975; 113m.

RETURN OF THE SECAUCUS 7 ★★★★½
DIR: John Sayles. **CAST:** Mark Arnott, Gordon Clapp, Maggie Cousineau, Adam Lefevre, Bruce MacDonald, Jean Passanante, Maggie Renzi.
Here's an absolute gem of a movie. Written, produced, and directed by John Sayles, it's a story about the reunion of seven friends ten years after they were wrongfully busted in Secaucus, New Jersey, while on their way to the last demonstration against the Vietnam war in Washington, D.C. It is a delicious blend of characterization, humor, and insight. No MPAA rating, but *Secaucus 7* has nudity, profanity, and implicit sex. 1980; 100m.

RETURN TO MAYBERRY ★★½
DIR: Bob Sweeney. **CAST:** Andy Griffith, Don Knotts, Ron Howard, Jim Nabors, George Lindsey, Aneta Corseaut, Betty Lynn.
Nostalgia time. Andy, Barney, and most of the gang are reunited in this TV-movie valentine to *The Andy Griffith Show*. The many plot lines include Opie's impending fatherhood, Barney's campaign for sheriff, and the appearance of a monster in the lake. 1986; 95m.

REUBEN, REUBEN ★★★★½
DIR: Robert Ellis Miller. **CAST:** Tom Conti, Kelly McGillis, Roberts Blossom, Cynthia Harris, E. Katherine Kerr, Joel Fabiani, Lois Smith.
A funny, touching, and memorable character study about an irascible Scottish poet, this film, directed by Robert Ellis Miller (*The Heart Is a Lonely Hunter*) and written by Julius J. Epstein (*Casablanca*), ranges from romantic to ribald, and from low-key believability to blistering black comedy. In short, it's a rare cinematic treat. First and foremost among the picture's assets is a superb leading performance by Tom Conti. Rated R for profanity and suggested sex. 1983; 101m.

REVENGE OF THE CHEERLEADERS 🦃
DIR: Richard Lerner. **CAST:** Jerii Woods, Rainbeaux Smith, Carl Ballantine, David Hasselhoff.
There were never any good *Cheerleaders* movies, but this one is about the worst of a bad bunch. Sleazy cheerleaders at an out-of-control school combat plans to close down the school by putting drugs into the cafeteria food. Pretty funny, huh? Garbage! Rated R for nudity and profanity. 1976; 88m.

REVENGE OF THE NERDS ★★★
DIR: Jeff Kanew. **CAST:** Robert Carradine, Anthony Edwards, Julie Montgomery, Curtis Armstrong, Ted

McGinley, Michelle Meyrink, James Cromwell, Bernie Casey, Timothy Busfield.

The title characters, Lewis (Robert Carradine) and Gilbert (Anthony Edwards), strike back at the jocks who torment them in this watchable, fitfully funny comedy. Rated R. 1984; 90m.

REVENGE OF THE NERDS II: NERDS IN PARADISE ★½

DIR: Joe Roth. **CAST:** Robert Carradine, Timothy Busfield, Curtis Armstrong, Larry B. Scott, Courtney Thorne-Smith, Anthony Edwards, Ed Lauter.

With this sequel, one assumes that the filmmakers were out for revenge against their audience. The story is lame, and the direction is perfunctory at best. The story has the Tri-Lambs being harassed by the jocks of the Alpha fraternity at a conference in Fort Lauderdale, Florida. Rated PG for profanity and brief nudity. 1987; 95m.

REVENGE OF THE PINK PANTHER, THE ★★★★½

DIR: Blake Edwards. **CAST:** Peter Sellers, Dyan Cannon, Robert Webber, Marc Lawrence, Herbert Lom, Burt Kwouk, Robert Loggia, Paul Stewart.

This is arguably the best of the slapstick series about an inept French police inspector. It contains inspired bits penned by director Blake Edwards and played to perfection by Peter Sellers. Rated PG. 1978; 99m.

RHINESTONE ★½

DIR: Bob Clark. **CAST:** Sylvester Stallone, Dolly Parton, Richard Farnsworth, Ron Leibman.

Dolly Parton plays a country singer who bets her lascivious manager that she can take an average guy off the street and turn him into a country star in two weeks. What she gets stuck with is a New York cabbie (Sylvester Stallone), who, when she first meets him, can't carry a tune in a bag. The hokey premise eventually does it in. Rated PG for profanity, sexual innuendo, and violence. 1984; 111m.

RICH HALL'S VANISHING AMERICA ★★★

DIR: Steve Rash. **CAST:** Rich Hall, M. Emmet Walsh, Peter Isacksen, Harry Anderson, Wilt Chamberlain.

Rich Hall goes in search of the Junior Seed Sales Club. (When he was 8, he joined the club. He sold the seeds, but never got his prize of a Wilt Chamberlain basketball and hoop.) A number of guest stars are on hand for this look at a nostalgic era—a vanishing America. This enjoyable film was made for cable and is recommended for general audience viewing. 1986; 50m.

RICH LITTLE—ONE'S A CROWD ★★½

DIR: Thomas E. Engel. **CAST:** Rich Little.

Rich Little is both host and entire cast in a sort of "Greatest Hits" video album. Little is, of course, very good at his craft, but his self-written material is not always the best, and his unique talent wears a little thin after an hour or so. Not rated, but with mild profanity. 1988; 86m.

RICHARD LEWIS—I'M IN PAIN CONCERT ★★½

DIR: Charles Braverman. **CAST:** Richard Lewis, Billy Crystal, Robin Williams, Harold Ramis, Rob Reiner.

Richard Lewis is a bold, daring comic who tends to turn his mind inside out on stage. Reckless and risky, his neurotic improvisation seems honest, but Lewis's stream-of-consciousness lacks the manic mimicking of Robin Williams, a skill that would make this comedy concert far more entertaining. 1986; 60m.

RICHARD PRYOR—HERE AND NOW ★★★★½

DIR: Richard Pryor. **CAST:** Richard Pryor.

The popular comedian doing what he does best, stand-up comedy. Rated R for profanity. 1983; 83m.

RICHARD PRYOR—LIVE AND SMOKIN' ★★½
DIR: Michael Blum. **CAST:** Richard Pryor.
Disappointing comedy concert film featuring Richard Pryor. It's not boring, but Pryor is clearly unnerved by the presence of the film crew. While there are some nice bits, the laughs are few. Unrated, the film has profanity. 1985; 45m.

RICHARD PRYOR—LIVE IN CONCERT ★★★★★
DIR: Jeff Margolis. **CAST:** Richard Pryor.
Richard Pryor's first live comedy performance film is still the best. Life has never been so sad and funny at the same time. Rated R for profanity. 1979; 78m.

RICHARD PRYOR LIVE ON THE SUNSET STRIP ★★★
DIR: Joe Layton. **CAST:** Richard Pryor.
Richard Pryor's second concert film (and first film after his accidental burning) is highly watchable. *Live in Concert* and *Here and Now*, however, are superior. Rated R for nonstop profanity and vulgarity. 1982; 82m.

RIDERS OF THE STORM ★
DIR: Maurice Phillips. **CAST:** Dennis Hopper, Michael J. Pollard, Eugene Lipinski.
This lame parody strikes out at far too many targets to effectively sink any. The plot has Dennis Hopper as the captain of an ancient B-29 that, with a crew of Vietnam veterans, has been circling the country for fifteen years to broadcast an illegal television network. The constant music-video effects are headache-inducing. Rated R for nudity. 1987; 92m.

RIDING ON AIR ★★★
DIR: Edward Sedgwick. **CAST:** Joe E. Brown, Florence Rice, Vinton Haworth, Guy Kibbee.
Lots of thrills and laughs in this topically dated comedy adventure about two small-town newspaper correspondents vying for the same girl and the scoop on a story involving aerial smugglers and a device for flying airplanes by a remote control radio beam—a reality today, but not when the film was made. Joe E. Brown is, as always, warm, winning, and wholesome. 1937; B&W; 58m.

RIKKI AND PETE ★★★
DIR: Nadia Tass. **CAST:** Nina Landis, Stephen Kearny, Bruce Spence, Bruno Lawrence.
An offbeat comedy from Australia. A geologist and her crazy brother abandon the city for the Australian Outback. This film is a great crash course in living your own life. Highly engaging! Rated R for nudity and language. 1988; 101m.

RIPPING YARNS ★★★½
DIR: Jim Franklin, Alan Bell, Terry Hughes. **CAST:** Michael Palin.
Wildly funny series featuring excellent writing by Monty Python members Michael Palin and Terry Jones. Palin is well cast in different roles as he romps through six vignettes that comically parody the social structure and history of the British empire. Originally produced for British TV, this double cassette features the following episodes: "Tomkin's Schooldays," "Escape from Stalag Luft 112B," "Golden Gordon," "The Testing of Eric Olthwaite," "Whinfrey's Last Case," and "The Curse of the Claw." Not rated. 1978; 180m.

RISKY BUSINESS ★★★★
DIR: Paul Brickman. **CAST:** Tom Cruise, Rebecca DeMornay, Curtis Armstrong, Bronson Pinchot, Raphael Sbarge, Joe Pantoliano, Nicholas Pryor, Richard Masur.
An ordinarily well-behaved boy (Tom Cruise) goes wild when his parents are on vacation. His troubles begin when a gorgeous hooker (Rebecca DeMornay) who doesn't exactly have a heart of gold makes a house call at his request and he doesn't have enough in his piggy bank to cover the cost of her services. It's stylish, funny, and sexy—everything, in fact,

that most movies of this kind generally are not. Rated R for nudity, profanity, and suggested sex. 1983; 99m.

RITA, SUE AND BOB TOO ★½
DIR: Alan Clarke. **CAST:** George Costigan, Siobhan Finneran, Michelle Holmes.

In a promising twist on all those crude coming-of-age films, this cheeky British flick follows a pair of best friends who lose their virginity to a man whose children they both babysit. But this romp rapidly becomes vulgar, filling time with gratuitous glimpses of lower-class life and the racial strife of England. Rated R for language. 1986; 90m.

RITZ, THE ★★★★
DIR: Richard Lester. **CAST:** Jack Weston, Rita Moreno, Jerry Stiller, Kaye Ballard, F. Murray Abraham, Treat Williams.

This film is brimful of belly laughs that will leave you exhausted. After the death of his father-in-law, Jack Weston (as Geatano Proclo) flees Cleveland. His brother-in-law has put out a contract on him to prevent his inheriting any part of the family garbage business. His escape takes him to New York City and, by accident, a gay hotel called The Ritz. Rated R for profanity. 1976; 91m.

ROAD TO BALI ★★★½
DIR: Hal Walker. **CAST:** Bob Hope, Bing Crosby, Dorothy Lamour, Murvyn Vye.

Excellent entry in the Bob Hope/Bing Crosby *Road* series. In this one the boys play a pair of vaudeville performers in competition for Dorothy Lamour, pursuing her to the South Seas island of Bali, where they must contend with all sorts of jungle dangers, from cannibalistic natives to various Hollywood stars who appear in hilarious (though very brief) cameos. The Humphrey Bogart scene is a classic. 1952; 90m.

ROAD TO RIO ★★★
DIR: Norman Z. McLeod. **CAST:** Bob Hope, Bing Crosby, Dorothy Lamour, Gale Sondergaard, Frank Faylen, Jerry Colonna, The Andrews Sisters.

More a straight comedy than the madcap mayhem that marked its predecessors, this fifth *Road* show has Bob Hope and Bing Crosby hopping a boat south to Rio de Janeiro. On board they meet and fall for Dorothy Lamour, who runs hot and cold because her wicked aunt (Gale Sondergaard) is hypnotizing her so she will accept an arranged marriage. Lots of laughs. 1947; B&W; 100m.

ROAD TO UTOPIA ★★★
DIR: Hal Walker. **CAST:** Bob Hope, Bing Crosby, Dorothy Lamour, Hillary Brooke, Douglass Dumbrille, Jack LaRue, Robert Benchley.

The Klondike and a hunt for an Alaskan gold mine provide the background for this fourth of the seven *Roads* Bob Hope, Bing Crosby, and Dorothy Lamour traveled between 1940 and 1962. Rated the best of the bunch by fans, it's a mix of songs, sight gags, wisecracks, inside jokes, hoke, and the usual love triangle. 1945; B&W; 90m.

ROBIN WILLIAMS LIVE ★★★★
DIR: Bruce Cowers. **CAST:** Robin Williams.

An always funny and sometimes hilarious live performance by one of comedy's premier talents. Irreverent and vulgar, Williams doesn't so much shock as he carefully picks sensitive factors of the human condition. He will then immediately switch to impressions of Jack Nicholson debating Clint Eastwood. In the funniest portion of the show, he attacks our sexual practices and mocks radio sex therapists. Not rated, but contains profanity and many sexual references. Recommended for adult audiences. 1986; 65m.

ROCK 'N' ROLL HIGH SCHOOL ★★★½
DIR: Allan Arkush. **CAST:** P. J. Solés, Vincent Van Patten, Clint Howard, Dey Young, The Ramones.

The stern new principal tries to turn a school into a concentration camp. The popular Riff (P. J. Soles) goes against the principal by playing loud Ramones music all the time. Meanwhile, boring Tom (Vincent Van Patten) has a crush on Riff. The film includes lots of laughs and good rock 'n' roll music—a cult favorite. Rated PG. 1979; 93m.

ROCK 'N' ROLL WRESTLING WOMEN VS. THE AZTEC MUMMY

DIR: René Cardona Jr., Manuel San Fernando. **CAST:** Lorena Velazquez, Armand Silvestre.

Some folks found this old Mexican horror flick and attempted to turn it into a comedy by redubbing the dialogue, giving it a comical rock 'n' roll soundtrack, and retitling it. In the dumb story, two female wrestlers assist an archeologist in foiling a madman's plans of ruling the world by possessing the secrets of an ancient mummy's tomb. Not rated; has violence. 1986; B&W; 88m.

RODNEY DANGERFIELD: "IT'S NOT EASY BEING ME" ★★

DIR: Walter C. Miller. **CAST:** Rodney Dangerfield, Jeff Altman, Roseanne Barr, Sam Kinnison, Bob Nelson, Jerry Seinfeld, Robert Townsend.

Humdrum comic showcase for a new bunch of stand-up comedians performing at Rodney Dangerfield's night club in New York. The show is hosted by Dangerfield, whose contributions are limited to a short vintage routine at the start of the show, and screamingly unfunny buffer vignettes between the acts. Most of the show is badly edited to boot. Not rated; the movie contains vulgar language. 1986; 59m.

RODNEY DANGERFIELD—NOTHIN' GOES RIGHT ★★

DIR: Walter C. Miller. **CAST:** Rodney Dangerfield.

Rodney Dangerfield introduces several aspiring standup comics at his comedy club, Dangerfield's, and provides "cameo" jokes between the acts. Robert Schimmel and Barry Sobel are the best of the bunch, but none of them is very funny, and much of the humor will be offensive to blacks, gays, foreigners, and especially women. Not rated, but there is much profanity and some very frank discussions of sex. 1988; 83m.

ROMANCE WITH A DOUBLE BASS ★★★½

DIR: Robert Young. **CAST:** John Cleese, Connie Booth, Graham Crowden, Desmond Jones, Freddie Jones, Andrew Sachs.

Monty Python madman John Cleese stars in this delightfully silly vignette about a double-bass player and a princess who are caught naked in a pond when a thief makes off with their clothes. The ensuing romance will tickle and charm most adult viewers with its refreshing subtlety, but a word of caution for parents: This short will not win any awards for costume design. 1974; 40m.

ROMANTIC COMEDY ★★★

DIR: Arthur Hiller. **CAST:** Dudley Moore, Mary Steenburgen, Frances Sternhagen, Janet Eilber, Robyn Douglass, Ron Leibman.

In this enjoyable comedy, based on the 1979 Broadway play, Dudley Moore and Mary Steenburgen star as two collaborating playwrights who, during their long association, suffer from "unsynchronized passion." Rated PG for profanity and suggested sex. 1983; 103m.

RON REAGAN IS THE PRESIDENT'S SON ★

DIR: Jim Yukich. **CAST:** Ron Reagan.

Junior should leave the acting to papa. This pathetic character does not get us to sympathize with the trials of being the president's son, if that was the intent. It's half of a one-hour tape whose better half is entitled *The New Homeowner's Guide to Happiness*. 1987; 60m.

ROOM SERVICE ★★★
DIR: William A. Seiter. **CAST:** The Marx Brothers, Lucille Ball, Ann Miller.
After leaving his brothers (Groucho, Harpo, and Chico) to try movie producing, Zeppo Marx came up with this Broadway play about a foundering stage production and attempted to have it rewritten to suit his siblings' talents. He wasn't completely successful, but this romp does have its moments. Look for Lucille Ball and Ann Miller in early supporting roles. 1938; B&W; 78m.

ROSEANNE BARR SHOW, THE ★★★½
DIR: Rocco Urbishi. **CAST:** Roseanne Barr.
This HBO comedy special showcases Roseanne Barr in her standup routine and mixes in scenes with her family in the old mobile home. Made before her meteoric rise to stardom, this could have served as the inspiration for her hit TV series. Rated R for language not allowed on her weekly sitcom. 1987; 60m.

ROSEBUD BEACH HOTEL, THE 💔
DIR: Harry Hurwitz. **CAST:** Colleen Camp, Peter Scolari, Christopher Lee, Hamilton Camp, Eddie Deezen, Chuck McCann, Hank Garrett.
An absolutely awful attempt to combine comedy with soft-core porn. Colleen Camp and Peter Scolari take over her father's failing hotel and hire prostitutes as bellgirls to improve business. Stay away from this mess. Rated R. 1985; 82m.

ROXANNE ★★★★½
DIR: Fred Schepisi. **CAST:** Steve Martin, Daryl Hannah, Shelley Duvall, Rick Rossovich, Michael J. Pollard, Fred Willard.
Steve Martin's most effective and rewarding comedy since *All of Me*. Martin, who wrote the screenplay, based on Rostand's *Cyrano de Bergerac*, plays the big-nosed fire chief of a small town who befriends a professional firefighter (Rick Rossovich) who has come to help train the inept local firemen. While doing so, he meets and falls in love with the title character (Daryl Hannah) and soon enlists Martin's aid in wooing her with words. Rated PG for profanity and suggested sex. 1987; 107m.

RSVP ★★★
DIR: John Amero, Lem Amero. **CAST:** Ray Colbert, Veronica Hart, Carey Hayes.
This is an out-and-out sex comedy with lots of nudity and sexual situations. The plot concerns an author who has written a novel that turns out to be based on fact. The people who inspired the "characters" have been invited to a Hollywood party to celebrate the making of a movie from the book and discover the truth. The writing is lively, and the puns and gags are funny. Rated R for sexual situations and language that will be offensive to some. 1984; 87m.

RUDE AWAKENING ★★★★
DIR: Aaron Russo. **CAST:** Cheech Marin, Eric Roberts, Julie Hagerty, Robert Carradine, Buck Henry, Louise Lasser, Cindy Williams, Andrea Martin, Cliff De Young.
The premise sounds dreadful: In 1969 two draft dodgers (Cheech Marin and Eric Roberts) flee from the F.B.I. and drop out to Central America until a twist of fate fans their liberal fires and propels them to New York City in 1989. But wait! This movie is hilarious! Cheech, naturally, is brain-dead and at his best; Roberts sends out sexual flares with his pearly whites and long mane and fringed leather jacket (which housemom Louise Lasser kept for him); Julie Hagerty is Roberts's once-meek flower-child love, now turned into Signature Artist From Hell; and SCTV's Andrea Martin here redefines the standard for drunken housewives. Swell, nostalgic soundtrack, too. Rated R for language. 1989; 100m.

RUGGLES OF RED GAP ★★★★½

DIR: Leo McCarey. **CAST:** Charles Laughton, Mary Boland, Charlie Ruggles, ZaSu Pitts, Roland Young, Leila Hyams.

Charles Laughton is superb as Ruggles, the valet who is lost in a poker game by a continental gentleman (Roland Young) to Americans (Charlie Ruggles and Mary Boland). The latter take him from Paris to the wilds of 1908 Washington State. Hilarious. 1935; B&W; 92m.

RULING CLASS, THE ★★★★

DIR: Peter Medak. **CAST:** Peter O'Toole, Alastair Sim, Arthur Lowe, Harry Andrews, Coral Browne.

Superbly irreverent satire about upper-crust British eccentricities. Peter O'Toole plays the heir to a peerage who proves problematic because of his insane belief that he is Jesus Christ. Rated PG. 1972; 154m.

RUNNING WILD ★★

DIR: Gregory La Cava. **CAST:** W. C. Fields, Mary Brian, Claude Buchanan.

W. C. Fields is miscast and overplays his role of a toady worm suddenly turned (by hypnotism) into a coarse, violent lion—mean to family, friends, and dog. Far from vintage Fields, this film is a disappointing outing for his comic genius. Silent with titles. 1927; B&W; 68m.

RUSSIANS ARE COMING, THE RUSSIANS ARE COMING, THE ★★★½

DIR: Norman Jewison. **CAST:** Alan Arkin, Carl Reiner, Paul Ford, Theodore Bikel, Brian Keith, Jonathan Winters, Eva Marie Saint.

A Russian submarine runs aground off Nantucket Island, and the townspeople go gaga, not knowing what to do first, get guns or pour vodka. Cued by Alan Arkin's engaging portrayal of an out-of-his-depth Russian sailor, the cast delivers a solid comedy as cultures clash. With Jonathan Winters aboard, think wacky. 1966; 120m.

RUSSKIES ★★½

DIR: Rick Rosenthal. **CAST:** Whip Hubley, Leaf Phoenix, Peter Billingsley, Charles Frank.

A sweet-natured Russian sailor (Whip Hubley) becomes stranded in Key West, Florida, when a raft capsizes and aborts a secret Soviet mission to pick up a stolen American defense weapon. He finds three youngsters who eventually agree to help him escape. This is essentially a formula teen comedy with a humanitarian theme. The cast is appealing, but the laughs aren't frequent enough. Rated PG-13 for slight violence and profanity. 1987; 90m.

RUSTLER'S RHAPSODY ★★★

DIR: Hugh Wilson. **CAST:** Tom Berenger, G. W. Bailey, Marilu Henner, Andy Griffith, Fernando Rey, Patrick Wayne.

In this fun spoof of the singing cowboy movies of the 1930s, 1940s, and 1950s, Tom Berenger plays the "greatest" horseback crooner of them all, Rex O'Herlihan, who must face his greatest challenge. There's only one problem: Viewers need to be familiar with the old B westerns to get the jokes. If you are, it's a hoot. Rated PG for mild violence and slight profanity. 1985; 88m.

RUTHLESS PEOPLE ★★★★½

DIR: Jim Abrahams, David Zucker, Jerry Zucker. **CAST:** Danny DeVito, Bette Midler, Judge Reinhold, Helen Slater, Anita Morris, Bill Pullman.

Hollywood's only three-man directing team comes up with another comedy classic. Danny DeVito portrays a man who decides to murder his obnoxious but rich wife, played by Bette Midler. But when he arrives home to carry out the deed, he discovers she has been abducted. The kidnappers demand fifty thousand dollars "or else." *Or else* is exactly what DeVito has in mind, so he refuses to pay a cent. Rated R for nudity and profanity. 1986; 90m.

SABRINA ★★★★
DIR: Billy Wilder. **CAST:** Audrey Hepburn, Humphrey Bogart, William Holden, John Williams.

Elfin Audrey Hepburn shines in the title role. She's the simple chauffeur's daughter who is swept off her feet by wealthy rake William Holden. Humphrey Bogart, as Holden's business-minded brother, attempts to save her from the ne'er-do-well. Director Billy Wilder paces things with his usual deft touch. 1954; B&W; 113m.

SAM KINISON LIVE! ★★★½
DIR: Walter C. Miller. **CAST:** Sam Kinison.

Once a balls-of-fire preacher, Sam Kinison, the crazed screaming comic, still divides audiences squarely in half. His fans, the believers, idolize him. Detractors think him loud, crude, and one-dimensional. His routines are anything but subtle, slamming women, religion, and homosexuals. It's gonzo, frontal-assault humor, an aggressive take-no-prisoners approach that will leave you livid or laughing out loud. Rated R. 1987; 50m.

SAME TIME NEXT YEAR ★★★★
DIR: Robert Mulligan. **CAST:** Ellen Burstyn, Alan Alda.

Funny, touching film begins with an accidental meeting in 1951 between two married strangers at a rural California inn. Doris (Ellen Burstyn) is a young housewife from California, and George (Alan Alda) an accountant from New Jersey. Their meetings become an annual event. And through them, we see the changes in America and its people as we return to the same cottage every five years until 1977. Rated PG. 1978; 117m.

SAMMY AND ROSIE GET LAID ★★★★
DIR: Stephen Frears. **CAST:** Shashi Kapoor, Frances Barber, Claire Bloom, Ayub Khan Din.

Excellent sexual farce set in riot-torn east London concerns a young married couple who receive an unexpected visit from Sammy's father, an arrogant politician who is fleeing from a Middle Eastern country. His world becomes shaken up by the couple's sexually liberated, anarchic friends. Outrageous comedy from the creators of *My Beautiful Laundrette.* Not rated, but contains nudity and violence. 1987; 97m.

SAPS AT SEA ★★★
DIR: Gordon Douglas. **CAST:** Oliver Hardy, Stan Laurel, Ben Turpin.

Oliver Hardy contracts "hornophobia," and the only cure is rest and sea air. The boys rent a houseboat, but an escaped killer strands them all at sea to avoid the police. Comedic timing is off and some of the jokes misfire, but enough of them work to make the movie enjoyable. 1940; B&W; 57m.

SATURDAY NIGHT LIVE ★★★½
DIR: Dave Wilson. **CAST:** John Belushi, Chevy Chase, Dan Aykroyd, Bill Murray, Gilda Radner, Jane Curtin, Laraine Newman, Garrett Morris, Steve Martin, Lily Tomlin, George Carlin, Richard Pryor, Ray Charles, Rodney Dangerfield.

Saturday Night Live was to the 1970s what *Your Show of Shows* was to the 1950s and *Rowan & Martin's Laugh-In* to the 1960s—a hit comedy-variety show that reflected the times. Its nucleus was The Not Ready For Prime Time Players, a group of talented yet struggling comedians assembled by producer Lorne Michaels. John Belushi, Chevy Chase, Dan Aykroyd, Bill Murray, and Jane Curtin all based successful careers on their initial fame earned on the show. 1975–1980; 64–120 minutes.

SAVAGES (1973) ★★★
DIR: James Ivory. **CAST:** Lewis J. Stadlen, Anne Francine, Thayer David, Salome Jens.

James Ivory's offbeat look at society, in which a naked group of primitives find their sacrificial rites disrupted by a croquet ball. This discovery leads then to a deserted mansion where an odd cluster of events culminates in a transformation in which they are civilized. Unrated, contains nudity and violence. 1973; 108m.

SAVING GRACE ★★★★

DIR: Robert M. Young. **CAST:** Tom Conti, Fernando Rey, Edward James Olmos, Giancarlo Giannini, Erland Josephson.

The pope (Tom Conti), frustrated with his lack of freedom, finds himself in the small, depressed Italian village of Montepetra where he gets back to helping people on a one-on-one basis. All this is done with only a couple of people knowing who he really is. *Saving Grace* is very good, showing moments of conflict with the human element exposed in all its emotions. Rated PG for violence and profanity. 1986; 112m.

SAY ANYTHING ★★★½

DIR: Cameron Crowe. **CAST:** John Cusack, Ione Skye, John Mahoney.

So many things are right with this comedy-drama about two teens' first love that one can't help wincing when it takes a wrong turn. Yet everything else is honest in its depiction of a well-meaning, unexceptional guy (John Cusack) who falls in love with a seemingly unattainable beauty with brains (Ione Skye). It's a minor gem from first-time director Cameron Crowe, who wrote the excellent book about teens, *Fast Times at Ridgemont High*. Rated PG-13 for suggested sex and profanity. 1989; 100m.

SAY YES ★★½

DIR: Larry Yust. **CAST:** Art Hindle, Lissa Layng, Logan Ramsey, Jonathan Winters, Maryedith Burrell, Anne Ramsey.

A multimillionaire (Jonathan Winters) dies, leaving his estate to his son (Art Hindle) on the condition that he marry before his thirty-fifth birthday—only a day away. The comedy doesn't work most of the time, but the story is cute enough to tolerate. Rated PG-13 for sex, nudity, and profanity. 1986; 87m.

SCANDALOUS ★★

DIR: Rob Byrum. **CAST:** Robert Hays, Pamela Stephenson, John Gielgud, Jim Dale, M. Emmet Walsh.

Robert Hays plays an investigative reporter who gets mixed up with spies, con men, and murder in London. The cast, who seem to be working at feverish pitch to keep things interesting, includes Pamela Stephenson and John Gielgud, as a pair of con artists. Gielgud seems to be having a grand old time playing everything from an old Chinese man to the world's oldest punk rocker, while Jim Dale is embarrassing as an eccentric detective chasing Hays. Rated PG for profanity, nudity, and brief violence. 1983; 93m.

SCAVENGER HUNT

DIR: Michael Schultz. **CAST:** Richard Benjamin, James Coco, Scatman Crothers, Ruth Gordon, Cloris Leachman, Roddy McDowall, Cleavon Little, Robert Morley, Richard Mulligan, Tony Randall, Vincent Price.

It's a Mad Mad Mad Mad World writhes again as a bunch of wackos run hither, thither, and yawn to reap a dead man's inheritance in this "comedy." Rated PG. 1979; 117m.

SCAVENGERS ★

DIR: Duncan McLachlan. **CAST:** Kenneth Gilman, Brenda Bakke, Ken Gampu.

This inane comedy-adventure pits a Miami University professor and his ex-girlfriend against the CIA, KGB, and a local African drug kingpin. It seems that the pair have stumbled upon information which would prove the KGB gave the CIA secrets in exchange for drugs. Rated PG-13 for violence. 1988; 94m.

SCHLOCK ★★★

DIR: John Landis. **CAST:** John Landis, Saul Kahan, Joseph Plantadosi.

Directed by and starring John Landis, this film is a spoof of not only "missing link" monster movies but other types of horror and science-fiction films. It involves the discovery of a prehistoric man (still alive) and his "rampages" in the world of modern man. This is Landis's first film, and while it doesn't have the laughs of his later effort, *Animal House*, it does include some chuckles of its own. Rated PG. 1971; 80m.

SCHOOL DAZE ★★★½
DIR: Spike Lee. **CAST:** Larry Fishburne, Giancarlo Esposito, Tisha Campbell, Spike Lee, Ossie Davis.

Writer-director Spike Lee tries to get people to wake up not only to the conflict in South Africa, but also the problems that exist among different factions of the black community. This message is cloaked in some inventive comedy bits. Too much time is spent on a silly subplot involving a college fraternity; however, the film features some first-rate production numbers and a fine musical score by the filmmaker's father, Bill Lee. Rated R for profanity and nudity. 1988; 120m.

SCHOOL SPIRIT
DIR: Alan Holleb. **CAST:** Tom Nolan, Elizabeth Foxx, Larry Linville.

Stupid highschool flick about an obnoxious libido case (Tom Nolan) who dies in an auto accident and returns as a ghost. Now he can see all the naked girls he wants, and director Alan Holleb doesn't pull the punches in that department. Not rated, but an easy R for sex, nudity, and profanity. 1985; 90m.

SCREEN TEST
DIR: Sam Auster. **CAST:** Michael Allan Bloom, Robert Bundy.

Unfunny comedy about a group of teenage boys who pose as film producers in order to audition beautiful women nude for a bogus sex comedy. When one of their "stars" turns out to be the daughter of a big-time gangster, they have to come up with a real movie or else. It's as stupid and tasteless as it sounds. Rated R. 1986; 84m.

SCREWBALL ACADEMY ★½
DIR: Reuben Rose. **CAST:** Colleen Camp, Ken Welsh.

When a production company tries to make a movie in a small beachfront town, assorted loonies come out of the closet. Some of the lowbrow jokes raise a giggle, though the overall effort disappoints. Reuben Rose is former *SCTV* director John Blanchard under a pseudonym. Rated R for profanity. 1987; 90m.

SCREWBALLS
DIR: Rafal Zielinski. **CAST:** Peter Keleghan, Linda Speciale, Linda Shayne.

Set in 1965, this dreadful teen-lust comedy takes place at Taft and Adams Educational Center, otherwise know as "T&A High." The ads say it features "the nuts who always score" in the game of getting girls. It should have been rained out. Rated R for nudity, sex, and profanity. 1983; 80m.

SCROOGED ★★½
DIR: Richard Donner. **CAST:** Bill Murray, Karen Allen, John Forsythe, John Glover, Bob Goldthwait, Carol Kane, Robert Mitchum, Alfre Woodard.

The power of Charles Dickens's uncredited source material and an energetic turn by Carol Kane as the Ghost of Christmas Present save this bloated comedy from total disaster. Bill Murray waltzes through his role as a venial television executive with no time or patience for life's finer attractions. His confrontations with his past, present, and future serve less to awaken his conscience and more to allow the viewer to play Spot That Guest Star. Rated PG-13 for language. 1988; 101m.

SECRET ADMIRER ★★½
DIR: David Greenwalt. **CAST:** C. Thomas Howell, Lori Laughlin, Kelly Preston, Dee Wallace, Cliff De Young, Fred Ward, Leigh Taylor-Young.

A sweet-natured sex comedy that suffers from predictability, this stars teen heartthrob C. Thomas Howell as a 16-year-old who, on the last day of school before summer vacation, receives an anonymous letter from a female who swears undying love. He hopes it's from the girl of his dreams (Kelly Preston) and decides to find out. Meanwhile, the letter falls into a number of other hands, the owners of which each interpret the letter differently. Rated R for nudity, light violence, and profanity. 1985; 100m.

SECRET DIARY OF SIGMUND FREUD, THE ★★★½

DIR: Danford B. Greene. **CAST:** Bud Cort, Carol Kane, Klaus Kinski, Marisa Berenson, Carroll Baker, Ferdinand Mayne, Dick Shawn.

The Secret Diary of Sigmund Freud is a consistently humorous satire on the early life of Sigmund Freud. Everyone in the cast looks to be having a swell time. Needless to say, sexual and psychological jokes abound. That they are flamboyantly funny is no small feat. Rated PG. 1984; 129m.

SECRET LIFE OF AN AMERICAN WIFE, THE ★★

DIR: George Axelrod. **CAST:** Walter Matthau, Anne Jackson, Patrick O'Neal, Edy Williams, Richard Bull.

To see if she still has sex appeal, bored wife Anne Jackson decides to moonlight as a call girl. Her first client is her husband's employer. Husband walks in on wife and employer, etc. Director and writer George Axelrod had a cute idea, but it really doesn't gel. 1968; 93m.

SECRET LIFE OF WALTER MITTY, THE ★★★★

DIR: Norman Z. McLeod. **CAST:** Danny Kaye, Virginia Mayo, Boris Karloff, Reginald Denny, Florence Bates, Ann Rutherford, Thurston Hall.

Based on James Thurber's story, this comedy presents Danny Kaye as a timid man who dreams of being a brave, glory-bound hero. This comedy provides plenty of laughs and enjoyable moments. 1947; 105m.

SECRET OF MY SUCCESS, THE ★★★½

DIR: Herbert Ross. **CAST:** Michael J. Fox, Helen Slater, Margaret Whitton, Richard Jordan, Christopher Murney, John Pankow, Fred Gwynne.

The secret of this movie's success can be found in its ingredients: a witty script, vibrant direction, bouncy pop score, ingratiating star, and gifted supporting cast. Michael J. Fox is terrifically likable as a wildly ambitious Kansas lad who heads for New York City with plans to conquer the corporate world overnight. This is a slick, 1980s version of a Molière-style farce. Rated PG-13. 1987; 110m.

SECRET POLICEMAN'S PRIVATE PARTS, THE ★★★

DIR: Roger Graef, Julien Temple. **CAST:** John Cleese, Michael Palin, Terry Jones, Graham Chapman, Peter Cook, Terry Gilliam, Pete Townshend, Phil Collins, Donovan, Bob Geldof.

Monty Python fans will find some of their favorite sketches in this Amnesty International production, but they have been executed elsewhere in better form. The whole film seems lackluster, with so-so performances by the musical guests. If you are a fan, you probably will enjoy it, but if you're less of an enthusiast, you might check out *Monty Python Live at the Hollywood Bowl* first. Rated R. 1984; 77m.

SECRET POLICEMEN'S OTHER BALL, THE ★★★★

DIR: Julien Temple, Roger Graef. **CAST:** John Cleese, Graham Chapman, Michael Palin, Terry Jones, Eric Clapton, Jeff Beck, Pete Townshend, Peter Cook.

British comedians John Cleese, Graham Chapman, Michael Palin, and Terry Jones (of Monty Python) join with rock performers Sting, Eric Clapton, Jeff Beck, and Pete Townshend (of the Who) in a live performance to benefit Amnesty International. The comedy bits—which also feature Dudley Moore's former partner, Peter Cook—go from funny to hilarious, and the music is surprisingly effective. Rated R for profanity and adult themes. 1982; 91m.

SECRET WAR OF HARRY FRIGG, THE ★★

DIR: Jack Smight. **CAST:** Paul Newman, Sylva Koscina, Andrew Duggan, James Gregory.

A group of Allied generals has been captured by the Italians. Strangely, they make no attempt to escape. In their vast wisdom, the high command chooses a disgruntled private (Paul Newman) to go behind the lines and free them if possible. This is a very basic comedy, with few original laughs. Rated PG. 1968; 110m.

SEE NO EVIL, HEAR NO EVIL ★★★½

DIR: Arthur Hiller. **CAST:** Gene Wilder, Richard Pryor, Joan Severance, Kevin Spacey.

Richard Pryor and Gene Wilder play two handicapped buddies – one deaf, one blind – who find themselves running from cops and killers alike when they "witness" a murder. Forget the contrived, stale plot and enjoy the marvelous interplay between the stars. Rated R for profanity, nudity, and violence. 1989; 103m.

SEEMS LIKE OLD TIMES ★★★

DIR: Jay Sandrich. **CAST:** Goldie Hawn, Chevy Chase, Charles Grodin, Robert Guillaume, Harold Gould.

This slick, commercial package is much better than it deserves to be. It's another predictable Neil Simon sitcom packed with one-liners. But at least it's funny most of the time. Rated PG. 1980; 121m.

SEMI-TOUGH ★★

DIR: Michael Ritchie. **CAST:** Burt Reynolds, Jill Clayburgh, Kris Kristofferson, Robert Preston, Bert Convy, Lotte Lenya.

Semihumorous love triangle set in a professional football background is just not as funny as it should be. Some inspired moments and very funny scenes make it a highly watchable film (especially Lotte Lenya's guest bit as an untemptable masseuse), and the character actors are fine, but the film is mean-spirited at times and much of the humor relies on profanity and cruel situations. Rated R. 1977; 108m.

SENATOR WAS INDISCREET, THE ★★★

DIR: George S. Kaufman. **CAST:** William Powell, Ella Raines, Peter Lind Hayes, Arleen Whelan, Hans Conried.

A staid and irreproachable U.S. senator's diary disclosures cause considerable embarrassment in this satire. Urbane and suave as always, William Powell is perfect in the title role. 1947; B&W; 81m.

SEND ME NO FLOWERS ★★★

DIR: Norman Jewison. **CAST:** Rock Hudson, Doris Day, Tony Randall, Paul Lynde, Clint Walker, Hal March, Edward Andrews.

Typically bright and bubbly Doris Day vehicle has Rock Hudson as her hypochondriacal hubby, who, believing he is dying, keeps trying to find a mate for his increasingly flustered wife. This is a light, frothy comedy that asks for no more than a smile. It also provokes some solid chuckles, thanks to the two leads and Tony Randall's supporting turn. 1964; 100m.

SENIORS, THE ★

DIR: Rod Amateau. **CAST:** Jeffrey Bryon, Gary Imhoff, Dennis Quaid, Priscilla Barnes, Edward Andrews, Alan Reed.

In order to meet girls, a group of college buddies open a sex clinic. To their surprise, it becomes a big success. The movie is called *Seniors*, but it's pretty sophomoric. Given the subject matter, it's also pretty tame, with only slight nudity. 1978; 87m.

SEPARATE VACATIONS ★★★½

DIR: Michael Anderson. **CAST:** David Naughton, Jennifer Dale, Mark Keyloun, Tony Rosato.

This comedy about Richard, a bored husband (David Naughton) suddenly seeking romance outside his marriage, has some hilarious, if contrived, moments. When Richard goes to Mexico alone, he constantly strikes out with the beautiful women he meets. Rated R for nudity and sexual situations. 1985; 92m.

SERIAL ★★★½
DIR: Bill Persky. **CAST:** Martin Mull, Tuesday Weld, Jennifer McAlister, Bill Macy, Tom Smothers, Christopher Lee.

At the center of this farce is the Holroyd family. Harvey Holroyd (Martin Mull) finds it difficult to go with the flow, especially when he finds out his wife, Kate (Tuesday Weld), is having an affair with a Cuban poodle-groomer while his daughter, Joan (Jennifer McAlister), has joined a religious cult. That's when the problems really begin. Rated R. 1980; 86m.

SEVEN LITTLE FOYS, THE ★★★
DIR: Melville Shavelson. **CAST:** Bob Hope, Milly Vitale, George Tobias, Billy Gray, James Cagney.

Deftly tailored to Bob Hope, this biography of famed vaudevillian Eddie Foy and his performing offspring is gag-filled entertainment until death makes him a widower at odds with his talented brood. A classic scene with James Cagney as George M. Cohan has Hope dancing on a tabletop. All's well that ends well—in church! 1955; 95m.

SEVEN MINUTES IN HEAVEN ★★½
DIR: Linda Feferman. **CAST:** Jennifer Connelly, Byron Thames, Maddie Corman, Michael Zaslow.

When her only parent leaves town on business, 15-year-old Natalie (Jennifer Connelly) allows classmate Jeff (Byron Thames) to move into her home. Their relationship is purely platonic, but no one will believe them. Average but well-meant teen comedy. Rated PG for tastefully suggested sex. 1986; 95m.

SEVEN YEAR ITCH, THE ★★★★
DIR: Billy Wilder. **CAST:** Tom Ewell, Marilyn Monroe, Oscar Homolka, Carolyn Jones.

This movie is Marilyn Monroe's most enjoyable comedy. Marilyn lives upstairs from average American Tom Ewell. It seems his wife has escaped the heat of their New York home by going on vacation. This leaves Tom alone and unprotected, and one visit from luscious neighbor Marilyn leads him on a Walter Mitty–style adventure that is a joy to behold. 1957; 105m.

SEX ON THE RUN 🦃
DIR: François Legrand. **CAST:** Tony Curtis, Marisa Berenson, Britt Ekland.

This story of a sexually voracious Arabian sheik is amazingly bad. Grotesque and in shockingly bad taste. 1978; 88m.

SEX WITH A SMILE ★½
DIR: Sergio Martino. **CAST:** Marty Feldman, Edwige Fenech, Sydne Rome, Barbara Bouchet, Dayle Haddon.

Silly, badly dubbed Italian film featuring five short stories on sexual misunderstandings. Marty Feldman's section produces some laughs, but the film is too broad and too dependent on sexism Italian-style. Rated R for nudity and sex. 1976; 100m.

SEXTETTE ★
DIR: Ken Hughes, Irving Rapper. **CAST:** Mae West, Timothy Dalton, Dom DeLuise, Tony Curtis, Ringo Starr, George Hamilton, George Raft.

A dreadful movie only *barely* worth a viewing on fast-forward to witness the vulgar campiness of the nearly 80-year-old Mae West barely able to move through a bevy of barely clad beefcake—and certainly unable to shock or amuse. Her famous way with innuendo, her sexy purr, her let's-see-if-whàtcha-got-measures-up and come-hither-with-it look—the whole package is decades past its expiration date. Rated R. 1978; 91m.

SHADEY ★★½

DIR: Phillip Saville. **CAST:** Antony Sher, Billie Whitelaw, Patrick Macnee, Katherine Helmond.

Mildly entertaining British comedy about Shadey (Antony Sher), a man who has the ability to "think pictures onto film." When these little movies turn out to be prophecies that are ultimately fulfilled, Shadey becomes a hot item in the defense department. Plodding one moment, all-out bizarre the next. Rated PG-13 for violence and profanity. 1987; 90m.

SHAKIEST GUN IN THE WEST, THE ★★

DIR: Alan Rafkin. **CAST:** Don Knotts, Barbara Rhoades, Jackie Coogan, Don Barry.

This picture is a remake of *The Paleface* with Don Knotts in the Bob Hope role. A Philadelphia dentist goes West and gets himself involved in gunfights and trysts with buxom beauties. A fun family film. 1968; 100m.

SHANGHAI SURPRISE ★

DIR: Jim Goddard. **CAST:** Sean Penn, Madonna, Paul Freeman, Richard Griffiths, Philip Sayer, Victor Wong.

The only surprise here is the amount of money poured into this silly farce. Madonna plays an uptight missionary in Shanghai, 1938. She recruits a con artist (Sean Penn) to help her recover eleven hundred pounds of opium to ease the pain of the suffering. Rated PG for occasional obscenities and partial nudity. 1986; 93m.

SHE COULDN'T SAY NO ★★

DIR: Lloyd Bacon. **CAST:** Robert Mitchum, Jean Simmons, Arthur Hunnicutt, Edgar Buchanan.

An oil-rich woman (Jean Simmons) wishes to repay the citizens of her hometown of Progress, Arkansas, for the kindnesses shown her in childhood. Her idea of showering the town with money is charitable, but disrupts the day-to-day life of the citizenry. Robert Mitchum, as the town doctor, seems out of place in this picture. 1954; B&W; 89m.

SHE DONE HIM WRONG ★★★★

DIR: Lowell Sherman. **CAST:** Mae West, Cary Grant, Gilbert Roland, Noah Beery Sr., Rochelle Hudson, Louise Beavers.

Mae West woos Cary Grant in this comedy classic. She is a lady saloon keeper in the Gay Nineties. He is the undercover cop assigned to bring her in. She says, "Come up and see me sometime." He does, and the result is movie magic. 1933; B&W; 66m.

SHE'S GOTTA HAVE IT ★★★★

DIR: Spike Lee. **CAST:** Tracy Camilla Johns, Redmond Hicks, John Terrell, Spike Lee.

A movie about a randy young woman who's "gotta have it" might seem a bit iffy. But independent filmmaker Spike Lee—who wrote, directed, and edited this unique narrative-quasi-documentary—set up the challenge for himself and then set out to succeed *con gusto*. The beautiful lady in question, Nola Darling, is played by Tracy Camilla Johns. Rated R for language and nudity. 1986; B&W; 100m.

SHE'S HAVING A BABY ★½

DIR: John Hughes. **CAST:** Kevin Bacon, Elizabeth McGovern, William Windom, James Ray, Holland Taylor.

Director John Hughes, champion and glorifier of the teenage set, advanced from the breakfast club to the breakfast table in this concoction. The joys and tribulations of domesticity are the subject of this bland account of a young newlywed couple, played by Kevin Bacon and Elizabeth McGovern. A major (and deserved) failure. Rated PG. 1988; 110m.

SHE'S OUT OF CONTROL ★

DIR: Stan Dragoti. **CAST:** Tony Danza, Catharine Hicks, Wallace Shawn, Ami Dolenz.

In this brain-dead comedy, Tony Danza overplays the father of a fifteen-year-old girl (Ami Dolenz) who suddenly blossoms into a sexy young woman. Director Stan Dragoti made similarly slight premises work well in

Mr. Mom and *Love at First Bite*, but here he is strapped with a screenplay filled with absurd situations and grotesque characters. Rated PG for very brief violence. 1989; 97m.

SHOCK TREATMENT
DIR: Jim Sharman. **CAST:** Jessica Harper, Cliff De Young, Richard O'Brien.

Forgettable sequel to *The Rocky Horror Picture Show* that bombed out even with the rabid *Rocky Horror* crowd. Plot concerns two heroes, Janet and Brad, going on a TV game show and ending up trying to escape from it. Avoid this one at all costs. Rated PG. 1981; 94m.

SHOOT LOUD, LOUDER...I DON'T UNDERSTAND ★½
DIR: Eduardo De Filippo. **CAST:** Marcello Mastroianni, Raquel Welch, Leopoldo Trieste.

The last part of the title is indicative of this confusing jumble, which is alternately surreal and pedestrian as antique dealer Marcello Mastroianni confronts wooden Raquel Welch and inept gunmen. Unrated, this film contains some violence and adult situations, and even at 100 minutes it runs too long. 1966; 100m.

SHOP AROUND THE CORNER, THE ★★★★
DIR: Ernst Lubitsch. **CAST:** James Stewart, Margaret Sullavan, Frank Morgan, Joseph Schildkraut.

A charming period comedy dealing with the lives of two people who work in the same Budapest shop and become loving pen pals. MGM later remade this picture as *In the Good Old Summertime*, and it formed the basis of the stage musical *She Loves Me*. 1939; B&W; 98m.

SHOT IN THE DARK, A ★★★★
DIR: Blake Edwards. **CAST:** Peter Sellers, Elke Sommer, George Sanders, Burt Kwouk, Herbert Lom.

A Shot in the Dark is a one-man show, with Peter Sellers outdoing himself as the character he later reprised in *The Return of the Pink Panther*, *The Pink Panther Strikes Back*, and *The Revenge of the Pink Panther*. In this slapstick delight, Clouseau attempts to discover whether or not a woman (Elke Sommer) is guilty of murdering her lover. 1964; 101m.

SHOW PEOPLE ★★★★
DIR: King Vidor. **CAST:** Marion Davies, William Haines, Polly Moran.

Loosely based on the career of Gloria Swanson, this was the justly fabled Marion Davies's last silent film. Davies is warm and genuinely touching as innocent Polly Pepper, a young actress whose ambitions are thwarted at nearly every turn. As a satire on the industry, this is a glittering gem, right on the money. Charlie Chaplin, John Gilbert, May Murray, and Norma Talmadge are among a coterie of stars appearing as themselves. Silent. 1928; B&W; 81m.

SILENT MOVIE ★★★½
DIR: Mel Brooks. **CAST:** Mel Brooks, Marty Feldman, Dom DeLuise, Bernadette Peters, Sid Caesar, James Caan, Burt Reynolds, Paul Newman, Liza Minnelli, Anne Bancroft, Marcel Marceau, Harry Ritz, Ron Carey.

Mel Brooks's *Silent Movie* is another kitchen-sink affair, with Brooks going from the ridiculous to the sublime with a beautiful idea that bears more exploring. Silent films were the best for comedy, and Brooks, along with co-stars Marty Feldman, Dom DeLuise, and Sid Caesar, supplies numerous funny moments. Rated PG. 1976; 86m.

SILVER BEARS ★★
DIR: Ivan Passer. **CAST:** Michael Caine, Cybill Shepherd, Louis Jourdan, Martin Balsam, Stéphane Audran, Tom Smothers, David Warner.

If *Silver Bears* was meant to be a comedy, it isn't funny. If it was meant to be a drama, it isn't gripping. It's boring. Michael Caine stars as a Mafia henchman sent to Switzerland to buy a bank for a Las Vegas gambler (Martin Balsam). He's swindled and ends up buying two rooms over a pizza parlor. Rated PG. 1978; 113m.

SILVER STREAK ★★★★½
DIR: Arthur Hiller. **CAST:** Gene Wilder, Jill Clayburgh, Richard Pryor, Patrick McGoohan, Ray Walston, Ned Beatty, Richard Kiel.

A fast-paced, action story laced with comedy and stars such as Gene Wilder, Jill Clayburgh, and Richard Pryor. It will have you cheering, laughing, gasping, and jumping. *Streak* pits neurotic Wilder, sexy Clayburgh, and shifty Pryor against cool millionaire villain Patrick McGoohan and his evil henchman, Ray Walston, in a wild high-speed chase that brings back the train as a modern-day source for good thrillers. Rated PG. 1976; 113m.

SIMON ★★
DIR: Marshall Brickman. **CAST:** Alan Arkin, Madeline Kahn, Austin Pendleton, William Finley, Fred Gwynne.

Weird, weird comedy about an average guy (Alan Arkin) who is brainwashed into thinking he's a visitor from outer space. The film has some funny moments, as well as a few interesting things to say, but it just doesn't work as a whole. Rated PG. 1980; 97m.

SIN OF HAROLD DIDDLEBOCK (AKA MAD WEDNESDAY) ★★★½
DIR: Preston Sturges. **CAST:** Harold Lloyd, Frances Ramsden, Jimmy Conlin, Raymond Walburn, Edgar Kennedy, Arline Judge, Lionel Stander, Margaret Hamilton, Rudy Vallee.

The result of a disastrous joint effort of director Preston Sturges, silent-screen great Harold Lloyd, and backer Howard Hughes is a much better film than popular Hollywood legend implies. This story about a middle-aged man fired from his job and set adrift with nothing but unfulfilled potential doesn't sound like a scream. However, Lloyd's bizarre antics redeem the character. Hughes rereleased it in 1950 as *Mad Wednesday* and edited it down to seventy-nine minutes. 1947; B&W; 90m.

SINGLETON'S PLUCK ★★★
DIR: Richard Eyre. **CAST:** Ian Holm, Penelope Wilton.

In this gentle British comedy, a goose farmer, whose business has been shut down by a strike, decides to herd his gaggle to the slaughterhouse himself. Television reporters begin to cover his hundred-mile trip and he becomes a national figure. 1984; 93m.

SITTING DUCKS ★½
DIR: Henry Jaglom. **CAST:** Michael Emil, Zack Norman, Patrice Townsend, Richard Romanus.

Largely improvised comedy about a mafia accountant and his pal who steal a day's payroll and hit the road. Director Henry Jaglom's low-budget movies are an acquired taste; in this case, we really don't see why you would want to bother. Michael Emil (the director's brother) is especially annoying. Rated R for nudity and language. 1980; 90m.

SIX PACK ★
DIR: Daniel Petrie. **CAST:** Kenny Rogers, Diane Lane, Erin Gray, Barry Corbin.

In this unimaginative retread of *Rocky*, *Smokey and the Bandit*, and every bachelor-father comedy ever made, country crossover king Kenny Rogers plays a footloose stock-car racer who is latched on to by six homeless, sticky-fingered kids ranging in age from 7 to 16. In his feature-film debut, Rogers is wooden and unconvincing, but then so is the whole movie. Rated PG for profanity. 1982; 110m.

SIXTEEN CANDLES ★★★★
DIR: John Hughes. **CAST:** Molly Ringwald, Paul Dooley, Blanche Baker, Edward Andrews, Anthony Michael Hall, Billie Bird.

Molly Ringwald stars in this fast and funny teen comedy as a high-school student who is crushed when the whole family forgets her sixteenth birthday. Things, it seems to her, go downhill from there—that is, until the boy of her dreams suddenly starts showing some interest. Sort of the female flip side of *Risky Business*. Rated PG for profanity. 1984; 93m.

SKIN DEEP ★★
DIR: Blake Edwards. **CAST:** John Ritter, Vincent Gardenia, Alyson Reed, Joel Brooks, Julianne Phillips, Don Gordon, Nina Foch.

Writer-director Blake Edwards tries for another sex farce in the *10* vein, but this one fails to rise to its potential. John Ritter's undeniable charm and boyish good looks cannot compensate for the fact that his character—a womanizing alcoholic—is selfish, thoughtless, egocentric, and utterly lacking in redeeming social qualities. Viewers with raised consciousnesses are advised to stay away from this one. Rated R for nudity, profanity, and explicit sexual themes. 1989; 98m.

SKYLINE ★★★
DIR: Fernando Colombo. **CAST:** Antonio Resines, Susana Ocana.

Antonio Resines plays a Spanish photographer named Gustavo who comes to New York seeking international fame. Once there, he struggles to learn English, find work, and pursue friendship and romance. In Spanish and English, with subtitles it would be excellent for bilingual viewers. The twist ending really gives one a jolt. We'd rate it PG for slight profanity. 1984; 84m.

SLAMMER GIRLS ★★
DIR: Chuck Vincent. **CAST:** Devon Jenkin, Jeff Eagle, Jane Hamilton.

Spoof of women's prison films. A male reporter disguises himself as a woman to get a story and prove the heroine's innocence. A few funny bits, but many more that are plain stupid. Rated R for nudity and profanity. 1987; 82m.

SLAP SHOT ★★★★
DIR: George Roy Hill. **CAST:** Paul Newman, Strother Martin, Jennifer Warren, Lindsay Crouse, Melinda Dillon.

When released in 1977, this comedy about a down-and-out hockey team was criticized for its liberal use of profanity. The controversy tended to obscure the fact that *Slap Shot* is a very funny, marvelously acted movie. Paul Newman, as an aging player-coach who's a loser in love and on the ice until he instructs the members of his team to behave like animals during their matches, has never been better. Rated R. 1977; 122m.

SLAPSTICK OF ANOTHER KIND
DIR: Steven Paul. **CAST:** Jerry Lewis, Madeline Kahn, Marty Feldman.

Jerry Lewis hasn't made a funny film in years, and this sci-fi spoof is no exception. The gags are old, predictable, and forced. It seems the harder Jerry tries, the fewer laughs he generates. All of the elaborate costumes and props and the help of the usually funny Marty Feldman and Madeline Kahn cannot save this turkey based on a Kurt Vonnegut story. Rated PG. 1983; 85m.

SLAVE GIRLS FROM BEYOND INFINITY ★★
DIR: Ken Dixon. **CAST:** Elizabeth Cyton, Cindy Beal, Brinke Stevens.

A pair of space bimbos in bikinis scuttle off a slave ship only to find themselves in hotter water on a weird planet whose sole occupant hunts intergalactic visitors. Low budget, but with decent effects and lighting. The patter is sporadically funny, but not nearly campy enough. Rated R for nudity. 1987; 80m.

SLAVES OF NEW YORK ★
DIR: James Ivory. **CAST:** Bernadette Peters.

James Ivory's film is curiously old-fashioned and seems out of step for a supposedly up-to-date film about Manhattan's downtown art scene. The film technique is all cutesy gimmicks, and the content is shopworn situation-comedy and girl-needs-boy romance, despite the exotic, colorful settings and supposedly aimless amoral characters. Rated R, with profanity and sexual situations. 1989; 125m.

SLEEPER ★★★★
DIR: Woody Allen. **CAST:** Woody Allen, Diane Keaton, John McLiam, John Beck.
Writer-star-director Woody Allen finally exhibited some true film-making talent with this 1973 sci-fi spoof. The frenetic gag-a-minute comedy style of Allen's earlier films was replaced by some nice bits of character comedy. This makes *Sleeper* the most enjoyable of Allen's pre–*Annie Hall* creations. Rated PG. 1973; 88m.

SLIGHTLY HONORABLE ★★★
DIR: Tay Garnett. **CAST:** Pat O'Brien, Edward Arnold, Broderick Crawford, Evelyn Keyes, Phyllis Brooks, Eve Arden.
Wisecracks and red herrings provide the drawing cards in this fast-paced comedy-thriller. The plot's muddy, but basically it concerns a lawyer, Pat O'Brien, who is set up for a murder by crooked politician Edward Arnold. O'Brien ends up clearing himself and netting the real killer in the bargain. 1939; B&W; 85m.

SLUGGER'S WIFE, THE ★★
DIR: Hal Ashby. **CAST:** Michael O'Keefe, Rebecca DeMornay, Martin Ritt, Randy Quaid, Cleavant Derricks.
The most shallow of Neil Simon's works to date, this is bad television situation comedy blown up to big-screen size. Darryl Palmer (Michael O'Keefe) is a self-centered baseball player who bullies his way into the affections of Debby Palmer (Rebecca De Mornay), a would-be rock star. Rated PG-13 for nudity and profanity. 1985; 105m.

SLUMBER PARTY 57
DIR: William E. Levey. **CAST:** Noelle North, Debra Winger, Rainbeaux Smith, Joe E. Ross.
In this sleazy, smutty movie, six girls sit around a campfire and tell about the first time they "did it." It's really embarrassing to see a young Debra Winger involved in such garbage, and her fans are advised to avoid it. Rated R—you'd better believe it! 1977; 89m.

SMALLEST SHOW ON EARTH, THE ★★★½
DIR: Basil Dearden. **CAST:** Peter Sellers, Bill Travers, Margaret Rutherford.
Warm, often hilarious comedy about a couple who inherit a run-down movie theater and its wacky attendants. Excellent performances by Peter Sellers and Margaret Rutherford. 1957; B&W; 80m.

SMOKEY AND THE BANDIT ★★★½
DIR: Hal Needham. **CAST:** Burt Reynolds, Pat McCormick, Jerry Reed, Sally Field, Mike Henry, Jackie Gleason, Paul Williams.
Smokey and the Bandit may strain credibility, but it never stops being fun. The Bandit (Burt Reynolds) is an infamous independent trucker who is hired to transport four hundred cases of Coors beer from Texarkana, Texas, where it is legal, to Atlanta, Georgia, where it is not. Hold on to your hat. Rated PG for profanity. 1977; 97m.

SMOKEY AND THE BANDIT II ★★
DIR: Hal Needham. **CAST:** Burt Reynolds, Jerry Reed, Pat McCormick, Paul Williams, Mike Henry, Jackie Gleason, Dom DeLuise.
Smokey II is just more proof that "sequels aren't equal." But it isn't a total loss. If you find yourself sitting through this pale imitation, don't turn it off until the credits roll (although you may want to fast-forward). Outtakes featuring the stars flubbing their lines are spliced together at the end, and they're hilarious. Rated PG. 1980; 101m.

SMOKEY AND THE BANDIT III
DIR: Dick Lowry. **CAST:** Jerry Reed, Jackie Gleason, Paul Williams, Pat McCormick.

The Bandit may be back, but it ain't Burt. Instead, Jerry Reed, who played Reynolds's buddy Cletus in the first two films, takes over that half of the title roles, with Jackie Gleason returning for the other as Sheriff Buford T. Justice. An embarrassing waste of celluloid and money. Rated PG for nudity, profanity, and scatological humor. 1983; 86m.

SMOKEY BITES THE DUST ★★½
DIR: Charles B. Griffith. **CAST:** Jimmy McNichol, Walter Barnes, John Blythe Barrymore, William Forsythe.
Jimmy McNichol stars as a mischievous teenager who takes great delight in stealing cars and making buffoons out of the sheriff and his deputies. To make matters worse, he takes the sheriff's daughter along for the ride. This is pretty standard car-chase action, but it does move along and there are some laughs along the way. Rated PG. 1981; 85m.

SO FINE ★
DIR: Andrew Bergman. **CAST:** Ryan O'Neal, Jack Warden, Richard Kiel, Fred Gwynne, Mike Kellin, David Rounds.
This so-called sex comedy—about a fashion house (run by Ryan O'Neal and Jack Warden) that introduces a new line of designer jeans with see-through plastic inserts in the seat—is little more than a television situation comedy with leers. Rated R because of nudity and profanity. 1981; 91m.

SO THIS IS WASHINGTON ★★½
DIR: Ray McCarey. **CAST:** Charles Lauck, Norris Goff, Alan Mowbray, Minerva Urecal.
From a park bench in Washington, D.C., Charles Lauck and Norris Goff, radio's crackerbarrel philosophers Lum and Abner, dispense common sense to senators and congressmen. Third in a series, this product of wartime mentality is a simpleminded feature aimed at warming the heart. 1943; B&W; 65m.

S.O.B. ★★★
DIR: Blake Edwards. **CAST:** Julie Andrews, William Holden, Robert Preston, Richard Mulligan, Robert Vaughn, Loretta Swit, Larry Hagman, Craig Stevens, Shelley Winters, Rosanna Arquette.
Director Blake Edwards vents his resentment over Hollywood's treatment of him in the early 1970s in this failed attempt at satire. There are some good moments, but they are too few to make this potent satire. Self-indulgent. Rated R. 1981; 121m.

SOME GIRLS ★★★
DIR: Michael Hoffman. **CAST:** Patrick Dempsey, Jennifer Connelly, Lila Kedrova, Florinda Bolkan.
European tale about a young man (Patrick Dempsey) invited to join a girl and her very strange family over the Christmas season. Concentrates more on character and dramatic depth than story development. Rated R for language, nudity, and simulated sex. 1988; 95m.

SOME KIND OF HERO ★½
DIR: Michael Pressman. **CAST:** Richard Pryor, Margot Kidder, Ronny Cox, Olivia Cole.
This Richard Pryor movie can't decide whether it should tell the story of a Vietnam prisoner of war and his problems returning to American society or be another comedy caper film. As a result, it's neither very funny nor worth thinking about. Rated R for profanity, nudity, and violence. 1982; 97m.

SOME KIND OF WONDERFUL ★★★★
DIR: Howard Deutch. **CAST:** Eric Stoltz, Mary Stuart Masterson, Lea Thompson, Craig Sheffer, John Ashton.
Eric Stoltz stars as an affable lad who can't seem to make any headway with women. Unaware of the deep affection hurled in his direction by constant companion Mary Stuart Masterson (who all but steals the show), Stoltz sets his sights high on Lea

Thompson, who mingles with the school's upper-echelon social caste. Perceptive, thoughtful viewing. Rated PG-13 for mature situations. 1987; 93m.

SOME LIKE IT HOT ★★★★★

DIR: Billy Wilder. **CAST:** Marilyn Monroe, Jack Lemmon, Tony Curtis, Joe E. Brown, George Raft, Pat O'Brien, Nehemiah Persoff, Mike Mazurki.

Billy Wilder's *Some Like It Hot* is the outlandish story of two men (Jack Lemmon and Tony Curtis) who accidentally witness a gangland slaying. They pose as members of an all-girl band in order to avoid the gangsters, who are now trying to silence them permanently. Marilyn Monroe is at her sensual best as the band's singer. Joe E. Brown is also hilarious as a wealthy playboy who develops an attraction for an obviously bewildered Lemmon. 1959; B&W; 119m.

SOMETHING SHORT OF PARADISE ★★★

DIR: David Helpern Jr. **CAST:** Susan Sarandon, David Steinberg, Marilyn Sokol, Jean-Pierre Aumont.

This romantic comedy is something short of perfect but still manages to entertain. Two New Yorkers (Susan Sarandon and David Steinberg) manage to find love and happiness together despite distractions from other conniving singles. Marilyn Sokol is great as one of the obstacles. Rated PG. 1979; 91m.

SOMETHING SPECIAL ★★★

DIR: Paul Schneider. **CAST:** Patty Duke, Pamela Segall, Eric Gurry, Mary Tanner, John Glover, Seth Green.

Offbeat but surprisingly pleasant comedy about a 15-year-old girl named Milly (Pamela Segall) who is convinced that life would be easier if she were a boy. With the help of a magical potion and a solar eclipse, she manages to grow a penis. Forced to choose between the sexes, she changes her name to Willy to please her father and to satisfy her own curiosity. Rated PG-13. 1987; 90m.

SOMETHING WILD ★★★★½

DIR: Jonathan Demme. **CAST:** Jeff Daniels, Melanie Griffith, Ray Liotta, Margaret Colin, Tracey Walter.

Jeff Daniels stars as a desk-bound investment type whose idea of yuppie rebellion is stiffing a local diner for the price of a lunch. This petty larceny is observed by a mysterious woman (Melanie Griffith) who, to Daniels's relief and surprise, takes him not to the local police but to a seedy motel, where they share an afternoon that justifies the film's R rating. This moves from hilarious beginnings to true edge-of-the-seat terror. Rated R. 1986; 113m.

SON OF PALEFACE ★★★½

DIR: Frank Tashlin. **CAST:** Bob Hope, Jane Russell, Roy Rogers, Douglass Dumbrille, Bill Williams, Harry Von Zell, Iron Eyes Cody.

Bob Hope is in top shape as he matches wits with smooth villain Douglass Dumbrille and consistently loses, only to be aided by gun-totin' Jane Russell and government agent Roy Rogers. 1952; 95m.

SONS OF THE DESERT ★★★★★

DIR: William A. Seiter. **CAST:** Stan Laurel, Oliver Hardy, Charlie Chase.

In *Sons of the Desert*, Stan Laurel and Oliver Hardy scheme to get away from their wives and attend a lodge convention in Chicago. After persuading the wives that Ollie needs to sail to Honolulu for his health, they go to Chicago. The boat sinks on the way back from Hawaii, and the boys end up having to explain how they got home a day earlier than the other survivors (they ship-hiked). 1933; B&W; 69m.

SORORITY BABES IN THE SLIMEBALL BOWL-O-RAMA ★★★½

DIR: David DeCoteau. **CAST:** Linnea Quigley, Andras Jones, Robin Rochelle.

A spoof of horror films. A group of kids break into a bowling alley and accidentally release a murderous little demon. Silly and with low production values, but it's a lot of gory fun. Rated R for nudity, violence, and profanity. 1987; 77m.

SORROWFUL JONES ★★★
DIR: Sidney Lanfield. **CAST:** Bob Hope, Lucille Ball, Mary Jane Saunders, Thomas Gomez, William Demarest, Bruce Cabot.

Bob Hope's first semiserious film, this is a remake of the 1934 Shirley Temple hit, *Little Miss Marker*. Bob, as a bookie, gets tangled up with nightclub singer Lucille Ball and an assortment of gangsters while babysitting a gambler's baby daughter. A good mix of wisecracks, fast action, and sentiment. 1949; B&W; 88m.

SOUL MAN ★★★
DIR: Steve Miner. **CAST:** C. Thomas Howell, Rae Dawn Chong, James Earl Jones, Arye Gross, James B. Sikking, Leslie Nielsen.

Los Angeles preppie Mark Watson (C. Thomas Howell) masquerades as a needy black to gain entrance to Harvard Law School. Director Steve Miner keeps things moving so fast one doesn't have time to consider how silly it all is. Rated PG-13 for profanity, suggested sex, and violence. 1986; 101m.

SOUP FOR ONE ★★★
DIR: Jonathan Kaufer. **CAST:** Saul Rubinek, Marcia Strassman, Teddy Pendergrass.

Marcia Strassman (formerly the wife on *Welcome Back Kotter*) stars as the dream girl to an often disappointed lover. When he finds her, he tries to persuade her to marry him. Although there are a few slow-moving parts, it is a generally enjoyable comedy. Rated R for sexual themes. 1982; 87m.

SPACEBALLS ★★
DIR: Mel Brooks. **CAST:** Mel Brooks, John Candy, Rick Moranis, Bill Pullman, Daphne Zuniga, Dick Van Patten, George Wyner, Michael Winslow, Lorene Yarnell.

The plot loosely concerns planet Spaceball's attempt to "steal" the atmosphere from neighbor Druidia by kidnapping and ransoming off the royally spoiled Princess Vespa. The wacky Dark Helmet (Rick Moranis) is responsible for this dastardly plot, and he is opposed by rogue trader Lone Starr (Bill Pullman) and his human-canine sidekick, John Candy's Barf the Mawg ("I'm my own best friend"). Rated PG for mild profanity. 1987; 96m.

SPACED OUT ★★★
DIR: Norman J. Warren. **CAST:** Barry Stokes, Tony Maiden, Glory Annen.

In this spoof of science-fiction films, the Earth is visited by an all-female crew on a broken-down spaceship. Three men and a woman are taken hostage. The testing of these hostages and the discovery of the differences between men and women make for a watchable but raunchy comedy. This film is rated R for nudity and implied sex. 1985; 85m.

SPACESHIP
DIR: Bruce Kimmel. **CAST:** Cindy Williams, Bruce Kimmel, Leslie Nielsen, Gerrit Graham.

This "comedy" is all about an unwanted alien tagging along on a rocket full of idiots. Tries to be another *Airplane!*, even going as far as to steal that film's co-star (Leslie Nielsen), but there's not one funny moment in this dud. A complete failure. Original title: *The Creature Wasn't Nice*. Rated PG. 1981; 88m.

SPALDING GRAY: TERRORS OF PLEASURE ★★★★
DIR: Thomas Schlamme. **CAST:** Spalding Gray.

Spalding Gray, the master storyteller, relates the humorous adventure of finding the perfect retreat and piece of land to call his own. This HBO special was filmed in concert, but some terrific editing takes you to the scenes he describes. The star of *Swimming to*

Cambodia also describes his brief encounter with Hollywood. 1988; 60m.

SPIES LIKE US ★★½
DIR: John Landis. **CAST:** Chevy Chase, Dan Aykroyd, Bruce Davison, William Prince, Steve Forrest, Bernie Casey, Donna Dixon.
Chevy Chase and Dan Aykroyd, who were co-stars on the original *Saturday Night Live* television show, appeared together on the big screen for the first time in this generally enjoyable comedy about two inept recruits in a U.S. intelligence organization's counterespionage mission. Rated PG for violence and profanity. 1985; 104m.

SPIKE OF BENSONHURST ★
DIR: Paul Morrissey. **CAST:** Sasha Mitchell, Ernest Borgnine, Sylvia Miles.
Haphazard mess about life in a mafia-run neighborhood in New York City. Sasha Mitchell stars as a young Italian boxer trying to get his big break in a sport that's fixed inside and outside of the ring. Meandering nonsense conveys contempt for its audience. Rated R for nudity, violence, and profanity. 1989; 102m.

SPLASH ★★★★★
DIR: Ron Howard. **CAST:** Tom Hanks, Daryl Hannah, John Candy, Eugene Levy, Dody Goodman, Richard B. Shull.
An uproarious comedy about a young man (Tom Hanks) who unknowingly falls in love with a mermaid (Daryl Hannah). John Candy and Eugene Levy add some marvelous bits of comedy. Rated PG for profanity and brief nudity. 1984; 111m.

SPOOKS RUN WILD ★½
DIR: Phil Rosen. **CAST:** Bela Lugosi, The East Side Kids, Dave O'Brien, Dennis Moore.
Bottom-of-the-barrel "entertainment" wastes a rapidly deteriorating Bela Lugosi in another silly role that gives the aging East Side Kids a chance to humiliate him on-screen. Inane, laughless, and overlong at sixty-nine minutes, this film fails on all levels. 1941; B&W; 69m.

SPRING BREAK ★
DIR: Sean S. Cunningham. **CAST:** David Knell, Steve Bassett, Perry Lang, Paul Land.
Here's a numbingly stupid movie about four guys on the make in Fort Lauderdale. It's reminiscent of the old "Beach Party" films, with one major exception—Annette Funicello never took off her top. Parents of the teenagers it's directed at may be shocked by the nudity, implied sex, and profanity that rightfully earned *Spring Break* its R rating. 1983; 101m.

SPRING FEVER ★
DIR: Joseph L. Scanlan. **CAST:** Jessica Walter, Susan Anton, Frank Converse, Carling Bassett, Stephen Young.
In spite of an advertising come-on that promised another beach romp in the tradition of *Where the Boys Are*, this limp Canadian production is an unbelievably dull story about a rising young tennis star (Carling Bassett). Even the tennis sequences are boring, making the film seem to run an hour too long. Rated PG. 1983; 100m.

SPY WITH A COLD NOSE, THE ★★★
DIR: Daniel Petrie. **CAST:** Laurence Harvey, Daliah Lavi, Lionel Jeffries, Eric Sykes, Paul Ford.
This cute British spy spoof features Lionel Jeffries as an un-Bond-like counterintelligence agent. His plan to implant a microphone in the goodwill gift to the Soviets goes awry. The gift, a bulldog, may require an operation, and then the Soviets would be outraged. Thus, our agent seeks the help of a womanizing vet (Laurence Harvey). They go to Moscow to remove the microphone. 1966; 113m.

SQUEEZE, THE (1987) ★
DIR: Roger Young. **CAST:** Michael Keaton, Rae Dawn Chong, Meat Loaf.
Michael Keaton can always be counted on for at least a few laughs,

but a few laughs is about all you get in this dreary comedy-thriller. Keaton is an urban wiseguy, Rae Dawn Chong is a bill collector, and together they try to stop a plot to defraud the New York lottery. It's rated PG-13 for language and violence. 1987; 101m.

STAGE DOOR ★★★★
DIR: Gregory La Cava. **CAST:** Katharine Hepburn, Ginger Rogers, Eve Arden, Lucille Ball, Ann Miller.

A funny and tender taste of New York theatrical life. Katharine Hepburn and Ginger Rogers are two aspiring actresses who undergo the stifling yet stimulating life of a lodging house that caters to a vast array of prospective actresses trying any avenue to break into the big time. Eve Arden, Lucille Ball, and Ann Miller also take residence in this overcrowded and active boardinghouse. 1937; B&W; 92m.

STAND-IN ★★★
DIR: Tay Garnett. **CAST:** Leslie Howard, Humphrey Bogart, Joan Blondell, Jack Carson, Alan Mowbray.

This send-up of Hollywood rubbed more than one Tinsel Town mogul the wrong way by satirizing front office studio manipulators. Eastern financial genius Leslie Howard is sent west to "stand in" for stockholders and find out why Colossal Pictures is heading for skidsville. 1937; B&W; 91m.

STARDUST MEMORIES ★
DIR: Woody Allen. **CAST:** Woody Allen, Charlotte Rampling, Jessica Harper, Marie-Christine Barrault.

Absolutely unwatchable Woody Allen film, his most chaotic and Bergmanesque attempt to claim that he can't stand his fans. Boring, self-indulgent, and completely lacking the charm and perception of Allen's other films. And if this all was intended, as he has claimed, then he should be smacked for maiming the hand that feeds him. Rated PG—profanity. 1980; B&W; 88m.

STARS AND BARS ★★
DIR: Pat O'Connor. **CAST:** Daniel Day Lewis, Harry Dean Stanton, Maury Chaykin, Joan Cusack, Keith David, Spalding Gray, Will Patton, Martha Plimpton, Steven Wright.

Inept comedy about a well-groomed British art expert who finds himself in a culture clash when he is sent to rural Georgia to acquire a priceless Renoir from an eccentric businessman. His task becomes complicated as he is pursued by menacing rednecks, vicious gangsters, and various amorous females. Pretty disappointing considering the fine cast. Rated R for nudity and profanity. 1988; 99m.

START THE REVOLUTION WITHOUT ME ★★★★
DIR: Bud Yorkin. **CAST:** Gene Wilder, Donald Sutherland, Hugh Griffith, Jack MacGowran.

Gene Wilder and Donald Sutherland star in this hilarious comedy as two sets of twins who meet just before the French Revolution. Cheech and Chong's *The Corsican Brothers* covered pretty much the same ground. Only trouble was, it wasn't funny. If you want to see the story done right, check this one out. Rated PG. 1970; 98m.

STARTING OVER ★★★★
DIR: Alan J. Pakula. **CAST:** Burt Reynolds, Jill Clayburgh, Candice Bergen, Charles Durning, Frances Sternhagen.

Burt Reynolds and Jill Clayburgh are delightful in this Alan Pakula film about two lonely hearts trying to find romance in a cynical world. Candice Bergen is superb as Reynolds's off-key singer/ex-wife, whom he has trouble trying to forget in this winner. Rated R. 1979; 106m.

STATUE, THE ★
DIR: Rod Amateau. **CAST:** David Niven, Virna Lisi, Robert Vaughn, John Cleese.

David Niven plays a Nobel Prize-winning linguist whose wife, a sculptor, is commissioned to do a statue of him for the United Nations. But when he sees the nether regions of the nude statue, he feels certain that someone else posed for it. He sets off in search of the model, whom he presumes has been making love to his wife. A smutty comedy with a nonetheless skillful cast, which includes Monty Pythonite Graham Chapman in a tiny role. Rated R for innuendos and nudity. 1971; 84m.

STEAGLE, THE ★★★
DIR: Paul Sylbert. **CAST:** Richard Benjamin, Cloris Leachman, Chill Wills, Susan Tyrrell, Peter Hobbs.

Black comedy about how a daydreaming college professor (Richard Benjamin) deals with his mortality during the Cuban missile crisis. The week-long living spree he goes on over the fear that it might be his last has some hilarious consequences, but the screenplay is not handled very well despite the excellent cast. Rated PG for profanity and sex. 1971; 94m.

STEAMBOAT BILL JR. ★★★★½
DIR: Charles F. Reisner. **CAST:** Buster Keaton, Ernest Torrence, Marion Byron.

Buster Keaton is at his comedic-genius best in this delightful silent film as an accident-prone college student who is forced to take over his father's old Mississippi steamboat. The climax features spectacular stunts by Keaton. It is truly something to behold—and to laugh with. Silent. 1928; B&W; 71m.

STEELYARD BLUES ★★★½
DIR: Alan Meyerson. **CAST:** Jane Fonda, Donald Sutherland, Peter Boyle, Alan Myerson, Garry Goodrow.

This is a quirky little film about a group of social misfits who band together to help one of their own against his government-employed brother. Jane Fonda, Donald Sutherland, and Peter Boyle seem to have fun playing the misfits. Boyle's imitation of Marlon Brando is a highlight. Rated PG for language. 1973; 93m.

STEVE MARTIN LIVE ★★★½
DIR: Carl Gottlieb, Gary Weis. **CAST:** Steve Martin, Buck Henry, Teri Garr, David Letterman, Paul Simon, Alan King, Henny Youngman, Henry Winkler.

Though the bulk of this video offers a 1979 live performance that you've probably already seen in part on television, there are a number of reasons you'll enjoy this comedy video. If you're a fan of Martin's on-stage bits, such as "King Tut" and "Happy Feet," the live segment is for you. Viewers are also offered a tasty helping of Martin's satirical wit in his comedic short, *The Absent Minded Waiter*, which was nominated for an Academy Award. 1986; 60m.

STEVEN WRIGHT LIVE ★★★½
DIR: Walter C. Miller. **CAST:** Steven Wright.

For fans of the low-octane, extremely cerebral comic Steven Wright, this performance film is paradise. Wright delivers an endless stream of odd observations. He's funny, but an hour of deadpan is almost an eternity. 1985; 60m.

STICK-UP, THE ★
DIR: Jeffrey Bloom. **CAST:** David Soul, Pamela McMyler.

The alternate title, *Mud*, seems more appropriate for this dreary romance-adventure set in 1935 England. David Soul is trying to get to London, where he and a friend plan to rob an armored truck. His progress is slowed considerably by a runaway waitress who lands him in a heap of predicaments. Unreleased in the U.S. before its video incarnation, the British film is unrated, with some very brief nudity. 1977; 101m.

STICKY FINGERS
DIR: Catlin Adams. **CAST:** Helen Slater, Melanie Mayron, Eileen Brennan, Christopher Guest, Stephen McHattie, Shirley Stoler, Gwen Welles, Danitra Vance, Carol Kane.

Flat, awesomely unfunny film about two struggling female musicians who are handed $900,000 in dirty money by a drug-dealing friend. A lack of clever writing and two stars who have no charisma make this attempt at comedy aggravating. Rated PG-13 for language and sexual allusions. 1988; 89m.

STILL SMOKIN

DIR: Thomas Chong. **CAST:** Cheech and Chong, Hansman In't Veld, Carol Van Herwijnen.

Richard "Cheech" Marin and Thomas Chong, who also directed, hit rock bottom with this humorless shambles about a film festival in Amsterdam, Holland. It seems to indicate Cheech and Chong's disrespect for their audience. Rated R for nudity and scatological humor. 1983; 91m.

STIR CRAZY ★★★½

DIR: Sidney Poitier. **CAST:** Richard Pryor, Gene Wilder, Georg Stanford Brown, JoBeth Williams.

Richard Pryor and Gene Wilder work something close to a miracle in this comedy, making something out of nothing or, at least, close to nothing. It's a simpleminded spoof of crime and prison movies with, of all things, a little *Urban Cowboy* thrown in. You've seen it all before, but you have so much fun watching the stars, you don't mind. Rated R. 1980; 111m.

STITCHES

DIR: Alan Smithee. **CAST:** Parker Stevenson, Geoffrey Lewis, Eddie Albert.

Stitches is a formula bomb in which three med school students spend 92 minutes playing pranks on classmates and teachers. The humor isn't as aggressive or mean-spirited as in other *Porky's*-style movies, but a turkey by any other name is still a turkey. Rated R. 1985; 92m.

STOOGEMANIA ★

DIR: Chuck Workman. **CAST:** Josh Mostel, Melanie Chartoff, Sid Caesar, Moe Howard, Curly Howard, Larry Fine, Shemp Howard.

Don't be fooled by the title. The Three Stooges had very little to do with this movie. It's the story of Howard F. Howard (Josh Mostel), a man whose life is controlled by watching Three Stooges films, making him a Stoogemaniac. The movie is incredibly unfunny. Not rated, suitable for all ages. 1985; 83m.

STORM IN A TEACUP ★★★

DIR: Victor Saville, Ian Dalrymple. **CAST:** Vivien Leigh, Rex Harrison, Cecil Parker, Sara Allgood.

The refusal of an old lady to pay for a dog license touches off this amusing farrago on love, politics, and life. Rex Harrison is, of course, smashing. The dialogue is the thing. 1937; B&W; 87m.

STRANGE BREW ★★★½

DIR: Dave Thomas, Rick Moranis. **CAST:** Rick Moranis, Dave Thomas, Max von Sydow, Paul Dooley, Lynne Griffin.

Okay, all you hosers and hoseheads, here come those *SCTV* superstars from the Great White North, Bob and Doug McKenzie (Rick Moranis and Dave Thomas) in their first feature film. Beauty, eh? A mad scientist employed by a brewery controls a group of mental patients by feeding them beer laced with a mind-controlling drug. Rated PG. 1983; 90m.

STRANGER THAN PARADISE ★★★★½

DIR: Jim Jarmusch. **CAST:** John Lurie, Richard Edson, Eszter Balint.

In this superb independently made comedy, three oddball characters go on a spontaneous road trip through the United States, where they encounter boredom, routine problems, bad luck, and outrageous good fortune. The film, which won acclaim at the Cannes and New York film festivals, plays a lot like a Woody Allen comedy. It's a silly film for smart people. Rated R for profanity. 1985; B&W; 90m.

STRIKE UP THE BAND ★★★
DIR: Busby Berkeley. **CAST:** Mickey Rooney, Judy Garland, June Preisser, Paul Whiteman.

This encore to *Babes in Arms* has ever-exuberant Mickey Rooney leading a high-school band that would shade Glenn Miller's, going for the gold in a nationwide radio contest hosted by Paul Whiteman. Second banana Judy Garland sings. "Come on, kids, let's put on a show" in a different setting. 1940; B&W; 120m.

STRIPES ★★★★
DIR: Ivan Reitman. **CAST:** Bill Murray, Harold Ramis, John Candy, Warren Oates, P. J. Soles, Sean Young, John Larroquette.

It's laughs aplenty when *Saturday Night Live* graduate Bill Murray enlists in the army. But hey, as Murray might say, after a guy loses his job, his car, and his girl all in the same day, what else is he supposed to do? Thanks to Murray, Harold Ramis, and John Candy, the U.S. Army may never be the same. The late Warren Oates also is in top form as the boys' no-nonsense sergeant. Rated R. 1981; 105m.

STROKER ACE ★★★
DIR: Hal Needham. **CAST:** Burt Reynolds, Ned Beatty, Jim Nabors, Loni Anderson, Parker Stevenson.

Film critics all over the country jumped on this car-crash-and-cornpone comedy. It's not all that bad. About an egotistical, woman-chasing race-car driver, it's the same old predictable nonsense. Yet it's certain to please the audience it was intended for. Rated PG for sexual innuendo and violence. 1983; 96m.

STUCK ON YOU ★½
DIR: Michael Herz, Samuel Weil. **CAST:** Professor Irwin Corey, Virginia Penta, Mark Mikulski.

A dewinged Angel Gabriel (Professor Irwin Corey) is sent to Earth to help bring a couple back together. Gabriel becomes the judge in their palimony case and relates all their problems to events in history. The best and funniest parts of the film are when Carol (Virginia Penta) and Bill (Mark Mikulski) discuss their early relationship. Rated R for nudity, obscenities, and simulated sex. 1982; 86m.

STUDENT CONFIDENTIAL ★★½
DIR: Richard Horian. **CAST:** Eric Douglas, Marlon Jackson, Ronee Blakley.

A new school counselor helps some problem children with high IQs. *Student Confidential* does not speak to teens with the self-satisfaction of *The Breakfast Club* or the brutality of *River's Edge*, but it is far better than most teen films. Rated R for violence, profanity, and nudity. 1987; 92m.

SULLIVAN'S TRAVELS ★★★★★
DIR: Preston Sturges. **CAST:** Joel McCrea, Veronica Lake, Robert Warwick, William Demarest, Franklin Pangborn, Porter Hall, Eric Blore, Jimmy Conlin.

Pure genius produced this social comedy. It's the most beautifully witty and knowing spoof of Hollywood ever realized. Director Joel McCrea decides to find out what life outside the Tinseltown fantasyland is really like. With only ten cents in his pocket, he sets out on his travels. Along the way, he acquires a fellow wanderer in the form of the lovely Veronica Lake. This is a genuine Hollywood classic. 1941; B&W; 90m.

SUMMER CAMP
DIR: Chuck Vincent. **CAST:** Michael Abrams, Jake Barnes.

One of about two zillion *Animal House* ripoffs that littered drive-in screens in the late Seventies, replacing humor with nudity and sex jokes. The madcaps in this case are teens invited to a reunion of their old summer camp. What is it that makes us suspect that the actor billed as Dustin Pacino Jr. wasn't born with that name? Rated R. 1979; 85m.

SUMMER RENTAL ★★½
DIR: Carl Reiner. **CAST:** John Candy, Richard Crenna, Karen Austin, Rip Torn, Kerri Green.

John Candy is watchable in his first film as star. Unfortunately, the film itself does not live up to his talents. It starts off well enough—with air traffic controller Candy exhibiting the kind of stress that causes his superiors to suggest a vacation—but after a fairly funny first hour, it sinks into the mire of plot resolution as our hero decides to take up sailing and take on snobbish Richard Crenna. After Candy hooks up with sailing expert Rip Torn, the film rarely provides a chuckle. Rated PG for profanity. 1985; 88m.

SUMMER SCHOOL ★★★★
DIR: Carl Reiner. **CAST:** Mark Harmon, Kirstie Alley, Nels Van Patten, Carl Reiner, Courtney Thorne-Smith, Lucy Lee Flippin, Shawnee Smith.

This teen comedy does something almost unheard of for its genre—it bridges the generation gap and entertains young and old alike. Director Carl Reiner knows how to milk every scene for a laugh. Mark Harmon stars as a P.E. coach forced to teach remedial English in summer school. Rated PG-13 for obsenities and gore. 1987; 95m.

SUNSET LIMOUSINE ★½
DIR: Terry Hughes. **CAST:** John Ritter, Susan Dey, Martin Short, Paul Reiser, Audrie Neenan, Lainie Kazan.

John Ritter plays an out-of-work comic who must make something of himself before his girlfriend (Susan Dey) will take him back. As a limo driver he gets involved with a nerd (Martin Short) who is being pursued by thugs. Made for TV. 1983; 92m.

SUNSHINE BOYS, THE ★★★★
DIR: Herbert Ross. **CAST:** Walter Matthau, Richard Benjamin, George Burns, Lee Meredith, Carol Arthur, Howard Hesseman, Ron Rifkin.

The Sunshine Boys tells the story of two feuding ex–vaudeville stars who make a TV special. Walter Matthau, Richard Benjamin, and (especially) George Burns give memorable performances. Director Herbert Ross turns this adaptation of the successful Broadway play by Neil Simon into a celluloid winner. Rated PG. 1975; 111m.

SUPERGRASS, THE ★★
DIR: Peter Richardson. **CAST:** Adrian Edmondson, Jennifer Saunders, Peter Richardson.

The reluctant hero (Adrian Edmondson) of this English farce pretends to be an important drug dealer in order to impress his girlfriend. Ultimately, the bloke is in way over his head. So-so comedy. 1987; 96m.

SUPPOSE THEY GAVE A WAR AND NOBODY CAME? ★★
DIR: Hy Averback. **CAST:** Brian Keith, Ernest Borgnine, Suzanne Pleshette, Tom Ewell, Tony Curtis, Bradford Dillman, Ivan Dixon, Arthur O'Connell, Don Ameche.

In this comedy involving a confrontation between a rural town and a nearby military base, Brian Keith, Tony Curtis, and Ivan Dixon play three army buddies who take it upon themselves to stop the fighting. Ernest Borgnine plays a nasty police chief. Some funny moments and good acting. Rated PG for adult themes. 1970; 113m.

SURE THING, THE ★★★½
DIR: Rob Reiner. **CAST:** John Cusack, Daphne Zuniga, Anthony Edwards, Boyd Gaines, Lisa Jane Persky.

This enjoyable romantic comedy, about two college freshmen who discover themselves and each other through a series of misadventures on the road, is more or less director Rob Reiner's updating of Frank Capra's *It Happened One Night.* John Cusack and Daphne Zuniga star as the unlikely protagonists. Rated PG-13 for profanity and suggested sex. 1985; 100m.

SURRENDER ★★★
DIR: Jerry Belson. **CAST:** Sally Field, Michael Caine, Steve Guttenberg, Peter Boyle, Julie Kavner, Jackie Cooper.
Sally Field gives a sparkling performance as a confused woman in love with Michael Caine, Steve Guttenberg, and money, not necessarily in that order. Caine and Guttenberg are superb. At times contrived and a bit forced, overall, this is an enjoyable light comedy. Rated PG-13 for language and sex. 1987; 105m.

SURVIVORS, THE ★★★½
DIR: Michael Ritchie. **CAST:** Robin Williams, Walter Matthau, Jerry Reed, James Wainwright.
This is an often funny movie about a goofy "survivalist" (Robin Williams), who is "adopted" by a service station owner (Walter Matthau) and pursued by a friendly but determined hit man (Jerry Reed). Generally a black comedy, this movie features a variety of comedic styles, and they all work. Rated R for vulgar language and violence. 1983; 102m.

SUSAN SLEPT HERE ★★½
DIR: Frank Tashlin. **CAST:** Dick Powell, Debbie Reynolds, Anne Francis, Glenda Farrell.
Screenwriter Dick Powell must keep a tight leash on the ultra-high-spirited vagrant teenager he protects and falls for in the course of researching a script on juvenile delinquency. Amusing dialogue and lots of innuendo mark this otherwise pedestrian sex comedy. 1954; 98m.

SWEATER GIRLS ★
DIR: Don Jones. **CAST:** Harry Moses, Meegan King, Noelle North, Kate Sarchet, Charlene Tilton.
One of the silliest of the teen sexcapade movies, this concerns a club called "Sweater Girls" that Meegan King and Noelle North decide to form because they are fed up with their drinking, pawing boyfriends. Rated R for sex and language. 1984; 84m.

SWEET LIBERTY ★★★★
DIR: Alan Alda. **CAST:** Alan Alda, Michael Caine, Michelle Pfeiffer, Bob Hoskins, Lise Hilboldt, Lillian Gish, Saul Rubinek, Lois Chiles, Linda Thorson.
Writer-director-star Alan Alda strikes again, this time with the story of a small-town historian (Alda) whose prize-winning saga of the Revolutionary War is optioned by Hollywood and turned into a movie. When the film crew descends on Alda's hometown for location shooting, predictable chaos erupts. Quite entertaining. Rated PG for mild sexual situations. 1986; 107m.

SWEET WILLIAM ★★★½
DIR: Claude Whatham. **CAST:** Sam Waterston, Jenny Agutter, Anna Massey, Tim Pigott-Smith.
Sam Waterston and Jenny Agutter shine in this low-key adult comedy, which, while concerned with sex, doesn't feel the need to display any of it. They have an affair. She is attracted to his frenetic romanticism but slowly realizes that that same trait gets him into bed with every woman in sight. The women get the last laugh in this gentle British farce. Rated R for talk, not action. 1980; 92m.

SWIMMING TO CAMBODIA ★★★★
DIR: Jonathan Demme. **CAST:** Spalding Gray.
This low-budget movie consists of nothing more than actor-monologist Spalding Gray sitting at a desk while he tells about his experiences as a supporting actor in *The Killing Fields*. But seldom has so much come from so little. Gray is an excellent storyteller and his extended anecdotes—covering the political history of Cambodia, the filming of the movie, the sex and drugs available in Southeast Asia, and life in New York City—are often hilarious. Unrated. 1987; 87m.

SWING HIGH, SWING LOW ★★½
DIR: Mitchell Leisen. **CAST:** Carole Lombard, Fred MacMurray, Dorothy

Lamour, Charles Butterworth, Franklin Pangborn, Anthony Quinn.

Entertainers Carole Lombard and Fred MacMurray, stranded in Panama, get married, split, and fight ennui and a variety of troubles. This is a slanted-for-comedy remake of 1929's highly successful tearjerking backstage drama, *The Dance of Life*. 1937; B&W; 95m.

SWING IT, SAILOR ★★
DIR: Raymond Connon. **CAST:** Wallace Ford, Isabel Jewell, Ray Mayer.

Envision two gobs after one gal, or make it two swabs after one skirt, and you've got this film figured out. Broad, roughhouse humor is the order of the day. The story is stale, but this neighborhood-theater programmer moves along at a decent clip. 1937; B&W; 61m.

SWINGIN' SUMMER, A ★★
DIR: Robert Sparr. **CAST:** Raquel Welch, James Stacy, William Wellman Jr., Quinn O'Hara, Martin West.

This is one of those swingin' sixties flicks where three swingin' teens move to a swingin' summer resort for a swingin' vacation. They start up their own swingin' dance concert schedule and book big-name acts like Gary and the Playboys, the Rip Tides, and the Righteous Brothers. Raquel Welch debuts here and also sings. 1965; 82m.

SWISS MISS ★★★
DIR: John G. Blystone. **CAST:** Stan Laurel, Oliver Hardy, Della Lind, Walter Woolf King, Eric Blore.

Here we have Stan Laurel and Oliver Hardy in the Swiss Alps. A weak and uneven script is overcome by the stars, who seize several opportunities for brilliant comedy. For the most part, however, the film is mediocre. 1938; B&W; 72m.

SWITCHING CHANNELS ★★★
DIR: Ted Kotcheff. **CAST:** Kathleen Turner, Burt Reynolds, Christopher Reeve, Ned Beatty, Henry Gibson, Joe Silver.

Effective performances by Kathleen Turner, Burt Reynolds, and Christopher Reeve enliven this fourth big-screen version of Ben Hecht and Charles MacArthur's *The Front Page*. More specifically a remake of Howard Hawks's 1940 comedy classic, *His Girl Friday*, *Switching Channels* switches the setting from newspapers to television but keeps many of the elements of the original's plot. Rated PG for profanity. 1988; 113m.

TAKE DOWN ★★½
DIR: Kleth Merrill. **CAST:** Edward Herrmann, Kathleen Lloyd, Lorenzo Lamas, Maureen McCormick, Kevin Hooks, Stephen Furst.

Earnest comedy-drama set in the arena of high-school wrestling. It centers on two initially reluctant participants: an intellectual teacher-turned-coach and a fiery student. The movie has enough heart to carry it to victory. Rated PG. 1978; 107m.

TAKE THE MONEY AND RUN ★★★★
DIR: Woody Allen. **CAST:** Woody Allen, Janet Margolin, Marcel Hillaire.

Woody Allen's first original feature is still a laugh-filled delight as the star-director plays an inept criminal in a story told in pseudo-documentary-style (à la *Zelig*). It's hilarious. Rated PG. 1969; 85m.

TAKE THIS JOB AND SHOVE IT ★★★½
DIR: Gus Trikonis. **CAST:** Robert Hays, Art Carney, Barbara Hershey, Martin Mull, Eddie Albert.

Robert Hays stars as a rising corporate executive who returns, after a ten-year absence, to his hometown to take charge of a brewery where he once worked, and winds up organizing a revolt among his fellow employees. This contemporary comedy-drama is out to raise one's spirits, and it does just that. Rated PG. 1981; 100m.

TALK OF THE TOWN, THE ★★★★
DIR: George Stevens. **CAST:** Ronald Colman, Jean Arthur, Cary Grant,

Edgar Buchanan, Glenda Farrell, Emma Dunn, Charles Dingle, Tom Tyler, Don Beddoe, Rex Ingram.

Falsely accused of arson and murder, parlor radical Cary Grant escapes jail and holes up in a country house Jean Arthur is readying for law professor Ronald Colman. The radical and the egghead take to one another. Gifted direction and a brilliant cast make this intelligent comedy topflight entertainment. 1942; B&W; 118m.

TALKING WALLS ★★

DIR: Stephen F. Verona. **CAST:** Stephen Shellen, Marie Laurin, Sybil Danning, Sally Kirkland, Barry Primus.

Offbeat, mildly interesting comedy-drama about a sociology student who decides to do his thesis on human sexual relationships by videotaping unwitting guests as they cavort in the rooms of a sleazy Hollywood motel. Not rated, contains nudity, sex, and vulgar language. 1987; 85m.

TAMING OF THE SHREW, THE (1929) ★★★

DIR: Sam Taylor. **CAST:** Mary Pickford, Douglas Fairbanks Sr., Dorothy Jordan.

The first royal couple of Hollywood co-starred in this film while under the duress of a failing marriage. Mary Pickford is properly shrewish as Katharina; Douglas Fairbanks is smug, commanding, and virile as Petruchio. Critics liked it and the public flocked to see the famous duo have at the Bard. Director Sam Taylor gave Hollywood one of its enduring anecdotes by taking screen credit for additional dialogue. 1929; B&W; 66m.

TAMING OF THE SHREW, THE (1966) ★★★★½

DIR: Franco Zeffirelli. **CAST:** Richard Burton, Elizabeth Taylor, Cyril Cusack, Michael York.

This is a beautifully mounted comedy of the battle of the sexes. Petruchio (Richard Burton), a spirited minor nobleman of the Italian Renaissance, pits his wits against the man-hating Kate (Elizabeth Taylor) in order to win her hand. The zest with which this famous play is transferred to the screen can be enjoyed even by those who feel intimidated by Shakespeare. 1966; 126m.

TAPEHEADS ★★★

DIR: Bill Fishman. **CAST:** John Cusack, Tim Robbins, Mary Crosby, Connie Stevens, Doug McClure, Lyle Alzado.

In this off-the-wall *Night Shift*, John Cusack plays a pretentious and obnoxious con man who convinces Tim Robbins, a video genius, to make music videos. The overblown characters and situations they encounter in the Los Angeles rock-music scene make for weird and funny viewing, and the chemistry between the two leads is perfect. Not rated; contains offensive language and sexual situations. 1988; 94m.

TEACHERS ★★

DIR: Arthur Hiller. **CAST:** Nick Nolte, JoBeth Williams, Judd Hirsch, Richard Mulligan, Ralph Macchio.

This satirical look at a contemporary urban high school flunks as a film. Teachers will hate it because it's not serious enough; students will hate it because it's just terrible. It promised to "do for high school what *Network* did for television." Actually, it's no more interesting than a dull day in high school. Rated R for sexual innuendo, violence, and profanity. 1984; 106m.

TEACHER'S PET ★★★

DIR: George Seaton. **CAST:** Clark Gable, Doris Day, Gig Young, Mamie Van Doren, Nick Adams, Jack Albertson, Marion Ross.

Winsome journalism instructor Doris Day fascinates and charms hard-boiled city editor Clark Gable in this near plotless but most diverting comedy of incidents. The two are terrific, but Gig Young, as the teacher's erudite but liquor-logged boyfriend, is the one to watch. 1958; B&W; 120m.

TEEN VAMP

DIR: Samuel Bradford. **CAST:** Clu Gulager, Karen Carlson.

In this grade-Z horror-comedy, a high-school nerd is transformed into a vampire by a bloodsucking prostitute. He then proceeds to wreak revenge on his former tormentors. You'll be tormented, too. Rated R for violence and profanity. 1988; 87m.

TEEN WITCH ★★

DIR: Dorian Walker. **CAST:** Robyn Lively, Zelda Rubinstein, Dick Sargent, Shelley Berman.

Robyn Lively plays Louise, a high-school wallflower who discovers on her sixteenth birthday that she has the powers of witchcraft. Rob Menken and Vernon Zimmerman's script is a live-action adaptation of *Sabrina the Teenage Witch* with a large measure of *Bell, Book and Candle* and *Cinderella* thrown in. Some blandly catchy songs (by Larry Weir) are patched in for the music-video market. Rated PG-13 for mild profanity. 1989; 90m.

TELEPHONE, THE ★★

DIR: Rip Torn. **CAST:** Whoopi Goldberg, Elliott Gould, Amy Wright, John Heard, Severn Darden.

It's hard to like, but even harder to walk away from, this uneven comedy-drama. Whoopi Goldberg stars as an out-of-work actress who is more than a little nuts. Definitely for the mid-night-movie junkie who will enjoy the bizarre ending. Rated R for profanity. 1987; 96m.

10 ★★★½

DIR: Blake Edwards. **CAST:** Dudley Moore, Bo Derek, Julie Andrews, Robert Webber.

Ravel's "Bolero" enjoyed a renewed popularity, and Bo Derek rocketed to stardom because of this uneven but generally entertaining sex comedy, directed by Blake Edwards (*The Pink Panther*). Most of the film's funny moments come from the deftly timed physical antics of Dudley Moore, who plays a just-turned-40 songwriter who at long last meets the girl (Bo Derek) of his dreams—on her wedding day. Rated R. 1979; 122m.

10 FROM YOUR SHOW OF SHOWS ★★★★

DIR: Max Liebman. **CAST:** Sid Caesar, Imogene Coca, Carl Reiner, Howard Morris, Louis Nye.

Ten skits from the early 1950s television program that set the pace for all variety shows. Granted, the style is dated and far from subtle, but as a joyful look at television's formative years, it can't be beat. Unrated. 1973; B&W; 92m.

THAT LUCKY TOUCH ★★★

DIR: Christopher Miles. **CAST:** Roger Moore, Susannah York, Shelley Winters, Lee J. Cobb, Sydne Rome.

This romantic comedy features unlikely neighbors falling in love. Roger Moore plays Michael Scott, a weapons merchant who wheels and deals with everyone from Arabs to NATO. Susannah York, on the other hand, is an antimilitary writer. Shelley Winters provides a few laughs as the air-head wife of a NATO general (Lee J. Cobb). Comparable with a PG, but basically pretty tame. 1975; 93m.

THAT SINKING FEELING ★★★★

DIR: Bill Forsyth. **CAST:** Robert Buchanan, John Hughes, Billy Greenlees, Gordon John Sinclair.

Following Scottish director Bill Forsyth's box-office success with *Gregory's Girl* and *Local Hero*, his first feature was resurrected for release in America. It's a typically wry and dry comic affair about a group of unemployed young men deciding on a life of crime. The result is engaging silliness. Rated PG. 1979; 92m.

THAT TOUCH OF MINK ★★★½

DIR: Delbert Mann. **CAST:** Doris Day, Cary Grant, Gig Young, Audrey Meadows, John Astin.

This 1962 romantic comedy is enjoyable, but only as escapist fare. Doris Day stars as an unemployed girl pursued by a wealthy businessman (Cary Grant). 1962; 99m.

THAT UNCERTAIN FEELING ★★½
DIR: Ernst Lubitsch. **CAST:** Merle Oberon, Melvyn Douglas, Alan Mowbray, Burgess Meredith, Eve Arden, Sig Ruman.

This is an amusing film about marital unrest until somewhere around the midpoint, when the time-tried romantic triangle plot thins rather than thickens. Burgess Meredith all but filches the film in a supporting role. Merle Oberon is devastatingly beautiful, even when she has the hiccups—an important plot device. 1941; B&W; 86m.

THAT'S LIFE ★★★
DIR: Blake Edwards. **CAST:** Julie Andrews, Jack Lemmon, Sally Kellerman, Robert Loggia, Jennifer Edwards, Chris Lemmon.

Jack Lemmon and Julie Andrews play a married couple enduring a torrent of personal and family crises during one fateful weekend. The film is a mixture of good and bad, funny and sad, tasteful and tasteless. That it ends up on the plus side is more to the credit of its lead players than to its theme or handling. Rated PG-13 for profanity and scatological humor. 1986; 102m.

THERE'S A GIRL IN MY SOUP ★★½
DIR: Roy Boulting. **CAST:** Peter Sellers, Goldie Hawn, Diana Dors, Tony Britton.

Goldie Hawn hadn't completely shed her *Laugh-In* image when this British sex farce came out, and it didn't do her career any good. Quite a letdown, after her Oscar-winning performance in *Cactus Flower*. Peter Sellers is a middle-aged boob who falls in lust with flower child Hawn. A low point for all concerned. Rated R. 1970; 95m.

THESE GIRLS WON'T TALK ★½
DIR: Mack Sennett. **CAST:** Colleen Moore, Carole Lombard, Betty Compson.

As a series of three silent short stories, this Mack Sennett–produced series is woefully short of inspiration. The shorts are called *Her Bridal Nightmare, Campus Carmen*, and *As Luck Would Have It*. The most interesting thing about this compilation is seeing Carole Lombard long before she was a star. 1920; B&W; 50m.

THEY ALL LAUGHED ★★★★
DIR: Peter Bogdanovich. **CAST:** Audrey Hepburn, Ben Gazzara, John Ritter, Dorothy Stratten.

This is director Peter Bogdanovich at his best. A very offbeat comedy that looks at four New York private eyes' adventures and love lives. Final film of ex–Playboy bunny Dorothy Stratten. Worth a look. Rated PG. 1981; 115m.

THEY CALL ME BRUCE? ★★
DIR: Elliot Hong. **CAST:** Johnny Yune, Ralph Mauro, Margaux Hemingway.

In this unsophisticated kung-fu comedy, Johnny Yune portrays an Asian immigrant who, because of his "resemblance" to Bruce Lee and an accidental exhibition of craziness (misinterpreted as martial arts expertise), gets a reputation as a mean man with fists and feet. But it is Ralph Mauro, playing Bruce's chauffeur, who steals the show. Rated PG. 1982; 88m.

THEY GOT ME COVERED ★★½
DIR: David Butler. **CAST:** Bob Hope, Dorothy Lamour, Lenore Aubert, Otto Preminger, Eduardo Ciannelli, Marion Martin, Donald MacBride, Donald Meek, Philip Ahn.

Typical Bob Hope vehicle of the 1940s is full of gals, gags, goofy situations, snappy dialogue, and one-line zingers, and boasts an incredible supporting cast of great character actors and actresses. Thin story about spy nonsense in Washington, D.C., is secondary to the zany antics of Paramount's ski-nosed comedian. 1943; B&W; 95m.

THEY STILL CALL ME BRUCE
DIR: Johnny Yune, James Orr. **CAST:** Johnny Yune, David Mendenhall, Joey Travolta.

Perhaps one of the least-anticipated sequels ever, this attempt by Korean comic Johnny Yune to follow up his 1982 nonhit *They Call Me Bruce?* is completely hopeless. It's rated PG for Yune's occasionally off-color humor. 1987; 91m.

THIEF WHO CAME TO DINNER, THE ★★★
DIR: Bud Yorkin. **CAST:** Ryan O'Neal, Jacqueline Bisset, Warren Oates, Jill Clayburgh, Charles Cioffi, Ned Beatty.

Silly stuff about Ryan O'Neal leading a double life: as a bookish computer programmer by day and a jewel thief by night. The film's most interesting performance comes from Jill Clayburgh in an early screen role. It's mindless fluff and inoffensive. Rated PG. 1973; 102m.

THINGS ARE TOUGH ALL OVER ★
DIR: Tom Avildsen. **CAST:** Cheech and Chong, Rikki Marin, Rip Taylor.

If cheap laughs are worthless, then so is this romp starring Cheech and Chong. This time around, Richard "Cheech" Marin and Tommy Chong play dual roles: as their usual spaced-out characters, plus two Arab brothers up to no good. Rated R for profanity and scatological humor. 1982; 92m.

THINGS CHANGE ★★★★
DIR: David Mamet. **CAST:** Don Ameche, Joe Mantegna, Robert Prosky.

Director David Mamet and his co-screenwriter, Shel Silverstein, have fashioned a marvelously subtle and witty comedy about an inept, low-level gangster (Joe Mantegna). He goes against orders to take an old shoeshine "boy" (Don Ameche) on one last fling before the latter goes to prison for a crime he didn't commit. Rated PG for profanity and violence. 1988; 100m.

THINGS WE DID LAST SUMMER ★★½
DIR: Gary Weis. **CAST:** John Belushi, Dan Aykroyd, Bill Murray, Gilda Radner, Garrett Morris, Laraine Newman.

A mixed bag used to supplement *Saturday Night Live* episodes in the show's first golden era, this features some of The Not Ready For Prime Time Players in skits of varying quality. The highlights are provided by John Belushi and Dan Aykroyd performing live in concert as the Blues Brothers. 1977; 50m.

THINKIN' BIG ★★
DIR: S. F. Brownrigg. **CAST:** Bruce Anderson, Nancy Buechler.

Soft-core beach romp with the usual horny teens heading for spring-break fun in the sun. About all that's unusual here is that they vacation on the gulf coast of Texas rather than in Florida. Rated R for nudity. 1986; 94m.

30 FOOT BRIDE OF CANDY ROCK, THE ★★
DIR: Sidney Miller. **CAST:** Lou Costello, Dorothy Provine, Gale Gordon, Charles Lane, Doodles Weaver.

A nebbish inventor turns his girlfriend into a giant. A mild comedy with a certain amount of charm, this was the last film made by Columbia's B-picture unit, and Lou Costello's only feature film after breaking up with Bud Abbott. He died before the film was released. 1959; B&W; 75m.

30 IS A DANGEROUS AGE, CYNTHIA ★½
DIR: Joseph McGrath. **CAST:** Dudley Moore, Suzy Kendall, Eddie Fox Jr., John Bird, Patricia Routledge.

Dated British comedy features Dudley Moore as a pianist-composer who intends to find a bride and write a musical before he turns 30. Unfortunately, he has only six weeks. Much of the action takes place in Moore's fantasies about his success and happiness. Suzy Kendall plays the object of his affections. A few chuckles here, but not enough. 1967; 83m.

THIS HAPPY FEELING ★★
DIR: Blake Edwards. **CAST:** Debbie Reynolds, Curt Jurgens, John Saxon,

Alexis Smith, Mary Astor, Estelle Winwood, Troy Donahue.

Curt Jurgens is an aging actor, Debbie Reynolds is the young girl who develops a crush on him, and John Saxon is Jurgens's handsome young neighbor who falls hard for Reynolds. The film is truly reflective of the 1950s, with its unreal colors and a musical score inundating every scene. Alexis Smith as "the other woman" is enjoyable. 1958; 92m.

THIS IS SPINAL TAP ★★★★½
DIR: Rob Reiner. **CAST:** Michael McKean, Christopher Guest, Harry Shearer, Rob Reiner.

This is one of the funniest movies ever made about rock 'n' roll. This is a satire of rock documentaries that tells the story of Spinal Tap, an over-the-hill British heavy-metal rock group that's fast rocketing to the bottom of the charts. *This Is Spinal Tap* isn't consistently funny, but does it ever have its moments. Some of the song lyrics are hysterical, and the performances are perfect. Rated R for profanity. 1984; 82m.

THOSE ENDEARING YOUNG CHARMS ★★★
DIR: Lewis Allen. **CAST:** Robert Young, Laraine Day, Bill Williams, Ann Harding, Anne Jeffreys, Lawrence Tierney.

Heroine Laraine Day brings smoothie Robert Young to bay and then to heel in this cliché-plotted, but sprightly played, romantic comedy. Public hunger for wholesome laughter and sentimental tears as World War II wound down made this a box-office bonanza. Ann Harding is perfect as the wise mother. 1945; B&W; 82m.

THOSE MAGNIFICENT MEN IN THEIR FLYING MACHINES ★★★★
DIR: Ken Annakin. **CAST:** Terry-Thomas, Stuart Whitman, Sarah Miles, Gert Fröbe.

An air race between London and Paris in the early days of flight is this comedy's centerpiece. Around it hang an enjoyable number of rib-tickling vignettes. A large international cast each get their chance to shine as the contest's zany participants. Terry-Thomas stands out as the hapless villain. His ingenious evil schemes continually go wrong, with hilarious results. 1965; 132m.

THOUSAND CLOWNS, A ★★★★
DIR: Fred Coe. **CAST:** Jason Robards Jr., Barry Gordon, Barbara Harris, Martin Balsam, Gene Saks, William Daniels.

Famous Broadway play comes to the screen with memorable performances by all the principals and standout jobs by Jason Robards as a talented nonconformist and Barry Gordon as his precocious ward. They struggle against welfare bureaucracy in order to stay together. Very funny in spots and equally poignant in others. 1965; B&W; 118m.

THREE AGES, THE ★★★½
DIR: Buster Keaton, Eddie Cline. **CAST:** Buster Keaton, Wallace Beery, Oliver Hardy.

Frozen-faced Buster Keaton coproduced and codirected this parody on the films of that master of excessiveness, Cecil B. DeMille. A funny and very enjoyable silent film. It's not Keaton's best, but it's far from mundane. 1923; B&W; 89m.

THREE AMIGOS ★★½
DIR: John Landis. **CAST:** Steve Martin, Chevy Chase, Martin Short, Alfonso Arau, Patrice Martinez, Joe Mantegna, Jon Lovitz.

In this send-up of *The Magnificent Seven*, Steve Martin, Chevy Chase, and Martin Short play three silent-screen cowboys who attempt to save a Mexican village from bloodthirsty banditos. Steve Martin, in particular, has some very funny moments. Overall, it's pleasant—even amusing—but nothing more. Rated PG. 1986; 105m.

THREE BROADWAY GIRLS ★★★
DIR: Lowell Sherman. **CAST:** Joan Blondell, Ina Claire, Madge Evans, David Manners, Betty Grable.

Three streetwise gold-diggers stalk their prey among New York's socially prominent in this comedy adapted from Zoe Atkins's 1930 Broadway hit about avarice. Also titled *The Greeks Had a Word for Them.* 1932; B&W; 78m.

THREE FOR BEDROOM C ★★★
DIR: Milton H. Bren. **CAST:** Gloria Swanson, James Warren, Fred Clark, Hans Conried, Margaret Dumont.
Adequate farce that was the first film made by Gloria Swanson after her stunning comeback in *Sunset Boulevard.* She portrays a movie star who books a compartment on a train that is also occupied by a Harvard scientist. The resulting romance is predictable. 1952; 74m.

THREE FOR THE ROAD ★
DIR: Bill L. Norton. **CAST:** Charlie Sheen, Kerri Green, Alan Ruck, Sally Kellerman.
Dull comedy about a senator's aide (Charlie Sheen) who is assigned to take his employer's difficult daughter (Kerri Green) to a reform school. The cast tries hard, but the result is an amiable, yet generally tedious, rehash of all the road movies that have gone before. Rated PG. 1987; 95m.

THREE FUGITIVES ★★★
DIR: Francis Veber. **CAST:** Nick Nolte, Martin Short, James Earl Jones, Kenneth McMillan.
France's current master of film comedy, Francis Veber, makes his American debut with this overly sentimental but often hilarious comedy about a hardened criminal (Nick Nolte) just released from prison. He finds himself thrown together with a mute girl (Sarah Rowland Doroff) and her down-and-out dad (Martin Short) when the latter robs a bank and takes Nolte hostage. Rated PG for profanity and violence. 1989; 90m.

THREE IN THE CELLAR
DIR: Theodore J. Flicker. **CAST:** Wes Stern, Joan Collins, Larry Hagman, David Arkin, Judy Pace.
This dated, unfunny comedy features Wes Stern as a college student who has just lost his scholarship due to a computer error. Larry Hagman plays the college president who refuses to help. To get revenge, Stern decides to seduce Hagman's wife (Joan Collins), daughter, and mistress. Unrated, this low-budget yawner contains nudity and sexual situations. 1970; 93m.

THREE MEN AND A BABY ★★★½
DIR: Leonard Nimoy. **CAST:** Tom Selleck, Steve Guttenberg, Ted Danson, Nancy Travis, Margaret Colin.
Tom Selleck, Steve Guttenberg, and Ted Danson are three carefree bachelors in this energetic remake of the French *Three Men and a Cradle.* The trio find an unexpected bundle at the door of their impeccably furnished apartment. There's a silly subplot involving drugs, and the conclusion (changed from the French original) is hopelessly hokey, but getting there's a lot of fun. Rated PG for language. 1987; 102m.

THREE MUSKETEERS, THE (1939) ★★★
DIR: Allan Dwan. **CAST:** Don Ameche, The Ritz Brothers, Lionel Atwill, Binnie Barnes.
The Ritz Brothers as Dumas's famous trio? Yes, it's true. As a comedy-musical, this picture rides a moderate course, sticking closely to the original story but never taking anything too seriously. Don Ameche is very sharp as D'Artagnan and Binnie Barnes is charming as Lady DeWinter. 1939; B&W; 73m.

THREE NUTS IN SEARCH OF A BOLT ★
DIR: Tommy Noonan. **CAST:** Mamie Van Doren, Tommy Noonan, Paul Gilbert, Ziva Rodann.
Three loonies, too poor to see a psychiatrist on their own, hire an out-of-work actor to pretend he has each of their symptoms. Why this dreadful B comedy from the sixties was released for home viewing is unknown. Filmed

in both color and black-and-white for no apparent reason other than economy. Rated R for nudity and adult situations. 1964; 78m.

THREE O'CLOCK HIGH ★★½
DIR: Phil Joanou. **CAST:** Casey Siemaszko, Anne Ryan, Richard Tyson, Jeffrey Tambor, Phillip Baker Hall, John P. Ryan.

Director Phil Joanou leaves no doubt of his technical skill in his first film. Too bad his story is just a teen variation on *High Noon.* Jerry Mitchell (Casey Siemaszko) is an average high-schooler who ends up having the worst day of his life. Rated PG-13 for profanity and violence. 1987; 95m.

THREE STOOGES, THE (VOLUMES 1–10) ★★★★
DIR: Various. **CAST:** Moe Howard, Curly Howard, Larry Fine.

The Three Stooges made 190 two-reel short subjects between 1934 and 1959. For over fifty years, people have either loved them or hated them. Those in the latter category should, of course, avoid these tapes. But if you are a fan, you'll find these collections the answer to a knucklehead's dream. Each cassette features three shorts of impeccable quality, transferred from brand-new, complete 35-mm prints. All of the films are from the classic "Curly" period, when the team was at the peak of its energy and originality. 1934; B&W; 60m.

THRILL OF IT ALL, THE ★★★
DIR: Norman Jewison. **CAST:** Doris Day, James Garner, Arlene Francis, Edward Andrews, ZaSu Pitts, Elliott Reid, Reginald Owen, Alice Pearce.

Married life is perfect for housewife and mother Doris Day and doctor James Garner until she accepts a high-paying television commercial job. Family and career clash in this witty observation of television, advertising, the servant problem and domestic bliss, as scripted by Carl Reiner. 1963; 103m.

THROW MOMMA FROM THE TRAIN ★★★
DIR: Danny DeVito. **CAST:** Danny DeVito, Billy Crystal, Anne Ramsey, Kim Greist, Kate Mulgrew.

Gravel-voiced Anne Ramsey, as the titular Momma, is by far the best element of this comedy, which marks the directing debut of star Danny DeVito. He's a would-be writer in novelist Billy Crystal's class, and the two concoct a scheme to trade murders *à la* Hitchcock's *Strangers on a Train.* The finished film just doesn't provide the manic delight promised by its two stars, however, and the result is only occasionally amusing. Rated PG-13 for language. 1987; 88m.

TIGER'S TALE, A ★
DIR: Peter Douglas. **CAST:** Ann-Margret, C. Thomas Howell, Charles Durning, Kelly Preston, William Zabka, Ann Wedgeworth, Tim Thomerson.

Grievously unfunny comedy about a not-so-bright teenage stud from Texas (C. Thomas Howell) who switches his affections from tease Kelly Preston to her much-more-willing mom (Ann-Margret). Rated R for nudity, profanity, and simulated sex. 1988; 97m.

TIGHT LITTLE ISLAND ★★★★
DIR: Alexander Mackendrick. **CAST:** Basil Radford, Joan Greenwood, James Robertson Justice, Gordon Jackson.

A World War II transport laden with whiskey founders just off the shore of a Scottish island. Hilarious hell breaks loose as dram-delirious lads and lassies seek to salvage the water of life before authorities can claim it and put it under government control. One of the great comedies that revived the British film industry after the war. 1949; B&W; 82m.

TILT
DIR: Rudy Durand. **CAST:** Brooke Shields, Ken Marshall, Charles Durning, Geoffrey Lewis.

Brooke Shields's third movie (after *Alice, Sweet Alice* and *Pretty Baby*) is a mess. Co-starring Ken Marshall (*Krull*), Charles Durning, and Geoffrey Lewis, this film is pitiful at best and unbearable at worst. The dialogue is laughable, and the performances are generally putrid. Rated PG. 1978; 104m.

TIN MEN ★★★★
DIR: Barry Levinson. **CAST:** Richard Dreyfuss, Danny DeVito, Barbara Hershey.
Writer-director Barry Levinson takes a simple subject—the vendetta between two aluminum-siding salesmen in the 1950s—and fashions it into an insightful, witty comedy. The tone is similar to Levinson's earlier *Diner*. He has elicited top-notch performances from his trio of stars. Barbara Hershey is convincing as she transforms her character from mousy pawn to attractive, assertive woman. Rated R. 1987; 110m.

TO BE OR NOT TO BE (1942) ★★★★½
DIR: Ernst Lubitsch. **CAST:** Carole Lombard, Jack Benny, Robert Stack.
After gaining early stardom in *Twentieth Century*, Carole Lombard returned to another black comedy and another role as an oddball theater performer, for the last film of her life. One of Hollywood's premier comedy directors, Ernst Lubitsch, coached excellent performances from Carole Lombard and co-star Jack Benny in this hilarious farce about a theater couple who outwit the Nazis. 1942; B&W; 99m.

TO BE OR NOT TO BE (1983) ★★★★
DIR: Alan Johnson. **CAST:** Mel Brooks, Anne Bancroft, Charles Durning, Tim Matheson.
In this hilarious remake of the Jack Benny–Carole Lombard classic from 1942, Mel Brooks and Anne Bancroft are Polish actors who foil the Nazis at the outbreak of World War II. It's producer-star Brooks' best film since *Young Frankenstein* and was directed by Alan Johnson, who choreographed *Springtime for Hitler* for Brooks' first film, *The Producers*. Rated PG. 1983; 108m.

TO PARIS WITH LOVE ★★½
DIR: Robert Hamer. **CAST:** Alec Guinness, Odile Versois, Austin Trevor, Vernon Gray.
Alec Guinness stands out like a pumpkin in a pea patch in this average comedy about a rich and indulgent father who takes his son to gay Paree to learn the facts of life. 1955; 78m.

TO SEE SUCH FUN ★★
DIR: Jon Scoffield. **CAST:** Peter Sellers, Marty Feldman, Benny Hill, Eric Idle, Margaret Rutherford, Alec Guinness, Dirk Bogarde, Spike Milligan, Norman Wisdom.
This is a compilation of a vast number of comedy film clips from 1930 to 1970. Many of the clips illustrate the British love of puns, rhymes, and slapstick. Included are many phone gags, famous recurring lines, men in drag, student and teacher skits, wild car rides, and male-female conflicts. Viewers hoping to see a lot of Peter Sellers, Benny Hill, and Marty Feldman clips will be disappointed because most of the footage comes from films of the 1930s and 1940s. 1977; 90m.

TOM, DICK AND HARRY ★★★½
DIR: Garson Kanin. **CAST:** Ginger Rogers, George Murphy, Burgess Meredith, Alan Marshal, Phil Silvers.
An energetic comic delight has Ginger Rogers trying to decide which very eligible bachelor to have for her beau. The entire cast comes through with solid performances, but Phil Silvers almost walks off with the show in his role as an obnoxious ice-cream man. Garson Kanin's direction is sharp. 1941; B&W; 86m.

TOM JONES ★★★★★
DIR: Tony Richardson. **CAST:** Albert Finney, Susannah York, Hugh Griffith, Edith Evans.
Rarely has a movie captured the spirit and flavor of its times or the novel on which it was based. This is a ram-

bunctious, witty, and often bawdy tale of a youth's misadventures in eighteenth-century England. Albert Finney is a perfect rascal as Tom. We joyously follow him through all levels of British society as he tries to make his fortune and win the lovely Sophie (Susannah York). The entire cast is brilliant. 1963; 129m.

TOMMY CHONG ROAST, THE ★
DIR: Barry Glazer. **CAST:** Tommy Chong, Dick Shawn, Richard Belzer, Slappy White, Jerry Seinfeld, David Steinberg.

When a gang of subpar talents gather to celebrate the skills of a comedian whose chief claim to fame is bringing drug and flatulence jokes to the big screen, the result is predictably low-level humor: dumb jokes about sex, drugs, and going to the bathroom. Rated R for language. 1986; 60m.

TONIGHT FOR SURE ★
DIR: Francis Ford Coppola. **CAST:** Don Kenney.

One of two nudie movies that Francis Ford Coppola made while he was still a student at UCLA, this gives no indication of the director's talents. The loose story about two men discussing their grudges against women while at a burlesque show only serves as a frame to display a lot of naked (and often flabby) flesh. 1962; 66m.

TOOTSIE ★★★★★
DIR: Sydney Pollack. **CAST:** Dustin Hoffman, Bill Murray, Jessica Lange, Teri Garr, Dabney Coleman, Sydney Pollack, George Gaynes.

Dustin Hoffman is Michael Dorsey, an out-of-work actor who disguises himself as a woman—Dorothy Michaels—to get a job and becomes a big star on a popular television soap opera. An absolute delight, *Tootsie* is hilarious, touching, and marvelously acted. Rated PG for adult content. 1982; 119m.

TOP SECRET ★★½
DIR: Jim Abrahams, David Zucker, Jerry Zucker. **CAST:** Val Kilmer, Omar Sharif, Peter Cushing, Lucy Gutteridge.

By the makers of *Airplane!*, this film makes up for its flimsy plot with one gag after another. Nick Rivers (Val Kilmer) is the main character who, as a rock 'n' roll star, visits East Germany. There he falls in love with Hilary and becomes involved in the plot to free her scientist father. The soundtrack features lots of lively old Beach Boys and Elvis Presley tunes. Rated PG for some profanity and sexually oriented gags. 1984; 90m.

TOPPER ★★★★
DIR: Norman Z. McLeod. **CAST:** Cary Grant, Constance Bennett, Roland Young, Billie Burke.

This is the original feature of what became a delightful fantasy movie series and television series. Cary Grant and Constance Bennett are the Kirbys, a duo of social high livers who, due to an unfortunate auto accident, become ghosts. They now want to transfer their spirit of living the good life to a rather stodgy banker, the fellow they are now haunting, one Cosmo Topper (Roland Young). Good fun all around. 1937; B&W; 97m.

TOPPER RETURNS ★★★
DIR: Roy Del Ruth. **CAST:** Roland Young, Joan Blondell, Eddie Anderson, Carole Landis, Dennis O'Keefe, H. B. Warner.

Cary Grant and Constance Bennett have gone on to their heavenly rewards, but Roland Young, as Cosmo Topper, is still seeing ghosts. This time the spooky personage is that of Joan Blondell, who helps our hero solve a murder in this entertaining comedy. 1941; B&W; 87m.

TOPPER TAKES A TRIP ★★★
DIR: Norman Z. McLeod. **CAST:** Constance Bennett, Roland Young, Billie Burke, Alan Mowbray, Franklin Pangborn.

Second film in the original series finds Cosmo and Henrietta Topper on the French Riviera accompanied by their ghostly friend Marion Kirby, portrayed by the star of the original film, Constance Bennett. Topper and Marion pool forces to stop Mrs. Topper from being victimized by a smooth-talking confidence man. Marion's new companion is a pet dog, but Cary Grant makes a brief appearance in a flashback sequence. Harmless fun. 1939; B&W; 85m.

TOUCH AND GO ★★½
DIR: Robert Mandel. **CAST:** Michael Keaton, Maria Conchita Alonso, Ajay Naidu.
A comedy that sat on the shelf for two years. Chicago hockey player falls in love with the mother of a young delinquent who mugged him. Michael Keaton is appealing, Maria Conchita Alonso is fiery, and the script contains sharp dialogue, a few good laughs, and a number of sweet moments. Rated PG for profanity. 1984; 101m.

TOUCH OF CLASS, A ★★★★★
DIR: Melvin Frank. **CAST:** George Segal, Glenda Jackson, Paul Sorvino, Hildegard Neil.
In one of the best romantic comedies of recent years, George Segal and Glenda Jackson are marvelously paired as a sometimes loving—sometimes bickering—couple who struggle through an extramarital affair. They begin their oddball romance when he runs over one of her children while chasing a fly ball in a baseball game. Fine acting and witty dialogue. Rated PG. 1972; 105m.

TOUGH GUYS ★★★
DIR: Jeff Kanew. **CAST:** Burt Lancaster, Kirk Douglas, Charles Durning, Alexis Smith, Dana Carvey, Darlanne Fluegel, Eli Wallach.
This enjoyable movie features Burt Lancaster and Kirk Douglas as two flamboyant train robbers who are released from prison after thirty years to find they have no place in society. Angered by being relegated to the nonperson status suffered by many older people, they decide to strike back by doing what they do best. It's featherweight, but the stars make it fun. Rated PG for light profanity, suggested sex, and mild violence. 1986; 103m.

TOY, THE ★★
DIR: Richard Donner. **CAST:** Richard Pryor, Jackie Gleason, Scott Schwartz, Ned Beatty.
You would think any comedy that combines the talents of Richard Pryor and Jackie Gleason would have to be exceptionally good, to say nothing of funny. But that's simply not true of this movie, about a spoiled rich kid (Scott Schwartz) whose father (Gleason) allows him to buy the ultimate toy (Pryor). Rated PG for profanity and adult themes. 1982; 99m.

TRADING PLACES ★★★★
DIR: John Landis. **CAST:** Dan Aykroyd, Eddie Murphy, Ralph Bellamy, Don Ameche, Jamie Lee Curtis.
Here's an uproarious comedy about what happens when uptight Philadelphia broker (Dan Aykroyd) and dynamic black street hustler (Eddie Murphy) change places. Rated R for nudity and profanity. 1983; 117m.

TRAIL OF THE PINK PANTHER, THE ★★½
DIR: Blake Edwards. **CAST:** Peter Sellers, David Niven, Herbert Lom, Capucine, Robert Wagner.
Through the magic of editing, the late Peter Sellers "stars" as the bumbling Inspector Clouseau, in this late entry in the comedy series. Writer-director Blake Edwards uses outtakes of Sellers from previous films and combines them with new footage featuring David Niven, Herbert Lom, and Capucine. The results are disappointing. Rated PG for nudity and scatological humor. 1982; 97m.

TRANSYLVANIA 6-5000 ★★
DIR: Rudy DeLuca. **CAST:** Jeff Goldblum, Ed Begley Jr., Joseph Bologna, Carol Kane, Jeffrey Jones, John Byner, Michael Richards.
Sometimes amusing but ultimately silly horror spoof focusing on an inept

pair of tabloid reporters (Jeff Goldblum and Ed Begley Jr.) sent to Transylvania to investigate the possible resurgence of the Frankenstein monster. Rated PG for mild profanity. 1985; 93m.

TRAVELS WITH MY AUNT ★★½
DIR: George Cukor. **CAST:** Maggie Smith, Alec McCowen, Louis Gossett Jr., Robert Stephens, Cindy Williams.

Director George Cukor's screen version of Graham Greene's comic novel is only slightly above average. Maggie Smith's overbearing and overplayed Aunt knocks what could have been a delightful *Auntie Mame*–style farce completely off-kilter. Alec McCowen gives an affecting performance as the bank executive who finds his tidy world disrupted when his mother dies. Rated PG. 1972; 109m.

TRENCHCOAT ★½
DIR: Michael Tuchner. **CAST:** Margot Kidder, Robert Hays, Daniel Faraldo.

No one is what he appears to be in this inept spoof of the detective genre. Margot Kidder plays Mickey Raymond, a would-be writer of hard-boiled detective fiction who is ensnared in a scheme that involves drugs (perhaps), stolen plutonium (most likely), and murder (definitely). While there are moments that will evoke some chuckles, *Trenchcoat* rarely hits the mark as being the spontaneous, unpredictable madcap chase film it was meant to be. Rated PG. 1983; 91m.

TROOP BEVERLY HILLS ★
DIR: Jeff Kanew. **CAST:** Shelley Long, Craig T. Nelson, Betty Thomas, Mary Gross.

In this stupendously awful comedy, Shelley Long embarrasses herself as a ditsy Beverly Hills mom who agrees to act as the troop leader for her daughter's Wilderness Girls group. Of course, Long's idea of camping out is renting a bungalow at the Beverly Wilshire. Rated PG for slight profanity. 1989; 105m.

TROUBLE IN THE GLEN ★★
DIR: Herbert Wilcox. **CAST:** Orson Welles, Margaret Lockwood, Victor McLaglen, Forrest Tucker.

A white-haired, cigar-chomping Orson Welles in Scots kilts is far-fetched, to say the least. The film turns on a feud over a closed road. What was projected as a Highland comedy is thoroughly scotched by poor pacing and a script that misses the mark. Deep-dyed Welles fans will like it. 1953; 91m.

TROUBLE WITH ANGELS, THE ★★★
DIR: Ida Lupino. **CAST:** Rosalind Russell, Hayley Mills, June Harding.

Rosalind Russell stars as the Mother Superior at the St. Francis Academy for Girls. Her serenity and the educational pursuits of the institution are coming apart at the seams due to the pranks of two rambunctious teenagers, Hayley Mills and June Harding. This comedy's humor is uninspired, but the warmth and humanity of the entire production make it worthwhile family viewing. 1966; 112m.

TROUBLE WITH HARRY, THE ★★★★
DIR: Alfred Hitchcock. **CAST:** John Forsythe, Edmund Gwenn, Shirley MacLaine, Mildred Natwick, Jerry Mathers.

Shirley MacLaine made her film debut in this wickedly funny black comedy, directed by Alfred Hitchcock. This is the last of long-unseen screen works by the master of suspense to be rereleased, and the most unusual, because the accent is on humor instead of tension-filled drama. In it, a murdered man causes no end of problems for his neighbors in a peaceful New England community. Rated PG when it was rereleased. 1955; 100m.

TROUBLE WITH SPIES, THE ★★
DIR: Burt Kennedy. **CAST:** Donald Sutherland, Ned Beatty, Ruth Gordon, Lucy Gutteridge, Michael Hordern, Robert Morley.

Even Donald Sutherland's amiable charm can't save this inept secret-agent spoof, which piles double crosses on top of plot twists until the whole muddled mess makes no sense at all. Producer-director Burt Kennedy, who also adapted the script from Marc Lovell's *Apple Spy in the Sky*, lacks the simplest knowledge of pacing, shading, or tonal consistency. Rated PG-13 for partial nudity. 1984; 91m.

TRUE STORIES ★★½
DIR: David Byrne. **CAST:** David Byrne, John Goodman, Annie McEnroe, Swoosie Kurtz, Spalding Gray.

True Stories is Talking Heads leader David Byrne's satirical look at the imaginary town of Virgil, Texas. It's a mixture of *The National Enquirer* and deadpan cinematic humor. Some of the bits are truly funny, but the lethargic tone becomes an aggravating artistic conceit. Rated PG. 1986; 89m.

TRULY TASTELESS JOKES ★★
DIR: Peter Robert. **CAST:** John Fox, Larry Reeb, Marsha Warfield, Ollie Joe Prater, Denny Johnston, The Legendary Wid.

Not really as raunchy as the title suggests, this short video pretends to to be a live version of the book of the same name. In reality it's merely a marketing ploy for the brief performances of many minor league comics. The format gives a nice, short sampling of a variety of routines, but there is neither continuity nor purpose. Rated R for language. 1987; 30m.

TULIPS ★
DIR: Stan Ferris. **CAST:** Gabe Kaplan, Bernadette Peters, Henry Gibson, Al Waxman.

Awful Canadian-made comedy casts Gabe Kaplan and Bernadette Peters as would-be suicides. They fall in love and decide that life *is* worth living after all—if they can just call off the hitman that Kaplan hired to kill him. The plot is ancient, and the movie (which went through numerous rewrites and different directors) is a labored mess. Rated PG. 1981; 91m.

TUNNELVISION ★★½
DIR: Neal Israel, Brad Swirnoff. **CAST:** Chevy Chase, Howard Hesseman, Betty Thomas, Laraine Newman.

Here is a lightweight spoof of television. Sometimes it is funny, and other times it is just gross. The "stars," like Chevy Chase, have small bits, and it is not at all what one would expect from the billing. Still, there are some funny moments. *Tunnelvision* is like *The Groove Tube* in most respects, the good equally in proportion to the bad. Rated R. 1976; 67m.

TURNER AND HOOCH ★★★
DIR: Roger Spottiswoode. **CAST:** Tom Hanks, Mare Winningham.

K-9 redux! Tom Hanks is a fussy police detective who finds himself stuck with a mean junkyard dog who is the only witness to a murder. Once again the Hanks magic elevates a predictable story into a fun film. Rated PG. 1989; 110m.

TURTLE DIARY ★★★★½
DIR: John Irvin. **CAST:** Glenda Jackson, Ben Kingsley, Richard Johnson, Michael Gambon, Rosemary Leach, Eleanor Bron, Harriet Walter, Jeroen Krabbé.

Glenda Jackson and Ben Kingsley are absolutely delightful in this deliciously offbeat bit of British whimsy about urban life—of people living side by side but rarely touching. Jackson is Neaera Duncan, an author of children's books, while Kingsley is William Snow, a bookstore assistant. Both share an obsession for turtles and devise a plan to kidnap the shelled creatures, who are imprisoned in a nearby zoo, and release them into their natural habitat. Rated PG for nudity. 1986; 97m.

TUTTLES OF TAHITI, THE ★★★
DIR: Charles Vidor. **CAST:** Charles Laughton, Jon Hall, Peggy Drake, Mala, Florence Bates, Alma Ross,

Victor Francen, Curt Bois, Gene Reynolds.

Captain Bligh goes native in this comedy of arch indolence and planned sloth in beautiful, bountiful Tahiti. Impoverished Charles Laughton and Florence Bates are rivals whose son Jon Hall and daughter Peggy Drake respectively fall in love. A good-natured, congenial film of leisure life. 1942; B&W; 91m.

TWELVE CHAIRS, THE ★★★
DIR: Mel Brooks. **CAST:** Mel Brooks, Dom DeLuise, Frank Langella, Ron Moody.

Based on a Russian comedy-fable about an impoverished nobleman seeking jewels secreted in one of a dozen fancy dining room chairs. Ron Moody is the anguished Russian, Dom DeLuise his chief rival in the hunt. Mel Brooks's direction keeps things moving with laughs. Rated G. 1970; 94m.

TWENTIETH CENTURY ★★★★
DIR: Howard Hawks. **CAST:** Carole Lombard, John Barrymore, Roscoe Karns, Walter Connolly, Edgar Kennedy.

A screwball-comedy masterpiece, scripted from the hit play by Ben Hecht and Charles MacArthur. Egocentric Broadway producer, John Barrymore, turns shopgirl Carole Lombard into a star, gets dumped, and pulls out all stops to win her back during a cross-country train trip. The fun is fast and furious as the miles fly by. Barrymore and Lombard couldn't be funnier. 1934; B&W; 91m.

TWINS ★★★★
DIR: Ivan Reitman. **CAST:** Arnold Schwarzenegger, Danny DeVito, Kelly Preston, Chloe Webb.

Arnold Schwarzenegger and Danny DeVito play the title roles in this marvelously silly movie, which has the far-from-identical twins—products of a supersecret scientific experiment—meeting as adults after being separated at birth. This could easily have been a one-joke movie, but director Ivan Reitman and the stars keep it warm, funny, and fast-paced right up to the nicely satisfying conclusion. Rated PG for profanity and violence. 1988; 105m.

TWO FOR THE ROAD ★★★★
DIR: Stanley Donen. **CAST:** Audrey Hepburn, Albert Finney, Jacqueline Bisset.

Clever editing and Frederic Raphael's inventive script highlight this delightful study of a marriage on the rocks, illuminated by deftly inserted flashbacks that occur each time the vacationing couple passes another car on the road. Albert Finney and Audrey Hepburn are the tempestuous lovers; the sweetly romantic score comes from Henry Mancini. 1967; 112m.

TWO OF A KIND (1983) ★★
DIR: John Herzfeld. **CAST:** John Travolta, Olivia Newton-John, Charles Durning.

John Travolta and Olivia Newton-John, who first teamed on screen in the box-office smash *Grease*, are reunited in this 1980s-style screwball comedy, which mixes clever ideas with incredibly stupid ones. The result is a movie that the young viewers it was made for probably won't rave about, but neither will they be too disappointed. Others, however, should stay away. Rated PG for profanity and violence. 1983; 87m.

TWO TOP BANANAS ★★½
DIR: Phil Olsman. **CAST:** Don Rickles, Don Adams, Carol Wayne, Murray Langston.

Don Rickles and Don Adams bring burlesque back in this production of sketches, sight gags, one-liners, and song and dance. The two Dons are suited to this unsophisticated brand of comedy. Rated R for nudity and profanity. 1982; 45m.

TWO WEEKS TO LIVE ★★½
DIR: Malcolm St. Clair. **CAST:** Chester Lauck, Norris Goff, Franklin Pangborn, Kay Linaker, Irving Bacon, Herbert Rawlinson.

This second of the Lum and Abner series has Abner (Norris Goff) agreeing to pilot a rocket ship to Mars because he thinks he is dying. Coupled with this are a bomb in a violin case, the foiling of a Nazi spy plot, and a haunted house. Director St. Clair, who began in silent slapstick with Mack Sennett, keeps the pace breakneck with sight gags galore. 1943; B&W; 65m.

UFORIA ★★★★

DIR: John Binder. **CAST:** Cindy Williams, Harry Dean Stanton, Fred Ward, Harry Carey Jr., Darrell Larson.

Like *Repo Man* and *Stranger Than Paradise*, this low-budget American film deserved better treatment than the limited theatrical release it was given. Cindy Williams is hilarious as a born-again Christian who believes that salvation will come to Earth in the form of a flying saucer. Fred Ward is equally humorous as a truck-driving Waylon Jennings look-alike. Harry Dean Stanton plays a crooked evangelist who exploits the Jesus-in-a-spaceship concept for every penny he can get. Rated PG for profanity. 1984; 100m.

UHF ★★★½

DIR: Jay Levey. **CAST:** "Weird Al" Yankovic, Victoria Jackson, Kevin McCarthy, Michael Richards, David Bowie, Anthony Geary, Billy Barty.

Daydreamer George Newman (Weird Al Yankovic) finally lands in the right habitat: Channel 62, a UHF station with the lowest ratings in the country. What this station needs is fewer reruns of *Mister Ed* and *The Beverly Hillbillies* and more local talent! Like Emo Philips, the local woodshop instructor who loses a digit in the buzzsaw, and Stanley Spadowski (Michael Richards as the movie's real hero), station janitor turned kid-show host. Partway through your viewing of this tastelessly innocent and funny film, you may run to the medicine cabinet to see if your prescription drugs are way past their expiration date. Rated PG for mild profanity. 1989; 95m.

UNDER THE RAINBOW ★★½

DIR: Steve Rash. **CAST:** Chevy Chase, Carrie Fisher, Eve Arden, Joseph Maher.

While this comedy is not quite jam-packed with laughs, it certainly keeps your interest. Set in 1938, the improbable story centers around the making of *The Wizard of Oz*, assassination attempts on a duke and duchess, the nefarious doings of Nazi and Japanese spies prior to World War II, and the lifespan of a dog named Streudel. Rated PG because of slight nudity and suggestive dialogue. 1981; 98m.

UNDERGROUND ACES 🦃

DIR: Robert Butler. **CAST:** Dirk Benedict, Melanie Griffith, Karlo Salem, Robert Hegyes, Audrey Landers, Frank Gorshin.

In this stupid comedy *à la Car Wash*, a bunch of obnoxious big-city hotel parking attendants run amok. They don't spend much time parking cars, because that would be boring. So they do a lot of wild and crazy things like wrecking the customers' vehicles, having sex, and poking fun at the hotel management. Rated PG for profanity and nudity. 1980; 93m.

UNFAITHFULLY YOURS (1948) ★★★

DIR: Preston Sturges. **CAST:** Rex Harrison, Linda Darnell, Kurt Kreuger, Barbara Lawrence, Rudy Vallee, Lionel Stander.

Symphony conductor Rex Harrison suspects his wife of infidelity and contemplates several solutions to his "problem." This film follows all the prerequisites of screwball comedies—mistaken identities, misinterpreted remarks. Harrison has fun as a sort of manic Henry Higgins, but his energy cannot sustain a film that runs about fifteen minutes too long. Unrated—family fare. 1948; B&W; 105m.

UNFAITHFULLY YOURS (1984) ★★★

DIR: Howard Zieff. **CAST:** Dudley Moore, Nastassja Kinski, Armand Assante, Albert Brooks.

In this entertaining and sometimes hilarious remake of Preston Sturges's 1948 comedy, Dudley Moore plays a symphony orchestra conductor who suspects his wife (Nastassja Kinski) of fooling around with a violinist (Armand Assante) and decides to get revenge. Rated PG for nudity and profanity. 1984; 96m.

UNKISSED BRIDE

DIR: Jack H. Harris. **CAST:** Tom Kirk, Danica d'Hondt, Anne Helm, Jacques Bergerac, Joe Pyne.

The theme song of this forgettable comedy is "Mother Goose A-Go-Go." That should tell you something! Tom Kirk plays the groom who passes out every time he and his wife (Anne Helm) contemplate lovemaking. His beautiful psychiatrist (played by Danica d'Hondt) says he has a hang-up about the tales of Mother Goose as she uses a psychedelic drug to take him back to his childhood. Though this is unrated, the use of drugs and alcohol, as well as the sexual topic, should make this one a no-no for children. 1966; 82m.

UP! ★★★

DIR: Russ Meyer. **CAST:** Robert McLane.

One of Russ Meyer's most bizarre efforts, combining lumberjacks, a mad killer, and Adolf Hitler in a small town—with the director's usual Amazonian women. It's a pointless but amusing parody loaded with extreme (though unbelievable) violence and sex. Like all of his films, it's edited faster than any MTV video. Unrated, but better hide it from the kids. 1976; 80m.

UP IN ARMS ★★½

DIR: Elliott Nugent. **CAST:** Danny Kaye, Dinah Shore, Dana Andrews, Constance Dowling.

Danny Kaye's first film will certainly not disappoint his fans, as he sings and mugs his way through the war. Dinah Shore loves the hypochondriac Kaye; he loves Constance Dowling, and she loves Dana Andrews. They all end up in the service together, and the war takes a backseat to entertainment. 1944; 105m.

UP IN SMOKE ★★★★

DIR: Lou Adler. **CAST:** Cheech and Chong, Strother Martin, Stacy Keach, Edie Adams, Tom Skerritt.

This is Cheech and Chong's first, and best, film. Forget about any plot as Cheech and Chong go on the hunt for good weed, rock 'n' roll, and good times. Several truly hysterical moments, with Stacy Keach's spaced-out cop almost stealing the show. Rated R for language, nudity, and general raunchiness. 1978; 87m.

UP THE ACADEMY ★½

DIR: Robert Downey. **CAST:** Ron Leibman, Wendell Brown, Ralph Macchio, Tom Citera, Tom Poston, Stacey Nelkin, Barbara Bach.

This was *MAD* magazine's first and only attempt to emulate *National Lampoon*'s film success. Set in a strict military academy, the movie holds promise but is quickly done in by tasteless gags and gross over-acting. Ron Leibman, who had his name taken off the credits, is the best thing about it. The film originally ran 96 minutes, but various people have been hacking it up over the years. Even *MAD* has disowned it. Rated R for profanity and general disgustingness. 1980; 88m.

UP THE CREEK ★★★

DIR: Robert Butler. **CAST:** Tim Matheson, Stephen Furst, Dan Monahan, John Hillerman, James B. Sikking.

Two stars from *Animal House*, Tim Matheson ("Otter") and Stephen Furst ("Flounder"), are reunited in this mostly entertaining raft-race comedy. It doesn't beg you to laugh at it the way *Police Academy* does. Matheson is charismatic enough—in his own audacious way—to carry the film. Rated R for nudity, profanity, suggested sex, scatological humor, and violence. 1984; 95m.

UP THE DOWN STAIRCASE ★★★½

DIR: Robert Mulligan. **CAST:** Sandy Dennis, Eileen Heckart, Jean Stapleton.

Sandy Dennis perfectly captures the flighty teacher of Bel Kaufman's hilarious novel about the New York City high school scene, but the students and minor plot crises do not wear as well as her performance. Although Dennis smoothly enacts the teacher we'd all like to have, Tad Mosel's script never quite catches the book's inspired lunacy. 1967; 124m.

UP THE SANDBOX ★

DIR: Irvin Kershner. **CAST:** Barbra Streisand, David Selby, Jane Hoffman.

A weird, uneven comedy about a neglected housewife (Barbra Streisand). Its fantasy sequences are among the strangest ever put on film. Rated R. 1972; 97m.

UP YOUR ANCHOR ★

DIR: Dan Wolman. **CAST:** Yftach Katzur, Zachi Nay.

Ever wonder what one of the beach films of the 1960s or *Love Boat* would be like with nudity and rampant sexual encounters? Pick up this video and find out. Unrated, this Israeli film would be comparable to an R. 1985; 89m.

UPHILL ALL THE WAY ★

DIR: Frank Q. Dobbs. **CAST:** Roy Clark, Mel Tillis, Glen Campbell.

Ridiculous film concerns two down-and-outers, Roy Clark and Mel Tillis, mistaken for bank robbers. The standard clichés are all here, and they have been done better so many times before. A good lesson here: Keep the boys playin' guitars instead of trying to be movie stars. Rated PG. 1985; 86m.

UPTOWN SATURDAY NIGHT ★★★½

DIR: Sidney Poitier. **CAST:** Sidney Poitier, Bill Cosby, Harry Belafonte, Richard Pryor, Flip Wilson.

Sidney Poitier (who also directed), Bill Cosby, Harry Belafonte, Richard Pryor, and Flip Wilson head an all-star cast in this enjoyable comedy about a couple of buddies (Poitier and Cosby) who get into all sorts of trouble during a night on the town. Rated PG. 1974; 104m.

USED CARS ★★★★

DIR: Robert Zemeckis. **CAST:** Jack Warden, Kurt Russell, Frank McRae, Gerrit Graham, Deborah Harmon.

This is a riotous account of two feuding used-car businesses. Jack Warden and Kurt Russell are both excellent in this overlooked comedy. Fine support is offered by Frank McRae, Gerrit Graham, and Deborah Harmon. Rated R for language, nudity, and some violence. 1980; 111m.

UTILITIES ★★★½

DIR: Harvey Hart. **CAST:** Robert Hays, Brooke Adams, John Marley.

Despite some rather crude humor once in a while, this modest comedy has a lot of charm and the heart of a Frank Capra film. Robert Hays plays a fed-up social worker who turns vigilante against the public utility companies. Rated PG for profanity and sex. 1983; 94m.

VACATION

DIR: Harold Ramis. **CAST:** Chevy Chase, Beverly D'Angelo, Anthony Michael Hall, Dana Barron, Christie Brinkley, John Candy.

One of the unfunniest comedies ever made, *Vacation* contains one laugh. Count 'em...one. That's when Clark Griswold (Chevy Chase), who goes on a disastrous vacation with his wife, Ellen (Beverly D'Angelo), and kids, Rusty (Anthony Michael Hall) and Audrey (Dana Barron), falls asleep at the wheel and the family station wagon careens hilariously out of control. Rated R for nudity and profanity. 1983; 98m.

VALLEY GIRL ★★★½

DIR: Martha Coolidge. **CAST:** Nicolas Cage, Deborah Foreman, Colleen Camp, Frederic Forrest, Lee Purcell.

The story of a romance between a San Fernando Valley girl and a Hollywood punker, *Valley Girl* claims the distinction of being one of the few teen movies directed by a woman: Martha Coolidge. And, perhaps for that reason, it's a little treasure: a funny, sexy, appealing story that makes fun of no one but contains something for nearly everyone. Rated R. 1983; 95m.

VAN, THE ★

DIR: Sam Grossman. **CAST:** Stuart Getz, Danny DeVito.

Inept light comedy about a shy teenager (Stuart Getz) who uses his impressive new van to seduce bimbos in Southern California. Innocuous idiocy of L.A. youth culture; a real stinker. Rated PG. 1976; 92m.

VASECTOMY ★★½

DIR: Robert Burge. **CAST:** Paul Sorvino, Abe Vigoda, Cassandra Edwards, Lorne Greene.

A bank vice-president (Paul Sorvino) is having plenty of family problems. After bearing their eighth child, his wife urges him to have a vasectomy while other family members are stealing from his bank. This comedy is rated R for nudity and obscenities. 1986; 92m.

VICE VERSA ★★★½

DIR: Brian Gilbert. **CAST:** Judge Reinhold, Fred Savage, Swoosie Kurtz, Jane Kaczmarek, David Proval, William Prince.

Young Fred Savage nearly steals the show from Judge Reinhold in this surprisingly entertaining comedy about a father who changes bodies with his son. We've seen it all many times before in lesser films such as *Freaky Friday* and *Like Father, Like Son.* However, the writing of Dick Clement and Ian De Frenais and the chemistry of the players make it seem almost fresh. Rated PG for profanity. 1988; 98m.

VICTOR/VICTORIA ★★★★

DIR: Blake Edwards. **CAST:** Julie Andrews, James Garner, Robert Preston, Lesley Ann Warren.

Director Blake Edwards takes us on a funny, off-the-wall romp through 1930s Paris. Julie Andrews plays a down-on-her-luck singer who poses as a gay Polish count to make ends meet. Rated PG because of adult situations. 1982; 133m.

VIRGIN QUEEN OF ST. FRANCIS HIGH, THE ★★★

DIR: Francesco Lucente. **CAST:** Joseph R. Straface, Stacy Christensen.

The title is sexploitive in this teen market release, but the film has more depth and interest than most in its genre. There's nothing much new in the first half hour, but the two leads, Joseph R. Straface and Stacy Christensen, have such winning personalities that you want to see them develop. The ending is too pat and saccharine, though. Rated PG for profanity. 1988; 89m.

VIVA MAX! ★★★

DIR: Jerry Paris. **CAST:** Peter Ustinov, Jonathan Winters, Keenan Wynn, Pamela Tiffin.

Skip credibility and enjoy. Peter Ustinov is a contemporary Mexican general who leads his men across the border to reclaim the Alamo as a tourist attraction. Jonathan Winters all but steals this romp, playing a bumbling, confused National Guard officer in the face of an audacious "enemy." Rated G. 1969; 92m.

VIVACIOUS LADY ★★★

DIR: George Stevens. **CAST:** Ginger Rogers, James Stewart, Charles Coburn, Frances Mercer, James Ellison, Beulah Bondi, Franklin Pangborn, Grady Sutton, Jack Carson, Willie Best.

Cultures clash when small-town college botany professor James Stewart impulsively weds New York nightclub singer Ginger Rogers, brings her back to the campus, and cannot find the time or the words to tell his father, upright and stuffy college president Charles Coburn, who the new lady is. 1938; B&W; 90m.

VIXEN ★★½
DIR: Russ Meyer. **CAST:** Erica Gavin, Garth Pillsbury, Harrison Page.

Russ Meyer, functioning simultaneously as producer, scriptwriter, director and camerman, turns out one of his best films with this bizarre satirical farce concerning a voluptuous young woman called Vixen (Erica Gavin) who has an unlimited appetite for sex. Contains a great deal of nudity and profanity. Recommended for adult viewing only. 1968; 70m.

VOLUNTEERS ★★
DIR: Nicholas Meyer. **CAST:** Tom Hanks, John Candy, Rita Wilson, Tim Thomerson, Gedde Watanabe.

At first glance, this comedy seems to have everything going for it: It reunites Tom Hanks and John Candy, who were so marvelously funny together in Ron Howard's *Splash*. In truth, however, this film about high jinks in the Peace Corps in Thailand circa 1962 has very little going for it. Hanks and Candy do their best, but the laughs are few and far between. Rated R for profanity, violence, and sexual innuendo. 1985; 105m.

WACKIEST SHIP IN THE ARMY, THE ★★★
DIR: Richard Murphy. **CAST:** Jack Lemmon, Ricky Nelson, John Lund, Chips Rafferty, Tom Tully, Joby Baker, Warren Berlinger.

A battered ship becomes an unlikely implement for World War II heroism. The situation is played mostly for laughs, but dramatic moments are smoothly included. Jack Lemmon sets his performance at just the right pitch. Ricky Nelson is amiable and amusing. 1960; 99m.

WACKO
DIR: Greydon Clark. **CAST:** Joe Don Baker, Stella Stevens, George Kennedy, Jeff Altman.

This excruciating parody of *Halloween* features Joe Don Baker as a no-nonsense cop who diligently pursues the deranged lawnmower killer who terrorized a town ten years earlier. Pretty bad spoof that works hard for laughs without managing even a chuckle. Rated PG. 1981; 90m.

WAITRESS
DIR: Samuel Weil, Michael Herz. **CAST:** Jim Harris, Carol Drake, Carol Bever.

This awful comedy features three waitresses working in a most unsanitary restaurant. The girls include a would-be actress, a would-be writer, and a spoiled brat who's been kicked out of her prep school. Rated R for nudity, profanity, and simulated sex. 1981; 85m.

WALK, DON'T RUN ★★★
DIR: Charles Walters. **CAST:** Cary Grant, Samantha Eggar, Miiko Taka, Jim Hutton, John Standing, George Takei.

During the summer Olympics in Tokyo, Samantha Eggar agrees to share her apartment in the crowded city with businessman Cary Grant and athlete Jim Hutton. Happy, wholesome havoc results. Cary Grant's last film, a remake of 1943's *The More the Merrier*. 1966; 114m.

WALK LIKE A MAN ★
DIR: Melvin Frank. **CAST:** Howie Mandel, Christopher Lloyd, Cloris Leachman, Amy Steel.

Unfunny, forced attempt at a comic version of *The Jungle Book*. Howie Mandel plays a young boy lost in the woods, raised by wolves, then returning to make life difficult for his jerk brother (Christopher Lloyd). Overblown. Rated PG-13 for language and adult ideas. 1987; 86m.

WALTZ OF THE TOREADORS ★★★★
DIR: John Guillermin. **CAST:** Peter Sellers, Margaret Leighton, Dany Robin.
The unique Peter Sellers is superb as a retired military officer who can't subdue his roving eye. Margaret Leighton is fine, as always. Dany Robin is adorable. It's saucy and sex-shot, but intellectually stimulating nonetheless. A charming film, and not just for Sellers's fans. 1962; 105m.

WALTZES FROM VIENNA ★
DIR: Alfred Hitchcock. **CAST:** Jessie Matthews, Esmond Knight, Edmund Gwenn.
Alfred Hitchcock...directing a musical? Not really. This undistinguished biopic of the Strauss family is more of a romantic comedy. By any category, it's a misfire. Hitchcock's boredom is plainly evident; he had his mind on other things—specifically his next picture, which would make his reputation: *The Man Who Knew Too Much*. Unrated; suitable for family viewing. 1933; B&W; 80m.

WATER ★★★
DIR: Dick Clement. **CAST:** Michael Caine, Brenda Vaccaro, Valerie Perrine, Fred Gwynne.
In this delightful British comedy, Michael Caine is the governor of the small English colony located on the island of Cascara. The governor's wife (Brenda Vaccaro) is bored with life on Cascara until an oil company headed by Fred Gwynne sends out a famous actor to film a commercial. What ensues is pleasant craziness accompanied by a great soundtrack featuring the music of Eddy Grant, and a jam session with Ringo Starr, George Harrison, and Eric Clapton. Rated PG-13. 1986; 91m.

WATERMELON MAN ★★
DIR: Melvin Van Peebles. **CAST:** Godfrey Cambridge, Estelle Parsons.
The life of a bigoted white man is turned inside-out when he wakes up one morning and finds himself black. Using the late, great black comedian Godfrey Cambridge in the title role shows that someone in production had his head on right. The film makes a statement. Trouble is, it makes it over and over and over again. Rated R. 1970; 97m.

WAY OUT WEST ★★★★★
DIR: James W. Horne. **CAST:** Stan Laurel, Oliver Hardy, Sharon Lynn.
Stan Laurel and Oliver Hardy travel west to deliver a gold mine map to the daughter of a friend. The map is given to an imposter, and the boys have to retrieve it and ensure correct delivery. A delightful, marvelous film that demonstrates the team's mastery of timing and characterization. 1937; B&W; 65m.

WE THINK THE WORLD OF YOU ★★★½
DIR: Colin Gregg. **CAST:** Alan Bates, Gary Oldman, Frances Barber, Max Wall.
A bittersweet British comedy, set in the 1950s, and based on the autobiographical novel by Joseph R. Ackerley. Alan Bates plays a frustrated and emotionally abused homosexual who can't seem to reconcile his relationship with an ex-sailor/ex-con (Gary Oldman). Bates finally finds a degree of warmth in his friendship with Oldman's dog. This is a quirky, gentle, offbeat film, elevated by strong performances. Rated PG. 1988; 100m.

WEDDING, A ★★★
DIR: Robert Altman. **CAST:** Carol Burnett, Desi Arnaz Jr., Geraldine Chaplin, Vittorio Gassman, Lillian Gish, Lauren Hutton, Paul Dooley, Howard Duff, Pam Dawber, Dina Merrill, John Considine.
This is one of those *almost* movies—one that has enough good things about it to recommend, but that could have been so much better. During the late 1970s, director Robert Altman's films had begun to lose their focus, and any kind of coherence had largely disappeared, as this film demonstrates. The

story deals with a wedding between two relatively wealthy families and the comic implications that follow. Fine acting keeps things afloat. Rated PG. 1978; 125m.

WEDDING PARTY, THE ★
DIR: Cynthia Munroe, Wilford Leach, Brian De Palma. **CAST:** Robert De Niro, Jill Clayburgh, Jennifer Salt.

Plodding and irksome, this is about a groom who develops cold feet after meeting his prospective father and mother-in-law. It's the screen debut of Jill Clayburgh and, as it's spelled out in the credits, Robert De Niro. Filmed in 1963, but not released until1969. Yawn. 1969; B&W; 92m.

WEDDING REHEARSAL ★★
DIR: Alexander Korda. **CAST:** Roland Young, George Grossmith, John Loder, Lady Tree, Wendy Barris, Maurice Evans, Merle Oberon.

There's not much magic or comedy in this shaky farce. Director Alexander Korda shows poor directorial technique in this story of an officer whose grandmother plans to get him married. You can catch the whole thing with one eye closed and your favorite radio station on. 1932; B&W; 84m.

WEEKEND AT BERNIE'S ★★½
DIR: Ted Kotcheff. **CAST:** Andrew McCarthy, Jonathan Silverman, Catherine Mary Stewart, Terry Kiser.

In this tolerable comedy with some hilarious moments, Andrew McCarthy and Jonathan Silverman play upwardly mobile young executives all set to have a wild, wild weekend at their boss's swank beach house—until they find the murdered body of said boss and realize they could be the next victims. Terry Kiser steals the show as the dead man, which gives you an idea of how silly it all is. Rated PG. 1989; 110m.

WEEKEND PASS ★
DIR: Lawrence Bassoff. **CAST:** D. W. Brown, Peter Ellenstein, Patrick Hauser, Chip McAllister.

A quartet of stupid sailors on shore leave cavorts uncomically in Los Angeles, in this tired and lewd low-budget sex comedy. Rated R. 1984; 92m.

WEIRD SCIENCE ★★★
DIR: John Hughes. **CAST:** Anthony Michael Hall, Kelly LeBrock, Ilan Mitchell-Smith.

In this wacky comedy by writer-director John Hughes, two put-upon nerds (Anthony Michael Hall and Ilan Mitchell-Smith), desperate for a date, cop an idea from James Whale's *Frankenstein* (which is playing on television) and create a sexy woman via computer. Thus begins a roller coaster ride of hit-and-miss humor as the nerds get class fast. Rated PG-13 for slight violence, partial nudity, and profanity. 1985; 94m.

WELCOME TO 18
DIR: Terry Carr. **CAST:** Mariska Hargitay, Courtney Thorne-Smith, Jo Ann Willette.

This low-budget film's only point of interest is that it marks the big-screen debut of Mariska Hargitay, the daughter of Jayne Mansfield—and she can't act. Otherwise, it's an unrelentingly awful movie about three typically pert female high-school graduates who take summer jobs at a Lake Tahoe dude ranch and soon find themselves at the mercy of a drug-dealing pimp. Rated PG-13 for profanity and nudity. 1986; 91m.

WE'RE NO ANGELS ★★½
DIR: Michael Curtiz. **CAST:** Humphrey Bogart, Peter Ustinov, Aldo Ray, Basil Rathbone, Joan Bennett, Leo G. Carroll.

The *New York Times* dubbed this "a slow, talky reprise of the delightful stage comedy" and was right. Three Devil's Island convicts "adopt" an island family and protect it against an uncle it can do without. There is a roguishness about the trio that almost makes them endearing, and there is humor, but the film does drag. 1955; 106m.

WHAT DO YOU SAY TO A NAKED LADY? ★
DIR: Allen Funt. **CAST:** Allen Funt, Richard Roundtree.
Allen Funt's R-rated version of *Candid Camera* is a bust from the start. Imagine the same candid camera gags only with naked women and you've pretty well figured this dud out. Pass on this one. Rated R for nudity. 1970; 90m.

WHAT PRICE GLORY ★★★
DIR: John Ford. **CAST:** James Cagney, Dan Dailey, Corinne Calvet, William Demarest, Robert Wagner, Marisa Pavan, James Gleason.
James Cagney is Captain Flagg, Dan Dailey is Sergeant Quirt in this rough-and-tumble tale of rivalry in romance set against the sobering background of World War I in France. The feisty pair of marines vies for the affections of adorable Charmaine (Corinne Calvet). Between quarrels, they fight in the trenches. 1952; 109m.

WHAT'S NEW, PUSSYCAT? ★★★
DIR: Clive Donner. **CAST:** Peter Sellers, Peter O'Toole, Woody Allen, Ursula Andress, Romy Schneider, Capucine, Paula Prentiss.
Peter O'Toole is a fashion editor who can't stop becoming romantically involved with his models. In spite of a strong supporting cast, this dated 1960s "hip" comedy has few genuine laughs. Mostly, it's just silly. 1965; 108m.

WHAT'S UP, DOC? ★★★★
DIR: Peter Bogdanovich. **CAST:** Ryan O'Neal, Barbra Streisand, Kenneth Mars, Austin Pendleton.
A virtual remake of Howard Hawks's classic *Bringing Up Baby*, with Ryan O'Neal and Barbra Streisand representing the Cary Grant and Katharine Hepburn roles, this manages to recapture much of the madcap charm and nonstop action of the original story. O'Neal is the studious scientist delightfully led astray by a dizzy Streisand, who keeps forcing herself into his life. The zany final chase through the streets of San Francisco is one of filmdom's best. Rated G. 1972; 94m.

WHAT'S UP FRONT ★
DIR: Bob Whealing. **CAST:** Tommy Holden, Marilyn Manning.
Silly, dated, and bizarre comedy features a determined nerd (Tommy Holden) selling bras door-to-door. Amazingly, he's successful, but his orders are stolen by a two-timing cad at the office. Unrated; this features women wearing very *un*sexy bras. 1963; 90m.

WHAT'S UP, TIGER LILY? ★★★
DIR: Woody Allen. **CAST:** Tatsuya Mihashi, Miya Hana, Woody Allen.
A dreadful Japanese spy movie has been given a zany English-language soundtrack by Woody Allen in one of his earliest movie productions. You are left with an offbeat spoof of the whole genre of spy films. The results are often amusing, but its one-joke premise gets rather tedious before it's over. 1966; 80m.

WHEEL OF FORTUNE ★★½
DIR: John H. Auer. **CAST:** John Wayne, Frances Dee, Ward Bond.
John Wayne in a screwball comedy? Yep. Also titled *A Man Betrayed*, the surprise is that this low-budget production is watchable. 1941; B&W; 83m.

WHEN HARRY MET SALLY ★★★★½
DIR: Rob Reiner. **CAST:** Billy Crystal, Meg Ryan, Carrie Fisher, Bruno Kirby.
Wonderful character comedy stars Billy Crystal and Meg Ryan as long-time acquaintances who drift from mild animosity to friendship to love. Director Rob Reiner skillfully tickles our funnybones and touches our hearts with this semiautobiographical tale, which was scripted by Nora Ephron. Rated R for profanity and suggested sex. 1989; 110m.

WHEN THINGS WERE ROTTEN ★★★

DIR: Coby Ruskin, Marty Feldman, Peter Bonerz. **CAST:** Dick Gautier, Dick Van Patten, Bernie Kopell, Richard Dimitri, Henry Polic II, Misty Rowe, David Sabin.

This compilation of three episodes from the short-lived television series of the same name is sure to please fans of *Blazing Saddles*–style humor. Dick Gautier's nearly serious portrayal of Robin Hood is a perfect foil for the slapstick antics of the rest of the cast. 1975; 78m.

WHEN WOMEN HAD TAILS ★★

DIR: Pasquale Festa Campanile. **CAST:** Senta Berger, Frank Wolff, Giuliano Gemma, Lando Buzzanca.

This Italian comedy is a prehistoric romp about five cavemen discovering the delightful difference of the sexes when pretty Senta Berger suddenly appears in their midst. Despite plenty of potential, this farce falls flat. Rated R for language and nudity. 1970; 99m.

WHEN WOMEN LOST THEIR TAILS ★★½

DIR: Pasquale Festa Campanile. **CAST:** Senta Berger, Frank Wolff, Lando Buzzanca, Francesco Mule.

Most of the cast of *When Women Had Tails* returns in a much more sophisticated sex comedy set in prehistoric times. Where the first film focused entirely on the discovery of sex, this slapstick sequel takes a broader view, poking fun at the earliest manifestations of civilization. The stone-age jabs are still silly, but many of the observations are surprisingly enlightening. Rated R. 1971; 94m.

WHEN'S YOUR BIRTHDAY? ★★★

DIR: Harry Beaumont. **CAST:** Joe E. Brown, Marian Marsh, Edgar Kennedy, Margaret Hamilton.

Joe E. Brown stars as a student of astrology who doubles as a boxer. The stars tell him when he'll win in the ring. Unfortunately, a gangster gets wind of his abilities and tries to turn them to his own ends. It's all a showcase for Brown, though Edgar Kennedy steals his scenes with his hilarious slow burn. 1937; B&W; 76m.

WHERE THE BOYS ARE ★★★

DIR: Henry Levin. **CAST:** Dolores Hart, George Hamilton, Yvette Mimieux, Jim Hutton, Barbara Nichols, Connie Francis.

Connie Francis warbled the title tune and made her movie debut in this frothy, mildly entertaining film about teenagers doing what's natural during Easter vacation in Fort Lauderdale. It's miles ahead of the idiotic remake. 1960; 99m.

WHERE THE BOYS ARE '84

DIR: Hy Averback. **CAST:** Lisa Hartman, Russell Todd, Lorna Luft, Lynn-Holly Johnson, Wendy Schaal, Howard McGillin, Louise Sorel.

No, this isn't a rerelease of the 1960 film about teens tearin' it up in Fort Lauderdale, which Connie Francis immortalized in the song of the same name. It's a poorly made remake by Mr. "Can't Stop the Music" himself: producer Allan Carr. Rated R. 1984; 96m.

WHERE THE BUFFALO ROAM

DIR: Art Linson. **CAST:** Bill Murray, Peter Boyle, Bruno Kirby, René Auberjonois, R. G. Armstrong, Rafael Campos, Leonard Frey.

Director Art Linson's horrendous film about the exploits of gonzo journalist Hunter S. Thompson. Bill Murray turns in one of his few bad performances as the consistently stoned-out writer. Thompson has reportedly sworn "to rip Murray's throat out" if they ever meet. It's our feeling it would have been better if this movie had never been released on video. Rated R. 1980; 96m.

WHERE'S POPPA? ★★★★

DIR: Carl Reiner. **CAST:** George Segal, Ruth Gordon, Trish Van Devere, Ron Leibman, Rae Allen, Vincent Gardenia, Barnard Hughes, Rob Reiner, Garrett Morris.

One of George Segal's best comic performances is found in this cult favorite. Ruth Gordon co-stars as the senile mother whom Segal tries to scare into having a cardiac arrest. Director Carl Reiner's son, Rob, makes a short appearance as a fervent draft resister. Rated R. 1970; 82m.

WHICH WAY IS UP? ★★★★
DIR: Michael Schultz. **CAST:** Richard Pryor, Lonette McKee, Margaret Avery, Dolph Sweet, Morgan Woodward.
This irreverent, ribald farce reunites the talented comedy team of director Michael Shultz and star Richard Pryor (*Greased Lightning*) for one of the funnier movies of the 1970s. Pryor plays three major roles. His ability to create totally separate and distinctive characters contributes greatly to the success of this oft-tried but rarely believable gimmick. Rated R. 1977; 94m.

WHICH WAY TO THE FRONT? 🦃
DIR: Jerry Lewis. **CAST:** Jerry Lewis, John Wood, Jan Murray, Kaye Ballard, Robert Middleton, Paul Winchell, Gary Crosby.
Mention this film to even the staunchest of Jerry Lewis fans and they're likely to blanch or bristle. Even they usually admit that this is a *bad* film. Jerry Lewis directs and stars in this pathetic story about a rich 4-F American who enlists other such unfortunates into a military unit to combat Nazi Germany. 1970; 96m.

WHIFFS ★
DIR: Ted Post. **CAST:** Elliott Gould, Eddie Albert, Jennifer O'Neal, Harry Guardino.
Dull, listless comedy starring Elliot Gould as an army private who is a human guinea pig suffering annoying side-effects from biological and chemical-weapons testing. Drummed out of the service on a medical discharge and thoroughly screwed by the army, Gould devises a scheme of revenge. No need to take a whiff of this mess. Not rated. 1975; 92m.

WHO AM I THIS TIME? ★★★½
DIR: Jonathan Demme. **CAST:** Susan Sarandon, Christopher Walken, Robert Ridgely.
The new girl in town, Helene Shaw (Susan Sarandon), gets a part in the local theater group production of *A Streetcar Named Desire* opposite Harry Nash (Christopher Walken). Dreadfully shy, Harry only comes to life in every part he plays on the stage. Helene, an introvert herself, falls for both sides of his persona and sets out to win him. This is a pleasing Kurt Vonnegut Jr. story played by a capable cast. 1982; 60m.

WHO FRAMED ROGER RABBIT ★★★★½
DIR: Robert Zemeckis. **CAST:** Bob Hoskins, Christopher Lloyd, Joanna Cassidy, Stubby Kaye.
In this innovative and vastly entertaining motion picture, which seamlessly blends animated characters with live action, cartoon character Roger Rabbit (voice by Charles Fleischer) is accused of murder and turns to a hard-boiled private detective (Bob Hoskins) for help. As with his *Back to the Future* and *Romancing the Stone*, director Robert Zemeckis has come up with a wonderful movie for all ages. Rated PG for vulgar language. 1988; 103m.

WHOLLY MOSES! ★★½
DIR: Gary Weis. **CAST:** Dudley Moore, Richard Pryor, Laraine Newman, James Coco, Paul Sand, Jack Gilford, Dom DeLuise, John Houseman, Madeline Kahn, David L. Lander, John Ritter.
Wholly Moses! pokes fun at Hollywood biblical epics in a rapid-fire fashion. While the film is sometimes very funny, it is also loaded with a fair share of predictable, flat, and corny moments. It's so-so viewing fare. Rated R. 1980; 109m.

WHOOPEE BOYS, THE 🦃
DIR: John Byrum. **CAST:** Michael O'Keefe, Paul Rodriguez, Lucinda

Jenney, Denholm Elliott, Eddie Deezen.

Not since *Mad* magazine's *Up the Academy* has a so-called outrageous comedy been so unrelentingly awful. Stand-up comic Paul Rodriguez seems to have trouble in choosing his film properties. In this one, Rodriguez teams up with Michael O'Keefe in a clichéd story about a pair of obnoxious—and supposedly lovable—misfits who attempt to save a school for needy children. Rated R for profanity. 1986; 94m.

WHOOPS APOCALYPSE ★★½
DIR: John Reardon. **CAST:** John Barron, John Cleese, Richard Griffiths, Peter Jones, Barry Morse.

This overlong but sometimes rewarding British comedy consists of a news coverage spoof on events leading up to World War III. There are some funny parts as the newscasters interview world leaders. The plot centers around the theft of a U.S. nuclear bomb. Many viewers may get fidgety during the second, less successful half. Unrated, it contains nudity and obscene language. 1981; 137m.

WHO'S HARRY CRUMB?
DIR: Paul Flaherty. **CAST:** John Candy, Jeffrey Jones, Annie Potts, Tim Thomerson, Barry Corbin.

John Candy's *Who's Harry Crumb?* is such a crummy comedy that it will move some people to drop Candy from their film-watching diet. There are absolutely no laughs as inept private eye Harry Crumb bumbles his way through the case of a kidnapped heiress. Candy acted as executive producer on this moronic mess. Rated PG-13 for profanity and suggested sex. 1989; 87m.

WHO'S MINDING THE MINT? ★★★½
DIR: Howard Morris. **CAST:** Milton Berle, Jim Hutton, Dorothy Provine, Joey Bishop, Walter Brennan, Jamie Farr, Victor Buono.

When a U.S. Mint employee (Jim Hutton) accidentally destroys thousands of newly printed bills, a group of misfits bands together to help him out. This film is often hilarious and always enjoyable. 1967; 97m.

WHO'S THAT GIRL
DIR: James Foley. **CAST:** Madonna, Griffin Dunne, Haviland Morris, John McMartin, John Mills.

A warped, pseudoremake of the 1938 comedy classic *Bringing Up Baby*. Griffin Dunne plays a spectacled stuffed shirt whose life is turned upside down by the impervious Madonna. The movie is a disaster. Rated PG for profanity. 1987; 95m.

WILD LIFE, THE ★★
DIR: Art Linson. **CAST:** Christopher Penn, Lea Thompson, Rick Moranis, Randy Quaid, Ilan Mitchell-Smith.

From some of the same people who brought you *Fast Times at Ridgemont High* comes a film set in a world where your "cool" is measured by how many cigarettes you can smoke (and eat) and how many girls you can bed. Christopher Penn offers a believable performance as the leader of a pack of teens trying to grow up too fast. Rated R for suggested sex and language. 1984; 96m.

WILDCATS ★★
DIR: Michael Ritchie. **CAST:** Goldie Hawn, Swoosie Kurtz, James Keach, Nipsy Russell, Woody Harrelson, M. Emmet Walsh.

Standard Goldie Hawn vehicle, with her playing high-school football coach to a rowdy group of inner-city kids who need to prove their worth as much as she needs to raise her self-esteem and prove her skill to chauvinistic athletic directors. Director Michael Ritchie shows little of the tension he brought to *The Bad News Bears*. Rated R for nudity and language. 1986; 107m.

WIMPS ★
DIR: Chuck Vincent. **CAST:** Louie Bonanno, Deborah Blaisdell, Jim Abele, Jane Hamilton.

Animal House meets *Cyrano de Bergerac*. Louis Bonanno portrays the wimp son of a football great who is trying to pledge the same fraternity and ends up helping the star quarterback woo a brainy sorority girl. Neither plot is handled well. A dull attempt at updating a classic situation. Rated R for language, nudity, and sexual situations. 1986; 94m.

WIN, PLACE OR STEAL 🦃

DIR: Richard Bailey. **CAST:** Dean Stockwell, Russ Tamblyn, Alex Karras, McLean Stevenson.

Slow, boring comedy about three aging adolescents who prefer playing the ponies to working. Strapped for money, they steal a racetrack betting machine and decide to print their own winning tickets. McLean Stevenson provides a few chuckles. Unrated, it features brief nudity comparable to a PG. 1972; 88m.

WISE GUYS ★★★½

DIR: Brian De Palma. **CAST:** Danny DeVito, Joe Piscopo, Harvey Keitel, Ray Sharkey, Dan Hedaya.

Director Brian De Palma, apparently tired of derivative Hitchcockian thrillers, returned to his roots with this send-up of gangster movies. Danny DeVito and Joe Piscopo play Harry and Moe, a couple of goofball syndicate gofers trusted with little above the boss's laundry. The reason for this becomes obvious when they muck up a bet on the ponies; as punishment, the boss secretly instructs each to kill the other. Inexplicably rated R for language. 1986; 91m.

WISH YOU WERE HERE ★★★★

DIR: David Leland. **CAST:** Emily Lloyd, Tom Bell, Jesse Birdsall, Geoffrey Durham, Pat Heywood.

The heroine of this British production is a foulmouthed, promiscuous 16-year-old (superbly played by Emily Lloyd), who raises hackles in the straitlaced world of 1940s England. Her story is shocking, funny, and ultimately touching. Writer-director David Leland has created a hilarious comedy. Rated R for profanity, nudity, and simulated sex. 1987; 92m.

WITCHES' BREW ★★

DIR: Richard Shoor, Herbert L. Strock. **CAST:** Richard Benjamin, Teri Garr, Lana Turner, Kathryn Leigh Scott.

Margret (Teri Garr) and her two girlfriends have been dabbling in witchcraft to help their university professor husbands to succeed. When a coveted chairmanship opens up, the two friends use their powers against Margret and her husband Josh (Richard Benjamin). It's supposed to be a horror spoof but turns out to be more of a horror ripoff of *Burn Witch Burn*! Lana Turner has a small role as the witchcraft mentor to the three young women. Rated PG. 1980; 98m.

WITCHES OF EASTWICK, THE ★★★★½

DIR: George Miller. **CAST:** Jack Nicholson, Cher, Susan Sarandon, Michelle Pfeiffer, Veronica Cartwright, Richard Jenkins.

In this wickedly funny comedy, Jack Nicholson gives one of his finest—and funniest—performances as a self-described "horny little devil" who comes to a tiny hamlet at the behest of three women (Cher, Susan Sarandon, and Michelle Pfeiffer). Only trouble is, these "witches" have no idea of what they've done until it is very nearly too late. Rated R for profanity and suggested sex. 1987; 121m.

WITH SIX YOU GET EGGROLL ★★

DIR: Howard Morris. **CAST:** Doris Day, Brian Keith, Barbara Hershey.

Widow Doris Day has three kids; widower Brian Keith has a daughter. They get together. Awwwww! *Bachelor Father* meets *Mother Knows Best*. The two stars refer to Doris and Brian, neither of whom helped their cause with this turkey. Strictly a picture for the 1960s. Unrated. 1968; 99m.

WITHNAIL AND I ★★★★

DIR: Bruce Robinson. **CAST:** Richard E. Grant, Paul McGann, Richard Griffiths.

A funny but sometimes grim comedy set in the Great Britain of the late 1960s. Two friends, whose decadent lifestyle of booze and drugs has hit bottom, try to make a new start by taking a holiday in the country. The performances are excellent, period details are perfect, and the movie is well made. Rated R for profanity and adult themes. 1987; 110m.

WITHOUT A CLUE ★★★★

DIR: Thom Eberhardt. **CAST:** Michael Caine, Ben Kingsley, Jeffrey Jones, Lysette Anthony, Paul Freeman, Nigel Davenport, Peter Cook.

In this delightful send-up of Conan Doyle's Sherlock Holmes mysteries, it is revealed that Holmes was nothing more than a fictional creation of the real crime-fighting genius, Dr. John H. Watson (Ben Kingsley). The man everyone thought was the Great Detective was actually an inept, clumsy, and often inebriated actor, Reginald Kincaid (Michael Caine), hired by Watson. An overlooked gem of a comedy. Rated PG for violence. 1988; 106m.

WITHOUT RESERVATIONS ★★★

DIR: Mervyn LeRoy. **CAST:** John Wayne, Claudette Colbert, Don DeFore, Phil Brown, Thurston Hall, Louella Parsons.

Wartime comedy about authoress Claudette Colbert and her plan to turn soldier John Wayne into the leading man of her filmed novel is light and enjoyable and sprinkled with guest appearances by Hollywood celebrities. This is hardly the kind of war film in which one would expect to find John Wayne, but the Duke makes the best of a chance to act under top director Mervyn LeRoy (who was in a slump during this period). 1946; B&W; 107m.

WOMAN IN RED, THE ★★★★

DIR: Gene Wilder. **CAST:** Gene Wilder, Charles Grodin, Joseph Bologna, Gilda Radner, Judith Ivey, Michael Huddleston, Kelly LeBrock.

Gene Wilder's funniest film in years, this is best described as a bittersweet romantic comedy. Wilder, who also adapted the screenplay and directed, plays an advertising executive and heretofore happily married man who becomes obsessed with a beautiful woman he happens to see one day in a parking garage. The results are hilarious. Rated PG-13 for partial nudity, brief violence, and profanity. 1984; 87m.

WOMAN OF DISTINCTION, A ★★★½

DIR: Edward Buzzell. **CAST:** Rosalind Russell, Ray Milland, Edmund Gwenn, Janis Carter, Francis Lederer.

Though minor, this is really a quite enjoyable film. Rosalind Russell portrays a college dean who must face a tough decision involving a professor (Ray Milland). Familiar but fun. 1950; B&W; 85m.

WOMAN OF THE YEAR ★★★★★

DIR: George Stevens. **CAST:** Spencer Tracy, Katharine Hepburn, Fay Bainter, Reginald Owen, William Bendix.

This is the film that first teamed Spencer Tracy and Katharine Hepburn, and it's impossible to imagine anybody else doing a better job. He's a sports reporter; she's a famed political journalist who needs to be reminded of life's simple pleasures. Like baseball...and her attempts to learn the game are priceless. The witty script garnered an Oscar for Ring Lardner Jr. and Michael Kanin. Unrated—family fare. 1942; B&W; 112m.

WOMEN, THE ★★★★½

DIR: George Cukor. **CAST:** Norma Shearer, Joan Crawford, Rosalind Russell, Joan Fontaine, Paulette Goddard.

Director George Cukor and some of Hollywood's finest female stars combine for a winning screen version of Claire Booth's stage hit. This look at the state of matrimony is great entertainment. The script is full of witty, stinging dialogue. 1939; B&W; 132m.

WOMEN'S CLUB, THE ★
DIR: Sandra Weintraub. **CAST:** Michael Paré, Maud Adams, Eddie Velez.
In this poor comedy, Eddie Velez provides the few comic moments as Michael Paré's zany buddy. Paré has just started working for Maud Adams, servicing her rich and powerful clients. What at first seems like heaven quickly turns into a nightmare. Rated R for profanity, brief nudity, and excessive sexual situations. 1986; 89m.

WONDER MAN ★★★
DIR: H. Bruce Humberstone. **CAST:** Danny Kaye, Vera-Ellen, Virginia Mayo, Donald Woods, S. Z. Sakall, Allen Jenkins, Edward Brophy.
Deftly doubling, Danny Kaye plays identical twins with personalities as far apart as the polar regions. One, Buzzy Bellew, is a brash, irrepressible nightclub comic; his mirror, Edwin Dingle, is a mousy double-dome full of tongue-twisting erudition. Identities are switched, of course. Thin on plot, this is mostly a tailored showcase for Kaye's brilliant talents. 1945; 98m.

WORKING GIRL ★★★★
DIR: Mike Nichols. **CAST:** Harrison Ford, Sigourney Weaver, Melanie Griffith, Alec Baldwin, Joan Cusack.
A clever, sophisticated comedy with grit, *Working Girl* makes up for a lack of all-out belly laughs with the ring of truth. Melanie Griffith is terrific as the good-hearted gal attempting to work her way up in the brokerage business. She is thwarted in this by her scheming boss, Sigourney Weaver, until Harrison Ford, as a high-powered dealmaker rides to the rescue. Weaver is marvelously sinister and Ford is properly perplexed, but it is Griffith who steals the show. Rated R for nudity and profanity. 1988; 120m.

WORLD OF ABBOTT AND COSTELLO, THE ★★★
DIR: Jack E. Leonard. **CAST:** Bud Abbott, Lou Costello, various guest stars.
Compilation of Abbott and Costello's best film footage is well handled, with many of their classic scenes intact: the frog in the soup, Lou in the wrestling ring, Lou meeting Dracula, and of course "Who's on First?" Would've been better without the narration, but the film never fails to entertain. Add one star if you're a fan. 1965; B&W; 79m.

WORLD OF HENRY ORIENT, THE ★★★★
DIR: George Roy Hill. **CAST:** Peter Sellers, Paula Prentiss, Angela Lansbury, Phyllis Thaxter.
A quirky comedy for the whole family. Peter Sellers is a woman-crazy New York pianist who finds himself being followed by two teen-age girls who have come to idolize him. Loads of fun, with a great performance by Angela Lansbury. 1964; 106m.

WORLD'S GREATEST LOVER, THE ★★½
DIR: Gene Wilder. **CAST:** Gene Wilder, Carol Kane, Dom DeLuise, Fritz Feld, Carl Ballantine, Michael Huddleston, Matt Collins, Ronny Graham.
Gene Wilder plays a would-be silent-movie star who tests for the part of the "new Valentino" while his wife (Carol Kane) runs off with the real Rudolph. Dom DeLuise is around to brighten things up, but writer-director Wilder's ideas of what's funny and well-timed aren't quite right. Rated PG. 1977; 89m.

WRONG ARM OF THE LAW, THE ★★★★
DIR: Cliff Owen. **CAST:** Peter Sellers, Lionel Jeffries, Bernard Cribbins, Davy Kaye, Nanette Newman.
Peter Sellers is hilarious as Pearly Gates, the Cockney leader of a group of bandits. Sellers and his gang join forces with police inspector Parker

(Lionel Jeffries) after a group of Australians pose as police and capture Sellers' stolen goods. This British comedy contains enough of the wacky zaniness that Sellers built his reputation on to keep most viewers in stitches. 1962; B&W; 94m.

WRONG BOX, THE ★★★★
DIR: Bryan Forbes. **CAST:** John Mills, Ralph Richardson, Dudley Moore, Peter Sellers, Peter Cook, Michael Caine, Nanette Newman, Wilfrid Lawson, Tony Hancock.
Some of Britain's best-known comics appear in this screwball farce about two zany families who battle over an inheritance in Victorian England. The film borders on black humor as the corpse of a wealthy brother is shuffled all over London by the contending parties—headed by John Mills and Ralph Richardson. Dudley Moore, Peter Sellers, and Peter Cook are just a few of the funnymen who give cameo performances in the delightful comedy. 1966; 105m.

WRONG GUYS, THE ★½
DIR: Danny Bilson. **CAST:** Louie Anderson, Richard Lewis, Richard Belzer, Franklin Ajaye, Tim Thomerson, John Goodman, Brion James, Ernie Hudson, Alice Ghostley, Kathleen Freeman.
Flat, no-energy comedy that teams some of the giants of stand-up in a film about the camping-trip reunion of a 1962 Cub Scout Troop. The troop is mistaken for FBI agents by a crazed convict, and therein lies the comedy. A disappointment. Rated PG for language and comic-book violence. 1988; 86m.

WRONG IS RIGHT ★★★★
DIR: Richard Brooks. **CAST:** Sean Connery, Robert Conrad, George Grizzard, Katharine Ross, G. D. Spradlin, John Saxon, Henry Silva, Léslie Nielsen, Robert Webber, Rosalind Cash, Hardy Krüger, Dean Stockwell, Ron Moody.
Sean Connery, as a globe-trotting television reporter, gives what may be the best performance of his career, in this outrageous, thoroughly entertaining end-of-the-world black comedy, written, produced, and directed by Richard Brooks It's an updated combination of *Network* and *Dr. Strangelove*, and wickedly funny. Rated R because of profanity and violence. 1982; 117m.

YELLOWBEARD ★★½
DIR: Mel Damski. **CAST:** Graham Chapman, Eric Idle, John Cleese, Peter Cook, Cheech and Chong, Peter Boyle, Madeline Kahn, Marty Feldman, Kenneth Mars.
This pirate comedy has a shipload of comedians; unfortunately, it barely contains a boatload of laughs under the directorship of first-timer Mel Damski. Rated PG for profanity, nudity, violence, gore, and scatological humor. 1983; 101m.

YO-YO MAN ★★★★
DIR: David Grossman. **CAST:** Tom Smothers, Dick Smothers, Daniel Volk.
This is ostensibly an instruction video on the development of yo-yo skills, but it is much more. The actual instruction consists of the basic tricks, tips on using the yo-yo, plus advanced skills that are great fun to watch and can be accomplished with practice. There are clips from *The Smothers Brothers Comedy Hour* series and new footage with Tommy Smothers and yo-yo expert Daniel Volk. Dick Smothers adds narrative and humor, and there is a catchy soundtrack. 1988; 38m.

YOU BET YOUR LIFE (TELEVISION SERIES) ★★★½
DIR: Robert Dwan, Bernie Smith. **CAST:** Groucho Marx, George Fenneman.
Over the years, two different game formats were devised for this show, but it was the interview segment that made the program a winner. In grilling the contestants, who ranged from average folks to celebrities to bizarre characters, Groucho Marx invariably

got off a number of clever quips. 1950–1961; B&W; 30m.

YOU CAN'T CHEAT AN HONEST MAN ★★★½

DIR: George Marshall. **CAST:** W. C. Fields, Edgar Bergen and Charlie McCarthy, Constance Moore, Mary Forbes, Thurston Hall, Eddie Anderson.

Nearly plotless, this is, star W. C. Fields admitted, "a jumble of vaudeville skits"—which, nonetheless, brings together, with hilarious results, a cast of exquisite comedians. Fields fans will relish it all, of course. 1939; B&W; 76m.

YOU CAN'T FOOL YOUR WIFE ★★★

DIR: Ray McCarey. **CAST:** Lucille Ball, Robert Coote, James Ellison.

A disillusioned Lucille Ball leaves her husband (James Ellison) and then tries to patch things up at a costume party. This is an average comedy with Ball playing two parts. 1940; B&W; 68m.

YOU CAN'T HURRY LOVE ★½

DIR: Richard Martini. **CAST:** David Leisure, Scott McGinnis, Anthony Geary, Bridget Fonda, Frank Bonner, Kristy McNichol.

Yet another teen comedy-romance. After being dumped by his bride, a young man leaves Ohio to live with his hep cousin in Los Angeles. There he meets assorted women through a video dating service. Rated R for nudity and profanity. 1987; 92m.

YOU'LL FIND OUT ★★★

DIR: David Butler. **CAST:** Kay Kyser, Peter Lorre, Boris Karloff, Bela Lugosi, Dennis O'Keefe, Helen Parrish.

Three titans of terror—Boris Karloff, Peter Lorre, and Bela Lugosi—menace bandleader Kay Kyser and heiress Helen Parrish in this silly but amiable comedy. Kyser isn't much of a screen personality, but director David Butler keeps the comedy, music, and suspense nicely balanced. 1940; B&W; 97m.

YOUNG DOCTORS IN LOVE ★★★

DIR: Garry Marshall. **CAST:** Michael McKean, Sean Young, Harry Dean Stanton, Patrick Macnee, Hector Elizondo, Dabney Coleman, Pamela Reed, Michael Richards, Taylor Negron, Saul Rubinek, Titos Vandis.

This comedy attempts to do for medical soap operas what *Airplane!* did for disaster movies—and doesn't quite make it. That said, director Garry Marshall (of television's *Laverne and Shirley*) has nevertheless created an enjoyable movie for open-minded adults. The R-rated film is a bit too raunchy and suggestive for the younger set. 1982; 95m.

YOUNG EINSTEIN ★

DIR: Yahoo Serious. **CAST:** Yahoo Serious.

Touted as the next *Crocodile Dundee*, this silly and self-absorbed blank check of a movie is a perfect example of the downfall of Australian cinema. Young Einstein discovers how to split the atom and thus puts the bubbles into beer. During his travels he meets and falls in love with Madame Curie. Yahoo Serious sports a huge hairdo that is probably the major lasting impression this movie makes. Rated PG. 1989; 91m.

YOUNG FRANKENSTEIN ★★★★½

DIR: Mel Brooks. **CAST:** Gene Wilder, Marty Feldman, Peter Boyle, Teri Garr, Madeline Kahn, Cloris Leachman, Kenneth Mars, Richard Haydn.

This is one of Mel Brooks's best. *Young Frankenstein* is the story of Dr. Frankenstein's college professor descendant who abhors his family history. This spoof of the old Universal horror films is hilarious from start to finish. Rated PG. 1974; B&W; 105m.

YOUNG NURSES IN LOVE ★

DIR: Chuck Vincent. **CAST:** Jeanne Marie.

A foreign spy poses as a nurse to steal the sperm from the sperm bank that was donated by world leaders, celebrities, and geniuses. It is presumed this will create a superior race. Silly low-budget sex farce. Rated R for nudity. 1989; 82m.

YOU'RE A BIG BOY NOW ★★★★½

DIR: Francis Ford Coppola. **CAST:** Peter Kastner, Elizabeth Hartman, Geraldine Page, Julie Harris, Rip Torn, Michael Dunn, Tony Bill, Karen Black.

Francis Ford Coppola not only directed this (his first) film but also wrote the screenplay. Peter Kastner, the product of overprotective parents, learns about life from street-wise go-go dancer Elizabeth Hartman. Fast-paced and very entertaining. 1966; 96m.

YOURS, MINE AND OURS ★★★

DIR: Melville Shavelson. **CAST:** Lucille Ball, Henry Fonda, Van Johnson, Tom Bosley.

A widow with eight children marries a widower with ten of his own. This works as a harbinger of *The Brady Bunch.* Wholesome but never sterile or overly sentimental, this comedy-drama is probably Lucille Ball's best post–*I Love Lucy* vehicle. Rated G. 1968; 111m.

ZANY ADVENTURES OF ROBIN HOOD, THE ★★

DIR: Ray Austin. **CAST:** George Segal, Morgan Fairchild, Roddy McDowall, Janet Suzman.

Made-for-TV spoof of the legendary hero of Sherwood Forest who must rob from the rich to raise ransom money to free King Richard. George Segal is likable as Robin Hood. Numerous references to future inventions are meant to be funny but aren't. Okay time-passer but nothing more. 1984; 90m.

ZAPPED! ★★

DIR: Robert J. Rosenthal. **CAST:** Scott Baio, Willie Aames, Felice Schachter, Heather Thomas, Scatman Crothers, Robert Mandan, Greg Bradford.

A campy takeoff on high-school movies that doesn't work. *Zapped* is a bore. Rated R for nudity and sexual situations. 1982; 96m.

ZELIG ★★★★★

DIR: Woody Allen. **CAST:** Woody Allen, Mia Farrow.

Woody Allen plays Leonard Zelig, a remarkable man who can fit anywhere in society because he can change his appearance at will. The laughs come fast and furious in this account of his adventures in the 1920s, when he became all the rage and hung out with the likes of F. Scott Fitzgerald, Jack Dempsey, and Babe Ruth. Allen seamlessly weds black-and-white newsreel footage with his humorous tale, allowing Zelig to be right in the thick of history. Rated PG. 1984; B&W; 79m.

ZORRO, THE GAY BLADE ★★★★

DIR: Peter Medak. **CAST:** George Hamilton, Lauren Hutton, Brenda Vaccaro, Ron Leibman, Donovan Scott.

Here's another delight from (and starring) actor-producer George Hamilton. As with *Love at First Bite,* in which Hamilton played a slightly bent and bewildered Count Dracula to great effect, the accent in *Zorro, the Gay Blade* is on belly-wrenching laughs...and there are plenty of them. Rated PG because of sexual innuendo. 1981; 93m.

ZOTZ! ★★★½

DIR: William Castle. **CAST:** Tom Poston, Jim Backus, Julia Meade.

Charming, underrated little fantasy about a college professor (Tom Poston) who finds a magical coin blessed with three bizarre powers: sudden pain, slow motion, and explosive destruction. Good adaptation of the novel by Walter Karig, and an excellent opportunity for Poston to control a film in one of his rare leading parts. Give this a try; you won't be disappointed. 1962; B&W; 87m.

DOCUMENTARIES

AFRICA BLOOD AND GUTS ★★
DIR: Gualtiero Jacopetti.

Another shockumentary from the production team that created *Mondo Cane*. This film crudely explores tribal violence, the slaughter of wild animals, and the racial and political turbulence throughout Africa. It contains scenes of graphic, realistic violence; sensitive viewers should exercise caution. 1983; 90m.

ALWAYS FOR PLEASURE ★★★★½
DIR: Les Blank.

Les Blank has beautifully captured the true spirit of the Mardi Gras festival, a celebration of life through the rollicking, sensual ritual of music and dance. This remarkable piece of filmmaking features great traditional American ethnic music in the form of Dixieland jazz, blues, and rock 'n' roll. Blank's cinematography is a standout, creating the mood of a surreal funhouse. 1979; 58m.

ANIMALS ARE BEAUTIFUL PEOPLE ★★★½
DIR: Jamie Uys.

South African filmmaker Jamie Uys takes a pixilated perspective on wildlife documentaries in this sporadically hilarious film. Rated G. 1974; 92m.

ATHENS, GA. ★★★½
DIR: Tony Gayton.

The right mixture of interviews and raw live footage, plus a pounding rock soundtrack and a dash of trash make this documentary must-viewing. Playful and witty, the film is tightly edited with a focus that flows gracefully from stage to Georgia street scenes, providing a grand view not only of the bands but also of the essence of Athens. 1987; 82m.

ATOMIC CAFE, THE ★★
DIR: Kevin Rafferty, Jayne Loader, Pierce Rafferty.

Beyond being an interesting cultural document, this feature-length compilation of post–World War II propaganda, documentary, and newsreel footage on official and unofficial American attitudes toward the atomic bomb has little to offer, especially as entertainment. No MPAA rating. The film has no objectionable material, though some of the footage featuring casualties of atomic bomb explosions is quite graphic. 1982; B&W; 88m.

BACKSTAGE AT THE KIROV ★★★★
DIR: Derek Hart.
Documentary about Leningrad's Kirov Ballet, where dancers are rigorously trained for their art from an early age. Even nonfans will find themselves led to a better appreciation of ballet through interviews with the dancers. In fact, if you're looking for an introduction to ballet, you can't do better than this. 1983; 78m.

BORNEO ★★★★
DIR: Martin Johnson, Osa Johnson.
Husband and wife explorers Martin and Osa Johnson spent twenty-five years exploring and making documentary films about then-uncharted areas of the world. In this one, their last (Martin Johnson was killed in a plane crash when they returned), the pair explore the primitive island of Borneo. Comic commentary in some sequences will help hold the kids' attention, and the unusual animals (flying snakes, land-roving fish, and some very odd-looking monkeys) will delight the whole family. 1937; B&W; 76m.

BURDEN OF DREAMS ★★★★★
DIR: Les Blank. **CAST:** Werner Herzog, Klaus Kinski, Mick Jagger, Jason Robards Jr., Claudia Cardinale.
Documentary specialist Les Blank unearthed a rare treasure in Ecuador, where Werner Herzog was laboring for years to make *Fitzcarraldo*, a lavish film depicting a man's obsessive quest to bring fine opera to the jungle. Shooting on location, among fighting tribes and without any modern conveniences, Herzog's task becomes a parallel quest of compulsion. This would be dreamlike material for any documentary, but Blank logged the overtime to make the metaphors meaningful, more powerful even than Herzog did in *Fitzcarraldo*. Unrated. 1982; 94m.

CALIFORNIA REICH ★★★
DIR: Walter F. Parkes, Keith F. Critchlow.
Fascinating, unsettling documentary about the Nazi organization in California. Made by two Stanford University grads, the film ultimately connects today's resurgence of Nazism to the brand practiced by Hitler. Not rated; contains rough language and gang violence. 1977; 55m.

CHARIOTS OF THE GODS ★★
DIR: Harald Reinl.
Based on Erich Von Daniken's bestselling book, this German production presents the theory that centuries ago Earth was visited by highly advanced space folks. These strange visitors showed our ancestors how to add, subtract, divide, and subdivide. The film is a nice travelogue, but its theories are never proved. Of minor interest only. Rated G. 1974; 98m.

CHICKEN RANCH ★★★
DIR: Nick Broomfield, Sandi Sissel.
This documentary about the brothel that was the setting for the musical *The Best Little Whorehouse in Texas* presents a different picture of prostitution. Although shot in a cinéma vérité style—the workers and customers speak for themselves, with no passing of judgment by the filmmakers—the movie paints a relentlessly grim picture of the oldest profession. Unrated. 1983; 84m.

CHILDREN OF THEATRE STREET, THE ★★★½
DIR: Robert Dornhelm.
Grace Kelly narrates this documentary about the Kirov School of Ballet, where children who meet rigorous criteria are isolated from the world (including their families) and trained intensively. Bring this home with *Backstage at the Kirov* for the perfect ballet double-feature. 1978; 92m.

COMIC BOOK CONFIDENTIAL ★★★½
DIR: Ron Mann. **CAST:** Lynda Barry, Robert Crumb, Will Eisner, William M. Gaines, Stan Lee, Jack Kirby.
The history and pop-culture charms of the comic book are explored in this entertaining documentary by a Cana-

dian filmmaker and comic-book buff. The leading lights of comic books—Marvel's Stan Lee, Robert Crumb, Jack Kirby, etc.—are interviewed about their creations, artistic style, influence, and beliefs. 1988; 90m.

COVER UP ★★★
DIR: Barbara Trent.

This leftist political propaganda piece puts together news clips and interviews to paint a picture of deception on the part of U.S. government officials in Central America. The scope is narrow and conclusions are often farfetched and forced, yet the low-budget documentary offers an eye-opening overview of covert operations and makes a case for controls against any more Iran-Contra scandals. Unrated. 1988; 76m.

CRY OF REASON, THE ★★★★★
DIR: Robert Bilheimer. **CAST:** Beyers Naude, Desmond Tutu.

An impassioned and enlightening documentary about courage and sacrifice in the face of South Africa's apartheid policies. The Oscar-nominated film profiles Beyers Naude, a white Afrikaner minister who gave up a promising career and a powerful position in the white community to stand with the blacks against apartheid. 1988; 60m.

DEAR AMERICA: LETTERS HOME FROM VIETNAM ★★★★
DIR: Bill Couturie.

This docudrama traces the Vietnam conflict from 1964 to 1973 through the eyes of American soldiers writing to their loved ones at home. The live footage has been so carefully selected that you forget that the letter you are hearing is being read by an actor instead of the person on the screen. Offscreen narration by a *Who's Who* of actors, including Robert De Niro, Ellen Burstyn, Tom Berenger, Michael J. Fox, Sean Penn, Martin Sheen, and Robin Williams. Rated PG. 1988; 86m.

DECLINE OF WESTERN CIVILIZATION, PART II—THE METAL YEARS ★★★
DIR: Penelope Spheeris. **CAST:** Ozzy Osbourne, Alice Cooper.

An unrevealing but fun documentary about the jaded world of heavy-metal music, as seen in statements and actions by the large cast of musicians and fans. Director Penelope Spherris, who previously explored punk, takes a safe, unchallenging stance here as she explores the music and its makers. 1988; 90m.

DISTANT HARMONY: PAVAROTTI IN CHINA ★★★
DIR: DeWitt Sage.

This documentary of Luciano Pavarotti's 1986 tour of the People's Republic of China has all the predictably superb music and scenery one would expect. Director DeWitt Sage cleverly juxtaposes Chinese and Western cultures and includes a plethora of bright, optimistic Chinese children in doing so. Nevertheless, the unbelievably mediocre sound and film print and Pavarotti's own all-too-intrusive ego mar this production. 1987; 90m.

DOPE MANIA ★½
DIR: Johnny Legend, Jeff Vilencia.

Collectively, this odd grouping of exploitation films deserves a higher rating than any of them could muster individually, meaning this is a cream-of-the-crap collection. Previews and snippets from 1950s antidrug films provide most of the fun in this mishmash of low-budget junk, but it gets bogged down along the way. Fun for a while, but this oddity seems long even at 60 minutes. 1987; B&W; 60m.

FACES OF DEATH I & II 🦃
DIR: Rosilyn T. Scott.

These two gruesome video programs are the ultimate in tasteless exploitation. Both feature graphic, uncensored footage of death autopsies, suicides, executions, and the brutal slaughter of animals. You'll have to have a strong stomach to sit through it, and even would-be thrill seekers may find they get more than they bargained for. 1983; 88/84 minutes.

FANTASY FILM WORLDS OF GEORGE PAL, THE ★★★
DIR: Arnold Leibovit. **CAST:** Rod Taylor, Charlton Heston, Yvette Mimieux, Ray Bradbury, Roy Disney, Walter Lantz, Ray Harryhausen, Gene Roddenberry.

Documentary of the film career of George Pal, the father of screen sci-fi. Poorly written and edited, the film is more than saved by the excellent interviews and film clips, dating back to vintage Pal *Puppetoons*, produced in the Thirties for Paramount. *Destination Moon* is extensively covered, as well as the classic *When Worlds Collide* and *The War of the Worlds*. Narrated by Paul Frees. 1985; 93m.

GIZMO! ★★★★½
DIR: Howard Smith.

A collection of short films of daredevils, flying machines, and enthusiastic inventors demonstrating their questionable benefits to mankind. It's up to the audience to decide whether these people were complete morons or just ahead of their time. A delightful, often hysterical celebration of the American spirit. Rated G. 1977; B&W; 77m.

HAPPY ANNIVERSARY 007: 25 YEARS OF JAMES BOND ★★★★
DIR: Mel Stuart. **CAST:** Sean Connery, Roger Moore, George Lazenby, Timothy Dalton.

Roger Moore hosts this engaging tribute to superspy James Bond, which scripter Richard Schickel cleverly divides into segments reflecting 007's diverse experiences: dangerous train trips, briefings with Q and his gadgets, deadly skiing excursions, bizarre death-traps, and his limitless fund of arcane knowledge. 1987; 59m.

HARLAN COUNTY, U.S.A. ★★★★½
DIR: Barbara Kopple.

This Oscar-winning documentary concerning Kentucky coal miners is both tragic and riveting. Its gripping scenes draw the audience into the world of miners and their families. Superior from start to finish. Rated PG. 1977; 103m.

HELLSTROM CHRONICLE, THE ★★★★
DIR: Walon Green. **CAST:** Lawrence Pressman.

This 1971 pseudodocumentary features fantastic close-up cinematography of insects and their ilk underpinning a storyline by Dr. Hellstrom (Lawrence Pressman), which contends the critters are taking over and we humans had better wise up before it's too late. Despite the dumb premise, *The Hellstrom Chronicle* remains a captivating film. Rated G. 1971; 90m.

HOLLYWOOD ★★★★
DIR: David Gill, Kevin Brownlow.

First-class documentary series on the silent-film era was made for British television. It includes interviews with Gloria Swanson, Lillian Gish, Douglas Fairbanks Jr., Buster Keaton and King Vidor. The titles in this thirteen-cassette release include *The Pioneers, In the Beginning, Single Beds and Double Standards, Hollywood Goes to War, Hazard of the Game, Swanson and Valentino, The Autocrats, Comedy—A Serious Business, Out West, The Man with the Megaphone, Star Treatment* and *End of an Era*. 1979; B&W/color; 52 minutes each.

IMPROPER CONDUCT ★★★★½
DIR: Nestor Almendros, Orlando Jimenez Leal.

An astonishing view of Fidel Castro's terrifying regime is found in this uncompromising documentary by Academy Award–winning cinematographer Nestor Almendros. Cuban refugees discuss their experiences within the labor concentration camps and jails. This provocative work is undoubtedly the best film to date on the Cuban revolution. Not rated. In

Spanish with English narration and subtitles. 1984; 112m.

JOHN HUSTON—THE MAN, THE MOVIES, THE MAVERICK ★★★★★

DIR: Frank Martin.

A wonderful, robust, and entertaining documentary biography of the great director, compiled from rare home movies, film clips, and interviews, narrated by Robert Mitchum (who speaks from a fantasy attic of engrossing Huston memorabilia). John Huston was an utterly fascinating eccentric and adventurer. This TV biography is a superb tribute. 1989; 129m.

KOYAANISQATSI ★★★★

DIR: Godfrey Reggio.

The title is a Hopi Indian word meaning "crazy life, life in turmoil, life disintegrating, life out of balance, a state of life that calls for another way of living." In keeping with this, director Godfrey Reggio contrasts scenes of nature to the hectic life of the city. There is no plot or dialogue. Instead, the accent is on the artistic cinematography, by Ron Fricke, and the score, by Philip Glass. It's a feast for the eyes and ears. No MPAA rating. 1983; 87m.

LEGEND OF LOBO, THE ★★★

DIR: Not credited.

An animal adventure film told from the perspective of Lobo, a wolf, this is one of the excellent nature films produced by Disney in the 1950s and 1960s. Although the story is highly fictionalized to create dramatic impact, this is both an entertaining and informative film. 1962; 67m.

LET'S GET LOST ★★★★★

DIR: Bruce Weber. **CAST:** Chet Baker.

The music and the volatile, self-destructive personality of Chet Baker are explored in this artful, invigorating, and controversial documentary feature from photographer-filmmaker Bruce Weber. This film, which justifiably earned an Oscar nomination, depicts Baker in what turned out to be the last year of his life, as he meanders through performances, recording sessions, and self-centered encounters with women, fans, and family. 1989; B&W; 120m.

MAKING OF A LEGEND—*GONE WITH THE WIND* ★★★★

DIR: David Hinton.

Though some film purists object to Ted Turner's colorization of film classics, they have to acknowledge that he's supported the creation of first-rate documentaries *about* Hollywood. This feature documentary uses David O. Selznick's many memos, other letters, and the remembrances of survivors to reconstruct the creation of the most popular Hollywood film of all time. Produced by Selznick's sons, and written by David Thomson, it's must viewing for *GWTW's* many fans. 1989; 120m.

MAN WHO SAW TOMORROW, THE ★★★½

DIR: Robert Guenette. **CAST:** Orson Welles (narrator).

Orson Welles narrates and appears in this fascinating dramatization of the prophecies of sixteenth-century poet, physician, and psychic Michel de Nostradamus. Nostradamus was astonishingly accurate and, in some cases, actually cited names and dates. His prediction for the future is equally amazing—and, sometimes, terrifying. Rated PG. 1981; 90m.

MAN WITH A MOVIE CAMERA ★★★★

DIR: Dziga Vertov.

Russian directors pioneered the use of inventive editing techniques in the Twenties. This experimental documentary shows off many of those methods. The subject matter here is the making of a movie about the city of Moscow, and we follow from initial production to public screening. Sixty years later, the craft demonstrated here is still impressive. 1927; B&W; 60m.

MANCE LIPSCOMB: A WELL-SPENT LIFE ★★★★
DIR: Les Blank.

Les Blank's stirring portrait of Texas songster Mance Lipscomb is a moving tribute to a legendary bluesman. Discovered during the early Sixties folk boom, Lipscomb's crafty, bottleneck-slide guitar style is reminiscent of country-blues giant Furry Lewis and contemporary Texas-blues great Lightnin' Hopkins. 1981; 44m.

MONDO CANE ★★★
DIR: Gualtiero Jacopetti.

One of the oldest movies ever made (the title means *A Dog's World*), this Italian film inspired a deluge of shockumentaries throughout the 1960s and the 1970s. In many vignettes—some scenes are real while others are patently staged—we are given a cook's tour of human eccentricities, from the "cargo cults" of New Guinea to a Southern California pet cemetery. Believe it or not, the beautiful song "More" was introduced in this movie. Not rated; unsuitable for children. 1963; 105m.

MONDO CANE II ★★
DIR: Gualtiero Jacopetti.

Disappointing sequel to the controversial and bizarre cult documentary released in 1963. Again the strange and fascinating world of human ritual is explored in its various forms of grotesque deviation, but without the intensity or the humor that the first film managed to create. Not rated; contains violence and nudity. 1964; 90m.

MONDO TOPLESS ★★½
DIR: Russ Meyer.

Silly Russ Meyer "documentary" is nothing more than scenes of various topless dancers going through their paces in various outdoor locations. What makes it amusing are the inane narration (a Meyer trademark) and the combination of superb photography and frenetic editing, which makes it look like an hour-long MTV video. Unrated; there is no sex or even sexual suggestiveness, just nonstop toplessness. 1966; 60m.

NANOOK OF THE NORTH ★★★★
DIR: Robert Flaherty.

Crude and primitive as the conditions under which it was made, this direct study of Eskimo life set the standard for and has remained the most famous of the early documentary films. A milestone in stark realism; the walrus hunt sequence is especially effective. 1922; B&W; 55m.

NIGHT AND FOG, THE ★★★★
DIR: Alain Resnais.

Graphic footage of the Nazi death camps makes this sad, shockingly painful documentary one of the most personal and effective of all studies of Hitler's final solution. Beautifully composed by director Alain Resnais, this film juxtaposes still photographs and Allied footage of gruesome spectacles. French, subtitled in English. 1955; 32m.

PORTRAIT OF JASON ★★★★
DIR: Shirley Clarke.

Celebrated independent filmmaker Shirley Clarke's penetrating glimpse into the life of a street hustler is a provocative, daring study in human tragedy. Not rated, but contains profanity and violence. 1967; B&W; 105m.

POWAQQATSI ★★★★
DIR: Godfrey Reggio.

Director's Godfrey Reggio's followup to *Koyaanisqatsi* is a sumptuous treat for the eyes and the ears. Subtitled *Life in Transformation*, it combines gorgeous cinematography with exquisite music by Philip Glass. The movie takes its title from a Hopi Indian word that refers to a sorceror who lives at the expense of others. Like its predecessor, it's an engaging but sobering look at the cost of what some call progress. 1988; 99m.

POWER OF MYTH, THE ★★★★
DIR: Bill Moyers.

Author-philosopher Joseph Campbell explores the world of mythology and its reflection on contemporary society in these six absorbing one-hour episodes originally aired on PBS and hosted by Bill Moyers. Campbell discusses the importance of accepting death as rebirth as in the myth of the buffalo and the story of Christ. The individual episodes are *The Heroes Adventure, The Message of the Myth, The First Storytellers, Sacrifice and Bliss, Love and the Goddess*, and *Mask of Eternity*. 1988; 360m.

SENSE OF LOSS, A ★★
DIR: Marcel Ophuls.

Marcel Ophuls (*The Sorrow and the Pity*) turns his attention to the troubles in Northern Ireland with diminished effect. This documentary fails to provide an historically clear picture of all sides of the issue, and as it was made over fifteen years ago, it will confuse more than illuminate viewers. Unrated. 1972; 135m.

STATE OF THE ART OF COMPUTER ANIMATION, THE ★★½
DIR: Various. **CAST:** Animated.

Lack of structure hurts this collection of the best in computer animation from around the world. Prime segments are a minidocumentary about the making of a computer-animated commercial and a *Dire Straits* music video. Interesting if you're a fan of computer animation. 1988; 60m.

STREETWISE ★★★★★
DIR: Martin Bell, Mary Ellen Mark, Cheryl McCall.

A powerful, emotionally compelling glimpse into the lives of displaced homeless youths surviving as pimps, prostitutes, muggers, panhandlers, and small-time drug dealers on the streets of Seattle. This Oscar nominee explores its disturbing theme with great sensitivity while creating a portrait of a teenage wasteland. Highly recommended. Not rated, but contains violence and profanity. 1985; 92m.

THIN BLUE LINE, THE ★★★★
DIR: Errol Morris.

Fascinating look into the 1976 murder of a Dallas policeman that led to a highly debated conviction of a drifter. Filmmaker Errol Morris's terrifying account of this incident raises some serious questions about the misuse of our current justice system. Not rated. 1988; 90m.

TIBET ★★★
DIR: Stanley Dorfman.

Splendid cinematography and an arresting score by New Age artist Mark Isham turn this travelogue into a stunning tour de force in the style of *Koyaanisqatsi*. Sticklers for plot will be disappointed, for this is a visual and audio masterpiece of mystical images. 1988; 50m.

UNDERGROUND ★★★
DIR: Emile De Antonio, Mary Lampson, Haskell Wexler.

This documentary features interviews with members of the radical Weather Underground. Whether or not you agree with their views, they are discussed intelligently, making this an invaluable document for any study of recent radical politics. 1976; 88m.

VANISHING PRAIRIE, THE ★★★½
DIR: James Algar.

Award-winning true-life adventure from Walt Disney is a landmark documentary that ranks with *The Living Desert* as the finest (and certainly most widely seen) nature film of the 1950s. Beautifully photographed, this is a fun but sobering movie and one that literally the whole family can enjoy. 1954; 75m.

VERNON, FLORIDA ★★★
DIR: Errol Morris.

Weirdos of the world seem to have united and set up housekeeping in Vernon, Florida. This unique and off-the-wall film comes from the strange vision of director Errol Morris. In this slice of life, Morris lets his camera and the viewers become acquainted with (and amused by) the citizens of this slightly off-center small town. Not rated. 1988; 60m.

VINCENT: THE LIFE AND DEATH OF VINCENT VAN GOGH ★★★★

DIR: Paul Cox.

Australian filmmaker Paul Cox combines painter Vincent van Gogh's "Dear Theo" letters with stunning visuals—juxtaposing van Gogh's paintings with luscious scenery—for a deeply satisfying portrait of the brilliant but tortured artist. John Hurt does an excellent job of narrating. Truly impressive. 1987; 110m.

VOICES OF SARAFINA ★★★★

DIR: Nigel Noble. **CAST:** Hugh Masakela.

A robust, feature-length documentary that details the personal stories of the performers and creators of *Sarafina*, the anti-apartheid Broadway hit musical from South Africa. Directed by English filmmaker Nigel Noble, it's not only a record of the unique stage show but also a gentle, affecting portrayal of the performers and their amazing ability to maintain hope and strength in the face of racism at home. The music is by Hugh Masakela and other South Africans. 1988; 90m.

WONDER OF IT ALL ★★★½

DIR: Arthur R. Dubs.

This nature documentary takes you on an armchair cruise around the world. You will observe animals in their natural environment interacting with members of their own and other species. While Disney nature films include superior photography, this is still worth a watch by animal and nature lovers. Rated G. 1982; 47m.

DRAMA

AARON LOVES ANGELA ★★★
DIR: Gordon Parks Jr. **CAST:** Moses Gunn, Kevin Hooks, Irene Cara, Ernestine Jackson, Robert Hooks.

This Harlem love affair features a black youth (Kevin Hooks) falling for a sweet Puerto Rican girl (Irene Cara). Their relative innocence contrasts with the drug-dealing violence around them. Rated R for violence and profanity. 1975; 99m.

ABDUCTION (1975) ★★
DIR: Joseph Zito. **CAST:** Gregory Rozakis, Leif Erickson, Dorothy Malone, Lawrence Tierney.

This film comes across as a cheap exploitation of the Patty Hearst kidnapping. It includes theories and conclusions that may or may not be true. As in the real incident Patty is kidnapped from the house she shares with her boyfriend. Rated R for profanity, violence, nudity, and sex. 1975; 100m.

ABE LINCOLN IN ILLINOIS ★★★★
DIR: John Cromwell. **CAST:** Raymond Massey, Ruth Gordon, Gene Lockhart, Mary Howard.

Based on Sherwood Anderson's Broadway play, this is a reverent look at the early career and loves of the sixteenth president. As contrasted to John Ford's *Young Mr. Lincoln*, this is a more somber, historically accurate, and better-acted version. 1934; B&W; 110m.

ABOUT LAST NIGHT ★★★★
DIR: Edward Zwick. **CAST:** Rob Lowe, Demi Moore, James Belushi, Elizabeth Perkins, George DiCenzo.

A slick adaptation of David Mamet's play, *Sexual Perversity in Chicago*, which focuses on the difficulties involved in "making a commitment." Demi Moore and Rob Lowe, as the central couple, meet for a one-night stand and then realize they *like* each other. Jim Belushi and Elizabeth Perkins turn in solid performances, but the film belongs to Moore, who finally has found a role worthy of her talent. Rated R for nudity and explicit adult situations. 1986; 113m.

ABRAHAM LINCOLN ★★★★
DIR: D. W. Griffith. **CAST:** Walter Huston, Una Merkel, Kay Hammond, Ian Keith, Hobart Bosworth, Jason Robards Sr., Henry B. Walthall.

A milestone in many ways, this episodic film is legendary director Griffith's first "talkie," Hollywood's first sound biography of an American, the first attempt to cover Lincoln's life from cradle to grave, and the first about the martyred president to include the Civil War. Walter Huston's peerless performance in the title role dominates throughout. 1930; B&W; 91m.

ABSENCE OF MALICE ★★★★
DIR: Sydney Pollack. **CAST:** Paul Newman, Sally Field, Bob Balaban, Melinda Dillon, Wilford Brimley.

Sally Field is a Miami reporter who writes a story implicating an innocent man (Paul Newman) in the mysterious disappearance—and possible murder—of a union leader in this taut, thoughtful drama about the ethics of journalism. It's sort of *All the President's Men* turned inside out. Rated PG because of minor violence. 1982; 116m.

ABSOLUTION ★★½
DIR: Anthony Page. **CAST:** Richard Burton, Dominic Guard, Andrew Keir, Billy Connolly.

Slow-moving but interesting tale of a priest's emotional and physical battle with one of his students at an English school for boys. As the priest, Richard Burton gives his usual compelling performance. Nice plot twist at the end. Not rated, but contains violence. 1977; 91m.

ACCIDENT ★★★★
DIR: Joseph Losey. **CAST:** Dirk Bogarde, Stanley Baker, Jacqueline Sassard, Michael York.

Harold Pinter's complicated play retains its subtleties in this sometimes baffling British film. Dirk Bogarde is excellent as a married professor pursuing an attractive student. There are enough twists and turns in the characters' actual desires to maintain your complete attention. 1967; 105m.

ACCIDENTAL TOURIST, THE ★★★★
DIR: Lawrence Kasdan. **CAST:** William Hurt, Kathleen Turner, Geena Davis, Bill Pullman, Amy Wright, David Ogden Stiers, Ed Begley Jr.

William Hurt and Kathleen Turner team again with director Lawrence Kasdan (they worked together on *Body Heat*) for this compelling adaptation of Anne Tyler's masterful novel. Hurt's the writer of travel guides who distances himself from everybody—including wife Kathleen Turner—after the death of their young son; Geena Davis is the earthy, colorful free spirit who tries to break through his wall of self-imposed isolation. Filled with strong emotional highs and lows, and highlighted by a superb supporting cast, this intelligent drama is a must for those bored with mindless action fare. Rated PG. 1988; 120m.

ACCUSED, THE ★★★★
DIR: Jonathan Kaplan. **CAST:** Jodie Foster, Kelly McGillis, Bernie Coulson, Steve Antin, Leo Rossi, Woody Brown.

Superb, emotionally intense retelling of the precedent-setting New Bedford, Massachusetts, gang-rape case, with Jodie Foster as an innocent but definitely not saintly victim, and Kelly McGillis as a tough D.A. An excellent and wrenching film. Rated R for adult themes, language, nudity, and sexual violence. 1988; 105m.

ACT, THE ★★★
DIR: Sig Shore. **CAST:** Robert Ginty, Sarah Langenfeld, Jill St. John, Eddie Albert, Pat Hingle.

A comedy-drama with a convoluted plot of political chicanery, double-cross, and robbery. The overall quality is erratic and yet this ends up being a good effort from a veteran cast. Trivia fans may note John Sebastian's involvement in the musical score. Rated R for sexual situations and language. 1982; 90m.

ACT OF PASSION ★★

DIR: Simon Langton. **CAST:** Marlo Thomas, Kris Kristofferson, Jon De Vries, David Rasche, Linda Thorson, Edward Winter, George Dzundza.

In this made-for-television movie, Marlo Thomas plays a single woman who picks up a stranger (Kris Kristofferson) at a party. She is subsequently subjected to harassment by the police and the press when the man turns out to be a suspected terrorist. The filmmakers attempt to examine the potential for mistreatment by law enforcement and the press. But the siren here is harsh and blatantly exaggerated. 1984; 95m.

ACT OF VENGEANCE ★★★★

DIR: John Mackenzie. **CAST:** Charles Bronson, Ellen Burstyn, Wilford Brimley, Hoyt Axton, Ellen Barkin.

In this first-rate drama, a suprisingly effective Charles Bronson plays Jock Yablonski, an honest man who wants to turn his coal-miners union around. When he runs for union president against the thoroughly corrupt incumbent (played brilliantly by Wilford Brimley), the threatened leader resorts to strong-arm tactics. Excellent supporting cast. Not rated, but contains violence and profanity. 1985; 97m.

ACTORS AND SIN ★★½

DIR: Ben Hecht, Lee Garmes. **CAST:** Edward G. Robinson, Eddie Albert, Marsha Hunt, Alan Reed, Dan O'Herlihy.

Actors and Sin is actually two short films. *Actor's Blood* is a drama starring Edward G. Robinson as the devoted father of a successful Broadway actress (Marsha Hunt) whose prima donna attitude earns her a reputation that catches up with her when her talents start to wane. *Woman's Sin* is a comedy starring Eddie Albert as an irrepressible Hollywood agent who finds a winning screenplay but loses its author. 1952; B&W; 86m.

ADAM ★★★★

DIR: Michael Tuchner. **CAST:** Daniel J. Travanti, JoBeth Williams, Richard Masur.

Daniel J. Travanti and JoBeth Williams deliver fine performances in this chillingly real account of John and Reve Williams's search for their missing 6-year-old son, Adam. A quite believable picture, detailing the months of uncertainty and anguish that surrounded the child's disappearance from a department store. This ordeal resulted in the formation of the Missing Children's Bureau. Made for television. 1983; 97m.

ADAM HAD FOUR SONS ★★★★

DIR: Gregory Ratoff. **CAST:** Ingrid Bergman, Warner Baxter, Susan Hayward.

This classic has it all: good acting, romance, seduction, betrayal, tears, and laughter. Ingrid Bergman plays the good governess, and Susan Hayward plays the seductive hussy who tries to turn brother against brother. Warner Baxter offers a fine performance as Adam, the father. 1941; B&W; 81m.

ADULTRESS, THE

DIR: Norbert Meisel. **CAST:** Tyne Daly, Eric Braeden, Greg Morton.

Gobble, gobble, gobble...this is an abysmal film about an impotent husband (Greg Morton) who hires a gigolo (Eric Braeden) to service his physically deprived wife (Tyne Daly). 1973; 85m.

ADVENTURES OF GALLANT BESS ★★

DIR: Lew Landers. **CAST:** Cameron Mitchell, Audrey Long, Fuzzy Knight.

Minor melodrama about a man who seems to be more in love with his horse than he is with the woman in his life. The photography is quite good and the performances are passable, but it is still only fair. 1948; 73m.

ADVENTURES OF NELLIE BLY, THE ★★
DIR: Henning Schellerup. **CAST:** Linda Purl, Gene Barry, John Randolph, Raymond Buktenica, J. D. Cannon.
In this made-for-television film, Linda Purl shines as a reporter who uncovers serious problems in places such as factories and insane asylums. The script unfortunately is weak and the direction is uninspired. 1981; 100m.

ADVISE AND CONSENT ★★★½
DIR: Otto Preminger. **CAST:** Henry Fonda, Don Murray, Charles Laughton, Franchot Tone, Lew Ayres, Walter Pidgeon, Peter Lawford, Paul Ford, Burgess Meredith, Gene Tierney.
An engrossing adaptation of Allen Drury's bestseller about behind-the-scenes Washington. Fine performances abound among the familiar faces that populate Otto Preminger's vision of the U.S. Senate as it is called upon to confirm a controversial nominee for Secretary of State (Henry Fonda). Easily the most riveting is Charles Laughton, at his scene-stealing best, as a smiling old crocodile of a Southern senator. 1962; B&W; 140m.

AFFAIR, THE ★★★
DIR: Gilbert Cates. **CAST:** Natalie Wood, Robert Wagner, Bruce Davison, Kent Smith, Pat Harrington.
Touching, honest story of a crippled songwriter (Natalie Wood) tentatively entering into her first love affair—with an attorney (Robert Wagner). This is an unusually well-acted, sensitively told TV movie. 1973; 74m.

AFFAIR IN TRINIDAD ★★★
DIR: Vincent Sherman. **CAST:** Glenn Ford, Rita Hayworth, Alexander Scourby, Torin Thatcher.
Sultry, enticing café singer Rita Hayworth teams with brother-in-law Glenn Ford to trap her husband's murderer. The two fall in love en route. 1952; 98m.

AFRICAN QUEEN, THE ★★★★★
DIR: John Huston. **CAST:** Humphrey Bogart, Katharine Hepburn, Peter Bull, Robert Morley, Theodore Bikel.
Humphrey Bogart and Katharine Hepburn star in this exciting World War I adventure film. Bogart's a drunkard, and Hepburn's the spinster sister of a murdered missionary. Together they take on the Germans and, in doing so, are surprised to find themselves falling in love. 1951; 106m.

AGAINST ALL ODDS ★★★½
DIR: Taylor Hackford. **CAST:** Jeff Bridges, Rachel Ward, Alex Karras, James Woods.
A respectable remake of *Out of the Past*, a 1947 *film noir* classic, this release stars Jeff Bridges as a man hired by a wealthy gangster (James Woods) to track down his girlfriend (Rachel Ward), who allegedly tried to kill him and made off with forty thousand dollars. Bridges finds her, they fall in love, and that's when the plot's twists really begin. Rated R for nudity, suggested sex, violence, and profanity. 1984; 128m.

AGATHA ★★½
DIR: Michael Apted. **CAST:** Dustin Hoffman, Vanessa Redgrave, Celia Gregory.
Supposedly based on a true event in the life of mystery author Agatha Christie (during which she disappeared for eleven days in 1926), this is a moderately effective thriller. Vanessa Redgrave is excellent in the title role, but co-star Dustin Hoffman is miscast as the American detective on her trail. Rated PG. 1979; 98m.

AGENCY ★★
DIR: George Kaczender. **CAST:** Robert Mitchum, Lee Majors, Saul Rubinek, Valerie Perrine.
Despite the presence of Robert Mitchum, this Canadian feature about a power struggle in the world of advertising doesn't convince. Nor do the supporting performances by wooden Lee Majors and lovely, but wasted,

Valerie Perrine. Rated PG. 1981; 94m.

AGNES OF GOD ★★★
DIR: Norman Jewison. **CAST:** Jane Fonda, Anne Bancroft, Meg Tilly, Anne Pitoniak, Winston Rekert.
This fascinating drama features tour-de-force performances by Jane Fonda, Anne Bancroft, and Meg Tilly. Tilly's character, the childlike novice of an extremely sheltered convent, is discovered one night with the bloodied body of a baby she claims not to recognize. Psychiatrist Fonda is sent to determine Tilly's sanity in anticipation of a court hearing; Bancroft, as the Mother Superior, struggles to prevent the young girl's loss of innocence. Rated PG-13 for subject matter. 1985; 101m.

AGONY AND THE ECSTASY, THE ★★★
DIR: Carol Reed. **CAST:** Charlton Heston, Rex Harrison, Diane Cilento, Harry Andrews.
Handsomely mounted but plodding historical drama based on Irving Stone's bestselling novel about Pope Julius II (Rex Harrison) engaging Michelangelo (Charlton Heston) to paint the ceiling of the Sistine Chapel. Heston overacts and the direction is heavy-handed. 1965; 140m.

AIRPORT ★★★★
DIR: George Seaton. **CAST:** Burt Lancaster, Dean Martin, Helen Hayes, Jacqueline Bisset, Van Heflin, Jean Seberg.
The daddy of them all, this *Grand Hotel* in the air is slick, enjoyable entertainment. Taking place on a fateful winter night, it miraculously rises above some stiff performances and an often hackneyed plot. Rated G. 1970; 137m.

AIRPORT 1975 ★½
DIR: Jack Smight. **CAST:** Charlton Heston, George Kennedy, Karen Black, Sid Caesar, Helen Reddy.
Universal waited four years after the release of the original *Airport* but could resist the temptation no longer. Released at the height of the disaster film craze, this second entry in the series profits from a strong performance by Charlton Heston and very little else. Rated PG—moderate tension. 1974; 106m.

AIRPORT '77 ★
DIR: Jerry Jameson. **CAST:** Jack Lemmon, Lee Grant, George Kennedy, Christopher Lee.
This movie is, at best, an inoffensive diversion and, at worst, a regurgitation of all the clichéd situations and stereotyped characters we have come to expect from a disaster flick. If you've seen one *Airport*, you've seen them all. Rated PG for violence. 1977; 113m.

AIRPORT '79: THE CONCORDE ★
DIR: David Lowell Rich. **CAST:** Alain Delon, Robert Wagner, Susan Blakely, George Kennedy, Eddie Albert, Cicely Tyson.
This is another in the seemingly endless *Airport* series. Robert Wagner is a ruthless tycoon with a scheme to destroy the aircraft to cover up for some of his dirty business affairs soon to be revealed by another affair, one with his mistress, Susan Blakely, a top newscaster with a hot story. Bring your own air sickness bag. Rated PG. 1979; 113m.

ALAMO BAY ★★★★
DIR: Louis Malle. **CAST:** Ed Harris, Amy Madigan, Ho Nquyen, Donald Moffat.
French director Louis Malle once again looks at the underbelly of the American dream. This time, he takes us to the Gulf Coast of Texas in the late 1970s where Vietnamese refugees arrived, expecting the land of opportunity, and came face to face, instead, with the Ku Klux Klan. Rated R for nudity, violence, and profanity. 1985; 105m.

ALEXANDER THE GREAT ★★★½
DIR: Robert Rossen. **CAST:** Richard Burton, Fredric March, Claire Bloom, Danielle Darrieux.

The strange, enigmatic, self-possessed Macedonian conqueror of Greece and most of the civilized world of his time rides again. Richard Burton, with his enthralling voice and uniquely hypnotic eyes, dominates an outstanding cast in this lavish epic of life and love among the upper crust from 356 to 323 B.C. 1956; 141m.

ALICE ADAMS ★★★★
DIR: George Stevens. **CAST:** Katharine Hepburn, Fred MacMurray, Evelyn Venable, Fred Stone, Frank Albertson, Hattie McDaniel, Charley Grapewin, Hedda Hopper.

Life and love in a typical mid-American small town when there were still such things as concerts in the park and ice cream socials. Hepburn is a social-climbing girl wistfully seeking love while trying to overcome the stigma of her father's lack of money and ambition. High point of the film is the dinner scene, at once a comic gem and painful insight into character. 1935; B&W; 99m.

ALICE DOESN'T LIVE HERE ANYMORE ★★★★½
DIR: Martin Scorsese. **CAST:** Ellen Burstyn, Kris Kristofferson, Harvey Keitel, Billy Green Bush, Alfred Lutter, Jodie Foster, Vic Tayback.

The feature film that spawned the television series *Alice* is a memorable character study about a woman (Ellen Burstyn, who won an Oscar for her performance) attempting to survive after her husband's death has left her penniless and with a young son to support. The hard-edged direction by Martin Scorsese adds grit to what might have been a lightweight yarn. Rated PG for profanity and violence. 1975; 113m.

ALICE'S RESTAURANT ★★★½
DIR: Arthur Penn. **CAST:** Arlo Guthrie, Pat Quinn, James Broderick, Michael McClanathan, Geoff Outlaw, Tina Chen.

This film was based on Arlo Guthrie's hit record of the same name. Some insights into the 1960s counterculture can be found in this story of Guthrie's attempt to stay out of the draft. There is some fine acting by a basically unknown cast. Rated PG for language and some nudity. 1969; 111m.

ALL ABOUT EVE ★★★★★
DIR: Joseph L. Mankiewicz. **CAST:** Bette Davis, Anne Baxter, Marilyn Monroe, George Sanders, Celeste Holm, Gary Merrill.

The behind-the-scenes world of the New York theater is the subject of this classic. The picture won several Academy Awards, including best picture, but it is Bette Davis as Margo Channing whom most remember. The dialogue sparkles, and the performances are of high caliber. 1950; B&W; 138m.

ALL GOD'S CHILDREN ★★
DIR: Jerry Thorpe. **CAST:** Richard Widmark, Ned Beatty, Ossie Davis, Ruby Dee.

Forced busing to achieve educational integration is the crux of this story of two families, one white and one black, whose sons are friends. The cast is excellent, but a wandering script makes comprehension difficult. Rated PG for violence. 1980; 107m.

ALL MINE TO GIVE ★★★
DIR: Allen Reisner. **CAST:** Glynis Johns, Cameron Mitchell, Patty McCormack, Hope Emerson.

Reaching for the heartstrings, this melodrama follows the lives of a Scottish family in 1850s Wisconsin. The backwoods life is brutal and by the film's midpoint both the mother and father have died and left the oldest child the task of parceling out his little brothers and sisters to the far-flung neighbors. A fairly decent weeper. 1957; 102m.

ALL MY SONS ★★★½
DIR: Jack O'Brien. **CAST:** James Whitmore, Aidan Quinn, Michael Learned, Joan Allen.

An excellent adaptation of the Arthur Miller play. A family must deal with the death of one son in World War II and the father's profit made by selling plane parts during the war. James Whitmore is the guilt-ridden father, Michael Learned his distraught wife. Made for TV. 1986; 122m.

ALL QUIET ON THE WESTERN FRONT ★★★½

DIR: Delbert Mann. **CAST:** Richard Thomas, Ernest Borgnine, Donald Pleasence, Ian Holm, Patricia Neal.

This is a television remake of the 1930 film, which was taken from Erich Maria Remarque's classic antiwar novel. It attempts to recall all the horrors of World War I, but even the great detail issued to this film can't hide its TV mentality and melodramatic characters. Despite this major flaw, the film is watchable for its rich look and compelling story. 1979; 126m.

ALL THE KING'S MEN ★★★★

DIR: Robert Rossen. **CAST:** Broderick Crawford, Joanne Dru, John Ireland, Mercedes McCambridge, John Derek.

Broderick Crawford and Mercedes McCambridge won Academy Awards for their work in this adaptation of Robert Penn Warren's Pulitzer Prize–winning novel about a corrupt politician's ascension to power. Seen today, the film retains its relevance and potency. 1949; B&W; 109m.

ALL THE PRESIDENT'S MEN ★★★★★

DIR: Alan J. Pakula. **CAST:** Dustin Hoffman, Robert Redford, Jason Robards Jr., Jane Alexander, Jack Warden, Martin Balsam.

Robert Redford, who also produced, and Dustin Hoffman star in this gripping reenactment of the exposure of the Watergate conspiracy by reporters Bob Woodward and Carl Bernstein. What's so remarkable about this docudrama is, although we know how it eventually comes out, we're on the edge of our seats from beginning to end. That's inspired movie-making. Rated PG. 1976; 136m.

ALL THE RIGHT MOVES ★★★½

DIR: Michael Chapman. **CAST:** Tom Cruise, Craig T. Nelson, Christopher Penn.

Tom Cruise (*Risky Business*) stars in this entertaining coming-of-age picture as a blue-collar high-school senior trying to get out of a Pennsylvania mill town by way of a football scholarship. Rated R for profanity, sex, and nudity. 1983; 91m.

ALL THIS AND HEAVEN TOO ★★★★

DIR: Anatole Litvak. **CAST:** Bette Davis, Charles Boyer, Jeffrey Lynn, Barbara O'Neill, Virginia Weidler, Henry Daniell, Ann Todd, June Lockhart, Harry Davenport.

Based on a true murder case, this film, set in Paris in 1840, casts Bette Davis as the governess who wins Charles Boyer's heart. Barbara O'Neill is the uncaring mother and obsessed wife who becomes jealous of Davis and the attention given her by both the children and her husband. When she is found murdered, Davis and Boyer become prime suspects. A classic. 1940; B&W; 121m.

ALLIGATOR SHOES ★★

DIR: Clay Borris. **CAST:** Gary Borris, Clay Borris, Ronalda Jones, Rose Mallais-Borris.

This is pretty much a home movie by two brothers, Gary and Clay Borris. Although their characters here are grown-up, they still live at home. When their mentally disturbed aunt moves in, trouble arises. How each deals with the problem forms the basis for this drama, which becomes strained before its fatal conclusion. This Canadian film is unrated. 1982; 98m.

ALMOS' A MAN ★★½

DIR: Stan Lathan. **CAST:** LeVar Burton, Madge Sinclair, Robert DoQui, Christopher Brooks, Garry Goodrow.

You'll have trouble finding firm moral ground in this adaptation of Richard Wright's short story about a boy (LeVar Burton) impatient to achieve adulthood. The conclusion leaves an unpleasant taste. Introduced by Henry Fonda; unrated and suitable for family viewing. 1976; 51m.

ALOHA SUMMER ★★★½
DIR: Tommy Lee Wallace. **CAST:** Chris Makepeace, Don Michael Paul, Tia Carrere.

In this coming-of-age film, Chris Makepeace stars as a middle-class, Italian-American teenager who goes to the Hawaiian islands with his family in 1959. Once there, he learns important lessons about life and love. Instead of being just another empty-headed teen exploitation flick, *Aloha Summer* is a drama blessed with sensitivity and insight. Rated PG for violence. 1988; 97m.

ALPHABET CITY ★½
DIR: Amos Poe. **CAST:** Vincent Spano, Kate Vernon, Michael Winslow, Zohra Lampert, Raymond Serra.

Talented Vincent Spano plays a "sympathetic" drug dealer in this pretentious movie set in Manhattan's Lower East Side. Rated R for profanity, sex, nudity, and violence. 1984; 98m.

AMATEUR, THE ★★★½
DIR: Charles Jarrott. **CAST:** John Savage, Christopher Plummer, Marthe Keller, John Marley.

A CIA computer technologist (John Savage) blackmails The Company into helping him avenge the terrorist murder of his girlfriend, only to find himself abandoned—and hunted—by the CIA. Rated R because of violence. 1982; 111m.

AMAZING GRACE AND CHUCK ★
DIR: Mike Newell. **CAST:** Jamie Lee Curtis, Alex English, Gregory Peck, William L. Petersen, Dennis Lipscomb, Lee Richardson.

Paranoid fantasy about what happens when a 12-year-old Little Leaguer (Joshua Zuehlke) decides to give up baseball in protest of nuclear arms. This well-intentioned antiwar movie is almost impossible to watch. Rated PG for suspense. 1987; 115m.

AMAZING HOWARD HUGHES, THE ★½
DIR: William A. Graham. **CAST:** Tommy Lee Jones, Ed Flanders, Tovah Feldshuh, Sorrell Booke, Lee Purcell, Arthur Franz.

Howard Hughes was amazing, but little in this lackluster account of his life and career would so indicate. Best portrayal is Ed Flanders as longtime, finally turned-upon associate Noah Dietrich. An ambitious TV production that falls short of the mark. 1977; 215m.

AMAZING TRANSPLANT, THE
DIR: Louis Silverman. **CAST:** Juan Fernandez.

Preposterous, sleazy melodrama about a penis transplant that turns a young man into a rapist and murderer. There isn't that much plot, just a lot of murkily filmed murders and soft-core trysts. Not worth passing up a rerun of *The Love Boat* for. Not rated. 1970; 80m.

AMBASSADOR, THE ★★★½
DIR: J. Lee Thompson. **CAST:** Robert Mitchum, Rock Hudson, Ellen Burstyn, Fabio Testi, Donald Pleasence.

The Ambassador confronts the Arab-Israeli conflict with a clear head and an optimistic viewpoint. Robert Mitchum plays the controversial U.S. ambassador to Israel, who tries to solve the Palestinian question while being criticized by all factions. Rock Hudson (in his last big-screen role) is the security officer who saves the ambassador's life. Rated R for violence, profanity, sex, and nudity. 1984; 97m.

AMERICAN ANTHEM ★
DIR: Albert Magnoli. **CAST:** Mitch Gaylord, Janet Jones, Michelle Phillips.

Starring 1984 Olympic gold medal gymnast Mitch Gaylord, this film features superb gymnastics. Otherwise, it is hard to find anything likable. The screenplay is amateurish, and the acting, except for a few brief moments by Gaylord, is even worse. Rated PG. 1986; 100m.

AMERICAN FLYERS ★★★½
DIR: John Badham. **CAST:** Kevin Costner, David Grant, Rae Dawn Chong, Alexandra Paul, Janice Rule, John Amos.

Another bicycle-racing tale from writer Steve Tesich (*Breaking Away*), who correctly decided he could milk that theme at least one more time. Kevin Costner and David Grant star as estranged brothers who get to know and like each other again during their participation in a grueling three-day overland race. Rated PG-13 for brief nudity and language. 1985; 113m.

AMERICAN GIGOLO ★★
DIR: Paul Schrader. **CAST:** Richard Gere, Lauren Hutton, Hector Elizondo, Nina Van Pallandt.

This story of a male hooker, Julian Kay (Richard Gere), who attends to the physical needs of bored, rich, middle-aged women in Beverly Hills, may be something different. But who needs it? This is sensationalism in the guise of social comment, though it has some incidental humor and impressive performances by Gere and Lauren Hutton. Rated R for explicit depictions of a low lifestyle. 1980; 117m.

AMERICANA ★★½
DIR: David Carradine. **CAST:** David Carradine, Barbara Hershey, Michael Greene, Bruce Carradine, John Barrymore III.

Strange, offbeat film about a Vietnam veteran (director David Carradine) who attempts to rebuild a merry-go-round in a rural Kansas town and meets with hostility from the locals. Carradine attempts to make a statement about rebuilding America and reinstating its simple, honest values, but this gets lost in the impressionistic haze of his film. Rated PG for violence and profanity. 1981; 90m.

AMIN: THE RISE AND FALL ♥
DIR: Richard Fleischer. **CAST:** Joseph Olita.

Putrid garbage isn't strong enough to describe this awful movie about the atrocities committed by Idi Amin during his reign of terror in Uganda. But it'll have to do. It's exploitation in the worst sense—and boring, to boot. Rated R for violence, nudity, sex, and profanity. 1981; 101m.

AMONG THE CINDERS ★★½
DIR: Rolf Haedrick. **CAST:** Paul O'Shea, Derek Hardwick.

A teenager (Paul O'Shea) holds himself responsible for the accidental death of a friend, and it takes a trip to the wilds with his grandfather (Derek Hardwick) to pull him out of it. This coming-of-age drama from New Zealand has its good moments, but these are outnumbered by the unremarkable ones. Rated R for nudity, profanity, suggested sex, and brief gore. 1985; 105m.

ANATOMY OF A MURDER ★★★★
DIR: Otto Preminger. **CAST:** James Stewart, Arthur O'Connell, Lee Remick, Ben Gazzara, Eve Arden, Kathryn Grant, George C. Scott, Joseph Welch, Orson Bean, Murray Hamilton.

A clever plot, realistic atmosphere, smooth direction, and sterling performances from a topflight cast make this frank and exciting small-town courtroom drama first-rate fare. For the defense, it's James Stewart at his best vs. prosecuting attorney George C. Scott. Ben Gazzara plays a moody young army officer charged with killing the man who raped his wife, Lee Remick. Real-life lawyer Joseph Welch, of McCarthy hearings fame, plays the judge. Honest realism saturates throughout. 1959; B&W; 160m.

AND BABY MAKES SIX ★★★
DIR: Waris Hussein. **CAST:** Colleen Dewhurst, Warren Oates, Mildred Dunnock, Maggie Cooper, Timothy Hutton.

Colleen Dewhurst is a middle-aged mother who becomes pregnant. It's too much for her loving husband (Warren Oates), who just doesn't want the responsibility of another child. A wonderful cast proved this made-for-TV movie good enough to produce a sequel, *Baby Comes Home*. 1979; 104m.

AND GOD CREATED WOMAN (1987) ★
DIR: Roger Vadim. **CAST:** Rebecca DeMornay, Vincent Spano, Frank Langella, Donovan Leitch.
This hodgepodge "feel good" movie induces a nauseated feeling instead. Rebecca DeMornay is unbelievable as a convict who tries to go straight by concentrating on her rock-music career. Hokey. Rated R for language, nudity, and simulated sex. 1987; 97m.

AND I ALONE SURVIVED ★★½
DIR: William A. Graham. **CAST:** Blair Brown, David Ackroyd, Vera Miles, G. D. Spradlin.
In this TV movie Blair Brown stars as Lauren Elder, the only survivor of a plane crash in California's Sierra Nevada mountains. Based on a true event, the film tends toward the overdramatic and begs for better characterizations. Still, Brown does give a fine performance. 1978; 100m.

AND JUSTICE FOR ALL ★★★½
DIR: Norman Jewison. **CAST:** Al Pacino, Jack Warden, John Forsythe, Craig T. Nelson.
This is a bristling black comedy starring Al Pacino as a lawyer who becomes fed up with the red tape of our country's legal system. It's both heartrending and darkly hilarious—but not for all tastes. Rated R. 1979; 117m.

AND NOTHING BUT THE TRUTH ★★★
DIR: Karl Francis. **CAST:** Glenda Jackson, Jon Finch, Kenneth Colley.
This is a British film about a TV news magazine—an Anglo *A Current Affair*. Glenda Jackson stars as a documentary filmmaker who must confront a sometimes exploitative reporter (well played by Jon Finch). Superficial but interesting. 1982; 90m.

AND THEN THERE WERE NONE ★★★★★
DIR: René Clair. **CAST:** Barry Fitzgerald, Walter Huston, Richard Haydn, Roland Young, Judith Anderson, Louis Hayward, June Duprez, C. Aubrey Smith.
One of the best screen adaptations of an Agatha Christie mystery. A select group of people is invited to a lonely island and murdered one by one. René Clair's inspired visual style gives this release just the right atmosphere and tension. 1945; B&W; 98m.

ANDERSONVILLE TRIAL, THE ★★★★½
DIR: George C. Scott. **CAST:** Martin Sheen, William Shatner, Buddy Ebsen, Richard Basehart, Cameron Mitchell, Jack Cassidy.
Based on MacKinley Kantor's Pulitzer Prize novel, this made-for-TV play tells the story of Andersonville, the notorious Georgia prison where 50,000 Northern soldiers suffered and close to 14,000 died. This is one of the great accounts of the Civil War. 1970; 150m.

ANDY WARHOL'S BAD ★★★½
DIR: Jed Johnson. **CAST:** Carroll Baker, Perry King, Susan Tyrrell.
Carroll Baker stars in this nasty and very sick outing from producer Andy Warhol. She plays a tough mama who runs a squad of female hit men out of her cheery suburban home while disguising it as an electrolysis operation. Into this strange company comes Perry King as a mysterious stranger who boards there until he completes his "mission." The film has gore, violence, and nudity. 1977; 107m.

ANGEL ON MY SHOULDER ★★★★
DIR: Archie Mayo. **CAST:** Paul Muni, Anne Baxter, Claude Rains, George Cleveland, Onslow Stevens.
In a break from his big-budget prestige screen biographies of the period,

Paul Muni stars in this entertaining fantasy as a murdered gangster who makes a deal with the devil. He wants to return to his human form. He gets his wish and spends his time on Earth—as a judge—trying to outwit Satan. 1946; B&W; 101m.

ANGELO, MY LOVE ★★★★
DIR: Robert Duvall. **CAST:** Angelo Evans, Michael Evans.
Robert Duvall wrote and directed this loosely scripted, wonderfully different movie about a street-wise 11-year-old gypsy boy. Duvall reportedly conceived the project when he spotted the fast-talking, charismatic Angelo Evans on a New York street and decided he ought to be in pictures. Rated R for profanity. 1983; 115m.

ANGELS OVER BROADWAY ★★★
DIR: Ben Hecht, Lee Garmes. **CAST:** Douglas Fairbanks Jr., Rita Hayworth, Thomas Mitchell, John Qualen.
Codirected by legendary newsmen and playwrights Ben Hecht and Lee Garmes, this tale of street-wise Douglas Fairbanks's efforts to save would-be suicide John Qualen and provide him with a reason for living is full of great dialogue and pithy comments on life and the human condition. But it lacks the charm that would mark it as a true classic. Recommended for its dialogue, as well as its odd tone. 1940; B&W; 80m.

ANIMAL FARM ★★½
DIR: John Halas, Joy Batchelor. **CAST:** Animated.
Serious, sincere animated adaptation of George Orwell's ingenious satire concerning the follies of government. The treatment would have benefited from greater intensity. The attempt at creating an optimistic ending was ill-advised. Keep in mind the film isn't children's fare. 1954; 72m.

ANN VICKERS ★★★★
DIR: John Cromwell. **CAST:** Irene Dunne, Bruce Cabot, Walter Huston, Conrad Nagel, Edna May Oliver, J. Carrol Naish.
Rebuffed by Bruce Cabot, noble and self-sacrificing Irene Dunne scorns all men and turns to social service. Against all odds she seeks penal reform. A somewhat unique women's prison film in that the heroine is not a victimized inmate. 1933; B&W; 72m.

ANNA ★★★★
DIR: Yurek Bogasyevicz. **CAST:** Sally Kirkland, Paulina Porizkova, Robert Fields, Stefan Schnabel.
In this wonderfully offbeat turn on *All About Eve*, Sally Kirkland plays a former Czech film star struggling to find work in New York. Model Paulina Porizkova is fine as the refugee who remembers Kirkland's former glories and insinuates herself into the older woman's life only to surpass her successes in America. In English and Czech with subtitles. Rated PG-13 for nudity and profanity. 1987; 100m.

ANNA CHRISTIE ★★★★
DIR: Clarence Brown. **CAST:** Greta Garbo, Charles Bickford, Marie Dressler.
Greta Garbo is mesmerizing and Marie Dressler hilariously memorable in this early sound classic adapted from Eugene O'Neill's play. The tag line for it in 1930 was "Garbo speaks!" And speak she does, uttering the famous line, "Gif me a viskey, ginger ale on the side, and don't be stingy, baby," while portraying a woman with a shady past. 1930; B&W; 90m.

ANNA KARENINA (1935) ★★★★
DIR: Clarence Brown. **CAST:** Greta Garbo, Fredric March, Basil Rathbone, Freddie Bartholomew, Maureen O'Sullivan, Reginald Denny, May Robson, Reginald Owen.
The forever fascinating, peerless Greta Garbo, a superb supporting cast headed by Fredric March, and the masterful direction of Clarence Brown make this film one of the

actress's greatest, a true film classic. 1935; B&W; 95m.

ANNA KARENINA (1947) ★★½
DIR: Julien Duvivier. **CAST:** Vivien Leigh, Kieron Moore, Ralph Richardson, Sally Ann Howes, Michael Gough.

In this version of Tolstoy's classic story of a married woman madly in love with a military officer, Vivien Leigh is miscast as the heroine. Though she tries valiantly, she is overwhelmed by the role. An overly sentimental script doesn't help. 1947; B&W; 139m.

ANNE OF GREEN GABLES ★★★★
DIR: Kevin Sullivan. **CAST:** Megan Follows, Richard Farnsworth, Colleen Dewhurst.

This delightful film, based on L. M. Montgomery's classic novel, is set in 1908 on Canada's Prince Edward Island. Anne (Megan Follows) is a foster child taken in by Matthew (Richard Farnsworth) and Marilla Cuthbert (Colleen Dewhurst), who mistakenly expects her to be the boy they need for a farmhand. Unrated; suitable for family viewing. 1985; 240m.

ANNE OF THE THOUSAND DAYS ★★★
DIR: Charles Jarrott. **CAST:** Genevieve Bujold, Richard Burton, Anthony Quayle.

The story of Anne Boleyn, Henry VIII's second wife and mother of Queen Elizabeth I, is given the big-budget treatment. Luckily, the tragic tale of a woman who is at first pressured into an unwanted union with England's lusty king, only to fall in love with him and eventually lose her head to court intrigue, is not lost beneath the spectacle. Genevieve Bujold's well-balanced performance of Anne carries the entire production. 1969; 146m.

ANOTHER COUNTRY ★★★½
DIR: Marek Kanievska. **CAST:** Rupert Everett, Colin Firth, Cary Elwes.

For this film, Julian Mitchell adapted his stage play about Guy Burgess, an Englishman who became a spy for Russia in the 1930s. Little in this story reportedly was based on fact. Still, Mitchell's postulations provide interesting viewing, and Rupert Everett's lead performance—as Guy "Bennett"—is stunning. Rated PG for suggested sex and profanity. 1984; 90m.

ANOTHER TIME, ANOTHER PLACE (1958) ★
DIR: Lewis Allen. **CAST:** Lana Turner, Barry Sullivan, Glynis Johns, Sean Connery, Sidney James.

Ho-hum melodrama about American newspaperwoman whose brief affair with British journalist ends in tragedy when he dies during World War II. Flat and unconvincing, this indifferent weeper is notable mainly for the appearance of a young and sturdy-looking Sean Connery and an older, worldly-wise Lana Turner. 1958; B&W; 98m.

ANOTHER TIME, ANOTHER PLACE (1984) ★★★
DIR: Michael Radford. **CAST:** Phyllis Logan, Paul Young.

In this British import set in 1944, a woman (Phyllis Logan) lives on a small farm in Scotland with her husband (Paul Young), fifteen years her senior. As part of a war rehabilitation program, the couple welcomes three Italian POW's onto their place, and Janie, infatuated with their accents and cultural differences, falls in love. Rated PG. 1984; 118m.

ANOTHER WOMAN ★★★★
DIR: Woody Allen. **CAST:** Gena Rowlands, Gene Hackman, Ian Holm, Mia Farrow, John Houseman, Blythe Danner, Sandy Dennis.

A subtle, purposely enigmatic yet engrossing portrait of a woman reassessing her own identity and purpose. Gena Rowlands is superb as a college professor whose life is not as solid or emotionally stable as she assumes. When she overhears another woman (Mia Farrow) in a session with her psychoanalyst, Rowlands begins to have doubts. Rated PG. 1988; 81m.

ANTHONY ADVERSE ★★★½

DIR: Mervyn LeRoy. **CAST:** Fredric March, Olivia De Havilland, Anita Louise, Donald Woods, Edmund Gwenn, Claude Rains, Louis Hayward, Gale Sondergaard, Henry O'Neill.

Fredric March, in the title role, wanders around early nineteenth-century America and Mexico, growing to manhood, sowing oats, and buckling swash, in this all-stops-out romantic blockbuster. 1936; B&W; 136m.

ANTONY AND CLEOPATRA ★★

DIR: Charlton Heston. **CAST:** Charlton Heston, Hildegard Neil, Eric Porter, Fernando Rey, John Castle.

Marginal film interpretation of Shakespeare's play. Obviously a tremendous amount of work on Charlton Heston's part, casting himself as Antony, but the film is lacking in energy. Rated PG. 1973; 160m.

ANZACS ★★★★

DIR: George Miller. **CAST:** Andrew Clark, Paul Hogan, Megan Williams.

The ANZACS (Australian/New Zealand Army Corps) join the British in World War I to stir up a few stuffed shirts among the very stiff English. Emphasis is upon the friendship and loyalty among the Australians. Paul Hogan provides a few moments of comic relief. A powerful war film that dwells on the people involved, not the machinery. Made for television, this is unrated but deals with mature subject matter. 1985; 165m.

APPLAUSE ★★★★½

DIR: Rouben Mamoulian. **CAST:** Helen Morgan, Joan Peers.

This is a remarkable early sound-era movie. Filmed at actual New York locations, it tells the story of a fading vaudeville star (Helen Morgan) who loses the love of her daughter and is jilted by her lowly boyfriend. A smashing success. 1929; B&W; 78m.

APPRENTICESHIP OF DUDDY KRAVITZ, THE ★★★

DIR: Ted Kotcheff. **CAST:** Richard Dreyfuss, Jack Warden, Micheline Lanctot, Denholm Elliott, Randy Quaid.

Richard Dreyfuss, in an early starring role, is the main attraction in this quirky little comedy about the rise of a poor Jewish lad from a Montreal ghetto. The story is full of cruel and smartassed humor, a trait that haunts Dreyfuss to this day. Ultimately, the film is too long and too shrill. Rated PG for sexual content. 1974; 121m.

ARCH OF TRIUMPH ★★★

DIR: Lewis Milestone. **CAST:** Ingrid Bergman, Charles Boyer, Charles Laughton, Louis Calhern.

In Paris before the Nazis arrive, a refugee doctor meets and falls in love with a woman with a past in this long, slow-paced, emotionless drama. It's sad, frustrating, tedious, and sometimes murky, but fans of the principal players will forgive and enjoy. 1948; B&W; 120m.

ARENA BRAINS ★

DIR: Robert Longo. **CAST:** Ray Liotta, Eric Bogosian, Sean Young.

This experimental film short is a disorganized mess. Nothing is clearly defined in the juxtaposition of characters and events. Not rated, but contains nudity and profanity. 1988; 34m.

ARRANGEMENT, THE ★

DIR: Elia Kazan. **CAST:** Kirk Douglas, Deborah Kerr, Faye Dunaway, Richard Boone.

The cast is the only real reason for watching this tedious talkfest between Kirk Douglas and whoever will listen after he botches a suicide attempt and reevaluates his life. Very nicely produced, but sets and style contribute only so much to a film. Rated R for adult themes, language. 1969; 127m.

ARROGANT, THE

DIR: Philippe Blot. **CAST:** Garry Graham, Sylvia Kristel.

The title best describes writer-producer-director Philippe Blot: he not only made this inane, unbearably pretentious movie about a waitress and a philosophy-spouting motorcyclist, he then had the nerve to release it. Although not cheaply made, it is full of astoundingly obvious blunders, and the actors read their dialogue in voices so bored they sound dubbed. There's enough profanity, violence, and nudity to earn an R rating. 1987; 86m.

ARROWSMITH ★★★★
DIR: John Ford. **CAST:** Ronald Colman, Helen Hayes, Richard Bennett, DeWitt Jennings, Beulah Bondi, Myrna Loy.

Mellifluous-voiced Ronald Colman is a young, career-dedicated research doctor tempted by the profits of commercialism in this faithful rendering of Sinclair Lewis's noted novel of medicine. Helen Hayes is his first wife—doomed to die before he sees the light. This is the first film to center seriously on a doctor's career and raise the question of professional integrity and morality versus quick money and social status. 1931; B&W; 101m.

ARTHUR'S HALLOWED GROUND ★
DIR: Freddie Young. **CAST:** Michael Elphick, Jimmy Jewel, David Swift.

An elderly British gent stands his ground against the system in order to protect his beloved land. A good premise, until one realizes the bit of turf in question is a field on which to play cricket! Silly. 1973; 88m.

AS IS ★★½
DIR: Michael Lindsay-Hogg. **CAST:** Robert Carradine, Jonathan Hadary, Joanna Miles, Alan Scarfe, Colleen Dewhurst.

How AIDS affects family and loved ones is dealt with in a thoughtful manner as Robert Carradine portrays a homosexual who contracts the disease. Jonathan Hadary is the lover who stands by him. Although not preachy, the film does suffer from staginess, as it was adapted from a Broadway play. Not rated, but the whole concept is adult in nature, and some coarse language is used. 1986; 86m.

AS SUMMERS DIE ★★★½
DIR: Jean-Claude Tramont. **CAST:** Scott Glenn, Jamie Lee Curtis, Bette Davis, John Randolph, Ron O'Neal, Bruce McGill, John McIntire, Beah Richards.

A very leisurely story set in Georgia, 1959, concerns a southern aristocratic family's attempt to wrest control of land given to a black woman years earlier, because oil deposits have been found on it. Plot line is nothing new but the performances by a veteran cast carry this HBO film. Bette Davis has some touching moments as a woman whose mental competency is challenged. 1987; 87m.

ASPHALT JUNGLE, THE ★★★★½
DIR: John Huston. **CAST:** Sterling Hayden, Sam Jaffe, Louis Calhern, Marilyn Monroe, Jean Hagen, James Whitmore, Marc Lawrence, Anthony Caruso.

One of the greatest crime films of all time. This realistic study of a jewel robbery that sours, lets the audience in early on what the outcome will be while building tension for any unexpected surprises that might pop up. Sterling Hayden and a near-perfect cast charge the film with an electric current that never lets up and only increases in power as they scheme their way closer to their fate. John Huston broke new ground with this landmark drama. 1950; B&W; 112m.

ASSASSIN OF YOUTH (A.K.A. MARIJUANA) ★
DIR: Elmer Clifton. **CAST:** Luana Walters, Arthur Gardner, Earl Dwire.

This silly, low-budget exploitation film tells the story of a courageous young reporter who goes undercover to infiltrate the marijuana cult that has been wreaking havoc with a local town. Cornball humor in the form of "Pop" Brady and the scooter-riding

Henrietta Frisbie, the town snoop, gives this an extra edge on most films of this nature, but not much. 1936; B&W; 67m.

ASSASSINATION OF TROTSKY, THE ★

DIR: Joseph Losey. **CAST:** Richard Burton, Alain Delon, Romy Schneider.

This dramatic tale of international intrigue wastes a solid peformance from Richard Burton as the exiled Soviet leader. The plot is confused and the pacing staggers. Instead of a gripping thriller, it's a chaotic yawner. Rated R. 1972; 102m.

AT CLOSE RANGE ★★★★

DIR: James Foley. **CAST:** Christopher Walken, Sean Penn, Christopher Penn.

A powerful thriller based on true events that occurred in Pennsylvania during the summer of 1978. A rural gang leader returns to the family he abandoned years ago. His two sons try to prove themselves worthy of joining the gang. Events beyond their control lead to a brutal showdown between father and sons. Rated R for violence and profanity. 1986; 115m.

ATLANTIC CITY ★★★★★

DIR: Louis Malle. **CAST:** Burt Lancaster, Susan Sarandon, Kate Reid.

This superb motion picture has all of the elements that made the films of Hollywood's golden age great—with a few appropriately modern twists tossed in. The screenplay, by John Guare—about a struggling casino worker (Susan Sarandon) who becomes involved in a drug deal—gives us powerful drama, wonderful characters, memorable dialogue, and delightfully funny situations. And the performances by Burt Lancaster, Sarandon, and Kate Reid, in particular, are top-notch. Rated R because of brief nudity and violence. 1981; 104m.

ATTICA ★★★★

DIR: Marvin J. Chomsky. **CAST:** Charles Durning, George Grizzard, Anthony Zerbe, Glynn Turman, Henry Darrow.

This made-for-TV account of the horrifying Attica prison riots of 1971 is a very detailed translation of Tom Wicker's bestselling book *A Time to Die*. Screenwriter James Henerson deserves kudos for this adaptation. The performances are uniformly excellent. 1980; 100m.

AUTOBIOGRAPHY OF MISS JANE PITTMAN, THE ★★★★★

DIR: John Korty. **CAST:** Cicely Tyson, Richard Dysart, Odetta, Michael Murphy, Thalmus Rasulala.

This terrific television movie traces black history in America from the Civil War years to the turbulent civil rights movement of the 1960s. All this is seen through the eyes of 110-year-old ex-slave Jane Pittman (Cicely Tyson). The entire cast is superb, but Tyson still manages to tower above the others in the title role. There is no rating, but it should be noted that there are some violent scenes. 1974; 110m.

AUTUMN LEAVES ★★½

DIR: Robert Aldrich. **CAST:** Joan Crawford, Cliff Robertson, Vera Miles, Lorne Greene.

Troubled middle-aged typist Joan Crawford is further anguished after marrying a younger man (Cliff Robertson) who proves to be mentally disturbed and already married. Run-of-the-mill Crawford fare. 1956; B&W; 108m.

AVIATOR, THE ★★

DIR: George Miller. **CAST:** Christopher Reeve, Rosanna Arquette, Jack Warden, Scott Wilson, Tyne Daly, Sam Wanamaker.

This film, about a grumpy flyer (Christopher Reeve) during the 1920s who is forced to take a feisty passenger (Rosanna Arquette) on his mail route, is too similar to *High Road to China*. It has neither the high adventure nor the humor of the latter. What we're left with is a predictable boy-meets-girl drama that takes a left turn into a danger-in-the-wilderness cliché. Rated PG. 1984; 102m.

BABY DOLL ★★★★
DIR: Elia Kazan. **CAST:** Carroll Baker, Eli Wallach, Karl Malden, Mildred Dunnock, Lonny Chapman, Rip Torn.

Set in hot, humid, sleazy Mississippi, this is the story of a child bride (Carroll Baker) who sleeps in a crib, her lusting, short-on-brains husband (Karl Malden), and a scheming business rival (Eli Wallach) determined to use and abuse them both. What else but a Tennessee Williams story? Tepid stuff today, but when first released, the film was condemned by the Legion of Decency. Baker's skimpy pajamas became fashionable. 1956; B&W; 114m.

BABY MAKER, THE ★★
DIR: James Bridges. **CAST:** Barbara Hershey, Colin Wilcox-Horne, Scott Glenn, Sam Groom, Jeannie Berlin.

Still timely if overwrought drama of a couple who hire Barbara Hershey to have a baby when it is discovered the wife is barren. Mediocre dialogue, too many beach scenes, and some not-so-interesting subsidiary characters drag this potentially exciting drama to a halt. One of Hershey's first roles. 1970; 109m.

BABY THE RAIN MUST FALL ★★½
DIR: Robert Mulligan. **CAST:** Steve McQueen, Lee Remick, Don Murray.

This confusing character study of a convict who is paroled and reunited with his family raises a lot of questions but answers none of them. 1965; B&W; 100m.

BACK FROM ETERNITY ★★
DIR: John Farrow. **CAST:** Robert Ryan, Anita Ekberg, Rod Steiger, Phyllis Kirk.

No surprises in this rehash of similar films about a handful of people who survive a calamity (in this case, an airplane crash) and have to learn to cope with their predicament as well as with each other. Basically a potboiler that depends on stock footage and phony studio sets, this tired story limps along through the jungles of South America and gives Anita Ekberg plenty of opportunity to show off her torn blouse. 1956; B&W; 97m.

BACK ROADS ★★★
DIR: Martin Ritt. **CAST:** Sally Field, Tommy Lee Jones, David Keith.

Pug (Tommy Lee Jones) and prostitute (Sally Field) hitch and brawl down the back roads of the South in this sometimes raunchy, often hilarious romance-fantasy. Though it drags a bit, the performances by the two stars and an earthy, down-home charm make it worthwhile. Rated R. 1981; 94m.

BACK STREET ★★★
DIR: David Miller. **CAST:** Susan Hayward, John Gavin, Vera Miles.

Third version of novelist Fannie Hurst's romantic tearjerker about clandestine love, with Susan Hayward as the noble mistress who sacrifices all and stands by her lover even when he stupidly marries another woman. 1961; 107m.

BACKDOOR TO HEAVEN ★★★½
DIR: William K. Howard. **CAST:** Aline MacMahon, Wallace Ford, Stu Erwin, Van Heflin.

With superb performances from a talented cast, this strong social drama is somewhat dated but still compelling. A poor young man must make a choice: a lifetime of toil and repression or a career of crime. 1939; B&W; 86m.

BAD AND THE BEAUTIFUL, THE ★★★★½
DIR: Vincente Minnelli. **CAST:** Lana Turner, Kirk Douglas, Gloria Grahame, Dick Powell, Barry Sullivan, Walter Pidgeon, Gilbert Roland.

Dynamite story of a Hollywood producer (Kirk Douglas) and his turbulent relations with a studio actress (Lana Turner). Along the way there are fine performances by all of the cast. It's old Hollywood gloss, and very good, indeed. Five Oscars for this gem. 1952; B&W; 118m.

BAD BOYS ★★★★½

DIR: Rick Rosenthal. **CAST:** Sean Penn, Esai Morales, Reni Santoni, Ally Sheedy, Jim Moody, Eric Gurry.

This is a grimly riveting vision of troubled youth. Sean Penn and Esai Morales are featured as Chicago street hoods sworn to kill each other in prison. It's exciting, thought-provoking, and violent, but the violence, for once, is justified and not merely exploitative. Rated R for language, violence, and nudity. 1983; 123m.

BAD DAY AT BLACK ROCK ★★★★

DIR: John Sturges. **CAST:** Spencer Tracy, Robert Ryan, Anne Francis, Walter Brennan, Lee Marvin, Ernest Borgnine.

Spencer Tracy gives one of his greatest performances in this suspenseful, action-packed drama as a one-armed man who stirs up trouble when he arrives at a Western town whose citizens have a guilty secret. Robert Ryan is superb as the main villain. Lee Marvin and Ernest Borgnine ooze menace as brutal, sadistic henchmen. 1955; 81m.

BAD SEED, THE ★★½

DIR: Mervyn LeRoy. **CAST:** Patty McCormack, Nancy Kelly, Henry Jones, Eileen Heckart, William Hopper.

Despite the contrived ending and pathetically cutesy "curtain call," this story of a perfectly wicked child protected by her image is still capable of generating chills. Nancy Kelly may be more than a bit melodramatic as the concerned mother on a constant crying jag, but young Patty McCormack has that special cold beauty that makes her crimes all the more hideous. 1956; B&W; 129m.

BADLANDS ★★★★

DIR: Terence Malick. **CAST:** Martin Sheen, Sissy Spacek, Warren Oates, Ramon Bieri, Alan Vint.

Featuring fine performances by Sissy Spacek, Martin Sheen, and Warren Oates, this is a disturbing recreation of the Starkweather-Fugate killing spree of the 1950s. It is undeniably a work of intelligence and fine craftsmanship. However, as with Martin Scorsese's *Taxi Driver* and Bob Fosse's *Star 80*, *Badlands* is not an easy film to watch. Rated PG. 1973; 95m.

BAJA OKLAHOMA ★★

DIR: Bobby Roth. **CAST:** Lesley Ann Warren, Peter Coyote, Swoosie Kurtz, Billy Vera.

Lesley Ann Warren plays a tired bartender who dreams of success as a country and western songwriter. When one of the many men who walked out on her returns, she is reluctant to give him a second chance. Willie Nelson and Emmylou Harris make cameo appearances as themselves. Made for HBO, this contains profanity, violence, and partial nudity. 1988; 100m.

BALBOA

DIR: James Polakof. **CAST:** Tony Curtis, Carol Lynley, Steve Kanaly, Chuck Connors.

Tacky soap about a ruthless millionaire (Tony Curtis) who has the hots for his ex-girlfriend (Carol Lynley). Steve Kanaly plays an honest politician who also loves Lynley. Unrated, this film contains nudity and sexual situations. 1982; 92m.

BANG THE DRUM SLOWLY ★★★★

DIR: John Hancock. **CAST:** Robert De Niro, Michael Moriarty, Vincent Gardenia.

Robert De Niro and Michael Moriarty are given a perfect showcase for their acting talents in this poignant film, and they don't disappoint. The friendship of two baseball players comes alive as the team's star pitcher (Moriarty) tries to assist journeyman catcher (De Niro) in completing one last season before succumbing to Hodgkin's disease. The story may lead to death, but it is filled with life, hope, and compassion. Rated PG. 1973; 98m.

BARABBAS ★★½
DIR: Richard Fleischer. **CAST:** Anthony Quinn, Jack Palance, Ernest Borgnine, Katy Jurado.
Early Dino De Laurentis opus is long on production, short on credibility. Standard gory religious spectacle follows the life of the thief Barabbas, whom Pilate freed when Jesus was condemned to die. Good cast of veteran character actors attempts to move this epic along, but fails. 1962; 144m.

BARBARIAN AND THE GEISHA, THE ★
DIR: John Huston. **CAST:** John Wayne, Sam Jaffe, Eiko Ando.
John Wayne is horribly miscast as an American ambassador to Japan during the nineteeth century who finds romance with geisha Eiko Ando. Wayne made his share of bad films, and this one is close to the top of the list. 1958; 105m.

BARBARY COAST, THE ★★★½
DIR: Howard Hawks. **CAST:** Edward G. Robinson, Miriam Hopkins, Joel McCrea, Walter Brennan, Brian Donlevy, Frank Craven.
Big-budget Hollywood hokum drew its inspiration from Herbert Asbury's colorful history of early San Francisco, but tailored the book to fit the unique talents of its great cast. This story of femme fatale Miriam Hopkins and the men in her life is fun for the whole family and a treat for film buffs who like the look of the past as created on studio backlots. Look for David Niven in his first recognizable bit as a drunken tramp who gets thrown out of a tavern. 1935; B&W; 90m.

BAREFOOT CONTESSA, THE ★★★
DIR: Joseph L. Mankiewicz. **CAST:** Humphrey Bogart, Ava Gardner, Edmond O'Brien, Marius Goring, Rossano Brazzi.
A gaggle of Hollywood vultures headed by director Humphrey Bogart picks naïve dancer Ava Gardner out of a Madrid nightclub and proceeds to mold her into a film star. A simple unpretentious soul who never really comes to grips with all that transpires, she marries an impotent Italian nobleman (Rossano Brazzi), dies, and is buried by her chief mentor who tells her tragic story in flashback. A cynical, bizarre tale that never delivers what it promises. 1954; 128m.

BARFLY ★★★★
DIR: Barbet Schroeder. **CAST:** Mickey Rourke, Faye Dunaway, Alice Krige, J. C. Quinn, Frank Stallone.
Superb performances by Mickey Rourke and Faye Dunaway, as well as a dynamite jazz and R&B score, highlight this hip, flip, and often gruesomely funny semiautobiographical film written by Charles Bukowski. Rourke and Dunaway drink their way from one sodden, sleazy misadventure to another, and director Barbet Schroeder makes it all seem to truly take place on the street—or is that the gutter? Rated R for profanity, suggested sex, and violence. 1987; 97m.

BARN BURNING ★★★★
DIR: Peter Werner. **CAST:** Tommy Lee Jones, Diane Kagan, Shawn Whittington.
A sterling adaptation of William Faulkner's short story. Oscar-winning scripter Horton Foote is responsible for this teleplay. Tommy Lee Jones is grand in a role that oozes menace. Introduced by Henry Fonda; unrated and suitable for family viewing. 1980; 40m.

BARRY LYNDON ★★★
DIR: Stanley Kubrick. **CAST:** Ryan O'Neal, Marisa Berenson, Patrick Magee, Hardy Krüger, Steven Berkoff, Gay Hamilton.
This period epic directed by Stanley Kubrick will please only the filmmaker's most fervent admirers. Although exquisitely photographed

and meticulously designed, this three-hour motion picture adaptation of William Makepeace Thackeray's novel about an eighteenth-century rogue is a flawed masterpiece at best and is far too drawn out. However, it is worth watching for the lush cinematography by John Alcott. Rated PG for brief nudity and violence. 1975; 183m.

BARTLEBY ★★★½
DIR: Anthony Friedman. **CAST:** Paul Scofield, John McEnery.

Herman Melville's tale of a man who "would prefer not to" seems especially timely now. Paul Scofield is the unfortunate boss who, stuck with the inert Bartleby, is forced to fire him. Superior acting makes this thought-provoking tale both moving and believable. 1970; 79m.

BATTERED ★★½
DIR: Peter Werner. **CAST:** Mike Farrell, LeVar Burton, Karen Grassle, Joan Blondell, Howard Duff, Diana Scarwid.

This TV docudrama will have you believing there are wife beaters lurking around every corner. The script is somewhat stiff and uninventive at times, but does offer a fairly accurate picture of the few alternatives open to the women in this desperate situation. 1978; 95m.

BAY BOY, THE ★★★★½
DIR: Daniel Petrie. **CAST:** Liv Ullmann, Kiefer Sutherland, Joe MacPherson.

The story of a brief period in an adolescent boy's life while growing up in a small mining town on the Nova Scotia coast during the mid-1930s. This film develops the character, including the sexual awakening, guilt, and terror, of Donald Campbell (Kiefer Sutherland). Liv Ullmann is well cast as Donald's mother. Donald becomes the sole witness to a tragic murder and is forced to endure in silence the knowledge the murderer is behind virtually every step he takes. 1985; 104m.

BAYOU ROMANCE ★½
DIR: Alan Myerson. **CAST:** Annie Potts, Michael Ansara, Barbara Horan.

Louis Jourdan plays host to this low-budget Romantic Theatre entry. In it, Lily (played by Annie Potts), a successful artist, inherits a Louisiana plantation. There, she is pursued by a handsome, well-educated gypsy as well as a scheming doctor. Avoid if possible! Not rated but has no offensive language or nudity. 1982; 105m.

BEACHCOMBER, THE ★★★
DIR: Erich Pommer. **CAST:** Charles Laughton, Elsa Lanchester, Tyrone Guthrie, Robert Newton.

This Somerset Maugham story of a dissolute South Seas beachcomber and the lady missionary who reforms him is sculptor's clay in the expert dramatic hands of Charles Laughton and Elsa Lanchester. He is delightful as the shiftless, conniving bum; she is clever and captivating as his Bible-toting nemesis. There's a scene at a bar that is Charles Laughton at his wily, eye-rolling, blustering best. 1938; B&W; 80m.

BEACHES ★★★★
DIR: Garry Marshall. **CAST:** Bette Midler, Barbara Hershey, John Heard, Spalding Gray.

Here's a terrific tearjerker that casts Bette Midler and Barbara Hershey as two unlikely friends who enjoy a thirty-year relationship that's full of ups and downs. Fans of five-handkerchief films will love it. Midler is often hilarious as the show-biz-crazy Jewish gal who both loves and competes with WASPish heiress Hershey. See it if only for the mind-boggling performance of look-alike Mayim Bialik as the 11-year-old Midler, but be prepared to suspend your disbelief. Rated PG-13 for profanity and suggested sex. 1988; 120m.

BEAU BRUMMELL ★★★★
DIR: Harry Beaumont. **CAST:** John Barrymore, Mary Astor, Irene Rich, Carmel Myers.

John Barrymore scores a great success as the handsome dandy who works his way into the good graces of the Prince of Wales. Mary Astor is wonderful as Lady Alvanley. This is a must-see film for admirers of the silent film nearing its peak of perfection. Silent. 1924; B&W; 92m.

BECKET ★★★★
DIR: Peter Glenville. **CAST:** Richard Burton, Peter O'Toole, Martita Hunt, Pamela Brown.

Magnificently acted spectacle of the stormy relationship between England's King Henry II (Peter O'Toole) and his friend and nemesis Archbishop Thomas Becket (Richard Burton). This visually stimulating historical pageant, set in twelfth-century England, garnered Oscar nominations for both its protagonists. 1964; 148m.

BECKY SHARP ★★½
DIR: Rouben Mamoulian. **CAST:** Miriam Hopkins, Frances Dee, Cedric Hardwicke, Billie Burke, Alison Skipworth, Nigel Bruce.

Well-mounted historical drama of a callous young woman who lives for social success is lovely to look at in its original three-strip Technicolor. Fine performances by a veteran cast bolster this first sound screen adaptation of Thackeray's *Vanity Fair*. 1935; 83m.

BEDFORD INCIDENT, THE ★★★
DIR: James B. Harris. **CAST:** Richard Widmark, Sidney Poitier, Martin Balsam, Wally Cox, Eric Portman.

A battle of wits aboard a U.S. destroyer tracking Soviet submarines off Greenland during the Cold War. Richard Widmark is a skipper with an obsession to hunt and hound a particular sub. A conflict develops between the captain and Sidney Poitier, a cocky magazine reporter along for the ride. 1965; B&W; 102m.

BEETHOVEN'S NEPHEW ★★½
DIR: Paul Morrissey. **CAST:** Wolfgang Reichmann, Dietmar Prinz, Jane Birkin, Nathalie Baye, Mathieu Carrière.

This surreal drama by Paul Morrissey takes an incisive look at the dark side of Beethoven's genius. It's a convoluted period piece that follows the bizarre exploits of Beethoven's young nephew, Karl. Interesting performances, beautiful settings, and great costumes carry this film over the slow spots. Rated R. 1985; 103m.

BEGUILED, THE ★★★★
DIR: Don Siegel. **CAST:** Clint Eastwood, Geraldine Page, Jo Ann Harris.

An atmospheric, daring change of pace for director Don Siegel and star Clint Eastwood, this production features the squinty-eyed actor as a wounded Yankee soldier taken in by the head (Geraldine Page) of a girls' school. He becomes the catalyst for incidents of jealousy and hatred among its inhabitants, and this leads to a startling, unpredictable conclusion. Rated R. 1971; 109m.

BEHOLD A PALE HORSE ★
DIR: Fred Zinnemann. **CAST:** Gregory Peck, Anthony Quinn, Omar Sharif.

Gregory Peck is miscast in this slow, talky, vague drama of a Loyalist holdout in post–Civil War Spain who continues to harass the Franco regime. Everyone tries hard, but the film steadily sinks. 1963; 118m.

BELFAST ASSASSIN ★★½
DIR: Lawrence Gordon Clark. **CAST:** Derek Thompson, Ray Lonnen, Benjamin Whitrow.

This film, about an IRA hit man and a British antiterrorist who is ordered to track down the Irish assassin on his own turf, could have used a clipper-happy editor; the same statement could have been said in much less than two hours plus. The film takes a pro-IRA stand, yet is open-minded enough to see the other side of the story without resorting to self-righteouness. Not rated, but the equivalent of a PG for sex, violence, and profanity. 1982; 130m.

BELIZAIRE THE CAJUN ★★★★
DIR: Glen Pitre. **CAST:** Armand Assante, Gail Youngs, Michael Schoeffling, Stephen McHattie, Will Patton.

Belizaire the Cajun is a film that is atmospheric in the best sense of the word. The Louisiana bayou of the 1850s is richly re-created in a cadence of texture and deep, dark swampland colors, along with the rhythms of Cajun accents and full-bodied folk music (score by Michael Doucet). Armand Assante is Belizaire, an herbal doctor who finds himself in a mess of trouble because of his affection for his childhood sweetheart and his efforts to save a friend from persecution. 1986; 114m.

BELL JAR, THE ★★★
DIR: Larry Peerce. **CAST:** Marilyn Hassett, Julie Harris, Anne Jackson, Barbara Barrie, Robert Klein.

Based on the novel by Sylvia Plath about the mental breakdown of an overachiever in the world of big business in the 1950s, this film has a strong lead performance by Marilyn Hassett and thoughtful direction by her husband, Larry Peerce. But the overriding melancholy of the subject matter makes it difficult to watch. Barbara Barrie is also memorable in a key supporting role. Rated R. 1979; 107m.

BELLMAN AND TRUE ★★★★
DIR: Richard Loncraine. **CAST:** Bernard Hill, Derek Newark, Richard Hope, Ken Bones, Frances Tomelty.

This gripping crime drama centers around a British computer genius who is forced to aid thugs in a bank heist after his son is kidnapped. Fascinating characters and suspenseful plot twists give this film depth and realism. Rated R. 1988; 114m.

BELLS OF ST. MARY'S, THE ★★★★½
DIR: Leo McCarey. **CAST:** Bing Crosby, Ingrid Bergman, Ruth Donnelly.

An effective sequel to *Going My Way*, also directed by Leo McCarey, this film has Bing Crosby returning as the modern-minded priest once again up against a headstrong opponent, Mother Superior (played by Ingrid Bergman). While not as memorable as his encounter with hard-headed older priest Barry Fitzgerald in the first film, this relationship—and the movie as a whole—does have its viewing rewards. 1945; B&W; 126m.

BELLY OF AN ARCHITECT, THE ★★
DIR: Peter Greenaway. **CAST:** Brian Dennehy, Chloe Webb, Lambert Wilson.

Dreamlike, symbolism-laced story of an American architect (Brian Dennehy) trying to deal with hypocrisy in his art and in his life while working on a project in Italy. His efforts take on an urgency when he begins to suspect that he's dying of cancer. Alternately artful and pretentious, simple and enigmatic, the film is most interesting as a showcase for Dennehy. 1987; 108m.

BELOVED ENEMY ★★★½
DIR: H. C. Potter. **CAST:** Merle Oberon, Brian Aherne, Karen Morley, David Niven.

This stylish film concerns a beautiful woman (Merle Oberon) in love with a young leader in the Irish revolution (Brian Aherne). Great supporting cast adds panache to this crackerjack Samuel Goldwyn production. 1936; B&W; 86m.

BELOW THE BELT ★★★½
DIR: Robert Fowler. **CAST:** Regina Baff, Mildred Burke, John C. Becher, Shirley Stoler, Dolph Sweet, Ric Mancini.

This agreeable low-budget feature is short on technical polish but long on heart. It's a semidocumentary about a waitress (Regina Baff) who tries to become a professional wrestler, taking advice from ex-champ Mildred Burke (playing herself). There's even a *Rocky*ish finale. Made in 1974, but not released until 1980. Rated R. 1980; 91m.

BEN-HUR (1926) ★★★★
DIR: Fred Niblo. **CAST:** Ramon Novarro, Francis X. Bushman, May McAvoy, Betty Bronson, Carmel Myers.
Colossal in every sense of the word, this greatest of silent film spectacles is still a winner today. Years in production, it cost a staggering $4 million and was two years being edited. The chariot-race and sea-battle scenes are unsurpassed. Ramon Novarro as Ben-Hur and Francis X. Bushman as Messala gave the performances of their careers. 1926; B&W; 116m.

BENNY GOODMAN STORY, THE ★★★
DIR: Valentine Davies. **CAST:** Steve Allen, Donna Reed, Teddy Wilson, Herbert Anderson, Gene Krupa, Robert F. Simon.
If you enjoy good big-band music and don't mind a few errors in biographical fact, then this big brassy picture is a must for you. Steve Allen as Benny Goodman does a fine job. Watch for some other great performers in cameos. 1955; 116m.

BERLIN AFFAIR, THE ★★
DIR: Liliana Cavani. **CAST:** Gudrun Landgrebe, Kevin McNally, Mio Takaki.
Uneven erotic psychodrama about a Japanese art student in pre-war 1938 Germany who becomes involved in a bizarre love triangle with the wife of a politically affluent German diplomat and her husband. Though heavy on eroticism, the film is lean on story and character motivation. Rated R for nudity and profanity. 1985; 97m.

BEST LITTLE GIRL IN THE WORLD, THE ★★★★½
DIR: Sam O'Steen. **CAST:** Jennifer Jason Leigh, Charles Durning, Eva Marie Saint, Jason Miller.
This gut-wrenching teleplay about a girl, portrayed by Jennifer Jason Leigh who suffers from anorexia nervosa pulls no punches; some of the drama is hard to take, but if you can make it through the film's end, you'll feel rewarded. This was originally an after-school special. The entire cast turns in great performances. The equivalent of a PG for intense drama. 1986; 90m.

BEST SELLER ★★★★
DIR: John Flynn. **CAST:** James Woods, Brian Dennehy, Victoria Tennant, Paul Shenar.
James Woods and Brian Dennehy give superb performances in this gripping character study about a ruthless hitman (Woods) who convinces a Joseph Wambaugh–type cop-turned-author (Dennehy) to help him write a book. Because the book threatens to expose the illegal empire of a wealthy industrialist, the authors soon find their lives in danger. The story by Larry Cohen is outrageous at times, but the electricity generated by the stars is undeniable. Rated R for profanity and violence. 1987; 110m.

BEST YEARS OF OUR LIVES, THE ★★★★★
DIR: William Wyler. **CAST:** Myrna Loy, Fredric March, Teresa Wright, Dana Andrews, Virginia Mayo, Harold Russell, Cathy O'Donnell.
What happens when the fighting ends and warriors return home is the basis of this eloquent, compassionate film. Old master William Wyler takes his time and guides a superb group of players through a tangle of postwar emotional conflicts. Harold Russell's first scene has lost none of its impact. Keep in mind World War II had just ended when this film debuted. 1946; B&W; 170m.

BETHUNE ★★★½
DIR: Eric Till. **CAST:** Donald Sutherland, Kate Nelligan, David Gardner, James Hong.
This biographical teleplay gets off to a slow start, but delivers an absorbing story and masterful acting. It's the biography of Norman Bethune, the Canadian hero who served as a doctor in

the combat between China and Japan. 1984; 88m.

BETRAYAL (1978) ★★½
DIR: Paul Wendkos. **CAST:** Lesley Ann Warren, Rip Torn, Richard Masur, Peggy Ann Garner, Ron Silver, Bibi Besch.

Based on a true incident, this soapy TV movie concerns a young woman who has an affair with her psychiatrist. What could have been a revealing and vital picture breaks down into conventional melodrama. 1978; 100m.

BETRAYAL (1983) ★★★★★
DIR: David Jones. **CAST:** Jeremy Irons, Ben Kingsley, Patricia Hodge.

Harold Pinter's play about the slow death of a marriage has been turned into an intelligent and innovative film that begins with the affair breaking apart and follows it backward to the beginning. Jeremy Irons and Patricia Hodge are superb. Rated R for profanity. 1983; 95m.

BETRAYED ★★★½
DIR: Constantin Costa-Gavras. **CAST:** Debra Winger, Tom Berenger, John Heard, Betsy Blair, Ted Levine.

A searing performance from Debra Winger surmounts baffling inconsistencies in Joe Eszterhas's script. She's sent by mentor John Heard to infiltrate a comfortably homespun rural American community that might conceal a nest of white supremacists. The horrifying premise is credible enough, but its gut-wrenching impact is repeatedly dampened by the naïve and foolish actions taken by Winger. Focus on the message and forget the story. Rated R for violence and language. 1988; 127m.

BETSY, THE ★★
DIR: Daniel Petrie. **CAST:** Laurence Olivier, Tommy Lee Jones, Robert Duvall, Katharine Ross, Lesley-Anne Down, Jane Alexander.

Here is a classic example of how to waste loads of talent and money. The Harold Robbins novel about a wealthy family in the auto manufacturing business was trashy to start with, but after Hollywood gets done with it, not even the likes of Laurence Olivier can save this debacle. Rated R. 1978; 125m.

BETWEEN FRIENDS ★★½
DIR: Lou Antonio. **CAST:** Elizabeth Taylor, Carol Burnett, Barbara Rush, Stephen Young, Henry Ramer.

Two middle-aged divorcées meet and gradually form a life-sustaining friendship. This made-for-cable feature occasionally gets mired in melodramatic tendencies, but the dynamic performances of its two charismatic stars make it well worth watching. Unrated. 1983; 100m.

BETWEEN WARS
DIR: Michael Thornhill. **CAST:** Corin Redgrave, Arthur Dingham, Judy Morris.

What seems innocent enough on the cassette box turns into a soft-core porn flick, so keep an eye out for little ones in the room if you decide to rent. For most adults, though, this Australian offering about an idealistic doctor will be a deadly bore. Adult situations. 1985; 97m.

BEULAH LAND ★★★½
DIR: Virgil Vogel, Harry Falk. **CAST:** Lesley Ann Warren, Michael Sarrazin, Eddie Albert, Hope Lange, Don Johnson, Meredith Baxter Birney.

A generational look at the life of a southern plantation family. The saga carries you through the Civil War and its aftermath. A polished TV production with a strong cast, all of whom turn in fine performances. 1980; 267m.

BEYOND A REASONABLE DOUBT ★★★
DIR: Fritz Lang. **CAST:** Dana Andrews, Joan Fontaine, Sidney Blackmer, Shepperd Strudwick.

To reveal the faults of the justice system, novelist Dana Andrews allows himself to be incriminated in a murder. The plan is to reveal his innocence and discredit capital punishment at the last minute. But the one man who can exonerate him is killed. Don't expect surprise, but shock! 1956; B&W; 80m.

BEYOND REASON ★★★
DIR: Telly Savalas. **CAST:** Telly Savalas, Diana Muldaur, Marvin Laird.

Telly Savalas shows his stuff in this sensitve film, which he wrote and directed. He plays an iconoclastic psychologist who slowly loses touch with reality. Though thought-provoking and touching throughout, the story gets a little muddy from time to time and finishes unsatisfyingly. 1985; 88m.

BEYOND THE LIMIT ★★
DIR: John Mackenzie. **CAST:** Michael Caine, Richard Gere, Bob Hoskins, Elpidia Carrillo.

A dull, unconvincing adaptation of *The Honorary Consul*, Graham Greene's novel about love and betrayal in an Argentinian town stars Michael Caine as a kidnapped diplomat and Richard Gere as the doctor in love with his wife. It'll take you beyond your limit. Rated R. 1983; 103m.

BEYOND THE VALLEY OF THE DOLLS
DIR: Russ Meyer. **CAST:** Dolly Read, Cynthia Myers, Marcia McBroom.

Like all other films by Russ Meyer, *Dolls* dabbles in petty political ideas and contains enough 1960s hip talk to make you lose your lunch. This was rated X when it came out, but by today's standards it's an R for gratuitous nudity and profanity. 1970; 109m.

BIBLE, THE ★★★
DIR: John Huston. **CAST:** Michael Parks, Ulla Bergryd, Richard Harris, John Huston, Ava Gardner.

An overblown all-star treatment of five of the early stories in the Old Testament. Director John Huston gives this movie the feel of a Cecil B. De Mille spectacle, but there is little human touch to any of the stories. This expensively mounted production forgets that in the Bible, individual accomplishments are equally relevant to grandeur. 1966; 174m.

BIG BLUFF, THE ★
DIR: W. Lee Wilder. **CAST:** John Bromfield, Martha Vickers, Robert Hutton, Rosemarie Bowe.

A good cast sinks under the weight of an overfamiliar plot. Martha Vickers plays a young woman with a terminal disease married to a gigolo who plots to murder her for her money if she should linger too long. 1955; B&W; 70m.

BIG CHILL, THE ★★★★½
DIR: Lawrence Kasdan. **CAST:** Tom Berenger, William Hurt, Glenn Close, Jeff Goldblum, JoBeth Williams, Kevin Kline, Mary Kay Place, Meg Tilly.

As with John Sayles's superb *Return of the Secaucus 7*, this equally impressive and thoroughly enjoyable film by writer-director Lawrence Kasdan concerns a weekend reunion of old friends, all of whom have gone on to varied lifestyles after once being united in the hip, committed 1960s. It features a who's-who of today's hot young stars as the friends. Rated R for nudity and profanity. 1983; 103m.

BIG LIFT, THE ★★½
DIR: George Season. **CAST:** Montgomery Clift, Paul Douglas, Cornell Borchers, O. E. Hasse.

Montgomery Clift gives an emotionally charged performance as an Air Force pilot who becomes romantically involved with a young German girl in post–World War II Berlin. Excellent location photography gives a lift to this uneven melodrama. 1950; B&W; 120m.

BIG PARADE, THE ★★★★★
DIR: King Vidor. **CAST:** John Gilbert, Renée Adorée, Hobart Bosworth.

A compelling depiction of World War I, this silent film has long been recognized as one of the era's greatest. Moreover, it is King Vidor's masterpiece. As the saying goes, it has everything: romance, humor, love, tragedy, and suspense. 1925; B&W; 126m.

BIG STREET, THE ★★½

DIR: Irving Reis. **CAST:** Henry Fonda, Lucille Ball, Hans Conried, Barton MacLane, Agnes Moorehead, Ray Collins, Sam Levene, Louise Beavers.

Though somewhat too sentimental at times, this Damon Runyon story of a busboy's (Henry Fonda) sincere devotion to a couldn't-care-less-for-him nightclub singer (Lucille Ball) is often touching and lively. Lucille Ball gives her best big-screen performance and you couldn't ask for a better gangster than Barton MacLane. 1942; B&W; 88m.

BIG TOWN, THE ★★

DIR: Ben Bolt. **CAST:** Matt Dillon, Diane Lane, Tommy Lee Jones, Bruce Dern, Tom Skerritt, Lee Grant, Suzy Amis.

Chicago, circa 1957. The story starts off well: a talented small-town boy (Matt Dillon) with a penchant for crap shooting goes off to the Big City. But the production loses focus and drive. Rated R for language, nudity, and sex. 1987; 110m.

BIG WEDNESDAY ★★

DIR: John Milius. **CAST:** Jan-Michael Vincent, Gary Busey, William Katt, Lee Purcell, Patti D'Arbanville.

Only nostalgic surfers with more than a little patience will enjoy this ode to the beach set and that perfect wave by writer-director John Milius. Rated PG. 1978; 120m.

BIG WHEEL, THE ★★½

DIR: Edward Ludwig. **CAST:** Mickey Rooney, Thomas Mitchell, Spring Byington, Allen Jenkins, Michael O'Shea.

Smart-mouthed Mickey Rooney rises from garage mechanic to champion racing-car driver, losing respect and friends along the way in this well-worn story worn thinner by a poor script and poorer direction. More than 20 of the film's 92 minutes are given over to ear-splitting scenes of high-speed racing. 1949; B&W; 92m.

BILL ★★★★½

DIR: Anthony Page. **CAST:** Mickey Rooney, Dennis Quaid, Largo Woodruff.

Extremely moving drama based on the real-life experiences of Bill Sackter, a retarded adult forced to leave the mental institution that has been his home for the past forty-five years. Mickey Rooney won an Emmy for his excellent portrayal of Bill. Dennis Quaid plays a filmmaker who offers kindness and employment to Bill as he tries to cope with life on the "outside." Unrated. 1981; 100m.

BILL: ON HIS OWN ★★★½

DIR: Anthony Page. **CAST:** Mickey Rooney, Helen Hunt, Teresa Wright, Dennis Quaid, Largo Woodruff.

This is the sequel to the 1981 drama *Bill*. Mickey Rooney continues his role as Bill Sackter, a mentally retarted adult forced to live on his own after spending forty-five years in an institution. Helen Hunt co-stars as the college student who tutors him. It doesn't have quite the emotional impact that *Bill* carried, but it's still good. 1983; 104m.

BILLY BUDD ★★★½

DIR: Peter Ustinov. **CAST:** Terence Stamp, Robert Ryan, Peter Ustinov.

Herman Melville's brooding, allegorical novel of the overpowering of the innocent is set against a backdrop of life on an eighteenth-century British warship. The plight of a young sailor subjected to the treacherous whims of his ship's tyrannical first mate is well-acted throughout. It is powerful filmmaking and succeeds in leaving its audience unsettled and questioning. 1962; B&W; 112m.

BILLY GALVIN ★★★½

DIR: John Gray. **CAST:** Karl Malden, Lenny Von Dohlen, Toni Kalem, Keith Szarabajka, Alan North, Barton Haymon, Joyce Van Patten.

Surprisingly good slice-of-life drama about steelworkers in Boston. Karl Malden is excellent as Jack Galvin, a hard-bitten steelworker who doesn't want his son, Billy (Lenny Von Dohlen, also excellent), to follow in his footsteps. Billy has other ideas, though. Rated PG for language. 1986; 99m.

BILLY LIAR ★★★★
DIR: John Schlesinger. **CAST:** Tom Courtenay, Julie Christie, Finlay Currie, Ethel Griffies, Mona Washbourne.

Poignant slices of English middle-class life are served expertly in this finely played story of a lazy young man who escapes dulling routine by retreating into fantasy. The eleven minutes Julie Christie is on-screen are electric and worth the whole picture. 1963; B&W; 96m.

BIRD MAN OF ALCATRAZ ★★★★
DIR: John Frankenheimer. **CAST:** Burt Lancaster, Karl Malden, Thelma Ritter, Telly Savalas.

In one of his best screen performances, Burt Lancaster plays Robert Stroud, the prisoner who became a world-renowned authority on birds. 1962; B&W; 143m.

BIRDY ★★★★½
DIR: Alan Parker. **CAST:** Matthew Modine, Nicolas Cage, John Harkins, Sandy Baron, Karen Young, Bruno Kirby.

Matthew Modine and Nicolas Cage give unforgettable performances in this dark, disturbing, yet somehow uplifting study of an odd young man named Birdy (Modine) from South Philadelphia who wants to be a bird. That way he can fly away from all his troubles—which worsen manifold after a traumatic tour of duty in Vietnam. Rated R for violence, nudity, and profanity. 1985; 120m.

BIRTH OF A NATION, THE ★★★★
DIR: D. W. Griffith. **CAST:** Lillian Gish, Mae Marsh, Henry B. Walthall, Miriam Cooper.

Videotape will probably be the only medium in which you will ever see this landmark silent classic. D. W. Griffith's epic saga of the American Civil War and its aftermath is today considered too racist in its glorification of the Ku Klux Klan ever to be touched by television or revival theaters. This is filmdom's most important milestone (the first to tell a cohesive story) but should only be seen by those emotionally prepared for its disturbing point of view. 1915; B&W; 158m.

BITCH, THE ★
DIR: Gerry O'Hara. **CAST:** Joan Collins, Kenneth Haigh, Michael Coby.

Joan Collins has the title role in this fiasco, an adaptation of sister Jackie Collins's book. Unfortunately, much was lost when transferred to the screen. It's about two "users," Fontaine (Collins) and Niko (Michael Coby), who find each other when she's in need of money because her disco almost goes under and he's fencing stolen jewels for the mob. Rated R. 1979; 93m.

BITTER HARVEST ★★★★
DIR: Roger Young. **CAST:** Ron Howard, Art Carney, Richard Dysart.

In this made-for-television film based on a true incident, Ron Howard gives an excellent performance as an at-first panicky and then take-charge farmer whose dairy farm herd becomes sick and begins dying. His battle against bureaucracy, as he earnestly tries to find out the cause of the illness (chemicals in the feed), provides for scary, close-to-home drama. Good supporting cast. 1981; 104m.

BITTERSWEET LOVE ★½
DIR: David Miller. **CAST:** Lana Turner, Robert Lansing, Celeste Holm, Robert Alda, Meredith Baxter Birney.

A stellar cast is wasted in a talk-you-to-death film about a young married couple who discover that they are a half-brother and sister. The other problem is that they are expecting a baby. After the revelations everyone sits around and dissects the problem. Rated PG. 1976; 92m.

BLACK FURY ★★★★
DIR: Michael Curtiz. **CAST:** Paul Muni, Karen Morley, William Gargan, Barton MacLane.
Paul Muni is excellent as Joe Radek, an apolitical eastern European immigrant coal miner who unwittingly falls into the middle of a labor dispute that ends up leaving the impoverished miners out of work. The acting is good, but the film doen't reach its happy ending in a logical manner, so things just seem to fall into place without any reason. 1935; B&W; 95m.

BLACK HAND, THE ★★
DIR: Richard Thorpe. **CAST:** Gene Kelly, J. Carrol Naish, Teresa Celli.
Gene Kelly offers a fine dramatic performance as a young man who must avenge the murder of his father. He becomes embroiled in the machinations of the Black Hand, (a.k.a. the Mafia) at the turn of the century. 1950; 93m.

BLACK LIKE ME ★★★
DIR: Carl Lerner. **CAST:** James Whitmore, Roscoe Lee Browne, Will Geer, Sorrell Booke.
Based on the book by John Griffin, this film poses the question: What happens when a white journalist takes a drug that turns his skin black? The interesting premise almost works. James Whitmore plays the reporter, who wishes to experience racism firsthand. Somewhat provocative at its initial release, but by today's standards, a lot of the punch is missing. 1964; B&W; 107m.

BLACK MAGIC ★★½
DIR: Gregory Ratoff. **CAST:** Orson Welles, Akim Tamiroff, Nancy Guild, Raymond Burr, Frank Latimore.
Orson Welles revels in the role of famous eighteenth-century charlatan Count Cagliostro—born Joseph Balsamo, a peasant with imagination and a flair for magic, hypnosis, and the power of superstition. The story is of his tempestuous life and career, and Cagliostro's attempt to gain influence and clout in Italy using his strange and sinister talents. The star co-directed (without credit). 1949; B&W; 105m.

BLACK MARBLE, THE ★★★
DIR: Harold Becker. **CAST:** Paula Prentiss, Harry Dean Stanton, Robert Foxworth.
A Los Angeles cop (Robert Foxworth) and his new partner (Paula Prentiss) attempt to capture a dog snatcher (Harry Dean Stanton) who is demanding a high ransom from a wealthy dog lover. Along the way, they fall in love. Based on Joseph Wambaugh's novel. Rated PG—language, some violence. 1980; 110m.

BLACK NARCISSUS ★★★½
DIR: Michael Powell. **CAST:** Deborah Kerr, Jean Simmons, David Farrar, Flora Robson, Sabu.
Worldly temptations, including those of the flesh, create many difficulties for a group of nuns starting a mission in the Himalayas. Superb photography makes this early postwar British effort a visual delight. Unfortunately, key plot elements in this unusual drama were cut from the American prints by censors. 1947; 99m.

BLACK ORCHID, THE ★★½
DIR: Martin Ritt. **CAST:** Sophia Loren, Anthony Quinn, Ina Balin, Mark Richman.
Sophia Loren plays the widow of a criminal and Anthony Quinn is the businessman who is romancing her in this patchy weeper. The two principals spend the vast majority of the film trying to persuade their children that all will be better if they marry. 1959; B&W; 96m.

BLACK PANTHER, THE ★★½
DIR: Ian Merrick. **CAST:** Donald Sumpter, Debbie Farrington, Marjorie Yates, David Swift.
In 1974 Donald Neilson (Donald Sumpter), known as the Black Panther, robbed a series of post offices and killed their employees. Neilson also plotted the kidnapping of a wealthy teenage heiress that went awry. *The Black Panther* portrays

Neilson's actions in such a matter-of-fact fashion that it removes all the horror. Still, some good action and a few intense scenes. Not rated, has violence and nudity. 1977; 90m.

BLACK SISTER'S REVENGE ★★½
DIR: Jamaa Fanaka. **CAST:** Jerri Hayes, Ernest Williams II.

Shamefully, the video distributor has given this drama a new title and cover art that imply that the movie is a blaxploitation action-adventure. In reality, it's a serious drama, originally titled *Emma Mae*, about a black girl from Georgia struggling to fit in with her cousins and the other kids in an L.A. ghetto. It's a low-budget movie lacking technical flair, but it deserves more attention than the misleading advertising is going to bring it. Not rated. 1976; 100m.

BLACKMAIL ★★★
DIR: Alfred Hitchcock. **CAST:** Anny Ondra, Sara Allgood, John Longden, Charles Paton, Donald Calthrop, Cyril Ritchard.

Hitchock's first sound film stands up well when viewed today and was responsible for pushing Great Britain into the world film market. Many bits of film business that were to become Hitchcock trademarks are evident in this film, including the first of his cameo appearances. Story of a woman who faces the legal system as well as a blackmailer for murdering an attacker in self-defense was originally shot as a silent film but partially reshot and converted into England's first sound release. 1929; B&W; 86m.

BLADES OF COURAGE ★★★½
DIR: Randy Bradshaw. **CAST:** Christianne Hirt, Colm Feore, Stuart Hughes, Rosemary Dunsmore.

Christianne Hirt is a Canadian ice skater with a promising future in the Olympics. Unfortunately she is assigned a coach who employs ruthless methods to achieve what he desires. Aside from the stereotyped pushy mother, this is a realistic film that reveals the effort involved in developing a champion. It is well acted with some choice figure-skating numbers. Unrated. 1988; 98m.

BLAME IT ON THE NIGHT ★½
DIR: Gene Taft. **CAST:** Nick Mancuso, Byron Thames, Leslie Ackerman, Dick Bakalyan.

Mick Jagger cowrote the original story for this movie but wisely chose not to appear in it. It's a trite tale of a rock singer who discovers he has a 13-year-old son. After the straitlaced boy's mother dies, the singer decides that he and the boy should get to know each other. Gets an extra half star for some good tunes (by Ted Neeley, not Jagger). Rated PG-13. 1984; 85m.

BLESS THE BEASTS AND THE CHILDREN ★
DIR: Stanley Kramer. **CAST:** Billy Mumy, Barry Robins, Miles Chapin, Ken Swofford, Jesse White, Vanessa Brown.

Stanley Kramer's heavy-handed allegory is about as subtle as a brick through a plate-glass window. A group of misfit teenagers at a western ranch-resort rebel against their moronic counselors to save a nearby herd of buffalo from being slaughtered. A major waste of a good cast and an intriguing premise. Rated R for explicit violence. 1972; 109m.

BLIND HUSBANDS ★★★
DIR: Erich Von Stroheim. **CAST:** Sam de Grasse, Francis Billington, Erich Von Stroheim, Gibson Gowland.

A doctor and his wife are in an Alpine village so that he can do some mountain climbing. His wife falls prey to the attentions of a suave Austrian army officer who seduces her. The doctor and the officer go climbing together. In addition to directing and starring, Erich Von Stroheim adapted the screenplay from his own story and designed the sets. A shocker when first released. Silent. 1919; B&W; 98m.

BLOCKHOUSE, THE ★
DIR: Clive Rees. **CAST:** Peter Sellers, Charles Aznavour, Peter Vaughan, Jeremy Kemp.
Set during World War II, this hideous drama follows the exploits of a group of workers who become trapped in a German army bunker as the Allies invade France. Depressing, dull, and for the most part inept. 1973; 90m.

BLONDE ICE ★★
DIR: Jack Bernhard. **CAST:** Leslie Brooks, Robert Paige, Walter Sands, John Holland, James Griffith.
Odd, obscure melodrama about an unbalanced woman who makes a career of killing her husbands and boyfriends because she likes the attention she gets. (Not to mention the money.) Another long-forgotten curiosity revived for video. 1949; 73m.

BLONDE VENUS ★
DIR: Josef von Sternberg. **CAST:** Marlene Dietrich, Cary Grant, Herbert Marshall.
This is a rambling, incomprehensible piece of glitzy fluff. Only diehard fans of Marlene Dietrich will find it worth watching. In this, we witness Miss Dietrich descend from being a loving wife to becoming involved in distasteful activities because she must pay the medical costs for her sick husband. Ludicrous. 1932; B&W; 90m.

BLOOD AND SAND ★★★
DIR: Rouben Mamoulian. **CAST:** Tyrone Power, Rita Hayworth, Anthony Quinn, Linda Darnell, Nazimova, John Carradine.
The "Moment of Truth" is not always just before the matador places his sword, as Tyrone Power learns in this classic story of a poor boy who rises to fame in the bullring. Linda Darnell loves him, Rita Hayworth leads him on, in this colorful remake of a 1922 Valentino starrer. 1941; 123m.

BLOOD MONEY ★★★
DIR: Rowland Brown. **CAST:** George Bancroft, Frances Dee, Judith Anderson, Chick Chandler, Blossom Seeley.
This highly engaging film features an excellent cast in a story about an underworld bail-bondsman who falls for a thrill-seeking socialite. His life becomes complicated by another female cohort. 1933; B&W; 65m.

BLOOD OF OTHERS, THE 💔
DIR: Claude Chabrol. **CAST:** Jodie Foster, Sam Neill, Michael Ontkean, John Vernon, Kate Reid.
Jodie Foster is terribly miscast as a fashion designer in France during the German occupation of World War II. She plays both sides of the fence in this dull, plodding film. Inane plot, empty performances, inept direction, terrible dialogue, and stupid stereotypes all add up to a bloody bore. Not rated, but equivalent to a PG for violence and adult situations. 1984; 130m.

BLOOD TIES ★
DIR: Giacomo Battiato. **CAST:** Brad Davis, Tony Lo Bianco, Vincent Spano, Barbara de Rossi, Ricky Tognazzi, Michael Gazzo.
Brad Davis and Tony LoBianco are wasted in this pointless ripoff of *The Godfather*. Davis is an innocent American engineer blackmailed into assassinating his cousin, an anticrime justice in Sicily. Bad writing and bad direction are the culprits. Not rated, but contains strong language, violence, and nudity. 1987; 98m.

BLOOD VOWS: THE STORY OF A MAFIA WIFE ★★★½
DIR: Paul Wendkos. **CAST:** Melissa Gilbert, Joe Penny, Talia Shire, Eileen Brennan.
A fairy-tale romance between a beautiful orphan (Melissa Gilbert) and a dashing lawyer (Joe Penny) results in a nightmarish prison for her after they marry. It seems his clan needs him back home for a war between mafia families and she can't deal with the violence or the restrictions put on mob women. Some chilling moments. Originally shown as a TV movie. 1987; 104m.

BLOODBROTHERS ★★★½
DIR: Robert Mulligan. **CAST:** Richard Gere, Paul Sorvino, Tony Lo Bianco, Marilu Henner.
Richard Gere and Marilu Henner take top honors in this drama. Plot revolves around a family of construction workers and the son (Gere) who wants to do something else with his life. Rated R. 1978; 116m.

BLOODLINE 🦃
DIR: Terence Young. **CAST:** Audrey Hepburn, Ben Gazzara, James Mason, Omar Sharif.
This is an inexcusably repulsive montage of bad taste, predictability, and incoherence. Fans of Audrey Hepburn will be sickened to see her in such a travesty. Rated R for graphic sex scenes. 1979; 116m.

BLUE COLLAR ★★★★½
DIR: Paul Schrader. **CAST:** Richard Pryor, Harvey Keitel, Yaphet Kotto.
This film delves into the underbelly of the auto industry by focusing on the fears, frustrations, and suppressed anger of three factory workers, superbly played by Richard Pryor, Harvey Keitel, and Yaphet Kotto. It is the social comment and intense drama that make this a highly effective and memorable film. Good music, too. Rated R for violence, sex, nudity, and profanity. 1978; 114m.

BLUE HEAVEN ★
DIR: Kathleen Dowdey. **CAST:** Leslie Denniston, James Eckhouse.
This slow-paced drama depicts a New York TV executive whose job and marriage are threatened by a severe problem with alcohol. After several brutal beatings, his young wife is forced to leave him. This film lacks plot and originality. Not rated, but contains violence and strong language. 1984; 100m.

BLUE HOTEL ★★
DIR: Ján Kadár. **CAST:** David Warner, James Keach, John Bottoms, Rex Everhart.
Unsatisfying interpretation of Stephen Crane's short story. David Warner chews the scenery as a stranger in town who fears his life will be taken by the other guests of the hotel he occupies. The entire silly affair, which flirts with the notion of predestination, revolves around a card game. Introduced by Henry Fonda; unrated and suitable for family viewing. 1984; 55m.

BLUE KNIGHT, THE (1973) ★★★½
DIR: Robert Butler. **CAST:** William Holden, Lee Remick, Joe Santos, Sam Elliott, David Moody, Jamie Farr.
William Holden gives an excellent, Emmy-winning performance as the hero of Joseph Wambaugh's bestselling novel. *The Blue Knight* chronicles the last four days in the life of an aging L.A. street cop who pursues a sadistic killer responsible for the murder of a prostitute. Lee Remick is superb as Holden's girlfriend. Originally made for television and cut down from a four-part, 200-minute presentation. Not rated. 1973; 103m.

BLUE KNIGHT, THE (1975) ★★
DIR: J. Lee Thompson. **CAST:** George Kennedy, Alex Rocco, Verna Bloom, Glynn Turman.
This is the second made-for-TV production based on Joseph Wambaugh's bestselling book. In this rendering, George Kennedy assumes the role of tough L.A. cop Bumper Morgan, who is searching frantically for a cop killer. The story is average, but Kennedy gives a typically strong portrayal. 1975; 78m.

BLUE LAGOON, THE ★★½
DIR: Randal Kleiser. **CAST:** Brooke Shields, Christopher Atkins, Leo McKern, William Daniels.
Two things save *The Blue Lagoon* from being a complete waste: Nestor Almendros's beautiful cinematography and the hilarious dialogue. Unfortunately, the laughs are unintentional. The screenplay is a combination of *Swiss Family Robinson* and the story of Adam and Eve, focusing on the

growing love and sexuality of two children stranded on a South Sea island. Rated R for nudity and suggested sex. 1980; 101m.

BLUE SKIES AGAIN ★★

DIR: Richard Michaels. **CAST:** Harry Hamlin, Robyn Barto, Mimi Rogers, Kenneth McMillan, Dana Elcar.

A sure-fielding, solid-hitting prospect tries to break into the lineup of a minor league team. There's just one problem: The determined ballplayer is a female. This "triumph of the underdog" story, set on a baseball diamond, aims at the skies but is nothing more than a routine grounder. Rated PG. 1983; 96m.

BLUME IN LOVE ★★★★

DIR: Paul Mazursky. **CAST:** George Segal, Susan Anspach, Kris Kristofferson, Marsha Mason, Shelley Winters.

Sort of the male version of *An Unmarried Woman*, this Paul Mazursky film is the heartrending, sometimes shocking tale of a lawyer (George Segal) who can't believe his wife (Susan Anspach) doesn't love him anymore. He tries everything to win her back (including rape), and the result is a drama the viewer won't soon forget. Superb performances by Segal, Anspach, and Kris Kristofferson (as the wife's new beau) help immensely. Rated R for suggested sex, profanity, and violence. 1973; 117m.

BOBBY DEERFIELD ★★★½

DIR: Sydney Pollack. **CAST:** Al Pacino, Marthe Keller, Romolo Valli.

In this film, a racing driver (Al Pacino) becomes obsessed with the cause of how a competitor was seriously injured in an accident on the track. In a visit to the hospitalized driver, he meets a strange lady (Marthe Keller) and has an affair. Rated PG. 1977; 124m.

BODY AND SOUL (1947) ★★★★★

DIR: Robert Rossen. **CAST:** John Garfield, Lilli Palmer, Hazel Brooks, Anne Revere, William Conrad.

The best boxing film ever, this is an allegorical work that covers everything from the importance of personal honor to corruption in politics. It details the story of a fighter (John Garfield) who'll do anything to get to the top—and does, with tragic results. Great performances, gripping drama, and stark realism make this a must-see. 1947; B&W; 104m.

BODY AND SOUL (1981) ★★★

DIR: George Bowers. **CAST:** Leon Isaac Kennedy, Jayne Kennedy, Perry Lang.

Okay remake of the 1947 boxing classic. It's not original, deep, or profound, but entertaining, and for a movie like this, that's enough. However, the original, with John Garfield, is better. Rated R for violence and profanity. 1981; 100m.

BODY HEAT ★★★★½

DIR: Lawrence Kasdan. **CAST:** William Hurt, Kathleen Turner, Richard Crenna, Mickey Rourke.

This is a classic piece of *film noir*; full of suspense, characterization, atmosphere, and sexuality. Lawrence Kasdan makes his directorial debut with this top-flight 1940s-style entertainment about a lustful romance between an attorney (William Hurt) and a married woman (Kathleen Turner) that leads to murder. Rated R because of nudity, sex, and murder. 1981; 113m.

BOGIE ★★½

DIR: Vincent Sherman. **CAST:** Kevin J. O'Connor, Kathryn Harrold, Ann Wedgeworth, Patricia Barry.

Boring biography of Humphrey Bogart unconvincingly enacted by Bogie and Bacall look-alikes. Too much time is spent on the drinking and temper problems of Bogie's third wife, Mayo Methot, and not enough time is spent on Lauren Bacall. Kathryn Harrold, as Bacall, is so bad, however, that it's probably a blessing her part is small. 1980; 100m.

BOLERO (1984)
DIR: John Derek. **CAST:** Bo Derek, George Kennedy, Andrea Occhipinti, Ana Obregon, Olivia D'Abo.
Bo Derek stars in this simply awful soft-core porno flick as an American heiress in the 1920s trying to lose her viginity. What follows is stupid, boring, and amateurish. Unrated, the film has explicit sex, profanity, and nudity. 1984; 106m.

BONJOUR TRISTESSE ★★★
DIR: Otto Preminger. **CAST:** Deborah Kerr, David Niven, Jean Seberg, Mylene Demongeot.
Jean Seberg is a spoiled teenager who tries to ruin the affair between her widowed father (David Niven) and his mistress (Deborah Kerr) in this dated soap opera. Kerr gives a fine performance and Niven is just right as the suave playboy, but Otto Preminger failed again to make a star of Seberg. Not rated. 1958; 94m.

BOOST, THE ★★
DIR: Harold Becker. **CAST:** James Woods, Sean Young, Steven Hill.
The controversy surrounding the off-screen, *Fatal Attraction*-style relationship between James Woods and Sean Young is certainly more interesting than the movie itself. Woods gives a typically high-powered performance in this uncomfortably intense drama as a Beverly Hills investment broker who begins to use cocaine to keep up his energy level and predictably loses control. The story lacks coherence. Rated R for nudity, profanity and drug use. 1989; 96m.

BORDER RADIO ★
DIR: Allison Anders, Dean Lent, Kurt Voss. **CAST:** Chris D., Luana Anders.
A disillusioned rock star steals a large sum of performance money owed to him by a sleazy club owner. With three thugs and a record producer hot on his heels, he splits to Mexico. An attempt at cult filmmaking in the style of *Stranger than Paradise*, this movie achieves something closer to the campy excesses of John Waters. Not rated, but contains profanity and violence. 1988; B&W; 89m.

BORN AGAIN
DIR: Irving Rapper. **CAST:** Dean Jones, Anne Francis, Jay Robinson, Dana Andrews.
This is a shallow, ponderous, and pandering account of the religious "rebirth" of President Nixon's special council Charles Colson. Inspirational it's supposed to be. Dull and phony is what it is. Rated PG. 1978; 110m.

BORN INNOCENT ★★★
DIR: Donald Wyre. **CAST:** Linda Blair, Kim Hunter, Joanna Miles.
Rape with a broomstick marked this made-for-television film a shocker when first aired. The scene has been toned down, but the picture still penetrates with its searing story of cruelty in a juvenile detention home. Linda Blair does well as the runaway teenager. Joanna Miles is excellent as a compassionate teacher whose heart lies with her charges. It's strong stuff. 1974; 100m.

BORN OF FIRE ★★
DIR: Jamil Dehlaui. **CAST:** Peter Firth, Suzan Crowley, Stefan Kalipha.
A classical concert flutist (Peter Firth) journeys to the Middle East in hopes of finding the reason for his father's death. The flutist only becomes embroiled in the same drama that befell his father. A boring, confusing story. Contains sex, nudity, and violence. 1987; 84m.

BORN TO KILL ★★★½
DIR: Robert Wise. **CAST:** Lawrence Tierney, Claire Trevor, Walter Slezak, Elisha Cook Jr., Audrey Long, Phillip Terry.
Tough film about two bad apples whose star-crossed love brings them both nothing but grief is one of the best examples of American *film noir*. Lawrence Tierney's aggressive pursuit of his wife's sister (Claire Trevor) defies description. This hard-boiled crime melodrama is an early surprise

from director Robert Wise. 1947; B&W; 97m.

BOSS' SON, THE ★★★

DIR: Bobby Roth. **CAST:** Asher Brauner, Rita Moreno, Rudy Solari, Henry G. Sanders, James Darren, Piper Laurie.

Enjoyable drama about a young man's passage to adulthood. Our hero jumps at the chance to follow in his father's footsteps and run the family factory. But when Dad decides his son must earn his way to the top, the boy learns what it truly means to earn a living. A little slow but rewarding. Unrated. 1978; 102m.

BOSTONIANS, THE ★★★

DIR: James Ivory. **CAST:** Christopher Reeve, Vanessa Redgrave, Jessica Tandy, Madeleine Potter, Nancy Marchand, Wesley Addy, Linda Hunt, Nancy New, Jon Van Ness, Wallace Shawn.

A visually striking but dry production from Merchant Ivory Productions. Most of the sparks of conflict come not from the tortured love affair between Christopher Reeve and Madeleine Potter or the main theme of women's fight for equality, but from the few scenes of direct confrontation between Reeve and Vanessa Redgrave. The setting is Boston during the Centennial. 1984; 120m.

BOULEVARD NIGHTS ★★

DIR: Michael Pressman. **CAST:** Richard Yniguez, Marta Du Bois, Danny De La Paz, Carmen Zapata, Victor Millan.

Well-intentioned but dramatically dull account of a Chicano youth's desire to break out of East Los Angeles. Richard Yniguez is sincere in the lead role and Danny De La Paz is sympathetic as his brother, but the whole thing comes across like a preachy soap opera. Rated R for violence and profanity. 1979; 102m.

BOUND FOR GLORY ★★★★

DIR: Hal Ashby. **CAST:** David Carradine, Ronny Cox, Melinda Dillon, Randy Quaid, Gail Strickland, Ji-Tu Cumbuka, John Lehne.

David Carradine had one of the best roles of his career as singer-composer Woody Guthrie. Film focuses on the depression years when Guthrie rode the rails across America. Director Hal Ashby explores the lives of those hit hardest during those times. Haskell Wexler won the Oscar for his beautiful cinematography. Rated PG. 1976; 147m.

BOXOFFICE ★½

DIR: Josef Bogdanovich. **CAST:** Robin Clark, Monica Lewis, Carole Cortne, Eddie Constantine, Aldo Ray, Edie Adams, Peter Hurkos.

Bizarre movie tracing the career of Eve Chandler (Carole Cortne) from lousy nightclubs to the big time. Unfortunately the acting and writing aren't up to the striking cinematography. Not rated, but contains language and nudity. 1981; 92m.

BOY IN BLUE, THE ★★★

DIR: Charles Jarrott. **CAST:** Nicolas Cage, Christopher Plummer, Cynthia Dale, David Naughton.

Nice little screen biography of Ned Hanlan (Nicolas Cage), the famed Canadian lad who owned the sport of international sculling (rowing) for ten years during the end of the nineteenth century. Although the picture plays like a thin retread of *Rocky*—particularly with respect to its music—the result is no less inspirational. Inexplicably rated R for very brief nudity and coarse language. 1986; 97m.

BOY IN THE PLASTIC BUBBLE, THE ★

DIR: Randal Kleiser. **CAST:** John Travolta, Glynnis O'Connor, Ralph Bellamy, Robert Reed, Diana Hyland, Buzz Aldrin.

John Travolta has his hands full in this significantly altered television adaptation of the boy who, because of an immunity deficiency, must spend every breathing moment in a sealed environment. Vapid stuff needlessly mired with sci-fi jargon and an embarrassing romance with Glynnis O'Connor. Considering the heroic struggles of the true David (who was much younger), this film is a grotesque insult. Unrated. 1976; 100m.

BOY WHO COULD FLY, THE ★★★★

DIR: Nick Castle. **CAST:** Lucy Deakins, Jay Underwood, Bonnie Bedelia, Fred Savage, Colleen Dewhurst, Fred Gwynne, Mindy Cohn.

Writer-director Nick Castle has created a marvelous motion picture which speaks to the dreamer in all of us. His heroine, Milly (Lucy Deakins), is a newcomer to a small town where her neighbor, Eric (Jay Underwood), neither speaks nor responds to other people. All he does is sit on his roof and pretend to fly. Rated PG for dramatic intensity. 1986; 114m.

BOY WITH GREEN HAIR, THE ★★★

DIR: Joseph Losey. **CAST:** Dean Stockwell, Robert Ryan, Barbara Hale, Pat O'Brien.

A young war orphan's hair changes color, makes him a social outcast, and brings a variety of bigots and narrow minds out of the woodwork in this food-for-thought fable. The medium is the message in this one. 1948; 82m.

BOYS IN THE BAND, THE ★★★

DIR: William Friedkin. **CAST:** Kenneth Nelson, Peter White, Leonard Frey, Cliff Gorman.

Widely acclaimed film about nine men who attend a birthday party and end up exposing their lives and feelings to one another in the course of the night. Eight of the men are gay; one is straight. One of the first American films to deal honestly with the subject of homosexuality. Sort of a large-scale *My Dinner with André* with the whole film shot on one set. Rated R. 1970; 119m.

BOYS NEXT DOOR, THE ★★★

DIR: Penelope Spheeris. **CAST:** Charlie Sheen, Maxwell Caulfield, Hank Garrett, Patti D'Arbanville, Christopher McDonald, Moon Zappa.

This story of two alienated teenage youths, Charlie Sheen and Maxwell Caulfield, going on a killing spree in Los Angeles, makes for some tense viewing. Having been rejected by their peers, Sheen and Caulfield decide to go to L.A. for the weekend before graduation. Once in the city, things turn ugly as one violent encounter spawns another. Beware: This one is extremely graphic in its depiction of violence. Rated R. 1985; 88m.

BOYS' TOWN ★★★★

DIR: Norman Taurog. **CAST:** Spencer Tracy, Mickey Rooney, Henry Hull.

Spencer Tracy gives one of his most memorable performances in this MGM classic about Father Flanagan and his struggle to give orphans and juvenile delinquents a chance at life. Overtly manipulative, but rewarding. 1938; B&W; 93m.

BRAINWASHED ★★½

DIR: Gerd Oswald. **CAST:** Curt Jurgens, Claire Bloom, Hansjor Felmy, Albert Lieven.

Disquieting psychological thriller about a man who is imprisoned by Nazis during World War II. Story documents his struggle to remain rational while being brainwashed by his captors. 1961; 102m.

BRASS ★★

DIR: Corey Allen. **CAST:** Carroll O'Connor, Lois Nettleton, Jimmy Baio, Paul Shenar.

Routine made-for-TV cop thriller starring Carroll O'Connor as a top New York City police officer caught between the City Hall brass and a politically sensitive kidnap-murder case. The pilot for a proposed series. 1985; 94m.

BREAKFAST AT TIFFANY'S ★★★★

DIR: Blake Edwards. **CAST:** Audrey Hepburn, George Peppard, Patricia Neal, Buddy Ebsen, Mickey Rooney, Martin Balsam.

An offbeat yet tender love story of a New York writer and a fey party girl. Strong performances are turned in by George Peppard and Audrey Hepburn. Hepburn's Holly Golightly is a masterful creation that blends the sophistication of her job as a Manhattan "escort" with the childish country girl of her roots. Henry Mancini's score is justly famous, as it creates much of the mood for this wistful story. 1961; 115m.

BREATHLESS (1983)
DIR: Jim McBride. **CAST:** Richard Gere, Valerie Kaprisky, Art Metrano, John P. Ryan.
In this rambling, repulsive remake of Jean-Luc Godard's 1961 French film classic, Richard Gere plays a car thief hunted by police, and Valerie Kaprisky is the college student who is both attracted and repelled by the danger he represents. Watching these two aimless, amoral jerks fooling around for nearly two hours is not the proverbial good time at the movies. Rated R for sex, nudity, profanity, and violence. 1983; 100m.

BRIAN'S SONG ★★★★★
DIR: Buzz Kulik. **CAST:** James Caan, Billy Dee Williams, Jack Warden, Judy Pace, Shelley Fabares.
This is one of the best movies ever made originally for television. James Caan is Brian Piccolo, a running back for football's Chicago Bears. His friendship for superstar Gale Sayers (Billy Dee Williams) becomes a mutually stimulating rivalry on the field and inspirational strength when Brian is felled by cancer. As with any quality film that deals with death, this movie is buoyant with life and warmth. Rated G. 1970; 73m.

BRIDESHEAD REVISITED ★★★★
DIR: Charles Sturridge, Michael Lindsay-Hogg. **CAST:** Jeremy Irons, Anthony Andrews, Diana Quick, Laurence Olivier, Claire Bloom, John Gielgud, Stéphane Audran, Mona Washbourne, John Le Mesurier, Simon Jones.
Evelyn Waugh's massive novel of British upper-class decadence gets royal treatment in this adaptation from John Mortimer (*Rumpole of the Bailey*), who captures every nuance of Waugh's often scathing indictment of the wealthy. Jeremy Irons stars as the impressionable Oxford youth bedazzled by Sebastian Flyte (Anthony Andrews), youngest of the ill-fated Marchmain family. Irons quickly falls in love with this odd group, but their embrace nearly proves more than he can handle. Unrated; includes frank sexual themes and brief nudity. 1981; 388m.

BRIDGE AT REMAGEN, THE ★★★
DIR: John Guillermin. **CAST:** George Segal, Ben Gazzara, Robert Vaughn, E. G. Marshall, Bradford Dillman, Peter Van Eyck.
Solid World War II drama concerns the German attempt to hold or blow up one of the last remaining bridges leading into the fatherland. Well-done action sequences keep things moving along at a good pace. Not a great film, but it should fill the bill for fans of the genre. 1969; 115m.

BRIDGE OF SAN LUIS REY, THE ★★½
DIR: Rowland V. Lee. **CAST:** Lynn Bari, Nazimova, Louis Calhern, Akim Tamiroff, Francis Lederer, Blanche Yurka, Donald Woods.
Five people meet death when an old Peruvian rope bridge collapses. This snail's-pace, moody version of Thornton Wilder's fatalistic 1920s novel traces their lives. Not too hot, and neither was the 1929 version. 1944; B&W; 85m.

BRIDGE TO NOWHERE ★★½
DIR: Ian Mune. **CAST:** Bruno Lawrence, Alison Routledge, Margaret Umbers, Philip Gordon.
When five street-wise city kids head to the rough-and-rugged country for a fun-filled weekend, they are not prepared to end up fighting for their lives. Once they trespass on the land

of an extremely vicious and violent man (Bruno Lawrence), they are forced to fight for survival. Parental discretion advised. 1986; 87m.

BRIEF ENCOUNTER (1945) ★★★★½

DIR: David Lean. **CAST:** Celia Johnson, Trevor Howard, Stanley Holloway, Joyce Carey, Cyril Raymond.

In this evergreen classic, a chance meeting in a railroad station results in a doomed, poignant love affair between two lonely people married to others. Celia Johnson is the woman, Trevor Howard the man. A compassionate look at the innocence of sudden, unforeseen romance. David Lean's direction results in a moving, memorable film for all time. 1945; B&W; 85m.

BRIEF ENCOUNTER (1974) ★★½

DIR: Alan Bridges. **CAST:** Richard Burton, Sophia Loren.

This is a remake of the 1946 classic film that was based on Noel Coward's play *Still Life*. It tells the story of two married strangers who meet in a British train terminal and fall into a short-lived but intense romance. This made-for-television production suffers in comparison. 1974; 103m.

BRIGHT LIGHTS, BIG CITY ★

DIR: James Bridges. **CAST:** Michael J. Fox, Kiefer Sutherland, Phoebe Cates, Swoosie Kurtz, Frances Sternhagen, John Houseman, Jason Robards Jr., Dianne Wiest, William Hickey.

Films grappling with the evils of substance abuse run the risk of glamorizing the subject they intend to criticize, and that is precisely the problem with this abysmal adaptation of Jay McInerney's novel (even though he wrote his own screenplay). The supporting cast is excellent, but star Michael J. Fox simply cannot carry this vehicle. Rated R for language and graphic drug emphasis. 1988; 110m.

BROKEN BLOSSOMS ★★★½

DIR: D. W. Griffith. **CAST:** Lillian Gish, Richard Barthelmess, Donald Crisp.

The tragic story of a young Chinese boy's unselfish love for a cruelly mistreated white girl. Lillian Gish is heart-twisting as the girl; Richard Barthelmess's portrayal of the Chinese boy made him an overnight star. Donald Crisp, later famous in warm and sympathetic roles, is the unfortunate girl's evil tormentor. Trivia note: This is the first film made and released by United Artists. Silent. 1919; B&W; 68m.

BROTHER JOHN ★★

DIR: James Goldstone. **CAST:** Sidney Poitier, Paul Winfield, Will Geer, Beverly Todd, Bradford Dillman.

In this not-so-heavenly melodrama, Sidney Poitier stars as an angel who returns to his Alabama hometown to see how things are going. He steps into bigotry and labor troubles. Not one of Poitier's best. Rated PG. 1971; 94m.

BROTHER SUN, SISTER MOON ★★★★

DIR: Franco Zeffirelli. **CAST:** Graham Faulkner, Judi Bowker, Alec Guinness.

Alec Guinness stars as the Pope in this movie about religious reformation. This film shows a young Francis of Assisi starting his own church. He confronts the Pope and rejects the extravagant and pompous ceremonies of the Catholic Church, preferring simple religious practices. Rated PG. 1973; 121m.

BROTHERHOOD, THE ★★

DIR: Martin Ritt. **CAST:** Kirk Douglas, Alex Cord, Irene Papas, Luther Adler, Susan Strasberg, Murray Hamilton.

A *Godfather* predecessor, *The Brotherhood* stars Kirk Douglas and Alex Cord as Italian brothers who inherit their father's criminal empire. Douglas doesn't make a convincing Italian, but the story is good and overcomes the poor casting and cinematography.

Not rated, contains violence and mild profanity. 1968; 96m.

BROTHERS KARAMAZOV, THE ★★★
DIR: Richard Brooks. **CAST:** Yul Brynner, Claire Bloom, Lee J. Cobb, Maria Schell, Richard Basehart, William Shatner, Albert Salmi.

Director Richard Brooks, who also scripted, and a fine cast work hard to give life to Russian novelist Fyodor Dostoyevsky's turgid account of the effect of the death of a domineering father on his disparate sons: a fun-lover, a scholar, a religious zealot, and an epileptic. Studio promotion called it absorbing and exciting. It is, but only in flashes. 1957; 146m.

BRUBAKER ★★★
DIR: Stuart Rosenberg. **CAST:** Robert Redford, Yaphet Kotto, Jane Alexander, Murray Hamilton.

Robert Redford stars as Henry Brubaker, a reform-minded penologist who takes over a decrepit Ohio prison, only to discover the state prison system is even more rotten than its facilities. The film begins dramatically enough, with Redford arriving undercover at the prison, masquerading as one of the convicts. After that, its dramatic impact lessens. Rated R. 1980; 132m.

BUDDY SYSTEM, THE ★★
DIR: Glenn Jordan. **CAST:** Richard Dreyfuss, Susan Sarandon, Nancy Allen, Wil Wheaton.

In the middle of this movie, the would-be novelist (Richard Dreyfuss) takes his unbound manuscripts to the edge of the sea and lets the wind blow the pages away. He should have done the same thing with the screenplay for this mediocre romantic comedy. The plot is that old chestnut about a fatherless little kid (Wil Wheaton) who helps his mom (Susan Sarandon) and an eligible man (Dreyfuss) get together. Rated PG for profanity. 1984; 110m.

BURKE AND WILLS ★★
DIR: Graeme Clifford. **CAST:** Jack Thompson, Nigel Travers, Greta Scacchi.

Like most Australian period movies, this historical drama about a failed attempt to travel through the uncharted interior of 19th century Australia is meticulously produced. But the story follows the trip through the desert with numbing detail and it ends up being more exhausting than entertaining. It's also about 45 minutes too long. It's rated PG-13 for language and brief nudity. 1987; 140m.

BURN! ★★★★
DIR: Gillo Pontecorvo. **CAST:** Marlon Brando, Evaristo Marquez, Renato Salvatori.

Marlon Brando's performance alone makes *Burn!* worth watching. Seldom has a star so vividly and memorably lived up to his promise as an acting great, and that's what makes this film a must-see. Brando plays Sir William Walker, an egotistical mercenary sent by the British to instigate a slave revolt on a Portuguese-controlled sugar-producing island. He succeeds all too well by turning José Dolores (Evaristo Marquez) into a powerful leader and soon finds himself back on the island, plotting the downfall of his Frankenstein monster. Rated PG. 1969; 112m.

BURNING BED, THE ★★★★
DIR: Robert Greenwald. **CAST:** Farrah Fawcett, Paul LeMat, Richard Masur, Grace Zabriskie.

Farrah Fawcett is remarkably good in this made-for-TV film based on a true story. She plays a woman reaching the breaking point with her abusive and brutish husband, well played by Paul LeMat. Fawcett not only proves she can act, but that she has the capacity to pull off a multilayered role. Believable from start to finish, this is a superior television film. 1985; 105m.

BURNING SECRET ★★
DIR: Andrew Birkin. **CAST:** Faye Dunaway, Klaus Maria Brandauer.

A cool, overly restrained mystery-romance, set in an Austrian health spa in the years between the world wars. Faye Dunaway and Klaus Maria Brandauer star as emotionally crippled strangers who meet when Brandauer befriends her young son. They then carry out a game of seduction that is remarkably short on passion. Rated PG. 1988; 110m.

BUS IS COMING, THE ★★★
DIR: Wendell J. Franklin. **CAST:** Mike Sims, Stephanie Faulkner, Burl Bullock.

The message of this production is: racism (both black and white) is wrong. In this film, Billy Mitchell (Mike Sims) is a young black soldier who returns to his hometown after his brother is murdered. Billy's white friend encourages him to investigate the death of his brother, while his black friends want to tear the town down. The acting is not the greatest, but the film does succeed in making its point. Rated PG for violence. 1971; 102m.

BUSTED UP ★★½
DIR: Conrad E. Palmisano. **CAST:** Irene Cara, Paul Coufos, Tony Rosato, Stan Shaw.

A story about a local-circuit barefisted fighter and a nightclub singer. The neighborhood is being targeted by some big-money boys trying to buy up all the property. Typical plot, average acting, but professionally produced and technically polished. Rated R for violence and language. 1986; 93m.

BUSTER ★★★
DIR: David Green. **CAST:** Phil Collins, Julie Walters, Sheila Hancock.

Pop star Phil Collins makes his film debut in this enjoyable story about the British Great Train Robbery of 1963. Collins is Buster Edwards, who became a folk hero after he and his cronies pulled off the greatest robbery in the history of England. It's enjoyable and an interesting character study. Rated R for language and brief nudity. 1988; 93m.

BUSTER AND BILLIE ★★
DIR: Daniel Petrie. **CAST:** Jan-Michael Vincent, Joan Goodfellow, Pamela Sue Martin, Clifton James.

A handsome high-school boy falls in love with a homely but loving girl in the rural South. Set in the 1940s, the film has an innocent, sweet quality until it abruptly shifts tone and turns into a mean-spirited revenge picture. Rated R for violence and nudity. 1974; 100m.

BUTTERFIELD 8 ★★★
DIR: Daniel Mann. **CAST:** Elizabeth Taylor, Laurence Harvey, Eddie Fisher, Dina Merrill, Mildred Dunnock, Betty Field.

Severe illness helped sway votes her way when Elizabeth Taylor copped an Oscar for her by-the-numbers portrayal of a big-ticket call girl who wants to go straight after finding someone she thinks is Mr. Right. Adapted from the John O'Hara novel. 1960; 109m.

BUTTERFLIES ARE FREE ★★★★
DIR: Milton Katselas. **CAST:** Goldie Hawn, Edward Albert, Eileen Heckart, Mike Warren.

Edward Albert is a blind youth determined to be self-sufficient in spite of his overbearing mother and the distraction of his will-o'-the-wisp next-door neighbor (Goldie Hawn). This fast-paced comedy benefits from some outstanding performances, none better than that by Eileen Heckart. Her concerned, protective, and sometimes overloving mother is a treasure to behold. Rated PG. 1972; 109m.

BUTTERFLY ★★
DIR: Matt Climber. **CAST:** Pia Zadora, Stacy Keach, Orson Welles, Lois Nettleton.

Sex symbol Pia Zadora starts an incestuous relationship with her father (played by Stacy Keach). Orson Welles, as a judge, is the best thing about this film. Rated R. 1982; 107m.

CABIN IN THE SKY ★★★

DIR: Vincente Minnelli. **CAST:** Eddie Anderson, Lena Horne, Ethel Waters, Rex Ingram, Louis Armstrong.

One of Hollywood's first general-release black films and Vincente Minnelli's first feature. Eddie Anderson shows acting skill that was sadly and too long diluted by his playing foil for Jack Benny. Ethel Waters, as always, is superb. The film is a shade racist, but bear in mind that it was made in 1943, when Tinsel Town still thought blacks did nothing but sing, dance, and love watermelon. 1943; B&W; 100m.

CACTUS ★★★½

DIR: Paul Cox. **CAST:** Isabelle Huppert, Robert Menzies, Norman Kaye.

Have patience with this warm and witty tale of a French lady (Isabelle Huppert), who is injured in an auto accident while visiting friends in Australia. She meets a young blind man who helps her adjust to her diminishing eyesight. The supporting cast and Australian locale add to this story of growth and awareness. 1986; 96m.

CADDIE ★★★★

DIR: Donald Crombie. **CAST:** Helen Morse, Takis Emmanuel, Jack Thompson, Jacki Weaver.

This is an absorbing character study of a woman who struggles to support herself and her children in Australia in the 1920s. Thanks greatly to the star's performance, it is yet another winner from Down Under. MPAA unrated, but contains mild sexual situations. 1976; 107m.

CAESAR AND CLEOPATRA ★½

DIR: Gabriel Pascal. **CAST:** Claude Rains, Vivien Leigh, Stewart Granger, Francis L. Sullivan, Flora Robson.

George Bernard Shaw's wordy play about Rome's titanic leader and Egypt's young queen. Claude Rains and Vivien Leigh are brilliant, but talk alone does not save the film from slowly sinking into the sands surrounding the Sphinx. 1946; 127m.

CAINE MUTINY, THE ★★★★

DIR: Edward Dmytryk. **CAST:** Humphrey Bogart, José Ferrer, Van Johnson, Robert Francis, Fred MacMurray.

Superb performances by Humphrey Bogart, Van Johnson, José Ferrer, and Fred MacMurray, among others, make this adaptation of Herman Wouk's classic novel an absolute must-see. This brilliant film concerns the hard-nosed Captain Queeg (Bogart), who may or may not be slightly unhinged, and the subsequent mutiny by his first officer and crew, who are certain he is. Beautifully done, a terrific movie. 1954; 125m.

CAL ★★★★

DIR: Pat O'Connor. **CAST:** Helen Mirren, John Lynch, Donal McCann.

This superb Irish film, which focuses on "the troubles" in Northern Ireland, stars John Lynch as Cal, a teenage boy who wants to sever his ties with the IRA. This turns out to be anything but easy, as the leader tells him, if he isn't for them, he's against them. Cal hides out at the home of Marcella (Helen Mirren, in a knockout of a performance). She's the widow of a policeman he helped murder. Nevertheless, they fall in love. Rated R for sex, nudity, profanity, and violence. 1984; 102m.

CALIFORNIA DREAMING ★★

DIR: John Hancock. **CAST:** Glynnis O'Connor, Seymour Cassel, Dennis Christopher, Tanya Roberts.

Wimpy film about a dork from Chicago trying to fit into the California lifestyle. The cast is good, but the story is maudlin and slow-moving. Rated R for partial nudity. 1979; 93m.

CALIGULA

DIR: Tinto Brass. **CAST:** Malcolm McDowell, Peter O'Toole, Teresa Ann Savoy, Helen Mirren.

A $15 million porno flick with big stars, this is a disgusting historical piece that follows the ruthless Roman ruler through an endless series of decapitations and disembowelments.

Not satisfied with the amount of nudity and sex put into the film by director Tinto Brass, *Penthouse* magazine publisher and film producer Bob Guccione inserted other sex acts. Rated X for every excess imaginable. 1980; 156m.

CALL IT MURDER ★★★

DIR: Chester Erskine. **CAST:** Sidney Fox, Humphrey Bogart, Lynne Overman, Henry Hull, O. P. Heggie, Margaret Wycherly, Henry O'Neill, Richard Whorf.

An inflexible jury foreman casts the vote that sends a young girl to her death in the electric chair. Hounded by the press, he nevertheless says he would do it again—even if a loved one were involved. Then he learns his daughter has committed murder under the same circumstances. Originally released under the title *Midnight*. 1934; B&W; 73m.

CALL TO GLORY ★★★½

DIR: Thomas Carter. **CAST:** Craig T. Nelson, Cindy Pickett, Keenan Wynn, Elisabeth Shue, David Hollander.

Engrossing pilot episode for what was to be a short-lived TV series. Set in the early 1960s, it follows an Air Force officer's family through the events of the Kennedy presidency. The taut script ably balances the story of their struggle to deal with military life and still retains the flavor of a historical chronicle of the times. This uniformly well-acted and -directed opening show promised much quality that was unfortunately unfulfilled in later episodes. 1984; 97m.

CALLIE AND SON ★★½

DIR: Waris Hussein. **CAST:** Lindsay Wagner, Jameson Parker, Dabney Coleman, Andrew Prine, Michelle Pfeiffer, James Sloyan.

Syrupy drama about a poor waitress who becomes the queen of a Texas publishing empire. On the way, she is reunited with her long-lost son. Sometimes halfway engrossing; sometimes really disturbing. 1981; 150m.

CAMILLE ★★★★

DIR: George Cukor. **CAST:** Greta Garbo, Robert Taylor, Lionel Barrymore, Henry Daniell, Laura Hope Crews, Elizabeth Allan, Lenore Ulric, Jessie Ralph.

Metro-Goldwyn-Mayer's lavish production of the Dumas classic provided screen goddess Greta Garbo with one of her last unqualified successes and remains the consummate adaptation of this popular weeper. The combined magic of the studio and Garbo's presence legitimized this archaic creaker about a dying woman and her love affair with a younger man (Robert Taylor, soon to be one of MGM's biggest stars). 1936; B&W; 108m.

CAN YOU HEAR THE LAUGHTER? THE STORY OF FREDDIE PRINZE ★★½

DIR: Burt Brinckerhoff. **CAST:** Ira Angustain, Kevin Hooks, Randee Heller, Julie Carmen.

Freddie Prinze was a Puerto Rican comedian who rose from the barrio to television superstardom in a relatively brief time. His premiere achievement was a starring role in *Chico and The Man*, with Jack Albertson. This is a sympathetic handling of his story, but no punches are pulled on the facts surrounding his death. 1979; 106m.

CANDIDATE, THE ★★★½

DIR: Michael Ritchie. **CAST:** Robert Redford, Peter Boyle, Don Porter, Allen Garfield.

Michael Ritchie expertly directed this release, an incisive look at a political hopeful (Robert Redford) and the obstacles and truths he must confront on the campaign trail. Rated PG. 1972; 109m.

CANDY MOUNTAIN ★★★★

DIR: Robert Frank, Rudy Wurlitzer. **CAST:** Kevin J. O'Connor, Harris Yulin, Tom Waits, Bulle Ogier, David Johansen, Leon Redbone, Joe Strummer, Dr. John.

Mediocre musician Kevin J. O'Connor takes to the highway in search of a legendary guitar craftsman Elmore Silk. He encounters some eccentric characters who have populated Silk's past. Celebrated photographer and underground filmmaker Robert Frank joins screenwriter Rudy Wurlitzer to create an engaging, offbeat, visually beautiful film. Rated R for nudity and profanity. 1987; 90m.

CANDYMAN, THE
DIR: Herbert J. Leder. **CAST:** George Sanders, Leslie Parrish.
Terrible story of an English drug peddler (George Sanders) in Mexico City who plots to kidnap the child of an American movie star. A waste of a once great star. 1968; 98m.

CAPTAIN NEWMAN, M.D. ★★★
DIR: David Miller. **CAST:** Gregory Peck, Angie Dickinson, Tony Curtis, Eddie Albert, Jane Withers, Bobby Darin, Larry Storch.
The movie fluctuates between meaningful laughter and heavy drama. An excellent ensemble neatly maintains the balance. Gregory Peck is at his noble best as a sympathetic army psychiatrist. The film's most gripping performance comes from Bobby Darin, who plays a psychotic. 1963; 126m.

CAPTAINS COURAGEOUS ★★★★★
DIR: Victor Fleming. **CAST:** Spencer Tracy, Freddie Bartholomew, Lionel Barrymore, Melvyn Douglas, Mickey Rooney.
This is an exquisite adaptation of Rudyard Kipling's story about a spoiled rich kid who falls from an ocean liner and is rescued by fishermen. Through them, the lad learns about the rewards of hard work and genuine friendship. Spencer Tracy won a well-deserved best-actor Oscar for his performance as the fatherly fisherman. 1937; B&W; 116m.

CAPTIVE HEART ★★★★½
DIR: Basil Dearden. **CAST:** Michael Redgrave, Rachel Kempson, Basil Radford, Jack Warner.
Exciting, well-written, marvelously performed story that examines the plight of British POWs and their Nazi captors. A superior job by all involved. 1948; B&W; 108m.

CAPTIVE HEARTS ★★½
DIR: Paul Almond. **CAST:** Noriyuki "Pat" Morita, Chris Makepeace, Michael Sarrazin.
Quiet little drama about two bomber crewmen (Chris Makepeace and Michael Sarrazin) shot down over a small Japanese town in the waning days of World War II. Makepeace is in over his head with this role, but Pat Morita, as the village elder who adopts Makepeace, and Sarrazin, as Makepeace's abrasive and abusive chum, carry the picture. Rated PG for language and violence. 1988; 102m.

CARAVAGGIO ★★★★
DIR: Derek Jarman. **CAST:** Nigel Terry, Sean Bean, Tilda Swinton, Spencer Leigh, Michael Gough.
Derek Jarman's extraordinary and revealing film is based on the life and art of Caravaggio, perhaps the greatest of Italian post-Renaissance painters. This controversial biography explores the artist's life, which was troubled by extremes of passion and artistic radicalism. Not rated; contains nudity, profanity, and violence. 1986; 97m.

CARAVANS ★
DIR: James Fargo. **CAST:** Anthony Quinn, Michael Sarrazin, Jennifer O'Neill, Christopher Lee, Joseph Cotten, Barry Sullivan, Jeremy Kemp.
An American diplomat is sent to the Middle East to bring back the daughter of an American politician who has joined an Arab caravan. Weak plot, talky script. The performances are only passable. Rated PG. 1978; 123m.

CARDINAL, THE ★★★
DIR: Otto Preminger. **CAST:** Tom Tryon, Romy Schneider, Carol Lynley, John Huston.
Director Otto Preminger's epic view of a vital and caring young Catholic priest's rise from a backwoods clergyman to cardinal. Alternately compelling and shallow. Watch for the late Maggie McNamara in her last role. 1963; 175m.

CAREFUL HE MIGHT HEAR YOU ★★★★½
DIR: Carl Schultz. **CAST:** Robyn Nevin, Nicholas Gledhill, Wendy Hughes, John Hargreaves.
A child's-eye view of the harsh realities of life, this Australian import is a poignant, heartwarming, sad, and sometimes frightening motion picture. A young boy named P.S. (played by 7-year-old Nicholas Gledhill) gets caught up in a bitter custody fight between his two aunts. While the movie does tend to become a tearjerker on occasion, it does so without putting off the viewer. Rated PG for suggested sex and violence. 1983; 116m.

CARNAL KNOWLEDGE ★★★★
DIR: Mike Nichols. **CAST:** Jack Nicholson, Candice Bergen, Art Garfunkel, Ann-Margret.
The sexual dilemmas of the modern American are analyzed and come up short in this thoughtful film. Jack Nicholson and singer Art Garfunkel are college roommates whose lives are followed through varied relationships with the opposite sex. Nicholson is somewhat of a stinker, and one finds oneself more in sympathy with the women in the cast. Rated R. 1971; 96m.

CARNIVAL STORY ★½
DIR: Kurt Neumann. **CAST:** Anne Baxter, Steve Cochran, Jay C. Flippen, George Nader.
Familiar story of rivalry between circus performers over the affections of the girl they both love. No real surprises in this production, which was filmed in Germany on a limited budget, with the cast simply going through the motions. 1954; 95m.

CARNY ★★★★
DIR: Robert Kaylor. **CAST:** Gary Busey, Jodie Foster, Robbie Robertson, Meg Foster, Bert Remsen.
This film takes us behind the bright lights into the netherworld of the "carnies," people who spend their lives cheating, lying, and stealing from others yet consider themselves superior to their victims. Gary Busey, Jodie Foster, Robbie Robertson are all outstanding. The accent in *Carny* is on realism with disenchanted losers who live only from day to day. Rated R. 1980; 107m.

CARPETBAGGERS, THE ★★★
DIR: Edward Dmytryk. **CAST:** George Peppard, Alan Ladd, Audrey Totter, Carroll Baker, Robert Cummings, Lew Ayres, Martin Balsam, Archie Moore.
Howard Hughes–like millionaire George Peppard makes movies, love, and enemies in the Hollywood of the 1920s and 1930s. Alan Ladd, as a Tom Mix clone, helps in this, his last picture. Carroll Baker is steamy. Very tame compared with the porno-edged Harold Robbins novel. 1964; 150m.

CARRINGTON, V. C. ★★★
DIR: Anthony Asquith. **CAST:** David Niven, Margaret Leighton, Noelle Middleton, Laurence Naismith, Victor Maddern, Maurice Denham.
Everybody's Englishman David Niven gives one of the finest performances of his long film career in this story of a stalwart British army officer, accused of stealing military funds, who undertakes to conduct his own defense at court-martial proceedings. This is a solid, engrossing drama. Filmed in England and released heavily cut in the United States under the title *Court Martial*. 1955; B&W; 105m.

CASABLANCA ★★★★★
DIR: Michael Curtiz. **CAST:** Humphrey Bogart, Ingrid Bergman,

Claude Rains, Paul Henreid, Peter Lorre, Sydney Greenstreet.

A kiss may be just a kiss and a sigh just a sigh, but there is only one *Casablanca.* Some misguided souls tried to remake this classic in 1980 as *Caboblanco*, but film lovers are well advised to accept no substitutes. The original feast of romance and pre–World War II intrigue is still the best. Superb performances by Humphrey Bogart and Ingrid Bergman, Paul Henreid, Claude Rains, Peter Lorre, and Sydney Greenstreet, and the fluid direction of Michael Curtiz combined to make it an all-time classic. 1942; B&W; 102m.

CASE OF LIBEL, A ★★★★★

DIR: Eric Till. **CAST:** Edward Asner, Daniel J. Travanti, Gordon Pinsent, Lawrence Dane.

Slick, superb made-for-cable adaptation of Henry Denker's famed Broadway play, which itself is taken from the first portion of Louis Nizer's excellent biography, *My Life in Court.* The story closely follows the legendary Westbrook Pegler–Quentin Reynolds libei suit, wherein columnist Pegler had attempted to smear Reynolds's reputation with a series of vicious lies. Ed Asner plays the lawyer and Daniel Travanti the columnist, and the verbal give-and-take ranks with the finest courtroom dramas on film. Unrated. 1984; 92m.

CASINO ★★

DIR: Don Chaffey. **CAST:** Mike Connors, Gene Evans, Barry Van Dyke, Gary Burghoff, Joseph Cotten, Lynda Day George, Robert Reed, Barry Sullivan.

This pedestrian telemovie features former *Mannix* star Mike Connors as the action-oriented owner of a plush hotel and casino. The resort is populated by shady types who are played with little enthusiasm by TV-series stars and former silver-screen luminaries. 1980; 100m.

CASSANDRA CROSSING, THE

DIR: George Pan Cosmatos. **CAST:** Richard Harris, Sophia Loren, Burt Lancaster, Ava Gardner, Martin Sheen.

One of the worst all-star disaster pictures, this involves a plague-infested train heading for a weakened bridge. The star power of Burt Lancaster, Sophia Loren, Richard Harris, Martin Sheen, and Ava Gardner, among others, does little to relieve its boredom. Rated PG. 1977; 127m.

CASTAWAY ★★

DIR: Nicolas Roeg. **CAST:** Oliver Reed, Amanda Donohoe.

Nicolas Roeg adds some surreal touches to this otherwise mediocre film about a wealthy publisher (Oliver Reed) who advertises for a woman to live with him for a year on a deserted tropical island. His dreams of animal passion turn into domestic doldrums when his companion (Amanda Donohoe) opts for celibacy. Rated R for profanity, nudity, and simulated sex. 1987; 118m.

CASTLE, THE ★★★½

DIR: Rudolf Noelte. **CAST:** Maximillian Schell, Cordula Trantow, Trudik Daniel.

This highly metaphorical story from Franz Kafka's incomplete novel is translated literally here and makes for a very strange and humorous affair. Maximillian Schell is a land surveyor who is employed by the mysterious inhabitants of a castle, only to be denied access to the place once he arrives there. Not rated, has sex and nudity. 1983; 89m.

CAT ON A HOT TIN ROOF (1958) ★★★★

DIR: Richard Brooks. **CAST:** Elizabeth Taylor, Paul Newman, Burl Ives, Jack Carson.

This heavy drama stars Elizabeth Taylor as the frustrated Maggie and Paul Newman as her alcoholic, ex-athlete husband. They've returned to his father's (Big Daddy, played by

Burl Ives) home upon hearing he's dying. They are joined by Newman's brother, Gooper, and his wife, May, and their many obnoxious children. Maggie struggles against May and Gooper to get a larger share in Big Daddy's will. 1958; 108m.

CAT ON A HOT TIN ROOF (1985) ★★★½
DIR: Jack Hofsiss. **CAST:** Jessica Lange, Tommy Lee Jones, Rip Torn, Kim Stanley, David Dukes, Penny Fuller.

Updated rendition of the famed Tennessee Williams play strikes to the core in most scenes but remains oddly distanced in others. The story itself is just as powerful as it must have been in 1955, with its acute examination of a family under stress. Jessica Lange is far too melodramatic as Maggie the Cat; it's impossible to forget she's acting. Things really come alive, though, when Big Daddy (Rip Torn) and Brick (Tommy Lee Jones) square off. The play ends on what is for Williams an uncharacteristically optimistic note. A near miss. Unrated—sexual situations. 1985; 140m.

CATHERINE THE GREAT ★★
DIR: Paul Czinner. **CAST:** Elisabeth Bergner, Douglas Fairbanks Jr., Flora Robson, Joan Gardner, Gerald Du Maurier.

Stodgy spectacle from Great Britain is sumptuously mounted but takes its own time in telling the story of the famed czarina of Russia and her (toned-down) love life. Elisabeth Bergner in the title role lacks a real star personality, and dashing Douglas Fairbanks Jr. and sage Flora Robson provide the only screen charisma evident. Fair for a historical romance, but it won't keep you on the edge of your seat. 1934; B&W; 92m.

CATHOLICS ★★★★½
DIR: Jack Gold. **CAST:** Trevor Howard, Martin Sheen, Raf Vallone, Andrew Keir.

This film has Martin Sheen playing the representative of the Father General (the Pope). He comes to Ireland to persuade the Catholic priests there to conform to the "new" teachings of the Catholic Church. The Irish priests and monks refuse to discard traditional ways and beliefs. Trevor Howard is excellent as the rebellious Irish abbot. 1973; 78m.

CAUGHT ★★★
DIR: Max Ophuls. **CAST:** Robert Ryan, Barbara Bel Geddes, James Mason, Natalie Schafer, Ruth Brady, Curt Bois, Frank Ferguson.

Starry-eyed model Barbara Bel Geddes marries neurotic millionaire Robert Ryan, who proceeds to make her life miserable. His treatment drives her away and into the arms of young doctor James Mason. Upon learning she is pregnant, she returns to her husband, who refuses to give her a divorce unless she gives him the child. 1949; B&W; 88m.

CEASE FIRE ★★★½
DIR: David Nutter. **CAST:** Don Johnson, Lisa Blount, Robert F. Lyons, Richard Chaves, Chris Noel.

An answer to the comic book–style heroism of *Rambo* and the *Missing in Action* movies, *Cease Fire* is a heartfelt, well-acted, and touching drama about the aftereffects of Vietnam and the battle still being fought by some veterans. Don Johnson stars as Tim Murphy, a veteran whose life begins to crumble after fifteen years of valiant effort at fitting back into society. Rated R for profanity and violence. 1985; 97m.

CELEBRITY ★★★½
DIR: Paul Wendkos. **CAST:** Michael Beck, Joseph Bottoms, Ben Masters.

Three high-school buddies go too far on a drunken binge, with one of them raping a country girl. This crime binds the three as they go on with their lives. Each gains fame in a different medium (writing, acting and preaching). Twenty-five years later, they're reunited in a highly publicized trial. This sudsy TV miniseries will have you glued to your set. 1984; 313m.

CENTERFOLD GIRLS
DIR: John Peyser. **CAST:** Andrew Prine, Tiffany Bolling, Aldo Ray, Ray Danton, Jeremy Slate.
This is a silly and utterly exploitative film about an insane brute (Andrew Prine) who spends his time killing beautiful, exotic models. Rated R. 1974; 93m.

CERTAIN SACRIFICE, A
DIR: Stephen Jon Lewicki. **CAST:** Jeremy Pattnosh, Madonna.
Avoid this one at all costs. A thoroughly inept film about two drifters who fall in love, are assaulted by a bigot, and then get revenge on him. Rated R for language, sex, nudity, violence. 1985; 58m.

CHAINED FOR LIFE ★
DIR: Harry Fraser. **CAST:** Daisy Hilton, Violet Hilton.
This murder drama featuring Siamese twins Daisy and Violet Hilton is certainly one of the saddest and most exploitative feature films of all. Cheap and embarrassing, this tawdry attempt to cash in on a physical deformity is long, boring, and in terrible taste. 1951; B&W; 81m.

CHALK GARDEN, THE ★★★
DIR: Ronald Neame. **CAST:** Deborah Kerr, Edith Evans, Hayley Mills, John Mills, Elizabeth Sellars.
Adapted from the play of the same name by Enid Bagnold. The plot centers around a spoiled brat (Hayley Mills) who is the bane of her grandmother's (Edith Evans) life until she is made to see the light of day by the new governess (Deborah Kerr). Sensational acting all around. 1964; 106m.

CHAMP, THE (1931) ★★★★
DIR: King Vidor. **CAST:** Wallace Beery, Jackie Cooper, Irene Rich.
Wallace Beery is at his absolute best in the Oscar-winning title role of this tearjerker, about a washed-up fighter and his adoring son (Jackie Cooper) who are separated against their will. King Vidor manages to make even the hokiest bits of hokum work in this four-hankie feast of sentimentality. 1931; B&W; 87m.

CHAMP, THE (1979) ★★★½
DIR: Franco Zeffirelli. **CAST:** Jon Voight, Faye Dunaway, Ricky Schroder, Jack Warden.
This remake is a first-class tearjerker. Billy Flynn (Voight), a former boxing champion, works in the back-stretch at Hialeah when not drinking or gambling away his money. His son, T.J. (Schroder), calls him "Champ" and tells all his friends about his father's comeback, which never seems to happen. Rated PG. 1979; 121m.

CHAMPAGNE ★
DIR: Alfred Hitchcock. **CAST:** Betty Balfour, Gordon Harker.
Alfred Hitchcock regarded this silent feature as one of his worst films, and who are we to disagree? The insipid love story unfolds interminably—with overwrought performances making the boy-meets-and-loses-girl story even more laughable. For Hitchcock completists only. Unrated; suitable for family viewing. 1928; B&W; 69m.

CHAMPION ★★★★
DIR: Stanley Kramer. **CAST:** Kirk Douglas, Arthur Kennedy, Ruth Roman.
One of Hollywood's better efforts about the fight game. Kirk Douglas is a young boxer whose climb to the top is accomplished while forsaking his friends and family. He gives one of his best performances in an unsympathetic role. 1949; B&W; 100m.

CHAMPIONS ★★★★
DIR: John Irvin. **CAST:** John Hurt, Edward Woodward, Jan Francis, Ben Johnson.
The touching true story of English steeplechase jockey Bob Champion (John Hurt), who fought a desperate battle against cancer through chemotherapy to win the 1981 Grand National. Rated PG. 1984; 113m.

CHANEL SOLITAIRE ★★
DIR: George Kaczender. **CAST:** Marie-France Pisier, Timothy Dalton, Rutger Hauer, Karen Black, Brigitte Fossey.
This half-hearted rendering of the rise to prominence of French designer Coco Chanel (played by fragile Marie-France Pisier) is long on sap and short on plot. Timothy Dalton and Rutger Hauer, as two of Coco's well-heeled suitors, fare best; Miss Pisier wears a sour pout throughout. For the terminally romantic only. Rated R. 1981; 120m.

CHANGE OF HABIT ★★
DIR: William A. Graham. **CAST:** Elvis Presley, Mary Tyler Moore, Barbara McNair, Jane Elliot, Edward Asner.
In direct contrast to the many comedy-musicals that Elvis Presley starred in, this drama offers a more substantial plot. Elvis plays a doctor helping the poor in his clinic. Mary Tyler Moore plays a nun who is tempted to leave the order to be with Elvis. Rated G. 1970; 93m.

CHAPTER TWO ★★★½
DIR: Robert Moore. **CAST:** James Caan, Marsha Mason, Valerie Harper, Joseph Bologna.
In *Chapter Two*, writer Neil Simon examines the problems that arise when a recently widowed author courts and marries a recently divorced actress. George Schneider (James Caan) is recovering from the death of his wife when he strikes up a whirlwind courtship with actress Jennie MacLaine (Marsha Mason). They get married, but George is tormented by the memory of his first, beloved wife. Rated PG. 1979; 124m.

CHARIOTS OF FIRE ★★★★★
DIR: Hugh Hudson. **CAST:** Ben Cross, Ian Charleson, Nigel Havers, Nicolas Farrell, Alice Krige.
Made in England, this is the beautifully told and inspiring story of two runners (Ian Charleson and Ben Cross) who competed for England in the 1924 Olympics. An all-star supporting cast—Ian Holm, John Gielgud, Dennis Christopher (*Breaking Away*), Brad Davis (*Midnight Express*), and Nigel Davenport—and taut direction by Hugh Hudson help make this a must-see motion picture. Rated PG, the film has no objectionable content. 1981; 123m.

CHASE, THE (1946) ★★
DIR: Arthur Ripley. **CAST:** Robert Cummings, Michele Morgan, Peter Lorre, Steve Cochran.
If the tempo were faster and the writing tighter, this film might have been interesting. As it is, it staggers along. The plot is quite predictable as Michele Morgan runs away from her husband. 1946; B&W; 86m.

CHASE, THE (1966) ★★½
DIR: Arthur Penn. **CAST:** Robert Redford, Jane Fonda, Marlon Brando, Angie Dickinson, Janice Rule, James Fox, Robert Duvall, E. G. Marshall, Miriam Hopkins, Martha Hyer.
Convoluted tale of prison escapee (Robert Redford) who returns to the turmoil of his Texas hometown. The exceptional cast provides flashes of brilliance, but overall, the film is rather dull. Redford definitely showed signs of his superstar potential here. 1966; 135m.

CHEERS FOR MISS BISHOP ★★★
DIR: Tay Garnett. **CAST:** Martha Scott, William Gargan, Edmund Gwenn, Sterling Holloway, Sidney Blackmer.
Nostalgic, poignant story of a schoolteacher in a midwestern town who devotes her life to teaching. A warm reassuring film in the tradition of *Miss Dove* and *Mr. Chips*. 1941; B&W; 95m.

CHERRY, HARRY AND RAQUEL ★★★½
DIR: Russ Meyer. **CAST:** Charles Napier.
One of Russ Meyer's best movies, even though he lost several reels after he finished shooting and had to pad the film out at the last minute with

purposely silly commentary by a woman wearing nothing but an Indian headdress. Forget the plot about a drug-running sheriff (the wonderful Charles Napier) in New Mexico. Novelist Tom Wolfe wrote the screenplay. Rated X in 1969, though it would get an R nowadays. 1969; 71m.

CHIEFS ★★★★

DIR: Jerry London. **CAST:** Charlton Heston, Wayne Rogers, Billy Dee Williams, Brad Davis, Keith Carradine, Stephen Collins, Tess Harper, Paul Sorvino, Victoria Tennant.

An impressive cast turns in some excellent performances in this, one of the better TV miniseries. A string of unsolved murders in 1920 in a small southern town is at the base of this engrossing suspense drama. The story follows the various police chiefs from the time of the murders to 1962 when Billy Dee Williams, the town's first black police chief, is intrigued by the case and the spell it casts over the town and its political boss (Charlton Heston). Some material not suitable for children. 1985; 200m.

CHILD BRIDE OF SHORT CREEK ★★

DIR: Robert Michael Lewis. **CAST:** Christopher Atkins, Diane Lane, Conrad Bain, Dee Wallace.

Based on a true account, this is the story of a polygamist community in Arizona disbanded by the police. Christopher Atkins plays a boy outraged by his father's desire to add a fifteen-year-old girl to his harem of wives. Made for TV. 1981; 100m.

CHILDREN OF A LESSER GOD ★★★★★

DIR: Randa Haines. **CAST:** William Hurt, Marlee Matlin, Piper Laurie, Philip Bosco.

Based on the Tony Award–winning play by Mark Medoff, this superb film concerns the love that grows between a teacher (William Hurt) for the hearing-impaired and a deaf woman (Oscar-winner Marlee Matlin). The performances are impeccable, the direction inspired, and the story unforgettable. Considering the problems inherent in telling its tale, this represents a phenomenal achievement for first-time film director Randa Haines. Rated R for suggested sex, profanity, and adult themes. 1986; 118m.

CHILDREN OF AN LAC, THE ★★★★

DIR: John Llewellyn Moxey. **CAST:** Ina Balin, Shirley Jones, Beulah Quo, Alan Fudge, Ben Piazza.

Just before the fall of Saigon in 1975, three women did the next to impossible: They managed the escape of hundreds (perhaps thousands) of Vietnamese children. One of these women was actress Ina Balin, who plays herself here. The performances and production values of this made-for-television film are very good. 1980; 100m.

CHILDREN OF RAGE ★★½

DIR: Arthur Allan Seidelman. **CAST:** Helmut Greim, Olga Georges-Picot, Cyril Cusack, Simon Ward.

This little-seen film deserves credit for doing something that few were willing to do at the time it was made: look beyond the actions of Palestinian terrorists to try to understand their motives. Unfortunately, good intentions don't compensate for lack of drama in this talky story about an Israeli doctor who attempts to open lines of communications with terrorists. Unrated, the film contains violence. 1975; 106m.

CHILDREN OF SANCHEZ, THE ★★★

DIR: Hall Bartlett. **CAST:** Anthony Quinn, Dolores Del Rio.

Anthony Quinn stars as a poor Mexican worker who tries to keep his large family together. This well-intentioned film is slightly boring. Rated PG. 1978; 126m.

CHILLY SCENES OF WINTER ★★★★

DIR: Joan Micklin Silver. **CAST:** John Heard, Mary Beth Hurt, Peter

Riegert, Kenneth McMillan, Gloria Grahame.

You'll probably find this excellent little film in the comedy section of your local video store, but don't be fooled; it's funny all right, but it has some scenes that evoke the true pain of love. John Heard plays a man in love with a married woman (Mary Beth Hurt). She also loves him, but is still attached to her husband. Rated PG for language and sex. 1979; 96m.

CHINA SYNDROME, THE ★★★★★

DIR: James Bridges. **CAST:** Jane Fonda, Jack Lemmon, Michael Douglas, Scott Brady.

This taut thriller, about an accident at a nuclear power plant, has no real competition. It's superb entertainment with a timely message. Rated PG. 1979; 123m.

CHOCOLATE WAR, THE ★★★½

DIR: Keith Gordon. **CAST:** John Glover, Ilan Mitchell-Smith, Wally Ward, Adam Baldwin, Bud Cort.

Actor Keith Gordon makes an impressive directorial debut with this comedy-drama about a bereaved student (Ilan Mitchell-Smith) facing the horrors of a sadistic teacher (John Glover) and a secret society of students at his Catholic high school. A bit heavy-handed at times, it still delivers some excellent performances and a story that keeps you fascinated. Rated R for profanity and violence. 1989; 103m.

CHOICE, THE ★★

DIR: David Greene. **CAST:** Susan Clark, Mitchell Ryan, Jennifer Warren.

Abortion is the controversy in this made-for-television film. Susan Clark stars as a mother who must help her daughter make the critical decision on whether to have an abortion or not. Too sentimental, but the performances are commendable. 1981; 100m.

CHOOSE ME ★★★★

DIR: Alan Rudolph. **CAST:** Lesley Ann Warren, Keith Carradine, Genevieve Bujold.

A feast of fine acting and deliciously different situations, this stylish independent film works on every level and proves that inventive, non-mainstream entertainment is still a viable form. Written and directed by Alan Rudolph, *Choose Me* is a funny, quirky, suspenseful, and surprising essay on love, sex, and the wacky state of male-female relationships in the 1980s. Rated R for violence and profanity. 1984; 110m.

CHOSEN, THE ★★★★★

DIR: Jeremy Paul Kagan. **CAST:** Robby Benson, Rod Steiger, Maximilian Schell.

The Chosen is a flawless, arresting drama illustrating the conflict between friendship and family loyalty experienced by two young men. Based on the novel of the same name by Chaim Potok, the story, centering on Jewish issues, transcends its setting to attain universal impact. Rated G. 1978; 105m.

CHRISTMAS TO REMEMBER, A ★★★★

DIR: George Englund. **CAST:** Jason Robards Jr., Eva Marie Saint, Joanne Woodward.

Grandpa Larson (Jason Robards), who never got over his son's death, resents his grandson's visit. His unkind manner toward the boy convinces the youngster that he must run away. Eva Marie Saint plays Grandma Larson, who rebuffs her husband for his cruelty. Joanne Woodward makes a cameo appearance as the boy's impoverished mom. Unrated, this provides fine family entertainment comparable with a G rating. 1979; 96m.

CHRISTMAS WITHOUT SNOW, A ★★★★

DIR: John Korty. **CAST:** John Houseman, Ramon Bieri, James Cromwell, Valerie Curtin.

John Houseman and the entire cast shine in this beautiful made-for-TV story about a dictatorial choirmaster, a newly divorced woman, a church choir, and their combined problems while rehearsing for a performance of Handel's *Messiah* oratorio. Definitely worth viewing. 1980; 100m.

CHRISTOPHER STRONG ★★½
DIR: Dorothy Arzner. **CAST:** Katharine Hepburn, Colin Clive, Billie Burke, Helen Chandler, Jack LaRue.

Katharine Hepburn's second film, this one gave her her first starring role. She is a record-breaking flyer who falls passionately in love with a married man she cannot have. Pregnancy complicates things further. High-plane soap opera. Kate's legions of fans will love it, however. 1933; B&W; 77m.

CIAO! MANHATTAN
DIR: John Palmer, David Weisman. **CAST:** Edie Sedgwick, Isabel Jewell, Baby Jane Holzer, Roger Vadim, Viva, Paul America.

Far more pornographic than any skin flick, this sleazy, low-budget release features Edie Sedgwick, a one-time Andy Warhol "superstar," in a grotesque parody of her life. Sedgwick, who, at the age of 28, died shortly after the film's completion, is most often topless and slurs her way through this near-documentary of the last days of an aimless self-indulgent young woman. No MPAA rating, but rife with objectionable material. 1983; 84m.

CINDERELLA LIBERTY ★★★½
DIR: Mark Rydell. **CAST:** James Caan, Marsha Mason, Eli Wallach.

Marsha Mason earned an Oscar nomination as a feisty Seattle hooker with a worldly-wise 11-year-old son in this quirky little romance, which also stars James Caan as a sailor who learns to love them both. The plot is predictable, but the performances are genuinely touching. Rated R for profanity and sexual themes. 1973; 117m.

CIRCLE OF LOVE ★
DIR: Roger Vadim. **CAST:** Jane Fonda, Jean-Claude Brialy, Maurice Ronet, Jean Sorel, Anna Karina.

This is a terrible rehash of Max Ophuls's *La Ronde*. The irony of the original is missing. Roger Vadim's direction lacks vision and wit and the performances are quite dull. Stick with the original 1950 masterpiece. 1964; 105m.

CIRCLE OF TWO ★½
DIR: Jules Dassin. **CAST:** Richard Burton, Tatum O'Neal, Kate Reid, Robin Gammell.

Thoroughly ludicrous tale of an eccentric artist (Richard Burton) who develops a romantic—but somehow platonic—relationship with a teenage girl (Tatum O'Neal). Laughable dialogue throughout, punctuated by heavy sighs and fluttering eyelashes. O'Neal has a painfully embarrassing nude scene that is out of place in this story with its gentle tone. Rated PG for nudity. 1980; 105m.

CIRCUS WORLD ★
DIR: Henry Hathaway. **CAST:** John Wayne, Rita Hayworth, Claudia Cardinale, John Smith, Lloyd Nolan, Richard Conte.

Even the presence of John Wayne can't help this sappy soap opera set under the big top. It's a Cinerama extravaganza that does not survive the transfer to videotape (less than a third of the three-screen picture remains). But that's okay—the story is dreadful. 1964; 135m.

CITADEL, THE ★★★½
DIR: King Vidor. **CAST:** Robert Donat, Rosalind Russell, Ralph Richardson, Rex Harrison, Emlyn Williams, Francis L. Sullivan, Felix Aylmer, Mary Clare, Cecil Parker.

Superb acting by a fine cast marks this adaptation of novelist A. J. Cronin's story of an impoverished doctor who temporarily forsakes his ideals but comes to his senses when tragedy strikes. 1938; B&W; 112m.

CITIZEN KANE ★★★★★

DIR: Orson Welles. **CAST:** Orson Welles, Joseph Cotten, Everett Sloane, Agnes Moorehead, Ray Collins, George Coulouris, Ruth Warrick.

What can you say about the film considered by many to be the finest picture ever made in America? The story of a reporter's quest to find the "truth" about the life of a dead newspaper tycoon closely parallels the life of William Randolph Hearst. To 1940s audiences, the plot may have seemed obscured by flashbacks, unusual camera angles, and lens distortion. After forty years, however, most of these film tricks are now commonplace, but the story, the acting of the Mercury Company cast, Gregg Toland's camera work, and Bernard Herrmann's score haven't aged a bit. This picture is still a very enjoyable experience for first-time viewers, as well as for those who have seen it ten times. 1941; B&W; 119m.

CITY IN FEAR ★★★

DIR: Jud Taylor (Allen Smithee). **CAST:** David Janssen, Robert Vaughn, Susan Sullivan, William Prince, Perry King, William Daniels.

David Janssen is excellent in his last role, a burned-out writer goaded by a ruthless publisher (Robert Vaughn). The plot concerns a mad killer on the loose in a big city. High-quality made-for-TV feature. 1980; 150m.

CITY THAT NEVER SLEEPS ★★★½

DIR: John H. Auer. **CAST:** Gig Young, Mala Powers, Edward Arnold, William Talman.

Dated but delectable film about a Chicago policeman (Gig Young) who decides to leave his wife and the force to run away with a cheap showgirl. In a corny device, the city talks to us—via an off-screen narrator—to introduce its citizens and explain its purpose in society. Unrated, it contains violence. 1953; B&W; 90m.

CIVILIZATION ★★★

DIR: Thomas Ince. **CAST:** Howard Hickman, Enid Markey, Lola May.

Though little-known today, Thomas Ince was one of the first great American film producers and *Civilization* was his crowning effort. Seeing the overwhelming response to D. W. Griffith's epic *Birth of a Nation*, Ince decided to abandon the short westerns and dramas that made him wealthy. Instead, he put all his efforts into this moralistic antiwar blockbuster. Unfortunately for Ince, America entered Word War I after the sinking of the *Lusitania* and *Civilization* died at the box office. Silent with intertitles. 1916; B&W; 102m.

CLARA'S HEART ★★½

DIR: Robert Mulligan. **CAST:** Whoopi Goldberg, Michael Ontkean, Kathleen Quinlan, Spalding Gray, Beverly Todd, Neil Patrick Harris.

Despite a wonderful performance by Whoopi Goldberg, this is a strangely unaffecting drama about a Jamaican maid who helps a youngster (Neil Patrick Harris) come to terms with life. His parents (Michael Ontkean and Kathleen Quinlan) are too concerned with themselves after the death of their baby, which soon results in the collapse of their marriage. The characters are so unsympathetic, though, that the viewer cannot help but lose interest. PG-13 for profanity. 1988; 107m.

CLASH BY NIGHT ★★★½

DIR: Fritz Lang. **CAST:** Barbara Stanwyck, Paul Douglas, Robert Ryan, Marilyn Monroe, Keith Andes, J. Carrol Naish.

Intense, adult story is a dramatist's dream but not entertainment for the masses. Barbara Stanwyck gives another of her strong characterizations as a woman with a past who marries amiable Paul Douglas only to find herself gravitating toward tough but sensual Robert Ryan. Gritty realism and outstanding performances make this a slice-of-life tragedy that lingers in the memory. 1952; B&W; 105m.

CLASS OF MISS MACMICHAEL, THE ★★

DIR: Silvio Narizzano. **CAST:** Glenda Jackson, Oliver Reed, Michael Murphy.

British film about obnoxious students battling obnoxious teachers. Mixes *The Blackboard Jungle*, *To Sir with Love*, and *Teachers* without expanding on them. Loud and angry, but doesn't say much. Rated R for profanity. 1978; 91m.

CLASS OF '44 ★★★

DIR: Paul Bogart. **CAST:** Gary Grimes, Jerry Houser, William Atherton, Deborah Winters.

Sequel to the very popular *Summer of '42* proves once again it's tough to top the original. Gary Grimes and Jerry Houser are back again. This time we follow the two through college romances. No new ground broken, but Grimes is very watchable. Rated PG. 1973; 95m.

CLEAN AND SOBER ★★★★

DIR: Glenn Gordon Caron. **CAST:** Michael Keaton, Morgan Freeman, M. Emmet Walsh, Kathy Baker.

Michael Keaton gives a brilliant performance in this highly effective drama as a hotshot executive who wakes up one morning to find that his life is totally out of control. The woman he picked up at a bar the night before is dead in his bed from an allergic reaction to cocaine and he is in trouble for stealing money from business accounts to fuel his drug habit. He checks into a drug rehabilitation center to dry out and discovers the shocking truth about himself. An impressive filmmaking debut for Glenn Gordon Caron, creator of television's *Moonlighting*. Rated R for violence and profanity. 1988; 124m.

CLEOPATRA (1934) ★★★★

DIR: Cecil B. DeMille. **CAST:** Claudette Colbert, Warren William, Henry Wilcoxon, C. Aubrey Smith.

One of the most opulent and intelligent films Cecil B. De Mille ever directed. Its success arises in large part from historical accuracy and the superb peformances by all the principals. 1934; B&W; 95m.

CLEOPATRA (1963) ★★★★

DIR: Joseph L. Mankiewicz. **CAST:** Elizabeth Taylor, Richard Burton, Rex Harrison, Roddy McDowall, Pamela Brown.

This multimillion-dollar, four-hour-long extravaganza created quite a sensation when released. Its all-star cast includes Elizabeth Taylor (as Cleopatra) and Richard Burton (as Marc Antony). The story begins when Caesar meets Cleopatra in her native Egypt and she has his son. Later she comes to Rome to join Caesar when he becomes the lifetime dictator of Rome. Marc Antony gets into the act as Cleopatra's Roman lover. 1963; 243m.

CLOAK AND DAGGER (1946) ★★½

DIR: Fritz Lang. **CAST:** Gary Cooper, Lilli Palmer, Robert Alda, James Flavin, J. Edward Bromberg, Marc Lawrence.

Director Fritz Lang wanted to make *Cloak and Dagger* as a warning about the dangers of the atomic age. But Warner Bros. reedited the film into a standard spy melodrama. The story has American scientist Gary Cooper, working for the OSS, sneaking into Nazi Germany to grab an Italian scientist who is helping the Nazis build the atom bomb. 1946; B&W; 106m.

CLOCK, THE ★★★

DIR: Vincente Minnelli. **CAST:** Judy Garland, Robert Walker, James Gleason, Keenan Wynn.

Dated but still entertaining film directed by Judy Garland's then-husband, Vincente Minnelli. Judy stars as a working girl who meets and falls in love with soldier Robert Walker. He's on a forty-eight-hour leave, so they decide to make the most of the time they have together. 1945; 90m.

CLOUD WALTZING ★★★

DIR: Gordon Flemyng. **CAST:** Kathleen Beller, François-Eric Gendron.

Beautiful photography and a respectable performance by Kathleen Beller are the highlights of this telefilm. The story is only marginal. Beller stars as an American journalist who is sent to France to do an exclusive interview with a hardnosed French winemaker. She uses many ploys, including a hot-air balloon ride, to get her interview and finally her man. 1987; 103m.

CLOUDS OVER EUROPE ★★½
DIR: Tim Whelan. **CAST:** Laurence Olivier, Valerie Hobson, Ralph Richardson.
Handsome test pilot Laurence Olivier teams up with a man from Scotland Yard to discover why new bombers are disappearing in this on-the-verge-of-war thriller. 1939; B&W; 82m.

CLOWN, THE ★★★
DIR: Robert Z. Leonard. **CAST:** Red Skelton, Jane Greer, Tim Considine, Loring Smith.
Red Skelton in a dramatic role? Yes, it's true. In this film, a reworking of *The Champ*, he portrays a comedian who wins the love of his estranged son. Skelton is commendable and Tim Considine is excellent as the son. This film has an average storyline but is well performed. 1953; B&W; 91m.

CLUB, THE ★★★
DIR: Bruce Beresford. **CAST:** Jack Thompson, Harold Hopkins, Graham Kennedy, John Howard.
A highly paid rookie joins an Australian football team whose last championship was twenty years ago. A powerful story of winning and losing, of business and loyalty, and of determination. Intense and polished. Rated PG for profanity and violence. 1985; 93m.

CLUB MED ★½
DIR: Bob Giraldi. **CAST:** Jack Scalia, Linda Hamilton, Patrick Macnee, Bill Maher.
Yet another tired retread of the *Fantasy Island/Love Boat/Hotel* scenario: the romantic ups and downs of guests at a fashionable vacation resort. Music-video director Bob Giraldi's style dissipates quickly in this made-for-TV movie. Not rated. 1986; 104m.

COACH ★½
DIR: Bud Townsend. **CAST:** Cathy Lee Crosby, Michael Biehn, Keenan Wynn.
What do you get when you cross *Hoosiers* with *Private Lessons*? Not much. *Coach* is an exploitation flick devoid of titillation, a root-for-the-underdog basketball saga without heart. The interesting element here is the performance of Michael Biehn as a star student. Overall, though, the movie is about as appealing as unwashed gym socks. 1978; 100m.

COCAINE FIENDS ★½
DIR: William A. O'Connor. **CAST:** Lois January, Sheila Manners, Noel Madison.
Grim drama about drug addiction follows two women down their path to dependency. Better acted than most cheap morality tales, this one even uses symbolism to convey the heroines' tragedy. Melodramatic, yes, but not as funny as *Reefer Madness* and more outlandish exploitation films that went for bawdier, more sensational footage. 1936; B&W; 74m.

COCAINE: ONE MAN'S SEDUCTION ★★★½
DIR: Paul Wendkos. **CAST:** Dennis Weaver, Karen Grassle, Pamela Bellwood, James Spader, David Ackroyd, Jeffrey Tambor.
Though this is not another *Reefer Madness*, the subject could have been handled a little more subtly. Still, the melodrama is not obtrusive enough to take away from Dennis Weaver's brilliant performance as a real estate salesman who gets hooked. Not rated, but the equivalent of a PG for adult subject matter. 1983; 97m.

COCKTAIL ★
DIR: Roger Donaldson. **CAST:** Tom Cruise, Bryan Brown, Elisabeth Shue, Laurence Luckinbill.
Only Bryan Brown's rendition of a seasoned bartender saves this turgid

mess from becoming a complete turkey. Tom Cruise, as the fast-rising newcomer of the glass-and-bottle set, substitutes vacuous grins for acting and manages the impressive feat of failing to project *any* credibility in the entire picture. Rated R for language and brief nudity. 1988; 104m.

COLD ROOM, THE ★½
DIR: James Dearden. **CAST:** George Segal, Amanda Pays, Warren Clarke, Anthony Higgins.

This made-for-television movie, based on a superior Jeffrey Caine novel, is a waste of good material. George Segal plays a writer who, accompanied by his daughter, travels to East Germany, only to run into trouble with the secret police and radicals of all kinds. 1984; 95m.

COLDITZ STORY, THE ★★★½
DIR: Guy Hamilton. **CAST:** John Mills, Eric Portman, Lionel Jeffries, Bryan Forbes, Ian Carmichael, Theodore Bikel, Anton Diffring, Richard Wattis.

Tight direction, an intelligent script, and a terrific cast make this one of the most compelling British dramas of the 1950s and one of the best prison films of all time. John Mills is outstanding as the glue that keeps the escape plans together, but the entire crew works well together. 1957; B&W; 97m.

COLLECTOR'S ITEM ★★★½
DIR: Giuseppe Patroni Griffi. **CAST:** Tony Musante, Laura Antonelli, Florinda Bolkan.

This erotic suspense-drama is a surprise sleeper. Tony Musante meets up with gorgeous Laura Antonelli whom he had seduced sixteen years earlier. The actors give intense performances and Antonelli just may have found a role model in Glenn Close of *Fatal Attraction* fame. Unrated but strictly adult fare with nudity and profanity. 1988; 99m.

COLOR ME DEAD ★★½
DIR: Eddie Davis. **CAST:** Tom Tryon, Carolyn Jones, Rick Jason.

An innocent accountant (Tom Tryon) gets caught in the middle of an illegal uranium robbery and is poisoned with a deadly slow-working drug. With his days numbered, he adopts the methods of a detective and tries to find out why he was murdered. Carolyn Jones is effective as Tryon's girlfriend-secretary and gives the story poignancy; but the screenplay is wanting. Not rated, the film contains violence. 1969; 91m.

COLOR OF MONEY, THE ★★★★
DIR: Martin Scorsese. **CAST:** Paul Newman, Tom Cruise, Mary Elizabeth Mastrantonio, Helen Shaver, John Turturro.

A sequel to *The Hustler*, this film features outstanding performances by Paul Newman as the now-aging pool champion and Tom Cruise as his protégé. The story may be predictable, even clichéd, but the actors make it worth watching. Rated R for nudity, profanity, and violence. 1986; 117m.

COLOR PURPLE, THE ★★★★★
DIR: Steven Spielberg. **CAST:** Whoopi Goldberg, Danny Glover, Adolph Caesar, Margaret Avery, Oprah Winfrey, Rae Dawn Chong, Akosua Busia.

Steven Spielberg's adaptation of Alice Walker's Pulitzer Prize–winning novel about the growth to maturity and independence of a mistreated black woman is one of those rare and wonderful movies that can bring a tear to the eye, a lift to the soul, and joy to the heart. Walker's story, set between 1909 and 1947 in a small town in Georgia, celebrates the qualities of kindness, compassion, and love. Rated PG-13 for violence, profanity, and suggested sex. 1985; 130m.

COLORS ★★★★
DIR: Dennis Hopper. **CAST:** Sean Penn, Robert Duvall, Maria Conchita Alonso, Randy Brooks, Don Cheadle.

Robert Duvall gives a powerhouse performance in this hard-hitting police drama. He's a cool, experienced cop who attempts to teach his young, hotheaded partner (Sean Penn) how to survive in the violence-ridden streets of East Los Angeles. Penn manages to match Duvall scene for scene, and director Hopper skillfully holds it all together, although he does go overboard in the sex and violence department. 1988; 119m.

COME BACK AFRICA ★★★½
DIR: Lionel Rogosin.

Lionel Rogosin, director of the extraordinary *On the Bowery*, has created another overwhelming portrait of human tragedy in this drama about a black South African who loses a series of jobs while trying to keep his residency in Johannesburg. Exploited by a racist bureaucracy, the central character is forced to endure the horrible conditions of the hazardous coal mines. Not rated, but recommended to adult viewers. 1959; B&W; 83m.

COME BACK TO THE FIVE AND DIME, JIMMY DEAN, JIMMY DEAN ★★★½
DIR: Robert Altman. **CAST:** Sandy Dennis, Cher, Karen Black, Sudie Bond, Kathy Bates, Marta Heflin.

This film concerns the twenty-year reunion of the Disciples of James Dean, a group formed by high-school friends from a small Texas town after *Giant* was filmed on location nearby. Their get-together ends up being a catalyst that forces the members to confront the lies they have been living since those innocent days. Though a surreal work that deals with broken dreams and crippling illusions, *Jimmy Dean* is highlighted by some excellent comedy and a terrific performance by Cher. Unrated, the film contains profanity and mature subject matter. 1982; 110m.

COMEBACK KID, THE ★★
DIR: Peter Levin. **CAST:** John Ritter, Doug McKeon, Susan Dey, Jeremy Licht, James Gregory.

John Ritter plays a down-and-out major leaguer who ends up coaching a group of street kids. Mediocre made-for-TV movie. 1980; 97m.

COMEDIAN, THE ★★★★★
DIR: John Frankenheimer. **CAST:** Mickey Rooney, Mel Torme, Edmond O'Brien, Kim Hunter.

Originally aired live as a *Playhouse 90* drama, this film features Mickey Rooney as Sammy Hogarth, a ruthless, egomaniacal comedy star. His insatiable desire for unconditional adoration and obedience from those closest to him makes life a nightmare for his humiliated brother Lester (Mel Torme) and gag writer (Edmond O'Brien). Rod Serling's tight screenplay and the outstanding performances combine to make this an undated classic. 1957; B&W; 90m.

COMEDIANS, THE ★★
DIR: Peter Glenville. **CAST:** Elizabeth Taylor, Richard Burton, Alec Guinness, Peter Ustinov, Paul Ford, Lillian Gish, James Earl Jones, Cicely Tyson.

In this drama, Elizabeth Taylor and Richard Burton inadvertently become involved in the political violence and unrest of Haiti under Papa Doc Duvalier. The all-star cast does little to improve an average script—based on Graham Greene's novel. 1967; 160m.

COMIC, THE (1969) ★★★★
DIR: Carl Reiner. **CAST:** Dick Van Dyke, Mickey Rooney, Michele Lee, Cornel Wilde, Nina Wayne, Pert Kelton, Jeannine Riley.

There's a bit of every famous silent film funny man—Chaplin, Keaton, Arbuckle, Langdon, and Lloyd—in this engrossing account of a beloved reel comedian who's an egocentric heel in real life. Dick Van Dyke is peerless in the title character. Well planned and executed, this is a gem of its genre. Beautifully handled, the closing minutes alone are worth the entire film. Rated PG. 1969; 96m.

COMIC, THE (1985) ★
DIR: Richard Driscoll. **CAST:** Steve Munroe.

Set in a police state of the near future, an aspiring comic kills a popular entertainer in order to get a chance to perform in his stead. He soon becomes a star on the nightclub circuit, taking on his victim's mistress. Despite the subject matter, there are no jokes—or anything else you'd want to see—in this muddled hodgepodge. Unrated; brief nudity. 1985; 90m.

COMING HOME ★★★★½
DIR: Hal Ashby. **CAST:** Jane Fonda, Jon Voight, Bruce Dern, Robert Carradine, Robert Ginty, Penelope Milford.

Jane Fonda, Jon Voight, and Bruce Dern give superb performances in this thought-provoking drama about the effect the Vietnam War has on three people. Directed by Hal Ashby, it features a romantic triangle with a twist: Fonda, the wife of a gung-ho officer, Dern, finds real love when she becomes an aide at a veteran's hospital and meets a bitter but sensitive paraplegic, Voight. Rated R. 1978; 127m.

COMING OUT OF THE ICE ★★★½
DIR: Waris Hussein. **CAST:** John Savage, Willie Nelson, Ben Cross, Francesca Annis.

An engrossing made-for-television movie based on a true story. An American spends thirty-eight years in a Soviet prison camp for not renouncing his American citizenship. He is jailed and then banished to a remote northern village where he learns the meaning of freedom and finally is allowed to go home. 1987; 97m.

COMMON LAW CABIN ★★
DIR: Russ Meyer. **CAST:** Ken Swofford.

Melodrama set at an isolated fishing cabin on the Colorado River, where the guests include sex-starved women, ineffectual husbands, and an escaped bank robber. Not as over the top as such later Russ Meyer films as *Vixen*, *Cherry*, and *Harry and Raquel*, which it resembles, this is for Meyer historians only. Unrated, but a mild R equivalent for brief nudity and violence. 1967; 70m.

COMPETITION, THE ★★★½
DIR: Joel Oliansky. **CAST:** Richard Dreyfuss, Amy Irving, Lee Remick, Sam Wanamaker.

Richard Dreyfuss and Amy Irving star in this exquisitely crafted and completely enjoyable romance about two classical pianists who, while competing for top honors in a recital program, fall in love. Lee Remick and Sam Wanamaker add excellent support. Watch it with someone you love. Rated PG. 1980; 129m.

CON ARTISTS, THE ★½
DIR: Sergio Corbucci. **CAST:** Anthony Quinn, Capucine.

What could have been a lark turns into a ho-hum caper. Anthony Quinn is released from jail and attempts to swindle beautiful Capucine. Both leads are worthy of better vehicles. Look elsewhere. 1977; 87m.

CONCRETE ANGELS ★★
DIR: Carlo Liconti. **CAST:** Joseph Dimambro, Luke McKeehan.

Set in 1964 Toronto, this downbeat teen drama revolves around several friends trying to put together a band to enter in a competition. First prize is an opening spot at a Beatles concert. Separate stories of the boys are spun off, told with more realism than most teen films about the early Sixties. Unrated, but an R equivalent. 1987; 97m.

CONCRETE JUNGLE, THE (A.K.A. THE CRIMINAL) ★★★
DIR: Joseph Losey. **CAST:** Stanley Baker, Margit Saad, Sam Wanamaker, Gregoire Aslan, Jill Bennett, Laurence Naismith, Edward Judd.

Grim, claustrophobic prison drama is tightly directed and well acted (especially by the underrated Stanley Baker), and remains one of the best films of its kind as well as one of director Joseph Losey's most satisfying works. Often referred to in filmographies as *The Criminal*, this uncompromising look at life "inside" boasts gutsy, believable performances by a fine crew of veteran British character actors. 1962; B&W; 86m.

CONFESSIONS OF A POLICE CAPTAIN ★½
DIR: Damiano Damiani. **CAST:** Martin Balsam, Franco Nero, Marilu Tolo.
Heavy-handed melodrama wastes a fine performance by Martin Balsam as a good cop trying to close a tough case amid an avalanche of bureaucratic corruption. This Italian-made film is given to excess, and the confusing story fails to sustain interest. Rated PG. 1971; 102m.

CONFESSIONS OF A VICE BARON ★
DIR: Harvey Thew. **CAST:** Willy Castello.
Fly-by-night film chronicling the rise and fall of vice baron Lombardo isn't quite as bad as it could have been. The shoddy production values of this basement opus don't get in the way of the sleazy story of Lombardo's world of flesh peddling and illegal operations (not to mention dope!) that fell apart when he went sappy and fell in love. Some nudity thrown in, but overall pretty tame. Last part of tape features previews of other exploitation titles. 1942; B&W; 70m.

CONNECTION ★★★½
DIR: Tom Gries. **CAST:** Charles Durning, Ronny Cox, Zohra Lampert, Dennis Cole, Dana Wynter.
Charles Durning steals the show in this made-for-television movie. As an out-of-work newspaperman desperately in need of money, he becomes the intermediary between an insurance company and a high-priced jewel thief. Taut direction and a literate script help. 1973; 73m.

CONRACK ★★★★
DIR: Martin Ritt. **CAST:** Jon Voight, Paul Winfield, Hume Cronyn, Madge Sinclair.
In this sleeper, based on a true story, Jon Voight plays a dedicated white teacher determined to bring the joys of education to deprived blacks inhabiting an island off the coast of South Carolina. Rated PG. 1974; 107m.

CONSOLATION MARRIAGE ★★★
DIR: Paul Sloane. **CAST:** Irene Dunne, Pat O'Brien, John Halliday, Myrna Loy.
Slow-moving but well-made (for early talkie) soap opera about two jilted sweethearts (Irene Dunne and Pat O'Brien) who marry each other on the rebound, then find themselves tested when their old lovers come back. Stilted dialogue is a drawback, but the film remains interesting for the early performances of the stars. No rating; suitable for all audiences. 1931; B&W; 81m.

CONTRACT FOR LIFE: THE S.A.D.D. STORY ★★★½
DIR: Joseph Pevney. **CAST:** Stephen Macht.
Based on the work of real-life hockey coach Bob Anastas, this chronicles the creation of Students Against Driving Drunk. After two of his all-stars are killed while driving drunk, Anastas (beautifully played by Stephen Macht) inspires his students to band together to prevent similar tragedies. Well done! 1984; 46m.

CONVERSATION, THE ★★★★★
DIR: Francis Ford Coppola. **CAST:** Gene Hackman, John Cazale, Allen Garfield, Cindy Williams, Harrison Ford.
Following his box-office and artistic triumph with *The Godfather*, director Francis Ford Coppola made this absorbing character study about a bugging-device expert (Gene Hackman) who lives only for his work but finds himself developing a conscience. Although not a box-office hit when originally released, this is a fine little film. Rated PG. 1974; 113m.

CORN IS GREEN, THE (1945) ★★★★
DIR: Irving Rapper. **CAST:** Bette Davis, John Dall, Joan Lorring, Nigel Bruce, Rhys Williams, Mildred Dunnock.

Bette Davis leads a winning cast in this well-mounted film of British playwright-actor Emlyn Williams' drama of education vs. coal in a rough-edged Welsh mining village. John Dall is the young miner whom schoolteacher Davis grooms to win a university scholarship. 1945; B&W; 114m.

CORN IS GREEN, THE (1979) ★★★½

DIR: George Cukor. **CAST:** Katharine Hepburn, Ian Saynor, Bill Fraser, Patricia Hayes, Anna Massey.

Based on Emlyn Williams's play and directed by George Cukor, this telefilm stars Katharine Hepburn. She gives a tour-de-force performance as the eccentric spinster-teacher who helps a gifted young man discover the joys of learning. 1979; 100m.

CORNBREAD, EARL AND ME ★★½

DIR: Joseph Manduke. **CAST:** Moses Gunn, Bernie Casey, Rosalind Cash, Madge Sinclair.

A fine cast of black performers is ill served by this overdone drama about racism. A gifted basketball player is mistakenly killed by the police. It's a familiar plot directed with little inspiration by Joseph Manduke. Rated R. 1975; 95m.

COUNTDOWN ★★★

DIR: Robert Altman. **CAST:** James Caan, Robert Duvall, Charles Aidman.

This lesser-known Robert Altman film finds James Caan and Robert Duvall as American astronauts preparing for a moonshot. The realistic scenes and great acting raise this film high above most films of this kind—well worth watching. Unrated. 1968; 101m.

COUNTRY ★★★★

DIR: Richard Pearce. **CAST:** Jessica Lange, Sam Shepard, Wilford Brimley, Matt Clark.

A quietly powerful movie about the plight of farmers struggling to hold on while the government and financial institutions seem intent on fostering their failure. *Country* teams Jessica Lange and Sam Shepard on screen, for the first time since the Oscar-nominated *Frances*, in a film as topical as today's headlines. Rated PG. 1984; 109m.

COUNTRY GIRL, THE (1954) ★★★★½

DIR: George Seaton. **CAST:** Bing Crosby, Grace Kelly, William Holden, Anthony Ross.

Bing Crosby and Grace Kelly give terrific performances in this little-seen production. Crosby plays an alcoholic singer who wallows in self-pity until he seizes a chance to make a comeback. Kelly won an Oscar for her sensitive portrayal of his wife. 1954; B&W; 104m.

COUNTRY GIRL, THE (1982) ★★★½

DIR: Gary Halvorson. **CAST:** Faye Dunaway, Dick Van Dyke, Ken Howard.

Cable TV remake of Clifford Odets's tragic play pales somewhat compared to the Bing Crosby–Grace Kelly rendition. In this filmed stage-play version Dick Van Dyke is the alcoholic actor who has one last chance at a comeback. Ken Howard is the brash young director who blames Van Dyke's wife (Faye Dunaway) for the actor's decline. 1982; 137m.

COUNTRYMAN ★★★½

DIR: Dickie Jobson. **CAST:** "Countryman" Hiram Keller, Kristian Sinclair.

A strange and fun film following the adventures of a young marijuana-smuggling woman (Kristian Sinclair) whose airplane crash-lands in Jamaica. She is rescued by Countryman and led to safety. Lots of Rasta humor and supernatural happenings keep the viewer entertained. *Countryman* also has a great reggae music soundtrack. Rated R for nudity and adult themes. 1984; 103m.

COURAGEOUS DR. CHRISTIAN, THE ★★½

DIR: Bernard Vorhaus. **CAST:** Jean Hersholt, Dorothy Lovett, Robert Baldwin, Tom Neal.

In this episode in the Dr. Christian series, Jean Hersholt again plays the saintlike physician. Predictable but pleasing. 1940; B&W; 67m.

COURTMARTIAL OF BILLY MITCHELL, THE ★★★

DIR: Otto Preminger. **CAST:** Gary Cooper, Rod Steiger, Charles Bickford, Ralph Bellamy, Elizabeth Montgomery, Jack Lord, Peter Graves, Darren McGavin.

In 1925, Army General Billy Mitchell was court-martialed for calling the army and the navy almost treasonous for their neglect of military air power after World War I. Gary Cooper is marvelous as Mitchell, but the show is almost stolen by prosecuting attorney Rod Steiger. 1955; 100m.

COURTNEY AFFAIR, THE ★★★

DIR: Herbert Wilcox. **CAST:** Anna Neagle, Michael Wilding, Coral Browne.

British family saga stretching across four and a half decades: 1900–1945. Classy soap opera in which a housemaid marries money and trades the back stairs for the drawing room. 1947; B&W; 112m.

COURTSHIP ★★★★

DIR: Howard Cummings. **CAST:** Hallie Foote, Amanda Plummer, Rochelle Oliver, Michael Higgins, William Converse-Roberts.

A touching and engrossing period play (set in 1915) from the pen of Horton Foote, whose superb dialogue makes this tale of a young woman's coming of age easy to believe. A wonderful transport back to the more chivalrous days of yesteryear. No rating. 1987; 85m.

COWARD OF THE COUNTY ★★★

DIR: Dick Lowry. **CAST:** Kenny Rogers, Frederic Lehne, Largo Woodruff, Mariclare Costello, Ana Alicia.

This made-for-TV film is based on Kenny Rogers's hit song. He plays a World War II Georgia preacher with a pacifist nephew. When the nephew's girlfriend is raped, he's put to the ultimate test of his nonviolent beliefs. The acting and setting are believable, making this a film worth viewing. 1981; 110m.

COWBOY AND THE BALLERINA, THE ★★

DIR: Jerry Jameson. **CAST:** Lee Majors, Leslie Wing, Christopher Lloyd, Anjelica Huston.

This telemovie is romance at its most basic: hero rescues damsel in distress and love naturally follows. Lee Majors plays a former world-champion rodeo rider who meets a Russian ballerina (Leslie Wing) who is attempting to defect. Corny but adequate time-passer. 1984; 100m.

CRACKER FACTORY ★★★★

DIR: Burt Brinckerhoff. **CAST:** Natalie Wood, Peter Haskell, Shelley Long, Vivian Blaine, Perry King.

This made-for-TV drama features Natalie Wood as Cassie Barrett, an alcoholic housewife who loses her grip on reality. Her long-suffering husband, Charlie (Peter Haskell), silently offers support while she spends her rehabilitation in the Cracker Factory, a mental institution. Perry King plays the handsome psychiatrist that fellow patient Cara (Shelley Long) falls in love with. Unrated, but the mature topic warrants parental discretion. 1979; 95m.

CRADLE WILL FALL, THE ★

DIR: John Llewellyn Moxey. **CAST:** Lauren Hutton, Ben Murphy, James Farentino, Charlita Bauer, Carolyn Ann Clark.

This made-for-television suspense movie falls flat. Lauren Hutton is an attorney who gets entangled with a doctor (Ben Murphy). Along comes another doctor—straight out of Dachau, one would think—who turns things upside down. The story is silly and the direction uninspired. 1983; 100m.

CRAIG'S WIFE ★★★
DIR: Dorothy Arzner. **CAST:** Rosalind Russell, John Boles, Billie Burke, Jane Darwell, Thomas Mitchell, Alma Kruger.
In her first film success, Rosalind Russell is brilliant as Harriet Craig, the wife of the title, a heartless domestic tyrant whose neurotic preference for material concerns over human feelings alienates all around her. John Boles is her long-suffering, slow-to-see-the-light husband. 1936; B&W; 75m.

CRAZY MOON ★½
DIR: Allan Eastman. **CAST:** Kiefer Sutherland, Vanessa Vaughan.
This is another entry in the *Harold and Maude* genre: Neurotic, alienated young man gets his act together when he falls in love with a spunky older woman who is managing to cope with real problems. Here, though, the eccentricities of Brooks (Kiefer Sutherland), a gentle withdrawn teenager who dresses and acts as if he were living in the Big Band era, are too pathetic and extreme to be amusing. Rated PG-13. 1986; 89m.

CREATOR ★★
DIR: Ivan Passer. **CAST:** Peter O'Toole, Mariel Hemingway, Vincent Spano, Virginia Madsen, David Ogden Stiers, John Dehner.
This film, about a scientist (Peter O'Toole) who is attempting to bring back to life the wife who died thirty years before, during childbirth, is, at first, a very witty and occasionally heart-tugging comedy. However, in its last third, it turns into a sort of second-rate tearjerker. Rated R for nudity, profanity, and simulated sex. 1985; 108m.

CRIMES OF PASSION
DIR: Ken Russell. **CAST:** Kathleen Turner, Anthony Perkins, John Laughlin.
Kathleen Turner stars in this disgusting and perverse sex film as Joanna Crane, a woman who leads a double life. By day she's a highly paid fashion designer; by night, she's a kinky high-priced hooker called China Blue. Anthony Perkins (in a role reminiscent of his famous *Psycho* turn) is a sleazy street-corner preacher who becomes obsessed with her. Rated R for nudity, suggested sex, profanity, and violence. 1984; 107m.

CRIMINAL CODE, THE ★★★★
DIR: Howard Hawks. **CAST:** Boris Karloff, Walter Huston, Phillips Holmes.
A powerful performance by Boris Karloff as a revenge-minded convict, elevates this Howard Hawks release from interesting to memorable. It's a lost classic that deserves its release on video. The story involves a district attorney (impressively played by Walter Huston) who over-zealously pursues his job, with the result that an innocent man (Phillips Holmes) is sent to prison. 1931; B&W; 83m.

CRISIS AT CENTRAL HIGH ★★★★½
DIR: Lamont Johnson. **CAST:** Joanne Woodward, Charles Durning, Henderson Forsythe, William Russ.
In the late Fifties Little Rock, Arkansas, was rocked by the integration of the school system. This television film is a retelling of those events as seen through the eyes of teacher Elizabeth Huckaby, one of the principal characters involved. Joanne Woodward is simply wonderful as the caught-in-the-middle instructor. 1981; 125m.

CRISS CROSS ★★★
DIR: Robert Siodmak. **CAST:** Burt Lancaster, Yvonne De Carlo, Dan Duryea, Stephen McNally, Richard Long.
A less than riveting plot mars this otherwise gritty *film noir*. Burt Lancaster plays an armored-car guard who, along with his less than trustworthy wife, gets involved with a bunch of underworld thugs. 1948; B&W; 87m.

CROMWELL ★★
DIR: Ken Hughes. **CAST:** Richard Harris, Alec Guinness, Robert Morley, Frank Finlay, Dorothy Tutin, Timothy Dalton, Patrick Magee.
Richard Harris hams it up again in this overblown historical melodrama. A fine cast founders amid tradition-soaked locations and beautiful backgrounds. The accoutrements and design are splendid, but the story is lacking and Harris's performance is inept. 1970; 145m.

CROSS COUNTRY ★★
DIR: Paul Lynch. **CAST:** Richard Beymer, Nina Axelrod, Michael Ironside, Brent Carver.
Michael Ironside plays Detective Ed Roersch, who pursues Richard Beymer following the murder of an expensive call girl. Although this movie involves prostitution, blackmail, murder, and deceit, it still manages to bore. Rated R for nudity, sex, profanity, and violence. 1983; 95m.

CROSS CREEK ★★★½
DIR: Martin Ritt. **CAST:** Mary Steenburgen, Rip Torn, Peter Coyote, Dana Hill.
About the life of 1930s author Marjorie Kinnan Rawlings (Mary Steenburgen), this watchable release illustrates how Rawlings's relationships with backwoods folks inspired her novels, particularly *The Yearling* and *Jacob's Ladder*. Rated PG for brief violence. 1983; 122m.

CROSSFIRE ★★★½
DIR: Edward Dmytryk. **CAST:** Robert Ryan, Robert Mitchum, Robert Young, Sam Levene, Gloria Grahame, Paul Kelly, Steve Brodie.
While on leave from the army, psychopathic bigot Robert Ryan meets Sam Levene in a nightclub and later murders him during an argument. An army buddy is blamed; another is also murdered. Often billed as a *film noir*, this interesting film is more of a message indicting anti-Semitism, and it was the first major Hollywood picture to explore racial bigotry. 1947; B&W; 86m.

CROSSING DELANCEY ★★★★½
DIR: Joan Micklin Silver. **CAST:** Amy Irving, Peter Riegert, Reizl Bozyk, Jeroen Krabbé, Sylvia Miles.
Amy Irving has the role of her career as the independent New Yorker scrutinized by Susan Sandler's deft and poignant screenplay (adapted from her own stage play). Irving has a bookstore job that brings her into close contact with the pretentious members of the Big Apple's literary scene; she fulfills deeper needs with visits to her feisty grandmother (Reizl Bozyk). Grandmother has matchmaking plans, specifically involving Irving with street-vendor Peter Riegert, whose flawless timing is one of the many highlights here. Rated PG for language and mild sexual themes. 1988; 97m.

CROWD, THE ★★★★½
DIR: King Vidor. **CAST:** James Murray, Eleanor Boardman.
Director King Vidor's pioneering slice-of-life story of a working class family in a big city during the jazz age still holds up beautifully after sixty years. James Murray, in his only major movie, gives an extraordinary performance as a hard-working clerk who never seems to get ahead. Not rated; suitable for all but the youngest children. 1928; B&W; 90m.

CRUEL SEA, THE ★★★½
DIR: Charles Frend. **CAST:** Jack Hawkins, Virginia McKenna, Stanley Baker, Donald Sinden.
The ever-changing and unpredictable wind-lashed sea is the star of this gripping documentary-style adventure about a stalwart British warship and its crew during World War II. 1953; B&W; 121m.

CRUISING ★★
DIR: William Friedkin. **CAST:** Al Pacino, Paul Sorvino, Karen Allen, Richard Cox, Don Scardino.

Cruising, which was based on a series of brutal murders in New York City between 1962 and 1979, is horror in the real sense of the word. Friedkin throws in everything you can think of to make it a grisly ordeal for the viewer: dismembered body parts, graphic stabbing scenes, and the like. The film begins when a rotted, bloated forearm is found floating in the East River. Rated R. 1980; 106m.

CRY DANGER ★★★
DIR: Robert Parrish. **CAST:** Dick Powell, Rhonda Fleming, William Conrad, Richard Erdman.
Dick Powell plays a wisecracking ex-con who has been framed for a robbery. Upon his release, he sets out to take revenge on the people who set him up. Rhonda Fleming is the woman he loves. Not bad! Unrated, this contains violence. 1950; B&W; 80m.

CRY FOR LOVE, A ★★★½
DIR: Paul Wendkos. **CAST:** Susan Blakely, Powers Boothe, Gene Barry, Edie Adams, Lainie Kazan, Charles Siebert.
Taut teledrama about two people—one an alcoholic, the other addicted to uppers—who, through some very real difficulties, fall in love. Their attempts to help each other over the crises of substance abuse draw them closer together. 1980; 100m.

CRY FREEDOM ★★★★½
DIR: Richard Attenborough. **CAST:** Kevin Kline, Penelope Wilton, Denzel Washington, Ian Richardson.
Director Richard Attenborough and screenwriter John Briley's superb film about South African apartheid begins by chronicling the growing friendship between nonviolent black leader Steve Biko (Denzel Washington) and white newspaperman Donal Woods (Kevin Kline). When Biko is brutally murdered, Woods must fight to tell the truth about his friend's death to the rest of the world. Rated PG for violence. 1987; 130m.

CRY IN THE DARK, A ★★★★½
DIR: Fred Schepisi. **CAST:** Meryl Streep, Sam Neill, Charles Tingwell.
A chilling, superbly acted true-life drama set in 1980 Australia, this film features Meryl Streep and Sam Neill as the parents of an infant who is stolen by a wild dog while they are camping out—or so they say. The authorities begin to doubt their story and the Australian people begin spreading rumors that the baby was killed in a sacrificial rite. Thus begins this harrowing motion picture. Rated PG-13 for mature themes. 1988; 120m.

CRY VENGEANCE ★
DIR: Mark Stevens. **CAST:** Mark Stevens, Martha Hyer, Skip Homeier, Joan Vohs, Douglas Kennedy.
Another formula revenge story. An ex-cop set up as a fall guy seeks revenge against the villains who framed him and killed his family. Sound familiar? Stevens's perpetual suit and tie are laughably out of place against the rough-hewn setting of an Alaskan fishing village. 1954; B&W; 83m.

CRYSTAL HEART
DIR: Gil Bettman. **CAST:** Tawny Kitaen, Lee Curreri, Lloyd Bochner.
A young man with a rare illness falls in love with an aspiring rock singer in this brainless weeper with awful music video sequences. The viewer suffers more than the characters. Avoid this preposterous tearjerker. Rated R. 1987; 103m.

CUT AND RUN
DIR: Ruggero Deodato. **CAST:** Lisa Blount, Leonard Mann, Willie Aames, Richard Lynch, Richard Bright, Michael Berryman, John Steiner, Karen Black.
Lisa Blount plays a television journalist in search of the ultimate scoop. She finds it in South America, while covering a bloody cocaine war. She finally encounters the conquering army led by one of Jim Jones's hit men. It is quite difficult to like anyone or anything in this miserable outing. Rated

R for violence, profanity, sex, and nudity. 1985; 87m.

CUTTER'S WAY ★★★★
DIR: Ivan Passer. **CAST:** Jeff Bridges, John Heard, Lisa Eichhorn, Ann Dusenberry.

Cutter's Way comes very close to being a masterpiece. The screenplay, by Jeffrey Alan Fiskin, adapted from the novel *Cutter and Bone* by Newton Thornburg, is a murder mystery. The three lead performances are first-rate. Rated R because of violence, nudity, and profanity. 1981; 105m.

CYRANO DE BERGERAC ★★★★
DIR: Michael Gordon. **CAST:** José Ferrer, Mala Powers, William Prince.

Charming, touching story of steadfast devotion and unrequited love done with brilliance and panache. As the fearless soldier of the large nose, José Ferrer superbly dominates this fine film. Mala Powers is beautiful as his beloved Roxanne. William Prince, who now often plays heavies, makes Christian a proper, handsome, unimaginative nerd. 1950; B&W; 112m.

DA ★★★★
DIR: Matt Clark. **CAST:** Barnard Hughes, Martin Sheen, William Hickey, Doreen Hepburn.

New York City playwright Martin Sheen returns to his Irish home when his adoptive father (Barnard Hughes) dies. While in the house in which he was raised, Sheen relives his less-than-idyllic youth with the help of his father's cantankerous ghost. Both sentimental and uncompromising, this special film benefits from a performance of a lifetime by Hughes and one of nearly equal merit by Sheen. Rated PG for profanity. 1988; 96m.

DADDY'S GONE A-HUNTING ★★★
DIR: Mark Robson. **CAST:** Carol White, Paul Burke, Scott Hylands, Mala Powers.

Veteran director Mark Robson knows how to get the best out of the material he has to work with. And this is an exciting, neatly crafted psychological drama—in which Carol White gets involved with a psychotic photographer (Scott Hylands). If you get a chance to go a-hunting for this one at your local video store, you won't go unrewarded. Not rated, but with some violent content. 1969; 108m.

DAISY MILLER ★
DIR: Peter Bogdanovich. **CAST:** Cybill Shepherd, Barry Brown, Cloris Leachman, Mildred Natwick, Eileen Brennan.

Even a world-class director has a bad outing now and then. Peter Bogdanovich seems to have lost his edge on this effort. This limp screen adaptation of a story by the great novelist Henry James is more a study on rambling dialogue than on the clashing of two cultures. Cybill Shepherd plays a young American visiting Europe in the 1880s who sets the Victorian high society on its ear with her gauche behavior. She babbles her way through the film without really saying anything. Rated G. 1974; 93m.

DAKOTA (1988) ★★★
DIR: Fred Holmes. **CAST:** Lou Diamond Phillips, Dee Dee Morton.

Outstanding cinematography highlights this run-of-the-mill story of a troubled teen on the run. Lou Diamond Phillips is the teen who works off a debt by training horses on a Texas farm. In the process he learns he must also face his past. Rated PG-13. 1988; 90m.

DANCE HALL RACKET ★½
DIR: Phil Tucker. **CAST:** Lenny Bruce.

Inane dance scenes, cheap sets, and ham acting take up a lot of this film, and screenplay writer Lenny Bruce takes up the rest of the scenes. Bruce plays creepy killer Vincent, bodyguard to a vice lord who enjoys hurting women. This is a genuine sleazy exploitation film from the 1950s underground. 1953; B&W; 60m.

DANCE WITH A STRANGER ★★★★½

DIR: Mike Newell. **CAST:** Miranda Richardson, Rupert Everett, Ian Holm, Matthew Carroll.

A superbly acted, solidly directed import, this British drama is a completely convincing tale of tragic love. Newcomer Miranda Richardson makes a stunning film debut as the platinum-blond hostess in a working-class nightclub who falls in love with a self-indulgent, upperclass snob (Rupert Everett). The screenplay was based on the true story of Ruth Ellis, who, on July 13, 1955, was hanged at London's Holloway prison for shooting her lover outside a pub. Rated R for profanity, nudity, sex, and violence. 1985; 102m.

DANCING IN THE DARK ★★½

DIR: Leon Marr. **CAST:** Martha Henry, Neil Munro, Rosemary Dunsmore.

Interesting drama about Edna Cormick (Martha Henry) who—after twenty years of being the ideal housewife, finds her life torn apart in a few short hours. From her hospital bed, Edna reconstructs the events that led up to her act of vengeance. Although this film is extremely slow-moving, feminists are likely to appreciate it. Rated PG-13. 1986; 93m.

DANGER LIGHTS ★★★

DIR: George B. Seitz. **CAST:** Louis Wolheim, Jean Arthur, Robert Armstrong, Hugh Herbert.

Louis Wolheim plays a tough-as-nails rail-yard boss who befriends hobo Robert Armstrong and jeopardizes his chances with a young Jean Arthur, who is "almost" a fiancée. This story, done many times before and since, works well against the backdrop of a railroad world that is now largely gone. 1930; B&W; 73m.

DANGEROUS COMPANY ★★

DIR: Lamont Johnson. **CAST:** Beau Bridges, Carlos Brown, Karen Carlson, Kene Holliday, Ralph Macchio.

The true story of convict Ray Johnson, who lived in and out of prison for years until his reform. Excellent acting saves what would otherwise be a tedious biography. 1982; 100m.

DANGEROUS LIAISONS ★★★★

DIR: Stephen Frears. **CAST:** Glenn Close, John Malkovich, Michelle Pfeiffer, Mildred Natwick.

Based on the classic French novel *Les Liaisons Dangereuses,* this exquisitely filmed story of competitive sexual gamesmanship between two ex-lovers is charged with sensual energy. The cast, led by a marvelously brittle Glenn Close and John Malkovich, is first rate. There's a sumptuous rhythm to the language and a lush setting that beautifully captures upper-class, sixteenth-century France. Rated R. 1989; 120m.

DANGEROUS SUMMER, A ★

DIR: Quentin Masters. **CAST:** James Mason, Tom Skerritt, Ian Gilmour, Wendy Hughes.

Set in Australia, this film deals with a posh resort—owned in part by American Howard Anderson (Tom Skerritt)—damaged by fire and the subsequent investigation by insurance troubleshooter George Engels (James Mason), sent by Lloyds of London to discover whether the incident was an accident or arson. Cheaply made, unimaginatively photographed, and poorly directed. Unrated, the film has violence and profanity. 1984; 100m.

DANIEL ★★½

DIR: Sidney Lumet. **CAST:** Timothy Hutton, Mandy Patinkin, Lindsay Crouse, Edward Asner, Amanda Plummer.

Sidney Lumet directed this disappointing and ultimately depressing screen version of E. L. Doctorow's thinly veiled account of the Rosenberg case of thirty years ago, in which the parents of two young children were electrocuted as spies. If it weren't for Timothy Hutton's superb performance in the title role (as one of the children), *Daniel* would be much less effective. Rated R for profanity and violence. 1983; 130m.

DANNY BOY (1941) ★★
DIR: Oswald Mitchell. **CAST:** Ann Todd, Wilfrid Lawson.

Estranged from her husband and small son, a singer searches for them, only to find that they have become street musicians. Overly sentimental, but the music is nice enough. 1941; B&W; 80m.

DANNY BOY (1982) ★★★★
DIR: Neil Jordan. **CAST:** Stephen Rea, Marie Kean, Ray McAnally, Donal McCann.

A young saxophone player witnesses the brutal murder of two people and becomes obsessed with understanding the act. Set in Ireland, this movie is enhanced by haunting musical interludes that highlight the drama of the people caught up in the Irish "troubles." There are flaws, most notably in some of the coincidences, but the overall effect is mesmerizing. Rated R. 1982; 92m.

DARK JOURNEY ★★★
DIR: Victor Saville. **CAST:** Vivien Leigh, Conrad Veidt, Joan Gardner, Anthony Bushell.

Espionage with a twist. A British and a German spy fall in love in Stockholm during World War I. 1937; B&W; 82m.

DARK PAST, THE ★★★½
DIR: Rudolph Maté. **CAST:** William Holden, Lee J. Cobb, Nina Foch, Adele Jergens.

A psychotic killer escapes from prison and a psychologist attempts to convince the hood to give himself up. Lee J. Cobb is marvelous as the psychiatrist and William Holden is wonderful as the bad guy. Nina Foch is top-notch as Holden's moll. A remake of *Blind Alley*. 1948; 75m.

DARK VICTORY ★★★★
DIR: Edmund Goulding. **CAST:** Bette Davis, George Brent, Humphrey Bogart, Ronald Reagan, Geraldine Fitzgerald.

This Warner Bros. release gave Bette Davis one of her best roles, as a headstrong heiress who discovers she has a brain tumor. A successful operation leads to a love affair with her doctor (George Brent). In the midst of all this bliss, Davis learns the tragic truth: surgery was only a halfway measure, and she will die in a year. Sure it's corny. But director Edmund Goulding, Davis, and her co-stars make it work. 1939; B&W; 106m.

DARK WATERS ★★½
DIR: André de Toth. **CAST:** Merle Oberon, Franchot Tone, Thomas Mitchell, Fay Bainter, Rex Ingram, John Qualen, Elisha Cook Jr.

Muddled story of orphaned girl(?), Merle Oberon, and her strange and terrifying experiences with her aunt and uncle in the bayou backwaters of Louisiana is atmospheric and properly chilling at times, but fails to deliver enough of a story to justify its moody build-up. The leads are all right, but the supporting players (along with the misty bogs) really carry the ball in this film. 1944; B&W; 90m.

DARLING ★★★★
DIR: John Schlesinger. **CAST:** Julie Christie, Dirk Bogarde, Laurence Harvey, Jose Luis de Villalonga.

John Schlesinger's direction is first-rate, and Julie Christie gives an Oscar-winning portrayal of a ruthless model who bullies, bluffs, and claws her way to social success, only to find life at the top depressing and meaningless. 1965; B&W; 122m.

DAVID AND LISA ★★★½
DIR: Frank Perry. **CAST:** Keir Dullea, Janet Margolin, Howard DaSilva, Neva Patterson, Clifton James.

Mentally disturbed teenagers (Keir Dullea and Janet Margolin) meet and develop a sensitive emotional attachment while institutionalized. Abetted by Howard Da Silva as their understanding doctor, Dullea and Margolin make this study highly watchable. Independently produced, this one was a sleeper. 1962; B&W; 94m.

DAVID COPPERFIELD ★★★★½
DIR: George Cukor. **CAST:** Freddie Bartholomew, Frank Lawton, Lionel Barrymore, W. C. Fields, Edna May Oliver, Basil Rathbone.

A first-rate production of Charles Dickens's rambling novel about a young man's adventures in nineteenth-century England. W. C. Fields and Edna May Oliver are standouts in an all-star cast. 1935; B&W; 100m.

DAY OF THE LOCUST, THE ★★★★½
DIR: John Schlesinger. **CAST:** Donald Sutherland, Karen Black, Burgess Meredith, Bo Hopkins.

This drama is both extremely depressing and spellbinding. It shows the unglamorous side of Hollywood in the 1930s. The people who don't succeed in the entertainment capital are the focus of the film. Rated R. 1975; 144m.

DAYS OF HEAVEN ★★★★½
DIR: Terence Malick. **CAST:** Richard Gere, Brooke Adams, Sam Shepard, Linda Manz.

Each frame of *Days of Heaven* looks like a page torn from an exquisitely beautiful picture book. The film begins in the slums of Chicago, where Bill (Richard Gere) works in a steel mill. He decides to take Abby (Brooke Adams), his girl, and Linda (Linda Manz), his young sister, to the Texas Panhandle to work in the wheat fields at harvest time. That's the beginning of an idyllic year that ends in tragedy. Rated PG. 1978; 95m.

DAYS OF WINE AND ROSES ★★★½
DIR: Blake Edwards. **CAST:** Jack Lemmon, Lee Remick, Charles Bickford, Jack Klugman.

In this saddening film, Jack Lemmon and Lee Remick shatter the misconceptions about middle-class alcoholism. 1962; B&W; 117m.

DAYS OF WINE AND ROSES, THE (TELEVISION) ★★★½
DIR: John Frankenheimer. **CAST:** Cliff Robertson, Piper Laurie.

Unpolished but still excellent television original from which the 1962 film was adapted. Cliff Robertson is the up-and-coming executive and Piper Laurie, his pretty wife, whose lives are shattered by alcoholism. Written for the *Playhouse 90* series, *The Days of Wine and Roses* is introduced by Julie Harris and framed with interviews with the featured players. 1958; B&W; 90m.

D-DAY THE SIXTH OF JUNE ★½
DIR: Henry Koster. **CAST:** Robert Taylor, Richard Todd, Dana Wynter, Edmond O'Brien.

Slow-moving account of the Normandy invasion in World War II. Story concentrates on Allied officers Robert Taylor's and Richard Todd's romantic and professional problems. The actual invasion scenes are good, but come way too late to save this poor excuse for a war film. 1956; 106m.

DEAD, THE ★★★★★
DIR: John Huston. **CAST:** Anjelica Huston, Donal McCann, Ingrid Craigie, Dan O'Herlihy, Marie Kean, Donal Donnelly, Sean McClory.

John Huston's final bow is an elegant adaptation of James Joyce's short story about a party given by three women for a group of their dearest friends. During the evening, conversation drifts to those people, now dead, who have had a great influence on the lives of the guests and hostesses at the party. Huston, who died before the film was released, seems to be speaking to us from beyond the grave. This is one of his best. Rated PG. 1987; 81m.

DEAD EASY ★★½
DIR: Bert Dilling. **CAST:** Scott Burgess, Rosemary Paul, Tim McKenzie.

George, Alexa, and Armstrong are three friends who try to break into the big-city night life. In doing so they anger a crime boss whose overreaction sets off a chain of events that results in every small-time hood and paid killer chasing them. Well-done contemporary crime thriller. Rated R for nudity, violence, language. 1978; 90m.

DEAD END ★★★
DIR: William Wyler. **CAST:** Humphrey Bogart, Sylvia Sidney, Joel McCrea, Claire Trevor.

Many famous names combined to film this story of people trying to escape their oppressive slum environment. Humphrey Bogart is cast in one of his many gangster roles from the 1930s. Joel McCrea conforms to his Hollywood stereotype by playing the "nice guy" architect, who dreams of rebuilding New York's waterfront. 1937; B&W; 93m.

DEAD POETS SOCIETY, THE ★★★½
DIR: Peter Weir. **CAST:** Robin Williams, Robert Sean Leonard, Norman Lloyd, Ethan Hawke.

Robin Williams offers an impressive change-of-pace performance as an unorthodox English teacher. He inspires a love of poetry and intellectual freedom in his students at a strict, upscale New England prep school. Though not entirely satisfying in its resolution, the film offers much of the heart and mood of *Goodbye, Mr. Chips* and *The Prime of Miss Jean Brodie*. Richly textured by Australian filmmaker Peter Weir. 1989; 124m.

DEADLINE (1987) ★★★
DIR: Nathaniel Gutman. **CAST:** Christopher Walken, Hywel Bennett.

Christopher Walken is good as a reporter covering the conflict in Beirut, finding himself becoming personally involved when he falls for a German nurse working for the rebels. This film is very much in the vein of *Salvador* and *Under Fire*, but cannot duplicate their tension. Rated R. 1987; 100m.

DEADLINE USA ★★★★
DIR: Richard Brooks. **CAST:** Humphrey Bogart, Kim Hunter, Ethel Barrymore.

In this hard-hitting newspaper drama, Humphrey Bogart plays an editor who has to fight the city's underworld while keeping the publisher (superbly portrayed by Ethel Barrymore) from giving in to pressure and closing the paper down. While Kim Hunter is wasted in the small role as Bogart's ex-wife, the picture has much to recommend it. 1952; B&W; 87m.

DEADLY ENCOUNTER (1975) ★
DIR: R. John Hugh. **CAST:** Dina Merrill, Carl Betz, Leon Ames.

A rich woman invites her friends and business associates to a dinner at which she is to reveal details of a new business venture. Her real purpose, though, is to provoke dissent. Full of enough overwrought situations for a month's worth of soap operas, and appropriately hammy acting. Originally released as *The Meal*. Rated R for sexual talk and situations. 1975; 90m.

DEATH DRUG ★★
DIR: Oscar Williams. **CAST:** Philip Michael Thomas, Vernee Watson, Rosalind Cash.

A truthful yet cliché-filled movie about a promising young musician who starts using angel dust. Although the drug PCP deserves any bad rap it gets, this movie is a mediocre effort. Not rated, but fairly inoffensive. 1986; 73m.

DEATH IN VENICE ★★
DIR: Luchino Visconti. **CAST:** Dirk Bogarde, Marisa Berenson, Mark Burns, Silvana Mangano.

This slow, studied film based on Thomas Mann's classic novel is about an artist's life and quest for beauty and perfection. The good cast seems to move through this movie without communicating with one another or the audience. Visually absorbing, but lifeless. Adult language, adult situations throughout. Rated PG. 1971; 130m.

DEATH OF A CENTERFOLD ★★
DIR: Gabrielle Beaumont. **CAST:** Jamie Lee Curtis, Robert Reed, Bruce Weitz.

This made-for-TV film chronicles the brutal murder of Playboy playmate Dorothy Stratten. Bob Fosse's *Star 80* does a much better job of getting inside the characters of Stratten and her power-crazy husband. Unrated. 1981; 100m.

DEATH OF A SALESMAN ★★★★
DIR: Volker Schlondorff. **CAST:** Dustin Hoffman, Kate Reid, John Malkovich, Stephen Lang, Charles Durning.
Impressive TV version of the Arthur Miller play. Dustin Hoffman is excellent as the aging, embittered Willy Loman, who realizes he has wasted his life and the lives of his family. Kate Reid is his long-suffering wife and Charles Durning is the neighbor. Thoughtful and well produced. 1985; 135m.

DEATH OF A SCOUNDREL ★★★
DIR: Charles Martin. **CAST:** George Sanders, Zsa Zsa Gabor, Tom Conway, Yvonne De Carlo, Nancy Gates, Coleen Grey, Victor Jory, John Hoyt.
If anyone could portray a suave, debonair, conniving, ruthlessly charming, amoral, despicable, notorious, manipulating cad, it was George Sanders. He does so to a *tee* in this portrait of the ultimate rake—based on the life of financier Serge Rubenstein. 1956; 119m.

DEATH OF A SOLDIER ★★½
DIR: Phillippe Mora. **CAST:** James Coburn, Bill Hunter, Reb Brown, Maurie Fields.
Based on a true story that changed the procedures of military court-martial. In 1942 an American GI stationed in Australia murdered three Melbourne women. The incident aggravated U.S.–Australian relations, and General MacArthur ordered the execution of the serviceman to firm up Allied unity. James Coburn plays a major who believes the GI isn't sane enough to stand trial. Rated R for profanity, violence, and nudity. 1985; 93m.

DEATH OF ADOLF HITLER, THE ★★★
DIR: Rex Firkin. **CAST:** Frank Finlay, Caroline Mortimer, Ray McAnally.
Made-for-British-television dramatization of the last ten days of the dictator's life, all spent in the underground bunker where he received the news of Germany's defeat. Frank Finlay is excellent as Hitler, avoiding the usual stereotypes. The low-key nature of the production renders it eerie, but strangely unmoving. Not rated. 1972; 107m.

DEATHTRAP ★★★
DIR: Sidney Lumet. **CAST:** Michael Caine, Christopher Reeve, Dyan Cannon, Irene Worth, Henry Jones.
An enjoyable mystery-comedy based on the long-running Broadway play, this Sidney Lumet film stars Michael Caine, Christopher Reeve, and Dyan Cannon. Caine plays a once-successful playwright who decides to steal a brilliant murder mystery just written by one of his drama students (Reeve), claim it as his own, murder the student, and collect the royalties. Rated PG for violence and adult themes. 1982; 116m.

DEDICATED MAN, A ★★
DIR: Robert Knights. **CAST:** Alec McCowen, Joan Plowright, Christopher Irving.
Haunting British romance about a workaholic who asks a lonely spinster to pose as his wife. All goes well until she starts asking questions about his past. The *Romance Theatre* presentation will disappoint viewers hoping for high passions. 1982; 50m.

DEER HUNTER, THE ★★★★★
DIR: Michael Cimino. **CAST:** Robert De Niro, John Cazale, John Savage, Meryl Streep, Christopher Walken.
Five friends—Michael (Robert De Niro), Stan (John Cazale), Nick (Christopher Walken), Steven (John Savage), and Axel (Chuck Aspergen)—work at the dangerous blast furnace in a steel mill of a dingy Midwestern industrial town in 1968. At

quitting time, they make their way to their favorite local bar to drink away the pressures of the day. For Michael, Nick, and Steven it is the last participation in the ritual. In a few days, they leave for Vietnam, where they find horror and death. What follows is a gripping study of heroism and the meaning of friendship. Rated R for profanity and violence. 1978; 183m.

DEFENSE OF THE REALM ★★★★
DIR: David Drury. **CAST:** Gabriel Byrne, Greta Scacchi, Denholm Elliott, Ian Bannen, Bill Paterson, Fulton MacKay.

In London, two reporters (Gabriel Byrne and Denholm Elliott) become convinced that a scandal involving a government official (Ian Bannen) may be a sinister coverup. Acting on this belief puts both their lives in danger. *Defense of the Realm* is a tough-minded British thriller that asks some thought-provoking questions about what the public has a right to know. Rated PG for suspense. 1986; 96m.

DEFIANT ONES, THE ★★★★
DIR: Stanley Kramer. **CAST:** Tony Curtis, Sidney Poitier, Theodore Bikel, Charles McGraw, Lon Chaney Jr.

Director Stanley Kramer scored one of his few artistic successes with this compelling story about two escaped convicts (Tony Curtis and Sidney Poitier) shackled together—and coping with mutual hatred—as they run from the authorities in the South. 1958; B&W; 97m.

DEJA VU ★
DIR: Anthony Richmond. **CAST:** Jaclyn Smith, Shelley Winters, Claire Bloom, Nigel Terry.

Jaclyn Smith and Nigel Terry put in equally lame performances in this stupid story about reincarnation. Shelley Winters' portrayal of a stereotypical Russian gypsy is so bad, it's laughable. The film's only good point is Claire Bloom. Rated R for some sex, nudity, and violence. 1984; 91m.

DELINQUENT DAUGHTERS ★½
DIR: Albert Herman. **CAST:** June Carlson, Fifi D'Orsay, Teala Loring.

A reporter and a cop decide to find out just what's going on with today's kids after a high-school girl commits suicide. Slow-moving cheapie that is merely a hyped-up dud. 1944; B&W; 71m.

DEMPSEY ★★★
DIR: Gus Trikonis. **CAST:** Treat Williams, Sam Waterston, Sally Kellerman, Victoria Tennant, Peter Mark Richman, Jesse Vint.

Treat Williams plays Jack Dempsey, World Heavyweight Champion boxer from 1919 to 1926. Stylish and with riveting plot twists. As Dempsey's first wife, Sally Kellerman is particularly effective. Not rated, contains violence and profanity. 1983; 110m.

DESERT BLOOM ★★★
DIR: Eugene Corr. **CAST:** Jon Voight, JoBeth Williams, Ellen Barkin, Allen Garfield, Annabeth Gish.

This poignant study of awakening adolescence and family turmoil is effectively set against a backdrop of 1950 Las Vegas, as the atomic age dawns. The story unfolds slowly but sensitively. Thirteen-year-old Annabeth Gish gives a remarkably complex performance as a brilliant girl who must cope with an abusive stepfather, an ineffectual mother, and a sexpot aunt. Rated PG. 1986; 106m.

DESERT HEARTS ★★★½
DIR: Donna Deitch. **CAST:** Helen Shaver, Patricia Charbonneau, Audra Lindley, Gwen Welles, Dean Butler.

A sensitive portrayal of the evolving relationship between a young, openly lesbian woman and a quiet university professor ten years her senior. Set on a Reno "divorce ranch" in 1959. The excellent acting by Patricia Charbonneau and Helen Shaver superbly sets off the development of their individual and joint characters. Some may find the explicit love scenes upsetting, but the humor and characterization entirely overrule any objection on this basis, and the bonus of 1950s props and sets is a treat. Rated R for profanity and sex. 1986; 90m.

DESIRE UNDER THE ELMS ★★
DIR: Delbert Mann. **CAST:** Sophia Loren, Anthony Perkins, Burl Ives, Frank Overton.

There is not much to recommend in this adaptation of Eugene O'Neill's play. Burl Ives brings home a new wife, Sophia Loren, and sparks are supposed to ignite with the stepson, Anthony Perkins. But this film merely proves that good actors, when miscast, make for tedious viewing and disappointment. 1958; B&W; 114m.

DESIRÉE ★★
DIR: Henry Koster. **CAST:** Marlon Brando, Jean Simmons, Merle Oberon, Michael Rennie, Cameron Mitchell, Isabel Epsom, John Hoyt, Cathleen Nesbitt.

A romantic tale of Napoleon's love for 17-year-old seamstress Desirée Clary. Marlon Brando bumbles about as Napoleon in this tepid travesty of history. 1954; 110m.

DESPERATE HOURS, THE ★★★★
DIR: William Wyler. **CAST:** Humphrey Bogart, Fredric March, Arthur Kennedy, Martha Scott, Gig Young.

Three escaped convicts terrorize a suburban Indiana family; based on Joseph Hayes's novel and play. Humphrey Bogart is too old for the part that made a star of Paul Newman on Broadway, but the similarity to the *The Petrified Forest* must have been too good to pass up. Frederic March takes top acting honors. Not rated. 1955; B&W; 112m.

DETECTIVE, THE (1968) ★★★
DIR: Gordon Douglas. **CAST:** Frank Sinatra, Lee Remick, Al Freeman Jr., Jacqueline Bisset, Ralph Meeker, Jack Klugman, Robert Duvall, William Windom.

A disgusted NYPD detective (Frank Sinatra), carrying an overload of both professional and personal problems, railroads the wrong man into the electric chair while seeking a homosexual's killer. He loses his job and leaves his nympho wife (Lee Remick). Filmed on location in New York, this is one of the first hard-look-at-a-cop's life films. 1968; 114m.

DETOUR ★★★
DIR: Edgar G. Ulmer. **CAST:** Tom Neal, Ann Savage, Claudia Drake, Tim Ryan.

This routine story about a drifter enticed into crime is skillfully constructed, economically produced, and competently acted; it has long been considered one of the best (if not *the* best) low-budget film ever made. Ann Savage as the beguiling, destructive enchantress playing off Tom Neal's infatuation rings just as true in this bargain-basement production as it does in the highly acclaimed adult crime dramas produced by the major studios. 1945; B&W; 69m.

DEVIL AND DANIEL WEBSTER, THE ★★★★
DIR: William Dieterle. **CAST:** Edward Arnold, Walter Huston, James Craig, Anne Shirley, Jane Darwell, Simone Simon, Gene Lockhart.

This wickedly witty tale, based on a Stephen Vincent Benét story, delivers some potent messages. Edward Arnold, so often cast as a despicable villain, is riveting as the noble Webster. This eloquent hero must defend ingenuous James Craig in a bizarre courtroom. Both of their immortal souls are at stake. Opposing Webster is Mr. Scratch, also known as the Devil. Walter Huston gives a dazzling performance in the role. 1941; B&W; 85m.

DEVIL AT 4 O'CLOCK, THE ★★★
DIR: Mervyn LeRoy. **CAST:** Spencer Tracy, Frank Sinatra, Kerwin Mathews, Jean-Pierre Aumont.

This script may be weak and predictable, but the acting of Spencer Tracy and Frank Sinatra make this a watchable motion picture. Tracy is a priest who is in charge of an orphanage.

When their island home is endangered by an impending volcanic eruption, he seeks the aid of a group of convicts headed by Sinatra. 1961; 126m.

DEVIL THUMBS A RIDE, THE ★
DIR: Felix Feist. **CAST:** Lawrence Tierney, Ted North, Nan Leslie.
This third-rate crime melodrama features Lawrence Tierney as a bank robber who gets a ride with Ted North and enlists his help in a series of holdups. A poor script, poor production values, and muddled performances. 1947; B&W; 62m.

DEVILS, THE ★★★★
DIR: Ken Russell. **CAST:** Oliver Reed, Vanessa Redgrave, Dudley Sutton, Max Adrian, Gemma Jones.
Next to *Women in Love*, this is director Ken Russell's best film. Exploring witchcraft and politics in France during the seventeenth century, it's a mad mixture of drama, horror, camp, and comedy. Ugly for the most part (with several truly unsettling scenes), it is still fascinating. Rated R. 1971; 109m.

DEVIL'S PARTY, THE ★
DIR: Ray McCarey. **CAST:** Victor McLaglen, Paul Kelly, William Gargan.
Insipid melodrama about a group of friends from a bad neighborhood who run around starting fires and engaging in crime with a bunch of stereotypical mobsters. Yawn! 1938; B&W; 65m.

DEVLIN CONNECTION III, THE ★★
DIR: Christian Nyby. **CAST:** Rock Hudson, Jack Scalia, Leigh Taylor-Young, Tina Chen.
One of the *Devlin Connection* TV episodes entitled "Love, Sex, Sin and Death at Point Dume" features Rock Hudson and Jack Scalia as a father-son duo who try to find a murderer before he kills their friend (Leigh Taylor-Young). Nothing special here, folks. 1982; 50m.

D.I., THE ★★★
DIR: Jack Webb. **CAST:** Jack Webb, Don Dubbins, Lin McCarthy, Monica Lewis, Jackie Loughery, Virginia Gregg.
Jack Webb embodies the tough, no-nonsense drill instructor so commonly associated with the Marine Corps in this straightforward story of basic training and the men that it makes (or breaks). Don Dubbins plays the troublesome recruit who makes life miserable for Webb; many other roles are played by real-life members of the armed services. 1957; B&W; 106m.

DIAMOND HEAD ★★
DIR: Guy Green. **CAST:** Charlton Heston, Yvette Mimieux, George Chakiris, France Nuyen, James Darren.
Domineering Hawaiian plantation boss Charlton Heston comes close to ruining his family with his dictatorial ways. The lush scenery is the only credible thing in this pineapple opera. 1963; 107m.

DIARY OF A MAD HOUSEWIFE ★★★
DIR: Frank Perry. **CAST:** Richard Benjamin, Carrie Snodgress, Frank Langella.
Most women will detest Jonathan (Richard Benjamin), the self-centered, social climber husband of Tina (Carrie Snodgress). He has had an affair and also lost all their savings in a bad investment. Tina, a college graduate, has been unhappily stuck at home for years with their two children. She finally finds happiness in an affair with George (Frank Langella). Profanity, sex, and nudity are included in this film. 1970; 94m.

DIARY OF A TEENAGE HITCHHIKER ★★
DIR: Ted Post. **CAST:** Charlene Tilton, Dick Van Patten, Katherine Helmond, James Carroll Jordan, Katy Kurtzman, Dominique Dunne, Craig T. Nelson.
Trite dialogue and an inappropriate score lessen the impact of this made-for-TV drama documenting the dan-

gers of hitchhiking for young women. Inferior. 1979; 96m.

DIARY OF ANNE FRANK, THE ★★★★½

DIR: George Stevens. **CAST:** Millie Perkins, Joseph Schildkraut, Shelley Winters.

Excellent adaptation of the Broadway play dealing with the terror Jews felt during the Nazi raids of World War II. Two families are forced to hide in a Jewish sympathizer's attic to avoid capture by the Nazis. Anne (Millie Perkins) is the teenage girl who doesn't stop dreaming of a better future. Shelley Winters won an Oscar for her role as the hysterical Mrs. Van Daan, who shares sparse food and space with the Frank family. 1959; B&W; 170m.

DIARY OF FORBIDDEN DREAMS ★★½

DIR: Roman Polanski. **CAST:** Hugh Griffith, Marcello Mastroianni, Sydne Rome.

A bizarre variation on the classic fantasy *Alice In Wonderland*, this concerns a beautiful young woman (Sydne Rome) who becomes lost in a remote area of the Italian Riviera. The film suffers from too many diversions that create a complete mess out of this highly unlikely story. Rated R for nudity and language. 1981; 94m.

DIFFERENT STORY, A ★★★½

DIR: Paul Aaron. **CAST:** Perry King, Meg Foster, Valerie Curtin, Peter Donat.

Perry King and Meg Foster play homosexuals who realize their romances are just not clicking. They fall in love with each other, marry, grow rich, and, eventually, dissatisfied. King and Foster are genuinely funny and appealing as the most modern of young adult couples. Rated PG. 1979; 107m.

DIM SUM: A LITTLE BIT OF HEART ★★★★

DIR: Wayne Wang. **CAST:** Laureen Chew, Kim Chew, Victor Wong.

Dim Sum is an independently made American movie about the tension and affection between a Chinese mother and daughter living in San Francisco's Chinatown. The film moves quietly, but contains many moments of humor. The restraint of the mother, who wants her daughter to marry, and the frustration of the daughter, who wants to live her life as she chooses, are beautifully conveyed by real-life mother and daughter Laureen and Kim Chew. Victor Wong, as a rambunctious uncle, is a gas. Rated PG. 1985; 88m.

DINGAKA ★★★½

DIR: Jamie Uys. **CAST:** Stanley Baker, Juliet Prowse, Ken Gampu, Bob Courtney.

Cultures collide in this South African film as Masai warrior Ken Gampu tracks his daughter's killer to a metropolis and comes face to face with civilized justice. Spectacularly filmed by writer-producer Jamie Uys, this impressive movie features knockout performances by African film star Gampu as the accused and Stanley Baker as his attorney. 1965; 98m.

DINO ★★

DIR: Thomas Carr. **CAST:** Sal Mineo, Brian Keith, Susan Kohner, Frank Lovejoy, Joe De Santis.

Sal Mineo plays a troubled teen filled with hate and confusion after spending nearly four years in reform school. Brian Keith is the savvy psychologist who helps him understand his emotions in this utterly predictable film. The street jargon is strained. 1957; B&W; 96m.

DISAPPEARANCE OF AIMEE, THE ★★★½

DIR: Anthony Harvey. **CAST:** Faye Dunaway, Bette Davis, James Woods, Severn Darden.

Strong performers and taut direction made this one made-for-television movie that is way above average. Faye Dunaway plays preacher Aimee Semple McPherson, whose mysterious disappearance in 1926 gave rise to all sorts of speculation. A literate script, solid supporting performances by Bette Davis and James Woods, and plenty of period flavor make this one a winner. 1976; 110m.

DISPLACED PERSON, THE ★★★★

DIR: Glenn Jordan. **CAST:** Irene Worth, John Houseman, Shirley Stoler, Lane Smith, Robert Earl Jones.

Man's cruel, ugly side is exposed in this adaptation of Flannery O'Connor's brutal short story. Irene Worth is a struggling Georgia farm widow who allows a Polish World War II refugee and his family to live and work on her land. The woman's initially sympathetic feelings gradually mirror those of her other worthless laborers, who fear that their lives of relative laziness are jeopardized by this "unwanted foreigner." Introduced by Henry Fonda; unrated and suitable for family viewing. 1976; 58m.

DISTANT THUNDER (1988) ★★½

DIR: Rick Rosenthal. **CAST:** John Lithgow, Ralph Macchio.

After roaming the wilds of the Pacific Northwest with his Vietnam-vet buddies for several years, emotionally scarred ex-soldier John Lithgow decides to return to civilization and find the son (Ralph Macchio) he hasn't seen in over a decade. Lithgow struggles valiantly with the downbeat material, but Macchio is miscast and no help at all. Rated R for violence and profanity. 1988; 114m.

DISTANT VOICES/STILL LIVES ★★★★★

DIR: Terence Davies. **CAST:** Freda Dowie, Pete Postlethwaite, Angela Walsh, Dean Williams.

An impressionistic memory film, based on the director's family memories and history. Set in England in the late 1940s, it explores the relationships and emotions of a middle-class family as they undergo domestic brutality, failed marriages, and the pains of life. The film's rich humanity and its unique use of a robust musical score overcome its cynicism. Off-beat and original. 1988; 85m.

DIVORCE HIS: DIVORCE HERS ★★½

DIR: Waris Hussein. **CAST:** Richard Burton, Elizabeth Taylor, Carrie Nye, Barry Foster, Gabriele Ferzetti.

This less-than-exceptional TV movie follows the breakup of a marriage in which both partners are allowed to explain what they think led to the failure of their marriage. Although its soap-opera format is mildly interesting, the talents of Elizabeth Taylor and Richard Burton are barely tapped. 1972; 144m.

D.O.A. (1949) ★★★½

DIR: Rudolph Maté. **CAST:** Edmond O'Brien, Pamela Britton, Luther Adler, Lynne Baggett, Neville Brand.

CPA Edmond O'Brien, slowly dying from radiation poisoning, seeks those responsible in this fast-paced, stylized *film noir* thriller. Most unusual is the device of having the victim play detective and hunt his killers as time runs out. Neville Brand takes honors as a psychopath who tries to turn the tables on the victim before he can inform the police. 1949; B&W; 83m.

D.O.A. (1988) ★★

DIR: Rocky Morton, Annabel Jankel. **CAST:** Dennis Quaid, Meg Ryan, Charlotte Rampling, Daniel Stern, Jane Kaczmarek.

This failed update of the 1949 *film noir* classic makes the crippling mistake of hauling its Chandleresque storyline into the 1980s. Dennis Quaid is the hard-drinking college professor who wakes to find he's been fatally poisoned; with mere hours to live, he drags lovestruck college student Meg Ryan along on the hunt for his killer. Rated R for language and violence. 1988; 96m.

DOCKS OF NEW YORK, THE ★★★★

DIR: Josef von Sternberg. **CAST:** George Bancroft, Betty Compson, Olga Baclanova, Mitchell Lewis.

A solid drama of love and death on a big-city waterfront. Rough-edged George Bancroft rescues would-be suicide Betty Compson, marries her, clears her of a murder charge, and goes to jail for her. The direction is masterful, the camerawork and lighting superb in this, one of the last silent films to be released. 1928; B&W; 60m.

DR. CHRISTIAN MEETS THE WOMEN

DIR: William McGann. **CAST:** Jean Hersholt, Dorothy Lovett, Edgar Kennedy, Frank Albertson, Veda Ann Borg, Rod La Rocque.

Kindly old Dr. Christian (Jean Hersholt) takes on a diet charlatan in this stanza of the film series. 1940; B&W; 60m.

DR. FAUSTUS ★★

DIR: Richard Burton. **CAST:** Richard Burton, Elizabeth Taylor.

Richard Burton is the man who sells his soul for gain and Elizabeth Taylor is Helen of Troy in this weird adaptation of Christopher Marlowe's retelling of the ancient Greek legend. Strictly fodder for Taylor and Burton fans. 1968; 93m.

DR. ZHIVAGO ★★★★

DIR: David Lean. **CAST:** Omar Sharif, Julie Christie, Geraldine Chaplin, Rod Steiger, Alec Guinness.

An epic treatment was given to Boris Pasternak's novel of romance and revolution in this film. Omar Sharif is Zhivago, a Russian doctor and poet whose personal life is ripped apart by the upheaval of the Russian Revolution. The screenplay is choppy and overlong and is often sacrificed to the spectacle of vast panoramas, detailed sets, and impressive costumes. These artistic elements, along with a beautiful musical score, make for cinema on a grand scale, and it remains a most watchable movie. 1965; 176m.

DOCTORS' WIVES

DIR: George Schaefer. **CAST:** Gene Hackman, Richard Crenna, Carroll O'Connor, Janice Rule, Dyan Cannon, Cara Williams.

Trashy film that focuses on the seedy side of being a doctor's wife. Dyan Cannon, Cara Williams, and Janice Rule star as the unhappy spouses who turn to sex and substance abuse to cope with their feelings of loneliness and inadequacy. Rated PG. 1971; 100m.

DODSWORTH ★★★★

DIR: William Wyler. **CAST:** Walter Huston, Ruth Chatterton, Mary Astor, David Niven, Spring Byington, Paul Lukas, John Payne, Maria Ouspenskaya.

Walter Huston, in the title role, heads an all-star cast in this outstanding adaptation of the Sinclair Lewis novel. Auto tycoon Samuel Dodsworth is the epitome of the classic American self-made man. His wife is an appearance-conscious *nouveau riche* snob. An intelligent, mature script, excellent characterizations, and sensitive cinematography make this film a modern classic. 1936; B&W; 101m.

DOG DAY AFTERNOON ★★★★½

DIR: Sidney Lumet. **CAST:** Al Pacino, John Cazale, Charles Durning, Carol Kane.

Dog Day Afternoon is a masterpiece of contemporary commentary. Al Pacino once again proves himself to be in the front rank of America's finest actors. Director Sidney Lumet scores high with masterful pacing and real suspense. This is an offbeat drama about a gay man who's involved in bank-robbing. Highly recommended. Rated R. 1975; 130m.

DOLLMAKER, THE ★★★★

DIR: Daniel Petrie. **CAST:** Jane Fonda, Levon Helm, Amanda Plummer, Susan Kingsley, Ann Hearn, Geraldine Page.

Jane Fonda won an Emmy for her intensely quiet portrayal of a mother of five in 1940s Kentucky. As a devoted mother, her only personal happiness is sculpting dolls out of wood. When her husband is forced to take work in Detroit, their relocation causes many personal hardships and setbacks. The story is beautifully told.

This made-for-TV movie is unrated, but it provides excellent family entertainment. 1984; 140m.

DOLL'S HOUSE, A ★★★

DIR: Joseph Losey. **CAST:** Jane Fonda, David Warner, Trevor Howard.

Jane Fonda is quite good in this screen version of Henrik Ibsen's play about a liberated woman in the nineteenth century, and her struggles to maintain her freedom. Pacing is a problem at times, but first-class acting and beautiful sets keep the viewer interested. 1973; 103m.

DOMINICK AND EUGENE ★★★★½

DIR: Robert M. Young. **CAST:** Tom Hulce, Ray Liotta, Jamie Lee Curtis, Robert Levine.

Fraternal twin brothers Dominick and Eugene Luciano have big plans for the future. Eugene (Ray Liotta), an ambitious medical student, plans to take care of Dominick (Tom Hulce), who is considered "slow" but nonetheless has been supporting them by working as a trash collector. All "Nicky" wants is to live in a house by a lake where he and his brother can be together. This is a deeply touching film; superbly directed and acted. Rated PG-13 1988; 103m.

DOMINO ★★

DIR: Ivana Massetti. **CAST:** Brigitte Nielsen.

Artsy Italian film delves into the surreal as it follows Brigitte Nielsen in her quest for love. She's been looking in all the wrong places and now think she's found it in the voice of an obscene caller. Rated R for nudity and countless sexual situations. 1989; 96m.

DOMINO PRINCIPLE, THE ★

DIR: Stanley Kramer. **CAST:** Gene Hackman, Richard Widmark, Candice Bergen, Eli Wallach, Mickey Rooney.

Never have so many been wasted on so little. The only true victims in this assassination/double cross/conspiracy thriller are the viewers tricked into watching it. Even Gene Hackman can't do anything as a confused convict busted out of prison with the intent to kill somebody. R for violence. 1977; 100m.

DON'T CRY, IT'S ONLY THUNDER ★★★★

DIR: Peter Werner. **CAST:** Dennis Christopher, Susan Saint James.

Here is one of those "little" movies that slipped by without much notice yet so satisfying when discovered by adventurous video renters. A black market wheeler-dealer (Dennis Christopher), lining his pockets behind the lines during the Vietnam War is forced to aid some Asian nuns and their ever-increasing group of Saigon street orphans. The results are predictably heartwarming and occasionally heartbreaking, but the film never drifts off into sentimental melodrama. Rated PG. 1982; 108m.

DON'T MESS WITH MY SISTER ★

DIR: Meir Zarchi. **CAST:** Joe Perce, Jeannine Lemay.

This low-budget creation from Meir (*I Spit on Your Grave*) Zarchi features a handsome young man trapped in a forced marriage. He's also tired of working in a junkyard with his wife's two brothers. Her family retaliates after his one-night affair with a belly dancer. Unrated; contains profanity, violence, and sexual situations. 1985; 85m.

DOOMSDAY FLIGHT, THE ★★★

DIR: William A. Graham. **CAST:** Jack Lord, Edmond O'Brien, Van Johnson, John Saxon, Michael Sarrazin.

Rod Serling wrote the script for this made-for-television movie, the first to depict the hijacking of an airliner. A distraught Edmond O'Brien blackmails an airline company by planting a bomb aboard a passenger plane. *The Doomsday Flight* offered good suspense at the time, but may not be as provocative today. Still, good acting is on hand as the search for the bomb is carried out. 1966; 100m.

DOUBLE LIFE, A ★★★★
DIR: George Cukor. **CAST:** Ronald Colman, Edmond O'Brien, Shelley Winters, Ray Collins.
Ronald Colman gives an Oscar-winning performance as a famous actor whose stage life begins to take over his personality and private life, forcing him to revert to stage characters, including Othello, to cope with everyday situations. Clever, brilliantly written by Garson Kanin and Ruth Gordon, and impressively acted by a stand-out cast of top character actors and actresses. Top treatment of a fine story. 1947; B&W; 104m.

DOWN TO THE SEA IN SHIPS ★★★
DIR: Elmer Clifton. **CAST:** William Walcott, Marguerite Courtot, Clara Bow.
The plot involving a romantic conflict within a family of whalers has a beard, but vivid scenes filmed at sea aboard real New England whalers out of Bedford make it worthwhile. 1922; B&W; 83m.

DOWNHILL RACER ★★★½
DIR: Michael Ritchie. **CAST:** Robert Redford, Gene Hackman, Camilla Sparv.
Robert Redford struggles with an unappealing character, in this study of an Olympic skier. But Gene Hackman is excellent as the coach who tries to turn him around, and the exciting scenes of this snow sport hold the film together. Rated PG. 1969; 101m.

D.P. ★★★★
DIR: Alan Bridges. **CAST:** Stan Shaw, Rosemary Leach, Julius Gordon.
The shattering loss of innocence by war's true victims—children—is examined in this Emmy-winning adaptation of Kurt Vonnegut's poignant story. Julius Gordon is one of many orphans cared for by nuns in post—World War II Germany, a truly "displaced person" because he is the only boy with black skin. Unrated; suitable for family viewing. 1985; 60m.

DRAGON SEED ★★½
DIR: Jack Conway, Harold S. Bucquet. **CAST:** Katharine Hepburn, Walter Huston, Turhan Bey, Hurd Hatfield.
This study of a Chinese town torn asunder by Japanese occupation is taken from the novel by Nobel Prize winner Pearl S. Buck. It's occasionally gripping but in general too long. 1944; B&W; 145m.

DREAM OF KINGS, A ★★★★
DIR: Daniel Mann. **CAST:** Anthony Quinn, Irene Papas, Inger Stevens, Sam Levene, Val Avery.
Anthony Quinn turns in an unforgettable performance in this powerful and touching drama set in Chicago's Greek community. He plays an earthy, proud father determined to raise enough money to flee from America to Greece with his ailing young son. A moving character study. Not rated. 1969; 111m.

DREAM OF PASSION, A ★★★½
DIR: Jules Dassin. **CAST:** Melina Mercouri, Ellen Burstyn, Andreas Voutsinas, Despo Diamantidou.
Melina Mercouri plays a Greek actress who is preparing to play Medea. As a publicity stunt, she goes to a prison to meet a real-life Medea. Ellen Burstyn is brilliant as the American prisoner who has killed her three children in order to take revenge on her husband. Rated R. 1978; 106m.

DREAM STREET ★★
DIR: D. W. Griffith. **CAST:** Carol Dempster, Charles Emmett Mack, Ralph Graves, Tyrone Power Sr., Morgan Wallace.
Good struggles with evil in this sentimental morality tale of London's infamous Limehouse slum. Two brothers, in love with the same girl, vie for her attentions while a wily, blackmailing Chinese gambler plans to take her by force. Good eventually wins. Silent. 1921; B&W; 138m.

DREAM TO BELIEVE ★★★
DIR: Paul Lynch. **CAST:** Olivia D'Abo, Rita Tushingham, Keanu Reeves.

If you like *Flashdance*, *Rocky*, and the *World Gymnastics Competition*, you'll love this Cinderella story. It's the soap drama of a teenage girl who, against physical odds, turns herself into an accomplished gymnast. No rating. 1985; 96m.

DRESSER, THE ★★★★★
DIR: Peter Yates. **CAST:** Albert Finney, Tom Courtenay, Edward Fox, Zena Walker.

Peter Yates directed this superb screen treatment of Ronald Harwood's play about an eccentric stage actor (Albert Finney) in wartime England and the loyal valet (Tom Courtenay) who cares for him, sharing his triumphs and tragedies. Rated PG for language. 1983; 118m.

DRUM 🦃
DIR: Steve Carver. **CAST:** Ken Norton, Warren Oates, Pam Grier, John Colicos, Yaphet Kotto.

Sweaty, sexed-up continuation of *Mandingo*, Kyle Onstott's lurid tale of plantation life in the pre–Civil War South. An abomination. 1976; 110m.

DRYING UP THE STREETS ★½
DIR: Robin Spry. **CAST:** Sarah Torov, Don Francks, Len Cariou, Calvin Butler.

This Canadian exposé of street people, drugs and prostitution does not translate well for the American viewer. Attenuated and predictable. Unrated. 1984; 90m.

DUDES ★★
DIR: Penelope Spheeris. **CAST:** Jon Cryer, Catherine Mary Stewart, Daniel Roebuck, Flea, Lee Ving.

Billed as the first punk-rock western, this film starts off well as a comedy about three New York City rockers (Jon Cryer, Daniel Roebuck and Flea) who decide to go to California in hopes of finding a better life. After the first goofy 20 minutes, *Dudes* abruptly turns violent. Rated R for violence and profanity. 1988; 90m.

DUET FOR ONE ★★★
DIR: Andrei Konchalovsky. **CAST:** Julie Andrews, Alan Bates, Max von Sydow, Rupert Everett.

As an English virtuoso violinist with multiple sclerosis, Julie Andrews gives an outstanding performance in this high-class tearjerker. Alan Bates is her sympathetic but philandering husband. Max von Sydow is the psychiatrist who atttempts to help her. And Rupert Everett plays her protégé who shuns the classical world for big time showbiz. Rated R. 1987; 110m.

DUNERA BOYS, THE ★★★★
DIR: Greg Snedon. **CAST:** Joe Spano, Bob Hoskins, Warren Mitchell.

Bob Hoskins is sensational in this harrowing war drama about a group of Jewish refugees who are ironically suspected of being German informants by the British army. They are shipped to a prison camp in Australia on the HMT *Dunera*. A film of great intelligence and humanity. Rated R for violence and profanity. 1987; 150m.

DUST ★★
DIR: Marion Hansel. **CAST:** Jane Birkin, Trevor Howard.

A Bergmanesque tale of a lonely South African farmer's daughter and her descent into madness after she kills her abusive father. Jane Birkin does a commendable job as the bitter farm maid, but the film is very moody, with lots of mumbled lines and long still shots. Not rated, but contains violence and suggested sex. 1985; 87m.

DUTCH GIRLS ★
DIR: Giles Foster. **CAST:** Bill Paterson, Colin Firth, Timothy Spall.

Another coming-of-age movie, this time showing a British field-hockey team grappling with rites of puberty as they try to score off the field during a visit to Amsterdam. Dreary. Rated R for suggested sex. 1985; 83m.

D. W. GRIFFITH TRIPLE FEATURE ★★★
DIR: D. W. Griffith. **CAST:** Mae Marsh, Lillian Gish, Charles West, Blanche Sweet, Mary Pickford.
Kentucky dreamer and failed playwright David Wark Griffith was the American film industry's first great mover and shaker. Three fine examples of his early short films make up this feature: *The Battle of Elderbush Gulch, Iola's Promise,* and *The Goddess of Sagebrush Gulch.* Silent. 1912–1922; B&W; 50m.

EARLY FROST, AN ★★★★½
DIR: John Erman. **CAST:** Gena Rowlands, Ben Gazzara, Aidan Quinn, Sylvia Sidney, John Glover.
This timely, extremely effective drama focuses on a family's attempt to come to grips with the fact that their son is not only gay but has AIDS as well. Gena Rowlands, one of Hollywood's most neglected actresses, and Aidan Quinn take the acting honors as mother and son. One of those rare television movies that works on all levels, it is highly recommended. 1985; 100m.

EAST OF EDEN (1955) ★★★★★
DIR: Elia Kazan. **CAST:** James Dean, Jo Van Fleet, Julie Harris, Raymond Massey, Burl Ives.
The final portion of John Steinbeck's renowned novel of miscommunication and conflict between a father and son was transformed into a powerful, emotional movie. James Dean burst onto the screen as the rebellious son in his first starring role. Jo Van Fleet received an Oscar for her role as Kate, a bordello madam and Dean's long-forgotten mother. 1955; 115m.

EAST OF EDEN (1982) ★★★½
DIR: Harvey Hart. **CAST:** Jane Seymour, Timothy Bottoms, Bruce Boxleitner, Warren Oates, Anne Baxter, Lloyd Bridges, Howard Duff.
This above-average television miniseries maintains the integrity of the source material by John Steinbeck without dipping too far into pathos. One major change: the focus shifts from the two sons who crave Papa's affection, to the deliciously evil woman—Jane Seymour—who twists them all around her little finger. Stick with the 1955 original. Unrated. 1982; 240m.

EAST OF ELEPHANT ROCK ★★
DIR: Don Boyd. **CAST:** John Hurt, Jeremy Kemp, Judi Bowker.
This story of the 1948 British struggle to maintain a Far Eastern colony focuses on a new governor general's takeover after his predecessor is murdered by terrorists. The film is slow-paced and burdened with soap-opera overtones. Rated R. 1981; 93m.

EASY LIVING ★★★½
DIR: Jacques Tourneur. **CAST:** Victor Mature, Lucille Ball, Lizabeth Scott, Sonny Tufts.
Shorn of the clichés one usually expects from movies about over-the-hill athletes, this picture offers a realistic account of an aging professional football player (Victor Mature) coming to terms with the end of a long career and a stormy home life. Lucille Ball and Lizabeth Scott are wonderful as the understanding secretary and shrewish wife, respectively. 1949; B&W; 77m.

EASY RIDER ★★★½
DIR: Dennis Hopper. **CAST:** Peter Fonda, Dennis Hopper, Jack Nicholson, Karen Black, Luana Anders.
Time has not been kind to this 1969 release, about two drifters (Peter Fonda and Dennis Hopper) motorcycling their way across the country only to be confronted with violence and bigotry. Jack Nicholson's keystone performance, however, still makes it worth watching. Rated R. 1969; 94m.

EASY VIRTUE ★★
DIR: Alfred Hitchcock. **CAST:** Isabel Jeans, Franklyn Dyall, Ian Hunter.
In this melodrama, based loosely on a Noel Coward play, the wife of an alcoholic falls in love with a younger man who commits suicide. Her past

life prevents her from leading a normal life. Considering the directorial credit, this is close to dull. A British production. 1927; B&W; 73m.

EBONY TOWER, THE ★★★
DIR: Robert Knights. **CAST:** Laurence Olivier, Greta Scacchi.

Sir Laurence Olivier is well cast as an aging artist who shields himself from the world outside his estate in this fine screen adaptation of the John Fowles novel. This absorbing British TV drama is not rated, but it contains some partial nudity. 1986; 80m.

ECHO PARK ★★★
DIR: Robert Dornhelm. **CAST:** Susan Dey, Tom Hulce, Michael Bowen, Christopher Walker, Shirley Jo Finney, John Paragon, Richard "Cheech" Marin, Cassandra Peterson.

Tom Hulce, Susan Dey and Michael Bowen star as three young show-biz hopefuls living in one of Los Angeles's seedier neighborhoods and waiting for stardom to strike. Director Robert Dornhelm and screenwriter Michael Ventura have some interesting things to say about the quest for fame, and the stars provide some memorable moments. Rated R for nudity, profanity, and violence. 1986; 93m.

EDUCATION OF SONNY CARSON, THE ★★★
DIR: Michael Campus. **CAST:** Rony Clanton, Don Gordon, Joyce Walker, Paul Benjamin.

This grim but realistic movie is based on the autobiography of Sonny Carson, a ghetto-raised black youth whose life was bounded by gangs, drugs, and crime. There's no upbeat happy ending and no attempt to preach, either; the film simply shows ghetto life for the frightening hell it is. Rated R. 1974; 104m.

EIGHT MEN OUT ★★★★½
DIR: John Sayles. **CAST:** Charlie Sheen, John Cusack, Christopher Lloyd, D. B. Sweeney, David Straithairn, Michael Lerner, Clifton James, John Sayles, Studs Terkel.

Writer-director John Sayles scores a home run with this baseball drama about the 1919 Black Sox scandal—when members of the Chicago White Sox conspired to throw the World Series. A superb ensemble cast, which includes Sayles as Ring Lardner, shines in this true-life shocker, with David Straithairn and John Cusack giving standout performances. Rated PG for profanity. 1988; 120m.

84 CHARING CROSS ROAD ★★½
DIR: David Jones. **CAST:** Anne Bancroft, Anthony Hopkins, Judi Dench, Maurice Denham.

Anne Bancroft manages to act manic even while reading books in this true story based on the life of Helene Hanff, a writer and reader who begins a twenty-year correspondence with a London bookseller (Anthony Hopkins). Along with her orders for first editions, Hanff sends witty letters and care packages to the employees during the hard postwar times. Hanff and the bookseller begin to rely on the correspondence, yet never get to meet. Rated PG for language. 1986; 99m.

ELECTRIC HORSEMAN, THE ★★★
DIR: Sydney Pollack. **CAST:** Robert Redford, Jane Fonda, Valerie Perrine, Willie Nelson, John Saxon, Nicolas Coster.

Directed by Sydney Pollack, *The Electric Horseman* brought the third teaming of Jane Fonda and Robert Redford on the screen. The result is a winsome piece of light entertainment. Redford plays Sonny Steele, a former rodeo star who has become the unhappy spokesman for Ranch Breakfast, a brand of cereal. He's always in trouble and in danger of blowing the job—until he decides to rebel. Rated PG. 1979; 120m.

ELENI ★★★
DIR: Peter Yates. **CAST:** Kate Nelligan, John Malkovich, Linda Hunt.
Interesting film adaptation of Nicholas Gage's factual book *Eleni*. In 1948, during the civil war in Greece, a small mountain village is terrorized by a group of communist guerrillas. Eleni Gatzoyiannis (Kate Nelligan) defies the communists and their attempts to abduct her children and is subsequently tortured and executed in cold blood. Eleni's son Nicholas Gage (John Malkovich) returns to Greece after many years as a reporter for the *New York Times*, devoting his life there to unmasking her killers. Rated PG for language and violence. 1985; 116m.

ELEPHANT MAN, THE ★★★★
DIR: David Lynch. **CAST:** Anthony Hopkins, John Hurt, Anne Bancroft, Wendy Hiller, Freddie Jones.
Though it has its flaws, this film is a fascinating and heartbreaking study of the life of John Merrick, a hopelessly deformed but kind and intelligent man who struggles for dignity. John Hurt is magnificent in the title role. Rated PG. 1980; B&W; 125m.

ELLIS ISLAND ★★★
DIR: Jerry London. **CAST:** Richard Burton, Faye Dunaway, Ben Vereen, Melba Moore, Ann Jillian, Greg Martyn, Peter Riegert.
This TV miniseries, of the soap-opera variety, follows the lives of three immigrants who come to the United States at the turn of the century. All struggle to find acceptance, happiness, and success in the promised land. 1984; 310m.

ELMER GANTRY ★★★★
DIR: Richard Brooks. **CAST:** Burt Lancaster, Jean Simmons, Dean Jagger, Arthur Kennedy, Shirley Jones.
Burt Lancaster gives one of his most memorable performances in this release as a phony evangelist who, along with Jean Simmons, exploits the faithful with his fire-and-brimstone sermons. Arthur Kennedy is the reporter out to expose their operation in this screen version of Sinclair Lewis' story set in the Midwest of the 1920s. 1960; 145m.

ELVIS—THE MOVIE ★★★★
DIR: John Carpenter. **CAST:** Kurt Russell, Shelley Winters, Pat Hingle, Melody Anderson, Season Hubley, Charlie Hodge, Ellen Travolta, Ed Begley Jr.
A fictional account of Elvis Presley's rise to stardom, it probes deeply into the family life of rock 'n' roll's king. This TV movie should rate highly with fans of Elvis, as well as those just interested in a good story. Excellent voice re-creation by Ronnie McDowell. 1979; 117m.

EMILY ★★
DIR: Henry Herbert. **CAST:** Koo Stark.
This British film was Koo Stark's premiere in soft-core porn. She plays a teenager returning home from boarding school who finds out that her mother is a well-paid prostitute. This bit of news upsets Emily momentarily, but she manages to create her own sexual world with a female painter, the painter's husband, and her boyfriend, James. Lots of nudity and sex. Rated R. 1982; 87m.

EMPEROR JONES, THE ★★★½
DIR: Dudley Murphy. **CAST:** Paul Robeson, Dudley Digges, Frank Wilson.
This liberal version of Eugene O'Neill's prize-winning play invents entire sections that were written to capitalize on star Paul Robeson's fame as a singer as well as an introductory piece that provides a background for Robeson's character, the doomed Jones. This is still an interesting and sometimes strong film despite the drastic changes. Surviving prints that have been transferred to tape are not always in the best of condition, so quality will vary on this title. 1933; B&W; 72m.

EMPIRE OF THE SUN ★★★½

DIR: Steven Spielberg. **CAST:** Christian Bale, John Malkovich, Miranda Richardson, Nigel Havers.

J. G. Ballard's harrowing autobiographical examination of life in a World War II Japanese prison camp has been given the Hollywood treatment by director Steven Spielberg, who took his film crew to Shanghai for some stunning location work. Young Christian Bale stars as Ballard's boyhood self, who is separated from his parents during the Japanese invasion of Shanghai and winds up in a concentration camp for four years. Too much surface gloss prevents this from being a genuine classic, but it nonetheless contains scenes of surprising power and poignancy. Rated PG for language and intensity. 1987; 145m.

EMPTY CANVAS, THE

DIR: Damiano Damiani. **CAST:** Bette Davis, Horst Buchholz, Catherine Spaak, Daniela Rocca, Georges Wilson.

Would-be painter Horst Buchholz falls for gold-digging model Catherine Spaak, brings her home to his mother, Bette Davis, hoping family wealth will persuade her to marry him. Spurned, he suffers a mental breakdown. Maudlin pap. 1964; B&W; 118m.

ENCHANTED COTTAGE, THE ★★★½

DIR: John Cromwell. **CAST:** Dorothy McGuire, Robert Young, Herbert Marshall, Spring Byington, Hillary Brooke.

An engrossing blend of romance, fantasy, and melodrama. Robert Young gives one of his best big-screen performances as a battle-scarred World War II veteran. Dorothy McGuire offers a beautifully realized portrayal of a young woman whose inner loveliness is hidden beneath a painfully plain exterior. As the blind friend who sees so much more than everyone else, Herbert Marshall is as suave as ever. 1945; B&W; 91m.

ENCORE ★★★

DIR: Harold French, Pat Jackson, Anthony Pelissier. **CAST:** Glynis Johns, Nigel Patrick, Kay Walsh, Roland Culver, Ronald Squire, Peter Graves.

Somerset Maugham introduces three of his short stories in this sequel to *Trio*. The best of the three is "Gigolo and Gigolette" in which trapeze artist Glynis Johns begins to feel used by her husband as he promotes her death-defying act. The other two ("The Ant and the Grasshopper" and "Winter Cruise") are more humorous. 1952; B&W; 85m.

END OF THE LINE ★★★

DIR: Jay Russell. **CAST:** Wilford Brimley, Levon Helm, Kevin Bacon, Bob Balaban, Barbara Barrie, Mary Steenburgen, Holly Hunter, Bruce McGill, Howard Morris.

Financed as a labor of love by executive producer and co-star Mary Steenburgen, this first film by director Jay Russell features Wilford Brimley as a railroad worker who, with buddy Levon Helm, steals a train engine to protest the closing of the freight depot where he has worked for thirty-eight years. The skilled peformances will keep you interested right to the end of the line. Rated PG for profanity. 1988; 105m.

END OF THE ROAD ★★

DIR: Aram Avakian. **CAST:** Stacy Keach, Harris Yulin, Dorothy Tristan, James Earl Jones.

Stacy Keach plays a college graduate who falls out of society, receives help from an unorthodox psychotherapist named Doctor D (James Earl Jones), then becomes intimately involved with a married couple. The imagery can be compelling, but the finale is too graphic. Rated X (by 1960s standards) but more like a hard R for sex, nudity, and adult themes. 1969; 110m.

ENDLESS LOVE ★★

DIR: Franco Zeffirelli. **CAST:** Brooke Shields, Martin Hewitt, Shirley Knight, Don Murray.

Though this story of a teenage love affair has all the elements of a great romance, it is marred by implausibility and inconsistency. The film improves as it progresses and even offers some compelling moments, but not enough to compensate for its flaws. Rated R because of sex and nudity. 1981; 115m.

ENOLA GAY: THE MEN, THE MISSION, THE ATOMIC BOMB ★★★
DIR: David Lowell Rich. **CAST:** Billy Crystal, Kim Darby, Patrick Duffy, Gary Frank, Gregory Harrison.

In this made-for-TV drama, Patrick Duffy plays Paul Tibbets, the man in charge of the plane that dropped the atomic bomb over Hiroshima. The film delves into the lives and reactions of the crew members in a fairly effective manner. 1980; 150m.

EQUUS ★★★★
DIR: Sidney Lumet. **CAST:** Richard Burton, Peter Firth, Colin Blakely, Joan Plowright, Harry Andrews, Eileen Atkins, Jenny Agutter.

Peter Firth plays a stableboy whose mysterious fascination with horses results in an act of meaningless cruelty and violence. Richard Burton plays the psychiatrist brought in to uncover Firth's hidden hostilities. The expanding of Peter Shaffer's play leaves the film somewhat unfocused but the scenes between Burton and Firth are intense, riveting, and beautifully acted. This was Burton's last quality film role; he was nominated for best actor. Rated R for profanity and nudity. 1977; 137m.

ERIC ★★★★
DIR: James Goldstone. **CAST:** Patricia Neal, John Savage, Claude Akins, Sian Barbara Allen, Mark Hamill, Nehemiah Persoff.

This made-for-TV movie is the true story of Eric Lund, a teenager with a promising athletic future who becomes terminally ill. John Savage, in the title role, gives a meaningful portrayal of a young man who refuses to give up. Patricia Neal, as the mother, gives the kind of warm, sensitive performance she is noted for, and there is a fine supporting cast. 1975; 100m.

ESCAPE TO BURMA ★
DIR: Allan Dwan. **CAST:** Barbara Stanwyck, Robert Ryan, David Farrar, Murvyn Vye.

This features a tea plantation, wild animals, and a hunted man seeking refuge. Every great star makes a turkey, and this is Barbara Stanwyck's. But some films are so bad they are good. This may be one. 1955; B&W; 87m.

ESCAPE TO LOVE ★★★
DIR: Herb Stein. **CAST:** Clara Perryman.

This adventurous romance pits a beautiful American student (Clara Perryman) and her lover against the Polish KGB as they speed on a train toward Paris. Their passion increases to a point where they must both reach a life-changing decision. 1982; 105m.

ESCAPE TO THE SUN ★★★
DIR: Menahem Golan. **CAST:** Laurence Harvey, Josephine Chaplin, John Ireland, Jack Hawkins.

Two young university students try to escape from the oppressive Soviet Union under the watchful eyes of the KGB. They try first for an exit visa; only one visa is issued, and one of the students is taken into custody. The two are forced to make a heroic escape to the West. Rated PG for violence. 1972; 94m.

ESCAPIST, THE ★
DIR: Eddie Beverly Jr. **CAST:** Bill Shirk, Peter Lupus.

Real-life escape artist, Bill Shirk, plays himself in this exhibition of his talents through multiple escapes. The thin plot encasing his feats has him as a radio station owner threatened by a big-business takeover. To keep his station known, he performs stunts for publicity, leading to a frightening climax. Many of the players, including Shirk, have limited acting ablility. The script also lacks a professional touch. Unrated, the film contains nudity and simulated sex. 1983; 87m.

ETERNALLY YOURS ★★★
DIR: Tay Garnett. **CAST:** Loretta Young, David Niven, C. Aubrey Smith, ZaSu Pitts, Billie Burke, Eve Arden, Hugh Herbert, Broderick Crawford.

A stellar cast of accomplished scene-stealers deftly brings off this iffy story of a magician (David Niven) and his wife (Loretta Young), who thinks his tricks are overshadowing their marital happiness. 1939; B&W; 95m.

EUREKA ★★★★½
DIR: Nicolas Roeg. **CAST:** Gene Hackman, Theresa Russell, Rutger Hauer, Jane Lapotaire, Mickey Rourke, Ed Lauter, Joe Pesci.

Another stunner from Nicolas Roeg. *Eureka* is about an ambitious gold miner (Gene Hackman) who makes his fortune in the snowbound Canadian wilderness, then retires to his very own Caribbean island. Rated R for sex, nudity, violence, and profanity. 1983; 130m.

EUROPEANS, THE ★★★★
DIR: James Ivory. **CAST:** Lee Remick, Robin Ellis, Wesley Addy, Tim Choate, Lisa Eichhorn, Tim Woodward, Kristin Griffith.

This intelligent, involving adaptation of the Henry James novel is another wonder from director James Ivory. Lee Remick is one of two free-thinking, outspoken foreigners who descend on their Puritan relatives in nineteenth-century New England. The result is a character-rich study of a clash of cultures. Rated PG. 1979; 90m.

EVERY TIME WE SAY GOODBYE ★★★
DIR: Moshe Mizrahi. **CAST:** Tom Hanks, Cristina Marsillach, Benedict Taylor.

A change-of-pace role for Tom Hanks, who stars as an American pilot in WWII Jerusalem who falls in love with a young Jewish girl. The Jewish girl's family is dead set against a gentile-Jew match. Hanks brings a certain well-rounded realism to this dramatic part, injecting the seriousness with humor, and Cristina Marsillach is very subtle as the Jewish girl. Rated PG-13 for mild profanity, brief nudity, and mature themes. 1987; 97m.

EVERYBODY'S ALL-AMERICAN ★★★½
DIR: Taylor Hackford. **CAST:** Dennis Quaid, Jessica Lange, Timothy Hutton, John Goodman.

Though a bit long-winded at times, this story (based on a book by *Sports Illustrated*'s Frank Deford) is a must-see for anyone who believes professional athletes have it made. Dennis Quaid is the college football hero who believes he can go on catching passes as a professional forever. Since he can't, and catching passes pays the bills, he soon finds himself unable to cope. Jessica Lange (as Quaid's wife) and Timothy Hutton round out an unnecessary love triangle. Rated R for profanity and suggested sex. 1988; 122m.

EXECUTION, THE ★★
DIR: Paul Wendkos. **CAST:** Jessica Walter, Barbara Barrie, Sandy Dennis, Valerie Harper, Michael Lerner, Robert Hooks.

Five women survivors of the Holocaust, now living in Los Angeles, have a chance meeting with a former Nazi doctor from their camp. They plot to seduce and then kill him. There is some suspense in this made-for-TV movie, but it is too melodramatic to be believable. 1985; 100m.

EXECUTIONER'S SONG, THE ★★★½
DIR: Lawrence Schiller. **CAST:** Tommy Lee Jones, Rosanna Arquette, Christine Lahti, Eli Wallach.

Pulitzer Prize novelist Norman Mailer's made-for-television adaptation of his engrossing account of convicted killer Gary Gilmore's fight to get Utah to carry out his death sentence. The performances of Tommy

Lee Jones and Rosanna Arquette are electrifying. Unrated. 1982; 200m.

EXECUTIVE ACTION ★★★★
DIR: David Miller. **CAST:** Burt Lancaster, Robert Ryan, Will Geer, Gilbert Green, John Anderson.
This forceful film, based on Mark Lane's book *Rush to Judgment*, features a fascinating look at possible reasons for the assassination of John F. Kennedy. Rated PG. 1973; 91m.

EXECUTIVE SUITE ★★★★
DIR: Robert Wise. **CAST:** William Holden, June Allyson, Barbara Stanwyck, Fredric March, Louis Calhern, Walter Pidgeon, Shelley Winters, Dean Jagger, Nina Foch, Paul Douglas.
An all-star cast is topnotch in this film about the world of corporate life. Based on Cameron Hawley's novel, the drama examines the intense power struggles in big business with honesty and panache. 1954; B&W; 104m.

EXODUS ★★½
DIR: Otto Preminger. **CAST:** Paul Newman, Eva Marie Saint, Ralph Richardson, Peter Lawford, Lee J. Cobb, Sal Mineo, Jill Haworth.
The early days of Israel are seen through the eyes of various characters, in this epic, adapted from the novel by Leon Uris. Directed by the heavy-handed Otto Preminger, its length and plodding pace caused comic Mort Sahl to quip, "Otto, let my people go," at a preview. 1960; 213m.

EXTREMITIES ★★½
DIR: Robert M. Young. **CAST:** Farrah Fawcett, James Russo, Diana Scarwid, Alfre Woodard.
This well-meant but difficult-to-watch thriller casts Farrah Fawcett (in a first-rate performance) as a single woman who is brutalized and terrorized in her own home by a homicidal maniac (James Russo). When she manages to outwit her attacker and render him helpless, she must decide between bloody revenge and human compassion. Robert M. Young directs this adaptation by William Mastrosimone of his play with authority and realism. Rated R for violence. 1986; 100m.

FACE IN THE CROWD, A ★★★★
DIR: Elia Kazan. **CAST:** Andy Griffith, Patricia Neal, Lee Remick, Anthony Franciosa, Walter Matthau, Kay Medford.
A sow's ear is turned into a silk purse in this Budd Schulberg story, scripted by the author, of a television executive who discovers gold in a winsome hobo she molds into a tube star. But all that glitters is not gold. A fine cast makes this a winning film, which brought Andy Griffith and Lee Remick to the screen for the first time. 1957; B&W; 125m.

FAIL-SAFE ★★★★
DIR: Sidney Lumet. **CAST:** Henry Fonda, Walter Matthau, Fritz Weaver, Larry Hagman, Dom DeLuise, Frank Overton.
In this gripping film, a United States aircraft is mistakenly assigned to drop the big one on Russia, and the leaders of the two countries grapple for some kind of solution as time runs out. 1964; B&W; 111m.

FAKEOUT ★½
DIR: Matt Cimber. **CAST:** Telly Savalas, Pia Zadora, Desi Arnaz Jr., Larry Storch.
In this melodrama a Las Vegas singer goes to jail instead of ratting on her loanshark boyfriend. Later, agreeing to falsely testify in exchange for her freedom, she becomes a target for death. The cast is much better than the movie. Not rated, but contains violence and mild sex scenes. 1982; 89m.

FALCON AND THE SNOWMAN, THE ★★★★★
DIR: John Schlesinger. **CAST:** Timothy Hutton, Sean Penn, Pat Hingle, Lori Singer, Richard Dysart.
In this powerful motion picture, Timothy Hutton and Sean Penn give stunning performances as two childhood friends who decide to sell United States secrets to the Russians. Based

on a true incident, this release—to its credit—makes no judgments. The viewer is left to decide what's right and wrong, and whether Boyce met with justice. It is not an easy decision to make. Rated R for violence and profanity. 1985; 131m.

FALL OF THE ROMAN EMPIRE, THE ★★★★
DIR: Anthony Mann. **CAST:** Sophia Loren, James Mason, Stephen Boyd, Alec Guinness, Christopher Plummer, John Ireland, Mel Ferrer.

During the early and mid-1960s, Hollywood looked to the history books for many of its films. Director Anthony Mann has fashioned an epic that is a feast for the eyes and does not insult the viewers' intelligence. *The Fall of the Roman Empire* has thrilling moments of action and characters the viewer cares about. 1964; 149m.

FALLEN ANGEL ★★★½
DIR: Robert Michael Lewis. **CAST:** Dana Hill, Richard Masur, Melinda Dillon, Ronny Cox, David Hayward.

This made-for-television drama deals with the controversial topic of child pornography. A young girl, Jennifer (played by Dana Hill), is pushed into pornography by a so-called adult friend, Howard (played by Richard Masur). Jennifer sees no hope of getting out of her predicament, because she can't communicate with her mother (played by Melinda Dillon). Very timely topic! 1981; 100m.

FALLEN IDOL, THE ★★★★
DIR: Carol Reed. **CAST:** Ralph Richardson, Michele Morgan, Bobby Henrey, Jack Hawkins, Bernard Lee.

A small boy hero-worships a household servant suspected of murdering his wife in this quiet Graham Greene thriller. Largely told from the child's point of view, this one is pulse-raising. As always, the late Ralph Richardson is great. Bernard Lee later became "M" in the Bond films. 1948; B&W; 94m.

FALLEN SPARROW, THE ★★★
DIR: Richard Wallace. **CAST:** John Garfield, Maureen O'Hara, Walter Slezak, Patricia Morison, Martha O'Driscoll.

In this sometimes confusing but generally engrossing film, John Garfield is a veteran of the Spanish Civil War whose wartime buddy is later murdered by Fascists in New York City. Maureen O'Hara is Garfield's girlfriend. Walter Slezak is the head Fascist out to get Garfield. Many powerful scenes and strong performances make this one of Garfield's best films. 1943; 94m.

FALLING IN LOVE ★★★
DIR: Ulu Grosbard. **CAST:** Robert De Niro, Meryl Streep, Harvey Keitel.

Robert De Niro and Meryl Streep are fine as star-crossed lovers who risk their marriages for a moment of passion. Thanks to the uneven direction of Ulu Grosbard and an unbelievable story by Michael Cristofer, the stars' performances are the only outstanding features in this watchable love story. Rated PG for profanity and adult situations. 1984; 107m.

FAMILY UPSIDE DOWN, A ★★★
DIR: David Lowell Rich. **CAST:** Helen Hayes, Fred Astaire, Efrem Zimbalist Jr., Patty Duke Astin.

A touching, all too real drama about a previously self-sufficient couple whose age makes them dependent on their grown children. Hayes, Astin, and Zimbalist were nominated, and Astaire won an Emmy for this affecting made-for-television film. 1978; 100m.

FANNY (1961) ★★★★
DIR: Joshua Logan. **CAST:** Leslie Caron, Maurice Chevalier, Charles Boyer, Horst Buchholz, Baccaloni, Lionel Jeffries.

Leslie Caron is a beautiful and lively Fanny in this 1961 film. She plays a young girl seeking romance with the boy she grew up with. Unfortunately, he leaves her pregnant as he pursues a life at sea. 1961; 133m.

FANNY HILL: MEMOIRS OF A WOMAN OF PLEASURE

DIR: Russ Meyer. **CAST:** Letitia Roman, Miriam Hopkins.

Tame, boring adaptation of the famous erotic novel about an innocent girl who finds shelter in a house of prostitution. Thirties star Miriam Hopkins does what she can as a madam, but she looks embarrassed. Cult director Russ Meyer only worked on this as a hired gun for another producer. Unrated, but expect no cheap thrills here. 1965; B&W; 104m.

FANTASIES

DIR: John Derek. **CAST:** Bo Derek, Peter Hotten, Anna Alexiadis.

Bo Derek stars in this ridiculous story of a woman who lives life like a female Walter Mitty. This has to be one of the worst films ever made, though it does have gorgeous cinematography. Rated R for brief nudity and adult situations. 1984; 81m.

FAR FROM THE MADDING CROWD ★★★★

DIR: John Schlesinger. **CAST:** Julie Christie, Terence Stamp, Alan Bates, Peter Finch.

The combination of the world-class director and a stellar British cast makes this Thomas Hardy adaptation a lovely, intelligent epic. Julie Christie plays a country girl who becomes entangled in the lives of three diverse men. Cinematographer-now-director Nicolas Roeg beautifully captured the rustic countryside. 1967; 169m.

FAR PAVILIONS, THE ★★★

DIR: Peter Duffell. **CAST:** Ben Cross, Amy Irving, Omar Sharif, Christopher Lee, Benedict Taylor, Rossano Brazzi.

In this romantic adventure, Ben Cross plays Ash, a young British officer in Imperial India. Oddly enough, he had been raised as an Indian until he was eleven. As an adult, he is reunited with his childhood friend the Princess Anjuli (Amy Irving). Despite her impending marriage to the elderly Rajaha (Rossano Brazzi), Ash and Anjuli fall in love. Rated PG for sex and violence. 1983; 108m.

FAREWELL TO ARMS, A ★★★★

DIR: Frank Borzage. **CAST:** Helen Hayes, Gary Cooper, Adolphe Menjou, Mary Phillips, Jack LaRue.

Ernest Hemingway's well-crafted story of doomed love between a wounded ambulance driver and a nurse in Italy during World War I. Adolphe Menjou is peerless as the Italian army officer, Helen Hayes dies touchingly, and Gary Cooper strides away in the rain. 1932; B&W; 78m.

FAST-WALKING ★★★½

DIR: James B. Harris. **CAST:** James Woods, Kay Lenz, Tim McIntire, Robert Hooks, Susan Tyrrell.

This one is definitely not for everyone, but if you are adventurous, it may surprise you. James Woods plays a prison guard whose yearning for the good life leads him into a jail-break scheme. Film plays for black comedy and generally succeeds. Rated R for violence, language, nudity. 1983; 116m.

FAT CITY ★★★★½

DIR: John Huston. **CAST:** Stacy Keach, Jeff Bridges, Susan Tyrrell, Nicholas Colasanto, Candy Clark.

This neglected treasure is perhaps the best film ever made about boxing. Tank-town matches between hopefuls and has-beens along California's Central Valley keep Stacy Keach and Jeff Bridges in hamburger and white port. A classic piece of Americana and one of John Huston's greatest achievements. Rated PG. 1972; 96m.

FATAL VISION ★★★★½

DIR: David Greene. **CAST:** Karl Malden, Gary Cole, Eva Marie Saint, Gary Grubbs, Mitchell Ryan, Andy Griffith.

This excellent TV miniseries is based on the actual case of convicted murderer, Dr. Jeffrey MacDonald. In 1970, MacDonald (Gary Cole) murdered his pregnant wife and two daughters. Although he denies the charges, his father-in-law (Karl Malden) becomes suspicious and helps to convict him. 1984; 198m.

FEAR (1955) ★★
DIR: Roberto Rossellini. **CAST:** Ingrid Bergman, Kurt Kreuger, Mathias Wiemann.

The plot has interesting twists, but neither star Ingrid Bergman nor her then husband-director Roberto Rossellini are able to save this tired drama of an indiscreet wife being blackmailed by her lover's ex. As ever, Bergman scores personally. 1955; B&W; 91m.

FEVER PITCH
DIR: Richard Brooks. **CAST:** Ryan O'Neal, Catharine Hicks, Giancarlo Giannini, Bridgette Anderson, Chad Everett, John Saxon, William Smith.

Ryan O'Neal plays a sports journalist writing about gambling. To research his story, O'Neal becomes a gambler, loses his wife, endangers his job, and becomes involved with a sleazy bookie. What we get are too many shots of gambling in casinos and not enough about the characters. A real disappointment. Rated R for profanity and violence. 1985; 95m.

55 DAYS AT PEKING ★★
DIR: Nicholas Ray. **CAST:** Charlton Heston, Ava Gardner, David Niven, John Ireland.

A lackluster big-screen adventure about the Boxer Revolt in 1900. The story about a group of multinational embassy officials who become besieged within the Peking embassy compound takes no time to develop any rounded characterizations. Charlton Heston, David Niven, and the rest of the large cast seem made of wood. 1963; 150m.

52 PICK-UP ★½
DIR: John Frankenheimer. **CAST:** Roy Scheider, Ann-Margret, Vanity, John Glover, Clarence Williams III, Kelly Preston.

Generally unentertaining tale of money, blackmail, and pornography, as adapted from Elmore Leonard's story. Roy Scheider's secret fling with Kelly Preston leads to big-time blackmail and murder. It's more cards than Scheider could ever pick up, and a more mean and nasty movie than most people will want to watch. Rated R for nudity, profanity, simulated sex, and violence. 1986; 111m.

FIGHTING MAD ★★★
DIR: Jonathan Demme. **CAST:** Peter Fonda, Lynn Lowry, John Doucette, Philip Carey, Scott Glenn, Kathleen Miller.

A quiet, unassuming farmer (Peter Fonda) is driven to distraction by a ruthless businessman who wants to assume his property. Instead of a free-for-all of violence and car crashes (as in other Fonda films of the time), this ranks as an in-depth character study. Rated R for violence. 1976; 90m.

FINDERS KEEPERS, LOVERS WEEPERS ★
DIR: Russ Meyer. **CAST:** Paul Lockwood.

Producer-director Russ Meyer's least idiosyncratic (and therefore least interesting) movie. It's a trite melodrama about two adulterous couples tormented by thugs who are robbing the bar owned by one of the captives. Unrated, but an R equivalent for some nudity. 1968; 71m.

FINGERS ★★★★
DIR: James Toback. **CAST:** Harvey Keitel, Jim Brown, Tisa Farrow, Michael Gazzo.

Harvey Keitel gives an electric performance as a would-be concert pianist who is also a death-dealing collector for his loan-sharking dad. Film is extremely violent and not for all tastes, but there is an undeniable fascination one feels toward the Keitel character and his tortured life. Rated R. 1978; 91m.

FIRE DOWN BELOW ★★★
DIR: Robert Parrish. **CAST:** Rita Hayworth, Robert Mitchum, Jack Lemmon, Herbert Lom, Anthony Newley.

Rita Hayworth is a lady of dubious background and virtue on a voyage between islands aboard a tramp steamer owned by adventurers Robert Mitchum and Jack Lemmon, both of whom chase her. A below-decks explosion traps one of the partners. The plot is familiar, contrived, but entertaining just the same. 1957; 116m.

FIRE WITH FIRE ★★
DIR: Duncan Gibbins. **CAST:** Craig Sheffer, Virginia Madsen, Jon Polito, Kate Reid, Jean Smart.
What hath Shakespeare wrought? The true story of a girl's Catholic school that invited the residents of a neighboring boy's reform school to a dance has been turned into another of those good girl/bad boy melodramas wherein misunderstood teens triumph against all odds. Craig Sheffer and Virginia Madsen are appealing, but the plot is laughable. Rated PG-13 for mild sex and language. 1986; 103m.

FIRST AFFAIR ★★★
DIR: Gus Trikonis. **CAST:** Loretta Swit, Melissa Sue Anderson, Joel Higgins, Charley Lang, Kim Delaney, Amanda Bearse.
Melissa Sue Anderson stars as a naïve Harvard scholarship student. She finds herself romantically inclined toward her English professor's husband. A strong entourage of actors helps make this an insightful commentary about the difficulties of keeping a marriage together, and the pain of losing one's innocence. Made for television. 1983; 100m.

FIRST LOVE ★★
DIR: Joan Darling. **CAST:** William Katt, Susan Dey, John Heard, Beverly D'Angelo, Robert Loggia.
A somber movie about a college student who is unlucky in love. While the film has a lot going for it—an interesting cast, sharp dialogue, and a refreshingly honest story—it's basically muddleheaded. Rated R for nudity and language. 1977; 92m.

FIRST MONDAY IN OCTOBER ★★★
DIR: Ronald Neame. **CAST:** Walter Matthau, Jill Clayburgh, Barnard Hughes, Jan Sterling.
This is a Walter Matthau picture, with all the joys that implies. As he did in *Hopscotch*, director Ronald Neame allows Matthau, who plays a crusty Supreme Court justice, to make the most of every screen moment. *The First Monday in October* also had the advantage of perfect timing: Jill Clayburgh plays the first woman appointed to the Supreme Court (mirrored in real life the same year by the appointment of Sandra Day O'Connor). Rated R for nudity and profanity. 1981; 98m.

FIRSTBORN ★★★★
DIR: Michael Apted. **CAST:** Teri Garr, Peter Weller.
An emotionally charged screen drama that deftly examines some topical, thought-provoking themes, this stars Teri Garr as a divorced woman who gets involved with the wrong man (Peter Weller) to the horror of her two sons. Rated PG for profanity and violence. 1984; 100m.

FISH HAWK ★★★
DIR: Donald Shebib. **CAST:** Will Sampson, Don Francks, Charles Fields, Chris Wiggins.
Excellent drama about an Indian (Will Sampson) who befriends a young farm boy in turn-of-the-century rural America. Sampson has a drinking problem, which he kicks in an effort to return to his former life. Rated G; contains very mild profanity. 1984; 95m.

F.I.S.T. ★★
DIR: Norman Jewison. **CAST:** Sylvester Stallone, Rod Steiger, Peter Boyle, Melinda Dillon, David Huffman, Tony Lo Bianco.
It's too bad that *F.I.S.T.* is so predictable and cliché-ridden, because Sylvester Stallone gives a fine performance. As Johnny Kovak, organizer and later leader of the Federation of

Interstate Truckers, he creates an even more poignant character than his Rocky Balboa. It is ironic that Stallone, after being favorably compared with Marlon Brando, should end up in a film so similar to *On the Waterfront*...and with Rod Steiger yet! Rated PG. 1978; 145m.

FIVE CAME BACK ★★★
DIR: John Farrow. **CAST:** Chester Morris, Wendy Barrie, John Carradine, Allen Jenkins, Joseph Calleia, C. Aubrey Smith, Patric Knowles, Lucille Ball.

A plane carrying the usual mixed bag of passengers goes down in the jungle. Only five of the group will survive. The cast, fine character players all, makes this melodrama worthwhile, though it shows its age. 1939; B&W; 75m.

FIVE CORNERS ★★★½
DIR: Tony Bill. **CAST:** Jodie Foster, Tim Robbins, John Turturro.

Most viewers will feel a little *Moonstruck* after watching this bizarre comedy-drama writen by John Patrick Shanley. Jodie Foster stars as a young woman who attempts to get help from the tough-guy-turned-pacifist (Tim Robbins) who saved her from being raped by an unhinged admirer (John Turturro) when the latter is released from prison. Moments of suspense and hard-edged realism are effectively mixed with bits of offbeat comedy. Rated R for violence and adult themes. 1988; 92m.

FIVE DAYS ONE SUMMER ★★★
DIR: Fred Zinnemann. **CAST:** Sean Connery, Anna Massey, Betsy Brantley, Lambert Wilson.

This is an old-fashioned romance, with Sean Connery as a mountain climber caught in a triangle involving his lovely niece and a handsome young guide. Two handkerchiefs and a liking for soap opera are suggested. Rated PG for adult situations. 1983; 108m.

FIVE EASY PIECES ★★★★½
DIR: Bob Rafelson. **CAST:** Jack Nicholson, Karen Black, Susan Anspach, Billy Green Bush, Sally Struthers, Ralph Waite, Fannie Flagg.

Shattering drama concerns Jack Nicholson's return to his family home after years of self-imposed exile. Playing a once promising pianist who chose to work in the oil fields, Nicholson has rarely been better; his fully shaded character with its explosions of emotion are a wonder to behold. One of the gems of the Seventies. The chicken-salad scene in the diner is now a classic. Rated R. 1970; 90m.

FLASH OF GREEN, A ★★★½
DIR: Victor Nunez. **CAST:** Ed Harris, Blair Brown, Richard Jordan, George Coe, Isa Thomas, William Mooney, Joan Goodfellow, Helen Stenborg, John Glover.

This is a compelling adaptation of John D. MacDonald's novel about a small-town Florida reporter (Ed Harris) whose boredom, lust, and curiosity lead him into helping an ambitious, amoral county official (Richard Jordan) win approval for a controversial housing project. Their tactics of deceit, blackmail, and coercion soon grow uglier than they expected. The acting is superb. 1984; 118m.

FLESH
DIR: Paul Morrissey. **CAST:** Joe Dallesandro, Geraldine Smith, Patti D'Arbanville, Candy Darling.

If you wish to experience an exercise in truly bad cinema, look no further than Andy Warhol's *Flesh*. Once again, tattoo-riddled beefcake Joe Dallesandro is cast as a street hustler who can't stay away from transvestites, sleazy women, and drugs. Not rated; contains nudity and profane language. 1968; 90m.

FLESH AND THE DEVIL ★★★
DIR: Clarence Brown. **CAST:** Greta Garbo, John Gilbert.

Story of a woman who flouts moral conventions at every turn by pursuing a third man while married to two others. The sensual pairing of sultry Greta Garbo with suave John Gilbert electrifies this film. 1927; B&W; 103m.

FLIGHT FROM VIENNA ★★★
DIR: Denis Kavanagh. **CAST:** Theodore Bikel, John Bentley, Donald Gray.

Theodore Bikel gets to demonstrate the range of his acting abilities as a Hungarian official trying to defect to the West. British officials make him perform an undercover rescue mission, which proves his commitment but also places his life in jeopardy. 1956; B&W; 54m.

FLIM-FLAM MAN, THE ★★★
DIR: Irvin Kershner. **CAST:** George C. Scott, Michael Sarrazin, Sue Lyon, Harry Morgan, Jack Albertson.

A con man (George C. Scott) teaches an army deserter (Michael Sarrazin) the art of fleecing yokels. Scott is an altogether charming, wry, winning rascal in this improbable, clever film, which is highlighted by a spectacular car-chase scene. 1967; 104m.

FOOL FOR LOVE ★★★½
DIR: Robert Altman. **CAST:** Sam Shepard, Kim Basinger, Harry Dean Stanton, Randy Quaid.

Writer-star Sam Shepard's disturbing, thought-provoking screenplay is about people who, as one of his characters comments, "can't help themselves." Shepard plays a cowboy-stuntman who is continuing his romantic pursuit of Kim Basinger in spite of her objections. For open-minded adults who appreciate daring, original works. Rated R for profanity and violence. 1986; 107m.

FOOLISH WIVES ★★★★
DIR: Erich Von Stroheim. **CAST:** Erich Von Stroheim, Mae Busch, Rudolph Christians.

Anticipating Orson Welles by two decades, director and star Erich Von Stroheim also wrote, produced, codesigned, and cocostumed this stark and unsettling account of a sleazy rogue's depraved use of women to achieve his aims. Von Stroheim is brilliant as the oily, morally corrupt, bogus nobleman plying his confidence game against the naïve rich in post–World War I Monaco and Monte Carlo. The final scene is a masterful simile. Silent. 1921–1922; B&W; 107m.

FOOLS ★½
DIR: Tom Gries. **CAST:** Jason Robards Jr., Katharine Ross, Scott Hylands.

An aging star of horror pictures falls in love with the beautiful wife of an attorney. San Francisco is picturesque, but the acting is wretched and the screenplay juvenile. Rated PG. 1970; 97m.

FOR KEEPS
DIR: John G. Avildsen. **CAST:** Molly Ringwald, Randall Batinkoff, Kenneth Mars, Conchata Ferrell, Miriam Flynn.

The serious issue of teen pregnancy is irresponsibly trivialized in this ludicrous effort. Molly Ringwald and Randall Batinkoff are in love. Because both are cursed with moronic parents—who exist only in movies like this—they abandon plans for college and get married when Ringwald turns up pregnant. Rated PG-13 for frank language and sexual themes. 1988; 98m.

FOR LADIES ONLY ★★★
DIR: Mel Damski. **CAST:** Gregory Harrison, Lee Grant, Louise Lasser, Dinah Manoff.

A young, good-looking farm-belt guy goes to New York to become a star. He ends up nearly starving and finally turns to stripping to make more money. This stale, TV film is a predictable morality play made fresher with the role reversal. 1981; 94m.

FOR LOVE ALONE ★★★½
DIR: Stephen Wallace. **CAST:** Helen Buday, Sam Neill, Hugo Weaving.

An Australian girl is frustrated by the romantic double standard of the 1930s. Helen Buday plays the lovelorn student willing to waste her life on her selfish professor (Hugo Weaving) until she meets a dashing banker (Sam Neill). Buday and Neill are excellent, but Weaving offers a very wooden performance. Rated PG for partial nudity and simulated sex. 1985; 102m.

FOR LOVE OF ANGELA ★★
DIR: Rudy Vejar. **CAST:** Sarah Rush, Barbara Mallory, David Winn, Margaret Fairchild, Dr. Joyce Brothers.

A beautiful jewelry clerk falls in love with the store owner's son. His meddling mom tries to break them up. Meanwhile, our heroine's best friend must struggle with an unwanted pregnancy. Originally made for commercial TV, this film has numerous cuts and breakaways that are most distracting. 1982; 105m.

FOR QUEEN AND COUNTRY ★★★½
DIR: Martin Stellman. **CAST:** Denzel Washington, Amanda Redman, George Baker.

A taut, tragic combination of social commentary and ghetto thriller focusing on racism in contemporary England. American actor Denzel Washington is superb as a black working-class British soldier who returns home from military service to find himself restricted to a second-class life. Rated R. 1989; 108m.

FOR US THE LIVING: THE MEDGAR EVERS STORY ★★★★
DIR: Michael Schultz. **CAST:** Howard Rollins Jr., Irene Cara, Margaret Avery, Roscoe Lee Browne.

Assassinated civil-rights activist Medgar Evers is profiled in this inspirational drama. Adapted from Evers's wife's biography, this film gives a look at the total person, not just the legends surrounding him. Originally made for television, this is unrated. 1983; 90m.

FOR YOUR LOVE ONLY ★★
DIR: Wolfgang Petersen. **CAST:** Nastassja Kinski, Christian Quadflieg.

European beauty Nastassja Kinski stars as a young student who has an affair with her teacher, which leads to murder and blackmail. Pretty dull soap opera made for German television and released theatrically in 1982. Not rated, but contains sexual situations and violence. 1976; 97m.

FORBIDDEN ★★★
DIR: Anthony Page. **CAST:** Jacqueline Bisset, Jurgen Prochnow, Irene Worth, Peter Vaughan.

Made-for-cable film about a gentile woman who falls in love with a Jewish man during World War II: a crime in Hitler's Germany. Enough suspense here to keep the viewer attentive, but not enough atmosphere to make it as intense as the melodramatic soundtrack assumes it to be. Not rated, but the equivalent of a PG for some violence and light sex. 1984; 114m.

FORBIDDEN LOVE ★
DIR: Steven H. Stern. **CAST:** Yvette Mimieux, Andrew Stevens, Lisa Lucas, John Considine.

Silly made-for-TV love story involving a sexy older woman (Yvette Mimieux) and handsome young man (Andrew Stevens). It has a sudsy beautiful-people glitz but that just isn't enough. 1982; 100m.

FORCE OF EVIL ★★★
DIR: Abraham Polonsky. **CAST:** John Garfield, Thomas Gomez, Roy Roberts, Marie Windsor.

A lawyer (John Garfield) abandons his principles and goes to work for a racketeer in this somber, downbeat story of corruption and loss of values. Compelling story and acting compensate for some of the heavy-handedness of the approach. A good study of ambition and the different paths it leads the characters on. 1948; B&W; 78m.

FOREVER YOUNG ★★
DIR: David Drury. **CAST:** James Aubrey, Nicholas Gecks, Alec McCowen.

This slow-moving British soap opera features a handsome priest who is idolized by a lonely boy. When the priest's old friend returns, the viewer learns (through black-and-white flashbacks) that the priest had betrayed his friend. The plot thickens when the friend decides to take revenge on the priest. Unrated, but brief nudity and mature themes would make it comparable with a PG. 1983; 85m.

FORMULA, THE ★★
DIR: John G. Avildsen. **CAST:** George C. Scott, Marlon Brando, Marthe Keller, John Gielgud, G. D. Spradlin.
Take a plot to conceal a method producing enough synthetic fuel to take care of the current oil shortage and add two superstars like George C. Scott and Marlon Brando. Sounds like the formula for a real blockbuster, doesn't it? Unfortunately, it turns out to be the formula for a major disappointment. Rated R. 1980; 117m.

FORT APACHE—THE BRONX ★★★½
DIR: Daniel Petrie. **CAST:** Paul Newman, Ken Wahl, Edward Asner, Kathleen Beller, Rachel Ticotin.
Jarring violence surfaces throughout this story about New York's crime-besieged South Bronx, but absorbing dramatic elements give this routine cops-and-criminals format gutsy substance. Paul Newman, as an idealistic police veteran, proves his screen magnetism hasn't withered with time. The supporting cast is top-notch. Rated R for violence, profanity, and sexual references. 1981; 125m.

FORTRESS ★★½
DIR: Arch Nicholson. **CAST:** Rachel Ward, Sean Garlick, Rebecca Rigg.
In this drawn-out story of a mass kidnapping in the Australian Outback, Rachel Ward is passable as a teacher in a one-room school. She is abducted along with her students, ranging in age from about six to fourteen. The story centers around their attempts to escape. 1985; 90m.

49TH PARALLEL, THE ★★★★
DIR: Michael Powell. **CAST:** Laurence Olivier, Anton Wallbrook, Eric Portman, Leslie Howard, Raymond Massey, Finlay Currie, Glynis Johns.
Rich suspense drama about a World War II German U-boat sunk off the coast of Canada whose crew makes it to shore and tries to reach safety in neutral territory. The cast is first-rate, the characterizations outstanding. Original story won an Oscar. 1941; B&W; 105m.

FOUNTAINHEAD, THE ★★½
DIR: King Vidor. **CAST:** Gary Cooper, Patricia Neal, Raymond Massey, Kent Smith, Robert Douglas.
Gary Cooper tries his best in this Ayn Rand novel, brought to the screen without any of the book's vitality or character development. "Coop" is cast as Howard Roark, a Frank Lloyd Wright–type architect whose creations are ahead of their time and therefore go unappreciated. Patricia Neal is the love interest. 1949; B&W; 114m.

FOUR FRIENDS ★★
DIR: Arthur Penn. **CAST:** Craig Wasson, James Leo Herlihy, Jodi Thelen.
Arthur Penn directed and Steve Tesich (*Breaking Away*) wrote this interesting but ultimately disappointing film about America as seen through the eyes of a young immigrant (Craig Wasson) and the love he shares with two friends for a free-thinking young woman (Jodi Thelen). Rated R because of violence, nudity, and profanity. 1981; 114m.

FOUR IN A JEEP ★★½
DIR: Leopold Lindtberg. **CAST:** Viveca Lindfors, Ralph Meeker.
Just after World War II, Vienna was a city divided into four nationally divided zones. This picture deals with a police patrol made up of American, Soviet, British, and French troops who clash over cases with which they must deal. It's not a terribly exciting film, but it does evoke some emotion about this tragic episode in postwar history. 1951; B&W; 96m.

FOUR SEASONS, THE ★★★½
DIR: Alan Alda. **CAST:** Alan Alda, Carol Burnett, Len Cariou, Sandy Dennis, Rita Moreno, Jack Weston.

Written and directed by Alan Alda, this film focuses on the pains and joys of friendship shared by three couples who are vacationing together. Despite a flawed and uneven script, the characters have been skillfully drawn by Alda and convincingly played by an excellent cast. *Four Seasons* is by no means a perfect film, yet it is an appealing, uplifting piece of entertainment. Rated PG. 1981; 117m.

FOURTH WISH, THE ★★★★
DIR: Don Chaffey. **CAST:** John Meillon, Robert Bettles, Robyn Nevin.

This moving Australian tearjerker features a 12-year-old boy dying of leukemia. His father's desire to grant his final wishes gets progressively harder to arrange. Wonderful story of a father's love, but be prepared with a box of Kleenex nearby. Not rated. 1976; 120m.

FOXES ★★★
DIR: Adrian Lyne. **CAST:** Jodie Foster, Sally Kellerman, Cherie Currie, Randy Quaid, Scott Baio.

Adrian Lyne directed this fitfully interesting film, about four young women who share an apartment in Los Angeles. The cast is good and the film has some interesting things to say about young society, but somehow it all falls flat. Rated R. 1980; 106m.

FOXFIRE LIGHT ★
DIR: Allen Baron. **CAST:** Leslie Nielsen, Tippi Hedren, Lara Parker, Barry Van Dyke, Burton Gilliam.

Sappy romantic melodrama about a girl (Lara Parker) who overemotes her way through a love triangle in the Ozarks. Badly written. Rated PG for adult situations. 1982; 102m.

FOXTROT ★★½
DIR: Arturo Ripstein. **CAST:** Peter O'Toole, Charlotte Rampling, Max von Sydow, Jorge Luke, Helena Rojo, Claudio Brook.

Peter O'Toole plays a European aristocrat who escapes World War II when he takes a yacht to a deserted island in the Black Sea and sets up residence with his wife (Charlotte Rampling), his ship's captain (Max von Sydow), and his servant (Jorge Luke). Tension builds when visiting aristocrats hunt down all the wild game on the island purely for sport. *Foxtrot* centers on the wastes of the leisure class even in a time of war. Rated R for sex, nudity, and violence. 1975; 91m.

FRANCES ★★★★½
DIR: Graeme Clifford. **CAST:** Jessica Lange, Kim Stanley, Sam Shepard, Jeffrey DeMunn.

Director Howard Hawks called Frances Farmer "the best actress I ever worked with." However, the Seattle-born free-thinker was never allowed to reign as a star in Hollywood. This chilling, poignant motion picture explains why. Jessica Lange is superb as the starlet who snubs the power structure at every turn and pays a horrifying price for it. Kim Stanley is also impressive as Frances's mother, a money- and fame-hungry hag who uses her daughter. Sam Shepard is the one person who loves Frances for who and what she really is. An unforgettable film. Rated R. 1982; 139m.

FRANCIS GARY POWERS: THE TRUE STORY OF THE U-2 SPY INCIDENT ★★★½
DIR: Delbert Mann. **CAST:** Lee Majors, Noah Beery Jr., Nehemiah Persoff, Brooke Bundy, William Daniels, James Gregory, Lew Ayres.

In this made-for-television movie, the infamous 1960 U-2 spy plane shootdown over Russia is dramatized. The best performances in this true story are supplied by the supporting cast. Based on U-2 pilot Francis Gary Powers's book, it's worth viewing. 1976; 120m.

FRANKIE AND JOHNNY (1934)
DIR: Chester Erskine. **CAST:** Helen Morgan, Chester Morris, Lilyan Tashman.
Poorly acted costume drama which shows that even Helen Morgan, a great singer-actress, cannot save a bad production. Inspired by the now-legendary love-triangle title song. 1934; B&W; 66m.

FREE, WHITE, AND 21 ★★
DIR: Larry Buchanan. **CAST:** Frederick O'Neal, Annalena Lund.
A southern black man is accused of raping a white woman who is working for the civil rights movement. The main attraction of this dated movie is that it is made in a pseudodocumentary style—as a trial during which the testimony is shown in the form of flashbacks. Interesting, though very overlong. 1963; B&W; 102m.

FRENCH LIEUTENANT'S WOMAN, THE ★★★★★
DIR: Karel Reisz. **CAST:** Meryl Streep, Jeremy Irons, Leo McKern, Hilton McRae, Emily Morgan.
A brilliant adaptation of John Fowles' bestseller, starring Meryl Streep as the enigmatic title heroine and Jeremy Irons as her obsessed lover. Victorian and modern attitudes on love are contrasted in this intellectually and emotionally engrossing film. Rated R because of sexual references and sex scenes. 1981; 123m.

FRENCH QUARTER ★★½
DIR: Dennis Kane. **CAST:** Bruce Davison, Virginia Mayo.
Everyone in the cast plays two characters, one in modern times and one at the turn of the century, in this drama set in New Orleans. Both stories are connected by voodoo magic, as a woman discovers she is the reincarnation of a prostitute. Slow moving but intriguing. Rated R for sexual situations. 1977; 101m.

FRESH HORSES ★½
DIR: David Anspaugh. **CAST:** Molly Ringwald, Andrew McCarthy, Patti D'Arbanville.
Adult version of *Pretty in Pink* that's obsessive, masochistic, and luridly manipulative. Molly Ringwald continues as the kid from the wrong side of the tracks, only this time there's nothing upbeat about her character. Andrew McCarthy is once again typecast as a middle-class nice guy who is consumed by an obsessive desire. Rated PG-13 for profanity and violence. 1988; 106m.

FRIENDLY FIRE ★★★★
DIR: David Greene. **CAST:** Carol Burnett, Ned Beatty, Sam Waterston, Timothy Hutton.
A gripping account of an American couple who run into government indifference when they attempt to learn the truth about their son's death—by American artillery fire—in Vietnam. Based on a true story. Both Carol Burnett and Ned Beatty give smashing performances as the grieved couple. Picture won four Emmy awards. Not rated; made for TV. 1979; 180m.

FRIENDLY PERSUASION ★★★★
DIR: William Wyler. **CAST:** Gary Cooper, Dorothy McGuire, Marjorie Main, Anthony Perkins, Robert Middleton, Richard Eyer.
Jessamyn West's finely crafted novel of a Quaker family beset by the realities of the Civil War in southern Indiana is superbly transferred to film by an outstanding cast guided by gifted direction. 1956; 140m.

FRINGE DWELLERS, THE ★★★★
DIR: Bruce Beresford. **CAST:** Justine Saunders, Kristina Nehm, Bob Maza.
Bruce Beresford, the Austrialian filmmaker who directed *Breaker Morant* and *Tender Mercies*, has a tendency to make movies that have rambling stories but fascinating characters and rich performances. That description fits this production, which follows the domestic problems of a family of Aborigines who move from

a shantytown to a clean and proper suburban neighborhood. It's an intriguing, touching, but nonsentimental look at a race of people unfamiliar to most Americans. It's rated PG for language. 1987; 98m.

FROM HERE TO ETERNITY ★★★★★

DIR: Fred Zinnemann. **CAST:** Burt Lancaster, Montgomery Clift, Deborah Kerr, Frank Sinatra, Donna Reed, Ernest Borgnine.

This smoldering drama, depicting the demands of military life just before America's involvement in World War II, earned the Academy Award for best picture of 1953. This riveting classic includes the historic on-the-beach love scene that turned a few heads during its time. And no wonder! Director Fred Zinnemann took chances with this realistic portrait of the U.S. military. 1953; B&W; 118m.

FRONT, THE ★★★★

DIR: Martin Ritt. **CAST:** Woody Allen, Zero Mostel, Andrea Marcovicci, Joshua Shelley, Georgann Johnson.

Focusing on the horrendous blacklist of entertainers in the 1950s, this film manages to drive its point home with wit and poignance. Joseph McCarthy started finding communists under every bed right after World War II and was able to destroy careers. This film is about writers who find a man to submit their scripts to after they have been blacklisted. Woody Allen plays the title role. Rated PG. 1976; 94m.

FUGITIVE KIND, THE ★★

DIR: Sidney Lumet. **CAST:** Marlon Brando, Joanne Woodward, Anna Magnani, Victor Jory.

This picture takes Tennessee Williams's stage play *Orpheus Descending*, shakes it up, and lets a new storyline fall out. Marlon Brando, with his hair dyed blond, is a wanderer who woos southern belles while strumming a guitar. As one of the wooed, Joanne Woodward gives a fine performance. 1959; B&W; 135m.

FULL METAL JACKET ★★★★

DIR: Stanley Kubrick. **CAST:** Matthew Modine, Adam Baldwin, Vincent D'Onofrio, Lee Ermey, Dorian Harewood, Arliss Howard, Ed O'Ross.

Stanley Kubrick and Vietnam? How can that combination miss? Well, it does and it doesn't. Kubrick scores higher in smaller moments than in scenes seemingly intended to be climactic. Don't be surprised if days later, fragments of what you saw and heard are still with you. Particularly memorable is Lee Ermey as Gunnery Sgt. Hartman. Rated R for violence and some inventive and colorful profanity. 1987; 120m.

GABY, A TRUE STORY ★★★★

DIR: Luis Mandoki. **CAST:** Liv Ullmann, Norma Aleandro, Robert Loggia, Rachel Levin, Lawrence Monoson, Robert Beltran.

Rachel Levin gives a smashing portrayal of a brilliant young woman trapped in a body incapacitated by cerebral palsy. Based on the true-life drama of Gabriela Brimmer. Assisted by a screenplay that steers clear of maudlin situations, the cast delivers powerful performances. Rated PG-13. 1987; 120m.

GAL YOUNG 'UN ★★★

DIR: Victor Nunez. **CAST:** Dana Peru, David Peck, J. Smith-Cameron.

Set in the early 1900s when bootlegging was a popluar source of income, this charming low-budget film focuses on a young man, unable to pay his debts, who woos a lonely, elderly (and comparatively rich) widow. He cons her into marriage with his boyish charm and uses her money to set up his own moonshine still. Featuring fine performances and good use of locations, this film is not rated. 1986; 105m.

GALLIPOLI ★★★★½

DIR: Peter Weir. **CAST:** Mark Lee, Mel Gibson, Robert Grubb, Tim McKenzie, David Argue.

Add this to the list of outstanding motion pictures from Australia and the very best films about war. Directed by Peter Weir this appealing character study, which is set during World War I, manages to say more about life on the battlefront than many of the more straightforward pictures in the genre. Rated PG because of violence. 1981; 110m.

GAMBLE ON LOVE ★★
DIR: Jim Balden. **CAST:** Beverly Garland.
Las Vegas provides the backdrop for this slow-moving film. Liz (Beverly Garland) inherits a casino from her father and falls in love with the brash casino manager. This relationship leads to an explosive climax. 1982; 105m.

GAMBLER, THE ★★★½
DIR: Karel Reisz. **CAST:** James Caan, Paul Sorvino, Lauren Hutton, Jacqueline Brooks, Morris Carnovsky.
This gritty film features James Caan in one of his best screen portrayals as a compulsive, self-destructive gambler. Director Karel Reisz keeps the atmosphere thick with tension. Always thinking he's on the edge of a big score, Caan's otherwise intelligent college professor character gets him deeper and deeper into trouble. It's a downer, but still worth watching. Rated R. 1974; 111m.

GAMBLER AND THE LADY, THE ★
DIR: Patrick Jenkins. **CAST:** Dane Clark, Kathleen Byron, Naomi Chance.
This British production dramatizes the troubles of a gambler who falls in love with a beautiful woman, forcing a change in his lifestyle. Not recommended. 1952; B&W; 71m.

GANDHI ★★★★★
DIR: Richard Attenborough. **CAST:** Ben Kingsley, Candice Bergen, Edward Fox, John Gielgud, Martin Sheen, John Mills, Trevor Howard, Saeed Jaffrey, Roshan Seth.
One of the finest screen biographies in the history of motion pictures, this film, by Richard Attenborough, chronicles the life of the deceased Indian leader (Ben Kingsley). Running three hours, it is an old-style "big" picture, with spectacle, great drama, superb performances, and, as they used to say, a cast of thousands. Yet for all its hugeness, *Gandhi* achieves a remarkable intimacy. Afterward, viewers feel as if they have actually known—and, more important, been touched by—the man Indians called the "Great Soul." Rated PG for violence. 1982; 188m.

GANGSTER'S LAW ★
DIR: Siro Marcellini. **CAST:** Klaus Kinski, Maurice Poli, Suzy Andersen, Max Delys.
This is a routine Mafia story filmed in Italy. Klaus Kinski, who is sometimes in interesting and distinguished films, is reduced to playing a con man double-crossing another bank-robbing gang. The acting is poor. Dubbed. 1986; 89m.

GARDEN OF ALLAH, THE ★★
DIR: Richard Boleslawski. **CAST:** Marlene Dietrich, Charles Boyer, Tilly Losch, John Carradine, Basil Rathbone, Joseph Schildkraut.
Gloriously photographed, yawnable yarn of romance in the Algerian boondocks. Tepid, silly, and full of clichéd dialogue. However, the early Technicolor—which won a special Oscar—is outstanding. Could be retitled: *Marlene's Manhunt*. 1936; 80m.

GARDENS OF STONE ★★★½
DIR: Francis Ford Coppola. **CAST:** James Caan, Anjelica Huston, James Earl Jones, D. B. Sweeney, Dean Stockwell, Mary Stuart Masterson, Dick Anthony Williams, Lonette McKee, Sam Bottoms.
A poignant drama examining the self-described toy soldiers who officiate at military funerals at Virginia's Fort Myer, adjacent to Arlington National Cemetery. The setting is the Vietnam 1960s, and James Caan stars as a dis-

illusioned sergeant who'd rather be training recruits. D. B. Sweeney is excellent as the young recruit who is taken under Caan's wing, but James Earl Jones walks away with his every scene as the poetically foul-mouthed Sergeant Major "Goody" Nelson. Rated R for profanity. 1987; 111m.

GATHERING, THE ★★★★
DIR: Randal Kleiser. **CAST:** Edward Asner, Maureen Stapleton, Lawrence Pressman.
Winner of the Emmy for outstanding TV drama special of 1977–1978, this powerful tearjerker features Ed Asner as Adam Thornton. He returns to the family he abandoned after learning that he's dying. The reunion with his family occurs at Christmas and succeeds mainly because his estranged wife (Maureen Stapleton) encourages her children to forgive and forget the past. 1977; 104m.

GATHERING, PART II, THE ★★★½
DIR: Charles S. Dubin. **CAST:** Maureen Stapleton, Rebecca Balding, Efrem Zimbalist Jr., Jameson Parker.
Picking up two years after *The Gathering*, this sequel opens with Kate (Maureen Stapleton) managing her late husband's business. When she falls in love with a business tycoon, she decides to break the news to her grown children over Christmas dinner. 1979; 104m.

GATHERING STORM ★
DIR: Herbert Wise. **CAST:** Richard Burton, Virginia McKenna, Robert Hardy, Ian Bannen.
Richard Burton tries his best to bring some life to this dull movie, which covers Winston Churchill's life from 1937 to the start of World War II. Filmed almost entirely on a few indoor stages, this film plays more like an episode of *Masterpiece Theater* than a motion picture. Only for Churchill buffs. 1974; 72m.

GENE KRUPA STORY, THE ★
DIR: Don Weis. **CAST:** Sal Mineo, Susan Kohner, Susan Oliver, James Darren, Yvonne Craig, Red Nichols.
A fictionalized biography of the late great drummer Gene Krupa. The film borrows facts when needed, integrating them in a hodgepodge of musical hokum. Krupa's addiction to drugs is handled with delicacy. 1959; B&W; 101m.

GENTLEMAN BANDIT, THE ★★★
DIR: Jonathan Kaplan. **CAST:** Ralph Waite, Julie Bovasso, Jerry Zaks, Joe Grifasi, Estelle Parsons, Vincent Spano.
Ralph Waite gives a convincing portrait of Father Pagano, who was accused of a series of armed robberies in 1978. This made-for-TV biography chronicles his ordeal when mistakenly identified by seven eyewitnesses. Good viewing. 1981; 96m.

GENTLEMAN JIM ★★★★½
DIR: Raoul Walsh. **CAST:** Errol Flynn, Jack Carson, Alan Hale, Alexis Smith.
Errol Flynn has a field day in this beautifully filmed biography of heavyweight champion Jim Corbett. Always cocky and light on his feet, Flynn is a joy to behold and will make those who considered him a star instead of a actor think twice. Ward Bond is equally fine as John L. Sullivan. Said to have been Flynn's favorite role. 1942; B&W; 104m.

GEORGIA, GEORGIA ★★
DIR: Stig Bjorknan. **CAST:** Diana Sands, Dirk Benedict, Minnie Gentry, Roger Furman.
This film, adapted by Maya Angelou from one of her stories, is a dated but fairly interesting study of racism. The story centers around the relationship between a white photographer and a black singer, whose motherly touring companion is adamantly antiwhite. If you get mildly involved with this movie, stay with it. Rated R. 1972; 91m.

GETTING OF WISDOM, THE ★★★★

DIR: Bruce Beresford. **CAST:** Susannah Fowle, Sheila Helpmann, Patricia Kennedy, Hilary Ryan.

Out of Australia, this better-than-average rites-of-passage story of an unrefined country girl (Susannah Fowle) who gets sent off to school in the city displays all the qualities of top-notch directing. The girl is easy prey for her more sophisticated, yet equally immature classmates. The story takes place in the mid-1800s and is taken from the classic Australian novel by Henry Handel Richardson. Not rated but the equivalent of a G. 1980; 100m.

GETTING OVER

DIR: Bernie Rollins. **CAST:** John Daniels, Gwen Brisco, Paulette Gibson.

This low-budget black exploitation flick is so poorly lit that it's often hard to discern the facial expressions of the actors. A would-be music producer (John Daniels) is adopted by a huge music corporation as a tax write-off. Unrated, it contains profanity. 1980; 108m.

GETTING PHYSICAL ★★★½

DIR: Steven H. Stern. **CAST:** Alexandra Paul, Sandahl Bergman, David Naughton.

Alexandra Paul plays Nadine, a pudgy junk-food addict who decides to toughen up after her purse is stolen. Most couch potatoes can vicariously experience the joy of Nadine's transformation from chubby wimp to lean body builder without lifting a muscle themselves. A must-see for everyone who dreams about a fitter lifestyle. Made for television, this is unrated and very mild. 1984; 95m.

GETTING STRAIGHT ★★½

DIR: Richard Rush. **CAST:** Elliott Gould, Candice Bergen, Max Julien, Jeff Corey, Robert F. Lyons.

During the campus riots of the 1960s, Hollywood jumped on the bandwagon with such forgettable films as *The Strawberry Statement* and *R.P.M.* Add *Getting Straight* to the list. Elliott Gould plays a "hip" graduate student caught up in campus unrest. Somewhat effective during its initial release, it now seems like an odd curio. Rated PG. 1970; 124m.

GIANT ★★★½

DIR: George Stevens. **CAST:** James Dean, Rock Hudson, Elizabeth Taylor, Carroll Baker, Dennis Hopper.

The third part of director George Stevens's American Trilogy, which also included *Shane* and *A Place in the Sun*, this 1956 release traces the life of a cattle rancher through two generations. Although the lead performances by Elizabeth Taylor, Rock Hudson, and James Dean are unconvincing when the stars are poorly "aged" with make-up, *Giant* is still a stylish, if overlong movie that lives up to its title. 1956; 198m.

GIDEON'S TRUMPET ★★★★

DIR: Robert Collins. **CAST:** Henry Fonda, John Houseman, José Ferrer.

Henry Fonda is the chief delight in this factual account of Clarence Earl Gideon, who was thrown into prison in the early 1960s for a minor crime—and denied a legal counsel because he could not afford to pay for one. Gideon boned up on the laws of our land and concluded that everybody was entitled to a lawyer, whether or not such was affordable. This made-for-TV movie accurately follows Anthony Lewis's source book. Unrated; suitable for family viewing. 1980; 104m.

GILDA ★★★★

DIR: Charles Vidor. **CAST:** Glenn Ford, Rita Hayworth, George Macready, Joseph Callela, Steven Geray.

Glenn Ford plays a small-time gambler who goes to work for a South American casino owner and his beautiful wife, Gilda (Rita Hayworth). When the casino owner disappears and is presumed dead, Ford marries Hayworth and they run the casino together. All goes well until the husband returns, seeking revenge against them. There is some violence in this film. 1946; B&W; 110m.

GIN GAME, THE ★★★★½
DIR: Mike Nichols. **CAST:** Jessica Tandy, Hume Cronyn.

A sensitive, insightful, and touchingly funny, award-winning Broadway play taped live in London with its two original stars. The enchanting performances are highlighted with superb simplicity in this two-character play that explores the developing relationship between two senior citizens. Unrated, but freely sprinkled with profanity. 1984; 82m.

GINGER IN THE MORNING ★★½
DIR: Gordon Wiles. **CAST:** Sissy Spacek, Monte Markham, Slim Pickens, Susan Oliver, Mark Miller.

A lonely salesman, Monte Markham, picks up a hitchhiker, Sissy Spacek, and romance blossoms in this okay romantic comedy. No great revelations about human nature will be found in this one, just harmless fluff that will be forgotten soon after it's been viewed. 1973; 89m.

GIRL, THE ★★★
DIR: Arne Mattson. **CAST:** Franco Nero, Bernice Stegers, Clare Powney, Christopher Lee.

A strange and disturbing European film analyzing the seduction of a powerful attorney by a 14-year-old school girl. This paves the way for a variety of settings in which lust, passion, and murder become the norm. Unfortunately, what might have been a very powerful film becomes slow and plods to the finish. Though no rating is available, there is ample sex and nudity throughout the film. 1986; 104m.

GIRL FROM PETROVKA, THE ★★★
DIR: Robert Ellis Miller. **CAST:** Goldie Hawn, Hal Holbrook, Anthony Hopkins.

American journalist Hal Holbrook falls in love with Russian Goldie Hawn while on assignment in the Soviet Union. The manipulative script often becomes overly melodramatic, but the film still works as an effective tearjerker. Something about Hawn's guileless, resourceful character is impossible to resist, and the story's conclusion packs a surprising punch. Rated PG for adult situations. 1974; 104m.

GIRL IN BLUE, THE ★★½
DIR: George Kaczender. **CAST:** David Selby, Maud Adams.

Trifling romantic drama about a man obsessed with a woman he glimpsed fleetingly years before. When he begins to have trouble with his current girlfriend, he goes to seek the woman whose face he can't forget. Filmed in Montreal. Unrated, the movie contains brief nudity and sexual situations. 1973; 105m.

GIRLFRIENDS ★★★★
DIR: Claudia Weill. **CAST:** Melanie Mayron, Anita Skinner, Eli Wallach, Christopher Guest, Viveca Lindfors.

Realistic film about a young Jewish woman who learns to make it on her own after her best friend/roommate leaves to get married. Melanie Mayron's performance is the highlight of this touching and offbeat comic-drama. Rated PG. 1978; 88m.

GIRLS OF HUNTINGTON HOUSE ★½
DIR: Alf Kjellin. **CAST:** Shirley Jones, Sissy Spacek, Mercedes McCambridge, Pamela Sue Martin.

With Shirley Jones as the teacher in a halfway house for unwed young mothers-to-be, this made-for-TV story explores the plight of a group of young women trying to make a most difficult decision. Simplistic dialogue and plot developments help to water down the impact of this one. 1973; 73m.

GIVE 'EM HELL, HARRY! ★★★★
DIR: Steve Binder. **CAST:** James Whitmore.

This is the film version of James Whitmore's wonderful portrayal of President Harry S. Truman. Taken from the stage production, the film is a magnificent tribute and entertainment. Rated PG. 1975; 102m.

GLASS HOUSE, THE ★★★★
DIR: Tom Gries. **CAST:** Vic Morrow, Clu Gulager, Billy Dee Williams, Dean Jagger, Alan Alda.

This powerful prison drama is based on a story by Truman Capote. An idealistic new prison guard (Clu Gulager) is overwhelmed by the gang violence within the prison. Alan Alda plays a new prisoner who becomes the target of a violent gang leader (Vic Morrow). R for sex and violence. 1972; 89m.

GLASS MENAGERIE, THE ★★★★
DIR: Paul Newman. **CAST:** Joanne Woodward, John Malkovich, Karen Allen, James Naughton.

Director Paul Newman made this impressive screen drama to immortalize wife Joanne Woodward's excellent portrayal of faded southern belle Amanda Winfield, whose strong opinions tend to make her adventure-hungry son (John Malkovich) miserable, and drive her shy daughter (Karen Allen) deeper within herself. This is the best film version to date of Tennessee Williams's semi-autobiographical play. Rated PG. 1987; 134m.

GLEN OR GLENDA
DIR: Edward D. Wood Jr. **CAST:** Bela Lugosi, Dolores Fuller, Daniel Davis (director Ed Wood Jr.), Lyle Talbot, Timothy Farrell, George Weiss.

Incredible film by the incomparably *inept* Edward D. Wood Jr., tells the powerful story of a young transvestite who finally summons up the courage to come out of the closet and ask his fiancée if he can wear her sweater. 1953; B&W; 67m.

GODDESS, THE ★★★
DIR: John Cromwell. **CAST:** Kim Stanley, Lloyd Bridges, Betty Lou Holland, Joyce Van Patten, Steven Hill.

A lonely girl working in a Maryland five-and-dime dreams of film stardom, goes to Hollywood, clicks in a minor role, and makes the big time, only to find it all bittersweet. Stage star Kim Stanley, largely ignored by Hollywood, does well in the title role, though she was far from suited for it. Paddy Chayefsky supposedly based his screenplay on Marilyn Monroe. 1958; B&W; 105m.

GODFATHER, THE ★★★★
DIR: Francis Ford Coppola. **CAST:** Marlon Brando, Al Pacino, James Caan, Richard Castellano, John Cazale, Diane Keaton, Talia Shire, Robert Duvall, Sterling Hayden, John Marley, Richard Conte, Al Lettieri.

Mario Puzo's popular novel comes to life in artful fashion. Filmed in foreboding tones, the movie takes us into the lurid world of the Mafia. Marlon Brando won an Oscar for his performance, but it's Al Pacino who grabs your attention with an unnerving intensity. Rated R. 1972; 175m.

GODFATHER, THE, PART II ★★★★
DIR: Francis Ford Coppola. **CAST:** Al Pacino, Robert Duvall, Diane Keaton, Robert De Niro, John Cazale, Talia Shire, Lee Strasberg, Michael Gazzo.

This is a sequel that equals the quality of the original, an almost unheard-of circumstance in Hollywood. Director Francis Ford Coppola skillfully meshes past and present, intercutting the story of young Don Corleone (Robert De Niro), an ambitious, immoral immigrant, and his son Michael (Al Pacino), who lives up to his father's expectations, turning the family's crime organization into a sleek, cold, modern operation. This gripping film won seven Academy Awards. Rated R. 1974; 200m.

GODFATHER EPIC, THE ★★★★★
DIR: Francis Ford Coppola. **CAST:** Marlon Brando, Talia Shire, James Caan, Robert Duvall, John Cazale, Al Pacino, Diane Keaton, Robert De Niro.

Few screen creations qualify as first-class entertainment and cinematic art.

Francis Ford Coppola's *The Godfather* series unquestionably belongs in that category. Yet as good as *The Godfather* and *The Godfather, Part II* are, they are no match for *The Godfather Epic*. A compilation of the two films with extra scenes added, it is nothing less than a masterwork. By editing the two films together in chronological order, for the videotape release of *The Godfather Epic*, Coppola has created a work greater than the sum of its parts. See it! Rated R. 1977; 380m.

GOD'S LITTLE ACRE ★★★★
DIR: Anthony Mann. **CAST:** Robert Ryan, Aldo Ray, Tina Louise, Jack Lord, Fay Spain, Buddy Hackett.

This is a terrific little film focusing on poor Georgia farmers. Robert Ryan gives one of his best performances as an itinerant farmer. Aldo Ray, Jack Lord, and Buddy Hackett lend good support. 1958; B&W; 110m.

GOING MY WAY ★★★★½
DIR: Leo McCarey. **CAST:** Bing Crosby, Barry Fitzgerald, Rise Stevens, Gene Lockhart, Frank McHugh.

Bing Crosby won the best-actor Oscar in 1944 for his delightful portrayal of the easygoing priest who finally wins over his strict superior (Barry Fitzgerald, who also won an Oscar for his supporting role). Leo McCarey wrote and directed this funny, heartwarming character study and netted two Academy Awards for his efforts, as well as crafting the year's Oscar-winning best picture. 1944; B&W; 130m.

GOLD OF NAPLES, THE ★★★½
DIR: Vittorio De Sica. **CAST:** Sophia Loren, Vittorio De Sica, Toto, Silvana Mangano.

A charming quartet of vignettes: Sophia Loren as a wife who cheats on her pizza-baker husband; demon cardplayer Vittorio De Sica being put down by a clever child; Toto as a henpecked husband; and Silvana Mangano playing a married whore whose marital arrangement is more than passing strange. 1954; B&W; 107m.

GOLDEN BOY ★★★★
DIR: Rouben Mamoulian. **CAST:** William Holden, Barbara Stanwyck, Adolphe Menjou, Lee J. Cobb.

William Holden made a strong starring debut in this screen adaptation of Clifford Odet's, play about a musician who becomes a boxer. Though a bit dated today, Holden and co-star Barbara Stanwyck still shine. 1939; B&W; 100m.

GOLDEN HONEYMOON, THE ★★★★
DIR: Noel Black. **CAST:** James Whitmore, Teresa Wright, Stephen Elliott, Nan Martin.

Delightful adaptation of Ring Lardner's deft and biting story. James Whitmore steals the show as talkative Charley Tate, a crusty old windbag married fifty happy years to his patient wife, Lucy (Teresa Wright). While celebrating their golden anniversary in Florida, she meets up with an old flame, and suddendly Charley feels the need to prove—once again—that Lucy didn't choose the wrong fella fifty years back. Introduced by Henry Fonda; unrated and suitable for family viewing. 1980; 52m.

GONE WITH THE WIND ★★★★★
DIR: Victor Fleming. **CAST:** Clark Gable, Vivien Leigh, Leslie Howard, Olivia De Havilland, Thomas Mitchell, Hattie McDaniel.

The all-time movie classic with Clark Gable and Vivien Leigh as Margaret Mitchell's star-crossed lovers in the final days of the Old South. Need we say more? 1939; 222m.

GOOD EARTH, THE ★★★★
DIR: Sidney Franklin. **CAST:** Paul Muni, Luise Rainer, Keye Luke, Walter Connolly, Jessie Ralph.

Nobel Prize novelist Pearl Buck's engrossing, richly detailed story of a simple Chinese farm couple whose lives are ruined by greed is impressively brought to life in this milestone film. Luise Rainer won the second of her back-to-back best-actress Oscars for her portrayal of the ever-patient wife. The photography and special effects are outstanding. 1937; B&W; 138m.

GOOD FATHER, THE ★★★★½

DIR: Mike Newell. **CAST:** Anthony Hopkins, Jim Broadbent, Harriet Walter, Simon Callow, Joanne Whalley.

In this brilliant British import, Anthony Hopkins is a walking time bomb. A separation from his wife has left him on the outside of his son's life. Hopkins's reaction is so extreme that he is haunted by nightmares. Director Mike Newell lays on the suspense artfully with this device while detailing the revenge Hopkins plots against the wife of a friend who is in similar circumstances. Rated R for profanity, suggested sex, and stylized violence. 1986; 90m.

GOOD MORNING...AND GOODBYE! ★★

DIR: Russ Meyer. **CAST:** Alaina Capri, Stuart Lancaster.

One of Russ Meyer's more obscure movies, and one of the duller ones as well. Unsatisfied wife Alaina Capri fools around with everyone in sight until her older husband (Stuart Lancaster) is magically cured of his impotence. Dated—and unrated. 1967; 78m.

GOOD MORNING, BABYLON ★★★

DIR: Paolo Taviani, Vittorio Taviani. **CAST:** Vincent Spano, Joaquim de Almeida, Greta Scacchi, Charles Dance.

This follows the misadventures of two brothers who come to America to find their fortunes as artists and find jobs on the production of D. W. Griffith's silent classic, *Intolerance*. The movie has moments of lyrical beauty and its story is sweet. But the dialogue has been translated from Italian in an occasionally awkward fashion. Rated PG-13 for nudity and profanity. 1987; 115m.

GOOD MORNING, VIETNAM ★★★½

DIR: Barry Levinson. **CAST:** Robin Williams, Forest Whitaker, Tung Thanh Tran, Chintara Sukapatana, Bruno Kirby, Robert Wuhl, J. T. Walsh.

Robin Williams stars as disc jockey Adrian Cronauer, who briefly ruled Saigon's Armed Forces Radio in 1965. Williams's improvisational monologues are the high points in a film that meanders too much, but Forest Whitaker also shines as Cronauer's aide-de-camp. Rated R for language and violence. 1987; 120m.

GOOD MOTHER, THE ★★★½

DIR: Leonard Nimoy. **CAST:** Diane Keaton, Jason Robards Jr., Ralph Bellamy, Liam Neeson, James Naughton.

Single mom Anna (Diane Keaton) finds romance with an irresistible Irish artist (Liam Neeson). Their dreamy affair becomes a nightmare when Anna's ex-husband accuses the artist of sexually abusing his daughter. This film will make you squirm and speculate on the rightness or wrongness of Anna's sexually open child-rearing techniques. Rated R for nudity and obscenities. 1988; 104m.

GOOD WIFE, THE ★

DIR: Ken Cameron. **CAST:** Rachel Ward, Bryan Brown, Sam Neill, Steven Vidler.

The Good Wife is about one woman's yearning for sexual fulfillment. Rachel Ward as the wife is given to obsessive behavior and made to humble herself before her husband, whom she must say is too good for her. This tremendous oversight of the central problem is bad enough, but the film has a bigger problem because Ward lacks the tension of repressed lust. Rated R. 1987; 97m.

GOODBYE, MR. CHIPS (1939) ★★★★½

DIR: Sam Wood. **CAST:** Robert Donat, Greer Garson, John Mills.

Robert Donat creates one of filmdom's most heartwarming roles as Chips, the Latin teacher of an English boys' school. The poignant movie follows Chips from his first bumbling, early teaching days until he becomes a beloved school institution. Greer Garson was introduced to American audiences in the rewarding role of Chips' loving wife. 1939; B&W; 114m.

GOODBYE, NORMA JEAN ★★★
DIR: Larry Buchanan. **CAST:** Misty Rowe, Terrence Locke, Patch Mckenzie.
A depiction of Norma Jean Baker's travels along the rocky road to superstardom as Marilyn Monroe. The film begins in 1941 with a naïve and vulnerable teenage Norma Jean, orphaned and alone. Her only motivation in life is her dream of becoming a star. Rated R for nudity. 1975; 95m.

GOODBYE PEOPLE, THE ★★★★
DIR: Herb Gardner. **CAST:** Judd Hirsch, Martin Balsam, Pamela Reed, Ron Silver, Michael Tucker, Gene Saks.
This unashamedly sentimental film is a delight. Martin Balsam is memorable as a man attempting to realize the dream of many years by rebuilding his Coney Island hot-dog stand. Pamela Reed and Judd Hirsch, as the young people who help him, turn in outstanding performances, and the hot-dog stand itself is a fantastic structure. 1984; 104m.

GORILLAS IN THE MIST ★★★★
DIR: Michael Apted. **CAST:** Sigourney Weaver, Bryan Brown, Julie Harris, John Omirah Miluwi.
Sigourney Weaver stars in this impressive biopic about Dian Fossey, the crusading primatologist whose devotion to the once-nearly extinct mountain gorillas of central Africa led to her murder. Rather than present Fossey as a saint, director Michael Apted, screenwriter Anna Hamilton Phelan, and Weaver take great pains to show her complexity. There are some truly unforgettable scenes of Fossey's interaction with the gorillas. Rated PG-13 for profanity, suggested sex, and violence. 1988; 129m.

GRADUATE, THE ★★★★½
DIR: Mike Nichols. **CAST:** Dustin Hoffman, Anne Bancroft, Katharine Ross.
Mike Nichols won an Academy Award for his direction of this touching, funny, unsettling, and unforgettable release about a young man (Dustin Hoffman, in his first major role) attempting to chart his future and develop his own set of values. He falls in love with Katharine Ross, but finds himself seduced by her wily, sexy mother, Anne Bancroft (as Mrs. Robinson). Don't forget the superb soundtrack of songs by Paul Simon and Art Garfunkel. 1967; 105m.

GRAND HOTEL ★★★★
DIR: Edmund Goulding. **CAST:** John Barrymore, Greta Garbo, Wallace Beery, Joan Crawford, Lionel Barrymore, Lewis Stone.
World War I is over. Life in the fast lane has returned to Berlin's Grand Hotel, crossroads of a thousand lives, backdrop to as many stories. This anthology of life at various levels won an Oscar for best picture. 1932; B&W; 113m.

GRAND PRIX ★★½
DIR: John Frankenheimer. **CAST:** James Garner, Eva Marie Saint, Yves Montand, Toshiro Mifune, Brian Bedford, Jessica Walter, Antonio Sabato, Adolfo Celi.
The cars, the drivers, and the race itself are the real stars of this international epic, beautifully filmed on locations throughout Europe. The four inter-related stories of professional adversaries and their personal lives intrude on the exciting footage of the real thing. Yves Montand, though, does a credible job in what is basically a big-budget soap opera with oil stains. 1966; 179m.

GRANDVIEW, U.S.A ★
DIR: Randal Kleiser. **CAST:** Jamie Lee Curtis, C. Thomas Howell, Patrick

Swayze, Jennifer Jason Leigh, Ramon Bieri, Carole Cook, Troy Donahue, William Windom.

Jamie Lee Curtis is one of the finest actresses in movies today. Therefore, to see her talents wasted in *Grandview, U.S.A.*, another of director Randal Kleiser's blatantly commercial, light-headed entertainments, made our blood boil. *Grandview, U.S.A.* is a coming-of-age study totally lacking in depth and characterization. Rated R for nudity, violence, and profanity. 1984; 97m.

GRAPES OF WRATH, THE ★★★★★

DIR: John Ford. **CAST:** Henry Fonda, John Carradine, Jane Darwell, Russell Simpson, Charley Grapewin, John Qualen.

Henry Fonda stars in this superb screen adaptation of the John Steinbeck novel about farmers from Oklahoma fleeing the Dust Bowl and poverty of their home state only to be confronted by prejudice and violence in California. It's a compelling drama beautifully acted by the director's stock company. 1940; B&W; 129m.

GREASER'S PALACE ★★½

DIR: Robert Downey. **CAST:** Allan Arbus, Luana Anders, Herve Villechaize, Don Calfa.

You'll either love or hate this one, a retelling of the passion of Christ set in a small western town. In typical post-Sixties style, director Robert Downey throws in every allegorical point he can think of. Sometimes inventive, sometimes maddening. Not rated. 1972; 91m.

GREAT DAN PATCH, THE ★★★

DIR: Joseph M. Newman. **CAST:** Dennis O'Keefe, Gail Russell, Ruth Warrick, Charlotte Greenwood.

The story of the greatest trotting horse of them all. Good racing scenes. An opera for horse lovers. 1949; B&W; 94m.

GREAT EXPECTATIONS (1946) ★★★★½

DIR: David Lean. **CAST:** John Mills, Alec Guinness, Valerie Hobson, Bernard Miles, Finlay Currie, Martita Hunt, Jean Simmons.

A penniless orphan becomes a gentleman through the generosity of a mysterious patron. The second of three film versions of Charles Dickens's classic story. Made at the close of World War II, this version is by far the finest from all standpoints: direction, script, cast, photography, art direction. 1946; B&W; 118m.

GREAT EXPECTATIONS (1988) ★★★★

DIR: Julian Amyes. **CAST:** Stratford Johns, Gerry Sundquist, Joan Hickson.

Fine BBC production of Charles Dickens's classic tale about a boy named Pip. This broadcast takes special care to include every plot convolution (and there are many!). While literary enthusiasts will rejoice in this, most casual viewers will be fidgeting with impatience. Best to watch this in two sittings! 1988; 300m.

GREAT GABBO, THE ★★★½

DIR: James Cruze. **CAST:** Erich Von Stroheim, Betty Compson, Don Douglas.

Cinema giant Erich Von Stroheim gives a tour de force performance as a brilliant but cold ventriloquist whose disregard for the feelings of others comes back to haunt him when he realizes that he has lost the affection of a girl he has come to love. Von Stroheim and his little wooden pal are a compelling couple—this is a film that lingers in the memory and rates with other fine films about ventriloquism like *Dead Of Night* and *Magic*. 1929; B&W; 89m.

GREAT GATSBY, THE ★★★

DIR: Jack Clayton. **CAST:** Robert Redford, Mia Farrow, Karen Black, Sam Waterston, Bruce Dern.

This is a well-mounted, well-acted film that is, perhaps, a bit overlong.

However, Robert Redford, the mysterious title character, is marvelous as Gatsby. Bruce Dern is equally memorable as the man who always has been rich and selfish. Rated PG. 1974; 144m.

GREAT GUY ★★
DIR: John G. Blystone. **CAST:** James Cagney, Mae Clarke, Edward Brophy.
Depression film about a feisty inspector crusading against corruption in the meat-packing business. Not vintage James Cagney...but okay. 1936; B&W; 75m.

GREAT IMPOSTOR, THE ★★★½
DIR: Robert Mulligan. **CAST:** Tony Curtis, Edmond O'Brien, Arthur O'Connell, Gary Merrill.
The amazing story of Ferdinand Demara is told in engrossing style by director Robert Mulligan. Demara, with natural charm and uncanny adaptability, successfully managed to pose as everything from a clergyman to a doctor. The role is a tour de force for Tony Curtis. Compelling and seasoned with dark humor. 1960; 112m.

GREAT SANTINI, THE ★★★★
DIR: Lewis John Carlino. **CAST:** Robert Duvall, Blythe Danner, Michael O'Keefe.
Robert Duvall's superb performance in the title role is the most outstanding feature of this fine film. The story of a troubled family and its unpredictable patriarch (Duvall), it was released briefly in early 1980 and then disappeared. But thanks to the efforts of the New York film critics, it was re-released with appropriate hoopla and did well at the box office. Rated PG for profanity and violence. 1980; 116m.

GREAT WALLENDAS, THE ★★★
DIR: Larry Elikann. **CAST:** Lloyd Bridges, Britt Ekland, Taina Elg, John van Dreelen, Cathy Rigby, Michael McGuire.
In this made-for-television movie, Lloyd Bridges stars as the head of the Wallenda family of high-wire artists. Bridges gives one of his most convincing performances as he keeps the spirit and determination of the family alive through their many tragedies. 1978; 104m.

GREATEST, THE ★★
DIR: Tom Gries. **CAST:** Muhammad Ali, Ernest Borgnine, John Marley, Robert Duvall, James Earl Jones, Roger E. Mosley.
Muhammad Ali plays himself in this disjointed screen biography, which is poorly directed by Tom Gries. Even the supporting performances don't help much. Only *Magnum, P.I.* regular Roger E. Mosley shines, as Sonny Liston—and steals the movie from its star. Rated PG. 1977; 101m.

GREATEST SHOW ON EARTH, THE ★★★★
DIR: Cecil B. DeMille. **CAST:** Betty Hutton, James Stewart, Charlton Heston, Cornel Wilde, Dorothy Lamour, Gloria Grahame.
The 1952 Oscar winner for best picture succeeds in the same manner as its subject, the circus; it's enjoyable family entertainment. Three major stories of backstage circus life all work and blend well in this film. 1952; 153m.

GREATEST STORY EVER TOLD, THE ★★★
DIR: George Stevens. **CAST:** Max von Sydow, Charlton Heston, Carroll Baker, Angela Lansbury, Sidney Poitier, Telly Savalas, José Ferrer, Van Heflin, Dorothy McGuire, John Wayne, Ed Wynn, Shelley Winters.
Although this well-meant movie is accurate to the story of Jesus, the viewer tends to be distracted by its long running time and the appearance of Hollywood stars in unexpected roles. 1965; 141m.

GREED ★★★★★
DIR: Erich Von Stroheim. **CAST:** Gibson Gowland, ZaSu Pitts, Jean Hersholt.
One of the greatest silent films, this is the stark, brilliant study of the corruption of a decent, simple man by the

specter of poverty and failed dreams. Gibson Gowland is superb as the bumbling self-taught dentist who marries spinster ZaSu Pitts, loses his trade, and succumbs to avarice-based hatred leading to murder. A masterpiece. Silent. 1924; B&W; 133m.

GREEK TYCOON, THE ★★½
DIR: J. Lee Thompson. **CAST:** Anthony Quinn, Jacqueline Bisset, Raf Vallone, Edward Albert, Charles Durning, Camilla Sparv, James Franciscus.

When this film was first shown, it stimulated much controversy and interest, because it promised to tell all about the Aristotle Onassis and Jackie Kennedy romance. Anthony Quinn borrows from his *Zorba the Greek* role to be a convincingly macho and callous Greek shipping tycoon. Unfortunately, the plot was neglected and the story comes across as grade-B soap. Rated R. 1978; 106m.

GREEN DOLPHIN STREET ★★
DIR: Victor Saville. **CAST:** Lana Turner, Donna Reed, Van Heflin, Edmund Gwenn, Frank Morgan, Richard Hart.

Tedious, plodding drama about two sisters, Lana Turner and Donna Reed, in romantic pursuit of the same man, Van Heflin, in nineteenth-century New Zealand. Special effects, including a whopper of an earthquake, won an Oscar, but do not a film make. 1947; B&W; 141m.

GREEN PROMISE, THE ★★★
DIR: William D. Russell. **CAST:** Marguerite Chapman, Walter Brennan, Robert Paige, Natalie Wood.

The hard life of farmers and their families is explored in this surprisingly involving and well-acted film. Walter Brennan gives his usual first-rate performance as the patriarch who toils over and tills the land. 1949; B&W; 93m.

GRIEVOUS BODILY HARM ★★½
DIR: Mark Joffe. **CAST:** Colin Friels, John Waters, Bruno Lawrence, Shane Briant.

This Australian drama is a well-woven tale about a police detective trying to find his missing wife. The acting is first-rate, as is the script, but director Mark Joffe lets the pace drag from time to time. Rated R. 1988; 135m.

GRIFFIN AND PHOENIX: A LOVE STORY ★★★½
DIR: Daryl Duke. **CAST:** Peter Falk, Jill Clayburgh, Dorothy Tristan.

Strange, haunting tearjerker about two dying people in love with one another and with life. Jill Clayburgh and Peter Falk in the title roles win hearts hands-down and lift spirits as gloom and doom close in. Made for TV. 1976; 100m.

GRISSOM GANG, THE ★★★
DIR: Robert Aldrich. **CAST:** Kim Darby, Scott Wilson, Irene Dailey, Tony Musante, Robert Lansing.

Lurid crime drama set in the 1920s. A wealthy heiress (Kim Darby) is kidnapped by a family of grotesque rednecks whose leader (Scott Wilson) falls in love with her. This gritty, violent film receives comically uneven direction from Robert Aldrich. Rated R. 1971; 127m.

GROUP, THE ★★★
DIR: Sidney Lumet. **CAST:** Joan Hackett, Elizabeth Hartman, Shirley Knight, Joanna Pettet, Jessica Walter, James Broderick, Larry Hagman, Richard Mulligan, Hal Holbrook.

Based on the book by Mary McCarthy about the lives and loves of eight female college friends. Overlong, convoluted semi-sleazy fun. The impressive cast almost makes you forget it's just a catty soap opera. So watch it anyway. 1966; 150m.

GROWN-UPS ★★
DIR: John Madden. **CAST:** Charles Grodin, Martin Balsam, Marilu Henner, Jean Stapleton.

Originally made for cable TV, this theatre piece by cartoonist Jules Feiffer revolves around a writer (Charles Grodin) and his difficulties with his family. Feiffer's dialogue is sharply observed, but there's no real story, and the characters' continual bickering never leads anywhere. 1985; 106m.

GUARDIAN, THE ★★★½
DIR: David Greene. **CAST:** Martin Sheen, Louis Gossett Jr., Arthur Hill.
When the tenants of an upper-class New York City apartment house become fed up with the violence of the streets intruding on their building, they hire a live-in guard (Louis Gossett Jr.). While he does manage to rid the building of lawbreakers, some begin to question his methods. This HBO made-for-cable film is notches above most cable fare. Profanity and violence. 1984; 102m.

GUESS WHO'S COMING TO DINNER ★★★
DIR: Stanley Kramer. **CAST:** Spencer Tracy, Katharine Hepburn, Sidney Poitier, Katharine Houghton, Cecil Kellaway, Beah Richards, Virginia Christine.
This final film pairing of Spencer Tracy and Katharine Hepburn was also one of the first to deal with interracial marriage. Though quite daring at the time of its original release, this movie, directed by the heavy-handed Stanley Kramer, seems rather quaint today. Still, Tracy and Hepburn are fun to watch, and Sidney Poitier and Katharine Houghton (Hepburn's niece) make an appealing young couple. 1967; 108m.

GUEST IN THE HOUSE ★★★
DIR: John Brahm. **CAST:** Anne Baxter, Ralph Bellamy, Aline MacMahon, Ruth Warrick, Jerome Cowan.
This grim melodrama features Anne Baxter as an emotionally disturbed girl who turns an idyllic household into a chaotic nightmare. An engrossing psychological thriller. 1944; B&W; 121m.

GULAG ★★½
DIR: Roger Young. **CAST:** David Keith, Malcolm McDowell.
This engrossing tale of an American athlete shipped to a Soviet prison camp works at odd moments in spite of a preposterous script. On the other hand, the escape sequence is clever and quite exciting. 1985; 120m.

GUN IN THE HOUSE, A ★★★½
DIR: Ivan Nagy. **CAST:** Sally Struthers, David Ackroyd, Jeffrey Tambor, Dick Anthony Williams, Millie Perkins.
This TV movie stars Sally Struthers as a woman being tried for the handgun murder of a man who broke into her house. Struthers excels in the role. An above-average drama. 1981; 100m.

GUY NAMED JOE, A ★★★★
DIR: Victor Fleming. **CAST:** Spencer Tracy, Van Johnson, Irene Dunne, Ward Bond, Lionel Barrymore, James Gleason.
Enchanting film has a dead WWII pilot (Spencer Tracy) coming back to Earth from heaven to aid a young aviator (Van Johnson) with his love life and combat missions. MGM pulls out all the stops with a blockbuster cast and high production values. Tracy's performance is sublime. 1943; B&W; 120m.

HAIRY APE, THE ★★★
DIR: Alfred Santell. **CAST:** William Bendix, Susan Hayward, John Loder.
Eugene O'Neill's play about an animallike coal stoker on an ocean liner. The hairy ape falls in love with a heartless socialite passenger who at once is captivated and repulsed by his coarse approach to life. William Bendix is fascinating in the title role. 1944; B&W; 90m.

HALF-MOON STREET ★★
DIR: Bob Swaim. **CAST:** Sigourney Weaver, Michael Caine, Patrick Kavanagh.
Half-baked adaptation of Paul Theroux's *Doctor Slaughter*, which was equally flawed as a novel. Sigourney Weaver stars as an American abroad who decides to supplement her academic (but low-paid) government position by moonlighting as a sophisticated "escort." Rated R for nudity and sexual themes. 1986; 90m.

HAMBONE AND HILLIE ★★★
DIR: Roy Watts. **CAST:** Lillian Gish, Timothy Bottoms, Candy Clark, O. J. Simpson, Robert Walker.

A delightful story of love and loyalty between an old woman (Lillian Gish) and her dog and constant companion, Hambone. While boarding a flight in New York to return to Los Angeles, Hambone is accidentally set loose from his travel cage and becomes lost. And so begins a three-thousand-mile cross-country trip filled with perilous freeways, wicked humans, and dangerous animals. Rated PG. 1984; 97m.

HAMBURGER HILL ★★½
DIR: John Irvin. **CAST:** Anthony Barrile, Michael Patrick Boatman, Don Cheadle, Michael Dolan, Don James, Dylan McDermott, M. A. Nickles, Harry O'Reilly, Tim Quill, Courtney P. Vance, Steven Weber.

In dealing with one of the bloodiest battles of the Vietnam War, director John Irvin and screenwriter Jim Carabatsos have made a film so brutally real that watching it is an endurance test. Although well acted and well made, it is more like a shocking documentary than a work of fiction. Rated R for violence and profanity. 1987; 112m.

HAMLET (1948) ★★★★★
DIR: Laurence Olivier. **CAST:** Laurence Olivier, Basil Sydney, Eileen Herlie, Jean Simmons, Felix Aylmer, Terence Morgan, Peter Cushing, Stanley Holloway.

In every way a brilliant presentation of Shakespeare's best-known play masterminded by England's foremost player. Superb in the title role, Laurence Olivier won the 1948 Oscar for best actor, and (as producer) for best picture. A high point among many is Stanley Holloway's droll performance as the First Gravedigger. 1948; B&W; 150m.

HAMLET (1969) ★★★
DIR: Tony Richardson. **CAST:** Nicol Williamson, Gordon Jackson, Anthony Hopkins, Judy Parfitt, Marianne Faithfull, Mark Dignam.

Nicol Williamson gives a far more energetic portrayal of the famous Dane than the noted Oscar-winning performance of Laurence Olivier. Worth seeing for comparison of interpretations. An exceptional supporting cast adds to the allure of this low-budget adaptation. 1969; 113m.

HANDFUL OF DUST, A ★★★★
DIR: Charles Sturridge. **CAST:** James Wilby, Rupert Graves, Kristin Scott Thomas, Anjelica Huston, Alec Guinness.

Based on Evelyn Waugh's masterpiece, *A Handful of Dust* is a deliciously staged drama of actions and fate. Set in post–World War I England and the jungles of South America, this film presents two aristocrats searching along different paths for happiness. Superb ensemble playing. 1988; 118m.

HANGING ON A STAR ★½
DIR: Mike MacFarland. **CAST:** Lane Caudell, Deborah Raffin, Wolfman Jack.

Yet another production from Cannon International's sappy and syrupy department. Deborah Raffin is the persistent and savvy road agent for a promising group of unknown musicians. This comes off more like an extended episode of *Star Search*. Rated PG. 1978; 93m.

HANOI HILTON, THE ★
DIR: Lionel Chetwynd. **CAST:** Michael Moriarty, Paul LeMat, David Soul, Jeffrey Jones, Lawrence Pressman.

This overly long, poorly directed and acted drama is set in a prisoner-of-war camp during the Vietnam War. We witness eight long years of torture and confinement suffered by American prisoners at the hands of the enemy. Rated R for profanity and extreme violence. 1987; 130m.

HANOVER STREET ♥
DIR: Peter Hyams. **CAST:** Harrison Ford, Lesley-Anne Down, Christopher Plummer, Alec McCowen.

This inept story of a romance during World War II features Harrison Ford as an American soldier and Lesley-Anne Down as a British nurse who meet by accident and fall in love. There are complications. She won't tell him her name. Later we find that she's married to a British intelligence officer (Christopher Plummer). Naturally, Plummer and Ford end up on a secret mission behind German lines, becoming friends while they fend off bullets and tanks. Dumb. Rated PG. 1979; 109m.

HARDCORE ★★
DIR: Paul Schrader. **CAST:** George C. Scott, Peter Boyle, Season Hubley, Dick Sargent.

This film stars George C. Scott as Jake Van Dorn, whose family leads a church-oriented life in their home in Grand Rapids, Michigan. When the church sponsors a youth trip to California, Van Dorn's daughter Kristen (Ilah Davis) is allowed to go. She disappears, so Van Dorn goes to Los Angeles and learns she's now making porno flicks. *Hardcore* is rated R but is closer to an X. 1979; 108m.

HARDER THEY FALL, THE ★★★½
DIR: Mark Robson. **CAST:** Humphrey Bogart, Rod Steiger, Jan Sterling, Mike Lane, Max Baer, Jersey Joe Walcott.

This boxing drama is as mean and brutal as they come. A gentle giant is built up, set up, and brought down by a collection of human vultures while sports writer Humphrey Bogart flip-flops on the moral issues. The ring photography is spectacular. Don't expect anything like *Rocky*. 1956; B&W; 109m.

HARDHAT AND LEGS ★★★
DIR: Lee Philips. **CAST:** Kevin Dobson, Sharon Gless.

The scene is New York City. Kevin Dobson is a horse-playing Italian construction worker who whistles at nice gams. Sharon Gless is democratic upper-class. The twain meet, and sparks fly as he tries to make it work despite educational and cultural differences. It's all cheerful and upbeat and works because of first-rate acting. Made for television. 1980; 104m.

HAREM ★★★½
DIR: Arthur Joffe. **CAST:** Nastassja Kinski, Ben Kingsley, Robbin Zohra Segal.

Nastassja Kinski is a stockbroker who is abducted by a wealthy OPEC oil minister (Ben Kingsley) and taken to his Middle Eastern palace where she becomes a part of his harem. A bittersweet tale of a lonely dreamer and his passion for a modern woman. Not rated, but has violence, profanity, and nudity. 1985; 107m.

HARLOW ★★
DIR: Gordon Douglas. **CAST:** Carroll Baker, Peter Lawford, Red Buttons, Michael Connors, Raf Vallone, Angela Lansbury, Martin Balsam, Leslie Nielsen.

One of two films made in 1965 that dealt with the life of the late film star and sex goddess Jean Harlow. Carroll Baker simply is not the actress to play Harlow, and the whole thing is a trashy mess. 1965; 125m.

HARRAD EXPERIMENT, THE ★★
DIR: Ted Post. **CAST:** Don Johnson, James Whitmore, Tippi Hedren, Bruno Kirby, Laurie Walters.

Uninvolving adaptation of Robert Rimmer's well-intentioned bestseller about an experimental college that makes exploration of sexual freedom the primary hands-on curriculum of the student body. The film is attractive as a novelty item today because of its erotic scenes between Don Johnson and Lauri Walters. Rated R. 1973; 88m.

HARRY AND SON ★★★
DIR: Paul Newman. **CAST:** Paul Newman, Robby Benson, Joanne Woodward, Ellen Barkin, Ossie Davis, Wilford Brimley.

A widower (Paul Newman) can land a wrecking ball on a dime but can't seem to make contact with his artistically inclined son, Howard (Robby Benson), in this superb character study. Directed, coproduced, and cowritten by Newman, it's sort of a male *Terms of Endearment*. Rated PG for nudity and profanity. 1984; 117m.

HARRY AND TONTO ★★★★
DIR: Paul Mazursky. **CAST:** Art Carney, Ellen Burstyn, Chief Dan George, Geraldine Fitzgerald, Larry Hagman, Arthur Hunnicutt.

Art Carney won an Oscar for his tour-de-force performance in this character study, directed by Paul Mazursky. In a role that's a far cry from his Ed Norton on Jackie Gleason's *The Honeymooners*, the star plays an older gentleman who, with his cat, takes a cross-country trip and lives life to the fullest. Rated R. 1974; 115m.

HASTY HEART ★★★½
DIR: Martin Speer. **CAST:** Gregory Harrison, Cheryl Ladd, Perry King.

Made for Showtime pay cable, this version of the 1949 movie with Ronald Reagan is corny as all get-out, but is still pretty effective. In an army hospital in Burma during WWII, a proud Scottish soldier (Gregory Harrison) doesn't know that he has only a few weeks to live. He refuses to accept the hospitality of the other soldiers in the ward, all of whom know of his approaching death. Get out your handkerchiefs! 1983; 135m.

HAUNTING OF JULIA, THE ★★
DIR: Richard Loncraine. **CAST:** Mia Farrow, Keir Dullea, Tom Conti.

A vague, confused story of a young mother whose daughter chokes to death. The mother's emotional breakdown is followed by a long and strange recovery period. In this otherwise pedestrian film there are sporadic spots of quality, mostly in Tom Conti's scenes. Rated R for profanity. 1981; 96m.

HAWAII ★★★★
DIR: George Roy Hill. **CAST:** Julie Andrews, Max von Sydow, Richard Harris, Gene Hackman, Carroll O'Connor.

All-star epic presentation of Part III of James Michener's six-part novel of the same title. Excellent performances by Max von Sydow and Julie Andrews as the early 1800s missionaries to Hawaii, as well as by Richard Harris as the sea captain who tries to woo Andrews away. 1966; 171m.

HEART ★★
DIR: James Lemmo. **CAST:** Brad Davis, Jesse Doran, Sam Gray, Robinson Frank Adu, Steve Buscemi, Frances Fisher.

A down-and-out boxer (Brad Davis) makes a comeback while the rest of his peers are ready to write him off. This is well-worn territory and *Heart* has little new to offer. Rated R for violence, profanity. 1987; 93m.

HEART BEAT ★★★★
DIR: John Byrum. **CAST:** Nick Nolte, Sissy Spacek, John Heard, Ray Sharkey, Ann Dusenberry.

Heart Beat is a perfect title for this warm, bittersweet visual poem on the beat generation by writer-director John Byrum. It pulses with life and emotion, intoxicating the viewer with a rhythmic flow of stunning images and superb performances by Nick Nolte, Sissy Spacek, and John Heard. The story begins with the cross-country adventure that inspired Jack Kerouac's *On the Road*. Rated R. 1980; 109m.

HEART IS A LONELY HUNTER, THE ★★★★
DIR: Robert Ellis Miller. **CAST:** Alan Arkin, Sondra Locke, Laurinda Barrett, Stacy Keach, Chuck McCann, Cicely Tyson.

This release features Alan Arkin in a superb performance, which won him an Academy Award nomination. In it, he plays a sensitive and compassionate man who is also a deaf-mute. Rated G. 1968; 125m.

HEART OF A CHAMPION: THE RAY MANCINI STORY ★★★
DIR: Richard Michaels. **CAST:** Robert Blake, Doug McKeon, Mariclare Costello.

Made-for-TV movie of the life of Ray "Boom Boom" Mancini focuses on his quest for the lightweight boxing title. His drive is intensified by his desire to bring pride to his father, who could have had a shot at the title had he not been called to serve in World War II. Fight sequences staged by Sylvester Stallone. 1985; 100m.

HEART OF DIXIE, THE ★★
DIR: Martin Davidson. **CAST:** Ally Sheedy, Virginia Madsen, Phoebe Cates, Don Michael Paul, Treat Williams.

With its heart in the right place but its head lost in the clouds *The Heart of Dixie* only manages to satisfy on two levels: its 1957 period details of the South, which is struggling to maintain its slipping grip on antebellum grandeur; and a small, tight performance by Treat Williams (as a wire-service photographer, a dispassionate observer of the emerging new consciousness whose victories lie in spurring others on to action). The film centers on the activities of a group of sorority sisters at Alabama's Randolph University and their Big-Daddy-in-training lugs of boyfriends. Rated PG for mild violence and reasonably oblique sexual discussions. 1989; 110m.

HEART OF THE STAG ★★★★
DIR: Michael Firth. **CAST:** Bruno Lawrence, Terence Cooper, Mary Regan.

The shocking subject matter of *Heart of the Stag*—forced incest—could have resulted in an uncomfortable film to watch. However, New Zealander Michael Firth, who directed the movie and conceived the story, handles it expertly, and the result is a riveting viewing experience. Rated R for violence, profanity, and sexual situations. 1983; 94m.

HEARTACHES ★★★
DIR: Donald Shebib. **CAST:** Robert Carradine, Margot Kidder, Annie Potts, Winston Rekert, George Touliatos.

A touching, yet lighthearted, film about love, friendship, and survival, *Heartaches* follows the trials and tribulations a young pregnant woman (Annie Potts), who is separated from her husband (Robert Carradine), and the kooky girlfriend she meets on the bus (Margot Kidder). Although the two women are total opposites, they wind up rooming together and share a variety of experiences. The Canadian film is rated R for a minimal amount of sex, which is handled discreetly. 1981; 93m.

HEARTBREAK HOTEL ★★★
DIR: Chris Columbus. **CAST:** David Keith, Tuesday Weld, Charlie Schlatter, Chris Mulkey.

In this bit of none-too-convincing whimsy, Charlie Schlatter plays an aspiring rock guitarist who kidnaps Elvis Presley (David Keith) in an attempt to buoy the self-esteem of his alcoholic, divorced mother (Tuesday Weld). Keith does a terrific job of impersonating Presley, and director Chris Columbus's script has some warmly funny moments, but the movie cannot overcome its preposterous premise. Rated PG-13 for profanity and violence. 1988; 100m.

HEARTBREAKERS ★★★½
DIR: Bobby Roth. **CAST:** Peter Coyote, Nick Mancuso, Max Gail, Kathryn Harrold.

Two men in their thirties, Arthur Blue (Peter Coyote) and Eli Kahn (Nick Mancuso), friends since childhood, find their relationship severely tested when each is suddenly caught up in his own fervent drive for success. Rated R for simulated sex and profanity. 1984; 106m.

HEARTS OF THE WORLD ★★★
DIR: D. W. Griffith. **CAST:** Lillian Gish, Dorothy Gish, Robert Harron, Ben Alexander.

This World War I epic, a propaganda film, was made to convince the United States to enter the conflict and aid Britain and France. Actual battle footage from both sides in the conflict is interwoven with the story of a young man going to war and the tragic effects on his family and village. Silent. 1918; B&W; 122m.

HEAT (1972) ★★★
DIR: Paul Morrissey. **CAST:** Sylvia Miles, Joe Dallesandro, Andrea Feldman, Pat Ast.
One of Andy Warhol's better film productions is this steamy tale of an unemployed actor (Joe Dallesandro) whose involvement with a neurotic has-been actress (Sylvia Miles) has tragicomic results. A low-budget homage to *Sunset Boulevard* that even non-Warhol fans may enjoy. Excellent music score composed and performed by John Cale. Rated R for nudity and language. 1972; 100m.

HEAT AND DUST ★★★★
DIR: James Ivory. **CAST:** Julie Christie, Greta Scacchi, Shashi Kapoor, Christopher Cazenove, Julian Glover, Susan Fleetwood.
Two love stories—one from the 1920s and one from today—are entwined in this classy, thoroughly enjoyable soap opera about two British women who go to India and become involved in its seductive mysteries. Julie Christie stars as a modern woman retracing the steps of her great-aunt (Greta Scacchi), who fell in love with an Indian ruler (played by the celebrated Indian star Shashi Kapoor). Rated R for nudity and brief violence. 1983; 130m.

HEATWAVE ★★★
DIR: Phillip Noyce. **CAST:** Judy Davis, Richard Moir, Chris Haywood, Bill Hunter, Anna Jemison.
Judy Davis plays an idealistic liberal opposed to proposed real estate developments that will leave some people homeless. In this political thriller, Davis's crusade leads to her involvement in a possible kidnap-murder and a love affair with the young architect of the housing project she's protesting. Unrated. 1983; 99m.

HEAVY TRAFFIC ★★★
DIR: Ralph Bakshi. **CAST:** Animated.
Ralph Bakshi's follow-up to *Fritz the Cat* is a mixture of live action and animation. Technically outstanding, but its downbeat look at urban life is rather unpleasant to watch. Rated R for profanity, nudity, and violence. 1973; 76m.

HEIRESS, THE ★★★★½
DIR: William Wyler. **CAST:** Olivia De Havilland, Montgomery Clift, Ralph Richardson, Miriam Hopkins, Vanessa Brown, Mona Freeman, Ray Collins.
This moving drama takes place in New York City around 1900. Olivia De Havilland is excellent (she won an Oscar for this performance) as a plain but extraordinarily rich woman who is pursued by a wily gold digger (played by Montgomery Clift). Ralph Richardson is great as her straitlaced father. 1949; B&W; 115m.

HELL TO ETERNITY ★★★
DIR: Phil Karlson. **CAST:** Jeffrey Hunter, David Janssen, Vic Damone, Patricia Owens, Sessue Hayakawa.
A trimly told and performed anti-prejudice, antiwar drama based on the life of World War II hero Guy Gabaldon, a Californian raised by Japanese-American parents. Jeffrey Hunter and Sessue Hayakawa share acting honors as the hero and the strong-minded Japanese commander who confronts him in the South Pacific. Lots of battle scenes. 1960; B&W; 132m.

HELTER SKELTER ★★★★
DIR: Tom Gries. **CAST:** George DiCenzo, Steve Railsback, Nancy Wolfe, Marilyn Burns.
The story of Charles Manson's 1969 murder spree is vividly retold in this excellent TV movie. Steve Railsback is superb as the crazed Manson. Based on prosecutor Vincent Bugliosi's novel, this is high-voltage stuff. Un-

rated and too intense for the kids. 1976; 114m.

HENRY V ★★★★★
DIR: Laurence Olivier. **CAST:** Laurence Olivier, Robert Newton, Leslie Banks, Felix Aylmer, Renée Asherson, Leo Genn.
The first of Olivier's three major film forays into Shakespeare (the others are *Hamlet* and *Richard III*), this production blazed across screens like a meteor. A stirring, colorful film, full of sound and fury, and all the pageantry one expects from English history brought to vivid life. Olivier won an honorary Oscar for acting, directing, and producing. In a word: superb. 1944; 137m.

HERO, THE ★★
DIR: Richard Harris. **CAST:** Richard Harris, Romy Schneider, Kim Burfield.
Richard Harris distinguishes himself neither as actor nor as director in this mawkish sports drama. He plays a soccer star getting on in years who agrees to throw a game for money. But will doing so lose him the respect of a young boy who idolizes him? Not the freshest of storylines. Not rated. 1971; 97m.

HEROES ★★★½
DIR: Jeremy Paul Kagan. **CAST:** Henry Winkler, Sally Field, Harrison Ford, Val Avery.
Henry Winkler is excellent in this compelling story of a confused Vietnam vet traveling cross-country to meet a few of his old war buddies who are planning to start a worm farm in California. One important note: MCA Home Video has elected to alter the film's closing theme for this release. Removing the emotionally charged "Carry on Wayward Son" by Kansas in favor of a teary generic tune somewhat diminishes the overall impact of the movie. Rated PG for mild language and violence. 1977; 113m.

HESTER STREET ★★★★
DIR: Joan Micklin Silver. **CAST:** Carol Kane, Steven Keats, Mel Howard.
Beautifully filmed look at the Jewish community in nineteenth-century New York City. Film focuses on the relationship of a young couple, he turning his back on the old Jewish ways while she fights to hold on to them. Fine performances and great attention to period detail make this very enjoyable. Rated PG. 1975; B&W; 92m.

HEY GOOD LOOKIN' ★
DIR: Ralph Bakshi. **CAST:** Animated.
This boring animated film follows the street gangs of New York City during the 1950s. It tends to put the viewer to sleep with its poor storyline and lousy animation. Rated R. 1983; 86m.

HIDE IN PLAIN SIGHT ★★★½
DIR: James Caan. **CAST:** James Caan, Jill Eikenberry, Robert Viharo, Joe Grifasi.
James Caan is a tire factory laborer whose former wife marries a two-bit hoodlum who pulls a robbery and gets busted. The hood turns informant and, under the government's Witness Relocation Program, is given a secret identity. Caan's former wife and their two children are spirited off to points unknown. Caan's subsequent quest for his kids becomes a one-man-against-the-system crusade in this watchable movie. Rated PG. 1980; 98m.

HIDING PLACE, THE ★★½
DIR: James F. Collier. **CAST:** Julie Harris, Eileen Heckart, Arthur O'Connell.
A professional cast gives depth and feeling to this true story of two Dutch women who are sent to a concentration camp for hiding Jews from the Nazis during World War II. This film was produced by Reverend Billy Graham's Evangelistic Association. 1975; 145m.

HIGH SCHOOL CONFIDENTIAL! ★★½
DIR: Jack Arnold. **CAST:** Russ Tamblyn, Jan Sterling, John Drew Barrymore, Mamie Van Doren.
A narcotics officer sneaks into a tough high school to bust hop-heads.

Incredibly naïve treatment of drug scene is bad enough, but it's the actors' desperate attempts to look "hip" that make the film an unintentional laugh riot. 1958; B&W; 85m.

HIGH TIDE ★★★★
DIR: Gillian Armstrong. **CAST:** Judy Davis, Jan Adele, Claudia Karvan, Colin Friels.

Judy Davis gives a superb performance as a rock 'n' roll singer stranded in a small Australian town when she loses her job in a band and her car breaks down all in the same day. She winds up staying in a trailer park only to encounter by accident the teenage daughter she deserted following the death of her husband. The offbeat but moving *High Tide* reunites Davis with her *My Brilliant Career* director, Gillian Armstrong, for some truly impressive results. Rated PG. 1987; 102m.

HINDENBURG, THE ★
DIR: Robert Wise. **CAST:** George C. Scott, Anne Bancroft, William Atherton, Roy Thinnes, Burgess Meredith, Charles Durning.

Another disaster movie whose major disaster is its own script. It is a fictionalized account of the German airship *Hindenburg*, which exploded over New Jersey in 1937. George C. Scott portrays a German official who suspects sabotage and races against time to prevent a catastrophe. Rated PG. 1975; 125m.

HISTORY IS MADE AT NIGHT ★★★
DIR: Frank Borzage. **CAST:** Charles Boyer, Jean Arthur, Colin Clive, Leo Carrillo.

A preposterous film, but...Colin Clive is a sadistic jealous husband whose wife, Jean Arthur, falls for Parisian headwaiter Charles Boyer. He tries to frame the headwaiter for a murder he himself committed. He fails. Insanely determined to destroy the lovers, he arranges for his superliner to hit an iceberg! 1937; B&W; 97m.

HITLER ★★
DIR: Stuart Heisler. **CAST:** Richard Basehart, Cordula Trantow, Maria Emo, John Mitchum.

Richard Basehart plays Adolf Hitler in this rather slow-moving, shallow account of *der Führer*'s last years. You're better off watching a good documentary on the subject. 1962; 107m.

HITLER, THE LAST TEN DAYS ★★
DIR: Ennio DeConcini. **CAST:** Alec Guinness, Simon Ward, Adolfo Celi, Diane Cilento.

This film should hold interest only for history buffs. It is a rather dry and tedious account of the desperate closing days of the Third Reich. Alec Guinness gives a capable, yet sometimes overwrought, performance as the Nazi leader from the time he enters his underground bunker in Berlin until his eventual suicide. Rated PG. 1973; 108m.

HOLD THE DREAM ★★★
DIR: Don Sharp. **CAST:** Jenny Seagrove, Deborah Kerr, Stephen Collins, James Brolin.

This made-for-TV sequel to *A Woman of Substance* finds an aging Emma Harte (Deborah Kerr) turning over her department-store empire to her granddaughter, Paula (Jenny Seagrove). The rest of the family, in an uproar after being slighted, has plans to steal away much of the business for themselves. Not as captivating as *Woman of Substance*, this sequel will still manage to entertain patrons of the soaps. 1986; 180m.

HOLOCAUST ★★★★½
DIR: Marvin J. Chomsky. **CAST:** Tom Bell, Michael Moriarty, Tovah Feldshuh, Meryl Streep, Fritz Weaver, David Warner.

This Emmy-winning miniseries is one of the finest programs ever produced for television. The story follows the lives of two German families during the reign of Hitler's Third Reich. Everyone in front of and behind the camera does a stunning job. This is a must-see. 1978; 570m.

HOME OF THE BRAVE ★★★

DIR: Mark Robson. **CAST:** James Edwards, Steve Brodie, Jeff Corey, Douglas Dick.

This is one of the first films dealing with blacks serving in the military during World War II. The story finds James Edwards on a mission in the Pacific and deals with the racial abuse that he encounters from his own men. The good plot of this film could use some more action, yet it is still worth watching. 1949; B&W; 85m.

HOME, SWEET HOME ★★½

DIR: D. W. Griffith. **CAST:** Henry B. Walthall, Lillian Gish, Dorothy Gish, Mae Marsh, Spottiswoode Aitken, Miriam Cooper, Robert Harron, Donald Crisp, Blanche Sweet, Owen Moore.

Henry B. Walthall is John Howard Payne in this fanciful biography of the famous composer of the song from which the title is taken. Lillian Gish is his faithful, long-suffering sweetheart. Denied happiness in life, the lovers are united as they "fly" to heaven. Silent. 1914; B&W; 80m.

HOMECOMING, THE ★★★★

DIR: Peter Hall. **CAST:** Cyril Cusack, Ian Holm, Michael Jayston, Vivien Merchant, Terrence Rigby, Paul Rogers.

Michael Jayston brings his wife, Vivien Merchant, home to meet the family after several years of separation. His father and two brothers are no-holds-barred Harold Pinter characters. If you like drama and Pinter, you'll want to check out this American Film Theater production, which has outstanding direction by Peter Hall. 1973; 111m.

HOMEWORK

DIR: James Beshears. **CAST:** Joan Collins, Shell Kepler, Wings Hauser, Betty Thomas.

Terrible film, about a high-school teacher who seduces one of her students, does its best to cash in on the Joan Collins craze, but it's a total ripoff. Since a double was used in Joan's nude scene, the poor sucker watching this trash is left with nothing but horrendous acting by all. Rated R for nudity. 1982; 90m.

HONKYTONK MAN ★★★★

DIR: Clint Eastwood. **CAST:** Clint Eastwood, Kyle Eastwood, John McIntire.

Clint Eastwood stars as an alcoholic, tubercular country singer headed for an audition at the Grand Ole Opry during the depths of the Depression. A bittersweet character study, it works remarkably well. You even begin to believe Eastwood in the role. The star's son, Kyle Eastwood, makes an impressive film debut. Rated PG for strong language and sexual content. 1982; 122m.

HONOR THY FATHER ★★

DIR: Paul Wendkos. **CAST:** Joseph Bologna, Brenda Vaccaro, Raf Vallone.

A movie version of the real-life internal Mafia war that took place during the late 1960s among members of the Bonanno crime family. A weak film based on a strong book by Gay Talese. Not rated but contains violence. 1973; 97m.

HOOSIERS ★★★★½

DIR: David Anspaugh. **CAST:** Gene Hackman, Barbara Hershey, Dennis Hopper, Sheb Wooley.

Hoosiers is the most satisfying high-school basketball movie in years. Gene Hackman is the new coach—with a mysterious past—at Hickory High. His unorthodox methods rankle the locals and his fellow teachers (particularly frosty Barbara Hershey), not to mention the undisciplined team members. But before you can say hoosiermania, the team is at the 1951 state championships. It doesn't hurt, either, that the realistic script is based on a true Indiana Cinderella story. Rated PG. 1986; 114m.

HOPE AND GLORY ★★★★½
DIR: John Boorman. **CAST:** Sarah Miles, David Hayman, Derrick O'Connor, Susan Wooldridge, Sammi Davis, Ian Bannen, Sebastian Rice Edwards, Jean-Marc Barr.

Writer-producer-director John Boorman's much-praised film chronicles his boyhood experiences during the London blitz. Rather than the horror story one might expect, it is a marvelously entertaining, warm, and thoughtful look backward. Blessed with vibrant characters, cultural richness, and a fresh point of view, it never fails to fascinate. Rated PG-13 for profanity and suggested sex. 1987; 113m.

HOT SHOT ★★★½
DIR: Rick King. **CAST:** Jim Youngs, Pelé, Billy Warlock, Weyman Thompson, Mario Van Peebles.

More than just a soccer version of *The Karate Kid*, this film of a young man's conquest of adversity stands on its own. Jim Youngs is a rich kid who runs away to Rio de Janeiro, where he pursues his idol, Pelé, the greatest soccer player of all time. An enjoyable family film and a must for soccer fans. Rated PG. 1986; 94m.

HOT SPELL ★★★
DIR: Daniel Mann. **CAST:** Shirley Booth, Anthony Quinn, Shirley MacLaine, Earl Holliman, Eileen Heckart.

Entertaining thoughts of leaving her for a younger woman, macho husband Anthony Quinn has anguishing housewife Shirley Booth sweating out this and younger-generation problems in this near remake of *Come Back, Little Sheba*. The impact of that film is lost here, however. Booth invokes empathy, Quinn again proves his depth of talent, Shirley MacLaine shows why stardom soon was hers; but a soap opera is a soap opera. 1958; B&W; 86m.

HOTEL ★★½
DIR: Richard Quine. **CAST:** Rod Taylor, Catherine Spaak, Melvyn Douglas, Karl Malden, Richard Conte, Michael Rennie, Merle Oberon, Kevin McCarthy.

This film is based on Arthur Hailey's bestseller, which eventually spawned a TV series. In its *Airport*-style story, a number of characters and events unfold against the main theme of Melvyn Douglas's attempt to keep from selling the hotel to a tycoon who would modernize and change the landmark. 1967; 125m.

HOTEL NEW HAMPSHIRE, THE ★
DIR: Tony Richardson. **CAST:** Beau Bridges, Jodie Foster, Rob Lowe, Nastassja Kinski, Amanda Plummer.

Based on John Irving's novel, this muddled motion picture has its moments, but very few of them. The story seems to jump from one incident to another in a totally illogical manner. Beau Bridges stars as the head of a family that weathers all sorts of disasters and keeps going in spite of it all. Rated R for profanity, violence, and sex. 1984; 110m.

HOUSE ACROSS THE BAY, THE ★★½
DIR: Archie Mayo. **CAST:** George Raft, Joan Bennett, Lloyd Nolan, Gladys George, Walter Pidgeon.

An airplane designer (Walter Pidgeon) swipes the waiting wife (Joan Bennett) of a gangster (George Raft) while Raft is paying his dues in the joint. Then he gets out.... Classic Raft film. Tense, exciting, but familiar. Lloyd Nolan plays a shyster very well. 1940; B&W; 86m.

HOUSE BY THE RIVER ★★★
DIR: Fritz Lang. **CAST:** Louis Hayward, Jane Wyatt, Lee Bowman, Ann Shoemaker, Kathleen Freeman.

Fritz Lang explores one of his favorite themes: obsession. A moody chamber work about a man who kills his maid out of passionate rage, then implicates his own brother to relieve his guilt. Full of fascinating psychological touches that manage to create a disturbing atmosphere. 1950; B&W; 88m.

HOUSE ON GARIBALDI STREET ★★
DIR: Peter Collinson. **CAST:** Martin Balsam, Topol, Janet Suzman, Leo McKern.
Run-of-the-mill suspense tale chronicling the abduction of Nazi war criminal Adolf Eichmann by Israelis in South America. Effectively performed, though. 1979; 104m.

HOUSEKEEPING ★★★
DIR: Bill Forsyth. **CAST:** Christine Lahti, Andrea Burchill, Sara Walker.
Director Bill Forsyth makes superbly quirky movies, and *Housekeeping*, based on Marilynne Robinson's novel, is a worthy addition to his body of work. Christine Lahti plays a contented transient who comes to the Pacific Northwest to care for her two orphaned nieces. Lahti makes the offbeat moments resound with weird humor. Rated PG. 1987; 112m.

HOWARDS OF VIRGINIA, THE ★★
DIR: Frank Lloyd. **CAST:** Cary Grant, Martha Scott, Cedric Hardwicke, Alan Marshal, Richard Carlson, Paul Kelly, Anne Revere, Irving Bacon.
Tiring, too-long retelling of the Revolutionary War centering on an aristocratic Virginia family. In the Cary Grant filmography, it is just plain awful. 1940; B&W; 117m.

HUD ★★★★★
DIR: Martin Ritt. **CAST:** Paul Newman, Patricia Neal, Melvyn Douglas, Brandon de Wilde.
In one of his most memorable performances, Paul Newman stars as the arrogant ne'er-do-well son of a Texas rancher (Melvyn Douglas) who has fallen on hard times. Instead of helping his father, Hud drunkenly pursues the family's housekeeper (Patricia Neal), who wants nothing to do with him. When asked, Newman dubbed this one "pretty good." An understatement. 1963; B&W; 112m.

HUMAN COMEDY, THE ★★★½
DIR: Clarence Brown. **CAST:** Mickey Rooney, Frank Morgan, "Butch" Jenkins, Ray Collins, Darryl Hickman, Marsha Hunt, Fay Bainter, Donna Reed, James Craig, Van Johnson.
California author William Saroyan's tender and touching story of life in a small valley town during World War II is a winner all around in this compassionate, now nostalgic film. Mickey Rooney shines as the Western Union messenger verging on manhood. A sentimental slice of life, comic and tragic. 1943; B&W; 118m.

HUNTER'S BLOOD ★
DIR: Robert C. Hughes. **CAST:** Sam Bottoms, Clu Gulager, Kim Delaney, Mayf Nutter, Ken Swofford, Joey Travolta.
This film has an amazing resemblance to *Deliverance*, but without any of that film's tension or acting. Several Yuppie deer hunters from Oklahoma go to Arkansas. Of course, they have a run-in with some backwoods boys, and blood starts flowing. The script is an insult to any intelligent viewer. Rated R for language, violence, and adult content. 1987; 101m.

HURRICANE, THE (1937) ★★★
DIR: John Ford. **CAST:** Jon Hall, Dorothy Lamour, Raymond Massey, Mary Astor.
One of early Hollywood's disaster films. The lives and loves of a group of stereotyped characters on a Pacific island are interrupted by the big wind of the title. The sequences involving people are labored, but the special effects of the hurricane make this picture worth watching. 1937; B&W; 102m.

HUSTLER, THE ★★★★★
DIR: Robert Rossen. **CAST:** Paul Newman, Jackie Gleason, Piper Laurie, George C. Scott, Myron McCormick, Murray Hamilton.
This film may well contain Paul Newman's best screen performance. As pool shark Eddie Felson, he's magnificent. A two-bit hustler who travels from pool room to pool room taking suckers—whom he allows to win until the stakes get high enough,

then wipes them out—Felson decides to take a shot at the big time. He challenges Minnesota Fats (nicely played by Jackie Gleason) to a big money match. 1961; B&W; 135m.

HUSTLING ★★★★
DIR: Joseph Sargent. **CAST:** Lee Remick, Jill Clayburgh, Alex Rocco, Monte Markham.
An investigative report delves into the world of big city prostitution in this adult TV movie. Fine performances and a good script place this above the average TV film. 1975; 100m.

I AM A CAMERA ★★★½
DIR: Henry Cornelius. **CAST:** Julie Harris, Laurence Harvey, Shelley Winters, Ron Randell, Patrick McGoohan.
Julie Harris is perfect as the easy, good-time English bohemian Sally Bowles in this finely honed film clone of the play adapted by John Van Druten from novelist Christopher Isherwood's autobiographical stories about pre–World War II Berlin. The Broadway and screen versions ultimately became the musical *Cabaret*. 1955; 98m.

I AM A FUGITIVE FROM A CHAIN GANG ★★★★
DIR: Mervyn LeRoy. **CAST:** Paul Muni, Glenda Farrell, Helen Vinson, Preston Foster.
Dark, disturbing, and effective Paul Muni vehicle. The star plays an innocent man who finds himself convicted of a crime and brutalized by a corrupt court system. An unforgettable film. 1932; B&W; 90m.

I AM THE CHEESE ★★½
DIR: Robert Jiras. **CAST:** Robert MacNaughton, Hope Lange, Don Murray, Robert Wagner, Cynthia Nixon, Lee Richardson.
A teenager who has witnessed the death of his parents retreats from reality into a fantasy world. He is confined to a psychiatric hospital where doctors try to get him to deal with his tragedy. The dime-store psychology is the only drawback to this well-played movie. Rated PG. 1983; 95m.

I HEARD THE OWL CALL MY NAME ★★★½
DIR: Daryl Duke. **CAST:** Tom Courtenay, Dean Jagger, Paul Stanley.
In this mystical tale of love and courage, Tom Courtenay beautifully portrays Father Mark Brian, a young Anglican priest whose bishop, played by Dean Jagger, sends him to make his mark. He finds himself among the proud Indians of the Northwest. Rated G. 1973; 79m.

I KNOW WHY THE CAGED BIRD SINGS ★★★½
DIR: Fielder Cook. **CAST:** Diahann Carroll, Ruby Dee, Esther Rolle, Roger E. Mosley.
Based on writer Maya Angelou's memoirs of her early life in the Depression years in the South. Often very touching and effective, this made-for-TV film details the author's reaction to her parents' divorce and the struggle of her grandparents to raise her and her brother. 1979; 100m.

I LIVE WITH ME DAD ★★★
DIR: Paul Moloney. **CAST:** Peter Henir, Haydon Samuels, Rebecca Gibney.
Yes, the title is correct. That's what a poor Australian boy keeps repeating to the various child-welfare and police authorities who try to take him from his father. Unrated. 1985; 86m.

I MARRIED A CENTERFOLD ★★½
DIR: Peter Werner. **CAST:** Teri Copley, Timothy Daly, Diane Ladd, Anson Williams.
When a nerdish engineer bets $500 that he can meet Miss November, a centerfold, he not only finds her, but the two fall in love. Made for TV. 1984; 100m.

I NEVER PROMISED YOU A ROSE GARDEN ★★★½
DIR: Anthony Page. **CAST:** Bibi Andersson, Kathleen Quinlan, Diane Varsi.

Kathleen Quinlan plays a schizophrenic teenager seeking treatment from a dedicated psychiatrist in this well-acted but depressing drama. Rated R. 1977; 96m.

I NEVER SANG FOR MY FATHER ★★★★½
DIR: Gilbert Cates. **CAST:** Melvyn Douglas, Gene Hackman, Estelle Parsons, Dorothy Stickney.

A depressing but finely crafted film about a man (Gene Hackman) who must deal with the care of his elderly father (Melvyn Douglas). Everyone in this touching film does a superb job. Based on a play of the same name by Robert Anderson. Rated PG. 1970; 93m.

I REMEMBER MAMA ★★★½
DIR: George Stevens. **CAST:** Irene Dunne, Barbara Bel Geddes, Oscar Homolka, Philip Dorn, Ellen Corby.

Irene Dunne is Mama in this sentimental drama about an engaging Norwegian family in San Francisco. Definitely a feel-good film for the nostalgic-minded. Hearts of gold all the way! 1948; B&W; 148m.

I STAND CONDEMNED ★★★
DIR: Anthony Asquith. **CAST:** Harry Baur, Laurence Olivier, Robert Cochran.

A jealous suitor frames a rival in order to have a clear field for the affections of the woman both love. Not much here, except a young and dashing Laurence Olivier in one of his first films. 1935; B&W; 75m.

I WANT TO LIVE! ★★★
DIR: Robert Wise. **CAST:** Susan Hayward, Simon Oakland, Virginia Vincent, Theodore Bikel.

Pulling all stops out, Susan Hayward won an Oscar playing antiheroine B-girl Barbara Graham in this shattering real-life drama. Stupidly involved in a robbery-murder, Graham was indicted, railroaded to conviction, and executed at California's infamous San Quentin State Prison in 1955. To sit through this one you have to be steel-nerved or supremely callous, or both. The film is all the more devastating for being based on a true story. 1958; B&W; 120m.

I WANT WHAT I WANT ★★
DIR: John Dexter. **CAST:** Anne Heywood, Harry Andrews, Jill Bennett, Michael Coles, Nigel Flatley.

The search for emotional and sexual identity is the focal point of this British production about a man who undergoes a sex-change operation and falls in love. Although the subject matter is still controversial today, this film is remarkably tame. 1972; 97m.

ICE CASTLES ★★½
DIR: Donald Wrye. **CAST:** Robby Benson, Lynn-Holly Johnson, Colleen Dewhurst, Tom Skerritt.

Alexis Wintson (Lynn-Holly Johnson) is a girl from a small Midwestern town who dreams of skating in the Olympics. No matter how fetching and believable Johnson may be, nothing can surmount the soggy sentimentality of this cliché-ridden work. Rated PG. 1979; 109m.

ICE PALACE ★★★½
DIR: Vincent Sherman. **CAST:** Richard Burton, Robert Ryan, Carolyn Jones, Martha Hyer, Jim Backus.

Film adaptation of Edna Ferber's soap-opera saga about Alaska's statehood. Zeb Kennedy (Richard Burton) fights against statehood while Thor Storm (Robert Ryan) devotes his life to it. Beautifully acted, particularly by Carolyn Jones as the woman both men love. 1960; 144m.

IDIOT'S DELIGHT ★★★½
DIR: Clarence Brown. **CAST:** Clark Gable, Norma Shearer, Edward Arnold, Charles Coburn, Burgess Meredith, Laura Hope Crews, Joseph Schildkraut, Virginia Grey.

An all-star cast makes memorable movie history in this, the last anti-war film produced before World War II erupted. Norma Shearer is at her best as a Garbo-like fake-Russian-accented mistress companion of munitions tycoon Edward Arnold. Clark Gable is her ex, a wise-cracking vaudeville hoofer who's slipped while she's climbed. With other types, they are stranded in a European luxury hotel as war looms. 1938; B&W; 105m.

IF EVER I SEE YOU AGAIN
DIR: Joseph Brooks. **CAST:** Joe Brooks, Shelley Hack, Jimmy Breslin, George Plimpton.

Fresh from his success with *You Light Up My Life*, writer-director-composer Joe Brooks threw together this celluloid love poem to model Shelley Hack. It's blatantly autobiographical and incredibly egotistical. Rated PG. 1978; 105m.

IF YOU COULD SEE WHAT I HEAR ★
DIR: Eric Till. **CAST:** Marc Singer, R. H. Thompson, Sarah Torgov, Shari Belafonte Harper, Douglas Campbell.

The film is supposedly the biography of blind singer/composer Tom Sullivan. You'd have to be not only blind but deaf and, most of all, dumb to appreciate this one. Rated PG. 1982; 103m.

IKE: THE WAR YEARS ★½
DIR: Melville Shavelson, Boris Sagal. **CAST:** Robert Duvall, Lee Remick, J. D. Cannon, Darren McGavin.

Robert Duvall is D-day commander General Dwight Eisenhower, and Lee Remick is his wartime romance Kay Summersby, in this tedious retelling of high-echelon soldiering and whitewashed hanky-panky during the European phase of World War II. Trimmed drastically from an original six-hour miniseries. Boring if you're not a history buff. 1978; 196m.

ILL MET BY MOONLIGHT ★★★
DIR: Michael Powell. **CAST:** Dirk Bogarde, Marius Goring, David Oxley, Cyril Cusack.

In 1944 on the island of Crete, the British hatch a plot to kidnap a German general and smuggle him to Cairo. This sets off a manhunt with twenty thousand German troops and airplanes pursuing the partisans through Crete's mountainous terrain. 1957; B&W; 105m.

ILLEGALLY YOURS
DIR: Peter Bogdanovich. **CAST:** Rob Lowe, Colleen Camp, Kenneth Mars, Kim Myers.

Only the most devoted fan of director Peter Bogdanovich could possibly bear this painful experience. Rob Lowe's performance as a bumbling jury member who falls for the plaintiff in a murder case (Colleen Camp) is as awkward as the script. Bogdanovich sees this as a 1930s screwball comedy. Rated PG for language. 1988; 102m.

I'M A FOOL ★★★
DIR: Noel Black. **CAST:** Ron Howard, Amy Irving, John Light.

Ron Howard stars as a naïve young man who abandons his Ohio home for life on the road as a horse trainer. His desperate attempts to make himself worthy in the eyes of the opposite sex escalate until he's passing himself off as the son of a fabulously wealthy man. From a Sherwood Anderson story. Introduced by Henry Fonda; unrated and suitable for family viewing. 1976; 38m.

I'M DANCING AS FAST AS I CAN ★
DIR: Jack Hofsiss. **CAST:** Jill Clayburgh, Nicol Williamson, Geraldine Page.

Based on documentary filmmaker Barbara Gordon's bestselling autobiography, which dealt with her valiant—and sometimes horrifying—struggle with Valium addiction, this film seems more like a *Saturday Night Live* parody of the subject than a serious examination of it. It's one movie that belongs on a shelf—permanently. Rated PG for profanity and violence. 1981; 107m.

IMAGE OF PASSION
DIR: Susan Orlikoff-Simon. **CAST:** James Horan, Susan Damante-Shaw.
In this unimpressive romance, a young advertising executive (Susan Damante-Shaw), begins a passionate affair with a male stripper she has hired for a new account. He's married, she's engaged to another, and a choice must be made. 1982; 105m.

IMAGEMAKER, THE ★★★½
DIR: Hal Weiner. **CAST:** Michael Nouri, Anne Twomey, Jerry Orbach, Jessica Harper, Farley Granger.
Intriguing exposé on the selling of American politicians. Michael Nouri plays a deposed political powermaker whose life is threatened when he plans to tell all. Anne Twomey plays the TV reporter who had ruined his previous career. Rated R for nudity, violence, and profanity. 1985; 93m.

IMITATION OF LIFE ★★★½
DIR: Douglas Sirk. **CAST:** Lana Turner, John Gavin, Sandra Dee, Dan O'Herlihy, Susan Kohner, Troy Donahue, Robert Alda, Juanita Moore.
Earnest performances and gifted direction make this soap-operaish, Fannie Hurst tearjerker tolerable viewing. Lana Turner is a fame-greedy actress who neglects her daughter for her career. Juanita Moore is her black friend whose daughter repudiates her heritage and breaks her mother's heart by passing for white. 1959; 124m.

IMMORTAL BATTALION, THE (A.K.A. THE WAY AHEAD) ★★★½
DIR: Carol Reed. **CAST:** David Niven, Stanley Holloway, Raymond Huntley, Peter Ustinov, Trevor Howard, Leo Genn, James Donald.
Based on an idea conceived by Lt. Col. David Niven, this highly effective wartime semidocumentary follows his attempts to turn a group of newly activated civilians into a combat team capable of fighting the Germans on any terrain. This gem skillfully mixes training and combat footage with filmed sequences to create a powerful mood while delicately balancing great performances. 1944; 91m.

IMMORTAL SERGEANT, THE ★★★½
DIR: John Stahl. **CAST:** Henry Fonda, Maureen O'Hara, Thomas Mitchell, Allyn Joslyn, Reginald Gardiner, Melville Cooper.
Henry Fonda gives a solid performance as a corporal in the Canadian Army, attached to the British Eighth Army in North Africa during World War II. During a battle with Nazi troops, his squad sergeant is killed and he is forced into command. From a novel by John Brophy. 1943; B&W; 91m.

IMPOSTER, THE ★
DIR: Michael Pressman. **CAST:** Anthony Geary, Billy Dee Williams, Lorna Patterson, Penny Johnson, Jordan Charney.
Unbelievable account of a tough con artist who smooth-talks his way into the job of a high school principal in order to wage a private war against juvenile drug dealers. This ridiculous drama was originally produced for television by Gloria Monty, who was responsible for many daytime soap operas. Not rated. 1984; 95m.

IN A LONELY PLACE ★★★★
DIR: Nicholas Ray. **CAST:** Humphrey Bogart, Gloria Grahame, Frank Lovejoy, Robert Warwick.
Humphrey Bogart gives one of his finest performances in this taut psychological thriller. He plays a hard-drinking, fiercely opinionated screenwriter whose violent temper has more than once landed him in trouble. He has an affair with a sexy neighbor (Gloria Grahame) who begins to fear for her life when Bogart becomes the prime suspect in a murder case. 1950; B&W; 91m.

IN A SHALLOW GRAVE ★★

DIR: Kenneth Bowser. **CAST:** Michael Biehn, Patrick Dempsey, Michael Beach, Maureen Mueller.

Michael Biehn stars as a disfigured World War II vet who returns to an empty home and life. Patrick Dempsey is a drifter who becomes a messenger between Biehn and his ex-fiancée (Maureen Mueller). The resulting love triangle, both heterosexual and homosexual, is too short on plot, and the movie ends without an ending. Rated R. 1988; 92m.

IN COLD BLOOD ★★★★★

DIR: Richard Brooks. **CAST:** Robert Blake, Scott Wilson, John Forsythe, Jeff Corey.

A chilling documentarylike recreation of the senseless murder of a Kansas farm family. This stark black-and-white drama follows two ex-convicts (Robert Blake and Scott Wilson) from the point at which they hatch their plan until their eventual capture and execution. This is an emotionally powerful film that is not for the faint of heart. 1967; B&W; 134m.

IN DANGEROUS COMPANY ★

DIR: Reuben Preuss. **CAST:** Tracy Scoggins, Cliff De Young, Chris Mulkey, Henry Darrow, Richard Portnow, Steven Keats.

Unexciting, glitzy Sidney Sheldon–ish piece has Tracy Scoggins as a beautiful woman who uses her body to square one bad guy off against the other. Basic banal trash. Rated R for nudity, simulated sex, violence, and language. 1988; 92m.

IN LOVE WITH AN OLDER WOMAN ★★½

DIR: Jack Bender. **CAST:** John Ritter, Karen Carlson, Jamie Rose, Jeff Altman.

San Francisco lawyer John Ritter falls in love with a new employee at his firm, a woman fifteen years older than him. They move in together, to the displeasure of her daughter, who is the same age as Ritter. Made-for-TV movie (can't you tell?), though not bad. 1982; 96m.

IN NAME ONLY ★★★½

DIR: John Cromwell. **CAST:** Carole Lombard, Cary Grant, Kay Francis, Charles Coburn, Helen Vinson, Peggy Ann Garner.

This is a classic soap opera. Cary Grant is desperately in love with sweet and lovely Carole Lombard. Unfortunately, he's married to venomous Kay Francis, who sadistically refuses to give him a divorce. You can't help but get completely wrapped up in the skillfully executed story. 1939; B&W; 102m.

IN PRAISE OF OLDER WOMEN

DIR: George Kaczender. **CAST:** Tom Berenger, Karen Black, Susan Strasberg, Alexandra Stewart.

This dull film about a man's reflections on the past two decades and his various affairs along the way goes nowhere fast with uninteresting characterizations and plot line. Rated R. 1978; 108m.

IN SEARCH OF ANNA ★

DIR: Esben Storm. **CAST:** Richard Moir, Judy Morris, Chris Hayward, Bill Hunter.

Pseudo-art movie about an ex-con and a flaky model traveling across Australia in an old car looking for the girlfriend who wrote to him while he was in prison. Nice-looking but pointless. 1977; 94m.

IN THE HEAT OF THE NIGHT ★★★★

DIR: Norman Jewison. **CAST:** Sidney Poitier, Rod Steiger, Warren Oates, Lee Grant.

This film is a rousing murder mystery elevated by the excellent acting of Rod Steiger and Sidney Poitier. Racial tension is created when a rural Southern sheriff (Steiger) and a black Northern detective reluctantly join forces to solve the crime. The picture received Oscars for best picture and Steiger's performance. 1967; 109m.

IN TROUBLE
DIR: Gilles Carle. **CAST:** Julie Lachapelle, Jacques Cohen, Daniel Pilon.
An incomprehensible Canadian film, this seems to be about a young woman who finds herself pregnant and unmarried. Not rated but contains brief nudity, adult situations, and profanity. 1967; 82m.

IN WHICH WE SERVE ★★★★★
DIR: Noel Coward, David Lean. **CAST:** Noel Coward, John Mills, Michael Wilding.
Noel Coward wrote, produced, directed, and acted in this, one of the most moving wartime portrayals of men at sea. It is not the stirring battle sequences that make this film stand out but the intimate human story of the crew, their families, and the ship they love. A great film in all respects. 1942; B&W; 115m.

INCREDIBLE JOURNEY OF DR. MEG LAUREL, THE ★★★½
DIR: Guy Green. **CAST:** Lindsay Wagner, Jane Wyman, Dorothy McGuire, James Woods, Gary Lockwood, Charles Tyner, Andrew Duggan, Brock Peters, John Reilly.
In this made-for-television film, Lindsay Wagner gives her usual solid performance as Meg Laurel. From humble beginnings as an orphan from the Appalachian Mountains, she becomes a doctor. After graduating from Harvard Medical School, she sets up practice in 1930s Boston. But Wagner decides to return to the mountain people and administer the latest in medical procedures. 1978; 150m.

INCREDIBLE SARAH, THE ★
DIR: Richard Fleischer. **CAST:** Glenda Jackson, Daniel Massey, Yvonne Mitchell.
As the legendary French actress Sarah Bernhardt—in her time the toast of Paris, London, and New York—Glenda Jackson tears passions to tatters, to very rags. Theater history buffs may like this pseudobiography. 1976; 106m.

INDECENT OBSESSION, AN ★★★
DIR: Lex Marinos. **CAST:** Wendy Hughes, Gary Sweet, Richard Moir.
A bleak, intense view of the results of war. Wendy Hughes is the compassionate nurse in Ward X, the psycho ward for shell-shocked British soldiers and other war-torn crazies. A sensitive adaptation of Colleen McCullough's bestseller. Not rated but contains violence and profanity. 1985; 100m.

INDEPENDENCE DAY ★★★★
DIR: Robert Mandel. **CAST:** David Keith, Kathleen Quinlan, Richard Farnsworth, Frances Sternhagen, Cliff De Young, Dianne Wiest.
Excellent little story about a young woman (Kathleen Quinlan) who wants to leave the stifling environment of her home town to become a big-city photographer. She's helped and hindered by a growing attachment to David Keith, a garage mechanic with his own problems. His sister, Dianne Wiest, is the uncomplaining victim of her wife-beating husband. Rated R for violence and sex. 1983; 110m.

INDISCRETION OF AN AMERICAN WIFE ★★½
DIR: Vittorio De Sica. **CAST:** Jennifer Jones, Montgomery Clift, Gino Cervi, Richard Beymer.
One hour and three minutes of emotional turmoil played out against the background of Rome's railway station as adultress Jennifer Jones meets her lover, Montgomery Clift, for the last time. 1954; B&W; 63m.

INFORMER, THE ★★★★
DIR: John Ford. **CAST:** Victor McLaglen, Heather Angel, Preston Foster.
John Ford's classic about a slow-witted Irish pug (Victor McLaglen), who turns his friend in for money to impress his ladylove and gets his comeuppance from the IRA, has lost none of its atmospheric punch over the years. McLaglen is superb, and the

movie lingers in your memory long after the credits roll. 1935; B&W; 91m.

INHERIT THE WIND ★★★★★

DIR: Stanley Kramer. **CAST:** Spencer Tracy, Fredric March, Gene Kelly, Dick York, Claude Akins.

In this superb film based on the stage play of the notorious Scopes monkey trial, a biology teacher is put on trial for teaching the theory of evolution. The courtroom battle that actually took place between Clarence Darrow and William Jennings Bryan could not have been more powerful or stimulating than the acting battle put on by two of America's most respected actors—Spencer Tracy and Fredric March. 1960; B&W; 127m.

INN OF THE SIXTH HAPPINESS, THE ★★★★

DIR: Mark Robson. **CAST:** Ingrid Bergman, Curt Jurgens, Robert Donat.

Superb acting marks this heartwarming biography of China missionary Gladys Aylward (Ingrid Bergman). The movie opens with her determined attempt to enter the missionary service and follows her to strife-torn China. The highlight is her cross-country adventure as she leads a group of orphans away from the war zone. 1958; 158m.

INQUIRY, THE ★★

DIR: Damiano Damiani. **CAST:** Keith Carradine, Harvey Keitel, Phyllis Logan.

Italian-made film about the investigation by a Roman official (Keith Carradine) into the resurrection of Christ. Carradine is fine as the ascetic and fanatical investigator, but Harvey Keitel makes an uneasy Pontius Pilate because of his tough-guy accent. Not rated; contains some nudity and violence. 1986; 106m.

INSERTS

DIR: John Byrum. **CAST:** Richard Dreyfuss, Jessica Harper, Bob Hoskins, Veronica Cartwright.

Even Richard Dreyfuss can't save this dreary film about a once-great 1930s film director now making porno movies. Rated R. 1976; 99m.

INSIDE MOVES ★★★★

DIR: Richard Donner. **CAST:** John Savage, David Morse, Amy Wright, Tony Burton.

This is a film that grows on you as the heartwarming story unfolds. With a unique blend of humor and insight, director Richard Donner and screenwriters Valerie Curtin and Barry Levinson provide a captivating look into a very special friendship. John Savage plays a man who, after failing at suicide, succeeds at life with the help of some disabled friends. Rated PG. 1980; 113m.

INSIDE THE THIRD REICH ★★★½

DIR: Marvin J. Chomsky. **CAST:** Rutger Hauer, Derek Jacobi, Blythe Danner, John Gielgud, Ian Holm, Elke Sommer, Trevor Howard, Robert Vaughn.

This made-for-TV miniseries is based on the autobiography of Albert Speer, the German architect who became Hitler's chief builder. Rutger Hauer portrays Speer as a man obsessed with the opportunity to build extensively while being blissfully unaware of the horrors of war around him. 1982; 250m.

INSIGNIFICANCE ★★

DIR: Nicolas Roeg. **CAST:** Michael Emil, Theresa Russell, Gary Busey, Tony Curtis, Will Sampson.

Michael Emil's absolutely wonderful impersonation of Albert Einstein makes this film worth seeing. Director Nicholas Roeg has envisioned a night in 1954 New York where Marilyn Monroe comes to visit Einstein in his hotel room to explain the theory of relativity to him. The encounter is a charming one, but it eventually loses its uniqueness as it incorporates disjunctive symbolic flashbacks into the narrative. Rated R. 1985; 110m.

INTERIORS ★★★★

DIR: Woody Allen. **CAST:** Diane Keaton, E. G. Marshall, Geraldine

Page, Richard Jordan, Sam Waterston.

Woody Allen tips his hat to Swedish director Ingmar Bergman with this very downbeat drama about a family tearing itself apart. Extremely serious stuff, with fine performances by all. Allen shows he can direct more than comedy. Rated R for language. 1978; 99m.

INTERMEZZO ★★★★

DIR: Gregory Ratoff. **CAST:** Leslie Howard, Ingrid Bergman, Cecil Kellaway.

A love affair between a married concert violinist and a young woman doesn't stray very far from the standard eternal love triangle. This classic weeper has more renown as the English-language debut of Ingrid Bergman. 1939; B&W; 70m.

INTERNS, THE ★★★

DIR: David Swift. **CAST:** Cliff Robertson, Michael Callan, James MacArthur, Nick Adams, Suzy Parker, Buddy Ebsen, Telly Savalas.

This melodrama of the lives of interns in an American hospital has it all. The new doctors must deal with death, drugs, abortions, and personal problems. Competently acted and directed. 1962; B&W; 130m.

INTERVAL ★★

DIR: Daniel Mann. **CAST:** Merle Oberon, Robert Wolders, Claudio Brook, Russ Conway.

Merle Oberon's last feature film is a weepy story of a woman who tours the world trying to find her one true love while attempting to forget her own unfortunate past. Filmed in Mexico, this melodrama is passable, but hardly a distinguished finale for Oberon's career. Rated PG. 1973; 84m.

INTIMATE CONTACT ★★★

DIR: Waris Hussein. **CAST:** Claire Bloom, Daniel Massey, Sylvia Syms, Mark Kingston, Maggie Steed.

Claire Bloom and Daniel Massey are wonderful as an affluent couple whose lives are shattered when they are confronted with the specter of AIDS. A sobering account of a family's attempt to deal with this tragic disease. Rate PG. 1987; 159m.

INTIMATE STRANGERS ★★

DIR: John Llewellyn Moxey. **CAST:** Dennis Weaver, Sally Struthers, Tyne Daly, Larry Hagman, Melvyn Douglas.

Dennis Weaver and Sally Struthers are a husband and wife who permit a lack of self-esteem to drag them into the dark areas of psychological warfare and wife beating. Melvyn Douglas is outstanding and Tyne Daly was nominated for an Emmy Award for her work in this made-for-TV film. 1977; 120m.

INTO THE NIGHT ★★½

DIR: John Landis. **CAST:** Jeff Goldblum, Michelle Pfeiffer, Paul Mazursky, Kathryn Harrold, Richard Farnsworth, Irene Papas, David Bowie, Dan Aykroyd.

Packed with cinematic in-jokes and guest appearances by more than a dozen film directors, this is a film fan's dream. Unfortunately, it might also be a casual viewer's nightmare. Jeff Goldblum and Michelle Pfeiffer stumble into international intrigue and share a bizarre and deadly adventure in the night world of contemporary Los Angeles. Rated R for violence and profanity. 1985; 115m.

INTOLERANCE ★★★★

DIR: D. W. Griffith. **CAST:** Lillian Gish, Bessie Love, Mae Marsh, Elmo Lincoln, Tully Marshall, Eugene Pallette, Tod Browning, Monte Blue, Robert Harron, Constance Talmadge, Erich Von Stroheim.

This milestone silent epic tells and blends four stories of injustice, modern and ancient. The sets for the Babylonian sequence were the largest ever built for a film. One scene alone involved 15,000 people and 250 chariots. The acting is dated, but the picture presents a powerful viewing experience. 1916; B&W; 123m.

IRISHMAN, THE ★★★½
DIR: Donald Crombie. **CAST:** Michael Craig, Simon Burke, Robyn Nevin, Lou Brown.
Excellent Australian drama set in the 1920s. An immigrant Irish worker, who has made a living in rough territory with his team of horses, refuses to recognize progress in the form of a gas-driven truck that will put him out of business. His unwillingness to adapt tears apart his family, who wants to back him up but recognizes that he is wrong. 1978; 108m.

IRON DUKE, THE ★★★★
DIR: Victor Saville. **CAST:** George Arliss, A. E. Matthews, Emlyn Williams, Felix Aylmer, Gladys Cooper.
A thoroughly English stage actor, George Arliss did not make this, his first British film, until late in the decade he spent in the Hollywood studios. His Duke of Wellington, victor over Napoleon at Waterloo, is picture perfect. Buffs will particularly enjoy a younger Felix Aylmer, later Polonius in Laurence Olivier's 1948 *Hamlet*. 1936; B&W; 88m.

IRON TRIANGLE, THE ★★★
DIR: Eric Weston. **CAST:** Beau Bridges, Haing S. Ngor, Johnny Hallyday.
The Vietnam War seen through the eyes of a hardboiled American captain (Beau Bridges, fine as always). Haing S. Ngor (Oscar winner for *The Killing Fields*) plays a small part as a Cong officer. Solid, blood-and-guts war drama bogs down in the middle but ends with a well-staged climactic battle. Rated R for graphic combat scenes and profanity. 1988; 94m.

IRONWEED ★★★★½
DIR: Hector Babenco. **CAST:** Jack Nicholson, Meryl Streep, Carroll Baker, Michael O'Keefe, Tom Waits, Fred Gwynne.
William Kennedy's adaptation of his Pulitzer Prize–winning novel turns into a showcase for Jack Nicholson and Meryl Streep, both playing skid-row alcoholics. Director Hector Babenco superbly captures the grinding, hand-to-mouth dreariness of this Depression Era tale, which traces the relationship of opportunity and convenience between the two leads. This may be Streep's finest hour; her complete descent into the part is riveting. Rated R for language, violence, and brief nudity. 1987; 144m.

IRRECONCILABLE DIFFERENCES ★★½
DIR: Charles Shyer. **CAST:** Drew Barrymore, Ryan O'Neal, Shelley Long.
Drew Barrymore plays a little girl who sues her self-centered, career-conscious parents—Ryan O'Neal and Shelley Long—for divorce. This uneven comedy-drama was written by the creators of *Private Benjamin*, Nancy Meyers and Charles Shyer, who also directed. The laughs are few, but there are some effective scenes of character development. Rated PG for profanity and nudity. 1984; 101m.

ISADORA ★★★
DIR: Karel Reisz. **CAST:** Vanessa Redgrave, James Fox, Jason Robards Jr.
A straightforward biography of American modern dance pioneer Isadora Duncan. Vanessa Redgrave ably carries the burden of bringing this eccentric, early flower child to life. Unfortunately she is often undone by a script that drags, becomes repetitious, and rambles. 1969; 138m.

ISLAND OF DESIRE ★½
DIR: Stuart Heisler. **CAST:** Linda Darnell, Tab Hunter, Donald Gray.
Dull film about a trio who become involved in a romantic triangle when they are marooned on an island during World War II. The whole thing is substandard, but Linda Darnell is still worth watching. 1952; 103m.

ISLAND OF THE BLUE DOLPHINS ★★★
DIR: James B. Clark. **CAST:** Celia Kaye, George Kennedy, Larry Domasin.
Alone on an island, a girl and her brother struggle to survive. When at-

tacked by wild dogs, the girl manages to befriend the fiercest one. This adventure will be especially interesting for 7- to 12-year-olds. 1964; 93m.

ISLANDS IN THE STREAM ★★★
DIR: Franklin J. Schaffner. **CAST:** George C. Scott, Julius W. Harris, David Hemmings, Brad Savage, Hart Bochner, Claire Bloom.

Islands in the Stream is really two movies in one. The first part is an affecting and effective look at a broken family. The second is a cheap action adventure. Thomas Hudson (George C. Scott), a famous painter and sculptor, lives the life of a recluse in the Bahamas. His only companions are his seagoing crew of Joseph and Eddy. One summer, his three sons Tom, Andy, and Davy arrive to see him for the first time in four years. Rated PG for violence and profanity. 1977; 105m.

IT RAINED ALL NIGHT THE DAY I LEFT ★★½
DIR: Nicolas Gessner. **CAST:** Louis Gossett Jr., Sally Kellerman, Tony Curtis.

Tony Curtis and Louis Gossett Jr. play two small-time weapons salesmen who are ambushed in Africa. They go to work for a recently widowed woman (Sally Kellerman) who controls all the water in this extremely hot and dry region. Because she blames the natives for her husband's death, she rations their water. Rated R for sex and violence. 1978; 100m.

IT'S A WONDERFUL LIFE ★★★★½
DIR: Frank Capra. **CAST:** James Stewart, Donna Reed, Lionel Barrymore, Thomas Mitchell, Ward Bond, Henry Travers.

Have you ever wished you'd never been born? What if that wish were granted? That's the premise of Frank Capra's heartbreaking, humorous, and ultimately heartwarming *It's a Wonderful Life*. James Stewart was tapped for the lead role right after he left the service at the end of World War II. The story is about a good man who is so busy helping others that life seems to pass him by. 1946; B&W; 129m.

IT'S GOOD TO BE ALIVE ★★★½
DIR: Michael Landon. **CAST:** Paul Winfield, Louis Gossett Jr., Ruby Dee, Ramon Bieri, Lloyd Gough.

The tragedy of a great athlete being struck down in the prime of his career is dealt with in this story of Brooklyn Dodgers catcher Roy Campanella (Paul Winfield). Campanella had two spectacular seasons with the Dodgers before being permanently crippled from the waist down in a car accident in 1958. *It's Good to Be Alive* focuses on Campanella's struggle with self-respect after the wreck. A good companion piece to *Brian's Song*. 1974; 100m.

IT'S MY TURN ★★
DIR: Claudia Weill. **CAST:** Jill Clayburgh, Michael Douglas, Beverly Garland, Charles Grodin.

Jill Clayburgh is a college professor confused about her relationship with live-in lover Charles Grodin, a Chicago real-estate salesman. Then she meets baseball player Michael Douglas. They fall in love. The viewer yawns. Rated R. 1980; 91m.

JACK LONDON ★★
DIR: Alfred Santell. **CAST:** Michael O'Shea, Susan Hayward, Osa Massen, Harry Davenport, Frank Craven, Virginia Mayo.

Episodic, fictionalized account of the life of one of America's most popular authors is entertaining enough, but one wishes that a more accurate, detailed biography of this fabulous man were available on film. Heavily influenced by the anti-Japanese sentiment rampant at the time of its release, the colorful and tragic tale of the poor boy who gained and alienated the love of America and the world cries out to be remade in today's more permissive and investigative atmosphere. 1943; B&W; 94m.

JACKIE ROBINSON STORY, THE ★★★★

DIR: Alfred E. Green. **CAST:** Jackie Robinson, Ruby Dee, Minor Watson, Louise Beavers.

This is one of the best baseball films ever—the biography of Jackie Robinson, first black to play in the major leagues. The performances (including Mr. Robinson as himself) are very good, and the direction is sharp. 1950; B&W; 76m.

JACKKNIFE ★★★★

DIR: David Jones. **CAST:** Robert De Niro, Ed Harris, Kathy Baker.

Ed Harris and Kathy Baker star as brother and sister in this drama about veterans who suffer from post-Vietnam stress syndrome. Robert De Niro plays another vet who comes into their lives, causing volatile changes in Harris and unexpected romance for Baker. Rated R, with profanity and violence. 1989; 102m.

JAGGED EDGE ★★½

DIR: Richard Marquand. **CAST:** Glenn Close, Jeff Bridges, Peter Coyote, Robert Loggia, Leigh Taylor-Young.

A publishing magnate (Jeff Bridges) is accused of the ritualistic slaying of his wife; an attorney (Glenn Close) is hired to defend him. They fall in love, conduct an affair during the trial(!), which is not noticed by the ambitious prosecutor (Peter Coyote) (!), and generally behave like total fools; during this, we and Close ponder the burning question: Did Bridges do the dirty deed? Too bad the story doesn't measure up. Rated R for violence. 1985; 108m.

JAMAICA INN ★★★

DIR: Alfred Hitchcock. **CAST:** Charles Laughton, Maureen O'Hara, Leslie Banks, Emlyn Williams, Robert Newton, Mervyn Johns.

Not one of Alfred Hitchcock's best directorial efforts. But the cast makes it, just the same. Charles Laughton is Squire Pengallon, the evil chief of a band of cutthroats who lures ships onto the rocks of the Cornish Coast in Victorian England. Maureen O'Hara is a beautiful damsel in distress who must contend with his madness. 1939; B&W; 98m.

JAMES DEAN—A LEGEND IN HIS OWN TIME ★★½

DIR: Robert Butler. **CAST:** Michael Brandon, Stephen McHattie, Candy Clark, Amy Irving, Meg Foster, Jayne Meadows, Brooke Adams.

Lackluster dramatization of actor James Dean's life as seen through the eyes of a friend. Stephen McHattie qualifies as a James Dean look-alike and gives a solid performance. This film features a fine supporting cast. 1976; 99m.

JAMES JOYCE'S WOMEN ★★★★½

DIR: Michael Pearce. **CAST:** Fionnula Flanagan, Timothy E. O'Grady, Chris O'Neill.

James Joyce's Women is a delicious, verbally erotic movie. With Joyce as the writer and Fionnula Flanagan (writer and producer) as interpreter, things are bound to be intense. The film is virtually a one-woman show, with Flanagan portraying seven different characters from Joyce's life and works. The humor and sensuality will thrill Joyce fans. Rated R for nudity and sexual situations. 1985; 89m.

JANE DOE ★★½

DIR: Ivan Nagy. **CAST:** Karen Valentine, William Devane, Eva Marie Saint, David Huffman.

A passable suspense movie about a woman who is brutally attacked and left for dead in a shallow grave. She survives with amnesia, so she can't identify her attacker, believed to be a local serial killer. Made for TV. 1983; 96m.

JANE EYRE ★★★★

DIR: Julian Amyes. **CAST:** Timothy Dalton, Zelah Clarke.

This marvelous BBC production honors Charlotte Brontë's classic tale of courage and romance. A thrilling and thorough adaptation. Zelah Clarke plays the orphaned, mistreated, and unloved Jane who later falls for the darkly mysterious Mr. Rochester (Timothy Dalton). 1983; 239m.

JAYNE MANSFIELD STORY, THE ★½

DIR: Dick Lowry. **CAST:** Loni Anderson, Arnold Schwarzenegger, Kathleen Lloyd.

Loni Anderson gives only an average performance as 1950s blonde sex bomb Mansfield. She portrays Mansfield as a ruthless starlet who puts publicity stunts and fame ahead of all other life goals. Arnold Schwarzenegger is more convincing as her body-building mate, Mickey Hargitay. Unrated. Made for television. 1980; 100m.

JERICHO MILE, THE ★★★★

DIR: Michael Mann. **CAST:** Peter Strauss, Roger E. Mosley, Brian Dennehy, Billy Green Bush, Ed Lauter, Beverly Todd.

This tough, inspiring TV movie tells the story of a man, serving a life sentence at Folsom Prison, who dedicates himself to becoming an Olympic-caliber runner. Director Michael Mann makes sure the film is riveting and realistic at all times. Peter Strauss, in a powerful performance, gives the character an edge, never letting him appear too noble or sympathetic. 1979; 100m.

JESSIE OWENS STORY, THE ★★★

DIR: Richard Irving. **CAST:** Dorian Harewood, Debbi Morgan, George Kennedy, Georg Stanford Brown, Tom Bosley, LeVar Burton.

This made-for-TV movie of the Olympic hero provides a provocative insight into the many behind-the-scenes events that plague people who are thrust into public admiration. Dorian Harewood is perfect in his performance of the not-always-admirable hero, a victim of his own inabilities and the uncontrollable events surrounding him. This film also holds up a mirror to our society's many embarrassing racial attitudes. 1984; 180m.

JESUS ★★

DIR: Peter Sykes, John Kirsh. **CAST:** Brian Deacon, Rivka Noiman.

More a Bible study than entertainment; this film is narrated by Alexander Scourby and the words are taken from the Good News Bible, the Book of Luke. Filmed in the Holy Land. 1979; 117m.

JESUS OF NAZARETH ★★★★

DIR: Franco Zeffirelli. **CAST:** Robert Powell, Anne Bancroft, James Mason, Rod Steiger.

This vivid TV movie of the life of Jesus is beautifully directed by the poetic genius Franco Zefferelli. An outstanding cast gives warm and sensitive performances in what is the finest film to date of the familiar Bible story. It fills *three* cassettes but well worth the time. 1976; 371m.

JEWEL IN THE CROWN, THE ★★★★★

DIR: Christopher Morahan, Jim O'Brien. **CAST:** Tim Pigott-Smith, Geraldine James, Peggy Ashcroft, Charles Dance, Susan Wooldridge, Art Malik, Judy Parfitt.

Based on Paul Scott's *Raj Quartet*, this Emmy Award–winning series first aired on the BBC in fourteen episodes. It is a wonderful epic that depicts Britain's last years of power in India (1942–1947). The story revolves around the love of an Indian man, Hari Kumar (Art Malik), for a white woman, Daphne Manners (Susan Wooldridge), and the repercussions of their forbidden romance. The love-hate relationship of the English and the Indians is well depicted. Fine entertainment! 1984; 700m.

JEZEBEL ★★★★

DIR: William Wyler. **CAST:** Bette Davis, Henry Fonda, George Brent, Spring Byington.

Bette Davis gives one of her finest performances as a spoiled Southern belle in this release. Devised by Warner Bros. as a consolation prize for their star, who was turned down when she tried for the role of Scarlett O'Hara, it's not as good a film as *Gone with the Wind*. But then, how many are? Directed by William Wyler, it brought Davis her second Best Actress Oscar—and a well-deserved one at that. She's superb as the self-centered "Jezebel" who takes too long in deciding between a banker (Henry Fonda) and a dandy (George Brent) and loses all. 1938; B&W; 103m.

JILTING OF GRANNY WEATHERALL, THE ★
DIR: Randa Haines. **CAST:** Geraldine Fitzgerald, Lois Smith.

This relentlessly depressing adaptation of the Katherine Anne Porter short story will appeal only to those with an insatiable desire to see an old woman sink into delirium and die. Corinne Jacker's screenplay never sufficiently explains the thoughtless lover supposedly responsible for the lead character's acrimonious nature, which leaves Geraldine Fitzgerald acting up a storm in a vacuum. Introduced by Henry Fonda; suitable for family viewing. 1980; 57m.

JIM THORPE—ALL AMERICAN ★★★
DIR: Michael Curtiz. **CAST:** Burt Lancaster, Charles Bickford, Steve Cochran, Phyllis Thaxter, Dick Wesson.

This well-intentioned bio-pic stretches much of the truth in the sad story of great American Indian athlete Jim Thorpe, Olympic medalist and professional baseball, football, and track star. Veteran director Michael Curtiz places most of the audience sympathy with toothy Burt Lancaster, hinting at but sidestepping Thorpe's own personal demons and presenting him as a victim of a cold system. Burt himself is in fine physical shape as he recreates some of Thorpe's feats for the camera. 1951; B&W; 107m.

JO JO DANCER, YOUR LIFE IS CALLING ★★★★½
DIR: Richard Pryor. **CAST:** Richard Pryor, Debbie Allen, Art Evans, Fay Hauser, Barbara Williams, Carmen McRae, Paula Kelly, Diahnne Abbott, Scoey Mitchill, Billy Eckstine, Wings Hauser, Michael Ironside.

In this brilliant show-biz biography, Richard Pryor plays Jo Jo Dancer, a well-known entertainer at the peak of his popularity and the depths of self-understanding and love. A drug-related accident puts Jo Jo in the hospital and forces him to reexamine his life. Rated R for profanity, nudity, suggested sex, drug use, violence, and unflinching honesty. 1986; 100m.

JOAN OF ARC ★★★
DIR: Victor Fleming. **CAST:** Ingrid Bergman, José Ferrer, Francis L. Sullivan, J. Carrol Naish, Ward Bond.

Ingrid Bergman is touching and devout in this by-the-book rendering of Maxwell Anderson's noted play, but too much talk and too little action strain patience and buttocks. 1948; 100m.

JOE ★★★
DIR: John G. Avildsen. **CAST:** Peter Boyle, Dennis Patrick, Susan Sarandon.

Peter Boyle stars in this violent film about a bigot who ends up associating much more closely with the people he hates. Falling short in the storytelling, *Joe* is nevertheless helped along by top-notch acting. Rated R. 1970; 107m.

JOHN AND THE MISSUS ★★★
DIR: Gordon Pinsent. **CAST:** Gordon Pinsent, Jackie Burroughs, Timothy Webber.

The beautiful coast of Newfoundland provides the backdrop for this otherwise depressing Canadian film. A town loses its source of income when the local mine is closed. Gordon Pinsent plays a stubborn, courageous man who refuses the meager resettlement money the goverment offers.

Rated PG for mature themes. 1987; 98m.

JOHNNY BELINDA ★★★★
DIR: Jean Negulesco. **CAST:** Jane Wyman, Lew Ayres, Charles Bickford, Agnes Moorehead.

Jane Wyman won an Oscar for her remarkable performance as a deaf-mute farm girl. Her multidimensional characterization lifts this movie over mere melodrama. The many disasters that befall its put-upon heroine, including rape and trying to raise the resulting offspring in the face of community pressure, would be scoffed at in a lesser actress. 1948; B&W; 103m.

JOHNNY GOT HIS GUN ★★½
DIR: Dalton Trumbo. **CAST:** Timothy Bottoms, Marsha Hunt, Jason Robards Jr., Donald Sutherland, Diane Varsi, David Soul, Anthony Geary.

Featuring Timothy Bottoms as an American World War I soldier who loses his legs, eyes, ears, mouth, and nose after a German artillery shell explodes, this is a morbid, depressing anti-war film with flashes of brilliance. Rated PG. 1971; 111m.

JOHNNY TIGER ★★½
DIR: Paul Wendkos. **CAST:** Robert Taylor, Geraldine Brooks, Chad Everett.

Chad Everett is a half-breed Seminole, Robert Taylor is a sympathetic teacher, and Geraldine Brooks is a sympathetic doctor, all trying to reach some valid conclusion about the American Indians' role in the modern world. It's nothing to get excited about. 1966; 102m.

JOLLY CORNER, THE ★★★
DIR: Arthur Barron. **CAST:** Fritz Weaver, Salome Jens.

The uncertainties of diverging career paths lie at the heart of this TV adaptation of the moody Henry James short story. Fritz Weaver returns to turn-of-the-century America after having lived abroad for thirty-five years, and he becomes obsessed by the memories contained within his ancestral home. Introduced by Henry Fonda; unrated and suitable for family viewing. 1975; 43m.

JONATHAN LIVINGSTON SEAGULL ★
DIR: Hall Bartlett.

You may have been convinced that a man can fly, but you'll never believe that a bird can talk. This misfired adaptation of Richard Bach's bestseller used real locations and actual seagulls, rather than infinitely more expressive animated counterparts. Needless to say, seagulls aren't the world's best method actors. Overblown and laughable. Rated G. 1973; 120m.

JOURNEY INTO FEAR ★★
DIR: Daniel Mann. **CAST:** Sam Waterston, Zero Mostel, Yvette Mimieux, Scott Marlowe, Ian McShane, Joseph Wiseman, Shelley Winters, Stanley Holloway, Donald Pleasence, Vincent Price.

This Canadian remake of Orson Welles's 1942 spy drama is occasionally intriguing but ultimately ambiguous and lacking in dramatic punch. Sam Waterston's portrayal of a research geologist, and wide-ranging European locations help sustain interest. Rated PG. 1975; 103m.

JOY HOUSE ★★½
DIR: René Clement. **CAST:** Jane Fonda, Alain Delon, Lola Albright, Sorrell Booke.

Spooky and interesting, but ultimately only mildly rewarding, this film features Jane Fonda in one of her sexy French roles as a free-spirited waif attempting to seduce her cousin's chauffeur (Alain Delon). Meanwhile, said cousin (Lola Albright) tries to help her criminal lover hide from the authorities. You could do worse. 1964; 98m.

JOYRIDE ★★½
DIR: Joseph Ruben. **CAST:** Desi Arnaz Jr., Robert Carradine, Melanie Griffith, Anne Lockhart, Tom Ligon.

Four second-generation actors acquit themselves fairly well in this loosely directed drama about a quartet of youngsters who start off in search of adventure and find themselves turning to crime. Rated R. 1977; 92m.

JUAREZ ★★★★
DIR: William Dieterle. **CAST:** Paul Muni, Bette Davis, Brian Aherne, Claude Rains, John Garfield.

Warner Bros. in the 1930s and '40s seemed to trot out veteran actor Paul Muni every time they attempted to film a screen biography. This re-creation of the life of Mexico's famous peasant leader was no exception. Surrounded by an all-star cast, including Bette Davis and Brian Aherne, this big budget bio is well-mounted and well-intentioned. 1939; B&W; 132m.

JUDGE PRIEST ★★★½
DIR: John Ford. **CAST:** Will Rogers, Anita Louise, Stepin Fetchit, Henry B. Walthall, Tom Brown, Hattie McDaniel.

A slice of Americana, and a good one. Life and drama in an old southern town, with all the clichés painted brilliantly. Will Rogers is fine. Stepin Fetchit is properly Uncle Tom. John Ford's sensitive direction makes this film one for the books. A touching, poignant portrait of community life lost and gone forever. 1934; B&W; 71m.

JUDGMENT AT NUREMBERG ★★★★
DIR: Stanley Kramer. **CAST:** Spencer Tracy, Burt Lancaster, Maximilian Schell, Richard Widmark, Marlene Dietrich, Montgomery Clift, Judy Garland.

An all-star cast shines in this thoughtful social drama. During the late stages of the Nazi war crimes trial, an American judge (Spencer Tracy) must ponder the issue of how extensive is the responsibility of citizens for carrying out the criminal orders of their governments. 1961; B&W; 178m.

JUDGMENT IN BERLIN ★★★
DIR: Leo Penn. **CAST:** Martin Sheen, Sam Wanamaker, Max Gail, Sean Penn.

Intelligent courtroom drama in the *Inherit the Wind* and *Judgment at Nuremberg* vein. An East German hijacks a Polish airliner and has it fly to West Berlin, where he seeks political asylum. Instead of offering safety, the U.S. government puts him on trial for terrorism. Martin Sheen as the nononsense judge carries the film. Rated PG for language. 1988; 110m.

JULIA ★★★★½
DIR: Fred Zinnemann. **CAST:** Jane Fonda, Vanessa Redgrave, Jason Robards Jr., Maximilian Schell.

Alvin Sargent won an Oscar for his taut screen adaptation of the late Lillian Hellman's best-selling memoir *Pentimento*. It's a harrowing tale of Hellman's journey into Germany to locate her childhood friend who has joined in the resistance against the Nazis. Great performances by all cast members. Rated PG. 1977; 118m.

JULIUS CAESAR ★★
DIR: Stuart Burge. **CAST:** Charlton Heston, Jason Robards Jr., John Gielgud, Robert Vaughn, Richard Chamberlain, Diana Rigg, Christopher Lee.

A good cast, but Shakespeare loses in this so-so rendering of ambition, greed, jealousy, and politics in toga Rome. 1970; 117m.

JUNO AND THE PAYCOCK ★★½
DIR: Alfred Hitchcock. **CAST:** Sara Allgood, Edward Chapman, Sidney Morgan.

Sean O'Casey's famous play gets the Hitchcock treatment, and the result is an intriguing blend of Irish melodrama and sinister moods. The setting is the Dublin uprising, the characters members of a poor family with more than its share of grief. A young unwed mother, an anticipated inheritance, and an unwise young man are the focus for various sorts of tragedy. 1929; B&W; 85m.

JUST A GIGOLO ★
DIR: David Hemmings. **CAST:** David Bowie, Sydne Rome, Kim Novak, David Hemmings, Marlene Dietrich, Maria Schell, Curt Jurgens.

Rock star David Bowie gives a lifeless performance in this bizarre, rambling study of a proud Prussian aristocrat who ends up as a disillusioned male prostitute. A strong cast cannot do much to save this failed attempt at black comedy. 1978; 96m.

JUST BETWEEN FRIENDS ★★★½
DIR: Allan Burns. **CAST:** Mary Tyler Moore, Christine Lahti, Sam Waterston, Ted Danson, Mark Blum.

Mary Tyler Moore stars in this big-screen soap opera as a homemaker happily married to Ted Danson. One day at an aerobics class, she meets TV news reporter Christine Lahti and they become friends. They have a lot in common—including being in love with the same man. Rated PG-13 for profanity and suggested sex. 1986; 115m.

JUST THE WAY YOU ARE ★★½
DIR: Edouard Molinaro. **CAST:** Kristy McNichol, Michael Ontkean, Kaki Hunter.

Kristy McNichol gives a fine performance as a pretty flautist who cleverly overcomes the need to wear a leg brace and fulfills her wish to "be like other people." But this deception brings an unexpected moment of truth. Even the plodding direction of Edouard Molinaro can't prevent this well-written work from occasionally being witty, and touching. Rated PG. 1984; 95m.

JUSTINE ★★
DIR: George Cukor. **CAST:** Anouk Aimée, Dirk Bogarde, Robert Forster, Anna Karina, Philippe Noiret, Michael York, John Vernon, Jack Albertson, Cliff Gorman, Michael Constantine, Severn Darden.

Compressing all four volumes of Laurence Durrell's *Alexandria Quartet* into one film was an all-but-impossible task; to say that it was done here as well as it could be is faint praise. It is the story of a Middle Eastern prostitute who rises by marriage to a position of power in her country while retaining many of her lovers. Fans of the novels will be disappointed; those unfamiliar with the story will be confused. Rated R for nudity and sexual situations. 1969; 117m.

KANDYLAND ★★★
DIR: Robert Schnitzer. **CAST:** Sandahl Bergman, Kim Evenson.

Fairly interesting story centers around a girl's desire to make a living at exotic dancing. The nice thing about this film is that it concentrates on the people involved, not the dances. Sandahl Bergman is good as the young girl's mentor and lonely friend. Rated R for nudity, profanity, and violence. 1987; 94m.

KANGAROO ★★★★
DIR: Tim Burstall. **CAST:** Colin Friels, Judy Davis, John Walton, Hugh Keays-Byrne.

Real-life husband and wife Colin Friels and Judy Davis give superb performances in this Australian film adaptation of the semiautobiographical novel by D. H. Lawrence. Writer Richard Somers (Friels), a thinly veiled version of Lawrence, finds himself vilified by critics in his native England for writing sexually suggestive novels and, with his German-born wife Harriet (Davis), journeys Down Under in search of a better life. Rated R for violence, nudity, and profanity. 1986; 100m.

KANSAS ★½
DIR: David Stevens. **CAST:** Matt Dillon, Andrew McCarthy, Leslie Hope, Kyra Sedgwick.

Lethargic, predictable melodrama has fresh-faced Andrew McCarthy teaming up with sleazy Matt Dillon, who cons him into robbing a bank. In one of several preposterous plot twists, McCarthy takes the time to rescue the governor's daughter while escaping from the police. When *Kansas* isn't being ridiculous, it's mind-numbingly routine. Rated R for profanity and violence. 1988; 105m.

KARATE KID, THE ★★★★½
DIR: John G. Avildsen. **CAST:** Ralph Macchio, Noriyuki "Pat" Morita, Elisabeth Shue.
A heartwarming, sure-fire crowd pleaser, this believable and touching work about the hazards of high-school days and adolescence will have you cheering during its climax and leave you with a smile on your face. You'll find yourself rooting for the put-upon hero, Daniel (Ralph Macchio), and booing the bad guys. Rated PG for violence and profanity. 1984; 126m.

KARATE KID PART II, THE ★★★½
DIR: John G. Avildsen. **CAST:** Ralph Macchio, Noriyuki "Pat" Morita, Nobu McCarthy, Martin Kove, William Zabka.
This second in the *Karate Kid* series begins moments after the conclusion of the first film. Mr. Miyagi (Noriyuki "Pat" Morita) receives word that his father, residing in Okinawa, is dying, so he drops everything and heads for home, with young Daniel (Ralph Macchio) along for the ride. Once in Okinawa, Miyagi encounters an old rival and an old love, while Daniel makes a new enemy and a new love. Rated PG for mild violence. 1986; 113m.

KARATE KID PART III, THE ★★
DIR: John G. Avildsen. **CAST:** Ralph Macchio, Noriyuki "Pat" Morita, Martin Kove.
Back for the third time as Daniel "The Karate Kid" LaRusso, Ralph Macchio prepares to defend his valley championship with training from a new mentor who is secretly in cahoots with the kid's old arch-enemy Crease (Martin Kove) to ensure our hero's defeat. The story is interlarded with forced sentiment and tired homilies, and even the watchable Pat Morita can't make this one a winner. Rated PG. 1989; 111m.

KATHERINE ★★★
DIR: Jeremy Paul Kagan. **CAST:** Sissy Spacek, Art Carney, Henry Winkler, Jane Wyatt, Julie Kavner.
This television movie follows Sissy Spacek from a middle-class young student to a social activist and finally to an underground terrorist. Spacek is very convincing in this demanding role. The movie tends to remind one of the Patty Hearst case and features good, solid storytelling. 1975; 100m.

KENNEDY (TELEVISION MINISERIES) ★★★★
DIR: Jim Godard. **CAST:** Martin Sheen, John Shea, Blair Brown, E. G. Marshall, Geraldine Fitzgerald, Vincent Gardenia.
This outstanding made-for-TV miniseries is even more enjoyable when viewed in one sitting. This upfront portrait of John F. Kennedy from presidential campaign to assassination shows the warts as well as the charm and mystique of the entire Kennedy clan. The cast is excellent, with Martin Sheen as JFK, John Shea as RFK, and Vincent Gardenia particularly chilling as J. Edgar Hoover. An easy-to-swallow history lesson on the Bay of Pigs, Cuba, Vietnam, and Camelot. 1983; 278m.

KENNETH ANGER—VOLUME ONE ★★½
DIR: Kenneth Anger. **CAST:** Kenneth Anger, Gordon Gray.
Filmmaker Kenneth Anger's collection of movie shorts are a bizarre invocation of his fusion of dreams and sexual desire. The works presented in this middling program are "Fireworks," "Rabbit's Moon," and "Eaux d'Artifice." Not rated, but contains explicit sexuality. 1953; 21m.

KENNETH ANGER—VOLUME TWO ★★★
DIR: Kenneth Anger. **CAST:** Marjorie Cameron, Anais Nin, Kenneth Anger.

Kenneth Anger's "Inauguration of the Pleasure Dome" is a surreal opera of mystical awakening inspired by the literary works of author Aleister Crowley. It is by far one of the avant-garde filmmaker's most hypnotic works. Not rated, but contains explicit sex. 1954; 38m.

KENNETH ANGER—VOLUME THREE ★★★
DIR: Kenneth Anger. **CAST:** Bruce Byron, Johnny Sapienza.

Kenneth Anger's third volume of collected film shorts are surreal comical reflections on Hollywood, decadence, and masculinity. Titles included in this program are "Kustom Kar," "Kommandos," "Puce Moment," and "Scorpio Rising." 1965; 37m.

KENNETH ANGER—VOLUME FOUR ★★
DIR: Kenneth Anger. **CAST:** Leslie Huggins, Marianne Faithfull, Donald Cammell.

Kenneth Anger's fourth volume of film shorts focuses on paganism and satanic rituals. Music by Mick Jagger and Bobby Beausoleil. Program titles are "Invocation of My Demon Brother" and "Lucifier Rising." Not rated, but contains sex and violence. 1980; 39m.

KEY, THE ★★½
DIR: Carol Reed. **CAST:** William Holden, Sophia Loren, Trevor Howard, Oscar Homolka, Bernard Lee.

A strange, moody curio, directed in somber tones by British filmmaker Carol Reed, and noteworthy as the first British film to star Sophia Loren. She plays a kept woman who comes with the London flat belonging to a succession of tugboat captains during World War II. 1958; B&W; 125m.

KEY EXCHANGE ★★★
DIR: Barnet Kellman. **CAST:** Brooke Adams, Ben Masters, Daniel Stern, Danny Aiello, Tony Roberts.

This movie is a good study of modern-day relationships. Brooke Adams and Ben Masters play a couple who confront the idea of making a firm commitment in their relationship. Daniel Stern is hilarious as a friend of the couple who is going through his own domestic crisis. Rated R for language, sex, and nudity. 1985; 96m.

KILLING, THE ★★★★
DIR: Stanley Kubrick. **CAST:** Sterling Hayden, Coleen Gray, Jay C. Flippen, Marie Windsor, Timothy Carey, Vince Edwards, Elisha Cook Jr.

Strong *noir* thriller from Stanley Kubrick has Sterling Hayden leading a group of criminals in an intricately timed heist at a racetrack. Excellent performances and atmospheric handling of the subject matter mark Kubrick, even at this early stage of his career, as a filmmaker to watch. 1956; B&W; 83m.

KILLING AFFAIR, A ★★★
DIR: David Saperstein. **CAST:** Peter Weller, Kathy Baker, John Glover, Bill Smitrovich.

Exceptional psychological drama about a young woman (Kathy Baker) who befriends a stranger (Peter Weller). As it turns out, he killed her husband to avenge the death of his own wife and family. The relationship between the two intensifies to an unexpected, terrifying conclusion. Rated R for nudity and violence. 1988; 100m.

KILLING 'EM SOFTLY ★★
DIR: Max Fischer. **CAST:** George Segal, Irene Cara, Joyce Gordon, Barbara Cook.

George Segal is a down-and-out musician who kills the friend of a young singer (Irene Cara) in an argument over the death of his dog. While attempting to prove that Segal is not the killer, Cara falls in love with him. An interesting and well-acted story bogs down in the attempt to turn this film into a music video. The music is good, but it overpowers the story and causes the whole to lose focus. Filmed in Canada. 1985; 90m.

KILLING FIELDS, THE ★★★★★
DIR: Roland Joffe. **CAST:** Sam Waterston, Haing S. Ngor, John

Malkovich, Julian Sands, Craig T. Nelson.

Here's an unforgettable motion picture. Based on the experiences of *New York Times* correspondent Sidney Schanberg during the war in Cambodia and his friendship with Cambodian guide and self-proclaimed journalist Dith Pran (whom Schanberg fights to save from imprisonment), it is a tale of love, loyalty, political intrigue, and horror. The viewer cannot help but be jarred and emotionally moved by it. Rated R for violence. 1984; 142m.

KILLING HEAT ★★½

DIR: Michael Raeburn. **CAST:** Karen Black, John Thaw, John Kani.

Uneven acting and a general lack of atmosphere hinder the screen adaptation of Doris Lessing's novel *The Grass is Singing*. Karen Black plays a city woman who marries a small-time farmer and slowly goes insane while trying to adapt herself to the rural lifestyle. Set in South Africa in the early 1960s. Not rated but contains nudity and violence. 1984; 104m.

KILLING OF ANGEL STREET, THE ★

DIR: Donald Crombie. **CAST:** Liz Alexander, John Hargreaves, Reg Lye.

The misleading title and packaging of *The Killing of Angel Street* makes it look like a teenage slasher flick, but the title refers to an actual street in a neighborhood in Australia. The plot involves the citizens' struggle to keep their homes from demolition by corrupt businessmen. The movie is alternately dull and unbelievable. 1981; 100m.

KILLING OF RANDY WEBSTER, THE ★★

DIR: Sam Wanamaker. **CAST:** Hal Holbrook, Dixie Carter, Jennifer Jason Leigh, Sean Penn.

Hal Holbrook and Dixie Carter, his real-life wife, portray parents searching desperately for meaning in the death of their troubled teenage son. The boy steals a van, then leads Houston police on a wild chase. They fire as the boy pulls a gun. Or did he? Made for television. 1985; 90m.

KILLING OF SISTER GEORGE, THE ★★½

DIR: Robert Aldrich. **CAST:** Beryl Reid, Susannah York, Coral Browne.

Now that the initial controversy that swirled around this film's honest depiction of a lesbian relationship has died away, a retrospective viewing shows us a film with a passable yet uninspired story and wooden acting in its central performances. This stage play of an aging actress whose career and relationships are crumbling around her was not brought to the screen with much spirit. Rated R for nudity. 1968; 140m.

KIND OF LOVING, A ★★

DIR: John Schlesinger. **CAST:** Alan Bates, Thora Hird, June Ritchie.

This British romance features Alan Bates as a young man infatuated with a cute blonde at work. When she gets pregnant, he marries her and realizes how ill-prepared he was for this commitment. Unrated, this contains nudity and adult themes equivalent to an R. 1962; B&W; 107m.

KING ★★★★

DIR: Abby Mann. **CAST:** Paul Winfield, Cicely Tyson, Ossie Davis, Roscoe Lee Browne, Howard Rollins Jr., Cliff De Young, Dolph Sweet, Lonny Chapman.

Paul Winfield and Cicely Tyson star as the Rev. Martin Luther King Jr. and Coretta Scott King in this outstanding docudrama of the martyred civil rights leader's murder-capped battle against segregation and for black human dignity. Director Abby Mann, who also scripted, interpolated actual newsreel footage with restaged confrontation incidents for maximum dramatic impact. 1978; 272m.

KING DAVID ★★★

DIR: Bruce Beresford. **CAST:** Richard Gere, Edward Woodward, Alice Krige, Denis Quilley.

Only biblical scholars will be able to say whether the makers of *King David* remained faithful to the Old Testament. As a big-screen production, however, it is impressive. Directed by Australian filmmaker Bruce Beresford, it is one of the few responsible attempts at filming the Bible. Rated PG-13 for nudity and violence. 1985; 115m.

KING LEAR ★★★½
DIR: Peter Brook. **CAST:** Paul Scofield, Irene Worth, Jack MacGowran, Alan Webb, Cyril Cusack, Patrick Magee.

Sturdy but truncated film adaptation of Shakespeare's play about a mad king and his cruel, power-hungry children. The Danish set location lends a disturbing air to this production, which features a powerful portrayal from Paul Scofield. 1971; 137m.

KING OF COMEDY, THE ★★★★
DIR: Martin Scorsese. **CAST:** Robert De Niro, Jerry Lewis, Sandra Bernhard.

This is certainly one of the most unusual movies of all time; a sort of black-comedy variation on creator Martin Scorsese's *Taxi Driver*. The star of that film, Robert De Niro, stars as aspiring comic Rupert Pupkin. In order to get his big break on television, Pupkin kidnaps a talk-show host (Jerry Lewis). Rated PG. 1983; 109m.

KING OF KINGS, THE ★★★
DIR: Cecil B. DeMille. **CAST:** H. B. Warner, Ernest Torrence, Jacqueline Logan, William Boyd, Joseph Schildkraut.

Cecil B. De Mille was more than ready when he made this one. It's silent, but Hollywood's greatest showman displays his gift for telling a story with required reverence. Naturally, since it's by De Mille, the production is a lavish one. 1927; B&W; 115m.

KING OF THE GYPSIES ★★★
DIR: Frank Pierson. **CAST:** Eric Roberts, Sterling Hayden, Susan Sarandon, Annette O'Toole, Brooke Shields, Shelley Winters.

Dave Stepanowicz (Eric Roberts) is the grandson of King Zharko Stepanowicz (Sterling Hayden), the patriarch of a gypsy tribe who is both intelligent and violent. Though Dave renounces his gypsy heritage, he is unable to escape it. The performances are uniformly excellent. Director Frank Pierson is the only one who can be held responsible for the film's lack of power. Rated R. 1978; 112m.

KING OF THE MOUNTAIN ★½
DIR: Noel Nosseck. **CAST:** Harry Hamlin, Richard Cox, Joseph Bottoms, Dennis Hopper.

The quest for success and peer group immortality by a trio of buddies leads mostly to unexciting night races on Hollywood's winding Mulholland Drive and cliché back-stabbing in the music business. Dennis Hopper provides the film with a few good moments as a spaced-out 1960s hasbeen. Rated PG. 1981; 90m.

KING, QUEEN AND KNAVE
DIR: Jerzy Skolimowski. **CAST:** David Niven, Gina Lollobrigida, John Moulder-Brown, Mario Adorf.

Even with the wonderful grace and charm of David Niven, this story authored by Vladimir Nabokov is a dud. The plot concerns a fumble-fingered young man who falls under the romantic spell of his aunt (Gina Lollobrigida). Not rated. 1972; 92m.

KING RAT ★★★★
DIR: Bryan Forbes. **CAST:** George Segal, Tom Courtenay, James Fox, John Mills.

A Japanese prison camp in World War II is the setting for this stark drama of survival of the fittest, the fittest in this case being "King Rat" (George Segal), the opportunistic head of black market operations within the compound. In this camp the prisoners fight one another for the meager necessities of existence. 1965; B&W; 133m.

KING'S ROW ★★★★★
DIR: Sam Wood. **CAST:** Ann Sheridan, Robert Cummings, Ronald Reagan, Claude Rains, Charles Coburn, Betty Field, Judith Anderson.
A small American town at the turn of the century is the setting where two men (Ronald Reagan and Robert Cummings) grow up to experience the corruption and moral decay behind the facade of a peaceful, serene community. This brilliantly photographed drama is close to being a masterpiece, thanks to exceptional performances by many of Hollywood's best character actors. 1941; B&W; 127m.

KIPPERBANG ★★½
DIR: Michael Apted. **CAST:** John Albasiny, Alison Steadman.
This is another World War II coming-of-age saga, in the same category as *Hope and Glory*, *Empire of the Sun*, and *Au Revoir les Enfants*. Charming and wistful at times, it doesn't quite reach the heights attained by the other three films. Rated PG. 1982; 80m.

KISS OF THE SPIDER WOMAN ★★★★
DIR: Hector Babenco. **CAST:** William Hurt, Raul Julia.
This first English-language film by Hector Babenco is a somber, brilliantly acted tale about a gay window dresser, Molina (William Hurt), and a revolutionary, Valentin (Raul Julia), who slowly begin to care for each other and understand each other's viewpoint while imprisoned together in a South American prison. It is stark, violent, and daring. Rated R for profanity, violence, and suggested sex. 1985; 119m.

KITCHEN TOTO, THE ★★★★
DIR: Harry Hook. **CAST:** Bob Peck, Phyllis Logan.
Powerful, uncompromising drama about a ten-year-old black boy who becomes hopelessly caught in the middle of racial violence between East African tribesmen and white British colonists in 1952 Kenya. Brilliantly performed and directed. Rated PG; contains violence and nudity. 1988; 90m.

KITTY FOYLE ★★★★½
DIR: Sam Wood. **CAST:** Ginger Rogers, Dennis Morgan, James Craig, Eduardo Ciannelli.
Ginger Rogers won an Oscar for her outstanding performance in this drama. She plays a poor girl who falls in love with a wealthy socialite. 1940; B&W; 107m.

KLUTE ★★★★
DIR: Alan J. Pakula. **CAST:** Jane Fonda, Donald Sutherland, Roy Scheider.
Jane Fonda dominates every frame in this study of a worldly call girl. Her Oscar-winning performance looks into the hidden sides of a prostitute's lifestyle; the dreams, fears, shame, and loneliness of Klute's world are graphically illustrated. Donald Sutherland costars as an out-of-town cop looking for a missing friend. He feels Fonda holds the key to his whereabouts. Rated R. 1971; 114m.

KNIGHT WITHOUT ARMOUR ★★★
DIR: Jacques Feyder. **CAST:** Robert Donat, Marlene Dietrich, Miles Malleson, David Tree.
This melodrama, about a British national caught up in the Russian revolution and his attempts to save aristocrat Marlene Dietrich, is filled with beautiful photography but remains basically a curiosity, one of the few American films to depict communism in the 1930s. Robert Donat is an unassuming, gentle hero. 1937; B&W; 107m.

KNOCK ON ANY DOOR ★★★½
DIR: Nicholas Ray. **CAST:** John Derek, Humphrey Bogart, Susan Perry, Allene Roberts.
Before John Derek became a Svengali for Ursula Andress, Linda Evans, and Bo Derek, he was an actor—and a pretty good one, too, as he proves in this courtroom drama directed by

Nicholas Ray. He's a kid who can't help having gotten into trouble, and Humphrey Bogart is the attorney who attempts to explain his plight to the jury. 1949; B&W; 100m.

KNUTE ROCKNE—ALL AMERICAN ★★★
DIR: Lloyd Bacon. **CAST:** Ronald Reagan, Pat O'Brien, Donald Crisp.

This is an overly sentimental biography of the famous Notre Dame football coach. But if you like football or you want to see Ronald Reagan show off his moves, it could hold your interest. Pat O'Brien has the central role, and he plays it with real gusto. 1940; B&W; 84m.

KOSTAS ★★½
DIR: Paul Cox. **CAST:** Takis Emmanuel, Wendy Hughes.

A tormented Greek-Cypriot tries to find love with an Australian girl in England. Director Paul Cox has created a character study with little depth and too much tedium. Not for the easily bored. Rated R for suggested sex. 1979; 110m.

KRAMER VS. KRAMER ★★★★
DIR: Robert Benton. **CAST:** Dustin Hoffman, Meryl Streep, Jane Alexander, Howard Duff, JoBeth Williams.

Dustin Hoffman and Meryl Streep star in the Academy Award–winning drama about a couple who separate, leaving their only son in the custody of the father, who is a stranger to his child. Just when the father and son have learned to live with each other, the mother fights for custody of the child. *Kramer vs. Kramer* jerks you from tears to laughs and back again—and all the while you're begging for more. Rated PG. 1979; 104m.

L.A. LAW ★★★½
DIR: Gregory Hoblit. **CAST:** Harry Hamlin, Susan Dey, Jimmy Smits, Michael Tucker, Jill Eikenberry, Richard Dysart, Corbin Bernsen, Alan Rachins, Susan Ruttan.

Above-average television movie introduced the cast of characters of the new successful series. Set in a high-powered Los Angeles law firm, *L.A. Law* is both compelling and humorous. A must for fans of the series. 1987; 97m.

LBJ: THE EARLY YEARS ★★★★
DIR: Peter Werner. **CAST:** Randy Quaid, Patti LuPone, Morgan Brittany, Pat Hingle, Kevin McCarthy, Charles Frank.

This superlative made-for-TV movie is the story of Lyndon Johnson from 1934, when he was first entering politics as a congressman's aide, to his swearing-in as president aboard *Air Force One*. Randy Quaid and Patti LuPone as LBJ and Lady Bird are outstanding. 1986; 144m.

LADY CAROLINE LAMB 🦃
DIR: Robert Bolt. **CAST:** Sarah Miles, Richard Chamberlain, John Mills, Laurence Olivier, Ralph Richardson, Margaret Leighton, Jon Finch.

Without shame, this banal film victimizes the wife of an English politician who openly carried on with poet and womanizer Lord Byron. Writer-director Robert Bolt created this fiasco. 1972; 118m.

LADY CHATTERLEY'S LOVER (1959) ★
DIR: Marc Allegret. **CAST:** Danielle Darrieux, Leo Genn, Erno Crisa.

This is a poor cinematic telling of D. H. Lawrence's risqué novel. It concerns the wife of a crippled and impotent mine owner who has an affair with a handsome gamekeeper. It's not very good in any respect. A British-French coproduction. 1959; B&W; 101m.

LADY CHATTERLEY'S LOVER (1981) ★
DIR: Just Jaeckin. **CAST:** Sylvia Kristel, Nicholas Clay.

A beautifully staged, but banal, version of the D. H. Lawrence classic. The sometimes compelling score is the only force to help this creep along. Viewers should compare other, always difficult attempts to portray Lawrence (*Sons and Lovers*, 1963;

Women in Love, 1970). Rated R. 1981; 105m.

LADY FOR A NIGHT ★½
DIR: Leigh Jason. **CAST:** John Wayne, Joan Blondell, Ray Middleton.
John Wayne plays second fiddle to Joan Blondell. She's a saloon singer fighting for a measure of respectability in this release. If you plan to watch it, have some coffee brewed—you'll need it to help you stay awake. 1941; B&W; 87m.

LADY GREY
DIR: Worth Keeter. **CAST:** Ginger Alden.
Ginger Alden, Elvis Presley's girlfriend at the time of his death, stars in this umpteenth version of the story of the woman who makes the long, hard climb to the top of the show-biz ladder, only to lose her soul along the way. It's like *The Lonely Lady* with country music. Made for the southern drive-in circuit, where it should have stayed. Not rated, but an R equivalent for sexual situations. 1980; 100m.

LADY ICE ★½
DIR: Tom Gries. **CAST:** Donald Sutherland, Robert Duvall, Jennifer O'Neill, Patrick Magee.
Donald Sutherland is an investigator for an insurance firm and Jennifer O'Neill is his romantic interest. The catch is that her father is a crook who sells stolen gems. It's a good idea. It's a good cast. It's a below-average screenplay. Rated PG. 1973; 93m.

LADY JANE ★★★½
DIR: Trevor Nunn. **CAST:** Helena Bonham Carter, Cary Elwes, John Wood, Michael Hordern, Jill Bennett, Jane Lapotaire, Sara Kestleman, Patrick Stewart.
Excellent costume political soap opera about Lady Jane Grey, accidental successor to the English throne after the deaths of Henry VIII and his son, Edward VI. Helena Bonham Carter glows as Lady Jane, the strong-willed suffragist who engages in a power struggle with Mary I for the throne of England. Rated PG-13 for adult situations and violence. 1985; 140m.

LADY OF THE HOUSE ★½
DIR: Ralph Nelson, Vincent Sherman. **CAST:** Dyan Cannon, Armand Assante, Zohra Lampert, Susan Tyrrell.
Dyan Cannon stars in this TV dramatization of the life of Sally Stanford, Mayor of Sausalito, California. Cannon gives a better performance than usual, and Armand Assante is even better. Quite a bit of footage was cut from the original TV broadcast, leaving the audience lost between scenes. 1978; 90m.

LADY WINDERMERE'S FAN ★★★★½
DIR: Ernst Lubitsch. **CAST:** Ronald Colman, May McAvoy, Irene Rich.
This is a dynamite version of Oscar Wilde's play. The very enigmatic Mrs. Erlynne comes close to scandalizing all of London society. This is one of Ernst Lubitsch's best silent films. 1925; B&W; 80m.

LAS VEGAS STORY, THE
DIR: Robert Stevenson. **CAST:** Jane Russell, Victor Mature, Vincent Price, Hoagy Carmichael, Jay C. Flippen, Brad Dexter.
Neither the robbery nor the murder it leads to in fast-paced and glittering Las Vegas can give this loser any sort of shine. The acting is so uniformly bad, it's hard to tell who's worse, Jane Russell, Victor Mature or Vincent Price. 1952; B&W; 88m.

LAST ANGRY MAN, THE ★★★½
DIR: Daniel Mann. **CAST:** Paul Muni, David Wayne, Betsy Palmer, Luther Adler, Joby Baker.
Paul Muni, one of Hollywood's most respected actors, gave his final screen performance in this well-made version of Gerald Greene's novel about an aging family doctor in a poor neighborhood of Brooklyn. The sentiment gets a little thick occasionally, but Muni's performance keeps it all watchable. Look for Godfrey Cam-

bridge in a small role. Unrated, but suitable for the whole family. 1959; B&W; 100m.

LAST COMMAND, THE (1928) ★★★★

DIR: Josef von Sternberg. **CAST:** Emil Jannings, William Powell, Evelyn Brent.

German star Emil Jannings's second U.S. film has him portraying a Czarist army commander who flees the Russian revolution to America. Here, he sinks into poverty and winds up as a Hollywood extra. Art imitates life when he is cast to play a Russian general in a film directed by a former revolutionary (and former rival in love). William Powell plays the director, a stiff, unbending sadist bent upon humiliating Jannings. Silent. 1928; B&W; 80m.

LAST DAYS OF POMPEII, THE ★★★

DIR: Ernest B. Schoedsack. **CAST:** Preston Foster, Basil Rathbone, Alan Hale, Louis Calhern.

Roman blacksmith Preston Foster becomes a gladiator after tragedy takes his wife and baby. En route to fortune, he adopts the young son of one of his victims. In Judea, he sees but refuses to help Christ, who cures the boy following serious injury. Touched by Jesus, the boy grows up to help runaway slaves. Tremendous special effects. 1935; B&W; 96m.

LAST DETAIL, THE ★★★★

DIR: Hal Ashby. **CAST:** Jack Nicholson, Otis Young, Randy Quaid, Michael Moriarty, Nancy Allen.

Two veteran Navy men (Jack Nicholson and Otis Young) are assigned to transport a young sailor to the brig for theft. They take pity on the naïve loser (Randy Quaid) and decide to show him one last good time. By opening the youngster's eyes to the previously unknown world around him, their kindness is in danger of backfiring in this drama. Rated R. 1973; 105m.

LAST EMPEROR, THE ★★★★★

DIR: Bernardo Bertolucci. **CAST:** John Lone, Peter O'Toole, Joan Chen, Ying Ruocheng, Victor Wong, Dennis Dun.

An awe-inspiring epic that tells a heartrending, intimate story against a backdrop of spectacle and history. The screenplay by Mark Peploe and director Bernardo Bertolucci dramatizes the life of Pu Yi (John Lone), China's last emperor. When he was taken from his home at the age of 3 to become the all-powerful Qing Emperor, the youngster was ironically condemned to a lifetime of imprisonment. Rated R for suggested sex, nudity, and violence. 1987; 160m.

LAST GAME, THE ★★

DIR: Martin Beck. **CAST:** Howard Segal, Ed L. Grady, Terry Alden, Joan Hotchkis.

Maudlin tale of an attractive and responsible clean-cut college kid who works two jobs, goes to school, and takes care of his blind father while his father dreams that one day his boy will play pro football. Video shoppers could do a lot worse, but this movie is just too banal for recommendation. No MPAA rating, but equal to a PG for sex and profanity. 1980; 107m.

LAST HURRAH, THE ★★★★

DIR: John Ford. **CAST:** Spencer Tracy, Jeffrey Hunter, Dianne Foster, Pat O'Brien, Basil Rathbone, Donald Crisp, James Gleason, Edward Brophy, John Carradine, Wallace Ford, Frank McHugh, Jane Darwell.

Spencer Tracy gives a memorable performance as an Irish-Catholic mayor running for office one last time. Jeffrey Hunter is Tracy's newphew, a cynical reporter who comes to respect the old man's values and integrity. 1958; B&W; 111m.

LAST INNOCENT MAN, THE ★★★★

DIR: Roger Spottiswoode. **CAST:** Ed Harris, Roxanne Hart, David Suchet, Bruce McGill.

When a talented and up-and-coming young district attorney meets a mysterious and beautiful woman in a bar, their ensuing affair entangles him in a web of deceit. This suspenseful courtroom drama provides a number of intriguing plot twists and makes for a delicious combination of action and suspense. Produced by Home Box Office; has brief nudity and sexual situations. 1987; 114m.

LAST MAN STANDING ★★★★

DIR: Damian Lee. **CAST:** Vernon Wells, William Sanderson, Franco Columbu.

Surprisingly good prizefight film in which Vernon Wells plays a down-and-out boxer who attempts to find work outside the ring. The brutality of the fight game is well captured. Rated R for profanity and violence. 1988; 92m.

LAST MILE, THE ★★★

DIR: Sam Bischoff. **CAST:** Preston Foster, Howard Phillips, George E. Stone, Paul Fix.

No-win prison film (based on a then-current stage play) is a claustrophobic foray into death row, where cons talk tough and the audience better listen. This archetypal prison-break melodrama has a quiet dignity that elevates the dialogue between the inmates to high drama. Preston Foster as Killer Miles plays the toughest con in the block and the leader of the break attempt. 1932; B&W; 70m.

LAST OF MRS. LINCOLN, THE ★★★★

DIR: George Schaefer. **CAST:** Julie Harris, Michael Cristofer, Robby Benson, Patrick Duffy, Denver Pyle, Priscilla Morrill.

Julie Harris shines in her portrayal of Mary Todd Lincoln during the last seventeen years of her life. Bearing enormous debts accumulated during her stay in the White House and denied a pension by the Senate because of her Southern heritage, she eventually falls into penury and insanity. Michael Cristofer and Robby Benson play the two surviving Lincoln sons. Made for television. 1984; 117m.

LAST OF PHILIP BANTER, THE ★★½

DIR: Herve Hachuel. **CAST:** Scott Paulin, Irene Miracle, Gregg Henry, Kate Vernon, Tony Curtis.

Scott Paulin gives a stunning performance in this lurid psychodrama. He's a self-destructive alcoholic whose life degenerates into madness after the discovery of some mysterious manuscripts. Rated R; contains profanity and violence. 1986; 100m.

LAST PICTURE SHOW, THE ★★★★★

DIR: Peter Bogdanovich. **CAST:** Timothy Bottoms, Ben Johnson, Jeff Bridges, Cloris Leachman, Cybill Shepherd, Randy Quaid.

Outstanding adaptation of Larry McMurtry's novel about a boy's rites of passage in a small Texas town during the 1950s. Virtually all the performances are excellent due to the deft direction of Peter Bogdanovich, who assured his fame with this picture. Ben Johnson, as a pool hall owner, and Cloris Leachman, as a lonely wife, deservedly won Oscars for their supporting performances. Rated R for brief nudity and adult situations. 1971; B&W; 118m.

LAST SUMMER ★★½

DIR: Frank Perry. **CAST:** Richard Thomas, Barbara Hershey, Bruce Davison, Cathy Burns, Ralph Waite, Conrad Bain.

Engrossing tale of teen desires, frustrations, and fears, played out in disturbingly dark fashion. Bruce Davison and Cathy Burns are especially memorable in unusual roles. Rated R. 1969; 97m.

LAST TANGO IN PARIS ★★★

DIR: Bernardo Bertolucci. **CAST:** Marlon Brando, Maria Schneider, Jean-Pierre Léaud.

A middle-aged man (Marlon Brando) and a young French girl (Maria Schneider) have a doomed love affair. This pretentious sex melodrama was mainly notable for being banned when it first came out. Rated R for sex. 1972; 129m.

LAST TEMPTATION OF CHRIST, THE ★★★

DIR: Martin Scorsese. **CAST:** Willem Dafoe, Harvey Keitel, Barbara Hershey, Harry Dean Stanton, David Bowie, Verna Bloom, Andre Gregory.

Martin Scorsese's well-intentioned adaptation of Nikos Kazantzakis's controversial novel suffers from the filmmaker's excesses at some times, as well as the quirks of screenwriter Paul Schrader. There are some unnecessary scenes of nudity and simulated sex. Nevertheless, what emerges is a heartfelt work that has some moments of true power—especially when the story's reluctant savior (Willem Dafoe) accepts his divine nature and begins to perform miracles. Rated R for nudity and violence. 1988; 164m.

LAST TIME I SAW PARIS, THE ★★★

DIR: Richard Brooks. **CAST:** Van Johnson, Elizabeth Taylor, Donna Reed, Walter Pidgeon, Eva Gabor.

The Metro-Goldwyn-Mayer glitter shows clearly in this dramatic account of post–World War II Paris. This Paris, though, is filled with divorce, domestic quarrels, and jaded lives. Donna Reed gives the best performance. 1954; 116m.

LAST TYCOON, THE ★★★

DIR: Elia Kazan. **CAST:** Robert De Niro, Robert Mitchum, Tony Curtis, Jeanne Moreau, Jack Nicholson, Donald Pleasence, Peter Strauss, Ray Milland, Ingrid Boulting, Dana Andrews, John Carradine.

Tantalizing yet frustrating, this slow-moving attempt to film F. Scott Fitzgerald's last (and unfinished) book is a blockbuster conglomeration of talent at all levels, but fails to really capture the imagination of the average film-goer and appears to be a somewhat confusing collection of scenes and confrontations. Robert DeNiro as Monroe Starr, the sickly motion picture magnate and the "last tycoon" of the story, gives another fine, understated performance. 1976; 125m.

LAST WINTER, THE ★

DIR: Riki Shelach. **CAST:** Kathleen Quinlan, Yona Elian, Stephen Macht.

Kathleen Quinlan and Yona Elian are wives of Israeli soldiers missing in action during the Yom Kippur War of 1973. Over the prospect of both women becoming widows, their friendship grows intense, with hints of homosexuality. 1984; 92m.

LAST WORD, THE ★★★

DIR: Roy Boulting. **CAST:** Richard Harris, Karen Black, Martin Landau, Dennis Christopher, Biff McGuire, Christopher Guest, Penelope Milford, Michael Pataki.

When police try to evict him and his family from a run-down apartment building, inventor Danny Travis (Richard Harris) takes a police officer hostage. His goal is to get the attention of the newspapers so that he can expose the governor's crooked real-estate racket and save his home. Likable comedy-drama in the Frank Capra mold. Rated PG. 1979; 105m.

LATINO ★½

DIR: Haskell Wexler. **CAST:** Robert Beltran, Annette Cardona, Tony Plana.

Master cinematographer Haskell Wexler tries his hand at writing and directing in this story of a Chicago Green Beret who questions the morality of the activities required of him in the Nicaraguan war. This is a fairly routine war story, with the exception of the protagonist being a Latin American. 1985; 108m.

LAUGHING AT LIFE ★★½

DIR: Ford Beebe. **CAST:** Victor McLaglen, Regis Toomey, Tully Marshall, Noah Beery Sr.

Fleeing the police, gun runner Victor McLaglen deserts his family to knock about the world. Years later he meets his son. For McLaglen, this drama of sacrifice was practically drawn from his life before he took up acting. Two years later, he won an Oscar for best actor in *The Informer*. 1933; B&W; 68m.

LAZARUS SYNDROME, THE ★★
DIR: Jerry Thorpe. **CAST:** Louis Gossett Jr., Ronald Hunter, E. G. Marshall, Sheila Frazier.

When the illicit practices of a hospital administrator drive another practitioner to distraction, he joins forces with a patient who just happens to be a journalist in order to expose the bad guy and his lackeys. Made for television. 1976; 90m.

LEAN ON ME ★★★★
DIR: John G. Avildsen. **CAST:** Morgan Freeman, Robert Guillaume, Beverly Todd.

Morgan Freeman gives a superb performance as real-life high-school principal Joe Clark, who almost singlehandedly converted Eastside High in Paterson, New Jersey, from a den of drugs, gangs, and corruption into an effective place of learning. Director John Avildsen has created a feel-good movie that conveys a timely message. Rated PG-13 for profanity and violence. 1989; 104m.

LEATHER BOYS, THE ★★
DIR: Sidney J. Furie. **CAST:** Rita Tushingham, Dudley Sutton, Colin Campbell.

Considered adult and controversial when first released in England, this slice-of-life drama about teenagers who marry for sex and settle into drab existences doesn't carry the weight it once did. Rather depressing, this film is an interesting look at life in London in the early 1960s, but it has dated badly. 1963; B&W; 108m.

LEAVE 'EM LAUGHING ★★★★½
DIR: Jackie Cooper. **CAST:** Mickey Rooney, Anne Jackson, Red Buttons, William Windom, Elisha Cook Jr.

Mickey Rooney is outstanding portraying real-life Chicago clown Jack Thum. Thum and his wife (played by Anne Jackson) cared for dozens of unwanted children. When Thum realizes he has terminal cancer, he falls apart and his wife must help him regain his inner strength and deal with reality. A real tearjerker! Made for TV, this is unrated. 1981; 104m.

LEFT FOR DEAD
DIR: Murray Markowitz. **CAST:** Elke Sommer, Donald Pilon, Chuck Shamata, George Toullatos.

Contrived murder drama, staged in a series of flashbacks. All in all, a collection of reprehensible characters involved in a story that often makes no sense. Not rated, but contains violence, profanity, sex, and nudity. 1978; 88m.

LEGEND OF VALENTINO ★★
DIR: Melville Shavelson. **CAST:** Franco Nero, Suzanne Pleshette, Judd Hirsch, Lesley Ann Warren, Milton Berle, Yvette Mimieux, Harold J. Stone.

TV movie released close to the fiftieth anniversary of the fabled actor's death adheres to some facts concerning the archetypal Latin lover, but still presents an unsatisfying and incomplete portrait. But this film still leaves too many questions either unanswered or glossed over. Not too bad for a TV movie. 1975; 100m.

LENNY ★★★★★
DIR: Bob Fosse. **CAST:** Dustin Hoffman, Valerie Perrine, Jan Miner.

Bob Fosse brilliantly directed this stark biography of self-destructive, controversial persecuted comic talent Lenny Bruce. Dustin Hoffman captures all those contrary emotions in his portrayal of the late 1950s and '60s stand-up comedian. Valerie Perrine is a treasure in her low-key role as Bruce's stripper wife. Rated R. 1974; B&W; 112m.

LEOPARD IN THE SNOW ★★
DIR: Gerry O'Hara. **CAST:** Keir Dullea, Susan Penhaligon, Kenneth More, Billie Whitelaw, Jeremy Kemp.

Silly romance between a spoiled rich girl and a maimed former race-car driver. The dialogue is slow and some scenes lead nowhere. The pluses include the driver's pet leopard and his butler Bolt (Jeremy Kemp). Rated PG for one scene in which our lovebirds *almost* become passionate. 1977; 89m.

LES MISERABLES (1935) ★★★★
DIR: Richard Boleslawski. **CAST:** Fredric March, Charles Laughton, Cedric Hardwicke, Florence Eldridge.

The most watchable and best acted of the many versions of Victor Hugo's story of good and evil. Fredric March is Hugo's nineteenth-century common man. He steals a loaf of bread in order to survive, only to undergo a lifetime of torment. Charles Laughton is absolutely frightening as the personification of an uncaring legal system. 1935; B&W; 108m.

LES MISERABLES (1978) ★★★½
DIR: Glenn Jordan. **CAST:** Richard Jordan, Anthony Perkins, John Gielgud, Cyril Cusack, Flora Robson, Claude Dauphin.

Lavish television version of Victor Hugo's classic tale of a petty thief's attempt to forget his past only to be hounded through the years by a relentless police inspector. Richard Jordan as the thief turned mayor and Anthony Perkins as his tormentor are extremely good. 1978; 150m.

LESS THAN ZERO
DIR: Marek Kanievska. **CAST:** Andrew McCarthy, Jami Gertz, Robert Downey Jr., James Spader, Tony Bill, Nicholas Pryor, Michael Bowen.

There has never been a more aptly named movie. A movie meant to illuminate the meaninglessness of Los Angeles's post-college-crowd cool becomes a real yawner. Character development goes no deeper than Andrew McCarthy's constant smirks. Rated R for violence and profanity. 1987; 100m.

LET IT ROCK ★½
DIR: Roland Klick. **CAST:** Dennis Hopper, Terrance Robay, David Hess.

This ludicrous behind-the-scenes view of the music business features Dennis Hopper as a manic rock-music promoter who turns pop-star hopeful Terrance Robay's bid for fame into a nightmare. Rated R for nudity, profanity, and violence. 1988; 75m.

LET'S GET HARRY ★★½
DIR: Alan Smithee. **CAST:** Robert Duvall, Gary Busey, Mark Harmon, Glenn Frey, Michael Schoeffling.

When an American (Mark Harmon) is kidnapped during a South American revolution, a group of his friends decide that they are going to bring him home. When the government doesn't respond, they hire a soldier of fortune (Robert Duvall) to lead them into the jungles of Colombia where, against all odds, they fight to bring Harry home. Rated R for violence and language. 1986; 98m.

LETTER, THE ★★★★
DIR: William Wyler. **CAST:** Bette Davis, Herbert Marshall, James Stephenson.

Bette Davis stars in this screen adaptation of Somerset Maugham's play as the coldly calculating wife of a rubber plantation owner (Herbert Marshall) in Malaya. In a fit of pique, she shoots her lover and concocts elaborate lies to protect herself. With tension mounting all the way, we wonder if her evil ways will eventually lead to her downfall. 1940; B&W; 95m.

LETTER OF INTRODUCTION ★★★★
DIR: John Stahl. **CAST:** Adolphe Menjou, Andrea Leeds, Edgar Bergen and Charlie McCarthy, George Murphy, Eve Arden, Rita Johnson, Ernest Cossart, Ann Sheridan.

An essentially enjoyable melodrama, *Letter of Introduction* is the story of a young actress (Andrea Leeds) who seeks out the advice of an old actor (Adolphe Menjou). The aging star encourages her in her various endeavors. The relationship between the two lead characters is so real, so warm that it carries the film. 1938; B&W; 100m.

LETTERS TO AN UNKNOWN LOVER ★★★
DIR: Peter Duffell. **CAST:** Cherie Lunghi, Yves Beneyton, Mathilda May.
A soldier who has been carrying on a romance through the mails with a Frenchwoman he has never met dies. When his friend escapes from a Nazi prison camp, he pretends to be the dead man in order to get the woman and her sister to hide him. This engrossing tale, a French and British co-production, is unrated; it contains some nudity and sexual situations. 1985; 100m.

LIANNA ★★★★
DIR: John Sayles. **CAST:** Linda Griffiths, Jane Halloren, Jon De Vries, Jo Henderson.
The problem with most motion pictures about gays is they always seem to be more concerned with sex than love. In comparison, this film, written and directed by John Sayles stands as a remarkable achievement. About a married housewife named Lianna (Linda Griffiths) who decides to have an affair with, and eventually move in with, another woman (Jane Halloren), it is a sensitive study of one woman's life and loves. Rated R for nudity, sex, and profanity. 1983; 110m.

LIAR'S MOON ★★★½
DIR: David Fisher. **CAST:** Matt Dillon, Cindy Fisher, Christopher Connelly, Hoyt Axton, Yvonne De Carlo, Susan Tyrrell.
Two young lovers encounter unusually hostile resistance from their parents. Their elopement produces many of the expected problems faced by youths just starting out: limited finances, inexperience and incompatibility. Rated PG for language. 1983; 106m.

LIBERATION OF L. B. JONES, THE ★
DIR: William Wyler. **CAST:** Lola Falana, Roscoe Lee Browne, Lee J. Cobb, Lee Majors, Barbara Hershey.
In what starts as a movie effort to portray race relations gone asunder, all we are given is cardboard cutout stereotypes and a confusing plot. This story, of a wealthy black man who is deluded into divorcing his wife (Lola Falana) because of her believed infidelity with a white cop, never gains our sympathy or interest. Rated R. 1970; 102m.

LIES ★★★★
DIR: Ken Wheat, Jim Wheat. **CAST:** Ann Dusenberry, Gail Strickland, Bruce Davison, Clu Gulager, Terence Knox, Bert Remsen.
Ann Dusenberry plays a starving actress who gets sucked into a complicated and treacherous plan to gain the inheritance of a rich patient in a mental hospital. The plot is complicated and the good acting balances the intensity. The best part: a great performance by Gail Strickland, who plays a character you'll love to hate. Rated R for violence, sex, nudity, and profanity. 1986; 93m.

LIFE AND ASSASSINATION OF THE KINGFISH, THE ★★★
DIR: Robert Collins. **CAST:** Edward Asner, Nicholas Pryor.
A docudrama chronicling the life of flamboyant Louisiana politician Huey Long (Edward Asner) from his early days through stints as governor and senator. Told as a flashback, during the time Long lay dying from an assassin's bullet, this is an insightful look at an unforgettable time in U.S. history. 1976; 96m.

LIFE AND DEATH OF COLONEL BLIMP, THE ★★★★★
DIR: Michael Powell, Emeric Pressburger. **CAST:** Roger Livesey, Deborah Kerr, Anton Walbrook.
A truly superb film chronicling the life and times of a staunch for-king-and-country British soldier. Sentimentally celebrating the human spirit, it opens during World War II and unfolds through a series of flashbacks that reach as far back as the Boer War. Roger Livesey is excellent in the title

role. Deborah Kerr portrays the four women in his life across four decades with charm and insight. Definitely a keeper. 1943; 163m.

LIFE OF EMILE ZOLA, THE ★★★★

DIR: William Dieterle. **CAST:** Paul Muni, Joseph Schildkraut, Gale Sondergaard, Gloria Holden, Donald Crisp, Louis Calhern.

Paul Muni is excellent in the title role of the nineteenth-century novelist who championed the cause of the wrongly accused Captain Dreyfus (Joseph Schildkraut). A lavish production! 1937; B&W; 93m.

LIFEBOAT ★★★½

DIR: Alfred Hitchcock. **CAST:** Tallulah Bankhead, John Hodiak, William Bendix, Walter Slezak, Henry Hull, Cañada Lee, Hume Cronyn, Heather Angel.

A microcosm of American society, survivors of a World War II torpedoing, adrift in a lifeboat, nearly come a cropper when they take a Nazi aboard. Dumbly dismissed as an artistic failure by most critics, it has some ridiculous flaws, but is nonetheless an interesting and engrossing film. Tunnel-voiced Tallulah Bankhead is tops in this sea-going *Grand Hotel*. Look for Hitchcock's pictorial trademark in a newspaper. 1944; B&W; 96m.

LIFEGUARD ★★½

DIR: Daniel Petrie. **CAST:** Sam Elliott, Anne Archer, Kathleen Quinlan, Parker Stevenson, Stephen Young.

After his fifteen-year high-school reunion, Sam Elliott begins to feel twinges of fear and guilt. How long can he go on being a lifeguard? Shouldn't he be making the move into a career with a future? Shouldn't he be chasing the almighty dollar like everyone else? The film is likable and easygoing, like its star. If your interest starts to drift, Elliott's charisma will pull you back. Rated PG. 1976; 96m.

LIGHT OF DAY ★★½

DIR: Paul Schrader. **CAST:** Michael J. Fox, Gena Rowlands, Joan Jett, Jason Miller, Michael McKean.

Director Paul Schrader tends toward the perverse and seedy, and in *Light of Day* the dregs lure him once again. The object of his obsessive gaze is the dead-end lives of a Cleveland bar band. There's Michael J. Fox as the guitarist willing to compromise in life for some stability. And there's his nihilistic sister (Joan Jett), the leader of the group who says that the beat of the music is all-important. 1987; 107m.

LIGHTNING OVER WATER ★★★½

DIR: Wim Wenders. **CAST:** Nicholas Ray, Wim Wenders.

This haunting film chronicles the final days in the life of American film director Nicholas Ray, whose movies include *Rebel Without a Cause*, *Johnny Guitar*, and *In a Lonely Place*. Wim Wenders presents a warm and gentle portrait of the director as he slowly dies from cancer. Filmed on location in Ray's loft in New York City. Poignant and unforgettable. 1980; 91m.

LIGHTSHIP, THE ★★

DIR: Jerzy Skolimowski. **CAST:** Robert Duvall, Klaus Maria Brandauer, Michael Lyndon.

The chief interest in this allegorical suspense drama is in seeing Robert Duvall play an over-the-top villain. But the story itself—a trio of sadistic bank robbers hijack a floating, anchored lighthouse and the ship's pacifist captain (Klaus Maria Brandauer) tries to stop his crew from fighting back—is short on suspense. Rated R. 1986; 90m.

LILIES OF THE FIELD ★★★★

DIR: Ralph Nelson. **CAST:** Sidney Poitier, Lilia Skala.

Sidney Poitier won an Academy Award for his portrayal of a handyman who happens upon a group of nuns who have fled from East Germany and finds himself building a chapel for them. With little or no build-up, the movie went on to become a big hit. 1963; B&W; 93m.

LILITH ★★
DIR: Robert Rossen. **CAST:** Warren Beatty, Jean Seberg, Peter Fonda, Kim Hunter, Anne Meacham, Jessica Walter, Gene Hackman.

This is an intriguing, somber, frequently indecipherable journey into the darker depths of the human psyche. Warren Beatty is a young psychiatric therapist at a mental institute who falls in love with a beautiful schizophrenic patient (Jean Seberg), with tragic results. Visually impressive, it remains dramatically frustrating due to its ambiguous blending of sanity and madness. 1964; B&W; 114m.

LINDBERGH KIDNAPPING CASE, THE ★★★
DIR: Buzz Kulik. **CAST:** Cliff De Young, Anthony Hopkins, Joseph Cotten, Denise Alexander, Sian Barbara Allen, Martin Balsam, Peter Donat, Dean Jagger, Walter Pidgeon.

Still another look at one of this century's most famous and fascinating tragedies, this made-for-television version is above average. Anthony Hopkins rates four stars as Bruno Hauptmann, the man convicted and executed for the crime. 1976; 150m.

LION IN WINTER, THE ★★★★½
DIR: Anthony Harvey. **CAST:** Katharine Hepburn, Peter O'Toole, Anthony Hopkins, John Castle, Timothy Dalton.

Acerbic retelling of the clash of wits between England's King Henry II (Peter O'Toole) and Eleanor of Aquitaine (Katharine Hepburn), adapted by James Goldman from his Broadway play. Hepburn won an Oscar for her part, and it's quite well played. The story's extended power struggle rages back and forth, with Henry and Eleanor striking sparks throughout. Rated PG. 1968; 135m.

LISTEN TO ME ★
DIR: Douglas Day Stewart. **CAST:** Kirk Cameron, Jami Gertz, Roy Scheider, Anthony Zerbe.

In yet another of the endless series of subpar variations on the *Rocky* formula, Kirk Cameron and Jami Gertz play members of a college debating team who take time out to find romance. Roy Scheider, co-starring as their coach, deserves a better script. Rated R. 1989; 107m.

LITTLE ANNIE ROONEY ★★★
DIR: William Beaudine. **CAST:** Mary Pickford, Spec O'Donnell, Hugh Fay.

The title character is a teen-aged street kid in braids, but America's Sweetheart, Mary Pickford, who played her, was 32 at the time. Pickford gets away with it—as she did in many of her films. As the daughter of a widowed New York cop, Annie keeps house, runs a street gang, and anguishes when her father is killed and her boyfriend is wrongly accused of the crime. Silent. 1925; B&W; 60m.

LITTLE BOY LOST ★★★
DIR: George Seaton. **CAST:** Bing Crosby, Claude Dauphin, Nicole Maurey.

Newspaperman Bing Crosby can't tell which kid is his as he searches for his son in a French orphanage following World War II. Get out the Kleenex. 1953; 95m.

LITTLE DORRIT ★★★★★
DIR: Christine Edzard. **CAST:** Alec Guinness, Derek Jacobi, Sarah Pickering, Joan Greenwood, Roshan Seth.

Told in two parts "Nobody's Fault" and "Little Dorritt's Story," this is a splendid six-hour production of Charles Dickens's most popular novel of his time. Derek Jacobi plays Arthur Clennam, a businessman whose life is forever changed when he meets the good-hearted heroine of the title (newcomer Sarah Pickering). An epic of human suffering, compassion, and triumph. Rated G. 1988; 356m.

LITTLE FOXES, THE ★★★★
DIR: William Wyler. **CAST:** Bette Davis, Herbert Marshall, Teresa Wright, Richard Carlson, Dan Duryea.
The ever-fascinating, ever-unique Bette Davis dominates this outstanding rendering of controversial playwright Lillian Hellman's drama of amoral family greed and corruption down South. Davis's ruthless matriarch, Regina, is the ultimate Edwardian bitch, for whom murder by inaction is not beyond the pale when it comes to achieving her desires. 1941; B&W; 116m.

LITTLE GLORIA...HAPPY AT LAST ★★★★
DIR: Waris Hussein. **CAST:** Martin Balsam, Bette Davis, Michael Gross, Lucy Gutteridge, Glynis Johns, Angela Lansbury, Maureen Stapleton.
This TV miniseries focuses on the unhappy childhood of Gloria Vanderbilt and the tug-of-war surrounding her custody trial in 1934. It's hard not to pitty the poor little rich girl as portrayed in William Haney's bestseller and adapted in this teleplay. Definitely worth a watch! 1982; 208m.

LITTLE LADIES OF THE NIGHT ★½
DIR: Marvin J. Chomsky. **CAST:** Linda Purl, David Soul, Louis Gossett Jr., Carolyn Jones, Paul Burke, Dorothy Malone.
Linda Purl plays a teenage runaway who is forced into a life of prostitution. When a vice cop tries to help her, he realizes her parents don't want her back. TV-movie sexploitation. 1977; 100m.

LITTLE LORD FAUNTLEROY (1936) ★★★★
DIR: John Cromwell. **CAST:** Freddie Bartholomew, C. Aubrey Smith, Dolores Costello, Jessie Ralph, Mickey Rooney, Guy Kibbee.
Far from a syrupy-sweet child movie, this is the affecting tale of a long-lost American heir (Freddie Bartholomew) brought to live with a hard-hearted British lord (C. Aubrey Smith) whose icy manner is warmed by the cheerful child. 1936; B&W; 98m.

LITTLE MEN ★½
DIR: Norman Z. McLeod. **CAST:** Jack Oakie, Kay Francis, George Bancroft, Jimmy Lydon, Ann Gillis, William Demarest, Sterling Holloway, Isabel Jewell.
Louisa May Alcott's classic of childhood turned into a travesty. Poor writing and second-rate histrionic endeavors by mediocre cast stifled the charm and sentiment of the novel, making the production one of cheap jokes and dialogue from the Ice Age. Film was a box-office loser. 1940; B&W; 84m.

LITTLE MINISTER, THE ★★★½
DIR: Richard Wallace. **CAST:** Katharine Hepburn, Donald Crisp, John Beal, Andy Clyde.
An early effort in the career of Katharine Hepburn. This charming story, of a proper Scottish minister who falls in love with what he believes is a gypsy girl, is not just for Hepburn fans. 1934; B&W; 110m.

LITTLE WOMEN (1933) ★★★★½
DIR: George Cukor. **CAST:** Katharine Hepburn, Spring Byington, Joan Bennett, Frances Dee, Jean Parker.
George Cukor's *Little Women* is far and away the best of the four film versions of Louisa May Alcott's timeless story of the March family. Katharine Hepburn is excellent as the tomboyish Jo. 1933; B&W; 115m.

LITTLE WOMEN (1949) ★★½
DIR: Mervyn LeRoy. **CAST:** June Allyson, Peter Lawford, Elizabeth Taylor, Mary Astor, Janet Leigh, Margaret O'Brien.
Textbook casting and intelligent performances make this a safe second rendering of Louisa May Alcott's famous story of maturing young women finding romance in the nineteenth century. Technicolor is an enhancement, but the 1933 original is vastly superior. 1949; 121m.

LIVING PROOF: THE HANK WILLIAMS, JR., STORY
DIR: Dick Lowry. **CAST:** Richard Thomas, Clu Gulager, Allyn Ann McLerie.

John-Boy gone bad. Richard Thomas is totally unconvincing as the troubled country-western star, whose life is dominated by the memory of his infamous father. A miscast made-for-television stink bomb. 1983; 100m.

LOLITA ★★★
DIR: Stanley Kubrick. **CAST:** James Mason, Sue Lyon, Shelley Winters, Peter Sellers.

A man's unconventional obsession for a "nymphet" is the basis for this bizarre satire. James Mason and Sue Lyon are the naughty pair in this film, which caused quite a stir in the 1960s but seems fairly tame today. 1962; B&W; 152m.

LONELY HEARTS ★★★★½
DIR: Paul Cox. **CAST:** Norman Kaye, Wendy Hughes, Julia Blake.

A funny, touching Australian romantic comedy about two offbeat characters who fall in love. Peter (Norman Kaye) is a 50-year-old mama's boy who doesn't know what to do with his life when his mother dies. Then he meets Patricia (Wendy Hughes), a woman who has never had a life of her own. It's a warmly human delight. Rated R. 1981; 95m.

LONELY LADY, THE
DIR: Peter Sasdy. **CAST:** Pia Zadora, Lloyd Bochner, Bibi Besch.

Adapted from the novel by Harold Robbins, this film stars Pia Zadora as an aspiring writer who is used and abused by every man she meets. You never believe it for a moment. As a result, it's a hilarious mixture of bad dialogue, campy performances, and outrageous situations. Rated R for sex, violence, nudity, and profanity. 1983; 92m.

LONELY PASSION OF JUDITH HEARNE, THE ★★★★
DIR: Jack Clayton. **CAST:** Maggie Smith, Bob Hoskins, Marie Kean, Wendy Hiller.

Maggie Smith gives a superb, seamless performance as Judith Hearne, an Irish spinster in the 1950s sequestered from the carnal world by plainness and Catholicism. When she meets an Americanized Irishman (brilliantly portrayed by Bob Hoskins, New York accent and all), parts of her character's dormant personality spring to life. Rated R 1987; 115m.

LONELYHEARTS ★★
DIR: Vincent J. Donahue. **CAST:** Montgomery Clift, Robert Ryan, Myrna Loy, Maureen Stapleton, Dolores Hart, Jackie Coogan, Mike Kellin, Frank Overton, Onslow Stevens.

A perfect example of how Hollywood can ruin great material. Montgomery Clift is tortured as only he could be, Robert Ryan is cynical, and Maureen Stapleton is pitifully sex-starved in this disappointing adaptation of Nathaniel West's brilliant novel about an agony columnist who gets too caught up in a correspondent's life. Baloney! 1958; B&W; 101m.

LONG AGO TOMORROW ★★★
DIR: Bryan Forbes. **CAST:** Malcolm McDowell, Nanette Newman, Georgia Brown, Gerald Sim, Bernard Lee, Michael Flanders.

Malcolm McDowell stars in this in-depth story about an arrogant soccer player who is paralyzed by a mysterious disease. In an attempt to escape from the sympathy of friends and family, he admits himself to a countryside home for the disabled, where a pretty young woman who shares the same disability is able to help him adapt. McDowell keeps the plot alive with a very believable performance. Rated PG. 1970; 116m.

LONG DAY'S JOURNEY INTO NIGHT (1962) ★★★★★
DIR: Sidney Lumet. **CAST:** Katharine Hepburn, Ralph Richardson, Jason Robards Jr., Dean Stockwell.

This superb film was based on Eugene O'Neill's play about a troubled turn-of-the-century New England family. Katharine Hepburn is brilliant as the drug-addict wife. Ralph Richardson is equally good as her husband, a self-centered actor. One of their sons is an alcoholic, while the other is dying of tuberculosis. Although depressing, it is an unforgettable viewing experience. 1962; B&W; 136m.

LONG DAY'S JOURNEY INTO NIGHT (1987) ★★★★
DIR: Jonathan Miller. **CAST:** Jack Lemmon, Bethel Leslie, Peter Gallagher, Kevin Spacey.

Excellent television adaptation of Eugene O'Neill's harrowing drama about a New England family in deep crisis. The stunning direction by Jonathan Miller makes this almost the equal of the 1962 film. Jack Lemmon turns in another powerful performance. Recommended for mature audiences. 1987; 169m.

LONG GONE ★★★★
DIR: Martin Davidson. **CAST:** William L. Petersen, Virginia Madsen, Henry Gibson.

This very likable film follows the exploits of a minor-league baseball team and their manager (William Petersen) during one magical season in Florida during the early Fifties. Insightful HBO-produced movie is not unlike *Bull Durham* in that both take a loving look at Americas's favorite pastime while dissecting other societal concerns. 1987; 110m.

LONG HOT SUMMER, THE ★★★½
DIR: Stuart Cooper. **CAST:** Don Johnson, Jason Robards Jr., Cybil Shepherd, Judith Ivey, Ava Gardner, Wings Hauser.

Don Johnson is a drifter who comes to a small Southern town and upsets the routine of a family clan headed by patriarch Jason Robards. As well as being a moving, steamy tale of lust and greed, it also shows that director Stuart Cooper can get above-average performances from the likes of Johnson and Cybill Shepherd. This telemovie was originally shown in two parts. 1985; 208m.

LONG VOYAGE HOME, THE ★★★★½
DIR: John Ford. **CAST:** John Wayne, Barry Fitzgerald, Thomas Mitchell, Mildred Natwick.

Life in the merchant marine as experienced and recalled by Nobel Prize–winning playwright Eugene O'Neill. The hopes and dreams and comradeship of a group of seamen beautifully blended in a gripping, moving account of men, a ship, and the ever-enigmatic sea. The major characters are superbly drawn by those playing them. Definitely a must-see, and see-again, film. Classic. 1940; B&W; 105m.

LONGSHOT ★
DIR: E. W. Swackhamer. **CAST:** Leif Garrett, Ralph Seymour, Zoe Chaveau, Linda Manz.

A promising soccer star turns down a scholarship at a prestigious university in order to attend the football championships in Europe. He falls in love with a French girl who is incredibly rich and sweet. Silly and soporific. 1981; 100m.

LOOK BACK IN ANGER (1958) ★★★★½
DIR: Tony Richardson. **CAST:** Richard Burton, Claire Bloom.

This riveting look into one of the "angry young men" of the 1950s has Richard Burton and Claire Bloom at their best. Burton exposes the torment and frustration these men felt toward their country and private life with more vividness than you may want to deal with, but if you're looking for a realistic recreation of the period, look no further. 1958; B&W; 99m.

LOOK BACK IN ANGER (1980) ★★

DIR: Lindsay Anderson. **CAST:** Malcolm McDowell, Lisa Banes, Fran Brill, Robert Brill, Raymond Hardie.

Jimmy Porter is a failed trumpet player and lower-class intellectual who turns his dashed hopes into a symphony of verbal abuse played upon his wife and best friend. McDowell serves up a Porter who is smug and easy to despise, but his portrayal lacks the powerful rage of Richard Burton in the 1958 film version of this mid-Fifties stage smash. 1980; 101m.

LOOKING FOR MR. GOODBAR ★

DIR: Richard Brooks. **CAST:** Diane Keaton, Tuesday Weld, Richard Gere, LeVar Burton, Richard Kiley, Tom Berenger.

A strong performance by star Diane Keaton can't save this dismal character study about a woman drawn to sleazy sex and lowlifes. Tuesday Weld and Richard Gere also are memorable in support, but director Richard Brooks obviously intended to revolt the audience through the main character's aimless immorality and untimely end—and did so to the detriment of his picture. Rated R. 1977; 135m.

LOOKING GLASS WAR, THE ★★

DIR: Frank R. Pierson. **CAST:** Christopher Jones, Pia Degermark, Ralph Richardson, Anthony Hopkins.

This plodding adaptation of John Le Carré's espionage novel about a Pole sent to get the scam on a rocket in East Berlin is replete with spy slang and the usual covert and clandestine operations. But it never gets off the ground. Most of the acting is as wooden as bleacher seating. Where's Smiley when we need him? Rated PG. 1970; 106m.

LORD OF THE FLIES ★★★★

DIR: Peter Brook. **CAST:** James Aubrey, Hugh Edwards, Tom Chapin.

William Golding's grim allegory comes to the screen in a near-perfect adaptation helmed by British stage director Peter Brook. English schoolboys, stranded on an island and left to their own devices, gradually revert to the savage cruelty of wild animals. Visually hypnotic and powerful, something you just can't tear your eyes away from. The cast is outstanding, and what the film fails to take from Golding's symbolism, it compensates for with raw energy. 1963; B&W; 91m.

LORDS OF DISCIPLINE, THE ★★★½

DIR: Franc Roddam. **CAST:** David Keith, Robert Prosky, G. D. Spradlin, Rick Rossovich.

A thought-provoking film, *Lords* contains many emotionally charged and well-played scenes. David Keith stars as a student at a military academy who puts his life in danger by helping a black cadet being hazed by The Ten, a secret group of white students dedicated to the "purification" of the campus. Rated R for profanity, nudity, and violence. 1983; 102m.

LORDS OF FLATBUSH, THE ★★½

DIR: Stephen F. Verona, Martin Davidson. **CAST:** Perry King, Sylvester Stallone, Henry Winkler, Paul Mace, Susan Blakely.

Of all the leads, only Paul Mace didn't go on to bigger things. A stocky Sylvester Stallone shows promise as a character actor. Perry King is dashing. Susan Blakely is lovely. And Henry Winkler is particularly winning, playing an unexaggerated Fonzie-type character. The film provides a fairly satisfying blend of toughness and sentimentality, humor and pathos, as it tells a story of coming of age in 1950s New York. Rated PG. 1974; 88m.

LORNA ★★½
DIR: Russ Meyer. **CAST:** Lorna Maitland.

A sexually frustrated backwoods wife finds satisfaction with an escaped convict while her husband is away at work. Adult director Russ Meyer's first "serious" movie after his earlier nudie films, this atmospheric morality play will interest his fans, but may seem campy to some and dull to others. Unrated, it includes brief nudity and sexual situations. 1964; B&W; 78m.

LOST! ★★★½
DIR: Peter Rowe. **CAST:** Kenneth Walsh, Helen Shaver, Michael Hogan.

Even though it contains no nudity or violence, this is a movie that you should be careful about letting children see. Based on a true incident, it tells of three people adrift in the Pacific Ocean on an overturned boat. Complicating the efforts of the others to survive is the fact that one, a religious zealot, feels that their plight is a test of God, and that they should do nothing to try to help themselves. Not rated. 1986; 94m.

LOST ANGELS ★★★★
DIR: Hugh Hudson. **CAST:** Adam Horovitz, Donald Sutherland, Amy Locane, Don Bloomfield, Celin Weston, Graham Beckel.

Adam Horovitz ("King Ad Rock" of the Beastie Boys) makes an impressive dramatic debut as Tim Doolan, a misguided teenager who winds up in a Los Angeles psychiatric counseling center, where one of the staff psychiatrists (Donald Sutherland) wants to see the troubled youngsters properly treated. Director Hugh Hudson, who scored big with *Chariots of Fire* and failed to connect with *Revolution,* is once again blessed with a good script. Rated R for language and violence. 1989; 121m.

LOST HORIZON ★★★★
DIR: Frank Capra. **CAST:** Ronald Colman, Jane Wyatt, John Howard, Edward Everett Horton, Margo, Sam Jaffe, Thomas Mitchell, Isabel Jewell, H. B. Warner.

Novelist James Hilton's intriguing story of a group of disparate people who survive an air crash and stumble on to a strange and haunting Tibetan land. One of the great classic films of the late 1930s. Long-missing footage has recently been restored, along with so-called lost scenes. 1937; B&W; 132m.

LOST MOMENT, THE ★★★½
DIR: Martin Gable. **CAST:** Robert Cummings, Susan Hayward, Agnes Moorehead, Eduardo Ciannelli.

A low-key, dark, offbeat drama based on Henry James's novel *The Aspern Papers*, which was based on a true story. A publisher (Robert Cummings), seeking love letters written by a long-dead great poet, goes to Italy to interview a very old lady and her niece. The old lady is spooky, the niece neurotic, the film fascinating. Those who know Cummings only from his TV series will be pleasantly surprised with his serious acting. 1947; B&W; 88m.

LOST WEEKEND, THE ★★★★★
DIR: Billy Wilder. **CAST:** Ray Milland, Jane Wyman, Phillip Terry, Howard DaSilva, Frank Faylen.

Gripping, powerful study of alcoholism and its destructive effect on one man's life. Arguably Ray Milland's best performance (he won an Oscar) and undeniably one of the most potent films of all time. Forty years after its release, the movie has lost none of its importance or effectiveness. Additional Oscars for best picture, director, and screenplay. 1945; B&W; 101m.

LOUISIANA ★
DIR: Philippe de Broca. **CAST:** Margot Kidder, Ian Charleson, Victor Lanoux, Andrea Ferreol.

Margot Kidder plays a conniving, self-centered southern belle who manages to destroy the lives of all around her. Her character is so hard that she makes Scarlet O'Hara look like a saint. The scenery is the only plus in this sudsy epic. Made for television, this is unrated. 1984; 206m.

LOVE AT THE TOP ★★★★

DIR: John Bowab. **CAST:** Janis Paige, Richard Young, Jim McKrell.

In this delightful film set in New York, Glynnis (Janis Paige) is at the top of her career as a lingerie designer. While being considered for promotion, she finds herself pitted against the son-in-law of the boss, a very romantic young man. Excellent. 1982; 105m.

LOVE CHILD ★★★★

DIR: Larry Peerce. **CAST:** Amy Madigan, Beau Bridges, Mackenzie Phillips.

Although its ads gave *Love Child* the appearance of a cheapo exploitation flick, this superb prison drama is anything but. Directed by Larry Peerce it is the gripping story of a young woman, Terry Jean Moore (Amy Madigan), who became pregnant by a guard in a women's prison in Florida and fought for the right to keep her baby. Rated R for profanity, nudity, sex, and violence. 1982; 96m.

LOVE IS A MANY-SPLENDORED THING ★★★

DIR: Henry King. **CAST:** Jennifer Jones, William Holden, Isobel Elsom, Richard Loo.

Clichéd story of ill-starred lovers from two different worlds who don't make it. Jennifer Jones is a Eurasian doctor who falls in love with war correspondent William Holden during the Korean conflict. 1955; 102m.

LOVE LEADS THE WAY ★★★★

DIR: Delbert Mann. **CAST:** Timothy Bottoms, Eva Marie Saint, Arthur Hill, Susan Dey.

This Disney TV movie features Timothy Bottoms in the true story of Morris Frank, the first American to train with a seeing-eye dog. Blinded while boxing, Frank at first refuses to accept his handicap and later resents the dog who offers to be his eyes. Fortunately, he adapts and later lobbies for acceptance of seeing-eye dogs throughout the United States. Bottoms turns in an exceptional performance as the struggling Frank. 1984; 99m.

LOVE LETTERS ★★★★

DIR: Amy Jones. **CAST:** Jamie Lee Curtis, Amy Madigan, Bud Cort, James Keach.

In this impressive character study, the heroine, played by Jamie Lee Curtis, wonders aloud to her friend (Amy Madigan): "Sometimes it's right to do the wrong thing, isn't it?" Probing the emotions that lead to infidelity, *Love Letters* is a true adult motion picture. This concept is intelligently explored by writer-director Amy Jones. Rated R for graphic sex. 1983; 98m.

LOVE MACHINE, THE ★★

DIR: Jack Haley Jr. **CAST:** Dyan Cannon, John Phillip Law, Robert Ryan, Jackie Cooper, David Hemmings, Shecky Greene, William Roerick.

A lust for power drives a television newscaster into the willing arms of the network president's wife. Pessimistic tale of the motivations that move the wheels of television news. Sexy, soapy adaptation of the Jacqueline Susann novel. Rated R. 1971; 108m.

LOVE ON THE DOLE ★★★½

DIR: John Baxter. **CAST:** Deborah Kerr, Clifford Evans, Mary Merrall.

Based on Walter Greenwoods's novel, this film is about a London family trying to subsist during the Depression. A classy cast gives top-notch performances. 1941; 89m.

LOVE STORY ★★★★

DIR: Arthur Hiller. **CAST:** Ryan O'Neal, Ali MacGraw, Ray Milland, John Marley.

Unabashedly sentimental and manipulative, this film was a box-office smash. Directed by Arthur Hiller and adapted by Erich Segal from his bestselling novel, it features Ryan O'Neal and Ali MacGraw as star-crossed lovers who meet, marry, make it, and then discover she is dying. Rated PG. 1970; 99m.

LOVE STREAMS ★★
DIR: John Cassavetes. **CAST:** John Cassavetes, Gena Rowlands, Diahnne Abbott, Seymour Cassel.

A depressing story of a writer who involves himself in the lives of lonely women for inspiration, and his emotionally unstable sister, whom he takes in after a difficult divorce has left her without possession of her child. There are some funny moments and some heartfelt scenes, as well, but John Cassavetes's direction is awkward. Rated PG-13 for language and adult situations. 1984; 122m.

LOVE WITH THE PROPER STRANGER ★★★★
DIR: Robert Mulligan. **CAST:** Natalie Wood, Steve McQueen, Edie Adams, Herschel Bernardi, Tom Bosley.

This neatly crafted tale of a pregnant young woman (Natalie Wood) and a restless trumpet player (Steve McQueen) offers generous portions of comedy, drama, and romance. Wood is at her most captivating. McQueen, veering a bit from his trademark cool, gives a highly engaging performance. Their relationship creates ample sparks. 1963; 100m.

LOVELESS, THE ★★
DIR: Kathryn Bigelow, Monty Montgomery. **CAST:** Willem Dafoe, Robert Gordon, Marin Kanter.

This could have been called *The Senseless* thanks to its lack of plot and emphasis on violence. It's a biker picture set in the 1950s and stars Willem Dafoe, who gives a good performance with the scant dialogue he's given. Though a poor tribute to *The Wild One*, this film does have a cult following. Rated R for violence, nudity and sex scenes. 1984; 85m.

LOVERS OF THEIR TIME ★★
DIR: Robert Knights. **CAST:** Edward Petherbridge, Cheryl Prime.

In this passable film, a married man (Edward Petherbridge) leads a boring life until he meets his dream love. 1986; 60m.

LOVES OF CARMEN, THE ★★
DIR: Charles Vidor. **CAST:** Rita Hayworth, Glenn Ford, Ron Randell, Victor Jory, Luther Adler, Arnold Moss.

Rita Hayworth plays an immoral gypsy hussy who ruins the life of a young Spanish officer (Glenn Ford). It's melodramatic and corny at times but still fun to see sparks fly between Hayworth as the beautiful vixen and an ever-so-handsome Ford. 1948; 98m.

LOVE'S SAVAGE FURY ★
DIR: Joseph Hardy. **CAST:** Jennifer O'Neill, Perry King, Raymond Burr, Connie Stevens.

TV-movie attempt to re-create the passion of *Gone With the Wind* is a dismal failure. Jennifer O'Neill plays the spoiled Southern belle who is imprisoned by Yankees. She escapes and begins a search for her family's gold. 1979; 100m.

LOVING ★★★½
DIR: Irvin Kershner. **CAST:** George Segal, Eva Marie Saint, Keenan Wynn, Sterling Hayden, Roy Scheider.

George Segal stars as a free-lance artist who becomes bored with his lifestyle and begins exploring some rather outrageous alternatives. Director Irvin Kershner brings out the best in his cast and material, thus providing a thought-provoking work for open-minded adults. Rated R for profanity and nudity. 1970; 90m.

LOYALTIES ★½
DIR: Anne Wheeler. **CAST:** Susan Wooldridge, Tantoo Cardinal, Kenneth Welsh.

In this Canadian-made drama, an upper-class Englishwoman reluctantly moves to a small town in one of the northwest provinces, where she becomes friends with her housekeeper, a hell-raising half-Indian woman. The story of the two women is well handled, but the movie turns into an unbelievable melodrama about the wife having to suffer for her husband's indiscretions. Rated R for violence and sexual situations. 1987; 98m.

LUCAS ★★★★
DIR: David Seltzer. **CAST:** Corey Haim, Kerri Green, Charlie Sheen, Courtney Thorne-Smith, Winona Ryder.
Charming tale of young love, leagues above the usual teen-oriented fare due to an intelligent and compassionate script by writer/director David Seltzer. Corey Haim stars as a 14-year-old whiz kid "accelerated" into high school who falls in love, during the summer between terms, with 16-year-old Kerri Green. Rated PG-13 for language. 1986; 100m.

LYDIA ★★★½
DIR: Julien Duvivier. **CAST:** Merle Oberon, Joseph Cotten, Edna May Oliver, Alan Marshal.
This sentimental treatment of the highly regarded French film *Carnet du Bal* is well acted and directed. It's the story of an elderly woman who has a reunion with four of her former loves. Merle Oberon's performance is one of her best. 1941; B&W; 104m.

M.A.D.D.: MOTHERS AGAINST DRUNK DRIVING ★★½
DIR: William A. Graham. **CAST:** Mariette Hartley, Paula Prentiss, Bert Remsen, John Rubinstein, Cliff Potts, David Huddleston, Grace Zabriskie, Nicolas Coster.
True story of Candy Lightner and her struggle to establish M.A.D.D., the national anti-drunk driving organization. A convincing performance by Mariette Hartley as the California housewife whose life is thrown into turmoil and tragic heartbreak when her daughter is killed by a drunk driver. Above-average TV movie. 1983; 100m.

MACARTHUR ★★★
DIR: Joseph Sargent. **CAST:** Gregory Peck, Dan O'Herlihy, Ed Flanders.
Gregory Peck is cast as the famous general during the latter years of his long military career. It begins with his assumption of command of the Philippine garrison in World War II and continues through his sacking by President Truman during the Korean Conflict. The film takes a middle ground in its depiction of this complex man and the controversy that surrounded him. Peck's performance is credible but the film remains uneven. Rated PG. 1977; 130m.

MACBETH (1948) ★★★
DIR: Orson Welles. **CAST:** Orson Welles, Roddy McDowall, Jeanette Nolan, Edgar Barrier, Dan O'Herlihy.
Shakespeare's noted tragedy, filmed according to a script by Orson Welles. Interesting movie—made on a budget of $700,000 in three weeks. Welles is an intriguing MacBeth, but Jeanette Nolan as his lady is out of her element. Edgar Barrier and Dan O'Herlihy are fine as Banquo and MacDuff. 1948; B&W; 105m.

MACBETH (1971) ★★★½
DIR: Roman Polanski. **CAST:** Jon Finch, Francesca Annis, Martin Shaw, Nicholas Selby, John Stride.
The violent retelling of this classic story was commissioned and underwritten by publisher Hugh Hefner. Shakespeare's tragedy about a man driven to self-destruction by the forces of evil is vividly brought to life by director Roman Polanski. Grim yet compelling, this version of one of our great plays is not for everyone and contains scenes that make it objectionable for children (or sequeamish adults). 1971; 140m.

MAD BULL ★★½
DIR: Walter Doniger, Len Steckler. **CAST:** Alex Karras, Susan Anspach, Nicholas Colasanto, Elisha Cook Jr., Danny Dayton.
A wrestler struggles to escape the sensationalism of his profession. Alex Karras is believable as a man haunted by the assassination of his tag-team

brother. Schmaltzy at times, but enjoyable nonetheless. 1977; 100m.

MADAME BOVARY ★★★

DIR: Vincente Minnelli. **CAST:** Jennifer Jones, Louis Jourdan, Van Heflin, James Mason.

Emma Bovary is an incurable romantic whose affairs of the heart ultimately lead to her destruction. Jennifer Jones is superb as Emma. Louis Jourdan plays her most engaging lover. Van Heflin portrays her betrayed husband. James Mason portrays Gustave Flaubert, on whose classic French novel the film is based. 1949; B&W; 115m.

MADAME SOUSATZKA ★★★

DIR: John Schlesinger. **CAST:** Shirley MacLaine, Navin Chowdhry, Peggy Ashcroft, Twiggy.

A flamboyant star turn from Shirley MacLaine fuels this gentle story about an eccentric piano teacher and the gifted prodigy (Navin Chowdhry) who comes to her for lessons in both music and life. As was true with Ruth Prawer Jhabvala's Oscar-winning script for *Room With a View,* her adaptation this time (of Bernice Rubens's novel) devotes equal time to richly drawn supporting characters: Peggy Ashcroft's wistful landlady and Twiggy's aspiring singer, among others. Rated PG-13 for language. 1988; 122m.

MADAME X ★★★

DIR: David Lowell Rich. **CAST:** Lana Turner, John Forsythe, Constance Bennett, Ricardo Montalban, Burgess Meredith.

In this sentimental old chestnut, filmed six times since 1909, a woman is defended against murder charges by an attorney who is not aware he is her son. Lana Turner is good and is backed by a fine cast, but Technicolor and a big budget make this one of producer Ross Hunter's mistakes. Constance Bennett's last film. 1966; 100m.

MADE IN USA ★★½

DIR: Ken Friedman. **CAST:** Adrian Pasdar, Christopher Penn, Lori Singer.

Bonnie and Clyde–style drama about a couple of drifters who leave their brutal job as coal miners in Pennsylvania for the sunny horizon of California. While en route west they encounter sexy hitchhiker Lori Singer and embark on a crime spree. Good cast fails to lift this overdone crime drama above mediocrity. Pretty disappointing. Rated R. 1988; 82m.

MAE WEST ★★★½

DIR: Lee Philips. **CAST:** Ann Jillian, James Brolin, Roddy McDowall, Piper Laurie.

This TV biography features a very convincing Ann Jillian as siren Mae West. (Some poetic license has been taken in order to make this complimentary to West.) Roddy McDowall, as a female impersonator, trains West to be sultry, alluring, and ultra-desirable while James Brolin plays the long-time love who offers her stability. 1982; 100m.

MAFIA PRINCESS ★½

DIR: Robert Collins. **CAST:** Tony Curtis, Susan Lucci, Kathleen Widdoes, Chuck Shamata.

A substandard plot can't be saved by Susan Lucci and Tony Curtis. Lucci plays the spoiled daughter of a Mafia crime lord (Curtis) who can't cope with the fact that money won't make her socially accepted. Made for TV, this is unrated. 1986; 100m.

MAGIC TOWN ★★

DIR: William Wellman. **CAST:** James Stewart, Jane Wyman, Ned Sparks.

After successfully collaborating with Frank Capra on some of his finest films, writer Robert Riskin teamed with director William Wellman for this mildly entertaining but preachy tale. An advertising executive (James Stewart) finds the perfect American community, which is turned topsy-turvy when the secret gets out. 1947; B&W; 103m.

MAGICIAN OF LUBLIN, THE ★½
DIR: Menahem Golan. **CAST:** Alan Arkin, Louise Fletcher, Valerie Perrine, Shelley Winters, Lou Jacobi, Warren Berlinger, Lisa Whelchel.

Superficial adaptation of Isaac Bashevis Singer's novel about a Jewish traveling magician in nineteenth-century Europe. Director Menahem Golan encourages his players to overact, a real mistake with a cast that includes Alan Arkin and Shelley Winters. Rated R for nudity. 1979; 105m.

MAGNIFICENT AMBERSONS, THE ★★★★★
DIR: Orson Welles. **CAST:** Joseph Cotten, Tim Holt, Agnes Moorehead.

Orson Welles's legendary depiction of the decline of a wealthy Midwestern family and the comeuppance of its youngest member is a definite must-see motion picture. Much has been made about the callous editing of the final print by studio henchmen, but that doesn't change the total impact. It's still a classic. Special notice must be given to Welles and cameraman Stanley Cortez for the artistic, almost portraitlike, look of the film. 1942; B&W; 88m.

MAGNIFICENT OBSESSION ★★★
DIR: Douglas Sirk. **CAST:** Jane Wyman, Rock Hudson, Agnes Moorehead, Otto Kruger.

Rock Hudson, a drunken playboy, blinds Jane Wyman in an auto accident. Stricken, he reforms and becomes a doctor in order to restore her sight in this melodramatic tearjerker from the well-known Lloyd C. Douglas novel. First filmed in 1935, with Irene Dunne and Robert Taylor. 1954; 108m.

MAHLER ★★½
DIR: Ken Russell. **CAST:** Robert Powell, Georgina Hale, Richard Morant.

Ken Russell's fantasy film about the biography of composer Gustav Mahler. Robert Powell's portrayal of Mahler as a man consumed with passion and ambition is a brilliant one. Georgina Hale as Alma, Mahler's wife, is also well played. Unfortunately, the cast cannot give coherence to the script. 1974; 115m.

MAHOGANY ★★
DIR: Berry Gordy. **CAST:** Diana Ross, Anthony Perkins, Billy Dee Williams.

The highlight of this unimpressive melodrama is Diana Ross's lovely wardrobe. She plays a poor girl who makes it big as a famous model and, later, dress designer after Anthony Perkins discovers her. That's when she leaves boyfriend Billy Dee Williams behind to pursue a world of glamour and success. This one jerks more yawns than tears. Rated PG. 1975; 109m.

MAKE A WISH 🦃
DIR: Kurt Neumann. **CAST:** Bobby Breen, Basil Rathbone, Marion Claire, Henry Armetta, Leon Errol, Donald Meek.

Young Bobby Breen is a prodigy. Basil Rathbone is a jolly good composer. Henry Armetta, Leon Errol, and Donald Meek want to steal Basil's latest operetta. The whole sweet, wholesome thing is enough to curdle milk. 1937; B&W; 80m.

MAKE ME AN OFFER ★
DIR: Jerry Paris. **CAST:** Susan Blakely, Patrick O'Neal, Stella Stevens, John Rubinstein.

A young woman makes her way to the top by becoming a quick study in the California real-estate business. Too cutesy to digest. Made for television. 1980; 100m.

MAKING LOVE ★
DIR: Arthur Hiller. **CAST:** Kate Jackson, Michael Ontkean, Harry Hamlin.

A wife (Kate Jackson) discovers that her husband (Michael Ontkean) is in love with another…man (Harry Hamlin) in this contrived soap opera, directed by Arthur Hiller. Rated R because of adult subject matter, profanity, and implicit sexual activity. 1982; 113m.

MALTA STORY, THE ★★★
DIR: Brian Desmond Hurst. **CAST:** Alec Guinness, Jack Hawkins, Anthony Steel, Muriel Pavlow.

Set in 1942, this is about British pluck on the island of Malta while the British were under siege from the Axis forces and the effect the war has on private lives. Flight Lieutenant Ross's (Alec Guinness) love for a native girl (Muriel Pavlow) goes unrequited when his commanding officer (Anthony Steel) sends him on a dangerous mission. 1953; B&W; 103m.

MAN CALLED ADAM, A ★
DIR: Leo Penn. **CAST:** Sammy Davis Jr., Louis Armstrong, Peter Lawford, Mel Torme, Frank Sinatra Jr., Lola Falana, Ossie Davis, Cicely Tyson.

Sammy Davis Jr. is Adam Johnson, a world-class jazz trumpet player who can't live with the guilt of accidentally killing his wife and child. Almost unwatchable. 1966; B&W; 103m.

MAN FOR ALL SEASONS, A ★★★★★
DIR: Fred Zinnemann. **CAST:** Paul Scofield, Wendy Hiller, Robert Shaw, Orson Welles, Susannah York.

This splendid film, about Sir Thomas More's heartfelt refusal to help King Henry VIII break with the Catholic Church and form the Church of England, won the best-picture Oscar in 1966. Paul Scofield, who is magnificent in the title role, also won best actor. Directed by Fred Zinnemann and written by Robert Bolt, the picture also benefits from memorable supporting performances by an all-star cast. 1966; 120m.

MAN IN GREY, THE ★★★
DIR: Leslie Arliss. **CAST:** Margaret Lockwood, James Mason, Phyllis Calvert, Stewart Granger, Martita Hunt.

A tale of attempted husband-stealing that worked well to make the prey, James Mason, a star. Margaret Lockwood is the love thief who proves to intended victim Phyllis Calvert that with her for a friend she needs no enemies. Mason is a stand-out as the coveted husband. 1943; B&W; 116m.

MAN IN LOVE, A ★
DIR: Diane Kurys. **CAST:** Peter Coyote, Greta Scacchi, Peter Riegert, Jamie Lee Curtis, Claudia Cardinale, John Barry.

Generally awful tearjerker from the normally perceptive and clever French writer-director Diane Kurys. Greta Scacchi stars as an aspiring European actress who finds herself involved in an affair with an egotistical American film star (stridently played by Peter Coyote). Rated R for nudity, profanity, and simulated sex. 1987; 108m.

MAN WHO BROKE 1000 CHAINS, THE ★★★★½
DIR: Daniel Mann. **CAST:** Val Kilmer, Sonia Braga, Charles Durning, Kyra Sedgwick, James Keach.

An excellent retelling of *I am a Fugitive from a Chain Gang* with Val Kilmer in the Paul Muni role. Kilmer's performance is as sharp as Muni's, and the supporting players, notably Charles Durning, are superb. Not rated, has violence and profanity. 1987; 113m.

MAN WHO HAD POWER OVER WOMEN, THE ★★
DIR: John Krish. **CAST:** Rod Taylor, James Booth, Carol White.

This British picture, adapted from Gordon Williams's novel, takes a semiserious look at a talent agency in London and the man who operates it. A passable time-filler, with some unexpected touches. Rated R. 1970; 89m.

MAN WITH THE GOLDEN ARM, THE ★★★
DIR: Otto Preminger. **CAST:** Frank Sinatra, Eleanor Parker, Kim Novak, Arnold Stang, Darren McGavin, Robert Strauss.

This dated film attempts to be *The Lost Weekend* of drug-addiction movies. Frank Sinatra is the loser on the needle and the nod in sleazy Chicago surroundings. Eleanor Parker is his crippled wife. Kim Novak, in an early role, is the girl who saves him. As a study of those who say yes, it carries a small jolt. 1955; B&W; 119m.

MAN, WOMAN AND CHILD ★★★½

DIR: Dick Richards. **CAST:** Martin Sheen, Blythe Danner, Sebastian Dungan.

Here's a surprisingly tasteful and well-acted tearjerker directed by Dick Richards and written by Erich Segal. Martin Sheen stars as a married college professor who finds out he has a son in France, the result of an affair that took place there ten years before. Sheen decides to bring his son to America, which causes complications. Rated PG language and adult situations. 1983; 99m.

MANCHURIAN CANDIDATE, THE ★★★★½

DIR: John Frankenheimer. **CAST:** Frank Sinatra, Laurence Harvey, Janet Leigh, Angela Lansbury, James Gregory, Leslie Parrish.

This cold-war black comedy is still topical, chilling, and hilarious. Frank Sinatra gives a superbly controlled performance as a Korean War veteran who begins to believe that the honored heroics of a former member of his squad (Laurence Harvey) may be the product of brainwashing by an enemy with even more sinister designs. Harvey has some moments of true brilliance, and Angela Lansbury, whose role is perhaps best described as the Republican mother from hell, is also memorable. Director John Frankenheimer and screenwriter George Axelrod (*The Seven Year Itch, The Loved One*) maintain a delicate balance between hilarity and horror. Unrated, the film has violence. 1962; B&W; 126m.

MANDELA ★★★

DIR: Philip Saville. **CAST:** Danny Glover, Alfre Woodard, Warren Clarke, Julian Glover.

Although Danny Glover and Alfre Woodard put heart and soul into their interpretations of South African activists Nelson and Winnie Mandela, Ronald Harwood's poorly balanced script sets events in a one-sided vacuum. While there's no question of the self-sacrificing integrity of the Mandelas, the virtual absence of any sympathetic white characters makes this a less involving drama than Richard Attenborough's *Cry Freedom*. Unrated; suitable for family viewing. 1987; 135m.

MANDINGO ★

DIR: Richard Fleischer. **CAST:** James Mason, Susan George, Perry King, Richard Ward, Brenda Sykes.

Sick film concerning the southern plantations before the Civil War and the treatment of the black slaves. The top-name cast should have known better. Rated R. 1975; 127m.

MANIPULATOR, THE ★

DIR: Yabo Yablonsky. **CAST:** Mickey Rooney, Luana Anders, Keenan Wynn.

Mickey Rooney plays a schizophrenic movie makeup man who abducts an actress (Luana Anders) and forces her to act in his own make-believe movie. Bizarre and pointless. Rated R for violence, profanity, and nudity. 1971; 91m.

MANXMAN, THE ★

DIR: Alfred Hitchcock. **CAST:** Carl Brisson, Malcolm Keen, Anny Ondra.

Afternoon soap operas are nothing compared to this howler, the last of director Alfred Hitchcock's silent films. Pert Anny Ondra is in love with humble Carl Brisson, but her father insists that his daughter's husband must be more financially secure. Brisson goes off to seek his fortune, Ondra courts Malcolm Keen when Brisson is lost and presumed dead, Brisson returns and...well, you get the idea. Not rated; suitable for family viewing. 1929; B&W; 70m.

MARCIANO ★★
DIR: Bernard Kowalski. **CAST:** Tony Lo Blanco, Belinda J. Montgomery, Vincent Gardenia, Richard Herd.

This made-for-TV bio-film concentrates far too much on the private life of the only boxer ever to retire from the pugilistic sport world undefeated—Rocky Marciano. More footage should have been devoted to his professional fighting career. There's nothing special here. 1979; 100m.

MARIA'S LOVERS ★
DIR: Andrei Konchalovsky. **CAST:** Nastassja Kinski, John Savage, Keith Carradine, Robert Mitchum, Vincent Spano, Bud Cort.

The story details the unhappy marriage of a former World War II prisoner of war (John Savage) and his loving wife (Nastassja Kinski). While Savage was in the Japanese P.O.W. camps he fantasized about being married to Kinski. Once he comes home and actually weds her, all he can think about when they're together are the horrors of imprisonment. Can their marriage survive this? Who cares? Rated R for profanity, nudity, suggested sex, and violence. 1985; 105m.

MARIE ★★★
DIR: Roger Donaldson. **CAST:** Sissy Spacek, Jeff Daniels, Keith Szarabajka.

Sissy Spacek plays real-life heroine Marie Ragghianti, whose courage and honesty brought about the fall of a corrupt administration in Tennessee. Marie is a battered housewife who leaves her cruel husband. Struggling to raise her three children and get an education at the same time, eventually works her way up to becoming the state's first female parole board head, and this is where she discovers some ugly truths. Rated PG-13 for violence and profanity. 1986; 100m.

MARIJUANA ★
DIR: Dwain Esper. **CAST:** Harley Wood, Hugh McArthur.

A woman's addiction to marijuana forces her into prostitution and other crimes that culminate in her kidnapping an infant. But as all aficionados of bad exploitation films know, there's always something worse in store for the main character. In this case, the child that the drug-crazed woman steals turns out to be her own, put up for adoption shortly after birth. A lame cheapie. 1937; B&W; 58m.

MARJOE ★★★½
DIR: Howard Smith, Sarah Kernochan. **CAST:** Marjoe Gortner.

The life of evangelist-turned-actor Marjoe Gortner is traced in this entertaining documentary. Film offers the viewer a peek into the world of the traveling evangelist. When Marjoe gets his act going, the movie is at its best. At times a little stagy, but always interesting. Rated PG for language. 1972; 88m.

MARJORIE MORNINGSTAR ★★★
DIR: Irving Rapper. **CAST:** Gene Kelly, Natalie Wood, Ed Wynn, Claire Trevor, Everett Sloane, Martin Milner, Carolyn Jones.

Natalie Wood and Gene Kelly give fine performances in this adaptation of the novel by Herman Wouk. Wood falls for show biz and for carefree theatrical producer Kelly. As Wood's eccentric uncle, Ed Wynn almost steals the show. A fine score by Max Steiner. 1958; 123m.

MARK OF THE HAWK, THE ★½
DIR: Michael Audley. **CAST:** Sidney Poitier, Juano Hernandez, Eartha Kitt, John McIntire.

This is an unfocused, off-balanced drama about a literate and educated African man who, through peaceful means, struggles to integrate his people into the societal mainstream. A snooze. 1958; 84m.

MARLENE ★★★★
DIR: Maximilian Schell. **CAST:** Marlene Dietrich, Maximilian Schell.

In this documentary, director Maximilian Schell pulls off something close to a miracle: he creates an absorbing and entertaining study of

Marlene Dietrich without ever having her on camera during the interviews. (She refused to be photographed.) Instead, we hear her famous husky voice talking about her life, loves, and movies as scenes from the latter—as well as newsreels and TV clips—play onscreen. 1985; 95m.

MARRIED MAN, A ★★
DIR: John Davies. **CAST:** Anthony Hopkins, Ciaran Madden, Lise Hilboldt, John Le Mesurier.

A love triangle leads to murder in this oh-so-British boudoir-and-drawing-room tale of a success-weary barrister, his very proper wife, and, of course, the other woman. Expect to yawn frequently during this made-for-TV feature. 1984; 200m.

MARTY ★★★★★
DIR: Delbert Mann. **CAST:** Ernest Borgnine, Betsy Blair.

This heartwarming movie about a New York butcher captured the Academy Award for best picture and another for Ernest Borgnine's poignant portrayal. Two lonely people manage to stumble into romance in spite of their own insecurities and the pressures of others. 1955; B&W; 91m.

MARTY (TELEVISION) ★★★★
DIR: Delbert Mann. **CAST:** Rod Steiger, Nancy Marchand, Esther Minciotti, Joe Mantell, Betsy Palmer, Nehemiah Persoff.

The original *Marty*, written for the *Goodyear Playhouse* by Paddy Chayefsky in 1953. Rod Steiger is tremendously sincere in his first starring role as the lonely butcher who meets a plain schoolteacher (Nancy Marchand) one night at the Waverly ballroom. Powerful, low-key drama, hardly hurt by the poor technical standards of the time. Hosted by Eva Marie Saint; interviews with the stars and the director thrown in for good measure. 1953; B&W; 60m.

MARVIN AND TIGE ★★★★
DIR: Eric Weston. **CAST:** John Cassavetes, Gibran Brown, Billy Dee Williams, Denise Nicholas, Fay Hauser.

Touching story of a runaway (Gibran Brown) who finds a friend in a poor and lonely man (John Cassavetes). Cassavetes's beautiful loser character works so well with Brown's streetwise pomp that the tension created by the clash of personalities makes their eventual deep relationship that much more rewarding. Rated PG for a few profane words. 1982; 104m.

MARY OF SCOTLAND ★★★★
DIR: John Ford. **CAST:** Katharine Hepburn, Fredric March, John Carradine.

Katharine Hepburn plays one of history's tragic figures in director John Ford's biography of the Sixteenth-century queen of Scotland. Fredric March is Bothwell, her supporter (and eventual lover) in her battle for power. The last scene, where Mary confronts her English accusers in court, is so well acted and photographed, it alone is worth the price of the rental. 1936; B&W; 123m.

MASADA ★★★★
DIR: Boris Sagal. **CAST:** Peter O'Toole, Peter Strauss, Barbara Carrera.

A spectacular TV movie based on the famous battle of Masada during the Roman domination of the known world. Fine acting, especially by Peter O'Toole, and excellent production values elevate this one far above the average small-screen movie. Unrated. 1984; 131m.

MASK ★★★★★
DIR: Peter Bogdanovich. **CAST:** Cher, Sam Elliott, Eric Stoltz, Laura Dern.

They used to call them moving pictures, and few films fit this phrase as well as this one, starring Cher, Sam Elliott, and Eric Stoltz. The story of a teenage boy coping with a disfiguring disease, it touches the viewer's heart as few movies have ever done. *Mask* rises above simple entertainment with its uplifting true-life tale. Rated PG-13. 1985; 120m.

MASS APPEAL ★★★★½
DIR: Glenn Jordan. **CAST:** Jack Lemmon, Zeljko Ivanek, Charles Durning, Louise Latham, James Ray.
A first-rate discussion of the dichotomy between private conscience and mass appeal, this film finds a mediocre and worldly priest, Father Tim Farley (Jack Lemmon), walking a political tightrope between the young seminarian (Zeljko Ivanek) he has befriended and his superior, Monsignor Burke (Charles Durning). At times both comic and tragic, it is not only a fine memorial but also a splendid motion picture. Rated PG. 1984; 99m.

MASSACRE IN ROME ★★★½
DIR: George Pan Cosmatos. **CAST:** Richard Burton, Marcello Mastroianni, Leo McKern, John Steiner.
Chilling drama about a priest (Marcello Mastroianni) opposing a Nazi colonel (Richard Burton) who must execute hundreds of Roman citizens in retaliation for the death by partisans of some Nazi troops. Rated PG for violence. 1973; 103m.

MASTER HAROLD AND THE BOYS ★★★★
DIR: Michael Lindsay-Hogg. **CAST:** Matthew Broderick, Zakes Mokae, John Kani.
An intense movie filmed in a single setting with a cast of three. Matthew Broderick gives a moving performance as a white English boy in 1950s South Africa. Zakes Mokae, in a brilliant portrayal as a back servant, tries to lead the boy gently toward manhood. Not rated, but contains profanity. 1984; 90m.

MASTER RACE, THE ★★★
DIR: Herbert J. Biberman. **CAST:** George Coulouris, Stanley Ridges, Osa Massen, Lloyd Bridges.
Hitler's Third Reich collapses. A dedicated Nazi officer escapes. His refusal to accept defeat becomes an engrossing study of blind obedience to immorality. 1944; B&W; 96m.

MATEWAN ★★★★½
DIR: John Sayles. **CAST:** Chris Cooper, Will Oldham, Mary McDonnell, James Earl Jones, David Straithairn, Josh Mostel.
Writer-director John Sayles's masterpiece about the massacre of striking West Virginia coal miners in 1920 has both heart and humor. Chris Cooper is the soft-spoken union organizer who tries to avoid violence. James Earl Jones is the leader of a group of black workers who were shocked to find, too late, that they were brought in as scabs. And David Straithaim is memorable as the town sheriff who attempts to keep the peace. Rated PG-13 for violence and profanity. 1987; 132m.

MATTER OF TIME, A ★
DIR: Vincente Minnelli. **CAST:** Liza Minnelli, Ingrid Bergman, Charles Boyer, Spiro Andros, Isabella Rossellini.
A penniless countess takes a country-bumpkin-come-to-the-big-city hotel chambermaid in hand and feeds her dreams of becoming a famous movie star. Skipping between present and past, this is a film of small consequence made palatable by adroit editing. Rated PG. 1976; 99m.

MAURICE ★★★
DIR: James Ivory. **CAST:** James Wilby, Hugh Grant, Rupert Graves, Denholm Elliott.
Based on E. M. Forster's long-suppressed, semiautobiographical novel, this film details the love of a middle-class college student (James Wilby) for his aristocratic classmate (Hugh Grant). A minor, but handsome and thoughtful film. Rated R for nudity and implied sex. 1987; 140m.

MAX DUGAN RETURNS ★★½
DIR: Herbert Ross. **CAST:** Jason Robards Jr., Marsha Mason, Donald Sutherland.
After spending many years in jail and gambling to big winnings, Max

Dugan (Jason Robards) seeks his widowed daughter (Marsha Mason) to bestow gifts upon her and her son. Though grateful for her new-found wealth, she finds it difficult to explain to her policeman-boyfriend, Donald Sutherland. The charm of this Neil Simon fable wears thin through repetition. Rated PG. 1983; 98m.

MAYFLOWER MADAM ★★
DIR: Lou Antonio. **CAST:** Candice Bergen, Chris Sarandon, Chita Rivera.

TV-movie bio of Mayflower descendant and debutante Sydney Biddle Barrows. Barrows (Candice Bergen), finding her cash supply inadequate, begins a classy call-girl service. Though allegedly based on fact, the events depicted here seem strictly soap-operaish. 1987; 96m.

MCVICAR ★★★
DIR: Tom Clegg. **CAST:** Roger Daltrey, Adam Faith, Jeremy Blake.

In this interesting British film, Roger Daltrey (lead singer for the Who) portrays John McVicar, whose real-life escape from the high-security wing of a British prison led to him being named "public enemy No. 1." Rated R. 1980; 111m.

MEAN STREETS ★★★★½
DIR: Martin Scorsese. **CAST:** Robert De Niro, Harvey Keitel, Amy Robinson, Robert Carradine, David Carradine.

This impressive film by director Martin Scorsese has criminal realism and explosive violence. Robert De Niro gives a high-energy performance as a ghetto psycho in New York's Little Italy who insults a Mafia loan shark by avoiding payment. He then rips off the friend who tries to save him. This study of street life at its most savage is a cult favorite. Rated R. 1973; 110m.

MEDIUM COOL ★★★★½
DIR: Haskell Wexler. **CAST:** Robert Forster, Verna Bloom, Peter Bonerz.

Robert Forster stars as a television news cameraman in Chicago during the 1968 Democratic convention. All the political themes of the 1960s are here—many scenes were filmed during the riots. Cinematographer Haskell Wexler's first try at directing is a winner. Highly recommended. Rated R for nudity and language. 1969; 110m.

MEET DR. CHRISTIAN ★★
DIR: Bernard Vorhaus. **CAST:** Jean Hersholt, Dorothy Lovett, Robert Baldwin, Paul Harvey, Marcia Mae Jones, Jackie Moran.

Folksy Jean Hersholt enacts the title role, meeting and besting medical crisis after medical crisis, in this first of six films translated from the popular 1930s radio series. He is wise, witty, kindly, and beloved by all, including Dorothy Lovett as his faithful nurse. 1939; B&W; 63m.

MEET JOHN DOE ★★★★
DIR: Frank Capra. **CAST:** Gary Cooper, Barbara Stanwyck, Walter Brennan, Spring Byington.

A penniless drifter (Gary Cooper) gets caught up in a newspaper publicity stunt. He is groomed and presented as the spokesman of the common man by powerful men who manipulate his every action for their own purposes. When he finally resists, he is exposed as a fraud. His fellow common men turn against him, or do they? Barbara Stanwyck is the newspaperwoman who first uses him and with whom he predictably falls in love. 1941; B&W; 132m.

MEETINGS WITH REMARKABLE MEN ★★★★
DIR: Peter Brook. **CAST:** Dragan Maksimovic, Mikica Dimitrijevic, Terence Stamp, Athol Fugard, Gerry Sundquist, Warren Mitchell.

The quest for spiritual truth and self-realization by Russian philosopher G. I. Gurdjieff (Dragan Maksimovic) is the subject of this intriguing work. Director Peter Brook concentrates on Gurdjieff's early days. Not rated. 1979; 102m.

MELANIE ★★★
DIR: Rex Bromfield. **CAST:** Glynnis O'Connor, Burton Cummings, Paul Sorvino, Don Johnson.
This drama about an illiterate Arkansas woman trying to regain custody of her son from her ex-husband in California is full of clichés but works anyway thanks to sincere direction and performances. Singer Burton Cummings plays a washed-up rock star who helps Melanie and is redeemed in the process; he also contributed the musical score. Not rated, but the equivalent of a PG-13. 1982; 109m.

MELODY IN LOVE
DIR: Hubert Frank. **CAST:** Melody O'Bryan, Sasha Hehn.
Who can guess what the original language was for this inane and badly dubbed exercise in sex play? An innocent young girl comes to a fiery tropical island, where promiscuity seems to be the order of the day for just about everyone. Save your money; this will inevitably be offered on TV around 3 A.M. 1978; 81m.

MELODY MASTER ★★
DIR: Reinhold Schunzel. **CAST:** Alan Curtis, Ilona Massey, Albert Basserman, Binnie Barnes, Billy Gilbert, Sterling Holloway, John Qualen, Sig Arno, Forrest Tucker.
This film, also known under the title of *New Wine* and *The Great Awakening* is another one in a long line of tortured-composer melodramas. Alan Curtis gives a bland portrayal of Franz Schubert. His real-life wife Ilona Massey, playing a Hungarian countess, comes to the composer's aid by attempting to prove to the world his greatness. There are some good comedy spots supplied by Binnie Barnes and Billy Gilbert. 1941; B&W; 80m.

MEMBER OF THE WEDDING, THE ★★★★
DIR: Fred Zinnemann. **CAST:** Julie Harris, Ethel Waters, Brandon de Wilde, Arthur Franz.
Julie Harris plays an awkward 12-year-old who is caught between being a child and growing up. She yearns to belong and decides to join her brother and his bride on their honeymoon. Her total introversion allows her to ignore the needs of her motherly nanny (brilliantly played by Ethel Waters) and her loyal cousin (Brandon deWilde). Depressing but riveting. 1953; B&W; 91m.

MEMORIAL DAY ★★★
DIR: Joseph Sargent. **CAST:** Mike Farrell, Shelley Fabares, Robert Walden, Edward Hermann, Danny Glover, Bonnie Bedelia.
Made-for-TV movie with stirring, sensitive performances by Mike Farrell, Robert Walden, and Edward Hermann. Farrell portrays a successful attorney who has a reunion with his former Vietnam combat buddies. The reunion awakens painful memories and a dark secret. Shelley Fabares plays Farrell's psychologist wife. Rated PG. 1988; 95m.

MEN, THE ★★★★
DIR: Fred Zinnemann. **CAST:** Marlon Brando, Jack Webb, Teresa Wright.
Marlon Brando's first film, this is about a paralyzed World War II vet trying to deal with his injury. A sensitive script and good acting make this film a classic. Better than *Coming Home* in depicting vets' feelings and attitudes about readjusting to society. 1950; B&W; 85m.

MEN'S CLUB, THE ★★★
DIR: Peter Medak. **CAST:** Roy Scheider, Frank Langella, Harvey Keitel, Treat Williams, Richard Jordan, David Dukes, Craig Wasson, Stockard Channing, Ann Wedgeworth, Jennifer Jason Leigh, Cindy Pickett.
Fine performances by an all-star cast are the main draw in this offbeat and disturbing film about a boy's night out that is turned into an exploration of men's attitudes toward women. The changes remain hidden inside the characters, although we can guess

what has happened by their actions. Rated R for nudity, profanity, suggested sex, and violence. 1986; 93m.

MERRY CHRISTMAS, MR. LAWRENCE ★★★½
DIR: Nagisa Oshima. **CAST:** David Bowie, Ryuichi Sakamoto, Tom Conti.

Set in a prisoner-of-war camp in Java in 1942, this film, by Nagisa Oshima, focuses on a clash of cultures—and wills. Oshima's camera looks on relentlessly as a British officer (David Bowie), who refuses to cooperate or knuckle under, is beaten and tortured by camp commander Ryuichi Sakomoto. Rated R for violence, strong language, and adult situations. 1983; 122m.

MESSAGE, THE (MOHAMMAD, MESSENGER OF GOD) ★★½
DIR: Moustapha Akkad. **CAST:** Anthony Quinn, Irene Papas, Michael Ansara, Johnny Sekka.

Viewers expecting to see Mohammad in this three-hour epic will be disappointed.... He never appears on the screen. Instead, we see Anthony Quinn, as Mohammad's uncle, struggling to win religious freedom for Mohammad. The film tends to drag a bit and is definitely overlong. Rated PG. 1977; 180m.

MIDNIGHT (1934) ★★
DIR: Chester Erskine. **CAST:** O. P. Heggie, Sidney Fox, Henry Hull, Lynne Overman, Margaret Wycherly, Humphrey Bogart, Richard Whorf.

Based on a well-recieved stage play, this rather implausible melodrama concerns a jury foreman who insists on a death verdict in the case of a young woman who killed a cruel lover. The juror then has to turn his own daughter over to the authorities for the same crime. Its main appeal now is Humphrey Bogart in a supporting role as a slick gangster. 1934; B&W; 74m.

MIDNIGHT COWBOY ★★★★★
DIR: John Schlesinger. **CAST:** Jon Voight, Dustin Hoffman, Sylvia Miles, Barnard Hughes, Brenda Vaccaro.

In this tremendous film, about the struggle for existence in the urban nightmare of New York's Forty-second Street area, Jon Voight and Dustin Hoffman deliver brilliant performances. The film won Oscars for best picture, best director and best screenplay. Voight plays handsome Joe Buck, who arrives from Texas to make his mark as a hustler, only to be out-hustled by everyone else, including the crafty, sleazy "Ratso," superbly played by Hoffman. Rated R. 1969; 113m.

MIDNIGHT DANCER ★★★
DIR: Pamela Gibbons. **CAST:** Deanne Jeffs, Mary Regan.

A young ballerina balances her artistic yearning with a night job in the chorus line of Club Paradise. Only hints of gangsters, drugs, and seedy sex, but enough to give this Australian film an honest coating of grit—rare among recent dance movies. Rated R. 1987; 97m.

MIDNIGHT EXPRESS ★★★★½
DIR: Alan Parker. **CAST:** Brad Davis, John Hurt, Randy Quaid.

This is the true story of Billy Hayes, who was busted for trying to smuggle hashish out of Turkey and spent five years in the squalor and terror of a Turkish prison. *Midnight Express* is not an experience easily shaken. Yet it is a film for our times that teaches a powerful and important lesson. Rated R. 1978; 121m.

MIKE'S MURDER ★★★
DIR: James Bridges. **CAST:** Debra Winger, Mark Keyloun, Darrell Larson.

This could have been an interesting tale of a small-time Los Angeles drug dealer and part-time tennis pro who becomes involved in a drug rip-off. But a string of confusing plot devices, doesn't work. Rated R for violence, language, and nudity. 1984; 97m.

MILAGRO BEANFIELD WAR, THE ★★★

DIR: Robert Redford. **CAST:** Rubén Blades, Richard Bradford, Sonia Braga, Julie Carmen, James Gammon, Melanie Griffith, John Heard, Daniel Stern, Christopher Walken, Chick Vennera.

There are fine perfomances in this slight, but enjoyable comedy-drama in which a group of citizens from a small town attempt to save their way of life by fighting big-money interests. The story is simplistic but, as with the films of Frank Capra, this mixture of fable and wish fulfillment can be a real spirit-lifter. Rated R for violence and profanity. 1988; 117m.

MILDRED PIERCE ★★★★

DIR: Michael Curtiz. **CAST:** Joan Crawford, Jack Carson, Zachary Scott, Eve Arden, Ann Blyth, Bruce Bennett, George Tobias, Lee Patrick.

Bored housewife Joan Crawford parlays waiting tables into a restaurant chain and an infatuation with Zachary Scott. Her spoiled daughter, Ann Blyth, hits on him. Emotions run high and taut as everything unravels in this A-one adaptation of James M. Cain's novel of murder and cheap love. Her performance in the title role won Joan Crawford an Oscar for best actress. 1945; B&W; 109m.

MILES FROM HOME ★★

DIR: Gary Sinise. **CAST:** Richard Gere, Kevin Anderson.

Richard Gere and Kevin Anderson star as brothers in this uneven drama about tragic rural figures. The brothers' farm is lost to foreclosure. They respond by torching the place and heading off on a confused odyssey of crime and misadventure. Rated R, for profanity and violence. 1988; 103m.

MILL ON THE FLOSS, THE ★★★½

DIR: Tim Whelan. **CAST:** Geraldine Fitzgerald, James Mason.

Geraldine Fitzgerald is Maggie and James Mason is Tom Tolliver in this careful and faithful adaptation of novelist George Eliot's story of ill-starred romance in a tradition-bound English village. 1939; B&W; 77m.

MIN AND BILL ★★★

DIR: George Hill. **CAST:** Marie Dressler, Wallace Beery, Dorothy Jordan, Marjorie Rambeau.

Their first picture together as a team puts Marie Dressler and Wallace Beery to the test when the future of the waif (Dorothy Jordan) she has reared on the rough-and-tumble waterfront is threatened by the girl's disreputable mother, Marjorie Rambeau. Her emotional portrayal won Marie Dressler an Oscar for best actress and helped make the film the box-office hit of its year. 1931; B&W; 70m.

MINE OWN EXECUTIONER ★★★

DIR: Anthony Kimmins. **CAST:** Burgess Meredith, Kieron Moore, Dulcie Gray.

Noted psychiatrist Burgess Meredith accepts ex–fighter pilot and Japanese prisoner of war Kieron Moore as a patient. He finds himself in the thick of a schizophrenic's hell, resulting in murder and suicide. Top-notch suspense. 1948; B&W; 105m.

MIRACLE OF OUR LADY OF FATIMA, THE ★★★½

DIR: John Brahm. **CAST:** Gilbert Roland, Frank Silvera, Sherry Jackson.

Remarkably well-told story of the famous appearance of the Virgin Mary in the small town of Fatima, Portugal. The Virgin appears to some farm children and they try to spread her word to a skeptical world. Not rated, but equivalent to a G. 1952; 102m.

MIRACLE OF THE BELLS, THE ★★★

DIR: Irving Pichel. **CAST:** Fred MacMurray, Alida Valli, Frank Sinatra, Lee J. Cobb.

A miracle takes place when a movie star is buried in her coal-mining hometown. Hard-bitten press agent Fred MacMurray turns mushy to see "the kid" gets the right send-off. The story is trite and its telling too long, but the cast is earnest and the film has a way of clicking. 1948; B&W; 120m.

MIRACLE OF THE HEART ★★★
DIR: Georg Stanford Brown. **CAST:** Art Carney, Casey Siemaszko, Jack Bannon, Darrell Larson.

Made-for-TV sequel to the 1938 *Boys Town*, which featured Spencer Tracy as Father Flanagan. This time, Art Carney plays one of Flanagan's boys, who is now an older priest. Touching and heartwarming. 1986; 96m.

MIRACLE WORKER, THE (1962) ★★★★½
DIR: Arthur Penn. **CAST:** Anne Bancroft, Patty Duke, Andrew Prine.

Anne Bancroft and Patty Duke are superb when re-creating their acclaimed Broadway performances in this production. Patty Duke is the untamed and blind deaf-mute Helen Keller and Bancroft is her equally strong-willed, but compassionate, teacher. Their harrowing fight for power and the ultimately touching first communication make up one of the screen's great sequences. 1962; B&W; 107m.

MIRACLE WORKER, THE (1979) ★★★½
DIR: Paul Aaron. **CAST:** Patty Duke Astin, Melissa Gilbert, Charles Siebert.

This made-for-TV biography features Patty Duke Astin as Anne Sullivan, teacher and friend of a disturbed deaf and blind girl. Melissa Gilbert takes the role of Helen Keller, which garnered an Oscar for Duke in 1962. This version is not quite as moving as the earlier one, but it's still worth watching. 1979; 100m.

MIRAGE ★★★
DIR: Edward Dmytryk. **CAST:** Gregory Peck, Diane Baker, Walter Matthau, Kevin McCarthy, Jack Weston, George Kennedy, Leif Erickson, Walter Abel.

Some really fine scenes and top-notch actors enliven this slow but ultimately satisfying mystery thriller. Gregory Peck is David Stillwell, a man who has lost his memory and becomes the victim of numerous murder attempts. Occasionally snappy dialogue, with an interesting but overdone use of flashbacks. 1965; B&W; 108m.

MISFITS, THE ★★★
DIR: John Huston. **CAST:** Marilyn Monroe, Clark Gable, Montgomery Clift, Thelma Ritter, Eli Wallach, Estelle Winwood.

Arthur Miller's parable of a hope-stripped divorcée and a gaggle of her boot-shod cowpoke boyfriends shagging wild horses in the Nevada desert, this film was the last hurrah for Marilyn Monroe and Clark Gable. The acting is good, but the storyline is mean. 1961; B&W; 124m.

MISHIMA: A LIFE IN FOUR CHAPTERS ★★★★
DIR: Paul Schrader. **CAST:** Ken Ogata, Ken Swada, Yasusuka Brando.

By depicting this enigmatic writer's life through his art, filmmaker Paul Schrader has come close to illustrating the true heart of an artist. This is not a standard narrative biography but a bold attempt to meld an artist's life with his life's work. The movie is, as suggested in the title, divided into four parts: "Beauty," "Art," "Action," and the climactic "A Harmony of Pen and Sword." Rated R for sex, nudity, violence, and adult situations. 1985; 121m.

MISS SADIE THOMPSON ★★½
DIR: Curtis Bernhardt. **CAST:** Rita Hayworth, José Ferrer, Aldo Ray.

A remake of *Rain*, the 1932 adaptation of Somerset Maugham's novel with Joan Crawford and Walter Huston, this production (with music) is notable only for the outstanding performance by Rita Hayworth in the title role. 1953; 91m.

MISSILES OF OCTOBER, THE ★★★★½
DIR: Anthony Page. **CAST:** William Devane, Ralph Bellamy, Martin Sheen, Howard DaSilva.

This is a superbly cast, well-written, excitingly directed made-for-TV film dealing with the crucial decisions that were made during the Cuban missile crisis of October 1962. It follows the hour-by-hour situations that occurred when the U.S. government discovered that the Soviet Union was installing offensive missiles in Cuba. Gripping and realistic. 1974; 175m.

MISSING ★★★★★
DIR: Constantin Costa-Gavras. **CAST:** Jack Lemmon, Sissy Spacek, John Shea, Melanie Mayron, Janice Rule, David Clennon.

A superb political thriller directed by Costa-Gavras, this stars Jack Lemmon and Sissy Spacek as the father and wife of a young American journalist who disappears during a bloody South American coup. Rated R for violence, nudity, and profanity. 1982; 122m.

MISSION, THE ★★★½
DIR: Roland Joffe. **CAST:** Jeremy Irons, Robert De Niro, Philip Bosco, Aidan Quinn.

Jeremy Irons plays a Spanish Jesuit who goes into the South American wilderness to build a mission in the hope of converting the Indians of the region. Robert De Niro plays a slave hunter who is converted and joins Irons in his mission. When Spain sells the colony to Portugal, they are forced to defend all they have built against the Portuguese aggressors. Rated PG for violence and sex. 1986; 125m.

MISSION TO GLORY ★
DIR: Ken Kennedy. **CAST:** Ricardo Montalban, Cesar Romero, Rory Calhoun, Michael Ansara, Keenan Wynn, Richard Egan.

The true story of Father Francisco Kin, the Spanish padre who helped develop California in the late seventeenth century. This film has all the dullness of one of those elementary-school movies you were forced to suffer through. Rated PG for violence. 1979; 97m.

MISSISSIPPI BURNING ★★★★
DIR: Alan Parker. **CAST:** Gene Hackman, Willem Dafoe, Frances McDormand, Brad Dourif, Lee Ermey.

Proving once again—as with *Midnight Express*—that he's the master of dramatic propaganda, Alan Parker presents this hair-raising account of what *might* have happened back in 1964 when three civil-rights activists turned up missing in Mississippi. Laid-back Gene Hackman and by-the-book Willem Dafoe are the FBI agents in charge of the investigation that generates its own share of racial tension. If good intentions excuse execution, then this is worthy fiction; at the very least, it allows Hackman to demonstrate his considerable range. Definitely not for the squeamish. Rated R for language and brutal violence. 1988; 125m.

MRS. MINIVER ★★★★
DIR: William Wyler. **CAST:** Greer Garson, Walter Pidgeon, Teresa Wright, May Whitty, Richard Ney, Henry Travers, Henry Wilcoxon, Reginald Owen.

This highly sentimental story of the English home front during the early years of World War II is one of the best examples of cinematic propaganda ever produced. It follows the lives of the Miniver family, especially Mrs. Miniver (Greer Garson), as they become enmeshed in a series of attempts to prove that there will always be an England. It won seven Academy Awards, including best picture. 1942; B&W; 134m.

MR. ARKADIN (A.K.A. CONFIDENTIAL REPORT) ★★½
DIR: Orson Welles. **CAST:** Orson Welles, Michael Redgrave, Akim Tamiroff, Patricia Medina, Mischa Auer.

Actor-writer-director Orson Welles confuses the audience more than he entertains them in this odd story of an amnesiac millionaire financier who hires an investigator to find his past. The intriguing story fails to translate effectively to the screen; even the efforts of a fine cast couldn't help Welles turn this into a critical or commerical success. 1955; B&W; 99m.

MR. HALPERN AND MR. JOHNSON ★★★

DIR: Alvin Rakoff. **CAST:** Laurence Olivier, Jackie Gleason.

Laurence Olivier plays a recently widowed Jewish manufacturer who, to his surprise, is asked to join a seemingly well-off stranger named Johnson (Jackie Gleason) for a drink after the funeral. It seems that Johnson was once in love with the late Mrs. Halpern. What's more, they carried on a friendship (and monthly platonic get-togethers) for a number of years right up to just before her death. Mr. Halpern is, of course, shocked. And therein lies the drama of this slight tale. 1983; 57m.

MR. SKEFFINGTON ★★★

DIR: Vincent Sherman. **CAST:** Bette Davis, Claude Rains, Walter Abel, George Coulouris, Jerome Cowan, Gigi Perreau.

Selfish and self-centered Bette Davis goes from reigning society beauty to hag in this typical soap opera of the upper crust—ranging across decades through feast and famine, indulgence and deceit. Time takes its toll on her beauty, her marriage fails, the stag line dwindles to zero. Then comes her one chance to do the right thing. Davis's performance is splendid. 1944; B&W; 127m.

MR. SMITH GOES TO WASHINGTON ★★★★★

DIR: Frank Capra. **CAST:** James Stewart, Jean Arthur, Claude Rains.

This Frank Capra classic is the story of a naïve senator's fight against political corruption. James Stewart stars as Jefferson Smith, the idealistic scoutmaster who is appointed to fill out the term of a dead senator. Upon arriving in the capitol, he begins to get a hint of the corruption in his home state. His passionate filibuster against this corruption remains one of the most emotionally powerful scenes in film history. 1939; B&W; 129m.

MISTRAL'S DAUGHTER ★★

DIR: Douglas Hickox. **CAST:** Stefanie Powers, Stacy Keach, Lee Remick, Timothy Dalton, Robert Urich, Stéphane Audran.

This sudsy adaptation of Judith Krantz's novel features Stefanie Powers as a French girl who becomes the model and then mistress of a cynical artist (Stacy Keach). When he chooses his wealthy sponsor (Lee Remick) over Powers, she becomes the mistress of a handsome married man (Timothy Dalton). Made for television, this miniseries is unrated but contains partial nudity and simulated sex. 1984; 300m.

MRS. SOFFEL ★★½

DIR: Gillian Armstrong. **CAST:** Diane Keaton, Mel Gibson, Matthew Modine, Edward Herrmann, Trini Alvarado.

We assume Australian director Gillian Armstrong's intent was to make more than a simple entertainment of this story about a warden's wife (Diane Keaton) who helps two prisoners (Mel Gibson and Matthew Modine) escape. But she creates, instead, a shapeless "statement" about the plight of women at the turn of the century. Even the stars' excellent performances can't save it. Rated PG-13 for violence, suggested sex, and profanity. 1984; 112m.

MRS. WIGGS OF THE CABBAGE PATCH ★★

DIR: Norman Taurog. **CAST:** Pauline Lord, W. C. Fields, ZaSu Pitts, Evelyn Venable, Kent Taylor, Charles Middleton, Donald Meek.

This sentimental twadle about a poor but optimistic family from the wrong side of the tracks is a throwback to nineteenth-century stage melodrama, saved only by the presence of the great W. C. Fields, ZaSu Pitts, and a fine cast of character actors. If you are a Fields fan, beware—the much-put-upon comedian only appears in the last part of the film. Creaky. 1934; B&W; 80m.

MISUNDERSTOOD (1984) ★
DIR: Jerry Schatzberg. **CAST:** Gene Hackman, Henry Thomas, Huckleberry Fox.

A rich businessman (Gene Hackman) has to cope with the problem of raising two young sons who are traumatized by the sudden death of their mother. This is a dull, almost unbearable, tearjerker. Rated PG for profanity. 1984; 91m.

MISUNDERSTOOD (1988) ★★
DIR: Luigi Comencini. **CAST:** Anthony Quayle, Stefano Colagrande, Georgia Moll.

This is an Italian production of the U.S. film release that starred Gene Hackman. The slow, depressing story did not need to be done twice. In this version, Anthony Quayle is a British consul in Italy. He is trying to raise his two sons following the death of his wife. The focus is on the father's relationship with the older son, which lacks understanding and compassion. The director, Luigi Comencini, takes far too long to reach the too late conclusion. Rated PG for adult themes. 1988; 101m.

MOLLY MAGUIRES, THE ★★★
DIR: Martin Ritt. **CAST:** Sean Connery, Richard Harris, Samantha Eggar, Frank Finlay, Art Lund.

The Molly Maguires were a group of terrorists in the 1870s who fought for better conditions for the Pennsylvania coal miners. In this dramatization, Sean Connery is their leader and Richard Harris is a Pinkerton detective who infiltrates the group. The film gives a vivid portrayal of the miners' dreadful existence. Performances are first-rate. A little long, but worth checking out. 1970; 123m.

MOMMIE DEAREST ★★★½
DIR: Frank Perry. **CAST:** Faye Dunaway, Diana Scarwid, Steve Forrest.

At times this trashy screen version of Christine Crawford's controversial autobiography—which stars Faye Dunaway in an astounding performance as Joan Crawford—is so harrowing and grotesque you're tempted to stop the tape. But it's so morbidly fascinating you can't take your eyes off the screen. Rated PG. 1981; 129m.

MONA LISA ★★★★½
DIR: Neil Jordan. **CAST:** Bob Hoskins, Cathy Tyson, Michael Caine, Clark Peters.

Bob Hoskins is Britain's answer to Humphrey Bogart and James Cagney. In this crime thriller, Hoskins plays a simple but moral man whose less than honest endeavors have landed him in prison. Upon his release, he goes to his former boss (Michael Caine) in search of a job. Unrated the film has profanity, suggested sex, and violence. 1986; 100m.

MONDO NEW YORK ★
DIR: Harvey Keith. **CAST:** Joey Arias, Rick Aviles, Charlie Barnett.

Raunchy docudrama in which a young girl impartially observes the depravity and senselessness of New York City. Achieves new depths of tastelessness. Not rated; contains vile language and nudity. 1987; 83m.

MONSIGNOR ★½
DIR: Frank Perry. **CAST:** Christopher Reeve, Genevieve Bujold, Fernando Rey, Jason Miller.

Christopher Reeve stars in the highly implausible story of a Vatican priest who seduces a student nun and makes deals with the Mafia to help the Church's finances. It's an outrageous melodrama that will have you groaning in no time at all. Rated R for profanity, nudity, sex, and violence. 1982; 122m.

MONTENEGRO ★★★★
DIR: Dusan Makavejev. **CAST:** Susan Anspach, John Zacharias.

Susan Anspach stars as a discontented housewife who wanders into a Yugoslavian nightclub, finds herself surrounded by sex and violence, and discovers she rather likes it, in this outlandish, outrageous, and sometimes shocking black comedy. The laughs come with the realization that everyone in this movie is totally bonkers. Rated R because of profanity, nudity, sex, and violence. 1981; 98m.

MONTH IN THE COUNTRY, A ★★★

DIR: Pat O'Connor. **CAST:** Colin Firth, Kenneth Branagh, Natasha Richardson.

Two emotionally scarred World War I veterans find themselves working for a month in a small Yorkshire village. The acting is flawless, but a gripping plot never quite materializes. Rated PG. 1987; 96m.

MOON IN SCORPIO ★

DIR: Gary Graver. **CAST:** Britt Ekland, John Phillip Law, William Smith.

Three Vietnam War vets and their girlfriends go on a sailing trip that turns to horror. Another post-traumatic stress syndrome film where one of the vets has flashbacks about the war. The film's limp ending, with its unanswered questions, will leave you feeling cheated. Not rated; has violence, profanity, sex, and nudity. 1987; 90m.

MOON OVER HARLEM ★★½

DIR: Edgar G. Ulmer. **CAST:** Bud Harris.

Uneven melodrama featuring an all-black cast. The unlikely director is German émigré Edgar G. Ulmer, the visionary film poet who worked with F. W. Murnau and other German expressionists. Considered a great cult filmmaker, Ulmer has a considerable reputation among French critics. 1939; B&W; 77m.

MORNING GLORY ★★½

DIR: Lowell Sherman. **CAST:** Katharine Hepburn, Adolphe Menjou, Douglas Fairbanks Jr., C. Aubrey Smith.

A naïve young actress comes to New York to find fame and romance. Based on the Zoe Akins play, the stagy film version hasn't aged well. But C. Aubrey Smith adds dignity to the piece in a supporting role and Katharine Hepburn is charismatic as the actress. She won her first Academy Award for this showy performance. 1933; B&W; 74m.

MOROCCO ★★★

DIR: Josef von Sternberg. **CAST:** Gary Cooper, Adolphe Menjou, Marlene Dietrich.

The fabulous and fabled Marlene Dietrich in her first Hollywood film. She's a cabaret singer stranded in exotic, sinister Morocco, who must choose between suave, rich Adolphe Menjou, or dashing French Legionnaire Gary Cooper. The scene at the oasis is classic 1930s cinematography. 1930; B&W; 92m.

MOSES ★★★

DIR: Gianfranco De Bosio. **CAST:** Burt Lancaster, Anthony Quayle, Irene Papas, Ingrid Thulin, William Lancaster.

This biblical screen story of the Hebrew lawgiver is fairly standard as such films go. Burt Lancaster is well-suited to play the stoic Moses. However, in trimming down this six-hour T.V. miniseries for video release, its makers lost most of the character development in the supporting roles. 1975; 141m.

MOSQUITO COAST, THE ★★★

DIR: Peter Weir. **CAST:** Harrison Ford, Helen Mirren, River Phoenix, Conrad Roberts, Andre Gregory, Martha Plimpton.

In spite of the top-notch talent involved, this remains a flawed endeavor. Theroux's Allie Fox (Ford) is a monomaniacal genius who can't bear what he perceives to be the rape of the United States, so he drags his wife and four children on one of the most outrageous picnics of all time, to the untamed wilderness of the Mosquito Coast in a self-indulgent attempt to mimic the Swiss Family Robinson. Rated PG. 1986; 117m.

MOUNTAIN, THE ★★★

DIR: Edward Dmytryk. **CAST:** Spencer Tracy, Robert Wagner, Claire

Trevor, William Demarest, Richard Arlen, E. G. Marshall.

Though this moralistic drama lacks punch, the fine performances of Spencer Tracy and Robert Wagner make it worth watching. They play mountaineering brothers risking a treacherous climb to find the wreckage of a passenger plane. 1956; 105m.

MUDHONEY ★★★★

DIR: Russ Meyer. **CAST:** Hal Hopper, Antoinette Cristiani.

A cult favorite from Russ Meyer about the exploits of some rural folks involved in the pursuit of cheap thrills and the meaning of life. Considered an adults-only film when released, it now seems quite tame. Plot has a local scum terrorizing Antoinette Cristiani, a deaf-and-dumb beautiful blonde until her rescue by Hal Hopper. Unrated, but an R rating would be in order because of some nudity and adult themes. 1965; B&W; 92m.

MURDER ELITE ★★

DIR: Claude Whatham. **CAST:** Ali MacGraw, Billie Whitelaw, Hywel Bennett, Ray Lonnen.

Ali MacGraw plays a woman who, after losing all her money in America, comes back to her native England to start fresh. Meanwhile, there is a killer on the loose. The two stories ultimately collide, but MacGraw's uninspired acting and the poor direction make the film rather plodding. Not rated. 1985; 104m.

MURDER IN COWETA COUNTY ★★★½

DIR: Gary Nelson. **CAST:** Andy Griffith, Johnny Cash, Earl Hindman.

Andy Griffith is outstanding as a Georgia businessman who thinks he can get away with murder. Johnny Cash plays the determined sheriff who's willing to go to any lengths to prove Griffith's guilt. This made-for-TV suspense-drama was based on an actual Georgia murder that took place in 1948. 1983; 104m.

MURPHY'S ROMANCE ★★★★

DIR: Martin Ritt. **CAST:** Sally Field, James Garner, Brian Kerwin, Corey Haim.

This sweet little love story also marks the finest performance given on film by James Garner. He's a crusty small-town pharmacist, a widower with no shortage of home-cooked meals but little interest in anything more permanent. Garner and Sally Field are great together, and the result is a complete charmer. Rated PG-13. 1985; 107m.

MURROW ★★★★

DIR: Jack Gold. **CAST:** Daniel J. Travanti, Dabney Coleman, Edward Herrmann, John McMartin, David Suchet, Kathryn Leigh Scott.

Compassionate HBO film about the famous radio and television journalist Edward R. Murrow, played brilliantly by Daniel Travanti. The film devotes most of its running time to the journalist's struggle against McCarthyism. 1985; 114m.

MUSIC SCHOOL, THE ★★★

DIR: John Korty. **CAST:** Ron Weyand, Dana Larsson, Cathleen Bauer.

The mathematical precision of music as a metaphor for the ideal life unattainable by mere mortals is the driving force behind this John Updike story. Ron Weyand stars as a typically *angst*-ridden Updike hero. The story unfolds through Updike's off-camera commentary. Introduced by Henry Fonda; aside from fleeting nudity, suitable for family viewing. 1974; 30m.

MUSSOLINI AND I ★★★

DIR: Alberto Negrin. **CAST:** Anthony Hopkins, Susan Sarandon, Bob Hoskins, Annie Girardot, Barbara de Rossi, Vittorio Mezzogiorno, Fabio Testi, Kurt Raab.

A weak and confusing narrative hinders this HBO film about the Fascist leader and his family's struggle with power. Bob Hoskins plays the Italian premier with a British accent; ditto for Anthony Hopkins who portrays Galeazzo Ciano, Italy's minister of foreign affairs and the dictator's brother-in-law. Still, the story is kept interesting despite its length. Not rated, but the equivalent of a PG for violence. 1985; 130m.

MY BEAUTIFUL LAUNDRETTE ★★★★½

DIR: Stephen Frears. **CAST:** Saeed Jaffrey, Roshan Seth, Daniel Day Lewis, Gordon Warnecke, Shirley Anne Field.

In modern-day England, a young Pakistani immigrant is given a launderette by his rich uncle and, with the help of his punk-rocker boyfriend turns it into a showplace. Everything goes along reasonably well until a racist gang decides to close them down. British director Stephen Frears keeps things from becoming too heavy by adding deft touches of comedy. Rated R for profanity, suggested and simulated sex, and violence. 1985; 103m.

MY BODYGUARD ★★★★★

DIR: Tony Bill. **CAST:** Chris Makepeace, Matt Dillon, Martin Mull, Ruth Gordon, Adam Baldwin.

This is a wonderfully funny and touching movie. Fifteen-year-old Clifford Peache (Chris Makepeace) must face the challenges of public high school after nine years of private education. His classes are easy. It's his schoolmates who cause problems. Specifically, there's Moody (Matt Dillon), a nasty young thug who extorts money from the other students. Rated PG. 1980; 96m.

MY BOYS ARE GOOD BOYS ★★

DIR: Bethel Buckalew. **CAST:** Ralph Meeker, Ida Lupino, Lloyd Nolan, David Doyle.

It's good to see veteran actors Ralph Meeker and Ida Lupino again, but it's too bad the occasion is this low-budget effort. They play parents of juvenile delinquents who rob an armored car. The movie has a serious side—the second half examines the results of the thieves' actions—but the whole affair is pretty mediocre. Rated PG. 1978; 90m.

MY BRILLIANT CAREER ★★★★½

DIR: Gillian Armstrong. **CAST:** Judy Davis, Sam Neill, Wendy Hughes.

A superb Australian import, *My Brilliant Career* is about a young woman clearly born before her time. It is the waning years of the nineteenth century, when the only respectable status for a woman is to be married. Sybylla Melvyn (Judy Davis), who lives with her family in the Australian bush, does not want to marry. She has "immortal longings." Rated G. 1979; 101m.

MY DINNER WITH ANDRE ★★★★★

DIR: Louis Malle. **CAST:** Andre Gregory, Wallace Shawn.

One of the most daring films ever made, this fascinating work consists almost entirely of a dinner conversation between two men. It's a terrific little movie. You'll be surprised how entertaining it is. No MPAA rating. The film has no objectionable material. 1981; 110m.

MY FIRST WIFE ★★★½

DIR: Paul Cox. **CAST:** John Hargreaves, Wendy Hughes.

In the tradition of *Ordinary People*, *Kramer vs Kramer*, *Shoot the Moon*, and *Smash Palace* comes another film about the dissolution of a marriage. The story deals with a classical music programmer/composer who finds that his wife doesn't love him anymore. Rated PG for adult situations and language. 1985; 95m.

MY FORBIDDEN PAST ★★

DIR: Robert Stevenson. **CAST:** Robert Mitchum, Ava Gardner, Janis Carter, Melvyn Douglas, Lucile Watson.

Set in steamy New Orleans in 1890, this one's about Ava Gardner's cold-blooded attempts to buy married-man Robert Mitchum's affections with the help of an unexpected inheritance. His wife is killed. He's accused of her murder. Gardner, revealing her unsavory past in order to save him, wins his love. 1951; B&W; 81m.

MY LITTLE GIRL ★★
DIR: Connie Kaiserman. **CAST:** James Earl Jones, Geraldine Page, Mary Stuart Masterson, Anne Meara.
Familiar tale of a do-good rich kid's introduction to the real world. Mary Stuart Masterson stars as a 16-year-old high school student who volunteers to spend a summer working with runaway, homeless, and abused girls at a state-run shelter. The performances raise this (just barely) to the tolerable level. Rated R for violence and profanity. 1986; 118m.

MY OLD MAN ★★★★
DIR: John Erman. **CAST:** Warren Oates, Kristy McNichol, Eileen Brennan.
Excellent made-for-television adaptation of a short story by Ernest Hemingway about a down-on-his-luck horse trainer (Warren Oates) and the daughter (Kristy McNichol) who loves him even more than horses. Oates gives a fabulous performance; certainly one of the best of his too-brief career. Eileen Brennan lends support as a sympathetic waitress. Unrated; suitable for family viewing. 1979; 104m.

MY OLD MAN'S PLACE ★★
DIR: Edwin Sherin. **CAST:** Arthur Kennedy, Mitchell Ryan, William Devane, Michael Moriarty.
Outdated cliché-ridden melodrama about a soldier's return home from Vietnam bringing two army friends with him. The inevitable clash of wills and personalities leads to the film's deadly conclusion. Rated R for nudity, profanity, and violence. 1973; 92m.

MY SWEET CHARLIE ★★★★
DIR: Lamont Johnson. **CAST:** Patty Duke, Al Freeman Jr., Ford Rainey.
The fine performances of Patty Duke and Al Freeman Jr. make this made-for-TV drama especially watchable. Duke plays a disowned, unwed mom-to-be who meets a black lawyer being pursued by the police. They hit it off and manage to help each other. A must-see for viewers interested in drama with a social comment. 1969; 97m.

MY WICKED, WICKED WAYS ★★
DIR: Don Taylor. **CAST:** Duncan Regehr, Barbara Hershey, Darren McGavin, Hal Linden.
Errol Flynn's fast-paced life—as related in his autobiography—is slowed down a bit for this TV movie. It seems to have lost its zest in the translation. But choosing Duncan Regehr to play Flynn was an inspiration. 1984; 142m.

MYSTERY OF THE MARIE CELESTE, THE ★★★
DIR: Denison Clift. **CAST:** Bela Lugosi, Shirley Grey.
On December 4, 1872, the brigantine *Marie Celeste*, said to have been jinxed by death, fire, and collision since its launching in 1861, was found moving smoothly under halfsail, completely deserted, east of the Azores. No trace of the crew was ever found. To this day, what happened remains a true mystery of the sea. This account offers one explanation. Also released as *The Phantom Ship*. 1937; B&W; 64m.

MYSTIC PIZZA ★★★½
DIR: Amy Jones. **CAST:** Annabeth Gish, Julia Roberts, Lili Taylor, Vincent D'Onofrio, William R. Moses, Adam Storke.
This coming-of-age picture has all of the right ingredients of a main-course favorite. Instead of gangly guys, the antics involve three women—two sisters and a friend—who work at a pizza parlor in the resort town of Mystic, Connecticut. The superb young players and the dazzling New England scenery are a slice of heaven. Rated R for language. 1988; 102m.

NAIROBI AFFAIR ★½
DIR: Marvin J. Chomsky. **CAST:** John Savage, Maud Adams, Charlton Heston.

Poor acting, particularly Charlton Heston's—he seems to be sleepwalking throughout the entire film—mar what could have made a powerful melodrama. Heston plays a safari photographer who is having an affair with his son's ex-wife (Maud Adams). His spoiled son (John Savage) tries to break up their relationship while drawing Heston into a duel against the ruthless ivory hunters. Rated PG for violence. 1986; 95m.

NAKED HEART, THE ★½
DIR: Marc Allegret. **CAST:** Michele Morgan, Kieron Moore, Françoise Rosay.
After five years in a convent, a young woman returns to her home in the frozen Canadian north and tries to decide which of her three suitors to marry. Filmed in Europe, this slow, somewhat depressing tale has little going for it. 1950; B&W; 96m.

NAPOLEON (1955) ★
DIR: Sacha Guitry. **CAST:** Orson Welles, Maria Schell, Yves Montand, Erich Von Stroheim.
It seems inconceivable that Napoleon, who towered historically over Patton, MacArthur, and Rommel, could be the subject of such an insignificant little film. This offering mumbles its way from nowhere to nowhere with little along the way. It's boring. 1955; 115m.

NAPOLEON AND JOSEPHINE: A LOVE STORY ★
DIR: Richard T. Heffron. **CAST:** Jacqueline Bisset, Armand Assante, Anthony Perkins, Stephanie Beacham.
This boring saga was an unpopular TV miniseries. Armand Assante plays Napoleon from his pregeneral days until his exile. Jacqueline Bisset is his loving Josephine. 1987; 300m.

NASHVILLE ★★★★★
DIR: Robert Altman. **CAST:** Keith Carradine, Lily Tomlin, Ned Beatty, Henry Gibson, Karen Black, Ronee Blakley.
Robert Altman's classic study of American culture is, on the surface, a look into the country-western music business. But underneath, Altman has many things to say about all of us. Great ensemble acting by Keith Carradine, Lily Tomlin, Ned Beatty, and Henry Gibson, to name just a few, makes this one of the great films of the 1970s. Rated R for language and violence. 1975; 159m.

NATIVE SON ★★½
DIR: Jerrold Freedman. **CAST:** Victor Love, Geraldine Page, Elizabeth McGovern, Matt Dillon, Oprah Winfrey, Akosua Busia, Carroll Baker, Art Evans, David Rasche, Lane Smith, John McMartin.
In this well-meant but muddled screen adaptation of Richard Wright's 1940 novel, a 19-year-old black youth (Victor Love) takes a job as a chauffeur to a wealthy white couple. His hopes for a brighter future are shattered when a tragic accident leads to the death of their daughter (Elizabeth McGovern) and he is accused of murder. Rated R for nudity, suggested sex, violence, and gore. 1986; 101m.

NATIVITY, THE ★★
DIR: Bernard Kowalski. **CAST:** John Shea, Madeleine Stowe, Jane Wyatt, Paul Stewart, Leo McKern, John Rhys-Davies, Kate O'Mara.
Nicely filmed but dramatically unimpressive TV movie about Joseph's (John Shea) wooing of Mary (Madeline Stowe). Leo McKern is the mad King Herod. Not one of the top Biblical epics by a long shot. 1978; 97m.

NATURAL, THE ★★★★
DIR: Barry Levinson. **CAST:** Robert Redford, Robert Duvall, Glenn Close, Kim Basinger, Wilford Brimley, Richard Farnsworth, Robert Prosky, Joe Don Baker.
A thoroughly rewarding, old-fashioned screen entertainment, this adaptation of Bernard Malamud's novel about an unusually gifted baseball player is a must-see. With its brilliant all-star cast, superb story, unforgettable characters, sumptuous cinematography, and sure-handed direction, this

film recalls the Golden Age of Hollywood at its best. Rated PG for brief violence. 1984; 134m.

NATURAL ENEMIES ★★★★
DIR: Jeff Kanew. **CAST:** Hal Holbrook, Louise Fletcher, Viveca Lindfors, José Ferrer, Patricia Elliott.

Excellent study of domestic murder. Hal Holbrook plays a successful magazine editor who murders his wife and three children. Louise Fletcher is great as Holbrook's emotionally unstable wife. Depressing, to be certain, but worth watching, Rated R for violence, profanity, sex, nudity, and adult subject matter. 1979; 100m.

NETWORK ★★★★★
DIR: Sidney Lumet. **CAST:** Peter Finch, William Holden, Faye Dunaway, Robert Duvall, Ned Beatty.

"I'm mad as hell and I'm not going to take it anymore!" Peter Finch (who won a posthumous Academy Award for best actor), William Holden, Faye Dunaway, Robert Duvall, and Ned Beatty give superb performances in this black comedy about the world of television as penned by Paddy Chayefsky. It's a biting satire on the inner workings of this century's most powerful medium. Rated R. 1976; 121m.

NEVER LET GO ★★
DIR: John Guillermin. **CAST:** Peter Sellers, Richard Todd, Elizabeth Sellars, Carol White, Mervyn Johns.

Peter Sellers bombs out in his first dramatic role as a ruthless criminal in this thin story about car stealing. The sure acting of Mervyn Johns, longtime dependable supporting player, helps things but cannot begin to save the film. Nor can Richard Todd's efforts. 1960; B&W; 90m.

NEVER LOVE A STRANGER ★
DIR: Robert Stevens. **CAST:** John Drew Barrymore, Lita Milan, Steve McQueen.

Insulting his theatrical heritage, John Drew Barrymore struggles to portray one of novelist Harold Robbins's sleazy gangster types: a young hustler whose success puts him on a collision course with his old boss and an eager district attorney. 1958; 91m.

NEVER ON SUNDAY ★★★★
DIR: Jules Dassin. **CAST:** Melina Mercouri, Jules Dassin.

A wimpy egghead tries to make a lady out of an earthy, fun-loving prostitute. The setting is Greece; the dialogue and situations are delightful. Melina Mercouri is terrific. 1960; 91m.

NEW CENTURIONS, THE ★★★★
DIR: Richard Fleischer. **CAST:** George C. Scott, Stacy Keach, Jane Alexander, Erik Estrada.

The New Centurions is a blend of harsh reality and soap opera. The moral seems to be "It is no fun being a cop." Watching George C. Scott and Stacy Keach get their lumps, we have to agree. Rated R. 1972; 103m.

NEWSFRONT ★★★★
DIR: Phillip Noyce. **CAST:** Bill Hunter, Wendy Hughes, Gerald Kennedy.

A story of a newsreel company from 1948 until technology brought its existence to an end, this is a warm and wonderful film about real people. It's an insightful glimpse at the early days of the news business, with good character development. Rated PG. 1978; 110m.

NICHOLAS AND ALEXANDRA ★★
DIR: Franklin J. Schaffner. **CAST:** Michael Jayston, Janet Suzman, Tom Baker, Laurence Olivier, Michael Redgrave.

This is an overlong, overdetailed depiction of the events preceding the Russian Revolution until the deaths of Czar Nicholas (Michael Jayston), his wife (Janet Suzman) and family. Some of the performances are outstanding, and the sets and costumes are top-notch. However, the film gets mired in trying to encompass too much historical detail. Rated PG. 1971; 183m.

NICHOLAS NICKLEBY ★★★½
DIR: Alberto Cavalcanti. **CAST:** Derek Bond, Cedric Hardwicke, Sally Ann Howes, Cathleen Nesbitt.

Proud but penniless young Nicholas Nickleby struggles to forge a life for himself and his family while contending with a money-mad scheming uncle and lesser villains. Good acting and authentic Victorian settings bring this classic Dickens novel to vivid screen life. Not quite in the mold of *Great Expectations*, but well above average. 1947; B&W; 108m.

NIGHT AND DAY ★★
DIR: Michael Curtiz. **CAST:** Cary Grant, Alexis Smith, Jane Wyman, Monty Woolley, Eve Arden.

The life of composer Cole Porter, told with cloying pretension. The story vaguely resembles truth and is mostly song-stuffed baloney. The film is too long, too smug, and too deceiving. Cary Grant sings, Alexis Smith tries, and Monty Woolley is funny now and then. 1946; 128m.

NIGHT GAMES ★★★
DIR: Don Taylor. **CAST:** Barry Newman, Susan Howard, Albert Salmi, Luke Askew, Ralph Meeker, Stefanie Powers.

This film, which was originally made for television, led to the *Petrocelli* TV series for Barry Newman. He plays a lawyer who defends Stefanie Powers when she's accused of her husband's murder. There's enough intrigue and suspense in this film to capture most viewers' attention. Rated R. 1974; 78m.

NIGHT IN HEAVEN, A
DIR: John G. Avildsen. **CAST:** Lesley Ann Warren, Christopher Atkins, Robert Logan, Carrie Snodgress.

Lesley Ann Warren plays a respectable college teacher who falls in lust with student-male stripper Christopher Atkins. All in all, it's a movie to forget. Rated R for nudity, slight profanity, and simulated sex. 1983; 80m.

'NIGHT, MOTHER ★★
DIR: Tom Moore. **CAST:** Sissy Spacek, Anne Bancroft.

'Night, Mother, playwright Marsha Norman's argument in favor of suicide, is incredibly depressing material. Sissy Spacek plays a woman who has chosen to end her life. She decides to commit the act in her mother's house, with her mother there. We are only shown Spacek's unhappiness, and this limited manipulative view leaves us with nothing to do but wait uncomfortably for the outcome. Rated PG-13. 1986; 97m.

NIGHT OF THE IGUANA, THE ★★★
DIR: John Huston. **CAST:** Richard Burton, Ava Gardner, Deborah Kerr, Sue Lyon.

In this film, based on Tennessee Williams's play, Richard Burton is a former minister trying to be reinstated in his church. Meanwhile, he takes a menial job as a tour guide, from which he gets fired. His attempted suicide is foiled and confusing. Finally, he finds other reasons to continue living. Sound dull? If not for the cast it would be. 1964; B&W; 118m.

NIGHT PORTER, THE ★
DIR: Liliana Cavani. **CAST:** Dirk Bogarde, Charlotte Rampling, Philippe Leroy, Gabriele Ferzetti, Isa Miranda.

Sordid little outing about a sadomasochistic relationship between an ex-Nazi and the woman he used to abuse sexually in a concentration camp. Lots of kinky scenes, including lovemaking on broken glass. Rated R for violence, nudity, and profanity. 1974; 115m.

NIGHT THE LIGHTS WENT OUT IN GEORGIA, THE ★★★½
DIR: Ronald F. Maxwell. **CAST:** Kristy McNichol, Mark Hamill, Dennis Quaid, Don Stroud.

Gutsy, lusty, and satisfying film about a country singer (Dennis Quaid) with wayward appetites and his level-headed sister-manager (Kristy Mc-

Nichol) who run into big trouble while working their way to Nashville. The gritty deep-South settings, fine action, a cast of credible extras, some memorable musical moments, and a dramatic script with comic overtones add up to above-average entertainment. Rated PG. 1981; 120m.

NIGHT TO REMEMBER, A (1958) ★★★★

DIR: Roy Baker. **CAST:** Kenneth More, Jill Dixon, David McCallum, Laurence Naismith, Honor Blackman, Frank Lawton, Alec McCowen, George Rose.

Authenticity and credibility mark this documentarylike enactment of the sinking of the luxury passenger liner H.M.S. *Titanic* in deep icy Atlantic waters in April, 1912. Novelist Eric Ambler scripted from historian Walter Lord's meticulously detailed account of the tragedy. 1958; B&W; 123m.

NIGHT TRAIN TO KATMANDU ★★

DIR: Robert Wiemer. **CAST:** Pernell Roberts, Eddie Castrodad.

Standard family fare about two youngsters who are uprooted from their comfortable suburban home in the United States to live with their anthropologist parents in Nepal. There they get involved in the quest for the legendary City That Never Was. Nothing special. Not rated. 1988; 102m.

NIGHT VISITOR, THE (1970) ★★★

DIR: Laslo Benedek. **CAST:** Max von Sydow, Liv Ullmann, Trevor Howard, Per Oscarsson, Rupert Davies.

Revenge is the name of the game in this English-language Danish production. Max von Sydow plays an inmate in an insane asylum who comes up with a plan to escape for a single night and take revenge on the various people he believes are responsible for his current predicament. Performances are fine. Rated PG. 1970; 106m.

NIGHT ZOO ★★★

DIR: Jean-Claude Lauzon. **CAST:** Gilles Maheu, Roger Le Bel.

An impressive, quirky French-Canadian film that brings together the unlikely combination of a tough, visceral, urban thriller about drug dealers and corrupt cops and a sensitive, bittersweet story about the renewed love between a dying father and his grown son. The film moves from the dark streets of nighttime Montreal to a strange encounter with an elephant during a nocturnal visit to the zoo. Rated R, with strong violence and profanity. 1987; 107m.

NIGHTS IN WHITE SATIN ★★½

DIR: Michael Bernard. **CAST:** Kenneth David Gilman, Priscilla Harris.

Hokey Cinderella story has Prince Charming as an ace fashion photographer. The glass slippers are snapshots of a rags-dressed beauty who lives among the poor just a motorcycle ride from the photographer's elegant loft. Of course, this gorgeous streetwise Cinderella has hidden talent as a model. Rated R for nudity. 1987; 99m.

NIJINSKY ★★★

DIR: Herbert Ross. **CAST:** Alan Bates, George de la Pena, Leslie Browne, Jeremy Irons.

George de la Pena stars as the legendary dancer and Alan Bates is his lover, a Ballet Russe impresario. Herbert Ross (*The Turning Point*) is no stranger to ballet films. Here, he has assembled an outstanding cast and filmed them beautifully. Rated R. 1980; 125m.

9 1/2 WEEKS ★★

DIR: Adrian Lyne. **CAST:** Mickey Rourke, Kim Basinger, Margaret Whitton, David Branski, Karen Young.

Somewhere between toning down the bondage and liberating the heroine in this adaptation, this movie's story definitely loses out to the imagery. Mickey Rourke is quite believable in the lead role of the masochistic seducer, but Kim Basinger does little more than look pretty. However, together this couple makes steamy work of simple things like dressing and eating. Rated R for sex and violence. 1986; 113m.

NINE DAYS A QUEEN ★★★

DIR: Robert Stevenson. **CAST:** Cedric Hardwicke, Nova Pilbeam, John Mills, Sybil Thorndike, Leslie Perrins, Felix Aylmer, Miles Malleson.

This well-acted historical drama picks up after the death of Henry VIII and follows the frenzied and often lethal scramble for power that went on in the court of England. Lovely Nova Pilbeam plays Lady Jane Grey, the heroine of the title who is taken to the headsman's block by Mary Tudor's armies after a pathetic reign of only nine days. Tragic and moving, this British film was well received by critics when it premiered but is practically forgotten today. 1936; B&W; 80m.

1918 ★★★

DIR: Ken Harrison. **CAST:** William Converse-Roberts, Hallie Foote, Matthew Broderick, Rochelle Oliver, Michael Higgins.

Minor-key slice-of-life film focuses on the denizens of a small Texas town in 1918. After introducing the main characters (including some based on members of his own family), screenwriter Horton Foote details the effects of a devastating epidemic of influenza that ravaged the town that year. The result is an almost academic but well-acted look at a bygone era. Rated PG. 1984; 94m.

1900 ★★

DIR: Bernardo Bertolucci. **CAST:** Robert De Niro, Gerard Depardieu, Dominique Sanda, Burt Lancaster.

This sprawling, self-conscious, exhausting film seems to revel in violence for its own sake. An insincere mishmash of scenes, *1900* chronicles the adventures of two young men set against the backdrop of the rise of fascism and socialism in Italy. The performances of Gerard Depardieu, Robert De Niro, and Dominique Sanda are lost in the all flashiness and bravado of Bernardo Bertolucci's direction. Rated R. 1976; 240m.

1969 ★★★

DIR: Ernest Thompson. **CAST:** Kiefer Sutherland, Robert Downey Jr., Bruce Dern, Mariette Hartley, Winona Ryder, Joanna Cassidy.

Writer-director Ernest Thompson's reminiscences of the flower-power era feature Kiefer Sutherland and Robert Downey Jr. as high-school buddies who face the challenges of college and the abyss of military service in Vietnam. Thompson, who did such a fine job writing *On Golden Pond* and *Sweet Hearts Dance*, goes for too many larger-than-life moments in his directorial debut. But Sutherland and Bruce Dern create sparks as son and father, and the other actors are fine, too. Rated R for profanity, nudity, and violence. 1988; 105m.

NINTH CONFIGURATION, THE ★★★★½

DIR: William Peter Blatty. **CAST:** Stacy Keach, Scott Wilson, Jason Miller, Ed Flanders, Neville Brand, George DiCenzo, Moses Gunn, Robert Loggia, Joe Spinell, Alejandro Rey, Tom Atkins.

This terse, intense film is not for everyone; a barroom brawl near the film's close is one of the most uncomfortable scenes in all of flickdom, but the plot, screenplay, and acting are top-notch. Stacy Keach plays a psychiatrist caring for Vietnam War veterans who suffer from acute emotional disorders. Rated R for profanity and violence. 1979; 115m.

NO DRUMS, NO BUGLES ★★★

DIR: Clyde Ware. **CAST:** Martin Sheen.

Because he refuses to kill, a West Virginia farmer (Martin Sheen) spends three years during the Civil War hiding in the Blue Ridge Mountains. Generally the movie is excellent;

Sheen commands your interest in what is essentially a one-man show, and the nature photography is striking. It's ruined for the home viewer, though, by a terrible film-to-video transfer in which much of the widescreen dimension has been compressed into the square television ratio. What a waste! Rated PG. 1971; 85m.

NO LOVE FOR JOHNNIE ★★★
DIR: Ralph Thomas. **CAST:** Peter Finch, Stanley Holloway, Mary Peach, Donald Pleasence, Billie Whitelaw, Dennis Price.

This oddly titled drama is about a member of the British Parliament beset by problems in his personal and professional lives. The political issues may be a bit vague to American audiences, but this is still enjoyable for the performances by the outstanding character actors. 1961; B&W; 111m.

NO ONE CRIES FOREVER ★★★
DIR: Jans Rautenbach. **CAST:** Elke Sommer, Howard Carpendale, James Ryan.

Don't let the confusing start discourage you—this one gets better! An innocent South African girl is forced into prostitution. When she falls in love with a charming conservationist, her madam has her face disfigured and her boyfriend sets out in search of her. Contains violence and gore. 1985; 96m.

NO TIME FOR SERGEANTS (TELEVISION) ★★½
DIR: Alex Segal. **CAST:** Andy Griffith, Harry Clark, Robert Emhardt, Eddie Le Roy, Alexander Clark.

Andy Griffith turns in a good performance as Will Stockdale, a Georgia hick drafted into the army in this 1955 comedy written especially for television by Ira Levin. Unfortunately, this type of physical comedy needs lots of rehearsal, something to which live television did not lend itself. Also, modern audiences have now been inundated with the innocent-turning-the-establishment-on-its-ear storyline, thereby dating the play. In this case, the theatrical movie is better. 1955; B&W; 60m.

NO WAY TO TREAT A LADY ★★★★
DIR: Jack Smight. **CAST:** Rod Steiger, George Segal, Lee Remick, Eileen Heckart, Michael Dunn, Murray Hamilton.

Excellent thriller with a tour-de-force performance by Rod Steiger, who dons various disguises and personas to strangle women and imprint them with red lipstick lips. Superb script, adapted from William Goldman's novel, and a skilled supporting cast: George Segal as a mothered cop, Eileen Heckart as his delightfully pick-pick-picking mother, and Lee Remick as the attractive love interest. Rated PG for violence. 1968; 108m.

NONE BUT THE LONELY HEART ★★★
DIR: Clifford Odets. **CAST:** Cary Grant, Ethel Barrymore, Barry Fitzgerald, Jane Wyatt, June Duprez, Dan Duryea.

Old pro Ethel Barrymore won an Oscar for her sympathetic portrayal of moody, whining Cockney Cary Grant's mother Ma Mott in this murky drama of broken dreams, thwarted hopes, and petty crime in the slums of London in the late 1930s. Nothing else like it in the Grant filmography. 1944; B&W; 113m.

NOON WINE ★★★★½
DIR: Michael Fields. **CAST:** Fred Ward, Lise Hilboldt, Stellan Skarsgard, Pat Hingle, Jon Cryer.

The fickle nature of human opinion and its ability to savage a victim already down on his luck are the bitter lessons in this adaptation of Katharine Anne Porter's perceptive tale. Porter establishes a stable protagonist (Fred Ward) whose life eventually collapses after he generously provides work on his turn-of-the-century Texas farm for a taciturn loner (Stellan Skarsgard). Suitable for family viewing. 1985; 81m.

NORMA RAE ★★★★
DIR: Martin Ritt. **CAST:** Sally Field, Ron Leibman, Pat Hingle, Beau Bridges.
Sally Field won her first Oscar for her outstanding performance as a southern textile worker attempting to unionize the mill with the aid of organizer Ron Leibman. Film is based on a true story and has good eyes and ears for authenticity. Entire cast is first-rate. Rated PG, some language, minor violence. 1979; 113m.

NORTH DALLAS FORTY ★★★★½
DIR: Ted Kotcheff. **CAST:** Nick Nolte, Bo Svenson, G. D. Spradlin, Dayle Haddon, Mac Davis.
Remarkably enough, *North Dallas Forty* isn't just another numbingly predictable sports film. It's an offbeat, sometimes brutal, examination of the business of football. A first-rate Nick Nolte stars. Rated R. 1979; 119m.

NORTH SHORE ★★½
DIR: William Phelps. **CAST:** Matt Adler, Nia Peeples, John Philbin, Gregory Harrison.
Matt Adler plays an Arizona teen who desperately wants to make it in Hawaii's North Shore surfing pipeline. Gregory Harrison is his mentor, a Sixties burnout case. The pipeline shots are terrific. Rated PG-13 for mild violence. 1987; 92m.

NOT MY KID ★★★
DIR: Michael Tuchner. **CAST:** George Segal, Stockard Channing, Andrew Robinson, Tate Donovan.
Not just another disease-of-the-week vehicle. This telefilm is a well-written look at teenage drug abuse and the havoc it wreaks in a family. 1985; 100m.

NOTHING IN COMMON ★★★½
DIR: Garry Marshall. **CAST:** Tom Hanks, Jackie Gleason, Eva Marie Saint, Hector Elizondo, Barry Corbin, Bess Armstrong, Sela Ward.
Tom Hanks plays a hotshot advertising executive who must deal with his increasingly demanding parents, who are divorcing after thirty-four years of marriage. Jackie Gleason gives a subtle, touching portrayal of the father. The film succeeds at making the difficult shift from zany humor to pathos. Rated PG for profanity and suggested sex. 1986; 120m.

NOW AND FOREVER ★
DIR: Adrian Carr. **CAST:** Cheryl Ladd, Robert Coleby, Carmen Duncan.
In this sappy romance flick, Cheryl Ladd is a boutique owner who comes back from a clothes-buying trip to New York to find that her husband (Robert Coleby) has been accused of rape. This Australian production has a good first half, and a perfectly awful second half. Rated R for violence, profanity, and sex. 1983; 93m.

NOW, VOYAGER ★★★½
DIR: Irving Rapper. **CAST:** Bette Davis, Claude Rains, Paul Henreid.
Bette Davis plays a neurotic, unattractive spinster named Charlotte Vail; an ugly duckling, who, of course, blossoms into a beautiful swan. And it's all thanks to the expert counsel of her psychiatrist (Claude Rains) and a shipboard romance with a married man (Paul Henreid). Directed by Irving Rapper, it features the famous cigarette-lighting ritual that set a trend in the 1940s. 1942; B&W; 117m.

NUN'S STORY, THE ★★★
DIR: Fred Zinnemann. **CAST:** Audrey Hepburn, Edith Evans, Peter Finch, Dean Jagger, Beatrice Straight, Colleen Dewhurst, Peggy Ashcroft, Mildred Dunnock.
A record of a devoted nun's ultimate rebellion against vows of chastity, obedience, silence, and poverty, this Audrey Hepburn starrer was one of the big box-office hits of the 1950s. The wistful and winning Miss Hepburn shines. The supporting cast is excellent. 1959; 152m.

NURSE EDITH CAVELL ★★★
DIR: Herbert Wilcox. **CAST:** Anna Neagle, Edna May Oliver, George Sanders, ZaSu Pitts, H. B. Warner, May Robson, Robert Coote, Martin Kosleck, Mary Howard.

The story of England's second most famous nurse, who helped transport refugee soldiers out of German-held Belgium during World War I. The film delivered a dramatically satisfying antiwar message just as World War II got under way. 1939; B&W; 95m.

NUTS ★★★★
DIR: Martin Ritt. **CAST:** Barbra Streisand, Richard Dreyfuss, Maureen Stapleton, Eli Wallach, Robert Webber, James Whitmore, Karl Malden.

Star-producer Barbra Streisand chaperoned Tom Topor's deft play to the big screen and gave herself a meaty starring role in the process. She's a high-toned prostitute facing a murder charge who may not get her day in court, because her mother and stepfather would rather bury her in an insane asylum. Rated R for language and sexual themes. 1987; 116m.

O LUCKY MAN! ★★★★
DIR: Lindsay Anderson. **CAST:** Malcolm McDowell, Rachel Roberts, Ralph Richardson, Alan Price, Lindsay Anderson.

Offbeat, often stunning story of a young salesman (Malcolm McDowell) and his efforts and obstacles in reaching the top rung of the success ladder. Allegorical and surrealistic at times, this film takes its own course like a fine piece of music. Great acting by a great cast (many of the principals play multiple roles) makes this a real viewing pleasure. Some adult situations and language. Rated R. 1973; 173m.

OCTAVIA ★
DIR: David Beaird. **CAST:** Susan Curtis, Neil Kinsella, Jake Foley.

Octavia starts out like a ridiculously sappy fairy tale that quickly falls into an exploitation mode. The girl in the film is blind and her father likes to abuse her. Then a criminal seeks shelter in their yard and the girl instantly falls in love with him. Rated R. 1982; 93m.

ODD ANGRY SHOT, THE ★★★
DIR: Tom Jeffrey. **CAST:** Bryan Brown, John Hargreaves, Graham Kennedy.

This low-key film about Australian soldiers stationed in Vietnam during the undeclared war is a good attempt to make sense out of a senseless situation as Bryan Brown and his comrades attempt to come to grips with the morality of their involvement in a fight they have no heart for. Odd, sometimes highly effective blend of comedy and drama characterize this offbeat war entry. Some violence; adult situations and language. 1979; 89m.

ODD MAN OUT ★★★★
DIR: Carol Reed. **CAST:** James Mason, Robert Newton, Kathleen Ryan, Dan O'Herlihy.

Carol Reed directed this suspenseful drama about a wounded IRA gunman (James Mason) on the run in Belfast and the people who help and hinder his escape. One of the hallmarks of postwar British cinema. 1946; B&W; 113m.

ODE TO BILLY JOE ★★★
DIR: Max Baer. **CAST:** Robby Benson, Glynnis O'Connor, Joan Hotchkis.

For those who listened to Bobbie Gentry's hit song and wondered why Billy Joe jumped off the Talahachi Bridge, this movie tries to provide one hypothesis. Robby Benson plays Billy Joe with just the right amount of innocence and confusion to be convincing as a youth who doubts his sexual orientation. Rated PG. 1976; 108m.

OEDIPUS REX ★★½
DIR: Tyrone Guthrie. **CAST:** Douglas Rain, Douglas Campbell.

Good adaptation of Sophocles's tragedy. Douglas Rain plays Oedipus, the doomed hero, who kills his father and marries his mother in fulfillment of the prophecy. 1957; 87m.

OF HUMAN BONDAGE (1934) ★★★★½

DIR: John Cromwell. **CAST:** Bette Davis, Leslie Howard, Alan Hale, Frances Dee.

A young doctor (Leslie Howard) becomes obsessed with a sluttish waitress (Bette Davis), almost causing his downfall. Fine acting by all, with Davis an absolute knockout. No rating, but still a little adult for the kiddies. 1934; B&W; 83m.

OF HUMAN BONDAGE (1964) ★★★★½

DIR: Ken Hughes. **CAST:** Kim Novak, Laurence Harvey, Robert Morley, Siobhan McKenna, Roger Livesey, Nanette Newman, Ronald Lacey.

Excellent remake of the 1934 film with Bette Davis. This time Kim Novak plays Mildred Rogers, the promiscuous free spirit who becomes the obsession of Philip Carey (Laurence Harvey). Harvey's performance is wonderfully understated, and Novak plays the slut to the hilt without overdoing it. 1964; B&W; 100m.

OF MICE AND MEN ★★★½

DIR: Reza Badiyi. **CAST:** Robert Blake, Randy Quaid, Lew Ayres, Pat Hingle, Cassie Yates.

Robert Blake is George, Randy Quaid is big, dim-witted Lenny in this Blake-produced TV remake of the classic 1939 Burgess Meredith/Lon Chaney Jr. rendition of John Steinbeck's morality tale of migrant-working life on a California ranch during the Depression. While not as sensitive as the original, this version merits attention and appreciation. 1981; 125m.

OFFICE ROMANCES ★★

DIR: Mary McMurray. **CAST:** Judy Parfitt, Ray Brooks.

Slow-moving British soap. A plain, lonely country girl comes to work in London and is seduced by a selfish, married coworker. Ironically, she feels lucky to have been chosen by him. Unrated. 1981; 48m.

OFFICER AND A GENTLEMAN, AN ★★★★½

DIR: Taylor Hackford. **CAST:** Richard Gere, Debra Winger, Louis Gossett Jr., David Keith, Harold Sylvester.

Soap opera has never been art. However, this funny, touching, corny, and predictable movie, starring Richard Gere and Debra Winger, takes the genre as close to it as any of the old three-handkerchief classics. Director Taylor Hackford keeps just the right balance between the ridiculous and the sublime, making *An Officer and a Gentleman* one of the best of its kind. Rated R for nudity, profanity, and simulated sex. 1982; 125m.

OH, ALFIE ★

DIR: Ken Hughes. **CAST:** Alan Price, Jill Townsend, Joan Collins, Rula Lenska, Hannah Gordon.

Alan Price is an uncaring ladies' man who beds every woman he comes in contact with and then goes on to the next conquest. But there's always one who resists, isn't there? This time it's Jill Townsend, a successful businesswoman. Little of interest here. Rated R for nudity, language, and sex. 1975; 99m.

O'HARA'S WIFE ★★

DIR: William Bartman. **CAST:** Edward Asner, Mariette Hartley, Jodie Foster, Tom Bosley.

Trite little tale about a businessman whose dead wife returns from the grave to help him along in life. More than reminiscent of films like *Topper* and *Kiss Me Goodbye*. Made for television. 1982; 87m.

OLD BOYFRIENDS ★½

DIR: Joan Tewkesbury. **CAST:** Talia Shire, Richard Jordan, Keith Carradine, John Belushi, John Houseman, Buck Henry.

A muddled morass about a woman who decides to exact some revenge on those men who made her past miserable. The viewer is miserable, too, within a very few minutes of this picture, which can't be saved even by

John Belushi. Rated R for profanity and violence. 1979; 103m.

OLD ENOUGH ★
DIR: Marisa Silver. **CAST:** Sarah Boyd, Rainbow Harvest, Neill Barry, Danny Aiello.

A pre-pubescent "coming of age" movie. The two principal characters live on opposite sides of the tracks. It is their curiosity about each other and their radically different lifestyles that spark their friendship, or so we are led to believe. This film fails to deliver. Rated PG. 1984; 91m.

OLD GRINGO, THE ★★★
DIR: Luis Puenzo. **CAST:** Jane Fonda, Gregory Peck, Jimmy Smits, Jessica Tandy.

Based on the novel by Carlos Fuentes. Jane Fonda hesitantly portrays an American schoolteacher on a quest for adventure with Pancho Villa's army during the 1910 Mexican revolution. Gregory Peck is an aging expatriate journalist traveling along for the last ride of his life. This project, long plagued with production difficulties, shows more aesthetic sensitivity during battle scenes than in dialogue sequences. Rated R for adult language. 1989; 120m.

OLD MAID, THE ★★★½
DIR: Edmund Goulding. **CAST:** Bette Davis, Miriam Hopkins, George Brent, Donald Crisp.

Tearjerking film version of the Zoe Akins play based on the Edith Wharton novel about an unwed mother (Bette Davis) who gives up her daughter to be raised by a married cousin (Miriam Hopkins), and suffers the consequences. Hopkins works hard to upstage Davis. A solid box-office winner. 1939; B&W; 95m.

OLD SWIMMIN' HOLE, THE ★★
DIR: Robert McGowan. **CAST:** Marcia Mae Jones, Jackie Moran, Leatrice Joy, Charles Brown.

Easygoing homage to small-town America focuses on young Jackie Moran's plans to become a doctor and his and his mother's life in simpler times. Modest and pleasant enough, this Monogram production came out at the same time as *Our Town* and other films about heartland America and bears some similarities to them. 1940; B&W; 78m.

OLDEST LIVING GRADUATE, THE ★★★★
DIR: Jack Hofsiss. **CAST:** Henry Fonda, George Grizzard, Harry Dean Stanton, Penelope Milford, Cloris Leachman, David Ogden Stiers, Timothy Hutton.

The Oldest Living Graduate features a memorable performance by Henry Fonda as the oldest living member of a prestigious Texas military academy. Cloris Leachman shines in her role of the Colonel's daughter-in-law. The final moments of this teleplay are poignantly realistic. 1983; 90m.

OLIVER TWIST (1922) ★★★
DIR: Frank Lloyd. **CAST:** Jackie Coogan, Lon Chaney Sr., Gladys Brockwell, Esther Ralston.

Young Jackie Coogan, teamed with the legendary "Man of a Thousand Faces" Lon Chaney to portray, respectively, abused orphan Oliver Twist and literature's great manipulator of thieving children, Fagin, in this loose adaptation of Charles Dickens's enduring classic. Something of an oddity, this is one of at least eight film versions of the world-famous novel. Silent. 1922; B&W; 77m.

OLIVER TWIST (1933) ★½
DIR: William Cowen. **CAST:** Dickie Moore, Irving Pichel, William "Stage" Boyd, Barbara Kent.

Low-budget, forgotten version of the popular Charles Dickens story features some interesting performances and a few effective moments. This is a curiosity for students of literature or early sound film. Print quality is marginal. 1933; B&W; 77m.

OLIVER TWIST (1948) ★★★★
DIR: David Lean. **CAST:** Alec Guinness, Robert Newton, John Howard Davies.

Alec Guinness and Robert Newton give superb performances as the villains in this David Lean adaptation of the Charles Dickens story about a young boy who is forced into a life of thievery until he's rescued by a kindly old gentleman. 1948; B&W; 105m.

OLIVER'S STORY ★

DIR: John Korty. **CAST:** Ryan O'Neal, Candice Bergen, Nicola Pagett, Edward Binns, Ray Milland.

Even if you loved *Love Story* you'll find it difficult to like this lame sequel. O'Neal's character apparently decides money's not so bad after all and courts an heiress. Movies like this mean always having to say you're sorry. Rated PG. 1978; 92m.

ON GOLDEN POND ★★★★★

DIR: Mark Rydell. **CAST:** Henry Fonda, Katharine Hepburn, Jane Fonda, Doug McKeon.

Henry Fonda, Katharine Hepburn, and Jane Fonda are terrific in this warm, funny, and often quite moving film, written by Ernest Thompson, about the conflicts and reconciliations among the members of a family that take place during a fateful summer. Rated PG because of brief profanity. 1981; 109m.

ON THE BOWERY ★★★★

DIR: Lionel Rogosin. **CAST:** Ray Sayler, Gorman Hendricks, Frank Mathews.

Gritty, uncompromising docudrama, dealing with life among the tragic street people of the Lower East Side in New York City. An extraordinary, agonizing glimpse into the world of the depraved alcoholic nomads whose lives become a constant daily struggle. Excellent black-and-white cinematography. 1956; B&W; 65m.

ON THE EDGE ★★★½

DIR: Rob Nilsson. **CAST:** Bruce Dern, Bill Bailey, Jim Haynie, John Marley, Pam Grier.

Bruce Dern gives a solid performance as a middle-aged runner hoping to regain the glory that escaped him twenty years earlier when he was disqualified from the 1964 Olympic trials. The race to test his ability is the grueling 14.2-mile annual Cielo Sea Race over California's Mount Tamalpais. The mobile camera action in the training and race sequences is very effective. Rated PG. 1985; 95m.

ON THE NICKEL ★★½

DIR: Ralph Waite. **CAST:** Donald Moffat, Ralph Waite, Hal Williams, Jack Kehoe, Ellen Geer.

Ralph Waite, of TV's *The Waltons*, wrote, produced, and directed this drama about derelicts on L.A.'s skid row. It's a well-intentioned effort that is too unfocused and sentimental to work, though Donald Moffat's performance as a cleaned-up drunk is worth seeing. Rated R for rough language. 1980; 96m.

ON THE WATERFRONT ★★★★★

DIR: Elia Kazan. **CAST:** Marlon Brando, Eva Marie Saint, Karl Malden, Lee J. Cobb, Rod Steiger.

Tough, uncompromising look at corruption on the New York waterfront. Marlon Brando is brilliant as Terry Malloy, a one-time fight contender who is now a longshoreman. Led into crime by his older brother (Rod Steiger), Terry is disgusted by the violent tactics of boss Lee J. Cobb. Yet if he should turn against the crooks, it could mean his life. A classic American film with uniformly superb performances. 1954; B&W; 108m.

ON VALENTINE'S DAY ★★½

DIR: Ken Harrison. **CAST:** William Converse-Roberts, Hallie Foote, Michael Higgins, Steven Hill, Rochelle Oliver, Matthew Broderick.

Horton Foote created this small-town love story about his own parents. A young couple (William Converse and Hallie Foote) to make ends meet after eloping. Her wealthy parents haven't spoken to her since they ran away, but all that is about to change. Rated PG. 1986; 106m.

ONCE IN PARIS ★★★

DIR: Frank D. Gilroy. **CAST:** Wayne Rogers, Gayle Hunnicutt, Jack Lenoir, Tanya Lopert, Doris Roberts.

Effervescent romantic comedy about a script doctor (Wayne Rogers) called to Paris to repair a screenplay. Once there, he falls in love and ends up ignoring his work. Sparkling writing perks up an old story. Rated PG for adult situations. 1978; 100m.

ONCE IS NOT ENOUGH

DIR: Guy Green. **CAST:** Kirk Douglas, Alexis Smith, David Janssen, Deborah Raffin, George Hamilton, Melina Mercouri, Brenda Vaccaro.

Trash based on trash, this film of the late Jacqueline Susann's novel of jet-set sex and shenanigans is still being lived down by all concerned. Rated R. 1975; 121m.

ONE AND ONLY, THE ★★★

DIR: Carl Reiner. **CAST:** Henry Winkler, Kim Darby, Herve Villechaize, Harold Gould, Gene Saks, William Daniels.

Writer Steve Gordon got started with this tale of an obnoxious college show-off who eventually finds fame as a wrestling showboater. Henry Winkler was still struggling to find a big-screen personality, but his occasional character flaws often are overshadowed by Gordon's deft little script. The material has become more timely, considering the current fascination with big-time wrestling. Rated PG. 1978; 98m.

ONE DAY IN THE LIFE OF IVAN DENISOVICH ★★★

DIR: Caspar Wrede. **CAST:** Tom Courtenay, Espen Skjonberg, James Maxwell, Alfred Burke.

Tom Courtenay does a fine job as the title character, a prisoner in a Siberian labor camp. The famed novel by Alexander Solzhenitsyn is beautifully and bleakly photographed. Not an uplifting story, but a significant one. 1971; 100m.

ONE FLEW OVER THE CUCKOO'S NEST ★★★★★

DIR: Milos Forman. **CAST:** Jack Nicholson, Louise Fletcher, Will Sampson, Danny DeVito, Christopher Lloyd, Scatman Crothers.

Not since Capra's *It Happened One Night* had a motion picture swept all the major Academy Awards. Jack Nicholson sparkles as Randall P. McMurphy, a convict who is committed to a northwestern mental institution for examination. While there, he stimulates in each of his ward inmates an awakening spirit of self-worth and frees them from their passive acceptance of the hospital authorities' domination. Louise Fletcher is brilliant as the insensitive head nurse. Rated R. 1975; 133m.

ONE MAGIC CHRISTMAS ★★★★½

DIR: Phillip Borsos. **CAST:** Mary Steenburgen, Harry Dean Stanton, Gary Basaraba, Arthur Hill, Ken Pogue.

Mary Steenburgen stars in this touching, feel-good movie as a young mother who has lost the spirit of Christmas. She regains it with the help of a Christmas angel (played by that terrific character actor Harry Dean Stanton). Rated G. 1985; 95m.

ONE NIGHT STAND

DIR: Allan Winton King. **CAST:** Chapelle Jaffe, Brent Carver.

This Canadian made-for-TV adaptation of a stage play isn't a horror movie at all, though it's being sold as such. It's a comedy-drama about a woman who picks up a young man in a nightclub and takes him home. But instead of an evening's *amour*, she gets a lot of talk, talk, talk. It's so badly edited that at several points you'd swear they got the reels mixed up while transferring it to video. Unrated, it's all talk and no action. 1977; 93m.

ONE ON ONE ★★★★
DIR: Lamont Johnson. **CAST:** Robby Benson, Annette O'Toole, G. D. Spradlin.

The harsh world of big-time college athletics is brought into clearer focus by this unheralded "little film." Robby Benson is a naïve small-town basketball star who has his eyes opened when he wins a scholarship to a large western university. He doesn't play up to his coach's expectations, and the pressure is put on to take away his scholarship. Rated R. 1980; 98m.

ONE RUSSIAN SUMMER ★
DIR: Antonio Calenda. **CAST:** Oliver Reed, John McEnery, Claudia Cardinale, Carole André, Raymond Lovelock.

Another movie we'd never have seen in this country if not for home video, and a good example of what a mixed blessing that is. In czarist Russia of the eighteenth century, an anarchist peasant (John McEnery) arrives at the estate of a brutish landowner (Oliver Reed at his loudest) to stir up trouble and seek revenge. The film gets progressively sillier and more lurid. Rated R. 1973; 112m.

ONION FIELD, THE ★★★★
DIR: Harold Becker. **CAST:** John Savage, James Woods, Franklyn Seales, Ted Danson, Ronny Cox, Dianne Hull.

Solid screen version of Joseph Wambaugh's book about a cop (John Savage) who cracks up after his partner is murdered. James Woods and Franklyn Seales are memorable as the criminals. While not for all tastes, this film has a kind of subtle power and an almost documentarylike quality that will please those fascinated by true crime stories. Rated R. 1979; 124m.

ONLY WHEN I LAUGH ★★★
DIR: Glenn Jordan. **CAST:** Marsha Mason, Kristy McNichol, James Coco, Joan Hackett.

A brilliant but self-destructive actress (Marsha Mason) and her daughter (Kristy McNichol) reach toward understanding in this sometimes funny, sometimes tearful, but always entertaining adaptation by Neil Simon of his play *The Gingerbread Lady.* Rated R for profanity. 1981; 121m.

ORDEAL OF DR. MUDD, THE ★★★½
DIR: Paul Wendkos. **CAST:** Dennis Weaver, Susan Sullivan, Richard Dysart, Arthur Hill.

The true story of Dr. Samuel Mudd, who innocently aided the injured, fleeing John Wilkes Booth following Lincoln's assassination and was sent to prison for alleged participation in the conspiracy. Dennis Weaver's fine portrayal of the ill-fated doctor makes this film well worthwhile. More than a century passed before Mudd was cleared, thanks to the efforts of a descendant, newscaster Roger Mudd. Rated PG. 1980; 143m.

ORDINARY HEROES ★★★
DIR: Peter H. Cooper. **CAST:** Richard Dean Anderson, Valerie Bertinelli, Doris Roberts.

A moving love story about a young couple torn apart when the man (Richard Dean Anderson) is drafted into the army and sent to Vietnam. He returns from combat blinded and attempts to piece his broken life back together with his former girlfriend (Valerie Bertinelli). This absorbing drama gets its strength from strong performances by both leads. Rated PG. 1986; 90m.

ORDINARY PEOPLE ★★★★½
DIR: Robert Redford. **CAST:** Mary Tyler Moore, Donald Sutherland, Timothy Hutton, Judd Hirsch, Elizabeth McGovern, Dinah Manoff, James B. Sikking.

This moving human drama, which won the Academy Award for best picture of 1980, marked the directorial debut of Robert Redford...and an auspicious one it is, too. Redford elicits memorable performances from Mary Tyler Moore, Donald Sutherland, Timothy Hutton, and Judd Hirsch and makes the intelligent, powerful script by Alvin Sargent seem even better. Rated R for adult situations. 1980; 123m.

ORPHAN TRAIN ★★★½

DIR: William A. Graham. **CAST:** Jill Eikenberry, Kevin Dobson, Linda Manz, Glenn Close.

Inspirational tale of a young woman's desire to help thousands of orphans who were roaming the streets of New York in the 1850s. Realizing that her soup kitchen can't keep the kids out of trouble, she takes a group out west in hopes of finding farming families willing to adopt them. Originally shown on TV. 1979; 150m.

ORPHANS ★★★★

DIR: Alan J. Pakula. **CAST:** Albert Finney, Matthew Modine, Kevin Anderson.

Based on the play by Lyle Kessler, this compact drama is a psychological thriller with a poignant twist. Albert Finney effectively portrays an affluent American gangster who does more than merely befriend two homeless young men—Treat, an angry delinquent (Matthew Modine), and Phillips (Kevin Anderson), his helpless younger brother. In a short time, he changes their lives. Rated R. 1987; 115m.

ORPHANS OF THE STORM ★★★½

DIR: D. W. Griffith. **CAST:** Lillian Gish, Dorothy Gish, Sidney Herbert, Sheldon Lewis, Monte Blue, Joseph Schildkraut, Creighton Hale, Morgan Wallace.

Film's first master director blends fact and fiction, mixing the French Revolution with the trials and tribulations of two sisters—one blind and raised by thieves, the other betrayed by self-saving aristocrats. The plot creaks with age, but the settings and action spell good entertainment. Silent. 1922; B&W; 125m.

OSCAR, THE

DIR: Russell Rouse. **CAST:** Stephen Boyd, Elke Sommer, Tony Bennett, Eleanor Parker, Ernest Borgnine, Joseph Cotten.

Take a trite story of an unscrupulous actor trying to advance his career at the expense of others. Add some acting that is so embarrassing it makes you slump in your seat. What you get is a real stinker. 1966; 119m.

OTHER SIDE OF MIDNIGHT, THE ★½

DIR: Charles Jarrott. **CAST:** Marie-France Pisier, John Beck, Susan Sarandon, Raf Vallone, Clu Gulager.

Glossy, tasteless soap opera derived from schlockmaster Sidney Sheldon's best-selling novel. The story runs from 1939 to 1947 and the movie seems to last that long. Rated R. 1977; 165m.

OTHER SIDE OF THE MOUNTAIN, THE ★★★

DIR: Larry Peerce. **CAST:** Marilyn Hassett, Beau Bridges.

Absolutely heart-wrenching account of Jill Kinmont, an Olympic-bound skier whose career was cut short by a fall that left her paralyzed. Marilyn Hassett, in her film debut, makes Kinmont a fighter whose determination initially backfires and prompts some to have unreasonable expectations of her limited recovery. Rated PG. 1975; 103m.

OTHER SIDE OF THE MOUNTAIN, PART II, THE ★★

DIR: Larry Peerce. **CAST:** Marilyn Hassett, Timothy Bottoms, Nan Martin, Belinda Montgomery.

A sequel to the modest 1975 hit, the film continues the story of Jill Kinmont, a promising young skier who was paralyzed from the shoulders down in an accident. The tender romance, well played by Hassett and Bottoms, provides some fine moments. Rated PG. 1978; 100m.

OUR DAILY BREAD ★★½

DIR: King Vidor. **CAST:** Tom Keene, Karen Morley, John Qualen, Addison Richards.

This vintage Depression social drama about an idealistic man organizing community farms and socialistic society is pretty creaky despite sincere effort by director King Vidor. Lead actor Tom Keene did better in cowboy films. 1934; B&W; 74m.

OUR FAMILY BUSINESS ★★
DIR: Robert Collins. **CAST:** Ted Danson, Sam Wanamaker, Vera Miles, Ray Milland.
Two sons take different tacks in surviving within a Mafia family. Sam Wanamaker and Ray Milland give strong performances in this generally slow, uninspired twist on the *Godfather* theme. Made for television. 1981; 74m.

OUR TOWN (1940) ★★★★
DIR: Sam Wood. **CAST:** Frank Craven, William Holden, Martha Scott, Thomas Mitchell, Fay Bainter.
Superb performances from a top-flight cast add zest to this well-done adaptation of Thornton Wilder's play about life in a small town. 1940; B&W; 90m.

OUR TOWN (1980) ★★★½
DIR: Franklin Schaeffer. **CAST:** Ned Beatty, Sada Thompson, Ronny Cox, Glynnis O'Connor, Robby Benson, Hal Holbrook, John Houseman.
Not as good as the 1940s theatrical version, this TV version of the award-winning play by Thornton Wilder is notable for the fine performance of Hal Holbrook. The simple telling of the day-to-day life of Grover's Corners is done with remarkable restraint. 1980; 100m.

OUT OF AFRICA ★★★★½
DIR: Sydney Pollack. **CAST:** Robert Redford, Meryl Streep, Klaus Maria Brandauer, Michael Kitchen, Malick Bowens, Michael Gough, Suzanna Hamilton.
Robert Redford and Meryl Streep are at the peaks of their considerable talents in this 1985 Oscar winner for best picture, a grand-scale motion picture also blessed with inspired direction, gorgeous cinematography, and a haunting score. An epic romance, it was based by Kurt Luedtke on the life and works of Isak Dinesen and concerns the love of two staunch individualists for each other and the land in which they live. Rated PG for a discreet sex scene. 1985; 160m.

OUT OF SEASON ★★
DIR: Alan Bridges. **CAST:** Vanessa Redgrave, Cliff Robertson, Susan George.
This British mood piece is full of atmosphere, but its strange love story, about a man who returns to England to find the woman with whom he had an affair twenty years before, is nothing more than average. The woman now has a beautiful daughter who may be the product of their affair. Rated R. 1975; 90m.

OUTSIDE THE LAW ★★★
DIR: Tod Browning. **CAST:** Priscilla Dean, Lon Chaney Sr., Ralph Lewis, Wheeler Oakman.
Director Tod Browning's long association with the greatest of all character actors and one of the biggest stars of the silent screen began in 1921 when Lon Chaney supported female star Priscilla Dean in this crime drama. The incomparable Chaney plays Black Mike, the meanest and smarmiest of hoodlums, as well as an old Chinese man, the faithful retainer to Miss Dean. Silent. 1921; B&W; 77m.

OUTSIDERS, THE ★½
DIR: Francis Ford Coppola. **CAST:** C. Thomas Howell, Matt Dillon, Ralph Macchio, Emilio Estevez, Tom Cruise, Leif Garrett.
Based on S. E. Hinton's popular novel, which has sold some four million copies, this is a fairly simple—and simplistic—movie about kids from the wrong side of the tracks. The pace is slow, and watching it soon becomes a trial—even though it was directed by Francis Ford Coppola. Rated PG for profanity and violence. 1983; 91m.

OVER THE EDGE ★★★★
DIR: Jonathan Kaplan. **CAST:** Matt Dillon, Michael Kramer, Pamela Ludwig.

An explosive commentary on the restlessness of today's youth, this film also serves as an indictment against America's hypocritically permissive society. The violence that was supposedly caused by the release of gang films like *The Warriors*, *Boulevard Nights*, and *The Wanderers* caused the movie's makers to shelve it. However, Matt Dillon, who made his film debut herein, is now a hot property, and that's why this deserving movie is out on video. Rated R. 1979; 95m.

OVER THE TOP ★★
DIR: Menahem Golan. **CAST:** Sylvester Stallone, Robert Loggia, Susan Blakely, David Mendenhall.
Thoroughly silly effort. Sylvester Stallone stars as a compassionate trucker who only wants to spend time with the son (David Mendenhall) whom he left, years before, in the custody of his wife (Susan Blakely, in a thankless role) and her rich, iron-willed father (Robert Loggia, as a one-note villain). This clichéd story has little of interest. Rated PG for mild violence. 1987; 94m.

OVERINDULGENCE ★★
DIR: Ross Devenish. **CAST:** Denholm Elliott, Holly Aird, Michael Bryne, Kathryn Pogson.
Rather tame rendition of the scandalous 1940s South African murder trial that shocked the world. A sordid tale of adultery, drugs, and child abuse is told by Juanita Carberry, one of the daughters of the decadent British settlers. Sir Jock Broughton is the accused murderer, and only Juanita knows the truth behind the sensational killing. A good dramatic story is done in by a lightweight script, amateurish direction, and mediocre acting. For substance, sophistication, and style covering the subject, check out *White Mischief*. Rated PG-13. 1987; 95m.

OXFORD BLUES ★★
DIR: Robert Boris. **CAST:** Rob Lowe, Amanda Pays.
Rob Lowe plays a brash American who attempts to woo the beautiful Lady Victoria while attending England's Oxford University. Writer-director Robert Boris has even worked in the sports angle, by making Lowe a rowing champ who has to prove himself. A formula picture. Rated PG-13. 1984; 93m.

PALM BEACH ★★★
DIR: Albie Thomas. **CAST:** Nat Young, Ken Brown, Amanda Berry, Bryan Brown.
Four different stories concerning troubled Australian teens converge at the title location, a popular Aussie beach. Fans of the new Australian cinema will want to take a look, though the accents may be a bit thick for others. Not rated. 1979; 88m.

PALOOKA ★★½
DIR: Ben Stoloff. **CAST:** Jimmy Durante, Stu Erwin, Lupe Velez, Marjorie Rambeau, Robert Armstrong, William Cagney, Thelma Todd, Mary Carlisle.
First filmed version of Ham Fisher's popular *Joe Palooka* is an okay little film about country bumpkin Stu Erwin's rise to the top in the fight game. This film shares a niche with the other seldom-seen comic-strip film adaptations of the 1930s, and its availability on video is a pleasant gift to the fan who loves those tough and slightly goofy movies of the early 1930s. 1934; B&W; 86m.

PAPA'S DELICATE CONDITION ★★½
DIR: George Marshall. **CAST:** Jackie Gleason, Glynis Johns, Charlie Ruggles, Laurel Goodwin, Charles Lane, Elisha Cook Jr., Juanita Moore, Murray Hamilton.
Somewhat stolid but pleasant enough story of family life in a small Texas town and the sometimes unpleasant notoriety brought to a family by their alcoholic patriarch, Jackie Gleason. Not as good a film as it was considered when released, this is still an enjoyable movie. 1963; 98m.

PAPER CHASE, THE ★★★★
DIR: James Bridges. **CAST:** Timothy Bottoms, John Houseman, Lindsay Wagner.
John Houseman won the Oscar for best actor in a supporting role in 1973 with his first-rate performance in this excellent film. Timothy Bottoms stars as a law student attempting to earn his law degree in spite of a stuffy professor (Houseman). Rated PG. 1973; 111m.

PAPER LION ★★★½
DIR: Alex March. **CAST:** Alan Alda, Lauren Hutton, Alex Karras, David Doyle, Ann Turkel, Roger Brown.
Based on George Plimpton's book, this film tells the story of the author's exploits when he becomes an honorary team member of the Detroit Lions pro football team. Alan Alda is fine as Plimpton and Alex Karras is a standout in his support. 1968; 107m.

PARADISE ALLEY 🦃
DIR: Sylvester Stallone. **CAST:** Sylvester Stallone, Armand Assante, Lee Canalito.
Sylvester Stallone wrote, directed (his debut), and starred in this turgid mess about three brothers hoping for a quick ride out of the slums and into high society. The dialogue is infantile, the delivery mawkish, the direction completely inept. Rated PG for violence. 1978; 107m.

PARALLAX VIEW, THE ★★★★
DIR: Alan J. Pakula. **CAST:** Warren Beatty, Paula Prentiss, William Daniels.
This fine film offers a fascinating study of a reporter, played by Warren Beatty, trying to penetrate the cover-up of an assassination in which the hunter becomes the hunted. Rated R. 1974; 102m.

PARIS BLUES ★★★½
DIR: Martin Ritt. **CAST:** Paul Newman, Joanne Woodward, Diahann Carroll, Sidney Poitier, Louis Armstrong, Serge Reggiani.
Duke Ellington's superb jazz score enhances this boys-meet-girls drama. The action takes place in Paris where two jazz musicians (Paul Newman and Sidney Poitier) fall for two lovely tourists (Joanne Woodward and Diahann Carroll). What the plot lacks in originality is amply made up for by the fine music and outstanding cast. 1961; 98m.

PARIS, TEXAS ★★★★½
DIR: Wim Wenders. **CAST:** Harry Dean Stanton, Nastassja Kinski, Dean Stockwell, Aurore Clement, Hunter Carson.
Paris, Texas is a haunting vision of personal pain and universal suffering, with Harry Dean Stanton impeccable as the weary wanderer who returns after four years to reclaim his son (Hunter Carson) and search for his wife (Nastassja Kinski). It is the kind of motion picture we rarely see, one that attempts to say something about our country and its people—and succeeds. Rated R for profanity and adult content. 1984; 144m.

PARK IS MINE, THE ★★½
DIR: Steven H. Stern. **CAST:** Tommy Lee Jones, Helen Shaver, Yaphet Kotto.
After his friend is killed, unstable Vietnam vet (Tommy Lee Jones) invades New York's Central Park and proclaims it to be his. Using combat tactics, Jones holds off the authorities until the predictable ending. Pretty far-fetched stuff. An HBO Film. 1985; 102m.

PARKER ADDERSON, PHILOSOPHER ★★★★
DIR: Arthur Barron. **CAST:** Harris Yulin, Douglas Watson, Darren O'Connor.
Man's ability to inflict torment even on those with nothing left to lose is the theme of this deft adaptation of the Ambrose Bierce short story. Harris Yulin stars as a Yankee spy caught red-handed by the ragtag troops of Douglas Watson's Confederate general. Introduced by Henry Fonda; suitable for family viewing. 1974; 39m.

PARTING GLANCES ★★★★
DIR: Bill Sherwood. **CAST:** Richard Ganoung, John Bolger, Steve Buscemi, Adam Nathan, Kathy Kinney, Patrick Tull.

Nick (Steve Buscemi), a rock singer, discovers he is dying of AIDS. Writer-director Bill Sherwood charts the effect this discovery has on Nick and his estranged lover, Michael (Richard Ganoung), who now lives with Robert (John Bolger). Subject matter aside, *Parting Glances* has a number of funny moments and is a life-affirming look at the gay lifestyle. 1986; 90m.

PASCALI'S ISLAND ★★★★
DIR: James Dearden. **CAST:** Ben Kingsley, Helen Mirren, Charles Dance.

A quietly enigmatic film about town loyalties, hypocrisy, and broader philosophical issues of art and romanticism, as represented by three characters on a Greek island in 1908. Ben Kingsley is brilliant as a low-level bureaucrat and semispy who will never challenge what he does or why, even when it threatens to destroy everything he cares about. Rated PG-13. 1988; 101m.

PASSAGE TO INDIA, A ★★★★★
DIR: David Lean. **CAST:** Judy Davis, Victor Banerjee, Alec Guinness, Peggy Ashcroft.

After an absence from the screen of fourteen years, British director David Lean returned triumphantly, with the brilliant *A Passage to India*. Based on the 1924 novel by E. M. Forster, it is a work that compares favorably with the filmmaker's finest. Ostensibly about the romantic adventures of a young Englishwoman in "the mysterious East" that culminate in a court trial (for attempted rape), it is also a multi-layered, symbolic work about, in the words of Forster, "the difficulty of living in the universe." Rated PG. 1984; 163m.

PASSENGER, THE ★★
DIR: Michelangelo Antonioni. **CAST:** Jack Nicholson, Maria Schneider, Jenny Runacre, Ian Hendry.

Billed as a suspense drama, *The Passenger* is a very slow-moving tale about a disillusioned TV reporter (Jack Nicholson) working in Africa. He exchanges identities with a dead Englishman and thereby becomes involved with underworld international arms smugglers. Rated R. 1975; 119m.

PATHS OF GLORY ★★★★★
DIR: Stanley Kubrick. **CAST:** Kirk Douglas, Adolphe Menjou, George Macready, Timothy Carey, Ralph Meeker.

A great antiwar movie! Kirk Douglas plays the compassionate French officer in World War I who must lead his men against insurmountable enemy positions, and then must defend three of them against charges of cowardice when the battle is lost. Adolphe Menjou and George Macready perfectly portray Douglas's monstrous senior officers. 1957; B&W; 86m.

PATTERNS ★★★½
DIR: Fielder Cook. **CAST:** Van Heflin, Everett Sloane, Ed Begley Sr., Beatrice Straight.

Ed Begley dominates this Rod Serling drama of manipulation and machinations in the executive suite. The classic corporate-power-struggle story has changed in recent years, dating this film somewhat, but the game people play to climb to the top is still fascinating. 1956; B&W; 83m.

PATTI ROCKS ★★★★
DIR: David Morris. **CAST:** Chris Mulkey, John Jenkins, Karen Landry.

Controversial sequel to 1975's *Loose Ends* picks up twelve years later. Bill (Chris Mulkey) has been having an affair with Patti Rocks (Karen Landry), who has informed him that she is pregnant. A very human story with a genuine twist. Rated R for profanity, nudity, and simulated sex. 1987; 86m.

PATTON ★★★★★
DIR: Franklin J. Schaffner. **CAST:** George C. Scott, Karl Malden, Stephen Young, Tim Considine.
Flamboyant, controversial General George S. Patton is the subject of this Oscar-winning picture. George C. Scott is spellbinding in the title role. Scott's brilliant performance manages to bring alive this military hero, who strode a fine line between effective battlefield commander and demigod. Rated PG. 1970; 169m.

PATTY HEARST ★★★
DIR: Paul Schrader. **CAST:** Natasha Richardson, William Forsythe, Ving Rhames, Frances Fisher.
Paul Schrader provides a restless, relentless, and often moving story of revolutionary idealism gone amok in this documentary-style drama of the kidnapping and subversion of Patty Hearst (Natasha Richardson). Richardson's rendition of Hearst is captivating, and William Forsythe and Frances Fisher are outstanding as Bill and Emily Harris. Yet the film leaves one with a lot of unanswered questions. Rated R for profanity, nudity, and violence. 1988; 108m.

PAUL'S CASE ★★
DIR: Lamont Johnson. **CAST:** Eric Roberts, Michael Higgins, Lindsay Crouse.
Eric Roberts's impassioned portrayal of the working-class youth from turn-of-the-century Pittsburgh is the only draw in this interpretation of Willa Cather's dreary story. The outcome will leave viewers wondering about the point of it all. Introduced by Henry Fonda; suitable for family viewing. 1980; 52m.

PAWNBROKER, THE ★★★★★
DIR: Sidney Lumet. **CAST:** Rod Steiger, Geraldine Fitzgerald, Brock Peters.
This is a somber and powerfully acted portrayal of a Jewish man who survived the Nazi holocaust, only to find his spirit still as bleak as the Harlem ghetto in which he operates a pawnshop. Rod Steiger gives a tour-de-force performance as a man with dead emotions who is shocked out of his zombielike existence by confronting the realities of modern urban life. 1965; B&W; 116m.

PAY OR DIE ★★★½
DIR: Richard Wilson. **CAST:** Ernest Borgnine, Zohra Lampert, Al Austin.
Ernest Borgnine plays the fabled leader of the Italian Squad, New York's crack police detectives who dealt with the turn-of-the-century Black Hand. Borgnine and his fellow Italian-Americans use force and intimidation to combat the savage Mafia-connected hoodlums who extort and murder their own people in Little Italy. An underrated crime film. 1960; B&W; 110m.

PAYDAY ★★★★
DIR: Daryl Duke. **CAST:** Rip Torn, Ahna Capri, Elayne Heilveil, Michael C. Gwynne.
Bravura performance by Rip Torn as a hard-drinking, ruthless country singer who's bent on destroying himself and everyone around him. Gripping, emotionally draining drama. Rarely seen in theaters, this one is definitely worth viewing on tape. Rated R for language, nudity, sexual situations. 1973; 103m.

PEARL, THE ★★
DIR: Emilio Fernandez. **CAST:** Pedro Armendariz, Maria Elena Marques.
John Steinbeck's heavy-handed parable about the true riches in life and the value of wealth when compared with natural treasures is beautifully photographed and effectively presented, but the film suffers from the same shortcoming inherent in the book. The tragic plight of the loving couple and their desperately ill son is relentlessly hammered home. 1948; 77m.

PEARL OF THE SOUTH PACIFIC ★½
DIR: Allan Dwan. **CAST:** Virginia Mayo, Dennis Morgan, David Farrar, Murvyn Vye.

Allan Dwan guides another one down the tubes. A dull film about murder in the tropics that tries to be intriguing and exotic but fails on both counts. 1955; 86m.

PEDESTRIAN, THE ★★★½
DIR: Maximilian Schell. **CAST:** Gustav Rudolph Sellner, Peter Hall, Maximilian Schell.

The directorial debut for Maximilian Schell, this is a disturbing near masterpiece of drama exploring the realm of guilt and self-doubt that surrounds ex–World War II Nazis. Gustav Rudolph Sellner's haunting and quiet performance as an aging industrialist who is exposed as an ex-Nazi is a little tedious but thought-provoking in the outcome—much like the film itself. 1974; 97m.

PENITENT, THE ★★
DIR: Cliff Osmond. **CAST:** Raul Julia, Armand Assante, Julie Carmen.

Raul Julia is a member of the Penitents, a religious cult that remembers the suffering of Christ by affixing one of its members to a cross and leaving him in the desert sun for an entire day—often to die as "God's will." Exploration of this intriguing milieu is set aside in favor of a silly soap opera about Julia's problem with his young wife and lusty pal. Rated PG for suggested sex. 1988; 90m.

PENNY SERENADE ★★★★
DIR: George Stevens. **CAST:** Cary Grant, Irene Dunne, Edgar Buchanan.

Cary Grant and Irene Dunne are one of the most fondly remembered comedy teams in films such as *The Awful Truth* and *My Favorite Wife*. This 1941 film is a radical change of pace, for it is a ten-hankie tearjerker about a couple's attempt to have children. They are excellent in this drama far removed from their standard comic fare. 1941; B&W; 125m.

PEOPLE VS. JEAN HARRIS ★★
DIR: George Schaefer. **CAST:** Ellen Burstyn, Martin Balsam, Richard Dysart, Peter Coyote.

A sedate, dramatic reenactment of a lengthy trial transcript, shot entirely inside a courtroom. Although everyone underplays their roles perfectly, it is still a long, long, boring trial. Made for TV. 1981; 147m.

PERFECT ★½
DIR: James Bridges. **CAST:** John Travolta, Jamie Lee Curtis, Jann Wenner, Marilu Henner, Laraine Newman.

In this irritatingly uneven and unfocused film, John Travolta stars as a *Rolling Stone* reporter out to do an exposé on the current health-club boom. Jamie Lee Curtis is the uncooperative aerobics instructor he attempts to spotlight in his story. Just another moralizing mess about journalistic ethics. Rated R for profanity, suggested sex, and violence. 1985; 120m.

PERFORMANCE ★★★★
DIR: Nicolas Roeg, Donald Cammell. **CAST:** Mick Jagger, James Fox, Anita Pallenberg.

Mick Jagger, the leader of the Rolling Stones rock group, stars in this bizarre film as Turner, a rock singer who decides to switch identities with a hunted hit man (James Fox). Co-directed by Nicolas Roeg and Donald Cammell, *Performance* is a chilling, profoundly disturbing cinematic nightmare about the dark side of man's consciousness. Rated R for profanity, nudity, violence. 1970; 105m.

PERMANENT RECORD ★★½
DIR: Marisa Silver. **CAST:** Keanu Reeves, Alan Boyce, Richard Bradford.

This drama stars Keanu Reeves as Chris, whose best friend, a popular, talented, seemingly well-adjusted high-school senior, commits suicide. The film focuses on the effects the suicide has on his closest friends and how they come to accept it. Rated PG-13. 1988; 92m.

PERSECUTION
DIR: Don Chaffey. **CAST:** Lana Turner, Trevor Howard, Ralph Bates.

Even with pros like Lana Turner and Trevor Howard, this tale of murder and deception never shows minimal signs of life. A sorry waste of film. Rated R. 1974; 92m.

PERSONAL BEST ★★★★
DIR: Robert Towne. **CAST:** Mariel Hemingway, Patrice Donnelly, Scott Glenn.

Oscar-winning screenwriter Robert Towne wrote, directed, and produced this tough, honest, and nonexploitive story about two women who are friends, teammates, and sometimes lovers (Mariel Hemingway, Patrice Donnelly) preparing for the 1980 Olympics. Hemingway's and Donnelly's stunning performances make the film an impressive achievement. Rated R for nudity, strong language, and drug use. 1982; 124m.

PETRIFIED FOREST, THE ★★★★½
DIR: Archie Mayo. **CAST:** Humphrey Bogart, Leslie Howard, Bette Davis, Dick Foran.

This adaptation of the Robert Sherwood play seems a bit dated at first. It's about a gangster (Humphrey Bogart, in one of his first important screen roles) who holds a writer (Leslie Howard), a waitress (Bette Davis), and others hostage in a diner. The first-rate story, exquisite ensemble acting and taut direction by Archie Mayo soon mesmerize the viewer. 1936; B&W; 83m.

PETULIA ★★★★
DIR: Richard Lester. **CAST:** George C. Scott, Julie Christie, Richard Chamberlain, Shirley Knight, Joseph Cotten, Arthur Hill.

A story of complex relationships that centers around a prominent doctor (George C. Scott) who gets involved with a kooky young socialite (Julie Christie). A brilliant tragicomedy, one of Richard Lester's major achievements. Rated R. 1968; 105m.

PHAR LAP ★★★★½
DIR: Simon Wincer. **CAST:** Tom Burlinson, Ron Leibman, Martin Vaughn.

Absolutely chilling (and true) account of the superb Australian racehorse that chewed up the track in the 1920s and early 1930s. Tom Burlinson, stars as the stableboy who first believed in, and then followed to fame, the indefatigable Phar Lap. This film's indictment of early horse-racing practices will make you shudder. Rated PG—very intense for younger children. 1984; 106m.

PHILBY, BURGESS AND MACLEAN: SPY SCANDAL OF THE CENTURY ★★★★
DIR: Gordon Flemyng. **CAST:** Anthony Bates, Derek Jacobi, Michael Culver, Ingrid Hafner, Elizabeth Seal.

Yes, you can have an exciting spy story without James Bond chases and gimmicks. This riveting film spins the quiet, chilling tale of three of Britain's most notorious spies. They attended college together, were recruited by the Russians, and held high government security posts for thirty years before their discovery. Unrated. 1986; 83m.

PHONE CALL FROM A STRANGER ★★★
DIR: Jean Negulesco. **CAST:** Shelley Winters, Gary Merrill, Michael Rennie, Keenan Wynn, Bette Davis, Craig Stevens, Hugh Beaumont.

Fine acting by a stellar cast lifts this soap opera above the bubbles. Gary Merrill plays confessor to various fellow passengers on an ill-fated airline flight, and brings comfort and understanding to their families when most are killed in the crash. 1952; B&W; 96m.

PIANO FOR MRS. CIMINO, A ★★★★
DIR: George Schaefer. **CAST:** Bette Davis, Keenan Wynn, Alexa Kenin, Penny Fuller, Christopher Guest, George Hearn.

Blessed with great humor and a terrific performance by Bette Davis, this made-for-television film about growing old with dignity is manipulative at times. In light of all the wonderful moments, however, the contrivances don't seem so bad. Davis plays a widow who is institutionalized for senility. The film follows her through her recovery and her rebirth as a single, self-sufficient woman. 1982; 96m.

PILOT, THE ★★½
DIR: Cliff Robertson. **CAST:** Cliff Robertson, Frank Converse, Diane Baker, Gordon MacRae, Dana Andrews, Milo O'Shea, Edward Binns.

Cliff Robertson directed and starred in this film about an airline pilot's struggle with alcohol. A lot of heart went into this film. Just the same, Robertson's directing is not as convincing as his acting, and the screenplay is sometimes sickeningly sweet. Rated PG for profanity. 1979; 98m.

PIPE DREAMS ★
DIR: Stephen F. Verona. **CAST:** Gladys Knight, Barry L. Hankerson, Bruce French, Wayne Tippitt.

While writer-director-producer Stephen F. Verona may have had good intentions, the story is trite, and the poor acting and weak direction only aggravate the problem. Gladys Knight plays a wife who moves to Alaska to win back her estranged man who is working on the pipe line. Rated PG for sex, violence, profanity, and adult subject matter. 1976; 89m.

P.K. & THE KID ★★★
DIR: Lou Lombardo. **CAST:** Paul LeMat, Molly Ringwald, Alex Rocco, Esther Rolle, John Madden.

Molly Ringwald, in one of her earliest films, is running away from her abusive father, Alex Rocco. She hitches up with Paul LeMat, who is driving to California for the annual arm-wrestling championships. They strike up an interesting companionship in what is a far better movie than Sylvester Stallone's similar *Over the Top*. The characters are well developed and you can see a star in the making. 1985; 90m.

PLACE CALLED TODAY, A
DIR: Don Schain. **CAST:** J. Herbert Kerr Jr., Lana Wood, Cheri Caffaro.

Political drama laid in a city beset by racial strife. A black man running for mayor uses rioters to stir up controversy. All of the characters are repulsive in this cynical and sanctimonious movie, the type of hyped-up stupidity that gives liberalism a bad name. Also on video as *City in Fear*. Rated R for nudity and violence. 1972; 103m.

PLACE IN THE SUN, A ★★★★
DIR: George Stevens. **CAST:** Elizabeth Taylor, Montgomery Clift, Shelley Winters, Keefe Brasselle, Raymond Burr, Anne Revere.

Elizabeth Taylor, Montgomery Clift, and Shelley Winters are caught in a tragic love triangle in this picture, based on Theodore Dreiser's *An American Tragedy*. All three artists give first-rate performances. The story of a working-class man who falls for a wealthy girl is a traditional one, yet the eroticism conveyed in the scenes between Taylor and Clift keeps this production well above the standard. 1951; B&W; 122m.

PLACE OF WEEPING ★★★½
DIR: Darrell Roodt. **CAST:** James Whylie, Gcina Mhlope, Charles Comyn.

The first film about the South African struggle made by South Africans, this drama follows the battle of one woman who, with the help of a white reporter, stands against the system of apartheid. Although this film is a bit slow-moving and obviously made on a low budget, its political importance cannot be denied. Rated PG. 1986; 88m.

PLACES IN THE HEART ★★★★★
DIR: Robert Benton. **CAST:** Sally Field, Ed Harris, Lindsay Crouse, John Malkovich, Danny Glover.

Writer-director Robert Benton's *Places in the Heart* is a great film. Based on Benton's childhood memories in Waxahachie, Texas, the film stars Sally Field, Ed Harris, Lindsay Crouse, with special performances by John Malkovich and Danny Glover. Field plays Edna Spalding, a mother of two who is suddenly widowed. Almost immediately, she is pressured by the bank to sell her home and the surrounding property. Rated PG for suggested sex, violence, and profanity. 1984; 110m.

PLATOON ★★★★★
DIR: Oliver Stone. **CAST:** Tom Berenger, Willem Dafoe, Charlie Sheen, Forest Whitaker, Francesco Quinn, John C. McGinley, Richard Edson.

Writer-director Oliver Stone's Oscar-winning work is not just the best film made on the subject of Vietnam; it is a great cinematic work that stands high among the finest films ever made. Charlie Sheen is the well-meaning youth who volunteers for military service to become a real person instead of, in his words, "a fake human being." Not only does every step and noise bring the threat of death, but there is an intercompany war going on between the brutal Tom Berenger and the humanistic Willem Dafoe. Rated R for profanity, gore, and violence. 1986; 120m.

PLAYERS
DIR: Anthony Harvey. **CAST:** Ali MacGraw, Dean Paul Martin, Maximilian Schell.

It boggles the mind to consider that the man responsible for this unrelenting bomb also directed *The Lion in Winter*. Ali MacGraw is the bored mistress of Maximilian Schell; she falls for tennis pro Dean-Paul Martin. Rated PG—sexual situations. 1979; 120m.

PLAYING FOR TIME ★★★★
DIR: Daniel Mann. **CAST:** Vanessa Redgrave, Jane Alexander, Maud Adams, Viveca Lindfors, Shirley Knight.

This outstanding TV drama won numerous Emmy awards. It's the true story of Fania Fenelon (Vanessa Redgrave) and a group of women prisoners in Auschwitz who survived by forming a small orchestra and performing for the Nazi officers. 1980; 148m.

PLEASURE PALACE ★★
DIR: Walter Grauman. **CAST:** Omar Sharif, Victoria Principal, Walter Grauman, J. D. Cannon, Gerald S. O'Loughlin, José Ferrer, Hope Lange.

No, this is not a porno flick—in fact, the characters in this made-for-TV movie are more like old-fashioned melodrama icons. Hope Lange plays an honest widowed casino owner (yea!) who is afraid she will loose her casino to an influential oil baron (boo!). Omar Sharif portrays a high-rolling international gambler who comes to the rescue—gambler's style. Despite the lack of subtlety in characters, some of the gambling scenes have real tension in them. Not rated, but the equivalent of a PG for violence. 1980; 92m.

PLENTY ★★★★
DIR: Fred Schepisi. **CAST:** Meryl Streep, Charles Dance, Sam Neill, Tracey Ullman, John Gielgud, Sting, Ian McKellen.

In this difficult but rewarding film, Meryl Streep is superb as a former member of the French Resistance who finds life in her native England increasingly maddening during the postwar reconstruction period. Rated R for profanity, suggested sex, and violence. 1985; 120m.

PLOUGHMAN'S LUNCH, THE ★½
DIR: Richard Eyre. **CAST:** Jonathan Pryce, Tim Curry, Rosemary Harris, Frank Finlay, Charlie Dore.

The Ploughman's Lunch is a morality piece about opportunism and exploitation portrayed through the world of journalism. The problem is that almost everyone in the film is a weasel; they're all users. The point is to call attention to this fact, but it doesn't make for very enjoyable movie watching. Rated R. 1984; 107m.

POINT BLANK ★★★★
DIR: John Boorman. **CAST:** Lee Marvin, Angie Dickinson, Lloyd Bochner, Keenan Wynn, Carroll O'Connor, John Vernon.

Brutal crime drama is one of the finest films of its type. Gangster Lee Marvin is double-crossed by his wife and crime partner, who shoot him and leave him for dead on Alcatraz Island—only to have him turn up a few years later, bent on revenge. Entire cast pulls out all of the stops; it's one of Lee Marvin's strongest performances. Rated R. 1967; 92m.

POINTSMAN, THE ★★★
DIR: Jos Stelling. **CAST:** Stephane Excoffier.

A lady from Holland mysteriously disembarks from a train in the Scottish Highlands. The only person at the depot is the pointsman who resides at this isolated outpost. This most unusual film requires patience in viewing, but it has a strangely compelling attraction. The interesting characters, the fine photography, and the sensual development between the two leads keep you rapt until the end. Rated R for nudity and adult situations. 1988; 95m.

POOR WHITE TRASH ★
DIR: Harold Daniels. **CAST:** Peter Graves, Lita Milan, Douglas Fowley, Timothy Carey, Jonathan Haze.

According to the cassette box, this film was considered so racy in the 1960s that armed guards were posted at the entrance to the drive-ins where it played to mostly teen crowds. Peter Graves stars as a Yankee architect who clashes with the business (and moral) ethics of Louisiana developers. Unrated but with nudity and violence. 1961; B&W; 90m.

POOR WHITE TRASH II
DIR: S. F. Brownrigg. **CAST:** Gene Ross.

Not really a sequel to *Poor White Trash*, just another lousy thriller about an insane Vietnam veteran who starts slaughtering people in his hometown, in this case the members of a hillbilly family. The title was tacked on by the producer simply to trick people into the theatre. And yes, the movie is bad enough that customers had to be tricked. Rated R for violence. 1976; 83m.

POPE OF GREENWICH VILLAGE, THE ★★★½
DIR: Stuart Rosenberg. **CAST:** Eric Roberts, Mickey Rourke, Daryl Hannah, Geraldine Page.

This watchable film focuses on the hard-edged misadventures of two Italian cousins, Paulie (Eric Roberts) and Charlie (Mickey Rourke). Paulie is a not-so-bright dreamer who's obviously headed for trouble, and Charlie, who is smart enough to know better, always seems to get caught up in the middle of his cousin's half-baked and dangerous rip-off schemes. Rated R for profanity and violence. 1984; 120m.

PORK CHOP HILL ★★★★
DIR: Lewis Milestone. **CAST:** Gregory Peck, Harry Guardino, Rip Torn, Woody Strode, George Peppard, Bob Steele, James Edwards.

This no-win look at the Korean conflict features tough yet vulnerable Gregory Peck as the man forced to hold an insignificant mound of earth against overwhelming hordes of communist Chinese. A great cast and master director Lewis Milestone elevate this story to epic status. 1959; B&W; 97m.

PORT OF NEW YORK ★★½
DIR: Laslo Benedek. **CAST:** Scott Brady, Richard Rober, K. T. Stevens, Yul Brynner.

A female narcotics smuggler decides to play ball with the police and deliver her former colleagues to them. Scott Brady plays the cop eager to make the arrest while protecting his lovely informant. Yul Brynner is the head smuggler who wants to stop the squealing—fast. Gritty and engrossing. 1949; B&W; 82m.

PORTFOLIO 🦃

DIR: Robert Guralnick. **CAST:** Carol Alt, Julie Wolfe, Patty Owen, Kelly Emberg, Paulina Porizkova.

Don't let the box fool you! This has no plot—just a series of interviews endeavoring to make modeling look appealing. A feeble attempt to make a top model out of a young girl from Long Island doesn't get off the ground before you've nodded off. Rated R for profanity. 1983; 83m.

PORTNOY'S COMPLAINT ★

DIR: Ernest Lehman. **CAST:** Richard Benjamin, Karen Black, Lee Grant, Jack Somack, Jeannie Berlin, Jill Clayburgh.

Amazing that anyone had the nerve to attempt to translate Philip Roth's infamous novel to the screen. The neurotic Jewish boy, who has a strange relationship with his mother and an obsession with sex, should be neutered. It's worth viewing only as a curiosity. Rated R for profanity and sex. 1972; 101m.

PORTRAIT OF A SHOWGIRL ★½

DIR: Steven H. Stern. **CAST:** Lesley Ann Warren, Rita Moreno, Dianne Kay, Tony Curtis, Barry Primus, Howard Morris.

This subpar made-for-television film is another attempt to chronicle the life of Las Vegas showgirls. They meet men, they lose men. They lose jobs, they get jobs. Ho Hum! 1982; 100m.

PORTRAIT OF A STRIPPER ★★

DIR: John A. Alonzo. **CAST:** Lesley Ann Warren, Edward Herrmann, Vic Tayback, Sheree North.

A dancer is forced to strip in order to support her fatherless son, causing the authorities to label her an unfit mother. Since this was originally made for TV, its timid presentation will, no doubt, disappoint many drooling video renters. 1979; 100m.

POSSESSED (1931) ★★★½

DIR: Clarence Brown. **CAST:** Joan Crawford, Clark Gable, Wallace Ford.

Wonderful melodrama featuring Joan Crawford as a beautiful gold digger who becomes Clark Gable's mistress. When he has a chance to run for governor, she must choose between her luxurious life-style and his chance for a political career. Don't confuse this with Crawford's efforts as a schizophrenic in the 1947 *Possessed*. This gem was released to celebrate MGM's Diamond Jubilee. 1931; B&W; 77m.

POSSESSED (1947) ★★★

DIR: Curtis Bernhardt. **CAST:** Van Heflin, Joan Crawford, Raymond Massey, Geraldine Brooks, Stanley Ridges.

A cold and clinical account of loveless marriage, mysterious suicide, frustrated love for a scoundrel, murder, and schizophrenia. The much-maligned Joan Crawford heads a fine, mature cast and gives one of her finer performances as a mentally troubled nurse whose head and heart problems destroy her life. Extremely watchable. The opening scene is a real grabber. 1947; B&W; 108m.

POSTMAN ALWAYS RINGS TWICE, THE (1946) ★★★★

DIR: Tay Garnett. **CAST:** John Garfield, Lana Turner, Cecil Kellaway, Hume Cronyn.

If you wondered what went wrong in the sometimes steamily sexy and all too often soggy 1981 screen version of James M. Cain's celebrated novel, you need only watch this 1946 adaptation. John Garfield and Lana Turner play the lovers who murder the husband who stands in the way of their lust and suffer the consequences. 1946; B&W; 113m.

POSTMAN ALWAYS RINGS TWICE, THE (1981) ★★★

DIR: Bob Rafelson. **CAST:** Jessica Lange, Jack Nicholson, John Col-

Icos, Michael Lerner, John P. Ryan, Anjelica Huston.

Jack Nicholson plays the drifter whose lust for a married woman (Jessica Lange) leads to murder in this disappointing remake based on James M. Cain's hard-boiled novel of sex and violence. After an electric first hour, it begins to ramble and ends abruptly, leaving the viewer dissatisfied. Rated R for graphic sex and violence. 1981; 123m.

POT O' GOLD ★★
DIR: George Marshall. **CAST:** James Stewart, Paulette Goddard, Horace Heidt, Charles Winninger, Mary Gordon.

An amusing time-passer based on a one-time popular radio show. The plot concerns an enthusiastic young man's effort to get Horace Heidt and his orchestra on his uncle's radio program. Gee! 1941; B&W; 86m.

POWER ★★★★
DIR: Sidney Lumet. **CAST:** Richard Gere, Julie Christie, Gene Hackman, Kate Capshaw, Denzel Washington, E. G. Marshall, Beatrice Straight.

Sidney Lumet, who directed *Network*, once again takes viewers into the bowels of an American institution with this hard-edged study of the manipulation of the political process by market research and advertizing. Richard Gere gives one of his better performances as a ruthless hustler who is given pause when the one politician he believes in (E. G. Marshall) becomes a pawn in the political power trade. Rated R for profanity, violence, and suggested sex. 1986; 111m.

PRAY TV (1982) ★★½
DIR: Robert Markowitz. **CAST:** John Ritter, Ned Beatty, Richard Kiley, Madolyn Smith, Louise Latham.

Interesting TV movie about a young minister (John Ritter) who comes under the spell of a charismatic televangelist (Ned Beatty). Beatty is superb, but Ritter's performance is lackluster. 1982; 96m.

PRAYER FOR THE DYING, A ★★
DIR: Mike Hodges. **CAST:** Mickey Rourke, Bob Hoskins, Alan Bates, Sammi Davis.

An overwrought adaptation of Jack Higgins's exciting thriller which sounds preachy even when trying to be suspenseful. Mickey Rourke is an IRA assassin who finds his conscience after unintentionally killing some schoolchildren; he flees to London and engages natty Alan Bates to help him out of the country. Rated R for language and violence. 1987; 107m.

PRESENTING LILY MARS ★½
DIR: Norman Taurog. **CAST:** Judy Garland, Van Heflin, Richard Carlson, Marta Eggerth, Connie Gilchrist, Fay Bainter, Spring Byington, Marilyn Maxwell, Tommy Dorsey, Bob Crosby.

Stagestruck girl plugs her way to stardom. High points are when Judy Garland sings and has a nostalgic backstage conversation with has-been actress Connie Gilchrist. The Tommy Dorsey and Bob Crosby bands help keep audiences awake. 1943; B&W; 104m.

PRESIDENT'S PLANE IS MISSING, THE ★★★
DIR: Daryl Duke. **CAST:** Buddy Ebsen, Peter Graves, Arthur Kennedy, Raymond Massey, Mercedes McCambridge, Rip Torn, Dabney Coleman.

Crisis after crisis occurs when *Air Force One* disappears with the president on board. This story of indecision and desire for control against a background of international crisis is an engaging suspense yarn. A very good story is helped by a veteran cast. 1971; 100m.

PRETTY BABY ★★★★
DIR: Louis Malle. **CAST:** Brooke Shields, Susan Sarandon, Keith Carradine, Frances Faye, Antonio Fargas.

Forcing the audience to reexamine accepted concepts is just one of the effects of this brilliant work by Louis

Malle. He is fascinated by Violet (Brooke Shields), the girl we see growing up in a whorehouse in New Orleans. For Violet, all that goes on around her is normal. Rated R. 1978; 109m.

PRETTY IN PINK ★★★★
DIR: Howard Deutch. **CAST:** Molly Ringwald, Harry Dean Stanton, Jon Cryer, Andrew McCarthy, Annie Potts, James Spader.

Molly Ringwald is wonderful to watch as a young woman "from the poor side of town" who falls in love with rich kid Andrew McCarthy. The feeling is mutual, but their peers do everything they can to keep them apart. It is that rare teenage-oriented release that can be enjoyed by teens and adults. Rated PG-13 for profanity and violence. 1986; 96m.

PRETTY POISON ★★★★
DIR: Noel Black. **CAST:** Anthony Perkins, Tuesday Weld, Beverly Garland.

Anthony Perkins gives one of his finest screen performances in this bizarre drama about a troubled arsonist who enlists the aid of a sexy high school girl (Tuesday Weld) in a wild scheme. This surreal black comedy is sparked by Weld's vivid performance and a highly original screenplay by Lorenzo Semple Jr. Not rated. 1968; 89m.

PRICK UP YOUR EARS ★★★★
DIR: Stephen Frears. **CAST:** Gary Oldman, Alfred Molina, Vanessa Redgrave, Julie Walters, Wallace Shawn.

The poignant love story at the center of *Prick Up Your Ears* will be touching to some and shocking to others. But this film about the rise to prominence of British playwright Joe Orton (Gary Oldman) and his relationship with Kenneth Halliwell (Alfred Molina) never fails to fascinate. Rated R for profanity and scenes of graphic sex. 1987; 110m.

PRIDE AND PREJUDICE ★★★★
DIR: Robert Z. Leonard. **CAST:** Greer Garson, Laurence Olivier, Maureen O'Sullivan, Marsha Hunt.

This film is an accurate adaptation of Jane Austen's famous novel. The story takes place in nineteenth-century England with five sisters looking for suitable husbands. 1940; B&W; 116m.

PRIDE AND THE PASSION, THE ★★
DIR: Stanley Kramer. **CAST:** Frank Sinatra, Cary Grant, Sophia Loren, Theodore Bikel.

Here is a supreme example of how miscasting can ruin a movie's potential. Frank Sinatra is horrible as the Spanish peasant leader of a guerrilla army during the Napoleonic era. He secures the services of a gigantic cannon and a British Navy officer (Cary Grant) to fire it. Sophia Loren is also in the cast, primarily as window dressing. 1957; 132m.

PRIDE OF JESSE HALLMAN, THE ★★
DIR: Gary Nelson. **CAST:** Johnny Cash, Brenda Vaccaro, Eli Wallach, Ben Marley, Guy Boyd.

This is a well-meant but sluggish account of the quest for literacy by the title character, who is played by country singer–songwriter Johnny Cash. Made for television. 1981; 99m.

PRIDE OF THE BOWERY ★
DIR: Joseph H. Lewis. **CAST:** Leo Gorcey, Bobby Jordan, Donald Haines, Carleton Young, Kenneth Howell, David Gorcey.

This offshoot of the famous Dead End Kids features Leo Gorcey and Bobby Jordan, two of the original "kids," along with Gorcey's brother David, who continued on and off for the rest of the series. Not quite as bad as their later efforts, this film still needs a dyed-in-the-wool East Side Kids fan to really enjoy it. 1940; B&W; 63m.

PRIDE OF THE YANKEES, THE ★★★★★
DIR: Sam Wood. **CAST:** Gary Cooper, Teresa Wright, Babe Ruth, Walter Brennan, Dan Duryea, Ludwig Stossel.

Gary Cooper gives one of his finest performances as he captures the courageous spirit of New York Yankee immortal Lou Gehrig. This 1942 drama is a perfect blend of an exciting sports biography and a touching melodrama as we follow Gehrig's baseball career from its earliest playground beginnings until an illness strikes him down in his prime. Teresa Wright is just right in the difficult role of his loving wife. 1942; B&W; 127m.

PRIEST OF LOVE ★★★★
DIR: Christopher Miles. **CAST:** Ian McKellen, Janet Suzman, Ava Gardner, John Gielgud, Penelope Keith, Jorge Rivero, Maurizio Merli.

The culmination of a decade-long quest to film the life of D. H. Lawrence (Ian McKellen) by producer-director Christopher Miles, *Priest of Love* is absorbing, brilliantly acted, and stunningly photographed. It deals with Lawrence's exile from his native England, where his books were generally reviled; his relationship with wife Frieda (Janet Suzman); and their final time together in Italy, where Lawrence wrote *Lady Chatterley's Lover*. Rated R for profanity and sex. 1981; 125m.

PRIME SUSPECT ★½
DIR: Noel Black. **CAST:** Mike Farrell, Teri Garr, Veronica Cartwright, Lane Smith, Barry Corbin, James Sloyan, Charles Aidman.

A young girl is murdered. A decent, honest, hardworking citizen (Mike Farrell) becomes the prime suspect in the case. This is a precursor to the current run of media-bashing movies and is a bit too close to *Absence of Malice* for comfort. See *The Wrong Man* instead. 1982; 100m.

PRIMROSE PATH ★★★★
DIR: Gregory LaCava. **CAST:** Ginger Rogers, Joel McCrea, Marjorie Rambeau, Henry Travers.

In one of her best dramatic roles, Ginger Rogers stars as a young woman from the wrong side of the tracks who cons Joel McCrea into marriage. A fine film with a literate script, deftly crafted characters, fine production values—and heart. 1940; B&W; 93m.

PRINCE OF THE CITY ★★★★
DIR: Sidney Lumet. **CAST:** Treat Williams, Jerry Orbach, Richard Foronjy.

Director Sidney Lumet has created one of the screen's most intense character studies out of the true story of a corrupt New York narcotics cop, played wonderfully by Treat Williams. In becoming a government agent, the cop destroys the lives of his closest friends. Rated R because of violence and strong profanity. 1981; 167m.

PRINCESS DAISY ★★½
DIR: Waris Hussein. **CAST:** Lindsay Wagner, Paul Michael Glaser, Robert Urich, Claudia Cardinale, Ringo Starr, Merete VanKamp, Sada Thompson, Stacy Keach, Barbara Bach, Rupert Everett.

If you enjoy sleaze and glitter, then you should be tickled by this made-for-TV rendition of Judith Krantz's novel of a poor little rich girl. Merete Van Kamp as the heroine is able to fend off the lustful advances of her half brother and learn to control great wealth and power. Eventually she realizes the emptiness and loneliness of her life without a true love. Stacy Keach and Claudia Cardinale give the best performances. 1983; 188m.

PRINCIPAL, THE ★★
DIR: Christopher Cain. **CAST:** James Belushi, Louis Gossett Jr., Rae Dawn Chong, Michael Wright, Esai Morales.

Unrealistic treatment and poor writing sabotage this story of a renegade teacher (James Belushi) who, as punishment, is made principal of a high school where all the hardship cases from the other schools are relegated. Belushi doesn't do justice to his role, but Louis Gossett Jr. is good as the school's security chief. Rated R for language and violence. 1987; 110m.

PRISONER, THE ★★★★
DIR: Peter Glenville. **CAST:** Alec Guinness, Jack Hawkins.
Gripping political drama with outstanding performances by Alec Guinness and Jack Hawkins. Guinness portrays a cardinal being held as a political prisoner in a communist country. Jack Hawkins is the head of the secret police in charge of breaking down and brainwashing Guinness. Not rated. 1955; 91m.

PRIVATE HELL 36 ★★½
DIR: Don Siegel. **CAST:** Ida Lupino, Steve Cochran, Howard Duff, Dean Jagger, Dorothy Malone.
Tight, well-constructed story of two cops who skim money from a haul they have intercepted and have trouble living with it, is nicely acted by veteran performers. Ida Lupino, equally adept on either side of the camera, cowrote and produced this grim drama. 1954; B&W; 81m.

PRIVATE LIFE OF DON JUAN, THE ★★
DIR: Alexander Korda. **CAST:** Douglas Fairbanks Sr., Merle Oberon, Binnie Barnes, Benita Hume, Joan Gardner, Melville Cooper.
A vehicle for the aging Douglas Fairbanks, his last picture is set in seventeenth-century Spain. A famous lover (Fairbanks) fakes a suicide in order to make a comeback in disguise. It is somewhat tragic that the first great hero of the screen should have ended up in this disappointment. The supporting cast seems idle, as if the whole picture is just a party to humor Fairbanks. 1934; B&W; 90m.

PRIVATE LIFE OF HENRY THE EIGHTH, THE ★★★★
DIR: Alexander Korda. **CAST:** Charles Laughton, Robert Donat, Merle Oberon, Elsa Lanchester, Binnie Barnes.
This well-paced historical chronicle of England's bluebeard monarch and his six wives was to be Britain's first successful entry into worldwide movie-making. Charles Laughton's tour-de-force as the notorious king remains one of filmdom's greatest portrayals. Laughton's real-life spouse, Elsa Lanchester, plays Anne, the fourth wife. She manages to keep her head off the chopping block by humoring the volatile king during a memorable game of cards. 1933; B&W; 87m.

PRIVATE LIVES OF ELIZABETH AND ESSEX, THE ★★★½
DIR: Michael Curtiz. **CAST:** Bette Davis, Errol Flynn, Olivia De Havilland, Vincent Price, Donald Crisp, Nanette Fabray, Henry Daniell, Alan Hale, Robert Warwick, Henry Stephenson.
Bette Davis is Queen Elizabeth and Errol Flynn is her dashing suitor in this enjoyable costume drama. 1939; 106m.

PROMISED LAND ★★
DIR: Michael Hoffman. **CAST:** Kiefer Sutherland, Meg Ryan, Jason Gedrick.
Promised Land shows a segment from the lives of four young people, three of whom have just graduated from high school. Their "promised land" is ultimately only a wasteland. And the film is all exposition and not much insight. Kiefer Sutherland is convincing as an insecure, misguided wanderer. Rated R for profanity. 1988; 101m.

PROMISES IN THE DARK ★★★½
DIR: Jerome Hellman. **CAST:** Marsha Mason, Ned Beatty, Susan Clark, Michael Brandon, Kathleen Beller, Paul Clemens, Donald Moffat.
This film is about a young girl dying of cancer. Marsha Mason co-stars as her sympathetic doctor. Good movie, but very depressing! Rated PG. 1979; 115m.

PROVIDENCE ★★★★
DIR: Alain Resnais. **CAST:** Dirk Bogarde, John Gielgud, Ellen Burstyn, David Warner, Elaine Stritch.
Director Alain Resnais's first English-language film includes the great cast of Dirk Bogarde, John Gielgud,

Ellen Burstyn, and David Warner. An old and dying writer (Gielgud) completing his last novel invites his family up for the weekend. The fast cutting between the writer's imagined thoughts and real life makes this film difficult to follow for some. Rated R. 1977; 104m.

PSYCH-OUT ★★½
DIR: Richard Rush. **CAST:** Susan Strasberg, Jack Nicholson, Adam Roarke, Dean Stockwell, Bruce Dern.
The psychedelic Sixties couldn't have been more outrageous than this film about a pretty, deaf runaway who ends up in Haight-Ashbury while searching for her missing brother. She encounters a rock musician (Jack Nicholson) with whom she falls in love. Too self-important to be taken seriously. Rated PG. 1968; 82m.

PT 109 ★★½
DIR: Leslie Martinson. **CAST:** Cliff Robertson, Robert Culp, Ty Hardin, James Gregory, Robert Blake, Grant Williams.
Cliff Robertson is John F. Kennedy in this monument to the former president's war adventures on a World War II PT boat. Robertson is credible, but the story is only interesting because of the famous people and events it represenrts. 1963; 140m.

PUBERTY BLUES ★★★½
DIR: Bruce Beresford. **CAST:** Neil Schofield, Jad Capelja.
This film takes a frank look at the coming of age of two teenagers as they grow up on the beaches of Australia. The two girls become temporary victims of peer group pressure that involves drugs, alcohol, and sex. Unlike many other teenage films, *Puberty Blues* offers interesting insights into the rite of passage as seen from a female point of view. Rated R. 1981; 86m.

PUDD'NHEAD WILSON ★★★½
DIR: Alan Bridges. **CAST:** Ken Howard, Lise Hilboldt.
Mark Twain's sometimes humorous but always entertaining tale of deceit is faithfully re-created in this *American Playhouse* production. When a rash of crimes are committed in a Midwest town, only Pudd'nhead Wilson and his newfangled fingerprinting theory can unearth the culprit. Fine slice of Americana! 1984; 90m.

PUMPING IRON ★★★★
DIR: George Butler, Robert Fiore. **CAST:** Arnold Schwarzenegger, Lou Ferrigno, Matty and Victoria Ferrigno, Mike Katz.
Very good documentary concerning professional body building. Arnold Schwarzenegger and Lou Ferrigno ("The Hulk") are at the forefront as they prepare for the Mr. Universe contest. Always interesting and at times fascinating. Rated PG for language. 1977; 85m.

PUMPING IRON II: THE WOMEN ★★★★½
DIR: George Butler. **CAST:** Lori Bowen, Carla Dunlap, Bev Francis, Rachel McLish.
This documentary on the 1983 Women's World Cup held at Caesar's Palace is more than just beauty and brawn. While it does seem to side with one contestant (and when you see Bev Francis's massive body, you'll know why), the film has all the passion and wit of a first-rate narrative. Not rated, but an equivalent of a PG. 1985; 107m.

PUNCHLINE ★★★
DIR: David Seltzer. **CAST:** Tom Hanks, Sally Field, John Goodman, Mark Rydell.
An energetic performance from Tom Hanks can't quite compensate for the bewildering miscasting of Sally Field in this tribute to the hellishly difficult life of stand-up comics. Although Hanks superbly conveys the anguish of a failed med-school student with comedy in his blood, Field never convincingly captures the conservative housewife who yearns for more out of life than fixing dinners and washing

clothes. Inexplicably rated R for language. 1988; 128m.

PURPLE HEART, THE ★★★★
DIR: Lewis Milestone. **CAST:** Dana Andrews, Richard Conte, Farley Granger, Sam Levene, Tala Birell, Nestor Paiva.

Dana Andrews and Richard Conte are leaders of a group of American fliers who are captured by the Japanese after they bomb Tokyo and put on trial for war crimes. This fascinating film is a minor classic. 1944; B&W; 99m.

PURPLE HEARTS ★
DIR: Sidney J. Furie. **CAST:** Ken Wahl, Cheryl Ladd.

Anyone who can sit all the way through this Vietnam war–film romance deserves a medal. Ken Wahl stars as a surgeon in the United States Navy Medical Corps who falls in love with a nurse (Cheryl Ladd). Halfway through this film, directed by Sidney J. Furie, there's a natural and satisfying ending. But does it end there? Noooo. There's an additional forty minutes of unnecessary and unoriginal story tacked on. Rated R for nudity, profanity, violence, and gore. 1984; 115m.

PURPLE TAXI, THE ★★★
DIR: Yves Boisset. **CAST:** Fred Astaire, Edward Albert, Philippe Noiret, Peter Ustinov, Charlotte Rampling, Agostina Belli.

Fred Astaire, Edward Albert, and Philippe Noiret star in this exploration of angst, love, and friendship in Ireland, where a collection of expatriate characters impaled on memories and self-destructive compulsions work out their kinks before returning to various homelands. Fine backdrops in Ireland's "curtain of rain" and impressive acting. Rated R. 1977; 107m.

PURSUIT OF HAPPINESS, THE ★★★½
DIR: Robert Mulligan. **CAST:** Michael Sarrazin, Barbara Hershey, Robert Klein, Arthur Hill, E. G. Marshall, David Doyle, Barnard Hughes, Sada Thompson, Rue McClanahan, William Devane, Charles Durning.

Although it will seem dated to many, this heartfelt drama about a young man standing up for his ideals is still worth a look. Michael Sarrazin is good as a student who runs afoul of the judicial system more for a bad attitude than for his actual crime. Robert Mulligan's direction is excellent, and the cast features many now-familiar faces in small roles. Rated PG. 1971; 85m.

QB VII ★★★★
DIR: Tom Gries. **CAST:** Anthony Hopkins, Ben Gazzara, Leslie Caron, Lee Remick, Anthony Quayle.

Leon Uris's hefty bestseller is vividly brought to life in this five-hours-plus made-for-television drama about a Polish expatriate doctor living in England who sues an American writer for libel when the writer accuses him of carrying out criminal medical activities for the Nazis during World War II. Anthony Hopkins is brilliant as the physician, Ben Gazzara is outraged and tenacious as the writer. Expect a powerful, engrossing ending. 1974; 312m.

QUACKSER FORTUNE HAS A COUSIN IN THE BRONX ★★★★
DIR: Waris Hussein. **CAST:** Gene Wilder, Margot Kidder, Eileen Colga.

This comedy-drama falls into the category of sleeper. Gene Wilder is delightful as an Irishman who marches to the beat of a different drummer. Margot Kidder is a rich American going to university in Dublin who meets and falls in love with him. Filmed in Ireland and rated R for nudity and language. 1970; 88m.

QUALITY STREET ★★½
DIR: George Stevens. **CAST:** Katharine Hepburn, Joan Fontaine, Eric Blore, Franchot Tone.

In early nineteeth-century England, a schoolteacher (Katharine Hepburn) worries about whether her youthful flame (Eric Blore) will return from war. When he does return, she wonders if all he ever saw in her was her beauty. A familiar story, but a fine cast elevates the proceedings. 1937; B&W; 84m.

QUARTERBACK PRINCESS ★★½
DIR: Noel Black. **CAST:** Helen Hunt, Don Murray, Barbara Babcock, Dana Elcar, John Stockwell.

True story of Tami Maida, the Canadian girl who came to a small Oregon town and managed to become a star on the football team as well as being chosen the homecoming queen. Helen Hunt is adequate as Tami; Don Murray is better as her supportive dad. Made for television. 1983; 96m.

QUARTET (1948) ★★★★
DIR: Ken Annakin, Arthur Crabtree, Harold French, Ralph Smart. **CAST:** Dirk Bogarde, Hermione Baddeley, Mervyn Johns, Cecil Parker, Basil Badford, Françoise Rosay, Susan Shaw, Naunton Wayne, Mai Zetterling.

A dramatization of W. Somerset Maugham's favorite stories: "The Facts of Life," "The Alien Corn," "The Kite," and "The Colonel's Lady." All four are immensely watchable. 1948; B&W; 120m.

QUARTET (1981) ★★
DIR: James Ivory. **CAST:** Isabelle Adjani, Alan Bates, Anthony Higgins, Maggie Smith.

In terms of acting, this is a first-rate film. Unfortunately, the pathetic characters that mope around in this period piece drag down any positive points. Isabelle Adjani plays the wife of a convicted criminal who ends up in a *ménage à trois* with a married couple, played by Alan Bates and Maggie Smith. Rated R for nudity. 1981; 101m.

QUEEN KELLY ★★★
DIR: Erich Von Stroheim. **CAST:** Gloria Swanson.

Gloria Swanson used her clout to keep Erich Von Stroheim's *Queen Kelly* buried for nearly sixty years. This reconstructed version is but a shadow of the five-hour epic Von Stroheim had intended to make. The sumptuously mounted melodrama is fascinating—and often hilarious—for its indulgences, decadence, and outright perversity. Swanson plays a rebellious schoolgirl who is kidnapped from a convent and introduced to the pleasures of life by a debauched prince. Silent. 1928; B&W; 95m.

QUEEN OF THE STARDUST BALLROOM ★★★★
DIR: Sam O'Steen. **CAST:** Maureen Stapleton, Charles Durning, Michael Brandon, Michael Strong.

Touching love story about a lonely widow (Maureen Stapleton) who finally finds Mr. Right (Charles Durning). Stapleton is outstanding. 1975; 100m.

QUESTION OF HONOR, A ★★★★
DIR: Jud Taylor. **CAST:** Ben Gazzara, Robert Vaughn, Paul Sorvino, Tony Roberts, Danny Aiello.

Superior made-for-TV movie tells the true story of an honest New York narcotics officer who got caught in the middle of a federal drug scam and found himself accused of corruption. Based on a book by Sonny Grosso, the cop portrayed by Roy Scheider in *The French Connection*. Not rated. 1982; 134m.

QUICKSILVER ★
DIR: Tom Donnelly. **CAST:** Kevin Bacon, Jami Gertz, Paul Rodriguez, Rudy Ramos.

Wretched mess of a film. Kevin Bacon stars as a Wall Street wizard who blows it all one day—including his parents' savings account—and then puts his natural talents to work by becoming...a bicycle messenger! Rated PG for mild violence. 1986; 101m.

QUIET DAY IN BELFAST, A ★★★½
DIR: Milad Bessada. **CAST:** Margot Kidder, Barry Foster.

This fine Canadian message film reveals the hopelessness and insanity of Ireland's civil war. Margot Kidder plays Catholic twins, one in love with a British soldier. Unrated, but contains profanity, nudity, and violence. 1978; 92m.

QUO VADIS (1951) ★★★
DIR: Mervyn LeRoy. **CAST:** Robert Taylor, Deborah Kerr, Peter Ustinov, Leo Genn, Finlay Currie, Patricia Laffan, Abraham Sofaer, Felix Aylmer, Buddy Baer.
Colossal! Roman soldier Robert Taylor loves and pursues Christian maiden Deborah Kerr. It's Christians versus Nero and the lions in the eternal fight between good and evil. 1951; 171m.

QUO VADIS? (1985) ★★★
DIR: Franco Rossi. **CAST:** Klaus Maria Brandauer, Frederic Forrest, Cristina Raines, Francesco Quinn.
Lavish adaptation of Henryk Sienkiewicz's novel set during the reign of Nero. Klaus Maria Brandauer gives a brilliant performance as Nero in this made-for-Italian-television production. 1985; 200m.

RABBIT RUN ★★
DIR: Jack Smight. **CAST:** James Caan, Carrie Snodgress, Jack Albertson, Henry Jones, Anjanette Comer.
John Updike's novel concerning an ex–high school athlete's trouble adjusting to life off the playing field is brought to the screen in a very dull fashion. James Caan has the title role as the lost ex-jock who can't find out why life is so hard. Supporting cast is good, but the script sinks everyone involved. 1970; 74m.

RACHEL, RACHEL ★★★½
DIR: Paul Newman. **CAST:** Joanne Woodward, James Olson, Kate Harrington, Estelle Parsons.
Paul Newman's directorial debut focuses on a spinsterish schoolteacher (Joanne Woodward) and her awakening to a world beyond her job and her elderly mother's influence. This bittersweet story is perfectly acted by Woodward, with strong support by James Olson as her short-term lover and Estelle Parsons as her friend. Rewarding on all levels. Rated R. 1968; 101m.

RACING WITH THE MOON ★★★½
DIR: Richard Benjamin. **CAST:** Sean Penn, Elizabeth McGovern, Nicolas Cage, John Karlen, Rutanya Alda, Carol Kane.
Sean Penn and Elizabeth McGovern star in this thoroughly entertaining and touching comedy-romance set during World War II. He's just a regular town boy who discovers he's fallen in love with one of the area's rich girls. But that doesn't stop him from trying to win her heart. Rated PG for nudity, profanity, suggested sex, and brief violence. 1984; 108m.

RACKET, THE ★★★
DIR: John Cromwell. **CAST:** Robert Mitchum, Robert Ryan, Lizabeth Scott, William Talman, Ray Collins, Robert Hutton.
This pessimistic look at political corruption focuses on the steps honest police captain Robert Mitchum takes in order to bring underworld figure Robert Ryan to justice. Mitchum is a man alone as he confronts seemingly insurmountable opposition from both police and political higher-ups who want to keep things just as crooked as they are. 1951; B&W; 88m.

RAGE ★★★
DIR: George C. Scott. **CAST:** George C. Scott, Martin Sheen, Richard Basehart, Barnard Hughes.
This pits a lone man against the impersonal Establishment (in this instance the U.S. Army). This is not a happy film by any means, but it is an interesting one. Making his directorial debut, George C. Scott plays a peaceful sheep rancher whose son is the victim of military chemical testing. Seeking revenge, he sets out to nail those responsible. Rated PG. 1972; 104m.

RAGE OF ANGELS ★

DIR: Buzz Kulik. **CAST:** Jaclyn Smith, Ken Howard, Armand Assante, Ron Hunter, Kevin Conway.

If you enjoyed Sidney Sheldon's bestseller about a beautiful lawyer in love with a married politician but cornered by a mobster, don't ruin it by watching this trashy TV movie. Acting prowess is nonexistent, and the changes made from the novel rob it of its original flair. Unrated. 1986; 200m.

RAGGEDY RAWNEY, THE ★★½

DIR: Bob Hoskins. **CAST:** Bob Hoskins, Dexter Fletcher.

A quaint, modest effort most notable because its first-time writer-director is the superb Cockney actor, Bob Hoskins. Fresh from *Who Framed Roger Rabbit?* he created this folk fable about Gypsies and a myth about a speechless madwoman with magical powers who follows the caravans about. In this case, though, the *rawney* is actually an AWOL British soldier who is hiding in drag. 1988; 102m.

RAGING BULL ★★★★½

DIR: Martin Scorsese. **CAST:** Robert De Niro, Cathy Moriarty, Joe Pesci, Frank Vincent, Nicholas Colasanto, Theresa Saldana.

This is a tough, compelling film...in fact, a great one. Directed by Martin Scorsese and starring the incredible Robert De Niro, it's one movie you won't want to miss. In playing prize fighter Jake La Motta from his twenties through to middle age, De Niro undergoes a transformation that takes him from his normal weight of 150 to 212 pounds. That is startling in itself, but the performance he gives is even more startling—see it. Rated R. 1980; B&W; 128m.

RAGTIME ★★★★½

DIR: Milos Forman. **CAST:** James Cagney, Brad Dourif, Pat O'Brien, Donald O'Connor, Elizabeth McGovern, Mary Steenburgen.

James Cagney returned to the screen after an absence of twenty years in this brilliant screen adaptation of E. L. Doctorow's bestselling novel about New York City at the turn of the century. It's a bountifully rewarding motion picture. Rated PG because of violence. 1981; 155m.

RAID ON ENTEBBE ★★★

DIR: Irvin Kershner. **CAST:** Peter Finch, Charles Bronson, Horst Buchholz, Martin Balsam, John Saxon, Jack Warden, Yaphet Kotto.

Second of three dramas filmed in 1976–1977 about the daring Israeli commando assault on the Entebbe airport in Uganda, this TV movie avoids the soap-opera tone of the earlier *Victory at Entebbe* (also made for TV) and focuses on the action and power struggle between the Israelis and Idi Amin. The timeliness of the subject matter made it more effective when it was initially shown, but it's still worth a watch. 1977; 150m.

RAILROADED ★★★

DIR: Anthony Mann. **CAST:** John Ireland, Sheila Ryan, Hugh Beaumont, Jane Randolph, Keefe Brasselle.

Future TV father Hugh Beaumont has his hands full as a police detective trying to run interference between gangster John Ireland and his intended victim Sheila Ryan. Tough, tight, and deadly, this early effort from director Anthony Mann oozes suspense and remains a fine example of American *film noir*, modestly budgeted and effectively conveyed. 1947; B&W; 71m.

RAIN ★★★★

DIR: Lewis Milestone. **CAST:** Joan Crawford, Walter Huston, William Gargan, Guy Kibbee, Walter Catlett, Beulah Bondi.

Joan Crawford plays island hussy Sadie Thompson in this depressing drama. Walter Huston is the preacher who wants to "save" her—for himself. 1932; B&W; 93m.

RAIN MAN ★★★★★

DIR: Barry Levinson. **CAST:** Dustin Hoffman, Tom Cruise, Valeria Golino.

Dustin Hoffman gives the performance of his career as the autistic older brother of Tom Cruise, who plays (once again) a thoughtless, self-centered hustler with no room in his life for anything but money. Greed propels him to take a cross-country road trip with Hoffman, who inherited the bulk of Dad's vast estate. Barry Levinson deftly blends pathos with gentle humor that allows us to laugh with, but never at, Hoffman's autistic savant. Inexplicably rated R for occasional profanity. 1988; 140m.

RAIN PEOPLE, THE ★★★★
DIR: Francis Ford Coppola. **CAST:** James Caan, Shirley Knight, Robert Duvall, Tom Aldredge.

James Caan plays a retired football star who is picked up by a bored pregnant woman (played by Shirley Knight). She felt trapped as a housewife and ran away from her husband to be free. Directed by Francis Ford Coppola, this is an interesting, well-acted character study. Rated R. 1969; 102m.

RAINBOW, THE ★★★★
DIR: Ken Russell. **CAST:** Sammi Davis, Paul McGann, Glenda Jackson, Amanda Donohoe, David Hemmings, Christopher Gable.

After a series of increasingly bizarre gothic films in the 1980s, director Ken Russell returns to D. H. Lawrence, the source of his great success, *Women in Love*. This time, he focuses on the companion novel, a prequel. Sammi Davis is wonderful as an adolescent English girl who is exposed to the ways of love at the hands of both a soldier and her teacher, and makes a decision to seek a more satisfying life for herself. Rated R. 1989; 102m.

RAINMAKER, THE ★★★½
DIR: Joseph Anthony. **CAST:** Burt Lancaster, Katharine Hepburn, Wendell Corey, Lloyd Bridges, Earl Holliman, Wallace Ford, Cameron Prud'homme.

Based on N. Richard Nash's play, the movie adaptation could easily have seemed confined, but the boundless intensity and energy of Burt Lancaster's performance as the smooth-talking con man gives the whole film an electric crackle. Katharine Hepburn has the magnetism to hold her own in the role of the spinster. 1956; 121m.

RAINTREE COUNTY ★★★
DIR: Edward Dmytryk. **CAST:** Elizabeth Taylor, Montgomery Clift, Eva Marie Saint, Nigel Patrick, Lee Marvin, Rod Taylor, Agnes Moorehead, Walter Abel, Rhys Williams.

Civil War melodrama with Elizabeth Taylor as a southern belle is two and one-half hours of showy tedium that wastes a fine cast and miles of film. Bestselling novel comes to the screen as an extended soap opera with little promise and fewer results. 1957; 168m.

RAISIN IN THE SUN, A ★★★★
DIR: Daniel Petrie. **CAST:** Sidney Poitier, Claudia McNeil, Ruby Dee, Diana Sands, Ivan Dixon, John Fiedler, Louis Gossett Jr.

A black family tries to escape from their crowded apartment life by moving to a house in an all-white neighborhood. Sidney Poitier delivers his usual outstanding performance in this film with a message about the limited opportunities open to blacks in the 1950s. 1961; B&W; 128m.

RANDOM HARVEST ★★★★
DIR: Mervyn LeRoy. **CAST:** Ronald Colman, Greer Garson, Philip Dorn, Henry Travers, Reginald Owen.

Ronald Colman and Greer Garson are at their best in this touching, tearful story. A shell-shocked World War I veteran is saved from oblivion by the compassion of a music-hall entertainer. A stellar cast supports. 1942; B&W; 124m.

RAPPACCINI'S DAUGHTER ★★★★½
DIR: Dezso Magyar. **CAST:** Kristoffer Tabori, Kathleen Beller, Michael Egan, Leonardo Cimino.

This Nathaniel Hawthorne tale concerns a university student who accepts new lodgings overlooking a beautiful and mysterious garden. What follows is a particularly spellbinding tale of love and tragedy. Introduced by Henry Fonda; unrated and suitable for family viewing. 1980; 57m.

RATBOY ★★

DIR: Sondra Locke. **CAST:** Sondra Locke, Robert Townsend, Louie Anderson, Gerrit Graham, Christopher Hewett.

Not a horror film but a satirical allegory directed by and starring Sondra Locke. Eugene, a boy with the face of a rat, is torn out of his peaceful existence in a dump by an unemployed window dresser (Locke). She sees him as her ticket to the big time. With her two brothers, she sets out to market the ratboy as a media star. Rated PG-13 for profanity and some violence. 1986; 104m.

RATTLE OF A SIMPLE MAN ★★★

DIR: Muriel Box. **CAST:** Harry H. Corbett, Diane Cilento, Michael Medwin.

One of the realistic, kitchen-sink dramas that were in vogue in England at the time, this resembles a British version of *Marty*. Middle-aged Percy, a virgin who lives with his mother, is goaded by his friends into a bet that he can't pick up and spend the night with an attractive waitress. In his attempt to do so, he finds love for the first time. 1964; B&W; 96m.

RAZOR'S EDGE, THE (1946) ★★★★½

DIR: Edmund Goulding. **CAST:** Tyrone Power, Gene Tierney, Clifton Webb, Herbert Marshall, Anne Baxter, John Payne, Elsa Lanchester.

A long but engrossing presentation of Somerset Maugham's philosophical novel about a young man seeking the goodness in life. Full of memorable characterizations and scenes. Herbert Marshall steers the plot, playing the author. 1946; B&W; 146m.

RAZOR'S EDGE, THE (1984) ★★★½

DIR: John Byrum. **CAST:** Bill Murray, Theresa Russell, Catharine Hicks, James Keach, Brian Doyle-Murray.

Bill Murray gives a finely balanced comic and dramatic portrayal as a man searching for meaning after World War I in this adaptation of W. Somerset Maugham's novel. The result is a richly rewarding film, which survives the unevenness of John Byrum's direction. Rated PG-13 for suggested sex, violence, and profanity. 1984; 128m.

REAL AMERICAN HERO, THE ★½

DIR: Lou Antonio. **CAST:** Brian Dennehy, Forrest Tucker, Brian Kerwin, Ken Howard, Sheree North.

Below average TV movie does not do justice to slain Sheriff Buford Pusser. Brian Dennehy plays Pusser, a frustrated law enforcer who will do anything—even risk his own life—to get the bad guys. Ken Howard plays a ruthless bar owner who kills two teenagers with his illegal moonshine. *Walking Tall* says it all better. Not rated, but contains profanity and violence. 1978; 94m.

REBECCA ★★★★★

DIR: Alfred Hitchcock. **CAST:** Laurence Olivier, Joan Fontaine, George Sanders, Nigel Bruce, Reginald Denny, Judith Anderson.

Rebecca won an Oscar for best picture and nominations for its stars, Laurence Olivier and Joan Fontaine. The popular Daphne du Maurier novel was transferred to the screen without losing any of its gothic blend of romance and mystery. Judith Anderson as the sinister housekeeper is one of the most compelling figures in film history. 1940; B&W; 130m.

REBECCA OF SUNNYBROOK FARM ★★½

DIR: Marshall Neilan. **CAST:** Mary Pickford, Eugene O'Brien, Helen Jerome Eddy.

Once again, the adult Mary Pickford successfully portrays a saucy teenager who wins love, respect, and prosperity in this rags-to-riches tearjerker based on the famous Kate Douglas Wiggin bestseller. Shirley Temple starred in a talkie version in 1938. Silent. 1917; B&W; 77m.

REBEL (1985) ★
DIR: Michael Jenkins. **CAST:** Matt Dillon, Debbie Byrne, Bryan Brown, Bill Hunter, Ray Barrett.

During World War II, a marine sergeant in Australia goes AWOL and falls in love with a nightclub singer. He is torn between trying to get home to the States and staying Down Under. This soap opera quickly gets mired in sludge. Rated R for profanity and adult situations. 1985; 93m.

REBEL LOVE 🦃
DIR: Milton Bagby Jr. **CAST:** Jamie Rose, Terence Knox, Fran Ryan, Charles Hill.

Overblown romantic drama set during the Civil War about a Yankee widow who falls in love with a Confederate spy. The widow's name is Columbine Cromwell; that alone should clue you in to what a stinker this is. Unrated, there is some very mild sexual content. 1986; 84m.

REBEL WITHOUT A CAUSE ★★★★★
DIR: Nicholas Ray. **CAST:** James Dean, Natalie Wood, Sal Mineo, Jim Backus, Ann Doran, Corey Allen, Edward Platt, Dennis Hopper, Nick Adams.

This is the film that made James Dean a legend. Directed by Nicholas Ray, it is undoubtedly the classic film about juvenile delinquency. Featuring fine performances by Dean, Natalie Wood, and Sal Mineo as the teens in trouble, it has stood up surprisingly well over the years. 1955; 111m.

RECKLESS ★
DIR: James Foley. **CAST:** Aidan Quinn, Daryl Hannah, Kenneth McMillan, Cliff De Young, Lois Smith, Adam Baldwin, Dan Hedaya.

A 1980s version of the standard 1950s "angry young man" movie, this features Aidan Quinn as a motorcycle-riding, mumbling (à la James Dean and Marlon Brando) outcast and Daryl Hannah as the "good girl." She is the A-student cheerleader both attracted and repelled by the danger he represents. Wait a minute...wasn't that the synopsis of *Breathless*? It was, and that should give you an idea of how original this movie is. Rated R for nudity, profanity, violence, and suggested sex. 1984; 90m.

RED BADGE OF COURAGE, THE ★★★½
DIR: John Huston. **CAST:** Audie Murphy, Bill Mauldin, Royal Dano, Arthur Hunnicutt, Douglas Dick.

Natural performances mark this realistic treatment of Stephen Crane's famous Civil War novel of a young soldier's initiation to battle. A John Huston classic, and a major film achievement by any standard. 1951; B&W; 69m.

RED DUST ★★★★
DIR: Victor Fleming. **CAST:** Clark Gable, Jean Harlow, Mary Astor, Donald Crisp, Gene Raymond, Tully Marshall.

Red Dust is one of those remarkable films where the performances of its stars propel a movie to classic status despite a rather uninspired story. A hackneyed story of a rubber plantation boss (Gable) who dallies with another man's wife only to return to the arms of a shady lady (Harlow) with the proverbial heart of gold. 1932; B&W; 83m.

RED KIMONO, THE ★½
DIR: Walter Lang. **CAST:** Priscilla Bonner, Nellie Bly Baker, Mary Carr, Tyrone Power Sr.

The Red Kimono is a tawdry story about a young lady who is abandoned by her philandering husband and forced to become a scarlet woman. The story is told in flashbacks. Cheap and corny, this exploitation film exists in versions of different lengths. Silent. 1925; B&W; 95m.

RED LIGHT STING, THE ★★

DIR: Rod Holcomb. **CAST:** Farrah Fawcett, Beau Bridges, Harold Gould, Paul Burke, Alex Henteloff, Conrad Janis, James Luisi, Philip Charles MacKenzie.

Pale TV film about a young district attorney (Beau Bridges) who is assigned to buy a whorehouse to bring out an elusive big-time crook (Harold Gould). Not rated, but the equivalent of a PG for adult subject matter. 1984; 96m.

RED NIGHTS ★

DIR: Izhak Hanooka. **CAST:** Christopher Parker, Brian Matthews, Jack Carter, William Smith.

A New England youth with stars in his eyes heads out to Hollywood. His dream of becoming a cowboy star (in the Eighties? Good luck!) is shattered when he finds that people in Tinseltown just aren't nice. In other words, this is another excuse to trot out all the standard exploitation clichés about drugs, porn, and mob influence in the movie business. The one plus is the score by Tangerine Dream, which is better than the movie deserves. Rated R. 1988; 89m.

RED TENT, THE ★★½

DIR: Mikhail K. Kalatozov. **CAST:** Sean Connery, Claudia Cardinale, Hardy Krüger, Peter Finch, Massimo Girotti.

Sean Connery heads an international cast in this slow-moving reconstruction of a polar expedition that ended in tragedy in 1928. The scope of the film and the trials faced by the party in their struggles for survival are enthralling, but too much reliance on flashbacks works against this one. 1970; 121m.

REDS ★★★★★

DIR: Warren Beatty. **CAST:** Warren Beatty, Diane Keaton, Jack Nicholson, Gene Hackman, Edward Herrmann, Maureen Stapleton, Jerzy Kosinski.

Warren Beatty produced, directed, cowrote, and starred in this $33 million American film masterpiece. This three-hour-plus film biography of left-wing American journalist John Reed (Beatty) and Louise Bryant (Diane Keaton) also features brilliant bits from Jack Nicholson, Gene Hackman, and Maureen Stapleton. Rated PG because of profanity, silhouetted sex scenes, and war scenes. 1981; 200m.

REFLECTIONS IN A GOLDEN EYE ★★½

DIR: John Huston. **CAST:** Marlon Brando, Elizabeth Taylor, Brian Keith, Julie Harris, Robert Forster.

Very bizarre film concerning a homosexual army officer (Marlon Brando) stationed in the South. This very strange film very rarely works—despite a high-powered cast. 1967; 108m.

REMBRANDT ★★★★

DIR: Alexander Korda. **CAST:** Charles Laughton, Gertrude Lawrence, Elsa Lanchester.

This is one of the few satisfying movie biographies of an artist. The depiction of the famous Dutch painter and his struggle to maintain his artistic integrity is related with respectful restraint and attention to factual detail. Charles Laughton, as Rembrandt, is brilliant in what was for him an atypically low-key performance. 1936; B&W; 90m.

RENO AND THE DOC ★★½

DIR: Charles Dennis. **CAST:** Kenneth Walsh, Henry Ramer, Linda Griffiths.

Though it has a slow start, this tale of two middle-aged men brought together by mental telepathy soon gains momentum. Ken Walsh plays Reno, a solitary mountain man who is induced by Doc (Henry Ramer) to enter the pro-ski tour. Reno's surprising success leads to his romance with Savannah, a *Sports Illustrated* writer (Linda Griffiths). Mild nudity and obscenities. 1984; 88m.

REPORT TO THE COMMISSIONER ★★★★

DIR: Milton Katselas. **CAST:** Michael Moriarty, Yaphet Kotto, Susan Blakely, Hector Elizondo, Tony King, William Devane, Richard Gere.

One of the best of the urban crime films to come out in the early Seventies. Michael Moriarty plays an innocent rookie in the New York Police Department. Not understanding the politics of the cop on the beat he commits a series of errors that leads to his downfall. Look for Richard Gere in a small part as a pimp. Rated PG for violence, profanity, and nudity. 1974; 113m.

REQUIEM FOR A HEAVYWEIGHT ★★★½

DIR: Ralph Nelson. **CAST:** Anthony Quinn, Julie Harris, Jackie Gleason, Mickey Rooney.

Anthony Quinn, Julie Harris, Jackie Gleason, Mickey Rooney, and Muhammad Ali (at that time Cassius Clay) give fine performances in this watchable film about boxing corruption. An over-the-hill boxer (Quinn) receives career counseling from a social worker (Harris). 1962; B&W; 100m.

REQUIEM FOR A HEAVYWEIGHT (TELEVISION) ★★★★

DIR: Ralph Nelson. **CAST:** Jack Palance, Keenan Wynn, Kim Hunter, Ed Wynn, Ned Glass.

Superb drama written for *Playhouse 90* by Rod Serling, about a washed-up heavyweight boxer (Jack Palance) who is forced to find a life outside the ring. Keenan Wynn is magnificent as his gruff, self-centered manager, and Ed Wynn is perfect as the trainer. One of the best live dramas to come out of the Golden Age of Television. Hosted by Jack Klugman, with interviews with the stars and background information on the show. 1956; B&W; 89m.

RESTLESS ★

DIR: George Pan Cosmatos. **CAST:** Raquel Welch, Richard Johnson, Flora Robson.

This Greek movie with Raquel Welch, originally titled *The Beloved,* was all but unknown until it appeared on video, and if you watch it, you'll know why. There's a lot of pretty island scenery, but the plot about housewife Raquel (who doesn't even get any dialogue until the midpoint) having an affair with a childhood friend is a guaranteed sleep-inducer. Unrated, the film contains sexual situations and violence. 1972; 75m.

RESURRECTION ★★★★½

DIR: Daniel Petrie. **CAST:** Ellen Burstyn, Sam Shepard, Richard Farnsworth, Roberts Blossom, Clifford David, Pamela Payton-Wright, Eva LeGallienne.

Ellen Burstyn's superb performance is but one of the topflight elements in this emotional powerhouse. After Burstyn loses her husband and the use of her legs in a freak automobile accident, she discovers she has the power to heal not only herself but anyone who is sick or crippled. Pulitzer Prize–winning playwright Sam Shepard is also memorable as the young hell-raiser who begins to believe she is Jesus reborn. Rated PG. 1980; 103m.

RETURN ★★

DIR: Andrew Silver. **CAST:** Karlene Crockett, John Walcutt, Anne Lloyd Francis, Frederic Forrest.

Right before her father's bid for the Arkansas governorship, Diana (Karlene Crockett) decides to find out about her grandfather's mysterious death. She meets a young man who relives her grandfather's life through hypnosis. Below-par mystery. Rated R for profanity, violence, and partial nudity. 1984; 78m.

RETURN OF THE SOLDIER, THE ★★★★★

DIR: Alan Bridges. **CAST:** Glenda Jackson, Julie Christie, Ann-Margret,

Alan Bates, Ian Holm, Frank Finlay, Jeremy Kemp.

During World War I, a soldier (Alan Bates) suffers shell shock and forgets the last twenty years of his life. His doctors must decide whether he should be allowed to enjoy what has resulted in a carefree second youth, or be brought back to real life and the responsibilities that go with it. Everyone in the cast is superb. Not rated, the film contains adult situations. 1985; 105m.

RETURN TO EDEN ★★★

DIR: Karen Arthur. **CAST:** Rebecca Gilling, James Reyne, Wendy Hughes.

This four-and-one-half-hour miniseries, originally made for Australian television, is a bit much to watch at one sitting. Fans of soaps, however, will find it holds their interest. A wealthy woman discovers that her handsome husband only married her for her money when he feeds her to the crocodiles. He thinks she's dead. Miraculously surviving, she alters her appearance and sets about gaining revenge. Unrated, but with brief nudity. 1983; 259m.

REVOLUTION ★★

DIR: Hugh Hudson. **CAST:** Al Pacino, Nastassja Kinski, Donald Sutherland.

Director Hugh Hudson must have had good intentions going into this project, examining what it might have been like to be involved in the American Revolution. Unfortunately, his actors are so miscast and the script so ragged that Hudson's project stalls almost before it gets started. Rated R. 1986; 125m.

RICH AND FAMOUS ★★★★

DIR: George Cukor. **CAST:** Jacqueline Bisset, Candice Bergen, David Selby, Hart Bochner, Steven Hill, Meg Ryan, Matt Lattanzi, Michael Brandon.

Jacqueline Bisset and Candice Bergen star in this warm, witty, and involving chronicle of the ups, downs, joys, and heartbreak experienced by two friends during a twenty-year relationship. Hollywood great George Cukor directed in his inimitable style. Rated R because of profanity and sex. 1981; 117m.

RICH AND STRANGE ★★½

DIR: Alfred Hitchcock. **CAST:** Henry Kendall, Joan Barry, Percy Marmont.

This quirky little drama from Alfred Hitchcock concerns a bickering couple (Henry Kendall and Joan Barry) who come into money, take a world cruise, and suffer through a few minor adventures. The domestic squabbling, which forms the story's only true conflict, is far from Hitchcock's forte; this probably will be of interest only to the director's devotees. Not rated; suitable for family viewing. 1932; B&W; 83m.

RICH KIDS ★★

DIR: Robert M. Young. **CAST:** Trini Alvarado, Jeremy Levy, John Lithgow, Kathryn Walker, Terry Kiser, Paul Dooley.

A poor screenplay plagues this movie about two kids going through puberty at the same time they are experiencing the dissolution of their parents' marriages. A great cast helps. Also, there is an unforgettable heartfelt moment between mother and daughter (Kathryn Walker and Trini Alvarado). Rated PG for language. 1979; 97m.

RICHARD III ★★★★

DIR: Laurence Olivier. **CAST:** Laurence Olivier, Ralph Richardson, John Gielgud, Claire Bloom.

Once again, as in *Henry V* and *Hamlet*, England's foremost player displays his near-matchless acting and directing skills in bringing Shakespeare to life on film. His royal crookback usurper is beautifully malevolent, a completely intriguing, smiling villain. The film fascinates from first to last. 1955; 161m.

RICHARD'S THINGS ★★

DIR: Anthony Harvey. **CAST:** Liv Ullmann, Amanda Redman, David Markham.

Gloomy drama about a widow who gets seduced by her late husband's girlfriend. Liv Ullmann plays the patsy as if she were on depressants. 1980; 104m.

RIGHT HAND MAN, THE ★

DIR: Di Drew. **CAST:** Rupert Everett, Hugo Weaving, Arthur Dignam, Jennifer Claire.

Too bad the pace, plot, and character development did not get the same attention as period detail and visual beauty in this Australian import. A would-be romantic epic about a dying, disabled, nobleman's (Rupert Everett) repressed love for his doctor's daughter. Barely watchable. Rated R for nudity and suggested sex. 1987; 101m.

RIGHT OF WAY ★★★★

DIR: George Shaefer. **CAST:** James Stewart, Bette Davis, Melinda Dillon, Priscilla Morrill, John Harkins.

This made-for-cable work deals with a rather unusual decision made by an old married couple, (Bette Davis and James Stewart) who have decided to commit suicide. Thus begins a battle between daughter (Melinda Dillon) and parents. The result is a surprisingly gripping character study. 1983; 106m.

RIGHT STUFF, THE ★★★★★

DIR: Phil Kaufman. **CAST:** Sam Shepard, Scott Glenn, Ed Harris, Dennis Quaid, Barbara Hershey, Fred Ward, Kim Stanley, Veronica Cartwright, Pamela Reed, Donald Moffat, Levon Helm, Scott Wilson, Jeff Goldblum, Harry Shearer.

From Tom Wolfe's bestseller about the early years of the American space program, writer-director Phil Kaufman has created an epic screen tribute to, and examination of the men (both test pilots and astronauts) who "pushed the outside of the envelope," and the women who watched and waited while the world watched them. Rated PG for profanity. 1983; 193m.

RING, THE ★½

DIR: Alfred Hitchcock. **CAST:** Carl Brisson, Lillian Hall-Davies, Ian Hunter.

Long before Sylvester Stallone turned boxing into a filmic event, Alfred Hitchcock toyed with the sports medium in this unremarkable melodrama. The story is little more than a love triangle between two boxing champions (Carl Brisson and Ian Hunter) and the woman loved by both (Lillian Hall-Davies). Not rated; suitable for family viewing. 1927; B&W; 73m.

RITA HAYWORTH: THE LOVE GODDESS ★★½

DIR: James Goldstone. **CAST:** Lynda Carter, Michael Lerner, John Considine, Alejandro Rey.

This lifeless attempt to re-create pinup queen Rita Hayworth's exciting life falls short of its goal. Beautiful Lynda Carter as Hayworth, however, keeps the viewer's attention. Made for television. 1983; 100m.

RIVER, THE (1951) ★★★½

DIR: Jean Renoir. **CAST:** Nora Swinburne, Arthur Shields.

Beautiful locations enhance this lyrical drama about English children growing up in Bengal. This well-orchestrated character study is brilliantly directed by cinema master Jean Renoir and is equally blessed with rich color photography by his brother Claude. 1951; 99m.

RIVER, THE (1984) ★★★½

DIR: Mark Rydell. **CAST:** Mel Gibson, Sissy Spacek, Scott Glenn.

Following as it does on the heels of two other first-rate farmer films, this work by director Mark Rydell often seems hopelessly unoriginal and, as a result, boring. As with *Country*, it deals with a farming family who must battle a severe storm and foreclosure proceedings. It simply has little new to say. Rated PG for nudity, violence, and profanity. 1984; 122m.

RIVER OF UNREST ★★

DIR: Brian Desmond, Walter Summers. **CAST:** John Lodge, John

Loder, Antoinette Cellier, Niall MacGinnis, Clifford Evans.

Melodrama about the Sinn Fein rebellion in Ireland bears a strong resemblance to John Ford's classic *The Informer*, but there's more emphasis on the love story between Antoinette Cellier and the two men in her life. Good performances by a capable cast help this slow-moving story, which was based on a stage play. 1937; B&W; 69m.

RIVER RAT, THE ★★★½

DIR: Tom Rickman. **CAST:** Tommy Lee Jones, Martha Plimpton, Brian Dennehy.

Although essentially the story of the growing love between a long-separated father (Tommy Lee Jones), who has been in prison for thirteen years, and daughter (newcomer Martha Plimpton), this release is much more than a simple tearjerker. Writer-director Tom Rickman has invested his story with a grit and realism that set it apart from similar works. As a result, he's created a powerful, thought-provoking motion picture. Rated R for profanity and violence. 1984; 109m.

RIVER'S EDGE ★★★½

DIR: Tim Hunter. **CAST:** Dennis Hopper, Crispin Glover, Keanu Reeves, Ione Skye Leitch, Roxana Zal, Daniel Roebuck, Tom Bower, Leo Rossi.

This is a deeply disturbing film based on a real-life 1980 murder case. The teenage murderer in *River's Edge* takes his friends to see the corpse of his classmate-victim. The death becomes a secret bond among them until two decent kids (Keanu Reeves, Ione Skye Leitch) decide to do something about it. Rated R for violence, profanity, nudity, and simulated sex. 1987; 99m.

ROAD TO RUIN, THE ★½

DIR: Norton S. Parker. **CAST:** Helen Foster, Grant Withers, Charles Miller.

A classic exploitation feature, this silent quickie is creaky and heavily moralistic. Obligatory punishment is meted out to the wrongdoers, while virtue is bountifully rewarded. Unintentionally funny. Silent. 1928; B&W; 45m.

ROBE, THE ★★★★

DIR: Henry Koster. **CAST:** Richard Burton, Victor Mature, Jean Simmons, Michael Rennie, Richard Boone, Dean Jagger, Dawn Addams, Jay Robinson.

Richard Burton is the Roman tribune charged with overseeing the execution of Christ in this story of his involvement with the followers of Christ and the effect the robe of Jesus has on all involved. It is a well-made film, and although it revolves around a religious subject, it is not heavy-handed in its approach. 1953; 135m.

ROCKET GIBRALTAR ★★★

DIR: Daniel Petrie. **CAST:** Burt Lancaster, Suzy Amis, John Glover, Bill Pullman.

A bittersweet comedy-drama about the reunion of an eccentric family in the Hamptons, drawn by the 77th birthday of the patriarch. Burt Lancaster plays the elder, giving this slight, sentimental film credibility and prestige. Rated PG. 1988; 100m.

ROCKY ★★★★★

DIR: John G. Avildsen. **CAST:** Sylvester Stallone, Burgess Meredith, Talia Shire, Burt Young, Carl Weathers.

Those put to sleep by the endless sequels in this series probably have forgotten the gentleness and dignity of this initial entry. Star Sylvester Stallone wrote the original script about Rocky Balboa, the painfully shy boxer who only "wants to go the distance" with champ Apollo Creed (Carl Weathers). The supporting cast is excellent—Burgess Meredith as the feisty trainer, Talia Shire as Rocky's girlfriend, and Burt Young as her brother. One of the ultimate feel-good films, and it works every time. Rated PG for violence. 1976; 119m.

ROCKY II ★★

DIR: Sylvester Stallone. **CAST:** Sylvester Stallone, Carl Weathers, Talia Shire, Burgess Meredith, Burt Young.

The weakest entry in Sylvester Stallone's boxing series, about a down-and-out fighter attempting to prove himself through a rematch with the champ (Carl Weathers). Talia Shire, Burgess Meredith, and Burt Young reprise their series roles in this soaper in the ring. Rated PG. 1979; 119m.

ROCKY III ★★★
DIR: Sylvester Stallone. **CAST:** Sylvester Stallone, Talia Shire, Burgess Meredith, Mr. T, Carl Weathers.

Writer-director-star Sylvester Stallone's third entry in the Rocky Balboa series is surprisingly entertaining. Though we've seen it all before, Stallone manages to make it work one more time—and even better than in *Rocky II*. Rated PG for violence and mild profanity. 1982; 99m.

ROCKY IV ★★★
DIR: Sylvester Stallone. **CAST:** Sylvester Stallone, Talia Shire, Burt Young, Carl Weathers, Brigitte Nielsen, Tony Burton, Michael Pataki, Dolph Lundgren.

Sylvester Stallone's Everyman boxing hero returns to take on a massive Russian fighter (Dolph Lundgren) trained via computer and programmed to kill. The result is deliciously corny, enjoyably predictable entertainment. Even though we know the *Rocky* formula, the movie works. Rated PG for violence and profanity. 1985; 90m.

RODEO GIRL ★★★★
DIR: Jackie Cooper. **CAST:** Katharine Ross, Bo Hopkins, Candy Clark, Jacqueline Brooks, Wilford Brimley.

Katharine Ross is Sammy, the wife of rodeo champ Will Garrett (Bo Hopkins). When she decides to try her hand at roping and bronco riding, she finds that she has the potential to be a rodeo champ. But complications arise when she discovers she is pregnant. Based on a true story. 1980; 92m.

ROLLOVER ★★★½
DIR: Alan J. Pakula. **CAST:** Jane Fonda, Kris Kristofferson, Hume Cronyn, Josef Sommer, Bob Gunton.

Jane Fonda plays an ex–film star who inherits a multimillion-dollar empire when her husband is mysteriously murdered in this gripping, but not great, film. Kris Kristofferson is the financial troubleshooter who joins forces with her to save the company. Soon both their lives are in danger. Rated R because of profanity. 1981; 118m.

ROMAN HOLIDAY ★★★★★
DIR: William Wyler. **CAST:** Gregory Peck, Audrey Hepburn, Eddie Albert.

Amid the beauty and mystique of Rome, an American newspaperman (Gregory Peck) is handed a news scoop on the proverbial silver platter. A princess (Audrey Hepburn) has slipped away from her stifling royal lifestyle. In her efforts to hide as one of Rome's common people, she encounters Peck. Their amiable adventures provide the basis for a charming fantasy-romance. 1953; B&W; 119m.

ROMAN SPRING OF MRS. STONE, THE ★★
DIR: Jose Quintero. **CAST:** Vivien Leigh, Warren Beatty, Lotte Lenya, Jill St. John.

A sensitive, elegant middle-aged actress (Vivien Leigh) has retreated to Rome to get a new focus. Warren Beatty plays a sleek, surly, wet-lipped Italian gigolo out for what he can get with the help of a crass, waspish procuress (Lotte Lenya). It's all banal. 1961; 104m.

ROMANTIC ENGLISHWOMAN, THE ★★★★
DIR: Joseph Losey. **CAST:** Glenda Jackson, Michael Caine, Helmut Berger.

Though not a completely successful adaptation of Thomas Wiseman's novel this is likely to be vastly more engaging than anything on television on any given night. Casual infidelity among the wealthy intelligentsia is always at least voyeuristically satisfying. And here pulp novel writer Michael Caine actually impels his discontented, but presumably faithful, wife Glenda Jackson into an affair with gigolo Helmut Berger. Rated R for language, adult situations. 1975; 115m.

ROMEO AND JULIET ★★★★½
DIR: Franco Zeffirelli. **CAST:** Olivia Hussey, Leonard Whiting, John McEnery, Michael York, Milo O'Shea.

Franco Zeffirelli directed this excellent version of *Romeo and Juliet.* When it was filmed, Olivia Hussey was only 15 and Leonard Whiting was only 17, keeping their characters in tune with Shakespeare's hero and heroine. Rated PG. 1968; 138m.

ROOM 43 ★★
DIR: Alvin Rakoff. **CAST:** Eddie Constantine, Diana Dors, Odile Versois, Herbert Lom.

Cabbie Eddie Constantine battles a ring of white slavers after he falls in love with one of their victims, a French girl who needs his help to remain in England. Lukewarm crime tale, featuring Michael Caine and future trash novelist Jackie Collins in small roles. 1959; B&W; 85m.

ROOM AT THE TOP ★★★★★
DIR: Jack Clayton. **CAST:** Laurence Harvey, Simone Signoret, Heather Sears, Hermione Baddeley.

John Braine's powerful novel, adapted for the screen by Neil Patterson, is a smashing success. Laurence Harvey is an opportunist who will stop at nothing, including a dalliance with his boss's daughter, to get to the top in the business world. A great cast and superb direction. This is a must-see film. 1959; B&W; 115m.

ROOM WITH A VIEW, A ★★★★★
DIR: James Ivory. **CAST:** Maggie Smith, Helena Bonham Carter, Denholm Elliott, Julian Sands, Daniel Day Lewis, Simon Callow, Judi Dench, Rosemary Leach.

This is a triumph of tasteful, intelligent filmmaking. Director James Ivory painstakingly re-creates the mood, manners, and milieu of 1908 Edwardian England as he explores the consequence of a tour of Florence, Italy, taken by an innocently curious young woman (Helena Bonham Carter) and her persnickety, meddling aunt (Maggie Smith, in top form). Unrated, the film has one brief scene of violence and some male frontal nudity. 1986; 115m.

ROSELAND ★★½
DIR: James Ivory. **CAST:** Christopher Walken, Geraldine Chaplin, Teresa Wright, Lou Jacobi, Don DeNatale, Lilia Skala.

A somewhat overly respectful triptych set in the famous, now-tattered, New York dance palace. The three stories about aging people seeking a haven of nostalgia are quietly compelling, but only Christopher Walken (certainly a good enough dancer) and Don DeNatale (who was an emcee at Roseland) give the film any vim. 1977; 103m.

R.P.M. (REVOLUTIONS PER MINUTE) ★★
DIR: Stanley Kramer. **CAST:** Anthony Quinn, Ann-Margret, Gary Lockwood.

In this story set on a small-town college campus in the late 1960s, a liberal professor (Anthony Quinn) and his coed mistress (Ann-Margret) become involved in the efforts of a liberal student (Gary Lockwood) to have the professor made president of the university. Good intentions turn into campus unrest and violence. Rated R for violence. 1970; 92m.

RUBY GENTRY ★★★
DIR: King Vidor. **CAST:** Jennifer Jones, Charlton Heston, Karl Malden, Tom Tully.

An excellent cast and sensitive direction make this drama of a Carolina swamp girl's social progress better than might be expected. Its focus is the caste system and prejudice in a picturesque region of the great melting pot. 1952; B&W; 82m. .

RUMBLE FISH ★★

DIR: Francis Ford Coppola. **CAST:** Christopher Penn, Tom Waits, Matt Dillon, Dennis Hopper, Vincent Spano, Mickey Rourke.

Francis Ford Coppola's black-and-white screen portrait of S. E. Hinton's second-rate novel about a teenage boy (Matt Dillon) seeking to escape his hellish life is a disappointing misfire. Rated R. 1983; B&W; 94m.

RUMOR MILL, THE ★★

DIR: Gus Trikonis. **CAST:** Elizabeth Taylor, Jane Alexander, Richard Dysart, Joyce Van Patten.

Hokey soap opera played to the hilt by Elizabeth Taylor and Jane Alexander as rival gossip queens Louella Parsons and Hedda Hopper. Plenty of cat fights, complete with claws baring, teeth flashing, and eye-piercing high camp. Made-for-TV melodrama that originally aired as *Malice in Wonderland*. 1988; 94m.

RUN IF YOU CAN

DIR: Virginia Lively Stone. **CAST:** Martin Landau, Yvette Napir, Jerry Van Dyke.

An incomprehensible police thriller about a woman who is able to view women being brutally murdered on her TV. Jerry Van Dyke and Martin Landau play the cops in charge of the murder investigation. Preposterous. This is a movie to run from. Rated R for nudity and violence. 1987; 92m.

RUNNER STUMBLES, THE ★★★

DIR: Stanley Kramer. **CAST:** Dick Van Dyke, Kathleen Quinlan, Maureen Stapleton, Beau Bridges.

A good adaptation of Milan Stitt's play, which certainly did not deserve the scorching hatred generated during its brief box-office appearance. Dick Van Dyke plays a priest who falls in love with Kathleen Quinlan's appealing nun. The subject may make viewers uneasy, but the film is by no means tacky or exploitative. Rated PG for adult subject matter. 1979; 99m.

RUNNING BRAVE ★★★★

DIR: Donald Shebib. **CAST:** Robby Benson, Pat Hingle, Jeff McCracken.

Robby Benson stars as Billy Mills, whose winning the ten-thousand meter race in the 1964 Olympics was one of the biggest upsets in sports history. The direction is pedestrian at best. But Benson's fine performance and the true-life drama of Mills's determination to set a positive example of achievement for his people—the Sioux and all Native Americans—is affecting enough to carry the film. Rated PG for profanity. 1983; 105m.

RUNNING HOT ★★★

DIR: Mark Griffiths. **CAST:** Eric Stoltz, Stuart Margolin, Monica Carrico, Virgil Frye.

Eric Stoltz gives a very good performance as a 17-year-old convicted of killing his father and sentenced to death row. The publicity of his case arouses the interest of 30-year-old Monica Carrico, who sends him love letters in prison. His escape and bizarre affair with her have serious consequences in this fast-paced drama. Rated R for sex, violence, language, and nudity. 1983; 88m.

RUNNING MATES ★★

DIR: Thomas L. Neff. **CAST:** Gregg Webb, Barbara Howard.

Stereotyped characters populate this story of two teenagers who fall in love, only to be torn apart when their respective fathers run against each other in an election. A sometimes interesting picture of how outside events can shape a relationship. Rated PG for adult situations. 1985; 90m.

RUNNING ON EMPTY ★★★★

DIR: Sidney Lumet. **CAST:** Christine Lahti, Judd Hirsch, River Phoenix, Martha Plimpton.

Extremely well-made film looks at a fugitive family that has been on the lam from the F.B.I. for years. Unable to establish roots anywhere because of the constant fear of detection, parents Christine Lahti and Judd Hirsch must decide what to do when their son, River Phoenix, is accepted to the Julliard School of Music. Rated PG-13. 1988; 116m.

RUNNING WILD ★★
DIR: Abner Biberman. **CAST:** William Campbell, Mamie Van Doren, Keenan Wynn, Katherine Case, Jan Merlin, John Saxon.

Rookie cop William Campbell pretends to be a young tough in order to go undercover and get the goods on an auto theft gang headed by Keenan Wynn. Made to catch the teenage rock 'n' roll crowd. 1955; 81m.

RYAN'S DAUGHTER ★★½
DIR: David Lean. **CAST:** Sarah Miles, Christopher Jones, Robert Mitchum, Trevor Howard, John Mills, Leo McKern.

Acclaimed director David Lean took a critical beating with this release, about a spoiled woman (Sarah Miles) who shamelessly lusts after an officer (Christopher Jones). Robert Mitchum, as Miles's long-suffering husband, is the best thing about this watchable misfire. Rated R. 1970; 176m.

SADIE THOMPSON ★★★
DIR: Raoul Walsh. **CAST:** Gloria Swanson, Raoul Walsh, Lionel Barrymore.

Screen legend Gloria Swanson is Somerset Maugham's famous South Seas floozy in this silent predecessor of the better-known 1932 Joan Crawford sound remake. Director-writer-costar Raoul Walsh more than holds his own against her, as reformer Lionel Barrymore resists but eventually succumbs to the sins of the flesh. 1928; B&W; 97m.

SAILOR WHO FELL FROM GRACE WITH THE SEA, THE ★★
DIR: Lewis John Carlino. **CAST:** Sarah Miles, Kris Kristofferson, Margo Cunningham, Earl Rhodes.

Much of Japanese culture remains misunderstood, and this inept adaptation of Yukio Mishima's novel is a perfect example. Kris Kristofferson doesn't have to stretch his limited abilities as an amiable sailor who falls in love with Sarah Miles. Her son, unfortunately, views the relationship with less than delight. Rated R for violence and sex. 1976; 104m.

ST. BENNY THE DIP ★★
DIR: Edgar G. Ulmer. **CAST:** Dick Haymes, Nina Foch, Roland Young, Lionel Stander, Freddie Bartholomew.

A good cast is about all that recommends this time-worn story of con artists who disguise their larceny behind clerics' robes and find themselves thinking clearer and walking the straight and narrow as a result of their contact with religion. 1951; B&W; 79m.

ST. ELMO'S FIRE ★★★
DIR: Joel Schumacher. **CAST:** Emilio Estevez, Rob Lowe, Andrew McCarthy, Demi Moore, Judd Nelson, Ally Sheedy, Mare Winningham, Martin Balsam, Andie MacDowell, Joyce Van Patten.

This film would have us believe a group of college graduates are, at the age of 22, all suffering from mid-life crises. It's a little hard to believe. However, the fine acting by some of the screen's hottest young stars helps us forgive this off-kilter premise. The movie succeeds almost in spite of itself. Rated R for suggested sex, violence, nudity, and profanity. 1985; 110m.

ST. HELENS ★★½
DIR: Ernest Pintoff. **CAST:** Art Carney, David Huffman, Cassie Yates, Albert Salmi, Ron O'Neal.

Very shallow look at the Mount St. Helens volcanic eruption and the following disasters. Art Carney plays Harry, the old man who refuses to move from his home as the upcoming fiasco is about to take place. Pretty bland stuff. Rated PG for no particular reason. 1981; 90m.

SAINT JACK ★★★
DIR: Peter Bogdanovich. **CAST:** Ben Gazzara, Denholm Elliott, James Villiers, Joss Ackland, Peter Bogdanovich, George Lazenby.

Although an interesting film, *Saint Jack* lacks power and a sense of wholeness. Ben Gazzara plays an oddly likable pimp plying his trade in Singapore in the 1970s who wants to become rich and powerful by running the classiest whorehouse in the Far East. Rated R. 1979; 112m.

SAINT JOAN ★★
DIR: Otto Preminger. **CAST:** Jean Seberg, Richard Widmark, Richard Todd, John Gielgud, Anton Walbrook, Harry Andrews, Felix Aylmer.

Even a screenplay by Graham Greene can't salvage Otto Preminger's dull screen version of George Bernard Shaw's intriguing play. Jean Seberg seems at a loss to convey the complexity of her character, and the presence of such perfomers as Richard Widmark and John Gielgud, just remind one what a great production this could have been. 1957; B&W; 110m.

SAKHAROV ★★★★
DIR: Jack Gold. **CAST:** Jason Robards Jr., Glenda Jackson, Michael Bryant, Paul Freeman, Anna Massey, Joe Melia, Jim Norton.

Compassionate story of the nuclear physicist and designer of the H-bomb, Andrei Sakharov (Jason Robards), who won the Nobel Peace Prize after waking up to the global terror of the nuclear gambit and contributing to the budding human rights movement in the Soviet Union during the late 1960s. 1984; 118m.

SALLY OF THE SAWDUST ★★★★
DIR: D. W. Griffith. **CAST:** Carol Dempster, W. C. Fields, Alfred Lunt.

W. C. Fields is at his brilliant best as the lovable con-man guardian of pretty Carol Dempster in this early film of his Broadway hit, *Poppy*. Knowing the identity of her wealthy grandparents, he works to restore her to her rightful place in society, does so after a variety of problems, and says farewell with the now classic line—Fields's accepted credo—"Never give a sucker an even break." Silent. 1925; B&W; 91m.

SALOME (1953) ★★
DIR: William Dieterle. **CAST:** Rita Hayworth, Stewart Granger, Judith Anderson, Charles Laughton, Cedric Hardwicke.

Biblical belly dancer Salome (Rita Hayworth) offers herself up as a sacrifice to save John the Baptist (Stewart Granger). Inane. 1953; 103m.

SALOME (1985) ★½
DIR: Claude D'Anna. **CAST:** Jo Ciampa, Tomas Milian, Tim Woodward.

This is a strange mixture. It is the story of the famous temptress Salome, but in director Claude D'Anna's version the Roman soldiers are in World War II overcoats, there is an elevator in the palace, and the slaves are listening to portable radios. Whatever he had in mind, it doesn't make it. Rated R. 1985; 105m.

SALOME, WHERE SHE DANCED
DIR: Charles Lamont. **CAST:** Yvonne De Carlo, Rod Cameron, Walter Slezak, David Bruce, Albert Dekker, Marjorie Rambeau.

Yvonne DeCarlo plays an exotic dancer in Austria. The authorities suspect her of espionage, so she packs her fancy duds and escapes to the American West. Pure hokum. 1945; 90m.

SALOME'S LAST DANCE ★★★★
DIR: Ken Russell. **CAST:** Glenda Jackson, Stratford Johns, Nickolas Grace, Douglas Hodge, Imogen Millais Scott.

Ken Russell pays homage to Oscar Wilde in this outrageous dark comedy that takes place in 1895 London. A group of eccentric actors enact Wilde's play *Salome* in the most bizarre setting imaginable: a brothel. Glenda Jackson is simply remarkable and she's supported by an equally gifted cast in this brilliant staged surreal fantasy. Rated R for nudity and profanity. 1988; 93m.

SALUTE JOHN CITIZEN! ★★½
DIR: Maurice Elvey. **CAST:** Edward Rigby, Mabel Constanduroos, Stanley Holloway, Peggy Cummins.

World War II home-front propaganda about how an ordinary British family copes with deprivations and does its part to pull for the war effort. Sort of a low-rent *Mrs. Miniver*. 1942; B&W; 74m.

SALVADOR ★★★★
DIR: Oliver Stone. **CAST:** James Woods, John Savage, James Belushi, Michael Murphy, Elpidia Carrillo, Tony Plana, Cynthia Gibb.

James Woods plays screenwriter-photojournalist Richard Boyle in the latter's semiautobiographical account of the events that occurred in El Salvador circa 1980–81. It is a fascinating movie despite its flaws and outrageousness. Rated R for profanity, nudity, suggested sex, drug use, and violence. 1986; 120m.

SALVATION ★★★½
DIR: Beth B. **CAST:** Stephen McHattie, Dominique Davalos, Exene Cervenka.

A punk's weird wife sends the family cash to a televangelist. Angered, the punk has his teenage sister-in-law seduce the boob-tube preacher and then blackmails him into sharing his religious revenues. Beth B., who directed and shares writing and production credits, has delivered a raw, insightful film. Rated R for nudity, profanity. 1986; 80m.

SAM'S SON ★★★½
DIR: Michael Landon. **CAST:** Timothy Patrick Murphy, Eli Wallach, Anne Jackson.

Written and directed by Michael Landon, this sweetly nostalgic semiautobiographical family film features Timothy Patrick Murphy as the young Eugene Orowitz (Landon's real name), whose parents, Sam (Eli Wallach) and Harriet (Anne Jackson), seem destined never to realize their fondest dreams until their son lends a hand. Rated PG for brief violence. 1984; 104m.

SAMSON AND DELILAH (1949) ★★★★
DIR: Cecil B. DeMille. **CAST:** Hedy Lamarr, Victor Mature, George Sanders, Angela Lansbury.

This Cecil B. De Mille extravaganza still looks good today. Hedy Lamarr plays the beautiful vixen Delilah, who robs Samson (Victor Mature) of his incredible strength. Dumb but fun. 1949; 128m.

SAMSON AND DELILAH (1984) ★★½
DIR: Lee Philips. **CAST:** Antony Hamilton, Belinda Bauer, Max von Sydow, Stephen Macht, Maria Schell, José Ferrer, Victor Mature.

An okay TV remake of the De Mille classic that had Victor Mature in the lead. This time, Mature plays Samson's father. Mature and the other veteran actors (Max von Sydow and José Ferrer) help to save the movie. Lots of action—lions, chains, and crumbling masonry. 1984; 100m.

SAN FRANCISCO ★★★★
DIR: W. S. Van Dyke. **CAST:** Clark Gable, Jeanette MacDonald, Spencer Tracy.

In its heyday, MGM boasted it had more stars than were in the heavens, and it made some terrific star-studded movies as a result. Take this 1936 production, starring Clark Gable, Jeanette MacDonald, and Spencer Tracy, for example. It's entertainment of the first order, with special effects—of the San Francisco earthquake—that still stand up today. 1936; B&W; 115m.

SANDPIPER, THE ★½
DIR: Vincente Minnelli. **CAST:** Richard Burton, Elizabeth Taylor, Eva Marie Saint, Charles Bronson.

Corny love triangle involves barefoot Elizabeth Taylor, who loves Richard Burton, who is married to Eva Marie

Saint. Lots of surf and birds in this so-what star vehicle, which capitalizes on its location shooting off the California coast. Watch for Charles Bronson in his pre-star days. 1965; 116m.

SARA DANE ★½
DIR: Rod Hardy, Gary Conway. **CAST:** Harold Hopkins, Brenton Whittle.
Headstrong eighteenth-century girl manages to raise her status through marriages to a naval officer and a French aristocrat as well as through her wise business decisions. This Australian film's premise is very similar to *A Woman of Substance* but not nearly as watchable. 1981; 150m.

SATURDAY NIGHT AT THE PALACE ★★★
DIR: Robert Davies. **CAST:** Paul Slabolepszy, John Kani.
The fears and hatreds behind South Africa's policy of apartheid are explored in a microcosm in this intense South African film. It expands upon a real-life incident, a late-night confrontation between a white man and a black at a suburban hamburger joint. Paul Slabolepszy, who plays the white antagonist, also wrote the screenplay. 1988; 87m.

SAVAGE IS LOOSE, THE
DIR: George C. Scott. **CAST:** George C. Scott, Trish Van Devere, John David Carson, Lee Montgomery.
Kill it before it multiplies. In addition to acting and directing, George C. Scott also produced and distributed this pretentious disaster. The tedious tale strands a young man and his parents on an island for many years. They explore a recreational activity the Swiss Family Robinson never considered: incest. Rated R. 1974; 114m.

SAVE THE TIGER ★★★
DIR: John G. Avildsen. **CAST:** Jack Lemmon, Jack Gilford, Thayer David.
Jack Lemmon won the Academy Award for best actor for his portrayal in this 1973 film as a garment manufacturer who is at the end of his professional and emotional rope. His excellent performance helps offset the fact that the picture is essentially a downer. Rated R. 1973; 101m.

SAYONARA ★★★★
DIR: Joshua Logan. **CAST:** Marlon Brando, Red Buttons, Miyoshi Umeki, Ricardo Montalban, James Garner.
Marlon Brando is an American airman who engages in a romance with a Japanese actress while stationed in Japan after World War II. His love is put to the test by each culture's misconceptions and prejudices. James A. Michener's thought-provoking tragedy-romance still holds up well. Red Buttons and Miyoshi Umeki deservedly won Oscars for their roles as star-crossed lovers "American Occupation"–style. 1957; 147m.

SCANDAL ★★★★½
DIR: Michael Caton-Jones. **CAST:** John Hurt, Joanne Whalley, Bridget Fonda, Ian McKellen.
A remarkable motion picture, this British production takes on the Profumo affair of the 1960s and emerges as an uncommonly satisfying adult-oriented drama, rich in character and insight. John Hurt is superb as Stephen Ward, the London osteopath who groomed teenage Christine Keeler (Joanne Whalley-Kilmer) into the femme fatale who brought down the British Conservative government. Rated R for nudity, simulated sex, violence, and profanity. 1989; 105m.

SCAR, THE ★★★★
DIR: Steve Sekely. **CAST:** Paul Henreid, Joan Bennett, Eduard Franz, Leslie Brooks, John Qualen.
Fans of hardboiled *film noir* will want to look for this lesser-known but memorable example of the genre. Paul Henreid plays two parts: a gambler fleeing from the police and a psychiatrist who is his exact double. The gambler plans to escape the law by killing the doctor and assuming his

identity. Look for Jack Webb in a small role. 1948; B&W; 83m.

SCARECROW ★★★
DIR: Jerry Schatzberg. **CAST:** Al Pacino, Gene Hackman, Eileen Brennan, Richard Lynch.
A real downer about two losers (Al Pacino and Gene Hackman) trying to make something of themselves, this drama is made watchable by the performances. Rated R. 1973; 115m.

SCARLET LETTER, THE (1926) ★★★
DIR: Victor Seastrom. **CAST:** Lillian Gish, Henry B. Walthall, Karl Dane, Lars Hanson.
Hester Prynne wears the scarlet letter A for adultery. Only her sadistic husband Roger knows that minister Arthur Dimmesdale is the father of her daughter, Pearl. Roger taunts Arthur, who plans to flee with Hester and the child but finally confesses his sin publicly. Silent. 1926; B&W; 80m.

SCARLET LETTER, THE (1934) ★★★
DIR: Robert Vignola. **CAST:** Colleen Moore, Hardie Albright, Henry B. Walthall.
Twenties flapper star Colleen Moore proved she had acting skill in this second version (first sound) of Nathaniel Hawthorne's great classic of love, hate, jealousy, and emotional blackmail in Puritan New England. As in the 1926 silent version, D. W. Griffith star Henry B. Walthall portrays the heartless persecutor Roger Chillingworth. 1934; B&W; 69m.

SCARLET STREET ★★★½
DIR: Fritz Lang. **CAST:** Edward G. Robinson, Joan Bennett, Dan Duryea, Margaret Lindsay, Rosalind Ivan.
The director (Fritz Lang) and stars (Edward G. Robinson, Joan Bennett, and Dan Duryea) of the excellent *Woman in the Window* reteamed with less spectacular results for this film about a mild-mannered fellow (Robinson) seduced into a life of crime by a temptress (Bennett). 1945; B&W; 103m.

SCENES FROM THE GOLDMINE ★★½
DIR: Marc Rocco. **CAST:** Catherine Mary Stewart, Cameron Dye, Steve Railsback, Joe Pantoliano, Lee Ving, Lesley-Anne Down.
Music industry exposé with Catherine Mary Stewart as a musician-composer who joins a rock band and falls in love with the lead singer. Realistic story won't appeal much to nonrock fans, and even rock fans will find the band's performances somewhat synthetic (most of the actors do their own singing and playing). Rated R for sexual situations and profanity. 1987; 105m.

SCOTT OF THE ANTARCTIC ★½
DIR: Charles Frend. **CAST:** John Mills, Derek Bond, Christopher Lee, Kenneth More, James Robertson.
This is a plodding, straightforward account of British explorer Robert Scott, complete with fake atmosphere (i.e., painted backdrops). You'd do much better to rent the superior expedition film, *Flight of the Eagle*. 1948; 110m.

SCROOGE (1935) ★★★
DIR: Henry Edwards. **CAST:** Seymour Hicks, Donald Calthrop, Robert Cochran, Maurice Evans.
This little-known British version of Charles Dickens's classic *A Christmas Carol* is faithful to the original story and boasts a standout performance by Seymour Hicks, who also cowrote the screenplay. A truly enjoyable film, unjustly overshadowed by Alistair Sim's bravura performance as Scrooge in the venerated 1951 version. 1935; B&W; 78m.

SEA LION, THE ★★½
DIR: Rowland V. Lee. **CAST:** Hobart Bosworth, Bessie Love, Richard Morris.
Stern sea story with hard-bitten Hobart Bosworth as a tyrannical ship's master who vents his pent-up hatred on the men in his charge. But just

when the old boy is really hitting his stride, romance rears its head and we find out that he's not all bad; he was just acting like a sadist because he had a broken heart. Silent. 1921; B&W; 50m.

SECOND WOMAN, THE ★★★
DIR: James V. Kern. **CAST:** Robert Young, Betsy Drake, John Sutton.
Is Robert Young paranoid, or is the whole world crazy? Strange and violent occurrences are plaguing the life of this talented architect. Betsy Drake, smitten with the confused fellow, is the only onlooker who doesn't doubt his sanity. This dark drama maintains a steady undercurrent of suspense. 1951; B&W; 91m.

SECRET CEREMONY ★★½
DIR: Joseph Losey. **CAST:** Elizabeth Taylor, Mia Farrow, Robert Mitchum, Peggy Ashcroft, Pamela Brown.
Typical Joseph Losey psychodrama about a psychotic girl (Mia Farrow) semikidnapping an aging streetwalker (Elizabeth Taylor) who reminds her of her dead mother. Robert Mitchum plays Farrow's lecherous stepfather who disrupts the relationship. With its strong sexual undertones, this film is not for kids (and probably not for some adults). 1968; 108m.

SECRET HONOR ★★★★
DIR: Robert Altman. **CAST:** Philip Baker Hall.
This one-man show features Philip Baker Hall as Richard Nixon—drinking, swearing, and going completely over the top in his ravings, on such subjects as Castro, Kennedy, and Henry Kissinger. Fascinating, with Hall's performance a wonder. A one-of-a-kind movie from Robert Altman. Rated PG. 1984; 90m.

SECRET OBSESSIONS (turkey)
DIR: Henri Vart. **CAST:** Julie Christie, Ben Gazzara, Patrick Bruel, Jean Carmet.
Maudlin, morose, melodramatic yawner with Julie Christie and Ben Gazzara sleepwalking through their performances. Gazzara, as a wealthy landowner, and Christie are forced to flee from their home when the North African state they live in gains independence. Rated PG. 1988; 82m.

SECRETS ★★
DIR: Philip Saville. **CAST:** Jacqueline Bisset, Per Oscarsson, Shirley Knight Hopkins, Robert Powell.
Jacqueline Bisset's torrid sex scene is about the only interesting thing in this turgid soap opera about the romantic secrets of a husband, wife, and daughter. Rated R for nudity, suggested sex, and profanity. 1971; 86m.

SEDUCERS, THE ★
DIR: Peter Traynor. **CAST:** Sondra Locke, Seymour Cassel, Colleen Camp.
Bizarre, misogynist parable about a San Francisco architect who takes in two young women one rainy night and then can't get rid of them for the next two days. They seduce him, destroy his house, kill a delivery boy, and generally display behavior that would give Miss Manners a stroke. Noisy and obnoxious. Also on video under its original title, *Death Game*. Rated R for nudity and profanity. 1977; 90m.

SEDUCTION OF JOE TYNAN, THE ★★★
DIR: Jerry Schatzberg. **CAST:** Alan Alda, Barbara Harris, Meryl Streep, Rip Torn, Charles Kimbrough, Melvyn Douglas.
Alan Alda plays Senator Joe Tynan in this story of behind-the-scenes romance and political maneuvering in Washington, D.C. Tynan must face moral questions about himself and his job. It's familiar ground for Alda but still entertaining. Rated PG for language, brief nudity. 1979; 107m.

SEE YOU IN THE MORNING ★★★★
DIR: Alan J. Pakula. **CAST:** Jeff Bridges, Alice Krige, Farrah Fawcett, Drew Barrymore, Lukas Haas, David Dukes, Frances Sternhagen, Linda Lavin.

Writer-director Alan J. Pakula spent ten years refining his screenplay *See You in the Morning*, and the result is a touching character study with numerous memorable and believable moments. Jeff Bridges is a New York psychiatrist whose first marriage to model Farrah Fawcett crumbles, catching him off guard. A second marriage, to Alice Krige, seems more promising, but our hero has a number of obstacles to overcome. Rated PG-13 for profanity. 1989; 115m.

SEIZE THE DAY ★★★
DIR: Fielder Cook. **CAST:** Robin Williams, Joseph Wiseman, Jerry Stiller, Glenne Headly, John Fiedler, Tom Aldredge, Tony Roberts.

Robin Williams is watchable in this drama, but like so many comedians who attempt serious acting, he is haunted by his madcap persona. This PBS *Great Peformances* entry casts Williams as Wilhelm "Tommy" Adler, the Jewish ne'er-do-well son of wealthy, unsympathetic Joseph Wiseman. The story concerns the disintegration of Tommy's life. 1986; 87m.

SENSATIONS ★½
DIR: Chuck Vincent. **CAST:** Rebecca Lynn, Blake Bahner.

Ex–porno director Chuck Vincent continues to grind out a half-dozen or so movies every year, which is probably why most of them seem so uninspired. This one is an odd-couple love story between a prostitute and a male stripper; it features too many dumb subplots and disagreeable main characters. Rated R for strong sexual situations. 1988; 91m.

SENSE OF FREEDOM, A ★★★
DIR: John Mackenzie. **CAST:** David Hayman, Alex Norton, Jake D'Arcy, Fulton Mackay.

The true story of Jimmy Boyle, a violent Scottish criminal who refused to temper his viciousness during over a decade in various prisons. The film never attempts to make a hero out of Boyle, but neither does it offer any insight into his personality. A very well-made film from John Mackenzie, whose excellent *The Long Good Friday* featured a similar protagonist. Rated R. 1983; 81m.

SEPARATE PEACE, A ★★★
DIR: Larry Peerce. **CAST:** John Heyl, Parker Stevenson, Peter Brush.

Based on John Knowles's bestselling novel, this involving story of a young man's first glimpse of adult emotions and motivations—some say homosexual frustration—is watchable for plot and performance. Gene and Finny are prep-school roommates at the beginning of World War II. Jealous of Finny's popularity, Gene betrays his roommate in a moment of anger and treachery, and is responsible for a crippling accident. Rated PG. 1972; 104m.

SEPARATE TABLES ★★★★★
DIR: John Schlesinger. **CAST:** Julie Christie, Alan Bates, Claire Bloom.

This is a cable-television remake of the 1958 film with Burt Lancaster and Wendy Hiller. This time the work achieves a remarkable intimacy on tape with a top-notch British cast. Divided into two segments, this is a sort of British *Grand Hotel* room with Alan Bates and Julie Christie in dual roles. Richly engrossing adult entertainment. Rated PG for adult subject matter. 1983; 108m.

SEPTEMBER ★★★½
DIR: Woody Allen. **CAST:** Mia Farrow, Dianne Wiest, Sam Waterston, Denholm Elliott, Elaine Stritch, Jack Warden.

Woody Allen in his serious mode. Mia Farrow is superb as a troubled woman living in Vermont. Her houseguests are her hard-living mother (Elaine Stritch), her stepfather (Jack Warden), her best friend (Diane Wiest), and an aspiring writer (Sam Waterston). What transpires are subtle yet intense love-hate relationships. Rated PG. 1987; 82m.

SEPTEMBER AFFAIR ★★½

DIR: William Dieterle. **CAST:** Joseph Cotten, Joan Fontaine, Françoise Rosay, Jessica Tandy, Robert Arthur, Jimmy Lydon.

Superficial romantic tale about two married people who are reported dead after a plane crash. This gives them their chance to conduct a love affair. Bonuses: nice photography on the isle of Capri and the famous Walter Huston recording of the title song. 1950; B&W; 104m.

SERGEANT RYKER ★★★

DIR: Buzz Kulik. **CAST:** Lee Marvin, Bradford Dillman, Vera Miles, Peter Graves, Lloyd Nolan, Murray Hamilton.

This film revolves around the court-martial of Sergeant Ryker (Lee Marvin), a Korean War soldier. Ryker, accused of treason, is valiantly defended by his attorney (Bradford Dillman in a superb performance). Originally shown on television as *The Case Against Sergeant Ryker*, then released theatrically under the shortened title. 1968; 86m.

SERPENT'S EGG, THE ★½

DIR: Ingmar Bergman. **CAST:** Liv Ullmann, David Carradine, Gert Fröbe, James Whitmore.

Two trapeze artists are trapped in Berlin during pre-Nazi Germany. They find work in a strange clinic, where they discover a satanic plot. Director Ingmar Bergman's nightmare vision is disappointing at best. Sven Nykvist's cinematography is the one redeeming element. 1977; 120m.

SERPICO ★★★★

DIR: Sidney Lumet. **CAST:** Al Pacino, Tony Roberts, John Randolph, Biff McGuire, Jack Kehoe.

Al Pacino is magnificent in this poignant story of an honest man who happens to be a cop. The fact that this is a true story of one man's fight against corruption adds even more punch. Rated R. 1973; 130m.

SERVANT, THE ★★★★

DIR: Joseph Losey. **CAST:** Dirk Bogarde, Sarah Miles, James Fox.

A conniving manservant (Dirk Bogarde) gradually dominates the life of his spoiled master in this psychological horror story. By preying on his sexual weaknesses, he is able to easily maneuver him to his will. The taut, well-acted adult drama holds your interest throughout, mainly because the shock value is heightened for the audience because of its plausibility. 1963; B&W; 115m.

SESSIONS ★★★

DIR: Richard Pearce. **CAST:** Veronica Hamel, Jeffrey DeMunn, Jill Eikenberry.

Veronica Hamel poses as a career woman who also takes pleasure in being a high-priced call girl in the evening. Soap-opera drama? Yes, but that's what you expect in this made-for-TV movie. And it's done with class. 1983; 100m.

SET-UP, THE ★★★★

DIR: Robert Wise. **CAST:** Robert Ryan, Audrey Totter, George Tobias, Alan Baxter, James Edwards, Wallace Ford.

Taut *film noir* boxing flick takes the simple story of an over-the-hill boxer who refuses to disregard his principles and throw the big fight and elevates it to true tragedy. Robert Ryan as the has-been fighter gives another of the finely drawn and fiercely independent portrayals that marked his illustrious career as one of Hollywood's finest character actors. 1949; B&W; 72m.

SEVEN CITIES OF GOLD ★★★

DIR: Robert D. Webb. **CAST:** Michael Rennie, Richard Egan, Anthony Quinn, Jeffrey Hunter, Rita Moreno.

Michael Rennie plays an incredibly pious Father Junípero Serra, struggling to set up his first mission in California. His love of the Indians contrasts sharply with the ruthless greed of the Spanish military leaders (played by Anthony Quinn and Richard Egan). Unrated, this contains violence. 1955; 103m.

SEVEN DAYS IN MAY ★★★★
DIR: John Frankenheimer. **CAST:** Burt Lancaster, Fredric March, Kirk Douglas, Ava Gardner, Edmond O'Brien, Martin Balsam.

A highly suspenseful account of an attempted military takeover of the U.S. government. After a slow buildup, the movie's tension snowballs toward a thrilling conclusion. This is one of those rare films that treat their audiences with respect. A working knowledge of the political process is helpful for optimum appreciation. Fredric March, as a president under pressure, heads an all-star cast, all of whom give admirable performances. 1964; B&W; 120m.

SEVEN MINUTES, THE ★
DIR: Russ Meyer. **CAST:** Wayne Maunder, Marianne McAndrew, Jay C. Flippen, Edy Williams, Yvonne De Carlo, John Carradine.

Pornography is put on trial when a young man claims that he was driven to commit rape after reading a sexy novel. This talky movie was based on a potboiler by novelist Irving Wallace, so don't expect an insightful examination of the issues. Slow-moving and unbelievably dreary. Look for Tom Selleck in a small role. Rated R. 1971; 115m.

SEVENTH VEIL, THE ★★★½
DIR: Compton Bennett. **CAST:** James Mason, Ann Todd, Herbert Lom, Hugh McDermott, Albert Lieven.

A young woman forsakes her family and chooses to become a musician, encountering many men along the way. Safe and satisfying, this middlebrow entertainment owes much of its success to a strong performance by James Mason and an Oscar-winning screenplay. Ann Todd is just right as the free-thinking heroine. 1945; B&W; 94m.

SEX MADNESS ★
DIR: Dwayne Vesper. **CAST:** Not Credited.

"Educational" film about the dangers of syphilis is long on melodrama and morality and surprisingly short on graphic footage of disease victims. Several stories about youth gone wrong tie together in this sometimes hilarious exploitation film, but the exaggerated clichés and inept burlesque scenes can't lighten the heavy-handed story. 1934; B&W; 50m.

SHACK-OUT ON 101 ★★★½
DIR: Edward Dein. **CAST:** Frank Lovejoy, Terry Moore, Lee Marvin, Keenan Wynn, Whit Bissell.

This odd blend of character study and espionage thriller, which takes place at a highway hash-house, involves some of the most colorful patrons you'll ever run across. Perky Terry Moore plays the waitress who helps the authorities close in on the men who have sabotage plans for a local chemical plant, and Lee Marvin is at his most audacious as Slob, a name he does his best to live up to. 1955; B&W; 80m.

SHADES OF LOVE: CHAMPAGNE FOR TWO ★★
DIR: Lewis Furey. **CAST:** Nicholas Campbell, Kirsten Bishop.

Comedy and romance are blended in this so-so story about a young architect (Kirsten Bishop) who falls in love with her roommate (Nicholas Campbell). This modern romance is complicated by the choice she must make between love and a career. 1987; 82m.

SHADES OF LOVE: LILAC DREAM ★½
DIR: Marc Voizard. **CAST:** Dack Rambo, Susan Almgren.

Mystery and romance combine in this tale of a young woman left brokenhearted by a former lover. Then a storm leaves a man with no memory on the shore of her island. She nurses him back to health. Gradually, his past comes back to haunt him. 1987; 83m.

SHADES OF LOVE: THE ROSE CAFE ★½

DIR: Daniele J. Suissa. **CAST:** Parker Stevenson, Linda Smith.

Dreams can sometimes hide the truth, and in the case of Courtney Fairchild (Linda Smith), her dream of opening a restaurant has hidden her feelings for the men in her life. When trouble hits her restaurant, Courtney finds she must solve her man problems before she can find happiness. 1987; 84m.

SHADES OF LOVE: SINCERELY, VIOLET ★½

DIR: Mort Ransen. **CAST:** Simon MacCorkindale, Patricia Phillips.

In this mediocre story of love and romance, a professor (Patricia Phillips) becomes a cat burglar named Violet. She is caught in the act by Mark Janson (Simon MacCorkindale) who tries to reform her. 1987; 86m.

SHADOWS ★★★

DIR: Tom Forman. **CAST:** Lon Chaney Sr., Harrison Ford, Marguerite de la Motte, Walter Long.

A zealous young minister takes it upon himself to convert the local Chinese laundrymen. Lon Chaney as Yen Sin gives a moving performance as the man who must confront the self-righteous churchman, played by Harrison Ford (no relation to today's star). A colorful cast of good character actors help to make this a thought-provoking film. Silent. 1922; B&W; 70m.

SHAKA ZULU ★★★½

DIR: William C. Faure. **CAST:** Edward Fox, Robert Powell, Trevor Howard, Fiona Fullerton, Christopher Lee, Henry Cole, Roy Dotrice, Gordon Jackson.

A tremendously staged epic chronicling the rise of Shaka (Henry Cole) as the king of the Zulus. Set against the emergence of British power in Africa during the early nineteenth century, this film provides some valuable insights into comparative cultures. Despite some poor editing and an overly dramatic, inappropriate musical score, *Shaka Zulu* is quite rewarding. Unrated, this release contains graphic violence and frequent nudity. 1986; 300m.

SHAKESPEARE WALLAH ★★★★

DIR: James Ivory. **CAST:** Shashi Kapoor, Geoffrey Kendall, Laura Liddell, Felicity Kendall, Madhur Jaffrey.

A family troupe of Shakespearean players performs to disinterested, dwinding audiences in the new India (*wallah* is Hindustani for *peddler*). Frustrated sensuality, social humiliation, dedication to a dying cause, and familial devotion are rendered here with the sensitivity and delicacy that we have come to expect from director James Ivory. Madhur Jaffrey won the best actress award at the Berlin Festival for her satiric rendering of a Bombay musical star, the personification of narcissism and oversized vulgarity. 1964; B&W; 114m.

SHAMING, THE ★★

DIR: Marvin J. Chomsky. **CAST:** Anne Heywood, Donald Pleasence, Robert Vaughn, Carolyn Jones, Dorothy Malone, Dana Elcar.

A spinster schoolteacher seeks psychiatric help because of extreme emotional problems relating to her virginity. She is then raped by a janitor and continues to have sex with him until she is exposed and then ostracized by the school. This film is rated R for sex. 1975; 90m.

SHAMPOO ★★★★

DIR: Hal Ashby. **CAST:** Warren Beatty, Julie Christie, Lee Grant, Jack Warden, Goldie Hawn, Carrie Fisher.

Star Warren Beatty and Robert Towne cowrote this perceptive comedy of morals, most of them bad, which focuses on a hedonistic Beverly Hills hairdresser played by Beatty. Although portions come perilously close to slapstick, the balance is an insightful study of the pain caused by people who try for no-strings-attached relationships. Rated R—sexuality and adult themes. 1975; 112m.

SHANGHAI GESTURE, THE ★★
DIR: Josef von Sternberg. **CAST:** Gene Tierney, Ona Munson, Walter Huston, Albert Basserman, Eric Blore, Victor Mature, Maria Ouspenskaya, Mike Mazurki.

Camp melodrama—an excursion into depravity in mysterious Shanghai. Walter Huston wants to close the gambling casino run by Ona Munson, who has a hold over his daughter Gene Tierney. Atmospheric idiocy. 1942; B&W; 106m.

SHATTERED ★★
DIR: Alistair Reid. **CAST:** Peter Finch, Shelley Winters, Colin Blakely, John Stride, Linda Hayden.

Peter Finch plays a mild-mannered, neurotic businessman who picks up a hitchhiker (Linda Hayden) only to have her attach herself to him. As a result, he slowly begins to lose his sanity. Shelley Winters plays Finch's obnoxious wife. Like a lot of British thrillers, this one has little action until it explodes in the final fifteen minutes. Rated R for profanity and violence. 1972; 100m.

SHE'S DRESSED TO KILL ★★
DIR: Gus Trikonis. **CAST:** Eleanor Parker, Jessica Walter, John Rubinstein, Jim McMullan, Corinne Calvet.

Acceptable murder mystery concerning the deaths of high-fashion models. Eleanor Parker is excellent as a garish, once-renowned designer trying to stage a comeback. This made-for-TV movie was retitled *Someone's Killing the World's Greatest Models*. 1979; 100m.

SHE'S IN THE ARMY NOW ★★★
DIR: Hy Averback. **CAST:** Kathleen Quinlan, Jamie Lee Curtis, Melanie Griffith, Janet MacLachlan.

The distributor has labeled this made-for-TV film as a comedy, but there is very little to laugh about in the story of seven weeks of basic training in a women's squadron. Some fine character studies emerge as the various recruits are introduced. Kathleen Quinlan as the appointed squadron leader and Jamie Lee Curtis as the streetwise recruit with additional problems forced upon her by a drug-dealing boyfriend are both very good. 1981; 97m.

SHINING SEASON, A ★★★
DIR: Stuart Margolin. **CAST:** Timothy Bottoms, Allyn Ann McLerie, Ed Begley Jr., Rip Torn, Mason Adams.

Fact-based story of track star and Olympic hopeful John Baker, (Timothy Bottoms) who, when stricken by cancer, devoted his final months to coaching a girls' track team. This is very familiar territory, but director Stuart Margolin keeps things above water most of the time. Bottoms is an engaging hero-victim. Made for television. 1979; 100m.

SHIP OF FOOLS ★★★★★
DIR: Stanley Kramer. **CAST:** Vivien Leigh, Oskar Werner, Simone Signoret, José Ferrer, Lee Marvin, George Segal, Michael Dunn, Elizabeth Ashley, Lilia Skala, Charles Korvin.

In 1933, a vast and varied group of characters take passage on a German liner sailing from Mexico to Germany amidst impending doom. The all-star cast features most memorable performances by Vivien Leigh (her last film) as the neurotic divorcée, Oskar Werner as the ship's doctor, who has an affair with the despairing Simone Signoret, Lee Marvin as the forceful American baseball player, and Michael Dunn as the wise dwarf. Superb screen adaptation of the Katherine Anne Porter novel of the same name. 1965; B&W; 150m.

SHOCK, THE ★★★
DIR: Lambert Hillyer. **CAST:** Lon Chaney Sr., Christine Mayo.

The legendary Lon Chaney Sr. added yet another grotesque character to his growing closet of skeltons when he played Wilse Dilling. This decent crime melodrama, no different in plot than dozens of other films over the years, has the advantage of Chaney and an exciting climax consisting of a bang-up earthquake. Corny at times, this one is still a good bet if you're interested in silent films. 1923; B&W; 96m.

SHOES OF THE FISHERMAN ★½
DIR: Michael Anderson. **CAST:** Anthony Quinn, Laurence Olivier, Oskar Werner, David Janssen, Vittorio De Sica, John Gielgud, Leo McKern, Barbara Jefford.

A truly memorable cast is about all there is to recommend this improbable and boring film about an enthusiastic pope who singlehandedly attempts to stop nuclear war, starvation, world strife, and people who think that the pontiff should stay in Rome and say Mass. David Janssen plays a journalist with a direct line to the action, but too much of this "topical" film is spent following Janssen as he tries to straighten out his love life. 1968; 157m.

SHOOT THE MOON ★★
DIR: Alan Parker. **CAST:** Albert Finney, Diane Keaton, Karen Allen, Dana Hill, Tracey Gold.

Why didn't they just call it *Ordinary People Go West*? Of course, this film isn't really a sequel to the 1980 Oscar winner. It's closer to a rip-off; another somber movie about the disintegration of a marriage and a family. Yet it has none of the style, believability, or consistency of its predecessor. Rated R because of profanity, violence, and adult themes. 1982; 123m.

SHOOTING PARTY, THE ★★★★
DIR: Alan Bridges. **CAST:** James Mason, Edward Fox, Dorothy Tutin, John Gielgud, Gordon Jackson, Cheryl Campbell, Robert Hardy.

This meditation on the fading English aristocracy is an acting showcase. All main characters are played with verve, or at least the verve one would expect from English nobility in the years preceding World War I. While nothing much happens here, the rich texture of the characters, the highly stylized sets, and the incidental affairs in the plot are enough to sustain the viewer. Not rated, but equivalent to a PG for partial nudity. 1985; 97m.

SHORT EYES ★★★★
DIR: Robert M. Young. **CAST:** Bruce Davison, Jose Perez.

Film version of Miguel Pinero's hard-hitting play about a convicted child molester at the mercy of other prisoners. A brutal and frightening film. Excellent, but difficult to watch. Rated R for violence and profanity. 1977; 104m.

SHY PEOPLE ★★★
DIR: Andrei Konchalovsky. **CAST:** Barbara Hershey, Jill Clayburgh, Martha Plimpton, Merritt Butrick, John Philbin, Mare Winningham.

Moody drama about a New York writer (Jill Clayburgh) who journeys to the Louisiana bayous to get family-background information from distant Cajun relatives. Barbara Hershey, in an offbeat role, plays a dominating Cajun mother. Clayburgh gives a strong performance, and Martha Plimpton as her troublemaking daughter is fine too. Rated R for language and sexual content. 1987; 118m.

SID AND NANCY ★★★½
DIR: Alex Cox. **CAST:** Gary Oldman, Chloe Webb, Drew Schofield, David Hayman.

Leave it to Alex Cox, director of the suburban punk classic *Repo Man*, to try to make sense out of deceased punk rocker Sid Vicious and his girlfriend Nancy Spungen. Its compassionate portrait of the two famed nihilists is a powerful one, which nevertheless is not for everyone. Rated R for violence, sex, nudity, and adult subject matter. 1986; 111m.

SIDEWALKS OF LONDON ★★★★
DIR: Tim Whelan. **CAST:** Vivien Leigh, Charles Laughton, Rex Harrison, Tyrone Guthrie.

Street entertainer Charles Laughton puts pretty petty thief Vivien Leigh in his song-and-dance act, then falls in love with her. Befriended by successful songwriter Rex Harrison, she puts the streets and old friends behind her and rises to stage stardom while her rejected and dejected mentor hits the skids. Vivien Leigh is entrancing, and Charles Laughton is compelling and touching, in this dramatic sojourn in London byways. 1940; B&W; 85m.

SIESTA ★★★½

DIR: Mary Lambert. **CAST:** Ellen Barkin, Gabriel Byrne, Julian Sands, Jodie Foster, Martin Sheen, Isabella Rossellini, Grace Jones.

Oddly fascinating and sexually intense drama. Ellen Barkin plays a stuntwoman in love with a former trainer (Gabriel Byrne), a man who loved her but married someone else. *Siesta* plays with time, reality, and consciousness, turning them into something suspenseful. Rated R for language and sex. 1987; 90m.

SILAS MARNER ★★★★

DIR: Giles Foster. **CAST:** Ben Kingsley, Jenny Agutter, Patrick Ryecart, Patsy Kensit.

Fate is the strongest character in this BBC-TV adaptation of George Eliot's novel, although Ben Kingsley gives an excellent performance as the cataleptic eighteenth-century English weaver. Betrayed by his closest friend and cast out of the church, Marner disappears into the English countryside and becomes a bitter miser, only to have his life wonderfully changed when fate brings an orphan girl to his hovel. 1985; 97m.

SILENCE OF THE NORTH ★★

DIR: Allan Winton King. **CAST:** Ellen Burstyn, Tom Skerritt, Gordon Pinsent.

There are some of us at the *Video Movie Guide* who would follow Ellen Burstyn anywhere. But Burstyn's narration here is pure melodrama, and ninety minutes of one catastrophe after the next is more tiring than entertaining. Burstyn portrays a woman who falls in love with a fur trapper, played by Tom Skerritt, and moves into the Canadian wilderness. Rated PG for violence. 1981; 94m.

SILENT NIGHT, LONELY NIGHT ★★½

DIR: Daniel Petrie. **CAST:** Lloyd Bridges, Shirley Jones, Carrie Snodgress, Robert Lipton.

Slow-moving, but fairly interesting TV film about two lonely people (Lloyd Bridges and Shirley Jones) who share a few happy moments at Christmas time. Flashbacks to previous tragedies are distracting. Unrated. 1969; 98m.

SILENT REBELLION ★★

DIR: Charles S. Dubin. **CAST:** Telly Savalas, Michael Constantine, Keith Gordon.

Telly Savalas plays a naturalized American who goes back to his hometown in Greece to visit. He finds that the old ways in the village where he was born are too outdated for him and tries to introduce his kin to the American way of life. But the cross-cultural experience is not always pleasant. Some poignant moments, but lots of dull ones, too. Not rated 1982; 90m.

SILENT VICTORY: THE KITTY O'NEIL STORY ★★★

DIR: Lou Antonio. **CAST:** Stockard Channing, James Farentino, Colleen Dewhurst, Edward Albert, Brian Dennehy.

Better-than-average TV biography of ace stuntwoman Kitty O'Neil, who overcame the handicap of being deaf to excel in her profession. Proof positive is O'Neil doubling Channing in the stunt scenes. 1979; 100m.

SILKWOOD ★★★★

DIR: Mike Nichols. **CAST:** Meryl Streep, Kurt Russell, Cher, Craig T. Nelson, Fred Ward, Sudie Bond.

At more than two hours, *Silkwood* is a shift-and-squirm movie that's worth it. The fine portrayals by Meryl Streep, Kurt Russell, and Cher keep the viewer's interest. Based on real events, the story focuses on 28-year-old nuclear worker and union activist Karen Silkwood, who died in a mysterious car crash while she was attempting to expose the alleged dangers in the Oklahoma plutonium plant where she was employed. Rated R for nudity, sex, and profanity. 1984; 128m.

SILVER CHALICE, THE ★★
DIR: Victor Saville. **CAST:** Jack Palance, Joseph Wiseman, Paul Newman, Virginia Mayo, Pier Angeli, E. G. Marshall, Alexander Scourby, Natalie Wood, Lorne Greene.

Thomas Costain's historical novel about the cup used at the Last Supper comes off third best in this ripe Technicolor presentation. Full of intrigue and togas, this film is notable only for two unnotable screen debuts by Paul Newman and Lorne Greene. 1954; 144m.

SILVER DREAM RACER ★★½
DIR: David Wickes. **CAST:** David Essex, Beau Bridges, Cristina Raines, Clark Peters, Harry Corbett.

This so-so British drama features David Essex as a mechanic turned racer. He is determined to win not only the World Motorcycle Championship but another man's girlfriend as well. Rated PG. 1980; 110m.

SILVER STREAK ★★
DIR: Thomas Atkins. **CAST:** Charles Starrett, Sally Blane, Hardie Albright, William Farnum, Irving Pichel, Arthur Lake.

Interesting primarily for the vintage locomotives and the railway system as well as a good cast of unique personalities, this slowly paced drama follows a high-speed train on a mission of mercy. 1934; B&W; 72m.

SINCERELY YOURS 🦃
DIR: Gordon Douglas. **CAST:** Liberace, Joanne Dru, Dorothy Malone, William Demarest, Lurene Tuttle, Richard Eyer.

Written by Irving Wallace, who should have known better, this tepid, camp remake of George Arliss's classic *The Man Who Played God* may earn cult status because the leading man is Liberace. Ridiculous, sincerely. 1955; 115m.

SINGLE BARS, SINGLE WOMEN 🦃
DIR: Harry Winer. **CAST:** Tony Danza, Paul Michael Glaser, Keith Gordon, Shelley Hack, Christine Lahti, Frances Lee McCain, Kathleen Wilhoite, Mare Winningham.

A dated film that pretends to know all about the singles scene. Imagine a bevy of unattached chicks and a herd of macho dudes mixing it up in a typical pick-up joint. See *Looking for Mr. Goodbar* instead. Made for TV. 1984; 100m.

SINGLE ROOM FURNISHED ★
DIR: Matt Cimber. **CAST:** Jayne Mansfield, Dorothy Keller, Fabian Dean.

Jayne Mansfield's last movie was this lurid overwrought melodrama. She plays a woman who is constantly being seduced and abandoned, eventually sinking into a life of prostitution. 1968; 93m.

SISTER KENNY ★★
DIR: Dudley Nichols. **CAST:** Rosalind Russell, Alexander Knox, Dean Jagger, Charles Dingle, Philip Merivale, Beulah Bondi, John Litel.

Rosalind Russell is noble and sincere in the title role of the Australian nurse who fought polio in the bush. Her pioneering treatment methods finally prevailed over a skeptical medical community jealous of allowing her recognition. But the telling of her life in this dull and slow box-office flop is tiresome. 1946; B&W; 116m.

SIX WEEKS ★★★½
DIR: Tony Bill. **CAST:** Dudley Moore, Mary Tyler Moore, Katherine Healy, Joe Regalbuto.

Dudley Moore and Mary Tyler Moore star as two adults trying to make the dreams of a young girl—who has a very short time to live—come true in this tearjerker. Directed by Tony Bill, it's enjoyable for viewers who like a good cry. Rated PG for strong content. 1982; 107m.

SIZZLE

DIR: Don Medford. **CAST:** Loni Anderson, John Forsythe, Michael Goodwin, Leslie Uggams, Roy Thinnes, Richard Lynch, Phyllis Davis.

This TV movie should be called *Fizzle*, which is what it does. A small-town songbird chirps her way into the heart of a mobster to protect her man. Loni Anderson tries to sizzle for John Forsythe (the suave mobster), but this is so badly cast that it's laughable. 1981; 100m.

SKAG ★★★½

DIR: Frank Perry. **CAST:** Karl Malden, Piper Laurie, Craig Wasson, Peter Gallagher, George Voskovec.

Home-ridden to recuperate after being felled by a stroke, veteran steelworker Pete Skagska must deal with family problems, his own poor health, and the chance his illness may leave him impotent. In the title role, Karl Malden gives a towering, hard-driving performance as a man determined to prevail, no matter what the emotional cost. TV movie. 1980; 152m.

SKEEZER ★★½

DIR: Peter R. Hunt. **CAST:** Karen Valentine, Dee Wallace, Tom Atkins, Mariclare Costello.

Made-for-TV movie about a lonely young woman and her friendship with a mutt named Skeezer. This dog eventually helps her to reach emotionally disturbed children in a group home where she is a volunteer. Good for family viewing. 1982; 100m.

SKY IS GRAY, THE ★★★

DIR: Stan Lathan. **CAST:** Olivia Cole, James Bond III, Margaret Avery, Cleavon Little, Clinton Derricks-Carroll.

Generosity comes from unexpected quarters in this languid TV adaptation of Ernest J. Gaines's melancholy study of a young boy's first exposure to racism, poverty, and pride in 1940s Louisiana. James Bond III is the youth, dragged to town by his strong-willed mother (Olivia Cole) to have an infected tooth removed. Introduced by Henry Fonda; suitable for family viewing. 1980; 46m.

SLATE, WYN, AND ME

DIR: Don McLennan. **CAST:** Sigrid Thornton, Simon Burke, Martin Sacks.

The plot here, if you can call it that, involves two sociopaths who kidnap a woman who witnessed a murder they committed. When she falls in love with one killer the other goes on a rampage. If this sounds interesting, forgive us, because it isn't. Rated R for endless profanities and violence. 1987; 90m.

SLAYGROUND ★½

DIR: Terry Bedford. **CAST:** Peter Coyote, Billie Whitelaw, Philip Sayer, Bill Luhr.

Based on the hardboiled Parker series of crime novels, *Slayground* will disappoint fans of the books. The character of Parker, a tough, no-nonsense professional criminal who shoots first and walks away, has been softened into a whiny thief named Stone (Peter Coyote). When a heist he masterminds goes awry because of a lead-footed getaway driver, Stone finds himself hunted by a sadistic hit man. Rated R. 1984; 89m.

SLEEPING TIGER, THE ★★★½

DIR: Joseph Losey. **CAST:** Alexis Smith, Alexander Knox, Dirk Bogarde.

A woman finds herself caught up in a tense triangular love affair with her psychiatrist husband and a cunning crook out on parole and released in her husband's custody. Dirk Bogarde gives a stunning performance as the ex-con. 1954; B&W; 89m.

SLEUTH ★★★★★

DIR: Joseph L. Mankiewicz. **CAST:** Michael Caine, Laurence Olivier.

Michael Caine and Laurence Olivier engage in a heavyweight acting *bataille royal* in this stimulating mystery. Both actors are brilliant as the characters engage in the struggle of one-upmanship and social game-playing. Without giving away the movie's twists and turns, we can let on that the ultimate game is being played on its audience. Rated PG. 1972; 138m.

SLIGHTLY SCARLET ★½
DIR: Allan Dwan. **CAST:** John Payne, Arlene Dahl, Rhonda Fleming, Kent Taylor.

Confused blend of romance, crime, and political corruption focuses on good girl falling for gang leader. The fact that she's the mayor's secretary mucks the plot of this one up even further. Forget the story. Just watch the character actors and actresses interplay. 1956; 99m.

SLOW BULLET
DIR: Allen Wright. **CAST:** Jim Baskin.

Inept amateurs with a video camera made this incoherent mess about a Vietnam veteran who allows his haunting memories of combat prevent him from living in the present. Rated R for violence and nudity. 1988; 95m.

SLOW BURN ★★
DIR: Matthew Chapman. **CAST:** Eric Roberts, Beverly D'Angelo, Dennis Lipscomb.

Newspaper reporter Eric Roberts is hired as a private investigator to find the son of a Palm Springs artist. Beverly D'Angelo plays the lost son's mother who may or may not know what happened to him. A muddled plot and apprenticelike direction. This made-for-cable movie is equivalent to a PG-13 for violence and profanity. 1986; 88m.

SMALL CIRCLE OF FRIENDS, A ★½
DIR: Rob Cohen. **CAST:** Karen Allen, Brad Davis, Jameson Parker, Shelley Long, John Friedrich.

Despite a solid cast, this story of campus unrest during the 1960s never comes together. As college students at Harvard, Karen Allen, Brad Davis, and Jameson Parker play three inseparable friends living and loving their way through protests and riots. Rated PG. 1980; 112m.

SMALL KILLING, A ★★★½
DIR: Steven H. Stern. **CAST:** Edward Asner, Jean Simmons, Sylvia Sidney, Andrew Prine.

This above-average made-for-TV movie gains some of its appeal from the casting. Ed Asner is a cop going undercover as a wino and Jean Simmons is a professor posing as a bag lady. They're out to bust a hit man but manage to fall in love along the way. The supporting cast is equally wonderful. 1981; 100m.

SMASH PALACE ★★★★
DIR: Roger Donaldson. **CAST:** Bruno Lawrence, Anna Jemison, Greer Robson, Desmond Kelly.

A scrap yard of crumpled and rusting automobiles serves as a backdrop to the story of a marriage in an equally deteriorated condition in this well-made, exceptionally acted film from New Zealand. Explicit sex and nude scenes may shock some viewers. It's a *Kramer vs. Kramer*, *Ordinary People*–style of movie that builds to a scary, nail-chewing climax. No MPAA rating; this has sex, violence, nudity, and profanity. 1981; 100m.

SMASH-UP: THE STORY OF A WOMAN ★★★
DIR: Stuart Heisler. **CAST:** Susan Hayward, Lee Bowman, Marsha Hunt, Eddie Albert, Carleton Young, Carl Esmond.

Night-club songbird Susan Hayward puts her songwriter husband's (Lee Bowman) career first. As he succeeds, she slips. His subsequent neglect and indifference make her a scenery-shedding bottle baby until near tragedy restores her sobriety and his attention. 1947; B&W; 103m.

SMITHEREENS ★★★
DIR: Susan Siedelman. **CAST:** Susan Berman, Brad Rinn, Richard Hell, Roger Jett.

An independently made feature (its budget was only $100,000), this work by producer-director Susan Siedelman examines the life of an amoral and aimless young woman (Susan

Berman) living in New York. Rated R. 1982; 90m.

SMOOTH TALK ★★★★

DIR: Joyce Chopra. **CAST:** Laura Dern, Treat Williams, Mary Kay Place, Elizabeth Berridge, Levon Helm.

Coltish Laura Dern owns this film, an uncompromising adaptation of the Joyce Carol Oates short story "Where Are You Going, Where Have You Been?" Dern hits every note as a sultry woman-child poised on the brink of adulthood and sexual maturity. Mary Kay Place does well as an exasperated mom, and Elizabeth Berridge is a sympathetic older sister. Rated PG-13 for language and sexual situations. 1985; 92m.

SOLDIER IN THE RAIN ★★★

DIR: Ralph Nelson. **CAST:** Steve McQueen, Tony Bill, Jackie Gleason, Tuesday Weld, Tom Poston.

My Bodyguard director Tony Bill is among the featured performers in this fine combination of sweet drama and rollicking comedy starring Steve McQueen, Jackie Gleason, and Tuesday Weld. Gleason is great as a high-living, worldly master sergeant, and McQueen is equally good as his protégé. 1963; B&W; 88m.

SOLDIER'S HOME ★★★½

DIR: Robert Young. **CAST:** Richard Backus, Nancy Marchand, Robert McIlwaine, Lisa Essary, Mark La Mura, Lane Binkley.

Melancholy adaptation of an Ernest Hemingway story. The war in question is World War I, "the war to end all wars," and young Harold Krebs (Richard Backus) learns, almost to his shame, that he'd prefer that the fighting continue; without it, he has no sense of purpose. Introduced by Henry Fonda; unrated and suitable for family viewing. 1976; 41m.

SOLO ★

DIR: Tony Williams. **CAST:** Vincent Gil, Perry Armstrong.

An uninteresting love story with forgettable characters. This movie will cure the most serious case of insomnia. Rated PG. 1977; 90m.

SOLOMON AND SHEBA ★★★

DIR: King Vidor. **CAST:** Yul Brynner, Gina Lollobrigida, George Sanders.

High times in biblical times as Sheba vamps Solomon. Don't look for too much of a script, because the emphasis is on lavish spectacle. Eyewash, not brain food. 1959; 139m.

SOME CALL IT LOVING ★

DIR: James B. Harris. **CAST:** Zalman King, Carol White, Tisa Farrow, Richard Pryor, Logan Ramsey.

Herein lies the bizarre tale of a rich jazz musician, who buys a "Sleeping Beauty" from a circus side show for his own perverse enjoyment. A rambling, incoherent mess. Rated R for nudity, sex, and language. 1974; 103m.

SOME CAME RUNNING ★★★½

DIR: Vincente Minnelli. **CAST:** Frank Sinatra, Dean Martin, Shirley MacLaine, Arthur Kennedy, Martha Hyer.

Based on James Jones's novel of life in a midwestern town, this film offers an entertaining study of some rather complex characters. Shirley MacLaine gives a sparkling performance as the town's loose woman who's in love with Frank Sinatra. The story is not strong, but the performances are fine. 1958; 136m.

SOMEBODY UP THERE LIKES ME ★★★★½

DIR: Robert Wise. **CAST:** Paul Newman, Pier Angeli, Everett Sloane, Sal Mineo, Eileen Heckart, Robert Loggia, Steve McQueen.

This is a first-rate biography. Boxer Rocky Graziano's career is traced from the back streets of New York to the heights of fame in the ring. It's one of the very best fight films ever made and features a sterling performance by Paul Newman. 1956; B&W; 113m.

SOMEONE TO LOVE ★★

DIR: Henry Jaglom. **CAST:** Henry Jaglom, Michael Emil, Andrea

Marcovicci, Sally Kellerman, Orson Welles.

Not understanding why his girlfriend of six months (Andrea Marcovicci) won't ever let him spend the night, Danny (Henry Jaglom) decides to have a filmmaking–Valentine's Day party with single people explaining directly into the camera why they are alone. Orson Welles (in his last screen appearance) sits on the balcony, commenting. One small problem: This movie wallows in all there is to detest about the Los Angeles art scene. Rated R for language. 1986; 112m.

SOMETHING FOR EVERYONE ★★★

DIR: Harold Prince. **CAST:** Michael York, Angela Lansbury, Anthony Corlan, Jane Carr.

This sleeper about a manipulative, amoral young man (Michael York) and the lengths he goes to in order to advance himself might not be to everyone's tastes. Angela Lansbury gives one of her best performances as the down-on-her-luck aristocrat who falls victim to York's charms and ends up regretting their association. Mature themes and situations make this film more suitable for an older audience. 1970; 112m.

SOMETIMES A GREAT NOTION ★★★

DIR: Paul Newman. **CAST:** Paul Newman, Henry Fonda, Lee Remick, Michael Sarrazin, Richard Jaeckel.

Paul Newman plays the elder son of an Oregon logging family that refuses to go on strike with the other lumberjacks in the area. The family pays dearly for its unwillingness to go along. One scene in particular, which features Newman aiding Richard Jaeckel, who has been pinned in the water by a fallen tree, is unforgettable. Rated PG. 1971; 114m.

SONG OF BERNADETTE, THE ★★★★

DIR: Henry King. **CAST:** Jennifer Jones, Charles Bickford, William Eythe, Vincent Price, Lee J. Cobb, Gladys Cooper, Anne Revere.

Four Oscars, including one to Jennifer Jones for best actress, went to this beautifully filmed story of the simple nineteenth-century French peasant girl, Bernadette Soubirous, who saw a vision of the Virgin Mary in the town of Lourdes. 1943; B&W; 156m.

SOONER OR LATER ★★

DIR: Bruce Hart. **CAST:** Denise Miller, Rex Smith, Morey Amsterdam, Judd Hirsch, Lynn Redgrave, Barbara Feldon.

This made-for-TV romance may fascinate preteens. A 13-year-old girl (Denise Miller) sets her sights on a 17-year-old rock guitarist (Rex Smith). She pretends to be older and gets caught up in her lies. 1978; 100m.

SOPHIA LOREN: HER OWN STORY ★★½

DIR: Mel Stuart. **CAST:** Sophia Loren, John Gavin, Rip Torn.

Sophia Loren portrays herself in this television drama that chronicles her life from obscurity to international stardom. At times, it appears more like a self-parody. Interesting, but not compelling enough to justify its extreme length. 1980; 150m.

SOPHIE'S CHOICE ★★★★★

DIR: Alan J. Pakula. **CAST:** Meryl Streep, Kevin Kline, Peter MacNicol.

A young, inexperienced southern writer named Stingo (Peter MacNicol) learns about love, life, and death in this absorbing, wonderfully acted, and heartbreaking movie. One summer, while observing the affair between Sophie (Meryl Streep), a victim of a concentration camp, and Nathan (Kevin Kline), a charming, but sometimes explosive biologist, Stingo falls in love with Sophie, a woman with deep, dark secrets. Rated R. 1982; 157m.

S.O.S. TITANIC ★★★

DIR: William Hale. **CAST:** David Janssen, Cloris Leachman, Susan Saint James, David Warner.

The "unsinkable" pride of the Ismay Line once again goes to her watery grave deep beneath the cold Atlantic in this made-for-television docudrama compounded of fiction and fact. 1979; 105m.

SOUNDER ★★★★★
DIR: Martin Ritt. **CAST:** Cicely Tyson, Paul Winfield, Kevin Hooks, Carmen Mathews, Taj Mahal, James Best, Janet MacLachlan.
Beautifully made film detailing the struggle of a black sharecropper and his family. Director Martin Ritt gets outstanding performances from Cicely Tyson and Paul Winfield. When her husband is sent to jail, Tyson must raise her family and run the farm by herself while trying to get the eldest son an education. A truly moving and thought-provoking film. Don't miss this one. Rated G. 1972; 105m.

SOUTH OF RENO ★★★
DIR: Mark Rezyka. **CAST:** Jeff Osterhage, Lisa Blount, Lewis Van Bergen, Joe Phelan.
This surreal psychodrama offers a compelling look at one man's struggle with desperation in a broiling Nevada backroads community. When he learns that his wife is carrying on an extramarital affair, he goes over the edge. Rated R; contains nudity, profanity, and violence. 1987; 98m.

SOUTHERNER, THE ★★★★
DIR: Jean Renoir. **CAST:** Zachary Scott, Betty Field, J. Carrol Naish.
Stark life in the rural South before civil rights. Dirt-poor tenant farmer (Zachary Scott) struggles against insurmountable odds to provide for his family while maintaining his dignity. Visually a beautiful film, but uneven in dramatic continuity. Nonetheless, its high rating is deserved. 1945; B&W; 91m.

SPARROWS ★★★
DIR: William Beaudine. **CAST:** Mary Pickford, Gustav von Seyffertitz.
The legendary Mary Pickford—"Our Mary" to millions during her reign as Queen of Hollywood when this film was made—plays the resolute, intrepid champion of a group of younger orphans besieged by an evil captor. Silent melodrama at its best, folks. 1926; B&W; 84m.

SPIRIT OF ST. LOUIS, THE ★★★★
DIR: Billy Wilder. **CAST:** James Stewart, Patricia Smith, Murray Hamilton, Marc Connelly.
Jimmy Stewart always wanted to portray Charles Lindbergh in a re-creation of his historic solo flight across the Atlantic. When he finally got his chance, at age 48, many critics felt he was too old to be believable. Stewart did just fine. The action does drag at times, but this remains a quality picture for the whole family. 1957; 138m.

SPITFIRE ★★★½
DIR: John Cromwell. **CAST:** Katharine Hepburn, Robert Young, Ralph Bellamy, Sara Haden, Sidney Toler.
A girl (Katharine Hepburn) believes herself to have healing powers and is cast out from her Ozark Mountain home as a result. It's an interesting premise, and well-acted. 1934; B&W; 88m.

SPLENDOR IN THE GRASS ★★★★
DIR: Elia Kazan. **CAST:** Warren Beatty, Natalie Wood, Pat Hingle, Audrey Christie.
Warren Beatty made his film debut in this 1961 film, as a popular, rich high-school boy. Natalie Wood plays his less prosperous girlfriend who has a nervous breakdown when he dumps her. A few tears shed by the viewer make this romantic drama all the more intriguing. 1961; 124m.

SPLIT DECISIONS ★★
DIR: David Drury. **CAST:** Gene Hackman, Craig Sheffer, Jeff Fahey, Jennifer Beals, John McLiam.
Gene Hackman might have been hoping for an audience-pleasing sports film on a par with *Hoosiers* when he agreed to do this fight picture, but the result is another failed takeoff on the *Rocky* series. The final fight scenes

are good, but the story leading up to them is pure melodrama: Hackman attempts to groom one son (Craig Sheffer) for the Olympics while fearing that he, like his older brother (Jeff Fahey), will opt for the easy money offered by sleazy fight promoters. Rated R for violence and profanity. 1988; 95m.

SPLIT IMAGE ★★★★
DIR: Ted Kotcheff. **CAST:** Peter Fonda, James Woods, Karen Allen, Michael O'Keefe.

This is a very interesting, thought-provoking film about religious cults and those who become caught up in them. Michael O'Keefe plays a young man who is drawn into a pseudo-religious organization run by Peter Fonda. The entire cast is good, but Fonda stands out in one of his best roles. Rated R for language and nudity. 1982; 113m.

SPLIT SECOND ★★★
DIR: Dick Powell. **CAST:** Stephen McNally, Alexis Smith, Jan Sterling, Paul Kelly, Richard Egan.

Tense film about an escaped convict who holds several people hostage in a deserted town has a lot working for it, including the fact that the place they're holed up in is a nuclear test site. 1953; B&W; 85m.

SPORTING CLUB, THE ★
DIR: Larry Peerce. **CAST:** Robert Fields, Nicolas Coster, Maggie Blye, Jack Warden, Richard Dysart.

This adaptation of a Thomas McGuane novel caused quite an uproar when it was first released to unanimously negative reviews. It's an allegory of America in the late Sixties that takes place at an exclusive hunting club, where several younger members set out to destroy the Establishment by wreaking social havoc. It's all quite heavyhanded. Look for Linda Blair in a small role. 1971; 104m.

SPY IN BLACK, THE ★★★
DIR: Michael Powell. **CAST:** Conrad Veidt, Valerie Hobson, Sebastian Shaw, June Duprez, Marius Goring.

Unusual espionage-cum-romance story of German agent Conrad Veidt and his love affair with British agent Valerie Hobson. British director Michael Powell brings just the right blend of duty and tragedy to this story, set in the turmoil of World War I. 1939; B&W; 82m.

SPY OF NAPOLEON ★★
DIR: Maurice Elvey. **CAST:** Richard Barthelmess, Dolly Hass.

Heavy-handed historical hokum finds Emperor Napoleon III using his illegitimate daughter to ferret out dissidents and enemies. This harmless fact-bender is amusing enough and stars former silent-screen good guy Richard Barthelmess in a meaty role. 1936; B&W; 77m.

SPY WHO CAME IN FROM THE COLD, THE ★★★★
DIR: Martin Ritt. **CAST:** Richard Burton, Claire Bloom, Oskar Werner, Bernard Lee, George Voskovec, Peter Van Eyck, Sam Wanamaker.

Realism and stark authenticity mark this sunless drama of the closing days in the career of a British cold-war spy in Berlin. Richard Burton is matchless as embittered, burnt-out Alec Leamas, the sold-out agent. No 007 glamour and gimmicks here. 1965; 112m.

SQUARE DANCE ★★★★
DIR: Daniel Petrie. **CAST:** Jason Robards Jr., Jane Alexander, Winona Ryder, Rob Lowe, Gulch Koock.

A coming-of-age drama about a 13-year-old Texas girl (Winona Ryder), *Square Dance* has so much atmosphere that you can almost smell the chicken-fried steaks. When the girl's loose-living mother (well played by Jane Alexander) takes her away from the comfort and care of her grandfather's (Jason Robards) ranch, the youngster's life goes from idyllic to hard-edged. Rated PG-13 for profanity and suggested sex. 1987; 110m.

SQUEEZE, THE (1977) ★★½
DIR: Michael Apted. **CAST:** Stacy Keach, David Hemmings, Edward Fox, Stephen Boyd, Carol White.

Stacy Keach plays an alcoholic detective whose ex-wife is kidnapped for a large ransom. As he plots to save her from the brutal kidnappers, he is forced to confront his drinking problem. Good performances do not save this mediocre film. Rated R for nudity and language. 1977; 106m.

STACKING ★★★½
DIR: Martin Rosen. **CAST:** Christine Lahti, Frederic Forrest, Megan Follows, Jason Gedrick, Ray Baker, Peter Coyote.

A cut above the righteous save-the-farm films that abound these days, because it doesn't allow for an overblown triumphant outcome and the performances are exquisite. Frederic Forrest is wonderful as a hard-drinking hired hand, and Christine Lahti really gets under the skin of her restless character. Rated PG. 1988; 95m.

STAGE DOOR CANTEEN ★★
DIR: Frank Borzage. **CAST:** William Terry, Cheryl Walkers, Katharine Hepburn, Harpo Marx, Helen Hayes, Count Basie, Edgar Bergen and Charlie McCarthy.

An all-star cast play themselves in this mildly amusing romance about the behind-the-scenes world of Broadway. Unless you enjoy looking at the many stage luminaries during their early years, you will find this entire film to be ordinary, predictable, and uninspired. 1943; B&W; 85m.

STAGE STRUCK ★★
DIR: Sidney Lumet. **CAST:** Henry Fonda, Susan Strasberg, Joan Greenwood, Herbert Marshall, Christopher Plummer.

Despite a fine cast—Susan Strasberg excepted—this rehash of *Morning Glory* is flat and wearisome. You don't really care to pull for the young actress trying to make her mark. The late Joan Greenwood's throaty voice, however, is sheer delight. 1958; 95m.

STAND AND DELIVER ★★★★½
DIR: Ramon Menendez. **CAST:** Edward James Olmos, Lou Diamond Phillips, Rosana De Soto, Andy Garcia.

A *Rocky*esque interpretation of high-school math teacher Jaime Escalante's true-life exploits. Edward James Olmos stars as Escalante, a man who gave up a high-paying job in electronics to make a contribution to society. Recognizing that his inner-city students need motivation to keep them from a lifetime of menial labor, he sets them a challenge: preparation for the state Advanced Placement Test…in calculus. Rated PG for language. 1988; 105m.

STAND BY ME ★★★★½
DIR: Rob Reiner. **CAST:** Wil Wheaton, River Phoenix, Corey Feldman, Jerry O'Connell, Kiefer Sutherland, John Cusack, Richard Dreyfuss.

Based on Stephen King's novella, *The Body*, the story involves four young boys in the last days of summer and their search for the missing body of a young boy believed hit by a train. Morbid as it may sound, this is not a horror movie. Rather, it is a story of ascending to manhood. Sometimes sad and often funny. Rated R. 1986; 90m.

STANLEY AND LIVINGSTONE ★★★
DIR: Henry King. **CAST:** Spencer Tracy, Cedric Hardwicke, Richard Greene, Nancy Kelly.

When Spencer Tracy delivers the historic line, "Doctor Livingstone, I presume," to Cedric Hardwicke in this production, you know why he was such a great screen actor. It is primarily his performance, as a reporter who journeys to Africa in order to find a lost Victorian explorer, that injects life and interest into what could have been just another stodgy prestige picture from the 1930s. 1939; B&W; 101m.

STAR CHAMBER, THE ★★★★
DIR: Peter Hyams. **CAST:** Michael Douglas, Hal Holbrook, Yaphet Kotto, Sharon Gless, Jack Kehoe.

A model group of Superior Court judges lose faith in the constitutional bylaws that they have sworn to uphold and decide to take the law into their own hands. Michael Douglas plays the idealistic young judge who uncovers the organization. Rated PG for profanity and violence. 1983; 109m.

STAR 80 ★★★★
DIR: Bob Fosse. **CAST:** Mariel Hemingway, Eric Roberts, Cliff Robertson, Carroll Baker.

A depressing, uncompromising, but brilliantly filmed and acted portrait of a tragedy. Mariel Hemingway stars as Dorothy Stratten, the Playboy playmate of the year who was murdered in 1980 by the husband (an equally impressive portrayal by Eric Roberts) she had outgrown. The movie paints a bleak portrait of her life, times, and death. Rated R for nudity, violence, profanity, and sex. 1983; 102m.

STAR IS BORN, A (1937) ★★★★
DIR: William Wellman. **CAST:** Fredric March, Janet Gaynor, Adolphe Menjou, May Robson.

The first version of this thrice-filmed in-house Hollywood weeper, this is the story of an aging actor (Fredric March) whose career is beginning to go on the skids while his youthful bride's (Janet Gaynor) career is starting to blossom. Great acting and a tight script keep this poignant movie from falling into melodrama. 1937; 111m.

STAR IS BORN, A (1954) ★★★★½
DIR: George Cukor. **CAST:** Judy Garland, James Mason, Charles Bickford, Jack Carson, Tommy Noonan.

Judy Garland's acting triumph is the highlight of this movie, which is considered to be the best version of this classic romantic tragedy. This one is well worth watching. James Mason is also memorable in the role originated by Fredric March. Be sure to get the full restored version. 1954; 154m.

STAR IS BORN, A (1976) ★★
DIR: Frank Pierson. **CAST:** Barbra Streisand, Kris Kristofferson, Gary Busey, Oliver Clark.

The third and by far least watchable version of this venerable Hollywood warhorse has been sloppily crafted into a vehicle for star Barbra Streisand. The rocky romance between a declining star (Kris Kristofferson) and an up-and-coming new talent (Streisand) has been switched from the world of the stage to that of rock 'n' roll. Rated R. 1976; 140m.

STARLIGHT HOTEL ★★
DIR: Sam Pillsbury. **CAST:** Peter Phelps.

Familiar tale, although with a new setting: 1929 New Zealand. A 12-year-old runaway bound for Australia heads across the New Zealand countryside. Rated PG for profanity and violence. 1987; 91m.

STARS LOOK DOWN, THE ★★★★
DIR: Carol Reed. **CAST:** Michael Redgrave, Margaret Lockwood, Edward Rigby, Emlyn Williams, Cecil Parker.

Classic film about a Welsh coal miner and his struggle to rise above his station and maintain his identity and the respect of his community is every bit as good today as it was when released. A coup for director Carol Reed and another great performance by Michael Redgrave as a man of quiet dignity and determination. Well worth the watching. 1939; B&W; 110m.

STATE OF THE UNION ★★★
DIR: Frank Capra. **CAST:** Spencer Tracy, Katharine Hepburn, Adolphe Menjou, Van Johnson, Angela Lansbury.

This is a political fable about an American businessman who is encouraged by opportunities to run for the presidency, and leave his integrity behind in the process. Spencer Tracy and Katharine Hepburn are a joy to watch, as usual. 1948; B&W; 124m.

STATIC ★★★
DIR: Mark Romanek. **CAST:** Keith Gordon, Amanda Plummer, Bob Gunton.

This highly offbeat drama explores isolation and alienation in human experience and the need to believe in something greater. The story centers around a would-be inventor (Keith Gordon) who attempts to enlighten people through a device that monitors images of Heaven. Surreal film falls somewhere between *Eraserhead* and *True Stories*. Rated R. 1985; 93m.

STAY AS YOU ARE ★★★★
DIR: Alberto Lattuada. **CAST:** Nastassja Kinski, Marcello Mastroianni, Francisco Rabal.

This film begins conventionally but charmingly as the story of a romance between a 20-year-old girl, Francesca (Nastassja Kinski), and Giulio (Marcello Mastroianni), a man old enough to be her father. It remains charming, but the charm becomes mingled with a controlled anguish when it becomes evident that Giulio may indeed be her father. No MPAA rating. 1978; 95m.

STAY HUNGRY ★★★★½
DIR: Bob Rafelson. **CAST:** Jeff Bridges, Sally Field, R. G. Armstrong, Arnold Schwarzenegger.

An underrated film dealing with a young southern aristocrat's (Jeff Bridges) attempt to complete a real estate deal by purchasing a bodybuilding gym. Bridges begins to appreciate those who work and train at the gym as well as getting some insights into his own life. Rated R for violence, brief nudity, and language. 1976; 103m.

STEAL THE SKY ★★
DIR: John Hancock. **CAST:** Ben Cross, Mariel Hemingway.

In this pretentious, melodramatic misfire, first telecast on HBO, Ben Cross is an Iraqi jet pilot who is targeted by Israeli intelligence for its own purposes. Mariel Hemingway is the agent assigned to seduce him into cooperating. Not rated. 1988; 110m.

STEALING HEAVEN ★★
DIR: Clive Donner. **CAST:** Derek De-Lint, Kim Thomson, Denholm Elliott.

Middle Ages story of a forbidden love between a member of the clergy and a beautiful young aristocrat—Abelard and Heloise. Lots of lust and guilt but little else to sustain the film. Rated R for nudity. 1988; 108m.

STEALING HOME ★★★½
DIR: Steven Kampmann, Will Aldis. **CAST:** Mark Harmon, Jodie Foster, Blair Brown, John Shea, Jonathan Silverman, Harold Ramis.

Enjoyable and sporadically disarming character study about a gifted athlete (Mark Harmon) who renews his commitment to baseball after several years of aimless drifting. His life is suddenly brought into focus when news reaches him that his one-time baby-sitter (Jodie Foster)—a free-thinking rebel who was the one person who believed in him—has committed suicide. An ensemble cast does a fine job with this bittersweet tale. Jodie Foster is unforgettable. Rated PG-13 for profanity and suggested sex. 1988; 98m.

STEAMING ★½
DIR: Joseph Losey. **CAST:** Vanessa Redgrave, Sarah Miles, Diana Dors, Brenda Bruce, Felicity Dean.

Nell Dunn's play, *Steaming*, takes place in an English Turkish-style bathhouse where a group of women share their feelings about life. The play has some interesting structural symbolism, but also a lot of stale dialogue. Joseph Losey's film version is minus the connective structure but full of the banal colloquies. Vanessa

Redgrave lends some needed reality to this sweaty gabfest. Rated R. 1984; 112m.

STELLA DALLAS ★★★★
DIR: King Vidor. **CAST:** Barbara Stanwyck, Anne Shirley, John Boles, Alan Hale, Tim Holt, Marjorie Main.
Barbara Stanwyck's title-role performance as the small-town vulgar innocent who sacrifices everything for her daughter got her a well-deserved Oscar nomination and set the standard for this type of screen character. John Boles is the elegant wealthy heel who does her wrong. Anne Shirley is Laurel, the object of her mother's completely self-effacing conduct. 1937; B&W; 111m.

STEPPENWOLF ★★½
DIR: Fred Haines. **CAST:** Max von Sydow, Dominique Sanda, Pierre Clementi.
In this United States–Switzerland coproduction, director Fred Haines gives us an almost literal adaptation of Hermann Hesse's most widely read novel. It's a good try, but given the heady themes involved, the source really isn't filmable. Rated PG. 1974; 105m.

STERILE CUCKOO, THE ★★★★
DIR: Alan J. Pakula. **CAST:** Liza Minnelli, Wendell Burton, Tim McIntire.
Painfully poignant story about a dedicated young college lad (Wendell Burton) and the loopy young woman (Liza Minnelli) who, unable to handle people on their own terms, demands too much of those with whom she becomes involved. Minnelli's Pookie Adams won the actress a well-deserved Academy Award nomination. Rated PG for sexual situations. 1969; 107m.

STEVIE ★★★★
DIR: Robert Enders. **CAST:** Glenda Jackson, Mona Washbourne, Trevor Howard, Alec McCowen.
Glenda Jackson gives a brilliant performance as reclusive poet Stevie Smith in this stagy, but still interesting, film. Mona Washbourne is the film's true delight as Smith's doting—and slightly dotty—aunt. Trevor Howard narrates and costars in this British release. Rated PG for brief profanity. 1978; 102m.

STIGMA ★
DIR: David E. Durston. **CAST:** Philip Michael Thomas.
A 23-year-old Philip Michael Thomas is not sufficient reason to suffer through this potboiler. As an ex–medical student just out of prison, he battles prejudice and an epidemic of VD in a sheltered island community. Close-up photos of advanced-syphilis sufferers are not for the squeamish. Those photos and some nudity earn this an R. 1972; 93m.

STOCKS AND BLONDES
DIR: Arthur Greenstands. **CAST:** Leigh Wood, Veronica Hart.
A female college student researches a term paper on hostile corporate takeovers and unearths some dirty work. She zeros in on an affluent businesswoman and soon she is stalked by a violent stranger bent on keeping her quiet. Rated R. 1984; 79m.

STONE BOY, THE ★★★★★
DIR: Christopher Cain. **CAST:** Robert Duvall, Frederic Forrest, Glenn Close, Wilford Brimley.
A superb ensemble cast elevates this rural *Ordinary People*–style film about a boy who accidentally shoots the older brother he adores and begins losing touch with reality. It's a tough subject, exquisitely handled. For some reason, this fine film was never theatrically released on a wide scale. Rated PG for brief violence and some profanity. 1984; 93m.

STORY OF LOUIS PASTEUR, THE ★★★½
DIR: William Dieterle. **CAST:** Paul Muni, Joseph Hutchinson, Anita Louise, Donald Woods, Porter Hall, Akim Tamiroff.
Master actor Paul Muni won an Oscar for his restrained portrayal of the famous French founder of bacteriology

in this well-honed film biography. This is an honest, engrossing character study that avoids sentimentality. 1936; B&W; 85m.

STRAIGHT TIME ★★★★
DIR: Ulu Grosbard. **CAST:** Dustin Hoffman, Harry Dean Stanton, Gary Busey, Theresa Russell, M. Emmet Walsh.

Well-told story of an ex-convict (Dustin Hoffman) attempting to make good on the outside only to return to crime after a run-in with his parole officer (M. Emmet Walsh). Hoffman's performance is truly chilling. A very grim and powerful film that was sadly overlooked on its initial release. Rated R for violence, nudity, and language. 1978; 114m.

STRANGE INTERLUDE ★★★★
DIR: Herbert Wise. **CAST:** Glenda Jackson, José Ferrer, David Dukes, Ken Howard, Edward Petherbridge.

Eugene O'Neill's complex love story is not for viewers seeking mindless entertainment, but for those willing to endure the considerable length, it offers ample rewards. Glenda Jackson plays a neurotic woman who, in the course of twenty-five years, manages to control the lives of the three men who love her. High-class soap opera. Unrated, this PBS production contains adult themes. 1988; 190m.

STRANGE LOVE OF MARTHA IVERS, THE ★★★
DIR: Lewis Milestone. **CAST:** Barbara Stanwyck, Van Heflin, Kirk Douglas, Lizabeth Scott, Judith Anderson, Darryl Hickman.

Terrible title doesn't do this well-acted drama justice. Woman-with-a-past Barbara Stanwyck excels in this story of a secret that comes back to threaten her now-stable life and the lengths she must go to in order to ensure her securtiy. Young Kirk Douglas in his film debut already charges the screen with electricity. 1946; B&W; 117m.

STRANGERS IN THE CITY ★★★★
DIR: Rick Carrier. **CAST:** Robert Gentile, Camilo Delgado.

This forceful film set in a Manhattan slum paints a vivid picture of a Puerto Rican family struggling to adjust to life in a new country. When the proud father loses his job, other family members have to go to work to support themselves. The final third gives way to cheap melodrama, but the film is still well worth seeing. 1961; B&W; 83m.

STRANGERS KISS ★★½
DIR: Matthew Chapman. **CAST:** Peter Coyote, Victoria Tennant, Blaine Novak, Dan Shor.

Offbeat film about the making of a low-budget movie, circa 1955. A strange romantic relationship between the male and female leads develops off camera. A good script inspired by Stanley Kubrick's *Killer's Kiss* is quite absorbing despite some production flaws. Rated R for sexual situations. 1984; 94m.

STRANGERS: THE STORY OF A MOTHER AND A DAUGHTER ★★★½
DIR: Milton Katselas. **CAST:** Bette Davis, Gena Rowlands, Ford Rainey, Royal Dano.

Bette Davis won an Emmy Award in this taut, made-for-television drama about a long-estranged daughter's sudden reentry into the life and home of her bitter, resentful mother. Gena Rowlands, as the daughter, holds her own against the old pro, matching Davis scene for scene. 1979; 100m.

STRANGERS WHEN WE MEET ★★½
DIR: Richard Quine. **CAST:** Kirk Douglas, Kim Novak, Ernie Kovacs, Barbara Rush, Walter Matthau, Virginia Bruce, Kent Smith, Helen Gallagher.

An all-star cast fails to charge this overblown soap opera about an unhappily married architect who falls in love with his beautiful neighbor. Evan Hunter derived the screenplay from his novel of the same name. Not rated. 1960; 117m.

STRATEGIC AIR COMMAND ★★½

DIR: Anthony Mann. **CAST:** James Stewart, June Allyson, Frank Lovejoy, Barry Sullivan, Bruce Bennett, Rosemary DeCamp.

Aviation and sports come together as professional baseball player Jimmy Stewart is called back to active service and forced to leave his career, his teammates, and his wife (June Allyson). Air Force veterans will love the footage of the "new" aircraft of the day, and baseball fans will enjoy the all-too-brief glimpses of real games, but, otherwise, this is just routine studio fare. 1955; 114m.

STRAWBERRY BLONDE, THE ★★★

DIR: Raoul Walsh. **CAST:** James Cagney, Olivia De Havilland, Rita Hayworth, Alan Hale, Jack Carson, George Tobias, Una O'Connor, George Reeves.

Sentimental flashback story of young man's unrequited love for *The Strawbery Blonde* (Rita Hayworth) is a change of pace for dynamic James Cagney and one of the most evocative period pieces produced in America about the innocent "Gay Nineties." Winsome Olivia De Havilland and a great cast of characters (including Alan Hale as Cagney's father) breathe life into this tragicomic tale. 1941; B&W; 97m.

STRAWBERRY STATEMENT, THE ★½

DIR: Stuart Hagman. **CAST:** Kim Darby, Bruce Davison, Bob Balaban, James Kunen.

Inane message film attempts to make some sense (and money) out of student dissidents and rebellion, focusing on the Columbia University riots of the late 1960s. Some good performances in this hodgepodge of comedy, drama, and youth-authority confrontations and clichés. Rated R. 1970; 103m.

STREAMERS ★★★½

DIR: Robert Altman. **CAST:** Matthew Modine, Michael Wright, Mitchell Lichtenstein.

This tense film is about four recruits and two veterans awaiting orders that will send them to Vietnam. The six men are a microcosm of American life in the late 1960s and early 1970s. A powerful, violent drama, this film is not suitable for everyone. Rated R. 1984; 118m.

STREET SCENE ★★★½

DIR: King Vidor. **CAST:** Sylvia Sidney, William Collier Jr., Beulah Bondi, David Landau, Estelle Taylor, Walter Miller.

Playwright Elmer Rice wrote the screenplay for this fine film version of his Pulitzer Prize–winning drama of life in the New York tenements and the yearning and anguish of the young and hopeful who are desperate to get out. The cast is excellent, the score classic Alfred Newman, the camera work outstanding. 1931; B&W; 80m.

STREET SMART ★★½

DIR: Jerry Schatzberg. **CAST:** Christopher Reeve, Kathy Baker, Mimi Rogers, Andre Gregory, Morgan Freeman.

Christopher Reeve gives a listless performance as a magazine writer under pressure who fabricates the life story of a New York pimp. Problems arise when parallels with a real pimp under investigation by the D.A. surface. In order not to lose credibility, Reeve must play both sides against the middle. Morgan Freeman plays the pimp Fast Black with an electrifying mesh of elegance and sleaze. Rated R for language and theme. 1986; 97m.

STREET WARRIORS

DIR: Anthony Loma. **CAST:** Victor Petit, Frank Brana.

Although a tacked-on American narration tries to pass this off as a serious statement about the horrors of juvenile delinquency, it's merely a sleazy exploitation movie about some Barcelona teens who rob and kill, secure in the knowledge that because they're under age they're all but immune to punishment. No opportunity to insert repulsive violence or nudity is passed up. 1977; 105m.

STREET WARRIORS II

DIR: Anthony Loma. **CAST:** Angel Fernandez Franco, Veronica Miriel.

This sequel is even worse; if there was ever any merit to this trash, it's been lost in the terrible dubbing. The filmmakers idly shift from portraying the teen characters as heroes to involving them in rape and robbery, just for the sake of cheap exploitation. Contains nudity, simulated rape, and violence. 1981; 105m.

STREETCAR NAMED DESIRE, A ★★★★★

DIR: Elia Kazan. **CAST:** Vivien Leigh, Marlon Brando, Kim Hunter, Karl Malden.

Virtuoso acting highlights this powerful and disturbing drama based on the Tennessee Williams play. Vivien Leigh once again is the southern belle. Unlike Scarlett O'Hara, however, her Blanche DuBois is no longer young. She is a sexually disturbed woman who lives in a world of illusion. Her world begins to crumble when she moves in with her sister and brutish brother-in-law (Marlon Brando). 1951; B&W; 122m.

STREETFIGHT ★★

DIR: Ralph Bakshi. **CAST:** Barry White, Scatman Crothers, Philip Michael Thomas.

Originally released in 1975 as *Coonskin*, this mixture of animation and live action was labeled racist by many. The animation tells the tale in almost *Song of the South* characterizations of a young black country rabbit caught up in Harlem's drug world. Definitely a curiosity. Rated R. 1987; 89m.

STREETS OF GOLD ★★★

DIR: Joe Roth. **CAST:** Klaus Maria Brandauer, Adrian Pasdar, Wesley Snipes, Angela Molina.

This is a pleasant story about an ex-boxer (Klaus Maria Brandauer) who decides to regain his self-worth by passing on his skills to a pair of street-boxers. Brandauer puts a lot of energy into his role, demonstrating shading and character depth far beyond what you'd expect from a routine story. Inexplicably rated R for mild language and violence. 1986; 95m.

STREETS OF L.A., THE ★★★½

DIR: Jerrold Freedman. **CAST:** Joanne Woodward, Robert Webber, Michael C. Gwynne, Audrey Christie, Isela Vega, Pepe Serna, Miguel Pinero, Tony Plana.

Joanne Woodward plays a struggling real-estate saleswoman who gets her new tires slashed by a group of angry Hispanics and decides to pursue them in the hopes of getting reimbursed for the damage. The acting is quite good even if the film is a low-budget production. A sensitive, rather quiet drama. Not rated, but contains violence. 1979; 94m.

STREETWALKIN' ★

DIR: Joan Freeman. **CAST:** Julie Newmar, Melissa Leo, Leon Robinson, Antonio Fargas.

As a lesson on why not to become a prostitute, this film has a lot to say. As entertainment, it is unsuccessful. Good acting cannot save an incoherent and pointless script. Rated R for simulated sex, profanity, and violence. 1985; 84m.

STRIPPER, THE ★★½

DIR: Franklin J. Schaffner. **CAST:** Joanne Woodward, Richard Beymer, Claire Trevor, Carol Lynley, Robert Webber, Gypsy Rose Lee, Louis Nye.

Somewhat engrossing account of an aging stripper (Joanne Woodward) falling in love with a teenager (Richard Beymer). Good performances by all, but the film tends to drag and become too stagy. Based on William Inge's play. 1963; 95m.

STUD, THE

DIR: Quentin Masters. **CAST:** Joan Collins, Oliver Tobias.

Joan Collins reaches new lows in this boring, sordid soft-core porn film concerning a young man's rise to fortune through his various affairs. This one will be tough to get through, even for hard-core Collins fans. Rated R. 1978; 95m.

STUDS LONIGAN ★★
DIR: Irving Lerner. **CAST:** Christopher Knight, Frank Gorshin, Jack Nicholson, Venetia Stevenson, Dick Foran, Jay C. Flippen, Carolyn Craig.
Film version of James T. Farrell's landmark first novel is a major disappointment to those familiar with the *Studs Lonigan* trilogy. Depressing tale of a young man's slide into drunkenness and debauchery pulls most of the punches that the books delivered and ends up candy-coating the message and drastically changing the ending to a more conventional Hollywood fadeout. Memorable mainly for Jack Nicholson, miscast as the coldhearted Weary Reilly. 1960; B&W; 95m.

STUNT MAN, THE ★★★★½
DIR: Richard Rush. **CAST:** Peter O'Toole, Steve Railsback, Barbara Hershey, Chuck Ball, Allen Garfield, Adam Roarke, Alex Rocco.
Nothing is ever quite what it seems in this fast-paced, superbly crafted film. It's a Chinese puzzle of a movie and, therefore, may not please all viewers. Nevertheless, this directorial tour de force by Richard Rush has ample thrills, chills, suspense, and surprises for those with a taste for something different. Rated R. 1980; 129m.

SUBURBIA ★★★
DIR: Penelope Spheeris. **CAST:** Chris Pederson, Bill Coyne, Jennifer Clay.
Penelope Spheeris, who directed the punk-rock documentary *Decline of Western Civilization*, did this low-budget film of punk rockers versus local rednecks and townspeople in a small suburban area. Not for all tastes, but a good little film for people who are bored with releases like *Cannonball Run II*. Rated R. 1983; 96m.

SUCCESS IS THE BEST REVENGE ★★★½
DIR: Jerzy Skolimowski. **CAST:** Michael York, Anouk Aimée, Michael Lyndon, John Hurt, Jane Asher, Michel Piccoli.
Polish exile filmmaker hustles to make a film about the growing unrest in his native country while ignoring his own family problems. Director Jerzy Skolimowski, who dazzled us with the 1982 film *Moonlighting* is in good form with this biting drama. Not rated, has violence, profanity, and nudity. 1984; 95m.

SUDDENLY ★★★★
DIR: Lewis Allen. **CAST:** Frank Sinatra, Sterling Hayden, James Gleason, Nancy Gates.
Here's top-notch entertainment with Frank Sinatra perfectly cast as a leader of a gang of assassins out to kill the President of the United States. *Suddenly* has gone largely unnoticed over the last few years, but thanks to home video, we can all enjoy this gem of a picture. 1954; B&W; 77m.

SUDDENLY, LAST SUMMER ★★★
DIR: Joseph L. Mankiewicz. **CAST:** Elizabeth Taylor, Montgomery Clift, Katharine Hepburn.
Another one of those unpleasant but totally intriguing forays of Tennessee Williams. Elizabeth Taylor is a neurotic girl being prodded into madness by the memory of her gay cousin's bizarre death, a memory that Katharine Hepburn, his adoring mother, wants to remain vague if not submerged. She prevails upon Montgomery Clift to make sure it does. 1959; B&W; 114m.

SUGAR COOKIES
DIR: Michael Herz. **CAST:** Mary Woronov, Monique Van Vooren, Lynn Lowry.
Abysmal sexploitation movie about two women who are set up to be murdered by a porno filmmaker. Bizarre, convoluted, incoherent mess that should have remained on the shelf.

Rated R for nudity, profanity, and violence. 1988; 89m.

SUGARLAND EXPRESS, THE ★★★★

DIR: Steven Spielberg. **CAST:** Goldie Hawn, Ben Johnson, Michael Sacks, William Atherton.

A rewarding film in many respects, this was Steven Spielberg's first feature effort. Based on an actual incident in Texas during the late 1960s, a prison escapee and his wife try to regain custody of their infant child. Their desperation results in a madcap chase across the state with a kidnapped state trooper. Rated PG. 1974; 109m.

SUMMER CAMP NIGHTMARE ★★

DIR: Bert L. Dragin. **CAST:** Chuck Connors, Charles Stratton.

Based on *The Butterfly Revolution* and misleadingly retitled to cash in on the teen-horror market, this is actually an antifascist parable similar to *Lord of the Flies*. A young counselor at a preteen summer camp stages a revolution, overthrowing the strict director and setting himself up in charge. The ambitious premise is never resolved satisfactorily, with a particularly anticlimactic ending. Rated PG-13, with violence and nudity. 1986; 88m.

SUMMER HEAT (1983) ★

DIR: Jack Starrett. **CAST:** Bruce Davison, Susan George, Anthony Franciosa.

Bruce Davison stars as Dolin Pike, a young sheepherder who, upon being sentenced to prison, attempts to escape with his new love, Baby (Susan George). Although the acting is fine, the film falls flat due to predictability, implausibility, and corniness. Rated R for violence, profanity, and implied sex. 1983; 101m.

SUMMER HEAT (1987) ★

DIR: Michie Gleason. **CAST:** Lori Singer, Bruce Abbott, Anthony Edwards, Clu Gulager, Kathy Bates.

This is a barely lukewarm sex-and-soap sizzler about the complications that ensue when plantation wife Lori Singer cheats on husband Anthony Edwards with farmhand Bruce Abbott. They should have called it *Sex with a Yawn*. Rated R. 1987; 95m.

SUMMER LOVERS

DIR: Randal Kleiser. **CAST:** Peter Gallagher, Daryl Hannah, Valerie Quennessen, Barbara Rush, Carole Cook.

The director of *Grease* and *Blue Lagoon*, Randal Kleiser, returns with more young lust in this self-penned study of a *ménage à trois* in Greece. *Summer Lovers* is really little more than a two-hour commercial for teenage promiscuity. Rated R for nudity, profanity, and implied sex. 1982; 98m.

SUMMER OF '42 ★★★★

DIR: Robert Mulligan. **CAST:** Gary Grimes, Jennifer O'Neill, Jerry Houser, Oliver Conant, Christopher Norris, Lou Frizell.

Set against the backdrop of a vacationers' resort island off the New England coast during World War II. An inexperienced young man (Gary Grimes) has a crush on the 22-year-old bride (Jennifer O'Neill) of a serviceman. His stumbling attempts to acquire sexual knowledge are handled tenderly and thoughtfully. Rated PG. 1971; 102m.

SUMMER TO REMEMBER, A ★★★½

DIR: Robert Lewis. **CAST:** James Farentino, Louise Fletcher, Burt Young.

Heartwarming story about a deaf-mute boy who distrusts Mom's new husband. When the boy befriends an intelligent orangutan, he begins to see beyond his closed world. Rated PG for no apparent reason. 1984; 98m.

SUMMER WISHES, WINTER DREAMS ★

DIR: Gilbert Cates. **CAST:** Joanne Woodward, Martin Balsam, Sylvia Sydney, Dori Brenner.

This is one of those all-too-well-intentioned films about a Manhattan housewife's depression. The movie feels dated and stale. The characters are either screaming at each other or reciting banalities. Rated PG. 1973; 95m.

SUMMERTIME ★★★★
DIR: David Lean. **CAST:** Katharine Hepburn, Rossano Brazzi, Edward Andrews, Darren McGavin, Isa Miranda.

Katharine Hepburn is a sensitive, vulnerable spinster on holiday in Venice. She falls in love with unhappily married shopkeeper Rossano Brazzi, and the romantic idyll is beautiful. David Lean's direction is superb, Jack Hildyard's cinematography excellent. 1955; 99m.

SUNDAY, BLOODY SUNDAY ★★★
DIR: John Schlesinger. **CAST:** Peter Finch, Glenda Jackson, Murray Head, Peggy Ashcroft, Maurice Denham.

Brilliant performances by Peter Finch and Glenda Jackson are the major reason to watch this very British three-sided love story; the sides are a bit different, though...both love Murray Head. Difficult to watch at times, but intriguing from a historical standpoint. Rated R for sexual situations. 1971; 110m.

SUNDAY TOO FAR AWAY ★★★½
DIR: Ken Hannam. **CAST:** Jack Thompson, Max Cullen, John Ewart, Reg Lye.

An Australian film about the life and lot of a sheepshearer Down Under circa 1956. Jack Thompson stars as Foley, a champion shearer who finds his mantle challenged. Unrated, the film has profanity, nudity, and violence. 1983; 100m.

SUNDOWN ★★½
DIR: Henry Hathaway. **CAST:** Gene Tierney, Bruce Cabot, George Sanders, Harry Carey, Cedric Hardwicke, Joseph Calleia, Reginald Gardiner, Marc Lawrence.

Fairly entertaining stiff-upper-lip British drama in Africa features Bruce Cabot as a Canadian and George Sanders as the army officer who replaces him and prepares their desert outpost for action. It seems that the local tribesmen are being armed by the Germans. Although there are some bursts of energy this is still slow going. 1941; B&W; 90m.

SUNDOWNERS, THE (1960) ★★★★
DIR: Fred Zinnemann. **CAST:** Robert Mitchum, Deborah Kerr, Peter Ustinov, Glynis Johns, Dina Merrill, Chips Rafferty.

Robert Mitchum and Deborah Kerr were one of the great screen teams, and this is our choice as their best film together. The story of Australian sheepherders in the 1920s, it is a character study brought alive by Fred Zinnemann's sensitive direction and attention to detail, as well as by the fine acting of a superb cast. 1960; 113m.

SUNRISE AT CAMPOBELLO ★★★★★
DIR: Vincent J. Donehue. **CAST:** Ralph Bellamy, Greer Garson, Alan Bunce, Hume Cronyn.

Producer-writer Dore Schary's inspiring and heartwarming drama of Franklin Delano Roosevelt's public political battles and private fight against polio. Ralph Bellamy is FDR; Greer Garson is Eleanor. Both are superb. The acting is tops, the entire production sincere. Taken from Schary's impressive stage play, with all the fine qualities intact. 1960; 143m.

SUNSET BOULEVARD ★★★★★
DIR: Billy Wilder. **CAST:** William Holden, Gloria Swanson, Erich Von Stroheim, Fred Clark, Jack Webb, Hedda Hopper, Buster Keaton.

Sunset Boulevard is one of Hollywood's strongest indictments against its own excesses. It justly deserves its place among the best films ever made. William Holden plays an out-of-work gigolo-screenwriter who attaches himself to a faded screen star attempting a comeback. Gloria Swanson, in a stunning parody, is brilliant as the tragically deluded Norma Desmond. 1950; B&W; 110m.

SURROGATE, THE ★★½
DIR: Don Carmody. **CAST:** Art Hindle, Carole Laure, Shannon Tweed, Michael Ironside, Marilyn Lightstone, Jim Bailey.

This bizarre film concerns a couple with marriage problems who seek counseling. A surrogate sex partner enters the picture. A kinky tale that twists and turns before its violent conclusion. Fortunately, the stars are attractive. Rated R for nudity, simulated sex, profanity, and violence. 1984; 100m.

SWAP, THE 🦃
DIR: John Shade, John Broderick, Jordon Leondopoulos. **CAST:** Robert De Niro, Jennifer Warren, Lisa Blount, Sybil Danning.

Robert De Niro fans, don't waste your time. This hodgepodge uses a few minutes of film from an unreleased movie De Niro made in 1969 called *Sam's Song* to pad out a story about an ex-con looking for his brother's murderer. Rated R. 1980; 87m.

SWEET HEARTS' DANCE ★★★
DIR: Robert Greenwald. **CAST:** Don Johnson, Susan Sarandon, Jeff Daniels, Elizabeth Perkins, Justin Henry.

From Ernest (*On Golden Pond*) Thompson, a delightful little movie about love and relationships. High school sweethearts Don Johnson and Susan Sarandon are a married couple whose marriage has stagnated into routine and complacency. At the same time there are subplots about male bonding, best friends, and father-son relationships. Rated R for profanity. 1988; 101m.

SWEET LORRAINE ★★★★
DIR: Steve Gomer. **CAST:** Maureen Stapleton, Trini Alvarado, Lee Richardson, John Bedford Lloyd, Giancarlo Esposito.

There's a lot to like in this nostalgic stay at The Lorraine, a hotel in the Catskills. Maureen Stapleton is the owner of the 80-year-old landmark that may be seeing its last summer. It needs extensive repairs and developers are offering a tempting price. A perfect cast makes this small-scale film a huge success. Rated PG. 1987; 91m.

SWEET SMELL OF SUCCESS ★★★½
DIR: Alexander Mackendrick. **CAST:** Burt Lancaster, Tony Curtis, Martin Milner, Sam Levene, Barbara Nichols, Susan Harrison.

Burt Lancaster is superb as a ruthless newspaper columnist. Tony Curtis is equally great as the seedy press agent who will stop at nothing to please him. Outstanding performances by a great cast and brilliant cinematography by James Wong Howe perfectly capture the night life in Manhattan. Screenplay by Clifford Odets and Ernest Lehman. 1957; B&W; 96m.

SWIMMER, THE ★★★★
DIR: Frank Perry. **CAST:** Burt Lancaster, Janet Landgard, Janice Rule, Joan Rivers, Tony Bickley, Marge Champion, Kim Hunter.

A middle-aged man in a gray flannel suit who has never achieved his potential swims from neighbor's pool to neighbor's pool on his way home on a hot afternoon in social Connecticut. Each stop brings back memories of what was and what might have been. Burt Lancaster is excellent in the title role. Rated PG. 1968; 94m.

SWING SHIFT ★½
DIR: Jonathan Demme. **CAST:** Goldie Hawn, Kurt Russell, Ed Harris, Fred Ward, Christine Lahti, Sudie Bond.

Goldie Hawn stars in this disappointing 1940s-era romance as Kay Walsh, the girl who's left behind when her husband, Jack (Ed Harris), goes off to fight in World War II. Kay goes to work and, despite a few misgivings, finds she has all sorts of hidden talents—including an untapped potential for passion, fulfilled by co-worker Lucky Lockhart (Kurt Russell). Rated PG for profanity and suggested sex. 1984; 100m.

SYBIL ★★★★
DIR: Daniel Petrie. **CAST:** Joanne Woodward, Sally Field, William Prince.
Sally Field is outstanding in this deeply disturbing but utterly fascinating made-for-TV drama of a young woman whose intense pyschological childhood trauma has given her seventeen distinct personalities. Joanne Woodward is the patient, dedicated psychiatrist who sorts it all out. 1976; 116m.

SYLVESTER ★★★★
DIR: Tim Hunter. **CAST:** Melissa Gilbert, Richard Farnsworth, Michael Schoeffling, Constance Towers.
Director Tim Hunter does an admirable job with this hard-edged *National Velvet*–style drama about a tomboy (Melissa Gilbert) who rides her horse, Sylvester, to victory in the Olympics' Three-Day Event in Lexington, Kentucky. Gilbert is first-rate as the aspiring horsewoman, and Richard Farnsworth is his reliable, watchable self as her cantankerous mentor. Rated PG-13 for profanity and violence. 1985; 109m.

SYLVIA ★★
DIR: Michael Firth. **CAST:** Eleanor David, Nigel Terry, Tom Wilkinson, Mary Regan.
Sylvia is about as underwhelming as a film can get and still have some redeeming qualities. Were it not for the fine performance by Eleanor David in the title role, this film about seminal educator Sylvia Ashton-Warner would be a muddled bore. It jumps from one event to another with little or no buildup or continuity. Rated PG for graphic descriptions of violence. 1985; 97m.

TABLE FOR FIVE ★★★
DIR: Robert Lieberman. **CAST:** Jon Voight, Richard Crenna, Millie Perkins.
Had it up to here with *Kramer vs. Kramer* clones about single parents coping with their kids? If you have, you'll probably decide to skip this movie—and that would be a shame, because it's a good one. Jon Voight stars as J. P. Tannen, a divorcé who takes his three youngsters on a Mediterranean cruise in hopes of getting back into their lives full-time. Rated PG for mature situations. 1983; 122m.

TALE OF TWO CITIES, A ★★★★★
DIR: Jack Conway. **CAST:** Ronald Colman, Basil Rathbone, Edna May Oliver, Elizabeth Allan.
A Tale of Two Cities is a satisfactory rendition of Charles Dickens's novel. It is richly acted, with true Dickens flavor. Ronald Colman was ideally cast in the role of Sydney Carton, the English no-account who finds purpose in life amid the turmoil of the French Revolution. The photography in this film is one of its most outstanding features. The dark shadows are in keeping with the spirit of this somber Dickens story. 1935; B&W; 121m.

TALES OF ORDINARY MADNESS ★
DIR: Marco Ferreri. **CAST:** Ben Gazzara, Ornella Muti, Susan Tyrrell, Tanya Lopert.
Abysmal film features Ben Gazzara in the role of infamous drunken poet Charles Bukowski, who interacts with a strange assortment of women during binges of sexual excess. The film is pretentious and just plain dull, and Gazzara seems totally lost. Rated R for profanity and nudity. 1983; 107m.

TALK RADIO ★★★★
DIR: Oliver Stone. **CAST:** Eric Bogosian, Alec Baldwin, Ellen Greene, John Pankow, John C. McGinley.
Powerful story centers on a controversial Dallas radio talk-show host's rise

to notoriety—and the ultimate price he pays for it. Eric Bogosian repeats his acclaimed Broadway stage performance as the radio host who badgers and belittles callers and listeners alike. Filmed mainly in the confines of a radio studio, this is a highly cinematic, fascinating film. Director Oliver Stone keeps his camera moving and the pace rapid throughout. Rated R. 1989; 110m.

TAMMY AND THE BACHELOR ★★★

DIR: Joseph Pevney. **CAST:** Debbie Reynolds, Leslie Nielsen, Walter Brennan, Mala Powers, Fay Wray, Sidney Blackmer, Mildred Natwick, Louise Beavers.

Like Debbie Reynolds's number-one hit song *Tammy*, the movie is corny but irresistible. Ingenuous country girl Reynolds falls in love with injured pilot Leslie Nielsen and nurses him back to health. The romance and humor are sweet and charming. The movie's success led to sequels and a TV series. 1957; 89m.

TAMMY AND THE DOCTOR ★

DIR: Harry Keller. **CAST:** Sandra Dee, Peter Fonda, Macdonald Carey, Beulah Bondi, Margaret Lindsay, Reginald Owen, Adam West.

Thanks to the video revolution, closet Sandra Dee fans can enjoy this undemanding fare without the snickers that would accompany a public screening. Cutesy romance between country gal Sandra Dee and young Peter Fonda is relatively harmless, but this is definitely a film with a limited audience. No muss, no fuss—in fact, not much of anything at all. 1963; 88m.

TAPS ★★★½

DIR: Harold Becker. **CAST:** George C. Scott, Timothy Hutton, Ronny Cox, Tom Cruise.

George C. Scott is an iron-jawed commander of a military academy and Timothy Hutton a gung-ho cadet who leads a student revolt in this often exciting but mostly unbelievable and unnecessarily violent drama. Rated R. 1981; 118m.

TARTUFFE ★★★

DIR: Bill Alexander. **CAST:** Antony Sher, Nigel Hawthorne, Alison Steadman.

Let's be upfront about this one: It's a sophisticated version of Molière's play about religious hypocrisy. The satire is funny and biting, but this Royal Shakespeare Company production is not for everyone. The performances, especially Antony Sher's interpretation of Tartuffe, are brilliant, but very subtle. 1984; 110m.

TASTE OF HONEY, A ★★★½

DIR: Tony Richardson. **CAST:** Rita Tushingham, Dora Bryan, Murray Melvin, Robert Stephens.

Offbeat comedy-drama memorably tells the story of a lower-class teenager (Rita Tushingham) made pregnant by a black sailor. Tough but tender, this piece of attempted social realism by new-wave British director Tony Richardson is based on a successful stage play. 1961; B&W; 100m.

TATTOO

DIR: Bob Brooks. **CAST:** Bruce Dern, Maud Adams, John Getz.

Simply the most vile, reprehensible, sexist, and misogynistic piece of tripe ever released under the guise of a mainstream film. Bruce Dern is a demented tattoo artist who kidnaps Maud Adams to use as a "living tableau." The film concludes with her scarred for life, and we're supposed to believe it's an upbeat ending. Rated R for gross violence and kinky sex. 1981; 103m.

TAXI DRIVER ★★★★★

DIR: Martin Scorsese. **CAST:** Robert De Niro, Harvey Keitel, Cybill Shepherd, Jodie Foster, Peter Boyle.

Robert De Niro plays an alienated Vietnam-era vet thrust into the nighttime urban sprawl of New York City. In his despair after a romantic rejection by an attractive political campaign aide, he focuses on "freeing" a

12-year-old prostitute by unleashing violent retribution on her pimp. It's unnerving and realistic. Rated R for violence and profanity. 1976; 113m.

TEARAWAY ★★
DIR: Bruce Morrison. **CAST:** Matthew Hunter, Mark Pilisi.

In this film from Australia, the young streetwise son of an alcoholic father rescues a rich girl from a gang of lecherous toughs. Regrettably, tragic but predictable events cause this otherwise gritty study of desperate youth going nowhere to degenerate into another ordinary tale of revenge. Rated R for violence and strong language. 1987; 100m.

TELL ME A RIDDLE ★★★½
DIR: Lee Grant. **CAST:** Melvyn Douglas, Lila Kedrova, Brooke Adams, Dolores Dorn, Zalman King.

Melvyn Douglas and Lila Kedrova give memorable performances as an elderly married couple whose relationship has grown bitter over the years. Their love for each other is rekindled when they take a cross-country trip to see the far-flung members of their family. This poignant drama marked the directorial debut of actress Lee Grant. Rated PG. 1980; 94m.

TEMPEST (1928) ★★½
DIR: Sam Taylor. **CAST:** John Barrymore, Camilla Horn, Louis Wolheim, George Fawcett.

Set during the 1914 Bolshevik uprising in Russia, this richly romantic drama has Army officer John Barrymore stepping out of place to court his aristocratic commandant's daughter. As a result, both are undone and must flee for their lives and love. Silent, with music track. 1928; B&W; 105m.

TEMPEST (1982) ★
DIR: Paul Mazursky. **CAST:** John Cassavetes, Gena Rowlands, Vittorio Gassman, Molly Ringwald, Susan Sarandon.

This isn't a movie; it's an endurance test. About an architect (John Cassavetes) who has prophetic dreams and is going through a mid-life crisis but nothing ever really happens. Rated PG, the film has nudity and profanity. 1982; 140m.

TEN COMMANDMENTS, THE (1923) ★★★
DIR: Cecil B. DeMille. **CAST:** Theodore Roberts, Charles de Roche, Estelle Taylor, James Neill, Noble Johnson, Richard Dix, Rod La Rocque, Leatrice Joy, Nita Naldi.

Master showman Cecil B. De Mille's monumental two-phase silent version of the Book of Exodus and the application of the Ten Commandments in modern life. Part One, set in ancient times, is in early color; Part Two, set in the modern (1923) period, is in black and white. Impressive special effects, including the parting of the Red Sea. In scope, this is the film that foreshadows De Mille's great spectacles of the sound era. 1923; B&W; 140m.

TEN COMMANDMENTS, THE (1956) ★★★½
DIR: Cecil B. DeMille. **CAST:** Charlton Heston, Yul Brynner, Edward G. Robinson, Cedric Hardwicke, John Derek, Anne Baxter.

A stylish, visually stunning, epic-scale biblical study as only Cecil B. DeMille could make 'em (until William Wyler came along three years later with *Ben Hur*). Charlton Heston, as Moses, takes charge of "God's people" and wrests them from Egypt's punishing grasp. Heston's utter conviction holds the lengthy film together. Then, of course, there's the parting of the Red Sea—an effect that *still* looks great. Unrated; suitable for family viewing. 1956; 219m.

10 RILLINGTON PLACE ★★★★
DIR: Richard Fleischer. **CAST:** Richard Attenborough, Judy Geeson, John Hurt, Andre Morell.

This bleak true-crime drama is based on one of England's most famous murder cases and was actually shot in the house and the neighborhood where the crimes took place. The seamy squalor of the surroundings perfectly mirrors the poverty of mind and soul that allowed John Christy to murder and remain undetected for over ten years. 1971; 111m.

TENDER MERCIES ★★★★★
DIR: Bruce Beresford. **CAST:** Robert Duvall, Tess Harper, Ellen Barkin.
Robert Duvall more than deserved his best-actor Oscar for this superb character study about a down-and-out country singer trying for a comeback. His Mac Sledge is a man who still has songs to sing, but barely the heart to sing them. That is, until he meets up with a sweet-natured widow (Tess Harper) who gives him back the will to live. Rated PG. 1983; 89m.

TENDER YEARS, THE ★★½
DIR: Harold Schuster. **CAST:** Joe E. Brown, Josephine Hutchinson, Charles Drake.
The fight against cruelty to animals is at the heart of this sentimental film about a small-town minister who steals the dog his son loves to save it from being used in illicit dog fighting. 1948; B&W; 81m.

TENTH MONTH, THE ★★½
DIR: Joan Tewkesbury. **CAST:** Carol Burnett, Keith Michell, Dina Merrill.
Tiresome overlong drama about a middle-aged divorcee who has an affair with a married man and becomes pregnant. Good performances by Carol Burnett and Keith Michell are the only bright spots in this made-for-TV film. 1979; 130m.

TERMS OF ENDEARMENT ★★★★
DIR: James L. Brooks. **CAST:** Shirley MacLaine, Debra Winger, Jack Nicholson, Danny DeVito.
This stylish soap opera, written, produced, and directed by James L. Brooks, covers thirty years in the lives of a Houston matron, played by Shirley MacLaine, and her daughter, played by Debra Winger, who marries an English teacher with a wandering eye. Jack Nicholson is also on hand, to play MacLaine's neighbor, an astronaut with the wrong stuff. Rated PG for profanity and suggested sex. 1983; 132m.

TERRY FOX STORY, THE ★★★
DIR: Ralph Thomas. **CAST:** Eric Fryer, Robert Duvall, Chris Makepeace, Rosalind Chao, Michael Zelniker.
This made-for-HBO film chronicles the "Marathon of Hope" undertaken by amputee Terry Fox (Eric Fryer), who lost a leg to cancer. Fox jogged 3,000 miles across Canada before collapsing from exhaustion in Ontario. Based on a true story, this uplifting film is helped by solid performances, direction, and writing. 1983; 96m.

TESS ★★★★½
DIR: Roman Polanski. **CAST:** Nastassja Kinski, Peter Firth, John Bett.
A hypothetically beautiful adaptation of Thomas Hardy's late-nineteenth-century novel *Tess of the D'Urbervilles*, this is director Roman Polanski's finest artistic achievement. Nastassja Kinski is stunning as the country girl who is "wronged" by a suave aristocrat and the man she marries. The story unfolds at the pace of a lazy afternoon stroll, but Polanski's technical skills and the cinematography are spellbinding. Rated PG. 1979; 170m.

TEST OF LOVE, A ★★
DIR: Gil Brealey. **CAST:** Angela Punch McGregor, Drew Forsythe, Tina Arhondis.
This tearjerker, taken from the Australian best selling novel *Annie's Coming Out*, vividly displays the love and determination a therapist (Angela Punch McGregor) has in fighting for the rights of Anne O'Farrell, a severely disabled teenager who was misdiagnosed as being retarded. In that sense the film is a winner. Yet the makers of this movie lack the finesse it takes to make the antagonists of this story more than one-dimensional. Rated PG for profanity. 1984; 93m.

TEX ★★★★½
DIR: Tim Hunter. **CAST:** Matt Dillon, Jim Metzler, Ben Johnson, Emilio Estevez, Meg Tilly.
Matt Dillon, Jim Metzler, and Ben Johnson star in this superb coming-of-age adventure about the struggles and conflicts of two teenage brothers growing up in the Southwest without parental guidance. Rated PG for violence and mature situations. 1982; 103m.

THAT CHAMPIONSHIP SEASON ★★½
DIR: Jason Miller. **CAST:** Bruce Dern, Stacy Keach, Martin Sheen, Paul Sorvino, Robert Mitchum.
Former high-school basketball stars (Bruce Dern, Stacy Keach, Martin Sheen, and Paul Sorvino) and their coach (Robert Mitchum) get together for the twenty-fourth annual celebration of their championship season. However, it turns out to be a fiasco as the longtime friendships begin disintegrating. While there's nothing wrong with a sobering look at broken dreams and the pain of mid-life crisis, we've seen it all on screen before. Rated R for profanity, racial epithets, violence, and adult content. 1982; 110m.

THAT COLD DAY IN THE PARK ★★
DIR: Robert Altman. **CAST:** Sandy Dennis, Michael Burns, Suzanne Benton, John Garfield Jr., Luana Anders, Michael Murphy.
This claustrophobic study of an emotionally disturbed woman and her obsessive interest in a young man who frequents the park across from her house is just about as strange as they come. It nonetheless gives gifted Sandy Dennis one of her most memorable roles. This film focuses on repressed sexuality, but also hints at incest and other subjects considered taboo when this Canadian-made movie was released. 1969; 113m.

THAT HAMILTON WOMAN ★★★½
DIR: Alexander Korda. **CAST:** Vivien Leigh, Laurence Olivier.
The legendary acting duo of Mr. and Mrs. Laurence Olivier re-creates one of England's legendary romantic scandals: the love of naval hero Horatio Nelson for the alluring Lady Emma Hamilton. The affair between these two already married lovers caused quite a stir in early nineteenth-century Britain. 1941; B&W; 128m.

THAT WAS THEN...THIS IS NOW ★★★★
DIR: Christopher Cain. **CAST:** Emilio Estevez, Craig Sheffer, Kim Delaney, Morgan Freeman, Larry B. Scott, Barbara Babcock.
The best film to be adapted from a novel by S. E. Hinton (*The Outsiders*; *Rumble Fish*), this work, directed by Christopher Cain, has a resounding ring of truth. The cuteness and condescension that mar most coming-of-age films are laudably absent in its tale of two working-class teenagers (Emilio Estevez and Craig Sheffer) coming to grips with adulthood. This is a work that teens and adults alike can appreciate. Rated R for violence and profanity. 1985; 103m.

THESE THREE ★★★★
DIR: William Wyler. **CAST:** Miriam Hopkins, Merle Oberon, Joel McCrea, Bonita Granville, Marcia Mae Jones.
A superb cast brings alive this story of two upright and decent schoolteachers victimized by the lies of a malicious student. Miriam Hopkins and Merle Oberon are the pair brutally slandered; Bonita Granville is the evil liar. Script by Lillian Hellman, loosely based on her play *The Children's Hour*, under which title the film was remade in 1961. 1936; B&W; 93m.

THEY CAME TO CORDURA ★★
DIR: Robert Rossen. **CAST:** Gary Cooper, Rita Hayworth, Van Heflin, Tab Hunter, Richard Conte.

This film, which examines the true character of the war hero, is not one of Gary Cooper's best. The story has Cooper in Mexico during World War I as one of six military men returning to base. The hardships they encounter on the way create the drama. The movie has a nice look, but just not enough action. 1959; 123m.

THEY KNEW WHAT THEY WANTED ★★★
DIR: Garson Kanin. **CAST:** Charles Laughton, Carole Lombard, William Gargan, Harry Carey.

This film is a fine example of offbeat casting that somehow succeeds. Charles Laughton and Carole Lombard were required to submerge their usual histrionics in order to bring off a low-key little tragedy. The story is of the unrequited love of an Italian wine grower for the opportunistic hash house waitress that he marries. 1940; B&W; 96m.

THEY LIVE BY NIGHT ★★★½
DIR: Nicholas Ray. **CAST:** Farley Granger, Cathy O'Donnell, Howard DaSilva, Jay C. Flippen.

A seminal film dealing with youth, alienation, and the concept of the loner who operates outside the confines of conventional behavior and morality. This postwar crime drama gave American youth a minor cultural folk hero in Farley Granger and began the directing career of young Nicholas Ray, who would in turn provide the world with the ultimate image of teenage alienation: *Rebel Without a Cause.* 1949; B&W; 95m.

THEY MADE ME A CRIMINAL ★★½
DIR: Busby Berkeley. **CAST:** John Garfield, Claude Rains, Ann Sheridan, Gloria Dickson, The Dead End Kids, Ward Bond.

John Garfield's film persona is a direct result of this Warner Bros. story about the redemption of a loner on the lam from the law for a crime he didn't commit. A great cast still doesn't change the fact that this remake of 1933's *The Life of Jimmy Dolan* is muddled and not too solidly constructed. 1939; B&W; 92m.

THEY MEET AGAIN ★½
DIR: Erle C. Kenton. **CAST:** Jean Hersholt, Robert Baldwin, Neil Hamilton, Dorothy Lovett, Arthur Hoyt.

In this film, the last in the popular Dr. Christian series about a snoopy small-town doctor, genial Jean Hersholt is upset because a man he feels is innocent is serving time in prison. Spurred on by the plight of the convicted man's young daughter, the good doctor finds out who embezzled the missing money and leads the authorities to them. 1941; B&W; 69m.

THEY MIGHT BE GIANTS ★★★★
DIR: Anthony Harvey. **CAST:** George C. Scott, Joanne Woodward, Jack Gilford.

Stylish and engaging study of a retired judge (George C. Scott) who imagines himself to be Sherlock Holmes. With visions of dollar signs floating before his eyes, the judge's brother hopes to have this ersatz detective committed; to this end, the brother brings in a female psychiatrist whose name happens to be—you guessed it—Watson. This unlikely duo embarks on a series of adventures, real and imagined. Rated PG. 1971; 88m.

THEY SHOOT HORSES, DON'T THEY? ★★★★★
DIR: Sydney Pollack. **CAST:** Jane Fonda, Gig Young, Michael Sarrazin.

The desperation and hopelessness of the Great Depression are graphically shown in this powerful drama, through a pitiful collection of marathon dancers. Some of the group will endure this physical and mental assault on their human spirit; some will not. Jane Fonda, as a cynical casualty of the Depression, and Gig Young, as the uncaring master of ceremonies, give stunning performances. Rated PG. 1969; 121m.

THEY WON'T BELIEVE ME ★★★½
DIR: Irving Pichel. **CAST:** Robert Young, Susan Hayward, Jane Greer, Rita Johnson, Tom Powers, Don Beddoe, Frank Ferguson.
Robert Young is a grade-A stinker in this classic *film noir* of deceit, mistaken murder, suicide, and doomed romance. Rita Johnson is especially fine as the wronged wife. 1947; B&W; 95m.

THEY'RE PLAYING WITH FIRE
DIR: Howard Avedis. **CAST:** Sybil Danning, Eric Brown, Andrew Prine.
A high school student is seduced by a teacher in this gobbler which eventually leads to some extracurricular fraud and murder. Rated R. 1983; 96m.

THIEF OF HEARTS ★★★
DIR: Douglas Day Stewart. **CAST:** Steven Bauer, Barbara Williams.
A young, upwardly mobile married woman loses her intimate diary of sexual fantasies to a thief who has broken into her home. In an interesting premise, the woman becomes a willing participant in the thief's sexual manipulations without knowing that he is the man who stole her secrets. Rated R. 1984; 100m.

THIS LAND IS MINE ★★★
DIR: Jean Renoir. **CAST:** Charles Laughton, Maureen O'Hara, George Sanders, Walter Slezak.
Charles Laughton performs another fine characterization, this time as a timid French teacher who blossoms as a hero when he is incited to vigorous action by the Nazi occupation. Time has dulled the cutting edge of this obviously patriotic wartime film, but the artistry of the director and players remains sharp. 1943; B&W; 103m.

THIS PROPERTY IS CONDEMNED ★★½
DIR: Sydney Pollack. **CAST:** Natalie Wood, Robert Redford, Charles Bronson, Kate Reid, Robert Blake.
Marginal film interpretation of Tennessee Williams's play. Owen Legate (Robert Redford) is a stranger in town, there for the purpose of laying off local railroaders. Alva (Natalie Wood) is a flirtatious southern girl who casts her spell of romance on the stranger, who is staying at her mother's boardinghouse. 1966; 109m.

THIS SPORTING LIFE ★★★½
DIR: Lindsay Anderson. **CAST:** Rachel Roberts, Richard Harris, Colin Blakely.
Richard Harris and Rachel Roberts shine in this stark, powerful look into the life and dreams of a Yorkshire coal miner who seeks to become a professional rugby player. The squeamish will not like all the game scenes. 1963; 129m.

THORNBIRDS, THE ★★★
DIR: Daryl Duke. **CAST:** Richard Chamberlain, Rachel Ward, Christopher Plummer, Bryan Brown, Barbara Stanwyck, Richard Kiley, Jean Simmons, John Friedrich.
Originally a ten-hour TV miniseries, this much-edited film is still worth a watch. Richard Chamberlain plays an ambitious priest who falls in love with an innocent, trusting young woman (Rachel Ward). It's all played out against shifting backgrounds of outback Australia, Vatican Rome, and idyllic Greece. This has been released for a limited time and copies may be hard to locate. 1983; 150m.

THREE CAME HOME ★★★
DIR: Jean Negulesco. **CAST:** Claudette Colbert, Patric Knowles, Sessue Hayakawa.
During World War II, British families residing in Borneo are forced into prison camps by Japanese troops. The courage and suffering of the confined women make for compelling drama. Claudette Colbert delivers one of her finest performances. 1950; 106m.

THREE FACES WEST ★★★
DIR: Bernard Vorhaus. **CAST:** John Wayne, Charles Coburn, Sigrid Gurie, Spencer Charters.

John Wayne is the leader of a group of Dust Bowl farmers attempting to survive in this surprisingly watchable Republic release. Sigrid Gurie and Charles Coburn co-star as the European immigrants who show them what courage means. 1940; B&W; 79m.

THREE SOVEREIGNS FOR SARAH ★½
DIR: Philip Leacock. **CAST:** Vanessa Redgrave, Ronald Hunter, Patrick McGoohan, Will Lyman, Kim Hunter.

Though Vanessa Redgrave does her part to carry along this slow-moving film about the Salem witch trials, a ponderous script and unimaginative direction destroy all hope for what surely began as an interesting story. Supposedly a true story about the real motivations that led to this dark spot in American history. 1987; 171m.

THUNDER IN THE CITY ★½
DIR: Marion Gering. **CAST:** Edward G. Robinson, Nigel Bruce, Ralph Richardson.

Time severely dates this comedy-drama about a brash, fast-talking American promotor (Edward G. Robinson) who goes to staid London to promote modern U.S. advertising methods. Nigel Bruce fared far better as Holmes's Dr. Watson. 1937; B&W; 85m.

THURSDAY'S GAME ★★★
DIR: Robert Moore. **CAST:** Gene Wilder, Bob Newhart, Ellen Burstyn, Cloris Leachman, Rob Reiner, Nancy Walker, Valerie Harper.

Engaging made-for-television film about two ordinary guys (Gene Wilder and Bob Newhart) who continue to get together on Thursday nights after their weekly poker game collapses. Both have reasons for wanting to leave the house, and both make the most of this small rebellion. The supporting cast is excellent. Unrated; adult themes. 1974; 74m.

TICKET TO HEAVEN ★★★
DIR: Ralph Thomas. **CAST:** Nick Mancuso, Saul Rubinek, Meg Foster, Kim Cattrall, R. H. Thompson.

This Canadian film presents a lacerating look at the frightening phenomenon of contemporary religious cults. Nick Mancuso is riveting as the brainwashed victim. Saul Rubinek and Meg Foster are splendid in support. But R. H. Thompson almost steals the show as a painfully pragmatic deprogrammer. Nice touches of humor give the movie balance. Rated PG. 1981; 107m.

TIGER BAY ★★★½
DIR: J. Lee Thompson. **CAST:** John Mills, Horst Buchholz, Hayley Mills, Yvonne Mitchell, Anthony Dawson.

Young Hayley Mills began her film career—in a part originally written for a boy—as an imaginative girl who witnesses a murder and then befriends the killer. Since the child is a known liar, nobody believes her until events escalate to the point of desperation. Horst Buchholz is excellent as the remorseful murderer. A thoughtful drama for all ages. Unrated; suitable for family viewing. 1959; B&W; 105m.

TIGER WARSAW ★★
DIR: Amin Q. Chaudhri. **CAST:** Patrick Swayze, Barbara Williams, Lee Richardson, Piper Laurie.

Members of a family torn apart by a tragic incident struggle through their lives—all the while unable to forgive and forget. Patrick Swayze is Tiger Warsaw, a man haunted by the memory of shooting his father and the scandal he caused his family. Vague film lacking in substance and direction. Rated R for violence and profanity. 1987; 92m.

TILL THE END OF TIME ★★★
DIR: Edward Dmytryk. **CAST:** Dorothy McGuire, Guy Madison, Robert Mitchum, Jean Porter.

Three veterans of World War II come home to find life, in general and how it was when they left, considerably changed. Readjustment is tough, and the love they left has soured. A good drama. 1946; B&W; 105m.

TIM ★★★★½
DIR: Michael Pate. **CAST:** Mel Gibson, Piper Laurie, Alwyn Kurts.

An unforgettable character study from Down Under, this features Mel Gibson in his film debut as a simple-minded young adult and Piper Laurie as the older woman who finds herself falling in love with him. Superb supporting performances by the Australian cast—especially Alwyn Kurts and Pat Evison, as Tim's parents. Rated PG for suggested sex. 1979; 108m.

TIME OF DESTINY, A ★★½
DIR: Gregory Nava. **CAST:** William Hurt, Timothy Hutton, Melissa Leo, Stockard Channing.

Old-fashioned tale of love, hate, and revenge set against the backdrop of World War II. William Hurt is the guilt-ridden son of a Basque family in San Diego out to avenge the accidental death of his father. Timothy Hutton is the subject of Hurt's revenge. Beautiful photography, terrific editing, and pacing help keep you from noticing the weak spots in the familiar plot. Rated PG-13 for violence and profanity. 1988; 118m.

TIME OF YOUR LIFE, THE ★★★½
DIR: H. C. Potter. **CAST:** James Cagney, Wayne Morris, Broderick Crawford, Jeanne Cagney, Ward Bond, James Lydon, Gale Page.

Originally a prize-winning play by the brilliant William Saroyan. Director H. C. Potter and a talented group of actors have created a pleasing film about the diverse characters who are regulars at Nick's Saloon, Restaurant and Entertainment Palace on San Francisco's Barbary Coast. A charmer, this picture grows on you. 1948; B&W; 109m.

TIME TO LOVE AND A TIME TO DIE, A ★★½
DIR: Douglas Sirk. **CAST:** John Gavin, Lilo Pulver, Jock Mahoney, Don DeFore, Keenan Wynn, Erich Maria Remarque, Jim Hutton, Klaus Kinski.

A well-intentioned but preachy and largely unsatisfying antiwar film adapted from the novel by Erich Maria Remarque who also portrays the Professor. John Gavin is a German soldier who receives a furlough from the Russian front in 1944. He returns home to find his town a bombed-out shell and his parents missing. 1958; 133m.

TIN MAN ★★★
DIR: John C. Thomas. **CAST:** Timothy Bottoms, Deana Jurgens, John Phillip Law, Troy Donahue.

For the most part, this is an intriguing drama about a deaf auto mechanic who invents a computer with which he can hear and speak. When he attempts to get the device manufactured, the computer company sets out to exploit him. Timothy Bottoms is extraordinary, and the story holds your attention, but the film is hurt by cardboard villains and a pat ending. Unrated. 1983; 95m.

T-MEN ★★½
DIR: Anthony Mann. **CAST:** Dennis O'Keefe, Alfred Ryder, Mary Meade, Wallace Ford, June Lockhart, Charles McGraw, Jane Randolph.

Two undercover operatives for the Treasury Department infiltrate a master counterfeiting ring and find themselves on opposite sides when the lead starts to fly. Unable to save the life of his partner without exposing himself, agent Dennis O'Keefe courageously continues the work of both men. 1948; B&W; 92m.

TO KILL A MOCKINGBIRD ★★★★★
DIR: Robert Mulligan. **CAST:** Gregory Peck, Mary Badham, Phillip Alford, John Megna.

To Kill a Mockingbird is a leisurely paced, flavorful filming of Harper Lee's bestselling novel. Gregory Peck earned an Oscar as a small-town southern lawyer who defends a black man accused of rape. Mary Badham, Philip Alford, and John Megna are superb as Peck's children and a visiting friend who are trying to understand life in a small town. 1962; B&W; 129m.

TO SIR WITH LOVE ★★★★
DIR: James Clavell. **CAST:** Sidney Poitier, Judy Geeson, Christian Roberts, Suzy Kendall, Lulu.

A moving, gentle portrait of the influence of a black teacher upon a classroom of poverty-ridden teenagers in London's East End, this stars Sidney Poitier, in one of his finest performances, as the teacher. He instills in his pupils a belief in themselves and respect for one another. 1967; 105m.

TOAST OF NEW YORK, THE ★★★
DIR: Rowland V. Lee. **CAST:** Edward Arnold, Cary Grant, Frances Farmer, Jack Oakie, Donald Meek, Clarence Kolb, Billy Gilbert.

Semiaccurate biography of legendary post–Civil War Wall Street wheeler-dealer James Fisk. But, even so, it is a good film. Edward Arnold superbly plays Fisk. Jack Oakie does a fine turn. Don't expect the Cary Grant you know and love, however. 1937; B&W; 109m.

TODD KILLINGS, THE ★★½
DIR: Barry Shear. **CAST:** Robert F. Lyons, Richard Thomas, Belinda Montgomery, James Broderick, Gloria Grahame, Holly Near, Edward Asner, Barbara Bel Geddes.

Harrowing fact-based drama about a rebellious young murderer (Robert F. Lyons) and the alienated kids who protect him. This film offers a penetrating look into the pathological mind of 23-year-old killer who seeks out teenage girls for drug escapades and sexual pleasure. Shocking, disturbing portrait of a thrill-seeking psychopath. Rated R, contains nudity and violence. 1971; 93m.

TOL'ABLE DAVID ★★½
DIR: King Vidor. **CAST:** Richard Barthelmess, Gladys Hulette, Ernest Torrence, Warner Richmond.

Though it creaks a bit with age, this stalwart tale of good besting evil deserves attention and rewards it. Silent. 1921; B&W; 80m.

TOM BROWN'S SCHOOL DAYS ★★½
DIR: Robert Stevenson. **CAST:** Cedric Hardwicke, Freddie Bartholomew, Gale Storm, Jimmy Lydon, Josephine Hutchinson, Polly Moran, Billy Halop.

"Old school tie" story mixes top Hollywood production values and minor classic of British secondary schools into an enjoyable froth filled with all the clichés that have since been completely overexposed in ludicrous movie and television treatments. Better than one would think and not the creaky old groaner it could have been. 1940; B&W; 86m.

TOM BROWN'S SCHOOLDAYS ★★★½
DIR: Gordon Parry. **CAST:** Robert Newton, John Howard Davies, James Hayter, Hermione Baddeley.

Tom, played by John Howard Davies, brings a civilizing influence to his peers in this engaging account of life in a Victorian England boys' school. Robert Newton, of course, is superb. An excellent cast, under good direction, makes this a particularly fine film. 1950; B&W; 93m.

TOMORROW ★★★★★
DIR: Joseph Anthony. **CAST:** Robert Duvall, Olga Bellin, Sudie Bond.

Robert Duvall gives yet another sensitive, powerful, and completely convincing performance in this superb black-and-white character study about a caretaker who finds himself caring for—in both senses—a pregnant woman (Olga Bellin) who turns up one day at the lumber mill where he works. Rated PG for violence. 1972; B&W; 103m.

TOMORROW AT SEVEN ★★
DIR: Ray Enright. **CAST:** Chester Morris, Vivienne Osborne, Allen Jenkins, Frank McHugh, Henry Stephenson, Grant Mitchell, Charles Middleton.

Obscure murder drama pits crime novelist Chester Morris and bumbling policemen Allen Jenkins and Frank McHugh against the mysterious Ace, who sends his victims a calling card and tells them where to go to die, which they inevitably do. This routine whodunit has little to offer. 1933; B&W; 62m.

TOO OUTRAGEOUS ★★
DIR: Richard Benner. **CAST:** Craig Russell, Hollis McLaren, David McIlwraith.

In this disappointing sequel to 1977's suprise hit *Outrageous*, Craig Russell reprises his role as the gay hairdresser, now having realized his dreams of becoming a successful female impersonator. Hollis McLaren is his schizophrenic friend. Rated R for language and sexual content. 1987; 100m.

TORCH SONG TRILOGY ★★★
DIR: Paul Bogart. **CAST:** Harvey Fierstein, Anne Bancroft, Matthew Broderick, Brian Kerwin.

Harvey Fierstein's prize-winning play of the same title couldn't be better suited to film, but this comedy-drama is not for everyone. Fierstein plays Arnold Beckoff, an insecure female impersonator looking for that one, all-encompassing relationship. Anne Bancroft is his unbending Jewish mama. The musical numbers in the gay nightclub are classy and clever. Rated R. 1988; 120m.

TORCHLIGHT
DIR: Tom Wright. **CAST:** Pamela Sue Martin, Steve Railsback, Ian McShane, Al Corley.

Pamela Sue Martin produced, co-wrote, and starred in this less-than-memorable film. In it, her successful but insecure husband, Jake (Steve Railsback), becomes hopelessly addicted to cocaine. Naturally their marriage suffers as a result of his addiction. Rated R for explicit drug use and sadism. 1985; 90m.

TORN BETWEEN TWO LOVERS ★★★½
DIR: Delbert Mann. **CAST:** Lee Remick, Joseph Bologna, George Peppard, Giorgio Tozzi.

This made-for-TV romantic triangle features a married Lee Remick who finds herself having an affair with a divorced architect. She must finally tell her husband the truth and choose between the two. Nothing boring about this soap! 1979; 100m.

TOUCHED ★★★
DIR: John Flynn. **CAST:** Robert Hays, Kathleen Beller, Gilbert Lewis, Ned Beatty.

This sensitive drama involves the struggle of two young psychiatric patients who try to make it outside the hospital walls. Robert Hays and Kathleen Beller are terrific as the frightened couple who must deal with numerous unforeseen obstacles. Rated R for mature topic. 1982; 89m.

TOUCHED BY LOVE ★★★
DIR: Gus Trikonis. **CAST:** Deborah Raffin, Diane Lane, Michael Learned, Cristina Raines, Mary Wickes, Clu Gulager, John Amos.

Strong performances make this affecting sentimental drama about a teenage cerebral palsy victim given hope through correspondence with singer Elvis Presley. Deborah Raffin is excellent as the nurse who nurtures patient Diane Lane from cripple to functioning teenager. Originally titled *From Elvis with Love*. Rated PG. 1980; 95m.

TOUGH GUYS DON'T DANCE ★★
DIR: Norman Mailer. **CAST:** Ryan O'Neal, Isabella Rossellini, Wings Hauser, Debra Sundland, Frances Fisher.

Interesting but uneven attempt at *film noir*. Strenuous dialogue and bizarre acting make this excursion into experimental filmmaking too confusing.

Ryan O'Neal is an ex-con who wants to be a writer. In his path are Wings Hauser as a psychotic, drug-dealing policeman, and Isabella Rossellini. Newcomer Debra Sundland is stunning as an obnoxious southern belle. Rated R for nudity, language, and violence. 1987; 110m.

TOWN LIKE ALICE, A ★★★★½
DIR: David Stevens. **CAST:** Helen Morse, Bryan Brown, Gordon Jackson.

This outstanding PBS series is even more enjoyable to watch in one viewing than during a six-week period. It is the story of female British POWs in Malaysia and their incredible struggle. Helen Morse is wonderful as the one who takes charge to help maintain the sanity and welfare of the group. Bryan Brown is the soldier who risks his life to help the women and falls in love with Morse. 1980; 301m.

TRACK 29 ★
DIR: Nicolas Roeg. **CAST:** Theresa Russell, Gary Oldman, Christopher Lloyd, Colleen Camp, Sandra Bernhard, Seymour Cassel.

British director Nicolas Roeg continues his downhill creative slide with this psycho-silly story of a bored, alcoholic housewife (Theresa Russell) who takes up with a strange hitchhiker (Gary Oldman) who may or may not be her son. Roeg and screenwriter Dennis Potter stubbornly refuse to engage the viewer in any real way, creating an artsy, weird, open-ended movie that plays like a bad joke without a punchline. Rated R for violence, profanity and gore. 1988; 90m.

TRACKS
DIR: Henry Jaglom. **CAST:** Dennis Hopper, Taryn Power, Dean Stockwell, Topo Swope, Michael Emil.

Dennis Hopper plays a Vietnam War veteran who escorts his dead buddy on a train across country and goes crazy in the process. Rated R. 1977; 90m.

TRAIN KILLER, THE ★★
DIR: Sandor Simo. **CAST:** Michael Sarrazin, Towje Kleiner.

The true story of Sylvester Matushka, the Hungarian businessman who was responsible for a number of train wrecks in 1931. What is frustrating about this film is that it prepares the viewer for political intrigue that is never fully explained by the end of the film. Towje Kleiner is superb as Dr. Epstein, investigator of the train wrecks. Not rated, but contains sex, nudity, and violence. 1983; 90m.

TRAMP AT THE DOOR ★★★★
DIR: Allan Kroeker. **CAST:** Ed McNamara, August Schellenberg, Monique Mercure.

Poignant story of a transient who poses as a distant relative of a family to gain shelter and food from them. The script is solid, especially the stories that the tramp (played brilliantly by Ed McNamara) weaves for the astonished family. Not rated; for all ages. 1985; 81m.

TRAPEZE ★★½
DIR: Carol Reed. **CAST:** Burt Lancaster, Tony Curtis, Gina Lollobrigida, Katy Jurado, Thomas Gomez.

Overly familiar tale of professional (Burt Lancaster) who takes young protégé (Tony Curtis) under his wing and teaches him all he knows about aerial acrobatics only to have scheming opportunist Gina Lollobrigida come between them is okay but nothing out of the ordinary. Solid performances and competent stunts peformed by the stars themselves highlight this international effort set in European circus circuit. 1956; 105m.

TRASH ★★½
DIR: Andy Warhol. **CAST:** Joe Dallesandro, Holly Woodlawn, Jane Forth.

Favorite Andy Warhol actor Joe Dallesandro faces the squalor of New York once again. This is one of Warhol's more palatable productions. It contains some truly amusing scenes and insightful dialogue, as well as good performances by Dallesandro and Holly Woodlawn, whose relationship is the highlight of the film. Nudity, language, and open drug use fill the frames of this freewheeling life study. 1970; 110m.

TREE GROWS IN BROOKLYN, A ★★★★

DIR: Elia Kazan. **CAST:** Dorothy McGuire, James Dunn, Joan Blondell, Peggy Ann Garner, Lloyd Nolan, James Gleason.

A richly detailed and sentimental evocation of working class Brooklyn at the turn of the century. The story focuses on the happiness and tragedies of a poor family ruled by a kindly but alcoholic father and a strong-willed mother. 1945; B&W; 128m.

TRESPASSES

DIR: Adam Roarke, Loren Bivens. **CAST:** Ben Johnson, Robert Kuhn, Mary Pillot, Van Brooks, Adam Roarke.

You'll spend an hour tying to figure out what's happening in this ridiculous drama and then realize it wasn't worth the wait. A beautiful woman is raped by two degenerate transients while her banker husband watches. She falls in love with a drifter who comes to her rescue. Rated R for nudity and violence. 1986; 90m.

TRIAL, THE ★★★½

DIR: Orson Welles. **CAST:** Anthony Perkins, Jeanne Moreau, Romy Schneider, Orson Welles, Elsa Martinelli, Akim Tamiroff.

A man in an unnamed country is arrested for an unexplained crime he is never told about. It is never made too clear to the audience, either. Orson Welles's unique staging and direction nevertheless make it all fascinating, if disturbing, entertainment. 1963; B&W; 118m.

TRIAL OF THE CANTONSVILLE NINE, THE ★

DIR: Gordon Davidson. **CAST:** Ed Flanders, Douglas Watson, William Schallert, Peter Strauss, Richard Jordan, Barton Heyman.

This film is a claustrophobic adaptation of a play about nine Baltimore antiwar protesters (two are priests), who faced trial for burning draft records in 1968. It's high-minded and too self-righteous. William Schallert as the judge is a complete annoyance. 1972; 85m.

TRIBES ★★★½

DIR: Joseph Sargent. **CAST:** Jan-Michael Vincent, Darren McGavin, Earl Holliman.

Long-haired peacenik Jan-Michael Vincent is drafted into the marines and faces a tough time from drill instructor Darren McGavin. TV movie is far above the usual television schlock, with insightful script and solid acting. One of Vincent's best performances. Seems a bit dated by today's standards, but still worth a look. 1970; 74m.

TRIBUTE ★★★½

DIR: Bob Clark. **CAST:** Jack Lemmon, Robby Benson, Lee Remick, Colleen Dewhurst, John Marley.

A moving portrait of a man in crisis, *Tribute* bestows a unique gift to its audience: the feeling that they have come to know a very special man. Jack Lemmon stars as a Broadway press agent who has contracted a terminal blood disease and is feted by his friends in show business. Though adjusted to his fate, Lemmon finds that he has some unfinished business: to make peace with his son, Robby Benson. Rated PG. 1980; 121m.

TRIO ★★★★

DIR: Ken Annakin, Harold French. **CAST:** Jean Simmons, Michael Rennie, Nigel Patrick, Wilfred Hyde-White.

Wonderful collection of Somerset Maugham's short stories, introduced by Maugham. Each has a nice twist ending. "The Verger" centers on a man's decisions after being fired for his illiteracy. "Mr. Know-All" is an obnoxious bore who is shunned by the others on his cruise. Finally, Michael Rennie and Jean Simmons co-star as TB patients who fall in love while they live in the sanitorium. 1950; B&W; 88m.

TRIP, THE ★★

DIR: Roger Corman. **CAST:** Peter Fonda, Susan Strasberg, Bruce Dern, Dennis Hopper, Dick Miller, Luana Anders, Peter Bogdanovich.

Peter Fonda plays a director of TV commercials who discovers the kaleidoscopic pleasures of LSD. This curio of the psychedelic era features outdated special effects and sensibilities. Screenplay by Jack Nicholson. 1967; 85m.

TRIP TO BOUNTIFUL, THE ★★★★½

DIR: Peter Masterson. **CAST:** Geraldine Page, John Heard, Carlin Glynn, Richard Bradford, Rebecca DeMornay.

In 1947, an elderly widow (wonderfully played by Oscar-winner Geraldine Page) leaves the cramped apartment where she lives with her loving but weak son (John Heard) and his demanding wife (Carlin Glynn) to return to Bountiful, the small town where she had spent her happy youth...unaware that it no longer exists. Along the way, she meets a kindred spirit (Rebecca DeMornay) and the film becomes a joyous celebration of life. Rated PG. 1986; 105m.

TROJAN WOMEN, THE ★½

DIR: Michael Cacoyannis. **CAST:** Katharine Hepburn, Vanessa Redgrave, Genevieve Bujold, Irene Papas.

This Greek-American film is worth seeing only for the four female leads: Katharine Hepburn, Vanessa Redgrave, Genevieve Bujold, and Irene Papas. Unfortunately, the plot (revolving around the Trojan War and their defeat) is lost. Rated PG. 1972; 105m.

TROUBLE IN MIND ★★★★

DIR: Alan Rudolph. **CAST:** Kris Kristofferson, Keith Carradine, Genevieve Bujold, Lori Singer, Joe Morton, Divine.

An ex-cop, Kris Kristofferson, is paroled from prison and returns to Rain City, hoping to rekindle his romance with café owner Genevieve Bujold. Once there, he falls in love with the wife (Lori Singer) of a thief (Keith Carradine). Director Alan Rudolph's ultrabizarre, semifuturistic tale is a free-form character study, an unusual screen experience that almost defies description. Rated R. 1986; 111m.

TRUE BELIEVER ★★★★

DIR: Joseph Rubin. **CAST:** James Woods, Robert Downey Jr., Margaret Colin, Kurtwood Smith.

James Woods gives a powerhouse performance in this gripping thriller, tautly directed by Joseph Rubin. Woods plays a maverick lawyer who takes on the case of a convicted killer, only to find himself bucking the powers-that-be in New York City. Robert Downey Jr. gives a subdued and effective performance as Woods's assistant. Rated R for violence and profanity. 1989; 103m.

TRUE CONFESSIONS ★★★★½

DIR: Ulu Grosbard. **CAST:** Robert De Niro, Robert Duvall, Charles Durning, Burgess Meredith.

This is the thoughtful, powerful story of two brothers (Robert De Niro and Robert Duvall)—one a priest, the other a jaded detective—caught in the sordid world of power politics in post–World War II Los Angeles. It's a brilliant and disturbing film. Rated R. 1981; 108m.

TRUE HEART SUSIE ★★★

DIR: D. W. Griffith. **CAST:** Lillian Gish, Robert Herron, Wilbur Higby, George Fawcett, Carol Dempster.

Lillian Gish and Robert Herron are sweethearts in a small, rural, bedrock-solid American town in this sentimental silent film account of a young girl's transition from scatterbrained, uninhibited adolescent to dignified, self-assured woman. Sensitive acting and directing make what could have been cloying mush a touching, charming excursion back to what are nostalgically recalled as "the good old days." 1919; B&W; 62m.

TRUE WEST ★★★★
DIR: Gary Sinise. **CAST:** John Malkovich, Gary Sinise.
Sam Shepard's powerful play about sibling rivalry and responsibility is masterfully performed by members of the Steppenwolf Theater Company for public television. John Malkovich stars as a reclusive drifter who returns home to make his brother, a Hollywood screenwriter, sit up and take notice. Not rated. 1983; 110m.

TRUEBLOOD ★★½
DIR: Frank Kerr. **CAST:** Jeff Fahey, Chad Lowe.
Writer-director Frank Kerr gives a 1980s spin to urban underworld dramas of the 1940s like *The Naked City* and *Kiss of Death.* Jeff Fahey and Chad Lowe are brothers, estranged for ten years, who try to rebuild their relationship on the mean streets of Brooklyn. Rated R for profanity and graphic violence. 1989; 100m.

TRUTH ABOUT WOMEN, THE ★★½
DIR: Muriel Box. **CAST:** Laurence Harvey, Julie Harris, Eva Gabor, Diane Cilento, Mai Zetterling, Wilfrid Hyde-White.
Playboy Laurence Harvey flirts with every woman in sight in this comedy-drama. This British production has a fine cast, especially Julie Harris, and the production design is also quite good, but it's sooo slow. 1958; 98m.

TUCKER: A MAN AND HIS DREAM ★★★½
DIR: Francis Ford Coppola. **CAST:** Jeff Bridges, Frederic Forrest, Joan Allen, Dean Stockwell, Martin Landau, Mako, Lloyd Bridges, Christian Slater.
Francis Ford Coppola has always admired Preston Tucker, entrepreneurial genius and designer of the Tucker, a Forties automobile built to challenge the big three auto makers. This homage to dreams stars Jeff Bridges, played with an almost comic-strip-style enthusiasm. This movie truly catches the spirit of postwar times when everything seemed possible. Rated PG-13 for language. 1988; 130m.

TUFF TURF ★★
DIR: Fritz Kiersch. **CAST:** James Spader, Kim Richards, Paul Mones.
A forgettable movie about young love as the new kid in town falls for a street-wise young woman with a dangerous lover. Rated R for violence, profanity, and suggested sex. 1984; 112m.

TULSA ★★½
DIR: Stuart Heisler. **CAST:** Susan Hayward, Robert Preston, Pedro Armendariz, Chill Wills, Ed Begley Sr.
Typical potboiler has feisty Susan Hayward as a strong-willed woman intent on drilling oil wells on her property no matter who tries to interfere. Standard stock situations made more palatable by fine cast of character actors typify this story of a hard-headed businesswoman humanized during the course of the action. 1949; 90m.

TUNES OF GLORY ★★★★
DIR: Ronald Neame. **CAST:** Alec Guinness, John Mills, Susannah York, Dennis Price, Duncan Macrae, Kay Walsh, Gordon Jackson, John Fraser, Allan Cuthbertson.
Gripping drama of rivalry between embittered older soldier Alec Guinness and his younger replacement John Mills is a classic study of cruelty as Guinness loses no opportunity to bully and belittle the competent but less aggressive Mills. Superb acting highlights this tragic story. 1960; 107m.

TURK 182 ★★
DIR: Bob Clark. **CAST:** Timothy Hutton, Robert Urich, Kim Cattrall, Robert Culp, Darren McGavin, Peter Boyle.
Timothy Hutton stars as a young man who embarks on a personal crusade

against injustice. His older brother (Robert Urich), a fireman, has been denied his pension after being injured while saving a child from a burning building when he was off-duty. *Turk 182* is one of those manipulative movies thought by their makers to be surefire hits. It's anything but. Rated PG-13 for violence, profanity, and suggested sex. 1985; 102m.

TURNING POINT, THE ★★★★½
DIR: Herbert Ross. **CAST:** Anne Bancroft, Shirley MacLaine, Mikhail Baryshnikov, Leslie Browne, Tom Skerritt.

Anne Bancroft and Shirley MacLaine have the meaty scenes in this well-crafted drama, as a pair of dancers both blessed and cursed with the aftermaths of their own personal turning points. Bancroft, forsaking family and stability, became a ballet star; MacLaine, forsaking fame and personal expression, embraced family and stability. Blended with the story is a series of beautifully rendered ballet sequences featuring Mikhail Baryshnikov, in his film debut. Great stuff, played with strength and conviction by all concerned. Rated PG for intensity of theme. 1977; 119m.

12 ANGRY MEN ★★★★★
DIR: Sidney Lumet. **CAST:** Henry Fonda, Lee J. Cobb, Ed Begley Sr., E. G. Marshall, Jack Klugman, Jack Warden, Martin Balsam, John Fiedler, Robert Webber, George Voskovec, Edward Binns, Joseph Sweeney.

A superb cast under inspired direction makes this film brilliant in every aspect. Henry Fonda is the holdout on a jury who desperately seeks to convince his eleven peers to reconsider their hasty conviction of a boy accused of murdering his father. The struggle behind closed doors is taut, charged, and fascinating. 1957; B&W; 95m.

TWICE IN A LIFETIME ★★★★★
DIR: Bud Yorkin. **CAST:** Gene Hackman, Ann-Margret, Ellen Burstyn, Amy Madigan, Ally Sheedy, Brian Dennehy.

Superior slice-of-life drama about a Washington mill worker (Gene Hackman) who reaches a mid-life crisis and decides that he and wife Ellen Burstyn can't sustain the magic anymore. That decision is helped by a sudden interest in local barmaid Ann-Margret, but the script isn't that simplistic. The cast is uniformly fine, the story poignant without being sugary. Rated R for adult situations. 1985; 111m.

TWO MOON JUNCTION ★½
DIR: Zalman King. **CAST:** Sherilyn Fenn, Richard Tyson, Louise Fletcher, Burl Ives, Kristy McNichol.

Two weeks before her marriage, a young, well-to-do Southern woman falls for a muscular carnival worker. A pattern in their relationship soon develops. They argue, they make love, and then she cries. The film wastes the talents of Louise Fletcher and Burl Ives. Rated R for nudity, profanity, and violence. 1988; 104m.

TWO OF A KIND (1982) ★★★★
DIR: Roger Young. **CAST:** George Burns, Robby Benson, Cliff Robertson, Barbara Barrie, Ronny Cox.

This heartwarming TV film features George Burns as a discarded senior citizen and Robby Benson as his retarded grandson. The two come together when the boy decides to help his seemingly disabled grandpa play golf again. Cliff Robertson and Barbara Barrie play Benson's parents. All in all, this is a fine film with a positive message about family unity. 1982; 102m.

UGLY AMERICAN, THE ★★½
DIR: George Englund. **CAST:** Marlon Brando, Pat Hingle, Sandra Church, Arthur Hill, Eiji Okada, Jocelyn Brando.

With Marlon Brando playing an American ambassador newly arrived at his Asian post, more is expected of this film than just a routine potboiler. However, the film attempts to focus on the political interworkings of Brando's struggle with rising communist elements, but fails to generate any excitement. 1963; 120m.

UN CHIEN ANDALOU ★★★★★
DIR: Luis Buñuel, Salvador Dali.

Possibly the only film ever made completely according to surrealist principles, this famous short consists of a series of shocking and humorous images designed to have no point or connection. Luis Buñuel and Salvador Dali wrote down some of their dreams, selected random incidents from them, and then photographed them. Sixty years later this seventeen-minute film retains the power to startle, with images of an eyeball being slit open by a razor, a hand crawling with ants, and many others, all set to a silly tango score that Buñuel later added. The videotape includes three other avant-garde shorts: *Ballet Mechanique, Regen (Rain), Uberfall,* and *The Hearts of Age,* by 19-year-old Orson Welles—all of interest to the serious cinema student. 1928; B&W; 74m.

UNAPPROACHABLE, THE
DIR: Krzysztof Zanussi. **CAST:** Leslie Caron, Daniel Webb, Leslie Magon.

A completely unwatchable film about a young man obsessed with a reclusive aging starlet. Do not approach this one. Not rated, but contains profanity and adult situations. 1982; 100m.

UNBEARABLE LIGHTNESS OF BEING, THE ★★★★★
DIR: Phil Kaufman. **CAST:** Daniel Day-Lewis, Juliette Binoche, Lena Olin, Derek de Lint, Erland Josephson.

Philip Kaufman's *The Unbearable Lightness of Being* is one of the most playfully alive films ever made. Kaufman calls his film a "variation" of Milan Kundera's novel about Tomas, the womanizing neurosurgeon from Prague. What results is something poetic, erotic, funny, and exuberant. Rated R for sexual content. 1988; 164m.

UNDER CAPRICORN ★★★
DIR: Alfred Hitchcock. **CAST:** Michael Wilding, Ingrid Bergman, Joseph Cotten.

This film is about a nineteenth-century Australian household that is hiding some dark secrets. Michael Wilding is drawn into solving the family's mystery because of his attraction to the lady of the house, Ingrid Bergman. This is not a typical Alfred Hitchcock movie. It lacks his customary suspense, and its pace could be called leisurely at best. 1949; 117m.

UNDER MILK WOOD ★★
DIR: Andrew Sinclair. **CAST:** Elizabeth Taylor, Richard Burton, Peter O'Toole, Glynis Johns, Vivien Merchant, Sian Phillips.

The late, great Welsh poet Dylan Thomas's play loses its charm, vitality, and message in this slow, stuffy, dry, pretentious, image-burdened film version. All the queen's men (Richard Burton and Peter O'Toole), plus the beautiful Elizabeth Taylor, cannot deliver the lusty verve required to infuse it with life. Dull, plodding, murky. A photo buff's picture. 1973; 90m.

UNDER THE CHERRY MOON ★★
DIR: Prince. **CAST:** Prince, Jerome Benton, Steven Berkoff, Alexandra Stewart, Kristin Scott Thomas, Francesca Annis.

Although this film is slow moving, it may appeal to teenagers, especially Prince fans. Prince plays a gigolo-type singer who pursues a debutante, Mary (Kristin Scott Thomas). Mary's greedy father has planned a marriage for Mary that will merge two large fortunes. When Mary realizes her dad is using her, she takes off with Prince. Rated PG for language and mature theme. 1986; B&W; 100m.

UNDER THE SUN ★
DIR: James Sbardellati. **CAST:** Vanessa Williams, Sam Jones, John Russell.

A hotheaded St. Louis cop (Sam Jones) comes to Los Angeles to investigate the murder of his brother, where he runs afoul of the local police (of course!) and a shady saloon owner (veteran John Russell) involved with some stolen plutonium. Former Miss America Vanessa Williams shows that acting is not her strong suit. Rated R for language, violence, and nudity. 1988; 90m.

UNDER THE VOLCANO ★★★★
DIR: John Huston. **CAST:** Albert Finney, Jacqueline Bisset, Anthony Andrews.

Brilliant, but disturbing, adaptation of the Malcolm Lowry novel about a suicidal, alcoholic British consul in Mexico on the eve of World War II. Albert Finney's performance is superb, as is that by co-star Jacqueline Bisset, who plays Finney's wife. Rated R for suggested sex, violence, and profanity. 1984; 109m.

UNDERWORLD U.S.A. ★★★½
DIR: Samuel Fuller. **CAST:** Cliff Robertson, Dolores Dorn.

Impressive crime drama from writer-director Sam Fuller about a man (Cliff Robertson) who, after witnessing his father's death at the hands of mobsters, develops a lifetime obsession to get even with the murderers. Great cinematography and exceptional performances rise above the weak script. 1961; B&W; 99m.

UNHOLY ROLLERS
DIR: Vernon Zimmerman. **CAST:** Claudia Jennings, Louis Quinn, Roberta Collins, Alan Vint.

Searching for something extremely raunchy and cheaply made? If so, look no further. This roller-derby flick will fit the bill. A sexually harassed cannery worker (Claudia Jennings) quits her job to join the Avengers, a tough skating team. Unrated, this has enough profanity, nudity, and simulated sex to make it comparable to an R. 1972; 88m.

UNION CITY ★★★
DIR: Mark Reichert. **CAST:** Deborah Harry, Dennis Lipscomb, Pat Benatar.

Called the "punk rock *film noir*," *Union City* is a quietly disturbing tale of murder and paranoia circa 1953. Deborah Harry (of the rock group Blondie) stars as a bored housewife; Dennis Lipscomb is her high-strung, paranoid husband. The mood, tone, and feel of the film are spooky, though it may be too oblique for some. Rated PG for adult themes and violence. 1980; 87m.

UNMARRIED WOMAN, AN ★★★★★
DIR: Paul Mazursky. **CAST:** Jill Clayburgh, Michael Murphy, Alan Bates, Pat Quinn.

Jill Clayburgh's Erica has settled into a comfortable rut and barely notices it when things begin to go wrong. One day, after lunch with her husband, Martin (Michael Murphy), she is shocked by his sobbing admission that he is in love with another woman. Her world is shattered. This first-rate film concerns itself with her attempts to cope with the situation. Rated R for sex, nudity, and profanity. 1978; 124m.

UNNATURAL CAUSES ★★★★
DIR: Lamont Johnson. **CAST:** John Ritter, Alfre Woodard, Patti LaBelle, John Sayles.

Alfre Woodard stars in this made-for-TV movie about a Veterans Administration counselor who takes up the cause of linking Agent Orange to stricken vets under her care. John Ritter gives a sensitive performance as one of the Vietnam vets. This fact-based story is given maximum impact thanks to the intelligent script of John Sayles. 1986; 100m.

UNSETTLED LAND ★
DIR: Uri Barbash. **CAST:** Kelly McGillis, John Shea.

Israeli-made production concerning a commune of young Jews from Europe establishing a settlement in the Sinai

Desert after World War I. The film chronicles their fears and dreams as they struggle through their first year. Overblown saga that travels already familiar territory. Rated PG for violence. 1987; 109m.

UNTIL SEPTEMBER ★½

DIR: Richard Marquand. **CAST:** Karen Allen, Thierry Lhermitte, Christopher Cazenove.

A midwestern divorcée (Karen Allen) falls in love with a married Parisian banker (Thierry Lhermitte) during the summer vacation in this unabashed soap opera. Rated R. 1984; 95m.

UPTOWN NEW YORK ★★

DIR: Victor Schertzinger. **CAST:** Jack Oakie, Shirley Grey.

Sobby melodrama about a doctor whose family forces him to jilt the girl he loves and marry for money. She bounces into marriage with a bubble gum machine salesman who nobly offers her a divorce when he learns the truth. 1932; B&W; 80m.

URBAN COWBOY ★★★

DIR: James Bridges. **CAST:** John Travolta, Debra Winger, Scott Glenn, Madolyn Smith, Charlie Daniels Band.

The film is a slice-of-life *Saturday Night Fever*–like look at the after-hours life of blue-collar cowboys. Overall, the film works because of excellent directing by James Bridges and the fine acting of John Travolta, Debra Winger, and Scott Glenn. Rated PG. 1980; 132m.

URGE TO KILL ★★★★

DIR: Mike Robe. **CAST:** Karl Malden, Holly Hunter, Alex McArthur, Paul Sorvino, Catherine Mary Stewart, William Devane.

A top-notch cast shines in this drama about a convicted killer who, upon release from a mental institution, comes home to face prejudice and violent recriminations. Well written and acted, the film's focus is on the quality of justice versus the quality of mercy and what people will do to subvert both. Holly Hunter is outstanding as the sister of the murder victim. Not rated, but contains mature themes. 1984; 96m.

USERS, THE ★★

DIR: Joseph Hardy. **CAST:** Jaclyn Smith, Tony Curtis, Joan Fontaine, Red Buttons.

Another bloated TV movie boasts a fine cast and little else. Jaclyn Smith stars as a beautiful girl who plays a major role in the resurgence of a down-and-out movie star's career. Standard "television" production values and "television" dialogue do this one in. 1978; 125m.

VANISHING ACT ★★★½

DIR: David Greene. **CAST:** Mike Farrell, Margot Kidder, Elliott Gould, Fred Gwynne, Graham Jarvis.

A tense psychological drama with a knockout ending. Mike Farrell's wife of one week is missing. He routinely reports this to town cop Elliot Gould. Before the investigation begins, the wife reappears. But there's a catch: Farrell says she's not his wife. Rated PG. 1987; 95m.

VANITY FAIR

DIR: Chester M. Franklin. **CAST:** Myrna Loy, Conway Tearle, Barbara Kent, Anthony Bushell.

Old stories in modern settings can be successful, but in updating Thackeray's classic novel *Vanity Fair*, screenwriter F. Hugh Herbert and director Chester M. Franklin have created a disaster. An unmitigated stinker. 1938; B&W; 78m.

VELVET TOUCH, THE ★★★★½

DIR: John Gage. **CAST:** Rosalind Russell, Leo Genn, Claire Trevor, Leon Ames, Sydney Greenstreet, Frank McHugh, Lex Barker.

This is a marvelous suspense drama featuring Rosalind Russell as a stage actress. In a fit of rage, she kills her jealous producer, a blackmailer. Leo Rosten's screenplay crackles with spirit and polish. 1948; B&W; 97m.

VERDICT, THE ★★★★½
DIR: Sidney Lumet. **CAST:** Paul Newman, James Mason, Charlotte Rampling, Jack Warden.

In this first-rate drama, Paul Newman brilliantly plays an alcoholic Boston lawyer who redeems himself by taking on slick James Mason in a medical malpractice suit. Rated R for profanity and adult situations. 1982; 129m.

VERY EDGE, THE ★★★
DIR: Cyril Frankel. **CAST:** Anne Heywood, Richard Todd, Jack Hedley, Maurice Denham, Patrick Magee.

An ex-model loses the child she is carrying after she is raped. Her trauma puts a strain on her marriage, while her attacker is still on the loose. Effective psychological suspense, marred slightly by a contrived ending. 1963; B&W; 82m.

VICTIM ★★★
DIR: Basil Dearden. **CAST:** Dirk Bogarde, Sylvia Syms, Dennis Price, John Barrie.

One of the first films to deal with homosexuality, this well-made British effort has Dirk Bogarde as a lawyer who risks his job and reputation by confronting a gang of blackmailers who killed his lover. It was daring then, but not now. The story, though, is still interesting. 1961; B&W; 100m.

VIETNAM WAR STORY ★★★★
DIR: Kevin Hook, Georg Stanford Brown, Ray Danton. **CAST:** Eriq La Salle, Nicholas Cascone, Tony Becker.

This is a collection of three outstanding episodes from HBO's short-term series. *The Pass* dramatizes one soldier's reluctance to return to duty. *The Mine* is about an independent soldier's reliance on others when he is trapped on a land mine. *Home* concerns disabled veterans in a hospital. All are heart-wrenching. There are no stars in the cast, but all performances are top-rate. Unrated, but for mature audiences. 1988; 90m.

VIETNAM WAR STORY—PART TWO ★★★★
DIR: Michael Toshiyuki Uno, David Morris, Jack Sholder. **CAST:** Tom Guinee, Cynthia Bain.

Three more segments of the HBO series: *An Old Ghost Walks the Earth*; *R&R* and *The Flagging*. Unrated, but for mature audiences. 1988; 90m.

VIOLETS ARE BLUE ★★★½
DIR: Jack Fisk. **CAST:** Sissy Spacek, Kevin Kline, Bonnie Bedelia, Augusta Dabney.

In this watchable screen soap opera, former high-school sweethearts Sissy Spacek and Kevin Kline are reunited when she, a successful photojournalist, returns to her hometown. Their romance is rekindled although he is now married (to Bonnie Bedelia, who is terrific in her all-too-brief onscreen bits) and has a 13-year-old son. Rated PG for suggested sex and light profanity. 1986; 89m.

VIRGIN AND THE GYPSY, THE ★★★½
DIR: Christopher Miles. **CAST:** Franco Nero, Joanna Shimkus, Honor Blackman, Mark Burns, Maurice Denham.

The title tells the tale in this stylish, effective screen adaptation of the D. H. Lawrence novella. Franco Nero and Joanna Shimkus exude sexual tension as the gypsy and his love, a minister's daughter. Rated R for nudity. 1970; 95m.

VIRGIN QUEEN, THE ★★★
DIR: Henry Koster. **CAST:** Bette Davis, Richard Todd, Joan Collins, Herbert Marshall.

Bette Davis reprises her memorable 1939 *Elizabeth and Essex* portrayal of Elizabeth I of England in this rehashing of majestic might and young love. This time around the queen dotes on Sir Walter Raleigh, who crosses her up, but survives to sail away to happiness. A fine example of Hollywood film history. 1955; 92m.

VIRGIN SOLDIERS, THE ★★★★
DIR: John Dexter. **CAST:** Hywel Bennett, Nigel Patrick, Lynn Redgrave, Nigel Davenport.
This outstanding drama of young British recruits in 1950 Singapore has some great performances. Hywel Bennett is one of the recruits who is as green with his first sexual encounter as he is on the battlefield. 1969; 96m.

VISION QUEST ★★★½
DIR: Harold Becker. **CAST:** Matthew Modine, Linda Fiorentino, Michael Schoeffling, Ronny Cox, Harold Sylvester.
Here's yet another movie in which a young athlete makes good against all odds. If you can get past the familiarity of the plot, it isn't bad. It benefits particularly from a charismatic lead performance by Matthew Modine. Rated R for nudity, suggested sex, violence, and profanity. 1985; 96m.

VIVA ZAPATA! ★★★★½
DIR: Elia Kazan. **CAST:** Marlon Brando, Anthony Quinn, Jean Peters, Joseph Wiseman.
This film chonicles Mexican revolutionary leader Emiliano Zapata from his peasant upbringing until his death as a weary, disillusioned political liability. Marlon Brando won an Oscar nomination for his insightful portrayal of Zapata. Anthony Quinn, as Zapata's brother, did manage to hold his own against the powerful Brando characterization and was rewarded with a supporting actor Oscar. 1952; B&W; 113m.

VOICES ★★★
DIR: Robert Markowitz. **CAST:** Amy Irving, Michael Ontkean, Herbert Berghof, Viveca Lindfors.
A sentimental love story that manages to maintain a sensitive tone that ultimately proves infectious. Amy Irving stars as a deaf young woman who wants to become a dancer; Michael Ontkean is a young man who would rather be a singer. They meet, fall in love. The material is sugary, but Irving and Ontkean make it work. Rated PG for language and adult themes. 1979; 107m.

VOYAGE OF THE DAMNED ★★★★
DIR: Stuart Rosenberg. **CAST:** Oskar Werner, Faye Dunaway, Max von Sydow, Orson Welles, Malcolm McDowell, James Mason, Julie Harris, Lee Grant.
This fine drama takes place in 1939 as a shipload of Jewish refugees are refused refuge in Havana and are forced to return to Germany for certain imprisonment or death. Rated PG. 1976; 134m.

WAITING FOR THE MOON ★★
DIR: Jill Godmilow. **CAST:** Linda Hunt, Linda Bassett, Bruce McGill, Andrew McCarthy, Bernadette Lafont.
Linda Hunt is Alice B. Toklas and Linda Bassett is Gertrude Stein in this idiosyncratic, self-indulgent, and frustrating film. The stars' performances are fine, but the impressionistic style of cowriter-director Jill Godmilow, who plays with the sequence of events in a way that will thoroughly confuse most viewers, tends to be more irritating than artistic. Rated PG-13 for profanity and adult themes. 1987; 88m.

WALK IN THE SPRING RAIN, A ★★½
DIR: Guy Green. **CAST:** Anthony Quinn, Ingrid Bergman, Fritz Weaver, Katherine Crawford.
Two well-into-middle-age people find romance while on vacation in the country. Their problem is that both are married to other people. Average soap opera, but from such a fine cast you expect more. Rated PG. 1970; 100m.

WALK ON THE WILD SIDE ★★
DIR: Edward Dmytryk. **CAST:** Laurence Harvey, Jane Fonda, Capucine, Barbara Stanwyck, Anne Baxter.
Trashy tale of a young man's attempt to find his girlfriend, only to discover she's working in a New Orleans

brothel. Extremely slow-paced film wastes a first-rate cast and a great musical score by Elmer Bernstein. For lovers of soap operas only. 1962; B&W; 114m.

WALKER ★★★
DIR: Alex Cox. **CAST:** Ed Harris, Richard Masur, René Auberjonois, Marlee Matlin, Sy Richardson, Peter Boyle.
This true story of William Walker and his takeover of Nicaragua in 1855 in the name of U.S. democracy is mixed with modern elements and satire by director Alex Cox. Ed Harris has a great time with the broad character of Walker and makes clear that power corrupts. For those with a taste for something out of the ordinary, *Walker* is worth viewing. Rated R for language nudity, and simulated sex. 1988; 98m.

WALL STREET ★★★★
DIR: Oliver Stone. **CAST:** Michael Douglas, Charlie Sheen, Daryl Hannah, Martin Sheen, Terence Stamp, Sean Young, Hal Holbrook, James Spader.
The same energy and insight that propelled writer-director Oliver Stone's Oscar-winning *Platoon* helps make this look at double-dealing in the stock market much more entertaining than one would expect. Chief among its pleasures is Michael Douglas's deliciously evil character of Gordon Gekko, a hotshot financier who takes novice Bud Fox (Charlie Sheen) under his wing and quickly corrupts him. Rated R for profanity, nudity and violence. 1987; 120m.

WALLS OF GLASS ★★★½
DIR: Scott Goldstein. **CAST:** Philip Bosco, Geraldine Page, Olympia Dukakis, William Hickey.
A New York cab driver who aspires to be an actor exposes us to the many characters of his life: his gambling family, his troubled youth, and the colorful customers in his cab. A truly warm and insightful drama with a bravura performance by Philip Bosco. Rated R for language. 1988; 85m.

WANDERERS, THE ★★★★
DIR: Phil Kaufman. **CAST:** Ken Wahl, John Friedrich, Karen Allen, Tony Ganios.
This enjoyable film is set in the early 1960s and focuses on the world of teenagers. Though it has ample amounts of comedy and excitement, because it deals with life on the streets of the Bronx there is an atmosphere of ever-present danger and fear. The Wanderers are a gang of Italian-American youths who have banded together for safety and good times. Rated R. 1979; 113m.

WAR AND PEACE (1956) ★★½
DIR: King Vidor. **CAST:** Henry Fonda, Audrey Hepburn, Mel Ferrer, John Mills.
Mammoth international effort to film this classic novel results in an overlong, unevenly constructed melodrama. The massive battle scenes and outdoor panoramas are truly impressive, as are the performers on occasion. But the whole production seems to swallow up the principals and the action, leaving a rather lifeless film. 1956; 208m.

WAR LOVER, THE ★★½
DIR: Philip Leacock. **CAST:** Steve McQueen, Robert Wagner, Shirley Anne Field.
This is a very slow-moving account of pilots (Steve McQueen and Robert Wagner) in England during World War II. Both pilots are seeking the affections of the same woman. Nothing in the film raises it above the level of mediocrity. 1962; B&W; 105m.

WASH, THE ★★★
DIR: Michael Toshiyuki Uno. **CAST:** Mako, Nobu McCarthy.
A straightforward story of a fading marriage and the rekindling of love, unusual for the advanced age of its characters and the film's offbeat setting among Asian-Americans in California. The talented Mako is memorable as a gruff, seemingly

unaffectionate retiree who can't understand why his wife (Nobu McCarthy) wants a separation. Rated PG. 1988; 100m.

WASHINGTON AFFAIR, THE ★★★

DIR: Victor Stoloff. **CAST:** Tom Selleck, Barry Sullivan, Carol Lynley.

Jim Hawley (Tom Selleck) is an incorruptible federal agent who must award a government contract. Walter Nicholson (Barry Sullivan) is a wheeler-dealer who tries to blackmail Hawley into giving him the contract. There are enough surprises in this film to keep most viewers on the edge of their couch. Rated R for simulated sex. 1977; 104m.

WATCH ON THE RHINE ★★★★

DIR: Herman Shumlin. **CAST:** Paul Lukas, Bette Davis, Geraldine Fitzgerald.

Lillian Hellman's expose of Nazi terrorism was brought from Broadway to the screen in first-rate form. Paul Lukas won a best-actor Oscar for his role of an underground leader who fled Germany for the U.S., only to be hunted down by Nazi agents. Bette Davis is wonderful in what was one of her few small supporting roles. 1943; B&W; 114m.

WATERFRONT ★★

DIR: Steve Sekely. **CAST:** John Carradine, J. Carrol Naish, Terry Frost.

Classic film villains John Carradine and J. Carrol Naish are properly menacing as Nazi spies who try to convert German-Americans to their cause in this low-budget wartime espionage drama. Uninspired. 1944; B&W; 68m.

WATERLOO BRIDGE ★★★★

DIR: Mervyn LeRoy. **CAST:** Vivien Leigh, Robert Taylor, Lucile Watson.

A five-hanky romance about the lives of two people caught up in the turmoil of World War II. This is a poignant tale of a beautiful ballerina (Vivien Leigh) who falls in love with a British officer (Robert Taylor) and how her life is altered when he leaves for the battlefields of Europe. This is one of Leigh's best performances, although she rarely gave a bad one. 1941; B&W; 103m.

WAY DOWN EAST ★★★

DIR: D. W. Griffith. **CAST:** Lillian Gish, Richard Barthelmess, Lowell Sherman.

Classic story of a young woman ostracized by her family and community for moral reasons was an audience favorite of the early part of this century but old hat even by 1920, when this melodrama was released. Justly famous for the exciting and dangerous flight of the beautiful Lillian Gish across the ice floes, pursued and eventually rescued by stalwart yet sensitive Richard Barthelmess, this was one of classic director D. W. Griffith's best-remembered films, but was also one of his last solid critical and commercial blockbusters. Silent. 1920; B&W; 119m.

WAY WE WERE, THE ★★★½

DIR: Sydney Pollack. **CAST:** Barbra Streisand, Robert Redford, Patrick O'Neal, Viveca Lindfors, Bradford Dillman, Lois Chiles.

The popular theme song somewhat obscures the fact that this is a rather slow-moving romance about a Jewish girl (Barbra Streisand) who marries a WASPish writer (Robert Redford). The film has its moments, but a portion dealing with the McCarthy communist witch hunt falls flat. Rated PG. 1973; 118m.

WEDDING IN WHITE ★½

DIR: William Fruet. **CAST:** Donald Pleasence, Carol Kane, Doris Petrie.

It's World War II and Carol Kane is the young naïve daughter of an authoritative father who only shows affection for his son. When Kane becomes pregnant as a result of being raped by her brother's soldier friend, her father sets out to maintain the family honor by destroying his daughter's future. *Wedding in White* is a study of the effects of intolerance that stem from sexual double standards and male pride. The film succeeds in making you feel outrage, but is bleak from beginning to end. 1972; 103m.

WEDDING MARCH, THE ★★★½
DIR: Erich Von Stroheim. **CAST:** Erich Von Stroheim, Fay Wray, ZaSu Pitts, George Fawcett.
The story is simple: the corrupt, money-hungry family of an Austrian prince forces him to forsake his true love, a penniless musician, and marry a dull, crippled heiress. The telling is incredibly overblown and long beyond belief. Critics and big-city audiences acclaimed this film, but it laid eggs by the gross in the hinterlands. Silent. 1928; B&W; 140m.

WEEDS ★★★
DIR: John Hancock. **CAST:** Nick Nolte, Lane Smith, William Forsythe, Joe Mantegna, Ernie Hudson.
Nick Nolte gives one of his finest performances in this uneven but generally rewarding film as a San Quentin inmate doing "life without possibility" until he secures his release by writing a play that impresses a reporter. Rated R for profanity, nudity, and violence. 1987; 115m.

WELCOME TO L.A. ★★★½
DIR: Alan Rudolph. **CAST:** Keith Carradine, Geraldine Chaplin, Harvey Keitel, Sally Kellerman, Sissy Spacek, Lauren Hutton.
Extremely well made film concerning the disjointed love lives of several of Los Angeles's nouveaux riche. The film's focal point is songwriter Keith Carradine, whose romantic interludes set the wheels in motion. Entire cast is first-rate, with Richard Baskin's musical score the only drawback. Rated R. 1977; 106m.

WETHERBY ★★½
DIR: David Hare. **CAST:** Vanessa Redgrave, Ian Holm, Judi Dench, Marjorie Yates, Joely Richardson, Tom Wilkinson, Stuart Wilson.
Buried under *Wetherby*'s dismally portentous attitudes about England and loneliness is a pretty interesting story. The film unfolds like a thriller, but it doesn't satisfy in the end. Vanessa Redgrave in the lead is characteristically excellent. 1985; 104m.

WHALE FOR THE KILLING, A ★★★
DIR: Richard T. Heffron. **CAST:** Peter Strauss, Richard Widmark, Dee Wallace, Kathryn Walker, Bruce McGill.
Peter Strauss's dramatic, powerful personal statement against the slaughter of whales off the rugged coast of Newfoundland. Based on Canadian environmentalist–nature writer Farley Mowat's noted book indicting the practice. Overlong, but engrossing, TV movie. 1981; 150m.

WHALES OF AUGUST, THE ★★★
DIR: Lindsay Anderson. **CAST:** Bette Davis, Lillian Gish, Vincent Price, Ann Sothern, Harry Carey Jr., Mary Steenburgen.
The joy of seeing two screen legends, Bette Davis and Lillian Gish, together in a film tailor-made for them is considerably muted by the uneventfulness of playwright David Barry's story. Essentially, we watch Davis and Gish play two elderly sisters who cope, bicker, and reminisce at their summer home on an island off the coast of Maine. Rated PG for profanity. 1987; 90m.

WHAT COMES AROUND ★★
DIR: Jerry Reed. **CAST:** Jerry Reed, Bo Hopkins, Barry Corbin, Arte Johnson.
Jerry Reed stars as a world-famous country-western singer who is strung out on booze and pills. Bo Hopkins plays the younger brother who kidnaps Reed to save him from his own self-destruction. This all-American action-comedy-drama features the country music of Jerry Reed. A must-see for his fans. Rated PG. 1985; 92m.

WHAT PRICE HOLLYWOOD? ★★★★
DIR: George Cukor. **CAST:** Constance Bennett, Lowell Sherman, Neil Hamilton, Gregory Ratoff.

This first production of *A Star Is Born* packs the same punch as the two more famous versions and showcases Constance Bennett as a tough but tender girl who wants to reach the top. Lowell Sherman plays the man with the connections who starts Constance on her way, but who eventually becomes a hindrance to her. Bennett seems somehow less martyred and long-suffering than either Janet Gaynor or Judy Garland, and that gives this version an edge that the others lack. 1932; B&W; 88m.

WHEN WOLVES CRY ★
DIR: Terence Young. **CAST:** William Holden, Virna Lisi, Brook Fuller, Bourvil.

Poorly directed melodrama about a 10-year-old boy, Pascal, who is diagnosed as being terminally ill. His father, Laurent (William Holden), dedicates himself to indulging his son's every whim—including stealing two wild wolves from the Paris zoo. Originally titled *The Christmas Tree*. Rated G. 1983; 108m.

WHEN YOUR LOVER LEAVES
DIR: Jeff Bleckner. **CAST:** Valerie Perrine, Betty Thomas, David Ackroyd, Edward O'Neill, Dwight Schultz.

Valerie Perrine plays the other woman who's just lost out to her lover's wife. She proceeds to fall apart, making herself a selfish burden for those around her. Hideous TV movie. 1983; 96m.

WHITE LEGION ★★
DIR: Karl Brown. **CAST:** Ian Keith, Tala Birell, Snub Pollard.

The White Legion were doctors who fought to find a cure for the yellow fever that plagued workers building the Panama Canal. Unfortunately, their story doesn't make for much of a movie; it's artificially padded with melodramatic situations. 1936; B&W; 81m.

WHITE MAMA ★★★
DIR: Jackie Cooper. **CAST:** Bette Davis, Ernest Harden, Eileen Heckart, Lurene Tuttle, Virginia Capers.

Aging widow Bette Davis, living on a shoestring in a condemned tenement, is befriended by streetwise black (Ernest Harden) and becomes the mother he can't remember when she provides him with a home in return for protection. A good story, touchingly told. Made for TV. 1980; 105m.

WHITE MISCHIEF ★★½
DIR: Michael Radford. **CAST:** Charles Dance, Sarah Miles, Greta Scacchi, John Hurt, Joss Ackland.

In the early Forties while Britain was being pounded to rubble by German bombs, a group of wealthy colonials carried on with alcohol, drugs, and spouse swapping in Kenya as if there were no tomorrow—and no England. A stunning backdrop—complete with giraffes roaming in the backyards of opulent mansions—is the film's greatest asset. But James Fox's script is flat. Rated R for language and explicit sex scenes. 1987; 100m.

WHITE NIGHTS ★★★½
DIR: Taylor Hackford. **CAST:** Mikhail Baryshnikov, Gregory Hines, Geraldine Page, Jerzy Skolimowski, Isabella Rossellini.

Russian defector and ballet star Mikhail Baryshnikov, finding himself back in the U.S.S.R., joins forces with American defector Gregory Hines to escape to freedom in this soap opera–styled thriller. The plot is contrived, but the dance sequences featuring the two stars together and separately are spectacular. Rated PG-13 for violence and profanity. 1985; 135m.

WHITE TOWER, THE ★★½
DIR: Ted Tetzlaff. **CAST:** Glenn Ford, Claude Rains, Alida Valli, Oscar Homolka, Cedric Hardwicke, Lloyd Bridges.

Symbolic melodrama of a weird group of people who attempt the ascension of an Alpine mountain. The action scenes are good, but the actors seem to walk through their parts. 1950; 98m.

WHO IS THE BLACK DAHLIA? ★★★★

DIR: Joseph Pevney. **CAST:** Lucie Arnaz, Efrem Zimbalist Jr., Ronny Cox, MacDonald Carey, Gloria De Haven, Tom Bosley, Mercedes McCambridge, Donna Mills, June Lockhart.

An above-average semidocumentary crime drama based on one of the Los Angeles Police Department's most famous unsolved cases: the 1947 murder and gruesome dissection of a mysterious young woman whose lifestyle and mode of dress earned her the nickname of Black Dahlia. An excellent cast performs a first-rate script in this gripping telemovie. 1975; 100m.

WHO'S AFRAID OF VIRGINIA WOOLF? ★★★★★

DIR: Mike Nichols. **CAST:** Elizabeth Taylor, Richard Burton, Sandy Dennis, George Segal.

Edward Albee's powerful play about the love-hate relationship of a college professor and his bitchy wife was brilliantly transferred to the screen by director Mike Nichols. Elizabeth Taylor gives one of her best acting performances as Martha, a screeching bitch caught in an unfulfilled marriage. Richard Burton is equally stunning as the quiet, authoritative professor who must decide between abandoning or salvaging their marriage after a night of bitter recriminations and painful revelations. 1966; B&W; 129m.

WHOSE CHILD AM I?

DIR: Lawrence Britten. **CAST:** Kate O'Mara, Paul Freeman, Edward Judd.

Artificial insemination is the pitiful excuse for this ridiculously sordid film. A woman whose husband is sterile tries both real and artificial means of impregnation. This low-budget time-waster is unrated but comparable with an X. 1974; 90m.

WHOSE LIFE IS IT, ANYWAY? ★★★★

DIR: John Badham. **CAST:** Richard Dreyfuss, John Cassavetes, Christine Lahti, Bob Balaban, Kenneth McMillan, Kaki Hunter, Janet Eilber.

Richard Dreyfuss is superb as a witty and intellectually dynamic sculptor who is paralyzed after an auto accident and fights for his right to be left alone to die. John Cassavetes and Christine Lahti co-star as doctors in this surprisingly upbeat movie. Rated R. 1981; 118m.

WHY SHOOT THE TEACHER? ★★★

DIR: Silvio Narizzano. **CAST:** Bud Cort, Samantha Eggar, Chris Wiggins, Gary Reineke.

Bud Cort stars in this intimate and simple film about a young instructor whose first teaching position lands him in the barren plains of Canada. Lean realism and bright dashes of humor give the picture some memorable moments, but this story of an outsider trying to adapt to the lifestyle of an isolated community develops with a disengaging slowness. Rated PG. 1977; 101m.

WICKED LADY, THE (1945) ★★

DIR: Leslie Arliss. **CAST:** Margaret Lockwood, James Mason, Patricia Roc, Michael Rennie, Martita Hunt.

Margaret Lockwood's scruples dip as low as her neckline in this somewhat tedious period piece about a vixen who masquerades as an outlaw. James Mason is appropriately evil as her companion in crime. 1945; B&W; 104m.

WILBY CONSPIRACY, THE ★★★½

DIR: Ralph Nelson. **CAST:** Michael Caine, Sidney Poitier, Nicol Williamson.

This underappreciated political thriller tackled the issue of apartheid years before its worldwide recognition as a serious problem. Michael Caine stars as an apolitical Brit who gains social consciousness after encountering an idealistic revolutionary (Sidney Poitier). Somewhat implausible, but entertaining nonetheless. Rated PG. 1975; 104m.

WILD DUCK, THE ★★½
DIR: Henri Safran. **CAST:** Liv Ullmann, Jeremy Irons, Lucinda Jones, Arthur Dignam, John Meillon, Michael Pate.
Despite the cast, or maybe because of it, this poignant story of love and tragedy falls short of its ambitious mark. Jeremy Irons and Liv Ullmann are struggling parents whose child is slowly going blind. An idealistic friend (Arthur Dignam) complicates matters by unearthing truths that were better off buried. Rated PG for profanity. 1983; 96m.

WILD GUITAR
DIR: Ray Dennis Steckler. **CAST:** Arch Hall Jr., Nancy Czar, William Watters (Arch Hall Sr.), Cash Flagg (Ray Dennis Steckler).
An exploitative record company gets their comeuppance from hell-raising Arch Hall Jr., a motorcycle-riding rock 'n' roller who sings up a storm on cue and couldn't act if his life depended on it. Incredibly bad, this film and others of its ilk still have a unique charm because of the sheer audacity displayed by barely talented people. 1962; 87m.

WILD IN THE COUNTRY ★★★
DIR: Philip Dunne. **CAST:** Elvis Presley, Hope Lange, Tuesday Weld, Millie Perkins, John Ireland.
Elvis Presley is encouraged to pursue a literary career when counseled during his wayward youth. Most viewers will find it interesting to see Elvis in such a serious role. The supporting cast also has something to add to the okay script. 1961; 114m.

WILD ORCHIDS ★★★
DIR: Sidney Franklin. **CAST:** Greta Garbo, Lewis Stone, Nils Asther.
A young Greta Garbo is the highlight of this familiar story of tropic love. Plantation owner Lewis Stone busies himself with overseeing his property in Java, but local prince Nils Asther finds himself overseeing the owner's wife and the usual complications ensue. Silent. 1928; B&W; 103m.

WILD PARTY, THE ★★★½
DIR: James Ivory. **CAST:** James Coco, Raquel Welch, Perry King, David Dukes.
This is a very grim look at how Hollywood treats its fading stars. James Coco plays a one-time comedy star trying to come back with a hit film. Raquel Welch plays Coco's longtime girlfriend who plans a party for Hollywood's elite in order to push his film. The film is based on the career of Fatty Arbuckle and provides some interesting insights into the Hollywood power structure. Rated R. 1975; 107m.

WILD RIDE, THE ★
DIR: Harvey Berman. **CAST:** Jack Nicholson, Robert Bean.
Abysmal low-budget film featuring Jack Nicholson as a hedonistic hotrodder who casually kills people. Unless you're curious about early Nicholson, this inept movie should be avoided. 1960; B&W; 63m.

WILD ROSE ★★
DIR: John Hanson. **CAST:** Lisa Eichhorn, Tom Bower.
This low-budget film, shot in and around the Wisconsin coal mine fields, floats between being a love story and a social commentary on mining conditions. By trying to cover all the bases, writer-director John Hanson fails to cover even one satisfactorily. 1984; 96m.

WILL, G. GORDON LIDDY ★★★½
DIR: Robert Leiberman. **CAST:** Robert Conrad, Katherine Cannon, Gary Bayer, James Rebhorn.
Robert Conrad is transformed into the fanatic, strong-willed Watergate mastermind Liddy. The first half lacks excitement or revelation for viewers who remember the Watergate scandal. Liddy's stay in prison, however, is a fascinating study. 1982; 100m.

WILMA ★★½
DIR: Bud Greenspan. **CAST:** Cicely Tyson, Shirley Jo Finney, Joe Seneca, Jason Bernard.

This made-for-TV film chronicles the early years of Olympic star Wilma Rudolph (Cicely Tyson) and follows her career up to her winning the gold. Film fails to do justice to its subject matter. Lackluster production. 1977; 100m.

WIND, THE (1928) ★★★★
DIR: Victor Sjöström. **CAST:** Lillian Gish, Lars Hanson, Montague Love.

A gentle girl marries a brutish farmhand in order to escape from relatives who do not understand her sensitive nature. She finds no peace. As the girl, Lillian Gish joined Victor Seastrom (né Sjöström) in scoring an artistic triumph. An incredible film. Silent. 1928; B&W; 82m.

WINDOM'S WAY ★★★
DIR: Ronald Neame. **CAST:** Peter Finch, Mary Ure, Natasha Parry, Robert Flemyng, Michael Hordern, Marne Maitland, Gregoire Aslan.

In this British drama set on an island in the Far East, a struggle ensues between the natives and plantation owners over civil rights. A doctor (Peter Finch) is enlisted as the spokesperson for the natives. Set against the backdrop of World War II, *Windom's Way* is enjoyable entertainment. 1957; 104m.

WINDS OF JARRAH, THE ★★
DIR: Mark Egerton. **CAST:** Terence Donovan, Sue Lyon, Harold Hopkins.

At the close of World War II, an Englishwoman on the rebound from a bad love affair takes a position in Australia as a nanny. Her employer is a bitter, lonely man who hates women because his mother ran out on his father when he was a child. Readers of paperback romances will guess what happens within the first two minutes, and the rest of the audience won't be far behind. Not rated. 1983; 78m.

WINDS OF KITTY HAWK, THE ★★★★
DIR: E. W. Swackhamer. **CAST:** Michael Moriarty, David Huffman, Kathryn Walker.

This made-for-TV movie is beautifully photographed, quietly acted and gives a wonderful insight into the lives of the Wright brothers and the period in which they lived. A treat for the entire family. 1978; 100m.

WINDY CITY ★★
DIR: Armyan Bernstein. **CAST:** John Shea, Kate Capshaw, Josh Mostel, Jeffrey DeMunn, Lewis J. Stadlen, James Sutorius.

Very uneven, very frustrating attempt to chronicle the story of a group of young adults who have known one another since they were kids. Told through the eyes of one of their own, a writer (John Shea), it has the feel of being based on real-life experiences but is embarrassingly true to some of the more rude and off-putting behavior most people would rather have private memories of. Rated R. 1984; 103m.

WINSLOW BOY, THE ★★★★
DIR: Anthony Asquith. **CAST:** Robert Donat, Margaret Leighton, Cedric Hardwicke, Basil Radford, Frank Lawton, Wilfrid Hyde-White, Neil North.

Robert Donat is superb as the proper British barrister defending a young naval cadet, wrongly accused of theft, against the overbearing pomp and indifferent might of the Crown. At stake in this tense Edwardian courtroom melodrama is the long-cherished and maintained democratic right to be regarded as innocent until proven guilty by a fair trial. Based on an actual 1912 case. 1950; B&W; 118m.

WINTER KILLS ★★★★
DIR: William Richert. **CAST:** Jeff Bridges, John Huston, Belinda Bauer, Richard Boone, Anthony Perkins, Toshiro Mifune, Sterling Hayden, Eli Wallach, Ralph Meeker, Dorothy Malone, Tomas Milian, Elizabeth Taylor.

An all-star cast is featured in this sometimes melodramatic, but often wry, account of a presidential assassination. Rated R. 1979; 97m.

WINTER OF OUR DREAMS ★★
DIR: John Duigan. **CAST:** Judy Davis, Bryan Brown, Cathy Downes.

An all-too-typical soaper about a married man (Bryan Brown) who tries to help a lost soul (Judy Davis). This downbeat film has good acting but less-than-adequate direction. Rated R. 1981; 90m.

WINTER PEOPLE ★★★½
DIR: Ted Kotcheff. **CAST:** Kurt Russell, Kelly McGillis, Lloyd Bridges, Mitchell Ryan.

Kelly McGillis's outstanding performance in this drama elevates what is essentially a Hatfields-and-McCoys rehash. Kurt Russell stars as a clockmaker in the Depression who leaves his hometown to find work and ends up in the Blue Ridge Mountains, where unwed mother McGillis is about to stir up the feudin' locals. Somehow, director Ted Kotcheff and his cast help us forget how silly *Winter People* is for most of its running time. Rated PG-13 for violence. 1989; 110m.

WINTERSET ★★½
DIR: Alfred Santell. **CAST:** Burgess Meredith, Margo, Eduardo Ciannelli, John Carradine, Paul Guilfoyle, Stanley Ridges, Mischa Auer.

Heavy-duty drama of a bitter young man's efforts to clear his father's name lacks the punch it must have possessed as a top stage play in the 1930s but boasts a great cast of distinguished character actors and marks the screen debut of the versatile Burgess Meredith. Long on moralizing and short on action. 1936; B&W; 78m.

WISE BLOOD ★★★★
DIR: John Huston. **CAST:** Brad Dourif, Harry Dean Stanton, Ned Beatty, Amy Wright, Dan Shor.

While there are many laughs in this fascinating black comedy about a slow-witted country boy (Brad Dourif) who decides to become a man of the world, they tend to stick in your throat. This searing satire on southern do-it-yourself religion comes so close to the truth, it is almost painful to watch at times. Rated PG. 1979; 108m.

WITHOUT A TRACE ★★★
DIR: Stanley Jaffe. **CAST:** Kate Nelligan, Judd Hirsch, David Dukes, Stockard Channing, Jacqueline Brooks, Kathleen Widdoes.

A drama about a boy who vanishes and his mother's unrelenting faith that he will return, this is yet another entry in the family-in-trouble movie genre. If you didn't get your fill of that from *Kramer vs. Kramer*, *Ordinary People*, *Shoot the Moon*, and the rest, you might enjoy this well-acted but sometimes overwrought and predictable film. Rated PG for mature content. 1983; 120m.

WITNESS FOR THE PROSECUTION (1957) ★★★★★
DIR: Billy Wilder. **CAST:** Tyrone Power, Charles Laughton, Marlene Dietrich, Elsa Lanchester, John Williams, Henry Daniell, Una O'Connor.

Superb performances help make this gripping courtroom drama an enduring favorite of film buffs. The screenplay was adapted from a play by Agatha Christie and features Laughton as an aging lawyer called upon to defend an alleged murderer (Power). It is Dietrich, in one of her greatest screen performances, who nearly steals the show. 1957; B&W; 114m.

WITNESS FOR THE PROSECUTION (1982) ★★★
DIR: Alan Gibson. **CAST:** Ralph Richardson, Beau Bridges, Diana Rigg, Deborah Kerr.

An enjoyable made-for-television remake of Agatha Christie's courtroom drama that director Billy Wilder fashioned into a screen classic in 1957. Ralph Richardson and Deborah Kerr are adequate as the wily yet ailing barrister and his continually frustrated nurse. Unfortunately, they lack the rich humor brought to the roles by

Charles Laughton and Elsa Lanchester in the original. Beau Bridges is particularly outstanding as the defendant. 1982; 100m.

WOMAN CALLED GOLDA, A ★★★½

DIR: Alan Gibson. **CAST:** Ingrid Bergman, Judy Davis, Leonard Nimoy.

Ingrid Bergman won an Emmy for her outstanding performance as Israeli Prime Minister Golda Meir. Leonard Nimoy co-stars in this highly watchable film, which was originally made for TV. 1982; 200m.

WOMAN OF PARIS, A ★★★★

DIR: Charles Chaplin. **CAST:** Edna Purviance, Adolphe Menjou, Henry Bergman.

In this now-classic silent, a simple country girl (Edna Purviance) goes to Paris and becomes the mistress of a wealthy philanderer (Adolphe Menjou). In her wake follow her artist sweetheart and his mother. Director Charles Chaplin surprised everyone with this film by suddenly forsaking, if only momentarily, his Little Tramp comedy for serious caustic drama. 1923; B&W; 112m.

WOMAN OF SUBSTANCE, A ★★★½

DIR: Don Sharp. **CAST:** Jenny Seagrove, Deborah Kerr, Barry Bostwick, John Mills, Barry Morse.

This TV mini-series retells Barbara Taylor Bradford's bestselling novel of love and revenge. Multimillionairess Emma Hart (Deborah Kerr) recalls her humble beginnings as a poor servant girl (Jenny Seagrove). Due to the length of this film it's broken down into three volumes (tapes). Volume I ("A Nest of Vipers") finds young Emma employed by the wealthy Fairleys. Volume II ("Fighting for the Dream") centers around Emma's struggle to survive in a new city, building a business for herself. In the final volume ("The Secret Is Revealed"), Emma finds the love of her life. Overall, this is fine entertainment. 1984; 300m.

WOMAN REBELS, A ★★★★

DIR: Mark Sandrich. **CAST:** Katharine Hepburn, Herbert Marshall, Donald Crisp, Elizabeth Allan, Van Heflin.

Surprisingly valid today despite its 1936 vintage. Katharine Hepburn plays a rebellious woman of Victorian England who flaunts convention and becomes a fighter for women's rights. Van Heflin makes his film debut. 1936; B&W; 88m.

WOMAN TIMES SEVEN ★★

DIR: Vittorio De Sica. **CAST:** Shirley MacLaine, Peter Sellers, Alan Arkin, Rossano Brazzi, Robert Morley, Michael Caine, Vittorio Gassman, Anita Ekberg.

Shirley MacLaine assays seven different roles in this episodic stew and is not as good as she could have been in any of them—even when playing opposite Peter Sellers and Michael Caine. There are some funny moments, but they do not a film make. 1967; 99m.

WOMAN'S FACE, A ★★★½

DIR: George Cukor. **CAST:** Joan Crawford, Conrad Veidt, Melvyn Douglas, Osa Massen, Reginald Owen, Albert Basserman, Marjorie Main, Charles Quigley, Henry Daniell, George Zucco, Robert Warwick.

Joan Crawford is the heroine accused of villain Conrad Veidt's murder. Her personality undergoes an amazing transformation following plastic surgery in this taut, strongly plotted melodrama. 1941; B&W; 105m.

WOMEN IN LOVE ★★★★½

DIR: Ken Russell. **CAST:** Glenda Jackson, Oliver Reed, Alan Bates, Eleanor Bron, Jennie Linden, Alan Webb.

Glenda Jackson won an Oscar for her performance in this British film. Two love affairs are followed simultaneously in this excellent adaptation of D. H. Lawrence's novel. Rated R. 1970; B&W; 129m.

WOMEN OF VALOR ★★½

DIR: Buzz Kulik. **CAST:** Susan Sarandon, Kristy McNichol, Alberta Watson, Valerie Mahaffey.

This made-for-television feature about a group of army nurses who are captured by the invading Japanese in the Philippines of early World War II is merely average. The script and direction are off-base, but the stars raise it up a notch. 1986; 100m.

WOODEN HORSE, THE ★★★
DIR: Jack Lee. **CAST:** Leo Genn, David Tomlinson, Anthony Steel, Peter Finch.

Good casting and taut direction make this tale of British POWs tunneling out of a Nazi prison camp well worth watching. Made when memories were fresh, the film glows with reality as English cunning, grit, and timing vie with Nazi suspicion, assumed superiority, and complacency. 1950; B&W; 101m.

WORD, THE ★★★
DIR: Richard Lang. **CAST:** David Janssen, John Huston, James Whitmore.

In a catacomb beneath Ostia, Italy, an archeologist discovers an ancient manuscript that could cause chaos in the Christian world. The manuscript is said to contain the writings of Christ's younger brother, James the Just. The writings contain heretofore unknown fragments of Jesus's life and death. A good story, with wonderful actors. Unrated. 1978; 188m.

WORKING GIRLS ★★★★
DIR: Lizzie Borden. **CAST:** Louise Smith, Ellen McElduff.

The sex in this feminist docudrama about prostitution is about as appealing as the smell of dirty socks. The story, on the other hand, is compelling, thought-provoking, oddly touching, and often funny. The main character, Molly (Louise Smith), is a Yale graduate who lives with a female lover and is working toward becoming a professional photographer. Unrated, the film has simulated sex, profanity, nudity, and violence. 1987; 90m.

WORLD ACCORDING TO GARP, THE ★★★★½
DIR: George Roy Hill. **CAST:** Robin Williams, Glenn Close, John Lithgow, Mary Beth Hurt, Hume Cronyn, Jessica Tandy, Swoosie Kurtz, Amanda Plummer.

Director George Roy Hill and screenwriter Steven Tesich have captured the quirky blend of humor and pathos of John Irving's bestseller. The acting is impressive, with first-rate turns by Robin Williams (in the title role), Glenn Close as his mother, Jenny Fields, and John Lithgow as a kindly transsexual. Rated R for nudity, profanity, sexual situations, and violence. 1982; 136m.

WORLD APART, A ★★★½
DIR: Chris Menges. **CAST:** Barbara Hershey, Jodhi May.

Based on a true story, *A World Apart* is an emotionally charged drama about an anti-apartheid South African journalist (Barbara Hershey) who becomes the first white woman to be held under that country's infamous ninety-day detention law. Seen largely through the half-understanding eyes of the woman's daughter. The musical score enhances the searing brutality of this "world apart." Rated PG. 1988; 135m.

WORLD GONE MAD, THE ★½
DIR: Christy Cabanne. **CAST:** Pat O'Brien, Evelyn Brent, Neil Hamilton, Mary Brian, Louis Calhern, J. Carrol Naish.

This features Wall Street types of questionable character versus a district attorney and his investigators during the Prohibition era. A great cast, but the viewers lose interest. 1933; B&W; 73m.

WORLD OF SUZIE WONG, THE ★★
DIR: Richard Quine. **CAST:** William Holden, Nancy Kwan, Sylvia Syms, Michael Wilding, Laurence Naismith, Jackie Chan.

William Holden is an artist living a bohemian life in Hong Kong. He falls in love with Nancy Kwan, a prostitute who poses for him. Tepid and without much action. Nancy Kwan is very good, but she can't save the slow romantic melodrama. 1960; 129m.

WRITTEN ON THE WIND ★★★½

DIR: Douglas Sirk. **CAST:** Rock Hudson, Lauren Bacall, Robert Stack, Dorothy Malone, Robert Keith.

Tame by today's standards, *Written on the Wind* still provides quite a few good moments and an Academy Award–winning performance by Dorothy Malone. Rock Hudson and Robert Stack play good friends who meet, respectively, Dorothy Malone who has a problem just saying no and Lauren Bacall who is nice and loves Stack but loves his oil-dipped money even more. High-quality Hollywood soap opera. 1956; 99m.

WUTHERING HEIGHTS (1939) ★★★★

DIR: William Wyler. **CAST:** Merle Oberon, Laurence Olivier, Flora Robson, David Niven.

Taken from the Emily Brontë novel, this is a haunting, mesmerizing film. Set on the murky, isolated moors, it tells the tale of Heathcliff, a foundling Gypsy boy who loves Cathy, the spoiled daughter of the house. Their affair, born in childhood, is doomed. As the star-crossed lovers, Laurence Olivier and Merle Oberon are impressive. 1939; B&W; 103m.

WUTHERING HEIGHTS (1971) ★★★½

DIR: Robert Fuest. **CAST:** Timothy Dalton, Anna Calder-Marshall, Harry Andrews, Hugh Griffith.

Inventive but not great rendition of Emily Brontë's classic about the star-crossed lovers, Heathcliff (Timothy Dalton) and Cathy (Anna Calder-Marshall). Dalton is especially good as Cathy's smoldering, much abused, and later vengeful love. The 1939 version is still the best overall. Rated G. 1971; 105m.

X, Y AND ZEE

DIR: Brian G. Hutton. **CAST:** Elizabeth Taylor, Michael Caine, Susannah York, Margaret Leighton, John Standing.

Pointless, tasteless tale of sexual and interpersonal relationships among the three principals is aptly described by the last three letters of the alphabet used to name this mess—X for sick sexual content, Y for why was it made, and Z for the sounds of sleep that emanate from everywhere this mess is playing. Rated R. 1972; 110m.

YEAR MY VOICE BROKE, THE ★★★★

DIR: John Duigan. **CAST:** Noah Taylor.

A likable Australian coming-of-age drama with echoes of *The Last Picture Show* and the novels of S. E. Hinton. Though the film market's been saturated with adolescent dramas circa 1962, this movie's Down Under locale and refreshing honesty make it a welcome addition to the genre. Rated PG-13, with profanity and some mild sexual situations. 1988; 103m.

YESTERDAY'S HERO ★★★

DIR: Neil Leifer. **CAST:** Ian McShane, Adam Faith, Paul Nicholas, Suzanne Somers.

Ian McShane plays a washed-up alcoholic ex-soccer star who wants to make a comeback. He gets assistance from his old flame (Suzanne Somers), a pop star, and her singing partner (Paul Nicholas). Not rated. 1979; 95m.

YOLANDA AND THE THIEF ★★

DIR: Vincente Minnelli. **CAST:** Fred Astaire, Lucille Bremer, Frank Morgan, Mildred Natwick, Ludwig Stossel, Leon Ames, Gigi Perreau.

An exotic fantasy, staged with near-cloying opulence, and now a cult favorite. Down on his luck con man Fred Astaire finds beautiful, rich, convent-bred Lucille Bremer praying to her guardian angel. His eye on her money, he claims to be the angel come to earth to protect her. 1945; 108m.

YOU LIGHT UP MY LIFE ★★½
DIR: Joseph Brooks. **CAST:** Didi Conn, Michael Zaslow, Joe Silver, Stephen Nathan.

Pretty weak story concerning a young girl, Didi Conn, trying to make it in show business. Notable for the title song, film proves it's tough to make a hit song stretch into a feature film. Rated PG. 1977; 90m.

YOU ONLY LIVE ONCE ★★
DIR: Fritz Lang. **CAST:** Henry Fonda, Sylvia Sidney, William Gargan, Barton MacLane, Jerome Cowan, Margaret Hamilton, Ward Bond, Guinn Williams.

About a three-time loser (Henry Fonda) who can't even be saved by the love of a good woman (Sylvia Sidney) because society won't allow him to go straight. This film is a real downer—recommended for Fonda fans only. 1937; B&W; 86m.

YOUNG AND WILLING ★★½
DIR: Edward H. Griffith. **CAST:** William Holden, Susan Hayward, Eddie Bracken, Barbara Britton, Robert Benchley.

Hope springs eternal in the hearts of a gaggle of show business neophytes living and loving in a New York theatrical boardinghouse. Cute and entertaining, but formula. Summer stock in Manhattan. 1943; B&W; 82m.

YOUNG GRADUATES
DIR: Robert Anderson. **CAST:** Patricia Wymer, Tom Stewart, Dennis Christopher.

Stupid youth film that follows the misadventures of a high-school girl who falls in love with her teacher and gets into various problematic situations. Don't waste your time. 1971; 99m.

YOUNG LIONS, THE ★★★½
DIR: Edward Dmytryk. **CAST:** Marlon Brando, Montgomery Clift, Dean Martin, Hope Lange, Barbara Rush, May Britt, Maximilian Schell, Arthur Franz.

The impact of love and war on young lives is the focus of this gripping drama of World War II told from the German and American points of view. Marlon Brando is superb as the Aryan soldier who comes to question his Nazi beliefs. Recommended. 1958; 167m.

YOUNG LOVE, FIRST LOVE ★★
DIR: Steven H. Stern. **CAST:** Valerie Bertinelli, Timothy Hutton.

Boy loves girl, girl loves boy. Does girl love boy enough to go all the way? Nothing better to do? Then watch and find out. Valerie Bertinelli is super-cute as the girl in the quandary of whether to or not. Timothy Hutton is wasted as the boy with the sweats. Unrated. 1979; 100m.

YOUNG MR. LINCOLN ★★★★½
DIR: John Ford. **CAST:** Henry Fonda, Alice Brady, Marjorie Weaver, Donald Meek, Richard Cromwell, Eddie Quillan, Milburn Stone, Ward Bond.

Director John Ford's tribute to the Great Emancipator is splendidly acted by Henry Fonda in the title role, with typically strong support from a handpicked supporting cast. This homespun character study develops into a suspenseful courtroom drama for a rousing conclusion. 1939; B&W; 100m.

YOUNG PHILADELPHIANS, THE ★★★★
DIR: Vincent Sherman. **CAST:** Robert Vaughn, Paul Newman, Barbara Rush, Alexis Smith, Brian Keith, Adam West, Billie Burke, John Williams, Otto Kruger.

In this excellent film, Robert Vaughn stars as a rich young man accused of murder. Paul Newman, a young lawyer, defends Vaughn while pursuing society girl Barbara Rush. 1959; B&W; 136m.

YOUNG WINSTON ★★★
DIR: Richard Attenborough. **CAST:** Simon Ward, Anne Bancroft, Robert Shaw, John Mills, Jack Hawkins, Rob-

ert Flemyng, Patrick Magee, Laurence Naismith.

Rousing and thoroughly entertaining account of this century's man for all seasons, England's indomitable Winston Churchill. The film takes him from his often wretched school days to his beginnings as a journalist of resource and daring in South Africa during the Boer War, up to his first election to Parliament. Simon Ward is excellent in the title role. Rated PG. 1972; 145m.

YOUNGBLOOD ★½
DIR: Peter Markle. **CAST:** Rob Lowe, Patrick Swayze, Cynthia Gibb, Ed Lauter, Jim Youngs, Fionnula Flanagan.

A bit of silliness about a sensitive kid who tries to make it in the world of hockey. Lowe's character can race around anyone to score a goal. The problem is, he lacks the killer instinct this movie would have us believe is an integral part of the game. Rated R for profanity, nudity, simulated sex, and violence. 1986; 110m.

YURI NOSENKO, KGB ★★★½
DIR: Mick Jackson. **CAST:** Tommy Lee Jones, Josef Sommer, Ed Lauter, Oleg Rudnik.

This ably directed spy drama is based on the transcripts of public hearings, interviews, and published sources relating to the defection of KGB agent Yuri Nosenko in 1962. The filmmakers have filled in the gaps where direct evidence was unavailable. Tommy Lee Jones gives a tremendous performance as CIA agent Steve Daley. Oleg Rudnik is also good as Nosenko. 1986; 89m.

ZABRISKIE POINT ★★½
DIR: Michelangelo Antonioni. **CAST:** Mark Frechette, Daria Halprin, Rod Taylor.

An interesting but confusing story of a young college radical who shoots a policeman during a campus demonstration in the late 1960s. This film examines subjects such as Vietnam, black power, and government repression but does not really say too much. Rated R. 1970; 112m.

ZELLY AND ME ★★
DIR: Tina Rathborne. **CAST:** Isabella Rossellini, Alexandra Johnes, Glynis Johns, Kaiulani Lee.

In this drama, we witness the turbulent life of a rich orphan played by Alexandra Johnes. She is overprotected and minus the knowledge of the ways of the real world. Isabella Rossellini and Glynis Johns are outstanding in secondary leads. The basic problem with this film, though, is that we never learn what happens to our orphan. Rated PG. 1988; 87m.

ZORBA THE GREEK ★★★★
DIR: Michael Cacoyannis. **CAST:** Anthony Quinn, Alan Bates, Irene Papas, Lila Kedrova.

A tiny Greek village in Crete is the home of Zorba, a zesty, uncomplicated man whose love of life is a joy to his friends and an eye-opener to a visiting stranger. Anthony Quinn is a delight as Zorba. Lila Kedrova was to win an Oscar for her poignant role as an aging courtesan in this drama. 1963; B&W; 146m.

FOREIGN LANGUAGE FILMS

A COEUR JOIE (HEAD OVER HEELS)
DIR: Serge Bourguignon. **CAST:** Brigitte Bardot, Laurent Terzieff.

This piece of swinging Sixties fluff about a woman torn between two men has plenty of wide belts, black eyeliner, and bad acting by Brigitte Bardot. Original title in its American release: *Two Weeks in September*. In French with English subtitles. 1967; 89m.

A NOS AMOURS ★★★
DIR: Maurice Pialat. **CAST:** Sandrine Bonnaire, Dominique Besnehard, Maurice Pialat.

Winner of the Cesar (French Oscar) for best film of 1983, *A Nos Amours* examines the life of a working-class girl of 15 (Sandrine Bonnaire) who engages in one sexual relationship after another because, as she says, "I'm only happy when I'm with a guy." In French with English subtitles. Rated R for nudity. 1983; 110m.

A NOUS LA LIBERTE ★★½
DIR: René Clair. **CAST:** Raymond Cordy, Henri Marchand.

Louis and Emile are two prisoners who plan an escape. Only Louis gets away and, surprisingly, he becomes a rich, successful businessman. There are some slapstick segments, and many believe that this film was the inspiration for Charlie Chaplin's *Modern Times*. In French, with English subtitles. 1931; B&W; 87m.

AFTER THE REHEARSAL ★★★½
DIR: Ingmar Bergman. **CAST:** Erland Josephson.

This Ingmar Bergman movie—which was originally made for Swedish television—is about a director (Erland Josephson) who is approached by a young actress with a proposition: she wants to have an affair with him. The approach takes place at the end of their rehearsal of Strindberg's *Dream Play*. In Swedish with English subtitles. 1984; 72m.

AGE OF GOLD ★★★
DIR: Luis Buñuel. **CAST:** Pierre Prevert, Gaston Modot, Lya Lys, Max Ernst.

Filmmaker Luis Buñuel's surrealist masterpiece is a savage assault on organized religion, the bourgeoisie, and social ethics. Salvador Dali contributed a few ideas to the production. In French with English subtitles. 1930; B&W; 62m.

AGUIRRE: WRATH OF GOD ★★★★

DIR: Werner Herzog. **CAST:** Klaus Kinski, Ruy Guerra, Del Negro, Helena Rojo.

Klaus Kinski gives one of his finest screen performances in the title role as the mad, traitorous Spanish conquistador who leads an expedition through the South American wilds in a quest for the lost golden city of El Dorado. It's a spectacular adventure story. In German with English subtitles. Unrated, the film has violence. 1972; 94m.

ALEXANDER NEVSKY ★★★★

DIR: Sergei Eisenstein. **CAST:** Nikolai Cherkassov, Dmitri Orlov.

Another classic from the inimitable Russian director Sergei Eisenstein (*Ivan the Terrible*; *Battleship Potemkin*), this film is a Soviet attempt to prepare Russia for the coming conflict with Hitlerian Germany via portrayal of Alexander Nevsky, a thirteenth-century Russian prince, and his victories over the Teutonic knights of that era. As with all state-commissioned art, the situations can be corny, but the direction is superb. In Russian with English subtitles. 1938; B&W; 105m.

ALICE IN THE CITY ★★★

DIR: Wim Wenders. **CAST:** Rudiger Vogler, Yella Rottlander, Lisa Kruezer.

Another road movie from Wim Wenders. While touring Western Europe, a journalist from the United States stumbles upon a precocious nine-year-old girl who has been abandoned by her mother. Excellent eccentric tragicomedy about the problems of two people from completely different cultural backgrounds. In German with English subtitles. 1974; B&W; 110m.

ALLEGRO NON TROPPO ★★★★

DIR: Bruno Bozzetto. **CAST:** Animated.

An animated spoof of Disney's *Fantasia* by Italian filmmaker Bruno Bozzetto, this release entertainingly weds stylish slapstick with the music of Debussy, Ravel, Vivaldi, Stravinsky, Dvorak, and Sibelius. Rated PG. 1976; 75m.

ALPHAVILLE ★★★

DIR: Jean-Luc Godard. **CAST:** Eddie Constantine, Anna Karina, Akim Tamiroff.

Eddie Constantine portrays Lemmy Caution, French private eye extraordinaire, who is sent into the future to rescue a trapped scientist. The future is Alphaville, a logic-constricted city run by a computer. It's a Dick Tracy–type of story with sci-fi leanings. In French, with English subtitles. 1965; 98m.

ALSINO AND THE CONDOR ★★

DIR: Miguel Littin. **CAST:** Alan Esquivel, Dean Stockwell, Carmen Bunster.

This is an earnest attempt to dramatize the conflict between the Central American governments and the Sandinista rebels in Nicaragua. The film revolves around the story of one young boy caught in the turmoil. Alan Esquivel is Alsino, the boy who escapes into a fantasy world of flight. 1983; 90m.

AMARCORD ★★★★★

DIR: Federico Fellini. **CAST:** Magali Noel, Bruno Zanin, Pupella Maggio.

This landmark film is based on director Federico Fellini's reflections of his youth in a small town in prewar Italy. While celebrating the kinship that exists in the town, Fellini examines the serious shortcomings that would pave the route for fascism. Brilliantly photographed by Giuseppe Rotunno. Italian dubbed in English. 1974; 127m.

AMERICAN FRIEND, THE ★★★★½

DIR: Wim Wenders. **CAST:** Dennis Hopper, Bruno Ganz, Lisa Kreuzer, Gerard Blain.

Tense story of an American criminal (Dennis Hopper) in Germany talking a picture framer into murdering a gangster. Extremely well done, with lots of surprises. Cameo appearances by American film directors Sam Fuller and Nicholas Ray. Rated R—language, violence. 1977; 127m.

AND GOD CREATED WOMAN (1957) ★★½
DIR: Roger Vadim. **CAST:** Brigitte Bardot, Curt Jurgens, Jean-Louis Trintignant, Christian Marquand.

Brigitte Bardot rose to international fame as the loose-moraled coquette who finds it hard to say no to an attractive male, especially a well-heeled one. Shot with as much of Bardot exposed as the law then allowed, this rather slight story works well and is peopled with interesting characters. In French, with English subtitles. 1957; 92m.

AND NOW, MY LOVE ★★★½
DIR: Claude Lelouch. **CAST:** Marthe Keller, André Dussolier, Charles Denner.

In biography-documentary style, director Claude Lelouch juxtaposes three generations of a family while depicting the moral, political, and artistic events that shaped the members' lives. All this is wonderfully designed to show how inevitable it is for two young people (played by André Dussolier and Marthe Keller) from different backgrounds to fall in love. Dubbed. 1974; 121m.

AND THE SHIP SAILS ON ★★
DIR: Federico Fellini. **CAST:** Freddie Jones, Barbara Jefford, Victor Poletti.

Federico Fellini's heavily symbolic parable about a luxury liner filled with eccentric beautiful people sailing the Adriatic on the eve of World War I was called by one critic "a spellbinding, often magical tribute to the illusions and delusions of art." That's one way of looking at it. We found it boring. However, Fellini fans may find it rewarding. In Italian with English subtitles. 1984; 138m.

ANGELE ★★★½
DIR: Marcel Pagnol. **CAST:** Orane Demazis, Fernandel, Jean Servais.

Absorbing character study that blends comedy with drama in a story about a young French girl who becomes bored with life in the country and is lured into a sleazy existence in Paris with an older street hustler. A poignant drama in the tradition of Jean Renoir. In French with English subtitles. 1934; B&W; 132m.

ANGRY HARVEST ★★★★
DIR: Agnieszka Holland. **CAST:** Armin Mueller-Stahl, Elisabeth Trissenaar.

This drama from director Agnieszka Holland features Fassbinder veterans Armin Mueller-Stahl and Elisabeth Trissenaar in a wartime story that is an absorbing character study and a mesmerizing thriller about a Jewish woman who escapes from a train bound for the Nazi death camps. The film features brilliant performances. Not rated, but contains nudity and violence. In German with English subtitles. 1986; 102m.

ANTARCTICA ★
DIR: Koreyoshi Kurahara. **CAST:** Ken Takakura, Tsunehiko Watase.

Antarctica is the true story of a 1958 expedition. While in Antarctica, Japanese scientists encounter complications and are forced to return home, leaving their team of dogs behind to fend for themselves. The dogs are pretty good naturalistic actors, but you're not drawn to them as you are to the wolves of Carroll Ballard's *Never Cry Wolf*. Dubbed in English. 1984; 112m.

ARABIAN NIGHTS ★★½
DIR: Pier Paolo Pasolini. **CAST:** Franco Citti.

Pier Paolo Pasolini re-creates some of Scheherezade's original tales in this uneven but breathtaking film. Set in various Middle Eastern locales, *Arabian Nights* offers some memorable tales of trust, betrayal, and sorrow. Nudity is plentiful; violence is heavyhanded. In Italian with English subtitles. Rated X. 1974; 128m.

ARSENAL ★★
DIR: Alexander Dovzhenko. **CAST:** Semyon Svashenko.
This imaginative, symbolic denoucement of war is rich in visual images, but takes too long to make its point. More a collection of episodes that take place during the last part of World War I than a character-dominated drama, this Russian offering lacks fire. 1929; B&W; 70m.

ASHES AND DIAMONDS ★★★★
DIR: Andrzej Wajda. **CAST:** Zbigniew Cybulski.
The conflict between idealism and instinct is explored with great intensity in this story of a Polish resistance fighter who assassinates the wrong man at the end of World War II. Director Andrzej Wajda captures all the bitterness and disillusionment of political fanaticism in this powerful testament of the Polish people during the struggle that followed the war's end. In Polish with English subtitles. 1958; B&W; 102m.

ASSASSINS DE L'ORDRE, LES (LAW BREAKERS) ★★
DIR: Marcel Carné. **CAST:** Jacques Brel, Catherine Rouvel, Michel Lonsdale, Charles Denner, Didier Haudepin.
Marcel Carné, who directed the 1944 classic *Children of Paradise*, slips into innocuousness with this less than riveting tale. Jacques Brel plays a judge who is trying to get to the bottom of corrupt police practices. 1971; 107m.

ASSAULT, THE ★★★★½
DIR: Fons Rademakers. **CAST:** Derek de Lint, Marc van Uchelen, Monique van de Ven.
This Academy Award winner for best foreign language film deserves its praise. It is a tale of war and its inevitable impact. In Holland in 1945, a Nazi collaborator is murdered and the lives of the witnesses, a small boy in particular, are changed forever. Dubbed. 1986; 126m.

AU REVOIR, LES ENFANTS ★★★★★
DIR: Louis Malle. **CAST:** Gaspard Manesse, Raphael Fejto, Philippe Morier-Genoud, Francine Racette.
Louis Malle may have created his masterpiece with this autobiographical account of a traumatic incident in his youth that occurred in World War II France. Certainly this heartfelt and heartbreaking work about man's inhumanity to man is likely to remain his most unforgettable creation. Rated PG for strong themes. In French with English subtitles. 1987; 104m.

AUTUMN SONATA ★★★★★
DIR: Ingmar Bergman. **CAST:** Ingrid Bergman, Liv Ullmann, Lena Nyman.
Ingmar Bergman directed this superb Swedish release about the first meeting in seven years of a daughter (Liv Ullmann) with her difficult concert pianist mother (Ingrid Bergman). A great film. In Swedish and English. Rated PG. 1978; 97m.

AVIATOR'S WIFE, THE ★★★½
DIR: Eric Rohmer. **CAST:** Philippe Marlaud, Marie Riviere, Anne-Laure Marie.
Not much happens in a film by French director Eric Rohmer, at least not in the traditional sense. In this typically Rohmer character study, a young law student named François (Philippe Marlaud) is crushed when he discovers his lover, Anne (Marie Riviere), in the company of another man and decides to spy on them. In French, with English subtitles. Unrated, the film has no objectionable material. 1981; 104m.

BABETTE'S FEAST ★★★★
DIR: Gabriel Axel. **CAST:** Stéphane Audran, Jean-Philippe Lafont, Jarl Kulle, Bibi Andersson.
Writer-director Gabriel Axel's Oscar-winning adaptation of Isak Dinesen's short story has the kind of wistful warmth that makes it seem like a tale told by a wise old storyteller. It also has a pixilated quality that makes it good fun even when the characters are

being deadly serious. The finale is a sumptuous dinner prepared by an expatriate French chef (Stéphane Audran) for a group of devout Dutch Lutherans. It may be the funniest meal ever put on screen. In French and Dutch with English subtitles. Rated G. 1987; 102m.

BAD SLEEP WELL, THE ★★★★
DIR: Akira Kurosawa. **CAST:** Toshiro Mifune, Masayuki Mori, Takashi Shimura.

A man seeks revenge for the murder of his father in this suspenseful tale of corruption in high places. Akira Kurosawa remarkably captures the spirit of Forties crime dramas in this engrossing film, based on an Ed McBain story. In Japanese with English subtitles. 1960; B&W; 152m.

BAKER'S WIFE, THE ★★★★
DIR: Marcel Pagnol. **CAST:** Raimu, Ginette Leclerc, Charles Moulin.

The new baker is coming to a town that has been without fresh-baked goods for too long. With great fanfare, the baker and his new wife arrive, but she has a roving eye. This comedy is a gem. In French with English subtitles. 1938; B&W; 124m.

BALLAD OF A SOLDIER ★★★½
DIR: Grigori Chukhrai. **CAST:** Vladimir Ivashov, Shanna Prokhorenko.

A soldier finds love and adventure on a ten-day pass to see his mother. This import features excellent cinematography and acting, and despite the always obvious Soviet propaganda, some piercing insights into the Russian soul. In Russian with English subtitles. 1959; B&W; 89m.

BATTLE OF ALGIERS ★★★★
DIR: Gillo Pontecorvo. **CAST:** Yacef Saadi, Jean Martin, Brahim Haggiag.

This gut-wrenching Italian-Algerian pseudodocumentary about the war between Algerian citizens and their French "protectors" was released when America's involvement in Vietnam was still to reach its peak, but the parallels between the two stories are obvious. Covering the years from 1954 to 1962, this film is an emotional experience—it is not recommended for the casual viewer and is too strong for children. 1965; B&W; 123m.

BATTLESHIP POTEMKIN, THE ★★★★★
DIR: Sergei Eisenstein. **CAST:** Alexander Antonov, Vladimir Barsky.

One of a handful of landmark motion pictures. This silent classic, directed by the legendary Sergei Eisenstein, depicts the mutiny of the crew of a Russian battleship and its aftermath. The directorial technique expanded the threshold of what was then standard cinema story-telling. The massacre of civilians on the Odessa Steps remains one of the most powerful scenes in film history. Silent. 1925; B&W; 65m.

BEATRICE ★★
DIR: Bertrand Tavernier. **CAST:** Bernard Pierre Donnadieu, Julie Delpy, Nils Tavernier.

In creating *Beatrice*, writer-director Bertrand Tavernier set out to demythologize the Middle Ages, which is generally portrayed as a time of chivalry, valiant knights, and ladies fair. He succeeds all too well with this repulsive, nightmarish movie in which the angelic title character (Julie Delpy) is raped and tortured by the demented father (Bernard Pierre Donnadieu) she once idolized. In French with English subtitles. Unrated, the film has nudity, violence, and simulated sex. 1987; 128m.

BEAU PERE ★★★★
DIR: Bertrand Blier. **CAST:** Patrick Dewaere, Ariel Besse, Maurice Ronet, Nicole Garcia.

Patrick Dewaere stars again for French director Bertrand Blier (*Get Out Your Handkerchiefs*) in this film, about a stepfather who falls in love with his adopted pubescent daughter. It could have been shocking—or just plain perverse. But *Beau Pere* is a bittersweet, thoroughly charming motion picture. In French, with English subtitles. Unrated, the film has nudity, profanity, and adult themes. 1982; 120m.

BEAUTY AND THE BEAST (1946) ★★★★★
DIR: Jean Cocteau. **CAST:** Josette Day, Jean Marais.
This French classic goes far beyond mere retelling of the well-known fairy tale. Its eerie visual beauty and surrealistic atmosphere mark it as a genuine original. The tragic love story between Beauty (Josette Day) and the all-too-human Beast (Jean Marais) resembles a moving painting. In French with English subtitles. 1946; B&W; 90m.

BELLISSIMA ★★★
DIR: Luchino Visconti. **CAST:** Anna Magnani, Walter Chiari, Tina Apicella.
Luchino Visconti is known for such pioneering works as *Rocco and His Brothers*, *The Damned*, and *Death in Venice*. As for *Bellissima,* if you are programming an Anna Magnani festival, you might be interested in this oddly and determinedly lightweight comedy. The story is set in the Cinecitta Studios, where a search is on for the prettiest child in Rome. In Italian with English subtitles. 1951; B&W; 95m.

BERLIN ALEXANDERPLATZ ★★★½
DIR: Rainer Werner Fassbinder. **CAST:** Gunter Lamprecht, Hanna Schygulla, Barbara Sukowa.
Remember the scene in *A Clockwork Orange* in which Malcolm McDowell's eyes are wired open and he is forced to watch movies? That's how we often felt when wading through the fifteen-and-a-half hours of Rainer Werner Fassbinder's magnum opus, *Berlin Alexanderplatz*. Not that this much-praised German television production doesn't have its moments of interest, fascination, and yes, even genius. But as with all of Fassbinder's films, *Berlin Alexanderplatz* also has its excesses and false notes. Unrated. In German with English subtitles. 1983; 930m.

BETTY BLUE ★★
DIR: Jean-Jacques Beineix. **CAST:** Jean-Hugues Anglade, Beatrice Dalle.
Betty Blue is about Betty, who is radically spontaneous and a bit wacko (we don't know why), and Zorg, the man she inspires to continue writing. The trick is not to think too much about the ridiculousness of the film but instead to bask in Jean-Jacques Beineix's sensuous visual flair. In French with English subtitles. Rated R. 1986; 117m.

BEYOND FEAR ★★★
DIR: Yannick Andrei. **CAST:** Michel Bouquet, Michael Constantine, Marilu Tolo.
A man's wife and child are taken hostage by a band of outlaws and he must work with the police to ensure the safety of his family in this compelling film. Rated R by mid-1970s standards due to violence and profanity (very little of both, actually). 1975; 92m.

BEYOND OBSESSION ★★
DIR: Liliana Cavani. **CAST:** Tom Berenger, Marcello Mastroianni, Eleonora Giorgi, Michel Piccoli.
Marcello Mastroianni and Eleonora Giorgi are strange bedfellows for American Tom Berenger in this confusing Italian film about hustling, obsession, and seduction. Not rated, has profanity and nudity. Dubbed. 1982; 116m.

BEYOND THE WALLS ★★½
DIR: Uri Barbash. **CAST:** Arnon Zadok, Muhamad Bakri.
This Israeli film pits Jewish and Arab convicts against each other with explosive consequences. Finally, though, it dwindles into a standard prison drama. Nominated for a best foreign film Oscar, it lost to *Dangerous Moves*. 1984; 103m.

BICYCLE THIEF, THE ★★★★
DIR: Vittorio De Sica. **CAST:** Lamberto Maggiorani, Lianella Carell, Enzo Staiola.
Considered by critics an all-time classic, this touching, honest, beautifully human film speaks realistically to the heart with simple cinematic eloquence. A bill poster's bicycle, on which his job depends, is stolen. Ignored by the police, who see nothing special in the loss, the anguished worker and his young son search Rome for the thief. In Italian with English subtitles. 1949; B&W; 90m.

BIG DEAL ON MADONNA STREET ★★★★
DIR: Mario Monicelli. **CAST:** Marcello Mastroianni, Vittorio Gassman, Toto, Renato Salvatori, Claudia Cardinale.
Mario Monicelli directed this tale as a classic spoof of the perfect-crime film that depicts in great detail the elaborate planning and split-second timing involved in huge thefts. Monicelli's characters—who are attempting to burglarize a safe—also formulate intricate plans and employ precise timing, but everything they do results in humiliating disaster—providing a hilarious comedy of errors. In Italian with English subtitles. 1960; B&W; 91m.

BILITIS ★★★★
DIR: David Hamilton. **CAST:** Patti D'Arbanville, Bernard Giraudeau, Mathieu Carriere.
A surprisingly tasteful and sensitive soft-core sex film, this details the sexual awakening of the title character, a 16-year-old French girl while she spends the summer with a family friend. Rated R for nudity and simulated sex. 1982; 93m.

BIRGIT HAAS MUST BE KILLED ★★★★★
DIR: Laurent Heynemann. **CAST:** Philippe Noiret, Jean Rochefort, Lisa Kreuzer.
It is hard to imagine a more perfect film than this spellbinding, French thriller-drama. Though its plot revolves around the assassination of a German terrorist (Birgit Haas) by a French counterspy organization, this film says as much about human relationships as it does espionage. Unrated, the film contains well-handled violence and nudity. In French with English subtitles. 1981; 105m.

BIZET'S CARMEN ★★★★★
DIR: Francesco Rosi. **CAST:** Placido Domingo, Julia Migenes-Johnson.
Julia Migenes-Johnson and Placido Domingo excel in this film adaptation of the opera by Georges Bizet based on the short story by Prosper Mérimée. It is about a poor girl whose fierce independence maddens the men who become obsessed with her. In French, with English subtitles. Rated PG for mild violence. 1985; 152m.

BLACK AND WHITE IN COLOR ★★★★
DIR: Jean-Jacques Annaud. **CAST:** Jean Carmet, Jacques Dufilho, Catherine Rouvel, Jacques Spiesser, Dora Doll.
This whimsical film concerns a group of self-satisfied Frenchmen at a remote African trading post. The expatriates become stung by a fever of patriotism at the outbreak of World War I, and they organize a surprise assault on a nearby German fort. Excellent cast turns in outstanding performances in this sleeper that won an Oscar for best foreign film. Not rated, but contains nudity, profanity, and violence. In French with English subtitles. 1977; 90m.

BLACK ORPHEUS ★★★★★
DIR: Marcel Camus. **CAST:** Breno Mello, Marpessa Dawn, Lea Garcia, Lourdes de Oliveira.
The Greek myth of Orpheus, the unrivaled musician, and his ill-fated love for Eurydice has been updated and set in Rio de Janeiro during carnival for this superb film. A Portuguese-French coproduction, it has all the qualities of a genuine classic. Its stunning photography captures both the magical spirit

of the original legend and the tawdry yet effervescent spirit of Brazil. 1959; 98m.

BLACK VENUS ★

DIR: Claude Mulot. **CAST:** Josephine Jacqueline Jones, Emiliano Redondo.

Lavish 19th-century Parisian costumes and settings can't salvage this endless sex romp for the former Miss Bahamas (Josephine Jacqueline Jones, who plays Venus). She becomes involved with a starving artist. Very loosely based on stories by Honoré de Balzac, this European film is poorly dubbed. Rated R. 1983; 80m.

BLIND TRUST (POUVOIR INTIME) ★★★★

DIR: Yves Simoneau. **CAST:** Marie Tifo, Pierre Curzi, Jacques Robert Gravel.

Four misfit robbers drive away with an armored car only to find a guard locked in the back with the money. Intense and fascinating. In French with English subtitles. Rated PG-13 for profanity and violence. 1987; 86m.

BLOOD FEUD ★★½

DIR: Lina Wertmuller. **CAST:** Sophia Loren, Marcello Mastroianni, Giancarlo Giannini.

Marcello Mastroianni, a lawyer, and Giancarlo Giannini, a sleazy hood, compete for the romantic attentions of a beautiful Sicilian widow (Sophia Loren) in this abrasive, overblown potboiler set during the rise of fascism in 1920s Italy. Not rated, but contains profanity and violence. Dubbed in English. 1979; B&W; 112m.

BLOOD OF A POET ★★½

DIR: Jean Cocteau. **CAST:** Jean Cocteau.

This pretentious and self-centered first film by France's multitalented Jean Cocteau is also intriguing, provoking, and inventive. Cocteau stars in and narrates this highly personal excursion into a poet's inner life: his fears and obsessions, his relation to the world about him, and the classic poetic preoccupation with death. In French with English subtitles. 1930; B&W; 55m.

BLOOD WEDDING ★★★

DIR: Carlos Saura. **CAST:** Antonio Gades, Cristina Hoyos.

Excellent ballet adaptation of Federico Garcia Lorca's classic tragedy is impeccably performed by a great, lavishly costumed cast in an empty rehearsal hall. Carlos Saura's direction gives this production a great sense of power and beauty. In Spanish with English subtitles. 1981; 72m.

BLUE ANGEL, THE ★★★★★

DIR: Josef von Sternberg. **CAST:** Emil Jannings, Marlene Dietrich, Kurt Gerron.

This stunning tale about a straitlaced schoolteacher's obsession with a striptease dancer in Germany is the subject of many film classes. The photography, set design, and script are all top-notch, and there are spectacular performances by all. In German, with English subtitles. 1930; B&W; 98m.

BLUE COUNTRY ★★★½

DIR: Jean-Charles Tacchella. **CAST:** Brigitte Fossey, Jacques Serres, Ginette Garcin, Armand Meffre, Ginett Mathieu.

A lighthearted comedy involving a nurse who leaves the city to enjoy a free and independent life in the country. She meets up with a bachelor who equally enjoys his freedom. Their encounters with the local townspeople provide amusing glimpses of French folk life. In French with English subtitles. 1977; 90m.

BLUEBEARD (1963) ★★★½

DIR: Claude Chabrol. **CAST:** Charles Denner, Michele Morgan, Danielle Darrieux, Hildegarde Neff.

Claude Chabrol, justifiably known as the Gallic Hitchcock, tells the story of the Frenchman who married and murdered eleven women in order to support his real family. Chabrol approaches the material in the same manner that Chaplin did in *Monsieur Verdoux*—as a satirical parable of capitalism. He also sets it against the backdrop of World War I, which killed many more people for less defensible motives. Not for all tastes, obviously, but well worth a look. Screenplay by Françoise Sagan. Original title *Landru*. Dubbed in English. 1963; 114m.

BOAT IS FULL, THE ★★★
DIR: Markus Imhoof. **CAST:** Tina Engel, Marin Walz.

Markus Imhoof's film about refugees from the Nazis trying to obtain refuge in Switzerland is tragic and extraordinarily effective. It could have been a better movie, but it could hardly have been more heartbreaking. No MPAA rating. 1983; 100m.

BOB LE FLAMBEUR ★★★★★
DIR: Jean-Pierre Melville. **CAST:** Roger Duchesne, Isabel Corey, Daniel Cauchy, Howard Vernon.

This is an exquisite example of early French *film noir*. In it are all the trappings of the classic gangster movie. The most fascinating element of this import is the title character, Bob Montagne (Roger Duchesne), who plans to rob a casino of $800 million. In French with English subtitles. 1955; B&W; 102m.

BOCCACCIO 70 ★★★★
DIR: Federico Fellini, Luchino Visconti, Vittorio De Sica. **CAST:** Anita Ekberg, Sophia Loren, Romy Schneider, Tomas Milian.

As with its Renaissance namesake, this film tells stories—three of them, in fact, by three of Italy's greatest directors. Federico Fellini's entry, "The Temptation of Dr. Antonio," showcases Anita Ekberg. The second playlet, by Luchino Visconti, is "The Bet," which features Romy Schneider as a not-so-typical housewife. "The Raffle," by Vittorio De Sica, is reminiscent of a dirty joke told badly, and it tends to cheapen the panache of the first two. In Italian with English subtitles. 1962; 165m.

BOLERO (1982) ★★
DIR: Claude Lelouch. **CAST:** James Caan, Geraldine Chaplin, Robert Hossein, Nicole Garcia, Daniel Olbrychski, Richard Bohringer.

Like American Alan Rudolph, French director Claude Lelouch is an obsessive romantic whose admirers (a small cult in this country) seem to admire his fervent style more than his plots. In this case, even though *Bolero* is almost three hours long, there's little plot to speak of. The film spans fifty years in the lives of a number of characters who live for music. To confuse matters, most of the cast plays multiple roles. You'll either be mesmerized or bored stiff. 1982; 173m.

BOMBAY TALKIE ★★
DIR: James Ivory. **CAST:** Shashi Kapoor, Jennifer Kendal, Zia Mohyeddin.

An early effort from the team of producer Ismail Merchant, writer Ruth Prawer Jhabvala, and director James Ivory, who have been working together exclusively for over twenty-five years. (They finally hit it big in 1986 with *A Room With a View*.) In this drama, a British novelist (Jennifer Kendal) travels to India in search of romance, which she finds in the person of an Indian movie star (Shashi Kapoor). Pretty dull; the most fascinating parts have to do with the Indian film industry. 1970; 112m.

BORDER STREET ★★★★
DIR: Alexander Ford. **CAST:** M. Cwiklinska.

This hard-hitting Polish film is set in the ghettos into which Nazis forced Jews during the Third Reich and where many of them died for lack of food and medicine. There are a few lapses into low-grade melodrama, but mostly this is a gripping story that retains its power. 1950; 75m.

BOUDU SAVED FROM DROWNING ★★★★★
DIR: Jean Renoir. **CAST:** Michel Simon, Charles Granval, Max Dalban, Jean Dasté.

This is the original *Down and Out in Beverly Hills,* except that the tramp (the beloved Michel Simon) is saved by an antiquarian bookseller after a suicide attempt in the Seine—down and out in Paris. Unlike the play on which it was based and unlike the Hollywood version—both of which have the bum accept his responsibilities—*Boudu* is a celebration of joyful anarchy. A masterpiece. In French, with English subtitles. 1932; B&W; 88m.

BREATHLESS (1959) ★★★★★
DIR: Jean-Luc Godard. **CAST:** Jean-Paul Belmondo, Jean Seberg.

Richard Gere or Jean-Paul Belmondo? The choice should be easy after you see the Godard version of this story of a carefree crook and his "along for the ride" girlfriend. See it for Belmondo's performance as the continent's most charming crook, but while you're along for the ride, note just how well-made a film can be. 1959; B&W; 89m.

BRINK OF LIFE ★★★
DIR: Ingmar Bergman. **CAST:** Eva Dahlbeck, Ingrid Thulin, Bibi Andersson, Max von Sydow, Erland Josephson.

Early Ingmar Bergman film set entirely in a hospital maternity ward, where three women ponder their pregnancies and the relationships that preceded them. Rather bleak and naturalistic, this is an actors' piece, though Bergman still controls the film emotionally in subtle ways. In Swedish with English subtitles. 1957; B&W; 82m.

BUFFET FROID (COLD CUTS) ★★★★
DIR: Bertrand Blier. **CAST:** Gerard Depardieu, Bernard Blier, Jean Carmet.

Outrageously funny surreal black comedy about three hapless murderers. This whimsical study in madness is laced with brilliant performances and great direction by Bertrand Blier. Highly engaging. Not rated, but contains nudity, profanity, and violence. In French with English subtitles. 1979; 95m.

BYE BYE BRAZIL ★★★½
DIR: Carlos Diegues. **CAST:** Jose Wilker, Betty Faria.

This is a bawdy, bizarre, satiric, and sometimes even touching film that follows a ramshackle traveling tent show—the Caravana Rolidei—through the cities, jungle, and villages of Brazil. In Portuguese with English subtitles. Rated R. 1980; 110m.

CABINET OF DOCTOR CALIGARI, THE ★★★½
DIR: Robert Wiene. **CAST:** Werner Krauss, Conrad Veidt, Lil Dagover.

A nightmarish story and surrealistic settings are the main ingredients of this early German classic of horror and fantasy. Cesare, a hollow-eyed sleepwalker (Conrad Veidt), commits murder while under the spell of the evil hypnotist Dr. Caligari (Werner Krauss). Ordered to kill Jane, a beautiful girl (Lil Dagover), Cesare defies Caligari, and instead abducts her. Silent. 1919; B&W; 51m.

CAFE EXPRESS ★★★½
DIR: Nanni Loy. **CAST:** Nino Manfredi, Adolfo Celi, Vittorio Mezzogiorno.

Chaplinesque comedy starring Nino Manfredi, best known in this country for *Bread and Chocolate*. He plays a similar character here, a vendor selling coffee on a commuter train. Because such sales are illegal, he is hounded by conductors and other petty types trying to keep him from earning a living. A bit lightweight, but Manfredi is always fun to watch. 1980; 105m.

CAGED HEART, THE (L'ADDITION) ★★★
DIR: Denis Amar. **CAST:** Richard Berry, Richard Bohringer, Victoria Abril.
This absorbing French film has Bruno Winkler (Richard Berry) arrested for shoplifting when he tries to help a beautiful young woman (Victoria Abril). Once behind bars, he's accused of aiding a crime lord in his escape and shooting a guard. Though the video is poorly dubbed, one can't help but get caught up in the story. Rated R for violence and profanity. 1985; 85m.

CAMILA ★★★½
DIR: Maria Luisa Bemberg. **CAST:** Susu Pecoraro, Imanol Arias, Hector Alterio, Mona Maris.
A romantic and true story of forbidden love in the classic tradition. Susu Pecoraro is Camila O'Gorman, the daughter of a wealthy aristocrat in Buenos Aires in the mid-1800s. Imanol Arias plays Ladislao Gutierrez, a Jesuit priest who falls in love with Camila. Not rated, but with sex, nudity, and violence. In Spanish with English subtitles. 1984; 105m.

CAMORRA ★★
DIR: Lina Wertmuller. **CAST:** Angela Molina, Francisco Rabal, Harvey Keitel.
Lina Wertmuller lacks her usual bite in this well-intentioned but conventional crime story. The Camorra is an organized-crime outfit in Italy, and the movie details the efforts of an ex-prostitute to band the women of Naples together against the mobsters. Rated R for violence and sexual situations. 1986; 115m.

CARNIVAL IN FLANDERS ★★★★
DIR: Jacques Feyder. **CAST:** Françoise Rosay, Andre Alerme, Jean Murat, Louis Jouvet, Micheline Cheirel.
This sly drama about a village that postpones its destruction by collaborating with their conquerors was considered a poor statement to make to the rest of the world in light of what Nazi Germany and Italy were attempting to do to their neighbors. A clever, subtle work and one of Jacques Feyder's finest achievements, this classic is a conscious effort to re-create on celluloid the great paintings of the masters depicting village life during carnival time. Interesting on many levels. In French with English subtitles. 1936; B&W; 92m.

CAT AND MOUSE ★★★★½
DIR: Claude Lelouch. **CAST:** Michele Morgan, Jean-Pierre Aumont, Serge Reggiani, Valerie Lagrange.
Written, produced, and directed by Claude Lelouch, *Cat and Mouse* is a deliciously urbane and witty whodunit guaranteed to charm and deceive while keeping you marvelously entertained. The plot has more twists and turns than a country road, and the characters are...well...just slightly corrupt and totally fascinating. In French with English subtitles. Rated PG. 1975; 107m.

CATHERINE & CO. ★★½
DIR: Michel Boisrone. **CAST:** Jane Birkin, Patrick Dewaere, Jean-Claude Brialy, Jean-Pierre Aumont.
British-born Jane Birkin is one of France's most popular actresses, though this, one of her typical softcore sex comedies, hardly shows why. She plays a young woman who, having drifted into an innocent sort of prostitution, decides to incorporate herself with four regular "stockholders." Rated R. 1975; 99m.

CÉSAR ★★★★½
DIR: Marcel Pagnol. **CAST:** Raimu, Orane Demazis, Pierre Fresnay.
The final and best part of the Marseilles trilogy that includes *Marius* and *Fanny*. You can watch it on its own, but you won't enjoy it nearly as much unless you see all three parts: the cumulative effect is resoundingly emotional. In French with English subtitles. 1933; B&W; 117m.

CÉSAR AND ROSALIE ★★★½
DIR: Claude Sautet. **CAST:** Yves Montand, Romy Schneider, Sami Frey, Umberto Orsini, Eva Marie Meineke.
Beautifully orchestrated story of human passion about a woman (Romy Schneider) and her relationship with two lovers over a period of years. Excellent cast and a subtle screenplay and direction give strength to this comedy-drama. In French with English subtitles. Not rated. 1972; 104m.

CHAPAYEV ★★★
DIR: Sergei Vasiliev, Georgi Vasiliev. **CAST:** Boris Bobochkin.
Although this was obviously designed as propaganda for the Bolshevik revolution, it is still well-made and entertaining, with a minimum of proselytizing. The film follows the overthrow of the czar from the point of view of Chapayev, a Russian general. In Russian with English subtitles. 1934; B&W; 95m.

CHEATERS, THE ★
DIR: Sergio Martino. **CAST:** Dayle Haddon, Luc Merenda, Lino Troisi, Enrico Maria Salerno.
From the director of such gems as *Screamers*, *Sex With a Smile*, and *Slave of the Cannibal God* comes another dumb Italian flick. *The Cheaters* is about a top-notch card cheat who makes his way to the top working for a Milan crimelord. Rated R for profanity, sex, and violence. 1976; 91m.

CHINA IS NEAR ★★★½
DIR: Marco Bellocchio. **CAST:** Glauco Mauri, Elda Tattoli.
Marco Bellocchio, infamous recently for the tiresome *Devil in the Flesh*, displays a talent for both sardonic humor and political satire in this early film. The main characters plot against each other to gain political office, sexual satisfaction, and financial security. Their various connivings eventually bring them together as a sort of large, squabbling family. In Italian with English subtitles. 1968; B&W; 110m.

CHLOE IN THE AFTERNOON ★★★★
DIR: Eric Rohmer. **CAST:** Bernard Verley, Zouzou, Francoise Verley, Françoise Fabian, Beatrice Romand.
This film concludes director Eric Rohmer's series of "moral fables." It is a trifle, featherweight and utterly charming. Will the faithful hero have an affair with bohemian Chloe (played deftly by singer-actress Zouzou)? No rating. In French with English subtitles. 1972; 97m.

CHOCOLAT ★★★
DIR: Claire Dennis. **CAST:** Cecile Ducasse.
A subtle, sophisticated, overly restrained French look at the colonial life of the past in Africa, as viewed from the innocent perspective of an 8-year-old girl. Cecile Ducasse is memorable as the girl, whose story of growing racial awareness is told in flashback. Rated PG-13, with profanity. In French with English subtitles. 1989; 105m.

CHOICE OF ARMS, A ★★★
DIR: Alain Corneau. **CAST:** Yves Montand, Gerard Depardieu, Catherine Deneuve, Michel Galabru, Gerard Lanvin.
Yves Montand is a retired gangster who has chosen a peaceful life raising stud horses and giving his beautiful wife, Catherine Deneuve, all she could hope for. Gerard Depardieu is the convict who arrives with an old friend of Montand's seeking asylum. In French with subtitles, this film is unrated. 1983; 114m.

CHRIST STOPPED AT EBOLI ★★
DIR: Francesco Rosi. **CAST:** Gian Maria Volonté, Irene Papas, Alain Cuny, Lea Massari, François Simon.
Christ Stopped at Eboli is based on a renowned Italian novel about Carlo Levi, a political exile who was punished in 1935 for his antifascist writings and exiled to a village in southern

Italy. Irene Papas livens things up with her resounding laugh, but ultimately this quiet tale is forgettable. In Italian with English subtitles. 1983; 118m.

CHRISTIANE F. ★½
DIR: Ulrich Edel. **CAST:** Natja Brunkhorst, Thomas Haustein.

Although quite interesting in places, this West German film dealing with young heroin addicts ultimately becomes a bore. Too many repetitive scenes of kids shooting dope, and bad acting, make this a yawn. In German with English subtitles. 1981; 124m.

CIAO FEDERICO! ★★★
DIR: Gideon Bachmann. **CAST:** Federico Fellini, Martin Potter, Hiram Keller, Roman Polanski, Sharon Tate.

A revealing portrait of Federico Fellini at work, directing the actors who populate the unreal world of *Satyricon*. Immersed in the creative process, Fellini is captured by documentary filmmaker Gideon Bachmann as he interacts with his English and American actors. Not rated. In English and Italian with English subtitles. 1971; 55m.

CLAIRE'S KNEE ★★★★★
DIR: Eric Rohmer. **CAST:** Jean-Claude Brialy, Aurora Cornu, Beatrice Romand.

There is no substitute for class, and director Eric Rohmer exhibits a great deal of it in this fifth film in a series entitled *Six Moral Tales*. The plot is simplicity itself. Jerome (Jean-Claude Brialy) renews his friendship with a writer (Aurora Cornu) whose roommate has two daughters; one is Claire. Jerome is intrigued by Claire but is obsessed with her knee—her right knee, to be specific. In French with English subtitles. PG rating. 1971; 103m.

CLEAN SLATE (COUP DE TORCHON) ★★★★
DIR: Bertrand Tavernier. **CAST:** Philippe Noiret, Isabelle Huppert, Stéphane Audran.

Set during 1938 in a French West African colonial town, this savage and sardonic black comedy is a study of the circumstances under which racism and fascism flourish. Philippe Noiret stars as a simple-minded sheriff who decides that it's time to wipe out the corruption. In French, with English subtitles. Unrated, the film has nudity, implied sex, violence, profanity, and racial epithets. 1981; 128m.

CLOSELY WATCHED TRAINS ★★★★½
DIR: Jirí Menzel. **CAST:** Vaclav Neckar, Jitka Bendova.

A bittersweet coming-of-age comedy-drama against a backdrop of the Nazi occupation of Czechoslovakia. A naïve young train dispatcher is forced to grow up quickly when asked to help the Czech underground. This gentle film is one of the more artistic efforts to come from behind the Iron Curtain. 1966; B&W; 91m.

CLOWNS, THE ★★★★½
DIR: Federico Fellini. **CAST:** Mayo Morin, Lima Alberti.

Federico Fellini's television documentary is a three-ring spectacle of fun and silliness, too. Here, style is substance, and the only substance worth noting is the water thrown onto the journalist who asks the cast of circus crazies, "What does it all mean?" In Italian with English subtitles. 1971; 90m.

COLONEL REDL ★★½
DIR: Istvan Szabo. **CAST:** Klaus Maria Brandauer, Armin Mueller-Stahl.

The ponderous and deliberate nature of *Colonel Redl*, which tells the story of how the title character became a pawn in a struggle for power in the Austro-Hungarian Empire just prior to World War I, keeps it from becoming a fully satisfying film. Rated R for profanity, nudity, simulated sex, and violence. In German with English subtitles. 1985; 144m.

COMING UP ROSES ★★½
DIR: Stephen Bayly. **CAST:** Dafydd Hywel, Lola Gregory, Bill Paterson.

This offbeat comedy is about the efforts of a projectionist in a small mining village in south Wales to keep a local movie theatre open during an economic crisis. Endearing characters performed with zest by an all–Welsh-speaking cast but the movie never rises above the poor film direction. In Welsh with English subtitles. Not rated. 1986; 90m.

COMMISSAR, THE ★★★★
DIR: Aleksandr Askoldov. **CAST:** Nonna Mordyukova.

A cinematic gift from Glasnost, it's a long-repressed Soviet film about a female Soviet officer and her relationship with a family of Jewish villagers. Challenging and innovative, it's a pro-Semitic film from the mid-Sixties that languished on a shelf for two decades before being freed by changing times. It surfaced in the U.S. in 1988. In Russian with English subtitles. 1988; 115m.

CONFIDENTIALLY YOURS ★★½
DIR: François Truffaut. **CAST:** Fanny Ardant, Jean-Louis Trintignant, Jean-Pierre Kalfon.

François Truffaut's last film is a stylized murder mystery in the tradition of Hitchcock. Truffaut might have had a jolly time making this homage, but it's only a lighthearted soufflé. Jean-Louis Trintignant plays a real estate agent framed for murder. Rated PG. In French with English subtitles. 1983; B&W; 110m.

CONFORMIST, THE ★★★★
DIR: Bernardo Bertolucci. **CAST:** Jean-Louis Trintignant, Stefania Sandrelli, Dominique Sanda, Pierre Clementi.

Fascinating character study of Marcello Clerici (Jean-Louis Trintignant), a follower of Mussolini. He becomes increasingly obsessed with conformity as he tries to suppress a traumatic homosexual experience suffered as a youth. He is forced to prove his loyalty to the fascist state by murdering a former professor who lives in exile. Rated R for language and subject matter. In French with English subtitles. 1971; 107m.

CONTEMPT ★★★½
DIR: Jean-Luc Godard. **CAST:** Brigitte Bardot, Jack Palance, Fritz Lang, Jean-Luc Godard, Michel Piccoli.

A cult film to be, if it isn't already, this one takes a tongue-in-cheek, raised-eyebrow look at European moviemaking. Jack Palance is a vulgar producer; Fritz Lang, playing himself, is his director; Jean-Luc Godard plays Lang's assistant, and in directing this film turned it into an inside joke—in real (not reel) life, he held the film's producer Joseph E. Levine in contempt. 1963; 103m.

CONTRABAND ★★
DIR: Lucio Fulci. **CAST:** Fabio Testi, Ivana Monti.

A mediocre Italian gangster movie, dubbed into English. This time the main vice is contraband goods rather than hard drugs or prostitution. But the story is the same. Each gang is vying for complete control and is killing and undermining the other's operations. 1987; 87m.

CONVERSATION PIECE ★
DIR: Luchino Visconti. **CAST:** Burt Lancaster, Silvana Mangano, Helmut Berger, Claudia Cardinale.

All the talent collected to produce this film can't save it from being mundane, wordy, and phlegmatic. Burt Lancaster portrays a bewildered, reclusive professor whose life changes direction when he encounters a countess and her children. In Italian with English subtitles. 1974; 122m.

COP AND THE GIRL, THE ★
DIR: Peter Keglevic. **CAST:** Jurgen Prochnow, Annette Von Klier.

Something is lost in the translation of this dubbed German film. A policeman (Jurgen Prochnow) chases an 18-year-old girl who has stolen his gun. Both of them become fugitives. Unrated, but contains profanity and violence. 1987; 95m.

COUSIN, COUSINE ★★★½
DIR: Jean-Charles Tacchella. **CAST:** Marie-Christine Barrault, Victor Lanoux, Marie-France Pisier, Guy Marchand.
Marie-Christine Barrault and Victor Lanoux star in this ever-popular French comedy. Both married to others, they become cousins by marriage. Once the kissing starts, their relationship expands beyond the boundaries of convention. In French with English subtitles. 1975; 95m.

CRAZY RAY, THE ★★★½
DIR: René Clair. **CAST:** Henri Rollan, Madeline Rodrigue, Albert Préjean.
René Clair's classic fantasy about a scientist's paralyzing ray is basically an experimental film. A handful of people who have not been affected by the ray take advantage of the situation and help themselves to whatever they want but eventually begin to fight among themselves. 1923; B&W; 60m.

CRIES AND WHISPERS ★★★★★
DIR: Ingmar Bergman. **CAST:** Harriet Andersson, Liv Ullmann, Ingrid Thulin, Kari Sylwan.
Directed and written by Ingmar Bergman and hauntingly photographed by Sven Nykvist, this Swedish language film tells a story of a dying woman, her two sisters, and a servant girl. Faultless performances make this an unforgettable film experience. Rated R. 1972; 106m.

CRIME OF MONSIEUR LANGE, THE ★★★★
DIR: Jean Renoir. **CAST:** René Lefévre, Jules Berry.
Jean Renoir's compelling masterpiece sprang from the director's belief that the common man, by united action, could overcome tyranny. When the head of a printing press disappears with all of the firm's funds, the employees band together and raise enough money to go into business as a publisher of popular novelettes. In French with English subtitles. 1935; B&W; 90m.

CRIMINAL LIFE OF ARCHIBALDO DE LA CRUZ, THE ★★★★
DIR: Luis Buñuel. **CAST:** Ernesto Alonso, Miroslava Stern.
Luis Buñuel's violently erotic satire about a perverted young aristocrat who believes a music box he owned as a child has the power to kill. This surreal black comedy is an uncompromising attack on the social, religious, and political ramifications of contemporary society. A must-see! In Spanish with English subtitles. Not rated. 1955; B&W; 91m.

DAMNED, THE ★★★½
DIR: Luchino Visconti. **CAST:** Dirk Bogarde, Ingrid Thulin, Helmut Griem, Helmut Berger.
Deep, heavy drama about a German industrialist family that is destroyed under Nazi power. This film is difficult to watch, as the images are as bleak as the story itself. In German, with English subtitles. Rated R for sex. 1969; 155m.

DANDELIONS ★
DIR: Adrian Hoven. **CAST:** Rutger Hauer, Dagmar Lassander.
This German-made soft-porn film stars Rutger Hauer as a cold, sadistic leather boy in pursuit of his fantasy girl. Made in 1974, it is obviously being released to cash in on Hauer's current popularity. Dubbed in English. 1987; 92m.

DANGEROUS MOVES ★★★★½
DIR: Richard Dembo. **CAST:** Michel Piccoli, Leslie Caron, Alexandre Arbatt, Liv Ullmann.
Worthy of its Oscar for best foreign film of 1984, this French film about a chess match between two grand masters in Geneva is not just for fans of the game. Indeed, the real intensity that is created here comes from the sidelines: the two masters' camps, the psych-out attempts, the political stakes, and the personal dramas. Rated PG for adult situations and language. 1984; 95m.

DANTON ★★★½
DIR: Andrzej Wajda. **CAST:** Gerard Depardieu, Wojiech Pszoniak, Patrice Chereau.
Polish director Andrezej Wajda takes the French revolutionary figure (well played by Gerard Depardieu) and the events surrounding his execution by one-time comrades and turns it into a parable of modern life. It may not be good history, but the film does provide food for thought. In French. Rated PG. 1982; 136m.

DARK EYES ★★★½
DIR: Nikita Mikhalkov. **CAST:** Marcello Mastroianni, Marthe Keller, Silvana Mangano.
Based on several short stories by Anton Chekhov, *Dark Eyes* takes its title from a Russian ballad that fills the sound track. Marcello Mastroianni is wonderfully endearing as a dapper, love-struck Italian who meets a young Russian woman at a spa and later in her village. The Russian scenery, replete with rolling hills at dawn and singing Gypsies, is a tourist's dream. In Italian with English subtitles. 1987; 118m.

DAS BOOT (THE BOAT) ★★★★★
DIR: Wolfgang Petersen. **CAST:** Jurgen Prochnow, Herbert Gronemeyer.
During World War II, forty thousand young Germans served aboard Nazi submarines. Only ten thousand survived. This West German film masterpiece recreates the tension and claustrophobic conditions of forty-three men assigned to a U-boat in 1941. This is the English-dubbed version. 1981; 150m.

DAY FOR NIGHT ★★★★★
DIR: François Truffaut. **CAST:** Jacqueline Bisset, Jean-Pierre Léaud, François Truffaut.
One of the best of the film-within-a-film movies ever made, this work by the late François Truffaut captures the poetry and energy of the creative artist at his peak. In French with English subtitles. Rated PG. 1973; 120m.

DAY IN THE COUNTRY, A ★★★★
DIR: Jean Renoir. **CAST:** Sylvia Bataille, Georges Darnoux.
A young girl who was seduced on an afternoon outing returns to the scene fourteen years later, an unhappily married woman. Jean Renoir's lyrical impressionistic tragedy is based on a story by Guy de Maupassant. Mesmerizing cinematography by Claude Renoir and Henri Cartier-Bresson. In French with English subtitles. 1935; 40m.

DAY OF WRATH ★★★½
DIR: Carl Dreyer. **CAST:** Lisbeth Movin, Thorkild Roose.
Slow-moving, intriguing story of a young woman who marries an elderly preacher but falls in love with his son is an allegorical indictment on the appearances of evil. Visually effective and well acted by all the principals, this film relies too much on symbolism but is still worthy as a study of hysteria and the motivations behind fear. 1944; B&W; 98m.

DEBAJO DEL MUNDO (UNDER EARTH) ★★★★
DIR: Beda Docampo Feijoo, Juan Bautista Stagnaro. **CAST:** Sergio Renan.
A Polish family's prosperous life is shattered when the German army invades their small farming community. This Spanish film captures the spirit of a family torn apart by war. A great cast gives compelling performances in this poignant drama. Dubbed in English. Rated R for profanity and graphic violence. 1988; 100m.

DECLINE OF THE AMERICAN EMPIRE, THE ★★★★
DIR: Denys Arcand. **CAST:** Dominique Michel, Dorothee Berryman, Louise Portal.
Writer-director Denys Arcand focuses on two groups, one male and one female. Both reveal intimate secrets about their lives. Rated R for

profanity, nudity, and simulated sex. In French with English subtitles. 1986; 101m.

DERSU UZALA ★★★★½
DIR: Akira Kurosawa. **CAST:** Maxim Munzuk, Yuri Solomin.
This epic about the charting of the Siberian wilderness (circa 1900) is surprisingly as intimate in relationships and details as it is grand in vistas and scope. A Japanese-Russian coproduction, the second half of this Oscar winner is much better than the first. In Russian and Japanese with English subtitles. 1974; 140m.

DESPAIR ★★★★
DIR: Rainer Werner Fassbinder. **CAST:** Dirk Bogarde, Klaus Lowitsch.
Karlovich (Dirk Bogarde), a Russian living in Germany in 1930, runs an unsuccessful chocolate factory. The stock market crash in America pushes his business into even deeper trouble, and he begins to lose touch with himself in a major way. Black comedy at its blackest. Rated R. 1979; 119m.

DESTINY ★★★½
DIR: Fritz Lang. **CAST:** Lil Dagover, Walter Janssen, Bernhard Goetzke, Rudolf Klein-Rogge.
Fritz Lang's first important success is a triumph of style that delves into the nature of love. Consisting of interlocking stories, dream sequences, and nightmarish associations, Lang's fable tells the story of a young woman who challenges Death for the life of her lover but cannot bring herself to offer the sacrifices the grim one demands. Silent. 1921; B&W; 114m.

DEVI (THE GODDESS) ★★★★
DIR: Satyajit Ray. **CAST:** Chhabi Biswas, Soumitra Chatterjee.
Excellent social satire from India's gifted Satyajit Ray. A deeply religious landowner becomes convinced that his beautiful daughter-in-law is the incarnation of the Hindu goddess Kali, to whom he becomes fanatically devoted. In Bengali with English subtitles. 1960; B&W; 96m.

DEVIL IN THE FLESH ★
DIR: Marco Bellocchio. **CAST:** Maruschka Detmers, Federico Pitzalis.
A story of two young lovers—a lanky student and a *Betty Blue*–like madwoman. Both are deeply unsympathetic. When the graphic sex finally arrives, it's anticlimactic. Rated X. In Italian with English subtitles. 1987; 120m.

DEVIL'S EYE, THE ★★
DIR: Ingmar Bergman. **CAST:** Jarl Kulle, Bibi Andersson, Gunnar Björnstrand.
Disappointing comedy based on the Danish radio play *Don Juan Returns*. In order to cure the sty in his eye, the devil sends Don Juan (Jarl Kulle) from hell to breach a woman's chastity. Bibi Andersson plays Britt-Marie, the pastor's virgin daughter. 1960; 90m.

DIABOLICALLY YOURS ★★★
DIR: Julien Duvivier. **CAST:** Alain Delon, Senta Berger.
How would you like to wake up after an accident to find a beautiful wife and a luxurious mansion that you have no recollection of? Sound great? Unfortunately, it's the start of a nightmare. This French film is unrated but contains violence. 1967; 94m.

DIABOLIQUE ★★★★
DIR: Henri-Georges Clouzot. **CAST:** Simone Signoret, Vera Clouzot, Charles Vanel, Paul Meurisse.
This classic thriller builds slowly but rapidly gathers momentum along the way. Both wife and mistress of a headmaster conspire to kill him. This twisted plot of murder has since been copied many times. In French, with English subtitles. 1955; B&W; 107m.

DIARY OF A CHAMBERMAID ★★★★
DIR: Luis Buñuel. **CAST:** Jeanne Moreau, Michel Piccoli, Georges Geret, Daniel Ivernel.
Excellent remake of Jean Renoir's 1946 film concerns the personal dilemma of a maid (Jeanne Moreau) caught in the grip of fascism in 1939

France. Director Luis Buñuel paints a cynical portrait of the bourgeoisie—a stunning character study. French dialogue with English subtitles. 1964; B&W; 95m.

DIARY OF A COUNTRY PRIEST ★★★★

DIR: Robert Bresson. **CAST:** Claude Laydu, Nicole Ladmiral, Nicole Maurey.

The slow pace at the beginning of this tale about a priest trying to minister to his parish might tend to put some viewers off. However, with Bresson's poetic style and camera work, the wait is well worth it. In French with English subtitles. 1950; B&W; 120m.

DIARY OF A LOST GIRL ★★★★

DIR: G. W. Pabst. **CAST:** Louise Brooks, Joseph Rovensky, Fritz Rasp, André Roanne, Valeska Gert.

In this silent classic, Louise Brooks plays a young girl who is raped by her father's business partner (Fritz Rasp). Banished to a girls' reformatory, she eventually escapes, falling prey to the false sanctuary provided by a whorehouse madame. Those who maintain there is a docility to silent films may be surprised by the relatively mature subject matter in this film. 1929; B&W; 99m.

DIRTY DISHES ★★

DIR: Joyce Buñuel. **CAST:** Pierre Santini, Liliane Roveryre, Liza Braconnier.

The American-born daughter-in-law of Luis Buñuel makes her directorial debut with this mediocre comedy about domestic madness. A beautiful French housewife finds herself trapped in an uneventful marriage. This leads to an explosive encounter with a lecherous neighbor. This comedy-drama takes its theme from the superior *Diary of a Mad Housewife*. Not rated. In French with English subtitles. 1982; 99m.

DISCREET CHARM OF THE BOURGEOISIE, THE ★★★★

DIR: Luis Buñuel. **CAST:** Fernando Rey, Delphine Seyrig, Stéphane Audran, Bulle Ogier, Jean-Pierre Cassel, Michel Piccoli.

Dinner is being served in this Louis Buñuel masterpiece, but the food never gets a chance to arrive at the table. Every time the hosts and guests try to begin the meal, some outside problem rises. Typically French, typically Buñuel, topically hilarious. Winner of the best foreign film Oscar for 1972. 1972; 100m.

DISTANT THUNDER (1974) ★★★★

DIR: Satyajit Ray. **CAST:** Soumitra Chatterjee.

Outstanding drama by Satyajit Ray about the effects of a famine on the lives of various family members in World War II India. Beautiful cinematography sweeps the viewer through the desert landscapes of India. In Bengali with English subtitles. 1974; 92m.

DIVA ★★★★

DIR: Jean-Jacques Beineix. **CAST:** Frederic Andrei, Wilhemenia Wiggins Fernandez.

In this stunningly stylish suspense film by first-time director Jean-Jacques Beineix, a young opera lover unknowingly becomes involved with the underworld. Unbeknownst to him, he's in possession of some very valuable tapes—and the delightful chase is on. In French, with English subtitles. Rated R for profanity, nudity, and violence. 1982; 123m.

DIVINE NYMPH, THE ★★½

DIR: Giuseppe Patroni Griffi. **CAST:** Laura Antonelli, Terence Stamp, Marcello Mastroianni.

This story of love and passion resembles an Italian soap opera at best. Laura Antonelli is the young beauty who is unfaithful to her fiancé. She has an affair with Terence Stamp, who coerces her into having another affair with Marcello Mastroianni. In Italian, with English subtitles. Rated R for nudity. 1977; 89m.

DODES 'KA-DEN ★★★★
DIR: Akira Kurosawa. **CAST:** Yoshitaka Zushi.

Akira Kurosawa's first color film is a spellbinding blend of fantasy and reality. The film chronicles the lives of a group of Tokyo slum dwellers that includes children, alcoholics, and the disabled. Illusion and imagination are their weapons as they fight for survival. In Japanese with English subtitles. 1970; 140m.

DONA FLOR AND HER TWO HUSBANDS ★★★★
DIR: Bruno Barreto. **CAST:** Sonia Braga, José Wilker, Mauro Mendonca.

A ribald Brazilian comedy about a woman (Sonia Braga) haunted by the sexy ghost of her first husband (José Wilker), who's anything but happy about her impending remarriage, this film inspired the Sally Field vehicle *Kiss Me Goodbye*. The original is better all around. In Portuguese, with English subtitles. Unrated, the film has nudity. 1978; 106m.

DONKEY SKIN (PEAU D'ÂNE) ★★★★
DIR: Jacques Demy. **CAST:** Catherine Deneuve, Jean Marais, Jacques Perrin, Delphine Seyrig.

Looking for something different? The creator of *The Umbrellas of Cherbourg* also made this charming, colorful fairy tale for an adult audience. A princess, about to be forced to marry her own father, escapes with the aid of her fairy godmother and hides out as a scullery maid. Before long, though, the local Prince Charming sees through her drab disguise. *Donkey Skin* is a delightful combination of the real and the dreamlike that could easily have been unbearably cute in less skilled hands. Okay for kids, but not really intended for them. In French with English subtitles. 1970; 90m.

DONNA HERLINDA AND HER SON ★★★
DIR: Jaime Humberto Hermosillo. **CAST:** Guadalupe Del Toro, Marco Antonio Trevino.

This highly enjoyable, raunchy comedy explores the bizarre relationship a mother has with her sexually liberated homosexual son. It's a delightful comedy of manners featuring a memorable cast and a director with a great touch for deadpan humor. In Spanish with English subtitles. 1986; 90m.

DOUBLE SUICIDE ★★★★
DIR: Masahiro Shinoda. **CAST:** Kichiemon Nakamura, Shima Iwashita.

Stunning portrait of erotic obsession and passion in turn-of-century Japan. Director Masahiro Shinoda explores sexual taboos in his story of a merchant and a geisha whose illfated love affair is orchestrated entirely by outside forces. This poignant drama is presented in the style of a Bunraku puppet play. Not rated. In Japanese with English subtitles. 1969; B&W; 105m.

DOWN AND DIRTY ★★★★
DIR: Ettore Scola. **CAST:** Nino Manfredi, Francesco Anniballi.

Brutal but brilliant black comedy about a slumlord of a shantytown in Rome. Nino Manfredi is excellent as a money-hoarding patriarch whose obsession with his stash leads to a plot by his wife and delinquent sons to kill him. Not rated, but contains violence, profanity, and nudity. In Italian with English subtitles. 1976; 115m.

DRUNKEN ANGEL ★★★★
DIR: Akira Kurosawa. **CAST:** Toshiro Mifune, Takashi Shimura.

Master director Akira Kurosawa here displays an early interest in good guys and bad guys. Toshiro Mifune is a petty gangster who learns from an idealistic slum doctor (Takashi Shimura) that he is dying of tuberculosis. In Japanese with English subtitles. 1949; B&W; 102m.

EARLY SUMMER ★★★½
DIR: Yasujiro Ozu. **CAST:** Setsuko Hara.
Involved and involving story about a young woman rebelling against an arranged marriage in post–World War II Tokyo. Yasujiro Ozu, one of Japan's most respected directors, deftly presents this tale of culture clash, which won the Japanese Film of the Year Award in 1951. In Japanese with English subtitles. 1951; B&W; 135m.

EARTH ★★★★
DIR: Alexander Dovzhenko. **CAST:** Semyon Svashenko.
One of the last classic silent films, this short homage to the spirit of the collective farmer and his intangible ties to the land employs stunning camera shots. Certain scenes from the original print no longer exist, but what remains of this film tells a beautiful, moving story. Russian, silent. 1930; B&W; 56m.

ECSTASY ★★½
DIR: Gustav Machaty. **CAST:** Hedy Lamarr, Arlbert Mog.
Completely overshadowed since its release by the notoriety of Hedy Lamarr's nude scenes, this new packaging in video should shift the emphasis back to the film itself, which is basically a romance of illicit love between a married woman and a stranger to whom she is attracted. Filmed in pre-Hitler Czechoslovakia, this version is subtitled in English. 1933; B&W; 88m.

EDITH AND MARCEL ★★★★
DIR: Claude Lelouch. **CAST:** Evelyne Bouix, Marcel Cerdan Jr., Jacques Villeret, Francis Huster.
Based on the real life of famous torch singer Edith Piaf (Evelyn Bouix), this powerful musical-drama follows the passionate affair she had with champion boxer Marcel Cerdan (Marcel Cerdan Jr.). Director Claude Lelouch brings to life the stormy romance that at one time captured the attention of the world. In French with English subtitles. 1983; 170m.

8½ ★★★★★
DIR: Federico Fellini. **CAST:** Marcello Mastroianni, Anouk Aimée, Claudia Cardinale, Barbara Steele, Sandra Milo.
Perhaps one of Federico Fellini's strongest cinematic achievements. *8 1/2* is the loose portrayal of a film director making a personal movie and finding himself trapped in his fears, dreams, and irresolutions. This brilliant exercise features outstanding performances, especially by Marcello Mastroianni. Not rated. Dubbed into English. 1963; B&W; 135m.

EL AMOR BRUJO ★★
DIR: Carlos Saura. **CAST:** Antonio Gades, Cristina Hoyos, Laura Del Sol.
This occasionally brilliant big-screen production of Manuel de Falla's ballet will appeal primarily to flamenco fans. The cast is excellent and some of the scenes rivet the viewer, but overall the movie fails to fascinate. In Spanish with English subtitles. Rated PG for brief, stylized violence and references to sex in lyrics. 1986; 100m.

EL BRUTO (THE BRUTE) ★★★½
DIR: Luis Buñuel. **CAST:** Pedro Armendariz, Katy Jurado, Andres Soler.
Exceptional surreal drama from Luis Buñuel about a tough slaughterhouse laborer who is exploited by a tyranical landowner. Some strange melodramatic twists laced with moments of irony make this Mexican film one of Buñuel's stronger efforts. Spanish dialogue with English subtitles. Not rated. 1952; B&W; 83m.

EL NORTE ★★★★★
DIR: Gregory Nava. **CAST:** Zaide Silvia Gutierrez, David Villalpando.
A rewarding story about two Guatemalans, a young brother and sister, whose American dream takes them on a long trek through Mexico to El Norte—the United States. This American-made movie is funny, frightening, poignant, and sobering—a movie

that stays with you. Rated R for profanity and violence. In Spanish with subtitles. 1983; 139m.

EL PROFESSOR HIPPIE ★★½
DIR: Fernando Ayala. **CAST:** Luis Sandrini.
Veteran comedian Luis Sandrini plays a college professor who, because of his free-thinking attitudes and concerns for moral questions over matters of business, has more in common with his students than his colleagues. This gentle comedy is a real audience-pleaser. In Spanish. 1969; 91m.

ELENA AND HER MEN ★★★
DIR: Jean Renoir. **CAST:** Ingrid Bergman, Jean Marais, Mel Ferrer, Juliette Greco.
One of Jean Renoir's personal favorites, this musical fantasy is about the power of love, the folly of progress, the beauty of laziness, and the evil of dictators. Ingrid Bergman is supported by a fine cast in this enjoyable comedy-drama. Originally released in America as *Paris Does Strange Things*. In French with English subtitles. 1956; 98m.

ELUSIVE CORPORAL, THE ★★★★½
DIR: Jean Renoir. **CAST:** Jean-Pierre Cassel, Claude Brasseur, Claude Rich.
Twenty-five years after he made his greatest masterpiece, *La Grande Illusion,* Renoir reexamines men in war with almost equally satisfying results. This time the soldiers are Frenchmen in a World War II prison camp. *The Elusive Corporal* is a delicate drama infused with considerable wit. In French with English subtitles. 1962; 108m.

ELVIRA MADIGAN ★★★★
DIR: Bo Widerberg. **CAST:** Pia Degermark, Thommy Berggren.
This is a simple and tragic story of a young Swedish officer who falls in love with a beautiful circus performer. Outstanding photography makes this film. Try to see the subtitled version. 1967; 89m.

EMMANUELLE ★★★
DIR: Just Jaeckin. **CAST:** Sylvia Kristel, Marika Green, Daniel Sarky, Alain Cuny.
Sylvia Kristel became an international star as a result of this French screen adaptation of Emmanuelle Aran's controversial book about the initiation of a diplomat's young wife into the world of sensuality. In the soft-core sex film genre, this stands out as one of the best. Rated R for nudity. 1974; 92m.

END OF ST. PETERSBURG, THE ★★★½
DIR: V. I. Pudovkin. **CAST:** Ivan Chuvelov.
The story of a worker who gradually becomes aware of his duty to his class. He becomes a part of the 1917 revolution. Although pure propaganda, this powerful indictment of czarist Russia has a fervor and sweep that transcends its message. Silent, with English intertitles. 1927; B&W; 75m.

ENTRE NOUS (BETWEEN US) ★★★★★
DIR: Diane Kurys. **CAST:** Miou-Miou, Isabelle Huppert, Guy Marchand.
This down-to-earth, highly human story by director Diane Kurys concentrates on the friendship between two women, Madeline (Miou-Miou) and Lena (Isabelle Huppert), who find they have more in common with each other than with their husbands. It is an affecting tale the viewer won't soon forget. Rated PG for nudity, suggested sex, and violence. 1983; 110m.

ERENDIRA ★★½
DIR: Ruy Guerra. **CAST:** Irene Papas, Claudia Ohana, Michel Lonsdale.
In this disturbing and distasteful black comedy, Irene Papas stars as a wealthy old woman who loses everything in a fire accidentally set by her sleepwalking granddaughter, Erendira (Claudia Ohana). To regain her lost riches, the grandmother turns

her charge into a prostitute and insists that she earn back over $1 million. In Spanish, with English subtitles. Unrated, the film has nudity, profanity, simulated sex, and violence. 1983; 103m.

EVERY MAN FOR HIMSELF AND GOD AGAINST ALL ★★★★
DIR: Werner Herzog. **CAST:** Bruno S., Walter Ladengast, Brigitte Mira.

Based on a real incident, the story of Kasper Hauser (Bruno S.) tells of a man who had been kept in confinement since birth. Hauser's appearance in Nuremberg in the 1920s was a mystery. He was a man who tried to adjust to a new society while maintaining his own vision. Also released as *The Mystery of Kasper Hauser*. In German, with English subtitles. No MPAA rating. 1975; 110m.

EXTERMINATING ANGEL, THE ★★★★★
DIR: Luis Buñuel. **CAST:** Silvia Pinal, Enrique Rambal.

Luis Buñuel always did love a good dinner party. In *The Discreet Charm of the Bourgeoisie*, the dinner party never could get under way, and here the elite *aprѐs-opéra* diners find they cannot escape the host's sumptuous music room. This is a very funny film—in a very black key. In Spanish with English subtitles. 1962; B&W; 95m.

EYES, THE MOUTH, THE ★
DIR: Marco Bellocchio. **CAST:** Lou Castel, Angela Molina, Emmanuelle Riva.

This movie presumes to tell the story of a man (Lou Castel) who liberates his soul from the past and embraces life after his twin brother commits suicide. It founders so much that your mind soon drifts. In Italian with English subtitles. Rated R for language and nudity. 1983; 100m.

EYES WITHOUT A FACE ★★★★½
DIR: Georges Franju. **CAST:** Pierre Brasseur, Alida Valli, Edith Scob, Juliette Mayniel.

Georges Franju, one of the underrated heroes of French cinema, creates an austerely beautiful horror film about a plastic surgeon who, in systematic experiments, removes the faces of beautiful young women and tries to graft them onto the ruined head of his daughter. Imaginative cinematography by Eugen Shuftan with music by Maurice Jarre. Subtitled, not rated. (Originally released in America as *The Horror Chamber of Dr. Faustus*.) 1960; B&W; 102m.

FAMILY, THE (1987) ★★★
DIR: Ettore Scola. **CAST:** Vittorio Gassman, Fanny Ardant, Stefania Sandrelli.

This bustling, good-natured film, thick with anecdotes, covers the life of a man growing up in Italy from the turn of the century to the present. It is a theatrical account focusing on a celebration of family life. In Italian with English subtitles. The film has no objectionable material. 1987; 140m.

FAMILY GAME, THE ★★★★½
DIR: Yoshimitsu Morita. **CAST:** Yusaku Matsuda, Juzo Itami.

This is a very funny film about a modern Japanese family faced with the same problems as their Western counterparts. A teen with school problems, a father striving for middle-class affluency, and a new tutor who shakes things up result in what was voted best film of 1983 in Japan. With English subtitles. 1983; 107m.

FANNY (1932) ★★★★
DIR: Marc Allegret. **CAST:** Raimu, Orane Demazis, Pierre Fresnay.

The middle part of a trilogy that began with *Marius* and ended with *César*, this can nevertheless be viewed on its own. Young Marius leaves Marseilles to become a sailor, not knowing that his fiancée, Fanny, is pregnant. In his absence, she marries another man, who agrees to raise the child as his own. The film itself is static—it was conceived for the stage—but the performances are superb, particularly Raimu as Marius's father. The entire trilogy was condensed and remade in America as *Fanny* (1961). In French with English subtitles. 1932; B&W; 120m.

FANNY AND ALEXANDER ★★★★★
DIR: Ingmar Bergman. **CAST:** Pernilla Allwin, Bertil Guve.

Set in Sweden around the turn of the century, this movie follows the adventures of two children. Some have called this Ingmar Bergman's first truly accessible work. It is undeniably his most optimistic. In Swedish, with English subtitles. Rated R for profanity and violence. 1983; 197m.

FATHER ★★★
DIR: Istvan Szabo. **CAST:** Andras Balint, Miklos Gabor.

Istvan Szabo, best known for the Oscar-winning *Mephisto*, directed this drama. It concerns a boy who creates an elaborate fantasy about the heroism of his father, who was killed in World War II. As an adult, he is led by the uprising of 1956 and the love of a Jewish girl to abandon his fantasies and examine the reality of his heritage. Slow-moving but provocative. In Hungarian with English subtitles. 1966; B&W; 89m.

FAUST ★★★★★
DIR: F. W. Murnau. **CAST:** Emil Jannings, Gosta Ekman, Camilla Horn.

The undisputed master of early German cinema, Friedrich W. Murnau triumphs once again with the legendary story of Faust. Gosta Ekman gives an excellent performance as Faust and Emil Jannings plays the Devil with comic pathos. Silent, with English intertitles. 1926; B&W; 100m.

FEARLESS
DIR: Stelvio Massi. **CAST:** Joan Collins, Maurizio Merli.

This confusing, raunchy Italian film features Joan Collins as a rather inept striptease artist in Vienna. On the side, she induces young girls to meet with her wealthy clients. The only interesting thing here is the laughable dubbing. Unrated, it contains violence and nudity. 1978; 89m.

FELLINI SATYRICON ★★★½
DIR: Federico Fellini. **CAST:** Martin Potter, Hiram Keller, Gordon Mitchell, Capucine.

Federico Fellini's visionary account of ancient Rome before Christ is a bizarre, hallucinatory journey. Imaginative art direction, lavish costumes, and garish makeup create a feast for the eyes. Composer Nino Rota's brilliant score is another plus. Not rated, contains nudity and violence. Italian dialogue with English subtitles. 1969; 129m.

FELLINI'S ROMA ★★★★
DIR: Federico Fellini. **CAST:** Peter Gonzales, Marne Maitland, Federico Fellini.

Federico Fellini's odyssey through Rome is the director's impressionistic account of the city of his youth. With the help of a small film crew, Fellini explores the Italian capital with his own unique brand of visionary wit. A brilliant piece of moviemaking. Not rated. In Italian with English subltitles. 1972; 128m.

FERNANDEL THE DRESSMAKER ★★
DIR: Jean Boyer. **CAST:** Fernandel, Suzy Delair, Françoise Fabian.

Using Fernandel as the hub, the film is a bit of whimsy about a gentleman's tailor who desires to become a world-famous couturier. Even with a lightweight plot, watching this famous comedian is certainly worth the time and effort to wade through the nonsense. In French with English subtitles. 1957; B&W; 84m.

FIELD OF HONOR (1988) ★★
DIR: Jean-Pierre Denis. **CAST:** Cris Campion.

A nineteenth-century French saga about young men at war, with aspirations to the classic status of *The Red Badge of Courage*. Despite its aim at tragic symmetry, the film's muddled and meandering script causes it to fall short. Strangely uninvolving. In

French with English subtitles. 1988; 89m.

FIREMAN'S BALL, THE ★★½
DIR: Milos Forman. **CAST:** Jan Vostrcil.

Highly acclaimed comedy of a small-town firemen's gathering that turns into a sprawling, ludicrous disaster. Fairly weak considering direction by Milos Forman. In Czech with English subtitles. 1968; 73m.

FIRES ON THE PLAIN ★★★★
DIR: Kon Ichikawa. **CAST:** Eiji Funakoshi.

Kon Ichikawa's classic uses World War II and malnourished soldiers' cannibalism as symbols for the brutality of man. *Fires on the Plain* is uncomplicated and its emotion intensely focused. It is a stark and disturbing vision. In Japanese with English subtitles. 1959; 105m.

FITZCARRALDO ★★★½
DIR: Werner Herzog. **CAST:** Klaus Kinski, Claudia Cardinale.

For Werner Herzog, the making of this film was reportedly quite an ordeal. Watching it may be an ordeal for some viewers as well. In order to bring Caruso, the greatest voice in the world, to the backwater town of Iquitos, the title character (Klaus Kinski) decides to haul a large boat over a mountain from a good river to a navigable portion of the bad one. Unrated, this film has profanity. In German, with English subtitles. 1982; 157m.

FLIGHT OF THE EAGLE ★★★½
DIR: Jan Troell. **CAST:** Max von Sydow.

This Swedish production presents the true adventure of three foolhardy 1897 polar explorers (one played by Max von Sydow) who tried to conquer the Arctic in a balloon. Unrated, the film has some gore. In Swedish with English subtitles. 1982; 139m.

FLOATING WEEDS ★★★★
DIR: Yasujiro Ozu. **CAST:** Ganjiro Nakamura, Machiko Kyo.

An aging leader of a troupe of actors takes his company to a small town where he pays a visit to a woman with whom he had an affair twenty years before. Her son believes him to be his uncle. The actor's mistress jealously plots to have the company seduce the boy in order to create a scandal. In Japanese with English subtitles. 1959; 128m.

FLOR SYLVESTRE ★★★½
DIR: Emilio Fernandez. **CAST:** Dolores Del Rio, Pedro Armendariz, Emilio Fernandez.

Mexican-born beauty Dolores Del Rio made many schlocky movies in America but had to return to her native country to appear in quality productions. This tale of two families torn apart by the Mexican revolution is one of the best. The story is a little corny, but the film has been beautifully photographed and directed. In Spanish with English subtitles. 1945; B&W; 94m.

FORBIDDEN GAMES ★★★★★
DIR: René Clement. **CAST:** Brigitte Fossey, Georges Poujouly.

It has been said that *Forbidden Games* is to World War II what *Grand Illusion* is to World War I. The horror of war has never been more real than as portrayed here against the bucolic surroundings of the French countryside. At the nucleus of the plot is Paulette, played by five-year-old Brigitte Fossey. Witnessing German troops kill her parents twists the girl, who acquires an attraction for the symbols of death. A truly tragic, must-see work. In French with English subtitles. 1951; B&W; 87m.

FORGOTTEN TUNE FOR THE FLUTE, A ★★★
DIR: Eldar Ryazanov. **CAST:** Tatyana Dogileva.

This Glasnost romantic comedy is a little long and stumbles with a somewhat contrived ending, but it's a joy otherwise. It introduces to the West the vivacious and talented Tatyana Dogileva and is a perfect remedy for

American movie-watchers who think all Russian films are solemn enterprises at best, epic drags at worst. In Russian with English subtitles. 1988; 131m.

FORTUNE'S FOOL ★★½
DIR: Reinhold Schunzel. **CAST:** Emil Jannings, Daguey Servaes, Reinhold Schunzel.
Best known for his dramatic roles, Emil Jannings hams it up in this German comedy about a profiteering meat-packer. Jannings was years away from *The Blue Angel* and international stardom when this was filmed, but he displays the gifts that made him a dominating screen figure. Silent. 1925; B&W; 60m.

400 BLOWS, THE ★★★★★
DIR: François Truffaut. **CAST:** Jean-Pierre Léaud, Patrick Auffay, Claire Maurier, Albert Remy.
Poignant story of a boy and the world that seems to be at odds with him is true and touching as few films have ever been. Powerful, tender, and at times overwhelmingly sad, this great film touches all the right buttons without being exploitative. In French with English subtitles. 1959; B&W; 99m.

FOURTH MAN, THE ★★★½
DIR: Paul Verhoeven. **CAST:** Jeroen Krabbé, Renee Soutenduk.
Jeroen Krabbe plays a gay alcoholic writer prone to hallucinations. Invited to lecture at a literary society, he meets a mysterious woman who he becomes convinced intends to kill him. *The Fourth Man* emerges as an atmospheric, highly original chiller. In Dutch, with English subtitles. Unrated, the film has nudity, simulated sex, violence, and profanity. 1984; 128m.

FRANZ
DIR: Jacques Brel. **CAST:** Jacques Brel.
Franz is a royal mess. A shy man named Leon falls in love with a woman named Leonie. He is tortured by his oppressive mother and his war memories. Leonie is just aloof and strange-looking, sort of like a mix of the Wicked Witch and Dracula. In French with English subtitles. 1972; 88m.

FRENCH CAN CAN ★★★
DIR: Jean Renoir. **CAST:** Jean Gabin.
Jean Renoir's rich cinematic style is evident in this comedy-drama starring Jean Gabin as a nightclub owner. Renoir tosses his can-can artists at the viewer, seducing us with the consuming spectacle. In French with English subtitles. 1955; 93m.

FRENCH DETECTIVE, THE ★★★★
DIR: Pierre Granier-Deferre. **CAST:** Lino Ventura, Patrick Dewaere, Victor Lanoux, Jacques Serres.
Suspenseful police drama featuring Lino Ventura as a tough, independent veteran cop who pursues a hood working for a corrupt politician. Solid performances by Ventura and Patrick Dewaere. In French with English subtitles. 1975; 93m.

FRENCH WAY, THE ★
DIR: Jacques De Baroncelli. **CAST:** Josephine Baker, Micheline Presle, Georges Marshall.
Famed burlesque dancer Josephine Baker appears as a café singer in this underdressed comedy about a boy and a girl who want to marry but can't because his father and her mother hate each other. Baker begins to do her famous feather dance, but the ending is edited out. That sexy tease aside, there's nothing of interest here. In French with English subtitles. 1952; B&W; 73m.

FROM THE LIVES OF THE MARIONETTES ★★
DIR: Ingmar Bergman. **CAST:** Robert Atzorn, Christine Buchegger, Heinz Bennent.
This Ingmar Bergman film, which details the vicious sex murder of a prostitute by an outwardly compassionate and intelligent man, is a puzzle that never really resolves itself. Nevertheless, fans of the acclaimed Swedish director's works will no doubt consider it another triumphant essay on

the complexities of the human condition. 1980; B&W; 104m.

FULL HEARTS AND EMPTY POCKETS ★½

DIR: Camillo Mastrocinque. **CAST:** Thomas Fritsch, Alexandra Stewart, Gino Cervi, Senta Berger, Linda Christian, Françoise Rosay.

A German youth in Rome begins with nothing and, through luck and happy coincidence, rises to a position of wealth and power. Forgettable European production will appeal only to those who can't resist another look at the streets of Rome. Dubbed in English. 1963; B&W; 88m.

FULL MOON IN PARIS ★★

DIR: Eric Rohmer. **CAST:** Pascale Ogier, Fabrice Luchini, Tcheky Karyo.

This French film from Eric Rohmer, does not sustain its momentum with it's this tale of a young girl's disillusionment with her live-in lover. Perhaps the problem is her self-absorption and lack of commitment, but you just don't seem to care about what happens. In French with English subtitles. 1984; 102m.

FUNERAL, THE ★★★½

DIR: Juzo Itami. **CAST:** Nobuko Miyamoto, Tsutomu Yamazaki.

An old man's sudden death creates hilarious havoc for his surviving family members in this engagingly offbeat comedy directed by Juzo Itami. The Japanese burial ritual becomes the stage where the younger generation struggles with the complex rituals of the traditional Buddhist ceremony. In Japanese with English subtitles. 1987; 124m.

FUNNY DIRTY LITTLE WAR (NO HABRA MAS PENAS NI OLVIDO) ★★★

DIR: Hector Olivera. **CAST:** Federico Luppi, Hector Bidonde.

This allegorical, comedic piece begins in the small town of Colonia Vela. The comedy centers around the struggle between the Marxists and the Peronistas in 1974, shortly before the death of Juan Perón. The action quickly builds from a series of foolish misunderstandings to a very funny confrontation. Not rated. Spanish with English subtitles. 1985; 80m.

GABRIELA ★★★

DIR: Bruno Barreto. **CAST:** Sonia Braga, Marcello Mastroianni, Antonio Cantafora.

Sexy Sonia Braga is both cook and mistress for bar owner Marcello Mastroianni in this excellent adaptation of Brazilian novelist Jorge Amado's comic romp *Gabriela, Clove and Cinnamon.* In Portuguese, with English subtitles. Rated R. 1983; 102m.

GAME IS OVER, THE ★★★

DIR: Roger Vadim. **CAST:** Jane Fonda, Peter McEnery, Michel Piccoli, Tina Marquand.

Emile Zola's novel *La Curée* was the basis for this adult story of a young woman who marries an older man but finds herself attracted to (and eventually sharing a bed with) his son. Well-acted and intelligently scripted, this film by Jane Fonda's then-husband Roger Vadim was considered daring at the time and holds up well for today's audiences. In French. 1966; 96m.

GARDEN OF THE FINZI-CONTINIS, THE ★★★★

DIR: Vittorio De Sica. **CAST:** Dominique Sanda, Helmut Berger, Lino Capolicchio, Fabio Testi.

Vittorio De Sica's adaptation of a Giorgio Bassani novel views the life of an aristocratic Jewish family's misfortune in fascist Italy. Flawless acting by Dominique Sanda and Helmut Berger. One of De Sica's best. Rated R. 1971; 95m.

GATE OF HELL ★★★★

DIR: Teinosuke Kinugasa. **CAST:** Machiko Kyo.

Beautiful, haunting tale about a samurai who becomes a monk in twelfth-century Japan in order to atone for his crime of driving a married woman to suicide. Winner of the Academy

Award for best foreign film of 1954. Director Teinosuke Kinugasa brilliantly re-creates medieval Japan. In Japanese with English subtitles. 1953; 86m.

GERVAISE ★★★
DIR: René Clement. **CAST:** Maria Schell, François Perier, Suzy Delair.

Soap-opera fans will be the best audience for this adaptation of an Emile Zola novel. Set in 1850 Paris, the movie follows the sad life of a woman who is abandoned by her lover, unlucky in business, and sent into penury by her drunken husband. In French with English subtitles. 1956; B&W; 120m.

GET OUT YOUR HANDKERCHIEFS ★★★½
DIR: Bertrand Blier. **CAST:** Gerard Depardieu, Patrick Dewaere, Carole Laure.

Winner of the 1978 Academy Award for best foreign film, this stars Gerard Depardieu as a clumsy husband so desperate to make his melancholic wife happy and pregnant that he provides her with a lover (Patrick Dewaere). A mostly improbable existential drama. Unrated, contains nudity. In French. 1978; 108m.

GIFT, THE ★★★
DIR: Michel Lang. **CAST:** Clio Goldsmith, Pierre Mondy, Claudia Cardinale.

A 55-year-old bank worker (Pierre Mondy) decides to take early retirement. So his coworkers give him an unusual retirement gift, an expensive hooker (Clio Goldsmith), who is asked to seduce him without his knowing her profession. An amiable sex comedy that most adult viewers will find diverting. In French with English subtitles. Rated R for nudity and profanity. 1982; 105m.

GINGER AND FRED ★★★★
DIR: Federico Fellini. **CAST:** Marcello Mastroianni, Giulietta Masina, Franco Fabrizi.

Set in the bizarre world of a modern-television supernetwork, this Fellini fantasy presents Giulietta Masina and Marcello Mastroianni as Ginger and Fred—a dance couple of the late Forties who copied the style of Fred Astaire and Ginger Rogers. The two are reunited for *Here's to You*, a television extravaganza. *Ginger and Fred* is a brillant satire of television and modern life. Rated PG-13 for profanity and adult themes. 1986; 127m.

GO-MASTERS, THE ★★★★
DIR: Junya Sato, Duan Ji-Shun. **CAST:** Sun Dao-Lin.

An impressive coproduction from Japan and China. *The Go-Masters*, set primarily during the Sino-Japanese War, details the odyssey of a young man who becomes a champion player in the ancient art of competition called Go, the precursor of chess, checkers, and other board games. His mastery of the game comes at a heart-rending price. A fascinating tale of obsession, heartbreak, and the tragedies of war. In Chinese and Japanese with English subtitles. Unrated, the film has violence. 1984; 123m.

GOALIE'S ANXIETY AT THE PENALTY KICK ★★★
DIR: Wim Wenders. **CAST:** Arthur Brauss, Erika Pluhar.

An athlete suffering from alienation commits a senseless murder for no apparent reason in this slow-moving, existential thriller. Arthur Brauss gives a moody performance as a man who is isolated by the end of his professional effectiveness. Excellent adaptation by Wim Wenders of the Peter Handke novel. In German with English subtitles. 1971; B&W; 101m.

GOING PLACES ★★
DIR: Bertrand Blier. **CAST:** Gerard Depardieu, Patrick Dewaere, Miou-Miou, Jeanne Moreau, Isabelle Huppert, Brigitte Fossey.

Memorable only as one of Gerard Depardieu's first screen appearances. He and Patrick Dewaere play a couple of amiable lowlifes who dabble in petty thievery and have their way with all the local women. Contains one of filmdom's most acutely uncomfortable scenes, when one of the young lads gets shot in the testicles. In French with English subtitles. Rated R for sex. 1974; 117m.

GOLDEN COACH, THE ★★★★
DIR: Jean Renoir. **CAST:** Anna Magnani.

Jean Renoir's little-known Franco-Italian masterpiece features Anna Magnani in a stunning performance as the leading lady of an eighteenth-century acting troupe touring South America. Magnani finds herself caught in a complex love triangle with a soldier, a vain bullfighter, and a viceroy who gives her a golden coach. In English. 1952; 95m.

GOLDEN DEMON ★★★
DIR: Koji Shima. **CAST:** Jun Negami.

As a rule, most Japanese love stories are sad. *Golden Demon*, a story of true love broken by pride, tradition, and avarice, is an exception. The story of a poor young man, in love with his adopted parents' daughter, who loses her to a rich entrepreneur (an arranged marriage), is richly entertaining. In Japanese, with English subtitles. 1953; 91m.

THE GOLEM (HOW HE CAME INTO THE WORLD) (DER GOLEM, WIE ER IN DIE WELT KAM) ★★★★
DIR: Paul Wegener. **CAST:** Paul Wegener.

Director Paul Wegener plays the lead role as the Golem, an ancient clay figure from Hebrew mythology that is brought to life by means of an amulet activated by the magic word "Aemaet" (the Hebrew word for truth). In a story similar to *Frankenstein,* the man of clay roams through medieval Prague in a mystic atmosphere created by the brilliant camerman Karl Freund. Silent. 1920; B&W; 70m.

GOLGOTHA ★
DIR: Julien Duvivier. **CAST:** Robert le Vigan, Jean Gabin, Harry Baur.

Early, seldom-seen depiction of the passion of Jesus Christ was reverently filmed in France, where it was a big box-office success. Adapted from the four gospels of the New Testament, using only direct quotes for the lines spoken by Jesus. In French with English subtitles. 1935; B&W; 100m.

GOODBYE EMMANUELLE ★★
DIR: François Letterier. **CAST:** Sylvia Kristel, Umberto Orsini, Jean Pierre Bouvier.

One of the *Emmanuelle* soft-core series, *Goodbye Emmanuelle* takes place on a tropical island and concerns a succession of personal and sexual relationships among half a dozen men and women. The dubbing is tolerable. Rated R for sexual situations. 1979; 92m.

GOSPEL ACCORDING TO SAINT MATTHEW, THE ★★★★
DIR: Pier Paolo Pasolini. **CAST:** Enrique Irazoque.

Pier Paolo Pasolini's visionary account of Jesus Christ's spiritual struggle against the afflictions of social injustice. Shot on location throughout southern Italy with a cast of nonprofessional actors who possess a natural quality. This highly acclaimed film received a special jury prize at the Venice Film Festival. In Italian with English subtitles. 1964; B&W; 136m.

GRAND ILLUSION ★★★★★
DIR: Jean Renoir. **CAST:** Jean Gabin, Pierre Fresnay, Erich Von Stroheim, Marcel Dalio, Julien Carette.

Shortly before Hitler plunged Europe into World War II, this monumental French film tried to examine why men submit to warfare's "grand illusions." We are taken to a German prison camp in World War I, where it becomes quite easy to see the hypocrisy of war while watching the day-to-day miniworld of camp life. This classic by Jean Renoir is a must-see for anyone who appreciates great art. 1937; B&W; 95m.

GRANDE BOURGEOISE, LA ★½
DIR: Mauro Bolognini. **CAST:** Catherine Deneuve, Giancarlo Giannini, Fernando Rey.
This should be a suspenseful film about a brother who murders his sister's lackluster husband. However, the movie's primary concern is with costume and soft-focus lenses so that even the lukewarm emotions are overshadowed. In Italian with English subtitles. 1974; 115m.

GREEN ROOM, THE ★★
DIR: François Truffaut. **CAST:** François Truffaut, Nathalie Baye, Jean Dasté.
Based on the writings of Henry James, this is a lifeless and disappointing film by François Truffaut about a writer obsessed with death who turns a dilapidated chapel into a memorial for World War I soldiers. Not the French filmmaker at his best. In French, with English subtitles. Rated PG. 1978; 93m.

HAIL MARY ★★★★
DIR: Jean-Luc Godard. **CAST:** Myriem Roussel, Thierry Lacoste, Philippe Lacoste.
This story of the coming of Christ in modern times will offend only the most dogmatic Christians, or narrow-minded religious zealots who have only heard a sketchy outline of the plot. Godard's eye for the aesthetic gives this film a compassionate feel. *The Book of Mary*, a film by Anne-Marie Mieville, is the prologue and is equally beautiful. In French with English subtitles. Not rated; the equivalent of an R for nudity. 1985; 107m.

HALF OF HEAVEN ★★★★
DIR: Manuel Gutierrez Aragon. **CAST:** Angela Molina, Margarita Lozano, Fernando Fernan-Gomez.
A woman works her way up from poverty to power in this unusual import from Spain. Rosa (Angela Molina) almost seems to drift her way to the top as Madrid's most successful restaurateur, but there are deeper meanings in this often funny and always fascinating mix of magic, politics, and romance. Unrated, the film has brief violence. In Spanish with English subtitles. 1987; 127m.

HANNA K. ★½
DIR: Constantin Costa-Gavras. **CAST:** Jill Clayburgh, Jean Yanne, Gabriel Byrne, David Clennon.
An intriguing premise that fails to live up to its promise. Jill Clayburgh is an Israeli lawyer appointed to defend a man who entered the country illegally in an attempt to reclaim the land where he grew up. Alas, the man is an Arab, which complicates matters between Clayburgh and her Israeli lover...not to mention her French Catholic husband. Rated R for coarse language. 1984; 110m.

HAPPILY EVER AFTER ★★
DIR: Bruno Barreto. **CAST:** Regina Duarte, Paulo Castelli.
For some unknown reason, a seemingly happy wife and mother takes off with a bisexual male prostitute in this Brazilian film. After *Dona Flor and Her Two Husbands*, director Bruno Baretto again presents a woman who seems to need two very different men in her life. Unrated, but contains nudity and simulated sex. In Portuguese with English subtitles. 1986; 108m.

HAPPY NEW YEAR (LA BONNE ANNEE) ★★★★
DIR: Claude Lelouch. **CAST:** Lino Ventura, Françoise Fabian, Charles Gerard.
Delightful French crime caper mixed with romance and comedy. As two thieves plot a jewel heist, one (Lino Ventura) also plans a meeting with the lovely antique dealer (Françoise Fabian) who runs the shop next door to their target. Director Claude Lelouch's film blends suspense with engaging wit. Rated PG for profanity and sex. Available in French version or dubbed. 1974; 114m.

HEAT OF DESIRE ★★
DIR: Luc Beraud. **CAST:** Patrick Dewaere, Clio Goldsmith, Jeanne Moreau, Guy Marchand.

So many sex comedies are about married men who discover adultery brings new vitality, this plot has become a cinematic cliché. But this didn't stop director Luc Beraud from using it again in this disappointing film about a writer (Patrick Dewaere) who dallies with an unpredictable flirt (Clio Goldsmith). In French, with English subtitles. Unrated, the film has nudity and suggested sex. 1984; 91m.

HENRY IV ★★★

DIR: Marco Bellocchio. **CAST:** Marcello Mastroianni, Claudia Cardinale, Leopoldo Trieste.

This Italian TV film is based on a Luigi Pirandello play. A modern aristocrat is thrown from his horse and then believes he is Emperor Henry IV. Twenty years pass and his past lover and a psychiatrist devise a plan to shake him back to reality. It's interesting, but long. In Italian with English subtitles. 1984; 95m.

HEY, BABU RIBA ★★★½

DIR: Javan Acin. **CAST:** Gala Videnovic.

Yugoslav version of *American Graffiti*. The title comes from an American song popular in the swing era, which its characters dance to in this poignant, funny reminiscence of four boys and a girl growing up in the early 50s. The film has an easy charm. In Serbo-Croatian with English subtitles. Rated R for mild profanity, violence, and sex. 1986; 109m.

HIDDEN FORTRESS, THE ★★★★★

DIR: Akira Kurosawa. **CAST:** Toshiro Mifune, Minoru Chiaki.

Toshiro Mifune stars in this recently reconstructed, uncut, and immensely entertaining 1958 Japanese period epic directed by Akira Kurosawa. George Lucas has openly admitted the film's influence on his *Star Wars* trilogy. *Hidden Fortress* deals with the adventures of a strong-willed princess (à la Carrie Fisher in the space fantasy) and her wise, sword-wielding protector (Mifune in the role adapted for Alec Guinness). In Japanese with English subtitles. Unrated, the film has violence. 1958; B&W; 126m.

HIGH AND LOW ★★★★★

DIR: Akira Kurosawa. **CAST:** Toshiro Mifune, Tatsuya Nakadai, Tatsuya Mihashi, Tsutomu Yamazaki, Takashi Shimura.

From a simple, but exquisitely devised detective story, Akira Kurosawa builds a stunning work of insight, humor, suspense, and social commentary. Toshiro Mifune is the businessman who must decide if he will pay a ransom to kidnappers who have taken his chauffeur's young son by mistake. A masterwork, featuring superb acting by two of the giants of Japanese cinema, Mifune and Tatsuya Nakadai. Based on Ed McBain's 87th Precinct novel *King's Ransom*. In Japanese with English subtitles. 1963; B&W; 143m.

HIGH HEELS ★★

DIR: Claude Chabrol. **CAST:** Laura Antonelli, Jean-Paul Belmondo, Mia Farrow.

A French comedy to make you chuckle more often than not. The story involves a medical student who marries the homely daughter of a hospital president to ensure himself of a job after graduation. Not rated, but recommended for viewers over 18 years of age. In French with English subtitles. 1972; 90m.

HIMATSURI ★★★★½

DIR: Mitsuo Yanagimachi. **CAST:** Kinya Kitaoji.

Metaphysical story about man's lustful and often destructive relationship with nature. Kinya Kitaoji plays a lumberjack in a beautiful seaboard wilderness which is about to be marred by the building of a marine park. Rated R for nudity, and violence. 1985; 120m.

HIROSHIMA, MON AMOUR ★★★★

DIR: Alain Resnais. **CAST:** Emmanuelle Riva, Bernard Fresson, Eiji Okada.

A mind-boggling tale about two people: one, a French woman, the other, a male survivor of the blast at Hiroshima. They meet and become lovers. Together they live their pasts, present, and futures in a complex series of fantasies, and nightmares. In French, with English subtitles. 1959; B&W; 88m.

HOLIDAY HOTEL ★★★

DIR: Michel Lang. **CAST:** Sophie Barjac, Daniel Ceccaldi, Michel Greiller, Guy Marchand.

It's August, and all of France is going on vacation for the entire month. The cast of this fast-paced comedy is heading toward the Brittany coast. Michel Lang keeps the tempo moving with clever farcical bits and dialogue. Partially in English, the movie has an R rating due to nudity and profanity. 1978; 109m.

HOLY INNOCENTS ★★★★

DIR: Mario Camus. **CAST:** Alfredo Landa, Francisco Rabal.

This moving drama explores the social class struggles in a remote farming community during Franco's rule of Spain. It's a sensitive and compelling look into the struggle of the rural lower class against the wealthy landowners. This critically acclaimed film earned acting awards at the Cannes Film Festival for Alfredo Landa and Francisco Rabal. In Spanish with English subtitles. 1984; 108m.

HOME AND THE WORLD ★★★★★

DIR: Satyajit Ray. **CAST:** Soumitra Chatterjee, Victor Banerjee.

Satyajit Ray's critically acclaimed, harrowing account of the coming of age of an Indian woman. She falls in love with her husband's best friend, an organizer against British goods. This fascinating portrait of Bengali life was based on the Nobel Prize–winning novel by Rabindranath Tagore. Not rated. In Bengali with English subtitles. 1984; 130m.

HOUR OF THE WOLF ★★★★

DIR: Ingmar Bergman. **CAST:** Max von Sydow, Liv Ullmann, Ingrid Thulin.

Ingmar Bergman's surreal, claustrophobic look into the personality of a tormented artist. Bizarre hallucinations shape the artist's world, creating a disturbing vision that seems at times completely out of control. Probably the closest Bergman has ever come to creating a horror film. In Swedish with English subtitles. 1968; B&W; 89m.

HUMAN CONDITION, PART ONE: NO GREATER LOVE, THE ★★★★

DIR: Masaki Kobayashi. **CAST:** Tatsuya Nakadai, Michiyo Aratama, Chikage Awashima.

Based on a popular Japanese bestseller, *The Human Condition* tells the story of a sensitive, compassionate man who tries to maintain his humanity through the spiraling horrors of World War II. Part One opens in 1943, just as the war is beginning to go badly for Japan. The film is quite long, but never dull, with breathtaking wide-screen photography (the film is available in a letterbox video format). The fractured-English subtitles are the only drawback. Unrated. 1958; B&W; 200m.

HUMAN CONDITION, PART TWO: THE ROAD TO ETERNITY, THE ★★★½

DIR: Masaki Kobayashi. **CAST:** Tatsuya Nakadai.

Director Masaki Kobayashi's epic film trilogy continues, with hero Kaji entering the imperial army in the closing months of World War II. Despite his doubts about Japanese war aims, which earn him the suspicion of his superiors, he proves a good soldier and acquits himself bravely. Unlike the first film in the trilogy, *No Greater Love*, this one ends with a cliffhanger. Not rated, but not for children or squeamish adults. 1959; B&W; 180m.

HUMAN CONDITION, PART THREE: A SOLDIER'S PRAYER, THE ★★★★

DIR: Masaki Kobayashi. **CAST:** Tatsuya Nakadai.

Director Masaki Kobayashi's magnum opus comes to its shattering conclusion as Kaji, his unit wiped out in battle, leads a band of stragglers and refugees through the Manchurian wilderness. Acting, cinematography, and editing are all first-rate in this heartwrenching tale of Japan's darkest days. Not rated. 1961; B&W; 190m.

HUNGARIAN FAIRY TALE, A ★★★★½

DIR: Gyula Gazdag. **CAST:** David Vermes.

An imaginative and affecting tale from Hungary, blending myth, social satire, and a Dickensian story of a Budapest orphan. Filmed in stunning black and white and employing little dialogue. In Hungarian with English subtitles. 1988; 97m.

I AM CURIOUS BLUE ★★

DIR: Vilgot Sjoman. **CAST:** Lena Nyman, Vilgot Sjoman, Borje Ahlstedt.

Both *I Am Curious Yellow* and *Blue* were derived from the same footage, shot by director Vilgot Sjoman in the late Sixties. When the finished product turned out to be too long, he turned it into two movies instead. Ergo, *Curious Blue* is less a sequel than simply more of the same meandering inquiry into social issues, punctuated by an occasional naked body. Unrated, the movie features frank but unerotic sex. In Swedish with English subtitles. 1968; B&W; 103m.

I AM CURIOUS YELLOW ★½

DIR: Vilgot Sjoman. **CAST:** Lena Nyman, Borje Ahlstedt.

This Swedish import caused quite an uproar when it was released in the mid-1960s, because of its frontal nudity and sexual content. It seems pretty tame and dull today. There isn't much of a plot built around the escapades of a young Swedish sociologist whose goal in life appears to be having sex in as many weird places as she can. 1967; B&W; 121m.

I KILLED RASPUTIN ★

DIR: Robert Hossein. **CAST:** Gert Fröbe, Peter McEnery, Geraldine Chaplin, Ivan Desny.

It can't have been easy, but they actually managed to make a completely boring movie about Rasputin, the peasant monk who gained control over the czar of Russia in the period prior to the Russian revolution. Actually, Rasputin isn't in it that much, and when he is they've cleaned up his act. Dubbed in English. 1967; 95m.

I LOVE YOU (EU TE AMO) ★★★

DIR: Arnaldo Jabor. **CAST:** Sonia Braga, Paulo Cesar Perelo.

This release, starring Brazilian sexpot Sonia Braga *Dona Flor and Her Two Husbands*,is a high-class hard-core—though not close-up—sex film with pretensions of being a work of art. And if that turns you on, go for it. Unrated, the film has nudity and profanity. 1982; 104m.

I SENT A LETTER TO MY LOVE ★★★

DIR: Moshe Mizrahi. **CAST:** Simone Signoret, Jean Rochefort, Delphine Seyrig.

Simone Signoret and Jean Rochefort star as sister and brother in this absorbing study of love, devotion, loneliness, and frustration. After Signoret places a personal ad (requesting male companionship) in the local paper, Rochefort responds—and they begin a correspondence, via mail, that brings passion and hope to their otherwise empty lives. In French with English subtitles. 1981; 96m.

I VITELLONI ★★★★

DIR: Federico Fellini. **CAST:** Franco Interlenghi, Alberto Sordi, Franco Fabrizi.

Five men in a small town on the Adriatic become discontented and restless. Stunning cinematography highlights this consideration of rootlessness, a central theme that runs throughout Fellini's work. In Italian with English subtitles. 1953; B&W; 104m.

IKIRU ★★★★½
DIR: Akira Kurosawa. **CAST:** Takashi Shimura.

Ikiru is the Japanese infinitive *to live*. The film opens with a shot of an X-ray; a narrator tells us the man—an Everyman—is dying of cancer. But a dream flickers to life, and his last years are fulfilled by a lasting accomplishment. *Ikiru* packs a genuine emotional wallop. In Japanese with English subtitles. 1952; B&W; 143m.

IMMORTAL BACHELOR, THE ★★
DIR: Marcello Fondato. **CAST:** Giancarlo Giannini, Monica Vitti, Vittorio Gassman, Claudia Cardinale.

A female juror hearing the case of a cleaning woman who killed her cheating husband fantasizes about the dead man, who seems to her much more interesting than her own dullard spouse. But for the well-known cast, this Italian comedy would never have been imported. Unrated, but a PG equivalent. Dubbed in English. 1979; 95m.

INHERITORS, THE
DIR: Walter Bannert. **CAST:** Nicholas Vogel.

A teenage boy with a troubled family life stumbles into a neo-Nazi group, which trains him in the use of weapons and how and who to hate. What could have been a work of some social significance is instead a muddled mess. A German film, this production didn't survive its trip overseas. 1984; 90m.

INNOCENT, THE ★★★★
DIR: Luchino Visconti. **CAST:** Laura Antonelli, Giancarlo Giannini.

Some rate this as the most beautiful of all Luchino Visconti's films. Set in a nineteenth-century baronial manor, it's the old tale of the real versus the ideal, but beautifully done. Rated R due to some explicit scenes. In Italian with English subtitles. 1976; 115m.

INVESTIGATION ★★★
DIR: Etienne Perier. **CAST:** Victor Lanoux, Jean Carmet, Valerie Mairesse, Michel Robin.

When the village tannery owner (Victor Lanoux) kills his wife to marry his pregnant girlfriend (Valerie Mairesse), a meticulous inspector comes to investigate. His Columbo-ish tactics pick up the film's pace and turn a so-so melodrama into a delightful winner. In French with English subtitles. Rated R for violence. 1979; 116m.

INVITATION AU VOYAGE ★★★½
DIR: Peter Del Monte. **CAST:** Laurent Malet, Aurore Clement, Mario Adorf.

Here is a strange but watchable French import with plenty of suspense and surprises for those willing to give it a chance to work its unusual magic. Peter Del Monte's film allows the viewer to make assumptions and then shatters those conceptions with a succession of inventive twists and revelations. In French, with English subtitles. Rated R for adult content. 1982; 100m.

IPHIGENIA ★★★★★
DIR: Michael Cacoyannis. **CAST:** Irene Papas.

A stunning film interpretation of the Greek classic *Iphigenia in Aulis*. Irene Papas is brilliant as Clytemnestra, the caring and outraged mother. Intense score by Mikos Theodorakis. In Greek, with English subtitles. No MPAA rating. 1978; 127m.

IREZUMI (SPIRIT OF TATTOO) ★★★★½
DIR: Yoichi Takabayashi. **CAST:** Masayo Utsunomiya, Tomisaburo Wakayama.

An erotic tale of obsession that calls forth the rebirth of a near-dead art. A woman defies cultural taboos and gets her back elaborately tattooed to fulfill her mate's obsession. Rated R for nudity. 1983; 88m.

ISTANBUL ★½
DIR: Marc Didden. **CAST:** Brad Dourif, Dominique Deruddere, Ingrid De Vos.
A grungy American with a mysterious past meets a penniless student in Belgium and involves him in a kidnapping. This English-dubbed thriller from France is worth watching only for the hammy overacting of Brad Dourif. Rated R for nudity, profanity, and sexual situations. 1985; 90m.

ITALIAN STRAW HAT, THE ★★★
DIR: René Clair. **CAST:** Albert Préjean, Olga Tschechowa.
The future happiness of newlyweds is threatened when the groom must find a replacement for a straw hat eaten by a horse. Failure means fighting a duel with the lover of the married woman who was wearing the hat. A silent classic with English intertitles and musical score. 1927; B&W; 72m.

IVAN THE TERRIBLE—PART I & PART II ★★★★★
DIR: Sergei Eisenstein. **CAST:** Nikolai Cherkassov, Ludmila Tselikovskaya.
Considered among the classics of world cinema, this certainly is the most impressive film to come out of the Soviet Union. This epic biography of Russia's first tsar was commissioned personally by Joseph Stalin to encourage acceptance of his harsh and historically similar policies. World-renowned director Sergei Eisenstein, instead, transformed what was designed as party propaganda into a panoramic saga of how power corrupts those seeking it. 1945; B&W; 188m.

JACKO AND LISE ★
DIR: Walter Bal. **CAST:** Laurent Malet, Annie Girardot, Michel Montanary, Evelyne Bouix, Françoise Arnoul.
This film should have been called *Jacko and Freddie* because most of it concerns Jacko and his pal Freddie escaping responsibility and adulthood by doing juvenile things. When Jacko finally does meet Lise, the movie falls apart. In French. Rated PG. 1975; 92m.

JE VOUS AIME (I LOVE YOU ALL) ★★
DIR: Claude Berri. **CAST:** Catherine Deneuve, Jean-Louis Trintignant, Serge Gainsbourg.
Some films are so complicated and convoluted you need a viewer's guide while watching them. So it is with this flashback-ridden French import. About a 35-year-old woman, Alice (Catherine Deneuve), who finds it impossible to keep a love relationship alive, it hops, skips, and jumps back and forth through her life. No MPAA rating; the film has sexual situations and nudity. 1981; 105m.

JEAN DE FLORETTE ★★★★
DIR: Claude Berri. **CAST:** Yves Montand, Gerard Depardieu, Daniel Auteuil.
This is a sort of French *Days of Heaven*, an epic set close to the land, specifically the hilly farm country of Provence. Land is the central issue around which the action swirls. Yves Montand is spellbinding as an ambitious, immoral farmer who dupes his city-bred neighbor Jean de Florette (played by the equally impressive Gerard Depardieu). The rest of the story is told in *Manon of the Spring*. In French with English subtitles. Rated PG. 1987; 122m.

JOKE OF DESTINY ★★
DIR: Lina Wertmuller. **CAST:** Ugo Tognazzi, Piera Degli Esposti, Gastone Moschin.
Italian audiences may have laughed uproariously at this new film by director Lina Wertmuller. However, American viewers are unlikely to get the joke. The elements of social satire are unfathomable for those unfamiliar with political events in Italy. Rated PG for profanity. In Italian with English subtitles. 1984; 105m.

JOUR DE FETE ★★½
DIR: Jacques Tati. **CAST:** Jacques Tati, Guy Decomble, Paul Frankeur.

Jacques Tati is the focal point of this light comedy loosely tied to the arrival of a carnival in a small village. As François, the bumbling postman, Tati sees a film on the heroism of the American postal service and tries to emulate it on his small rural route. In French, with subtitles. 1949; B&W; 81m.

JUD SUSS
DIR: Veidt Harlan. **CAST:** Ferdinand Marian, Werner Krauss.

Jud Suss (The Jew, Suss) is infamous as the most rabid of the anti-Semitic films made by the Nazis under personal supervision of propaganda minister Joseph Goebbels. It depicts "the Jewish menace" in both symbolic and overt terms in a story about a wandering Jew who enters a small European country and nearly brings it to ruin. Any serious student of cinema should see it as an example of the medium's enormous power to proselytize; it's an extreme and hateful version of what art does every day. In German with English subtitles. 1940; B&W; 97m.

JUDEX ★★★½
DIR: Georges Franju. **CAST:** Channing Pollock, Jacques Jouanneau, Edith Scob, Michel Vitold, Francine Berge.

This remake of a serial from the early days of cinema will make you laugh out loud one moment and become misty-eyed with nostalgia the next. Based on an old potboiler by Feuillade and Bernede, *Judex* ("the judge") is an enjoyable adventure of a superhero who is lovable, human, and fallible. In French with English subtitles. 1963; B&W; 103m.

JULES AND JIM ★★★★★
DIR: François Truffaut. **CAST:** Oskar Werner, Jeanne Moreau, Henri Serre.

Superb character study, which revolves around a bizarre ménage à trois. It is really a film about wanting what you can't have and not wanting what you think you desire once you have it. In French with English subtitles. 1961; B&W; 104m.

JULIET OF THE SPIRITS ★★★★★
DIR: Federico Fellini. **CAST:** Giulietta Masina, Sandra Milo, Valentina Cortese, Sylva Koscina.

The convoluted plot in this classic centers around a wealthy wife suspicious of her cheating husband. Giulietta Masina (in real life, Mrs. Fellini) has never been so tantalizingly innocent with her Bambi eyes. This is Fellini's first attempt with color. 1965; 148m.

JUPITER'S THIGH ★★★★½
DIR: Philippe de Broca. **CAST:** Annie Girardot, Philippe Noiret.

The delightful *Dear Inspector* duo is back in this delicious sequel directed by Philippe de Broca (*King of Hearts*). This time, the lady detective (Annie Girardot) and her Greek archeologist lover (Philippe Noiret) get married and honeymoon—where else?—in Greece. But they aren't there long before they find themselves caught up in mayhem. It's great fun, served up with sophistication. In French with English subtitles. 1983; 90m.

KAGEMUSHA ★★★★★
DIR: Akira Kurosawa. **CAST:** Tatsuya Nakadai.

The 70-year-old Akira Kurosawa outdoes himself in this epic masterpiece about honor and illusion. Kurosawa popularized the samurai genre—which has been described as the Japanese equivalent of the western—in America with his breathtaking, action-packed films. *Kagemusha* is yet another feast for the eyes, heart, and mind. Rated PG. 1980; 159m.

KAMERADSCHAFT ★★★½
DIR: G. W. Pabst. **CAST:** George Challa, David Mendaille, Ernest Busch.

In this classic, the story development is slow, but the concept is so strong, and the sense of cross-cultural camaraderie so stirring that the film remains impressive. The story concerns

French miners getting trapped by a mine disaster, with German miners attempting a daring rescue. In German and French, with English subtitles. 1931; B&W; 87m.

KAMIKAZE 89 ★★★
DIR: Wolf Gremm. **CAST:** Rainer Werner Fassbinder, Gunther Kaufmann, Brigitte Mira, Franco Nero.

The late Rainer Werner Fassbinder stars in this bizarre fantasy-thriller set in a decadent German city in 1989. A bomb has been planted in the headquarters of a giant conglomerate that controls all media and a police lieutenant (Fassbinder) has very little time to locate it. In German with English subtitles. 1983; 90m.

KANAL ★★★★
DIR: Andrzej Wajda. **CAST:** Teresa Izewska.

Andrzej Wajda's compelling war drama about the Polish resistance fighters during World War II brought international acclaim to the Polish cinema. This film explores the dreams, the despair, and the struggle of a generation who refused to be held captive in their own land by the Nazi war machine in 1944. In Polish with English subtitles. 1957; B&W; 96m.

KAOS ★★★½
DIR: Paolo Taviani, Vittorio Taviani. **CAST:** Margarita Lovano, Enrica Maria Mudugno, Omero Antonutti.

Italian writer-directors Paolo and Vittorio Taviani adapted four short stories by Luigi Pirandello for this sumptuously photographed film about peasant life in Sicily. For all its beauty and style, this is a disappointing, uneven work. The first two stories are wonderful, but the final pair leave a lot to be desired. In Italian, with English subtitles. Rated R for nudity and violence. 1986; 188m.

KATIE'S PASSION ★
DIR: Paul Verhoeven. **CAST:** Rutger Hauer, Monique van de Ven.

The story of a poor country girl's struggle to survive in Holland during the economic crisis of the 1880's. Director Paul Verhoeven, whose previous successes (*Spetters* and *Soldier of Orange*) gave us some quality entertainment, completely misses the mark with this uninspired saga. Rutger Hauer delivers a rather lackluster performance as a vain, shallow banker. Not much passion, or anything else here. In Dutch with English subtitles. 1988; 107m.

KIDNAP SYNDICATE, THE ★
DIR: Fernando Di Leo. **CAST:** James Mason, Luc Merenda, Valentina Cortese.

James Mason plays a millionaire whose child has been kidnapped. Luc Merenda is the poor father of a child who has been taken along with Mason's. Director Fernando DiLeo tries to juxtapose the irony of the two fathers but it comes off like a trite melodrama with lots of blood spilling and profanity. 1976; 105m.

KING OF HEARTS ★★★★½
DIR: Philippe de Broca. **CAST:** Alan Bates, Genevieve Bujold.

Philippe de Broca's wartime fantasy provides delightful insights into human behavior. A World War I Scottish infantryman (Alan Bates) searching for a hidden enemy bunker enters a small town that, after being deserted by its citizens, has been taken over by inmates of an insane asylum. In French, with English subtitles. No MPAA rating. 1966; 102m.

KINGS OF THE ROAD ★★★★
DIR: Wim Wenders. **CAST:** Rudiger Vogler, Hanns Zischler, Lisa Kreuzer.

This is the film that put the new wave German cinema on the map. Wim Wenders's classic road tale of wanderlust in Deutschland centers on a traveling movie projectionist/repairman who encounters a hitchhiker who is depressed following the collapse of his marriage. The men form an unusual relationship while en route from West to East Germany. A truly astonishing film with a great rock 'n' roll score. In German with English subtitles. 1976; B&W; 176m.

KNIFE IN THE WATER ★★★★
DIR: Roman Polanski. **CAST:** Leon Niemczyk, Jolanta Umecka, Zygmunt Malanowicz.
Absolutely fascinating feature-film debut for director Roman Polanski, who immediately demonstrated his strength with character studies. A couple off for a sailing holiday encounter a young hitchhiker and invite him along. The resulting sexual tension is riveting, the outcome impossible to anticipate. In many ways, this remains one of Polanski's finest pictures. In Polish, with English subtitles. Unrated, the film has sexual situations. 1962; B&W; 94m.

KOJIRO ★★★★
DIR: Hiroshi Inagaki. **CAST:** Kikunosuke Onoe, Yuriko Hoshi, Tatsuya Nakadai.
This first-rate semisequel to director Hiroshi Inagaki's *Samurai Trilogy* casts Tatsuya Nakadai as the fabled master swordsman, Musashi Miyamoto, whose exploits made up the three previous films. But he is not the main character here. Instead, the focus is on Kojiro (Kikunosuke Onoe), whose goal is to become the greatest swordsman in all Japan and thus follow the trail blazed by Miyamoto. Unrated, the film contains violence. In Japanese with English subtitles. 1967; 152m.

KRIEMHILDE'S REVENGE ★★★★
DIR: Fritz Lang. **CAST:** Margarete Schon, Rudolf Klein-Rogge, Paul Richter, Bernhard Goetzke.
This is a perfect sequel to the splendid *Siegfried.* Watch them both in one sitting if you get the chance. Siegfried's vengeful lover Kriemhilde raises an army to atone for his death. Beautifully photographed and edited, this international success placed German cinema in the vanguard of filmmaking. Silent. 1925; B&W; 95m.

KWAIDAN ★★★★
DIR: Masaki Kobayashi. **CAST:** Michiko Aratama, Keiko Kishi, Tatsuya Nakadai.
An anthology of ghost stories adapted from books by Lafcadio Hearn, an American writer who lived in Japan in the late nineteenth century. Colorful, eerie, and quite unique, it's one of the most visually stunning horror films ever produced. The movie isn't for children, though—it could induce nightmares. In Japanese with English subtitles. 1963; 164m.

L'ANNÉE DES MEDUSES ★
DIR: Christopher Frank. **CAST:** Valerie Kaprisky, Bernard Giraudeau, Caroline Cellier.
If Jackie Collins were French, she'd probably be churning out stuff like this. On the Riviera, where people drop their inhibitions as quickly as their bathing suits, a young girl competes with her mother for the pick of the season's hunk crop. Unrated, but loaded with nudity and soft-core sex. In French with English subtitles. 1986; 110m.

L'ATALANTE ★★★
DIR: Jean Vigo. **CAST:** Michel Simon, Jean Dasté, Dita Parlo.
The ocean and the elements form a backdrop for director Jean Vigo's surrealistic exercise. A disjointed but intriguing journey into the mind of an artist. Vigo died before his thirtieth birthday, shortly after completing *L'Atalante*, robbing the world of a promising filmmaker. In French, with English subtitles. 1934; B&W; 82m.

L'AVVENTURA ★★★★
DIR: Michelangelo Antonioni. **CAST:** Monica Vitti, Gabriele Ferzetti, Lea Massari.
A girl disappears on a yachting trip, and while her lover and best friend search for her, they begin a wild romantic affair. Antonioni's penetrating study of Italy's bored and idle bourgeoisie contains some staggering observations on spiritual isolation and love. Winner of the Special Jury Award at Cannes. Italian with English subtitles. 1960; B&W; 145m.

L'HOMME BLESSÉ (THE WOUNDED MAN) ★★★½
DIR: Patrice Chereau. **CAST:** Jean-Hugues Anglade, Vittorio Mezzogiorno, Roland Bertin, Lisa Kreuzer.
Lurid sexual psychodrama about a withdrawn young man's obsession for a street hustler he meets by chance. His frustrated lust builds until it finds its shocking release. A powerful and disturbing piece of cinema for adults only. Not rated; contains profanity, nudity, and violence. In French with English subtitles. 1988; 90m.

L'ODEUR DES FAUVES (SCANDAL MAN) ★
DIR: Richard Balducci. **CAST:** Maurice Ronet, Josephine Chaplin, Vittorio De Sica.
This is a real slipshod movie about a hack photographer-reporter who earns his living digging up *National Enquirer*–type stories. He eventually and unintentionally hits on a real scoop involving an affair between a black man and a white woman whose father is a Ku Klux Klan leader. 1986; 86m.

LA BALANCE ★★★★
DIR: Bob Swaim. **CAST:** Nathalie Baye, Philippe Léotard, Richard Berry, Maurice Ronet.
La Balance is an homage of sorts to the American cop thriller. It turns the genre inside out, however, by focusing on the plight of two unfortunates—a prostitute (Nathalie Baye) and a petty criminal (Philippe Léotard)—who get caught in a vise between the cops and a gangland chief. The result is a first-rate crime story. In French with English subtitles. Rated R for nudity, profanity, and violence. 1982; 102m.

LA BÊTE HUMAINE ★★★★½
DIR: Jean Renoir. **CAST:** Jean Gabin, Julien Carette, Fernand Ledoux, Jean Renoir, Simone Simon.
Remarkable performances by Jean Gabin, Fernand Ledoux, and Simone Simon, along with Jean Renoir's masterful editing and perfectly simple visuals, elevate a middling and grim Emile Zola novel to fine cinema. The artistry of *La Bête Humaine*, a film about duplicity and murder, transcends what could have been a seedy little tale. In French with English subtitles. 1938; B&W; 99m.

LA BOUM ★★★
DIR: Claude Pinoteau. **CAST:** Sophie Marceau, Brigitte Fossey, Claude Brasseur.
A teenager (Sophie Marceau) discovers a whole new world open to her when her parents move to Paris. Her new set of friends delight in giving "boums"—French slang for big parties. Although this film seems overly long for the subject matter and strains to hang together, many scenes are nevertheless tender and lovingly directed by Claude Pinoteau. No MPAA rating. In French with English subtitles. 1980; 100m.

LA CAGE AUX FOLLES ★★★★
DIR: Edouard Molinaro. **CAST:** Ugo Tognazzi, Michel Serrault.
A screamingly funny French comedy and the biggest-grossing foreign-language film ever released in America, this stars Ugo Tognazzi and Michel Serrault as lovers who must masquerade as husband and wife so as not to obstruct the marriage of Tognazzi's son to the daughter of a stuffy bureaucrat. In French with English subtitles. Rated PG for mature situations. 1978; 110m.

LA CAGE AUX FOLLES II ★★
DIR: Edouard Molinaro. **CAST:** Ugo Tognazzi, Michel Serrault.
This follow-up to the superb French comedy is just more proof sequels aren't equals. Though it reunites Ugo Tognazzi and Michel Serrault it has little of the original's special charm and unbridled hilarity. Rated PG for mature situations. In French with English subtitles. 1981; 101m.

LA CAGE AUX FOLLES III, THE WEDDING

DIR: Georges Lautner. **CAST:** Michel Serrault, Ugo Tognazzi, Stéphane Audran.

Pathetic and dreadful second sequel to *La Cage Aux Folles*. The two gay entrepreneurs are back, and in an effort to save their financially failing night club, Renato (Ugo Tognazzi) sends Albin (Michel Serrault) to the reading of a distant relative's will in which he stands to inherit a fortune. In French with English subtitles. Rated PG-13. 1986; 88m.

LA DOLCE VITA ★★★★

DIR: Federico Fellini. **CAST:** Marcello Mastroianni, Anouk Aimée, Anita Ekberg, Barbara Steele, Nadia Gray.

Federico Fellini's surreal journey through Rome follows a society journalist (Marcello Mastroianni) as he navigates a bizarre world in which emotions have been destroyed by surface realities, moral conventions, and unresolved guilts. This film, considered a landmark in cinematic achievement, won the Academy Award for best foreign language film. Not rated. In Italian with English subtitles. 1960; B&W; 175m.

LA LECTRICE (THE READER) ★★★

DIR: Michel Deville. **CAST:** Miou-Miou, Maria Casares, Patrick Chesnais.

Clever comedy for ultraliterary types, with Miou-Miou at her charming best as a woman who hires herself out as a professional reader. Selecting appropriate books from world literature, she becomes a confidante, booster, advisor, and friend to a successive collection of loners, loonies, and emotionally unstable individuals. In French with English subtitles. 1989; 98m.

LA MARSEILLAISE ★★★★

DIR: Jean Renoir. **CAST:** Pierre Renoir, Louis Jouvet, Julien Carette.

Though its plot is somewhat uneven, *La Marseillaise* contains many beautiful sequences. This documentarylike story (and Jean Renoir's call to his countrymen to stand fast against the growing threat of Hitler) parallels the rise of the French Revolution with the spread of the new rallying song as 150 revolutionary volunteers from Marseilles march to Paris and join with others to storm the Bastille. In French with English subtitles. 1937; B&W; 130m.

LA NUIT DE VARENNES ★★½

DIR: Ettore Scola. **CAST:** Marcello Mastroianni, Jean-Louis Barrault, Harvey Keitel.

An ambitious and imaginative, but ultimately disappointing, film of King Louis XVI's flight from revolutionary Paris in 1791 as seen through the ideologically opposed sensibilities of Casanova (Marcello Mastroianni), Restif de la Bretonne (Jean-Louis Barrault), and Tom Paine (Harvey Keitel). All these folks do is talk, talk, talk. In French, with English subtitles. Rated R for nudity, sex, and profanity. 1983; 133m.

LA PASSANTE ★★½

DIR: Jaques Rouffio. **CAST:** Romy Schneider, Michel Piccoli, Maria Schell.

Romy Schneider is featured in a dual role as Elsa, a German refugee, and as Lina, the wife of a contemporary world leader. This story centers on the relationship of two lovers caught up in a drama of political intrigue in France. Both Schneider and Michel Piccoli give excellent performances in this otherwise slow-moving thriller. In French with English subtitles. Contains nudity and violence; recommended for adult viewing. 1983; 106m.

LA RONDE ★★★

DIR: Max Ophuls. **CAST:** Anton Walbrook, Serge Reggiani, Simone Simon, Simone Signoret, Daniel Gelin, Danielle Darrieux.

It would be hard to imagine any film more like a French farce than *La Ronde*, in spite of its Austrian origins from the play by Arthur Schnitzler. This fast-paced, witty, and sometimes wicked look at amours and indiscretions begins with the soldier (Serge Reggiani) and lady of easy virtue (Simone Signoret). Their assignation starts a chain of events that is charmingly risqué. In French with English subtitles. 1950; B&W; 97m.

LA STRADA ★★★★★
DIR: Federico Fellini. **CAST:** Giulietta Masina, Anthony Quinn, Richard Basehart.
This is Fellini's first internationally acclaimed film. Gelsomina (Giulietta Masina), a simpleminded peasant girl, is sold to a circus strongman (Anthony Quinn), and as she follows him on his tour through the countryside, she falls desperately in love with him. She becomes the victim of his constant abuse and brutality until their meeting with an acrobat (Richard Basehart) dramatically changes the course of their lives. 1954; B&W; 94m.

LA TRAVIATA ★★★★
DIR: Franco Zeffirelli. **CAST:** Teresa Stratas, Placido Domingo.
Franco Zeffirelli set out to make an opera film of Verdi's *La Traviata* that would appeal to a general audience as well as opera buffs, and he has handsomely succeeded. He has found the right visual terms for the pathetic romance of a courtesan compelled to give up her aristocratic lover. The score is beautifully sung by Teresa Stratas, as Violetta and Placido Domingo, as Alfredo. In Italian, with English subtitles. Rated G. 1982; 112m.

LA TRUITE (THE TROUT) ★★★
DIR: Joseph Losey. **CAST:** Lissette Malidor, Isabelle Huppert, Jacques Spiesser.
Sometimes disjointed story of a young girl who leaves her rural background and arranged marriage to climb the rocky path to success in both love and business. Although director Joseph Losey generally has the right idea, *La Truite*, in the end, lacks warmth and a sense of cohesion. In French, with English subtitles. Rated R. 1982; 100m.

LADY ON THE BUS ★★
DIR: Neville D'Almeida. **CAST:** Sonia Braga.
Story of a shy bride who is frigid on her wedding night. She first turns to her husband's friends and then goes on to sample strangers she meets on buses. Her psychiatrist thinks she is normal, although she is driving her husband mad. Marginal comedy. Rated R for sex. In Portuguese with English subtitles. 1978; 102m.

LAST LAUGH, THE ★★★★
DIR: F. W. Murnau. **CAST:** Emil Jannings.
Historically recognized as the first film to exploit the moving camera, this silent classic tells the story of a lordly luxury hotel doorman who is abruptly and callously demoted to the menial status of a washroom attendant. Deprived of his job and uniform, his life slowly disintegrates. Emil Jannings gives a brilliant performance. 1924; B&W; 74m.

LAST METRO, THE ★★★½
DIR: François Truffaut. **CAST:** Catherine Deneuve, Gerard Depardieu, Jean Poiret.
Catherine Deneuve and Gerard Depardieu star in this drama about a Parisian theatrical company that believes "the show must go on" despite the restrictions and terrors of the Nazis during their World War II occupation of France. This film has several nice moments and surprises that make up for its occasional dull spots and extended running time. Rated PG. 1980; 133m.

LAST YEAR AT MARIENBAD ★★★
DIR: Alain Resnais. **CAST:** Delphine Seyrig, Giorgio Albertazzi, Sacha Pitoeff.
This film provides no middle ground—you either love it or you hate it. The confusing story is about a young man (Giorgio Albertazzi) find-

ing himself in a monstrous, baroque hotel trying to renew his love affair with a woman who seems to have forgotten that there is an affair to renew. The past, present, and future all seem to run parallel, cross over, and converge. In French with English subtitles. 1962; B&W; 93m.

LAW OF DESIRE ★★★
DIR: Pedro Almodóvar. **CAST:** Eusebio Poncela, Carmen Maura, Antonio Banderas, Miguel Molina.
Spain's Pedro Almodóvar can perhaps best be described as R. W. Fassbinder with a sunnier disposition; he likes to play with the clichés of movie melodrama in a manner that endears him to movie buffs. In this, the film that first gained him wide attention in the U.S., the protagonist is a gay movie director who longs to live as passionately as his transsexual brother (now his sister). He gets his wish in this topsy-turvy farce. Unrated, but an R equivalent. In Spanish with English subtitles. 1986; 100m.

LE BAL ★★★★
DIR: Ettore Scola.
European history of the last half-century is reduced to some fifty popular dance tunes—and a variety of very human dancers—in this innovative and entertaining film. This unusual import eschews dialogue for tangos, fox trots, and jazz to make its points. Scola chronicles the dramatic changes in political power, social behavior, and fashion trends from the 1930s to the present without ever moving his cameras out of an art deco ballroom. No MPAA rating; the film has brief violence. 1983; 109m.

LE BEAU MARIAGE ★★★★
DIR: Eric Rohmer. **CAST:** Beatrice Romand, Arielle Dombasle, André Dussolier.
A young woman decides it is high time she got married. She chooses the man she wants, a busy lawyer, and tells her friends of their coming wedding. He knows nothing of this, but she is confident. That is the premise in this film by French director Eric Rohmer. In French with English subtitles. Rated R. 1982; 100m.

LE BOURGEOIS GENTILHOMME ★★
DIR: Jean Meyer. **CAST:** Jean Meyer, Louis Seigner, Jacques Charon.
This adaptation of Molière's satire about a *nouveau riche* social climber was presented theatrically by the prestigious Comédie-Française. The film is merely a recording of the stage performance, and will seem static and overacted to most viewers. Worth checking out for Molière enthusiasts and French language classes, but not recommended for general audiences. In French with English subtitles. 1958; 97m.

LE CAS DU DR. LAURENT ★★½
DIR: Jean-Paul Le Chanois. **CAST:** Jean Gabin, Nicole Courcel, Sylvia Monfort.
Dated tale about a kindly old doctor who tries to introduce modern methods of medicine and sanitation to the residents of a small farming village. In particular, he tries to ease the suffering of women as they endure childbirth. Noteworthy for the performance of Gabin as the doctor and for footage of an actual childbirth. In French. 1957; B&W; 88m.

LE CAVALEUR ★★★★
DIR: Philippe de Broca. **CAST:** Jean Rochefort, Annie Girardot.
A poignantly philosophical, yet witty and often hilarious farce about the perils of the middle-aged heartbreak kid. Our cad about town is unerringly portrayed by Jean Rochefort as a classical pianist trying to juggle his art and the many past, present, and possible future women in his life. Nudity but generally innocent adult situations. 1980; 106m.

LE CHEVRE (THE GOAT) ★★½
DIR: Francis Veber. **CAST:** Pierre Richard, Gerard Depardieu, Michel Robin, Pedro Armendariz Jr.
The stars of *Les Comperes*, Pierre Richard and Gerard Depardieu, romp

again in this French comedy as two investigators searching for a missing girl in Mexico. While this import may please staunch fans of the stars, it is far from being a laugh riot. Unrated, the film has profanity and violence. In French with English subtitles. 1981; 91m.

LE DÉPART ★★★
DIR: Jerzy Skolimowski. **CAST:** Jean-Pierre Léaud, Catherine Isabelle Duport.

Jean-Pierre Léaud, best known from François Truffaut's semiautobiographical films *The 400 Blows* and *Love on the Run*, stars as another disaffected youth. He's desperately trying to borrow or rent a Porsche so that he can enter a race. Zany comedy is noteworthy for Léaud's performance and as an early effort by Polish director Jerzy Skolimowski. In French with English subtitles. Unrated. 1967; B&W; 89m.

LE DOULOS ★★★★
DIR: Jean-Pierre Melville. **CAST:** Jean-Paul Belmondo, Serge Reggiani, Michel Piccoli.

Outstanding, complex crime drama about a police informer who attempts to expose a violent underworld crime ring. An excellent homage to American gangster films of the 1940s. Brilliant cinematography and sizzling performances by a great cast make this suspenseful thriller a film classic. In French with English subtitles. 1961; B&W; 105m.

LE GENTLEMAN D'ESPOM, (DUKE OF THE DERBY) ★★★
DIR: Jacques Juranville. **CAST:** Jean Gabin, Madeleine Robinson, Paul Frankeur.

This lighthearted look at the sport of kings gives veteran French film star Jean Gabin ample chance to shine as the title character, an aged, suave snob living by his wits and luck handicapping and soliciting bets from the rich. Everything is fine until, eager to impress an old flame, he passes a bad check. 1962; B&W; 83m.

LE GRAND CHEMIN (THE GRAND HIGHWAY) ★★★★
DIR: Jean-Loup Hubert. **CAST:** Vanessa Guedj, Antoine Hubert, Richard Bohringer, Anemone.

A delightful film about an 8-year-old Parisian boy's summer in the country. Along with his friend Martine (Vanessa Guedj), Louis (played by director Jean-Loup Hubert's son Antoine) learns about the simple pleasures and terrors of life and love. This is great cinema for old and young alike, despite some nudity. In French with English subtitles. 1988; 104m.

LE JOUR SE LEVE (DAYBREAK) ★★★
DIR: Marcel Carné. **CAST:** Jean Gabin, Jules Berry, Arletty, Jacqueline Laurent.

An affecting, atmospheric French melodrama by the director of the classic *Children of Paradise*. Jean Gabin plays a man provoked to murder his lover's seducer, who then barricades himself in his room through the night. There is some brilliant, sensuous moviemaking here. The existing print lacks sufficient subtitling but is still worth viewing. 1939; B&W; 85m.

LE MAGNIFIQUE ★★★
DIR: Philippe de Broca. **CAST:** Jean-Paul Belmondo, Jacqueline Bisset.

A writer of spy novels imagines himself as his own character, a James Bond type, with the girl next door as his trusty sidekick. Though it never builds up a full head of steam, this French comedy holds your interest through the dull stretches. Written by Francis Verber (*La Cage Aux Folles, Three Fugitives*). In French with English subtitles. 1974; 93m.

LE MILLION ★★★★
DIR: René Clair. **CAST:** Annabella, Rene Lefevre.

Made more than fifty years ago, this delightful comedy about the efforts of a group of people to retrieve an elusive lottery ticket is more applicable to American audiences of today than it was when originally released. René

Clair's classic fantasy-adventure is freewheeling and fun. Subtitled in English. 1931; B&W; 85m.

LE PLAISIR ★★½
DIR: Max Ophuls. **CAST:** Jean Gabin, Danielle Darrieux, Simone Simon.

Max Ophuls (*La Ronde*) adapts three ironic stories by Guy de Maupassant with his customary style, most evident in his extremely mobile camera work. However, the stories themselves are mediocre and not really up to the elaborate treatment. In French with English subtitles. 1952; B&W; 97m.

LE REPOS DU GUERRIER (WARRIOR'S REST) ★★★★
DIR: Roger Vadim. **CAST:** Brigitte Bardot, Robert Hossein, James Robertson Justice, Jean-Marc Bory.

Brigitte Bardot plays a proper French girl who rescues a sociopathic drifter from a suicide attempt. The drifter immediately takes over Bardot's life, ruining her reputation and abusing her verbally and emotionally, yet denying her attempts to form a real relationship. This is a precursor of *The Servant, 9 1/2 Weeks*, and other frank observations of sexual obsession. In French. 1962; 98m.

LE SECRET ★★★
DIR: Robert Enrico. **CAST:** Jean-Louis Trintignant, Marlene Jobert, Philippe Noiret.

Jean-Louis Trintignant plays an escapee from a psychiatric prison who finds shelter with a reclusive writer and his wife by persuading them that he has been tortured for information. Fine performances, a tense atmosphere, and music by Ennio Morricone make this worth your while. Unrated. In French with English subtitles. 1974; 100m.

LEGEND OF THE EIGHT SAMURAI ★★
DIR: Haruki Kaduwara. **CAST:** Hiroku Yokoshimaru, Sonny Chiba.

Shizu is the princess who leads her warriors into battle against a giant centipede, ghosts, and a nearly immortal witch. This Japanese fantasy features an interesting storyline, but is derivative, slow in spots, badly dubbed, and disappointing. Unrated, has moderate violence. 1984; 130m.

LES COMPERES ★★★★
DIR: Bertrand Blier. **CAST:** Pierre Richard, Gerard Depardieu.

Pierre Richard and Gerard Depardieu star in this madcap French comedy as two strangers who find themselves on the trail of a runaway teenager. Both think they're the father—it was the only way the boy's mother could think of to enlist their aid. In French with English subtitles. Rated PG for profanity and brief violence. 1984; 90m.

LES GRANDES GUEULES (JAILBIRDS' VACATION) ★★½
DIR: Robert Enrico. **CAST:** Lino Ventura, Bourvil, Marie Dubois.

This comedy-drama about parolees working on a backwoods sawmill would be better if it were shorter and the extended fistfight scenes were cut measurably. Otherwise, the "jailbirds" are a lively, entertaining bunch. In French with English subtitles. 1965; 125m.

LESSON IN LOVE, A ★★★
DIR: Ingmar Bergman. **CAST:** Gunnar Björnstrand, Eva Dahlbeck, Harriet Andersson.

Gunnar Björnstrand plays a philandering gynecologist who realizes that his long-suffering wife is the woman he loves the most, and he sets out to win her back. This is a little ponderous for a true romantic comedy, but good writing and good acting move the film along and provide some funny yet realistic situations. In Swedish, with subtitles. 1954; B&W; 97m.

LIFE OF OHARU ★★★★½
DIR: Kenji Mizoguchi. **CAST:** Kinuyo Tanaka, Toshiro Mifune.

All but unknown in this country, Japanese director Kenji Mizoguchi was one of the great artists of the cinema. This story, of a woman in feudal

Japan who, after disgracing the honor of her samurai father, is sold into prostitution, may seem somewhat melodramatic to Western audiences. But Mizoguchi's art rested in his formalistic visual style, consisting of carefully composed shots, long takes, and minimal editing. In Japanese with English subtitles. 1952; B&W; 136m.

LITTLE VERA ★★★
DIR: Vasily Pichul. **CAST:** Natalya Negoda.

Glasnost takes a front-row-center seat in this angst-ridden drama about the thoroughly modern Moscowite Vera. Her alcoholic father and ineffectual mother constantly worry about Vera's untraditional ways. She falls in love and moves her fiancé into the family's tight quarters. This is the first widely released Soviet film to show present-day teenage culture—plus—simulated sex. Not rated. In Russian with English subtitles. 1989; 130m.

LIVING ON TOKYO TIME ★★★★
DIR: Steven Okazaki. **CAST:** Minako Ohashi, Ken Nakagawa.

Living on Tokyo Time explores an Asian-American culture clash from the Japanese point of view. Kyoko (Minako Ohashi), a young woman, comes from Japan to San Francisco. When her visa expires, she agrees to a marriage of convenience with a junk-food-eating Japanese-American who wants to be a rock star. The result is a warmhearted character study blessed with insight and humor. In English and Japanese with subtitles. 1987; 83m.

LOS OLVIDADOS ★★★★★
DIR: Luis Buñuel. **CAST:** Alfonso Mejia, Roberto Cobo.

Luis Buñuel marks the beginning of his mature style with this film. Hyperpersonal, shocking, erotic, hallucinogenic, and surrealistic images are integrated into naturalistic action: two youths of the Mexican slums venture deeper and deeper into the criminal world until they are beyond redemption. In Spanish with English subtitles. 1950; B&W; 88m.

LOST HONOR OF KATHARINA BLUM, THE ★★★
DIR: Volker Schlondorff. **CAST:** Angela Winkler.

Angela Winkler's performance as Katharina Blum is the central force behind Schlondörff's interpretation of Heinrich Boll's novel. Katharina Blum is a poor, young housekeeper who spends one night with a suspected political terrorist. Her life is thereby ruined by the police and the media. In German, with English subtitles. Rated R. 1977; 97m.

LOVE AND ANARCHY ★★★★★
DIR: Lina Wertmuller. **CAST:** Giancarlo Giannini, Mariangela Melato.

Giancarlo Giannini gets to eat up the screen with this role. Comic, tragic, and intellectually stimulating, this is Wertmuller's best film. Giannini is bent on assassinating Mussolini right after the rise of Fascism but somehow gets waylaid. A classic. Rated R for sexual situations, language, and some nudity. 1973; 117m.

LOVE IN GERMANY, A ★★
DIR: Andrzej Wajda. **CAST:** Hanna Schygulla, Marie-Christine Barrault, Bernhard Wicki.

During World War II, the Germans bring in Polish POWs to do menial labor. While grocer Frau Kopp's (Hanna Schygulla) husband is off fighting, she hires a young Polish POW. The first half of the film is effective, but the second half receives an excessively sensational treatment, ultimately diminishing the flavor and appeal. In French with English subtitles. Rated R for violence and nudity. 1984; 107m.

LOVE ON THE RUN ★★★½
DIR: François Truffaut. **CAST:** Jean-Pierre Léaud, Claude Jade, Marie-France Pisier.

Francois Truffaut's tribute to himself. *Love on the Run* is the fifth film (*400 Blows*; *Love at Twenty*; *Stolen Kisses*;

Bed & Board) in the series for character Antoine Doinel (Jean-Pierre Léaud). Now in his thirties and on the eve of divorce, Doinel rediscovers women. Light romantic work filled with humor and compassion. In French, with English subtitles. Rated PG. 1979; 93m.

LOVE SONGS (PAROLES ET MUSIQUE) ★★
DIR: Elie Chouraqui. **CAST:** Catherine Deneuve, Christopher Lambert, Nick Mancuso, Richard Anconina, Jacques Perrin.
Christopher Lambert plays a bisexual rock singer having an affair with a woman (Catherine Deneuve) recently separated from her husband (Nick Mancuso). Pointless and frequently incomprehensible. Dubbed (execrably) into English. 1985; 107m.

LOVERS, THE ★★
DIR: Louis Malle. **CAST:** Jeanne Moreau, Alain Cuny, Jean-Marc Bory.
Notorious in the early Sixties, when it was prosecuted in the U.S. for obscenity, this French drama looks mighty tame now. All the fuss was over an extended lovemaking scene between rich wife Jeanne Moreau and a young man she has just met, who revives her interest in life. What little interest the film retains is in its widescreen photography, which is lost in the transfer to home video, anyway. In French with English subtitles. 1958; B&W; 90m.

LOVES OF A BLONDE ★★★
DIR: Milos Forman. **CAST:** Hana Brejchova, Josef Sebanek.
This dark comedy from Milos Forman centers on a young girl working in a small-town factory who pursues a musician to his home in Prague. Often hilarious. In Czechoslovakian with English subtitles. 1965; B&W; 88m.

LOWER DEPTHS (1936) ★★★★
DIR: Jean Renoir. **CAST:** Jean Gabin, Louis Jouvet.
Another poignant observation by Jean Renoir about social classes. This time the director adapts Maxim Gorky's play about an impoverished thief (brilliantly performed by Jean Gabin) who meets a baron and instructs him in the joys of living without material wealth. In French with English subtitles. 1936; 92m.

LUMIERE ★
DIR: Jeanne Moreau. **CAST:** Jeanne Moreau, Francine Racette, Bruno Ganz, François Simon, Lucia Bose, Keith Carradine.
The only thing this film illuminates is Jeanne Moreau's pretentiousness. The famed French actress fares poorly behind the camera as writer and director of this self-conscious story about the life of an actress (Moreau herself). In French. 1976; 95m.

M ★★★★★
DIR: Fritz Lang. **CAST:** Peter Lorre, Gustav Grundgens.
A child-killer is chased by police, and by other criminals who would prefer to mete out their own justice. Peter Lorre, in his first film role, gives a striking portrayal of a man driven by uncontrollable forces. A classic German film, understated, yet filled with haunting images. Beware of videocassettes containing badly translated, illegible subtitles. Unrated. In German, with English subtitles. 1931; B&W; 99m.

MACARTHUR'S CHILDREN ★
DIR: Masahiro Shinoda. **CAST:** Takaya Yamauchi, Yoshiyuki Omori.
This import deals with effects of Japan's defeat during World War II, and its subsequent occupation by America, on a group of youngsters and adults living on a tiny Japanese island. While there are some brilliant touches by director Masahiro Shinoda, the film as a whole fails. Rated PG for profanity and suggested sex. In Japanese with English subtitles. 1984; 120m.

MADAME ROSA ★★★★★
DIR: Moshe Mizrahi. **CAST:** Simone Signoret, Sammy Den Youb, Claude Dauphin.

This superbly moving motion picture features Simone Signoret in one of her greatest roles. It is a simple, human story that takes place six flights up in a dilapidated building where a once-beautiful prostitute and survivor of Nazi concentration camps cares for the children of hookers. No MPAA rating. 1977; 105m.

MAEDCHEN IN UNIFORM ★★★★

DIR: Leontine Sagan. **CAST:** Emilia Unda, Dorothea Wieck.

At once a fascinating and emotionally disturbing film, this German classic turns mainly on the love of a sexually repressed young girl for a compassionate female teacher in a state-run school. Remade in 1958 with Romy Schneider and Lili Palmer. In German with English subtitles. 1931; B&W; 90m.

MAGIC GARDEN, THE ★★★

DIR: Donald Swanson. **CAST:** Tommy Ramokgopa.

Charming South African comedy featuring an amateur cast. A sum of money stolen from a church keeps finding its way into the hands of people who need it; when they transfer it to the less deserving to repay their debts, the same thief manages to steal it back! A good family movie. Also known as *Pennywhistle Blues*. 1952; B&W; 63m.

MAGICIAN, THE ★★★

DIR: Ingmar Bergman. **CAST:** Max von Sydow, Ingrid Thulin, Gunnar Björstrand, Bibi Andersson.

Dark and somber parable deals with the quest for an afterlife by focusing on confrontation between a mesmerist and a magician. This shadowy allegory may not be everyone's idea of entertainment, but the richness of ideas and the excellent acting of director Ingmar Bergman's fine stable of actors make this a compelling film. Subtitled in English. 1959; B&W; 102m.

MAKE ROOM FOR TOMORROW ★★★

DIR: Peter Kassovitz. **CAST:** Victor Lanoux, Jane Birkin, Georges Wilson.

More a collection of mildly humorous events than an out-and-out comedy. Victor Lanoux plays a father going through a mid-life crisis. Rated R for language and nudity. 1982; 104m.

MALICIOUS ★★★½

DIR: Salvatore Samperi. **CAST:** Laura Antonelli, Turi Ferro, Alessandro Momo, Tina Aumont.

Italian beauty Laura Antonelli is hired as a housekeeper for a widower and his three sons. Not surprisingly, she becomes the object of affection for all four men—particularly 14-year-old Nino. Rated R. 1974; 98m.

MALOU ★★★

DIR: Jeanine Meerapfel. **CAST:** Ingrid Caven, Helmut Griem.

Moving drama of a woman's search for the truth about the marriage between her French mother and a German-Jew during Hitler's terrifying reign. The story unfolds through a rich tapestry of flashbacks that draws out the mystery of the mother, Malou, and her daughter. Not rated. In German with English subtitles. 1983; 94m.

MAN AND A WOMAN, A ★★★★

DIR: Claude Lelouch. **CAST:** Anouk Aimée, Jean-Louis Trintignant, Pierre Barouh, Valerie Lagrange.

This is a superbly written, directed, and acted story of a young widow and widower who fall in love. Anouk Aimee and race-car driver Jean-Louis Trintignant set this film on fire. A hit in 1966 and still a fine picture. Dubbed into English. 1966; 102m.

MAN AND A WOMAN: 20 YEARS LATER, A

DIR: Claude Lelouch. **CAST:** Anouk Aimée, Jean-Louis Trintignant, Richard Berry.

This may be the most narcissistic bad film ever made. The director of this movie took his 1966 *A Man and a*

Woman and, after twenty years, assembled the original lead actors and created a monster. *A Man and a Woman: 20 Years Later* is a tedious piece of nostalgic self-admiration. In French. Rated PG. 1986; 112m.

MAN FACING SOUTHEAST ★★★½

DIR: Eliseo Subiera. **CAST:** Lorenzo Quinteros, Hugo Soto.

A haunting, eerie mystery in which an unknown man—possibly an alien—inexplicably appears in the midst of a Buenos Aires psychiatric hospital. Rich with Christian symbolism, this film leaves one wondering who is really sick—society or those society finds insane. Some nudity and sexual situations. In Spanish with English subtitles. 1987; 105m.

MAN WHO LOVED WOMEN, THE (1977) ★★★★

DIR: François Truffaut. **CAST:** Charles Denner, Brigitte Fossey, Leslie Caron, Nathalie Baye.

The basis for a 1983 Blake Edwards film starring Burt Reynolds, this comedy-drama from François Truffaut has more irony and bite than the remake. Beginning with the protagonist's funeral, the movie examines why he wants and needs women so much, and why they respond to him as well. Like most Truffaut films, it has a deceptively light tone. In French with English subtitles. 1977; 119m.

MANON OF THE SPRING ★★★★★

DIR: Claude Berri. **CAST:** Yves Montand, Daniel Auteuil, Emmanuelle Beart, Elisabeth Depardieu.

For its visual beauty alone, this sequel to *Jean de Florette* is a motion picture to savor. But it has a great deal more to offer. Chief among its pleasures are superb performances by Yves Montand and Daniel Auteuil. A fascinating tale of revenge and unrequited love. Rated PG-13 for nudity. In French with English subtitles. 1987; 113m.

MARIUS ★★★

DIR: Alexander Korda. **CAST:** Raimu, Pierre Fresnay, Orane Demazis, Alida Rouffe.

This French movie is a marvelous view of the working class in Marseilles between the wars. The story revolves around Marius (Pierre Fresnay) and his love for Fanny (Orane Demazis), the daughter of a fish store proprietess. The poetic essence of the film is captured with style as Marius ships out to sea, unknowingly leaving Fanny with child. In French with English subtitles. 1931; B&W; 125m.

MARRIAGE OF MARIA BRAUN, THE ★★½

DIR: Rainer Werner Fassbinder. **CAST:** Hanna Schygulla, Klaus Lowitsch, Ivan Desny.

The Marriage of Maria Braun is probably Rainer Werner Fassbinder's easiest film to take because it's basically straightforward and stars the sensual and comedic Hanna Schygulla. She plays Maria Braun, a tough cookie who marries a Wehrmacht officer whom she loses to the war and then prison. The film is full of Fassbinder's overly dramatic, sordid sexual atmosphere. It can be both funny and perverse. In German. Rated R. 1979; 120m.

MASCULINE FEMININE ★★★

DIR: Jean-Luc Godard. **CAST:** Jean-Pierre Léaud, Chantal Goya, Catherine Isabelle Duport, Marlene Jobert.

Jean-Luc Godard's eleventh film is an uneven attempt at exploring the relationship between a young Parisian radical, effectively portrayed by Jean-Pierre Leaud, and a slightly promiscuous woman (Chantal Goya) in fifteen discontinuous, contrapuntal vignettes. Good camera work and interesting screenplay lose strength in a muddled and disjointed story. In French with English subtitles. 1966; B&W; 103m.

MASTER OF THE HOUSE (DU SKAL AERE DIN HUSTRU) ★★★★
DIR: Carl Dreyer. **CAST:** Johannes Meyer, Astrid Holm.

In this funny satire of middle-class life, a wife runs away from her husband, a chauvinist pig who treats her brutally. Later, the wife is reunited with her husband after an old nurse has taught him a lesson. Silent. 1925; B&W; 81m.

MAYERLING ★★★
DIR: Anatole Litvak. **CAST:** Charles Boyer, Danielle Darrieux, Suzy Prim.

Fine-tuned, convincing performances mark this French-made romantic tragedy based upon one of history's most dramatic personal incidents: Austrian Crown Prince Rudolph's ill-starred clandestine love for court lady-in-waiting Countess Marie Vetsera, in 1889. Mayerling is the royal hunting lodge where it all comes together—and falls apart. A 1969 British remake stinks by comparison. In French with English subtitles. 1936; B&W; 91m.

MELO ★★★
DIR: Alain Resnais. **CAST:** Sabine Azema, Pierre Arditi, Fanny Ardant, André Dussollier.

An offering of quiet, subtle charms, one of those typically French chamber romances in which small gestures or glances speak volumes. It's a straightforward exploration of a romantic triangle, set in the world of contemporary classical music, and features a memorable, César-winning performance by Sabine Azema. In French with English subtitles. 1988; 112m.

MELODIE EN SOUS-SOL (THE BIG GRAB) ★★★
DIR: Henri Verneuil. **CAST:** Jean Gabin, Alain Delon, Viviane Romance, Carla Marlier.

Fresh from prison, aging gangster Jean Gabin makes intricate and elaborate plans to score big by robbing a major Riviera gambling casino. Alain Delon joins him in conniving their way to the casino vault by seducing a showgirl to gain vital backstage access. Suspense builds as delays threaten the plan. Crime ultimately pays, but a clever twist of fate resolves the usual moral dilemma of right versus wrong. Gabin, as the cool, experienced ex-convict, and Delon, as his young, upstart, eager partner, are part-perfect. In French, with English subtitles. Originally released in U.S. as *Any Number Can Win*. 1963; B&W; 118m.

MEN... ★★★★
DIR: Doris Dörrie. **CAST:** Uwe Ochenknecht, Ulrike Kriener, Heiner Lauterbach.

In this tongue-in-cheek anthropological study by German writer-director Doris Dörrie, a hotshot advertising executive, who has been having a fling with his secretary, is outraged to discover that his wife has a lover. Devastated at first, he finally decides to get even, and his revenge is one of the most inventive and hilarious ever to grace the screen. In German with English subtitles. Unrated, the film has profanity. 1985; 99m.

MENAGE ★★★
DIR: Bertrand Blier. **CAST:** Gerard Depardieu, Michel Blanc, Miou-Miou, Bruno Cremer.

Two down-and-outers (Michel Blanc and Miou-Miou) are taken in by a flamboyant thief (Gerard Depardieu), who introduces them to a life of crime, and kinky sex in this alternately hilarious and mean-spirited comedy. The first half of this bizarre work is enjoyable, but the acceptance of the last part will depend on the taste—and tolerance—of the viewer. In French, with English subtitles. Unrated, the film has profanity, violence, nudity, and simulated sex. 1986; 84m.

MEPHISTO ★★★★★
DIR: Istvan Szabo. **CAST:** Klaus Maria Brandauer, Krystyna Janda.

Winner of the 1981 Academy Award for best foreign-language film, this brilliant movie, by Hungarian writer-director Istvan Szabo, examines the conceits of artists with devastating honesty and insight. Klaus Maria Brandauer, in a stunning performance, plays an actor whose overwhelming desire for artistic success leads to his becoming a puppet of the Nazi government. The film has nudity and violence. In German, with English subtitles. 1981; 135m.

MILKY WAY, THE (1970) ★★★★
DIR: Luis Buñuel. **CAST:** Paul Frankeur, Laurent Terzieff, Alain Cuny, Bernard Verley, Michel Piccoli, Delphine Seyrig.
Haunting comedy about two men making a religious pilgrimage through France. Excellent supporting cast and outstanding direction by Luis Buñuel. French dialogue with English subtitles. Not rated. 1970; 102m.

MISS MARY ★★★½
DIR: Maria Luisa Bemberg. **CAST:** Julie Christie, Nacha Guevara, Tato Pavlovsky.
A good knowledge of the history of Argentina—specifically between the years 1930 and 1945—will help viewers appreciate this biting black comedy. Julie Christie gives a marvelous performance as a British governess brought to the South American country to work for a wealthy family. Through her eyes, in a series of flashbacks, we see how the corrupt aristocracy slowly falls apart. In both English and Spanish. Rated R for profanity, nudity, and suggested and simulated sex. 1987; 100m.

MR. HULOT'S HOLIDAY ★★★½
DIR: Jacques Tati. **CAST:** Jacques Tati, Nathale Pascaud.
A delightfully lighthearted film about the natural comedy to be found in vacationing. Jacques Tati plays the famous Monsieur Hulot, who has some silly adventures at a seaside resort. Although partially dubbed in English, this film has a mime quality that is magical. 1953; B&W; 86m.

MR. KLEIN ★★★½
DIR: Joseph Losey. **CAST:** Alain Delon, Jeanne Moreau, Juliet Berto, Michel Lonsdale, Jean Bouise, Francine Berge.
Dark-sided character study of a Parisian antique dealer who buys artwork and personal treasures from Jews trying to escape Paris in 1942. He (Alain Delon) finds himself mistaken for a missing Jew of the same name. This thriller builds around the search to reveal the identity of the second Mr. Klein. Rated PG. Available in French version. 1976; 123m.

MON ONCLE D'AMERIQUE ★★★★
DIR: Alain Resnais. **CAST:** Gerard Depardieu, Nicole Garcia, Roger Pierre.
In this bizarre French comedy, director Alain Resnais works something close to a miracle: he combines intelligence with entertainment. On one level, *Mon Oncle d'Amerique* is a delectable farce with the requisite ironies, surprise complications, and bittersweet truths. Underneath, it is a thought-provoking scientific treatise—by biologist Henri Laborit—on the human condition. Rated PG. In French with English subtitles. 1980; 123m.

MONSIEUR VINCENT ★★★★
DIR: Maurice Cloche. **CAST:** Pierre Fresnay, Aimée Clairiond, Jean Debucourt.
Winner of a special Academy Award, this is a moving, beautifully photographed biography of St. Vincent de Paul, patron saint of social workers. Even if you don't think you'd be interested in the subject matter, it's worth seeing for the performance of Pierre Fresnay, one of France's greatest actors. In French with English subtitles. 1949; 73m.

MOON IN THE GUTTER, THE ★
DIR: Jean-Jacques Beineix. **CAST:** Gerard Depardieu, Nastassja Kinski, Victoria Abril.
A pretentious, self-consciously artistic bore that seems to defy any viewer to sit through it. Shortly after the film was completed, Gerard Depardieu

complained the movie didn't make any sense and had serious problems in pacing. He was absolutely right. Rated R for profanity, nudity, and violence. In French with subtitles. 1983; 126m.

MOONLIGHTING (1983) ★★★★½
DIR: Jerzy Skolimowski. **CAST:** Jeremy Irons, Eugene Lipinski.
This film, a political parable criticizing the Soviet Union's suppression of Solidarity in Poland, may sound rather heavy, gloomy, and dull. It isn't. Written and directed by Jerzy Skolimowski, it essentially focuses on four Polish construction workers remodeling a flat in London. Give it a look. In Polish, with English subtitles. Rated PG for very brief nudity. 1983; 97m.

MOSCOW DOES NOT BELIEVE IN TEARS ★★★★
DIR: Vladimir Menshov. **CAST:** Vera Alentova, Irina Muravyova.
For all its rewards, *Moscow Does Not Believe in Tears* requires a bit of patience on the part of the viewer. The first hour of this tragic comedy is almost excruciatingly slow. You're tempted to give up on it. But once it gets deeper into the story, you're very glad you toughed it out. MPAA unrated, but contains brief nudity and brief violence. 1980; 152m.

MOTHER ★★★★
DIR: Mikio Naruse. **CAST:** Kinuyo Tanaka.
This is a beautifully shot black-and-white movie about a working-class mother who must raise her family after her husband's death in post–World War II. While the story appears to be simple, there is great depth in each character. This was voted Japan's best film in 1952. In Japanese with English subtitles. 1952; B&W; 98m.

MOZART BROTHERS, THE ★★½
DIR: Suzanne Osten. **CAST:** Étienne Glaser, Philip Zanden.
This surrealistic film about a zany director's insane production of *Don Giovanni* owes far more to the madcap antics of the Marx Brothers than the music of Mozart. Étienne Glaser is splendid as the spacy director with vague, but grand plans to reinterpret the opera. However refreshing, the plot is not developed beyond the initial sniggers. Unrated. In Swedish with English subtitles. 1988; 111m.

MY BEST FRIEND'S GIRL ★★★
DIR: Bertrand Blier. **CAST:** Isabelle Huppert, Thierry Lhermitte, Coluche.
A philosophical comedy about two best but very different friends who find themselves in love with the same girl. Isabelle Huppert marvelously plays the sultry and amoral object of both men's desire, but the real gem of this film is the performance of Coluche, who falls in love with his best friend's girl. Nudity and simulated sex. In French with English subtitles. 1984; 99m.

MY LIFE AS A DOG ★★★★★
DIR: Lasse Hallström. **CAST:** Anton Glanzelius.
This charming, offbeat, and downright lovable import from Sweden is a big surprise. It tells of a young boy in 1950s Sweden who's shipped off to a country village when his mother becomes seriously ill. There, as he tries to come to terms with his new life, he encounters a town filled with colorful eccentrics and a young tomboy who becomes his first love. In Swedish, with English subtitles. 1987; 101m.

MY LIFE TO LIVE ★★★
DIR: Jean-Luc Godard. **CAST:** Anna Karina, Saddy Rebbot, André S. Labarthe.
Twelve vignettes in the life of a woman who leaves her husband to become an actress but eventually turns to prostitution. As with any Jean-Luc Godard film, the point is not so much the plot as the director's relentless experimentation with film technique and probing of social is-

sues. In French with English subtitles. 1963; B&W; 85m.

MY NEW PARTNER ★★★★
DIR: Claude Zidi. **CAST:** Philippe Noiret, Thierry Lhermitte, Regine.

Walrus-faced Philippe Noiret is hilarious in this French comedy that swept the César Awards (the French Oscars). He plays a corrupt but effective police detective who is saddled with a new partner, an idealistic young police-academy graduate. Hollywood would never make a comedy this cynical about police work; they've seldom made one as funny either. Rated R for nudity and sexual situations. In French with English subtitles. 1984; 106m.

MY NIGHT AT MAUD'S ★★★★
DIR: Eric Rohmer. **CAST:** Jean-Louis Trintignant, Françoise Fabian, Marie-Christine Barrault.

My Night At Maud's was the first feature by Eric Rohmer to be shown in the United States. It is the third film of the cycle he called *Six Moral Tales*. A man is in love with a woman, but his eyes wander to another. However, the transgression is only brief, for, according to Rohmer, the only true love is the love ordained by God. Beautifully photographed in black and white, the camera looks the actors straight in the eye and captures every nuance. In French with English subtitles. 1970; B&W; 105m.

MY OTHER HUSBAND ★★★★
DIR: Georges Lautner. **CAST:** Miou-Miou, Roger Hanin, Eddy Mitchell.

At first, this French import starring the marvelous Miou-Miou seems rather like a scatterbrained, faintly funny retread of the old person-with-two-spouses comedy plot. But it goes on to become an affecting, sweetly sad little treasure. In French with English subtitles. Rated PG-13 for profanity. 1981; 110m.

MY UNCLE (MON ONCLE) ★★★★
DIR: Jacques Tati. **CAST:** Jacques Tati, Jean-Pierre Zola.

The second of Jacques Tati's cinematic romps as Mr. Hulot (the first was the famous *Mr. Hulot's Holiday*), this delightful comedy continues Tati's recurrent theme of the common man confronted with an increasingly mechanized and depersonalized society. (It's also the only Tati film to win the Academy Award for best foreign film.) 1958; 116m.

MYSTERIES ★★★
DIR: Paul de Lussanet. **CAST:** Sylvia Kristel, Rutger Hauer, David Rappaport, Rita Tushingham, Andrea Ferreol.

Rutger Hauer plays an affluent foreigner in a seaside village who becomes obsessed by a local beauty. His love drives him to progressively stranger behavior. This intriguing drama is hampered by poorly dubbed dialogue. Not rated, but has sex and nudity. 1984; 93m.

NAPOLEON (1927) ★★★★★
DIR: Abel Gance. **CAST:** Albert Dieudonné, Antonin Artaud.

Over a half century after its debut, *Napoleon* remains a visual wonder, encompassing a number of film-making techniques, some of which still seem revolutionary. The complete film—as pieced together by British film historian Kevin Brownlow over a period of twenty years—is one motion picture event no lover of the art form will want to miss even on the small screen without the full effect of its spectacular three-screen climax. 1927; B&W; 235m.

NEA (A YOUNG EMMANUELLE) ★★★
DIR: Nelly Kaplan. **CAST:** Sami Frey, Ann Zacharias, Micheline Presle.

In this French sex comedy, a young girl, Sybille Ashby (Ann Zacharias), stifled by the wealth of her parents, turns to anonymously writing erotic literature via firsthand experience. Her anonymity betrayed, she perfects her novel, *Nea*, by the sweetest revenge she can devise. A relatively successful and entertaining film of its kind, this has sex and adult themes. In French, with English subtitles. Rated R. 1978; 103m.

NEST, THE (1981) ★★½
DIR: Jaime De Arminan. **CAST:** Hector Alterio, Ana Torrent.

The Nest is the story of a tragic relationship between a 60-year-old widower and a 12-year-old girl. The movie takes a far too romantic view of the widower's sacrifices to the friendship, and Ana Torrent is a bit too austere and worldly-wise for her own good. Hector Alterio as the older man has a warm and inviting face and voice. He is the one who enlists our sympathies. In Spanish, with English subtitles. 1981; 109m.

NEXT SUMMER ★★★
DIR: Nadine Trintignant. **CAST:** Claudia Cardinale, Fanny Ardant, Philippe Noiret, Marie Trintignant, Jean-Louis Trintignant.

This romantic comedy features some of France's top stars in a story about a family in which personal frustrations conflict with passions in the quest for power and beauty. Excellent performances by a top-notch cast made this film a major box-office hit in France. In French with English subtitles. Not rated. 1986; 100m.

NIGHT IS MY FUTURE ★★★½
DIR: Ingmar Bergman. **CAST:** Mai Zetterling, Birger Malmsten.

In this early Ingmar Bergman film, a film that at the same time is dark in mood but bright with promise of things to come, we meet a blinded military veteran (Birger Malmsten) who is at war with the world and with himself due to his handicap. Through the selfless efforts of a maid, he learns to accept his problems and make a new life for himself. In Swedish with English subtitles. 1947; B&W; 87m.

NIGHT OF THE SHOOTING STARS ★★½
DIR: Paolo Taviani, Vittorio Taviani. **CAST:** Omero Antonutti, Margarita Lozano.

Made by Paolo and Vittorio Taviani, this Italian import is about the flight of peasants from their mined village in pastoral Tuscany during the waning days of World War II. Despite its subject matter, the horrors of war, it is a strangely unaffecting—and ineffective—motion picture. In Italian, with English subtitles. Unrated, the film has violence. 1982; 116m.

NIGHTS OF CABIRIA ★★★★
DIR: Federico Fellini. **CAST:** Giulietta Masina, Amadeo Nazzari, François Perier.

Federico Fellini's seventh film can be hailed as a tragicomic masterpiece. The story focuses on an impoverished prostitute (Giulietta Masina) living on the outskirts of Rome, who is continuously betrayed by her faith in human nature. Masina gives an unforgettable performance. In Italian with English subtitles. 1957; B&W; 110m.

NOSFERATU ★★★★
DIR: F. W. Murnau. **CAST:** Max Schreck, Gustav von Waggenheim.

A product of the German expressionist era, *Nosferatu* is a milestone in the history of world cinema. Director F. W. Murnau seems to make the characters jump out at you. With his skeletal frame, rodent face, long nails, and long, pointed ears, Max Schreck is the most terrifying of all screen vampires. Silent. 1922; B&W; 63m.

NOUS N' IRONS PLUS AU BOIS ★★
DIR: Georges Dumoulin. **CAST:** Marie-France Pisier, Siegfried Rauch, Richard Leduc.

A group of young French Resistance fighters harass German troops in a forest held by the Germans. They capture a young German soldier who joins them when he falls in love with a French girl. Aside from the presence of Marie-France Pisier, there's nothing here likely to interest an American audience. In French with English subtitles. 1969; 90m.

NUDO DI DONNA (PORTRAIT OF A WOMAN, NUDE) ★★★
DIR: Nino Manfredi. **CAST:** Nino Manfredi, Eleonora Giorgi.
Nino Manfredi stars in this Italian comedy as a husband shocked to discover his wife (Eleonora Giorgi) may have posed nude for a painting. Told the model was a hooker, the skeptical Manfredi attempts to discover the truth in this madcap import. In Italian, with English subtitles. Unrated. 1982; 112m.

OBLOMOV ★★★★
DIR: Nikita Mikhalkov. **CAST:** Oleg Tabakov, Elena Soloyei.
This thoroughly delightful film has as its main character Oblomov, a man who has chosen to sleep his life away. Then along comes a childhood friend who helps him explore a new meaning of life. A beautifully crafted triumph for director Nikita Mikhalkov (*A Slave of Love*). In Russian with English subtitles. MPAA unrated. 1980; 146m.

OCCURRENCE AT OWL CREEK BRIDGE, AN ★★★½
DIR: Robert Enrico. **CAST:** Roger Jacquet, Anne Cornaly.
This fascinating French film looks at the last fleeting moments of the life of a man being hanged from the bridge of the title during the American Civil War. This memorable short film works on all levels. 1962; B&W; 22m.

ODD OBSESSION ★½
DIR: Kon Ichikawa. **CAST:** Machiko Kyo, Tatsuya Nakadai.
An aging man hopes to revive his waning potency. Too slow moving to maintain interest. In Japanese with often incomplete or confusing English subtitles. Unrated, it contains off-camera sex. 1960; 107m.

OFFICIAL STORY, THE ★★★★★
DIR: Luis Puenzo. **CAST:** Norma Aleandro, Hector Alterio, Analia Castro.
This winner of the Oscar for best foreign language film unforgettably details the destruction of a middle-class Argentinian family. The beginning of the end comes when the wife (brilliantly played by Norma Aleandro) suspects that her adopted baby daughter may be the orphan of parents murdered during the "dirty war" of the 1970s. In Spanish with English subtitles. Unrated, the film has violence. 1985; 110m.

OLD TESTAMENT, THE ★
DIR: Gianfranco Parolini. **CAST:** Susan Paget, Brad Harris, Bridgette Corey.
In this boring Italian epic, the Jews of Jerusalem are ruled by cruel Syrians. They flee, gather strength in the desert, and return to reclaim their city. What could have been inspirational has been reduced to a viewing sedative. Unrated, this contains violence. 1963; 88m.

ONE DEADLY SUMMER ★★★
DIR: Jean Becker. **CAST:** Isabelle Adjani, Alain Souchon, François Cluzet, Suzanne Flon, Manuel Gelin.
Isabelle Adjani stars as a promiscuous young woman who returns to a small village to seek revenge on three men who beat and raped her mother many years before. Exceptionally well acted, especially by Alain Souchon as her sympathetic boyfriend, and veteran European actress Suzanne Flon as his slightly crazy aunt. Rated R for nudity and violence. In French with English subtitles. 1983; 133m.

ONE SINGS, THE OTHER DOESN'T ★★½
DIR: Agnes Varda. **CAST:** Valerie Mairesse, Thérèse Liotard.
Labeled early on as a feminist film, this story is about a friendship between two different types of women spanning 1962 to 1976. When they meet again at a women's rally after ten years, they renew their friendship by discussing events in their lives. 1977; 105m.

ONE WILD MOMENT ★★★★
DIR: Claude Berri. **CAST:** Jean-Pierre Marielle, Victor Lanoux.

In French director Claude Berri's warm and very sensitive film, a middle-aged man (Jean-Pierre Marielle) is told by his best friend's daughter that she's in love with him. Enjoy the story (which was adapted by director Stanley Donen for *Blame it on Rio*) as it should be told, as delicately and thoughtfully handled by Berri. In French with English subtitles. Unrated, the film has nudity, and profanity. 1980; 90m.

ONE WOMAN OR TWO ★★★½
DIR: Daniel Vigne. **CAST:** Sigourney Weaver, Gerard Depardieu, Dr. Ruth Westheimer.

Gerard Depardieu plays an anthropologist digging for "the missing link." Dr. Ruth debuts as a philanthropist whose money will continue the search. And Sigourney Weaver is the advertising executive who, almost ruins the entire project. Wonderful acting and superb dialogue are the highlights of this French turn on *Bringing Up Baby*. In French with English subtitles. 1987; 95m.

OPEN CITY ★★★★½
DIR: Roberto Rossellini. **CAST:** Aldo Fabrizi, Anna Magnani.

Stunning study of resistance and survival in World War II Italy was the first important film to come out of postwar Europe and has been considered a classic in realism. Co-scripted by a young Federico Fellini, this powerful story traces the threads of people's lives as they interact and eventually entangle themselves in the shadow of their Gestapo-controlled "open city." In Italian with English subtitles. 1946; B&W; 105m.

OPERA DO MALANDRO ★★★
DIR: Ruy Guerra. **CAST:** Edson Celulari, Claudia Ohana.

A homage to the Hollywood musicals of the Forties, this vibrant, stylish film is set in Rio's seedy back streets on the eve of the Pearl Harbor invasion. The story is about a gangster whose search for the American dream is disrupted by his love for a beautiful Brazilian girl. In Portuguese with English subtitles. 1987; 108m.

ORDET ★★★★½
DIR: Carl Dreyer. **CAST:** Henrik Malberg.

Possibly the greatest work of Carl Dreyer, the Danish director whose films (*The Passion of Joan of Arc, Day of Wrath*) demonstrate an intellectual obsession with the nature of religious faith in the modern world. In this drama, based on a play written by a priest who was murdered by the Nazis, characters in a small, God-fearing town wrestle between two varieties of faith, one puritanical, the other life-affirming. In Danish with English subtitles. 1955; B&W; 125m.

ORPHEUS ★★★½
DIR: Jean Cocteau. **CAST:** Jean Marais, Maria Casares.

Jean Cocteau's surreal account of the Greek myth with Jean Marais as Orpheus, the successful, envied, and despised poet who thrusts himself beyond mortality. Maria Casares co-stars as the lonely, troubled, passionate Death. Cocteau's poetic imagery will pull you deep into the fantasy. In French with English subtitles. 1949; B&W; 86m.

OVERCOAT, THE ★★★
DIR: Alexi Batalov. **CAST:** Rolan Bykov.

Based on a story by Gogol, this Russian film tells the story of an office clerk who is content with his modest life and ambitions until he buys a new overcoat and enters on an upward track. Entertaining satire. In Russian with English subtitles. 1960; B&W; 78m.

PADRE PADRONE ★★★½
DIR: Vittorio Taviani, Paolo Taviani. **CAST:** Omero Antonutti, Saverio Marioni.

Although slow-moving, this low-budget film is a riveting account of a young Sardinian's traumatizing relationship with his overbearing father in a patriarchal society. The son bears the brutality, but eventually breaks the emotional bonds. This quietly powerful film depends on the actors for its punch. In Sardinian (Italian dialect) with English subtitles. 1977; 114m.

PAIN IN THE A—, A ★★
DIR: Edouard Molinaro. **CAST:** Lino Ventura, Jacques Brel.

A professional hit man (Lino Ventura) arrives in Montpellier, Italy, to kill a government witness who is set to testify against the mob. This unfunny slapstick comedy was adapted by director Billy Wilder for the equally disappointing *Buddy, Buddy* with Jack Lemmon and Walter Matthau. In French, with English subtitles. Rated PG for light violence. 1973; 90m.

PAISAN ★★★½
DIR: Roberto Rossellini. **CAST:** Carmela Sazio, Robert Van Loon, Gar Moore.

Six separate stories of survival are hauntingly presented by writer Federico Fellini and director Roberto Rossellini in this early postwar Italian film. Shot on the streets and often improvised, this strong drama exposes the raw nerves brought on by living in a battleground and drags the audience into the lives of these victims. 1946; B&W; 90m.

PANDORA'S BOX ★★★★½
DIR: G. W. Pabst. **CAST:** Louise Brooks, Fritz Kortner.

Here is a gem from the heyday of German silent screen expressionism. The film follows a winning yet amoral temptress, Lulu (a sparkling performance by Louise Brooks). Without concerns or inhibitions, Lulu blissfully ensnares a variety of weak men, only to contribute to their eventual downfall. 1929; B&W; 131m.

PANIQUE ★★★½
DIR: Julien Duvivier. **CAST:** Michel Simon, Viviane Romance.

Based on a thriller by Georges Simenon, this gripping story features Michel Simon as a stranger who is framed for murder by a couple covering their own crime. This is a taut film comparable to the best of the chase *noir* genre so prevalent in French and American cinema of the mid-1940s. In French, with English subtitles. 1946; B&W; 87m.

PARDON MON AFFAIRE ★★★★
DIR: Yves Robert. **CAST:** Jean Rochefort, Claude Brasseur, Anny Duperey, Guy Bedos, Victor Lanoux.

Enjoyable romantic comedy about a middle-class, happily married man (Jean Rochefort) who pursues his fantasy of meeting a beautiful model (Anny Duperey) and having an affair. Later remade in America as *The Woman in Red.* In French with English subtitles. Rated PG. 1976; 105m.

PARDON MON AFFAIRE, TOO! ★½
DIR: Yves Robert. **CAST:** Jean Rochefort, Claude Brasseur, Guy Bedos, Victor Lanoux, Daniele Delorme.

Lukewarm comedy of infidelity and friendship. The focus is on four middle-aged men who share their troubles and feelings about their marriages and sex lives. A sequel to *Pardon Mon Affaire*, the movie elicits no real laughs. In French with English subtitles. 1977; 110m.

PARDON MY TRUNK ★★½
DIR: Gianni Franciolini. **CAST:** Vittorio De Sica, Maria Mereader, Sabu, Nando Bruno.

An Italian schoolteacher (Vittorio De Sica), struggling against poverty to raise his family in a tenement building, does a good deed for a visiting Hindu prince. In gratitude, the Indian sends him a gift: a baby elephant. De Sica's performance elevates what otherwise would have been merely a silly slapstick exercise. Also known as *Hello Elephant*! Dubbed in English. 1952; B&W; 85m.

PASSION (1919) ★★★
DIR: Ernst Lubitsch. **CAST:** Pola Negri, Emil Jannings.

Combining realism with spectacle, this account of famous eighteenth-century French courtesan Madame Du Barry was the first German film to earn international acclaim after World War I. As a result, the director and the stars received Hollywood contracts. The film is still recognized as the best of seven made about the subject between 1915 and 1954. Silent. 1919; B&W; 134m.

PASSION OF JOAN OF ARC, THE ★★★★★

DIR: Carl Dreyer. **CAST:** Maria Falconetti, Eugene Silvain, Antonin Artaud.

This is simply one of the greatest films ever made. Its emotional intensity is unsurpassed. Faces tell the tale of this movie. Maria Falconetti's Joan is unforgettable. Silent. 1928; B&W; 114m.

PASSION OF LOVE ★★★★

DIR: Ettore Scola. **CAST:** Valeria D'Obici, Bernard Giraudeau, Laura Antonelli, Bernard Blier, Jean-Louis Trintignant, Massimo Girotti.

In 1862 Italy just after the war, a decorated captain (Bernard Giraudeau) is transferred to a faraway outpost, where he becomes the love object of his commander's cousin (Valeria D'Obici). What follows is a fascinating study of torment. Dubbed in English and unrated. 1982; 117m.

PASSIONATE THIEF, THE ★½

DIR: Mario Monicelli. **CAST:** Ben Gazzara, Anna Magnani, Toto, Fred Clark, Edy Vessel.

This less-than-hilarious Italian comedy is poorly dubbed. Ben Gazzara plays a thief at a New Year's Eve party. His suave attempts at removing the jewels are thwarted when Anna Magnani shows up and decides that he's interested in her. Monotonous. 1961; B&W; 100m.

PAULINE AT THE BEACH ★★★★

DIR: Eric Rohmer. **CAST:** Amanda Langlet, Arielle Dombasle, Pascal Greggory, Feodor Atkine.

The screen works of French writer-director Eric Rohmer are decidedly unconventional. In this, one of his "Comedies and Proverbs," the 14-year-old title character (Amanda Langlet) shows herself to have a better sense of self and reality than the adults around her. In French, with English subtitles. Rated R for nudity. 1983; 94m.

PELLE THE CONQUEROR ★★★★★

DIR: Bille August. **CAST:** Max von Sydow, Pelle Hvenegaard.

Bille August's superb drama casts Max von Sydow as a Swedish widower who takes his young son to Denmark in the hope of finding a better life. Once there, they must endure even harder times. In Danish and Swedish with English subtitles. Unrated, the film has nudity, violence, and profanity. 1988; 138m.

PEPE LE MOKO ★★★½

DIR: Julien Duvivier. **CAST:** Jean Gabin, Mireille Balin, Gabriel Gario, Marcel Dallo.

Algiers criminal Pepe Le Moko (Jean Gabin) is safe just as long as he remains in the city's picturesque, squalid native quarter, the Casbah, a sanctuary for fugitives where the police have no power. His passionate infatuation with a beautiful visitor from his beloved Paris, however, spells his doom. In French with English subtitles. 1937; B&W; 93m.

PERIL ★★

DIR: Michel Deville. **CAST:** Christophe Malavoy, Nicole Garcia, Richard Bohringer, Anemone, Michel Piccoli.

Nicole Garcia plays the wife of a wealthy businessman who is having an affair with their daughter's guitar instructor (Christophe Malavoy). Filmmaker Michel Deville aims too high in his direction with French New Wave–like scene cuts; they come off more amateurish than artistic. Rated R for nudity, violence, profanity, and adult subject matter. In French with English subtitles. 1985; 100m.

PERSONA ★★★
DIR: Ingmar Bergman. **CAST:** Liv Ullmann, Bibi Andersson, Gunnar Björnstrand.
Liv Ullmann gives a haunting performance as an actress who suddenly becomes mute and is put in the charge of a nurse (Bibi Andersson). The two women become so close that they change personalities. Ingmar Bergman's use of subtle split-screen effects dramatizes the metaphorical quality of this quiet film. In Swedish with English subtitles. 1966; B&W; 81m.

PETIT CON ★½
DIR: Gerard Lauzier. **CAST:** Guy Marchand, Caroline Cellier, Bernard Brieux, Souad Amidou.
France's equivalent of our American teenage-boy-in-heat flicks, with a few differences. The film tries for a serious side involving the trauma that Michel (Bernard Brieux) is causing his family. Rated R. In French with English subtitles. 1986; 90m.

PHANTOM OF LIBERTY, THE ★★
DIR: Luis Buñuel. **CAST:** Jean-Claude Brialy, Adolfo Celi, Michel Piccoli, Monica Vitti.
A kaleidoscope of satirical vignettes composed of outrageous riddles, jokes, and associations all mocking mankind's inexplicable willingness to enslave itself in order to be "free." A big disappointment from Luis Buñuel whose use of tricks from his other films make this one seem clichéd. In French with English subtitles. 1974; 104m.

PHEDRE ★★½
DIR: Pierre Jourdan. **CAST:** Marie Bell, Jacques Dacqumine, Claude Giraud.
The performance of Marie Bell, the great French tragedienne, is the only reason to dig out this abbreviated adaptation of the seventeenth-century drama by Racine. Taken from the Greek myth about the queen who fell in love with her stepson and caused her husband's death, the production is stagy, the supporting cast is not up to Bell's abilities, and Racine's Alexandrine verse is poorly served by the subtitles. In French with English subtitles. 1968; 93m.

PIXOTE ★★★★
DIR: Hector Babenco. **CAST:** Fernando Ramos Da Silva, Marilia Pera.
In Rio, half the population is younger than 18. Kids, only 10- or 12-year-olds, become thieves, beggars, and prostitutes. *Pixote* is the story of one of these unfortunates. For some viewers it may be too powerful and disturbing, yet it is not the least bit exploitative or exaggerated. Rated R for violence, explicit sex, and nudity. 1981; 127m.

PLAYTIME ★★★½
DIR: Jacques Tati. **CAST:** Jacques Tati.
Mr. Hulot is back again in this slapstick comedy as he attempts to keep an appointment in the big city. Paris and all of its buildings, automobiles, and population seem to conspire to thwart Mr. Hulot at every turn, and there are plenty of visual gags. The subtitled American release version is over thirty minutes shorter than the original French release. 1967; 108m.

PORT OF CALL ★★★
DIR: Ingmar Bergman. **CAST:** Nine-Christine Jonsson, Bengt Eklund.
When a seaman begins working on the docks, he falls in love with a suicidal young woman. The woman has had an unhappy childhood and a wild past, which has given her a bad reputation. This drama seems dated today. In Swedish with English subtitles. 1948; B&W; 100m.

QUERELLE ★★½
DIR: Rainer Werner Fassbinder. **CAST:** Rainer Werner Fassbinder, Brad Davis, Franco Nero, Jeanne Moreau.
In this depressing rendering of Jean Genet's story, Brad Davis stars in the title role as a young sailor whose good looks set off a chain reaction. This is a disturbing and depressing portrait of

terminally unhappy people doomed to destroy either themselves, one another, or both. In German with English subtitles. Rated R for nudity and obscenity. 1982; 120m.

QUESTION OF SILENCE, A ★★★★½

DIR: Marleen Gorris. **CAST:** Cox Habbema, Nelly Frijda.

After an unusual murder is committed, three women, all strangers to one another, stand trial for the same crime. A woman psychiatrist is appointed to the case after the three openly display their hostilities toward male-dominated society. Rated R for profanity. Available in original Dutch or dubbed. 1983; 92m.

QUI ETES-VOUS, MR. SORGE? (SOVIET SPY) ★

DIR: André Girard. **CAST:** Thomas Holtzman, Keiko Kishi.

This is a docudrama about the case of Richard Sorge, a German WWII journalist who, records show, was hanged as a Soviet spy in 1944. The movie spends the time offering up differing opinions of various witnesses as to the accuracy of the information. *Qui Etes-Vous, Mr. Sorge* is nothing but a treacherously long, very dry film. In French with English subtitles. 1961; 130m.

RAMPARTS OF CLAY ★★★★

DIR: Jean-Louis Bertucelli. **CAST:** Leila Schenna and the villagers of Tehouda, Algeria.

Terse but hauntingly beautiful documentary-style film set against the harsh background of a poor North African village. A young woman (Leila Schenna) struggles to free herself from the second-class role imposed on her by the village culture, much as the village tries to liberate itself from subservience to the corporate powers that control its salt mines. In Arabic, with English subtitles. Rated PG. 1970; 87m.

RAN ★★★★★

DIR: Akira Kurosawa. **CAST:** Tatsuya Nakadai, Akira Terao.

This superb Japanese historical epic tells the story of a sixteenth-century warlord's time of tragedy. Based on Shakespeare's *King Lear,* this is yet another masterwork from Akira Kurosawa. It is stunningly photographed and acted, and blessed with touches of glorious humor and hair-raising battle sequences. In Japanese with English subtitles. Rated R for violence and suggested sex. 1985; 160m.

RAPE OF LOVE (L'AMOUR VIOLÉ) ★★★★

DIR: Yannick Bellon. **CAST:** Nathalie Nell, Alain Foures.

A graphic rape scene may scare some viewers away from this French export, but that would be unfortunate. *Rape of Love* is a telling account of one woman's quest to come to terms with her tragic experience. Not rated, but has graphic violence, nudity, and profanity. In French with English subtitles. 1979; 111m.

RASCALS, THE ★★★

DIR: Bernard Revon. **CAST:** Bernard Brieux, Thomas Chabrol, Pascale Rocard.

Two kids (Bernard Brieux and Thomas Chabrol) go through school together trying to beat the system. Taking place in the German-occupied France of 1942, *The Rascals* deals with the coming-of-age themes we have seen many times: cheating on school exams, peer group pressure, sexual curiosity, etc. But the film's nationalistic subtext, which results in a triumphant ending, is, perhaps, a new one. In French, with English subtitles. Rated R for sex and nudity. 1979; 93m.

RASHOMON ★★★★★

DIR: Akira Kurosawa. **CAST:** Toshiro Mifune, Machiko Kyo, Masayuki Mori.

After a violent murder and rape is committed by a bandit, four people tell their own different versions of what happened. Set in medieval Japan, this examination of truth and guilt is charged with action. The combination of brilliant photography, stellar acting, direction, and script won this Japanese classic the Oscar for best foreign film. 1951; B&W; 83m.

RED BEARD ★★★★½
DIR: Akira Kurosawa. **CAST:** Toshiro Mifune.

In the early nineteenth-century, a newly graduated doctor, hopes to become a society doctor. Instead, he is posted at an impoverished clinic run by Dr. Niide (Toshiro Mifune), whose destitute patients affectionately call him "Red Beard." Akira Kurosawa, at one of his directorial pinnacles, describes his film as a "monument to the goodness in man." In Japanese with English subtitles. 1965; B&W; 185m.

RED DESERT ★★★★
DIR: Michelangelo Antonioni. **CAST:** Monica Vitti, Richard Harris.

An acutely depressed married woman (Monica Vitti) finds her life with an industrial-engineer husband to be demanding and unrealistic. Photographed in the industrial wasteland of northern Italy by Carlo Di Palma, this film remains one of the most beautiful of director Michelangelo Antonioni's works. Italian with English subtitles. 1964; 116m.

RED SORGHUM ★★★★★
DIR: Zhang Yimou. **CAST:** Gong Li, Jian Weng, Liu Ji.

A superb pastoral epic from the People's Republic of China and the winner of the Golden Bear at the 1988 Berlin Film Festival. The story relates a passionate folk tale about village winemakers who fight against interloping Japanese invaders. Lyrical and affecting drama. In Chinese with English subtitles. 1988; 91m.

REGINA ★★★
DIR: Jean-Yves Prate. **CAST:** Anthony Quinn, Ava Gardner, Ray Sharkey, Anna Karina.

This strange psychological drama features Ava Gardner as a nagging wife and mother who is obsessed with keeping her 36-year-old son at home with her. Anthony Quinn is the much-put-upon husband. An Italian film, this is unrated but contains mature themes. 1983; 86m.

REPENTANCE ★★★
DIR: Tenghiz Abuladze. **CAST:** Avtandil Makharadze.

Set in Georgia in the Soviet Union, this richly varied film presents a central character who personifies all European villains—a cross, most obviously, between Stalin and Hitler. The film is not only a brutally direct comment on evil in politics, but a marvelous study of Georgian life. No rating but there are violent scenes. In Russian with English subtitles. 1987; 151m.

RETURN OF MARTIN GUERRE, THE ★★★★½
DIR: Daniel Vigne. **CAST:** Gerard Depardieu, Nathalie Baye, Roger Planchon.

Brilliantly absorbing account of an actual sixteenth-century court case in which a man returns to his family and village after years away at the wars, only to have his identity questioned. Gerard Depardieu and Nathalie Baye give outstanding, carefully restrained performances. In French with English subtitles. No MPAA rating. 1982; 111m.

RETURN OF THE TALL BLOND MAN WITH ONE BLACK SHOE, THE ★★½
DIR: Yves Robert. **CAST:** Pierre Richard, Mireille Darc, Jean Rochefort.

This sequel to the original *Tall Blond Man...*is, unfortunately, inferior. But it's still a delight to watch Pierre Richard go through his comic paces. Once again our hero is caught up in intrigue and derring-do, and his reactions to what he's faced with are the reason to see this or the original. In French with English subtitles. No MPAA rating. 1974; 84m.

REVOLT OF JOB, THE ★★★★
DIR: Imre Gyongyossy. **CAST:** Ferenc Zenthe, Hedi Tenessy.

In this moving account of the Holocaust in rural Hungary, an old Jewish couple awaiting the inevitable Nazi takeover adopt a gentile orphan boy to survive them. Nominated for best foreign language film in 1983's Academy Awards. In Hungarian, with English subtitles. No rating. 1983; 97m.

ROBERT ET ROBERT ★★★★½
DIR: Claude Lelouch. **CAST:** Charles Denner, Jacques Villeret, Jean-Claude Brialy, Macha Meril, Regine.

A brilliant French film about two lonely but very different men (Charles Denner and Jacques Villeret) who strike up a tenuous friendship while waiting for their respective computer dates. It is a bittersweet tale of loneliness and compassion. No MPAA rating. 1978; 105m.

RULES OF THE GAME, THE ★★★★★
DIR: Jean Renoir. **CAST:** Marcel Dalio, Nora Gregor, Mila Parely.

This is Jean Renoir's masterful comedy-farce that deftly exposes the moral bankruptcy of the French upper classes. A manor house is the location for a party as the shallowness of each guest is brilliantly exposed. 1939; B&W; 110m.

SACCO AND VANZETTI ★★★★
DIR: Giuliano Montaldo. **CAST:** Gian Maria Volonté, Riccardo Cucciolla, Cyril Cusack, Milo O'Shea.

Excellent historical drama recounts the trial and eventual execution of Sacco and Vanzetti, the Italian immigrants who were convicted of murder in 1921. The case was a *cause célèbre* at the time, since many felt that they were condemned on the basis of their politics rather than on the weak evidence against them. Whether or not the film persuades you, it poses powerful questions about the American system of justice. Dubbed in English. Rated PG. 1971; 121m.

SACRIFICE, THE ★★★★
DIR: Andrei Tarkovsky. **CAST:** Erland Josephson, Susan Fleetwood, Valerie Mairesse, Allan Edwall.

In this Andrei Tarkovsky film, the actors do most of the work that expensive special effects would accomplish in an American film with a similar theme. During an approaching world holocaust, we don't see anything as unsubtle as bombs bursting, bloodshed, or devastation. Rather, the camera carefully records the various emotional reactions of six people in a house in the secluded countryside. Actors' faces and unpredictable actions mirror horror, pathos, and even grim humor as the plot twists in a surprisingly supernatural direction. In Swedish, with English subtitles. Unrated, the film has suggested sex. 1986; 145m.

SALAAM BOMBAY! ★★★★½
DIR: Mira Nair. **CAST:** Shafiq Syed, Sarfuddin Qurrassi.

In the most potent film about street children since Hector Babenco's *Pixote*, director Mira Nair takes us on a sobering, heartrending tour of the back alleys and gutters of India. It is there that young Krishna (Shafiq Syed) must struggle to survive among the drug dealers, pimps, and prostitutes. In Hindi with English subtitles. Unrated, the film has profanity, violence, and suggested sex. 1988; 113m.

SAMURAI TRILOGY, THE ★★★★★
DIR: Hiroshi Inagaki. **CAST:** Toshiro Mifune, Koji Tsuruta.

This brilliant and cinematically beautiful three-deck epic by director Hiroshi Inagaki tells the story of the legendary Japanese hero Musashi Miyamoto, a sixteenth-century samurai who righted wrongs in the fashion of Robin Hood and Zorro. Toshiro Mifune is impeccable as Miyamoto, whom we follow from his wild youth through spiritual discovery to the final battle with his archenemy, Sasaki Kojiro (Koji Tsuruta). The Samurai film for the uninitiated. In Japanese with English subtitles. 1954; B&W; 303m.

SANJURO ★★★★½
DIR: Akira Kurosawa. **CAST:** Toshiro Mifune, Tatsuya Nakadai, Takashi Shimura.

First-rate sequel to *Yojimbo* has the original "Man With No Name" (Toshiro Mifune) again stirring up trouble in feudal Japan. He is recruited by several young would-be samurai as their teacher and leader in exposing corruption in their clan. In his usual gentle manner, Mifune wreaks all sorts of havoc while occasionally warning, "Watch it, I'm in a bad mood." In Japanese with English subtitles. 1962; B&W; 96m.

SANSHO THE BAILIFF ★★★
DIR: Kenji Mizoguchi. **CAST:** Kinuyo Tanaka.

This beautifully photographed tale presents the suffering and heroism of a mother who is separated from her two children by a brutal man called Sansho. A poetic film that exhibits the humanism for which director Kenji Mizoguchi is well known. In Japanese with English subtitles. 1954; B&W; 125m.

SARDINE: KIDNAPPED ★★★
DIR: Gianfranco Mingozzi. **CAST:** Franco Nero, Charlotte Rampling.

Intriguing adventure set on the Italian island of Sardinia. Peasants have traditionally obtained land for raising sheep by kidnapping members of wealthy families and ransoming them for land. One family has the courage to stand up to the bandits and informs the police. Directed by a former documentary filmmaker, this English-dubbed film benefits from a realistic look. 1968; 110m.

SAWDUST AND TINSEL ★★★½
DIR: Ingmar Bergman. **CAST:** Harriet Andersson, Anders Ek.

A traveling circus is the background for this study of love relationships between a circus manager, the woman he loves, and her lover. Director Ingmar Bergman scores some emotional bull's-eyes in this early effort with many haunting scenes. Love triangles lead to powerful climax, somewhat reminiscent of *The Blue Angel*. 1953; B&W; 95m.

SCARLET LETTER ★★★½
DIR: Wim Wenders. **CAST:** Senta Berger, Lou Castel, Hans-Christian Blech, Yella Rottlander.

Wim Wender's stunning psychological portrait of bigotry and isolation, this follows a story about the social sanctions imposed upon a woman suspected of adultery in seventeenth-century Salem, Massachusetts. Based on Nathaniel Hawthorne's classic novel, this film version is given some fine contemporary touches by Wenders. In German with English subtitles. 1973; 90m.

SCENE OF THE CRIME (1987) ★★★
DIR: André Téchiné. **CAST:** Catherine Deneuve, Danielle Darrieux, Wadeck Stanczak, Victor Lanoux.

Scene of the Crime is a romantic thriller with an Oedipal angle. A nightclub owner (Catherine Deneuve) and her son get caught up in an increasingly dangerous attempt to safeguard a criminal. This watchable movie could use fast pacing and less obvious camera pyrotechnics. In French, with English subtitles. 1987; 90m.

SCENES FROM A MARRIAGE ★★★★★
DIR: Ingmar Bergman. **CAST:** Liv Ullmann, Erland Josephson, Bibi Andersson.

Director Ingmar Bergman successfully captures the pain and emotions of a marriage that is disintegrating. Several scenes are extremely hard to watch because there is so much truth to what is being said. Originally a six-part film for Swedish television, the theatrical version was edited by Bergman. Believable throughout, this one packs a real punch. In Swedish. No rating (contains some strong language). 1973; 168m.

SECRETS OF WOMEN (OR WAITING WOMEN) ★★★½

DIR: Ingmar Bergman. **CAST:** Anita Bjork, Jarl Kulle, Eva Dahlbeck, Gunnar Björnstrand, Maj-Britt Nilsson, Birger Malmsten.

Infidelity is the theme of this early Ingmar Bergman film. Three wives (Anita Bjork, Maj-Britt Nilsson, and Eva Dahlbeck) who are staying at a summer house recount adventures from their marriages while they are waiting for their husbands' return. Clearly illustrates Bergman's talent for comedy and was his first commercial success. 1952; B&W; 107m.

SEDUCED AND ABANDONED ★★★½

DIR: Pietro Germi. **CAST:** Saro Urzi, Stefania Sandrelli.

This raucous Italian film takes wonderfully funny potshots at Italian life and codes of honor. It centers on a statute of Italian law that absolves a man for the crime of seducing and abandoning a girl if he marries her. This is one of the funniest movies exposing the strategems of saving face. In Italian with English subtitles. 1964; B&W; 118m.

SEDUCTION OF MIMI, THE ★★★★

DIR: Lina Wertmuller. **CAST:** Giancarlo Giannini, Mariangela Melato, Agostina Belli.

Giancarlo Giannini gives an unforgettable performance as the sad-eyed Mimi, a Sicilian who migrates to the big city as a member of the working class. He soon gets into trouble because of his obstinate character and his simple mind. Like all Wertmuller's films, sex and politics are at the heart of her dark humor. Includes one of the funniest love scenes ever filmed. Rated R for language and sex. 1974; 89m.

SENSUOUS NURSE, THE ★

DIR: Nello Rossati. **CAST:** Ursula Andress, Jack Palance, Duilio Del Prete, Luciana Paluzzi.

A wealthy aristocrat has a heart attack and his two fortune-hunting, conniving nephews decide to help their lecherous uncle meet his maker. They send for a voluptuous night nurse (Ursula Andress) and.... You can guess the rest. This dubbed Italian comedy is a dud. Rated R for nudity and simulated sex. 1978; 76m.

SEVEN BEAUTIES ★★★★★

DIR: Lina Wertmuller. **CAST:** Giancarlo Giannini, Fernando Rey, Shirley Stoler.

Winner of many international awards, this Italian film classic is not what the title might suggest. *Seven Beauties* is actually the street name for a small-time gangster, played by Giancarlo Giannini. We watch him struggle and survive on the streets and in a World War II German prisoner-of-war camp. Excellent! Rated R. 1976; 115m.

SEVEN SAMURAI, THE ★★★★★

DIR: Akira Kurosawa. **CAST:** Toshiro Mifune, Takashi Shimura.

This Japanese release—about seven swordsmen coming to the aid of a besieged peasant village—is one of those rare screen wonders that seems to end much too soon. It's timeless and appealing story, which served as the basis for *The Magnificent Seven* and other American films. Unrated, the film has violence. In Japanese, with English subtitles. 1954; B&W; 197m.

SEVENTH SEAL, THE ★★★★½

DIR: Ingmar Bergman. **CAST:** Max von Sydow, Bibi Andersson, Gunnar Bjornstrand.

This is considered by many to be Ingmar Bergman's masterpiece. It tells the story of a knight coming back from the Crusades. He meets Death, who challenges him to a chess match, the stakes being his life. The knight is brilliantly played by Max von Sydow. In Swedish with English subtitles. 1956; B&W; 96m.

SEX SHOP, LE ★★★½
DIR: Claude Berri. **CAST:** Claude Berri, Juliet Berto, Jean-Pierre Marielle.
This French sex comedy stars and was directed by Claude Berri. He plays a bookstore owner. Unable to make ends meet, he converts his store into a sex shop specializing in pornography and sex gadgets. Rated R for nudity and sexual reference. 1974; 93m.

SHAOLIN TEMPLE ★★★★
DIR: Chang Hsin Yen. **CAST:** Li Lin Jei.
The best kung-fu film since *Enter the Dragon*, this period piece, set in seventh-century China, traces the history of the Shaolin Temple. It stars the country's top martial arts experts, yet characterization and plot are not slighted. Unrated, the film has violence. In Chinese, with English subtitles. 1982; 111m.

SHOGUN ASSASSIN ★★★
DIR: (Japan) Kenji Masuni; (United States) David Weisman, Robert Hous. **CAST:** Tomisaburo Wakayama.
This film will rate a zero for the squeamish and close to five for fans of the nineteen-film "Baby Cart" series, so popular in Japan in the 1970s. The color red predominates in this meticulously reedited, rescripted, rescored (by Mark Lindsay), and English-dubbed version of the original *Baby-Cart at the River Styx*: swords enter bodies at the most imaginative angles; a body-count is impossible; all records are broken for bloodletting. Rated R for the violence, which really is fairly aesthetic. 1980; 90m.

SHOOT THE PIANO PLAYER ★★★½
DIR: François Truffaut. **CAST:** Charles Aznavour, Marie Dubois, Nicole Berger, Michele Mercier.
Singer Charles Aznavour plays to perfection the antihero of this minor masterpiece directed by François Truffaut. Don't look for plot, unity of theme, or understandable mood transitions. This one's a brilliantly offbeat mix of crime, melodrama, romance, and slapstick. In French, with English subtitles. 1962; B&W; 85m.

SHOP ON MAIN STREET, THE ★★★★
DIR: Ján Kadár. **CAST:** Elmar Klos, Josef Kroner, Ida Kaminska.
This film finds a Jewish woman removed from her small business and portrays her growing relationship with the man who has been put in charge of her shop. Set among the turbulent and depressing days of the Nazi occupation of Czechoslovakia, this tender film depicts the instincts of survival among the innocent pawns of a brutal war. A moving film. 1964; B&W; 128m.

SIEGFRIED ★★★★
DIR: Fritz Lang. **CAST:** Paul Richter, Margarete Schon, Theodor Loos, Bernhard Goetzke.
Vivid, spectacular story of young god Siegfried, whose conquests and eventual murder form an intrinsic part of Teutonic legend, this nationalistic triumph for German director Fritz Lang was the most ambitious attempt to transfer folklore to film and proved an international success. Moody sets and photography give this movie an otherworldly feeling and evoke just the right atmosphere. Silent. 1923; B&W; 100m.

SILENCE, THE ★★
DIR: Ingmar Bergman. **CAST:** Ingrid Thulin, Gunnel Lindblom, Birger Malmsten.
The Silence is one of Ingmar Bergman's more pretentious and claustrophobic films. Two sisters who are traveling together stop for a time in a European hotel. The film is laden with heavy-handed symbolism and banal dialogue concerning repression, sexuality, guilt, and hate. In Swedish with English subtitles. 1963; 95m.

SIMON OF THE DESERT ★★★★½
DIR: Luis Buñuel. **CAST:** Claudio Brook, Silvia Pinal.

One has the feeling that *Simon of the Desert* is a short film because Luis Buñuel simply ran out of money (and tacked on a fairly unsatisfactory ending). It is, however, impossible to deny the sly pleasure we have with St. Simon Stylites, the desert anchorite who spent thirty-seven years atop a sixty-foot column (circa A.D. 400) preaching to Christian flocks and avoiding temptation—particularly with knockout Silvia Pinal, as the devil, who comes along to tempt him. Good nasty fun for aficionados and novices alike. In Spanish with English subtitles. 1965; B&W; 40m.

SIMPLE STORY, A ★★★½

DIR: Claude Sautet. **CAST:** Romy Schneider, Bruno Cremer, Claude Brasseur, Roger Pigaut.

Marie (Romy Schneider) is pregnant and decides to have an abortion. At forty, she is forced to reevaluate her life and her relationships with men. Rewarding film is paced very slowly and plot is interwoven with subplots of other characters in distress. One of Romy Schneider's best performances. In French, with English subtitles. No MPAA rating. 1978; 110m.

SINCERELY CHARLOTTE ★★★

DIR: Caroline Huppert. **CAST:** Isabelle Huppert, Neils Arestrup, Christine Pascal, Luc Beraud.

Caroline Huppert directs her sister Isabelle in this intriguing tale of a woman with a shady past. Isabelle finds herself in trouble with the law and seeks the help of her old lover, who's now married. It's the interaction between these three characters that is fun and enticing. In French, with English subtitles. 1986; 92m.

SLAVE OF LOVE, A ★★★★½

DIR: Nikita Mikhalkov. **CAST:** Elena Soloyei, Rodion Nakhapetov, Alexandar Kalyagin.

Shortly after the Bolshevik revolution, a crew of silent filmmakers attempt to complete a melodrama while fighting the forces of the changing world around them. This examines the role of the Bourgeois as Olga (Elena Solovei) changes from matinee idol to revolutionary. Politically and emotionally charged. In Russian, with English subtitles. Unrated. 1978; 94m.

SLEEPING CAR MURDERS, THE ★★★★

DIR: Constantin Costa-Gavras. **CAST:** Yves Montand, Simone Signoret, Pierre Mondy, Michel Piccoli, Jean-Louis Trintignant, Charles Denner.

An all-star French cast and crisp direction from Costa-Gavras (his first film) make this a first-rate thriller. Yves Montand stars as the detective investigating the case of a woman found dead in a sleeping compartment of a train when it pulls into Paris. Soon other occupants of the car are found murdered as well. In French with English subtitles. 1966; B&W; 92m.

SLIGHTLY PREGNANT MAN, A ★★

DIR: Jacques Demy. **CAST:** Catherine Deneuve, Marcello Mastroianni, Mireille Mathieu.

This French comedy features Marcello Mastroianni as the first pregnant man. The reversal of parenting roles provides a few laughs and the surprise ending is worth the wait in an otherwise ho-hum film. Unrated, this film contains adult subject matter. In French, with subtitles. 1973; 92m.

SMALL CHANGE ★★★★★

DIR: François Truffaut. **CAST:** Geary Desmouceaux, Philippe Goldman.

One of François Truffaut's best pictures, this is a charming and perceptive film viewing the joys and sorrows of young children's lives in a small French town. Wonderfully and naturally acted by a cast of young children. French. 1976; 104m.

SMILES OF A SUMMER NIGHT ★★★★★

DIR: Ingmar Bergman. **CAST:** Ulla Jacobsson, Gunnar Björnstrand, Eva

Dahlbeck, Harriet Andersson, Jarl Kulle.

Nowhere in Ingmar Bergman's amazing *oeuvre*, perhaps nowhere in cinema, is there such a classic of carnal comedy. An elegant roundelay that is, at heart, an enlightened boudoir farce. Used as the basis of Stephen Sondheim's *A Little Night Music*. In Swedish with English subtitles. 1955; B&W; 106m.

SNOW COUNTRY ★★★½

DIR: Shiro Toyoda. **CAST:** Ryo Ikebe.

A painter's romance with a lovely geisha is complicated by various friends and acquaintances. Fine Japanese love story set amidst the snow banks of an isolated village. In Japanese with English subtitles. 1957; B&W; 134m.

SOFT SKIN, THE ★★★½

DIR: François Truffaut. **CAST:** Jean Desailly, Nelly Benedetti, Françoise Dorleac.

For some critics, *The Soft Skin* ranks as one of the New Wave master's worst; for some it remains one of his best. As usual, the truth lies in between. What keeps this from being at least a minor classic is the less-than-fresh plot. In French with English subtitles. 1964; 118m.

SOIS BELLE ET TAIS-TOI (JUST ANOTHER PRETTY FACE) ★★★

DIR: Marc Allegret. **CAST:** Mylene Demongeot, Henri Vidal, René Lefévre, Jean-Paul Belmondo, Alain Delon.

This French import tries to be a lighthearted, romantic adventure, but doesn't focus itself properly. Mylene Demongeot is Virginie, an 18-year-old orphan who runs away from a reformatory and falls in with a jewel-smuggling gang. Jean-Paul Belmondo and Alain Delon, both in their first film roles, are members of the teenage gang. In French, with English subtitles. 1958; B&W; 110m.

SOLDIER OF ORANGE ★★★★★

DIR: Paul Verhoeven. **CAST:** Rutger Hauer, Peter Faber, Jeroen Krabbé.

Rutger Hauer became an international star as a result of his remarkable performance in this Dutch release, in which he plays one of four college buddies galvanized into action when the Nazis invade the Netherlands. This is an exceptional work; an exciting, suspenseful, and intelligent war-adventure. In several languages and subtitled. Rated R for nudity, profanity, implied sex, and violence. 1979; 165m.

SOLDIER OF THE NIGHT

DIR: Dan Wolman. **CAST:** Iris Kaner, Hellel Neeman, Yftach Katzur.

This Israeli movie about a man who kills soldiers by night while working in a toy store by day has some psychological thriller elements, but its plodding storyline and poor dubbing make it almost impossible to watch. Not rated, has nudity, violence, and profanity. 1984; 89m.

SOTTO SOTTO ★★★

DIR: Lina Wertmuller. **CAST:** Enrico Montesano, Veronica Lario.

A sexy, raucous, hilarious farce about a woman who finds herself romantically drawn to her best friend's husband. This leads to comically disastrous results. Good entertainment, especially for hard-core fans of Lina Wertmuller. In Italian with English subtitles. 1984; 104m.

SPAGHETTI HOUSE ★★

DIR: Giulio Paradisi. **CAST:** Nino Manfredi, Rita Tushingham.

Five Italian restaurant employees are held hostage in a food storage room by three crooks who resort to desperate measures. Most of the film is lighthearted, though—and, unfortunately, light-headed. In Italian with English subtitles. Not rated, contains violence and profanity. 1985; 103m.

SPECIAL DAY, A ★★★★

DIR: Ettore Scola. **CAST:** Sophia Loren, Marcello Mastroianni.

Antonietta (Sophia Loren), a slovenly housewife, and Gabriele (Marcello Mastroianni), a depressed homosexual, meet in the spring of 1938—the same day Hitler arrives in Rome. Their experience together enriches but does not change the course of their lives. In Italian, with English subtitles. No MPAA rating. 1977; 106m.

SPETTERS ★★★★½
DIR: Paul Verhoeven. **CAST:** Hans Van Tongeren, Toon Agterberg, Renee Soutenduk.

A study of the dreams, loves, discoveries, and tragedies of six young people in modern-day Holland, this is yet another tough, uncompromising motion picture from Paul Verhoeven. Though the sex scenes are more graphic than anything we've ever had in a major American movie, *Spetters* is never exploitative. MPAA-unrated, it contains violence, profanity, nudity. 1980; 115m.

SPIES ★★★★
DIR: Fritz Lang. **CAST:** Rudolph Klein-Rogge, Gerda Maurus, Willy Fritsch, Fritz Rasp.

Thrilling, imaginative drama of the underworld and the dark doings of espionage agents is one of the finest of all such films and remains a classic of the genre as well as a terrific adventure movie. The camera moves in and out among the shadowy doings of the spies and their pursuers like a silent spider weaving all the components together. The final chase provides a fitting climax to this topflight entertainment from Fritz Lang. Silent. 1928; B&W; 90m.

SPIRIT OF THE BEEHIVE, THE ★★★★
DIR: Victor Erice. **CAST:** Fernando Fernán Gomez, Ana Torrent.

A disturbing cinematic study of the isolation of an individual. Ana Torrent gives an unforgettable performance as a lonely girl who enters the world of fantasy when she sees the 1931 *Frankenstein* and falls in love with the monster. By far one of the most haunting films ever made about children. In Spanish with English subtitles. Not rated. 1974; 95m.

SPRING SYMPHONY ★
DIR: Peter Schamoni. **CAST:** Nastassja Kinski, Herbert Gronemeyer, Bernhard Wicki.

Spring Symphony is a routine presentation of the lives of German composer Robert Schumann and celebrated pianist Clara Wieck, who wooed and wed despite the objections of Clara's father. The film portrays emotion in fairy-tale fashion, simplistic and overstated. The music is the star of this show. Dubbed in English. Rated PG. 1984; 102m.

SPUTNIK ★★★
DIR: Jean Dreville. **CAST:** Noel-Noel, Denise Grey, Mischa Auer.

The memorable character actor Mischa Auer (remember the artist who imitated a gorilla in *My Man Godfrey*?) co-stars in this French comedy about an animal lover trying to protect a dog and a mouse that escaped from a Russian satellite. Pleasant family comedy. 1960; B&W; 80m.

STATE OF SIEGE ★★★★
DIR: Constantin Costa-Gavras. **CAST:** Yves Montand, O. E. Hasse, Renato Salvatori.

This is a highly controversial but brilliant film about the kidnapping of an American A.I.D. official by left-wing guerrillas in Uruguay. The film follows step-by-step how U.S. aid is sent to fascist countries through the pretext of helping the economy and strengthening democracy. No MPAA rating. 1973; 120m.

STATE OF THINGS, THE ★★★★½
DIR: Wim Wenders. **CAST:** Allen Garfield, Samuel Fuller, Paul Getty III, Viva, Roger Corman, Patrick Bauchau.

Absorbing account of a film crew stranded on an island in Portugal during the production of a movie dealing with the aftermath of a nuclear holocaust. Running out of money and film stock, the German director, who is a parody of Wim Wenders, attempts to locate an American producer who is on the lam from loan sharks. In German and English. 1983; B&W; 120m.

STATELINE MOTEL ★★
DIR: Maurizio Lucidi. **CAST:** Ursula Andress, Eli Wallach, Barbara Bach, Fabio Testi, Massimo Girotti.
This Italian-made film involves a jewelry store robbery by a ruthless killer (Eli Wallach) and his handsome partner, Floyd (Fabio Testi). When Wallach suspects a double cross, he goes to the Stateline Motel to collect his jewels. Not much else to the film except the surprise ending featuring Barbara Bach. The film is dubbed and rated R for nudity, violence, sexual situations, and obscenities. 1975; 87m.

STILTS, THE (LOS ZANCOS) ★★★½
DIR: Carlos Savrat. **CAST:** Laura Del Sol, Fernando Fernán Gomez, Francisco Rabal, Antonio Banderas.
This film, about an aged playwright and professor (Fernando Fernán Gomez) who falls in love with a young actress (Laura Del Sol), is occasionally melodramatic. Her unwillingness to commit herself to him gives the film its tension, and the acting is good enough to overcome most of the overwrought moments. In Spanish with English subtitles. Not rated, but contains nudity. 1984; 95m.

STOLEN KISSES ★★★★★
DIR: François Truffaut. **CAST:** Jean-Pierre Léaud, Delphine Seyrig, Michel Lonsdale, Claude Jade, Daniel Ceccaldi.
This is François Truffaut's third film in the continuing story about Antoine Doinel (Jean-Pierre Leaud) which began with *400 Blows*. Like the other films in the series, this work resembles Truffaut's autobiography as he romantically captures the awkwardness of Doinel and his encounters with women. This delightful comedy is often considered one of Truffaut's best movies. In French with English subtitles. 1968; 90m.

STORM OVER ASIA ★★★★
DIR: V. I. Pudovkin. **CAST:** Valeri Inkizhinov.
Also known as *The Heir to Genghis Khan*, this masterpiece is from the great Russian director, Vsevolod Pudovkin. It tells the story of a young Mongol hunter who is discovered to be the heir of the great Khan. A superb example of the formal beauty of the silent film. Silent. 1928; B&W; 102m.

STORMY WATERS ★★★★
DIR: Jean Gremillon. **CAST:** Jean Gabin, Michele Morgan, Madeleine Renaud, Fernand Ledoux.
Tough rescue-ship captain Jean Gabin braves stormy waters to save hauntingly beautiful Michele Morgan. They then have a passionate love affair. This film is a fine example of French cinema at its pre–WWII zenith. 1941; 75m.

STORY OF ADELE H, THE ★★★½
DIR: François Truffaut. **CAST:** Isabelle Adjani, Bruce Robinson.
This basically simple story of author Victor Hugo's daughter, who loves a soldier in vain, is surprisingly textured and intriguing. Slow, exquisite unfolding of many-layered love story is arresting and pictorially beautiful. Nicely done. Some adult situations. Rated PG. In French with English with subtitles. 1975; 97m.

STRAY DOG ★★★★
DIR: Akira Kurosawa. **CAST:** Toshiro Mifune, Takashi Shimura.
In a fascinatingly detailed portrait of postwar Tokyo, a young detective (Toshiro Mifune) desperately searches the underworld for his stolen service revolver. Akira Kurosawa has created a tense thriller in the tradition of early Forties crime dramas. Not rated. In Japanese with English subtitles. 1949; B&W; 122m.

STRIKE ★★★★
DIR: Sergei Eisenstein. **CAST:** Grigori Alexandrov, Alexander Antonov.
Shot in a documentarylike style, this drama about a labor dispute during

the czarist era was Sergei Eisenstein's first feature film. Advanced for its time and using techniques Eisenstein would perfect in his later masterpieces, *Strike* remains a remarkable achievement and still holds one's interest today. Silent. 1924; B&W; 82m.

STROMBOLI ★★
DIR: Roberto Rossellini. **CAST:** Ingrid Bergman, Mario Vitale.

This potboiler from the director of *Open City* is a brooding, sometimes boring movie about an attractive woman who marries a fisherman and attempts to adjust to the isolation and tedium of the life. Even Ingrid Bergman (by this time married to Rossellini) couldn't salvage this film. Subtitled. 1950; B&W; 81m.

SUBWAY ★★
DIR: Luc Besson. **CAST:** Isabelle Adjani, Christopher Lambert, Richard Bohringer.

The stunning Isabelle Adjani plays a young wife who becomes involved with a streetwise rogue played by Christopher Lambert. The plot is not very clear and the bad jokes don't help. Fast-paced action scenes keep the film interesting, but they all lead nowhere. In French with English subtitles. Rated R for profanity and violence. 1985; 110m.

SUGAR CANE ALLEY ★★★★★
DIR: Euzhan Paloy. **CAST:** Garry Cadenat, Darling Legitimus.

Set in Martinque of the 1930s, this superb French import examines the lives led by black sugar cane plantation workers. Specifically, it focuses on the hopes and dreams of José (Garry Cadenat), an 11-year-old orphan with a brilliant mind, which just may be the key to his breaking the bonds of slavery. In French with English subtitles. Unrated, the film has some scenes of violence. 1983; 100m.

SUGARBABY ★★★½
DIR: Percy Adlon. **CAST:** Marianne Sägebrecht.

In this decidedly offbeat comedy-drama from West German filmmaker Percy Adlon, an overweight morgue attendant (Marianne Sägebrecht) finds new meaning in her life when she falls in love with a subway driver. In German with English subtitles. Unrated; the film has nudity. 1986; 86m.

SUMMER ★★★★
DIR: Eric Rohmer. **CAST:** Marie Riviere, Lisa Heredia, Beatrice Romand.

Eric Rohmer's fifth of his six-part *Comedies and Proverbs* is the slight but emotionally resonant tale of Delphine (Marie Riviere), a Paris secretary whose vacation plans are suddenly ruined. Like the previous films in the series, *Summer* requires a commitment on the part of the viewer. Ultimately, the story touches your heart. In French with English subtitles. Rated R for nudity and profanity. 1986; 98m.

SUMMER NIGHT ★★★
DIR: Lina Wertmuller. **CAST:** Mariangela Melato, Michele Placido.

The full title is *Summer Night, with Greek Profile, Almond Eyes and Scent of Basil*, and it's a semisequel-reprise of Wertmuller's *Swept Away...*, with Mariangela Melato in a similar role as a rich industrialist who captures a terrorist and holds him prisoner on a secluded island. Wertmuller fans will be disappointed; it covers nothing she hasn't done better before. Nonfans with lower expectations can enjoy it as a pleasingly sexy comedy set against some gorgeous Greek backgrounds. Rated R for nudity and sexual situations. In Italian with English subtitles. 1987; 94m.

SUNDAY IN THE COUNTRY, A ★★★★
DIR: Bertrand Tavernier. **CAST:** Louis Ducreux, Michel Aumont, Sabine Azema.

Filmed like an Impressionist painting, this is a romantic look at French family life in pre-World War II France.

Bertrand Tavernier won the best director prize at the 1984 Cannes Film Festival for this delightful drama. In French, with English subtitles. Rated G. 1984; 94m.

SUNDAYS AND CYBÈLE ★★★★
DIR: Serge Bourguignon. **CAST:** Hardy Krüger, Patricia Gozzi.
A shell-shocked soldier, who feels responsible for the death of a young girl in the war, seeks redemption through a friendship with a 12-year-old orphan. But he fails to see the suspicion with which the authorities view their relationship. Superb acting and direction mark this Oscar winner for best foreign film. In French with English subtitles. 1962; B&W; 110m.

SUSANNA ★★
DIR: Luis Buñuel. **CAST:** Rosita Quintana, Fernando Soler.
This lurid soap opera from Luis Buñuel concerns a voluptuous young girl who escapes from a reformatory and hides out with a plantation family; her sexual prowess turns the conservative religious household inside out. Unfortunately, this movie lacks Buñuel's great comic surreal touch in exploiting his characters' obsessions. Not rated. In Spanish with English subtitles. 1951; B&W; 82m.

SWANN IN LOVE ★★★★
DIR: Volker Schlondorff. **CAST:** Jeremy Irons, Ornella Muti, Alain Delon, Fanny Ardant, Marie-Christine Barrault.
Slow-moving but fascinating film portrait of a Jewish aristocrat (Jeremy Irons) totally consumed by his romantic and sexual obsession with an ambitious French courtesan (Ornella Muti). It's definitely not for all tastes. However, those who can remember the overwhelming ache of first love may find it worth watching. In French with English subtitles. Rated R for nudity and suggested sex. 1985; 110m.

SWEPT AWAY ★★★½
DIR: Lina Wertmuller. **CAST:** Giancarlo Giannini, Mariangela Melato.
The full title is *Swept Away by an Unusual Destiny in the Blue Sea in August*, and what this Italian import addresses is a condescending, chic goddess who gets hers on a deserted island. In Italian with English subtitles. Rated R. 1975; 116m.

SWIMMING POOL, THE ★
DIR: Jacques Deray. **CAST:** Alain Delon, Romy Schneider, Maurice Ronet, Jane Birkin.
This slow-moving French film features Alain Delon, Romy Schneider, and Maurice Ronet in a love triangle that leads to homicide. An overabundance of meaningful glances and heavy breathing. Unrated, but contains nudity. Dubbed into English. 1970; 85m.

SWORD OF DOOM ★★★
DIR: Kihachi Okamoto. **CAST:** Tatsuya Nakadai, Toshiro Mifune.
Tatsuya Nakadai gives a fascinating performance as a brutal samurai, whose need to kill alienates even his once devoted father. Several stories are interwoven in this film, but, suprisingly, at least two are left unresolved at film's end. This will make it disappointing—and confusing—for all but the most devoted fans of Japanese action movies. In Japanese with English subtitles. 1967; 122m.

SYLVIA AND THE PHANTOM ★★★★
DIR: Claude Autant-Lara. **CAST:** Odette Joyeux, François Perier, Julien Carette.
A delightful story concerning hosts and the fantasies of a young lady living with her family in a castle. As the story begins, we meet Sylvia on the eve of her sixteenth birthday and find that she fantasizes about the portrait of her grandmother's lover and the rumors that he haunts the castle. In French, with English subtitles. 1950; 97m.

TALL BLOND MAN WITH ONE BLACK SHOE, THE ★★★★
DIR: Yves Robert. **CAST:** Pierre Richard, Bernard Blier, Mireille Darc.
If you're looking for an entertaining, easy-to-watch comedy, this is one of the best. Pierre Richard plays the bumbling blond man to hilarious perfection, especially when it comes to physical comedy. The story involves spies, murder, a mysterious sexy woman, and plenty of action. Highly recommended, but try to see the original version, with subtitles, not the dubbed version. Rated PG. 1972; 90m.

TAMPOPO ★★★★
DIR: Juzo Itami. **CAST:** Nobuko Miyamoto.
This Japanese spoof of the Italian spaghetti western (which was, in turn, a spinoff of the samurai movie) shows a female diner owner (Nobuko Miyamoto) learning how to make perfect noodles. As silly as it sounds, this is a wonderful movie full of surprises. Unrated but with nudity and brief violence. In Japanese with English subtitles. 1987; 95m.

TANGO BAR ★★★
DIR: Marcos Zurinaga. **CAST:** Raul Julia, Valeria Lynch, Ruben Juarez.
Part musical, part documentary, part romantic-triangle love story, this film employs all those elements to detail the historical and cultural importance of the tango. Raul Julia and Ruben Juarez play two tango performers who are reunited for a nightclub show, despite their split over a woman years before. In Spanish with English subtitles. 1988; 90m.

TAXI ZUM KLO (TAXI TO THE TOILET) ★★★½
DIR: Frank Ripploh. **CAST:** Frank Ripploh, Bernd Broaderup.
Sexually explicit film by and about Frank Ripploh, a restless and promiscuous gay elementary-school teacher in Berlin. Ripploh pulls absolutely no punches in his portrait of his sexual encounters, and that should be a fair warning. Get through the sex, however, and the humor will seem refreshing compared to a lot of other films that try to capture gay life. Not rated, but contains profanity and frank sexual content. In German with English subtitles. 1981; 92m.

TAXING WOMAN, A ★★★
DIR: Juzo Itami. **CAST:** Nobuko Miyamoto, Tsutomu Yamazaki.
After exposing the world to the inner workings of the noodle business in *Tampopo*, director Juzo Itami focused on Japan's nasty Internal Revenue Service. Nobuko Miyamoto plays a hard-line tax inspector. Nicely offbeat. Unrated, with adult themes. In Japanese with English subtitles. 1988; 118m.

TAXING WOMAN'S RETURN, A ★★★
DIR: Juzo Itami. **CAST:** Nobuko Miyamoto, Rentaro Mikuni.
Though the wonderfully wacky food comedy *Tampopo* was a smash hit in America, Japanese director Juzo Itami had even greater success in his homeland with his two *Taxing Woman* comedies. Both deal with Japan's harsh, complex, and frustrating tax laws, and the bungling bureaucracy doesn't always translate well for U.S. viewers. In this sequel the title character tackles unscrupulous real-estate developers. In Japanese with English subtitles. 1988; 127m.

TCHAO PANTIN ★★★★½
DIR: Claude Berri. **CAST:** Coluche, Richard Anconina, Philippe Léotard.
Violent *film noir* about an ex-cop suffering from alienation as a result of the tragic death of his son from narcotics. He befriends a young stranger who deals heroin. The two form an odd relationship that eventually leads to disaster. This movie swept the French Oscars. In French with English subtitles. 1985; 94m.

TENDRES COUSINES ★★
DIR: David Hamilton. **CAST:** Thierry Tevini, Anja Shute.

Okay soft-core sex comedy about the amorous adventures of two pubescent cousins. Directed by renowned photographer, David Hamilton. In French, with English subtitles. Rated R. 1980; 90m.

THAT OBSCURE OBJECT OF DESIRE ★★★★½
DIR: Luis Buñuel. **CAST:** Fernando Rey, Carole Bouquet, Angela Molina.

Luis Buñuel's last film cunningly combines erotic teasing, wit, and social comment. Mathieu (Fernando Rey) is a 50-year-old man who falls hopelessly in love with a young woman. Buñuel, a master of surrealism, tantalizes the viewer by casting two actresses to play the heroine and a third actress to do the voice of both. Rated R for profanity and nudity. 1977; 100m.

THERESE ★★★★½
DIR: Alain Cavalier. **CAST:** Catherine Mouchet, Helene Alexandridis.

French director Alain Cavalier's breathtakingly beautiful *Therese* is the story of St. Theresa of Lisieux, who entered a Carmelite nunnery in the late nineteenth century at the age of 15 and lived there for eight years until she died of tuberculosis. She was declared a saint by Pope Pius XI in 1925, twenty-eight years after her death. In French with English subtitles. 1986; 90m.

THERESE AND ISABELLE ★½
DIR: Radley Metzger. **CAST:** Essy Persson, Anna Gael, Barbara Laage, Anne Vernon.

Two French schoolgirls keep their growing sexual attraction for each other a secret until they take a holiday together. Considered daring at the time of its release, this adult story takes the form of a flashback as one of the girls revisits the locations where she and her lover met. Unrated, but this might earn an R rating today because of nudity and story content. In French, with English subtitles. 1968; 102m.

36 FILLETTE ★★★
DIR: Catherine Breillat. **CAST:** Delphine Zentout, Etienne Chicot.

A sexually charged comedy-drama from France, about a 14-year-old girl and her frustrated efforts to cast off her virginity. Delphine Zentout is most impressive as the girl. The title is a reference to a French adolescent dress size. In French with English subtitles. 1988; 92m.

THIS MAN MUST DIE ★★★★
DIR: Claude Chabrol. **CAST:** Michel Duchaussoy, Jean Yanne, Caroline Cellier.

Claude Chabrol pays homage to Alfred Hitchcock with this outstanding thriller about a man who sets out to find the hit-and-run driver responsible for the death of his son. Complications ensue as the father encounters the murderer's sister, whom he seduces. A riveting shocker with a startling climax. Dubbed into English. 1970; 112m.

THREE BROTHERS ★★★★★
DIR: Francesco Rosi. **CAST:** Philippe Noiret, Michele Placido, Vittorio Mezzogiorno.

Francesco Rosi directed this thoughtful, emotionally powerful movie that details the effect of a mother's recent death on her family. A drama with great insight and compassion. Unrated, the film has a few scenes of violence. In Italian with English subtitles. 1980; 113m.

THREE MEN AND A CRADLE ★★★★
DIR: Coline Serreau. **CAST:** Roland Giraud, Michel Boujenah, André Dussollier.

In this sweet-natured character study from France, three high-living bachelors become the guardians of a baby girl. In addition to turning their lifestyles inside out, she forces them to confront their values—with heartwarming results. Rated PG for profanity and nudity. In French with English subtitles. 1985; 105m.

THREE STRANGE LOVES ★★½
DIR: Ingmar Bergman. **CAST:** Eva Henning, Birger Malmsten.

Three former ballerinas struggle to find happiness in their private lives. Ingmar Bergman's gloomy style is the perfect backdrop for the disappointment and heartache the women face. In Swedish with subtitles that flicker by at a pace suitable only for a speed reader. 1949; B&W; 84m.

THREEPENNY OPERA, THE ★★★★
DIR: G. W. Pabst. **CAST:** Rudolph Forster, Lotte Lenya, Reinhold Schunzel, Carola Neher.

Classic gangster musical features mob leader Mack the Knife, his moll, and the hordes of the underworld. This Bertolt Brecht satire (with music by Kurt Weill), although not too popular with the Nazis or their predecessors, is always a favorite with the audience and has been filmed under its original title at least twice and in many subsequent guises. 1931; B&W; 113m.

THRONE OF BLOOD ★★★★★
DIR: Akira Kurosawa. **CAST:** Toshiro Mifune, Minoru Chiaki, Takashi Shimura.

Japanese director Akira Kurosawa's retelling of *Macbeth* may be the best film adaptation of Shakespeare ever made. Kurosawa uses the medium to present Shakespeare's themes in visual images. When Birnam Wood literally comes to Dunsinane, it is a truly great moment you would have believed could only happen in the limitless landscapes of a dream. In Japanese with English subtitles. 1957; B&W; 105m.

THROUGH A GLASS DARKLY ★★
DIR: Ingmar Bergman. **CAST:** Harriet Andersson, Gunnar Björnstrand, Max von Sydow.

Two siblings compete for their father's love. The father, who happens to be a famous writer, sits back and observes. Ingmar Bergman goes overboard this time with endless monologues on God and love. In Swedish with English subtitles, this film is unrated but contains mature themes. 1961; B&W; 90m.

TILL MARRIAGE DO US PART ★★
DIR: Luigi Comencini. **CAST:** Laura Antonelli.

Although a slight Italian sex comedy, its star, Laura Antonelli, is as delicious as ever. It's a treat for her fans only. Rated R. 1974; 97m.

TIME STANDS STILL ★★½
DIR: Peter Gothar. **CAST:** Ben Barenholtz, Albert Schwartz.

This Hungarian export dwells so much on the "art for art's sake" credo that it nearly destroys some of the life the film tries to depict. *Time Stands Still* is about restless youths at the threshold of adulthood in Hungary. The film is presented in the original language with subtitles. Not rated, but the equivalent of an R for nudity and language. 1982; 99m.

TIN DRUM, THE ★★★★½
DIR: Volker Schlondorff. **CAST:** David Bennent, Mario Adorf, Angela Winkler, Daniel Olbrychski.

Günter Grass's bizarre tale of three-year-old Oskar, who stops growing as the Nazis rise to power in Germany. Oskar expresses his outrage by banging on a tin drum. This unique film has a disturbing dreamlike quality, while its visuals are alternately startling and haunting. *The Tin Drum* won an Academy Award for best foreign film. In German, with English subtitles. Rated R for nudity and gore. 1979; 142m.

TOKYO-GA ★★★
DIR: Wim Wenders. **CAST:** Chishu Ryu, Yuharu Atsuta, Werner Herzog.

German filmmaker Wim Wenders presents an absorbing film diary of his visit to Japan, where he attempts to define his relationship to a culture and city he knows only through the cinematic work of Yasujiro Ozu, the director of *Tokyo Story*. A great introspective account of Ozu's career is much of the film's focus. In Japanese with English subtitles. 1983; 92m.

TONI ★★★★
DIR: Jean Renoir. **CAST:** Charles Blavette, Max Dalban.

Of the Italian neorealists, only Luchino Visconti is known to have been aware of this film before 1950, but in story, style, and mood, *Toni* anticipates the methods of the future master postwar directors. A love quadrangle, a murder, a trial, an execution, a confession—these are the everyday elements director Jean Renoir chose to show as objectively as possible. No studio sets were used, and many citizens of the town where *Toni* was shot filled out the cast. Renoir was proud of his film (something of an experiment), and it holds up well. In French with English subtitles. 1934; B&W; 90m.

TONIO KROGER ★★
DIR: Rolf Thiele. **CAST:** Jean-Claude Brialy, Najda Tiller, Werner Heinz, Gert Fröbe.

This adaptation of Thomas Mann's semiautobiographical novel, about a young writer wandering Europe while trying to choose between bourgeois comfort and the excitement of the unchained life, never comes alive on screen. It works best as an illustrated version of the novel for those already familiar with it. In German with English subtitles. 1965; 92m.

TOPSY TURVY ★★
DIR: Edward Fleming. **CAST:** Lisbet Dahl, Ebbe Rode.

A conservative young man finds his world turned topsy-turvy when a swinging neighbor girl takes him on vacation. This European sex comedy, dubbed into English is mediocre. 1984; 90m.

TURKISH DELIGHT ★★★½
DIR: Paul Verhoeven. **CAST:** Rutger Hauer, Monique van de Ven.

Those already familiar with the work of Dutch director Paul Verhoeven (*Spetters, The 4th Man*) will be the most appreciative audience for this drama about a bohemian artist and his wife who learn the hard way what it means to create and honor a commitment to each other. Others may be put off by the graphic sexuality and crude behavior of the characters. Dubbed in English. 1974; 96m.

TWENTY-FOUR EYES ★★★½
DIR: Teinosuke Kinugasa. **CAST:** Keisuke Kinoshita, Chishu Ryu.

Beauty and innocence are lost as war and progress intrude upon a rural village in this poignant, touching drama. The story concerns a progressive schoolteacher from Tokyo who changes the lives of students in an elementary school on a remote island off Japan in the late 1920s. In Japanese with English subtitles. 1954; B&W; 158m.

TWIST AND SHOUT ★★★★½
DIR: Bille August. **CAST:** Adam Tonsberg, Lars Simonsen.

An exceptional coming-of-age story about two friends, a drummer with a pseudo-Beatles group, and a quiet sort with severe problems at home, circa 1964. It is a true-to-life movie that will leave no viewer unmoved. Unrated, the film has profanity, nudity, and suggested sex. In Danish with English subtitles. 1986; 99m.

TWO DAUGHTERS ★★★★
DIR: Satyajit Ray. **CAST:** Anil Chatterjee, Chandana Bannerjee, Soumitra Chatterjee.

Satyajit Ray's beautiful two-part film is based on tales by Nobel Prize–winning author Rabindranath Tagore. With Chekhovian delicacy and pathos, Ray explores the hopes and disappointments of two young women experiencing first love. Ray's stories transcend the surface of Indian culture while creating a universally felt character study. In Bengali with English subtitles. 1961; B&W; 114m.

TWO ENGLISH GIRLS ★★★★½
DIR: François Truffaut. **CAST:** Jean-Pierre Léaud, Kiki Markham, Stacey Tendeter.

Twenty-two minutes were recently added to this very civilized and rewarding film. Set in pre–World War I Europe and based on the Henri-Pierre Roché novel (his only other being *Jules et Jim,* the modern flip-side of the arrangement here), Truffaut's work has Frenchman Léaud the object of two English sisters' desire. In French with English subtitles. 1972; 130m.

TWO MEN AND A WARDROBE ★★½

DIR: Roman Polanski. **CAST:** Henlyk Kluga, Jakub Goldberg.

Roman Polanski's award-winning short made while he was a student at the Polish Film Institute is a bitter parable blending slapstick and the absurd. It concerns two men who emerge from the sea sporting a single wardrobe. Also included in the package is a second short, *The Fat and the Lean,* an outrageously funny attack on governmental tyranny. Silent. 1958; B&W; 35m.

TWO OF US, THE ★★★½

DIR: Claude Berri. **CAST:** Alain Cohen, Michel Simon.

This story of generational and religious differences joins an 8-year-old Jewish boy (Alain Cohen) and an irascible Catholic grandpa (Michel Simon). The boy is fleeing Nazi-occupied France in 1944 and comes to live with the anti-Semitic old man who is a family friend's relative. Beautifully acted, this is a different kind of movie for parents to enjoy with their older children. In French with English subtitles. 1968; 86m.

TWO WOMEN ★★★★

DIR: Vittorio De Sica. **CAST:** Sophia Loren, Eleanora Brown, Jean-Paul Belmondo, Raf Vallone.

In the performance that won her an Oscar, Sophia Loren is a widow who, with her 13-year-old daughter, escapes war-torn Rome, eventually finding solace in her native village. This uncompromising drama was a Grand Prize winner at the Cannes Film Festival. Not rated. In Italian with English subtitles. 1960; 99m.

UGETSU ★★★★½

DIR: Kenji Mizoguchi. **CAST:** Machiko Kyo, Masayuki Mori.

Set in sixteenth-century Japan, this film follows the lives of two Japanese peasants as their quest for greed and ambition brings disaster upon their families. There is a fine blending of action and comedy in this ghostly tale. In Japanese, with English subtitles. 1953; 94m.

UMBERTO D ★★★★★

DIR: Vittorio De Sica. **CAST:** Carlo Battisti, Maria Pia Casilio.

Umberto D seems as poignant now as when it was initially released. Quite simply, the plot centers upon a retired civil servant trying to maintain some sort of dignity and life for himself and his dog on his meager government pension. The film is agonizingly candid. A Vittorio De Sica masterpiece. In Italian with English subtitles. 1955; B&W; 89m.

UMBRELLAS OF CHERBOURG, THE ★★★★

DIR: Jacques Demy. **CAST:** Catherine Deneuve, Nino Castelnuovo, Marc Michel.

Simply the most romantic film to come from France in the 1960s. Catherine Deneuve made her first popular appearance, and we've been madly in love with her ever since. Simple story—boy meets girl—but played against a luxuriously photographed backdrop. Exquisite score from Michel Legrand. Watch this with somebody you love. 1964; 91m.

UN SINGE EN HIVER (A MONKEY IN WINTER) ★★½

DIR: Henri Verneuil. **CAST:** Jean Gabin, Jean-Paul Belmondo, Suzanne Flon, Paul Frankeur, Noel Roquevert.

Alcoholic Jean Gabin vows to swear off if he and his wife survive the bombing of their village during World War II. They do, and he does. Years pass. A young version of Gabin arrives and rekindles the older man's memories of drink and dreams, fostering regret and making him feel he has lost the golden opportunity of his youth. In French, with English subtitles. Originally released in the U.S. as *A Monkey in Winter*. Marred by murky photography. 1962; B&W; 105m.

VAGABOND ★★★½
DIR: Agnes Varda. **CAST:** Sandrine Bonnaire, Macha Meril.

French New Wave writer-director Agnes Varda's dispassionate but beautifully photographed "investigation"—via flashbacks—of a young misfit's meandering trek through the French countryside features a superb performance by Sandrine Bonnaire. Her *Vagabond* is presented as rude, lazy, ungrateful. Yet in some subliminal way the film draws one into the alienation that fuels this outsider's journey into death. In French with English subtitles. Rated R for profanity and suggested sex. 1986; 105m.

VAMPYR ★★★★★
DIR: Carl Dreyer. **CAST:** Julian West, Sybille Schmitz.

Director Carl Dreyer believed that horror is best implied. By relying on the viewer's imagination, he created a classic. A young man arrives at a very bizarre inn, where he discovers an unconscious woman who had been attacked by a vampire in the form of an old woman. This outstanding film is one of the few serious films of the macabre. 1931; B&W; 68m.

VARIETY ★★★★★
DIR: E. A. Dupont. **CAST:** Emil Jannings, Lya de Putti.

A milestone of cinema art. It tells a simple, tragic tale of a famous and conceited vaudeville acrobat whose character flaw is cowardice; a clever and entirely unscrupulous girl; and a trusting waterfront circus boss—made a fool of by love—who murders because of that hollow love. The cast is incredible, the cinematography superb. Silent. 1926; B&W; 104m.

VERY PRIVATE AFFAIR, A ★★★
DIR: Louis Malle. **CAST:** Brigitte Bardot, Marcello Mastroianni.

Bardot fan, or just never had a chance to see her? In this romantic drama she plays a famous movie star who can no longer cope with notoriety, so she retreats from public scrutiny. Marcello Mastroianni is equally appealing as a director coming to her aid. In French with English subtitles. 1962; 95m.

VIRGIN SPRING, THE ★★★★★
DIR: Ingmar Bergman. **CAST:** Max von Sydow, Birgitta Pettersson, Gunnel Lindblom.

Ingmar Bergman's scenario is based on a fourteenth-century Swedish legend. Accompanied by her jealous older stepsister, a young girl is raped and killed while on a journey to her church—and the three killers make the mistake of seeking shelter with the parents. Won an Oscar for best foreign language film. In Swedish, with English subtitles. 1960; B&W; 87m.

VIRIDIANA ★★★★★
DIR: Luis Buñuel. **CAST:** Silvia Pinal, Fernando Rey, Francisco Rabal, Margarita Lozano.

Angelic Viridiana (Silvia Pinal) visits her sex-obsessed uncle (Fernando Rey) prior to taking her religious vows. The film was an amazing cause célèbre at the time. *Viridiana*—much to Spain's and the Catholic Church's consternation—won the Palme d'Or at Cannes. In Spanish with English subtitles. 1961; B&W; 90m.

VOLPONE ★★★★
DIR: Maurice Tourneur. **CAST:** Harry Baur, Louis Jouvet.

Filmed in 1939, this superb screen version of Shakespeare contemporary Ben Jonson's classic play of greed was not released until after World War II, by which time star Harry Baur, a titan of French cinema, was mysteriously dead, having been, it is supposed, erased by the Nazis in 1941. Aided by his avaricious and parasitic servant, Mosca, Volpone, an old Venetian, pretends he is dying and convinces his greedy friends that each of them is his heir. Volpone and Mosca spin a web of lies until they are caught. In French with English subtitles. 1939; B&W; 80m.

VOULEZ VOUS DANSER AVEC MOI? (WILL YOU DANCE WITH ME?)

DIR: Michel Boisrone. **CAST:** Brigitte Bardot, Henri Vidal, Dawn Addams, Noel Roquevert.

This is another interminable Brigitte Bardot film, one in which a marital squabble lands her in the center of a murder investigation. It's supposed to be flirtatious, cute, and lighthearted, but it's just junky. In French with English subtitles. 1959; 89m.

VOYAGE EN BALLON (A.K.A. STOWAWAY TO THE STARS) ★★★

DIR: Albert Lamorisse. **CAST:** Andregrave Gille, Maurice Baquet, Pascal Lamorisse.

This endearing little French film is somewhat of a follow-up to *The Red Balloon* (also directed by Albert Lamorisse and starring son Pascal, this time allowing that small boy to ascend into the clouds—in the basket of a hot-air balloon). Unfortunately, Lamorisse *père* is a far better director than writer, and this film lacks the drama needed to sustain its greater length. Unrated; suitable for family viewing. 1959; 82m.

WAGES OF FEAR, THE ★★★★★

DIR: Henri-Georges Clouzot. **CAST:** Yves Montand, Charles Vanel, Peter Van Eyck, Vera Clouzot.

This masterpiece of suspense pits four seedy and destitute men against the challenge of driving two nitroglycerin-laden trucks over crude and treacherous Central American mountain roads to quell a monstrous oil well fire. Incredible risk and numbing fear ride along as the drivers, goaded by high wages, cope with dilemma after dilemma. In French with English subtitles. 1953; B&W; 128m.

WANNSEE CONFERENCE, THE ★★★★

DIR: Heinz Schirk. **CAST:** Dietrich Mattausch.

This is a fascinating historical drama about a meeting held on January 20, 1942, with the fourteen members of Hitler's hierarchy. Wannsee is the Berlin suburb where they met to decide "the final solution" to the Jewish problem. Chillingly told from the actual minutes taken at the conference. A must-see film. In German with subtitles. 1984; 87m.

WANTON CONTESSA, THE ★★★★½

DIR: Luchino Visconti. **CAST:** Alida Valli, Farley Granger, Massimo Girotti.

Luchino Visconti—aristocrat by birth, Marxist by conviction—offers one of the lushest and most expressive Italian films ever made (known there as *Senso*). The large-budget spectacular is operatic in scope and look. Venice, 1866. A countess (the alluring Alida Valli) finds herself passionately in love with a young Austrian officer (Farley Granger). Dubbed in English (with dialogue by Tennessee Williams and Paul Bowles). 1954; 120m.

WAR AND PEACE (1968) ★★★★★

DIR: Sergei Bondarchuk. **CAST:** Lyudmila Savelyeva, Sergei Bondarchuk.

Many film versions of great books take liberties that change important plot situations, and more. This Academy Award–winning Soviet production stays as close to the book as possible, making it terribly long, but one of the greatest re-creations of great literature ever done. It took five years to make at enormous cost; it is a cinematic treasure. Poorly dubbed. 1968; 373 minutes (originally 507 minutes).

WE ALL LOVED EACH OTHER SO MUCH ★★★★

DIR: Ettore Scola. **CAST:** Nino Manfredi, Vittorio Gassman, Stefania Sandrelli.

Exceptional high-spirited comedy about three friends and their lives and loves over the course of three decades. A wonderful homage to Fellini, De Sica, and postwar neorealism. In Italian with English subtitles. 1977; 124m.

WHAT HAVE I DONE TO DESERVE THIS? ★★★★
DIR: Pedro Almodóvar. **CAST:** Carmen Maura.
Outrageously funny black comedy about a working-class housewife who struggles to maintain her sanity while keeping her crazy family afloat. This perverse fable on contemporary life is superbly directed by Pedro Almodovar and features a brilliant performance by Carmen Maura. In Spanish with English subtitles. Not rated, but contains nudity and profanity. 1984; 100m.

WHEN FATHER WAS AWAY ON BUSINESS ★★★
DIR: Emir Kusturica. **CAST:** Moreno D'e Bartolli, Miki Manojlovic.
Seen through the eyes of a young boy, the film deals with the sudden disappearance of a father from a family because of a few minor yet commonly held opinions of the party in power and the party in disfavor. Tension mounts when it becomes clear that it is the father's brother-in-law who turned him in and had him sent to a work camp. The film received the Gold Palm at the 1985 Cannes Film Festival. Rated R for sex and nudity. In Slavic with English subtitles. 1985; 144m.

WHERE THE GREEN ANTS DREAM ★★★★
DIR: Werner Herzog. **CAST:** Bruce Spence, Ray Barrett, Norman Kaye.
Another stark, yet captivating vision from perhaps the most popular director of current German cinema. The film is basically an ecological tug of war between progress and tradition, namely uranium mining interests against aborigines and their practices. 1984; 100m.

WHITE ROSE, THE ★★★
DIR: Michael Verhoeven. **CAST:** Lena Stolze, Wulf Kessler, Martin Benrath.
The White Rose is based on a true story about a group of youths in wartime Germany who revolted against Hitler by printing and distributing subversive leaflets to the public. All of the young actors are good, especially Lena Stolze, who plays the main protagonist. In German. 1983; 108m.

WHITE SHEIK, THE ★★★
DIR: Federico Fellini. **CAST:** Brunella Bovo, Leopoldo Trieste, Alberto Sordi, Giulietta Masina.
A warm salute to romantic movie heroes. When a recently wed couple go to Rome for their honeymoon, the bride sneaks off to a movie set where her idol, the White Sheik, is making a film. Federico Fellini manages to create an original cinematic piece with great satirical precision. In Italian English with subtitles. 1952; B&W; 86m.

WIFEMISTRESS ★★★½
DIR: Marco Vicario. **CAST:** Marcello Mastroianni, Laura Antonelli, Leonard Mann.
Marcello Mastroianni stars as a husband in hiding, and Laura Antonelli as his repressed wife. When Mastroianni is falsely accused of murder, he hides out in a building across the street from his own home. His wife, not knowing where he is, begins to relive his sexual escapades. There are some comic moments as the former philandering husband must deal with his wife's new sexual freedom. 1977; 110m.

WILD STRAWBERRIES ★★★★
DIR: Ingmar Bergman. **CAST:** Victor Sjöström, Ingrid Thulin, Bibi Andersson, Gunner Björstrand.
This film is probably Ingmar Bergman's least ambiguous. Superbly photographed and acted, the film tells the story of an elderly professor facing old age and reviewing his life's

disappointments. The use of flashbacks is very effective. 1957; B&W; 90m.

WINGS OF DESIRE ★★★★
DIR: Wim Wenders. **CAST:** Bruno Ganz, Solveig Dommartin, Curt Bois, Peter Falk.

Angels see in black-and-white; mortals see in color. Wim Wenders's follow-up to *Paris, Texas* is a stark and moving story set in Berlin about two angels (Ganz and Dommartin) who travel through the city listening to people's thoughts. Ganz grows weary of comforting others and decides to reenter the world as a human. Rated PG-13 for adult subject matter. In German and French with English subtitles. 1988; 130m.

WINTER LIGHT ★★★
DIR: Ingmar Bergman. **CAST:** Ingrid Thulin, Gunnar Björstrand, Max von Sydow, Gunnel Lindblom.

Second film in director Bergman's "faith" trilogy (it follows *Through a Glass Darkly* and precedes *The Silence*) centers on a disillusioned priest who attempts to come to grips with his religion and his position in the inner workings of the church. This effort to explore the psyche of a cleric and answer the questions that have troubled the "spiritual" side of man for centuries is a thoughtful, incisive drama with great performances. In Swedish with English subtitles. 1962; B&W; 80m.

WITCHCRAFT THROUGH THE AGES (HAXAN) ★★★½
DIR: Benjamin Christensen. **CAST:** Maren Pedersen.

After almost seventy years of notoriety, this controversial film is still unique as one of the most outrageous movies of all time. Envisioned by director Benjamin Christensen as a study of black magic, witchcraft, and demonology from the Middle Ages to the present, this silent Scandinavian epic fluctuates between lecture material and incredibly vivid footage that gave the censors ulcers in the 1920s. There is a version available with William Burroughs reading the narration; other prints are captioned in English. 1921; B&W; 82m.

WOLF AT THE DOOR ★★
DIR: Henning Carlsen. **CAST:** Donald Sutherland, Fanny Bastien.

Pompous and heavy-handed, *Wolf at the Door* gnaws away at painter Paul Gauguin's life in a rather self-conscious fashion, despite some beautiful photography. Donald Sutherland is honest enough as the French painter, but the script is predictable and ponderous, and Gauguin's love life with 13-year-old girls is downright depressing. English-dubbed. 1987; 94m.

WOMAN IN FLAMES, A ★★★★
DIR: Robert Van Ackeren. **CAST:** Gudrun Landgrebe, Mathieu Carriere.

A male and a female prostitute fall in love and decide to set up shop in the same household, insisting that their business trysts will not interfere with their personal relationship. If erotic drama and bizarre twists are your fancy, this should be your film. Rated R for sexual situations and language. 1984; 104m.

WOMAN IN THE DUNES ★★★★★
DIR: Hiroshi Teshigahara. **CAST:** Eiji Okada.

An entomologist collecting beetles on the dunes misses his bus back to the city. Some locals offer him assistance, and he is lowered by a ladder down into a sand pit where he finds a woman willing to provide food and lodging in her shack. The ladder is removed, however, and he is trapped. A classic thriller. In Japanese with English subtitles. 1964; B&W; 123m.

WOMAN IN THE MOON (A.K.A. GIRL IN THE MOON; BY ROCKET TO THE MOON) ★★★
DIR: Fritz Lang. **CAST:** Gerda Maurus, Willy Fritsch, Fritz Rasp, Gustav von Waggenheim.

Fritz Lang's last silent film is actually a futuristic melodrama written by his wife and collaborator, Thea von Harbou. Although much of the action takes place on the moon, (and is obviously shot on indoor sets) this film remains stuck to a story that could have taken place just as easily on Earth. Admired by science-fiction aficionados for Lang's imaginative visual sense, not the content of the story. German, silent. 1929; B&W; 115m.

WOMAN NEXT DOOR, THE ★★★★½

DIR: François Truffaut. **CAST:** Gerard Depardieu, Fanny Ardant, Henri Garcin.

François Truffaut is on record as one of the greatest admirers of Alfred Hitchcock, and the influence shows in his gripping, well-made film about guilt, passion, and the growing influence of a small sin that grows. In French with English subtitles. MPAA unrated but contains nudity and violence. 1981; 106m.

WOMAN WITHOUT LOVE, A ★★★

DIR: Luis Buñuel. **CAST:** Rosario Granados, Julio Villarreal.

Absorbing melodrama about a neglected housewife who indulges in an affair with an engineer only to return to her wealthy old husband. Twenty years later, the husband leaves a fortune to her son's lover, causing a family castastrophe. This cynical portrait of the bourgeoisie was adapted from a short story by Guy de Maupassant. Not rated. In Spanish with English subtitles. 1952; B&W; 91m.

WORLD OF APU, THE ★★★★

DIR: Satyajit Ray. **CAST:** Soumitra Chatterjee, Sharmila Tagore, Alok Charkravarty, Swapan Mukherji.

This is the concluding part of director Satyajit Ray's famed *Apu* trilogy covering the life and growth of a young man in India. In this last film, Apu marries and helps bring life into the world himself, completing the cycle amid realizations about himself and his limitations in this world. This movie and its predecessors form a beautiful tapestry of existence in a different culture and were among the most influential of all Indian films for many years. In Bengalese, with English subtitles. 1959; B&W; 103m.

WRONG MOVE, THE ★★

DIR: Wim Wenders. **CAST:** Rudiger Vogler, Hanna Schygulla, Nastassja Kinski.

Rudiger Vogler is cast as a would-be writer in this slow-moving character drama. It concerns a soul-searching odyssey across Germany by a diverse group of misfits. Initially absorbing, yet too disconcerting to recommend. German with English subtitles. 1978; 103m.

WUTHERING HEIGHTS (1953) ★★½

DIR: Luis Buñuel. **CAST:** Iraseme Dillan, Jorge Mistral.

This is Luis Buñuel's film of the Emily Brontë classic. This Spanish version, although beautifully photographed and with easy-to-read subtitles, in no way measures up to the 1939 original. The Richard Wagner music, however, is perfect for the melodramatic performances. 1953; 90m.

YEAR OF THE QUIET SUN ★★★★

DIR: Krzysztof Zanussi. **CAST:** Scott Wilson, Maja Komorowska.

A beautifully orchestrated meditation on the nature of love, this import is about a Polish widow after World War II who becomes romantically involved with an American soldier during a war-crimes investigation. In Polish with English subtitles. 1985; 106m.

YESTERDAY, TODAY AND TOMORROW ★★★½

DIR: Vittorio De Sica. **CAST:** Sophia Loren, Marcello Mastroianni, Tina Pica.

Hilarious three-vignette romp teaming Sophia Loren and Marcello Mastroianni. The first (and best) story features Loren as an impoverished woman who continues to have babies in order to avoid a jail sentence, with Mastroianni as her husband who gives in to the scheme. Italian dubbed into English. 1964; 119m.

YOJIMBO ★★★★½
DIR: Akira Kurosawa. **CAST:** Toshiro Mifune, Eijiro Tono.

Viewed from different perspectives, *Yojimbo* ("bodyguard") is: the most devastating comedy ever made; Kurosawa's parody of the American western; or his satire on the United States and Soviet Union's achieving peace through nuclear proliferation. Toshiro Mifune, an unemployed samurai in nineteenth-century Japan, sells his services to two rival merchants, each with killer gangs that are tearing the town apart. The film is boisterous—*lots* of bones crunching and samurai swords flashing and slashing—and exuberant. (Remade by Sergio Leone as *A Fistful of Dollars*.) No rating, but very violent. 1961; B&W; 110m.

YOL ★★★½
DIR: Serif Goren. **CAST:** Tarik Akin, Serif Sezer.

Winner of the Grand Prix at the Cannes Film Festival, this work, by Turkish filmmaker and political prisoner Yilmaz Gurney, follows several inmates of a minimum-security prison who are granted a few days' leave, telling their stories in parallel scenes. Gurney—who smuggled instructions out of prison to his trusted assistants, then escaped from prison and edited the film—was hailed at Cannes for creating an eloquent protest against suppression and totalitarian government. Unrated, the film has violence and suggested sex. 1982; 111m.

Z ★★★★
DIR: Constantin Costa-Gavras. **CAST:** Yves Montand, Irene Papas, Jean-Louis Trintignant, Charles Denner.

Director Costa-Gavras first explored political corruption in this taut French thriller. Yves Montand plays a political leader who is assassinated. Based on a true story. Academy Award for best foreign film. Well worth a try. No rating, with some violence and coarse language. 1969; 127m.

ZATOICHI VS. YOJIMBO ★★★½
DIR: Kihachi Okamoto. **CAST:** Shintaro Katsu, Toshiro Mifune.

Two of the giants of the Japanese samurai genre square off in this comic entry in the long-running blind-swordsman series. Shintaro Katsu is Zatoichi, an almost superhuman hero. The story is a send-up of Akira Kurosawa's *Yojimbo*, with Toshiro Mifune doing a comedic turn on his most famous character. It's fun for fans, but far from classic. In Japanese with English subtitles. 1970; 116m.

ZERO FOR CONDUCT ★★★★½
DIR: Jean Vigo. **CAST:** Jean Dasté.

This unique fantasy about the rebellion of boys in a French boarding school is told from the point of view of the students and provides perhaps the purest picture in the history of cinema of what authority appears to be to young minds. This all too short gem was sadly one of only four films made by terminally ill director Jean Vigo, at the age of 29. Banned across the Continent when first released, this 50-year-old film provided much of the storyline for Lindsay Anderson's 1969 update *If*... In French with English subtitles. 1933; B&W; 44m.

HORROR/ SUSPENSE

ABOMINABLE DR. PHIBES, THE ★★★½

DIR: Robert Fuest. **CAST:** Vincent Price, Joseph Cotten, Hugh Griffith, Terry-Thomas.

Stylish horror film features Vincent Price in one of his best latter-day roles as a man disfigured in a car wreck taking revenge on those he considers responsible for the death of his wife. Rated PG. 1971; 93m.

AFTER DARKNESS ★

DIR: Dominique Othenin-Girard. **CAST:** John Hurt, Julian Sands, Victoria Abril.

An odd thriller about twin brothers who share visions of their parents' death. This movie takes forever to make its point. John Hurt gives a strong performance, but not strong enough to redeem the cinematic doldrums. Not rated, but contains nudity and profanity. 1985; 105m.

AGAINST ALL ODDS (KISS AND KILL, BLOOD OF FU MANCHU) ★

DIR: Jess (Jesus) Franco. **CAST:** Christopher Lee, Richard Greene, Shirley Eaton.

The evil Fu Manchu hatches another dastardly plan for world domination. This time he saturates ten beautiful slave girls with a deadly poison and sends them out to kiss his enemies to death. The stars of the film disappear for long stretches, no doubt to keep their fees down. A complete bore. Rated PG. 1968; 93m.

ALBINO ★

DIR: Jurgen Goslar. **CAST:** Christopher Lee, Trevor Howard, James Faulkner, Sybil Danning.

African terrorists, led by an albino chief, frighten natives into aiding their battle against the white settlers. Don't let the box fool you; this isn't really a horror movie, and top-billed Christopher Lee and Trevor Howard only have small parts. Unrated, give it a B for boring. 1976; 96m.

ALICE, SWEET ALICE (COMMUNION AND HOLY TERROR) ★★

DIR: Alfred Sole. **CAST:** Brooke Shields, Tom Signorelli, Paula E. Sheppard, Lillian Roth.

A 12-year-old girl goes on a chopping spree. No, it's not Brooke Shields. She only has a small role in this, her first film. But after the success of *Pretty Baby* the following year, the distributor changed the title, gave Brooke top billing, and rereleased this uninteresting thriller. Rated R for violence. 1977; 96m.

ALIEN PREY

DIR: Norman J. Warren. **CAST:** Barry Stokes, Sally Faulkner.

This savage alien is on a protein mission. Unfortunately the vegetarian dinner served up by his two lesbian hosts does not satisfy him. This film contains sexual and cannibalistic scenes, making it unsuitable for the squeamish. 1984; 85m.

ALISON'S BIRTHDAY ★★½

DIR: Ian Coughlan. **CAST:** Joanne Samuel, Lou Brown.

A slow but interesting Australian horror story involving curses and possession. A young girl is told by her father's ghost to leave home before her nineteenth birthday, but as you may guess, she's summoned back days before the big day, and things get nasty. 1984; 99m.

ALL THE KIND STRANGERS ★★

DIR: Burt Kennedy. **CAST:** Stacy Keach, Samantha Eggar, John Savage, Robby Benson, Arlene Farber.

This made-for-TV thriller lacks the overt terror present in most fright films today. A family of orphans lures kind strangers to their isolated home and then forces them to act as their parents. If the strangers don't measure up, they're murdered. Interesting in an eerie way. 1974; 74m.

ALLIGATOR ★★★½

DIR: Lewis Teague. **CAST:** Robert Forster, Michael Gazzo, Robin Riker, Perry Lang, Jack Carter, Bart Braverman, Henry Silva, Dean Jagger.

The wild imagination of screenwriter John Sayles invests this comedy-horror film with wit and style. It features Robert Forster as a cop tracking down a giant alligator. It's good, unpretentious fun, but you have to be on your toes to catch all the gags (be sure to read the hilarious graffiti). Rated R. 1980; 94m.

ALONE IN THE DARK

DIR: Jack Sholder. **CAST:** Jack Palance, Donald Pleasence, Martin Landau, Dwight Schultz, Deborah Hedwall, Erland Van Lidth.

The inmates of a New Jersey mental institution (played by Jack Palance, Martin Landau, and Erland Van Lidth) break out during a blackout (with a little help from psychiatrist Donald Pleasence) to terrorize a doctor and his family. No matter how quickly they're all killed, it isn't soon enough. Rated R. 1982; 92m.

AMERICAN GOTHIC ★★★½

DIR: John Hough. **CAST:** Rod Steiger, Yvonne De Carlo, Michael J. Pollard.

Inventive, chilling, and atmospheric horror film pits a group of vacationers on a remote island against a grotesque, creepy family headed by Ma and Pa (Rod Steiger and Yvonne De Carlo). The latter's children, middle-aged adults who act and dress like kids, delight in killing off the newcomers one by one. An absence of gore and an emphasis on characterization make this an uncommonly satisfying film for horror buffs. Rated R for violence and profanity. 1988; 90m.

AMERICAN WEREWOLF IN LONDON, AN ★★★½

DIR: John Landis. **CAST:** David Naughton, Jenny Agutter, Griffin Dunne.

Director John Landis weaves humor, violence, and the classic horror elements of suspense in the tale of the two American travelers who find more than they bargained for on the English moors. Rated R for violence, nudity, and gore. 1981; 97m.

AMITYVILLE HORROR, THE

DIR: Stuart Rosenberg. **CAST:** James Brolin, Margot Kidder, Rod Steiger.

A better title for this turgid mishmash would be *The Amityville Bore*. Based on a supposedly true story, it's a hackneyed, unbelievable horror flick. Avoid it. Rated R. 1979; 117m.

AMITYVILLE II: THE POSSESSION ★★½
DIR: Damiano Damiani. **CAST:** Burt Young, Rutanya Alda, James Olson, Moses Gunn.
Okay, so it's not a horror classic. But thanks to tight pacing, skillful special effects, and fine acting, *Amityville II: The Possession* is a fairly suspenseful flick. Rated R for violence, implied sex, light profanity, and adult themes. 1982; 104m.

AMITYVILLE III: THE DEMON
DIR: Richard Fleischer. **CAST:** Tony Roberts, Robert Joy, Tess Harper, Lori Laughlin, Meg Ryan.
In this soggy second sequel to *The Amityville Horror*, Tony Roberts plays a reporter who investigates the spooky goings-on at the infamous house in Amityville, New York. It's hack horror. Rated PG for violence and gore. 1983; 105m.

AMSTERDAMNED ★
DIR: Dick Maas. **CAST:** Huub Stapel, Monique van de Ven.
When a psycho killer comes up from the depths of the Amsterdam canals seeking prey, a Dutch cop and his buddy, a scuba-diving expert, try to reel him in. It's pure slice-and-dice raunch. Rated R for violence. 1988; 114m.

AND NOW THE SCREAMING STARTS ★★★
DIR: Roy Ward Baker. **CAST:** Peter Cushing, Stephanie Beacham, Herbert Lom, Patrick Magee, Ian Ogilvy.
Frightening British horror film about a young newlywed couple moving into a house haunted by a centuries-old curse on the husband's family. Well done, with a great cast, but occasionally a bit too bloody. Rated R. 1973; 87m.

AND SOON THE DARKNESS ★★½
DIR: Robert Fuest. **CAST:** Pamela Franklin, Michele Dotrice, Sandor Eles.
Two young English college girls decide to go bicycle touring through the French countryside. But when the more vivacious of the two suddenly disappears in the same spot where a young girl was killed the year before, the foundation is laid for a tale of suspense. Rated PG. 1970; 94m.

ANDY WARHOL'S DRACULA ★
DIR: Paul Morrissey. **CAST:** Udo Kier, Joe Dallesandro, Vittorio De Sica, Roman Polanski.
Companion piece to Andy Warhol's equally revolting version of *Frankenstein*. The "joke" this time is that Dracula (Udo Kier) can survive only on the blood of "were-gins" and vomits that which comes from more experienced ladies. Rated X for excessive violence and kinky sex. 1974; 93m.

ANDY WARHOL'S FRANKENSTEIN
DIR: Paul Morrissey. **CAST:** Joe Dallesandro, Monique Van Vooren, Udo Kier.
A stupendously awful horror film by Warhol's New York Pop Art crowd. Blood and gore gush at every opportunity. This turkey should have been left on the shelf. Rated R for obvious reasons. 1974; 94m.

ANGEL HEART ★★★½
DIR: Alan Parker. **CAST:** Mickey Rourke, Lisa Bonet, Robert De Niro, Charlotte Rampling.
Mickey Rourke stars as a down-and-out private investigator who is given a rather bizarre case to solve. The elegant, dapper, and more than slightly sinister Louis Cyphre (Robert De Niro) wants a missing singer found in order to settle a vague "debt." Absolutely not for the squeamish or for children; rated R for violence, sex, and language. 1987; 113m.

ANGUISH ★★★★
DIR: Bigas Luna. **CAST:** Zelda Rubinstein, Michael Lerner.
This horror thriller is actually a movie within a movie. The first portion deals with a mother and son's odd relationship that has him murdering people for their eyes, while the second portion is actually about an audience watching the film and being terrorized by an unknown killer. *Not* recommended for those with weak stomachs. Rated R. 1988; 85m.

ANTS! ★
DIR: Robert Sheerer. **CAST:** Robert Foxworth, Lynda Day George, Suzanne Somers, Myrna Loy, Brian Dennehy.
From its abrupt beginning to its predictable conclusion, *Ants!* is just another haunting remnant of boring filmmaking from the *Movie of the Week* closet. Wretched. 1977; 88m.

APE, THE ★★
DIR: William Nigh. **CAST:** Boris Karloff, Gertrude Hoffman.
Boris Karloff finished out his contract with Monogram Studios with this story about a doctor who discovers a cure for polio that requires spinal fluid from a human being. Not too many thrills, but Karloff is always worth watching. 1940; B&W; 61m.

APE MAN, THE ★★
DIR: William Beaudine. **CAST:** Bela Lugosi, Louise Currie, Wallace Ford, Minerva Urecal.
Bela Lugosi was one of the great horror film stars. However, the monster-movie boom stopped short in 1935, leaving the Hungarian actor out of work. When shockers came back in vogue four years later, Lugosi took any and every role he was offered. The result was grade-Z pictures such as this one, about a scientist (Lugosi) attempting to harness the physical power of apes for humankind. Too bad. 1943; B&W; 64m.

APOLOGY ★★★
DIR: Robert Bierman. **CAST:** Lesley Ann Warren, Peter Weller, George Loros, John Glover, Christopher North.
This psycho-suspense film features Lesley Ann Warren as a bizarre artist who starts an anonymous phone service to get ideas for her latest project. People call the recording and confess a sin they've committed. All goes well until a caller falls in love with the confessional idea and begins killing people in order to have something to be sorry for. Made for cable TV, this is unrated but it contains obscenities, gore, and simulated sex. 1986; 98m.

APPOINTMENT, THE ★
DIR: Lindsey C. Vickers. **CAST:** Edward Woodward, Jane Merrow.
Only the distinguished acting of Edward Woodward prevents this British-made supernatural thriller from being rated as a turkey. Writer-director Lindsey C. Vickers shows very little talent with this story of a father (Woodward) cursed by his evil daughter (Samantha Weysom). Unrated, the film has some violence. 1982; 90m.

APPRENTICE TO MURDER ★★½
DIR: R. L. Thomas. **CAST:** Donald Sutherland, Chad Lowe, Mia Sara, Rutanya Alda, Eddie Jones, Mark Burton.
This film of the occult was inspired by a true story in Pennsylvania in 1927. Donald Sutherland appears as a religious leader with healing and mystical powers. Chad Lowe, in his desperation to get help for his alcoholic father, falls prey to Sutherland's powers. Rated PG-13 for language and violence. 1987; 97m.

APRIL FOOL'S DAY ★★★
DIR: Fred Walton. **CAST:** Jay Baker, Deborah Foreman, Griffin O'Neal, Amy Steel.
A group of college kids on spring break are invited to a mansion on a desolate island by a rich girl named Muffy St. John. They read Milton, quote Boswell, play practical jokes, and get killed off in a nice, orderly fashion. Not really a horror film; more

of a mystery à la *Ten Little Indians*. Rated R for violence and profanity. 1986; 90m.

ARNOLD ★½
DIR: Georg Fenady. **CAST:** Roddy McDowall, Elsa Lanchester, Stella Stevens, Farley Granger, Victor Buono, John McGiver, Shani Wallis.

A delightful cast cannot save this rather muddled mess of murder and mirth. Stella Stevens, married to a corpse, suddenly discovers her co-stars meeting their maker in a variety of strange ways reminiscent of *The Abominable Dr. Phibes*. Pretty ho-hum. Rated PG for violence. 1973; 100m.

ASTRO-ZOMBIES
DIR: Ted V. Mikels. **CAST:** Wendell Corey, John Carradine, Rafael Campos.

A grade-Z horror film that wastes the talent of star John Carradine as a standard mad scientist who kills to obtain body parts for his new creation. 1967; 83m.

ASYLUM ★★★★
DIR: Roy Ward Baker. **CAST:** Barbara Parkins, Sylvia Syms, Peter Cushing, Barry Morse, Richard Todd, Herbert Lom, Patrick Magee.

A first-rate horror anthology from England featuring fine performances. Four seemingly unrelated stories of madness by Robert Bloch are interwoven, leading to a nail-biting climax. Rated PG. 1972; 92m.

ATOM AGE VAMPIRE
DIR: Anton Giulio Masano. **CAST:** Alberto Lupo, Susanne Loret.

Badly dubbed Italian time-waster with cheese-ball special effects and a tired premise. A mad professor restores the face of a scarred accident victim. To keep her beautiful, he must kill other women and swipe their glands. Every so often, just for fun, the doc transforms into something resembling that troll doll your sister used to have. 1960; B&W; 71m.

ATTACK OF THE CRAB MONSTERS ★★★
DIR: Roger Corman. **CAST:** Richard Garland, Pamela Duncan, Mel Welles, Russell Johnson, Ed Nelson.

Neat Roger Corman low-budget movie, seemed scarier when you were a kid, but it's still a lot of fun. A remote Pacific atoll is besieged by a horde of giant land crabs that, upon devouring members of a scientific expedition, absorb their brains and acquire the ability to speak in their voices. 1957; B&W; 64m.

ATTACK OF THE 50-FOOT WOMAN ★★★
DIR: Nathan Juran. **CAST:** Allison Hayes, William Hudson, Yvette Vickers.

One of the best "schlock" films from the 1950s. Allison Hayes stars as a woman who's kidnapped by a tremendous bald alien and transformed into a giant herself. Duddy special effects only serve to heighten the enjoyment of this kitsch classic. 19[illegible] B&W; 66m.

ATTACK OF THE SWAMP CREATURE
DIR: Arnold Stevens. **CAST:** Frank Crowell, Patricia Robertson.

In one of Elvira's Thriller Video movies, we're subjected to the story of a mad scientist who turns himself into a giant, man-eating, walking catfish. Need we go further? 1985; 96m.

ATTIC, THE ★½
DIR: George Edwards. **CAST:** Carrie Snodgress, Ray Milland.

Rather slow-moving and routine story concerning a young woman (Carrie Snodgress) fighting to free herself from the clutches of her crippled, almost insane, father. Tries to be deep and psychological and falls flat on its face. Rated PG. 1979; 97m.

AUDREY ROSE ★
DIR: Robert Wise. **CAST:** Marsha Mason, Anthony Hopkins, John Beck.

Plodding melodrama about a man (Anthony Hopkins) who constantly annoys a couple by claiming that his dead daughter has been reincarnated as their live one. Bad script is only one problem in one of director Wise's few duds. Rated PG. 1977; 113m.

AUTOPSY ★
DIR: Armando Crispino. **CAST:** Mimsy Farmer, Raymond Lovelock, Barry Primus.
Never has a film dwelled so lovingly upon the dissection of the human body. The story involves a young medical student doing graduate study in a morgue. She slowly becomes unbalanced by all the disfigured bodies. When her father's girlfriend shows up on a slab as a murder victim, she snaps. Not recommended for the squeamish. Rated R for nudity and graphic violence. 1976; 90m.

AVENGING CONSCIENCE, THE ★★½
DIR: D. W. Griffith. **CAST:** Henry B. Walthall, Blanche Sweet, Mae Marsh, Robert Harron, Ralph Lewis.
Edgar Allan Poe's short stories provide the inspiration for this tale of a young writer (Henry B. Wathall) obsessed with Poe. Faced with the choice of continued patronage from his strict uncle or marriage with the "Annabel Lee" (Blanche Sweet) of his dreams, our tortured hero subjects his uncle to the tortures suggested by Poe's stories. Interesting historically, this silent feature is most effective in atmospheric chills. 1914; B&W; 78m.

AWAKENING, THE ★★½
DIR: Mike Newell. **CAST:** Charlton Heston, Susannah York, Jill Townsend, Stephanie Zimbalist.
In this mediocre horror flick, Charlton Heston plays an Egyptologist who discovers the tomb of a wicked queen. The evil spirit escapes the tomb and is reincarnated in Heston's newborn daughter. A bit hard to follow. Rated R for gore. 1980; 102m.

BABY, THE ★★★
DIR: Ted Post. **CAST:** Ruth Roman, Marianna Hill.
Extremely odd film by veteran director Ted Post about a teenager who has remained an infant all his life (yes, he still lives in his crib) and his insane, overprotective mother. Eerily effective chiller is entertaining, though many will undoubtedly find it repulsive and ridiculous. Rated PG. 1974; 80m.

BABYSITTER, THE ★★★½
DIR: Peter Medak. **CAST:** Patty Duke Astin, William Shatner, Quinn Cummings, David Wallace, Stephanie Zimbalist, John Houseman.
Outside of some glaring plot flaws, *The Babysitter* is an effectively eerie film. Stephanie Zimbalist is Joanna, a woman hired as a housekeeper (not a baby-sitter). But after a series of mysterious accidents and some rather ominous behavior, we find that Joanna is no Mary Poppins. Not rated; has violence. 1980; 96m.

BAD DREAMS ★
DIR: Andrew Fleming. **CAST:** Jennifer Rubin, Bruce Abbott, Richard Lynch, Harris Yulin.
Director-coscriptor Andrew Fleming brings the viewer to spasms of nausea as he unfolds this tale of a young woman (Jennifer Rubin) awakened from a thirteen-year coma only to be haunted and hunted by the ghost of a maniacal leader (Richard Lynch) of a hippie cult. Rated R for violence, gore, and profanity. 1988; 90m.

BAD RONALD ★★
DIR: Buzz Kulik. **CAST:** Scott Jacoby, Kim Hunter, Pippa Scott, Dabney Coleman.
Scott Jacoby plays a slowly degenerating teen who lives secretly in a hidden room his mother builds for him after he kills a taunting peer. When Mama passes on, a new family moves into the place, unaware that someone is watching them all the while. Intriguing but tedious made-for-TV movie. 1978; 72m.

BASKET CASE ★★★
DIR: Frank Henenlotter. **CAST:** Kevin Vanhentryck, Terri Susan Smith.

Comedy and horror are mixed beautifully in this weird tale of a young man and his deformed Siamese twin out for revenge against the doctors who separated them. Gruesomely entertaining and highly recommended for shock buffs. Rated R. 1982; 91m.

BAT PEOPLE ★
DIR: Jerry Jameson. **CAST:** Stewart Moss, Marianne McAndrew, Michael Pataki.

A young biologist on his honeymoon is bitten by a bat and is slowly transformed into a flying, blood-hungry rodent. His bride gets annoyed. Originally titled *It Lives by Night*. It sucks under any name. Rated R. 1974; 95m.

BATTLE SHOCK ★★
DIR: Paul Henreid. **CAST:** Ralph Meeker, Janice Rule, Rosenda Monteros, Paul Henreid.

Ralph Meeker portrays an artist who becomes involved in a murder while working in Mexico. Janice Rule is his doting wife. An uneven suspenser also known under the title of *A Woman's Devotion*. 1956; 88m.

BEAKS THE MOVIE ★
DIR: Rene Cardona Jr. **CAST:** Christopher Atkins, Michelle Johnson.

Hitchcock made birds menacing. *Beaks* makes them at times unintentionally funny and at other times too gruesome to watch. Christopher Atkins is a TV cameraman and Michelle Johnson a TV reporter assigned to investigate reports of attacking birds. It is rated unsuitable for anyone under 17. That goes for anyone over 17 as well. 1987; 86m.

BEAR ISLAND ★
DIR: Don Sharp. **CAST:** Donald Sutherland, Richard Widmark, Vanessa Redgrave, Christopher Lee, Lloyd Bridges.

Alistair MacLean writes some of the best thrillers around; why can't they be turned into better films? This is one of the worst, a pointlessly melodramatic tale mixing gold fever, murder, and other incidental intrigue. Rated PG for mild violence. 1980; 118m.

BEAST IN THE CELLAR, THE ★½
DIR: James Kelly. **CAST:** Beryl Reid, Flora Robson, T. P. McKenna, John Hamill.

Boring story about a pair of aging sisters (well played by veterans Beryl Reid and Flora Robson) with something to hide. Only, instead of a skeleton in the closet, they've got a beast in the cellar. More specifically, their deranged, deformed brother is down there, and he wants out! Weak. Rated R. 1971; 87m.

BEAST MUST DIE, THE ★★
DIR: Paul Annett. **CAST:** Calvin Lockhart, Peter Cushing, Charles Gray, Anton Diffring.

A millionaire hunter invites a group of guests to an isolated mansion. One of them is a werewolf he intends to destroy. A tame, talky reworking of Agatha Christie's *Ten Little Indians*. Rated PG. 1974; 98m.

BEAST WITHIN, THE ★
DIR: Phillippe Mora. **CAST:** Ronny Cox, Bibi Besch, Paul Clemens, Don Gordon.

This unbelievably gory movie consists mainly of one grisly murder after another. Phillippe Mora, an Australian documentary filmmaker, tries his best to create an atmosphere of intelligent horror (as does top-billed Ronny Cox), but there's no competing with the excessive gore. Rated R. 1982; 90m.

BEDLAM ★★★
DIR: Mark Robson. **CAST:** Boris Karloff, Anna Lee, Ian Wolfe, Richard Fraser, Jason Robards Sr.

One of the lesser entries in the Val Lewton–produced horror film series at RKO, this release still has its moments as the courageous Anna Lee tries to expose the cruelties and inadequacies of an insane asylum run by Boris Karloff, who is first-rate, as usual. 1946; B&W; 79m.

BEDROOM WINDOW, THE ★★★
DIR: Curtis Hanson. **CAST:** Steve Guttenberg, Elizabeth McGovern, Isabelle Huppert, Paul Shenar.

Upwardly mobile architect Steve Guttenberg has it made until his boss's wife (Isabelle Huppert) sees a murder being committed—from his bedroom window. When Guttenberg goes to the police in her place, he becomes the prime suspect. This is a tense thriller that manages to stay interesting despite some wildly unbelievable plot twists. Rated R for profanity, nudity, and violence. 1987; 112m.

BEES, THE ★½
DIR: Alfredo Zacharias. **CAST:** John Saxon, John Carradine.
Despite all temptation to label this a honey of a picture, it's a drone that will probably give viewers the hives. Rated PG. 1978; 83m.

BEETLEJUICE ★★★
DIR: Tim Burton. **CAST:** Alec Baldwin, Geena Davis, Michael Keaton, Jeffrey Jones, Catherine O'Hara, Winona Ryder.
Like a cinematic trip through the Haunted Mansion, this film may require two viewings just to catch all the complex action and visual jokes. Alec Baldwin and Geena Davis play a young couple who accidentally drown and return as novice ghosts. The family that moves into their pretty little Connecticut farmhouse seem intent on destroying it aesthetically, and the ghostly couple are forced to call on the evil spirit Betelguese (Michael Keaton) to scare the intruders away. Rated PG for shock action and language. 1988; 93m.

BEFORE I HANG ★★★
DIR: Nick Grindé. **CAST:** Boris Karloff, Evelyn Keyes, Bruce Bennett, Pedro de Cordoba, Edward Van Sloan.
Neat little thriller has Boris Karloff as a goodhearted doctor who creates an age-retardant serum. Trouble begins when he tests it on himself, with horrible side effects. Nicely done, the film benefits from a good supporting performance by horror veteran Edward Van Sloan. 1940; B&W; 71m.

BEING, THE
DIR: Jackie Kong. **CAST:** Martin Landau, José Ferrer, Dorothy Malone, Ruth Buzzi.
This inept little horror film must have taxed the funds or patience of its producers, since gaping hunks of plot are missing and replaced with laughable narration. Water contaminated with nuclear waste spawned a beast that likes to shove itself *through* people...or maybe the monster is the deformed child of Dorothy Malone; the story's that confusing. Unwatchable. Rated R for gore and nudity. 1984; 82m.

BELIEVERS, THE ★★★½
DIR: John Schlesinger. **CAST:** Martin Sheen, Helen Shaver, Robert Loggia, Richard Masur, Elizabeth Wilson, Lee Richardson, Harris Yulin, Jimmy Smits.
Martin Sheen portrays a recently widowed father whose son is chosen as a sacrifice to a voodoo cult running rampant in New York. John Schlesinger is not the best director for a thriller of this type, but in this case the quality of the acting, the snap of the writing, and the strength of the story build the suspense nicely and provide a striking climax. Rated R for language, nudity, and nightmarism. 1987; 110m.

BEN ★
DIR: Phil Karlson. **CAST:** Arthur O'Connell, Lee Montgomery, Rosemary Murphy.
The only thing going for this silly sequel to *Willard* is an awkwardly charming title song performed by a young Michael Jackson (a love song for a rat, no less). Turgid entry in the beasts-get-even subgenre of horror films. Where's a better rattrap when you need one? Rated PG—violence. 1972; 95m.

BERSERK ★★★½
DIR: Jim O'Connolly. **CAST:** Joan Crawford, Ty Hardin, Michael Gough, Diana Dors, Judy Geeson.
Effectively staged thriller stars Joan Crawford as the owner of a once-great circus now on its last legs—until a

number of accidental deaths of the performers starts packing 'em in. Joan comes under suspicion immediately when the cops begin counting the box-office receipts. Could she be guilty? 1967; 96m.

BERSERKER ★
DIR: Jeff Richard. **CAST:** Joseph Alan Johnson.
Silly slasher in which a Viking demon, the berserker, is reincarnated in his descendants. Said demon meets up with a group of college students who are vacationing at a lonely campsite. Rated R for nudity, violence, gore, and simulated sex. 1987; 85m.

BEST OF SEX AND VIOLENCE ★★
DIR: Ken Dixon. **CAST:** Hosted by John Carradine.
A quickie video production containing unrelated clips and preview trailers from low-budget exploitation films. A rip-off, to be sure, but not without laughs and a certain sleazy charm. Unrated, the film has profanity, nudity, and, of course, sex and violence. 1981; 76m.

BEWARE, MY LOVELY ★★★★
DIR: Harry Horner. **CAST:** Ida Lupino, Robert Ryan, Taylor Holmes, Barbara Whiting.
Robert Ryan is terrifyingly right as an amnesiac psycho who can fly into a strangling rage one minute, then return to his simpleminded handyman guise the next. Ida Lupino is also superb as the widow who hires Ryan to clean her floors, a mistake she soon regrets. Dark suspense remains taut right up to the ending. 1952; B&W; 77m.

BEYOND EVIL ★
DIR: Herb Freed. **CAST:** John Saxon, Lynda Day George, Michael Dante.
Larry Andrews (John Saxon) and his wife, Barbara (Lynda Day George), travel to a tropical island to mix business with their honeymoon. Andrews is to supervise a construction project for Barbara's ex-spouse, and the former husband lodges the newlyweds in a luxurious mansion, which happens to be haunted. Rated R. 1980; 94m.

BEYOND THE DOOR ★
DIR: Ovidio Assonitis (Oliver Hellman). **CAST:** Juliet Mills, Richard Johnson, David Colin Jr.
Sick ripoff of *The Exorcist* has Juliet Mills as a woman possessed by guess what. Or should we say guess who? Disgusting production only serves to induce nausea. Made in Italy. Rated R. 1975; 94m.

BEYOND THE DOOR 2 ★★
DIR: Mario Bava. **CAST:** Daria Nicolodi, John Steiner, David Colin Jr.
Why, why, why? Actually, this semisequel is much better than the original mainly because its director was the famed Mario Bava. This time a young boy becomes possessed by the unseen power of Hell, and many die. Alternate title: *Shock*. Rated R. 1979; 92m.

BIG FOOT 🦃
DIR: Robert F. Slatzer. **CAST:** John Carradine, Joi Lansing, John Mitchum, Chris Mitchum.
Legendary monster comes down from the hills and beats the hell out of everybody. Laughable film is worthless, one of John Carradine's worst and that's saying something. 1971; 94m.

BILLY THE KID VS. DRACULA ★½
DIR: William Beaudine. **CAST:** John Carradine, Chuck Courtney, Melinda Plowman, Virginia Christine, Harry Carey Jr.
Hokey horror film casts John Carradine as the famous vampire, on the loose in a small western town. From the director of *Bela Lugosi Meets a Brooklyn Gorilla*, another so-bad-it's-funny film. 1966; 95m.

BIRD WITH THE CRYSTAL PLUMAGE, THE ★★★
DIR: Dario Argento. **CAST:** Tony Musante, Suzy Kendall, Eva Renzi, Enrico Maria Salerno.
Stylish thriller weaves a complex story thread in adventure of an American writer who witnesses a murder

and is drawn into the web of mystery and violence. Minor cult favorite, well photographed and nicely acted by resilient Tony Musante and fashion plate Suzy Kendall. Rated PG. 1969; 98m.

BIRDS, THE ★★★★
DIR: Alfred Hitchcock. **CAST:** Rod Taylor, Tippi Hedren, Jessica Tandy, Suzanne Pleshette, Veronica Cartwright, Ethel Griffies.

Alfred Hitchcock's *The Birds* is an eerie, disturbing stunner, highlighted by Evan Hunter's literate adaptation of Daphne Du Maurier's ominous short story. Rod Taylor and Tippi Hedren are thrown into an uneasy relationship while our avian friends develop an appetite for something more substantial than bugs and berries. Although quite fantastic, the premise is made credible by Hitchcock's unswerving attention to character; the supporting cast is excellent. Unrated, but may be too intense for younger viewers. 1963; 120m.

BLACK CAT, THE ★★★★
DIR: Edgar G. Ulmer. **CAST:** Boris Karloff, Bela Lugosi, Jacqueline Wells.

A surrealistic, strikingly designed horror-thriller that has become a cult favorite thanks to its pairing of Boris Karloff and Bela Lugosi. Lugosi has one of his very few good-guy roles as a concerned citizen who gets drawn into a web of evil that surrounds Karloff's black magic. Available on a videocassette double feature with *The Raven*. 1934; B&W; 70m.

BLACK CHRISTMAS ★★★
DIR: Bob Clark. **CAST:** Olivia Hussey, Keir Dullea, Margot Kidder, John Saxon.

During the holiday season, members of a sorority house fall victim to the homicidal obscene phone-caller living in their attic. Margot Kidder, fresh from Brian De Palma's *Sisters*, is quite convincing as a vulgar, alcoholic college kid with asthma. Atmospheric and frightening. If the film seems somewhat derivative today, try to remember that it came before *Halloween* and *When A Stranger Calls*. Rated R. 1975; 99m.

BLACK DRAGONS ★
DIR: William Nigh. **CAST:** Bela Lugosi, Joan Barclay, Clayton Moore.

A silly film about Japanese agents who are surgically altered to resemble American businessmen and chiefs of industry. This low-budget bore gives former horror film champion Bela Lugosi little to do but eavesdrop and appear unexpectedly from behind doors. 1949; B&W; 62m.

BLACK MAGIC TERROR ★
DIR: L. Sujio. **CAST:** Suzanna.

This Japanese horror story is very reminiscent of badly dubbed Japanese science-fiction films. It's the story of a young woman jilted by her lover who turns to black magic for her violent revenge. Enlisting the aid of evil spirits, she wreaks havoc on the village that cast her out. Not rated but contains some nudity and violence. 1985; 85m.

BLACK ROOM, THE (1935) ★★★
DIR: Roy William Neill. **CAST:** Boris Karloff, Marian Marsh, Robert Allen, Katherine DeMille, Thurston Hall.

Boris Karloff is excellent as twin brothers with an age-old family curse hanging over their heads. Well-handled thriller never stops moving. 1935; B&W; 67m.

BLACK ROOM, THE (1985) ★
DIR: Norman Thaddeus Vane. **CAST:** Stephen Knight, Cassandra Gavioca.

A philandering husband rents an apartment from a couple who spy on his extramarital trysts, then kill the adulterous man's girlfriends. The movie is filled with poor performances and bad dialogue. Rated R for nudity. 1985; 88m.

BLACK ROSES ★★½
DIR: John Fasano. **CAST:** John Martin, Ken Swofford.

Black Roses is the name of a hard rock group that comes to sleepy Mill Basin for a live concert. Soon, demonic things begin to happen, the audience is turned into hypnotic slaves, and the concert hall becomes a hell on Earth. Want to see a guy get sucked into a wall-mounted stereo speaker? It's here. Rated R for violence, nudity and language. 1988; 90m.

BLACK SABBATH ★★★½
DIR: Mario Bava. **CAST:** Boris Karloff, Mark Damon, Suzy Andersen.

Above-average trio of horror tales given wonderful atmosphere by director Mario Bava. Boris Karloff plays host and stars in the third story, a vampire opus entitled "The Wurdalak." One of the others, "A Drop of Water," is based on a story by Chekhov; the third, "The Telephone," involves disconnected calls of the worst sort. 1964; 99m.

BLACK WIDOW ★★★★
DIR: Bob Rafelson. **CAST:** Debra Winger, Theresa Russell, Sami Frey, Dennis Hopper, Nicol Williamson, Terry O'Quinn.

A superb thriller from director Bob Rafelson that recalls the best of the Bette Davis–Joan Crawford "bad girl" films of earlier decades. Debra Winger stars as an inquisitive federal agent who stumbles upon an odd pattern of deaths by apparently natural causes: the victims are quite wealthy, reclusive, and leave behind a young—and very rich—widow. Rated R for nudity, adult situations. 1987; 103m.

BLACKENSTEIN
DIR: William A. Levy. **CAST:** John Hart, Joe DiSue.

Tasteless and grotesque entry in the subgenre of blaxploitation horror films. Mad doctor John Hart takes a maimed Vietnam veteran (Joe DiSue) and transforms him into a shambling nightmare. Rated R for violence and nudity. 1973; 92m.

BLACKOUT (1985) ★★★½
DIR: Douglas Hickox. **CAST:** Richard Widmark, Keith Carradine, Kathleen Quinlan, Michael Beck.

A police detective (Richard Widmark) becomes obsessed with an unsolved murder. Six years after the incident he begins to find valuable clues. This superior made-for-HBO movie has violence and profanity. 1985; 99m.

BLACULA ★★★½
DIR: William Crain. **CAST:** William Marshall, Denise Nicholas, Vonetta McGee, Thalmus Rasulala.

An old victim (William Marshall) of Dracula's bite is loose in modern L.A. Surprisingly well-done shocker. Fierce and energetic, with a solid cast. Rated R for violence. 1972; 92m.

BLOB, THE (1958) ★★★
DIR: Irvin S. Yeaworth Jr. **CAST:** Steve McQueen, Aneta Corseaut, Olin Howlin.

This was Steve McQueen's first starring role. He plays a teenager battling parents and a voracious hunk of protoplasm from outer space. Long surpassed by more sophisticated sci-fi, it's still fun to watch. 1958; 86m.

BLOB, THE (1988) ★★★★
DIR: Chuck Russell. **CAST:** Kevin Dillon, Shawnee Smith, Donovan Leitch, Jeffrey DeMunn, Candy Clark, Joe Seneca.

Frightening and occasionally comedic remake of the 1958 cult classic. This time around, Kevin Dillon and Shawnee Smith battle the gelatinous ooze as it devours the inhabitants of a small ski resort. The best horror remake since *The Fly*. A thrill ride for those with the stomach to take it. Rated R for profanity and state-of-the-art gruesomeness. 1988; 95m.

BLOOD AND BLACK LACE ★★½
DIR: Mario Bava. **CAST:** Cameron Mitchell, Eva Bartok.

This sometimes frightening Italian horror film features a psychotic killer eliminating members of the modeling industry with gusto. Decent entry in the genre from specialist Mario Bava. 1964; 88m.

BLOOD BEACH ★
DIR: Jeffrey Bloom. **CAST:** John Saxon, Marianna Hill, Otis Young.
Poor horror story of mysterious forces sucking people down into the sand isn't nearly as fun as it sounds. Bad acting, bad writing, and bad special effects. Rated R. 1981; 89m.

BLOOD DINER
DIR: Jackie Kong. **CAST:** Rick Burks, Carl Crew.
Like *Bloodsucking Freaks*, this horror-comedy is likely to offend even the most avid gore fan. Two brothers kill women in various "amusing" ways in order to obtain body parts for a demonic ceremony. They serve the "leftovers" in their diner. Offensive and moronic. Director Jackie Kong (yes, a woman) should really be ashamed. Unrated, but filled with violence, nudity, and gore. 1987; 88m.

BLOOD FEAST
DIR: Herschell Gordon Lewis. **CAST:** Connie Mason, Thomas Wood.
First and most infamous of the drive-in gore movies bolsters practically nonexistent plot of crazed murderer with gallons of director Herschell Gordon Lewis's patented stage blood as well as props like a sheep's tongue and a power saw. Crude, vulgar, and ineptly acted, this bargain-basement production was one of the low-budget bonanzas of the 1960s and set the tone for dozens of subsequent nauseating hack-and-slash films. 1963; 75m.

BLOOD FRENZY ★½
DIR: Hal Freeman. **CAST:** Wendy MacDonald, Hank Garrett, Lisa Loring.
In this made-for-video horror thriller, a psychotherapist takes a group of her patients into the desert for a retreat. Predictably, someone starts killing them off one by one. Who is the killer? Who cares? Unrated, the movie contains violence. 1987; 90m.

BLOOD HOOK
DIR: James Mallon. **CAST:** Mark Jacobs, Lisa Todd.
While attending a fishing tournament, several teenagers are murdered by a killer who uses a giant fishhook to reel in his catch. He grinds up his victims and feeds them to the fish. Not rated, but contains graphic violence and brief nudity. 1986; 85m.

BLOOD LINK
DIR: Alberto De Martino. **CAST:** Michael Moriarty, Penelope Milford, Cameron Mitchell.
All his life, a prominent physician has had strange hallucinations about older women being brutally murdered. He discovers that he is seeing through the eyes of his Siamese twin (who was separated from him during infancy) as he kills his victims. The film starts off contrived and becomes even more so. Rated R for nudity and violence. 1983; 98m.

BLOOD OF DRACULA'S CASTLE
DIR: Al Adamson, Jean Hewitt. **CAST:** John Carradine, Paula Raymond, Alex D'Arcy, Robert Dix.
Quite possibly the worst Dracula movie ever made. The count and countess spend most of the film sitting around, rambling incoherently, sipping blood cocktails provided by their butler (John Carradine). The film has a werewolf, a hunchback, women in chains, human sacrifices, a laughable script, and a ten-dollar budget. Rated PG. 1967; 84m.

BLOOD ON SATAN'S CLAW ★★★
DIR: Piers Haggard. **CAST:** Patrick Wymark, Barry Andrews, Linda Hayden, Simon Williams.
Fun, frightening horror film set in seventeenth-century England. A small farming community is besieged by the devil himself, who succeeds in turning the local children into a coven of witches. Familiar story is presented in a unique manner by director Piers Haggard, helped by excellent period

detail and clever effects. Not for the kids, though. Rated R. 1971; 93m.

BLOOD ORGY OF THE SHE DEVILS ★
DIR: Ted V. Mikels. **CAST:** Lila Zaborin, Tom Pace.
Despite the title, which seems to offer all sorts of luridly sexual and violent cheap thrills, *Blood Orgy of the She Devils* is tame and oh-so-boring. The plot is nothing more than California witch queen Mara (Lila Zaborin) leading her followers in several ritualistic murders before the forces of good put an end to her schemes. Rated PG. A near turkey. 1972; 73m.

BLOOD RAGE ★
DIR: John Grissmer. **CAST:** Louise Lasser, Mark Soper.
When a 10-year-old boy kills a stranger at a drive-in movie, he escapes punishment by blaming his twin brother, who is sent to an institution. Eight years later, when the innocent boy escapes, the murderous twin starts killing everyone in sight so that those deaths will be blamed on his brother as well. It's just another slasher movie, distinguished only by the presence of Louise Lasser. It played movie houses and cable TV as *Nightmare at Shadow Woods*. So don't get tricked into watching it twice! Rated R. 1983; 83m.

BLOOD SISTERS 🦃
DIR: Roberta Findlay. **CAST:** Amy Brentano, Shannon McMahon.
A poorly produced excuse for a slasher film, this has a wonderfully lurid idea: a group of sorority girls must spend the night in a haunted house with a maniac. But the film never delivers any shocks or thrills. Rated R for nudity. 1987; 85m.

BLOOD SPELL ★
DIR: Deryn Warren. **CAST:** Anthony Jenkins.
A modern-day evil sorcerer possesses his son in an attempt to gain immortality. The son is placed in a halfway house for emotionally disturbed teenagers. There he begins slaughtering the patients in graphic and grotesque fashion. Rated R for graphic violence. 1987; 87m.

BLOOD SUCKERS FROM OUTER SPACE ★★
DIR: Glenn Coburn. **CAST:** Thom Meyer, Pat Paulsen.
Low-budget horror spoof about an alien virus that causes people to vomit up their guts, turning them into sneaky zombies out to suck the innards from hapless victims. Although sometimes funny, the film is an uneven mix of comedy and suspense. Not rated, but contains profanity and partial nudity. 1984; 79m.

BLOODBEAT ★
DIR: Fabrice A. Zaphiratos. **CAST:** Helen Benton, Terry Brown.
This cheap supernatural flick tries to pass off the idea that a samurai ghost is haunting the backwoods of an American wilderness because of an old war debt—we think. The plot is not at all clear, and the bad acting and poor direction only aggravate the problem. 1985; 84m.

BLOODSUCKERS, THE ★★½
DIR: David L. Hewitt. **CAST:** Lon Chaney Jr., John Carradine.
Lots of blood, gory special effects, and some good humor. Not bad for this type of film. Also known as *Return from the Past* and *Dr. Terror's Gallery of Horrors*. Not for the squeamish. 1967; 84m.

BLOODSUCKING FREAKS A.K.A. THE INCREDIBLE TORTURE SHOW 🦃
DIR: Joel M. Reed. **CAST:** Seamus O'Brian, Niles McMaster.
Any movie with a title this outrageous just has to be fun, right? *Wrong!* This putrid film is an endurance test for even the most hard-core horror buffs. The scene where one of the maniacs sucks a woman's brains out with a straw has to be one of the most repulsive moments ever put on film. Rated R for nudity and violence. 1978; 89m.

BLOODTHIRSTY BUTCHERS
DIR: Andy Milligan. **CAST:** John Miranda, Annabella Wood.

As the title suggests, an extremely violent series of murders is committed in very gruesome fashion. A dreadful ripoff of *The Demon Barber of Fleet Street*, with Sweeney Todd and his baker friend selling human meat pies. Nothing new here. Rated R. 1970; 80m.

BLOODTIDE
DIR: Richard Jeffries. **CAST:** James Earl Jones, José Ferrer, Lila Kedrova.

Cheap horror film about bizarre rituals on a Greek isle involving cannibalism, wastes a talented cast. Rated R. 1984; 82m.

BLOODY BIRTHDAY
DIR: Edward Hunt. **CAST:** Susan Strasberg, José Ferrer, Lori Lethin, Joe Penny.

Actually filmed six years before its release, this monumental waste of time is one of the worst terror films ever made. Three children, born during an eclipse of the moon, run amok, killing everyone in sight. It's sickening. Rated R. 1986; 85m.

BLOODY NEW YEAR ★★½
DIR: Norman J. Warren. **CAST:** Suzy Aitchison, Colin Heywood, Cathrine Roman.

Five teenagers become stranded on an abandonded island resort that's caught in a time warp. Zombie ghosts begin to pop up, first taunting the kids, then terrorizing, and finally killing them. Fairly well produced and boasting some decent special effects. Rated R for violence and nudity. 1987; 90m.

BLOODY WEDNESDAY ★★½
DIR: Mark G. Gilhuis. **CAST:** Raymond Elmendorf, Pamela Baker.

A peculiar psychological horror story whose prime attraction is that it never gets predictable. After a man suffers a nervous breakdown, his brother sets him up as the caretaker of a vacant hotel. He encounters strange attackers who may or may not be real. Unfortunately, the story is never satisfactorily resolved. Not rated. 1985; 97m.

BLOW OUT ★★★★
DIR: Brian De Palma. **CAST:** John Travolta, Nancy Allen, John Lithgow, Dennis Franz.

John Travolta and Nancy Allen are terrific in this thriller by director Brian De Palma. The story concerns a motion picture sound man (Travolta) who becomes involved in murder when he rescues a young woman (Allen) from a car that crashes into a river. It's suspenseful, thrill-packed, adult entertainment. Rated R because of sex, nudity, profanity, and violence. 1981; 107m.

BLOW-UP ★★★★★
DIR: Michelangelo Antonioni. **CAST:** Vanessa Redgrave, David Hemmings, Sarah Miles.

Director Michelangelo Antonioni's first English-language film was this stimulating examination into what is or is not reality. On its surface, a photographer (David Hemmings) believes he has taken a snapshot of a murder taking place. Vanessa Redgrave arrives at his studio and tries to seduce him out of the photo. 1966; 108m.

BLUE MONKEY ★★★
DIR: William Fruet. **CAST:** Steve Railsback, Susan Anspach, Gwyneth Walsh, John Vernon, Joe Flaherty, Robin Duke.

A small city hospital becomes contaminated by a patient infected by an unknown insect that causes terminal gangrene as it gestates eggs. One of these insects becomes mutated and grows to huge proportions. A low-budget film, this movie sometimes has the charm, humor, and suspense of classics like *The Thing* and *Them.* Rated R for violence and language. 1987; 98m.

BLUE VELVET ★★★★½
DIR: David Lynch. **CAST:** Kyle MacLachlan, Isabella Rossellini, Dennis Hopper, Laura Dern, Dean Stockwell.

In this brilliant but disturbing film, Kyle MacLachlan and Laura Dern play youngsters who become involved in the mystery surrounding night-club singer Isabella Rossellini. It seldom lets the viewer off easy, yet it is nevertheless a stunning cinematic work. Rated R for violence, nudity, and profanity. 1986; 120m.

BLUEBEARD (1944) ★★★
DIR: Edgar G. Ulmer. **CAST:** John Carradine, Jean Parker, Nils Asther, Ludwig Stossel, Iris Adrian.

Atmospheric low-budget thriller by resourceful German director Edgar G. Ulmer gives great character actor John Carradine one of his finest leading roles as a strangler who preys on women. 1944; B&W; 73m.

BLUEBEARD (1972) ★★½
DIR: Edward Dmytryk. **CAST:** Richard Burton, Raquel Welch, Karin Schubert, Joey Heatherton.

Richard Burton stars in *Bluebeard*, a film with its tongue planted firmly in cheek. The legend of the multiple murderer is intermingled with Nazi lore to come out as a reasonably convincing foray into a combination of black comedy and classic horror films. Rated R. 1972; 125m.

BODY COUNT ★½
DIR: Paul Leder. **CAST:** Bernie White, Marilyn Hassett, Dick Sargent, Greg Mullavey.

An unexceptional thriller about a man committed to a mental institution by relatives who want his money. He escapes, and the title should clue you in as to what happens next. *Body Count* aims for suspense rather than slasher horror, but fails to achieve either. Not rated. 1988; 93m.

BODY DOUBLE ★★★½
DIR: Brian De Palma. **CAST:** Craig Wasson, Melanie Griffith, Gregg Henry, Deborah Shelton.

This Brian De Palma thriller is often gruesome, disgusting, and exploitative. But you can't take your eyes off the screen. Craig Wasson is first-rate as a young actor who witnesses a brutal murder, and Melanie Griffith is often hilarious as the porno star who holds the key to the crime. Rated R for nudity, suggested sex, profanity, and violence. 1984; 110m.

BODY SNATCHER, THE ★★★★
DIR: Robert Wise. **CAST:** Henry Daniell, Boris Karloff, Bela Lugosi.

Boris Karloff gives one of his finest performances in the title role of this Val Lewton production, adapted from the novel by Robert Louis Stevenson. Karloff is a sinister grave robber who provides dead bodies for illegal medical research and then uses his activities as blackmail to form a bond of "friendship" with the doctor he services, Henry Daniell (in an equally impressive turn). 1945; B&W; 77m.

BOG 🦃
DIR: Don Keeslar. **CAST:** Gloria De Haven, Aldo Ray, Marshall Thompson.

Extremely low-budget film is entertaining for just that reason. Unlucky group of people on an excursion into the wilderness run into the recently defrosted monster Bog. Needless to say, things go downhill from there. Rated PG. 1983; 87m.

BOOGEYMAN, THE ★★★½
DIR: Ulli Lommel. **CAST:** Suzanna Love, Michael Love, John Carradine.

Despite the lame title, this is an inventive, atmospheric fright flick about pieces of a broken mirror causing horrifying deaths. Good special effects add to the creepiness. Rated R for violence and gore. 1980; 86m.

BOOGEYMAN 2, THE ★
DIR: Bruce Star. **CAST:** Suzanna Love, Shana Hall, Ulli Lommel.

Not nearly as good as *The Boogeyman*, this cheapo sequel uses footage from the original and a substandard plot to cash in on success of its predecessor. Don't be fooled. Rated R for violence and gore. 1983; 79m.

BOSTON STRANGLER, THE ★★★
DIR: Richard Fleischer. **CAST:** Tony Curtis, Henry Fonda, Mike Kellin, Murray Hamilton, Sally Kellerman, Hurd Hatfield, George Kennedy, Jeff Corey.

True account, told in semidocumentary-style, of Beantown's notorious deranged murderer, plumber Albert De Salvo. Tony Curtis gives a first-class performance as the woman-killer. 1968; 120m.

BOWERY AT MIDNIGHT ★
DIR: Wallace Fox. **CAST:** Bela Lugosi, John Archer, Wanda McKay, Tom Neal.

Very cheaply made story about a maniac on a killing spree in the Bowery area of New York City. Bela Lugosi fans may want to award this an additional star; others, be forewarned. 1942; B&W; 63m.

BOYS FROM BRAZIL, THE ★★½
DIR: Franklin J. Schaffner. **CAST:** Gregory Peck, Laurence Olivier, James Mason, Lilli Palmer.

In this thriller, Gregory Peck plays an evil Nazi war criminal with farfetched plans to resurrect the Third Reich. Laurence Olivier as a Jewish Nazi-hunter pursues him. Rated R. 1978; 123m.

BOYS FROM BROOKLYN, THE
DIR: William Beaudine. **CAST:** Bela Lugosi, Duke Mitchell, Sammy Petrillo.

Absolutely hilarious bomb with Bela Lugosi as a mad scientist turning people into apes on a forgotten island. Standout performance by Sammy Petrillo as a Jerry Lewis clone will have you rolling in the aisles! Better known as *Bela Lugosi Meets a Brooklyn Gorilla*, a much more appropriate title. 1952; B&W; 72m.

BRAIN, THE ★★½
DIR: Edward Hunt. **CAST:** Tom Breznahan, Cyndy Preston, David Gale.

Hokey special effects take away from this shocker about a TV psychologist (David Gale) and his alien brain who attempt to use the doctor's TV program to take over the minds of people in a small town before going national. The brain (eyes, nose, and long, sharp teeth added) starts munching anyone who gets in the way. Occasionally entertaining, this is one film that never reaches its potential. Rated R for violence and mild gore. 1988; 94m.

BRAIN DAMAGE ★★½
DIR: Frank Henenlotter. **CAST:** Rich Herbst, Gordon MacDonald.

A wisecracking giant worm escapes from its elderly keepers and forces a teenager to kill people. Although the low budget hampers the special effects, the offbeat execution makes this worth a look for horror fans. Rated R for sexual situations and graphic violence. 1988; 90m.

BRAIN OF BLOOD
DIR: Al Adamson. **CAST:** Kent Taylor, John Bloom, Regina Carroll, Grant Williams.

Really awful horror movie, shot in the Philippines (which is not exactly Hollywood south) by Al Adamson, one of the all-time worst. (He's made even tackier movies than this one, which you'll find hard to believe if you actually sit through it.) It's about a mad doctor who performs brain transplants and who creates a hulking monster. And there's a dwarf assistant to torture underdressed women. 1971; 83m.

BRAIN THAT WOULDN'T DIE ★★
DIR: Joseph Green. **CAST:** Jason Evers, Virginia Leith, Adele Lamont.

A surgeon keeps the head of his decapitated fiancée alive while searching for a shapely secondhand torso. This talky, laughably cheap thriller is notable only for two moments of outrageous violence rarely seen in films of its era. Inexplicably, those scenes have been edited out of the video release. Since the film runs fairly regularly on after-hours TV, you might want to wait until it's broadcast in your area. 1963; B&W; 81m.

BRAINIAC, THE ★★★
DIR: Chano Urveta. **CAST:** Abel Salazar.

Mexi-monster stuff about a nobleman, executed as a warlock in 1661, who comes back to life to seek revenge on the descendants of those who killed him. Every so often he transforms himself into a monster with a long, snaky tongue that he uses to suck out people's brains. With their low production values and indifferent dubbing, most Mexican horror films are good only for camp value. This one has those same flaws, but you'll also find it has some eerily effective moments. 1961; 77m.

BRAINWAVES ★★★
DIR: Ulli Lommel. **CAST:** Keir Dullea, Suzanna Love, Vera Miles, Percy Rodrigues, Paul Wilson, Tony Curtis.

A young San Francisco wife and mother undergoes brain surgery as a result of an accident. An experimental brain wave transfer is performed in an attempt to restore her to a normal life, producing startling results since the brain waves came from a murder victim. Rated R for some nudity and mild violence. 1982; 83m.

BRIDE, THE ★½
DIR: Franc Roddam. **CAST:** Sting, Jennifer Beals, Geraldine Page, Clancy Brown, Anthony Higgins, David Rappaport.

This remake of James Whale's classic 1935 horror comedy of the macabre, *Bride of Frankenstein*, has some laughs. But these, unlike in the original, are unintentional. Rock singer Sting makes a rather stuffy, unsavory Dr. Charles (?!) Frankenstein, and Jennifer Beals is terribly miscast as his second creation. Rated PG-13 for violence, suggested sex, and nudity. 1985; 119m.

BRIDE OF FRANKENSTEIN ★★★★★
DIR: James Whale. **CAST:** Boris Karloff, Colin Clive, Valerie Hobson, Dwight Frye, Ernest Thesiger, Elsa Lanchester.

This is a first-rate sequel to *Frankenstein*. This time, Henry Frankenstein (Clive) is coerced by the evil Dr. Praetorius (Ernest Thesiger in a delightfully weird and sinister performance) into creating a mate for the monster. 1935; B&W; 75m.

BRIDE OF THE MONSTER 🦃
DIR: Edward D. Wood Jr. **CAST:** Bela Lugosi, Tor Johnson, Tony McCoy, Loretta King.

Another incredibly inept but hilarious film from Ed Wood Jr., this stinker uses most of the mad scientist clichés and uses them poorly as a cadaverous-looking Bela Lugosi tries to do fiendish things to an unconscious (even while alert) Loretta King. This bottom-of-the-barrel independent monstrosity boasts possibly the worst special-effects monster of all time, a rubber octopus that any novelty store would be ashamed to stock. 1955; B&W; 69m.

BRIGHTON STRANGLER, THE ★★½
DIR: Max Nosseck. **CAST:** John Loder, June Duprez, Miles Mander, Rose Hobart, Ian Wolfe.

John Loder runs amok after a Nazi bomb destroys the London theater where he has been playing a murderer in a drama. Stunned in the explosion, he confuses his true identity with the character he has been playing. A chance remark by a stranger sends him off to the seaside resort of Brighton, where he performs his stage role for real! 1945; B&W; 67m.

BRIMSTONE AND TREACLE ★★★
DIR: Richard Loncraine. **CAST:** Denholm Elliott, Joan Plowright, Suzanna Hamilton, Sting.

Sting plays an angelic-diabolic young drifter who insinuates himself into the home lives of respectable Denholm Elliott and Joan Plowright in this British-made shocker. Rated R. 1982; 85m.

BROOD, THE ★★
DIR: David Cronenberg. **CAST:** Oliver Reed, Samantha Eggar, Art Hindle.
Fans of director David Cronenberg will no doubt enjoy this offbeat, grisly horror tale about genetic experiments. Others need not apply. Rated R. 1979; 90m.

BROTHERHOOD OF SATAN ★
DIR: Bernard McEveety. **CAST:** Strother Martin, L. Q. Jones, Charles Bateman, Ahna Capri.
Strong cast is wasted in this ridiculous thriller about a small town taken over by witches and devil worshipers, led by maniacal Strother Martin. Boring. Rated PG. 1971; 92m.

BROTHERLY LOVE ★★★½
DIR: Jeff Bleckner. **CAST:** Judd Hirsch, Karen Carlson, George Dzundza, Barry Primus, Lori Lethin, Josef Sommer.
A revenge melodrama. Judd Hirsch plays twin brothers; one a respectable businessman, the other a sociopath. When the latter is released from a mental ward, he vows to ruin his brother. This TV movie is not rated, but contains some violence. 1985; 94m.

BRUTE MAN, THE ★½
DIR: Jean Yarbrough. **CAST:** Tom Neal, Rondo Hatton, Jane Adams.
A homicidal maniac escapes from an asylum. Unmemorable, standard B-movie stuff, notable mainly as a showcase for actor Rondo Hatton. Hatton appeared in several low-budget thrillers in the 1940s, usually as a menacing thug. *The Brute Man* was Hatton's last film. He died in the year of its release, at the age of 42. 1946; B&W; 60m.

BUG ★★½
DIR: Jeannot Szwarc. **CAST:** Bradford Dillman, Joanna Miles, Richard Gilliland.
Weird horror film with the world, led by Bradford Dillman, staving off masses of giant mutant beetles with the ability to commit arson, setting fire to every living thing they can find. Rated PG for violence. 1975; 100m.

BULLIES ★
DIR: Paul Lynch. **CAST:** Jonathon Crombie, Janet Laine Green, Olivia D'Abo.
A frustrating film about a family who moves to a small town that happens to be run by a murderous family of moonshiners. Although not badly acted, the brutality portrayed in this film makes it hard to sit through. Rated R for graphic violence and profanity. 1985; 96m.

BURIAL GROUND
DIR: Andrea Bianchi. **CAST:** Karin Well, Gian Luigi Chirizzi, Simone Mattioli.
A scientist's study inadvertently unearths the burial place of the living dead. He becomes one of them. Awful. Not rated, it contains nudity and extreme violence. 1979; 85m.

BURNING, THE
DIR: Tony Maylam. **CAST:** Brian Matthews, Leah Ayres, Brian Backer.
This tedious film is just one more stab at the horror genre that trades surprises and suspense for buckets of blood and severed limbs. Similar to many other blood feasts of late, it's the story of a summer camp custodian who, savagely burned as a result of a teenage prank, comes back years later for revenge. Rated R. 1981; 90m.

BURNT OFFERINGS ★½
DIR: Dan Curtis. **CAST:** Oliver Reed, Karen Black, Burgess Meredith, Bette Davis, Lee Montgomery, Eileen Heckart.
Good acting cannot save this predictable horror film concerning a haunted house. More of a made-for-television type of film than a true motion picture. Rated PG. 1976; 115m.

CALL ME ★½
DIR: Sollace Mitchell. **CAST:** Patricia Charbonneau, Patti D'Arbanville, Sam Freed, Boyd Gaines, Stephen McHattie, Steve Buscemi.

In this silly suspense thriller, a New York newspaper columnist (Patricia Charbonneau) mistakenly believes an obscene phone caller to be her boyfriend and soon finds herself involved with murder and mobsters. Rated R for violence, profanity, nudity, and simulated sex. 1988; 96m.

CAMERON'S CLOSET ★★★
DIR: Armand Mastroianni. **CAST:** Cotter Smith, Mel Harris, Tab Hunter, Chuck McCann, Leight McCloskey.
A young boy with psychic powers unwittingly unleashes a demon in his closet. The above-par special effects, by Oscar winner Carlo Rambaldi, (*E.T.* and *Alien*), and an ever-growing tension makes this a neat little supernatural thriller. Not rated, but contains violence. 1989; 90m.

CAMPUS CORPSE, THE ★
DIR: Douglas Curtis. **CAST:** Jeff East, Brad Davis, Charles Martin Smith.
College fraternity hazing gets out of hand when a pledge is accidentally killed. The story is contrived and the acting is amateurish at best. In addition, the overall look of the film is cheap and uninspired. Rated PG for mild violence and language. 1977; 92m.

CANDLES AT NINE ★★
DIR: John Harlow. **CAST:** Jessie Matthews, John Stuart, Beatrix Lehmann.
Old-dark-house mystery about a young woman who inherits a fortune from a great-uncle she hardly knew, with the stipulation that she has to spend a month living in his gloomy mansion. This gives his other relatives a chance to try to relieve her of some of the money, with tactics that range from devious to deadly. Musical star Jessie Matthews was the draw for this British film that is competently made but unexceptional. 1944; B&W; 84m.

CAPE FEAR ★★★★
DIR: J. Lee Thompson. **CAST:** Gregory Peck, Polly Bergen, Robert Mitchum, Lori Martin, Martin Balsam, Telly Savalas, Jack Kruschen.
Great cast in a riveting tale of a lawyer (Gregory Peck) and his family menaced by a vengeful ex-con (Robert Mitchum), who Peck helped to send up the river eight years earlier. Now he's out, with big plans for Peck's wife and especially his daughter. 1962; B&W; 106m.

CAPTAIN KRONOS: VAMPIRE HUNTER ★★★½
DIR: Brian Clemens. **CAST:** Horst Janson, John David Carson, Caroline Munro, Shane Briant.
British film directed by the producer of *The Avengers* television show. It's an unconventional horror tale about a sword-wielding vampire killer. An interesting mix of genres. Good adventure, with high production values. Rated PG for violence. 1974; 91m.

CARNIVAL OF BLOOD 🦃
DIR: Leonard Kirman. **CAST:** Earle Edgerton, Judith Resnick, Burt Young.
Boring horror mystery about a series of murders committed at New York's Coney Island. Way too much time is taken up with people sitting around talking; given the liveliness of the Coney Island area, couldn't they at least have had the characters walking the streets and talking? Noteworthy only as the debut of Burt Young, this was made in 1971 but not released until 1976, presumably to cash in on Young's success in *Rocky*. 1976; 87m.

CARNIVAL OF SOULS ★★★½
DIR: Herk Harvey. **CAST:** Candace Hilligoss, Sidney Berger.
Creepy film made on shoestring budget in Lawrence, Kansas, concerns a girl who, after a near-fatal car crash, is haunted by a ghoulish, zombielike character. Extremely eerie, with nightmarish photography, this little-known gem has a way of getting to you. Better keep the lights on. 1962; B&W; 80m.

CARPATHIAN EAGLE ★★
DIR: Francis Meahy. **CAST:** Anthony Valentine, Suzanne Danielle, Sian Phillips.

Murdered men begin popping up with their hearts cut out. A police detective scours the town and racks his brain looking for the killer, not realizing how close he is. What all this has to do with the title is never resolved in this addition to Elvira's Thriller Video. 1982; 60m.

CARRIE ★★★★½
DIR: Brian De Palma. **CAST:** Sissy Spacek, Piper Laurie, John Travolta, Nancy Allen, Amy Irving.

Carrie is the ultimate revenge tale for anyone who remembers high school as a time of rejection and ridicule. The story follows the strange life of Carrie White (Sissy Spacek), a student severely humiliated by her classmates and stifled by the Puritan beliefs of her mother (Piper Laurie), a religious fanatic. Rated R for nudity, violence, and profanity. 1976; 97m.

CARRIER ★
DIR: Nathan J. White. **CAST:** Gregory Fortescue, Steve Dixon.

Small-town teenage outcast suddenly becomes a carrier of an unknown disease that consumes living organisms on contact. A sudden storm isolates the community, leading to mass hysteria and paranoia. Innoculate yourself against this dud. Rated R for violence, profanity, and adult situations. 1987; 99m.

CARS THAT EAT PEOPLE (THE CARS THAT ATE PARIS) ★★★
DIR: Peter Weir. **CAST:** John Meillon, Terry Camilleri, Kevin Miles.

Peter Weir began with this weird black comedy/horror film about an Outback Australian town where motorists and their cars are trapped each night. Rated PG. 1975; 90m.

CASSANDRA
DIR: Colin Eggleston. **CAST:** Tessa Humphries, Shane Briant.

Lifeless psychic thriller about an Australian woman plagued by a nightmare of her mother's gruesome suicide. Suddenly, the nightmares depict the brutal slayings of friends and family members. Rated R for violence and nudity. 1987; 94m.

CASTLE OF EVIL
DIR: Francis D. Lyon. **CAST:** Virginia Mayo, Scott Brady, David Brian, Hugh Marlowe.

Take an electronic humanoid, a dead scientist, some faulty wiring, what appears to be a good cast, and throw them together with a budget that must have run into the tens of dollars and you get this terrible, clumsy, uninteresting, pathetic suspense movie. 1966; 81m.

CASTLE OF FU MANCHU
DIR: Jess (Jesus) Franco. **CAST:** Christopher Lee, Richard Greene, Maria Perschy.

The exotic location is Istanbul. The evil character is Fu Manchu (Christopher Lee). The budget is nonexistent. The result is the worst Fu Manchu film ever made. 1968; 92m.

CASTLE OF THE LIVING DEAD ★★
DIR: Herbert Wise. **CAST:** Christopher Lee, Gaia Germani, Philippe Leroy, Donald Sutherland.

A French-Italian horror film about a troupe of performers who perform at a castle owned by the crazed Count Drago. Drago's atrocities include murder, freezing people by injection, and wearing too much eye makeup. Another atmospheric but slow-moving thriller made by Christopher Lee between his Dracula films at Hammer Studios. 1964; B&W; 90m.

CASTLE OF THE WALKING DEAD ★★½
DIR: Herbert Wise. **CAST:** Christopher Lee, Philippe Leroy, Donald Sutherland.

What makes this otherwise run-of-the-mill horror yarn worth watching are some impressive scenes toward the end. They were added by Michael Reeves, a young Englishman who directed several powerful horror films before his suicide. Christopher Lee plays a count who preserves people with an embalming formula. Donald Sutherland, in his film debut, plays two parts, including an old witch woman! 1964; B&W; 90m.

CAT AND THE CANARY, THE (1978) ★★★½
DIR: Radley Metzger. **CAST:** Honor Blackman, Michael Callan, Edward Fox, Wendy Hiller, Carol Lynley, Olivia Hussey.
This is a surprisingly entertaining remake of the 1927 period thriller about a group of people trapped in a British mansion and murdered one by one. Rated PG. 1978; 90m.

CAT PEOPLE (1942) ★★★★
DIR: Jacques Tourneur. **CAST:** Simone Simon, Kent Smith, Tom Conway.
Simone Simon, Kent Smith, and Tom Conway are excellent in this movie about a shy woman (Simon) who believes she carries the curse of the panther. Jacques Tourneur knew the imagination was stronger and more impressive than anything filmmakers could show visually and played on it with impressive results. 1942; B&W; 73m.

CAT PEOPLE (1982) ★
DIR: Paul Schrader. **CAST:** Nastassja Kinski, Malcolm McDowell, John Heard, Annette O'Toole, Ed Begley Jr., Ruby Dee, Scott Paulin.
While technically a well-made film, *Cat People* spares the viewer nothing—incest, bondage, bestiality—for no worthy purpose. It makes one yearn for the films of yesteryear, which achieved horror through implication. Rated R for nudity, profanity, and gore. 1982; 118m.

CATAMOUNT KILLING, THE ★
DIR: Krzysztof Zanussi. **CAST:** Horst Buchholz, Ann Wedgeworth, Polly Holliday.
Choppy and clichéd film about the perfect crime gone sour. A bank manager is transferred to the sticks (the town is aptly named Pittsville). Desperate to escape from tedium, the newcomer decides to run off with the bank deposits, paving the way for murder and violence. Dull, nevertheless. 1985; 82m.

CATHY'S CURSE ★
DIR: Eddy Matalon. **CAST:** Alan Scarfe, Randi Allen.
Drive-in screens in the late 1970s saw an unending wave of cheap ripoffs of *The Exorcist*, and this is one of the duller ones. When a young girl moves with her parents into the old family house, she is possessed by the spirit of her aunt, who died in an automobile accident as a child. Nothing new or interesting here, unless you crave snowy Canadian landscapes. 1976; 90m.

CAT'S EYE ★★★½
DIR: Lewis Teague. **CAST:** James Woods, Robert Hays, Kenneth McMillan, Drew Barrymore, Candy Clark, Alan King.
Writer Stephen King and director Lewis Teague, who brought us *Cujo*, reteam for this even better horror release: a trilogy of terror in the much-missed *Night Gallery* anthology style. It's good, old-fashioned, tell-me-a-scary-story fun. Rated PG-13 for violence and gruesome scenes. 1985; 98m.

CAULDRON OF BLOOD ★
DIR: Edward Mann (Santos Alocer). **CAST:** Boris Karloff, Viveca Lindfors, Jean-Pierre Aumont.
One of several films Boris Karloff made outside the U.S. shortly before his death, this is far from one of his best. Boris plays a blind sculptor who uses the skeletons of women his wife has murdered as the foundations for his projects. 1968; 95m.

CAVE OF THE LIVING DEAD ★
DIR: Akos von Ratony. **CAST:** Adrian Hoven, Karin Field, Erika Remberg, Wolfgang Preiss, John Kitzmiller.
This is a boring West German–Yugoslavian spooker that was only released in America with its present title in the late 1960s to cash in on the success of

George Romero's *Night of the Living Dead.* An Interpol inspector and a witch join forces to locate some missing girls. Their search leads them to an old castle where a mad doctor-vampire has turned the girls into zombies. 1964; 89m.

CELLAR DWELLER ★
DIR: John Carl Buechler. **CAST:** Deborah Mullowney, Vince Edwards, Yvonne De Carlo.
Typical junk about a hideous, satanic monster called up by comic-book artists to wreak havoc on the main characters. The film looks like it was lit and directed as a TV sitcom, and one set was used throughout. Low budget, and it shows. Not rated, but contains violence. 1987; 78m.

CHAMBER OF FEAR
DIR: Juan Ibanez, Jack Hill. **CAST:** Boris Karloff.
Another of the Mexican films featuring footage of Boris Karloff shot in Los Angeles just before his death (see *Sinister Invasion*). He plays a scientist who dies early on in the movie. His assistants continue his work with a living rock that requires the blood of living women. The story is about as vague as it sounds. 1968; 87m.

CHAMBER OF HORRORS ★★½
DIR: Hy Averback. **CAST:** Patrick O'Neal, Cesare Danova, Wilfrid Hyde-White, Suzy Parker, Tony Curtis, Jeanette Nolan.
A mad killer stalks 1880s Baltimore. Two wax museum owners attempt to bring him to justice. Originally produced as a television pilot titled House of Wax, but it was considered too violent. Tame and silly. 1966; 99m.

CHANGELING, THE ★★★★
DIR: Peter Medak. **CAST:** George C. Scott, Trish Van Devere, Melvyn Douglas, Jean Marsh, Barry Morse.
This ghost story is blessed with everything a good thriller needs: a suspenseful story, excellent performances by a top-name cast, and well-paced solid direction by Peter Medak. The story centers around a composer whose wife and daughter are killed in a tragic auto accident. Rated R. 1979; 109m.

CHARLIE BOY
DIR: Robert Young. **CAST:** Leigh Lawson, Angela Bruce.
Charlie Boy is an African fetish, inherited by a young British couple, that will take care of all your problems—usually by killing them. Unfortunately, the couple curses themselves and races to destroy the fetish and break the curse. It sounds interesting enough, but poor acting and bad direction hamper what could have been a worthwhile film. 1982; 60m.

CHEERLEADER CAMP
DIR: John Quinn. **CAST:** Betsy Russell, Leif Garrett, Lucinda Dickey.
Another dumb teenage slasher flick, this time set at a resort for cheerleaders. Youngsters gather to train and polish their favorite cheer routines for a national competition, not realizing they're going to be eliminated permanently. Give me an *A*; give me a *V*; give me an *O*; give me an *I*; give me a *D. Avoid, avoid, avoid.* Rated R for nudity and violence. 1987; 89m.

CHILDREN, THE
DIR: Max Calmanowicz. **CAST:** Martin Shaker, Gil Rogers, Gale Garnett.
This is really a terrible film about kids marked by a radioactive accident while they were on a school bus. This picture should be avoided. Rated R. 1980; 89m.

CHILDREN OF THE CORN
DIR: Fritz Kiersch. **CAST:** Peter Horton, Linda Hamilton, R. G. Armstrong, John Franklin.
Yet another adaptation of a Stephen King horror story. This time, it's a total mess. Peter Horton and Linda Hamilton play a young couple who come to a Midwestern farming town where a young preacher with mesmerizing powers has instructed all the children to slaughter adults in order to appease a satanic demon. Rated R for violence and profanity. 1984; 93m.

CHILDREN OF THE FULL MOON
DIR: Tom Clegg. **CAST:** Christopher Cazenove, Celia Gregory, Diana Dors.
Even the curvaceous horror hostess Elvira and her off brand of humor can't salvage this cross between *Rosemary's Baby* and *The Wolfman.* Fans of truly bad films won't want to waste their time on this one. 1982; 60m.

CHILDREN SHOULDN'T PLAY WITH DEAD THINGS ★
DIR: Bob Clark. **CAST:** Alan Ormsby, Anya Ormsby, Jeffrey Gillen.
Typical "evil dead" entry; amateur filmmakers work in a spooky graveyard and make enough noise to, well, wake the dead. Poor, washed-out cinematography and an all-but-unintelligible soundtrack make this more trouble than it's worth. Rated PG for violence. 1972; 85m.

CHILD'S PLAY ★★½
DIR: Tom Holland. **CAST:** Catharine Hicks, Chris Sarandon, Brad Dourif.
Hokey, violent horror film finds a dying criminal putting his soul into a doll. When a mother buys the doll for her son's birthday, predictable mayhem occurs. Good special effects and some humorous dialogue keep this one from becoming routine. Rated R. 1988; 87m.

CHOPPING MALL ★★½
DIR: Jim Wynorski. **CAST:** Kelli Maroney, Tony O'Dell, John Terlesky, Russell Todd.
A group of teenagers hold the ultimate office party at the store in which they work in the local shopping mall. At midnight it is impenetrably sealed and security droids, armed with high-tech weaponry, go on patrol, incapacitating any unauthorized personnel. This film has a good sense of humor and good visual effects. Rated R for nudity, profanity, and violence. 1986; 77m.

CHRISTINE ★★★½
DIR: John Carpenter. **CAST:** Keith Gordon, John Stockwell, Alexandra Paul, Harry Dean Stanton, Robert Prosky, Christine Belford, Roberts Blossom.
Novelist Stephen King and director John Carpenter team up for top-flight, tasteful terror with this movie about a 1958 Plymouth Fury with spooky powers. It's scary without being gory; a triumph of suspense and atmosphere. Rated R for profanity and violence. 1983; 111m.

CHRISTMAS EVIL ★½
DIR: Lewis Jackson. **CAST:** Brandon Maggart, Jeffrey DeMunn.
This film about a toy factory employee who goes slowly insane has some great black comedy moments but not enough to save the rest of the boring narrative from putting the viewer to sleep. Not rated, but the equivalent of an R rating for sex and violence. 1983; 91m.

C.H.U.D. ★
DIR: Douglas Cheek. **CAST:** John Heard, Daniel Stern, Christopher Curry.
The performances by John Heard and Daniel Stern are all that make this cheapo horror film even barely watchable. C.H.U.D. (Cannibalistic Humanoid Underground Dwellers) are New York City bag people who have been exposed to large doses of radiation and start treating the other inhabitants of the city as lunch. Rated R for violence, profanity, and gore. 1984; 88m.

CIRCUS OF HORRORS ★★★
DIR: Sidney Hayers. **CAST:** Anton Diffring, Erika Remberg, Yvonne Romain, Donald Pleasence.
British thriller about a renegade plastic surgeon using a circus as a front. After making female criminals gorgeous, he enslaves them in his Temple of Beauty. When they want out, he colorfully offs them. Well made with good performances. This is the more violent European version. 1960; 87m.

CITY IN PANIC
DIR: Robert Bouvier. **CAST:** Dave Adamson.
A brutal killer stalks the city streets, murdering homosexuals. A controversial radio talk-show host helps the police lure the killer out into the open. Poor acting and ultragross murders place this movie in the halls of bad taste. Not rated, but contains nudity and graphic violence. 1987; 85m.

CITY OF THE WALKING DEAD ★½
DIR: Umberto Lenzi. **CAST:** Hugo Stiglitz, Laura Trotter, Francisco Rabal, Mel Ferrer.
Yet another Italian *Dawn of the Dead* ripoff, this one has a strong opening and then goes to sleep. A radiation leak at an atomic power plant turns people into monsters who must drink the blood of the living to stay alive. The ending is particularly infuriating. Originally released as *Nightmare City*. Rated R. 1980; 92m.

CLASS OF 1984 ★★½
DIR: Mark L. Lester. **CAST:** Perry King, Merrie Lynn Ross, Roddy McDowall, Timothy Van Patten.
Violent punkers run a school, forcing teachers to arm and security to be hired. A new teacher arrives and tries to change things, but he's beaten, and his pregnant wife is raped. He takes revenge by killing all the punkers. Rated R for violence. 1982; 93m.

CLASS OF NUKE 'EM HIGH
DIR: Richard W. Haines, Samuel Weil. **CAST:** Janelle Brady, Gilbert Brenton.
The makers of *The Toxic Avenger* strike again in this poor black comedy–monster movie. A sloppily managed nuclear power plant is located next door to a high school and begins to have harmful radioactive effects on the students. Rated R for nudity, profanity, and graphic violence. 1987; 84m.

CLOWN MURDERS, THE ★
DIR: Martyn Burke. **CAST:** Stephen Young, John Candy, Lawrence Dane, Al Waxman.
Nothing funny or interesting in this confusing mess about four friends attempting to stage a Halloween prank. John Candy appears in a straight dramatic role. Be warned: This is not a comedy—or anything else. Not rated, but equivalent to an R for violence, profanity, and nudity. 1975; 94m.

COLLECTOR, THE ★★★★½
DIR: William Wyler. **CAST:** Terence Stamp, Samantha Eggar, Maurice Dallimore, Mona Washbourne.
In this chiller, Terence Stamp plays a disturbed young man who, having no friends, collects things. Unfortunately, one of the things he collects is beautiful Samantha Eggar. He keeps her as his prisoner and waits for her to fall in love with him. Extremely interesting profile of a madman. 1965; 119m.

COLOR ME BLOOD RED
DIR: Herschell Gordon Lewis. **CAST:** Don Joseph.
An artist discovers the perfect shade of red for his paintings. (Take a guess.) Another low-budget gore film from the people who brought you *Blood Feast*. Everything about this movie is absolutely awful. Unrated, the film has violence. 1965; 70m.

COMA ★★★½
DIR: Michael Crichton. **CAST:** Genevieve Bujold, Michael Douglas, Richard Widmark, Rip Torn.
A doctor (Genevieve Bujold) becomes curious about several deaths at a hospital where patients have all lapsed into comas. Very original melodrama keeps the audience guessing. One of Michael Crichton's better film efforts. Rated PG for brief nudity and violence. 1978; 113m.

COMING OUT ALIVE ★★★
DIR: Don McBrearty. **CAST:** Helen Shaver, Scott Hylands, Michael Ironside, Anne Ditchburn, Monica Parker.

Enjoyable suspense chiller involving one mother's search for her child after he's abducted by her estranged husband. Scott Hylands is wonderful in his role as a soldier-for-hire who helps her out. 1984; 77m.

COMING SOON ★★★½
DIR: John Landis. **CAST:** Jamie Lee Curtis.

A compilation of scenes and trailers from Universal Studio's most famous and infamous horror and suspense films. There's also some behind-the-scenes interviews and production clips. A must for anyone who loves going to the movies and seeing those coming attractions. Not rated, but suitable for all audiences. 1983; 55m.

CONQUEROR WORM, THE ★★★
DIR: Michael Reeves. **CAST:** Vincent Price, Ian Ogilvy, Hilary Dwyer.

In this graphic delineation of witch-hunting in England during the Cromwell period, Vincent Price gives a sterling performance as Matthew Hopkins, a self-possessed and totally convincing witch finder. The production values are very good considering the small budget. A must-see for thriller fans. 1968; 88m.

CONTAGION ★★
DIR: Karl Zwicky. **CAST:** John Doyle, Nicola Bartlett.

When a traveling salesman is trapped in a rural mansion for a night, he comes under the influence of its reclusive owner, who offers him riches and sexual pleasures in exchange for his complete obedience. First, he must prove himself worthy by committing a murder. Rambling, unsatisfying thriller. Not rated. 1988; 90m.

CORPSE GRINDERS, THE ★
DIR: Ted V. Mikels. **CAST:** Sean Kenney, Monika Kelly.

This silly horror comedy about two cat-food makers who use human corpses in their secret recipe has a cult reputation as one of those so-bad-it's-good movies. Really, though, it's just boring. Even the corpse-grinding machine itself, a cardboard box with some flashing lights, seems perfectly at home in the cheapo surroundings. Rated R, but pretty tame by 1980s standards. 1972; 72m.

CORPSE VANISHES, THE ★
DIR: Wallace Fox. **CAST:** Bela Lugosi, Luana Walters, Tristram Coffin, Minerva Urecal, Elizabeth Russell.

Hokey pseudoscientific thriller about crazed scientist Bela Lugosi and his efforts to keep his elderly wife young through transfusions from young girls. Another cheap quickie. 1942; B&W; 64m.

CORRIDORS OF BLOOD ★★★
DIR: Robert Day. **CAST:** Boris Karloff, Francis Matthews, Adrienne Corri, Betta St. John, Nigel Green, Christopher Lee.

Kindly surgeon (Boris Karloff) in nineteeth-century London tries to perfect anesthesia and becomes addicted to narcotics. In a mental fog, he is blackmailed by grave robbers. A suprisingly effective thriller originally withheld from release in the United States for five years. 1957; 86m.

COSMIC MONSTERS, THE ★★
DIR: Gilbert Gunn. **CAST:** Forrest Tucker, Gaby André.

Low-budget horror from Great Britain. Giant carnivorous insects invade our planet. An alien in a flying saucer arrives to save the day. The effects are cheap but the English accents do give the picture a partial dignity. 1958; B&W; 75m.

COUNT DRACULA ★★½
DIR: Jess (Jesus) Franco. **CAST:** Christopher Lee, Herbert Lom, Klaus Kinski.

Christopher Lee dons the cape once again in this mediocre version of the famous tale about the undead fiend terrorizing the countryside. Rated R. 1970; 98m.

COUNT YORGA, VAMPIRE ★★★
DIR: Bob Kelljan. **CAST:** Robert Quarry, Roger Perry, Donna Anders, Michael Murphy.

Contemporary vampire terrorizes Los Angeles. Somewhat dated, but a sharp and powerful thriller. Stars Robert Quarry, an intense, dignified actor who appeared in several horror films in the early 1970s, then abruptly left the genre. Rated R for violence. 1970; 91m.

CRATER LAKE MONSTER, THE ★
DIR: William R. Stromberg. **CAST:** Richard Cardella, Glenn Roberts.
Inexpensive, unimpressive film about a prehistoric creature emerging from the usually quiet lake of the title and raising hell. Rated PG. 1977; 89m.

CRAVING, THE ★½
DIR: Jack Molina. **CAST:** Paul Naschy.
A witch burned at the stake hundreds of years ago comes back to life and resurrects her werewolf henchman to do her dirty work. This Italian-made film loses something in the translation. Only fans of truly bad films will enjoy this. Rated R for violence and nudity. 1980; 93m.

CRAWLING EYE, THE ★★★
DIR: Quentin Lawrence. **CAST:** Forrest Tucker, Janet Munro.
Acceptable horror thriller about an unseen menace hiding within the dense fog surrounding a mountaintop. A nice sense of doom builds throughout, and the monster remains unseen (always the best way) until the very end. 1958; B&W; 85m.

CRAWLING HAND, THE ★
DIR: Herbert L. Strock. **CAST:** Peter Breck, Rod Lauren, Kent Taylor.
Low-budget tale of a dismembered hand at large in a small town, killing off the local residents in a psychotic reign of terror. Goofy film really is as dumb as it sounds. 1963; B&W; 89m.

CRAWLSPACE
DIR: David Schmoeller. **CAST:** Klaus Kinski, Talia Balsam.
Terrible imitation of the classic *Peeping Tom*, with Klaus Kinski as a sadistic landlord who engages in murder and voyeurism while using the building's crawl space in pursuing his female tenants. Kinski fans may find his pathological performance amusing, but the film is an exercise in stupidity. Rated R. 1986; 82m.

CRAZED
DIR: Richard Cassidy. **CAST:** Laslo Papas, Belle Mitchell, Beverly Ross.
A demented man living in a boardinghouse becomes obsessed with a young woman. This obsession turns to murder, and he finds he must kill to keep his dark secret safe. Slow-moving and without a lick of suspense, this film is better than a sleeping pill. Not rated, but contains violence and profanity. 1984; 88m.

CRAZIES, THE ★★
DIR: George A. Romero. **CAST:** Lane Carroll, W. G. McMillan, Lynn Lowry, Richard Liberty.
A military plane carrying an experimental germ warfare virus crashes near a small midwestern town, releasing a plague of murderous madness. George Romero attempts to make a statement about martial law while trying to capitalize on the success of his cult classic, *Night of the Living Dead*. Rated R. 1975; 103m.

CRAZY FAT ETHEL II
DIR: Nick Phillips. **CAST:** Priscilla Alden, Michael Flood.
Schlocky, sophomoric attempt at a slasher film with Priscilla Alden in the title role as an obese lunatic released from an asylum and terrorizing a halfway house. Not rated, but contains (ridiculous) violence. The same cast and crew also assembled for another gobbler: *Death Nurse*. 1987; 70m.

CREATURE FROM BLACK LAKE ★★
DIR: Joy N. Houck Jr. **CAST:** Jack Elam, Dub Taylor, Dennis Fimple, John David Carson.
This is another forgettable, cliché-ridden horror film. Dennis Fimple and John David Carson play two college students who go to the swamps of Louisiana in search of the missing link. Through the reluctant help of the

locals, they come face to face with a man in an ape suit. Rated PG. 1979; 97m.

CREATURE FROM THE BLACK LAGOON ★★★½

DIR: Jack Arnold. **CAST:** Richard Carlson, Julie Adams, Richard Denning, Nestor Paiva, Antonio Moreno, Whit Bissell.

In the remote backwaters of the Amazon, members of a scientific expedition run afoul of a vicious prehistoric man-fish inhabiting the area and are forced to fight for their lives. Excellent film (first in a trilogy) features true-to-life performances, a bone-chilling score by Joseph Gershenson, and beautiful, lush photography that unfortunately turns to mud in the murky 3-D video print. 1954; 79m.

CREEPERS ★★

DIR: Dario Argento. **CAST:** Jennifer Connelly, Donald Pleasence, Daria Nicolodi, Dalila Di Lazzaro.

Plodding Italian production casts Jennifer Connelly as a young girl with the ability to communicate with, and control, insects. This unique power comes into play when she must use her little friends to track down the maniac who's been murdering students at the Swiss girls' school she's attending, as bugs are attracted to rotting corpses. Rated R for gore. 1985; 82m.

CREEPING FLESH, THE ★★★

DIR: Freddie Francis. **CAST:** Peter Cushing, Christopher Lee, Lorna Heilbron.

Peter Cushing and Christopher Lee are top-notch, in this creepy tale about an evil entity accidentally brought back to life by an unsuspecting scientist. While not as good as the stars' Hammer Films collaborations this will still prove pleasing to their fans. Rated PG. 1972; 91m.

CREEPOZOIDS

DIR: David DeCoteau. **CAST:** Linnea Quigley, Ken Abraham.

A post-apocalyptic sci-fi–horror yarn about military deserters who find an abandoned science lab that has a bloodthirsty monster wandering in the halls. With its poor special effects and lousy acting, this film is a waste of time. Rated R for violence, nudity, and profanity. 1987; 72m.

CREEPSHOW ★★★★

DIR: George A. Romero. **CAST:** Hal Holbrook, Adrienne Barbeau, Fritz Weaver, Leslie Nielsen, Stephen King.

Stephen King, the modern master of printed terror, and George Romero, the director who frightened unsuspecting moviegoers out of their wits with *Night of the Living Dead*, teamed for this funny and scary tribute to the E.C. horror comics of the 1950s. Like *Vault of Horror* and *Tales from the Crypt*, two titles from that period, it's an anthology of ghoulish bedtime stories. Rated R for profanity and gore. 1982; 120m.

CREEPSHOW 2 ★★

DIR: Michael Gornick. **CAST:** Lois Chiles, George Kennedy, Dorothy Lamour.

Three tales of horror and terror based on short stories by Stephen King and a screenplay by George Romero should have turned out a lot better than this. "Ode to Chief Wooden Head" stars George Kennedy and Dorothy Lamour as senior citizens in a slowly dying desert town. "The Raft" concerns four friends whose vacation at a secluded lake turns into a nightmare. "The Hitchhiker" features Lois Chiles as a hit-and-run driver. Rated R for nudity, violence, and profanity. 1987; 92m.

CRIMINAL LAW ★★½

DIR: Martin Campbell. **CAST:** Gary Oldman, Kevin Bacon, Karen Young, Tess Harper, Joe Don Baker.

Gary Oldman gives a strong performance in this suspense thriller as an attorney who successfully defends accused killer Kevin Bacon. It is only after proving his client's innocence by discrediting eyewitnesses that Oldman discovers Bacon is guilty—and intends to kill again. At first, the film bristles with tension and intelligence, yet it goes on to become predictable and ludicrous. Rated R for violence, simulated sex, and profanity. 1989; 112m.

CRITTERS ★★★½
DIR: Stephen Hereck. **CAST:** Dee Wallace, M. Emmet Walsh, Scott Grimes, Don Opper, Terrence Mann.
This mild horror film with its hilarious spots could become a cult classic. In it, eight ravenous critters escape from a distant planet and head for earth. Two futuristic bounty hunters pursue them, and the fun begins. Rated PG for gore and profanity. 1986; 90m.

CRITTERS 2: THE MAIN COURSE ★★
DIR: Mick Garris. **CAST:** Scott Grimes, Liane Curtis, Don Opper, Barry Corbin, Terrence Mann.
The charm begins to wear thin in this sequel to the 1986 original. *Critters 2: The Main Course* takes off where the first one ended, but dwells too much on a dopey subplot. Rated PG-13 for violence and profanity. 1987; 87m.

CROCODILE
DIR: Sompote Sands. **CAST:** Nat Puvanai.
An island paradise is turned into a hellhole by a giant crocodile. Poorly dubbed and badly edited, the film is almost incomprehensible at times. Not rated, but contains profanity and violence. 1981; 95m.

CRUCIBLE OF HORROR ★★★½
DIR: Viktors Ritelis. **CAST:** Michael Gough, Yvonne Mitchell.
Intense story of a violent, domineering man (Michael Gough in one of his better roles) who drives his passive wife and nubile daughter to murder. The suspense and terror build unrelentingly. Keep the lights on! Rated R. 1971; 91m.

CRUISE INTO TERROR ★
DIR: Bruce Kessler. **CAST:** Dirk Benedict, John Forsythe, Lynda Day George, Christopher George, Stella Stevens, Ray Milland, Frank Converse, Lee Meriwether, Hugh O'Brian.
Dreadful suspense flick made for the tube. When a band of TV old-timers assemble on one boat for a cruise, you know something dull is going to take place. This one is about an ancient Egyptian sarcophagus that is haunting the small ocean liner and the poor souls on board. 1977; 100m.

CRY OF THE BANSHEE ★★
DIR: Gordon Hessler. **CAST:** Vincent Price, Elisabeth Bergner, Hugh Griffith.
Uninspired film casts Vincent Price as a witch-hunting magistrate whose family is threatened when a curse is placed upon his house by practitioners of the old religion. Price fared much better in the similar *The Conqueror Worm*. Rated R for violence and nudity. 1970; 87m.

CUJO ★★★½
DIR: Lewis Teague. **CAST:** Dee Wallace, Danny Pintauro, Daniel Hugh-Kelly, Christopher Stone.
Stephen King's story of a mother and son terrorized by a rabid Saint Bernard results in a movie that keeps viewers on the edge of their seats. Rated R for violence, language. 1983; 91m.

CURSE, THE
DIR: David Keith. **CAST:** Wil Wheaton, John Schneider, Claude Akins.
A meteor crashes and infects the water of a small town with alien parasites, which, once consumed, do gruesome things to human bodies. A TVA troubleshooter and his boy sidekick crusade to rid the community of these monstrosities. Rated R for violence. 1987; 92m.

CURSE OF FRANKENSTEIN, THE ★★★½
DIR: Terence Fisher. **CAST:** Peter Cushing, Christopher Lee, Robert Urquhart.
Hammer Films' version of the Frankenstein story about a scientist who

creates a living man from the limbs and organs of corpses. Peter Cushing gives a strong performance as the doctor, with Christopher Lee his equal as the sympathetic creature. Some inspired moments are peppered throughout this well-handled tale. 1957; 83m.

CURSE OF KING TUT'S TOMB, THE ★½

DIR: Philip Leacock. **CAST:** Eva Marie Saint, Robin Ellis, Raymond Burr, Harry Andrews, Tom Baker.

Made-for-TV misfire concerning the mysterious events surrounding the opening of King Tut's tomb. Dumb film made even more ridiculous by Paul Scofield's uninspired narration. Close the lid and bury this one. 1980; 100m.

CURSE OF THE BLUE LIGHTS 🦃

DIR: John H. Johnson. **CAST:** Brent Ritter.

Abysmal horror film about a group of teenagers who must find a way to escape from an underground world populated by demons and ruled by the flesh-eating Muldoon Man. This one's so awful the actors appear to be reading—badly—their lines off cue cards. Unrated, but gory enough for an R rating. 1989; 96m.

CURSE OF THE CAT PEOPLE, THE ★★★

DIR: Gunther Von Fristch, Robert Wise. **CAST:** Simone Simon, Kent Smith, Jane Randolph, Elizabeth Russell.

When Val Lewton was ordered by the studio to make a sequel to the successful *Cat People*, he came up with this gentle fantasy about a child who is haunted by spirits. Not to be confused with the 1980s version of *Cat People*. 1944; B&W; 70m.

CURSE OF THE DEMON ★★★★½

DIR: Jacques Tourneur. **CAST:** Dana Andrews, Peggy Cummins, Niall MacGinnis, Maurice Denham.

Horrifying tale of an American occult expert, Dr. Holden (Dana Andrews), traveling to London to expose a supposed devil cult led by sinister Professor Karswell (Niall MacGinnis). Unfortunately for Holden, Karswell's cult proves to be all too real as a demon from hell is dispatched by the professor to put an end to the annoying investigation. Riveting production is a true classic of the genre. 1958; B&W; 96m.

CURSE OF THE WEREWOLF, THE ★★★½

DIR: Terence Fisher. **CAST:** Oliver Reed, Clifford Evans, Yvonne Romain, Anthony Dawson.

After being brutally raped in a castle dungeon by an imprisoned street beggar, a young woman gives birth to a son with a strange appetite for blood. His heritage remains a mystery until adulthood, whereupon he begins transforming into a wolf as the full moon rises. Oliver Reed is fine in the role of the werewolf, one of his earliest screen performances. 1961; 91m.

CURTAINS ★

DIR: Jonathan Stryker. **CAST:** John Vernon, Samantha Eggar, Linda Thorson, Anne Ditchburn.

Samantha Eggar stars in this mediocre splatter flick as a movie actress who gets herself committed to a mental institution as preparation for an upcoming film. However, she is left in the funny farm while the movie goes on without her. She escapes, and, one by one, the actresses trying out for her role are murdered. Rated R for nudity, profanity, violence, and sex. 1983; 89m.

CYCLOPS, THE ★★½

DIR: Bert I. Gordon. **CAST:** James Craig, Lon Chaney Jr., Gloria Talbott.

Low-budget whiz Bert I. Gordon does it again with this cheaply made but effective film about a woman (Gloria Talbott) whose brother is transformed into a big, crazy monster by—what else?—radiation. Neat little movie. 1957; B&W; 75m.

DAMIEN: OMEN II ★★★½
DIR: Don Taylor. **CAST:** William Holden, Lee Grant, Lew Ayres, Sylvia Sidney.

In this first sequel to *The Omen*, William Holden plays the world's richest man, Richard Thorn. In the previous picture, Richard's brother is shot by police while attempting to kill his son, who he believed to be the Antichrist, son of Satan. *Damien: Omen II* picks up seven years later. Rated R. 1978; 107m.

DANCE OF DEATH
DIR: Juan Ibanez. **CAST:** Boris Karloff, Andres Garcia.

Like most Mexican-made horror movies, this one has not worn well. Boris Karloff invites his relatives over to talk about his will. Then spooky things begin to happen all in a dull fashion. Don't waste your time. Not rated. 1971; 75m.

DANGER ★★★
DIR: Sidney Lumet. **CAST:** Don Hammer, Olive Deering, Kim Stanley, Eli Wallach.

Three *film noir* espisodes created for television: "The Lady on the Rock," "The System," and "Death Among the Relics." Sophisticated Alfred Hitchcock–like suspense chillers. Turn down the lights. 1952; B&W; 77m.

DANGEROUSLY CLOSE ★★
DIR: Albert Pyun. **CAST:** John Stockwell, Carey Lowell, Bradford Bancroft, Madison Mason.

In this disappointing modern-day vigilante film, a group of students, led by a Vietnam veteran teacher, tries to purge their school of "undesirable elements" by any means necessary—including murder. Film starts out promising enough but soon loses focus with its rambling script and stereotypical situations. Rated R for profanity, violence, and brief nudity. 1986; 95m.

DARK, THE ★½
DIR: John "Bud" Cardos. **CAST:** William Devane, Cathy Lee Crosby, Richard Jaeckel, Keenan Wynn, Vivian Blaine.

If your parents told you there was nothing frightening about the dark, you should have listened to them. This unthrilling thriller pits writer William Devane and TV reporter Cathy Lee Crosby against a deadly alien. Little tension and few surprises. Rated R. 1979; 92m.

DARK FORCES ★★★
DIR: Simon Wincer. **CAST:** Robert Powell, Broderick Crawford, David Hemmings, Carmen Duncan, Alyson Best.

Robert Powell plays a modern-day conjurer who gains the confidence of a family by curing their terminally ill son; or does he? The evidence stacks up against Powell as we find he may be a foreign spy and stage magician *extraordinaire*. While uneven in pacing at times, this film is decent entertainment. Rated PG for brief nudity and some violence. 1984; 96m.

DARK MIRROR, THE ★★★½
DIR: Robert Siodmak. **CAST:** Olivia De Havilland, Lew Ayres, Thomas Mitchell, Richard Long.

Olivia De Havilland, who did this sort of thing extremely well, plays twin sisters—one good, one evil—enmeshed in murder. Lew Ayres is the shrink who must divine who is who as the evil sibling deftly connives to muddy the waters. Good suspense. 1946; B&W; 85m.

DARK NIGHT OF THE SCARECROW ★★★
DIR: Frank di Felitta. **CAST:** Charles Durning, Tonya Crowe, Jocelyn Brando.

Despite its hasty beginning that fails to set up a strong premise for the pivotal scene of the movie, *Dark Night of the Scarecrow* is a chilling film that mixes the supernatural with a moral message. The film borrows some ideas from such films as *To Kill a Mockingbird* and *Of Mice and Men.* 1981; 100m.

DARK PLACES ★★★½
DIR: Don Sharp. **CAST:** Christopher Lee, Joan Collins, Herbert Lom, Robert Hardy, Jane Birkin, Jean Marsh.
Christopher Lee and Joan Collins play two fortune hunters trying to scare away the caretaker (Robert Hardy) of a dead man's mansion so they can get to the bundle of cash stashed in the old house. The film has a sophisticated psychological twist to it that is missing in most horror films of late, but the cardboard bats on clearly visible wires have got to go! Rated PG for gore and profanity. 1973; 91m.

DARK POWER, THE ★
DIR: Phil Smoot. **CAST:** Lash LaRue, Anna Lane Tatum.
Cowboy star Lash LaRue plays the sheriff in a town where a contractor has built a house over the graveyard of some ancient Mexican warriors. As anyone who's ever seen a horror movie knows, this causes the dead to rise and slaughter anyone foolish enough to occupy the house. It's pretty dull, except when Lash brings out his trademark whip. Not rated. 1985; 87m.

DARK SANITY 🦃
DIR: Martin Greene. **CAST:** Aldo Ray.
A formerly institutionalized housewife comes home and almost immediately begins to have dark psychic visions of doom. Can she convince everyone she's not insane? Low production quality and poor acting kill this one. Not rated, but contains violence. 1982; 89m.

DARK SECRET OF HARVEST HOME, THE ★★½
DIR: Leo Penn. **CAST:** Bette Davis, Rosanna Arquette, David Ackroyd, Michael O'Keefe.
Novelist-actor Tom Tryon's bewitching story of creeping horror gets fair treatment in this dark and foreboding film of Janus personalities and incantations in picturesque New England. 1978; 118m.

DARK TOWER ★
DIR: Ken Barnett. **CAST:** Michael Moriarty, Jenny Agutter, Theodore Bikel, Carol Lynley, Anne Lockhart, Kevin McCarthy.
Jenny Agutter stars as the head of a construction company putting up a skyscraper in Barcelona, Spain. Just as the project is about to be completed, a supernatural entity moves in and starts killing people. Dumb script and cornball performances provide the shaky foundation for this wasted effort. Rated R for violence and profanity. 1987; 91m.

DAUGHTER OF DR. JEKYLL ★★
DIR: Edgar G. Ulmer. **CAST:** Gloria Talbott, John Agar, Arthur Shields, John Dierkes.
Okay horror film about a girl (Gloria Talbott) who thinks she's inherited the famous dual personality after several local citizens turn up dead. 1957; B&W; 71m.

DAWN OF THE DEAD ★★★★
DIR: George A. Romero. **CAST:** David Emge, Ken Foree, Scott Reiniger, Tom Savini.
This film is the sequel to *Night of the Living Dead*. The central characters are three men and one woman who try to escape from man-eating corpses. As a horror movie, it's a masterpiece, but if you have a weak stomach, avoid this one. Rated R. 1979; 126m.

DAWN OF THE MUMMY 🦃
DIR: Frank Agrama. **CAST:** Brenda King.
A lame thriller about archaeologists who open up an accursed tomb. A sleeping pharoah awakens and wreaks bloody vengeance. Bad acting and stupid situations highlight this truly wretched film. Not rated, but contains graphic violence. 1981; 93m.

DAY OF THE ANIMALS 🦃
DIR: William Girdler. **CAST:** Christopher George, Lynda Day George, Richard Jaeckel, Leslie Nielsen, Michael Ansara, Ruth Roman.
Nature goes nuts after being exposed to the sun's radiation when the

Earth's ozone layer is destroyed. Another solidly laughable piece of nonsense from the star of *Pieces* and *Grizzly*, Christopher George. Rated R for violence, profanity, and gore. 1977; 98m.

DAY OF THE DEAD ★½
DIR: George A. Romero. **CAST:** Lori Cardille, Terry Alexander, Richard Liberty.

The third film in George A. Romero's *Dead* series doesn't hold up to its predecessors. Like earlier films in the series, *Day of the Dead* portrays graphic scenes of cannibalism, dismemberment, and other gory carnage. Unlike the other films this one has no truly likable characters to root for. Not rated, but contains scenes of violence. 1985; 100m.

DEAD AND BURIED ★★
DIR: Gary A. Sherman. **CAST:** James Farentino, Melody Anderson, Jack Albertson, Dennis Redfield.

This muddled venture by the creators of *Alien* (Ronald Shusett and Dan O'Bannon) involves a series of gory murders, and the weird part is that the victims seem to be coming back to life. The puzzle is resolved during the suspenseful, eerie ending—definitely the high point of the movie. Rated R for sex and violence. 1981; 92m.

DEAD CALM ★★★½
DIR: Phillip Noyce. **CAST:** Sam Neill, Nicole Kidman, Bill Zane.

A married couple (Sam Neill and Nicole Kidman) are terrorized at sea by a maniac (Bill Zane) in this intelligent, stylish thriller from Australian director Phillip Noyce. Although impressive overall, the movie has some unnecessarily explicit scenes. A near classic. Rated R for violence, profanity, nudity, and simulated sex. 1989; 95m.

DEAD DON'T DIE, THE ★½
DIR: Curtis Harrington. **CAST:** George Hamilton, Ray Milland, Joan Blondell, Linda Cristal, Ralph Meeker.

This rather unfrightening horror film features George Hamilton, who must take on the Zombie Master in order to clear his dead brother's name. The unbelievable story is set in the 1930s. Made for TV, this film bores more than it entertains. 1975; 76m.

DEAD EYES OF LONDON ★★½
DIR: Alfred Vohrer. **CAST:** Klaus Kinski, Karin Baal.

A German remake of the Bela Lugosi chiller *The Human Monster*. Once again the director of a home for the blind uses the place as a front for criminal activities ranging from murder to robbery. Interesting vehicle for Klaus Kinski, who gives a great maniacal performance. Even so, the film lacks the eerie atmosphere of the original. 1961; B&W; 104m.

DEAD HEAT ★★
DIR: Mark Goldblatt. **CAST:** Treat Williams, Joe Piscopo, Lindsay Frost, Darren McGavin, Vincent Price, Keye Luke.

In this so-so but gory spoof of the living-dead genre, Treat Williams and Joe Piscopo star as a pair of L.A. police detectives who find the mastermind behind a group of robberies that are being committed by criminals brought back from the dead. The special effects are pretty good, but 60 percent of the jokes fall flat. Rated R for violence and profanity. 1988; 86m.

DEAD KIDS ★★★
DIR: Michael Laughlin. **CAST:** Michael Murphy, Louise Fletcher, Dan Shor, Fiona Lewis, Arthur Dignam, Dey Young, Marc McClure, Scott Brady, Charles Lane.

Atmospheric horror flick about weird experiments at a small-town college that get out of hand. The test subjects, local teenagers, turn into homicidal maniacs. Not for the squeamish. Rated R for violence and language. 1981; 97m.

DEAD MEN WALK ★★
DIR: Sam Newfield. **CAST:** George Zucco, Mary Carlisle, Nedrick Young, Dwight Frye.
Master character actor George Zucco makes the most of one of his few leading roles, a dual one at that, in this grade-Z cheapie. Zucco is two brothers, one good, one evil, in this spooky tale about vampires and zombies. 1943; B&W; 67m.

DEAD OF NIGHT (1945) ★★★★½
DIR: Alberto Cavalcanti, Basil Dearden, Robert Hamer, Charles Crichton. **CAST:** Mervyn Johns, Michael Redgrave, Sally Ann Howes, Miles Malleson, Googie Withers, Basil Radford.
The granddaddy of the British horror anthologies still chills today, with the final sequence—in which ventriloquist Michael Redgrave fights a losing battle with his demonic dummy—rating as an all-time horror classic. The other stories are told almost as effectively. 1945; B&W; 104m.

DEAD OF NIGHT (1977) ★½
DIR: Dan Curtis. **CAST:** Ed Begley Jr., John Hackett, Patrick Macnee.
This trilogy of shockers written by Richard Matheson has some suspense and interesting twists, but is far inferior to his other achievements. Elvira is host on this, another in her "Thriller Video" series. 1977; 76m.

DEAD OF WINTER ★★★
DIR: Arthur Penn. **CAST:** Mary Steenburgen, Roddy McDowall, Jan Rubes, William Russ, Ken Pogue.
When aspiring actress Mary Steenburgen steps in at the last minute to replace a performer who has walked off the set of a film in production, she is certain it is the chance of a lifetime. But once trapped in a remote mansion with the creepy filmmakers, she begins to believe it may be the last act of her lifetime. The story is a bit contrived, but one only realizes it after the film is over. Rated R for profanity and violence. 1987; 98m.

DEAD RINGERS ★★½
DIR: David Cronenberg. **CAST:** Jeremy Irons, Genevieve Bujold, Heidi Von Palleske, Stephen Lack.
Director and co-scripter David Cronenberg toys intriguingly with the connective link between identical twins until the film sinks into a depressing spiral of depravity and gratuitous gore. Jeremy Irons is superb as both halves of twin gynecologists specializing in fertility; the performance rests in a vacuum, however, because the story self-destructs midway. Rated R for graphic medical procedures, sexual themes, and unsettling violence. 1988; 115m.

DEAD ZONE, THE ★★★★
DIR: David Cronenberg. **CAST:** Christopher Walken, Brooke Adams, Tom Skerritt, Herbert Lom, Martin Sheen.
This is an exciting adaptation of the Stephen King suspense novel about a man who uses his psychic powers to solve multiple murders and perhaps prevent the end of the world. Rated R for violence and profanity. 1983; 103m.

DEADLY ALLIANCE ★
DIR: Paul Salvatore Parco. **CAST:** Mike Lloyd Gentry.
This pretentious suspense film has higher aspirations toward being an exposé of international politics. Two shoestring filmmakers get caught up in the dealings of a secret cartel composed of the world's seven largest oil companies. The movie struggles to be cynical while the viewer struggles to stay awake. Not rated. 1975; 90m.

DEADLY BLESSING ★
DIR: Wes Craven. **CAST:** Maren Jensen, Susan Buckner, Sharon Strone, Lois Nettleton, Ernest Borgnine, Jeff East.
If beautiful women were enough to make a horror film succeed, this one would rate a 10. Unfortunately, that's all this film—about a strange religious sect—has going for it. Rated R

because of nudity and bloody scenes. 1981; 102m.

DEADLY COMPANION ★½
DIR: George Bloomfield. **CAST:** Anthony Perkins, Michael Sarrazin, Susan Clark, Howard Duff.

Slow-moving, confusing film has Michael Sarrazin trying to find his wife's killer. All clues point to Anthony Perkins but...? Ending is inconclusive and unsatisfying. Unrated, but contains violence and nudity. 1986; 90m.

DEADLY DREAMS ★½
DIR: Kristine Peterson. **CAST:** Mitchell Anderson.

Run-of-the-mill suspenser about a writer who dreams that the psychotic murderer who slew his parents is coming after him. Soon his dreams spill over into reality. Poorly written and acted and manages to hit every dream-sequence cliché there is. Rated R for violence, nudity and language. 1988; 79m.

DEADLY EYES ★
DIR: Robert Clouse. **CAST:** Sam Groom, Sara Botsford, Scatman Crothers.

Grain full of steroids creates rats the size of small dogs in this familiar horror tale adapted from British author James Herbert's novel *The Rats*. This is a B movie, all right—but the B stands for Boring. Rated R for gore, nudity, and simulated sex. 1982; 87m.

DEADLY FRIEND ★½
DIR: Wes Craven. **CAST:** Matthew Laborteaux, Michael Sharrett, Kristy Swanson.

A teenage whiz revives his murdered girlfriend by inserting a computer chip into her brain. The girl becomes a robot-zombie and kills people. This would-be thriller has much in common with its title character. It's cold, mechanical, and brain-dead. Rated R for violence. 1986; 99m.

DEADLY OBSESSION ★½
DIR: Jeno Hodi. **CAST:** Jeffrey R. Iorio.

This contrived, uneven thriller is about a disfigured psychopath who dwells in the tunnels and caves beneath a wealthy private college. He terrorizes the campus inhabitants in an effort to extort large sums of money. Pretty dull attempt at horror moviemaking. Rated R; contains nudity and violence. 1988; 93m.

DEADLY SANCTUARY
DIR: Jess (Jesus) Franco. **CAST:** Sylva Koscina, Mercedes McCambridge, Jack Palance, Klaus Kinski, Akim Tamiroff.

Based on the writings of the Marquis de Sade, this poor excuse for a horror film follows the tragic lives of two newly orphaned sisters as they fall prey to prison, prostitution, murder, and a torturous hellfire club led by Jack Palance. 1970; 93m.

DEADTIME STORIES
DIR: Jeffrey S. Delman. **CAST:** Scott Valentine.

Bizarre, ghoulish versions of fairy tales—including "Little Red Riding Hood" and "Goldilocks and the Three Bears"—make up this tacky, low-budget horror anthology. 1987; 89m.

DEAR DEAD DELILAH ★
DIR: John Farris. **CAST:** Agnes Moorehead, Will Geer, Michael Ansara, Dennis Patrick.

Delilah (Agnes Moorehead) is about to die, but there's a fortune buried somewhere on her property that her loony relatives will do anything to get ahold of. Idiotic from the outset, with many well-known stars wasted. Rated R for blood. 1972; 90m.

DEATH AT LOVE HOUSE ★★
DIR: E. W. Swackhamer. **CAST:** Robert Wagner, Kate Jackson, Sylvia Sidney, Joan Blondell, Dorothy Lamour, John Carradine, Bill Macy, Marianna Hill.

Much tamer than the lurid title would suggest. Robert Wagner plays a writer who becomes obsessed with a movie queen who died years earlier. He investigates the link between her and his own past. This mildly suspenseful hokum is made palatable by the engaging cast. Made for TV. 1976; 78m.

DEATH BY DIALOGUE
DIR: Tom DeWier. **CAST:** Ken Sagoes.
The title tells the tale. The incoherent plot centers around a group of teenagers who find a script from an old film project that was plagued with mysterious tragic accidents. Rated R for violence, profanity, and nudity. 1988; 90m.

DEATH NURSE
DIR: Nick Phillips. **CAST:** Priscilla Alden, Michael Flood.
Infantile, microscopically budgeted flick about a fat nurse and her psychotic brother. They run a clinic where the patients are murdered for their support money. This one is so bad it might break your VCR. Not rated, but contains hokey violence. 1987; 70m.

DEATH VALLEY ★★
DIR: Dick Richards. **CAST:** Paul Le-Mat, Catharine Hicks, Stephen Mc-Hattie, Wilford Brimley.
Paul Le Mat and Catharine Hicks star in this okay horror film about a vacation that turns into a nightmare. Rated R for violence and gore. 1982; 87m.

DEATH WEEKEND ★★
DIR: William Fruet. **CAST:** Brenda Vaccaro, Don Stroud, Chuck Shamata.
Don Stroud is chillingly convincing as a vicious sadist who, with the help of two demented pals, terrorizes lovers Brenda Vaccaro and Chuck Shamata at their *House by the Lake*, which was the film's theatrical title. Director William Fruet dwells too much on the cruelty and offers little hope for the protagonists. As a result, the film is uncomfortable to watch. Rated R for violence and profanity. 1977; 89m.

DEATHDREAM ★★★½
DIR: Bob Clark. **CAST:** John Marley, Richard Backus, Lynn Carlin, Anya Ormsby.
The underrated director Bob Clark made some interesting low-budget movies in his native Canada before gaining commercial success (and critical scorn) with the *Porky's* Series. This unsettling horror tale, an update of "The Monkey's Paw" as a comment on the Vietnam War and modern family life, is one of his best. It's a creepy mood piece, also known as *Dead of Night*. Rated R. 1972; 88m.

DEATHMOON
DIR: Bruce Kessler. **CAST:** Robert Foxworth, Charles Haid, France Nuyen.
A simple-minded telefilm about a businessman who is cursed by an old crone and turns into a werewolf. Sleep-inducing rather than thrill-making. Not rated, but is suitable for most audiences. 1985; 90m.

DEATHSHIP ★★
DIR: Alvin Rakoff. **CAST:** George Kennedy, Richard Crenna, Nick Mancuso, Sally Ann Howes, Kate Reid, Saul Rubinek.
This story of a modern-day lost *Dutchman* involves a World War II battleship—haunted by the ghosts of those who died on it. The ship seeks out and destroys any seagoing vessels it can find because it needs blood to continue running. There are a few chills along the way, but not enough. Rated R for violence and brief nudity. 1980; 91m.

DEEP END ★★★½
DIR: Jerzy Skolimowski. **CAST:** John Moulder-Brown, Jane Asher, Diana Dors.
A young man working in a London bathhouse becomes obsessed with a beautiful female coworker, which eventually leads to disaster. Offbeat drama with realistic performances by the cast. Rated R. 1970; 88m.

DEEP RED ★★★
DIR: Dario Argento. **CAST:** David Hemmings, Daria Nicolodi, Gabriele Lavia.
Another stylish and brutal horror-mystery from Italian director Dario Argento. His other works include *The Bird with the Crystal Plummage* and *Suspiria*. Like those, this film is slim on plot and a bit too talky, but

Argento builds tension beautifully with rich atmosphere and driving electronic music. Rated R for violence. 1975; 98m.

DEEPSTAR SIX
DIR: Sean S. Cunningham. **CAST:** Taurean Blacque, Nancy Everhard, Greg Evigan, Miguel Ferrer, Nia Peeples, Matt McCoy, Cindy Pickett.

A secret navy underwater colonization project goes awry when the undersea laboratory is attacked by a monster from the center of the Earth. The predictable plot, unimaginative special effects, and uninteresting dialogue make this one to leave on the shelf. Rated R for violence and profanity. 1989; 105m.

DELUSION ★
DIR: Alan Beattie. **CAST:** Patricia Pearcy, David Hayward, John Dukakis, Joseph Cotten.

A nurse relates a series of murders that occurred while she cared for an elderly invalid (Joseph Cotten). Throughout her rendition, you wonder why she opens every mysterious door in the gloomy mansion. The solution to this whodunit is completely unbelievable. Rated R for violence and gore. 1980; 83m.

DEMENTIA 13 ★★★
DIR: Francis Ford Coppola. **CAST:** William Campbell, Luana Anders, Patrick Magee.

Early Francis Coppola film is a low-budget shocker centering on a family plagued by violent ax murders that are somehow connected with the death of the youngest daughter many years before. Acting is standard, but the photography, creepy locations, and weird music are what make this movie click. Produced by Roger Corman. 1963; B&W; 75m.

DEMON BARBER OF FLEET STREET, THE ★★½
DIR: George King. **CAST:** Tod Slaughter, Bruce Seton.

Long before Vincent Price was the embodiment of evil, there was Tod Slaughter, master of the Grand Guignol school of lip-smacking villainy and star of many bloody thrillers. Partially based on a true occurrence, this popular folk tale tells the story of Sweeney Todd, an amoral barber who cuts the throats of his clients. Seldom seen in America since World War II, this influential film was a great success for the flamboyant Slaughter and provides the basis for the recent musical theater hit. 1936; B&W; 76m.

DEMON LOVER, THE
DIR: Donald B. Jackson. **CAST:** Christmas Robbins, Gunnar Hansen, Sonny Bell.

A bunch of college kids and bikers get involved with a Satanist who raises a demon that tears almost everyone apart. Not only is the acting rotten, but half the incantations are stolen from Robert Howard's Conan stories. Rated R for nudity, profanity, and violence. 1976; 87m.

DEMON OF PARADISE
DIR: Cirio H. Santiago. **CAST:** Kathryn Witt, William Steis, Laura Banks.

An unexciting monster flick about an ancient sea creature awakened from its slumber by drunken fishermen. A disjointed storyline and below-average effects make this a film to skip. Rated R for brief nudity and violence. 1987; 84m.

DEMONOID ★
DIR: Alfredo Zacharia. **CAST:** Samantha Eggar, Stuart Whitman.

Insipid horror film about a couple who unearth a severed hand while working in a Mexican mine. Awful direction and laughable special effects destroy any attempts at suspense. Rated R for graphic violence. 1981; 78m.

DEMONS ★★★
DIR: Lamberto Bava. **CAST:** Urbano Barberini.

Selected at random, people on the street are invited to an advance screening of a new horror film. When the members of the audience try to escape, they find themselves trapped. Although much of the acting is poor and some story elements are plain stupid, this actually is a very frightening movie. Not rated, but features graphic violence and adult language. 1986; 89m.

DEMONS 2
DIR: Lamberto Bava. **CAST:** David Knight, Nancy Brilli.

It's impossible to believe that this English-language version of *Demons 2* bears much resemblance to the Italian original. The story is incoherent, whole subplots are dropped and the dialogue is so meaningless you'd swear it was improvised. It's all about monsters resembling a cross between George Romero's zombies and *The Evil Dead* attacking the inhabitants of a high-rise apartment building. Not rated, but an R equivalent for violence and gore. 1987; 88m.

DEMONS OF LUDLOW, THE
DIR: Bill Rebane. **CAST:** Paul Von Hausen.

Regrettable little horror flick about an eastern seaboard community haunted by an old piano that is possessed. Terrible special effects and an ending that leaves a few questions unanswered. But by that time, will you really care? Not rated, but the equivalent of an R for nudity, profanity, violence, and gore. 1983; 83m.

DESTROYER ★
DIR: Robert Kirk. **CAST:** Lyle Alzado, Anthony Perkins, Deborah Foreman, Clayton Rohner.

Overblown attempt to create a camp classic slasher film. Lyle Alzado has the title role as a maniacal serial killer that the electric chair can't stop. Anthony Perkins, Deborah Foreman, and Clayton Rohner are on a film crew that is using Alzado's now deserted prison as a shooting location for a sleazy women's-prison film. The demoniacal Alzado has a field day destroying each one of the film-crew members in different and disgusting ways. Rated R for gratuitous violence, language, and nudity. 1988; 93m.

DEVIL BAT, THE ★★
DIR: Jean Yarbrough. **CAST:** Bela Lugosi, Suzanne Kaaren, Dave O'Brien, Guy Usher.

Pretty fair thriller from PRC, gives us Bela Lugosi as yet another bloodthirsty mad scientist who trains oversize rubber bats to suck blood from selected victims by use of a scent. 1941; B&W; 69m.

DEVIL BAT'S DAUGHTER ★½
DIR: Frank Wisbar. **CAST:** Rosemary La Planche, Michael Hale, Molly Lamont.

Unimaginative sequel to *Devil Bat* finds heroine Rosemary La Planche fearing for her sanity as her father spends more and more of his time experimenting with those darn bats.... Low-budget bore. 1946; B&W; 66m.

DEVIL DOG: THE HOUND OF HELL
DIR: Curtis Harrington. **CAST:** Richard Crenna, Yvette Mimieux, Victor Jory, Ken Kercheval.

This made-for-television movie is even more ridiculous than the title implies. Richard Crenna tries to save the wife and kids from the family pooch, which is actually a demon in disguise. It gets worse as Crenna uses Indian magic to battle lousy acting and poor special effects. 1976; 95m.

DEVIL DOLL, THE ★★★½
DIR: Tod Browning. **CAST:** Lionel Barrymore, Maureen O'Sullivan, Frank Lawton, Henry B. Walthall.

This imaginative fantasy thriller pits crazed Lionel Barrymore and his tiny "devil dolls" against those who have done him wrong. Although not as original an idea now as it was then, the acting, special effects, and director Tod Browning's odd sense of humor make this worth seeing. 1936; B&W; 79m.

DEVIL DOLL (1963) ★★
DIR: Lindsay Shonteff. **CAST:** Bryant Halliday, William Sylvester, Yvonne Romain.

Isn't it amazing how many horror movies have been made with the same story of a ventriloquist's dummy occupied by a human soul? This low-key British version has some creepy moments as Hugo the dummy stalks his victims with a knife, but lackadaisical direction holds the movie back. 1963; B&W; 80m.

DEVIL GIRL FROM MARS ★
DIR: David McDonald. **CAST:** Patricia Laffan, Hazel Court, Hugh McDermott.

This ridiculous story of a lanky messenger (the Devil Girl) sent from her native planet to kidnap Earthmen for reproductive purposes is lacking in thrills, special effects, tension, and just about everything else a good horror film should have. 1955; B&W; 76m.

DEVIL WITHIN HER, THE ★½
DIR: Peter Sasdy. **CAST:** Joan Collins, Donald Pleasence, Eileen Atkins, Ralph Bates, Caroline Munro, John Steiner.

One could only expect (and hope for) low-camp trash from a movie that rips off the title of a porno flick, *The Devil in Miss Jones*, takes its plot from *Rosemary's Baby*, and stars Joan Collins as the mother. Hilariously bad at times, plodding the rest. Rated R for violence, nudity, and profanity. 1975; 90m.

DEVIL'S COMMANDMENT, THE ★★★
DIR: Riccardo Freda. **CAST:** Gianna Maria Canale, Antoine Balpetre, Paul Muller.

Serious horror fans should make an effort to find this movie, which marked the beginning of the revival of the gothic horror film in Europe. Another version of the story of Countess Bathory, who tried to salvage her youth with the blood of young women, the film was sliced up by both its Italian and American distributors. The distinctive visual sense of director Riccardo Freda (assisted by cinematographer Mario Bava) is still compelling. Dubbed in English. 1956; B&W; 71m.

DEVIL'S GIFT, THE
DIR: Kenneth Berton. **CAST:** Bob Mendlesolin.

Ultra-low-budget and uncredited ripoff of Stephen King's short story "The Monkey." Lousy production values and the fact that the producers should be sued for plagiarism make this movie an all-time low. Not rated. 1984; 112m.

DEVIL'S RAIN, THE ★★½
DIR: Robert Fuest. **CAST:** Ernest Borgnine, Ida Lupino, William Shatner, Eddie Albert, Tom Skerritt, Keenan Wynn.

Great cast in a fair shocker about a band of devil worshipers at large in a small town. Terrific makeup, especially Ernest Borgnine's! Rated PG for language, violence. 1975; 85m.

DEVIL'S UNDEAD, THE ★★★½
DIR: Peter Sasdy. **CAST:** Christopher Lee, Peter Cushing, Georgia Brown, Diana Dors.

A surprisingly entertaining and suspenseful release starring the two kings of British horror, Christopher Lee and Peter Cushing, as a sort of modern-day Holmes and Watson in a tale of demonic possession. Rated PG. 1979; 91m.

DEVONSVILLE TERROR, THE ★★★
DIR: Ulli Lommel. **CAST:** Paul Wilson, Suzanna Love, Donald Pleasence.

Three witches are killed in Devonsville in 1683, and one of them places a curse on the townspeople. Flash forward to the present. Although this may sound like pure exploitation, this film has good performances, high production values, and a scary script that is not based on special effects. Rated R for nudity, violence, mild gore. 1983; 97m.

DIAL M FOR MURDER ★★★★
DIR: Alfred Hitchcock. **CAST:** Grace Kelly, Robert Cummings, Ray Milland, John Williams.

Alfred Hitchcock imbues this classic thriller with his well-known touches of sustained suspense. Ray Milland is a rather sympathetic villain whose desire to inherit his wife's fortune leads him to one conclusion: murder. His plan for pulling off the perfect crime is foiled temporarily. Undaunted, he quickly switches to Plan B, with even more entertaining results. 1954; 105m.

DIE! DIE! MY DARLING! ★★½
DIR: Silvio Narizzano. **CAST:** Tallulah Bankhead, Stefanie Powers, Peter Vaughan, Donald Sutherland.

This British thriller was Tallulah Bankhead's last movie. She plays a crazed woman who kidnaps her late son's fiancée for punishment and salvation. Grisly fun for Bankhead fans, but may be too heavy-handed for others. Unrated, the film has violence. 1965; 97m.

DIE, MONSTER, DIE! ★
DIR: Daniel Haller. **CAST:** Boris Karloff, Nick Adams, Suzan Farmer.

A slow-moving H. P. Lovecraft adaptation about a young man (Nick Adams) visiting his fiancée's family estate. Not rated, but may not be suitable for younger viewers. 1965; 80m.

DIE SCREAMING, MARIANNE 🦃
DIR: Pete Walker. **CAST:** Susan George, Barry Evans.

Graphic horror film concerns a young girl (Susan George), who is pursued by numerous crazies who try their best to prevent her from reaching her twenty-first birthday. Full of clichés and bad acting. Rated R. 1972; 99m.

DINOSAURUS! ★★½
DIR: Irvin S. Yeaworth Jr. **CAST:** Ward Ramsey, Paul Lukather.

Workers at a remote construction site accidentally stumble upon a prehistoric brontosaurus, tyrannosaurus rex, and a caveman (all quite alive) while excavating the area. Sure, the monsters look fake, and most of the humor is unintentional, but this film is entertaining nonetheless. 1960; 85m.

DISTORTIONS ★★½
DIR: Armand Mastroianni. **CAST:** Steve Railsback, Olivia Hussey, Piper Laurie, Rita Gam, Edward Albert, Terence Knox, June Chadwick.

The crazy plot developments in the final 15 minutes of the film—about a widow (Olivia Hussey) being held captive by her wicked aunt (Piper Laurie)—make this rather contrived film interesting. Rated PG for violence. 1987; 98m.

DR. ALIEN ★
DIR: David DeCoteau. **CAST:** Billy Jacoby, Judy Landers, Arlene Golonka, Troy Donahue.

Juvenile, low-budget horror spoof with a few chuckles and not much else. Visiting aliens assume human form and conduct experiments on a high-school boy. As a result, the student becomes the most sought-after man on campus. Rated R for nudity and profanity. 1988; 90m.

DOCTOR AND THE DEVILS, THE ★★★
DIR: Freddie Francis. **CAST:** Timothy Dalton, Jonathan Pryce, Twiggy, Julian Sands, Stephen Rea, Phyllis Logan, Beryl Reid, Sian Phillips.

This film, based on a true story, with an original screenplay by Dylan Thomas, is set in England in the 1800s. Dr. Cook (Timothy Dalton) is a professor of anatomy, who doesn't have enough corpses to use in class demonstrations. Not for the squeamish. Rated R for language, simulated sex, and violence. 1985; 93m.

DR. BLACK AND MR. HYDE ★
DIR: William Crain. **CAST:** Bernie Casey, Rosalind Cash.

Even though it was intended to be a horror film, *Dr. Black and Mr. Hyde* is more of a comedy because of all the unintentional laughs. Either way, it's pretty dreadful as Bernie Casey, a.k.a. Dr. Black, develops a serum to cure his kidney ailment only to find that the potion turns him into a monster with white skin. Rated R. 1976; 88m.

DR. BUTCHER, M. D. (MEDICAL DEVIATE) ★
DIR: Frank Martin. **CAST:** Ian McCulloch, Alexandra Cole.

Italian cannibal-zombie movie, and you know what that means—gore galore. The American distributor changed the name (from *Queen of the Cannibals*) and tacked on new footage left over from a NYU student film. There's a jungle island, a mad doctor, and lots of disgusting special effects. What else do you need to know? Rated R. Dubbed in English. 1979; 80m.

DR. CYCLOPS ★★★
DIR: Ernest B. Schoedsack. **CAST:** Albert Dekker, Janice Logan, Charles Halton, Thomas Coley, Victor Killian.

Oscar-nominated special effects dominate this tale of a brilliant physicist (Albert Dekker) in the remote jungles of Peru. He shrinks a group of his colleagues to miniature size in order to protect his valuable radium discovery. Entertaining film is best remembered as one of the earliest Technicolor horror movies, with lush photography and an effective performance by Dekker. 1940; 75m.

DR. DEATH: SEEKER OF SOULS ★★½
DIR: Eddie Saeta. **CAST:** John Considine, Barry Coe, Cheryl Miller, Florence Marly, Jo Morrow.

The ironically named Dr. Death can't die. He discovered how to cheat death one thousand years ago by periodically transferring his soul into another body. He's willing to share his talents with others, too. It's not really a comedy, but the makers of this low-rent terror tale had a tongue-in-cheek sense of humor, and it shows. Look for a cameo by head Stooge, Moe Howard. Rated R, though pretty tame by current standards. 1973; 87m.

DOCTOR GORE ★
DIR: Pat Patterson. **CAST:** J. G. "Pat" Patterson.

Cheap horror movie about a demented surgeon who, after the death of his wife, sets about assembling the perfect woman with parts taken from other women. Horror fans may want to see the introduction by director Herschell Gordon Lewis, the man who invented the gore movie. But *Doctor Gore*, made by one of Lewis's protégés and unreleased until it came to video, is indistinguishable from other junk littering the horror section of your video store. Rated R. 1975; 91m.

DOCTOR HACKENSTEIN
DIR: Richard Clark. **CAST:** David Muir, Stacey Travis.

Boring ripoff of *Re-Animator*, as well as all those Frankenstein flicks. Mad, goofy scientist, Doctor Hackenstein, is trying to bring his wife Sheila back from the dead. The doc borrows spare parts from donors living and dead. The hacks that put this turkey together should be sued for malpractice. Rated R for nudity and violence. 1988; 88m.

DR. JEKYLL AND MR. HYDE (1920) ★★★½
DIR: John S. Robertson. **CAST:** John Barrymore, Martha Mansfield, Nita Naldi, Louis Wolheim, Charles Lane.

Still considered one of the finest film versions of Robert Louis Stevenson's story, this features John Barrymore in a bravura performance as the infamous doctor who becomes a raging beast. Barrymore always prided himself on changing into the dreadful Hyde by contorting his body rather than relying on heavy makeup. Silent. 1920; B&W; 63m.

DR. JEKYLL AND MR. HYDE (1941) ★★★
DIR: Victor Fleming. **CAST:** Spencer Tracy, Ingrid Bergman, Lana Turner, Donald Crisp, C. Aubrey Smith, Sara Allgood.

A well-done version of Robert Louis Stevenson's classic story about a good doctor who dares to venture into the unknown. The horror of his transformation is played down in favor of the emotional and psychological consequences. Spencer Tracy and Ingrid Bergman are excellent, the production lush. 1941; B&W; 114m.

DR. JEKYLL AND SISTER HYDE ★★

DIR: Roy Ward Baker. **CAST:** Ralph Bates, Martine Beswick, Gerald Sim.

One of many variations on a Jack the Ripper theme, this one has a mad scientist driven to terrible deeds with slightly different results. Contains far too many midnight scenes in foggy old London Town. No rating, but contains violence and nudity. 1971; 94m.

DR. JEKYLL'S DUNGEON OF DEATH 🦃

DIR: James Woods. **CAST:** James Mathers.

The great-grandson of the original Dr. Jekyll spends the entire movie in his basement, injecting the family serum (which has been "improved" by Nazi scientists) into unwilling specimens. The result: They go crazy and have kung-fu battles while the doc watches gleefully. Pretty stupid. Rated R. 1982; 88m.

DR. PHIBES RISES AGAIN ★★★½

DIR: Robert Fuest. **CAST:** Vincent Price, Robert Quarry, Peter Jeffrey, Fiona Lewis, Peter Cushing, Hugh Griffith, Terry-Thomas, Beryl Reid.

Good-natured terror abounds in this fun sequel to *The Abominable Dr. Phibes*, with Vincent Price reprising his role as a disfigured doctor desperately searching for a way to restore his dead wife to life. Entertaining. Rated PG for mild violence. 1972; 89m.

DR. TARR'S TORTURE DUNGEON ★★½

DIR: Juan Lopez Moctezuma. **CAST:** Claudio Brook, Ellen Sherman.

A reporter investigating an insane asylum in nineteenth-century France discovers that the director, whose therapy includes having patients act out their obsessions, is really one of the inmates. Loosely based on an Edgar Allan Poe story, this surreal Mexican film is much better than the usual Mexican schlock. Rated R for sex and violence. 1972; 88m.

DR. TERROR'S HOUSE OF HORRORS ★★★

DIR: Freddie Francis. **CAST:** Peter Cushing, Christopher Lee, Roy Castle, Donald Sutherland.

Good anthology horror entertainment about a fortune teller (Peter Cushing) who has some frightening revelations for his clients. A top-flight example of British genre movie making. 1965; 98m.

DOCTOR X ★★★½

DIR: Michael Curtiz. **CAST:** Lionel Atwill, Preston Foster, Fay Wray, Lee Tracy.

From mayhem to murder, from cannibalism to rape—this picture offers it all. Dr. X is played with panache by Lionel Atwill. Lee Tracy is the reporter who tries valiantly to uncover and expose the mysterious doctor. This piece of vintage horror is a sure bet for the terror-loving fan. 1932; 80m.

DOGS OF HELL 🦃

DIR: Worth Keeter. **CAST:** Earl Owensby.

Low-budget thriller about a rural North Carolina sheriff (played by Earl Owensby) and his attempts to eliminate a pack of rottweilers terrorizing a Carolina mountain resort. The dogs, programmed to kill in a military experiment, run rampant after escaping from a tractor-trailer crash. Originally filmed in 3-D, the movie is rated R for profanity and graphic violence. 1982; 90m.

DOLLS ★★½

DIR: Stuart Gordon. **CAST:** Stephen Lee, Guy Rolfe, Hilary Mason.

During a fierce storm, six people are stranded at the home of a kindly old dollmaker and his wife. One by one, they are attacked by malevolent little creatures in funny outfits. (No, not Campfire Girls.) *Dolls* is from the same people who made *Re-Animator* and *From Beyond.* Rated R for violence. 1987; 77m.

DOMINIQUE IS DEAD ★★½
DIR: Michael Anderson. **CAST:** Cliff Robertson, Jean Simmons, Jenny Agutter, Flora Robson, Judy Geeson.
Weird film from England about a greedy man attempting to rid himself of his wife in order to get his hands on her money. Of course, things don't quite work out as planned. Mildly interesting movie, also known as *Dominique*. Rated PG. 1978; 98m.

DON'T ANSWER THE PHONE ★★
DIR: Robert Hammer. **CAST:** James Westmoreland.
Also known as *The Hollywood Strangler*, this unpleasantly brutal exploitation quickie might have been better in more competent hands. Rated R for violence and nudity. 1981; 94m.

DON'T BE AFRAID OF THE DARK ★★★
DIR: John Newland. **CAST:** Kim Darby, Jim Hutton, Pedro Armendariz Jr., William Demarest.
Scary TV movie as newlyweds Kim Darby and Jim Hutton move into a weird old house inhabited by eerie little monsters who want Kim for one of their own. The human actors are okay, but the creatures steal the show. 1973; 74m.

DON'T LOOK IN THE BASEMENT ★★½
DIR: S. F. Brownrigg. **CAST:** William McGee.
When the director of an insane asylum is murdered by one of the inmates, his assistant takes over. But that doesn't put an end to the murders. This is one horror movie in which the low budget actually helps; the lack of professionalism in the production gives it a disturbingly eerie aura. Rated R for violence. 1973; 95m.

DON'T LOOK NOW ★★★★
DIR: Nicolas Roeg. **CAST:** Julie Christie, Donald Sutherland.
Excellent psychic thriller about a married couple who, just after the accidental drowning of their young daughter, start having strange occurrences in their lives. Beautifully photographed by director Nicolas Roeg. Strong performances by Julie Christie and Donald Sutherland make this film a must-see. Rated R. 1973; 110m.

DON'T OPEN TILL CHRISTMAS ★★½
DIR: Edmund Purdom. **CAST:** Edmund Purdom, Caroline Munro, Gerry Sundquist.
A crazed maniac mutilates and kills bell-ringing Santas, and no one has a clue to the killer's identity, not even the filmmakers. But even with this problem, there is still a good bit of suspense. The British location adds the right amount of gothic atmosphere. Not rated, but contains graphic violence and profanity. 1985; 86m.

DOOM ASYLUM
DIR: Richard Friedman. **CAST:** Patty Mullen, Ruth Collins.
A man responsible for his wife's accidental death inhabits an old abandoned asylum. When a bunch of college kids decide to spend the night, the guilt-ridden man systematically knocks them off. A cheap and unoriginal slasher flick. Not rated, but contains nudity and graphic violence. 1987; 77m.

DORIAN GRAY
DIR: Massimo Dallamano. **CAST:** Helmut Berger, Richard Todd, Herbert Lom.
Horrid updating of the Oscar Wilde classic novel. Helmut Berger plays the title role this time as the man who remains eternally young while a painting of him grows increasingly decrepit. Fascinating story has never been more boring, with some good actors wasted. Alternate title: *The Secret of Dorian Gray*. Rated R. 1970; 93m.

DORM THAT DRIPPED BLOOD, THE

DIR: Jeffrey Obrow, Stephen Carpenter. **CAST:** Pamela Holland, Stephen Sachs.

The only good thing about this film is the title, and the producers got the idea for it from a memorable genre film starring Christopher Lee and Peter Cushing from the 1970s, *The House That Dripped Blood*. It turns out this mess was originally titled *Pranks*. Whatever they want to call it, this low-budget flick is just another excuse to serve up gratuitous violence. Rated R for violence. 1981; 84m.

DOUBLE EXPOSURE ★★★½

DIR: William Byron Hillman. **CAST:** Michael Callan, Joanna Pettet, James Stacy, Pamela Hensley, Cleavon Little, Seymour Cassel, Robert Tessier.

This psychological thriller about a photographer (Michael Callan) who has nightmares of murders that come true has some pretty ghoulish scenes. The cast puts in solid performances. Not rated, the film contains violence, profanity, nudity, and adult subject matter. 1982; 95m.

DOUBLE INDEMNITY ★★★★★

DIR: Billy Wilder. **CAST:** Fred MacMurray, Barbara Stanwyck, Edward G. Robinson, Porter Hall.

This is one of the finest suspense films ever made. Fred MacMurray is an insurance salesman who, with Barbara Stanwyck, concocts a scheme to murder her husband and collect the benefits. The husband's policy, however, contains a rider that states that if the husband's death is caused by a moving train the policy pays double face value. Edward G. Robinson is superb as MacMurray's suspicious boss. 1944; B&W; 106m.

DRACULA (1931) ★★★★

DIR: Tod Browning. **CAST:** Bela Lugosi, Dwight Frye, David Manners, Helen Chandler, Edward Van Sloan.

Bela Lugosi found himself forever typecast after brilliantly bringing to life the bloodthirsty Transylvanian vampire of the title in this 1931 genre classic, directed by Tod Browning. His performance and that of Dwight Frye as the spider-eating Renfield still impress even though this early talkie seems somewhat dated today. 1931; B&W; 75m.

DRACULA (1973) ★★★★

DIR: Dan Curtis. **CAST:** Jack Palance, Simon Ward, Nigel Davenport, Pamela Brown, Fiona Lewis.

Surprisingly effective made-for-television version of Bram Stoker's classic tale has Jack Palance as a sympathetic count trapped by his vampirism. Director Dan Curtis and scripter Richard Matheson had previously collaborated on the excellent *The Night Stalker* telefilm and work together equally well here. 1973; 99m.

DRACULA (1979) ★★½

DIR: John Badham. **CAST:** Frank Langella, Laurence Olivier, Donald Pleasence, Jan Francis.

This *Dracula* is a film of missed opportunities. Frank Langella makes an excellent Count Dracula. It's a pity he has so little screen time. The story, for the uninitiated, revolves around the activities of a bloodthirsty vampire who leaves his castle in Transylvania for fresh hunting in London. Rated R. 1979; 109m.

DRACULA VS. FRANKENSTEIN ★

DIR: Al Adamson. **CAST:** J. Carrol Naish, Lon Chaney Jr., Jim Davis.

This dud rates higher than a bomb simply for the presences of J. Carrol Naish and Lon Chaney Jr., but even they can't save this piece of junk about Dracula's eternal search for blood, eventually leading to a showdown with a dumb-looking Frankenstein monster. Pretty bad. Rated R. 1971; 90m.

DRACULA'S LAST RITES ★½

DIR: Domonic Paris. **CAST:** Patricia Lee Hammond, Gerald Fielding.

Give this one an extra half-star for attempting a novel approach; the vampires here (none named Dracula) are the mortician, police chief, and doctor in a small town who conspire to relieve accident victims of their last few pints of blood. But aside from that, the movie is a complete bore. Originally called *Last Rites*. Rated R. 1980; 88m.

DRACULA'S WIDOW ★★

DIR: Christopher Coppola. **CAST:** Josef Sommer, Sylvia Kristel, Lenny Van Dohlen, Stefan Schnabel.

The blood-sucking lord of Transylvania is dead, but his estranged wife doesn't believe it. She tracks down the last remaining descendant of Jonathan Harker, who assures her of her spouse's demise. She then goes on a rampage, slaughtering a satanic vampire cult in hopes of finding Dracula's remains. Rated R for violence and nudity. 1988; 86m.

DREAM LOVER ★½

DIR: Alan J. Pakula. **CAST:** Kristy McNichol, Ben Masters, Paul Shenar, Justin Deas, John McMartin, Gayle Hunnicutt.

This pretentious psychological thriller presents Kristy McNichol as a struggling musician living alone, in New York City no less, for the first time. After barely escaping from a knife-wielding maniac her first night in a new apartment, she suffers bloodcurdling nightmares. Rated R for violence. 1986; 104m.

DRESSED TO KILL ★★★½

DIR: Brian De Palma. **CAST:** Michael Caine, Angie Dickinson, Nancy Allen, Keith Gordon.

Director Brian De Palma again borrows heavily from Alfred Hitchcock in this story of sexual frustration, madness, and murder set in New York City. Angie Dickinson plays a sexually active housewife whose affairs lead to an unexpected conclusion. Rated R for violence, strong language, nudity, and simulated sex. 1980; 105m.

DRIFTER, THE ★★

DIR: Larry Brand. **CAST:** Kim Delaney, Timothy Bottoms, Miles O'Keeffe.

A successful businesswoman picks up a hitchhiker and they have a one-night stand. Afterward he refuses to leave her alone and her life is in jeopardy. Perhaps with a better script this could have been a reverse *Fatal Attraction*. Rated R for violence, nudity, and profanity. 1988; 89m.

DRILLER KILLER, THE

DIR: Abel Ferrara. **CAST:** Carolyn Mare, Jimmy Laine.

A maniac named Reno (who happens to be a total loser) falls for his roommate. When rejected by her, he goes out to do something crazy. The intro to this splatter flick states "Play this video loud." Follow our directions instead: "Don't play this video!" Not rated; contains violence, gore, and profanity. 1979; 84m.

DRIVE-IN MASSACRE ★★½

DIR: Stuart Segall. **CAST:** Jake Barnes, Adam Lawrence.

If you're in the mood for a slasher movie, you could do worse than this ultra-low-budget gorefest. The title says it all: Psycho killer bumps off patrons at a drive-in movie, but there are some bits that will please anyone who has ever spent summer nights at an outdoor cinema. Rated R for gore and nudity. 1976; 78m.

DRIVER'S SEAT, THE ★

DIR: Giuseppe Patroni Griffi. **CAST:** Elizabeth Taylor, Ian Bannen, Guido Mannari, Mona Washbourne, Andy Warhol.

Based on Muriel Spark's bestselling novel. Elizabeth Taylor stars as a psychotic spinster who is seeking her mysterious lover through a maze of strange adventures. Taylor would probably rather forget this one. Weird. 1973; 101m.

DUEL ★★★★★

DIR: Steven Spielberg. **CAST:** Dennis Weaver, Eddie Firestone.

Duel, an early Spielberg film, was originally a 73-minute ABC made-for-TV movie, but this full-length version was released theatrically overseas. The story is a simple one: a mild-mannered businessman (Dennis Weaver) alone on a desolate stretch of highway suddenly finds himself the unwitting prey of the maniacal driver of a big, greasy, oil tanker. 1971; 91m.

DUNWICH HORROR, THE ★

DIR: Daniel Haller. **CAST:** Sandra Dee, Dean Stockwell, Sam Jaffe, Ed Begley Sr., Talia Shire.

Torpid horror thriller made back in the good ol' days when folks didn't know that it's impossible to adapt H. P. Lovecraft. Dean Stockwell foreshadowed his hammy role in *Dune* with this laughable portrayal of a warlock whose talents run more toward hooded expressions than magical incantations. Rated PG for violence. 1970; 90m.

EATEN ALIVE ★★

DIR: Tobe Hooper. **CAST:** Neville Brand, Mel Ferrer, Carolyn Jones, Marilyn Burns, William Finley, Stuart Whitman, Robert Englund.

Director Tobe Hooper's follow-up to *The Texas Chainsaw Massacre* has a similar theme but is less successful. The owner of a run-down Louisiana Motel kills whoever wanders into his corner of the swamp, with the aid of a large, hungry alligator. Hooper was one of the inventors of the modern horror film, which emphasizes random violence, but this is often as sloppy as the dozens of imitations that followed *Massacre* and *Halloween*. Horror buffs will want to see it, anyway, for a cast that includes Neville Brand, Mel Ferrer, Stuart Whitman, and the future Freddy Krueger, Robert Englund. Rated R for strong violence. 1976; 97m.

EEGAH! ★

DIR: Nicholas Merriwether (Arch W. Hall Sr.). **CAST:** Arch Hall Jr., Richard Kiel, Marilyn Manning, William Watters (Arch W. Hall Sr.).

Teenage caveman gets the hots for brain-dead babe. A truly wretched film, but it rates one star for unintentional humor. 1962; 90m.

ENDLESS NIGHT ★

DIR: Sidney Gilliat. **CAST:** Hayley Mills, Hywel Bennett, Britt Ekland, George Sanders.

Routine suspense from the pen of Agatha Christie. Hywel Bennett plays a young British gold digger who marries heiress Hayley Mills, ostensibly out of love. Very British and with a twist ending that's not very twisty. Not rated; contains slight nudity and some violence. 1972; 95m.

ENTITY, THE

DIR: Sidney J. Furie. **CAST:** Barbara Hershey, Ron Silver, Jacqueline Brooks.

Barbara Hershey stars in this reprehensible horror flick as a woman who is sexually molested by an invisible, sex-crazed demon. Director Sidney J. Furie has created what amounts to a two-hour celebration of rape and the degradation of women. Rated R for nudity, profanity, violence, and rape. 1983; 115m.

EQUINOX (THE BEAST) ★★

DIR: Jack Woods. **CAST:** Edward Connell, Barbara Hewitt.

Good special effects save this unprofessional movie about college students searching for their archeology professor. On their search, they must face monsters and the occult. Rated PG. 1971; 82m.

ERASERHEAD ★★★

DIR: David Lynch. **CAST:** John Nance, Charlotte Stewart, Jeanne Bates.

Weird, weird movie…director David Lynch created this nightmarish film about Henry Spencer (John Nance), who, we assume, lives in the far (possibly post-apocalyptic) future when everyone is given a free lobotomy at birth. Nothing else could explain the bizarre behavior of its characters. 1978; B&W; 90m.

EVIL, THE ★★★
DIR: Gus Trikonis. **CAST:** Richard Crenna, Joanna Pettet, Andrew Prine, Cassie Yates, Victor Buono, Mary Louise Weller.

Psychologist Richard Crenna, his wife, and some of his students are trapped in an old mansion where an unseen force kills them off one by one. It's your basic haunted-house story with one added twist: the devil himself makes a memorable appearance in the person of Victor Buono, a choice bit of casting. Rated R for violence and nudity. 1978; 89m.

EVIL DEAD, THE ★★★★
DIR: Sam Raimi. **CAST:** Bruce Campbell, Ellen Sandweiss.

Five college students spending the weekend at a cabin in the Tennessee woods accidentally revive demons who possess their bodies. This low-budget wonder isn't much in the plot department, but it features lots of inventive, energetic camera work and plenty of hysterically gruesome special effects. Most of the violence is committed against unfeeling demons, so it's not that hard to take, though a sequence in which a woman is molested by a tree (!) is in poor taste. Unrated, but the black-humored violence isn't for children. 1982; 86m.

EVIL DEAD 2 ★★★½
DIR: Sam Raimi. **CAST:** Bruce Campbell, Sarah Barry.

The original *Evil Dead* didn't have a lot of plot, and the sequel has even less. Ash, the survivor of the first film, continues to battle demons in the cabin in the woods. A few lost travelers happen by to provide additional demon fodder. It's more of a remake than a sequel, except that this time director Sam Raimi has explicitly fashioned it as a tribute to one of his greatest influences: the Three Stooges. The overt slapstick may turn off some horror fans. Unrated, it contains nonstop violence and gore. 1987; 85m.

EVIL LAUGH ★
DIR: Dominick Brascia. **CAST:** Steven Bad, Dominick Brascia.

A typical slasher film about a group of college students spending the weekend in an abandoned house while a crazed serial killer stalks and kills them in various stages of undress. Gratuitous nudity abounds and spurts of blood stain the screen. Hack writing and an uninspired ending deliver this film into the halls of loserdom. Rated R for violence and nudity. 1986; 90m.

EVIL MIND, THE (A.K.A. THE CLAIRVOYANT) ★★★
DIR: Maurice Elvey. **CAST:** Claude Rains, Fay Wray, Mary Clare.

Nicely mounted story of fake mentalist who realizes that his phony predictions are actually coming true. The elegant Claude Rains gives a fine performance as a man who has inexplicably acquired a strange power and finds himself frightened by it. Interesting and fun. 1934; B&W; 80m.

EVIL OF FRANKENSTEIN, THE ★★½
DIR: Freddie Francis. **CAST:** Peter Cushing, Duncan Lamont, Peter Woodthorpe.

A weaker entry in Hammer Films' popular Frankenstein series pits Dr. Frankenstein (Peter Cushing) against an underhanded hypnotist (Peter Woodthorpe). Good production values and handsome set pieces, but the monster makeup is silly and the script convoluted. 1964; 98m.

EVIL SPAWN
DIR: Kenneth J. Hall. **CAST:** Bobbie Bresee, John Carradine.

Veteran actor John Carradine makes a token appearance in this laughably cheap horror movie about an anti-aging serum that turns a vain actress into a giant werebug. It's every bit as bad as it sounds. Not rated, with nudity, violence, and sexual situations. 1987; 88m.

EVIL TOWN
DIR: Edward Collins. **CAST:** James Keach, Dean Jagger, Robert Walker, Michele Marsh.

In a quaint mountain town, a mad doctor is keeping the citizens from aging at the expense of young tourists. When a young doctor stumbles on the town's secret, he attempts to end the madness. Unfortunately, he can't stop the mindless dialogue, rotten acting, and hack story. Rated R for violence, nudity, and language. 1987; 88m.

EVILS OF THE NIGHT
DIR: Mardi Rustam. **CAST:** Neville Brand, Aldo Ray, John Carradine, Tina Louise, Julie Newmar, Karrie Emerson, Tony O'Dell.

Despite a great trash-movie cast, this is just another bore about maniacs chasing nubile teens through the woods. Vampires from outer space hire two idiot mechanics (Neville Brand and Aldo Ray) to kidnap teenagers for them. Rated R for nudity, simulated sex, and violence. 1985; 85m.

EVILSPEAK
DIR: Eric Weston. **CAST:** Clint Howard, R. G. Armstrong, Joseph Cortese, Claude Earl Jones.

The alleged script centers on a devil-worshiping medieval Spanish priest brought into modern times by a student (Clint Howard) on a computer. Everything goes downhill—three minutes into the story—when the reborn father lops off the head of a topless female. Ick! Rated R for nudity, violence, and gore. 1982; 89m.

EXORCIST, THE ★★★★½
DIR: William Friedkin. **CAST:** Ellen Burstyn, Max von Sydow, Linda Blair, Jason Miller, Lee J. Cobb.

A sensation at the time of its release, this horror film—directed by William Friedkin (*The French Connection*)—has lost some of its punch because of the numerous imitations it spawned. An awful sequel, *Exorcist II: The Heretic*, didn't help much either. Rated R. 1973; 121m.

EXORCIST II: THE HERETIC
DIR: John Boorman. **CAST:** Richard Burton, Linda Blair, Louise Fletcher, James Earl Jones, Max von Sydow.

The script is bad, the acting poor, and the direction lacking in pace or conviction. The story concerns a priest, (Richard Burton), assigned by the Vatican to investigate the work of Father Merrin (Max von Sydow), who died freeing Regan MacNeil from possession by the devil. Rated R for violence and profanity. 1977; 110m.

EXPERIMENT IN TERROR ★★★½
DIR: Blake Edwards. **CAST:** Glenn Ford, Lee Remick, Stefanie Powers, Ross Martin, Ned Glass.

A sadistic killer (Ross Martin) kidnaps the teenage sister (Stefanie Powers) of a bank teller (Lee Remick). An FBI agent is hot on the trail, fighting the clock. The film crackles with suspense. The acting is uniformly excellent. Martin paints an unnerving portrait of evil. 1962; B&W; 123m.

EXPOSED ★
DIR: James Toback. **CAST:** Nastassja Kinski, Rudolph Nureyev, Harvey Keitel, Ian McShane.

Nastassja Kinski stars in this mediocre and confusing film as a high-priced fashion model whose constant exposure in magazines and on television has made her the target for the sometimes dangerous desires of two men. Former ballet star Rudolph Nureyev is also featured. Rated R. 1983; 100m.

EYEBALL
DIR: Umberto Lenzi. **CAST:** John Richardson.

Vacationers on a tour bus are murdered one by one, their bodies horribly mutilated with one eye cut out. The story is silly, the acting sillier, and the direction is unforgivable. Rated R for violence and nudity. 1977; 87m.

EYES OF A STRANGER ★★
DIR: Ken Weiderhorn. **CAST:** Lauren Tewes, Jennifer Jason Leigh.

The Love Boat's Julie, Lauren Tewes, makes an unexpected appearance in this blood-and-guts horror film. She plays a reporter who decides to track down a psychopathic killer. Lots of blood and some sexual molestation. Rated R. 1981; 85m.

EYES OF LAURA MARS, THE ★★
DIR: Irvin Kershner. **CAST:** Faye Dunaway, Tommy Lee Jones, Brad Dourif, René Auberjonois.

Laura Mars (Faye Dunaway) is a kinky commercial photographer whose photographs, which are composed of violent scenes, somehow become the blueprints for a series of actual killings. It soon becomes apparent the maniac is really after her. Although well-acted and suspenseful, *The Eyes of Laura Mars* is an unrelentingly cold and gruesome movie. Rated R. 1978; 103m.

EYEWITNESS ★★★★
DIR: Peter Yates. **CAST:** William Hurt, Sigourney Weaver, Christopher Plummer, James Woods.

A humdinger of a movie. William Hurt plays a janitor who, after discovering a murder victim, meets the glamorous television reporter (Sigourney Weaver) he has admired from afar. In order to prolong their relationship, he pretends to know the killer's identity—and puts both their lives in danger. Rated R for violence, and profanity. 1981; 102m.

FADE TO BLACK ★★★
DIR: Vernon Zimmerman. **CAST:** Dennis Christopher, Linda Kerridge, Tim Thomerson, Morgan Paull, Marya Small.

Movie buffs and horror fans will especially love *Fade to Black*, a funny, suspenseful, and entertaining low-budget film that features Dennis Christopher in a tour-de-force performance. Christopher plays Eric Binford, an odd young man who spends most of his time absorbing films. His all-night videotaping sessions and movie orgies only make him out of step with other people his age, and soon Eric goes over the edge. Rated R. 1980; 100m.

FALL OF THE HOUSE OF USHER, THE (1960) ★★★½
DIR: Roger Corman. **CAST:** Vincent Price, Mark Damon, Myrna Fahey.

Imagination and a chilling sense of the sinister make this low-budget Roger Corman version of Edgar Allan Poe's famous haunted-house story highly effective. Vincent Price is without peer as Usher. 1960; 79m.

FALL OF THE HOUSE OF USHER, THE (1979) ★
DIR: Stephen Lord. **CAST:** Martin Landau, Robert Hays, Charlene Tilton, Ray Walston..

Despite a name cast, this low-budget remake of the Edgar Allan Poe tale is tacky, inept, and dull. Stick with the Roger Corman version and its delicious performance by Vincent Price. Rated PG. 1979; 101m.

FAMILY PLOT ★★★★
DIR: Alfred Hitchcock. **CAST:** Karen Black, Bruce Dern, Barbara Harris, William Devane, Ed Lauter, Cathleen Nesbitt, Katherine Helmond.

Alfred Hitchcock's last film proved to be a winner. He interjects this story with more humor than in his other latter-day films. A seedy medium and her ne'er-do-well boyfriend (Barbara Harris and Bruce Dern) encounter a sinister couple (Karen Black and William Devane) while searching for a missing heir. They all become involved in diamond theft and attempted murder. Rated PG. 1976; 120m.

FAN, THE ★★★½
DIR: Edward Bianchi. **CAST:** Lauren Bacall, James Garner, Maureen Stapleton, Michael Biehn.

In this fast-moving suspense yarn, a young fan is obsessed with a famous actress (Lauren Bacall). When his love letters to her are ignored, he embarks on a murder spree. *The Fan* is an absorbing thriller. The acting is first-rate, the camera work breathtaking. Rated R. 1981; 95m.

FATAL ATTRACTION (1985) ★★★½

DIR: Michael Grant. **CAST:** Sally Kellerman, Stephen Lack, Lawrence Dane, John Huston.

In this suspenseful film, two people get caught up in sexual fantasy games so intense that they begin to act them out—in public. *Fatal Attraction* would receive a higher rating if it had a smoother transition from the innocent flirting to the heavy-duty sexual activity that leads to the film's thrilling and ironic close. Rated R for nudity, violence, and profanity. 1985; 90m.

FATAL ATTRACTION (1987) ★★★★

DIR: Adrian Lyne. **CAST:** Glenn Close, Michael Douglas, Anne Archer.

This adult shocker works beautifully as a nail-biting update of *Play Misty for Me*. It's the married man's ultimate nightmare. Glenn Close chews up the screen as Michael Douglas's one-night stand; when he (very married, to Anne Archer, an under-appreciated talent) backs away and tries to resume his ordinary routine, Close becomes progressively more dangerous. Rated R for nudity and language. 1987; 119m.

FATAL GAMES

DIR: Michael Elliot. **CAST:** Sally Kirkland, Lynn Banashek, Teal Roberts.

At first, it's difficult to determine whether or not this one is a comedy or a horror film. Then it becomes evident that this is just another slasher-type flick that is so stupid it's funny. In a school for young athletes, a murderer begins eliminating the students, using a javelin. Not rated, but contains explicit nudity and violence. 1984; 88m.

FATAL PULSE

DIR: Anthony Christopher. **CAST:** Michelle McCormick, Ken Roberts.

A house full of sorority girls get brutally picked off one by one in this sleazy slasher thriller. Barebreasted shower scenes take up more time than plot. The supposedly original murder methods are just silly: in one scene a girl's throat is slashed by a phonograph record. Not rated, but contains nudity, violence, and profanity. 1988; 90m.

FEAR IN THE NIGHT (DYNASTY OF FEAR) ★★★½

DIR: Jimmy Sangster. **CAST:** Ralph Bates, Judy Geeson, Peter Cushing, Joan Collins.

Effective British shocker about a teacher and his off-balance bride encountering lust, jealousy, and murder at a desolate boys' school. Another suspensful offering from Hammer Films. Rated PG. 1972; 94m.

FEAR NO EVIL

DIR: Frank LaLoggia. **CAST:** Stephan Arngrim, Elizabeth Hoffman.

Advertised as an exercise in horrific thrills and special effects, this is no horror movie. It's just plain horrible. The story of the satanic high-school student hell-bent on destroying a senior class, this film tries to be a male *Carrie*, a punk rock *The Exorcist*, and a contemporary *Night of the Living Dead*, all in one. Rated R. 1981; 96m.

FER-DE-LANCE ★★

DIR: Russ Mayberry. **CAST:** David Janssen, Hope Lange, Jason Evers, Ivan Dixon.

Made-for-TV suspense film is mildly entertaining as a cargo of poisonous snakes escape aboard a crippled submarine at the bottom of the sea, making life unpleasant for all concerned. 1974; 100m.

FIEND WITHOUT A FACE ★★★½

DIR: Arthur Crabtree. **CAST:** Marshall Thompson, Kim Parker, Terence Kilburn.

Surprisingly effective little horror chiller with slight overtones of the "Id" creature from *Forbidden Planet*. Scientific thought experiment goes awry and creates nasty creatures that look like brains with coiled tails. Naturally, they eat people. Story builds to a great climax. 1958; B&W; 74m.

FIFTH FLOOR, THE
DIR: Howard Avedis. **CAST:** Bo Hopkins, Dianne Hull, Patti D'Arbanville, Mel Ferrer, Sharon Farrell.

Thoroughly contemptible and completely unbelievable tale of an attractive college lass who is mistakenly popped into an insane asylum. Weak script is a poor excuse for disgusting treatment of women. Rated R for violence and nudity. 1980; 90m.

FINAL CONFLICT, THE ★★
DIR: Graham Baker. **CAST:** Sam Neill, Rossano Brazzi, Don Gordon, Lisa Harrow, Mason Adams.

The third and last in the *Omen* trilogy, this disturbing but passionless film concerns the rise to power of the son of Satan, Damien Thorn (Sam Neill), and the second coming of the Saviour. It is a crassly commercialized version of the ultimate clash between good and evil that depends more on shocking spectacle than gripping tension for its impact. Rated R. 1981; 108m.

FINAL EXAM
DIR: Jimmy Huston. **CAST:** Joel S. Rice.

A mad slasher hacks his way through a college campus in this *Friday the 13th* rip-off; and a bad rip-off it is. Even gore fans will find this film a bore. Rated R. 1981; 90m.

FINAL TERROR, THE ★½
DIR: Andrew Davis. **CAST:** Rachel Ward, Daryl Hannah, John Friedrich, Adrian Zmed.

Rachel Ward and Daryl Hannah weren't big stars when they made this mediocre low-budget slasher flick for one-time B-movie king Sam Arkoff and now they probably wish they hadn't. Rated R for brief nudity and violence. 1981; 82m.

FIRE! ★★
DIR: Earl Bellamy. **CAST:** Ernest Borgnine, Vera Miles, Alex Cord, Donna Mills, Lloyd Nolan, Ty Hardin, Neville Brand, Gene Evans, Erik Estrada.

Another of producer Irwin Allen's suspense spectaculars involving an all-star cast caught in a major calamity. This one concerns a mountain town in the path of a forest fire set by an escaped convict. Worth watching once. 1977; 100m.

FIRESTARTER ★★★½
DIR: Mark L. Lester. **CAST:** David Keith, Drew Barrymore, George C. Scott, Martin Sheen.

Stephen King writhes again. This time, Drew Barrymore stars as the gifted (or is that haunted) child of the title, who has the ability—sometimes uncontrollable—to ignite objects around her. David Keith is the father who tries to protect her from the baddies. *Firestarter* is suspenseful, poignant, and sometimes frightening entertainment that goes beyond its genre. Rated PG for violence. 1984; 115m.

FLESHBURN ★★★½
DIR: George Gage. **CAST:** Sonny Landham, Steve Kanaly, Karen Carlson.

An Indian who left five men in the desert to die breaks out of an insane asylum to hunt down and wreak his revenge against the psychiatrists who sentenced him. This film promises to be more than exploitation, and it does not let you down. Rated R for profanity, violence. 1983; 91m.

FLOOD! ★★★
DIR: Earl Bellamy. **CAST:** Robert Culp, Martin Milner, Barbara Hershey, Richard Basehart, Carol Lynley, Roddy McDowall, Cameron Mitchell, Teresa Wright.

Bureaucratic peevishness is responsible for a small town being caught short when a dam bursts. The resulting flood threatens to wipe out everybody and everything. Slick and predictable, but interesting just the same. If you like this, you'll like its sister film, *Fire!* 1976; 100m.

FLY, THE (1958) ★★★★
DIR: Kurt Neumann. **CAST:** David Hedison, Patricia Owens, Vincent Price, Herbert Marshall.

Classic horror film builds slowly but really pays off. A scientist (Al Hedison, soon to become David) experimenting with unknown forces turns himself into the hideous title character. Impressive production with top-notch acting and real neat special effects. 1958; 94m.

FLY, THE (1986) ★★★½
DIR: David Cronenberg. **CAST:** Jeff Goldblum, Geena Davis, John Getz.
A brilliant research scientist, Seth Brundle (Jeff Goldblum) has developed a way to transport matter. One night, thoroughly gassed, he decides to test the device on himself. Unfortunately, a pesky housefly finds its way into the chamber with the scientist. It must also be said that this otherwise entertaining update simply falls apart at the conclusion. Rated R for gore and slime. 1986; 100m.

FLY II, THE ★½
DIR: Chris Walas. **CAST:** Eric Stoltz, Daphne Zuniga, Lee Richardson, John Getz.
This sequel to David Croneberg's masterfully crafted 1986 horror remake *The Fly* doesn't have the right chemistry. The weak, unbelievable story centers around the birth of an heir (Eric Stoltz) to the original fly. He's kept in a secret laboratory, closely watched and monitored by a team of scientists who wait for his metamorphosis. This one doesn't fly. Rated R for violence, adult situations, and profanity. 1989; 104m.

FOG, THE ★★★
DIR: John Carpenter. **CAST:** Adrienne Barbeau, Jamie Lee Curtis, John Houseman, Hal Holbrook, Janet Leigh.
This is one of those *almost* movies. Director John Carpenter is on familiar ground with this story of eighteenth-century pirates back from the dead, terrorizing a modern-day fishing village. There's plenty of blood and gore, but the lack of any real chills or surprises makes this one a nice try but no cigar. Rated R. 1980; 91m.

FORBIDDEN WORLD ★★
DIR: Allan Holzman. **CAST:** Jesse Vint, Dawn Dunlap, June Chadwick, Linden Chiles.
Jesse Vint was rescued from the obscurity of his deep-space death in *Silent Running*, and his reward was a starring role in this ripoff of *Alien* in which an experimental food stuff starts killing the inhabitants of a space colony. Rated R for violence. 1982; 77m.

FORCED ENTRY ★
DIR: Jim Sotos. **CAST:** Ron Max, Tanya Roberts, Nancy Allen.
Sloppily made slasher film would be long forgotten had it not featured early appearances by Tanya Roberts and Nancy Allen. They're two of the victims of a gas-station attendant who kills women because his mother beat him when he was young. Original title: *The Last Victim*. Rated R. 1975; 88m.

FOREIGN CORRESPONDENT ★★★★★
DIR: Alfred Hitchcock. **CAST:** Joel McCrea, Laraine Day, Herbert Marshall, George Sanders, Edmund Gwenn.
Classic Alfred Hitchcock thriller still stands as one of his most complex and satisfying films. Joel McCrea stars as an American reporter in Europe during the war, caught up in all sorts of intrigue, romance, etc., in his dealings with Nazi spies, hired killers, and the like as he attempts to get the truth to the American public. 1940; B&W; 120m.

FOREST, THE ★
DIR: Don Jones. **CAST:** Dean Russell, Michael Brody.
This is an extremely amateurish attempt at a horror film. A very low budget coupled with an unprofessional cast makes this film a boorish waste of time. Unrated. 1983; 90m.

FOREVER EVIL ★
DIR: Roger Evans. **CAST:** Red Mitchell, Tracey Hoffman.

After his friends are massacred at a country cabin, the sole survivor tracks down the cult of the demon god who killed them. There are a few good special effects, but it's not worth suffering through this overlong, amateurish movie to see them. Not rated. 1987; 107m.

FRANKENSTEIN (1931) ★★★★
DIR: James Whale. **CAST:** Colin Clive, Mae Clarke, Boris Karloff, John Boles.

Despite all the padding, grease paint, and restrictive, awkward costuming, Boris Karloff gives a strong, sensitive performance in this 1931 horror classic—with only eyes and an occasional grunt to convey meaning. It still stands as one of the great screen performances. 1931; B&W; 71m.

FRANKENSTEIN (1973) ★★½
DIR: Glenn Jordan. **CAST:** Robert Foxworth, Susan Strasberg, Bo Svenson, Willie Aames.

Bo Svenson's sympathetic portrayal of the monster is the one saving grace of this essentially average made-for-TV retelling of Mary Wollstonecraft Shelley's horror tale. 1973; 130m.

FRANKENSTEIN (1984) ★★★
DIR: James Ormerod. **CAST:** Robert Powell, David Warner, Carrie Fisher, John Gielgud, Terence Alexander, Susan Wooldridge.

Solid made-for-TV adaptation of Mary Shelley's often filmed tale. Robert Powell gives a believable performance as a young Dr. Frankenstein, whose creation (David Warner) runs amok. Fine period flavor, crisp direction, and an excellent cast headed by Warner and John Gielgud. 1984; 81m.

FRANKENSTEIN ISLAND
DIR: Jerry Warren. **CAST:** John Carradine, Robert Clarke, Steve Brodie, Cameron Mitchell, Andrew Duggan.

A group of men stranded on a remote island stumble upon a colony of young women in leopard-skin bikinis. Sounds like fun until they run up against a relative of the famous doctor, who's creating a monster of his very own. Worse than you'd think. Rated PG. 1981; 89m.

FRANKENSTEIN MEETS THE SPACE MONSTER
DIR: Robert Gaffney. **CAST:** James Karen, Nancy Marshall, Robert Reilly.

The Frankenstein here is actually an android named Frank sent into outer space by NASA. He crash-lands near Puerto Rico, where evil aliens are kidnapping rock 'n' rolling teenyboppers to replenish their "breeding stock." One of the aliens is named Nadir, which could easily be an alternate title for this mess. Also known as *Mars Invades Puerto Rico*. 1965; B&W; 75m.

FRANKENSTEIN MEETS THE WOLF MAN ★★★½
DIR: Roy William Neill. **CAST:** Lon Chaney Jr., Patric Knowles, Bela Lugosi, Ilona Massey, Maria Ouspenskaya.

As the title suggests, two of Universal's most famous monsters clash in this series horror film. Very atmospheric, with beautiful photography, music, set design, and special effects. Only drawback is Bela Lugosi's overblown portrayal of the Frankenstein Monster. 1943; B&W; 73m.

FRANKENSTEIN—1970 ★
DIR: Howard W. Koch. **CAST:** Boris Karloff, Tom Duggan, Jana Lund, Don Barry.

This poor excuse for a movie wastes Boris Karloff as the great-grandson of the famous doctor, attempting to create a monster of his own. Unfortunately, the only ones who succeeded were the producers of this movie. Rates higher than a turkey solely because of Karloff's appearance. 1958; B&W; 83m.

FRANKENSTEIN'S DAUGHTER
DIR: Richard Cunha. **CAST:** John Ashley, Sandra Knight, Donald Murphy, Harold Lloyd Jr.

There's very little to redeem this inept attempt to cash in on the good name of Dr. Frankenstein and his creation. The makeup is ridiculous, the sets are cheap, and the performers need to be oiled. 1958; B&W; 85m.

FREAKS ★★★★
DIR: Tod Browning. **CAST:** Wallace Ford, Leila Hyams, Olga Baclanova, Roscoe Ates.

This legendary "horror" movie by Tod Browning is perhaps the most unusual film ever made and certainly one of the most unsettling. Based on Tod Robbins's *Spurs*, this is the story of a circus midget who falls in love with a statuesque trapeze artist and nearly becomes her victim as she attempts to poison him for his money. Incensed by her betrayal and near murder of their little friend, the armless, legless, pinheaded "freaks" exact their revenge. 1932; B&W; 64m.

FREEWAY MANIAC 🦃
DIR: Paul Winters. **CAST:** Loren Winters, James Courtney.

Just another low-budget splatter flick, long on gore and minuscule on plot. Matricidal maniac escapes from an insane asylum, not once but twice. The first time he's recaptured with the help of an actress. The second time he's out to get his own twisted revenge on the actress. *Playboy* cartoonist Gahan Wilson wrote this turkey. 1988; 94m.

FRENCHMAN'S FARM ★★½
DIR: Ron Way. **CAST:** Tracy Tainsh, Ray Barrett, Norman Kaye, John Meillon.

Don't be fooled by the lurid video-box illustration—this is really a fairly tame Australian import about a female law student who has a psychic experience and witnesses a murder that took place forty years earlier. Some good suspense, but the psychic-encounter scene is overdone. Rated R for language and violence. 1986; 86m.

FRENZY ★★★★½
DIR: Alfred Hitchcock. **CAST:** Jon Finch, Barry Foster, Barbara Leigh-Hunt, Anna Massey, Alec McCowen.

Frenzy marks a grand return to one of Hitchcock's favorite themes: that of a man accused of a murder he did not commit and all but trapped by the circumstantial evidence. Rated R. 1972; 116m.

FRIDAY THE 13TH ★★½
DIR: Sean S. Cunningham. **CAST:** Betsy Palmer, Adrienne King, Harry Crosby, Kevin Bacon.

The original slasher flick. A group of Crystal Lake camp counselors are systematically murdered by a masked maniac. Not much of a plot, just the killer hacking and slashing his way through the dwindling counselor population. Fine makeup effects by master Tom Savini highlight this spatterfest that has fostered many imitations and a series of (to date) eight Jason Voorhees slice-and-dicers. Rated R for gore. 1980; 95m.

FRIDAY THE 13TH, PART II ★★
DIR: Steve Miner. **CAST:** Amy Steel, John Furey, Adrienne King, Betsy Palmer.

This sequel to the box-office hit of the same name is essentially the *Psycho* shower scene repeated ad nauseum. A group of young people are methodically sliced and diced by Jason, the masked maniac. Though the makeup effects in this rehash were reportedly toned down, there is still enough blood for gore hounds. Rated R for gruesomeness, no matter how toned-down. 1981; 87m.

FRIDAY THE 13TH, PART III ★★
DIR: Steve Miner. **CAST:** Dana Kimmel, Paul Kratka.

More gruesome axe, knife, and meat-cleaver murders occur at sunny Crystal Lake. Works the same as the first two, though for the theatrical release it had the hook of being in 3-D. The video isn't in 3-D, so Jason is just his old two-dimensional self hacking and hewing his way through another unlucky group of campers. Won't they ever learn? Rated R for obvious reasons. 1982; 96m.

FRIDAY THE 13TH—THE FINAL CHAPTER ★★★
DIR: Joseph Zito. **CAST:** Kimberly Beck, Corey Feldman, Peter Barton, Joan Freeman.

It has been said that the only reason makeup master Tom Savini agreed to work on this film was that it gave him a chance to kill Jason, the maniacal killer whom he created in the original film. Well, Jason does die. Oh, boy! Does he ever! But not before dispatching a new group of teenagers. Savini's work is the highlight of this flick, which is really just a rehash of the first three. Rated R for extreme gruesomeness. 1984; 90m.

FRIDAY THE 13TH, PART V: A NEW BEGINNING
DIR: Danny Steinmann. **CAST:** John Shepherd, Melanie Kinnaman, Richard Young.

Well, they did it. The producers promised *Friday the 13th—The Final Chapter* would be the last of its kind. They lied. Rated R for graphic violence and simulated sex. 1985; 92m.

FRIDAY THE 13TH, PART VI: JASON LIVES ★★★
DIR: Tom McLoughlin. **CAST:** Thom Mathews, Jennifer Cooke.

It may be hard to believe, but this fifth sequel to the unmemorable *Friday the 13th* is actually better than all those that preceded it. Of course this thing is loaded with violence, but it is also nicely buffered by good comedy bits and one-liners. Rated R for language and violence. 1986; 85m.

FRIDAY THE 13TH, PART VII: THE NEW BLOOD ★★½
DIR: John Carl Buechler. **CAST:** Lar Park Lincoln, Terry Kiser.

Jason returns, only this time someone's waiting for him: a mentally disturbed teenage girl with telekinetic powers. The result is a bloodbath as the two battle to decide who will star in Part VIII. A decent sequel with above-average special effects and a little less gore than usual. Rated R for violence, language, and nudity. 1988; 90m.

FRIGHT NIGHT ★★★★
DIR: Tom Holland. **CAST:** Chris Sarandon, William Ragsdale, Roddy McDowall, Amanda Bearse, Stephen Geoffreys.

Charley Brewster (William Ragsdale) is a fairly normal teenager save one thing: he's convinced his new next-door neighbor, Jerry Dandrige (Chris Sarandon), is a vampire—and he is! So Charley enlists the aid of former screen vampire hunter Peter Vincent (Roddy McDowall), and the result is a screamingly funny horror spoof. Rated R for nudity, profanity, and gore. 1985; 105m.

FRIGHTMARE ★
DIR: Norman Thaddeus Vane. **CAST:** Luca Bercovici, Jennifer Starret, Nita Talbot.

Buried in his cape, Bela Lugosi–style, an eccentric horror-movie star is called back from the dead to destroy those who stole his body from his coffin. A weak plot line and poor lighting don't do much to improve this imitative chiller. Not rated, this film contains some violence. 1982; 86m.

FROGS ★★
DIR: George McCowan. **CAST:** Ray Milland, Sam Elliott, Joan Van Ark.

In this fair horror film, Ray Milland has killed frogs, so frogs come to kill his family. Milland accurately imitates Walter Brennan, and the whole cast dies convincingly. Rated PG. 1972; 91m.

FROM BEYOND ★★★
DIR: Stuart Gordon. **CAST:** Jeffrey Combs, Barbara Crampton, Ken Foree.

A lecherous scientist and his assistant create a machine that stimulates a gland in the brain that allows one to see into another dimension. Then the fun begins—with better-than-average special effects, scary-looking monsters, and suspenseful horror. Made by the creators of *Reanimator*. Not rated, but contains graphic violence and brief nudity. 1986; 89m.

FROM BEYOND THE GRAVE ★★★

DIR: Kevin Connor. **CAST:** Peter Cushing, Margaret Leighton, Ian Bannen, David Warner, Donald Pleasence, Lesley-Anne Down, Diana Dors.

One of the best Amicus horror anthologies, this features Peter Cushing as the owner of a curio shop, Temptations Ltd., where customers get more than they bargain for. A strong cast of character actors enlivens this fine adaptation of four R.Chetwynd-Hayes stories: "The Gate Crasher," "An Act of Kindness," "The Elemental," and "The Door." Rated PG. 1973; 97m.

FUNHOUSE, THE ★★½

DIR: Tobe Hooper. **CAST:** Elizabeth Berridge, Cooper Huckabee, Miles Chapin, Largo Woodruff, Sylvia Miles.

Looking for a watchable modern horror film? Then welcome to *The Funhouse*. This film about a group of teens trapped in the carnival attraction of the title proves that buckets of blood and severed limbs aren't essential elements to movie terror. Rated R. 1981; 96m.

FURY, THE ★★★

DIR: Brian De Palma. **CAST:** Kirk Douglas, Andrew Stevens, Amy Irving, Fiona Lewis, John Cassavetes, Charles Durning.

The Fury is a contemporary terror tale that utilizes the average-man-against-the-unknown approach that made Hitchcock's suspense films so effective. In the story, Kirk Douglas is forced to take on a super-powerful government agency which has kidnapped his son (Andrew Stevens), who has psychic powers. It's a chiller. Rated R. 1978; 118m.

FUTURE HUNTERS

DIR: Cirio H. Santiago. **CAST:** Robert Patrick.

A warrior from the future travels back to the present, seeking the other half of a religious artifact. He's killed, but before he dies, he persuades a young couple to continue the mission for him. Cheapo ripoff of almost every popular adventure film of the last ten years. Rated R for violence, profanity, and nudity. 1985; 96m.

FUTURE-KILL

DIR: Ronald W. Moore. **CAST:** Edwin Neal, Marilyn Burns.

Thoroughly rotten film about some obnoxious frat boys who get stuck on the wrong side of town and run into a gang of punks—one of whom has been exposed to radiation. This is as cheap as B movies get. Rated R for profanity, nudity, and gallons of gore. 1984; 83m.

GANJASAURUS REX

DIR: Ursi Reynolds. **CAST:** Paul Bassis, Dave Fresh, Rosie Jones.

A prodrug propaganda film about a prehistoric monster that awakens when the authorities begin burning marijuana crops. The heroes, of course, are the drug growers. The film's production values are so low that even its intended audience will have difficulty enjoying it. Not rated. 1988; 88m.

GASLIGHT ★★★★

DIR: George Cukor. **CAST:** Ingrid Bergman, Joseph Cotten, Charles Boyer.

Ingrid Bergman won her first Academy Award as the innocent young bride who, unfortunately, marries Charles Boyer. Boyer is trying to persuade her she is going insane. Many consider this the definitive psychological thriller. 1944; B&W; 114m.

GATE, THE ★★

DIR: Tibor Takacs. **CAST:** Stephen Dorff.

A film that insists that children shouldn't play heavy metal records with satanic messages. The kids in this film do and so unlock a gate to an ancient netherworld with an ancient evil more powerful than the devil.

Though not very scary, this film exhibits outstanding special effects. Rated PG-13 for mild violence and profanity. 1987; 85m.

GATES OF HELL ★
DIR: Lucio Fulci. **CAST:** Christopher George, Janet Agren.

Wanna see something *really* gross? Then rent this tape, fast forward, and stop almost any place. Otherwise, this Italian imitation of *Dawn of the Dead* is not likely to fit your idea of an evening's entertainment. Unrated, it played in theatres with an unofficial X rating. 1983; 93m.

GHASTLY ONES, THE
DIR: Andy Milligan. **CAST:** Don Williams, Maggie Rogers.

Ghastly is right. Members of a family, reunited for the reading of their dead father's will, are murdered by a mysterious killer. Bet you can't stay awake all the way to the end! Unrated, the movie has lots of fake-looking gore. 1969; 81m.

GHIDRAH, THE THREE-HEADED MONSTER ★★★
DIR: Inoshiro Honda. **CAST:** Yosuke Natsuki, Yuriko Hoshi, Hiroshi Koizumi.

A giant egg from outer space crashes into Japan and hatches the colossal three-headed flying monster of the title. It takes the combined forces of Godzilla, Rodan, and Mothra to save Tokyo from Ghidrah's rampage of destruction. Good Japanese monster movie is marred only by dumb subplot of evil agent out to kidnap a Martian princess. 1965; 85m.

GHOST STORY ★
DIR: John Irvin. **CAST:** John Houseman, Douglas Fairbanks Jr., Melvyn Douglas, Fred Astaire, Alice Krige, Craig Wasson, Patricia Neal.

Ghost stories are supposed to be scary, aren't they? Then what happened here? This film, based on the best selling novel by Peter Straub, is about as frightening as an episode of *Sesame Street,* and much less interesting. Rated R because of shock scenes involving rotting corpses and violence. 1981; 110m.

GHOST TOWN ★★
DIR: Richard Governor. **CAST:** Franc Luz, Catherine Hickland, Bruce Glover.

A passable time-waster mixing two genres, the horror film and the Western. Modern-day deputy (Franc Luz) with a penchant for the Old West stumbles into a satanic netherworld: ghost town in the middle of the Arizona desert. Around the turn of the century the town and its citizens are cursed by their sheriff after they fail to assist him in ridding the town of some nasty demonic outlaws and he winds up dead. The town becomes suspended in a supernatural purgatory of fear and hate. Rated R for nudity, violence, and profanity. 1988; 85m.

GHOSTRIDERS ★★
DIR: Alan L. Stewart. **CAST:** Bill Shaw.

Just before being hanged in 1886, a notorious criminal puts a curse on the preacher responsible for his execution. One hundred years later he and his gang return to wreak vengeance on the preacher's descendants. Rated R for violence and language. 1987; 85m.

GHOUL, THE (1933) ★★½
DIR: T. Hayes Hunter. **CAST:** Boris Karloff, Cedric Hardwicke, Ernest Thesiger, Ralph Richardson, Kathleen Harrison.

Trading on the success he achieved in *Frankenstein* and *The Mummy,* Boris Karloff plays an Egyptologist seeking eternal life through a special jewel. He dies and the jewel is stolen, bringing him back from the dead to seek revenge on the thief. 1933; B&W; 73m.

GHOUL, THE (1975) ★★½
DIR: Freddie Francis. **CAST:** Peter Cushing, John Hurt, Gwen Watford.

"Stay out of the garden, dear, there's a flesh-eating monster living there." One of Peter Cushing's many horror films. No gore, but not boring, either. Rated R. 1975; 88m.

GHOULIES
DIR: Luca Bercovici. **CAST:** Peter Liapis, Lisa Pelikan, John Nance.
The ad for this low-budget horror film featured a gruesome little reptilian creature—in a jumpsuit, no less—poking his head out of a toilet under the tag line, "They'll get you in the end." Could the movie be as tasteless as its promotion? Yes! Rated PG-13 for violence and sexual innuendo. 1985; 87m.

GHOULIES II ★
DIR: Albert Band. **CAST:** Damon Martin, Royal Dano.
Uneven sequel that dramatizes the further adventures of those mischievous little demons. This time, they help out some down-and-out carnies. The acting is bad, and the heavy-metal sound track distracts more than it enhances. Rated PG-13 for violence. 1987; 89m.

GIRL SCHOOL SCREAMERS ★
DIR: John P. Finegan. **CAST:** Mollie O'Mara.
An all-girls Catholic school inherits a wealthy benefactor's estate and sends its brightest (and rowdiest) pupils to catalogue the contents. But the mansion is inhabited by demonic spirits, led by the dead philanthropist. Only recommended for true horror fans. Not rated, but contains nudity and violence. 1985; 85m.

GIRLY
DIR: Freddie Francis. **CAST:** Vanessa Howard, Michael Bryant, Ursula Howells, Pat Heywood, Robert Swann.
A bizarre, almost laughable tale about the killing exploits of a demented English family. Girly and her brother Sonny visit a local park to bring an odd collection of drunks, playboys and street people home as their new friends. Once there, mumsy and nanny plot the murder of their new houseguests. Rated R for suggested sex. 1987; 101m.

GODZILLA 1985
DIR: Kohji Hashimoto, R. J. Kizer. **CAST:** Raymond Burr, Keiji Kobayashi.
Once again, the giant Japanese lizard tramples cars and crushes tall buildings in his search for radioactive nutrition. What was okay in the 1950s and '60s in the giant-monster genre is totally out of place today. Rated PG for gore. 1985; 91m.

GODZILLA, KING OF THE MONSTERS ★★★½
DIR: Inoshiro Honda (original version); Terry Morse (U.S. version). **CAST:** Raymond Burr, Takashi Shimura.
First, and by far the best, film featuring the four-hundred-foot monstrosity that was later reduced to a superhero. Here he's all death and destruction, and this movie really works, thanks to some expert photographic effects and weird music. 1956; B&W; 80m.

GODZILLA VS. GIGAN ★
DIR: Jun Fukuda. **CAST:** Hiroshi Ishikawa.
A basic rehash of previous Godzilla movies, only this time much more boring. Aliens from outer space hope to take over the world by calling forth destructive monsters. The people of Earth call up their own bad guy in the form of Godzilla, and the battle begins. Not rated. 1972; 89m.

GODZILLA VS. MECHAGODZILLA ★★
DIR: Jun Fukuda. **CAST:** Masaaki Daimon.
For Godzilla fans only. An enemy from space builds a metal Godzilla in an effort to take over the world. Godzilla is pressed into action to destroy the beast. Rated PG. 1975; 82m.

GODZILLA VS. MONSTER ZERO ★★★
DIR: Inoshiro Honda. **CAST:** Nick Adams, Akira Takarada.
Pretty good monster movie has an alien civilization "borrowing" Godzilla and Rodan to help defeat the hometown menace Monster Zero

(known previously and since as Ghidrah). 1966; 90m.

GODZILLA VS. MOTHRA ★★★
DIR: Inoshiro Honda. **CAST:** Akira Takarada, Yuriko Hoshi, Hiroshi Koizumi.
Fine Godzilla movie pits the "king of the monsters" against archenemy Mothra for its first half, later has him taking on twin caterpillars recently hatched from the moth's giant egg that had been incubating on a nearby beach. Excellent battle scenes in this one, with Godzilla's first appearance a doozy. 1964; 90m.

GODZILLA VS. THE SEA MONSTER ★
DIR: Jun Fukuda. **CAST:** Not Credited.
Godzilla must tackle a giant, rotten-looking crab monster that can throw boulders in this weak entry in the series. Boring as all-get-out, mainly because our hero doesn't even appear until the film is half over. 1966; 85m.

GOODNIGHT, GOD BLESS
DIR: John Eyres. **CAST:** Emma Sutton, Frank Rozelaar Goleen.
British entry in the slasher sweepstakes has a maniacal killer dressed in priest's garb starting off with a schoolyard massacre, then moving on to senseless murders and slaughter. The film is so slow-moving it's stillborn. Not rated, but contains violence and sexual suggestion. 1988; 100m.

GORATH ½
DIR: Inoshiro Honda. **CAST:** Not Credited.
An out-of-control planet headed for Earth is the subject of this Japanese science-fiction flick. Low-grade production with cheesy special effects by the usually exceptional Eiji Tsuburaya, boosted by some ridiculous dialogue and post-dubbing. 1964; 77m.

GORGO ★★★½
DIR: Eugene Lourie. **CAST:** Bill Travers, William Sylvester, Vincent Winter, Martin Benson.
Unpretentious thriller from England has a dinosaur-type monster captured and put on display in London's Piccadilly Circus, only to have its towering two-hundred-foot parent destroy half the city looking for it. Brisk pacing and well-executed effects. 1961; 76m.

GORGON, THE ★★★
DIR: Terence Fisher. **CAST:** Peter Cushing, Christopher Lee, Richard Pasco, Barbara Shelley.
Peter Cushing and Christopher Lee take on a Medusa-headed monster in this British Hammer Films chiller. A good one for horror buffs. 1964; 83m.

GOTHAM ★★
DIR: Lloyd Fonvielle. **CAST:** Tommy Lee Jones, Virginia Madsen, Frederic Forrest.
A *film noir* thriller that's confusing, slow, and tediously melodramatic. Tommy Lee Jones is a Marlowesque detective hired as a go-between for a well-to-do husband and his murdered wife. As Jones muddles his way through the investigation, he becomes strangely obsessed with the haunting reappearance of the dead wife (Virginia Madsen). Romantically atmospheric and beautifully photographed, the film is marred by terrible dialogue and anemic acting. Rated R for nudity, simulated sex, violence, and profanity. 1988; 92m.

GOTHIC ★★
DIR: Ken Russell. **CAST:** Gabriel Byrne, Julian Sands, Natasha Richardson, Timothy Spall.
Director Ken Russell returns to his favorite subject—the tortured artist—for this look at what may have happened that spooky evening in 1816 when Lord Byron, poet Percy Shelley, his fiancée Mary, her stepsister Claire, and Byron's ex-lover Dr. Polidori spent the evening together, attempting to scare each other. What the viewer gets is the usual Russell bag of tricks: insane hallucinations, group sex, scenes of gruesome murders, and much, much more. Rated R. 1986; 90m.

GRADUATION DAY ★★
DIR: Herb Freed. **CAST:** Christopher George, Michael Pataki, E. J. Peaker.
A high-school runner dies during a competition. Soon someone begins killing all her teammates. Christopher George, as the coach, becomes a suspect along with the principal and the victim's sister. Plenty of violence in this one. Rated R. 1981; 96m.

GRAVE OF THE VAMPIRE ★½
DIR: John Hayes. **CAST:** William Smith, Michael Pataki.
Although it's far from the classic it's reputed to be, this film was groundbreaking for its day. The story involves a vampire who interrupts a couple's first date, killing the boyfriend and raping the girl. She eventually gives birth to a baby bloodsucker who grows up to search for his father and discover his birthright. 1972; 95m.

GRAVEYARD SHIFT ★
DIR: Gerard Ciccoritti. **CAST:** Silvio Oliviero, Helen Papas.
This is the story of a New York cabbie who expects more than a tip. The cabbie is actually a vampire who goes around the city nibbling on various full-figured victims. Plenty of blood and lots of nudity. Rated R. 1987; 90m.

GRIZZLY ★★
DIR: William Girdler. **CAST:** Christopher George, Andrew Prine, Richard Jaeckel.
Another "nature runs amok" film with Christopher George going up against an eighteen-foot killer bear this time out. Some taut action, but the movie has no style or pizzazz. Rated PG for violence. 1976; 92m.

GROTESQUE ★
DIR: Joe Tornatore. **CAST:** Linda Blair, Tab Hunter, Charles Dierkop.
A college coed and a friend head up to the mountains for a weekend with Mom and Dad. It's meant to be a quiet gathering away from school, but soon it's interrupted by a gang of psychotic punks looking for a treasure rumored to be hidden in the house. As they knock off members of the family, something begins knocking them off and the hunters become the hunted. Rated R for violence and nudity. 1987; 80m.

GROUND ZERO ★★½
DIR: Micheal Pattinson, Bruce Myles. **CAST:** Colin Friels, Jack Thompson, Donald Pleasence.
Political thriller that lacks the strike capability to give it a complete victory. While a cameraman investigates his father's death, he stumbles onto a coverup by the British and Australian governments involving nuclear testing in the Fifties. Aborigines, political influence, corruption, murder, and genocide are just some of the fallout from his investigation. Just enough to keep you interested, but, ultimately misses the target. Rated PG-13 for violence and profanity. 1988; 100m.

GUARDIAN OF THE ABYSS ★½
DIR: Don Sharp. **CAST:** Ray Lonnen.
Uneventful devil-worship flick from England; the kind that winds up on the late late show. An antiques broker buys a mirror that is actually a window to hell. Few surprises and an anticlimactic ending. Not rated, but the equivalent of a PG for some sex. 1985; 50m.

H-MAN, THE ★★★
DIR: Inoshiro Honda. **CAST:** Yumi Shirakawa.
Unintentional humor makes this low-budget Japanese monster movie a near comedy classic. A commercial fishing boat wanders into a nuclear-test zone, mutating a crew member into a horrible water monster. When this soggy menace makes its way to Tokyo, police and organized crime alike try to destroy it. With some of the lamest special effects ever filmed, this is guaranteed to make even the most humorless individual crack a smile. Not rated, but suitable for all ages. 1959; 79m.

HALLOWEEN ★★★★½
DIR: John Carpenter. **CAST:** Jamie Lee Curtis, Donald Pleasence, Nancy Loomis, P. J. Soles, Charles Cyphers.

This is a surprisingly tasteful and enjoyable slasher film. Director John Carpenter puts the accent on suspense and atmosphere rather than blood and guts, as in other films of this kind. The story revolves around the escape of a soulless maniac who returns to the town where he murdered his sister. Rated R. 1978; 93m.

HALLOWEEN II ★★★
DIR: Rick Rosenthal. **CAST:** Jamie Lee Curtis, Donald Pleasence, Charles Cyphers, Jeffrey Kramer, Lance Guest.

This respectable sequel picks up where the original left off: with the boogeyman on the prowl and Jamie Lee Curtis running for her life. Rated R because of violence and nudity. 1981; 92m.

HALLOWEEN III: SEASON OF THE WITCH ★★½
DIR: Tommy Lee Wallace. **CAST:** Tom Atkins, Stacey Nelkin, Dan O'Herlihy.

A maniacal mask manufacturer in Northern California provides kiddies with devilishly designed pumpkin masks. Not a true sequel to the gruesome *Halloween* twosome, but still watchable. Rated R. 1983; 96m.

HALLOWEEN 4: THE RETURN OF MICHAEL MYERS ★★★
DIR: Dwight H. Little. **CAST:** Donald Pleasence, Ellie Cornell, Danielle Harris.

The makers of this third sequel to John Carpenter's ground-breaking *Halloween* obviously tried to create a quality horror film and for the most part they've succeeded. Director Dwight H. Little commendably puts the accent on atmosphere and suspense in detailing the third killing spree of Michael Myers (a.k.a. The Shape). Donald Pleasence returns as Myers's nemesis, Dr. Loomis, to hunt down this fiendish foe. Rated R for violence and profanity. 1988; 88m.

HAND, THE
DIR: Oliver Stone. **CAST:** Michael Caine, Andrea Marcovicci, Annie McEnroe, Bruce McGill.

Thumbs down on this dull film. It's the story of a successful cartoonist (Michael Caine) whose life is shattered when he loses his drawing hand in a car accident. Pretty soon he begins to think that the missing hand has a life of its own. Too bad this film doesn't have a life of its own. Rated R. 1981; 104m.

HAPPY BIRTHDAY TO ME ★
DIR: J. Lee Thompson. **CAST:** Melissa Sue Anderson, Glenn Ford, Matt Craven.

After surviving a tragic car accident that killed her mother, a young woman (Melissa Sue Anderson) suffers recurrent blackouts. During these lapses of consciousness, other—more popular and more intelligent—students at her exclusive prep school are murdered in bizarre and vicious ways. Story coherence and credibility take a backseat to all the bloodletting. Rated R. 1981; 108m.

HARD ROCK ZOMBIES ★★½
DIR: Krishna Shah. **CAST:** E. J. Curcio, Sam Mann.

The title pretty much says it all: After being murdered while on the road, the members of a heavy metal band are brought back from the dead as zombies. Half horror movie, half spoof of heavy metal music, the movie is sometimes amusing in a goofy way, though shoddy special-effects makeup brings it down a notch. Rated R for violence and gore. 1985; 94m.

HATCHET FOR THE HONEYMOON
DIR: Mario Bava. **CAST:** Stephen Forsythe, Dagmar Lassander, Laura Betti.

The man who brought you such substandard chillers as *Beyond the Door 2* and *The House of Exorcism* strikes again with another forgettable fright flick. This one is about a psychotic killer fashion mogul who hacks up brides with a...guess what. It is good for a couple of laughs, thanks to the poorly dubbed voices. Rated PG for violence. 1974; 90m.

HAUNTED CASTLE ★★★

DIR: F. W. Murnau. **CAST:** Paul Hartmann, Olga Tschechowa.

Based on the novel by Rudolf Stratz, this complex chiller takes place in a northern German castle shrouded in a mysterious, haunting atmosphere. Great cinematography and set design make for an impressive spectacle. Silent. 1921; B&W; 56m.

HAUNTED STRANGLER, THE ★★★½

DIR: Robert Day. **CAST:** Boris Karloff, Anthony Dawson, Elizabeth Allan.

Boris Karloff is well cast in this effective story of a writer who develops the homicidal tendencies of a long-dead killer he's been writing about. Gripping horror film. 1958; B&W; 81m.

HAUNTING, THE ★★★★

DIR: Robert Wise. **CAST:** Julie Harris, Claire Bloom, Richard Johnson, Russ Tamblyn, Fay Compton, Lois Maxwell.

Long considered one of the most masterly crafted tales of terror ever brought to the screen, this gripping triumph for Robert Wise still packs a punch. Julie Harris and Claire Bloom are outstanding as they recognize and finally confront the evil that inhabits a haunted house. Based on Shirley Jackson's classic *The Haunting of Hill House*. 1963; B&W; 112m.

HE KNOWS YOU'RE ALONE

DIR: Armand Mastroianni. **CAST:** Don Scardino, Caitlin O'Heany, Elizabeth Kemp, Tom Hanks.

There's a killer on the loose, specializing in brides-to-be. His current target for dismemberment is pretty Amy (Caitlin O'Heany), who can't decide whether to marry her male-chauvinist fiancé or return to her former admirer (Don Scardino), a lively lad who works in the morgue and is given to playing practical jokes. While stalking his special prey, the killer keeps his knife sharp by decimating the population of Staten Island. Rated R. 1981; 94m.

HE WALKED BY NIGHT ★★★★½

DIR: Alfred Werker. **CAST:** Richard Basehart, Scott Brady, Jack Webb, Roy Roberts, Whit Bissell.

Richard Basehart is superb in this documentary-style drama as a killer stalked by methodical policemen. A little-known cinematic gem, it's first-rate in every department and reportedly inspired Jack Webb to create *Dragnet*. 1948; B&W; 79m.

HEARSE, THE

DIR: George Bowers. **CAST:** Trish Van Devere, Joseph Cotten, David Gautreaux, Donald Hotton.

This film is about a satanic pact between an old woman and her lover. When Jane (Trish Van Devere) discovers this pact in her aunt's diary, the house starts shaking...literally. What does Satan want with Jane? This film fails to answer that question. Rated PG. 1980; 100m.

HEART OF MIDNIGHT ★★★

DIR: Matthew Chapman. **CAST:** Jennifer Jason Leigh, Peter Coyote, Frank Stallone, Brenda Vaccaro.

What begins as a disturbing haunted-house movie becomes a chilling whodunit. Jennifer Jason Leigh inherits a dilapidated ballroom with a steamy past; it seems her uncle ran a sex club on the premises and has left her an assortment of suitably decorated rooms, all of which seem to be alive. Grippingly weird. Rated R. 1989; 95m.

HELL NIGHT ★

DIR: Tom DeSimone. **CAST:** Linda Blair, Vincent Van Patten, Peter Barton, Jenny Neuman.

Linda Blair (*The Exorcist*) returns to the genre that spawned her film career in this poor low-budget horror flick about fraternity and sorority pledges spending the night in a mansion "haunted" by a crazed killer. Rated R. 1981; 101m.

HELLBOUND: HELLRAISER II ★★½

DIR: Tony Randel. **CAST:** Clare Higgins, Ashley Laurence, Kenneth Cranham.

People without skin! If that doesn't either pique your interest or turn you away, nothing will. A psychiatric patient, who is lost in a world of puzzles, unleashes the nasty Cenobites (introduced in *Hellraiser*). Clive Barker protégé Tony Randel makes everything a bit overwhelming, but it's all good, clean, gruesome fun. Rated R for gore. 1988; 96m.

HELLHOLE ★

DIR: Pierre DeMoro. **CAST:** Ray Sharkey, Judy Landers, Marjoe Gortner, Edy Williams.

A young woman witnesses her mother's murder and psychosomatically loses her memory. She is placed in an asylum where doctors perform illegal experiments involving chemical lobotomies. A poor script and stale acting make this a nearly suspenseless thriller. Rated R for violence and nudity. 1985; 90m.

HELLO, MARY LOU: PROM NIGHT II ★

DIR: Bruce Pittman. **CAST:** Lisa Schrage, Wendy Lyon, Michael Ironside.

Another tedious exploitation flick about a girl who returns from the grave to get revenge on her killers, who now run the school where she was murdered. Only redeeming features are the visual effects. Rated R for violence, nudity, and language. 1987; 96m.

HELLRAISER ★★½

DIR: Clive Barker. **CAST:** Andrew Robinson, Clare Higgins, Ashley Laurence.

In his directing debut, Clive Barker adapts his short story and proves even the author can't necessarily bring his work to life on the screen. The story is about a man who acquires a demonic Rubik's Cube. Although imbued with marvelous visuals, the film has little of the intensity of a Barker novel. Rated R for violence, sex, and adult language. 1987; 90m.

HIDE AND GO SHRIEK ★★

DIR: Skip Schoolnik. **CAST:** George Thomas, Brittain Frye.

Slasher film that's a cut above the others because of the acting. Eight high-school seniors, four boys and four girls, celebrate their graduation by partying in a deserted furniture store. Their plans for casual sex are interrupted by a psychotic killer. Not rated; contains nudity, and extreme violence. 1987; 94m.

HIDEOUS SUN DEMON, THE ★

DIR: Robert Clarke. **CAST:** Robert Clarke, Patricia Manning.

Everyone who saw this Fifties horror film as a kid probably remembers it as one of the scariest movies ever made. But look again—it's dreadful and just plain silly. Robert Clarke directed and also stars as the scientist turned into a lizardlike monster by radiation. 1959; B&W; 74m.

HILLS HAVE EYES, THE

DIR: Wes Craven. **CAST:** Susan Lamer, Robert Houston, Virginia Vincent, Russ Grieve, Dee Wallace.

The first scenes of this horror film reek of cheapness, and it gets worse. Foolish city folk have inherited a silver mine and are stopping on their way to California to check it out. That's when a ghoulish family comes crawling out of the rocks. Rated R for violence and profanity. 1977; 89m.

HILLS HAVE EYES: PART TWO, THE

DIR: Wes Craven. **CAST:** John Laughlin, Michael Berryman.

This really lame sequel wouldn't scare the most timid viewer. Teenagers are traveling to a motorcross meet in a schoolbus that breaks down in the desert. They battle the surviving members of the cannibal family from part one. A waste of everyone's time, especially yours. Rated PG-13 for violence (mild by horror standards). 1984; 86m.

HITCHER, THE ★★★
DIR: Robert Harmon. **CAST:** Rutger Hauer, C. Thomas Howell, Jeffrey DeMunn, Jennifer Jason Leigh.

C. Thomas Howell plays a young, squeamish California-bound motorist who picks up a hitchhiker, played by Rutger Hauer, somewhere in the barren Northwest. What transpires is action that will leave you physically and emotionally drained. If you thought *The Terminator* was too violent, this one will redefine the word for you. Rated R. 1986; 96m.

HITCHHIKERS
DIR: Ferd Sebastian. **CAST:** Misty Rowe, Norman Klar, Linda Avery.

Awful piece of trash about female hitchhikers who rob the motorists who stop to pick them up. Don't stop for this no-hitter! Rated R for nudity, profanity, and simulated sex. 1971; 87m.

HOLLYWOOD STRANGLER MEETS THE SKID ROW SLASHER
DIR: Wolfgang Schmidt. **CAST:** Pierre Agostino, Carolyn Brandt.

For a little over an hour, a psycho wanders around L.A. taking photos of amateur models and then strangling them, babbling all the while about his ex-girlfriend. This is occasionally interrupted by scenes of a woman who works at a magazine store stabbing bums to death. There's no dialogue, just voice-overs and a *lot* of canned music. Rated R for nudity, violence, and gore. 1982; 72m.

HOLOCAUST 2000
DIR: Alberto De Martino. **CAST:** Kirk Douglas, Agostina Belli, Simon Ward, Anthony Quayle.

This is a shameless rip-off of *The Omen.* The Antichrist plans to destroy the world, using nuclear reactors. This movie stinks. Rated R. 1978; 96m.

HOMEBODIES ★★★
DIR: Larry Yust. **CAST:** Douglas Fowley, Ruth McDevitt, Ian Wolfe.

A cast of aging screen veterans liven up this offbeat thriller about a group of senior citizens who turn into a hit squad when faced with eviction. Director Larry Yust keeps things moving at a lively pace and even manages a few bizarre twists in the final scenes. Rated PG for violence, language. 1974; 96m.

HONEYMOON ★★★½
DIR: Patrick Jamain. **CAST:** Nathalie Baye, John Shea, Richard Berry, Peter Donat.

A Frenchwoman (Nathalie Baye) goes on what appears to be a carefree New York vacation with her boyfriend (Richard Berry). However, he is busted for smuggling cocaine, and she is set for deportation. She goes to an agency that arranges marriages of convenience. She is assured that she will never see her new American "husband"—only to have him show up and refuse to leave her alone. Rated R for profanity, nudity and violence. 1987; 98m.

HONEYMOON KILLERS, THE ★★★
DIR: Leonard Kastle. **CAST:** Tony LoBlanco, Shirley Stoler, Mary Jane Higby.

Grim story of a smooth-talking Lothario and his obese lover who befriend and murder vulnerable older women for their money is based on the infamous "lonely hearts killers" of the 1940s and 1950s. Not for the squeamish, but a solid entry in the growing file of true-crime films. 1970; 108m.

HORROR EXPRESS ★★★
DIR: Eugenio Martin. **CAST:** Peter Cushing, Christopher Lee, Telly Savalas.

Director Eugenio Martin creates a neat shocker about a prehistoric manlike creature terrorizing a trans-Siberian train when he is awakened from his centuries-old tomb. Lively cast includes a pre-Kojak Telly Savalas in the role of a crazed Prussian officer intent on killing the thing. Rated R. 1972; 88m.

HORROR HOSPITAL ★★
DIR: Anthony Balch. **CAST:** Michael Gough, Robin Askwith, Dennis Price.
A crazy doctor (Michael Gough) performing gruesome brain experiments at a remote English hospital runs into trouble when a nosy young couple checks in and begins snooping around. Slow-moving gorefest. Rated R for violence and blood. 1973; 84m.

HORROR OF DRACULA ★★★★½
DIR: Terence Fisher. **CAST:** Christopher Lee, Peter Cushing, Michael Gough, Melissa Stribling, Miles Malleson.
This is the one that launched Hammer Films's popular Dracula series, featuring Christopher Lee in the first—and best—of his many appearances as the Count and Peter Cushing as his arch-nemesis Van Helsing. A stylish, exciting reworking of Bram Stoker's classic story of a bloodthirsty vampire on the prowl from Transylvania to London and back again. Genuinely scary film, with a hell of an ending, too. 1958; 82m.

HORROR OF FRANKENSTEIN ★★★★
DIR: Jimmy Sangster. **CAST:** Ralph Bates, Kate O'Mara, Veronica Carlson, Dennis Price.
Young medical student, fed up with school, decides to drop out and continue his studies alone. So what if his name just happens to be Frankenstein and he just happens to be making a monster? Good entry in the series has many ghoulish sequences, along with some welcome touches of humor. Recommended. Rated R. 1970; 95m.

HORROR OF PARTY BEACH, THE
DIR: Del Tenney. **CAST:** John Scott, Alice Lyon.
A really horrendous horror film about radioactive waste creating lizardlike monsters, who emerge from the sea and menace a group of carefree young beach revelers. Imagine *Frankie and Annette Meet the Creature from the Black Lagoon* and you've pegged this strictly-for-Thanksgiving gobbler. Unrated, but should be a Z. 1964; 72m.

HOSPITAL MASSACRE ★½
DIR: Boaz Davidson. **CAST:** Barbi Benton, Chip Lucia, Jon Van Ness.
Another *Halloween* clone, this one is set in a hospital where a psycho killer murders everyone in an attempt to get revenge on the girl who laughed at his Valentine's Day card twenty years before. Slow-moving and witless. We preferred the original title: *Be My Valentine, Or Else*. Rated R for nudity and gore. 1982; 88m.

HOUSE ★★½
DIR: Steve Miner. **CAST:** William Katt, George Wendt, Kay Lenz, Richard Moll.
A comedy-thriller about an author who moves into an old mansion left to him by an aunt who committed suicide. He's looking for solitude, but instead he finds an assortment of slimy monsters. The cast is good, but the shocks are predictable, crippling the suspense. Rated R for violence and profanity. 1986; 93m.

HOUSE II: THE SECOND STORY ★★
DIR: Ethan Wiley. **CAST:** Arye Gross, Jonathan Stark, Royal Dano, Bill Maher, John Ratzenberger.
In this unwarranted sequel to *House*, a young man inherits a mansion and invites his best friend to move in with him. A series of humorous and mysterious events lead the two to exhume the grave of the young man's great-grandfather, who is magically still alive. Rated PG-13 for foul language and some violence. 1987; 88m.

HOUSE OF EXORCISM, THE
DIR: Mickey Lion, Mario Bava. **CAST:** Telly Savalas, Robert Alda, Elke Sommer.

Early in this incomprehensible film, which has something to do with a woman possessed by the spirit of *Exorcist* rip-offs, one of the characters prophetically proclaims, "It's awful." That it is. Rated R for profanity, nudity, gore, and violence. 1975; 93m.

HOUSE OF GAMES ★★★★½
DIR: David Mamet. **CAST:** Lindsay Crouse, Joe Mantegna, Lilia Skala.
Pulitzer Prize–winning playwright David Mamet makes an impressive directorial debut with this suspense thriller. Lindsay Crouse, the writer-director's wife, gives an effective performance as a psychiatrist who attempts to intercede with a con man (Joe Mantegna) on behalf of one of her patients, a compulsive gambler who owes him several thousand dollars. She is sucked into a world of mirrors where nothing is what it seems. Rated R for profanity and violence. 1987; 102m.

HOUSE OF SEVEN CORPSES, THE ★★½
DIR: Paul Harrison. **CAST:** John Ireland, Faith Domergue, John Carradine.
Veteran cast almost saves this minor yarn about the grisly events that happen to the members of a film crew shooting a horror movie in a foreboding old mansion. Semi-entertaining nonsense. Rated PG. 1973; 90m.

HOUSE OF TERROR
DIR: Sergei Goncharff. **CAST:** Jenifer Bishop, Arell Blanton, Mitchell Gregg.
A private nurse and her ex-con boyfriend try to bilk a millionaire out of his riches upon the death of his wife. The nurse and the millionaire marry and a woman who looks exactly like the dead wife appears on the scene. It doesn't work. Rated PG for violence and adult situations. 1987; 90m.

HOUSE OF THE DEAD
DIR: Knute Allmendinger. **CAST:** John Erickson, Charles Aldman, Bernard Fox.
A young man stranded in a haunted house finds he is not alone. Don't ask why anyone would watch or enjoy this bomb. 1980; 90m.

HOUSE OF THE LONG SHADOWS ★★★
DIR: Pete Walker. **CAST:** Vincent Price, John Carradine, Christopher Lee, Desi Arnaz Jr., Peter Cushing.
This is the good old-fashioned–type horror film that doesn't rely on blood and gore to give the viewer a scare. This gothic thriller is a great choice for horror fans who still like to use their imaginations. Rated PG. 1984; 102m.

HOUSE OF WAX ★★★½
DIR: André de Toth. **CAST:** Vincent Price, Phyllis Kirk, Carolyn Jones.
Vincent Price stars as a demented sculptor who, after losing the use of his hands in a fire, turns to murder to continue his work in this above-average horror film. 1953; 88m.

HOUSE ON CARROLL STREET, THE ★★★
DIR: Peter Yates. **CAST:** Kelly McGillis, Jeff Daniels, Jessica Tandy, Mandy Patinkin.
Commendable suspense film about a young accused Communist (Kelly McGillis) who becomes involved in a Nazi smuggling ring in 1951 Washington, D.C. Jeff Daniels is one of the investigating F.B.I. men who falls for McGillis. A good costume piece, and McGillis and Daniels turn in solid performances, along with Jessica Tandy as McGillis's crusty employer. Rated PG for language, violence, and slight nudity. 1988; 111m.

HOUSE ON HAUNTED HILL ★★★
DIR: William Castle. **CAST:** Vincent Price, Carol Ohmart, Richard Long, Elisha Cook Jr., Carolyn Craig, Alan Marshal.
Vincent Price is at his most relaxed and confident in this fun fright flick about the wealthy owner of a creepy old fortress who offers a group a fortune if they can survive a night there.

Humorous at times, deadly serious at others. 1958; B&W; 75m.

HOUSE ON SKULL MOUNTAIN
DIR: Ron Honthaner. **CAST:** Victor French, Mike Evans.

The one thing you could say for a lot of the so-called blaxploitation movies of the Seventies was that they were at least fast-moving and energetic. Not so this creaky spooker. Relatives gathered in an old, dark house for the reading of a will are killed off one by one. Who's the killer? Stay tuned for the not very surprising answer. Rated PG. 1974; 89m.

HOUSE ON SORORITY ROW
DIR: Mark Rosman. **CAST:** Eileen Davidson.

In this low-budget horror film, a group of college girls takes over their sorority and kills the house mother. While the house mother may be down, she's not out—at least not out of the picture—as she comes back from the dead to wreak havoc. Rated R. 1983; 90m.

HOUSE THAT BLED TO DEATH, THE ★★
DIR: Tom Clegg. **CAST:** Nicolas Ball.

Marginally scary horror film about a house that is possessed. Possessed by what or who? Don't ask us—the film refuses to give up the reason for all the blood that keeps shooting out of the pipes, or the various bloody members that show up in the fridge now and then. Not rated, but would probably merit a PG for violence and gore. 1985; 50m.

HOUSE THAT DRIPPED BLOOD, THE ★★★½
DIR: Peter Duffell. **CAST:** Christopher Lee, Peter Cushing, Denholm Elliott, Jon Pertwee, Ingrid Pitt.

All-star horror-anthology high jinks adapted from the stories of Robert Bloch. It's not quite on a par with the pioneering British release *Dead of Night*, but it'll do. Best segment: a horror star (Jon Pertwee) discovers a vampire's cape and finds himself becoming a little too convincing in the role of a bloodsucker. Rated PG. 1970; 102m.

HOUSE THAT VANISHED, THE ★½
DIR: Joseph Larraz. **CAST:** Andrea Allan.

Exploitative suspense tale about a woman who sees a murder but can't convince anyone that it happened because she can't find the house. There's a lot of nudity and an underdeveloped plot in this British-made film, which was fifteen minutes longer when it was originally released as *Scream and Die*. Rated R. 1973; 84m.

HOUSE WHERE EVIL DWELLS, THE ★★
DIR: Kevin O'Connor. **CAST:** Edward Albert, Susan George, Doug McClure.

Depressing little horror romp with a Japanese background. In a savagely violent opening, a young samurai swordsman discovers the amorous activities of his less-than-faithful wife, and a gory fight ensues. This traps some really angry spirits in the house, which Edward Albert and Susan George move into centuries later. Rated R for nudity, violence, language. 1985; 91m.

HOWLING, THE ★★★★
DIR: Joe Dante. **CAST:** Dee Wallace, Christopher Stone, Patrick Macnee, Dennis Dugan, Slim Pickens, John Carradine.

The Howling has every spooky scene you've ever seen, every horror movie cliché that's ever been overspoken, and every guaranteed-to-make-'em-jump, out-of-the-dark surprise that Hollywood ever came up with for its scary movies. It also has the best special effects since *Alien* and some really off-the-wall humor. Rated R for gruesome adult horror. 1981; 91m.

HOWLING II...YOUR SISTER IS A WEREWOLF
DIR: Philippe Mora. **CAST:** Christopher Lee, Reb Brown, Annie McEnroe, Sybil Danning.

Poor follow-up to *The Howling* concerns the plight of Ben White (Reb Brown) to uncover and destroy the colony of werewolves that infected his sister. An awful sequel; even Sybil Danning as the Leader of the Pack can't save it. Rated R for nudity, blood, and gore. 1984; 91m.

HOWLING III ★★½
DIR: Phillippe Mora. **CAST:** Barry Otto.
Werewolves turn up in Australia, only these are marsupials. A sociologist falls in love with one of them and tries to save the whole tribe. The story focuses more on character than gore and you find yourself strangely engrossed. Rated R for brief nudity and violence. 1987; 95m.

HOWLING IV
DIR: John Hough. **CAST:** Romy Windsor, Michael Weiss, Antony Hamilton.
Werewolves are scarce in this third sequel about a woman haunted by the ghost of a nun who was killed by one of the lycanthropes. The woman moves to the same small town that was seen in the original *Howling*. From that point on we're bored to tears as she unravels this supernatural mystery. Rated R for violence and nudity. 1988; 94m.

HUMAN MONSTER, THE (DARK EYES OF LONDON) ★★★
DIR: Walter Summers. **CAST:** Bela Lugosi, Hugh Williams, Greta Gynt, Edmon Ryan.
Creaky but sometimes clever suspense thriller about a humanitarian (Bela Lugosi) who may not be as philanthropic as he seems. Strange murders have been occurring in the vicinity of his charitable facility. This preposterous Edgar Wallace story has its moments. 1939; B&W; 73m.

HUMANOIDS FROM THE DEEP ★★★
DIR: Barbara Peters. **CAST:** Doug McClure, Ann Turkel, Vic Morrow.
As in *Jaws*, beachgoers are terrified by water beasts in this science-fiction film. This time, it's underwater vegetable monsters who attack seaside frolickers. This is a never-a-dull-moment thriller. Rated R. 1980; 80m.

HUMONGOUS ★
DIR: Paul Lynch. **CAST:** Janet Julian, David Wallace.
A group of idiotic teenagers become shipwrecked on an island whose only inhabitant is a hairy, murderous mutant. What follows is just a variation of the shopworn *Friday the 13th* plot, incredibly dull. Rated R for violence. 1982; 90m.

HUNCHBACK OF NOTRE DAME, THE (1923) ★★★★½
DIR: Wallace Worsley. **CAST:** Lon Chaney Sr., Patsy Ruth Miller, Ernest Torrence.
Although it has been remade, with varying degrees of success, in the sound era, no film has surpassed the Lon Chaney version in screen spectacle or in the athletic excellence of moviedom's "man of a thousand faces." A musical score has been added. 1923; B&W; 108m.

HUNCHBACK OF NOTRE DAME, THE (1939) ★★★★
DIR: William Dieterle. **CAST:** Charles Laughton, Thomas Mitchell, Maureen O'Hara, Edmond O'Brien.
In this horror classic, Charles Laughton gives a tour-de-force performance as the deformed bell-ringer who comes to the aid of a pretty gypsy (Maureen O'Hara). Cedric Hardwicke, and Edmond O'Brien also give strong performances in this remake of the silent film. 1939; B&W; 117m.

HUNGER, THE ★
DIR: Tony Scott. **CAST:** Catherine Deneuve, David Bowie, Susan Sarandon, Cliff De Young.
Arty and visually striking yet cold, this kinky sci-fi horror film features French actress Catherine Deneuve as a seductive vampire. Her centuries-old boyfriend (David Bowie) is about to disintegrate, so she picks a new lover (Susan Sarandon). Rated R for gore, profanity, and nudity. 1983; 94m.

HUSH...HUSH, SWEET CHARLOTTE ★★★
DIR: Robert Aldrich. **CAST:** Bette Davis, Olivia De Havilland, Joseph Cotten, Agnes Moorehead, Cecil Kellaway, Mary Astor, Bruce Dern.

Originally planned as a sequel to *What Ever Happened to Baby Jane?*, reuniting stars of that movie, Bette Davis and Joan Crawford, this effort was filmed with Bette opposite her old Warner Bros. cellmate—Olivia De Havilland. This time they're on opposite sides of the magnolia bush, with Olivia trying to drive poor Bette, who's not all there to begin with, mad. 1965; B&W; 133m.

HYSTERIA ★★½
DIR: Freddie Francis. **CAST:** Robert Webber, Lelia Goldoni, Maurice Denham, Jennifer Jayne.

After their success in remaking old Universal horror movies, the folks at England's Hammer Films decided to try their luck with Hitchcockian suspense. This film is one of the results. Robert Webber plays an American amnesia victim in England. Released from the hospital, he begins to see mysterious women, hear strange noises, and imagine bloody knives and corpses. This unrated film contains some mild violence. 1964; B&W; 85m.

I CONFESS ★★★
DIR: Alfred Hitchcock. **CAST:** Montgomery Clift, Karl Malden, Anne Baxter, Brian Aherne.

In spite of shortcomings, this is the film that best reflects many of Hitch's puritanical ethics. Clift stars as a priest who takes confession from a man who—coincidentally—killed a blackmailer who knew of Clift's pre-vows relationship with Baxter. (Whew!) Moody and atmospheric. 1953; B&W; 95m.

I DISMEMBER MAMA ★
DIR: Paul Leder. **CAST:** Zooey Hall, Greg Mullavey.

Great title—horrible movie. Mama's boy escapes from institution and goes on a "purifying" spree. In a sick plot turn, he falls in love with an 11-year-old girl after carving up her mother. A low-budget bore. Rated R for violence and nudity. 1972; 86m.

I, MADMAN ★★
DIR: Tibor Takacs. **CAST:** Jenny Wright, Clayton Rohner.

A bookstore employee (Jenny Wright) becomes so engrossed in a horror novel that she begins living its terrors. Director Tibor Takacs says that the laughs are intentional in this film, which provides the same kind of tacky entertainment found in such masterpieces of ineptitude as *Plan 9 from Outer Space* and *Robot Monster*. Rated R for violence, simulated sex, and profanity. 1989; 95m.

I MARRIED A VAMPIRE
DIR: Jay Raskin. **CAST:** Rachel Golden, Brendan Hickey.

Boring nonsense, more about a country girl's adventures in the big city than a horror flick. Rachel Gordon is the girl, and Brendan Hickey is the supposed vampire. This one's better than Sominex. Not rated. 1983; 85m.

I SPIT ON YOUR CORPSE
DIR: Al Adams. **CAST:** Georgina Spelvin.

A team of larcenous females goes on a killing spree across the country, at the behest of their male mob boss. This is one of the worst sex and violence exploitation flicks ever made. The acting and scripting is lower than low. Not rated, but contains nudity and violence. 1974; 88m.

I SPIT ON YOUR GRAVE
DIR: Meir Zarchi. **CAST:** Camille Keaton.

After being brutally raped by a gang of thugs (one of whom is retarded), a young woman takes sadistic revenge. This is, beyond a doubt, one of the most tasteless, irresponsible, and disturbing movies ever made. Most videotapes of this title contain the longer X-rated version. Rated R or X. 1981; 88m.

I WAKE UP SCREAMING ★★★
DIR: H. Bruce Humberstone. **CAST:** Betty Grable, Victor Mature, Carole Landis, Laird Cregar, William Gargan.
Laird Cregar's performance as a menacing and sinister detective bent on convicting an innocent Victor Mature for the murder of Carole Landis dominates this suspense-filled *film noir*. Betty Grable is surprisingly effective in her first nonmusical role as the victim's sister, who finds herself attracted to the chief suspect. A classy whodunit. 1941; B&W; 82m.

I WALKED WITH A ZOMBIE ★★★★½
DIR: Jacques Tourneur. **CAST:** Frances Dee, Tom Conway, James Ellison.
Director Jacques Tourneur made this classic horror film, involving voodoo and black magic, on an island in the Pacific. One of the best of its kind, this is a great Val Lewton production. 1943; B&W; 69m.

I WAS A TEENAGE ZOMBIE
DIR: John Elias Michalakis. **CAST:** Michael Rubin, Steve McCoy.
A drug pusher is murdered and his body thrown into a river contaminated by a nuclear power plant. He returns as a green zombie and avenges himself upon his teenage killers, turning them into flesh-eating maniacs. Really foul. Not rated but contains violence, adult language, and brief nudity. 1986; 90m.

ILSA, SHE WOLF OF THE SS
DIR: Don Edmonds. **CAST:** Dyanne Thorne.
A disturbing portrait of a Nazi concentration-camp commandant and her insatiable need for both sex and violent torture. Sicko filmmaking not for the faint of heart or weak of stomach. (Sequels *Ilsa, Harmen Keeper of the Oil Sheiks* and *Ilsa, Wicked Warden* heap it on *ad nauseum*.) Not rated, but contains nudity and extreme violence. 1974; 92m.

IMPACT ★★
DIR: Arthur Lubin. **CAST:** Brian Donlevy, Helen Walker, Tony Barrett, Ella Raines, Charles Coburn, Anna May Wong.
Shades of *Double Indemnity*! Unfaithful wife and lover plot to kill rich husband, but lover gets bumped instead. Interesting, but don't believe the title. 1948; B&W; 111m.

IMPULSE (1974) ★
DIR: William Grefe. **CAST:** William Shatner, Ruth Roman, Harold Sakata.
William Shatner plays an emotionally disturbed ex–mental patient with a penchant for murder. Overfamiliar story made unintentionally comical by super-cheapie production. Not rated, but with several unconvincing murders and lots of phony blood. 1974; 85m.

IMPULSE (1984) ★★
DIR: Graham Baker. **CAST:** Tim Matheson, Meg Tilly, Hume Cronyn.
This mildly interesting thriller takes place in a town where the inhabitants find they have increasing difficulties in controlling their urges. The film attempts to tie up its plot in a hasty, unconvincing final ten minutes. Rated R for profanity and violence. 1984; 91m.

IN THE SHADOW OF KILIMANJARO ★
DIR: Raju Patel. **CAST:** John Rhys-Davies, Timothy Bottoms, Irene Miracle, Michele Carey.
This is the gory but supposedly true story of what happened in Kenya when ninety thousand baboons went on a killing spree because of the 1984 drought. They were hungry, and people were the only readily available source of food. Rated R for violence. 1986; 97m.

INCREDIBLE TWO-HEADED TRANSPLANT, THE ★
DIR: Anthony M. Lanza. **CAST:** Bruce Dern, Pat Priest, Casey Kasem.
A sadistic killer's head is grafted to the body of a dim-witted giant, creat-

ing a threat to well-built women and motorcycle gangs everywhere. This low-budget yawn is a complete waste of time. Rated PG. 1971; 88m.

INCREDIBLY STRANGE CREATURES WHO STOPPED LIVING AND BECAME MIXED-UP ZOMBIES, THE ★½
DIR: Ray Dennis Steckler. **CAST:** Cash Flagg, Brett O'Hara, Carolyn Brandt, Atlas King.

This movie doesn't live up to its title; how could it? It was later released as *Teenage Psycho Meets Bloody Mary.* Under any name it's a most peculiar horror-comedy about a young dropout (Cash Flagg, who is really producer-director Ray Dennis Steckler) running afoul of a carnival gypsy. Bad acting and laughable special effects. What do you expect on a budget of $38,000? 1965; 81m.

INCUBUS, THE 🦃
DIR: John Hough. **CAST:** John Cassavetes, Kerrie Keane, Helen Hughes, John Ireland.

About a spate of sex murders in a small town, this is a vile and mean-spirited film, a nightmare of bad taste and burdensome plotting, and a depressing example of movie-making at its most prurient. Rated R for all manner of gruesome goings-on. 1982; 90m.

INDESTRUCTIBLE MAN ★★
DIR: Jack Pollexfen. **CAST:** Lon Chaney Jr., Marian Carr, Ross Elliott, Casey Adams.

Lon Chaney looks uncomfortable in the title role of an electrocuted man brought back to life who seeks revenge on the old gang who betrayed him. Nothing new has been added to the worn-out story, unless you want to count the awful narration, which makes this passable thriller seem utterly ridiculous at times. 1956; B&W; 70m.

INFERNO ★★
DIR: Dario Argento. **CAST:** Eleonora Giorgi, Leigh McCloskey, Gabriele Lavia.

This Italian horror flick is heavy on suspense but weak on plot. Leigh McCloskey is the hero who comes to help his sister when she discovers that her apartment is inhabited by an ancient evil spirit. Voices are dubbed, even American actor McCloskey's, and something may have been lost in the translation. Rated R for gore. 1978; 83m.

INITIATION, THE ★★
DIR: Larry Stewart. **CAST:** Vera Miles, Clu Gulager, James Read, Daphne Zuniga.

A particularly gruesome story involving psychotic terror and lots of blood and gore. In a quest to rid herself of a recurring nightmare, a young coed becomes involved in a bloody reality, unlocking a twisted past that was blotted from her memory at a young age. Rated R. 1984; 97m.

INITIATION OF SARAH, THE ★★
DIR: Robert Day. **CAST:** Kay Lenz, Shelley Winters, Kathryn Crosby, Morgan Brittany, Tony Bill.

Adequate TV movie features Kay Lenz as a young college girl being victimized by other students during initiation, and her subsequent revenge upon acquiring supernatural powers. Hokey thriller should have been better, judging from the cast. 1978; 100m.

INTERNECINE PROJECT, THE ★★★
DIR: Ken Hughes. **CAST:** James Coburn, Lee Grant, Harry Andrews, Ian Hendry, Michael Jayston, Keenan Wynn.

James Coburn plays an ambitious business tycoon who finds he has to kill four associates to meet a business agreement. The fashion in which he does this proves to be interesting. Worth a look for the trick ending. Rated PG. 1974; 89m.

INTRUDER ★½
DIR: Scott Spiegel. **CAST:** Elizabeth Cox, Danny Hicks, Rene Estevez.

A bloodthirsty killer is locked in a supermarket with employees preparing for a going-out-of-business sale. Slasher fans should find this amusing. Rated R for violence and profanity. 1988; 90m.

INVASION EARTH: THE ALIENS ARE HERE ★

DIR: George Maitland. **CAST:** Janis Fabian, Christian Lee.

Comedic aliens take over a cinema presenting a sci-fi film festival, subverting humans into blank-eyed underwear-clad zombies. But some kids get wise to the scheme and try to put a stop to it before it's too late. Unfunny as comedy, but with great clips of classic SF and horror films from years past. Not rated, but suitable for most age groups. 1987; 84m.

INVASION OF THE BLOOD FARMERS ★

DIR: Ed Adlum. **CAST:** Cynthia Fleming.

The residents of a secluded New York town are really modern-day Druids. They attack travelers and drain their blood, looking for a rare blood type that will revive their quenn. Pure fertilizer. Rated PG. 1972; 84m.

INVISIBLE GHOST ★

DIR: Joseph H. Lewis. **CAST:** Bela Lugosi, Polly Ann Young, John McGuire, Betty Compson, Jack Mulhall.

This low-budget Monogram programmer features Bela Lugosi as an unwitting murderer, used by his supposedly dead wife to further her schemes—much the same as Lugosi himself was killed in films by overexposure in exploitative poverty row productions like this. 1941; B&W; 64m.

INVISIBLE MAN, THE ★★★★½

DIR: James Whale. **CAST:** Claude Rains, Gloria Stuart, Una O'Connor, Henry Travers, E. E. Clive, Dwight Frye.

Claude Rains goes unseen until the finish in his screen debut. He plays Jack Griffin, the title character in H. G. Wells's famous story of a scientist who creates an invisibility serum—with the side effect of driving a person slowly insane. Frightening film could initially be mistaken for a comedy, with large chunks of humor in the first half, turning deadly serious thereafter. 1933; B&W; 71m.

INVISIBLE RAY, THE ★★★

DIR: Lambert Hillyer. **CAST:** Boris Karloff, Bela Lugosi, Frances Drake, Frank Lawton.

Boris Karloff and Bela Lugosi are teamed in this interesting story. A brilliant research scientist (Karloff), experimenting in Africa, is contaminated by a hunk of radioactive meteor landing nearby and soon discovers that his mere touch can kill. Neat Universal thriller features first-rate effects and good ensemble acting. 1936; B&W; 81m.

INVISIBLE STRANGLER 🦃

DIR: John Florea. **CAST:** Robert Foxworth, Stefanie Powers, Elke Sommer.

A murderer on death row discovers he has a psychic power to make himself invisible. He escapes from prison and begins killing the witnesses who testified against him. Poorly acted. Not rated, but contains graphic violence. 1984; 85m.

INVITATION TO HELL 🦃

DIR: Wes Craven. **CAST:** Robert Urich, Joanna Cassidy, Susan Lucci, Kevin McCarthy.

A family visits a posh vacation resort, only to be seduced by a beautiful Satan worshiper who takes them down into the bowels of hell. This bland telefilm never really gets off the ground. The acting is lackluster and the plot ill-conceived. 1984; 96m.

ISLAND, THE ★½

DIR: Michael Ritchie. **CAST:** Michael Caine, David Warner, Angela Punch McGregor.

Dreadful horror-adventure movie featuring Michael Caine as a reporter investigating the mysterious disappearances of pleasure craft and their owners in an area of the Caribbean. Caine discovers that the force behind the phenomenon is a band of pirates who have remained untouched by progress for three centuries. Rated R. 1980; 113m.

ISLAND CLAWS ★★
DIR: Hernan Cardenas. **CAST:** Robert Lansing, Barry Nelson, Steve Hanks, Nita Talbot.
As science-fiction horror thrillers go, this one is about average. *Attack of the Killer Crabs* would have been a more appropriate title, though. Dr. McNeal (Barry Nelson) is a scientist who is experimenting to make larger crabs as a food source. Rated PG for violence. 1980; 91m.

ISLE OF THE DEAD ★★★½
DIR: Mark Robson. **CAST:** Boris Karloff, Ellen Drew, Jason Robards Sr.
Atmospheric goings-on dominate this typically tasteful horror study from producer Val Lewton. A group of people are stranded on a Greek island during a quarantine. Star Boris Karloff is, as usual, outstanding. 1945; B&W; 72m.

IT CAME FROM BENEATH THE SEA ★★★★
DIR: Robert Gordon. **CAST:** Kenneth Tobey, Faith Domergue, Donald Curtis, Ian Keith.
Ray Harryhausen's powerhouse special effects light up the screen in this story of a giant octopus from the depths of the Pacific that causes massive destruction along the North American coast as it makes its way toward San Francisco. A little talky at times, but the brilliantly achieved effects make this a must-see movie even on the small screen. 1955; B&W; 80m.

IT LIVES AGAIN ★★★
DIR: Larry Cohen. **CAST:** Frederic Forrest, Kathleen Lloyd, John P. Ryan, John Marley, Andrew Duggan.
In an effort to outdo the original *It's Alive!*, this film has three mutated babies on the loose, and everybody in a panic. Doesn't quite measure up to its predecessor, but still successful due to another fine make up job on the monsters by Rick Baker. Rated R. 1978; 91m.

IT'S ALIVE! ★★★½
DIR: Larry Cohen. **CAST:** John P. Ryan, Sharon Farrell, Andrew Duggan, Guy Stockwell, Michael Ansara.
This camp classic about a mutated baby with a thirst for human blood has to be seen to be believed. Convincing effects work by Rick Baker and a fantastic score by Bernard Herrmann make this film one to remember. Rated PG. 1974; 91m.

IT'S ALIVE III: ISLAND OF THE ALIVE ★★½
DIR: Larry Cohen. **CAST:** Michael Moriarty, Karen Black, Gerrit Graham, James Dixon.
In this sequel, the mutant babies are sequestered on a desert island, where they reproduce and make their way back home to wreak havoc. Although this is a surprisingly strong entry in the *Alive* series, it suffers from some sloppy effects and mediocre acting. Rated R for violence. 1986; 95m.

JACK THE RIPPER ★★
DIR: Jess (Jesus) Franco. **CAST:** Klaus Kinski, Josephine Chaplin.
Klaus Kinski plays Jack the Ripper, and Josephine Chaplin is Cynthia, the Scotland Yard inspector's girlfriend. Jack the Ripper is terrorizing London by killing women and disposing of their bodies in the Thames River. Rated R for violence and nudity. 1979; 82m.

JACK'S BACK ★★★
DIR: Rowdy Herrington. **CAST:** James Spader, Cynthia Gibb, Robert Picardo, Rod Loomis, Chris Mulkey.
Not a splatter film, but a fairly thoughtful suspense melodrama. James Spader portrays twin brothers in this tale of a Jack-the-Ripper copycat killer operating in modern-day Los Angeles. Rated R for gore. 1988; 90m.

JANUARY MAN, THE ★★★
DIR: Pat O'Connor. **CAST:** Kevin Kline, Susan Sarandon, Mary Elizabeth Mastrantonio, Harvey Keitel, Danny Aiello, Rod Steiger.

Whew! We've seen some weird movies in our time, but this one deserves a special place in some museum. John Patrick Shanley (*Moonstruck*) wrote this goofy mystery about a former police detective (Kevin Kline) who is drafted back into service when a serial killer begins to terrorize New York City. Kline starts working on the case while romancing Mary Elizabeth Mastrantonio, the daughter of NYC mayor Rod Steiger. This is a silly movie for smart people and will repel as many people as it entertains. Rated R for profanity and violence. 1989; 110m.

JAR, THE
DIR: Bruce Toscano. **CAST:** Gary Wallace, Karen Sjoberg.

Utterly boring horror film about a man who is haunted by a demon in a jar given to him by an old man on the street. Now he is stuck with the thing; even when he shatters the jar, it keeps coming back. The film has all the flair of a home movie, but is insufferably longer. 1984; 90m.

JAWS ★★★★★
DIR: Steven Spielberg. **CAST:** Roy Scheider, Robert Shaw, Richard Dreyfuss, Lorraine Gary, Murray Hamilton.

A young Steven Spielberg (27 at the time) directed this 1975 scare masterpiece based on the Peter Benchley novel. A large shark is terrorizing the tourists at the local beach. The eerie music by John Williams heightens the tension to underscore the shark's presence and scare the audience right out of their seats. Roy Scheider, Robert Shaw, and Richard Dreyfuss offer outstanding performances. Rated PG. 1975; 124m.

JAWS 2 ★★★
DIR: Jeannot Szwarc. **CAST:** Roy Scheider, Lorraine Gary, Murray Hamilton, Jeffrey Kramer.

Even though it's a sequel, *Jaws 2* delivers. Police chief Martin Brody (Roy Scheider) believes there's a shark in the waters off Amity again, but his wife and employers think he's crazy. Rated PG. 1978; 120m.

JAWS 3 ★★
DIR: Joe Alves. **CAST:** Louis Gossett Jr., Dennis Quaid, Bess Armstrong, Simon MacCorkindale.

Among those marked for lunch in this soggy, unexciting sequel are Louis Gossett Jr., Dennis Quaid, and Bess Armstrong. They look bored. You'll be bored. Rated PG. 1983; 97m.

JAWS THE REVENGE
DIR: Joseph Sargent. **CAST:** Lorraine Gary, Lance Guest, Michael Caine, Mario Van Peebles, Karen Young.

This third sequel is lowest-common-denominator filmmaking, a by-the-numbers effort. Lorraine Gary returns as Mom Brody, who inanely blames the *same animal*—conveniently forgetting all the others which were blown up and electrocuted—when her now-grown son becomes fish-food. Rated PG. 1987; 89m.

JAWS OF DEATH, THE ★½
DIR: William Grefe. **CAST:** Richard Jaeckel, Jenifer Bishop, Harold Sakata.

Low-rent *Jaws* clone features Jaeckel as a shark breeder who rents his finny friends out to Florida aquariums. But when he finds out that the sharks are being exploited he seeks revenge. Better than *Jaws: The Revenge*, but not by much. 1976; 93m.

JENNIFER ★★
DIR: Brice Mack. **CAST:** Lisa Pelikan, Bert Convy, Nina Foch, John Gavin, Wesley Eure.

A carbon copy of *Carrie*—but with snakes. Jennifer is a sweet, innocent child on a poor-kids scholarship at an uppity school for rich girls. She is tormented by one particularly sadistic girl and her cohorts until she is harassed into a frenzy. What's the catch? Jennifer was raised by a cult of religious fanatics who believe that God has given her the power to command reptiles. Rated PG. 1978; 90m.

JESSE JAMES MEETS FRANKENSTEIN'S DAUGHTER 🦃
DIR: William Beaudine. **CAST:** John Lupton, Estelita, Cal Bolder, Jim Davis.

At last! The one we've all been waiting for! The one they said couldn't be made! Well, they were almost right. From the director of *Bela Lugosi Meets a Brooklyn Gorilla* comes a film that *shouldn't* have been made. The feeble plot pits hero Jesse James against the evil daughter of the infamous doctor of the title. Watch if you must. 1966; 88m.

JIGSAW MAN, THE ★★★★
DIR: Freddie Francis. **CAST:** Michael Caine, Laurence Olivier, Susan George, Robert Powell, Charles Gray.

In this suspense film, Michael Caine plays a British secret agent who has defected, under orders, to Russia. Before leaving, he discovered a list of Soviet spies operating in England and hid it. After forty years, he returns to England in order to get the list with spies from both countries hot on his trail. This is a wonderfully entertaining puzzle of a movie. Rated PG for violence and profanity. 1984; 90m.

JUGGERNAUT (1936) ★★½
DIR: Henry Edwards. **CAST:** Boris Karloff.

In this low-budget mystery-drama filmed in England, Boris Karloff plays Dr. Sartorius, a brilliant (but cracked) specialist on the verge of perfecting a cure for paralysis. He makes a deal with a patient to murder her husband. 1936; B&W; 64m.

JUNIOR 🦃
DIR: Jim Henley. **CAST:** Linda Singer.

We can't figure out what's more despicable about this film—its exploitation of women or its shameless theft of ideas from *Psycho* and *The Texas Chainsaw Massacre*. Not rated, but contains violence, nudity, and profanity. 1984; 80m.

KEEP, THE ★½
DIR: Michael Mann. **CAST:** Ian McKellen, Alberta Watson, Scott Glenn, Jurgen Prochnow.

This is a visually impressive but otherwise flat and disappointing horror film set during World War II. Ian McKellen and Alberta Watson play Jewish prisoners freed by the Nazis when a centuries-old presence awakens in an old castle. After an impressive beginning with good special effects, this ends up being no more than an interesting curio. Rated R for nudity and violence. 1983; 96m.

KEEPER, THE 🦃
DIR: T. Y. Drake. **CAST:** Christopher Lee, Sally Gray.

You'd probably be more entertained by watching commercials on TV. Bad, bad, bad. Christopher Lee plays the title role of the owner of an insane asylum who preys on the wealthy families of his charges. Rated R. 1984; 96m.

KIDNAPPING OF THE PRESIDENT, THE ★★★★
DIR: George Mendeluk. **CAST:** William Shatner, Hal Holbrook, Van Johnson, Ava Gardner.

As the title implies, terrorists kidnap the president and hold him hostage in this excellent action thriller. The acting is excellent, the suspense taut, and the direction tightly paced. 1979; 120m.

KILLER INSIDE ME, THE ★★★
DIR: Burt Kennedy. **CAST:** Stacy Keach, Susan Tyrrell, Tisha Sterling, Keenan Wynn, Charles McGraw, John Dehner, Pepe Serna, Royal Dano, John Carradine, Don Stroud.

Stacy Keach plays a schizophrenic sheriff in a small town. A tightly woven plot offers the viewer plenty of surprises. Rated R for violence and profanity. 1975; 99m.

KILLER KLOWNS FROM OUTER SPACE ★★★½
DIR: Stephen Chiodo. **CAST:** Grant Cramer, Suzanne Snyder, John Allen Nelson, Royal Dano, John Vernon.

Lon Chaney once opined that "there is nothing more frightening than a clown after midnight." This low-budget sci-fi–horror thriller from the Chiodo brothers proves that claim with this high-style mixture of camp, comedy, and chills. The title pretty much says it all, but the results are more entertaining than one might expect. Rated PG-13 for profanity and violence. 1988; 90m.

KILLING HOUR, THE ★½
DIR: Armand Mastroianni. **CAST:** Perry King, Elizabeth Kemp, Norman Parker, Kenneth McMillan.

Elizabeth Kemp plays a clairvoyant art student who, through her drawings, becomes involved in a series of murders. The story is a blatant rip-off of *The Eyes of Laura Mars*. With that said, suspense is achieved during the last fifteen minutes of the film. Rated R for violence, nudity, and profanity. 1984; 97m.

KINDRED, THE ★
DIR: Jeffrey Obrow, Stephen Carpenter. **CAST:** David Allen Brooks, Amanda Pays, Rod Steiger, Kim Hunter.

A senseless script and an unsatisfactory ending mar this derivative horror film, which steals its creature from *Alien* and its plot from any one of a hundred run-of-the-razor slasher flicks. Rod Steiger, Kim Hunter, and Amanda Pays give strong performances. Rated R for profanity, violence, and gore. 1987; 95m.

KING KONG (1933) ★★★★★
DIR: Merian C. Cooper, Ernest B. Schoedsack. **CAST:** Robert Armstrong, Fay Wray, Bruce Cabot, Frank Reicher, Noble Johnson.

This classic was one of early sound film's most spectacular successes. The movie, about the giant ape who is captured on a prehistoric island and proceeds to tear New York City apart until his final stand on the Empire State Building, is the stuff of which legends are made. Its marriage of sound, music, image, energy, pace, and excitement made *King Kong* stand as a landmark film. 1933; B&W; 100m.

KING KONG (1976) ★★
DIR: John Guillermin. **CAST:** Jeff Bridges, Jessica Lange, Charles Grodin.

This remake, starring Jeff Bridges and Jessica Lange, is a pale imitation of the 1933 classic. For kids only. Rated PG for violence. 1976; 135m.

KING KONG LIVES
DIR: John Guillermin. **CAST:** Brian Kerwin, Linda Hamilton, John Ashton, Peter Michael Goetz.

A moronic sequel to director John Guillermin's regrettable 1976 remake of *King Kong*, this features Brian Kerwin and Linda Hamilton as human witnesses to the romance of the resuscitated Kong and his new love, Lady Kong. Rated PG-13 for violence. 1986; 105m.

KING KONG VS. GODZILLA ★
DIR: Inoshiro Honda. **CAST:** Michael Keith, Tadao Takashima, Keji Sahaka.

King Kong and Godzilla duke it out atop Mount Fuji in this East meets West supermonster movie. Here, though, Kong is a junkie hooked on some wild jungle juice. The bouts are quite humorous. Not rated. 1963; 91m.

KING OF THE ZOMBIES ★
DIR: Jean Yarbrough. **CAST:** Dick Purcell, Joan Woodbury, Mantan Moreland, John Archer.

Typical mad scientist–zombie movie with evil genius attempting to create an invulnerable army of mindless slaves to further the cause of evil. 1941; B&W; 67m.

KINGDOM OF THE SPIDERS ★★★

DIR: John "Bud" Cardos. **CAST:** William Shatner, Tiffany Bolling, Woody Strode.

William Shatner stars in this unsuspenseful thriller with lurid special effects. The title tells it all. Rated PG. 1977; 94m.

KISS, THE ★½

DIR: Pen Densham. **CAST:** Joanna Pacula, Meredith Salenger.

An African voodoo priestess (Joanna Pacula) is looking for an heir. So she invades the lives of her dead sister's family. That old black magic just ain't there. Rated R for nudity and violence. 1988; 105m.

KISS DADDY GOODNIGHT ★★

DIR: Peter Ily Huemer. **CAST:** Uma Thurman, Paul Dillon, Paul Richards.

Uma Thurman stars as a struggling model who survives by picking up wealthy men in bars, then drugging and robbing them. She finds the situation reversed when an obsessive suitor decides that he wants her all to himself. Moody, ultimately incomprehensible thriller. Rated R for nudity and violence. 1988; 89m.

KISS OF THE TARANTULA ★

DIR: Chris Munger. **CAST:** Suzanne Ling, Eric Mason.

Boring, unpleasant story of an unhinged girl who obliterates her enemies with the help of some eight-legged friends. Rated PG for mild gore. 1972; 85m.

LADY BEWARE ★★

DIR: Karen Arthur. **CAST:** Diane Lane, Michael Woods, Cotter Smith.

Decent but unriveting film along the lines of *Fatal Attraction*, with a psychotic pursuing a pretty window dresser. Diane Lane is pretty but unspectacular as the small-town window dresser who storms the Big City, and the rest of the cast and situations are stereotypical and fairly mundane. Rated R for nudity and violence. 1987; 108m.

LADY FRANKENSTEIN ★

DIR: Mel Welles. **CAST:** Joseph Cotten, Mickey Hargitay.

Bottom-rung horror film with Joseph Cotten ill-used as Baron Frankenstein attempting once again to create life in yet another silly-looking assemblage of spare parts. The twist to this one is that the Baron's daughter takes over the duties and does her best to animate the lump on the operating table. Rated R for violence. 1971; 84m.

LADY IN A CAGE ★★★★

DIR: Walter Grauman. **CAST:** Olivia De Havilland, James Caan, Ann Sothern.

Superb shocker may finally get the recognition it deserves, thanks to home video. Olivia De Havilland is terrorized by a gang of punks when she becomes trapped in an elevator in her home. Good acting, especially by a young James Caan, and excellent photography help make this film really something special. Very violent at times. 1964; B&W; 93m.

LADY IN WHITE ★★★★

DIR: Frank LaLoggia. **CAST:** Lukas Haas, Len Cariou, Alex Rocco, Katherine Helmond.

A high-grade suspenser. A grade-school boy (Lukas Haas) is locked in his classroom closet. While there, he sees the ghost of one of ten children who've been molested and killed in the past ten years. He also sees (but not clearly) the murderer, who then begins pursuing him. Now the question: Who did it? Well worth a watch! Rated PG-13 for violence and obscenities. 1988; 112m.

LADY VANISHES, THE (1938) ★★★★★

DIR: Alfred Hitchcock. **CAST:** Margaret Lockwood, Michael Redgrave, May Whitty.

Along with *The Thirty-nine Steps*, this is the most admired film from Alfred Hitchcock's early directorial career. The comedy-suspense thriller centers around a group of British types on a train trip from England to central Europe. A young woman (Margaret Lockwood) seeks the aid of a fellow passenger (Michael Redgrave) in an attempt to locate a charming old lady (May Whitty) she had met earlier on the train and now is apparently missing. 1938; B&W; 97m.

LADY VANISHES, THE (1979) ★½

DIR: Anthony Page. **CAST:** Elliott Gould, Cybill Shepherd, Angela Lansbury, Herbert Lom, Arthur Lowe, Ian Carmichael.

A better title for this remake of the classic Alfred Hitchcock suspense film might be *The Plot Vanishes*. All sense and suspense is virtually cast aside as Elliott Gould and Cybill Shepherd cavort through a series of "comedy" scenes with some fine supporting players. Rated PG. 1979; 95m.

LAIR OF THE WHITE WORM

DIR: Ken Russell. **CAST:** Amanda Donohoe, Hugh Grant, Sammi Davis, Catherine Oxenberg, Peter Capaldi.

Ken Russell writhes again with this disgustingly perverse and snidely campy adaptation of the novel by Bram Stoker. Amanda Donohoe is the centuries-old bloodsucker who is hunting a virgin to sacrifice in order to restore life to the ultimate creature of evil, the White Worm. Russell loves to wallow in decadence and indulges in infantile sexual imagery mixed with brutality and gore. Rated R. 1988; 99m.

LAST HORROR FILM, THE

DIR: David Winters. **CAST:** Caroline Munro, Joe Spinell.

Mama's boy obsessed with a horror movie actress goes on a killing spree at the Cannes Film Festival. This one is really sick. Even gore fans may find it overwhelming. Rated R for violence. 1984; 87m.

LAST HOUSE ON THE LEFT

DIR: Wes Craven. **CAST:** David Hess, Lucy Grantham, Sandra Cassel.

This is a sick slasher movie in which two teenage girls are tortured and killed by a sadistic trio. Later, one of the girls' parents take revenge. This movie will probably turn your stomach and keep you awake at night. Graphic torture and humiliation scenes rate this one an R at best. 1972; 91m.

LAST WAVE, THE ★★★½

DIR: Peter Weir. **CAST:** Richard Chamberlain, Olivia Hamnett.

In this suspenseful, fascinating film, Richard Chamberlain plays a lawyer defending a group of aborigines on trial for murder. His investigation into the incident leads to a frightening series of apocalyptic visions. Rated PG. 1977; 106m.

LEGACY, THE ★★

DIR: Richard Marquand. **CAST:** Katharine Ross, Sam Elliott, John Standing, Roger Daltrey.

A young American couple (Katharine Ross and Sam Elliott) staying at a mysterious English mansion discover that the woman has been chosen as the mate for some sort of ugly, demonic creature upstairs. The bulk of the action surrounds their attempts to escape from this bizarre "legacy." Rated R for violence and language. 1979; 100m.

LEGEND OF BOGGY CREEK ★★

DIR: Charles B. Pierce. **CAST:** Willie E. Smith, John P. Nixon.

One of the better "mystery of" docudramas, which were the rage of the early 1970s, this supposedly true story focuses on a monster that lurks in the swamps of Arkansas. Included are interviews with people who have come in contact with the creature and reenactments of said encounters. Rated PG. 1972; 95m.

LEGEND OF HELL HOUSE, THE ★★★½

DIR: John Hough. **CAST:** Roddy McDowall, Pamela Franklin, Gayle Hunnicutt, Clive Revill.

Richard Matheson's riveting suspense tale of a group of researchers attempting to survive a week in a haunted house in order to try to solve the mystery of the many deaths that have occurred there. Jarring at times, with very inventive camera shots and a great cast headed by Roddy McDowall as the only survivor of a previous investigation. Rated PG for violence. 1973; 95m.

LEGEND OF THE WEREWOLF ★½
DIR: Freddie Francis. **CAST:** Peter Cushing, Ron Moody, Hugh Griffith.

Peter Cushing's ever-professional performance is the only noteworthy element of this subpar British werewolf movie. It's set in nineteenth-century Paris, where the lycanthrope runs the Paris zoo and murders the clientele of a brothel during the full moon. Unrated but the equivalent of PG-13. 1974; 90m.

LEOPARD MAN, THE ★★★½
DIR: Jacques Tourneur. **CAST:** Dennis O'Keefe, Isabel Jewell.

This Val Lewton–produced thriller depicts the havoc and killing that begin when a leopard (used for publicity) escapes and terrorizes a New Mexico village. 1943; B&W; 59m.

LET'S SCARE JESSICA TO DEATH ★★
DIR: John Hancock. **CAST:** Zohra Lampert, Barton Heyman.

A young woman staying with some odd people out in the country witnesses all sorts of strange things, like ghosts and blood-stained corpses. Is it real, or some kind of elaborate hoax? The title tells it all in this disjointed terror tale, though it does contain a few spooky scenes. Rated PG. 1971; 89m.

LEVIATHAN ★★
DIR: George Pan Cosmatos. **CAST:** Peter Weller, Richard Crenna, Amanda Pays, Daniel Stern, Ernie Hudson, Meg Foster, Lisa Eilbacher, Hector Elizondo.

The crew of an undersea mining platform comes across a sunken Soviet ship that has been scuttled in an effort to keep some genetic experiment gone awry away from the world. What the miners encounter is part *Alien,* part *20,000 Leagues Under the Sea,* part *The Thing*. Since these other films are so much better, it's best to leave this one alone. Rated R for violence. 1989; 98m.

LIFT, THE ★★★
DIR: Dick Maas. **CAST:** Huub Stapel.

An inquisitive mechanic (Huub Stapel) discovers that an elevator is possessed by some dark power and is killing the people who ride in it. The authorities don't believe him, and he alone is left to battle the unholy force. Competent acting and good production values lend considerable suspense to this dubbed-to-English Dutch production. 1985; 95m.

LINK ★★½
DIR: Richard Franklin. **CAST:** Terence Stamp, Elisabeth Shue.

A student (Elizabeth Shue) takes a job with an eccentric anthropology professor (Terence Stamp) and finds herself menaced by a powerful, intelligent ape named Link. The story leaves a number of questions unanswered, but the film can be praised for taking the old cliché of an ape being on the loose and making it surprisingly effective. Rated R for profanity, brief nudity, and violence. 1986; 103m.

LIPSTICK 🦃
DIR: Lamont Johnson. **CAST:** Margaux Hemingway, Mariel Hemingway, Anne Bancroft, Perry King, Chris Sarandon.

This film proved that acting was not the career for model Margaux Hemingway. She is sexually molested by a composer. When Margaux gets no justice in court and it looks as if her little sister (Mariel Hemingway) is next, she takes matters into her own hands. Rated R. 1976; 89m.

LITTLE GIRL WHO LIVES DOWN THE LANE, THE ★★★½
DIR: Nicolas Gessner. **CAST:** Jodie Foster, Martin Sheen, Alexis Smith.

The Little Girl Who Lives Down the Lane is a remarkably subdued film from a genre that has existed primarily on gore, violence, and audience manipulation. Jodie Foster gives an absorbingly realistic performance in the title role. Martin Sheen is the child molester who menaces her. It's a well-acted chiller. Rated PG. 1976; 94m.

LITTLE SHOP OF HORRORS, THE (1960) ★★★★
DIR: Roger Corman. **CAST:** Jonathan Haze, Mel Welles, Jackie Joseph, Jack Nicholson, Dick Miller.

Dynamite Roger Corman super-quickie about a meek florist shop employee (Jonathan Haze) who inadvertently creates a ferocious man-eating plant. This horror-comedy was filmed in two days and is one of the funniest ever made. 1960; B&W; 72m.

LOCH NESS HORROR, THE
DIR: Larry Buchanan. **CAST:** Barry Buchanan, Sandy Kenyon.

Japan isn't the only country that has monsters that look like muppets. Unless you're looking for laughs, avoid this one. Rated PG. Has some violence. 1982; 93m.

LODGER, THE ★★★★
DIR: Alfred Hitchcock. **CAST:** Ivor Novello, Malcolm Keen, Marie Ault.

Alfred Hitchock's first signature thriller remains a timeless piece of wonder, showcasing the unique visual and stylistic tricks that would mark Hitchcock's work for years to come. Ivor Novello stars as a man who checks into a boardinghouse and becomes the object of scrutiny when a series of murders plague the area. Silent. 1926; B&W; 75m.

LONG WEEKEND ★★★½
DIR: Colin Eggleston. **CAST:** John Hargreaves, Briony Behets.

This Australian film is a must-see for environmentalists. We are introduced to a couple who carelessly start a forest fire, run over a kangaroo, senselessly destroy a tree, shoot animals for the sport of it, and break an eagle's egg. Then nature avenges itself on the unsuspecting couple. Unrated, this contains obscenities, nudity, and gore. 1986; 95m.

LOST BOYS, THE ★★
DIR: Joel Schumacher. **CAST:** Jason Patric, Dianne Wiest, Corey Haim, Barnard Hughes, Edward Herrmann, Kiefer Sutherland, Jami Gertz, Corey Feldman.

In this vampire variation on *Peter Pan*, director Joel Schumacher seems more interested in pretty shots and fancy costumes than atmosphere and plot. The story has Jason Patric falling in with a group of hip bloodsuckers led by Kiefer Sutherland. Rated R for violence, suggested sex and profanity. 1987; 98m.

LOST TRIBE, THE
DIR: John Laing. **CAST:** John Bach, Darien Takle, Emma Takle.

A boring and disjointed story about twin brothers involved in smuggling, adultery, and murder. Along the way comes the discovery of a mystical lost tribe. Not rated but contains adult themes and violence. 1983; 96m.

LOVE BUTCHER
DIR: Mikel Angel, Don Jones. **CAST:** Erik Stern.

A series of grisly murders of young women are committed by a deranged psycho. Pretty original, huh? Poorly conceived thriller Rated R. 1983; 84m.

LOVE FROM A STRANGER ★★★
DIR: Richard Whorf. **CAST:** Sylvia Sidney, John Hodiak, John Howard, Isobel Elsom, Ernest Cossart.

Just-married woman suspects her new husband is a murderer and that she will be his next victim in this suspense thriller in the vein of *Suspicion*. 1947; B&W; 81m.

LOVELY BUT DEADLY
DIR: David Sheldon. **CAST:** Lucinda Dooling, John Randolph, Marie Windsor, Mark Holden.

A teen age boy dies by drowning while under the influence of illegal drugs. Soon afterward, a teen age girl appears, beating up pushers and giving them heavy doses of their own dope. When it's discovered that she's the older sister of the boy who drowned, the drug suppliers call in the mob to get rid of her. From that contrived point, this piece of low-budget tripe goes further than downhill. Rated PG. 1981; 88m.

LURKERS ★

DIR: Robert Findlay. **CAST:** Christine Moore, Gary Warner.

Hopelessly meandering tale about an abused young girl haunted by the forces of Evil but protected by the powers of Good, who grows up to become caught up in their eternal battle. The filmmakers lack both the intelligence to make this kind of pseudometaphysical bushwah plausible and the budget to make it believable. Rated R for violence and nudity. 1988; 95m.

LUST FOR A VAMPIRE ★★★

DIR: Jimmy Sangster. **CAST:** Suzanna Leigh, Michael Johnson, Ralph Bates, Barbara Jefford.

All-girls school turns out to be a haven for vampires, with a visiting writer (Michael Johnson) falling in love with one of the undead students (Yvette Stensgaard). Atmospheric blending of chills and fleshy eroticism combined with a terrific ending. Rated R. 1970; 95m.

MACABRE SERENADE ★

DIR: Juan Ibanez, Jack Hill. **CAST:** Boris Karloff.

One of the four Mexican films featuring footage of Boris Karloff but assembled after his death (see *Sinister Invasion*), this is the best of a bad lot. He plays a toymaker whose creations seek revenge on his evil relatives after his death. There's a sloppily cut version also on video called *Dance of Death*; it originally played theatres as *House of Evil*. 1968; 75m.

MAD BOMBER, THE ★

DIR: Bert I. Gordon. **CAST:** Vince Edwards, Chuck Connors, Neville Brand.

Bert I. Gordon wrote, produced, and directed this mess. It's not even up to his usual low standards. Vince Edwards stars as a Los Angeles police detective subtly named Geronimo. For some reason not explained in the script, he's obsessed with the case of a psycho (Chuck Connors) who likes to bomb high schools, mental hospitals, and women's lib meetings. Rated R for violence. 1973; 91m.

MAD DOCTOR OF BLOOD ISLAND, THE ★

DIR: Eddie Romero, Gerardo de Leon. **CAST:** John Ashley.

You'll be even madder than the doctor if you waste your time on this Filipino-made junk. He's experimenting with a chlorophyll-based fountain-of-youth solution—which turns people into green monsters instead. Rated PG. 1968; 88m.

MAD MONSTER ★½

DIR: Sam Newfield. **CAST:** Johnny Downs, George Zucco, Anne Nagel, Glenn Strange.

Scientist George Zucco is mad and Glenn Strange is the monster he creates in order to get even with disbelievers. This five-day wonder shows every corner it cut before the last cheap foot of film was in the can. 1942; B&W; 77m.

MADHOUSE ★★½

DIR: Ovidio Assonitis. **CAST:** Trish Everly, Michael Macrae.

When a woman's deranged twin escapes from the loony bin and crashes her sibling's party, you can imagine the blood fest that results. Although the story sounds simple, there are some surprises. Stylishly filmed and well acted, with a bigger budget this might have been a classic. As it is, it's worth a look. Not rated, but contains violence. 1987; 93m.

MAGIC ★★★½

DIR: Richard Attenborough. **CAST:** Anthony Hopkins, Burgess Meredith, Ed Lauter, Ann-Margret.

Magic will make your skin crawl. The slow descent into madness of the main character, Corky (Anthony Hopkins), a ventriloquist-magician, is the most disturbing study in terror to hit the screens since *Psycho*. Rated R. 1978; 106m.

MAKE THEM DIE SLOWLY

DIR: Umberto Lenzi. **CAST:** John Morghen, Lorainne DeSelle.

Thoroughly despicable film about a group of Americans who exploit and torture a village of South American Indians only to discover that the natives are cannibals. Not rated, contains nudity, profanity, and extreme violence. 1984; 92m.

MAMMA DRACULA ★

DIR: Boris Szulzinger. **CAST:** Louise Fletcher, Maria Schneider, Marc-Henri Wajnberg, Alexander Wanberg, Jess Hahn.

A horror–black comedy that fails on both counts. A blood specialist is hired by a vampire (Louise Fletcher) to help find virgin's blood that will keep Fletcher immortally young. The only humor comes from transvestite twin brothers and their zany antics. Not rated, but contains nudity and adult situations. 1988; 93m.

MAN THEY COULD NOT HANG, THE ★★★

DIR: Nick Grindé. **CAST:** Boris Karloff, Lorna Gray, Robert Wilcox.

Boris Karloff's fine performance carries this fast-paced tale of a scientist executed for murder and brought back to life, and his bizarre plan of revenge on the judge and jury who convicted him. 1939; B&W; 72m.

MAN WHO HAUNTED HIMSELF, THE ★★★½

DIR: Basil Dearden. **CAST:** Roger Moore, Hildegard Neil.

Freaky melodrama about a car crash with unexpected side effects. Recovering from the wreck, a man (Roger Moore) begins to question his sanity when it appears that his exact double has assumed his position in the world. Imaginative film keeps the viewer involved from start to finish. Rated PG. 1970; 94m.

MAN WHO KNEW TOO MUCH, THE (1934) ★★★★★

DIR: Alfred Hitchcock. **CAST:** Leslie Banks, Peter Lorre, Edna Best, Nova Pilbeam.

The remake with James Stewart can't hold a candle to this superb suspense film about a man (Leslie Banks) who stumbles on to a conspiracy and then is forced into action when his child is kidnapped to ensure his silence. This is Hitchcock at his best, with Peter Lorre in fine fettle as the sneering villain. 1934; B&W; 83m.

MAN WHO KNEW TOO MUCH, THE (1955) ★★★

DIR: Alfred Hitchcock. **CAST:** James Stewart, Doris Day, Carolyn Jones.

James Stewart and Doris Day star in this fairly entertaining Hitchcock thriller as a married couple who take a vacation trip to Africa and become involved in international intrigue when they happen on the scene of a murder. It's no match for the original, but the director's fans no doubt will enjoy it. 1955; 120m.

MAN WITH TWO HEADS

DIR: Scott Williams.

This semi remake of *Dr. Jekyll & Mr. Hyde* is loaded with gore and guts. Another piece of slime that has nothing going for it. Rated R. 1982; 80m.

MANHATTAN PROJECT, THE ★★★

DIR: Marshall Brickman. **CAST:** John Lithgow, Christopher Collet, Cynthia Nixon, Jill Eikenberry.

This contemporary comedy-adventure-thriller concerns a high-school youth (Christopher Collet) who, with the aid of his idealistic girlfriend (Cynthia Nixon), steals some plutonium and makes his own nuclear bomb. Though the film is sometimes far-fetched, there's a pleasing balance of humor and suspense. Rated PG for violence. 1986; 115m.

MANIAC (1934) ★½
DIR: Dwain Esper. **CAST:** Bill Woods, Horace Carpenter.

Legendary film about a mad doctor and his even madder assistant knocked 'em dead at the men's clubs and exploitation houses in the 1930s and 1940s, but it seems pretty mild compared to today's color gore-feasts. Not rated. 1934; B&W; 52m.

MANIAC (1962) ★★★
DIR: Michael Carreras. **CAST:** Kerwin Mathews, Nadia Gray, Donald Houston.

Spooky mystery film about a madman on the loose in France, with Kerwin Mathews perfect as an American artist whose vacation there turns out to be anything but. Chilling atmosphere. 1962; B&W; 86m.

MANIAC (1980)
DIR: William Lustig. **CAST:** Joe Spinell, Caroline Munro, Gail Lawrence, Kelly Piper, Tom Savini.

For maniacs only. A plethora of shootings, stabbings, decapitations, and scalpings sadistically depicted in graphic detail will send even those with strong stomachs rushing out for airsick bags. Rated R for every excess imaginable. 1980; 87m.

MANITOU, THE
DIR: William Girdler. **CAST:** Tony Curtis, Susan Strasberg, Michael Ansara, Ann Sothern, Burgess Meredith, Stella Stevens.

Hilariously hokey film about a woman (Susan Strasberg) who by some strange trick of chance, is growing an ancient Indian out of her neck! It's apparently supposed to be scary, but wait until you see the birth scene. You'll be rolling on the floor in a puddle of tears! Rated PG. 1978; 104m.

MARK OF CAIN ★★★
DIR: Bruce Pittman. **CAST:** Robin Crew, Wendy Crewson, August Schellenberg.

Though this film overdoes the eerie music and protracted conversations, it is a compelling tale about twin brothers. A graphic murder sets the plot in motion. A lovely old home surrounded by breathtaking winter scenery is the principal setting. 1984; 90m.

MARK OF THE DEVIL
DIR: Michael Armstrong. **CAST:** Herbert Lom, Udo Kier, Reggie Nalder.

A sadistic German-British film about an impotent, overachieving witch finder. Originally produced in 70mm and stereo, it's a depressing slaughterfest filled with nudity, brutality, and outrageous scenes of torture. Notorious as the only movie in history to offer free stomach-distress bags to every patron. Rated R. 1970; 96m.

MARK OF THE VAMPIRE ★★★½
DIR: Tod Browning. **CAST:** Lionel Barrymore, Elizabeth Allan, Bela Lugosi, Lionel Atwill, Carol Borland.

MGM's atmospheric version of *Dracula*, utilizing the same director and star. This time, though, it's Count Mora (Bela Lugosi) terrorizing the residents of an old estate along with his ghoulish daughter (Carol Borland). Lionel Barrymore is the believer who tries to put an end to their nocturnal activities. 1935; B&W; 61m.

MARNIE ★★★½
DIR: Alfred Hitchcock. **CAST:** Sean Connery, Tippi Hedren, Diane Baker, Martin Gabel, Bruce Dern.

Unsung Alfred Hitchcock film about a strange young woman (Tippi Hedren) who isn't at all what she appears to be, and Sean Connery as the man determined to get under the surface and find out what makes her tick. Compelling, if overlong, but in the best Hitchcock tradition. 1964; 129m.

MARTIN ★★★
DIR: George A. Romero. **CAST:** John Amplas, Lincoln Maazel.

Director George Romero creates a good chiller with a lot of bloodcurdling power about a young man who thinks he's a vampire. This is very well done. Rated R. 1978; 95m.

MARY, MARY, BLOODY MARY ★★
DIR: Juan Lopez Moctezuma. **CAST:** Cristina Ferrare, David Young, Helena Rojo, John Carradine.
A bloody and grisly film depicting the horror of vampirism and mass murder. A beautiful vampire and artist, Mary (Cristina Ferrare), goes to Mexico to fulfill her need for blood. This film is rated R for nudity, violence, and gore. 1987; 95m.

MASQUE OF THE RED DEATH, THE ★★★
DIR: Roger Corman. **CAST:** Vincent Price, Hazel Court, Jane Asher, David Weston, Patrick Magee.
The combination of Roger Corman, Edgar Allan Poe, and Vincent Price meant first-rate (though low-budget) horror films in the early 1960s. This was one of the best. Price is deliciously villainous. 1964; 86m.

MASQUERADE ★★½
DIR: Bob Swaim. **CAST:** Rob Lowe, Meg Tilly, Kim Cattral, Doug Savant, John Glover, Dana Delaney.
Overblown variation on Hitchcock's *Suspicion* with Rob Lowe playing the devious but attractive husband who may be after heiress Meg Tilly's money. Some new plot twists are introduced to Hitchcock's original vehicle, but unfortunately these don't save *Masquerade* from playing a lot like *Dallas*. Rated R for language, nudity, simulated sex, and violence. 1988; 98m.

MASSACRE AT CENTRAL HIGH ★★★
DIR: Renee Daalder. **CAST:** Andrew Stevens, Kimberly Beck, Derrel Maury, Robert Carradine.
Low-budget production has a teenager exacting his own brand of revenge on a tough gang who are making things hard for the students at a local high school. This violent drama has a lot going for it, except for some goofy dialogue. Otherwise, nicely done. Rated R. 1976; 85m.

MAUSOLEUM ★½
DIR: Jerry Zimmerman, Michael Franzese. **CAST:** Bobbie Bresee, Marjoe Gortner.
A reasonably spooky supernatural shocker about a rich, sexy housewife (Bobbie Bresee) who wreaks devastation on assorted victims because of a demonic possession dating back to 1682. Evangelist-turned-actor Marjoe Gortner plays her timid husband. Rated R. 1983; 96m.

MAXIMUM OVERDRIVE
DIR: Stephen King. **CAST:** Emilio Estevez, Pat Hingle, Laura Harrington, Yeardley Smith, Ellen McElduff, J. C. Quinn.
This boring, turgid, chaotic mess, loosely based on Stephen King's short story "Trucks," is a waste from start to finish. As a director, King hasn't the faintest idea how to elicit good performances from his cast, and the picture is paced abysmally. Rated R for violence. 1986; 97m.

MAZES AND MONSTERS ★
DIR: Steven H. Stern. **CAST:** Tom Hanks, Chris Makepeace, Wendy Crewson, David Wallace, Lloyd Bochner, Peter Donat, Louise Sorel, Susan Strasberg.
Mazes and Monsters, a TV movie, portrays the lives of several college students whose interest in a Dungeons and Dragons type of role-playing game becomes hazardous. The familiar faces of Tom Hanks, Chris Makepeace, and others are only that—familiar faces. If you're into this sword-and-sorcery stuff, rent *Ladyhawke* instead. 1982; 103m.

MCGUFFIN, THE ★★★
DIR: Colin Bucksey. **CAST:** Charles Dance, Brian Glover, Ritza Brown, Francis Matthews, Phyllis Logan, Jerry Stiller.
This British suspense drama begins like Alfred Hitchcock's *Rear Window*, which is well and good, considering its title is taken from a phrase

coined by Hitchcock himself! Charles Dance offers an excellent portrayal of a movie critic who becomes embroiled in a government cover-up. Brief nudity and sexual situations. 1985; 104m.

MEATEATER, THE
DIR: Derek Savage. **CAST:** Peter M. Spitzer.

An abandoned movie house is haunted by a mad killer who doesn't take kindly to efforts to reopen it. For some reason, this extremely peculiar horror movie is filled with pointless bits of dialogue and references to eating meat. It seems as if it's trying to be campy; if it is, it missed by a mile. Unrated, the film contains violence and gore. 1979; 85m.

MEDUSA TOUCH, THE ★★★
DIR: John Gold. **CAST:** Richard Burton, Lee Remick, Gordon Jackson, Lino Ventura, Harry Andrews.

Born with the power to kill by will, Richard Burton goes completely out of control after someone almost beats him to death. This is a strange, disturbing film. Burton is effective, but Lee Remick is out of place as his psychiatrist. Rated R. 1978; 110m.

MEPHISTO WALTZ, THE ★½
DIR: Paul Wendkos. **CAST:** Alan Alda, Jacqueline Bisset, Curt Jurgens.

Satanism and the transfer of souls are at the heart of this needlessly wordy and laughably atmospheric chiller involving a dying musician (Curt Jurgens) and a reporter (Alan Alda). The thin material—and the viewer's patience—are stretched about twenty minutes too long. Rated R for violence. 1971; 108m.

MICROWAVE MASSACRE
DIR: Wayne Berwick. **CAST:** Jackie Vernon.

The title says it all. Lounge comedian Jackie Vernon makes his movie debut in this pile of sludge about a henpecked husband who does away with his wife and feeds her to his mysterious microwave. Once he starts, there is no stopping, and he gets hooked on murder as a form of sexual gratification. Rated R for violence, nudity, and profanity. 1979; 75m.

MIDNIGHT (1980) ★
DIR: John Russo. **CAST:** Lawrence Tierney, Melanie Verlin, John Amplas.

On their way to Florida, two college guys and a female hitchhiker end up in a southern town plagued by racial prejudice and a family of Satan worshipers. That may sound like an interesting premise, but, unfortunately, what unfolds is a muddled mess of sadism. Rated R for violence and profanity. 1980; 91m.

MIDNIGHT HOUR ★★★
DIR: Jack Bender. **CAST:** Shari Belafonte Harper, LeVar Burton, Lee Montgomery, Dick Van Patten, Kevin McCarthy.

High-school students recite an ancient curse as a Halloween prank and unintentionally release demons from hell and the dead from their graves. Enjoyable cross between *Night of the Living Dead* and *An American Werewolf in London*, helped along by humor and a lively cast. Rated R for gore, violence and profanity. 1986; 87m.

MIND KILLER ★★
DIR: Michael Krueger. **CAST:** Joe McDonald.

A nerdy library worker uncovers a manuscript about the power of positive thinking. Soon he has the power to control minds and to lift objects mentally. But the power has its drawbacks, turning him into a monster. The movie is low-budget, but the filmmakers try hard. Not rated, but contains adult language and situations. 1987; 84m.

MIND SNATCHERS, THE ★★★
DIR: Bernard Girard. **CAST:** Christopher Walken, Ronny Cox, Joss Ackland, Ralph Meeker.

Christopher Walken plays a nihilistic U.S. soldier in West Germany who is admitted to a mental institution. He finds out later the hospital is actually a laboratory where a German scientist is testing a new form of psychological control. Walken's performance is excellent and the idea is an interesting one, but the film moves slowly. Rated PG for violence and profanity. 1972; 94m.

MIRACLE MILE ★★★★
DIR: Steve DeJarnatt. **CAST:** Anthony Edwards, Mare Winningham, John Agar.

A fascinatingly frightful study of mass hysteria centered on a spreading rumor that a nuclear holocaust is imminent. Anthony Edwards stars as a young man who accidentally overhears a phone conversation that "the button has been pushed." He learns that Los Angeles is seventy minutes from destruction and must scramble about, trying to discover the truth and possibly save himself and others. Superb. Rated R. 1989; 87m.

MIRROR OF DEATH ★½
DIR: Deryn Warren. **CAST:** Julie Merrill.

An abused woman takes up voodoo as therapy only to find that a vicious ghost is released from her bedroom mirror when she begins to chant. Not rated, but has violence, gore, and profanity. 1987; 85m.

MONGREL
DIR: Robert A. Burns. **CAST:** Terry Evans, Aldo Ray.

Deservedly obscure horror movie whose title serves equally well as a critical assessment: it's a dog, all right. Young Jerry has dreams in which he turns into a weredog and mutilates innocent people. When he wakes up, he finds they really have died. Unrated, with lots of fake gore. 1982; 90m.

MONKEY SHINES: AN EXPERIMENT IN FEAR ★★★
DIR: George A. Romero. **CAST:** Jason Beghe, Kate McNeil, John Pankow, Joyce Van Patten.

A virile young man doesn't take too readily to becoming a paralytic overnight, immobilized and wheelchair-bound. Enter Ella, a superintelligent (through the miracle of modern science) monkey who is brought in to help with absolutely everything, including revenge upon those Ella's master feels have done him injustice. Genuine amusement—and some decent chills—for aficionados of the genre. Rated R for violence, sex, and terror. 1988; 115m.

MONSTER CLUB, THE ★★★½
DIR: Roy Ward Baker. **CAST:** Vincent Price, John Carradine, Donald Pleasence, Stuart Whitman, Britt Ekland, Simon Ward.

Better-than-average series of horror tales by Ronald Chetwynd-Hayes linked by a sinister nightclub where the guys 'n' ghouls can hang out. All the stories keep tongue firmly in cheek and involve imaginary creatures of mixed parentage, such as a "shadmonk," borne of a vampire and werewolf. Rated PG for violence. 1981; 97m.

MONSTER DOG
DIR: Clyde Anderson. **CAST:** Alice Cooper, Victoria Vera.

Alice Cooper's music video, shown in the first five minutes of the film, is the only part of this release worth watching. This incoherent attempt to make a werewolf film using a pack of tail-wagging, playful German shepherds with poorly dubbed growls hasn't enough gore to please slasher-flick fans and no plot with which to entertain fans of classical horror. The title is a perfect review. Unrated, the film has violence. 1986; 88m.

MONSTER FROM GREEN HELL ★★
DIR: Kenneth Crane. **CAST:** Jim Davis, Barbara Turner, Eduardo Ciannelli.

Giant rubber wasps on the rampage in Africa. Our heroes battle a lethargic script to the death. In an attempt to revive the audience, the last reel of the movie was filmed in color. Big deal. 1957; B&W; 71m.

MONSTER FROM THE OCEAN FLOOR, THE ★
DIR: Wyott Ordung. **CAST:** Anne Kimball, Stuart Wade, Wyott Ordung.

A legendary sea monster is discovered off the coast of Mexico. The first film produced by Roger Corman. He made the movie in six days, on a budget of only $12,000. You can tell. It's slow-moving, endlessly talky, and the monster is almost impossible to see. 1954; B&W; 64m.

MONSTER IN THE CLOSET ★★½
DIR: Bob Dahlin. **CAST:** Donald Grant, Denise Dubarry, Claude Akins, Henry Gibson, John Carradine, Stella Stevens.

Horror spoof about a music-loving, bloodthirsty mutant that inhabits people's closets. This film pokes good-natured fun at films in and out of the horror genre. Some jokes bomb, but most hit home. John Carradine is priceless in his short role. Rated PG for profanity and brief nudity. 1987; 100m.

MONSTER MAKER, THE ★½
DIR: Sam Newfield. **CAST:** J. Carrol Naish, Ralph Morgan, Wanda McKay, Sam Flint, Glenn Strange.

A scientist conducting experiments in glandular research accidentally injects a pianist with a serum that causes his body to grow abnormally large, especially his hands. Low-budget thriller revamps the old gland-operation theme but does very little with it this time around. 1944; B&W; 64m.

MONSTER OF PIEDRAS BLANCAS, THE ★
DIR: Irvin Berwick. **CAST:** Les Tremayne, Forrest Lewis.

This low-budget monstrosity features a human-shaped sea creature with a penchant for separating humans from their heads. Film stock is poor, the action takes place at night, and most of the mayhem takes place off camera. 1958; B&W; 71m.

MONSTER SQUAD, THE ★★★
DIR: Fred Dekker. **CAST:** Andre Govan, Duncan Regehr, Stan Shaw, Tommy Noonan.

A group of kids form a club to help combat an infiltration of monsters in their town. The kids have something the monsters want and vice versa. What unfolds is a clever mixture of Hollywood sci-fi monster effects and a well-conceived spoof of horror movies, past and present. Rated PG-13 for violence. 1987; 82m.

MONSTER WALKS, THE ★★½
DIR: Frank Strayer. **CAST:** Rex Lease, Vera Reynolds, Mischa Auer, Sheldon Lewis, Willie Best.

This independently produced creaker contains most of the elements popular in old-house horror shows of the late 1920s and early 1930s, including deadly apes, secret passages, gloomy storms, and thoroughly petrified ethnic types. Tolerably funny if you overlook the racist portrayal by Sleep 'n Eat (Willie Best). 1932; B&W; 57m.

MOON OF THE WOLF ★★
DIR: Daniel Petrie. **CAST:** David Janssen, Barbara Rush, Bradford Dillman, John Beradino.

Another ABC Movie of the Week makes it to video. Disappointing yarn of the search for a werewolf on the loose in Louisiana. Good acting by the leads, but there's not enough action or excitement to sustain interest. 1972; 73m.

MORNING AFTER, THE ★★★½
DIR: Sidney Lumet. **CAST:** Jane Fonda, Jeff Bridges, Raul Julia, Diane Salinger, Richard Foronjy.

An alcoholic ex–movie star (Jane Fonda) wakes up one morning in bed next to a dead man and is unable to remember what happened the night before. Fonda is terrific as the heroine-victim, and Jeff Bridges gives a solid performance as the ex-cop who comes to her aid. The result is an enjoyable thriller in the style of *Jagged*

Edge. Rated R for profanity. 1986; 103m.

MORTUARY
DIR: Howard Avedis. **CAST:** Christopher George, Lynda Day George.

Christopher George and Lynda Day George are featured in this low-budget horror flick; one of the sickest entries in what has come to be called the knife-kill genre. All the standard commercial elements of profanity, gore, nudity, blood, and sex have been thrown together. Rated R. 1984; 91m.

MOST DANGEROUS GAME, THE ★★★½
DIR: Ernest B. Schoedsack, Irving Pichel. **CAST:** Joel McCrea, Fay Wray, Leslie Banks, Robert Armstrong.

This sister production to *King Kong* utilizes the same sets, same technical staff, and most of the same cast to tell the story of Count Zaroff, the insane ruler of a secret island who spends his time hunting the victims of the ships that he wrecks. Filmed many times since and used as a theme for countless television plots, this original is still the standard to measure all the others by. Non-stop action for sixty-three tight minutes. 1932; B&W; 63m.

MOTEL HELL ★★½
DIR: Kevin Connor. **CAST:** Rory Calhoun, Nancy Parsons, Paul Linke, Nina Axelrod, Elaine Joyce.

"It takes all kinds of critters to make Farmer Vincent Fritters!" Ahem! This above average horror-comedy stars Rory Calhoun (who overplays grandly) as a nice ol' farmer who has struck gold with his dried pork treats. What the public doesn't know—and, frankly, wouldn't *want* to know—is that his secret ingredient happens to be human flesh. Rated R for violence. 1980; 102m.

MOTHER'S DAY ★
DIR: Charles Kaufman. **CAST:** Nancy Hendrickson, Deborah Luce.

This slasher has a twist: a "loving" mother has trained her sons to kidnap and torture innocent victims. When the boys kidnap three women celebrating their college reunion, the women decide to fight back. Rated R for nudity, profanity, and violence. 1980; 98m.

MOUNTAINTOP MOTEL MASSACRE
DIR: Jim McCullough. **CAST:** Bill Thurman, Anna Chappell.

A deranged widow accidentally kills her daughter, and she takes her guilt out on the guests who stay at her hotel. Even splatter-film fans will be disappointed at the lack of bloodletting and poor special effects. Rated R for violence and brief nudity. 1983; 95m.

MULTIPLE MANIACS
DIR: John Waters. **CAST:** Divine, Mink Stole, Paul Swift, Cookie Mueller, David Lochary, Mary Vivian Pearce, Edith Massey.

A homage to gore king Herschell Gordon Lewis's *Two Thousand Maniacs*, *Multiple Maniacs* is director John Waters's favorite film. You can expect plenty of bad taste in this black-and-white movie, which trashes Christianity (Divine is seduced in a Catholic church) and just about any other established and respected institution that crosses Waters's viewfinder. Unrated, but the equivalent of an X. 1971; B&W; 70m.

MUMMY, THE (1932) ★★★★
DIR: Karl Freund. **CAST:** Boris Karloff, Zita Johann, David Manners, Edward Van Sloan.

First-rate horror thriller about an Egyptian mummy returning to life after 3,700 years. Boris Karloff plays the title role in one of his very best performances. Superb makeup, dialogue, atmosphere, and direction make this one an all-time classic. 1932; B&W; 73m.

MUMMY, THE (1959) ★★★½
DIR: Terence Fisher. **CAST:** Peter Cushing, Christopher Lee, Yvonne Furneaux.

Excellent updating of the mummy legend. Christopher Lee is terrifying as the ancient Egyptian awakened from his centuries-old sleep to take revenge on those who desecrated the tomb of his beloved princess. Well-photographed, atmospheric production is high-quality entertainment. 1959; 88m.

MUNCHIES
DIR: Bettina Hirsch. **CAST:** Harvey Korman, Charles Stratton, Alix Elias.

This mindless rip-off of *Gremlins* attempts to amuse but fails. Harvey Korman has dual parts as an archaeologist who discovers a junk-food-eating creature, and as a con artist who kidnaps the little critters. Rated PG for sexual innuendo. 1987; 83m.

MURDER ★★★
DIR: Alfred Hitchcock. **CAST:** Herbert Marshall, Norah Baring.

An early Alfred Hitchcock thriller, and a good one, although it shows its age. Herbert Marshall, a producer-director, is selected to serve on a murder-trial jury. He believes the accused, an aspiring actress, is innocent of the crime and takes it upon himself to apprehend the real killer. 1930; B&W; 92m.

MURDER BY PHONE ★★★
DIR: Michael Anderson. **CAST:** Richard Chamberlain, John Houseman.

In this okay shocker, Richard Chamberlain is cast as an environmentalist whose lecture engagement in New York City turns out to be an opportunity to investigate the gruesome death of one of his students. Chamberlain, a one-time radical, must resort to his old rock-the-establishment methods in order to solve the mystery. Rated R. 1980; 79m.

MURDER BY TELEVISION ★½
DIR: Clifford Sanforth. **CAST:** Bela Lugosi, June Collyer, George Meeker, Hattie McDaniel.

Bela Lugosi plays an inventor in this low-budget murder mystery. Television was still something out of *Science and Invention* back in 1935, so it was fair game as a contrivance used to commit the crime. Slow and creaky. 1935; B&W; 60m.

MURDER IN TEXAS ★★★★
DIR: William Hale. **CAST:** Farrah Fawcett, Sam Elliott, Katharine Ross, Andy Griffith, Bill Dana.

Absorbing TV docudrama based on a true story. Sam Elliott is Dr. John Hill, a prominent plastic surgeon accused of murdering his socialite wife. At times a gripping study of psychopathic behavior. Good performances all around, including Farrah Fawcett and Andy Griffith, who reaped an Emmy nomination. 1983; 200m.

MURDERS IN THE RUE MORGUE ★★
DIR: Gordon Hessler. **CAST:** Jason Robards Jr., Herbert Lom, Michael Dunn, Lilli Palmer, Christine Kaufmann, Adolfo Celi.

Members of a horror theater troupe in nineteenth-century Paris are dispatched systematically by a mysterious fiend. Good cast, nice atmosphere, but confusing and altogether too artsy for its own good. Rated PG. 1971; 87m.

MUTANT ★★½
DIR: John "Bud" Cardos. **CAST:** Bo Hopkins, Wings Hauser, Jennifer Warren, Cary Guffey, Lee Montgomery.

An incredibly frustrating film that displays well-crafted mood and tension during the first half and then lapses into the idiocy of yet another *Night of the Living Dead* rip-off. Too bad; this could—and should—have been much better. Rated R for violence. 1983; 100m.

MUTILATOR, THE ★
DIR: Buddy Cooper. **CAST:** Matt Mitler.

More gore galore as a psycho kills off his sons' friends when they visit the family island. The cheap splatter effects aren't very good, but they're plentiful, more so in the unrated version of the cassette than in the R version; neither one is advised for the weak-stomached. 1984; 86m.

MY BLOODY VALENTINE ★½
DIR: George Mihalka. **CAST:** Paul Kelman, Lori Hallier, Neil Affleck.
Candy boxes stuffed with bloody human hearts signal the return of a legendary murderous coal miner to Valentine Bluffs. Another variation on the *Halloween* holiday horror formula, this film provides a few doses of excitement and a tidal wave of killings. Unfortunately, it relies more on manipulative shocks than suspense for its impact. Rated R. 1981; 91m.

MY SISTER, MY LOVE ★★★
DIR: Karen Arthur. **CAST:** Carol Kane, Lee Grant, Will Geer, James Olson.
Offbeat story concerns two loving, but unbalanced, sisters who eliminate anyone who tries to come between them. Good acting all around and a perverse sense of style are just two elements that make this movie click. Alternate title—*The Mafu Cage.* Rated R. 1979; 99m.

MYSTERY OF THE WAX MUSEUM ★★★
DIR: Michael Curtiz. **CAST:** Lionel Atwill, Fay Wray, Glenda Farrell, Frank McHugh.
Dated but interesting tale of a crippled, crazed sculptor (the ever-dependable Lionel Atwill) who murders people and displays them in his museum as his own wax creations. Humorous subplot really curbs the attention, but stick with it. One of the earliest color films, it is often shown on television in black and white. 1933; 77m.

NAKED FACE, THE ★★★
DIR: Bryan Forbes. **CAST:** Roger Moore, Rod Steiger, Elliott Gould, Art Carney, Anne Archer.
A psychiatrist (Roger Moore) finds himself the target of murder in this enjoyable suspense film. Only trouble is the police think he's the killer, as the first attempt on his life results in the death of a patient who had borrowed his raincoat. Rated R for violence, and profanity. 1984; 98m.

NAVY VS. THE NIGHT MONSTERS, THE 🦃
DIR: Michael Hoey. **CAST:** Mamie Van Doren, Anthony Eisley, Pamela Mason, Bobby Van.
Excruciatingly poor horror film is for diehards only, as homicidal plants scheme to take over the world. The overused term *low-budget* has been truly redefined here. 1966; 90m.

NEAR DARK ★★★½
DIR: Kathryn Bigelow. **CAST:** Adrian Pasdar, Jenny Wright, Tim Thomerson, Jenette Goldstein, Lance Henriksen, Bill Paxton.
A stylish story of nomadic vampires. A girl takes a fancy to a young stud and turns him into a vampire, forcing him to join the macabre family. His problem is that he can't bring himself to make his first kill. It's the character development and acting that make this movie worthwhile. Rated R for violence and language. 1987; 95m.

NECROMANCER ★★
DIR: Dusty Nelson. **CAST:** Elizabeth Cayton, Russ Tamblyn.
A sorceress possesses a young woman, using her to kill men and steal their life forces. Violence and bloodshed abound unfortunately, but not much suspense. Rated R for graphic violence and nudity. 1988; 88m.

NECROPOLIS ★
DIR: Bruce Hickey. **CAST:** Lee Anne Baker.
A 300-year-old witch, looking pretty good for her age, is resurrected in New York City so that she can provide eternal life for her followers. Sole point of interest: the special effects people have outfitted the New Wave witch with six breasts, beating the previous record of four on the dancing girl in *The Warrior and the Sorceress.* (We hope this isn't an escalating trend!) Rated R. 1987; 96m.

NEON MANIACS ★★½
DIR: Joseph Mangine. **CAST:** Allan Hayes, Leilani Sarelle.

Ancient evil beings are released into present-day New York, killing everyone in their path. Three teenagers learn the demons' weakness and go on a crusade to destroy them. With good special effects, original creatures, and lots of scares, this film is worth a look. Rated R for violence. 1985; 90m.

NEST, THE (1988) ★★★½
DIR: Terence H. Winkless. **CAST:** Robert Lansing, Lisa Langlois, Franc Luz, Stephen Davies, Nancy Morgan.

A skin-rippling tale of a genetic experiment gone awry. Flesh-eating cockroaches are on the verge of overrunning a small island and they are not about to let anything stand in their way. What's worse, they're mutating into a form of whatever they consume. Special effects are above par and definitely not for the squeamish. Rated R. 1988; 88m.

NESTING, THE ★★
DIR: Armand Weston. **CAST:** Robin Groves, Christopher Loomis, John Carradine, Gloria Grahame.

Tolerable haunted house film about a writer (Robin Groves) who rents a house in the country so as to get some peace and quiet. But guess what. You got it—the house is plagued with undead spirits who seek revenge for their untimely deaths many years ago. Rated R for nudity and violence. 1980; 104m.

NEW KIDS, THE
DIR: Sean S. Cunningham. **CAST:** Shannon Presby, Lori Laughlin, James Spader.

In this horror film, two easygoing kids try to make friends at a new high school. Their attempt is thwarted by the town bully, who is angry because they refuse to bow to his superiority. Exploitative teen trash. Rated R for profanity, nudity, and violence. 1985; 96m.

NEW YEAR'S EVIL
DIR: Emmett Alston. **CAST:** Roz Kelly, Kip Niven, Chris Wallace.

Resolve right now to avoid this derivative holiday slasher movie. A crazy killer stalks victims at a televised New Year's Eve party, claiming a victim every hour. Most annoying of all, after the formula plot, is the stupid pseudopunk music. Rated R for all the usual reasons. 1980; 90m.

NEXT OF KIN ★
DIR: Tony Williams. **CAST:** Jackie Kerin, John Jarratt.

Boring Australian suspense film along the lines of *The Shining* has a young heiress inheriting her mother's mansion, which comes complete with unsettling memories. Don't they all? Not rated; contains nudity, simulated sex, and violence. 1987; 90m.

NIAGARA ★★★½
DIR: Henry Hathaway. **CAST:** Marilyn Monroe, Joseph Cotten, Jean Peters.

A sexy, slightly sleazy, and sinister Marilyn Monroe plots the murder of husband Joseph Cotten in this twisted tale of infidelity and greed, shot against the pulsing scenic grandeur of Niagara Falls. But plans go awry and the falls redeem a killer. Excellent location camerawork adds to the thrills. 1953; 89m.

NIGHT CREATURE
DIR: Lee Madden. **CAST:** Donald Pleasence, Nancy Kwan, Ross Hagen.

Grade Z film has Donald Pleasence playing a half-crazed adventurer who captures a killer leopard and brings the creature to his private island. He then decides to release the leopard so that the two of them can have a showdown. Nancy Kwan plays his daughter who is trapped on the island along with her husband and child. Rated PG for language. 1978; 83m.

NIGHT GALLERY ★★★
DIR: Boris Sagal, Steven Spielberg, Barry Shear. **CAST:** Roddy McDowall, Joan Crawford, Richard Kiley.

Pilot for the TV series. Three tales of terror by Rod Serling told with style and flair. Segment one is the best, with Roddy McDowall eager to get his hands on an inheritance. Segment two features Joan Crawford as a blind woman with a yearning to see. Segment three, involving a paranoid war fugitive, is the least of the three. 1969; 98m.

NIGHT HAS EYES, THE ★★★½
DIR: Leslie Arliss. **CAST:** James Mason, Joyce Howard, Wilfrid Lawson.

This suspense film from war-weary Great Britain focuses on a schoolmarm who searches for a colleague who is missing on a mist-shrouded moor. Joyce Howard is excellent as the teacher-sleuth and the young James Mason does a credible job as a disturbed composer. 1942; B&W; 79m.

NIGHT OF BLOODY HORROR 🦃
DIR: Joy N. Houck Jr. **CAST:** Gerald McRaney.

When a young man is released from a mental institution, a series of gory murders begins. Is he the culprit? The only suspense is in wondering if the bad gore effects will get any better. (They don't.) You can bet that *Simon & Simon* star Gerald McRaney would like to forget this one. Not rated. 1969; 89m.

NIGHT OF THE BLOODY APES ★
DIR: René Cardona Sr. **CAST:** José Elias Moreno.

A doctor revives his son with a heart transplant from a gorilla. Naturally, the boy becomes a murdering half-ape monster. This Mexican-made movie would be enjoyably campy were it not for the explicit gore and actual scenes of open-heart surgery. 1968; 82m.

NIGHT OF THE CREEPS ★★★½
DIR: Fred Dekker. **CAST:** Jason Lively, Steve Marchall, Jill Whitlow, Tom Atkins, Dick Miller.

A film derived from virtually every horror movie ever made, this does a wonderful job paying homage to the genre. The story involves an alien organism that lands on Earth in 1958 and immediately infects someone. Some thirty years later when this contaminated individual is accidentally released from cryogenic freeze, he wanders into a college town spreading these organisms in some rather disgusting ways. Not rated, but contains violence. 1986; 89m.

NIGHT OF THE DEMON 🦃
DIR: James C. Wasson. **CAST:** Michael Cutt, Jay Allen.

This is a boring little bomb of a movie with an intriguing title and nothing else. Not to be confused with the 1958 classic *Curse of the Demon.* 1983; 97m.

NIGHT OF THE DEATH CULT ★★½
DIR: Amando de Ossorio. **CAST:** Victor Petit, Maria Kosti.

This is one of a popular series of Spanish horror movies concerning the Templars, blind medieval priests who rise from the dead when their tombs are violated. In this one, the new doctor in a fishing village comes upon the Templars' human sacrifices. He sets about sending the priests back to their graves. The film contains nudity, violence, and gore, though as a whole it is more subdued and more atmospheric than American zombie movies. 1975; 85m.

NIGHT OF THE DEMONS ★★★
DIR: Kevin S. Tenney. **CAST:** William Gallo.

A great creaky-house movie about a group of teenagers who hold a séance in an abandoned mortuary. What they conjure up from the dead is more than they bargained for. Rated R for violence and nudity. 1989; 90m.

NIGHT OF THE GHOULS ★
DIR: Edward D. Wood Jr. **CAST:** Kenne Duncan, Criswell.

From the director of *Plan 9 from Outer Space* and *Glen or Glenda* comes a film so bad it was never released. Not nearly as enjoyably bad as Edward Wood's other work, but definitely worth a look for movie buffs. For the record, two young innocents stumble upon a haunted house (filled with some very tiresome bad actors). 1958; B&W; 75m.

NIGHT OF THE HOWLING BEAST

DIR: Miguel Iglesias Bonns. **CAST:** Paul Naschy, Grace Mills.

One of the all-time worst! Paul Naschy stars in this mess as a guy who has a slight problem whenever the full moon rises. Lon Chaney Jr. and Universal Pictures did it better—much better. Rated R. 1984; 87m.

NIGHT OF THE HUNTER ★★★★½

DIR: Charles Laughton. **CAST:** Robert Mitchum, Shelley Winters, Lillian Gish, James Gleason.

Absolutely the finest film from star Robert Mitchum, who is cast as a suave, smooth-talking—and absolutely evil—preacher determined to catch and kill his stepchildren. The entire film is eerie, exquisitely beautiful, and occasionally surreal; watch for the graceful, haunting shot of the children's freshly killed mother. 1955; B&W; 93m.

NIGHT OF THE LIVING DEAD ★★★★

DIR: George A. Romero. **CAST:** Duane Jones, Judith O'Dea, Keith Wayne.

This gruesome low-budget horror film still packs a punch for those who like to be frightened out of their wits. It is an unrelenting shock-fest laced with touches of black humor that deserves its cult status. 1968; B&W; 96m.

NIGHT OF THE ZOMBIES

DIR: Vincent Dawn. **CAST:** Frank Garfield, Margie Newton.

A low-budget horror film about the dead coming back to life (à la George Romero's *Night of the Living Dead*) and feasting on the living, this is a thoroughly disgusting motion picture. It's just one long cannibal feast—who needs this kind of trash? Rated R for violence and gore. 1983; 101m.

NIGHT SCREAMS ★

DIR: Allen Plone. **CAST:** Janette Allyson Caldwell, Joe Manno, Ron Thomas.

Three escaped convicts crash a teenage party and terrorize the kids. But the kids start turning up dead and so do the convicts. Figuring out who's killing who isn't tough, and there are only a few chills along the way. Not rated, but contains graphic violence and nudity. 1986; 85m.

NIGHT STALKER, THE (1971) ★★★★

DIR: John Llewellyn Moxey. **CAST:** Darren McGavin, Carol Lynley, Claude Akins.

A superb made-for-television chiller about a modern-day vampire stalking the streets of Las Vegas. Richard Matheson's teleplay is tight and suspenseful, with Darren McGavin fine as the intrepid reporter on the bloodsucker's trail. 1971; 73m.

NIGHT STALKER, THE, (1986) ★★★

DIR: Max Kleven. **CAST:** Charles Napier, Michelle Reese, Joe Gian, Leka Carlin.

A Vietnam veteran practicing martial-arts mysticism hits the street, brutally murdering prostitutes. An over-the-hill, alcoholic police detective pursues him. The acting is uneven, but the suspense is solid. Worth a look. Rated R for nudity, profanity, and graphic violence. 1986; 91m.

NIGHT VISITOR (1989) ★★

DIR: Robert Hitzig. **CAST:** Derek Rydall, Allen Garfield, Michael J. Pollard, Shannon Tweed, Elliott Gould, Richard Roundtree.

When a compulsive liar (Derek Rydall) witnesses a satanic murder committed by his history teacher, no one believes him. Rydall's childish whining is inconsistent with his role. Rated R for nudity, violence, and profanity. 1989; 93m.

NIGHT WARNING ★★

DIR: William Asher. **CAST:** Jimmy McNichol, Bo Svenson, Susan Tyrrell.

As in many gory movies, the victims and near-victims have a convenient and unbelievable way of hanging around despite clear indications they are about to get it. Consequently, *Night Warning*, in spite of good performances, is an unremarkable splatter film. Rated R for violence. 1982; 96m.

NIGHT WATCH ★★
DIR: Brian G. Hutton. **CAST:** Elizabeth Taylor, Laurence Harvey, Billie Whitelaw, Robert Lang, Tony Britton.

In this so-so suspense thriller, Elizabeth Taylor stars as a wealthy widow recovering from a nervous breakdown. From her window, she seems to witness a number of ghoulish goings-on. But does she? The operative phrase here after a while is "Who cares?" Rated PG. 1973; 98m.

NIGHTCOMERS, THE ★★½
DIR: Michael Winner. **CAST:** Marlon Brando, Stephanie Beacham, Thora Hird, Harry Andrews.

Strange prequel to *The Turn of the Screw*, this uneven effort contains some fine acting and boasts some truly eerie scenes, but is hampered by Michael Winner's loose direction and a nebulous storyline. Marlon Brando is in good form as the mysterious catalyst, but this murky melodrama still lacks the solid story and cohesiveness that could have made it a true chiller. Rated R. 1971; 96m.

NIGHTMARE AT NOON
DIR: Nico Mastorakis. **CAST:** Wings Hauser, Bo Hopkins, George Kennedy, Brion James.

A retread thriller about a group of renegade scientists testing a germ-warfare virus. A chemical is dumped into the water supply of a small Southwestern town, causing the inhabitants to turn green and shoot everyone in sight. Wings Hauser and Bo Hopkins play the heroes—who never get thirsty enough to drink the water. This film is so cheap the same effects shots are used over and over. Rated R for violence. 1987; 96m.

NIGHTMARE HOUSE ★
DIR: Joseph Adler. **CAST:** Ross Harris.

The main plot of this dated horror movie concerns an artist with a warped way of getting models for his grotesque paintings. But most of the running time is taken up with boring scenes of the love lives of four college kids. Previously available on video under its original title *Scream, Baby, Scream*, the movie is rated R for violence and brief nudity. 1969; 83m.

NIGHTMARE IN BLOOD ★★
DIR: John Stanley. **CAST:** Jerry Walter, Barrie Youngfellow, Kerwin Mathews.

A film that's fun for genre fans only. A horror-movie star appears at a horror convention that people are dying to get into. The twist is he isn't just playing a vampire in his films; he *is* one. The cassette box says "filmed in and around picturesque San Francisco," and most viewers will think that's the best thing about it. Not rated, but contains mild bloodletting. 1975; 92m.

NIGHTMARE IN WAX (CRIMES IN THE WAX MUSEUM) ★½
DIR: Bud Townsend. **CAST:** Cameron Mitchell, Anne Helm, Scott Brady.

Cameron Mitchell plays a disfigured ex–makeup man running a wax museum in Hollywood. His idea of a good time is to inject movie stars with a formula that turns them into statues. Low-grade, barely watchable mess with an unsatisfying ending. Rated PG. 1969; 91m.

NIGHTMARE ON ELM STREET, A ★★★★
DIR: Wes Craven. **CAST:** John Saxon, Ronee Blakley, Heather Langenkamp, Robert Englund.

Wes Craven directed this clever shocker about a group of teenagers afflicted with the same bad dreams. Horror movie buffs, take note. Rated R for nudity, violence, and profanity. 1985; 91m.

NIGHTMARE ON ELM STREET 2: FREDDY'S REVENGE, A ★
DIR: Jack Sholder. **CAST:** Mark Patton, Kim Myers, Clu Gulager, Hope Lange.
The only thing this substandard horror film has in common with its far superior predecessor is the title and gruesome old Freddy Krueger. Outside of the obvious, it is dull and lacks tension. Another teen exploitation film. Rated R for nudity, language, and gore. 1985; 83m.

NIGHTMARE ON ELM STREET 3: THE DREAM WARRIORS ★★
DIR: Chuck Russell. **CAST:** Robert Englund, Heather Langenkamp, Patricia Arquette, Craig Wasson.
Freddy is at it again, forcing his way into the dreams of unsuspecting teenage girls and twisting those dreams into demented nightmares. This one is only slightly better than the second entry. Rated R. 1987; 97m.

NIGHTMARE ON ELM STREET 4: THE DREAM MASTER, A ★★★½
DIR: Renny Harlin. **CAST:** Robert Englund, Lisa Wilcox.
America's favorite child-molesting burn victim Freddy Kruger (Robert Englund) is back in this fourth installment of the hit series. Freddy's favorite pastime, killing teenagers in their dreams, is played to the hilt with fantastic special effects. Rated R for violence and gore. 1988; 97m.

NIGHTMARE SISTERS 🦃
DIR: David DeCoteau. **CAST:** Linnea Quigley.
Leering horror flick with a comic undercurrent. The spirit of a succubus possesses three straitlaced sorority girls and turns them into monstrous nymphos. This film was given the bare bones of a plot just so the director could get three comely women naked on screen and not have it labeled porn. Rated R for nudity and simulated sex. 1988; 83m.

NIGHTMARE WEEKEND 🦃
DIR: H. Sala. **CAST:** Debbie Laster, Debra Hunter, Lori Lewis.
An incomprehensible film about a scientist who invents a computer system that can transform solid inorganic objects into deadly weapons. The computer is run by a hand puppet that is in love with the scientist's daughter, and is always using the computer to protect her from the male population of the town. Rated R for graphic violence and nudity. 1985; 88m.

NIGHTMARES ★★
DIR: Joseph Sargent. **CAST:** Cristina Raines, Emilio Estevez, Lance Henriksen.
Four everyday situations are twisted into tales of terror in this mostly mediocre horror film in the style of *Twilight Zone–the Movie* and *Creepshow*. Rated R for violence and profanity. 1983; 99m.

NIGHTWING 🦃
DIR: Arthur Hiller. **CAST:** David Warner, Kathryn Harrold, Nick Mancuso, Strother Martin.
Absolutely laughable tale, derived from an abysmal Martin Cruz Smith novel, about a flock (herd? pack?) of vampire bats—the real ones, not the two-legged cousins that prey on nubile young women—terrorizing a small community. Rated PG. 1979; 105m.

976-EVIL ★★★½
DIR: Robert Englund. **CAST:** Jim Metzler, Stephen Geoffreys, Sandy Dennis, Robert Picardo.
Actor Robert Englund makes his directorial debut with this tale of a wimpish teenager who slowly becomes possessed by a 976 "Horrorscope" number. Englund gives his film a genuinely eerie feel without missing his chance to throw in a little comedy. Rated R for violence. 1989; 92m.

NO WAY OUT ★★★½
DIR: Roger Donaldson. **CAST:** Kevin Costner, Gene Hackman, Sean Young, Will Patton, Howard Duff, Iman.
In this gripping, sexy and surprising suspense thriller, Kevin Costner stars

as a morally upright naval hero who accepts a position with the secretary of defense (Gene Hackman) and his somewhat overzealous assistant (Will Patton, who walks away with the film). Things become a bit sticky when the secretary becomes involved in murder. Rated R for nudity, sexual situations, language, and violence. 1987; 116m.

NOMADS ★★★
DIR: John McTiernan. **CAST:** Lesley-Anne Down, Pierce Brosnan, Adam Ant, Mary Woronov.
In this thought-provoking and chilling shocker, Pierce Brosnan is a French anthropologist who discovers a secret society of malevolent ghosts living in modern-day Los Angeles. In doing so, he incurs their wrath and endangers the life of a doctor (Lesley-Anne Down) fated to share his terrifying experiences. Rated R for profanity, nudity, and violence. 1986; 95m.

NORTH BY NORTHWEST ★★★★★
DIR: Alfred Hitchcock. **CAST:** Cary Grant, Eva Marie Saint, James Mason, Martin Landau.
Cary Grant and Eva Marie Saint star in this classic thriller by the master himself, Alfred Hitchcock, who plays (or preys) on the senses and keeps the action at a feverish pitch. The story is typical Hitchcock fare—a matter of mistaken identity embroils a man in espionage and murder. 1959; 136m.

NOT OF THIS EARTH ★★★
DIR: Jim Wynorski. **CAST:** Traci Lords, Arthur Roberts.
Purposely trashy remake of a Roger Corman sci-fi classic from the Fifties. Plenty of action, campy comedy, and sex to hold your interest. Traci Lords is a private nurse assigned to administer blood transfusions to a mysterious, wealthy patient. Once she starts nosing around, the fun starts. Rated R for nudity, simulated sex, and violence. 1988; 82m.

NOTHING UNDERNEATH ★
DIR: Carlo Vanzina. **CAST:** Tom Schanley, Renée Simonson, Donald Pleasence.
Completely predictable suspense yarn in which a ranger from Yellowstone goes to Florence, Italy, to investigate the disappearance of his kid sister, a top model. Of course, police captain Donald Pleasence lets the ranger in on all of the secrets of the Florence police handling the case. Pretty stupid. Not rated, but contains violence and nudity. 1987; 96m.

NOTORIOUS ★★★★½
DIR: Alfred Hitchcock. **CAST:** Cary Grant, Ingrid Bergman, Claude Rains, Louis Calhern.
Notorious is among the finest Alfred Hitchcock romantic thrillers. Cary Grant, as an American agent, and Ingrid Bergman, as the "notorious" daughter of a convicted traitor, join forces to seek out Nazis in postwar Rio. Claude Rains gives one of his greatest performances. 1946; B&W; 101m.

NUMBER 17 ★★½
DIR: Alfred Hitchcock. **CAST:** Leon M. Lion, Anne Grey, Donald Calthrop, Barry Jones.
Seldom-seen thriller from Alfred Hitchcock is a humorous departure from his later more obsessive films, but it still maintains his wry touches and unusual characters. Once again an unsuspecting innocent (in this case, a hobo) accidentally comes across something that places him in jeopardy (a gang of jewel thieves). 1932; B&W; 83m.

OBLONG BOX, THE ★★
DIR: Gordon Hessler. **CAST:** Vincent Price, Christopher Lee, Rupert Davies, Sally Geeson.
This little gothic horror is nothing to shiver about. Although it is taken from an Edgar Allan Poe short story, it can't escape the clichés of its genre: grave robbers, screaming women (with close-up shots of their widening eyes), lots of cleavage, and of course,

the hero's bride-to-be, who is unaware of her betrothed's wrongdoings. Sound familiar? Rated R (but more like a PG by today's standards) for violence. 1969; 91m.

OBSESSION ★★★★
DIR: Brian De Palma. **CAST:** Cliff Robertson, Genevieve Bujold, John Lithgow.
This is director Brian De Palma's tour de force. Bernard Hermann scores again, his music as effective as that in *Taxi Driver*. The script, about a widower who meets his former wife's exact double, was written by Paul Schrader (in collaboration with De Palma). Critics enthusiastically compare this with prime Hitchcock, and it more than qualifies. Rated PG. 1976; 98m.

OCTAMAN ★½
DIR: Harry Essex. **CAST:** Kerwin Mathews, Pier Angeli, Jeff Morrow.
Dull low-budget effort with a group of vacationers under attack by a funny-looking walking octopus-man created by a very young Rick Baker, who has since gone on to much bigger and better things. Rated PG for mild violence. 1971; 90m.

OF UNKNOWN ORIGIN ★★½
DIR: George Pan Cosmatos. **CAST:** Peter Weller, Jennifer Dale, Lawrence Dane.
Flashes of unintentional humor enliven this shocker, about a suburban family terrorized in their home by a monstrous rat. Contains some inventive photography and effects, but mediocre acting and forgettable music keep this film well away from classic status. Bring on the exterminator! Rated R. 1983; 88m.

OFFSPRING, THE ★★★★
DIR: Jeff Burr. **CAST:** Vincent Price, Clu Gulager, Terry Kiser.
Four scary and original short stories are tied together by the narration of an old man (Vincent Price) who lives in a small town that seems to make people kill. Well written and acted, with decent special effects. Horror fans will love this. Rated R for violence and brief nudity. 1986; 99m.

OMEN, THE ★★★★
DIR: Richard Donner. **CAST:** Gregory Peck, Lee Remick, Billie Whitelaw, David Warner.
This, first of a series of movies about the return to Earth of the devil, is a real chiller. In the form of a young boy, Damien, Satan sets about reestablishing his rule over man. A series of bizarre deaths points to the boy. Rated R. 1976; 111m.

ONE DARK NIGHT ★★½
DIR: Tom McLoughlin. **CAST:** Meg Tilly, Adam West, Robin Evans, Elizabeth Dally.
Meg Tilly and Adam "Batman" West star in this story of a young woman (Tilly) who is menaced by an energy-draining ghost. Rated R. 1983; 89m.

ONE FRIGHTENED NIGHT ★★
DIR: Christy Cabanne. **CAST:** Wallace Ford, Mary Carlisle, Hedda Hopper, Charley Grapewin.
A stormy night, a spooky mansion, an eccentric millionaire, and a group of people stranded together was about all it used to take to make a scary movie. A good cast and some witty dialogue help, but there's only so much that can be done with this kind of mystery. 1935; B&W; 69m.

OPEN HOUSE ★
DIR: Jag Mundhra. **CAST:** Joseph Bottoms, Adrienne Barbeau, Rudy Ramos, Tiffany Bolling.
Upset that rich people are spending millions of dollars on expensive Los Angeles real estate while other people are homeless and starving, a maniac starts killing potential purchasers and the real-estate agents who are helping them. This slasher movie features some particularly repellent and sadistic murders, along with nudity and sexual situations. A definite R. 1987; 95m.

ORACLE, THE ★★
DIR: Roberta Findlay. **CAST:** Caroline Capers Powers, Roger Neil.

A woman discovers that the last occupant of her new apartment was a murder victim. Reaching out from beyond the grave, he tries to force her to avenge his death. Better than average for this sort of low-budget chiller, with some effective shocks and a few interesting plot twists. Rated R for gore. 1985; 94m.

ORCA ★★★
DIR: Michael Anderson. **CAST:** Richard Harris, Keenan Wynn, Will Sampson, Bo Derek, Robert Carradine, Charlotte Rampling.

Where *Jaws* was an exaggerated horror story, *Orca* is based on the tragic truth. Motivated by profit, Richard Harris and his crew go out with a huge net and find a family of whales. He misses the male and harpoons the female, who dies and aborts, leaving her huge mate to wreak havoc on the tiny seaport. Rated PG. 1977; 92m.

ORGY OF THE DEAD 🦃
DIR: A. C. Stephen. **CAST:** Criswell, Pat Barringer, William Bates.

You'll find it in the horror section of your video store, but it's really trying to be a comedy. There's no plot to speak of, as the "Emperor of the Dead" (Criswell) holds court in a graveyard while dead souls dance for his amusement. They're all played by topless dancers who simply perform their nightclub routines while a fog machine works overtime. Not rated. 1965; 82m.

OTHER, THE ★★★½
DIR: Robert Mulligan. **CAST:** Uta Hagen, Diana Muldaur, Chris Udvarnoky, Martin Udvarnoky, John Ritter.

Screenwriter Thomas Tryon, adapting his bestselling novel, raises plenty of goose bumps. This supernatural tale of good and evil, as personified by twin brothers, creates a genuinely eerie mood. Legendary acting coach Uta Hagen contributes a compelling performance. Director Robert Mulligan, keeping the emphasis on characterizations, never allows the suspense to lag. 1972; 100m.

OTHER HELL, THE 🦃
DIR: Stephan Oblowsky. **CAST:** Franca Stoppi, Carlo De Melo.

An Italian film about a convent inhabited by the devil. The church sends a psychologist-priest to prove the strange goings-on are a case of mass hysteria. He's horrified to learn the nature of the supernatural events. We, however, are bored stiff by a stupid story and schlock effects. Rated R for graphic violence and nudity. 1980; 88m.

OUTING, THE ★
DIR: Tom Daley. **CAST:** Deborah Winters, James Huston, Danny D. Daniels.

A teenage girl is possessed by a demon and convinces her friends to spend the night in her father's museum. Murder follows bloody murder, building toward an anticlimactic ending filled with poor special effects. Cheap and poorly written. Not rated but contains brief nudity and graphic violence. 1986; 87m.

PACK, THE ★★
DIR: Robert Clouse. **CAST:** Joe Don Baker, Hope Alexander Willis, Richard B. Shull, R. G. Armstrong.

Slightly above average horror film about a pack of dogs that goes wild and tries to kill two families. Rated R. 1977; 99m.

PAPERHOUSE ★★★★
DIR: Bernard Rose. **CAST:** Charlotte Burke, Glenne Headly, Ben Cross.

In this original film from England, a lonely, misunderstood 11-year-old girl (Charlotte Burke) begins retreating into a fantasy world. Her world turns nightmarish when it starts to take over her dreams and a flulike disease keeps making her faint. Visually impressive, well-acted, and intelligent fare. Rated PG-13 for violence. 1989; 94m.

PARADINE CASE, THE ★★
DIR: Alfred Hitchcock. **CAST:** Gregory Peck, Ann Todd, Charles Laughton, Ethel Barrymore, Charles Coburn, Louis Jourdan, Alida Valli, Leo G. Carroll, John Williams.
Even the Master of Suspense can't win 'em all. Obviously chafing under the rein of mentor David O. Selznick, Alfred Hitchcock produced one of his few failures—a boring, talky courtroom drama that stalls long before its conclusion. Unrated; suitable for family viewing. 1947; B&W; 112m.

PARANOIA ★
DIR: Umberto Lenzi. **CAST:** Carroll Baker, Lou Castel, Colette Descombes.
Pretentious suspenser made in Italy about a rich American widow (Carroll Baker) who makes the mistake of taking an evil young couple into her isolated villa. First they seduce her, then they try to drive her insane so that they can get her money. Originally rated X for nudity and sexual situations, but a tame R equivalent now. 1969; 91m.

PARASITE ★★½
DIR: Charles Band. **CAST:** Robert Glaudini, Demi Moore, Luca Bercovici, Vivian Blaine.
If director Charles Band intended a film that would sicken its audience, he succeeded with this futuristic monster movie. Memorable scenes include parasites bursting through the stomach of one victim and the face of another. Rated R. 1982; 85m.

PATRICK ★★½
DIR: Richard Franklin. **CAST:** Susan Penhaligon, Robert Helpmann.
This film revolves around Patrick, who has been in a coma for four years. He is confined to a hospital, but after a new nurse comes to work on his floor he begins to exhibit psychic powers. Some violence, but nothing extremely bloody. Rated PG. 1979; 96m.

PEEPING TOM ★★★½
DIR: Michael Powell. **CAST:** Carl Boehm, Moira Shearer, Anna Massey.
Carl Boehm gives a chilling performance as a lethal psychopath who photographs his victims as they are dying. This film outraged both critics and viewers alike when it was first released, and rarely has been revived since. Not for all tastes, to be sure, but if you're adventurous, give this one a try. Rated R. 1960; 109m.

PET SEMATARY ★★★½
DIR: Mary Lambert. **CAST:** Dale Midkiff, Fred Gwynne, Denise Crosby.
This scarefest is the most faithful film adaptation of a Stephen King novel yet. A young doctor moves his family to an idyllic setting in the Maine woods. The calm is shattered when first the family's cat and then their son are killed on the nearby highway. If you can bear this, you'll love the all-out terror that follows. Rated R for violence. 1989; 102m.

PHANTASM ★★½
DIR: Don Coscarelli. **CAST:** Michael Baldwin, Bill Thornbury, Reggie Bannister.
This strange mixture of horror and science-fiction, while not an outstanding film by any account, does provide viewers with several thrills and unexpected twists. If you like to jump out of your seat, watch this alone with all the lights out. R-rated after scenes were cut from the original X-rated version. 1979; 87m.

PHANTASM II ★★
DIR: Don Coscarelli. **CAST:** James Le Gros, Reggie Bannister, Angus Scrimm.
After ten years, the Tall Man (Angus Scrimm) is back, and he's nastier than ever. No longer is he merely looting cemeteries to enslave the dead for his fiendish purposes. He's also going after the living. But the heroes from the first film are hot on his trail, intent on putting an end to his reign of terror. Lacks the wit, style, and originality of

its predecessor. Rated R for nudity, profanity, and graphic violence. 1988; 90m.

PHANTOM CREEPS, THE ★★½
DIR: Ford Beebe, Saul Goodkind. **CAST:** Bela Lugosi, Regis Toomey.

This Saturday-afternoon crowd-pleaser features a crazed scientist, a giant robot, an invisibility belt, and a meteorite fragment that can render an entire army immobile—just about anything a kid can ask for in a serial. Good fun. 1939; B&W; 12 chapters.

PHANTOM OF DEATH ★★
DIR: Ruggero Deodato. **CAST:** Michael York, Edwige Fenech, Donald Pleasence.

A concert pianist, dying of a rare disease that causes rapid aging, takes out his frustration on women from his past by hacking them to pieces. He stays one step ahead of the police because no description of him is ever the same. Donald Pleasence and Michael York are old pros, but the direction is flat and any suspense is worn quickly into the ground. Not rated, but contains nudity and violence. 1987; 95m.

PHANTOM OF THE OPERA (1925) ★★★★★
DIR: Rupert Julian. **CAST:** Lon Chaney Sr., Mary Philbin, Norman Kerry.

Classic silent horror with Lon Chaney Sr. in his most poignant and gruesome role. This 1925 sample of Chaney's brilliance—he was truly the "man of a thousand faces"—still has enough power to send chills up your spine. Enjoy. 1925; B&W; 79m.

PHANTOM OF THE OPERA (1943) ★★★
DIR: Arthur Lubin. **CAST:** Claude Rains, Susanna Foster, Nelson Eddy, Edgar Barrier, Miles Mander, Hume Cronyn.

Overabundance of singing hurts this otherwise good remake of the 1925 silent. The well-known story concerns a Paris opera house being terrorized by a disfigured composer (Claude Rains) whose best works have been stolen. Acting is great, production values are high, but that singing has got to go! 1943; 92m.

PHOBIA ★
DIR: John Huston. **CAST:** Paul Michael Glaser, Susan Hogan, John Colicos, Patricia Collins.

Exhibit A in the argument that even the great filmmakers occasionally make turkeys. The master, John Huston, had occasional lapses between masterpieces. This Canadian-financed film is surely one. An almost-unwatchable nonthrilling thriller that combines psychobabble with murder. Rated R. 1980; 90m.

PICNIC AT HANGING ROCK ★★★★½
DIR: Peter Weir. **CAST:** Rachel Roberts, Dominic Guard, Helen Morse, Jacki Weaver.

Surreal, hypnotic suspense story revolves around the mysterious disappearance of a group of students from an all-girls' school at the turn of the century in Australia. Director Peter Weir fashions a truly unsettling motion picture. His fans will rank it among his best. 1975; 110m.

PICTURE MOMMY DEAD ★★
DIR: Bert I. Gordon. **CAST:** Don Ameche, Martha Hyer, Zsa Zsa Gabor, Signe Hasso, Susan Gordon.

The tragic death of her mother causes a young girl to lose her memory. Afterward, she is possessed by the spirit of her late mommy. Ooh! Meanwhile the father, Don Ameche, marries again. Thus a rather silly battle ensues between stepmom and stepdaughter. Good acting; too bad the script isn't better. 1966; 88m.

PICTURE OF DORIAN GRAY, THE ★★★★
DIR: Albert Lewin. **CAST:** George Sanders, Hurd Hatfield, Donna Reed, Angela Lansbury, Peter Lawford.

The classic adaptation of Oscar Wilde's famous novel, this features Hurd Hatfield giving a restrained performance in the title role of a young man whose portrait ages while he remains eternally youthful. Though talky and slow-moving, this film nevertheless keeps you glued to the screen. A few key scenes shot in Technicolor for effect. 1945; B&W; 110m.

PIECES 🦃

DIR: Juan Piquer Simon. **CAST:** Christopher George, Lynda Day George, Edmund Purdom.

Christopher George and Lynda Day George, who were fast becoming the Lunt and Fontane of sicko horror flicks, star in this movie, which promises, "You don't have to go to Texas for a chainsaw massacre!" Sounds lovely. While not rated by the MPAA, the picture would probably qualify for an X rating. 1983; 85m.

PIRANHA ★★★

DIR: Joe Dante. **CAST:** Bradford Dillman, Kevin McCarthy, Heather Menzies, Keenan Wynn.

Director Joe Dante and writer John Sayles sent up *Jaws* in this nifty, gag-filled horror film. Full of scares and chuckles. Rated R. 1978; 92m.

PIRANHA PART TWO: THE SPAWNING ★

DIR: James Cameron. **CAST:** Tricia O'Neil, Steve Marachuk, Lance Henriksen, Leslie Graves.

Sorry sequel to *Piranha* by the man who would later grace us with *The Terminator*. A mutated strain of piranha (with the ability to fly, no less) launches an air and sea tirade of violence against a group of vacationers at a tropical resort. Interesting idea poorly executed. Rated R for mild gore. 1981; 88m.

PIT AND THE PENDULUM, THE ★★★

DIR: Roger Corman. **CAST:** Vincent Price, John Kerr, Barbara Steele, Luana Anders, Anthony Carbone.

More stylish, low-budget Edgar Allan Poe–inspired terror with star Vincent Price and director Roger Corman reteaming for this release. This is for fans of the series only. 1961; 80m.

PLANET OF THE VAMPIRES ★★

DIR: Mario Bava. **CAST:** Barry Sullivan, Norma Bengell, Angel Aranda.

After landing on a mysterious planet, astronauts are possessed by formless alien vampires trying to reach Earth. An Italian-Spanish production, also known as *Demon Planet*. The film is plodding and poorly dubbed. Watch director Mario Bava's *Black Sunday* instead. 1965; 86m.

PLAY MISTY FOR ME ★★★★

DIR: Clint Eastwood. **CAST:** Clint Eastwood, Jessica Walter, Donna Mills, John Larch, Irene Hervey.

A suspenseful shocker in which director-star Clint Eastwood, playing a disc jockey, is stalked by a crazed fan (Jessica Walter). It puts goosebumps on your goosebumps and marked an auspicious directorial debut for the squinty-eyed star. Rated R. 1971; 102m.

PLAYGIRL KILLER, THE 🦃

DIR: Enrick Santamaran. **CAST:** William Kirwin, Jean Christopher, Neil Sedaka.

An insane painter kills his models and stores them in deep freeze. In between those merry scenes, Neil Sedaka (prior to his Seventies comeback) sings a few awful songs, lounges by a pool, and generally gives no evidence of being involved with the plot. This Canadian film is unrated. 1969; 90m.

PLUMBER, THE ★★★½

DIR: Peter Weir. **CAST:** Ivar Kants, Judy Morris, Robert Coleby.

A slightly unhinged plumber completely destroys a young couple's bathroom and begins to terrorize the woman of the house during his visits to make the repairs. A very black comedy-horror-film from the director of *Witness*. Originally made for Australian television. No rating (contains some strong language). 1980; 76m.

PLUTONIUM BABY 🦃

DIR: Ray Hirschman. **CAST:** Patrick Molloy, Danny Guerra.

A heroic, shape-changing mutant squares off with his evil counterpart, leaving death and destruction behind them in the heart of New York City. This is a cheap comic-book rip-off, slow moving and so poorly acted, one can't help laughing. Not rated, but contains violence and nudity. 1987; 85m.

POLTERGEIST ★★★★★
DIR: Tobe Hooper. **CAST:** Craig T. Nelson, JoBeth Williams, Beatrice Straight, Dominique Dunne.
The ultimate screen ghost story, *Poltergeist* is guaranteed to raise goosepimples while keeping viewers marvelously entertained. A sort of *Close Encounters* of the supernatural, it's a scary story about the plight of a suburban family whose home suddenly becomes a house of horrors. Rated PG for tense situations. 1982; 114m.

POLTERGEIST II: THE OTHER SIDE ★★
DIR: Brian Gibson. **CAST:** JoBeth Williams, Craig T. Nelson, Heather O'Rourke, Oliver Robins, Zelda Rubinstein, Will Sampson, Geraldine Fitzgerald.
Mere months (screen time) after their last film adventure, the stalwart Freeling family is up to its eyeballs in spooks again—although the ghosts stay backstage while another collection of effects parades before the audience. Coherence and common sense aren't in much evidence, and the whole project collapses under its own weight. Rated PG-13 for violence. 1986; 92m.

POLTERGEIST III ★
DIR: Gary A. Sherman. **CAST:** Tom Skerritt, Nancy Allen, Heather O'Rourke, Zelda Rubinstein.
Little Carol Ann (Heather O'Rourke) moves to Chicago to attend a school for gifted children with mental disorders. It seems all of her supernatural experiences have just about sent her over the edge. The acting in this film is stale and uninspired, while the special effects are surprisingly low-budget. Rated PG-13 for violence. 1988; 90m.

POOR GIRL, A GHOST STORY ★★
DIR: Michael Apted. **CAST:** Lynne Miller, Angela Thorne, Stuart Wilson.
Strange, mildly interesting tale of a young governess being pursued by both her young pupil and his father. Soon a ghost takes over her actions and it becomes impossible for her to carry on her teaching duties. Made for Canadian TV, this is unrated but contains sexual situations. 1975; 52m.

POSITIVE I.D. ★★½
DIR: Andy Anderson. **CAST:** Stephanie Rascoe, John Davies, Steve Fromholz.
Slow-developing story about a suburban housewife (Stephanie Rascoe) who, after being raped, assumes another identity to escape her past life. Rascoe makes a remarkable transformation from plain housewife to knockout, and the twist ending is ample reward for those patient enough to sit through the first hour of the film. Rated R for language and nudity. 1988; 93m.

POSSESSION
DIR: Andrzej Zulawski. **CAST:** Isabelle Adjani, Sam Neill, Heinz Bennent.
Enjoy confusion, a lack of plot, unanswered questions, accents so thick that the words can't be understood? If so, this French-German coproduction is a must-see for you. Sam Neill's talent is wasted as the husband of a woman who's possessed by the devil. Rated R for nudity, violence, and gore. 1984; 80m.

POWER, THE ★½
DIR: Jeffrey Obrow, Stephen Carpenter. **CAST:** Susan Stokey, Warren Lincoln, Lisa Erickson.
Nearly incomprehensible movie in which a centuries-old Aztec idol that holds the culture's forces of evil is unearthed by some youngsters, who must face the consequences. Rated R for profanity, violence, and gore. 1980; 87m.

PREMATURE BURIAL, THE ★★
DIR: Roger Corman. **CAST:** Ray Milland, Hazel Court, Richard Ney, Heather Angel.

A medical student's paranoia about being buried alive causes his worst fears to come true. Roger Corman's only Poe-derived film without Vincent Price. Lacking Price's playful and hammy acting style, it all seems too serious. 1962; 81m.

PREMONITION, THE ★★½
DIR: Robert Schnitzer. **CAST:** Sharon Farrell, Richard Lynch, Jeff Corey, Danielle Brisebois.

Well-written but turgidly directed terror film about a young adopted girl kidnapped by her natural mother. The girl's adoptive parents turn to ESP to locate her, and fall into a strange world. Not rated, but has intense situations and some violence. 1975; 94m.

PRETTY KILL
DIR: George Kaczender. **CAST:** David Birney, Season Hubley, Yaphet Kotto.

A madam involved with a police detective hires a hooker who just happens to have a multiple-personality disorder. The main problem with this film, besides being ludicrous, is that it has too many subplots, which don't add up to one strong story. Rated R for violence and nudity. 1987; 95m.

PREY, THE ★
DIR: Edwin Scott Brown. **CAST:** Debbie Thurseon, Steve Bond, Lori Lethin, Jackie Coogan.

Six young hikers go up into the woods, where they run into a ghoul who hunts them down and has them for dinner. Yum. Rated R for nudity and violence. 1980; 80m.

PRIME EVIL ★★½
DIR: Roberta Findlay. **CAST:** William Beckwith, Christine Moore.

A band of priests in New York City are actually disciples of Satan. A bloody sacrifice every thirteen years grants them immortality. Passable horror film has decent suspense and contains violent acts without being awash in gore. Rated R. 1989; 87m.

PRINCE OF DARKNESS ★
DIR: John Carpenter. **CAST:** Donald Pleasence, Jameson Parker, Victor Wong, Lisa Blount, Dennis Dun, Alice Cooper.

Horror impresario John Carpenter tried to return to his *Halloween*-ish roots with this scientific chiller, but wound up with a leaden bore more appropriate to Thanksgiving. Priest Donald Pleasence learns about a canister hidden below an unused church and suspects he's found Satan's resting place. B-o-o-o-ring. Rated R for violence and language. 1987; 110m.

PRISON ★½
DIR: Renny Harlin. **CAST:** Lane Smith, Chelsea Field, Andre de Shields, Lincoln Kilpatrick.

An old prison is haunted by the vengeful ghost of a man executed in 1964. Unfortunately, that plot is made toothless by a confused storyline, and the horror of the situation is lost. Rated R for language and violence. 1988; 102m.

PROM NIGHT ★★
DIR: Paul Lynch. **CAST:** Jamie Lee Curtis, Leslie Nielsen, Casey Stevens.

This okay slasher flick has a group of high-school students being systematically slaughtered as payment for the accidental death of one of their friends when they were all children. Rated R. 1980; 92m.

PROPHECY
DIR: John Frankenheimer. **CAST:** Talia Shire, Robert Foxworth, Armand Assante, Richard Dysart, Victoria Racimo.

Dull ecological horror film about a mutated beast that inhabits a northeastern American forest. The monster looks quite stupid, the special effects are laughable, and the cast sleepwalks through the whole event. Rated PG. 1979; 95m.

PSYCHIC KILLER ★
DIR: Ray Danton. **CAST:** Jim Hutton, Paul Burke, Julie Adams, Nehemiah Persoff, Neville Brand, Aldo Ray, Della Reese.
This is a completely ordinary thriller about a man who acquires psychic powers in a mental institution and then utilizes them for revenge. *Psychic Killer* doesn't take itself seriously and that's a plus, but it's not sufficiently engrossing. Rated PG. 1975; 89m.

PSYCHO ★★★★★
DIR: Alfred Hitchcock. **CAST:** Anthony Perkins, Janet Leigh, Vera Miles, John Gavin, John McIntire, Simon Oakland, John Anderson, Frank Albertson, Patricia Hitchcock.
The quintessential shocker, which started a whole genre of films about psychotic killers enacting mayhem on innocent victims, still holds up well today. If all you can remember about this film is its famous murder of Janet Leigh in the shower, you might want to give it a second look. Anthony Perkins's performance and the ease with which Hitchcock maneuvers your emotions make *Psycho* far superior to the numerous films that tried to duplicate it. 1960; B&W; 109m.

PSYCHO II ★★★
DIR: Richard Franklin. **CAST:** Anthony Perkins, Vera Miles, Meg Tilly, Robert Loggia, Dennis Franz, Hugh Gillin.
Picking up where Alfred Hitchcock's original left off, this sequel begins with Norman Bates (Anthony Perkins) being declared sane after twenty-two years in an asylum. Old Normie goes right back to the Bates Motel, and strange things begin to happen. Directed with exquisite taste and respect for the old master by Richard Franklin. It's suspenseful, scary, and funny. Rated R for profanity and violence. 1983; 113m.

PSYCHO III ★★
DIR: Anthony Perkins. **CAST:** Anthony Perkins, Diana Scarwid, Jeff Fahey, Hugh Gillin.
Second follow-up to *Psycho* works mainly because actor-director Anthony Perkins understands poor Norman Bates inside and out. Although lensed beautifully by Bruce Surtees, the film fails in the most critical area: creating suspense. Rated R for gory violence. 1986; 93m.

PSYCHO GIRLS ★★★
DIR: Gerard Ciccoritti. **CAST:** John Haslett Cuff, Darlene Wignacci.
Over-the-top horror parody will appeal most to avid horror fans, who will appreciate the black humor. A writer of mystery novels holds a dinner party that turns into a nightmare when it is disrupted by a psychotic woman. Not a great movie by any means, but a change of pace for genre fans. Rated R for violence and nudity. 1986; 90m.

PSYCHO SISTERS ★★★★
DIR: Reginald LeBorg. **CAST:** Susan Strasberg, Faith Domergue, Charles Knox Robinson.
After her husband is killed, a woman goes to stay with her sister—her sister who has only recently emerged from an insane asylum and is still hearing their dead mother's voice. This film is a classic of the early 1970s horror/gore/exploitation cycle. Rated PG for mild violence. 1972; 76m.

PSYCHOMANIA ★★
DIR: Don Sharp. **CAST:** George Sanders, Nicky Henson, Mary Larkin, Patrick Holt, Beryl Reid.
This British-made film is about a motorcycle gang. They call themselves the Living Dead because they committed a group suicide and only came back to life through a pact with the devil. The film moves slowly and includes lots of violence. Rated R. 1971; 95m.

PSYCHOPATH, THE ★
DIR: Larry Brown. **CAST:** Tom Basham, John Ashton.
The host of a children's television show spends his spare time killing parents who abuse their kids. The best that can be said for this is that it's not

nearly as tasteless as the premise portends. On the other hand, this is an edited version of the movie in which most of the reportedly gory murders have been cut out, so who knows how bad the original was? Rated PG. 1973; 84m.

PSYCHOS IN LOVE ★★½
DIR: Gorman Bechard. **CAST:** Carmine Capobianco, Debi Thibeault, Frank Stewart.

This film is an *Eating Raoul*–style horror comedy. Joe is a bar owner who has no trouble meeting women and getting dates. The problem is that he is a psychopath who ends up killing them—generally when he finds out they like grapes! This made-for-video movie has lots of gore and nudity. 1985; 88m.

PULSE ★
DIR: Paul Golding. **CAST:** Cliff DeYoung, Roxanne Hart, Joey Lawrence, Matthew Lawrence, Charles Tyner, Dennis Redfield.

Cinema families have been terrorized by evil demons, evil animals, evil people, and...evil electricity? That's the premise of this mediocre thriller that doesn't know when to pull the plug. Cliff DeYoung leads his family against some incredibly vicious electrical pulses. These pulses, never fully explained, lend themselves to interesting special effects, but not enough to add power to the dull story. Rated PG-13. 1988; 90m.

PUMA MAN, THE ★
DIR: Alberto De Martino. **CAST:** Donald Pleasence, Sydne Rome.

Humorless Italian junk about a man given extraordinary powers to fight evil. Low-budget and low-brow, with insulting special effects. Thankfully, the movie was never released in the U.S. 1980; 80m.

PUMPKINHEAD ★
DIR: Stan Winston. **CAST:** Lance Henriksen, Jeff East.

A typical revenge picture wherein Lance Henriksen (*Aliens*) convinces a backwoods witch to conjure up a demon to wreak havoc on a group of teenagers involved in the accidental death of his son. When he decides to stop the violence, he finds he is more involved than he thought. Special-effects wizard turned director Stan Winston has little to work with. Rated R for violence. 1989; 87m.

Q ★★★★
DIR: Larry Cohen. **CAST:** Michael Moriarty, David Carradine, Candy Clark, Richard Roundtree, James Dixon.

This is an old-fashioned giant monster film. The stop-motion animation is excellent, the acting (done tongue-in-cheek) is perfect. The story revolves around the arrival of a giant flying lizard in New York City. A series of ritualistic murders follow and point to the monster being Quetzelcoatl (the flying serpent god of the Aztecs). Rated R. 1982; 93m.

QUEST, THE ★½
DIR: Brian Trenchard-Smith. **CAST:** Henry Thomas, Tony Barry, John Ewart.

Henry Thomas plays a young boy living in Australia who has reason to believe that a monster lives in a small lake not far from his home. He sets out to prove the creature's existence—or to expose it as a fraud. Though slow, this film has decent acting. Rated PG. 1985; 94m.

RABID ★★
DIR: David Cronenberg. **CAST:** Marilyn Chambers, Joe Silver, Patricia Gage.

This horror flick has become a cult favorite despite many repulsive scenes. In it, porn queen Marilyn Chambers lives on human blood after a motorcycle accident operation. For fans of director David Cronenberg only. Rated R. 1977; 90m.

RACE WITH THE DEVIL ★★
DIR: Jack Starrett. **CAST:** Warren Oates, Peter Fonda, Loretta Swit, Lara Parker.

Good cast and exciting chase sequences can't save this muddled yarn.

It's about two couples who accidentally intrude on a witches' sacrificial ceremony while on a vacation that literally becomes "hell on Earth" when they're discovered observing the proceedings. Rated PG for violence. 1975; 88m.

RAGGEDY MAN ★★★½
DIR: Jack Fisk. **CAST:** Sissy Spacek, Eric Roberts, William Sanderson, Tracey Walter, Sam Shepard, Henry Thomas.
Sissy Spacek gives another outstanding performance as a World War II divorcée trying to raise two sons and improve their lives in a small Texas Gulf Coast town. *Raggedy Man* is a curious mixture of styles. It begins as a character study and ends like a horror film. But it works. Rated PG for violence. 1981; 94m.

RATS ★½
DIR: Vincent Dawn. **CAST:** Richard Raymond, Alex McBride.
Italian-made gore-a-thon set in the future after The Bomb has destroyed civilization. Survivors who have remained alive in underground shelters emerge, only to find that the world is overrun with rats that have fed on multitudes of human carcasses. Dubbed in English. Unrated, but loaded with violence. 1983; 97m.

RATS ARE COMING!, THE WEREWOLVES ARE HERE!, THE ★
DIR: Andy Milligan. **CAST:** Hope Stansbury, Jackie Skarvellis.
England is besieged by a pack of werewolves in the 1800s. Boring horror film was made on shoestring budget, and it shows. Also featured in this nonsense are the pets of one of the werewolves' daughters—killer rats! Good title, bad movie. Rated R. 1972; 92m.

RAVEN, THE (1935) ★★★★
DIR: Louis Friedlander. **CAST:** Boris Karloff, Bela Lugosi, Irene Ware, Lester Matthews, Samuel S. Hinds.
Solid Universal Pictures horror thriller casts Bela Lugosi as a mad scientist who is obsessed with the writings of Edgar Allan Poe. Boris Karloff is the hapless fugitive Lugosi deforms in order to carry out his evil schemes. Unlike many of the 1930s horror classics, this one has retained its suspense and drama. Available on a double-feature video cassette with *Black Cat*. 1935; B&W; 62m.

RAVEN, THE (1963) ★★★★
DIR: Roger Corman. **CAST:** Boris Karloff, Vincent Price, Peter Lorre, Jack Nicholson, Hazel Court.
The best of the Roger Corman–directed Edgar Allan Poe adaptations, this release benefits from a humorous screenplay by Richard Matheson and tongue-in-cheek portrayals by Boris Karloff, Vincent Price, and Peter Lorre. Look for Jack Nicholson in an early role as Lorre's son. 1963; 86m.

RAWHEAD REX ★★½
DIR: George Pavlou. **CAST:** David Dukes, Kelly Piper, Niall Toibin.
A satanic demon is accidentally unearthed and begins to wreak havoc on a small village in Ireland. The acting and script are both low caliber, but ye ol' Rawhead and his nasty eating habits are worth watching if you like raunch. Rated R for profanity, nudity, and plenty-o-gore. 1986; 89m.

RAZORBACK ★★★½
DIR: Russell Mulcahy. **CAST:** Gregory Harrison.
This Australian film, concerning a giant pig that is terrorizing a small Aussie village, surprises the viewer by turning into a great little film. The special effects, photography, editing, and acting are great. Rated R. 1983; 95m.

RE-ANIMATOR ★★★★
DIR: Stuart Gordon. **CAST:** Bruce Abbott, Barbara Crampton, David Gale, Robert Sampson, Jeffrey Combs.
Stylishly grotesque and gory filming of H. P. Lovecraft's "Herbert West, Reanimator" hits the mark. This is Grand Guignol in the classic sense as we follow brilliant young medical student Herbert West in his deranged ef-

forts to bring the dead back to life. Some outrageous scenes highlight this terror entry and, although very well done, it's not for the squeamish. 1985; 86m.

REAR WINDOW ★★★★★
DIR: Alfred Hitchcock. **CAST:** James Stewart, Raymond Burr, Grace Kelly, Wendell Corey, Thelma Ritter, Judith Evelyn.

James Stewart plays a magazine photographer who, confined to a wheelchair because of a broken leg, seeks diversion in watching his neighbors, often with a telephoto lens. He soon becomes convinced that one neighbor (Raymond Burr) has murdered his spouse and dismembered the body. One of the director's best. 1954; 112m.

RED HEAT (1985) ★★
DIR: Robert Collector. **CAST:** Linda Blair, Sylvia Kristel, William Ostrander, Sue Kiel.

Linda Blair goes to Germany to see her fiancé, who is stationed at a military base. She is mistakenly arrested as a spy and sentenced to prison. Lurid and excessively violent. 1985; 104m.

RED HOUSE, THE ★★★½
DIR: Delmer Daves. **CAST:** Edward G. Robinson, Lon McCallister, Allene Roberts, Julie London, Judith Anderson, Rory Calhoun, Ona Munson.

A gripping suspense melodrama enhanced by a musical score by Miklos Rozsa. Edward G. Robinson employs Rory Calhoun to keep the curious away from a decaying old house deep in the woods. But his niece and a young hired hand *must* learn the secret. 1947; B&W; 100m.

REFLECTIONS OF MURDER ★★★
DIR: John Badham. **CAST:** Tuesday Weld, Joan Hackett, Sam Waterston.

A wife and a mistress set out to kill their abusive mate. They set up a foolproof trap to lure him to his death. The "accident" that kills him leads to more terror and horror than either woman expected. A TV-movie version of the French classic *Diabolique*. 1987; 98m.

REINCARNATE, THE
DIR: Don Haldane. **CAST:** Jack Creley, Jay Reynolds.

A lawyer belongs to an ancient cult that guarantees that he will live forever, as long as he can find a new body to inhabit when his present one dies. The bulk of this Canadian film is about his attempts to persuade a young artist to volunteer. If you find this video version boring, imagine sitting through the original, which was over half an hour longer! Rated PG. 1971; 89m.

REINCARNATION OF PETER PROUD, THE ★
DIR: J. Lee Thompson. **CAST:** Michael Sarrazin, Jennifer O'Neill, Margot Kidder, Cornelia Sharpe.

Laughably melodramatic tale of bewildered Michael Sarrazin, who—through dream research—recalls having been murdered in a previous life. Much to the dismay of girlfriend Cornelia Sharpe (bad, as always), he returns to the scene of the crime. Turgid direction, contrived plot, adapted by Max Erlich from his not-much-better book. Rated R for considerable nudity. 1975; 104m.

REJUVENATOR, THE ★★★
DIR: Brian Thomas Jones. **CAST:** Vivian Lanko, John MacKay.

This flick begins by resembling *Re-Animator* in more than just name, but it soon takes on a life of its own. A rich woman funds a doctor's research into reversing the aging process in hopes he will discover a way to make her young again. Some very nasty side effects occur. Above-average special effects make this a must for horror film fans. Rated R for extreme violence. 1988; 90m.

REMOTE CONTROL ★★½
DIR: Jeff Lieberman. **CAST:** Kevin Dillon, Jennifer Tilly, Deborah Goodrich.

The manager of a video rental outlet learns that many of his customers are being brutally murdered after watching a certain cassette. He and his friends go on a crusade to find out who's responsible. Rated R for violence and profanity. 1987; 88m.

REPULSION ★★★★½
DIR: Roman Polanski. **CAST:** Catherine Deneuve, Ian Hendry, Yvonne Furneaux, John Fraser, Patrick Wymark.
This brilliant British production, the first English-language film directed by Roman Polanski, is a classic chiller. Catherine Deneuve plays a sexually repressed, mentally ill young girl who is terrified of men. Left alone at her sister's home for a weekend, she suffers a series of severe hallucinations that finally lead her to commit murder. 1965; B&W; 105m.

REST IN PIECES ★
DIR: Joseph Braunsteen. **CAST:** Scott Thompson, Lorin Jean, Dorothy Malone, Patty Shepard.
An unimpressive ghost story about a young couple who inherit an old Spanish estate occupied by a bizarre cult of murderous satanists. It seems they want to resurrect their leader in a living body. Gory mayhem makes up the bulk of this cheap slasher flick. Not rated, but contains graphic violence and nudity. 1987; 90m.

RETRIBUTION ★★
DIR: Guy Magar. **CAST:** Dennis Lipscomb, Leslie Wing, Hoyt Axton.
In this supernatural thriller, a mild-mannered, down-and-out artist attempts suicide at the same moment a small-time hood is tortured to death. The artist becomes possessed by the soul of the hood and then proceeds to avenge his murder. Low-budget shocker with an inadequate script. Rated R for violence and profanity. 1988; 109m.

RETURN OF THE ALIEN'S DEADLY SPAWN, THE ★★
DIR: Douglas McKeown. **CAST:** Charles George Hildebrandt.
Blood-filled horror film about alien creatures from outer space who kill and destroy anyone and everything that gets in their way. Lots of gore, ripped flesh, and off-the-wall humor. For people who like sick movies. Rated R for profanity and gore. 1984; 90m.

RETURN OF THE FLY, THE ★★★
DIR: Edward L. Bernds. **CAST:** Vincent Price, Brett Halsey, David Frankham.
In this fine sequel to *The Fly*, the son of the original insect makes the same mistake as his father...with identical results. Effective film benefits from stark black-and-white photography and solid effects. Watch out for the guinea pig scene! 1959; B&W; 80m.

RETURN OF THE LIVING DEAD, THE ★★★★
DIR: Dan O'Bannon. **CAST:** Clu Gulager, James Karen, Don Calfa, Thom Mathews.
Extremely gory horror film produced with a great deal of style and ample amounts of comedy as well. The residents of a small New Orleans cemetery are brought back to life after accidental exposure to a strange chemical, and they're hungry...for human brains. Rated R for violence, nudity, and language. 1985; 91m.

RETURN OF THE LIVING DEAD PART II ★★
DIR: Ken Wiederhorn. **CAST:** James Karen, Thom Mathews, Dan Ashbrook.
The dead have once again risen from their long slumber and are hungry for human brains. A drum of special gas that seems to reanimate the dead has been discovered by a trio of children. They unwittingly loose the gas on the unsuspecting town. Definitely an R rating for the violence and language. 1988; 90m.

RETURN OF THE SWAMP THING ★★★
DIR: Jim Wynorski. **CAST:** Louis Jourdan, Heather Locklear, Dick Durock.

The big, green monster-hero comes out of the swamp to do battle once again with evil scientist Louis Jourdan, while Heather Locklear is the object of his affections. Unlike the first film, which was also based on the DC Comics character created by Berni Wrightson, you're not supposed to take this sequel seriously. Rated PG. 1989; 87m.

RETURN OF THE VAMPIRE, THE ★★★
DIR: Lew Landers, Kurt Neumann. **CAST:** Bela Lugosi, Frieda Inescort, Nina Foch, Miles Mander, Matt Willis.

Set during World War II, this surprisingly good vampire tale has the supposedly destroyed fiend, Armand Tesla (Bela Lugosi), unearthed by a German bombing raid on London. He resumes his reign of terror after twenty-three years of undead sleep. 1943; B&W; 69m.

RETURN TO BOGGY CREEK
DIR: Tom Moore. **CAST:** Dawn Wells.

A cheap and boring sequel about a mysterious creature that stalks the swamps of a small fishing community. There's nothing scary about this so-called horror film. Rated PG. 1978; 87m.

RETURN TO HORROR HIGH
DIR: Bill Froechlich. **CAST:** Vince Edwards, Alex Rocco, Brendan Hughes, Scott Jacoby, Lori Lethin, Philip McKeon.

A group of filmmakers go back to a high school where a series of murders took place. The confusing screenplay proves frustrating. Rated R for sex, nudity, profanity, and violence. 1987; 95m.

RETURN TO SALEM'S LOT, A
DIR: Larry Cohen. **CAST:** Michael Moriarty, Samuel Fuller, Andrew Duggan, Evelyn Keyes.

Don't let the title fool you. Stephen King had nothing to do with this mess. Writer-director Larry Cohen ignores King's horror classic and creates a story that has nothing to do with the original *Salem's Lot*. The story involves a divorced father, recently reunited with his teenage son, who goes back to the town of his birth to find that its inhabitants are vampires. Rated R for nudity and violence. 1987; 101m.

REVENGE ★★
DIR: Jud Taylor. **CAST:** Shelley Winters, Stuart Whitman, Bradford Dillman, Roger Perry.

Made for television, this has Shelley Winters out for—you guessed it—revenge for her daughter's rape. Not as bad as it could have been. 1971; 78m.

REVENGE ★★
DIR: Sidney Hayers. **CAST:** Joan Collins, James Booth, Sinead Cusack.

When a little girl is abducted and murdered, her family kidnaps the man they believe responsible, torturing and finally killing him. Interesting suspense film, but it lacks the intensity it should have. Not rated. 1971; 85m.

REVENGE OF THE DEAD
DIR: Pupi Avati. **CAST:** Gabriele Lavia, Anne Canovas.

Talky Italian film with misleading title. It's not part of George Romero's series, or even a bad imitation. It's an incredibly dull movie. Impossible to tell what it's about or why it was made. Rated R for violence and profanity. 1984; 98m.

REVENGE OF THE STEPFORD WIVES
DIR: Robert Fuest. **CAST:** Arthur Hill, Don Johnson, Sharon Gless, Mason Adams, Audra Lindley.

A TV sequel to the suspense classic. A new family moves to Stepford and finds the same problem with the women in the town. Pass up this cheap and unscary follow-up and see the original. Not rated, but may not be suitable for children. 1980; 95m.

REVENGE OF THE ZOMBIES ★★½
DIR: Steve Sekely. **CAST:** John Carradine, Robert Lowery, Gale Storm,

Veda Ann Borg, Mantan Moreland, Bob Steele.

As soon as the Hollywood back-lot native walks across the foggy bog in baggy underwear and begins to wail "Whoooooo," you know this is going to be one of those films. And it sure is, with mad scientist John Carradine, his zombie wife Veda Ann Borg (in her best role), do-gooders Gale Storm and Robert Lowery, and "feets do yo' stuff" Mantan Moreland aiding escaping zombies and Nazis in this low-budget howler. 1943; B&W; 61m.

REVOLT OF THE ZOMBIES ★½

DIR: Victor Halperin. **CAST:** Dean Jagger, Roy D'Arcy, Dorothy Stone, George Cleveland.

Following the unexpected success of their independently produced *White Zombie* in 1932, brothers Edward and Victor Halperin found themselves making another zombie movie in 1936. Lacking the style and imagination of their earlier effort, this quasi-supernatural story involves the use of a stupor-inducing potion that turns Cambodian troops into dull-eyed slaves. For curiosity seekers only. 1936; B&W; 65m.

RIPPER, THE

DIR: Christopher Lewis. **CAST:** Tom Schreier, Wade Tower.

In this poorly filmed modernization of the Jack the Ripper legend, a college professor finds a ring, originally belonging to the nineteenth-century killer, which when worn turns him into—yes, you guessed it! Amateurish throughout, this film has nothing to recommend it, even to die-hard fans of the genre. 1985; 104m.

RITUALS ★

DIR: Peter Carter. **CAST:** Hal Holbrook, Lawrence Dane, Robin Gammell.

Several middle-aged men head up to the wilds on a camping trip, only to be stalked by a relentless killer. This cheap ripoff of *Deliverance* offers little in the way of entertainment. Rated R for violence and profanity. 1981; 100m.

ROAD GAMES ★★

DIR: Richard Franklin. **CAST:** Stacy Keach, Jamie Lee Curtis, Marion Howard, Grant Page.

An elusive latter-day Jack the Ripper is loose in Australia. He cruises desolate areas in a mysterious, customized van, picking up female hitchhikers and then raping, killing, and dismembering them. Even though director Richard Franklin (*Psycho II*) actually studied under Alfred Hitchcock at USC's renowned film school, he doesn't show any of his mentor's ability here. Rated PG. 1981; 100m.

ROBOT MONSTER

DIR: Phil Tucker. **CAST:** George Nader, Gregory Moffett, Claudia Barrett.

Take a desolate-looking canyon outside of Los Angeles, borrow Lawrence Welk's bubble machine, and add a typical family on an outing and a man dressed in a gorilla suit wearing a diving helmet, and you have a serious competitor for the worst movie of all time. This absurd drama of the last days of Earth and its conquest by robot gorillas has long been considered the most inept of all science-fiction films. A must-see for all fans of truly terrible films. 1953; B&W; 63m.

ROCK 'N' ROLL NIGHTMARE ★

DIR: John Fasano. **CAST:** Jon-Miki Thor, Paula Francescatto, Rusty Hamilton.

Members of a heavy metal band are killed by a mysterious presence while rehearsing a new album at a farmhouse. This Canadian horror movie is pretty dull most of the way through, but it does have a heckuva surprise ending that almost makes it worth sitting through. Well...almost. Unrated, the film contains violence and nudity. 1987; 89m.

ROCKTOBER BLOOD ★★

DIR: Ferd Sebastian, Beverly Sebastian. **CAST:** Tray Loren.

The ghost of a rock star, executed for murder, returns from the dead to avenge himself upon his former band members who helped to convict him. The film starts off well and ends decently, but the middle wanders aimlessly. Non-horror fans will probably find this tedious. Rated R for violence, nudity, and profanity. 1984; 88m.

ROLLERCOASTER ★★★★½
DIR: James Goldstone. **CAST:** George Segal, Richard Widmark, Timothy Bottoms, Susan Strasberg, Henry Fonda.

Fast-paced suspense film about an extortionist (Timothy Bottoms) blowing up rides in some of the nation's most famous amusement parks, and the efforts of a county safety inspector (George Segal) and an FBI agent (Richard Widmark) to nab him. Very well done, this much-maligned film has great action, crisp dialogue, and a brilliant, nail-biting climax. Rated PG for language and violence. 1977; 119m.

ROPE ★★★★½
DIR: Alfred Hitchcock. **CAST:** James Stewart, John Dall, Farley Granger, Cedric Hardwicke.

This recently resurrected Alfred Hitchcock film is based in part on the famous Leopold-Loeb thrill-murder case in Chicago in the 1920s. In it, the two killers divulge clues to their horrific escapade at a dinner party, to the growing suspicion of the other guests. It's one of Hitchcock's best. 1948; 80m.

ROSEMARY'S BABY ★★★★
DIR: Roman Polanski. **CAST:** Mia Farrow, John Cassavetes, Ruth Gordon, Ralph Bellamy, Elisha Cook Jr., Maurice Evans, Patsy Kelly.

Mia Farrow is a young woman forced by her husband (John Cassavetes) into an unholy arrangement with a group of devil-worshipers. The suspense is sustained as she is made aware that those friendly people around her are not what they seem. Ruth Gordon is priceless in her Oscar-winning role as one of the seemingly normal neighbors. Rated R. 1968; 136m.

RUBY ★★
DIR: Curtis Harrington. **CAST:** Piper Laurie, Stuart Whitman, Roger Davis.

A sleazy drive-in is the setting for this unexciting horror film about a young girl possessed by the homicidal ghost of a dead gangster. Rated R for gore. 1977; 84m.

RUDE AWAKENING ★★½
DIR: Peter Sasdy. **CAST:** Denholm Elliott, James Laurenson, Pat Heywood.

In another of Elvira's "Thriller Video" series, and one of the best, a real estate broker finds himself sucked into dreams that seem like reality; or is it the other way around? It sounds standard, but it's better than you would think. 1982; 60m.

RUN STRANGER RUN ★★★½
DIR: Darren McGavin. **CAST:** Patricia Neal, Cloris Leachman, Ron Howard, Bobby Darin.

Ron Howard plays a teenager searching for his biological parents in a seaside town. Once there, he discovers that some of the town inhabitants have been disappearing. Unfortunately, the disappearances are closely linked to his past. Overall, this film keeps viewer interest without dwelling on the slash-'em-up theme. Rated PG for gore. 1973; 92m.

SABOTAGE ★★★
DIR: Alfred Hitchcock. **CAST:** Sylvia Sidney, Oscar Homolka, John Loder.

One of the first of Alfred Hitchcock's characteristic thrillers. London's being terrorized by an unknown bomber, and movie theater cashier Sylvia Sidney begins to fear that her husband (Oscar Homolka) is behind it all. Hitch was still experimenting, and his use of shadows and sound effects betrays the influence of German silent films. 1936; B&W; 76m.

SABOTEUR ★★★★½
DIR: Alfred Hitchcock. **CAST:** Robert Cummings, Priscilla Lane, Norman Lloyd, Otto Kruger.
Outstanding Alfred Hitchcock film about a World War II factory worker (Robert Cummings) turned fugitive after he's unjustly accused of sabotage. The briskly paced story follows his efforts to elude police while he tries to unmask the real culprit. A humdinger of a climax. 1942; B&W; 108m.

SADIST, THE
DIR: James Landis. **CAST:** Arch Hall Jr., Helen Hovey, Marilyn Manning.
A lame chiller about a serial killer and his girlfriend as they terrorize three teachers stranded in the middle of nowhere. There are no thrills here, just melodramatic acting and unimaginative direction. The story is predictable and tired, and the video quality is excessively poor. Not rated, but contains some violence. 1963; B&W; 90m.

SALEM'S LOT ★★★★
DIR: Tobe Hooper. **CAST:** David Soul, James Mason, Reggie Nalder, Lance Kerwin, Elisha Cook Jr., Ed Flanders.
This story of vampires in modern-day New England is one of the better adaptations of Stephen King's novels on film. Some real chills go along with an intelligent script in what was originally a two-part TV movie. 1979; 112m.

SATAN'S CHEERLEADERS
DIR: Greydon Clark. **CAST:** Kerry Sherman, John Ireland, Yvonne De Carlo, John Carradine, Jack Kruschen.
Sure, from a cast like this you wouldn't expect *Hamlet*. But you might hope for an entertainingly campy movie. Instead, this yawner about a busload of cheerleaders who run afoul of a cult of Satanists has no blood, no sex, no laughs—nothing whatsoever. Rated PG. 1977; 92m.

SATAN'S SCHOOL FOR GIRLS ★★½
DIR: David Lowell Rich. **CAST:** Pamela Franklin, Kate Jackson, Roy Thinnes, Cheryl Ladd.
Originally made as an ABC Movie of the Week, this decent shocker concerns a series of apparent suicides at a prominent girls' school, but we all know better. Interesting story has good acting and some creepy atmosphere, but the typical TV ending falls flat. 1973; 74m.

SATURDAY THE 14TH ★
DIR: Howard R. Cohen. **CAST:** Richard Benjamin, Paula Prentiss, Jeffrey Tambor, Rosemary DeCamp.
Richard Benjamin and Paula Prentiss (who are husband and wife in real life) star in this low-budget horror comedy about a family that moves into a haunted house. Thanks to the curiosity of their son, Billy, they find themselves at the mercy of the Book of Evil and its onslaught of terrors. The jokes are tired, the monsters insipid, and the plot weak. Rated PG. 1981; 75m.

SAVAGE ATTRACTION ★★★★
DIR: Frank Shields. **CAST:** Kerry Mack, Ralph Schicha.
A psychotic German becomes sadistically obsessed with a lovely Australian girl in this bizarre but true tale. He uses both mental and physical cruelty to keep her with him. The suspense is never lacking. Rated R for sadism, nudity, and violence. 1983; 93m.

SAVAGE BEES, THE ★★½
DIR: Bruce Geller. **CAST:** Ben Johnson, Michael Parks, Horst Buchholz.
Above-average thriller about a plague of African killer bees wreaking havoc on New Orleans during Mardi Gras. Oscar-winner Ben Johnson gives dramatic punch to this made-for-TV chiller. Some good thrills. 1976; 99m.

SAVAGE INTRUDER, THE ★
DIR: Donald Wolfe. **CAST:** Miriam Hopkins, John David Garfield, Gale Sondergaard.

Nothing fancy about this lurid splatterfest. An aging film star (Miriam Hopkins)—a loon herself— hires a male nurse (John David Garfield) who turns out to be a psycho. Hopkins overacts terribly. 1977; 90m.

SAVAGE WEEKEND ★
DIR: John Mason Kirby. **CAST:** Christopher Allport, James Doerr, Marilyn Hamlin, William Sanderson.
Several couples head out from the big city into the backwoods to watch a boat being built, but they are killed off one by one. The only reason this movie earns any stars is for talented actor William Sanderson's performance as a demented lunatic who may or may not be the killer. Rated R for nudity, simulated sex, violence. 1979; 88m.

SAVAGES (1974) ★★★
DIR: Lee H. Katzin. **CAST:** Andy Griffith, Sam Bottoms, Noah Beery Jr., James Best.
Man hunts man! Sam Bottoms is guiding Andy Griffith on a hunt in the desert when Griffith goes bananas and begins a savage, relentless pursuit of Bottoms. A sandy rendition of the famous short story, "The Most Dangerous Game." Thrilling, suspenseful, intriguing to watch. Made for TV. 1974; 78m.

SCALPEL ★
DIR: John Grissmer. **CAST:** Robert Lansing, Judith Chapman, Arlen Dean Snyder, Sandy Martin.
Robert Lansing is a cunning, unscrupulous plastic surgeon who transforms a young accident victim into the spitting image of his missing daughter to pull an inheritance swindle. A rather dull melodrama sinks to deplorable depths when it uses graphic, repulsive scenes of surgery. Rated R. 1976; 96m.

SCANNERS ★★★½
DIR: David Cronenberg. **CAST:** Jennifer O'Neill, Patrick McGoohan, Stephen Lack, Lawrence Dane.
From its first shocking scene—in which a character's head explodes, spewing blood, flesh, and bone all over—*Scanners* poses a challenge to its viewers: How much can you take? Shock specialist David Cronenberg wrote and directed this potent film, about a bloody war among a group of people with formidable extrasensory powers. Rated R. 1981; 102m.

SCARECROWS ★★★★
DIR: William Wesley. **CAST:** Ted Vernon, Michael Simms, Richard Vidan.
This is something rare—a truly frightening horror film, loaded with suspense, intelligent writing, and decent acting. The story involves a group of military deserters who have ripped off a federal money exchange and are flying south in a stolen cargo plane. They land in a secluded wilderness of cornfields filled with…scarecrows. Not recommended for the squeamish, but horror fans will find this to be a feast. Not rated, but contains graphic violence. 1988; 88m.

SCARED STIFF ★
DIR: Richard Friedman. **CAST:** Andrew Stevens, Mary Page Keller.
A newly married couple move into an old house cursed by a voodoo priest. Soon the newlyweds become possessed and are forced to relive a bloody historical incident. This retread story has decent acting but poor writing and skimpy special effects. Rated R for violence. 1986; 85m.

SCARED TO DEATH ★★
DIR: Christy Cabanne. **CAST:** Bela Lugosi, Douglas Fowley, Joyce Compton, George Zucco, Nat Pendleton.
This tepid thriller is noteworthy primarily because it is Bela Lugosi's only color film, not for the lukewarm story about a woman who dies without a traceable cause. Plenty of hocus-pocus, red herrings, and hypnosis in this also-ran horror film directed by Christy Cabanne, a silent film pioneer. 1946; 65m.

SCARS OF DRACULA ★★★
DIR: Roy Ward Baker. **CAST:** Christopher Lee, Dennis Waterman, Christopher Matthews.

A young couple searching for the husband's brother follow the trail to Dracula's castle, and soon regret it. Compares well with other films in the series, thanks primarily to Christopher Lee's dynamite portrayal of the Count, and the first-rate direction of horror veteran Roy Ward Baker. Rated R. 1970; 94m.

SCHIZO
DIR: Pete Walker. **CAST:** Jack Watson, Lynne Frederick, John Leyton.

A deranged night worker freaks out when his favorite figure skater announces her wedding plans. An obvious plot twist is used in an attempt to salvage the ridiculous premise, but this fails miserably. Rated R. 1978; 109m.

SCHIZOID ★½
DIR: David Paulsen. **CAST:** Klaus Kinski, Marianna Hill, Craig Wasson, Christopher Lloyd.

This is an unimaginative slasher flick with typically gory special effects. Not for the squeamish. Rated R. 1980; 91m.

SCREAM
DIR: Byron Quisenberry. **CAST:** Woody Strode, John Ethan Wayne, Hank Worden, Alvy Moore, Gregg Palmer.

A group of vacationing friends spend the night in a ghost town. Bad move. One by one, the buddies are murdered by a maniac lurking in the shadows. Amateurish plot, no suspense, no intrigue, no blood, no good. Rated R. 1982; 86m.

SCREAM AND SCREAM AGAIN ★★★½
DIR: Gordon Hessler. **CAST:** Vincent Price, Peter Cushing, Christopher Lee, Christopher Matthews, Michael Gothard.

A top-notch cast excels in this chilling, suspenseful story of a crazed scientist (Vincent Price) attempting to create a race of superbeings while a baffled police force copes with a series of brutal murders that may or may not be related. Complex film benefits from polished performances. Based on the novel *The Disoriented Man*, by Peter Saxon. Rated PG for violence, language, brief nudity. 1970; 95m.

SCREAM, BLACULA, SCREAM ★
DIR: Bob Kelljan. **CAST:** William Marshall, Pam Grier, Michael Conrad.

William Marshall returns as the black vampire, Blacula, in this unimpressive sequel to the 1972 original. Blacula is resurrected by a voodoo priest and uses his rebirth to pursue a beautiful woman (Pam Grier). Bob Kelljan also directed *Count Yorga, Vampire*, but is unable to do much with this low-budget mess. Rated R. 1973; 96m.

SCREAM FOR HELP
DIR: Michael Winner. **CAST:** Rachel Kelly, David Brooks.

A frustratingly simple and poorly acted suspense thriller about a teenage girl whose stepfather is trying to kill her and her mother. Of course, no one believes her, even when the evidence is abundantly clear. Rated R for nudity, profanity, and violence. 1986; 95m.

SCREAM GREATS, VOL. 1 ★★★
DIR: Damon Santostefano.

The first in a projected series by *Starlog Magazine*. A documentary on horror effects master Tom Savini. Gory highlights are featured from many of his movies, including *Friday the 13th*, *Creepshow*, and *Dawn of the Dead*. Savini shows his secrets, explains his techniques. Unrated, contains massive but clinical gore. 1986; 60m.

SCREAMERS
DIR: Sergio Martino, Dan T. Miller. **CAST:** Claudio Cassinelli, Richard Johnson, Joseph Cotten.

Just what we needed, another low-budget horror film. Claudio Cassinelli finds himself stranded on an uncharted island and at the mercy of a mad doctor (Richard Johnson), a crazy inventor (Joseph Cotten), and a bunch of underpaid extras in native costumes. Rated R. 1979; 90m.

SEANCE ON A WET AFTERNOON ★★★★½
DIR: Bryan Forbes. **CAST:** Kim Stanley, Richard Attenborough, Patrick Magee, Nanette Newman.

This is an absolutely fabulous movie. An unbalanced medium (Kim Stanley) involves her meek husband (Richard Attenborough) in a kidnapping scheme that brings about their downfall. Brilliant acting by all, working from a superb script. No rating, but some intense sequences. 1964; B&W; 115m.

SEASON OF THE WITCH ★
DIR: George A. Romero. **CAST:** Jan White, Ray Lane.

A slow-moving tale of an aging woman who is unable to cope with the disappointments of her daily routine. She seeks an answer to her boredom and disillusionment in witchcraft with disastrous results. Slim on plot as well as on dialogue. Also known as *Hungry Wives*. Rated R. 1972; 90m.

SEDUCTION, THE ★
DIR: David Schmoeller. **CAST:** Morgan Fairchild, Andrew Stevens, Vince Edwards, Michael Sarrazin.

This is a silly suspense film about a lady newscaster (Morgan Fairchild) stalked by an unbalanced admirer (Andrew Stevens) patched together from *The Fan* and all those Brian De Palma movies combining implausible menace with soapy eroticism. Rated R for nudity and violence. 1982; 104m.

SEE NO EVIL ★★★½
DIR: Richard Fleischer. **CAST:** Mia Farrow, Dorothy Alison, Robin Bailey.

Chilling yarn follows a young blind woman (Mia Farrow) as she tries to escape the clutches of a ruthless killer who has done away with her entire family at their quiet country farm. Mia Farrow is very convincing as the maniac's next target. Rated PG for tense moments. 1971; 90m.

SEIZURE ★★★½
DIR: Oliver Stone. **CAST:** Jonathan Frid, Martin Beswicke, Herve Villechaize, Troy Donahue.

In Oliver Stone's directorial debut, an author of horror stories has a recurring dream about the murder of his houseguests by a trio of diabolical characters. Dream and reality intersect. Definitely a respectable chiller. Rated PG. 1974; 93m.

SENDER, THE ★★★
DIR: Roger Christian. **CAST:** Kathryn Harrold, Zeljko Ivanek, Shirley Knight, Paul Freeman.

Those who like their horror movies with a little subtlety should have a look at this low-key but effective yarn. A young man brought to a hospital after he attempts suicide is discovered to have telepathic powers. Because of his emotional disturbances, he is unable to control himself and unleashes his nightmares into the minds of doctors and patients. Rated R for violence. 1982; 91m.

SENTINEL, THE ★
DIR: Michael Winner. **CAST:** Chris Sarandon, Cristina Raines, Martin Balsam, John Carradine, José Ferrer, Ava Gardner, Arthur Kennedy, Burgess Meredith, Sylvia Miles, Deborah Raffin, Eli Wallach.

This is a dismal genre piece about a woman (Cristina Raines) who unknowingly moves into an apartment building over the gates of hell. *The Sentinel* doesn't have much suspense, nor does it deliver many shocks. Instead, it has a sort of nauseating relentlessness. Rated R for nudity, profanity, and violence. 1977; 93m.

SERPENT AND THE RAINBOW, THE ★★★½
DIR: Wes Craven. **CAST:** Bill Pullman, Cathy Tyson, Zakes Mokae, Paul Winfield.

Loosely based on the nonfiction book of the same name, this is about a sociologist who goes to Haiti to bring back a potion that reportedly resurrects the dead. What he discovers is oppression, corrupt politicians, an abusive police state, and the horror of voodoo. Rated R for violence, language, and nudity. 1988; 98m.

SEVEN BROTHERS MEET DRACULA, THE ★★½
DIR: Roy Ward Baker. **CAST:** Peter Cushing, David Chaing, Julie Ege.

Hammer Films' last Dracula movie was a coproduction with the Shaw Brothers of Hong Kong, known mainly for their kung-fu films. A martial arts-horror-fantasy about Professor Van Helsing fighting a vampire cult in China. An interesting attempt to revive the series, but unless you are a kung-fu fan, this entry will seem all too silly. Rated R, this feature was originally titled *Legend of the Seven Golden Vampires*. 1973; 88m.

SEVENTH SIGN, THE ★★★½
DIR: Carl Schultz. **CAST:** Demi Moore, Michael Biehn, Jurgen Prochnow, John Heard.

Finely crafted suspense film with Demi Moore portraying a woman whose unborn baby is threatened by the Biblical curse of the Apocalypse. Moore is superb and Jurgen Prochnow is perfect as the avenging angel. Rated R for language and shock effects. 1988; 94m.

SEVENTH VICTIM, THE ★★★
DIR: Mark Robson. **CAST:** Tom Conway, Kim Hunter, Jean Brooks, Evelyn Brent, Hugh Beaumont, Isabel Jewell, Barbara Hale.

Innocent Kim Hunter stumbles onto a New York City coven of devil-worshippers in this eerie thriller-chiller ancestor of *Rosemary's Baby* and kindred horror stories of the bizarre and occult. Leave the lights on. 1943; B&W; 71m.

SEVERED ARM, THE ★★½
CAST: Paul Carr, Deborah Walley, Marvin Kaplan.

Before being rescued from a cave-in, a group of trapped mine explorers cut off the arm of one of the men as food for the others. Many years later, the survivors of the expedition are systematically slaughtered by an unseen psychopath. This low-budget independent production is fairly suspenseful, though the acting is often listless and the gore a bit excessive. Rated R. 1973; 86m.

SEXTON BLAKE AND THE HOODED TERROR ★★½
DIR: George King. **CAST:** George Curzon, Tod Slaughter, Greta Gynt.

One of a series of British mysteries featuring Sexton Blake, a detective in the Sherlock Holmes tradition. He's on the trail of an international gang known as the Hooded Terror, led by a millionaire (Tod Slaughter). Slaughter, Britain's king of Grand Guignol, is the best reason to see this, even though he's relatively restrained in a supporting role. 1938; B&W; 69m.

SHADOW OF A DOUBT ★★★★½
DIR: Alfred Hitchcock. **CAST:** Joseph Cotten, Teresa Wright, Macdonald Carey, Henry Travers, Hume Cronyn.

This disturbing suburban drama, regarded by Alfred Hitchcock as the personal favorite among his films, probes the hidden facets of a family with a secret. Teenager Charlie (Teresa Wright) adores the uncle (Joseph Cotten) after whom she was named and is delighted when he comes to stay for an indefinite period. Her love grows tainted, however, as she begins to suspect that "dear Uncle Charlie" may be the killer wanted by the police for having sent several widows to their premature reward. Unrated; a bit intense for younger viewers. 1943; B&W; 108m.

SHADOW PLAY ★
DIR: Susan Shadburne. **CAST:** Dee Wallace, Cloris Leachman, Ron Kuhlman, Barry Laws.

Described as a romantic mystery by its makers, this pitiful excuse for a movie presents Dee Wallace Stone as a Manhattan playwright who is obsessed by the tragic death of her fiancé seven years earlier. Indeed, she becomes possessed by his ghost, which inspires her to write awful poetry. Rated R for profanity and violence. 1986; 101m.

SHE BEAST, THE ★
DIR: Michael Reeves. **CAST:** Barbara Steele, Ian Ogilvy.

Laughable Italian chiller featuring the exquisite Barbara Steele as a witch who comes back from the grave to avenge her death. Ridiculous, tacky filmmaking. 1966; 74m.

SHE DEMONS 🦃
DIR: Richard Cunha. **CAST:** Irish McCalla, Tod Griffin, Victor Sen Yung, Gene Roth.

This low-rent chiller is like an issue of a 1930s shudder pulp combined with a 1950s men's adventure magazine. A crazed Nazi scientist holds an uncharted island in a grip of terror as he conducts unnatural experiments that transform shapely Hollywood extras into shapely extras with ugly masks. Voluptuous monstrosities, obsessed madmen, erupting volcanoes—this film has it all. 1958; B&W; 80m.

SHE FREAK, THE ★½
DIR: Byron Mabe. **CAST:** Claire Brennan, Lee Raymond.

An uncredited remake of the classic *Freaks*, with waitress Claire Brennan marrying a carnival owner for his money while maintaining a lover. Her fatal mistake, however, is in mistreating the members of the carnival's freak show. Compared to the original, this is merely exploitative, and not very good at that. 1966; B&W; 87m.

SHE WAITS ★★
DIR: Delbert Mann. **CAST:** Patty Duke, David McCallum, Lew Ayres, Beulah Bondi, Dorothy McGuire.

Producer-director Delbert Mann tries hard but cannot breathe any real thrills into this pedestrian tale of a young wife (Patty Duke) who becomes possessed by the spirit of her husband's first wife. Made-for-TV mediocrity. 1971; 74m.

SHINING, THE ★★½
DIR: Stanley Kubrick. **CAST:** Jack Nicholson, Shelley Duvall, Scatman Crothers.

A struggling writer (Jack Nicholson) accepts a position as the caretaker of a large summer resort hotel during the winter season. The longer he and his family spend in the hotel, the more Nicholson becomes possessed by it. Considering the talent involved, this is a major disappointment. Director Stanley Kubrick keeps things at a snail's pace, and Nicholson's performance approaches high camp. Rated R for violence and language. 1980; 146m.

SHOCK ★★★
DIR: Alfred Werker. **CAST:** Vincent Price, Lynn Bari, Reed Hadley, Pierre Watkin, Frank Latimore.

Highly effective thriller features Vincent Price in an early performance as a murderer—in this case he's a psychiatrist who murders his wife and is then forced to silence a witness through drugs and hypnosis. This minor classic provided the framework for many subsequent suspense movies. 1946; B&W; 70m.

SHOCK! SHOCK! SHOCK! 🦃
DIR: Todd Rutt. **CAST:** Brad Isaac.

A sorry spoof of slasher flicks about an escaped mental patient who gets involved in a jewel theft—only the thieves are aliens with strange and stupid powers. Only for fans of truly bad films. Not rated but contains profanity and violence. 1988; B&W; 60m.

SHOCK WAVES (DEATH CORPS) ★½
DIR: Ken Wiederhorn. **CAST:** Peter Cushing, Brooke Adams, John Carradine.

Vacationers stumble upon a crazed ex-Nazi controlling an army of underwater zombies. It's just as stupid as it sounds. The sopping-wet zombies wear full dress uniforms, perky little swimming goggles, and a stunning complement of seaweed accessories. They're a riot. Rated PG. 1977; 86m.

SHOUT, THE ★★★
DIR: Jerzy Skolimowski. **CAST:** Alan Bates, Susannah York, John Hurt, Robert Stephens, Tim Curry.

Enigmatic British chiller about a wanderer's chilling effect on an unsuspecting couple. He possesses the ancient power to kill people by screaming. Well made, with an excellent cast. The film may be too offbeat for some viewers. Rated R. 1979; 87m.

SHRIEK OF THE MUTILATED
DIR: Michael Findlay. **CAST:** Alan Brock, Jennifer Stock.

College students looking for the Yeti on an obscure island (funny, we thought they inhabited the Himalayas!) find cannibals instead. The lurid title is the best part of this otherwise inept shocker. Rated R. 1974; 92m.

SIDE SHOW ★★½
DIR: William Conrad. **CAST:** Lance Kerwin, Anthony Franciosa, Red Buttons, Connie Stevens.

A young boy runs away to join the circus and discovers alcoholism, sex, and racial prejudice. When he witnesses a murder, he has to stay one step ahead of the killer. Not rated, but may not be suited for younger audiences. 1986; 98m.

SILENT NIGHT, BLOODY NIGHT ★★★
DIR: Theodore Gershuny. **CAST:** Patrick O'Neal, John Carradine, Mary Woronov.

Give this one an extra star for originality, even if it's not that well produced. Lawyer Patrick O'Neal and girlfriend Mary Woronov spend a few nights in an old house that he is trying to sell. But the place used to be an insane asylum, and it has quite an interesting history. Rated R, it may be a bit too strong for kids. 1973; 88m.

SILENT NIGHT, DEADLY NIGHT ★
DIR: Charles E. Sellier Jr. **CAST:** Lilyan Chauvin, Gilmer McCormick, Robert Brian Wilson, Toni Nero.

This is the one that caused such a commotion among parents' groups for its depiction of Santa Claus as a homicidal killer. A kid sees his parents slaughtered by a hitchhiker in a Santa Claus suit and is, understandably, haunted by the memory for years. No rating, but contains gobs of nudity and violent bloodshed. 1984; 92m.

SILENT NIGHT, DEADLY NIGHT PART 2
DIR: Lee Harry. **CAST:** Eric Freeman, James L. Newman, Elizabeth Cayton.

The first half of this sequel is composed almost entirely of flashback scenes lifted whole from the earlier movie. The second half, in which the brother of the original slashing Santa Claus carries on in his sibling's footsteps, is treated pretty much as a joke, with Eric Freeman overacting outrageously. Rated R for nudity and gore. 1987; 88m.

SILENT PARTNER, THE ★★★★½
DIR: Daryl Duke. **CAST:** Elliott Gould, Christopher Plummer, Susannah York, John Candy.

This suspense thriller is what they call a sleeper. It's an absolutely riveting tale about a bank teller (Elliott Gould) who, knowing of a robbery in advance, pulls a switch on a psychotic criminal (Christopher Plummer) and might not live to regret it. *Silent Partner* is a real find for movie buffs. But be forewarned; it has a couple of truly unsettling scenes of violence. Rated R. 1978; 103m.

SILENT SCREAM ★★½
DIR: Denny Harris. **CAST:** Yvonne De Carlo, Barbara Steele, Avery Schreiber, Rebecca Balding.

This is a well-done shock film with a semi-coherent plot and enough thrills to satisfy the teens. Rated R. 1980; 87m.

SILVER BULLET ★★★★
DIR: Daniel Attias. **CAST:** Gary Busey, Everett McGill, Corey Haim, Megan Follows, James Gammon, Robin Groves.

A superior Stephen King horror film, this release moves like the projectile after which it was named. From the opening scene, in which a railroad worker meets his gruesome demise at the claws of a werewolf, to the final confrontation between our heroes (Gary Busey and Corey Haim) and the hairy beast, it's an edge-of-your-seat winner. Rated R for violence and gore. 1985; 90m.

SIMON, KING OF THE WITCHES ★½
DIR: Bruce Kessler. **CAST:** Andrew Prine, Brenda Scott.

Modern-day warlock lives in a Los Angeles sewer, casting spells and grasping for power. Underrated actor Andrew Prine does his best, but the movie is hopelessly dated and about as scary as a dead Smurf. Originally cobilled with *Werewolves on Wheels*. Rated R. 1971; 90m.

SINISTER INVASION
DIR: Juan Ibanez, Jack Hill. **CAST:** Boris Karloff.

Boris Karloff filmed scenes for this Mexican horror film just before his death, but they were inserted into movies that were substantially different from the scripts he had approved. It's embarrassing to see him struggling through this garbage about a depraved maniac possessed by aliens from outer space. Also available in a truncated version, *Alien Terror*. 1968; 88m.

SINS OF DORIAN GRAY, THE ★½
DIR: Tony Maylam. **CAST:** Anthony Perkins, Belinda Bauer, Joseph Bottoms, Olga Karlatos, Michael Ironside.

This modern-day version of Oscar Wilde's famous horror tale, with a portrait of dear old Dorian in female form, manages to disappoint at nearly every turn. Only the plot—about a beautiful woman who sells her soul for eternal youth and then watches a video screen test of herself age and decay—manages to fascinate. Made for television. 1983; 98m.

SISTER, SISTER ★★★
DIR: Bill Condon. **CAST:** Eric Stoltz, Jennifer Jason Leigh, Judith Ivey, Dennis Lipscomb, Anne Pitoniak.

A gothic thriller set in the Louisiana bayou. Jennifer Jason Leigh is a frail lass who is haunted by a demon lover and taken care of by an overprotective older sister (Judith Ivey), who just may harbor a dark secret. Rated R for violence, nudity, simulated sex, and profanity. 1988; 91m.

SISTERS ★★★★½
DIR: Brian De Palma. **CAST:** Margot Kidder, Charles Durning, Jennifer Salt, Barnard Hughes.

A terrifying tale of twin sisters (Margot Kidder). One is normal; the other is a dangerous psychopath. It's an extremely effective thriller on all levels. Charles Durning and Jennifer Salt give the stand-out performances in this Brian De Palma release. Rated R for violence, nudity, and language. 1973; 93m.

SKETCHES OF A STRANGLER ★½
DIR: Paul Leder. **CAST:** Allen Garfield, Meredith MacRae.

Allan Garfield, in the days when he was billing himself as Allan Goorwitz, stars as a painter with a fixation on his dead mother. He takes out his frustrations by hiring Hollywood hookers as models and then strangling them after he paints them. The sister of one of his victims helps the police track him down. Garfield is vastly superior to his material here. Not rated. 1978; 91m.

SKULLDUGGERY ★
DIR: Ota Richter. **CAST:** Thom Haverstock, Wendy Crewson.

Thom Haverstock plays a costume store employee who inherits a satanic curse that sends him on a killing rampage. Too odd to be taken seriously as a horror flick and not odd enough to be interesting. Terrible attempts at humor, too. Not rated, but would earn a PG for violence and profanity. 1983; 95m.

SLAUGHTER HIGH ★★
DIR: George Dugdale. **CAST:** Caroline Munro, Simon Scuddamore.
Ten years after disfiguring a schoolmate, several former high-school friends attend a deadly reunion. The rest of the film is fairly predictable. The ending is a welcome change from the norm, though, and it's nice to see horror queen Caroline Munro still working. Not rated, but contains graphic violence and adult situations. 1986; 91m.

SLAUGHTER OF THE VAMPIRES ★
DIR: Roberto Mauri. **CAST:** Walter Brandy.
A hunted vampire bites the neck of a beautiful victim, making her a fellow bloodsucker. In this Italian would-be thriller, any decent performances are lost in inept dubbing. Not rated, but should be suitable for most viewers. 1971; B&W; 81m.

SLAUGHTERHOUSE
DIR: Rick Roessler. **CAST:** Joe Barton, Sherry Rendorf.
A typical slasher film about a disturbed man who butchers people as if they were farm animals. The film includes your average stupid teenagers and has special effects that amount to how much blood can be splashed onto the camera. Rated R for violence and profanity. 1987; 85m.

SLAUGHTERHOUSE ROCK ★
DIR: Dimitri Logothetis. **CAST:** Nicholas Celozzi.
Typical schlock shocker about a kid who becomes possessed by a spirit from Alcatraz. He and some rather simpleton friends go to Alcatraz on a stormy night to find out why. Lo and behold, they wind up getting slaughtered one after another. Rated R for nudity and violence. 1988; 90m.

SLEEPAWAY CAMP
DIR: Robert Hiltzik. **CAST:** Mike Kellin, Paul DeAngelo.
This bloody, disgusting film, written and directed by Robert Hiltzik, is one that will make you appreciate the fast-forward feature on your VCR. 1983; 88m.

SLEEPAWAY CAMP II: UNHAPPY CAMPERS ★★½
DIR: Michael A. Simpson. **CAST:** Pamela Springsteen, Rene Estevez, Brian Patrick Clarke.
Gory and funny sequel about naughty kids being slaughtered by a puritanical camp counselor. The film pokes fun at various other horror films with a fairly good sense of humor. Rated R for nudity, violence, and profanity. 1988; 81m.

SLITHIS ★★
DIR: Stephen Traxler. **CAST:** Alan Blanchard, Judy Motulsky.
Okay horror tale of a gruesome monster, derived from garbage and radiation in Southern California, and his reign of terror in and around the L.A. area. While earnestly done, the film just can't overcome its budget restrictions. Actual on-screen title: *Spawn of the Slithis*. Rated PG. 1978; 92m.

SLUGS, THE MOVIE
DIR: Juan Piquer Simon. **CAST:** Michael Garfield, Kim Terry, Patty Shepard.
Mutated slugs infest a small town, devouring anyone they can crawl across. A public-health official tackles the slithering creatures and some greedy bureaucrats as well. No one even thinks to pour salt on the hungry little devils. Rated R for violence and brief nudity. 1988; 90m.

SLUMBER PARTY MASSACRE ★
DIR: Amy Jones. **CAST:** Michele Michaels, Robin Stille, Michael Villella.
A typical exploitation film about a mass murderer who has escaped from a mental hospital and is killing young girls with a power drill. In between the bloodletting, the girls find enough time to disrobe, take showers, and

have sex with their boyfriends. The acting is atrocious, the writing insipid, and the direction uninspired. Rated R for nudity and graphic violence. 1982; 77m.

SLUMBER PARTY MASSACRE II ★★

DIR: Deborah Brock. **CAST:** Crystal Bernard.

The driller killer is back, but this time he appears as the ghost of a 1950s rock star. His weapon: a heavy metal guitar with a high-powered drill extending from the neck. The producers tried to be original, but they didn't go far enough. Maybe next time. Rated R for violence, nudity, and profanity. 1987; 90m.

SNAKE PEOPLE

DIR: Juan Ibanez, Jack Hill. **CAST:** Boris Karloff.

In this Mexican movie with scenes of Boris Karloff shot just before his death, the ailing actor plays a rich man whose niece is kidnapped by demon worshippers. Better than Karloff's other Mexican movies (see *Sinister Invasion*), but still nothing worth looking for. 1968; 90m.

SNOW CREATURE, THE ★½

DIR: W. Lee Wilder. **CAST:** Paul Langton, Leslie Denison.

Bargain-basement abominable snowman movie is one of the weakest of the batch that hit American theaters in the mid-1950s, but it did have one different gimmick: the yeti is captured and brought to Los Angeles. In the best tradition of captured snowmen, this one escapes and wreaks havoc on the terror-stricken metropolis. 1954; B&W; 70m.

SNOWBEAST ★

DIR: Herb Wallerstein. **CAST:** Bo Svenson, Yvette Mimieux, Robert Logan, Clint Walker, Sylvia Sidney.

Hokey white sasquatch/abominable snowman makes life miserable on the slopes for Bo Svenson and Yvette Mimieux's ski resort during a winter festival. Clint Walker and Sylvia Sidney almost make this predictable comic-book thriller worth watching, but it's too poor to be a passable horror film and not bad enough to be funny. 1977; 100m.

SOLE SURVIVOR ★★

DIR: Thom Eberhardt. **CAST:** Anita Skinner, Kurt Johnson.

A gory remake of a fine English suspense thriller of the same title—about the lone survivor of an airplane crash, haunted by the ghosts of those who died in the tragedy. A psychic tries to help this haunted woman by keeping the ghosts from killing her. Although there are some chills, this version pales in comparison to its predecessor—with Robert Powell and Jenny Agutter. Rated R for sexual situations and violence. 1985; 85m.

SOMEONE BEHIND THE DOOR ★★½

DIR: Nicolas Gessner. **CAST:** Charles Bronson, Anthony Perkins, Jill Ireland, Henri Garcin.

A brain surgeon takes an amnesiac into his home and, during the course of his treatment, conditions him to murder his wife. Intense suspense drama with a decent cast. The story contains too many plot twists though. Not rated but contains violence. 1971; 93m.

SOMEONE TO WATCH OVER ME ★★★★

DIR: Ridley Scott. **CAST:** Tom Berenger, Mimi Rogers, Lorraine Bracco, Andreas Katsulas.

This first-rate thriller benefits from director Ridley Scott's visual dynamics and an intelligent script. Ultra-rich lady Mimi Rogers witnesses a horrible murder and barely escapes with her life; Tom Berenger is the down-home cop from the Bronx assigned to protect her. Rated R for language, nudity, and violence. 1987; 106m.

SOMETHING WEIRD ★

DIR: Herschell Gordon Lewis. **CAST:** Tony McCabe, Elizabeth Lee.

Tedious and bloodless time-waster about a burn victim who finds he has gained extrasensory powers. There's also a subplot about a witch who restores his looks on the condition that he become her lover. None of it makes much sense. 1967; 83m.

SOMETIMES AUNT MARTHA DOES DREADFUL THINGS ★½
DIR: Thomas Casey. **CAST:** Abe Zwick, Scott Lawrence, Robin Hughes.
Weird obscurity about a killer hiding out from the police by holing up in a Miami beach house dressed as a woman. He has an indecisive young male lover whom he passes off as his nephew. There are a few touches of black comedy, but not enough for the movie to succeed. Rated R for nudity. 1971; 95m.

SON OF BLOB (BEWARE! THE BLOB) ★★
DIR: Larry Hagman. **CAST:** Robert Walker, Godfrey Cambridge, Carol Lynley, Larry Hagman, Cindy Williams, Shelley Berman, Gerrit Graham, Dick Van Patten.
Larry Hagman made this sequel to *The Blob* in his low period between *I Dream of Jeannie* and *Dallas*. It looks like he just got some friends together and decided to have some fun. The result is rather lame. Rated PG. 1972; 88m.

SON OF DRACULA ★★★½
DIR: Robert Siodmak. **CAST:** Lon Chaney, Louise Allbritton, Robert Paige, Evelyn Ankers, Frank Craven, J. Edward Bromberg.
Moody horror film features Lon Chaney's only turn as the Count, this time stalking a southern mansion as Alucard (spell it backward). Compelling, highly original Univeral chiller boasts several eye-catching effects, dazzling camerawork by George Robinson. 1943; B&W; 80m.

SON OF FRANKENSTEIN ★★★★½
DIR: Rowland V. Lee. **CAST:** Boris Karloff, Basil Rathbone, Bela Lugosi, Lionel Atwill, Josephine Hutchinson.
A strong cast (including Boris Karloff in his last appearance as the monster) makes this second sequel to *Frankenstein* memorable. This time, Henry Frankenstein's son Wolf (Basil Rathbone) revives the dormant monster with the help of insane shepherd Ygor (Bela Lugosi, in his most underrated performance). Impressive, intelligent production scores highly in all departments, with the stark lighting and photography rating a special mention. 1939; B&W; 99m.

SON OF GODZILLA ★★
DIR: Jun Fukuda. **CAST:** Tadao Takashima, Kenji Sahara.
Juvenile production has the cute offspring of one of Japan's biggest stars taking on all sorts of crazy-looking monsters, with a little help from Dad. Good special effects and miniature sets make this at least watchable, but the story is just too goofy for its own good. Recommended viewing age: 2 and under. Rated PG. 1969; 86m.

SON OF KONG, THE ★★★½
DIR: Ernest B. Schoedsack. **CAST:** Robert Armstrong, Helen Mack, Victor Wong, John Marston, Frank Reicher.
To cash in on the phenomenal success of *King Kong*, the producers hastily rushed this sequel into production using virtually the same cast and crew. This time out, Carl Denham (Robert Armstrong) returns to Skull Island only to find King Kong's easygoing son trapped in a pool of quicksand. Denham saves the twelve-foot albino gorilla, who becomes his protector. 1933; B&W; 70m.

SORORITY HOUSE MASSACRE ★
DIR: Carol Frank. **CAST:** Angela O'Neill, Wendy Martel.
This particularly flagrant *Halloween* ripoff features, as the title indicates, a vengeful killer slashing the sexy residents of a sorority house. It gets a star only because the filmmakers are obviously talented; too bad they wasted their time with this tired retread. Rated R for profanity, nudity, and violence. 1986; 74m.

SORRY, WRONG NUMBER ★★★★
DIR: Anatole Litvak. **CAST:** Barbara Stanwyck, Burt Lancaster, Wendell Corey, Ed Begley Sr., Ann Richards.
Slick cinema adaptation, by the author herself, of Lucille Fletcher's famed radio drama. Barbara Stanwyck is superb—and received an Oscar nomination—as an invalid who, due to those "crossed wires" so beloved in fiction, overhears two men plotting the murder of a woman. Gradually Stanwyck realizes that she is the target. 1948; B&W; 89m.

SPASMS ★★★
DIR: William Fruet. **CAST:** Peter Fonda, Oliver Reed, Kerrie Keane, Al Waxman, Marilyn Lightstone.
If it were not for the poor acting, this would be a top-notch horror film. Oliver Reed plays a millionaire trophy hunter who, on a hunting trip in a tropical jungle, becomes cursed by a giant monsterlike snake. Peter Fonda plays the special psychologist who is hired to examine him. When the serpent is brought back to the hunter, the tension rises as the body count goes up. Not rated but contains profanity, nudity, and gore. 1982; 92m.

SPECIAL EFFECTS ★
DIR: Larry Cohen. **CAST:** Zoe Tamerlis, Eric Bogosian, Brad Rijn, Kevin J. O'Connor.
Low-budget, rather sick horror film about a film director (Eric Bogosian) who, in a fit of rage, murders a would-be actress (Zoe Tamerlis) and attempts to pin the rap on her holier-than-thou husband. An ugly, repulsive film. Unrated, the film has nudity and violence. 1984; 90m.

SPECTERS ★
DIR: Marcello Avallone. **CAST:** Donald Pleasence, John Pepper, Erna Schurer.
Archeologists uncover an ancient tomb in Rome. When the seal is broken, the door to hell is opened, and murderous demons are unleashed upon the world. Although the production values are decent, the plot is a muddled rehash. Not rated, but contains violence and brief nudity. 1987; 95m.

SPELLBINDER 🦃
DIR: Janet Greek. **CAST:** Timothy Daly, Kelly Preston, Rick Rossovich, Audra Lindley.
Awful horror flick revolves around the obsession of a lawyer (Timothy Daly) for a young woman (Kelly Preston) who is a Satanist. Her cult is suspected of being responsible for mysterious disappearances and murders in the Los Angeles area. Rather than a spellbinder, this repulsive ripoff is a gutbinder. Rated R for profanity, nudity, and violence. 1988; 99m.

SPELLBOUND ★★★★
DIR: Alfred Hitchcock. **CAST:** Ingrid Bergman, Gregory Peck, Leo G. Carroll, John Emery, Wallace Ford, Rhonda Fleming, Bill Goodwin.
Hitchcock said in his usual, understated manner that *Spellbound* "is just another manhunt story wrapped up in pseudo-psychoanalysis." The story is more than just another manhunt story; of that we can assure you. We can divulge that Ingrid Bergman plays the psychiatrist, Gregory Peck is the patient, and Salvador Dalí provides the nightmare sequences. 1945; B&W; 111m.

SPHINX ★★
DIR: Franklin J. Schaffner. **CAST:** Lesley-Anne Down, Frank Langella, Maurice Ronet, John Gielgud.
This is a watchable film...but not a good one. Taken from the tedious novel by Robin Cook (*Coma*), it concerns the plight of an Egyptologist (Lesley-Anne Down) who inadvertently runs afoul of the underworld. Directed by Franklin J. Schaffner. Rated PG. 1981; 117m.

SPIRAL STAIRCASE, THE (1946) ★★★★
DIR: Robert Siodmak. **CAST:** George Brent, Dorothy McGuire, Ethel Barry-

more, Kent Smith, Elsa Lanchester, Sara Allgood.

Dorothy McGuire gives what some call the performance of her career as a mute servant in a hackle-raising household harboring a killer. Watch this one late at night, but not alone. 1946; B&W; 83m.

SPIRAL STAIRCASE, THE (1975) ★

DIR: Peter Collinson. **CAST:** Jacqueline Bisset, Christopher Plummer, Sam Wanamaker, Gayle Hunnicutt.

A mute woman is stalked by a deranged killer who preys upon handicapped females. This is a sad remake. The editing is poor and the dialogue worse. Watch the original instead. Not rated, but contains mild violence. 1975; 89m.

SPIRIT OF THE DEAD ★★★½

DIR: Peter Newbrook. **CAST:** Robert Stephens, Robert Powell, Jane Lapotaire.

Originally titled *The Asphyx*, slightly edited for videocassette. Interesting tale of a scientist who discovers the spirit of death possessed by all creatures. If the spirit is trapped, its owner becomes immortal. Well-made British film with sincere performances. Rated PG for mild violence. 1972; 82m.

SPLATTER UNIVERSITY 🦃

DIR: Richard W. Haris. **CAST:** Francine Forbes, Ric Randig.

Typical slasher film featuring students having sex and then getting hacked to pieces. Rated R for profanity, brief nudity, and violence. 1985; 78m.

SPOOKIES 🦃

DIR: Eugine Joseph, Thomas Doran, Brenden Faulkner. **CAST:** Felix Ward, Dan Scott.

Zombies of all varieties maim and kill people trapped in an old mansion. Cheesy effects, rotten acting, and unintentional humor mark this film as a member of the turkey club. Rated R for violence and profanity. 1985; 85m.

SQUIRM ★

DIR: Jeff Lieberman. **CAST:** Don Scardino, Patricia Pearcy.

Ugly, disgusting horror film has hordes of killer worms attacking a small town. Only serves to nauseate. Rated PG. 1976; 92m.

STAGE FRIGHT ★★★

DIR: Alfred Hitchcock. **CAST:** Marlene Dietrich, Jane Wyman, Michael Wilding, Alastair Sim, Richard Todd, Kay Walsh, Patricia Hitchcock.

Another winner from Alfred Hitchcock. Drama student Jane Wyman spies on actress Marlene Dietrich to prove she murdered her husband. Alastair Sim steals his moments as Wyman's protective parent, but most of the other moments go to the hypnotic Dietrich. 1950; B&W; 110m.

STANLEY ★★

DIR: William Grefe. **CAST:** Chris Robinson, Alex Rocco, Susan Carroll, Steve Alaimo.

A crazy Vietnam vet (Chris Robinson) uses an army of deadly snakes to destroy his enemies in this watchable, though rather grim, horror yarn. Rated PG for violence and unpleasant situations. 1972; 106m.

STEPFATHER, THE ★★★★

DIR: Joseph Ruben. **CAST:** Terry O'Quinn, Shelley Hack, Jill Schoelen, Charles Lanyer, Stephen Shellen.

Jerry Blake (Terry O'Quinn) is so relentlessly cheerful that his stepdaughter, Stephanie Maine (Jill Schoelen), complains to a friend, "It's just like living with Ward Cleaver." Little does she know that the accent should be on the cleaver. Jerry, you see, is a raving maniac. A thriller of a chiller. Rated R for violence, profanity, and brief nudity. 1987; 90m.

STEPHEN KING'S NIGHT SHIFT COLLECTION ★

DIR: Frank Durabont, Jeffrey C. Schiro. **CAST:** Michael Cornelison, Dee Croxton, Brion Libby.

In this so-called collection, featuring two short-story adaptations from Stephen King's book, *Night Shift*, we see again how hard it is to bring King's writing to the screen. Although this film has its moments, do yourself a favor: check *Night Shift* out of the library and *read* the stories. 1986; 61m.

STILL OF THE NIGHT ★★★½
DIR: Robert Benton. **CAST:** Roy Scheider, Meryl Streep, Jessica Tandy, Joe Grifasi, Sara Botsford.

In this well-crafted thriller by writer-director Robert Benton a psychiatrist (Roy Scheider) falls in love with an art curator (Meryl Streep) who may have killed one of his patients and may be after him next. If you like being scared out of your wits, you won't want to miss it. Rated PG for violence and adult themes. 1982; 91m.

STONES OF DEATH
DIR: James Bagle. **CAST:** Zoe Carides, Tom Jennings, Eric Oldfield.

Nothing new here: teenagers getting knocked off one by one by supernatural forces. One difference is that instead of Hometown, U.S.A., the location is Mate City, Australia. Seems a real-estate developer has built a subdivision over an Aboriginal burial site. This triggers a curse against whites. You'll feel cursed if you watch this bore. Rated R for nudity, profanity, and violence. 1988; 95m.

STORMY MONDAY ★★★½
DIR: Mike Figgis. **CAST:** Melanie Griffith, Tommy Lee Jones, Sting, Sean Bean.

In this stylish British thriller, Melanie Griffith and Sean Bean play unlikely lovers who attempt to stop ruthless American businessman Tommy Lee Jones from taking over a jazz nightclub owned by Sting. The generally strong performances, inventive filmmaking techniques, and offbeat sensibilities of *Stormy Monday* make it worth watching. Rated R for violence. 1988; 93m.

STRAIT-JACKET ★★★½
DIR: William Castle. **CAST:** Joan Crawford, Diane Baker, Leif Erickson, George Kennedy.

Chilling vehicle for Joan Crawford as a convicted axe murderess returning home after twenty years in an insane asylum, where it appears she was restored to sanity. But was she? Genuinely frightening film features one of Joan's most powerful performances. George Kennedy is almost as good in an early role as a farm hand. 1964; B&W; 89m.

STRANGE BEHAVIOR ★★★½
DIR: Michael Laughlin. **CAST:** Michael Murphy, Marc McClure, Dan Shor, Fiona Lewis, Louise Fletcher, Arthur Dignam.

Michael Murphy stars as the police chief of Galesburg, Illinois, who suddenly finds himself inundated by unexplained knife murders. In all, this offbeat film is a true treat for horror movie fans and other viewers with a yen for something spooky. Rated R. 1981; 98m.

STRANGE CASE OF DR. JEKYLL AND MR. HYDE, THE ★★
DIR: Charles Jarrott. **CAST:** Jack Palance, Denholm Elliott, Torin Thatcher, Oscar Homolka, Leo Genn, Billie Whitelaw.

The offbeat casting of Jack Palance in the title role(s) is the main attraction in this taped-for-television production. Charles Jarrott directs with the same ponderous hand he brought to *Anne of the Thousand Days* and *Mary, Queen of Scots*, but the distinguished supporting cast is a plus. Not rated. 1968; 96m.

STRANGENESS, THE ★
DIR: David Michael Hillman. **CAST:** Dan Lunham, Terri Berland.

Extremely low-budget horror film shot mostly in the dark. The Gold Spike Mine is haunted by a creature from down deep inside the earth. Who of the wimpish cast will dare to challenge this "strangeness?" This film is not worth watching to find out. Unrated. 1985; 90m.

STRANGER, THE ★★★★
DIR: Orson Welles. **CAST:** Orson Welles, Edward G. Robinson, Loretta Young, Richard Long.
Nazi war criminal (Orson Welles) assumes a new identity in a Midwestern town following World War II, unaware that a government agent (Edward G. Robinson) is tailing him. Extremely well-done film, holds the viewer's interest from start to finish. 1946; B&W; 95m.

STRANGER IS WATCHING, A ★
DIR: Sean S. Cunningham. **CAST:** Kate Mulgrew, Rip Torn, James Naughton.
A psychotic killer kidnaps two young ladies and keeps them prisoner in the catacombs beneath Grand Central Station. This commuter's nightmare is directed by Sean S. Cunningham and is an ugly, dimly lit suspenser for horror buffs only. Rated R. 1982; 92m.

STRANGER, THE ★★★★
DIR: Adolfo Aristarian. **CAST:** Bonnie Bedelia, Peter Riegert.
Taut psychological thriller that keeps you on the edge of your seat. Bonnie Bedelia plays a woman with amnesia trying to put the pieces together after a car accident. She thinks she may or may not have witnessed a murder. Peter Riegert is her psychiatrist who may or may not be trying to help her. This unique sleeper is fast-paced and suspenseful. Rated R for brief nudity and violence. 1986; 93m.

STRANGER WITHIN, THE ★
DIR: Lee Philips. **CAST:** Barbara Eden, George Grizzard, Joyce Van Patten, David Doyle.
A housewife is mysteriously impregnated, and her unborn child begins to have a strange effect on her eating habits and personality. Typical TV tripe with a big buildup but a small payoff. Not rated. 1979; 74m.

STRANGERS ON A TRAIN ★★★★★
DIR: Alfred Hitchcock. **CAST:** Farley Granger, Robert Walker, Ruth Roman, Leo G. Carroll, Patricia Hitchcock, Marion Lorne.
One of the most discussed and analyzed of all of Alfred Hitchcock's films. *Strangers on a Train* was made during the height of Hitchcock's most creative period, the early 1950s. When you add a marvelous performance by Robert Walker as the stranger, you have one of the most satisfying thrillers ever. 1951; B&W; 101m.

STRANGLER, THE ★★½
DIR: Burt Topper. **CAST:** Victor Buono, David McLean, Ellen Corby, Jeanne Bates.
Victor Buono gives a good performance as corpulent, mother-fixated maniac who murders nurses and throws Chicago into a state of alarm. This low-budget thriller didn't get a lot of playdates as a result of the real-life horrors of Boston strangler Albert De Salvo and the senseless murder of eight nurses by Richard Speck. Not rated, but violent and gruesome. Also available at 80 minutes. 1964; B&W; 89m.

STRANGLER OF THE SWAMP ★★
DIR: Frank Wisbar. **CAST:** Rosemary La Planche, Robert Barrat, Blake Edwards, Charles Middleton.
Ghostly revenge story about a ferry man who was unjustly lynched and who hangs his murderers one by one is atmospheric and eerie but bogged down by a cheap budget and an unnecessary love story. Considered a minor classic among fantasy fans. 1946; B&W; 60m.

STRAW DOGS ★★★★
DIR: Sam Peckinpah. **CAST:** Dustin Hoffman, Susan George, Peter Vaughn, T. P. McKenna, Peter Arne, David Warner.
An American intellectual mathematician (played brilliantly by Dustin Hoffman) takes a wife (Susan

George) and returns to her ancestral village on the coast of England. She taunts her former boyfriends with her wealth and power, and soon she is viciously raped. This violent, controversial shocker by Sam Peckinpah is rated R. 1971; 113m.

STREET TRASH
DIR: Jim Muro. **CAST:** Bill Chepil, Jane Arakawa.
Immeasurably awful load of cinematic trash, should be avoided at all costs. Filmed in New York's Lower East Side, it focuses on a group of street transients who consume a new brew that's been spiked with a destructive substance created by the military and go on a gory killing spree. 1987; 90m.

STUDENT BODIES ★★½
DIR: Mickey Rose. **CAST:** Kristin Ritter, Matthew Goldsby, Joe Flood.
This comedy-horror release has something extra, because it is a parody of the blood-and-guts horror films. Rated R. 1981; 86m.

STUFF, THE
DIR: Larry Cohen. **CAST:** Michael Moriarty, Andrea Marcovicci, Garrett Morris, Paul Sorvino, Danny Aiello.
A scrumptious, creamy dessert devours from within all those who eat it in this not funny and not scary horror-comedy. It's as flat as month-old whipped cream and just as enjoyable. Rated R for gore and profanity. 1985; 93m.

SUICIDE CLUB, THE ★★
DIR: James Bruce. **CAST:** Mariel Hemingway, Robert Joy, Madeleine Potter, Michael O'Donoghue.
This uneven, contrived shocker features Mariel Hemingway as a bored heiress involved with a group of self-indulgent aristocrats who engage in bizarre ritualistic games. Hemingway turns in a compelling performance in this otherwise disappointing thriller. Rated R; contains nudity and violence. 1988; 90m.

SUPERNATURALS, THE ★★★½
DIR: Armand Mastroianni. **CAST:** Nichelle Nichols, Maxwell Caulfield, Talia Balsam, LeVar Burton.
A group of modern-day soldiers face off against Civil War Confederate zombies. The commanding officer (Nichelle Nichols) must find the secret to exorcise these evil spirits before they kill her and her men. Good scary entertainment. Rated R for graphic violence. 1988; 91m.

SUSPICION (1941) ★★★★
DIR: Alfred Hitchcock. **CAST:** Joan Fontaine, Cary Grant, Cedric Hardwicke, Nigel Bruce, May Whitty, Isabel Jeans.
A timid woman is gradually unnerved by apprehension. Bits of evidence lead her to believe that her charming husband is a killer and that she is the intended victim. Joan Fontaine played a similar role in *Rebecca* and eventually won a best-actress Oscar for her performance in *Suspicion*. Cary Grant is excellent too. 1941; B&W; 99m.

SUSPICION (1987) ★★
DIR: Andrew Grieve. **CAST:** Jane Curtin, Anthony Andrews, Betsy Blair, Michael Hordern, Vivian Pickles, Jonathan Lynn.
A plain country Jane (Curtin) grows suspicious of her hubby's intentions after piecing together the plot for a murder that would benefit her penniless mate. All the elements for a suspenseful evening are in place, but things move at a plodding pace. This Alfred Hitchcock remake lacks the subtle suspense of the original. Rated PG. 1987; 97m.

SVENGALI ★★★★
DIR: Archie Mayo. **CAST:** John Barrymore, Marian Marsh, Donald Crisp, Carmel Myers, Bramwell Fletcher.
This film is adapted from the George Du Maurier novel that put Svengali into the language as one who controls another. John Barrymore, plays Svengali, a demonic artist obsessed with Trilby, a young artist's model. Under his hypnotic influence, she becomes a

singer who obeys his every command. Bizarre sets and arresting visual effects make this a surrealistic delight. 1931; B&W; 76m.

SWAMP THING ★½

DIR: Wes Craven. **CAST:** Louis Jourdan, Adrienne Barbeau, Ray Wise, David Hess.

Kids will love this movie, about a monster-hero—part plant, part scientist—who takes on a supervillain (Louis Jourdan) and saves heroine Adrienne Barbeau. But adults will no doubt find it too corny and sloppily made for their tastes. *Swamp Thing* was based on the popular 1972 comic book of the same name. Rated PG, it has some tomato-paste violence and brief nudity. 1982; 91m.

SWARM, THE 🦃

DIR: Irwin Allen. **CAST:** Michael Caine, Katharine Ross, Richard Widmark, Henry Fonda, Olivia De Havilland, Richard Chamberlain' Fred MacMurray.

"Irwin Allen is still 'Lost in Space,' " science-fiction author Ray Bradbury once said of the notorious television and film producer who also fathered *The Poseidon Adventure* and *The Towering Inferno*. And there is no better proof of Allen's ineptitude than this dreadful, self-directed killer-bee rip-off of Alfred Hitchcock's *The Birds*. It wastes the talents of a top-flight cast. Rated PG. 1978; 116m.

SWISS CONSPIRACY, THE ★★½

DIR: Jack Arnold. **CAST:** David Janssen, Senta Berger, Ray Milland, Elke Sommer, John Ireland, John Saxon.

Swiss banker Ray Milland hires ex-fed David Janssen to thwart sophisticated blackmail scheme involving supposedly secret numbered accounts. Sexy Senta Berger and John Saxon, as a Chicago gangster double-crossing his friends, are among those being threatened with exposure and death. Rated PG. 1977; 92m.

TALES FROM THE CRYPT ★★★½

DIR: Freddie Francis. **CAST:** Peter Cushing, Joan Collins, Ralph Richardson.

Excellent anthology has five people gathered in a mysterious cave where the keeper (Ralph Richardson) foretells their futures, one by one, in gruesome fashion. Director Freddie Francis keeps things moving at a brisk pace, and the performances are uniformly fine, most notably Peter Cushing's in one of the better segments—"Poetic Justice." Don't miss it. Rated PG. 1972; 92m.

TALES OF TERROR ★★★

DIR: Roger Corman. **CAST:** Vincent Price, Basil Rathbone, Peter Lorre, Debra Paget.

An uneven anthology of horror stories adapted from the works of Edgar Allan Poe. Directed by cult favorite Roger Corman, it does have a few moments. 1962; 90m.

TARGETS ★★★★★

DIR: Peter Bogdanovich. **CAST:** Tim O'Kelly, Boris Karloff, Nancy Hsueh, Peter Bogdanovich.

The stunning film-making debut of critic-turned-director Peter Bogdanovich juxtaposes real-life terror, in the form of an unhinged mass murderer (Tim O'Kelly), with its comparatively subdued and safe screen counterpart, as represented by the scare films of Byron Orlock (Boris Karloff in a brilliant final bow). Rated PG. 1968; 90m.

TEEN ALIEN 🦃

DIR: Peter Senelka. **CAST:** Vern Adix.

A low-budget yawner about a group of kids putting on a Halloween spook show in an abandoned mining mill. The catch is, the place is haunted—by an alien disguised as a high-school student. Rotten. Rated PG for mild violence. 1988; 88m.

TEEN WOLF ★

DIR: Rod Daniel. **CAST:** Michael J. Fox, James Hampton, Scott Paulin.

Pitifully bad film about a teenager (Michael J. Fox) who discovers he has the ability to change into a werewolf, making him a hit at high school when he carries their losing basketball team to the championships. It's the same old story, even considering the "wolf" angle, with the usual cliché-ridden plot and "be yourself" message at the end. Boring and tiresome. Rated PG for mild language. 1985; 95m.

TEEN WOLF, TOO
DIR: Christopher Leitch. **CAST:** Jason Bateman, Kim Darby, John Astin, James Hampton.
In this painfully dull sequel, the original Teen Wolf's cousin goes to college on a sports scholarship, even though he never played high-school sports. Of course he is a werewolf, and the rest of this movie we've seen before. Rated PG for language. 1987; 95m.

TEENAGE ZOMBIES
DIR: Jerry Warren. **CAST:** Don Sullivan, Katherine Victor.
Not even bad enough to be fun, this is a stodgy tale of teenagers stranded on an island where a lady scientist is conducting experiments for an enemy government. The pseudohip dialogue is good for an occasional chuckle, but you can't possibly be *that* starved for entertainment! 1957; B&W; 71m.

TEMPTER, THE ★
DIR: Ennio Morricone. **CAST:** Carla Gravina, Mel Ferrer, Arthur Kennedy.
Lurid Italian demonic-possession flick about a crippled woman who is the reincarnation of a witch burned at the stake hundreds of years ago. In the course of this sickening romp, we see things that look like outtakes from *The Exorcist*. Rated R for profanity and violence. 1978; 96m.

TENANT, THE ★★★
DIR: Roman Polanski. **CAST:** Roman Polanski, Melvyn Douglas, Shelley Winters.
Roman Polanski is superb in this cryptic thriller about a bumbling Polish expatriate in France who leases an apartment owned previously by a young woman who committed suicide. Increasingly, Polanski believes the apartment's tenants conspired demonically to destroy the woman and are attempting to do the same to him. Rated R. 1976; 125m.

TENTACLES
DIR: Ovidio Assonitis (Oliver Hellman). **CAST:** John Huston, Shelley Winters, Henry Fonda, Bo Hopkins, Cesare Danova.
Rotten monster movie from Italy about a phony-looking octopus attacking and devouring some famous Hollywood stars, who should all be ashamed of themselves for appearing in this sleaze. Rated PG. 1977; 90m.

TERMINAL CHOICE ★★
DIR: Sheldon Larry. **CAST:** Joe Spano, Diane Venora, David McCallum, Robert Joy, Don Francks, Nicholas Campbell, Ellen Barkin.
If it's blood you want, you'll get your money's worth with this one—by the gallons! There's some real tension in this film about a hospital that has a staff that secretly bets on the mortality of its patients—not exactly family entertainment. Rated R for nudity, language, and plenty o'gore. 1984; 98m.

TERMINAL MAN, THE ★★
DIR: Mike Hodges. **CAST:** George Segal, Joan Hackett, Jill Clayburgh.
A dreary adaptation of the crackling novel by Michael Crichton, although George Segal tries hard to improve the film's quality. He stars as a paranoid psychotic who undergoes experimental surgery designed to quell his violent impulses; unfortunately (and quite predictably), he becomes even worse. Rated R for violence. 1974; 104m.

TERROR, THE
DIR: Roger Corman. **CAST:** Boris Karloff, Jack Nicholson, Sandra Knight.
This is an incomprehensible sludge of mismatched horror scenes even Boris Karloff can't save, but he does better than a miscast Jack Nicholson in this forgettable Roger Corman loser,

which was shot in three days and shows it. 1963; 81m.

TERROR AT LONDON BRIDGE ★
DIR: E. W. Swackhamer. **CAST:** David Hasselhoff, Stephanie Kramer, Randolph Mantooth, Adrienne Barbeau.

Jack the Ripper is mystically resurrected in contemporary Arizona and goes on a killing spree in the British-style tourist trap. Only one man suspects that this is more than the work of a serial killer, and he must convince someone before it's too late. Predictable made-for-TV movie with some schlock gore effects. Not rated, but contains some graphic violence. 1985; 96m.

TERROR AT THE RED WOLF INN ★★★
DIR: Bud Townsend. **CAST:** Linda Gillin, Arthur Space, John Neilson, Mary Jackson.

This is a sometimes ghoulishly funny horror/comedy about a college student who is chosen as the winner of a free vacation at an inn owned by a sweet old couple. Not all of the scenes work, but we guarantee it will give you the willies and the sillies. Rated R. (Also known as *The Folks at the Red Wolf Inn* and *Terror House*.) 1972; 98m.

TERROR IN THE AISLES ★★★
DIR: Andrew Kuehn. **CAST:** Donald Pleasence, Nancy Allen.

Donald Pleasence and Nancy Allen host this basically enjoyable compilation film of the most graphic scenes from seventy-five horror films. Rated R for violence, profanity, nudity, and suggested sex. 1984; 82m.

TERROR IN THE HAUNTED HOUSE ★★★
DIR: Harold Daniels. **CAST:** Gerald Mohr, Cathy O'Donnell.

Although the title of this movie makes it sound as if it's a horror film, it is actually a psychological thriller along the Hitchcock line. It is the story of a young newlywed woman who has a recurring nightmare about a house she has never seen. She fears that something in the attic will kill her. The terror starts when her new husband takes her from Switzerland, where she has been since childhood, to the United States and...the house in her horrid dream. 1958; 90m.

TERROR IN THE SWAMP
DIR: Joe Catalanotto. **CAST:** Billy Holliday.

A Sasquatch-like creature is stalking the swamp, preying upon innocent and not-so-innocent visitors. The local game warden is savvy to the situation, but the local bureaucrats don't want him causing a panic, so he's all on his own to stop the bloodthirsty monster. A low-budget waste in the extreme. Rated PG for violence. 1984; 87m.

TERROR IN THE WAX MUSEUM ★
DIR: Georg Fenady. **CAST:** Ray Milland, Broderick Crawford, Elsa Lanchester, Maurice Evans, Shani Wallis, John Carradine, Louis Hayward, Patric Knowles.

The all-star cast from yesteryear looks like a sort of Hollywood wax museum. Their fans will suffer through this unsuspenseful murder mystery. It belongs in a museum—of missed opportunities. Rated PG. 1973; 93m.

TERROR OF MECHAGODZILLA ★★
DIR: Inoshiro Honda. **CAST:** Katsuhiko Sasaki.

Another outlandish Godzilla epic from the 1970s with the big guy battling his own robot double, Mechagodzilla. Nothing special, but a lot of flashy effects and explosions help to make this an adequate time-passer, and, as always, the kids will love it. Rated G. 1978; 89m.

TERROR ON ALCATRAZ
DIR: Philip Marcus. **CAST:** Aldo Ray.

A group of teenagers split off from a tour of a former prison and end up locked in overnight. Then an escaped con returns to retrieve some loot he left there years before and systematically picks the kids off. This low-budget yawner is boring and predictable. Not rated, but contains violence. 1987; 96m.

TERROR ON THE 40TH FLOOR ★★

DIR: Jerry Jameson. **CAST:** John Forsythe, Joseph Campanella, Don Meredith.

A typical disaster film, this deals with a skyscraper fire that traps a group of office workers on the top floor. In the face of impending death, they recount their lives. Unrated. 1974; 100m.

TERROR OUT OF THE SKY ★★

DIR: Lee H. Katzin. **CAST:** Efrem Zimbalist Jr., Dan Haggerty, Tovah Feldshuh, Lonny Chapman, Ike Eisenmann, Steve Franken.

This made-for-television film is a sequel to *The Savage Bees* (1976). Here two bee experts and a gung-ho pilot try everything to stop another infestation of the flying killers in the United States. Stick with the original. 1978; 100m.

TERROR TRAIN ★★★★

DIR: Roger Spottiswoode. **CAST:** Ben Johnson, Jamie Lee Curtis, Hart Bochner, David Copperfield.

This is perhaps the best slasher film made in recent years. The story involves a New Year's Eve frat party taking place on a moving train, with everyone having a great time until students start showing up murdered. This film relies on true suspense and good performances for its thrills. Rated R for violence. 1980; 97m.

TESTAMENT OF DR. MABUSE ★★★½

DIR: Fritz Lang. **CAST:** Rudolf Klein-Rogge, Otto Wernicke.

In this sequel to *Dr. Mabuse the Gambler* by Thea Von Harboll and the director Fritz Lang, the infamous criminal mastermind dies in an asylum, and his assistant takes over his identity. It's a fast-moving picture, said by Lang to be a diatribe against Adolf Hitler. Whatever it is, it rates as slick entertainment. 1933; B&W; 122m.

TEXAS CHAINSAW MASSACRE, THE ★★★

DIR: Tobe Hooper. **CAST:** Marilyn Burns, Gunnar Hansen, Edwin Neal.

This, the first film about a cannibalistic maniac by horror specialist Tobe Hooper, went pretty much unnoticed in its original release. That's probably because it sounds like the run-of-the-mill drive-in exploitation fare. While it was made on a very low budget, it nevertheless has been hailed as a ground-breaking genre work by critics and film buffs and became a cult classic. Rated R for extreme violence. 1974; 83m.

TEXAS CHAINSAW MASSACRE 2, THE ★★½

DIR: Tobe Hooper. **CAST:** Dennis Hopper, Caroline Williams.

Leatherface is back! In fact, so is most of the family in this maniacal sequel to *The Texas Chainsaw Massacre.* Dennis Hopper stars as a retired lawman out to avenge the gruesome murder of his nephew, and Caroline Williams plays the disc jockey who helps him locate the butchers. Unrated, but loaded with repulsive gore. 1986; 95m.

THEATRE OF BLOOD ★★★★

DIR: Douglas Hickox. **CAST:** Vincent Price, Diana Rigg, Robert Morley.

Deliciously morbid horror-comedy about a Shakespearean actor (Vincent Price) who, angered by the thrashing he receives from a series of critics, decides to kill them in uniquely outlandish ways. He turns to the Bard for inspiration, and each perceived foe is eliminated in a manner drawn from one of Shakespeare's plays. Rated R for violence. 1973; 104m.

THEATRE OF DEATH ★★½

DIR: Samuel Gallu. **CAST:** Christopher Lee, Julian Glover, Lelia Goldoni.

Mildly interesting mystery succeeds mainly due to Christopher Lee's assured performance and some well-timed scares as a series of gruesome murders is committed in Paris with an apparent connection to the local theater company. Good title sequence deserves mention. 1967; 90m.

THEY CAME FROM WITHIN ★★★

DIR: David Cronenberg. **CAST:** Paul Hampton, Joe Silver, Lynn Lowry, Barbara Steele.

This is David Cronenberg's commercial feature-film debut. Even at this early stage in his career, his preoccupation with violence and biological rebellion is very much in evidence. Slimy, disgusting parasites invade the sterile orderliness of a high-rise apartment complex, turning the inhabitants into raving sex maniacs. Rated R. 1975; 87m.

THEY LIVE ★★½

DIR: John Carpenter. **CAST:** Roddy Piper, Keith David, Meg Foster.

The first two-thirds of the science fiction–horror hybrid is such harebrained fun that one is truly disappointed when it falls apart at the end. Roddy Piper is a drifter in the not-so-distant future who discovers that the human population of Earth is being hypnotized into subservience by alien-created television signals. Rated R for nudity and violence. 1988; 95m.

THEY SAVED HITLER'S BRAIN

DIR: David Bradley. **CAST:** Walter Stocker, Audrey Caire, Carlos Rivas, John Holland, Marshall Reed, Nestor Paiva.

This bargain-basement bomb is actually a used movie since a major portion of it was lifted from an entirely different film made ten years earlier. The story of a girl whose pursuit of her kidnapped scientist father leads her to an island teeming with Nazis is secondary to the question of *why* anybody would bother to save Hitler's brain. Fun to watch if you know what you're getting into. 1963; B&W; 74m.

THIRD MAN, THE ★★★★★

DIR: Carol Reed. **CAST:** Joseph Cotten, Orson Welles, Alida Valli, Trevor Howard.

Considered by many to be the greatest suspense film of all time, this classic inevitably turns up on every best-film list. It rivals any Hitchcock thriller as being the ultimate masterpiece of film suspense. A writer (Joseph Cotten) discovers an old friend he thought dead to be the head of a vicious European black market organization. Unfortunately for him, that information makes him a marked man. 1949; B&W; 104m.

THIRST ★½

DIR: Rod Hardy. **CAST:** Chantal Contouri, David Hemmings, Henry Silva, Rod Mullinar.

An innocent young woman is kidnapped by a satanic brotherhood and taken to a remote village where she is subjected to diabolical torture. This is a messy, contrived thriller, wasting the talents of veteran actors Henry Silva and David Hemmings. Rated R for nudity and violence. 1988; 96m.

THIRSTY DEAD, THE 🦃

DIR: Terry Becker. **CAST:** John Considine, Jennifer Billingsley.

John Considine plays a Charles Mansonesque figure who lives in the jungle and sacrifices young women in bloody rituals. Highly missable. Made in the Philippines. Rated PG. 1975; 90m.

13 GHOSTS ★★★

DIR: William Castle. **CAST:** Charles Herbert, Donald Woods, Martin Milner, Rosemary DeCamp, Jo Morrow, Margaret Hamilton.

Lighthearted horror tale of an average family inheriting a haunted house complete with a creepy old housekeeper (Margaret Hamilton) who may also be a witch, and a secret fortune hidden somewhere in the place. William Castle directs with his customary style and flair. Pretty neat. 1960; B&W; 88m.

THIRTY-NINE STEPS, THE (1935) ★★★★★

DIR: Alfred Hitchcock. **CAST:** Robert Donat, Madeleine Carroll, Lucie Mannheim.

Alfred Hitchcock was assigned to direct what was intended to be a simple, low-budget spy-chase thriller. Using the style and technique that were to make him famous, he gained immediate audience sympathy for the plight of his central character, an innocent Canadian (Robert Donat) who while visiting England is implicated in the theft of national secrets and murder. The result was a big hit. 1935; B&W; 87m.

THIRTY-NINE STEPS, THE (1959) ★★½
DIR: Ralph Thomas. **CAST:** Kenneth More, Taina Elg, Brenda de Banzie, Barry Jones, Sidney James.
Inferior remake of Alfred Hitchcock's suspense classic has Kenneth More as the hapless fellow who innocently becomes involved in a murder plot. The 1978 version with Robert Powell also has it beat. 1959; 93m.

THOU SHALT NOT KILL...EXCEPT 🦃
DIR: Josh Becker. **CAST:** Brian Schulz, Tim Quill, Sam Raimi.
Hilariously cheap horror film about a violent cult (complete with a Charles Manson look-alike) that goes on a killing spree only to run into heroic Vietnam vets. Not rated, but has violence, profanity, and comic-book gore. 1987; 84m.

THREAT, THE ★★★½
DIR: Felix Feist. **CAST:** Charles McGraw, Michael O'Shea, Frank Conroy, Virginia Grey, Julie Bishop, Robert Shayne, Anthony Caruso, Don McGuire.
This underrated suspense feature packs every minute with tension as vengeance-minded Charles McGraw escapes from jail and kidnaps the police detective and district attorney as well as snatches a singer he thinks may have told on him for good measure. The police put the pressure on the kidnapper and he puts the squeeze on his captives. 1949; B&W; 65m.

THRILL KILLERS, THE ★
DIR: Ray Dennis Steckler. **CAST:** Cash Flagg, Liz Renay, Carolyn Brandt, Atlas King.
Psycho killer Cash Flagg (a.k.a. writer-director Ray Dennis Steckler) and three escaped mental patients with a fondness for decapitations meet up at a diner, where they terrorize the patrons. Pretty dull. 1965; B&W; 69m.

THRILLKILL ★½
DIR: Anthony Kramreither, Anthony D'Andrea. **CAST:** Robin Ward, Gina Massey.
Slow-moving, boring melodrama about a woman who has a falling out with her partners after stealing $3 million via computer. The woman is killed for her troubles, but not before dragging her innocent sister into the fray. You've seen this one before. Not rated, but contains some violence and frank language. 1986; 88m.

THRONE OF FIRE, THE ★
DIR: Franco Prosperi. **CAST:** Sabrina Siani.
The son of Satan must overthrow the king and marry his daughter to sit upon the legendary Throne of Fire, from which he will be able to rule the world. Poor dubbing, bad acting, and outrageous dialogue make this worth watching just to see how bad a film can be. Not rated, but contains violence that might be unsuitable for younger viewers. 1973; 91m.

TICKET OF LEAVE MAN, THE ★★
DIR: George King. **CAST:** Tod Slaughter, John Warwick, Marjorie Taylor.
British horror star Tod Slaughter gleefully plays a maniacal killer who swindles rich philanthropists with a phony charity organization he has established. Slaughter, the original Sweeney Todd of the cinema, singlehandedly presided as Great Britain's unofficial hobgoblin during the 1930s and early 1940s. The majority of his films have been unavailable for years in America. 1937; B&W; 71m.

TIGHTROPE ★★★★★
DIR: Richard Tuggle. **CAST:** Clint Eastwood, Genevieve Bujold, Dan Hedaya, Alison Eastwood.

A terrific, taut suspense thriller, this ranks with the best films in the genre. Written and directed by Richard Tuggle, *Tightrope* casts Clint Eastwood as Wes Block, homicide inspector for the New Orleans Police Department. His latest assignment is to track down a Jack the Ripper–style sex-murderer. This case hits disturbingly close to home in more ways than one. Rated R for violence. 1984; 115m.

TIME WALKER 🦃
DIR: Tom Kennedy. **CAST:** Ben Murphy, Nina Axelrod, Kevin Brophy, Shari Belafonte-Harper.

Imagine sitting through a movie that isn't all that great to begin with and, as the story seems to be building up to a pretty good climax, the words "To Be Continued" flash on the screen. Outrageous, you say? Well, that's exactly what happens at the end of this horror rip-off, which features Ben Murphy as an Egyptologist who accidentally brings an ancient mummy back to life. Avoid it. Rated PG. 1982; 83m.

TO ALL A GOOD NIGHT ★★
DIR: David Hess. **CAST:** Jennifer Runyon, Forrest Swenson.

In this typical slasher film, a group of young teen age girls gets away from supervision, and the mad killer shows up with a sharp weapon. There is some build-up of terror and suspense. The camera work is good and the timing fair, adding up to a slightly above average film of its genre. Rated R; has nudity, violence, and profanity. 1983; 90m.

TO CATCH A KING ★★
DIR: Clive Donner. **CAST:** Robert Wagner, Teri Garr, Horst Janson, Barbara Parkins.

Made-for-cable spy thriller that fails to live up to its promising premise. In 1940, cunning Nazis plot to kidnap the Duke and Duchess of Windsor during the romantic couple's respite in Lisbon. Robert Wagner plays a café owner, a more debonair version of *Casablanca*'s Rick. Teri Garr is a nightclub singer. The film is neither convincing nor exciting. 1984; 113m.

TO CATCH A THIEF ★★★★
DIR: Alfred Hitchcock. **CAST:** Cary Grant, Grace Kelly, John Williams, Jessie Royce Landis.

John Robie (Cary Grant) is a retired cat burglar living in France in peaceful seclusion. When a sudden rash of jewel thefts hits the Riviera, he is naturally blamed. He sets out to clear himself, and the fun begins. This is certainly one of director Alfred Hitchcock's most amusing, films. 1955; 103m.

TO KILL A CLOWN ★
DIR: George Bloomfield. **CAST:** Alan Alda, Blythe Danner.

A husband and wife move from the big city to a remote island in an effort to save their marriage. Their new landlord (Alan Alda) appears at first to be a pleasant sort of fellow, but as time goes on, he is revealed to be a maniac bent on their destruction. *To Kill a Clown* is an unnecessarily depressing and essentially uninvolving drama. Rated R for violence. 1983; 82m.

TO THE DEVIL, A DAUGHTER ★★★½
DIR: Peter Sykes. **CAST:** Richard Widmark, Christopher Lee, Honor Blackman, Denholm Elliott, Nastassja Kinski.

Dennis Wheatley wrote a number of books on the occult. This film was based on one of them, and it is his influence that raises this above the average thriller. Another plus is the acting. Richard Widmark gives an understated and effective performance as occult novelist John Verney, who finds himself pitted against satanists. Rated R, the film contains nudity, profanity, and violence in small quantities. 1976; 95m.

TOMB OF LIGEIA ★★★
DIR: Roger Corman. **CAST:** Vincent Price, Elizabeth Shepherd.
A grieving widower is driven to madness by the curse of his dead wife. Filmed in England, this was Roger Corman's final Poe-inspired movie. The most subtle and atmospheric entry in the series, it was photographed by Nicolas Roeg on sets left over from *Becket.* The screenplay was by Robert Towne, who went on to write *Chinatown.* 1964; 81m.

TOMB OF TORTURE 🦃
DIR: Anthony Kristye. **CAST:** Annie Albert.
A young woman, haunted by dreams that she lived a past life as an evil countess, visits the abandoned castle of the countess. Needless to say, this is a mistake, as the place features a still-active torture chamber run by the countess's butler. You'll be making a mistake if you rent this slow-moving Italian shocker, which is dubbed in English. 1966; B&W; 88m.

TOO SCARED TO SCREAM 🦃
DIR: Tony Lo Bianco. **CAST:** Mike Connors, Anne Archer, Leon Isaac Kennedy, Ian McShane.
Pathetic "demented killer" movie features Mike Connors as a grizzled New York detective on the trail of a psychopath who's knocking off tenants at a posh Manhattan apartment building. No suspense, just tedium, in a film laced with bad acting, writing, photography. Rated R for nudity and gore. 1982; 104m.

TOOLBOX MURDERS, THE ★
DIR: Dennis Donnelly. **CAST:** Cameron Mitchell, Pamelyn Ferdin, Wesley Eure, Aneta Corseaut, Tim Donnelly.
Sick excursion into mayhem. What can you say about a film whose sole purpose is to show someone using screwdrivers, pliers, and hammers on another human being? Not Cameron Mitchell's shining hour. 1978; 93m.

TOPAZ ★★★
DIR: Alfred Hitchcock. **CAST:** John Forsythe, Frederick Stafford, Dany Robin, John Vernon.
Medium-to-rare Hitchcock suspense thriller about cloak-and-dagger intrigue concerning Russian involvement in Cuba and infiltration of the French government. Constant shift of scene keeps viewers on their toes. Rated PG. 1969; 127m.

TORMENT ★★
DIR: Samson Aslanian, John Hopkins. **CAST:** Taylor Gilbert.
This low-budget slasher film starts off slow and, if it weren't for one interesting plot twist halfway through, would be an exercise in boredom. The story revolves around a man who becomes a psychotic killer when he is rejected by a younger woman. R for violence and gore. 1986; 90m.

TORN CURTAIN ★★★
DIR: Alfred Hitchcock. **CAST:** Paul Newman, Julie Andrews, Lila Kedrova, David Opatoshu.
This just-okay film was directed by Alfred Hitchcock in 1966. Paul Newman plays an American scientist posing as a defector, with Julie Andrews as his secretary/lover. Somehow we aren't moved by the action or the characters. 1966; 128m.

TORTURE CHAMBER OF BARON BLOOD, THE ★★
DIR: Mario Bava. **CAST:** Joseph Cotten, Elke Sommer, Massimo Girotti.
Boring Italian production is basically nonsense as a long-dead nobleman (Joseph Cotten) is inadvertently restored to life, only to (naturally) embark on a horrendous killing spree. Worth watching for Mario Bava's unique directorial style. Originally titled *Baron Blood.* Rated R. 1972; 90m.

TORTURE CHAMBER OF DR. SADISM, THE ★½
DIR: Harald Reinl. **CAST:** Christopher Lee, Lex Barker, Karin Dor.

Based on Poe's "The Pit and the Pendulum," this German production has Christopher Lee as a count who lures Lex Barker and Karin Dor to his foreboding castle. Although containing some good shock scenes, *Torture Chamber* doesn't live up to its source material or title. Not rated, contains violence and torture. 1967; 90m.

TORTURE GARDEN ★★★½
DIR: Freddie Francis. **CAST:** Burgess Meredith, Jack Palance, Beverly Adams, Peter Cushing, Maurice Denham, Robert Hutton.

A group of patrons at a carnival sideshow has their possible futures exposed to them by a screwball barker (Burgess Meredith) who exclaims, "I've promised you horror...and I intend to keep that promise." He does more than this in this frightening film laced with plenty of shocks, plot twists, and intense situations. Rated PG. 1968; 93m.

TOUCH OF EVIL ★★★★½
DIR: Orson Welles. **CAST:** Orson Welles, Charlton Heston, Marlene Dietrich, Janet Leigh, Zsa Zsa Gabor.

In 1958, director-actor Orson Welles proved that he was still a film-making genius, with this dark and disturbing masterpiece about crime and corruption in a border town. 1958; B&W; 108m.

TOURIST TRAP ★
DIR: David Schmoeller. **CAST:** Chuck Connors, Jon Van Ness, Jocelyn Jones, Tanya Roberts.

Another in the endless stream of psycho-hack films with a lot of stupid actors wondering where all these life-size dummies in Chuck Connors's basement museum have come from. Some scary moments, and Connors carries a lethal axe. With Tanya Roberts in her pre-*Sheena* days. Rated R for violence, gore, nudity, and profanity. 1979; 83m.

TOWER OF LONDON ★★★
DIR: Roger Corman. **CAST:** Vincent Price, Michael Pate, Joan Freeman.

A bloody update of the 1939 classic. Vincent Price plays Richard III, who systematically murders everyone who stands in his way to the throne of England. One can feel the chills crawling up the spine. Roger Corman's melodramatic style works well in this gothic setting. Not rated. 1962; B&W; 79m.

TOWN THAT DREADED SUNDOWN, THE ★★★½
DIR: Charles B. Pierce. **CAST:** Ben Johnson, Andrew Prine, Dawn Wells.

The fact that *The Town that Dreaded Sundown* is based on actual events makes this effective little film all the more chilling. The story takes place in the year 1946 in the small border town of Texarkana. It begins in documentary style, with a narrator describing the post–World War II atmosphere, but soon gets to the unsettling business of the Phantom, a killer who terrorized the locals. Rated R for violence. 1977; 90m.

TOXIC AVENGER, THE ★★★
DIR: Michael Herz, Samuel Weil. **CAST:** Mitchell Cohen.

Just another "nerdy pool attendant tossed into a tub of toxic waste becomes mutant crimefighter" picture. Actually, this low-budget horror spoof has a number of inspired moments. If you are looking for sick humor and creative bloodshed, press play and enjoy. Rated R for violence. 1985; 100m.

TRACK OF THE MOON BEAST ★
DIR: Richard Ashe. **CAST:** Chase Cordell.

A mineralogist comes into contact with a fragment of a meteor. Next thing you know he becomes a lizard monster. Notable only for makeup effects by Oscar winner (not for this) Rick Baker; otherwise, a pathetic effort. Not rated. 1976; 90m.

TRANSMUTATIONS ★★
DIR: George Pavlou. **CAST:** Larry Lamb, Denholm Elliott, Nicola Cowper, Steven Berkoff, Miranda Richardson, Ingrid Pitt.

Much-lauded horror writer Clive Barker disowned this, the first of his stories to be filmed. A retired London mobster, searching for his missing girlfriend, discovers an underground society of mutants, the victims of drug experiments. The strong cast has little to do, and the story is more mystery than horror. Rated R. 1985; 103m.

TRAP, THE ★★★½
DIR: Norman Panama. **CAST:** Richard Widmark, Lee J. Cobb, Earl Holliman, Tina Louise, Lorne Greene.
Fast pace and taut suspense mark this thriller about as fine a gaggle of fleeing gangsters as ever menaced the innocent inhabitants of a small California desert town. This is edge-of-chair stuff. It was in films such as this that Richard Widmark made his name praisingly hissable. 1958; 84m.

TRICK OR TREAT (1982)
DIR: Gary Graver. **CAST:** Peter Jason, Chris Graver, David Carradine, Carrie Snodgress, Steve Railsback.
An unbelievably slow-moving mess about a baby-sitter and a spoiled brat on Halloween. The two are being stalked by the little boy's insane father. There isn't one exciting or suspenseful moment in the entire film. Not rated, but contains violence and profanity. 1982; 90m.

TRICK OR TREAT (1986) ★★½
DIR: Charles Martin Smith. **CAST:** Marc Price, Doug Savant, Elaine Joyce, Gene Simmons, Ozzy Osbourne.
Perhaps it was inevitable that someone would make a horror film about the supposed satanic messages found in heavy metal rock music. While not a classic of the genre, *Trick or Treat* is both clever and funny. Marc Price's performance is one of the film's pluses. Rated R for profanity, nudity, suggested sex, and violence. 1986; 97m.

TRILOGY OF TERROR ★★★
DIR: Dan Curtis. **CAST:** Karen Black, Robert Burton, John Karlen.
Karen Black stars in this trio of horror stories, the best of which is the final episode, about an ancient Indian doll coming to life and stalking Black. It's often very frightening, and well worth wading through the first two tales. This was originally made as an ABC Movie of the Week. 1974; 78m.

TWICE DEAD ★★★
DIR: Bert L. Dragin. **CAST:** Tom Breznahan, Jill Whitlow, Todd Bridges.
An all-American family moves into an old mansion inhabited by a street gang. The gang, furious about losing their clubhouse, starts terrorizing the family. This movie is highlighted by good performances, above-average effects, and a sharp wit. Rated R for violence and nudity. 1988; 90m.

TWICE-TOLD TALES ★★
DIR: Sidney Salkow. **CAST:** Vincent Price, Sebastian Cabot, Joyce Taylor, Brett Halsey, Beverly Garland, Mari Blanchard.
With all his usual feeling, Vincent Price lurks, leers, and hams his nefarious way through a trilogy of nineteenth-century novelist Nathaniel Hawthorne's most vivid horror stories, including *The House of the Seven Gables*. 1963; 119m.

TWILIGHT PEOPLE
DIR: Eddie Romero. **CAST:** John Ashley, Jan Merlin, Pam Grier.
Mad scientist on remote island dabbles with things better left unfilmed. A remake of *Island of Lost Souls* with batmen, tree women, antelope people, and other laughable creatures. Rated R for violence. 1972; 84m.

TWILIGHT ZONE—THE MOVIE ★★★
DIR: Steven Spielberg, John Landis, Joe Dante, George Miller. **CAST:** Vic Morrow, Scatman Crothers, Kathleen Quinlan, John Lithgow, Dan Aykroyd, Albert Brooks.
A generally enjoyable tribute to the 1960s television series created by Rod Serling, this film, directed by Steven Spielberg John Landis, Joe Dante and

George Miller, is broken into four parts. Miller brings us the best: a tale about a white-knuckled air traveler (John Lithgow) who sees a gremlin doing strange things on the wing of a jet. Rated PG. 1983; 102m.

TWINS OF EVIL ★★★
DIR: John Hough. **CAST:** Peter Cushing, Madeleine Collinson, Mary Collinson, Dennis Price.

Playboy magazine's first twin Playmates, Madeleine and Mary Collinson, were tapped for this British Hammer Films horror entry about a good girl and her evil, blood-sucking sister. Peter Cushing adds class to what should in theory have been a forgettable exploitation film but provides surprisingly enjoyable entertainment for genre buffs. Rated R for nudity, violence, and gore. 1972; 85m.

TWINSANITY ★★★
DIR: Alan Gibson. **CAST:** Judy Geeson, Martin Potter, Alexis Kanner, Michael Redgrave, Mike Pratt, Freddie Jones, Peter Jeffrey.

Twins (Judy Geeson and Martin Potter) who still play games together are lured into London's underbelly. Sleazy sexual encounters lead the twins to concoct a game of murder. Though dated by its music and costuming, this film (originally released as *Goodbye Gemini*) does include some fine acting and a complex storyline. Rated R for violence. 1970; 91m.

TWISTED NIGHTMARE ★
DIR: Paul Hunt. **CAST:** Rhonda Gray, Cleve Hall.

A group of young people at a camp near a lake are menaced by a mysterious homicidal maniac. Sound familiar? This flick is just another in a long line of *Friday the 13th* ripoffs. Same story, only less well done, with poor special effects and bad acting. Rated R for violence. 1982; 95m.

TWO OF A KIND ★★
DIR: Henry Levin. **CAST:** Edmond O'Brien, Lizabeth Scott, Terry Moore, Alexander Knox.

Average suspense drama concerning a con-artist team who attempt to steal the inheritance of two elderly people. Both the cast and script are okay, but that's just the problem. 1951; B&W; 75m.

2,000 MANIACS ★½
DIR: Herschell Gordon Lewis. **CAST:** Thomas Wood, Jeffrey Allen.

Flushed with the runaway success of his landmark gore film *Blood Feast*, producer-director Herschell Gordon Lewis whipped together this paean to pain about vacationers who become the victims of long-dead Confederate soldiers. Full of cruel tortures and mutilation, this drive-in hit was the prototype of today's sick-humor slasher films. 1964; 84m.

UNCANNY, THE ★
DIR: Denis Heroux. **CAST:** Peter Cushing, Ray Milland, Susan Penhaligon, Joan Greenwood, Donald Pleasence, Samantha Eggar, John Vernon.

A paranoid writer tells three tales of cat-related horror. He believes felines are trying to take over the world. Judging from this film, they're trying to bore us to death. Rated R. 1977; 88m.

UNEARTHLY, THE 🦃
DIR: Brooke L. Peters. **CAST:** John Carradine, Allison Hayes, Myron Healey.

Mad scientist John Carradine goes back into the lab to torture more innocent victims. The real sufferers, however, are not his human experiments but the video viewers unfortunate enough to watch this mess. 1957; 73m.

UNHOLY, THE ★
DIR: Camilo Vila. **CAST:** Ben Cross, Hal Holbrook, Ned Beatty, Trevor Howard, William Russ.

Even the presence of a talented cast does little to raise this story above the level of ludricous. A priest (Ben Cross) attempts to battle a demon that prolongs its existence by killing sinners in the act of sinning. The special effects are hokey—especially the stop-motion animated demon—and the screenplay is fashioned around shocks rather than sense. Rated R for gore, nudity, and profanity. 1988; 99m.

UNINVITED, THE 🦃
DIR: Greydon Clark. **CAST:** George Kennedy, Alex Cord, Clu Gulager, Toni Hudson.
A group of college kids take staff jobs on a yacht and spend their spring break cruising to the Caribbean. A mutant cat with a taste for human flesh causes more excitement than any of them counted on. Poor special effects and sloppy editing spoil any suspense potential. Rated R for violence and nudity. 1987; 92m.

UNION STATION ★★★
DIR: Rudolph Maté. **CAST:** William Holden, Nancy Olson, Allene Roberts, Barry Fitzgerald, Lyle Bettger, Jan Sterling.
A big, bustling railroad terminal is the backdrop of this suspense-thriller centering on the manhunt that ensues following the kidnapping of a blind girl for ransom. William Holden is the hero, Lyle Bettger is the villain, Allene Roberts is the victim. The plot's tired, but ace cinematographer-turned-director Rudolph Mate keeps everything moving fast and frantic. 1950; B&W; 80m.

UNNAMABLE, THE ★★★
DIR: Jean Paul Ouellette. **CAST:** Charles King, Mark Kinsey Stephenson, Alexandra Durrell.
College students spend the night in a haunted house in this adaptation of an H. P. Lovecraft short story. While there, the promiscuous teens must contend with a family curse and a monstrous she-beast that delights in tearing humans limb from limb. There's a fair amount of good humor and some genuine chills. Horror fans should have a good time. Not rated, but contains nudity and graphic violence. 1988; 87m.

UNSANE ★★★½
DIR: Dario Argento. **CAST:** Anthony Franciosa, Daria Nicolodi, John Saxon, Giuliano Gemma, John Steiner.
American fans of stylish Italian director Dario Argento have been awaiting his 1984 film *Tenebrae* for years. Although it never played theatrically in this country, it snuck on to video with a new title, *Unsane*. A mystery novelist on a promotional tour in Rome discovers that a series of killings seems to be based on those in his latest book. Argento's trademarks—violent murders, a complex plot, and a pulsing synthesizer score—are all here in abundance. Unrated, the film contains nudity and violence. 1984; 92m.

UNSEEN, THE 🦃
DIR: Peter Foleg. **CAST:** Barbara Bach, Sidney Lassick, Stephen Furst.
This awful horror film should remain unseen, in spite of the quaint Danish-style location of Solvang, California, and a cellar-dwelling invisible critter which does what you'd expect. Rated R. 1981; 89m.

VAMP ★★★
DIR: Richard Wenk. **CAST:** Chris Makepeace, Grace Jones, Robert Rusler, Sandy Baron, Gedde Watanabe, Dedee Pfeiffer.
Effective comedy-shocker concerns a pair of college kids (Chris Makepeace and Robert Rusler) who, in order to make it into the best fraternity on campus, must find a stripper for a big party being thrown that night. Upon arriving at the After Dark Club, the duo quickly decide on the outrageous Katrina (Grace Jones) as their unanimous choice, little realizing that she is actually a vicious, bloodthirsty vampire in disguise. Rated R for gore and brief nudity. 1986; 93m.

VAMPIRE AT MIDNIGHT ★★
DIR: Greggor McClatchy. **CAST:** Jason Williams, Gustav Vintas, Leslie Milne, Jenie Moore, Robert Random.

A young woman becomes the object of adoration of a brutal vampire posing as a motivational psychologist. As more blood-depleted bodies show up, a heroic cop figures out who the bloodsucker is. This tries hard to be a character study rather than a horror movie, but it misses the mark more often than not. Rated R for violence and nudity. 1988; 94m.

VAMPIRE BAT, THE ★★★
DIR: Frank Strayer. **CAST:** Lionel Atwill, Fay Wray, Melvyn Douglas, Dwight Frye, Maude Eburne.

Prolific director Frank Strayer gave low-rent Majestic Studios their biggest hit with this eerie thriller reminiscent of the great horror films. Lionel Atwill and Fay Wray reunite to share the screen with distinguished Melvyn Douglas as a skeptical magistrate out to solve several mysterious deaths. It seems the victims have all been drained of blood and great hordes of bats have been hovering about... 1933; B&W; 63m.

VAMPIRE HOOKERS ★
DIR: Cirio H. Santiago. **CAST:** John Carradine.

Aging vampire lords over a bevy of beauteous bloodsuckers. Come on now, did you really think this movie could live up to its title? (Also known as *Sensuous Vampires*.) Made in the Philippines. It should have stayed there. Rated R for violence and nudity. 1979; 82m.

VAMPIRE LOVERS, THE ★★★
DIR: Roy Ward Baker. **CAST:** Ingrid Pitt, Peter Cushing, Pippa Steele, Madeleine Smith, George Cole, Dawn Addams, Kate O'Mara.

Hammer Films of England revitalized the Frankenstein and Dracula horror series in the late 1950s. But by 1971, when *Vampire Lovers* was released, Hammer's horrors had become passé. Even adding sex to the mix, as the studio did in this faithful screen version of Sheridan LeFanu's *Camilla*, didn't help much. Nonetheless, sexy Ingrid Pitt makes a voluptuous vampire. Rated R for violence, nudity, suggested sex, and gore. 1971; 88m.

VAMPYRES ★★½
DIR: Joseph Larraz. **CAST:** Marianne Morris, Anulka, Murray Brown, Brian Deacon, Bessie Love.

This tale of two beautiful female vampires living in an old mansion and sharing their male victims sexually before drinking their blood was considered pornographic in its time. It's pretty tame by current standards, and also easier to appreciate as a piece of serious, if low-budget, erotica. There are two versions available on video; the longer, unrated one has elongated sexual situations, though both feature abundant nudity. 1974; 84/87 minutes.

VARAN, THE UNBELIEVABLE ★★½
DIR: Inoshiro Honda. **CAST:** Jerry Baerwitz, Myron Healey, Tsuruko Kobayashi.

Another Godzilla ripoff with better-than-average effects. 1962; B&W; 70m.

VAULT OF HORROR ★★
DIR: Roy Ward Baker. **CAST:** Daniel Massey, Anna Massey, Terry-Thomas, Glynis Johns, Curt Jurgens, Dawn Addams, Tom Baker, Denholm Elliott, Michael Craig, Edward Judd.

British sequel to *Tales from the Crypt* boasts a fine cast and five short stories borrowed from the classic EC comics line of the early 1950s but delivers very little in the way of true chills and atmosphere. Not nearly as effective as the earlier five-story thriller *Dr. Terror's House of Horrors* and not as much fun as the most recent homage to the EC horror story, *Creepshow*. Rated R. 1973; 87m.

VENOM ★
DIR: Piers Haggard. **CAST:** Nicol Williamson, Klaus Kinski, Susan George, Oliver Reed, Sterling Hayden, Sarah Miles.

This combination horror film and police thriller doesn't really work as either. The plot centers on the bungled kidnapping of a 10-year-old scion of a wealthy London family. Police trap the kidnappers in the boy's home, in which, unknown to either the police or criminals, a vicious black mamba snake stalks victims. Rated R for nudity and violence. 1982; 98m.

VERTIGO ★★★★
DIR: Alfred Hitchcock. **CAST:** James Stewart, Kim Novak, Barbara Bel Geddes.
The first hour of this production is slow, gimmicky, and artificial. However, the rest of this suspense picture takes off at high speed. James Stewart stars as a San Francisco detective who has a fear of heights and is hired to shadow an old friend's wife (Kim Novak). He finds himself falling in love with her—then tragedy strikes. 1958; 128m.

VIDEODROME ★★½
DIR: David Cronenberg. **CAST:** James Woods, Deborah Harry, Sonja Smits.
Director David Cronenberg strikes again with a clever, gory nightmare set in the world of television broadcasting. James Woods and Deborah Harry (of the rock group Blondie) star in this eerie, occasionally sickening horror film about the boss (Woods) of a cable TV station. Rated R for profanity, nudity, violence, gore, and pure nausea. 1983; 88m.

VILLAGE OF THE DAMNED ★★★★
DIR: Wolf Rilla. **CAST:** George Sanders, Barbara Shelley, Michael C. Gwynne.
A science-fiction thriller about twelve strangely emotionless children all born at the same time in a small village in England. Sanders plays their teacher, who tries to stop their plans for conquest. This excellent low-budget film provides chills. 1960; B&W; 78m.

VILLAGE OF THE GIANTS ★★
DIR: Bert I. Gordon. **CAST:** Tommy Kirk, Beau Bridges, Ron Howard, Johnny Crawford.
Utterly ridiculous story of a gang of teenage misfits taking over a small town after they ingest a bizarre substance created by a 12-year-old named "Genius" and grow to gigantic heights. What makes this worth watching, though, are the famous faces of the many young stars-to-be. 1965; 80m.

VIRGIN OF NUREMBERG ★
DIR: Anthony M. Dawson. **CAST:** Rossana Podesta, George Riviere, Christopher Lee.
Christopher Lee's contribution as the only recognizable face is not enough to save this film. It's a combination of no-name foreign actors, dubbed English, and cheesy special effects. The plot, involving a hooded killer lurking in an ancient German castle, has the potential for plenty of scare, but this ends up a horror movie without any horror. (Alternate title: *Horror Castle.*) 1963; 82m.

VISITING HOURS 🦃
DIR: Jean Claude Lord. **CAST:** Lee Grant, William Shatner, Linda Purl, Michael Ironside.
Here's a Canadian production that actually forces the viewer to wallow in the degradation, humiliation, and mutilation of women. What Lee Grant, William Shatner, and Linda Purl are doing in such an awful picture is anybody's guess. Rated R for blood, gore, violence, and general unrelenting ugliness. 1982; 103m.

VULTURES ★
DIR: Paul Leder. **CAST:** Stuart Whitman, Greg Mullavey, Carmen Zapata, Yvonne De Carlo, Marcia Perschy.
A murder mystery with slasher undertones about the heirs to a fortune being killed off one by one. Poorly written and acted, but has some suspense. Not rated, but contains graphic

violence and adult situations. 1983; 101m.

W ★★★½
DIR: Richard Quine. **CAST:** Twiggy, Michael Witney, Eugene Roche, John Vernon, Dirk Benedict.

Someone is trying to kill the Lewises, Katy (Twiggy) and Ben (Michael Witney). Each gets into a car and finds too late that it has been tampered with and nearly is killed in a headlong, high-speed crash. On each vehicle, the letter *W* is scrawled in the dust. Who could be after them? This is a highly involving, Hitchcockian thriller that will keep mystery lovers captivated. Rated PG. 1974; 95m.

WAIT UNTIL DARK ★★★★
DIR: Terence Young. **CAST:** Audrey Hepburn, Alan Arkin, Richard Crenna, Efrem Zimbalist Jr.

Suspense abounds in this chiller about a blind housewife (Audrey Hepburn) who is being pursued by a gang of criminals. She has inadvertently gotten hold of a doll filled with heroin. Alan Arkin is especially frightening as the psychotic gang's mastermind who alternates between moments of deceptive charm and sudden violence in his attempt to separate Hepburn from the doll. 1967; 108m.

WARNING SHADOWS ★★
DIR: Albert Herman, Colbert Clark. **CAST:** Bela Lugosi, Henry B. Walthall, Karl Dane, Roy D'Arcy, Bob Kortman, Tom London, Lafe McKee, Ethel Clayton.

Bela Lugosi hams it to the hilt as the curator of the House of Mystery. He's the tainted genius behind the lifelike wax figures that move and speak like human creatures. But is he the mysterious Whispering Shadow who jams the airwaves and can eavesdrop and even murder people by remote-control radio and television? This Mascot serial, though stilted and creaky, is worth a watch. 1933; B&W; 12 chapters.

WARNING SIGN ★★★
DIR: Hal Barwood. **CAST:** Sam Waterston, Kathleen Quinlan, Yaphet Kotto, Jeffrey DeMunn, Richard Dysart, G. W. Bailey, Rick Rossovich.

A sort of *The Andromeda Strain* meets *The Night of the Living Dead*, this is a passable science-fiction thriller about what happens when an accident occurs at a plant, producing a particularly virulent microbe for germ warfare. Rated R for violence and gore. 1985; 99m.

WATCH ME WHEN I KILL 🦃
DIR: Anthony Bido. **CAST:** Richard Stewart, Sylvia Kramer.

You've heard of the spaghetti western? Now here's the spaghetti slasher. Sylvia Kramer plays a woman who is witness to a murder and is now in danger of becoming one of the killer's next victims. Dubbed in English and stupid. Not rated; has violence and profanity. 1981; 94m.

WATCHER IN THE WOODS, THE ★★
DIR: John Hough. **CAST:** Bette Davis, Lynn-Holly Johnson, Carroll Baker, David McCallum.

This typical teenage gothic plot (family moves into old mansion and strange things begin to happen) is completely obscure and ends by defiantly refusing to explain itself. Rated PG because of minor violence. 1980; 84m.

WAXWORK ★★★
DIR: Anthony Hickox. **CAST:** Zack Galligan, Deborah Foreman, Michelle Johnson, Miles O'Keeffe, Patrick Macnee, David Warner.

In this thrilling tongue-in-cheek horror film, six college students are invited to a midnight show at a mysterious wax museum. The sets of wax figures, famous monsters and killers, are missing one ingredient that can bring them all back to life: a dead victim. The proprietors intend the six students to be the needed components to start their reign of terror. Rated R. 1988; 100m.

WEREWOLF OF WASHINGTON ★★

DIR: Milton Moses Ginsberg. **CAST:** Dean Stockwell, Biff McGuire, Clifton James, Michael Dunn.

Dean Stockwell plays the president's press secretary, who becomes a werewolf after a visit to eastern Europe. Although it was made at the height of the Watergate scandal, this satire is surprisingly lacking in bite. Stockwell gives a game performance, but the script doesn't give him much to work with. Rated PG. 1973; 90m.

WEREWOLVES ON WHEELS ★

DIR: Michel Levesque. **CAST:** Steven Oliver, Barry McGuire, Billy Gray.

Cursed bikers become werewolves. The worst of two genres. Give us a break. Rated R for nudity and violence. 1971; 85m.

WHAT EVER HAPPENED TO BABY JANE? ★★★½

DIR: Robert Aldrich. **CAST:** Bette Davis, Joan Crawford, Victor Buono.

One of the last hurrahs of screen giants Bette Davis and Joan Crawford in a chillingly unpleasant tale of two aged sisters. Davis plays a former child movie star who spends her declining years dreaming of lost fame and tormenting her sister (Crawford). Victor Buono deserves special notice in a meaty supporting role. 1962; B&W; 132m.

WHATEVER HAPPENED TO AUNT ALICE? ★★★½

DIR: Lee H. Katzin. **CAST:** Geraldine Page, Ruth Gordon, Rosemary Forsyth, Robert Fuller, Mildred Dunnock.

Entertaining black comedy about an eccentric woman (impeccably performed by Geraldine Page) who stays wealthy by killing off her housekeepers and stealing their savings. Ruth Gordon is equally impressive as an amateur sleuth trying to solve the missing-persons mystery. 1969; 101m.

WHEN A STRANGER CALLS ★★★

DIR: Fred Walton. **CAST:** Carol Kane, Charles Durning, Colleen Dewhurst, Tony Beckley, Rachel Roberts, Ron O'Neal.

A *Psycho II*–style atmosphere pervades this film when the murderer of two children returns after seven years to complete his crime. Rated R. 1979; 97m.

WHEN TIME RAN OUT! ★½

DIR: James Goldstone. **CAST:** Paul Newman, Jacqueline Bisset, William Holden, James Franciscus, Edward Albert, Red Buttons, Ernest Borgnine, Burgess Meredith, Valentina Cortese, Alex Karras, Barbara Carrera.

This disastrous disaster film runs out of plot and characterization after the first few scenes. Time never seems to run out as we wait and wait for a volcano to erupt and put the all-star cast out of its misery. Producer Irwin Allen deserves to have a molten lava shampoo for inflicting this one on the public. Rated PG. 1980; 121m.

WHERE ARE THE CHILDREN? ★★★½

DIR: Bruce Malmuth. **CAST:** Jill Clayburgh, Max Gail, Clifton James, Elizabeth Wilson, Barnard Hughes, Frederic Forrest.

On the ninth anniversary of the murder of her previous children, a mother's children from her new marriage disappear. Jill Clayburgh is very good as the mother attempting to piece together the reason for this second occurrence. This film has a crackerjack surprise ending. Rated R. 1988; 97m.

WHISTLE BLOWER, THE ★★★★

DIR: Simon Langton. **CAST:** Michael Caine, Nigel Havers, James Fox, Felicity Dean, John Gielgud, Kenneth Colley, Gordon Jackson, Barry Foster.

This taut suspense thriller from England combines the elements of a murder mystery with real-life human drama. Michael Caine, in one of his finest performances, stars as a stoic British subject whose tidy life is disrupted when his son (Nigel Havers) discovers what he believes are immoral acts on the part of the government. Rated PG for suspense. 1987; 100m.

WHITE OF THE EYE ★★★
DIR: Donald Cammell. **CAST:** David Keith, Cathy Moriarty, Art Evans.

Tense film deals with a serial killer on the loose in Arizona. David Keith plays a commercial-stereo whiz who finds his life being turned upside down when he becomes a suspect in a series of bizarre and brutal murders of affluent women. Cathy Moriarty plays his devoted wife. Director Donald Cammell avoids the usual slasher pitfalls, although this one is saddled with a truly abysmal finale. Rated R. 1988; 113m.

WHITE PONGO (A.K.A. BLOND GORILLA)
DIR: Sam Newfield. **CAST:** Richard Fraser, Lionel Royce, Al Ebon, Gordon Richards.

Reverently referred to by fans of genre films as the worst of all crazed-gorilla/missing link jungle movies, this imbecilic waste features a no-star cast and a man in a frosted gorilla suit. This is to jungle films what *Robot Monster* is to science-fiction movies. 1945; B&W; 74m.

WHITE ZOMBIE ★★★★
DIR: Victor Halperin. **CAST:** Bela Lugosi, Madge Bellamy, Robert Frazer.

This eerie little thriller is the consummate zombie film, with hordes of the walking dead doing the bidding of evil Bela Lugosi as their overseer and master. A damsel-in-distress story with a new twist, this independently produced gem features sets and production standards usually found in films by the major studios. A minor classic, with a standout role by Lugosi. 1932; B&W; 73m.

WHO SLEW AUNTIE ROO? ★★
DIR: Curtis Harrington. **CAST:** Shelley Winters, Mark Lester, Chloe Franks, Ralph Richardson, Lionel Jeffries, Hugh Griffith.

Ghoulish horror version of *Hansel and Gretel*, with Shelley Winters as the madwoman who lures two children (Mark Lester and Chloe Franks) into her evil clutches. Rated R for violence. 1971; 89m.

WICKED STEPMOTHER, THE
DIR: Larry Cohen. **CAST:** Bette Davis, Barbara Carrera, Richard Moll, Tom Bosley.

A lame horror-comedy about an old woman who moves in with a family and turns their lives upside-down with her evil powers. Originally intended as a straight horror flick, Bette Davis walked out before the film's completion, Larry Cohen had to rewrite the script. Rated PG-13 for profanity. 1989; 95m.

WICKER MAN, THE ★★★★½
DIR: Robin Hardy. **CAST:** Edward Woodward, Christopher Lee, Britt Ekland, Diane Cilento, Ingrid Pitt.

An anonymous letter that implies a missing girl has been murdered brings Sergeant Howie (Edward Woodward), of Scotland Yard, to Summerisle, an island off the coast of England. The islanders are anything but cooperative. Lord Summerisle (Christopher Lee), the ruler and religious leader of the island, seems to take it all as a joke, so Howie swears to find the truth. Rated R. 1973; 95m.

WILLARD ★★½
DIR: Daniel Mann. **CAST:** Bruce Davison, Ernest Borgnine, Sondra Locke.

This worked far better as a novel, although the film accurately follows the elements of Stephen Gilbert's *Ratman's Notebooks*. Bruce Davison plays a put-upon wimp who identifies more with rodents than people. When nasty Ernest Borgnine becomes too unpleasant, Davison decides to make him the bait in a better rattrap. Pretty cheesy stuff...but it was destined to get worse in the sequel, entitled *Ben*. Rated PG—mild violence. 1971; 95m.

WIND, THE (1986) ★★½
DIR: Nico Mastorakis. **CAST:** Meg Foster, Wings Hauser, Robert Morley.

There's some solid suspense in this tale of a mystery novelist on a secluded Mediterranean island who is terrorized by a psychopath. She can't call for help—and he knows that she is the only one who can identify him as the murderer. Director Nico Mastorakis makes good use of the Greek locations. Unfortunately, he lets his two stars overact. 1986; 92m.

WINDOW, THE ★★★½
DIR: Ted Tetzlaff. **CAST:** Bobby Driscoll, Arthur Kennedy, Barbara Hale, Paul Stewart, Ruth Roman.

This chilling drama about a young boy who witnesses a murder and finds himself unable to convince any authority figures of what he has seen is one of the classic nightmare films of the postwar period, Bobby Driscoll (who earned a special Academy Award for this film) is kidnapped by the murderers and the film becomes one taut encounter after another. 1949; B&W; 73m.

WITCHBOARD ★★
DIR: Kevin S. Tenney. **CAST:** Todd Allen, Tawny Kitaen, Stephen Nichols, Kathleen Wilhoite, Rose Marie.

Some good moments buoy this horror film about a group of people who play with a Ouija board at a party and find themselves haunted into becoming murderers and victims. Rated R for profanity and violence. 1987; 100m.

WITCHCRAFT ★
DIR: Robert Spera. **CAST:** Anat Topol-Barzilai.

A new mother can't understand the strange nightmares she begins to have after she moves in with her mother-in-law. If only she had seen *Rosemary's Baby, The Exorcist,* or *The Omen,* she would have understood. Lame special effects don't even warrant the R rating. The acting is worse. 1988; 90m.

WITCHING, THE (NECROMANCY) ★
DIR: Bert I. Gordon. **CAST:** Orson Welles, Pamela Franklin, Michael Ontkean, Lee Purcell.

Whenever he was making a movie just for the money, Orson Welles would disguise himself. In this piece of trash from director Bert I. Gordon, he wears both a false nose and a beard. But there can be no doubt that *Citizen Kane* himself is playing Cato, the head of a community whose one enterprise is the manufacture of occult toys. Cato, as it turns out, takes his witchcraft seriously and attempts to use it to bring his dead son back to life. Rated PG. 1972; 82m.

WITCHING TIME ★★
DIR: Don Leaver. **CAST:** Jon Finch, Patricia Quinn, Prunella Gee, Ian McCulloch.

Another entry from "Thriller Video," hosted by TV's Elvira, "Mistress of the Dark." The owner of an English farmhouse is visited by a previous occupant, a seventeenth-century witch. Unfortunately for him, after three hundred years, the old gal is hot to trot. Originally filmed for the British television series *Hammer House of Horror*. Unrated; nudity edited out of the print used for this cassette. 1985; 60m.

WIZARD OF GORE, THE ★½
DIR: Herschell Gordon Lewis. **CAST:** Ray Sager.

Herschell Gordon Lewis (*Blood Feast*) is at it again! Blood and guts galore as a sideshow magician takes the old "saw the girl in half" trick a bit too far. Disgusting. Rated R. 1982; 80m.

WOLF MAN, THE ★★★★★
DIR: George Waggner. **CAST:** Lon Chaney Jr., Evelyn Ankers, Claude Rains, Patric Knowles, Ralph Bellamy, Bela Lugosi, Maria Ouspenskaya, Warren William.

Classic horror film featuring a star-making performance by Lon Chaney Jr. as Lawrence Talbot (a role he would go on to play five times). Everyone knows the story: upon attempting to save a young woman from a wolf's vicious attack, Talbot is bitten by the animal. He discovers that it was not an ordinary wolf, but a werewolf, and that now he too will become a bloodthirsty creature of the night whenever the full moon rises. 1941; B&W; 70m.

WOLFEN ★★
DIR: Michael Wadleigh. **CAST:** Albert Finney, Diane Venora, Gregory Hines, Tommy Noonan, Edward James Olmos, Dick O'Neill.

The best features of this sluggish horror film are its innovative visual work and actors who make the most of an uneven script. Directed by Michael Wadleigh, *Wolfen* follows a sequence of mysterious murders that are sometimes disturbingly bloody. This explains the R rating. 1981; 115m.

WOLFMAN 🦃
DIR: Worth Keeter. **CAST:** Earl Owensby.

It's the werewolf schtick, but told a little differently. A young man inherits his ancestral home, only to be transformed into a wolfman by a cult of satanists who need a perfect killing machine. There's nothing to redeem this tired feature. Not rated, but contains violence. 1978; 91m.

WRAITH, THE ★★
DIR: Mike Marvin. **CAST:** Charlie Sheen, Randy Quaid, Clint Howard, Griffin O'Neal.

A small town in Arizona is visited by a spirit taking revenge on a gang of road pirates. Some nice car wrecks and explosions. Car buffs will like the Wraith Mobile. A typical shallow revenge picture without style, substance, or surprises. Rated PG. 1986; 93m.

WRONG MAN, THE ★★★★
DIR: Alfred Hitchcock. **CAST:** Henry Fonda, Vera Miles, Anthony Quayle, Harold J. Stone, Nehemiah Persoff.

In this frightening true-life tale, Henry Fonda plays a man falsely accused of robbery. Vera Miles is his wife, who can't handle the changes wrought in their lives by this gross injustice. Fonda is excellent. 1956; B&W; 105m.

XTRO ★
DIR: Harry Davenport. **CAST:** Philip Sayer, Bernice Stegers, Maryam D'Abo.

Grotesquely slimy sci-fi/horror flick with an idiotic plot—one that requires every character to behave like a jerk at all times—that revolves around a series of repulsive bladder effects. Average dad Philip Sayer is abducted by aliens; he returns three years later and, just to prove his love, infects his son, kills countless people, and turns the family *au pair* girl into an alien breeding chamber. Sick, sick, sick. Rated R. 1982; 84m.

ZERO BOYS, THE ★½
DIR: Nico Mastorakis. **CAST:** Daniel Hirsch, Kelli Maroney, Nicole Rio.

A survival-game team of three college buddies truck out to the backwoods for some serious partying and instead ride straight into a murderous game of hide-and-seek with a couple of homegrown psychotics. This movie has the current prerequisites of very sick killers, a lot of guns with a lot of lousy marksmanship, torture barns, mass graves, and stupid reasons for being alone so someone can kill you. Rated R. 1985; 89m.

ZOLTAN—HOUND OF DRACULA 🦃
DIR: Albert Band. **CAST:** Michael Pataki, Reggie Nalder, José Ferrer.

Dracula's faithful servant journeys to Los Angeles in search of the last surviving member of the Dracula clan. The film is amateurish in virtually every way and never suspenseful or frightening. Rated R for violence. 1977; 85m.

ZOMBIE ★
DIR: Lucio Fulci. **CAST:** Tisa Farrow, Ian McCulloch, Richard Johnson.

Gruesome, gory, and ghastly unauthorized entry in George Romero's zombie series. Richard Johnson is a mad scientist who reanimates the dead; the flesh-eating stiffs can be destroyed only by bullets in the brain...a chore that Johnson embraces lovingly and director Lucio Fulci's camera repeats *ad nauseum*. Rated X for gore and nudity. 1979; 91m.

ZOMBIE HIGH

DIR: Ron Link. **CAST:** Virginia Madsen, Richard Cox, James Wilder.

Low-rent horror movie set at a prep school where the administration consists of 100-year-old men who have kept their youth through a potion made with live brain tissue obtained from their students. The loss of the tissue also lobotomizes the students, giving the school a reputation for turning out decent, orderly graduates. No, it's not a comedy. The R rating is solely for a few uses of a certain word that has obviously been added expressly for that purpose. Sloppy and boring. 1987; 93m.

ZOMBIE ISLAND MASSACRE

DIR: John Carter. **CAST:** David Broadnax, Rita Jenrette.

Excruciatingly bad film about tourists in the Caribbean who run into a pack of natives practicing voodoo. Rated R for violence, profanity, and nudity. 1984; 89m.

ZOMBIE NIGHTMARE ★★

DIR: Jack Brauman. **CAST:** Adam West, Tia Carrere, Linda Singer.

This film—about an innocent boy who is killed by some "savage suburban teens" only to rise again as a zombie to avenge his murder—tries to be more mystical than gory. But it never becomes atmospheric enough to be interesting. Rated R for violence and profanity. 1986; 89m.

ZOMBIES OF MORA TAU ★

DIR: Edward Cahn. **CAST:** Gregg Palmer, Allison Hayes.

Laughable, low-budget time-waster about zombies and sunken treasure. Shows how dull zombies were before *Night of the Living Dead*. Unrated, but timid enough for your aunt Sally. 1957; B&W; 70m.

MUSIC/MUSICALS

ABSOLUTE BEGINNERS ★★★★
DIR: Julien Temple. **CAST:** Eddie O'Connell, Patsy Kensit, David Bowie, James Fox, Ray Davies, Anita Morris, Sade Adu, Mandy Rice Davies.

Absolute Beginners is based on the cult novel by Colin MacInnes, who chronicled the musical and social scene in London during the pivotal summer of 1958. Occasionally the accents are too thick and the references too obscure for Americans, but the overall effect is an unequivocal high. Rated PG-13 for stylized, but rather intense, violence and some profanity. 1986; 107m.

ALCHEMY LIVE ★★★★
DIR: Peter Sinclair. **CAST:** Dire Straits.

Before Dire Straits reached MTV popularity, there was *Alchemy*, a 95-minute romp into the world of Mark Knopfler. Because of Knopfler's talent with a guitar, songs such as "Water of Love," "Romeo and Juliet," and "Sultans of Swing," explode in this concert recorded before a hometown London audience. 1984; 95m.

ALICE ★
DIR: Jerzy Gruza, Jacek Bromski. **CAST:** Sophie Barjac, Jean-Pierre Cassel, Susannah York, Paul Nicholas.

In this bizarre adaptation of *Alice in Wonderland*, Alice falls for a jogger called Rabbit. When he must leave the country to get away from overdue debts, she contemplates suicide. Unrated. 1981; 80m.

ALICE THROUGH THE LOOKING GLASS ★★★½
DIR: Alan Handley. **CAST:** Ricardo Montalban, Judy Rolin, Nanette Fabray, Robert Coote, Agnes Moorehead, Jack Palance, Jimmy Durante, Tom Smothers, Dick Smothers, Roy Castle, Richard Denning.

What? Another version of Lewis Carroll's immortal classic? Why not? When you've got such a talented cast working with a great story, you've got a winner. In this made-for-TV version, Alice makes an attempt to become the Queen of Wonderland by visiting the Royal Castle. However, she must avoid the fire-breathing monster, the evil Jabberwock. 1966; 72m.

ALIVE NOW ★★½

DIR: Jim Yukich. **CAST:** Eric Clapton.

Eric Clapton is still one of the best guitarists in the business. But watching Clapton sleepwalk through the eleven songs from this 1985 concert, one only wishes there was a similar video taken of him in his prime. 1986; 56m.

ALL THAT JAZZ ★★★★

DIR: Bob Fosse. **CAST:** Roy Scheider, Ann Reinking, Jessica Lange.

While it may not be what viewers expect from a musical, this story of a gifted choreographer, Joe Gideon (Roy Scheider, in his finest performance), who relentlessly drives himself to exhaustion is daring, imaginative, shocking, and visually stunning. Rated R. 1979; 123m.

AMADEUS ★★★★★

DIR: Milos Forman. **CAST:** Tom Hulce, F. Murray Abraham, Elizabeth Berridge.

F. Murray Abraham, who won an Oscar for his performance, gives a haunting portrayal of Antonio Salieri, the court composer for Hapsburg Emperor Joseph II. A second-rate musician, Salieri felt jealousy and admiration for the young musical genius Wolfgang Amadeus Mozart (Tom Hulce), who died at the age of thirty-five—perhaps by Salieri's hand. It's a stunning film full of great music, drama, and wit. Rated PG for mild violence. 1984; 158m.

AMERICAN HOT WAX ★★★½

DIR: Floyd Mutrux. **CAST:** Tim McIntire, Fran Drescher, Jay Leno, John Lehne, Laraine Newman, Jeff Altman, Chuck Berry, Jerry Lee Lewis.

Though facts may be in short supply in this bio-pic of pioneer rock disc jockey Alan Freed, abundant energy and spirit make this movie a winner. The incredible excitement caused by the birth of rock'n'roll is captured here. Tim McIntire gives a remarkable performance as Freed. Rated PG. 1978; 91m.

AMERICAN IN PARIS, AN ★★★★★

DIR: Vincente Minnelli. **CAST:** Gene Kelly, Leslie Caron, Nina Foch, Oscar Levant.

One of Gene Kelly's classic musicals, this Oscar-winning best picture features the hoofer as the free-spirited author of the title. The picture is a heady mixture of light entertainment and the music of George Gershwin. 1951; 115m.

ANCHORS AWEIGH ★★★

DIR: George Sidney. **CAST:** Gene Kelly, Frank Sinatra, Kathryn Grayson, Dean Stockwell.

A somewhat tedious and overlong dance film that is perked up by a few truly impressive numbers, none finer than Gene Kelly's duet with an animated Jerry the mouse (of Tom and Jerry fame). Kelly and Frank Sinatra play a couple of sailors on leave. Unrated; suitable for family viewing. 1945; 140m.

ANNIE ★★★★

DIR: John Huston. **CAST:** Albert Finney, Carol Burnett, Bernadette Peters, Edward Herrmann, Aileen Quinn.

A sparkling $40 million movie musical based on the Broadway production of the long-running comic strip *Little Orphan Annie*. Ten-year-old Aileen Quinn is just fine in the title role. Rated PG for brief profanity. 1982; 128m.

ARIA ★½

DIR: Robert Altman, Bruce Beresford, Bill Bryden, Jean-Luc Godard, Derek Jarman, Franc Roddam, Nicolas Roeg. **CAST:** Buck Henry, John Hurt, Anita Morris, Bridget Fonda, Theresa Russell.

High expectations are dashed in this unexpectedly boring collection of vignettes made by ten different directors using opera segments as a creative springboard. A few good moments here and there, but the overall impression is about as memorable as a few hours of MTV. Rated R for nudity. 1988; 90m.

ART BLAKEY JAZZ AT THE SMITHSONIAN ★★★½

DIR: Clark Santee, Della Gravelle Santee. **CAST:** Art Blakey and the Jazz Messengers.

Art Blakey, one of the great bebop drumming masters, brings his special brand of hard-bopping jazz to the Smithsonian in Washington, D.C., in 1982. He is joined by two outstanding reedmen in trumpeter Wynton Marsalis and saxaphonist Branford Marsalis. A dynamite evening of jazz. 1983; 58m.

ART ENSEMBLE OF CHICAGO LIVE FROM THE JAZZ SHOWCASE ★★★★

DIR: William J. Mahin. **CAST:** Lester Bowie, Joseph Jarman, Roscoe Mitchell, Malachi Favors, Famoudou Don Moye.

This excellent concert features some of the most talented and innovative musicians to fill out the Afro-American avant-garde jazz scene since Sun-Ra. The band kicks out some powerful improvisational jazz while dressed in surreal, primitive costumes. Highly recommended. 1982; 52m.

BABES IN ARMS ★★★

DIR: Busby Berkeley. **CAST:** Mickey Rooney, Judy Garland, June Preisser, Guy Kibbee, Charles Winninger, Henry Hull, Margaret Hamilton.

Richard Rodgers and Lorenz Hart wrote the Broadway musical from which this film was taken—although most of the songs they wrote are absent. But never mind; Mickey and Judy sing, dance, and prance up a storm as the kids in town put on a show! 1939; B&W; 96m.

BABES ON BROADWAY ★★½

DIR: Busby Berkeley. **CAST:** Mickey Rooney, Judy Garland, Fay Bainter, Virginia Weidler, Richard Quine, Donna Reed.

Raising funds for underprivileged children is the excuse for this musical extravaganza showcasing Mickey Rooney and Judy Garland, both of whom shine despite a trite plot. See it for the songs. 1941; B&W; 118m.

BABY SNAKES ★½

DIR: Frank Zappa. **CAST:** Frank Zappa, Ron Delsner, Joey Psychotic, Donna U Wanna, Diva.

Overlong and overboard; this concert-tour film will be pure joy to Frank Zappa fans, and pure torment to others. A waste of time, this weird and sometimes vulgar ego trip contains brilliant sequences of Claymation. 1979; 166m.

BACK TO THE BEACH ★

DIR: Lyndall Hobbs. **CAST:** Frankie Avalon, Annette Funicello, Connie Stevens, Lori Laughlin.

Annette and Frankie are married, in their 40's, live in Ohio, and have two children with behavioral problems. The pressures of selling Fords convinced Frankie that a Hawaiian vacation is in order to rekindle fond memories and romance. A wipeout in terms of plot, dialogue, and acting. Cameo appearances by Don Adams, Bob Denver, and Pee-Wee Herman add interest. Rated PG for language. 1987; 88m.

BAND WAGON, THE ★★★★

DIR: Vincente Minnelli. **CAST:** Fred Astaire, Cyd Charisse, Jack Buchanan, Nanette Fabray, Oscar Levant.

One of Vincente Minnelli's best grand-scale musicals and one of Fred Astaire's most endearing roles. He plays a Hollywood has-been who decides to try his luck on stage. This is the film that gave us "That's Entertainment." Unrated—family fare. 1953; 112m.

BARKLEYS OF BROADWAY, THE ★★★

DIR: Charles Walters. **CAST:** Fred Astaire, Ginger Rogers, Oscar Levant.

As a film team, Ginger Rogers and Fred Astaire parted in 1939. This final pairing, the result of Judy Garland's inability to make the picture, does not favorably compare with earlier efforts. Harry Warren's score, while augmented by a great George Gershwin number, is not up to snuff. Nevertheless, the film was a critical and commercial hit. 1949; 109m.

BARYSHNIKOV BY THARP ★★★★★
DIR: Don Mischer, Twyla Tharp. **CAST:** Mikhail Baryshnikov.
Twyla Tharp, one of the most imaginative and versatile choreographers in theatre, matches her best work here with three amazing ballets that feature brilliant dancing by Mikhail Baryshnikov. The Sinatra Suite, is the highlight. Baryshnikov is at his dazzling best. 1984; 60m.

BEACH BLANKET BINGO ★★½
DIR: William Asher. **CAST:** Frankie Avalon, Annette Funicello, Paul Lynde, Harvey Lembeck, Don Rickles, Linda Evans, Jody McCrea, Marta Kristen, John Ashley, Deborah Walley, Buster Keaton.
The fifth in the series, and the last true "Beach Party" film. Basically, it's the same old stuff: stars on their way up (Linda Evans) or on their way down (Buster Keaton) or at their peak (Frankie and Annette), spouting silly dialogue and singing through echo chambers. But it's one of the best of the series, whether you're laughing with it or at it. 1965; 98m.

BEACH BOYS: AN AMERICAN BAND, THE ★★½
DIR: Malcolm Leo. **CAST:** The Beach Boys, Al Jardine, Bruce Johnston, Mike Love.
Even the most fervent fans of the country's number-one surf group are likely to be a bit disappointed by this "authorized biography," directed by Malcolm Leo (*This Is Elvis*). It skims the surface of the band's troubled but ultimately triumphant history and only occasionally catches a wave. Rated G. 1984; 90m.

BEACH PARTY ★★½
DIR: William Asher. **CAST:** Robert Cummings, Dorothy Malone, Frankie Avalon, Annette Funicello, Harvey Lembeck, Jody McCrea, John Ashley, Morey Amsterdam.
Bob Cummings, a bearded, sheltered anthropologist, studies the wild dating and mating habits of beach-bound teens. He ends up courting Annette Funicello to make Frankie Avalon jealous. This orgy of silly 1960s slapstick is intermittently fun. Cummings has his moments, as does Harvey Lembeck, as the biker Eric Von Zipper. 1963; 101m.

BEAT STREET ★½
DIR: Stan Lathan. **CAST:** Rae Dawn Chong, Guy Davis.
A hackneyed plot, about kids breaking into show biz, and just-okay acting overpower the dancing and undermine the excitement in this disappointing musical. Rated PG for profanity and violence. 1984; 106m.

BELINDA LIVE ★★
DIR: L. A. Johnson. **CAST:** Belinda Carlisle, Susie Davis, Rick Boston, Donna Delory, Bekka Bramlett, Eric Pressly, Denny Fonghelser.
Belinda Carlisle bounded to the top with the giggly girl group, the Go Gos. Now solo, she's slimmer and slicker. Like a Stepford singer, she's pretty and precise, yet lifeless, lacking any range or humor. Even the crack band cannot compensate for Carlisle's weak voice. 1988; 60m.

BELLE OF NEW YORK, THE ★★
DIR: Charles Walters. **CAST:** Fred Astaire, Vera-Ellen, Marjorie Main, Keenan Wynn.
A fantasy set at the turn of the century, this frothy film was a box office failure about which, in his autobiography, Fred Astaire snaps: "The less said about it the better." Harry Warren's score—assembled from earlier hits—is terrific, though none of the songs have survived as standards. 1952; 82m.

BELLS ARE RINGING ★★
DIR: Vincente Minnelli. **CAST:** Judy Holliday, Dean Martin, Fred Clark, Eddie Foy Jr.

This filmed version of the Broadway musical pits answering-service operator Judy Holliday against Dean Martin in an on-again, off-again love circle. Nothing new or exciting story-wise here, but Fred Clark and Eddie Foy ham it up enough to hold your interest. 1960; 127m.

BERT RIGBY, YOU'RE A FOOL ★★★★

DIR: Carl Reiner. **CAST:** Robert Lindsay, Cathryn Bradshaw, Robbie Coltrane, Jackie Gayle, Anne Bancroft, Corbin Bernsen.

Musical-comedy star Robert Lindsay, who won a Tony for *Me and My Girl*, plays an English coal miner obsessed with the great musicals of Fred Astaire and Gene Kelly. When a strike is called at the mine, he decides to take a shot at making it as a song-and-dance man. Director Carl Reiner also scripted, and he is at the peak of his powers on both counts, for this is his best film to date. There is some profanity, but the R rating seems excessive. 1989; 94m.

BEST FOOT FORWARD ★★★½

DIR: Edward Buzzell. **CAST:** Lucille Ball, William Gaxton, Virginia Weidler, Tommy Dix, June Allyson, Nancy Walker, Gloria De Haven.

Film star Lucille Ball accepts military cadet Tommy Dix's invitation to his school's annual dance. The film introduced June Allyson and Nancy Walker and gave numerous high schools a fight song by adapting its biggest hit, "Buckle Down, Winsocki." Wholesome family fun. 1943; 95m.

BEST LITTLE WHOREHOUSE IN TEXAS, THE ★★★½

DIR: Colin Higgins. **CAST:** Burt Reynolds, Dolly Parton, Dom DeLuise, Charles Durning.

Dolly Parton and Burt Reynolds in a so-so version of the Broadway play, whose title explains all. Rated R for nudity, profanity, and sexual situations. 1982; 114m.

BIG BROTHER AND THE HOLDING COMPANY—BALL AND CHAIN ★★★½

DIR: Robert Zagone. **CAST:** Janis Joplin.

During this 1967 studio recording session, drummer David Gertz confides that Big Brother is a band of "primitive musicians." Indeed, no other group from San Francisco in the Summer of Love could claim as strong a singer and such weak musicianship. This intimate archival treasure shows Janis Joplin in full glory and the group in glorious psychedelic sloppiness. Unrated. 1989; B&W; 30m.

BIG TIME ★★★

DIR: Chris Blum. **CAST:** Tom Waits.

The eccentric, gritty, funny, and highly theatrical concert style of singer-songwriter Tom Waits has been captured on film in this quirky documentary. It's a colorful fantasia of dreamland dementia by the highly regarded cult singer. The man's style ranges from Howlin' Wolf to Lenny Bruce, which is a considerable spread indeed. Rated PG. 1988; 100m.

BIKINI BEACH ★★

DIR: William Asher. **CAST:** Frankie Avalon, Annette Funicello, Keenan Wynn, Don Rickles.

This silly film captures Frankie Avalon and Annette Funicello in their best swim attire. There are lots of girls in bikinis and some drag-racing for an added diversion. A group of kids who always hang out at the beach try to prevent a man from closing it. Ho-hum. 1964; 100m.

BIRD ★★★★½

DIR: Clint Eastwood. **CAST:** Forest Whitaker, Diane Venora, Samuel E. Wright, Keith David.

Clint Eastwood's *Bird* soars with a majesty all its own. About the life of legendary saxophonist Charlie "Bird" Parker, it is the ultimate jazz movie. It features Parker's inspired improvised solos in abundance, while telling the story of the brilliant but troubled and drug-addicted artist. Parker is solidly played by Forest Whitaker. Rated R for profanity and drug use. 1988; 140m.

BLACK TIGHTS ★★★½
DIR: Terence Young. **CAST:** Cyd Charisse, Zizi Jeanmaire, Moira Shearer, Roland Petit Dance Company.
There are several attractive performers in this British film that aficionados of dance should not miss: Cyd Charisse, Zizi Jeanmaire, and in her last film before retirement, Moira Shearer. It's a good film that even those who are not dance groupies might enjoy. The film is also known under the French title *Un, Deux, Trois, Quatre!* 1960; 140m.

BLUE HAWAII ★★★½
DIR: Norman Taurog. **CAST:** Elvis Presley, Joan Blackman, Angela Lansbury, Iris Adrian.
In this enjoyable Elvis Presley flick, the star plays a returning soldier who works with tourists against his mom's (Angela Lansbury) wishes. 1962; 101m.

BOB DYLAN WITH TOM PETTY AND THE HEARTBREAKERS—HARD TO HANDLE ★★★★
DIR: Gillian Armstrong. **CAST:** Bob Dylan, Tom Petty.
This sensational concert features an emotionally charged Bob Dylan at his hottest during a single show from his 1986 tour of Australia with Tom Petty. Dylan's solo acoustic versions of "It's Alright Ma (I'm Only Bleeding)" and "Girl from the North Country" are memorable. 1986; 60m.

BOBBY MCFERRIN SPONTANEOUS INVENTIONS ★★★★
DIR: Bud Schaetzle. **CAST:** Bobby McFerrin.
Solo is the most challenging stage test, yet Grammy-winner Bobby McFerrin turns Hollywood's Aquarius Theatre into his own living room. He pounds on chairs, uses the audience for background harmonies, and plays every part of his body. This is a rare case of blockbuster concert talent translating superbly to video. 1986; 48m.

BODY ROCK 🦃
DIR: Marcelo Epstein. **CAST:** Lorenzo Lamas, Vicki Frederick, Cameron Dye, Ray Sharkey.
A boring pop musical, this features Lorenzo Lamas as a youngster from the South Bronx who sees the break-dancing subculture as his ticket to the big time. Rated PG-13. 1984; 93m.

BOY FRIEND, THE ★★★
DIR: Ken Russell. **CAST:** Twiggy, Christopher Gable, Max Adrian, Tommy Tune, Glenda Jackson.
Ken Russell, at his least self-indulgent and most affectionate, provides a plucky parody of Twenties musicals. The inventiveness and opulence call to mind the work of Busby Berkeley. Twiggy's performance is engaging. Rated G. 1971; 110m.

BREAKIN' ★½
DIR: Joel Silberg. **CAST:** Lucinda Dickey, Adolfo Quinones, Michael Chambers, Ben Lokey.
The dancing scenes are wonderful but as a whole, *Breakin'* is pretty lame. Sort of *Flashdance* meets street break-dancing, the film would have us believe that jazz dancer Kelly (Lucinda Dickey) could hook up with street dancers Ozone ("Shabba-Do") and Turbo ("Boogaloo Shrimp") to win dance contests and finally break (no pun intended) into big-time show biz. Rated PG for profanity and violence. 1984; 90m.

BREAKIN' 2 ELECTRIC BOOGALOO ★★½
DIR: Sam Firstenberg. **CAST:** Lucinda Dickey, Adolfo Quinones, Michael Chambers.
This sometimes exhilarating break-dancing movie is better than the original. This time, instead of trying to break into show business, Kelly (Lucinda Dickey), Ozone (Adolfo "Shabba-Doo" Quinones), and Turbo

(Michael "Boogaloo Shrimp" Chambers) put on a show to save a local arts center for children. Rated PG for brief violence and suggested sex. 1984; 90m.

BREAKING GLASS ★★½

DIR: Brian Gibson. **CAST:** Phil Daniels, Hazel O'Connor, Jon Finch, Jonathan Pryce.

British film about a New Wave singer's rise to the top, at the expense of personal relationships. Hazel O'Connor's heavy music isn't for all tastes, and the plot line is as old as film itself, but the actors are sincere, and the film contains some striking visual imagery. Rated PG. 1980; 104m.

BREAKING THE ICE ★½

DIR: Eddie Cline. **CAST:** Bobby Breen, Charlie Ruggles, Dolores Costello, Billy Gilbert, Margaret Hamilton.

In this improbable meld of music and ice skating, Bobby Breen ducks out on his Pennsylvania Dutch family, gets a job singing at a Philadelphia rink, and meets skating moppet Irene Dare. Not a turkey, but close. 1938; B&W; 79m.

BRIGADOON ★★★★

DIR: Vincente Minnelli. **CAST:** Gene Kelly, Van Johnson, Cyd Charisse, Elaine Stewart, Barry Jones.

This enchanting musical stars Van Johnson and Gene Kelly as two Americans who discover Brigadoon, a Scottish village with a lifespan of only one day for every hundred years. In the village, Kelly meets Cyd Charisse, and they naturally dance up a storm. 1954; 108m.

BRING ON THE NIGHT ★

DIR: Michael Apted. **CAST:** Sting, Omar Hakim, Darryl Jones, Kenny Kirkland, Branford Marsalis.

Obnoxious, self-serving documentary about popular rock star Sting (formerly of The Police) and the formation of his new band. The first three-quarters of the film features nothing more than a few rehearsal sessions and far too much of Sting talking about Sting, followed by a live concert finale which is intercut with unnecessary scenes of his son being born. Rated PG-13 for the birth scene. 1985; 97m.

BROADWAY MELODY OF 1936 ★★★

DIR: Roy Del Ruth. **CAST:** Jack Benny, Eleanor Powell, Robert Taylor, Una Merkel, Buddy Ebsen.

Backstage musical comedy. Obnoxious gossip columnist Jack Benny tries to use dancer Eleanor Powell to harass producer Robert Taylor. Forget the plot and enjoy the singing and dancing—including Taylor's rendition of "I've Got a Feelin' You're Foolin'," the only time he sang onscreen in his own voice. 1935; B&W; 110m.

BROADWAY MELODY OF 1938 ★★½

DIR: Roy Del Ruth. **CAST:** Robert Taylor, Eleanor Powell, George Murphy, Binnie Barnes, Sophie Tucker, Judy Garland, Buddy Ebsen, Willie Howard, Billy Gilbert.

Fifteen-year-old Judy Garland stops the show in this tuneful musical anthology when she sings the now legendary "Dear Mr. Gable" version of "You Made Me Love You." The finale stretches credibility until it snaps as Eleanor Powell, in top hat and tails, dances with a division of chorus boys before a neon skyline. 1937; B&W; 110m.

BROADWAY MELODY OF 1940 ★★★

DIR: Norman Taurog. **CAST:** Fred Astaire, Eleanor Powell, George Murphy, Frank Morgan, Ian Hunter.

Fine performances redeem this otherwise tired tale of friendship and professional rivalry between dancing partners. The dancing of course, is flawless; the Cole Porter songs are outstanding. 1940; B&W; 102m.

BRUCE SPRINGSTEEN VIDEO ANTHOLOGY/1978–88 ★★★★
DIR: John Sayles, Arthur Rosato, Meiert Avis, Carol Dodds, Arnold Levine, Brian De Palma. **CAST:** Bruce Springsteen, Nils Lofgren, Miami Steve Van Zandt, Clarence Clemons.

Bruce Springsteen is the total rock performer: inexhaustable, devoted, and utterly sincere. The concert footage catches him in intimate settings, while the video clips, of equally high quality, focus attention on the idealistic and romantic nature of his introspective compositions. On the downside, this eighteen-song package contains little archival material other than the poorly produced "Rosalita" from 1978. 1989; 100m.

BUDDY HOLLY STORY, THE ★★★★½
DIR: Steve Rash. **CAST:** Gary Busey, Don Stroud, Charles Martin Smith, Dick O'Neil.

Gary Busey's outstanding performance as Buddy Holly makes this one of the few great rock 'n' roll movies. Not only does he convincingly embody the legend from Lubbock, Texas, he also sings Holly's songs—including "That'll Be the Day," "Not Fade Away," and "It's So Easy"—with style and conviction. Backed by Don Stroud and Charles Martin Smith, who also play and sing impressively. Rated PG. 1978; 114m.

BYE BYE BIRDIE ★★★
DIR: George Sidney. **CAST:** Dick Van Dyke, Ann-Margret, Janet Leigh, Paul Lynde, Bobby Rydell.

A rock star's approaching appearance in a small town turns several lives upside down in this pleasant musical comedy. Based on the successful Broadway play, this is pretty lightweight stuff, but a likable cast and good production numbers make it worthwhile. No rating; okay for the whole family. 1963; 112m.

CABARET ★★★★½
DIR: Bob Fosse. **CAST:** Liza Minnelli, Michael York, Helmut Griem, Joel Grey.

This classic musical-drama takes place in Germany in 1931. The Nazi party has not yet assumed complete control, and the local cabaret unfolds the story of two young lovers, the ensuing mood of the country, and the universal touch of humanity. Everything is handled with taste—bisexual encounters, the horrors of the Nazi regime, and the bawdy entertainment of the nightclub. "Host" Joel Grey is brilliant. Michael York and Liza Minnelli are first-rate. So is the movie. Rated PG. 1972; 128m.

CALAMITY JANE (1953) ★★★
DIR: David Butler. **CAST:** Doris Day, Howard Keel, Allyn Ann McLerie, Philip Carey.

A legend of the Old West set to music for Doris Day, who mends her rootin', tootin' ways in order to lasso Howard Keel. The song "Secret Love" copped an Oscar. Cute 'n' perky. 1953; 101m.

CAMELOT ★★★
DIR: Joshua Logan. **CAST:** Richard Harris, Vanessa Redgrave, Franco Nero, David Hemmings, Lionel Jeffries.

The legend of King Arthur and the Round Table—from the first meeting of Arthur (Richard Harris) and Guinevere (Vanessa Redgrave) to the affair between Guinevere and Lancelot (Franco Nero), and finally the fall of Camelot—is brought to life in this enjoyable musical. 1967; 178m.

CAN-CAN ★★★
DIR: Walter Lang. **CAST:** Shirley MacLaine, Frank Sinatra, Maurice Chevalier, Juliet Prowse, Louis Jourdan.

Frank Sinatra plays an 1890's French attorney defending Shirley MacLaine's right to perform the risqué can-can in a Parisian nightclub. There's a lot of energy put into the production numbers by the dancers and peripheral performers, but the stars appear, at times, to be walking through their roles. Cole Porter songs include "I Love Paris," "C'est Magnifique" and the wonderful "Just One of Those Things." 1960; 131m.

CAN'T STOP THE MUSIC
DIR: Nancy Walker. **CAST:** The Village People, Valerie Perrine, Bruce Jenner, Steve Guttenberg, Paul Sand, Tammy Grimes, June Havoc, Jack Weston, Barbara Rush, Leigh Taylor-Young.
Despite the positive-thinking title, the music of the Village People ("Macho Man," "YMCA") was stopped cold by this basically awful musical about the world of show biz. The only thing happy about this irrepressibly sunny groaner are the members of the featured musical group, which has slipped into obscurity. Rated PG. 1980; 118m.

CAREFREE ★★★
DIR: Mark Sandrich. **CAST:** Fred Astaire, Ginger Rogers, Ralph Bellamy, Jack Carson.
In this blend of music, slapstick situations, and romantic byplay, Ginger Rogers is a crazy, mixed-up girl-child who goes to psychiatrist Fred Astaire for counsel. His treatment results in her falling in love with him. While trying to stop this, he falls in love with her. Of course they dance! It's more a Rogers film than an Astaire film, and more screwball comedy than musical. 1938; B&W; 80m.

CARNIVAL ROCK
DIR: Roger Corman. **CAST:** Susan Cabot, Dick Miller, Brian Hutton.
Laughable early effort of Roger Corman. This tedious tale about a nighclub and the people whose lives surround it offers little enjoyment. Great music, though, by the Platters and David Houston. 1958; 80m.

CATHERINE WHEEL, THE ★★★★★
DIR: Twyla Tharp. **CAST:** The Royal Ballet Company.
This is an astonishing dance piece about the symbolic self-destruction of man. It brings together celebrated choreographer Twyla Tharp and rock music composer David Byrne of Talking Heads for a unique brilliantly staged performance by the Royal Ballet Company. It features dancing of astonishing beauty and power. 1982; 90m.

CELEBRATING BIRD: THE TRIUMPH OF CHARLIE PARKER ★★★★
DIR: Gary Giddins, Kendrick Simmons. **CAST:** Charlie Parker.
Fascinating documentary that chronicles jazz legend Charlie Parker's career through interviews and live performances. Parker, nicknamed Bird, created a new style of jazz before his untimely death at 34. Other jazz greats—Dizzy Gillespie, Charles Mingus, and Thelonius Monk—add to the pleasure. 1987; 58m.

CHICK COREA AND GARY BURTON LIVE IN TOKYO ★★★★
DIR: Yatsusune Kikuchi. **CAST:** Chick Corea, Gary Burton.
Celebrated jazz pianist Chick Corea and vibist Gary Burton will simply amaze you with their extraordinary musical gifts in this impressive concert from 1982. These two gifted masters breeze through complex arrangements that shift in mood from bebop to Latin grooves. 1985; 60m.

CHOCOLATE SOLDIER, THE ★★
DIR: Roy Del Ruth. **CAST:** Nelson Eddy, Rise Stevens, Florence Bates, Nigel Bruce.
Nelson Eddy and Rise Stevens play husband and wife opera stars whose marriage is skidding in this clever, winning remake of the Lunt-Fontanne hit, *The Guardsman*. Delightful. 1941; B&W; 102m.

CHORUS LINE, A ★★★★
DIR: Richard Attenborough. **CAST:** Michael Douglas, Alyson Reed, Terrence Mann, Audrey Landers, Jan Gan Boyd.

The screen version of Michael Bennett's hit Broadway musical allows the viewer to experience the anxiety, struggle, and triumph of a group of dancers auditioning for a stage production. Director Richard Attenborough gracefully blends big production numbers with intimate moments. Rated PG for profanity and sexual descriptions. 1985; 120m.

CHUCK BERRY HAIL! HAIL! ROCK 'N' ROLL ★★★★★
DIR: Taylor Hackford. **CAST:** Chuck Berry, Keith Richards, Bo Diddley, Little Richard, Eric Clapton, Linda Ronstadt, Johnnie Johnson.
Put simply, this is the greatest rock 'n' roll concert movie ever made. Anyone who has ever kissed, danced, or just tapped feet to the classic songs written by Chuck Berry will love it. They're all here: "Maybellene," "Roll Over Beethoven," "Memphis," "Nadine," "No Particular Place to Go"...Keith Richards, Eric Clapton, Julian Lennon, and Linda Ronstadt are just some of the singers and players who back Berry during his sixtieth-birthday-tribute concert at St. Louis's Fox Theatre. 1987; 120m.

CINDERELLA (1964) ★★★
DIR: Charles S. Dubin. **CAST:** Lesley Ann Warren, Stuart Damon, Ginger Rogers, Walter Pidgeon, Celeste Holm.
This film is a reworking of the live 1957 CBS broadcast of the Rodgers and Hammerstein musical that featured the young Julie Andrews. The score is unchanged with the exception of an additional "Loneliness of Evening," which had been cut from *South Pacific*. A charming show for the entire family. 1964; 100m.

CINDERFELLA ★
DIR: Frank Tashlin. **CAST:** Jerry Lewis, Anna Maria Alberghetti, Ed Wynn.
This musical version of the oft-told fairy tale has little to recommend it. Adapted for the talents of star Jerry Lewis, it has no laughs to speak of and will only appeal to his fans. 1960; 91m.

CLAMBAKE ★★★
DIR: Arthur H. Nadel. **CAST:** Elvis Presley, Shelley Fabares, Will Hutchins, Bill Bixby, Gary Merrill, James Gregory.
This typical Elvis Presley musical romance has a *Prince and the Pauper* scenario. Elvis, an oil baron's son, trades places with Will Hutchins, a penniless water-ski instructor, in order to find a girl who'll love him for himself and not his money. When Elvis falls for a gold-digging Shelley Fabares, he must compete with Bill Bixby, the playboy speedboat racer. 1967; 100m.

COAL MINER'S DAUGHTER ★★★★½
DIR: Michael Apted. **CAST:** Sissy Spacek, Tommy Lee Jones, Beverly D'Angelo, Levon Helm.
Sissy Spacek gives a superb, totally believable performance in this film biography of country singer Loretta Lynn. The title role takes Spacek from Lynn's impoverished Appalachian childhood through marriage at thirteen up to her mid-thirties and reign as the "First Lady of Country Music." Rated PG. 1980; 125m.

COLOR ME BARBRA ★★
DIR: Dwight Hemion. **CAST:** Barbra Streisand.
Color Me Barbra, Streisand's second TV special, doesn't hold a candle to her first, *My Name Is Barbra*. The song selections can't compare and the skits aren't nearly as funny. 1966; 60m.

COMEBACK ★★★½
DIR: Christel Buschmann. **CAST:** Eric Burdon.
Real-life rock singer Eric Burdon (lead singer of the Animals) stars in this rock 'n' roll drama. Burdon plays a part that mirrors his own life: that of a white blues singer trying to get back on top. 1982; 96m.

COMPLEAT BEATLES, THE ★★★★

DIR: Patrick Montgomery. **CAST:** Malcolm McDowell, The Beatles.

Even experts on the life and times of the Fab Four are likely to find something new and enlightening in *The Compleat Beatles.* Furthermore, while not a consistent work, this film provides something of interest for fans and non-fans. 1982; 119m.

CROSSOVER DREAMS ★★★★

DIR: Leon Ichaso. **CAST:** Rubén Blades, Shawn Elliot, Elizabeth Peña, Tom Signorelli, Frank Robles.

Rubén Blades plays a popular Latino musician who tries his talents at the big time. The price he pays for his efforts is high. And while this may all sound like one big movie cliché, it's now time to add that the cast put in performances that redefine the story, giving this trite tale a bite that will surprise the viewer, who may expect nothing but music and laughs. 1985; 85m.

CROSSROADS ★★★½

DIR: Walter Hill. **CAST:** Ralph Macchio, Joe Seneca, Jami Gertz, Joe Morton, Dennis Lipscomb, Harry Carey Jr.

A superb blues score by guitarist Ry Cooder highlights this enjoyable fantasy about an ambitious young bluesman (Ralph Macchio) who "goes down to the crossroads," in the words of Robert Johnson, to make a deal with the devil for fame and fortune. Most viewers will enjoy the performances, the story, and the music in this all-too-rare big-screen celebration of the blues and its mythology. Rated R for profanity, suggested sex, and violence. 1986; 105m.

CURE IN ORANGE, THE ★

DIR: Tim Pope. **CAST:** Robert Smith, Simon Gallup, Pol Thompson, Boris Williams.

To many, the Cure sounds droning, repetitive, and largely lifeless, but fans feel primal power in the spare instrumentation and lack of melody. Perhaps someday this bleak, black and white band will warrant a big-screen revue, but even fans will be tested by this dreary, nearly two-hour concert film, shot almost straight ahead, with no visual diversions. 1987; 113m.

CURLY TOP ★★★

DIR: Irving Cummings. **CAST:** Shirley Temple, John Boles, Rochelle Hudson, Jane Darwell, Arthur Treacher.

Millionaire songwriter John Boles adopts moppet Shirley Temple who plays matchmaker when he falls in love with her sister Rochelle Hudson. Almost too-cute Shirley sings "Animal Crackers in My Soup." Arthur Treacher provides his usual droll humor. 1935; B&W; 74m.

CYNDI LAUPER IN PARIS ★★★½

DIR: Andy Morahan. **CAST:** Cyndi Lauper, Rick Derringer.

Whatever little Cyndi Lauper lacks in voice, she makes up in stage presence and energy. The Parisian audience is enthusiastic, the crack band features guitarist Rick Derringer, the sound is hi-fi stereo, and the visuals are exciting as Lauper romps through a fast-paced rendition of all her hits. 1987; 90m.

DAMES ★★★

DIR: Ray Enright. **CAST:** Joan Blondell, Dick Powell, Ruby Keeler, ZaSu Pitts, Guy Kibbee, Hugh Herbert.

Music, songs, dancing, great Busby Berkeley production numbers. Plot? Know the one about backing a Broadway musical? But, gee, it's fun to see and hear Joan Blondell, Dick Powell, Ruby Keeler, ZaSu Pitts, Guy Kibbee, and Hugh "Woo-woo" Herbert again. 1934; B&W; 90m.

DAMN YANKEES ★★★½

DIR: George Abbott, Stanley Donen. **CAST:** Gwen Verdon, Ray Walston, Tab Hunter.

A torrid, wiggling vamp teams with a sly, hissing Devil to frame the Yankees by turning a middle-aged baseball fan into a wunderkind and planting him on the team. Gwen Verdon is sensational as the temptress Lola, who gets whatever she wants. Hollywood called on her to reprise her role in the original Broadway musical hit. Lots of pep and zing in this one. 1958; 110m.

DAMSEL IN DISTRESS, A ★★★
DIR: George Stevens. **CAST:** Fred Astaire, Joan Fontaine, Gracie Allen, George Burns, Constance Collier, Reginald Gardiner.
By choice, Fred Astaire made this one without Ginger, who complemented him, but with Joan Fontaine—then a beginner—who did not, and who could not dance. Fred's an American popular composer in stuffy London. He mistakenly thinks heiress Joan is a chorus girl. 1937; B&W; 98m.

DANCE HALL ★½
DIR: Irving Pichel. **CAST:** Carole Landis, Cesar Romero, William Henry, June Storey.
This is a minor musical about a nightclub owner (Cesar Romero) who falls in love with one of his employees (Carole Landis). Not great. The cast saves this film from being a dud. 1941; B&W; 74m.

DANCE ON FIRE ★★★
DIR: Ray Manzarek. **CAST:** The Doors.
Doors leader Jim Morrison is captivating as the focal point in *Dance on Fire,* which succeeds in succinctly portraying one of the 1960s' top rock groups. A combination of Elektra Records promotional clips, new videos, TV-show appearances, and concert footage. The hi-fi stereo sound is outstanding, having been digitally mastered and mixed from the original master tapes. 1985; 65m.

DANCING LADY ★★★
DIR: Robert Z. Leonard. **CAST:** Joan Crawford, Clark Gable, Fred Astaire, Franchot Tone, May Robson, Grant Mitchell, Sterling Holloway, Ted Healy, The Three Stooges.
Joan Crawford goes from burlesque dancer to Broadway star in this backstage drama set to music. A good film, this was also one of her early moneymakers. Fred Astaire made his screen debut in one dance number. 1933; B&W; 94m.

DANGEROUS WHEN WET ★★
DIR: Charles Walters. **CAST:** Esther Williams, Fernando Lamas, Jack Carson, Charlotte Greenwood, Denise Darcel.
Fame and fortune await she who swims the English Channel. Esther Williams plays a corn-fed wholesome who goes for it, Fernando Lamas cheers her on. Semi-sour Jack Carson and high-kicking Charlotte Greenwood clown. Good music and a novel underwater Tom and Jerry cartoon sequence. 1953; 95m.

DATE WITH JUDY, A ★★½
DIR: Richard Thorpe. **CAST:** Jane Powell, Wallace Beery, Elizabeth Taylor, Carmen Miranda, Robert Stack, Xavier Cugat, Scotty Beckett, Leon Ames.
Ho-hum musical comedy about rival teenagers Jane Powell and Elizabeth Taylor fighting for the affections of Robert Stack. High point is Carmen Miranda teaching Wallace Beery to dance. 1948; 113m.

DAVID BOWIE—GLASS SPIDER ★★★
DIR: David Mallet. **CAST:** David Bowie, Peter Frampton, Carlos Alomar, Charlie Sexton.
This David Bowie concert was taped in 1987 in London and features guitarist-song-writer Peter Frampton in a lavishly staged event directed by David Mallet (who was responsible for the music video of "China Girl," "Ashes to Ashes" and "Loving the Alien"). Unfortunately, Bowie displays very little energy and drama in his performance and the band lacks the punch of earlier groups. Songs include "Day In Day Out," "Jean Genie," "Rebel-Rebel," "Modern Love," and "Heroes." 1988; 112m.

DAVID BOWIE—SERIOUS MOONLIGHT ★★★★

DIR: David Mallet. **CAST:** David Bowie, Carlos Alomar, Carmine Rojas, Frank Simms, George Simms, Earl Slick.

David Bowie, rock's most enigmatic and commanding performer is in top form as he slams into his best-known songs during his 1983 world tour. He is backed by a sizzling band in this electrifying concert that features some brilliant theatrical staging and highly imaginative video location direction by David Mallet. Songs included in this program are: "Golden Years," "Life on Mars," "Ashes to Ashes," and "Space Oddity." 1984; 90m.

DEAD KENNEDYS VIDEO DOCUMENTARY ★½

DIR: Dirk Dirksen. **CAST:** Jello Biafra, the Dead Kennedys.

The Dead Kennedys always claimed more mileage from poses, politics, and publicity than from the lame melodies and Jello Biafra's monotonous vocals. Yet the Kennedys were a competent band and this concert film shows the excitement of the punk performance at the closing night of San Francisco's landmark Mabuhay Gardens Club. 1986; 25m.

DEADMAN'S CURVE ★★★

DIR: Richard Compton. **CAST:** Richard Hatch, Bruce Davison, Pamela Bellwood, Susan Sullivan, Dick Clark, Wolfman Jack.

This made-for-TV biopic recounts the true story of Fifties rock stars Jan and Dean. An endearing sense of humor and their engaging surf sound propels them to the top. Then a near-fatal auto accident brings their career to a screeching halt. Courageously, they battle back. Richard Hatch and Bruce Davison deliver strong performances as Jan Berry and Dean Torrence. The use of Jan and Dean's original hits adds spark to the film. 1978; 100m.

DEEP IN MY HEART ★★

DIR: Stanley Donen. **CAST:** José Ferrer, Merle Oberon, Paul Henreid, Walter Pidgeon, Helen Traubel.

Most of the films presenting the lives of great composers have been tepid and silly. This biography of Sigmund Romberg is no exception. The songs are wonderful, but the rest is pure drivel. Along the way, Gene Kelly, Tony Martin, and Ann Miller drop by for brief musical visits, and that's it. Only fair. 1954; 132m.

DIMPLES ★★★

DIR: William A. Seiter. **CAST:** Shirley Temple, Frank Morgan, Helen Westley, Stepin Fetchit, John Carradine.

Dimpled darling Shirley Temple tries to care for her lovable rogue grandfather Frank Morgan, a street pickpocket who works the crowds she gathers with her singing and dancing. A rich patron takes her in hand, gets her off the street, and on the stage. 1936; B&W; 79m.

DIPLOMANIACS ★★½

DIR: William A. Seiter. **CAST:** Bert Wheeler, Robert Woolsey, Marjorie White, Hugh Herbert, Louis Calhern, Edgar Kennedy.

In this preposterous romp, Bert Wheeler and Robert Woolsey play Indian-reservation barbers sent to a peace convention in Switzerland. This is a musical comedy, so don't expect too much plot. Hugh Herbert is a delight. Woo-woo! 1933; B&W; 63m.

DIRTY DANCING ★★★★

DIR: Emile Ardolino. **CAST:** Jennifer Grey, Patrick Swayze, Cynthia Rhodes, Jerry Orbach, Jack Weston.

A surprise hit. Jennifer Grey stars as a teenager poised at the verge of adulthood in the early Sixties. She accompanies her family on a Catskills vacation and meets up with rhythm-and-blues in the form of dancers Patrick Swayze and Cynthia Rhodes. This coming-of-age tale contains nothing new, but the players present the material with exuberant energy.

Rated PG-13 for language and sexual themes. 1987; 97m.

DISORDERLIES ★
DIR: Michael Schultz. **CAST:** The Fat Boys, Tony Plana, Ralph Bellamy, Anthony Geary.

Ralph Bellamy and a few rap songs by The Fat Boys are all there is to recommend this embarrassingly bad film. A total waste of Bellamy's talents, and hopefully the last movie the flash-in-the-pan noisemakers will ever appear in. Rated PG. 1987; 87m.

DIVINE MADNESS ★★★½
DIR: Michael Ritchie. **CAST:** Bette Midler.

Here's the sassy, unpredictable Bette Midler as captured in concert by director Michael Ritchie. Some of it is great; some of it is not. It helps if you're a Midler fan. Rated R for profanity. 1980; 95m.

DIXIE JAMBOREE ★
DIR: Christy Cabanne. **CAST:** Guy Kibbee, Lyle Talbot, Eddie Quillan, Frances Langford, Fifi D'Orsay, Charles Butterworth.

Another B movie from lowly PRC Studios. The action takes place on the showboat *Ellabella* and the characters range from con men and lizard oil salesmen to various musicians and roustabouts. Not a total disaster, but it rides a fine line. 1945; B&W; 80m.

DIZZY GILLESPIE IN REDONDO BEACH ★★★★
DIR: Stanley Dorfman. **CAST:** Dizzy Gillespie.

One of the early trumpet masters of bebop jazz, Dizzy Gillespie has lost none of his touch in this spicy performance taped in Redondo Beach in 1981. Dizzy sails through a hot set of music that combines elements of Latin and bebop. 1986; 60m.

DR. JEKYLL AND MR. HYDE (1973) ★
DIR: David Winters. **CAST:** Kirk Douglas, Susan George, Stanley Holloway, Michael Redgrave, Donald Pleasence.

Kirk Douglas stars in this major misfire, a made-for-television musical based on Robert Louis Stevenson's classic tale of good and evil. It simply does not work on any level. 1973; 90m.

DOGS IN SPACE ★★
DIR: Richard Lowenstein. **CAST:** Michael Hutchence, Saskia Post, Chris Haywood.

Michael Hutchence, the lead singer of the Australian rock group INXS, stars in this film about the pop culture in Melbourne in 1978. Not unlike the druggy, hippie Haight-Ashbury scene, this is a trip through the sexually permissive commune that merely serves as a setting for the singing performances of Hutchence. This is really only for the enjoyment of his fans and not the general public. 1988; 109m.

DOLL FACE ★★★
DIR: Lewis Seiler. **CAST:** Vivian Blaine, Dennis O'Keefe, Perry Como, Carmen Miranda.

"Hubba Hubba Hubba." That's the song that launched Perry Como, and it was in this movie that it was first sung. Vivian Blaine is fine as a burlesque dancer who shoots to the top with the help of her boyfriend. It's one of those nice, often overlooked movies. 1945; B&W; 80m.

DON'T LOOK BACK ★★★
DIR: D. A. Pennebaker. **CAST:** Bob Dylan, Joan Baez, Donovan, Alan Price.

A documentary account directed by D. A. Pennebaker of folk singer/poet ("guitarist," he calls himself) Bob Dylan on a 1965 tour of England. The tedium of travel and pressures of performing are eased by relaxing moments with fellow travelers Joan Baez, Alan Price, and (briefly) Donovan. Shot in striking black and white, with excellent sound quality. Unrated, it contains some vulgarity. 1967; B&W; 96m.

DOORS: A TRIBUTE TO JIM MORRISON, THE ★★½
DIR: Ray Manzarek. **CAST:** Jim Morrison and The Doors.

The life of Jim Morrison, rock's dark visionary poet of the prepsychedelic Sixties gets a complete review through interviews, live performances, and conceptual footage in this fascinating music profile. But unless you're a die hard Doors fan, this hour-long journey through the music of Morrison and Ray Manzarek could seem excessive. The songs include "The End," "Moonlight Drive," "Touch Me," "When the Music's Over," and "Unknown Soldier." 1988; 60m.

DOUBLE TROUBLE ★½
DIR: Norman Taurog. **CAST:** Elvis Presley, Annette Day.

Typical Elvis Presley musical. This time he plays a rock 'n' roll singer touring England. When a teenage heiress (whose life is constantly threatened) falls for him, he gets caught up in the action. 1967; 92m.

DU BARRY WAS A LADY ★★½
DIR: Roy Del Ruth. **CAST:** Red Skelton, Lucille Ball, Gene Kelly, Zero Mostel, Virginia O'Brien, Donald Meek, Louise Beavers, Tommy Dorsey.

Despite the incredible collection of talent showcased in this film, the result is a slow-moving adaptation of a popular stage hit minus most of the music that made it popular in the first place. Set in the court of Louis XIV, this musical romp gives Red Skelton a chance to mug and Gene Kelly a chance to dance. 1943; 101m.

DU-BEAT-E-O ★★
DIR: Alan Sacks. **CAST:** Ray Sharkey, Derf Scratch.

More of a pastiche than a feature movie, *du-BEAT-e-o* has the air of something thrown together by a bunch of guys goofing around in a film-editing room. (Indeed, much of the movie's narration consists simply of random comments by some of the crew sitting around watching it.) The skeleton plot has underground L.A. filmmaker Dubeateo (Ray Sharkey) and his editor (Derf Scratch of the punk band Fear) trying to turn some scattered footage of rocker Joan Jett into a movie. Unrated, there is nudity and profanity. 1984; 84m.

DUKE ELLINGTON STORY, THE ★★★★
DIR: Various. **CAST:** Duke Ellington.

Jazz legend Duke Ellington is well captured in this film compilation. The composer-pianist is seen in a 1962 TV special, "Good Year Jazz," a 1930 musical *Tan and Black*, and in a concert at the Côte d'Azur in 1966. 1980; B&W; 86m.

EARTH GIRLS ARE EASY ★★★½
DIR: Julien Temple. **CAST:** Geena Davis, Jeff Goldblum, Julie Brown, Jim Carrey, Damon Wayans, Michael McKean, Charles Rocket.

A wacky but consistently funny musical comedy, *Earth Girls* is based on the bizarre premise of some extraterrestrial visitors crash-landing in the swimming pool behind Valley girl Geena Davis's house. Davis and friend Julie Brown decide to shave the hairy intruders, discover they are hunks, and embark on a California adventure to acquaint the visitors with the L.A. lifestyle. Rated PG for mild profanity. 1989; 100m.

EASTER PARADE ★★★★
DIR: Charles Walters. **CAST:** Judy Garland, Fred Astaire, Peter Lawford, Jules Munshin, Ann Miller.

Judy Garland and Fred Astaire team up for this thoroughly enjoyable musical. Irving Berlin provided the songs for the story, about Astaire trying to forget ex–dance partner Ann Miller as he rises to the top with Garland. The result is an always watchable—and repeatable—treat. 1948; 104m.

EASY COME, EASY GO ★★
DIR: John Rich. **CAST:** Elvis Presley, Elsa Lanchester, Dodie Marshal, Pat Priest.

For Elvis Presley fans, only. Elvis sings some snappy songs, but the plot is not going to be filed under great scripts—our star is a frogman searching for treasure on behalf of the United States Navy. 1967; 95m.

EASY TO LOVE ★★½
DIR: Charles Walters. **CAST:** Esther Williams, Tony Martin, Van Johnson, Carroll Baker, John Bromfield.
Tony Martin and Van Johnson vie for the love of mermaid Esther Williams in this most lavish of her numerous water spectacles. A toe-curling, high-speed sequence performed on water skis tops the Busby Berkeley numbers staged in lush Cypress Gardens at Winter Haven, Florida. 1953; 96m.

EDDIE AND THE CRUISERS ★★★½
DIR: Martin Davidson. **CAST:** Tom Berenger, Michael Paré, Ellen Barkin.
Long after his death, rock 'n' roll singer Eddie Wilson's (Michael Paré) songs become popular all over again. This revives interest in a long-shelved concept album. The tape for it has been stolen, and it's up to Wilson's one-time songwriting collaborator (Tom Berenger) to find them. Only trouble is, other people want the tapes, too, and they may be willing to kill to get them. The songs are great! Rated PG. 1983; 92m.

ELEPHANT PARTS ★★★½
DIR: William Dear. **CAST:** Mike Nesmith, Jonathan Nesmith, Bill Martin.
Mike Nesmith, formerly of The Monkees, is surprisingly versatile and talented in this video record. He sings five songs; especially memorable is "Tonight Is Magic," which dramatizes the romance of a roller-skating waitress at a hamburger stand. Between songs, Nesmith presents several funny spoofs. 1981; 60m.

ELVIS '56 ★★★★
DIR: Alan Raymond, Susan Raymond. **CAST:** Documentary.
Impressive documentary traces the evolution of Elvis Presley from naïve teenage rocker to jaded superstar—all in the space of one year. Narrated by Levon Helm (of the Band), the film uses television appearances, newsreel footage, publicity stills, and recordings to re-create the pivotal year in Elvis's career and life. 1987; 60m.

ELVIS AND ME ★
DIR: Larry Peerce. **CAST:** Dale Midkiff, Susan Walters, Billy Green Bush.
Originally a TV miniseries, this film version of Priscilla Presley's biography is disturbingly one-sided. As played by Susan Walters, Priscilla appears incredibly naïve, then manipulated, then put upon, and then finally triumphantly mature and free of Elvis, who—throughout the film—is made to look foolish, strange, and unable to deal with life. If you admire the King, avoid this sudsy desecration of his legend. 1988; 192m.

ERIC CLAPTON AND FRIENDS ★★★
DIR: Gavin Taylor. **CAST:** Eric Clapton, Phil Collins, Nathan East, Greg Phillinganes.
While the song selection is a marvelous blend of old and new, the playing is decidedly stale. E.C. and his buddies look and sound like road-weary rockers waiting for the end of the tour. But Clapton is still Clapton and until he forgets how to play that Stratocaster, he is worth seeing. 1986; 60m.

EUBIE! ★★★★
DIR: Julianne Boyd. **CAST:** Gregory Hines, Terri Burrell, Maurice Hines, Leslie Dockery.
Originally a Broadway tribute to legendary composer Eubie Blake, this is nonstop song, dance, and vaudeville entertainment. Gregory Hines and Maurice Hines are outstanding with their toe-stomping tap routines. About twenty of Blake's tunes are performed on this tape—including "I'm Just Wild About Harry," "I've Got the Low Down Blues," and "In Honeysuckle Time." Unrated. 1981; 85m.

EURYTHMICS LIVE, THE ★★★★
DIR: Geoff Wonfor. **CAST:** Annie Lennox, Dave Stewart, Patrick Seymour, Chucho Merchan, Jimmy Z' Zavala, Joniece Jamison.

Annie Lennox and Dave Stewart demonstrate their raw dynamic stage presence in this concert filmed during their 1987 tour in Australia. They are backed by some outstanding musicians who manage to create a high-energy performance. Songs include "Here Comes the Rain Again," "Sex Crime," "Missionary Man," "When Tomorrow Comes," and "There Must Be an Angel." 1988; 90m.

EURYTHMICS SAVAGE ★★½
DIR: Sophie Muller. **CAST:** Annie Lennox, Dave Stewart.

This video interpretation of the Eurythmics' album *Savage* has no concept or theme to connect the songs. The focus wisely moves to Annie Lennox, a striking singer who shows her sexy moves in a variety of settings. Her chameleonlike ability to adopt guises and personas almost carries the show. 1988; 52m.

EVENING WITH MARLENE DIETRICH, AN ★★★
DIR: Not credited. **CAST:** Marlene Dietrich.

The legendary Marlene Dietrich is captured in this unique concert, filmed in 1972 for British television at the New London Theatre. Performing here at 71, Dietrich still has the charismatic grace and eloquence that dazzled audiences for over four decades. This concert, her last performance before a live audience, will be a treat for her most devoted fans. 1988; 50m.

EVENING WITH RAY CHARLES, AN ★★★★
DIR: John Blanchard. **CAST:** Ray Charles.

In this superb event shot for British TV at the Jubilee Auditorium in Edmonton, Alberta, Ray Charles proves once again why he is the living definition of soul. This excellent show captures this gifted musical legend at his best. 1983; 50m.

FABULOUS DORSEYS, THE ★★
DIR: Alfred E. Green. **CAST:** Tommy Dorsey, Jimmy Dorsey, Janet Blair, William Lundigan, Paul Whiteman.

A mildly musical, plotless dual biography of the Dorsey brothers as they fight their way to the top while fighting with each other, trombone and clarinet at the ready. Janet Blair is cute, William Lundigan is personable, and Paul "Pops" Whiteman is along for the ride. 1947; B&W; 88m.

FABULOUS THUNDERBIRDS LIVE FROM LONDON, THE ★★★
DIR: Phillip Goodhand-Tait. **CAST:** Kim Wilson, Jimmie Vaughan, Fran Christina, Preston Hubbard.

These rocking bluesmen offer few frills, just solid, straight-ahead, smoking songs. Likewise, this concert video is an unpretentious showcase of a scorching show. Singer and harmonica player Kim Wilson is in hot form, but the best reason to rent this tape is for all of the close-ups of guitarist Jimmie Vaughan's nifty licks. 1985; 60m.

FAIRPORT CONVENTION—IT ALL COMES 'ROUND AGAIN ★★★★
DIR: Paul Kovit. **CAST:** Sandy Denny, Jerry Donahue, Ashley Hutchings, Martin Lamble, Trevor Lucas, Dave Mattacks, Richard Thompson, June Tabor, Dave Swarbrick.

This highly engaging music documentary traces the British folk rock band from 1968 to 1987. Some of Britain's finest musical talents have come together over the years to form various groups that have made this traveling musical feast one of the United Kingdom's most important bands. 1987; 110m.

FAME ★★★½
DIR: Alan Parker. **CAST:** Irene Cara, Lee Curreri, Eddie Barth, Laura Dean, Paul McCrane, Barry Miller, Gene Anthony Ray, Maureen Teefy.

Today everybody wants to be a star. *Fame* addresses that contemporary dream in a most charming and lively fashion. By focusing on the aspirations, struggles, and personal lives of a group of talented and ambitious students at New York City's High School of the Performing Arts, it manages to say something about all of us and the age we live in. Rated R. 1980; 130m.

FARMER TAKES A WIFE, THE ★★
DIR: Henry Levin. **CAST:** Betty Grable, Dale Robertson, Thelma Ritter, John Carroll, Eddie Foy Jr., Merry Anders.

Tiresome musical remake of a 1935 Janet Gaynor–Henry Fonda drama (filmed under the same title). This depiction of life along the Erie Canal in the early nineteenth century is a mistake from word one. 1953; 81m.

FAST FORWARD ★★
DIR: Sidney Poitier. **CAST:** John Scott Clough, Don Franklin.

This is an undisguised variation on the cliché of "let's put on a show so we can make it in show biz." In it, eight high-school kids from Sandusky, Ohio, journey to New York for a promised audition. *Fast Forward* is a bubbly bit of fluff that relies on sheer energy to patch up its plot and make up for the lack of an inspired score. Sometimes, it works. Rated PG. 1985; 100m.

FIDDLER ON THE ROOF ★★★★
DIR: Norman Jewison. **CAST:** Topol, Norman Crane, Leonard Frey, Molly Picon, Paul Mann, Rosalind Harris.

A lavishly mounted musical, this 1979 screen adaptation of the long-running Broadway hit, based on the stories of Sholem Aleichem, works remarkably well. This is primarily thanks to Topol's immensely likable portrayal of Tevye, the proud but put-upon father clinging desperately to the old values in a changing world. Rated G. 1971; 181m.

FINIAN'S RAINBOW ★★½
DIR: Francis Ford Coppola. **CAST:** Fred Astaire, Petula Clark, Tommy Steele, Keenan Wynn, Barbara Hancock, Don Francks.

Those who believe Fred Astaire can do no wrong haven't seen this little oddity. Francis Coppola's heavy direction is totally inappropriate for a musical and the story's concerns about racial progress, which were outdated when the film first appeared, are positively embarrassing now. The mix of Irish leprechauns and the American deep South is an uneasy vehicle for demonstrating the injustices of bigotry. Rated G. 1968; 145m.

FIRST NUDIE MUSICAL, THE ★★★
DIR: Mark Haggard. **CAST:** Bruce Kimmel, Stephen Nathan, Cindy Williams, Diana Canova.

A struggling young director saves the studio by producing the world's first pornographic movie musical à la Busby Berkeley. Pleasant but extremely crude little romp. Not as bad as it sounds, but definitely for the very open-minded, and that's being generous. Rated R for nudity. 1979; 100m.

FLASHDANCE ★★★
DIR: Adrian Lyne. **CAST:** Jennifer Beals, Michael Nouri, Lilia Skala.

Director Adrian Lyne explodes images on the screen with eye-popping regularity while the spare screenplay centers on the ambitions of Alex Owens (Jennifer Beals), a welder who dreams of making the big time as a dancer. Alex finds this goal difficult to attain—until contractor Nick Hurley (Michael Nouri) decides to help. Rated R for nudity, profanity, and implied sex. 1983; 96m.

FLOWER DRUM SONG ★★
DIR: Henry Koster. **CAST:** Jack Soo, Nancy Kwan, Benson Fong, Miyoshi Umeki, Juanita Hall, James Shigeta.

Set in San Francisco's colorful Chinatown, this Rogers and Hammerstein musical rings sour. It has its bright moments, but the score is largely second-rate. The plot is conventional: a modern son's views versus those of an old-fashioned father. Ingredients include the usual Oriental cliché of an arranged marriage. 1962; 131m.

FLYING DOWN TO RIO ★★½
DIR: Thornton Freeland. **CAST:** Dolores Del Rio, Ginger Rogers, Fred Astaire.
We're sure the joy of watching Fred Astaire and Ginger Rogers dance is the only thing that has prevented the negatives of this embarrassing movie from being burned. The ludicrous plot centers around an attempt to keep a Rio hotel afloat. The climactic dance number, in which chorus girls perform on airplane wings, is so corny it has now passed into the realm of camp. 1933; B&W; 89m.

FOLLOW THE FLEET ★★★★
DIR: Mark Sandrich. **CAST:** Fred Astaire, Ginger Rogers, Randolph Scott, Harriet Nelson, Betty Grable.
In this musical Fred Astaire and Ginger Rogers are at their best, as a dance team separated by World War II. However, sailor Astaire still has time to romance Rogers while shipmate Randolph Scott gives the same treatment to her screen sister Harriet Hilliard (Mrs. Ozzie Nelson). Look for Lucille Ball in a small part. 1936; B&W; 110m.

FOOTLIGHT PARADE ★★★½
DIR: Lloyd Bacon. **CAST:** James Cagney, Ruby Keeler, Joan Blondell, Dick Powell, Guy Kibbee, Hugh Herbert, Frank McHugh.
Brash and cocksure James Cagney is a hustling stage director bent upon continually topping himself with Busby Berkeley–type musical numbers, which, not surprisingly, are directed by Busby Berkeley. Another grand-scale musical from the early days of sound films. 1933; B&W; 100m.

FOOTLIGHT SERENADE ★★
DIR: Gregory Ratoff. **CAST:** John Payne, Betty Grable, Victor Mature, Jane Wyman, James Gleason, Phil Silvers.
Heavyweight boxing champion Victor Mature means trouble for Broadway entertainers John Payne and Betty Grable when he joins their stage show. So-so musical. One of a series Grable made to boost morale during World War II. 1942; B&W; 80m.

FOOTLOOSE ★★★★
DIR: Herbert Ross. **CAST:** Kevin Bacon, Lori Singer, John Lithgow, Dianne Wiest, Christopher Penn.
A highly entertaining film that combines the rock beat exuberance of *Flashdance* and *Risky Business* with an entertaining—and even touching—story. This features Kevin Bacon as a Chicago boy who finds himself transplanted to a small rural town where rock music and dancing are banned—until he decides to do something about it. Rated PG for slight profanity and brief violence. 1984; 107m.

FOR ME AND MY GAL ★★★
DIR: Busby Berkeley. **CAST:** Judy Garland, Gene Kelly, George Murphy, Stephen McNally, Keenan Wynn.
A colorful tribute to the great and grand days of vaudeville before World War I, this tuneful trip down memory lane boosted Judy Garland's stock out of sight and made a star of Gene Kelly, he of the fleet foot and beguiling smile. Flaws aside—the predictable plot needs a shave—this is a generally warm, invigorating picture rife with the nostalgia of happy times. 1942; B&W; 104m.

42ND STREET ★★★★
DIR: Lloyd Bacon. **CAST:** Dick Powell, Ruby Keeler, Ginger Rogers, Warner Baxter, Una Merkel.
Every understudy's dream is to get a big chance and rise to stardom. Such is the premise of *42nd Street*. This Depression-era musical of 1933 is lifted above cliché by its vitality and sincerity. 1933; B&W; 98m.

FRANKIE AND JOHNNY ★★★
DIR: Frederick de Cordova. **CAST:** Elvis Presley, Donna Douglas, Sue

Ane Langdon, Harry Morgan, Nancy Kovack, Audrey Christie.

As the song goes, Elvis, as a Mississippi riverboat singer-gambler, betrays his lady (Donna Douglas) with his roving heart. He easily captures the attention of beautiful young ladies but must suffer the consequences of his actions. Elvis fans won't be disappointed with this musical love story. 1966; 87m.

FRENCH LINE, THE ★★
DIR: Lloyd Bacon. **CAST:** Jane Russell, Gilbert Roland, Mary McCarty, Craig Stevens, Steven Geray, Arthur Hunnicutt.

This is a dull musical with forgettable songs. Ultrarich heroine Jane Russell can't find true love. She masquerades as a fashion model during a voyage on the French Line's luxury ship, *Liberté*, hoping her money won't show while she snags a man. Despite presenting Miss Russell in 3-D, the film was a bust. 1954; 102m.

FROM MAO TO MOZART ★★★★½
DIR: Murray Lerner. **CAST:** Isaac Stern, David Golub, Tan Shuzhen.

Violinist Isaac Stern's concert tour of Red China is the subject of this warm and perceptive Academy Award–winning documentary. 1980; 88m.

FUN IN ACAPULCO ★★½
DIR: Richard Thorpe. **CAST:** Elvis Presley, Ursula Andress, Paul Lukas, Alejandro Rey, Elsa Cardenas.

Beautiful Acapulco sets the stage for this sun-filled Elvis Presley musical. This time he's a lifeguard by day and a singer by night at a fancy beachfront resort. Typical of Elvis's films. 1963; 97m.

FUNNY FACE ★★★½
DIR: Stanley Donen. **CAST:** Fred Astaire, Audrey Hepburn, Kay Thompson, Michel Auclair, Ruta Lee.

One of the best of Fred Astaire's later pictures. This time he's a fashion photographer who discovers naïve Audrey Hepburn and turns her into a sensation. Typical fairy-tale plot, enlivened by Astaire's usual charm and a good score based on the works of George Gershwin. 1957; 103m.

FUNNY GIRL ★★★★
DIR: William Wyler. **CAST:** Barbra Streisand, Omar Sharif, Walter Pidgeon, Kay Medford.

The early years of Ziegfeld Follies star Fanny Brice were the inspiration for a superb stage musical. Barbra Streisand re-created her Broadway triumph in as stunning a movie debut in 1968 as Hollywood ever witnessed. She sings, roller-skates, cracks jokes, and tugs at your heart in a tour-de-force performance. Rated G. 1968; 155m.

FUNNY LADY ★★★
DIR: Herbert Ross. **CAST:** Barbra Streisand, James Caan, Omar Sharif, Ben Vereen.

The sequel to *Funny Girl* is not quite up to the original, but still worth seeing. We follow comedienne Fanny Brice after she became a stage luminary only to continue her misfortunes in private life. James Caan plays her second husband, producer Billy Rose, and Omar Sharif returns in his role of Fanny's first love. But Streisand's performance and a few of the musical numbers carry the day. 1975; 149m.

GAY DIVORCEE, THE ★★★★
DIR: Mark Sandrich. **CAST:** Fred Astaire, Ginger Rogers, Edward Everett Horton, Alice Brady, Erik Rhodes, Eric Blore, Betty Grable.

This delightful musical farce was the only Fred Astaire/Ginger Rogers film to be nominated for a best-picture Oscar. The outstanding score includes "Night and Day" and "The Continental." 1934; B&W; 107m.

GENESIS LIVE—THE MAMA TOUR ★★★½
DIR: Jim Yukich. **CAST:** Genesis.

Genesis is one of the strongest and most influential bands to emerge from Britain since the Beatles. This 1982 concert at the Nassau Coliseum on Long Island, New York, features the veteran British progressive-rock band with drummer-vocalist Phil Collins at the helm. Fans will not be disappointed. 1986; 102m.

GEORGE WHITE'S SCANDALS ★★

DIR: Felix Feist. **CAST:** Joan Davis, Jack Haley, Jane Greer, Philip Terry.

Joan Davis saves this fairly minor musical from collapsing. The slapstick routines come off with some verve, but the plot is not as sturdy as it could have been. 1945; B&W; 95m.

G.I. BLUES ★★★½

DIR: Norman Taurog. **CAST:** Elvis Presley, Juliet Prowse.

Juliet Prowse improves this otherwise average Elvis Presley film. The action takes place in Germany, where Elvis makes a bet with his G.I. buddies he can date the aloof Prowse, who plays a nightclub dancer. 1960; 104m.

GIGI ★★★★

DIR: Vincente Minnelli. **CAST:** Leslie Caron, Maurice Chevalier, Louis Jourdan, Hermione Gingold, Jacques Bergerac, Eva Gabor.

Hermione Gingold plays guardian to lovely Leslie Caron, who is coming of age in France in the early 1900s. Louis Jourdan plays her romantic interest. Maurice Chevalier adds class. 1959; 116m.

GIMME SHELTER ★★★★

DIR: David Maysles, Albert Maysles, Charlotte Zwerin. **CAST:** The Rolling Stones, Melvin Belli.

This documentary chronicles the events leading up to and including the now infamous free Rolling Stones concert in 1969 at the Altamont Speedway outside San Francisco. It's the dark side of Woodstock, with many unforgettable scenes, including the actual murder of a spectator by the Hell's Angels in front of the stage as the Stones are playing. Rated R for violence, language, and scenes of drug use. 1970; 91m.

GIRL CRAZY ★★★

DIR: Busby Berkeley, Norman Taurog. **CAST:** Mickey Rooney, Judy Garland, June Allyson, Rags Ragland, Guy Kibbee, Nancy Walker, Henry O'Neill.

Girls are driving the ever-ebullient Mickey Rooney bonkers. His family sends him to a small southwestern college, hoping the "craze" will fade, but he meets Judy Garland, and away we go into another happy kids-give-a-show musical with glorious George and Ira Gershwin tunes. 1943; B&W; 99m.

GIRL HAPPY ★★★

DIR: Boris Sagal. **CAST:** Elvis Presley, Shelley Fabares, Mary Ann Mobley.

This is *Where the Boys Are* in reverse, as Elvis plays chaperone to a Chicago mobster's daughter in Fort Lauderdale, Florida. While Elvis romances vixenish Mary Ann Mobley, his nerdish charge (Shelley Fabares) constantly gets into trouble with a sexy Italian. A romantic triangle develops when both girls fall for Elvis. 1964; 96m.

GIRL MOST LIKELY, THE ★★★½

DIR: Mitchell Leisen. **CAST:** Jane Powell, Cliff Robertson, Tommy Noonan, Una Merkel.

This musical, a remake of *Tom, Dick and Harry*, succeeds because it's light and breezy. The choreography is by the late Gower Champion and is wonderful to watch. This is a fine film for the entire family. 1957; 98m.

GIRL OF THE GOLDEN WEST, THE ★★½

DIR: Robert Z. Leonard. **CAST:** Jeanette MacDonald, Nelson Eddy, Walter Pidgeon, Leo Carrillo, Buddy Ebsen, Monty Woolley, H. B. Warner, Charley Grapewin.

Jeanette MacDonald is an 1850s saloon owner attracted to bold bandit Nelson Eddy in this sloppy, hitless musical version of a 1905 play (better known as a Puccini opera). Fans of filmdom's matchless duo will love the romance, music, and scenic splendor, despite a plot that creaks with age. 1938; B&W; 120m.

GIRLS! GIRLS! GIRLS! ★★
DIR: Norman Taurog. **CAST:** Elvis Presley, Stella Stevens, Benson Fong, Laurel Goodwin, Jeremy Slate.
In this musical comedy, Elvis Presley is chased by an endless array of beautiful girls. Sounds like the ideal situation? Not for poor Elvis as he tries to choose just one. 1962; 105m.

GIVE MY REGARDS TO BROAD STREET ★★
DIR: Peter Webb. **CAST:** Paul McCartney, Ringo Starr, Barbara Bach, Linda McCartney.
McCartney wrote and stars in this odd, but not really offensive, combination of great rock music and a truly insipid story as a rock singer who loses the master tapes for his album and finds his future seriously threatened. Forget the story and enjoy the songs. Rated PG for mild violence. 1984; 108m.

GLENN MILLER STORY, THE ★★★½
DIR: Anthony Mann. **CAST:** James Stewart, June Allyson, Charles Drake, Harry Morgan, Frances Langford, Gene Krupa, Louis Armstrong.
Follows the life story of famous trombonist and bandleader Glenn Miller, who disappeared in a plane during World War II. Jimmy Stewart delivers a convincing portrayal of the popular bandleader whose music had all of America tapping its feet. Miller's music is the highlight of the film, with guest appearances by Louis Armstrong and Gene Krupa. 1954; 113m.

GLORIFYING THE AMERICAN GIRL ★★½
DIR: Millard Webb. **CAST:** Mary Eaton, Edward Crandall, Eddie Cantor, Helen Mòrgan.
The only film produced by legendary showman Florenz Ziegfeld, this dreary backstage rags-to-riches story reeked of mothballs even in 1929. Recognizing that, Ziegfeld padded it out with Follies production numbers that provide the only reason to watch this. Highlights are an Eddie Cantor skit, a bevy of celebrity cameos, and torch singer Helen Morgan giving her all on "What I Wouldn't Do For That Man." 1929; B&W; 95m.

GO, JOHNNY, GO! ★½
DIR: Paul Landres. **CAST:** Jimmy Clanton, Alan Freed, Sandy Stewart, Chuck Berry, Jo-Ann Campbell, Eddie Cochran, Richie Valens, The Cadillacs, Jackie Wilson, The Flamingos.
Don't get your hopes up after reading the cast list. Despite the presence of some great rock 'n' roll and R&B acts, this story of a boy plucked from anonymity to become a star is about as dull as they come. One of the most disappointing of all 1950s teenage music films. 1958; B&W; 75m.

GOLD DIGGERS OF 1933 ★★★★
DIR: Mervyn LeRoy. **CAST:** Joan Blondell, Ruby Keeler, Dick Powell, Aline MacMahon, Ginger Rogers, Sterling Holloway.
This typical 1930s song-and-dance musical revolves around a Broadway show. Notable tunes include: "We're in the Money," sung by Ginger Rogers; "Forgotten Man," sung by Joan Blondell; and "Shadow Waltz," by the chorus girls. Enjoyable fare if you like nostalgic musicals. 1933; B&W; 96m.

GOLD DIGGERS OF 1935 ★★★
DIR: Busby Berkeley. **CAST:** Dick Powell, Adolphe Mènjou, Winifred Shaw, Glenda Farrell.
Classic Busby Berkeley musical production numbers dominate this absurd story of mercenary schemers swarming around the rich at a posh resort. Though the film sags and lags, the kitsch director's staging of "Lullaby of Broadway" is a piece of cinematic brilliance. 1935; B&W; 95m.

GOLDWYN FOLLIES, THE 🦃
DIR: George Marshall. **CAST:** Adolphe Menjou, Andrea Leeds, Kenny Baker, The Ritz Brothers, Vera

Zorina, Edgar Bergen and Charlie McCarthy.

Goldwyn's folly is a better title for this turkey. The cast must have been standing around doing nothing on contract, and someone said, "Hey, let's make a movie! Adolphe, you be a producer. Andrea can be the wholesome ingenue. The Ritz Brothers can act zany, Zorina can dance, Edgar can do his thing, and Kenny can sing and sing and sing." And so they all did, darn it! 1938; 120m.

GOOD NEWS ★★★

DIR: Charles Walters. **CAST:** June Allyson, Peter Lawford, Patricia Marshall, Joan McCracken, Mel Torme.

Football hero Peter Lawford resists the class vamp and wins the big game and the campus cutie who loves him in this quintessential musical of college life. The dialogue is painfully trite and trying, but energy and exuberance abound. 1948; 95m.

GOODBYE, MR. CHIPS (1969) ★½

DIR: Herbert Ross. **CAST:** Peter O'Toole, Petula Clark, Michael Redgrave, George Baker, Sian Phillips.

Herbert Ross's directional debut is dismal indeed. The only good idea here is casting Peter O'Toole as the stiff-upper-lip schoolteacher. Remaking a classic is always a dubious task, turning one into a musical is even riskier. Cash in this *Chips*. Rated G. 1969; 151m.

GOSPEL ★★★★

DIR: David Levick, Frederick A. Rizenberg. **CAST:** Mighty Clouds of Joy, Clark Sisters, Walter Hawkins and the Hawkins Family, Shirley Caesar, Rev. James Cleveland.

Featuring many of the top stars of black gospel music, this is a joyous, spirit-lifting music documentary that contains the highlights of a five-and-a-half-hour concert filmed in June 1981 at Oakland Paramount Theater. The spirited performances might even make a believer out of you—that is, if you aren't already. Rated G. 1982; 92m.

GRATEFUL DEAD MOVIE, THE ★★★½

DIR: Jerry Garcia, Leon Gast. **CAST:** Grateful Dead.

Dead Heads will undoubtedly love this combination of backstage, concert, and animated psychedelic scenes. Supervised by Dead lead guitarist-vocalist Jerry Garcia, it's a laughable look at the mechanics and magic of rock. But the uninitiated and unconverted may find it tedious after a while. 1976; 131m.

GREASE ★★★

DIR: Randal Kleiser. **CAST:** John Travolta, Olivia Newton-John, Stockard Channing, Jeff Conaway, Didi Conn, Eve Arden, Sid Caesar.

After they meet and enjoy a tender summer romance, John Travolta and Olivia Newton-John tearfully part. Surprisingly, they are reunited when she becomes the new girl at his high school. Around his friends, he must play Mr. Tough-Guy, and her goody-two-shoes image doesn't quite fit in. Slight, but fun. Rated PG. 1978; 110m.

GREASE 2 ★★★

DIR: Patricia Birch. **CAST:** Maxwell Caulfield, Michelle Pfeiffer, Adrian Zmed, Lorna Luft, Didi Conn.

A sequel to the most successful screen musical of all time, *Grease 2* takes us back to Rydell High for more 1950s adolescent angst. The result is a fun little movie that seems to work almost in spite of itself. Rated PG for suggestive gestures and lyrics. 1982; 115m.

GREAT BALLS OF FIRE ★★★★

DIR: Jim McBride. **CAST:** Dennis Quaid, Winona Ryder, Alec Baldwin, Trey Wilson.

A landmark music bio. It's obvious how hard talented Dennis Quaid has worked on his piano playing (with hands, feet, head, and tail) and on his Jerry Lee Lewis hellion-touched-by-God mannerisms and he's sublime in the role. So is Alec Baldwin, playing it straight and righteous as Jerry Lee's famous cousin, Jimmy Swaggart. Despite filmmaker Jim McBride's insistence on cutting too quickly from a supercharged song, *Great Balls of Fire* survives intact with some miraculous moments. Rated R for language and simulated sex. 1989; 110m.

GREAT CARUSO, THE ★★★★
DIR: Richard Thorpe. **CAST:** Mario Lanza, Ann Blyth, Dorothy Kirsten.

A number of factual liberties are taken in this lavish screen biography of the great Italian tenor, but no matter. Mario Lanza's voice is magnificent; Ann Blyth and Dorothy Kirsten sing like birds. Devotees of music will love the arias. 1950; 109m.

GREAT ZIEGFELD, THE ★★★★★
DIR: Robert Z. Leonard. **CAST:** William Powell, Myrna Loy, Luise Rainer, Frank Morgan, Fanny Brice, Virginia Bruce, Reginald Owen, Dennis Morgan.

This Academy Award–winning best picture is a marvelous film biography of legendary showman Florenz Ziegfeld. William Powell is perfect in the title role and Oscar winner Luise Rainer is tremendous as the fabulous Anna Held. The sets, costumes and production design are superb. This is Hollywood at its finest. 1936; B&W; 176m.

GUYS AND DOLLS ★★★
DIR: Joseph L. Mankiewicz. **CAST:** Marlon Brando, Frank Sinatra, Jean Simmons, Vivian Blaine, Stubby Kaye, Veda Ann Borg.

This passable musical stars Marlon Brando and Frank Sinatra as New York gamblers with a gangsterlike aura. Brando and Sinatra bet on whether or not a lovely Salvation Army soldier (Jean Simmons) is date bait. 1955; 150m.

GYPSY ★★★
DIR: Mervyn LeRoy. **CAST:** Natalie Wood, Rosalind Russell, Karl Malden.

Gypsy tries to surpass its hackneyed situation with an energetic musical score and a story about real people. In this case, the characters are stripper Gypsy Rose Lee and her backstage mother supreme, Rose. The music is excellent, but the characters are weakly defined. 1962; 149m.

HAIR ★★★★
DIR: Milos Forman. **CAST:** Treat Williams, John Savage, Beverly D'Angelo, Annie Golden, Charlotte Rae.

Neglected adaptation of the hit Broadway play about 1960s unrest. John Savage is the uptight Midwesterner who pals up with a group of (shudder) hippies celebrating the Age of Aquarius. Grand musical moments, due to Twyla Tharp's impressive choreography; particularly droll is Treat Williams's rendition of the title song at an upper-crust dinner party. Rated PG for nudity. 1979; 121m.

HANS CHRISTIAN ANDERSEN ★★★½
DIR: Charles Vidor. **CAST:** Danny Kaye, Farley Granger, Zizi Jeanmaire, John Qualen.

Danny Kaye is superb as the famous storyteller, and Frank Loesser composed some wonderful songs for this glossy oversweet musical. Ballet great Jeanmaire is a knockout. This is top-notch family entertainment. 1952; 120m.

HAPPY GO LOVELY ★★★
DIR: H. Bruce Humberstone. **CAST:** David Niven, Vera-Ellen, Cesar Romero.

Perky Vera-Ellen is a dancing darling in this lightweight musical with a very tired plot about a producer who hires a chorus girl with the idea that her boyfriend has money to invest in his show. It's all cute, but nothing startling. 1951; 87m.

HARD DAY'S NIGHT, A ★★★★★
DIR: Richard Lester. **CAST:** The Beatles, Wilfred Brambell, Victor Spinetti, Anna Quayle.

Put simply, this is the greatest rock 'n'roll comedy ever made. Scripted by Alan Owen as a sort of day in the life of the Beatles, it's fast-paced, funny, and full of great Lennon-McCartney songs. Even more than twenty years after its release, it continues to delight several generations of viewers. 1964; B&W; 85m.

HARD TO HOLD ★½
DIR: Larry Peerce. **CAST:** Rick Springfield, Janet Eilber, Patti Hansen, Albert Salmi.
In this highly forgettable, mostly mediocre film, Rick Springfield plays a music superstar who has everything except the one thing he really wants: the woman (Janet Eilber) he loves. The first half-hour, which is light and funny, is quite good, but from there it goes downhill into sappy soap opera. Rated PG for brief nudity and profanity. 1984; 93m.

HARDER THEY COME, THE ★★★★
DIR: Perry Henzell. **CAST:** Jimmy Cliff, Janet Barkley.
Made in Jamaica by Jamaicans, this film has become an underground cult classic. In it, a rural boy comes to the big city to become a singer. There, he is forced into a life of crime. Rated R. 1973; 98m.

HARMONY LANE ★
DIR: Joseph Santley. **CAST:** Douglass Montgomery, Evelyn Venable, Adrienne Ames, William Frawley.
Only the music saves this halfhearted account of composer Stephen Foster's tragic life from being classed a turkey. The sets are shoddy, the camera rarely moves, most of the acting is insipid, and the screenplay is one long string of music cues. 1935; B&W; 89m.

HARRY BELAFONTE GLOBAL CARNIVAL ★★★
DIR: John Fortenberry. **CAST:** Harry Belafonte.
Festive sounds of Africa are interspersed with Belafonte favorites like "Jamaica Farewell" in this spirited show from Zimbabwe. Belafonte augments the colorful concert scenes with brief interviews illuminating the problems of modern Africa. All in all, informative and entertaining. Unrated. 1988; 50m.

HARUM SCARUM ★★★
DIR: Gene Nelson. **CAST:** Elvis Presley, Mary Ann Mobley, Michael Ansara, Billy Barty.
When a swashbuckling film star (Elvis Presley) visits a primitive Arabian country, he is forced to aid assassins in their bid to destroy the king. Simultaneously, he falls in love with the king's beautiful daughter (Mary Ann Mobley) and must outwit the treacherous usurpers. Elvis manages to belt out nine tunes, including "Shake That Tambourine" and "Harem Holiday." His fans won't be disappointed. 1965; 85m.

HARVEY GIRLS, THE ★★★
DIR: Vincente Minnelli. **CAST:** Judy Garland, John Hodiak, Ray Bolger, Preston Foster, Virginia O'Brien, Angela Lansbury, Marjorie Main, Chill Wills, Cyd Charisse, Kenny Baker.
Rousing fun marks this big, bustling musical, which is loosely tied to the development of pioneer railroad-station restaurateur Fred Harvey's string of eateries along the Santa Fe right-of-way. Judy Garland is the innocent who goes West to grow up, Angela Lansbury is the wise bad girl, and John Hodiak is the requisite gambler. 1945; 102m.

HEAD ★★★
DIR: Bob Rafelson. **CAST:** Mickey Dolenz, David Jones, Mike Nesmith, Peter Tork, Teri Garr, Vito Scotti, Timothy Carey, Logan Ramsey.
They get the funniest looks from everyone they meet. And it's no wonder. This film is truly bizarre. The Monkees were hurtled to fame in the aftershock of the Beatles' success. Their ingratiating series was accused of imitating *A Hard Day's Night*, but their innovative feature-film debut, *Head*, was ahead of its time. A free-form product of the psychedelic era. 1968; 86m.

HEARTLAND REGGAE ★★★★½
DIR: J. P. Lewis. **CAST:** Bob Marley, Jacob Miller, Peter Tosh, Judy Mowatt, Dennis Brown, Junior Tucker.

Reggae fans will find this unique concert a mini-Woodstock, celebrating the finest bands to establish the reggae sound as a great moment in pop-music history. The One Love Peace Concert in Kingston, Jamaica, on April 22, 1978, was organized by the government to prevent riots from destroying the city. This astonishing music event captures Bob Marley and the Wailers at their best, along with Peter Tosh and Jacob Miller. 1984; 90m.

HEART'S DESIRE ★½
DIR: Paul Stein. **CAST:** Richard Tauber, Leonora Corbett.

Richard Tauber, a popular tenor in British operetta, stars in this ho-hum musical as a Viennese waiter who becomes a star in London. In the end, true love brings him back home. Lacking the gloss of Hollywood's Nelson Eddy or Mario Lanza vehicles, this will appeal only to diehard adenoid admirers. 1935; B&W; 79m.

HELLO, DOLLY! ★
DIR: Gene Kelly. **CAST:** Barbra Streisand, Walter Matthau, Michael Crawford, E. J. Peaker, Marianne McAndrew.

A multimillion-dollar disaster, this 1969 "spectacular" features a miscast Barbra Streisand as an intrepid matchmaker. Rated G. 1969; 146m.

HELP! ★★★★
DIR: Richard Lester. **CAST:** The Beatles, Leo McKern, Eleanor Bron, Victor Spinetti.

Though neither as inventive nor as charming as *A Hard Day's Night*, this second collaboration between director Richard Lester and the Fab Four has enough energy, fun, and memorable songs to make it worth viewing again. The slim plot has a bizarre religious cult trying to retrieve a sacrificial ring from Ringo. From the reverberating opening chord of the title tune, the movie sweeps you up in its irresistibly zesty spirit. 1965; 90m.

HERBIE HANCOCK AND THE ROCKIT BAND LIVE ★★★★
DIR: Ken O'Neill. **CAST:** Herbie Hancock.

Award-winning composer-musician Herbie Hancock brings his mix of electronic funk–jazz-fusion together in this dynamite performance taped before a live audience at the Hammersmith Odeon in 1983. This electrifying concert features some lightning percussion by Anton Fier and the rap turntable "scratching" of Grandmixer D. ST. Some of the robots used to create the music video "Rockit" fill the stage and are punctuated with breakdancers in this high-energy, pulsating music event. 1984; 73m.

HIGH SOCIETY ★★★½
DIR: Charles Walters. **CAST:** Bing Crosby, Frank Sinatra, Grace Kelly, Louis Armstrong.

The outstanding cast in this film is reason enough to watch this enjoyable musical remake of *The Philadelphia Story*. The film moves at a leisurely pace, helped by some nice songs by Cole Porter. 1956; 107m.

HIGHER AND HIGHER ★★
DIR: Tim Whelan. **CAST:** Frank Sinatra, Michele Morgan, Jack Haley, Leon Errol, Victor Borge, Mel Torme.

Frank Sinatra and the entire cast do a wonderful job in this practically plotless picture about a once-rich man teaming up with his servants in his quest to be wealthy once again. This is Sinatra's first major film effort, and he does a fine job with the first-rate songs. 1943; B&W; 90m.

HIT THE DECK ★★½
DIR: Roy Rowland. **CAST:** Jane Powell, Tony Martin, Debbie Reynolds, Vic Damone, Ann Miller, Russ Tamblyn, Walter Pidgeon, Gene Raymond.

Fancy-free sailors on shore leave meet girls, dance, sing, and cut up in this updated 1920s Vincent Youmans hit from Broadway. Nothing to rave about, just good, time-filling eyewash. 1955; 112m.

HOLIDAY INN ★★★★
DIR: Mark Sandrich. **CAST:** Bing Crosby, Fred Astaire, Marjorie Reynolds, Virginia Dale.
Irving Berlin's music and the delightful teaming of Bing Crosby and Fred Astaire are the high points of this wartime musical. The timeless renditions of "White Christmas" and "Easter Parade" more than make up for a script that at best could be called fluff. 1942; B&W; 101m.

HOLLYWOOD HOTEL ★★
DIR: Busby Berkeley. **CAST:** Dick Powell, Rosemary Lane, Lola Lane, Ted Healy, Alan Mowbray, Frances Langford, Hugh Herbert, Louella Parsons, Glenda Farrell, Edgar Kennedy.
Saxophonist Dick Powell wins a talent contest, gets a film contract, but gets the boot because he won't cozy up to bitchy star Lola Lane, preferring her sister instead. Songs by Johnny Mercer and Richard Whiting, including "Hooray for Hollywood," help bolster this otherwise average musical mishmash. 1937; B&W; 109m.

HONEYSUCKLE ROSE ★★½
DIR: Jerry Schatzberg. **CAST:** Willie Nelson, Dyan Cannon, Amy Irving, Slim Pickens.
For his first starring role, country singer Willie Nelson is saddled with a rather stodgy film that all but sinks in the mire of its unimaginative handling and sappy story. As a result, *Honeysuckle Rose* is something only his devoted fans will love. Rated PG. 1980; 119m.

HOT PEPPER ★★★★
DIR: Les Blank, Maureen Gosling. **CAST:** Clifton Chenier.
Penetrating look into the life of Louisiana zydeco–music legend Clifton Chenier. Filmmaker Les Blank follows the Cajun-French accordionist through the sweaty dance halls and along the streets and into the homes of family and friends. Another excellent documentary from Blank. 1980; 54m.

HOW TO STUFF A WILD BIKINI ★★
DIR: William Asher. **CAST:** Frankie Avalon, Annette Funicello, Dwayne Hickman, Mickey Rooney, Buster Keaton.
It's no surprise to see Frankie Avalon and Annette Funicello together in this beach party film. Dwayne Hickman (TV's Dobie Gillis) tries his hand at romancing Annette in this one. Not much plot, but lots of crazy (sometimes funny) things are going on. 1965; 90m.

HURRICANE IRENE: JAPAN AID CONCERT FOR PEACE ★★½
DIR: Hart Perry. **CAST:** Peter Gabriel, Howard Jones, Jackson Browne, Lou Reed, Nona Hendryx, Little Steven, Youssou N'Dour.
Jackson Browne, Little Steven, and Peter Gabriel are among the familiar singing stars taking an antiwar message to Japan in this benefit concert. The performances are solid, although not explosive. The video introductions and the political pitch for global peace tend to slow the pace. 1988; 78m.

I COULD GO ON SINGING ★★★
DIR: Ronald Neame. **CAST:** Judy Garland, Dirk Bogarde, Jack Klugman, Aline MacMahon.
In this, her last film, with a disturbing true-to-her-life plot, Judy Garland plays a successful concert singer beset by personal problems. When Judy sings, the film lives. When she doesn't, it's wistful, teary, and a bit sloppy. Strictly for Garland fanatics. 1963; 99m.

I DO! I DO! ★★★★
DIR: Gower Champion. **CAST:** Lee Remick, Hal Linden.
Lee Remick and Hal Linden step into the parts originally created on Broadway by Mary Martin and Robert Preston in this video of a performance

taped before an audience. The play is the musical version of *The Fourposter*, and deals with the marriage of Michael to Agnes—from the night before their wedding to the day when they leave their home of forty years. Solid entertainment. 1982; 116m.

I DREAM TOO MUCH ★★½
DIR: John Cromwell. **CAST:** Henry Fonda, Lily Pons, Lucille Ball, Eric Blore.
This picture is more of a showcase for Lily Pons's vocal abilities in the operetta form. Henry Fonda and Pons are two performers who face the standard career obstacles. The music is okay. 1935; B&W; 95m.

I MARRIED AN ANGEL ★½
DIR: W. S. Van Dyke. **CAST:** Jeanette MacDonald, Nelson Eddy, Edward Everett Horton, Binnie Barnes, Reginald Owen.
In this, their final film together, playboy Nelson Eddy dreams he courts and marries angel Jeanette MacDonald. *Leaden* and *bizarre* are but two of the words critics used to pan this rape of what had been a popular musical comedy on Broadway. Not quite a turkey, but cackling can be heard in the distance. 1942; B&W; 84m.

IDOLMAKER, THE ★★★★
DIR: Taylor Hackford. **CAST:** Ray Sharkey, Tovah Feldshuh, Peter Gallagher, Maureen McCormick.
This superior rock 'n'roll drama stands with a handful of pictures—*The Buddy Holly Story* and *American Hot Wax* among them—as one of the few to capture the excitement of rock music while still offering something in the way of a decent plot and characterization. Ray Sharkey is excellent as a songwriter-manager who pulls, pushes, punches, and plunders his way to the top of the music world. The score, by Jeff Barry, is top-notch. Rated PG. 1980; 119m.

IF YOU KNEW SUSIE ★★½
DIR: Gordon Douglas. **CAST:** Eddie Cantor, Joan Davis, Allyn Joslyn.
If you enjoy the comedy and musical stylings of Joan Davis and Eddie Cantor, you'll probably be pleased with this thin story of two entertainers who discover a will signed by George Washington. The film is dated and held together only by Cantor's sure touch and slick performance. 1948; B&W; 90m.

I'LL CRY TOMORROW ★★★½
DIR: Daniel Mann. **CAST:** Susan Hayward, Eddie Albert, Richard Conte, Jo Van Fleet, Don Taylor, Ray Danton.
In addition to giving one of the most professional performances of her career, Susan Hayward sang (and very well) the songs in this screen biography of Lillian Roth. Her masterful portrayal, supported by a solid cast, won her a Cannes Film Festival award. 1955; B&W; 117m.

IMAGINE: JOHN LENNON ★★★★★
DIR: Andrew Solt. **CAST:** John Lennon, Yoko Ono, George Harrison.
Superb documentary chronicles the life, times, and untimely death of rock 'n' roll icon John Lennon. Carefully selected footage from the career of the Beatles is combined with television interviews and never-before-seen film of Lennon's private life for a remarkably insightful and emotionally moving work. Rated R for nudity and profanity. 1988; 103m.

IN BERLIN ★★★★
DIR: Michael Lindsay-Hogg. **CAST:** Neil Young.
The ever-changing Neil Young shows all his facets at this highly entertaining concert filmed in West Berlin in 1983. A total of eleven songs, including samples from the beginning of his solo career ("Old Man") are combined with those from his ill-fated computer experiment ("Transformer Man"). Backed by an excellent band, Young's acoustical and electronic sets merge into a blaze of metal on the

rocking "Hurricane" and "Hey Hey My My." 1985; 60m.

IN THE GOOD OLD SUMMERTIME ★★★
DIR: Robert Z. Leonard. **CAST:** Judy Garland, Van Johnson, S. Z. Sakall, Buster Keaton, Spring Bylngton.

Despite its title, most of the action of this remake of the classic romantic comedy *The Shop Around the Corner* takes place in winter. Judy Garland and Van Johnson work in the same music store. They dislike each other, but are unknowingly secret pen pals who have much in common. Truth wins out, but by the time it does, love has struck. Buster Keaton is wasted as comic relief. 1949; 102m.

INVITATION TO THE DANCE ★★★
DIR: Gene Kelly. **CAST:** Gene Kelly.

Strictly for lovers of terpsichore, this film tells three stories entirely through dance. It sort of drags until Gene Kelly appears in a live action–cartoon sequence about "Sinbad" of Arabian Nights fame. 1957; 93m.

IT HAPPENED AT THE WORLD'S FAIR ★★½
DIR: Norman Taurog. **CAST:** Elvis Presley, Joan O' Brien, Gary Lockwood, Yvonne Craig.

Adorable tyke plays matchmaker for Elvis Presley and Joan O'Brien at Seattle World's Fair. It's a breezy romantic comedy with bouncy songs. Elvis hadn't yet reached the point where he was just going through the motions. He seems to be having fun and you will, too. 1963; 105m.

IT HAPPENED IN NEW ORLEANS ★½
DIR: Kurt Neumann. **CAST:** Bobby Breen, May Robson, Charles Butterworth, Louise Beavers, Alan Mowbray, Benita Hume, Henry O'Neill, Eddie "Rochester" Anderson.

Bobby Breen, the male Shirley Temple, stars as a Civil War orphan forced to leave his ex-slave mammy and go to New York. There, his Yankee relatives give him a hard time until his renditions of Stephen Foster tunes and his overwhelming cuteness win them over. For those with either a high tolerance for saccharin or a keen sense of the ridiculous. Also known as *Rainbow on the River*. 1936; B&W; 83m.

IT'S ALWAYS FAIR WEATHER ★★★
DIR: Gene Kelly, Stanley Donen. **CAST:** Gene Kelly, Dan Dailey, Michael Kidd, Cyd Charisse, Dolores Gray, David Burns.

World War II buddies Gene Kelly, Dan Dailey, and Michael Kidd meet a decade after discharge and find they no longer have anything in common and actively dislike one another. Enter romance, reconciliation ploys, and attempted exploitation of their reunion on televison. Don't be surprised to realize it recalls *On the Town*. 1955; 102m.

JAILHOUSE ROCK ★★★★
DIR: Richard Thorpe. **CAST:** Elvis Presley, Mickey Shaughnessy, Dean Jones, Judy Tyler.

Quite possibly Elvis Presley's best as far as musical sequences go, this 1957 film is still burdened by a sappy plot. Good-hearted Presley gets stuck in the slammer, only to hook up with a conniving manager (Mickey Shaughnessy). Forget the plot and enjoy the great rock 'n' roll songs. 1957; B&W; 96m.

JAMES BROWN—LIVE IN LONDON ★★★½
DIR: Martin Brierly. **CAST:** James Brown.

Superb evening of high-energy rhythm and blues from the Godfather of Soul, James Brown, who has stirred the emotions of audiences for over thirty years. He is supported by a terrific eleven-piece band in this concert taped in 1985 at London's Hammersmith Odeon. Among the songs: "Cold Sweat," "Prisoner of Love," and "I Feel Good." 1986; 56m.

JANIS ★★★
DIR: Howard Alk, Seaton Findlay. **CAST:** Documentary.
The most comprehensive documentary study of flower child Janis Joplin, this is filled with poignant memories and electrifying performances. Rated R for language. 1974; 96m.

JAZZ SINGER, THE (1927) ★★★½
DIR: Alan Crossland. **CAST:** Al Jolson, May McAvoy, Warner Oland, William Demarest, Roscoe Karns, Myrna Loy.
Generally considered the first talking film, this milestone in motion-picture history is really a silent film with a musical score and a few spoken lines. Al Jolson plays the son of an orthodox cantor who wants his son to follow in his footsteps. Jolson, though touched by his father's wishes, feels he must be a jazz singer. 1927; B&W; 89m.

JAZZ SINGER, THE (1980) ★
DIR: Richard Fleischer. **CAST:** Neil Diamond, Laurence Olivier, Lucie Arnaz.
Only Lucie Arnaz shines as a sexy show business manager in this film about a fifth-generation Jewish cantor (Neil Diamond) who leaves his wife, father, and synagogue to become a big rock 'n' roll star. It's a mushy mishmash that only Diamond's most devoted fans will love. Rated PG. 1980; 115m.

JESUS CHRIST, SUPERSTAR ★★★½
DIR: Norman Jewison. **CAST:** Ted Neeley, Carl Anderson, Yvonne Elliman.
Believe it or not, this could be the ancestor of such rock videos as Michael Jackson's "Thriller." The movie illustrates segments of Jesus Christ's later life by staging sets and drama to go along with the soundtrack. This will not offer any religious experiences in the traditional sense, but is interesting nonetheless. Rated G. 1973; 103m.

JIMI HENDRIX ★★★★
DIR: Gary Weis. **CAST:** Jimi Hendrix, Billy Cox, Mitch Mitchell, Eric Clapton, Pete Townshend, Little Richard, Dick Cavett.
Jimi Hendrix, the undisputed master of psychedelia, is captured brilliantly through concert footage and candid film clips in this excellent all-around 1973 rockumentary. The film explores Hendrix's career through interviews and rare concert footage of his performances from London's Marquee Club in 1967, and the Monterey Pop, Woodstock, and Isle of Wight festivals. Director Gary Weis was responsible for some great film shorts on *Saturday Night Live*. 1984; 103m.

JIMMY CLIFF—BONGO MAN ★★½
DIR: Stefan Paul. **CAST:** Jimmy Cliff.
This little-known documentary is a tribute to reggae singer-songwriter Jimmy Cliff. The film attempts, somewhat confusingly, to portray him as a man of the people, a champion of human rights during a period of racial and political turbulence in Jamaica. Cliff's other movie vehicle, *The Harder They Come*, a crudely shot musical drama, remains stronger than *Bongo Man*. 1985; 89m.

JIVE JUNCTION ★★½
DIR: Edgar G. Ulmer. **CAST:** Dickie Moore, Tina Thayer.
Weird World War II musical about high-school music students who give up playing the classics and turn to jazz in order to help the war effort! How? By opening up a canteen where solidiers can dance their troubles away. Written by future novelist Irving Wallace. 1943; B&W; 62m.

JOE JACKSON LIVE IN TOKYO ★★★★
DIR: Kaname Kawachi. **CAST:** Joe Jackson, Tom Teeley, Rick Ford, Greg Burke.
Unjustly overlooked pop-music artist Joe Jackson is captured in an explosive performance in Tokyo during his 1986 concert tour of Japan. He per-

forms some of his best material with a small ensemble of outstanding musicians who execute the music with tight precision. Songs include "Right and Wrong," "It's a Big World," "Soul Kiss," and "Steppin' Out." 1987; 112m.

JOHN LENNON LIVE IN NEW YORK CITY ★★★★

DIR: Steve Gebhardt, Carol Dysinger. **CAST:** John Lennon, Yoko Ono.

John Lennon's solo concert, a 1972 benefit at Madison Square Garden for mentally handicapped children, was one of only two shows he ever performed after the Beatles stopped touring in 1966. The music itself triumphs over the ill-prepared band who seem disjointed and out of synch. The durability of songs like "Imagine," "Instant Karma," "Mother," and "Woman Is the Nigger of the World" receive powerful and courageous energy from Lennon. 1986; 55m.

JOHN LENNON—THE DREAM IS OVER ★★★

DIR: Thomas Grimm. **CAST:** The Cullberg Ballet.

The Dream Is Over is a splendid dance performance piece that showcases the music of John Lennon. Dance pieces are presented in vignettes and performed by members of the Cullberg Ballet, choreographed and directed by Thomas Mann. The production seems faithful to the songs but lacks the power to give them their needed drama. Songs include "Love," "Imagine," "Mother," and "Working Class Hero." 1987; 101m.

JOLSON SINGS AGAIN ★★½

DIR: Henry Levine. **CAST:** Larry Parks, Barbara Hale, William Demarest, Bill Goodwin, Ludwig Donath, Myron McCormick.

Larry Parks again does the great and incomparable Al Jolson to a turn; Jolson himself again sings his unforgettable standards. But the film, trumped up to cash in, hasn't the class, charm, or swagger of the original. 1949; 96m.

JOLSON STORY, THE ★★★★

DIR: Alfred E. Green. **CAST:** Larry Parks, William Demarest, Evelyn Keyes, Bill Goodwin, Ludwig Donath.

The show business life story of vaudeville and Broadway stage great Al Jolson gets all-stops-out treatment in this fast-paced, tune-full film. Larry Parks acts and lip-syncs the hard-driving entertainer to a Tee. Jolson himself dubbed the singing. 1946; 128m.

JONI MITCHELL—SHADOWS AND LIGHT ★★★½

DIR: Joni Mitchell. **CAST:** Joni Mitchell, Pat Metheny, Jaco Pastorius, Michael Brecker.

Singer-songwriter Joni Mitchell is in top musical form in this outdoor concert filmed in 1979 at the Santa Barbara Bowl. She is joined by some highly gifted jazz musicians and the great backup chorus of the Persuasions in this emotionally charged music event that blends film clips from *Rebel Without a Cause* and some conceptual footage to complement the stage performance. 1982; 60m.

JUMBO ★½

DIR: Charles Walters. **CAST:** Doris Day, Stephen Boyd, Jimmy Durante, Martha Raye, Dean Jagger.

A big-budget circus-locale musical that flopped, despite Rodgers and Hart songs, William Daniels photography, a Sidney Sheldon script from a Hecht and MacArthur story, and a cast that should have known better. 1962; 125m.

JUST AROUND THE CORNER ★★★

DIR: Irving Cummings. **CAST:** Shirley Temple, Joan Davis, Charles Farrell, Bill Robinson, Bert Lahr.

This bucket of sap has nearly too-sweet Shirley Temple ending the Depression by charming a crusty sourpussed millionaire into providing new jobs. The ridiculous becomes sublime when Shirley dances with the incomparable Bill Robinson. 1938; B&W; 70m.

KATE BUSH LIVE AT HAMMERSMITH ODEON ★★★½
DIR: Keith "Keef" MacMillan. **CAST:** Kate Bush.

With her exotic beauty and remarkable woman-child voice, Kate Bush delivers a fine performance in this elaborately staged concert that features music from her first two albums released in the late Seventies. She has a large following in Britain and Europe, but has yet to receive major attention in the United States. This concert video may help to widen her appeal with American audiences. 1979; 52m.

KEITH JARRETT–LAST SOLO ★★★
DIR: Kaname Kawachi. **CAST:** Keith Jarrett.

Gifted jazz pianist Keith Jarrett is captured on video as he slides through ninety minutes of dazzling improvisational music. But unless you're a die-hard fan of Jarrett, this concert may become tedious. 1986; 92m.

KID CREOLE AND THE COCONUTS—THE LEISURE TOUR ★★★
DIR: Peter Orton. **CAST:** Kid Creole, Coatimundi, The Coconuts.

Wild, wacky, and zesty, Kid Creole cooks in this concert film, which also showcases the sexy moves of the camp Coconuts. The Kid and Coatimundi (a.k.a. August Darnell and Andy Hernandez) did duty with Dr. Buzzard's Original Savannah Band, and they concoct a rhythmic stew that ranges from funk to salsa to calypso. 1986; 60m.

KID GALAHAD ★★½
DIR: Phil Karlson. **CAST:** Elvis Presley, Gig Young, Lola Albright, Joan Blackman, Ned Glass.

Remake of a film of the same title made in 1937 starring Edward G. Robinson, Bette Davis, and Humphrey Bogart. In this version, Elvis Presley is a boxer who prefers life as a garage mechanic. Presley fans will enjoy this one, of course. 1962; 95m.

KID MILLIONS ★★
DIR: Roy Del Ruth. **CAST:** Eddie Cantor, Ethel Merman, Ann Sothern, George Murphy, Warren Hymer.

The fifth of six elaborate musicals produced with Eddie Cantor by Samuel Goldwyn. Banjo Eyes inherits a fortune and becomes the mark for a parade of con artists. Lavish Busby Berkeley musical numbers help to salvage an otherwise inane plot. 1934; B&W; 90m.

KIDS ARE ALRIGHT, THE ★★★½
DIR: Jeff Stein. **CAST:** The Who, Ringo Starr, Steve Martin, Tom Smothers.

More a documentary detailing the career of British rock group the Who than an entertainment, this film by Jeff Stein still manages to capture the essence of the trend-setting band and, in doing so, the spirit of rock 'n' roll. Rated PG. 1979; 108m.

KING AND I, THE ★★★★½
DIR: Walter Lang. **CAST:** Yul Brynner, Deborah Kerr, Rita Moreno.

Yul Brynner and Deborah Kerr star in this superb 1956 Rodgers and Hammerstein musicalization of *Anna and the King of Siam*. Kerr is the widowed teacher who first clashes, then falls in love with, the King (Brynner). 1956; 133m.

KING CREOLE ★★★★
DIR: Michael Curtiz. **CAST:** Elvis Presley, Carolyn Jones, Dolores Hart, Dean Jagger, Walter Matthau.

A surprisingly strong Elvis Presley vehicle, this musical, set in New Orleans, benefits from strong direction from Michael Curtiz. 1958; 116m.

KING CRIMSON—THREE OF A PERFECT PAIR ★★★★
DIR: Ryuji Sasaki. **CAST:** Robert Fripp, Bill Bruford, Adrian Belew, Tony Levin.

This legendary British art-rock band originally founded by guitarist Robert Fripp features a sensational group of veteran rock musicians in solid form during a 1983 concert tour of Japan.

The band plays a sophisticated, unusually eclectic form of trance music, modern-classical, and avant-garde jazz that is highly imaginative and powerful. This explosive quartet features some astonishing percussion by Bill Bruford, a former member of The Yes band, and some complex yet flowing guitar sounds by Robert Fripp. 1985; 82m.

KING OF JAZZ, THE ★★★
DIR: John Murray Anderson. **CAST:** Paul Whiteman and His Orchestra, John Boles, Bing Crosby.
Lavish big-budget musical revue chock-full of big production numbers and great songs. Shot in early two-color Technicolor. Imaginative settings and photography make this last of the all-star extravaganzas most impressive. 1930; 93m.

KISMET ★★½
DIR: Vincente Minnelli. **CAST:** Howard Keel, Ann Blyth, Monty Woolley, Vic Damone, Dolores Gray.
The Borodin-based Arabian Nights fantasy, a hit on Broadway, is stylishly staged and ripe with "Baubles, Bangles, and Beads" and Dolores Gray's show-stopping "Bagdad." Sadly, however, the shift to film loses the snap and crackle despite great singing by Howard Keel, Vic Damone, and Ann Blyth. The earlier Ronald Colman version (1944) is more fun and a star better. 1955; 113m.

KISS ME KATE ★★★
DIR: George Sidney. **CAST:** Howard Keel, Kathryn Grayson, Keenan Wynn, James Whitmore, Ann Miller, Tommy Rall, Bobby Van, Bob Fosse.
That which is Shakespeare's *Taming of the Shrew* in the original is deftly rendered by Cole Porter, scripter Dorothy Kingsley, and George Sidney's graceful direction, by way of some fine performances by Howard Keel and Kathryn Grayson as a married pair whose on-stage and off-stage lives mingle. Keenan Wynn and James Whitmore play as engaging a duo of low comic gangster types as ever brushed up on their Shakespeare. 1953; 109m.

KISSIN' COUSINS ★
DIR: Gene Nelson. **CAST:** Elvis Presley, Arthur O'Connell, Jack Albertson.
Would Elvis in dual roles double the fun? Divide it by two is closer to the truth. This time he is both an air force lieutenant and a *blond* hillbilly. As a soldier, he is sent to persuade some distant cousins to lease their mountain for a military missile site. He manages to fall in love while belting a few country tunes such as "Smokey Mountain Boy" and "Barefoot Ballad." 1964; 96m.

KNICKERBOCKER HOLIDAY ★★
DIR: Harry Brown. **CAST:** Nelson Eddy, Charles Coburn, Shelley Winters, Chester Conklin, Constance Dowling, Percy Kilbride.
A plodding, lackluster rendition of the Kurt Weill/Maxwell Anderson musical about Peter Stuyvesant and Dutch New York. The best song, "September Song," was originally sung by Walter Huston. Unfortunately, he's not in the film. 1944; B&W; 85m.

KNIGHTS OF THE CITY 🦃
DIR: Dominic Orlando. **CAST:** Leon Isaac Kennedy, Nicholas Campbell, John Mengatti, Wendy Barry, Stoney Jackson, The Fat Boys, Michael Ansara.
An absolutely ridiculous mishmash concerning a New York street gang that is also a pop musical group. In between defending its turf from a rival gang, the boys are also competing in a citywide talent contest. Nothing makes sense in this low-grade misfire. Rated R. 1987; 89m.

KRUSH GROOVE ★½
DIR: Michael Schultz. **CAST:** Blair Underwood, Sheila E., Kurtis Blow, The Fat Boys, Run DMC.
Lame rap musical featuring several performances by well-known artists and not much more. About a struggling record company, this movie is

little more than a series of musical numbers staged with very little imagination. Rated R. 1985; 95m.

LA BAMBA ★★★★
DIR: Luis Valdez. **CAST:** Lou Diamond Phillips, Rosana De Soto, Esai Morales, Danielle von Zerneck, Elizabeth Peña.

At the age of seventeen, with three huge hits under his belt, Ritchie Valens joined Buddy Holly and the Big Bopper on an ill-fated airplane ride that killed all three and left rock 'n' roll bereft of some giant talent. In this biography, *Zoot Suit* writer-director Luis Valdez achieves a fine blend of rock 'n' roll and soap opera. Rated PG-13 for language. 1987; 108m.

LADY SINGS THE BLUES ★★★½
DIR: Sidney J. Furie. **CAST:** Diana Ross, Billy Dee Williams, Richard Pryor.

Diana Ross made a dynamic screen debut in this screen biography of another singing great, Billie Holiday, whose career was thwarted by drug addiction. Rated R. 1972; 144m.

LAST WALTZ, THE ★★★★
DIR: Martin Scorsese. **CAST:** The Band, Bob Dylan, Neil Young, Joni Mitchell, Van Morrison, Eric Clapton, Neil Diamond, Muddy Waters.

Director Martin Scorsese's (*Taxi Driver*) superb film of the Band's final concert appearance is an unforgettable celebration of American music. Rated PG. 1978; 117m.

LES GIRLS ★★★★
DIR: George Cukor. **CAST:** Gene Kelly, Kay Kendall, Taina Elg, Mitzi Gaynor, Jacques Bergerac.

Gene Kelly is charming, Mitzi Gaynor is funny, Taina Elg is funnier, Kay Kendall is funniest in this tale of a libel suit over a published memoir. Three conflicting accounts of what was and wasn't emerge in flashback from the courtroom. A witty film with Cole Porter music and stylish direction by George Cukor. 1957; 114m.

LET IT BE ★★★½
DIR: Michael Lindsay-Hogg. **CAST:** The Beatles.

The last days of the Beatles are chronicled in this *cinéma vérité* production, which was originally meant to be just a documentary on the recording of an album. What emerges, however, is a portrait of four men who have outgrown their images and, sadly, one another. There are moments of abandon, in which they recapture the old magic but overall, the movie makes it obvious that the Beatles would never get back to where they once belonged. Rated G. 1970; 80m.

LET'S MAKE LOVE ★★★
DIR: George Cukor. **CAST:** Marilyn Monroe, Yves Montand, Tony Randall, Wilfrid Hyde-White.

A tasty soufflé filled with engaging performances. Yves Montand plays a millionaire who wants to stop a musical show because it lampoons him. When he meets cast member Marilyn Monroe, he changes his mind. He hires Milton Berle to teach him comedy, Gene Kelly to teach him dance, and Bing Crosby as a vocal coach. Monroe's "My Heart Belongs to Daddy" number is a highlight. 1960; 118m.

LET'S SPEND THE NIGHT TOGETHER ★★★½
DIR: Hal Ashby. **CAST:** The Rolling Stones.

In this concert film, directed by Hal Ashby, the Rolling Stones are seen rockin' and rollin' in footage shot during the band's 1981 American tour. It's a little too long—but Stone's fans and hard-core rockers should love it. Rated PG for suggestive lyrics and behavior. 1982; 94m.

LILI ★★★★
DIR: Charles Walters. **CAST:** Leslie Caron, Mel Ferrer, Zsa Zsa Gabor, Jean-Pierre Aumont.

"Hi Lili, Hi Lili, Hi Low," the famous song by composer Bronislau Kaper, is just one of the delights in this musical fantasy about a French orphan who tags along with a carnival and a self-centered puppeteer. A certified pleasure to keep your spirits up. 1953; 81m.

LISZTOMANIA
DIR: Ken Russell. **CAST:** Roger Daltrey, Sara Kestleman, Paul Nicholas, Fiona Lewis, Ringo Starr.
Ken Russell lets his lurid imagination run sickeningly wild in this hokey screen biography on the life of composer Franz Liszt (played by Roger Daltrey, lead singer for the rock group the Who). Rated R. 1975; 105m.

LITTLE COLONEL, THE ★★★½
DIR: David Butler. **CAST:** Shirley Temple, Lionel Barrymore, Evelyn Venable, Bill Robinson, Sidney Blackmer.
Grandpa Lionel Barrymore is on the outs with daughter Evelyn Venable as the South recovers from the Civil War. Adorable Shirley Temple smoothes it all over. Film's high point is her step dance with Mr. Bojangles, Bill Robinson. 1935; B&W; 80m.

LITTLE MISS BROADWAY ★★★
DIR: Irving Cummings. **CAST:** Shirley Temple, George Murphy, Jane Darwell, Edna May Oliver, Jimmy Durante, El Brendel, Donald Meek.
Orphan Shirley Temple is placed with the manager of a theatrical hotel whose owner, crusty Edna May Oliver, dislikes show people. When she threatens to ship Shirley back to the orphanage, nephew George Murphy sides with the actors. Along the way, Shirley dances with Murphy and clowns with hotel guest Jimmy Durante. 1938; B&W; 70m.

LITTLE NIGHT MUSIC, A ★★½
DIR: Harold Prince. **CAST:** Elizabeth Taylor, Diana Rigg, Lesley-Anne Down.
Based on Ingmar Bergman's comedy about sexual liaisons at a country mansion, this musical version doesn't quite come to life. Rated PG. 1978; 124m.

LITTLE PRINCE, THE ★½
DIR: Stanley Donen. **CAST:** Richard Kiley, Steven Warner, Bob Fosse, Gene Wilder.
Aviator Richard Kiley teaches an alien boy about life and love. This picture has a great cast, beautiful photography, and is based on the children's classic by Antoine de Saint-Exupéry. It also has a poor musical score by Alan J. Lerner and Frederick Loewe. Rated G. 1974; 88m.

LITTLE SHOP OF HORRORS (1986) ★★★★½
DIR: Frank Oz. **CAST:** Rick Moranis, Ellen Greene, Vincent Gardenia, Steve Martin, James Belushi, John Candy, Bill Murray, Christopher Guest.
This totally bent musical-horror-comedy was based on director Roger Corman's bizarre horror cheapie from 1961. Rick Moranis is wonderful as the schnook who finds and cares for a man-eating plant set on conquering the world. It's a little sick on one hand, and uproariously funny, marvelously acted, spectacularly staged, and tuneful on the other. Rated PG-13 for violence. 1986; 94m.

LITTLEST REBEL, THE ★★★½
DIR: David Butler. **CAST:** Shirley Temple, John Boles, Jack Holt, Bill Robinson, Karen Morley, Guinn Williams, Willie Best.
Prime Shirley Temple, in which, as the daughter of a Confederate officer during the Civil War, she thwarts a double execution by charming President Lincoln. The plot stops, of course, while she and Bojangles dance. 1935; B&W; 70m.

LIVE A LITTLE, LOVE A LITTLE ★½
DIR: Norman Taurog. **CAST:** Elvis Presley, Michele Carey, Don Porter, Dick Sargent.
The interesting thing about this Elvis vehicle is that the sexual innuendos are more blatant than in his other romantic comedies. Unfortunately, everything else about this entry is sub-

par. The King plays a photographer falling in love with an eccentric kook. As always, Elvis's songs ("Wonderful World," "A Little Less Conversation," and "Edge of Reality") are the film's highlights. Rated PG for mild profanity and sexual situations. 1968; 89m.

LIVE AT THE HOLLYWOOD BOWL ★★½

DIR: Ray Manzarek. **CAST:** The Doors.

On July 3, 1968, the Doors returned to their hometown to play the prestigious Hollywood Bowl, an outstanding achievement for a band only two years old. Unfortunately, though the Doors put on one of the most outrageous rock shows of its day, the passage of over twenty years has taken its toll. The band's antics, particularly those of lead singer Jim Morrison, seem contrived and, worst of all, boring. 1987; 55m.

LIVING INXS ★★★

DIR: Karl Steinberg. **CAST:** Michael Hutchence, Andrew Farriss, Kirk Pengilly, Tim Farriss, Jon Farriss, Garry Gary Beers, Jenny Morris.

Sexy singer Michael Hutchence does a great Jim Morrison—and his band is much better than the Doors. Still, the songs suffer from a sameness and this 1985 concert film from Inxs's own Australia could have benefitted from the brasher material of the 1987 breakthrough album, "Kick." 1985; 48m.

LOVE ME OR LEAVE ME ★★★★

DIR: Charles Vidor. **CAST:** James Cagney, Doris Day, Cameron Mitchell, Robert Keith, Tom Tully.

This musical bio-pic about ambitious singer Ruth Etting and her crude and domineering racketeer husband found usually cute Doris Day and old pro James Cagney scorching the screen with strong performances. Along with biting drama, a record-setting thirteen Doris Day solos, including the title song and "Ten Cents a Dance," are served. The story won an Oscar. 1955; 122m.

LOVING YOU ★★★

DIR: Hal Kanter. **CAST:** Elvis Presley, Lizabeth Scott, Wendell Corey, Dolores Hart.

This better-than-average Elvis Presley vehicle features him as a small-town country boy who makes good when his singing ability is discovered. It has a bit of romance but the main attraction is Elvis singing his rock 'n' roll songs, including the title tune. 1957; 101m.

MAD DOGS AND ENGLISHMEN ★★★½

DIR: Pierre Adidge. **CAST:** Joe Cocker, Leon Russell, Rita Coolidge.

Joe Cocker and friends, including Rita Collidge and Leon Russell, put together one of the zaniest rock tours ever in the early 1970s, leaving a legendary trail of drugs and groupies in their wake. Fortunately, the superstar group was also able to function on stage, and this movie effectively captures the spirit of the 1970 tour. Performances of "With a Little Help from My Friends," "Superstar," and "Feeling Alright" can be considered rock classics. 1972; 118m.

MAGICAL MYSTERY TOUR ★½

DIR: The Beatles. **CAST:** The Beatles, Bonzo Dog Band.

This is a tour by bus and by mind. Unfortunately, the minds involved must have been distorted at the time that the film was made. Occasional bursts of wit and imagination come through, but mostly this chunk of psychedelic pretension is a crashing bore. 1967; 60m.

MAME ★

DIR: Gene Saks. **CAST:** Lucille Ball, Robert Preston, Jane Connell, Beatrice Arthur.

You won't love Lucy in this one. Or Robert Preston, either. It's Roz Russell's boffo *Auntie Mame* with music, and the notes are all sour. Rated PG. 1974; 131m.

MAN OF LA MANCHA
DIR: Arthur Hiller. **CAST:** Peter O'Toole, Sophia Loren, James Coco, Harry Andrews.

For those who loved the hit Broadway musical and those who heard about it and looked forward to this film, this is a shameful and outrageous letdown. Rated G. 1972; 130m.

MANHATTAN MERRY-GO-ROUND ★★½
DIR: Charles F. Riesner. **CAST:** Gene Autry, Phil Regan, Leo Carrillo, Ann Dvorak, Tamara Geva, Ted Lewis, Cab Calloway and the Cotton Club Orchestra, Joe DiMaggio, Louis Prima, Henry Armetta, Max Terhune, Smiley Burnette, James Gleason.

Incredible line-up of popular performers and celebrities is the main attraction of this catch-all production about a gangster who takes over a recording company. Basically a collection of performances strung together by a romantic thread, this oddity runs the gamut from Gene Autry's country crooning to the jivin' gyrations of legendary Cab Calloway. 1938; B&W; 80m.

MAX ROACH IN WASHINGTON, D.C. ★★★½
DIR: Stanley Dorfman. **CAST:** Max Roach.

A sizzling hour of fusion jazz by celebrated percussionist Max Roach whose drumming style has influenced many of today's musicians. The music stands apart from the poor video production. 1986; 60m.

MAYTIME ★★★
DIR: Robert Z. Leonard. **CAST:** Jeanette MacDonald, Nelson Eddy, John Barrymore, Sig Ruman.

A curio of the past. A penniless tenor meets and falls in love with an opera star suffering in a loveless marriage to her adoring and jealous teacher and mentor. The hands Fate deals are not pat. See if you can tell that John Barrymore is reading his lines from idiot boards off camera. This film is one of the Eddy/MacDonald duo's best. 1937; B&W; 132m.

MEET ME IN ST. LOUIS ★★★★
DIR: Vincente Minnelli. **CAST:** Judy Garland, Margaret O'Brien, Tom Drake.

Here's a fun-filled entertainment package made at the MGM studios during the heyday of their musicals. This nostalgic look at a family in St. Louis before the 1903 World's Fair dwells on the tension when the father announces an impending transfer to New York. Judy Garland's songs remain fresh and enjoyable today. 1944; 112m.

MEET THE NAVY ★★★
DIR: Alfred Travers. **CAST:** Lionel Murton, Margaret Hurst.

This British musical fell into obscurity because the cast contains no star names. That's because they're all from the Royal Canadian Navy revue, a troupe of drafted performers who toured bases entertaining servicemen in WWII. However, there are enough talented singers, dancers, and funnymen here to make you wonder why none went on to greater success. 1946; B&W; 81m.

MERRY WIDOW, THE ★★★
DIR: Ernst Lubitsch. **CAST:** Maurice Chevalier, Jeanette MacDonald, Una Merkel, Edward Everett Horton.

A carefully chosen cast, a witty script, an infectious score, lavish sets, and the fabled Lubitsch touch at the helm make this musical comedy sparkle. Maurice Chevalier and Jeanette MacDonald are perfect. 1934; B&W; 99m.

METROPOLIS (MUSICAL VERSION) ★★★★★
DIR: Fritz Lang (and Giorgio Moroder). **CAST:** Brigitte Helm, Alfred Abel.

Fritz Lang's 1926 silent science-fiction classic has been enhanced with special individual coloring and tints, recently recovered scenes, storyboards and stills. The rock score, supervised by Giorgio Moroder, features Pat Benatar, Bonnie Tyler, Loverboy, Billy Squier, Adam Ant, Freddie Mercury, Jon Anderson, and Cycle V. 1984; 120m.

MICHAEL JACKSON MOONWALKER ★★★★½
DIR: Jerry Kramer, Collin Chivers. **CAST:** Michael Jackson, Sean Lennon.

Spectacle is what we expect of Michael Jackson, and he delivers a stunning twenty-first-century Saturday-morning special that runs the course from Disney to Claymation to sizzling sci-fi effects. But what makes it such a treat is the sensational show of humor as Jackson parodies his own treatment by the tabloids, his kooky fetishes, even his own success. 1988; 84m.

MILLION DOLLAR MERMAID ★★
DIR: Mervyn LeRoy. **CAST:** Esther Williams, Victor Mature, Walter Pidgeon, David Brian, Jesse White.

Esther William swims through her role as famous early distaff aquatic star Annette Kellerman, who pioneered one-piece suits and vaudeville tank acts. Victor Mature woos her in this highly fictionalized film biography. The Busby Berkeley production numbers are a highlight. 1952; 115m.

MRS. BROWN YOU'VE GOT A LOVELY DAUGHTER ★★
DIR: Saul Swimmer. **CAST:** Herman's Hermits, Stanley Holloway.

England's Herman's Hermits star in this film, named after one of their hit songs. The limited plot revolves around the group acquiring a greyhound and deciding to race it. Caution: Only for hard-core Hermits fans! Rated G. 1968; 110m.

MONTEREY POP ★★★★
DIR: D. A. Pennebaker. **CAST:** Jimi Hendrix, Otis Redding, The Who, The Animals, Jefferson Airplane, Janis Joplin, Country Joe and the Fish, The Mamas and the Papas, Booker T. and the MGs, Ravi Shankar.

Despite its ragged sound by today's digital standards, *Monterey Pop* is a historical masterpiece. A chance to see legendary Sixties soloists and groups in their prime far outweighs any technical drawbacks. This was the concert that kicked off 1967's Summer of Love, and with it, a generation of mega-performer shows that culminated in Woodstock. 1969; 72m.

MOON OVER MIAMI ★★★
DIR: Walter Lang. **CAST:** Don Ameche, Robert Cummings, Betty Grable, Carole Landis, Charlotte Greenwood, Jack Haley.

Texas sisters Betty Grable and Carole Landis arrive in Miami to hunt for rich husbands. After a suitable round of romantic adventures, they snare penniless Don Ameche and millionaire Robert Cummings. A fun film that helped establish Grable. 1941; 91m.

MOZART STORY, THE ★★½
DIR: Carl Hartl. **CAST:** Hans Holt, Winnie Markus, Curt Jurgens.

Though produced in Austria, this Mozart biography plays as loose with the facts as any Hollywood biopic. You'll only want to see it for the music, played by the Vienna Philharmonic Orchestra and Vienna State Opera. Includes excerpts from all of Mozart's best-known works. Curt Jurgens (billed as Curd Juergens) plays Emperor Joseph II. Dialogue dubbed in English. 1937; B&W; 95m.

MURDER AT THE VANITIES ★★★½
DIR: Mitchell Leisen. **CAST:** Jack Oakie, Kitty Carlisle, Victor McLaglen, Carl Brisson, Donald Meek, Gail Patrick, Jessie Ralph, Duke Ellington, Ann Sheridan.

A musical whodunit, this blend of comedy and mystery finds tenacious Victor McLaglen embroiled in a murder investigation at Earl Carroll's Vanities, a popular and long-running variety show of the 1930s and 1940s. Musical numbers and novelty acts pop up between clues in this stylish oddity. Lots of fun. 1934; B&W; 89m.

MUSIC MAN, THE ★★★★½
DIR: Morton Da Costa. **CAST:** Robert Preston, Shirley Jones, Buddy Hackett, Ron Howard, Paul Ford, Hermione Gingold.

They sure don't make musicals like this anymore, a smashing adaptation of Meredith Willson's Broadway hit. Robert Preston reprises the role of his life as a smooth-talkin' salesman who cajoles the parents of River City, Iowa, into purchasing band instruments and uniforms for their children. 1962; 151m.

MY FAIR LADY ★★★★½
DIR: George Cukor. **CAST:** Rex Harrison, Audrey Hepburn, Stanley Holloway.

Pygmalion, the timeless George Bernard Shaw play, has been a success in every form in which it has been presented. This Oscar-winning 1964 movie musical adaptation is no exception. Rex Harrison, as Professor Henry Higgins, is the perfect example of British class snobbishness. Audrey Hepburn gives a fine performance as Eliza Doolittle (with Marni Nixon supplying the singing). 1964; 170m.

MY NAME IS BARBRA ★★★★
DIR: Dwight Hemion. **CAST:** Barbra Streisand.

Barbra Streisand fans have a real treasure awaiting them in *My Name Is Barbra*. Shown in 1965, shot in black and white, and featuring no guests, it was Streisand's first television special. It's a wonderful opportunity to see this exceptional performer early in her career. Viewers will also be treated to knockout versions of "When the Sun Comes Out" and "My Man." 1965; 60m.

NAUGHTY MARIETTA ★★★
DIR: W. S. Van Dyke. **CAST:** Jeanette MacDonald, Nelson Eddy, Frank Morgan, Douglass Dumbrille, Elsa Lanchester, Akim Tamiroff.

This warm, vibrant rehash of Victor Herbert's tuneful 1910 operetta established leads Jeanette MacDonald and Nelson Eddy as the screen's peerless singing duo. The plot's next to nothing—a French princess flees to America and falls in love with an Indian scout—but the music is stirring, charming, and corny. 1935; B&W; 106m.

NEPTUNE'S DAUGHTER ★★½
DIR: Edward Buzzell. **CAST:** Esther Williams, Red Skelton, Keenan Wynn, Ricardo Montalban, Betty Garrett, Mel Blanc, Mike Mazurki, Ted de Corsia, Xavier Cugat.

Big-budgeted aquatic musical from MGM studios has Esther Williams playing a (what else?) swimsuit designer on holiday in South America floating in and out of danger with Red Skelton. The plot isn't too important to this film as long as you can keep time with Xavier Cugat's mamba beat and not lose your place in the conga line. Harmless, enjoyable nonsense. 1949; 93m.

NEVER STEAL ANYTHING SMALL ★★½
DIR: Charles Lederer. **CAST:** James Cagney, Shirley Jones, Roger Smith, Cara Williams, Nehemiah Persoff, Royal Dano, Horace MacMahon.

Unbelievable musical comedy-drama about a good-hearted union labor leader is saved by the dynamic James Cagney, who was always enough to make even the most hackneyed story worth watching. 1959; 94m.

NEW FACES ★★½
DIR: Harry Horner. **CAST:** Ronny Graham, Eartha Kitt, Paul Lynde, Robert Clary, Alice Ghostley, Carol Lawrence.

This is a filmed version of the 1952 smash Broadway revue with a thin storyline added. Ronny Graham is very good in a parody of *Death of a Salesman*. Eartha Kitt became a star through this vehicle and Robert Clary, Paul Lynde, and Alice Ghostley are used to good advantage. 1954; 99m.

NEW MOON ★★★
DIR: Robert Z. Leonard. **CAST:** Jeanette MacDonald, Nelson Eddy, Mary Boland, George Zucco.
This melodramatic romance, which takes place during the French Revolution, features Jeanette MacDonald as a spoiled aristocrat who falls for an extraordinary bondsman (Nelson Eddy). Some comic moments, and Eddy comes off looking much better than MacDonald in this one, one of eight love stories they brought to the screen. 1940; B&W; 106m.

NEW YORK, NEW YORK ★★★½
DIR: Martin Scorsese. **CAST:** Robert De Niro, Liza Minnelli, Lionel Stander, Georgie Auld, Mary Kay Place.
This is a difficult film to warm to, but worth it. Robert De Niro gives a splendid performance as an egomaniacal saxophonist who woos sweet-natured singer Liza Minnelli. The songs (especially the title tune) are great, and those with a taste for something different in musicals will find it rewarding. Rated PG. 1977; 163m.

NO NUKES ★★★½
DIR: Julian Schlossberg, Danny Goldberg, Anthony Potenza. **CAST:** Jackson Browne, Crosby Stills and Nash, The Doobie Brothers, John Hall, Gil Scott-Heron, Bonnie Raitt, Carly Simon, Bruce Springsteen, James Taylor, Jessie Colin Young.
Entertaining record of the MUSE concerts presented for five nights at Madison Square Garden to benefit the antinuclear movement. Your enjoyment will depend greatly on appreciation of the artists involved, but the rare footage of Bruce Springsteen in concert is electrifying. While the picture is grainy, the stereo soundtrack is excellent. Rated PG for profanity. 1980; 103m.

OKLAHOMA! ★★★★
DIR: Fred Zinnemann. **CAST:** Shirley Jones, Gordon MacRae, Rod Steiger, Eddie Albert, Gloria Grahame.
This movie adaptation of Rodgers and Hammerstein's Broadway musical stars Shirley Jones as a country girl (Laurie) who is courted by Curly, a cowboy (Gordon MacRae). Rod Steiger plays a villainous Jud, who also pursues Laurie. A very entertaining musical. 1956; 140m.

OLD CURIOSITY SHOP, THE ★★★
DIR: Michael Tuchner. **CAST:** Anthony Newley, David Hemmings, David Warner, Michael Hordern, Jill Bennett.
This enjoyable British-made follow-up to *Scrooge*, the successful musical adaptation of Charles Dickens's *A Christmas Carol*, adds tunes to the author's *The Old Curiosity Shop* and casts songwriter-singer Anthony Newley as the title villain. Rated PG. 1975; 118m.

OLIVER ★★★★★
DIR: Carol Reed. **CAST:** Ron Moody, Oliver Reed, Hugh Griffith, Shani Wallis, Mark Lester, Jack Wild.
Charles Dickens never was such fun. *Oliver Twist* has become a luxurious musical and multiple Oscar-winner (including best picture). Mark Lester is the angelic Oliver, whose adventures begin one mealtime when he pleads, "Please, sir, I want some more." Jack Wild is an impish Artful Dodger, and Ron Moody steals the show as the scoundrel Fagin. Oliver Reed prevents the tale from becoming *too* sugar-coated. Rated G. 1968; 153m.

ON A CLEAR DAY, YOU CAN SEE FOREVER ★
DIR: Vincente Minnelli. **CAST:** Barbra Streisand, Yves Montand, Bob Newhart, Larry Blyden, Jack Nicholson.
Crashing, thudding bore of a musical about a psychiatrist (Yves Montand) who discovers that one of his patients (Barbra Streisand) has lived a former life and can recall it under hypnosis. Pompous screenplay filled with its own importance interrupted by vacuous songs. Rated PG for violence. 1970; 129m.

ON THE TOWN ★★★★
DIR: Gene Kelly, Stanley Donen. **CAST:** Gene Kelly, Frank Sinatra, Ann Miller, Vera-Ellen, Jules Munshin, Betty Garrett.
This is a classic boy-meets-girl, boy-loses-girl fable set to music. Three sailors are on a twenty-four-hour leave and find themselves (for the first time) in the big city of New York. They seek romance and adventure during their leave—and find it. 1949; 98m.

ONE FROM THE HEART ★★
DIR: Francis Ford Coppola. **CAST:** Teri Garr, Frederic Forrest, Raul Julia, Nastassja Kinski, Harry Dean Stanton, Allen Garfield, Luana Anders.
This Francis Coppola film is a ballet of graceful and complex camera movements occupying magnificent sets—but the characters get lost in the process. Teri Garr and Frederic Forrest play a couple flirting with two strangers (Raul Julia and Nastassja Kinski), but they fade away in the flash and fizz. Rated R. 1982; 100m.

ONE TRICK PONY ★★★½
DIR: Robert M. Young. **CAST:** Paul Simon, Lou Reed, Rip Torn, Blair Brown, Joan Hackett.
This good little movie looks at life on the road with a has-been rock star. Paul Simon is surprisingly effective as the rock star who finds both his popularity slipping and his marriage falling apart. Rated R for nudity. 1980; 98m.

ORNETTE—MADE IN AMERICA ★★★★
DIR: Shirley Clark. **CAST:** Ornette Coleman.
This critically acclaimed documentary by film and video artist Shirley Clark is a revealing portrait of jazz musician Ornette Coleman, one of the most innovative forces in contemporary music. He is captured in performance in his hometown, Fort Worth, Texas. It's a sensational performance with the local symphony orchestra. The stunning music is juxtaposed with interviews and rare early performances that feature jazz musicians Charley Haden, Don Cherry, and Ornette's son Darnel. 1987; 80m.

ORPHAN BOY OF VIENNA, AN ★★
DIR: Max Neufeld. **CAST:** Ferdinand Materhofer.
The only reason to see this hokey tear-jerker about a boy who struggles to adjust to life in a German orphanage is the presence of the famous Vienna Boys' Choir, accompanied in several performances by the Vienna Philharmonic. In German with English subtitles. 1937; B&W; 90m.

OTELLO ★★★★★
DIR: Franco Zeffirelli. **CAST:** Placido Domingo, Katia Ricciarelli, Justino Diaz, Urbano Barberini.
As with his screen version of *La Traviata*, Franco Zeffirelli's *Otello* is a masterpiece of filmed opera. In fact, it may well be the best such motion picture ever made. Placido Domingo is brilliant in the title role, both as an actor and a singer. And he gets able support from Katia Ricciarelli as Desdemona and Justino Diaz as Iago. Rated PG for stylized violence. 1987; 122m.

PAGAN LOVE SONG ★½
DIR: Robert Alton. **CAST:** Esther Williams, Howard Keel, Minna Gombell, Rita Moreno.
Watered-down love story about American schoolteacher Howard Keel who falls for native girl Esther Williams is just another excuse for singing, swimming, and studio-bound rehash of a tired old plot line. 1950; 76m.

PAINT YOUR WAGON ★★★½
DIR: Joshua Logan. **CAST:** Clint Eastwood, Lee Marvin, Jean Seberg, Harve Presnell, John Mitchum.
Clint Eastwood and Lee Marvin play partners during the California gold rush era. They share everything, including a bride (Jean Seberg) bought from a Mormon traveler (John

Mitchum), in this silly, but fun musical. Rated PG. 1969; 166m.

PAL JOEY ★★★★
DIR: George Sidney. **CAST:** Frank Sinatra, Rita Hayworth, Kim Novak, Barbara Nichols.

Frank Sinatra plays the antihero of this Rodgers and Hart classic about a hip guy who hopes to open a slick nightclub in San Francisco. With love interests Rita Hayworth and Kim Novak vying for ol' blue eyes, and George Sidney's fast-paced direction, the picture is an enjoyable romp. The Rodgers and Hart score is perhaps their finest. 1957; 111m.

PARADISE HAWAIIAN STYLE ★★½
DIR: Michael Moore. **CAST:** Elvis Presley, Suzanna Leigh.

Elvis Presley returns to Hawaii after his 1962 film, *Blue Hawaii*. This time he plays a pilot who makes time for romance while setting up a charter plane service. Some laughs and lots of Elvis's songs. 1966; 91m.

PAUL MCCARTNEY AND WINGS—ROCK SHOW ★★½
DIR: Paul McCartney. **CAST:** Paul McCartney.

Paul McCartney covers most of his hits in this concert recorded at the Seattle King Dome during Wings' 1976 world tour. But unless you're a big fan of the famous ex-Beatle, this unimaginatively shot film (underlit and grainy) will probably put you to sleep. McCartney and his band perform most of the music in a lifeless manner. 1981; 102m.

PAUL SIMON—GRACELAND: THE AFRICAN CONCERT ★★★★
DIR: Michael Lindsay-Hogg. **CAST:** Paul Simon, Hugh Masekela, Ladysmith Black Mambazo, Miriam Makeba.

Emotion tends to be missing from most concert videos, but there is no lack of fire from Hugh Masekela, dripping with sweat, or Miriam Makeba, singing about the South African homeland that exiled her in 1960. Add to this Paul Simon's stunning songs from his Grammy-winning *Graceland*, a crack band playing rhythm-rich African pop, and outstanding backing vocals. A colorful concert film from Zimbabwe with sparkling hi-fi stereo sound. 1987; 90m.

PENNIES FROM HEAVEN ★★★½
DIR: Herbert Ross. **CAST:** Steve Martin, Bernadette Peters, Jessica Harper.

Steve Martin and Bernadette Peters star in this downbeat musical. The production numbers are fabulous, but the dreary storyline—with Martin as a down-and-out song-plugger in Depression-era Chicago—may disappoint fans of the genre. Rated R for of profanity and sexual situations. 1981; 107m.

PETE KELLY'S BLUES ★★½
DIR: Jack Webb. **CAST:** Jack Webb, Janet Leigh, Edmond O'Brien, Jayne Mansfield, Lee Marvin, Peggy Lee, Ella Fitzgerald, Martin Milner, Andy Devine.

Guys, gals, gangsters, gin, and gutbucket Dixieland jazz are done to a turn in this ultrarealistic re-creation of how it was in Kansas City and across the river in the Roaring Twenties. 1955; 95m.

PETE TOWNSHEND'S DEEP END ★★★½
DIR: Keith "Keef" MacMillan. **CAST:** Pete Townshend, Dave Gilmour, Simon Phillips, Rabbit, Peter Hope Evans.

For all his success as a songwriter, Pete Townshend never felt secure to step out as a singer with the Who. Nestled among a rave-up fourteen-piece band, powered by horns and backed by several singers, Townshend need not worry about vocal punch. This exciting concert film features Townshend's best songs. The players are brilliant, especially Pink Floyd guitarist Dave Gilmour and young harmonica discovery Peter Hope Evans. 1986; 87m.

PHANTOM OF THE PARADISE ★★½

DIR: Brian De Palma. **CAST:** Paul Williams, William Finley, Jessica Harper.

Before he became obsessed with Hitchcock *hommages* and ultraviolent bloodbaths, director Brian De Palma did this odd little blend of Faust and *Phantom of the Opera*. William Finley sells his soul to Paul Williams and learns the dangers of achieving fame too quickly. Wildly erratic, with tedious dialogue alternating with droll visual bits. Rated PG—mild violence. 1974; 92m.

PIN-UP GIRL ★★★

DIR: H. Bruce Humberstone. **CAST:** Betty Grable, John Harvey, Martha Raye, Joe E. Brown, Eugene Pallette.

Another in the series of happy musical comedies Betty Grable starred in during World War II, *Pin-Up Girl* logically took its title from her status with GIs. This time, a secretary falls for a sailor. To be near him, she pretends to be a Broadway star. 1944; 83m.

PINK FLOYD AT POMPEII ★★★½

DIR: Michele Arnaud. **CAST:** Pink Floyd.

This 1971 French film captures Pink Floyd during the departure from their early psychedelic period. This unique band performs their music live without an audience in the Pompeii Amphitheatre in Greece. Director Michele Arnaud's camera records this powerful music event through awesome panoramic tracking shots. 1981; 85m.

PINK FLOYD THE WALL ★½

DIR: Alan Parker. **CAST:** Bob Geldof, Christine Hargreaves, Bob Hoskins.

For all its apparent intent, this visually impressive film, which has very little dialogue but, rather, uses garish visual images to the accompaniment of the British rock band's music, ends up being more of a celebration of insanity and inhumanity than an indictment of it as intended. Rated R for violence. 1982; 99m.

PIRATE, THE ★★★★

DIR: Vincente Minnelli. **CAST:** Judy Garland, Gene Kelly, Gladys Cooper, Reginald Owen, Walter Slezak.

This splashy, though at times narratively weak, musical features Judy Garland and Gene Kelly singing and dancing their way through a Cole Porter score. It features a terrific dance sequence titled "Be a Clown" featuring clown-pirate-acrobat Kelly and the marvelous Nicholas Brothers. Watch it for the songs and the dances. 1948; 102m.

PIRATE MOVIE, THE ★★

DIR: Ken Annakin. **CAST:** Christopher Atkins, Kristy McNichol, Ted Hamilton, Bill Kerr.

This rock 'n' roll adaptation of Gilbert and Sullivan's *The Pirates of Penzance* is passable entertainment. Expect a lot of music, a lot of swashbuckling, and a little sappy romance. Directed by Ken Annakin, this film is rated PG for slight profanity and sexual innuendo. 1982; 99m.

PIRATES OF PENZANCE, THE ★★★★

DIR: Wilford Leach. **CAST:** Angela Lansbury, Kevin Kline, Linda Ronstadt, Rex Smith, George Ross.

Stylized sets and takeoffs of Busby Berkeley camera setups give *Pirates* a true cinematic quality. Add to that outstanding work by the principals, some nice bits of slapstick comedy, and you have an enjoyable film for the entire family. Rated G. 1983; 112m.

POLICE SYNCHRONICITY CONCERT, THE ★★★★½

DIR: Kevin Godley, Lol Creme. **CAST:** The Police.

The Police, one of the most exciting bands to surface in recent years, are brilliantly captured live at Atlanta's Omni during their 1984 U.S. tour. This exciting musical event receives a great visual treatment by the gifted filmmaking duo of Godley and

Creme, who are responsible for some great music videos from Herbie Hancock, Peter Gabriel, and Duran Duran. Songs include "Message in the Bottle," "Wrapped Around Your Finger," "Can't Stand Losing You," and "Every Breath You Take." 1984; 76m.

POOR LITTLE RICH GIRL ★★★★
DIR: Irving Cummings. **CAST:** Shirley Temple, Alice Faye, Jack Haley, Michael Whalen, Gloria Stuart, Henry Armetta, Sara Haden, Jane Darwell.

A strong supporting cast makes this Shirley Temple starrer one of her finest. She plays a motherless child who gets lost. Befriended by vaudevillians Alice Faye and Jack Haley, she joins the act, wows 'em, and wins 'em. The plot's full of soap, but as movie musicals go this one is tops. 1936; B&W; 72m.

PRINCE AND THE REVOLUTION LIVE ★★★½
DIR: Paul Becher. **CAST:** Prince and the Revolution.

Filmed May 1985 at the height of Prince's popularity, this exciting concert captures an engaging, aggressive, and extremely sexy performer in his prime. The costuming and theatrics add to the pop experience, which is powered by shattering stereo hi-fi sound. Not rated. 1985; 116m.

PRIVATE BUCKAROO ★★
DIR: Eddie Cline. **CAST:** The Andrews Sisters, Joe E. Lewis, Dick Foran, Jennifer Holt, Donald O'Connor, Peggy Ryan, Harry James.

Showcase vehicle for Patty, LaVerne, and Maxene, the Andrews Sisters, who decide to put on a show for soldiers. The Donald O'Connor/Peggy Ryan duo stands out. 1942; B&W; 68m.

PURPLE RAIN ★★½
DIR: Albert Magnoli. **CAST:** Prince, Apollonia, Morris Day, Olga Karlatos.

In his first movie, pop star Prince plays a struggling young musician searching for self-awareness and love while trying to break into the rock charts. The film unsuccessfully straddles the line between a concert release and a storytelling production. As it is, the music is great, but the plot leaves a lot to be desired. Rated R for nudity, suggested sex, and profanity. 1984; 113m.

QUADROPHENIA ★★★½
DIR: Franc Roddam. **CAST:** Phil Daniels, Mark Wingett, Philip Davis, Sting.

Based on the Who's rock opera, this is the story of a teenager growing up in the early 1960s and the decisions he is forced to make on the path to adulthood. The focus is on the conflict between two English youth cults, the Rockers, a typical bike gang outfit, and the Mods, who also ride bikes but are more responsible types. Rated R because the language is rough, the violence graphic. 1979; 115m.

RAGS TO RICHES ★★
DIR: Bruce Seth Green. **CAST:** Joseph Bologna, Tisha Campbell.

Joseph Bologna plays millionaire Nick Foley, who tries to soften his ruthless-businessman image by adopting six girls. His money can't solve the problems that the girls present him with. This was a pilot for the TV series of the same name. 1986; 96m.

RAINBOW BRIDGE ★★
DIR: Chuck Wein. **CAST:** Jimi Hendrix, Pat Hartley.

There was a time when many of us could relate to the nonsensical ramblings of the acid heads gathered at the Rainbow Bridge Occult Meditation Center on Maui, Hawaii. They consume much of the movie. But now only the power of Jimi Hendrix's guitar playing, exhibited in the final 30 minutes, saves this mess from a turkey rating. 1971; 74m.

RAPPIN' ★½
DIR: Joel Silberg. **CAST:** Mario Van Peebles, Tasia Valenza, Charles Flohe.

Rap songs get the *Breakin'* treatment in this uninspired formula musical. Once again, a street performer (rap singer Mario van Peebles) takes on the baddies and still has time to make it in show biz. Dumb stuff. Rated PG for profanity. 1985; 92m.

REBECCA OF SUNNYBROOK FARM (1938) ★★★½
DIR: Allan Dwan. **CAST:** Shirley Temple, Randolph Scott, Jack Haley, Gloria Stuart, Phyllis Brooks, Helen Westley, Slim Summerville, Bill Robinson.

Lightweight but engaging Shirley Temple vehicle has the 1930's superstar playing a child performer who wants to be on radio. While Temple hoofs with the likes of Jack Haley and Bill "Bojangles" Robinson, Randolph Scott, in one of his few screen appearances out of the saddle, romances Gloria Stuart. 1938; B&W; 80m.

RED SHOES, THE ★★★★
DIR: Michael Powell. **CAST:** Moira Shearer, Anton Walbrook.

Fascinating backstage look at the world of ballet manages to overcome its unoriginal, often trite, plot. A ballerina (Moira Shearer) is urged by her forceful and single-minded impresario (Anton Walbrook) to give up a romantic involvement in favor of her career, with tragic consequences. Good acting and fine camera work save this British film from its overlong standard story. 1948; 136m.

REET, PETITE AND GONE ★★★
DIR: William Forest Crouch. **CAST:** Louis Jordan.

Louis Jordan, the overlooked hero of prerock days, is well captured (along with his hot backup band, the Tympany Five) in this farcical all-black musical. Jordan's sound is a blues-pop fusion known as jumpin' jive, and it gets great film treatment in this little-known movie treasure. 1946; 67m.

REGGAE TRIBUTE ★★★
DIR: Karen Baxter, Robert H. Peltscher. **CAST:** Third World, Steel Pulse, Melody Makers, Judy Mowatt, Eek-A-Mouse, Sly and Robbie, I-Threes, Wailers, Mighty Diamonds.

The entire honor society of reggae performs a live rhythmic tribute to the late Bob Marley. The format makes it hard to focus on any one act, and none emerges as a show-stopper. Still, for rasta fans and the uninitiated alike, this live reggae songfest is a fabulous sampler. 1985; 103m.

RETURN OF BRUNO, THE ★★★
DIR: Jim Yukich. **CAST:** Bruce Willis, Phil Collins, Dick Clark, Elton John, Brian Wilson, Michael J. Fox, Joan Baez, The Bee Gees.

Fake documentary follows fictitious Sixties singer Bruno (Bruce Willis) from *American Bandstand* to Woodstock, acid rock, and disco. Cameos are funny, especially Ringo Starr, who says "If it hadn't been for Bruno, there'd have been no Beatles." This was done before, and better, by *This is Spinal Tap* and *The Rutles*, but remains a refreshing change from standard HBO specials. Unrated. 1987; 56m.

RETURN TO WATERLOO ★
DIR: Ray Davies. **CAST:** Ken Colley.

Ray Davies, leader of the Kinks, scripted, directed, and scored this short feature, demonstrating again the danger of giving rock stars a green light to race to another art form. Set on a commuter train, the film looks tough, making nightmarish cuts into the psyche of a working-class hero, played hauntingly by Ken Colley. But connecting the dots into a cohesive picture takes a different talent than strumming a few pleasing chords. 1985; 60m.

ROBERTA ★★★½
DIR: William A. Seiter. **CAST:** Irene Dunne, Fred Astaire, Ginger Rogers, Randolph Scott, Helen Westley.

This lighthearted story of a group of entertainers who find themselves operating a dress shop in Paris belongs to the second and third-billed Fred Astaire and Ginger Rogers. With the music of Jerome Kern and Otto Harbach, including those gems "Smoke Gets in Your Eyes" and "I Won't

Dance," this carefree film is very enjoyable. Later remade as *Lovely to Look At*. 1935; B&W; 85m.

ROBIN & THE SEVEN HOODS ★★★
DIR: Gordon Douglas. **CAST:** Frank Sinatra, Dean Martin, Sammy Davis Jr., Bing Crosby, Peter Falk, Barbara Rush, Victor Buono, Edward G. Robinson.

Musical reworking of the Robin Hood legend set in Jazz Age, gangster-ruled Chicago. Frank Sinatra, Dean Martin, *et al*, are the Merry Men, with Bing Crosby the silver-tongued spokesman Alan A. Dale. Sometimes stretches a point to be too Runyonesque, but good tunes and actors make it pleasant. 1964; 123m.

ROCK, PRETTY BABY ★★
DIR: Richard Bartlett. **CAST:** John Saxon, Sal Mineo, Rod McKuen, Luana Patten, Edward Platt, Fay Wray, Shelley Fabares.

John Saxon plays Jimmy Daley, 18-year-old leader of a struggling rock 'n' roll combo whose life is complicated by his doctor father who wants him to go into the medical profession and a difficult first-love relationship with Luana Patten. So laughably awful in spots that it becomes enjoyable. 1957; B&W; 89m.

ROCK, ROCK, ROCK ★★
DIR: Will Price. **CAST:** Tuesday Weld, Teddy Randazzo, Alan Freed, Frankie Lymon and the Teenagers, Chuck Berry, The Flamingos, The Johnny Burnette Trio.

If you love Tuesday Weld, Fifties rock, or entertainingly terrible movies, this nostalgic blast from the past is for you. The plot is so flimsy, Dobie Gillis would have rejected it. But watching a young Weld lip-synch to songs actually sung by Connie Francis is a wonderful treat. 1956; B&W; 83m.

ROMAN SCANDALS ★★★
DIR: Frank Tuttle. **CAST:** Eddie Cantor, Ruth Etting, Alan Mowbray, Edward Arnold.

Old Banjo Eyes dreams himself back to ancient Rome and a string of low-comedy situations. Busby Berkeley staged the requisite musical numbers, including one censor-baiting stanza featuring semi-nude chorus girls, Goldwyn Girl Lucille Ball among them. 1933; B&W; 92m.

ROOFTOPS ★★
DIR: Robert Wise. **CAST:** Jason Gedrick, Troy Beyer, Eddie Velez.

What a coincidence! *West Side Story* director Robert Wise returns to make a film about streetwise teenagers in New York who dance, rumble, and struggle to survive. This time, star-crossed lovers (Jason Gedrick and Troy Beyer) combine kung-fu with dirty dancing. Rated R for rampant profanity, violence, and brief nudity. 1989; 95m.

ROSALIE ★★½
DIR: W. S. Van Dyke. **CAST:** Eleanor Powell, Nelson Eddy, Frank Morgan, Edna May Oliver, Ray Bolger, Ilona Massey.

From those thrilling days of yesteryear at MGM comes this gigantic musical about hero Nelson Eddy and his winning of a disguised Balkan princess (Eleanor Powell). It's big, colorful, and has a nice music score by Cole Porter. 1937; B&W; 122m.

ROSE, THE ★★★★
DIR: Mark Rydell. **CAST:** Bette Midler, Alan Bates, Frederic Forrest, Harry Dean Stanton.

Bette Midler stars as a Janis Joplin–like rock singer who falls prey to the loneliness and temptations of superstardom. Mark Rydell directed this fine character study, which features memorable supporting performances by Alan Bates and Frederic Forrest, and a first-rate rock score. Rated R. 1979; 134m.

ROSE MARIE ★★
DIR: W. S. Van Dyke. **CAST:** Nelson Eddy, Jeanette MacDonald, James Stewart, Alan Mowbray.

If you enjoy MGM's perennial songbirds Nelson Eddy and Jeanette Mac-

Donald, you might have fun with this musical romp into the Canadian Rockies. Unintentionally funny dialogue is created by the wooden way Eddy delivers it. 1936; B&W; 110m.

ROSIE ★★★
DIR: Jackie Cooper. **CAST:** Sondra Locke, Tony Orlando, Katherine Helmond, Penelope Milford, Kevin McCarthy, John Karlen.
Rosemary Clooney sings behind Sondra Locke's acting in this vivid, no-holds-barred rendition of the famed singer's autobiography *This for Remembrance*. Always an upfront gal, Clooney let it all hang out in telling of her rise to stardom, mental breakdown, and successful uphill fight to regain star status. Made for TV. 1982; 100m.

ROUND MIDNIGHT ★★★★½
DIR: Bertrand Tavernier. **CAST:** Dexter Gordon, François Cluzet, Lonette McKee, Christine Pascal, Herbie Hancock.
French director Bertrand Tavernier's ode to American jazz is a long overdue celebration of that great American music and a tribute to its brilliant exponents. It tells a semifictionalized story of a friendship between a self-destructive, be-bop tenor saxophonist (Dexter Gordon) and an avid French fan of the jazzman's music (Francois Cluzet). Rated R. 1986; 133m.

ROUSTABOUT ★★½
DIR: John Rich. **CAST:** Barbara Stanwyck, Elvis Presley, Leif Erickson, Sue Ane Langdon.
Barbara Stanwyck, as the carnival owner, upgrades this typical Elvis Presley picture. In this release, Presley is a young wanderer who finds a home in the carnival as a singer. Naturally, Elvis combines romance with hard work on the midway. 1964; 101m.

ROXY MUSIC—THE HIGH ROAD ★★★½
DIR: Robin Nash. **CAST:** Roxy Music.
The pre–New Wave British rock band that launched the careers of Bryan Ferry and Brian Eno is captured in straight-ahead fashion at Frejus, France, during their 1983 world tour. Roxy Music fans will not be disappointed. 1983; 76m.

ROY ORBISON AND FRIENDS ★★★★
DIR: Tony Mitchell. **CAST:** Roy Orbison, Bruce Springsteen, Elvis Costello, Jackson Browne, Bonnie Raitt, Tom Waits, Jennifer Warnes, T-Bone Burnett, James Burton.
The late Roy Orbison captured hitting those startling highs. His subdued style never sets sparks flying, but this video is all class, thanks to the star support and the cool setting. With everyone wearing black ties in an elegant club setting, the entire affair resembles a period piece, but the playing and hi-fi stereo sound is strictly modern state of the art. 1988; B&W; 55m.

ROYAL WEDDING ★★★
DIR: Stanley Donen. **CAST:** Fred Astaire, Jane Powell, Sarah Churchill, Peter Lawford, Keenan Wynn.
Brother and sister Fred Astaire and Jane Powell are performing in London when Princess Elizabeth marries Philip, and manage to find their own true loves while royalty ties the knot. 1951; 92m.

RUNNING OUT OF LUCK ★★★
DIR: Julien Temple. **CAST:** Mick Jagger, Rae Dawn Chong, Dennis Hopper, Jerry Hall.
Video film built around Mick Jagger's solo album, *She's the Boss*, has Jagger and Jerry Hall going to Rio to shoot a musical video being directed by Dennis Hopper. After an evening shoot, Jagger is mugged, thrown into the back of a meat wagon, abandoned in the Brazilian jungle, and taken prisoner by an oversexed banana plantation owner. If this all sounds pretty hokey, that's because it is. Rated R. 1987; 80m.

RUST NEVER SLEEPS ★★★
DIR: Bernard Shakey. **CAST:** Neil Young, Crazy Horse.

The concept is silly, but the hooded *Star Wars*–style figures scurrying around the stage don't detract from the music. This is a very thorough journey through Neil Young's past, from the simple solo strums of "Sugar Mountain" to the excessive electric antics of Crazy Horse. Nicely filmed with superb stereo sound. 1979; 113m.

RUTLES, THE (A.K.A. ALL YOU NEED IS CASH) ★★★★
DIR: Eric Idle, Gary Weis. **CAST:** Eric Idle, Neil Innes, Ricky Fataar, John Halsey, Mick Jagger, Paul Simon, George Harrison, John Belushi, Dan Aykroyd, Gilda Radner.

Superb spoof of the Beatles has ex–Monty Python member Eric Idle in a dual role as a television reporter and one of the Rutles, whose songs include "Cheese and Onions" and "Doubleback Alley." It's great stuff for fans of the Fab Four—with cameos from rock stars (including Beatle George Harrison) and members of *Saturday Night Live*'s Not Ready for Prime-Time Players. 1978; 78m.

SALSA ★
DIR: Boaz Davidson. **CAST:** Robby Rosa, Rodney Harvey.

The music is hot, but the rest of this movie is laughably awful. Robby Rosa, a Michael Jackson look-alike, plays a dance-crazy Latino out to win a big dance contest. A second-rate rip-off of *Dirty Dancing*. Rated PG for profanity and violence. 1988; 92m.

SATISFACTION ★
DIR: Joan Freeman. **CAST:** Justine Bateman, Liam Neeson, Trini Alvarado, Julia Roberts, Deborah Harry, Chris Nash.

Even younger viewers will get no satisfaction from this mediocre coming-of-age movie. Justine Bateman is the leader of a rock band from the poor side of town hired to play in a ritzy resort. Rated PG-13 for profanity and suggested sex. 1988; 95m.

SATURDAY NIGHT FEVER ★★★★
DIR: John Badham. **CAST:** John Travolta, Donna Pescow, Karen Lynn Gorney.

From the first notes of "Stayin' Alive" by the Bee Gees over the opening credits, it is obvious that *Saturday Night Fever* is more than just another youth exploitation film. It is *Rebel Without a Cause* for the 1970s, with realistic dialogue and effective dramatic situations. Rated R for profanity, violence, partial nudity, and simulated sex. 1977; 119m.

SAY AMEN, SOMEBODY ★★★★
DIR: George T. Nierenberg. **CAST:** Thomas A. Dorsey, Willie Mae Ford Smith, Sallie Martin.

This is a joyful documentary about gospel singers Thomas A. Dorsey and Willie Mae Ford Smith. Two dozen gospel songs make this modest film a treat for the ears as well as the eyes and soul. Rated G. 1982; 100m.

SCROOGE ★★★
DIR: Ronald Neame. **CAST:** Albert Finney, Alec Guinness, Edith Evans, Kenneth More, Michael Medwin, Laurence Naismith, Kay Walsh.

Tuneful retelling of Charles Dickens's classic *A Christmas Carol* may not be the best acted, but it's certainly the liveliest. Albert Finney paints old curmudgeon Ebeneezer Scrooge with a broad brush, but he makes his character come alive just as he embodied Daddy Warbucks in *Annie*. Rated G. 1970; 118m.

SEASIDE SWINGERS ★½
DIR: James Hill. **CAST:** John Leyton, Michael Sarne, Freddie and the Dreamers, Ron Moody, Liz Fraser.

Only the most fanatic fan of the Sixties British invasion will want to sit through this comedy about a TV talent contest starring Freddie and the Dreamers. There are lots of songs by different groups, but no hits. Trivia buffs may want to see co-star Michael Sarne, who went on to direct *Myra Breckenridge*, an even worse movie. 1965; 94m.

SECOND CHORUS ★★★
DIR: H. C. Potter. **CAST:** Paulette Goddard, Fred Astaire, Burgess Meredith, Charles Butterworth.

Rival trumpet players Fred Astaire and Burgess Meredith vie for the affections of Paulette Goddard, who works for Artie Shaw. The two want into Shaw's orchestra and make a comic mess of Goddard's attempts to help them. 1940; B&W; 83m.

SENSATIONS OF 1945 ★★
DIR: Andrew L. Stone. **CAST:** Eleanor Powell, W. C. Fields, Sophie Tucker, Dennis O'Keefe, Cab Calloway, C. Aubrey Smith, Eugene Pallette.

Yet another one of those all-star jumbles so popular during the mid-1940s, this uninspired musical limps along, saddled with a stale story of a producer who wants to put on a show. The great W. C. Fields isn't in his best form here, but any chance to see him and Cab Calloway in action is worth something. 1944; B&W; 87m.

SGT. PEPPER'S LONELY HEARTS CLUB BAND
DIR: Michael Schultz. **CAST:** The Bee Gees, Peter Frampton, Donald Pleasence, George Burns.

Universally panned musical featuring the Bee Gees, Peter Frampton, etc., performing songs from the Beatles' famous album as they try to save the small town of Heartland from the rule of the evil Mr. Mustard. Rated PG. 1978; 111m.

SEVEN BRIDES FOR SEVEN BROTHERS ★★★★★
DIR: Stanley Donen. **CAST:** Howard Keel, Jane Powell, Russ Tamblyn, Julie Newmar, Marc Platt.

Delightful musical. Howard Keel takes Jane Powell as his wife. The fun begins when his six younger brothers decide they want to get married, too...immediately! 1954; 103m.

1776 ★★★★
DIR: Peter H. Hunt. **CAST:** William Daniels, Howard da Silva, Ken Howard, Blythe Danner.

Broadway's hit musical about the founding of the nation is brought to the screen almost intact. Original cast members William Daniels, as John Adams, and Howard da Silva, as Benjamin Franklin, shine anew in this unique piece. Rated G. 1972; 141m.

SHALL WE DANCE? ★★★★½
DIR: Mark Sandrich. **CAST:** Fred Astaire, Ginger Rogers, Eric Blore, Edward Everett Horton.

Fred Astaire and Ginger Rogers team up (as usual) as dance partners in this musical comedy. The only twist is they must pretend to be married in order to get the job. Great songs include "Let's Call the Whole Thing Off." 1937; B&W; 109m.

SHOW BOAT ★★★½
DIR: George Sidney. **CAST:** Kathryn Grayson, Howard Keel, Ava Gardner, Joe E. Brown, Agnes Moorehead, Marge Champion, Gower Champion.

This watchable musical depicts life and love on a Mississippi showboat during the early 1900s. Kathryn Grayson, Howard Keel, and Ava Gardner try but can't get any real sparks flying. 1951; 115m.

SHOW BUSINESS ★★★
DIR: Edwin L. Marin. **CAST:** Eddie Cantor, George Murphy, Joan Davis, Nancy Kelly, Constance Moore.

Based on incidents in Eddie Cantor's entertainment career, this slick, brassy, and nostalgic picture provides fun and good music. For Cantor and Joan Davis fans, this film is a peach. 1944; B&W; 92m.

SHOWBIZ, THE STYLE COUNCIL, LIVE! ★★★½
DIR: Vaughan, Anthea. **CAST:** Paul Weller, Mick Talbot.

Style Council, the cool cabaret rock act Paul Weller formed after the Jam, is expanded to a twelve-piece with a full horn section. The result is a slick, dynamic stage show, but nothing sweetens Weller's raspy bark. He even sings backed only by a string section. Nicely filmed with superb stereo sound. 1986; 55m.

SIGN O' THE TIMES ★★
DIR: Prince. **CAST:** Prince, Sheila E., Cat.

This two-hour fiesta of funk is exquisitely filmed (mainly during a Holland performance) and features superb sound. The concert sequences are connected by dreamlike vignettes that, while equally beautiful, add little to what is essentially an hour and a half of MTV. Rated PG-13 for suggested sex. 1987; 85m.

SILK STOCKINGS ★★★
DIR: Rouben Mamoulian. **CAST:** Fred Astaire, Cyd Charisse, Janis Paige, Peter Lorre, Barrie Chase.

In this remake, Greta Garbo's classic *Ninotchka* is given the Cole Porter musical treatment with a degree of success. Fred Astaire is a Hollywood producer who educates a Russian agent in the seductive allure of capitalism. Cyd Charisse plays the Garbo role. 1957; 117m.

SING ★★★
DIR: Richard Baskin. **CAST:** Peter Dobson, Jessica Steen, Lorraine Bracco, Patti LaBelle, Louise Lasser.

A teen film with a commendable twist: no car chases! Actually, this is a cross between *Lady and the Tramp* and *Fame*. A tough Italian punk is forced to work with an innocent Jewish girl on the class musical. You guessed it! They fall for each other. Rated PG-13 for profanity. 1989; 99m.

SINGIN' IN THE RAIN ★★★★★
DIR: Gene Kelly, Stanley Donen. **CAST:** Gene Kelly, Debbie Reynolds, Donald O'Connor, Jean Hagen, Cyd Charisse, Rita Moreno.

In the history of movie musicals, no single scene is more fondly remembered than Gene Kelly's song-and-dance routine to the title song of *Singin' in the Rain*. This picture has more to it than Kelly's well-choreographed splash through a wet city street. It has an interesting plot based on the panic that overran Hollywood during its conversion to sound and it has wonderful performances. 1952; 102m.

SKY'S THE LIMIT, THE ★★★★
DIR: Edward H. Griffith. **CAST:** Fred Astaire, Joan Leslie, Robert Benchley, Elizabeth Patterson, Clarence Kolb, Robert Ryan, Richard Davis, Peter Lawford, Eric Blore.

This rare blend of comedy and drama is more than just another Fred Astaire musical. He plays a Flying Tiger ace, on leave, who meets and falls in love with magazine photographer Joan Leslie, but nixes anything permanent. Both audiences and critics misjudged this film when it debuted, seeing it as light diversion rather than incisive comment on war and its effect on people. 1943; B&W; 89m.

SLIPSTREAM ★★½
DIR: David Mallet. **CAST:** Jethro Tull.

This concept film twists together concert footage and video segments with every special-effect trick in the music-video textbook. The strength of the material, touching on every phase of Jethro Tull's two decades, and the theatrical flair of singer-flautist Ian Anderson (who portrays Dracula, old Aqualung, and the minstrel in the woods) keep things flowing. But the live shots fail to convey any sense of urgency. 1984; 60m.

SMILIN' THROUGH ★★
DIR: Frank Borzage. **CAST:** Jeanette MacDonald, Gene Raymond, Brian Aherne, Ian Hunter.

If you can believe it, an orphaned and brave Jeanette MacDonald falls in love with the son of a murderer. Directed and played for tear value. Best thing to come out of the picture was Jeannette's marriage to Gene Raymond. 1941; 100m.

SO FAR ★★★
DIR: Len Dell'Amico, Jerry Garcia. **CAST:** Grateful Dead.

Modern video techniques make this Grateful Dead film a bit more lively than those past. The band's psychedelic music is accentuated with colorful visual effects and clever editing. Little attention is paid to the infamous "Dead Heads," but this is a movie about the band, not the scene that accompanies it. 1987; 55m.

SOMETHING TO SING ABOUT ★★

DIR: Walter Schertzinger. **CAST:** James Cagney, William Frawley, Evelyn Daw, Gene Lockhart.

Even the great talents of James Cagney can't lift this low-budget musical above the level of mediocrity. In it, he plays a New York bandleader who tests his mettle in Hollywood. 1937; B&W; 93m.

SONG OF NORWAY

DIR: Andrew L. Stone. **CAST:** Florence Henderson, Torval Maurstad, Edward G. Robinson, Robert Morley.

If he were not dead, Norwegian composer Edvard Grieg would expire upon seeing this insult to his life and career. Talk about butchering what was an engaging, tuneful stage musical! Pass the cranberry sauce. Rated G. 1970; 142m.

SONG OF THE ISLANDS ★★

DIR: Walter Lang. **CAST:** Betty Grable, Victor Mature, Jack Oakie, Thomas Mitchell.

A Hawaiian cattle baron feuds with a planter over land while his son romances the planter's daughter. Everyone quarrels, but love wins. En route, Betty Grable sings and dances in the standard grass skirt. Mainly a slick travelogue with singing and dancing. 1942; 75m.

SONG REMAINS THE SAME, THE ★★★

DIR: Peter Clifton, Joe Massot. **CAST:** Led Zeppelin, Peter Grant.

If any band is truly responsible for the genre of "heavy metal" music, it is Led Zeppelin. Although this movie is a must for Zeppelin fans, the untrained ear may find numbers such as the twenty-three-minute version of "Dazed and Confused" a bit tedious. Rated PG. 1976; 136m.

SONG TO REMEMBER, A ★★★

DIR: Charles Vidor. **CAST:** Cornel Wilde, Merle Oberon, Paul Muni, George Coulouris, Nina Foch, Sig Arno.

The music is superb, but the plot of this Chopin biography is as frail as the composer's health is purported to have been. Cornel Wilde received an Oscar nomination as the ill-fated tubercular Chopin, and Merle Oberon is resolute but vulnerable in the role of his lover, French female novelist George Sand. 1945; 113m.

SONGWRITER ★★★★

DIR: Alan Rudolph. **CAST:** Willie Nelson, Kris Kristofferson, Lesley Ann Warren, Melinda Dillon, Rip Torn.

Wonderfully wacky and entertaining wish-fulfillment by top country stars Willie Nelson and Kris Kristofferson, who play—what else?—top country stars who take on the recording industry and win. A delight. Rated R for profanity, nudity, and brief violence. 1984; 100m.

SOUND OF MUSIC, THE ★★★★½

DIR: Robert Wise. **CAST:** Julie Andrews, Christopher Plummer, Eleanor Parker.

Winner of the Academy Award for best picture, this musical has it all: comedy, romance, suspense. Julie Andrews plays the spunky Maria, who doesn't fit in at the convent. When she is sent to live with a large family as their governess, she falls in love with and marries her handsome boss, Baron Von Trapp (Christopher Plummer). Problems arise when the Nazi invasion of Austria forces the family to flee. 1965; 172m.

SOUTH PACIFIC ★★★

DIR: Joshua Logan. **CAST:** Mitzi Gaynor, Rossano Brazzi, Ray Walston, John Kerr.

This extremely long film, adapted from the famous Broadway play about sailors during World War II, seems dated and is slow going for the most part. Fans of Rodgers and Hammerstein will no doubt appreciate this one more than others. 1958; 150m.

SPARKLE ★★★

DIR: Sam O'Steen. **CAST:** Irene Cara, Dorian Harewood, Lonette McKee.

Largely forgotten but immensely appealing study of a Supremes–like girl group's rise to fame in the 1960s Motown era. Lots of good musical numbers from Curtis Mayfield and the luscious Lonette McKee. Rated PG for profanity and nudity. 1976; 100m.

SPEEDWAY ★★

DIR: Norman Taurog. **CAST:** Elvis Presley, Nancy Sinatra, Bill Bixby, Gale Gordon.

Elvis Presley plays a generous stock-car driver who confronts a seemingly heartless IRS agent (Nancy Sinatra). Not surprisingly, she melts in this unremarkable musical. Rated G. 1968; 94m.

SPLIT ENZ ★★

DIR: Bruce Gowers. **CAST:** Tim Finn, Neil Finn, Noel Crombie, Nigel Griggs, Eddie Rayner.

During the late Seventies, Split Enz was among rock's most ambitious, artsy, and playful popsters. This concert film from Ontario somehow misses all the offhand Enz magic. Ordinarily sparkling Split Enz songs have no punch in this low-budget video. 1982; 54m.

SPRINGTIME IN THE ROCKIES ★★★

DIR: Irving Cummings. **CAST:** Betty Grable, John Payne, Carmen Miranda, Cesar Romero, Edward Everett Horton, Charlotte Greenwood, Jackie Gleason, Harry James.

Lake Louise and other breathtaking Canadian scenic wonders provide backgrounds for this near-plotless show-business musical. Jealous Broadway entertainers Betty Grable and John Payne fight and make up with the help of Carmen Miranda, Cesar Romero, and a bushel of songs and dances. 1942; 90m.

STAGE STRUCK ★★

DIR: Busby Berkeley. **CAST:** Joan Blondell, Dick Powell, Warren William, Frank McHugh, Jeanne Madden, Carol Hughes, Hobart Cavanaugh, Spring Byington.

A no-talent singer-dancer, Joan Blondell, makes a bid for Broadway by financing a show for herself. She hires Dick Powell to direct. They clash, fall in love, clash, and depend on good old suave Warren William to smooth it all out. Not that anyone should care too much. Below par. 1936; B&W; 86m.

STARING AT THE SEA—THE IMAGES ★★★

DIR: Tom Pope, Piers Bedford, David Hillier, Bob Rickerd, Mike Mansfield, Chris Gabrin. **CAST:** The Cure.

The Cure's quirky ten-year career has been interesting, if not enormously successful. *Staring at the Sea*, which includes seventeen videos compiled prior to the the 1987 double album, *Kiss Me, Kiss Me, Kiss Me*, is a great way of getting acquainted with the band's dark, yet humorous and offbeat style. 1986; 82m.

STARSTRUCK ★★★½

DIR: Gillian Armstrong. **CAST:** Jo Kennedy, Ross O'Donovan, Max Cullen.

For this movie, about a 17-year-old (Jo Kennedy) who wants to be a star and goes after it at top speed, director Gillian Armstrong has taken the let's-put-on-a-show! plot and turned it into an affable punk-rock movie. Rated PG for nudity and profanity. 1982; 95m.

STATE FAIR ★½

DIR: José Ferrer. **CAST:** Pat Boone, Bobby Darin, Ann-Margret, Pamela Tiffin, Alice Faye, Tom Ewell.

Lesser remake of the 1933 and 1945 films focusing on a very wholesome family's visit to the Iowa State Fair. A bit too hokey as predictable romantic situations develop. Only comic moment has Tom Ewell singing to a pig. 1962; 118m.

STAY AWAY JOE ★½

DIR: Peter Tewksbury. **CAST:** Elvis Presley, Burgess Meredith, Joan Blondell.

A lesser Elvis vehicle, this entry has a number of non-Indians unconvincingly trying to portray members of the Navajo tribe. Elvis has just returned to the range with enough government cattle to make his dad rich. Unfortunately, the only bull is barbecued and the search is on to find a replacement. At every turn, women throw themselves at the King and he tirelessly tries to maintain his reputation. An all-around disappointment. Rated PG for countless sexual situations. 1968; 102m.

STAYING ALIVE ★

DIR: Sylvester Stallone. **CAST:** John Travolta, Cynthia Rhodes, Finola Hughes, Steve Inwood.

This sequel to the gutsy, effective *Saturday Night Fever* is a slick, commercial near–rip-off. Six years have passed since Tony Manero (John Travolta) was king of the local disco, and he now attempts to break into the competitive life of Broadway dancing. For fans only. Rated PG for language and suggested sex. 1983; 96m.

STEP LIVELY ★★★½

DIR: Tim Whelan. **CAST:** Frank Sinatra, George Murphy, Walter Slezak, Adolphe Menjou.

As a jazzy, bright musical remake of the Marx Brothers film *Room Service*, this film is a very enjoyable story about George Murphy's attempt to get his show produced on Broadway. It's in this film that Frank Sinatra receives his first screen kisses (from Gloria DeHaven), which caused swoons from numerous female Sinatraphiles. As the hotel manager, Walter Slezak almost steals the show. 1944; 89m.

STEWART COPELAND: THE RHYTHMATIST ★½

DIR: J. P. Dutilleux. **CAST:** Stewart Copeland.

Police drummer Stewart Copeland attempts to show the relationship between rhythm and style in African tribal society in this disappointing documentary produced and directed by J. P. Dutilleux, respected for his field work in the Amazon. Copeland's approach to his subject matter seems ridiculous and often works as bad self-parody; he roams the beautiful African landscape with a blond female companion in the style of a great white hunter. Copeland's cultural study of Africa appears to be a pretentious joke. 1985; 58m.

STOP MAKING SENSE ★★★★

DIR: Jonathan Demme. **CAST:** Talking Heads.

Jonathan Demme's *Stop Making Sense* has been called a star vehicle. Filmed over a three-night period in December 1983 at Hollywood's Pantages Theater, the movie is a straight recording of a Talking Heads concert that offers the movie audience front-row-center seats. It offers great fun for the band's fans. Rated PG for suggestive lyrics. 1984; 88m.

STORMY WEATHER ★★★★

DIR: Andrew L. Stone. **CAST:** Lena Horne, Bill Robinson, Cab Calloway, Fats Waller.

A delightful kaleidoscope of musical numbers. Lena Horne performs the title number and Fats Waller interprets his own "Ain't Misbehavin." Dooley Wilson of *Casablanca* fame and the Nicholas Brothers are also really great. This is an overlooked MGM classic. 1943; B&W; 77m.

STORY OF VERNON AND IRENE CASTLE, THE ★★★★

DIR: H. C. Potter. **CAST:** Fred Astaire, Ginger Rogers, Edna May Oliver, Walter Brennan.

Another fine film with the flying footsies of Fred Astaire and the always lovely Ginger Rogers. 1939; B&W; 93m.

STOWAWAY ★★★

DIR: William A. Seiter. **CAST:** Shirley Temple, Robert Young, Alice Faye, Allan "Rocky" Lane, Eugene Pallette, Helen Westley, Arthur Treacher, J. Edward Blomberg.

Tale of missionary ward Shirley Temple lost in Shanghai and befriended by American Robert Young. She holds her own against such seasoned scene snitchers as Eugene Pallette, Arthur Treacher, and J. Edward Blomberg, while bringing playboy Young and Alice Faye together romantically, singing in Chinese, and imitating Fred Astaire, Al Jolson, Eddie Cantor. 1936; B&W; 86m.

STRANGLERS LIVE '78, SF, THE ★★

DIR: John Rees. **CAST:** Jet Black, J. J. Burnel, Hugh Cornwell, Dave Greenfield.

Long before hitting the charts with catchy singles, the Stranglers were punk purists. This 1978 concert footage shows a raw, energetic band, but the quality is strictly archival and the sound is total trash. 1978; 20m.

SUMMER STOCK ★★★

DIR: Charles Walters. **CAST:** Judy Garland, Gene Kelly, Eddie Bracken, Gloria De Haven, Phil Silvers, Hans Conried, Marjorie Main.

An echo of the Mickey Rooney–Judy Garland talented-kids/let's-give-a-show films, this likable musical is built around a troupe of ambitious performers, led by Gene Kelly, who invade farmer Judy Garland's barn. Love blooms. Judy's "Get Happy" number, filmed long after the movie was completed and spliced in to add needed flash, is inspired. 1950; 109m.

SUNDAY IN THE PARK WITH GEORGE ★★★★★

DIR: James Lapine. **CAST:** Mandy Patinkin, Bernadette Peters, Barbara Byrne, Charles Kimbrough.

This is a taped version of a performance of one of the most honored musicals of the 1980s. A Pulitzer Prize winner, the entire play is a fabrication of plot and characters based on the Georges Seurat painting, "Sunday Afternoon on the Island of La Grande Jatte." The painting comes to life, and each of the figures has a story to tell. Seurat is played expertly by Mandy Patinkin. 1986; 147m.

SWEENEY TODD ★★★★★

DIR: Harold Prince. **CAST:** Angela Lansbury, George Hearn, Sara Woods.

This is not a film, but rather an eight-camera video of a Broadway musical taped during a performance before an audience. And what a musical it is, this 1979 Tony Award winner! George Hearn is terrifying as Sweeney Todd, the barber who seeks revenge on the English judicial system by slashing the throats of the unfortunate who wind up in his tonsorial chair. Angela Lansbury is spooky as Mrs. Lovett, who finds a use for Todd's leftovers by baking them into meat pies. 1982; 150m.

SWEET CHARITY ★★★★

DIR: Bob Fosse. **CAST:** Shirley MacLaine, Chita Rivera, Paula Kelly, Ricardo Montalban, Sammy Davis Jr.

This was a Broadway smash hit, and it lost nothing in transfer to the screen. Neil Simon adapted the story from Federico Fellini's *Nights of Cabiria*. Shirley MacLaine is a prostitute who falls in love with a naïve young man who is unaware of her profession. The score by Dorothy Fields and Cy Coleman is terrific. Bob Fosse, in his directorial debut, does an admirable job. Rated G. 1969; 133m.

SWEET DREAMS ★★★★½

DIR: Karel Reisz. **CAST:** Jessica Lange, Ed Harris, Ann Wedgeworth, David Clennon, Gary Basaraba.

Jessica Lange is Patsy Cline, one of the greatest country-and-western singers of all time, in this film that is much more than a response to the popularity of *Coal Miner's Daughter*. Lange's performance is flawless right down to the singing, where she perfectly mouths Clines's voice. Rated PG for profanity and sex. 1985; 115m.

SWEETHEARTS ★★½
DIR: W. S. Van Dyke. **CAST:** Jeanette MacDonald, Nelson Eddy, Frank Morgan, Ray Bolger, Mischa Auer.
Good acting, splendid singing, and a bright updated script make this version of the ancient Victor Herbert operetta a winning comedy about a temperamental stage duo on a collision course set by jealousy. The Technicolor cinematography won an Oscar. 1938; 120m.

SWING TIME ★★★★½
DIR: George Stevens. **CAST:** Ginger Rogers, Fred Astaire, Betty Furness, Victor Moore, Helen Broderick.
Fred Astaire is a gambler trying to save up enough money to marry the girl he left behind (Betty Furness). By the time he's saved the money, he and Ginger Rogers are madly in love with each other. 1936; B&W; 105m.

SYMPATHY FOR THE DEVIL
DIR: Jean-Luc Godard. **CAST:** The Rolling Stones.
Several uncompleted sessions on the title song and documentary-style footage of black guerrillas with machine guns and white women in slips seem to be all that compose this boring film from internationally acclaimed director Jean-Luc Godard. 1970; 92m.

TAKE IT BIG ★★
DIR: Frank McDonald. **CAST:** Jack Haley, Ozzie Nelson, Harriet Nelson.
In the early 1940s at Paramount Pictures, a B-movie unit was formed by William H. Pine and William C. Thomas. With a good track record, they tried to produce more elaborate films. This is one of those bigger productions. Jack Haley is at the wrong end in a horse act that inherits a dude ranch. Ozzie Nelson and his band supply the musical numbers. 1944; B&W; 75m.

TAKE ME OUT TO THE BALL GAME ★★★
DIR: Busby Berkeley. **CAST:** Gene Kelly, Frank Sinatra, Esther Williams, Betty Garrett, Jules Munshin.
Don't expect to see the usual Berkeley extravaganza in this one; this is just a run-of-the-mill musical. It does contain some entertaining musical numbers, such as "O'Brien to Ryan to Goldberg." 1949; 93m.

TAKING MY TURN ★★
DIR: Robert H. Livingston. **CAST:** Margaret Whiting, Marni Nixon, Sheila Smith, Cissy Houston.
This is a videotape of an off-Broadway musical. Unfortunately, you had to be there to really enjoy it. Sort of *A Chorus Line* for the Geritol generation, this features aging actors lamenting the way times have changed and how it feels to grow old. Their song-and-dance routines are good, but for the most part this is pretty depressing. 1984; 90m.

TAP ★★★★
DIR: Nick Castle. **CAST:** Gregory Hines, Sammy Davis Jr., Joe Morton, Dick Anthony Williams.
This *Flashdance*-style musical-drama about a gifted tap dancer (Gregory Hines) is so good, you'll want to watch it a second time—not for the silly jewel-heist story, but for the marvelous dance sequences. See it for the eye-popping choreography and a *cut* contest—featuring old pros Sammy Davis Jr., Harold Nicholas, Bunny Briggs, Sandman Sims, Steve Condos, Rico, and Arthur Duncan—that will make your jaw drop. Rated PG-13 for profanity and violence. 1989; 111m.

TELEVISION PARTS HOME COMPANION ★★★
DIR: William Dear, Alan Myerson. **CAST:** Mike Nesmith, Joe Allain, Bill Martin.
This is more of Mike Nesmith's *Elephant Parts* style of variety-show entertainment. Again, he has hilarious skits and mock commercials, as well as choreographed stories to accompany his songs. 1984; 40m.

TERENCE TRENT D'ARBY—INTRODUCING THE HARDLINE LIVE ★★★★

DIR: Nick Morris. **CAST:** Terence Trent D'Arby.

Whether the latest overnight sensation or simply an overinflated ego, Terence Trent D'Arby has certainly studied the best soul singers and strutters. He borrows from James Brown, Prince, and even Sam Cooke. He moves, he grooves. This Munich concert film catches D'Arby in red-hot form, scorching through a set of his own songs and surprises like "Under My Thumb." 1988; 65m.

THANK GOD IT'S FRIDAY ★★

DIR: Robert Klane. **CAST:** Donna Summer, The Commodores, Ray Vitte, Debra Winger, Jeff Goldblum.

This film is episodic and light in mood and features a cast primarily of newcomers. Donna Summer plays an aspiring singer who pesters a club's master of ceremonies and disc jockey, Bobby Speed (Ray Vitte), to let her sing. Rated PG. 1978; 90m.

THANK YOUR LUCKY STARS ★★★½

DIR: David Butler. **CAST:** Eddie Cantor, Dennis Morgan, Joan Leslie, Bette Davis, Olivia De Havilland, Ida Lupino, Ann Sheridan, Humphrey Bogart, Errol Flynn, John Garfield.

Practically nonexistent plot—involving banjo-eyed Eddie Cantor as a cab driver and the organizer of this gala affair—takes a backseat to the wonderful array of Warner Bros. talent gathered together for the first and only time in one film. Lots of fun for film fans. 1943; B&W; 127m.

THAT WAS ROCK ★★★★★

DIR: Steve Binder, Larry Peerce. **CAST:** The Rolling Stones, Chuck Berry, Tina Turner, Marvin Gaye, The Supremes, Smokey Robinson and the Miracles, James Brown, Ray Charles, Gerry and the Pacemakers, The Ronettes.

Compilation of two previous films, *The T.A.M.I. Show* and *The Big T.N.T. Show*, which were originally shot on videotape in the mid-1960s. It's black and white, but color inserts have been added, featuring Chuck Berry giving cursory introductions to each act. The video is muddy, the simulated stereo is annoying, and the audience nearly drowns out the performers, but it's one of the best collections of rock 'n' roll and R&B talent you will ever see. Unrated. 1984; 92m.

THAT'LL BE THE DAY ★★★★

DIR: Claude Whatham. **CAST:** David Essex, Ringo Starr, Rosemary Leach, James Booth, Billy Fury, Keith Moon.

Stardust offers some of filmdom's most fascinating glimpses into the rock 'n' roll world. It is the sequel to *That'll Be the Day*, itself a provocative character study. Charismatic David Essex stars as a British working-class youth whose adolescent restlessness points him toward the emotional release rock music provides. Ringo Starr contributes an engaging performance as a rough-hewn lad who eventually proves to be less morally suspect than the protagonist. 1974; 90m.

THAT'S DANCING ★★★★

DIR: Jack Haley Jr. **CAST:** Mikhail Baryshnikov, Ray Bolger, Sammy Davis Jr., Gene Kelly, Liza Minnelli.

This is a glorious celebration of dance on film. From ballet to breakin', from Fred Astaire to Busby Berkeley, from James Cagney (in *Yankee Doodle Dandy*) to Marine Jahan (Jennifer Beals's stand-in in *Flashdance*), this one has it all. Rated G. 1985; 105m.

THAT'S ENTERTAINMENT ★★★★★

DIR: Jack Haley Jr. **CAST:** Judy Garland, Fred Astaire, Frank Sinatra, Gene Kelly, Esther Williams.

That's Entertainment is a feast of screen highlights. Culled from twenty-nine years of MGM classics, this release truly has something for everybody. Taken from Metro-Goldwyn-Mayer's glory days when it boasted "more stars than there are in heaven," nearly every sequence is a showstopper. Rated G. 1974; 135m.

THAT'S ENTERTAINMENT PART II ★★★★

DIR: Gene Kelly. **CAST:** Gene Kelly, Fred Astaire.

More wonderful scenes from the history of MGM highlight this compilation, hosted by director Gene Kelly and Fred Astaire. It's a real treat for film buffs. Rated G. 1976; 132m.

THERE'S NO BUSINESS LIKE SHOW BUSINESS ★★

DIR: Walter Lang. **CAST:** Ethel Merman, Dan Dailey, Marilyn Monroe, Donald O'Connor, Johnnie Ray, Mitzi Gaynor, Hugh O'Brian, Frank McHugh.

Even the strength of the cast can't save this marginally entertaining musical-comedy about a show-biz family. Irving Berlin's tunes and Monroe's scenes are the only redeeming qualities in this one. 1954; 117m.

THEY SHALL HAVE MUSIC ★★★

DIR: Archie Mayo. **CAST:** Jascha Heifetz, Joel McCrea, Andrea Leeds, Walter Brennan, Marjorie Main, Porter Hall.

Good cast and great music help the appeal of this attempt to make concert violinist Jascha Heifetz a film star. Simple plot has a group of poor kids convincing him to play a benefit and save Walter Brennan's music school in the slums. 1939; B&W; 101m.

THIS IS ELVIS ★★★★

DIR: Malcolm Leo, Andrew Solt. **CAST:** Elvis Presley, David Scott, Paul Boensh III.

This Is Elvis blends film footage of the "real" Elvis with other portions, played by convincing stand-ins. The result is a warm, nostalgic, funny, and tragic portrait of a man who touched the hearts and lives of young and old throughout the world. Rated PG because of slight profanity. 1981; 101m.

THIS IS THE ARMY ★★★

DIR: Michael Curtiz. **CAST:** George Murphy, Joan Leslie, Ronald Reagan, George Tobias, Alan Hale, Joe Louis, Kate Smith, Irving Berlin, Frances Langford, Charles Butterworth.

Hoofer (later U.S. Senator) George Murphy portrays Ronald Reagan's father in this musical mélange penned by Irving Berlin to raise funds for Army Emergency Relief during World War II. It's a star-studded, rousing show of songs and skits from start to finish, but practically plotless. 1943; 121m.

THOMAS DOLBY LIVE: WIRELESS ★★★

DIR: Thomas Dolby. **CAST:** Thomas Dolby, Lene Lovich.

Thomas Dolby, the wire-rimmed techno-rock whiz kid delivers his unique brand of synthi-pop music in this well-produced concert originally aired on MTV. As a director, Dolby's gift for visual imagination is evident throughout. The high-energy music makes up for Dolby's weak stage presence and is most powerfully felt in his version of Joni Mitchell's "Jungle Line." Another standout is his "New Toy" duet with New Wave rocker Lene Lovich. 1983; 58m.

THOROUGHLY MODERN MILLIE ★★★

DIR: George Roy Hill. **CAST:** Julie Andrews, Mary Tyler Moore, Carol Channing, James Fox, Beatrice Lillie, John Saxon, Noriyuki "Pat" Morita, Jack Soo.

First-rate music characterizing America's jazz age dominates this harebrained-plotted, slapstick-punctuated spoof of the 1920s, complete with villains, a bordello, and a cooing flapper so smitten with her stuffed-shirt boss that she can't see her boyfriend for beans. It's toe-tapping entertainment, but a tad too long. 1967; 138m.

THOSE LIPS, THOSE EYES ★★

DIR: Michael Pressman. **CAST:** Frank Langella, Glynnis O'Connor, Tom Hulce, Jerry Stiller, Kevin McCarthy.

So-so "let's put on a show" musical features Frank Langella as a would-be stage star forced to play to small towns, though he longs to appear on Broadway. Tom Hulce is a boy who becomes enamored of the visiting troupe, especially a beautiful young dancer (Glynnis O'Connor). Rated R for profanity and brief nudity. 1980; 106m.

THOUSANDS CHEER ★★★
DIR: George Sidney. **CAST:** John Boles, Kathryn Grayson, Mickey Rooney, Judy Garland, Gene Kelly, Red Skelton, Lucille Ball, Ann Sothern, Eleanor Powell, Frank Morgan, Lena Horne, Virginia O'Brien.

The typical story about someone (in this case John Boles as an army officer) putting together a talent show for some good cause gets a major shot in the arm by the appearances of top MGM performers. 1943; 126m.

THREE LITTLE WORDS ★★½
DIR: Richard Thorpe. **CAST:** Fred Astaire, Red Skelton, Vera-Ellen, Gloria De Haven, Arlene Dahl, Debbie Reynolds, Keenan Wynn.

That this is supposedly Fred Astaire's favorite among his numerous films says little for his taste. He and Red Skelton thoroughly enjoyed playing ace songwriters Bert Kalmar and Harry Ruby in this semiaccurate bio-pic, but, overall, the film lacks lustre—though it did well at the box office. 1950; 102m.

THUNDER ALLEY ★
DIR: J. S. Cardone. **CAST:** Roger Wilson, Jill Schoelen, Scott McGinnis, Leif Garrett.

Midwestern teenagers form a rock band and set out for the big time. The clichés date back to Mickey Rooney and Judy Garland and beyond; putting them in a rock 'n' roll setting fails to make them appear fresh. And besides, the music is synthetic pseudorock at its worst. Rated R. 1985; 102m.

TICKLE ME ★★
DIR: Norman Taurog. **CAST:** Elvis Presley, Jocelyn Lane, Julie Adams, Jack Mullaney, Merry Anders.

The plot falls below that found in a standard Elvis vehicle in this unfunny comedy-musical, which has Elvis working and singing at an all-female health ranch. Viewers seeking thought-provoking entertainment should avoid this mindless piece of fluff. 1965; 90m.

TILL THE CLOUDS ROLL BY ★★½
DIR: Richard Whorf. **CAST:** Robert Walker, Van Heflin, Judy Garland, Lucille Bremer.

Biography of songwriter Jerome Kern is a barrage of MGM talent that includes Judy Garland, Frank Sinatra, Lena Horne, Dinah Shore, Kathryn Grayson, and many more in short, tuneful vignettes that tie this all-out effort together. Not too bad as musical bio-pics go, but singing talent is definitely the star in this production. 1946; 137m.

TIMES SQUARE ★½
DIR: Alan Moyle. **CAST:** Tim Curry, Robin Johnson, Trini Alvarado, Peter Coffield.

A totally unbelievable story involving two New York teens who hang out in Times Square. Film generates no energy at all. Rated R for profanity and subject matter. 1980; 111m.

TOAST OF NEW ORLEANS ★★½
DIR: Norman Taurog. **CAST:** Kathryn Grayson, Mario Lanza, Thomas Mitchell, David Niven, J. Carrol Naish, Rita Moreno.

Don't look for too much plot in this colorful showcase for the considerable vocal talent of the late Mario Lanza. Aided and abetted by the engaging soprano of Kathryn Grayson, Lanza sings up a storm. "Be My Love" was the film's and record stores' big number. 1950; 97m.

TOKYO POP ★★
DIR: Fran Rubel Kuzui. **CAST:** Carrie Hamilton, Yutaka Tadokoro.

If you want a gander at modern-day Japan and its pop-music world, *Tokyo Pop* is just the ticket. When Wendy (Carrie Hamilton) leaves her punk band in New York and flies to Tokyo, she finds herself pursued by a would-be rocker who has decided his group needs a Western girl. Despite a maudlin love story, the film is worth watching for its revealing depictions of Tokyo street life and Japanese traditions. Rated R. 1988; 101m.

TOMMY ★★½

DIR: Ken Russell. **CAST:** Roger Daltrey, Ann-Margret, Jack Nicholson, Oliver Reed, Elton John, Tina Turner.

In bringing the Who's ground-breaking rock opera to the screen, director Ken Russell let his penchant for bad taste and garishness run wild. The result is an outrageous movie about a deaf, dumb, and blind boy who rises to prominence as a "Pinball Wizard" and then becomes the new Messiah. Rated PG. 1975; 111m.

TONIGHT AND EVERY NIGHT ★★★

DIR: Victor Saville. **CAST:** Rita Hayworth, Lee Bowman, Janet Blair, Leslie Brooks, Marc Platt.

Another Forties song-and-dance extravaganza—this time in war-torn London. In spite of bomb raids and uncertainty in their private lives, a determined troupe keeps their show alive. Seems a bit dated now, but Rita Hayworth is worth watching. 1945; 92m.

TOO MANY GIRLS ★★★½

DIR: George Abbott. **CAST:** Lucille Ball, Richard Carlson, Eddie Bracken, Ann Miller, Desi Arnaz Sr.

Four young men are hired by prestigious Pottawatomie College in Stopgap, New Mexico, to keep an eye on carefree student Lucille Ball. This marked the debut of Eddie Bracken, Desi Arnaz, *and*, in the chorus, Van Johnson. A trivia lover's delight, this is pure fun to watch. 1940; B&W; 85m.

TOP HAT ★★★★★

DIR: Mark Sandrich. **CAST:** Fred Astaire, Ginger Rogers, Edward Everett Horton, Eric Blore, Helen Broderick.

Top Hat is the most delightful and enduring of the Fred Astaire–Ginger Rogers musicals of the 1930s. This movie has an agreeable wisp of a plot and amusing, if dated, comedy dialogue. 1935; B&W; 99m.

TRAFFIC LIVE AT SANTA MONICA ★★★

DIR: Allan L. Muir. **CAST:** Steve Winwood, Jim Capaldi, Chris Wood, Rebop Kwakubaah, Roger Hawkins, David Hood.

Traffic was among the earliest groups to bring jazz and folk to mainstream rock. A relic, this concert film captures the best and worst of the period, from the long hair and dyed shirts to endless instrumentals (the eight songs average eight minute's each) and lofty, but meaningless lyrics. The great hi-fi sound is rare for an early 1970s rock film. 1972; 65m.

TRANSATLANTIC MERRY-GO-ROUND ★½

DIR: Ben Stoloff. **CAST:** Gene Raymond, Nancy Carroll, Jack Benny, Mitzi Green, Boswell Sisters.

Jack Benny is the emcee of this transatlantic showboat, the S.S. *Progress*, en route from New York to Paris. This tub is loaded with romance, blackmail, chicanery, and murder. But it's rather lightweight overall. 1934; B&W; 90m.

TROUBLE WITH GIRLS, THE ★★★½

DIR: Peter Tewksbury. **CAST:** Elvis Presley, Sheree North, Vincent Price, Dabney Coleman.

First of all, forget the stupid title, which has nothing to do with this charming tale of the Chautaqua Players of 1927. It's sort of a *Music Man*–ish tale about a troupe of entertainers who recruit locals for bit parts in their show. Elvis is the manager of the troupe. Sheree North is the tainted woman who is ruthlessly pursued by her lecherous boss (Dabney Coleman). Refreshingly above the norm from Elvis's inane girly films. Rated G. 1969; 105m.

U2: RATTLE AND HUM ★★★★½
DIR: Phil Joanou. **CAST:** U2.
U2: Rattle and Hum is more than just a concert movie. It's an eloquent cry for change. The Irish rock quartet and 26-year-old director Phil Joanou have combined forces to create a remarkably moving screenwork. Filmed in black and white and color during the group's American tour in support of its ground breaking *Joshua Tree* album, it captures the excitement of the live shows while underlining U2's timely message. Rated PG-13 for profanity. 1988; 99m.

U2 LIVE AT RED ROCKS: UNDER A BLOOD RED SKY ★★★★
DIR: Gavin Taylor. **CAST:** U2.
This astonishing concert documentary captures the Irish rock band at their hottest—during a 1983 stint at the Red Rocks Amphitheatre outside Denver, Colorado. The band delivers a powerful set of music to a highly emotional crowd. 1983; 55m.

UB40'S CCCP, THE VIDEO MIX ★★
DIR: Brian Travers. **CAST:** UB40.
It was a smart move to film this pop-reggae band's tour of the Soviet Union. (Who can resist UB40 in the USSR?) The Russian footage provides an intriguing travelogue touch, but neither the playground and the skating-rink scenes, nor the rhythmic numbers can compensate for UB40's lack of stage dynamics. This is a great studio group, but the concert clips look stale. 1987; 60m.

UNCLE MEAT
DIR: Frank Zappa. **CAST:** Phyllis Smith, Don Preston, Frank Zappa, Carl Zappa, Ray Collins, Meredith Monk.
Frank Zappa may find these home movies of his former band, the Mothers of Invention, amusing, but most people (including his most devoted fans) will be bored throughout this self-indulgent mess. There isn't even enough great music to warrant a viewing here. 1987; 120m.

UNSINKABLE MOLLY BROWN, THE ★★★
DIR: Charles Waters. **CAST:** Debbie Reynolds, Harve Presnell, Ed Begley Sr., Hermione Baddeley, Jack Kruschen.
Noisy, big-budget version of hit Broadway musical has Debbie Reynolds at her spunkiest as the tuneful gal from Colorado who survives the sinking of the *Titanic* and lives to sing about it. High-stepping dance numbers and the performances by Reynolds and Harve Presnell make this a favorite with musicals fans, but it does drag a bit for the casual viewer. 1964; 128m.

URGH! THE MUSIC WAR ★★★½
DIR: Derek Burbidge. **CAST:** Various artists.
Various punk–New Wave bands are well captured in this concert film that features hot sets by the Police, XTC, Echo and the Bunnymen, Oingo Boingo, the Dead Kennedys, and many more. 1981; 124m.

VAGABOND LOVER, THE ★★★
DIR: Marshall Neilan. **CAST:** Rudy Vallee, Sally Blane, Marie Dressler.
Rudy Vallee portrays an orchestra conductor who has fallen deeply in love with the daughter (Sally Blane) of a dotty dowager (Marie Dressler). Conventional but entertaining. 1929; B&W; 69m.

VAN MORRISON IN IRELAND ★★½
DIR: Michael Radford. **CAST:** Van Morrison, Peter Bardens, Bobby Tench, Herbie Armstrong.
Van Morrison is music's mystery man, a soulful singer whose star status has suffered from his mood swings, mysticism, and reclusive nature. This film captures Morrison the singer in strong form on stage in Dublin and Belfast. Songs run from "Gloria" to "Wavelength" and include John Lee Hooker's "Don't Look Back." The

band is only adequate, the color bland, and the sound quality hardly qualifies for the hi-fi listing, but Morrison carries this show. 1979; 57m.

VIDEO FROM HELL ★★½
DIR: Frank Zappa. **CAST:** Frank Zappa, Moon Zappa, Kyle Richards, Keith Moon, Don Preston.
These weird video sequences and live footage from 1982 highlight some of Zappa's best music and preview projects on the drawing board. Zappa is a serious composer and an exceptional guitarist, but his true talent seems to be in tossing ideas and seeing what sticks. The low-budget look gives this an earthy appeal, but the music remains an acquired taste. 1987; 62m.

VIDEO REWIND: THE ROLLING STONES GREAT VIDEO HITS ★★★★
DIR: Julien Temple. **CAST:** The Rolling Stones.
This is a real score for lovers of the Rolling Stones or lovers of rock video in general. Mick Jagger and Bill Wyman take us on a tour of a "rock" museum, using flashbacks as a showcase for the band's videos. Included along with the videos are vintage clips of the Stones in concert. 1984; 60m.

VISION SHARED. A TRIBUTE TO WOODY GUTHRIE AND LEADBELLY, A ★★★★
DIR: Jim Brown. **CAST:** Bruce Springsteen, U2, John Cougar Mellencamp, Bob Dylan, Taj Mahal, Pete Seeger, Arlo Guthrie, Emmylou Harris, Willie Nelson, Little Richard.
This tribute to folk pioneers Leadbelly and Woody Guthrie starts slow with historical notations, but once it gets rolling, it's peak after peak. The performances are bright and endearing, from the backyard washboard bluegrass of Cougar's "Do Re Mi" and Springsteen's tender "I Ain't Got No Home" to Little Richard's rave-up "Rock Island Line" and the chilling end with all contributing to a video collage on "This Land Is Your Land." 1988; 72m.

VIVA LAS VEGAS ★★
DIR: George Sidney. **CAST:** Elvis Presley, Ann-Margret, Cesare Danova, William Demarest, Jack Carter.
In this romantic musical, Elvis Presley plays a race car driver who also sings. Ann-Margret is a casino dancer who becomes jealous when her father becomes interested in Elvis's race car. Eventually Elvis and Ann-Margret get together, which comes as no surprise to any viewer who didn't fall asleep within the first ten minutes of the film. 1964; 86m.

VIVA SANTANA ★★★★
DIR: Tom McQuade. **CAST:** Carlos Santana, Neal Schon, Gregg Rolle, Armando Peraza, Mike Shrieve, Jose Chepito Areas, Dave Brown.
This career retrospective works much better than the record that prompted it. Thin on archival material, the album is filled with concert recordings—which come alive in this video. Carlos Santana talks about all the changes in his landmark Latin-rock band. The live clips present a complete picture, from the Ed Sullivan opening to the montage of "Black Magic Woman" by various editions of Santana. 1988; 81m.

WAGNER ★★★
DIR: Tony Palmer. **CAST:** Richard Burton, Vanessa Redgrave, Gemma Craven, John Gielgud, Ralph Richardson, Laurence Olivier, Marthe Keller, Ronald Pickup.
This five-hour film gives you an idea of what the greatest opera composer may have been like, but it will not explain his behavior, and the legendary supporting cast, although credible, is not up to reputation. Not rated, but equal to an R for violence, profanity, and nudity. 1982; 300m.

WARREN ZEVON ★★★★
DIR: Len Dell'Amico. **CAST:** Warren Zevon, Randy Brown, Joe Daniels, Larry Larson, John Wood.
A simply filmed concert from 1982 runs the risk of seeming dated, even subdued. Yet Warren Zevon is in fine

form with a tight backing band. The show manages to suggest intimacy without sacrificing stage dynamics. 1982; 68m.

WASN'T THAT A TIME! ★★★★★
DIR: Jim Brown. **CAST:** The Weavers, Pete Seeger, Lee Hays, Ronnie Gilbert, Fred Hellerman, Arlo Guthrie, Don McLean, Holly Near, Mary Travers, Harry Reasoner, Studs Turkel.
This is a folk music documentary about the Weavers' last reunion, as narrated wryly by group member Lee Hays. What really sets this apart from all the rest is the wealth of superb archival footage, all used in the proper proportion and sequence. The finale is the final reunion concert, and what a glorious and joyful event that was. Rated G. 1981; 78m.

WEATHER REPORT—THE DOMINO THEORY ★★★★
DIR: Kaname Kawachi. **CAST:** Wayne Shorter, Joe Zawinul, Victor Bailey, Omar Hakim, Mino Cinelu.
Weather Report proves why they are the hottest jazz group in the past twenty years with this electrifying concert taped in 1984 before a stunned audience in Tokyo. Wayne Shorter and Joe Zawinul dominate the set with their special brand of genius in this highly engaging music event. 1984; 61m.

WEST SIDE STORY ★★★★★
DIR: Robert Wise, Jerome Robbins. **CAST:** Natalie Wood, Richard Beymer, Rita Moreno, George Chakiris.
The Romeo-and-Juliet theme (with Richard Beymer and Natalie Wood in the lead roles) is updated to 1950s New York and given an endearing music score. The story of rival white and Puerto Rican youth gangs first appeared as a hit Broadway musical. None of the brilliance of the play was lost in its transformation to the screen. It received Oscars for best picture and its supporting players, Rita Moreno and George Chakiris. (Wood's vocals were dubbed by Marni Nixon.) 1961; 151m.

WHITE CHRISTMAS ★★★
DIR: Michael Curtiz. **CAST:** Bing Crosby, Danny Kaye, Vera-Ellen, Rosemary Clooney.
This attempt to capitalize on the title tune is an inferior remake of 1942's *Holiday Inn* (in which the song "White Christmas" first appeared). It's another in that long line of let's-put-on-a-show stories, with the last several reels showcasing the singing, dancing, and mugging talents of the cast. 1954; 120m.

WHITE CITY ★★½
DIR: Richard Lowenstein. **CAST:** Pete Townshend.
Rather than simply shoot a few videos to promote his album *White City*, former Who leader Pete Townshend produced an hour of concept footage about the same bleak British neighborhood that served as a backdrop for so many of his compositions. Nicely filmed, this ambitious effort is hampered both by its high aims and the demand of working the songs into the story. 1985; 60m.

WHOOPEE ★★½
DIR: Thornton Freeland. **CAST:** Eddie Cantor, Eleanor Hunt, Paul Gregory, Ethel Shutta.
The first of six Eddie Cantor musical films of the 1930s, this one's a two-color draft of his 1928 Broadway hit of the same name. The big-eyed comic plays a superhypochondriac on an Arizona dude ranch. Cowpokes and chorines abound. Busby Berkeley production numbers make it palatable. 1930; B&W; 93m.

WINDHAM HILL IN CONCERT ★★★★
DIR: Stanley Dorfman. **CAST:** William Ackerman, Michael Hedges, Scott Cossu, Shadowfax.
This engaging sampler, filmed documentary-style without video enhancements, offers an intimate look at the Windham Hill roster. Whether you worship New Age ambience or dismiss it as hot-tub Muzak matters little, because all of these musicians are

clearly on the cutting edge, and many, like guitarist Michael Hedges, are undeniably unique stylists. Unrated. 1986; 67m.

WIZ, THE ★
DIR: Sidney Lumet. **CAST:** Diana Ross, Richard Pryor, Michael Jackson, Nipsey Russell, Ted Ross, Mabel King, Theresa Merritt, Thelma Carpenter, Lena Horne.

Ineffective updating of *The Wizard of Oz* with an all-black cast, including Diana Ross (who is too old for the part), Richard Pryor, and Michael Jackson. Adapted from a successful Broadway play, this picture should have been better. Rated G. 1978; 133m.

WIZARD OF OZ, THE ★★★★★
DIR: Victor Fleming. **CAST:** Judy Garland, Ray Bolger, Bert Lahr, Jack Haley, Frank Morgan, Billie Burke, Margaret Hamilton, Charley Grapewin, Clara Blandick.

The all-time classic for children of all ages, this MGM release, directed by Victor Fleming (*Gone with the Wind*) and based on the story by L. Frank Baum, takes us "off to see the wizard...the wonderful wizard of Oz." Sometimes "there's no place like home" for watching great movies! 1939; 101m.

WOODSTOCK ★★★½
DIR: Michael Wadleigh. **CAST:** Country Joe and the Fish, Jimi Hendrix, Jefferson Airplane.

Woodstock is probably, along with *Gimme Shelter*, the most important film documentation of the late 1960s counterculture in the United States. The bulk of the film consists of footage of the bands and various other performers who played at the festival. There are some great split-screen sequences and some imaginative interviews that make the film quite enjoyable today. Well worth viewing. Rated R. 1970; 184m.

WOODY GUTHRIE—HARD TRAVELIN' ★★★½
DIR: Jim Brown. **CAST:** Hoyt Axton, Joan Baez, Judy Collins, Pete Seeger, Arlo Guthrie.

Woody Guthrie's musical presence will be felt for many years. This tribute traces his brilliant songwriting career from the dust bowl of the Midwest to California in the early 1940's. Many performers, including Joan Baez and Arlo Guthrie, Woody's son, sing and discuss the Guthrie influence on their own music. 1984; 74m.

WORDS AND MUSIC ★★½
DIR: Norman Taurog. **CAST:** Mickey Rooney, Tom Drake, June Allyson, Betty Garrett, Judy Garland, Gene Kelly, Ann Sothern, Vera-Ellen, Cyd Charisse, Allyn Ann McLerie, Mel Torme, Janet Leigh, Perry Como.

Fictionalized biography of the songwriting team of Richard Rogers and Lorenz Hart, dwelling mostly on the short and tormented life of the latter, played to excess by Mickey Rooney. Tom Drake is a dull Rogers. As long as there's music, song, and dance, everything is great. The rest should have been silence. 1948; 119m.

X, THE UNHEARD MUSIC ★★★½
DIR: W. T. Morgan. **CAST:** John Doe, Exene Cervenka, Billy Zoom, D. J. Bonebrake.

Los Angeles's best early punk band, X, is chronicled through old haunts, tracking the movers and the music of the time in this fine documentary. The film, like the band, has a clear awareness of the times, a sense of the history of music, and a humorous perception of it all. 1985; 84m.

XANADU ★★½
DIR: Robert Greenwald. **CAST:** Olivia Newton-John, Gene Kelly, Michael Beck, James Sloyan, Sandahl Bergman.

This musical lacks inspiration and storyline. It is basically a full-length video that includes some good numbers by Olivia Newton-John and

Gene Kelly. See it for the musical entertainment, not for the story. Rated PG. 1980; 88m.

YANKEE DOODLE DANDY ★★★★★

DIR: Michael Curtiz. **CAST:** James Cagney, Joan Leslie, Walter Huston, Irene Manning, Rosemary DeCamp, Richard Whorf, Jeanne Cagney.

Magnetic James Cagney, stepping out of his gangster roles, gives a magnificent strutting performance in the life story of dancing vaudevillian George M. Cohan. An outstanding show-business story with unassuming but effective production. 1942; B&W; 126m.

YELLOW SUBMARINE ★★★★

DIR: George Dunning. **CAST:** Animated.

Clever cartoon versions of John, Paul, George, and Ringo journey into Pepperland to save it from the Blue Meanies in this delightful blend of psychedelic animation and top-flight Beatles music. "All You Need Is Love," "When I'm 64," "Lucy in the Sky with Diamonds," and "Yellow Submarine" provide the background and power the action in a film that epitomized the flower generation. 1968; 85m.

YENTL ★★½

DIR: Barbra Streisand. **CAST:** Barbra Streisand, Mandy Patinkin, Amy Irving, Nehemiah Persoff, Steven Hill.

Barbra Streisand, who also produced, coscripted, and directed, stars as a woman who must disguise herself as a man in order to pursue an education among Orthodox Jews in turn-of-the-century eastern Europe. The story is fine, but the songs all sound the same. Still, *Yentl* is, overall, a watchable work. Rated PG for brief nudity. 1983; 134m.

YES, GIORGIO ★

DIR: Franklin J. Schaffner. **CAST:** Luciano Pavarotti, Kathryn Harrold, Eddie Albert, James Hong.

In this old-fashioned star vehicle, Luciano Pavarotti makes a less-than-memorable screen debut as Giorgio Fini, a macho Italian tenor who meets a pretty Boston throat specialist (Kathryn Harrold) when his voice suddenly fails him during a rehearsal. They fall in love and the viewer falls asleep. Rated PG for adult themes. 1982; 110m.

YESSONGS ★★★

DIR: Peter Neal. **CAST:** Yes.

A favorite on the midnight-movie circuit, *Yessongs* provides an interesting look at the glittery overindulgences of rock in the early 1970s. Formed in 1968, Yes fought for credibility with its suitelike, classical brand of rock, which utilized high vocal harmonies. By the time this concert was filmed in 1973, the band, featuring Steve Howe, Jon Anderson, Chris Squire, and Rick Wakeman, was one of rock's top draws. 1974; 70m.

YOU WERE NEVER LOVELIER ★★★★

DIR: William A. Seiter. **CAST:** Fred Astaire, Rita Hayworth, Adolphe Menjou, Leslie Brooks, Adele Mara.

In this interesting story, Fred Astaire goes stepping about with the most glamorous of all the stars—Rita Hayworth. This film's worth seeing twice. 1942; B&W; 97m.

YOU'LL NEVER GET RICH ★★★½

DIR: Sidney Lanfield. **CAST:** Fred Astaire, Rita Hayworth, John Hubbard, Robert Benchley, Osa Massen, Frieda Inescort, Guinn Williams.

This musical-comedy has play producer Fred Astaire getting drafted right before his big show. Somehow he manages to serve his country and put the show on while romancing Rita Hayworth. 1941; B&W; 88m.

YOUNG AT HEART ★★★½

DIR: Gordon Douglas. **CAST:** Doris Day, Frank Sinatra, Gig Young, Ethel Barrymore, Dorothy Malone.

This is a glossy remake of the Warner Bros. 1938 success *Four Daughters*. The plot presents Doris Day as a refined New England lass from a respected family who marries a down-on-his-luck musician (Frank Sinatra). The two stars are especially engaging. 1955; 117m.

YOUNG MAN WITH A HORN ★★★½

DIR: Michael Curtiz. **CAST:** Kirk Douglas, Lauren Bacall, Doris Day, Hoagy Carmichael, Juano Hernandez.

Interesting dramatic portrayal of a young horn player who fights to fill his need for music. Story becomes too melodramatic as Kirk Douglas becomes trapped in a romantic web between Lauren Bacall and Doris Day. Based on the life of Bix Beiderbecke. Hornwork by Harry James. 1950; B&W; 112m.

ZIEGFELD FOLLIES ★★★

DIR: Vincente Minnelli. **CAST:** Fred Astaire, Lucille Ball, William Powell, Judy Garland, Fanny Brice, Lena Horne, Red Skelton, Victor Moore, Virginia O'Brien, Cyd Charisse, Gene Kelly, Edward Arnold, Esther Williams.

MGM tries to imitate a Ziegfeld-style stage show. Don't get confused; this is not the Oscar-winning *The Great Ziegfeld* (with William Powell). The Ziegfeld name is merely a contrivance to provide some unified method of showcasing some of its stars. 1946; 110m.

ZIEGFIELD GIRL ★★★

DIR: Robert Z. Leonard. **CAST:** Judy Garland, Hedy Lamarr, Lana Turner, Edward Everett Horton, Eve Arden, James Stewart, Jackie Cooper, Dan Dailey.

Judy Garland becomes a star, Hedy Lamarr weds rich, and poor Lana Turner hits the bottle. This all-stops-out musical drama is jammed with showgirls, lavish sets and costumes, and songs no one but trivia buffs recall. 1941; B&W; 131m.

ZIGGY MARLEY AND THE MELODY MAKERS LIVE ★★★

DIR: Leslie Libman, Larry Williams. **CAST:** Ziggy Marley, The Melody Makers.

Recapping most of the songs from Ziggy and the Melody Makers' breakthrough LP *Conscious Party*, this 1988 concert film offers solid playing and no surprises. While Ziggy never really catches fire, it's startling not only to see how much Ziggy resembles his father, Bob Marley, but also how young yet confident he is onstage. Very good stereo sound. 1988; 58m.

ZIGGY STARDUST AND THE SPIDERS FROM MARS

DIR: D. A. Pennebaker. **CAST:** David Bowie.

Only the most devoted David Bowie fans will enjoy this documentary, filmed July 3, 1973, at London's Hammersmith Odeon Theatre during the English singer-songwriter's last live performance as an androgynous king. Rated PG for suggestive lyrics. 1982; 90m.

SCIENCE-FICTION/ FANTASY

ABYSS, THE ★★★★
DIR: James Cameron. **CAST:** Ed Harris, Mary Elizabeth Mastrantonio, Michael Biehn.
After suffering the deep-sea disappointments in *Leviathan* and *Deep-Star Six*, viewers are likely to be a little cautious of getting back into the water with this thriller-adventure-fantasy film. They shouldn't be. The third time's the charm with the underwater plot, thanks to the inventiveness of director James Cameron (*The Terminator*, *Aliens*). Rated R. 1989; 110m.

ADVENTURES OF BARON MUNCHAUSEN, THE ★★★★
DIR: Terry Gilliam. **CAST:** John Neville, Robin Williams, Eric Idle, Oliver Reed, Uma Thurman, Sarah Polley.
Terry Gilliam, that inspired madman of the movies, completes the fantasy trilogy—which began with *Time Bandits* and *Brazil*—with this eye-popping phantasmagoria about the celebrated eighteenth-century liar. The film begins in the Age of Reason when a small theatrical troupe attempts to put on a play about Munchausen, only to have an old soldier (John Neville) turn up claiming to be the real thing. He goes on to prove his identity with a series of wild tales. Rated PG for violence. 1989; 126m.

ADVENTURES OF BUCKAROO BANZAI, THE ★★★★
DIR: W. D. Richter. **CAST:** Peter Weller, John Lithgow, Ellen Barkin, Jeff Goldblum.
Peter Weller plays Buckaroo Banzai, a skilled neurosurgeon and physicist who becomes bored with his scientific and medical work and embarks on a career as a rock star and two-fisted defender of justice. This offbeat genre film is a silly movie for smart people. Rated PG. 1984; 103m.

ADVENTURES OF HERCULES, THE
DIR: Lewis Coates. **CAST:** Lou Ferrigno, Milly Carlucci.
This is the sequel to *Hercules*, the 1983 bomb with Lou "the Hulk" Ferrigno. The first Ferrigno folly was a laughfest, one can only comment that this tiresome piece of junk would only benefit insomniacs. Rated PG for violence (yes, even *that* can be boring). 1984; 89m.

AFTER THE FALL OF NEW YORK 🦃

DIR: Martin Dolman. **CAST:** Michael Sopkiw, Valentine Monnier, Anna Kanakis.

Dumb, dubbed, and dreadful Italian-made rip-off of the *Mad Max* series, with Michael Sopkiw as a two-fisted, post-apocalypse hero whose job is to save the human race by finding the last normal woman (she's been freeze-dried) and getting her pregnant. Not much to root for here. Rated R for violence and profanity. 1983; 91m.

ALIEN ★★★★½

DIR: Ridley Scott. **CAST:** Tom Skerritt, Sigourney Weaver, John Hurt, Ian Holm, Harry Dean Stanton, Yaphet Kotto, Veronica Cartwright.

A superb cinematic combination of science-fiction and horror, this is a heart-pounding, visually astounding shocker. The players are all excellent as the crew of a futuristic cargo ship that picks up an unwanted passenger: an alien that lives on human flesh and continually changes form. Rated R. 1979; 116m.

ALIEN CONTAMINATION ★

DIR: Lewis Coates. **CAST:** Ian McCulloch, Marino Masé.

An Italian director better known for inept imitations of George Romero's zombie movies this time provides a ripoff of *Alien.* A malevolent monster from outer space tries to conquer Earth with the aid of slime-spurting alien eggs that cause people to blow up. Rated R. 1982; 90m.

ALIEN FACTOR, THE ★★★

DIR: Don Dohler. **CAST:** Don Leifert, Tom Griffith.

As an amateur film, this is pretty decent. The cast and production crew are one and the same. There are four aliens on the planet Earth. Only one alien is good, and the Earthlings have a hard time figuring out which one is on their side. Rated PG. 1977; 82m.

ALIEN NATION ★★★

DIR: Graham Baker. **CAST:** James Caan, Mandy Patinkin, Terence Stamp.

There are some slow moments in *Alien Nation,* but just sit back and enjoy the ride through familiar territory in this cop-buddy movie with a sci-fi slant. James Caan plays a detective in Los Angeles of the future where genetically bred slaves from another planet are having some problems adjusting to Earth. Mandy Patinkin is the "newcomer," as the aliens are called, who is teamed with Caan to ferret out the perpetrators of a series of mysterious murders among the aliens. Rated R for profanity, violence, and nudity. 1988; 96m.

ALIEN PREDATORS ★½

DIR: Deran Sarafian. **CAST:** Dennis Christopher, Martin Hewitt, Lynn-Holly Johnson.

In this muddled cross between *Invasion of the Body Snatchers* and *Alien,* three young American adventurers stumble into an alien invasion in a small Spanish town. The aliens have destroyed the original inhabitants and taken the bodies. The heroic three must then escape. Rated R for violence and gore. 1986; 92m.

ALIEN WARRIOR 🦃

DIR: Edward Hunt. **CAST:** Brett Clark, Pamela Saunders.

In this unwatchable film, a father on another planet sends his only remaining son (Brett Clark) to Earth to protect its people and confront the ultimate evil, who happens to be a pimp. If this story sounds at all familiar, it's because the only thing missing in this comic-book rip-off—besides an original idea—is Kryptonite. Rated R for nudity, violence, and profanity. 1985; 100m.

ALIENS ★★★★½

DIR: James Cameron. **CAST:** Sigourney Weaver, Carrie Henn, Michael Biehn, Paul Reiser, Lance Henriksen, Jenette Goldstein.

Fifty-seven years have passed during Warrant Officer Ripley's (Sigourney Weaver) deep-space sleep; when she wakes, the planet Acheron—where the crew of the ill-fated *Nostromo* first encountered the nasty extraterrestrial—has been colonized. Then, to everybody's surprise except Ripley's, contact is lost with the colonists. Equal to, although different from the original. Rated R for considerable violence and profanity. 1986; 137m.

ALPHA INCIDENT, THE ★★
DIR: Bill Rebane. **CAST:** Ralph Meeker.
A deadly organism from Mars, an attempted government cover-up, a radiation leak, panic, and havoc. Okay, if you like this sort of now-tired thing. Rated PG. 1977; 84m.

ALTERED STATES ★★★½
DIR: Ken Russell. **CAST:** William Hurt, Blair Brown, Bob Balaban, Charles Hald, Drew Barrymore.
At times in *Altered States*, you can't help but be swept along...and almost overwhelmed. William Hurt, Blair Brown, Bob Balaban, and Charles Haid star in this suspenseful film as scientists involved in the potentially dangerous exploration of the mind. Rated R for nudity, profanity and violence. 1980; 102m.

ANDROID ★★★★
DIR: Aaron Lipstadt. **CAST:** Klaus Kinski, Don Opper, Brie Howard, Norbert Weisser.
A highly enjoyable tongue-in-cheek sci-fi adventure, this takes place on a space station where a mad scientist, Dr. Daniel (played by a surprisingly subdued and effective Klaus Kinski), is trying to create the perfect android. As a group of criminal castaways arrives at the station, the doctor's current robot assistant, Max 404 (Don Opper), decides it is time to rebel. Rated PG for nudity, violence, and profanity. 1982; 80m.

ANDROMEDA STRAIN, THE ★★★★
DIR: Robert Wise. **CAST:** Arthur Hill, David Wayne, James Olson, Kate Reid, Paula Kelly.
A tense science-fiction thriller, this film focuses on a team of scientists attempting to isolate a deadly virus while racing against time and the possibility of nuclear war. Though not as flashy as other entries in the genre, it's highly effective. Rated G. 1971; 130m.

ANGRY RED PLANET, THE ★★½
DIR: Ib Melchior. **CAST:** Gerald Mohr, Nora Hayden, Les Tremayne, Jack Kruschen.
Entertaining (if unoriginal) science-fiction tale of an expedition to Mars running into all sorts of alien terrors, most notable of which is a terrifying kind of giant mouse/spider hybrid. A fun film, though it takes forever to get to the action. 1959; 83m.

ANNA TO THE INFINITE POWER ★★★★
DIR: Robert Wiemer. **CAST:** Martha Byrne, Dina Merrill, Mark Patton, Loretta Devine, Jack Gilford.
Is individuality determined purely by genetic code, or by some other factor beyond the control of science? This film explores the dimensions of that question via the struggles of a brilliant, troubled child—who is also the unwitting subject of a scientific experiment to establish her own identity. Brilliant. 1982; 107m.

ARCHER: FUGITIVE FROM THE EMPIRE ★★
DIR: Nick Corea. **CAST:** Lane Caudell, George Kennedy, Belinda Bauer.
This uninspired sword-and-sorcery movie was the pilot for a television series. Lane Caudell is the young warrior of the title who must overcome numerous challenges in his quest to gain a throne. 1981; 99m.

AT THE EARTH'S CORE ★★½
DIR: Kevin Connor. **CAST:** Doug McClure, Peter Cushing, Caroline Munro, Godfrey James.

At the Earth's Core, an Edgar Rice Burroughs adaptation, benefits enormously from an inspired performance by Peter Cushing. He even manages to make Doug McClure look good occasionally. It's mostly for the kiddies, but we found ourselves clutching the arm of the chair a couple of times at the height of suspense. Rated PG. 1976; 90m.

ATOMIC SUBMARINE, THE ★★★
DIR: Spencer Gordon Bennet. **CAST:** Arthur Franz, Dick Foran, Brett Halsey, Tom Conway, Bob Steele, Joi Lansing.

Solid little thriller about U.S. atomic submarine and its encounter with an alien flying saucer in the Arctic suffers from budgetary limitations but benefits from a decent script, good direction, and an effective and thoroughly believable cast of fine character actors. Entertaining and effective without taking itself too seriously. 1959; B&W; 72m.

ATOR: THE FIGHTING EAGLE ♥
DIR: David Hills. **CAST:** Miles O'Keeffe, Sabrina Siani, Warren Hillman.

A low-budget stupid sword-and-sorcery flick with Miles O'Keeffe, from Bo Derek's *Tarzan, the Ape Man*. Rated PG for violence and nudity. 1983; 98m.

AURORA ENCOUNTER ★★★½
DIR: Jim McCullough. **CAST:** Jack Elam, Peter Brown, Carol Bagdasarian, Dottie West.

Here's one of few science fiction films that can be enjoyed by the whole family. Jack Elam is outstanding in a story about a small Texas town visited by aliens in the late 1800s. Rated PG. 1985; 90m.

BABY...SECRET OF THE LOST LEGEND ★★½
DIR: Bill L. Norton. **CAST:** William Katt, Sean Young, Patrick McGoohan.

Set on the Ivory Coast of West Africa, this Disney story offers more than a cute fable about the discovery of a family of brontosauri. Violence and a hint of sex represent Disney's attempt to appeal to a wider audience. The special effects of the ancient critters make the show worth watching. Rated PG. 1985; 90m.

BACK TO THE FUTURE ★★★★½
DIR: Robert Zemeckis. **CAST:** Michael J. Fox, Christopher Lloyd, Lea Thompson, Crispin Glover, Thomas F. Wilson.

Michael J. Fox as a teenager who is zapped back in time courtesy of a souped-up Delorean modified by mad scientist Christopher Lloyd. Once there, Fox meets his parents as teenagers, an act that could result in disaster. The first fifteen minutes of this film are pretty bad, but once Fox gets back to where he doesn't belong, it's terrific entertainment. Rated PG. 1985; 116m.

BAMBOO SAUCER (A.K.A. COLLISION COURSE) ★★½
DIR: Frank Telford. **CAST:** Dan Duryea, John Ericson, Lois Nettleton, Nan Leslie.

America and the U.S.S.R. compete with each other as they investigate reports of a UFO crash in the People's Republic of China. More concerned with plot and substance than special effects, this low-budget effort is thought-provoking and succeeds where a more gimmicky, less suspenseful approach would have failed. 1968; 100m.

BARBARELLA ★★½
DIR: Roger Vadim. **CAST:** Jane Fonda, John Phillip Law, Anita Pallenberg, Milo O'Shea.

Futuristic fantasy has Jane Fonda in the title role of a space beauty being drooled over by various male creatures on a strange planet. Drags at times, but Jane's fans won't want to miss it. Rated PG for partial nudity, sexual content. 1968; 98m.

BARBARIAN QUEEN 🦃

DIR: Hector Olivera. **CAST:** Lana Clarkson, Latta Shea, Frank Zagarino, Dawn Dunlap.

Another one of those lame fantasy flicks à la *Yor*, the *Conan* films, and Lou Ferrigno's *Hercules* films. Stupid and exploitative, this one is about a group of women who survive an attack on their village only to band together to defeat the raiders. Although not rated, *Barbarian Queen* has lots of nudity and violence. 1985; 75m.

BARBARIANS, THE ★½

DIR: Ruggero Deodato. **CAST:** Peter Paul, David Paul, Richard Lynch, Michael Berryman.

Unconvincing fantasy film casts David and Peter Paul (wrestling's Barbarian Brothers) as twins trying to save the queen of their people and retrieve the "magic ruby." The acting and writing are trash-can quality, but at least the Barbarian Brothers have a good time. Not rated. 1987; 88m.

BARON MUENCHHAUSEN ★★★

DIR: Josef von Baky. **CAST:** Hans Albers, Brigitte Horney, Leo Slezak.

This lavish epic was intended to be a cinematic jewel in the crown of Hitler's Third Reich, a big-budget masterpiece designed to prove that Germany could compete with Hollywood. While the outlandish adventures of Baron Hieronymus Muenchhausen are at times amusing and quite clever (such as his trip to the moon), the incredible visual spectacle—huge and chaotic sets, overly ornate costumes—often overwhelms the story. Very brief nudity; otherwise suitable for family viewing. 1943; 110m.

BATTLE BEYOND THE STARS ★★★★

DIR: Jimmy T. Murakami. **CAST:** Richard Thomas, John Saxon, Robert Vaughn, George Peppard.

Here's something different: a space fantasy-comedy. Richard Thomas stars in this funny and often exciting movie as an emissary from a peaceful planet desperately searching for champions to save it from destruction and domination by an evil warlord. It's *Star Wars* meets *The Magnificent Seven*, with fine tongue-in-cheek performances. Rated PG. 1980; 104m.

BATTLE FOR THE PLANET OF THE APES ★★

DIR: J. Lee Thompson. **CAST:** Roddy McDowall, Severn Darden, John Huston, Claude Akins, Paul Williams.

Events come full circle in this final *Apes* film, with simian Roddy McDowall attempting peaceful coexistence with conquered humanity. Naturally, not everybody plays along with such a plan, and an impending nuclear threat adds little tension to a story whose outcome is known. Rated PG for violence. 1973; 92m.

BATTLESTAR GALACTICA ★

DIR: Richard A. Colla. **CAST:** Lorne Greene, Richard Hatch, Dirk Benedict, Lew Ayres, Jane Seymour.

This film, adapted from the television series, opens with the preparation for a peace treaty by President Adar (Lew Ayres). He has arranged to end a thousand years of war between mankind and the subhuman Cylons. Events go downhill from there. It's seventh-rate *Star Wars*. Rated PG. 1978; 125m.

BEASTMASTER, THE ★★★½

DIR: Don Coscarelli. **CAST:** Marc Singer, Tanya Roberts, Rip Torn, John Amos, Rod Loomis.

A young medieval warrior (Marc Singer) who possesses the ability to communicate psychically with animals takes revenge—with the help of a slave (Tanya Roberts) and a master warrior (John Amos)—on the evil sorcerer (Rip Torn). It's fun for kids of all ages. Rated PG for violence and brief nudity. 1982; 118m.

BEAUTY AND THE BEAST (TELEVISION SERIES) ★★★½

DIR: Richard Franklin, Victor Lobl. **CAST:** Ron Perlman, Linda Hamilton, Roy Dotrice, Jay Acovone.

The classic legend received an updated facelift with this popular cult television series, which teamed Linda Hamilton's crusading district attorney with Ron Perlman's underworld dweller. Some admire the Renaissance surroundings and unusually literate scripts; others simply yearn for the sort of deep, platonic love shared by the two central characters. This much is certain: You'll either roll with the poetic dialogue or find it outrageously melodramatic. Unrated; suitable for family viewing. 1987; 100m.

BENEATH THE PLANET OF THE APES ★★½
DIR: Ted Post. **CAST:** Charlton Heston, James Franciscus, Maurice Evans, Kim Hunter, Linda Harrison, James Gregory.

Charlton Heston let himself get sucked into this sequel to *Planet of the Apes.* Astronaut James Franciscus—sent to find out what happened to the first team sent to the planet—has more than simians to contend with; he also discovers a race of u-g-l-y mutants that worships an atomic bomb, since it made them what they are.... Some of the original's energy remains. Rated PG for violence. 1970; 95m.

BEYOND THE RISING MOON ★★
DIR: Philip Cook. **CAST:** Tracy Davis, Hans Bachmann.

In the twenty-first century, a genetically created troubleshooter rebels against her training when the corporation that designed her sends her on a mission to help them exploit alien technology. The same theme was handled much better in *Blade Runner*, though here the plot is secondary to the mediocre special effects and outer-space shootouts. 1988; 93m.

BEYOND TOMORROW ★★½
DIR: A. Edward Sutherland. **CAST:** Jean Parker, Richard Carlson, Helen Vinson, Charles Winninger, Harry Carey, C. Aubrey Smith, Maria Ouspenskaya, Rod La Rocque.

Sudden success goes to singer Richard Carlson's head. He switches his affections from fiancée Jean Parker to captivating stage star Helen Vinson. To see that right is done, three ghosts return from the grave and change his troubled mind. An interesting premise on paper, the film fails to live up to its possibilities. 1940; B&W; 84m.

BIGGLES—ADVENTURES IN TIME ★★★★
DIR: John Hough. **CAST:** Neil Dickson, Alex Hyde-White, Peter Cushing, Fiona Hutchison, William Hootkins.

Delightful fantasy film focuses on the adventures of a New York frozen-food merchandiser, Jim Ferguson (Neil Dickson), who discovers he has a time twin—a World War I British fighter ace named Biggles (Alex Hyde-White). Every time Biggles is in danger, Ferguson finds himself bouncing back through time to come to his twin's rescue. Rated PG for profanity and violence. 1985; 100m.

BIONIC WOMAN, THE ★★
DIR: Richard Moder. **CAST:** Lindsay Wagner, Lee Majors, Richard Anderson.

What we have here is the female equivalent of TV's *The Six Million Dollar Man.* Lindsay Wagner is the superwoman who annihilates the bad guys. But with all of her indestructible parts that are able to stand any strain, why does she always go through her stunts in slow motion? 1975; 96m.

BLACK HOLE, THE ★
DIR: Gary Nelson. **CAST:** Maximilian Schell, Anthony Perkins, Robert Forster, Joseph Bottoms, Yvette Mimieux, Ernest Borgnine.

Only the splendid special effects make this sappy science-fiction dud from the Disney Studios bearable. Complete with a cute little robot (á la *Star Wars*) and a colorful crew (like *Star Trek*), it's an uninspired collection of space movie clichés. Rated PG. 1979; 97m.

BLADE RUNNER ★★★★½
DIR: Ridley Scott. **CAST:** Harrison Ford, Rutger Hauer, Sean Young, Daryl Hannah, Joanna Cassidy, Edward James Olmos, M. Emmet Walsh.
This Ridley Scott (*Alien*) production is thought-provoking and visually impressive. Harrison Ford stars as a futuristic Philip Marlowe trying to find and kill the world's remaining rebel androids in 2817 Los Angeles. *Blade Runner* may not be for everyone, but those who appreciate something of substance will find it worthwhile. Rated R for brief nudity and violence. 1982; 118m.

BOY AND HIS DOG, A ★★★★½
DIR: L. Q. Jones. **CAST:** Don Johnson, Suzanne Benton, Jason Robards Jr.
Looking for intelligence and biting humor in a science-fiction satire? Try this Hugo Award–winning screen adaptation of Harlan Ellison's novel, which focuses on the adventures of a young scavenger (Don Johnson) and his telepathic dog as they roam the earth circa 2024 after a nuclear holocaust. Rated R for violence, sexual references, and nudity. 1976; 87m.

BRAIN FROM PLANET AROUS, THE ★★★
DIR: Nathan Juran. **CAST:** John Agar, Joyce Meadows, Robert Fuller.
Great little film is much better than the plot or title would suggest. Giant brain from outer space takes over John Agar's body in an attempt to conquer the world. Not far behind is another brain that inhabits the body of Agar's dog and tries to prevent it. Good stuff. 1958; B&W; 70m.

BRAIN THAT WOULDN'T DIE, THE ★
DIR: Joseph Green. **CAST:** Jason Evers (Herb Evers), Virginia Leith, Adele Lamont.
Only the most dedicated science-fiction fans will enjoy this story, which revolves around a doctor who experiments with human limbs. When his fiancée is decapitated in a car accident, he saves her head and searches for the perfect body to go with it. 1963; B&W; 81m.

BRAINSTORM ★★★½
DIR: Douglas Trumbull. **CAST:** Christopher Walken, Natalie Wood, Louise Fletcher.
Christopher Walken and Natalie Wood star in this sci-fi thriller about an invention that can read and record physical, emotional, and intellectual sensations as they are experienced by an individual and allow them to be reexperienced by another human being. The machine's potential for good is impressive. But what happens if it's used for evil? Rated PG for nudity and profanity. 1983; 106m.

BRONX EXECUTIONER, THE
DIR: Bob Collins. **CAST:** Margie Newton, Chuck Valenti, Woody Strode.
Who comes up with the money for pieces of junk such as this? A group of humans battle for their lives against cyborgs bent on their destruction. How original! This schlock doesn't even have any scenes filmed in the Big Apple, not that it would have helped. Not rated, but contains violence. 1989; 88m.

BROTHER FROM ANOTHER PLANET, THE ★★★★
DIR: John Sayles. **CAST:** Joe Morton, Darryl Edwards, Steve James.
In this thoughtful comic fantasy, a dark-skinned extraterrestrial (Joe Morton) on the lam from alien cops crash-lands his spaceship in New York harbor, staggers ashore on Ellis Island, then makes his way to Harlem. Unrated, the film has profanity and violence. 1984; 110m.

BUCK ROGERS: DESTINATION SATURN (A.K.A. PLANET OUTLAWS) ★★½
DIR: Ford Beebe, Saul Goodkind. **CAST:** Buster Crabbe, Constance Moore, Jackie Moran, Jack Mulhall, Anthony Warde, C. Montague Shaw, Philip Ahn.
Edited-down version of the popular serial loses much of the continuity of

the twelve-episode chapter play but still proves to be great fun as ideal hero Buster Crabbe enthusiastically goes after the vile Killer Kan in an effort to help the oppressed people of future Earth. 1939; B&W; 91m.

BUCK ROGERS IN THE 25TH CENTURY ★★

DIR: Daniel Haller. **CAST:** Gil Gerard, Erin Gray, Pamela Hensley, Tim O'Connor, Henry Silva.

Updating of the Buck Rogers legend finds Buck (Gil Gerard), after years of suspended animation, awakened in a future society under attack by the power-mad Princess Ardala (Pamela Hensley). Of course, it's up to our hero to save the day. Substandard space fare was originally made as a TV pilot. Rated PG. 1979; 89m.

CAPRICORN ONE ★★★★

DIR: Peter Hyams. **CAST:** Elliott Gould, James Brolin, Hal Holbrook, Sam Waterston, Karen Black, O. J. Simpson, Telly Savalas.

In this suspenseful release, the government stages a mock flight to Mars in a television studio, with astronauts James Brolin, Sam Waterston, and O. J. Simpson pretending to be in outer space and landing on the planet. Then the news is released by the Pentagon that the ship crashed upon reentry and all aboard were killed, which puts the lives of the astronauts in danger. Rated PG. 1978; 124m.

CAPTIVE PLANET ♥

DIR: Al Bradley. **CAST:** Sharon Baker, Chris Avran.

Earth is once again besieged by alien invaders in this very missable movie. There may have been an interesting idea at the heart of this film, but it was lost in wooden acting, poor script, and unimaginative, budget-priced special effects. 1986; 105m.

CAT WOMEN OF THE MOON ♥

DIR: Arthur Hilton. **CAST:** Sonny Tufts, Marie Windsor, Victor Jory.

Another ludicrous entry in the travel-to-a-planet-of-barely-dressed-women subgenre which so fascinated makers of cheap, grade Z flicks in the 1950s. 1954; 64m.

CAVE GIRL ♥

DIR: David Oliver. **CAST:** Daniel Roebuck, Cindy Ann Thompson.

Yet another insult to the intelligence. This one is about a high-school student who gets lost in a cave during a field trip and pops up in prehistoric times. There he finds a beautiful woman. Of course, he just has to have sex with her! And the first English words our hero teaches the Neanderthal nymphet are not suitable for this publication. Rated R for nudity and profanity. 1985; 85m.

CHARLY ★★★★

DIR: Ralph Nelson. **CAST:** Cliff Robertson, Claire Bloom, Lilia Skala, Dick Van Patten.

Cliff Robertson won the best-actor Oscar for his role in this excellent science-fiction film as a retarded man turned into a genius through scientific experiments. Claire Bloom is also excellent as the caseworker who becomes his friend. Rated PG. 1968; 103m.

CHERRY 2000 ★★½

DIR: Steve DeJarnatt. **CAST:** Melanie Griffith, David Andrews, Ben Johnson, Tim Thomerson, Brion James, Harry Carey Jr., Michael C. Gwynne.

Made before she graduated to better roles in *Stormy Monday* and *Working Girl*, Melanie Griffith starred in this barely released movie as a sort of female Mad Max. Set in the year 2017, this semiparody casts Griffith as a mercenary who guides yuppie David Andrews through the deserts of the Southwest, now the domain of psychotic terrorists, in search of a robot warehouse. Rated PG-13. 1988; 93m.

CITY LIMITS ♥

DIR: Aaron Lipstadt. **CAST:** Darrell Larson, John Stockwell, Kim Cattrall, Rae Dawn Chong, Robby Benson, James Earl Jones.

Another in the endless parade of life-after-the-apocalypse, *Mad Max* rip-off films. In this dud, we have two rival youth gangs fighting it out for control of a big city. A good cast is wasted. Rated PG-13 for brief nudity, violence, and language. 1984; 85m.

CLAN OF THE CAVE BEAR ★½
DIR: Michael Chapman. **CAST:** Daryl Hannah, Pamela Reed, Thomas G. Waites.

In this dreadfully dumb adaptation of Jean M. Auel's bestselling fantasy novel, Daryl Hannah plays a Cro-Magnon child who is grudgingly adopted by a tribe of Neanderthals, who, with a few exceptions, fear she is a dark spirit intent on destroying them. *Quest for Fire* did the caveman story best. Even fans of the book will be disappointed. Rated R. 1986; 100m.

CLASH OF THE TITANS ★★½
DIR: Desmond Davis. **CAST:** Laurence Olivier, Harry Hamlin, Judi Bowker, Burgess Meredith, Maggie Smith.

Perseus (Harry Hamlin), the son of Zeus (Laurence Olivier), mounts his flying horse, Pegasus, and fights for the hand of Andromeda (Judi Bowker) against an onslaught of mythological monsters. Plagued by corny situations and stilted dialogue, only the visual wonders by special-effects wizard Ray Harryhausen make this movie worth seeing. Rated PG for violence and gore. 1981; 118m.

CLOCKWORK ORANGE, A ★★★★
DIR: Stanley Kubrick. **CAST:** Malcolm McDowell, Patrick Magee, Adrienne Corri.

Not for every taste, this is a stylized, "ultraviolent" black comedy. Malcolm McDowell stars as the number-one "malchick," Alex, who leads his "droogs" through "a bit of the old ultraviolence" for a real "horror show." Rated R. 1971; 137m.

CLONES, THE ★★½
DIR: Paul Hunt, Lamar Card. **CAST:** Michael Greene, Bruce Bennett, Gregory Sierra, John Barrymore Jr.

In a sinister plot to control the weather, several government scientists are duplicated and placed in strategic meteorological stations. Basically silly film is made watchable by the believable performances of Michael Greene and Gregory Sierra, and there's a terrific roller coaster–chase finale. Rated PG for language and violence. 1973; 86m.

CLONUS HORROR, THE ★★½
DIR: Robert S. Fiveson. **CAST:** Tim Donnelly, Dick Sargent, Peter Graves, Keenan Wynn, Lurene Tuttle.

Government scientists are hard at work creating a master race of superhumans in a laboratory. One of them breaks free to warn the world. Made on an extremely low budget, this is just good enough that you're disappointed that it couldn't have been better. Not a bad time-waster for science-fiction fans. Also known as *Parts: The Clonus Horror*. Rated R. 1979; 90m.

CLOSE ENCOUNTERS OF THE THIRD KIND ★★★★
DIR: Steven Spielberg. **CAST:** Richard Dreyfuss, François Truffaut, Teri Garr, Melinda Dillon.

This is director Steven Spielberg's enchanting, pre-*E.T.* vision of an extraterrestrial visit to Earth. The movie goes against many long-nurtured conceptions about space aliens. The humans, such as Richard Dreyfuss, act more bizarre than the non-threatening childlike visitors. Spielberg never surrenders his role as storyteller to the distractions of special effects. Rated PG. 1977; 132m.

COCOON ★★★★★
DIR: Ron Howard. **CAST:** Don Ameche, Wilford Brimley, Hume Cronyn, Brian Dennehy, Jack Gilford, Steve Guttenberg, Barrett Oliver, Maureen Stapleton, Jessica Tandy, Gwen Verdon, Tahnee Welch.

Cocoon is a splendid entertainment about a group of people in a retirement home who find what they believe is the fountain of youth. Only trouble is the magic place belongs to a group of extraterrestrials, who may or may not be friendly. Rated PG-13 for suggested sex, brief nudity, and light profanity. 1985; 118m.

COCOON: THE RETURN ★★★½

DIR: Daniel Petrie. **CAST:** Don Ameche, Wilford Brimley, Courtney Cox, Hume Cronyn, Brian Dennehy, Jack Gilford, Steve Guttenberg, Maureen Stapleton, Jessica Tandy, Gwen Verdon, Tahnee Welch.

Daniel Petrie pulls off something of a minor miracle in this sequel, which has the elderly Earthlings returning home to help their alien friends rescue some cocoons that have been endangered by an earthquake. Ron Howard used all of the story's possibilities for suspense and humor in the first film, so Petrie keeps our interest by concentrating on the characters and getting uniformly splendid performances from his cast of veterans. Rated PG for slight profanity. 1988; 112m.

COLOSSUS: THE FORBIN PROJECT ★★★½

DIR: Joseph Sargent. **CAST:** Eric Braeden, Susan Clark, William Schallert.

Low-key thriller about a supercomputer designed for defense that becomes too big for its bytes. Colossus launches its own plan for world domination. This intelligent production is disturbing and very well made. Lack of stars and a downbeat story kept it from becoming the box-office hit it deserved, but the film should find new fans on video. Rated PG. 1969; 100m.

COMPANY OF WOLVES, THE ★★★½

DIR: Neil Jordan. **CAST:** Angela Lansbury, David Warner, Sarah Patterson.

Neither a horror film nor a fantasy for the kiddies, this dark, psychologically oriented rendering of the "Little Red Riding Hood" story is for thinking viewers only. Angela Lansbury stars as Grandmother, who turns the dreams of her granddaughter (Sarah Patterson) into tales of spooky terror. Rated R for violence and gore. 1985; 95m.

CONAN THE BARBARIAN ★★★½

DIR: John Milius. **CAST:** Arnold Schwarzenegger, Sandahl Bergman, James Earl Jones, Mako.

Featuring Arnold Schwarzenegger in the title role, this $19 million sword-and-sorcery epic is just as corny, raunchy, sexist, and unbelievably brutal as the original tales by Robert E. Howard. Therefore, it seems likely Conan fans will be delighted. Rated R for nudity, profanity and violence. 1982; 129m.

CONAN THE DESTROYER ★★★

DIR: Richard Fleischer. **CAST:** Arnold Schwarzenegger, Grace Jones, Wilt Chamberlain, Tracey Walter.

In this lightweight, violent sequel, Conan (Arnold Schwarzenegger) bests beasts and bloodthirsty battlers at every turn with the help of his sidekick (Tracey Walter), a wizard (Mako), a staff-wielding thief (androgynous Grace Jones), and a giant warrior (Wilt Chamberlain) as they go on a perilous mission to find a sacred stone. Rated PG for violence. 1984; 103m.

CONQUEST OF THE PLANET OF THE APES ★★

DIR: J. Lee Thompson. **CAST:** Roddy McDowall, Ricardo Montalban, Don Murray, Severn Darden.

Having been rescued by Ricardo Montalban at the end of his previous film adventure, simian Roddy McDowall matures and leads his fellow apes—now domesticated—in a freedom revolt that sets the stage for the events in the very first film. Very melodramatic and formulaic, with few clichés left unused. Rated PG for violence. 1972; 87m.

CREATION OF THE HUMANOIDS ★★

DIR: Wesley E. Barry. **CAST:** Don Megowan.

In this futuristic parable, Don Megowan plays a cop who is paranoid about the development of near-perfect androids. It's bad enough that the machines are smarter and more productive than humans, but when his sister falls in love with one, Megowan vows to spill oil and strip gears. This low-budget vision of the future is long on talk, short on action, and hard to take seriously. 1962; 75m.

CREATURE

DIR: William Malone. **CAST:** Stan Ivar, Wendy Schaal, Klaus Kinski, Marie Laurin, Lyman Ward.

An insulting-to-the-intelligence rip-off of *Alien*, this film features the reawakening of human-devouring life on one of Jupiter's moons. Rated R for violence. 1985; 97m.

CREATURE FROM THE HAUNTED SEA, THE ★½

DIR: Roger Corman. **CAST:** Anthony Carbone, Betsy Jones-Moreland.

A muddled horror-comedy about a Bogart-type crook planning to steal a treasure with the help of a mythical sea monster. 1960; B&W; 60m.

CREATURES THE WORLD FORGOT ★

DIR: Don Chaffey. **CAST:** Julie Ege, Tony Bonner.

Migrating cavemen battle for superiority of the tribe. All the while they are being pursued by bloodthirsty, cannibalistic rival tribes. There is no dialogue in this movie and it is hard to follow the story without reading the synopsis on the back of the box. Rated PG, but contains some nudity. 1970; 95m.

CYBORG

DIR: Albert Pyun. **CAST:** Jean Claude Van Damme, Deborah Richter, Dayle Haddon.

A study in bad. Bad script. Bad acting. Bad directing. Bad special effects. A soldier of the future (Jean-Claude Van Damme) seeks vengeance against the savage gang that killed his family. Along the way he is pressed into service to bring a cyborg home. Rated R for violence. 1989; 90m.

CYBORG: THE SIX MILLION DOLLAR MAN ★★★

DIR: Richard Irving. **CAST:** Lee Majors, Darren McGavin, Martin Balsam.

Pilot for the long-running ABC series is more serious and subdued than the episodes to follow. Col. Steve Austin (Lee Majors), after flying an experimental jet that crashes is turned into a superman with powerful robotic limbs capable of almost limitless strength. Very good. 1973; 73m.

DAGORA, THE SPACE MONSTER ★½

DIR: Inoshiro Honda. **CAST:** Yosuke Natsuki.

From the folks who brought you *Godzilla*. A cache of gems stolen by Japanese gangsters is ripped off by a giant, flying, diamond-eating jellyfish. Probably a true story. 1964; 80m.

DALEKS—INVASION EARTH 2150 A.D. ★★★

DIR: Gordon Flemyng. **CAST:** Peter Cushing, Bernard Cribbins, Andrew Keir, Ray Brooks.

The always watchable Peter Cushing revives his distinctive interpretation of the ever-popular Dr. Who in this honorable sequel to *Dr. Who and the Daleks*. This time, the title creatures are attempting to take over Earth. 1966; 84m.

DAMNATION ALLEY ★★

DIR: Jack Smight. **CAST:** Jan-Michael Vincent, George Peppard, Dominique Sanda, Jackie Earle Haley, Paul Winfield.

The nuclear holocaust movie, which disappeared after its heyday in the 1950s, was revived by *Damnation Alley*, complete with giant mutations and roaming survivors. While it's not a bad movie, it's not particularly good, either. The laser effects are awful. Rated PG. 1977; 91m.

DARK CRYSTAL, THE ★★★★
DIR: Jim Henson, Frank Oz. **CAST:** Animated.
Jim Henson of "The Muppets" fame created this lavish fantasy tale in the style of J .R .R. Tolkien (*The Lord of the Rings*), using the movie magic that brought E.T. and Yoda (*The Empire Strikes Back*) to life. It's a delight for children of all ages. Rated PG. 1983; 93m.

DARK STAR ★★★½
DIR: John Carpenter. **CAST:** Dan O'Bannon, Brian Narelle.
This is one of the strangest sci-fi films you are likely to run across. Four astronauts have been in space entirely too long as they seek and destroy unstable planets. Director John Carpenter's first film is very funny in spurts and always crazy. Rated PG because of language. 1974; 83m.

D.A.R.Y.L. ★★★★
DIR: Simon Wincer. **CAST:** Barrett Oliver, Mary Beth Hurt, Michael McKean, Josef Sommer.
In this delightful science-fiction film, Barret Oliver stars as a boy adopted by Mary Beth Hurt and Michael McKean. He turns out to be a perfect little fellow...maybe a little too perfect. *D .A .R .Y .L.* is a film the whole family can enjoy. Rated PG for violence and light profanity. 1985; 99m.

DAY AFTER, THE ★★★★
DIR: Nicholas Meyer. **CAST:** Jason Robards Jr., JoBeth Williams, Steve Guttenberg, John Cullum, John Lithgow.
This excellent made-for-TV movie special received much advance publicity because of its timely topic: the effects of a nuclear war. Jason Robards Jr. plays a hospital doctor who treats many of the victims after the nuclear attack. 1983; 126m.

DAY OF THE DOLPHIN, THE ★★★
DIR: Mike Nichols. **CAST:** George C. Scott, Trish Van Devere, Paul Sorvino, Fritz Weaver.
Fine film centering on a research scientist (George C. Scott) who teaches a pair of dolphins to speak, and how they're kidnapped and used in an assassination attempt. Rated PG for language. 1973; 104m.

DAY OF THE TRIFFIDS, THE ★★★½
DIR: Steve Sekely. **CAST:** Howard Keel, Nicole Maurey, Janette Scott, Kieron Moore, Mervyn Johns.
This British film has triffids—alien plants—arriving on Earth during a meteor shower. The shower blinds most of the Earth's people. Then the plants grow, begin walking, and eat humans. This one will grow on you. 1963; 95m.

DAY THE EARTH CAUGHT FIRE, THE ★★★★
DIR: Val Guest. **CAST:** Edward Judd, Janet Munro, Leo McKern.
Veteran director Val Guest helmed this near-classic film concerning the fate of the Earth following simultaneous nuclear explosions at both poles, sending the planet on a collision course with the sun. Incredibly realistic production is unsettling, with Edward Judd perfectly cast as an Everyman caught up in the mass panic and hysteria. 1962; B&W; 99m.

DAY THE EARTH STOOD STILL, THE ★★★★
DIR: Robert Wise. **CAST:** Michael Rennie, Patricia Neal, Hugh Marlowe, Sam Jaffe, Billy Gray.
The Day the Earth Stood Still is one of the better science-fiction films. Even though some of the space gimmicks are campy and not up to today's standards of special effects, the film holds up well because of a good adult script and credible performances by Michael Rennie and Patricia Neal. 1951; B&W; 92m.

DEAD END DRIVE-IN ★★
DIR: Brian Trenchard-Smith. **CAST:** Ned Manning, Natalie McCurry.
It's the year 1990. After widespread economic collapse, the world is in chaos. The Dead-End Drive-In is a relocation camp for the undesirable element that the authorities no longer wish to deal with. Rated R for language, violence, and nudity. 1986; 92m.

DEAD MAN WALKING ★★★
DIR: Gregory Brown. **CAST:** Wings Hauser, Brion James, Jeffrey Combs, Pamela Ludwig.
Surprisingly well-done low-budget science fiction in which a disease has divided the world's population into the haves and the have-nots. A young man (Jeffrey Combs) hires a daredevil mercenary (Wings Hauser) to rescue his girlfriend (Pamela Ludwig) from the plague zone. Rated R for violence. 1987; 90m.

DEADLY HARVEST
DIR: Timothy Bond. **CAST:** Clint Walker, Nehemiah Persoff, Kim Cattrall, David Brown.
Mankind's unrelenting industrialization of arable land and subsequent cold winters (and summers!) wreak havoc with America's ecological system, slinging society into barbarism. Clint Walker sleepwalks through this sappy futuristic thriller. Rated PG. 1976; 86m.

DEATH RACE 2000 ★★★
DIR: Paul Bartel. **CAST:** David Carradine, Sylvester Stallone, Louisa Moritz, Mary Woronov, Joyce Jameson, Fred Grandy.
Futuristic look at what has become our national sport: road racing where points are accumulated for killing people with the race cars. David Carradine and Sylvester Stallone star in this tongue-in-cheek sci-fi action film. Stallone is a howl as one of the competitors. Rated R—violence, nudity, language. 1975; 78m.

DEATH WATCH ★★★★
DIR: Bertrand Tavernier. **CAST:** Romy Schneider, Harvey Keitel, Harry Dean Stanton, Max von Sydow.
A thought-provoking look at the power and the misuse of the media in a future society. Harvey Keitel has a camera implanted in his brain. A television producer (Harry Dean Stanton) uses Keitel to film a documentary of a terminally ill woman (Romy Schneider) without her knowledge. Suspenseful science-fiction drama. Rated R for profanity and suggested sex. 1980; 117m.

DEATHSPORT ★★
DIR: Henry Suso, Allan Arkush. **CAST:** David Carradine, Claudia Jennings, Richard Lynch.
Not really a sequel to *Death Race 2000*, but cut from the same cloth. Both are low-budget action films centered around futuristic no-holds-barred road races. The first film, though, was a lot more fun. Rated R for violence and nudity. 1978; 82m.

DEATHSTALKER
DIR: John Watson. **CAST:** Robert Hill, Barbi Benton, Lana Clarkson.
This film has a muscle-bound warrior (Robert Hill) attempting to save a beautiful princess (Barbi Benton) from an evil wizard. If the plot sounds familiar, it should. It's an unabashed rip-off of *Star Wars*. Rated R for nudity, profanity, simulated rape, and violence. 1984; 80m.

DEATHSTALKER II: DUEL OF THE TITANS ★★½
DIR: Jim Wynorski. **CAST:** John Terlesky, Monique Gabrielle.
This tongue-in-cheek sword-and-sorcery tale has little to do with its inferior predecessor aside from the name of the lead character. Deathstalker and a feisty deposed princess battle the evil magician who has taken over her kingdom. Lowbrow fun is too busy making fun of itself to be taken seriously. The R rating is for nudity and violence. 1987; 85m.

DEEP SPACE ★
DIR: Fred Olen Ray. **CAST:** Charles Napier, Ann Turkel, Ron Glass, Julie Newmar, James Booth, Anthony Elsley, Bo Svenson.

A creature created by the air force runs amok, and two rebel policemen (Charles Napier, Ron Glass) track it down. The Thing looks like a preliminary drawing from *Alien*, and to save money the filmmakers might just as well have used outtakes from that film. Rated R for violence and language. 1988; 90m.

DEF-CON 4 ★★½
DIR: Paul Donovan. **CAST:** Maury Chaykin, Kate Lynch, Tim Choate, Lenore Zann.

The first half of this film contains special effects the equal of any in modern science fiction, an intelligent script, and excellent acting. The second half is one postholocaust yawn. The overall impression is that perhaps the filmmakers ran out of time or money or both. Rated R for language and violence. 1985; 85m.

DELUGE ★★
DIR: Felix Feist. **CAST:** Peggy Shannon, Sidney Blackmer, Lois Wilson, Matt Moore, Edward Van Sloan, Fred Kohler Sr., Samuel S. Hinds.

The destruction of much of New York by earthquakes and a tidal wave highlights this otherwise dull romance. Edward Van Sloan as the harbinger of doom is about all there is to recommend this otherwise dull attempt at science fiction. 1933; B&W; 70m.

DEMON (GOD TOLD ME TO) ★★★½
DIR: Larry Cohen. **CAST:** Tony LoBianco, Sandy Dennis, Sylvia Sidney, Deborah Raffin, Sam Levene, Mike Kellin.

A minor masterpiece, this movie opens with several mass murders. The only thing that connects these incidents is they are committed by pleasant, smiling people who explain their acts by saying, "God told me to." Rated R for nudity, profanity, and violence. 1977; 95m.

DEMON SEED ★★★
DIR: Donald Cammell. **CAST:** Julie Christie, Fritz Weaver, Gerrit Graham.

Good, but not great, science-fiction film about a superintelligent computer designed by scientist Fritz Weaver to solve problems beyond the scope of man. The computer, however, has other ideas: it wants to study and experiment on the strange Earth species known as man. Weaver's wife (Julie Christie) becomes its unwilling guinea pig and, eventually, mate. Rated R. 1977; 94m.

DESERT WARRIOR ★
DIR: Jim Goldman. **CAST:** Lou Ferrigno, Shari Shattuck.

After World War III, two warring factions fight for dominance and continued survival of the human race. When a man and a woman from each side fall in love, the two sides are brought together in a battle for world supremacy. This low-budget yawner is chock full of bad acting and laugh-producing special effects. Rated PG-13 for violence and nudity. 1988; 89m.

DESTINATION MOON ★★★½
DIR: Irving Pichel. **CAST:** Warner Anderson, John Archer, Tom Powers, Dick Wesson.

This story involves the first American spaceship to land on the moon. Even though the sets are dated today, they were what scientists expected to find when people did land on the moon. This film boasts the classic pointed spaceship and bubble helmets on the space travelers, but it is still great fun for fans of the genre. 1950; 91m.

DOC SAVAGE...THE MAN OF BRONZE ★★★
DIR: Michael Anderson. **CAST:** Ron Ely, Pamela Hensley, Darrell Zwerling, Michael Miller, Paul Gleason.

Perfectly acceptable—although campy—first appearance by the famed hero of pulp novels, Doc Savage. Ron Ely makes a suitable Savage, complete with torn shirt and deadpan delivery. Special effects and set design are minimal, a true shame since this is the last film produced by science-fiction pioneer George Pal. Rated PG—some violence. 1975; 100m.

DR. STRANGE ★★
DIR: Philip DeGuere. **CAST:** Peter Hooten, Clyde Kusatsu, Jessica Walter, Eddie Benton, John Mills.
Another Marvel Comics superhero comes to life in *Dr. Strange, Master of the Mystic Arts*. Dr. Strange is chosen by the guardian of the spirit world to protect Earth from the evil villainess who is set on invading Earth. The adventures of our hero are high on magic and sorcery for a fair rendition of the comic book hero. 1978; 94m.

DR. WHO AND THE DALEKS ★★★
DIR: Gordon Flemyng. **CAST:** Peter Cushing, Roy Castle, Jennie Linden, Barrie Ingham.
In this feature film derived from—but not faithful to—the long-running BBC television series, an eccentric old scientist (Peter Cushing) takes his friends on a trip through space and time. They end up on a planet that has been devastated by nuclear war and must help a peace-loving people fight the Daleks, a race of war-mongering mutants who have encased their fragile bodies in robot shells. This juvenile science-fiction adventure should please youngsters. Rated G. 1965; 83m.

DR. WHO: REVENGE OF THE CYBERMEN ★★★
DIR: Michael E. Briant. **CAST:** Tom Baker, Elizabeth Sladen.
This is the first video from the popular British TV series and stars the fourth Dr. Who, Tom Baker. In this film, the evil Cybermen attempt to destroy the planet Voga, which is made of solid gold, the only item that can kill them. A good introduction to *Dr. Who*, the longest-running science-fiction TV series. 1986; 92m.

DOG STAR MAN ★★★★
DIR: Stan Brakhage.
An abstract vision of the creation of the universe—an epic work consisting of a prelude and four parts, making brilliant use of superimpositions, painting on film, distorting lenses, and rhythmic montage. This feature makes for hypnotic experimenting in silent filmmaking. 1964; 78m.

DONOVAN'S BRAIN ★★★
DIR: Felix Feist. **CAST:** Lew Ayres, Nancy Davis, Gene Evans, Steve Brodie.
After his death in a plane crash, a powerful business magnate has his brain removed by a research scientist (Lew Ayres) who hopes to communicate with the organ by feeding it electricity. Before you know it, the brain is in control, forcing the doctor to obey its ever-increasing demands. Credible acting and tight pacing. 1953; B&W; 83m.

DOOMWATCH ★★½
DIR: Peter Sasdy. **CAST:** George Sanders, Ian Bannen, Judy Geeson.
Sci-fi for the *Masterpiece Theatre* crowd, with plenty of British reserve. A scientist aids the army in investigating an island where pollution has turned the population into mutants. Thoughtful, though not very scary. Based on a BBC miniseries. Unrated. 1972; 92m.

DRAGONSLAYER ★★½
DIR: Matthew Robbins. **CAST:** Peter MacNicol, Caitlin Clarke, Ralph Richardson.
Peter MacNicol plays a sorcerer's apprentice who, to save a damsel in distress, must face a fearsome fire-breathing dragon in this tale of romance and medieval magic. While the special effects are spectacular, the rest of the film doesn't quite live up to them. It's slow, and often too corny for older viewers. Rated PG for violence. 1981; 110m.

DREAMCHILD ★★★★
DIR: Gavin Millar. **CAST:** Coral Browne, Peter Gallagher, Ian Holm, Jane Asher, Nicola Cowper.
Some of those familiar with *Alice's Adventures in Wonderland* may be surprised to learn that there was a real Alice. Author Lewis Carroll, first told his fanciful stories to 10-year-old Alice Liddel on a summer boat ride down the River Isis on July 1, 1862. In 1932, at the age of 80, Alice went to New York City to participate in a Columbia University tribute to Carroll. From these facts, director Gavin Millar and writer Dennis Potter have fashioned this rich and thought-provoking film. Rated PG. 1986; 94m.

DREAMS COME TRUE ★
DIR: Max Kalamanowicz. **CAST:** Michael Sanville, Stephanie Shuford.
A restless young factory worker meets a young woman with whom he shares an unusual power, the ability to control and live in their dreams. It's a fanciful premise, but the script never does anything of interest. You'll be sitting there at the end saying, "Is that all?" Rated R. 1984; 95m.

DREAMSCAPE ★★★★
DIR: Joseph Ruben. **CAST:** Dennis Quaid, Max von Sydow, Christopher Plummer, Eddie Albert, Kate Capshaw.
If you can go along with its intriguing but far-fetched premise—that trained psychics can enter other people's nightmares and put an end to them—this film will reward you with top-flight special effects, thrills, chills, and surprises. Rated PG-13 for suggested sex, violence, and profanity. 1984; 99m.

DUNE ★½
DIR: David Lynch. **CAST:** Sting, Kyle MacLachlan, Max von Sydow, Jurgen Prochnow, Sean Young, Kenneth McMillan, Richard Jordan.
The only good thing about the movie version of *Dune* is it makes one want to read (or reread) the book. Otherwise, it's a $47 million mess. Writer-director David Lynch touches on most of the elements and events in Frank Herbert's celebrated science-fiction novel and adequately explores none. Rated PG-13 for gore, suggested sex, and violence. 1984; 145m.

DUNGEONMASTER, THE ★
DIR: Rosemarie Turko, John Carl Buechler, Charles Band, David Allen, Steve Ford, Peter Manoogian, Ted Nic. **CAST:** Jeffrey Byron, Richard Moll.
This could be a movie sci-fi/fantasy buffs might put on their guilty pleasures list. It's corny, it's bad, it's simplistic, and, if you don't take it seriously, it's fun; a Saturday-afternoon matinee-style adventure for youngsters. Rated PG-13 for mild violence. 1985; 73m.

EARTH VS. THE FLYING SAUCERS ★★★★
DIR: Fred F. Sears. **CAST:** Hugh Marlowe, Joan Taylor, Donald Curtis, Morris Ankrum.
Stunning special effects by Ray Harryhausen enhance this familiar 1950s plot about an invasion from outer space. After misinterpreting a message for peace from the initially easygoing aliens, the military opens fire—and then all hell breaks loose! 1956; B&W; 83m.

EAT AND RUN ★
DIR: Christopher Hunt. **CAST:** Ron Silver, R. L. Ryan.
This science-fiction spoof is about a four-hundred pound alien named Murry Creature (R. L. Ryan) who eats Italian—the people, not the food. Rated R for nudity. 1986; 85m.

ELIMINATORS, THE
DIR: Peter Manoogian. **CAST:** Andrew Prine, Denise Crosby, Patrick Reynolds, Roy Dotrice.
The makers of *The Eliminators* got so carried away with time travel, Cyborgs, mad scientists, kung fu, and fantastic weapons that they forgot to use a plot and a script. In the slight story, a mad scientist creates the perfect weapon, the "Mandroid," which

turns against him when the scientist uses it for evil purposes. Rated PG. 1986; 95m.

EMBRYO ★★½
DIR: Ralph Nelson. **CAST:** Rock Hudson, Barbara Carrera, Diane Ladd.

Rock Hudson plays a scientist who succeeds in developing a fetus into a full-grown woman in record time. But something isn't quite right. Adequate thriller with a good ending. Rated PG. 1976; 104m.

EMPIRE OF THE ANTS ★
DIR: Bert I. Gordon. **CAST:** Joan Collins, Robert Lansing, Albert Salmi, Robert Pine.

H. G. Wells must somersault in his grave every time somebody watches this insulting adaptation of one of his more intriguing sci-fi stories. Director Bert I. Gordon really hit bottom with this, a laughable blend of Joan Collins's terrible acting and giant hypnotic insects. This isn't good enough even to be considered camp. Rated PG for violence. 1977; 90m.

EMPIRE STRIKES BACK, THE ★★★★★
DIR: Irvin Kershner. **CAST:** Billy Dee Williams, Harrison Ford, Carrie Fisher, Mark Hamill, Anthony Daniels, Dave Prowse, James Earl Jones (voice).

In George Lucas's follow-up to *Star Wars*, Billy Dee Williams joins Mark Hamill (Luke Skywalker), Harrison Ford (Han Solo), Carrie Fisher (Princess Leia), and the gang in their fight against the forces of the Empire led by Darth Vader. It's more action-packed fun in that faraway galaxy a long time ago. Rated PG. 1980; 124m.

ENCOUNTER WITH THE UNKNOWN ★★★½
DIR: Harry Thomason. **CAST:** Rod Serling, Rosie Holotik, Gene Ross.

Rod Serling narrates a series of true events in psychic phenomena. The episodes are based on studies made by Dr. Jonathan Rankin between 1949 and 1970. Each deals with a person's encounter with the unknown or supernatural. Rated PG. 1973; 90m.

END OF THE WORLD 🖤
DIR: John Hayes. **CAST:** Christopher Lee, Sue Lyon, Lew Ayres, Dean Jagger, MacDonald Carey.

Impressive cast founders in this film about aliens plotting to destroy the Earth while disguised as religious figures. Laughably bad movie might be good for a few, if only it weren't so slowly paced. Rated PG. 1977; 87m.

ENDANGERED SPECIES ★★★½
DIR: Alan Rudolph. **CAST:** Robert Urich, JoBeth Williams, Paul Dooley, Hoyt Axton.

Everything about this nifty science-fiction suspense thriller is well done. The story deals with bizarre incidents involving cattle mutilation and is based on fact. In it, a country sheriff (JoBeth Williams) and a hard-boiled New York detective (Robert Urich) join forces to find out who or what is responsible. Rated R for discreetly handled nudity, violence, and profanity. 1982; 97m.

ENDGAME 🖤
DIR: Steven Benson. **CAST:** Al Cliver, Moira Chen, George Eastman, Gordon Mitchell.

Ho-hum, another *Road Warrior* rip-off—this one complete with mutants who communicate via telepathy. Well, at least they don't look as stupid as the rest of the cast, who suffer the dreaded postproduction humiliation of bad dubbing. Not rated, but the equivalent of a PG-13 for violence and partial nudity. 1985; 98m.

ENEMY FROM SPACE ★★★★
DIR: Val Guest. **CAST:** Brian Donlevy, William Franklyn.

Brian Donlevy makes his second appearance as Professor Quatermass, a scientist hero who discovers that aliens are slowly taking over the governments of Earth—starting with Britain. It's an uncommonly powerful film, which was based on the long-running British television series written by Nigel Kneale. The first entry in the theatrical trilogy was *The Creeping Unknown* and the last was *Five*

Million Years to Earth. 1957; B&W; 85m.

ENEMY MINE ★½
DIR: Wolfgang Petersen. **CAST:** Dennis Quaid, Louis Gossett Jr., Brion James, Richard Marcus, Lance Kerwin.

A would-be outer-space epic that manages to disappoint on nearly every level. The story details what happens when two futuristic foes, an Earthman (Dennis Quaid) and a reptilian alien (Louis Gossett Jr.), are stranded on a hostile planet and forced to rely on each other for survival. Rated PG-13 for violence and profanity. 1985; 108m.

ESCAPE FROM SAFEHAVEN ★
DIR: Brian Thomas Jones, James McCalmont. **CAST:** Rick Gianasi.

This futuristic film about a family that is terrorized by a ruthless government loses much of its message to excessive graphic violence and gratuitous nudity and sadism. Leather, whips, and chains distinguish the bad from the good in this exercise in poor taste. Rated R. 1988; 87m.

ESCAPE FROM THE PLANET OF THE APES ★★★
DIR: Don Taylor. **CAST:** Roddy McDowall, Kim Hunter, Eric Braeden, Bradford Dillman, William Windom, Ricardo Montalban.

Escaping the nuclear destruction of their own world and time, intelligent simians Roddy McDowall and Kim Hunter arrive on ours. This third *Apes* entry makes wonderful use of the *Strangers in a Strange Land* theme, which turns ugly all too quickly as humanity decides to destroy the apes to prevent them from breeding. Rated PG for violence. 1971; 98m.

ESCAPE 2000 🦃
DIR: Brian Trenchard-Smith. **CAST:** Steve Railsback, Olivia Hussey, Michael Craig, Carmen Duncan, Roger Ward.

A nauseating science-fiction film from Britain, this consists of a series of close-ups of people in the throes of death—garrotings, bludgeonings, gut-stabbings, shoulder-slashings, and assorted thrashings. Yuck! Rated R for—you guessed it—violence and gore. 1981; 92m.

ESCAPES ★★★
DIR: David Steensland. **CAST:** Vincent Price, Michael Patton-Hall, John Mitchum, Todd Fulton, Jerry Grisham, Ken Thorley.

Low-budget anthology in the *Twilight Zone* vein, featuring six stories of the bizarre and done with great style by director David Steensland. Top honors go to "A Little Fishy," a grimly funny tale, and "Who's There?" a neat yarn about an escaped laboratory experiment and a Sunday jogger. 1985; 71m.

E. T.—THE EXTRA-TERRESTRIAL ★★★★★
DIR: Steven Spielberg. **CAST:** Dee Wallace, Henry Thomas, Peter Coyote, Robert MacNaughton, Drew Barrymore.

The highest-grossing (and we think most entertaining) science-fiction film of all time, this is Steven Spielberg's gentle fairy tale about what happens when a young boy meets up with a very special fellow from outer space. Sheer wonder is joined with warmth and humor in this movie classic. Rated PG. 1982; 115m.

EXCALIBUR ★★★★
DIR: John Boorman. **CAST:** Nicol Williamson, Nigel Terry, Helen Mirren, Nicholas Clay, Cherie Lunghi, Corin Redgrave, Paul Geoffrey.

Swords cross and magic abounds in this spectacular, highly enjoyable version of the Arthurian legend. A gritty, realistic view of the rise to power of King Arthur, the forbidden love of Queen Guinevere and Sir Lancelot and the quest of the Knights of the Round Table for the holy grail. *Excalibur* is highlighted by lush photography and fine performances. Rated R. 1981; 140m.

EXPERIMENTAL FILMS OF MAYA DEREN VOL. I ★★★★★
DIR: Maya Deren. **CAST:** Not Credited.

From the early 1940s until her death in 1961 Maya Deren exemplified the American avant-garde film movement. This compilation of her fantasy film shorts, considered to be some of the finest examples of independent movie-making, is reminiscent of other great film surrealists such as Luis Buñuel, Jean Cocteau and René Clair. This collection contains *Meshes of the Afternoon, At Land, A Study in Choreography for Camera, Ritual in Transfigured Time, Meditation on Violence*, and *The Very Eye of Night*. Not rated. B&W; 76m.

EXPLORERS ★★★½
DIR: Joe Dante. **CAST:** Ethan Hawke, River Phoenix, Jason Presson, Dick Miller, Robert Picardo.

The young and the young at heart are certain to have a grand time watching *Explorers*. It's a just-for-fun fantasy about three kids (Ethan Hawke, River Phoenix, and Jason Presson) who share the same dream and soon find themselves taking off on the greatest adventure of all: a journey through outer space. Rated PG for minor violence and light profanity. 1985; 109m.

EXTERMINATORS OF THE YEAR 3000 ★
DIR: Jules Harrison. **CAST:** Robert Jannucci, Alicia Moro, Alan Collins, Fred Harris, Beryl Cunningham, Luca Venantini.

This one rips off George Miller's *The Road Warrior* almost to the letter. The only major difference is that instead of a gas shortage, the world suffers a drought. The action scenes are poorly directed and contain some wholly impossible incidents. Rated R for violence and profanity. 1983; 101m.

EYES BEHIND THE STARS ★½
DIR: Roy Garrett. **CAST:** Robert Hoffman, Nathalie Delon, Martin Balsam.

A reporter and a UFO specialist investigate reports that extraterrestrial beings have landed on Earth, but are stymied by government agents at every turn. This Italian-made SF film is almost as concerned with being a conspiracy thriller, though it's not very good as either. Unrated. 1972; 95m.

FAHRENHEIT 451 ★★★★
DIR: François Truffaut. **CAST:** Oskar Werner, Julie Christie, Cyril Cusack, Anton Diffring.

Still the best adaptation of a Ray Bradbury book to hit the screen (big or small). Oskar Werner is properly troubled as a futuristic "fireman" responsible for the destruction of books, who begins to wonder about the necessity of his work. This is director François Truffaut's first English-language film, and he treats the subject of language and literature with a dignity not found in most American films. Unrated—family fare. 1967; 111m.

FANTASTIC PLANET ★★★
DIR: René Laloux. **CAST:** Animated.

This French-Czechoslovakian production is an animated metaphor concerning the class struggles—and, eventually, war—between two races on an alien planet. Lovely animation and a non-preachy approach to the story combine to produce a fine little film that makes its points and sticks in the memory. Short, but sincere and effective. Voices of Barry Bostwick, Nora Heflin. Rated PG—intense subject matter, some violence. 1973; 71m.

FANTASTIC VOYAGE ★★★
DIR: Richard Fleischer. **CAST:** Stephen Boyd, Raquel Welch, Edmond O'Brien, Donald Pleasence, Arthur O'Connell, William Redfield, Arthur Kennedy.

Scientists journey into inner space—the human body—by being shrunk to microscopic size. They then are threatened by the system's natural defenses. This Richard Fleischer film still packs an unusually potent punch. 1966; 100m.

FANTASY ISLAND ★★½
DIR: Richard Lang. **CAST:** Ricardo Montalban, Bill Bixby, Sandra Dee, Peter Lawford, Carol Lynley, Hugh O'Brian.

Dreams and fantasies come true and then some on a mysterious millionaire's island paradise in this sub-average TV-er that spawned the hit series. Yawn. 1977; 100m.

FIELD OF DREAMS ★★★★★
DIR: Phil Alden Robinson. **CAST:** Kevin Costner, Amy Madigan, James Earl Jones, Burt Lancaster, Ray Liotta, Timothy Busfield.

A must-see motion picture, this spirit-lifting work stars Kevin Costner as an Iowa farmer who hears a voice telling him to build a baseball diamond in the middle of his corn field. Against all common sense, he does so and sets in motion a chain of wonderful events. Costner gets strong support from Amy Madigan, Burt Lancaster, James Earl Jones, and Ray Liotta in this all-ages delight adapted from the novel, *Shoeless Joe*, by W. P. Kinsella. Rated PG for brief profanity. 1989; 106m.

FINAL COUNTDOWN, THE ★★½
DIR: Don Taylor. **CAST:** Kirk Douglas, Martin Sheen, Katharine Ross.

Far-fetched but passable story about an aircraft carrier traveling backward in time to just before the start of World War II. The crew must then decide whether or not to change the course of history. Some good special effects and performances by the leads manage to keep this one afloat. Rated PG. 1980; 104m.

FINAL EXECUTIONER, THE ★
DIR: Romolo Guerrieri. **CAST:** William Mang, Marina Costa, Harrison Muller, Woody Strode.

Following a nuclear holocaust a small undamaged elite entertain themselves by hunting down the contaminated human leftovers, plus castouts from their own repressive clan. Not rated, but contains violence and sex. 1983; 95m.

FIRE AND ICE (1983) ★★★★
DIR: Ralph Bakshi. **CAST:** Animated.

This animated film is geared more to adults than children. Sword and sorcery fantasy keeps the action moving. The plot begins with evil sorcerer Nekron planning world domination. It thickens when he kidnaps the princess, Teegra, to force her father to turn his kingdom over to him as his daughter's ransom. Rated PG. 1983; 81m.

FIRE AND SWORD ★
DIR: Vieth von Furstenburg. **CAST:** Christopher Waltz, Antonia Presser, Peter Firth, Leigh Lawson.

Boring, turgid retèlling of the Tristan and Isolde legend of the Middle Ages. Christopher Waltz is uninspired as Tristan, the brave knight, and Antonia Presser is equally uncaptivating as his tragic love, Isolde. Not rated, but contains violence and nudity. 1985; 84m.

FIREBIRD 2015 AD ★½
DIR: David Robertson. **CAST:** Darren McGavin, Doug McClure, George Touliatos.

In the near future, gas is so scarce that the government outlaws private ownership of automobiles and sets up an agency to destroy them. One of their agents, however, takes his duties too seriously and starts destroying the auto owners as well. Tongue-in-cheek action pix doesn't have the panache of the Roger Corman car films that obviously inspired it. Rated PG. 1981; 97m.

FIRST MAN INTO SPACE, THE ★★½
DIR: Robert Day. **CAST:** Marshall Thompson.

An arrogant test pilot is mutated, by cosmic rays, into a blood-hungry monster. Although it's dated and scientifically incorrect, this S-F chiller still has some B-film fun. Not rated, but suitable for all viewers. 1958; B&W; 78m.

FIRST MEN *IN* THE MOON ★★★½

DIR: Nathan Juran. **CAST:** Edward Judd, Martha Hyer, Lionel Jeffries, Peter Finch.

This whimsical adaptation of an H.G. Wells novel benefits greatly from the imaginative genius of Ray Harryhausen, who concocts the critters—stop-motion and otherwise—which menace some turn-of-the-century lunar explorers who arrive via a Victorian-era spaceship. Although the tone is initially tongue-in-cheek, this adventurous plot eventually develops some rather chilling teeth. Great fun for the entire family. 1964; 103m.

FIRST SPACESHIP ON VENUS ★

DIR: Kurt Maetzig. **CAST:** Yoko Tani.

Low-budget, lackluster German science-fiction plants an international crew of astronauts on Venus with poor special effects and worse dialogue. There are some interesting questions raised in this "let's proceed with caution" story, but not enough to merit it a spot in the science-fiction hall of fame. 1960; 78m.

FLASH GORDON ★★★½

DIR: Mike Hodges. **CAST:** Sam Jones, Topol, Max von Sydow, Melody Anderson, Timothy Dalton.

If you don't take it seriously, this campy film based on the classic Alex Raymond comic strip of the 1930s is a real hoot. Sam Jones, as Flash, and Melody Anderson, as Dale Arden, race through the intentionally hokey special effects to do battle with Max von Sydow, who makes an excellent Ming the Merciless. Rated PG. 1980; 110m.

FLASH GORDON CONQUERS THE UNIVERSE ★★★

DIR: Ford Beebe, Ray Taylor. **CAST:** Buster Crabbe, Carol Hughes, Charles Middleton, Frank Shannon, Lee Powell.

The third and last of Universal's landmark Flash Gordon serials finds the Earth in jeopardy again as Ming the Merciless spreads an epidemic known as the Plague of the Purple Death in yet another attempt to rule the universe. Not as ingenious or spectacular as the original, this serial was still a strong competitor in that great period from 1937 to 1945 when the chapterplay market was important. 1940; B&W; 12 chapters.

FLASH GORDON: MARS ATTACKS THE WORLD (A.K.A. TRIP TO MARS; DEADLY RAY FROM MARS, THE) ★★½

DIR: Ford Beebe, Robert Hill. **CAST:** Buster Crabbe, Jean Rogers, Charles Middleton, Frank Shannon.

In this edited version of the second Flash Gordon serial, Buster Crabbe and the gang head out to Mars to put a halt to a ray that is drawing nitrogen away from the Earth. Of course, Ming the Merciless is behind it all. Hokey but fun, even trimmed of almost half its running time, this space romp from simpler times is worth a watch just for the character acting, including Charles Middleton as the greatest of all serial scoundrels. 1938; B&W; 99m.

FLASH GORDON: ROCKETSHIP (A.K.A. SPACESHIP TO THE UNKNOWN; PERILS FROM PLANET MONGO) ★★★

DIR: Frederick Stephani. **CAST:** Buster Crabbe, Jean Rogers, Frank Shannon, Charles Middleton, Priscilla Lawson.

This original feature version of the first *Flash Gordon* serial is one of the best reedited chapter plays ever released. Boyish Buster Crabbe is the perfect Flash Gordon; Jean Rogers is one of the loveliest of all serial queens; and classic character heavy Charles Middleton becomes the embodiment of malevolent villainy as the infamous Ming the Merciless. 1936; B&W; 97m.

FLIGHT OF THE NAVIGATOR ★★★

DIR: Randal Kleiser. **CAST:** Joey Kramer, Veronica Cartwright, Cliff De

Young, Sarah Jessica Parker, Howard Hesseman, Matt Adler.

This all-ages Disney delight concerns a youngster (Joey Kramer) who has the unique ability to communicate with machines and uses this to help a UFO find its way home. *Flight of the Navigator* has something for everyone. Kids will love its crazy creatures, special effects, and action-packed conclusion, while parents will appreciate its nice balance of sense and nonsense. Rated PG for mild cussing. 1986; 90m.

FOOD OF THE GODS 🦃

DIR: Bert I. Gordon. **CAST:** Marjoe Gortner, Ida Lupino, Pamela Franklin, Ralph Meeker.

H. G. Wells's story is thrashed in this typical Bert I. Gordon bomb. After ingesting an unknown substance, various animals become giant and threaten the occupants of a remote mountain cabin. Fakey special effects might have been acceptable in the 1950s, but they just don't cut it today. Rated PG for violence. 1976; 88m.

FORBIDDEN PLANET ★★★★½

DIR: Fred McLeod Wilcox. **CAST:** Walter Pidgeon, Anne Francis, Leslie Nielsen, Jack Kelly.

This is the most highly regarded sci-fi film of the 1950s. Its special-effects breakthroughs are rather tame today, but its story remains interesting. As a space mission from Earth lands on the Planet Altair-4 in the year 2200, they encounter a doctor (Walter Pidgeon) and his daughter (Anne Francis) who are all that remain from a previous colonization attempt. It soon becomes apparent that some unseen force on the planet does not bid them welcome. 1956; 98m.

FORBIDDEN ZONE 🦃

DIR: Richard Elfman. **CAST:** Herve Villechaize, Susan Tyrrell, Marie-Pascale Elfman, Viva.

Absurd, would-be "cult" film has Herve Villechaize as the ruler of a bizarre kingdom located in the "Sixth Dimension." A sort-of comedy, this should be avoided by all means. Rated R for nudity and adult content. 1980; B&W; 76m.

4D MAN ★★★

DIR: Irvin S. Yeaworth Jr. **CAST:** Robert Lansing, Lee Meriwether, James Congdon, Robert Strauss, Patty Duke.

A scientist (Robert Lansing) learns of a method of moving through objects (walls, doors, bank vaults, etc.), without realizing the terrible consequences, which eventually lead to madness and murder. Eerie sci-fi film hampered only by an often brash music. From the director of *The Blob*. 1959; 85m.

FROM THE EARTH TO THE MOON ★★★

DIR: Byron Haskin. **CAST:** Joseph Cotten, George Sanders, Debra Paget, Don Dubbins.

Entertaining tale based on Jules Verne's story of a turn-of-the-century trip to the Moon led by Joseph Cotten and sabotaged by George Sanders. 1958; 100m.

FUTUREWORLD ★★★

DIR: Richard T. Heffron. **CAST:** Peter Fonda, Blythe Danner, Arthur Hill, Yul Brynner, Stuart Margolin, John P. Ryan.

An amusement park of the future caters to any adult fantasy. Lifelike androids carry out your every whim. A fun place, right? Not so, as reporter Peter Fonda finds out in this sequel to *Westworld*. This is okay escapist fare. Rated PG. 1976; 104m.

GALAXINA ★

DIR: William Sachs. **CAST:** Avery Schreiber, Dorothy Stratten, Stephen Macht.

See Captain Cornelius Butt (Avery Schreiber), of the spaceship *Infinity*, consume a raw egg and regurgitate a rubbery creature that later calls him "Mommy." Visit an intergalactic saloon that serves humans (they're on the menu, not the guest list). And be amazed, then disgusted and bored by the general tackiness and idiocy of this low-budget space spoof. Rated R. 1980; 95m.

GALAXY OF TERROR ★★½
DIR: B. D. Clark. **CAST:** Erin Moran, Edward Albert, Ray Walston.
In this movie, which was also known as *Planet of Horrors*, the crew of a spaceship sent to rescue a crash survivor finds itself facing one horror after another on a barren planet. This chiller wastes no time in getting to the thrills. Rated R because of profanity, nudity, and violence. 1981; 82m.

GAMERA VERSUS BARUGON ★★
DIR: Shigeo Tanaka. **CAST:** Kojiro Hongo.
In this first sequel, the giant flying turtle becomes a good guy, as he was to remain for the rest of the series. The bad guy, Barugon, is a giant dinosaur. Of course, several Japanese cities are leveled as the two battle, but no problem—civilization was reconstructed in time for the next sequel. 1966; 101m.

GAMERA VERSUS GAOS ★★
DIR: Noriyaki Yuasa. **CAST:** Kojiro Hongo.
Ever the friend of little children, Gamera does his giant flaming Frisbee impression once again to save his little pals from Gaos, another giant monster. Opinion differs as to whether Gaos more closely resembles a bat or a fox, as if it mattered at all to the poor stuntman sweating it out inside that rubber suit. 1967; 87m.

GAMERA VERSUS ZIGRA ★½
DIR: Noriyaki Yuasa. **CAST:** Reiko Kasahara.
Fans of this kind of stuff will be disappointed to note that, in the last of the Gamera movies, the titanic turtle is the sole monster. Zigra is a planet whose inhabitants want to take over Earth before we pollute ourselves to death. Some film student somewhere should do a paper comparing this with the contemporary *Godzilla vs. the Smog Monster*. 1971; 87m.

GAMMA PEOPLE, THE ★½
DIR: John Gilling. **CAST:** Paul Douglas, Eva Bartok, Leslie Phillips, Walter Rilla.
Weak science-fiction tale about the children of the middle European country of Gudavia being transformed into homicidal monsters or geniuses by the all-powerful dictator Dr. Boronski (Walter Rilla). Even considering the year it was made, acting and effects just aren't up to snuff. 1956; B&W; 79m.

GAS-S-S-S ★½
DIR: Roger Corman. **CAST:** Robert Corff, Elaine Giftos, Bud Cort, Ben Vereen, Cindy Williams, Country Joe and the Fish.
A gas accidentally escapes from a chemical company doing military work and everyone in the world over the age of thirty dies, creating a society that is a twisted parody of certain aspects of the destroyed civilization. This is similar in concept to the underground world in *A Boy and His Dog*, a far better movie. Very Sixties in humor, music, and visual style. Rated PG for language and sexual situations. 1970; 78m.

GLEN AND RANDA ★★★
DIR: Jim McBride. **CAST:** Steven Curry, Shelley Plimpton, Woodrow Chambliss, Garry Goodrow.
As with all cult films, *Glen and Randa* will not appeal to everyone. The film, at times thought-provoking, is both depressing and satirical. Two young people, Glen (Steve Curry) and Randa (Shelley Plimpton), set out on a search for knowledge across postholocaust America. Rated R for nudity and violence. 1986; 94m.

GOLDEN VOYAGE OF SINBAD, THE ★★★★
DIR: Gordon Hessler. **CAST:** John Phillip Law, Tom Baker, Caroline Munro, Gregoire Aslan, John Garfield Jr.
This first-rate Arabian Nights adventure pits Captain Sinbad (John Phillip Law) against the evil Prince Koura (Tom Baker) for possession of a mag-

ical amulet with amazing powers. This is a superb fantasy, with some truly incredible effects by master animator Ray Harryhausen. Rated G. 1974; 105m.

GOLDENGIRL ♥

DIR: Joseph Sargent. **CAST:** Susan Anton, James Coburn, Curt Jurgens, Robert Culp, Leslie Caron, Jessica Walter.

This modern retread of *Frankenstein* fails on all counts. Scientist Curt Jurgens turns Susan Anton into a super-athlete for Olympic glory. Acting, writing, and direction are terrible; the splicing between genuine Olympic footage and storyline fiction is equally lame. Rated PG. 1979; 104m.

GOR ★★

DIR: Fritz Kiersch. **CAST:** Urbano Barberini, Rebecca Ferratti, Jack Palance, Paul Smith, Oliver Reed.

A mild-mannered college professor is thrust through time and space to help a simple tribe recover its magical stone in this Conan-inspired sword-and-sorcery flick. Oliver Reed is the evil ruler Sarm, whose domain must be infiltrated if the tribe is to regain the stone. Elaborate costumes and sets don't make up for the second-rate story. Rated PG for violence. 1987; 95m.

GREMLINS ★★★★

DIR: Joe Dante. **CAST:** Zack Galligan, Phoebe Cates, Hoyt Axton, Frances Lee McCain, Polly Holliday, Glynn Turman, Dick Miller, Keye Luke, Scott Brady.

This "Steven Spielberg Presentation" is highly wacky. It's one part *E.T.—The Extra-Terrestrial*, one part scary/funny horror film one part Muppet movie, and one part Bugs Bunny/Warner Bros. cartoon. Sound strange? You got it. In the story, Billy Peltzer (Zach Galligan) gets a cute little pet from his inventor-father (Hoyt Axton) for Christmas. But there's a catch. Rated PG for profanity and stylized violence. 1984; 111m.

GROUNDSTAR CONSPIRACY, THE ★★★½

DIR: Lamont Johnson. **CAST:** George Peppard, Michael Sarrazin, Christine Belford.

This nifty thriller has gone unrecognized for years. George Peppard stars as a government investigator sent to uncover the security leak that led to the destruction of a vital—and secret—space laboratory, and the amnesia-stricken Michael Sarrazin is his only lead. The clever plot and excellent character interactions build to a surprising climax. Rated PG. 1972; 103m.

HANDS OF STEEL ★

DIR: Martin Dolman. **CAST:** Daniel Greene, Janet Agren, Claudio Cassinelli, George Eastman, John Saxon.

Abominably written and acted film which camouflages a good idea. Daniel Greene is a cyborg assassin who goes wrong and is pursued by police and baddies when he botches an important assignment. What four screenwriters and a dialogue coach did to that concept is a cinematic crime. Rated R for language and violence. 1986; 94m.

HANGAR 18 ♥

DIR: James L. Conway. **CAST:** Darren McGavin, Robert Vaughn, Gary Collins, Joseph Campanella, James Hampton.

The story revolves around an alien spaceship that is accidentally disabled by a U.S. satellite. Two astronauts (Gary Collins and James Hampton) in a nearby rocket witness the accident—a fellow astronaut is decapitated during the event—and, when they return to Earth, are blamed for the death of their partner. Rated PG. 1980; 93m.

HARRY AND THE HENDERSONS ★★★½

DIR: William Dear. **CAST:** John Lithgow, Melinda Dillon, Don Ameche, Lainie Kazan, David Suchet.

A sort of a shaggy *E.T.* story, this focuses on the plight of a family (headed by John Lithgow and Melinda Dillon) that just happens to run into Bigfoot one day. It's silly, outrageously sentimental, and a gentle poke in the ribs of Steven Spielberg, whose Amblin Productions financed the film. Rated PG for profanity and violence. 1987; 110m.

HAUNTING PASSION, THE ★
DIR: John Korty. **CAST:** Jane Seymour, Gerald McRaney, Millie Perkins, Ruth Nelson.

An uneven made-for-TV supernatural romance in which a ghost seduces a housewife. Jane Seymour and the rest of the cast do the best they can with the bad romance-novel dialogue they're given. There are a few chills, but more often than not, it falls short of the mark. 1983; 98m.

HAUNTS OF THE VERY RICH ★
DIR: Paul Wendkos. **CAST:** Lloyd Bridges, Donna Mills, Edward Asner, Cloris Leachman, Anne Francis, Tony Bill, Robert Reed, Moses Gunn.

This TV movie brings together a handful of people, who have had close calls with death. They are thrown together on a trip to a secret vacation paradise. It's sort of a low-quality *Twilight Zone* version of *Fantasy Island*. 1972; 72m.

HEADLESS HORSEMAN, THE ★★½
DIR: Edward Venturini. **CAST:** Will Rogers, Lois Meredith.

The time-honored (but worn) story of lanky Yankee schoolmaster Icabod Crane's rube-ish efforts to wed wealthy Katrina Van Tassel, and his defeat by rival Brom Bones and the phantom headless horseman. Will Rogers looks the part of the homespun Crane and gives a fair impression of the character. Silent. 1922; B&W; 52m.

HELL COMES TO FROGTOWN ★
DIR: R. J. Kizer, Donald G. Jackson. **CAST:** Roddy Piper, Sandahl Bergman, Rory Calhoun.

This laughable poverty-row quickie is set in one of those post-apocalyptic futures that allow a minimum of set design. Men have become mostly sterile, so convict Sam Hell (wrestler Roddy Piper) is sent into a mutant-filled wasteland to rescue—and impregnate, as he's one of the few lucky ones—a bevy of fertile women held captive by frog-faced critters with multiple genitalia. Rated R for nudity, language, and violence. 1987; 88m.

HERCULES (1959) ★★½
DIR: Pietro Francisci. **CAST:** Steve Reeves, Sylva Koscina, Ivo Garrani.

The first and still the best of the Italian-made epics based on the mythical superhero. Steve Reeves looks perfect in the part as Hercules out to win over his true love, the ravishing Sylva Koscina. Some nice action scenes. 1959; 107m.

HERCULES (1983)
DIR: Lewis Coates. **CAST:** Lou Ferrigno, Sybil Danning, Brad Harris, Rossana Podesta.

Following the beefy footsteps of Conan, Ator, and Yor comes Lou Ferrigno (formerly TV's *The Incredible Hulk*) as the most famous muscle man of them all, in this cheap and dreadful venture into Greek mythology. It was inevitable, but did it have to be so awful? Rated PG for violence. 1983; 98m.

HERCULES UNCHAINED ★★
DIR: Pietro Francisci. **CAST:** Steve Reeves, Sylva Koscina, Primo Carnera, Sylvia Lopez.

When the god of muscles sets his little mind on something, don't get in his way! In this one, he's out to rescue his lady fair. It's a silly but diverting adventure. Steve Reeves is still the best Hercules on film, dubbed voice and all. 1960; 101m.

HIDDEN, THE ★★★½
DIR: Jack Sholder. **CAST:** Michael Nouri, Kyle MacLachlan, Ed O'Ross, Clu Gulager, Claudia Christian, Clarence Felder.

When a bizarre series of crimes wreaks havoc in Los Angeles, police detective Michael Nouri finds himself paired with an FBI agent (Kyle MacLachlan) whose behavior becomes increasingly strange as they pursue what may be an alien intruder. This hybrid science-fiction/adventure will delight those who like their entertainment upredictable. Rated R for violence, nudity, and profanity. 1987; 97m.

HIGHLANDER ★★
DIR: Russell Mulcahy. **CAST:** Christopher Lambert, Clancy Brown, Sean Connery.

A sixteenth-century Scottish clansman discovers he is one of a small group of immortals destined to fight each other through the centuries. The movie is a treat for the eyes, but you'll owe your brain an apology. Rated R for violence. 1986; 110m.

HOWARD THE DUCK ★
DIR: Willard Huyck. **CAST:** Lea Thompson, Jeffrey Jones, Tim Robbins, Ed Gale.

It requires truly monumental talent to botch the film debut of a character as clever as Steve Gerber's *Howard the Duck*, but writer-director Willard Huyck and writer-producer Gloria Katz managed to lay an extremely rotten egg. Sensible plot and characterization are replaced with bigger and louder explosions, car wrecks, slimy monster makeup, more car wrecks, inane acting, and even more car wrecks. Unwisely rated PG, considering some smarmy sex scenes and frightening monster makeup. 1986; 111m.

HUMANOID DEFENDER ★
DIR: Ron Satlof. **CAST:** Terence Knox, Gary Kasper, Aimee Eccles, Marie Windsor.

This movie is actually two episodes from a TV series that never made it, sort of a mix of *The Six Million Dollar Man* and *The Fugitive*. A government scientist has created an artificial superman, J.O.E., but when he finds out what the military wants to do with him, he and J.O.E. escape. They spend their time hiding from the army and doing good deeds. Even by TV standards it's pretty derivative. 1985; 94m.

I MARRIED A MONSTER FROM OUTER SPACE ★★★
DIR: Gene Fowler Jr. **CAST:** Tom Tryon, Gloria Talbott, Ken Lynch, Maxie Rosenbloom.

This riveting story is about aliens who duplicate their bodies in the form of Earth men in hopes of repopulating their planet. One Earth woman who unknowingly marries one of the aliens discovers the secret, but can't get anyone to believe her. 1958; B&W; 78m.

I MARRIED A WITCH ★★★½
DIR: René Clair. **CAST:** Veronica Lake, Fredric March, Cecil Kellaway, Robert Benchley.

The whimsy of humorist Thorne Smith (the author of *Topper*) shows its age, but watching Veronica Lake and Fredric March perform together is a treat in this very pre-*Bewitched* farce. Look for Susan Hayward in a small role. 1942; B&W; 76m.

ICE PIRATES ★★★½
DIR: Stewart Raffill. **CAST:** Robert Urich, Mary Crosby, John Matuszak, Anjelica Huston, John Carradine.

Essentially a pirate movie set in outer space, this entertaining and often funny sci-fi film takes place countless years from now, when the universe has run out of water. Rated PG for violence, profanity, scatological humor, and suggested sex. 1984; 91m.

ICEMAN ★★★½
DIR: Fred Schepisi. **CAST:** Timothy Hutton, Lindsay Crouse, John Lone, Josef Sommer.

Timothy Hutton stars in this often gripping and always watchable movie as an anthropologist who is part of an arctic exploration team that discovers the body of a prehistoric man (John Lone), who is still alive. The question of what to do with this piece of living human history comes up, and Hutton finds himself defending the creature from those who want to poke, prod, and even dissect their terrified subject. Rated PG for violence and profanity. 1984; 99m.

IDAHO TRANSFER ♥

DIR: Peter Fonda. **CAST:** Keith Carradine, Kelly Bohannon.

Director Peter Fonda uses a cast of amateurs, with the exception of Keith Carradine in his first screen role, to act in this story about a group of young scientists who invent a time-travel machine. They end up stranded in a post-apocalypse wasteland in the year 2044. Fonda attempts to say something about ecology and man's responsibility to his environment and ends up with a hopelessly dull film. No rating. 1973; 90m.

ILLUSTRATED MAN, THE ★½

DIR: Jack Smight. **CAST:** Rod Steiger, Claire Bloom, Robert Drivas.

Ponderous, dull, and overly talky adaptation of the work of Ray Bradbury. It is lifelessly paced by director Jack Smight, who doesn't know the first thing about the awe and wonder that should accompany fantasy. Rated PG for violence, partial nudity. 1969; 103m.

IN THE AFTERMATH: ANGELS NEVER SLEEP ★★

DIR: Carl Colpaert. **CAST:** Tony Markes, Rainbow Dolan.

Uneasy mixture of animation and live-action in this sci-fi story concerning an angel sent to assist an Earthman after the nuclear holocaust. The animation and the live action are good, but the two don't gel. A decent attempt to add life to an overworked genre, though. Contains rough language and violence. 1987; 85m.

INCREDIBLE HULK, THE ★★½

DIR: Kenneth Johnson. **CAST:** Bill Bixby, Susan Sullivan, Lou Ferrigno, Jack Colvin, Charles Siebert.

Bill Bixby is sincere in the role of Dr. Bob Banner, a scientist whose experiments with gamma rays result in his being transformed into a huge green creature (Lou Ferrigno) whenever something angers him. Pilot for the series is a lot of fun, with better production values than most TV efforts. Based on the Marvel Comics character. 1977; 100m.

INCREDIBLE MELTING MAN, THE ★★

DIR: William Sachs. **CAST:** Alex Rebar, Burr DeBenning, Myron Healey, Ann Sweeney.

Superb makeup by Rick Baker highlights this story of an astronaut (Alex Rebar) who contracts a strange ailment that results in his turning into a gooey, melting mess upon his return to Earth. Wild stuff. Rated R for terminal grossness. 1978; 86m.

INCREDIBLE SHRINKING MAN, THE ★★★★

DIR: Jack Arnold. **CAST:** Grant Williams, Randy Stuart, Paul Langton, April Kent.

Good special effects as a man (Grant Williams), exposed to a strange radioactive mist, finds himself becoming smaller...and smaller...and smaller. Well-mounted thriller from Universal with many memorable scenes, including the classic showdown with an ordinary house spider. 1957; B&W; 81m.

INDIANA JONES AND THE LAST CRUSADE ★★★★½

DIR: Steven Spielberg. **CAST:** Harrison Ford, Sean Connery, Denholm Elliott, John Rhys-Davies, River Phoenix.

Creator-producer George Lucas and director Steven Spielberg end their big-budget, Saturday-matinee cliffhanger series in style with this sublimely entertaining movie, in which Indiana Jones (Harrison Ford) embarks on a quest for the Holy Grail when his father (Sean Connery) disappears while on the same mission. Father and son, with the help of *Raiders of the Lost Ark* returnees Denholm Elliott and John Rhys-Davies, are soon slugging it out with some nasty

Nazis in this all-ages delight. Ford and Connery work beautifully together. Rated PG for violence and profanity. 1989; 138m.

INDIANA JONES AND THE TEMPLE OF DOOM ★★★★
DIR: Steven Spielberg. **CAST:** Harrison Ford, Kate Capshaw.

This sequel is almost as good as the original, *Raiders of the Lost Ark.* The story takes place before the events of *Raiders* with its two-fisted, whip-wielding hero, Dr. Indiana Jones (Harrison Ford) performing feats of derring-do in Singapore and India circa 1935. Parents may want to see this fast-paced and sometimes scary film before allowing their kids to watch it. Rated PG for profanity and violence. 1984; 118m.

INFRA-MAN ★★½
DIR: Hua-Shan. **CAST:** Wang Hsieh.

Mainly for kids, this *Ultraman* rip-off, about a giant superhero protecting the Earth from a bunch of crazy-looking monsters, still manages to succeed, despite the lame acting and hokey special effects. Ridiculous but enjoyable. Rated PG. 1976; 92m.

INNERSPACE ★★★★
DIR: Joe Dante. **CAST:** Dennis Quaid, Martin Short, Meg Ryan, Kevin McCarthy, Fiona Lewis, Henry Gibson.

Get this storyline: Dennis Quaid is a rebel astronaut who is miniaturized in order to be injected into the body of a rabbit. By accident the syringe carrying Quaid ends up being injected into the body of hypochrondriac Martin Short. Sound weird? It is. Sound funny? We thought so. Rated PG for profanity and violence. 1987; 130m.

INTRUDER WITHIN, THE 🦃
DIR: Peter Carter. **CAST:** Chad Everett, Joseph Bottoms, Jennifer Warren.

Cheesy rip-off of Ridley Scott's classic *Alien.* Action takes place on an ocean oil-drilling rig instead of commercial spacecraft. 1981; 100m.

INVADERS FROM MARS (1953) ★★★★
DIR: William Cameron Menzies. **CAST:** Helena Carter, Jimmy Hunt, Leif Erickson, Arthur Franz.

Everybody remembers this one. Kid sees a flying saucer land in a nearby field, only nobody will believe him. Some really weird visuals throughout this minor sci-fi classic. 1953; 78m.

INVADERS FROM MARS (1986) ★★★
DIR: Tobe Hooper. **CAST:** Karen Black, Hunter Carson, Timothy Bottoms, Laraine Newman, James Karen, Louise Fletcher, Bud Cort.

Director Tobe Hooper maintains the tone of the original; this *Invaders from Mars* feels like a 1950s movie made with 1980s production values. Rated PG-13 for rather intense situations and ugly beasties. 1986; 94m.

INVASION OF THE ANIMAL PEOPLE 🦃
DIR: Virgil Vogel, Jerry Warren. **CAST:** Robert Burton, Barbara Wilson, John Carradine (narrator).

This inept foreign science-fiction clinker is a borderline turkey, but lacks the presence of a John Agar to mire it firmly in the annals of truly terrible films. Nonsense about extraterrestrial visitors who assume various forms is as stale as a year-old cracker and just about as appealing. 1962; B&W; 73m.

INVASION OF THE BEE GIRLS ★★★
DIR: Denis Sanders. **CAST:** Victoria Vetri, William Smith, Cliff Osmond, Anitra Ford.

Enjoyable film about strange female invaders doing weird things to the male population of a small town in California. Plot is not too important in this wacky sci-fi spoof. Not for kids. Rated PG. 1973; 85m.

INVASION OF THE BODY SNATCHERS (1956) ★★★★★
DIR: Don Siegel. **CAST:** Kevin McCarthy, Dana Wynter, Carolyn Jones, King Donovan.

Quite possibly the most frightening film ever made, this stars Kevin McCarthy as a small-town doctor who discovers his patients, family, and friends are being taken over by cold, emotionless, human-duplicating pods from outer space. Not many films can be considered truly disturbing, but this one more than qualifies. Coming from the B-movie science-fiction boom of the 1950s, it has emerged as a cinema classic. 1956; B&W; 80m.

INVASION OF THE BODY SNATCHERS (1978) ★★★★
DIR: Phil Kaufman. **CAST:** Donald Sutherland, Brooke Adams, Leonard Nimoy, Jeff Goldblum, Veronica Cartwright.

Excellent semisequel to Don Siegel's 1956 classic of the same name, with Donald Sutherland fine in the role originally created by Kevin McCarthy (who has a cameo here). This time the story takes place in San Francisco, with mysterious "seeds" from outer space duplicating—then destroying—San Francisco Bay Area residents at an alarming rate. Rated PG. 1978; 115m.

INVASION UFO ★
DIR: Gerry Anderson, David Lane, David Tomblin. **CAST:** Ed Bishop, George Sewell, Michael Billington.

Strictly for fans of the short-lived science-fiction TV series, whose title explains all. Others will find the story trite, the acting second-rate, and the special effects primitive by today's standards. 1980; 97m.

INVISIBLE KID, THE ★½
DIR: Avery Crounse. **CAST:** Jay Underwood, Wally Ward, Mike Genovese, Karen Black.

Geared for preteens, this sci-fi comedy about a boy who accidentally discovers an invisibility potion might be a little too juvenile for all audiences. All of the high-school-type fantasies are explored to their fullest, and Karen Black as the dippy (and overdone) mother fits more into a teen comedy genre. Rated PG for language and nudity. 1988; 96m.

IRON WARRIOR
DIR: Al Bradley. **CAST:** Miles O'Keeffe, Savin Gersak, Tim Lane.

Conan-type action flick with plenty of sabers, smoke, and skin, but nothing new. Miles O'Keeffe plays a warrior who tries to save a kingdom from a wicked sorceress. Rated R for violence and nudity. 1987; 82m.

ISLAND AT THE TOP OF THE WORLD, THE ★★★
DIR: Robert Stevenson. **CAST:** David Hartman, Mako, Donald Sinden.

A rich man ventures into the Arctic in search of his son. Unbelievably, he finds a Viking kingdom. This is Disney director Robert Stevenson's second attempt (*In Search of the Castaways* was number one) to re-create a Jules Verne classic. Rated G. 1974; 93m.

ISLAND OF DR. MOREAU, THE ★★
DIR: William Witney. **CAST:** Burt Lancaster, Michael York, Barbara Carrera, Richard Basehart.

Remake of 1933's *Island of Lost Souls* isn't nearly as good. Burt Lancaster develops process of turning animals into half-humans on a desolate tropical island. Watchable only for Burt's sturdy performance and Richard Basehart's portrayal of one of the beasts. Rated PG. 1977; 104m.

IT CAME FROM OUTER SPACE ★★★★
DIR: Jack Arnold. **CAST:** Richard Carlson, Barbara Rush, Charles Drake.

Science-fiction author Ray Bradbury wrote the screenplay for this surprisingly effective 3-D chiller from the 1950s about creatures from outer space taking over the bodies of Earthlings. It was the first film to use this theme and still holds up today. 1953; B&W; 81m.

JASON AND THE ARGONAUTS ★★★★

DIR: Don Chaffey. **CAST:** Todd Armstrong, Gary Raymond, Honor Blackman.

The captivating special effects by master Ray Harryhausen are the actual stars of this movie. This is the telling of the famous myth of Jason (Todd Armstrong), his crew of derring-doers, and their search for the Golden Fleece. 1963; 104m.

JOURNEY TO THE CENTER OF THE EARTH ★★★

DIR: Henry Levin. **CAST:** James Mason, Pat Boone, Arlene Dahl, Diane Baker.

This Jules Verne story was impressive when first released, but it looks pretty silly these days. However, James Mason is always fascinating to watch, production values are high, and kids should enjoy its innocent fun. 1959; 132m.

JOURNEY TO THE CENTER OF TIME ★★½

DIR: David L. Hewitt. **CAST:** Scott Brady, Gigi Perreau, Anthony Eisley, Abraham Sofaer, Lyle Waggoner.

A group of scientists working on a time-travel device are accidentally propelled five thousand years into the future following an equipment malfunction. Once there, they discover an alien civilization (headed by a young Lyle Waggoner) attempting to take over the world. Low-budget film features passable special effects, but the dialogue and acting are sub-par. 1967; 82m.

JOURNEY TO THE FAR SIDE OF THE SUN ★★★½

DIR: Robert Parrish. **CAST:** Roy Thinnes, Lynn Loring, Herbert Lom, Patrick Wymark, Ian Hendry.

This extremely clever sci-fi thriller concerns the discovery of a planet rotating in Earth's orbit, but always hidden from view on the other side of the sun. Thoughtful, literate, and fascinating, this effort is marred only by a needlessly oblique and frustrating conclusion. Unrated; suitable for family viewing. 1969; 99m.

JULIA AND JULIA ★

DIR: Peter Del Monte. **CAST:** Kathleen Turner, Gabriel Byrne, Sting, Gabriele Ferzetti.

This dreary Italian-made, English-language movie is an uninspired rehash of the parallel-worlds plot from the old science-fiction pulp magazines. Kathleen Turner is a woman whose husband dies in a car crash on the day of their wedding only to have him pop up (complete with the son they wanted to have) six years later. A loser all the way around. Rated R for profanity, nudity, and violence. 1988; 95m.

KILLERS FROM SPACE ★

DIR: W. Lee Wilder. **CAST:** Peter Graves, James Seay.

Peter Graves takes on bug-eyed men from outer space in this bargain-basement S-F thriller. It's so bad it's funny, but we bet you can't watch the whole thing. 1954; B&W; 68m.

KILLING EDGE, THE ★★

DIR: Lindsay Shontoeff. **CAST:** Bill French, Marv Spencer.

Fairly decent low-budget account of one man's search through a nuclear wasteland for his wife and son. The acting is good and the writing is solid, but the film occasionally gets bogged down in repetition. Not rated; violence and language. 1986; 90m.

KRONOS ★★★

DIR: Kurt Neumann. **CAST:** Jeff Morrow, Barbara Lawrence.

In this alien invasion film, a giant, featureless robot is sent to Earth to test Earth's potential for supplying energy to an alien civilization. The robot absorbs all forms of energy and grows as it feeds. The scientists must find a way to destroy the giant before it reaches the high-population areas of Southern California. Although the special effects are nothing by today's filmmaking standards, this picture is one of best from a decade dominated by giant monsters and alien invaders. 1957; B&W; 78m.

KRULL ★½

DIR: Peter Yates. **CAST:** Ken Marshall, Freddie Jones, Lisette Anthony.

In this poor sci-fi/sword-and-sorcery film, a young man (Ken Marshall) is called upon by an old wizard (Freddie Jones) to take up an ancient weapon and do battle with a master of evil to save a beautiful princess (Lisette Anthony). An obvious and unimaginative rip-off of *Star Wars*. Rated PG for violence. 1983; 117m.

LABYRINTH ★★★

DIR: Jim Henson. **CAST:** David Bowie, Jennifer Connelly, Toby Froud.

A charming fantasy that combines live actors with another impressive collection of Jim Henson's Muppets. Jennifer Connelly stars as a young girl who wishes for the Goblin King (David Bowie) to kidnap her baby brother; when that idle desire is granted, she must journey to an enchanted land and solve a giant maze in order to rescue her little brother. Rated PG for mild violence. 1986; 101m.

LAND THAT TIME FORGOT, THE ★★

DIR: Kevin Connor. **CAST:** Doug McClure, Susan Penhaligon, John McEnery.

Poor Edgar Rice Burroughs, his wonderful adventure books for kids rarely got the right screen treatment. This British production tries hard, but the cheesy special effects eventually do it in. A sequel, *The People That Time Forgot*, fared no better. Rated PG. 1975; 90m.

LASERBLAST ★★

DIR: Michael Raye. **CAST:** Kim Milford, Cheryl Smith, Roddy McDowall, Keenan Wynn, Mark Hamill.

Dreadful low-budget film with some excellent special effects by David Allen. Story concerns a young man who accidentally lays his hands on an alien ray-gun and all sorts of bizarre things begin to happen. Rated PG. 1978; 90m.

LAST CHASE, THE ★★½

DIR: Martyn Burke. **CAST:** Lee Majors, Chris Makepeace, Burgess Meredith.

Made at the end of the OPEC oil crisis, this film assumes the crisis only got worse until there was a civil war in America and the eastern states banned all cars and planes. Lee Majors plays an aged race car driver who flees New York to California with a runaway (Chris Makepeace). Confusing at times, and the Orwellian touches have been done so often that all the scare has left them. Not rated. 1980; 106m.

LAST DAYS OF MAN ON EARTH, THE ★★★½

DIR: Robert Fuest. **CAST:** Jon Finch, Sterling Hayden, Patrick Magee, Jenny Runacre, Hugh Griffith.

Kinetic adaptation of Michael Moorcock's weird little novel, *The Final Programme*, the first of his adventures featuring Jerry Cornelius. Jon Finch plays Jerry as a smart-assed James Bond, and the prize he fights for is a microfilm containing the secret to self-replicating beings...highly useful in case of nuclear war. Finch encounters a variety of oddball characters, none stranger than Jenny Runacre, an enigmatic adversary who absorbs her lovers. Rated R for violence and sex. 1973; 73m.

LAST MAN ON EARTH, THE ★★★

DIR: Sidney Salkow. **CAST:** Vincent Price, Franca Bettoia, Emma Danieli, Giacomo Rossi-Stuart.

In this nightmarish tale, a scientist (Vincent Price) is a bit late in developing a serum to stem the tide of a plague epidemic. He becomes the last man on Earth and lives in fear of the walking dead, who crave his blood. This paranoid horror film (based on Richard Matheson's *I Am Legend*) is more chilling than its higher-budget remake, *The Omega Man.* 1964; B&W; 86m.

LAST STARFIGHTER, THE ★★★★
DIR: Nick Castle. **CAST:** Lance Guest, Robert Preston, Dan O'Herlihy, Catherine Mary Stewart, Barbara Bosson.

In this enjoyable comedy/science-fiction film, a young man (Lance Guest) beats a video game called the Starfighter and soon finds himself recruited by an alien (Robert Preston) to do battle in outer space. Thanks to its witty dialogue and hilarious situations, this hybrid is a viewing delight. Rated PG for violence and profanity. 1984; 100m.

LAWLESS LAND
DIR: Jon Hess. **CAST:** Nick Corri, Amanda Peterson.

Just another grade-Z turkey about survival in a post-apocalypse civilization with Romeo-Juliet undertones. The daughter of the head honcho falls for a handsome young rebel. Dad sends some bounty hunters after them when they take off on their own. Rated R for violence and nudity. 1988; 81m.

LEGEND
DIR: Ridley Scott. **CAST:** Tom Cruise, Tim Curry, Mia Sara, David Bennent, Billy Barty.

Legend is a sad triumph of style over substance, a gorgeously-lensed but absolutely empty fantasy. Tom Cruise simply looks embarrassed as a forest-living lad who joins a quest to save a unicorn, keeper of his world's Light, from the evil entity who prefers to plunge the land into eternal Darkness. Rated PG for mild violence. 1986; 89m.

LIFEFORCE ★
DIR: Tobe Hooper. **CAST:** Steve Railsback, Peter Firth, Mathilda May, Frank Finlay, Michael Gothard.

In this disappointing and disjointed science-fiction/horror film by director Tobe Hooper (*Poltergeist*), ancient vampires from outer space return to Earth via Halley's Comet to feed on human souls. Rated R for violence, gore, nudity, profanity, and suggested sex. 1985; 96m.

LIFESPAN
DIR: Alexander Whitelaw. **CAST:** Klaus Kinski, Hiram Keller, Tina Aumont, Fons Rademakers.

This Dutch-made science-fiction film is so slow you'll feel it takes a lifetime to watch. A young scientist tries to discover the secret of a long-life formula that belonged to a dead colleague. Along the way, he becomes involved with the deceased's girlfriend. There's nothing to recommend this plodding sci-fi attempt—certainly not the acting or plot. Unrated, it does have nudity and simulated sex. 1974; 85m.

LIGHT YEARS ★★½
DIR: Harvey Weinstein. **CAST:** Animated.

Imaginative and daring sci-fi–fantasy cartoon written by Issac Asimov and produced by René Laloux. Sylvain, a young warrior, seeks out the evil that is destroying his world and embarks on an adventure into the future. Strong story, but rather simplistic animation and poor characterization. Rated PG for nudity. 1988; 79m.

LIQUID SKY ★★★½
DIR: Slava Tsukerman. **CAST:** Anne Carlisle, Paula E. Sheppard.

An alien spaceship lands on Earth in search of chemicals produced in the body during sex. One of the aliens enters the life of a new-wave fashion model and feeds off her lovers, most of whom she's more than happy to see dead. *Liquid Sky* alternately shocks and amuses us with this unusual, stark, and ugly—but somehow fitting—look at an American sub-culture. Rated R for profanity, violence, rape, and suggested sex. 1983; 112m.

LOGAN'S RUN ★★★
DIR: Michael Anderson. **CAST:** Michael York, Jenny Agutter, Peter Ustinov, Richard Jordan.

Popular but overlong sci-fi film concerning a futuristic society where people are only allowed to live to the age of 30, and a policeman nearing the limit who searches desperately for a way to avoid mandatory extermination. Nice production is enhanced immeasurably by outlandish sets and beautiful, imaginative miniatures. Rated PG. 1976; 120m.

LOOKER ★★
DIR: Michael Crichton. **CAST:** Albert Finney, James Coburn, Susan Dey, Leigh Taylor-Young.

Writer-director Michael Crichton describes this movie as "a thriller about television commercials," but it's really a fairly simpleminded suspense film. Plastic surgeon Albert Finney discovers a plot by evil mastermind James Coburn to clone models for television commercials. This is fiction? Rated PG because of nudity and violence. 1981; 94m.

LORD OF THE RINGS, THE ★
DIR: Ralph Bakshi. **CAST:** Animated.

J. R. R. Tolkien's beloved epic fantasy is all but trashed in this animated film, directed by Ralph Bakshi (*Fritz the Cat*). It deals with the first half of the trilogy, in which Frodo Baggins takes up the Ring of Power in order to save his fellow hobbits and all of Middle Earth from the forces of evil. The movie suffers from too much gore and cut-rate animation techniques, spoiling what should have been a cinematic event. Rated PG. 1978; 133m.

LOST IN SPACE (TELEVISION SERIES) ★★★
DIR: Leo Penn, Alexander Singer, Tony Leader. **CAST:** Guy Williams, June Lockhart, Mark Goddard, Jonathan Harris, Marta Kristen, Angela Cartwright, Billy Mumy.

The Robinson family volunteers to help Earth solve its overpopulation problem by exploring space. That incessantly fussy saboteur, Colonel Zachary Smith, thwarts their mission. The crew vows to continue to search for the welcoming climes of the star Alpha Sentori, while cowardly Smith whines and connives to return to Earth. Terrifically tacky special effects and loads of campy humor earned the show a cult following. The robot proved to be the most endearing personality on board. 1965–1968; 60m.

LOST WORLD, THE ★★★★
DIR: Harry Hoyt. **CAST:** Bessie Love, Lewis Stone, Wallace Beery.

Silent version of Arthur Conan Doyle's classic story of Professor Challenger and his expedition to a desolate plateau roaming with prehistoric beasts. The movie climaxes with a brontosaurus running amok in London. An ambitious production, interesting as film history and quite entertaining, considering its age. 1925; B&W; 60m.

MAC AND ME ★½
DIR: Stewart Raffill. **CAST:** Jade Calegory, Christine Ebersole, Jonathan Ward.

Imagine the most product-friendly film ever made, one where even the title has commercial innuendo, and you have (Big) *Mac and Me*. To be fair, *Mac and Me* stars the courageous Jade Calegory, a paraplegic wheelchair-bound since birth, and a share of the producer's net profits will be donated to Ronald McDonald's Children's Charities. But the plot rips off everything in sight. Rated PG. 1988; 101m.

MAD MAX ★★★½
DIR: George Miller. **CAST:** Mel Gibson, Joanne Samuel, Hugh Keays-Byrne, Tim Burns, Roger Ward.

The most successful Australian film of all time ($100 million in worldwide rentals), this exciting sci-fi adventure features Mel Gibson as a fast-driving cop who has to take on a gang of crazies in the dangerous world of the future. Rated R. 1979; 93m.

MAD MAX BEYOND THUNDERDOME ★★★½
DIR: George Miller, George Ogilvie. **CAST:** Mel Gibson, Tina Turner, Helen Buday, Frank Thring, Bruce Spence.

Mad Max is back—and he's angrier than ever. Those who enjoyed *Road Warrior* will find more of the same in director George Miller's third post-apocalypse, action-packed adventure film. This time the resourceful futuristic warrior (Mel Gibson) begrudgingly confronts what is left of civilization (as run by evil ruler Tina Turner). Rated PG-13 for violence and profanity. 1985; 109m.

MADE IN HEAVEN ★

DIR: Alan Rudolph. **CAST:** Timothy Hutton, Kelly McGillis, Maureen Stapleton, Mare Winningham, Ellen Barkin, Debra Winger.

This mawkish fantasy moves so slowly that it often seems to stop. Timothy Hutton stars as a lad who dies heroically, winds up in Heaven, and falls in love with unborn spirit Kelly McGillis. Their idyllic romance is interrupted when she's sent Earthward to inhabit a newborn baby. The story is tedious and trivial. Rated PG for brief nudity. 1987; 103m.

MAKING CONTACT ★★

DIR: Roland Emerich. **CAST:** Joshua Morell, Eve Kryll.

After his father dies, a little boy begins to exhibit telekinetic powers and begins giving life to his favorite toys. Telling his classmates about this leads to ridicule, so with only his toys and a little girl who believes his stories, they set out on a frightening adventure. Obviously aimed at children, this film is quite imaginative. 1985; 82m.

MAN CALLED RAGE, A 🦃

DIR: Anthony Richmond. **CAST:** Conrad Nichols.

In this dreadful, dubbed, Italian science-fiction flick, Rage, a Mad Max–type of character, leads a team to find uranium deposits that are vital to the survival of the human race. While searching for the uranium, Rage is followed by an evil band bent on stopping him. Rated PG for violence. 1987; 90m.

MAN FROM ATLANTIS, THE ★★½

DIR: Lee H. Katzin. **CAST:** Patrick Duffy, Belinda Montgomery, Victor Buono, Art Lud, Lawrence Pressman.

The pilot for the 1977 TV sci-fi series. Patrick Duffy plays the man from beneath the waves, recruited by the navy to retrieve a top-secret submarine. Belinda Montgomery is the marine biologist who holds Duffy's reins. 1977; 60m.

MAN FROM BEYOND, THE ★★★

DIR: Burton King. **CAST:** Harry Houdini.

Legendary escape artist Harry Houdini wrote and starred in this timeless story of a man encased in a block of ice for one hundred years who is discovered, thawed out, and thrust into twentieth-century life. While the special effects lack sophistication and the acting seems pretty broad, this is still worth watching for its place in cinema history and one of the few existing examples of Houdini's film work. Silent. 1921; B&W; 50m.

MAN WHO COULD WORK MIRACLES, THE ★★★½

DIR: Lothar Mendes. **CAST:** Roland Young, Ralph Richardson, Joan Gardner, George Zucco.

A timid department store clerk steps out of a British pub one evening and suddenly finds he possesses the power to do whatever he desires. Roland Young is matchless as the clerk, and is supported by a first-rate cast in this captivating fantasy film based on a story by H. G. Wells. 1937; B&W; 82m.

MAN WHO FELL TO EARTH, THE ★★★★

DIR: Nicolas Roeg. **CAST:** David Bowie, Rip Torn, Candy Clark, Buck Henry.

A moody, cerebral science-fiction thriller about an alien (David Bowie) who becomes trapped on our planet. Its occasional ambiguities are overpowered by sheer mind-tugging bizarreness and directorial brilliance. Rated R. 1976; 140m.

MAROONED

DIR: John Sturges. **CAST:** Gregory Peck, Richard Crenna, David Janssen, Gene Hackman, James Franciscus, Lee Grant.

The special effects are the only thing this bomb has going for it. Several dollars' worth of Hollywood acting talent is wasted in this tale of three astronauts unable to return to Earth and the ensuing rescue attempt. Rated PG. 1969; 134m.

MARTIAN CHRONICLES, THE PARTS I-III ★★★

DIR: Michael Anderson. **CAST:** Rock Hudson, Darren McGavin, Gayle Hunnicutt, Bernadette Peters, Nicholas Hammond, Roddy McDowall.

Mankind colonizes Mars in this adaptation of the Ray Bradbury classic. As this was originally a TV miniseries, the budget was low and it shows in the cheap sets and poor special effects. The acting is very good, however. 1979; 314m.

MASTER OF THE WORLD ★★★

DIR: William Witney. **CAST:** Vincent Price, Charles Bronson, Henry Hull.

Jules Verne's tale brought excitingly to the screen. Vincent Price plays a self-proclaimed god trying to end all war by flying around the world in a giant airship, armed to the teeth, blowing ships from the water, etc. Lots of fun. 1961; 104m.

MAX HEADROOM ★★★½

DIR: Rocky Morton, Annabel Jankel. **CAST:** Matt Frewer, Nickolas Grace, Hilary Tindall, Morgan Shepherd, Amanda Pays.

The original British production, later remade as a short-lived American TV series. Post-apocalypse newsman discovers an insidious form of advertising that causes viewers to explode. After being murdered by network executives, he's reborn as a computer-generated figure named Max Headroom. A sly parody of ratings-hungry television, the film is visually superb. 1986; 60m.

MEGAFORCE

DIR: Hal Needham. **CAST:** Barry Bostwick, Michael Beck, Persis Khambatta, Henry Silva.

Director Hal Needham makes us groan and gag with his biggest dud ever. This deadly dull sci-fi adventure is about a rapid-deployment defense unit that galvanizes into action whenever and wherever freedom is threatened. But rather than gasps, their exploits produce only yawns. PG for no discernible reason. 1982; 99m.

MERLIN & THE SWORD ★

DIR: Clive Donner. **CAST:** Malcolm McDowell, Candice Bergen, Edward Woodward, Dyan Cannon, Rupert Everett.

What a disappointment! An all-star cast and a good director absolutely waste their time on this retelling of the King Arthur legend. Edward Woodward gives a good performance as Merlin but can't save the film from the depths of stupidity into which it plunges. Not rated; contains mild sex and violence. 1982; 94m.

METALSTORM: THE DESTRUCTION OF JARED-SYN

DIR: Charles Band. **CAST:** Jeffrey Byron, Mike Preston, Tim Thomerson, Kelly Preston.

Charles Band, who was responsible for such forgettable turkeys as *Laserblast*, *End of the World*, and *Parasite*, directed this dud. In it, Jeffrey Byron plays an outer space ranger who, in order to save a barren planet, takes on the powerful villain of the title, Jared-Syn (Mike Preston). Rated PG for violence. 1983; 84m.

METEOR ★

DIR: Ronald Neame. **CAST:** Sean Connery, Natalie Wood, Karl Malden, Brian Keith, Henry Fonda.

In this disaster film, which wastes an all-star cast, a comet strikes an asteroid, and sends a huge chunk of rock hurtling on a collision course with

Earth. The United States and the U.S.S.R. must join forces to deflect the destructive mass, but the viewer wonders why they bother. Rated PG. 1979; 103m.

METROPOLIS ★★★★★
DIR: Fritz Lang. **CAST:** Brigitte Helm, Alfred Abel.

Fritz Lang's 1926 creation embodies the fine difference between classic and masterpiece. Using some of the most innovative camerawork in film of any time, it's also an uncannily accurate projection of futuristic society. It is a silent screen triumph. 1926; B&W; 120m.

MIAMI HORROR ★½
DIR: Martin Herbert. **CAST:** David Warbeck, Laura Trotter, John Ireland.

Poorly dubbed Italian thriller about scientists who believe that Earth life originated from bacteria on meteorites from outer space. Gangster John Ireland steals their experimental work, hoping to create a superbeing that will aid him in his evil plans. Aliens from another dimension get in on the story as well, trying to halt these experiments before they go too far. Indifferently made. 1985; 88m.

MIDSUMMER NIGHT'S DREAM, A ★★★★
DIR: Max Reinhardt. **CAST:** James Cagney, Olivia De Havilland, Dick Powell, Mickey Rooney.

Warner Bros. rolled out many of its big-name contract stars during the studio's heyday for this engrossing rendition of Shakespeare's classic comedy. Enchantment is the key element in this fairy-tale story of the misadventures of a group of mythical mischief-makers. 1935; B&W; 117m.

MIGHTY JOE YOUNG ★★★½
DIR: Ernest B. Schoedsack. **CAST:** Terry Moore, Ben Johnson, Robert Armstrong, Frank McHugh.

In this timeless fantasy from the creator of *King Kong* (Willis O'Brien with his young apprentice, Ray Harryhausen), the story follows the discovery of a twelve-foot gorilla in Africa by a fast-talking, money-hungry night-club owner (Robert Armstrong), who schemes to bring the animal back to Hollywood. 1949; B&W; 94m.

MISFITS OF SCIENCE ★★½
DIR: James D. Parriott. **CAST:** Dean Paul Martin, Kevin Peter Hall, Mark Thomas Miller, Courteney Cox.

Dean Paul Martin stars as the ringleader of a group of individuals possessing unique abilities. He rallies them together to combine their powers of mind control, cryogenics, electric energy, and size manipulation to save the world from a terrible neutron cannon developed by the government. No rating. This was the first installment in the failed television series. 1986; 96m.

MISSILE TO THE MOON
DIR: Richard Cunha. **CAST:** Richard Travis, Cathy Downes, K. T. Stevens, Michael Whalen, Tommy Cook, Gary Clarke.

A scientist and two reform-school escapees experience dèjá vu as they find themselves in the same plot Sonny Tufts and Victor Jory suffered through in *Cat Women of the Moon*. Silly story of renegade expedition to the moon is full of leotard-clad space gals and every moronic cliché so dear to bad filmmakers. One of the worst. 1958; B&W; 78m.

MISSION MARS ★
DIR: Nick Webster. **CAST:** Darren McGavin, Nick Adams.

Run-of-the-mill danger-in-outer-space adventure has a trio of astronauts coping with mysterious forces while on the way to Mars. 1968; 95m.

MOTHRA ★★★
DIR: Inoshiro Honda. **CAST:** Lee Kresel, Franky Sakai, Hiroshi Koizumi.

Two six-inch-tall princesses are taken from their island home to perform in a Tokyo nightclub. A native tribe prays for the return of the princesses, and their prayers hatch a giant egg, releasing a giant caterpillar. The caterpillar goes to Tokyo searching for the princesses and turns into a giant moth while wrecking the city. Although the story may sound corny, this is one of the best of the giant-monster movies to come out of Japan. 1962; 100m.

MURDER IN SPACE ★★
DIR: Steven H. Stern. **CAST:** Wilford Brimley, Michael Ironside, Martin Balsam, Arthur Hill.

As you watch this made-for-TV whodunit, you must immediately look for clues. If not, you'll get bored and the long-awaited solution won't make sense to you. Wilford Brimley as the head of mission control tries to put the pieces together. 1985; 95m.

MY SCIENCE PROJECT ★
DIR: Jonathan Betuel. **CAST:** John Stockwell, Danielle von Zerneck, Fisher Stevens, Dennis Hopper, Richard Masur.

Writer-director Jonathan Betuel flubbed his research with this noisy bomb and wound up with a time-warp story containing about as much credibility as Dennis Hopper's ex-hippie high-school teacher. John Stockwell finds some UFO debris abandoned (!) by the military in 1959. The doohickey quickly rages out of control and messes up the time-stream, sending Stockwell and chums to battle dinosaurs and futuristic soldiers. Consider these words a message from *your* future: You won't like this one. Rated PG for profanity. 1985; 94m.

MYSTERIANS, THE ★★½
DIR: Inoshiro Honda. **CAST:** Kenji Sahara.

An alien civilization attempts takeover of Earth after its home planet is destroyed. Massive destruction from the director of *Godzilla*. Quaint Japanese-style special effects look pretty silly these days, but the film can be fun if seen in the right spirit. 1959; 85m.

MYSTERIOUS ISLAND ★★★★
DIR: Cy Endfield. **CAST:** Michael Craig, Joan Greenwood, Michael Callan, Gary Merrill, Herbert Lom.

Fantasy adventure based on Jules Verne's novel about a group of Civil War prisoners who escape by balloon and land on an uncharted island in the Pacific, where they must fight to stay alive against incredible odds. With fantastic effects work by Ray Harryhausen and a breathtaking Bernard Herrmann score. 1961; 101m.

NAVIGATOR: A MEDIEVAL ODYSSEY, THE ★★★★½
DIR: Vincent Ward. **CAST:** Bruce Lyons, Chris Haywood.

A visionary film from New Zealand that involves a medieval quest through time. The film opens in Cumbria in 1348, in the midst of the terrifying black plague. A village of miners tries to appease what they view as a vengeful God by vowing to travel a great distance to fulfill a child's vision. The adventurers travel through the center of the Earth—and surface in a modern-day New Zealand town. Astonishingly original. In B&W and color. 1989; 91m.

NEPTUNE FACTOR, THE ★
DIR: Daniel Petrie. **CAST:** Ben Gazzara, Yvette Mimieux, Walter Pidgeon, Ernest Borgnine.

Ben Gazzara stars as the commander of an experimental deep-sea submarine. He is called in to rescue an aquatic research team trapped in the remains of their lab on the ocean floor. Why they built it in the middle of a quake zone is the first in a series of dumb plot ideas. Rated G. 1973; 94m.

NEVER ENDING STORY, THE ★★★★½
DIR: Wolfgang Petersen. **CAST:** Barret Oliver, Noah Hathaway.

This is a superb fantasy about a sensitive 10-year-old boy named Bastian (Barrett Oliver) who takes refuge in the pages of a fairy tale. In reading it, he's swept off to a land of startlingly strange creatures and heroic adventures where a young warrior, Atreyu (Noah Hathaway), does battle with the Nothing, a force that threatens to obliterate the land of mankind's hope and dreams—and only Bastian has the power to save the day. Rated PG for slight profanity. 1984; 92m.

NEW GLADIATORS, THE
DIR: Lucio Fulci. **CAST:** Jared Martin, Fred Williamson, Claudio Cassinelli.

Italian fantasy about Rome in the twenty-first century. The gladiators of ancient Rome are back, but now they ride motorcycles. The special effects are dreadful, the acting and script rotten. Not rated, has violence. 1987; 90m.

NEXT ONE, THE ★
DIR: Nico Mastorakis. **CAST:** Keir Dullea, Adrienne Barbeau, Jeremy Licht, Peter Hobbs.

Keir Dullea stars as a prophet from the future. He suddenly appears on the beach of a Greek island, and Adrienne Barbeau, with her son, takes him in. No soul, no substance, and no need to see this one. Wait for the next one. Not rated. 1981; 105m.

NIGHT CALLER FROM OUTER SPACE ★★½
DIR: John Gilling. **CAST:** John Saxon, Maurice Denham, Patricia Haines, Alfred Burke.

Here's another one of those perennial sci-fi plots: outer space alien from a dying world comes to Earth looking for human women to serve as breeding stock. (With a planet named Ganymede, it's no wonder they're dying out!) A little British reserve keeps this in check; not bad of its type. 1965; B&W; 84m.

NIGHT OF THE COMET ★★★½
DIR: Thom Eberhardt. **CAST:** Geoffrey Lewis, Mary Woronov, Catherine Mary Stewart.

The passage of the comet, which last visited Earth 65 million years ago, when the dinosaurs disappeared, wipes out all but a few people on our planet. The survivors, mostly young adults, are hunted by a pair of baddies, played by Geoffrey Lewis and Mary Woronov. It all adds up to a zesty low-budget spoof of science-fiction movies. Rated PG-13. 1984; 94m.

NIGHTFALL ★
DIR: Paul Mayersberg. **CAST:** David Birney, Sarah Douglas.

David Birney is the ruler of a land that has never known night. This flick (based on a story by Isaac Asimov) starts promisingly, but soon becomes helplessly bogged down in its own pretentiousness. Rated PG-13, but contains abundant nudity and violence. 1988; 83m.

NIGHTFLYERS ★★★
DIR: T. C. Blake. **CAST:** Catherine Mary Stewart, Michael Praed, John Standing, Lisa Blount, Michael Des Barres.

A motley crew of space explorers search for an ancient and mysterious entity. Their ship is controlled by a computer, programmed from the brain patterns of an abused, jealous, and telepathic woman. This film's only weaknesses are inconsistent special effects and an ending that leaves you hanging. Sci-fi fans should find this entertaining. Rated R for violence and language. 1987; 90m.

1984 (1955) ★★
DIR: Michael Anderson. **CAST:** Edmond O'Brien, Jan Sterling, Michael Redgrave, Donald Pleasence.

Workmanlike adaptation of George Orwell's famous novel that, in spite of a good stab at Winston Smith by Edmond O'Brien, just doesn't capture the misery and desolation of the book. Frankly, this plays more like a postwar polemic than a drama, and great liberties have been taken with the storyline. This movie is currently out of circulation. 1955; B&W; 91m.

1984 (1984) ★★★★½
DIR: Michael Radford. **CAST:** John Hurt, Richard Burton, Suzanna Hamilton, Cyril Cusack.

A stunning adaptation of George Orwell's novel, which captures every mote of bleak despair found within those pages. John Hurt looks positively emaciated as the forlorn Winston Smith, the tragic figure who dares to fall in love in a totalitarian society where emotions are outlawed. Richard Burton, in his last film role, makes a grand interrogator. Rated R for nudity and adult themes. 1984; 123m.

1990: THE BRONX WARRIORS 🦃
DIR: Enzo G. Castellari. **CAST:** Vic Morrow, Christopher Connelly, Mark Gregory.

Near the end of the 1980s, the Bronx is abandoned by law enforcement and becomes a kind of no-man's-land ruled by motorcycle gangs. Vic Morrow plays a lone wolf cop who tries to clean up the town. Obviously inspired by *Escape from New York* and *The Warriors*, it is a prime example of bad writing, acting, and direction. Rated R for violence and language. 1983; 89m.

OMEGA MAN, THE ★★★½
DIR: Boris Sagal. **CAST:** Charlton Heston, Anthony Zerbe, Rosalind Cash.

Charlton Heston does a last-man-on-Earth number in this free adaptation of Richard Matheson's *I Am Legend.* The novel's vampirism has been toned down, but Chuck still is holed up in his high-rise mansion by night, and killing robed (and sleeping) zombies by day. Although this is no more faithful to Matheson's work than 1964's *The Last Man on Earth*, *The Omega Man* has enough throat-grabbing suspense to keep it moving. Rated PG—considerable violence. 1971; 98m.

ON THE BEACH ★★★★
DIR: Stanley Kramer. **CAST:** Gregory Peck, Ava Gardner, Fred Astaire, Anthony Perkins.

The effect of a nuclear holocaust on a group of people in Australia makes for engrossing drama in this film. Gregory Peck is a submarine commander who ups anchor and goes looking for survivors as a radioactive cloud slowly descends upon this apparently last human enclave. Director Stanley Kramer is a bit heavy-handed in his moralizing and the romance between Peck and Ava Gardner is distracting, yet the film remains a powerful antiwar statement. 1959; B&W; 133m.

ONE MILLION B.C. ★★
DIR: Hal Roach, Hal Roach Jr. **CAST:** Victor Mature, Carole Landis, Lon Chaney Jr.

D. W. Griffith reportedly directed parts of this prehistoric-age picture before producer Hal Roach and his son took over. Victor Mature, Carole Landis, and Lon Chaney Jr. try hard—and there are some good moments—but the result is a pretty dumb fantasy film. 1940; B&W; 80m.

OUTER LIMITS, THE (TELEVISION SERIES) ★★★½
DIR: Laslo Benedek, John Erman, James Goldstone, Charles Haas, Byron Haskin, Leonard Horn, Gerd Oswald, Leslie Stevens. **CAST:** Robert Culp, Bruce Dern, Robert Duvall, Cedric Hardwicke, Shirley Knight, Martin Landau, David McCallum, Vera Miles, Edward Mulhare, Donald Pleasence, Cliff Robertson, Martin Sheen, Robert Webber.

This well-remembered television classic of science fiction produced some fine morality plays. Assisted by the control voice which promised "there is nothing wrong with your television set," viewers experienced compelling drama from one of the few examples of *film noir* science fiction ever lensed. Quite a few noted writers cut their teeth on this hour-long weekly program; with literate and absorbing scripts, the episodes hold up quite well today. The best is Harlan Ellison's Hugo Award–winning "Demon with a Glass Hand," starring Robert Culp. Other noteworthy episodes include "The Sixth Finger," in which Welsh coal miner David McCallum takes a trip into his own biologic future, and "The Man Who Was Never Born," which sends

Martin Landau back in time (to *our* present). Suitable for family viewing, although a bit intense for small fry. 1964; B&W; 52 minutes each.

OUTLAND ★★★★
DIR: Peter Hyams. **CAST:** Sean Connery, Peter Boyle, Frances Sternhagen.

Sean Connery stars as the two-fisted marshal in this thoroughly enjoyable outer-space remake of *High Noon* directed by Peter Hyams. Much of the credit for that goes to Connery. As he has proved in many pictures, he is one of the few actors today who can play a fully credible adventure hero. Rated R. 1981; 109m.

PEOPLE, THE ★★
DIR: John Korty. **CAST:** William Shatner, Dan O'Herlihy, Diane Varsi, Kim Darby.

This TV movie is a fair interpretation of the science-fiction stories of Zenna Henderson about a group of psychically talented aliens whose home world has been destroyed and who must survive on Earth. The script gives Henderson's subtle themes a heavy-handed and unbalanced treatment. 1971; 74m.

PEOPLE THAT TIME FORGOT, THE ★
DIR: Kevin Connor. **CAST:** Doug McClure, Patrick Wayne, Sarah Douglas, Thorley Walters.

Edgar Rice Burroughs probably would have been outraged by this and its companion piece, *The Land That Time Forgot*. Doug McClure gets rescued by friend Patrick Wayne from a fate worse than death on a strange island circa 1919. Laughable rubber-suited monsters mix it up with ludicrous wire-controlled beasties. Rated PG. 1977; 90m.

PHASE IV ★★★½
DIR: Saul Bass. **CAST:** Nigel Davenport, Michael Murphy, Lynne Frederick.

An interesting sci-fi mood piece from 1973 about scientists (Nigel Davenport, Michael Murphy) attempting to outwit superintelligent mutant ants. Good effects and fine acting. Rated PG. 1974; 86m.

PHILADELPHIA EXPERIMENT, THE ★★★½
DIR: Stewart Raffill. **CAST:** Michael Paré, Nancy Allen, Bobby DiCicco, Eric Christmas.

Reportedly based on a true incident during World War II involving an antiradar experiment that caused a naval battleship to disappear in Virginia, this entertaining science-fiction film stars Michael Pare as a sailor on that ship. But instead of ending up in Virginia, he finds himself in the modern world of 1984. Rated PG for violence and profanity. 1984; 102m.

PHOENIX THE WARRIOR 🦃
DIR: Robert Hayes. **CAST:** Persis Khambatta.

A sickeningly dull flick set in the distant future where germ warfare has killed all the men, and women have become warriors. A waste of celluloid. Not rated, but contains violence. 1987; 90m.

PLAGUE DOGS, THE ★★★★½
DIR: Martin Rosen. **CAST:** Animated.

This animated film is definitely *not* for children. It is a powerfully disturbing film which makes an unforgettable statement about animal rights. In it, two dogs escape from an experimental veterinary lab in which they had both been subjected to cruel and senseless operations and tests. Once free, the joy they feel is short-lived as they are hunted by both the "white coats" (lab doctors) and the nearby sheep owners. Rated PG. 1984; 99m.

PLAN 9 FROM OUTER SPACE 🦃
DIR: Edward D. Wood Jr. **CAST:** Bela Lugosi, Gregory Walcott, Tom Keene, Duke Moore, Mona McKinnon.

Ever seen a movie that was so bad it was funny? Well, this low-budget 1950s program is considered to be the very worst picture ever made, and it's hilarious. Written and directed by Edward D. Wood, it's a ponderous science-fiction cheapie that attempts to deliver an antiwar message as well as thrills and chills. It does neither. The acting is atrocious, the sets are made of cardboard (and often bumped into by the stars), the dialogue moronic, and the filmmaking technique execrable. Even worse, Bela Lugosi is top-billed even though he died months before the film was made. Undaunted, Wood used silent home-movie footage of the once great horror film star. Get the idea? 1959; B&W; 79m.

PLANET OF THE APES ★★★★
DIR: Franklin J. Schaffner. **CAST:** Charlton Heston, Kim Hunter, Roddy McDowall, Maurice Evans.

Here is the first and best of the *Planet of the Ape* sci-fi series. Four American astronauts crash on a far-off planet and discover a culture where evolution has gone awry. The dominant form of primates are apes and gorillas. Man is reduced to a beast of burden. Much of the social comment is cutesy and forced, but this remains an enjoyable fantasy. Rated PG for violence. 1968; 112m.

PREDATOR ★★★★½
DIR: John McTiernan. **CAST:** Arnold Schwarzenegger, Carl Weathers, Elpidia Carrillo, Bill Duke, Sonny Landham, Richard Chaves, R. G. Armstrong, Kevin Peter Hall.

Sort of an earthbound *Alien*, *Predator* stars Arnold Schwarzenegger as a commando out to terminate a kill-crazy creature in a Latin American jungle. Although it sounds derivative, this film contains a number of inventive moments and delivers a pulse-pounding tale. Rated R for profanity and violence. 1987; 107m.

PREHISTORIC WOMEN 🦃
DIR: Gregg Tallas. **CAST:** Laurette Luez, Allan Nixon, Joan Shawlee.

One of the worst films ever made. A tribe of female bimbos runs into a tribe of male bimbos, and they bore each other to death. If you can watch this one without hitting the scan button, you are a very troubled person. 1950; 74m.

PRINCESS BRIDE, THE ★★★★½
DIR: Rob Reiner. **CAST:** Cary Elwes, Robin Wright, Mandy Patinkin, Andre the Giant, Chris Sarandon, Wallace Shawn, Billy Crystal, Carol Kane, Peter Falk.

This grand adaptation of William Goldman's cult novel owes its success to director Rob Reiner's understanding of gentle whimsy. In a land long ago and far away, strapping and resourceful Cary Elwes battles horrible monsters and makes unusual friends while fighting to save his beloved Buttercup (Robin Wright) from the clutches of the smarmy Prince Humperdinck (Chris Sarandon). The cast is uniformly excellent, with Mandy Patinkin a standout as the swordsman determined to find the man who killed his father. A wonderful fantasy for all ages. Rated PG for modest violence and language. 1987; 98m.

PRISONER, THE (TELEVISION SERIES) ★★★★
DIR: Patrick McGoohan, David Tomblin, Don Chaffey, Pat Jackson. **CAST:** Patrick McGoohan, Angelo Muscat, Leo McKern, Peter Bowles, Nigel Stock, Peter Wyngarde.

Probably the finest science-fiction series ever created for television, this was the brainchild of star Patrick McGoohan, who intended it to be an oblique follow-up to his successful *Danger Man* and *Secret Agent* series. The main character (McGoohan), whose name never is given—although he is believed to be *Secret Agent*'s John Drake—abruptly resigns from a sensitive Intelligence position without explanation. He is abducted and awakens one morning in a mysterious community known only as The Village. Now he is called Number Six—every resident is known only by a number, never by a name. McGoohan conceived the show as a limited series of seventeen episodes; it therefore was the *first* television miniseries. Superior episodes are "The Arrival," wherein the Prisoner is abducted and learns about his new surroundings; "The Chimes of Big Ben," which details his first complicated escape scheme; "Schizoid Man," wherein the Prisoner is brainwashed into a new identity and confronts another person claiming to be Number Six; "Many Happy Returns," wherein the Prisoner wakes one morning to find The Village completely deserted; "Living in Harmony," an episode never shown on American television, which finds the Prisoner replaying a weird parody of his life in a western setting; "The Girl Who Was Death," another parody, this time of supersecret agents; and "Once Upon a Time" and "Fallout," the two-parter that brings the story to a close. 1968; 52 minutes each.

PRISONERS OF THE LOST UNIVERSE ★★
DIR: Terry Marcel. **CAST:** Richard Hatch, Kay Lenz, John Saxon.

A low-budget science-fantasy adventure about three people transported to a parallel universe. Once there, they must use modern technology and archaic weaponry to battle an evil warlord. Although riddled with poor special effects, the film is actually a lot of good-natured fun. Made for Showtime cable network; contains some profanity and mild violence. 1983; 94m.

PROGRAMMED TO KILL ★½
DIR: Allan Holzman. **CAST:** Robert Ginty, Sandahl Bergman, James Booth.

Sandahl Bergman plays a terrorist who is killed by an American special agent only to be brought back to life as a computer-controlled antiterrorist weapon for the United States. The plan backfires and Sandahl turns on her re-creators. Acting is poor and so is the script. Rated R for violence, profanity, and nudity. 1987; 91m.

PROJECT MOON BASE ★★
DIR: Richard Talmadge. **CAST:** Ross Ford, Donna Martell, James Craven.

Futuristic story (set in far-off 1970!) chronicles the fate of an expedition that leaves a space station orbiting Earth and heads for the moon. Made by independent producer Robert Lippert, this dull space story was coauthored by the esteemed Robert E. Heinlein, but it doesn't reflect his touch. 1953; B&W; 53m.

PROJECT X ★½
DIR: Jonathan Kaplan. **CAST:** Matthew Broderick, Helen Hunt, Bill Sadler, Jonathan Stark, Robin Gammell, Stephen Lang.

A misguided attempt to turn a serious issue—the abuse of research animals—into a mainstream comedy-drama. Matthew Broderick is an Air Force misfit who winds up assigned to a secret project involving chimpanzees and air-flight simulators. Rated PG for intensity of theme. 1987; 108m.

QUATERMASS CONCLUSION, THE ★★
DIR: Piers Haggard. **CAST:** John Mills, Simon MacCorkindale, Barbara Kellerman, Margaret Tyzack.

It's sad to see a great premise destroyed by bad editing and sloppy script continuity. Of course, the fact that this film is an edited-down version of a British miniseries may be the cause. In the strange future world of the story, society seems to be suffering a terrible case of inertia. The world's teen population is committing mass suicide, and only Dr. Quatermass (John Mills), genius scientist, can save them. 1979; 105m.

QUEST FOR FIRE ★★★★½
DIR: Jean-Jacques Annaud. **CAST:** Everett McGill, Rae Dawn Chong, Ron Perlman.

In this movie, about the attempt to learn the secret of making fire by a tribe of primitive men, director Jean-Jacques Annaud (*Black and White in Color*) and screenwriter Gerard Brach

(*Tess*) have achieved what once seemed to be impossible: a first-rate, compelling film about the dawn of man. Rated R for violence, gore, nudity, and semi-explicit sex. 1981; 97m.

QUIET EARTH, THE ★★★★
DIR: Geoff Murphy. **CAST:** Bruno Lawrence, Alison Routledge.
First-rate science-fiction thriller from New Zealand. A scientific researcher (Bruno Lawrence) wakes one morning and discovers that all living beings—people and animals—have vanished. Fearful that the world-encircling energy grid on which he'd been working may have been responsible, he sets out to find other people. Intelligent and absorbing adaptation of the book by Craig Harrison. Rated R for nudity and sexual situations. 1985; 91m.

QUINTET ★★
DIR: Robert Altman. **CAST:** Paul Newman, Fernando Rey, Bibi Andersson.
This is about as pessimistic a view of the future as one is likely to see. Director Robert Altman has fashioned a murky, hard-to-follow film, concerning the ultimate game of death, set against the background of a frozen post-nuclear wasteland. An intriguing idea, but Altman doesn't pull this one off. Rated R. 1979; 110m.

R.O.T.O.R.
DIR: Cullen Blaine. **CAST:** Richard Gesswein.
Abysmal variation on the *Robocop* theme has a part-man, part-machine police officer going berserk and shooting citizens for slight offenses such as jaywalking and speeding. Most of the picture deals with attempts to stop the roboslop, but someone simply should have stopped the filmmakers. Rated R for violence and profanity. 1988; 91m.

RADIOACTIVE DREAMS ★★★
DIR: Albert Pyun. **CAST:** John Stockwell, Michael Dudikoff, George Kennedy, Don Murray, Michelle Little, Norbert Weisser, Lisa Blount.
This one has a little bit of everything: action, adventure, science fiction, fantasy, and an excellent score. Essentially a spoof, the story begins in a post-apocalypse fallout shelter where two boys, who read 1930s detective novels and think the stories are real, have lived most of their lives. They end up in the middle of a gang war with a mutant surfer, hippie cannibals, and biker women. Rated R for nudity and violence. 1984; 94m.

RAIDERS OF THE LOST ARK ★★★★★
DIR: Steven Spielberg. **CAST:** Harrison Ford, Karen Allen, Wolf Kahler, Paul Freeman, Ronald Lacey, John Rhys-Davies, Denholm Elliott.
For sheer spirit-lifting entertainment, you can't do better than this film, by director Steven Spielberg and writer-producer George Lucas. Harrison Ford stars as Indiana Jones, the roughest, toughest, and most unpredictable hero to grace the silver screen, who risks life and limb against a set of the nastiest villains you've ever seen. It's all to save the world—what else? Rated PG for violence and gore. 1981; 115m.

RESURRECTION OF ZACHARY WHEELER, THE ★★
DIR: Bob Wynn. **CAST:** Bradford Dillman, Angie Dickinson, Leslie Nielsen.
Disappointing science-fiction/mystery has a well-known senator (Bradford Dillman) taken to a bizarre out-of-the-way treatment center in New Mexico after a serious car accident, and an investigation of the incident by an intrepid reporter (Leslie Nielsen). Confusing movie. Rated G. 1971; 100m.

RETURN, THE ★
DIR: Greydon Clark. **CAST:** Jan-Michael Vincent, Cybill Shepherd, Martin Landau, Raymond Burr, Neville Brand.

Terminally boring science-fiction flick about a close encounter and the psychological impact it has on two children and an old man in a small New Mexico town. Rated PG. 1980; 91m.

RETURN OF THE JEDI ★★★★★
DIR: Richard Marquand. **CAST:** Mark Hamill, Harrison Ford, Carrie Fisher, Billy Dee Williams, Dave Prowse, Peter Mayhew, Anthony Daniels, James Earl Jones.

This third film in the *Star Wars* series more than fulfills the viewer's expectations. The story centers on the all-out attempt by the Rebel forces—led by Luke Skywalker (Mark Hamill), Han Solo (Harrison Ford), Princess Leia (Carrie Fisher), and Lando Calrissian (Billy Dee Williams)—to turn back the tidal wave of interplanetary domination by the evil Galactic Empire and its forces, led by Darth Vader (Dave Prowse—with the voice of James Earl Jones). Rated PG. 1983; 133m.

RETURN TO FANTASY ISLAND ★★
DIR: George McCowan. **CAST:** Ricardo Montalban, Joseph Campanella, Joseph Cotten, Adrienne Barbeau, Laraine Day, Herve Villechaize, Cameron Mitchell, Karen Valentine, France Nuyen, George Chakiris, Horst Buchholz, George Maharis.

If you liked the television series *Fantasy Island,* you'll like this made-for-TV movie. Ricardo Montalban is the suave operator of a wish-fulfillment island, assisted by his tiny friend Tattoo (Herve Villechaize). It's pure hokum, but it does offer a chance to watch some fine actors. 1977; 100m.

RIDING WITH DEATH ★½
DIR: Alan J. Levi, Don McDougall. **CAST:** Ben Murphy, Katherine Crawford, Richard Dysart, William Sylvester, Andrew Prine, Alan Oppenheimer, Don Galloway.

Compilation of two hour-long shows from *The Gemini Man* television series, edited together by some mysterious and unconvincing process. Ben Murphy plays a man who, through a scientific accident, can render himself invisible for short bursts of time. Dated and hokey, and the invisibility factor is not played up at all. Real comic-book stuff. 1976; 97m.

ROAD WARRIOR, THE ★★★★
DIR: George Miller. **CAST:** Mel Gibson, Bruce Spence, Vernon Wells, Mike Preston.

A sequel to *Mad Max,* the most successful Australian film of all time ($100 million in worldwide rentals), this exciting science-fiction adventure features Mel Gibson as a fast-driving, cynical Robin Hood in the desolate, dangerous, post-apocalypse world of the future. Good fun! Rated R for violence, nudity, and profanity. 1981; 94m.

ROBIN HOOD: HERNE'S SON ★★★
DIR: Robert Young. **CAST:** Jason Connery, Oliver Cotton, George Baker, Michael Craig, Nickolas Grace.

The third in this series from the BBC begins with the death of Robin of Locksley and the choosing of Robert of Hunnington (Jason Connery) as his successor by Herne the Hunter. The refusal of the new Robin to serve leads to the breakup of the band, followed by the abduction of Maid Marion. The new Robin must then unite his followers and save his love. 1986; 101m.

ROBIN HOOD: THE SWORDS OF WAYLAND ★★★★
DIR: Robert Young. **CAST:** Michael Praed, Rula Lenska, Nickolas Grace.

The second of the *Robin Hood* series from the BBC is as good as the first, if not better. This adventure pits Robin against the forces of darkness represented by the sorceress Morgwyn of Ravenscar (Rula Lenska). The story twists and turns as the sorceress gathers the seven swords of Wayland, one of which is in Robin's hands. 1986; 105m.

ROBOCOP ★★★★½
DIR: Paul Verhoeven. **CAST:** Peter Weller, Nancy Allen, Dan O'Herlihy, Ronny Cox, Kurtwood Smith, Miguel Ferrer.

RoboCop is the ultimate super-hero movie. A stylish and stylized cop thriller set in the far future, it concerns a mortally wounded policeman (Peter Weller) who is melded with a machine to become the ultimate defender of justice, RoboCop. One word of warning: this is an extremely violent motion picture. Rated R. 1987; 103m.

ROCKET ATTACK USA
DIR: Barry Mahon. **CAST:** John McKay.

American spies attempt to steal the plans for Sputnik from the Russians. In retaliation, the Russians nuke Manhattan. The brief running time is padded out with a ludicrous romantic subplot and a lot of stock footage. Don't waste your time. 1958; B&W; 71m.

ROCKETSHIP X-M ★★½
DIR: Kurt Neumann. **CAST:** Lloyd Bridges, Hugh O'Brian, Noah Beery Jr., Osa Massen, John Emery.

A rocket heading for the moon is knocked off course by a meteor storm and is forced to land on Mars. The crewmen find Mars to be very inhospitable, as it has been devastated by atomic war and has mutated creatures inhabiting the planet. While the story is weak and the acting only passable, this is one of the first of the science-fiction films that dominated the 1950s. 1950; B&W; 77m.

RODAN ★★★½
DIR: Inoshiro Honda. **CAST:** Kenji Sawara.

This minor classic was Japan's answer to the nuclear "big bug" films of the decade. Murderous insects are just a prelude to the main event featuring not one but *two* supersonic-speed giant pterodactyls. Released in the United States with a stock-footage preface concerning the danger of radioactive experiments, this well-constructed thriller boasts special effects by Eiji Tsuburaya that are superior to many of its American counterparts. 1956; 72m.

ROLLERBALL ★★★★
DIR: Norman Jewison. **CAST:** James Caan, John Houseman, Maud Adams, Ralph Richardson, John Beck.

Vastly underappreciated science-fiction film envisions a world controlled by business corporations; with no wars or other aggressive activities, the public gets its release in rollerball, a violent combination of basketball, ice hockey, and roller derby. James Caan is a top rollerball champ who refuses to quit the game in spite of threats from industrialist John Houseman, who fears that Caan may turn into a public folk hero. Rated R for violence. 1975; 128m.

ROLLERBLADE
DIR: Donald G. Jackson. **CAST:** Suzanne Solari, Jeff Hutchinson.

Imagine a poor rip-off of *Mad Max* meeting *Kansas City Bomber* and *Red Sonja*. Now, remove any and all redeeming qualities and add a religious order whose icon is the classic smiling face. If you enjoy laughing at ineptitude, this may be worth a rental. 1986; 88m.

RUNAWAY ★★★
DIR: Michael Crichton. **CAST:** Tom Selleck, Cynthia Rhodes, Gene Simmons, Kirstie Alley.

Tom Selleck is a futuristic cop trying to track down a bunch of killer robots controlled by the evil villain (Gene Simmons, from the rock band KISS). It's a cinematic comic book and, although meant to be a thriller, never really gets the viewer involved in the story. Rated PG for violence and profanity. 1984; 99m.

RUNNING MAN, THE ★★★½
DIR: Paul Michael Glaser. **CAST:** Arnold Schwarzenegger, Maria Con-

chita Alonso, Richard Dawson, Yaphet Kotto, Jim Brown.

In this silly but exciting outing, Arnold Schwarzenegger is an honest cop who is framed for a crime he didn't commit and forced to fight for his life on a bizarre twenty-first-century game show. Another successful variation on the big guy's standard film formula. Rated R for profanity and violence. 1987; 101m.

SAMSON ★½

DIR: Gianfranco Parolini. **CAST:** Brad Harris, Bridgette Corey.

This Italian mini-epic features muscle-bound Brad Harris as Samson. He uses his strength to restore peace in his kingdom. This dubbed film is a yawner. 1960; 99m.

SANTA CLAUS CONQUERS THE MARTIANS 🦃

DIR: Nicholas Webster. **CAST:** John Call, Leonard Hicks.

Sounds like a classic, doesn't it? Well, guess again. This film, about a bunch of aliens abducting St. Nick because they don't have one of their own, is actually pretty slow, and not much really happens, though Pia Zadora does show off her acting skills as one of the younger residents of the red planet. 1964; 80m.

SATURN 3 ★★

DIR: Stanley Donen. **CAST:** Kirk Douglas, Farrah Fawcett, Harvey Keitel.

Although this space shocker is endowed with a fair amount of chills and surprises, there's very little else to it. The story takes place in the distant future on the Eden-like space station Titan, which is happily inhabited by two chemists (Kirk Douglas and Farrah Fawcett). Their idyllic existence is thrown into turmoil when a strangely hostile newcomer (Harvey Keitel) unleashes a terror that threatens to destroy them all. Rated R. 1980; 88m.

7 FACES OF DR. LAO ★★★★

DIR: George Pal. **CAST:** Tony Randall, Barbara Eden, Arthur O'Connell.

A first-rate fantasy taken from Charles Finney's classic story, "The Circus of Dr. Lao." Tony Randall plays multiple roles as a mysterious Chinese gentleman and his many strange circus sideshow creatures. Fabulous makeup and special effects, surrounded by a heartwarming story. Perfect for all ages, one of the few films to capture the wonder and sinister overtones of a traveling circus. 1964; 100m.

7TH VOYAGE OF SINBAD, THE ★★★★

DIR: Nathan Juran. **CAST:** Kerwin Mathews, Kathryn Grant (Crosby), Torin Thatcher.

Sinbad battles an evil magician who has reduced the Princess, who is also Sinbad's fiancée, to six inches in height. Our hero must battle a sword-wielding skeleton, a roc (giant bird), and other dangers to restore his bride-to-be to her normal size. This film contains some of the best stop-motion animation ever created by the master in that craft, Ray Harryhausen. 1958; 87m.

SHE (1925) ★★½

DIR: G. B. Samuelson. **CAST:** Betty Blythe, Carlyle Blackwell, Mary Odette.

Statuesque vamp Betty Blythe portrays the ageless Queen Ayesha (She) to perfection in this seventh and final silent version of adventure novelist H. Rider Haggard's fantasy about a lost tribe and a flame of eternal life in darkest Africa. Filmed in London and Berlin. Silent, with background music. 1925; B&W; 77m.

SHE (1983) 🦃

DIR: Avi Nesher. **CAST:** Sandahl Bergman, Quin Kessler, Harrison Muller, Gordon Mitchell.

Sandahl Bergman is She, the leader of a postapocalyptic nation that looks upon men as second-class citizens. Nevertheless, She defies her country's wishes by helping a man defeat a gang of mutants. Not rated, but would be an R for violence and nudity. 1983; 90m.

SHORT CIRCUIT ★★★★
DIR: John Badham. **CAST:** Ally Sheedy, Steve Guttenberg, Fisher Stevens, Austin Pendleton, G. W. Bailey.

In this enjoyable sci-fi comedy-adventure, a sophisticated robot, Number Five, is zapped by lightning during a storm and comes alive (à la Frankenstein's monster) to the shock of his creator (Steve Guttenberg). Created as the ultimate war weapon, the mechanical man learns the value of life from an animal lover (Ally Sheedy) and sets off on his own—with the military in hot pursuit. Rated PG for profanity and violence. 1986; 95m.

SHORT CIRCUIT 2 ★★
DIR: Kenneth Johnson. **CAST:** Fisher Stevens, Michael McKean, Cynthia Gibb, Jack Weston.

If it weren't filled with profanity, *Short Circuit 2* might have been a good film for the kiddies. The silly story is a throwback to the Disney films of the '60s. Indian inventor Fisher Stevens, whose mangling of the English language isn't as funny—or as cleverly written—the second time, goes into the toy business with streetwise hustler Michael McKean and that lovable robot, No. 5. Rated PG for profanity and violence. 1988; 110m.

SILENT RUNNING ★★★★
DIR: Douglas Trumbull. **CAST:** Bruce Dern, Cliff Potts, Ron Rifkin.

True science-fiction is most entertaining when it is not just glittering special effects and is, instead, accompanied by a well-developed plot and worthwhile message. This is such a picture. Bruce Dern is in charge of a futuristic space station that is entrusted with the last living remnants of Earth's botanical heritage. His efforts to preserve those trees and plants in spite of an order to destroy them makes for thoughtful moviemaking. Rated G. 1971; 89m.

SINBAD AND THE EYE OF THE TIGER ★★½
DIR: Sam Wanamaker. **CAST:** Patrick Wayne, Jane Seymour, Damien Thomas, Margaret Whiting, Patrick Troughton, Taryn Power.

The story has Sinbad (Patrick Wayne) seeking the hand of Princess Farah (Jane Seymour) and permission from her brother, Prince Kassim (Damian Thomas), who has been turned into a baboon by his wicked stepmother. Sinbad must sail to a distant isle to find Melanthius (Patrick Troughton), the only wizard capable of breaking the spell. *Sinbad and the Eye of the Tiger* is not a terrible movie (children will love it), but it just provides more evidence that all the movie tricks in the world cannot disguise a bad story. Rated G. 1977; 113m.

SISTERHOOD, THE ★★½
DIR: Cirio H. Santiago. **CAST:** Rebecca Holden, Chuck Wagner, Lynn-Holly Johnson.

Futuristic tale set in a postapocalyptic society, where a secret society of female superwarriors battle the male establishment. Most of the story follows the warriors as they enter the Forbidden Zone (there's always a forbidden zone in these movies) in search of their captured sisters. Filipino-made movie is okay for fans of the genre. Rated R. 1988; 76m.

SLAUGHTERHOUSE FIVE ★★★★
DIR: George Roy Hill. **CAST:** Michael Sacks, Valerie Perrine, Eugene Roche, John Dehner, Holly Near.

This film, based on Kurt Vonnegut's novel, centers around the activities of Billy Pilgrim, who has become unstuck in time. This enables, or forces, him to jump back and forth among different periods in his life and even experience two separate time/space incidents simultaneously. Well done. Rated R. 1972; 104m.

SOLARBABIES

DIR: Alan Johnson. **CAST:** Richard Jordan, Jami Gertz, Jason Patric, Charles Durning, Lukas Haas.

In the far future, a group of sports teens (who play a hard-top variation of ice hockey on roller skates) join forces with a mystical force (which looks like a dining-room fixture) to wrest control of the world's water source from an evil empire. *Solarbabies* contains not one decent performance or moment of interest. Rated PG-13 for violence. 1986; 94m.

SOMETHING WICKED THIS WAY COMES ★★★

DIR: Jack Clayton. **CAST:** Jason Robards Jr., Jonathan Pryce, Pam Grier, Shawn Carson.

Ray Bradbury's classic fantasy novel has been fashioned into a good, but not great, movie by the Walt Disney Studios. Jason Robards Jr. stars as the town librarian whose task it is to save his family and friends from the evil temptations of Mr. Dark (Jonathan Pryce) and his Pandemonium Carnival. It's an old-fashioned, even gentle, tale of the supernatural; a gothic *Wizard of Oz* that seems likely to be best appreciated by pre-teens. Rated PG. 1983; 94m.

SOMEWHERE IN TIME ★★★

DIR: Jeannot Szwarc. **CAST:** Christopher Reeve, Jane Seymour, Christopher Plummer, Bill Erwin, Teresa Wright.

This gentle, old-fashioned film directed by Jeannot Szwarc celebrates tender passions with great style and atmosphere. The story by Richard Matheson does have a bit of a twist to it—instead of the lovers having to overcome such mundane obstacles as dissenting parents, terminal illness, or other tragedies, they must overcome time itself. Rated PG. 1980; 103m.

SORCERESS ★

DIR: Brian Stuart. **CAST:** Leigh and Lynette Harris.

Even if you like swords, sorcery, demons, and dragons, you probably still won't like this film. Though the story—about twin girls who are bestowed with the power of sorcery and the fighting skills of the masters—is fairly entertaining, it winds up looking something like *Charlie's Angels Return to the Dark Ages*. Rated R for nudity and simulated sex. 1982; 83m.

SOYLENT GREEN ★★★

DIR: Richard Fleischer. **CAST:** Charlton Heston, Edward G. Robinson, Joseph Cotten, Chuck Connors.

In this watchable science-fiction flick, the year is 2022, and New York City is grossly overcrowded with a population of 40 million. Food is so scarce the government creates a product, Soylent Green, for people to eat. Heston plays the policeman who discovers what it's made of. There is some violence. Rated PG. 1973; 97m.

SPACE 1999 (TELEVISION SERIES) ★★

DIR: Ray Austin, Lee H. Katzin. **CAST:** Martin Landau, Barbara Bain, Barry Morse.

An atomic explosion occurs on the moon, throwing it out of orbit and forcing the occupants of Moon Base Alpha to wander the stars aimlessly. Low production values on this TV series hold back the occasionally original stories. This show still has a small cult following, and the producers have managed to compile some of the better episodes. Not rated. 1974; 92m.

SPACE RAGE

DIR: Conrad E. Palmisano. **CAST:** Richard Farnsworth, Michael Paré, John Loughlin, Lee Purcell, William Windom.

Embarrassingly bad sci-fi flick wastes the talents of Richard Farnsworth as a retired twenty-first-century cop living on a prison planet. When bad boy Michael Paré stages an escape, kidnaps the governor (William Windom), and kills a bunch of bounty hunters, it's up to Farnsworth to bring him down. Rated R for violence galore. 1986; 78m.

SPACE RAIDERS ★★★½
DIR: Howard R. Cohen. **CAST:** Vince Edwards, David Mendenhall.

In this low-budget sci-fi flick from B-movie king Roger Corman, a 10-year-old boy (David Mendenhall) is kidnapped by a group of space pirates led by Vince Edwards, who becomes his mentor. It's an entertaining adventure film which not-too-young-youngsters will enjoy. Rated PG for profanity and violence. 1983; 82m.

SPACECAMP ★★★
DIR: Harry Winer. **CAST:** Kate Capshaw, Lea Thompson, Tom Skerritt, Kelly Preston, Tate Donovan, Leaf Phoenix.

Kate Capshaw is a reluctant instructor at the U.S. Space Camp in Alabama. She and her independent charges—four teens and a younger child—board a real space shuttle and are accidentally launched on a perilous journey. With an attractive cast, impressive special effects, and a noble heart, the movie should inspire the astronauts of the future. Rated PG for suspense. 1986; 104m.

SPACEHUNTER: ADVENTURES IN THE FORBIDDEN ZONE 🦃
DIR: Lamont Johnson. **CAST:** Peter Strauss, Molly Ringwald, Ernie Hudson, Andrea Marcovicci, Michael Ironside, Beeson Carroll.

The grade-Z science-fiction flick is not dead; it just costs $12 million to make today. The story is a compendium of cornball clichés and groan-worthy dialogue. Peter Strauss plays a futuristic hero who takes on an army of militant humanoids on a plague-infested planet in order to save a group of marooned women. Rated PG for violence. 1983; 90m.

STAR CRASH ★
DIR: Lewis Coates. **CAST:** Caroline Munro, Christopher Plummer, Joe Spinell, Marjoe Gortner, David Hasselhoff.

A vapid science-fiction space opera with but one redeeming quality: the scanty costumes worn by Caroline Munro as heroine Stella Star. An unbelievable waste of talent, most particularly Christopher Plummer, who seems embarrassed by the whole thing. Rated PG—some violence. 1979; 92m.

STAR CRYSTAL ★
DIR: Lance Lindsay. **CAST:** Juston Campbell.

In this second-rate *Alien* rip-off, two astronauts encounter a rock containing a monster that feeds on and destroys humans. Rated R for nudity and violence. 1986; 93m.

STAR TREK: THE CAGE ★★★★
DIR: Robert Butler. **CAST:** Jeffrey Hunter, Leonard Nimoy, Majel Barrett, John Hoyt, Susan Oliver.

This is the first pilot episode of the *Star Trek* television series, initially rejected by NBC for being "too cerebral" and "too good for TV." This is the only recorded story of Captain Christopher Pike (Jeffrey Hunter) and his quite different *Enterprise* crew. The plot concerns a planet of aliens who entrap various forms of animal life in their interplanetary "zoo." They decide that Pike would make a good companion for their human female. Unrated; suitable for family viewing. 1964; 65m.

STAR TREK: THE MENAGERIE ★★★★
DIR: Marc Daniels. **CAST:** William Shatner, Leonard Nimoy, Jeffrey Hunter, Susan Oliver, DeForest Kelley, James Doohan, Nichelle Nichols, George Takei.

Combining the original *Star Trek* pilot, which starred Jeffrey Hunter as the space-adventuring captain, with footage featuring the show's eventual stars, it tells a fascinating story of how Spock brings comfort to his former commander on a planet capable of fulfilling any fantasy. It's science-fiction entertainment of the first order. 1967; 100m.

STAR TREK—THE MOTION PICTURE ★★½

DIR: Robert Wise. **CAST:** William Shatner, Leonard Nimoy, DeForest Kelley, James Doohan, Nichelle Nichols, George Takei, Walter Koenig.

Even though it reunites the cast of the popular television series and was directed by Robert Wise, who made one of the best science-fiction films of all time (*The Day the Earth Stood Still*), this $35 million film is a real hit-and-miss affair. Fans of the series may find much to love, but others will be bewildered—and sometimes bored—by the overemphasis on special effects and the underemphasis on characterization. Rated G. 1979; 132m.

STAR TREK II: THE WRATH OF KHAN ★★★★

DIR: Nicholas Meyer. **CAST:** William Shatner, Leonard Nimoy, DeForest Kelley, Ricardo Montalban, James Doohan, George Takei, Nichelle Nichols, Walter Koenig.

James T. Kirk (William Shatner), Mr. Spock (Leonard Nimoy), Doc "Bones" McCoy (DeForest Kelley) and the entire crew of the Starship *Enterprise* once more "boldly go where no man has gone before" in this *Star Trek* adventure. It's no *Gone With the Wind*—or even *Raiders of the Lost Ark.* But it is fun to watch, and Trekkies are sure to love it. As Khan, Ricardo Montalban reprises his supervillain role from the 1967 "Space Seed" episode of the television series. Rated PG for violence and gore. 1982; 113m.

STAR TREK III: THE SEARCH FOR SPOCK ★★★★½

DIR: Leonard Nimoy. **CAST:** Leonard Nimoy, William Shatner, DeForest Kelley, James Doohan, George Takei, Nichelle Nichols, Walter Koenig.

In this thrill-packed release, the crew of the U.S.S. *Enterprise* goes looking for their lost shipmate, Spock who appeared to give his life to save his friends—at the end of *Star Trek II: The Wrath of Khan.* But is he dead? Finding out may be one of the most entertaining things you ever do in front of a TV set. Rated PG. 1984; 105m.

STAR TREK IV: THE VOYAGE HOME ★★★★½

DIR: Leonard Nimoy. **CAST:** William Shatner, Leonard Nimoy, DeForest Kelley, James Doohan, George Takei, Walter Koenig, Nichelle Nichols, Catharine Hicks.

Our stalwart heroes journey back to Earth in their "borrowed" enemy spacecraft just in time to witness a new tragedy in the making: an alien deep-space probe is disrupting our planet's atmosphere by broadcasting a message that nobody understands. When Spock identifies the "language" as that of the humpback whale, extinct in the twenty-third century, Kirk leads his crew back to the twentieth century in an attempt to locate two of the great mammals and utilize them for translation duty. Charming and lighthearted, though rated PG for somewhat intense themes. 1986; 119m.

STAR TREK V: THE FINAL FRONTIER ★★½

DIR: William Shatner. **CAST:** William Shatner, Leonard Nimoy, DeForest Kelley, James Doohan, Walter Koenig, Nichelle Nichols, George Takei, David Warner, Laurence Luckinbill.

In this entry of the big-screen series, a Vulcan (Laurence Luckinbill) takes control of the *Enterprise* to pursue his personal quest for spiritual enlightenment. Luckinbill delivers a strong performance, and the script features a number of witty exchanges between the stars. However, its ambitious, metaphysical premise is diluted by a weak, unsatisfying ending. Rated PG for profanity. 1989; 110m.

STAR TREK (TELEVISION SERIES) ★★★½

DIR: Marc Daniels, Joseph Pevney, James Goldstone, Gerd Oswald, Vincent McEveety. **CAST:** William

Shatner, Leonard Nimoy, DeForest Kelley, George Takei, Walter Koenig, Nichelle Nichols, Majel Barrett, Grace Lee Whitney, James Doohan.

These are the voyages of the Starship *Enterprise*. Her original five-year mission was given short shrift by television executives who pulled the plug after a mere three years from late 1966 to mid-1969, and then watched in horror as fans turned it into the single most popular television series ever made. Beginning in 1979, it begat a successful film series, and the end is nowhere in sight. Paramount has reissued the original shows on tapes made from 35-mm masters, and the *Enterprise* and her crew never have looked lovelier. Superior episodes are "The City on the Edge of Forever," scripted by fantasist Harlan Ellison, "The Trouble with Tribbles," "Court Martial," "Shore Leave," scripted by science-fiction writer Theodore Sturgeon, "A Piece of the Action," "Amok Time," also scripted by Sturgeon; "Menagerie," a two-parter that incorporates the program's original pilot, "Space Seed," which introduces the evil Khan (Ricardo Montalban) and sets up the events later resolved in the second big-screen film; "Wolf in the Fold," scripted by horror writer Robert Bloch, which postulates that Jack the Ripper was a malevolent force that never died ; and "Where No Man Has Gone Before," wherein two members of the *Enterprise* crew suddenly acquire incredible mental abilities at the expense of their humanity. 1966–1969; 50 minutes each.

STAR WARS ★★★★★

DIR: George Lucas. **CAST:** Mark Hamill, Harrison Ford, Carrie Fisher, Alec Guinness, Peter Cushing, Anthony Daniels.

May the Force be with you! Writer-director George Lucas blended the best of vintage pulp science-fiction, old-fashioned cliff-hangers, comic books, and classic fantasy to come up with the ultimate adventure "a long time ago in a galaxy far, far away." Rated PG. 1977; 121m.

STARFLIGHT ONE ★

DIR: Jerry Jameson. **CAST:** Lee Majors, Hal Linden, Lauren Hutton, Ray Milland, Gail Strickland, George DiCenzo, Tess Harper, Terry Kiser, Robert Webber.

Airport '82? A new supersonic jet experiences catastrophies, one after the other, and the action becomes split between the heroic people on board and the nervous ground crew looking at the little green bleeps on the radar screen. All the actors in this all-star line-up phone in their performances in the grand tradition of disaster films. 1982; 115m.

STARMAN ★★★★

DIR: John Carpenter. **CAST:** Jeff Bridges, Karen Allen, Charles Martin Smith, Richard Jaeckel.

Jeff Bridges stars as an alien who falls in love with Earthling, Karen Allen. *Starman* is best described as a fairy tale for adults, but the kiddies undoubtedly will enjoy it, too. Rated PG-13 for suggested sex, violence, and profanity. 1984; 115m.

STARSHIP ★½

DIR: Roger Christian. **CAST:** John Tarrant.

Even though director Roger Christian worked on such sci-fi classics as *Alien, Star Wars,* and *Return of the Jedi,* his own outer space adventure is dull, dull, dull. The plot's similar to *Star Wars,* too: Rebels on a mining planet strive to overcome the evil rulers, who want to replace the workers with robots. There's even a cute robot in the R2D2 tradition. But there are no thrills, nor any sense of adventure. Rated PG. 1985; 98m.

STEEL DAWN ★

DIR: Lance Hool. **CAST:** Patrick Swayze, Lisa Niemi, Christopher Neame, Brion James, Anthony Zerbe.

Brainless bore set in the postapocalyptic future has martial-arts warrior

Patrick Swayze joining in to help widow Lisa Niemi (Swayze's real-life wife) protect a colony of peaceful settlers and their precious wells from water-snatching creeps led by Anthony Zerbe. The performers do their best, but *Road Warrior* this isn't. Rated R for violence. 1987; 100m.

STORMQUEST ★
DIR: Alex Sessa. **CAST:** Brent Huff.

The only reason this turkey rates one star is the deadpan humor sparsely scattered throughout. The jokes enliven this sorry tale of a tribe of Amazon women battling a band of renegade men from a neighboring tribe. Not rated. 1987; 90m.

STRANDED ★★★
DIR: Tex Fuller. **CAST:** Ione Skye, Joe Morton, Cameron Dye, Brendan Hughes, Maureen O'Sullivan.

A story of bigotry and intolerance centered around aliens escaping from another world and landing in a small town. Cameron Dye is the young man who tries to help them escape from the local sheriff, a gang of good ol' boys, and an assassin from outer space. More character development and pacing than usual for a science-fiction film. Rated PG-13 for profanity and violence. 1987; 80m.

STRANGE INVADERS ★★★★
DIR: Michael Laughlin. **CAST:** Paul LeMat, Diana Scarwid, Nancy Allen, Louise Fletcher, Michael Lerner, Kenneth Tobey, June Lockhart.

A splendid parody of 1950s science-fiction movies, this film begins in 1958, with buglike aliens taking over a farm town called Centerville, Illinois. The story then jumps to New York City, twenty-five years later, where a college professor (Paul LeMat) is suddenly running off to Illinois after his ex-wife (Diana Scarwid), who has disappeared during a visit to Centerville. Rated PG for violence. 1983; 94m.

STRANGER FROM VENUS ★
DIR: Burt Balaban. **CAST:** Patricia Neal, Helmut Dantine, Derek Bond.

The same plot and the same star (Patricia Neal) as the classic *The Day the Earth Stood Still* does not guarantee the same quality. A visitor from Venus attempts to warn Earth of the dangers of nuclear weapons but meets with suspicion and hatred. Cheap and unimaginative. Get *Day* instead. 1954; B&W; 78m.

STRYKER ★
DIR: Cirio H. Santiago. **CAST:** Steve Sandor, Andria Savio.

A low-budget futuristic action thriller à la *Spacehunter* and *Road Warrior*, the story here deals with a soldier of fortune (Steve Sandor) attempting to wrest a group of warrior women from the clutches of an evil tribe. Rated R. 1983; 86m.

SUPER FUZZ ★★½
DIR: Sergio Corbucci. **CAST:** Terence Hill, Ernest Borgnine, Joanne Dru, Marc Lawrence.

For adults, this is a silly, mindless film...but it's great fun for the kids. Terence Hill stars as Dave Speed, a police officer with supernatural powers. He and his ornery, befuddled partner (Ernest Borgnine) make an amusing team. Rated PG. 1981; 94m.

SUPERGIRL ★★½
DIR: Jeannot Swarc. **CAST:** Faye Dunaway, Peter O'Toole, Helen Slater, Mia Farrow, Brenda Vaccaro, Simon Ward, Peter Cook, Hart Bochner.

Helen Slater makes a respectable film debut as Superman's cousin in this screen comic book, which should delight the kiddies and occasionally tickle the adults. The stellar supporting cast doesn't seem to take it seriously, so why should we? PG-rated. 1984; 105m.

SUPERMAN ★★★½
DIR: Richard Donner. **CAST:** Christopher Reeve, Margot Kidder, Jackie Cooper, Marc McClure, Marlon Brando, Glenn Ford.

After a somewhat overblown introduction, which encompasses the end of Krypton and Clark Kent's adolescence in Smallville, this film takes off to provide some great moments as Superman swings into action. The action is complemented by fine tongue-in-cheek comedy. Rated PG. 1978; 143m.

SUPERMAN II ★★★★
DIR: Richard Lester. **CAST:** Margot Kidder, Christopher Reeve, Gene Hackman, Ned Beatty, Jackie Cooper.

Even better than the original, this terrific adventure of the Man of Steel includes a full-fledged—and beautifully handled—romance between Lois Lane (Margot Kidder) and Superman (Christopher Reeve) and a spectacular battle that pits our hero against three supervillains (during which the city of Metropolis is almost completely destroyed). Rated PG. 1980; 127m.

SUPERMAN III ★★
DIR: Richard Lester. **CAST:** Christopher Reeve, Richard Pryor, Robert Vaughn, Annette O'Toole, Jackie Cooper, Marc McClure, Pamela Stephenson.

If it weren't for Christopher Reeve's excellent performance in the title role, *Superman III* would be a major disappointment. The story features a subdued Richard Pryor as a computer whiz who is hired by bad guy Robert Vaughn to do dastardly deeds with his magic programming. Rated PG. 1983; 125m.

SUPERMAN IV: THE QUEST FOR PEACE ★½
DIR: Sidney J. Furie. **CAST:** Christopher Reeve, Gene Hackman, Margot Kidder, Jackie Cooper, Mariel Hemingway, Jon Cryer, Marc McClure, Sam Wanamaker.

A well-intentioned plot about Superman (Christopher Reeve) attempting to rid the Earth of nuclear weapons cannot save this overlong, overwrought, confusing and sometimes downright dull third sequel. Rated PG for violence. 1987; 90m.

SUPERMAN AND THE MOLE MEN ★★
DIR: Lee Sholem. **CAST:** George Reeves, Phyllis Coates, Jeff Corey, Walter Reed.

George Reeves dons the tights and cape that he was to be identified with for the rest of his life. This story concerns a huge oil well that drills too far and yields fuzzy midgets from inside the Earth. This film led to the famous television series and was subsequently shown as a two-part episode. 1951; B&W; 67m.

SUPERMAN—THE SERIAL ★★½
DIR: Spencer Gordon Bennet, Thomas Carr. **CAST:** Kirk Alyn, Noel Neill, Tommy Bond, Carol Forman, Pierre Watkin, George Meeker, Charles King, Charles Quigley, Herbert Rawlinson.

The first live-action Superman serial was one of the highest grossing of all chapterplays ever made, as well as Columbia's most prestigious effort in that field. As Superman, wavy-haired serial and B-movie hero Kirk Alyn manfully strove to bring life to a story that centered around a female crime czar known as the Spider Lady and her plans to rule or ruin Earth through a reducer ray. The film relies on inept flying sequences and the by-now classic relationship between Clark Kent and Lois Lane for the bulk of its action. 1948; B&W; 0m.

SURVIVAL ZONE ★
DIR: Percival Rubens. **CAST:** Gary Lockwood, Morgan Stevens, Camilla Sparv.

Yet another in a long series of movies about nuclear-holocaust survivors battling evil. This time it's leftover good ranchers versus a leftover bad motorcycle gang. This story's been run so far into the ground it's surfacing in China. Not rated; contains violence and nudity. 1983; 90m.

SURVIVOR ★★
DIR: Michael Shackleton. **CAST:** Chris Mayer, Richard Moll, Sue Kiel, Richard Haines.

While on a space mission, an astronaut witnesses a full-scale nuclear war. Upon return to Earth he finds total destruction. Richard Moll, of TV's *Night Court*, plays a fine villain in this otherwise routine and violent science-fiction story. 1987; 92m.

SWORD AND THE SORCERER, THE ★★
DIR: Albert Pyun. **CAST:** Lee Horsley, Kathleen Beller, Simon MacCorkindale, George Maharis, Richard Lynch, Richard Moll.

But for the derring-do and bits of comedy provided by star Lee Horsley, this film would be a complete waste of time and talent. A soldier of fortune (Horsley) rescues a damsel in distress (Kathleen Beller) and her brother (Simon MacCorkindale) from an evil king and his powerful wizard. Rated R because of nudity, violence, gore, and sexual references. 1982; 100m.

TENTH VICTIM, THE ★★★½
DIR: Elio Petri. **CAST:** Marcello Mastroianni, Ursula Andress, Elsa Martinelli, Massimo Serato.

A weird little science-fiction film that has achieved minor cult status, thanks to droll performances from Marcello Mastroianni and Ursula Andress and an intriguing plot taken from the novel by Robert Sheckley. The setting is the near future, and pop culture has embraced an assassination game that is played for keeps: ten participants start the hunt against one another, and the sequential elimination of opponents results in one winner. Unrated, contains sexual situations. 1965; 92m.

TERMINAL ENTRY ★★
DIR: John Kincade. **CAST:** Edward Albert, Paul Smith, Yaphet Kotto, Patrick Laborteaux.

This *War Games* clone is only moderately entertaining. Three teenage couples tap into a computer game called Terminal Entry. It turns out that the game is real and they're caught in the middle of a U.S. antiterrorist strike force and foreign invaders. Edward Albert plays a macho U.S. captain. Rated R for nudity and violence. 1986; 95m.

TERMINATOR, THE ★★★½
DIR: James Cameron. **CAST:** Arnold Schwarzenegger, Linda Hamilton, Michael Biehn.

In this science-fiction/time-travel adventure, Arnold Schwarzenegger stars as a cyborg (part man, part machine) sent from the future to present-day Los Angeles to murder a woman (Linda Hamilton). Her offspring will play an important part in the world from which the killer came. Michael Biehn is the rebel soldier sent to thwart Schwarzenegger's plans. Rated R for nudity, simulated sex, violence, and profanity. 1984; 108m.

TERROR VISION ★★★
DIR: Ted Nicolaou. **CAST:** Diane Franklin, Gerrit Graham, Mary Woronov, Chad Allen.

An imaginative spoof of sci-fi films, with a hip slant. A family of swinging yuppies accidentally beam down a hostile alien through their satellite dish. The film carries on from there in black-comedic fashion. Horror fans will be delighted. Rated R for violence and adult situations. 1986; 84m.

TERRORNAUTS, THE ★★
DIR: Montgomery Tully. **CAST:** Simon Oates, Zena Marshall, Charles Hawtrey, Max Adrian.

A British scientist succeeds in contacting an alien civilization. They beam the entire building in which he works to their galaxy. British science fiction tends to be talky, and this is no exception. 1967; 75m.

TESTAMENT ★★★★★
DIR: Lynne Littman. **CAST:** Jane Alexander, William Devane, Ross Harris, Roxana Zal, Lukas Haas, Lila Kedrova, Leon Ames.

In its own quiet, unspectacular way, this film tells a simple story about what happens to one family when World War III begins and ends in a matter of minutes. Jane Alexander is superb as the mother attempting to cope with the unthinkable, and this fine movie is one you won't soon forget. Rated PG. 1983; 90m.

THEM! ★★★★
DIR: Gordon Douglas. **CAST:** Edmund Gwenn, James Arness, James Whitmore, Fess Parker.
Classic 1950s sci-fi about colossal mutant ants, at large in a New Mexico desert, threatening to take over the world. Frightening special effects and lightning pace make this a supercharged entertainment, with Edmund Gwenn delivering a standout performance as the scientist who foretells the danger. Great. 1954; B&W; 94m.

THEY CAME FROM BEYOND SPACE ★★★
DIR: Freddie Francis. **CAST:** Robert Hutton, Jennifer Jayne, Zia Mohyeddin, Bernard Kay, Michael Gough.
Enjoyable tale of formless aliens landing in Cornwall and taking over the minds and bodies of a group of scientists in an effort to preserve their dissipating race. Robert Hutton plays the one man who can't be controlled because of a metal plate in his skull. Based on *The Gods Hate Kansas* by Joseph Millard. 1967; 86m.

THIEF OF BAGDAD, THE (1924) ★★★½
DIR: Raoul Walsh. **CAST:** Douglas Fairbanks Sr., Julanne Johnson, Anna May Wong, Sojin.
The first of four spectacular versions of this classic Arabian Nights–ish fantasy adventure of derring-do with magically flying carpets, giant genies, and crafty evil sorcery. The now fabled Douglas Fairbanks Sr. is the thief, Julanne Johnson the beautiful princess he carries away on an airborne rug. Of all silent epics, this one is rated the most imaginative. The sets rival everything filmed before and since. Silent. 1924; B&W; 140m.

THIEF OF BAGDAD, THE (1940) ★★★★★
DIR: Ludwig Berger, Tim Whelan, Michael Powell. **CAST:** Sabu, John Justin, June Duprez, Rex Ingram.
With its flying carpets, giant genies, magic spells, and evil wizards, *Thief of Bagdad* ranks as one of the finest fantasy films of all time. John Justin plays a young king, Ahmad, who is duped by his Grand Vizier, Jaffar, and loses his throne. With the aid of a colossal genie (excellently played by Rex Ingram) and other magical devices, Ahmad must do battle with Jaffar in a rousing fairy tale of good versus evil. 1940; 106m.

THING (FROM ANOTHER WORLD), THE (1951) ★★★★★
DIR: Christian Nyby (Howard Hawks). **CAST:** Kenneth Tobey, Margaret Sheridan, James Arness.
A highly entertaining film, this was based on John W. Campbell's story "Who Goes There?" about a hostile visitor from space at large at an army radar station in the Arctic. Considered by many to be a classic, this relies on the unseen rather than the seen for its power, and as such it is almost unbearably suspenseful. Tight direction, deliberate pacing—not to mention exceptional performances by the entire cast—make this a viewing must. James Arness, in an early role, plays the monster. 1951; B&W; 87m.

THING, THE (1982) ★★★★
DIR: John Carpenter. **CAST:** Kurt Russell, Wilford Brimley, Richard Dysart.
The modern master of fright, John Carpenter, has created a movie so terrifying, it'll crawl right up your leg. Rather than a remake, this updated version of Howard Hawks's 1951 science-fiction–horror classic is closer to a sequel, with Kurt Russell and his crew arriving at the Antarctic encampment after the chameleonlike creature from outer space has finished off its inhabitants. It's good ol' "tell me a scary story" fun. Rated R for profanity and gore. 1982; 108m.

THINGS TO COME ★★★★
DIR: William Cameron Menzies. **CAST:** Raymond Massey, Cedric Hardwicke, Ralph Richardson.

The world of the future as viewed from the perspective of the 1930s, this is an interesting screen curio based on the book by H. G. Wells. Special effects have come a long way since then, but sci-fi fans will still enjoy the spectacular sets in this honorable, thoughtful production. 1936; B&W; 92m.

THIS ISLAND EARTH ★★★
DIR: Joseph M. Newman. **CAST:** Jeff Morrow, Rex Reason, Faith Domergue.

A fine 1950s sci-fi flick about scientists kidnapped by aliens to help them save their planet, this has good make-up and effects for the era. 1955; 86m.

THREE WORLDS OF GULLIVER, THE ★★★
DIR: Jack Sher. **CAST:** Kerwin Mathews, June Thorburn, Jo Morrow, Gregoire Aslan.

Following a violent storm at sea, Dr. Lemuel Gulliver (Kerwin Mathews) finds himself ashore on Lilliput, an island with miniature people. Disguised as a family adventure, this film is actually more of a biting satire on human nature than anything else, featuring seamless special effects by Ray Harryhausen and an ear-filling Bernard Herrmann score. Based on the classic by Jonathan Swift. Great fun. 1960; 100m.

THRESHOLD ★★
DIR: Richard Pearce. **CAST:** Donald Sutherland, John Marley, Jeff Goldblum, Michael Lerner.

Donald Sutherland stars in this film about the first artificial-heart transplant. Made before Barney Clark was the first recipient of such an organ, this Canadian film went from science-fiction to real-life drama during the period when it was being prepared for release. Rated PG. 1981; 106m.

THX 1138 ★★★½
DIR: George Lucas. **CAST:** Robert Duvall, Donald Pleasence, Maggie McOmie.

Science-fiction and movie buffs may want to rent this moody, atmospheric picture, starring Robert Duvall and Donald Pleasence, to see an example of the type of work director George Lucas was doing pre–*Star Wars*. It was the fabulously successful filmmaker's first. Interesting. Rated PG. 1971; 88m.

TIME AFTER TIME ★★★★
DIR: Nicholas Meyer. **CAST:** Malcolm McDowell, David Warner, Mary Steenburgen.

H. G. Wells (Malcolm McDowell) pursues Jack the Ripper (David Warner) into modern-day San Francisco via a time machine. It's an enjoyable pastiche that has quite a few nice moments. Rated PG. 1979; 112m.

TIME BANDITS ★★★★
DIR: Terry Gilliam. **CAST:** Sean Connery, Shelley Duvall, Ralph Richardson, Ian Holm, David Warner, John Cleese, Michael Palin.

Anyone with a sense of adventure will find a lot to like about this delightful tale of a boy and six dwarves—no, this isn't *Snow White*—who travel back in time via a map that charts a course through holes in the fabric of the universe. Rated PG for violence and adult themes. 1981; 110m.

TIME MACHINE, THE ★★★★
DIR: George Pal. **CAST:** Rod Taylor, Yvette Mimieux, Alan Young, Sebastian Cabot.

Rod Taylor plays a scientist in the early 1900s who invents a device that can transport him within the dimensions of time. He goes forward past three world wars and into the year 802,701, where he encounters a world very different from the one he left. This movie has all the elements that make up a classic in science-fiction. 1960; 103m.

TIME TRAVELERS, THE ★★★½
DIR: Ib Melchior. **CAST:** Preston Foster, Philip Carey, Merry Anders, Steve Franken, John Hoyt, Joan Woodbury.

Imaginative story of scientists who plunge into a time corridor to rescue a colleague and find themselves stuck in the wreckage of the Earth of the future. Similar in many respects to other survival-after-nuclear-holocaust films, this entertaining film boasts vicious mutants, intelligent survivors who live under the surface of Earth, and a trick ending that is unique and intriguing. 1964; 82m.

TIME WARP 🦃
DIR: David L. Hewitt. **CAST:** Scott Brady, Anthony Eisley, Gigi Perreau, Abraham Sofaer.

Absolutely awful low-budget film about a scientist engaged in time-travel research. Probably had his 5-year-old do the special effects. Not rated; so bland it contains nothing offensive at all. 1967; 86m.

TRANCERS ★
DIR: Charles Band. **CAST:** Tim Thomerson, Helen Hunt, Michael Stefani, Art Le Fleur, Telma Hopkins, Richard Herd, Anne Seymour.

Reprehensible rip-off of *Blade Runner* and *The Terminator* with none of the style or suspense of either. Tim Thomerson is Jack Death, a police officer in the 2280s who is sent into the past to bring back a violent cult leader who escaped into the twentieth century to cut off the bloodlines of his twenty-third-century leaders. Rated PG-13 for profanity and lots of violence. 1985; 76m.

TRANSATLANTIC TUNNEL ★★½
DIR: Maurice Elvey. **CAST:** Richard Dix, Leslie Banks, Madge Evans, C. Aubrey Smith, George Arliss, Walter Huston, Helen Vinson.

A truly splendid cast still manages to get bogged down a bit in this heavy-handed account of the building of a passageway under the Atlantic Ocean. Richard Dix plays the stalwart engineer who can get the job done and Walter Huston plays the president of the United States. 1935; B&W; 90m.

TRIPODS ★★½
DIR: Graham Theakston, Christopher Barry. **CAST:** John Shackley, Jim Baker, Ceri Seel, Richard Wordsworth.

Though a bit hard to follow because it is a compilation of episodes from the middle of a BBC science-fiction TV series, *Tripods* is an interesting release about a young man's attempts to escape programming by alien conquerors of Earth in the far future. Once free, our hero decides to join the rebel forces and fight to free the Earth. 1984; 150m.

TROLL 🦃
DIR: John Buechler. **CAST:** Noah Hathaway, Michael Moriarty, Shelley Hack, Jenny Beck, June Lockhart, Anne Lockhart, Sonny Bono, Brad Hall.

Michael Moriarty, who deserves better, plays the head of a family besieged by evil little creatures in this horrendous horror/fantasy film. Rated PG-13 for profanity, violence, and gore. 1986; 95m.

TRON ★★★
DIR: Steven Lisberger. **CAST:** Jeff Bridges, David Warner, Bruce Boxleitner, Cindy Morgan, Barnard Hughes.

An enjoyable, if somewhat light-headed, piece of escapism, this science-fiction adventure concerns a computer genius (Jeff Bridges) who suspects evil doings by a corporate executive (David Warner). During his investigation, Bridges is zapped into another dimension and finds himself a player in a gladiatorial video game. Rated PG. 1982; 96m.

TV'S BEST ADVENTURES OF SUPERMAN ★★★½
DIR: Thomas Carr, George Reeves, Harry Gerstad, Dave Fleischer. **CAST:** George Reeves, Noel Neill, Phyllis Coates, Jack Larson, John Hamilton.

Excellent series of tapes combines two episodes of the TV series from the 1950s, one color and one black and white, with a Superman cartoon from the Max Fleischer Studios. This series is highly collectible for fans. In general, the black-and-white episodes of the TV series were the best, but you'll be surprised at how entertaining they all are. George Reeves makes a fine Superman–Clark Kent, and Phyllis Coates and Noel Neill do fine jobs in their particular series as Lois Lane. 1950; B&W/color; 60 minutes each.

2001: A SPACE ODYSSEY ★★★★★

DIR: Stanley Kubrick. **CAST:** Keir Dullea, William Sylvester, Gary Lockwood.

There's no denying the visual magnificence of this highly overrated science-fiction epic. Ponderous, ambiguous, and arty, it's nevertheless considered a classic of the genre by many film buffs. The set design, costumes, cinematography, and Oscar-winning special effects combine to create unforgettable imagery. Rated G. 1968; 139m.

2010 ★★★★

DIR: Peter Hyams. **CAST:** Roy Scheider, John Lithgow, Helen Mirren, Bob Balaban, Keir Dullea.

The exciting sequel stars Roy Scheider, John Lithgow, Helen Mirren and Bob Balaban as participants in a joint American-Russian space mission. We finally find out what really happened to astronaut Dave Bowman (Keir Dullea); the computer, HAL 9000; and the spaceship, *Discovery*, near the planet Jupiter. Rated PG. 1984; 116m.

TWO WORLDS OF JENNIE LOGAN, THE

DIR: Frank DeFelitta. **CAST:** Lindsay Wagner, Marc Singer, Linda Gray, Alan Feinstein, Irene Tedrow, Henry Wilcoxon.

A young woman in a troubled marriage finds an old dress in her new house. When she dons this aged garment, she is magically transported one hundred years into the past. Made for TV, this standard prime-time soap opera has some moments for romance fans, but the rest of us will be bored. 1979; 99m.

UFO—VOLUMES I AND II ★★½

DIR: David Lane, Ken Turner. **CAST:** Ed Bishop, George Sewell, Michael Billington, Jean Marsh.

Four episodes of the sci-fi soap opera from England concerning SHADO, an organization set up to protect Earth from invading aliens. The first, "Exposed," has the top fighter pilot at SHADO convinced his craft was destroyed by a UFO, while the government tries to argue him out of it. In the second installment, the Earth is threatened by lethal flying saucers. "Conflict" has Earth ships being sabotaged by aliens. "A Dalotek Affair" deals with a mysterious communications lapse between SHADO-Earth and its moon colony. The stories are not as good as *Star Trek*, but SF buffs may want to see more. 1979; 102m.

ULTIMATE WARRIOR, THE ★★½

DIR: Robert Clouse. **CAST:** Yul Brynner, Max von Sydow, Joanna Miles, William Smith, Stephen McHattie.

The payoff doesn't match the promise of the premise in this less-than-thrilling science-fiction thriller. In the not-so-distant future, ragged residents of devastated New York City battle vicious gangs. Initially intriguing, the film stumbles to a ludicrous conclusion. Rated R. 1975; 94m.

UNDERSEA KINGDOM ★★½

DIR: B. Reeves "Breezy" Eason, Joseph Kane. **CAST:** Ray "Crash" Corrigan, Lois Wilde, Monte Blue, William Farnum, Lee Van Atta, Smiley Burnette, Lon Chaney Jr.

"Crash" Corrigan plays himself in this science-fiction serial of the 1930s as he attempts to thwart the evil plans of Sharad and his followers, who live under the ocean in the ancient city of Atlantis. Filled with gadgetry, robots, and futuristic machines, this cliffhanger was extremely popular with young audiences, and it's still a lot of fun today. 1936; B&W; 12 chapters.

UNKNOWN WORLD ★½

DIR: Terrel O. Morse. **CAST:** Victor Kilian, Bruce Kellogg, Marilyn Nash.

Low-budget science-fiction story about an inventor who builds a drill capable of exploring inner Earth seems to borrow from Edgar Rice Burroughs's *Pellucidar* series, but it is actually closer to the nuclear-holocaust films of the postwar period. Short on thrills, this effort uses extensive footage of Carlsbad Caverns to simulate the interior of our planet. 1950; B&W; 74m.

VIBES ★★
DIR: Ken Kwapis. **CAST:** Cyndi Lauper, Jeff Goldblum, Julian Sands, Peter Falk.

This sad misfire should have been much better, given the track record of scripters Lowell Ganz and Babaloo Mandel, but the talented parts simply don't make an impressive whole. Cyndi Lauper and Jeff Goldblum play psychic hotshots hired by shifty Peter Falk to find one of those Lost Temples Containing Forbidden Powers, but everything plods along to a foolish finale. Rated PG. 1988; 99m.

VINDICATOR ★½
DIR: Jean Claude Lord. **CAST:** Teri Austin, Richard Cox, Pam Grier, Maury Chaykin.

A comic-bookish story about a scientist who is blown up by his evil employers and put back together using Cybornetic systems and a nearly indestructible futuristic space suit. Overall, it's a pretty typical story with some thrills and a fair amount of action and graphic violence. Rated R for violence, adult language, and brief nudity. 1984; 92m.

VISITANTS, THE
DIR: Rick Sloane. **CAST:** Marcus Vaughter, Johanna Grika, Nicole Rio.

Annoying sci-fi flick complete with stupid humor and rotten directing. Two aliens move into a house in an American suburb, but the next-door kid (Marcus Vaughter) gets wise. Not rated. 1987; 93m.

VISITOR, THE ★★
DIR: Michael J. Paradise. **CAST:** Mel Ferrer, John Huston, Glenn Ford, Shelley Winters.

An 8-year-old girl, gifted with incredible powers, uses her abilities maliciously. As she formulates a plan that could lead the world toward destruction, an ancient alien mystic comes to Earth to stop her evil scheme. Great premise, flawed execution. Rated R for violence. 1979; 96m.

VOYAGE TO THE BOTTOM OF THE SEA ★★★
DIR: Irwin Allen. **CAST:** Walter Pidgeon, Joan Fontaine, Robert Sterling, Barbara Eden, Michael Ansara, Peter Lorre, Frankie Avalon, Henry Daniell.

An atomic submarine rushes to save Earth from destruction by a burning radiation belt. Intrigue, adventure, and hokey fun, with a low-level all-star cast. Much better than the subsequent television show. Unrated, the film has mild violence. 1961; 105m.

WAR OF THE WORLDS, THE ★★★★
DIR: Byron Haskin. **CAST:** Gene Barry, Les Tremayne, Ann Robinson.

This science-fiction film stars Gene Barry as a scientist who is among the first Earthlings to witness the Martian invasion of Earth. The film is an updated version of H. G. Wells's classic story, with the action heightened by excellent special effects. 1953; 85m.

WARGAMES ★★★★½
DIR: John Badham. **CAST:** Matthew Broderick, Dabney Coleman, Ally Sheedy, John Wood, Barry Corbin.

A young computer whiz (Matthew Broderick) who thinks he's hooking into a game manufacturer's computer to get the scoop on its latest line accidentally starts World War III when he decides to "play" a selection titled "Global Thermonuclear Warfare." Though the movie contains almost no violence or any other sensationalistic content (apart from a wee bit of vulgar language), it still grips the viewer. Rated PG. 1983; 114m.

WARLORDS OF THE 21ST CENTURY ★
DIR: Harley Cokliss. **CAST:** James Wainwright, Annie McEnroe, Michael Beck.
A cold-blooded killer leads his band of roving outlaws in a siege against a peaceful community, only to face his comeuppance by an equally cold-blooded mystery man. A predictable, uninspired film that has all the earmarks of a good old-fashioned shoot-'em-up without the action to back it up. Rated R for violence. 1982; 91m.

WARRIOR AND THE SORCERESS, THE 🦃
DIR: John Broderick. **CAST:** David Carradine, Luke Askew, Maria Socas.
Why does David Carradine do films like this? In this sword-and-sorcery version of *A Fistful of Dollars*, two warring houses on opposite sides of a well in the middle of a desert both seek to control the well and destroy the other house. Carradine plays a "Dark Warrior" who arrives and pits the houses against each other while getting paid for it. Rated R for gore and nudity. 1984; 81m.

WARRIORS OF THE APOCALYPSE ★½
DIR: Bobby A. Suarez. **CAST:** Michael James, Deborah Moore.
Another low-rent postapocalyptic adventure, this one set fifty years after war has killed most of the Earth's population. A band of nomads search for a mountain that is said to hold the secret of survival. When they arrive there, they discover a jungle civilization of women and male slaves. Rent *The Road Warrior* instead, even if you've already seen it. Rated R for violence and brief nudity. 1985; 96m.

WARRIORS OF THE WASTELAND ★
DIR: Enzo G. Castellari. **CAST:** Fred Williamson, Timothy Brent, George Eastman, Anna Kanakis, Thomas Moore.
Cheap Italian copy of *Road Warrior*, with a small group of nuclear-holocaust survivors battling the evil Templars. The most interesting thing about this film is to see how bad the dubbing can get. Not rated; contains violence and slight nudity. 1983; 92m.

WARRIORS OF THE WIND ★★★★
DIR: Tokuma Shoten Pub. Co. Ltd. **CAST:** Animated.
This movie-length Japanese animated feature easily ranks with the best of American animated films. The characters are believable, the action is convincing, and the plot delivers the positive message that not everything good is beautiful and that ugliness, like true beauty, may take more than looking to be seen. Definitely not for the kiddies only. 1984; 95m.

WATCHERS ★★★½
DIR: Jon Hess. **CAST:** Corey Haim, Barbara Williams, Michael Ironside.
Based on the award-winning science-fiction novel by Dean R. Koontz, *Watchers* is a refreshing sci-fi/horror film. About a boy (Corey Haim) who finds a superintelligent dog and becomes the target of a scientifically created monster, it plays fair with the viewer throughout. Director Jon Hess even leaves quite a bit to the imagination, building the kind of suspense so seldom seen in this age of gore-infested hack-'em-ups. Rated R for violence and profanity. 1988; 91m.

WATERSHIP DOWN ★★★★
DIR: Martin Rosen. **CAST:** Animated.
Although it's a full-length cartoon about the adventures of a group of rabbits, you'll find no cutesy, Disney-styled Thumpers à la *Bambi*. About the odyssey that a small group of rabbits undertakes after one of them has a vision of evil things coming to destroy their homes. Their arduous journey is full of surprises and rewards. Rated PG. 1978; 92m.

WAVELENGTH ★★★★

DIR: Mike Gray. **CAST:** Robert Carradine, Cherie Currie, Keenan Wynn.

You've seen it all many times before in science-fiction movies of wide-ranging quality: the innocent visitors from outer space, the callous government officials who see them as guinea pigs instead of guests, the handful of compassionate Earthlings, even the race to the mother ship. But rarely has the plot been used so effectively. Rated PG. 1983; 87m.

WESTWORLD ★★★★

DIR: Michael Crichton. **CAST:** Yul Brynner, Richard Benjamin, James Brolin.

This is another science-fiction yarn from the author (Michael Crichton) of *The Andromeda Strain.* The film concerns an expensive world for well-to-do vacationers. They can live out their fantasies in the Old West or King Arthur's Court with the aid of programmed robots repaired nightly by scientists so they can be "killed" the next day by tourists. Richard Benjamin and James Brolin are tourists who come up against a rebellious robot (Yul Brynner). Rated PG. 1973; 88m.

WHEN THE WIND BLOWS ★★★

DIR: Jimmy T. Murakami. **CAST:** Animated.

Ironic full-length British cartoon that chronicles the preparations of a retired English couple for the coming nuclear holocaust. Living in the countryside, all the old people have to go on is faint (and sometimes fond) memories of World War II and a government handbook. Their ignorance of the facts and innocent faith in the "powers that be" make *When the Wind Blows* a touching and moving statement about the nuclear Armageddon. 1988; 80m.

WHEN WORLDS COLLIDE ★★

DIR: Rudolph Maté. **CAST:** Richard Derr, Barbara Rush, Peter Hanson, Larry Keating, John Hoyt.

Interesting end-of-the-world sci-fi fable from George Pal has dated badly since its original release in 1951. Final scene of Earth pilgrims landing on the planet and walking into an obvious superimposed painting is laughable today, but many of the other Oscar-winning effects are still quite convincing. 1951; 81m.

WHERE THE RIVER RUNS BLACK ★★★½

DIR: Christopher Cain. **CAST:** Charles Durning, Peter Horton, Ajay Naidu, Conchata Ferrell.

About a primitive child who is snatched from his home in the Amazon rain forest and brought into the modern world of corruption and violence, this fantasy unfolds like a dream. Sumptuous images, courtesy of Juan Ruiz-Anchia's superb cinematography, fill the screen as its eerie, fanciful, and finally suspenseful tale is told. Rated PG for violence and suggested sex. 1986; 105m.

WILD IN THE STREETS ★★

DIR: Barry Shear. **CAST:** Christopher Jones, Shelley Winters, Hal Holbrook, Diane Varsi, Ed Begley Jr., Millie Perkins, Richard Pryor, Bert Freed.

Ridiculous what-if? film about future America when youth runs the show, the voting age is lowered to 14, and a rock singer involved in drug selling sits as president in the White House. This dated daydream of the 1960s was considered lame at the time of its release, but has gathered a following over the years. Rated PG. 1968; 97m.

WILD WOMEN OF WONGO

DIR: James L. Wolcott. **CAST:** Jean Hawkshaw, Johnny Walsh, Ed Fury, Pat Crowley.

Wongo's women aren't any wilder than the moron who gave this project the go-ahead and supplied color film and the few thousand dollars it took to make it. This early sex-exploitation adventure pits two primitive tribes against each other with a new twist—one tribe boasts buxom beauties like Pat Crowley, while the rival cave dwellers have the likes of muscle man

Ed Fury. Just about as silly as they come. 1958; 72m.

WILLOW ★★★
DIR: Ron Howard. **CAST:** Val Kilmer, Joanne Whalley, Jean Marsh, Warwick Davis, Patricia Hayes, Billy Barty.

A formulaic but entertaining fantasy epic, this focuses on the quest of an apprentice sorcerer, Willow (Warwick Davis), to keep a magicial child safe from the minions of the wicked queen (Jean Marsh) she is destined to destroy. The first half tends to drag as the characters and situations are somewhat laboriously introduced. However, things pick up midway. Rated PG for violence. 1988; 120m.

WIRED TO KILL ★
DIR: Franky Schaeffer. **CAST:** Emily Longstreth, Deven Holescher, Merritt Buttrick.

The year is 1998, and 120 million Americans are dead from a killer plague. The country has been split into quarantine areas, where the survivors are victimized by violent street gangs of demented, drug-crazed youth. There are far too many plot flaws and inconsistencies in this film to make it believable. Rated R for violence and raw language. 1986; 90m.

WITHOUT WARNING (turkey)
DIR: Greydon Clark. **CAST:** Jack Palance, Martin Landau, Cameron Mitchell, Larry Storch, Sue Ane Langdon.

A cast of Hollywood veterans battle with an intergalactic alien hunter (a rubber-faced leftover from the *Outer Limits* television series) and his hungry pets in this awful low-budget science-fiction effort. Guess who ends up as lunch. Moreover, who cares? Rated R. 1980; 89m.

WIZARD OF MARS, THE ★½
DIR: David Hewitt. **CAST:** John Carradine, Vic McGee, Roger Gentry.

Low-budget interplanetary version of *The Wizard of Oz* finds a rocketship full of earthlings on the planet Mars where magic and fantasy are the prevalent forces. Written, directed, and produced by David Hewitt, with technical assistance from famed science-fiction-fantasy expert Forrest J. Ackerman, this doesn't really compare to major science-fiction or fantasy films. 1964; 81m.

WIZARD OF THE LOST KINGDOM (turkey)
DIR: Hector Olivera. **CAST:** Bo Svenson, Vidal Peterson, Thom Christopher.

Abysmal fantasy film stars a woefully miscast Bo Svenson as a master swordsman who comes to the aid of a sorceror's son. Cheesy cinematography and amateurish editing mix with bad acting and inept direction. Rated PG for violence. 1985; 76m.

WIZARDS ★★★
DIR: Ralph Bakshi. **CAST:** Animated.

Director-animator Ralph Bakshi's cost-cutting corners, which had not been that evident in his *Fritz the Cat* films, become a bit too noticeable in this charming little tale of ultimate good versus ultimate evil. Our hero is an aged wizard who relies on magic for his good-deed doing; his evil doppelgänger resorts to the horrors of technology in a battle to wrest control of the universe. The conflict builds well until its climax, which (sadly) negates the premise of the entire battle. Rated PG for occasionally graphic violence. 1977; 81m.

WOMEN OF THE PREHISTORIC PLANET ★
DIR: Arthur C. Pierce. **CAST:** Wendell Cory, John Agar, Keith Larsen, Merry Anders, Paul Gilbert, Adam Roarke, Stuart Margolin, Gavin MacLeod, Lyle Waggoner.

Not only is this outer space saga incredibly cheap, it's also misleadingly titled. There is only one woman, and she's not from the prehistoric planet. Astronauts looking for survivors of a crash battle monsters (lizards made to look huge with bad trick photography) and other perils. Worth watching only to spot the future TV stars in bit parts. 1966; 92m.

WORLD GONE WILD ♥
DIR: Lee H. Katzin. **CAST:** Bruce Dern, Michael Paré, Catherine Mary Stewart, Adam Ant.

On Earth after the nuclear holocaust, a group of flower children, led by a mushroom-eating guru (Bruce Dern), live a carefree life in Lost Wells, a desert oasis where water is plentiful. Everywhere else, water is more precious than gold, as it has not rained for fifty years. This stupefyingly awful film turns out to be a retread of *The Seven Samurai/The Magnificent Seven.* Rated R for violence, profanity, and nudity. 1988; 84m.

X (THE MAN WITH THE X-RAY EYES) ★★★
DIR: Roger Corman. **CAST:** Ray Milland, Diana Van Der Vlis, Harold J. Stone, John Hoyt, Don Rickles.

Intriguing, offbeat tale of a scientist (Ray Milland) who discovers a drug that gives him the power to see through objects. He has a great time at first, but soon becomes addicted and begins seeing more and more, until.... This production is highly enjoyable, with a surprisingly effective role by comedian Don Rickles as a carnival barker. 1963; 80m.

YESTERDAY MACHINE, THE ♥
DIR: Russ Marker. **CAST:** Tim Holt, Jack Herman.

Cheap sci-fi about a mad Nazi scientist who has invented a time machine that can move people to the past and the future. His goal: to revive Hitler. Featuring what must be the longest, dullest pseudoscientific explanation ever filmed, as scientist Jack Herman explains the physics of time travel to cop Tim Holt. 1962; 85m.

YOR: THE HUNTER FROM THE FUTURE ♥
DIR: Anthony M. Dawson. **CAST:** Reb Brown, Corinne Clery, John Steiner, Carole André, Alan Collins.

In the glorious tradition of *Plan 9 from Outer Space* and *Robot Monster* comes *Yor, the Hunter from the Future*, a movie so incredibly awful that it's hilarious. A mighty warrior (Reb Brown) attempts to discover his true identity on a planet trapped in a time warp where the past and the future collide. You'll guffaw at the unbelievable situations. You'll groan out loud at the insipid dialogue. In other words, it's a real hoot. Rated PG for violence and profanity. 1983; 88m.

ZARDOZ ♥
DIR: John Boorman. **CAST:** Sean Connery, Charlotte Rampling.

Sorry sci-fi about a strange society of the future and Sean Connery's attempts to free the people from the evil rulers. Murky plot is hard to follow, and the viewer soon loses interest. Good photography is all but lost on the home screen, leaving nothing but Connery running around in a diaper for two hours. Rated R. 1974; 105m.

ZONE TROOPERS ★
DIR: Danny Bilson. **CAST:** Tim Thomerson, Timothy Van Patten.

This is a dumb comic-book tale about an American troop in World War II lost behind German lines. Eventually, soldiers encounter space aliens who have crash-landed in the woods. Rated PG for mild violence. 1985; 86m.

WESTERNS

ABILENE TOWN ★★★
DIR: Edwin L. Marin. **CAST:** Randolph Scott, Ann Dvorak, Rhonda Fleming, Lloyd Bridges, Edgar Buchanan.
Cattlemen and homesteaders are at loggerheads in the 1870s in this fast-paced shoot-'em-up. Randolph Scott is the trusty tall man with the star who tries to sort it all out. Edgar Buchanan is sly, as always. 1946; B&W; 89m.

ACE HIGH ★
DIR: Giuseppe Colizzi. **CAST:** Eli Wallach, Brock Peters, Terence Hill, Kevin McCarthy, Bud Spencer.
In this violent spaghetti Western written and directed by Giuseppe Colizzi, a condemned outlaw is offered a chance to save himself from the hangman's noose. Having just completed the entertaining *The Good, The Bad, and The Ugly,* Eli Wallach is wasted in this quasi–Sergio Leone clone. There is some humor, but the dialogue and dubbing are simply terrible. 1969; 123m.

ACES AND EIGHTS ★★½
DIR: Sam Newfield. **CAST:** Tim McCoy, Luana Walters.
Although lacking in action, this Tim McCoy Western nevertheless has its moments. McCoy plays an infamous gambler who comes to the aid of a young Mexican unfairly accused of murder. 1936; B&W; 62m.

AGAINST A CROOKED SKY ★★
DIR: Earl Bellamy. **CAST:** Richard Boone, Clint Ritchie, Henry Wilcoxon, Stewart Peterson.
Nothing new in this familiar tale of a boy searching for his sister, who has been kidnapped by Indians. No more than just another inferior reworking of John Ford's classic Western *The Searchers.* For fans who watch anything with a horse and a saddle. Rated PG for violence. 1975; 89m.

ALAMO, THE ★★★½
DIR: John Wayne. **CAST:** John Wayne, Richard Widmark, Frankie Avalon, Richard Boone, Chill Wills, Laurence Harvey.
This Western, directed by and starring John Wayne, may have seemed overlong when originally released. But today it's the answer to a Duke-deprived fan's dream. Of course, there's the expected mushy flag-waving here and there. However, once Davy Crockett (Wayne), Jim Bowie (Richard Widmark), Will Travis (Laurence

Harvey), and their respective followers team up to take on Santa Ana's forces, it's a humdinger of a period war movie. 1960; 161m.

ALLEGHENY UPRISING ★★★
DIR: William A. Seiter. **CAST:** John Wayne, Claire Trevor, George Sanders, Chill Wills, Brian Donlevy.

John Wayne and Claire Trevor were reteamed the same year of their costarring triumph in 1939's *Stagecoach* for this potboiler set in the pre-Revolutionary American colonies, but the results were hardly as auspicious. Still, it's a decent time-passer and features Brian Donlevy in one of his better villain roles. 1939; B&W; 81m.

ALONG CAME JONES ★★★★
DIR: Stuart Heisler. **CAST:** Gary Cooper, Loretta Young, Dan Duryea.

Highly watchable comic Western with Gary Cooper as an innocent cowboy who's mistaken for an infamous outlaw. Both lawmen and the real outlaw (Dan Duryea) pursue him. 1945; B&W; 90m.

ALONG THE GREAT DIVIDE ★★½
DIR: Raoul Walsh. **CAST:** Kirk Douglas, John Agar, Walter Brennan, Virginia Mayo.

With his usual determination and grit, lawman Kirk Douglas fights a sandstorm to capture an escaped criminal and return him to justice. The pace is slow, but the scenery is grand. 1951; B&W; 88m.

ALVAREZ KELLY ★★
DIR: Edward Dmytryk. **CAST:** William Holden, Richard Widmark, Janice Rule, Patrick O'Neal, Victoria Shaw.

Edward Dymtryk unimaginatively directed this plodding Western starring William Holden as a cattle driver supplying beef to the Yankees. He is kidnapped by Confederate officer Richard Widmark, who wants him to steal that much-needed food supply for the South. Dull. 1966; 116m.

AMBUSH VALLEY ★½
DIR: Raymond Samuels. **CAST:** Bob Custer, John Elliott.

Paradise Valley is turned into Ambush Valley when a rancher's son murders a nester's son. It's up to Marshal Bob Custer to restore peace and prevent a range war. Routine. 1936; B&W; 57m.

AMERICAN EMPIRE ★★★
DIR: William McGann. **CAST:** Richard Dix, Frances Gifford, Preston Foster, Leo Carrillo, Guinn Williams.

A formula film featuring the now standard grand opening, dramatic problem-posing center, and slam-bang breathtaking climax, but a good, entertaining Western nonetheless. Friends and Civil War veterans Richard Dix and Preston Foster team to found a cattle empire in Texas. Villain Leo Carrillo makes most of the trouble the pair encounter. Fans of the genre will love it. 1942; B&W; 82m.

AMERICANO, THE ★★½
DIR: William Castle. **CAST:** Glenn Ford, Cesar Romero, Frank Lovejoy, Abbe Lane.

Texas cowboy Glenn Ford gets embroiled with a bunch of Brazilian bad guys in this way-south-of-the-border Western. A change of scenery is commendable, but a familiar plot makes this film all but pedestrian. 1954; 85m.

ANGEL AND THE BADMAN ★★★★
DIR: James Edward Grant. **CAST:** John Wayne, Gail Russell, Harry Carey, Irene Rich, Bruce Cabot.

A fine low-budget Western with John Wayne as a gunman who sees the light through the love of Quaker girl Gail Russell. Harry Carey and Bruce Cabot also are memorable in this thoughtful action film directed by longtime Wayne screenwriter James Edward Grant. 1947; B&W; 100m.

ANOTHER MAN, ANOTHER CHANCE ★★
DIR: Claude Lelouch. **CAST:** James Caan, Genevieve Bujold, Francis Huster, Jennifer Warren, Susan Tyrrell.
In 1977, director Claude Lelouch, inexplicably, decided to remake his charming film *A Man and a Woman* and set it in the American West of the late 1800s. Widow Genevieve Bujold and widower James Caan fall in love. The whole movie seems to have been shot in slow motion. It's light on romance and heavy on tedium. 1977; 128m.

APACHE ★★
DIR: Robert Aldrich. **CAST:** Burt Lancaster, Jean Peters, Charles Bronson, John Dehner, Monte Blue.
Moralistic message Western features a hammy Burt Lancaster as an idealistic warrior who resents yet understands the encroachment of the whites and refuses to live on government reservations. Strangely typical of early-to-mid-1950s Hollywood Westerns, this entry is long on conscience and short on action. 1954; 91m.

APACHE ROSE ★★½
DIR: William Witney. **CAST:** Roy Rogers, Dale Evans, Bob Nolan and the Sons of the Pioneers, George Meeker, Minerva Urecal, LeRoy Mason.
Roy's an oil-well engineer, Dale's the skipper of a tugboat, and the fellow that's causing all the trouble runs a gambling ship. But it's still a Western because Trigger and the Sons of the Pioneers are close at hand. This is the first of the popular series to be shot in color. Same old story in different garb, with more of a water base. 1947; 75m.

APPALOOSA, THE ★★
DIR: Sidney J. Furie. **CAST:** Marlon Brando, John Saxon, Anjanette Comer, Frank Silvera.
This slight, often boring Western follows Marlon Brando's attempts to recover an Appaloosa horse stolen by a Mexican bandit. Brando's brooding, method-acting approach to the character only makes things worse in an already slow-moving film. 1966; 98m.

ARIZONA BOUND ★★★
DIR: Spencer Gordon Bennet. **CAST:** Buck Jones, Tim McCoy, Raymond Hatton, Dennis Moore, Luana Walters, Slim Whitaker.
The first of the Rough Riders movies, this entry keeps secret the fact that Buck Roberts (Buck Jones), Tim McCall (Tim McCoy), and Sandy Hopkins (Raymond Hatton) are Texas Rangers who work together—but fans of classic Westerns will be familiar with the best cowboy-trio series of them all. In this case, they're called upon to save a stagecoach line from crooks operating in Mesa City. 1941; B&W; 57m.

ARIZONA DAYS ★★
DIR: John English. **CAST:** Tex Ritter, Eleanor Stewart, Syd Saylor, William Faversham, Snub Pollard, Forrest Taylor, Glenn Strange, William Desmond, Earl Dwire, Budd Buster.
Entertaining shoot-'em-up as somber-voiced Tex Ritter exposes the villain while shyly wooing the girl of his dreams. Ritter's films usually contained a tune or three and healthy doses of knock-down, drag-out fighting and this early entry is no exception. 1937; B&W; 57m.

ARIZONA LEGION ★★★★
DIR: David Howard. **CAST:** George O'Brien, Laraine Day, Chill Wills.
In this energetic entry in his superior Western series for RKO Pictures, George O'Brien is a Texas Ranger who goes undercover to bring a bunch of baddies to bay. Chill Wills, as his sidekick, provides comic relief that is honestly funny. Fresh and enjoyable. 1939; B&W; 58m.

AT GUNPOINT ★★★
DIR: Alfred Werker. **CAST:** Fred MacMurray, Dorothy Malone, Walter Brennan, Tommy Rettig, John Qualen, Skip Homeier.

Fred MacMurray plays a mild-mannered storekeeper who becomes a hero when he accidentally foils a bank robbery. The grateful town makes him sheriff, then turns to him when the outlaws return. The story is a clever reworking of *High Noon* to match MacMurray's unique screen personality, and the supporting cast is uniformly fine. Not rated, but may be too violent for young children. 1955; 81m.

BAD COMPANY ★★★★
DIR: Robert Benton. **CAST:** Jeff Bridges, Barry Brown, Jim Davis, David Huddleston, John Savage, Jerry Houser, Geoffrey Lewis.

This is a much underrated Civil War–era Western. The cultured Barry Brown and the street-wise Jeff Bridges team up as robbers. Charming performances by the leads and an intriguing, intelligent script by Robert Benton and David Newman make this well worth watching. Rated R. 1972; 94m.

BAD MAN'S RIVER ★★
DIR: Gene Martin. **CAST:** Lee Van Cleef, Gina Lollobrigida, James Mason.

A humorous Western about the "dreaded" King gang, which robs banks along the Texas and Mexican borders. A Mexican revolutionary offers them a million dollars to blow up the arsenal used by the Mexican army, which the gang does, only to find that they have been double-crossed. 1959; 96m.

BADMAN'S TERRITORY ★★★
DIR: Tim Whelan. **CAST:** Randolph Scott, Ann Richards, George "Gabby" Hayes, Ray Collins, Chief Thundercloud.

Staunch and true marshal combats saddle scum when they flee across the border into territory beyond the government's reach. Good watching. 1946; B&W; 97m.

BALLAD OF A GUNFIGHTER ★½
DIR: Bill Ward. **CAST:** Marty Robbins, Joyce Redd, Bob Barron, Nestor Paiva, Laurette Luez.

Marty Robbins is a rough-and-ready rebel who robs stages and gives to the poor. He ends up battling guys even worse than himself. Stilted dialogue and acting interlaced with a couple of good old songs. Unrated and inoffensive. 1964; 84m.

BALLAD OF CABLE HOGUE, THE ★★★★½
DIR: Sam Peckinpah. **CAST:** Jason Robards Jr., Stella Stevens, Strother Martin, L. Q. Jones, David Warner.

Jason Robards has one of his finest roles as Hogue, a loner who discovers water in the desert and becomes a successful entrepreneur by opening a stagecoach stopover. Director Sam Peckinpah's deft eye for period detail and outstanding acting by all involved make this one a winner. Rated R. 1970; 121m.

BALLAD OF GREGORIO CORTEZ, THE ★★★★½
DIR: Robert M. Young. **CAST:** Edward James Olmos, James Gammon, Tom Bower, Alan Vint, Timothy Scott, Barry Corbin.

This superb independent production tells the powerful story of one man's courage, pain, tragedy, and heartbreak—all of which come as the result of a simple misunderstanding. Edward James Olmos (*Miami Vice*) gives a haunting portrayal of the title character, who becomes a fugitive through no fault of his own. Rated PG for violence. 1982; 99m.

BANDITS ★
DIR: Robert Conrad, Alfredo Zacharias. **CAST:** Robert Conrad, Jan-Michael Vincent, Roy Jensen, Pedro Armendariz Jr.

A boring horse opera about three outlaws rescued from the hangman's noose. They join their savior on a mission to Mexico and get themselves into all kinds of dumb predicaments.

Not rated, but equivalent to PG-13 for violence. 1967; 89m.

BANDOLERO! ★★★

DIR: Andrew V. McLaglen. **CAST:** James Stewart, Dean Martin, Raquel Welch, Will Geer, George Kennedy, Andrew Prine.

Escape south of the border with outlaw brothers James Stewart and Dean Martin (if you can buy this), who ride just a few furlongs ahead of the law (George Kennedy), taking Raquel Welch along as hostage. 1968; 106m.

BARBAROSA ★★★★

DIR: Fred Schepisi. **CAST:** Willie Nelson, Gary Busey, Isela Vega, Gilbert Roland, Danny De La Paz, George Voskovec.

This action-packed Western stars Willie Nelson and Gary Busey as a pair of outcasts on the run. Australian director Fred Schepisi has created an exciting, funny movie that combines the scenic majesty of the great John Ford Westerns with the light touch of George Roy Hill's *Butch Cassidy and the Sundance Kid.* Rated PG for violence. 1982; 90m.

BARON OF ARIZONA, THE ★★½

DIR: Samuel Fuller. **CAST:** Vincent Price, Ellen Drew, Beulah Bondi, Vladimir Sokoloff, Reed Hadley, Robert Barrat.

Vincent Price hams it up as a smooth con man who nearly succeeds in claiming most of the Arizona territory as his own. This early directorial effort by Samuel Fuller lacks the edge he gave his best films but it's well played by a good cast. Based on a real incident. 1950; B&W; 90m.

BATTLE OF ELDERBUSH GULCH, THE/THE MUSKETEERS OF PIG ALLEY ★★★

DIR: D. W. Griffith. **CAST:** Lillian Gish, Mae Marsh, Robert Harron, Dorothy Gish, Walter Miller.

Two of pioneer director D. W. Griffith's finest early works, a gripping Western and the first important gangster film. In the first, a baby gets caught in the crossfire between greenhorn settlers who have provoked an attack by Indians. In the second, clearly an ancestor of *Little Caesar* and *The Godfather*, the wife of a struggling musician finds herself the helpless object of a gangster's attention. Silent. 1912/1914; B&W; 50m.

BELLS OF CORONADO ★★½

DIR: William Witney. **CAST:** Roy Rogers, Dale Evans, Pat Brady, Grant Withers.

Grant Withers heads an evil gang of foreign agents out to smuggle uranium to unfriendly powers. Roy Rogers plays a modern-day heroic insurance agent who is able to thwart the heavies. Comic-book story is full of fast riding and action. 1950; 67m.

BELLS OF ROSARITA ★★½

DIR: Frank McDonald. **CAST:** Roy Rogers, Dale Evans, George "Gabby" Hayes, Bob Nolan and the Sons of the Pioneers, Don Barry, Allan "Rocky" Lane, Sunset Carson, William Elliott, Robert Livingston.

Movie cowboy Roy Rogers enlists the aid of Republic Studios' top Western stars in order to save Gabby Hayes's and Dale Evans's circus. A fun western. 1945; B&W; 54m.

BELLS OF SAN ANGELO ★★★½

DIR: William Witney. **CAST:** Roy Rogers, Dale Evans, Andy Devine, John McGuire.

This is a sharp and unusually violent Roy Rogers film. Roy portrays a lawman who attempts to capture a bunch of smugglers. With the help of Dale Evans and Andy Devine, he succeeds. 1947; B&W; 78m.

BELOW THE BORDER ★★★

DIR: Howard Bretherton. **CAST:** Buck Jones, Tim McCoy, Raymond Hatton, Linda Brent, Roy Barcroft, Charles King.

Energetic Rough Riders adventure has Buck Roberts (Buck Jones) going underground as a bandit while Tim McCall (Tim McCoy) poses as a cattle buyer. It's all to trap evil Roy Barcroft and put an end to his cattle rustling in Border City. 1942; B&W; 57m.

BEND OF THE RIVER ★★★★

DIR: Anthony Mann. **CAST:** James Stewart, Arthur Kennedy, Rock Hudson, Julie Adams.

James Stewart and director Anthony Mann teamed up during the early 1950s to make a series of exceptional Westerns that helped the genre return to popularity. This one deals with Stewart leading a wagon train across the country and his dealings with ex-friend Arthur Kennedy, who hijacks their supplies. Superior Western fare in every sense. 1952; 91m.

BETWEEN GOD, THE DEVIL AND A WINCHESTER

DIR: Dario Silvester. **CAST:** Richard Harrison, Gilbert Roland.

A treasure is stolen from a church in Texas and a band of outlaws and a holy man go on the trail to find it. Guaranteed to net only horselaughs thanks to the dubbed dialogue. 1972; 98m.

BEYOND THE LAW ★

DIR: Giorgio Stegani. **CAST:** Lee Van Cleef, Antonio Sabato, Lionel Stander, Bud Spencer.

A cliché-ridden, low-budget spaghetti Western, with Lee Van Cleef as a bad guy turned good. Lionel Stander is one of his henchmen, and provides the only bright spot in the movie. Unrated; contains adult language and some gratuitous, badly-staged violence. 1968; 90m.

BIG COUNTRY, THE ★★★

DIR: William Wyler. **CAST:** Gregory Peck, Jean Simmons, Charlton Heston, Carroll Baker, Burl Ives, Charles Bickford.

Big-budget Western pits Gregory Peck and Charlton Heston as adversaries in an ongoing feud between rival cowmen Burl Ives and Charles Bickford. This would-be epic looks good but lacks the punch and plot of the best and most famous Westerns. 1958; 163m.

BIG JAKE ★★★

DIR: George Sherman. **CAST:** John Wayne, Richard Boone, Maureen O'Hara, Patrick Wayne, Chris Mitchum, Bobby Vinton, Bruce Cabot.

Big John Wayne takes up the trail of a gang of no-goods who kidnapped his grandson and shot up Maureen O'Hara's homestead and hired hands. One wishes there had been more scenes with Wayne and O'Hara together in this film, their last together. 1971; 110m.

BIG SHOW, THE ★★

DIR: Mack V. Wright. **CAST:** Gene Autry, Smiley Burnette, Kay Hughes, Sally Payne, William Newell, Max Terhune.

Big-budget Gene Autry series film benefits from location shooting and the musical talent that appears on the show, including young Leonard Slye (soon to be known as Roy Rogers), with the Sons of the Pioneers. Autry plays a double role as a spoiled movie cowboy and the look-alike stunt man who steps into his boots when the star has a tantrum. 1936; B&W; 70m.

BIG SKY, THE ★★

DIR: Howard Hawks. **CAST:** Kirk Douglas, Arthur Hunnicutt, Dewey Martin.

Even the normally reliable director Howard Hawks can't enliven this average tale of early-day fur trappers on an expedition up the Missouri River. Action was Hawks's forte, and there just isn't enough to sustain the viewer's interest. Plenty of beautiful scenery, but that's about it. 1952; B&W; 122m.

BIG SOMBRERO, THE ★★½

DIR: Frank McDonald. **CAST:** Gene Autry, Elena Verdugo, Stephen Dunne, George J. Lewis, Martin Garralaga, Gene Roth.

An impoverished Gene Autry comes to the aid of Elena Verdugo and saves her from land swindlers as well as a money-grubbing fiancé in this south-of-the-border tale. This is more of a musical than a horse opera. 1949; 77m.

BIG TRAIL, THE ★★★½

DIR: Raoul Walsh. **CAST:** John Wayne, Marguerite Churchill, El Brendel, Ian Keith, Tyrone Power Sr.

John Wayne made his starring debut in this exciting, although somewhat dated epic. Contrary to Hollywood legend, the Duke acquits himself well enough as a revenge-minded scout leading a wagon train across the wilderness. His allegedly stiff acting was long thought to be the reason for the film's box-office failure. In truth, the film was shot in wide-screen 55mm and released at a time when cinema owners were recovering from the cost of converting to sound. They were unwilling to invest in the projection equipment needed to show the film in Fox Grandeur, as it was called, and Wayne found himself grinding out B Westerns for the next nine years—until John Ford picked him to play the Ringo Kid in *Stagecoach*. 1930; B&W; 110m.

BIG VALLEY, THE (TELEVISION SERIES) ★★★

DIR: Virgil Vogel. **CAST:** Barbara Stanwyck, Richard Long, Peter Breck, Lee Majors, Linda Evans.

Set in Stockton, California, circa 1878, this is the TV-born saga of the Barkleys, a family of cattle ranchers. Victoria (Barbara Stanwyck) is the iron-willed widow who heads the clan. Jarrod (Richard Long), her oldest son, is a suave attorney. His brother Nick (Peter Breck) is a rugged cowpoke. Their half-brother is Heath (Lee Majors), whose illegitimacy has bred a rebellious streak. All three are protective of Audra (Linda Evans), their gorgeous, haughty sister. A pair of two-part episodes are available on tape: "Legend of a General" and "Explosion." 1965–1969; 90m.

BILLY THE KID RETURNS ★★½

DIR: Joseph Kane. **CAST:** Roy Rogers, Smiley Burnette, Lynne Roberts, Morgan Wallace, Fred Kohler Sr., Trigger.

Rogers plays a look-alike to the dead Billy the Kid and restores the tranquillity of Lincoln County after subduing the criminal element. Fun for fans. 1938; B&W; 58m.

BITE THE BULLET ★★★★½

DIR: Richard Brooks. **CAST:** Gene Hackman, James Coburn, Candice Bergen, Ben Johnson, Jan-Michael Vincent, Dabney Coleman, Ian Bannen.

A six-hundred-mile horse race is the subject of this magnificent adventure, an epic in every sense of the word. A real sleeper, hardly noticed during its theatrical release. Rated PG. 1975; 131m.

BLOOD ON THE MOON ★★★½

DIR: Robert Wise. **CAST:** Robert Mitchum, Barbara Bel Geddes, Robert Preston.

Robert Mitchum is in top form in this atmospheric Western concerning cattle ranchers trying to terminate homesteaders on rangeland. 1948; B&W; 88m.

BLOODY TRAIL 🦃

DIR: Richard Robinson. **CAST:** Paul Harper, Rance Howard, John Mitchum.

This western has no plot, just an ex–Union soldier wandering through the recently defeated South meeting up with angry African tribesmen(?), stubborn Confederates, and women who are ready to show off some skin. Rated R for sex, nudity, profanity, and violence. 1972; 91m.

BLUE AND THE GRAY, THE ★★★½

DIR: Andrew V. McLaglen. **CAST:** Stacy Keach, John Hammond, Lloyd Bridges, Rory Calhoun, Colleen Dewhurst, Warren Oates, Geraldine Page, Rip Torn, Robert Vaughn, Sterling Hayden, Paul Winfield, Gregory Peck.

From the historic John Brown trial through the Civil War and beyond, this star-studded saga dramatizes many viewpoints of the only war in history pitting American against

American. Seen mostly through the eyes of an artist correspondent, this TV miniseries is a polished, if occasionally sanitized, version of the bloodiest and most bitter conflict in U.S. history. 1982; 295m.

BLUE CANADIAN ROCKIES ★½
DIR: George Archainbaud. **CAST:** Gene Autry, Pat Buttram, Gail Davis, Ross Ford, Tom London, John Merton, Don Beddoe, Gene Roth.

Processed stock footage of Canada forms the backdrop for this weak story about a young girl's strong-willed ambitions and her father's efforts to save her and her dreams from tragedy. Gene Autry and his pal Pat Buttram help both parties and expose the inevitable villains, as well as helping preserve a wild-game preserve. 1952; B&W; 58m.

BLUE STEEL ★★★
DIR: Robert N. Bradbury. **CAST:** John Wayne, Eleanor Hunt, George "Gabby" Hayes, Ed Peil, Yakima Canutt, George Cleveland.

Fun but undistinguished B Western with a very young John Wayne as a cowpoke who saves a town from extinction when he reveals a secret known only to an outlaw gang: there's gold in them thar hills. 1934; B&W; 60m.

BOLD CABALLERO, THE ★★½
DIR: Wells Root. **CAST:** Robert Livingston, Heather Angel, Sig Ruman, Robert Warwick, Charles Stevens, Slim Whitaker.

This little-known color film is the first sound Zorro movie and an early effort from Republic Studios, better known for their action-filled serials. Robert Livingston plays the masked avenger who sweeps tyranny out of his part of California, while clearing himself of a murder charge. 1936; 69m.

BONANZA (TELEVISION SERIES) ★★★
DIR: Edward Ludwig, William F. Claxton, Robert Gordon, Don McDougall. **CAST:** Lorne Greene, Pernell Roberts, Dan Blocker, Michael Landon, Victor Sen Yung.

This Western series dominated the Sunday-night ratings for over a decade. It's the story of patriarch Ben Cartwright (Lorne Greene) and his three sons, all from different mothers. Adam (Pernell Roberts) is suave and mature. Hoss (Dan Blocker) is a big man with a bigger heart. Little Joe (Michael Landon) is earnest and hot-tempered. Together they make the Ponderosa the most prosperous ranch in the Comstock Lode country. Week after week, the Cartwrights, noble gents that they were, used their position, their money, their fists, and their guns to help those in distress. Frequently, they'd take time out for romance. Volume I includes the pilot episode, "A Rose for Lotta," as well as "The Underdog," guest-starring Charles Bronson. Volume II features James Coburn in "The Dark Gate" and DeForest Kelley in "Honor of Cochise." 1959–1973; 120m.

BOOT HILL ★★
DIR: Giuseppe Colizzi. **CAST:** Terence Hill, Bud Spencer, Woody Strode, Lionel Stander, Victor Buono.

Once again, Terence Hill and Bud Spencer are teamed in a spaghetti Western. This one pits them against bad guy Victor Buono. It's violent, bloody, and far from good. Rated PG. 1969; 87m.

BOOTS AND SADDLES ★★
DIR: Joseph Kane. **CAST:** Gene Autry, Smiley Burnette, Judith Allen, William Elliott.

An English tenderfoot learns his lessons in the "code of the West" from no-nonsense Gene Autry and his not-so-subtle sidekick Smiley Burnette in this standard story of a foreigner who inherits a working ranch. 1937; B&W; 59m.

BORDER PATROL ★★★
DIR: Lesley Selander. **CAST:** William Boyd, Andy Clyde, Russell Simpson, Duncan Renaldo, Robert Mitchum.

In this Hopalong Cassidy serial, Hoppy must put a stop to the criminal atrocities committed by the owner of a silver mine who is using Mexicans as virtual slaves. Robert Mitchum makes his film debut as one of the bad guys. Not the best of the series, but still good, with plenty of action. 1943; B&W; 66m.

BORDER PHANTOM ★★½
DIR: S. Roy Luby. **CAST:** Bob Steele, Harley Wood, Don Barclay, Karl Hackett.

Although *Border Phantom*, like all B Westerns, looks pretty creaky today, it's entertaining, thanks to Bob Steele's energetic performance and an intriguing premise, which involves mysterious murders and slavery. 1937; B&W; 59m.

BORDERLAND ★★★½
DIR: Nate Watt. **CAST:** William Boyd, James Ellison, George "Gabby" Hayes.

Hopalong Cassidy, an outlaw! Well, sort of. In this B oater, Hoppy must pretend to be a bad guy to save the day. The characterizations are strong. The script is literate, and Morris Ankrum is great as the main outlaw. Good fun for all. 1937; B&W; 82m.

BORROWED TROUBLE ★★
DIR: George Archainbaud. **CAST:** William Boyd, Andy Clyde, Rand Brooks, Elaine Riley.

Hopalong Cassidy and his pals get bogged down in this comedy-drama about a town gone to seed and the outspoken (and obnoxious) schoolteacher who wants to run the bad element out and restore her idea of a real community. Cutesy at times and light on the action, this one is perked up occasionally by the dialogue. 1948; B&W; 58m.

BOSS ★★½
DIR: Jack Arnold. **CAST:** Fred Williamson, D'Urville Martin, R. G. Armstrong, William Smith, Barbara Leigh.

In the Old West, bounty hunter Fred Williamson and his sidekick D'Urville Martin ride into a town and set themselves up as the law. It's part of their plan to capture a bad guy with a hefty price on his head. Amazing how much mileage Williamson, who wrote the screenplay for himself, gets out of Western clichés in this familiar but entertaining oater. Original title: *Boss Nigger*. Not rated. 1975; 87m.

BOUNTY MAN, THE ★★★½
DIR: John Llewellyn Moxey. **CAST:** Clint Walker, Richard Basehart, Margot Kidder, John Ericson, Arthur Hunnicutt, Gene Evans.

Made-for-television Western is dark, complex, and quite good. Bounty hunter Clint Walker follows a murderer into a town but is set upon by a group of outlaws. Richard Basehart is particularly good as the outlaw leader. 1972; 73m.

BRANDED A COWARD ★★
DIR: Sam Newfield. **CAST:** Johnny Mack Brown, Billie Seward, Yakima Canutt.

A minuscule budget and uninspired handling sabotage a potentially top-notch series Western. Johnny Mack Brown is a brave man who cannot bring himself to shoot others—even villains who taunt him—after witnessing the massacre of his family as a child. 1935; B&W; 57m.

BREAKHEART PASS ★★★
DIR: Tom Gries. **CAST:** Charles Bronson, Ben Johnson, Ed Lauter, Richard Crenna, Charles Durning, Jill Ireland, John Mitchum.

Charles Bronson is a government agent on the trail of gun runners in the Old West. Most of the action of this modest Western takes place aboard a train, so the excited pitch needed to fully sustain viewers' interest is never reached. Rated PG—some violence, rough language. 1976; 95m.

BROADWAY TO CHEYENNE ★★½
DIR: Harry Fraser. **CAST:** Rex Bell, George "Gabby" Hayes, Marceline Day.

A New York mob moves west to set up a cattlemen's protection association, but a New York cop on vacation breaks up their racket. This was Rex Bell's first Western and it set the formula for many of his pictures. 1932; B&W; 60m.

BROKEN ARROW ★★★
DIR: Delmer Daves. **CAST:** James Stewart, Jeff Chandler, Debra Paget, Will Geer, Arthur Hunnicutt, Basil Ruysdael, Jay Silverheels.

Jeff Chandler is the Apache chief Cochise and James Stewart is a cavalry scout in this sympathetic look at Indians and white settlers struggling to coexist on the Western frontier in the 1870s. As usual, crooked traders and renegades thwart peace. Interesting aspect is the depiction of Indian life as it really was, complex and cultured. The film was the first to treat the Indian with respect and understanding. 1950; 93m.

BROTHERS IN THE SADDLE ★★★
DIR: Lesley Selander. **CAST:** Tim Holt, Richard Martin, Steve Brodie.

Steve Brodie is the ne'er-do-well brother of straight-shooter Tim Holt in this above-average Western. Some of the scenes seem a bit drawn out today, but the storyline was uncommonly hard-edged for a series Western of the late 1940s, when interest in the genre was flagging and most cowboy movies were lifeless remakes. 1949; B&W; 60m.

BUCK AND THE PREACHER ★★½
DIR: Sidney Poitier. **CAST:** Sidney Poitier, Harry Belafonte, Ruby Dee, Cameron Mitchell.

Harry Belafonte and director Sidney Poitier play two escaped slaves heading west. On the way, they meet up with "bad guy" Cameron Mitchell and lovely Ruby Dee. So-so Western. Rated PG. 1972; 102m.

BUCKEYE AND BLUE ★½
DIR: J. C. Compton. **CAST:** Robyn Lively, Jeff Osterhage, Rick Gibbs, Will Hannah.

Disappointing *Bonnie and Clyde*–style Western featuring Robin Lively and Jeff Osterhage as a couple of desperadoes who engage in a crime spree after the Civil War. No new twists on this tired theme. Rated PG. 1988; 94m.

BUCKSKIN FRONTIER ★★★
DIR: Lesley Selander. **CAST:** Richard Dix, Jane Wyatt, Lee J. Cobb, Albert Dekker, Joe Sawyer, Victor Jory, Lola Lane.

Railroad representative Richard Dix and freight line owner Lee J. Cobb fight over business and a crucial mountain pass in this big-budget, fast-action Western. 1943; B&W; 82m.

BUFFALO BILL AND THE INDIANS ★★
DIR: Robert Altman. **CAST:** Paul Newman, Joel Grey, Kevin McCarthy, Burt Lancaster, Harvey Keitel, Geraldine Chaplin, Will Sampson.

In this offbeat Western, Paul Newman, Burt Lancaster, Harvey Keitel, Geraldine Chaplin, Joel Grey, Kevin McCarthy, and Will Sampson are fun to watch as they interact like jazz musicians jamming on the theme of distorted history and the delusion of celebrity. Rated PG. 1976; 120m.

BUGLES IN THE AFTERNOON ★★½
DIR: Roy Rowland. **CAST:** Ray Milland, Hugh Marlowe, Helena Carter, Forrest Tucker, Barton MacLane, George Reeves.

In this modest Western a young army officer is made a victim by a jealous rival. Set in the time of Custer's last stand, it has fairly good scenery and cinematography. 1952; 85m.

BULLDOG COURAGE ★★½
DIR: Sam Newfield. **CAST:** Tim McCoy, Joan Woodbury, Paul Fix, Eddie Buzzard.

Tim McCoy is excellent in the dual role of father and son in this slow-paced series Western. When Slim Braddock (McCoy) is killed, it's up to his son, Tim (McCoy), to avenge his death after a period of several years. This was one of McCoy's last starring films. 1935; B&W; 66m.

BULLWHIP ★★½
DIR: Harmon Jones. **CAST:** Rhonda Fleming, Guy Madison, James Griffith, Don Beddoe.

In this agreeable movie, Guy Madison avoids the hangin' tree by agreeing to marry a fiery halfbreed (Rhonda Fleming). If the plot sounds familiar, it should. Jack Nicholson used a similar one in *Goin' South*. 1958; 80m.

BUTCH AND SUNDANCE: THE EARLY DAYS ★★
DIR: Richard Lester. **CAST:** William Katt, Tom Berenger, Brian Dennehy, John Schuck, Jeff Corey.

Director Richard Lester has made better films (see *A Hard Day's Night* and *Superman II*), and because his usual film is a comedy, this outing is especially disappointing. Nearly all of the jokes fall flat despite a screenplay that hints at the original film with Paul Newman and Robert Redford. Rated PG for some mildly crude language and (very little) violence. 1979; 111m.

BUTCH CASSIDY AND THE SUNDANCE KID ★★★★½
DIR: George Roy Hill. **CAST:** Paul Newman, Robert Redford, Katharine Ross.

George Roy Hill directed this gentle Western spoof featuring personal-best performances by Paul Newman, Robert Redford, and Katharine Ross. A spectacular box-office success, and deservedly so, the release deftly combines action with comedy. Rated PG. 1969; 112m.

CAHILL—US MARSHAL ★★½
DIR: Andrew V. McLaglen. **CAST:** John Wayne, George Kennedy, Gary Grimes, Neville Brand.

John Wayne was still making B Westerns in the 1970s—to the disappointment of those who (rightly) expected better. Although still enjoyable, this film about a lawman (Wayne) whose son (Gary Grimes) becomes a bank robber is routine at best. Still, the performances by the Duke and George Kennedy (as the chief baddie) do bring pleasure. Rated PG. 1973; 103m.

CALAMITY JANE (1984) ★★★★
DIR: James Goldstone. **CAST:** Jane Alexander, Frederic Forrest, David Hemmings, Ken Kercheval, Talia Balsam.

Director James Goldstone provides more than just the story of Annie Oakley, which is fascinating in itself as a tale of one of America's first feminists. His unglamorous production and straightforward storytelling give a true feeling of the Old West. Jane Alexander, in an Emmy-nominated performance, shows the many sides of this spirited lady. A made-for-TV movie. 1984; 100m.

CALIFORNIA GOLD RUSH ★
DIR: Jack B. Hively. **CAST:** Robert Hays, John Dehner, Ken Curtis, Henry Jones, Dan Haggerty.

The writer Bret Harte (Robert Hays) is in the right place at the right time to chronicle the Gold Rush days of California from Sutter's Fort. Harte tells the story of the discovery, the people who came to find the gold, and the greed, violence, and corruption that came with them. Rated PG. 1985; 100m.

CALL OF THE CANYON ★★
DIR: Joseph Santley. **CAST:** Gene Autry, Smiley Burnette, Ruth Terry, Thurston Hall, Pat Brady, Marc Lawrence, Budd Buster, Bob Nolan and the Sons of the Pioneers, Bob Burns.

Even-tempered Gene Autry sides with the local cattlemen in their struggle against an unscrupulous meat-packing company tycoon in this enjoyable Republic Western. 1942; B&W; 71m.

CALLING WILD BILL ELLIOTT ★★½
DIR: Spencer Gordon Bennet. **CAST:** William Elliott, Anne Jeffreys, George "Gabby" Hayes.

In his first assignment in an A picture for Republic Studios, Wild Bill Elliott pals up with Gabby Hayes to fight off evil robbers harassing the lovely

Anne Jeffreys. Gabby Hayes is supposed to be a funny sidekick, but here he is more of an anvil around the neck. Average. 1943; B&W; 78m.

CAPTAIN APACHE ★½
DIR: Alexander Singer. **CAST:** Lee Van Cleef, Stuart Whitman, Carroll Baker, Percy Herbert.
Muddled Western has Lee Van Cleef in title role gunning down dozens of one-dimensional characters who cross his path or appear likely to. Rated PG for violence. 1971; 94m.

CARAVAN TRAIL ★★★★
DIR: Robert Emmett. **CAST:** Eddie Dean, Lash LaRue, Charles King.
The leader (Eddie Dean) of a wagon train of settlers takes the job of marshal to restore homesteaders' land being stolen by outlaws. He enlists the aid of some not-so-bad outlaws to stop the landgrabbers. Lash LaRue (in his second supporting role to Dean) steals the picture. LaRue went on to star in his own series of well-received Bs. 1946; 57m.

CARSON CITY CYCLONE ★★★★
DIR: Howard P. Bretherton. **CAST:** Donald "Red" Barry, Noah Beery Sr., Roy Barcroft.
Donald "Red" Barry plays a cocky young defense attorney framed for the murder of his father (a judge and banker). Intricate plot that proves how good B westerns can be. 1943; B&W; 55m.

CAT BALLOU ★★★
DIR: Elliot Silverstein. **CAST:** Jane Fonda, Lee Marvin, Michael Callan, Jay C. Flippen.
In this offbeat, uneven but fun comedy-Western, Jane Fonda plays Cat, a former schoolteacher out to avenge her father's death. Michael Callan is her main romantic interest. Lee Marvin outshines all with his Oscar-winning performance in the dual roles of the drunken hired gun and his evil look-alike. 1965; 96m.

CATTLE QUEEN OF MONTANA ★★
DIR: Allan Dwan. **CAST:** Barbara Stanwyck, Ronald Reagan, Gene Evans, Jack Elam.
Barbara Stanwyck gives a strong performance in this otherwise routine Western. Plot revolves around Stanwyck trying to protect her farm from land grabbers, who also murdered her father. Meanwhile, the Indians are out to wipe out everybody. 1954; 88m.

CHEROKEE STRIP ★★
DIR: Noel Smith. **CAST:** Dick Foran, Jane Bryan, David Carlyle, Glenn Strange.
The Oklahoma land rush is the basis for this routine story of a bunch of landgrabbers who try to stake a claim before the land is opened for settling. Dick Foran is good as the hero who puts the crimp in their plan. 1937; B&W; 55m.

CHEYENNE AUTUMN ★★★½
DIR: John Ford. **CAST:** Richard Widmark, Karl Malden, Carroll Baker, James Stewart, Edward G. Robinson, Ricardo Montalban.
John Ford strays away from his traditional glorification of Western mythology to bring us this story of the mistreatment of the American Indian. His standard heroes, the U.S. cavalry, are placed in the role of the villains as they try to stop a group of desperate Cheyenne Indians from migrating back to their Wyoming homeland from a barren reservation in Oklahoma. This movie is uniformly well acted, and as with any John Ford Western, the scenery is breathtaking. 1964; 160m.

CHEYENNE SOCIAL CLUB, THE ★★★
DIR: Gene Kelly. **CAST:** James Stewart, Henry Fonda, Shirley Jones, Sue Ane Langdon.
This Western comedy has a number of pleasing moments. James Stewart, an itinerant cowhand, and his lowkey cohort Henry Fonda inherit some

property in Cheyenne—which turns out to be a bordello. The premise is good, but at times director Gene Kelly doesn't have a firm grip on the script or on these hugely talented actors. Rated PG. 1970; 103m.

CHINO ★★
DIR: John Sturges. **CAST:** Charles Bronson, Jill Ireland, Vincent Van Patten.
A surprisingly low-key Charles Bronson Western about a horse breeder who attempts to live a peaceful life. The film was trimmed of much of its violence, and all that's left is an above-average performance by Bronson and an adequate one by his wife, Jill Ireland, as Chino's love interest. Rated PG. 1973; 98m.

CHISHOLMS, THE ★★★
DIR: Mel Stuart. **CAST:** Robert Preston, Rosemary Harris, Ben Murphy, Brian Kerwin.
This made-for-TV oater is fairly well done. Robert Preston is very good as the patriarch of the Chisholm family. It is a vast saga of a family's trek west from Virginia to California. A bit talky, but worth a viewing. 1979; 300m.

CHISUM ★★★½
DIR: Andrew V. McLaglen. **CAST:** John Wayne, Forrest Tucker, Christopher George, Ben Johnson, Patric Knowles, Bruce Cabot, Glenn Corbett.
The best of the John Wayne Westerns directed by Andrew V. McLaglen, this sprawling epic centers around the revenge sought by Billy the Kid (Geoffrey Duel) after his mentor (Patric Knowles) is murdered by the corrupt, land-grabbing bad guys. Rated G. 1970; 111m.

CIMARRON ★★★
DIR: Wesley Ruggles. **CAST:** Richard Dix, Irene Dunne, Estelle Taylor, William Collier Jr., Roscoe Ates.
One of the panoramic, expensive early sound films, this Western based on Edna Ferber's novel presents the story of a pioneer family bent on building an empire out of the primitiveness of early Oklahoma. It won the Academy Award for best picture, but some scenes now seem dated. 1931; B&W; 124m.

COLORADO ★★
DIR: Joseph Kane. **CAST:** Roy Rogers, George "Gabby" Hayes, Milburn Stone.
Roy Rogers and "Gabby" Hayes settle comfortably into what became a profitable and highly successful series in this routine shoot-'em-up about the two riders who aid the embattled homesteaders and clean up the territory for decent folk. Not too imaginative, but enjoyable. 1940; B&W; 54m.

COMANCHEROS, THE ★★★★
DIR: Michael Curtiz. **CAST:** John Wayne, Stuart Whitman, Lee Marvin, Ina Balin, Bruce Cabot, Nehemiah Persoff, Bob Steele.
Big John Wayne is the laconic Texas Ranger assigned to bring in dandy gambler Stuart Whitman for murder. Along the way, Wayne bests bad guy Lee Marvin, and Whitman proves himself a hero by helping the big guy take on the ruthless gun- and liquor-running villains of the title, led by Nehemiah Persoff. It's a fine Western with lots of nice moments. 1961; 107m.

COMES A HORSEMAN ★★★★
DIR: Alan J. Pakula. **CAST:** Jane Fonda, James Caan, Jason Robards Jr., George Grizzard, Richard Farnsworth, Jim Davis.
Dark, somber, but haunting Western set in the 1940s about the efforts of a would-be land baron (Jason Robards Jr.) to cheat his long-suffering neighbor (Jane Fonda) out of her land. She fights back with the help of a World War II veteran (James Caan) and a crusty old-timer (Richard Farnsworth). Rated PG for violence. 1978; 118m.

CORONER CREEK ★★★★
DIR: Ray Enright. **CAST:** Randolph Scott, Marguerite Chapman,

George Macready, Forrest Tucker, Edgar Buchanan.

Solid Western marks the first film in the series produced by the company set up by Randolph Scott and Harry Brown. Their collaboration culminated in the superb series directed by Budd Boetticher *(Ride Lonesome, The Tall T)*. Even so, this film is no slouch, with Scott attempting to track down the man responsible for the murder of his fiancée. 1948; 90m.

COW TOWN ★★½

DIR: John English. **CAST:** Gene Autry, Gail Davis, Harry Shannon, Jock Mahoney.

Action and stunts as well as a good crew of familiar faces make this, Gene Autry's seventy-second film as himself, better than many of his earlier efforts. Grazing rights, stampedes, gunplay, and a song or two (or three) are packed into the film. 1950; B&W; 70m.

COWBOY MILLIONAIRE ★★★

DIR: Eddie Cline. **CAST:** George O'Brien, Edgar Kennedy.

The accent is on humor in this series Western, which has two-fisted George O'Brien and sidekick Edgar Kennedy acting as "colorful cowboy types" at a hotel out west. It's just a way to raise money to finance their mining operation. 1935; B&W; 65m.

COWBOYS, THE ★★★★½

DIR: Mark Rydell. **CAST:** John Wayne, Roscoe Lee Browne, Bruce Dern, Colleen Dewhurst, Slim Pickens.

Along with Don Siegel's *The Shootist*, this is the best of John Wayne's latter-day Westerns. The Duke plays a rancher whose wranglers get gold fever. He's forced to recruit a bunch of green kids in order to take his cattle to market. Bruce Dern is on hand as the outlaw leader who fights our hero in one of the genre's most memorable (and violent) scenes. Rated PG. 1972; 128m.

CROSSFIRE (1986) 🦃

DIR: Robert Conrad, Alfredo Zacharia. **CAST:** Robert Conrad, Jan-Michael Vincent, Manuel Lopez Ochoa.

Insufferable Western about three outlaws who are saved from execution by a gang of Mexican freedom fighters. The fugitives end up banding together with the rebels to fight the Spanish in the Mexican Revolution. Robert Conrad puts in a good performance. But as a director, he's better off selling flashlight batteries. 1986; 82m.

CULPEPPER CATTLE CO., THE ★★★½

DIR: Dick Richards. **CAST:** Gary Grimes, Billy Green Bush, Luke Askew, Bo Hopkins, Geoffrey Lewis, Royal Dano.

A strong supporting cast of character actors makes this coming-of-age story set in the Old West into a real treat for fans of shoot-'em-ups. Gary Grimes is a 16-year-old farm boy who dreams of becoming a cowboy, something which the cowboys cannot quite understand. "Cowboying is something you do when you can't do nothin' else," he is told. Rated R for violence. 1972; 92m.

DAKOTA (1945) ★★½

DIR: Joseph Kane. **CAST:** John Wayne, Vera Hruba Ralston, Walter Brennan, Ward Bond.

Any Western with John Wayne, Walter Brennan, and Ward Bond has to be a winner, right? Wrong. This substandard film may be interesting to see for their performances, but you also have to put up with the incredibly untalented Vera Ralston (she was the wife of Republic Studio head Herbert Yates). It's almost worth it. 1945; B&W; 82m.

DAKOTA INCIDENT ★★½

DIR: Lewis R. Foster. **CAST:** Dale Robertson, Linda Darnell, John Lund.

It's a fight to the finish in this fairly good Western as the Indians attack a stagecoach rolling through Dakota Territory in those thrilling days of yesteryear. 1956; 88m.

DANGEROUS VENTURE ★★½
DIR: George Archainbaud. **CAST:** William Boyd, Andy Clyde, Rand Brooks.
This better-than-average Hopalong Cassidy adventure finds our heroes searching for Aztec ruins in the Southwest and encountering hostile renegades and unscrupulous fortune hunters. 1947; B&W; 55m.

DANIEL BOONE ★★★★
DIR: David Howard. **CAST:** George O'Brien, Heather Angel, John Carradine.
Action-packed story of the early American frontier features rugged outdoor star George O'Brien in the title role and evil John Carradine as a renegade who aids the marauding Indians. This rousing film is great schoolboy adventure stuff. 1936; B&W; 77m.

DANIEL BOONE, TRAIL BLAZER ★★½
DIR: Albert C. Gannaway. **CAST:** Bruce Bennett, Lon Chaney Jr., Faron Young.
This is a slightly better-than-average Western that has Daniel Boone (Bruce Bennett) not only pathfinding for settlers but fighting off what seems to be the entire population of native Americans. Good performances and lots of action save it from being mundane. 1956; 76m.

DARK COMMAND ★★★★½
DIR: Raoul Walsh. **CAST:** John Wayne, Claire Trevor, Walter Pidgeon, Roy Rogers, George "Gabby" Hayes.
Raoul Walsh, who directed John Wayne's first big Western, *The Big Trail*, was reunited with the star after the latter's triumph in *Stagecoach* for this dynamic shoot-'em-up. Walter Pidgeon is Quantrill, a once-honest man who goes renegade and forms Quantrill's Raiders. It's up to the Duke, with help from his *Stagecoach* co-star Claire Trevor, Roy Rogers, and Gabby Hayes, to set things right. 1940; B&W; 94m.

DAWN ON THE GREAT DIVIDE ★★★
DIR: Howard P. Bretherton. **CAST:** Buck Jones, Raymond Hatton, Rex Bell, Mona Barrie.
With a bigger budget than usual and a story with more plot twists than the average B western, the result is a good shoot-'em-up in the series vein. Buck Jones, of course, dominates as the two-fisted leader of a wagon train who takes on Indians, bad guys, and corrupt officials with equal aplomb. It was the last movie made by Jones, who died heroically trying to save lives during a fire at Boston's Coconut Grove on November 28, 1942. 1942; B&W; 63m.

DAWN RIDER ★★
DIR: Robert N. Bradbury. **CAST:** John Wayne, Marion Burns, Yakima Canutt, Reed Howes.
John Wayne is out for revenge in this formula B Western with no budget to speak of. His loving father is killed during a robbery, and it's up to a gangly, slightly stilted Wayne to get the bad guys. 1935; B&W; 56m.

DAYS OF JESSE JAMES ★★
DIR: Joseph Kane. **CAST:** Roy Rogers, George "Gabby" Hayes, Donald "Red" Barry, Harry Woods.
In this B Western, Roy Rogers sets out to prove that Jesse James, as played by Donald Barry, didn't stage the famous Northfield, Minnesota, bank robbery. Yep! It was those corrupt bankers who set it up. A confusing plot line doesn't help. 1939; B&W; 63m.

DEAD DON'T DREAM, THE ★★
DIR: George Archainbaud. **CAST:** William Boyd, Andy Clyde, Rand Brooks, John Parrish.
Hopalong Cassidy's partner "Lucky" finally decides to tie the knot, but his wedding plans are dashed when his fiancée's father is murdered before the ceremony. Hoppy tries to get to the bottom of this mystery. Originally released at sixty-two minutes. 1948; B&W; 55m.

DEADLY COMPANIONS, THE ★★½

DIR: Sam Peckinpah. **CAST:** Brian Keith, Maureen O'Hara, Chill Wills, Steve Cochran.

When gunfighter Brian Keith accidentally kills the son of dance-hall hostess Maureen O'Hara, he attempts to make amends by escorting her through hostile Indian territory. A less than grade-A Western made notable because it was director Sam Peckinpah's first feature. 1961; 90m.

DEADLY TRACKERS, THE ★★½

DIR: Barry Shear. **CAST:** Richard Harris, Rod Taylor, Neville Brand, William Smith, Al Lettieri, Isela Vega.

Extremely violent Western follows sheriff Richard Harris's attempt to track down the outlaw gang responsible for killing his family during a bank robbery. Film starts out well, but quickly becomes a standard revenge tale and is far too long. Be warned: There are some truly brutal scenes throughout. Rated R. 1973; 110m.

DEATH OF A GUNFIGHTER ★★★

DIR: Alan Smithee. **CAST:** Richard Widmark, Lena Horne, Carroll O'Connor, John Saxon, Kent Smith.

Any time you see the name Allen Smithee in the directorial slot that means the real director had his name taken off the credits. In this case, Don Siegel and Robert Totten were alternately at the helm of what still emerges as a sturdy Western, which gives a new twist to the tough-lawman story. Richard Widmark is very good as the sheriff who has outlived his usefulness to the town but refuses to change, thus setting the stage for tragic results. Rated PG. 1969; 100m.

DEATH RIDES A HORSE 🦃

DIR: Giulio Petroni. **CAST:** Lee Van Cleef, John Phillip Law, Mario Brega, Anthony Dawson.

Needlessly tedious spaghetti Western about a young boy who witnesses the butchery of his family and then grows up to be John Phillip Law so he can take his revenge. He and Lee Van Cleef spend most of the film saving and running from each other, all in the interests of those ludicrous gunfighters' codes. Rated PG for violence. 1969; 114m.

DEEP IN THE HEART OF TEXAS ★★★½

DIR: Elmer Clifton. **CAST:** Johnny Mack Brown, Tex Ritter.

This is a well-directed, finely photographed film about post–Civil War land-snatching. It's the first in a series of seven films to co-star the two great Western stars, Johnny Mack Brown and Tex Ritter. This one has lots of black hats, a few white hats, and plenty of action. 1942; B&W; 74m.

DEERSLAYER, THE ★★½

DIR: Dick Friedenberg. **CAST:** Steve Forrest, John Anderson, Ned Romero, Joan Prather.

Made-for-TV movie, based on James Fenimore Cooper's classic, *The Deerslayer* is a film of adventure in early America. The heroes, Hawkeye (Steve Forrest) and Chingachgook (Ned Romero), attempt to save a Mohican princess and avenge the death of Chingachgook's son. 1978; 98m.

DESERT TRAIL ★★

DIR: Robert N. Bradbury. **CAST:** John Wayne, Mary Kornman, Paul Fix, Edward Chandler.

Rodeo fans might like this standard B Western about a big-time bronc rider (John Wayne) who fights on the side of justice, but others may want to ride in the opposite direction. 1935; B&W; 54m.

DESPERADOS, THE ★★

DIR: Henry Levin. **CAST:** Vince Edwards, Jack Palance, Neville Brand, George Maharis, Sylvia Syms, Christian Roberts.

After the Civil War, a paranoid parson heads a gang of cutthroats and outlaws, including his three sons, in a violent crime spree. Roughly made (in Spain) and quite savage. Rated PG. 1969; 90m.

DESPERATE WOMEN ★
DIR: Earl Bellamy. **CAST:** Dan Haggerty, Susan Saint James, Ronee Blakley, Ann Dusenberry.
Three convicted women crossing a desert on their way to prison meet up with an ol' softy (Dan Haggerty) who takes them under his wing after the convicts' guards die of water poisoning. The comedy in this film is too sickly sweet to laugh over—the singing narrator should be strung up—and the action isn't fast enough. 1978; 98m.

DESTRY RIDES AGAIN ★★★★
DIR: George Marshall. **CAST:** James Stewart, Marlene Dietrich, Brian Donlevy, Mischa Auer, Una Merkel.
Destry's plot may seem a trifle clichéd, but it is the classic Western that copycats imitate. The story of a mild-mannered citizen who finds himself grudgingly forced to stand up against the bad guys may seem familiar, especially with Jimmy Stewart in the lead. But this is the original. 1939; B&W; 95m.

DEVIL HORSE, THE ★★½
DIR: Otto Brower, Richard Talmadge. **CAST:** Harry Carey, Noah Beery Sr., Frankie Darro, Greta Granstedt, Barrie O'Daniels, Yakima Canutt, Lane Chandler.
One of the best Mascot serials and a real audience favorite, this top-notch adventure features Harry Carey as a man tracking his brother's killer, evil Noah Beery. Codirector Richard Talmadge was one of the most famous and popular of silent stuntmen, and his apt hand as well as a fine cast, good photography, and exciting stunts make this a memorable serial. 1932; B&W; 12 chapters.

DEVIL'S PLAYGROUND ★★
DIR: George Archainbaud. **CAST:** William Boyd, Andy Clyde, Rand Brooks, Elaine Riley.
This so-so entry in the long-running Hopalong Cassidy series concerns crooked politicians, rumors of gold, and a forbidding, rugged area that holds the secrets to strange goings-on in the adjoining valley. 1946; B&W; 65m.

DJANGO ★
DIR: Sergio Corbucci. **CAST:** Franco Nero.
This spaghetti Western lacks convincing performances. A border town is about to explode, and the stranger, Django (Franco Nero), lights the fuse. The battle of guns and wits between the stranger and the leaders of two rival gangs is a rousing end to a poor but action-filled movie. 1965; 90m.

DODGE CITY ★★★★
DIR: Michael Curtiz. **CAST:** Errol Flynn, Olivia De Havilland, Ann Sheridan, Bruce Cabot, Alan Hale, Ward Bond.
Swashbuckler Errol Flynn sets aside his sword for a pair of six-guns to clean up the wild, untamed frontier city of the title. The best of Flynn's Westerns, this release is beautifully photographed in color with an all-star supporting cast. 1939; 105m.

DONNER PASS: THE ROAD TO SURVIVAL ★★
DIR: James L. Conway. **CAST:** Robert Fuller, Diane McBain, Andrew Prine, John Anderson, Michael Callan.
This fair made-for-TV retelling of the true story of the Donner party is based on historical accounts and tells of the snowstorm that traps the party and the physical hardship and starvation that lead to the infamous conclusion. Made for TV. 1978; 98m.

DOWN DAKOTA WAY ★★½
DIR: William Witney. **CAST:** Roy Rogers, Dale Evans, Pat Brady, Monte Montana, Roy Barcroft.
Roy Rogers takes a harder line with the bad guys in this exciting B Western, tracking down the no-goods responsible for the death of his friend, a veterinarian who could finger the man responsible for flooding the market with diseased meat. 1949; 67m.

DOWN MEXICO WAY ★★
DIR: Joseph Santley. **CAST:** Gene Autry, Smiley Burnette, Fay McKenzie, Harold Huber, Sidney Blackmer.
Bland Gene Autry and his oafish sidekick Smiley Burnette head south and find themselves embroiled in trouble when they come up against a gang of thieves. Routine. 1941; B&W; 78m.

DOWN TEXAS WAY ★★½
DIR: Howard Bretherton. **CAST:** Buck Jones, Tim McCoy, Raymond Hatton, Luana Walters, Harry Woods, Glenn Strange.
An agreeable if undistinguished entry in the Rough Riders series, this feature has Rangers Buck Jones and Tim McCoy coming to the aid of their pal, Raymond Hatton, when he is accused of murder. 1942; B&W; 57m.

DRAW ★★½
DIR: Steven H. Stern. **CAST:** James Coburn, Kirk Douglas.
Kirk Douglas and James Coburn play outlaw and lawman respectively. Both appear on a collision course for a gunfight but, alas, what we are treated to is a trick ending. Lots of missed chances in this one. Made for HBO cable television. 1984; 98m.

DRUM BEAT ★★½
DIR: Delmer Daves. **CAST:** Alan Ladd, Audrey Dalton, Marisa Pavan, Robert Keith, Anthony Caruso, Warner Anderson, Elisha Cook Jr., Charles Bronson.
Indian fighter Alan Ladd is detailed to ensure peace with marauding Modocs on the California-Oregon border in 1869. His chief adversary, in beads and buckskins, is Charles Bronson. Modoc maiden Marisa Pavan loves the hero, but the code dictates he settle for Audrey Dalton. As usual, white man speaks with forked tongue, but everything ends well. 1954; 111m.

DUCHESS AND THE DIRTWATER FOX, THE ★
DIR: Melvin Frank. **CAST:** George Segal, Goldie Hawn, Conrad Janis, Thayer David.
This Western-comedy romp never clicks. George Segal and Goldie Hawn labor so hard to get a laugh it's almost painful to watch. There isn't much of a story behind them, just a frontier hooker and a saddle tramp trying to make a buck in the Old West. It gets tedious real fast. Rated PG. 1976; 103m.

DUDE RANGER ★★★★
DIR: Eddie Cline. **CAST:** George O'Brien, Irene Hervey.
In this sturdy, well-played, and skillfully directed adaptation of the Zane Grey story, George O'Brien is a city boy who heads west to claim his inheritance: a ranch he fully intends to sell the first chance he gets. As it turns out, rustlers have been depleting his stock, and O'Brien stays on to find the culprits. 1934; B&W; 65m.

DUEL IN THE SUN ★★★
DIR: King Vidor. **CAST:** Jennifer Jones, Gregory Peck, Joseph Cotten, Lionel Barrymore, Walter Huston, Lillian Gish, Harry Carey.
This sprawling, brawling Western has land baron Lionel Barrymore's sons, unbroken, short-fused Gregory Peck and solid-citizen Joseph Cotten, vying for the hand of hot-blooded, half-breed Jennifer Jones. Peck and Jones take a lusty love-hate relationship to the max in the steaming desert. A near epic with a great musical score. 1946; 130m.

DYNAMITE CANYON ★★½
DIR: Robert Emmett Tansey. **CAST:** Tom Keene, Evelyn Finley, Kenne Duncan.
Tom Keene infiltrates an outlaw gang that is attempting to grab Evelyn Finley's ranch for its copper deposits. It's a bit slower than other Keene oaters. 1941; B&W; 58m.

DYNAMITE PASS ★★½
DIR: Lew Landers. **CAST:** Tim Holt, Richard Martin, Regis Toomey, Lynne Roberts, John Dehner, Robert Shayne, Cleo Moore, Denver Pyle, Ross Elliott.

Unconventional shoot-'em-up has cowpoke Tim Holt and sidekick Richard Martin helping a construction engineer battle a tyrannical toll-road operator and his hired guns. Once you get beyond the storyline, the action is in the best Western tradition. All of the principals and supporting players give it their best shot, and this modest little oater has a nice edge to it. 1950; B&W; 61m.

EL CONDOR ★½

DIR: John Guillermin. **CAST:** Jim Brown, Lee Van Cleef, Patrick O'Neal.

A disappointing Western, this features cardboard performances by Jim Brown and Lee Van Cleef as two adventurers determined to take a fortress of gold called El Condor. Together with a band of renegade Apaches, they capture their prize. Not rated, but equivalent to an R for nudity and violence. 1970; 102m.

EL DORADO ★★★★½

DIR: Howard Hawks. **CAST:** John Wayne, Robert Mitchum, James Caan, Arthur Hunnicutt, Edward Asner, Michele Carey, Christopher George, Charlene Holt, Jim Davis, Paul Fix, R. G. Armstrong, Johnny Crawford.

Few stars could match John Wayne's ability to dominate a scene—and one of those few, Robert Mitchum, costars in this tale of a land war between bad, bad Edward Asner and family man R. G. Armstrong. Mitchum plays the drunk in this take-off on *Rio Bravo*, and Wayne is the gunfighter with whom he forms an uneasy alliance. It's basically an upscale B Western with some of the best scenes ever to be found in a cowboy movie. 1967; 126m.

ELFEGO BACA: SIX GUN LAW ★★½

DIR: Christian Nyby. **CAST:** Robert Loggia, James Dunn, Lynn Bari, James Drury, Jay C. Flippen, Kenneth Tobey, Annette Funicello, Patric Knowles, Audrey Dalton.

Two-fisted lawyer Elfego Baca is charismatically portrayed by top actor Robert Loggia in this compilation of episodes from *Walt Disney Presents* originally aired from 1958 to 1962. Defending justice in Tombstone, Arizona, Elfego Baca fights for the lives of an Englishman framed for murder and a rancher charged with bank robbery. 1962; 77m.

END OF THE TRAIL ★★★★

DIR: D. Ross Lederman. **CAST:** Tim McCoy, Luana Walter, Wheeler Oakman.

The great Western star Colonel Tim McCoy was a lifelong champion of the American Indian. *End of the Trail* is his magnum opus, a movie sympathetic to Native Americans made nearly twenty years before *Broken Arrow*. It's an ambitious, somewhat dated story of a cavalry officer (McCoy) falsely accused of treason and forced to prove his innocence by uncovering the true villain. 1932; B&W; 62m.

ENEMY OF THE LAW ★★★★

DIR: Harry Fraser. **CAST:** Tex Ritter, Dave O'Brien, Guy Wilferson, Charles King.

The Texas Rangers track down an outlaw gang who, years before, robbed a safe and hid the money. There are some hilarious escapades in this well-above-average oater. Tex Ritter's songs are always good. 1945; B&W; 59m.

FALSE COLORS ★★½

DIR: George Archainbaud. **CAST:** William Boyd, Andy Clyde, Jimmy Rogers, Claudia Drake, Douglass Dumbrille, Robert Mitchum.

Typical entry in the Hopalong Cassidy series places Hoppy on the side of the innocent people who are being terrorized and murdered by ace heavy Douglas Dumbrille, who wants their property and water rights. 1943; B&W; 65m.

FALSE PARADISE ★★
DIR: George Archainbaud. **CAST:** William Boyd, Andy Clyde, Rand Brooks, Joel Friedkin.

Straight-shooting Hopalong Cassidy comes to the aid of a girl in peril and finds himself inveigled in yet another situation involving crooked ranch owners and false mining claims. 1948; B&W; 59m.

FAR COUNTRY, THE ★★★½
DIR: Anthony Mann. **CAST:** James Stewart, Ruth Roman, Walter Brennan, Corinne Calvet, John McIntire, Jay C. Flippen, Steve Brodie, Harry Morgan.

James Stewart is a tough-minded cattleman intent on establishing himself in Alaska during the Klondike gold rush of 1896. The result is fine Western fare. 1955; 97m.

FARGO EXPRESS ★★
DIR: Alan James. **CAST:** Ken Maynard, Helen Mack, Paul Fix.

When Helen Mack's brother (Paul Fix) is accused of a crime he didn't commit, Ken Maynard attempts to clear his name by impersonating him at another robbery. Strange plot, dumb Western. 1933; B&W; 61m.

FIGHTING CARAVANS ★★★½
DIR: Otto Brower, David Burton. **CAST:** Gary Cooper, Lily Damita, Ernest Torrence, Eugene Pallette, Charles Winninger.

Despite the title, this is a Zane Grey Western—and a good one, full of intrigue, action, and, for leavening, a smattering of comedy. Lanky, taciturn Gary Cooper, wanted by the law, avoids arrest by conning a wagon-train girl to pose as his wife. Romance blooms as the train treks west, into the sights of hostile forces. 1931; B&W; 80m.

FIGHTING KENTUCKIAN, THE ★★★
DIR: George Waggner. **CAST:** John Wayne, Vera Hruba Ralston, Philip Dorn, Oliver Hardy.

Worth seeing if only for the rare and wonderful on-screen combination of John Wayne and Oliver Hardy, this period adventure casts the duo as frontiersmen who come to the aid of the homesteading Napoleonic French, in danger of being tricked out of their lands by the bad guys. If only Vera Hruba Ralston weren't the Duke's love interest, this could have been a real winner. 1949; B&W; 100m.

FIGHTING SHADOWS ★★★
DIR: David Selman. **CAST:** Tim McCoy, Ward Bond.

Royal Canadian Mountie Tim O'Farrell (Tim McCoy) returns to his former home to find out who is terrorizing fur trappers there. This puts him up against his old nemesis (Ward Bond). Standard fare is made watchable by the stars. 1935; B&W; 57m.

FISTFUL OF DOLLARS ★★★
DIR: Sergio Leone. **CAST:** Clint Eastwood, Mario Brega, Gian Maria Volonté.

Clint Eastwood parlayed his multi-year stint on television's *Rawhide* into international fame with this film, a slick remake of Akira Kurosawa's *Yojimbo*. Eastwood's laconic "Man With No Name" blows into a town nearly blown apart by two feuding families; after considerable manipulation by all concerned, he moves on down the road. 1964; 96m.

FISTFUL OF DYNAMITE, A ★★★
DIR: Sergio Leone. **CAST:** Rod Steiger, James Coburn, Maria Monti, Romolo Valli.

After his success with Clint Eastwood's "Man with No Name" Westerns, Italian director Sergio Leone made this sprawling, excessive film set during the Mexican Revolution. A thief, played by Rod Steiger, is drawn into the revolution by Irish mercenary James Coburn. Soon both are blowing up everything in sight and singlehandedly winning the war. 1972; 121m.

FIVE CARD STUD ★★½
DIR: Henry Hathaway. **CAST:** Dean Martin, Robert Mitchum, Inger Ste-

vens, Roddy McDowall, Katherine Justice, Yaphet Kotto, Denver Pyle.

Muddled Western with a whodunit motif. Gambler-gunfighter Dean Martin attempts to discover who is systematically murdering the members of a lynching party. Robert Mitchum adds some memorable moments as a gun-toting preacher, but most of the performances are lifeless, with Roddy McDowall's gunslinger the most ludicrous of all. This is far from top-notch Henry Hathaway. 1968; 103m.

FLAMING FRONTIERS ★★

DIR: Ray Taylor, Alan James. **CAST:** Johnny Mack Brown, Eleanor Hansen, Ralph Bowman, Charles Middleton.

Former football favorite Johnny Mack Brown rides into a long career as a Western star in this pretty standard serial. He plays Tex Houston, famous Indian scout. 1938; B&W; 15 chapters.

FLAMING STAR ★★★★

DIR: Don Siegel. **CAST:** Elvis Presley, Barbara Eden, Steve Forrest, Dolores Del Rio, John McIntire.

A solid Western directed by Don Siegel (*Dirty Harry*), this features Elvis Presley in a remarkably effective performance as a half-breed Indian who must choose sides when his mother's people go on the warpath. 1960; 101m.

FOR A FEW DOLLARS MORE ★★½

DIR: Sergio Leone. **CAST:** Clint Eastwood, Lee Van Cleef, Gian Maria Volonté, Klaus Kinski.

Plot-heavy and overlong sequel to *A Fistful of Dollars* finds Clint Eastwood's "Man With No Name" partnered with shifty Lee Van Cleef, with both in pursuit of badder guy Gian Maria Volonte. Eastwood has his hands full, but the story contains few surprises. 1965; 130m.

FORBIDDEN TRAIL ★★★½

DIR: Lambert Hillyer. **CAST:** Buck Jones, Barbara Weeks, Mary Carr, Al Smith.

In this superior series Western, one of several Buck Jones made for Columbia Pictures in the 1930s, the star and Al Smith play a couple of happy-go-lucky cowboys who find themselves in the middle of a range war. Jones, usually the stalwart, square-jawed defender of justice, takes a comedic approach to his part, and the results are quite pleasing. 1932; B&W; 71m.

FORBIDDEN TRAILS ★★

DIR: Robert N. Bradbury. **CAST:** Buck Jones, Tim McCoy, Raymond Hatton, Dave O'Brien, Tristram Coffin, Charles King.

In this, the least interesting of the Rough Riders Westerns, a pair of hardened criminals (Charles King and Bud Osborne) force a youngster (Dave O'Brien) to take part in their evil schemes. Robert N. Bradbury's direction lacks the energy brought to the series by Howard Bretherton, but the stars are as watchable as ever. 1941; B&W; 55m.

FORLORN RIVER ★★★

DIR: Charles Barton. **CAST:** Buster Crabbe, June Martel, Harvey Stephens.

Exciting Zane Grey story has horse thieves trying to buy army mounts with six guns. Good photography, literate script. 1937; B&W; 56m.

FORT APACHE ★★★★½

DIR: John Ford. **CAST:** John Wayne, Henry Fonda, Shirley Temple, Ward Bond, John Agar, George O'Brien.

The first entry in director John Ford's celebrated cavalry trilogy stars Henry Fonda as a post commandant who decides to make a name for himself by starting a war with the Apaches, against the advice of an experienced soldier (John Wayne). Great film. 1948; B&W; 127m.

FOUR FACES WEST ★★★
DIR: Alfred E. Green. **CAST:** Joel McCrea, Frances Dee, Charles Bickford, Joseph Calleia.

A small-scale Western that tends to be overlooked, it uses a standard formula (an outlaw is pursued by a determined sheriff). But the writing, acting, and direction find those nuances that can make a story fresh. 1948; B&W; 90m.

FOUR RODE OUT
DIR: John Peyser. **CAST:** Pernell Roberts, Sue Lyon, Julian Mateos, Leslie Nielsen.

Pernell Roberts plays a U.S. marshall in pursuit of a Mexican bank robber. This film is bad with a capital *B*. 1968; 90m.

FRISCO KID, THE ★★★
DIR: Robert Aldrich. **CAST:** Gene Wilder, Harrison Ford, William Smith, Ramon Bieri, Penny Peyser.

Gene Wilder and Harrison Ford make a surprisingly effective and funny team as a rabbi and outlaw, respectively, making their way to San Francisco. Good fun. Rated PG. 1979; 122m.

FRONTIER HORIZON ★★★
DIR: George Sherman. **CAST:** John Wayne, Ray "Crash" Corrigan, Raymond Hatton, Jennifer Jones.

In this modern-day Western, the Three Mesquiteers ride to the rescue when a group of ranchers battle unscrupulous land grabbers. Jennifer Jones makes an early screen appearance here under the name Phyllis Isley. 1939; B&W; 56m.

FRONTIER PONY EXPRESS ★★½
DIR: Joseph Kane. **CAST:** Roy Rogers, Lynne Roberts (Mary Hart), Raymond Hatton, Edward Keane.

Good action-packed Western finds Roy Rogers (in one of his early starring roles) coming to the aid of Pony Express riders who have been preyed on by robbers. 1939; B&W; 54m.

FRONTIERSMAN, THE ★★
DIR: Lesley Selander. **CAST:** William Boyd, George "Gabby" Hayes, Russell Hayden, Evelyn Venable.

Hopalong Cassidy (William Boyd) and his pals (George "Gabby" Hayes and Russell Hayden) take a break from upholding the law to help a schoolteacher (Evelyn Venable) educate a passel of young 'uns. 1938; B&W; 58m.

GENTLE SAVAGE ★★★½
DIR: Sean MacGregor. **CAST:** William Smith, Gene Evans, Barbara Luna, Joe Flynn.

In this well-paced Western, William Smith portrays an American Indian framed for the rape and beating of a white girl in a small town. The girl's stepfather, who actually committed the crime, incites the townsmen to go after the innocent man. When the townsmen kill the hapless fellow's brother, the American Indian community retaliates. Rated R for violence. 1978; 85m.

GHOST TOWN LAW ★★★
DIR: Howard Bretherton. **CAST:** Buck Jones, Tim McCoy, Raymond Hatton, Charles King.

Atmospheric B Western has the Rough Riders on the trail of a gang that murdered two of their colleagues. The gang, in a nice touch, hides out in a ghost town, where there might be more than just outlaws for our heroes to contend with. 1942; B&W; 62m.

GIT ALONG, LITTLE DOGIES ★★
DIR: Joseph Kane. **CAST:** Gene Autry, Smiley Burnette, Judith Allen, William Farnum.

Typical of Gene Autry's prewar films, this thin story of a spoiled, willful girl who is eventually tamed and socialized by the silver-voiced cowboy is heavy on the music and singing stars. 1937; B&W; 60m.

GOIN' SOUTH ★★★
DIR: Jack Nicholson. **CAST:** Jack Nicholson, Mary Steenburgen, John Belushi.

Star Jack Nicholson also directed this odd little Western tale of an outlaw (Nicholson) saved from the gallows by a spinster (Mary Steenburgen). The catch is he must marry her and work on her farm. Lots of attempts at comedy, but only a few work. Look for John Belushi in a small role as a Mexican cowboy. Rated PG; some violence and language. 1978; 109m.

GOLDEN STALLION, THE ★★½
DIR: William Witney. **CAST:** Roy Rogers, Dale Evans, Estelita Rodriguez, Pat Brady.

This offbeat entry to the Roy Rogers series places the emphasis on Trigger and his efforts to save a cute Palomino mare from a life of crime. Absolute hooey but fun to watch, and exciting for the kids and animal lovers in the audience. 1949; 67m.

GONE WITH THE WEST (A.K.A. BRONCO BUSTERS) ★
DIR: Bernard Gerard. **CAST:** James Caan, Stefanie Powers, Aldo Ray, Barbara Werle, Robert Walker Jr., Sammy Davis Jr., Michael Conrad.

With this excellent cast, one would expect more, but this is a confusing and vague tale about an Old West ex-con on the vengeance trail. 1972; 92m.

GOOD THE BAD AND THE UGLY, THE ★★★★
DIR: Sergio Leone. **CAST:** Clint Eastwood, Eli Wallach, Lee Van Cleef.

The best of Italian director Sergio Leone's spaghetti Westerns with Clint Eastwood, this release features the latter in the dubiously "good" role, with Lee Van Cleef as "the bad" and Eli Wallach as "the ugly." All three are after a cache of gold hidden in a Confederate army graveyard. For Leone fans, it's full of what made his movies so memorable. Others might find it a bit long, but no one can deny its sense of style. 1966; 161m.

GRAND CANYON TRAIL ★★
DIR: William Witney. **CAST:** Roy Rogers, Jane Frazee, Andy Devine, Robert Livingston.

Roy Rogers is saddled with what he thinks is a useless mine, and former serial hero Robert Livingston just about succeeds in swindling him out of what is actually a bonanza in silver. Fast-paced and almost tongue-in-cheek. 1948; B&W; 67m.

GRAYEAGLE ★½
DIR: Charles B. Pierce. **CAST:** Ben Johnson, Iron Eyes Cody, Lana Wood, Alex Cord, Jack Elam, Paul Fix.

Disappointing reworking of John Wayne's *The Searchers*, with Alex Cord as the Cheyenne warrior Grayeagle, who kidnaps Lana Wood and is pursued by the girl's father, Ben Johnson. A good story, but the writing and directing drag it down to an amateur level. Rated PG for violence and mild nudity. 1977; 104m.

GREAT GUNDOWN 🦃
DIR: Paul Hunt. **CAST:** Robert Padilla, Richard Rust.

Overly long, poorly photographed, tritely written, violent melodrama tries to be half spaghetti Western, half *Wild Bunch*, and is neither. Best thing is the cameos by Western vets Walter Barnes and Don Megowan. Filmed in New Mexico in the mid-Seventies and released sporadically under varying titles: *El Salvejo (The Savage)*, *Savage Red, Outlaw White*, and finally *Great Gundown*. 1976; 98m.

GREAT MISSOURI RAID, THE ★★
DIR: Gordon Douglas. **CAST:** Wendell Corey, Macdonald Carey, Ellen Drew, Ward Bond.

Another depiction of Frank and Jesse James and their pals the Younger brothers. This picture is good for a late-night view or while you're microwaving your dinner. Passable, but better accounts of the James boys are available. 1950; 83m.

GREAT NORTHFIELD MINNESOTA RAID, THE ★★★
DIR: Phil Kaufman. **CAST:** Cliff Robertson, Robert Duvall, Luke Askew, R. G. Armstrong, Dana Elcar, Donald

Moffat, Jack Pearce, Matt Clark, Elisha Cook Jr.

A strong cast of character actors propels this offbeat Western, which chronicles the exploits of the James-Younger gang. Cliff Robertson is an effectively world-weary and witty Cole Younger, and Robert Duvall sets off sparks as a crafty, calculating Jesse James. The film never quite satisfies as a whole though there are some terrific moments. Rated R for violence and profanity. 1972; 91m.

GREAT SCOUT AND CATHOUSE THURSDAY, THE ★★★
DIR: Don Taylor. **CAST:** Lee Marvin, Oliver Reed, Elizabeth Ashley, Robert Culp, Strother Martin, Kay Lenz.

Eccentric Western comedy involving a variety of get-rich-quick schemes concocted by an amusing band of rogues. Oliver Reed steals the show as a wacky American Indian whose double-crosses usually backfire. Not much plot and considerable silliness, but fun nonetheless. Rated PG for sexual situations. 1976; 102m.

GREY FOX, THE ★★★★★
DIR: Phillip Borsos. **CAST:** Richard Farnsworth, Jackie Burroughs, Ken Pogue, Timothy Webber.

Richard Farnsworth (*Comes a Horseman*) stars in this marvelously entertaining Canadian feature as the gentleman bandit Bill Miner who, as the movie poster proclaimed, "on June 17, 1901, after thirty-three years in San Quentin Prison for robbing stagecoaches, was released into the twentieth century." Rated PG for brief violence. 1982; 92m.

GUN CODE ★★★
DIR: Peter Stewart. **CAST:** Tim McCoy, Dave O'Brien.

When the residents of Miller's Flats find themselves being coerced into paying protection money, Tim Haines (Tim McCoy) rides to the rescue, guns a-blazing. Even the minuscule budgets of Producers Releasing Corporation couldn't stop McCoy from turning out above-average Westerns. 1940; B&W; 52m.

GUN FURY ★★★
DIR: Raoul Walsh. **CAST:** Rock Hudson, Donna Reed, Lee Marvin, Philip Carey, Neville Brand.

Donna Reed is kidnapped. Rock Hudson chases the badmen and saves her from a fate worse than death in Arizona's mesmerizing Red Rock country. Villainy abounds. 1953; 83m.

GUN RIDERS, THE ★★
DIR: Al Adamson. **CAST:** Robert Dix, Scott Brady, Jim Davis, John Carradine, Paula Raymond.

Genre fans may enjoy this violent adult Western, though others will find it nihilistic and sleazy, without the humor that graced Italian spaghetti Westerns. A sadistic gunman, nicknamed the Messenger of Death, is the center of a story pitting Indians, gunrunners, and settlers against each other. Photographed by Vilmos Zsigmond. Rated PG. 1969; 88m.

GUNDOWN AT SANDOVAL ★★★
DIR: Harry Keller. **CAST:** Tom Tryon, Dan Duryea, Beverly Garland, Lyle Bettger, Harry Carey Jr.

Texas John Slaughter faces overwhelming odds when he vows to avenge a friend's death and goes against the inhabitants of Sandoval, an infamous outlaw hideout. Featuring lots of hard riding and gunplay, this Disney television show was originally shown in Europe as a feature film. 1959; 72m.

GUNFIGHT, A ★½
DIR: Lamont Johnson. **CAST:** Kirk Douglas, Johnny Cash, Jane Alexander, Karen Black, Raf Vallone.

This lifeless Western features the acting debut of country singer Johnny Cash. He is teamed with Kirk Douglas in a story of two long-in-the-tooth gunslingers who hatch a plan to make money by staging a shoot-out. 1971; 90m.

GUNFIGHT AT THE O.K. CORRAL ★★★★
DIR: John Sturges. **CAST:** Burt Lancaster, Kirk Douglas, Rhonda Fleming, Jo Van Fleet, John Ireland, Lee Van Cleef, Frank Faylen.

The Wyatt Earp–Doc Holliday legend got another going-over in this rather good Western. Burt Lancaster and Kirk Douglas portray these larger-than-life gunfighters, who shoot it out with the nefarious Clanton family in 1881 Tombstone. The movie effectively builds up its tension until the climactic gunfight. 1957; 122m.

GUNMAN FROM BODIE ★★★½
DIR: Spencer Gordon Bennet. **CAST:** Buck Jones, Tim McCoy, Raymond Hatton, Dave O'Brien.

The best of the many trio series Westerns of the 1930s and '40s, "The Rough Riders" teamed two of the genre's most charismatic stars, Buck Jones and Tim McCoy, with one of the best sidekicks in the business, Raymond Hatton. The second film in the series, *Gunman from Bodie* is considered by most aficionados to be the best, and we agree. The plot, about a trio of marshals who set out to capture a gang of cattle thieves, may be old and worn-out, but the sheer star power and personality of Jones, McCoy, and Hatton make this formula B Western a first-rate example of its kind. 1941; B&W; 60m.

GUNS OF THE MAGNIFICENT SEVEN ★★★
DIR: Paul Wendkos. **CAST:** George Kennedy, Monte Markham, James Whitmore, Bernie Casey, Joe Don Baker, Michael Ansara.

George Kennedy, fresh from his success with *Cool Hand Luke*, steps in for Yul Brynner as Chris, a well-meaning gunfighter who has a bad habit of getting his friends killed while defending the downtrodden. This second sequel has some fine performances—particularly by Kennedy and James Whitmore—and some rousing action scenes, but the original *Seven* has yet to be equaled. Rated PG. 1969; 106m.

HANG 'EM HIGH ★★★
DIR: Ted Post. **CAST:** Clint Eastwood, Inger Stevens, Ed Begley Sr., Pat Hingle, Arlene Golonka, Ben Johnson.

Clint Eastwood's first stateside spaghetti Western is a good one, with the star out to get the vigilantes who tried to hang him for a murder he didn't commit. Pat Hingle is the hangin' judge who gives Clint his license to hunt, and Ben Johnson is the marshal who saves his life. Ed Begley Sr. is memorable as the leader of the vigilantes. Rated PG. 1968; 114m.

HARLEM RIDES THE RANGE ★★½
DIR: Richard Kahn. **CAST:** Herbert Jeffrey (Jeffries), Lucius Brooks.

Stale plot about stolen mine rights (to a radium mine this time) is secondary to the limited action and uniqueness of seeing an all-black cast in what has traditionally been the territory of white actors and actresses. 1939; B&W; 58m.

HARRY TRACY ★★★½
DIR: William A. Graham. **CAST:** Bruce Dern, Helen Shaver, Michael C. Gwynne, Gordon Lightfoot.

Bruce Dern plays the title role in this surprisingly amiable little Western, with the star as the last of a gentlemanly outlaw breed. Although he's a crafty character, Harry always seems to get caught. His mind is all too often on other things—in particular, a well-to-do woman (Helen Shaver). Rated PG. 1982; 100m.

HATFIELDS AND THE MCCOYS, THE ★★½
DIR: Clyde Ware. **CAST:** Jack Palance, Steve Forrest, Richard Hatch, Joan Caulfield.

The great American legend of backwoods feuding long celebrated in song and story. Jack Palance and Steve Forrest make the most of portraying the clan patriarchs. The feud was reason enough to leave the hills and head west in the 1880s. A guy could get killed for saying hello to the wrong face! Made for TV. 1975; 74m.

HEART OF THE GOLDEN WEST ★★½

DIR: Joseph Kane. **CAST:** Roy Rogers, Smiley Burnette, George "Gabby" Hayes, Ruth Terry.

This modern-day adventure pits Roy Rogers and his fellow ranchers against cheating city slickers intent on defrauding the cowboys and putting them out of business. Enjoyable Western hokum. 1942; B&W; 65m.

HEART OF THE RIO GRANDE ★★

DIR: William Morgan. **CAST:** Gene Autry, Smiley Burnette, Fay McKenzie.

Gene Autry and the gang sing some sense into a snooty, spoiled rich girl and manage to bring her and her too busy father back together again. Standard story is given standard, simple-minded treatment. 1942; B&W; 70m.

HEARTLAND ★★★★

DIR: Richard Pearce. **CAST:** Conchata Ferrell, Rip Torn, Lilia Skala, Megan Folsom.

This is an excellent and deceptively simple story, of a widow (Conchata Ferrell) who settled, with her daughter and a homesteader (Rip Torn), in turn-of-the-century Wyoming. The film deals with the complex problems of surviving in nature and society. It's well worth watching. Rated PG. 1979; 96m.

HEAVEN'S GATE ★★★

DIR: Michael Cimino. **CAST:** Kris Kristofferson, Christopher Walken, Isabelle Huppert, John Hurt, Sam Waterston, Brad Dourif, Jeff Bridges, Joseph Cotten.

Written and directed by Michael Cimino (*The Deer Hunter*), this $36 million epic Western about the land wars in Wyoming, between the cattle barons and immigrant farmers, is awkward and overlong but at least makes sense in the complete video version. Rated R for nudity, sex, and violence. 1980; 219m.

HELL TOWN ★★★½

DIR: Charles Barton. **CAST:** John Wayne, Marsha Hunt, Johnny Mack Brown, Alan Ladd, James Craig, Monte Blue, Lucien Littlefield.

Here's a real find for fans of John Wayne, a pre-*Stagecoach* Western of good quality. Stepping up from his low-budget programmers for Republic and Monogram, the Duke was cast in this, the last of Paramount's series of films based on the stories of Zane Grey. He plays a happy-go-lucky cowhand who falls in with rustlers much to the chagrin of his serious-minded relative, lawman Johnny Mack Brown. Also known as *Born to the West*. 1938; B&W; 50m.

HELLBENDERS, THE

DIR: Sergio Corbucci. **CAST:** Joseph Cotten, Norma Bengell, Julian Mateos, Angel Aranda.

Joseph Cotten fans will weep at this badly overdubbed spaghetti Western set in the post–Civil war era. It's the story of a washed-out Confederate and his band of sons who call themselves The Hellbenders. In this overly long film, they are pursued across the barren landscape with stolen currency that Cotten plans to use to reorganize the Confederacy. Sappy dialogue and unlikable characters. Rated PG. 1967; 92m.

HELLDORADO (1946) ★★

DIR: William Witney. **CAST:** Roy Rogers, George "Gabby" Hayes, Dale Evans, Bob Nolan and the Sons of the Pioneers, LeRoy Mason, Paul Harvey, Rex Lease, Eddie Acuff, Clayton Moore.

Roy and the boys swing into action (and break into song) as they exercise their fists and tonsils while breaking up a gang of black-market racketeers in postwar Las Vegas. The popular rodeo forms the backdrop as Roy, Dale, and Gabby entertain the likes of singer Eddie Acuff and future Lone Ranger Clayton Moore. 1946; B&W; 70m.

HELLER IN PINK TIGHTS ★★½
DIR: George Cukor. **CAST:** Sophia Loren, Anthony Quinn, Margaret O'Brien, Edmund Lowe, Steve Forrest, Eileen Heckart, Ramon Novarro.
The career of legendary nineteenth-century actress and love goddess Adah Issacs Menken inspired this odd film about a ragtag theatrical troupe wandering the West in the 1880s. Colorful but air-filled, it offers a busty blond Sophia Loren with lusty Tony Quinn fending off belligerent townfolk, creditors, and distrustful sheriffs. 1960; 100m.

HELLFIRE ★★★½
DIR: R. G. Springsteen. **CAST:** William Elliott, Marie Windsor, Forrest Tucker, Jim Davis, Grant Withers, Paul Fix, Denver Pyle.
Solid, offbeat Western in which a ne'er-do-well gambler, William ("Wild Bill") Elliott, is shoved onto the path of righteousness when a preacher saves his life. A bit preachy at times, *Hellfire* still packs a solid wallop of entertainment. 1949; 79m.

HELL'S HINGES ★★★
DIR: William S. Hart, Charles Swickard. **CAST:** William S. Hart, Clara Williams, Robert McKim.
William S. Hart's trademark character, the good-bad man, loses his heart to the new minister's sister when she arrives in Hell's Hinges. Hart switches his allegiance from the saloon to the church. Shortly after he leaves town, the minister is corrupted and the church burned down, causing Hart to seek revenge. This grim story is perhaps Hart's best film, and certainly his most imitated. Silent. 1916; B&W; 65m.

HIGH NOON ★★★★★
DIR: Fred Zinnemann. **CAST:** Gary Cooper, Grace Kelly, Lloyd Bridges, Thomas Mitchell, Katy Jurado, Otto Kruger, Lon Chaney Jr.
Gary Cooper won his second Oscar for his role of the abandoned lawman in this classic Western. It's the sheriff's wedding day, and the head of an outlaw band, who has sworn vengeance against him, is due to arrive in town at high noon. When Cooper turns to his fellow townspeople for help, no one comes forward. The suspense of this movie keeps snowballing as the clock ticks ever closer to noon. 1952; B&W; 84m.

HIGH NOON, PART TWO
DIR: Jerry Jameson. **CAST:** Lee Majors, David Carradine, J. A. Preston, Pernell Roberts, M. Emmet Walsh.
This is a poor attempt at a sequel. It begins in much the same way as the original, with a man standing against impossible odds. The difference is the actors and the director. The film also lacks the suspense of the original. 1980; 100m.

HIGH PLAINS DRIFTER ★★★
DIR: Clint Eastwood. **CAST:** Clint Eastwood, Verna Bloom, Marianna Hill, Mitchell Ryan, Jack Ging, Geoffrey Lewis, John Mitchum.
Star-director Clint Eastwood tried to revive the soggy spaghetti Western genre one more time, with watchable results. Eastwood comes to a frontier town just in time to make sure its sleazy citizens are all but wiped out by a trio of revenge-seeking outlaws. Although atmospheric, it's also confusing and sometimes just downright nasty. Rated R for violence, profanity, and suggested sex. 1973; 105m.

HILLS OF UTAH, THE ★★½
DIR: John English. **CAST:** Gene Autry, Pat Buttram, Elaine Riley, Onslow Stevens, Donna Martell.
Harking back to a classic theme, Gene returns to the town where his father was killed and manages to settle a local feud as well as uncover the truth about his father's murder. Even with Pat Buttram, this is somber for a Gene Autry film. 1951; B&W; 70m.

HIRED HAND, THE ★★★½
DIR: Peter Fonda. **CAST:** Peter Fonda, Warren Oates, Verna Bloom, Severn Darden.

This low-key Western follows two drifters, Peter Fonda and Warren Oates, as they return to Fonda's farm and the wife, Verna Bloom, he deserted seven years earlier. While working on the farm, Fonda and Bloom begin to rekindle their relationship, only to have it interrupted when Fonda must go to the aid of Oates, who is being held prisoner in a small town. Beautiful cinematography and fine performances, especially by Oates, add greatly to this worthy entry in the genre. Rated R. 1971; 93m.

HIS NAME WAS KING ★½
DIR: Don Reynolds. **CAST:** Richard Harrison, Klaus Kinski.

Spaghetti Western about a bounty hunter named King (Richard Harrison) who tracks down a ring of gunrunners near the Mexican border. Plenty of action, but like most Westerns from Italy, the bad guys are so bad that their psychotic behavior, coupled with stupid voice dubbing, comes off too close to comedy to be taken seriously. Not rated, but equal to a PG. 1983; 90m.

HOMBRE ★★★★
DIR: Martin Ritt. **CAST:** Paul Newman, Fredric March, Richard Boone, Diane Cilento, Cameron Mitchell, Barbara Rush, Martin Balsam.

Paul Newman gives a superb performance as a white man raised by Indians who is enticed into helping a stagecoach full of settlers make its way across treacherous country. Richard Boone is the baddie who makes this chore difficult, but the racism Newman encounters in this Martin Ritt film provides the real—and thought-provoking—thrust. 1967; 111m.

HOME IN OKLAHOMA ★★
DIR: William Witney. **CAST:** Roy Rogers, George "Gabby" Hayes, Dale Evans, Carol Hughes, Bob Nolan and the Sons of the Pioneers, George Meeker, Frank Reicher.

Roy Rogers and Dale Evans play a nervy newspaper editor and a nervier reporter who question the "accidental" death of a millionaire ranch owner. Adhering to the tried-and-true formula of all series films, Roy and his cohort risk their reputations and lives for the underdog, in this case the dead rancher's niece (Carol Hughes). An enjoyable example of what kids watched before there was television. 1946; B&W; 72m.

HOPALONG CASSIDY ENTERS ★★★½
DIR: Howard P. Bretherton. **CAST:** William Boyd, Jimmy Ellison, George "Gabby" Hayes, Charles Middleton.

Solid series Western marked the debut of William Boyd as novelist Clarence E. Mulford's fictional hero, who was considerably changed by the time he reached the screen. Boyd gives a strong performance as Cassidy, who, in his initial movie, is possessed of a hair-trigger temper. Jimmy Ellison is the hotheaded but basically decent kid whom Cassidy turns around. 1935; B&W; 62m.

HOPPY'S HOLIDAY ★★
DIR: George Archainbaud. **CAST:** William Boyd, Andy Clyde, Rand Brooks, Jeff Corey.

A weak entry in the last of twelve Hopalong Cassidy films pits Hoppy and the Bar-20 cowboys against mechanized bank robbers. 1947; B&W; 60m.

HORSE SOLDIERS, THE ★★★★
DIR: John Ford. **CAST:** John Wayne, William Holden, Constance Towers, Hoot Gibson.

Based on a true incident during the Civil War, this is a minor, but enjoyable, John Ford cavalry outing. John Wayne and William Holden play well-matched adversaries in the Union Army. 1959; 119m.

HOW THE WEST WAS WON ★★★½
DIR: John Ford, Henry Hathaway, George Marshall. **CAST:** Gregory Peck, Henry Fonda, James Stewart,

John Wayne, Debbie Reynolds, Walter Brennan, Karl Malden, Richard Widmark, Robert Preston, George Peppard.

Any Western with this cast is at least worth a glimpse. Sadly, this 1962 epic doesn't hold up that well on video because it was released on the three-screen Cinerama process. Much of the grandeur of the original version is lost. But shoot-'em-up fans won't want to miss a chance to see many of the genre's greats in one motion picture. 1962; 155m.

I SHOT BILLY THE KID ★★

DIR: William Berke. **CAST:** Donald "Red" Barry, Robert Lowery, Tom Neal, John Morton, Jack Perrin.

Pat Garrett (Robert Lowery) tells this sympathetic tale of a good young man who went bad. A standard but watchable rehash of familiar material. 1950; B&W; 59m.

I WILL FIGHT NO MORE FOREVER ★★★½

DIR: Richard T. Heffron. **CAST:** Ned Romero, James Whitmore, Sam Elliott, Linda Redfern.

Effective and affecting story of how the Nez Percé Indian tribe, under Chief Joseph, were driven to war with U.S. government in 1877. In the last great Indian campaign waged by the cavalry, the Nez Percé tied up five troops for more than eight months, even though fighting with only a hundred able-bodied warriors. Ned Romero is superb as the proud but wise Chief Joseph, and James Whitmore turns in a fine performance as the craggy General Howard. Made for TV. 1975; 106m.

IDAHO ★★

DIR: Joseph Kane. **CAST:** Roy Rogers, Smiley Burnette, Bob Nolan and the Sons of the Pioneers, Virginia Grey, Harry Shannon, Ona Munson, Dick Purcell, Onslow Stevens, Hal Taliaferro (Wally Wales), Rex Lease, Tom London, Jack Ingram.

The king of the Cowboys tangles with the local evil influences as he helps put an end to bad-girl Ona Munson's vice dens. Gene Autry was in the air force in 1943, so Roy found himself in the number-one spot with a bigger budget and ex-Autry sidekick Smiley Burnette. 1943; B&W; 70m.

IN EARLY ARIZONA ★★★½

DIR: Joseph Levering. **CAST:** William Elliott, Harry Woods, Charles King.

In this big-budget B, Wild Bill Elliott tames the town of Tombstone by getting rid of the evil Harry Woods. A fine example of this type of Western lore. Plenty of action and energy. 1938; B&W; 53m.

IN OLD CALIFORNIA ★★★

DIR: William McGann. **CAST:** John Wayne, Binnie Barnes, Albert Dekker, Helen Parrish, Patsy Kelly, Edgar Kennedy.

In one of his numerous B-plus pictures for Republic Studios, John Wayne plays a mild-mannered pharmacist who is forced to take up arms when he settles down in a Western town run by the corrupt Albert Dekker. Director William McGann keeps things moving at a sprightly pace, which is more than one can say of the other films in the series. 1942; B&W; 88m.

IN OLD CHEYENNE ★

DIR: Stuart Paton. **CAST:** Rex Lease, Dorothy Gulliver, Harry Woods, Jay Hunt.

Forgotten low-budget star Rex Lease takes a backseat to a smart stallion in this predictable old creaker. Primitive and cheaply produced; the animal footage remains about the best part of this shoot-'em-up. 1931; B&W; 60m.

IN OLD MEXICO ★★★

DIR: Edward Venturini. **CAST:** William Boyd, George "Gabby" Hayes, Russell Hayden, Jane Clayton, Glenn Strange.

In this suspense-Western, a sequel to *Borderland*, Hopalong Cassidy solves a murder while working in Mexico. A good script plus fine direction and acting make this a sure-bet B Western. 1938; B&W; 62m.

INVITATION TO A GUNFIGHTER ★★

DIR: Richard Wilson. CAST: Yul Brynner, George Segal, Janice Rule, Pat Hingle.

Studio-slick Western is short on action and long on dialogue as a hired professional killer comes to town and changes the balance of power. Everybody gets a chance to emote in this gabfest—which helps, since the story is so slim. Typical of a Stanley Kramer message film but not quite as heavy-handed as most. 1964; 92m.

JEREMIAH JOHNSON ★★★★

DIR: Sydney Pollack. CAST: Robert Redford, Will Geer, Charles Tyner, Stefan Gierasch, Allyn Ann McLerie.

Robert Redford plays Johnson, a simple man who has no taste for cities. We see him as he grows from his first feeble attempts at survival to a hunter who has quickened his senses with wild meat and vegetation—a man who is a part of the wildlife of the mountains. *Jeremiah Johnson* gives a sense of humanness to a genre that had, up until its release, spent time reworking the same myths. Rated PG. 1972; 107m.

JESSE JAMES ★★★½

DIR: Henry King. CAST: Tyrone Power, Henry Fonda, Nancy Kelly, Randolph Scott, Henry Hull, Jane Darwell, Brian Donlevy, Donald Meek, John Carradine, Slim Summerville, J. Edward Bromberg.

Tyrone Power is Jesse and Henry Fonda is Frank in this legend-gilding account of the life and misdeeds of Missouri's most famous outlaw. Bending history, the film paints Jesse as a peaceful man driven to a life of crime by heartless big business in the form of a railroad, and a loving husband and father murdered for profit by a coward. 1939; 105m.

JESSE JAMES AT BAY ★★½

DIR: Joseph Kane. CAST: Roy Rogers, George "Gabby" Hayes, Sally Payne.

Roy Rogers is a fictionalized Jesse James who rides not against the railroads, but against one evil bunch misrepresenting the railroad and stealing the land of poor, honest farmers. A top contender for *the* most far-fetched, fallacious frontier foolishness ever filmed. 1941; B&W; 56m.

JOE KIDD ★★★½

DIR: John Sturges. CAST: Clint Eastwood, Robert Duvall, John Saxon, Don Stroud.

While not exactly a thrill-a-minute movie, this Western has a number of memorable moments. Director John Sturges has been better, but Clint Eastwood and Robert Duvall are at the peak of their forms in this story of a gunman (Eastwood) hired by a cattle baron (Duvall) to track down some Mexican-Americans who are fighting back because they've been cheated out of their land. Rated PG. 1972; 88m.

JOHNNY GUITAR ★★★½

DIR: Nicholas Ray. CAST: Joan Crawford, Mercedes McCambridge, Sterling Hayden, Scott Brady, Ward Bond, Ernest Borgnine, John Carradine.

A positively weird Western, this Nicholas Ray film features the ultimate role reversal. Bar owner Joan Crawford and landowner Mercedes McCambridge shoot it out while their gun-toting boyfriends (Sterling Hayden and Scott Brady) look on. 1954; 110m.

JORY ★★★

DIR: Jorge Fons. CAST: Robby Benson, John Marley, B. J. Thomas, Linda Purl.

A surprisingly sensitive film for the genre finds Robby Benson, in his first film role, as a 15-year-old boy who must learn to go it alone in the Wild West after his father is senselessly murdered. While remaining exciting and suspenseful, the film takes time to make commentary about manhood and machismo in an adult, thoughtful manner. Rated PG. 1972; 97m.

JUBAL ★★★½

DIR: Delmer Daves. **CAST:** Glenn Ford, Ernest Borgnine, Valerie French, Rod Steiger, Charles Bronson, Noah Beery Jr., Felicia Farr.

Adult Western finds drifter Jubal Troop (Glenn Ford) enmeshed in just about everybody's problems when he signs on with rancher Ernest Borgnine. Beautifully photographed and well acted, this tale of jealousy and revenge is standout entertainment. 1956; 101m.

JUNIOR BONNER ★★★

DIR: Sam Peckinpah. **CAST:** Steve McQueen, Robert Preston, Ida Lupino, Ben Johnson, Joe Don Baker.

A rodeo has-been, Steve McQueen, returns home for one last rousing performance in front of the home folks. McQueen is quite good as the soft-spoken cowboy who tries to make peace with his family. Robert Preston is a real scene-stealer as his hard-drinking carouser of a father. Rated PG. 1972; 103m.

KANSAN, THE ★★★

DIR: George Archainbaud. **CAST:** Richard Dix, Jane Wyatt, Victor Jory, Albert Dekker, Eugene Pallette, Robert Armstrong.

Tough, two-fisted Richard Dix sets his jaw and routs the baddies in a wide-open prairie town but must then contend with a corrupt official in this enjoyable Western, the third to pair him with Jane Wyatt and heavies Victor Jory and Albert Dekker. 1943; B&W; 79m.

KANSAS PACIFIC ★★½

DIR: Ray Nazarro. **CAST:** Sterling Hayden, Eve Miller, Barton MacLane, Douglas Fowley, Myron Healey, Clayton Moore, Reed Hadley.

Railroad drama set in pre–Civil War days has rangy Sterling Hayden romancing Eve Miller and battling pro-Confederate saboteurs intent on hindering construction of the Kansas Pacific Railroad. 1953; 73m.

KENTUCKIAN, THE ★★★

DIR: Burt Lancaster. **CAST:** Burt Lancaster, Diana Lynn, Dianne Foster, Walter Matthau, John Carradine, Una Merkel.

Pushing west in the 1820s, Burt Lancaster bucks all odds to reach Texas and begin a new life. A good mix of history, adventure, romance, and comedy make this one worth a family watching. 1955; 104m.

KENTUCKY RIFLE ★★½

DIR: Carl K. Hittleman. **CAST:** Chill Wills, Jeanne Cagney, Cathy Downes, Lance Fuller, Sterling Holloway.

Pioneers going West are stranded in Comanche country. They must barter the Kentucky long rifles in their wagons for safe passage. Passable oater. 1955; 80m.

KING OF THE BULLWHIP ★★½

DIR: Ron Ormond. **CAST:** Lash LaRue, Al St. John, Jack Holt, Dennis Moore, Tom Neal, Anne Gwynne.

Looking every bit like Humphrey Bogart's twin brother in a black hat, Lash LaRue was the whip-wielding westerner in a series of low budget shoot-'em-ups in the 1950s. This, his first for a major distributor, was one of his better efforts. Lash and his sidekick Al St. John must go undercover when a bandit pretends to be our hero while robbing a bank. 1951; 60m.

KING OF THE TEXAS RANGERS ★★½

DIR: William Witney, John English. **CAST:** Sammy Baugh, Neil Hamilton, Pauline Moore, Duncan Renaldo.

Standard Republic Studios cliffhanger serial has some truly bizarre qualities. The lead, Slingin' Sammy Baugh, was a famous football star in the 1940s. Baugh plays Tom King, a football player who gives up a successful career in the sport to avenge the death of his father, a Texas Ranger who was killed by fifth columnists. Yes, this is a modern-day Western with cars, phones, Nazis, and even a zeppelin(!). 1941; B&W; 12 chapters.

KIT CARSON ★★★½
DIR: George B. Seitz. **CAST:** Jon Hall, Dana Andrews, Lynn Bari.
This lively Western about the two-fisted frontiersman gave Jon Hall one of his best roles. Good action scenes. 1940; B&W; 97m.

LADY FROM LOUISIANA ★★
DIR: Bernard Vorhaus. **CAST:** John Wayne, Ray Middleton, Osa Massen.
John Wayne is a crusading lawyer in this middling Republic period piece. 1941; B&W; 82m.

LADY TAKES A CHANCE, A ★★★
DIR: William A. Seiter. **CAST:** Jean Arthur, John Wayne, Phil Silvers, Charles Winninger, Grady Sutton, Hans Conried, Grant Withers, Mary Field.
John Wayne is a rough-'n'-ready, not the marrying kind, rodeo star. Jean Arthur is an innocent girl from New York City out West. He falls off a horse into her lap, she falls for him, and the chase is on. Played for comedy, this one's *It Happened One Night* with spurs. 1943; B&W; 86m.

LAST COMMAND, THE (1955) ★★½
DIR: Frank Lloyd. **CAST:** Sterling Hayden, Richard Carlson, Anna Maria Alberghetti, Ernest Borgnine, Arthur Hunnicutt, Jim Davis, J. Carrol Naish.
This is a watchable Western about the famed last stand at the Alamo during Texas's fight for independence from Mexico. Jim Bowie (Sterling Hayden), Davy Crockett (Arthur Hunnicutt), and Colonel Travis (Richard Carlson) are portrayed in a more realistic manner than they were in John Wayne's *The Alamo*, but the story is still mostly hokum. 1955; 110m.

LAST FRONTIER, THE ★★½
DIR: Spencer Gordon Bennet, Thomas L. Story. **CAST:** Lon Chaney Jr., Dorothy Gulliver, Mary Jo Desmond, Francis X. Bushman Jr., Yakima Canutt, LeRoy Mason, William Desmond.
Another serial set in the Old West. The mysterious Black Ghost helps newspaper editor Tom Kirby (Lon Chaney Jr.) fight a band of ruffians who are intent on provoking Indians to attack the settlers and drive them from their homes. As usual, there's gold at the bottom of all the trouble. The hero has his hands full escaping from one perilous situation after another. 1932; B&W; 12 chapters.

LAST GUN, THE ★
DIR: Serge Bergone. **CAST:** Cameron Mitchell, Frank Wolff, Carl Moher.
In this Italian Western dubbed into English, a gunfighter tired of killing hangs up his pistols and settles down in a small town. Outlaws appear and he must protect the townspeople by putting on his guns. The story is classic. The acting and directing are not. 1964; 98m.

LAST OF THE MOHICANS, THE (1936) ★★★★
DIR: George B. Seitz. **CAST:** Randolph Scott, Binnie Barnes, Heather Angel, Robert Barrat, Phillip Reed, Henry Wilcoxon, Bruce Cabot.
Blood, thunder, and interracial romance during the French and Indian War are brought to life from James Fenimore Cooper's novel. Randolph Scott is the intrepid Hawkeye; Robert Barrat is the noble Chingachgook; Binnie Barnes is Alice Monroe. The star-crossed lovers are Philip Reed, as Uncas, the title character, and Heather Angel, as Cora Monroe. 1936; B&W; 100m.

LAST OF THE MOHICANS (1985) ★★½
DIR: James L. Conway. **CAST:** Steve Forrest, Ned Romero, Andrew Prine, Robert Tessier.
In this TV film based on James Fenimore Cooper's classic, a small party headed for a fort is deserted by their guide and must turn to Hawkeye and Chingachgook to bring them to safety. When two of the party are cap-

tured, our heroes must rescue them and battle the leader of the Indians. 1985; 97m.

LAST OF THE PONY RIDERS ★½
DIR: George Archainbaud. **CAST:** Gene Autry, Smiley Burnette, Buzz Henry.

Gene Autry's last feature film is a limp addition to a genre—the series Western—on its last legs. Autry was reunited with his old sidekick Smiley Burnette for his last six films. 1953; B&W; 80m.

LAST OUTLAW, THE ★★★★½
DIR: Christy Cabanne. **CAST:** Harry Carey, Hoot Gibson, Henry B. Walthall, Tom Tyler.

Possibly Harry Carey's best film as a star, this is a delightful remake of a John Ford story of the silent era. Carey is a former outlaw released from prison, only to find that the West he knew is gone. Hoot Gibson is Carey's old saddle pal, and they soon take on a group of modern-day outlaws. 1936; B&W; 62m.

LAST RIDE OF THE DALTON GANG, THE ★★½
DIR: Dan Curtis. **CAST:** Jack Palance, Larry Wilcox, Dale Robertson, Bo Hopkins, Cliff Potts.

When two former Dalton Gang train robbers are reunited in Hollywood in 1934, they relive the early days of the Dalton Gang as they share a bottle of whiskey. 1979; 146m.

LAW AND ORDER ★★★★
DIR: Edward Cahn. **CAST:** Walter Huston, Harry Carey, Raymond Hatton, Andy Devine.

In a story coscripted by John Huston, Walter Huston gets one of the best roles of his career as a Wyatt Earp-style lawman. Harry Carey and Raymond Hatton are superb as his ready-for-anything sidekicks in an excellent Western that still seems fresh and innovative today. 1932; B&W; 70m.

LAW RIDES AGAIN, THE 🦃
DIR: Alan James. **CAST:** Ken Maynard, Hoot Gibson, Betty Miles, Jack LaRue, Kenneth Harlan, Chief Thundercloud.

Dismal low-budget entry in the "Trail Blazers" series has one-time cowboy greats Ken Maynard and Hoot Gibson bluffing their way through a formula story about lawmen catching a crooked Indian agent (Kenneth Harlan) with the unwitting help of an outlaw (Jack LaRue). 1943; B&W; 58m.

LAW WEST OF TOMBSTONE ★★★½
DIR: Glenn Tryon. **CAST:** Harry Carey, Tim Holt, Evelyn Brent, Ward Bond, Allan "Rocky" Lane.

Enjoyable, folksy Western has the marvelous Harry Carey starring as a con artist who becomes the law in Tombstone. Tim Holt, in a strong film debut, is the young hothead he befriends and reforms. Look for Allan "Rocky" Lane in a brief bit at the beginning as Holt's saddle pal. 1938; B&W; 72m.

LAWLESS FRONTIER ★★½
DIR: Robert N. Bradbury. **CAST:** John Wayne, Sheila Terry, George "Gabby" Hayes.

A Mexican bandit (Earl Dwire) manages to evade the blame for a series of crimes he's committed because the sheriff is sure that John Wayne is the culprit. The Duke, of course, traps the bad guy and clears his good name in this predictable B Western. 1935; B&W; 59m.

LAWLESS RANGE ★★
DIR: Robert N. Bradbury. **CAST:** John Wayne, Sheila Manners, Earl Dwire.

In this low, low, budget early John Wayne Western, a banker attempts to drive out the local ranchers and get his hands on some rich gold mines. Wayne, sent by the governor, soon sets things aright. 1935; B&W; 59m.

LAWLESS VALLEY ★★★★
DIR: Bert Gilroy. **CAST:** George O'Brien, Kay Sutton, Walter Miller, Fred Kohler Sr., Fred Kohler Jr., Chill Wills.

Prison parolee George O'Brien returns home to clear his name and put the true guilty parties behind bars in this solid series Western. In a nice touch, Fred Kohler Sr. and Fred Kohler Jr. play father-and-son heavies. 1938; B&W; 59m.

LAWMAN IS BORN, A ★★½
DIR: Sam Newfield. **CAST:** Johnny Mack Brown, Iris Meredith, Al St. John.

Former football star Johnny Mack Brown is a two-fisted good guy who foils the nefarious plans of an outlaw gang. This time, the baddies are after land (as opposed to the alternate formulas of cattle, money, gold, or horses). It's fun for fans. 1937; B&W; 58m.

LEATHER BURNERS, THE ★★½
DIR: Joseph E. Henabery. **CAST:** William Boyd, Andy Clyde, Victor Jory, Bobby Larson, Robert Mitchum.

In this oddball series Western, Hopalong Cassidy (William Boyd) and his sidekick, California (Andy Clyde), are framed for murder by a calculating cattle rustler (Victor Jory). It's up to a junior detective (Bobby Larson) to prove our heroes' innocence in time to allow them to participate in the final showdown. 1943; B&W; 58m.

LEFT-HANDED GUN, THE ★★★
DIR: Arthur Penn. **CAST:** Paul Newman, Lita Milan, John Dehner, Hurd Hatfield.

First film by director Arthur Penn (*Bonnie and Clyde*) follows the life of Billy the Kid (Paul Newman) after a group of his friends have been murdered and he seeks vengeance for their deaths. Paul Newman's use of method acting is a bit obvious. 1958; B&W; 102m.

LEGEND OF FRENCHIE KING, THE (turkey)
DIR: Christian Jaque. **CAST:** Brigitte Bardot, Claudia Cardinale, Guy Casaril, Michael J. Pollard.

This muddled attempt at creating a Western about a gang of female outlaws led by that gorgeous desperado Brigitte Bardot falls flat in the desert landscape of New Mexico. If you like to laugh at poor films, then this one is for you. Rated R for profanity, violence, and adult situations. 1971; 97m.

LEGEND OF THE LONE RANGER, THE (turkey)
DIR: William Fraker. **CAST:** Klinton Spilsbury, Michael Horse, Jason Robards Jr.

Let your children watch *The Legend of the Lone Ranger*, but don't bother to watch it yourself. While kids will undoubtedly love what the advertising blurbs said was "the untold story of the man behind the mask and the legend behind the man," adults—after the first hour of this often corny, slow-paced Western—will probably be falling asleep or, at least, daydreaming. Rated PG. 1981; 98m.

LEGEND OF WALKS FAR WOMAN, THE (turkey)
DIR: Mel Manski. **CAST:** Raquel Welch, Bradford Dillman, George Clutsel, Nick Mancuso, Nick Ramos.

Badly miscast Raquel Welch portrays an Indian heroine facing the perils of the Indian versus white man's culture clash. Her story leads to the climactic battle at Little Big Horn. Not even the scenery is enough to maintain interest. 1982; 150m.

LIFE AND TIMES OF JUDGE ROY BEAN, THE ★★★
DIR: John Huston. **CAST:** Paul Newman, Stacy Keach, Victoria Principal, Jacqueline Bisset, Ava Gardner.

Weird Western with Paul Newman as the fabled hanging judge. It has some interesting set-pieces among the strangeness. Stacy Keach is outstanding as Bad Bob. Rated PG. 1972; 120m.

LIGHTNIN' CRANDALL ★★★★
DIR: Sam Newfield. **CAST:** Bob Steele, Lois January, Dave O'Brien, Charles King.

Bob Steele buys a ranch that is sandwiched between two feuding cattle ranches. Terrific action and stuntwork make this one a cavalcade of fast thrills, and one of Steele's best. 1937; B&W; 60m.

LIGHTNING CARSON RIDES AGAIN ★★

DIR: Sam Newfield. **CAST:** Tim McCoy, Joan Barclay, Ted Adams, Forrest Taylor.

Captain Bill Carson (Tim McCoy) of the U.S. Justice Department rides to the rescue when his nephew is accused of robbery and murder. Made on a minuscule budget by the penny-pinching producer Sam Katzman, this is one of the least of McCoy's Westerns. 1938; B&W; 58m.

LITTLE BIG MAN ★★★★

DIR: Arthur Penn. **CAST:** Dustin Hoffman, Chief Dan George, Faye Dunaway, Martin Balsam, Jeff Corey, Richard Mulligan.

Dustin Hoffman gives a bravura performance as Jack Crabbe, a 121-year-old survivor of Custer's last stand. An offbeat Western-comedy, this film chronicles, in flashback, Crabbe's numerous adventures in the Old West. It's a remarkable film in more ways than one. Rated PG. 1970; 150m.

LITTLE MOON & JUD MCGRAW

DIR: Bernard Girard. **CAST:** James Caan, Stefanie Powers, Sammy Davis Jr., Aldo Ray, Barbara Werle, Robert Walker Jr.

Technically incompetent and generally awful comedy Western that has James Caan as a falsely accused man hunting for the real crook. That weak plot is constantly interrupted by an even weaker pseudodocumentary of the Old West, told with voice-over narration. And if those two stories aren't enough, there's a third story involving a modern-day magazine writer being told the legend of Jud McGraw by an old Indian woman. Rated R; nudity and violence. 1978; 92m.

LONE RANGER, THE (1938) ★★★½

DIR: William Witney, John English. **CAST:** Lee Powell, Chief Thundercloud, Bruce Bennett, Lynne Roberts (Mary Hart), William Farnum, Lane Chandler, George Montgomery, Hal Taliaferro (Wally Wales), George Cleveland.

One of America's most popular heroes rode out of the radio and onto the screen in one of the best and most fondly remembered serials of all time. The ballyhoo and merchandising that accompanied the release of this exciting chapterplay made it an overwhelming hit at the box office. Thought to be lost until recently, most versions of this serial feature two chapters in Spanish, the only copy available. 1938; B&W; 15 chapters.

LONE RANGER, THE (1956) ★★★½

DIR: Stuart Heisler. **CAST:** Clayton Moore, Jay Silverheels, Lyle Bettger, Bonita Granville.

The first color feature film based on the legend of the Lone Ranger is a treat for the kids and not too tough for the adults to sit through. Clayton Moore and Jay Silverheels reprise their television roles and find themselves battling white settlers, led by an evil Lyle Bettger, and the much put-upon Indians, riled up by a surly Michael Ansara. 1956; 86m.

LONE RANGER, THE (TELEVISION SERIES) ★★★½

DIR: Various. **CAST:** Clayton Moore, Jay Silverheels.

Emerging from a cloud of dust, with a hearty "Hi-yo Silver!" the Lone Ranger (Clayton Moore), with his faithful Indian companion, Tonto (Jay Silverheels), leads the fight for law and order in the Old West. Wearing a black mask fashioned from the vest of his murdered brother, the former Texas Ranger used silver bullets to remind him of the value of human life. He sought justice, not vengeance. His simplistic, moralistic adventures made him a hero to millions of youngsters. Now, these two-episode videocassettes enable you to return to those thrilling days of yesteryear, as the Lone Ranger rides again! A bonus is the Lone Ranger trivia segments presented by Clayton Moore. 1949–1965; 55 minutes each tape.

LONE STAR TRAIL ★★★½

DIR: Ray Taylor. **CAST:** Johnny Mack Brown, Robert Mitchum.

In this entertaining oater, Johnny Mack Brown is framed in a robbery case. Obviously upset, he hits the trail to find the real perpetrators. In the process, he meets up with outlaw Robert Mitchum, and one of the great fistfights in movie history is the result. Certainly worth a view. 1943; B&W; 77m.

LONELY ARE THE BRAVE ★★★★

DIR: David Miller. **CAST:** Kirk Douglas, Walter Matthau, Gena Rowlands.

A "little" Hollywood Western set in modern times has a lot to offer those who can endure its heavy-handed message. Kirk Douglas is just right as the cowboy out of step with his times. His attempts to escape from jail on horseback in contrast to the mechanized attempts to catch him by a modern police force are handled well. 1962; B&W; 107m.

LONELY MAN, THE ★★★

DIR: Henry Levin. **CAST:** Jack Palance, Anthony Perkins, Neville Brand, Robert Middleton, Elisha Cook Jr., Lee Van Cleef.

Interesting, but not exciting, this tautly directed oater is about a gunfighter, bent on reforming, who returns to his family after a seventeen-year hiatus. A brooding Jack Palance is the gunfighter. He is not warmly welcomed home by his deserted son, brooding Anthony Perkins. Two of a kind, the pair square off in a contest of wills and emotions. 1957; B&W; 87m.

LONG RIDERS, THE ★★★½

DIR: Walter Hill. **CAST:** David Carradine, Keith Carradine, Robert Carradine, Stacy Keach, James Keach, Nicholas Guest, Christopher Guest, Dennis Quaid, Randy Quaid.

Fans of Westerns will probably enjoy this release. However, this film about the James-Younger Gang has a few deficiencies. Character development and plot complexity are ignored in favor of lots of action. This is partly offset by the casting of real-life brothers. While it sounds like a gimmick, it actually works and adds a much-needed dimension of character to the picture. Rated R for violence. 1980; 100m.

LOVE ME TENDER ★★★

DIR: Robert D. Webb. **CAST:** Elvis Presley, Debra Paget, Richard Egan.

This Western drama takes place in Texas after the Civil War, with Elvis and his brother fighting over Debra Paget. The most distinguishing characteristic of this movie is the fact that it was Elvis's first film. Elvis fans will, of course, enjoy his singing the ballad "Love Me Tender." 1956; B&W; 89m.

LUCKY BOOTS (A.K.A. GUN PLAY) ★★

DIR: Albert Herman. **CAST:** Guinn Williams, Marion Shilling, Tom London.

A map to a hidden treasure is concealed in Guinn "Big Boy's" Williams's boot heel and everyone's after it. Low-budget independent starring Williams, who fared better as a sidekick. 1935; B&W; 59m.

LUCKY TEXAN ★★★

DIR: Robert N. Bradbury. **CAST:** John Wayne, Barbara Sheldon, George "Gabby" Hayes.

Gold miners John Wayne and "Gabby" Hayes strike it rich. But before they can cash in their claim, Hayes is falsely accused of robbery and murder. Of course, the Duke rides to his aid. Creaky, but fun for fans. 1934; B&W; 56m.

LUSTY MEN, THE ★★★★

DIR: Nicholas Ray. **CAST:** Robert Mitchum, Susan Hayward, Arthur Kennedy, Arthur Hunnicutt.

The world of rodeo cowboys is explored in this well-made film directed by cult favorite Nicholas Ray. Robert Mitchum has one of his best roles as a broken-down ex–rodeo star who gets a second chance at the big money by tutoring an egotistical newcomer on the circuit, well played by Arthur Kennedy. 1952; B&W; 113m.

MACHO CALLAHAN ★★★
DIR: Bernard Kowalski. **CAST:** David Janssen, Jean Seberg, Lee J. Cobb, James Booth, David Carradine, Bo Hopkins.

David Janssen convincingly portrays Macho Callahan, a man hardened by his confinement in a horrid Confederate prison camp. When he kills a man (David Carradine) over a bottle of champagne, the man's bride (Jean Seberg) seeks revenge. Rated R for violence and gore. 1970; 99m.

MACKENNA'S GOLD ★★
DIR: J. Lee Thompson. **CAST:** Gregory Peck, Omar Sharif, Telly Savalas, Julie Newmar, Lee J. Cobb.

Disappointing "big" Western follows search for gold in a big canyon. Impressive cast cannot overcome a poor script and uninspired direction. 1969; 128m.

MADRON ★★½
DIR: Jerry Hopper. **CAST:** Richard Boone, Leslie Caron, Paul Smith, Gabi Amrani.

You've heard of the spaghetti western. Well here's an Israeli Western. The story involves a nun and a gunslinger who, after a typical wagon train massacre, are thrown together in an attempt to cross the desert chased by a band of Apaches. The actors are good, but the story is pedestrian. Rated PG. 1970; 93m.

MAGNIFICENT SEVEN, THE ★★★★
DIR: John Sturges. **CAST:** Yul Brynner, Steve McQueen, Charles Bronson, James Coburn, Eli Wallach, Robert Vaughn.

Japanese director Akira Kurosawa's *The Seven Samurai* served as the inspiration for this enjoyable Western, directed by John Sturges (*The Great Escape*). It's the rousing tale of how a group of American gunfighters come to the aid of a village of Mexican farmers plagued by bandits. 1960; 126m.

MAJOR DUNDEE ★★★
DIR: Sam Peckinpah. **CAST:** Charlton Heston, Richard Harris, James Coburn, Jim Hutton, Warren Oates, Ben Johnson.

This is a flawed but watchable Western directed with typical verve by master filmmaker Sam Peckinpah. The plot follows a group of Confederate prisoners who volunteer to go into Mexico and track down a band of rampaging Apache Indians. 1965; 124m.

MAN ALONE, A ★★★
DIR: Ray Milland. **CAST:** Ray Milland, Mary Murphy, Ward Bond, Raymond Burr, Lee Van Cleef.

Ray Milland's first directorial effort finds him hiding from a lynch mob in a small western town. And who is he hiding with? The sheriff's daughter! Not too bad, as Westerns go. 1955; 96m.

MAN AND BOY ★★½
DIR: E. W. Swackhamer. **CAST:** Bill Cosby, Gloria Foster, George Spell, Leif Erickson, Yaphet Kotto, Douglas Turner Ward, John Anderson, Henry Silva, Dub Taylor.

Bill Cosby and his family try to make a go of it by homesteading on the prairie. The story provides ample opportunity for some Cosbyesque explanations about the facts of life and the black experience of that period. Rated G. 1971; 98m.

MAN CALLED HORSE, A ★★★
DIR: Elliot Silverstein. **CAST:** Richard Harris, Judith Anderson, Jean Gascon, Corinna Tsopei, Dub Taylor.

Richard Harris (in one of his best roles) portrays an English aristocrat who's enslaved and treated like a pack animal by Sioux Indians in the Dakotas. He loses his veneer of sophistication and finds the core of his manhood. This strong film offers an unusually realistic depiction of American Indian life. Rated PG. 1970; 114m.

MAN FROM LARAMIE, THE ★★★★½

DIR: Anthony Mann. **CAST:** James Stewart, Arthur Kennedy, Donald Crisp, Alex Nicol, Cathy O'Donnell, Jack Elam.

Magnificent Western has James Stewart as a stranger who finds himself at odds with a powerful ranching family. The patriarch (Donald Crisp) is going blind, so the running of the ranch is left to his psychotic son (Alex Nicol) and longtime ranch foreman (Arthur Kennedy). Possibly the summit of director Anthony Mann's career; certainly Stewart's finest Western performance. 1955; 101m.

MAN FROM MUSIC MOUNTAIN ★★

DIR: Joseph Kane. **CAST:** Gene Autry, Smiley Burnette, Carol Hughes, Sally Payne, Ivan Miller, Earl Dwire.

Warbling Gene Autry and his simple-minded sidekick Smiley Burnette stymie the efforts of a swindler in this routine series film. 1938; B&W; 54m.

MAN FROM SNOWY RIVER, THE ★★★★

DIR: George Miller. **CAST:** Tom Burlinson, Kirk Douglas, Jack Thompson, Bruce Kerr.

If you've been looking for an adventure film for the whole family, this Australian Western about the coming of age of a mountain man (Tom Burlinson) is it. Rated PG, the film has no objectionable material. 1982; 115m.

MAN FROM THE ALAMO, THE ★★★½

DIR: Budd Boetticher. **CAST:** Glenn Ford, Julie Adams, Victor Jory, Chill Wills, Hugh O'Brian, Neville Brand.

This is an exciting, well-acted story of a soldier (Glenn Ford) who escapes from the doomed Alamo in an effort to warn others about Santa Ana's invasion of Texas. After the Alamo falls, he is branded a traitor and deserter and must prove his mettle to the Texicans. Historically inaccurate, but exciting and fun. 1953; 79m.

MAN FROM UTAH, THE ★

DIR: Robert N. Bradbury. **CAST:** John Wayne, Polly Ann Young, George "Gabby" Hayes, Yakima Canutt, George Cleveland.

Low, low-budget Western with a very young John Wayne as a lawman going undercover to catch some crooks using a rodeo to bilk unsuspecting cowboys. The rodeo footage was used over and over again by the film company, Monogram Pictures, in similar films. The best part is the dialogue, with such classic lines as "I'm gonna cloud up and rain all over you" and "Yeah? You and what army?" 1934; B&W; 57m.

MAN OF THE FOREST ★★★★

DIR: Henry Hathaway. **CAST:** Randolph Scott, Harry Carey, Buster Crabbe, Noah Beery Sr., Guinn Williams.

This is one of two very good Westerns made by Randolph Scott in a year that produced many fine films. Based on Zane Grey's novel, Scott plays a cowboy who kidnaps a young woman to keep her from the clutches of a bad guy. Zesty and action-packed. 1933; B&W; 62m.

MAN OF THE FRONTIER (RED RIVER VALLEY) ★★½

DIR: B. Reeves "Breezy" Eason. **CAST:** Gene Autry, Smiley Burnette, Frances Grant.

This early entry in the Gene Autry series features Gene as an undercover agent out to stop a gang bent on sabotaging construction of a much-needed dam. Very enjoyable, and a nice example of the kind of film Autry could make but didn't have to after a while. 1936; B&W; 60m.

MAN WHO LOVED CAT DANCING, THE ★

DIR: Richard C. Sarafian. **CAST:** Burt Reynolds, Sarah Miles, George Hamilton, Lee J. Cobb, Jack Warden.

Don't waste your time on this uninspired Western. Burt Reynolds is wasted in this tale of a train robber who kidnaps a prim Sarah Miles and falls in love with her. Rated PG. 1973; 114m.

MAN WHO SHOT LIBERTY VALANCE, THE ★★★★★

DIR: John Ford. **CAST:** John Wayne, James Stewart, Vera Miles, Lee Marvin, Edmond O'Brien, Woody Strode, Andy Devine, Strother Martin, Lee Van Cleef.

This release was director John Ford's bittersweet farewell to the Western. John Wayne replays his role of the western man of action, this time with a twist. James Stewart's part could well be called *Mr. Smith Goes to Shinbone*, it draws so much on his most famous image. Combined with Ford's visual sense and belief in sparse dialogue, as well as fine ensemble playing in supporting roles, it adds up to a highly satisfying film. 1962; B&W; 119m.

MAN WITHOUT A STAR ★★★

DIR: King Vidor. **CAST:** Kirk Douglas, Jeanne Crain, Claire Trevor, Richard Boone, Jack Elam, Mara Corday.

With charm, fists, and guns, foreman Kirk Douglas swaggers through this stock story of rival ranchers. Jeanne Crain is his beautiful boss; Claire Trevor is, as usual, a big-hearted saloon hostess. 1955; 89m.

MARAUDERS ★★

DIR: George Archainbaud. **CAST:** William Boyd, Andy Clyde, Rand Brooks, Ian Wolfe, Harry Cording, Earle Hodgins.

Hopalong Cassidy and his two sidekicks take refuge in an abandoned church one rainy night and find themselves embroiled in a battle between a pious clergyman and mean-spirited Harry Cording. This later effort by William Boyd still packs the good-natured humor and action of the earlier entries, but the story is predictable. 1947; B&W; 63m.

MARSHAL OF CRIPPLE CREEK ★★★★

DIR: R. G. Springsteen. **CAST:** Allan "Rocky" Lane, Robert Blake, Gene Roth, Trevor Bardette.

Last of the Republic Red Ryder series is one of the fastest-paced, most action-packed of the twenty-three they produced. The discovery of gold in Cripple Creek causes the boom town to be overrun by a lawless element. 1947; B&W; 54m.

MARSHAL OF MESA CITY ★★★★

DIR: David Howard. **CAST:** George O'Brien, Virginia Vale, Leon Ames, Henry Brandon.

Outstanding series Western features George O'Brien as a retired lawman who rides into a town ruled by a corrupt sheriff (Leon Ames) and stays on to end his reign of terror. Excellent character development and plot twists. 1939; B&W; 62m.

MASSACRE AT FORT HOLMAN (REASON TO LIVE...A REASON TO DIE, A) ★½

DIR: Tonino Valerii. **CAST:** James Coburn, Telly Savalas, Bud Spencer.

Spaghetti Western of marginal interest. Eight condemned men led by James Coburn, who plays a traitor to the Union Army in the Civil War, get a chance to redeem themselves by overtaking a rebel fort. Like most Westerns of this sort, there is plenty of action, but that alone can't help the worn-out plot or Western clichés. Rated PG for violence and profanity. 1984; 90m.

MAVERICK QUEEN, THE ★★★

DIR: Joseph Kane. **CAST:** Barbara Stanwyck, Barry Sullivan, Scott Brady, Mary Murphy, Wallace Ford.

Sparks erupt when a Pinkerton detective works undercover at a Wyoming gambling hotel that is a hangout for an outlaw gang. Barbara Stanwyck is cast aptly as the beauty who owns the hotel and is caught between her jealous lover and her love for the lawman. 1955; 90m.

MCCABE AND MRS. MILLER ★★★★

DIR: Robert Altman. **CAST:** Warren Beatty, Julie Christie, Shelley Duvall, Keith Carradine.

Life in the turn-of-the-century Northwest is given a first-class treatment in director Robert Altman's visually perfect comedy-drama. Sparkling performances are turned in by Warren Beatty, as a small-town wheeler-dealer, and Julie Christie, as a whore with a heart that beats to the jingle of gold and silver coins. Rated R. 1971; 121m.

MEANEST MEN IN THE WEST, THE

DIR: Samuel Fuller, Charles S. Dubin. **CAST:** Charles Bronson, Lee Marvin, Lee J. Cobb, James Drury, Albert Salmi, Charles Grodin.

Beware! This is the biggest rip-off ever to hit the video store shelves. It consists of two episodes of the 1960s television series *The Virginian* edited together so it appears that Charles Bronson and Lee Marvin are starring in a Western together. In actuality, they were guest stars on two different episodes and never shared a scene. 1962; 92m.

MELODY RANCH ★★½

DIR: Joseph Santley. **CAST:** Gene Autry, Jimmy Durante, Ann Miller, Barton MacLane, George "Gabby" Hayes.

The creative forces at Republic Studios decided to team Gene Autry with Jimmy Durante and Ann Miller, replace Smiley Burnette with Gabby Hayes and pretend nothing was different. Venerable heavy Barton MacLane provides the menace as a local gangster intent on running honorary sheriff Gene Autry out of town, but there isn't enough action to qualify this bigger-budgeted series entry as anything other than a curio. 1940; B&W; 80m.

MELODY TRAIL ★★½

DIR: Joseph Kane. **CAST:** Gene Autry, Smiley Burnette, Ann Rutherford.

The fifth Gene Autry–Smiley Burnette film is a pleasant story about a rodeo rider who loses his winnings and is forced to work for a rancher with a romantic daughter. 1935; B&W; 60m.

MINUTE TO PRAY, A SECOND TO DIE, A ★★

DIR: Franco Giraldi. **CAST:** Alex Cord, Arthur Kennedy, Robert Ryan, Nicoletta Machiavelli.

This is a routine Western with Alex Cord as an outlaw trying to turn himself in when amnesty is declared by the governor of New Mexico (played by Robert Ryan). Arthur Kennedy, as the marshal, has other plans. Rated R for violence. 1967; 99m.

MIRACLE RIDER, THE ★★½

DIR: Armand Schaefer, B. Reeves "Breezy" Eason. **CAST:** Tom Mix, Jean Gale, Charles Middleton, Jason Robards Sr., Edward Hearn.

Tom Mix plays a Texas Ranger and friend of the Indian in this sometimes slow but enjoyable pseudoscience-fiction serial. Charles Middleton plays Zaroff, leader of a gang who preys on the superstitions of the Indians in order to scare them off their reservation. After this, Mix retired from the screen. 1935; B&W; 0m.

MISSOURI BREAKS, THE ★★

DIR: Arthur Penn. **CAST:** Marlon Brando, Jack Nicholson, Kathleen Lloyd, Harry Dean Stanton.

For all its potential, this Western really lets you down. Jack Nicholson is acceptable as the outlaw trying to ply his trade. Marlon Brando, on the other hand, is inconsistent as a relentless bounty hunter who's tracking Nicholson. Rated PG. 1976; 126m.

MR. HORN ★★★

DIR: Jack Starrett. **CAST:** David Carradine, Richard Widmark, Karen Black, Richard Masur, Jeremy Slate, Pat McCormick, Jack Starrett.

Mr. Horn is a bittersweet, near melancholy chronicle of the exploits of Horn (David Carradine), who is shown first as an idealistic young man helping an old-timer (Richard Widmark) track down Geronimo and later as a cynical gunman hired to eliminate some rustlers. 1979; 200m.

MOHAWK ★½

DIR: Kurt Neumann. **CAST:** Scott Brady, Rita Gam, Neville Brand, Lori Nelson, Allison Hayes, Ted de Corsia.

Cornball story about love between settler Scott Brady and Indian Rita Gam and their efforts to bring their people together must have been inspired by access to footage from John Ford's classic *Drums Along the Mohawk*. 1956; 79m.

MONTE WALSH ★★★½

DIR: William Fraker. **CAST:** Lee Marvin, Jack Palance, Jeanne Moreau, Mitchell Ryan, Jim Davis.

Sad but satisfying Western about a couple of saddle pals (Lee Marvin, Jack Palance) attempting to make the transition to a new age and century. Cinematographer William Fraker made an impressive directorial debut with this fine film. Rated R for violence. 1970; 106m.

MORE WILD WILD WEST ★★½

DIR: Burt Kennedy. **CAST:** Robert Conrad, Ross Martin, Jonathan Winters, Harry Morgan, René Auberjonois, Liz Torres, Victor Buono, Dr. Joyce Brothers, Emma Samms.

This TV movie is a pale reminder of the irresistible original series. The Old West's most invincible Secret Service agents, James West and Artemus Gordon, again come out of retirement, this time to rescue the world from an invisibility plot. Jonathan Winters hams it up as the villainous Albert Paradine II. There's too much silly comedy, not enough excitement. 1980; 94m.

MOUNTAIN MEN, THE ★

DIR: Richard Lang. **CAST:** Charlton Heston, Brian Keith, Victoria Racimo, Stephen Macht.

A buddy movie about two bickering fur trappers who get involved in Indian uprisings and so on, this dull and overly violent film wastes the talents of its stars. Rated R. 1980; 102m.

MY DARLING CLEMENTINE ★★★★½

DIR: John Ford. **CAST:** Henry Fonda, Victor Mature, Walter Brennan, Linda Darnell, Ward Bond, Tim Holt.

The epic struggle between good and evil is wrapped up in this classic retelling of the shootout at the O.K. Corral, between the Earps and the lawless Clanton family. Henry Fonda gives his Wyatt Earp a feeling of believability, perfectly matched by Walter Brennan's riveting portrayal of villainy as the head of the Clanton gang. 1946; B&W; 97m.

MY NAME IS NOBODY ★★★½

DIR: Tonino Valerii. **CAST:** Henry Fonda, Terence Hill, Leo Gordon, Geoffrey Lewis.

This is a delightful spoof of the Clint Eastwood spaghetti Westerns. Terence Hill is a gunfighter who worships old-timer Henry Fonda, who merely wishes to go away and retire. Rated PG. 1974; 115m.

MY PAL, THE KING ★★★

DIR: Kurt Neumann. **CAST:** Tom Mix, Mickey Rooney.

Cowboy Tom Mix befriends boy king Mickey Rooney and teaches him the ways of the West. Mix's Wild West Show takes center stage for some entertaining passages, and cliffhanger action keeps the story moving along. 1932; B&W; 74m.

MY PAL TRIGGER ★★★½

DIR: Frank McDonald. **CAST:** Roy Rogers, George "Gabby" Hayes, Dale Evans, Jack Holt.

One of the most fondly remembered and perhaps the best of all the Roy Rogers movies, this gentle story centers on Roy's attempts to mate his mare with a superb golden stallion. Villain Jack Holt is responsible for the death of the mare, and Roy is blamed and incarcerated. 1946; B&W; 79m.

MYSTERY MOUNTAIN ★★
DIR: Otto Brewer, B. Reeves "Breezy" Eason. **CAST:** Ken Maynard, Verna Hillie, Syd Saylor, Gene Autry, Smiley Burnette.

Cowboy great Ken Maynard stars in his only serial, the story of the mysterious master of disguise known as the "Rattler," who lives to wreck trains. Gene Autry and his silly sidekick Smiley Burnette make their second screen appearance in this chapterplay. 1934; B&W; 12 chapters.

MYSTERY OF THE HOODED HORSEMEN ★★½
DIR: Ray Taylor. **CAST:** Tex Ritter, Iris Meredith, Charles King, Forrest Taylor, Earl Dwire, Lafe McKee, Hank Worden, Joe Girard.

One of Tex Ritter's most popular oaters. A group of night riders in dark hoods and cloaks add just a touch of the supernatural to an otherwise standard story of land greed and cattle conniving. 1937; B&W; 60m.

NAKED IN THE SUN ★★½
DIR: R. John Hugh. **CAST:** James Craig, Barton MacLane, Lita Milan, Tony Hunter.

Osceola (James Craig), war chief of the Seminole Indians, must battle unscrupulous whites, the United States Government, and his own tribe in order to live in dignity. One of many films of the 1950s that dealt with the American Indian as a noble, persecuted people. This is well-acted and effective in evoking audience sympathy. 1957; 79m.

NAKED SPUR, THE ★★★★½
DIR: Anthony Mann. **CAST:** James Stewart, Janet Leigh, Robert Ryan, Ralph Meeker, Millard Mitchell.

Superb Western finds bounty hunter James Stewart chasing bad guy Robert Ryan through the Rockies. Once captured, Ryan attempts to cause trouble between Stewart and his sidekicks. 1953; 91m.

NARROW TRAIL, THE ★★★
DIR: Lambert Hillyer. **CAST:** William S. Hart.

"Better a painted pony than a painted woman" was the slogan selling this above-average Western about a cowboy's love for his horse. One of famous early-Western star William S. Hart's many pictures, this one was something of a paean to his great horse, Fritz. Like all Hart films, this one is marked by his scrupulous attention to authenticity of setting, scenery, and costume. Silent. 1917; B&W; 56m.

'NEATH ARIZONA SKIES ★★½
DIR: Henry Frazer. **CAST:** John Wayne, Sheila Terry, Yakima Canutt, George "Gabby" Hayes.

Formula B Western has John Wayne as the protector of the heir to rich oil lands, a little Indian girl. Of course, the baddies try to kidnap her and the Duke rides to the rescue. Low-budget and predictable. 1934; B&W; 57m.

NEVADA SMITH ★★★
DIR: Henry Hathaway. **CAST:** Steve McQueen, Karl Malden, Brian Keith, Arthur Kennedy, Suzanne Pleshette, Raf Vallone, Pat Hingle, Howard Da-Silva, Martin Landau.

Steve McQueen, in the title role, is butcher's-freezer-cold, calculating, and merciless in this hard-hitting, gripping Western. The focus is on a senseless, vicious double murder and the revenge taken by the son of the innocent victims. Story and characters are excerpted from a section of Harold Robbins's sensational novel *The Carpetbaggers* not used in the 1964 film. 1966; 135m.

NEW FRONTIER ★★½
DIR: Carl Pierson. **CAST:** John Wayne, Muriel Evans, Mary McLaren, Murdock McQuarrie, Warner Richmond, Sam Flint, Earl Dwire.

In a familiar plot, John Wayne is the son of a murdered sheriff out to find the baddies who did the dirty deed. Creaky but fun for fans. 1935; B&W; 59m.

NIGHT OF THE GRIZZLY, THE ★★½

DIR: Joseph Pevney. **CAST:** Clint Walker, Martha Hyer, Ron Ely, Jack Elam.

In order to maintain a peaceful standing in the rugged Old West, big Clint Walker must fight all the local bad guys (who should have known better) as well as a giant grizzly bear who moves in and out of camera range on a wheeled dolly. Nice outdoor sets and some good characterization help this no-frills family story. 1966; 102m.

NIGHT RIDERS, THE ★★½

DIR: George Sherman. **CAST:** John Wayne, Ray "Crash" Corrigan, Max Terhune, Doreen McKay, Ruth Rogers, Tom Tyler, Kermit Maynard.

The Three Mesquiteers (John Wayne, Ray Corrigan, and Max Terhune) make like Zorro by donning cape and mask to foil a villain's attempt to enforce a phony Spanish land grant. Good formula Western fun. 1939; B&W; 58m.

NIGHT STAGE TO GALVESTON ★★

DIR: George Archainbaud. **CAST:** Gene Autry, Pat Buttram, Virginia Huston, Robert Livingston.

Old-fashioned actioner set in post–Civil War South finds Gene Autry and his buddy Pat Buttram working for a crusading newspaperman who intends to expose corruption in the ranks of the Texas Rangers. This routine story is easy to watch and not too hard to forget. 1952; B&W; 61m.

NINE LIVES OF ELFEGO BACA, THE ★★★

DIR: Norman Foster. **CAST:** Robert Loggia, Robert F. Simon, Lisa Montell, Nestor Paiva.

Robert Loggia, as the long-lived hero of the Old West, faces one of his most harrowing perils as he confronts scores of gunmen determined to perforate him with lead and take away all of his lives. Lots of action and fun for the whole family. Rated G. 1958; 78m.

NORTH OF THE GREAT DIVIDE ★½

DIR: William Witney. **CAST:** Roy Rogers, Penny Edwards, Gordon Jones, Roy Barcroft.

No-good Roy Barcroft is at it again, this time as a greedy salmon cannery owner who overfishes the waters and forces the local Indians to go hungry or turn to a life of crime. Roy Rogers plays a variation on his government agent identity but lacks the familiar support of Dale Evans, "Gabby" Hayes, or even Pat Brady in this lesser entry to the popular series. 1950; 67m.

NORTH TO ALASKA ★★★★

DIR: Henry Hathaway. **CAST:** John Wayne, Stewart Granger, Capucine, Fabian, Ernie Kovacs.

Rather than a typical John Wayne Western, this is a John Wayne Northern. It's a rough-and-tumble romantic comedy. Delightfully tongue-in-cheek, it presents the Duke at his two-fisted best. 1960; 122m.

OKLAHOMA KID, THE ★★★

DIR: Lloyd Bacon. **CAST:** James Cagney, Humphrey Bogart, Rosemary Lane, Donald Crisp, Charles Middleton, Ward Bond, Harvey Stephens.

Definitely one of the oddest of all major sagebrush sagas, this film, about a feared gunman (James Cagney) taking revenge on the men who hanged his innocent father, boasts a great cast of familiar characters as well as a musical interlude with Cagney singing "I Don't Want to Play in Your Yard" to the accompaniment of a honky-tonk piano and pair of six-shooters. A competent curio. 1939; B&W; 85m.

OKLAHOMAN, THE ★★

DIR: Francis D. Lyon. **CAST:** Joel McCrea, Barbara Hale, Brad Dexter, Douglas Dick, Verna Felton.

Run-of-the-trail Western with Joel McCrea riding point to protect the rights of an outcast Indian against white-eyed crooks. 1957; 80m.

OLD BARN DANCE, THE ★½
DIR: Joseph Kane. **CAST:** Gene Autry, Smiley Burnette, Helen Valkis, Sammy McKim, Ivan Miller, Roy Rogers.

Typical Gene Autry hooey features the former railroad telegrapher as—what else?—a singing cowboy. He croons over the radio for a tractor company that's putting horse-dependent farmers and ranchers out of business. 1938; B&W; 60m.

OLD CORRAL, THE ★★★
DIR: Joseph Kane. **CAST:** Gene Autry, Smiley Burnette, Hope Manning, Roy Rogers.

Early Gene Autry film finds the spud-shaped singer fighting East Coast gangsters who have invaded the frontier in search of a girl who knows too much. 1936; B&W; 56m.

ON THE OLD SPANISH TRAIL ★½
DIR: William Witney. **CAST:** Roy Rogers, Tito Guizar, Jane Frazee, Andy Devine, Estelita Rodriguez, Charles McGraw.

This odd collaboration of Republic Studios contract players finds Roy Rogers sharing the screen with Tito Guizar and Estelita Rodriguez as they take on villainous Charles McGraw and his cohorts. 1947; 75m.

ON TOP OF OLD SMOKY ★½
DIR: George Archainbaud. **CAST:** Gene Autry, Smiley Burnette, Gail Davis, Sheila Ryan.

Gene Autry is reunited with old saddle pal Smiley Burnette in this familiar story of a singing cowpoke (Autry) who is mistaken for a Texas Ranger with a price on his head. 1953; B&W; 59m.

ONCE UPON A TIME IN THE WEST ★★★★★
DIR: Sergio Leone. **CAST:** Claudia Cardinale, Henry Fonda, Charles Bronson, Jason Robards Jr., Jack Elam, Woody Strode, Lionel Stander.

This superb film is the only spaghetti Western that can be called a classic. A mythic tale about the coming of the railroad and the exacting of revenge with larger-than-life characters, it is a work on a par with the best by great American Western film directors. Like *The Wild Bunch*, it has a fervent—and well-deserved—cult following in America. Rated PG. 1969; 165m.

ONE-EYED JACKS ★★★★
DIR: Marlon Brando. **CAST:** Marlon Brando, Karl Malden, Katy Jurado, Ben Johnson, Slim Pickens, Elisha Cook Jr.

Star Marlon Brando took over the reins of directing this Western from Stanley Kubrick midway through production, and the result is a terrific entry in the genre. Superb supporting performances help this beautifully photographed film about an outlaw seeking revenge on a double-dealing former partner. 1961; 141m.

100 RIFLES ★★
DIR: Tom Gries. **CAST:** Burt Reynolds, Raquel Welch, Jim Brown, Fernando Lamas, Dan O'Herlihy.

The picture stirred controversy over guerrilla leader Raquel Welch's interracial love scene with deputy Jim Brown. But at this point, who cares? We're left with a so-so Western yarn. Rated R. 1969; 110m.

ONLY THE VALIANT ★★½
DIR: Gordon Douglas. **CAST:** Gregory Peck, Ward Bond, Barbara Payton, Gig Young.

Cavalry captain Gregory Peck is saddled not only with problems with native Americans but irritability among his own troops. Eventually Peck puts the bridle on tight. Produced by Cagney Productions, this Western is conventional and predictable but entertaining. 1951; B&W; 105m.

OUTCAST, THE ★★
DIR: William Witney. **CAST:** John Derek, Joan Evans, Jim Davis.

Before he became disenchanted with acting and turned to still photography,

John Derek made a number of mostly mediocre films, this one among them. In this standard Western, he fights to win his rightful inheritance. Justice prevails, of course, but you know that going in. 1954; B&W; 90m.

OUTLAW, THE ★★
DIR: Howard Hughes, Howard Hawks. **CAST:** Jane Russell, Walter Huston, Thomas Mitchell, Jack Buetel.

This once-notorious Western now seems almost laughable. Jane Russell keeps her best attributes forward, but one wonders what Walter Huston and Thomas Mitchell are doing in this film. Only for those who want to know what all the fuss was about. 1943; 103m.

OUTLAW JOSEY WALES, THE ★★★★½
DIR: Clint Eastwood. **CAST:** Clint Eastwood, Sondra Locke, Chief Dan George, William McKinney, John Vernon, John Mitchum, John Russell.

This Western, a masterpiece of characterization and action, is Clint Eastwood's best film as both an actor and director. Josey Wales (Eastwood) is a farmer whose family is murdered by Red Legs, a band of pillaging cutthroats who have allied themselves with the Union Army. Wales joins the Confederacy to avenge their deaths. After the war, everyone in his troop surrenders to the victorious Union except Wales. Rated PG. 1976; 135m.

OVERLAND STAGE RAIDERS ★★½
DIR: George Sherman. **CAST:** John Wayne, Louise Brooks, Ray "Crash" Corrigan, Max Terhune.

Louise Brooks made her last big-screen appearance in this series Western, which has the Three Mesquiteers investing in an airport used by gold miners to ship ore. Of course, our heroes must battle a group of crooks attempting to rob the shipments. 1938; B&W; 55m.

OX-BOW INCIDENT, THE ★★★★½
DIR: William Wellman. **CAST:** Henry Fonda, Dana Andrews, Mary Beth Hughes, Anthony Quinn, William Eythe, Harry Morgan, Jane Darwell, Frank Conroy, Harry Davenport.

One of the finest Westerns ever made, this thought-provoking drama stars Henry Fonda and Harry Morgan as a pair of drifters who try to stop the lynching of three men (Dana Andrews, Anthony Quinn, and Francis Ford) who may be innocent. Seldom has the terror of mob rule been so effectively portrayed. 1943; B&W; 75m.

PAINTED DESERT, THE ★★½
DIR: Howard Higgin. **CAST:** William Boyd, Helen Twelvetrees, William Farnum, J. Farrell MacDonald, Clark Gable.

The future Hopalong Cassidy, William Boyd, plays a foundling who grows up on the other side of the range from his lady love and must decide between the family feud and the cattle or Helen Twelvetrees and the cattle. A young Clark Gable plays the dark cloud that is menacing the future of these two nice kids. 1931; B&W; 75m.

PAINTED STALLION, THE ★★
DIR: William Witney, Ray Taylor. **CAST:** Ray Corrigan, Hoot Gibson, Sammy McKim, Jack Perrin, Hal Tallaferro, Duncan Renaldo, LeRoy Mason, Yakima Canutt.

This history-bending serial finds Kit Carson, Davy Crockett, and Jim Bowie coming to the aid of Hoot Gibson as he leads a wagon train to Santa Fe. Lots of action and plot reversals highlight this chapter play. 1937; B&W; 12 chapters.

PALE RIDER ★★★½
DIR: Clint Eastwood. **CAST:** Clint Eastwood, Michael Moriarty, Carrie Snodgress, Christopher Penn, Richard Dysart, Richard Kiel, John Russell.

Star-producer-director Clint Eastwood donned six-guns and a Stetson for the first time since the classic *The Outlaw Josey Wales* (1976) for this enjoyable Western. The star is a mysterious avenger who comes to the aid of embattled gold prospectors in the Old West. *Pale Rider* is somewhat similar to Eastwood's 1973 *High Plains Drifter* in theme. Rated R for violence and profanity. 1985; 113m.

PALS OF THE SADDLE ★★½
DIR: George Sherman. **CAST:** John Wayne, Ray "Crash" Corrigan, Max Terhune, Doreen McKay, Frank Milan, Jack Kirk.

The Three Mesquiteers (John Wayne, Ray Corrigan, and Max Terhune) help a woman government agent (Doreen McKay) trap a munitions ring in this enjoyable B Western series entry. 1938; B&W; 60m.

PANCHO VILLA ★★
DIR: Eugenio Martin. **CAST:** Telly Savalas, Clint Walker, Chuck Connors, Anne Francis.

Telly Savalas plays the famous bandit to the hilt and beyond. Clint Walker runs guns for him. Chuck Connors postures as a stiff and stuffy military type. You'll soon see why the title role forever belongs to Wallace Beery. It all builds to a rousing head-on train wreck. Rated R. 1972; 92m.

PARADISE CANYON ★★
DIR: Carl Pierson. **CAST:** John Wayne, Marion Burns, Yakima Canutt, Reed Howes.

A very young and sometimes awkward John Wayne stars in this low, low-budget Western as an undercover agent on the trail of counterfeiters (led by Yakima Canutt). For staunch Wayne and Western fans only. 1935; B&W; 59m.

PAT GARRETT AND BILLY THE KID ★★½
DIR: Sam Peckinpah. **CAST:** James Coburn, Kris Kristofferson, Bob Dylan, Jason Robards Jr., Rita Coolidge.

This is an interesting but flawed Western. James Coburn, as Pat, and Kris Kristofferson, as Billy, are good as the title characters, and director Sam Peckinpah creates some fine action scenes. However, Bob Dylan is pitifully inept in an anachronistic supporting role as Alias, and the film simply fails to gel overall. Rated R. 1973; 106m.

PHANTOM OF THE WEST ★★
DIR: D. Ross Lederman. **CAST:** Tom Tyler, William Desmond, Tom Santschi.

This early sound serial featured a whole gallery of suspects that were just suspicious enough to be the mysterious Phantom, scourge of the territory. Tom Tyler is looking for his father's murderer as well as disproving rumors that he is the hooded villain. Primitive but virile. 1931; B&W; 10 chapters.

PIONEER WOMAN ★★½
DIR: Buzz Kulik. **CAST:** Joanna Pettet, William Shatner, David Janssen, Lance LeGault, Helen Hunt.

In this passable made-for-television movie, the trials and tribulations of homesteading in Wyoming during the 1860s are told through the point of view of a wife and mother. After her husband is killed, she must make the difficult decision about staying on or going back east. 1973; 78m.

PLAINSMAN, THE ★★★
DIR: Cecil B. DeMille. **CAST:** Gary Cooper, Jean Arthur, Charles Bickford, George "Gabby" Hayes.

If you can imagine a scenario uniting George Custer, Wild Bill Hickok, Calamity Jane, and Abraham Lincoln and you're willing to suspend historical disbelief, you should enjoy this stylish Cecil B. De Mille shoot-'em-up. Gary Cooper as Wild Bill Hickok does his best to keep Charles Bickford from selling guns to the Indians. 1936; B&W; 113m.

PONY EXPRESS ★★★
DIR: Jerry Hopper. **CAST:** Charlton Heston, Rhonda Fleming, Jan Sterling, Forrest Tucker.

Bigger than they were in life, western legends Buffalo Bill Cody and Wild Bill Hickok battle stagecoach station owners and Sioux Indians to establish the short-lived but glamorous Pony Express mail route between St. Joseph, Missouri, and Sacramento, California, in the early 1860s. Rousing good action for the historical Western fan who doesn't check every fact. 1953; 101m.

PONY EXPRESS RIDER ★★★★
DIR: Hal Harrison Jr. **CAST:** Stewart Peterson, Henry Wilcoxon, Buck Taylor, Joan Caulfield, Maureen McCormick, Ken Curtis, Slim Pickens, Dub Taylor, Jack Elam.
A young man joins the Pony Express to find those responsible for the murder of his father. A well-produced film that features solid performances from a host of veteran Western character actors. 1976; 100m.

POWDERKEG ★★
DIR: Douglas Heyes. **CAST:** Rod Taylor, Dennis Cole, Fernando Lamas, Michael Ansara, Tisha Sterling, Luciana Paluzzi.
Mildly entertaining Western about two barnstorming adventurers (Rod Taylor and Dennis Cole) hired by a railroad owner to liberate a train taken hostage by a Mexican bandit. This was the pilot for the mid-Seventies TV series *The Bearcats*. 1976; 88m.

POWDERSMOKE RANGE ★★½
DIR: Wallace Fox. **CAST:** Harry Carey, Hoot Gibson, Bob Steele, Tom Tyler, Guinn Williams, William Farnum, William Desmond.
Despite its impressive all-star cast of Western players, *Powdersmoke Range* is just an average B Western. Its significance lies in it being the first film to feature William Colt MacDonald's Three Mesquiteers. 1935; 71m.

PRAIRIE MOON ★★
DIR: Ralph Straub. **CAST:** Gene Autry, Smiley Burnette, Shirley Deane, Tommy Ryan, David Gorcey.
Well-worn story about a promise to a dying man is shifted to Gene Autry's West and puts him in a position to care for a gangster's three children on his ranch. The kids are city-tough and cause no end of trouble, but by the end they have reformed (naturally) and help Gene and Smiley bring in a gang of rustlers. 1938; B&W; 58m.

PROUD AND THE DAMNED, THE ★★
DIR: Ferde Grofe Jr. **CAST:** Chuck Connors, Jose Greco, Cesar Romero, Aron Kincaid.
Standard Western plot with a Latin accent results in a below-par account. The cast does a poor job, but the South American locales save this film from a lower rating. 1973; 94m.

PROUD REBEL, THE ★★★½
DIR: Michael Curtiz. **CAST:** Alan Ladd, Olivia De Havilland, David Ladd, Dean Jagger, Henry Hull.
A post–Civil War sentimental drama about a Confederate veteran searching for a doctor who can cure his mute son, with father and son playing father and son. The principals in this one are excellent, the chemistry great. Well worth the watching, this was the ill-fated Alan Ladd's last "class" film. 1958; 103m.

PURSUED ★★★
DIR: Raoul Walsh. **CAST:** Robert Mitchum, Teresa Wright, Judith Anderson, Dean Jagger, Harry Carey Jr., Alan Hale.
A cowboy, Robert Mitchum, searches for the murderer of his father in this taut, atmospheric Western. The entire cast is very good, and famed action director Raoul Walsh keeps things moving along at a brisk pace. 1947; B&W; 101m.

QUICK AND THE DEAD, THE ★★★★
DIR: Robert Day. **CAST:** Sam Elliott, Kate Capshaw, Tom Conti, Matt Clark, Kenny Morrison.
This made-for-HBO Western is the third in a trilogy of high-class shoot-'em-ups adapted from the stories by Louis L'Amour for star Sam Elliott. He is marvelous as a grizzled frontiersman who comes to the aid of a family (headed by Tom Conti and

Kate Capshaw) making its way across the American wilderness. 1987; 90m.

RACHEL AND THE STRANGER ★★★½

DIR: Norman Foster. **CAST:** William Holden, Loretta Young, Robert Mitchum.

The leisurely-paced Western is made easier to watch by a fine cast. William Holden's love for his wife Loretta Young finally comes to full blossom only after she is wooed by stranger Robert Mitchum. A nice story done with charm and class. 1948; B&W; 93m.

RADIO RANCH (MEN WITH STEEL FACES, PHANTOM EMPIRE) ★★½

DIR: Otto Brewer, B. Reeves "Breezy" Eason. **CAST:** Gene Autry, Frankie Darro, Betsy King Ross, Dorothy Christy, Smiley Burnette.

Condensed version of popular science-fiction serial *Phantom Empire*, this sketchily tells the story of Gene Autry and his fight against scientists who want his Radio Ranch for the precious ore it contains, and his strange adventures in the underground city of Murania. Running about one-third the length of the original serial, this version takes less time to view but doesn't make quite as much sense as the twelve-chapter serial. 1940; B&W; 80m.

RAGE AT DAWN ★★★★

DIR: Tim Whelan. **CAST:** Randolph Scott, Forrest Tucker, Mala Powers, J. Carrol Naish, Myron Healey, Edgar Buchanan.

Solid Western has granite-jawed Randolph Scott as an undercover agent out to trap the infamous Reno brothers (played with zest by Forrest Tucker, J. Carrol Naish, and Myron Healey). Scott takes time out to romance their pretty sister (Mala Powers) before bringing the boys to justice. 1955; 87m.

RANCHO NOTORIOUS ★★★½

DIR: Fritz Lang. **CAST:** Marlene Dietrich, Arthur Kennedy, Mel Ferrer, Lloyd Gough, William Frawley, Gloria Henry, Jack Elam, George Reeves.

Brooding revenge Western is a curio of the 1950s, one of those films that appears to mean something more than what the action implies. This film, while not a great Western, is fun to watch and a treat for Marlene Dietrich fans. 1952; 89m.

RANDY RIDES ALONE ★★★

DIR: Henry Frazer. **CAST:** John Wayne, Alberta Vaughan, George "Gabby" Hayes, Earl Dwire, Yakima Canutt.

John Wayne stars in this enjoyable B Western as a lawman who goes undercover to catch a gang that has been robbing an express office. The opening is particularly good. 1934; B&W; 60m.

RANGE WAR ★★½

DIR: Lesley Selander. **CAST:** William Boyd, Russell Hayden, Britt Wood.

Hopalong Cassidy (William Boyd) rounds up a gang that is trying to stop construction on the railroad. Lesser entry in the Cassidy series. Britt Wood is no replacement for George "Gabby" Hayes, who had just bowed out of the Cassidy films to become Roy Rogers's sidekick at Republic—or Andy Clyde who was yet to come. 1939; B&W; 64m.

RANGER AND THE LADY, THE ★★½

DIR: Joseph Kane. **CAST:** Roy Rogers, George "Gabby" Hayes, Jacqueline Wells, Harry Woods, Henry Brandon, Noble Johnson, Yakima Canutt, Art Dillard.

Buckskin-clad Roy Rogers is a Texas Ranger trying to clear up some trouble on the old Santa Fe Trail in the days before the Civil War. Fetching Jacqueline Wells plays the lady leading a wagon train to Texas. 1940; B&W; 59m.

RARE BREED, THE ★★★

DIR: Andrew V. McLaglen. **CAST:** James Stewart, Maureen O'Hara,

Brian Keith, Juliet Mills, Jack Elam, Ben Johnson.

This is a generally rewarding Western. Jimmy Stewart is a Texas cattle rancher who grudgingly assists an Englishwoman's (Maureen O'Hara) attempts to introduce a new line of short-horned cattle to the Texan range. The story is quite original and holds one's interest throughout. 1966; 108m.

RAWHIDE (1938) ★★

DIR: Ray Taylor. **CAST:** Smith Ballew, Lou Gehrig, Lafe McKee, Evalyn Knapp.

Lou Gehrig in a western? Yes, the Pride of the Yankees made one sagebrush adventure in support of former bandleader Smith Ballew. Gehrig plays a rancher at constant odds with the badmen and Ballew plays the two-fisted young lawyer who helps to organize the honest folk. Ballew is a rather bland lead, but the presence of Gehrig makes this one worth a watch. 1938; B&W; 58m.

RAWHIDE (1951) ★★★

DIR: Henry Hathaway. **CAST:** Tyrone Power, Susan Hayward, Dean Jagger, Hugh Marlowe, Jack Elam, Edgar Buchanan, Jeff Corey, George Tobias.

Sturdy Western concerns an outlaw gang holding hostages at a remote stagecoach station. Veteran director Henry Hathaway knows how to keep things clicking right along; the final shootout is electrifying. A good cast, loaded with great character actors, keeps this one on target. 1951; 86m.

RED RIVER ★★★★★

DIR: Howard Hawks. **CAST:** John Wayne, Montgomery Clift, Walter Brennan, Joanne Dru, John Ireland, Noah Beery Jr., Paul Fox, Coleen Gray, Harry Carey, Harry Carey Jr.

After seeing this Western, directed by Howard Hawks, John Ford remarked, "I didn't know the big lug could act." The "big lug" he was referring to was the picture's star, John Wayne, whom Ford had brought to stardom in 1939's *Stagecoach*. This shoot-'em-up adaptation of *Mutiny on the Bounty* definitely features Wayne at his best in the role of a tough rancher making a historic cattle drive. 1948; B&W; 133m.

RED SUN ★★½

DIR: Terence Young. **CAST:** Charles Bronson, Alain Delon, Toshiro Mifune, Ursula Andress, Capucine.

All-star, fitfully entertaining Western has an interesting premise—samurai vs. cowboys—but ultimately wastes the considerable talents of the great Japanese actor Toshiro Mifune. Charles Bronson has another of those offbeat-character parts that he underplays into a leading role. The action sequences in this Italian/French/Spanish coproduction are effective. Rated PG. 1972; 112m.

RED-HEADED STRANGER, THE ★★★

DIR: William Witliff. **CAST:** Willie Nelson, R. G. Armstrong, Morgan Fairchild, Royal Dano, Katharine Ross.

Willie Nelson's country "opera" served as the basis for this little-seen Western which most fans of the genre will enjoy. Nelson plays a right-thinking preacher who takes on an evil family (headed by Royal Dano) that is terrorizing the townspeople of this new parish. Rated R for violence and profanity. 1986; 105m.

RENEGADE RANGER ★★★★

DIR: David Howard. **CAST:** George O'Brien, Rita Hayworth, Tim Holt, Ray Whitley.

Star George O'Brien and director David Howard made some of the finest series Westerns in the Thirties and Forties. O'Brien, a member of director John Ford's stock company since starring in the classic *Iron Horse*, demanded good writing and got it. The star is in top form as a Texas Ranger who is assigned to bring in a female bandit (Rita Hayworth) accused of murder. 1938; B&W; 60m.

RETURN OF A MAN CALLED HORSE, THE ★★★
DIR: Irvin Kershner. **CAST:** Richard Harris, Gale Sondergaard, Geoffrey Lewis, Bill Lucking, Jorge Luke, Enrique Lucero.

The Return of a Man Called Horse is every bit as good as its predecessor, *A Man Called Horse*. Both films present an honest, and sometimes shocking, glimpse at the culture of the American Indian. The new film picks up with a bored and unhappy Morgan deciding to return to America. Rated PG for violence. 1976; 129m.

RETURN OF FRANK JAMES, THE ★★★
DIR: Fritz Lang. **CAST:** Henry Fonda, Gene Tierney, Donald Meek, John Carradine, Jackie Cooper, J. Edward Bromberg, Henry Hull.

Gene Tierney made her film debut in this inevitable sequel to *Jesse James* (1939). Henry Fonda reprises his role as brother Frank and attempts to avenge Jesse's death at the hands of "dirty little coward" Bob Ford, played by John Carradine. Thanks to Fonda's fine acting and Fritz Lang's sensitive direction, what could have been a pale rip-off is an enjoyable Western. 1940; 92m.

RETURN OF JESSE JAMES, THE ★★½
DIR: Arthur Hilton. **CAST:** John Ireland, Ann Dvorak, Hugh O'Brian, Henry Hull.

In this low-budget oater, John Ireland portrays a small-time outlaw who bears a striking resemblance to Jesse James. Taking advantage of this rumor, he sets out to prove to everyone that Jesse James, shot and killed by fellow gang-member Bob Ford, did not die and is still in business. Plodding, but fairly well acted. 1950; B&W; 75m.

RETURN OF THE BADMEN ★★★
DIR: Ray Enright. **CAST:** Randolph Scott, Anne Jeffreys, Robert Ryan, George "Gabby" Hayes, Lex Barker.

Randolph Scott has his hands full in this routine Western. No sooner does he settle down in Oklahoma than he must slap leather with Billy the Kid, the Dalton gang, the Younger brothers, and the Sundance Kid. As the latter, Robert Ryan shore ain't the appealing gunhand who rode with Butch Cassidy. 1948; B&W; 90m.

RETURN OF THE SEVEN ★★½
DIR: Burt Kennedy. **CAST:** Yul Brynner, Robert Fuller, Warren Oates, Claude Akins, Emilio Fernandez, Jordan Christopher.

This drab, inferior sequel to *The Magnificent Seven* follows Yul Brynner doing what he does best, getting six Yankee gunfighters fool enough to take on scores of Mexican bandits for no pay at all. 1966; 96m.

RETURN TO SNOWY RIVER, PART II ★★★★½
DIR: Geoff Burrowes. **CAST:** Tom Burlinson, Sigrid Thornton, Brian Dennehy, Nicholas Eadie, Bryan Marshall.

In this spectacular sequel to *The Man from Snowy River*, Tom Burlinson returns to right wrongs and romance Sigrid Thornton in rugged, Old West–style Australia. Director Geoff Burrowes, who produced the first film, outdoes the original at every turn. A movie the whole family can love. Rated PG for some violence. 1988; 100m.

RIDE 'EM COWGIRL ★
DIR: Samuel Diege. **CAST:** Dorothy Page, Milton Frome, Vince Barnett.

Singing cowgirl Dorothy Page and her horse Snowy battle the bad guys who bilked her father out of $5,000. The concept seems designed to prove that a woman can rope, ride, and yodel as well as any cowboy. Well, in this case, they were wrong. 1939; 52m.

RIDE IN THE WHIRLWIND ★½
DIR: Monte Hellman. **CAST:** Jack Nicholson, Cameron Mitchell, Millie Perkins, Harry Dean Stanton, Rupert Crosse.

Throwaway Western with good cast of characters goes nowhere in the muddled story of three riders wrongfully pursued by an unrelenting posse. This sister production to *The Shooting* appears to have lost the toss on the editing and uses variations of the same camera shots over and over. 1965; 83m.

RIDE, RANGER, RIDE ★★

DIR: Joseph Kane. **CAST:** Gene Autry, Smiley Burnette, Kay Hughes, Monte Blue, Max Terhune, Chief Thundercloud, Iron Eyes Cody.

Gene Autry, star graduate of the bland school of acting, plays the riding ranger in the title as he averts trouble with hostile Indians and patches things up between the red man and the settlers. 1936; B&W; 63m.

RIDE THE HIGH COUNTRY ★★★★½

DIR: Sam Peckinpah. **CAST:** Joel McCrea, Randolph Scott, Warren Oates, R. G. Armstrong, Mariette Hartley, John Anderson, James Drury, L. Q. Jones, Edgar Buchanan.

Joel McCrea and Randolph Scott play two old-time gunslingers who team up to guard a gold shipment. McCrea just wants to do a good job so he can "enter (his) house justified." Scott, on the other hand, cares nothing for noble purpose and tries to steal the gold. From that point on, they are friends no longer. The result is a picture so good that McCrea and Scott decided to retire after making it—both wanted to go out with a winner. 1962; 94m.

RIDE THE MAN DOWN ★★

DIR: Joseph Kane. **CAST:** Brian Donlevy, Rod Cameron, Ella Raines, Chill Wills, Jack LaRue.

A traditional Western shot in the traditional manner. While waiting for its new owners to arrive, a ranch manager fights to keep the property out of the greedy hands of land grabbers. 1952; 90m.

RIDERS OF DEATH VALLEY ★★★½

DIR: Ford Beebe, Ray Taylor. **CAST:** Dick Foran, Buck Jones, Leo Carrillo, Charles Bickford, Lon Chaney Jr., Noah Beery Jr., Guinn Williams, Monte Blue, Glenn Strange.

Dick Foran and his pals Buck Jones and Leo Carrillo head a group of men organized to police the mining districts and to fight it out with the thieves and murderers that flocked to the gold claims. A fine serial. 1941; B&W; 15 chapters.

RIDERS OF DESTINY ★★★

DIR: Robert N. Bradbury. **CAST:** John Wayne, Cecilia Parker, George "Gabby" Hayes, Forrest Taylor, Al St. John, Heinie Conklin, Earl Dwire.

The earliest low, low-budget John Wayne B Western available on tape, this casts an extremely young-looking Duke as Singin' Sandy, an undercover agent out to help ranchers regain their water rights. Fun for fans of the star. 1933; B&W; 50m.

RIDERS OF THE DEADLINE ★★

DIR: Lesley Selander. **CAST:** William Boyd, Andy Clyde, Jimmy Rogers, Richard Crane, Robert Mitchum.

Hopalong Cassidy pretends to befriend a smuggler in order to smoke out the real boss of the bad guys, who turns out to be an unsuspected pillar of the community, the local banker. Routine stuff, but better than the later films in the series and superior to many programmers of the time. 1943; B&W; 70m.

RIDERS OF THE RIO GRANDE ★★★★

DIR: Howard P. Bretherton. **CAST:** Bob Steele, Tom Tyler, Jimmie Dodd, Edward Van Sloan, Rick Vallin, Roy Barcroft, Charles King.

The last in an eight-year string of three Mesquiteers Westerns is one of the best. Involved plot line has the Mesquiteers mistaken for the Cherokee Boys, a trio of outlaws. Plenty of action and a tongue-in-cheek story that often spoofs the genre without belittling it. 1943; B&W; 55m.

RIDERS OF THE ROCKIES ★★½
DIR: Robert N. Bradbury. **CAST:** Tex Ritter, Louise Stanley, Charles King, Snub Pollard, Yakima Canutt.

Entertaining Tex Ritter Western finds the two-fisted singer joining a gang of rustlers in order to get the goods on them. Silent comedian Snub Pollard plays his comic sidekick and Charles King plays the man who has to face Ritter in a long, violent fight. One of Ritter's best Westerns. 1937; B&W; 56m.

RIDERS OF THE WHISTLING PINES ★½
DIR: John English. **CAST:** Gene Autry, Patricia White, Jimmy Lloyd, Douglass Dumbrille, Clayton Moore.

Even a fine cast of cowboy stars can't make a Gene Autry Western much more than passable. As usual, our bland hero comes to the aid of a female in danger of being cheated out of her rightful property, and, true to the code of the Western series film, the infinitely more interesting villains fold up and lose to the overweight yodeler. 1949; B&W; 70m.

RIDERS OF THE WHISTLING SKULL ★★½
DIR: Mack V. Wright. **CAST:** Robert Livingston, Ray Corrigan, Max Terhune, Mary Russell, Yakima Canutt, C. Montague Shaw, Chief Thundercloud.

The Three Mesquiteers gallop into one of their best adventures. They brave Indians and ghostly goings-on to find a fabled lost city and its fabulous treasure. An eerie story, a great cast of supporting character actors, and the easy camaraderie of the three saddle pals makes this outdoor adventure one of the most popular in the series. 1937; B&W; 58m.

RIDIN' ON A RAINBOW ★½
DIR: Lew Landers. **CAST:** Gene Autry, Smiley Burnette, Mary Lee.

Slow-moving, song-laden programmer spends too much time on a showboat focusing on Mary Lee (who also appeared opposite Roy Rogers) and ignores the sagebrush, cacti, and hoofbeats. There's a pretty fair chase and roundup of bank robbers at the climax, but there are too many tunes in the middle. 1941; B&W; 79m.

RIDING TORNADO, THE ★★★
DIR: D. Ross Lederman. **CAST:** Tim McCoy, Shirley Grey.

A strong series entry for Tim McCoy. He's a wandering cowboy hired by rancher Shirley Grey, whose cattle are being systematically stolen. Of course, our hero sets things right. 1932; B&W; 64m.

RIMFIRE ★★★
DIR: B. Reaves "Breezy" Eason. **CAST:** James Millican, Mary Beth Hughes, Reed Hadley, Henry Hull, Fuzzy Knight, Jason Robards Jr., Glenn Strange.

Better-than-average B Western has federal agent James Millican looking for stolen gold. He's aided in his search by the ghost of a gambler who was unjustly hanged for cheating! 1949; 64m.

RIO BRAVO ★★★★½
DIR: Howard Hawks. **CAST:** John Wayne, Walter Brennan, Ward Bond, Ricky Nelson, Dean Martin, John Russell, Claude Akins, Angie Dickinson, Bob Steele.

A super-Western, with John Wayne, Walter Brennan, Ward Bond, Ricky Nelson (aping Montgomery Clift's performance in *Red River*), and the scene-stealing Dean Martin taking on cattle baron John Russell, who's out to get his kill-crazy brother (Claude Akins) out of jail. 1959; 141m.

RIO CONCHOS ★★★
DIR: Gordon Douglas. **CAST:** Richard Boone, Stuart Whitman, Anthony Franciosa, Edmond O'Brien, Jim Brown.

Rip-roaring Western action ignites this briskly paced yarn set in post–Civil War Texas. Richard Boone and his pals go undercover to get the goods on outlaws responsible for stealing a shipment of rifles. Boone gives a wry performance. 1964; 107m.

RIO GRANDE ★★★★
DIR: John Ford. **CAST:** John Wayne, Maureen O'Hara, Claude Jarman Jr., Ben Johnson, Harry Carey Jr., Victor McLaglen, Chill Wills, J. Carrol Naish.

The last entry in director John Ford's celebrated cavalry trilogy (which also includes *Fort Apache* and *She Wore a Yellow Ribbon*), this stars John Wayne as a company commander coping with renegade Indians and a willful wife (Maureen O'Hara), who wants to take their soldier son (Claude Jarman Jr.) home. 1950; B&W; 105m.

RIO LOBO ★★★
DIR: Howard Hawks. **CAST:** John Wayne, Jack Elam, Jorge Rivero, Jennifer O'Neill, Chris Mitchum, Mike Henry.

Neither star John Wayne nor director Howard Hawks was exactly at the peak of his powers when this second reworking of *Rio Bravo* (the first being *El Dorado*) was released. If one adjusts the normally high expectations he or she would have for a Western made by these two giants, *Rio Lobo* is a fun show. Jack Elam is terrific in a delightful supporting role. Rated G. 1970; 114m.

RIVER OF NO RETURN ★★★
DIR: Otto Preminger. **CAST:** Robert Mitchum, Marilyn Monroe, Rory Calhoun, Tommy Rettig.

Rory Calhoun has deserted Marilyn Monroe, believe it or not. She hires Robert Mitchum to track him down. The storyline is predictable and sometimes plodding, under Otto Preminger's heavy directorial hand. Nevertheless, Mitchum's quirky strength and the gorgeous color shots of Monroe and western vistas make the film sufficiently entertaining. 1954; 91m.

ROAMIN' WILD ★★★
DIR: Bernard B. Ray. **CAST:** Tom Tyler, Carol Wyndham, Al Ferguson, George Chesebro.

Undercover marshal (Tom Tyler) goes after a gang of outlaws operating in the goldfields trying to take over a woman's stage line. Fast-moving; plenty of excitement. 1936; B&W; 56m.

ROARING GUNS ★★★
DIR: Sam Newfield. **CAST:** Tim McCoy, Rosalinda Price, Wheeler Oakman.

A ruthless cattle baron attempts to drive out the independent ranchers while using a phony feud with his main competitor as a cover-up. It's up to steely-eyed Tim McCoy to set things aright in this low-budget but enjoyable series Western. 1936; B&W; 66m.

ROBIN HOOD OF TEXAS ★★
DIR: Lesley Selander. **CAST:** Gene Autry, Lynne Roberts (Mary Hart), Sterling Holloway, Adele Mara.

More of a detective story than a formula Western, Gene Autry's last film for Republic Studios finds him accused of bank robbery and keeping one step ahead of the law in order to clear his name. Better than many of his films and one of the best of his post-WWII movies, with a nicely turned story and more action and fisticuffs than most of Autry's productions, 1947; B&W; 71m.

ROOSTER COGBURN ★★★½
DIR: Stuart Millar. **CAST:** John Wayne, Katharine Hepburn, Richard Jordan, Anthony Zerbe, Strother Martin, John McIntire.

Okay, so this sequel to *True Grit* is only *The African Queen* reworked, with John Wayne playing the Humphrey Bogart part opposite the incomparable Katharine Hepburn, but we like—no, love—it. Watching these two professionals playing off each other is what movie-watching is all about. The plot? Well, it's not much, but the scenes with Wayne and Hepburn are, as indicated, priceless. Rated PG. 1975; 107m.

ROOTIN' TOOTIN' RHYTHM ★½
DIR: Mack V. Wright. **CAST:** Gene Autry, Smiley Burnette, Armida, Monte Blue.

Gene Autry and his bumbling sidekick Smiley Burnette settle a range dispute and restore the peace to the prairie in this unimaginative programmer. Too many songs and too much Smiley. 1938; B&W; 55m.

ROUGH JUSTICE
DIR: Mario Costa. **CAST:** Klaus Kinski, Steven Tedd.

Thanks to videocassettes, another skeleton in Klaus Kinski's closet is revealed. This one is a cheap spaghetti Western, with Kinski as a sex-crazed outlaw who, along with a band of con artists, almost pulls off a $50,000 scam. Not rated, but contains violence. 1987; 95m.

ROUGH RIDERS' ROUNDUP ★★½
DIR: Joseph Kane. **CAST:** Roy Rogers, Lynne Roberts (Mary Hart), Raymond Hatton, Eddie Acuff.

The accent is more on action than music in this early Roy Rogers Western about the Rough Riders reuniting to rid the range of an outlaw gang. In all, it's better than most of the Rogers vehicles that followed. 1939; B&W; 58m.

ROUND-UP TIME IN TEXAS ★½
DIR: Joseph Kane. **CAST:** Gene Autry, Smiley Burnette, Maxine Doyle.

Gene Autry brings his usual air of contained energy to this fairly early entry in the long-running series. Filled with blank stares, lame humor, bland tunes, and insipid plot developments, this is a typical Autry programmer. 1937; B&W; 58m.

RUN OF THE ARROW ★★★
DIR: Samuel Fuller. **CAST:** Rod Steiger, Brian Keith, Ralph Meeker, Sarita Montiel, Tim McCoy, Jay C. Flippen, Charles Bronson.

One of the strangest of all adult Westerns of the 1950s, this film tells the story of a man who joins the Sioux tribe after the Civil War rather than accept the reality of the South's defeat. Rod Steiger does a good job in a difficult role. While not entirely successful, this thought-provoking film is worth watching. 1957; 85m.

RUSTLER'S VALLEY ★★
DIR: Nate Watt. **CAST:** William Boyd, George "Gabby" Hayes, Russell Hayden, Lee J. Cobb.

William Boyd as Hopalong Cassidy helps a rancher save his range while putting a stop to a villainous lawyer who is squeezing the locals dry with his thieving and legal shenanigans. 1937; B&W; 60m.

RUTHLESS FOUR, THE ★
DIR: Giorgio Capitani. **CAST:** Van Heflin, Gilbert Roland, Klaus Kinski, George Hilton.

This spaghetti Western could have been a lot worse, but that's no reason to watch it. Van Heflin plays a prospector who strikes gold, only to have to split the fortune with three other men less honest than he. 1969; 96m.

SACKETTS, THE ★★★★
DIR: Robert Totten. **CAST:** Sam Elliott, Tom Selleck, Glenn Ford, Ben Johnson, Ruth Roman, Gilbert Roland.

Fine made-for-TV Western adapted from two novels by Louis L'Amour, *The Daybreakers* and *The Sacketts.* Sam Elliott, Tom Selleck, Glenn Ford, and Ben Johnson are terrific in the lead roles, and there's plenty of action. 1979; 200m.

SACRED GROUND ★★★½
DIR: Charles B. Pierce. **CAST:** Tim McIntire, Jack Elam, Serene Hedin.

Interracial marriage between a white mountain man and an Apache woman is further complicated when they have their child on the ancient burial grounds of another Indian tribe. The couple's romance and the trials they endure should hold viewer interest. Rated PG. 1983; 100m.

SAGA OF DEATH VALLEY ★★½
DIR: Joseph Kane. **CAST:** Roy Rogers, George "Gabby" Hayes, Donald "Red" Barry.

Early Roy Rogers film finds him fighting a gang of outlaws led by a desperado who turns out to be his own brother! The hidden identity or look-a-like theme was a common one for Roy's films of the late 1930s, but this well-produced Western isn't lacking in action and excitement. 1939; B&W; 56m.

SAGEBRUSH TRAIL ★★★
DIR: Armand Schaefer. **CAST:** John Wayne, Nancy Shubert, Lane Chandler, Yakima Canutt.

Big John Wayne, almost before he was shaving, is sent to prison for a murder he didn't commit. Naturally, our hero breaks out of the big house to clear his name. In a nice twist, he becomes friends—unknowingly—with the killer, who dies bravely in a climactic shootout. Good B Western. 1933; B&W; 58m.

SAGINAW TRAIL ★½
DIR: George Archainbaud. **CAST:** Gene Autry, Connie Marshall, Smiley Burnette.

Similar in plot to a half dozen or more previous Gene Autry films, the only thing that's as tired as the story is Smiley Burnette, resurrected to co-star in the last six titles in the series. Overall, this is a pretty tame ending to a pretty lame run of ninety-three movies. 1953; B&W; 56m.

SANTA FE STAMPEDE ★★½
DIR: George Sherman. **CAST:** John Wayne, Ray "Crash" Corrigan, Max Terhune, William Farnum.

The Three Mesquiteers (John Wayne, Ray Corrigan, and Max Terhune) ride to the rescue of an old friend (William Farnum) who strikes it rich with a gold mine. A villain (LeRoy Mason) is trying to steal his claim. Lightweight Western with plenty of action. 1938; B&W; 58m.

SANTA FE TRAIL ★★★½
DIR: Michael Curtiz. **CAST:** Errol Flynn, Alan Hale, Olivia De Havilland, Ronald Reagan, Raymond Massey, Ward Bond, Van Heflin.

Errol Flynn, Alan Hale, and Olivia De Havilland save this muddled Western, with Ronald Reagan as one of Flynn's soldier buddies who go after John Brown (Raymond Massey). 1940; B&W; 110m.

SANTEE ★★½
DIR: Gary Nelson. **CAST:** Glenn Ford, Dana Wynter, Michael Burns, Robert Donner, Jay Silverheels, Harry Townes, John Larch.

Bounty hunter with a heart (Glenn Ford) loses his son and adopts the son of an outlaw he kills. A fine variety of old Western hands add zip to this otherwise average oater. As usual, Ford turns in a solid performance. PG. 1973; 93m.

SAVAGE JOURNEY ★
DIR: Tom McGowan. **CAST:** Maurice Grandmaison, Charles Moll.

Simplistic, whitewashed account of the formation of the Mormon Church. The writing is laughable and the characterizations are too hackneyed to be believable. Not rated; contains some violence. 1983; 96m.

SEARCHERS, THE ★★★★★
DIR: John Ford. **CAST:** John Wayne, Natalie Wood, Jeffrey Hunter, Ward Bond, Vera Miles, Harry Carey Jr., Lana Wood.

John Ford is without a doubt the most celebrated director of Westerns, and *The Searchers* is considered by many to be his masterpiece. In it, he and his favorite actor, John Wayne, reached the peak of their long and successful screen collaboration. This thoughtful film follows Ethan Edwards (Wayne), an embittered Indian-hating, ex–Confederate soldier as he leads the search for his niece (Natalie Wood), who was kidnapped years earlier by Indians. As time goes on, we begin to wonder whether Edwards is out to save the girl or kill her. 1956; 119m.

SERGEANT PRESTON OF THE YUKON (TELEVISION SERIES) ★★½

DIR: Various. **CAST:** Richard Simmons, Yukon King.

This syndicated adventure series, set in the 1890s, stars Richard Simmons as the Northwest Mounted Policeman. No, it's not *that* Richard Simmons; this character gets most of his exercise from chasing bad guys. In the wild, gold-rush days of Alaska, there were plenty of villains around. Preston could always count on the assistance of his husky, Yukon King. 1955; B&W; 55m.

SHALAKO

DIR: Edward Dmytryk. **CAST:** Sean Connery, Brigitte Bardot, Stephen Boyd, Jack Hawkins, Honor Blackman, Woody Strode.

Here's an awful British Western about European immigrants Sean Connery, Brigitte Bardot, Stephen Boyd, Jack Hawkins, and Honor Blackman menaced by Apaches in the Old West. Ugh! 1968; 113m.

SHANE ★★★★★

DIR: George Stevens. **CAST:** Alan Ladd, Jean Arthur, Jack Palance, Van Heflin, Ben Johnson, Elisha Cook Jr.

Shane is surely among the best Westerns ever made. Alan Ladd plays the title role, the mysterious stranger who helps a group of homesteaders in their struggle against the cattlemen. 1953; 118m.

SHE WORE A YELLOW RIBBON ★★★★★

DIR: John Ford. **CAST:** John Wayne, Ben Johnson, Victor McLaglen, Harry Carey Jr., George O'Brien.

Lest we forget, John Wayne was one of the screen's greatest actors. The Duke gave what was arguably his greatest performance in this gorgeous color Western made by John Ford. As the aging Captain Nathan Brittles, Wayne plays a man set to retire but unwilling to leave his command at a time of impending war with the Apaches. This is one of the great Westerns. 1949; 103m.

SHENANDOAH ★★★★

DIR: Andrew V. McLaglen. **CAST:** James Stewart, Doug McClure, Glenn Corbett, Patrick Wayne, Katharine Ross, George Kennedy, Strother Martin.

James Stewart gives a superb performance in this, director Andrew V. McLaglen's best Western. Stewart plays a patriarch determined to keep his family out of the Civil War. He ultimately fails and is forced into action to save his children from the ravages of war. It's an emotionally moving, powerful tale. 1965; 105m.

SHINE ON HARVEST MOON ★★

DIR: Joseph Kane. **CAST:** Roy Rogers, Lynne Roberts (Mary Hart).

Roy Rogers rides to the rescue once again as he aids the forces of law and order and brings a gang of robbers to justice while clearing an old man's name. 1938; B&W; 60m.

SHOOTING, THE ★★★

DIR: Monte Hellman. **CAST:** Warren Oates, Millie Perkins, Will Hutchins, Jack Nicholson.

This early Jack Nicholson vehicle, directed by cult figure Monte Hellman, is a moody Western about revenge and murder. An interesting entry into the genre, it may not be everyone's cup of tea. No rating; has some violence. 1967; 82m.

SHOOTIST, THE ★★★★½

DIR: Don Siegel. **CAST:** John Wayne, Lauren Bacall, James Stewart, Ron Howard, Richard Boone, Hugh O'Brian, John Carradine, Harry Morgan, Scatman Crothers.

The Shootist is a special film in many ways. Historically, it is John Wayne's final film. Cinematically, it stands on its own as an intelligent tribute to the passing of the era known as the "Wild West." Wayne's masterful performance is touching and bitterly ironic as well. He plays a famous gunfighter dying of cancer and seeking a place to die in peace, only to become a victim of his own reputation. Rated PG. 1976; 99m.

SHOWDOWN AT BOOT HILL ★★½

DIR: Gene Fowler Jr. **CAST:** Charles Bronson, Robert Hutton, John Carradine.

Stone-faced Charles Bronson does some impressive work as a lawman who finds that the criminal he has killed in the line of duty is actually a respected citizen in another community. 1958; B&W; 71m.

SILENT CONFLICT ★★

DIR: George Archainbaud. **CAST:** William Boyd, Andy Clyde, Rand Brooks, Virginia Belmont.

A traveling charlatan hypnotizes and drugs Lucky into stealing money and trying to kill Hoppy and California. A fair series Western. 1948; B&W; 61m.

SILVER QUEEN ★★

DIR: Lloyd Bacon. **CAST:** George Brent, Priscilla Lane, Bruce Cabot, Lynne Overman, Eugene Pallette, Guinn Williams.

Young and devoted daughter Priscilla Lane is determined to uphold her family's honor and pay her father's debts. She does so by gambling in San Francisco, where she develops a reputation as a real sharpie. 1942; B&W; 81m.

SILVERADO ★★★★½

DIR: Lawrence Kasdan. **CAST:** Kevin Kline, Scott Glenn, Kevin Costner, Danny Glover, Rosanna Arquette, John Cleese, Brian Dennehy, Linda Hunt, Jeff Goldblum.

Scott Glenn, Kevin Kline, Kevin Costner, and Danny Glover ride side by side to clean up the town of Silverado. Excitement, laughs, thrills, and chills abound in this marvelous movie. Even those who don't ordinarily like Westerns are sure to enjoy it. Rated PG-13 for violence and profanity. 1985; 133m.

SINGING BUCKAROO ★★

DIR: Tom Gibson. **CAST:** Fred Scott, William Faversham, Victoria Vinton.

Lesser-known Western hero Fred Scott yodels the range in this hard-ridin' horse opera about a frontier knight who pounds the prairie to help an innocent girl pursued by villains intent on relieving her of her money. Nothing special but full of action interrupted by a few tunes. 1937; B&W; 50m.

SINISTER JOURNEY ★★

DIR: George Archainbaud. **CAST:** William Boyd, Andy Clyde, Rand Brooks, Elaine Riley.

Coming to the aid of an old friend, Hoppy and his saddle pals find themselves involved in a mystery on a west-bound railroad. Standard Hopalong Cassidy film doesn't have the punch of the earlier ones. 1948; B&W; 58m.

SIOUX CITY SUE ★★

DIR: Frank McDonald. **CAST:** Gene Autry, Lynne Roberts (Mary Hart), Sterling Holloway.

Gene Autry's first film after World War II finds him in Hollywood, where he tries his luck in the movie business. Originally intended as the voice of an animated donkey, Autry wins the leading role in the picture when the big shots hear him stretch his tonsils. Rampaging rustlers throw a monkey wrench into the proceedings and provide Gene with an opportunity to show his stuff on the ground and on horseback. 1946; B&W; 69m.

SKIN GAME ★★★★

DIR: Paul Bogart. **CAST:** James Garner, Louis Gossett Jr., Susan Clark, Edward Asner, Andrew Duggan.

Perceptive social comedy-drama set during the slave era. James Garner and Louis Gossett Jr. are a pair of con artists; Garner "sells" Gossett to unsuspecting slave owners and later helps break him free. The fleecing continues until they meet up with evil Edward Asner, who catches on to the act...then the story takes a chilling turn toward realism. Excellent on all levels. Rated PG for light violence. 1971; 102m.

SMITH! ★★★
DIR: Michael O'Herlihy. **CAST:** Glenn Ford, Nancy Olson, Dean Jagger, Keenan Wynn, Warren Oates, Chief Dan George.

A fine cast and sensitive screenplay distinguish this story of a strong man's efforts to secure a fair trial for an Indian accused of murder. Glenn Ford is believably rugged and righteous as he struggles with prejudice and ignorance in America's Southwest, and Chief Dan George is highly effective as the stoic focal point of the territory's rage. Good fare for the whole family. Rated G. 1969; 101m.

SMOKEY TRAILS ★★★
DIR: Bernard B. Ray. **CAST:** Bob Steele, Jimmy Aubrey, Ted Adams, Carleton Young.

Once again Bob Steele is after the killer of his father—chasing him right into Lost Canyon, an outlaw den that he cleans out with plenty of fisticuffs and blazing six-shooters. Above average. 1939; B&W; 57m.

SOLDIER BLUE ★★½
DIR: Ralph Nelson. **CAST:** Candice Bergen, Peter Strauss, John Anderson, Donald Pleasence.

An extremely violent film that looks at the mistreatment of Indians at the hands of the U.S. Cavalry. This familiar subject has fared much better in films such as *Little Big Man.* Final attack is an exercise in excessive gore and violence. Rated R. 1970; 112m.

SONG OF NEVADA ★★½
DIR: Joseph Kane. **CAST:** Roy Rogers, Dale Evans, Mary Lee, Bob Nolan and the Sons of the Pioneers, Lloyd Corrigan, Thurston Hall, John Eldredge, Forrest Taylor, George Meeker, LeRoy Mason, Kenne Duncan.

Roy, Dale, and the boys at the ranch come to the aid of an innocent girl who has become prey of a crook and his henchmen. This tuneful, hard-riding horse opera is chock-full of former cowboys and familiar faces and was intended to get the blood tingling and the toes tapping. It's typical of Roy's mid-1940s movies. 1944; B&W; 75m.

SONG OF TEXAS ★★½
DIR: Joseph Kane. **CAST:** Roy Rogers, Sheila Ryan, Barton MacLane, Harry Shannon, Pat Brady, Arline Judge, Eve March, Hal Taliaferro (Wally Wales), Bob Nolan and the Sons of the Pioneers, Tom London.

Most of the action comes at the end of this songfest as Roy competes in a chuck-wagon race in order to win back yet another stolen ranch. Roy and the boys squeeze ten songs into this programmer, but good character actors like Barton MacLane and Harry Shannon fill the screen enough to satisfy those with less tolerance for yodeling and guitar strumming. 1943; B&W; 69m.

SONG OF THE GRINGO ★★
DIR: John P. McCarthy. **CAST:** Tex Ritter, Monte Blue, Fuzzy Knight, Joan Woodbury.

Tex Ritter's first Western for Grand National is a low-budget shoot-'em-up with the singing cowboy as a deputy sheriff bent on cleaning out a gang of ruthless claim-jumpers. Ritter's films for Grand National lack the pacing and budget that other studios added to their product. 1936; B&W; 62m.

SONS OF KATIE ELDER, THE ★★★
DIR: Henry Hathaway. **CAST:** John Wayne, Dean Martin, Earl Holliman, Michael Anderson Jr., James Gregory, George Kennedy, Martha Hyer, Jeremy Slate, Paul Fix.

John Wayne stars in this entertaining film about four brothers reunited after the death of their mother and forced to fight to get back their land. Although this Western rarely goes beyond the predictable, it's better than no Duke at all. There's plenty of action and roughhouse comedy. 1965; 122m.

SOUTH OF ST. LOUIS ★★★★
DIR: Ray Enright. **CAST:** Joel McCrea, Zachary Scott, Douglas Kennedy, Dorothy Malone, Alexis Smith.
Joel McCrea, Zachary Scott, and Douglas Kennedy seek revenge for the burning of their respective spreads. Dorothy Malone and Alexis Smith provide the love interest. If you like dusty, exciting ranch epics, this film should be high on your list. 1949; 88m.

SOUTH OF THE BORDER ★★½
DIR: George Sherman. **CAST:** Gene Autry, Smiley Burnette, Duncan Renaldo, June Storey.
Gene and Smiley mosey on down to Mexico as government operatives in order to quell a rebellion engineered by foreign powers who wish to control that country's oil resources. This patriotic film contains some good action scenes. 1939; B&W; 71m.

SOUTH OF THE RIO GRANDE ★
DIR: Lambert Hillyer. **CAST:** Duncan Renaldo, Martin Garralaga.
Viewers who fondly remember the *Cisco Kid* television series might get a mild kick out of seeing series star Duncan Renaldo in one of his first appearances as the Robin Hood of Mexico. Otherwise, this is a dreary effort with poor editing, mediocre acting, and far too many forgettable songs. 1945; B&W; 62m.

SPIRIT OF THE WEST ★★
DIR: Otto Brower. **CAST:** Hoot Gibson, Doris Hill, Lafe McKee, Hooper Atchley.
This entertaining but primitive Western employs a tired old gimick that Hoot Gibson had used in previous films—that of a tough hombre who masquerades as a silly fool in order to help the gal in distress and bring the greedy, land-grabbing varmints to justice. 1932; B&W; 60m.

SPOILERS, THE ★★★★
DIR: Ray Enright. **CAST:** Marlene Dietrich, Randolph Scott, John Wayne, Harry Carey, Russell Simpson, George Cleveland.
John Wayne is a miner who strikes gold in Nome, Alaska. An unscrupulous gold commissioner (Randolph Scott) and his cronies plot to steal the rich claim. But the Duke, his partner (Harry Carey), and their backer (Marlene Dietrich) have other ideas. This was the fourth of five screen versions of Rex Beach's novel. 1942; B&W; 87m.

SPRINGTIME IN THE SIERRAS ★★
DIR: William Witney. **CAST:** Roy Rogers, Jane Frazee, Andy Devine, Stephanie Bachelor.
Beady-eyed Roy Rogers sets his sights on stopping evil Stephanie Bachelor and her hulking henchman Roy Barcroft from shooting game animals out of season. There's more action than story in this fast-paced series entry. 1947; 75m.

STAGE TO CHINO ★★★½
DIR: Edward Killy. **CAST:** George O'Brien, Virginia Vale, Roy Barcroft, Hobart Cavanaugh, Carl Stockdale, William Haade, Glenn Strange.
In this first-rate B Western, George O'Brien is a postal inspector who goes undercover to investigate a gold-shipping scam. The always reliable Roy Barcroft is the leader of the baddies, and Virginia Vale is the not-so-helpless principal victim. O'Brien's Westerns were always marked by fine acting, lots of action, and snappy dialogue, and this is a good example of the high standards he set for himself and his films. 1940; B&W; 58m.

STAGECOACH (1939) ★★★★★
DIR: John Ford. **CAST:** John Wayne, Claire Trevor, Thomas Mitchell, John Carradine, Donald Meek, Andy Devine, George Bancroft, Tim Holt.
John Ford utilized the *Grand Hotel* formula of placing a group of unrelated characters together in some common setting or dangerous situation. A stagecoach trip across the Old West provides the common setting and plenty of shared danger. Riding together with the mysterious Ringo

Kid (John Wayne) is a grand assortment of some of Hollywood's best character actors. 1939; B&W; 99m.

STAGECOACH (1986) ★

DIR: Ted Post. **CAST:** Willie Nelson, Kris Kristofferson, Johnny Cash, Waylon Jennings, John Schneider, Elizabeth Ashley, Anthony Franciosa, Anthony Newley, Mary Crosby, Lash LaRue.

A cast of country-music performers makes the mistake of attempting to reinterpret John Ford's classic Western. The result is a totally forgettable genre piece with phoned-in performances and an overall air of boredom. Made for TV. 1986; 98m.

STALKING MOON, THE ★★★

DIR: Robert Mulligan. **CAST:** Gregory Peck, Eva Marie Saint, Robert Forster, Frank Silvera, Lou Frizell.

Gregory Peck is an army scout who takes in a white woman (Eva Marie Saint) and the child she bore while a captive of the Apaches. The Apache father kidnaps the child and starts a chase that lasts through most of the movie. Familiar, but captivating and with exceptional performances. 1969; 109m.

STAR PACKER, THE ★★★

DIR: Robert N. Bradbury. **CAST:** John Wayne, Verna Hillie, George "Gabby" Hayes, Yakima Canutt.

The Shadow and his band of outlaws have a group of ranchers cowed until John Wayne rides into town and turns the tables on the baddies. A good B Western that will be best appreciated by Wayne fans. 1934; B&W; 60m.

STATION WEST ★★★

DIR: Sidney Lanfield. **CAST:** Dick Powell, Jane Greer, Tom Powers, Raymond Burr, Agnes Moorehead, Burl Ives, Regis Toomey, Steve Brodie, Guinn Williams.

An army undercover agent (Dick Powell) attempts to find out who is responsible for a rash of gold robberies, eventually falling in love with the ringleader (Jane Greer). This sturdy Western boasts a fine supporting cast, good location cinematography, and nice action scenes. 1948; 92m.

STONE OF SILVER CREEK ★★★★

DIR: Nick Grindé. **CAST:** Buck Jones, Noel Francis.

Another of producer-star Buck Jones's superior Westerns for Universal, this offbeat, often funny movie casts Jones as a straight-shooting saloon owner who fights off a pair of persistent baddies, gives the town preacher an education in manliness, and weighs in as an all-around champion of justice. 1935; B&W; 62m.

STRAIGHT TO HELL ★

DIR: Alex Cox. **CAST:** Sy Richardson, Joe Strummer, Dennis Hopper, Elvis Costello.

Maybe—and we do mean maybe—you will find something of interest in this self-indulgent Western spoof, but only if you've drunk as much tequila as the performers in the movie seem to have. Director Alex Cox, who specializes in punk cinema has gathered together musicians and actors for an extended in-joke that has something to do with bank robbers and thugs shooting at each other in a desert town. 1987; 86m.

STRANGE GAMBLE ★★

DIR: George Archainbaud. **CAST:** William Boyd, Andy Clyde, Rand Brooks, Elaine Riley.

The crooked "boss" of a small town steals valuable mining rights from a drunken customer and leaves his sick sister without any money or place to stay. Hoppy and his pals intervene and encounter gunplay and fast riding as they attempt to return to the victim her rightful fortune. Last of the Hopalong Cassidy series. 1948; B&W; 61m.

STRANGER AND THE GUNFIGHTER, THE ★★½

DIR: Anthony M. Dawson. **CAST:** Lee Van Cleef, Lo Lieh, Patty Shepard.

The world may never be ready for this improbable mix, a tongue-in-cheek spaghetti Western by way of a standard kung-fu chop-chop flick. Lee Van Cleef, as another of his weary gunslingers, teams with martial arts master Lo Lieh to find a missing treasure. A classic this isn't, but the fast action and camp humor make it watchable. Rated PG for violence. 1976; 107m.

SUNDOWN RIDER, THE ★★★★
DIR: Lambert Hillyer. **CAST:** Buck Jones, Barbara Weeks, Wheeler Oakman, Ward Bond.

Solid, brooding Western has Buck Jones as an easygoing cowpoke who happens upon a band of rustlers. The baddies leave Jones to "guard" their camp, where he is caught and brutally branded by revenge-minded lawmen despite his protests of innocence. So Jones swears revenge. Rewarding shoot-'em-up. 1933; B&W; 66m.

SUNDOWN RIDERS ★★★
DIR: Lambert Hillyer. **CAST:** Russell Wade, Jay Kirby, Andy Clyde, Evelyn Finley, Jack Ingram, Marshall Reed.

First of a proposed trio series (Russell Wade, Jay Kirby, Andy Clyde) that never materialized. Too bad, because it has plenty of action. Good chance to see famed stuntman Henry Wills in an acting role. 1948; B&W; 56m.

SUNDOWNERS, THE (1950) ★★★
DIR: George Templeton. **CAST:** Robert Preston, Cathy Downes, Robert Sterling, John Drew Barrymore, Jack Elam.

Robert Preston is the good brother and Robert Sterling is the bad one in this tolerable Western. The siblings face each other in a climactic showdown. 1950; 83m.

SUNSET ON THE DESERT ★★
DIR: Joseph Kane. **CAST:** Roy Rogers, George "Gabby" Hayes, Lynne Garver, Frank M. Thomas, Bob Nolan, Beryl Wallace, Glenn Strange, Douglas Fowley, Roy Barcroft, Pat Brady.

Roy's strong resemblance to a notorious crook gives him a chance to infiltrate the gang, but the usual complications arise when the look-alike desperado returns. It's fun to watch Roy Rogers play the tough, but the cast is better than the story in this series entry. 1942; B&W; 63m.

SUNSET SERENADE ★★½
DIR: Joseph Kane. **CAST:** Roy Rogers, George "Gabby" Hayes, Helen Parrish, Onslow Stevens, Joan Woodbury.

Beady-eyed Roy Rogers and his ornery sidekick "Gabby" Hayes thwart the plans of a couple of no-goods who aim to murder the heir to a ranch and take it over for themselves. Enjoyable enough and not too demanding. 1942; B&W; 58m.

SUPPORT YOUR LOCAL SHERIFF! ★★★★½
DIR: Burt Kennedy. **CAST:** James Garner, Joan Hackett, Walter Brennan, Harry Morgan, Jack Elam, Bruce Dern, Henry Jones.

The time-honored backbone of the industry, the Western, takes a real ribbing in this all-stops-out send-up. If it can be parodied, it is—in spades. James Garner is great as a gambler "just passing through" who gets roped into being sheriff and tames a lawless mining town against all odds, including an inept deputy, fem-lib mayor's daughter, and snide gunman. A very funny picture. Rated G. 1969; 93m.

SUSANNA PASS ★½
DIR: William Witney. **CAST:** Roy Rogers, Dale Evans, Estelita Rodriguez, Martin Garralaga.

Another variation on the crooked newspaper publisher theme, this minor effort again teams Roy Rogers and Dale Evans, the "King and Queen of the Westerns," with "Cuban Fireball" Estelita Rodriguez. Too many tunes and production numbers, as well as Republic Studios' vain effort to promote their south-of-the-border discovery, detract from the action in this film. 1949; 67m.

TAKE A HARD RIDE ★★½
DIR: Anthony M. Dawson. **CAST:** Jim Brown, Lee Van Cleef, Fred Williamson, Catherine Spaak, Dana Andrews, Barry Sullivan, Jim Kelly, Harry Carey Jr.
When his friend and partner (Dana Andrews) dies of a heart attack, big Jim Brown is charged with taking the proceeds from a cattle sale to their homestead in Sonora, Mexico. On the way, a ruthless bounty hunter (Lee Van Cleef) attempts to take the money for himself. A good cast falls prey to the shortcomings of this spaghetti Western, but there is some enjoyable action and humor. Rated R. 1975; 103m.

TALION ★★
DIR: Michael Moore. **CAST:** Robert Lansing, Patrick Wayne, Slim Pickens, Gloria Talbott, Paul Fix, Strother Martin, Clint Howard.
Two bounty hunters (Robert Lansing and Patrick Wayne) go on the vengeance trail against a turncoat (Slim Pickens). The twist is that in an early gun battle, Wayne is blinded and Lansing's gun hand is crippled. Lansing as the title character looks vaguely uncomfortable in a cowboy hat, and the writing is sometimes ridiculous. 1966; 92m.

TALL IN THE SADDLE ★★★★
DIR: Edwin L. Marin. **CAST:** John Wayne, George "Gabby" Hayes, Ward Bond, Ella Raines.
A first-rate B Western that combines mystery with shoot-'em-up action. John Wayne is wrongly accused of murder and must find the real culprit. Helping him is "Gabby" Hayes, and hindering is Ward Bond. 1944; B&W; 87m.

TALL MEN, THE ★★
DIR: Raoul Walsh. **CAST:** Clark Gable, Jane Russell, Robert Ryan, Cameron Mitchell, Mae Marsh.
Confederate army veterans Clark Gable and Cameron Mitchell join cattle baron Robert Ryan to drive his herd to market through Indian country. All three fancy Jane Russell, brawl for her favor, along with fighting Indians and the fickle elements. 1955; 122m.

TELL THEM WILLIE BOY IS HERE ★★★
DIR: Abraham Polonsky. **CAST:** Robert Redford, Robert Blake, Katharine Ross.
Robert Redford is a southwestern sheriff in the early days of this country. He is pursuing an Indian (Robert Blake) who is fleeing to avoid arrest. The story is elevated from a standard Western chase by the dignity and concern shown to the Indian's viewpoint. Rated PG. 1969; 96m.

TENNESSEE'S PARTNER ★★½
DIR: Allan Dwan. **CAST:** John Payne, Ronald Reagan, Rhonda Fleming, Coleen Gray.
Allan Dwan directed this minor Western featuring Ronald Reagan as a stranger who steps into the middle of a fight between gamblers and ends up befriending one (John Payne). This is one of Payne's better roles. He plays a bad guy who gets turned around by Reagan. Good little drama; better than the title suggests. 1955; 87m.

TERROR OF TINY TOWN, THE ♥
DIR: Sam Newfield. **CAST:** Billy Curtis, Yvonne Moray, Little Billy.
The definitive all-midget Western, with action, gunplay, romance, and a happy ending to boot. Just about as odd as they come, this turkey is an entertaining, if mysterious bad movie. 1938; B&W; 63m.

TEXAS ★★★
DIR: George Marshall. **CAST:** William Holden, Glenn Ford, Claire Trevor, George Bancroft, Edgar Buchanan, Raymond Hatton.
Friends William Holden and Glenn Ford are rivals for the affections of Claire Trevor in this lively, action-jammed Western pitting cattleman against cattle rustler in the sprawling land of Sam Houston. It might have been an epic, but a cost-conscious

producer kept a tight rein. Good, though! 1941; B&W; 93m.

TEXAS CYCLONE ★★★★
DIR: D. Ross Lederman. **CAST:** Tim McCoy, Shirley Grey, John Wayne, Walter Brennan, Wheeler Oakman, Mary Gordon.

An easygoing cowpoke (Tim McCoy) is mistaken for a straight-shooting rancher and sticks around to help the rancher's wife (Shirley Grey) fight off cattle rustlers. A top-notch McCoy gets some solid support from a couple of newcomers, John Wayne and Walter Brennan. 1932; B&W; 63m.

TEXAS JOHN SLAUGHTER: GERONIMO'S REVENGE ★★½
DIR: James Neilson. **CAST:** Tom Tryon, Darryl Hickman, Betty Lynn, Brian Corcoran, Adeline Harris.

Peace-loving Texas John Slaughter is forced to take up arms against his Apache friends when renegade Geronimo goes on the warpath. Full of action and filmed in authentic-looking locations, this feature is composed of episodes originally broadcast on the popular television show *Walt Disney Presents*. 1960; 77m.

TEXAS JOHN SLAUGHTER: STAMPEDE AT BITTER CREEK ★★½
DIR: Harry Keller. **CAST:** Tom Tryon, Harry Carey Jr., Adeline Harris, Annette Gorman, Betty Lynn.

Former Texas Ranger John Slaughter is falsely accused of rustling as he attempts to drive his cattle into New Mexico despite threats from a rival rancher and his hired gun. Tom Tryon is ruggedly heroic as Texas John Slaughter in this Disney adventure Western culled from episodes originally featured on *Walt Disney Presents* from 1958 to 1962. 1962; 52m.

TEXAS JOHN SLAUGHTER: WILD TIMES ★★½
DIR: Harry Keller. **CAST:** Tom Tryon, Harry Carey Jr., Adeline Harris, Annette Gorman, Betty Lynn, Brian Corcoran, Robert Middleton.

This film is a compilation of episodes from the popular series starring future bestselling author Tom Tryon as the lawman-turned-rancher. Handsomely photographed and well acted. 1962; 77m.

TEXAS LADY ★★
DIR: Tim Whelan. **CAST:** Claudette Colbert, Barry Sullivan, John Litel.

An out-of-her-element Claudette Colbert is a crusading newspaper editor in the Old West. If you're a Western fan, you'll like it. 1955; 86m.

TEXAS TERROR ★★½
DIR: Robert N. Bradbury. **CAST:** John Wayne, Lucille Brown, LeRoy Mason, George "Gabby" Hayes, Yakima Canutt.

John Wayne hangs up his guns (for a while) in this Lone Star Western about a lawman falsely accused of the death of his friend. After the usual plot machinations and clues, Wayne finds the real culprits and gets a chance to do some hard ridin' and fancy sluggin'. 1935; B&W; 58m.

THERE WAS A CROOKED MAN ★★★½
DIR: Joseph L. Mankiewicz. **CAST:** Kirk Douglas, Henry Fonda, Hume Cronyn, Warren Oates, Burgess Meredith, Arthur O'Connell.

Crooked-as-they-come Kirk Douglas bides and does his time harried by holier-than-thou Arizona prison warden Henry Fonda, who has more than redemption on his mind. A good plot and clever casting make this oater well worth the watching. And, yes, rattlesnakes do make good watchdogs. Rated R. 1970; 123m.

THEY CALL ME TRINITY ★★½
DIR: E. B. Clucher. **CAST:** Terence Hill, Bud Spencer, Farley Granger.

This Western-comedy can be best described as an Italian *Blazing Saddles*. Terence Hill and Bud Spencer team up as half-brothers trying to protect a colony from cattle rustlers and a shady sheriff. Rated G. 1971; 109m.

THEY DIED WITH THEIR BOOTS ON ★★★★

DIR: Raoul Walsh. **CAST:** Errol Flynn, Olivia De Havilland, Arthur Kennedy, Gene Lockhart, Anthony Quinn, Sydney Greenstreet.

Errol Flynn gives a first-rate performance as General George Custer in this Warner Bros. classic directed by Raoul Walsh. The superb supporting cast adds to this Western epic. 1941; B&W; 138m.

3:10 TO YUMA ★★★★

DIR: Delmer Daves. **CAST:** Glenn Ford, Van Heflin, Felicia Farr, Leora Dana, Henry Jones, Richard Jaeckel, Robert Emhardt.

This first-rate adult Western draws its riveting drama and power from the interaction of well-drawn characters rather than gun-blazing action. A farmer (Van Heflin) captures a notorious gunman (Glenn Ford) and, while waiting for the train to take them to Yuma prison, must hole up in a hotel and overcome the killer's numerous ploys to gain his freedom. 1957; B&W; 92m.

THREE-WORD BRAND, THE ★★★

DIR: Lambert Hillyer. **CAST:** William S. Hart, Jane Novak.

Indians murder a homesteader, thus orphaning his twin sons. The brothers become separated—going their own ways—until circumstances reunite them many years later. William S. Hart deftly portrays the father and the sons in this silent sagebrush drama. 1921; B&W; 75m.

TIN STAR, THE ★★★★

DIR: Anthony Mann. **CAST:** Henry Fonda, Anthony Perkins, Betsy Palmer, John McIntire, Michel Ray, Neville Brand, Lee Van Cleef.

Solid Anthony Mann–directed adult Western has Anthony Perkins as the inexperienced sheriff of a wild-and-woolly town seeking the help of hardened gunfighter Henry Fonda. Although it contains some unconvincing moments, *The Tin Star* succeeds overall thanks to the skilled playing of its cast. 1957; B&W; 93m.

TO THE LAST MAN ★★★★

DIR: Henry Hathaway. **CAST:** Randolph Scott, Richard Dix, Esther Ralston, Noah Beery Sr., Buster Crabbe, Jack LaRue.

Feudin' and fussin' in the Old West, Zane Grey style. Based on an actual clan clash that took place in Arizona during the 1880s, this is a top-quality oater from Paramount Pictures' series of films based on Grey's novels. Randolph Scott was directed in several of these by Henry Hathaway, and they made a potent team. Look for Shirley Temple in one of her earliest roles. 1933; B&W; 61m.

TOM HORN ★★½

DIR: William Wiard. **CAST:** Steve McQueen, Richard Farnsworth, Billy Green Bush, Slim Pickens, Elisha Cook Jr.

Steve McQueen doesn't give a great performance in his next-to-last motion picture, about the last days of a real-life Wyoming bounty hunter, nor does director William Wiard craft a memorable Western. But this 1980 release does have its moments—most of them provided by supporting players. Rated R. 1980; 98m.

TRACKER, THE ★★★

DIR: John Guillerman. **CAST:** Kris Kristofferson, Scott Wilson, Mark Moses, David Huddleston, Karen Kopins.

In this generally effective made-for-HBO Western, Kris Kristofferson stars as famed tracker Noble Adams. He hunts down a bloodthirsty religious zealot–turned-outlaw (Scott Wilson) wanted for multiple murders and the kidnapping of a teenage girl. The film is sometimes slow and a bit too talky, but it's sporadically inventive. 1988; 90m.

TRACKERS, THE ★★

DIR: Earl Bellamy. **CAST:** Sammy Davis Jr., Ernest Borgnine.

Ernest Borgnine plays a vengeful rancher out to get the men who killed his son and kidnapped his daughter. He reluctantly enlists the aid of a black professional tracker (Sammy Davis Jr.). It's a mildly entertaining Western made for TV. 1971; 73m.

TRAIL BEYOND, THE ★★½
DIR: Robert N. Bradbury. **CAST:** John Wayne, Verna Hillie, Noah Beery Sr., Noah Beery Jr.

Once again, John Wayne rides to the rescue in a low-budget Western from the 1930s. It's pretty typical stuff as the Duke fights outlaws who are attempting to steal a gold mine. But this B Western has lots of action and a rare appearance of father and son actors Noah Beery Sr. and Noah Beery Jr. 1934; B&W; 55m.

TRAIL OF ROBIN HOOD ★★★
DIR: William Witney. **CAST:** Roy Rogers, Penny Edwards, Gordon Jones, Jack Holt, Emory Parnell, Clifton Young, Rex Allen, Allan "Rocky" Lane, Monte Hale, Kermit Maynard, Tom Keene, Ray "Crash" Corrigan, William Farnum.

This star-studded oddity finds Roy Rogers and a handful of contemporary Western heroes aiding screen great Jack Holt (playing himself) in his effort to provide Christmas trees to needy families in time for the holidays. Enjoyable film for all ages and a special treat for fans of the genre. 1950; 67m.

TRAIL STREET ★★★
DIR: Ray Enright. **CAST:** Randolph Scott, Robert Ryan, Anne Jeffreys, George "Gabby" Hayes, Steve Brodie.

Randolph Scott plays Bat Masterson in this well-acted story of conflicting western philosophies as Robert Ryan defends the farmers against gambler Steve Brodie and the cattle-rancher faction. "Gabby" Hayes lends some levity to this otherwise dramatic adult Western, and Anne Jeffreys plays the saloon girl who must choose between Scott and Brodie. Skillful repackaging of a familiar story. 1947; B&W; 84m.

TRAILING TROUBLE ★★
DIR: Arthur Rosson. **CAST:** Ken Maynard, Lona Andre, Vince Barnett, Roger Williams.

Cowboy great Ken Maynard is past his prime in this oater, but there's still enough vitality left to please genre fans. Straight-shootin' Ken clears a cloud over his name and rights the local wrongs. 1937; B&W; 57m.

TRAIN ROBBERS, THE ★★½
DIR: Burt Kennedy. **CAST:** John Wayne, Ben Johnson, Ann-Margret, Rod Taylor, Ricardo Montalban.

John Wayne and Ben Johnson join Ann-Margret in a search for a lost train and gold. Some nice moments but generally unsatisfying. For hardcore Wayne fans only. Rated PG for violence, but nothing extreme. 1973; 92m.

TRAITOR, THE ★★½
DIR: Sam Newfield. **CAST:** Tim McCoy, Frances Grant, Wally Wales, Karl Hackett.

Marshal Tim McCoy goes undercover to catch a gang of cutthroats. He succeeds in his plan of joining the outlaws, but his life is in constant danger. This routine Western features a game performance by McCoy, but the story is too typical and the direction is plodding. 1936; B&W; 56m.

TRAMPLERS, THE ★½
DIR: Albert Band. **CAST:** Gordon Scott, Joseph Cotten, Jim Mitchum, Franco Nero.

Gordon Scott returns from the Civil War to find his father (Joseph Cotten) trying to preserve the prewar South by burning out settlers and starting mass lynchings. Scott and his younger brother (Jim Mitchum), who is unable to abide his fathers actions, leave and join up with their father's enemies. Dull. 1966; 105m.

TREASURE OF PANCHO VILLA, THE ★★½
DIR: George Sherman. **CAST:** Rory Calhoun, Shelley Winters, Gilbert Roland, Joseph Calleia.

Rory Calhoun and Gilbert Roland pull off a gold robbery with the intention of giving the loot to the Mexican revolutionary forces. However, Calhoun begins to think the money would be better in his pocket. Complications ensue. Calhoun carries a great machine gun in this watchable Western, and Roland is fascinating as always. Good action scenes. 1955; 96m.

TRIGGER, JR. ★★★
DIR: William Witney. **CAST:** Roy Rogers, Dale Evans, Pat Brady, Gordon Jones, Grant Withers.

This Trucolor Roy Rogers film has everything going for it in the form of plot, songs, character actors, and hard ridin'. Roy, Dale, and the gang battle an unscrupulous gang of blackmailers as well as teach a young boy to overcome his fear of horses. 1950; 68m.

TRINITY IS STILL MY NAME ★★
DIR: E. B. Clucher. **CAST:** Bud Spencer, Terence Hill, Harry Carey Jr.

In this comedy sequel to *They Call Me Trinity*, Bud Spencer and Terence Hill again team up as the unlikely heroes of an Italian Western. Rated G. 1972; 117m.

TRIPLE JUSTICE ★★★½
DIR: David Howard. **CAST:** George O'Brien, Virginia Vale, Paul Fix, Glenn Strange.

Once again, star George O'Brien and director David Howard take a standard B-Western plot and infuse it with intelligence, character, and excitement. O'Brien is a peaceable cowpoke who innocently joins a gang of bank robbers. Silly, but surprisingly effective. 1940; B&W; 65m.

TRIUMPHS OF A MAN CALLED HORSE ★½
DIR: John Hough. **CAST:** Richard Harris, Michael Beck, Ana De Sade.

Richard Harris has his third go-round in the title role as John Morgan, an English nobleman who was captured by the Sioux in 1825 and eventually became their leader. In a real cheat, Harris is killed off in the first third of the film. That leaves the way clear for his gun-slinging son, Koda (Michael Beck), to take over the leadership of the tribe and battle the greedy gold prospectors invading their land. Yawn. Rated PG for violence and implied sex. 1983; 86m.

TROUBLE IN TEXAS ★★½
DIR: Robert N. Bradbury. **CAST:** Tex Ritter, Rita Hayworth, Earl Dwire, Yakima Canutt.

Two-fisted singing rodeo cowboy Tex Ritter investigates crooked rodeo contests and seeks the identity of the men responsible for the death of his brother. Future glamor girl Rita Hayworth appears on screen for the last time under her real name (Cansino) as an undercover agent who assists Ritter and his salty sidekick Earl Dwire. This enjoyable oater boasts a wild chase on a dynamite-laden wagon for a finale. 1937; B&W; 53m.

TRUE GRIT ★★★★
DIR: Henry Hathaway. **CAST:** John Wayne, Kim Darby, Robert Duvall, Glen Campbell.

John Wayne finally won his best-actor Oscar for his 1969 portrayal of a boozy marshal helping a tough-minded girl (Kim Darby) track down her father's killers. Well-directed by Henry Hathaway, it's still not one of the Duke's classics—although it does have many good scenes, the best of which is the final shootout between Wayne's Rooster Cogburn and chief baddie, Ned Pepper (Robert Duvall). Rated G. 1969; 128m.

TUMBLEWEEDS ★★★½
DIR: William S. Hart, King Baggott. **CAST:** William S. Hart, Barbara Bedford, Lucien Littlefield, Lillian Leighton.

One of silent films' greatest action sequences, the Oklahoma Land Rush along the Cherokee Strip, highlights this prestigious Western, famed cowboy star William S. Hart's final film. He retired to write novels. This version, which was introduced with a prologue spoken by Hart—his only venture into sound film—was released in 1939. Silent, with musical score. 1925; B&W; 114m.

TWILIGHT IN THE SIERRAS ★★
DIR: William Witney. **CAST:** Roy Rogers, Dale Evans, Estellita Rodriguez, Pat Brady, George Meeker, Fred Kohler Jr., House Peters Jr., Edward Keane, Bob Burns, Foy Willing and the Riders of the Purple Sage.

Roy Rogers and his sweetheart Dale Evans are weighed down by Estelita Rodriguez and moronic comedy relief Pat Brady in this story about state parole officer Roy and his two-fisted battles with a group of counterfeiters. Not as good as most of the series, this one runs a long (for a Roy Rogers) sixty-seven minutes and was filmed in Trucolor. 1950; 67m.

TWO MULES FOR SISTER SARA ★★★
DIR: Don Siegel. **CAST:** Clint Eastwood, Shirley MacLaine.

Clint Eastwood returns in his role of the "Man with No Name" (originated in Sergio Leone's Italian spaghetti Westerns) and Shirley MacLaine is an unlikely nun in this entertaining comedy-Western. Rated PG. 1970; 105m.

TWO RODE TOGETHER ★★★
DIR: John Ford. **CAST:** James Stewart, Richard Widmark, Shirley Jones, John McIntire, Woody Strode, Linda Cristal, Andy Devine.

In this variation of *The Searchers*, director John Ford explores the anguish of settlers over the children they have lost to Indian raiding parties and the racial prejudice that arises when one boy, now a full-blown warrior, is returned to his "people." It is not a fully effective film, but it does have its moments. 1961; 109m.

ULZANA'S RAID ★★★★
DIR: Robert Aldrich. **CAST:** Burt Lancaster, Bruce Davison, Jorge Luke, Richard Jaeckel, Lloyd Bochner.

A tense and absorbing film. Burt Lancaster and an expert cast and director take a fine screenplay penned by Alan Short and create a cavalry-Indians tale that is far from ordinary. Burt Lancaster plays an Indian scout who helps an inexperienced cavalry officer try to roust renegade Apache Ulzana and his tribe. Rated R. 1972; 103m.

UNDEFEATED, THE ★★
DIR: Andrew V. McLaglen. **CAST:** John Wayne, Rock Hudson, Bruce Cabot, Ben Johnson, Antonio Aguilar, Harry Carey Jr., Lee Meriwether, Jan-Michael Vincent.

Lumbering large-scale Western has Yankee colonel John Wayne forming an uneasy alliance with Confederate colonel Rock Hudson to sell wild horses to the French in Mexico during the war between Maximilian and Juarez. This film has little to recommend it—even to die-hard Wayne fans. The story is silly, and the direction is confused. Even the action is minimal. Rated PG. 1969; 119m.

UNDER CALIFORNIA STARS ★★½
DIR: William Witney. **CAST:** Roy Rogers, Jane Frazee, Andy Devine, Michael Chapin.

Trigger, the "Smartest Horse in the Movies," is the victim of a horsenapping plot in this enjoyable Roy Rogers oater. 1948; 71m.

UNEXPECTED GUEST ★★
DIR: George Archainbaud. **CAST:** William Boyd, Andy Clyde, Rand Brooks, Una O'Connor.

Hopalong Cassidy comes to the aid of his saddle pal and comic relief California (Andy Clyde) after they discover that someone is trying to murder the cantankerous old cuss and all of his relatives. Hoppy gets to the bottom of things and uncovers a plot that revolves around an inheritance due the family. 1947; B&W; 59m.

UNFORGIVEN, THE ★★★½
DIR: John Huston. **CAST:** Burt Lancaster, Audrey Hepburn, Audie Murphy, John Saxon, Charles Bickford, Lillian Gish, Doug McClure, Joseph Wiseman, Albert Salmi.

This tough Texas saga is filled with pride, prejudice, and passion. Audrey Hepburn, as a troubled Indian girl raised by Whites, is at the center of the turmoil. In addition to some intriguing relationships, the movie provides plenty of thrills with intense cowboy-versus-Indian action scenes. The cast is uniformly excellent. 1960; 125m.

VALLEY OF FIRE ★★
DIR: John English. **CAST:** Gene Autry, Pat Buttram, Gail Davis, Russell Hayden.

After dispersing or recruiting the bad elements in town, Gene Autry plays matchmaker and, delivers a flock of females just dying to marry up with smelly prospectors and settle down in greasy tents. Pretty good fun. 1951; B&W; 63m.

VANISHING AMERICAN, THE ★★★½
DIR: George B. Seitz. **CAST:** Richard Dix, Lois Wilson, Noah Beery Sr., Charles Stevens.

One of the few major studio releases of the silent era to treat the American Indian with compassion and dignity, this is a beautifully photographed silent gem from Paramount. Based on Zane Grey's popular melodramatic adventure, this landmark film is still historically important as well as being a fine job by director George Seitz. Silent. 1925; B&W; 114m.

VENGEANCE VALLEY ★★
DIR: Richard Thorpe. **CAST:** Burt Lancaster, Robert Walker, Joanne Dru, Ray Collins, John Ireland, Sally Forrest.

Slow-moving story of no-good cattle heir Robert Walker and his protective foster brother Burt Lancaster lacks suspense and doesn't have enough action. 1951; 83m.

VERA CRUZ ★★★
DIR: Robert Aldrich. **CAST:** Gary Cooper, Burt Lancaster, Denise Darcel, Ernest Borgnine.

Two American soldiers of fortune find themselves in different camps during one of the many Mexican revolutions of the 1800s. Gary Cooper is the good guy, but Burt Lancaster steals every scene as the smiling, black-dressed baddie. The plot is pretty basic but holds your interest until the traditional climactic gunfight. 1954; 94m.

VIGILANTES ARE COMINGI ★★½
DIR: Mack V. Wright, Ray Taylor. **CAST:** Robert Livingston, Kay Hughes, Guinn Williams, Raymond Hatton, Fred Kohler Sr., William Farnum, Bob Kortman, Ray Corrigan, Yakima Canutt.

This early Republic serial features Robert Livingston in a story suspiciously similar to the Zorro legend; a young man returns to 1840s California and finds that an evil despot has taken his family's lands so he dons a mask and robe and finds the oppressor under the name of The Eagle. Action-packed and with impressive stunts. 1936; B&W; 12 chapters.

VILLA RIDES ★★
DIR: Buzz Kulik. **CAST:** Yul Brynner, Robert Mitchum, Charles Bronson, Herbert Lom, Jill Ireland, Alexander Knox, Fernando Rey.

Uneven rehash of the Pancho Villa legend ignores the wealth of the real story and becomes yet another comic-book adventure of the lethal yet patriotic bandit-hero and the gringo he comes to depend on and grudgingly respect. Good cast, but this ill-fated production doesn't deliver what it should. 1968; 125m.

VIRGINIAN, THE ★★★★
DIR: Victor Fleming. **CAST:** Gary Cooper, Walter Huston, Mary Brian, Richard Arlen, Eugene Pallette, Chester Conklin.

"If you want to call me that—smile!" Although a bit slow in parts, this early Western still impresses today. Gary Cooper (with a drawl helped along by coach Randolph Scott) is terrific in the title role as a fun-loving but tough ranch foreman who has to face the worst task of his life when a friend (Richard Arlen) falls in with an outlaw (Walter Huston). Huston, in his first film, plays the role of Trampas with an air of easygoing menace. 1929; B&W; 90m.

WAGONMASTER ★★★★½
DIR: John Ford. **CAST:** Ben Johnson, Ward Bond, Harry Carey Jr., Joanne Dru, James Arness.

John Ford was unquestionably the greatest director of Westerns. This release ranks with the best of Ford's work. Ward Bond, who plays the elder in this story of a Mormon congregation migrating west, became a star, thanks to the popular television series it inspired: *Wagon Train*. And Ben Johnson, who won the best-supporting-actor Oscar in 1971 for *The Last Picture Show*, is excellent in his first starring role. 1950; B&W; 86m.

WANTED: DEAD OR ALIVE (TELEVISION SERIES) ★★★½
DIR: Thomas Carr, Richard Donner. **CAST:** Steve McQueen, Wright King.

The public was first captivated by Steve McQueen's cool, tough, intense persona with this top-notch Western series. McQueen plays dedicated bounty hunter Josh Randall, who travels the country searching for outlaws. The first video releases feature "Reunion for Revenge" with James Coburn and Ralph Meeker and "Medicine Man" with J. Pat O'Malley and Cloris Leachman. 1958–1961; 30m.

WAR OF THE WILDCATS ★★★
DIR: Albert S. Rogell. **CAST:** John Wayne, Martha Scott, Albert Dekker, George "Gabby" Hayes, Sidney Blackmer, Dale Evans.

Big John Wayne takes on bad guy Albert Dekker in this story of oil drillers at the turn of the century. "Gabby" Hayes adds a vintage touch to this standard-formula Republic feature. 1943; B&W; 102m.

WAR WAGON, THE ★★★
DIR: Burt Kennedy. **CAST:** John Wayne, Kirk Douglas, Howard Keel, Keenan Wynn.

While not John Wayne at his best, this Western, co-starring Kirk Douglas and directed by Burt Kennedy, does have plenty of laughs and action. It's guaranteed to keep fans of the Duke and shoot-'em-ups pleasantly entertained. 1967; 101m.

WARLOCK ★★★
DIR: Edward Dmytryk. **CAST:** Henry Fonda, Richard Widmark, Anthony Quinn, Dorothy Malone.

Even a high-voltage cast cannot energize this slow-paced "adult" Western. Lack of action hurts this film, which concentrates on psychological homosexual aspects of the relationship between gunfighter Henry Fonda and gambler Anthony Quinn. Richard Widmark is all but lost in the background as the town sheriff. 1959; 121m.

WATERHOLE #3 ★★★
DIR: William A. Graham. **CAST:** James Coburn, Carroll O'Connor, Margaret Blye, Bruce Dern, Claude Akins, Joan Blondell, James Whitmore.

This amusing Western-comedy follows the misadventures of three outlaws, led by James Coburn, who rob the Union Army of a fortune in gold and bury it by a waterhole in the desert. 1967; 95m.

WEST OF THE DIVIDE ★★★
DIR: Robert N. Bradbury. **CAST:** John Wayne, Virginia Brown Faire, George "Gabby" Hayes, Yakima Canutt, Earl Dwire.

John Wayne is on the trail of his father's murderer (again) in this standard B Western, which has the slight twist of having the Duke also searching for his younger brother, who has been missing since dear old Dad took the fatal bullet. Looks as if it was made in a day—and probably was. Good stunt work, though. 1934; B&W; 54m.

WEST OF THE LAW ★★★
DIR: Howard Bretherton. **CAST:** Buck Jones, Tim McCoy, Raymond Hatton, Evelyn Cooke, Harry Woods, Jack Daley, Roy Barcroft.

The last of the Rough Riders Westerns, this entry takes the series out in style. The heroes help the townspeople defeat a band of rustlers. Jones handles most of the horseback heroics while McCoy instills fear in the bad guys with his steely-eyed stare. 1942; B&W; 60m.

WESTERNER, THE ★★★★
DIR: William Wyler. **CAST:** Gary Cooper, Walter Brennan, Forrest Tucker, Chill Wills, Dana Andrews, Tom Tyler, Fred Stone.

The plot revolves around earnest settlers being run off their land. But the heart of this classic yarn rests in the complex relationship that entwines Judge Roy Bean (Walter Brennan) and a lanky stranger (Gary Cooper). Bean is a fascinating character, burdened with a strange sense of morality and an obsession for actress Lily Langtree. Brennan won an Oscar for his portrayal. Cooper is at his laconic best. 1940; B&W; 100m.

WHEN A MAN RIDES ALONE ★★
DIR: J. P. McGowan. **CAST:** Tom Tyler, Alan Bridge.

Whenever John Wayne needed a formidable screen opponent, Tom Tyler was a good choice. But mostly, Tyler was a star of B Westerns like this none too original entry about a Robin Hood–style good guy thwarting a crooked mine owner. 1933; B&W; 60m.

WHEN A MAN SEES RED ★★★★
DIR: Alan James. **CAST:** Buck Jones, Peggy Campbell, LeRoy Mason.

Writer-director Alan James gives producer-star Buck Jones a marvelous storyline, and Jones gives a breezy, authoritative performance. Peggy Campbell plays the spoiled, rich girl who is heir to the California ranch that Jones oversees, and he is charged with looking after her interests. 1934; B&W; 60m.

WHEN THE LEGENDS DIE ★★★½
DIR: Stuart Millar. **CAST:** Richard Widmark, Frederic Forrest.

A young Ute Indian is taken from his home in the Colorado Rockies after his parents die. In the modern white world he is taught the "new ways." His extraordinary riding abilities make him a target for exploitation as Red Dillon (Richard Widmark) trains him as a rodeo bronco rider, then proceeds to cash in on his protégé's success. A touching story that finds Widmark in one of his better roles and introduces a young Frederic Forrest. Rated PG for some mild profanity. 1972; 105m.

WILD BUNCH, THE ★★★★½
DIR: Sam Peckinpah. **CAST:** William Holden, Ernest Borgnine, Robert Ryan, Ben Johnson, Edmond O'Brien, Warren Oates, Strother Martin, L. Q. Jones, Emilio Fernandez.

The Wild Bunch, a classic Western, was brilliantly directed by Sam Peckinpah. He created a whole new approach to violence in this landmark film about men making a last stand. It is without a doubt Peckinpah's greatest film and is bursting with action, vibrant characters, and memorable dialogue. Good acting, too, by a first-rate cast. Rated R. 1969; 145m.

WILD ROVERS, THE ★★★★
DIR: Blake Edwards. **CAST:** William Holden, Ryan O'Neal, Karl Malden, Tom Skerritt, Lynn Carlin, Joe Don Baker, Moses Gunn.

Sadly overlooked Western tells the story of two cowboys, William Holden and Ryan O'Neal, running from the law after robbing a bank. Holden is perfect as the older and not so wiser of the two, and O'Neal gives one of his best performances as the young partner. Rich in texture and smoothly directed by Blake Edwards. Rated PG. 1971; 109m.

WILD TIMES ★★★
DIR: Richard Compton. **CAST:** Sam Elliott, Ben Johnson, Timothy Scott, Harry Carey Jr., Bruce Boxleitner, Penny Peyser, Dennis Hopper.

A two-cassette Western originally made for television. Sam Elliott plays sharp-shooter High Cardiff, whose life is anything but easy as he makes his way across the Old West. This could have been helped by some trimming. 1980; 200m.

WILD WILD WEST REVISITED, THE ★★★

DIR: Burt Kennedy. **CAST:** Robert Conrad, Ross Martin, Paul Williams, Harry Morgan, René Auberjonois, Robert Shields, Lorene Yarnell.

That diminutive genius, Miguelito Loveless, has a new plan for world domination. He's cloning heads of state. It's worked in England, Spain, and Russia. The United States and President Cleveland could be next. Those legendary agents James West and Artemus Gordon are called out of retirement to save the day. This revival of the Sixties series is breezily entertaining. 1979; 95m.

WILL PENNY ★★★★½

DIR: Tom Gries. **CAST:** Charlton Heston, Joan Hackett, Donald Pleasence, Lee Majors, Bruce Dern, Anthony Zerbe, Clifton James, Ben Johnson, Slim Pickens.

Charlton Heston gives the finest performance of his distinguished career in this gritty, unsentimental look at the life of an illiterate cowboy in the American West. Director Tom Gries's screenplay leans a bit too heavily on George Stevens's *Shane* and Henry Hathaway's *Rawhide*, but his film can stand the comparison, which is high praise, indeed. Lucien Ballard's fine cinematography is another plus. Equivalent to a PG-13. 1968; 108m.

WINCHESTER '73 ★★★

DIR: Anthony Mann. **CAST:** James Stewart, Shelley Winters, Dan Duryea, Stephen McNally, Will Geer, Rock Hudson, Tony Curtis, John McIntire.

Cowboy James Stewart acquires the latest iron from the East, a Winchester '73 rifle, loses it to a thief, and pursues the prized weapon as it passes from hand to hand. He finally corners the original thief on a precipice. Responsible for renewing the popularity of the Western as film fare, this oater is simple, brisk-paced, direct, action-packed, tongue-in-cheek, mean, sweaty, suspenseful, and entirely entertaining. 1950; B&W; 82m.

WINDS OF THE WASTELAND ★★★

DIR: Mack V. Wright. **CAST:** John Wayne, Phyllis Fraser, Yakima Canutt, Lane Chandler.

Big John Wayne is the head of a stagecoach company that competes for a government mail contract in the days after the pony express. Better than most B Westerns made by the Duke, because he was beginning to show more polish and confidence, but still no classic. 1936; B&W; 57m.

WINDWALKER ★★★★

DIR: Kieth Merrill. **CAST:** Trevor Howard, Nick Ramus, James Remar, Serene Hedin.

Trevor Howard plays the title role in this superb film which spans three generations of a Cheyenne Indian family. It refutes the unwritten rule that family entertainment has to be bland and predictable and is proof that films don't need to include sensationalism to hold the attention of modern filmgoers. Rated PG. 1980; 108m.

WINNING OF THE WEST ★★

DIR: George Archainbaud. **CAST:** Gene Autry, Smiley Burnette, Gail Davis, Robert Livingston.

Same old stuff about a brave newspaper publisher who wants to stop corruption and lawlessness and enlists the aid of no-nonsense Gene Autry and all-nonsense Smiley Burnette. 1953; B&W; 57m.

YELLOW ROSE OF TEXAS ★★

DIR: Joseph Kane. **CAST:** Roy Rogers, Dale Evans, George Cleveland, Harry Shannon, Grant Withers, Bob Nolan and the Sons of the Pioneers, Tom London, Rex Lease.

Roy Rogers plays an undercover insurance agent out to clear the name of an old man who has been accused of aiding a stage robbery. 1944; B&W; 55m.

YOUNG GUNS ★★
DIR: Christopher Cain. **CAST:** Emilio Estevez, Kiefer Sutherland, Charlie Sheen, Lou Diamond Phillips, Dermot Mulroney, Casey Siemaszko, Jack Palance, Brian Keith, Patrick Wayne.

The Brat Pack attempts to ape the Wild Bunch and ends up resembling a cowboy version of the Bowery Boys in this disappointing Western. Emilio Estevez seems to be having a great time playing Billy the Kid, while his brother Charlie Sheen makes a more convincing cowboy. But it's all for naught because the story lacks any authenticity. The only bright moments are provided by genre veterans Jack Palance, Brian Keith, and Patrick Wayne in all-too-brief supporting roles. Rated R for violence and profanity. 1988; 102m.

YUMA ★★½
DIR: Ted Post. **CAST:** Clint Walker, Barry Sullivan, Edgar Buchanan, Kathryn Hays, Peter Mark Richman, Morgan Woodward.

Big Clint Walker fights most of the rowdy elements of a tough town and has to expose a plan to undermine his authority as a lawman in this enjoyable made-for-television Western. 1970; 73m.

ZACHARIAH ★★½
DIR: George Englund. **CAST:** John Rubinstein, Pat Quinn, Don Johnson, Country Joe and the Fish, Doug Kershaw.

Forget the storyline in this midnight movie Western and sit back and enjoy the music and the images. Television performers, a variety of musicians and actors, (including a youthful Don Johnson), populate this minor cult favorite and take every opportunity to be cool and break into song. There are tunes for most tastes and the fast-moving nature of the film makes it a good choice for company or a party. 1971; 93m.

ZORRO RIDES AGAIN ★★★
DIR: William Witney, John English. **CAST:** John Carroll, Helen Christian, Reed Howes, Duncan Renaldo, Noah Beery Sr., Nigel de Brulier, Bob Kortman, Tom London.

A modern-day Zorro, played by John Carroll, lends his hand to a railway under siege by ruthless Noah Beery Sr., one of the cinema's greatest heavies. Beery makes life miserable for the railway's owners and their workers; their constant harassment keeps Zorro on his toes. A great cast keeps this serial moving at a rapid clip. 1937; B&W; 12 chapters.

ZORRO'S BLACK WHIP ★★
DIR: Spencer Gordon Bennet, Wallace Grissell. **CAST:** George J. Lewis, Linda Stirling, Lucien Littlefield, John Merton, Tom London, Jack Kirk.

Zorro never makes an appearance in this serial, but lovely-yet-lethal action star Linda Stirling dons a black outfit and becomes the Black Whip, riding in the hoofprints of her crusading father, who was killed for his just beliefs. After several setbacks, the lovely heroine and her boyfriend (George J. Lewis) help the good people of Idaho thwart the greedy plans of a meanie who stands in the way of statehood for the territory. 1944; B&W; 12 chapters.

ZORRO'S FIGHTING LEGION ★★★
DIR: William Witney, John English. **CAST:** Reed Hadley, Sheila Darcy, C. Montague Shaw, Budd Buster, Carleton Young, Charles King.

Quality serial places Reed Hadley (as Zorro) at the helm of a determined band of patriotic ranchers eager to ensure safe passage of the gold shipments needed to continue Juarez's rule. Zorro faces danger from corrupt officials as well as marauding Yaqui Indians. 1939; B&W; 12 chapters.

CAST INDEX

DIRECTOR INDEX

FAMILY VIEWING INDEX

ALPHABETICAL LISTING OF MOVIES

ABOUT THE AUTHORS

MICK MARTIN is the film critic for the *Sacramento Union* newspaper and the host and executive producer of the quarterly videocassette release "Mick Martin's Best on Video." He also reviews movies for KZAP-FM radio in Sacramento and is a singer-songwriter who performs with Mick Martin and the Blues Rockers in northern California.

MARSHA PORTER, author of several short stories, articles, and a teacher's handbook, holds a master's degree in educational administration. Currently, she does freelance writing and editing and is an English instructor in Sacramento. Formerly, she was a newspaper advisor and collegiate actress.